Footprint
South American Handbook 2003

Ben Box

One morning, after almost two years of crossing, they became the first mortals to see the western slope of the mountain range. From the cloudy summit they saw the immense aquatic expanse of the great swamp as it spread out toward the other side of the world.

Gabriel García Márquez
One Hundred Years of Solitude
(Jonathan Cape, London, 1970)

South American Handbook 2003
79th edition
© Footprint Handbooks Ltd
September 2002

Published by Footprint Handbooks
6 Riverside Court
Lower Bristol Road
Bath BA2 3DZ. England
T +44 (0)1225 469141
F +44 (0)1225 469461
Email discover@footprintbooks.com
Web www.footprintbooks.com

ISBN 1 903471 35 4
CIP DATA: A catalogue record for this
book is available from the British Library

Distributed in the USA by
Publishers Group West

Credits

Series editors
Patrick Dawson and Rachel Fielding

Editorial
Editor: Claire Boobbyer
Maps: Sarah Sorensen

Production
Page layout: Emma Bryers
Maps: Claire Benison, Robert Lunn,
Kevin Feeney
Colour maps: Kevin Feeney
Cover: Camilla Ford
Colour section: Robert Lunn

Design
Mytton Williams

Photography
Front cover: getty one Stone
Back cover: Jamie Marshall/Tribal Eye

Inside colour section:
Patricia Fogden: page 10 (centre)
getty one Stone: page 6 (top right), page
15 (centre and bottom left and right),
page 16
Jamie Marshall: page 6 (bottom right),
page: 15 (top)
Nature pl: page 10 (top right, bottom left
and right)
Pictures Colour Library: page 9: centre
PromPerú: page 12
Robert Harding: page 9 (bottom left)
South American Pictures: page 9 (top
right)
TRIP Photographic Library: page 4-5, 6
(centre and bottom left), page 9
(bottom right)

Print
Manufactured in Italy by LEGOPRINT

South America

See back of book for colour maps

❶

CARACAS □

VENEZUELA

Gran Sabana

GUYANA

GEORGETOWN □
PARAMARIBO □
CAYENNE □

❷

□ BOGOTA

COLOMBIA

San Agustín ∴

Kaieter Falls

SURI-NAME

GUYANE

QUITO □

❶a

ECUADOR

Cotopaxi ▲

❹

Amazon

❺

Gran ∴
Vilaya

PERU

BRAZIL

Manu Biosphere Reserve ◆

LIMA □

Madidi National Park ◆

Machu ∴
Picchu

❸

Lake Titicaca

□ LA PAZ

BOLIVIA

□ BRASILIA

○ Salvador

❻

Salar de Uyuni

Pantanal

PARAGUAY

Atacama Desert

CHILE

ASUNCION □

Iguazú Falls

Rio de Janeiro ○

Pacific Ocean

❼

❼inset

Atlantic Ocean

Aconcagua ▲

SANTIAGO □

BUENOS AIRES □

URUGUAY

MONTEVIDEO □

ARGENTINA

❽

Chiloé

❾

❾inset

Falkland Islands

PN Torres del Paine

Tierra del Fuego

Machu Picchu — Archaeological site

Pantanal — Natural feature/national park

Angel Falls — Water feature/salt lake

═══ National highway including Pan-American Highway

─── Paved road

─── Unpaved all weather including unpaved Pan-American Highway

─── Seasonal unpaved road, track

─── Rail

–·–·– International border

N

0 km 300
0 miles 300

ECUADOR

GALAPAGOS ISLANDS

Altitude in metres
4000
3000
2000
1000
500
200
0
Neighbouring Country

A foot in the door

Right Monument to South American
Independence leader Simon Bolivar
in Caracas, Venezuela
Below All the fun of the fair:
Carnival in Rio, Brazil

Above Snow clad Volcán Cotopaxi, Ecuador
Right Guinea pigs (cuy) are most definitely
on the menu in Peruvian restaurants
Previous page The steaming El Tatio
geysers at dawn, Chile

Journeying into South America

South America can be a larger-than-life experience where all your senses will be assaulted. At La Diablada festival in Oruro, Bolivia, dancers wear masks of the scariest monsters. Blazing rainbows glitter in the mists which hang over Iguazú, where 275 waterfalls cascade into a great gorge on the Argentina/Brazil border. Snow-capped volcanoes in the Lauca National Park in northern Chile seem close enough to touch in the rarefied air. Senses are overwhelmed: the smell of guava filling the countryside when the fruit is ripe; the fire of chilli from that innocent-looking bottle on the table; the heat of the sun which almost floors you as you step from the plane in a tropical airport; the bitterness of the wind as it blows off the southern ice fields. New archaeological discoveries are still being made in the jungles of the Incas' last retreat from the Spaniards. Here intrepid travellers can wade deeper into forest territory to see these vegetation-clad sites. Water tumbles over jasper rocks in Guyana and the Venezuela interior. The camouflage of certain moths makes them indistinguishable from the tree bark they rest on. *Estancias* with ancient trees and antique furnishings wait to welcome visitors to the pampas. There are intricate patterns to decipher on textiles, in a parrot's feathers and in the stars. When people get together to celebrate, an orchestra of rhythms pervades the air. Drummers of Bahia create a sound that is physical, inescapable. At carnival, how can you fail to enter the spirit of the samba, or, in the Andes, revel in the brashness of a brass band? By contrast, the quiet solemnity of a religious procession, with devotees in coloured robes straining under the weight of the Virgin's litter, is moving in a different way.

The Andes

Running the length of the western side of the continent is the Andean mountain chain. Avenues of volcanoes stride across the Equator and, in southern Peru, look down upon canyons deeper than any others on earth. Bleak high altitude plains, some blinding white with salt, gleam under a crystal-clear sky. This is a landscape of geysers and strata of rocks in colours you never knew existed in stone. Condors soar in the mountains, waterfowl dabble in the marshes and flamingos fly over red and green lakes. There is also the lush Andes, where the slopes dive down to the Amazon basin. Agricultural terraces cling to impossibly steep hillsides and there are acres of flowers, coffee, coca and corn. In this unstable but beautiful environment, minerals such as silver, gold, copper and nitrates have brought great riches and led to much exploitation. Traditions are kept alive by the descendants of the Incas and other cultures, mingling their beliefs and customs with those of the Spanish *conquistadors*.

Patagonia

Before the mountains disappear into the uttermost reaches of the Pacific Ocean, the Andes have a final, dramatic display. The peaks of the Chaitén Massif and the Parque Nacional Torres del Paine are a fabulous world of towers, spires, lakes and forests, a paradise for trekkers and birdwatchers. On the Pacific side of the mountains, Chilean Patagonia is wet and windy, a confusion of fjords and channels, with ancient woodlands and glaciers tumbling into the sea. On the Argentine side, the beech forests and lakes of the foothills give way to a treeless plateau, scoured by dust-laden winds for much of the year. Sheep farms huddle in valleys where there is water. Scattered communities established themselves in the 19th century, most notably the Welsh towns, where you can find tea and cakes as if brought to you straight from the Valleys of Wales.

Atlantic South America

On the Península Valdés, on the Atlantic coast of Argentine Patagonia, Southern right whales and elephant seals come to breed in the sheltered bays. Further south, penguins, orcas, dolphins and sea lions flourish in these waters. Travelling north towards Buenos Aires and Uruguay, the sea becomes warmer, the climate mild enough for resorts such as Mar del Plata and Punta del Este to burst at the seams each summer. The coast of Brazil, all 7,408 km of it, is an endless succession of beaches, in wooded coves, dotted with islands in the south, palm tree and dune-fringed in the north. You can surf, party, dune-buggy to exhaustion, or find a secluded cove to while away the hours. Great historical ports like Rio de Janeiro, Salvador and Belém have become major tourist destinations, epitomising the Brazilian mix of music, carnival and the colonial and modern.

The Caribbean North of the Amazon delta, Guyane, Suriname and Guyana are classed as Caribbean states, despite having many South American features: thick rainforest, ancient mountains and bronze-tinted rivers. Culturally, though, with their mixture of African, Amerindian, Hindu, Indonesian and European, they stand apart. North and west of the Orinoco in Venezuela, where the mainland almost touches Trinidad, is where the Caribbean truly begins, the land where Columbus made his first South American landfall. There is African influence here: listen to the drumming in some of Venezuela's coastal festivals. Colombia's Caribbean, which stretches to the Panamanian isthmus, is the inspiration for Gabriel Garcia Márquez' world of magic realism, it is the land of accordian-led *vallenato* music, the secretive Indians of the Guajira Peninsula and banana plantations. Its history of slavery and pirates can be seen in the fortifications of the beautiful city of Cartagena, Colombia, where today pelicans and frigate birds share the beaches with holiday-makers.

The Pacific deserts North of the fertile heartlands of Chile, the Pacific coast rapidly turns to desert as sea currents and mountains drive the rain far inland. The occasional shower will transform what looks like utter barrenness into a riot of colour as dormant flowers seize the moment to bloom. Some places receive no rain at all, ever. Others are covered in mist for over half the year. It sounds uninhabitable, yet prehispanic cultures thrived here. They left their monuments in sculptures etched into the surface of the desert, most famously at Nasca in Peru. Pyramid builders welcomed gods from the sea and irrigated the soil to feed great cities of adobe bricks. Irrigation today produces olives, asparagus, flowers and sugar and there is rich offshore fishing for man and seabirds. At islands such as the Ballestas, Peru, and Isla de la Plata, Ecuador, you can see much marine life, but the destination *par excellence* is the Galápagos. On the peaks of massive volcanoes, which jut into the ocean, albatross, boobies, giant tortoises and iguanas have evolved with little instinctive fear of man, a paradise for naturalists.

The heart of the continent East of the Andes, the highlands fall away to jungle and plains. Roads to the lowlands struggle over ridges and down through steep gorges to hot and humid forests. If you fly, the greenness of the Amazon Basin stretches ahead of you with no end in sight. Its secrets take patience to appreciate, for within the immensity of the trees is a world which truly confuses the senses. You can hear the songs of the birds and the chorus of the frogs and cicadas, but seeing them is another matter. The electric blue *morpho* butterfly settles and becomes as brown as dead leaves. At dawn the howler monkey bellows his wake-up call, but throws his voice so far you may not catch sight of him. Canopy walkways strung high-up in the trees reveal a lifestyle which never touches ground, while stalking in the undergrowth is the elusive jaguar, whose influence has spread through almost every religion that has come into contact with the rainforest. There are trees that strangle their neighbours, palms with a million thorns, plants that heal and vines that will blow your mind.

Waterworlds On the Amazon's perimeter are the *llanos* of the Orinoco and the Pantanal, both of which flood seasonally and where cattle and cowboys share the land with wild birds and animals. South of the jungle and the wetlands is yet more cowboy territory, the Argentine *pampas*, a vast but fertile emptiness where the *gaucho* rides, the windpumps raise water to the surface and the oven bird builds its nest, six times its own size, on the fence and telegraph posts.

Left *The Inca ceremonial centre of Sacsayhuamán, overlooking Cusco, Peru*
Below *The Devil's Throat, the thundering Iguaçu Falls, Brazil*

Left *The mysterious heads of Rapa Nui (Easter Island)*
Above *The Perito Moreno glacier, Patagonia, Argentina, which used to be one of the few advancing glaciers in the world*

Right This beautiful tree frog (Hyla Picturata) is probably eyeing up some prey in the rainforest of Ecuador
Below Butterflies puddling on a river bank in the Manu jungle reserve, southeast Peru

Above The Amazon river dolphin or Boto (Inia geoffrensis) makes his way down the tributaries of the Amazon in Bolivia
Right The crest and colour of this elusive male bird - Cock of the Rock, (Guyana) - is more attractive than his female mate

The Amazon

The Amazon can only be described with superlatives: the largest watershed in the world, the greatest area of tropical rainforest (6 million sq km), the greatest volume of water flowing into the ocean, more tributaries than any other river. From the altiplano at over 4,000 m in Peru, a mere 190 km from the Pacific, to the river's mouth it flows for 6,577 km (other estimates vary from 6,437 to 7,100 km, depending on which source is acknowledged); no bridge crosses the main course for its entire length. The Amazon Basin contains 20% of the world's plant and bird species, 10% of the mammals and an inestimable number of insects. The rivers are called blackwater or whitewater, according to the deposits they carry, and in these waters live some 2,000 species of fish, from the 3-m long arapaima, to the voracious piranha. Also in the waters are shy giant otters, caiman (alligators – a favourite night-time prey for tour boats, looking for their eyes glowing red in torch light) and two species of freshwater dolphin, the pink and the grey. The river dolphin is a creature of legend, reputed to become a suave gentleman at night who lures unwitting young girls into passionate encounters and unwanted pregnancies. In reality it is endangered and has become a symbol of the need to preserve one of the greatest integrated bio systems on the planet.

Fish & ships

The great waterway is a well-travelled route by all manner of craft, from canoes sidling up the creeks to ocean-going cargo ships navigating 3,640 km upstream, to Iquitos in Peru. Every morning, all the life of the river seems to concentrate at Belém's iron market, the Ver-o-Peso, when the giant river fish are landed and a frenzied wholesale buying ensues. On shore, every conceivable forest product is for sale, aromatic roots, medicinal plants, fruits, sweets and regional foods. Boats become a temporary city each 28-30 June at Parintins, an island 26 hours by boat downstream from Manaus, Brazil's capital of Amazônia. A hundred thousand people come to see the *Festa do Boi*, a festival celebrating the legends of the Amazon and the daily life of the fishermen and rubber tappers. In a celebrated dance contest, some 2,500 participants compete in two rival groups, the Caprichosos and the Garantidos, for the annual championship.

Jungle gems

When the Spaniard, Francisco de Orellana, floated across the South American continent via the Amazon in 1542, he and his crew brought back tales of royal highways, grand cities and ferocious women warriors (their resemblance to the Amazons of Greek myth gave the river its name). The highways and cities were probably mirages brought on by hunger and the sun on the water; the female warriors melted into the forest never to be seen again. Soon European explorers were seeking the fabulous El Dorado in what they called the `Green Hell', but the myths gradually evaporated as scientists began to uncover the Amazon's mysteries. After his journey down river in 1743, Charles Marie de la Condamine took back to France the coagulated sap of the rubber tree. This eventually opened the way for the great boom industry of the river, when rubber barons built opera houses on the river banks and sent their laundry to be cleaned in Paris. In the mid-19th century the plant-hunting of the English botanists Alfred Russel Wallace (between 1848-52) and Henry Walter Bates (between 1848-59) helped Darwin formulate the theory of evolution.

Irreplaceable loss

The Indian cultures who survive in this vast tissue of waterways have a knowledge of the environment unmatched by science. But it is under threat from road building, tree-felling and burning for unsustainable agriculture, gold prospecting and mining. Among the fears is that, before this immense plant repository is fully understood, it will have disappeared.

Adventure highs in South America

Reach the top of the highest peak in the Americas and travel down in the company of condors. Paragliding from the summit of **Aconcagua** (6,959 m) in Argentina accords the ultimate in South American views, with the Andean chain stretching far into the distance.

Jutting out from the high plateau of Venezuela's Gran Sabana, **Mount Roraima** (2,810 m) is the highest of the table-top mountain *tepuis*, and a challenging wilderness hike. The likely inspiration for Conan Doyle's *Lost World*, its strange rock formations and dense jungle seem to be from another planet.

The **Cordilleras Blanca** and **Huayhuash** in Peru are popular with climbers and trekkers alike, but hold many other possibilities. The spectacular mountains offer many new routes for ski mountaineering and the chance to bag a first descent.

Bolivia's **Madidi National Park** is one of the most biologically diverse and untouched areas of the **Amazon** basin. Rafting through steep-sided canyons in lush primary rainforest along the Río Tuichi is an exciting mix of white water action with time for wildlife spotting between rapids.

Kaieteur Falls in Guyana have been grouped with Victoria, Niagara and Iguazú for their beauty. With a sheer drop of 228 m the falls are totally unspoilt and surrounded by virgin forest teeming with wildlife. Guyana is one of the final frontiers of Latin America, with few visitors, plus a good chance of spotting some of the continent's more elusive big cats.

Kayak the emerald waters of one of the continent's top rivers. The **Futaleufú** cascades through lush, largely untouched forest on its way through Chilean Patagonia, providing some of the most exhilarating stretches of white water in the Southern Hemisphere. Rafting is another option, for those who prefer not to go solo.

Canter across the **Chilean páramo** and explore **Patagonia** riding with gauchos through Chile's **Torres del Paine National Park**. Huge granite towers, open pampas and lakes dotted with icebergs are home to a vast amount of wildlife, and travelling on horseback allows access to remote and scarcely visited areas.

Explore the **Macanao Peninsula** on Venezuela's Isla Margarita on horseback. Undeveloped hidden beaches and stretches of cactus forest make enjoyable riding country. Later take to the water and try the fast and furious sport of kite surfing. The world's fastest growing sport certainly makes for more than your average beach holiday.

Take to two wheels for thrilling descents of some of the world's highest mountains. **Chimborazo** (6,310 m) and **Cotopaxi** (5,897 m) are part of Ecuador's avenue of volcanoes and the near-perfect cones are ideal for mountain biking. Beautiful views and adrenaline rush are guaranteed.

Spending several days mountain biking through the **Urubamba Valley** in the popular Cusco region of Peru will get you away from the crowds. Cycle down to the valley through the **Maras salt pans** – still in use today – and visit the Inca sites of Ollantaytambo and Pisac. The ride from Pisac to the pass of Tres Cruces, gateway from Andes to Amazon, is sure to leave you breathless with incredible sunset views.

Left Sheer magic. Rock, ice and snow breach the cloud layer as a lone mountaineer traverses the slopes in the Cordillera Blanca, in northern Peru

Into the blue   Exploring the **reefs** and inquisitive sea life of the Galápagos Islands from underwater is a truly memorable experience. Snorkelling and diving around the islands is strictly controlled for minimum impact on wildlife, although sea lions, turtles, dolphins and numerous sea bird species seem impervious to the potential threat of man.

Head to the southern seas and explore the fjords of **Patagonia** and the **Chiloé archipelago** by sea kayak. Visit isolated communities dotted over the emerald islands or paddle the glassy waters of the fjords, where towering peaks plunge directly into the sea. The numerous albatross, penguin and petrel that patrol the waters are sometimes joined by pods of killer whales.

Diving in the waters of **Fernando de Noronha Islands**, Brazil you may be accompanied by spinner dolphins, but very few tourists. Access to the islands is restricted and their waters are a protected nature reserve. Afterwards, back on the mainland, join the local party and celebrate carnival in the colonial town of Olinda.

A wild time   For a close-up view of South America's fauna, try camping in the **Pantanal** wetlands of Brazil. This vast area is home to many spectacular birds and mammals, including macaw, jabiru stork, anteater and puma.

Nearby **Bonito** offers excellent snorkelling in beautiful underground caverns and crystal clear rivers alive with fish. Both areas should only be visited accompanied by a guide, and arriving in the Pantanal before the end of the wet season could involve wading across anaconda-inhabited marshes.

Experience a close encounter with the largest mammals on the planet, whale watching off Argentina's **Peninsula de Valdés**. Southern Right whales breed in the Patagonian waters every year, and the almost uninhabited area is home to a host of other wildlife. You may be able to get closer still – wildlife census are carried out by willing participants using sea kayaks to collect information.

The road less   One of the least travelled roads into Bolivia is the route across Paraguay's **Gran Chaco**. This
travelled   peculiar area of marshland extends over 24 million ha and has fewer than 100,000 inhabitants – many of them Mennonites. Copious supplies of water are essential for crossing the Chaco; fuel and food supplies are scarce and daytime temperatures can reach 45° C.

The Auracaria forests of **Conguillio National Park**, Chile are deserted in winter, and the slopes of **Llaima** and **Lonquimay** volcanoes provide perfect terrain for ski touring. Make fresh tracks among monkey puzzle trees, and carve turns through lava flows in landscapes that date from prehistoric times.

Go trekking in the **Gran Vilaya** region of northern Peru and you may stumble on an ancient city from the Chachapoyas culture. Large areas of the forested mountains remain unexplored, and several extensive archeological finds have been uncovered in the last few years. The cloud forest is dense and overgrown paths are difficult to find. The area is one of the remaining habitats of the Andean bear.

Brazil's **Chapada Diamantina National Park** has some beautiful trekking possibilities and the park is rich in its biodiversity. Waterfalls, hidden caves and table-top mountains abound in the extensive area. The nearby colonial town of Lençóis, established for diamond exploitation in the mid 1800s, is the perfect place to relax after several days hiking.

The bizarre scenery of the **Salar de Uyuni** can be explored on four-day jeep trips from Uyuni, Bolivia. The dazzling expanse of the world's largest salt flat and the surrounding desert are full of weird and wonderful scenery: lunar landscapes and cactus-covered islands. It's also possible by bike, but expert assistance is advised – losing your sense of direction is easy when crossing the salt.

Left *High altitude biking in Ecuador*
Below *The plunge of a lifetime: Base jumping off the Angel Falls, Venezuela*

Above *River trekking in Argentina*
Left *The monogamous lined seahorse lives in the Caribbean sea off the coast of Colombia, Venezuela and the Guianas*
Next page *Idle fishing boats, Isla Margarita, Venezuela*

Contents

Map symbols

Administration
‑‑`` International border
—‑—‑ State / Province border
□ CAPITAL CITY
○ Other town

Roads and travel
Urban
═══ Main through route
═══ Main street
═══ Minor street
═══ Pedestrianized street
→ One way street

Regional
═══ National Highway
　 including Pan-American
　 Highway
─── Paved road
─── Unpaved all weather
　 road (including
　 unpaved sections of
　 Pan-American
　 Highway)
‑‑`` Seasonal unpaved
　 road/track
·········· Footpath
—⊞ Railway with station

Sights and services
■ Sleeping
● Eating
□ Sight
▢ Building
⊪⊪⊪ Steps
⊡⊡⊡ Park, garden, stadium
⊡⊡⊡ Fortified wall
✈ Airport
🚌 Bus station
Ⓜ Metro station
✚ Hospital
Ⓜ Market
🏛 Museum
✝✝ Cathedral, church

✡ Synagogue
🕌 Mosque
⛽ Petrol station
🅟 Police station
Ⓢ Bank
✉ Post office
♪ Telephone office
@ Internet
🅑 Tourist office
⤬ Bridge
∴ Archaeological site
⛳ Golf course
❀ Viewing point
◆ National park, wildlife
　 sanctuary
▲ Camp site
⌂ Refuge
🌴 Palm trees
Ⓐ Detail map
◁ Related map

Water features
═══ River
〜 Lake, reservoir, tank
v Seasonal marshland
▦ Sand bank, beach
Ocean
𝍢 Waterfall
⛴ Ferry
⚓ Boat anchorage
⛵ Windsurfing

Topographical features
⬭ Contours (approx),
　 rock outcrop
⛰ Mountain
△ Volcano
⤳ Mountain Pass
▱ Glacier
▨ Gorge
⌇⌇ Escarpment
▦ Salt flat

Weights and measures

Weight
1 kilogram = 2.205 pounds
1 pound = 0.454 kilograms

Length
1 metre = 1.094 yards
1 yard = 0.914 metres

Capacity
1 litre = 0.220 gallons
1 gallon = 4.546 litres
1 pint = 0.863 litres

1 kilometre = 0.621 miles
1 mile = 1.609 kilometres

Essentials

2

Essentials

Planning your trip

South America is a magnificently varied part of the world and tremendously hospitable. It is a tantalizing mixture of enticing images and ambiguous press reports. Even though tourism is seen in many parts as an economic necessity, you will be welcomed for more than just the dollars you bring in. No South American country is in the top 20 earners from tourism in the world and the region is frequently omitted from lists of top destinations and world climate. This helps to retain the air of mystery and inspire a certain amount of trepidation about the place. In common with many other parts of the world, South America suffers from meteorological, geological and social uncertainties, but within that context you will find some of the most dramatic landscapes you will see anywhere, biological diversity in a dizzying range of habitats, historical monuments of strength and elegance and a deep cultural resilience. In addition, South America is not lagging behind in terms of adventure sports, nature tourism or volunteering. A negative press does persist (with justification in some areas), especially regarding drugs, crime and corruption, but no South America country poses a serious health risk or is very dangerous to visit.

Detailed planning information is given for each country in the relevant chapter

Essentials

The first section of this Handbook deals with the practicalities of how to get to the region together with what generally to expect. In the first pages of each country chapter, you will find an overview to help you start planning what to see and when to go (an important consideration for a continent stretching from the tropics almost to the South Pole). Over the years a Gringo Trail became firmly established, a network of places to which foreigners tended to gravitate for reasons of shared interests, lower prices, safety in numbers and so on. Some of these places have passed into legend, others are still going strong. New places are added as fashions change, or transport links are opened. Stating that a particular place is 'the best' for ruins, or hiking, or partying perpetuates the gringo trail mentality, which many seek to avoid. If you want the best, though, this Handbook has got it, but it also gives the alternatives. This helps local businesses to share in the tourist market and it leaves you, the traveller, free to choose.

Two to three week trips

You are unlikely to go to more than one country unless your trip involves the Guianas, or the far south or Lake District of Argentina and Chile, where crossing the border is simple and sometimes necessary. Alternatively, you can visit the north of one country and the southern part of another, for example, northern Peru and southern Ecuador.

A four week trip

In four weeks you can see much of what each country has to offer, especially one the size of Ecuador. (If including the Galápagos Islands in an Ecuador itinerary, allow eight days for this.) You could also combine Ecuador with either southern Colombia or northern Peru, travel between southern Peru and Bolivia, Colombia and Venezuela or Venezuela and Amazonian Brazil, go overland from Buenos Aires via Uruguay to southeastern Brazil, or do some thorough exploration of the cross-border possibilities between Argentina and Chile. Countries with as much variety and size as Brazil and Peru demand a month or more for an in-depth survey and it goes without saying that the more time you have, the more you can appreciate. Bolivia, too, although not as large, demands more time as its transport infrastructure is not as good as some other countries.

A two to six month trip

Two months in any of these three would provide a fantastic opportunity to see a good range of the different historical and natural attractions, with some time to relax. Two months would also allow greater scope for concentration on, say, the Andes, on a route from Bogotá to Lima, or Quito to Bolivia, with enough leeway for some side trips to the Amazon basin or the Pacific. Two months in the Southern Cone would permit travel beyond the Patagonian region of Argentina and Chile so that the north of each country, even Paraguay and southern Brazil, could be included. Much depends on how far you want to limit yourself to one particular type of terrain or cultural area. If flights permit, there is no reason why you should not spend a month in northeastern Brazil and a month in southern Chile for a real contrast, but if you want to see the continent that comes in between, other

Essentials

Specialist tour operators

Austral Tours, 20 Upper Tachbrook Street, London SW1V 1SH, T020-7233 5384, F020-7233 5385, www.latinamerica.co.uk

Destination South America, 51 Castle Street, Cirencester, Glos GL7 1QD, T01285 885333, www.destinationsouthamerica.co.uk

Discover Chile Tours, Discover Peru Tours, Discover Argentina Tours, 7325 West Flagler St, Miami, FL 33144, T305-266 5827, T1-800 826 4845, www.discoverchile.com

Dragoman, Camp Green, Debenham, Suffolk IP14 6LA, T01728-861133, www.dragoman.co.uk

eXito, 1212 Broadway Suite 910, Oakland, CA 94612, T1-800-655 4053, T510-655 4054 (worldwide), www.exito-travel.com

Exodus Travels, 9 Weir Road, London SW12 OLT, T020-8675 5550, www.exodus.co.uk

ExpeditionTrips.com, 4509 Interlake Avenue N No 179, Seattle, WA 98103-6773, T206-547 0700, F206-634 9104, www.ExpeditionTrips.com

GAP Adventures, 19 Duncan Street, Toronto, Ontario M5H 3H1, T1-800-465 5600, USA 1-800-692 5495, www.gap.ca

GoChileTours, 9300 South Dixie Highway, Suite 201, Miami, FL 33156. T1-800-228 0088, www.GoChiletours.com

Journey Latin America, 12-13 Heathfield Terrace, Chiswick, London W4 4JE, T020-8747 8315, F020-8742 1312 and 12 St Ann's Square, 2nd floor, Manchester M2 7HW, T0161-832 1441, F0161-832 1551, www.journeylatinamerica.co.uk

Ladatco, USA T800-327 6162, www.ladatco.com

Last Frontiers, Fleet Marston Farm, Aylesbury HP18 0QT, T01296-653000, www.lastfrontiers.co.uk

Latin Tours (USA), T800-254 7378, www.GoToLatinTours.com

MILA Tours, 100 S Greenleaf, Gurnee IL 60031, T1-800-367 7378, www.milatours.com

Myths and Mountains, 976 Tee Court, Incline Village, NV 89451, USA, T800- 670 6984, 775-832 5454, F775-832 4454, www.mythsandmountains.com

Reef and Rainforest Tours Ltd, 1 The Plains, Totnes, Devon TQ9 5DR, T01803-866965, F01803-865916, www.reefrainforest.co.uk

South American Experience, 47 Causton Street, London SW1P 4AT, T020-7976 5511, F020-7976 6908, www.southamericanexperience.co.uk

South American Tours, Hanauer Landstrasse 208-216, D-60314, Germany, T+49-69-405 8970, F+49-69-440432, sat.fre@t-online.de

Southtrip, Sarmiento 347, 4th floor, of 19, Buenos Aires, Argentina, T+54-11-4328 7075, www.southtrip.com

STA Travel, see Discount flight agents.

Trailfinders, 194 Kensington High Street, London W8 7RG, T020-7938 3939 and also Birmingham, T0121 236 1234, Bristol, T0117-929 9000, Manchester, T0161-839 6969, Newcastle, T0191-261 2345 and Dublin, T01-677 7888

Travelbag, 3-5 High Street, Alton, Hampshire, GU34 1TL, T0870 9001350, www.travelbag.co.uk

Travelbag Adventures, 15 Turk Street, Alton, Hants GU34 1AG, T01420-593001, F544272, www.travelbag-adventures.com

Trips Worldwide, 9 Byron Place, Clifton, Bristol BS8 1JT, T0117-311 4400, www.tripsworldwide.co.uk

Tucan, London, T020-8896 1600, london@tucantravel.com PO Box 806, Randwick, NSW 2031, Australia, T02-9326 4557, sydney@tucantravel.com www.tucantravel.com In Cusco, T51 84 241123, cuzco@tucantravel.com

Veloso Tours, 33-34 Warple Way, London W3 0RG, T020-8762 0616, F020-8762 0716, www.veloso.com

than fleetingly, your time-frame has to expand. To get a feel for the whole of South America then three to six months will begin to satisfy your needs. Then you will begin to have the flexibility to make choices from the options in each country and make the most of being able to get away from the crowds and explore off the beaten track.

Essentials

Essentials

Finding out more

Travel and safety information: South American Explorers is a non-profit educational organization staffed by volunteers and for 22 years has been the best place to go for information on South America. Highly recommended source for specialized information, member-written trip reports, maps, lectures, library resources. SAE publishes a 64-page quarterly journal, helps members plan trips and expeditions, stores gear, holds mail, hosts book exchanges, provides expert travel advice, etc. The SAE membership card is good for many discounts throughout Peru. Annual membership fee US$50 individual (US$80 couple) plus US$10 for overseas postage of its quarterly journal, *The South American Explorer*. Open Monday-Friday 0930-1700 (till 2000 on Wed), 0930-1300 Sat, and the staff are very helpful. The Clubhouses are attractive and friendly; it is not necessary to 'explore' to feel at home there. SAE will sell used equipment on consignment (donations of used equipment, unused medicines, etc are welcome). Good maps of Inca Trail (US$5) and Cordillera Huayhuash. SAE has clubhouses in Quito, Ecuador, Lima and Cusco, Peru. The SAE Headquarters are located in the USA: 126 Indian Creek Rd, Ithaca, NY, 14850, T607 277 0488, F607-277 6122, ithacaclub@saexplorers.org For information and travel tips on-line: www.saexplorers.org Official representatives in UK: Bradt Publications, 19 High Street, Chalfont St Peters, Bucks, SL9 9QE, T01753-893444, F01753-892333, Info@bradt-travelguides.com If signing up in UK please allow 4-6 weeks for receipt of membership card.

The Latin American Travel Advisor: This web site (**www.amerispan.com/lata/**) contains a varied collection of articles offering practical advice for travellers to South and Central America.

See also Ron Mader's website **www.planeta.com**, which contains masses of useful information on ecotourism, conservation, travel, news, links, language schools and articles. Information on travel and language schools is available from *AmeriSpan Unlimited*, one of several language school brokers in the USA (see under Language).

It is better to seek advice on security before you leave from your own consulate than from travel agencies. Before you travel you can contact: **British Foreign & Commonwealth Office**, Travel Advice Unit, T0117 9169000. *Footprint* is a partner in the Foreign and Commonwealth Office's *Know before you go* campaign www.fco.gov.uk/knowbeforeyougo US State Department's **Bureau of Consular Affairs**, Overseas Citizens Services, T202-647 4225, F202-647 3000, travel.state.gov/travel_warnings.html Australian **Department of Foreign Affairs**, T06-6261 3305, www.dfat.gov.au/consular/advice.html

For the lowdown on the latest Latin sounds contact *Putumayo*, www.putumayo.com

Essentials

First time visitors' guide

South America is a big place, so it's important not to be too ambitious on a first visit. Decide what type of holiday you want and research which countries offer what you are interested in. Then work out an itinerary in which the places you want to see and the distance between them coincides with the amount of time you have available.

Getting around

By plane you can visit many places and airpasses, both regional and domestic, will reduce the cost of flying, but if your travel budget does not stretch to air tickets, bus is the only economical alternative. Making long, or mountainous journeys by bus takes many hours, so you should build this factor into your itinerary. Trains are now few and far between and certainly cannot be relied upon as the main means of transport. Car hire is expensive and tiring. Having said that, those who like driving can do very well and many travellers take their own cars or motorcycles. Cycling, too, is a popular way to get around.

When to go

It all depends on latitude: the far south of Argentina and Chile is busiest in the southern hemisphere summer, December-February; in winter, June-August, it is cold and snow and

rain can disrupt transport. The further north you go the more the seasons fall into wet and dry. On the Pacific side, northern Chile, Peru, southern Ecuador are desert, hot and dry December-April, cool and foggy May-November. The rest of Ecuador is wet December-January and April-June. The Pacific coast of Colombia is one of the wettest places on earth. The Peruvian and Bolivian Andes are dry (and very cold at night) April-October, the rest of the year is rainy. The Sierras of Ecuador and Colombia are wet February-May and October-November. The Caribbean coast of the subcontinent is wet April-November. East of the Andes is wet November-April, wettest March-May in the Amazon Basin. Northeastern Brazil can be exceptionally hot and dry. Changes in world climate and periodic phenomena such as El Niño can play havoc with these general rules.

Language

The main language of the continent is Spanish, except Portuguese in Brazil, English in Guyana, Dutch in Suriname and French in Guiane. If you have no Spanish or Portuguese, learn some, either before you go, or on a course when you get there. People in the tourist trade often speak English and, to

Useful websites
Website addresses for individual countries are given in the relevant chapters, in Essentials and throughout the text. The following is a miscellaneous selection of sites, which may be of interest:

www.latinworld.com A Latin American portal.

www.terra.com Website of the telephone company which has sites for Argentina, Brazil, Colombia, Chile, Peru, Uruguay and Venezuela. Many channels, links, news, etc.

www.xlro.net/sc/e Website of Accelero Solutions which has a portal to every country.

www.gda.com *Grupo de Diarios América*: daily news headlines and links to national newspapers of Argentina, Brazil, Chile, Colombia, Ecuador, Mexico, Peru, Puerto Rico, Uruguay and Venezuela.

gibbons.best.vwh.net Cultures of the Andes and Quechua.

www.latinsynergy.org Ecotourism website with articles, travel tips, statistics, maps and links.

www.escapeartist.com/embassy1/embassy1.htm A World directory of every country's embassies, with links to their websites.

volcano.und.nodak.edu/vw.html and **www.geo.mtu.edu/volcanoes** Two websites for everything you ever wanted to know about things that erupt.

www.oanda.com Currency converter and for all your financial needs.

Language
See page 1531 for a full list of useful words and phrases
Without some knowledge of Spanish (or Portuguese) you will become very frustrated and feel helpless in many situations. English, or any other language, is absolutely useless off the beaten track. Some initial study, to get you up to a basic vocabulary of 500 words or so, and a pocket dictionary and phrase-book, are most strongly recommended: your pleasure will be doubled if you can talk to the locals. Not all the locals speak Spanish, of course; apart from Brazil's Portuguese, you will find that some Indians in the more remote highland parts of Bolivia and

a lesser degree German, French and Japanese – but you cannot guarantee it (see Language, page 28).

Money
There is no point in taking any currency other than US dollars, in cash or travellers' cheques. There is also an extensive network of ATMs for cash withdrawals with credit or debit cards.

Documents
Visa requirements vary a lot. Check with a consulate before you leave. Not every country has full South American representation, nor is every country represented in South America.

Health risks
The main health risks involve mosquitos (which transmit malaria and dengue fever); altitude sickness; tropical diseases and parasites which adequate precautions and information can help to prevent; stomach bugs; overexposure to the sun.

Safety
No entire country is a must to avoid. Colombia has most areas which should be treated with utmost caution, but also has parts which can be visited in safety. Also to be treated with respect are some isolated bits of Peru and sensitive border areas. In general, big cities are more dangerous than the countryside and in

busy places like bus stations and markets you need to keep your wits about you.

Where to stay and what to eat
There are hotels throughout the price range. The most variety will be found in cities and main tourist centres. Youth hostels may be affiliated internationally or nationally, or not at all. Availability of campsites varies from country to country. Living with families is possible, especially if you are on a language course.

Local food is generally good, with lots of regional specialities, even within countries. Stick to what is local wherever you are, you'll do much better than trying to find international food. Pizza is pretty ubiquitous, sometimes genuine, sometimes anything but. Chinese restaurants tend to offer good value. The menú del día (dish of the day, with different names in different countries) is usually served at lunchtime and is the best deal you'll find for eating. Vegetarians are best served in tourist areas, although many cities have "healthy eating" outlets.

Internet
Access to the internet gets better all the time and prices in cyber cafés are often very low. Many hotels now have email for bookings.

Essentials

Peru, and lowland Indians in Amazonia, speak only their indigenous languages, though there will usually be at least one person in each village who can speak Spanish (or Portuguese).

The basic Spanish of Hispanic America is that of southwestern Spain, with soft 'c's' and 'z's' pronounced as 's', and not as 'th' as in the other parts of Spain. There are several regional variations in pronunciation, particularly in the River Plate countries, which are noted in the Argentine section Essentials. Differences in vocabulary also exist, both between peninsular Spanish and Latin American Spanish, and between the usages of the different countries.

If you are going to Brazil, you should learn some Portuguese. Spanish is not adequate: you may be understood but you will probably not be able to understand the answers. Language classes are available at low cost in a number of centres in South America, for instance Quito. See the text for details, under Language Courses.

AmeriSpan, PO Box 40007, Philadelphia, PA 19106-0007, T215-751 1100 (worldwide), T1-800-879 6640 (USA, Canada), F215-751 1986, www.amerispan.com, offers Spanish immersion programmes, educational tours, volunteer and internship positions throughout Latin America. Language programmes are offered in Buenos Aires, Córdoba, Sucre, Santiago, Cuenca, Quito, Cusco, Montevideo, Caracas, Mérida and Puerto La Cruz. Portuguese courses can also be arranged in Maceió and Rio de Janeiro. In Ecuador, they also offer a discount card for use in hotels, restaurants and shops. *LanguagesAbroad.com*, 317 Adelaide St West, Suite 900, Toronto, Ontario, Canada, M5V 1P9, T416-925 2112, toll free 1-800-219 9924, F416-925 5990, www.languagesabroad.com, offers Spanish and Portuguese programmes in every South American country except Colombia and Paraguay. They also have language immersion courses throughout the world. Similarly, *Cactus*, 9 Foundry St, Brighton BN1 4AT, T01273-687697, www.cactuslanguage.com For a list of Spanish schools, see www.planeta.com/ecotravel/schools/schoolist.html

Essentials

 ## *Spanish and Portuguese pronounciation*

Spanish

*The stress in a Spanish word conforms to one of three rules: 1) if the word ends in a vowel, or in **n** or **s**, the accent falls on the penultimate syllable (ventana, ventanas); 2) if the word ends in a consonant other than **n** or **s**, the accent falls on the last syllable (hablar); 3) if the word is to be stressed on a syllable contrary to either of the above rules, the acute accent on the relevant vowel indicates where the stress is to be placed (pantal**ó**n, met**á**fora). Note that adverbs such as cuando, 'when', take an accent when used interrogatively: ¿cuándo?, 'when?'*

*Vowels: **a** not quite as short as in English 'cat'; **e** as in English 'pay', but shorter in a syllable ending in a consonant; **i** as in English 'seek'; **o** as in English 'shop', but more like 'pope' when the vowel ends a syllable; **u** as in English 'food'; after 'q' and in 'gue', 'gui', u is unpronounced; in 'güe' and 'güi' it is pronounced; **y** when a vowel, pronounced like 'i'; when a semiconsonant or consonant, it is pronounced like English 'yes'; **ai**, **ay** as in English 'ride'; **ei**, **ey** as in English 'they'; **oi**, **oy** as in English 'toy'*

*Unless listed below **consonants** can be pronounced in Spanish as they are in English. **b**, **v** their sound is interchangeable and is a cross between the English 'b' and 'v', except at the beginning of a word or after 'm' or 'n' when it is like English 'b'; **c** like English 'k', except before 'e' or 'i' when it is as the 's' in English 'sip'; **g** before 'e' and 'i' it is the same as j; **h** when on its own, never pronounced; **j** as the 'ch' in the Scottish 'loch'; **ll** as the 'g' in English 'beige'; sometimes as the 'lli' in 'million'; **ñ** as the 'ni' in English 'onion'; **rr** trilled much more strongly than in English;*

*x depending on its location, pronounced as in English 'fox', or 'sip', or like 'gs'; **z** as the 's' in English 'sip'.*

Portuguese

*There is no standard Portuguese and there are many differences between the Portuguese of Portugal and the Portuguese of Brazil. If learning Portuguese before you go, get lessons with a Brazilian, or from a language course which teaches Brazilian Portuguese. Within Brazil itself, there are variations in pronunciation, intonation, phraseology and slang. This makes for great richness and for the possibility of great enjoyment in the language. Describing the complex Portuguese vocalic system is best left to the experts; it would take up too much space here. A couple of points which the newcomer to the language will spot immediately however are: the use of the til (~) over **a** and **o**. This makes the vowel a nasal vowel. Vowels also become nasal when a word ends in **m** or **ns**, when a vowel is followed by **m** + consonant, or by **n** + consonant. Another important point of spelling is that words ending in **i** or **u** are accented on the last syllable, though unlike Spanish no accent is used there. This is especially important in place names: Buriti, Guarapari, Caxambu, Iguaçu. Note also the use of **ç**, which changes the pronunciation of **c** from hard [k] to soft [s].*

*NB In conversation, most people refer to **you** as "você", although in the south and in Pará "tu" is more common. To be more polite, use "O senhor/A Senhora". For **us**, "a gente" (people, folks) is very common when it includes **you** too.*

Disabled travellers — In most of South America, facilities for the disabled are severely lacking. For those in wheelchairs, ramps and toilet access are limited to some of the more upmarket, or most recently-built hotels. Pavements are often in a poor state of repair or crowded with street vendors. Most archaeological sites, even Machu Picchu, have little or no wheelchair access. Visually or hearing-impaired travellers are similarly poorly catered for, but there are experienced guides in some places who can provide individual attention. There are also travel companies outside South America who specialize in holidays which are tailor-made for the individual's level of disability. Some moves are being made to improve the situation. In Chile all new public buildings are supposed to provide access for the disabled by law; *PromPerú* has initiated a programme to provide facilities at airports, tourist sites, etc; Quito's trolley buses are supposed to have wheelchairaccess, but they are often too crowded to make this practical. While disabled South Americans have to rely on others to get around, foreigners will find that people are generally very helpful. A useful website is **Global Access - Disabled Travel Network**, www.geocities.com/Paris/1502

Gay & lesbian travellers Much of Latin America is quite intolerant of homosexuality. Rural areas tend to be more conservative in these matters than cities. It is therefore wise to respect this and avoid provoking a reaction. For the gay or lesbian traveller, however, certain cities have active communities and there are local and international organizations which can provide information. The best centres are Buenos Aires (Argentina), Santiago (Chile), Rio de Janeiro and other cities in Brazil, Lima (Peru) and Quito (Ecuador). Helpful websites include, **general**: www.bluway.com www.damron.com www.gayscape.com www.outandabout.com **Arg entina**: www.mundogay.com (in Spanish) **Brazil**: riogayguide.com (lots of information) **Chile**: www.gaychile.com (very useful, in Spanish, English, French and German) **Ecuador**: GALASouthamerica.com (in English) **Peru**: gaylimape.tripod.com (good site, in English, lots of links and information) www.deambiente.com and www.gayperu.com/gp.htm (both in Spanish) **Uruguay**: www.hartas.com/mprohib/index.html (site of Mujeres Prohibidas, Uruguayan lesbian organization, in Spanish, interesting articles on gay issues).

Student travellers Student cards must carry a photograph if they are to be of any use in Latin America for discounts. If you are in full-time education you will be entitled to an International Student Identity Card, which is distributed by student travel offices and travel agencies in 77 countries. The ISIC gives you special prices on all forms of transport such as air, sea, rail, and access to a variety of other concessions and services. If you need to find the location of your nearest ISIC office contact: The **ISIC Association**, Herengracht 479, 1017 BS Amsterdam, Holland T+31-20-421 2800, F+31-20-421 2810, www.istc.org

Travelling with children
Visit www.babygoes2.com

People contemplating overland travel in South America with children should remember that a lot of time can be spent waiting for public transport. On bus journeys, if the children are good at amusing themselves, or can readily sleep while travelling, the problems can be considerably lessened. If your child is of an early reading age, take reading material with you as it is difficult, and expensive to find. A bag of, say 30 pieces, of *Duplo* or *Lego* can keep young children occupied for hours, while a *GameBoy* is ideal for older children. Travel on trains, while not as fast or at times as comfortable as buses, allows more scope for moving about. Some trains provide tables between seats, so that games can be played. Beware of doors left open for ventilation especially if air-conditioning is not working. If hiring a car, check that it has rear seat belts.

Fares On all long-distance buses you pay for each seat, and there are no half-fares if the children occupy a seat each. For shorter trips it is cheaper, if less comfortable, to seat small children on your knee. Often there are spare seats which children can occupy after tickets have been collected. In city and local excursion buses, small children generally do not pay a fare, but are not entitled to a seat when paying customers are standing. On sightseeing tours you should *always* bargain for a family rate – often children can go free. (In trains, reductions for children are general, but not universal.)

All civil airlines charge half for children under 12, but some military services don't have half-fares, or have younger age limits. Children's fares on Lloyd Aéreo Boliviano are considerably more than half, and there is only a 7 kg baggage allowance. (LAB also checks children's ages on passports.) Note that a child travelling free on a long excursion is not always covered by the operator's travel insurance; it is advisable to pay a small premium to arrange cover.

Food can be a problem if the children are not adaptable. It is easier to take food such as biscuits, drinks and bread with you on longer trips than to rely on meal stops where the food may not be to taste. Avocados are safe and nutritious; they can be fed to babies as young as six months and most older children like them. A small immersion heater and jug for making hot drinks is invaluable, but remember that electric current varies. Try and get a dual-voltage one (110v and 220v).

Hotels In all hotels, try to negotiate family rates. If charges are per person, always insist that two children will occupy one bed only, therefore counting as one tariff. If rates are per bed, the same applies. In either case you can almost always get a reduced rate at cheaper hotels. Occasionally when travelling with a child you will be refused a room in a hotel that is 'unsuitable'. On river boat trips, unless you have very large hammocks, it may be more comfortable and cost effective to hire a two-berth cabin for two adults and a child. (In restaurants, you can normally buy children's helpings, or divide one full-size helping between two children.)

For health matters, see page 63. Nappies/diapers: buy them at every available opportunity, in case of short supply later on.

Travel with children can bring you into closer contact with South American families and, generally, presents no special problems – in fact the path is often smoother for family groups. Officials tend to be more amenable where children are concerned and they are pleased if your child knows a little Spanish or Portuguese. Moreover, thieves and pickpockets seem to have some traditional respect for families, and may leave you alone because of it!

Many women travel alone or in pairs in South America without undue difficulty. Attitudes and courtesy towards western women, especially those on their own, vary from country to country. The following hints have mainly been supplied by women, but most apply to any single traveller. First time exposure to countries where sections of the population live in extreme poverty or squalor and may even be starving can cause odd psychological reactions in visitors. So can the exceptional curiosity extended to visitors, especially women. Simply be prepared for this and try not to over-react. When you set out, err on the side of caution until your instincts have adjusted to the customs of a new culture. If, as a single woman, you can befriend a local woman, you will learn much more about the country you are visiting. Unless actively avoiding foreigners like yourself, don't go too far from the beaten track; there is a very definite 'gringo trail' which you can join, or follow, if seeking company. This can be helpful when looking for safe accommodation, especially if arriving after dark (which is best avoided). Remember that for a single woman a taxi at night can be as dangerous as wandering around on her own. At borders dress as smartly as possible. Travelling by train is a good way to meet locals, but buses are much easier for a person alone; on major routes your seat is often reserved and your luggage can usually be locked in the hold. It is easier for men to take the friendliness of locals at face value; women may be subject to much unwanted attention. To help minimize this, do not wear suggestive clothing and, advises Alex Rossi of Jawa Timur, Indonesia, do not flirt. By wearing a wedding ring, carrying a photograph of your 'husband' and 'children', and saying that your 'husband' is close at hand, you may dissuade an aspiring suitor. When asked how long you are travelling, say only for a short time because a long journey may give the impression that you are wealthy (even if you are not). If politeness fails, do not feel bad about showing offence and departing. When accepting a social invitation, make sure that someone knows the address and the time you left. Ask if you can bring a friend (even if you do not intend to do so). A good rule is always to act with confidence, as though you know where you are going, even if you do not. Someone who looks lost is more likely to attract unwanted attention. Do not disclose to strangers where you are staying.

If you are seeking more than casual work in any South American country, there will be income tax implications which you should research at the relevant consulate before leaving home. For information on voluntary work and working abroad, try: **www.workingabroad.com** (2nd floor Office Suite, 59 Lansdowne Rd, Hove, East Sussex, BN3 1FL, T01273-711406); **www.i-to-i.com** (One Cottage Road, Headingley, Leeds, LS6 4DD, T0870-333 2332); **www.questoverseas.org**; **www.raleighinternational.org**; **www.projecttrust.org.uk**; **www.gapyear.com**; **www.gapyearjobs.co.uk**; **www.vacationwork.co.uk** Also contact *South American Explorers*, see above. If you are looking for a paying job, visit the *International Career and Employment Center*, www.internationaljobs.org

Women travellers

Working in South America

Essentials

Before you travel

Getting in
*See the Essentials
section of each country
for particular details*

Essentials

Documents Passports: Latin Americans, especially officials, are very document-minded. You should always carry your passport in a safe place about your person, or if not going far, leave it in the hotel safe. If staying in a country for several weeks, it is worth while registering at your embassy or consulate. Then, if your passport is stolen, the process of replacing it is simplified and speeded up. Keeping photocopies of essential documents, including your flight ticket, and some additional passport-sized photographs, is recommended. An alternative, if you have an email account, is to send yourself before you leave home a message containing all important details, addresses, etc which you can access in an emergency.

It is your responsibility to ensure that your passport is stamped in and out when you cross borders. The absence of entry and exit stamps can cause serious difficulties: seek out the proper immigration offices if the stamping process is not carried out as you cross. Also, do not lose your entry card; replacing one causes a lot of trouble, and possibly expense. Citizens of countries which oblige visitors to have a visa can expect more delays and problems at border crossings. If planning to study in Latin America for a long period, make every effort to get a student visa in advance.

Identity and Membership Cards Membership cards of British, European and US motoring organizations can be useful for discounts off items such as hotel charges, car rentals, maps and towing charges. Business people should carry a good supply of visiting cards, which are essential for good business relations in Latin America. Identity, membership or business cards in Spanish or Portuguese (or a translation) and an official letter of introduction in Spanish or Portuguese are also useful. See above for Student cards.

Everybody has their own preferences, but listed here are those most often mentioned. These include an inflatable travel pillow for neck support and strong shoes (remember that footwear over 9½ English size, or 42 European size, is difficult to find in South America). You should also take waterproof clothing and waterproof treatment for leather footwear and wax earplugs, which are vital for those long bus trips or in noisy hotels. Also important are rubber-thong Japanese-type sandals, which can be worn in showers to avoid athlete's foot, and a sheet sleeping-bag to avoid sleeping on filthy sheets in cheap hotels.

What to take
A good principle is to take half the clothes, and twice the money, that you think you will need

Other useful things to take with you include: a clothes line, a nailbrush, a vacuum flask, a water bottle, a universal bath- and basin-plug of the flanged type that will fit any waste-pipe (or improvise one from a sheet of thick rubber), string, electrical insulating tape, a Swiss Army knife, an alarm clock for those early-morning bus departures, candles (for frequent power cuts), a torch/flashlight, pocket mirror, pocket calculator, an adaptor, a padlock for the doors of the cheapest hotels (or for tent zip if camping), a small first aid kit, sun hat, contraceptives, and a small sewing kit. The most security-conscious may also wish to include a length of chain and padlock for securing luggage to bed or bus/train seat, and a lockable canvas cover for your rucksack.

A list of useful medicines and health-related items is given in the Health section. To these might be added some lip salve with sun protection, waterless soap and pre-moistened wipes (such as *Wet Ones*). Always carry toilet paper, which is especially important on long bus trips. Contact lens wearers: should note that lens solution can be difficult to find in Bolivia and Peru. Ask for it in a chemist/pharmacy, rather than an optician's.

Money

The three main ways of keeping in funds while travelling are with US dollars cash, US dollars travellers' cheques (TCs), or credit cards/current account cards.

Sterling and other currencies are not recommended. Though the risk of loss is greater, the chief benefit of US dollar notes is that better rates and lower commissions can usually be obtained for them. In many countries, US dollar notes are only accepted if they are in excellent, if not perfect condition (likewise, do not accept local currency notes in poor condition). Take and accept 'new style' US dollar bills (US$20, 50, 100), with centre thread, microprinting and watermarks, as there are countless, forged 'old style' notes in circulation. Low-value US dollar bills should be carried for changing into local currency if arriving in a country when banks or *casas de cambio* are closed (US$5 or US$10 bills). They are very useful for shopping: shopkeepers and exchange shops (*casas de cambio*) tend to give better exchange rates than hotels or banks (but see below). The better hotels will normally change travellers' cheques for their guests (often at a rather poor rate), but if you are travelling on the cheap it is essential to keep in funds; at weekends and on public holidays never run out of local currency. Take plenty of local currency, in small denominations, when making trips into the interior.

Cash
See each country's Money section in Essentials for exchange rates as at July 2002
Visa ATM locations: www.internationalvisa.com; MasterCard: www.mastercard.com; for American Express information: www.americanexpress.com; for Western Union agents: www.westernunion.com

These are convenient but they attract thieves (though refunds can of course be arranged) and you will find that they are more difficult than dollar bills to change in small towns (denominations of US$50 and US$100 are preferable, though one does need a few of US$20). American Express, Visa or Thomas Cook US$ travellers' cheques are recommended, but less commission is often charged on Citibank travellers' cheques, if they are cashed at Latin American branches of that bank. It is a good idea to take two kinds of cheque: if large numbers of one kind have recently been forged or stolen, making people suspicious, it is unlikely to have happened simultaneously with the other kind. Several banks charge a high fixed commission for changing travellers' cheques because they don't really want to be bothered. Exchange houses (*casas de cambio*) are usually much better for this service. Some establishments may ask to see the customer's record of purchase before accepting.

Travellers' cheques

Plastic It is straightfoward to obtain a cash advance against a credit card and, in the text, we give the names of banks that do this.

Credit cards

Cost of travelling

The cost in US$, per person per day, for two people travelling together on an economy, but not the most basic, budget in 2002 was approximately:

Argentina	35	Chile	40	Paraguay	50	Uruguay	50
Bolivia	25	Colombia	25	Peru	35	Venezuela	40
Brazil	40	Ecuador	25				

In the Guianas, allow perhaps US$25 per person per day for Guyana but this will substantially increase if you venture into the interior. Suriname is impossible to estimate given the problems of its exchange rate. Guyane is French and expensive.

Emergency contact numbers for credit card loss or theft are given in the relevant country's Essentials section

There are two international **ATM** (automatic telling machine) acceptance systems, Plus and Cirrus. Many issuers of debit and credit cards are linked to one, or both. Many banks are linked usually to one, but coverage is not uniform throughout the continent (eg Cirrus is less common in Brazil than Plus) so it may be wise to take two cards. Frequently, the rates of exchange on ATM withdrawals are the best available. Find out before you leave what ATM coverage there is in the countries you will visit and what international 'functionality' your card has. Check if your bank or credit card company imposes handling charges. Obviously you must ensure that the account to which your debit card refers contains sufficient funds. With a credit card, obtain a credit limit sufficient for your needs, or pay money in to put the account in credit. If travelling for a long time, consider a direct debit to clear your account regularly. Do not rely on one card, in case of loss. If you do lose a card, immediately contact the 24-hour helpline of the issuer in your home country (keep this number in a safe place).

For purchases, credit cards of the Visa and MasterCard (Eurocard, Access) groups, American Express (Amex), Carte Blanche and Diners Club can be used. Credit card transactions are normally at an officially recognized rate of exchange; they are often subject to tax. For credit card security, insist that imprints are made in your presence and that any imprints incorrectly completed should be torn into tiny pieces. Also destroy the carbon papers after the form is completed (signatures can be copied from them).

Money can be transferred between banks. A recommended method is, before leaving, to find out which local bank is correspondent to your bank at home, then when you need funds, telex your own bank and ask them to telex the money to the local bank (confirming by fax). Give exact information to your bank of the routing number of the receiving bank. Cash in dollars, local currency depending on the country, can be received within 48 banking hours.

Exchange

If departing by air, do not leave yourself too little money to pay the airport departure tax, which is never waived

Most of the countries described in this book have freedom of exchange between US dollars and the local currency (in Ecuador the local currency is the US dollar). A few have a parallel rate of exchange, which is not always better than the official rate. Local conditions are described in the relevant chapters. Changing money on the street: if possible, do not do so alone. If unsure of the currency of the country you are about to enter, check rates with more than one changer at the border, or ask locals or departing travellers.

Whenever you leave a country, sell any local currency before leaving, because the further away you get, the less the value of a country's money.

Americans should know that if they run out of funds they can usually expect no help from the US Embassy or Consul other than a referral to some welfare organization. Find out before you go precisely what services and assistance your embassy or consulate can provide if you find yourself in difficulties.

Cost of travelling

A limited budget will restrict how much ground you can cover because, even if you eke our your céntimos, you will not be able to go too far because of the costs of getting back to where your homeward flight leaves from. Also bear in mind that the cost of living varies from country to country. Your dollars will go further in Ecuador or Bolivia than in Brazil, Paraguay or Uruguay. These cheaper countries are therefore good places to end your journey as lower prices will be better suited to dwindling travel funds. Costs for the traveller (but not the locals) have fallen dramatically in Argentina after the early-2002 devaluation, so it now joins those countries where an economy-budget traveller can expect to spend US$30-40 per day (see box, Cost of travelling). If you are happy to count every penny every night and pay as you go, your funds will last longer than if you indulge in the occasional night of luxury, or wish to spend a few days in a jungle lodge. Prebooking often means you will spend more because the security of knowing you have a bed reserved for the night must be weighed against the freedom to shop around. Usually, you do not have to book ahead (although it is comforting to have your night of arrival in the country arranged), except at major holiday times in popular resorts or for important festivals. It is wise to reserve flights in advance at all times (and reconfirm bookings) and to reserve bus seats in advance when a festival is in the offing. Also allow for price increases in high season (each chapter indicates when this may be) and around public holidays.

Getting there

Air All the main airlines flying to each country are given in the 'Essentials' sections. There is no standard baggage allowance to Latin America. If you fly via the USA you are allowed two pieces of luggage up to 32 kg per case. Brazil has adopted this system, but it is not uniformly applied by all airlines. On flights from Europe there is a weight allowance of 20 or 23 kg, although some carriers out of Europe use the two-piece system, but may not apply it in both directions. The two-piece system is gaining wider acceptance, but it is always best to check in advance. Excess baggage charges can be high. The weight limits for internal flights are often lower; best to enquire beforehand.

Prices & discounts It is possible to fly to most South American countries direct from France, Spain or UK. Main US gateways (also for connections from Europe) are Miami, Houston, Dallas, Atlanta and New York. On the west coast, Los Angeles has flights to several South American cities. If buying airline tickets routed through the USA, check that US taxes are included in the price. From the UK Caracas and Rio are generally the cheapest destinations (US$575-700 in low season). Lima is good value (US$600-800) except in July and at Christmas. From the USA, Lima, Caracas and Bogotá are generally the cheapest destinations (around US$300-450). From Australia, Buenos Aires offers the best value all year (US$950-1,000).

Most airlines offer discounted fares on scheduled flights through agencies who specialize in this type of fare. For a list of these agencies see box page 38). The very busy seasons are 7 December-15 January and 10 July-10 September. If you intend travelling during those times, book as far ahead as possible. Between February- May and September-November special offers may be available.

Other fares on scheduled services fall into three groups: **a) Excursion (return) fares** with restricted validity. Some carriers permit a change of dates on payment of a fee. **b) Yearly fares** These may be bought on a one-way or return basis. Some airlines require a specified return date, changeable upon payment of a fee. To leave the return completely open is possible for an extra fee. **c) Student (or under 26) fares** Do not assume that student tickets are the cheapest;

Essentials

Discount flight agents

In the UK and Ireland: **STA Travel**, 86 Old Brompton Road, London SW7 3LH, T0870 160 6070, www.statravel.co.uk They have other branches in London, as well as in Brighton, Bristol, Cambridge, Leeds, Manchester, Newcastle-Upon-Tyne and Oxford and on many University campuses. Specialists in low-cost student/youth flights and tours, also good for student IDs and insurance. **Trailfinders**, 194 Kensington High Street, London W8 7RG, T020-7938-3939. They also have other branches in London, as well as in Birmingham, Bristol, Cambridge, Glasgow, Manchester, Newcastle, Dublin and Belfast.

In North America: **Air Brokers International**, 323 Geary Street, Suite 411, San Francisco, CA94102, T01-800-883-3273, www.airbrokers.com Consolidator and specialist on RTW and Circle Pacific tickets. **Council Travel**, there are retail outlets throughout the country but in New York you will find this company at 205 E 42nd Street, New York, NY 10017, 254 Greene Street, NY 10003 and 895 Amsterdam Av, NY 10025. Otherwise call T1-800-2COUNCIL, or check out www.counciltravel.com A student/ budget agency with branches in many other US cities. **Discount Airfares Worldwide On-Line**, www.etn.nl/discount.htm A hub of consolidator and discount agent links. **International Travel Network/Airlines of the Web**, www.itn.net/airlines Online air travel information and reservations. **STA Travel**, 5900 Wiltshire Boulevard, Suite 2110, Los Angeles, CA 90036, T1-800-781-4040,

www.sta-travel.com Also branches in New York, San Francisco, Boston, Miami, Chicago, Seattle and Washington DC. **Travel CUTS**, 187 College Street, Toronto, ON M5T 1P7, T1-800-954-2666, www.travelcuts.com Specialist in student discount fares, IDs and other travel services. Branches in other Canadian cities as well as California, USA. **Travelocity**, www.travelocity.com Online consolidator.

In Australia and New Zealand: **Flight Centre**, with offices throughout Australia and other countries. In Australia call T133-133 or log on to www.flightcentre.com.au **STA Travel**, T1300-360960, www.statravel.com.au 702 Harris Street, Ultimo, Sydney, and 256 Flinders Street, Melbourne. In NZ: 10 High Street, Auckland, T09-366-6673. Also in major towns and university campuses. **Travel.com.au**, 76 Clarence Street, Sydney NSW Australia, T02-9249-5232, outside Sydney: T1300-130-482, www.travel.com.au **NB** Using the web for booking flights, hotels and other services directly is becoming an increasingly popular way of making holiday reservations. You can make some good deals this way. Be aware, though, that cutting out the travel agents is denying yourself the experience that they can give, not just in terms of the best flights to suit your itinerary, but also advice on documents, insurance and other matters before you set out, safety, routes, lodging and times of year to travel. A reputable agent will also be bonded to give you some protection if arrangements collapse while you are travelling.

though they are often very flexible, they are usually more expensive than a) or b) above. Some airlines are flexible on the age limit, others strict. One way and returns available. For people intending to travel a linear route and return from a different point from that at which they entered, there are 'Open Jaws' fares, which are available on student, yearly, or excursion fares.

If you buy discounted air tickets *always* check the reservation with the airline concerned to make sure the flight still exists. Also remember the IATA airlines' schedules change in March and October each year, so if you're going to be away a long time it's best to leave return flight coupons open. In addition, check whether you are entitled to any refund or re-issued ticket if you lose, or have stolen, a discounted air ticket. Some airlines require the repurchase of a ticket before you can apply for a refund, which will not be given until after the validity of the original ticket has expired. The *Iberia* group and *Air France*, for example, operate this costly system. Travel insurance in some cases covers lost tickets.

Air passes The *Mercosur Airpass* which applies to Brazil, Argentina, Chile, Uruguay and Paraguay, using several local carriers, is available to any passenger with a return ticket to a participating country. It must be bought in conjunction with an international flight; minimum stay is seven days,

Essentials

Essentials

www.journeylatinamerica.co.uk GO

JOURNEY
LATIN
AMERICA

BRITAIN'S FOREMOST LATIN AMERICAN SPECIALIST
20 YEARS
SINCE 1980

Flights

Escorted Groups

Tailor-made Tours

Cruises

Insurance

Spanish Courses

Active Adventure

Search: Favourites ▶ ▲

Amazon
Angel Falls
Atacama
Antarctica
Galapagos
Iguassu
Machu Picchu
Pantanal
Patagonia
Rio ▼

Rafting
Hiking
Kayaking
Biking
Riding

Search: Regions ▶ ▲

Argentina
Bolivia
Brazil
Caribbean ▶
Central America ▶
Chile
Colombia
Ecuador
Mexico
Peru
Uruguay
Venezuela ▼

FULLY
BONDED

ATOL
ABTA
IATA
ATOL
2828

JOURNEY
LATIN
AMERICA

12-13 Heathfield
Terrace Chiswick
LONDON
W4 4JE
020 8747 8315
Fax 020 8742 1312

12 St. Ann's Square
(2nd floor)
MANCHESTER
M2 7HW
0161 832 1441
Fax 0161 832 1551

Essentials

Essentials

maximum 30, at least two countries must be visited. Maximum number of coupons is eight, the maximum number of stops per country is two. Fares are calculated on a mileage basis and range from US$225 to US$870. The All America Airpass, a multi-carrier, multi-country facility put together by Hahn Air of Germany, is built up from individual sectors at specially negotiated rates which can be bought just as a single journey, or a multi-sector trip, as required and according to cost. It is valid for 90 days from the use of the first coupon. *Grupo Taca* and *Copa* both offer airpasses linking South, Central and North America and have an attractive programme of sector fares. See the respective country sections for airpasses operated by national airlines.

Sea Travelling as a passenger on a cargo ship to South America is not a cheap way to go, but if you have the time and want a bit of luxury, it makes a great alternative to flying. There has also been an upsurge of interest after 11 September 2001. There are sailings from Europe to the Caribbean, east and west coasts of South America. Likewise, you can sail from US ports to east and west coast South America. In the main, passage is round trip only.

Useful contacts for advice and tickets: Andy Whitehouse at **Strand Voyages**, Charing Cross Shopping Concourse, The Strand, London WC2N 4HZ, T020-7836 6363, F020-7497 0078, www.strandtravel.co.uk *Strand Voyages* are booking agents for all routes, and are the sole agents for Fyffes' banana boats to Guyana and Suriname. **Cargo Ship Voyages Ltd**, Hemley, Woodbridge, Suffolk IP12 4QF, T/F01473-736265. **The Cruise People**, 88 York Street, London W1H 1QT, T020-7723 2450 (reservations 0800-526313), cruisepeople@pipex.com In Europe, **SGV Reisezentrum Weggis** (Mr Urs Steiner), Seestrasse 7, CH-6353, Weggis, Switzerland, T041-390 1133, u.steiner@reisezentrum-weggis.ch In the USA, **Freighter World Cruises**, 180 South Lake Ave, Pasadena, CA 91101, T626-449 3106, www.freighterworld.com **Travltips Cruise and Freighter Travel Association**, PO Box 580188, Flushing, NY 11358, T800-8728584, www.travltips.com On the web www.contship.de, or the *Internet Guide to Freighter Travel*, www.geocities.com/freighterman.geo/mainmenu.html Do not try to get a passage on a non-passenger carrying cargo ship to South America from a European port; it is not possible.

Touching down

Appearance There is a natural prejudice in all countries against travellers who ignore personal hygiene and have a generally dirty and unkempt appearance. Most Latin Americans, if they can afford it, devote great care to their clothes and appearance; it is appreciated if visitors do likewise. Buying clothing locally can help you to look less like a tourist.

Courtesy Remember that politeness – even a little ceremoniousness – is much appreciated. Men should always remove any headgear and say "con permiso" ("com licença" in Brazil) when entering offices, and be prepared to shake hands (this is much more common in Latin America than in Europe or North America); always say "Buenos días" (until midday) or "Buenas tardes" ("Bom dia" or "Boa tarde" in Brazil) and wait for a reply before proceeding further. Always remember that the traveller from abroad has enjoyed greater advantages in life than most Latin American minor officials and should be friendly and courteous in consequence. Never be impatient. Do not criticize situations in public: the officials may know more English than you think and they can certainly interpret gestures and facial expressions. Be judicious about discussing politics with strangers. Politeness can be a liability, however, in some situations; most Latin Americans are disorderly queuers. In commercial transactions (such as buying a meal and goods in a shop), politeness should be accompanied by firmness, and always ask the price first (arguing about money in a foreign language can be very difficult).

Politeness should also be extended to street traders; saying "No, gracias" or "Não, obrigado/a" with a smile is better than an arrogant dismissal. Whether you give money to beggars is a personal matter, but your decision should be influenced by whether a person is begging out of need or trying to cash in on the tourist trail. In the former case, local people giving may provide an indication. Giving money to children is a separate issue, upon which most agree: don't do it. There are occasions where giving food in a restaurant may be appropriate, but first inform yourself of local practice.

Moira Chubb, from New Zealand, suggests that if you are a guest and are offered food that arouses your suspicions, the only courteous way out is to feign an allergy or a stomach ailment. If worried about the purity of ice for drinks, ask for a beer.

Photography Pre-paid Kodak slide film cannot be developed in South America; it is also very hard to find. Kodachrome is almost impossible to buy. Some travellers (but not all) have advised against mailing exposed films home; either take them with you, or have them developed, but not printed, once you have checked the laboratory's quality. Note that postal authorities may use less sensitive equipment for X-ray screening than the airports do. Modern controlled X-ray machines are supposed to be safe for any speed of film, but it is worth trying to avoid X-ray as the doses are cumulative. Many airport officials will allow film to be passed outside X-ray arches; they may also hand-check a suitcase with a large quantity of film if asked politely. Western camera shops sell double lead-lined bags which will protect new and used film from x-rays. Black and white is a problem. Often it is shoddily machine-processed and the negatives are ruined. Ask the store if you can see an example of their laboratory's work and if they hand-develop.

Always ask people before taking pics or videos

Exposed film can be protected in humid areas by putting it in a balloon and tying a knot. Similarly keeping your camera in a plastic bag may reduce the effects of humidity. Humidity absorbing sachets can also be bought.

Responsible tourism

Spend money on locally produced (rather than imported) goods and services and use common sense when bargaining – your few dollars saved may be a week's salary to others. Protect wildlife and other natural resources – don't buy souvenirs or goods made from wildlife unless they are clearly sustainably produced and are not protected under CITES legislation (CITES controls trade in endangered species)

Essentials

Travel to the furthest corners of the globe is now commonplace and the mass movement of people for leisure and business is a major source of foreign exchange and economic development in many parts of South America. In some regions (eg the Galápagos Islands and Machu Picchu) it is probably the most significant economic activity.

The benefits of international travel are self-evident for both hosts and travellers: employment, increased understanding of different cultures, business and leisure opportunities. At the same time there is clearly a downside to the industry. Where visitor pressure is high and/or poorly regulated, adverse impacts to society and the natural environment may be apparent. Paradoxically, this is as true in undeveloped and pristine areas (where culture and the natural environment are less 'prepared' for even small numbers of visitors) as in major resort destinations.

The travel industry is growing rapidly and increasingly the impacts of this supposedly 'smokeless' industry are becoming apparent. These impacts can seem remote and unrelated to an individual trip or holiday (eg air travel is clearly implicated in global warming and damage to the ozone layer, resort location and construction can destroy natural habitats and restrict traditional rights and activities) but, individual choice and awareness can make a difference in many instances (see box), and collectively, travellers are having a significant effect in shaping a more responsible and sustainable industry.

In an attempt to promote awareness of and credibility for responsible tourism, organizations such as **Green Globe** (greenglobe@compuserve.com, T44-20-7930 8333) and the **Centre for Environmentally Sustainable Tourism** (CERT) (T44-1268-795772) now offer advice on destinations and sites that have achieved certain commitments to conservation and sustainable development. Generally these are larger mainstream destinations and resorts but they are still a useful guide and increasingly aim to provide information on smaller operations.

Of course travel can have beneficial impacts and this is something to which every traveller can contribute. Many National Parks are part funded by receipts from visitors. Similarly, travellers can promote patronage and protection of important archaeological sites and heritage through their interest and contributions via entrance and performance fees. They can also support small-scale enterprises by staying in locally run hotels and hostels, eating in local restaurants and by purchasing local goods, supplies and arts and crafts. In fact, since the Responsible Travel section was first introduced in the South American Handbook in 1992 there has been a phenomenal growth in *tourism that promotes and supports the conservation of natural environments and is also fair and equitable to local communities*. This "ecotourism" segment is probably the fastest growing sector of the travel industry and provides a vast and growing range of destinations and activities in South America. For example, in Ecuador, award winning ecotourism developments can be found in the Napo river catchment (T593-6-887072, fesquel3@hoy.net) and similar initiatives can be found in São Paulo state in Brazil (amazonadv@aol.com) and the Bolivian Amazon at the *Chalalan Lodge* (T591-892 2419, chalalan@cibol.rds.org.bo)

While the authenticity of some ecotourism operators' claims need to be interpreted with care, there is clearly both a huge demand for this type of activity and also significant opportunities to support worthwhile conservation and social development initiatives. Organizations such as **Conservation International** (T001-202-429 5660, www.ecotour.org), the **Eco-Tourism society** (T001-802-447 2121, ecotourism.org), **Planeta** (www.planeta.com) and **Tourism Concern** (T44-20-7753 3330, www.tourismconcern.org.uk) have begun to develop and/or promote ecotourism projects and destinations and their web sites are an excellent source of information and details for sites and initiatives throughout South America. Additionally, organizations such as, *Earthwatch* T44-1865-311601, www.earthwatch.org) and **Discovery International** (T44-20-7229 9881, www.discoveryinitiatives.com) offer opportunities to participate directly in scientific research and development projects throughout the region.

South America offers unique and unforgettable experiences – often based on the natural environment, cultural heritage and local society. These are the reasons many of us choose to travel and why many more will want to do so in the future. Shouldn't we provide an opportunity for future travellers and hosts to enjoy the quality of experience and interaction that we take for granted?

Drugs Users of drugs, even of soft ones, without medical prescription should be particularly *Safety*
careful, as some countries impose heavy penalties – up to 10 years' imprisonment – for even
the simple possession of such substances. In this connection, the planting of drugs on
travellers, by traffickers or the police, is not unknown. If offered drugs on the street, make no
response at all and keep walking. Note that people who roll their own cigarettes are often
suspected of carrying drugs and subjected to intensive searches. Advisable to stick to
commercial brands of cigarettes.

Keeping safe Generally speaking, most places in South America are no more dangerous *For specific local*
than any major city in Europe or North America. In provincial towns, main places of interest, *problems, see under*
on day time buses and in ordinary restaurants the visitor should be quite safe. Nevertheless, in *the individual*
large cities (particularly in crowded places, eg bus stations, markets), crime exists, most of *countries in the text*
which is opportunistic. If you are aware of the dangers, act confidently and use your common
sense, you will lessen many of the risks. The following tips are all endorsed by travellers. Keep
all documents secure; hide your main cash supply in different places or under your clothes:
extra pockets sewn inside shirts and trousers, pockets closed with a zip or safety pin,
moneybelts (best worn under rather than outside your clothes at the waist), neck or leg
pouches, a thin chain for attaching a purse to your bag or under your clothes and elasticated
support bandages for keeping money and cheques above the elbow or below the knee have
been repeatedly recommended. Keep cameras in bags; take spare spectacles (eyeglasses);
don't wear expensive wrist-watches or jewellery. If you wear a shoulder-bag in a market, carry
it in front of you.

Ignore mustard smearers and paint or shampoo sprayers, and strangers' remarks like
"what's that on your shoulder?" or "have you seen that dirt on your shoe?" Furthermore, don't
bend over to pick up money or other items in the street. These are all ruses intended to
distract your attention and make you easy prey for an accomplice to steal from. Take local
advice about being out at night and, if walking after dark, walk in the road, not on the
pavement/sidewalk.

Be wary of 'plainclothes policemen'; insist on seeing identification and on going to the
police station by main roads. Do not hand over your identification (or money – which he
should not need to see anyway), until you are at the station. On no account take them directly
back to your lodgings. Be even more suspicious if he seeks confirmation of his status from a
passer-by. A related scam is for a 'tourist' to gain your confidence, then accomplices create a
reason to check your documents. If someone tries to bribe you, insist on a receipt. If attacked,
remember your assailants may well be armed, and try not to resist.

Leave any valuables you don't need in safe-deposit in your hotel when sightseeing locally.
Always keep an inventory of what you have deposited. If there is no safe, lock your bags and
secure them in your room (some people take eyelet-screws for padlocking cupboards or
drawers). If you lose valuables, always report to the police and note details of the report – for
insurance purposes.

When you have all your luggage with you, be careful. From airports take official taxis or
special airport buses. Take a taxi between bus station/railway station and hotel. Keep your
bags with you in the taxi and pay only when you and your luggage are safely out of the
vehicle. Make sure the taxi has inner door handles and do not share the ride with a stranger.
Avoid night buses; never arrive at night; and watch your belongings whether they are stowed
inside or outside the cabin (roof top luggage racks create extra problems, which are
sometimes unavoidable – make sure your bag is waterproof). Major bus lines often issue a
luggage ticket when bags are stored in the hold of the bus. Finally, never accept food, drink,
sweets or cigarettes from unknown fellow-travellers on buses or trains. They may be
drugged, and you would wake up hours later without your belongings.

Rape This can happen anywhere. If you are the victim of a sexual assault, you are advised in
the first instance to contact a doctor (this can be your home doctor if you prefer). You will
need tests to determine whether you have contracted any sexually-transmitted diseases; you
may also need advice on post-coital contraception. You should also contact your embassy,
where consular staff are very willing to help in such cases.

Essentials

Police Whereas in Europe and North America we are accustomed to law enforcement on a systematic basis, in general, enforcement in Latin America is achieved by periodic campaigns. The most typical is a round-up of criminals in the cities just before Christmas. In December, therefore, you may well be asked for identification at any time, and if you cannot produce it, you will be jailed. If a visitor is jailed his or her friends should provide food every day. This is especially important for people on a diet, such as diabetics. In the event of a vehicle accident in which anyone is injured, all drivers involved are automatically detained until blame has been established, and this does not usually take less than two weeks.

Never offer a bribe unless you are fully conversant with the customs of the country. (In Chile, for instance, it would land you in serious trouble if you tried to bribe a *carabinero*.) Wait until the official makes the suggestion, or offer money in some form which is apparently not bribery, for example "In our country we have a system of on-the-spot fines (*multas de inmediato*). Is there a similar system here?" Do not assume that an official who accepts a bribe is prepared to do anything else that is illegal. You bribe him to persuade him to do his job, or to persuade him not to do it, or to do it more quickly, or more slowly. You do not bribe him to do something which is against the law. The mere suggestion would make him very upset. If an official suggests that a bribe must be paid before you can proceed on your way, be patient (assuming you have the time) and he may relent.

Where to stay

Hotels For about US$10, a cheap but not bad hotel room can be found in most countries, although in some of the Andean countries you may not have to pay that much. For those on a really tight budget, it is a good idea to ask for a boarding house – *casa de huéspedes, hospedaje, pensión, casa familial* or *residencial*, according to country – they are normally to be found in abundance near bus and railway stations and markets. Good value hotels can also be found near truckers' stops/service stations; they are usually secure. There are often great seasonal variations in hotel prices in resorts. Remember, cheaper hotels don't always supply soap, towels and toilet paper; in colder (higher) regions they may not supply enough blankets, so take your own or a sleeping bag. To avoid price hikes for gringos, ask if there is a cheaper room.

See inside front cover for our hotel grade price guide. Unless otherwise stated, it is assumed that hotels listed are clean and friendly and that rooms have shower and toilet. In any class, hotel rooms facing the street may be noisy always ask for the best, quietest room

Experiment in International Living Ltd, 287 Worcester Rd, Malvern, Worcestershire WR14 1AB, T0800-018 4015 or 01684-562577, F562212, and offices worldwide, www.eiluk.org Can arrange stays with families from one to four weeks in Argentina, Chile, Ecuador and Brazil. This has been recommended as an excellent way to meet people and learn the language. They also offer gap year opportunities.

NB The electric showers used in innumerable hotels should be checked for obvious flaws in the wiring; try not to touch the rose while it is producing hot water.

Cockroaches These are ubiquitous and unpleasant, but not dangerous. Take some insecticide powder if staying in cheap hotels; *Baygon* (Bayer) has been recommended. Stuff toilet paper in any holes in walls that you may suspect of being parts of cockroach runs.

Toilets Many hotels, restaurants and bars have inadequate water supplies. **Almost without exception used toilet paper should not be flushed down the pan, but placed in the receptacle provided**. This applies even in quite expensive hotels. Failing to observe this custom will block the pan or drain, a considerable health risk. It is quite common for people to stand on the toilet seat (facing the wall – easier to balance).

Youth hostels Organizations affiliated to the Youth Hostels movement exist in Argentina, Brazil, Colombia, Chile, Peru and Uruguay. There is an associate organization in Ecuador. Further information in the country sections and from *Hostelling International* (formerly the International Youth Hostel Federation). A good independent site on hostelling is the *Internet Guide to Hostelling*, www.hostels.com

Camping Organized campsites are referred to in the text immediately below hotel lists, under each town. If there is no organized site in town, a football pitch or gravel pit might serve. Obey the following rules for 'wild' camping: (1) arrive in daylight and pitch your tent as it gets dark; (2)

ask permission to camp from the parish priest, or the fire chief, or the police, or a farmer regarding his own property; (3) never ask a group of people – especially young people; (4) never camp on a beach (because of sandflies and thieves). If you can't get information from anyone, camp in a spot where you can't be seen from the nearest inhabited place, or road, and make sure no one saw you go there. In Argentina and Brazil, it is common to camp at gas/petrol stations. As Béatrice Völkle of Gampelen, Switzerland, adds, camping wild may be preferable to those organized sites which are treated as discos, with only the afternoon reserved for sleeping.

If taking a cooker, the most frequent recommendation is a multifuel stove (eg MSR International, Coleman Peak 1), which will burn unleaded petrol or, if that is not available, kerosene, *benzina blanca*, etc. Alcohol-burning stoves are simple, reliable, but slow and you have to carry a lot of fuel: for a methylated spirit-burning stove, the following fuels apply, *alcohol desnaturalizado, alcohol metílico, alcohol puro (de caña)* or *alcohol para quemar*. Ask for 95%, but 70% will suffice. In all countries fuel can usually be found in chemists/pharmacies. Gas cylinders and bottles are usually exchangeable, but if not can be recharged; specify whether you use butane or propane. Gas canisters are not always available. The Camping Clube do Brasil gives 50% discounts to holders of international campers' cards.

Getting around

The continent has an extensive road system with frequent bus services. The buses are often comfortable; the difficulties of Andean terrain affect the quality of vehicles. In mountainous country do not expect buses to get to their destination after long journeys anywhere near on time. Do not turn up for a bus at the last minute; if it is full it may depart early. Tall travellers are advised to take aisle rather than window seats on long journeys as this allows more leg room. When the journey takes more than three or four hours, meal stops at country inns or bars, good and bad, are the rule. Usually, no announcement is made on the duration of a stop: ask the driver and follow him, if he eats, eat. See what the locals are eating – and buy likewise, or make sure you're stocked up well on food and drink at the start. For drinks, stick to bottled water or soft drinks or coffee (black). The food sold by vendors at bus stops may be all right: watch if locals are buying, though unpeeled fruit is of course reliable.

Where they still run, trains are slower than buses. They tend to provide finer scenery and you can normally see much more wildlife than from the road – it is less disturbed by one or two trains a day than by the more frequent road traffic.

Buses & trains
See Getting there for details of air transport including air passes

The machine A normal car will reach most places of interest, but high ground clearance is useful for badly surfaced or unsurfaced roads and for fording rivers. Four-wheel drive vehicles are recommended for greater flexibility in mountain and jungle territory. In Patagonia, main roads are gravel rather than paved: perfectly passable without four-wheel drive, just rough and dusty. Consider fitting wire guards for headlamps, and for windscreens too. Wherever you travel you should expect from time to time to find roads that are badly maintained, damaged or closed during the wet season, and delays because of floods, landslides and huge potholes. Diesel cars are much cheaper to run than petrol ones and the fuel is easily available, although in Venezuela you may have to look hard for it outside Caracas. Most towns can supply a mechanic of sorts and probably parts for Bosch fuel injection equipment. Watch the mechanics like a hawk, since there's always a brisk market in spares. That apart, they enjoy a challenge, and can fix most things, eventually. Standard European and Japanese cars run on fuel with a higher octane rating than is commonly available in North, South or Central America, and in Brazil petrol (gasolina) is in fact gasohol, with a 12% admixture of alcohol. A high compression fuel injection engine will not like this.

Car

Security Spare no ingenuity in making your car secure. Anything less than the Brink's armoured van can be broken into and unsecured parts on the exterior (wing mirrors, spot lamps, even wheels without locking nuts) are likely to be stolen too. Try never to leave the car unattended except in a locked garage or guarded parking space. Lock the clutch or accelerator to the steering wheel with a heavy, obvious chain or lock. Street children will generally protect your car fiercely in exchange for a tip.

Documents To drive your own vehicle in South America, you must have an international driver's licence. You must also have the vehicle's registration document in the name of the driver, or, in the case of a car registered in someone else's name, a notarized letter of authorization. Most countries give a limited period of stay, but allow an extension if requested in advance. Be very careful to keep **all** the papers you are given when you enter, to produce when you leave (see box, *Carnet de passages*).

Insurance Insurance for the vehicle against accident, damage or theft is best arranged in the country of origin. In Latin American countries it is very expensive to insure against accident and theft, especially as you should take into account the value of the car increased by duties calculated in real (ie non devaluing) terms. If the car is stolen or written off you will be required to pay very high import duty on its value. A few countries insist on compulsory third party insurance, to be bought at the border: in other countries it's technically required, but not checked up on (Venezuela seems to be the only country where it is easy to obtain). Get the legally required minimum cover, not expensive, as soon as you can, because if you should be involved in an accident and are uninsured, your car could be confiscated. If anyone is hurt, do not pick them up (you may become liable). Seek assistance from the nearest police station or hospital if you are able to do so.

Car hire The main international car hire companies operate in all countries, but they do tend to be very expensive, reflecting the high costs and accident rates. Hotels and tourist agencies will tell you where to find cheaper rates, but you will need to check that you have such basics as spare wheel, toolkit and functioning lights etc. You'll probably have more fun if you drive yourself, although it's always possible to hire a car with driver. If you plan to do a lot of driving and will have time at the end to dispose of it, investigate the possibility of buying a second hand car locally: since hiring is so expensive it may well work out cheaper and will probably do you just as well. Car rental websites: *Avis* www.avis.com (in all countries except Bolivia, Colombia, Guyana, Paraguay); *Budget* www.budget.com (in all countries except Bolivia, Paraguay, Suriname); *Hertz* www.hertz.com (in all countries except Guyana); *Localiza* www.localiza.com.br (Argentina, Bolivia, Brazil, Ecuador, Paraguay, Peru, Uruguay); *National* www.nationalcar.com (Chile, Colombia, Paraguay, Peru). **Car Hire Insurance** Check exactly what the hirer's insurance policy covers. In many cases it will only protect you against minor bumps and scrapes, not major accidents, nor 'natural' damage (eg flooding). Ask if extra cover is available. Also find out, if using a credit card, whether the card automatically includes insurance. Beware of being billed for scratches which were on the vehicle before you hired it. This includes checking the windscreen and what procedures are involved if a new one is needed.

Shipping a vehicle From Europe or the USA you can go to Panama and shop around for the best value sailing to whichever port best suits your travelling plans. Alternatively you can ship a vehicle direct from Europe or the USA.

A book containing much practical information on South American motoring conditions and requirements is *Driving to Heaven*, by Derek Stansfield (available from the author, Ropley,

Carnet de passages

There are two recognized documents for taking a vehicle through customs in South America: a carnet de passages *issued jointly by the* Fedération Internationale de l'Automobile *(FIA – Paris) and the* Alliance Internationale de Tourisme *(AIT-Geneva), and the* Libreta de Pasos por Aduana *issued by the* Federación Interamericana de Touring y Automóvil Clubs *(FITAC). The* libreta, *a 10-page book of three-part passes for customs, should be available from any South American automobile club member of FITAC, but in practice it is only available in Venezuela to non-residents (see pages 1363 and 1390 for addresses of the Touring y Automóvil Club). The cost is about US$350, but is more for those who are not members of automobile clubs; about a third of the cost is refundable. The* carnet de passages *is issued only in the country where the vehicle is registered (in the UK it costs £75 for 25 pages, £65 for 10 pages, valid 12 months, either bank indemnity or insurance indemnity, half of the premium refundable value of the vehicle and countries to be visited required), available from the* RAC *or the* AA. In the USA the AAA *does not issue the* carnet, although the HQ in Washington DC may give advice. It is available from the Canadian Automobile Association, who can give full details. Ask the motoring organization in your home country about availability of the carnet.*

The carnet de passages *is recognized by all South American customs authorities and, while entry to most countries may be possible without this document, passage through customs will be much quicker and easier with it.*

Essentials

Broad Oak, Sturminster Newton, Dorset DT10 2HG, UK, T/F01258-472534, £4.95 plus postage, if outside the UK, or from www.amazon.co.uk).

The motorcycle The bike should be off road capable. Buying a bike in the States and driving down works out cheaper than buying one in the UK. Get to know the bike before you go, ask the dealers in your country what goes wrong with it and arrange a link whereby you can get parts flown out to you.

Motorcycling
People are generally very amicable to motorcyclists

Security Try not to leave a fully laden bike on its own. An Abus D or chain will keep the bike secure. A cheap alarm gives you peace of mind if you leave the bike outside a hotel at night. Most hotels will allow you to bring the bike inside. Look for hotels that have a courtyard or more secure parking and never leave luggage on the bike overnight or while it is unattended. Also take a cover for the bike.

Documents A passport, International Driving Licence and bike registration document are necessary. Riders fare much better with a *carnet de passages* than without it.

Shipping Bikes may be sent from Panama to Colombia by cargo flight (eg *Girag Ltda Colombia*, offices at Tocumen airport – Panama, Bogotá and Barranquilla), or from Miami to Caracas. From South America to Europe, check all possibilities as it can be cheaper to fly a bike home than to ship it.

Border crossings If you do not have a *carnet*, do not try to cross borders on a Sunday or a holiday anywhere as a charge is levied on the usually free borders in South America. South American customs and immigration inspectors are mostly friendly, polite and efficient. If in doubt ask to see the boss and/or the rule book.

Unless you are planning a journey almost exclusively on paved roads – when a high quality touring bike such as a Dawes Super Galaxy would suffice – a mountain bike is strongly recommended. The good quality ones (and the cast iron rule is **never** to skimp on quality), are incredibly tough and rugged, with low gear ratios for difficult terrain, wide tyres with plenty of tread for good road-holding, V brakes, sealed hubs and bottom bracket and a low centre of gravity for improved stability. A chrome-alloy frame is a desirable choice over aluminium as it can be welded if necessary. Although touring bikes, and to a lesser extent mountain bikes and spares are available in the larger Latin American cities, remember that in the developing world most indigenous manufactured goods are shoddy and rarely last. If your bike is shock suspension equipped, take your own replacement parts and know how to

Cycling
Pace yourself; do not be too ambitious at the start of the journey and plan ahead for the type of terrain that you will covering each day

overhaul them. In some countries, such as Chile and Uruguay, imported components can be found but they tend to be extremely expensive. (Shimano parts are generally the easiest to find.) Buy everything you possibly can before you leave home. *Richard's New Bicycle Book* (Pan, £12.99) makes useful reading for even the most mechanically minded.

Useful tips Wind, not hills is the enemy of the cyclist. Try to make the best use of the times of day when there is little; mornings tend to be best but there is no steadfast rule. In parts of Patagonia there can be gusting winds of 80 kph around the clock at some times of year, whereas in other areas there can be none. Take care to avoid dehydration, by drinking regularly. In hot, dry areas with limited supplies of water, be sure to carry an ample supply. Take an effective water filtration pump (eg Pur Explorer). For food, carry the staples (such as sugar, salt, dried milk, tea, coffee, porridge oats, raisins and dried soups) and supplement these with whatever local foods can be found in the markets. Give your bicycle a thorough daily check for loose nuts or bolts or bearings. See that all parts run smoothly. A good chain should last 5,000 miles, 8,000 km or more, but be sure to keep it as clean as possible – an old toothbrush is good for this – and to oil it lightly from time to time. Carry 'zap-straps' to fasten components together quickly and securely when disassembling your bike for bus or train transport. Remember that thieves are attracted to towns and cities, so when sightseeing, try to leave your bicycle with someone such as a café owner or a priest. Country people tend to be more honest and are usually friendly and very inquisitive. However, don't take unnecessary risks; always see that your bicycle is secure (most hotels will allow bikes to be kept in rooms). In more remote regions dogs can be vicious; carry a stick or some small stones, or use your water bottle as a spray to frighten them off. Traffic on main roads can be a nightmare; it is usually far more rewarding to keep to the smaller roads or to paths if they exist. Most cyclists agree that the main danger comes from other traffic. Dismount and move off the road when two large vehicles are passing you on a narrow, shoulderless road. You will be heartily thanked with honks and waves, even a free meal at times. A rearview mirror has been frequently recommended to forewarn you of vehicles which are too close behind. You also need to watch out for hazards such as oncoming, overtaking vehicles, unstable loads on trucks and protruding loads. Make yourself conspicuous by wearing bright clothing and a helmet. Most towns have a bicycle shop of some description, but it is best to do your own repairs and adjustments whenever possible. If undertaking your own maintenance, make sure you know how to do it. Knowing how to do simple overhauls, and carrying extra bearings for bottom bracket and hub repairs for local bikes (usually BMX styles), will earn you much gratitude, especially in isolated villages.

Many cycle tourists are opting for rugged trailers as opposed to the old rack and pannier system. The end product may look a little unwieldy but little time is necessary to get used to the new feeling. The biggest advantage is that you still have a bike, instantly, not an over laden tank on two wheels. It would be a shame to miss out on the amazing trail riding that exists all over the continent. Trailers are also much more rugged than racks, which constantly break, and are much easier to weld.

The **Expedition Advisory Centre**, administered by the Royal Geographical Society, 1, Kensington Gore, London SW7 2AR, T020-7591 3008, www.rgs.org, has published a useful monograph entitled ***Bicycle Expeditions***, by **Paul Vickers**. Published in March 1990, can be downloaded from the RGS's website. (In the UK there is also the **Cyclist's Touring Club**, CTC, Cotterell House, 69 Meadrow, Godalming, Surrey GU7 3HS, T01483-417217, cycling@ctc.org.uk, for touring, and technical information.) A useful website is *Bike South America*, www.e-ddws.com/bsa/ Also recommended is *Cyclo Accueil Cyclo*, 3 rue Limouzin, 42160 Andrézieux, France, cacoadou@netcourier.com This is an organization of long-haul tourers who open their homes for free to passing cyclists.

Hiking & trekking A network of paths and tracks covers much of South America and is in constant use by the local people. In countries with a large Indian population – Ecuador, Peru and Bolivia, for instance – you can walk just about anywhere, but in the more European countries, such as Venezuela, Chile, and Argentina, you must usually limit yourself to the many excellent national parks with hiking trails. Most South American countries have an *Instituto Geográfico Militar* which sells topographical maps, scale 1:100,000 or 1:50,000. The physical features

---

Essentials

Remember that you can always stick your bike on a bus, canoe or plane to get yourself nearer to the heart of where you want your wheels to take you. This is especially useful when there are long stretches of major road ahead, where all that stretches before you are hours of turbulence as the constant stream of heavy trucks and long-haul buses zoom by

In almost any country it is possible to rent a bike for a few days, or join an organized tour for riding in the mountains. You should check, however, that the machine you are hiring is up to the conditions you will be encountering, or that the tour company is not a fly-by-night outfit without back-up, good bikes or maintenance

In Peru, Ecuador and Bolivia, mountain biking is relatively new, so there are routes to discover and little in the way of guide books to follow

shown on these are usually accurate; the trails and place names less so. National park offices also sell maps.

Hiking and backpacking should not be approached casually. Even if you only plan to be out a couple of hours you should have comfortable, safe footwear (which can cope with the wet) and a daypack to carry your sweater and waterproof (which must be more than showerproof). At high altitudes the difference in temperature between sun and shade is remarkable. The longer trips mentioned in this book require basic backpacking equipment. Essential items are: backpack with frame, sleeping bag, closed cell foam mat for insulation, stove, tent or tarpaulin, dried food (not tins), water bottle, compass. Some, but not all of these things, are available locally.

When planning treks in the Andes you should be aware of the effects and dangers of acute mountain sickness, and cerebral and pulmonary oedema (see Health, page 59). These can be avoided by spending a few days acclimatizing to the altitude before starting your walk, and by climbing slowly. Otherwise there are fewer dangers than in most cities. Hikers have little to fear from the animal kingdom apart from insects (although it's best to avoid actually stepping on a snake), and robbery and assault are very rare. You are much more of a threat to the environment than vice versa. Leave no evidence of your passing; don't litter and don't give gratuitous presents of sweets or money to rural villagers. Respect their system of reciprocity; if they give you hospitality or food, then is the time to reciprocate with presents.

For trekking in mountain areas, where the weather can deteriorate rapidly (eg in Torres del Paine), trekkers should consider taking the following equipment (list supplied by Andrew Dobbie of Swansea, who adds that it "is in no way finite"): **Clothing**: warm hat (wool or man-made fibre), thermal underwear, T-shirts/shirts, trousers (quick-drying and preferably windproof, never jeans), warm (wool or fleece) jumper/jacket (preferably two), gloves, waterproof jacket and over trousers (preferably Gore-Tex), shorts, walking boots and socks, change of footwear or flip-flops. Camping Gear: tent (capable of withstanding high winds), sleeping mat (closed cell – Karrimat – or inflatable – Thermarest), sleeping bag (three-season minimum rating), sleeping bag liner, stove and spare parts, fuel, matches and lighter, cooking and eating utensils, pan scrubber, survival bag. **Food**: very much personal preference but at least two days' more supplies than you plan to use; tea, coffee, sugar, dried milk; porridge, dried fruit, honey; soup, pasta, rice, soya (TVP); fresh fruit and vegetables; bread, cheese, crackers; biscuits, chocolate; salt, pepper, other herbs and spices, cooking oil. **Miscellaneous**: map and compass, torch and spare batteries, trowel for burying excreta (which can be done after toilet paper has been burnt in the excavated hole – but take care fire doesn't spread), pen and notebook, Swiss army knife, sunglasses, sun cream, lip salve and insect repellent, first aid kit, water bottle, toiletries and towel.

Boat

Because expanding air services have captured the lucrative end of the passenger market, passenger services on the rivers are in decline. Worst hit have been the upper reaches; rivers like the Ucayali in Peru, but the trend is apparent throughout the region. The situation has been aggravated for the casual traveller by a new generation of purpose-built tugs (all engine-room and bridge), that can handle up to a dozen freight barges but have no passenger accommodation. In Peru passenger boats must now supplement incomes by carrying cargo, and this lengthens their journey cycle. In the face of long delays, travellers might consider shorter 'legs' involving more frequent changes of boat; though the more local the service, the slower and more uncomfortable it will be.

Hammocks, mosquito nets (not always good quality), plastic containers for water storage, kettles and cooking utensils can be purchased in any sizeable riverside town, as well as tinned food. Fresh bread, cake, eggs and fruit are available in most villages. Cabin bunks are provided with thin mattresses but these are often foul. Replacements can be bought locally but rolls of plastic foam that can be cut to size are also available and much cheaper. Eye-screws for securing washing lines and mosquito nets are useful, and tall passengers who are not using a hammock and who may find insufficient headroom on some boats should consider a camp-chair.

In Venezuelan Amazonas hitching rides on boats is possible if you camp at the harbour or police post where all boats must register. Take any boat going in your direction as long as it reaches the next police post. See the special section on the Brazilian Amazon, page 532.

Essentials

Essentials

Maps & Those from the *Institutos Geográficos Militares* in the capitals are often the only good maps
guide books available in Latin America. It is therefore wise to get as many as possible in your home country
before leaving, especially if travelling by land. A recommended series of general maps is that
published by **International Travel Maps** (ITM), 345 West Broadway, Vancouver BC, V5Y 1P8,
Canada, T604-879 3621, F604-879 4521, www.itmb.com, several compiled with historical
notes, by the late Kevin Healey. Available (among others) are South America South, North East
and North West (1:4M), Ecuador (1:1M), The Galapagos Islands (1:500,000), Easter Island
(1:30,000), Argentina (1:4M), The Amazon (1:4M), Uruguay (1:800,000), Venezuela (1:1.75M),
Guyana (1:850,000) and Surinam (1:750,000). Another map series that has been mentioned is
that of **New World Edition**, Bertelsmann, Neumarkter Strasse 18, 81673 München, Germany,
Mittelamerika, Südamerika Nord, Südamerika Sud, Brasilien (all 1:4M). For information on **Bradt
Travel Guides**' Backpacking Series (covering Chile and Argentina, Peru and Bolivia, Ecuador,
Venezuela), other titles and imported maps and guides, contact 19 High St, Chalfont St Peter,
Bucks SL9 9QE, UK, T01753-893444, F01753-892333, www.bradt-travelguides.com   London's
Stanfords, 12-14 Long Acre, Covent Garden, WC2E 9LP, T020-7836 1321, F020-7836 0189,
www.stanfords.co.uk, also sells a wide variety of guides and maps. A very useful book, highly
recommended, aimed specifically at the budget traveller is **The Tropical Traveller**, by **John
Hatt** (Penguin Books, 3rd edition, 1993).

Keeping in touch

Internet Email is common and public access to the internet is becoming widespread with cybercafés
opening in both large and small towns. We list some cybercafés in the text. Two websites
which give information on cybercafés are: www.netcafeguide.com, and the search engine
www.latinworld.com (which also gives a directory of internet resources on Latin America and
the Caribbean).

Post Postal services vary in efficiency from country to country and prices are quite high; pilfering is
frequent. All mail, especially packages, should be registered. Check before leaving home if your
embassy will hold mail, and for how long, in preference to the Poste Restante/General Delivery
(*Lista de Correos*) department of a country's Post Office. (Cardholders can use American Express
agencies.) If there seems to be no mail at the Lista under the initial letter of your surname, ask
them to look under the initial of your forename or your middle name. Remember that there is
no W in Spanish; look under V, or ask. For the smallest risk of misunderstanding, use title, initial
and surname only. If having items sent to you by courier (such as DHL), do not use poste
restante, but an address such as a hotel: a signature is required on receipt.

Telephone AT&T's 'USA Direct', *Sprint* and *MCI* are all available for calls to the USA. It is much cheaper than
See inside front operator-assisted calls. Details given under individual countries. Other countries such as the UK
cover for telephone and Canada have similar systems; obtain details before leaving home. With privatization, more
dialling codes and more companies are coming onto the market; check prices carefully. Many places with
public fax machines (post offices, telephone companies or shops) will receive messages as well
as send. Fax machines are often switched off; you may have to phone to confirm receipt.

World Band South America has more local and community radio stations than practically anywhere else
Radio in the world; a shortwave (world band) radio offers a practical means to brush up on the
language, sample popular culture and absorb some of the richly varied regional music.
International broadcasters such as the *BBC World Service*, the *Voice of America*, Boston
(Mass)-based *Monitor Radio International* (operated by *Christian Science Monitor*) and the
Quito-based Evangelical station, *HCJB*, keep the traveller abreast of news and events, in both
English and Spanish.

Compact or miniature portables are recommended, with digital tuning and a full range of
shortwave bands, as well as FM, long and medium wave. Detailed advice on radio models
(£150 for a decent one) and wavelengths can be found in the annual publication, **Passport to
World Band Radio** (Box 300, Penn's Park, PA 18943, USA, £15.50). Details of local stations is
listed in **World Radio and TV Handbook** (WTRH), PO Box 9027, 1006 AA Amsterdam, The

Netherlands, £15.80 (www.amazon.co.uk, prices). Both of these, free wavelength guides and selected radio sets are available from the BBC World Service Bookshop, Bush House Arcade, Bush House, Strand, London WC2B 4PH, UK, T020-7557 2576.

Food and drink

In all countries except Brazil and Chile (where cold meats, cheese, eggs, fruit etc generally figure) breakfast usually means coffee or tea with rolls and butter, and anything more is charged extra. In Colombia and Ecuador breakfast usually means eggs, a roll, fruit juice and a mug of milk with coffee; say "breakfast without eggs" if you do not want that much. There is a paragraph on each nation's food under 'Essentials'. Vegetarians should be able to list all the foods they cannot eat; saying "Soy vegetariano/a" (I'm a vegetarian) or "no como carne" (I don't eat meat) is often not enough. Most restaurants serve a daily special meal, usually at lunchtime, which is cheap and good. Other than that you can expect to pay from US$7 in Peru, Ecuador or Bolivia, to US$15 in Uruguay on breakfast and dinner per day.

Shopping

Remember that handicrafts can almost invariably be bought more cheaply away from the capital, though the choice may be less wide. Bargaining seems to be the general rule in most countries' street markets, but don't make a fool of yourself by bargaining over what, to you, is a small amount of money.

You can also ship items home

If British travellers have no space in their luggage, they might like to remember *Tumi*, the Latin American Craft Centre, who specialize in Mexican and Andean products and who produce cultural and educational videos for schools: at 8/9 New Bond St Place, Bath BA1 1BH (T01225-480470, www.tumicrafts.com). *Tumi* (Music) Ltd specializes in different rhythms of Latin America. See *Arts and Crafts of South America*, by **Lucy Davies** and **Mo Fini**, published by Tumi (1994), for a fine introduction to the subject. There are similar shops in the USA.

Festival guide

End February: Fiesta de la Vendimia, **Mendoza** (Mendoza), grape harvest and wine festival.
15 August: El Toreo de la Vincha, **Casabindo** (Jujuy), celebration of Nuestra Señora del Rosario with the last remaining bullfight in Argentina.
15 September: El Cristo del Milagro, **Salta** (Salta), procession of the Lord and the Virgin of the Miracles to commemorate the cessation of earthquakes in 1692.
10 November: Día de la Tradición, **throughout Argentina**, gaucho parades, with traditional music, on the days leading up to the day itself.

Argentina
www.whatsonwhen. com, for worldwide information on festivals and events

24 January to first week in February: Alacitas Fair, **La Paz**, a celebration of Ekeko, the household god of good fortune and plenty.
2 February: La Virgen de la Candelaria, **Copacabana**, processions, fireworks, dancing and bullfights on the shores of Lake Titicaca (also celebrated in many rural communities).
February/March: La Diablada, **Oruro**, Carnival celebrations in the high Andes with tremendous masked dancers and displays. Carnival is also worth seeing in the lowland city of **Santa Cruz de la Sierra**.
Mid-March: Phujllay, **Tarabuco** (Sucre), a joint celebration of carnival and the Battle of Jumbate (12 March 1816), with music and dancing.
May/June: Festividad del Señor del Gran Poder, **La Paz**, thousands of dancers in procession through the centre of the city.
June-August (movable): Masked and costumed dances are the highlight of the four-day Fiesta de la Virgen de Urkupiña in **Quillacolla**, near Cochabamba.

Bolivia

February/March: Carnaval, **throughout Brazil**, but the most famous are **Rio de Janeiro**, **Salvador de Bahia**, **São Paulo** and **Pernambuco (Recife/Olinda)**, parades (sometimes competitive, as in Rio), dancing, music, balls and general revelry.

Brazil

June: Festas Juninhas, **throughout Brazil**, to celebrate various saints days in the month; also Bumba-meu-boi, in **Maranhão state**, drummers and dancers in a festival which mixes Portuguese, African and indigenous traditions; last three days of June, Festa do Boi, **Parintins** (Amazonas), another festival based on the bull, whose main event is the competition between two rival groups of dancers.

The weekend after 15 August: Festa da Boa Morte, **Cachoeira** (Bahia), the processions of the Sisterhood of Good Death; also in August (third week) is the Festa do Peão Boiadeiro, **Barretos** (São Paulo), the largest rodeo in the world.

October: Oktoberfest, **Blumenau**, modelled on the famous festival of Munich, with German beer, music and traditions, all in the context of German immigration to this part of Brazil. Also in this month is Círio, **Belém** (Pará), the festival of candles for Nossa Senhora de Nazaré.

31 December: Reveillon, on **many beaches in Brazil**, especially **Rio de Janeiro**, a massive party to celebrate New Year. Principally at this time, but also on other dates, a number of places hold the more solemn festival of flowers, boats and candles in honour of Yemenjá, the Afro-Brazilian goddess of the sea.

Chile **End-January to early February**: Semanas Musicales, **Frutillar**, 10 days of classical music on the shores of beautiful Lago Llanquihue.

January-February: Muestra Cultural Mapuche, **Villarrica**, a celebration of the Mapuche culture, with music, singing, dancing and handicrafts. Also in February in this region there are various sports events.

Mid-February: Semana Valdiviana, **Valdivia**, a festival of various events, including the arts, culminating in a grand carnival on the river, with a procession of boats, fireworks and the election of a beauty queen.

End-March: National Rodeo Championships, **Rancagua**, the climax of a series of popular events throughout the summer, with competitions, dancing and displays of *huaso* (cowboy) culture.

12-18 July: La Virgen del Carmen, **La Tirana** (Iquique), one of Chile's most famous religious festivals which draws thousands of pilgrims. Also celebrated in **Santiago** at the Templo Votivo de Maipú on 16 July.

Colombia **February/March**: Carnaval, **Barranquilla**, one of the best carnivals in South America, with parades of masked dancers, floats, street dancing and beauty contests. It is less commercialized than some of the Brazilian events.

March: Caribbean Music Festival, **Cartagena**, groups from all over the Caribbean region attend. Also in March or April, Cartagena holds a film festival. The city's other great festival is Independence, in the second week of November, which can be pretty riotous.

March/April: Semana Santa, **Popayán**, throughout Easter week, there are spectacular processions and, in the following week, child processions. There is also a major festival of religious music in Holy Week.

April: Festival de la Leyenda Vallenata, **Valledupar** (César), thousands attend the festival of accordian-based *vallenato* music.

First week of August: Fiesta de las Flores y Desfile de Silleteros, **Medellín**, a great flower fair with parades and music.

Ecuador **February**: Fiesta de las Frutas y las Flores, **Ambato**, a carnival with parades, festivities and bullfights; unlike other Andean carnivals, the throwing of water and other messy stuff is banned.

June: Los San Juanes, the combined festivals of, 21st: Inti Raymi, 24th: San Juan Bautista, and 29th: San Pedro y San Pablo, **Otavalo and Imbabura province**, mostly indigenous celebrations of the summer solstice and saints' days, music, dancing, bullfights, regattas on Laguna San Pablo.

Second week of September: Yamor and Colla Raimi, **Otavalo**, lots of festivities and events to celebrate the equinox and the festival of the moon.

6 December: Día de Quito, **Quito**, commemorating the founding of the city with parades, bullfights, shows and music. The city is busy right through Christmas up to the 31st, *Años Viejos*, the New Year celebrations which take place all over the country.

Christmas-time: **Cuenca**, many parades, the highlight being the *Pase del Niño Viajero*, the finest Christmas parade in the country.

February/March: Carnaval, **throughout the country**.   Paraguay
8 December: La Inmaculada Concepción, **Caacupé**, Paraguay's main religious festival at the shrine of Nuestra Señora de los Milagros, attended by people from Paraguay, Argentina and Brazil, processions, fireworks and displays by bottle-dancers.

First two weeks of February: La Virgen de la Candelaria, **Puno** and the shores of Lake   Peru
Titicaca, masked dancers and bands compete in a famous festival in which local legends and characters are represented.
March/April: Semana Santa, **Arequipa** and **Ayacucho**, both cities celebrate Holy Week with fine processions, but each has its unique elements: the burning of an effigy of Judas in Arequipa and beautiful floral 'paintings' in Ayacucho, where Easter celebrations are among the world's finest.
June: Semana de Andinismo, **Huaraz**, international climbing and skiing week. In late June in this region also, San Juan and San Pedro are celebrated.
June: there are several major festivals in and around **Cusco**: Corpus Christi, on the Thursday after Trinity; mid-June, Q'Olloriti, the ice festival at 4,700 m on a glacier; 24th, Inti Raymi, the Inca festival of the winter solstice at Sacsayhuaman (this is preceded by a beer festival and, one week later, the Ollanta-Raymi in Ollantaytambo). Also in mid-June is the Huiracocha dance festival at Raqchi.
Last week of September: Festival de la Primavera, **Trujillo**, with beauty pageant, Caballos de Paso horse shows and cultural events.

February/March: Carnaval, **Montevideo**, notable for its *camdombe* drummers.   Uruguay
March/April: Semana Santa, **throughout the country** Holy Week is celebrated, but especially in **Montevideo** where it coincides with the Semana Criolla, a traditional gaucho festival.

February: week preceding Ash Wednesday: Feria del Sol, **Mérida**, a popular festival in this   Venezuela
Andean city.
February/March: Carnaval, **throughout the country**, but most famous is the traditional pre-Lenten carnival in **Carúpano**, the last of its kind in the country, with costumed dancers, masked women, drinking, etc.
Early June, Corpus Christi: Diablos Danzantes, **San Francisco de Yare** (Miranda), dancers in red devil-masks parade with their drums and rattles.
24 June: San Juan Bautista, Bailes de Tambor: **Barlovento Coast** in villages such as Chua, Cata and Ocumare de la Costa, a magnificent celebration of drumming. The drums can also be heard on 29 June (San Pedro) and at Christmas.

23 February: Mashramani/Republic Day, **Georgetown**, a week-long carnival including this   Guyana
date, with steel band competitions, calypso, dances with masquerade characters and sporting events.
March/April: **Phagwah**, the Hindu Spring festival.
March/April: Easter, **Georgetown**, as well as the Christian ceremony, Easter marks the start of the kite-flying season.
November (usually): Deepavali (Divali), the Hindu festival of light.

Phagwah and **Divali** are celebrated as in Guyana.   Suriname
March/April: Easter celebrations include parades in **Paramaribo**.
End-December-early-January: Surifesta, **Paramaribo**, cultural shows, street parties, flower and art markets, New Year celebrations.

February/March: Carnaval, celebrations begin in January, leading up to the four days preceding   Guyane
Ash Wednesday, each of which has a specific theme, with parades, dancing and music.

Health

Local populations in South America are exposed to a range of health risks not encountered in the western world. Many of the diseases are major problems for the local poor and destitute. The risk to travellers is more remote but cannot be ignored. Obviously five-star travel is going to carry less risk than back-packing on a minimal budget. The health care in the region is varied. There are many excellent private and government clinics/hospitals. As with all medical care, first impressions count. If a facility is grubby, staff wear grey coats instead of white ones then be wary of the general standard of medicine and hygiene. A good tip is to contact the embassy or consulate on arrival and ask where the recommended clinics (those used by diplomats) are. Diseases you may be exposed to are caused by viruses, bacteria and parasites. Tropical South America (Bolivia, Brazil, Colombia, Ecuador, French Guiana, Guyana, Paraguay, Peru, Suriname and Venezuela) poses a greater disease risk than Temperate South America (Argentina, Chile, Falkland Islands (Malvinas), and Uruguay). Other health problems, such as altitude sickness, may affect you along the entire length of the Andes.

Disease risks The greatest disease risk in Tropical South America is caused by the greater volume of insect disease carriers in the shape of mosquitoes and sandflies. The parasitic diseases are many but the two key ones are **malaria** and South American trypanosomiasis (known as **Chagas Disease**). The key viral disease is **Dengue fever**, which is transmitted by a mosquito that bites in the day, see page 59. Bacterial diseases include tuberculosis (**TB**) and some causes of traveller's **diarrhoea**.

Before you go Ideally see your GP or travel clinic at least six weeks before departure for general advice on travel risks, malaria and **vaccinations**. Make sure you have **travel insurance**, get a **dental check**, know your own **blood group** and if you suffer a long-term condition such as diabetes or epilepsy make sure someone knows or that you have a Medic Alert bracelet/necklace with this information.

Vaccinations for your South American trip **Polio** Recommended if nil in last 10 years.
Tetanus Recommended if nil in last 10 years (but after 5 doses you have had enough for life).
Typhoid Recommended if nil in last 3 years.
Yellow Fever Obligatory for most areas except Chile, Paraguay, Argentina and Uruguay. However, if you are travelling around South America it is best to get this vaccine since you will need it for the northern areas.
Rabies Recommended if going to jungle and/or remote areas.
Hepatitis A Recommended – the disease can be caught easily from food/water.

Further Information When you arrive in each country let the Embassy or Consulate know. The information can be useful if a friend/relative gets ill at home and there is a desperate search for you around the globe. You can also ask them about locally recommended medical facilities and do's and don'ts.

Organizations & websites **Foreign and Commonwealth Office** (FCO)
This is a key travel advice site, with useful information on the country, people, climate and lists the UK embassies/consulates. The site also promotes the concept of 'Know Before You Go'. And encourages travel insurance and appropriate travel health advice. It has links to the Department of Health travel advice site, listed below. **www.fco.gov.uk**
Department of Health Travel Advice
This excellent site is also available as a free booklet, the **T6**, from Post offices. It lists the vaccine advice requirements for each country. **www.doh.gov.uk/traveladvice**
Medic Alert
This is the website of the foundation that produces bracelets and necklaces for those with existing medical problems. Once you have ordered your bracelet/necklace you write your key medical details on paper inside it, so that if you collapse, a medical person can identify you as someone with epilepsy or allergy to peanuts etc. **www.medicalalert.co.uk**

Blood Care Foundation

The Blood Care Foundation is a Kent based charity 'dedicated to the provision of screened blood and resuscitation fluids in countries where these are not readily available.' It will dispatch certified non-infected blood of the right type to your hospital/clinic. The blood is flown in from various centres around the world. **www.bloodcare.org.uk**

Public Health Laboratory Service (has malaria guidelines)

This site has the malaria advice guidelines for travel around the world. It gives specific advice about the right drugs for each location. It also has useful information for those who are pregnant, suffering from epilepsy or planning to travel with children. www.phls.org.uk

Centers for Disease Control and Prevention (USA)

This site from the US Government gives excellent advice on travel health, has useful disease maps and has details of disease outbreaks. **www.cdc.gov**

World Health Organization

The WHO site has links to the WHO Blue Book on travel advice. This lists the diseases in different regions of the world. It describes vaccination schedules and makes clear which countries have Yellow Fever Vaccination certificate requirements. www.who.int

Tropical Medicine Bureau

This Irish based site has a good collection of general travel health information and disease risks. **www.tmb.ie**

Fit for Travel

This site from Scotland provides a quick A-Z of vaccine and travel health advice requirements for each country. **www.fitfortravel.scot.nhs.uk**

British Travel Health Association

This is the official website of an organization of travel health professionals. **www.btha.org**

NetDoctor

This general health advice site has a useful section on travel and has an ask the expert, interactive chat forum. **www.Netdoctor.co.uk**

Travel Screening Services

This is the author's website. A private clinic dedicated to integrated travel health. The clinic gives vaccine, travel health advice, email and SMS text vaccine reminders and screens returned travellers for tropical diseases. **www.travelscreening.co.uk**

Books & leaflets

The Travellers Good Health Guide by **Dr Ted Lankester**.(ISBN 0-85969-827-0)

Expedition Medicine (The Royal Geographic Society) Editors **David Warrell** and **Sarah Anderson**. (ISBN 1 86197 040-4)

International Travel and Health, **World Health Organisation,** Geneva (ISBN 92 4 158026 7)

The World's Most Dangerous Places by **Robert Young Pelton**, **Coskun Aral** and **Wink Dulles.** (ISBN 1-566952-140-9)

The Travellers Guide to Health (T6) can be obtained by calling the Health Literature Line on 0800 555 777

Advice for travellers on avoiding the risks of HIV and AIDS (Travel Safe) available from Department of Health, PO Box 777, London SE1 6XH.

The Blood Care Foundation. Order from PO Box 7, Sevenoaks, Kent, TN13 2SZ, T 01732 742 427.

What to take

Mosquito repellents Remember that DEET (Di-ethyltoluamide) is the gold standard. Apply the repellent every 4-6 hours but more often if you are sweating heavily. If a non-DEET product is used check who tested it. Validated products (tested at the London School of Hygiene and Tropical Medicine) include *Mosiguard*, Non-DEET *Jungle formula* and non-DEET *Autan*. If you want to use citronella remember that it must be applied very frequently (ie hourly to be effective)

Anti-malarials Specialist advice is required as to which type to take. General principles are that all except *Malarone* should be continued for four weeks after leaving the malarious area. *Malarone* needs to be continued for only seven days afterwards (if a tablet is missed or vomited seek specialist advice). The start times for the anti-malarials vary in that if you have never taken *Lariam* (Mefloquine) before it is advised to start it at least 2-3 weeks before the

Essentials

entry to a malarial zone (this is to help identify serious side-effects early). *Chloroquine* and *Paludrine* are often started a week before the trip to establish a pattern but *Doxycycline* and *Malarone* can be started only 1-2 days before entry to the malarial area. It is risky to buy medicinal tablets abroad because doses may differ and there may be a trade in false drugs.

Insect bite relief If you are prone to insects' bites or develop lumps quite soon after being bitten, carry an Aspivenin kit. This syringe suction device is available from *Boots Chemists* and draws out some of the allergic materials and provides quick relief.

Painkillers Paracetomol or a suitable painkiller can have multiple uses for symptoms but remember that more than eight paracetamol a day can lead to liver failure.

Antibiotics Ciproxin (*Ciprofloxacin*) is a useful antibiotic for traveller's diarrhoea (which can affect up to 70% of travellers). It can be obtained by private prescription in the UK which is expensive or bought over the counter in South American pharmacies, but if you do this check that the pills are in date. You take one 500 mg tablet when the diarrhoea starts and if you do not feel better in 24 hours the diarrhoea is likely to have a non-bacterial cause and may be viral. Viral causes of diarrhoea will settle on their own. However, with all diarrhoeas try to keep hydrated by taking the right mixture of salt and water. This is available as Rehydration Salts in ready made sachets or can be made up by adding a teaspoon of sugar and a half teaspoon of salt to a litre of clean water. Flat carbonated drinks can also be used.

Diarrhoea treatment *Immodium* is a great standby for those diarrhoeas that occur at awkward times ie before a long coach/train journey or on a trek. It helps stop the flow of diarrhoea and in the author's view is of more benefit than harm. It was believed that letting the bacteria or viruses flow out had to be more beneficial. However, with *Immodium* they still come out but in a more solid form. *Pepto-Bismol* is used a lot by the Americans for diarrhoea. It certainly relieves symptoms but like *Immodium* it is not a cure for underlying disease. Be aware that it turns the stool black as well as making it more solid.

Sun block the Australian's have a great campaign, which has reduced skin cancer. It is called Slip, Slap, Slop. Slip on a shirt, Slap on a hat, slop on sun screen. SPF stands for Sunscreen Protection Factor. It is measured by determining how long a given person takes to "burn" with and without the sunscreen product on. If it takes 10 times longer with the sunscreen product then that product has an SPF of 10. If it only takes twice as long then that product has an SPF of 2. In reality, the testing labs don't really burn the test subjects. They give them just enough UVR to cause the skin to turn barely red. This minimum dose is called the MED (minimal erythemal dose). The higher the SPF the greater the protection. However, do not just use higher factors just to stay out in the sun longer. 'Flash frying' (desperate bursts of excessive exposure), as it is called, is known to increase the risks of skin cancer.

MedicAlert These simple bracelets, or an equivalent, should be carried or worn by anyone with a significant medical condition.

Washing Biodegradable soap for jungle areas or ordinary soap for emergencies. Handwashing is the safest way of preventing unwanted muck to mouth transmission before you eat.

For longer trips involving jungle treks take a clean needle pack, clean dental pack and water filtration device.

Travel With Care, Homeway, Amesbury, Wiltshire, SP4 7BH, T0870 7459261, www.travelwithcare.co.uk provides a large range of products for sale.

Essentials

An A-Z of health risks

Air pollution

Many large Latin American cities are notorious for their poor air quality. Expect sore throats and itchy eyes. Sufferers from asthma or bronchitis may have to increase their regular maintenance treatment.

Altitude sickness

Symptoms: This can creep up on you as just a mild headache with nausea or lethargy. The more serious disease is caused by fluid collecting in the brain in the enclosed space of the skull and can lead to coma and death. A lung disease with breathlessness and fluid infiltration of the lungs is also recognised.
Cures: The best cure is to descend as soon as possible.
Prevention: Get acclimatized. Do not try to reach the highest levels on your first few days of arrival. Try to avoid flying directly into the cities of highest altitude such as La Paz. Climbers like to take treatment drugs as protective measures but this can lead to macho idiocy and death. The peaks are still there and so are the trails, whether it takes you personally a bit longer than someone else does not matter as long as you come back down alive.

Chagas Disease

Symptoms: The disease occurs throughout South America, affects locals more than travellers, but travellers can be exposed by sleeping in mud-constructed huts where the bug that carries the parasite bites and defaecates on an exposed part of skin. You may notice nothing at all or a local swelling, with fever, tiredness and enlargement of lymph glands, spleen and liver. The seriousness of the parasite infection is caused by the long-term effects which include gross enlargement of the heart and/or guts.
Cures: Early treatment is required with toxic drugs.
Prevention: Sleep under a permethrin treated bed net and use insect repellents.

Dengue Fever

Symptoms: This disease can be contracted throughout South America. In travellers this can cause a severe flu like illness with fever, lethargy, enlarged lymph glands and muscle pains. It starts suddenly, lasts for 2-3 days, seems to get better for 2-3 days and then kicks in again for another 2-3 days. It is usually all over in an unpleasant week. The local children are prone to the much nastier haemorrhagic form of the disease, which causes them to bleed from internal organs, mucous membranes and often leads to their death.
Cures: The traveller's disease is self limiting and forces rest and recuperation on the sufferer.
Prevention: The mosquitoes that carry the Dengue virus bite during the day unlike the malaria mosquitoes. Sadly this means that repellent and covered limbs are a 24 hr issue. Check your accommodation for flower pots and shallow pools of water since these are where the Dengue-carrying mosquitoes breed.

Diarrhoea/ intestinal upset

This is almost inevitable. One study showed that up to 70% of all travellers may suffer during their trip.
Symptoms: Diarrhoea can refer either to loose stools or an increased frequency; both of these can be a nuisance. It should be short lasting. Persistence beyond two weeks, with blood or pain, require specialist medical attention.
Cures: *Ciproxin* will cure many of the bacterial causes but none of the viral ones. Immodium and *Pepto-Bismol* provide symptomatic relief. Dehydration can be a key problem especially in

hot climates and is best avoided by the early start of Oral Rehydration Salts (at least one large cup of drink for each loose stool).

Prevention: The standard advice is to be careful with water and ice for drinking. Ask yourself where the water came from. If you have any doubts then boil it or filter and treat it. There are many filter/treatment devices now available on the market. Food can also transmit disease. Be wary of salads (what were they washed in? who handled them?), re-heated foods or food that has been left out in the sun having been cooked earlier in the day. There is a simple adage that says 'wash it, peel it, boil it or forget it'. Also be wary of unpasteurised dairy products these can transmit a range of diseases from brucellosis (fevers and constipation), to listeria (meningitis) and tuberculosis of the gut (obstruction, constipation, fevers and weight loss).

Hanta virus Some forest and riverine rodents carry hanta virus, epidemics of which have occurred in Argentina and Chile, but do occur worldwide. Symptoms are a flu-like illness which can lead to complications. Try as far as possible to avoid rodent-infested areas, especially close contact with rodent droppings. Campers and parents with small children should be especially careful.

Hepatitis Symptoms: Hepatitis means inflammation of the liver. Viral causes of Hepatitis can be acquired anywhere in South America. The most obvious sign is if your skin or the whites of your eyes become yellow. However, prior to this all that you may notice is itching and tiredness.

Cures: Early on, depending on the type of Hepatitis, a vaccine or immunoglobulin may reduce the duration of the illness.

Prevention: Pre-travel Hepatitis A vaccine is the best bet. Hepatitis B is spread by a different route by blood and unprotected sexual intercourse, both of which can be avoided. Unfortunately there is no vaccine for Hepatitis C or the increasing alphabetical list of other Hepatitis viruses.

Leishmaniasis Symptoms: A skin form of this disease occurs in all countries of South America except Chile and Uruguay. The main disease areas are in Bolivia, Brazil and Peru. If infected, you may notice a raised lump, which leads to a purplish discoloration on white skin and a possible ulcer. The parasite is transmitted by the bite of a sandfly. Sandflies do not fly very far and the greatest risk is at ground levels, so if you can avoid sleeping on the jungle floor do so. Seek advice for any persistent skin lesion or nasal symptom.

Cures: Several weeks treatment is required under specialist supervision. The drugs themselves are toxic but if not taken in sufficient amounts recurrence of the disease is more likely.

Prevention: Sleep above ground, under a permethrin treated net, use insect repellent and get a specialist opinion on any unusual skin lesions soon after return.

Leptospirosis Various forms of leptospirosis occur throughout Latin America, transmitted by a bacterium which is excreted in rodent urine. Fresh water and moist soil harbour the organisms, which enter the body through cuts and scratches. If you suffer from any form of prolonged fever consult a doctor.

Malaria Malaria can cause death within 24 hrs. It can start as something just resembling an attack of flu. You may feel tired, lethargic, headachy or worse, develop fits, coma and then death. You should have a low index of suspicion because it is very easy to write off vague symptoms, which may actually be malaria. Whilst abroad and on return get tested as soon as possible, the test could save your life.

Cures: Treatment is with drugs and may be oral or into a vein depending on the seriousness of the infection.

Prevention: This is best summarised by the B and C of the ABCD, see below: Bite avoidance and Chemoprophylaxis. Some would prefer to take test kits for malaria with them and have standby treatment available. However, the field test of the blood kits has had poor results. When you have malaria you do not perform well enough to do the tests correctly to make the right diagnosis. Standby treatment (treatment that you carry and take yourself for malaria) should still ideally be supervised by a doctor since the drugs themselves can be toxic if taken incorrectly. The Royal Homeopathic Hospital in the UK does not advocate homeopathic options for malaria prevention or treatment.

A for Awareness

Tropical South America: Malaria exists in all 10 areas of Tropical South America. Although some areas have a low risk of the disease, Paraguay is the only country, which has the less **deadly vivax** form of malaria. The other nine have areas with a risk of the deadly **falciparum** malaria.

Temperate South America: Malaria is only of concern in some parts of north-western Argentina. Always check with your doctor or travel clinic for the most up to date advice.

B for Bite Avoidance

Wear clothes that cover arms and legs and use effective insect repellents in areas with known risks of insect-spread disease. Use a mosquito net dipped in permethrin as both a physical and chemical barrier at night in the same areas.

C for Chemoprophylaxis

Depending on the type of malaria and your previous medical condition/psychological profile take the right drug before, during and after your trip. Always check with your doctor or travel clinic for the most up to date advice.

D for Diagnosis

Remember that up to a year after your return an illness could be caused by malaria. Be forceful about asking for a malaria test, even if the doctor says it is 'only flu.' The symptoms of malaria are wide ranging from fever, lethargy, headache, muscle pains, flu-like illness, to diarrhoea and convulsions. Malaria can lead to coma and death.

Malaria precautions for your South American trip

Certain tropical sea fish when trodden upon inject venom into bathers' feet. This can be exceptionally painful. Wear plastic shoes if such creatures are reported. The pain can be relieved by immersing the foot in extremely hot water for as long as the pain persists.

Marine bites & stings

A very common intensely itchy rash is avoided by frequent washing and by wearing loose clothing. It is cured by allowing skin to dry off (through use of powder and spending two nights in an air-conditioned hotel!).

Prickly heat

Remember that rabies is endemic throughout Latin America, so avoid dogs that are behaving strangely and cover your toes at night from the vampire bats, which also carry the disease. If you are bitten by a domestic or wild animal, do not leave things to chance: scrub the wound with soap and water and/or disinfectant, try to at least determine the animal's ownership, where possible, and seek medical assistance at once. The course of treatment depends on whether you have already been satisfactorily vaccinated against rabies. If you have (this is worthwhile if you are spending lengths of time in developing countries) then some further doses of vaccine are all that is required. Human diploid vaccine is the best, but expensive: other, older kinds of vaccine, such as that derived from duck embryos may be the only types available. These are effective, much cheaper and interchangeable generally with the human derived types. If not already vaccinated then anti rabies serum (immunoglobulin) may be required in addition. It is important to finish the course of treatment.

Rabies

Symptoms: The *mansoni* form of this flat worm occurs in Suriname and Venezuela. The form that penetrates the skin after you have swum or waded through snail infested water can cause a local itch soon after, fever after a few weeks and much later diarrhoea, abdominal pain and spleen or liver enlargement.

Cures: A single drug cures this disease.

Prevention: Avoid infected waters, check the CDC, WHO websites and a travel clinic specialist for up to date information.

Schistosomiasis (bilharzia)

Unprotected sex can spread HIV, Hepatitis B and C, Gonorrhea (green discharge), chlamydia (nothing to see but may cause painful urination and later female infertility), painful recurrent herpes, syphilis and warts, just to name a few. You can cut down on the risks by using condoms, a femidom or if you want to be completely safe, by avoiding sex altogether.

Sexual health

Snake bite & other animal bites & stings It is a very rare event indeed for travellers, but if you are unlucky (or careless) enough to be bitten by a venomous snake, spider, scorpion or sea creature, try to identify the creature, without putting yourself in further danger. Snake bites in particular are very frightening, but in fact rarely poisonous – even venomous snakes bite without injecting venom. Victims should be taken to a hospital or a doctor without delay. Commercial snake bite and scorpion kits are available, but are usually only useful for the specific types of snake or scorpion. Most serum has to be given intravenously so it is not much good equipping yourself with it unless you are used to making injections into veins. It is best to rely on local practice in these cases, because the particular creatures will be known about locally and appropriate treatment can be given.

Treatment of snake bite: Reassure and comfort the victim frequently. Immobilize the limb by a bandage or a splint and get the person to lie still. Do not slash the bite area and try to suck out the poison because this sort of heroism does more harm than good. If you know how to use a tourniquet in these circumstances, you will not need this advice. If you are not experienced, do not apply a tourniquet. What you might expect if bitten are: fright, swelling, pain and bruising around the bite and soreness of the regional lymph glands, perhaps nausea, vomiting and a fever. Symptoms of serious poisoning would be: numbness and tingling of the face, muscular spasms, convulsions, shortness of breath or a failure of the blood to clot, causing generalized bleeding.

Precautions: Do not walk in snake territory in bare feet or sandals – wear proper shoes or boots. If you encounter a snake stay put until it slithers away and do not investigate a wounded snake. Spiders and scorpions may be found in the more basic hotels, especially in the Andean countries. If stung, rest and take plenty of fluids and call a doctor. The best precaution is to keep beds away from the walls and look inside your shoes and under the toilet seat every morning.

Other tropical diseases and problems found in jungle areas: These are usually transmitted by biting insects. They are often related to African diseases and were probably introduced by the slave labour trade. Onchocerciasis (river blindness) carried by blackflies is found in parts of Venezuela. Wearing long trousers and a long sleeved shirt in infected areas protects against these flies. DEET is also effective. Epidemics of meningitis occur from time-to-time. Be careful about swimming in piranha or caribe infested rivers. It is a good idea not to swim naked: the Candiru fish can follow urine currents and become lodged in body orifices. Swimwear offers some protection.

Sun protection Symptoms: People with white skin are notorious for becoming red in hot countries because they like to stay out longer than everyone else and do not use adequate skin protection factors. This can lead to sunburn, which is painful, followed by flaking of skin. Aloe vera gel is a good pain reliever for sunburn. Long-term sun damage leads to a loss of elasticity of skin and the development of pre-cancerous lesions. Many years later a mild or a very malignant form of cancer may develop. The milder basal cell carcinoma, if detected early, can be treated by cutting it out or freezing it. The much nastier malignant melanoma may have already spread to bone and brain at the time that it is first noticed.

Prevention: Follow the Australians with their Slip, Slap, Slop campaign.

Tapeworms Acquired through eating the cysts of the worm in undercooked beef or pork. Humans can also get the cystic stage of the pork tape worm (cysticercosis) through food or water contaminated by human faeces. The cysts get into the muscle and brain, and cause fits months or years later.

Ticks Ticks usually attach themselves to the lower parts of the body often after walking in areas where cattle have grazed. They take a while to attach themselves strongly, but swell up as they start to suck blood. The important thing is to remove them gently, so that they do not leave their head parts in your skin because this can cause a nasty allergic reaction some days later. Do not use petrol, vaseline, lighted cigarettes etc to remove the tick, but, with a pair of tweezers remove the beast gently by gripping it at the attached (head) end and rock it out in very much the same way that a tooth is extracted. Certain tropical flies which lay their eggs under the skin of sheep and cattle also occasionally do the same thing to humans with the unpleasant result that a maggot grows under the skin and pops up as a boil or pimple. The best way to remove these is to cover the boil with oil, vaseline or nail varnish so as to stop the maggot breathing, then to squeeze it out gently the next day.

Symptoms: TB can cause fever, night sweats and a chronic cough. Some people cough up blood. You may not know you have it but your friends will remark on your gradual weight loss and lack of energy. The lung type of TB is spread by coughs. Sometimes TB causes swelling of the lymph glands. TB can be spread by dairy products. Gut or pelvic TB can cause abdominal lumps, gut obstruction and even infertility. All parts of the body can be affected by TB.
Cures: After diagnosis at least 6 months continuous treatment with several drugs is required.
Prevention: Unfortunately BCG vaccine may not protect against lung TB. The best you can do is avoid unpasteurised dairy products and do not let anyone cough or splutter all over you.

Tuberculosis (TB)

Symptoms This a gut infection which can spread to the blood stream. You get it from someone else's muck getting into your mouth. A classic example would be the waiter who fails to wash his hands and then serves you a salad. The fever is an obvious feature, occasionally there is a mild red rash on the stomach and often you have a headache. Constipation or diarrhoea can occur. Gut pain and hearing problems may also feature. Deaths occur from a hole 'punched' straight through the gut.
Cures: Antibiotics are required and you are probably best managed in hospital.
Prevention: The vaccine is very effective and is best boosted every 3 years. Watch what you eat and the hygiene of the place or those serving your food.

Typhoid fever

This can still occur and is carried by ticks. There is usually a reaction at the site of the bite and a fever. Seek medical advice.

Typhus

If you go diving make sure that you are fit do so. The **British Scuba Association** (BSAC, Telford's Quay, South Pier Road, Ellesmere Port, Cheshire CH65 4FL, UK, T0151 350 6200, F0151 350 6215, www.bsac.com) can put you in touch with doctors who do medical examinations. Protect your feet from cuts, beach dog parasites (larva migrans) and sea urchins. The latter are almost impossible to remove but can be dissolved with lime or vinegar.
Cures: Antibiotics for secondary infections. Serious diving injuries may need time in a De-compression Chamber.
Prevention: Check that the dive company knows what it is doing, has appropriate certification from BSAC or PADI, the **Professional Association of Diving Instructors**, (www.padi.com) and that the equipment is well maintained.

Underwater Health

There are a number of ways of purifying water. Dirty water should first be strained through a filter bag and then boiled or treated. Bringing water to a rolling boil at sea level is sufficient to make the water safe for drinking, but at higher altitudes you have to boil the water for a few minutes longer to ensure all microbes are killed. There are sterilizing methods that can be used and there are proprietary preparations containing chlorine (eg *Puritabs*) or iodine (eg *Pota Aqua*) compounds. Chlorine compounds generally do not kill protozoa (eg Giardia). There are a number of water filters now on the market available in personal and expedition size. They work either on mechanical or chemical principles, or may do both. Make sure you take the spare parts or spare chemicals with you and do not believe everything the manufacturers say.

Water

The health section was written by **Dr Charlie Easmon** MBBS MRCP MPH DTM&H DOCCMed In addition to his time as a hospital physician, Dr Easmon's aid and development work has included: Raleigh International (Medical Officer in Botswana), MERLIN (in Rwanda his team set up a refugee camp for 12,000 people), Save the Children (as a consultant in Rwanda), ECHO (The European Community Humanitarian Office review of Red Cross work in Armenia, Georgia and Azerbaijan), board member of International Care and Relief and previously International Health Exchange. He has worked as a medical adviser to the Foreign and Commonwealth Office and as a locum consultant at the Hospital for Tropical Diseases Travel Clinic as well as being a Specialist registrar in Public Health. He now also runs Travel Screening Services (www.travelscreening.co.uk) based at 1 Harley Street.

Argentina

65

Argentina is geared up to thrill – from steamy nights tangoing in the chic quarters of Buenos Aires to long days riding with gauchos in the grasslands of the pampas. You can climb to the roof of the Americas, raft down Andean rivers, visit the birthplace of Che Guevara and the resting place of a dinosaur known to have been bigger than T Rex. There are unusual sights and sounds to sharpen every sense: the thundering Iguazú Falls, jagged peaks and splintering glaciers in the far south, the birdlife of the Iberá marshes and the marine life of the Península Valdez. To set the taste buds tingling are the vineyards of Mendoza and the traditional Welsh tearooms of the Chubut valley. And at the end of the road is Ushuaia, the southernmost city in the world.

Argentina

Essentials

Planning your trip

The capital, **Buenos Aires**, has a distinctly European feel. Its architecture is mostly 20th-century, but earlier buildings can be found in San Telmo district, while the old port area of La Boca, with its multicoloured houses, has a bohemian feel and is home to artists' markets. Across the Río de la Plata is Uruguay; just west is Tigre, on the Paraná delta, a popular spot for escaping the city; to the east are coastal resorts which lead round to the most famous, Mar del Plata. West and south of Buenos Aires stretch the grasslands of the pampas, home of the *gaucho* (cowboy) and large *estancias*.

Where to go

Through **Northwest Argentina** a string of cities gives access to the Andean foothills and the higher peaks. On the way to the mountains are Córdoba, an important industrial centre close to resorts in the Sierras de Córdoba, and Santiago del Estero, Argentina's oldest city. From Tucumán, in view of the Andes, there is a beautiful route through desert foothills around Cafayate and the Valles Calchaquíes to the fine city and tourist hub of Salta. It is the departure point for the Tren a Las Nubes (the Train to the Clouds), which climbs to 4,475 m on a railway to high altitude mining communities. From Salta there are routes to Bolivia, through an area of isolated villages and old churches, and to Paraguay across the Chaco. There are also bus services to Chile.

In the **Northeast**, the wetlands of Mesopotamia have some interesting wildlife zones, such as the Iberá Marshes, and in Misiones province, sandwiched between Brazil and Paraguay, are ruined Jesuit missions, principally San Ignacio Miní. The highlight of this region is the magnificent Iguazú Falls, usually included on any itinerary to the country.

Back in the Northwest, **Ruta 40** starts its long, frequently remote journey beside the Andes to the far south. Among the many attractions it passes are the city of Mendoza, on the main Buenos Aires-Santiago road, with its vineyards, climbing and skiing centres, and the strange lunar landscapes of San Juan province. It traverses the **Lake District**, renowned for its lovely scenery and good fishing. The main centres are San Martín de los Andes and Bariloche, but there are many smaller places to visit, like Esquel, the terminus of the Old Patagonian Express. From Bariloche, and a number of other points, there are crossings to Chile. Ruta 40 continues south to the stunning peaks and glaciers of Los Glaciares national park.

On the Atlantic side of **Patagonia**, a good place to break the journey is Puerto Madryn and the Península Valdés. Here you can see whales, elephant seals, guanaco and other wildlife at close quarters (but check on the best times to view the animals). Just south of here are the Welsh communities of the Chubut Valley and, south again, three areas of petrified forest. Río Gallegos is the most southerly town of any size on the mainland. One road goes west to the most visited part of Los Glaciares, El Calafate, near where the Perito Moreno glacier tumbles into Lago Argentino. This increasingly popular place now forms part of the circuit which includes the Torres del Paine national park in Chile. Beyond Río Gallegos is Tierra del Fuego, shared with Chile; on the Argentine side is what claims to be the southernmost town in the world, Ushuaia, on the shores of the Beagle Channel.

When to go

Climate ranges from sub-tropical in the north to cold temperate in Tierra del Fuego. It is temperate and quite healthy in the densely populated central zone. From mid-Dec to the end of Feb Buenos Aires can be oppressively hot and humid, with temperatures ranging from 27°C (80°F) to 35°C (95°F) and an average humidity of 70%. The city is half-closed in late Dec and early Janas many people escape on holiday. Autumn can be a good time to visit and spring in Buenos Aires (Sep-Oct) is often very pleasant indeed.

The Northeast is best visited in Argentine winter when it is cooler and drier. Corrientes and Misiones provinces are wet in Aug and especially Sep. The winter is also a good time to visit the Northwest, but routes to Chile across the Andes may be closed by snow at this time and

Argentina

 Argentina embassies and consulates

Australia *John McEwen House, 7 National Circuit, 2nd floor, Barton, ACT 2006, T6273 9111, F6273 0500, www.argentina.org.au*

Belgium *225 Avenue Louise B.3, 1050 Brussels, T2-647 7812, F2-647 9319, www.embargentina.be*

Canada *90 Sparks Street, Suite 910, Ottawa KIP 5B4, T613-236 2351, F613-235 2659, www.argentina-canada.net*

Denmark *Borgergade 16, 1 floor, 13000 Copenhagen, T3315 8082, F3315 5574, embardin@post1.tele.dk*

France *6 rue Cimarosa, 75116 Paris, T4405 2700, F4553 4633, www.argentine-en-france.org*

Germany *Dorotheestrasse 89, floor 3, 10117 Berlin, T30-226 6890, F30-229 1400, www.argentinische-botschaft.de*

Israel *Herzliya Business Park, Medinat Hayeudim 85, 3rd floor, Herzliya Pituah 46120, T9970 2743, F9970 2748.*

Italy *Piazza dell'Esquilino 2, 00185 Rome, T474 2551, F481 9787, www.ambasciata-argentina.it/*

Japan *Moto Azabu 2-14-14, Minato Ku, 1060046 Tokyo, T3-5420 7101, F3-5420 7109, www.embargentina.or.jp*

Netherlands *Javastraat 20, 2585 AN The Hague, T70-365 4836, F70-392 4900, fepbaj@mrecic.gov.ar*

New Zealand *142 Lambton Quay, 14th floor, Wellington, T4-472 8330, F4-472 8331, www.arg.org.nz*

Spain *C Pedro de Valdivia 21, 28006 Madrid, T562 2800, F563 5182, www.portalargentino.net*

Sweden *Grevgatan 5-2 TR, S-104 40 Stockholm, T663 1965, F661 0009, fesuec@mrecic.gov.ar*

Switzerland *Jungfraustrasse 1, 3005 Bern, T31-352 3565, F31-352 0519, resembar@pingnet.ch*

UK *65 Brooke Street, London W1K 4AH, T202-7318 1300, F020-7318 1301, www.argentine-embassy-uk.org*
Consulate: *27 Three Kings Yard, London W1Y 1FL, T020-7318 1340, F020-7318 1349*

USA *1600 New Hampshire Avenue, NW Washington DC, 20009, T202-238 6400, F202-332 3171, www.embajadaargentina-usa.org*
Consulates: *12 West 56th Street, New York, NY 100019, T212-6030400, F212-3973523; 800 Brickell Avenue, PH1, Miami, FL 33131, T305-3731889, F305-3717108*

spring and autumn may be better: summer rains, especially in Jujuy, can make roads impassable. In the winter months of Jun, Jul and Aug establishments may close in the far south, transport can be restricted and routes across the Andes to Chile may be blocked by snow. Spring and autumn are the best seasons for visiting the Lake District. Ideally Patagonia should be visited in Dec or Feb/Mar, avoiding the winter months when the weather is cold and many services are closed. Jan is best avoided as this is the Argentine summer holiday period and some destinations, notably in Patagonia, are very crowded. There are also school holidays in Jul and some facilities such as youth hostels may be heavily booked in this period. Note that Bariloche is a very popular destination for school groups in Jul and Dec/early Jan.

Business visitors are advised to avoid the main holiday period (Jan-Mar); Jun, Jul and Aug are best for a business visit.

Finding out more

The national office of the **Secretaría de Turismo** is at Santa Fe 883, Buenos Aires, T4312 2232/0800-555 0016, www.turismo.gov.ar Addresses of other tourist offices in the country are given in the text. For tourist information abroad, contact Argentine embassies and consulates (see box), or **Argentina National Tourist Office**, 12 West 56th St, New York, NY 10019, USA, T212-603 0443, F212-315 5545, www.sectur.gov.ar

Websites The website **www.grippo.com/** provides the addresses of all the daily newspapers and just about anything you may need, plus the weather forecast and other useful information. Another site with tourist information for the whole country is **www.liveargentina.com** Another site with the daily papers, plus lots more information is **www.cityofbuenosaires.com**; **www.expatvillage.com** has information on life in Buenos

Aires and useful travel information. **www.mercotour.com** contains information on travel and other matters in Argentina, Uruguay, Chile and Brazil. For a list of newspapers, see above.

Spanish, with variant words and pronunciation. English comes second; French and Italian (especially in Patagonia) may be useful. The chief variant pronunciations are the replacement of the 'll' and 'y' sounds by a soft 'j' sound, as in 'azure' (though note that this is not done in Mendoza, Santiago del Estero and several other northern provinces), the omission of the 'd' sound in words ending in '-ado' (generally considered uncultured), the omission of final 's' sounds, the pronunciation of 's' before a consonant as a Scottish or German 'ch', and the substitution in the north and west of the normal rolled 'r' sound by a hybrid 'rj'. In grammar the Spanish 'tú' is replaced by 'vos' and the second person singular conjugation of verbs has the accent on the last syllable eg *vos tenés, podés*, etc. In the north and northwest, though, the Spanish is more akin to that spoken in the rest of Latin America.

Language

Argentina

Before you travel

Check visa requirements in advance. Passports are not required by citizens of neighbouring countries who hold identity cards issued by their own governments. No visa is necessary for US citizens, British citizens and nationals of other western European countries, Canada, Bolivia, Brazil, Chile, Panama, Paraguay, Uruguay, Venezuela, Mexico, El Salvador, Guatemala, Nicaragua, Honduras, Costa Rica, Colombia, Ecuador, Peru, Dominican Republic, Haiti, Barbados, Jamaica, Hong Kong, Malaysia, Israel, Czech Republic, Hungary, Poland, Turkey, Croatia, Yugoslavia, Slovenia, South Africa, Australia, New Zealand, Singapore and Japan, who are given a tourist card on entry and may stay for three months, a period which can be renewed for another three months (fee US$100) at the **National Directorate of Migration**, Antártida Argentina 1365, Buenos Aires, T4312 8663. For all others there are three forms of visa: a business 'temporary' visa (US$25, valid one year), a tourist visa (US$25 approximately, fees change monthly), and a transit visa. **Tourist visas** are usually valid for three months and multiple entry. If leaving Argentina on a short trip, check on re-entry that border officials look at the correct expiry date on your visa, otherwise they will give only 30 days. Renewing a visa is difficult and can only be done for 30-day periods. Visitors should carry passports at all times; backpackers are particular targets for thorough searches – just stay calm; it is illegal not to have identification handy. When crossing land borders, remember that though the migration and customs officials are generally friendly, helpful and efficient, the police at the control posts a little further into Argentina tend to be extremely bureaucratic.

Visas & immigration

At land borders, 90 days permission to stay is usually given without proof of transportation out of Argentina. Make sure you are given a tourist card, otherwise you will have to obtain one before leaving the country. If you need a 90-day extension for your stay in Argentina, leave the country, at Iguazú or to Uruguay, and 90 further days will be given on return. Visa extensions may also be obtained from the address above, ask for 'Prorrogas de Permanencia': fee US$100. No renewals are given after the expiration date. To authorize an exit stamp if your visa or tourist stamp has expired, go to Yrigoyen 952 where a 10-day authorization will be given for US$50. Alternatively, you can forego all the paperwork by paying a US$50 fine at a border immigration post (queues are shorter than in Buenos Aires, but still allow 30 minutes).

NB At Argentine/Uruguayan borders one immigration official will stamp passports for both countries. Argentine immigration and customs officials wear civilian dress. The border patrol, *gendarmería*, in green combat fatigues, operate some borders.

Duty-free allowance No duties are charged on clothing, personal effects, toilet necessities, etc. Cameras, typewriters, binoculars, radios and other things which a tourist normally carries are duty-free if they have been used and only one of each article is carried. This is also true of scientific and professional instruments for personal use. Travellers may only bring in new personal goods up to a value of US$300 (US$100 from neighbouring countries); the amount of duty and tax payable amounts to 50% of the item's cost. Baggage claim tags are inspected at the exit from the customs inspection area.

Customs

Two litres of alcoholic drinks, 400 cigarettes and 50 cigars are also allowed in duty-free; for tourists originating from neighbouring countries the respective quantities allowed are one litre, 200, 20 and 2 kg. You can buy duty-free goods *on arrival* at Ezeiza airport.

If having packages sent to Argentina, do not use the green customs label unless the contents are of real value and you expect to pay duty. For such things as books or samples use the white label if available. A heavy tax is imposed on packages sent to Argentina by courier.

Money

Currency
Argentine peso exchange rate with US$: 3.82

The peso is divided into 100 centavos. Peso notes in circulation: 2, 5, 10, 20, 50 and 100. Coins in circulation: 1, 5, 10, 25 and 50 centavos and 1 peso. At the time of writing, the entire banking system was shut down while the government sought measures to end the country's financial crisis. In the first four months of 2002 there had been so many changes in the economy that it was impossible to predict what the situation would be by publication date. Foreigners are advised to use credit cards to withdraw cash, where possible, and for making payments. If paying in cash, do so in pesos because, away from the capital especially, dollars are often not accepted for fear of forgeries. Also be aware of any changes to foreign exchange regulations.

Since Jan 2002, withdrawal of money from private bank deposits was strictly limited (a system called 'el corralito' – the little pen). Nevertheless, because of legal challenges and other factors, by Apr there was rumoured to be practically no money in the financial system. For this reason, and because of provincial government debt, a wide variety of bonds were being issued in lieu of pesos. Despite IMF pressure to end the practice, there was a large amount of provincial currency in circulation which travellers are advised to avoid. Bonds are only valid in the province in which they are issued, except those called 'Lecop', which are issued by the central government. Only use pesos (or dollars if allowed to do so) and try to give the exact amount, otherwise you may get your change on bonds.

ATMs (known as Cajeros Automáticos) can be found everywhere throughout the country except small towns. They are usually *Banelco* or *Link*, accepting international cards. Until the banking system has been stabilized, using ATMs is far better than over the counter transactions.

When crossing a land border into Argentina, make sure you have some Argentine currency as there are normally no facilities at the border.

Credit cards
American Express, Diners Club, Visa and MasterCard cards are all widely accepted in the major cities and provincial capitals, though less so outside these. There is a high surcharge on credit card transactions in many establishments; many hotels offer reductions for cash. Credit cards are readily accepted in all main towns, even in the south, but outside main towns their use is limited. Many service stations accept credit cards (**Automóvil Club Argentino** (ACA) stations only take cards from members; YPF accepts Visa). All shops, hotels and places showing *Argencard* (head office, Perú 143, Buenos Aires, T4331 2088) signs will accept Eurocard and Access, but you must state that these cards are affiliated to MasterCard. *Argencard* will not permit cash advances on these cards in outlying regions, and is itself very slow in advancing cash. MasterCard emergency number T0800- 555 0507.

Cost of living
In 2002, devaluation of the peso made Argentina, formerly the most expensive country in South America, considerably cheaper for the foreign visitor. Budget travellers should allow about US$15-20 a day for food, accommodation and travel, but much depends on the effect of both devaluation and inflation on prices and services. For the traveller with dollars, things may become cheaper still if the peso continues to lose value against the dollar and prices do not rise significantly. Hotel prices in early 2002 started at about US$5-6 pp in uncategorized establishments, with many good rooms available from US$15-40. Breakfast will cost about US$1.75-3.50, while cheap meals range from US$4-7.50.

Value-added tax VAT is not levied on most medicines and some foodstuffs but on all other products and services at 21%.

Touching down

Business hours Banks, government offices, insurance offices and business houses are not open on Saturday; normal office hours are 0900-1200, 1400-1900. **Banks**: 1000-1500 but time varies according to the city, and sometimes according to the season. (See under names of cities in text.) **Government** Offices: 1230-1930 (winter) and 0730-1300 (summer). **Post Offices**: stamps on sale during working days 0800-2000 but 0800-1400 on Saturday. **Shops** 0900-2000, though many close at 1300 on Saturday. Outside the main cities many close for the daily afternoon siesta, reopening at about 1700. 24-hour opening is allowed except on Monday; this applies mainly to restaurants, foodshops, barbers, newspaper shops, art, book and record stores.

IDD 54 When ringing: equal tones with long pauses. If engaged equal tones with equal pauses.

Official time Three hours behind GMT.

Voltage 220 volts (and 110 too in some hotels), 50 cycles, AC, European Continental-type plugs in old buildings, Australian three-pin flat-type in the new. Adaptors can be purchased locally for either type (ie from new three-pin to old two-pin and vice-versa).

Weights and measures The metric system is used.

Argentina

Getting there

From Europe There are flights to Buenos Aires from London, Barcelona, Madrid, Frankfurt, Paris, Milan, Rome, Zurich with European carriers, plus *Aerolíneas Argentinas* from Madrid and Rome, and *United Airlines* from London via New York. **Air**

    From North America *AR* and/or other South American and North American airlines fly from Miami, New York, Los Angeles, San Francisco, Atlanta, Dallas and Chicago. *Air Canada* fly from Toronto.

    From Australasia and South Africa *Aerolíneas Argentinas/Qantas* fly from Sydney, Australia, via Auckland, New Zealand, four times a week.

    From Latin America *AR* and other national carriers fly between Buenos Aires and all the South American capitals, plus Santa Cruz and Cochabamba in Bolivia. Several flights between Buenos Aires and Rio de Janeiro and São Paulo stop over in Porto Alegre and Florianópolis. There are also flights from Salvador and Recife. See under Brazil for the *Mercosur* Air Pass. There are also flights from Havana, Mexico City and Cancún.

Tourists can take into Argentina their own cars, vehicles bought or hired in neighbouring countries for up to eight months under international documentation. In practice, no papers other than the car's title document is asked for, except at remote crossings where a *libreta de pasos por aduana* may be required. No specific papers are usually required to take a Brazilian registered car into Argentina. **Road**

Touching down

Do not send unaccompanied luggage to Argentina; it can take up to three days of form-filling to retrieve it from the airport. Paying overweight, though expensive, saves time. **Airport information**

US$31 for all international flights, except to Montevideo from Aeroparque, which is subject to US$16.80 tax; US$8.05, payable only in pesos also for internal flights. When in transit from one international flight to another, you may be obliged to pass through immigration and customs, have your passport stamped and be made to pay an airport tax on departure. There is a 5% tax on the purchase of air tickets. Airport tax can be prepaid. **Airport tax**

Clothing Shorts are worn in Buenos Aires and residential suburbs in spring, summer and autumn, but their use is not common outside the capital. In general, dress tends to be formal (unless casual wear is specified on an invitation) in Buenos Aires and for evening outings to shows, etc. Men wearing earrings can expect comments, even hostility, in the provinces. **Local customs & laws**

Argentina

Safety
Never carry weapons, or drugs without prescriptions

Argentina is one of the safest countries in South America but in Buenos Aires and other major cities beware of the common trick of spraying mustard, ketchup or some other substance on you and then getting an accomplice to clean you off (and remove your wallet). If you are sprayed, walk straight on. Do all you can to avoid looking like a tourist. Highways may be blocked by road pickets (often the unemployed). There is usually no threat to travellers, just hours of inconvenience.

Where to stay

Hotels
See inside the front cover for our hotel grade price guide

In the beach and inland resorts there are many good hotels and *pensiones*; names are therefore not always given. Bed and breakfast accommodation throughout Argentina can be booked via www.bedargentina.tripod.com, in English, Spanish and a small part in French and German. Look out for special accommodation deals, such as weekend packages, three nights for the price of two, etc, aimed at the domestic market. Discounts can be obtained by paying in cash.

Camping

Camping is very popular in Argentina (except in Buenos Aires) and there are sites with services, both municipal, free, and paying private campsites in most tourist centres. Most are very noisy and many are closed off-season. The average price throughout the country is US$1.50-2 per person if you have your own tent. Camping is allowed at the side of major highways and in all national parks (except at Iguazú Falls). Wild camping in deserted areas is possible, but note that in Patagonia strong winds make camping very difficult. Many *ACA* and *YPF* service stations have a site where one can camp (usually free) and in general service station owners are very friendly to campers, but ask first. Service stations usually have hot showers. A list of camping sites is available from *ACA* (labelled for members, but should be easily available) and from the national tourist information office in Buenos Aires, which has a free booklet, *1ra Guía Argentina de Campamentos*.

Regular (blue bottle) Camping Gaz International is available in Buenos Aires. White gas (*bencina blanca*) is readily available in hardware shops (*ferreterías*) but may not be known by that name; if not, try asking for *solvente*.

Youth hostels

Hostelling International Argentina, or *Red Argentina de Alojamiento para Jóvenes (RAAJ)*, Florida 835 p 3, of 319B, Buenos Aires, T4511 8712, F4312 0089, www.hostelslatinamerica.org Offers 10% discount to card-holders at their hostels throughout Argentina. **NB** A HI card in Argentina costs US$14, ISIC cards also sold. Other than in Buenos Aires, where there are many, there are few other youth hostels (many open only February to March). Some towns offer free accommodation to young travellers in the holiday season, on floors of schools or church halls; some fire stations will let you sleep on the floor for free (sometimes men only).

Getting around

Air
All local flights are fully booked way in advance for travel in Dec

Internal air services are run by *Aerolíneas Argentinas* (AR – www.aerolineas.com.ar), *Austral* (part of AR), AIRG, formerly called Lapa (www.08107777arg.com), *Dinar* (www.dinar.com.ar), *LAER* (Entre Ríos, Mesopotamia), *American Falcon* (www.americanfalcon.com.ar), *Southern Winds* (www.sw.com.ar) and the army airline *LADE* (in Patagonia – www.lade.com.ar), which provides a good extended schedule with new Fokker F-28 jets. Some airlines operate during the high season, or are air taxis on a semi-regular schedule. All airlines operate standby systems, at half regular price, buy ticket 2-3 hrs before flight. It is only worth doing this off season. Children under three travel free. *LADE* also operates discount spouse (65%) and children (35%) tickets. Don't lose your baggage ticket; you won't be able to collect your bags without it. Check in 2 hrs before flight to avoid being 'bumped off' from overbooking. Meals are rarely served on internal flights.

Visit Argentina fare *Aerolíneas Argentinas* sell a **Visit Argentina ticket**: three flight coupons costing US$339, with US$105 for each extra coupon up to a maximum of eight. It is valid for 60 days and must be purchased outside Argentina and in conjunction with an

Argentina

international flight ticket. Note that for children under two years *Visit Argentina* fare is 10%. The airpass is valid on *Austral*. Routing must be booked when the coupons are issued: one change of date and of destination is free (but subsequent changes cost US$50). One stop only is permitted per town; this includes making a connection (as many flights radiate from Buenos Aires, journeys to and from the capital count as legs on the airpass, so a four-coupon pass might not get you very far). If you start your journey outside Buenos Aires on a Sun, when *Aerolíneas Argentinas* offices are closed, you may have difficulty getting vouchers issued at the airport. If you wish to visit Tierra del Fuego and Lago Argentino it is better to fly on the *Visit Argentina* pass to Río Grande or Ushuaia and travel around by bus or *LADE* from there than to stop off in Río Gallegos, fly to Ushuaia and thence back to Buenos Aires, which will use three coupons. It is unwise to set up too tight a schedule because of delays which may be caused by bad weather. Flights between Buenos Aires and Río Gallegos are often fully booked two to three weeks ahead, and there may be similar difficulties on the routes to Bariloche and Iguazú. If you are 'wait-listed' they cannot ensure a seat. Reconfirmation at least 24 hours ahead of a flight is important and it is essential to make it at the point of departure. Extra charges are made for reconfirming *LADE* flights but they are not high.

Car

Most of Argentina is served by about 215,578 km of road, but only 29% are paved and a further 17% improved

All motorists are required to carry two warning triangles, a fire-extinguisher, a rigid tow bar, a first aid kit, full car documentation together with international driving licence (for non-residents, but see Car hire below), and the handbrake must be fully operative. Safety belts must be worn if fitted. Although few checks are made in most of the country, with the notable exceptions of roads into Rosario and Buenos Aires, checks have been reported on cars entering the country. Parking restrictions are strictly enforced: a tow truck tours the towns; the cost of recovery is US$75. You may not export fuel from Argentina, so use up fuel in spare jerry cans while you are in the country. Always fill up when you can in less developed areas like Chaco and Formosa and in parts of Patagonia as filling stations are infrequent. Fuel is subsidized in Patagonia where it is half the price of the rest of the country. Octane rating for gasoline ('*nafta*') is as follows: regular gasoline 83; super 93. Unleaded fuel is widely available in 93, 95 and 97 octane. ACA sells petrol vouchers (*vales de nafta*) for use in *ACA* stations. Shell and Esso stations are slightly more expensive.

To obtain documents for a resident (holder of resident visa, staying at least six months in the country) to take a car out of Argentina, you can go to *ACA* in Buenos Aires for advice and paperwork. **NB** Non-residents may buy a car in Argentina but are in no circumstances allowed to take it out of the country; it must be resold in Argentina, preferably in the province where it was purchased. Non-residents who take cars into Argentina are not allowed to sell them and will encounter problems trying to leave the country without the vehicle. Third party insurance is obligatory; best obtained from the *ACA*, for members only.

Most main roads are paved, if rather narrow (road maps are a good indication of quality), and roadside services are good. Road surface conditions vary once you leave main towns. On the dirt and gravel roads, to avoid flying stones, don't follow trucks too closely, overtake with plenty of room and pull well over and slow down for oncoming vehicles. Most main roads now have private tolls, ranging from US$1 to US$5; tolls are spaced about every 100 km. Secondary roads (which have not been privatized) are generally in poor condition. Sometimes you may not be allowed to reach a border if you do not intend to cross it, stopping, eg 20 km from the border.

Automóvil Club Argentino (ACA), Av Libertador Gen San Martín 1850, 1st floor, touring department on 3rd floor, 1425 Buenos Aires, T4802 6061/7061, www.aca.org.ar Open 1000-1800 (take colectivo 130 from LN Alem and Corrientes down Alem, Libertador and F Alcorta, alight opposite ACA and walk one block through park; to return take the 130 from corner of Libertador on left as you leave building), office in Oficina Plaza San Martín, Santa Fe 887, has a travel documents service, complete car service facilities, insurance facilities, hotel lists, camping information, road information, road charts (*hojas de ruta*, about US$1.20 each to members), and maps (of whole country, showing service stations and *hosterías*, US$2 to members, US$4.75 to non-members, and of each province). A tourist guide book is for sale at a discount to members and members of recognized foreign motoring organizations. Foreign automobile clubs with reciprocity with *ACA* are allowed to use *ACA* facilities and benefit from discounts (you must present a membership card). Non-members will not receive any help if in trouble. *ACA* membership is US$10 per month, permitting payment with Eurocard (Argencard) for fuel in its service stations, 20% discount on hotel rooms and maps, and discounts at associated hotels, campsites and 10% discount on meals.

ACA accommodation comes in four types: *Motel*, *Hostería*, *Hotel*, and *Unidad Turística*, and they also organize campsites. A *motel* may have as few as three rooms, and only one night's stay is permitted. *Hosterías* have very attractive buildings and are very friendly. *Hoteles* are smarter and more impersonal. All have meal facilities of some kind. Anyone, motorist or not, can get in touch with the organization to find out about accommodation or road conditions.

Touring Club Argentino, Esmeralda 605 and Tucumán 781, p 3, T4392 6742, has similar travel services but no service stations.

Car hire
See car rental web addresses in Essentials, page 48

Minimum age for renting is 25 (private arrangements may be possible). A credit card is useful. Highest prices are in Patagonia. Discounts are available for several days', or weekly rental. Check the insurance details carefully, especially the excess clause. You must ensure that the renting agency gives you ownership papers of the vehicle, which have to be shown at police and military checks. At tourist centres such as Salta, Posadas, Bariloche or Mendoza it may be more economical to hire a taxi with driver, which includes the guide, the fuel, the insurance and the mechanic. *Avis* offers an efficient service with the possibility of complete insurance and unlimited mileage for rentals of seven days or more, but you should prebook from abroad. No one-way fee if returned to another *Avis* office, but the car may not be taken out of the country. *Localiza*, a Brazilian company, accepts drivers aged at least 21 (according to Brazilian rules, but higher insurance). It also offers four-wheel drive vehicles, though only from Buenos Aires. Taking a rented car out of Argentina is difficult with any company.

Bus

Express buses between cities are dearer than the *comunes*, but well worth the extra money for the fewer stops. When buying tickets at a bus office, don't assume you've been automatically allotted a seat: make sure you have one. Bus companies may give a 20% student discount if you show an international student card; a YHA card is also useful. The same discount may also be given to foreign, as well as Argentine, teachers and professors but you must carry documentary proof of your employment. It can be difficult to get reductions between Dec and Mar. Buses have strong a/c, even more so in summer; take a sweater for night journeys. Note that luggage is handled by *maleteros*, who expect payment (theoretically US$0.50, but in practice you can offer less) though many Argentines refuse to pay.

Hitchhiking

Argentina is getting increasingly difficult and much less safe for this. Traffic can be sparse, especially at distances from the main towns, and in Patagonia.

Internal checkpoints

There are checkpoints to prevent food, vegetable and meat products entering Patagonia, the Western provinces of Mendoza and San Juan, and the Northwestern provinces of Catamarca, Tucumán, Salta and Jujuy. All vehicles and passengers entering these areas are searched and prohibited products are confiscated.

Train

Trains only run on 22,000 of its 42,000 km of track and most of its is used only by freight services. There are few passenger services outside the Buenos Aires area.

Maps

Several series of road maps are available including those of the *ACA*, *YPF* (the oil company) and the *Automapas* published by *Línea Azul* (regional maps, Michelin-style, high quality). Topographical maps are issued by the **Instituto Geográfico Militar**, Cabildo 301, Casilla 1426, Buenos Aires (one block from Subte Ministro Carranza, Line D, or take bus 152). 1:500,000 sheets cost US$3 each and are 'years old'; better coverage of 1:100,000 and 1:250,000, but no general physical maps of the whole country or city plans. Helpful staff, sales office accessible from street, no passport required, map series indices on counter, open Mon-Fri, 0800-1300. *ITMB* publishes a 1:4,000,000 map of Argentina.

Argentina

Keeping in touch

Internet Use of email is growing fast and access to the internet is easy to find in the big cities. Most phone offices (*locutorios*) have email facilities.

Post Letters from Argentina take 10-14 days to get to the UK and the USA. For assured delivery, register everything. Small parcels only of 1 kg at post offices; larger parcels from Encomiendas Internacionales, **Centro Postal Internacional**, Av Comodoro Py y Antártida Argentina, near Retiro Station, Buenos Aires, and in main provincial cities. Larger parcels must first be examined, before final packing, by Customs, then wrapped (up to 2 kg, brown paper; over 2 kg must be sewn in linen cloth), then sealed by Customs, then taken to Encomiendas Internacionales for posting. Cheap packing service available. Customs usually open in the morning only. All incoming packages are opened by customs. *Poste restante* is available in every town's main post office, fee US$0.50.

Telephone Two private companies operate telephone services, *Telecom* in the north and *Telefónica Argentina* in the south. Buenos Aires Federal District and the country as a whole are split roughly in two halves. For the user there is no difference and the two companies' phone cards are interchangeable. For domestic calls public phones operate on phone cards of various values, which are more convenient than *cospeles* (tokens), which can be purchased at news stands (different tokens for local and inland calls). Domestic phone calls are priced at three rates: normal 0800-1000, 1300-2200, Sat 0800-1300; peak 1000-1300, Mon-Fri; night rate 2200-0800, Sat 1300-0800 and all day Sun and holidays. Peak is most expensive; night rate is cheapest and at this time also international calls are reduced by 20%. Both companies also have fax and, often, internet services. In main cities there are also privately-run 'locutorios' (phone offices), offering a good telephone, fax and internet service. International public phones display the DDI sign (Discado Directo Internacional). DDN (Discado Directo Nacional) is for phone calls within Argentina. Provide yourself with enough phone cards (or tokens) in Buenos Aires because, in the regions, many phone booths exist, but the cards and tokens are harder to find. Most telephone company offices in principal cities have a phone for *USA Direct*; if they do not, they can direct you to one. *BT* Chargecard can be used to the UK via the operator (T0800-54401).

Media **Newspapers** Buenos Aires dailies: *La Nación* (www.lanacion.com.ar), *La Prensa*, *Clarín* (www.clarin.com.ar), *La Razón*. Evening paper: *Crónica*. English language daily: *Buenos Aires Herald*, www.buenosairesherald.com **Magazines**: *Noticias, Gente, Redacción, Mercado, El Gráfico* (sports). The daily, *Página Doce*, is very popular among students and intellectuals. English language magazines: *The Review of the River Plate* (commercial, agricultural, political and economic comment), and *The Southern Cross* (Irish community). German-language weekly, *Argentinisches Tageblatt*, available everywhere, very informative. There is a weekly international edition of *La Nación*, priced in Europe at US$1.30. Write for further information to: La Nación, Edición Internacional, Bouchard 557, 1106 Buenos Aires.

Radio English language radio broadcasts can be heard daily on short wave: 0100-0130 on 6060 KHz 49m, 0230-0300 on 11710 KHz 25m, 0430-0500 and 2230-2300 on 15345 KHz 19m; *Radiodifusión Argentina al Exterior*, Casilla de Correo 555, 1000, Buenos Aires. This is a government station and broadcasts also in Japanese, Arabic, German, French, Italian and Portuguese. Foreign radio stations (including the BBC) are receivable on short wave.

Food and drink

Food National dishes are based in the main upon plentiful supplies of beef. Many dishes are distinctive and excellent; the *asado*, a roast cooked on an open fire or grill; *puchero*, a stew, very good indeed; *bife a caballo*, steak topped with a fried egg; the *carbonada* (onions, tomatoes, minced beef), particularly good in Buenos Aires; *churrasco*, a thick grilled steak; *parrillada*, a mixed grill, mainly roast meat, offal, and sausages, *chorizos* (including *morcilla*, black pudding to the British, or blood sausage), though do not confuse this with *bife de chorizo*, which is a rump steak (*bife de lomo* is fillet steak). A *choripán* is a roll with a *chorizo* inside. *Arroz con pollo* is a delicious combination of rice, chicken, eggs, vegetables and strong sauce. *Puchero de gallina* is chicken, sausage, maize, potatoes and squash cooked together. *Empanada* is a tasty meat pie; *empanadas de humita* are filled with a thick paste of cooked corn/maize, onions, cheese and flour *Milanesa de pollo* (breaded, boneless chicken) is usually good value. Also popular is *milanesa*, a breaded veal cutlet. *Ñoquis* (gnocchi), potato dumplings normally served with meat and tomato sauce, are tasty and often the cheapest item on the menu; they are also a good vegetarian option when served with either *al tuco* or Argentine roquefort (note that a few places only serve them on the 29th of the month, when you should put a coin under your plate for luck). *Locro* is a thick stew made of maize, white beans, beef, sausages, pumpkin and herbs. Pizzas come in all sorts of exotic flavours, both savoury and sweet. **NB** Extras such as chips, *puré* (mashed potato), etc are ordered and served separately, and are not cheap. Almost uniquely in Latin America, salads are quite safe. A popular sweet is *dulce de leche* (especially from Chascomús), milk and sugar evaporated to a pale, soft fudge. Other popular desserts are *almendrado* (ice cream rolled in crushed almonds), *dulce de batata* (sweet potato preserve), *dulce de membrillo* (quince preserve), *dulce de zapallo* (pumpkin in syrup); these *dulces* are often eaten with cheese. *Postre Balcarce*, a cream and meringue cake and *alfajores*, maize-flour biscuits filled with *dulce de leche* or apricot jam, are also very popular. Note that *al natural* in reference to fruit means canned without sugar (fresh fruit is *al fresco*) Croissants (known as *media lunas*) come in two varieties: *de grasa* (dry) and *de mantequilla* (rich and fluffy). Sweets: the Havana brands have been particularly recommended. Excellent Italian-style ice cream with exotic flavours. For local recipes (in Spanish) *Las comidas de mi pueblo*, by Margarita Palacios, is recommended.

Offices close for 2-2½ hrs for lunch between 1200 and 1500. Around 1700, many people go to a *confitería* for tea, sandwiches and cakes. Dinner often begins at 2200 or 2230; it is, in the main, a repetition of lunch. The cheapest option is always to have the set lunch as a main meal of the day and then find cheap, wholesome snacks for breakfast and supper. Also good value are *tenedor libre* restaurants – eat all you want for a fixed price. Those wishing to prepare their own food will find supermarkets fairly cheap for basics.

Drink Argentine wines (including champagnes, both charmat and champenoise) are sound throughout the price range. The ordinary *vinos de la casa*, or *comunes* are wholesome and relatively cheap; reds better than the whites. The local beers, mainly lager-type, are quite acceptable. In restaurants wines are quite expensive. Hard liquor is relatively cheap, except for imported whisky. *Clericó* is a white-wine *sangría* drunk in summer. It is best not to drink the tap water; in the main cities it is often heavily chlorinated. It is usual to drink soda or mineral water at restaurants, and many Argentines mix it with their cheaper wine, with ice, as a refreshing drink in summer.

Shopping

Local leather goods in Buenos Aires, eg coats (leather or suede), handbags and shoes. **NB** Leather from the *carpincho* is from the capybara and should not be purchased. A gourd for drinking *yerba mate* and the silver *bombilla* which goes with it, perhaps a pair of *gaucho* trousers, the *bombachas*. Ponchos (red and black for men, all colours for women). Articles of onyx, especially in Salta. Silver handicrafts. Knitted woollens, especially in Bariloche and Mar del Plata.

Sport and special interest travel

Birdwatching At least 980 of the 2,926 species of birds registered in South America exist in Argentina, in places with easy access. Enthusiasts head for Península Valdés, Patagonia, the subtropical forests in the northwest, or the Iberá Marshes and Chaco savanna in the northeast. The pampas, too, have rich birdlife: flamingoes rise in a pink and white cloud, egrets gleam white against the blue sky, pink spoonbills dig in the mud and rheas stalk in the

Argentina

distance. Most fascinating are the oven birds, *horneros*, which build oven-shaped nests six times as big as themselves on the top of telegraph and fence posts. Details are available from **Asociación Ornitológica del Plata** (address under Buenos Aires).

Climbing The Andes offer great climbing opportunities. Among the most popular peaks are Aconcagua, in Mendoza province, Pissis in Catamarca, and Lanín and Tronador, reached from the Lake District. The northern part of Los Glaciares national park, around El Chaltén, has some spectacular peaks with very difficult mountaineering. Climbing clubs (**Club Andino**) can be found in Mendoza, Bariloche, Esquel, Junín de los Andes, Ushuaia and other cities and in some places equipment can be hired.

Estancia tourism An *estancia* is, generally speaking, a farm, but the term covers a wide variety of establishments and many have opened their doors to visitors. In the pampas, *estancias* tend to be cattle ranches extending for thousands of hectares; in the west they often have vineyards; northeastern *estancias* border swamps; those in Patagonia are sheep farms at the foot of the mountains or beside lakes. Wherever you choose, be it to relax, or observe the workings of the place, you will gain an insight into aspects of the culture and economy of Argentina. Many offer horse riding and other options such as fishing, canoeing, walking and birdwatching.

Fishing The three main areas for fishing are the Northern Zone, around Junín de los Andes, extending south to Bariloche; the Central Zone around Esquel; the Southern Zone around Río Gallegos and Río Grande. The first two of these areas are in the lake district. Among the best lakes are: Lagos Traful, Gutiérrez, Mascardi, Futalaufquen (in Los Alerces National Park), Meliquina, Falkner, Villarino, Nuevo, Lacar, Lolog, Curruhué, Chico, Huechulafquen, Paimún, Epulafquen, Tromen (all in Lanín National Park), and, in the far north, Quillén. The Río Limay has good trout fishing, as do the rivers further north, the Quilquihue, Malle, Chimehuín, Collón-Curá, Hermoso, Meliquina and Caleufú. The southern fishing zone includes the Ríos Gallegos, Chico, Grande, Fuego, Ewan, San Pablo and Lago Fagnano near Ushuaia. It is famous for runs of sea trout. All rivers are 'catch and release'. The best time for fishing is at the beginning of the season, that is, in November and December (the season runs from early November to the end of March). To fish anywhere in Argentina you need a permit, which costs US$5 per day, US$15 per week, US$50 per year. In the Northern Zone forestry commission inspectors are very diligent.

Off-roading Large areas of Argentina are ideal for offroading since there are wide expanses of flat land or gently rolling hills with no woods, snow or ice. The vegetation is sparse and there are few animals or people. Patagonia, with is endless steppes interrupted only by rivers, gorges and gullies, is recommended, but some of the Andean valleys of the west and northwest are worth exploring. There are also some rough roads in the Andes, such as San Antonio de los Cobres to Catamarca via Antofagasta de la Sierra and the Laguna Brava area in La Rioja that make for adventurous driving. Note that hiring four-wheel drive vehicles is easier in provincial cities than in Buenos Aires, but is certainly not cheap. Also, avoid the wettest and coldest months: Oct-Nov (spring) and Apr-May (autumn) are best.

Skiing The season is roughly from May to Oct, depending on the weather and the resort. Las Leñas, south of Mendoza, is of international standard. Major resorts exist on Cerro Catedral and Cerro Otto near Bariloche and Chapelco near San Martín de los Andes. Smaller resorts, with fewer facilities, can be found near Mendoza (Los Penitentes, Vallecitos and Manantiales), in the Lake District (Caviahue, Cerro Bayo; La Hoya – near Esquel) and near Ushuaia (Cerro Martial, Wallner).

Trekking There is ample scope for short and long-distance trekking, on foot and on horseback. The best locations are in the foothills and higher up in the Andes. Some suggestions are the valleys around Salta; San Juan and La Rioja; Mendoza and Malargüe; in the national parks of the Lake District; around El Chaltén in Los Glaciares national park.

Watersports Surfing, windsurfing and waterskiing are practised along the Atlantic coast south of Buenos Aires. There are some good whitewater rafting runs in Mendoza province, near the provincial capital and near San Rafael and Malargüe. In the Lake District there are possibilities in the Lanín, Nahuel Huapi and Los Alerces national parks.

Other suggestions: good wine is made in Argentina and **vineyards** can be visited in Mendoza province and Cafayate (in the south of Salta province). **Geology** and **palaeontology**: there are areas of fascinating rock formations, different coloured strata and strange landscapes, especially in the northwest. San Juan province has some of the most spectacular examples. A large number of dinosaur fossils have been discovered in various locations (Neuquén, La Rioja, Chubut and other parts of Patagonia) and there are museums displaying the finds (eg Plaza Huincul and Rincón de los Sauces, Neuquén; Trelew, Chubut).

Holidays and festivals

No work may be done on the national holidays (1 January, Good Friday, 1 May, 25 May, 10 June, 20 June, 9 July, 17 August, 12 October and 25 December) except where specifically established by law. There are limited bus services on 25 and 31 December. On Holy Thursday and 8 December employers are left free to decide whether their employees should work, but banks and public offices are closed. Banks are also closed on 31 December. There are gaucho parades throughout Argentina, with traditional music, on the days leading up to the *Día de la Tradición*, 10 November. On 30 December (not 31 because so many offices in the centre are closed) there is a ticker-tape tradition in downtown Buenos Aires: it snows paper and the crowds stuff passing cars and buses with long streamers.

Health

Argentina is generally a healthy country to visit, with good sanitary services. In Buenos Aires and in some provinces, like Neuquén and Salta, medical assistance, including operations, X-ray and medication, is free in provincial hospitals, even for foreigners. Sometimes, though, you must pay for materials. All private clinics, on the other hand, charge. Medicines are more expensive than in Europe. Smallpox vaccination is no longer required to enter Argentina. If intending to visit the low-lying tropical areas, it is advisable to take precautions against malaria. Chagas' disease is found in northwest Argentina. To counter the effects of altitude in the northwest, chew coca leaves or take *te de coca* (use of coca is legal, its trade is not). In the south take plenty of sunscreen to prevent burning owing to the thinning of the ozone layer. Certain shellfish from the Atlantic coast are affected once or twice a year by red tide (*Marea Roja*), an algae poisonous to humans, at which time the public is warned not to eat the shellfish. Buy seafood, if self-catering, from fishmongers with fridge or freezer. To be certain, soak fish for 30 minutes in water with a little vinegar.

See also the Health section in Essentials at the beginning of the book, page 63

Argentina

Buenos
Aires

Buenos Aires

Elegant and fashion-conscious, Buenos Aires is usually seen as more European than South American. In the centre are fine boulevards, parks, museums, theatres, public buildings, shopping centres and a lively and incredibly varied nightlife. Here you can eat in the finest restaurants in the country, find music and entertainment to suit most tastes including of course, the tango which the city claims as its own musical creation.

Phone code: 011
Colour map 8, grid B5
Population:
capital 2.73 million
Gran Buenos Aires
11.38 million

Extreme humidity and unusual pollen conditions may affect asthma sufferers

The Río de la Plata, or River Plate, on which Buenos Aires lies, is not a river but an estuary or great basin, 300 km long and from 37 to 200 km wide, into which flow the Ríos Paraná and Uruguay and their tributaries. It is muddy and shallow and the passage of ocean vessels is only made possible by continuous dredging. The capital has been virtually rebuilt since the beginning of the 20th-century and very few of the old buildings are left. In the centre, which has maintained the original lay-out since its foundation, the streets are often very narrow and are mostly one-way. Its original name, 'Santa María del Buen Ayre' was a recognition of the good winds which brought sailors across the ocean.

Federal District of Buenos Aires

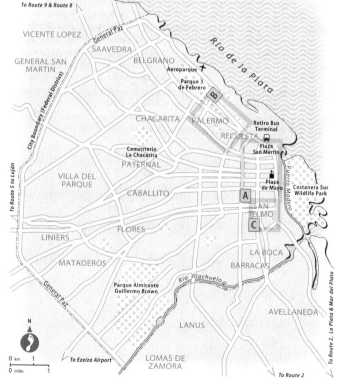

Related maps
A Buenos Aires centre, page 82
B Recoleta & Palermo, page 86
C San Telmo, page 88
Metro (Subte), page 101

Getting there Buenos Aires has 2 airports, Ezeiza, for international flights, and Aeroparque, for domestic flights, some services to Uruguay and to other neighbouring countries. Ezeiza is 35 km southwest of the centre by a good dual carriageway which links with the General Paz highway which circles the city. The safest way between airport and city is by the 2 airport bus services, *Manuel Tienda León* and *Transfer Express*, which have convenient offices and charge US$5.50-7.50 one way. Taxis charge US$10-15 (plus US$1.50 toll), but do not have a good reputation for security. *Remise* taxis (booked in advance), charge US$10-16 (including toll for a return journey) airport to town. Aeroparque is 4 km north of the city centre on the riverside; *Manuel Tienda León* and *Transfer Express* have buses between the airports. *Manuel Tienda León* and *Transfer Express* also run to the centre for US$2.50; remises charge US$4-5 and ordinary taxis US$3-4. As well as by air, travellers from Uruguay arrive by ferry (fast catamaran or slower vessels), docking in the port in the heart of the city, or by bus. All international and interprovincial buses use the Retiro bus terminal at Ramos Mejía y Antártida Argentina, which is next to the Retiro railway station. Both are served by city buses, taxis and Line C of the Subte (metro). Other train services, to the province of Buenos Aires and the suburbs use Constitución, Once and Federico Lacroze stations, all served by bus, taxi and Subte.

Ins & outs
For more detailed information, see Transport, page 100

Getting around The commercial heart of the city, from Retiro station and Plaza San Martín through Plaza de Mayo to San Telmo, east of Avenida 9 de Julio, can be explored on foot, but it is a large area and it would be best to take a couple of days to do so. Many places of interest lie outside this zone, so you will need to use public transport at some stage. City **buses** are plentiful, see below for city guides. The fare is US$0.40. The **metro**, or Subte, has five lines; a single fare is US$0.35. Yellow and black **taxis** are hailed on the street (make sure the meter is set), radio taxis can be booked by phone, while remise taxis, booked from an office, cost more but are usually more reliable. See Transport, below, for full details. Street numbers start from the dock side rising from east to west, but north/south streets are numbered from Av Rivadavia, 1 block north of Av de Mayo rising in both directions. Calle Juan D Perón used to be called Cangallo and Scalabrini Ortiz used to be Canning (the old names are still referred to). For tourist information, see Directory.

Sights

The heart of the city is the **Plaza de Mayo**. The **Casa de Gobierno** on the east side of the Plaza, and called the *Casa Rosada* because it is pink, contains the offices of the President of the Republic. It is notable for its statuary and the rich furnishing of its halls. ■ *Tours: Mon-Fri 1700, free (from Hipólito Yrigoyen 219; passport is required), T4344 3804.* The **Museo de los Presidentes** (in the basement) has historical memorabilia. ■ *Mon-Fri 1000-1800, T4344 3802. Guided visits at 1100 and 1600, free.* Behind the building, in the semicircular Parque Colón, is a large statue of Columbus. **Antiguo Congreso Nacional** (Old Congress Hall, 1864-1905) on the south of the Plaza, Balcarce 139, is a National Monument. ■ *Thu, 1500-1700, free.* The **Cathedral**, Rivadavia 437, on the north of Plaza, stands on the site of the first church in Buenos Aires. The current structure dates from 1758-1807. The 18th-century towers were never rebuilt, so that the architectural proportions have suffered. The imposing tomb (1880) of the Liberator, Gen José de San Martín, is guarded by soldiers in fancy uniforms. ■ *Masses: Mon-Fri 0900, 1100, 1230, 1800, Sat 1100, 1800, Sun 1100, 1200, 1300, 1800. Visiting hours Mon-Fri 0800-1900, Sat 0900-1230, 1700-1930, Sun 0900-1400, 1600-1930. For guided visits, T4331 2845.* **Museo del Cabildo y la Revolución de Mayo** is in the old Cabildo where the movement for independence from Spain was first planned. It contains paintings, documents, furniture, arms, medals, maps, all recording the May 1810 revolution, and memorabilia of the 1806 British attack; also Jesuit art. In the patio is La Posta del Cabildo café and stalls selling handicrafts. ■ *Temporarily closed during 2002. T4334 1782 for information. Library, Mon-Fri, 1100-1900.* Also on the Plaza is the Palacio de Gobierno de la Ciudad (City Hall). Within a few blocks are the main banks and business houses.

Around the Plaza de Mayo

Argentina

Buenos Aires centre

Argentina

To Palermo Parks & Aeroparque

To Recoleta

Montevideo
Quintana
Guido
Arroyo
Juncal

Av del Libertador

Basavilbaso

Palacio
San Martín

Gral
San Martín

Arenales

Av Sante Fe

MT de Alvear

Plaza
Libertad

Paraguay

Av Callao

Pizzurno

Av Córdoba

Cerrito

Viamonte

Plaza
Lavalle

Teatro
Colón

C Pellegrini

Suipacha

Tucumán

Tribunales

Libertad

Plaza de la
República &
Obelisco

Carlos
Pellegrini

Av Corrientes

Lavalle

Dellepiane
Paraná
Uruguay
Talcahuano

To La Chacarita
Cemetery

Callao
Rodríguez Peña
Montevideo

Uruguay
Av Corrientes

9 de Julio

Diagonal
Norte

Carabelas

Av R S Peña

Sarmiento

Juan D Perón

Bartolomé Mitre

Congreso

Riyadavia
Lima
Av de
Mayo
Piedras

Plaza del
Congreso

Sáenz
Peña

Av de Mayo

Palacio del
Congreso

H Yrigoyen

Av 9 de Julio

Piedras

Alsina

Av Entre Ríos
Solís
Virrey Ceballos
L Sáenz Peña

Moreno

Moreno

Belgrano

Roca

Bernado de Irigoyen

Venezuela

San José
Santiago del Estero
Salta

México

Chile

Independencia

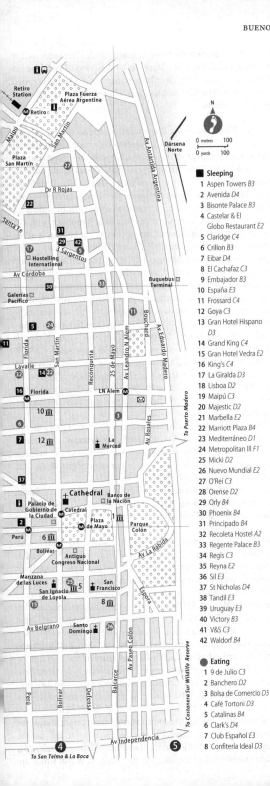

Argentina

■ Sleeping
1 Aspen Towers *B3*
2 Avenida *D4*
3 Bisonte Palace *B3*
4 Castelar & El Globo Restaurant *E2*
5 Claridge *C4*
6 Crillon *B3*
7 Eibar *D4*
8 El Cachafaz *C3*
9 Embajador *B3*
10 España *E3*
11 Frossard *C4*
12 Goya *C3*
13 Gran Hotel Hispano *D3*
14 Grand King *C4*
15 Gran Hotel Vedra *E2*
16 King's *C4*
17 La Giralda *D3*
18 Lisboa *D2*
19 Maipú *C3*
20 Majestic *D2*
21 Marbella *E2*
22 Marriott Plaza *B4*
23 Mediterráneo *D1*
24 Metropolitan III *F1*
25 Micki *D2*
26 Nuevo Mundial *E2*
27 O'Rei *C3*
28 Orense *D2*
29 Orly *B4*
30 Phoenix *B4*
31 Principado *B4*
32 Recoleta Hostel *A2*
33 Regente Palace *B3*
34 Regis *C3*
35 Reyna *E2*
36 Sil *E3*
37 St Nicholas *D4*
38 Tandil *E3*
39 Uruguay *E3*
40 Victory *B3*
41 V&S *C3*
42 Waldorf *B4*

● Eating
1 9 de Julio *C3*
2 Banchero *D2*
3 Bolsa de Comercio *D5*
4 Café Tortoni *D3*
5 Catalinas *B4*
6 Clark's *D4*
7 Club Español *E3*
8 Confitería Ideal *D3*
9 Criollo *C3*
10 Edelweiss *C2*
11 El Figón de Bonilla *C5*
12 El Gato Negro *C1*
13 El Imparcial *E2*
14 El Mundo *C3*
15 El Querandí *E4*
16 El Yatasto *B3*
17 Florida Garden *B4*
18 Güerrín *D2*
19 La Casona del Nonno *C3*
20 La Estancia *C3*
21 La Paz *C1*
22 La Pipeta *C4*
23 La Porcherie *B1*
24 La Posada de 1820 *C4*
25 La Puerto Rico *E4*
26 La Ventana *E4*
27 Las Nazarenas *A4*
28 Los Inmortales *C2/C3*
29 Los Troncos *C3*
30 Pepito & Pippo *D1*
31 Pizzería Roma *C3*
32 Richmond *C4*
33 Sabot *B4*
34 Tomo Uno *C3*

🏛 Museums
1 Casa de Gobierno (Casa Rosada) & Museo de los Presidentes *D5*
2 Museo de Armas *B3*
3 Museo de Arte Hispanoamericano Isaac Fernández Blanco *A3*
4 Museo de Arte Moderno & Teatro General San Martín *D1*
5 Museo de la Ciudad *E4*
6 Museo del Cabildo y la Revolución de Mayo *E4*
7 Museo del Teatro Nacional Cervantes *B2*
8 Museo Etnográfico JB Ambrosetti *E4*
9 Museo Judío *C2*
10 Museo y Biblioteca Mitre *D4*
11 Museo Nacional Ferroviario at Retiro Station *A3*
12 Museo Numismático Dr José Evaristo Uriburu *D4*

Argentina

On the Plaza de Mayo, the **Mothers of the Plaza de Mayo** march in remembrance of their children who disappeared during the 'dirty war' of the 1970s (their addresses are H Yrigoyen 1582 and Piedras 730). The Mothers march anti-clockwise round the central monument every Thursday at 1530, with photos of their disappeared loved-ones pinned to their chests.

West of the Plaza de Mayo Running west from the Plaza, the Av de Mayo leads 1½ km to the **Palacio del Congreso** (Congress Hall) in the Plaza del Congreso. This huge Greco-Roman building houses the seat of the legislature. Free access for public at sittings from Av Rivadavia 1850 (to check T4370 7100); passport essential. ■ *Guided tour on Mon, Tue and Fri at 1100 and 1700, when Congress is not sitting (T4953 3081).* Av de Mayo crosses the **Av 9 de Julio**, one of the widest avenues in the world, which consists of three major carriageways with heavy traffic, separated in some parts by wide grass borders. Five blocks north of Av de Mayo the great **Plaza de la República**, with a 67 m obelisk commemorating the 400th anniversary of the city's founding, is at the junction of Av 9 de Julio with Avs Roque Sáenz Peña and Corrientes. **Teatro Colón**, overlooking Av 9 de Julio with its main entrance on Libertad, between Tucumán and Viamonte, is one of the world's great opera houses. The Colón's interior is resplendent with red plush and gilt; the stage is huge, and salons, dressing rooms and banquet halls are equally sumptuous. The season runs from March to early December and there are concert performances most days. ■ *Guided tours front of house and to Museo del Teatro Colón from entrance at Toscanini 1168 (on C Viamonte side) Mon-Fri 1100 and 1500, Sat hourly 0900-1200; (Jan-Feb: Mon-Fri hourly 0900-1700), in Spanish, French (on request) and English. Recommended. US$2.50 (children or ISIC card US$1) T4378 7132/33, visitar@teatrocolon.org.ar Tickets sold 2 days before performance, from the C Tucumán or C Viamonte sides of the theatre. The cheapest seat is US$0.50 (available even on the same day) and 'El Paraíso' tickets are available for standing room in The Gods – queue for a good spot. There are free concerts quite regularly; visit www.teatrocolon.org.ar*

Close by is the **Museo del Teatro Nacional Cervantes**, Córdoba 1199, with history of the theatre in Argentina. ■ *Mon-Fri 1000-1830. The theatre also stages performances. T4815 8881 in advance.* **Museo Judío**, Libertad 769, has religious objects relating to Jewish presence in Argentina in a 19th-century synagogue. ■ *Tue and Thu 1500-1800; take identification. T4372 0014.*

La Chacarita, Guzmán 670, another well known cemetery, has the much-visited, lovingly-tended tombs of Juan Perón and Carlos Gardel, the tango singer. ■ *Daily 0700-1800, take Subte Line B to the Federico Lacroze station.*

North of the Plaza de Mayo The city's traditional shopping centre, C Florida, is reserved for pedestrians. Another shopping street is Av Santa Fe, which crosses Florida at Plaza San Martín. Av Corrientes, a street of theatres, restaurants and cafés, and nearby C Lavalle (part reserved to pedestrians), used to be the entertainment centre, but both are now regarded as faded. Recoleta, Palermo and Puerto Madero have become much more fashionable (see below). **La Merced**, J D Perón y Reconquista 207, was concluded in 1783 (façade renovated in 1905). One of the altars has a wooden figure of Christ carved during the 18th century by an Indian. It has one of the few fine carillons of bells in Buenos Aires; adjacent convent founded in 1604. On C San Martín, **Museo Numismático Dr José Evaristo Uriburu**, in the **Banco Central** library, No 216, 1st floor, is fascinating, well kept and overlooks a central foyer, ask guard for directions. ■ *Mon-Fri 1000-1500, free, T4348 3882.* **Museo y Biblioteca Mitre**, No 336, preserves intact the household of President Bartolomé Mitre; has a coin and map collection and historical archives. ■ *Mon-Fri 1300-1800, US$0.50, T4394 8240.*

The **Plaza San Martín** has a monument to San Martín in the centre and, at the north end, a memorial with an eternal flame to those who fell in the Falklands/Malvinas War of 1982. On the plaza, **Palacio San Martín**, Arenales 761, built 1905-09, is three houses linked together, the first floors of two of which are

shown on free guided tours. ■ *Thu 1100, Fri 1500,1600,1700, free, T4819 8092.*
Museo de Armas, Av Santa Fe 702 y Maipú, has all kinds of weaponry related to
Argentine history, including the 1982 Falklands/Malvinas War, plus Oriental weapons. ■ *Tue-Fri 1430-1900, closed 15 Dec-15 Mar, US$1, T4311 1071.*

Plaza Fuerza Aérea Argentina (formerly Plaza Británica) has the clock tower
presented by British and Anglo-Argentine residents (frequently vandalized), while
in the Plaza Canadá (in front of the Retiro Station) there is a Pacific Northwest
Indian totem pole, donated by the Canadian government. Behind Retiro station
Museo Nacional Ferroviario, Av del Libertador 405, is for railway fans: locomotives, machinery, documents of the Argentine system's history (building in very
poor condition). ■ *Mon-Fri 1030-1600. Archives 1030-1500, free, T4318 3343.*

Avenue 9 de Julio meets Avenue del Libertador, the principal way out of the city
to the north and west, between Retiro and La Recoleta. **Museo de Arte
Hispanoamericano Isaac Fernández Blanco,** Suipacha 1422 (three locks west of
Retiro) contains a most interesting and valuable collection of colonial art, especially
silver, in a beautiful neocolonial mansion (Palacio Noel, 1920s) with Spanish gardens. ■ *Tue-Sun, 1400-1900, Thu free; closed Jan, US$0.50. For guided visits in English or French contact Lía Guerrico at T4327 0228/0272. Guided tours in Spanish Sat,
Sun 1600.*

Nuestra Señora del Pilar, Junín 1898, is a jewel of colonial architecture dating from   Recoleta &
1732 (renovated in later centuries), facing onto the public gardens of Recoleta. A   Palermo
fine wooden image of San Pedro de Alcántara, attributed to the famous
17th-century Spanish sculptor Alonso Cano, is preserved in a side chapel on the left.

Next to it is the **Cemetery of the Recoleta,** entrance at Junín 1790, not far from
Museo de Bellas Artes (see below). It is one of the sights of Buenos Aires. With its
streets and alleys separating family mausoleums built in every imaginable architectural style, La Recoleta is often compared to a miniature city. Among the famous
names from Argentine history is Evita Perón who lies in the Duarte family mausoleum: to find it from the entrance go to the main plaza; turn left and where this avenue meets a main avenue (just past the Turriaca tomb, about 13 'blocks'), turn right;
take the third passage on the left. ■ *0700-1800. Tours last Sun of month, 1430, T4803
1594.* On Saturday and Sunday there is a good craft market near the entrance
(1100-1800), with street artists and performers. The **Centro Cultural Recoleta,**
next to the cemetery, specializes in contemporary local art. ■ *Tue-Fri 1400-2100,
Sat, Sun, holidays 1000-2100.* Also the Buenos Aires Design Centre, with furniture
shops and many restaurants. Several buses: 110, 102, 17, 60 (walk from corner of Las
Heras y Junín, two blocks); from downtown, eg Correo Central, 61/62, 93, to
Pueyrredón casi Av del Libertador, or 130 to Facultad de Derecho.

Museo de Bellas Artes (National Gallery), Av del Libertador 1473. In addition to
a fine collection of European works, particularly strong in the 19th century-French
school, there are many good Argentine works including new 19th and 20th-century
acquisitions, and wooden carvings from the Argentine hinterland. Film shows on
Friday 1830; classical music concerts on Sunday 1730. ■ *Tue-Fri 1230-1930,
Sat-Sun 0930-1930. Guided tours Tue-Sun 1700 for Argentine art, 1800 for European
art, tours for children Sat 1500, free, T4801 3390. Warmly recommended.* The **Museo
Nacional de Arte Decorativo,** Av del Libertador 1902, contains collections of
painting, furniture, porcelain, crystal, sculpture. ■ *Daily except Mon, 1400-1900.
Guided visits Thu and Wed 1630, US$1, half-price to ISIC holders, T4802 6606.* The
building is shared with the **Museo Nacional de Arte Oriental**; permanent exhibition of Chinese, Japanese, Hindu and Islamic art. ■ *Temporarily closed during 2002.*
Biblioteca Nacional (The National Library), is housed in a modern building at Av
del Libertador 1600 y Agüero 2502, where only a fraction of the extensive stock can
be seen. Art gallery, periodical and journal archives; cultural events held here.
■ *Mon-Fri 0900-2100, Sat and Sun 1200-1900. Guided tours in Spanish Mon-Sat
1500, T4806 6155.*

Argentina

Museo de Motivos Populares Argentinos José Hernández, Av Libertador 2373, widest collection of Argentine folkloric art, with rooms dedicated to Indian, colonial and Gaucho artefacts; handicraft shop and library. ■ *Wed-Sun 1300-1900, US$0.50, free Sun, T4802 7294/9967 for guided visits in English or French.*

The fine **Palermo Parks**, officially known as the Parque Tres de Febrero, are famous for their extensive rose garden, Andalusian Patio, Japanese garden (■ *Daily 1000-1800, US$1*), the Hipódromo Argentino (Palermo racecourse) (■ *Races 10 days per month, US$0.50-5, T4777 9001*). Opposite the parks are the Botanical and Zoological Gardens. At the entrance to the **Planetarium** (just off Belisario Roldán, in Palermo Park) are several large meteorites from Campo del Cielo (see page 170). ■ *Shows on weekends; small museum also Mon-Fri 1000-1800, US$2, T4771 9393.*

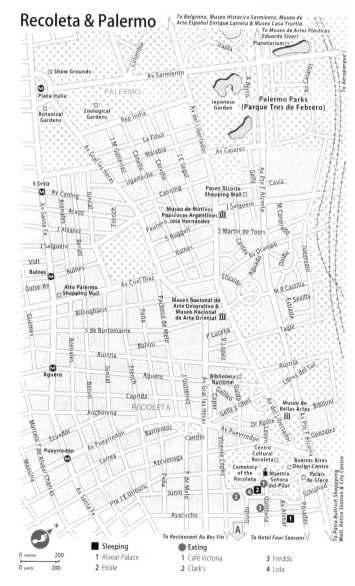

Recoleta & Palermo

Sleeping
1 Alvear Palace
2 Etoile

Eating
1 Café Victoria
2 Clark's
3 Freddo
4 Lola

0 metres 200
0 yards 200

Museo de Artes Plásticas Eduardo Sívori, Av Infanta Isabel 555 (Parque Tres de Febrero). Emphasis on 19th and 20th-century Argentine art, sculpture and tapestry. ■ *Tue-Fri 1200-1900, Sat and Sun 1000-1800, US$0.50, Wed free, T4774 9452.* The **Show Grounds** of the Argentine Rural Society, next to Palermo Park, entrance on Plaza Italia, stage the Annual Livestock Exhibition, known as Exposición Rural, in July. The **Botanical Gardens**, Santa Fe 3951, entrance from Plaza Italia (take Subte, line D) or from C República Arabe Siria, contain characteristic specimens of the world's vegetation. The trees native to the different provinces of Argentina are brought together in one section. ■ *The Gardens, daily 0800-1800, contain the Museo del Jardín Botánico, T4831 2951, whose collection of Argentine Flora is open Mon-Fri 0800-1500.*

There are three important museums in Belgrano: **Museo Histórico Sarmiento**, Juramento 2180 (Belgrano), the National Congress and presidential offices in 1880; documents and personal effects of Sarmiento; library of his work. ■ *Tue-Fri and Sun 1400-1830, US$0.50 Thu free, guided visits Sun 1600, T4783 7555, museosarmiento@fibertel.com.ar* **Museo de Arte Español Enrique Larreta**, Juramento 2291, Belgrano. The home of the writer Larreta, with paintings and religious art from the 13th to the 20th century. ■ *Daily 1000-1945, Tue closed, guided visits Sun 1500,1700, T4783 2640 for guided tour in language other than Spanish. US$0.50, Thu free.* **Museo Casa Yrurtia**, O'Higgins 2390, esq Blanco Encalada (Belgrano), an old house crammed with sculpture, paintings, furniture and the collections of artist Rogelio Yrurtia and his wife; peaceful garden. ■ *Tue-Fri 1300-1900, Sun 1500-1900, US$0.50, Fri free, guided visits Sun 1600, T/F4781 0385.*

The church of **San Ignacio de Loyola**, begun 1664, is the oldest colonial building in Buenos Aires (renovated in 18th and 19th centuries). It stands in a block of Jesuit origin, called the **Manzana de las Luces** (Enlightenment Square – Moreno, Alsina, Perú and Bolívar). Also in this block are the Colegio Nacional de Buenos Aires, formerly the Jesuits' Colegio Máximo (18th century), the Procuraduría de las Misiones and 18th-century tunnels. For centuries the whole block was the centre of intellectual activity. ■ *Church and School on C Bolívar. Guided tours to the tunnels from Perú 272. Mon-Fri 1600 (includes Church and School tour), Sat and Sun 1500, 1630, 1800, 2030 (candlelit tour, US$2) in Spanish (in English by prior arrangement), recommended, arrive 15 mins before tour, US$1, T4342 4655/9930.*

Museo de la Ciudad, Alsina 412. Permanent exhibition covering social history and popular culture, special exhibitions on daily life in Buenos Aires changed every two months, and a reference library open to the public. ■ *Mon-Fri, 1100-1900, Sun, 1500-1900, US$1, free on Wed, T4343 2123.* **San Francisco**, Alsina y Defensa, controlled by the Franciscan Order, was built 1730-1754 and given a new façade in 1911. **Santo Domingo**, Defensa y Belgrano, was founded in 1751. During the British attack on Buenos Aires in 1806 some of Whitelocke's soldiers took refuge in the church. The local forces bombarded it, the British capitulated and their regimental colours were preserved in the church. General Belgrano is buried here. There are summer evening concerts in the church.

Museo Etnográfico JB Ambrosetti, Moreno 350, has anthropological and ethnographic collections from around the world, including Bolivian and Mapuche silverwork. ■ *Wed-Sun 1430-1830, US$0.50.*

One of the few places which still has late colonial and Rosista buildings is the *barrio* of **San Telmo**, south of Plaza de Mayo, around Plaza Dorrego. It is an artistic centre, with cafés, antique shops and a pleasant atmosphere. There is a regular Sunday antiques market at the Plaza Dorrego (see page 99), with tango demonstrations on Sunday afternoon. The 29 bus connects La Boca with San Telmo. **Museo de Arte Moderno**, San Juan 350, with a salon at Av Corrientes 1530, 9th floor: international exhibitions and a permanent collection of 20th-century art in an old tobacco warehouse. ■ *Tue-Fri 1000-2000, Sat, Sun and holidays 1100-2000. Guided tours*

South of Plaza de Mayo

San Telmo & La Boca

Argentina

Tue-Sun 1700. US$0.50, Wed free, T4361 1121. **Museo del Cine Pablo Ducros Hicken**, Defensa 1220, dedicated to the history of Argentine cinema, with a library of over 600 sound films and newsreels from four decades. ■ *Mon-Fri 1000-1800, Sun 1530-1830, US$0.50, free on Wed. Film exhibitions on Wed and Sun 1600, US$0.50, T4361 2462.*

Parque Lezama, Defensa y Brasil, originally one of the most beautiful in the city, has an imposing statue of Pedro de Mendoza, who founded the original city in 1536 on this spot, according to tradition. In the park is the **Museo Histórico Nacional**, Defensa 1600.Trophies and mementoes of historical events, divided into halls depicting stages of Argentine history. Here are San Martín's uniforms, a replica of his sabre, and the original furniture and door of the house in which he died at Boulogne. ■ *Tue-Fri 1100-1800, Sat and Sun 1400-1900, US$0.50, guided tours Sat and Sun 1530, T4307 4457.*

East of the Plaza de Mayo, behind the Casa Rosada, a broad avenue, Paseo Colón, runs south towards San Telmo and the picturesque old port district known as **La Boca**, where the Riachuelo flows into the Plata. La Boca is reached by bus 152 from Av Santa Fe, or Alem, or bus 29 from Plaza de Mayo, US$0.40. For a tour of La Boca, start at Plaza Vuelta de Rocha, near Av Pedro de Mendoza and Dr Del Valle Iberlucea, then walk up Caminito, the little pedestrian street used as a theatre and art market. Visit the **Museo de Bellas Artes de la Boca**, Pedro de Mendoza 1835, with more than 1,000 works by Argentine artists, particularly Benito Quinquela Martín (1890-1977), who painted La Boca port life. Also sculptures and figureheads rescued from ships. ■ *Tue-Sun 1000-1730, free, T4301 1080.* La Boca, mostly Italian, has its own distinctive life and parts of it are very touristy. The area, with the adjacent industrial and meat-packing suburb of Avellaneda, is generally dirty and dangerous at night, but the tourist section, from the Avellaneda bridge to El Caminito, has been renovated. It is especially lively when the Boca Juniors football club is playing at home. **Museo de la Pasión Boquense**, Brandsen 805, T4362 1100 For Boca Juniors and football fans. ■ *Tue-Sun 1000-1900 (closed if a match at Boca Stadium), US$3.50.*

San Telmo

	Sleeping	4	La Casita de San Telmo	8	Youth Hostal	3	El Viejo Almacén
1	Bolívar	5	Oxford		Eating	4	La Casa de Esteban de Luca
2	Colonial	6	Res Carly	1	Bar Sur	5	La Convención de San Telmo
3	Hostal de San Telmo	7	Victoria	2	El Desnivel		

N

Not to scale

Fragata Presidente Sarmiento, dock 3, next to Av Alicia Moreau de Justo y Perón, Puerto Madero, a sailing ship used as a naval training ship until 1961; now a museum. ■ *Mon-Thu 0900-2300, Fri-Sun 0900-0200, US$1, T4334 9386.* Nearby, in dock 1, is the **Corbeta Uruguay**, the sailing ship which rescued Otto Nordenskjold's Antarctic expedition in 1903. ■ *Daily 0900-2100 all year, US$0.50, T4314 1090.* The **Puerto Madero** dock area has been renovated, the 19th-century warehouses being turned into restaurants and bars, a popular nightspot. East of San Telmo on the far side of the docks, the Av Costanera runs as a long, spacious boulevard. **Museo de Telecomunicaciones** in a magnificent art-deco building on the Costanera Sur, Av de los Italianos 851. ■ *Sat-Sun 1400-1800, T4968 3116/20.* A stretch of marshland reclaimed from the river forms the interesting **Costanera Sur Wildlife Reserve**, where there are many *coypu* (large rodents) and reptiles such as the *lagarto overo* (tupinambis). More than 200 species of birds have been identified, including the curve-billed reed hunter. ■ *Tue-Sun 0800-1900 (in summer, closes at 2000). The entrance is at Av Tristán Achával Rodríguez 1550, T4315 1320/4129; for pedestrians and bikers only. Free, guided tours available at weekends, but much can be seen from the road before then (binoculars useful). It is 30 mins walk from the entrance to the river shore, taking about 3 hrs to walk the whole perimeter. In summer it is very hot with little shade. For details (birdwatching, in particular) contact Aves Argentinas/AOP (see* Useful addresses *below). Take bus 4 or 2.*

Docks & Costanera Sur

Argentina

Excursions

This popular recreational centre on the Río Luján has an excellent fruit and handi-crafts market at nearby Canal San Fernando on Sunday. North of the town is the delta of the Río Paraná: innumerable canals and rivulets, with holiday homes and restaurants on the banks and a profitable fruit growing centre. The fishing is excellent and the peace is only disturbed by motor-boats at weekends. Regattas are held in November and March. Regular launch services (*lanchas colectivas*) run to all parts of the delta, including taxi launches – watch prices for these – from the wharf (*Estación Fluvial*). Tourist catamarans, two services a day from Mon to Fri, hourly at weekends, 1 to 2-hr trips, US$3.50-5, run by *Interisleña* (on Río Tigre, T4731 0261/63) and *Río Tur* (Puerto de Frutos, T4731 0280). Longer trips (4½ hrs) to the open Río de la Plata estuary are available only with *Catamarán Libertad* from Puerto de Olivos at weekends.

Tigre
Population: 40,000
29 km NW of Buenos Aires

The **Museo Naval**, Paseo Victorica 602, is worth a visit. ■ *Mon-Fri 0830-1730, Sat, Sun 1030-1830, US$1, 50% ISIC discount, T4749 0608.* Covers origins and development of Argentine navy. There are also relics of the 1982 Falklands/Malvinas War on display outside. **The Museo de la Reconquista**, Av Liniers 818 (y Padre Castañeda), near the location of Liniers' landing in 1806, celebrates the reconquest of Buenos Aires by the Argentines from the British in 1806-07. ■ *Wed-Sun 1000-1800, free, T4512 4496.* Tourist office at Av Italia y Mitre, T4512 4497, 0900-1800, www.tigre.gov.ar *Centro de Guías de Tigre y Delta*, T4749 0543, www.guiasdelta.com.ar For guided walks and launch trips.

Sleeping and eating There are no good hotels in Tigre itself. On the islands of the Delta: **B** pp *El Tropezón*, T4728 1012. An old inn on the Río Paraná de las Palmas island, including meals, formerly a haunt of Hemingway, now frequented by affluent *porteños*. Highly recommended despite the mosquitoes. **D** pp *l'Marangatú*, on Río San Antonio, T4728 0752. Includes breakfast and dinner, pool, sports facilities. **A** *Los Pecanes*, 90 mins by launch from Tigre, T4728 1932. Price is for 2 nights on weekends for a double room with breakfast, bath, fan, mosquito nets (20% discount on weekdays); Anglo-Argentine owners, meals extra, all vegetables home-grown, good *asados*. **F** pp *Delta Youth Hostel*, at Río Luján y Abra Vieja, T4728 0396/4717 4648 Clean, 3 ha park, hot showers (**B** double room with bath), table tennis, volleyball, canoes, restaurant, basic cooking facilities. Restaurants on the waterfront in Tigre across the Río Tigre from railway line; cheaper places on Italia and Cazón on the near side. There are also restaurants on islands in the delta to which excursions run.

Argentina

Transport Trains: Take train from Retiro station (FC Mitre section) to Tigre or to Bartolomé Mitre and change to the Maipú station (the stations are linked) for the Tren de la Costa, T4732 6000, US$1 one way (US$0.75 Mon-Fri), every 10 mins from 0700 to 2300 (Sat, Sun 0830-2400), 25 mins journey. (Buses to Tren de la Costa are 60 from Constitución, 19 or 71 from Once, 152 from centre.) Several stations on this line have shopping centres (eg San Isidro), as does the terminus, Estación Delta (*El Parque de la Costa*), T4732 6200. You can get off the train as many times as you want on the same ticket. **Buses** Take No 60 from Constitución: the 60 'bajo' takes a little longer than the 60 'alto' but is more interesting for sightseeing. **Ferries** To Carmelo, Uruguay leave from *Cacciola* dock (see page 104). Overnight trips to Carmelo (US$50-60 including accommodation) and bus connections to Montevideo are also available from Cacciola.

Isla Martín García
45 km N of Buenos Aires

This island in the Río de la Plata (Juan Díaz de Solís' landfall in 1516) used to be a military base. Now it is an ecological/historical centre and an ideal excursion from the capital, with many trails through the cane brakes, trees and rocky outcrops – interesting birds and flowers. Boat trips 3 to 4 weekly from Tigre at 0800, returning 1700, 3 hrs journey, US$18 including lunch and guide (US$14 transport only). Reservations can be made through *Cacciola* (address under Ferries to Uruguay, above), who also handle bookings for the inn and restaurant on the island. There is also camping and hostel accommodation.

Luján
Phone code: 02323
Population: 65,000
66 km W of Buenos Aires

This is a place of pilgrimage for devout Catholics throughout Argentina. An image of the Virgin was being taken from church to church in the area in 1630 by ox cart. The cart got stuck, in spite of strenuous efforts by men and oxen to move it. This was taken as a sign that the Virgin willed she should stay there. A chapel was built for the image, and around it grew Luján. The chapel has long since been superseded by an impressive neo-Gothic basilica and the Virgin now stands on the High Altar. Her days are 8 May and 8 December. Each arch of the church is dedicated to an Argentine province, and the transepts to Uruguay, Paraguay and Ireland. Behind the Cabildo is the river, with river walks, cruises and restaurants (an excellent one is **L'Eau Vive** on the road to Buenos Aires at Constitución 2112, run by nuns, pleasant surroundings). Luján is a very popular spot at weekends.

Museo Histórico Colonial, in the old Cabildo building, is one of the most interesting museums in the country. Exhibits illustrate its historical and political development. General Beresford, the commander of the British troops which seized Buenos Aires in 1806, was a prisoner here, as were Generals Mitre, Paz and Belgrano in later years. ■ *Thu, Fri 1215-1730, Sat, Sun 1015-1730. US$0.50.* Next to it are museums devoted to transport and to motor vehicles and there is also a poor **Museo de Bellas Artes**. ■ *Buses from Buenos Aires (Plaza Once) Bus 52 and 57, frequent, 1 hr 50 mins with direct service, US$2.25. To San Antonio de Areco, 5 a day, US$1.80, Empresa Argentina, 1 hr. Train to Once station, US$1 (change at Moreno).*

San Antonio de Areco
Phone code: 02326
Colour map 8, grid B5
113 km NW of Buenos Aires

San Antonio de Areco, with its single-storey buildings, tree-lined streets and popular *costanera*, is an attractive centre for visiting *estancias*. Many *gaucho* objects, ceramics, silver, leather and colonial furniture are sold. **Museo Gauchesco Ricardo Güiraldes**, on Camino Güiraldes y Aureliano, is a replica of a typical *estancia* of the late 19th century, containing artefacts associated with *gaucho* life and Güiraldes, the writer who described it. His best-known book is *Don Segundo Sombra*. ■ *Daily except Tue, 1100-1700, US$1.* There is also a **Parque de Flora y Fauna Carlos Merti** opposite the bridge ■ *0900-1200, 1400-1800, US$1.* Also the **Centro Cultural y Museo Usina Vieja**, Alsina 66, city museum ■ *Mon-Fri 0900-1545, Sat, Sun, holidays 1000-1700, free.*

Día de la Tradición, a *gaucho* festival with traditional parades, games, events on horseback, music and dance, is celebrated in the week up to 10 November each year (accommodation is hard to find). ■ *Tourist office, Zerboni y Arellano, T453165 or at Arellano 115, www.arecoturismo.com.ar Buses from Buenos Aires: from Plaza Once, 2 hrs, US$2, every hour; also Chevallier from Retiro bus terminal, US$4, 2 hrs.*

Sleeping and eating D *San Carlos*, Zerboni y Zapiola, T453106, www.hotel-sancarlos.com.ar Ask in advance for meals. **D** *Res San Cayetano*, Segundo Sombra y Rivadavia, T422166. Good, comfortable. **Camping** Near town centre, also *Auto-camping La Porteña*, 12 km from town on the Güiraldes estancia, good access roads. Many *parrillas* on the bank of the Río Areco. *La Olla de Cobre*, Matheu 433, is a good chocolate shop. **Estancias** The main *estancias* for day visits (about US$30 pp) or overnight stays (**LL**) are: *La Bamba*, T02326-456293, Buenos Aires T4732 1269, full board, www.la-bamba.com.ar *El Ombú*, T492080, Buenos Aires T4710 2795, elombu@sinectis.com.ar *La Porteña*, T453770, F454157, Buenos Aires T4822 1325, *La Cinacina*, T452045 or T452773, www.lacinacina.com.ar (principally a day *estancia*, but some accommodation), and *Don Silvano*, day visits only, T4767 2590/5289.

Essentials

The following list is only a selection; exclusion does not necessarily imply non-recommendation. All accommodation is graded by the number of beds available, and services supplied. Rates given below are generally the minimum rates. Room tax is 21% and is not always included in the price. Air conditioning is a must in high summer. Many of the cheaper hotels in the central area give large reductions on the daily rate for long stays. Hotels with red-green lights, or marked *Albergue Transitorio,* are hotels for homeless lovers (for stays of 1½-2 hrs).

Sleeping

5-star hotels in our LL range *Alvear Palace*, Alvear 1891, T/F4808 2100, www.alvearpalace.com Older-style, near Recoleta, roof garden, shopping gallery, elegant, extremely good. *Claridge*, Tucumán 535, T4314 7700, www.claridge-hotel.com.ar Highly recommended. *Etoile*, R Ortiz 1835 in Recoleta, T4805 2626, www.etoile.com.ar Outstanding location, rooftop pool, rooms with kitchenette. *Four Seasons*, Posadas 1086, T4321 1200, www.fourseasons.com/buenosaires Modern tower in Retiro district, pool, restaurant, including 7 suites at luxurious La Mansión residence. **L** *Hilton*, Av Macacha Güemes 351, Puerto Madero, T4891 0000, reservationsba@hilton.com A few blocks from banking district and located next to Costanera Sur; *El Faro* restaurant, health club and pool. *Marriott Plaza*, Florida 1005, T4318 3000, www.marriotthotels.com On Plaza San Martín, one of the most traditional hotels in town, opened in 1908. **4-star AL** *Crillon*, Santa Fe 796, T4312 8181, info@hotelcrillon.com.ar Comfortable, good breakfast. **AL** *Regente Palace*, Suipacha 964, T4328 6800, info@regente.com Very good, central, English spoken, buffet breakfast, sports facilities, stores luggage. **AL** *Aspen Towers*, Paraguay 857, T4313 1919, www.aspentowers.com.ar Small, spacious rooms, good breakfast. **AL** *Bisonte Palace*, MT de Alvear 910, T4328 4751, bispal@infovia.com.ar Very good, welcoming. **B** *Grand King*, Lavalle 560, T4393 4452, www.grandking.com.ar Helpful, English spoken. **B** *Principado*, Paraguay 481, T4313 3022, hotel@principado.com.ar With breakfast, central, helpful. **B** *Castelar*, Av de Mayo 1152, T4383 5001, F4383 8388. Elegant and attractive 1920s hotel, Turkish baths, good.

3-star B *Embajador*, Carlos Pellegrini 1185, T4326 5302 embajador@hotelnet.com.ar Good, with breakfast. **C** *Eibar*, Florida 328, T4325 0969, hoteleibar@redesdelsur.com.ar With breakfast, quiet, helpful, old fashioned. **B** *Phoenix*, San Martín 780, T4516 0507, phoenix@sinectis.com.ar Includes breakfast, a/c, well located, helpful, English spoken, lovely turn-of-the-century interior. **B** *Regis*, Lavalle 813, T4327 2605, regisventas@orho.hoteles.com.ar Good value, nice atmosphere. **B** *Waldorf*, Paraguay 450, T4312 2071, www.waldorf-hotel.com.ar Comfortable, rooms of varying standards, garage, a/c. **C** *Orly*, Paraguay 474, T/F4312 5344, www.orly.com.ar Good location, old fashioned, helpful, good lunches, English spoken, holds mail for guests, arranges tours and taxis, a/c. **C** *Victory*, Maipú 880, T4314 5440, www.victoryhotel.com.ar A/c, modern, heating, TV, comfortable, luggage store.

2-star C *Frossard*, Tucumán 686, T4322 1811, frossardh@uol.com.ar Renovated, comfortable, cable TV, convenient, good. **C** *Goya*, Suipacha 748, T4322 9269, goyahotel@infovia.com.ar A/c, quiet, **B** for luxurious double rooms. **C** *Nuevo Mundial*, Av de Mayo 1298, T4383 0011, mundial@house.com.ar A/c, luggage store, laundry service, comfortable, restaurant. **C** *Gran Hotel Hispano*, Av de Mayo 861, T4342 3472,

More expensive hotels can often be booked more cheaply through Buenos Aires travel agencies. Most hotels will give a discount for cash

Argentina

hhispano@hhispano.com.ar With breakfast, some a/c, spacious, pleasant patio, stores luggage, helpful.

1-star or below C *Avenida*, Av de Mayo 623, T4342 5664, F4343 7951. With breakfast, a/c, heating, simple but elegant, comfortable, bar. C *Lisboa*, B Mitre 1282, T4383 1141. With breakfast, central, cheaper for smaller double rooms. C *Majestic*, Libertad 121, T4382 1949. Subte Lima, colonial-style, safe, good value, includes breakfast. C *Marbella*, Av de Mayo 1261, T/F4383 3573, reservas@hotelmarbella.com.ar Modernized, quiet, breakfast, pricey, fans, English, French, Italian, Portuguese and German spoken. Highly recommended, no credit cards accepted. C *Gran Hotel Vedra*, Av de Mayo 1350, T4383 0584. Cheaper rooms with fan, stores luggage, small restaurant, English spoken. Recommended. D *King's*, Corrientes 623, T4322 8161, F4393 4452. With breakfast, a/c, helpful. D *La Giralda*, Tacuarí 17, T4345 3917, F4342 2142. Student discounts and for long stays. Recommended. D *Maipú*, Maipú 735, T4322 5142. Popular, hot water, basic, stores luggage, laundry facilities. D *Mediterráneo*, Rodríguez Peña 149, T4372 2852. Basic (E without bath), central, helpful, safe, stores luggage, laundry facilities. Recommended. D *O'Rei*, Lavalle 733, T4393 7186. E without bath, central, simple but comfortable, spotless, laundry facilities, helpful, fastidious staff. D *Orense*, B Mitre 1359, T4372 4441, informes@hotelorense.com.ar With breakfast, a/c, TV, laundry facilities. Recommended. D *Reyna*, Av de Mayo 1120, T4381 2496. Old fashioned, helpful, cheaper without bath, warm, noisy, ask for discounts. D *Tandil*, Av de Mayo 890, T4343 2597. Some rooms with bath (E without), TV, fan, central, good. D *Uruguay*, Tacuarí 83, T4334 3456. Central, good value. Recommended (opposite is D *España*, T4343 5541, old-fashioned and full of character). E *Micki*, Talcahuano 362, T4371 2376. No a/c, TV, basic, good value. E *Sil*, H Yrigoyen 775, T4331 8275. Nice but no heating. F pp *Metropolitan*, Medrano Station, Av Corrientes 3973, T4862 3366, www.hotelmetro.com.ar And *Metropolitan II*, Boedo 449, T4932 7547, F4931 1133 (Subte Line A to Castro Barros or Line E to Boedo), also *Metropolitan III*, Virrey Ceballos 411 3° G,, T4381 5239. All with breakfast, kitchen and laundry facilities, parking (D doubles with bath; E without), English spoken, good value. **Longer term accommodation** is offered by *Juan Carlos Dima*, Puan 551 C, T4432 4898, F4432 7101, juanka@sion.com (minimum 1 week), kitchen facilities, contacts with language and tango schools, accommodation also in San Telmo, English spoken. Also *Sra Anita*, Av Corrientes 2989, p 10c, T4864 4132. US$130 per month, shared rooms, good atmosphere, use of kitchen, laundry facilities. E pp at *Hotel San Román*, Moreno 1143, T4384 0582. Central, *Tía* supermarket nearby.

In San Telmo C *La Casita de San Telmo* Cochabamba 286 T/F4307 5073/8796, guimbo@pinos.com 6 rooms in restored colonial house, rooms rented by week or month. D *Oxford*, Chacabuco 719, T4361 8581. With breakfast, spacious rooms with bath, fan, good value, safe. E *Bolívar*, Bolívar 1356, T4300 6507. Good, shared bath, kitchen, laundry, helpful. E *Res Carly*, Humberto 1 464, T4361 7710. Cheaper without bath, fan, quiet, basic, kitchen facilities, good value. E *Colonial*, Bolívar 1357, near Constitución station. Rooms and dormitories, basic. E pp *Victoria*, Chacabuco 726, T/F4361 2135. With bath (F pp without), fan, kitchen and laundry facilities, popular with tango dancers, good meeting place.

Youth hostels E pp *Buenos Ayres*, Pasaje San Lorenzo 320, San Telmo, T4361 0694, www.buenosayreshostel.com New, with breakfast, also rooms with bath, hot water, kitchen, laundry. E pp *Che Lagarto*, Av San Juan 1836, T4304 7618 (subte line E to Entre Ríos; buses 37, 53, 126), www.chelagarto.com.ar Backpackers' hostel with special events to involve guests in local culture, including tango classes, lively atmosphere, breakfast, pool, internet access, self-catering. Highly recommended. E pp *El Cachafaz*, Viamonte 982, T4328 1445, www.elcachafaz.com.ar Shared rooms, internet access, laundry facilities. E pp *Recoleta Hostel*, Libertad 1216 (no sign), T4812 4419, F4815 6622, www.trhostel.com.ar Shared and C double rooms, cooking facilities, TV. E pp *St Nicholas*, B Mitre 1691 (y Rodríguez Peña), T4373 5920/8841, www.stnicholashostal.com.ar Beautifully restored old house, spotless, cooking facilities, large roof terrace, luggage store; also double rooms. Recommended. E pp *Hostal de San Telmo*, Carlos Calvo 614, T4300 6899, elhostal@satlink.com Dormitories, small double rooms, breakfast, kitchen, internet access, luggage store, English spoken (bus 126, 9, 70 or 45 from bus terminal, 86 from airport). E pp *V&S*, Viamonte 887, T4322 0994, www.hostelclub.com **B** in double room, central, some lovely rooms, a/c or fan, kitchen and laundry facilities, lounge, bar, mini gym, luggage storage, internet access, airport pick-up. Recommended. **F** pp *Del Aguila*, Espinosa 1628, T4581 6663, www.delaguilahostel.com Hot water, cooking and laundry facilities, large roof terrace, free transport to bus terminal and airport, internet access (buses 24, 105, 106, 109, 146; bus 86 from the airport). **F** pp and up *Milhouse Hostel*, Hipolito Yrigoyen 959, T/F4345 9694, www.milhousehostel.com In 1890 house, lovely rooms and dorms, central, comfortable, free breakfast, cooking facilities, laundry, internet, tango lessons. Recommended. See page 72 *Red Argentina de Alojamiento para Jóvenes*. Worldwide chain *Hostel-Inn* is opening hostels in Buenos Aires, www.hostel-inn.com, first at Humberto I 820, T4300 7992, **E**.

Argentina

Argentina

Student residences F pp *Dido*, Sarmiento 1343 T4373 5349, hosteldido@bigfoot.com.ar With kitchen, TV, roof terrace, single or shared rooms, monthly and ISIC discounts. Recommended. Accommodation for students and tourists with host families is arranged by *Argentina B&B*, run by Silvia Demetilla, www.bedargentina.tripod.com For accommodation in Buenos Aires and in other towns. Also *La Casa de Etty*, Luis Sáenz Peña 617, T4384 6378. Run by Esther Corcias, who also runs **Organización Coret** (host families), coret@ ciudad.com.ar *B&T Argentina*, Julián Alvarez 2850 p 7, T4804 1783, www.bytargentina.com Accommodation in residences and host families.

Apartments/self catering *BUENOSAIRESFLATRENTAL*, Araoz 2305 4-B C.P (1425), T155 183 5367, www.rioflatrental.com

Camping About 15 km out at Lomas de Zamora, US$3 pp per night, including swimming pool, 24-hr security, take drinking water; take bus 141 from Plaza Italia or 28 from Retiro to Puente La Noria then No 540 to Villa Albertina which passes the entrance. **G** *Burzaco*, off 25 de Mayo: leave the city on Autopista Ezeiza, exit at Ciudad Evita, south on Ruta 4 towards La Plata, at roundabout after 20 km turn south onto Av Espora then left on to 25 de Mayo by *Aspro* Station. Site is crowded at weekends, friendly, no showers, helpful staff.

Eating

The Buenos Aires Herald publishes a handy Guide to Good Eating in Buenos Aires with a guide to local wines) by Dereck Foster. There is also El Libro de los Restaurantes de Buenos Aires, published annually, describing the city's major restaurants

Eating out in Buenos Aires is very good but not cheap. Good restaurants charge US$20 pp and up; more modest places US$10-12 pp. **NB** In many mid to upper range restaurants, lunch is far cheaper than dinner. Lunch or dinner in a normal restaurant cost US$5-8 (cutlet, salad, ¼ of table wine, dessert); a portion at a *comidas para llevar* (take away) place cost US$1.50-2.50. Many cheaper restaurants are *tenedor libre*, eat as much as you like for a fixed price. The following list gives only those restaurants easily accessible for people staying in the city centre.

In the district between Plaza San Martín and Plaza de Mayo: *Clark's*, Sarmiento 645. In old English outfitter's shop. Recommended, well-cooked food, very expensive, busy, fish and lamb specialities, set lunch very good value. *Bolsa de Comercio*, 25 de Mayo 359. Downstairs at the Stock Exchange, good but expensive, lunch only. *Sabot*, 25 de Mayo 756. Very good business lunches. *La Pipeta*, San Martín 498, downstairs. Serving for 40 years, good, noisy, closed Sun. *La Posada de 1820*, Tucumán 501. Good value, steak and chips etc. *La Estancia*, Lavalle 941. Popular with business people, excellent grills and service, expensive. *La Casona del Nonno*, Lavalle 827. Popular, *parrilla* and pasta, not cheap. *El Palacio de la Papa Frita*, Lavalle 735 and 954, Corrientes 1612. 10% ISIC discount. Good value *parrilla* at *Criollo*, Maipú 442. *El Mundo*, Maipú 550. Good. *Pizzería Roma*, Lavalle 888. Cheap and good quality, delicious spicy *empanadas* and *ñoquis*, good breakfasts. *Los Inmortales*, Lavalle 746. Specializes in pizza, good, 10% ISIC discount. There are other locations: some serve *à la carte* dishes which are plentiful, and are open also from 1500-2000 when most other restaurants are closed. *El Figón de Bonilla*, Alem 673. Rustic style, good. *Dora*, Alem 1016. Huge steaks, get there early to beat the queue. *Los Troncos*, Suipacha 732. Good grills. *El Yatasto*, Suipacha 1015. Small, open till late, popular. *Catalinas*, Reconquista 850. Seafood, very expensive. *El Establo*, Paraguay 489, good *parrilla*, for eating at any time. **A few blocks from this district**: La Recova, an area on the 1000 block of Posadas, near *Four Seasons Hotel* and underneath the Autopista Arturo Illia, has several moderate to expensive restaurants, eg *El Mirasol*, No 1032, *parrilla*, *Piegari*, No 1042, and *La Tasca de Plaza Mayor*, No 1052. *Juana M*, Carlos Pellegrini 1535. Offers very good dishes at quite low prices in a spacious basement. *Las Nazarenas*, Reconquista 1132. Good for beef, expensive. *Natacha*, M T de Alvear 901. Steaks and wine good value. *Petit París*, Av Santa Fe 774. Popular with locals, good lunch.

In Recoleta *Lola*, Roberto M Ortiz 1805. Good pasta, lamb and fish but expensive. *Granda*, Junín 1281. French bistro, moderate to expensive, good. Nearby, 2 blocks from Recoleta towards Av Callao, *Au Bec Fin*, Vicente López 1827. Top quality, has fixed-price lunch and dinner, plus à la carte, reservations needed. *Rodi Bar*, Vicente López 1900. Excellent *bife* and other dishes. *Clark's* Junín 1777, T4801 9502. English atmosphere, excellent service. Recommended. *Grants*, Junín 1155. *Tenedor libre*, mainly Chinese, also barbecued meats, pasta, seafood, all-you-can-eat US$3.50, lunches US$2.50, go with an appetite, other locations. *El Sanjuanino*, Posadas y Callao. Dishes from San Juan, cheap.

In the San Telmo area *Calle de Angeles*, Chile 318. Nice setting in an old, covered street, high standards. *La Convención de San Telmo*, Carlos Calvo 375. Very good food, tango show. *La Casa de Esteban de Luca*, Defensa 1000. Very good food and wines. *El Desnivel*, Defensa 855. Popular, cheap, good atmosphere. For ice cream, *Sumo*, Independencia y Piedras.

The **Costanera Rafael Obligado** along the river front (far end of Aeroparque) is lined with eating places: try *Morena Beach* (good river views at Club Náutico Puerto Norte), or *Happening* Clo Clo, La Pampa y Costanera, T4788 0488. Good value for lunch, reservation required. Typical *parrilla* at *Rodizio*, Costanera Norte, opposite Balneario Coconor. Self-service and waiter service, other branches, for example Av Callao y Juncal, good value, popular.

Take taxi, or colectivo 45 from Plaza Constitución, Plaza San Martín or Retiro to Ciudad Universitaria

In **Puerto Madero**, along Av Alicia Moreau de Justo (from north to south), are *Katrine*, No 138. Pasta and fish. *Xcaret* No 164. *Bice*, No 192, mostly Italian, good. *El Mirasol del Puerto*, No 202. *Bahía Madero*, No 430. Highly recommended. *Las Lilas*, No 516. Excellent *parrilla*. Similar is *La Caballeriza* at No 580. Good service. *La Parolaccia*, Nos 1052 and 1160. Pasta and seafood, expensive, but does bargain executive lunch for US$5 Mon-Fri only. Branches of *Rodizio* and *Happening*. Many others. Cheapest places next to Fragata Sarmiento.

Near the Teatro Colón *Tomo Uno*, Carlos Pellegrini 521 (*Hotel Panamericano*). Expensive, trout, mignon, shrimp, home-made pasta, closed Sun. *9 de Julio*, C Pellegrini 587. Very good value. *Edelweiss*, Libertad 431. Tuna steaks, pasta, grill, expensive and famous. *El Cuartito*, Talcahuano 937, a traditional and good *pizzería*. **By Congreso**: *Plaza Mayor*, Venezuela 1399. Seafood, very popular. *Pepito*, Montevideo 383. Very good. *Pippo*, Montevideo 341. Large pasta house, simple food, very popular, also at Paraná 356. *Chiquilín*, Sarmiento 1599. Pasta and meat, good value. *La Porcherie*, Montevideo 966. Wide selection, good food and prices. *La María*, México 1316 Good *parrilla* and pasta.

La Boca *El Obrero*, Caffarena 64 y Av Pedro de Mendoza. For pasta. *El Puentecito*, Vieytes 1895. Cheap Argentine dishes.

Typical Boca restaurants on Necochea, but check the hygiene. All serve antipasto, pasta and chicken; no beef. All bands are loud

Palermo and Belgrano There are many in this area. A number of places have opened in the arches under the railway line that runs through Palermo park. *Grant's*, Scalabrini Ortiz 3170, see above. *Christophe*, Fitz Roy 1994. French, reasonably priced. *Cangas de Narcea*, Godoy Cruz 3108. Good local restaurant, steak, pasta. *La Cupertina*, Cabrera 5300 y Godoy Cruz. Small, good value regional dishes, homemade desserts, also take-away. *Garbis*, Monroe y 11 de Septiembre, near Barrancas de Belgrano. Armenian and Middle Eastern dishes, moderate prices. Several Tex/Mex places, eg *Xalapa*, El Salvador y Gurruchaga, *Cielito Lindo*, El Salvador 4999, and *Frida Kahlo*, Ciudad de La Paz 3093 (between Belgrano and Núñez).

Other Italian *Broccolino*, Esmeralda 776. Excellent, very popular, try *pechuguitas*. 4 famous *pizzerías* in the centre are on Corrientes: *Banchero*, No 1300; *Las Cuartetas*, No 838, *Güerrín*, No 1368 and *Los Inmortales*, No 1369, same chain as above. *Il Gatto*, Corrientes 959. Popular and reasonably priced. *Angelín*, Córdoba 5270. Popular pizzería, take away and eat in.

Latin American *Cumaná*, Rodríguez Peña 1149. *Empanadas, tamales, humitas*, etc, also pizzas, good value. *Status*, Virrey Cevallos e H Yrigoyen. Peruvian dishes. **Spanish**: *Club Español*, B de Irigoyen 180 (on Av 9 de Julio, near Av de Mayo). Luxurious ambience, fine building, quiet, very good food, not cheap. *El Imparcial*, H Yrigoyen 1201, and opposite, *El Globo*, No 1199. Both recommended. *Museo del Jamón*, Cerrito y Rivadavia. Good for tapas, seafood dishes and ham.

Oriental *Morizono*, Paraguay 3521 and Paraguay y Reconquista. Japanese, very good. *Lotus Bar*, Pasaje Tres Sargentos 427. Good Thai food and atmosphere, open for lunch and dinner Mon-Fri, dinner only Sat, closed Sun. *Chino Central*, Rivadavia 656. *Casa China*, Viamonte 1476. Many Taiwanese restaurants on Arribeños between Juramento and Mendoza (Barrancas de Belgrano). *Tulasi*, MT de Alvear 628. Indian and vegetarian, good.

Vegetarian *Granix*, Florida 165, p 1. *Tenedor libre* US$3, bland but filling, lunchtime Mon-Fri. *La Huerta*, Lavalle 895, p 2. *Tenedor libre*, reasonable. *La Ciboulette* Sarmiento 1810. Excellent value, *tenedor libre*, friendly staff. *Lotos*, Córdoba 1583. Open 1130-1800. *Dietética Córdoba*, Córdoba 1557. Also shop, open Mon-Fri 0900-2000, Sat 0900-1500.

Argentina

For quick cheap snacks the markets are recommended. See also Galerías Pacífico under Shopping, below

Cheap meals Some supermarkets have good, cheap restaurants: *Coto* supermarket, Viamonte y Paraná, upstairs. Many supermarkets have very good deli counters and other shops sell *fiambres* (smoked, cured meats) and cheeses and other prepared foods for quick, cheap eating. Good snacks all day and night at Retiro and Constitución railway termini. The snack bars in underground stations are also cheap. *Delicity* bakeries, several branches, very fresh pastries, sweets, breads, authentic American donuts. Another good bakery for breakfasts and salads is *Bonpler*, eg Florida 481, 0830-2200, daily papers, classical music. *Ugi's*, in many locations. For fast service and cheap pizza.

Tea rooms, cafés and bars *Richmond*, Florida 468 between Lavalle and Corrientes. Genteel (chess played between 1200-2400). Well-known are the *Confitería Suiza*, Tucumán 753, and the *Florida Garden*, Florida y Paraguay. Good coffee and cakes. *Confitería Ideal*, Suipacha 384. Old, faded, good service, cakes and snacks. Recommended. Many on Av del Libertador in the Palermo area. *El Querandí*, Perú y Moreno. Popular with intellectuals and students, good atmosphere, well known for its Gin Fizz. On Corrientes: *La Paz*, No 1599. *El Gato Negro*, No 1669. Old pharmacy, wide choice of coffees and teas, good cakes; branch at Galerías Pacífico (on Av Córdoba side). *Clásica y Moderna*, Callao 892. Bookshop at back, expensive but very popular, usually live music, open till late. *Café de la Biblioteca*, M T de Alvear 1155 (Asociación Biblioteca de Mujeres). Coffee and light snacks, books. *Freddo*, Pacheco de Melo y Callao, Ayacucho y Quintana, Santa Fe y Callao and at shopping malls, 'the city's best ice cream'. On Av Quintana 600 (Recoleta) is café *La Biela*, restaurant and *whiskería*, elegant. Also in Recoleta: *Café Victoria*, Roberto M Ortiz 1865, *whiskería/sandwichería*. Popular. *Hard Rock Café*, in Paseo del Pilar, Av Pueyrredón y Av Del Libertador, ISIC 15% discount. *Henry J Bean's*, Junín 1749 and Arce 907 (Las Cañitas), ISIC 10% discount. *Café Tortoni*, Av de Mayo 825-9. Delicious cakes, coffee, a haunt of artists, very elegant, over 100 years old, interesting *peña* evenings of poetry and music, see also Jazz and Tango, below. Good bars in San Telmo around Plaza Dorrego, for example *El Balcón de la Plaza*, and on Humberto I. *Mr Mate*, Estados Unidos 523. The only place dedicated to the national drink. *La Puerto Rico*, Alsina 420 One of the oldest *confiterías* in town. Another traditional place is *Las Violetas*, Av Rivadavia y Medrano. *Boquitas Pintadas*, Estados Unidos 1393, T4381 6064. Bar and hotel, German-run. Most cafés serve tea or coffee plus *facturas*, or pastries, for breakfast, US$1-1.50 (bakery shops sell 10 *facturas* for US$1). **Brew pubs**: *Buller Brewing Company*, Roberto M Ortiz 1827 (Recoleta). *Brewhouse Club*, Estados Unidos 745 (SanTelmo). **Pubs**: **British**: *The Alexandra*, San Martín 774. Curries, fish and seafood, nice bar, closed in evening. **Irish**: *The Kilkenny*, MT de Alvear 399 esq Reconquista. Open 1200-0600, happy hour 1900-2100, very popular. *The Shamrock*, Rodríguez Peña 1220. Irish-run, popular, expensive Guinness, happy hour for ISIC card holders. Also *Druid In*, Reconquista 1040. Live music weekly, English spoken. Next door is *Porto Pirata*. *Celta Bar*, Rodríguez Peña y Sarmiento. *The Temple Bar*, MT de Alvear 945.

Entertainment

Details of most events are given in Espectáculos section of main newspapers and in Guía Inrocks, published monthly by Los Inrockuptibles magazine

Cinemas The selection of films is as good as anywhere else in the world and details are listed daily in all main newspapers. Films are shown uncensored and most foreign films are subtitled. Tickets best booked early afternoon to ensure good seats (average price US$3.50 discount Wed and for first show daily; other discounts depending on cinema). Tickets obtainable, sometimes cheaper, from ticket agencies (*carteleras*), such as *Vea Más*, Paseo La Plaza, Corrientes 1660, local 2 (the cheapest), *Cartelera*, Lavalle 742, T4322 1559, *Cartelera Baires*, Corrientes 1382, local 24 and *Entradas con Descuento*, Lavalle 835, local 27, T4322 9263. Seats can also be booked by credit card in shopping centres for US$1. Many cinemas around Santa Fe and Callao, in Puerto Madero and in Belgrano (Av Cabildo and environs). On Fri and Sat nights many central cinemas have *transnoches*, late shows starting at 0100. At *Village Recoleta* (Vicente López y Junín) there is a cinema complex with *transnoche* programme on Wed. Independent foreign and national films are shown during the *Festival de Cine Independiente*, held every Apr.

Cultural events The *Luna Park* stadium holds pop/jazz concerts, ballet and musicals, at Bouchard 465, near Correo Central, T4311 5100, free parking at Corrientes 161. *Tango Week*,

Argentina

leading up to National Tango Day (11 Dec), has free events all over the city, details posted around the city and at tourist offices. *Teatro Gen San Martín*, Corrientes 1530, T4371 0111/8 or 0800-333 5254, www.teatrosanmartin.com.ar Organizes many cultural activities, many free, including concerts, 50% ISIC discount for Fri and Sun events (only in advance at 4th floor, Mon-Fri). The theatre's Sala Leopoldo Lugones shows international classic films, daily, US$1.50. *Centro Cultural Borges*, Galerías Pacífico, Viamonte y San Martín, p 1, T5555 5359/5449. Music and dance concerts, special exhibitions upstairs, some shows with discounts for students. *Centro Cultural Recoleta*, Junín 1930, next to the Recoleta cemetery. Has many free activities. *Palais de Glace*, Posadas 1725, T4804 1163/4805 4354. Temporary art exhibitions and other cultural events. *Fundación Proa*, Av Pedro de Mendoza 1929, T4303 0909. Contemporary art in La Boca.

Gay discos *Amerika*, Gascón 1040, www.ameri-k.com.ar *Xperiment*, Carlos Pellegrini 1083. Wed, Fri and Sun open at midnight. Most gay discos charge US$3-7 entry on door.

Tickets are much cheaper if bought from bars around Santa Fe y Pueyrredón from 0100

Jazz *Café Tortoni*, Av de Mayo 829, T4342 4328, classic tango spot, features the Creole Jazz Band (dixieland), Fri 2100, also tango (see below). Recommended. *Notorious*, Av Callao 966, T4813 6888 Live jazz at a music shop, Tue-Sat 2200. Live jazz also at *Tobago*, Alvarez Thomas 1368, T4553 5530; *Thelonius*, Salguero 1884, T4829 1562, *Jazz y algo más*, 3 de Febrero 1167.

Music Bars and restaurants in San Telmo, Palermo Viejo and Las Cañitas districts, with live music (usually beginning 2330-2400). Also at *El Samovar de Rasputín*, Del Valle Iberlucea 1251, Caminito, T4302 3190. Good blues and rock, dinner and/or show, Fri, Sat, Sun. Good and popular are *Club del Vino*, Cabrera 4737, T4833 0050/8300, live music, various styles including tango, *Niceto*, Niceto Vega 5510 (Palermo Hollywood district) and *La Cigale*, 25 de Mayo 722, T4312 8275.

For salsa: *La Salsera*, Yatay 961. Highly regarded. *Salsón*, Alvarez Thomas 1166, T4551 6551. Popular Fri and Sat late night. *Azúcar*, Av Corrientes 3330, T4865 3103. Clubs with 'tropical' music or *bailanta* on Plaza Once, near Av Rivadavia y Av Pueyrredón, *El Reventón* and *Fantástico Bailable*. *Maluco Beleza*, Sarmiento 1728, live Brazilian music. Classes at *La Trastienda*, Balcarce 460, Wed 2000, US$1, also some jazz shows.

Nightclubs and folklore Tango: *La Ventana*, Balcarce 431, T4331 0217. Daily dinner from 2000 (dinner and show US$35) or show with two drinks, 2200, US$22, very touristy but very good. *El Viejo Almacén*, Independencia y Balcarce, T4307 7388. Daily, dinner from 2000, show 2200, US$20 with all drinks, dinner and show US$30. *El Querandí*, Perú 302, T4345 0331. Tango show restaurant, Mon-Sat, show, 2200, US$25, dinner, 2100, and show US$35 including drink. In San Telmo: *La Cumparsita*, Chile 302,T4302 3387. Authentic, US$15 including drink and some food, 2230-0400. *Bar Sur*, Estados Unidos 299, T4362 6086. 2000-0300, US$7 including all-you-can-eat pizza, drinks extra. *La Casa de Aníbal Troilo*, Carlos Calvo 2540. Good singers and bands, for tourists. *Galería del Tango*, Boedo 722 y Independencia, T4523 9756 or 1540511562, www.tangodiscovery.com For non conventional tango lessons. *El Beso*, Riobamba 416, T4953 2794. Tango shows and lessons. Tango lessons at *Confitería Ideal*, address above, T4326 0521. Hours and teachers vary, dinner show Sat 2200, low price. Also at *Club Almagro*, Medrano 522, T4774 7454. Classes last 2 hrs. *Café Tortoni*, address above, daily evening tango shows, US$6 (a US$3 min expenditure at the bar is requested).

The best affordable tango bars are in La Boca, but it is difficult to find authentic tango for locals, most are tourist-oriented. Some shows are hugely overpriced and inauthentic; they usually have touts inviting tourists in

Milongas (gaucho music) are increasingly popular events among young dancers and take place in several locations: *La Viruta*, Armenia 1336, T4774 6357; *La Catedral*, Sarmiento 4006, T4342 4794; *La Calesita*, Comodoro Rivadavia 1350, T4744 5187; *Centro Cultural Torcuato Tasso*, Defensa 1575, T4307 6506. In all these places, information on lessons is given.

Argentina

Generally it is not worth going to discos before 0230 at weekends. Dress is usually smart

Recommended nightclub/discos The latest trend is the supper club, a fashionable restaurant serving dinner around 2200, which clears the table at 0100 for all-night dancing, eg *La Morocha*, Dorrego y Libertador, T4778 0050, *El Living*, M T de Alvear 1540, T4811 4730, *La Diosa*, Av Costanera Rafael Obligado 3731 (Costa Salguero), T4806 1079, for young people, and *Moliere*, Balcarce y Chile, T4343 2623. Very popular, cheap beer. Discos: *Cemento*, Estados Unidos 1234. Disco with live shows. Also *New York City*, Alvarez Thomas 1391, T4556 1700. Chic. *Tobago*, Alvarez Thomas 1368, T4553 5530. Live music, books and intellectuals. *Mitos Argentinos*, Humberto I 489, near Plaza Dorrego, T4362 7810. Dancing to 'rock national' music, in the daytime has tango and lunch with live music and public particip-ation. *El Dorado*, H Yrigoyen y 9 de Julio. Interesting, different. *Pacha*, Av Costanera Rafael Obligado y Pampa, T4788 4280. Electronic music. *El Divino*, Cecilia Grierson 225 (Puerto Madero, on dock 4), T4316 8400. *Buenos Aires News*, Paseo de la Infanta Isabel s/n, T4778 1500 *Luna Morena*, Av Chiclana 4118, T4925 7478.

Theatre About 20 commercial theatres play all year round. There are many amateur thea-tres. You are advised to book as early as possible for a seat at a concert, ballet, or opera. Tickets for most popular shows (including rock and pop concerts) are sold also through *Ticketek*, T4323 7200/7600 or *Ticketmaster*, T4321 9700, www.tm.com.ar For other ticket agencies, see Cinemas, above.

Shopping

Most shops close lunchtime on Sat. The main, fashionable shopping streets are Florida and Santa Fe (especially between 1,000 and 2,000 blocks)

Kelly's, Paraguay 431. A very large selection of reasonably priced Argentine handicrafts in wool, leather, wood, etc. *Regionales La Rueda*, Paraguay 730. Gaucho artefacts, woollen goods, silver, leather, good prices. *Plata Nativa*, Galería del Sol, Florida 860, local 41. For Latin American folk handicrafts. *Martín Fierro*, Santa Fe 908. Good handicrafts, stonework etc. Recommended. Very good aboriginal-style crafts at *Arte y Esperanza*, Balcarce 234, and *Artesanías Argentinas*, Montevideo 1386. *Campanera Dalla Fontana*, Reconquista 735. Leather factory, fast, efficient and reasonably priced for made-to-measure clothes. *Aida*, Galería de la Flor, local 30, Florida 670. Can make a leather jacket to measure in the same day. *Galería del Caminante*, Florida 844. Has a variety of good shops with leather goods, arts and crafts, souvenirs, etc. *XL*, in Paseo Alcorta, Alto Palermo, Unicenter, Abasto and Alto Avellaneda shopping malls. For leather goods, ISIC discount. *Marcelo Loeb*, galería at Maipú 466. For antique postcards from all over the world, not cheap, same *galería* has several phila-telic and numismatic shops. C Defensa in San Telmo is good for antique shops. *Pasaje de la Defensa*, Defensa 1179. A beautifully restored colonial house containing small shops. *Casa Piscitelli*, San Martín 450. Has a large selection of tapes and CDs, no rock or pop music.

Bookshops

Prices are very high for foreign books. For foreign newspapers try news stands on Florida, in Recoleta district and kiosk at Corrientes y Maipú

ABC, Av Córdoba 685 and Rawson 2105 in Martínez suburb, www.libreriasabc.com.ar Good selection of English and German books, expensive, also sells *Footprint Handbooks*. *Distal*, Corrientes 913 (sells *Footprint*) with branches at Florida 528 and 738. *Joyce Proust & Co*, Tucumán 1545, p 1. Paperbacks in English, Portuguese, French, Ital-ian; classics, language texts, etc, good prices. *Librería Rodríguez*, Sarmiento 835. Good selection of English books and magazines upstairs, has another branch at Florida 377. *Yenny*, Galerías Pacífico, Patio Bullrich, Buenos Aires Design and Unicenter Shopping, Paraná 3745, Martínez, stock *Footprint*, good selection of English classics. French bookshop at *Oficina del Libro Francés*, Esmeralda 861. *Librería Ensayo*, Lavalle 528. Good selection of English and German books. Italian books at *Asociación Dante Alighieri*, Tucumán 1646. *Asatej Book-shop*, see Useful addresses below. *El Ateneo*, Florida 340, basement. Has good selection of English books, other branches including Av Santa Fe 1860 (in a former sumptuous cinema) and Av Callao 1380, www.tematika.com *Kel Ediciones*, MT de Alvear 1369 and Conde 1990 (Belgrano). Good stock of English books. *Acme Agency*, Suipacha 245, p 1. For imported Eng-lish books, also Arenales 885. *Lola*, Viamonte 976, 2 p, T4322 3920. Mon-Fri 1200-1900, the only specialist in Latin American Natural History, birdwatching, most books in English. *El Viajero* Carlos Pellegrini 1233, T4394 7941, www.elviajero.com Large stock of travel books, library, information service, computer access for clients (not free), good place to research travel plans.

For used and rare books *The Antique Bookshop*, Libertad 1236. Recommended. Second-hand English language books from *British and American Benevolent Society* (BABS Bookstore), Av Santa Fe 512, Acassuso, T4747 3492 (take train from Retiro), Mon-Wed 0900-1800, Sat 1000-1230 (in summer, Wed mornings only). *Aquilanti*, Rincón 79, T4952 4546, especially good on Patagonia. *Entrelibros*, Av Cabildo 2280 and Santa Fe 2450, local 7, expensive. Several good used books shops at *Galería Buenos Aires*, Florida 835 (basement).

Every Apr the Feria del Libro is held at the Rural Society grounds, on Plaza Italia; exhibitions, shows and books for sale in all languages.

Camping equipment Good equipment and fuel from *Fugate* (no sign), Gascón 238 (off Rivadavia 4000 block), T4982 0203 or T5030 0838. Also repairs equipment. *Outside Mountain Equipment*, Plaza Este 3671 (estación Saavedra), T4541 2084. *Imperio Deportes*, Ecuador 696. Also repairs. Recommended. *Buenos Aires Sports*, Panamericana y Paraná, Martínez (Shopping Unicenter, 2nd level). Good camping stores also at Guatemala 5451. Camping gas available at *Britam*, B Mitre 1111, *Todo Gas*, Sarmiento 1540, and *El Pescador*, Paraguay y Libertad. Every kind of battery (including for Petzl climbing lamps) at Callao 373, T4375 1018. *Cacique Camping*, Esteban Echeverría 3360, Munro, T4762 4475. Manufacture clothing and equipment. *Ecrin*, Mendoza 1679, T4784 4799, info@escalada.com Imported climbing equipment.

Markets For souvenirs, antiques, etc, *Plaza Dorrego*, San Telmo. With food, dancers, buskers, Sun 1000-1700, entertaining, not cheap, an interesting array of 'antiques'. *Feria Hippie*, in Recoleta, near cemetery. Big craft and jewellery market, Sat and Sun, good street atmosphere, expensive. *Feria de Las Artes* (Fri, 1200-1700) on Defensa y Alsina. Sat craft, jewellery, etc market, at *Plaza Belgrano*, near Belgrano Barrancas station on Juramento, between Cuba y Obligado, 1000-2000. Handicraft market at weekends at *Parque Lezama*, San Telmo. *Plaza Italia*, Santa Fe y Uriarte (Palermo). Second hand textbooks and magazines (daily), handicrafts market on Sat 1200-2000, Sun 1000-2000. Plastic arts and expensive, imported Peruvian and Ecuadorean goods in the *Caminito*, Vuelta de Rocha (Boca), 1000-2000 summer, 0900-1900 winter. At *Parque Rivadavia*, Rivadavia 4900. Books and magazines (daily), records, toys, stamps and coins, Sun 0900-1300. Sat market in *Parque Centenario*, Díaz Vélez y L. Marechal, on weekends. Local crafts, good, cheap hand-made clothes. *Feria de Mataderos*, Lisandro de la Torre y Av de los Corrales, subte E to end of line then taxi (US$3), or buses 36, 92, 97, 126, 141. Long way but worth it: few tourists, fair of Argentine handicrafts and traditions, music and dance festivals, gaucho horsemanship skills, regional meals and games, every Sun and holiday from 1100; nearby *Museo de los Corrales*, Av de los Corrales 6436, T4687 1949, Sun 1200-1900. *Mercado de las Luces*, Perú y Alsina, Mon-Fri 1100-1900, Sun 1300-1900. Handicrafts. *Casi nuevo*, Av Santa Fe 512, Acassuso (train from Retiro). Thrift shop, Mon-Wed 0900-1800, Sat 1000-1230.

Shopping malls *Patio Bullrich*, Av Del Libertador 750 and Posadas 1245, has boutiques selling high quality leather goods but very expensive. *Alto Palermo*, Col Díaz y Santa Fe, very smart and expensive. *Paseo La Plaza*, at Corrientes 1660, also has theatres and a few restaurants. *Paseo Alcorta*, Salguero y Figueroa Alcorta, 4 levels, cinemas, supermarket, stores, many cheap restaurants (take colectivo 130 from Correo Central). *Galerías Pacífico*, on Florida, between Córdoba and Viamonte, is a beautiful mall with fine murals and architecture, many exclusive shops, cinemas and good food mall with wide choice and low prices in basement. Also good set-price restaurant on 2nd floor and free lunchtime concerts on lower-ground floor (details in the press). Guided visits Wed 1830 (desk on main floor). *Abasto de Buenos Aires*, Av Corrientes 3247, T4959 3400. In the former city's fruit and vegetables market building.

Association and rugby football: are both played to a very high standard. Soccer fans **Sport** should see Boca Juniors, matches Sun 1500-1900 (depending on time of year), cheapest entry US$4-5 (stadium La Bombonera, Brandsen 700, La Boca, open weekdays for visits – see the murals; buses 29, 33, 64, 86, 93, 152), or their arch-rivals, River Plate. Soccer season

Argentina

Argentina

Mar-Jun, Aug-Dec. Rugby season Apr-Oct/Nov. **Cricket**: is played at 4 clubs in Greater Buenos Aires between Nov and Mar. More information at **Asociación de Cricket Argentino**,
T4806 7306. **Golf**: visitors wishing to play at the leading private golf clubs should bring handicap certificate and make telephone booking. There are about a dozen such clubs. Weekend
play is possible only with a member. Good hotels may be able to make special arrangements.
Campo de Golf de la Ciudad in Palermo, open to anyone at any time. For information,
Asociación Argentina de Golf, T4325 1113. **Horse racing**: at Hipódromo Argentino de
Palermo, a large, modern racecourse, popular throughout the year, and at San Isidro. Riding
schools at both courses. **Motor racing**: There are rallies, stock racing and Formula 3 competitions, mostly from Mar to mid-Dec at the Oscar Alfredo Gálvez Autodrome, Av Coronel Roca
y Av General Paz, T4605 3333. **Polo**: the high handicap season is Sep to Dec, but it is played
all year round (low season Mar-May). Argentina has the top polo players in the world. A visit
to the national finals at Palermo in Nov and Dec is recommended. For information,
Asociación Argentina de Polo, T4342 8321. **Swimming**: public baths near Aeroparque,
Punta Carrasco (best, most expensive, also tennis courts), *Costa Salguero* and *Parque Norte*,
both popular. At *Club de Amigos*, Av Figueroa Alcorta y Av Sarmiento, T4801 1213, US$6
(including entrance), open all year round.

Tour operators
English is widely spoken

Tours: a good way of seeing Buenos Aires and its surroundings is by 3-hr tour. Longer tours
include dinner and a tango show, or a gaucho *fiesta* at a ranch (excellent food and dancing).
Bookable through most travel agents. *Autobuses Sudamericanos*, B de Irigoyen 1370, local
12, T4300 0528 (4648 0031 at night). City tour US$10, also longer tours, international buses,
sells Ameribus Pass. *BAT, Buenos Aires Tur*, Lavalle 1444, T4371 2304, city tours (US$7.50)
twice daily; Tigre and Delta, daily, 4 hrs (US$18). *Buenos Aires Vision*, Esmeralda 356 p 8,
T4394 4682. City tours, Tigre and Delta, Tango (US$35, cheaper without dinner) and Fiesta
Gaucha (US$35). *Eternautas*, Arcos 2514, T4781 8868, www.eternautas.com Historical, cul-
tural and artistic tours of the city and Pampas guided by university historians in English,
French or Spanish, flexible, also Tue and Sat walking tours from steps of Banco de la Nación,
Rivadavia y 25 de Mayo, 1600, 2 hrs. *Tripping*, Marcos Dartiguelongue, T4791 6769, T4993
3848 (mob), trippingbsas@hotmail.com Tours to dance clubs, football matches, city bike
tours. **Travel agents:** among those recommended are *ATI*, Esmeralda 567, T4329 9000.
Mainly group travel, very efficient, many branches. *Eves Turismo*, Tucumán 702, T4393 6151.
Helpful and efficient, recommended for flights. *Exprinter*, San Martín 170, T4341 6600,
Galería Güemes, info@exprinter-viajes.com.ar (especially their 5-day, 4-night tour to Iguazú
and San Ignacio Miní). *Turismo Feeling*, San Martín 969, T4311 9422. Excellent and reliable
horseback trips and adventure tourism. *Flyer*, Reconquista 621, p 8, T4312 9194/95. English,
Dutch, German spoken, repeatedly recommended, especially for *estancias*, fishing, polo,
motorhome rental. *Southdoors Group*, Maipú 971, T4313 9093, www.southdoors.com
Very helpful for *estancia* tours.

Transport
Colectivos cover a very wide radius and are clean, frequent, efficient and very fast (hang on tight)

Local Buses The basic fare for *colectivos* (city buses) is US$0.40, US$0.70 to the suburbs.
Have coins ready for ticket machine as drivers do not sell tickets, but may give change.
NB The bus number is not always sufficient indication of destination, as each number has a
variety of routes, but bus stops display routes of buses stopping there and little plaques are
displayed in the driver's window.

Car hire: driving in Buenos Aires is no problem, provided you have eyes in the back of your
head and good nerves. Note that traffic fines are high and police increasingly on the lookout
for drivers without the correct papers. See also Essentials and page 48 for international rental
agencies. *Al International*, Maipú 965, T4311 1000, aireservas@arnet.com.ar *Thrifty*, Av LN
Alem 699, T/F4315 0777, thrifty@thrifty.com.ar There are several national rental agencies,
eg *Express*, C Pellegrini 1576, T4326 0338 or T0800-999 8234, express-rentacar@
grupoexpress.com.ar **Motoring Associations**: see page 74 for details of service.

Metro ('**Subte**') five lines link the outer parts of the city to the centre. Line 'A' runs under C Rivadavia, from Plaza de Mayo to Primera Junta. Line 'B' from central Post Office, on Av L N Alem, under Av Corrientes to Federico Lacroze railway station at Chacarita. Line 'C' links Plaza Constitución with the Retiro railway station, and provides connections with all the other lines. Line 'D' runs from Plaza de Mayo (Catedral), under Sáenz Peña (Diagonal Norte), Córdoba, Santa Fe and Palermo to Congreso de Tucumán (Belgrano). Line 'E' runs from Plaza de Mayo (Cabildo, on C Bolívar) through San Juan to Plaza de los Virreyes (connection to Premetro train service to the southwest end of the city). Note that 3 stations, 9 de Julio (Line 'D'), Diagonal Norte (Line 'C') and Carlos Pellegrini (Line 'B') are linked by pedestrian tunnels. The fare is US$0.35, the same for any direct trip or combination between lines; magnetic cards (for 1, 2, 10 or 30 journeys) must be bought at the station before boarding; dollars not accepted. Trains are operated by *Metrovías*, T4555 1616 or T0800-555 1616. System operates 0500-2230 (Sun 0800-2200). Line A, the oldest was built in 1913, the earliest in South America. Backpacks and luggage allowed. Free map (if available) from stations and tourist office.

Many of the stations in the centre, especially on Line 'E', have fine tile-work designs and pictures. Some trains date from the early part of the century. The oldest and nicest station is Perú (line A)

Argentina

Taxis are painted yellow and black, and carry Taxi flags. Fares are shown in pesos. The meter starts at US$0.55 when the flag goes down; make sure it isn't running when you get in. A fixed rate of US$0.07 for every 200 m or 1-min wait is charged thereafter. A charge is sometimes made for each piece of hand baggage (ask first). **Security** Try always to phone a radio taxi. Check that the driver's licence is displayed. Lock doors on the inside. Four common taxi driver tricks are 1) to take you on a longer than necessary ride; 2) to switch low-denomination notes for higher ones preferred by the passenger (don't back down, demand to go to the police station); 3) to grab the passenger's baggage and prevent him/her from leaving the taxi (scream for help); 4) to quote 'old' prices for new, eg 'quince' (15) for 1.50 pesos, 'veinte y seis' (26) for 2.60 pesos, etc. If the driver says he has a puncture or mechanical problem, get out at once

Buenos Aires Metro (Subte)

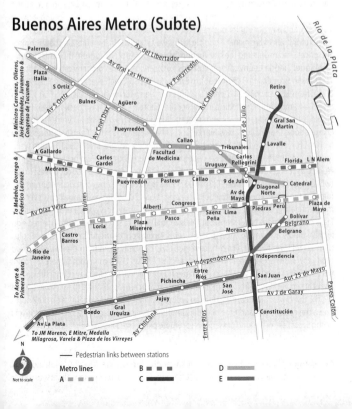

— Pedestrian links between stations

Metro lines

Not to scale

B · · · ·

A · · · ·

C ▬▬▬▬

D ▬▬▬▬

E ▬▬▬▬

Argentina

(unless you are in the middle of nowhere) and try to keep your luggage with you. Worst places are the two airports and Retiro; make sure you know roughly what the fare should be before the journey: eg from Aeroparque to: Ezeiza US$10 (plus toll), Congreso US$3.50, Plaza de Mayo US$3, Retiro US$2-2.50, La Boca US$4. In theory fares double for journeys outside city limits (Gen Paz circular highway), but you can often negotiate. **Radio Taxis** (same colours and fares) are managed by several different companies (eg *Del Plata*, T4504 7776; *Pídalo*, T4956 1200; *Llámenos*, T4815 3333) and are recommended as a safer alternative.

US$1 tip expected   *Remise* taxis operate all over the city, run from an office and have no meter. The companies are identified by signs on the pavement. Fares, which are fixed and can be cheaper than regular taxis, can be verified by phoning the office and items left in the car can easily be reclaimed. Good companies are *Le Coq*, T4963 9391/2, 4963 8532, and *Intercar*, T4867 2100, good airport service.

Tram: a green and white old-fashioned street car operates Apr-Nov on Sat and holidays 1600-1930 and Sun 1000-1300, 1600-1930 (not Easter Sun) and Dec-Mar on Sat and holidays 1700-2030, Sun 1000-1300, 1700-2030, free, on a circular route along the streets of Caballito district, from C Emilio Mitre 500, Subte Primera Junta (Line A) or Emilio Mitre (Line E), no stops en route. Operated by *Asociación de los Amigos del Tranvía*, T4372 0476.

Air   Ezeiza (officially Ministro Pistarini, T5480 6111), the international airport is 35 km southwest of the centre by a good dual carriageway, which links with the General Paz circular Highway round the city. The airport has two terminals: 'A' for all airlines except *Aerolíneas Argentinas*, which uses 'B'. 'A' has a very modern check-in hall. There are duty free shops (expensive), exchange facilities (*Banco de la Nación*, 1.5% commission; *Banco Piano*; *Global Exchange*) and ATMs (Visa and MasterCard), post office (open 0800-2000) and a left luggage office (US$4 per piece). No hotels nearby. There is a *Devolución IVA* desk (return of VAT) for purchases such as leather goods. Reports of pilfering from luggage, to discourage this have your bags sealed after inspection by Secure Bags, US$5 per piece (*British Airways* insists on, and pays for this for backpacks). Hotel booking service at Tourist Information desk – helpful, but prices are higher if booked in this way. A display in immigration shows choices and prices of transport into the city. **Airport buses**: special buses to/from the centre are run by **Manuel Tienda León** (office at customs exit), service to the company office at Santa Fe 790, next to *Hotel Crillon* (T4314 3636), to Ezeiza: 0400, 0500, then every 30 mins till 2030 and 21.30; from Ezeiza: 0630-2140 regular buses, then also for night arrivals, US$7.50 (US$13 return), 40-min journey, credit cards accepted. Santa Fe office has check-in desk for *AR* flights. Manuel Tienda León will also collect passengers from addresses in centre for no extra charge, book the previous day. Similar and cheaper services with *Transfer Express*, San Martín 1107, T0800-444 4872, airport office in front of you as you arrive, US$10 return (valid for one month, reconfirmation is needed before return journey). Minibus service run by *Hugo Guy*, Carlos Calvo 1931, T4942 2339, dorabritez@ciudad.com.ar   **Local buses**: No 86 (white and blue, Empresa Duvi, T4302 6067) runs to the centre from outside the airport terminal to the left as you leave the building, 2 hrs, US$0.70, coins only, runs all day, every 14 mins during the day. To travel to Ezeiza, catch the bus at Av de Mayo y Perú, 1 block from Plaza de Mayo (many other stops, but this is central) – make sure it has 'Aeropuerto' red sign in the window as many 86s stop short of Ezeiza. **Taxis**: from centre to Ezeiza US$10-15 (plus US$1.50 toll) but bargain. Fixed-price *remise taxis* can be booked from the *Manuel Tienda León* or *Transfer Express* counter at Ezeiza, US$17 (plus US$3 toll) from airport to town. **NB** Avoid unmarked cars at Ezeiza no matter how attractive the fare may sound; drivers are adept at separating you from far more money than you can possibly owe them. Always ask to see the taxi driver's licence. If you take an ordinary taxi the Policía Aeronáutica on duty notes down the car's licence and time of departure. There have been recent reports of taxi drivers taking Ezeiza airport-bound passengers to remote places, stealing all their luggage and leaving them there. If in doubt, take a *remise* or airport bus.

Aeroparque (Jorge Newbery Airport), 4 km north of the centre, T5480 6111, handles all internal flights, services to Punta del Este and Montevideo and few flights to other neighbouring countries The terminal is divided into 3 sections, 'A' for *AR*, *Austral* and *ARG* check-in desks and international arrivals, 'B' for *Dinar*, *LAER*, *Pluna* and *ARG Express* check-in desks, 'C' for *Southern Winds* check-in desk and *Dinar* arrivals. On the 1st floor there is a *patio de comidas* and many shops. At the airport also tourist information, car rental, bus companies, bank, ATMs, exchange facilities, post office, public phones and luggage deposit (between sections A-B), US$2 per piece a day. **Buses** *Manuel Tienda León* buses to/from centre (see above for address), 0710-2140 every 30 mins, US$2.50. *Transfer Express* (address above) buses charge the same. Local bus 45 runs from outside the airport to the Retiro railway station, then follows Av Alem and Paseo Colón to La Boca via Constitución. Nos 22, 27, 45 and 160 also run to Retiro. Bus 37C goes from Plaza del Congreso to Aeroparque but make sure it has 'Aeroparque' sign, US$0.70. **Remise taxis**: are operated by *Transfer Express* and *Manuel Tienda León*, US$6 to centre, US$20 to Ezeiza. Ordinary taxi to centre US$3-4.

Manuel Tienda León and *Transfer Express* operate buses between Ezeiza and Aeroparque airports, stopping in city centre, US$5.50-7.50.

Aerolíneas Argentinas, ARG, Austral, Dinar and *Southern Winds* offer daily flights to the main cities, for details see text under intended destination, see also page 72 for the Visit Argentina fare. If travelling in the south, book ahead if possible with *LADE*, whose flights are cheaper than buses in most cases but with several stops.

Trains There are 4 main terminals: **Retiro (3 lines: Mitre, Belgrano, San Martín in separate buildings):** Mitre line (run by *TBA*, T4317 4407 or T0800-333 3822, www.tbanet.com.ar Urban and suburban services: to Belgrano, Mitre (connection to Tren de la Costa, see below), Olivos, San Isidro, Tigre (see below), Capilla del Señor (connection at Victoria, US$1.30), Escobar and Zárate (connection at Villa Ballester, US$1.30); long distance services: to Rosario Norte, one weekly, 6 hrs, US$5.50-7, to Tucumán via Rosario, Mon and Fri, 2100, returning Mon and Fri 1000, 26 hrs, US$25 sleeper, US$20 pullman, US$15 1st (service run by *NOA Ferrocarriles*, T4893 2244). Belgrano line run by *Ferrovías*, T4511 8833. San Martín line run by *Metropolitano*, T0800-666 358736. Urban and suburban services: to Palermo, Chacarita, Devoto, Hurlingham and Pilar. Long distance services: to Junín, daily, 5hrs, US$4.50.

Constitución: Roca line (run by *Metropolitano*, T4959 0802 or T0800-666 358736). Urban and suburban services to La Plata (US$0.75), Ezeiza (US$0.50), Ranelagh (US$0.40) and Quilmes (US$0.30). Long distance services (run by *Ferrobaires*, T4304 0028/3165): Bahía Blanca, 3 weekly, 12½ hrs, US$12 pullman, US$9 1st, US$8 tourist, food mediocre; to Mar del Plata daily, US$8-15, 5 hrs; to Pinamar, 2 weekly, US$8-15, 6 hrs; to Miramar, in summer only, daily, 7 hrs, US$8-15; to Tandil, US$6-8, weekly, 6 hrs; to Quequén, 2 weekly, 12 hrs, US$8-15, and to Bolívar.

Federico Lacroze Urquiza line and Metro headquarters (run by *Metrovías*, T0800-555 1616 or T4555 1616, www.metrovias.com.ar). Suburban services: to General Lemos.

Once Sarmiento line (run by *TBA*, see above). Urban and suburban services: to Caballito, Flores, Merlo, Luján (connection at Moreno, US$1), Mercedes (US$1.50) and Lobos. Long distance services to Santa Rosa and General Pico can be seasonally interrupted by floods (T4861 0043). A fast service runs daily between Puerto Madero (station at Av Alicia Moreau de Justo y Perón) and Castelar.

Tickets checked before boarding and on train and collected at the end of the journey; urban and suburban fares are charge according different sections of each line; cheapest fare is around US$0.30 (depending on the company).

Buses Long distance bus terminal at Ramos Mejía y Antártida Argentina (Subte Line C), behind Retiro station, for information T4310 0700. Information desk for bus companies serving the destination you want is at the Ramos Mejía entrance. All ticket offices are upstairs (full list at the top of the escalator), as is the Buenos Aires city information desk, at office 83. There are left-luggage lockers, US$1 for 1 day (with two 1 peso coins); companies also store luggage. Large bags should be left at the bus office 'depositos' at the basement level. Fares may vary according to time of year and advance booking is essential Dec-Mar, Easter, Jul and long weekends. Travellers have reported getting discounts without showing evidence of status,

Argentina

so it's always worth asking. For further details of bus services and fares, look under proposed destinations. There are no direct buses to either of the airports.

International buses Direct buses to **Santiago, Chile**, 1,310 km, 23 hrs, 1,459 km; cheaper to book to Mendoza and then rebook. To **Bolivia**: there is no direct bus service from Buenos Aires to La Paz but through connections can be booked (*Sudamericanos*, goes via La Quiaca-Villazón, 48 hrs; *Atahualpa*, T4315 0601, goes via La Quiaca, or Pocitos, daily, then a new ticket to La Paz or Santa Cruz must be bought). Cheapest route to Pocitos is by bus to Tucumán, then re-book for Pocitos.

To **Asunción, Paraguay** , 1,370 km Clorinda (toll bridge): 11 bus companies, all close to each other at the Retiro bus terminal. You have choice between executive (luxury service, 15 hrs), *diferencial* (with food, drinks, 18 hrs) and *común* (without food, but a/c, toilet, 21 hrs). Also 5 companies to Ciudad del Este; *Caaguazú* goes to Villarrica, and *Expreso Río Paraná* and *La Encarnaceña* go to Encarnación. Tickets can be bought up to 30 days in advance. There area occasional occasional **river boats** to Asunción from May to Oct, 11 days, bed and private bath, food and nightly entertainment, US$400. Details from *Tamul*, Lavalle 388, T4393 2306/1533.

To **Peru** *Ormeño* (T4313 2259) and *El Rápido Internacional* (T4393 5057), direct service to Lima, Mon, Wed, Sat 1800, 3 days and 18 hrs, including all meals, 1 night spent in Santiago, Chile (if you need a visa for Chile, get one before travelling), the route is: Mendoza, Coquimbo, Arica, Tacna, Nasca, Ica, Lima.

Direct buses to **Brazil** via Paso de los Libres by *Pluma*: São Paulo, 40 hrs, Rio de Janeiro, 45 hrs, Porto Alegre, Curitiba, 38 hrs, Florianópolis, 32 hrs. To Rio, changing buses at Posadas and Foz do Iguaçu is almost half price, 50 hrs. A third route across the Río de la Plata and through Uruguay is a bit cheaper, not as long and offers a variety of transport and journey breaks. Tickets from *Buen Viaje*, Córdoba 415, T4311 2953, or *Pluma*, Córdoba 461, T4311 4871/4311 5986.

Boats and buses heavily booked Dec-Mar, especially at weekends

To Uruguay Direct **road** connections by means of 2 bridges over the Río Uruguay between Colón and Paysandú and between Puerto Unzué and Fray Bentos (much slower than the air or sea routes). Bus to Montevideo: *Bus de la Carrera*, 1000 and 2000 daily, 8½ hours, with a *dormibus* at 2300, via Zárate-Gualeguaychú-Puerto Unzué-Fray Bentos-Mercedes.

Boat connections: **1)** Direct to Montevideo, *Buquebus*, Terminal de Aliscafos, Av Córdoba y Madero and in Patio Bullrich shopping centre, p 1, loc 231, T4316 6500/4317 1017, F4313 7636, www.buquebus.com, twice a day, 0900 and 1530, 2½ hrs, US$59 tourist class, US$72 1st class one way including transport from office to port, vehicles US$100-122, motorcycles US$80, bus connection to Punta del Este, US$7. **2)** To Colonia, services by 3 companies: *Buquebus*: 3 hydrofoils a day, 50 mins or 2 hrs 40 mins, US$32-38 one way (fast service), US$20-27 (slow), with bus connection to Montevideo (US$7 extra). Motorcycles US$30-39, cars, US$46-78. *Ferrylíneas Sea Cat*, Córdoba 699, T4315 6800, port: Dársena Norte, Costanera y Córdoba: 0830 and 1930, 45 mins, US$30 one way. **3)** From Tigre to Carmelo, boats are operated by *Cacciola* at 0830, 1630, 3 hrs, US$13 (20 return) to Carmelo, and US$18.50 to Montevideo. *Cacciola* office: Lavalle y Florida 520, oficina 113, T4393 6100 and international terminal, Lavalle 520, Tigre, T4749 0320, credit cards accepted. It is advisable to book in advance; connecting bus from offices to port and from Carmelo to Montevideo. 4) From Tigre to Nueva Palmira, *Líneas Delta Argentina*, from Tigre 0730, also 1700 Fri and Sun 3 hrs, US$27 round trip, T4749 0537, information T4731 1236. **NB** No money changing facilities in Tigre, and poor elsewhere.

Do not buy Uruguayan bus tickets in Buenos Aires; wait till you get to Colonia

Beware of overcharging by taxis from the harbour to the centre of Buenos Aires. US$3 port tax is charged on all services to Colonia/Carmelo, US$10 port tax in Buenos Aires.

To Colonia by **air** from Jorge Newbery Airport (Aeroparque) 15 mins with *Air Class*. Buy tickets in advance especially at weekends when flights are fully booked. Continue by bus to Montevideo. Also from Jorge Newbery, shuttle service to Montevideo, known as Puente Aéreo and run by AR and Pluna, 40 mins. Book at Jorge Newbery Airport or T4393 5122/4773 0440. Other airlines fly this route. To Punta del Este, several flights daily 15 Dec-1 Mar with *AR*, 40 mins, *Pluna, Southern Winds* and *ARG* (out of season, Fri-Sun).

Airline offices *Aerolíneas Argentinas* (AR) and *Austral*, Perú y Rivadavia, Av LN Alem 1134 and Av Cabildo 2900, T0810-2228 6527, www.aerolineas.com.ar *Air Canada*, Av Córdoba 656, T4327 3640.*Air France*, San Martín 344 p 23, T4317 4700 or T0800-222 2600. *Alitalia*, Av Santa Fe 887, T4310 9910. *American*, Av Santa Fe 881, T4318 1000, Av Pueyrredón 1889 and branches in Belgrano and Acassuso. *AIRG* (ex Lapa), Carlos Pellegrini 1075, T0810-7777 2474, www.08107777arg.com Good service. *Avianca*, Carlos Pellegrini 1163 p 4, T4394 5990. *British Airways*, T4320 6600. *Dinar*, Carlos Pellegrini 675 p 9, T5371 1100. *Cubana*, Sarmiento 552 p 11, T4326 5291. *Iberia*, Carlos Pellegrini 1163, T4131 1000. *KLM*, Suipacha 268 p 9, T4326 8422. *LAB*, Carlos Pellegrini 141, T4323 1900. *LAER*, Suipacha 844, T4311 5237. *Lan Chile*, Cerrito y Paraguay, T4378 2200/0800-222 2424, www.lanchile.com *Líneas Aéreas del Estado* (LADE), Perú 710, T5129 9000, Aeroparque T4514 1524, reservas@lade.com.ar Erratic schedules, uninformed office. *Lufthansa*, M T Alvear 636, T4319 0610, www.lufthansa-argentina.com *Mexicana*, Av Córdoba 755 p 1, T4312 6152 *Pluna* and *Varig*, Florida 1, T4342 4420 or T4329 9211, www.plunavarig.com.ar, www.varig.com.br *Qantas*, Av Córdoba 673 p 13, T4514 4726, www.qantasargentina.com *Southern Winds*, Av Santa Fe 784, T0810-777 7979, www.sw.com.ar *Swissair* and *South African Airways*, Santa Fe 846 p 1, T4319 0000, www.swissair.com.ar *Taca*, Carlos Pellegrini 1275, T4325 8222. *TAM*, Cerrito 1026, T4819 4800 or T0810 333 3333. *United*, Av Madero 900, T0810-777 86148.

Banks Practices are constantly changing while the economy is in upheaval (early 2002). Most banks charge commission especially on TCs (as much as US$10). US dollar bills are often scanned electronically for forgeries, while TCs are sometimes very difficult to change and you may be asked for proof of purchase. American Express TCs are less of a problem than Thomas Cook. Banks open Mon-Fri 1000-1500, be prepared for long delays. *Lloyds TSB Bank*, Florida 999, T0800-555 6937, Visa cash advances. It has 14 other branches in the city, and others in Greater Buenos Aires. *Bank Boston*, Florida y B Mitre, T4820 2000, cash advances against credit cards. *Citibank*, B Mitre 502, T0810-444 2484, changes only Citicorps TCs cheques, no commission, also Visa, MasterCard; branch at Florida 199. *Bank of America*, 25 de Mayo 537, T4319 2600 changes Bank of America TCs morning only, US$ at very high commission. *HSBC*, 25 de Mayo 258, also at Florida 229, changes Thomas Cook TCs with US$10 commission. *American Express* offices are at Arenales 707 y Maipú, by Plaza San Martín, T4311 1906, where you can apply for a card, get financial services and change Amex TCs (1000-1500 only, no commission into US$ or pesos). Visa and MasterCard ATMs at branches of *Banco de la Nación Argentina, ABN Amro Bank, BNP, Itaú* and others. MasterCard/Cirrus also at *Argencard* offices. *Banco de San Juan*, Maipú 99, cash advance on MasterCard, very fast service. San Martín and Corrientes is where several *casas de cambio* may be found, eg *Banco Piano*, San Martín 345, T4322 0768 (has 24-hr exchange facility at Ezeiza airport), www.piano.com.ar Also *Forex*, MT de Alvear 540, opposite *Marriott Plaza Hotel*, and *Eves*, Tucumán 702, open until 1800. Major credit cards usually accepted but check for surcharges. General *MasterCard* office at Perú 151, T4348 7070, open 0930-1800, T0800-555 0507 for lost cards. *Visa*, Corrientes 1437, p 2, T4379 3300, for stolen cards. Other South American currencies can only be exchanged in *casas de cambio*. *Western Union*, branches in Correo Argentino post offices, eg Córdoba 917.

Communications Internet: Prices range from US$0.50 to US$1.50 per hr, shop around. Many *locutorios* (phone offices) have internet access. *CiberCity*, Lavalle 491, T4393 3360, Mon-Fri 0800-2200, Sat 1000-1400, US$0.50 per hour. *Cybercafé*, Maure 1886, Belgrano (bus 29), info@cyber.com.ar *M@gic-net*, Florida 578, US$1 per hr. *Sudat.com*, Maipú 486 (basement). Several PCs, good service, US$0.50 per hr. *Comunicar*, Lavalle y Cerrito, US$0.50 per hr at weekends. **General Post Office:** Correo Central – now privatized, **Correos Argentinos**, Sarmiento y Alem, Mon-Fri, 0800-2000, Sat 0900-1300. *Poste Restante* on ground floor (US$0.75 per letter). Philatelic section open Mon-Fri 0900-1900. Centro Postal Internacional, for all parcels over 1kg for mailing abroad, at Av Comodoro Py y Antártida Argentina, near Retiro station, helpful, many languages spoken, packaging materials available, open Mon-Fri 1000 to 1700 (see page 76.) Check both Correo Central and Centro Postal Internacional for *poste restante*. Post office without queues at Montevideo 1408 near Plaza V López, friendly staff, Spanish only. Also at Santa Fe 945. *UPS*, Bernardo de Irigoyen 974, T4339 2877. **Telephone:** the city is split into 2 telephone zones, owned by *Telecom* and *Telefónica Argentina*. Corrientes 705 (open 0800-2200) for international phone calls, fax, public telex in basement. International and local calls as well as fax also from phone offices (*locutorios* or *telecentros*), of which there are many in the city centre. Public telephone boxes operate with coins (US$0.12 min charge for local calls) and cards (available at *kioskos*). The cards of the 2 companies are interchangeable (no need to insert the card in the phone, simply dial the company's number). These cards are protected by a sealed wrapper: don't accept cards without a wrapper or with a broken seal. International telephone calls from hotels may incur a 40-50% commission in addition to government tax of about the same amount.

Argentina

Cultural and trade associations (see Libraries below) **British Council**, M T de Alvear 590, p 4, T4311 9814/7519, F4311 7747 (Mon-Thu 1100-1500). **British Arts Centre** (BAC), Suipacha 1333, T4393 6941, www.britishartscentre.org.ar English plays and films, music concerts, photography exhibitions. **Goethe Institut**, Corrientes 319, T4311 5338/8964, German library (Mon,Tue,Thu 1230-1930, Fri 1230-1600) and newspapers, free German films shown, cultural programmes, German language courses. In the same building, upstairs, is the German Club, Corrientes 327. **Alliance Française**, Córdoba 946, T4322 2350/0068. French library, temporary film and art exhibitions. **Instituto Cultural Argentino Norteamericano (ICANA)**, Maipú 686, T4322 3855/4557. **Biblioteca Centro Lincoln**, Maipú 686, T5382 1536, open Mon-Thu 1200-2000, library (borrowing for members only), English/US newspapers. **Clubs: American Club**, Viamonte 1133, T4371 6817, facing Teatro Colón, temporary membership available. **English Club**, 25 de Mayo 586, T4312 0689, open for lunch only, temporary membership available to British business visitors. The American and English Clubs have reciprocal arrangements with many clubs in USA and UK. **Swedish Club**, Tacuarí 147, T4331 7959. **Organización Hebrea Argentina Macabi**, Tucumán 3135, T4961 0449, social and sporting club for conservative Jews.

Embassies and consulates All open Mon-Fri unless stated otherwise. **Australia**, Villanueva y Zabala, T4777 6580, www.argentina.embassy.gov.au 0830-1100, ticket queuing system; take bus 29 along Av Luis María Campos to Zabala. **Austria**, French 3671, T4802 1400, www.austria.org.ar Mon-Thu 0900-1200. **Belgium**, Defensa 113 p 8, T4331 0066, 0800-1300. **Bolivian Consulate**, Belgrano 1670, p 2, T4381 4171, 0900-1400, visa while you wait or a month wait (depending on the country of origin), tourist bureau. **Brazilian Consulate**, C Pellegrini 1363, p 5, T4394 5255, www.brasil.org.ar 1000-1300, visa takes at least 72 hrs, US$12-52. **Canada**, Tagle 2828, T4805 3032, www.dfait-maeci.gc.ca/bairs Mon-Thu 1400-1600, tourist visa Mon-Thu 0845-1130 **Chilean Consulate**, San Martín 439, p 9, T4394 6582, 0900-1300. **Denmark**, Alem 1074, p 9, T4312 6901/6935, bueamb@um.dk Mon-Thu 0900-1200, 1400-1600, Fri 1400-1500. **Finland**, Santa Fe 846, p 5, T4312 0600, embajadadefinlandia@ arnet.com.ar Mon-Thu 0900-1200. **France**, Santa Fe 846, p 3, T4312 2409, 0900-1200. **Germany**, Villanueva 1055, T4778 2500, www.embalemana.com.ar 0830-1100. **Greece**, Av R Sáenz Peña 547, p 4, T4342 0528, 1000-1300. **Ireland**, Av Del Libertador 1068 p 6, T4325 8588, info@irlanda.org.ar 0900-1300, 1400-1530. **Israel**, Av de Mayo 701, p 10, T4338 2500, Mon-Thu 0900-1200, Fri 0900-1100. **Italy**, consulate at M T de Alvear 1149, T4816 6133/36, 0900-1300. **Japanese Consulate**, Bouchard 547 p 15, T4318 8200, 0915-1230, 1430-1630. **Netherlands**, Olga Cossentini 831 p 3, on dock 3 (across the bridge), Puerto Madero, T4338 0050, bue@minbuza.nl 0830-1230. **New Zealand**, C Pellegrini 1427 p 5, T4328 0301/5494 kiwiargentina@datamarket.com.ar 0900-1300, 1400-1730. **Norway**, Esmeralda 909, p 3 B, T4312 1904, 0930-1400. **Paraguayan Consulate**, Viamonte 1851, T4814 4803, 0800-1400. **Portugal**, Maipú 942 p 17, T4312 3524, 0900-1230. **Spain**, Guido 1760, T4811 0070, 0830-1400. **Sweden**, Tacuarí 147 p 6, T4342 1422, 1000-1200. **Switzerland**, Santa Fe 846, p 12, T4311 6491, open 0900-1200. **UK**, Luis Agote 2412/52 (near corner Pueyrredón y Guido), T4576 2222, F4803 1731, www.britain.org.ar 0900-1200. **Uruguay**, Av Las Heras 1907, consulate T4807 3040, F4805 8515, www.embajadauruguay.com.ar Open 0930-1730, visa takes up to 1 week. **US Embassy and Consulate General**, Colombia 4300, T5777 4533/34 or T4514 1830, 0900-1730.

Language schools *Encuentros*, Scalabrini Ortiz 2395 p 6 M, T/F4832 7794. *Argentina I.L.E.E*, Av Callao 339, p 3, T/F4782 7173, www.argentinailee.com Recommended by individuals and organizations alike. *Programa Tango* adds tango lessons to Spanish. Accommodation arranged. *PLS*, Carabelas 241 p 1, T4394 0543, F4394 0635, www.pls.com.ar Recommended for travellers and executives and their families; also translation and interpreting services. Spanish classes at *Instituto del Sur*, Bernardo de Irigoyen 668, p 1, T4334 1487, www.delsur.com.ar Individual and groups, cheap. *Universidad de Buenos Aires*, 25 de Mayo 221, T4334 7512 or T4343 1196, idlab@filo.uba.ar Offers cheap, coherent courses, including summer intensive courses. *Cedic*, Reconquista 715, p 11 E, T/F4315 1156. Recommended. For other schools teaching Spanish, and for private tutors look in *Buenos Aires Herald* in the classified advertisements. Enquire also at *Asatej* (see Useful addresses). **Schools which teach English to Argentines include:** *International House*, Pacheco de Melo 2555, T4805 6393, www.international-house.com.ar British-owned and run. *Berlitz*, Av de Mayo 847, T4342 0202, several branches. There are many others. Vacancies are advertised in the *Buenos Aires Herald* or search on www.inglesnet.com Before being allowed to teach, you must officially have a work permit (difficult to obtain) but schools may offer casual employment without one (particularly to people searching for longer-term employment). If unsure of your papers, ask at Migraciones (address below). A degree in education or TEFL/TESL is often required. 'Coordinadoras', usually women, who do not have an institute but run English 'schools' out of their homes, hire native English-speakers and send them out on jobs. Pay varies between US$5 and 10 per hour. Adverts occasionally appear in the *Herald*, but most contacts are by word of mouth.

Medical services Urgent medical service: for free municipal ambulance service to an emergency hospital department (day and night) **Casualty ward**, *Sala de guardia*, T107 or T4923 1051/58 (SAME). Inoculations: **Hospital Rivadavia**, Sánchez de Bustamante 2531 y Av Las Heras 2670, T4809 2000, Mon-Fri, 0800-1200 (bus 37, 38, 59, 60, 92, 93 or 102 from Plaza Constitución), or **Dirección de Sanidad de Fronteras y Terminales de Transporte**, Ing Huergo 690, T4343 1190, Mon 1400-1600, Tue 1000-1200, Wed 1230-1430, Thu and Fri 1500-1700, bus 20 from Retiro, no appointment required (yellow fever only; take syringe and needle). If not provided (unusually), buy the vaccines in *Laboratorio Biol*, Uriburu 153, or in larger chemists. Many chemists have signs indicating that they give injections. Any hospital with an infectology department will give hepatitis A. *Travel Medicine Service (Centros Médicos Stamboulian)*, 25 de Mayo 575, T4311 3000, French 3085, T4802 7772, www.viajeros.cei.com.ar Private health advice for travellers and inoculations centre. **Public Hospitals: Hospital Argerich**, Almte Brown esq Pi y Margall 750, T4362 5555/5811. **Hospital Juan A Fernández**, Cerviño y Bulnes, T4808 2600, good medical attention. If affected by pollen, asthma sufferers can receive excellent treatment at the **Hospital de Clínicas José de San Martín**, Av Córdoba 2351, T5950 8000, cheap treatment. **Children's Hospitals** (Ricardo Gutiérrez), Gallo 1330, T4962 9229/9232/9247, www.guti.gov.ar (Garrahan), Combate de los Pozos 1881, T4308 4300/4941. **British Hospital**, Perdriel 74, T4309 6400, www.hospitalbritanico.org.ar US$18 a visit. Cheap dental treatment at Solís 2180. **German Hospital**, Av Pueyrredón 1640, between Beruti and Juncal, T4821 1700 or T4827 7000, www.hospitalaleman.com.ar Both maintain first-aid centres (*centros asistenciales*) as do the other main hospitals. **French Hospital**, La Rioja 951, T4866 2546, www.cefran.com/site/hospital.htm **Dental Hospital**, M T de Alvear 2142, T4964 1259. **Eye Hospital**, Av San Juan 2021, T4941 5555. Fire accidents: **Hospital de Quemados**, Av Pedro Goyena 369, T4923 4082/3022. s, call T4658 7777, T4654 6648, T4962 6666.

For doctors and dentists, contact your consulate or the tourist office for recommendations

Security Buenos Aires is losing its reputation as a safe city. Street crime is on the rise, especially in the tourist season. Be particularly careful when boarding buses and near the Retiro train and bus stations. Beware of bagsnatching gangs in parks and markets, especially on Sun, and take care in La Boca. The authorities have announced an increase in uniformed police on the streets. See also Safety, page 72, on mustard-spraying gangs; these operate in main squares and tourist areas. Beware other distractions such as people asking directions. Do not change money on the street. If your passport is stolen, remember to get a new 'entrada' stamp at the **Dirección Nacional de Migraciones**.

Comisaría del Turista, Moreno 1417 p 9, T4346 5770 ext 1801, is a Policía Federal 24 hr service for travellers in case of theft or attack; English spoken

Tourist information National office at Santa Fe 883 with maps and literature covering the whole country. Open Mon-Fri 0900-1700, T4312 2232/5550, info@turismo.gov.ar, www.turismo.gov.ar There are kiosks at Aeroparque (*Aerolíneas Argentinas* section), and at Ezeiza Airport, daily 0900-2000. There are city-run tourist kiosks on Florida, junction with Roque Sáenz Peña, Mon-Fri 1000-1400, 1500-1800, at Torre Monumental (Plaza Fuerza Aérea Argentina, Retiro), Wed-Sat 1200-1900, in Puerto Madero, Dock 4, daily 1200-1500, 1600-2000, and at Retiro Bus Station (local 83), Mon-Sat 0700-1300. Free guided tours are usually organised by the city authorities. For free tourist information anywhere in the country T0800-555 0016 (0800-2000). Those overcharged or cheated can go to any tourist office or to **Casa del Consumidor**, Esmeralda 340 (Mon-Fri 1000-1700). For further information, see Tourist information in Directory.

Argentina

www.buenosaires.com A good guide to bus and subway routes is *Guía Peuser*; there is 1 for the city and 1 covering Greater Buenos Aires. Similar guides, *Filcar*, *Lumi* and *Guía T*, US$4-6, are available at news stands. Also handy is Auto Mapa's pocket-size *Plano guía* of the Federal Capital, available at news stands, US$2.50. *Viva Bue* is a free bimonthly tourist magazine with information on main tourist attractions, a city centre map and list of addresses; available at tourist kiosks and some hotels. Also free is *Buenos Aires Day & Night*, published quarterly, with useful information and a downtown map. *La Nación* has a Sun tourism section (very informative) and a *Vía Libre* entertainments section on Fri. Also on Fri, the youth section of *Clarín* (*Sí*) lists free entertainments; *Página 12* has a youth supplement on Thu called *NO*, the paper lists current events in *Pasen y Vean* section on Fri. The *Buenos Aires Herald* publishes *Get Out* on Fri, listing entertainments. Information on what's on at www.buenosairesherald.com *Guía Inrocks* is a free monthly supplement on entertainments usually available in tourist kiosks and some trendy shops.

In the capital, there are helpful *Casas de Provincia*, where tourist information is given (open Mon-Fri usually, 1000-1630/1730, depending on office): *Buenos Aires*, Av Callao 237, T4371 7045/7. Others on Callao are *Córdoba* 332, T4371 1668. *Chaco* 322, T4372 3045, casa.del.chaco@ecomchaco.com.ar *Mendoza* 445, T4371 7301/0835. *La Rioja* 745, T4815 1929, larioja@infovia.com.ar Others: *Catamarca*, Córdoba 2080, T/F4374 6891, casacata@sminter.gov.ar *Chubut*, Sarmiento 1172, T4382 2009/4383 7458, chubuturbue@ar.inter.net *Corrientes*, San Martín 333, p 4, T/F4394 2808. *Entre Ríos*, Suipacha 844, T/F4326 2573/2703. *Formosa*, H Yrigoyen 1429, T4381 2037, turismo@casadeformosa.gov.ar *Jujuy*, Santa Fe 967, T4394 2295, casadejujuy@yahoo.com.ar *La Pampa*, Suipacha 346, T/F4326 0511. *Mar del Plata*, Corrientes 1660, local 16, in La Plaza complex, T4384 5613, *Misiones*, Santa Fe 989, T4322 0686/1097. *Municipalidad de la Costa*, B Mitre 1135, T4381 0764. *Neuquén*, Perón 687, T4327 2454, casanqn_turismo@neuquen.gov.ar *Pinamar*, Florida 930 p 5, T4311 0693. *Río Negro*, Tucumán 1916, T4371 7078/5599, casaderionegro@infovia.com.ar *Salta*, Diagonal Norte 933, p 5 A, T4326 2456, F4326 0110, casasaltabaires@movi.com.ar *San Juan*, Sarmiento 1251, T4382 9241, F4382 9465. *San Luis*, Azcuénaga 1083, T4822 0426, F4823 9413. *Santa Cruz*, Suipacha 1120, T4325 3102/3098, infosantacruz@interlink.com.ar for information and reservations at *estancias* in Santa Cruz. *Santa Fe*, Montevideo 373, p 2, T/F4375 4570. *Santiago del Estero*, Florida 274, T4326 9418, F4326 5915. *Tierra del Fuego*, Marcelo T de Alvear 790, T4311 0233, infuebue@arnet.com.ar *Tucumán*, Suipacha 140, T4322 0564. *Villa Gesell*, B Mitre 1702, T4374 5098, F4374 5099, turismo@gesell.com.ar For tourist information on Patagonia and bookings for cheap accommodation and youth hostels, contact *Asatej*, see Useful addresses below.

Useful addresses **Migraciones:** (Immigration), Antártida Argentina 1335/55, edificios 3 y 4 (visas extended mornings only), T4317 0200, F4317 0282, 0800-1300 (see also Documents in Essentials). **Central Police Station:** Moreno 1550, Virrey Cevallos 362, T4370 5911/5800 (emergency, T101 from any phone, free). **Comisión Nacional de Museos y Monumentos y Lugares Históricos:** Av de Mayo 556, T4343 5835, heritage preservation official agency. **Administración de Parques Nacionales**, Santa Fe 690, opposite Plaza San Martín, T4311 0303, Mon-Fri 1000-1700, has leaflets on national parks. Also library (Biblioteca Perito Moreno), open to public Tue-Fri 1000-1700. **Aves Argentinas/AOP** (a BirdLife International partner), 25 de Mayo 749 p 2, T4312 8958, for information on birdwatching and specialist tours, good library open Wed and Fri 1500-2000.

Student organizations: *Asatej:* Argentine Youth and Student Travel Organization, runs a Student Flight Centre, Florida 835, p 3, oficina 320, T4114 7500, F4311 6158, www.asatej.com.ar Offering booking for flights (student discounts) including cheap one-way flights (long waiting lists), hotels and travel; information for all South America, noticeboard for travellers, the *Sleep Cheap Guide* lists cheap accommodation in Argentina, Bolivia, Chile, Brazil, Uruguay and Peru, ISIC cards sold (giving extensive discounts; Argentine ISIC guide available here), English and French spoken; also runs the following: *Red Argentino de Alojamiento Para Jovenes* (affiliated to HI), see page 72; *Asatej Travel Store*, ground floor and at Santa Fe 2450, p 3, loc 93, selling wide range of travel goods. *Oviajes*, Uruguay 385, p 6, T4371 6137 also at Echeverría 2498 p 1, T4785 7840/7884, www.oviajes.com.ar Offers travel facilities, ticket sales, information, and issues HI and Hostels of Europe, ISIC, ITIC, GO 25 and FIYTO cards, aimed at students, teachers and independent travellers. Cheap fares also at *TIJE*, San Martín 674 p 3, T4326 2036 or branch at Paraguay 1178, T5218 2800, www.tije.com **YMCA:** (Central), Reconquista 439, T4311 4785. **YWCA:** Tucumán 844, T4322 1550.

Argentina

South of Buenos Aires

The Atlantic Coast south of Buenos Aires with its many resorts, including Necochea, Bahía Blanca and Mar del Plata. This region also covers the hills of the Sierra de la Ventana. From Buenos Aires Autopista La Plata-Buenos Aires runs southeast to the city of La Plata. 30 km of Buenos Aires, Route 2 branches off and past the towns of Chascomús and Dolores to Mar del Plata, the most celebrated Argentine seaside resort.

La Plata

La Plata, on the Río de la Plata, was founded in 1882 as capital of Buenos Aires province after the city of Buenos Aires had become federal capital. It has a port and an oil refinery. The **Municipalidad**, an Italianate palace, and **Cathedral** ('a magnificent building with a classical Gothic interior') are in the **Plaza Moreno**. From here Av 51 and Av 53 run northeast to **Plaza San Martín**, which is bounded by the French-style **legislature** and the Italianate **Casa de Gobierno**. The **Teatro Argentino**, opera house, is at C53 y 10. Further northeast lies the **Paseo del Bosque**, a large park containing the **Museo de La Plata**. This houses an outstanding collection of extinct animals and artefacts from precolumbian peoples throughout the Americas. There are zoological, botanical, geological, mineralogical, palaeontological and archaeological sections. ■ *Daily 1000-1800, closed 1 Jan, 1 May, 25 Dec, US$1.50, free guided tours, weekdays 1400, 1600, Sat-Sun hourly, in Spanish and in English (phone first, T425 7744, F425 7527, www.fcnym.unlp.edu.ar Highly recommended.* There are free concerts during the summer in the *Teatro Martín Fierro* in the Paseo del Bosque. Tango and tropical music at *El Viejo Almacén*, at C 17 y 71. 8 km northwest of the city is the **República de los Niños**, an interesting children's village with scaled-down public buildings, built under the first Perón administration; take a green microbus 273 or a red and black 518 to República de los Niños from Plaza San Martín. At **Punta Lara**, a holiday resort 12 km north (bus 275 from La Plata, US$0.60), there is a nature reserve, slide show and tour. ■ *Open to public Sun only, 1000-1300 and 1400-1800, T0221-466 0396.* There is a *Foundation of the City* festival on 19 November. The Municipal tourist office is at C 50 between 6 and 7 (Pasaje Dardo Rocha), T427 1535.

Phone code: 0221
Colour map 8, grid B5
Population: 545,000
56 km SE of
Buenos Aires

Sleeping & eating **A** *Corregidor*, C 6 No 1026, T425 6800, F425 6805, informes@hotelcorregidor.com.ar 4-star, modern, a/c, snack bar, central. **C** *San Marco*, C 54 No 523, T422 9322. Good. Restaurants rarely open before 2100: *Don Quijote*, Plaza Paso. Good value, best in town, can get very crowded. The oldest restaurant in town is *Aguada*, C 50 entre 7 y 8. *El Gran Chaparral*, C 60 y C 117 (Paseo del Bosque). Good *parrillada*. Recommended bar, with steak sandwiches, *El Modelo*, C 54 y C5. Best *empanadas* at *La Madrileña*, a hole-in-the-wall on C 60 between Avs 5 and 6. Good bakeries: *El Globo*, C 43 y C 5, and *El Olmo*, C 48 entre 5 y 6.

Transport **Trains** To/from Buenos Aires (Constitución), frequent, US$0.75, 1 hr 10 mins (ticket office hidden behind shops opposite platform 6). **Buses** To **Buenos Aires**, 1½ hrs, US$2, about every 30 mins. From Buenos Aires, from Retiro day and night and from Plaza Constitución, daytime.

Colour map 8, grid B6 **San Clemente del Tuyú** (Phone code: 02252, 320 km from Buenos Aires) is the nearest Atlantic coastal resort to the capital. It is a family resort and cheaper than the more fashionable resorts further south. There are many places to stay along the promenade and several campsites. ■ *Buses to Mar del Plata are frequent*, Rápido del Sud, El Rápido Argentino, *US$7, 5 hrs. To Buenos Aires, several companies, US$8-12*.

At **Punta Rasa**, 9 km away, there is an old lighthouse and a nature reserve, which, in summer, is home to thousands of migratory birds from the northern hemisphere.

Pinamar & Villa Gesell About 89 km south of San Clemente is Pinamar (*Phone code*: 02254), a resort with a casino. The water-skiing is good. Fish may be bought on the beach from local fishermen. ■ *Bus terminal at Av Bunge e Intermédanos. To Buenos Aires, US$15, several companies. For trains, see under Buenos Aires.*

Villa Gesell (*Population*: 25,000. *Phone code*: 02255) is 22 km further south. A modern resort with a chocolate factory, it has fine beaches and over 100 hotels (most of which close at the beginning of March). It has become very popular although less crowded than Mar del Plata. ■ *Regular flights (in summer) to Buenos Aires. Buses direct to Buenos Aires, US$10-15, with several companies, book in advance at weekends.*

Sleeping **Pinamar**: **AL** *Del Bosque*, Av Bunge y Júpiter, T482480, F482179. With park, top class. **A** *Playas*, Bunge y de la Sirena, T482236, F482236. With breakfast, English spoken. **D** *Africa*, Av Libertador 500, T494443, hotelafrica@telpui.co.cr With breakfast, spotless, good atmosphere, small pool, near beach. Many others, all fully booked throughout Jan-Mar. Houses and apartments can be rented from Dec-Mar: 2-room flats about US$800 in January. Rates are increasingly cheaper in Feb and Mar. **Youth hostel** Mitre 149, T482908. **Camping** 5 sites (US$8-10 per day for a 4 people-tent) including *Moby Dick* at Ostende, Víctor Hugo 916, T486045, 5 km from beach. On beach at Ostende is *St Tropez*, Quintana 138, T482498, US$18 (take green *Montemar* bus from terminal).

Villa Gesell: **B** *Alpina Hostería*, C 307 y Alameda 206, T458066, alpinahosteria@ yahoo.com (Bs As T4791 9697). Includes breakfast, English, German, Italian, Slovenian and Croatian spoken, chalet style, 2 blocks from beach. **C** *ACA Hotel Villa Gesell*, Av 1 entre Paseos 112 y 113, T462272. **C** *Hostería Gran Chalet*, Paseo 105 No 447 y Av 4-5, T462913. Recommended. **D** *Mar Azul*, Av 4 y Paseo 106, T462457. **D** *Albatros*, Paseo 141 bis entre 3 y 4, T476179. Next to terminal, with breakfast and some meals provided. **E** pp *Hosp San Hector*, Av 8, No 641, T462052. Rates for apartment rental as Pinamar. **Camping sites** Many, a few open all year round. **Youth hostel** *Albergue Camping El Coyote*, Alameda 212 y 306, Barrio Norte, T458448.

Mar del Plata

Colour map 8, grid C5
Phone code: 0223
Population: 560,000
400 km from Buenos Aires

The greatest Argentine resort, dating from 1874, Mar del Plata is 110 km further south. There are 8 km of beaches. There are all classes of apartment blocks, boarding houses and lodgings but it is necessary to book in advance between late December and mid-March (when the night-life continues all night). Two million visitors stay during the summer months, but for the rest of the year the town is fairly quiet and good value. Local festivals include: **10 February** (Foundation of City); **10 November** (Day of Tradition); **22 November** (Santa Cecilia).

The most attractive area is around **Playa Bristol**: here are the fine casino (upper floor open to the public), the *Hotel Provincial*, and the Plaza Colón. Further north is the **Plaza San Martín**, flanked by the attractive cathedral. Southeast of Plaza Colón around C Colón y Gral Alvear at the top of a hill are some of the more 'eccentric' mansions of the early 20th century, and, 10 blocks southwest, in a neighbourhood called Los Troncos. These include the mock Tudor **Villa Blaquier** and, nearby, the Norman style **Villa Ortiz Basualdo** (1909), in which is the **Museo Municipal de Arte**, Av Colón 1189. Upper floors of the mansion can be visited, art exhibitions on the ground floor. ■ *Daily in summer 1700-2200, in winter 1200-1700, Wed closed, US$1.*

Beaches include fashionable **Playa Grande**, with its private clubs and the summer estates of wealthy *porteños,* and **Playa La Perla**, with moderately priced hotels. At **Punta Iglesia** there is a large rock carving of Florentino Ameghino, the palaeontologist who collected most of the fossils in the museum at La Plata. South of Playa Grande is the port, reached by bus, 15 mins from the terminal. There is a large fishing fleet, excursion boats, seafood restaurants and a huge sealion colony (walk along Escollera Sur-southern breakwater).

The wooded municipally-owned **Parque Camet** is 7 km north. It has polo grounds and playing fields. Visit the rocky promontory of **Cabo Corrientes** to watch the breakers, and **Punta Mogotes** lighthouse. ■ *Daily 1000-1700.* Fishing is good all along the coast and *pejerrey, corvina* and *pescadilla* abound.

Museo del Hombre del Puerto – Cleto Ciocchini, Padre J Dutto 383, shows the history of the port and its first Sicilian fishermen. ■ *Thu, Fri, Sat 1500-1900 (in summer, Tue-Sat 1700-2100), US$1.* **Museo Municipal de Ciencias Naturales**, Libertad 3099, small but interesting. **Centro Cultural Victoria Ocampo**, Matheu 1851, housed in the Villa Victoria, a beautiful early 20th-century wooden house prefabricated in England, where the famous author spent her summers until her death in 1979; inside are artefacts from her life and temporary exhibitions. ■ *Daily 1000-1300, 1700-2300, US$1, ISIC cards, free Wed.* Nearby is the **Villa Mitre**, in the former mansion of a son of Bartolomé Mitre; inside are an eclectic collection of artefacts including photos of the city at different points in its history. **Museo del Mar**, Av Colón 1114, T451 3553. A vast collection of 30,000 sea shells. ■ *From 0800 till late in the evening, US$1.50.* The tourist office is at Belgrano 2740, T495 1777, 0800-1500, English spoken, good information, including bus routes to all sites of interest.

B *Argentino*, Belgrano y Entre Ríos, T493 2223, also apartments. Highly recommended. Among the 3-star hotels (**C**) are: *Benedetti*, Av Colón 2198, T493 0031/2. Recommended. *O Sole Mío*, Independencia 1277, T495 6685. Half board, Italian run. Highly recommended. **D** *Alpino*, Balcarce y La Rioja, T493 1034. With breakfast, excellent, family run. **D** *Monterrey*, Lamadrid 2627, T15-683 9585. Good. **D** *Niza*, Santiago del Estero 1843, T495 1695. **E** out of season, shared bath, safe. Recommended. **Near the bus terminal D** *Europa*, Arenales 2735, T494 0436. Quiet, hot water. **D** *Paley*, Alberti 1752, T495 5036. Comfortable, open all year, good value restaurant. Recommended. **E** pp *Ushuaia*, Gascón 1561, T451 0911. With breakfast, pleasant. **Camping** *El Griego*, Av Edison 8000, Km 1.4 of Playa Serena (buses 581 or 511 G), T482 3471, www.elgriego.com.ar Reasonable prices. Several sites on the road south. **Youth hostel E** pp *Pergamino*, Tucumán 2728, T495 7927, near terminal, friendly, clean. **Apartment rental** There are many houses and apartments for rent. Monthly rates for summer exclude electricity, gas etc. Flats US$300-500, chalets US$500-800. The tourist office has a list of companies.

Sleeping
During summer months it is essential to book in advance. Many hotels open in season only. Out of season, bargain everywhere

El Caballito Blanco, Rivadavia 2534. Excellent, German decor. *La Paella*, Entre Ríos 2025. Good. Seafood restaurants in the Centro Comercial Puerto including *La Caracola*, good but not cheap. *La Piazzetta*, Plaza San Martín. Good pasta and salads, vegetarian options. *Los Vascos*, Av Martínez de Hoz 643 and *Taberna Baska*, 12 de Octubre 3301, both traditional places for seafood. *Tenedor libre* restaurants of all kinds along San Martín.

Eating
Many seafood restaurants near the fishing port

Argentina

Los Inmortales, Corrientes 1662. Good, moderately priced. Good value meals at *La Nueva Glorieta*, Alberti 1821. Cheap restaurants along Rivadavia. **Vegetarian** *La Huerta*, Santiago del Estero 1721. *Finca del Sol*, San Martin 2459. Both recommended.

Entertainment   **Bars**   Smart bars around C Alem and on C Güemes, popular in summer and weekends. *Mr Jones*, Alem 3738, near *Sheraton*, very good. **Casino** Open Dec to end-Apr, 1600-0330; 1600-0400 on Sat. Winter opening, May-Dec, Mon-Fri 1500-0230; weekends 1500-0300. Free; minimum bet US$0.50. **Cinemas** *Cine Arte* usually at Centro Cultural Pueyrredón, 25 de Mayo y Catamarca. Wed 50% discount at all cinemas. **Discos** Most are on Av Constitución.

Transport   **Air** Camet airport, T478 3990, 10 km north of town. Many flights daily to Buenos Aires, *AIRG* (T492 2112), *LADE* (T493 8220), *Southern Winds* (T486 6666) and *AR/Austral* (T496 0101/0810-2228 6527). *LADE* also to many Patagonian towns. *Remise* taxi from airport to town, mini bus US$2.

Trains To Buenos Aires (Constitución) 5¼ hrs, from Estación Norte, Luro 4599, T475 6076, about 13 blocks from the centre. See under Buenos Aires, Trains for details. To Miramar, from Estación Norte, only in summer.

Buses Terminal in former railway station at Alberti y Las Heras, T451 5404, central. To **Buenos Aires** 6 hrs, US$10-15, *Micromar, Empresa Argentina, Chevallier* and many others. *El Cóndor* and *Rápido Argentino* to La Plata, US$10-15. To **San Clemente del Tuyú**, *Rápido del Sud*, *El Rápido Argentino*, frequent, US$7, 5 hrs. To **Miramar** hourly, 45 mins, US$1.40. To **Bahía Blanca**, only *El Rápido*, US$14, 7 hrs. *La Estrella* and *Vía Bariloche* to **San Martín de los Andes**, US$38. To **Bariloche**, US$38 with *Vía Bariloche*. To **Puerto Madryn** and **Trelew**, bus connections at Bahía Blanca.

Directory   **Banks** *Lloyds TSB Bank*, Luro 3101, open 1000-1600, cash advances on Visa. *Casas de Cambio Jonestur*, San Martín 2574. *Amex*, at *Oti Internacional*, San Luis 1630, T494 5414. *La Moneta*, Rivadavia 2615. **Communications Internet:** Many places in town, US$0.50-1.50 per hour. **Post Office:** Luro 2460, poste restante, also international parcels office (open till 1200). **Telephone:** Many *locutorios* around the town. **Cultural centres** Cultural events: reduced price tickets are often available from *Cartelera Baires*, Santa Fe 1844, local 33, or from *Galería de los Teatros*, Santa Fe 1751. **Asociación Argentina de Cultura Inglesa**, San Luis 2498, friendly, extensive library. **Useful addresses** Immigration Office: Rivadavia 3820, T492 4271, open morning.

Inland, 68 km west of Mar de la Plata is the town of **Balcarce** (*Population*: 35,000). This is a centre for visits to the Cinco Cerros, five strangely shaped hills. Balcarce is also the birthplace of the great racing driver **Juan Fangio**; it has a racing circuit and the **Museo Juan Manuel Fangio** which houses all his racing cars and trophies (just off Plaza Libertad, open 1100-1800, US$3, recommended). Frequent buses from Mar de la Plata. **C** *Balcarce*, C 16 y 17, T422055, good. Excellent *parrillas* on the outskirts.

Mar del Plata to Bahia Blanca

Miramar
Phone code: 02291
Colour map 8, grid C5
Population: 22,000
53 km SW of Mar del Plata, along coast road

Cheaper than Mar del Plata, Miramar has higher cliffs backing the beach and more picturesque hills. There is a fine golf course at *Golf Club* (Ruta 11 Km 4) and a casino. The tourist office is on the central plaza. Immediately south of the city limits is an extensive forest park on the beach, the **Vivero Dunícola**, whose vegetation stays green and blooming throughout the year, despite winter night-time temperatures below freezing. There are dozens of hotels and apartments. **Camping G** pp *El Durazno*, on Ruta 11, 2 km from town, good facilities, shops, restaurant, take bus 501 marked 'Playas'. Many sites, reasonably priced. ■ *In summer only, there is a Ferrobaires train daily except Sun to Mar del Plata. There are 8 buses daily to Buenos Aires, Micromar, El Cóndor and many others, US$13-17; to Mar del Plata, US$1.40, Rápido del Sud; to Necochea, El Rápido, US$3.*

Necochea, 101 km further southwest along the coast, is another famous resort, second only to Mar del Plata. The town is in two parts, with the centre 2 km inland from the seafront area. There is a large Danish community with its own club and consulate. Its 24-km long beach is one of the best in the country. There is a municipal recreation complex, with a large casino deteriorating in the salt air (open summer daily and winter weekends 2200-0400), various sports facilities, a cinema, disco and children's play area. There is a language school, *Instituto Argentino de Idiomas*, Galería Monviso, local 8, C 62 y 63, recommended. A tourist office is on the beach front at Av 79 y Av 2, T430158, English spoken. It has a list of apartments for rent.

The **Parque Miguel Lillo** (named after the Argentine botanist) faces the beach, comprising 641 ha of conifers, nature park, swan lake with paddle boats, an amphitheatre, museum and go-cart track. About 3½ km across the mouth of the river from Necochea is **Quequén**, with an excellent beach, good bathing, and pleasant scenery.

Necochea
Phone code: 02262
Colour map 8, grid C5
Population: 65,000

Argentina

Sleeping The **Hotel Association** is at Av 79 y C 4. Most hotels close off-season when it is worth bargaining. **C** *Hostería del Bosque*, C 89 No 350, entre 8 y 10, T/F420002, 5 blocks from beach. Quiet, upper rooms better, nice bar and garden, parking next door. **C** *Perugia*, C 81, No 288, T422020. A/c, open all year. **D** *Doramar*, C 83, No 329, T425815. Family run, helpful. **D** *Hosp Solchaga*, C 62, No 2822, T425584. Excellent. Many more and several in Quequén. **Camping** *Río Quequén*, C 22 y Ribera Río Quequén, T422145/428051. Campsites on beach US$3 pp in season.

Most hotels are in the seafront area from C 2 (parallel with beach) north between Av 71-91. There are at least 100 within 700 m of the beach

Transport Buses Terminal at Av 58 y Jesuita Cardiel, T422470, 3 km from the beach area; bus 513, 517 from outside the terminal to the beach. Taxi to beach area US$1.50. To **Buenos Aires**, US$14-16, *La Estrella*, *El Cóndor* and few others. To **Mar del Plata**, *El Rápido*, US$4. To **Bahía Blanca**, *El Rápido* US$10. For **trains**, see under Buenos Aires.

Bahía Blanca

The most important centre south of Mar del Plata, Bahía Blanca stands at the head of a large bay at the mouth of the Río Napostá. Local holidays include Nuestra Señora de la *Merced* on 24 September and Day of Tradition on 10 November.

Phone code: 0291
Colour map 8, grid C4
Population: 300,000

The city is built back from the river front. The city has some fine buildings especially around the central **Plaza Rivadavia**, notably the ornate Italianate Municipalidad and the French-style Banco de la Nación. The **Barrio Inglés** (direction Ingeniero White) is where the foremen and technicians of the port and railway construction teams lived; Brickman St, just past the railway bridge, is a row of late Victorian semi-detached houses. Managers lived at nearby Harding Green. **Museo Histórico**, in the Teatro Municipal, Dorrego 116, has sections on the pre-conquest period, the conquest and interesting photos of early Bahía Blanca. Outside is a statue of Garibaldi, erected by the Italian community in 1928. **Museo del Puerto**, Torres y Carrega, Ingeniero White, excellent displays of domesic artefacts from the early 20th century. Serves as a *confitería* on Sunday. Bus 500, 504. The tourist office is in the Municipalidad on the main plaza, Alsina 65, T459 4007, turismo@ bb.mun.gba.gov.ar Very helpful. ■ *Mon-Fri 0800-1200*.

Excursions **Pehuén-Có**, 84 km east, is one of many fine beaches with camping places, well shaded by pine trees (beware of jellyfish when wind is in the south). Signs to it on the main road 24 km from Bahía Blanca. Another fine beach is **Monte Hermoso**, 106 km, two hours by bus (four a day in summer, two in winter) east of Bahía Blanca. Good cheap meals, several restaurants. (Its hotels are open only January-March, several campsites – including *Las Dunas*, T02921-482177, 30 minutes walk west along the beach, US$2 per person, a friendly spot run by an elderly German couple.)

B *Austral*, Colón 159, T456 1700, F455 3737, www.hoteles-austral.com.ar 4-star, restaurant. **Sleeping**
D *Barne*, H Yrigoyen 270, T453 0864, F453 0294. With breakfast, helpful, family run.

Argentina

Recommended. **D** *Belgrano*, Belgrano 44, T/F456 4404, hbelgrano@impsat1.com.ar Breakfast, restaurant. **D** *Victoria*, Gral Paz 82, T452 0522. Basic, hot water, **E** without bath, poor beds. **D** *Del Sur*, Rodríguez 80, T452 2452. With restaurant, noisy with traffic. Near railway station: **D** *Res Roma*, Cerri 759, T453 8500. **E** *Los Vascos*, Cerri 747, T452 9290. **Camping** Balneario Maldonado, 4 km from centre, US$3 per tent, US$0.50 pp, next to petrochemical plant, salt water swimming pool, bus 514 along Av Colón every hour but only when beach is open, that is when sunny and not in evening.

Eating *Gambrinus*, Arribeños 174. Founded in 1897, German specialities. *Paparazzi*, Lamadrid 9. For pizza and pasta. *Parrilla* at *La Bataraza*, Moreno y Güemes. A few good fish restaurants at the harbour, eg *El Royal*, at Ingeniero White. *North Western Café*, Alsina 236. American bar, pizzas, happy hour 1600-1800.

Transport **Local bus**: US$0.40, but you need to buy *tarjetas* (cards) from kiosks for 1, 2, 4 or 10 journeys. **Air** Comandante Espora, 11 km northeast of centre. *AR/Austral* (T456 0561/0810-2228 6527), *AIRG* (T452 6384/0810-7777 274) and *LADE* (T453 7697) to **Buenos Aires**. *LADE* to **Bariloche, Mar del Plata, Neuquén, Puerto Madryn, San Antonio Oeste, San Martín de los Andes, Trelew** and **Viedma**. **Trains** Station at Av Gral Cerri 780, T452 1571. To Buenos Aires 3 weekly, 12½ hrs, pullman US$12, 1st US$9, tourist US$8. **Buses** Terminal in old railway station 2½ km from centre at Estados Unidos y Brown, T481 9615, connected by buses 505, 514, 517, no hotels nearby. To **Buenos Aires** frequent, several companies, 8½ hrs, US$15, shop around. To **Mar del plata**, *El Rápido*, US$14, 7 hrs. To **Córdoba**, US$22, 12 hrs. To **Neuquén**, 6 a day, 8 hrs, US$12. To **Necochea**, *El Rápido*, 5 hrs, US$10. To **Zapala** 3 daily, 11 hrs, US$15, *El Valle* and few others. To **Río Colorado** US$4; *Viedma Ceferino, Plusmar* and *Río Paraná* (to Carmen de Patagones), 4 hrs, US$6-8. To **Trelew**, *Don Otto* and others, US$32, 10 ½ hrs. To **Río Gallegos**, *Don Otto* US$36. To **Tornquist**, US$2, *Río Paraná* and *La Estrella/El Cóndor*, 1 hr 20 min; to **Sierra de la Ventana** (town) *La Estrella/El Cóndor* and *Expreso Cabildo*, US$3.

Directory **Banks** *Lloyds TSB Bank*, Chiclana 299, T455 3563. *Citibank*, Chiclana 232. *Amex*, Fortur, Soler 38, T426290, English spoken. *Casas de Cambio*: *Pullman*, San Martín 171. All *casas de cambio* closed at weekends. **Communications** Post Office: Moreno 34. **Telephone**: 25 de Mayo 209.

Sierra de la Ventana Some 100 km to the north is the **Sierra de la Ventana**, the highest range of hills in the pampas and a favourite area for excursions from Bahía Blanca. **Tornquist**, 70 km north of Bahía Blanca by Route 33, with an attractive church on the central plaza, is a good starting point (**D** *San José*, Güemes 138, T0291-494 0152, small, quiet, modern; **G** campsite at *Parque Norte*, on Route 76). The **Parque Provincial Ernesto Tornquist** is 25 km east of Tornquist, with massive ornate gates from the Tornquist family home. Nearby is *Campamento Base*, camping, dormitory accommodation, T0291-491 0067, hospitable. From here it's a three-hour walk to the summit of Cerro de la Ventana, which has fantastic views from the 'window' in the summit ridge. 5 km further is the forestry station and a visitors centre, T0291-491 0039, with audio-visual display, from where a guided visit (only with own vehicle, 4-5 hours) is organised to natural caves (one with petroglyphs); also from here, short trail to cerro Bahía Blanca. Villa Ventana, 10 km further, is a wooden settlement with excellent teashop, *Casa de Heidi*, and wholefood available from *Jardín de Aylem*. Accommodation in cabins; municipal campsite by river with all facilities.

The town of **Sierra de la Ventana**, further east, is a good centre for exploring the hills. Tres Picos, rising bare and barren from the rich farmlands to 1,239 m, is only 6¼ km away. There is a 18-hole golf course, and good trout fishing in the Río Sauce Grande. Excellent tourist information. *Geotur*, San Martín 193, T0291-491 5355, for guided tours and horseback excursions. **B** *Provincial*, Drago y Malvinas, T491 5025. **D** *La Perlita*, San Martín y Roca, T4915 020. **F** pp *Yapay*, San Martín near bus terminal. Recommended, quiet.

Buenos
Aires

Córdoba and the Central Sierras

Córdoba, the second city in the country, has some historic, colonial buildings and is an important route centre, especially for road travel to the northwest. The Sierras de Córdoba contain many pleasant, small resorts in the hills.

Córdoba

Argentina

Capital of Córdoba Province, the city was founded in 1573. The site of the first university in the country, established in 1613 by the Jesuits, it now has two universities. It is an important industrial centre, the home of Argentina's motor industry, and a busy modern city with a flourishing shopping centre. Local holidays are 6 July, Foundation of the City; 30 September, St Jerome; and 7-10 October.

Phone code: 053
Colour map 8, grid A3
Population: 1.2 million
Altitude: 440 m

At the city's heart is the tranquil **Plaza San Martín**, with a statue of the Liberator. On the west side is the old **Cabildo**, Independencia 30, with the 'Red Hall', internal patios and subterranean prison cells. It now houses the Museos de la Ciudad, de Arqueología Urbana and Fotografías de Córdoba de Ayer. ■ *Tue-Sun 0900-1300, 1600-2100, Mon afternoon only.* Next to it stands the **Cathedral**, the oldest in Argentina (begun 1640, consecrated 1671), with attractive stained-glass windows and a richly-decorated ceiling: see the remarkable cupola (1753). Behind the cathedral is the pleasant Plaza del Fundador, with a statue to the city founder Jerónimo Luís de Cabrera. One of the features of this part of the city is its old churches. Near Plaza San Martín at Independencia 122 is the 16th-century **Carmelo convent** and chapel of **Santa Teresa**. The church of **La Compañía**, Obispo Trejo y Caseros, with a simple façade, dates from about 1650; its façade was rebuilt in the 20th century. The barrel vault and cupola of the Capilla Doméstica, built entirely of Paraguayan cedar, are unique. This church and two other former Jesuit institutions have been placed on UNESCO's World Heritage list. **La Merced** at 25 de Mayo 83, was built in the early 19th century, though its fine gilt wooden pulpit dates from the colonial period. On its exterior, overlooking Rivadavia, are fine murals in ceramic by local artist Armando Sica. Further east, at Blvd J D Perón, is the magnificent late 19th-century **Mitre railway station**, now closed though its beautiful tiled *confitería* is still in use.

Museo Marqués de Sobremonte, in the fine colonial house of this governor of Córdoba, Rosario de Santa Fe 218, one block east of San Martin, 18th and 19th provincial history. ■ *Tue-Fri 0900-1300, 1500-1900, Sat 0900-1300, Sun 1000-1300. US$1.* **Museo de Ciencias Naturales**, Yrigoyen 115. ■ *Mon-Fri 0830-1230, 1430-1800, Sat 0900-1200, good guided tours (in Spanish, 'interesting skeletons of prehistoric glyptodont'), US$1.* **Museo Provincial de Bellas Artes**, Plaza España, works from the precursors of Cordoban painters to the present in an early 20th-century mansion. ■ *Mon-Sun 0900-2100 (closed Jan).* **Museo de Arte Religioso**, in the Convent of Santa Teresa, Independencia 122. ■ *Wed-Sat 0930-1230.*

Sleeping

A *Panorama*, Alvear 251, T420 4000. Good, pool, central. **B** *Windsor*, Buenos Aires 214, T422 4012. Comfortable, very good. **D** *Res Mi Valle*, Corrientes 586, 5 mins from the bus terminal. Fan, small, nice, family-run. **On San Jerónimo   A** *Córdoba Plaza*, No 137, T426 8900. Large comfortable rooms, safe car park. **B** *Sussex*, No 125, T422 9071. Comfortable, roomy. **B** *Dallas*, No 339, T421 6091. With breakfast, parking, a/c. Recommended. **B** *Viña del Italia*, No 611, T/F422 6589. With breakfast, parking, restaurant, good value. **C** *Corona*, No 571, T422 8789. Comfortable. **D** *Rosa Mística*, No 532. Also monthly rates. **E** *La María*, No 628. Parking, good value. **E** *Res Thanoa*, No 479, T421 7297. Cheaper without bath (shared baths dirty), nice patio, noisy. **E** *Wonder*, No 519, T422 9321. With bath, good value, parking. On **Balcarce C** *Del Sol*, No 144, T424 2969. Fan, a/c extra. Recommended. **C** *Riviera*, No 74, T422 3969. With breakfast, parking. **Other hotels between Plaza San Martín and bus terminal D** *Roma Termini*, Entre Ríos 687, T421 8721. Fan, good value, welcoming. **D** *Nueva Florida*, Rosario de Santa Fe 459, T426373. Some rooms with a/c. Recommended. **E** *Entre Ríos*, Entre Ríos, 2 blocks from bus terminal. Recommended. **Other hotels C** *Alto Paraná*, Paraná 230, T428 1625, hotelaltoparana@arnet.com.ar Close to bus terminal, hot shower, TV, with breakfast, good value. **C** *Garden*, 25 de Mayo 35, T421 4729. Central, secure. Highly recommended. **D** *Harbor*, Paraná 126, T/F421 7300. Without breakfast, good value. **Youth hostel** Ituzaingó 1070, Nueva Córdoba, T468 7359, www.cordobahostel.com.ar **Camping** Municipal site, Gral San Martín, at the back of the Complejo Ferial (bus 31).

Eating

Numerous grills of all kinds on city outskirts, especially in the Cerro de las Rosas district, for outdoor meals when the weather is suitable

Mid-range: *Betos*, San Juan 494. Best *lomitos* in town, *parrilla*. Recommended. *Doña Anastasia*, San Juan 325. Good formal *churrascaría*. *Il Gatto*, Gral Paz 120. Great pasta and pizzas. *La Mamma*, Santa Rosa y Figueroa Alcorta. Excellent Italian. **Cheap**: *Minoliti*, Entre Ríos 358. Excellent homemade pastas, limited menu. *Da Piero*, Deán Funes y Belgrano. Good set lunch and dinner, pleasant atmosphere and owner. Many cheap restaurants along San Jerónimo including *San Carlos*, No 431, good food and service. *American Fast Food*, esq Chacabuco, self-service. *Sorocabana*, No 98, corner of Plaza San Martín, 24-hr café.

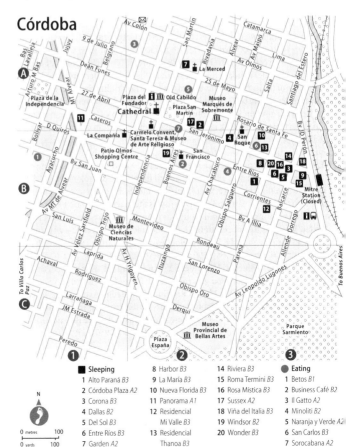

Córdoba

Others on Ituzaingó between Derqui and Obispo Oro. *Business Café*, Corrientes 161. Good set lunch, daily papers, CNN, internet access. Excellent fruit juices (*licuados*) at *Kiosco Americano*, Tucumán 185 and at Gral Paz 242. *Empanadería La Alameda*, Obispo Trejo 170, near University. Reasonable food, good student atmosphere, live music, best 2200-2400. Opposite is *Mandarina*, No 171. Salads, Chinese, meat, popular, good value. *Naranja y Verde*, Rivadavia 50. Vegetarian snack bar, cheap, clean, open Mon-Fri 0730-1600. Ice cream at branches of *Dolce Neve* throughout town. *Soppelsa's* ice cream is also recommended, with several outlets. **Pubs and bars**: *Rock & Feller's Bar*, Yrigoyen 320. Popular, fashionable bar and restaurant, reasonable prices. *Picadilly Pub*, Yrigiyen 464. British pub and restaurant, owner speaks good English, busy at lunchtime. *La Fenice*, Buenos Aires 779 e Yrigiyen, popular late night bar and *confitería* at weekends.

Entertainment

Argentina

Cinema   Many cinemas including *Teatro Córdoba*, 27 de Abril 275. Foreign language films. Programmes in local newspaper *La Voz del Interior*. **Discos**   Several discos, bars and restaurants on Av H Yrigoyen between Patio Olmos shopping centre and C Ituzaingó, popular at weekends, expensive. *La Luna*, Independencia e Yrigoyen. Crowded disco/bar. Several also in Cerro de las Rosas area. **Folk music**   At *Pulpería El Viejo Rincón*, Dumesnil y Mendoza. Excellent music till 0500. **Tango** in *Confitería Mitre*, Mitre railway station, Sun 2130.

Shopping

Main shopping area, with many galerías, is off Plaza San Martín

Patio Olmos, V Sarsfield y San Juan, is a large *galería* with varied shops. **Handicraft market** in Rodríguez y Cañada, Sat, Sun and holidays 1600-2300, worth a visit for the quantity and quality of goods. Health food shops in *galería* on 27 de Abril opposite Plaza Fundador. Shopping centres open daily 1000-2200, but their food courts open till 2400. In summer shops close at 1300 on Sat and don't reopen till Mon; in winter they open 0900-1830. *Americanos* supermarkets open on Sun, as does *Spar* at the bus terminal.

Transport

Local Bus: Municipal buses and electric buses (trolleys) do not accept cash. You have to buy tokens (*cospeles*) or cards from kiosks, normal US$0.55, *diferencial* US$1.

Long distance Air: Pajas Blancas airport, 13 km north of city, T481 0696, has shops, post office, a good restaurant and a *casa de cambio* (open Mon-Fri 1000-1500). Remise from airport to centre, US$8.50 with *Ecuador TAS*, T475 9111 or 0800-555 0224, who also run minibuses, US$2.50, 35 mins (starts at *Hotel Heidy*, Balcarce e Illia, from 0710 to 2045, pick up at *Heladería Armichi*, San Juan y Sarsfield, 10 mins later). Taxi US$6.50. Local bus No 55 from Chacabuco entre Rosario de Santa Fe y San Jerónimo, 40 mins to airport entrance. *Ciudad de Córdoba* bus from bus terminal, office 34, US$1, 40 mins to within 100 m of airport door. *AR/Austral* run a daily shuttle service to/from **Buenos Aires**, about 1 hr. Most major Argentine cities are served by *AR, Southern Winds, American Falcon* and *Dinar* usually via BsAs. International flights to **Bolivia** (Santa Cruz), **Brazil** and **Chile** direct, others via BsAs.

Buses: Large terminal conveniently situated at Blvd Perón 300, T421 2073. The ground floor has booking offices, tourist information, a *Banelco* ATM and left-luggage offices. There are bathrooms with showers, on the first floor, plus a restaurant, supermarket, pharmacy and *locutorio*. Very busy at peak travel periods.

To **Buenos Aires**, 10 companies, 9 hrs, US$18 *común*, US$30 *diferencial*: to **Salta** (US$18, *Panamericano*), 4 daily, *La Veloz del Norte* twice, about 12 hrs, and **Jujuy** (US$21, *Merco Bus*), 15 hrs. To **Mendoza**, 10 hrs, frequent with *TAC*, US$24, also 1 daily each *Chevallier, Jocolí, El Rápido*. To **Tucumán**, US$9-12, 8 hrs, about 8 a day, *Panamericano* has more than other companies. To **Posadas**, *Expreso Singer, Crucero del Norte* (very good buses), 15 hrs, US$21 including meals. To **Mar del Plata** US$22. To **La Rioja**, 4 a day, 6½ hrs, US$10.50. Some go on to **Catamarca**, US$12. To La Rioja-Aimogasta-**Tinogasta** (US$15)- **Fiambalá** with *El Cóndor*, Tue, Thu, Fri (see also page 160). To **Belén** (Catamarca) La Calera, Mon, Wed, Fri, 2100, US$17.50. *Satag*, efficient a/c buses, serve **Villa Carlos Paz** (1 hr, frequent service, every 15 mins, US$1.55), **Cosquín** (US$2.50) and **La Falda** (US$3.50) in the Sierras de Córdoba.

International services: To **Asunción** (Paraguay) direct, *Brújula*, Sat, and *Cacorba* Wed and Sun, 16 hrs. To **Montevideo** (Uruguay), Tue, Fri, Sun 1700, *Encon*, also *EGA*, Mon, Wed,

Sat 1745, 17 hrs. To **Santiago** (Chile), 16 hrs, *El Rápido* daily 2130 and *Tas-Choapa* 3 a week. Both continue to **Lima** (Peru) *El Rápido* Tue, Fri, Sun, *Tas-Choapa* Wed, Sun, via Mendoza and Chile, 65 hrs. To **Pocitos** (Bolivian border) with *Panamericano, CMP, Atahualpa* and *Andesmar* daily direct, US$30. It is best to travel from Córdoba if you are going north, as it may be hard to get a seat if boarding en route.

Directory **Airline offices** *Aerolíneas Argentinas/Austral*, Colón 520, T426 7601/2/0810-2228 6527. *Dinar*, Av Colón 533, T433 1700. *LAB*, Colón 119, p 3, T421 6458. *AIRG*, Av Colón 534, T425 8000. *Southern Winds*, Colón 540, T426 6626. **Banks** There are Link and Banelco ATMs at many locations. All ATMs take international credit cards. Many *cambios* as well as ATMs on Rivadavia 100 block, just off Plaza San Martín; shop around for best rate. For Visa problems, T424 3443. **Communications** Internet: *Business Café*, address above. *Cyber Cabildo*, in Cabildo, US$1.50 per hr, often full, Mon-Fri 0900-1800. Many others. **Post Office:** Colón 201, parcel service on the ground floor beside the customs office. **Telephone:** There are hundreds of *locutorios* throughout the city, many with a post office and internet access. **Cultural centres** Alliance Française, Ayacucho 46, cultural centre, French consulate in same building, internet access first 15 mins free, then US$4 per hr, 1600-2000. **Asociación Argentina de Cultura Británica**, Yrigoyen 496, good library (Mon-Fri 0900-2000), small reading room. **Goethe Institut**, Illia 356, T422 4358, open Tue-Fri 1700-2045 and Fri 0930-1230. **Embassies and consulates** Consulates: Austria, J Cortés 636, T472 0450. **Belgium**, F Posse 2533, T481 3298. **Bolivia**, San Juan 639, p 3, T423 1672. **Chile**, Crisol 280, T469 2010. **Denmark**, Núñez del Prado 2484, T481 0171. **Finland**, Chacabuco 716, T420 8200. **France** in *Alliance Française*, T422 1129. **Israel**, Vélez Sarsfield 84, p 2, No 1. **Italy**, Ayacucho 131, T422 1020. **Germany**, Eliseo Canton 1870, T489 0826 (Honorary Consul: Carlos Dechsle). **Paraguay**, 9 de Julio 573, then US$4 per hr, No 3, T422 6388. **Spain**, Chacabuco 875, T469 7490. **Sweden**, Alvear 10, T424 0111. **Switzerland**, Colón 184, p 1, No 6, T423 2170. **Language schools** *Aguas de la Cañada*, Independencia 595, T422 3314, US$150 per week, helpful. Recommended. *Casa de Lenguas*, T34-91-591 2393, www.casadelenguas.com *Comisión de Intercambio Educativo* (COINED), Artigas 220, planta alta, T429 9402, www.coined.com.ar Offers classes starting every Mon. In Germany classes can be pre-arranged through *Kommission für Bildungsaustausch*, Hoheluftchaussee 145, 20253 Hamburg, coined.@t-online.de). *Interswop*, Sucre 2828, Alta Cordoba, T471 0081, F422 0655. Organizes stays abroad, language classes and accommodation, also exchange programmes for any nationality. **Applications and details:** *Interswop*, Bornstrasse 16, 20146 Hamburg, Germany, T/F40-410 8029. **Medical services** Hospital Clínicas, T4337051. **Hospital de Urgencias**, T421 5001/422 7181. **Tourist offices** Dirección Provincial de Turismo, Tucumán 360, T423 3248. Provincial and municipal tourist offices in the old Cabildo, on Plaza San Martín, T433 1542/7542, open 0930-1200, 1630-1900 daily except Sun. Information office at the bus terminal, T433 1980/2, has free maps, extensive information on accommodation and camping in the province, very helpful. The tourist office desk at the airport is often unmanned. The tourist office has 3 city maps with self-guided tours in English and Spanish. Free guided tours start in front of the Cathedral at 1030, 1130 and 1630, led by guides in green suits, very interesting and thorough. For provincial tourist information T0800-40107. **Club Andino**, Deán Funes 2100, open Wed after 2100, closed Jan. **Useful addresses** *Asatej*, Belgrano 194, p 1, T426 5224/5, F424 7503, cordoba@asatej.com.ar

Sierras de Córdoba

Three ranges of undulating hills rise from the pampas, their lower slopes often wooded, particularly in the south. The Sierra Grande, the longest, lies between Sierra Chica to the east and Sierra de Guisapampa and its continuation, the Sierra de Pocho, to the west. The highest peak, Champaquí (2,975 m) has a small lake about 2,550 m up. The hills run roughly 500 km from north to south; west of Córdoba they are 150 km wide. A network of good roads gives pleasant contrasts of scenery. The region's climate is dry, sunny and exhilarating, especially in winter.

At the foot of the Sierra Chica are large dams to contain the waters of the Río Primero at San Roque, the Río Segundo at Los Molinos and Río Tercero. There are two other large dams in the hills, at Cruz del Eje and La Viña, providing power and irrigation. Sailing and fishing are popular on the lakes.

In the Punilla Valley is this large modern town on an artificial lake Lago San Roque. It is the nearest resort to Córdoba and is therefore often crowded. Tours available on catamarans to the two dams on the lake (US$10); launch trips also available. A chair-lift runs (0900-1900) to the summit of the Cerro de la Cruz, which offers splendid views. There is also a museum of meteorites. ■ *US$2*. The tourist office is at San Martín 400. North of Villa Carlos Paz, on Route 38, a road branches west to Tanti from where local buses go to Los Gigantes, a paradise for climbers, two-day treks possible. Club Andino has several *refugios*; details in Villa Carlos Paz.

Villa Carlos Paz
Phone code: 03541
Population: 46,000
Altitude: 642 m
36 km W of Córdoba

Sleeping D *El Monte*, Caseros 45, T422001, F422993. Very good. Recommended. **D** *Mar del Plata*, Esquiú 47, T422068. Recommended. **D** *Villa Carlos Paz Parque*, Santa Fe 50, T425128. Full board available. Recommended. **E** *Wanda*, Alvear 479, T/F421760. Nice garden. Recommended. **Youth hostel E** *Acapulco*, La Paz 39, T421929, acapulco@hostels.org.ar **Camping** At *ACA* site (Av San Martín y Nahuel Huapi, T422132) and several others including, *Club de Pescadores*, at lakeside. Recommended. *Los Pinos*, Curro Enríquez y Lincoln (open all year). Recommended.

Plenty of hotels, in all price categories

Transport Buses: To/from **Córdoba**, see above. To/from **Buenos Aires**, *Ablo*, US$15; also *Cacorba, Gen Urquiza*.

Situated on the banks of the Río Cosquín, it is the site of the most important **folklore festival**, beginning last week in January (recommended; accommodation is scarce but families rent out rooms or tent space; watch your belongings). There is also a national *artesanía* festival in the same month. **Museo de Artesanías**, Tucumán 1031. **Museo Camín Cosquín** at Km 760, out of town, minerals and archaeology, recommended. There is a tourist office on Plaza Próspero Molino; 0700-2100 daily in high season, 0800-2000 daily off season. Take a bus (or walk 2 hrs) to the Pan de Azúcar hill from where there is a good view over the Punilla valley. Chairlift to top (all year round). **D** *La Serrana*, P Ortiz 740, T451306, near bus terminal, good. **D** *Italia*, Ternengo y Vértiz, T452255, opposite bus terminal, recommended. Several campsites. ■ *Buses to Córdoba – see above, via Carlos Paz or La Calera via the San Roque dam.*

Cosquín
Population: 16,400
Altitude: 720 m
26 km N of Villa Carlos Paz

La Falda is a good touring centre. Visit the **Model Railway Museum** at **Las Murallas** at the end of Av 25 de Mayo. ■ *0900-1200, 1500-1800, US$5, German spoken.* **Museo Ambato Arqueológico**, Cuesta del Lago 1467, privately run, well displayed. ■ *Thu-Sun and public holidays 0900-2000, US$0.50.* Valle Hermoso (*Altitude*: 850 m) is 5 km away. The old restored chapel of San Antonio is a little gem. Horseriding and extensive hiking in surrounding hills. Round trip excursion to **Cascadas de Olaén** in a spectacular canyon – the water splashes into a small lake full of little fish. The tourist office is in the old railway station, open 0700-2000, maps available. ■ *Buses to Córdoba from La Falda hourly from 0500-2315, 2 hrs; to Buenos Aires, 12 hrs, US$24, Cacorba, Cita.*

La Falda
Phone code: 03548
Population: 30,000
Altitude: 933 m
82 km N of Córdoba

Sleeping and eating B *La Scala*, La Plata 59. Pool. Recommended. **E** *Hostería Los Abrojos*, Goya s/n, Valle Hermoso, T/F470430. Hot water, also full board, sports, excursions. Various campsites. Eating places include *El Cristal*, San Lorenzo 39, popular with locals, OK. *La Parilla de Raul*, Av Buenos Aires 111. Often *tenedor libre*, OK.

All 80 hotels are full in Dec-Feb La Falda is visited mostly by the elderly; most hotels belong to pension funds

Tour operators *Aventura Club*, 9 de Julio 541, T/F423809. Trekking, jeep tours, camping, birdwatching etc. *Wella Viajes*, Av Edén 412, loc 12, T054-821380. For trekking, climbing, etc.

Capilla del Monte (*Altitude*: 979 m), 106 km north of Córdoba and set in the heart of the Sierras, is a good centre for exploring this area. Sleeping: **C** *Hosp Roma*, Rivadavia 54, showers, opposite bus terminal, and **D** *Las Gemelas*, Alem 967, T481186, F481239, 7 blocks from centre, half board. Municipal campsite Calabalumba 600 m north of centre, **F** per tent, hot water, recommended. ■ *Buses to Córdoba, 3 hrs, US$6.50; to Buenos Aires, many companies, US$22.*

Argentina

Excursions in the hills, particularly to Cerro Uritorco, 1,979 m, 4 hrs via La Toma where there are medicinal waters and from where there are further walking opportunities (US$1.50). There is horse riding and tours to meditation and 'energy' centres: the location of many sightings of UFOs, the area is popular for '**mystical tourism**'. Tourist office in old railway station, open daily 0830-2030, some English spoken.

North from Córdoba

Jesús María
Colour map 8, grid A3
Population: 21,000
Altitude: 533 m
51 km N of Córdoba
on Route 9
(several hotels)

There is a good 18th-century Jesuit church and the remains of its once famous winery; in the cloister is an excellent **Museo Jesuítico**, said to be one of the best on the continent. ■ *Mon-Fri 0800-1200 and 1400-1900, Sat and Sun 1600-2000.* Each January there is a gaucho and folklore festival, lasting 10 nights from 2nd week; very popular. Good fishing in winter. 4 km north of Jesús María is **Sinsacate**, with an interesting church. There is also a fine colonial posting inn, now a museum, with long, deep verandah and chapel attached.

At Rayo Cortado, 114 km north of Jesús María, a turning leads west to **Cerro Colorado**, 160 km north of Córdoba, the former home of the late Argentine folklore singer and composer Atahualpa Yupanqui. His house is a museum, ask in the village for the curator. There are more than 30,000 rock paintings by the Comechingones Indians in the nearby Cerro Colorado archaeological park and a small archaeological museum. ■ *US$1, includes guide in English or Spanish. There is cheap accommodation with families and camping. Daily bus from Jesús María at 1610.*

Southwest of Córdoba

A scenic road southwest from Villa Carlos Paz passes **Ycho Cruz**, by the Río San Antonio (**D** *Hotel del Valle*, with bath; several campsites). Beyond is the **Camino de las Altas Cumbres**, the most spectacular route in the Sierras. 7 km north of the village of El Cóndor, a wide trail leads to Quebrada de los Condoritos (6-7 km), with superb landscape and the chance of seeing condors in their easternmost habitat. The road crosses the Pampa de Achala, a desert plateau of granite, before descending to another chain of resorts. ■ *Bus Córdoba-Ycho Cruz, US$2, Cotap; to El Cóndor US$5.*

Mina Clavero
Colour map 8, grid A3
Phone code: 035441
Population: 5,100
Altitude: 915 m
40 km W of Córdoba

This is a good centre for exploring the high *sierra* and the Traslasierra Valley. There is an intriguing museum, **Museo Rocsen**, 13 km south and about 5 km from the village of Nono; the personal collection of Sr Bouchón, it includes furniture, minerals, instruments, animals ('by far the best natural history and cultural museum, a whole day is needed to visit', Federico Kirbus). ■ *Daily 0900 till sunset, US$3. Taxi Mino Clavero-Nono, US$5.* The tourist office is at the *Municipalidad*, San Martín y 25 de Mayo, Plazoleta Merlo, T/F470171, with information on all accommodation, camping and tourist circuits. There are many hotels, *hosterías, hospedajes*, campsites and restaurants around Mina Clavero; others at Cura Brochero and Nono. ■ *Buses from Mina Clavero to Córdoba, US$6.50, 6 a day, 3 hrs; to Buenos Aires, TAC, US$24, 12 hrs; to Mendoza, 8½ hrs, US$16.*

Champaquí
2,884 m

The highest peak in the Sierras can be reached from Villa de las Rosas, 35 km south of Mina Clavero, or from San Javier, 20 km further southeast (an attractive village with accommodation in *hosterías*, eg *San Javier*, T/F03544-482006, www.hosteriasanjavier.com.ar also cabins for rent). The latter route goes by Capilla La Constancia, set in a river valley with pine and nut trees. To the summit takes eight to 10 hours, the descent to La Constancia four hours. Neither route should be attempted in misty weather. Take any Córdoba-Villa Dolores bus to Villa de las Rosas; at bus station look for the *pizzería* where taxis to Los Molles can be arranged. From Los Molles it's a three-hour walk to the house.

South from Córdoba

Alta Gracia, beside Lago Tajamar, has an interesting colonial church (a UNESCO World Heritage Site), finished about 1762. ■ *Open morning and after 1700.* The buildings housing the **Museo del Virrey Liniers**, on the Estancia de Alta Gracia, were founded in 1588 and taken over by the Jesuits in 1643. ■ *All day in summer. Tue-Fri 0900-1300, 1500-1830, Sat, Sun 0930-1230, 1530-1830, US$1.* The **Museo Manuel de Falla** on Pellegrini is where the Spanish composer spent his last years. ■ *Closed Mon, US$0.30.* Beautiful views from the Gruta de la Virgen de Lourdes, 3 km west of town. Tourist offices inside clock tower by Lago Tajamar. ■ *Buses to Córdoba, US$1.40, every 15 mins, 1 hr. Campsite at Alta Gracia.*

Alta Gracia
Phone code: 03547
Colour map 8, grid A3
Population: 39,000
Altitude: 580 m
39 km SW of Córdoba

The Bosque Alegre and Observatory, 24 km northwest, affords good views over Córdoba, Alta Gracia and the Sierra Grande. ■ *Thu 1600-1800, Sun 1000-1200, 1600-1800.* Che Guevara grew up in Alta Gracia after his parents left Rosario to live in the more refreshing environment in the foothills of the Andes. He had started to suffer from asthma, which would plague him for the rest of his life. See page 164.

This completely German town was founded by the surviving interned seamen from the *Graf Spee*, some of whom still live here. It is a good centre for excursions in the surrounding mountains. Genuine German cakes and smoked sausages are sold (eg at *Confitería Chocolate*, San Martín 8, owner, Héctor F de la Fuente, very informative on local hikes and activities; genuine German *wurst* at *Fritz's*, next to EG3 petrol station). Excursions can be made to **La Cumbrecita**, a charming German village 30 km west, from where Champaquí can be climbed (detailed map essential).

Villa General Belgrano
Phone code: 03546
85 km S of Córdoba

The **Museo Arqueológico Ambrosetti** has a collection of artefacts from the Comechingon Indians, the original inhabitants of the valley; **Museo del Carruaje** has old carriages and cars; **Museo Ovni**, Ruta 5 Km 743, on south outskirts, is dedicated to UFOs, but with archaeological exhibits and a good library. ■ *US$3.* There is an *Oktoberfest beer festival* in October and *Festival de las Tortas y las Masas Vienesas* around Easter. ■ *Villa General Belgrano tourist office, T461215.*

C *Edelweiss*, Ojo de Agua 295, T461317, F461387. Pool, excellent food. **C** *Hotel y Cabañas Halcón*, Cerro Negro 42, T461289, marilina@calamuchitanet.com.ar Pool, good views, with breakfast, quiet, German style. Recommended. Two **Youth hostels D** *El Rincón*, 600 m from bus terminal in beautiful surroundings, cooking and laundry facilities. Highly recommended (reservations: Patricia Mampsey, Casilla 64, T461323, F461761, cordoba1@hostels.org.ar). And at *Estancia Alta Vista*, T462238, 14 km from town on way to La Cumbrecita. Both offer discounts to ISIC and YHA card holders. **La Cumbrecita** has various hotels (**B-D**) and *hospedajes* in the **E** pp range. Restaurants *Tirol* and *Raices*, both good. Off the access to la Cumbrecita, to the right and uphill, is *La Colina*, good for trout.

Sleeping

Buses To/from **Córdoba**, 2 hrs, US$3.50, hourly. To **Mendoza**, US$17.50. To **Buenos Aires**, 1 a day, US$29. Gral Belgrano to **La Cumbrecita** by taxi (US$20, 1-1½ hrs) or by bus to Los Reales, 7 km, then walk, 28 km, US$6 (hitching impossible).

Transport

Argentina

Buenos
Aires

Argentina

The Northwest

This area includes routes to the major tourist centre of Salta, from where trips can be made into Andean regions, the Quebrada de Humahuaca and the Calchaquí and Cachi valleys. There are prehispanic ruins near Tafí del Valle, Quilmes, Santa Rosa de Tastil and others. This is also a region in which there are a number of Amerindian groups.

Background The first Spanish expedition from Bolivia entered Argentina in 1542. A little later, a better and lower route was discovered – the main route used today – descending from La Quiaca to Jujuy through the Quebrada de Humahuaca, with rugged and colourful mountain ranges closing in on both sides. Along this new route the Spaniards founded a group of towns in the northwest: Santiago del Estero (the first), Tucumán, Córdoba, Salta, La Rioja and Jujuy. Mendoza, San Juan and San Luis were all colonized by people who crossed the passes from Chile. All these colonies

The Northwest

were hemmed in by the warlike tribes of the Pampas, and until the war of extermination in 1880 the route from Buenos Aires to Córdoba was often unsafe. The Indians raided frequently for cattle, which they drove south and over the Andes for sale in Chile. Historically, Tucumán was always important, for the two river routes of the Salado and the Dulce across the dry belt forced the mule traffic to pass through it on the way to Salta. Tucumán still produces most of Argentina's sugar. Tobacco is a major crop, and an important factor in the northwest is the growth of tourism.

Santiago del Estero

Founded in 1553 by conquistadores pushing south from Peru, this is the oldest Argentine city. On the **Plaza Libertad** stand the **Municipalidad** and the **Cathedral** (the fifth on the site). The fine **Casa de Gobierno** is on Plaza San Martín, three blocks away. In the convent of **Santo Domingo**, Urquiza y 25 de Mayo, is one of two copies of the 'Turin Shroud', given by Philip II to his 'beloved colonies of America'. On Plaza Lugones is the church of **San Francisco**, the oldest surviving church in the city, founded in 1565. At the back of the church is the cell of San Francisco Solano, patron saint of Tucumán, who stayed in Santiago in 1593. Beyond the church is the pleasant **Parque Francisco de Aguirre**. **Museo de Ciencias Naturales y Antropología**, Avellaneda 353, an important collection of prehispanic artefacts from the Chaco; displays on cave paintings, funerary customs, ceramics and musical instruments. ■ *Mon-Fri 0800-1300, 1500-2000, Sat-Sun 0930-1200.* **Museo Histórico Provincial**, Urquiza 354, in a 200-year old mansion, containing a wide variety of 18th- and 19th-century artefacts from wealthy local families. ■ *Mon-Fri 0700-1300, 1400-1900, Sat-Sun 0930-1200.* There is a **carnival** in February, when virtually everything throwable gets thrown by everyone at everyone else. The tourist office is on Plaza Libertad, T421 3253/422 6777.

Phone code: 0385
Colour map 6, grid C4
Population: 212,000
Altitude: 200 m
395 km N of Córdoba
159 km SE of Tucumán

Argentina

Sleeping and eating **D** *Rodas*, Gallo 432, T421 8484. Safe. **E** *Res Emaus*, Av Moreno 673, T421 5893. Good value. **E** *Santa Rita*, Santa Fe 273, near bus terminal, T422 0625. Basic. **Camping** *Las Casuarinas*, Parque Aguirre. *Restaurant Sociedad Española*, Independencia 236. Popular, good value. *Centro de Viajantes*, Buenos Aires 49. Good value lunches. *Mía Mamma*, 24 de Septiembre 15, on Plaza. Good restaurant/salad bar, pricey.

Transport **Air** *AR* and *Dinar* to Buenos Aires. **Buses** To **Buenos Aires**, several daily, 12 hrs, US$20. To **Resistencia**, daily, several companies, 9 hrs, US$17-20. To **Córdoba**, several daily, 7 hrs, US$9. To **Tucumán** (via Río Hondo) US$4. To **Salta**, daily, US$8-10, 6 hrs, and to **Jujuy**, 7 hrs, US$9.

Bus information
T421 3746

Trains To/from Retiro (**Buenos Aires**), 20 hrs, US$10 1st, US$15 pullman, US$20 sleeper, and **Tucumán**, 5 hrs, with *NOA Ferrocarriles* (schedule given under Buenos Aires).

The thermal waters of this major spa town are recommended for blood pressure and rheumatism; good to drink, too, and used for the local soda water. There is swimming (free) in a public pool called La Olla near the bridge which crosses the Río Hondo (see Camping below). Tourist office at Caseros 132, T421721. There are over 170 hotels, but at national holiday periods, and especially in August, accommodation is hard to find, so book well in advance. **AL** *El Hostal del Abuelo*, Solano 168, T421489, elhostal@teletel.com.ar Half board (**A** in low season), thermal pool, sauna, gym, rooms with thermal bath. **B** *Los Pinos*, Maipú 201, T421043, info@lospinoshotel.com.ar Half board for standard double rooms, pleasant, pool, garden. **C** *Ambassador*, Libertad 184, T423396. Thermal pool. **E** *Charito*, Mar del Plata 376, T421034. With breakfast. **Camping** Two sites near river: *Del Río*, Av Yrigoyen y Ruta 9; *La Olla*, Av Yrigoyen y Lascano. Also *ACA*, on access to Dique Frontal (4 km from town), T421648; *El Mirador*, Ruta 9 y Urquiza. All charge about US$2 pp. ■ *Buses to Santiago del Estero, 1 hr, US$2 and to Tucumán, 2 hrs, US$2; several to Buenos Aires US$20.*

Termas de Río Hondo
Phone code: 03858
Population: 25,000
65 km N of Santiago del Estero
A sad place out of season

Tucumán

Argentina

Phone code: 0381
Colour map 6, grid C4
Population: 485,000
Altitude: 450 m

San Miguel de Tucumán was founded by Spaniards coming south from Peru in 1565. Capital of its province, it is the busiest and the most populous city in the north. It stands on a plain, but to the west towers the Sierra de Aconquija. Summer weather can be very hot and sticky.

On the west side of the main Plaza Independencia is the ornate **Casa de Gobierno**, across the road on San Martín is the church of **San Francisco**, with a picturesque façade. On the south side is the **Cathedral**, with an old rustic cross, kept inside on the left, used when founding the city. To the south, on C Congreso, is the **Casa Histórica** where, in 1816, the Congress of the United Provinces of Río de la Plata met to draft the country's Declaration of Independence. ■ *0900-1300,1500-1900, US$1; nightly (not Thu, except in Jul) at 2030, son et lumière programme at Casa Histórica, in garden, adults US$2, children US$1, tickets also from tourist office on Plaza Independencia, no seats.* There are good views over the city from *Cerro San Javier (reached by bus Empresa Ber Bus, US$1.50 from bus terminal).*

Several travel agencies offer half-day excursions, US$10-15 pp

East of the centre is the **Parque de Julio**, one of the finest urban parks in Argentina. Extending over 400 ha, it was the property of Bishop Colombres who played an important role in the development of the local sugar industry: his house is now the **Museo de la Industria Azucarera** ■ *Mon-Fri 0800-1200, 1500-1930, Sat-Sun 1430-2000, free.* The park contains a wide range of sub-tropical trees as well as a lake and sports facilities. There are several sugar mills near the city: check before if tours available during harvest period (Jun-Sep): **Ingenio Concepción**, T426 2528, Banda del Río Salí; **Ingenio La Florida**, T492 2011, Pedro G Méndez.

Museo Arqueológico, 25 de Mayo 265 in University building, fine collection. ■ *Mon-Fri 0800-1200.* **Casa Padilla (Museo de la Ciudad)**, Plaza Independencia, houses a collection of international art and antiques. ■ *Mon-Fri 0900-1230, 1600-1900 (in summer, mornings only).* **Museo Iramain**, Entre Ríos 27, memorial to the sculptor Juan Carlos Iramain. ■ *Mon-Fri 0800-1230, free.* **Fundación Miguel**

Tucumán

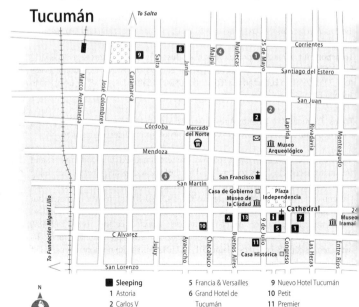

	Sleeping	5	Francia & Versailles	9	Nuevo Hotel Tucumán
	1 Astoria	6	Grand Hotel de	10	Petit
	2 Carlos V		Tucumán	11	Premier
	3 Colonial	7	Mediterráneo	12	Suites Garden Park
	4 Florida	8	Miami	13	Swiss Hotel Metropol

N

Not to scale

Lillo, Miguel Lillo 251, has a beautiful botanical garden, 12 blocks west of centre (bus 102 along C San Lorenzo), *Mon-Fri 0830-1230, 1500-1800.*

Sleeping

A *NH Grand Hotel del Tucumán*, Av Soldati 380, T450 2250, www.nh-hoteles.es 5-star, opposite Parque 9 de Julio, rooms with even numbers quieter, outstanding food and service, pool (open to non-residents), sauna, gym. A *Suites Garden Park*, Av Soldati 330, T431 0700, www.gardenparkhotel.com.ar 4-star, opposite Parque 9 de Julio, pool, gym, sauna, internet access, bar, restaurant. A *Swiss Hotel Metropol*, 24 de Septiembre 524, T431 1180, www.swisshotelmetropol.com With breakfast, restaurant, pool, parking, large rooms, central. C *Carlos V*, 25 de Mayo 330, T431 1666, www.redcarlosv.com.ar Central, good service, a/c, TV, bar, restaurant. Recommended. C *Premier*, Crisóstomo Alvarez 510, T/F431 0381, info@redcarlosv.com.ar With breakfast, restaurant, parking, a/c, good. C *Colonial*, San Martín 35, T431 1523. Modern, a/c, TV, pool, internet access, good breakfast, parking, near bus terminal. Recommended. C *Mediterráneo*, 24 de Septiembre 364, T431 0025, F431 0080, www.hotelmediterraneo.com.ar Good rooms, TV, a/c. D *Astoria*, Congreso 88, T/F421 3101. With breakfast, bar/restaurant, good beds, a/c, TV, convenient. D *Florida*, 24 de Septiembre 610, T422 6674. Without breakfast, a/c, basic, helpful. D *Francia*, Crisóstomo Alvarez 467, T/F431 0781. With breakfast, bar, restaurant, a/c, TV. D *Versailles*, Crisóstomo Alvarez 481, T422 9760, F422 9763. With breakfast, good beds, a/c. E *Petit*, Crisóstomo Alvarez 765, T421 3902. Spacious old house with patio, quiet, cheaper without bath, a/c or fan. **Near train station:** C *Miami*, Junín 580, T431 0265, F 422 2405. With breakfast, parking, discounts for *Hostelling International* members, pool, a/c, TV. D *Nuevo Hotel Tucumán*, Catamarca 573, T/F422 1809. E without bath, fan, *confitería*, good value. E *La Estrella*, Araoz 38, near bus terminal and opposite busy market. Basic rooms, also F pp without bath, no breakfast. Very hospitable. E *Independencia*, Balcarce 56, T421 7038. Basic budget option near bus terminal, with bath.

Eating
In this part of Argentina 'black beer' (eg Salta Negra) is available

There are several popular restaurants and cafés on Plaza Independencia and on Plaza Hipólito Yrigoyen (9 de Julio y General Paz). *Floreal*, 25 de Mayo 568. Expensive cuisine. *El Fondo*, San Martín 848, T422 2161. Superb steak house. *La Leñita*, 25 de Mayo 377. Expensive, smart, good meat, cheaper menus on offer. *La Parrilla del Centro*, San Martín 391. Excellent, reasonable prices. *Il Postino*, 25 de Mayo y Córdoba. Pizza bar, popular. *El Portal*, 24 de Septiembre 351, on patio. Cheap and excellent regional dishes, *empanadas* are recommended. *El Parravicini*, 24 de Septiembre 568. *Tenedor libre*. *La Sirio Libanesa*, Maipú 575. Middle Eastern specialities, also take away. Good coffee at *Bonafide*, San Martín 650. *La Mostaza*, San Martín 742. Lively and trendy café, cheap breakfasts. *Panadería Villecco*, Corrientes 751. Good bread, also 'integral'.

To Airport

Honduras
Haití
Guatemala
Cuba
A Jacques
Río de Janeiro
Francia
tiembre
Charcas
Díaz Vélez

Av Avellaneda
Av Sáenz Peña
Av Brígido Terán

Av Soldati

To Museo de la
Industria Azucarera

Parque
9 de Julio

Ruta 9 To Santiago del
Estero & Buenos Aires

Av B Araoz

6
12
3

● **Eating**
1 Floreal
2 La Leñita
3 La Parrilla del Centro
4 La Sirio Libanesa

Local holidays

9 Jul, *Independence Day*. 24 Sep, *Battle of Tucumán*. 29 Sep, *San Miguel*. 10 Nov, *Día de la Tradición*.

Shopping
All shops close 1230-1630

Artesanía El Cardón, Crisóstomo Alvarez 427. Excellent handicrafts. *Mercado Artesanal*, 24 de Septiembre 565. Small, but nice selection of lace, wood and leather work. Daily 0800-1300, 1700-2200 (in summer, mornings only). *Regionales del Jardín*, Congreso 18. Good selection of local jams, *alfajores* etc. *Lozano* supermarket, San Martín 344, just east of Plaza Independencia and 24 de Septiembre 651. *Tia* supermarket, Muñecas 137. Market: *Mercado del Norte*, on block bounded by Córdoba, Mendoza, Junín and Maipú.

Transport   **Local   Buses** operate on *cospeles*, US$0.35, which you have to buy in advance in kiosks. **Car hire**: *Movil Renta*, San Lorenzo 370, T431 0550, F0800-777 3682 (toll free), info@movilrenta.com and at airport (can leave vehicle in Salta). *AF Rent a Car*, 9 de Julio 79, T430 1849. *Donde Rent a Car*, Gob Gutiérrez 1384, T428 3626. **Car repairs**: *Rubén Boss*, Aconquija 947, T425 1940. Recommended especially for Volkswagen.

Long distance   Air: Airport at Benjamín Matienzo, 10 km east of town. Bus No 120 from terminal (*cospeles*, US$0.70, required). Taxi US$5. *Cielos del Norte*, T426 5555, vans to/from airport to/from any place in town, US$1.50. To **Buenos Aires**, *AR/Austral* (T431 1030/1419), *AIRG* (T430 2330, 0810-7777 274), *Dinar* (T452 2300/426 4200),also to **Salta** and *Southern Winds* (T422 5554/426 2630) also to Salta and several destinations via Córdoba and Buenos Aires.

   Buses: Modern terminal on Av Benjamín Araoz, T422 2221, beside a huge shopping complex, 6 blocks east of Plaza Independencia; bus 3 from outside terminal to San Lorenzo y 9 de Julio in centre. Taxi to centre US$0.50-1. To **Cafayate**, 5½, US$10, *Aconquija*, 1 to 2 daily (via **Tafí del Valle**, 2½ hrs, US$4). To **Salta** direct (not via Cafayate), 4½ hrs, several companies US$7-10. To **Jujuy**, several companies, 5 hrs, US$8. To **Buenos Aires**, many companies, US$20 *semi cama* 16 hrs, US$25 *cama* 15 hrs (*Empresa Argentina-General Urquiza*). To **Posadas**, *La Estrella, Vosa, Almirante Brown*, US$28, 19 hrs, daily. To **Mendoza**, US$18, 13 hrs, via Catamarca, La Rioja, and San Juan. To **La Rioja**, 5 hrs, US$9. To **Catamarca**, *Aconquija* and other companies, US$4-8, 3½-4 hrs. To **Tinogasta**, via **Andalgalá** and **Belén**, *Gutiérrez*, 3 a week, daily in high season. To **Córdoba**, US$9-12, 8 hrs, many companies. To **Santiago del Estero**, US$4, 2 hrs. To **La Quiaca** (border with Bolivia), *Balut*, US$15, 10 hrs. To **Pocitos** (border with Bolivia) US$10, 11 hrs. To **Santiago** (Chile) via Mendoza, *Andesmar* and *El Rápido Internacional*, daily, US$23-28, 24 hrs. To **Lima** (Perú), *El Rápido Internacional*, 3 a week, via Mendoza, US$100. **Left luggage**: next to *boleteria* 1, Mon-Sat 0600-2400, Sun 0700-2200, US$1-1.50 per day.

Trains   Service to **Buenos Aires** via Rosario run by *NOA Ferrocarriles*, T422 0861, departing Sun and Thu 0800, more information given under Buenos Aires.

Directory   **Banks**   Most banks along San Martín especially 700 block between Junín and Maipú. *Dinar*, Junín 58, T430 0652, cash only, and *Maguitur*, San Martín 765, T431 0032, good rates for cash, accepts TCs. *Maxicambio*, San Martín 779, T422 5399. **Communications**   Internet: *Cyber Noa*, 9 de Julio y San Lorenzo and *Centro Digital*, Chacabuco 32, US$1.25 including a coffee. **Post Office**: Córdoba y 25 de Mayo, open Mon-Fri 0800-2000. **Telephone:** Lots of *Telecom* call centres including *Telecentros*, at 24 de Septiembre 612, Buenos Aires y Lavalle, San Lorenzo 704, offering internet access, US$1 per hr. **Cultural centres**   *Alliance Française*, Laprida 456, T421 9651, free events in French. *Aticana* (North American Centre) including JF Kennedy Library, Salta 581, T430 3070, open Mon-Fri, 0800-1200, 1700-2100. **Tourist offices**   In Plaza Independencia at 24 de Septiembre 484, T/F422 2199 or T430 3644, daily 0800-2100. Also in the bus terminal and airport.

Tucumán to Salta

Via Rosario de la Frontera

Of the two routes to Salta, the more beautiful is via Tafí del Valle, Cafayate and the Quebrada de las Conchas. Quicker is via Rosario de la Frontera and Güemes

Rosario de la Frontera (*Altitude*: 769 m; *Phone code*: 03876), 130 km north of Tucumán, is a popular resort from June to September. 8 km away are thermal springs. About 20 km north is the historical post house, Posta de **Yatasto**, with museum, 2 km east of the main road; campsite. **C** *Termas*, Route 34, T481004, hoteltermas@hotmail.com (**A** full board), rambling place, good food but many rooms without private bath (6 km from bus station, taxi US$3.50). Thermal swimming pool, horse riding, golf, excursions. Baths US$2.50. About 1 km from *Hotel Termas* is **C** *ACA hostería*, T481143, opposite is artificial lake. **D** *Real*, Güemes 185, T481067, basic, clean, not all doors close.

About 70 km north of Rosario de la Frontera, at Lumbreras, a road branches off Route 9 and runs 90 km northeast to the **Parque Nacional El Rey**, which extends over 44,160 ha, a wildlife reserve set among 900-2,300 m hills with clear streams. Vegetation ranges from cloud forest to Chaco. It can also be reached from Salta (196 km) where there are park offices at Santa Fe 23 (helpful) and España 366, T0387-431 2683, pnaciorey@impsat1.com.ar Mosquitoes, ticks and chiggers thrive; take repellent. *Turismo San Lorenzo*, Juan Carlos Dávalos 960, San Lorenzo, Salta, T0387-492 1757, tsl@1turismosanlorenzo.com offers 3-day, 2-night packages staying at **C** *Hotel Las Lajitas*, Ruta 5 y 30, T03877-494131, with 4WD trips into the park. *Norte Trekking*, Av del Libertador 1151, Barrio Grand Bourg, Salta, T0387-4361 1844/46, fede@nortetrekking.com 1 or 2-day guided walks, from US$80 pp per day in small groups, leaving in 4WD vehicle from Salta. Camping is free, there are several tent sites, but few facilities. Horse riding. ■ *The access road is poor and fords the river 9 times; passable for ordinary cars except in the wet season. The best time to visit is winter (drier).*

There is no public transport to the park; ask the park offices in Salta about alternatives

Route 307 branches northwest, 46 km south of Tucumán, through a gorge with sub-tropical vegetation to Tafí del Valle, which has its own microclimate, much cooler than the lowlands in summer, often with the cloud formed by warm air moving up from the lowlands and wisps of white cloud rising like smoke over the artificial Embalse La Angostura. At Km 27 on this road is a statue to El Indio, with picnic area.

Via Cafayate

Tafí del Valle is known to archaeologists as a holy valley of the precolumbian Indian tribes. Ten minutes from Tafí is the **Capilla Jesuítica y Museo de La Banda** in the 18th-century chapel (mass Saturday 1830) and the 19th-century *estancia* (museum of archaeology and religious art). ■ *Mon-Sat 0900-1900, Sun 0900-1600 (closing early off season), US$0.50, includes a guided visit.* **Museo Los Tesoros de Tafí**, at La Banda, T421563, small archaeological museum. Juan Carlos Yapura, owner, guides day walks to aboriginal sites in nearby mountains, US$5 pp. **Museo Casa Duende**, 7 km south, ancient mythology. ■ *Daily 1000-1900, US$1.*

Tafí del Valle
Phone code: 03867
Population: 9,000
97 km from Tucumán
Altitude: 1,976 m

Not to be confused with Tafí Viejo which is 10 km N of the city

Some 10 km south of Tafí del Valle is the menhir park of **El Mollar**, with 129 standing stones with engraved designs of unknown significance (moved here from various sites in 1977) and good views (best to visit morning). ■ *Buses from Tafí, US$1, ask driver to let you off on hill by the entrance, not in El Mollar itself. Tucumán-Cafayate buses stop on request.*

Sleeping A *Castillo de Piedra*, at La Banda 1 km from Tafí, T421199. Cosy hotel, large park, pool, sauna, open all year round. **B** *Lunahuana*, Av Critto 540, 200 m from town, T/F421330, www.lunahuana.com.ar Half-board, good restaurant, gymnasium, solarium. **B** *Mirador del Tafí*, Ruta 307, Km 61.2, T/F421219, miradordeltafi@hotmail.com With breakfast, good beds, spacious, heating, restaurant, excellent views. **C** *Tafí*, Belgrano 177, T421007, F421452, hoteltafi@impsat1.com.ar With breakfast, bar, heating. **C** *La Rosada*, Belgrano 322, T421323/146, miguel_torres@sinectis.com.ar Lovely building, free use of cycles (US$7.50 per day), trekking expeditions. **C** *Huayra Puca*, Los Menhires 71, T421190, www.huayrapuca.com.ar With breakfast, cheaper off-season, large rooms, very attractive. Recommended. **C** *Hostería Los Cuartos*, Av Juan Calchaquí s/n, T/F421444. With breakfast, **B** half-board, restaurant, heating, good views, comfortable. **C** *Sumaj*, Ruta 307, Km 60, T421756, hotel_sumaj@yahoo.com Breakfast and guided walk included. **F** pp *Hostal Atep*, Los Menhires y Campero, T421061. Large, no breakfast, comfortable. **E** *Hospedaje El Valle*, Perón 56, T421641. With bath, cheaper without, no breakfast, good value. **F** *Hostal* of Celia Correa, Belgrano 443, T421170. Basic, no breakfast, heating. Recommended. **F** pp *La Cumbre*, Av Perón 120, T421768. Recently refurbished hostel, basic rooms for 2 to 5 people, cooking facilities, shared bathroom, owner is a tour operator. **Camping** *Los Sauzales*. Run down, US$2 pp plus tent. *La Mutual* at El Mollar. Also rooms with bath **F** pp.

Many places, including hotels, close off season

There is a cheese festival in Feb

Eating Most places are along Avenida Perón including: *El Rancho de Félix*, recommended; *Parador Tafinisto*, parrilla; *El Portal de Tafí*, very good food, excellent *empanadas*. Good breakfasts at *Panadería El Sol*, Av Critto y Av Perón. **Estancia** *Estancia Los Cuartos*, on Av Critto, T421124 or Tucumán (0381)-15587 4230, mercedes_chenaut@hotmail.com Offers a day at the *estancia*, lunch, excursion, and horse ride (US$18 all included), also *té criollo* (US$5). This *estancia* and *Estancia Las Carreras* run cheese shops on Av Miguel Critto.

Tour operators Tours to El Mollar and Tafí from travel agencies in Tucumán, US$20 each for 4 people minimum. *Daniel Carrazano*, T421768, lacumbreaventura@ciudad.com.ar, offers guided tours along the valley, mountains and archaeological sites, 4WD vehicle and trekking (from US$8 pp). Off season contact the *Casa del Turista* , T421477, in centre to arrange excursions by taxi, US$8 pp.

Transport **Buses**: To/from **Tucumán**, *Aconquija*, T421025, sit on left from Tucumán, several daily (fewer in winter), 2½ hrs, US$4. To **Cafayate** 3 a day, 2½ hrs, US$6 (an hour more if via Santa Maria, US$7). To **Santa María**, 2 hrs, US$3.50.

Directory **Banks** *Banco de Tucumán*, Miguel Critto 311, T421033, ATM, Visa, MasterCard.

From Tafí the road runs 56 km northwest over the 3,040 m Infiernillo Pass (Km 85) and through attractive arid landscape to **Amaichá del Valle** (Museo Casa de la Pachamama, T421004, overview of the Calchaquí culture, regional geology, tapestry and ceramics by Héctor Cruz for sale, entry US$2). From Amaichá the paved road continues north 15 km to the junction with Route 40. **Santa María** (*Population:* 10,000) , 22 km south of Amaichá by paved road, is a small town with a little archaeology museum on the plaza, hotels and a municipal campsite. (South of Santa María, Route 40 goes to Belén, see page 161).

At **Quilmes**, 32 km north, 5 km along a dirt road off the main Santa María-Cafayate road, 22 km from Amaichá del Valle, there are Inca ruins (dam, village and posting house – *tambo*), with splendid views and interesting cacti. ■ *Guide 0700-1730, US$1*. There is also a provincial archaeological museum. **B** *Parador Ruinas de Quilmes*, T03892-421075, at the site, comfortable, underfloor heating in winter, a/c in summer, owners are tapestry and ceramics experts; shop selling good indigenous crafts, particularly textiles; good restaurant, bar and free camping facilities. ■ *For a day's visit take 0600* Aconquija *bus from Cafayate to Santa María, alight at stop 5 km from site, or take 0700 bus from Santa María; take 1130 bus back to Cafayate, US$2. Taxi from Cafayate US$18 return.*

Cafayate

Phone code: 03868
Colour map 6, grid C3
Population: 12,000
Altitude: 1,660 m

Cafayate is a clean town, with low rainfall (none March-October), lying between two ranges of Andean foothills. A walk to Cerro San Isidro (three hours) takes you to a view of the Aconquija chain in the south to Nevado de Cachi in the north. There are 5 main *bodegas*: in town are **Nanni**, on Chavarría, one block east of the plaza, certified organic products, and **Domingo Hermanos**, three blocks south of the plaza on 25 de Mayo. North of town are **Vasija Secreta** (on outskirts, next to *ACA hostería*), T421503, the oldest in the valley, English spoken, and **La Rosa**, reached by turning right 500 m past the ACA *hostería*. ■ *Visits Mon-Thu 0800-1700, Fri 0800-1600, weekend mornings only, no need to book, 30-min tours and tasting.* **Etchart** is 2 km south on Route 40, T421310, F421529. ■ *Tours in Spanish Mon-Sat 0900-1700, Sun 0900-1300.* The **Museo de la Vid y El Vino** in an old *bodega* is on Av Güemes, two blocks south of the plaza, very well laid out. ■ *Mon-Fri 1000-1300, 1700-2000, US$0.50.* **Museo Arqueológico Rodolfo I Bravo**, one block from main plaza, local collection of the late Sr Bravo, pre-Inca funerary and religious artefacts, some dating back to the forth century, as well as Inca ceramics. ■ *Open on request, US$0.50, T421054.* On the main plaza is *Banco de la Nación* for cash, ATM, *Banco de Salta* and a tourist office kiosk. *Telecentro* is on the plaza, F421536/539.

C *Asturias*, Güemes Sur 154, T421328, asturias@infonoa.com.ar With breakfast, pool, restaurant. **C** *Hostería Cafayate* (ACA), T421296. With breakfast, colonial-style patio with gardens, pool, restaurant. **C** *Gran Real*, Güemes Sur 128, T421016/231, smr127@infonoa.com.ar With breakfast, pool, good beds, also apartments; owners have a *bodega*. **D** *Asembal*, Güemes Norte y Diego de Almagro, T421065. Nice rooms, good restaurant. **D** *Tinkunaku*, Diego de Almagro 12, 1 block from plaza, T421148. Breakfast provided at *Emperador* on plaza. Recommended. **D** *Los Sauces*, Calchaquí 62, T421158, lossauces@arnet.com.ar Modern, nice rooms on large garden, with breakfast. **E** *Confort*, Güemes Norte 232, T421091. Breakfast extra, fan, good value, very helpful, also has *cabañas* **B**, in town, sleep 6, with kitchen, pool, heating. **E** pp *Hospedaje Familiar* (run by school teacher Mirta Alcira Daruich), Rosario 165, T421098. Good rooms, lovely patio, kitchen, superb breakfast available. **F** pp *Colonial*, Diego de Almagro 134, T421655. Cheaper without bath in dormitory, colonial style, pool, parking, comfortable, use of kitchen, quiet, good value. **F** pp *Res Docente*, Güemes Norte 160, T421810. Dormitories, without breakfast, kitchen facilities. **F** pp *Hostal del Valle*, San Martín 243, T421039. Breakfast, nice patio, kitchen facilities. **F** pp *El Hospedaje*, Salta 13, T421680. With breakfast, shower, bicycle rental, cooking and laundry facilities, good advice. Recommended. **F** pp *Albergue Juvenil*, Güemes Norte 441, T421440. Rooms for 2 to 10 people, kitchen, camping facilities, hot water, stores luggage, tours arranged, English and Italian spoken.

Sleeping
Accommodation is hard to find at holiday periods. Off season, prices are much lower

Campsite Municipal site *Lorohuasi* at south access to town, T421051, US$2 pp plus tent. Hot water, pool, well maintained, bungalows for rent **E** for 4 people. *Luz y Fuerza*, on southern outskirts, quiet, good value, US$2 pp.

La Carreta de Don Olegario, Güemes 20. Recommended. *Comedor Criollo*, Güemes Norte 254. Recommended. *El Quincho de Cobra*, Mitre 151. Informal, good value. *El Rancho*, Toscano y Güemes. Very good. *Cafetería Santa Barbara*, Güemes Norte 151. Billiards, ice cream. *Helados Miranda*, Güemes Norte 170. Wine-flavoured ice cream.

Eating
Only the more expensive restaurants are open late

Handicrafts Locally woven tapestries are interesting, and very expensive; visit the Calchaquí tapestry exhibition of Miguel Nanni on the main plaza. Also *Platería* of Jorge Barraco, Colón 157, for silver craft work, and of Claudio Gómez and Mariana Araujo, La Banda de Arriba, agplateria@ciudad.com.ar Oil paintings, woodcarving, metalwork and ceramics by Calixto Mamani can be seen in his art gallery at Rivadavia 452, or contact him at home at Rivadavia 254. Handicrafts in wood and silver by Oscar Hipaucha near the *Bodega Domingo Hnos*. Pancho Silva and his family have a workshop at 25 de Mayo selling and displaying their own and locals' handicrafts. Souvenir prices are generally high. Local pottery in the *Mercado de Artesanos Cafayateños* on the main plaza.

Shopping

Calchaquí, Quintana de Niño 59, T1563 8085, calchaqui@hotmail.com For trekking, horseriding, bikes or 4WD vehicles tours to Quebrada de las Conchas (US$8pp), Cachi (US$18pp) and Quilmes (US$8pp). Taxis on main plaza charge US$4 return to San Carlos, driver José is recommended.

Tour operators

Local Rentals: Cycle hire on the plaza, another just off the plaza on Güemes Norte, US$0.75 per hr, US$5 per day. **Horses**: can be hired from *La Florida*, Bodega Etchart, 2 km south of Cafayate. **Buses** To Tucumán, *Aconquija*, 1 to 2 daily, 5½ hrs, US$10, alternatively take *El Indio* service to Santa María and change. To **Salta** via the Quebrada de las Conchas, *El Indio*, T421002, 2 to 4 daily, 3 ½ hrs, US$6 (worth travelling in daylight). To **Angastaco**, *El Indio*, 2 hrs, US$3, 1 daily.

Transport

Route 68 goes northeast from Cafayate to Salta through the gorge of the Río de las Conchas (also known as the **Quebrada de Cafayate**) with fascinating rock formations of differing colours, all signposted. The road goes through wild and semi-arid landscapes with many wild birds, including *ñandúes* (rheas).

Quebrada de las Conchas

Argentina

Argentina

North of Cafayate Route 40 runs 160 km through the Valles Calchaquíes to Cachi. The road is mainly gravel and can be difficult after rain, but the views of the Andean-foothill desert country with its strange rock formations and unexpected colours are fascinating. It passes interesting villages: **San Carlos, Angastaco**, just north of the spectacular **Quebrada de las Flechas**, and **Molinos** (hotels and bus services).

Cachi

Phone code: 03868
Colour map 6, grid C3
Altitude: 2,280 m

This is a beautiful little town renowned for its weaving, other crafts and invigorating climate. The church's roof and confessional are made from the wood of the *cardón* cactus. The **Museo Arqueológico** presents a small but interesting survey of pre-colonial Calchaquí culture. ■ *Mon-Fri 0900-1800, Sat 1000-1400, Sun, holidays 1000-1300, US$0.50.* There are fine views from the cemetery, 10 minutes' walk from the village. The Indian ruins at **Las Pailas**, 18 km west of Cachi, are barely excavated; in themselves, they are not especially impressive but the view is breathtaking, with huge cacti set against snow-topped Andean peaks. They can be reached on foot (four hours one way), or by bus from Cachi. Ask for directions or a guide.

Sleeping B-C *ACA Hostería Cachi*, T491905, on hill above the town. Good, pleasant. **E** pp *El Cortijo*, T491034. With good breakfast. **F** pp *Res Pajarito*, T491035. Basic. **E** *Albergue Municipal*, T491053, also has good municipal campsite with swimming pool and barbecue pits, on hill at south end of town. More accommodation at **Cachi Adentro**, 6 km west of Cachi, 3 buses a day from Cachi. Hire horses in the village, US$3 per hour.

Transport Buses To Salta, *Marcos Rueda*, 1 to 2 daily, 4-4½ hrs, US$7.

Cachi to Salta

Follow Route 40 for 11 km north to Payogasta (*Hostería*), then turn right to Route 33. This road (gravel) climbs continuously up the Cuesta del Obispo passing a dead-straight stretch of 14 km known as La Recta del Tin-Tin with magnificent views of the **Los Cardones National Park** with the huge candelabra cacti, which grow up to 6 m in height. (Visit by catching *Marcos Rueda* bus from Salta to Cachi, getting out at La Recta del Tin-Tin; then catch return bus.) It reaches the summit at Piedra de Molino (3,347 m) after 43 km. Then it plunges down through the Quebrada de Escoipe. The road rejoins Route 68 at El Carril, from where it is 37 km back to Salta.

Salta

Phone code: 0387
Colour map 6, grid C3
Population: 400,000
Altitude: 1,190 m
1,600 km N of B Aires

Situated on the Río Arias, in the Lerma valley, Salta lies in a mountainous and strikingly beautiful district. It was founded in 1582 and still possesses a number of fine colonial buildings. Capital of its province, it is a great handicraft centre and the major starting place for tours of the northwest.

Ins & outs

For more detailed information see Transport, page 134

Getting there There are regular flights to Salta, whose airport is a US$1.50 shuttle bus ride to town (taxi US$5). The bus terminal is eight blocks east of the centre.

Getting around The city centre is worth getting to know on foot and there are ceramic pavement plaques and maps from the tourist office for an interesting pedestrian tour. Many hotels are in or near the centre. Local buses in the city charge US$0.35. Taxis and remises charge US$1 per 1,500 m.

Tourist offices **Provincial Tourist Office**, Buenos Aires 93 (1 block from main plaza), T431 0950, www.turismosalta.com Open weekdays 0800-2100, weekends 0900-2000. Very helpful, gives free maps, arranges accommodation in private houses in high season (Jul), only when hotels are fully booked. Other websites: www.iruya.com and www.redsalta.com

Sights

The **Cathedral** (open mornings and evenings), on the north side of the central **Plaza 9 de Julio**, was built 1858-1878; it contains the much venerated images of the Cristo del Milagro and of the Virgin Mary, the first sent from Spain in 1592, and has a rich interior mainly in red and gold, as well as a huge late baroque altar. The miracle was the sudden cessation of a terrifying series of earthquakes when the images were paraded through the streets on 15 September 1692. They still are, each September.

On the opposite side of the Plaza is the **Cabildo**, built in 1783, now housing the **Museo Histórico del Norte**, Caseros 549, colonial, 19th-century exhibits and a fine 18th-century pulpit. Recommended. ■ *Tue-Sun 0930-1330, Tue-Fri 1530-2030, Sat 1630-2030. Guided tour in Spanish, US$0.50.* The Convent of **San Bernardo**, at Caseros y Santa Fe, was built in colonial style in the mid-19th century; it has a famous wooden portal of 1762. Nuns still live here so the inside of the convent is not open to visitors. **San Francisco** church, at Caseros y Córdoba (1882), rises above the city centre skyline with its magnificent façade and red, yellow and grey coloured tower. ■ *0700-1200, 1730-2100, in theory. Ask Sr Mamaní, for free guided visits.*

East of the city centre is the **Cerro San Bernardo** (1,458 m), accessible by cable car (*teleférico*), daily 1000-1945, US$3 return, children US$1.50, from Parque San Martín, fine views. Near the *teleférico* station is a lake where rowing boats can be hired. It takes about 30 minutes to walk back down the hill. Very beautifully set at the foot of the hill is an impressive **statue** by Víctor Gariño, 1931, **to Gen Güemes**, whose *gaucho* troops repelled seven powerful Spanish invasions from Bolivia between 1814 and 1821. A steep path (1,136 steps) behind the nearby Museo Antropológico leads to the top of the hill, where there is an old wooden cross, together with restaurant and artificial waterfalls.

Museo Antropológico, Paseo Güemes, behind the statue, contains many objects from Tastil (see page 136) and a mummy discovered high in the Andes. ■ *Mon-Fri 0800-1830, Sat 0900-1300, 1500-1800, US$0.50.* **Museo Histórico Uriburu**, Caseros 421, in the mansion of this distinguished *salteño* family. ■ *Tue-Sun 0930-1330, Tue-Fri 1530-2030, Sat 1630-2030, US$0.50.* **Museo de Ciencias Naturales**, in Parque San Martín, has a full display of over 20,000 specimens including more than 150 regional stuffed birds and an interesting collection of armadillos, recommended. ■ *Tue-Sun 1530-1930, US$0.25.* **Museo de Bellas Artes**, Florida 20, colonial, 17th to 20th-century art collections. ■ *Mon-Sat 0900-1300, 1630-2030, US$0.50.* **Museo de la Ciudad 'Casa de Hernández'**, Florida 91, in a 19th-century mansion, containing a collection of 18th and 19th-century furniture as well as plans and photographs which trace the development of the city. ■ *Mon-Fri 0900-1300, 1600-2030, Sat 1000-1300, US$0.50.*

Many museums are closed in the afternoons in summer; check museum opening times at tourist office

Essentials

A *El Lagar*, 20 de Febrero 877, T/F431 9439/421 7943, ellagar@arnet.com.ar Beautifully furnished, former Etchart home, close to train station but some way from centre. **B** *Salta*, Buenos Aires 1, in main plaza, T431 0740, www.hotelsalta.com 1st class, pool, good restaurant. **A** *Portezuelo*, Av Turística 1, T431 0104/105, reservas@portezuelohotel.com Breakfast extra, some rooms a/c, English, German, French, Italian spoken, pool, helpful, good restaurant. Recommended. **B** *Portal de Salta*, Alvarado 341, T431 3674, porsalta@infovia.com.ar A/c, pleasant, helpful, good breakfast, pool, restaurant./ Recommended. **B** *Posada del Sol*, Alvarado 646, T431 7300, salta@hotelposadadelsol.com A/c, TV. **B** *Victoria Plaza*, Zuviría 16, T431 8500/0634, vplaza@arnet.com.ar With buffet breakfast, expensive but good restaurant, the foyer overlooking the plaza is one of the centres of *salteño* life. **C** *Colonial*, Zuviría 6, T431 0805, F431 4249. With breakfast, a/c, restaurant, laundry service. Recommended. **C** *Petit*, H Yrigoyen 225, T421 3012. Pleasant, small, expensive breakfasts, rooms around courtyard with small swimming pool, a/c extra, French spoken, next to bus terminal.

Sleeping

Accommodation is scarce in Jul because of holidays, and around 10-16 Sep during celebrations of Cristo del Milagro

Argentina

Argentina

D *Las Lajitas*, Pasaje Calixto Gauna 336, T423 3796. Modern, good value. Recommended. **D** *Regidor*, Buenos Aires 8, T431 1305. Breakfast extra, a/c, English-speaking owner, good value, comfortable. **D** *Florida*, Urquiza 718, T421 2133, hotelflorida@salnet.com.ar Stores luggage, fan, no breakfast. Recommended. **D** *Astur*, Rivadavia 752, T421 2107. Basic, near train station. Recommended. **D** *Italia*, Alberdi 231, T421 4050, next to casino. Recommended. **D** *Res Elena*, Buenos Aires 256, T421 1529. Quiet, 'charming', safe. **D** *Res San Jorge*, Esteco 244 y Ruiz de los Llanos 1164 (no sign), T/F421 0443, hotelsanjorge@arnet.com.ar With bath (**E** without), parking, safe deposit, laundry and limited kitchen facilities, central heating, parking, homely, guide for climbing, horse-trekking advice by proprietor, also organizes local excursions by car, good value. Highly recommended (take buses 3 and 10 from bus station to San Martín y Malvinas). **D** *Hostal del Cerro*, Santa Fe 456, T431 8572, hostaldelcerro@hotmail.com Nice house on San Martín park, next to bus terminal, comfortable, with bath, TV, cooking and laundry facilities.

F pp *Rodó sisters*, Mendoza 915 (María), T432 0813 (about 10 blocks from bus station). Mendoza 917 (Amelia), T421 2233. Mendoza 919 (Natividad), T431 8948. Nice atmosphere, comfortable, roof terrace, cooking and laundry facilities, cosy. Highly recommended.

■ Sleeping	7 Hostal del Cerro	14 Salta	3 El Corredor de
1 Astur	8 Hostal Travellers	15 Terra Oculta	las Empanadas
2 Colonial	9 Italia	16 Victoria Plaza	4 El Palacio de
3 El Correcaminos	10 Portal de Salta		la Pizza
4 Elba Galleguillos	11 Posada del Sol	● Eating	5 El Solar del
5 El Lagar	12 Regidor	1 Doña Salta	Convento
6 Florida	13 Res Elena	2 Don José	6 La Terraza de la Posta

F pp *Elba Galleguillos*, Mendoza 509, T431 8985. Free transport from bus terminal, good showers, laundry, basic, with breakfast, friendly. **F** pp *Hosp Doll*, Pasaje Ruiz de los Llanos 1360 (7 blocks from centre). Safe. Recommended. **Youth hostel** **E** *Hostal Travellers*, San Martín 104, T/F431 9247, travellersalta@hotmail.com 5 mins from bus terminal, doubles or **F** pp dormitories, laundry, kitchen, English and German spoken, free use of cycles. Recommended. **F** pp *Backpackers*, Buenos Aires 930, T/F423 5910, hostelsalta@backpackerssalta.com (Hostelling International) Bus 12 from bus terminal or 30 mins walk, dormitories, laundry and kitchen facilities, stores luggage, budget travel information, bar, hot showers, English, Greek and Hebrew spoken, noisy, crowded, popular. Frequently recommended. **F** pp *El Correcaminos*, Vicente López 353, T422 0731, elcorrecaminoshostel@hotmail.com Nice location, patio, clean dormitories, cooking and laundry facilities. **F** pp *Terra Oculta*, Córdoba 361, T421 8769, www.terraoculta.com Hot showers, cooking facilities, TV, email, laundry, double rooms available, free coffee and tea, roof terrace with bar, very warm atmosphere. Recommended. **F** pp *El Portal de las Nubes*, Pasaje Zorrilla 244, T156-855564, hostal@portaldelasnubes.com Dormitories and double rooms, welcoming atmosphere, roof terrace, free coffee, English and French spoken.

Outside Salta At San Lorenzo, 11 km northwest of the centre, **AL** *Hostería El Castillo*, T/F492 1052, elcastillo@redsalta.com In a converted castle, very good. **B** *Hostal Selva Montana*, C Alfonsina Storni 2315, T492 1184, wernerg@arnet.com.ar Luxurious (**A**, VIP double rooms), also camping and picnicking beside rocky stream and natural woodland. Highly recommended. Hourly bus service from Salta terminal, *Empresa Chávez*, platform 15, 30 mins, US$0.40. Last bus back about 2330. **A** *Finca San Antonio*, Route 68 Km146, El Carril, T/F0387-490 2457, rcornejo@salnet.com.ar Offers accommodation on a farm dating from 17th century, pool, horseriding, farming activities. **A** pp *Finca El Manantial*, 25 km from Salta, T/F439 5506 or T156-858480, elmanantial@arnet.com.ar Beautiful views, full board (**C** pp half board), swimming, sports, farming activities, 'fabulous'. **C** *Hostería de Chicoana*, in Chicoana, 47 km south, T/F490 7009, nuevassendas@redsalta.com Pool, gardens, English and German spoken, excursions and horses for hire. Recommended. **Camping** *Camping Carlos Xamena*, by river, 300 m artificial lake (popular Dec-Feb but empty in winter). Bus 13 to grounds. There is no signposting: leave the city heading south on C Jujuy, after 3 km you will see the Coca Cola plant on your left; turn left before the plant and then take the second road right. Charges US$1.50 per tent plus US$1 pp. Free hot showers available if there is gas (not often), safe, bathrooms run-down. **Camping shops** *HR Maluf*, San Martín y Buenos Aires, and one at La Rioja 995. Also *Canigó*, Caseros 727 and *Status*, Zuviría 201.

Many estancias, known as fincas locally, offer accommodation and country activities

Argentina

El Solar del Convento, Caseros 444, half a block from plaza. Good quality and value for meat, good service. *La Terraza de la Posta*, España 456. Food and atmosphere both good, reasonable prices. Highly recommended. *El Viejo Jack*, Virrey Toledo 145. Good meat dishes, huge portions. *El Palacio de la Pizza*, Caseros 427. Not cheap. *El Corredor de las Empanadas*, Caseros 117. Good value for *empanadas, tamales, humitas, locros*, nice garden. Also *Patio de la Empanada*, Islas Malvinas y San Martín. Recommended. *9 de Julio*, Urquiza 1020. Excellent lunch. *Doña Salta*, Córdoba 46 (opposite San Francisco church). Excellent regional dishes and atmosphere. *Don José*, Urquiza 484. Good *parrilla*. *La Nueva Colonial*, Reyes Católicos 1602. Excellent pizzas, pricey. *La Nueva Cabaña*, Mendoza 1065. Good food, large portions, cheap. *Alvarez*, Buenos Aires y San Martín. Cafetería style, cheap and good. *Café del Paseo* at *Hotel Colonial*, Zuviría 6. Open 24 hrs, superb breakfast, good value (ask for Té Paseo). *Pan y Compañía*, on Plaza 9 de Julio. Bakery shop serving coffee, sandwiches and pizzas. Breakfasts also at traditional Café Tobías, Caseros 515.

Eating
Many restaurants are lunch only, especially on San Martín near the Municipal Market. Several good places on Plaza 9 de Julio. Cheapest food is from the numerous superpancho stalls

Music Folk music show and evening meal at *Boliche Balderrama*, San Martín 1126, T4211542, from 2200. *Gauchos de Güemes*, Uruguay 750, T492 1621. Some bars charge around US$3 pp for music, but don't display charges. The area of the railway station has become popular at nights with several bars and *peñas*. *La Vieja Estación*, Balcarce 885, T421 7727, live music and regional food, open also for lunch.

Entertainment

Local festivals 15 Sep, *Cristo del Milagro* (see above); 24 Sep, *Battles of Tucumán and Salta*. On **16-17 Jun**, folk music in evening and *gaucho* parade in morning around the Güemes statue. Salta celebrates **Carnival** with processions on the **4 weekends before Ash Wednesday** at 2200 in Ciudad de Salta Stadium, 4 km south of town (US$0.50); also *Mardi Gras* (**Shrove Tuesday**) with a procession of decorated floats and dancers with intricate masks of feathers and mirrors. Water is squirted at passers-by and *bombas de agua* (small balloons to be filled with water) are sold for dropping from balconies.

Shopping
Arts and handicrafts are often cheaper in surrounding villages

Mercado Municipal, corner of San Martín and Florida, for meat, fish, vegetables, *empanadas*, *humitas* and other produce and handicrafts, closed 1300-1700 and Sun. *Mercado Artesanal* on the western outskirts of the city, at San Martín 2555, T434 2808, daily 0900-2100, take bus 2, 3, or 7 from Av San Martín in centre and get off as bus crosses the railway line. Excellent range of goods but touristy and expensive. A wide variety of handicrafts at *El Convento*, Juramento 29. *Siwok Crafts*, Zuviría 30. Quality wood carvings by the Wichi indigenous people, and typical *yika* woven bags. Leather boots are made at *Torcivia*, Vicente López 1046. *Feria del Libro*, Buenos Aires 83. *Librería Rayuela*, Alvarado 570, also a *café*. Foreign-language books. *Plural Libros*, Buenos Aires 220. Helpful. *Shopping Alto Noa*, Virrey Toledo y Cornejo, modern shopping centre. Good supermarkets: *Disco*, Florida y Caseros and Mitre y Leguizamon; *Lozano*, Mendoza y Catamarca; *Tia*, 20 de Febrero y Caseros. 24-hr pharmacy, *San Francisco*, Dean Funes 596, T421 2984.

Tour operators
Out of season, tours often run only if there is sufficient demand; check carefully that tour will run on the day you want

All agencies charge similar prices for tours (though some charge extra for credit card payments): Salta city US$10; Quebrada del Toro US$15; Cachi US$25; Humahuaca US$30; San Antonio de los Cobres US$40; Cafayate (1 day) US$25; 2-day tour to Cafayate, Angastaco, Molinos, Cachi, US$50. *La Veloz Turismo*, Buenos Aires 44, T401 2000, info@ lavelozturismo.com.ar *Dinar*, Mitre 101, T/F432 2600, dinar@salnet.com.ar For Tren a las Nubes and full programme of tours. *Saltur*, Caseros 485, T421 2012, F432 1111, saltursalta@arnet.com.ar Very efficient and recommended for local tours. *Norte Trekking*, Av del Libertador 1151 Barrio Grand Bourg, T436 1844/46, or T156-832543, www.nortetrekking.com Tours with 4WD over Jama Pass to San Pedro de Atacama and to Salar de Uyuni, also to the dinosaur footprints at Tonco, hiking, horse riding, excursions to National Parks El Rey and Los Cardones, all with experienced guide Federico Norte. Recommended. *Puna Expediciones*, Agustín Usandivaras 230, T434 1875 or T154-030263, www.punaexpeditions.com Well-qualified and experienced guide Luis H Aguilar can also be contacted through the *Res San Jorge*, organizes treks in remote areas of Salta and Jujuy. Highly recommended. *Kollasuyo*, Mar Rojo 1051, T427 1687, or T156-837895, gary@impsat1.com.ar Specialists in cycle tours. *Ricardo Clark Expeditions*, Caseros 121, T/F421 5390, www.clarkexpediciones.com Specialist tours for bird watchers, English spoken, books on flora and fauna in several languages sold. Highly recommended. *Hernán Uriburu*, Leguizamón 446, T431 0605, www.nortetrekking.com/hru.htm Organizes horse or mule-riding expeditions to the mountains, sleeping at local's houses (US$85 pp per day, all included), highly professional. *Martin Oliver*, T432 1013. Adventure tourism guide for Cachi. *Movitrack*, Buenos Aires 28, T431 6749, www.movitrack.com.ar Offer a range of safaris in a 4x4 truck, to San Antonio de los Cobres, Humahuaca, Cafayate and Iruya, also over Paso de Sico to Chile, German, English spoken, very professional, book in advance direct from company, or through *Kraft Travel Service-American Express Travel Services*, Lamarca 359, Martínez, Buenos Aires, T/F4793 4062, mail@kraft-travel.com **Turismo San Lorenzo**, Dávalos 960, T/F492 1757 or 156-840400, San Lorenzo, www.1turismosanlorenzo.com For horseriding and adventure tourism. *José Adet*, T492 1620/421 0115. Guided walks through the cloud forest near San Lorenzo.

Transport **Local Car hire**: *Rentacar*, Buenos Aires 189, T156-853586, 24 hrs. *Marina Services*, at *Hotel Salta*, T431 2097, for all-terrain vehicles. *Ruiz Moreno*, Caseros 225, in *Hotel Salta*, good cars, helpful. *Europa*, Buenos Aires 186, T422 3609/0800-888 6699. It may be cheaper and more convenient to hire a taxi for a fixed fee. **Bicycles**: *Manresa*, Pellegrini y Corrientes, T423 3536. Large stock, imported equipment. *Parra*, Caseros 2154, T422 5326.

Long distance **Air**: *LAB* to Santa Cruz and Tarija (Bolivia) 2 weekly. *AR, Dinar* and *AIRG* fly to Bs As (2 hrs, minimum). *Southern Winds* to Córdoba, and Tucumán; *AIRG* to Jujuy and *Dinar* to São Paulo (Brasil). Bus 22 to access to airport from San Martín, US$0.35; don't be fooled by taxi touts who tell you there is no bus. Taxi from airport to bus station US$5.

Trains: Station at 20 de February y Ameghino, 9 blocks north of Plaza 9 de Julio, taxi US$1.

Buses: Terminal is 8 blocks east of the main plaza, T401 1143 for information. Behind terminal is a 24-hr Refinor station serving cheap snacks. To **Buenos Aires**, several daily, US$25 *semicama*, 20-22 hrs (*TAC, Panamericano, Brown, Chevallier, La Internacional* and others). To **Córdoba**, several daily, 12 hrs, US$12-18, *Panamericano* (T401 1118), twice daily, *Veloz del Norte*. To **Santiago del Estero**, 6 hrs, US$8-10. To **Tucumán**, 4½ hrs, several firms (*La Veloz del Norte* recommended), US$7-10. To **Mendoza** via Tucumán, several companies, daily, US$20-25, 17-20 hrs. To **Jujuy**, *Balut Hnos, La Veloz del Norte, Atahualpa* and others, hourly between 0600 and 2200, 'directo', US$2-3, 2 hrs. To **La Rioja**, US$12, 10 hrs. To **Puerto Iguazú**, US$32, 24 hrs, daily.

To **Cafayate**, US$6, 3½ hrs, 2-4 daily, to Santa María, US$17, daily, to **Angastaco**, daily, except on Thu and Sat, to **Belén**, Wed (*El Indio*, T431 9389*)*. To Cachi, US$7, 4-4½ hrs, 1-2 daily, to Molinos, US$10, 6½ hrs, every 2 days (sit on left) and to La Poma, US$9, 6½ hrs, 3 weekly (*Marcos Rueda*, T421 4447). To **Rosario de la Frontera**, US$3, 2½ hrs. To **San Antonio de Los Cobres**, 5 hrs, *El Quebradeño*, Mon-Sat 1500, Sun 1910, US$5.50.

International: To **Paraguay**: La Nueva Estrella, T422 4048, runs 3 services weekly to Clorinda (at the border), US$28, 17 hrs; buses or taxis will take you from there to Paraguay for a small fee. Alternatively travel to **Resistencia**, daily, US$18 with *La Veloz del Norte, Flecha Bus, La Nueva Estrella, Autotransportes Mendoza* or to **Formosa**, with *La Nueva Estrella*, US$25, 15 hrs, changing then, to a direct bus to Asunción. For description of border, see page 170.

To **Chile**: Services to **Calama, San Pedro de Atacama, Antofagasta, Iquique** and **Arica** with *Tur Bus* and *Geminis*, via Jujuy and the Jama Pass, Tue-Fri-Sun 0700, US$43, 18 hrs to Antofagasta and US$47, 24 hrs to Arica.

To **Bolivia**: To **La Quiaca**, on Bolivian border, *Balut*, 4 a day, US$12, 7½ hrs, and *Brown*, daily, US$10, 5 hrs. To **Orán**, 6 hrs, and Aguas Blancas with *Balut* and *La Veloz del Norte*, US$8-9, daily for Bermejo, Bolivia; thence road connection to Tarija. To Yacuiba, via **Pocitos** (Bolivian border, see page 143), for Santa Cruz, US$7-12 with several companies to Pocitos, 7-10 hrs, very full, road paved.

Directory

Airline offices *AR*, Caseros 475, T431 1331/0862. *Dinar*, Mitre 101, T432 2600/06. *AIRG*, Caseros 492, T431 7080/81. *Lloyd Aéreo Boliviano*, Deán Funes 29, T431 0320/1389. *Southern Winds*, Caseros 434, T422 5555. **Banks** Banks, open 0730-1300, all have ATMs (many on España). *Banco de la Nación*, Mitre y Belgrano, high commission. *Banco de Salta*, España 550 on main plaza, low commission on TCs. *Banca Nazionale del Lavoro*, Balcarce 1, cash on MasterCard. *HSBC* , Mitre 143, good rates, 1% commission on Amex TCs into US$, changes Thomas Cook TCs, recommended. *Amex*, *Chicoana Turismo*, Zuviría 255, changes TCs. *Dinar*, Mitre 101/109, 3% commission. *Golden Life*, Mitre 95 (Plaza 9 de Julio), local 1, first floor, best rates for cash. **Communications** Internet: *Chat Café*, Vicente López 117, US$0.75 per hr. *Intercafé*, Alvarado 537. *Cibercom*, Buenos Aires 97. *Every*, Deán Funes 141 (all charge US$0.50 per hour) Post Office: Deán Funes 160, between España and Belgrano. **Telephone:** Several *telecentros* in town, some offer internet access. **Cultural centres** Alliance Française, Santa Fe 20, T421 0827. **Consulates** Bolivia, Mariano Boedo 34, T421 1040, open Mon-Fri, 0900-1400 (unhelpful, better to go to Jujuy). **Chile**, Santiago del Estero 965, T431 1857. **Belgium**, Pellegrini 835, T423 4252. **Spain**, República de Israel 137, T431 2296, F431 0206. **Italy**, Santiago del Estero 497, T432 1532. **France**, Santa Fe 156, T431 2403. **Germany**, Urquiza 409, T421 6525, F431 1772, consul Juan C Kühl, helpful. **Immigration**: Maipú 35, 0730-1230.

Argentina

Argentina

Railway to the Clouds

The Argentine section of the railway to the Chilean border was engineered by Richard Maury, of Pennsylvania, who is commemorated by the station at Km 78 which bears his name. This remarkable project was built in stages between 1921 and 1948, by which time developments in road and air transport had already reduced its importance. No racks were used in its construction. The line includes 21 tunnels, 13 viaducts, 31 bridges, 2 loops and 2 zig-zags. From Salta the line climbs gently to Campo Quijano (Km 40, 1,520 m), where it enters the Quebrada del Toro, an impressive rock-strewn gorge. At El Alisal (Km 50) and Chorrillos (Km 66) there are zig-zags as the line climbs the side of the gorge before turning north into the valley of the Río

Rosario near Puerto Tastil (Km 101, 2,675 m), missing the archaeological areas around Santa Rosa de Tastil. At Km 122 and Km 129 the line goes into 360° loops before reaching Diego de Almagro (3,304 m). At Abra Muñano (3,952 m) the road to San Antonio can be seen zig-zagging its way up the end-wall of the Quebrada del Toro below. From Muñano (3,936 m) the line drops slightly to San Antonio, Km 196. The spectacular viaduct at La Polvorilla is 21 km further at 4,190 m, just beyond the branch line to the mines at La Concordia. The highest point on the line is reached at Abra Chorrillos (4,475 m, Km 231). From here the line runs on another 335 km across a rocky barren plateau 3,500-4,300 m above sea level before reaching Socompa (3,865 m).

From Salta to Chile

There is a 900 km, metre-gauge railway from Salta through the little town of San Antonio de los Cobres to Antofagasta, in northern Chile. San Antonio can also be reached by Route 51 from Salta, which is being upgraded. From Campo Quijano (**A-B** *Hostería Punta Callejas*, T0387-490 4086, with bath, comfortable, a/c, pool, tennis, riding, excursions; **D** *Hostería Finca Río Blanco*, T0387-431 4314; *Municipal Campsite*, at the entrance to Quebrada del Toro gorge, hot showers, bungalows, recommended) it runs along the floor of the Quebrada del Toro before climbing to Alto Blanco (paved section).

San Antonio de los Cobres
Phone code: 0387
Population: 4,000
Altitude: 3,775 m
196 km by rail
163 km by road from Salta

San Antonio de los Cobres is a squat, ugly mining town on a bleak, high desert. The inhabitants of this area are Coya Indians. Route 51 leads to La Polvorilla railway viaduct (see below), 20 km, ask in town for details and beware sudden changes in the weather. At **Santa Rosa de Tastil** there are important prehispanic ruins and a small museum (US$0.50), recommended. Basic accommodation next door to the museum, no electricity or heating, take food, water and candles. Take El Quebradeño bus (see below), a tour from Salta, or share a taxi. **C** *Hostería de las Nubes*, edge of San Antonio on Salta road (T0387-490 9059), or Bs As 4326 0126, Esmeralda 320), modern, includes breakfast, spacious, recommended. **E** *Hospedaje Belgrano*, T490 9025, welcoming, hot showers unreliable, evening meals. *Hospedaje El Palenque*, T490 9019, also café, main street, basic. **F** pp *Hostería Inti Huasi*, opposite the Aduana, T490 9041, restaurant. Try the *quesillo de cabra* (goat's cheese) from Estancia Las Cuevas.

On all train journeys on this line beware of soroche (altitude sickness): do not eat or drink to excess

Transport Trains The Tren a las Nubes (Train to the Clouds) runs between Salta and La Polvorilla viaduct (400 km round trip). The service operates from Apr to Nov, weather permitting, several times each month with most in the high season (Jul-Sep), depart 0700, return to Salta by 2200, US$105 (this price is only for non residents in the country; residents are charged 105 pesos), meals US$11, credit cards not accepted, a tour package can be sold at about US$250 from Buenos Aires. The train is well-equipped with oxygen facilities and medical staff as well as a restaurant car and snack bar. Translators on request. There is noisy entertainment on board. This service is operated privately and cannot be booked in advance at Salta railway station. Book in advance through *La Veloz Turismo* or *Dinar*, address under

Salta; in Buenos Aires, *La Veloz Turismo*, Esmeralda 320 4th floor, T4326 0126, F4326 0852, trenubes@arnet.com.ar, or *Dinar*, Av Roque Sáenz Peña 933, T4327 8000, F4326 0134, www.trenubes.com.ar Or through any good travel agency. **To Socompa** (Chilean border): a mixed train with 2 passenger carriages leaves Salta Wed about 0900 (in theory), ticket office opens 0800 (queue from 0600), US$5 one way to San Antonio, US$8 one way to Socompa, 27 hrs one way via San Antonio (14 hrs). There is a dining car and a bar. Long delays are common on this route and you may do most of the journey in the dark. Take water and warm clothing. Beyond Socompa there are irregular freight trains into Chile (Augusta Victoria, Baquedano or Antofagasta): officially the Chilean railway authorities do not permit passengers to travel on this line. To travel on by train or truck may involve a wait of several days. There are only 4 buildings in Socompa: no food or accommodation, but try the Chilean customs building. **Buses** From **San Antonio de los Cobres** to Salta, *El Quebradeño*, Mon-Sat 0900, Sun 1000, 5 hrs, US$5.50; stops at Santa Rosa de Tastil (book at *Telefónica* office). Same price by *remise*, but only 2 hrs.

The road from San Antonio de los Cobres to **San Pedro de Atacama**, Chile uses the **Sico** Pass (4,079 m). This is a very beautiful route: you cross salt lakes with flamingoes and impressive desert. It is well marked. There is a customs post at Paso Sico (you may be allowed to spend the night here), hours 0900-1900: check first in San Antonio de los Cobres if it is open. Police in San Antonio may be able to advise about road conditions but truck drivers using the route are more reliable. The road on the Argentine side is very good (police checkpoint beyond Catúa). On the Chilean side continue via Mina Laco and Socaire to Toconao (road usually very bad between these two points). Police checkpoint in Toconao but customs and immigration in San Pedro de Atacama. Note that fruit, vegetables and dairy products may not be taken into Chile (search 20 km after Paso Sico). Gasoline is available in San Pedro and Calama. Obtain sufficient drinking water for the trip in San Antonio.

Because of snowfalls, this route may be closed 2-3 times a year, for two or three days each time

Argentina

Jujuy

San Salvador de Jujuy (pronounced Hoo-hooey) often referred to by locals as San Salvador, is the capital of Jujuy province and is surrounded by partially wooded mountains. The city was founded first in 1561 and then in 1575, when it was destroyed by the Indians, and finally established in 1593. The province of Jujuy bore the brunt of fighting during the Wars of Independence. In August 1812 Gen Belgrano, commanding the republican troops, ordered the city to be evacuated and destroyed before the advancing Spanish army. This event is marked on 23-24 August by festivities known as El Exodo Jujeño with gaucho processions and military parades. Tourist office: Urquiza 354 (at the former railway station), T422 1325/6, very helpful. ■ *Mon-Fri 0730-2100, Sat-Sun 0900-2100*.

Phone code: 0388
Colour map 6, grid C4
Population: 237,000
Altitude: 1,260 m

In the eastern part of the city is the **Plaza Belgrano**, a fine square lined with orange trees. On the south side of the plaza stands the **Casa de Gobierno**, an elaborate French baroque-style palace. ■ *Daily 0800-1200, 1600-2000*. On the west side is the **Cathedral**, built in the late 19th century to replace the original (1598-1653) which was destroyed by earthquake in 1843. It retains fine 18th-century images and in the nave is a superb wooden pulpit, carved by Indians and gilded, a colonial treasure without equal in Argentina. On C Lavalle you can see the doorway through which Gen Lavalle, the enemy of Rosas, was killed by a bullet in 1841, but the door is a copy; the original is kept inside. The **Teatro Mitre** is at Alvear y Lamadrid.

Museo Histórico Provincial, Lavalle 250, includes a display of colonial art and history of Gen Lavalle. ■ *Mon-Sat 0800-1200, 1600-2000*. **Museo de Geología, Mineralogía y Paleontología**, part of the University of Jujuy, Avenida Bolivia 1661. ■ *Mon-Fri 0900-1230*. Beside is the **Estación Biológica de Fauna Silvestre**, very interesting. ■ *For more information, contact Dr Arturo A Canedi, T422 1520*. **Museo Arqueológico Provincial**, Lavalle 434, includes two mumified adults as well as ceramics from the Yavi and Humahuaca cultures. ■ *Daily 0900-1200, 1500-2000*.

Excursions At 19 km west of Jujuy is **Termas de Reyes**, with hot springs. This resort, with the *Hotel Termas de Reyes*, T0388-492 2522, is set among magnificent mountains one hour by bus *Empresa 19 de Abril (línea 14)* from Gorriti e Independencia or from C Segada (half block from Jujuy bus terminal), hourly, US$0.50. Municipal baths US$0.50 and pool US$1; also cabins with thermal water run by *Dirección de Recursos Hídricos*, US$5 pp.

Sleeping **B** *Augustus*, Belgrano 715, T423 0203. 3-star, modern, VIP section good, standard section overpriced, modern, comfortable but noisy. **B** *Fenicia*, 19 de Abril 427, T423 1800, www.quintar.com.ar Tower block on riverside, good views from upper floors, restaurant. **C** *Sumay*, Otero 232, T423 5065. Central. Recommended. **C** *Avenida*, 19 de Abril 469, T423 6136. On riverside, with good restaurant. **E** *Huaico*, Av Bolivia 3901, T423 5186, hotelhuaicojujuy@hotmail.com Breakfast extra, *confitería*, solarium, pool (buses 1, 2, 4, 9, 14 from Plaza Belgrano). **D** *Res San Carlos*, República de Siria 459, T422 2286. Modern, some rooms a/c (**E** without bath), parking. **D** *Ery Noa*, Güemes 1131, T402 0303/4. Breakfast, TV, good rooms. **E** *Chung King*, Alvear 627, T422 8142. Dark, very noisy, also without bath, good restaurant, live music and dancing at weekends at Alvear 628. **E** *Puerta del Sol*, San Antonio 659, T424 3422. With breakfast. **G** pp *Res Norte*, Alvear 444, T423 8475. Small dormitories, shared bath (**E** with bath), patio. Near the bus terminal only **E** *San Antonio*, Lisandro de la Torre 993 (opposite), T422 5998. Modern, with bath.

Outside the city: **A** *Altos De La Viña*, Route 56, Km 5, on northeastern outskirts, T426 1666/2626, lavina@imagine.com.ar Attractive, swimming pool. **C** *Hostería Posta de Lozano*, Route 9, Km 18 north, T498 0050, posta@imagine.com.ar Good restaurant, pools with fresh mountain water, covered parking. **E** *El Refugio*, in Yala, route 9, 14 km north, T/F490 9344, www.ar.geocities.com/refugio_jujuy Youth hostel, double rooms with bath, pool, camping (US$1.50 pp plus US$1 per tent), English spoken, restaurant, trekking and horseriding excursions.

Camping *Autocamping*, 3 km north outside city at Huaico Chico (opposite *Hotel Huaico*). Buses 4 or 9 frequent, hot showers (if you remind the staff), laundry facilities, very friendly. *Samiri*, Balcarce 569, T423 8425, samiri@cootepal.com.ar Also rooms, **F**.

Eating *Sociedad Española*, Belgrano y Senador Pérez. Elegant setting, good set price meals. *Bar La Royal*, Belgrano 766. Good but expensive. *El Oriente*, Güemes 723. Arab specialities. *Africana*, San Martín y Ramirez de Velasco. Pizzas. *El Socavón*, Belgrano 751. Live local music on Thu, Fri and Sat evenings. *Madre Tierra*, Belgrano y Otero. Vegetarian. Lunches only, closed on Sun. Recommended. *Krysys*, Balcarce 272. Excellent atmosphere, good food. *Ruta 9*, Lavalle 287. Good local food and home made pastas, Bolivian owners. *La Candelaria*, Alvear 1346, *parrilla*. *María Elena*, Balcarce 374, 1st floor. Light meals and vegetarian dishes. *Manos Jujeñas*, Senador Pérez 222, regional specialities. Cheaper places behind bus terminal on Santiago del Estero and Alem. *Confitería Carena*, Belgrano 899. Old-fashioned, good for breakfast. *El Humahuaqueño*, Güemes 920, pastries. Very good ice cream at *El Pingüino*, on C Belgrano. Good sandwiches at *Rada Tilly*, 2 locations on Belgrano.

Shopping Handicrafts are available at reasonable prices from vendors on *Paseo de las Artesanías* on the west side of the plaza. *Regionales Lavalle*, Lavalle 268. *Fundación Recrear*, Otero 220, T422 8653. Specialised workshop on historical religious paintings of the region. *Librería Rayuela*, Belgrano 636. *Farmacia Puente Lavalle*, Lavalle y 19 de Abril, 0800-2400. Municipal market at Dorrego y Alem, near bus terminal. Supermarkets: *Norte*, Belgrano 823 and *Lozano*, 19 de Abril y Necochea and Alvear y Balcarce.

Tour operators *NASA*, Senador Pérez 154, T/F422 3938, nasa@imagine.com.ar Guided tour to Quebrada de Humahuaca (US$30 pp, min 4 people); 4WD for rent. *Be Dor Turismo*, Lavalle 295, 10% discount for ISIC and youth card holders on local excursions. For information on bird watching, contact Mario Daniel Cheronaza, Peatonal 38, No 848-830, Viviendas 'El Arenal', Jujuy. *Marco Polo Expeditions*, T423 0751 or 156-854832, aventur@imagine.com.ar 4WD tours, English spoken, knowledgeable, trips to 10,000-year old petroglyphs in Quebrada de Humahuaca.

Colonial Churches of the North

Lovers of old churches will find Salta and Jujuy excellent centres. Franciscan and Dominican friars arrived in the area from Bolivia as early as 1550. The Jesuits followed about 1585. Some churches can be found along the old Camino de los Incas (now non-existent), eg Susques and Coranzulĵ. Many more are on or near the

Panamericana through the Quebrada de Iturbe. The padres, in the course of two centuries, built simple but beautiful churches, of which about 20 survive. They are marked by church symbols on the map on page 122. All of them can be visited by car from Salta or Jujuy, though some of the roads are very rough.

Air Airport T491 1101. Vans (US$2.50) to/from *Dinar* and *AIRG* offices; taxi, US$13. Flights to Buenos Aires by *AIRG* (T423 8666) and *Dinar*, T423 7100. *ARG* and *Dinar* also fly to **Salta**. **Buses** To Buenos Aires, US$20-30, 20-24 hrs, several daily with *TAC, La Estrella, Panamericano, Brown, Atahualpa, El Rápido* and *Balut*. Via Tucumán to Córdoba, *Panamericano* and *La Veloz del Norte*, daily to **Tucumán**, 5 hrs, US$8, and **Córdoba**, 14 hrs US$15. To **Salta** hourly, 2 hrs, US$2-3. To **La Quiaca**, 5-6½ hrs, US$8, *Panamericano, Balut, Jama Bus, El Quiaqueño* and *Atahualpa*, reasonably comfortable, but very cold at night. To **Humahuaca**, *Evelia* and others, US$3, 3 hrs, several daily, sit on left side. To **Orán** and **Aguas Blancas** (border with Bolivia), daily with *Balut* and *Brown*, via San Pedro and Ledesma. To **Purmamarca**, take buses to Susques or to Humahuaca (those calling at Purmamarca village). To Susques, *Purmamarca* and *Andes Bus*, US$6, 4-6½ hrs, daily (except Mon). To Tilcara 1½ hrs, US$2-2.50.

Transport
Airport at El Cadillal, 32 km SE
Bus terminal at Iguazú y Dorrego, 6 blocks S of centre

   To Chile: via the **Jama** pass (*Altitude*: 4,200 m), the route taken by most traffic, including trucks, crossing to northern Chile; hours 0900-1900. In this region, the only accommodation is at **Susques** (**E** pp *Res Las Vicuñitas*, T490207, opposite the outstanding church, without bath, thatched roof, hot water, breakfast), 105 km north of San Antonio de los Cobres on a road through utter desert. *Geminís* bus tickets sold at *Ortiz Viajes*, L N Alem 917, ortizviajes@latinmail.com

Banks *Banco de Jujuy*, Alvear 999, gives cash against MasterCard, no commission, also changes dollars. Amex TCs can only be changed at *Scotiabank Quilmes*, Belgrano y Balcarce, 1% commission while *Banco de Galicia*, Alvear y Necochea, charges US$10 commission. Visa and MasterCard ATMs at *Citibank*, Güemes y Balcarce; *Banco Río*, Alvear 802, *Banco Francés*, Alvear 992; *Banco Salta*, San Martín 785. Nowhere to change Thomas Cook TCs. *Horus*, Belgrano 722, good rates for cash. Travel agencies also change cash but not TCs. **Communications** Internet: *Cyber Explora*, Güemes 1049; *Ciber Nob*, Otero 317; *HVA*, Lavalle 390 (all US$0.50 per hour). *Telecom* centres at Alvear 870, Belgrano 730 and elsewhere. **Post Office**: at Independencia y Lamadrid. **Consulates**: Bolivia, Senador Pérez e Independencia, T424 0501, 0900-1300, price of visa should be US$5, pay no more. **Spain**, R de Velasco 362, T422 8139. **Italy**, Av Fascio 1056, T422 7398. **Immigration**: 19 de Abril 1057, T422 2638.

Directory

North from Jujuy to La Quiaca

Route 9, the Pan-American Highway, runs through the beautiful Quebrada de Humahuaca, which has a variety of rock colours and giant cacti in the higher, drier parts. In the rainy season (January-March) ask the highway police about flooding on the roads. All along the Quebrada de Humahuaca the pre-Lent carnival celebrations are picturesque and colourful. In Tilcara and Humahuaca pictures of the Passion are made of flowers, leaves, grasses and seeds at Easter and a traditional procession on Holy Thursday at night is joined by thousands. Beyond Tumbaya, where there is a church originally built in 1796 and rebuilt in 1873, a road runs 3 km west to **Purmamarca**, a very popular, picturesque village overlooked by a mountain: seven colours can be distinguished in the rock strata (best seen when sun is in the east). **A** *El Manantial del Silencio*, Route 52 Km 3.5, T0388-490 8080, restaurant, pool. **E** *Hospedaje Bebo Wilte*, T490 8038, above the church, pleasant, patio, breakfast extra, cooking facilities, camping in garden, hot shower. Recommended.

For drivers heading off main roads in this area, note that service stations are far apart: there are ACA stations at Jujuy, Humahuaca and La Quiaca, and YPF stations at Tilcara and Abra Pampa. Spare fuel and water must be carried

Argentina

F pp *Ranchito del Rincón*, Sarmiento, T0388-490 8023, owners Yolanda and Zulma are helpful. Highly recommended. *Comedor* on main plaza has good, cheap, local food. At the entrance to Purmamarca a right turn leads to a new gravel road, which leads through another *quebrada* over the 4,164 m Abra Potrerillos to the Salinas Grandes salt flats at about 3,400 m on the Altiplano (fantastic views especially at sunset). From here roads lead southwest past spectacular rock formations along the east side of the salt flats to San Antonio de los Cobres, and west across the salt flats via Susques to the Paso de Jama and Chile.

About 7 km north of the Purmamarca turning is **La Posta de Hornillos**, a museum in a restored colonial posting house, of which there used to be a chain from Buenos Aires to Lima. ■ *Open, in theory, Wed-Mon 0900-1800, free.* About 3 km further is **Maimará** (**C** *Posta del Sol*, Martín Rodríguez y San Martín, T499 7156, posta_del_sol@hotmail.com Restaurant, vehicles for rent, the owners' son is a tourist guide and has helpful information).

Tilcara

Phone code: 0388
Colour map 6, grid C3
Population: 3,500
Altitude: 2,460 m

Tilcara lies 22 km north of Purmamarca. The **Museo Arqueológico** here, attached to the University of Buenos Aires, contains a fine collection of precolumbian ceramics from the Andean regions of present day Argentina, Bolivia and Peru. ■ *Daily 0900-1230, 1400-1800, US$1, free entry Tue. Admission includes entry to a reconstruction of a pucará, or fortified village and a botanical garden, 2 km from the museum, recommended.* Beautiful mountain views. There are four art museums in town. A good guide for walks and car excursions is Oscar Branchesi, T495 5117, branchesi_guia@yahoo.com.ar Very knowledgeable, speaks some English. There are fiestas on weekends in January; carnival and Holy Week are very popular celebrations.

Sleeping and eating **C** *Villar del Ala*, Padilla 100, T495 5100, adriantilcara@hotmail.com Half-pension, good food, guided horse rides and 4WD excursions, pool. **D** *Malka*, San Martín s/n, 5 blocks from plaza, T495 5197, malka_tilcara@cootepal.com.ar Bungalows beautifully located with kitchen and laundry facilities, also **F** pp dormitory accommodation, kitchen facilities, Hostelling International affiliated, horse and bike rental, meals provided. **D** *El Antigal*, Rivadavia s/n, T495 5020. Good restaurant, stores luggage. **D** *Hosp Pucará*, Padilla s/n. 3 blocks from plaza, T495 5050. With bath, **F** pp without, run down. **D** *Posada con los Angeles*, Gorriti s/n, T495 5153, posada_conlosangeles@yahoo.com.ar Very nice rooms, family atmosphere, kitchen, BBQ, lovely garden, good views, laundry service, trekking and excursions on horseback or 4x4, 4-day guided walk to Calilegua. **F** pp *La Morada*, Debenedetti s/n, T/F495 5118, cds.api@imagine.com.ar Good rooms for 2 to 5 people with bath, heating, cooking facilities. **F** pp *Wiphala*, Jujuy 549, T495 5015, www.wiphala.com.ar Small, warm atmosphere, kitchen. **Camping** *Camping El Jardín*, access on Belgrano, T495 5128, US$2, clean, hot showers, also **D** double rooms at new hostel. Eating places include *El Patio*, Lavalle 352, very good meals and *San Jorge*, Belgrano y Villafañe, open when others are not.

At **Huacalera**, Km 90, is **D** *Hostal La Granja*, T0388-426 1766. Including breakfast, lunch and dinner US$8 each, pool, rustic, lovely atmosphere, outstanding food and service, good base for exploring the region.

Humahuaca

Phone code: 03887
Colour map 6, grid B3
Population: 8,700
Altitude: 2,940 m
129 km N of Jujuy

Although Humahuaca dates from 1594, it was almost entirely rebuilt in the mid-19th century. It is an attraction for coach trips from Salta and Jujuy, but is a peaceful centre for exploring the Quebrada de Humahuaca. On 2 February is *La Candelaria* festival. *Jueves de Comadres, Festival de las Coplas y de la Chicha*, at the beginning of carnival is worth attending.

The church, **La Candelaria**, originally built in 1631, was completely rebuilt in 1873-80; it has a bell from 1641. A mechanical figure of San Francisco Solano blesses the town from **El Cabildo**, the neo-colonial town hall, at 1200. Overlooking the town is the massive **Monumento a la Independencia Argentina**, weighing 60 tons, built in 1936-50 and sited here because the valley was the scene of the heaviest fighting in the country during the Wars of Independence. There is a good **Feria Artesanal** on Av San Martín (on the far side of the railway line and a **Fruit Market**, Tucumán y Belgrano.

Museo Ramoneda, Salta y Santa Fe, private collection of contemporary art. ■ *Daily 1030-1300, 1500-1830.* **Museo Nicasio Fernández Mar**, Buenos Aires, opposite *Hotel de Turismo*, memorial to the sculptor, open daily, free. **Museo Folklórico Regional**, Buenos Aires 435, run by Sixto Vásquez, traditional customs.

Excursions To **Coctaca**, 10 km northeast, where there is an impressive and extensive (40 ha) series of pre-colonial agricultural terraces.

Sleeping

C *Camino del Inca*, on the other side of the river, T421136, hosteriainca@imagine.com.ar New, pool, excursions. **D** *Res Humahuaca*, Córdoba y Corrientes, T421141, 1 block from bus terminal. **E** without bath, traditional, good. **E** *Res Colonial*, Entre Ríos 110, T421007. **E** without bath, laundry facilities. **F** pp *Cabaña El Cardón*, T156-29072, ask for owner Marcelo Núñez. Cabin with 4 beds, bath, hot water, kitchen, laundry service, regional foods, excursions, charming family. **F** pp *Posada El Sol*, over bridge from terminal, then 520 m, follow signs, T421466, elsolposada@imagine.com.ar Quiet rural area, very warm atmosphere, breakfast extra, laundry and cooking facilities, hot showers. Horse-riding. Warmly recommended. **F** pp *Albergue Humahuaca*, Buenos Aires 447, T421064. Laundry and limited cooking facilities, cafeteria, basic rooms and dormitories, tourist information. **G** pp *Res El Portillo*, Tucumán 69, T421288. Very good, dormitories and **E** rooms, shared bath, helpful, lively bar/restaurant. Ask for guided walks. **Camping** Across bridge by railway station, small charge including use of facilities.

Eating

Most restaurants open only during the day, the mediocre restaurant near bus terminal is often the only place open in evening. *La Cacharpaya*, Jujuy 317. Excellent, pricey, Andean music. *Humahuaca Colonial*, Tucumán 16. Good regional cooking, good value, but invaded by coach parties at midday. *El Rancho*, Belgrano s/n, just around the corner from market, lunches only, where the locals eat. *La Chichería*, Buenos Aires 435. Evenings only, regional dishes and *chicha*.

Directory

Banks To change money, try the handicraft shops on the main plaza for change, or the *farmacia* at Córdoba 99. ATM at **Banco de Jujuy** on main plaza, but establishments do not accept credit cards.

Iruya

Colour map 6, grid B3
Altitude: 2,600 m
66 km from Humahuaca

An unpaved road 25 km north of Humahuaca runs northeast from the Panamericana 8 km to **Iturbe** (also called Hipólito Irigoyen; **F** *Pensión El Panamericano*, basic) and then over the 4,000 m Abra del Cóndor before dropping steeply into the Quebrada de Iruya. The road is very rough and unsuited to hire cars. **Iruya** is a beautiful walled village wedged on a hillside. It has a colourful Rosario festival on first Sunday in October. Iruya is an extremely pleasant and friendly centre for horseback or walking trips (take sleeping bag). At Titiconte 4 km away, there are unrestored pre-Inca ruins (take guide). **C** *Hostería de Iruya*, T03887-156 29152, great views, comfortable. **F** *Albergue Belén*, very basic. **F** *Hosp Tacacho*, clean, *comedor*, on the plaza. Food at *Comedor Iruya*. Puna Expediciones (see Salta, page 134) runs (April-December, on Thursday) a 4-day excursion from Salta to Iruya and Salinas Grandes, including a 2-day walk from Iruya to Refugio Cóndor at San Juan (US$43 pp per day). A 7-day trek from Iruya to Nazareno and La Quiaca is organised upon request (minimum 8 people).

Transport

Buses Daily bus service from Jujuy and Humahuaca to **Iturbe**. *Empresa Mendoza* bus from Humahuaca (T03887-421016), 1030 daily, 3 hrs, US$4, US$6.50 return, returning 1515. Routine border police controls along Quebrada de Humahuaca can cause short delays on buses. Keep passport with you.

Argentina

Argentina

Tres Cruces & Some 62 km north of Humahuaca on the Panamericana, is Tres Cruces, where cus-
Abra Pampa toms searches are made on vehicles from Bolivia. **F** pp *El Aguilar* (no sign), without
bath, basic. **Abra Pampa** (*Population*: 6,000), 91 km north of Humahuaca, is an
important mining centre. **F** *Residencial El Norte*, Sarmiento 530, shared room, hot
water, good food. *Res y restaurante Cesarito*, one block from main plaza. At 15 km
southwest of Abra Pampa is the vicuña farm at Miraflores, the largest in Argentina.
Information offered, photography permitted; colectivos go morning Monday-Saturday Abra Pampa-Miraflores.

    Laguna de los Pozuelos (*Altitude*: 3,650 m), 50 km northwest of Abra Pampa, is
a flamingo reserve and natural monument. Bus Monday-Friday 0930, two hours,
US$3, dropping you at the park ranger station, 2 km from the Laguna. If driving, the
Laguna is 5 km from the road; walk last 800 m to reach the edge of the lagoon. Temperatures can drop to –25°C in winter.

    From a point 4 km north of Abra Pampa roads branch west to Cochinoca (25 km)
and southwest to **Casabindo** (62 km). On 15 August at Casabindo, the local saint's
day, the last and only *corrida de toros* (running with bulls) in Argentina is held
amidst a colourful popular celebration. The event is called *El Toreo de la Vincha*; in
front of the church a bull defies onlookers to take a ribbon and medal which it carries. The Casabindo church itself is a magnificent building, sometimes called 'the
cathedral of the Puna' (Federico Kirbus). **F** pp *Albergue*, T03887-491129. Buses to
Casabindo from Abra Pampa.

La Quiaca

Phone code: 03885
Altitude: 3,442 m
Colour map 6, grid B3
292 km N of Jujuy

Situated on the border with Bolivia, a concrete bridge links the town with Villazón
(see page 284) on the Bolivian side. Warm clothing is essential particularly in winter
when temperatures can drop to –15°C, though care should be taken against sunburn
during the day. On the third Sunday in October the *Manca Fiesta*, or the festival of
the pots, is held here, and the Colla Indians from Jujuy and the Bolivian *altiplano*
come, carrying all sorts of pots.

Excursions **Yavi**, with the fine church of San Francisco (1690), which has magnificent gold decoration and windows of onyx, is 16 km east of La Quiaca, reached by a good, paved
road; bus 4 times a day from La Quiaca, US$0.50. Taxi available – US$12 return,
including one hour wait. Find the caretaker at her house and she will show you
round the church. ■ *Tue-Sun 0900-1200 and Tue-Fri 1500-1800*. Opposite the
church is the house of the Marqués Campero y Tojo. **C** *Hostal de Yavi*,
T03887-490508, elportillo@cootepal.com.ar Bath, heating, restaurant. **F** *La
Casona 'Jatum Huasi'*, Sen Pérez y San Martín, T03885-422316,
mccalizaya@laquiaca.com.ar Owner Mónica Calizaya is very knowledgeable, with
breakfast, meals extra. Recommended.

Sleeping **C** *Turismo*, Siria y San Martín, T422243. Recommended, modern, comfortable, hot water
& eating 1800-2400, heating from 2030-2400 in winter, restaurant. **D** *Cristal*, Sarmiento 543,
T422255. Run down, without bath, hospitable. **D** *Victoria*, opposite railway station. Good
hot showers. **D** *La Frontera* hotel and restaurant, Belgrano y Siria, downhill from *Atahualpa*
bus stop. Good. **F** *Res Copacabana*, Pellegrini 141. Hot showers, luggage store, laundry
facilities. **Camping** Camping possible near the control post on the outskirts of town. Also at
the *ACA* service station about 300 m from the border.

Transport Bus terminal, España y Belgrano, luggage storage. 6-8 buses a day to **Salta** (US$10-12) with
Balut (7½ hrs), *Atahualpa* and *Brown*. Several daily to Humahuaca, US$5, 2½-3 hrs, and to
Jujuy, US$8, 5-6½ hrs. Take own food, as sometimes long delays. Buses may be stopped for
routine border police controls and searched for coca leaves. **NB** Buses from Jujuy may arrive
in the early morning when no restaurants are open and it is freezing cold outside.

Banks No facilities for changing TCs. Rates are better in Villazón. **Medical facilities** There is a good hospital in La Quiaca. *Farmacia Nueva*, ½ block from Church, has remedies for *soroche*.

Directory

The border bridge is 10 blocks from La Quiaca bus terminal, 15 minutes walk (taxi US$1). Argentine office open 24 hrs; on Saturday, Sunday, and holidays there is a special fee of US$1.50 which may or may not be charged. If leaving Argentina for a short stroll into Villazón, show your passport, but do not let it be stamped by Migración, otherwise you will have to wait 48 hours before being allowed back into Argentina. For immigration formalities in Bolivia, see page 304. Formalities on entering Argentina are usually very brief at the border but thorough customs searches are made 100 km south at Tres Cruces. Travellers who need a visa to enter Bolivia are advised to get it before arriving in La Quiaca.

Border with Bolivia
Argentine time is 1 hr later than Bolivia

Argentina

Parque Nacional Calilegua

Libertador Gen San Martín is a sugar town 113 km northeast of Jujuy on Route 34 to southeastern Bolivia. It is a base for exploring the **Parque Nacional Calilegua**, an area of peaks and sub-tropical valleys and cloud forest, reached by dirt road from just north of the town. In El Libertador there are several hotels, some **C** *Posada del Sol*, Los Ceibo y Pucará, T03886-424900, posadadelsol@cooperlib.com.ar, with breakfast, pool, to **D** *Artaza*, Victoria 891, T03886-423214, with breakfast, **E** without bath, and **E** *Residencial Gloria*, Urquiza 270, with hot water. For meals, try *Sociedad Boliviana*, Victoria 711, where the locals eat. Also *Del Valle*, Entre Ríos 793. There is a tourist offices at the bus terminal.

In the park, the best trek is to the summit of Cerro Amarillo (3,720 m), five days round trip from Aguas Negras. The first park ranger's house is at Aguas Negras (Guillermo Nicolossi). (Camping nearby; drinking water from river nearby, and some cooking facilities and tables.) 13 km further along the trail is the second ranger house (Walter Maciel), at Mesada de las Colmenas (ask permission at the first ranger house to camp here). 10 km from here is the north boundary of the park, marked by a monolith, and where the most interesting birds can be seen. Best time for visiting is outside the rainy season (November-March). ■ *Park headquarters are on San Lorenzo s/n, in Calilegua, 5 km from Libertador, T03886-422046, pncalilegua@cooperlib.com.ar   The park entrance is 10 km along the dirt road (hitching from Libertador possible), which climbs through the park and beyond to Valle Grande (basic accommodation and food supplies from shops), 90 km from Libertador.*

Colour map 6, grid C3

Over 300 species of bird including the red-faced guan and condors. Among the 60 species of mammal are tapir, puma, taruca or Andean deer and otters

Two bus companies leave Libertador daily at 0800 (except Wed) going across the park to **Valle Grande** (US$5, 6 hrs), returning the same day. *Remise* charges about US$3 from Libertador to Park entrance.

Transport

From Libertador, Route 34 runs northeast 244 km, to the Bolivian border at Pocitos (also called Salvador Mazza) and Yacuiba (see Eastern Bolivia, page 325). It passes through **Embarcación** and **Tartagal** (good regional museum, director Ramón Ramos very informative). In **Pocitos**, the border town, is **F** *Hotel Buen Gusto*, just tolerable. From Yacuiba, across the border, buses go to Santa Cruz de la Sierra. Customs at Pocitos is not to be trusted (theft reported) and overcharging for 'excess baggage' on buses occurs. ■ *Several bus companies including* Atahualpa *have services from the border to Salta, Tucumán and other cities.*

Routes to Bolivia

An alternative route is via Aguas Blancas. At Pichanal, 85 km northeast of Libertador, Route 50 heads north via **Orán**, an uninteresting place (*Population*: 60,000). **C** *Alto Verde*, Pellegrini 671, T421214, parking, pool, a/c. **D** *Res Crisol*, López y Planes, hot water. Recommended.

Aguas Blancas on the border is 53 km from Orán (restaurants, shops, but no accommodation, nowhere to change money and Bolivianos are not accepted south of Aguas Blancas). The passport office is open from 0700 to 1200 and 1500 to 1900. Insist on getting an exit stamp. Buses run from Bermejo, across the river (ferry US$0.50), to Tarija. Northwest of Aguas Blancas is the **Parque Nacional Baritú**, covering a mountainous area of pristine cloud forest. There are no facilities. Ranger post at Los Pozos, northwest of the park.

Transport **Buses** Between Aguas Blancas and Orán buses run every 45 mins, US$1, luggage checks on bus. Direct buses to Güemes, 8 a day, US$6.50; through buses to **Salta**, *La Veloz del Norte*, *Panamericano* and *Atahualpa*, several daily, US$7-9, 7-10 hrs. To **Tucumán**, *La Veloz del Norte*, *Panamericano* and *La Estrella*, 1 a day each company. To **Jujuy** with *Balut* and *Brown*, 3 daily. To **Embarcación**, US$2; some services from Salta and Jujuy call at Orán en route to **Tartagal** and **Pocitos**. Note that buses are subject to slow searches for drugs and contraband.

Argentina

Buenos
Aires

The West

From the Pampa to the heights of Aconcagua and the Uspallata Pass, en route to Santiago, Mendoza is a centre of wine making, fruit growing, winter sports (several ski resorts nearby) and climbing.

On route 7 to San Luis from Buenos Aires is **Junín** (*Population*: 63,700. *Phone code*: 02362), 256 km west of Buenos Aires across the pampa, close to lagoons from which fish are taken to the capital. Eva Perón was born near the city. There are hotels and restaurants.

San Luis Province

Phone code: 02652
Colour map 8, grid B2
Population: 150,000
Altitude: 765 m
770 km W of
Buenos Aires

The provincial capital, founded by Martín de Loyola, the governor of Chile, in 1596, **San Luis** stands at the south end of the Punta de los Venados hills. The area is rich in minerals including onyx. Visit the **Centro Artesanal San Martín de Porras**, run by the Dominican fathers, on Plaza Independencia, where rugs are woven. ■ *0700-1300 excluding Sat and Sun.* There is an excellent tourist office at Junín y San Martín and the Subsecretaría de Turismo is at 9 de Julio 934, T433853/0800-666 6176, www.sanluis.gov.ar

Sleeping **Several on Pres Illia** **A** *Quintana*, No 546, T/F438400. 4-star, best, without breakfast, large rooms, restaurant. **C** *Aiello*, No 431, T425609, F425694. With breakfast, a/c, spacious, garage. Recommended. **C** *Gran San Luis*, No 470, T425049, F430148. With breakfast, restaurant (closed weekends), pool. **C** *Grand Palace*, Rivadavia 657, T422059. With breakfast, parking, central, spacious, good lunches. **D** *Intihuasi*, La Pampa 815 (behind Casa de Cultura). Spotless, TV, lounge. Highly recommended. **E** *San Antonio*, Ejército de los Andes 1602, T422717. Without breakfast, restaurant. **Camping** Rio Volcán, 4 km from town.

16 km from San Luis is **L** *Potrero de los Funes*, T430125/420889, F423898 or BsAs 43134886, F3123876 (25 de Mayo 516, p 11), a luxury resort and casino on the lake of the same name, sports and watersports, lovely views.

Eating *El Cantón de Neuchatel*, San Martín 745, opposite Cathedral on main plaza. Open Sun, mod-
Most restaurants close est. *Michel*, Lafinur 1361. Good food and service. *Rotisería La Porteña*, Junín y Gral Paz.
at weekends. Hotel Good food, reasonable prices.
restaurants close Sun

Transport Bus terminal at Vía España between San Martín y Rivadavia. To **Buenos Aires**, US$21-27. To **Mendoza**, US$9, 3 hrs.

Northeast of the city are several ranges of hills, which are becoming more accessible **The Sierras** with the building of paved roads. The western edge of the sierras can be visited by **de San Luis** taking Route 9 northeast from San Luis via El Trapiche (bus from San Luis, US$4 return) to **Carolina**, where a disused goldmine can be seen. A statue of a gold miner overlooks the main plaza. There is *Hostería Las Verbenas*, T424425. Four-wheel drive vehicles can drive up Tomolasta mountain (2,000 m). From this road the Cuesta Larga descends to San Francisco del Monte de Oro, from where it is possible to follow Route 146 to Mina Clavero in Córdoba province.

The central part of the Sierras is best reached by Route 20 to **La Toma**, 70 km east of San Luís, the cheapest place to buy green onyx (**D** *Italia*, Belgrano 644, T421295, hot showers). North of La Toma a paved road runs as far as Libertador General San Martín (known as San Martín), 75 km, a good centre for exploring the rolling hills of the northern sierras (**E** *Hostería San Martín*, with bath and breakfast, meals served, good value, recommended).

Merlo (*Altitude*: 700 m. *Phone code*: 02656), almost at the San Luis-Córdoba border, is a small town on the western slopes of the Sierra de Comechingones. It enjoys a fresher climate than the pampas in summer, and the area is being promoted for its rich wildlife, particularly birds. There are many walks and excursions to *balnearios*, waterfalls and other attractions. Mountain biking, trekking, horse riding, fishing and jeep tours are all possible. *Valle del Sol*, T476109, has tours to Sierra de las Quijadas, minimum 6. The tourist office is at Mercau 605, T476078. There are many hotels, *hosterías* and *residenciales* both in the town and nearby. Most in Merlo are along Av del Sol. **A** *Altos del Rincón*, Av de los Césares 2977, T476333, very welcoming, nice rooms. ■ *Bus terminal 3 blocks from plaza. Frequent services to San Luis; to Buenos Aires*, TAC, Sierras Cordobesas *and* Chevallier, *US$21, 12 hrs; to Córdoba, TAC, 7 hrs.*

Mendoza

Situated at the foot of the Andes, **Mendoza** is a pleasant city at the centre of an expanding urban area. The city was colonized from Chile in 1561 and named in honour of the then governor of Chile. It was from here that the Liberator José de San Martín set out to cross the Andes, to help in the liberation of Chile. Mendoza was completely destroyed by fire and earthquake in 1861, so today it is essentially a modern city of low dwellings (as a precaution against earthquakes), thickly planted with trees and gardens. In the centre of the city is the **Plaza Independencia**, in the centre of which are the **Museo Municipal de Arte Moderno** and a theatre. On the west side are the Plaza Hotel, dating from the 1920s, and next door, the Teatro Independencia (seats US$10-15). Among the other pleasant squares nearby is the **Plaza España**, attractively tiled and with a mural displaying historical and literary scenes.

On the west side of the city is the great **Parque San Martín** containing watercourses and a 1 km-long artificial lake, where regattas are held. ■ *0900-1730 daily. US$3. Take bus 110 'Zoo'.* A new museum here is **Eureka**, a hands-on, interactive science park. ■ *In summer: Wed, Fri, Sun 0930-1230, 1630-2130, rest of year Tue-Fri 0930-1730, Sat-Sun 1030-1830, T425 3756. Take bus 30, 50, 60, 90, 100, 110.* There are views of the Andes (when the amount of floating dust will allow) rising in a blue-black perpendicular wall, topped off in winter with dazzling snow, into a china-blue sky. ■ *The park entrance is 10 blocks west of the Plaza Independencia, reached by bus 110 from the centre or the trolley from Sarmiento y 9 de Julio.* On a hill above the park is the Cerro de la Gloria, crowned by an astonishing monument to San Martín, a great rectangular stone block with bas-reliefs depicting various episodes in the equipping of the Army of the Andes and the actual crossing. ■ *An hourly bus ('Oro Negro') runs to the top of the Cerro de la Gloria from the information office at the entrance, US$3 – it's a long walk (45 mins).* **Plaza Pellegrini** (Avenue Alem y Av San Juan) is a beautiful small square where wedding photos are taken on Friday and Saturday nights.

Phone code: 0261
Colour map 8, grid B2
Population: city
148,000 (with suburbs,
600,000)
Altitude: 756 m
Annual mean
temperature: 19°C
1,060 km from
Buenos Aires
264 km from San Luis

Argentina

Argentina

Museums **Museo Histórico San Martín**, Av San Martín 1843, containing artefacts from San Martín's campaigns and other items, poorly organized. ■ *Mon-Fri 0930-1200, US$1.* **Museo del Pasado Cuyano**, Montevideo 544, large collection including sections on San Martín and history of Mendoza. ■ *Mon-Sat 0900-1300, 1600-2100, Sun 1600-2100, free.* The **Acuario Municipal** is underground at Buenos Aires e Ituzaingó, small but worth a visit. ■ *Daily 0900-1230, 1500-2030, US$0.50.* **Museo del Area Fundacional**, Alberdi y Videla Castillo, history of Mendoza, recommended. ■ *Tue-Sat 0800-1400, 1500-2100, Sun 1500-2100. Take bus 'T' or 110, US$1.50.* Across Ituzaingó from the museum (at Beltrán) are the ruins of the Jesuit church of **San Francisco**, part destroyed in the 1861 earthquake.

On the road south of the city to Luján de Cuyo (bus 200, 40 minutes) is the excellent Museo Provincial de Bellas Artes Emiliano Guiñazu, **Casa de Fader**, Carril San Martín 3671, Mayor Drummond, dedicated to Argentine artists, surrounded by sculpture in gardens. ■ *Tue-Fri 0830-1300, 1500-1930, Sat, Sun 1430-1930, US$1, T496 0224.*

Tours A large sign in Plaza Independencia shows a walking tour which takes about two hours. There is also a *Bus Turístico* which tours the city, with commentary from the driver. There are 14 stops and tourists can alight or join the bus at any point. Stops

www.mendoza.com.ar

Mendoza

Sleeping ■
1 Aconcagua *C1*
2 Argentino *B1*
3 Balbi *A1*
4 Campo Base *B1*
5 Del Sol *B2*
6 Escorial *A3*
7 Galicia *B3*
8 Horcones *A2*
9 Huentala *B2*
10 Mayo *B1*
11 Milena *C3*
12 Necochea *A1*
13 Nutibara *B1*
14 Pacífico *A2*
15 Palace & Restaurant Trevi *A2*
16 Petit *A1*
17 Plaza *B1*
18 Res Savigliano *B3*
19 RJ *A2*
20 San Martín *B1*
21 San Remo *A1*
22 Vendimia *A2*

Eating ●
1 Braserías & Mambrú *A1*
2 Centro Catalá *A2*
3 Green Apple *C1*
4 Las Tinajas *B2*
5 La Vuelta *C2*
6 Mesón Español *B2*
7 Montecatini *A1*
8 Nuevo Mundo *B1*
9 Pizzería Mi Querencia *A1*
10 Posta Las Marías *A1*
11 Sr Cheff *B2*

are clearly marked and the municipal tourist office issues a map. The bus waits for 15 minutes at Cerro de la Gloria. ■ *1000-1800 every 2 hrs, US$5 ticket valid for 24 hrs.*

Tourist offices Paseo Sarmiento/Garibaldi y San Martín, T420 1333, central, very helpful. Las Heras 670, T429 6298. At airport, T430 6484, helpful (0700-2300); at bus station, local D-1, T431 3001/431 5000, very helpful. The provincial office is at San Martín 1143, T420 2800. They have a list of reasonable private lodgings and a hotel booking service and other literature including lists of bodegas and an excellent free town and province map; the latter is also available at most kiosks.

Many bodegas welcome visitors (wine-making season March/April). To *La* **Wine** *Colina de Oro* winery, one of the world's biggest, take bus 150 (subnumber 151) marked 'Maipú' (every hour, 0900-1230, 1500-1800) from terminal platform 42 or 43, US$0.50, but check if winery is open before going, T497 2592, short tour, good tasting, restaurant. *La Rural* (*Ruttini*), Montecaseros s/n, Coquimbito, Maipú, T497 3590, a traditional bodega, is worth visiting, tours Monday-Saturday 1000-1630, Sunday 1000-1200, take bus 170 (173) from Rioja y Garibaldi, US$1. Its Museo del Vino (fascinating), T497 5004, is open Monday-Friday 0800-1100, 1500-1800 (sales oriented but no problem if you don't buy). (In Maipú itself, 15 km south of Mendoza, see the lovely square and eat at the Club Social, good simple food.) *Bodegas Escorihuela* (bus 'T' G Cruz from centre 9 de Julio, Godoy Cruz, or 170 (174)) T424 2744, tours Monday-Friday on the half-hour 0930-1530, but not 1330, has an international restaurant run by Francis Mallman. *Norton*, Ruta 15, Km 23.5, Perdriel, Luján, T488 0480, www.norton.com.ar Guided visits on the hour 0900-1700 (not 1300), take bus 380 from terminal. *Pequeña Bodega*, Ugarte 978, La Puntilla, Luján de Cuyo, with a small museum, T439 2094, Monday-Friday 0900-1300, 1600-2000, take bus 10 (Ugarte) on 25 de Mayo. The *Orfila* bodega in San Martín, T02623-420637, 40 km east, located in the house of the Liberator, also has a wine museum. Prices at the bodegas have roughly a 100% mark-up from supermarket prices. Many tourist agencies include the bodegas in their half-day or day-long tours but these visits are too short, with too few guides and little tasting – only of the cheaper wines, usually in plastic cups. Better are tours to micro-bodegas, which usually include three small wineries, such as *Domaine San Diego*, *Cabrini* and *Dolium*, with good a choice of tasting, explanations and extras like local olives and walnuts.

AL *Aconcagua*, 4-star, San Lorenzo 545, T420 4499, F420 2083. Good but expensive restau- **Sleeping** rant, pool, tourist advice and bookings available. **A** *Huentala*, Primitivo de la Reta 1007, T420 0766. 4-star, good. **B** *Nutibara*, Mitre 867, T429 6628, F429 6761. Central, a/c, parking, with breakfast, pool. Recommended. **C** *Argentino*, Espejo 455, Plaza Independencia, T/F425 4000. With breakfast, a/c, helpful, small restaurant, garage. **C** *Balbi*, Las Heras 340, T423 3500, F438 0626. Pool, a/c, nice rooms, helpful. **C** *Del Sol*, Garibaldi 80, T420 4296. Highly recommended, breakfast included. **C** *Palace*, Las Heras 70, T/F423 4200. A/c, with breakfast, good beds, central. **C** *San Martín*, Espejo 435, T438 0677. Recommended. **C** *Vendimia*, Godoy Cruz 101, T425 0675, F423 3099. Good.

All **C-D**: *Escorial*, San Luis 263, T425 4777. Recommended. *Horcones*, Av Las Heras 145, T425 0025. With breakfast, good value, helpful. *Mayo*, 25 de Mayo 1265, T425 4424. Includes breakfast, good value. Recommended. *Milena*, Pasaje Babilonia 17 (off San Juan near Don Bosco), T420 2490. Cosy, quiet, fan, nice atmosphere. *Necochea*, Necochea 541, T425 3501. Pleasant, cheerful, English spoken. *Pacífico*, San Juan 1407, T/F423 5444. Modern, comfortable, good value. *Petit*, Perú 1459, T423 2099. Without breakfast. Recommended. *RJ*, Las Heras 212, T/F438 0202. With breakfast, comfortable, helpful, English spoken. Recommended. *San Remo*, Godoy Cruz 477, T423 4068. Quiet, small rooms, TV, rooftop terrace, secure parking. Highly recommended.

E *Galicia*, Av San Juan 881, T420 2619. Convenient, cable TV, helpful, gloomy, kitchen facilites, a/c. **E** *Res Savigliano*, Palacios 944, T4237746, www.savigliano.com.ar Near bus terminal, without bath, shared rooms, with small breakfast, kitchen and laundry facilities, internet (strictly timed), rooftop terrace, popular, check out 1000, hot in summer. Recommended by many. **E** *Hosp Eben-Ezer*, Alberdi 580, T431 2635. Quiet, German spoken. **F** *Mariani*, Lamadrid 121, T431 9932. With breakfast, laundry, heating, good value. **Youth hostel E** *Campo Base*, Mitre 946, T429 0707, www.campo-base.com.ar Shared rooms, cooking and laundry facilities, very helpful, internet access, bike rental, information on climbing and permits for Aconcagua. **E** *Hostel Internacional Mendoza*, España 343, T424 0018, www.hostelmendoza.net Central, four beds per room and rooms with bath, cheaper for members, noisy, luggage store US$1 per day, internet access, laundry, climbing wall, good for outdoor activities.

Camping In Parque Gen San Martín, T/F4296656. At El Challao, open all year, 6 km west of the city centre, *Atsa*, friendly, swimming pool, good service, caters for families, noisy at weekends from disco; *Camping Suizo*, Av Champagnat s/n, T441 1406. Modern with pool, barbecues, hot showers. Recommended, but noisy at weekends. For both take bus 110 El Challao.

Eating

Tenedor libres are more expensive at weekends

Expensive: *Mesón Español*, Montevideo 244. Good food and atmosphere. *Montecatini*, Gral Paz 370. Wide variety, good food. *Posta Las Marías*, San Martín 914. English spoken, speciality is roast kid, good. *Trevi*, Las Heras 70. Good food and service. Recommended. **Mid-range**: *Boccaduro*, Mitre 1976. *Parrilla*, good. *Braserías*, Las Heras 510. Good for beef. *Centro Catalá*, San Juan 1436. Good fixed menu. Recommended. *Club Alemán*, Necochea 2261, Godoy Cruz. Recommended. *Il Tucco*, Emilio Civit 556, also in centre at Paseo Sarmiento 68. Excellent Italian restaurant. *Pizzería Mi Querencia*, Las Heras 523. Good pasta dishes and atmosphere. *La Vuelta*, San Lorenzo 65. *Parrilla libre*, good value, also pastas and other dishes, open at 1200 and 2100. Recommended. **Cheap**: *Mambrú*, Las Heras 510 y Chile. Good *tenedor libre*. *Nuevo Mundo*, Lavalle 126. Chinese, Italian, *parrilla*, good *tenedor libre*. *Sr Cheff*, de la Reta 1075. *Tenedor libre* for meat, fish, pastas. *Las Tinajas*, Lavalle 38. *Tenedor libre*, good variety. Recommended. *Trento*, Lavalle y San Juan. Recommended for pizza. Good value, and big 'super pancho' sandwiches in many places, including *Pizzería Sebastián*, Alem 431. *El Retamo*, Garibaldi 93. Vegetarian, take-away or sit outside only, cheap. *The Green Apple*, Colón 458. Excellent vegetarian with all-you-can-eat buffet. *Aranjuez*, Lavalle y San Martín. Nice café, good meeting place. Several good snack bars (known as *carrito* bars): *Tío Paco*, Salta y Alem; *Torombola*, San Juan 1348; *Don Claudio*, T Benegas 744. Also popular is the chain *Mr Dog*. Icecream at *Soppelsa*, Las Heras y España and at Sarmiento 55. Recommended.

Bars Calle Arístides Villanueva, the extension of Colón heading west, has several pleasant bars and pubs, eg *Blues Bar*, No 687, popular, reservations for eating T429 0240. Av Colón itself has also has bars and restaurants which are quieter than those on Av Las Heras. *Soul Café*, San Juan 456. Popular pub with jazz, lambada, blues, theatre performances, T432 0828.

Local holidays 18 Jan (*Crossing of the Andes*); 25 Jul (*Santiago Apóstol*); 8 Sep (*Virgin of Carmen de Cuyo*). The wine vintage festival, *Fiesta de la Vendimia*, is held in the amphitheatre of the Parque San Martín at the end of **Feb**. Hotels fill up fast. Prices rise at this time, and in Jul (the ski season) and **Sep** (*the spring festival*).

Shopping There are good souvenir, leather and handicraft shops on Av Las Heras. *Mercado Artesanal*, San Martín 1133, 0830-1930 daily, for traditional leather, baskets, weaving. Leather is good and cheap. *El Turista*, Las Heras 351, for regional souvenirs.

Sport **Bike rental**: *Piré*, Las Heras 615, T425 7699, US$4 per day. Also at *Campo Base*, see **Youth hostels**. **Mountain Climbing**: information from Tourist Office. *Club Andinista*, F L Beltrán 357, Gillén, T431 9870. There is a 3-day (Thu-Sat) climbing and trekking expedition via Godoy Cruz and Cacheuta to Cerro Penitentes (4,351 m), sleeping in mountain refuge, food included. See also page 151. **River rafting** is popular on the Río Mendoza; ask agencies for details.

Lots, especially on Paseo Sarmiento. *Aymara Turismo*, 9 de Julio 1023, T420 0607/420 5304, aymara@satlink.com Adventure tourism in general and Aconcagua climbs. *Casa Orviz*, Juan B Justo 550, T425 1281, www.orviz.com Guides, mules, transportation and hire of mountain trekking equipment. *Cuyo Travel*, Paseo Sarmiento 133, local 14. Discount for ISIC and youth card holders for trekking and climbing on Aconcagua. *Huentata*, Las Heras 695, T425 7444. Recommended. *Hunuc Huar Expediciones*, Av España 1340, p 8, oficina 7, and *Huera Pire*, Emilio Civit 320, specialize in assistance to climbers, especially on Aconcagua. *Inka Turismo Aventura*, Juan B Justo 343, Ciudad 5500, T/F425 0871, www.aconcagua.org.ar Private and programmed climbing expeditions. *Turismo Sepeán*, de la Reta 1088, T420 4162. Helpful. *Transport Star*, T423 4088, Roberto Gil. Good rates for excursions by van with driver.

Tour operators
Many agencies, including those in the terminal, run tours in summer to the Cristo Redentor statue via Puente del Inca, 12 hrs, only 15 mins at statue, city tours and bodega tours

Local Buses: most services have 2 numbers, a general number and a 'subnumber' in brackets which indicates the specific route. To travel on buses within and near the city you need a prepaid ticket, which is punched by a machine on the bus, sold in shops, the bus terminal and *Mendobus* ticket offices (eg Plaza Independencia at P Mendocinas y España): US$0.55 two trips, US$1.10 four, US$2.75 ten. A single ticket on the bus costs US$0.35. There are 2 trolley bus routes, red and blue, US$0.25. **Car hire**: *Herbst*, in *Hotel del Sol*, Garibaldi 82, T429 8403, reliable vehicles. Recommended. *Aires*, San Juan 1012, T4202666.

Transport

Long distance Air: El Plumerillo, 8 km north of centre, T448 0017, has *casa de cambio* and a few shops. Reached by *Manuel Tienda León*, remise, or taxi (US$5, US$4.50 and 4 respectively from airport to centre) and bus No 60 (subnumber 63) from Salta entre Alem y Garibaldi (US$0.55, 40 mins) which takes you close to the terminal (10 mins walk); make sure there is an 'Aeropuerto' sign on the driver's window. To **Buenos Aires**: 1 hr 50 mins, *AR, AIRG, Austral* and *Dinar*. *LanChile* to **Santiago**, daily. *Southern Winds* to **Córdoba** and many southern destinations. Airline information can be found at *TAC* office in the bus station (local D-16).

Buses: Terminal on east side of Av Videla, 15 mins walk from centre (go via Av Alem, which has pedestrian tunnel), T431 0543, with shops, post office, *locutorio*, tourist information and *Metro* supermarket (open till 2130). To **Bariloche**, *Andesmar* daily, *TAC*, 3 a week, US$35, 22 hrs, change in Neuquén, book well ahead. To **Córdoba**, several companies daily, 9 hrs, US$24. To **San Rafael**, many daily, US$6.50. To **San Juan** frequent, US$6.50, 2 hrs (several companies). To **La Rioja** US$12-14, 10 hrs, 5 a day, 3 companies; similarly to **Catamarca**, 12 hrs, daily, US$12-15. Several daily to **Tucumán**, US$18. To **Salta**, *Andesmar* 3 daily, and others, 20 hrs, US$20-25. To **Uspallata**, 5 a day with *Uspallata*, US$5.20, 2¼ hrs. To **Buenos Aires**, 2nd class US$18-24, 1st class daily, US$35 (lines including *Chevallier, TAC Coop, Jocoli*); *coche cama* daily at 1800 (*TAC, Emp Sendas*), US$50 including meals.

Transport to Santiago, Chile: Minibuses (US$15, 6 hrs) run by *Chi-Ar* and *Nevada* daily leave when they have 10 passengers. When booking, ensure that the receipt states that you will be picked up and dropped at your hotel; if not you will be dropped at the bus station. Buses to Santiago daily, several companies, *Chile Bus, Cata, Tur Bus, Tas Choapa* and *TAC* have been recommended, *Ahumada* has a *coche cama* at 0845; mixed reports on other companies. Most buses are comfortable, 6½-8 hrs, US$12, those with a/c and hostess service (includes breakfast) charge more, worth it when crossing the border as waiting time can be several hours. These companies also daily to **Viña del Mar** and **Valparaíso**, US$15. All companies in same part of Mendoza bus station: shop around. Children under 8 pay 60% of adult fare, but no seat; book at least 1 day ahead. Passport required, tourist cards given on bus. The ride is spectacular. Information at terminal. If you want to return, buy an undated return ticket Santiago-Mendoza; it is cheaper. For Chilean side, see under Santiago.

Other International buses: to **La Serena**, *Covalle, Cata* and others. To **Lima**, *El Rápido* Mon, Wed, Sat 0830, and *Ormeño*, T431 4913, Wed, Thu, Sun.

Airline offices *Aerolíneas Argentinas/Austral*, Paseo Sarmiento 82, T420 4143/0810-2228 6527. *AIRG*, Av España 1002 y Rivadavia, T4231000 (*Varig* also at this address). *Dinar*, Sarmiento 119, T/F420 4520. *Southern Winds*, España 943, T429 3200. *LanChile*, Rivadavia 135, T425 7900. **Banks** Many ATMs taking international cards. *American Express* agent, *Isc Viajes*, Av España 1016, T425 9259. Many

Directory

cambios along San Martín. *Casas de cambio* open till 2000 Mon-Fri, and some open Sat morning. **Communications** Internet: Several internet cafés in the centre and a number of *locutorios* have internet, eg Espejo 599, Sarmiento 202 and José Vicente Zapata 191, T4201934, English spoken. **Post Office:** San Martín y Colón, Mon-Fri 0800-2000, Sat 0900-1300, *poste restante* US$1.50 per item. *UPS*, 9 de Julio 803, T423 7861. **Telephone:** Chile 1584; San Martín 998. **Cultural centres** Alianza Francesa, Chile 1754, T423 4614. **Instituto Dante Alighieri** (Italy), Espejo 638, Mon, Wed, Fri 1730-2100. **Amicana** (Argentine-North American institute), Rivadavia 470, Mon-Fri 0830-1230, 1600-2030, very good library. **Goethe Institut**, San Martín y Morón, Mon-Fri, 0800-1200, 1600-2230, German newspapers, Spanish classes, very good. **Consulates** Bolivia, Garibaldi 380, T429 2458. **Chile**, Emilio Civit 599, T425 4344. **Spain**, Agustín Alvarez 455, T425 3947. **Italy**, Necochea 712, T423 1640. **France**, Houssay 828, T429 8339. **Germany**, Montevideo 127, p 1 D6, T429 6539. **Finland**, Boulogne Sur Mer 631, T424 0777. **Israel**, Lamadrid 738, T428 2140. **Language schools** *Sra Inés Perea de Bujaldon*, Rioja 620, T429 0429, teaches Spanish to German speakers. Recommended. **Medical facilities** Lamaggiore, Boulogne Sur Mer 2500, T429 9364, good public general hospital. Medical emergencies T428 0000. Pharmacies open 0800-2400: **Del Aguila**, San Martín y Buenos Aires, T423 3391, and **Del Puente**, Las Heras 201. **Useful addresses** *ACA*, Av San Martín 985, T420 2900, and Av Bandera de los Andes y Gdor Videla, T431 3510. *Asatej* , San Martín 1360, Loc 16, T/F429 0029, mendoza@asatej.com.ar Mon-Fri 0900-1300, Sat 0930-1330. **Migraciones**, San Martín 1859.

Ski resorts **Vallecito** (season July-September) is a small ski resort 21 km from Potrerillos (see below). It has a ski-lodge, four *refugios*, ski school and restaurant. **A** *Gran Hotel*, T423 3000, with meals. In summer you can hike from Potrerillos. On the first day you will see desert scenery, blooming cactus flowers, birds and an occasional goat or cow. The second day you walk surrounded by peaks, a steep but not difficult climb to the San Antonio refuge, usually open with beds and meals.

Los Penitentes, a small ski resort 165 km west of Mendoza, is named after the majestic mass of pinnacled rocks, passed on the highway to Chile. From their base (easily reached with a guide from Puente del Inca, see below), the higher rocks look like a church and the smaller, sharper rocks below give the impression of a number of cowled monks climbing upwards. Skiing is good with few people on slopes.

Sleeping B *Ayelén*, in middle of village, T425 9990. Comfortable. **D** *La Taberna del Gringo*, Km 151, Villa Los Penitentes. Recommended. And others. 5 km from Puente del Inca on the road to Mendoza is **C** *Cruz de Caña* ski club, only open in season, with comfortable dormitories, includes meals, and a good restaurant. The owner organizes trekking expeditions to Plaza de Mulas on Aconcagua.

Mendoza to Chile

The route to Chile is sometimes blocked by snow in winter: if travelling by car in June-October enquire about road conditions from *ACA* in Mendoza (see Useful addresses). Officially, driving without snow chains and a shovel is prohibited between Uspallata and the border, but this can be resolved in a friendly way with border police. Both *ACA* and Chilean Automobile Club sell, but do not rent, chains.

Uspallata
Phone code: 02624
Colour map 8, grid A1

Route 7 is the obligatory route for motorists to the Chilean border. It involves a detour while a dam is being built between Cacheuta and **Potrerillos**. Leave the city by Av J Vicente Zapata, which takes you onto Access Route 7. When you reach Route 40 (there is a statue of a condor here), carry on a further 17 km to a well-marked detour sign to Potrerillos, Uspallata and Chile. Take this until you get back onto Route 7. From Mendoza to the Chilean border is 234 km via the detour. At Potrerillos, **C** *Gran Hotel Potrerillos*, Ruta Nacional 7, Km 50, T02624-482010, with breakfast, faded resort hotel, nice location, pool. Good *ACA* campsite, T482013, well-shaded, with pool, clean. On this route, the only settlement of any size (and still expanding) is **Uspallata**, 52 km from Potrerillos. 5 km from Uspallata are the ruins of Las Bóvedas, built by the Huarpe Indians under the Jesuits, and an Inca *tambería*;

there is a small, interesting museum. They are just off the road which leads to Barreal and Calingasta (see page 156), unpaved for its first part, rough and tricky when the snow melts and floods it in summer. The tourist office in Uspallata keeps unreliable hours. **A** *Valle Andino*, Ruta 7, T420033, good rooms and restaurant, heating, pool, includes breakfast. **B** *Hotel Uspallata*, T420003, nice location, half board, good service and value. **D** *Hostería Los Cóndores*, T420002, good restaurant. Several *cabañas*. **Camping** Municipal site, US$4 per tent, hot water but dirty showers and toilets, poor. *La Estancia de Elias*, Km 1146, good cheap restaurant opposite Shell station. *Bodega del Gato*, in the centre, is a good bar with a knowledgeable owner. There are food shops (all closed in afternoon, reopen at 1800), bakeries, eating places, a post office and a Shell station with motel, restaurant, shop and *locutorio* open 0900-2200. *Desnivel Turismo Aventura*, Galería Comercial local 7, T420275, gustavomestre@infovia.com.ar Offers rafting, riding, mountain biking, trekking, climbing, skiing, recommended.

This is a base for exploring the surrounding mountains of great grandeur. The natural bridge after which the place is named is one of the wonders of South America; it crosses the Río Mendoza at a height of 19 m, has a span of 21 m, and is 27 m wide, and seems to have been formed by sulphur-bearing hot springs. Watch your footing on the steps; extremely slippery. There are hot thermal baths just under the bridge, very dilapidated, but a new bath has been built between the bridge and the small church, good for a soak with magnificent scenery. Horse treks go to Los Penitentes. Los Horcones, the Argentine customs post, is 1 km east: from here you can visit the green lake of Laguna los Horcones: follow signs to **Parque Provincial Aconcagua**, 2 km, where there is a Ranger station, excellent views of Aconcagua, especially morning; free camping, open climbing season only. From here a trail continues to the Plaza de Mulas base camp.

Puente del Inca
Colour map 8, grid B2
Altitude: 2,718 m
72 km W of Uspallata

Argentina

Sleeping **B** *Hostería Puente del Inca*, T438 0480. Less off-season, very pleasant atmosphere, but overpriced and more expensive if booked in Mendoza. **E** *Parador del Inca*. Dormitories, with breakfast, basic, cheap meals. Also in old railway station **E**, T432 1485 (only place open in low season – take a warm sleeping bag). Also meals. **F** *Refugio de Montaña*, small dormitories in the army barracks, helpful. **Camping** Possible next to the church, if your equipment can withstand the winds, also at Lago Horcones inside the park.

Transport **Buses**: *Expreso Uspallata* from Mendoza for **Uspallata** and **Puente del Inca**, US$6.25, 3½ hrs, 2 a day in the morning, returning from Puente del Inca in the afternoon. Uspallata-Puente del Inca US$2.50. Local buses also go on from Puente del Inca to **Las Cuevas**, *Expreso Uspallata*, US$6 return (**NB** take passport). You can go to Chile from Puente del Inca with *Tur Bus* at 1000 and 1400, US$10, but be sure to ask for an international ticket.

West of Puente del Inca (you can walk along the old railway, beware unsafe old planks at the end), on the right, there is a good view of Aconcagua, sharply silhouetted against the blue sky. In 1985, a complete Inca mummy was discovered at 5,300 m on the mountain.

The best time for climbing Aconcagua is from end-December to February. For trekking or climbing it is first necessary to obtain a permit: three-day trekking US$7.50 low season, US$15 high, five days' trekking US$15 low, US$20 high. For climbing a 20-day permit is required, US$40 15-30 November and 21 February-15 March, US$60 10-14 December and 1-20 February, US$80 15 December-31 January. Permits may be bought, in person, at **Subsecretaría de Turismo**, Avenue San Martín 1155, Mendoza, Monday-Friday 0800-1800, Saturday-Sunday 0900-1300.

There are two access routes: Río Horcones and Río Vacas, which lead to the two main base camps, Plaza de Mulas and Plaza Argentina respectively. Río Horcones starts a few kilometres from Puente del Inca, at the Horcones ranger station. About 80% of climbers use this route. From here you can go to Plaza de Mulas (4,370 m) for

Aconcagua
Colour map 8, grid B2
Altitude: 6,959 m
The highest peak in the Americas

the North Face, or Plaza Francia (4,200 m) for the South Face. The intermediate camp for either is Confluencia (3,300 m), four hours from Horcones. Río Vacas is the access for those wishing to climb the Polish Glacier. The Plaza Argentina base camp (200 m) is three hours from Horcones and the intermediate camps are Pampa de Leñas and Casa de Piedra. From Puente del Inca mules are available (list at the *Dirección de Recursos Naturales Renovables*, Parque Gral San Martín, 50 m from main gate, Mendoza, T425 2090, about US$250 for 60 kg of gear one way; arrange return before setting out for a reduced two-way price). This only takes you to Plaza de Mulas, near which is the highest hotel in the world (see below) and an accident prevention and medical assistance service (climbing season only); crowded in summer. The same service is offered at Plaza Argentina in high season. Climbers should make use of this service to check for early symptoms of mountain sickness and oedema. Take a tent able to withstand 100 mph/160 kmph winds, and clothing and sleeping gear for temperatures below –40° C. Allow at least one week for acclimatization at lower altitudes before attempting the summit (four days from Plaza de Mulas). Hotel *Plaza de Mulas*, **AL** pp full board, **C** without meals, good food, information, medical treatment, recommended, also camping area; closed in winter. In Mendoza you can book *refugio* reservations and programmes which include trekking, climbing to the summit, with hotel accommodation or camping, T/F Mendoza 0261-438 0383, 9 de Julio 1126. In Buenos Aires, representation at *Proterra Turismo*, Lavalle 750, p 20 D, T/F4326 2639.

Trekking and climbing programmes can be booked through agencies in Buenos Aires (eg *Proterra*, see above) and Mendoza. Treks and climbs are also organized by *Sr Fernando Grajales*, the famous climber, at Moreno 898, 5500 Mendoza, T493830, expediciones@grajales.net (or T421 4330 and ask for *Eduardo Ibarra* at *Hotel Plaza de Mulas* for further information), and by *Roger Cangiani* at *Campo Base* in Mendoza, T429 0707, www.campo-base.com.ar Near the Cementerio is *Los Puquios*, T461-317603, camping, mules, guides. Other guides can be found at the airport in Mendoza and further information from *Dirección de Recursos Naturales Renovables* (see also under Mendoza: **Travel agents**, for example *José Orviz* and *Aymara Turismo*; also *Aconcagua Trek – Rudy Parra*, T431 7003, aconcagua@rudyparra.com, and *Daniel Alessio Expediciones*, T496 2201, aconcagua@alessio.com.ar)

Las Cuevas & Cristo Redentor

Beyond **Las Cuevas**, an incomplete tourist complex 16 km from Puente del Inca, the road, fully paved, goes through the 3.2-km Cristo Redentor toll road tunnel to Chile (open 24 hours; US$1 for cars and VW buses, cyclists are not allowed to ride through, ask the officials to help you get a lift). The old road over La Cumbre pass via the statue of El Cristo Redentor (Christ the Redeemer) is now closed to through traffic. The 8 m statue was erected jointly by Chile and Argentina in 1904 to celebrate King Edward VII's decision in the boundary dispute of 1902, and is completely dwarfed by the spectacular landscape. (The road from the tunnel to the statue is closed for the season after the first snowfall in April.) To see the statue you must either go on a 12-hour excursion from Mendoza, worth it for the walk itself or walk from Las Cuevas, 4½ hours up, two hours down. You should be in good condition and the weather should be fine. In a private car you drive part of the way when the snow has melted; 4WD needed for the whole way.

Sleeping & transport

B *Hostel Internacional Aconcagua de Las Cuevas*. 70 beds, kitchens, affiliated to *Red Argentina de Alojamientos para Jóvenes*. *Campo Base* in Mendoza (**Youth hostels**) has *Hostal Las Cuevas*, **E**, T429 0707 in Mendoza to make a reservation, mendoza4@hostels.org.ar *Nido de Cóndores* restaurant. Communications centre with phones, fax and email. *Expreso Uspallata* buses to Mendoza (office serves meals).

Border with Chile

The Chilean border is beyond Las Cuevas, but all Argentine entry and exit formalities for cars and buses are dealt with at the Argentine customs post, Ingeniero Roque Carranza at Laguna Los Horcones, near Las Cuevas. Customs are open 0730-2300.

For Chilean immigration formalities, see page 635. Car drivers can undertake all formalities in advance at *migraciones* in Mendoza, or Uspallata while refuelling. For the Chilean consulate, see under Mendoza. **NB** No visas into Chile are available at the border. You can hitchhike, or possibly bargain with bus drivers for a seat, from Los Horcones to Santiago, but if you are dropped at the entrance to the tunnel, you cannot walk through. Customs officers may help by asking motorists to take hitchhikers through to Chile.

South of Mendoza

San Rafael lies in an area where irrigation makes possible fruit-growing in large quantities at the foot of the Andes. A road runs west over El Pehuenche pass to Talca (Chile). Two bodegas, *Suter* and *Bianchi* (Monte Caseros y E Civit, recommended) can be visited. There is a helpful tourist office at Av H Yrigoyen y Balloffet. Ask for Aldo or Hector Seguín at España 437 for trekking and climbing information. A small but interesting natural history museum is 6 km southeast of town at Isla Río Diamante ■ *Tue-Sun 0800-1200, 1500-1900, free;* Iselin *bus along Av JA Balloffet.* **D** *Kalton*, Yrigoyen 120, T430047, excellent, safe, good value; and others. **Youth hostel E** *Puesta del Sol*, Deán Funes 998, 3 km, T434881, mendoza3@hostels.org.ar **Campsites** Site at Isla Río Diamante, 15 km southeast. ■ *Buses to Mendoza, US$6.50; to Neuquén, US$14, 9 hrs.*

Southwest of San Rafael is the **Cañon de Atuel**, a spectacular gorge 20 km long with polychrome rocks. Buses go to the Valle Grande dam at the near end of the canyon on Thursday and Sunday, US$2. There is no public transport through the gorge to El Nihuel. Around Valle Grande there is plenty of accommodation and campsites, river rafting and horse riding. Travel agencies in Mendoza run all-day excursions to the canyon.

At 182 km southwest of San Rafael, a road heads west into the Andes. It passes **Los Molles**, Km 30, where there are thermal springs and accommodation in **B** range. Further along the Las Leñas road is the **Pozo de las Animas**, two natural pits, both filled with water (the larger is 80 m deep); when the wind blows across the holes, a ghostly wail is heard, hence the name (Well of the Spirits).

At the end of Valle Los Molles is **Las Leñas**, with 41 pistes for good skiing, and 11 ski-lifts. Beyond Las Leñas the road continues into Valle Hermoso, accessible December-March only. There are several hotels, **L** (T for all 471100) and a disco, shop renting equipment and expensive restaurant. For cheaper accommodation stay in Los Molles or Malargüe. ■ *Buses from San Rafael US$3.75, colectivo US$12.*

Further south on Route 40, Malargüe is developing as a centre for adventure tourism. Tourist information on Malargüe can be obtained at *Casa de Malargüe*, España 1075, Mendoza. The **Laguna Llancanelo**, 37 km southeast, is one of the main Argentine nesting areas of the Chilean flamingo. The lake is best visited in spring when the birds arrive. Details from the tourist office or the Natural Science Museum. Fishing licences from the Dirección de los Bosques, next to the tourist office. ■ *There are flights in the skiing season. Buses from Mendoza are* TAC *and* Expreso Uspallata, *while* Transporte Vuento Sur *run a minibus service, 4 hrs, US$12. Fare from* San Rafael, *US$9, 3 hrs.*

Sleeping B *Hotel del Turismo*, San Martín 224, T/F471042. With breakfast, heating, good restaurant. Recommended. **B** *Portal del Valle*, Ruta 40 Norte, T471294, F471811. Sauna, pool, restaurant, also suites. **C** *El Cisne*, Villegas 278, T471350. Good value. Recommended. **C** *Rioma*, Inalicán 68, T471065. With breakfast, heating. **D** *Llancanelo*, Av Rufino Ortega 158, T470689. With breakfast, use of kitchen, internet access, helpful, good value, discount for long stay. Several others.

Guides and tours *AGAPE Mendoza* (Asociación Grupo Antropo-Paleonto-Espeleológico); contact Dora de and Héctor Rofsgaard, Beltrán 414, T02627-471536.

San Rafael
Phone code: 0627
Colour map 8, grid B2
Population: 72,200
242 km S of Mendoza

Argentina

Altitude: 2,250 m
An international
ski resort

Malargüe
Phone code: 0627
Colour map 8, grid B2
Population: 8,600

Hotels issue guests
with a voucher for
50% discount on
Las Leñas lift pass

North of Mendoza

The oases of San Juan, La Rioja and Catamarca lie between the plains and the Andes. Interesting anthropomorphic rock formations and petroglyphs can be seen, especially in Valle de la Luna and Puerta de Talampaya. The skeletons of the oldest known dinosaurs on the planet were found in this region. Of the three oases in the more arid zone north of Mendoza, San Juan is the most prosperous, wine and olives support La Rioja, but Catamarca is economically depressed.

San Juan

Phone code: 02646
Colour map 8, grid A2
Population: 122,000
Altitude: 650 m
177 km N of Mendoza

San Juan was founded 1562 by Don Juan Jufré de Loaysa y Montese and is capital of its namesake province. Nearly destroyed by a 1944 earthquake, the centre is well laid-out, with a modern cathedral. The area is famous for its wine: 'to be between San Juan and Mendoza' is an Argentine expression for having drunk too much. One of the country's largest wine producers, *Bodegas Bragagnolo*, on the outskirts of town at Ruta 40 y Av Benavídez, Chimbas, can be visited (bus 20 from terminal; guided tours daily 0830-1330, 1530-1930, not Sunday). **Museo Casa Natal de Sarmiento**, Sarmiento Sur 21. Birthplace of Domingo Sarmiento (President of the Republic, 1868-1874, also an important historian/educator). ■ *Tue-Fri and Sun 0830-1330, 1500-2000, Mon and Sat 0830-1330, US$1, free Sun.* **Museo de Ciencias Naturales**, Predio Ferial, Av España y Maipú, includes fossils from Ischigualasto Provincial Park (see below). ■ *Mon-Sat 0830-1300, US$0.50.* **Museo Histórico Celda de San Martín**, Laprida 57 Este, including the restored cloisters and two cells of the Convent of Santo Domingo. San Martín slept in one of these cells on his way to lead the crossing of the Andes. ■ *Mon-Sat 0900-1400, US$1.* Tourist office is at Sarmiento Sur 24 y San Martín, T422 2431, F422 5778, www.ischigualasto.com Helpful, good brochures, open Mon-Fri, 0730-2030, Sat-Sun 0900-2000; also at bus terminal.

Excursions The **Museo Arqueológico** of the University of San Juan at La Laja, 20 km north, contains an outstanding collection of prehispanic indigenous artefacts, including several well-preserved mummies. Inexpensive thermal baths nearby. ■ *Daily 0930-1700, US$2. Bus 20 from San Juan, 2 a day: take the first (at 0830) to give time to return.*

Vallecito, 64 km east, has a famous shrine to the **Difunta Correa**, an unofficial saint whose infant, according to legend, survived at her breast even after the mother's death from thirst in the desert. During Holy Week, up to 100,000 pilgrims visit the site, some crawling 100 m on their knees. See the remarkable collection of personal items left in tribute, including number plates from all over the world and even one policeman's detective school diploma! (*Res Difunta Correa*). For information, consult Fundación Vallecito at Caucete.

Sleeping **A** *Alkázar*, Laprida 82 Este, T421 4965, www.alkazarhotel.com.ar Includes breakfast, garage, good. **A** *Nogaró*, de la Roza 132 Este, T422 7501/5. Pool, a/c, central, TV, parking. **B** *Capayan*, Mitre 31 Este, T421 4222. Very good. **B** *Jardín Petit*, 25 de Mayo 345 Este, T421 1825. Hot water, pricey, parking next door. **C** *Bristol*, Entre Ríos 368 Sur, T422 2629. A/c, hot water. **C** *Embajador*, Rawson 25 Sur, T422 5520. Large rooms, pleasant, café, good value. Several *residenciales* (**C-D**) along Av España, blocks 100-600 Sur. **D** *Hispano Argentino*, just outside bus station to the right. With breakfast, fan, a/c extra, snack bar, **F** with shared bath. **E** *Res 12 de Diciembre*, Sarmiento 272 Norte, no sign, ring bell beneath street number on wall. Fan, family atmosphere, laundry, also monthly rental. **E** *9 de Julio*, 9 de Julio 147 Oeste, no sign, owner Gregorio Romero. **F** without bath, quiet, family atmosphere, longer stays possible. **E** *Roy*, Entre Ríos 180 Sur, T422 4391. Reasonable, ask for room away from street. **Camping** At Chimbas, 7 km north.

Eating *Wiesbaden*, Circunvalación y San Martín. German-style, pleasant setting. *Soychú*, de la Roza 223 Oeste. Excellent vegetarian food. *Club Sirio Libanés 'El Palito'*, Entre Ríos 33 Sur. Pleasant decor, good food. *Las Leñas*, San Martín 1670 Ote. Parrilla, pricey. Recommended. *Listo El Pollo*, Av San

Martín y Santiago del Estero. Very good. *Amistad*, Rivadavia 47 Oeste. Chinese, good value, lots of choice. Many *pizzerías*, *confiterías*, and sidewalk cafés. *Fonon Bar*, Sarmiento Sur y Mitre Oeste. Snack bar, open 24 hrs, with *locutorio*. *Marilyn Bar*, San Martín y Mendoza. Late night drinks.

San Juan is known for its fine bedspreads, blankets, saddle cloths and other items made from sheep, llama and guanaco wool, fine leather, wooden plates and mortars and, of course, its wines. *Mercado Artesanal* at España y San Luis worth a visit. **Bicycle repairs**: *Petit Bicicletería*, San Martín y La Rioja, helpful.

Shopping

Fascinatur (Rafael Joliat), Rem esc de San Martín 1085 Oeste, Barrio Rivadavia, 5400 San Juan, T/F434 3014, fascinatur_dahu@arnet.com.ar Recommended for 4WD treks to remote areas, trekking, mountaineering, mountain biking, riding, speaks French, English, German. *Raul Horacio Despous*, Mendoza 4619 Sur, T424 2688, T156-606960 (mob). Car or van tours to Valle de la Luna and other parts of San Juan, very knowledgeable, excellent service.

Tour operators

Long distance Air: Chacritas Airport, 14 km southeast. From **Buenos Aires** with *AR/Austral* (Av San Martín 215 Oeste, T0810-2228 6527, or 425 0487) and *AIRG* (de la Roza 176 Este, T427 2744), who also fly from Mendoza. **Buses**: Terminal at Estados Unidos y Santa Fe, 9 blocks east of centre (buses 33 and 35 go through the centre), T422 1604. To **La Rioja**, 6 hrs, US$10, 4 companies. **Catamarca**, 4 companies, US$18. **Tucumán**, 5 companies, US$21. **Córdoba**, *Socasa, 20 de Julio, Autotransportes San Juan*, US$17 *coche cama*. **BsAs** (*Autotransporte San Juan, TAC* and others, US$27 *semi cama*, US$35 *coche cama*). To **San Agustín** with *Vallecito*, 3 a day, US$9. Hourly departures to and from **Mendoza** with *TAC* and *Media Agua* and others, 2 hrs, US$6.50, try to sit in the shade (on west side in the morning, east in evening). Also services to provincial tourist destinations.

Transport

Banks Many *Baneloc* and *Link* ATMs accepting international credit cards. *Cambio Santiago*, Gen Acha 52 Sur, weekdays until 2100, Sat until 1300. **Communications** Internet: Several *locutorios* have internet, those at Rivadavia y Acha, on the plaza, and Mendoza 139 Sur are open on Sun. Also *Cyber Café*, Rivadavia 12 Este, T420 1397. *Interredes*, Laprida 362 Este, T427 5790. *IAC*, Acha 142 Norte, T427 7104. **Cultural centres** Alianza Francesa, Mitre 202 Oeste. Library open Mon and Wed 0900-1300, 1800-2100. **Centro Cultural San Juan**, Gral Paz 737 Este. Concerts and other events. **Useful addresses** ACA, 9 de Julio y Rawson, T421 4205, information on routes, helpful.

Directory
Banks open 0700-1200

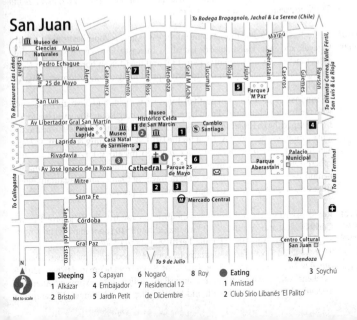

San Juan

Sleeping ■
1 Alkázar
2 Bristol
3 Capayan
4 Embajador
5 Jardín Petit
6 Nogaró
7 Residencial 12 de Diciembre
8 Roy

Eating ●
1 Amistad
2 Club Sirio Libanés 'El Palito'
3 Soychú

Not to scale

West of San Juan **Calingasta**, 135 km west of San Juan along scenic provincial route 12 (open westbound mornings, eastbound afternoons), lies in the valley of same name (annual cider festival in April). **C** *Calingasta*, T422014, pool, full board available. **D** *La Capilla*, T421033, includes breakfast, basic but very clean, family run, the family also sells the *TAC* bus tickets, and has the only public telephone in the village; *Hospedaje Nora*, Plaza Patricias Sanjuaninas, T421027, very simple; municipal campsite. Meals at *Comedor Doña Gorda*. Tourist information at the Municipalidad, Lavalle y Sarmiento, T421066. **NB** Ruta 12 from San Juan along the canyon of the Río San Juan has been disrupted by work on two dams and is only open after 2000 and Sunday (one-way system as above). When the lakes are full of water, this road will be permanently closed. Alternative, unpaved roads are in use, north via El Puntudo (Rutas 436/412), south via Los Berros, neither very good. Cyclists in this area should note that there is very little shade on any of these roads, fill up with water at every opportunity. The police should be consulted before cycling from Calingasta to San Juan.

40 km S of Calingasta on the road to Uspallata **Barreal** At El Leoncito (2,348 m), 26 km from Barreal there are two observatories (US$3, no public transport; tours can be arranged from San Juan, Av España 1512 Sur, T421 3653, or at *Hotel Barreal*) and a nature reserve with a semi-arid environment and interesting wildlife, ranger post at entrance, no facilities. For alternative tours, offroading, expeditions, *Fuga*, Sr Eduardo Conterno, Pres Roca s/n, T02648-441024/029, fugaevyt@infovia.com.ar Sr Ramón Luis Ossa, physical education teacher at Barreal's high school, runs mule treks into the Andes, crossing the foothills in summer, from 10 to 21 days between November and April; he can be reached at *Cabañas Doña Pipa*, Mariano Moreno s/n, 5405 Barreal, Pcia San Juan, T02648-441004. The *cabañas* sleep 5, with bath, kitchen, sitting room, comfortable. For tourist information, T02648-441066. **Sleeping and eating D** *Barreal*, San Martín s/n, T02648-441000, refurbished, good restaurant, pool, riding. **F** *Hotel Jorge*, clean, very simple. *Posada San Eduardo*, small, most rooms with bath, pleasant and relaxing. *Restaurante Isidoro*, Roca s/n, owned by local baker and sandyacht champion, reasonable, good set meals. ■ *Getting there: buses from San Juan daily,* El Triunfo, *0700, plus Mon, Wed, Fri, Sun at 2030 (return Sun, Mon 1330, 1600, Tue, Wed, Thu 1400, Fri, Sat 1600, and 0230 Mon, Wed), 5 hrs, US$6. No buses Barreal-Mendoza; ask for Sr Raul Escuela, Barrio Gendarmería, who runs a Renault Traffic to Mendoza, usually Sun afternoon.*

North of San Juan Route 40, the principal tourist route on the east Andean slope, heads north toward Cafayate and Salta, via San José de Jachal. At Talacasto, 55 km from San Juan, route 436 branches toward Las Flores (Km 180) and the Chilean border at Agua Negra pass (4,600 m; open only January to early April, immigration, customs and ACA at Los Flores).

San José de Jachal, 99 km north of Talacasto is a wine and olive-growing centre with many adobe buildings. From here, the undulating Route 40, paved but for the first 25 km to the La Rioja border, crosses dozens of dry watercourses. It continues to Villa Unión (see below), paved but for the last 15 km. **Sleeping & eating D** *Plaza*, San Juan 545, T420256. **F** *Doña Ilda Cañete*, Sarmiento 861, basic, family atmosphere, OK. *San Martín*, Juan de Echegaray 387, T420431, camping. Camping also behind ACA station at northeast edge of town. *El Chato Flores* restaurant, good. **Buses** *Expreso Argentino* bus from San Juan at 0730 arrives at 0940.

The parks of Ischigualasto & Talampaya *Colour map 8, grid A2 Home to the skeletons of the oldest known dinosaurs on earth and peculiar desert features* Route 141 runs across the south of the province towards La Rioja province and Córdoba. Just after Marayes (133 km), paved route 510 (poor in parts) goes north 135 km to **San Agustín del Valle Fértil** (**C** *Hostería Valle Fértil*, Rivadavia s/n, T02646-420015, vallefertil@alkazarhotel.com.ar Good, a/c, fine views, also has *cabañas*. *Hospedajes* include **F** pp *Los Olivos*, Santa Fe y Tucumán, T02646-420115, excellent value, with restaurant, and **F** pp *Ischigualasto*, Mitre y Aberstein, T02646-420146, both with bath and fan; families provide lodging; 2 campsites;

tourist information on plaza, *Empresa Mendoza* bus from Mendoza arrives 0200, better go from San Juan, *Vallecito*, 0700, 1900, four hours, a/c, US$9).

North of San Agustín, at a police checkpoint, 56 km by paved road, a side road goes northwest for 17 km to the 62,000 ha **Parque Provincial Ischigualasto** (a UNESCO World Heritage Site), also known as **Valle de la Luna** for its exotic desert landforms. Here the skeletons of the oldest known dinosaurs have been found (230 million years). ■ *US$2.50. Tours and access: There is one tour route, which lasts about 2½ hours, visiting only a part of the park but encompassing the most interesting sites. You have to go with a ranger and it can be crowded at holiday times. Tours from San Juan, US$25 (including breakfast, lunch and tour), 14 hrs; from San Agustín US$10 for a guide (in both towns, ask at tourist office). Taxi to park US$25 (recommended if there are four to five people), more out of season. You can camp opposite the ranger station, which has a small museum, but bring all food and water; expensive confitería next to ranger station.*

Just beyond the police checkpoint, near Los Baldecitos, paved Route 150 heads east to Patquía and then to La Rioja or Chilecito. From the junction provincial Route 26 heads north to Villa Unión. 58 km north of the junction a paved road goes east to the **Parque Nacional Talampaya**, another collection of spectacular desert landforms and a UNESCO World Heritage Site (*Refugio* near the entrance, sleeping bag essential). ■ *0900-1700. US$1.50*. Herbert Levi writes: "There are 600-year-old petroglyphs with pictures depicting animals. The whole area is said to have been covered with water long ago; now there are two visible strata, the *tarjado* and the *talampaya*. After that one enters a canyon with 'balconies', sheer overhanging walls. Coming out of the canyon there are rocks shaped like a cathedral, a bird, a castle, a chessboard, a monk, and three kings on a camel." ■ *Better to visit park in the morning to avoid strong winds in the afternoon. Free campsite next to park administration. Tours and access: Tours follow the dry bed of the Río Talampaya in 4WD vehicles operated by park rangers, three tours offered: 2- (US$20), 4- (US$45) and 6 hrs long (US$65), price depends on number of people, not including entrance. Also guided walks US$5 pp and very nice guided cycle tours, US$3 pp; cycles provided. Tours arranged at the park. Sr Páez (park director) can arrange accommodation in Pagancillo (eg with E pp Familia Flores, includes breakfast and dinner). Patquía-Villa Unión buses pass access to Talampaya (14 km far from park office) and Pagancillo. Ask the driver to let you off at park entrance.*

La Rioja

Founded 1591, La Rioja is the capital of its namesake province. It is known as 'City of the Orange Trees', but there are also many specimens of the contorted, thorn-studded *palo borracho* tree, whose ripened avocado-like pods release large brown seeds in a kapok-like substance. Despite a major earthquake in 1894, some colonial buildings survive. The **Convent of San Francisco**, 25 de Mayo/Bazán y Bustos, contains the Niño Alcalde, a remarkable image of the infant Jesus as well as the cell (*celda*) in which San Francisco Solano lived and the orange tree, now dead, which he planted in 1592. At **Las Padercitas**, 7 km from town, a stone temple protects the remains of the 16th-century adobe building where San Francisco converted the Indians of the Yacampis valley. The **Convent of Santo Domingo**, Luna y Lamadrid, dates from 1623. **Museo Arqueológico Inca Huasi**, Alberdi 650, owned by the Franciscan Order, contains a huge collection of fine Diaguita Indian ceramics. ■ *Tue-Sun, 0900-1200, US$0.50.* **Museo de Bellas Artes**, Pasaje Diaguita y Luna, works by local and national artists. ■ *Tue-Fri, 0900-1200, 1500-2000, Sat-Sun 0900-1200.* **Museo Folklórico**, Luna 811, includes displays on mythology, handicrafts and cooking. ■ *Tue-Fri, 0800-1200, 1600-2000, Sat-Sun 0800-1200.* There are good views of La Rioja from Cerro de la Cruz (1,680 m), 27 km west, now a centre for hang-gliding, where condors and falcons may be sighted. The tourist office is at Perón y Urquiza, T428839, turismolarioja@hotmail.com

Phone code: 03822
Colour map 8, grid A2
Population: 130,000
Avoid arriving on Sat night as most things are shut on Sun

Argentina

Argentina

Sleeping

Accommodation can be difficult to find, particularly in the lower price ranges

B *Plaza*, San Nicolás y 9 de Julio, T425215, turismo@plazahotel-larioja.com.ar Recommended but street noisy. **C** *Libertador*, Buenos Aires 253, T426052. Good value. **C** *Imperial*, Moreno 345, T422478. Helpful. **D** *Res Petit*, Lagos 427. Basic, hospitable. **D** *Savoy*, Roque A Luna 14, T426894. Excellent value, hot shower. **D** *Pensión 9 de Julio*, Copiapó y Vélez Sarsfield. Recommended. Tourist Office keeps a list of private lodgings, such as Sra Vera, Dávila 343. **Camping** At Balneario Los Sauces, 13 km west on route 75, *Camping de la Sociedad Sirio Libanesa*, hot showers, swimming-pool.

Eating

Aldea Virgen de Luján, Rivadavia 756. Cheap, good basic meals and Arab dishes. *Alike*, Vélez Sarsfield e Hipólito Yrigoyen, Chinese, *tenedor libre*. *Cavadini*, Av Quiroga 1145, good *parrilla*. *Los Palotes*, Hipólito Yrigoyen 128, offers *menú ejecutivo* at lower prices than its trendy menu *à la carte*. *Comedor Sociedad Española*, 9 de Julio 233. Excellent pastas, inexpensive. *La Vieja Casona*, Rivadavia 427. Very good and reasonably priced. Recommended.

Tour operators

For excursions to Talampaya, Valle de la Luna, Laguna Brava and Corona del Inca crater, city tours and horse riding in Velasco mountains: *Aguada*, T433695 or 15-515068, aguadatour@hotmail.com *Corona del Inca*, Luna 914, T435329 or 15-663811, expediciones@coronadelinca.com.ar *Terra Riojana*, Rivadavia y Dávila, T15661552, terralar@infovia.com.ar

Transport

Car hire Hotel King's, Av Quiroga 1170. **Air** To/from Buenos Aires, *AIRG* (T435197) and *Southern Winds* (T461717). **Buses** Terminal 7 blocks south of the Cathedral at Artigas y España (T425453). To Buenos Aires, *Gen Urquiza* and *Chevallier* US$25-30, 15 hrs. To Mendoza (US$12-14) and San Juan (US$10), *Socasa*, *Andesmar* and others, 6 hrs. To Tinogasta, daily, US$6. To Tucumán (US$9), with *Sol y Valle* and *La Estrella*. To Salta, *Andesmar*, 10 hrs, US$12. Also provincial services.

Directory

Banks US$ cash changed at *Banco de Galicia*, Plaza 25 de Mayo (no commission on Visa cash advance), and *BBVA Banco Francés*, San Nicolás 476. Change TCs before arriving. **Communications Internet:** Rivadavia 763, local 2, US$1.50 per hr, excellent service. **Telephone:** Perón 764, *telecentro* beside Cathedral, and others in town. **Post Office:** Perón 258.

Chilecito

Phone code: 03825
Colour map 8, grid A2
Population: 23,000

Chilecito, 129 km northwest of Patquía, is La Rioja province's second town. Founded in 1715, it has good views of Sierra de Famatina, especially from the top of El Portezuelo, an easy climb from the end of C El Maestro. The region is famous for its wines, olives and walnuts. **Samay Huasi**, 3 km south of town, was the house of Joaquín V González, founder of La Plata University. ■ *Mon-Fri 0800-1900, Sat-Sun 0800-1200, 1400-1800.* It contains the **Museo de Ciencias Naturales, Mineralogía y Arqueología**, pleasant gardens, and, from hills nearby, good views of Chilecito, the Famatina ridge and connecting valley. **Molino San Francisco y Museo de Chilecito**, at J de Ocampo 63, has archaeological, historical and artistic exhibits. ■ *Mon-Fri 0800-1300, 1400-1900.* La Mejicana mine via Santa Florentina road: a cable car system (built 1903, the highest and longest in Latin America) which brought ore 36 km to the railhead at Chilecito was reopened in 2001. The first station has a small museum (Av Perón 1300, acceso Sur). Tourist office at Castro y Bazán 52, T422688, very helpful.

Sleeping

C *Chilecito*, T Gordillo y A G Ocampo, T/F422201/2. ACA hotel, no credit cards, safe parking, pool. **C** *Riviera*, Castro Barros 158. Hot showers. Recommended. **C** *Belsavac*, Plaza Sarmiento above *Keops* bar, T422977, analuz@rcc.com.ar Good but thin walls. **D** *Wamatinag*, Galeria Victoria, west side of Plaza Sarmiento, T423419. Pleasant, best value in town. **D** *Hostal Mary Pérez*, Florencio Dávila 280, T/F423156, marymar@rcc.com.ar The Tourist Office has a list of families offering accommodation, but not for single travellers. Samay Huasi, T422629, also offers cheap accommodation, book in advance. **Camping** At Santa Florentina, 6 km northwest of Chilecito and Las Talas, 2 km beyond.

On Plaza Sarmiento are: *Chaplin*, expensive. *Creisy*, *tenedor libre* lunch, simple meals in evening, good. *Vanesa*, good home-made ice cream. Not far from Plaza Sarmiento are:*El Rancho de Ferrito*, Av Luna 547, very good. *Club Arabe*, 25 de Mayo 250.

Eating

For tours in the Reserva Natural Laguna Brava (see page 158) contact *Jorge and Adriana Llanos*, T422171, or Adolfo and Daniel at *Laguna Brava ETV*, T425238/423108. For guided walks to Mina La Mejicana and other excursions, contact *Alejo Piehl*, T425102, alejotur@rcc.com.ar

Tour operators

Buses To **San Juan** and Mendoza with *Vallecito*, US$11-13; to **La Rioja**, several times daily, US$3-4. To **Córdoba**, US$11 and **Buenos Aires**, US$28, *General Urquiza*. Connections with **Catamarca** via La Rioja only.

Transport

At Nonogasta 16 km south of Chilecito, the partly paved Route 40 heads west climbing through a deep narrow canyon in a series of hairpins to the Cuesta de Miranda (2,020 m). After the Cuesta is **Villa Unión**, 92 km from Nonogasta, *Hotel Centro*, on main plaza, has a restaurant. **B** *Hotel Pircas Negras*, on route 76, T03825-470611. **D** *Hotel Noryanepat*, JVGonzález 150, T03825-470372, small rooms with a/c, good. From Villa Unión, excursions can be made by four-wheel drive vehicle to the **Reserva Natural Laguna Brava**, 150 km north. The road goes through Vinchina (several basic *hospedajes* and new **D** *Hotel Corona del Inca*, T03825-494004, hotelcoronadelinca@ciudad.com.ar) and Jagüe. Further on, as you climb the Portezuelo del Peñón, the salt lake of Laguna Brava becomes visible with some of the mightiest volcanoes on earth in the background. From the left these are the perfect cone Veladero (6,436 m), Reclus (6,335 m), Los Gemelos (6,130 m), Pissis (6,882 m) the highest volcano in the world, though inactive, and Bonete (6,759 m) which is visible from Villa Unión and Talampaya. For tours in this area see under Chilecito and La Rioja.

Argentina

Catamarca

Officially San Fernando del Valle de Catamarca, Catamarca is capital of its province, on the Río del Valle, between the slopes of the Sierra de Ambato (to the west) and Ancasti (to the east). Cattle, fruit, grapes and cotton are the main agricultural products, but it is also renowned for hand-woven ponchos and fruit preserves. Pilgrimages are made to the church of the Virgen del Valle, while in July, regional handicrafts are sold at Festival del Poncho, a *feria* with four nights of music, mostly folklore of the northwest. There are traces of Indian civilizations, including extensive agricultural terraces (now mostly abandoned), throughout the province. There are six museums, including the **Museo Arqueológico Adán Quiroga**, Sarmiento 450, with one of the best collections in the country. ■ *Mon-Fri 0700-1300, 1430-2030, Sat-Sun 0830-1230, 1530-1830*. Provincial tourist office, Roca y Virgen del Valle, T/F437594, turismocatamarca@cedeconet.com.ar, daily 0900-2100. The same place houses a handicrafts market and a carpet and tapestry factory, Monday-Friday 0700-1300. There is also office in the airport. In small surrounding towns, go to municipal offices for information and maps.

Phone code: 03833
Colour map 8, grid A2
Population: 140,000
Altitude: 490 m
153 km NE of La Rioja
240 km S of Tucumán

The Zonda, a strong dry mountain wind, can cause dramatic temperature increases

B *Ancasti*, Sarmiento 520, T/F430617/435952, hotelancasti@cedeconet.com.ar Central, restaurant, gym and sauna, also apartments. **C** *Inti Huasi*, República 299, T435705. A/c, snack bar, parking. **C** *Pucará*, Caseros 501, T 430688. Good value. **C** *Suma Huasi*, Sarmiento 547, T435699, F432595. With breakfast, a/c, parking, good beds, but gloomy. **D** *Colonial*, República 802, T423502. Recommended, welcoming, good value. Several *residenciales* near bus terminal including: **D** *Res Ambato*, Güemes 841, T422142. **D** *Res Tucumán*, Tucumán 1040, T422209. Modern. **D** *Res Avenida*, Güemes 754, T422139. With and without bath. **E** *Hosp Menem*, Güemes 797, T424755, opposite terminal. Provincial tourist office has a list of families who rent rooms. **Camping** Municipal site 5 km from centre on road to El Rodeo/Las Juntas, US$1.50, clean, friendly, hot showers.

Sleeping

Argentina

Eating *Sociedad Española*, Virgen del Valle 725. *La Tinaja*, Sarmiento 533. Excellent, pricey, live music. Warmly recommended. *El Repulgue*, Sarmiento 555, nice atmosphere, excellent *empanadas* and other regional meals, also take-away. Several restaurants around Plaza 25 de Mayo including *Salsa Criolla*, República 546, *parrilla*, *Family*, Rivadavia 642, lively, good pizzas and *Montecarlo*, República 550, *trattoria*. Many cheap restaurants near bus terminal and around the Plaza 25 de Agosto. An interesting bar is *Richmond Bar*, Plaza 25 de Mayo, superb decor dating from 1920s with period furniture.

Shopping Catamarca specialities from: *Cuesta del Portezuelo*, Sarmiento 571 and *Valdez*, Sarmiento 578; *Mercado Artesanal*, Virgen del Valle 945 (beside Tourist office), T 437598, wide range of handicrafts. Supermarkets: *Lozano*, Plaza 25 de Agosto; *Tía*, Rivadavia 945.

Tour operators *Yokavil*, Rivadavia 916, local 14, T430066. Excursions to Cuesta de El Portezuelo and Dique Las Pirquitas, US$10, 4 hrs.

Transport **Air** Airport T453683/4. *Southern Winds* (San Martín 468, T0810-777 7979) to/from Buenos Aires. **Buses** Modern terminal 5 blocks southeast of plaza at Güemes y Tucumán T437578. Taxi to/from Plaza 25 de Mayo US$0.50. To **Tucumán**, several companies, 3½-4hrs, US$4-8. To **Buenos Aires**, 4 companies daily, 15 hrs, US$27-29. To **Córdoba**, 4 companies daily, 6 hrs, US$6-9. To **Santiago del Estero**, *Mendoza*, *La Estrella*, 4 hrs, US$8. To **Mendoza**, several companies, daily, 10 hrs, US$12-15. To **La Rioja**, several companies, daily, US$4-5, 2 hrs. To **Tinogasta**, 3 companies, US$6. To **Belén** via Aimogasta and Londres, several companies, 5 hrs, US$6-8; *Marín* (via Aconquija).

Directory **Banks** *Banco de Catamarca*, Plaza 25 Mayo, changes US$ cash but not TCs, ATM Visa and MasterCard. *Banco de Galicia*, Rivadavia 554 changes TCs, high commission, ATM. *BBVA Banco Francés*, Rivadavia 520. **Communications** Internet: *Cedecc*, Esquiú 414. *Taraj Net*, San Martín y Ayacucho. **Telephone:** most *telecentros* around Plaza 25 de Mayo, also at República 845 and Rivadavia 758, open 0700-2400, daily. **Post Office:** San Martín 753, slow, open 0800-1300, 1600-2000.

Tinogasta & Fiambalá Tinogasta (*Population*: 9,000; phone code 03837) is in an oasis of vineyards, olive groves, and poplars. **D** *Viñas del Sol*, Perón 231, T420028. **D** *Hostería Novel*, Córdoba 200, T420009, near airport, friendly. **E** *Res Don Alberto*, A del Pino y Rivadavia, T420323. *Restaurant Casa Grande*, Constitución y Moreno, good meals, try local wines. ■ *Buses to Tucumán*, Empresa Gutiérrez, 3 weekly (daily in high season). *To Catamarca*, Empresa Gutiérrez (connection to Buenos Aires), *Robledo* and *Rubimar*, US$6; *to La Rioja*, El Cóndor, *US$6*.

Tinogasta is the starting point for expeditions to the second highest mountain in South America. Most recent cartography has allowed for some corrections in altitude so that **Pissis** has been confirmed, at 6,882 m, higher than Ojos del Salado (6,879 m). To get there, take Route 60 which crosses Tinogasta in the direction of the San Francisco pass. You have to register at the police station outside Fiambalá, take passport. Expeditions organized and horse riding with Omar Monuey, La Espiga de Oro, 25 de Mayo 436 or *Varela Viajes*, T420428. At Fiambalá, contact Jonson and Ruth Reynoso, T496214.

Fiambalá is 49 km north of Tinogasta. Drive or take a taxi from here to **Termas de Fiambalá**, hot springs, 14 km east, temperatures from 30° C to 54° C (make sure taxi fare includes wait and return). There are vineyards in the valley. **D** *Hostería Municipal*, Almagro s/n, good value, also restaurant. Good *parrilla* and pizzas at *Roma*. At the Termas is a *Complejo Turístico* with cabins (**E** pp), T496016; also camping.

Transport **Buses** *Empresa Gutiérrez* to **Catamarca** via **Tinogasta**. For connections to Belén, change bus at Aimogasta. Four-wheel drive vehicles may be hired for approaching the Pissis-Ojos region; ask at the Intendencia.

Fiambalá is the starting-point for the crossing to Chile via Paso San Francisco (4,726 m), 203 km northwest along a paved road. The border is open 0830-1930. On the Chilean side roads run to El Salvador and Copiapó. This route is closed by snow between June and October; take enough fuel for at least 400 km as there are no service stations from Fiambalá to just before Copiapó.

Border with Chile – Paso San Francisco

The whole district is famous for weavings, ponchos, saddlebags and rugs. There are good views from the new statue of Virgin of Belén at the summit of the path beginning at C Gral Roca, and an interesting archaeological museum, Cóndor Huasi (San Martín y Belgrano, 1st floor, open daily). Festival: Nuestra Señora de Belén, 24 December-6 January. Belén is encircled by mountains, except to the southeast; lush vegetation along Río Belén. North of Belén Route 40 runs another 176 km, largely unpaved, to Santa María at Tucumán provincial border (see page 128), and on to Cafayate (page 128). A difficult road heads east, rough and sandy, to Andalgalá, a former-copper mining town (two archaeological museums; hotels **D** to **F**, for excursions and tourist information contact *Andalgalá Turismo*, T03835-422405, turandalgala@cotelbelen.com.ar, very helpful), from where roads go to southern Tucumán. South of Belén, Route 40 via Londres is paved to Chilecito. **D** *Samay*, Urquiza 349, T461320, recommended. **D** *Belén*, Belgrano y Cubas, T461501, hotel@cyberbelen.com.ar Good, recently refurbished. *Restaurant Dalesio*, near YPF gas station, excellent and cheap. *Remanzo*, Av Calchaquí 141, cheap and good basic dishes. *El Amigazo*, behind church, good. Good breakfast at bus terminal.
■ *Buses to Santa María*, San Cayetano *and* Parra *(connection there with other companies to Cafayate and Salta), daily, 5 hrs, US$6. To Tinogasta, Robledo, 3 weekly, 3hrs, US$6. To Antofagasta de la Sierra, El Antofagasteño, 5 weekly, 7 hrs, US$15. For more frequent services to Catamarca or La Rioja, take bus to Aimogasta, 1 hour, US$1.50.*

Belén
Phone code 0383
Population: 8,800

Argentina

The Northeast

Between the Ríos Uruguay and Paraná lies Argentine Mesopotamia: the provinces of Entre Ríos, Corrientes, and Misiones. The distance between the rivers is 390 km in northern Corrientes, but narrows to about 210 km in the latitude of Santa Fe. The province of Corrientes is marshy and deeply-wooded, with low grass-covered hills rising from the marshes. Entre Ríos has plains of rich pasture land not unlike those of Uruguay. Misiones is a hilly strip of land between the Uruguay and the Alto Paraná rivers, 80-100 km wide and about 400 km long; its capital is the river port of Posadas. Its boundary to the north is the Río Iguazú, which here tumbles over the great Iguazú Falls. Misiones is on the Paraná Plateau; much of it is covered with forests of pine and cedar and broad-leaved trees, and the land, with its red soil, is reminiscent of Brazil.

Argentine Mesopotamia was first colonized by Spaniards pushing south from Asunción to reoccupy Buenos Aires; Santa Fe was founded in 1573, Corrientes in 1588. From about 1880 there were Jewish agricultural settlements in Entre Ríos, promoted by Baron Hirsch for victims of pogroms in the Czarist Empire (see *Los gauchos judíos* by Alberto Gerchunoff). Vestiges of these settlements remain at Domínguez (museum) and Basavilbaso, and across the river in Moisesville (Santa Fe).

Background

Misiones Province was first occupied by the Jesuit Fathers, fleeing from the Brazilian Alto-Paraná region with their devoted Indian followers from the slave-hunting Bandeirantes. These missions and their history are described under Posadas (see page 171). The province has attracted immigrants from Eastern Europe, from Paraguay and from the rest of Mesopotamia.

Much of Entre Ríos and Corrientes is still pastoral, a land of large *estancias* raising cattle and sheep. Maize is largely grown in southern Entre Ríos, which is also the most important producer of linseed, citrus fruit and poultry in Argentina. In Corrientes, along the banks of the Paraná between the cities of Corrientes and Posadas, rice and oranges are grown. Misiones is a large producer of *yerba mate*, citrus, tobacco, timber and tung oil.

Climate
Winters are mild; summers are hot with rain falling in short, sharp storms. Both Entre Ríos and Corrientes often suffer from summer drought. In Misiones the rainfall is heavy: twice as heavy as in Entre Ríos. The days are hot, and the nights cool.

Gualeguaychú
Phone code: 03446
Colour map 8, grid B5
Population: 80,000
220 km N of Buenos Aires

Situated on the Río Gualeguaychú, 19 km above its confluence with the Río Paraná, this is a pleasant town with an attractive *costanera* and a lively pre-Lenten carnival. Some 33 km south the Libertador Gral San Martín Bridge (5.4 km long) provides the most southerly route across the Río Uruguay, to Fray Bentos (vehicles US$2; pedestrians and cyclists may cross only on vehicles, officials may arrange lifts). The Uruguayan consulate is at Rivadavia 510, T426168, conuruguale@infovia.com.ar

Museo Arqueológico, 25 de Mayo 734, with artefacts from indigenous cultures of the Uruguay basin. **Solar de los Haedo** (Museo de la Ciudad), San José y Rivadavia, is in the oldest house in the city, which served as Garibaldi's headquarters when he sacked the city in 1845. ■ *Guided tour, Wed-Sat 0900-1145, Fri-Sat also at 1600-1945, US$0.50.* **Museo Ferroviario**, Piccini y Rocamora, open-air, at the former station. The tourist office is at Av Costanera y 25 de Mayo, open 0800-2000. Also at 9 de Julio 844, T425820.

Accommodation is scarce at weekends (when few single rooms are to be found) and during carnival. The tourist office also has a list of family accommodation

Sleeping A *Berlín*, Bolívar 733, T/F425111. German spoken, with breakfast, comfortable. **B** *Alemán*, Bolívar 535, T426153. German spoken, without breakfast. Recommended. **B** *París*, Bolívar y Pellegrini, T423850, F426260. With breakfast, fan, restaurant, comfortable. **C** *Victoria*, Bolívar 565, T426469. Opposite terminal, small rooms, modern, with breakfast. **D** *Amalfi*, 25 de Mayo 571, T425677. With breakfast, good beds. **D** *Brutti*, Bolívar 591, T426048. Shabby, good value, without breakfast, fan. **E** *Mayo*, 3 de Febrero y Bolívar, T427661. Uncomfortable beds, with bath. **Camping** *La Delfina* in the Parque Unzué, T422293. Others near the river. *Ñandubaysal*, 15 km east, T426009, best.

Transport Bus terminal in centre of town at Bolívar y Chile. To **Fray Bentos**, 1 hr, US$3.50, 2 a day, *ETA*. To **Mercedes**, 1½ hrs, US$2.75, 2 a day, *ETA*; to **Buenos Aires**, US$10, 4 hrs, several daily.

Concepción del Uruguay
Phone code: 03442
Colour map 8, grid B5
Population: 65,000
74 km N of Gualeguaychú

The first Argentine port of any size on the Río Uruguay is known locally as Concepción. Founded in 1783, it was, until 1883, capital of Entre Ríos province. The old town is centred on Plaza Ramírez. Overlooking the main plaza is the church of the Immaculate Conception which contains the remains of Gen Urquiza. **Palacio San José**, Urquiza's former mansion, 35 km west of the town, is now a museum, with artefacts from Urquiza's life and a collection of period furniture, recommended. ■ *Mon-Fri 0900-1300, 1400-1800, Sat-Sun 0900-1245, 1400-1745, written explanations in Spanish, French and English, US$0.75. Itape buses to 3 km from the Palacio, US$1.50, 45 mins.* The **Museo Casa del Delio Panizza**, Galarza y Supremo Entrerriano, is in a mansion dating from 1793 and contains 19th-century furnishings and artefacts.

Sleeping and eating **L** *Estancia San Pedro*, outside Concepción, T427459, postal address: Moreno 122, Concepción del Uruguay, 3260 Pvca Entre Ríos. Owned by descendants of Urquiza, old rooms full of antiques, very good. **C** *Res Fiuri*, Sarmiento 779, T427016. Attractive. **D** *Ramírez*, Martínez 50, T425106, above bus terminal. **F** *Hosp Los Tres Nenes*, Galarza 1233, near terminal. Good. Restaurants: *El Canguro*, opposite terminal. Good food, reasonably priced. *Rocamora*, Rocamora y Millán, bus terminal bar for *tenedor libre* meals.

Transport Buses Terminal at Rocamora y Los Constituyentes (bus 1 to centre or remise, US$0.50). To **Buenos Aires**, frequent, 4½ hrs, US$10. To **Paysandú** (**Uruguay**) 1 hr, US$2.75.

Founded in 1863, Colón has an attractive *costanera* and five sandy beaches, with cliffs visible from a considerable distance. A road bridge links Colón and Paysandú, Uruguay. *Artesanía* shops line 12 de Abril and there is a large handicrafts fair at Carnival time (February). Just outside town is the Complejo Termal Colón, with open-air thermal pools, US$2. There is a tourist office at Av Costanera y Gouchón.

Colón
Colour map 8, grid A5
Population: 15,000
45 km N of Concepción
del Uruguay

Sleeping B *Plaza*, 12 de Abril y Belgrano, T421043. With breakfast, a/c, modern. C *Holimasú*, Belgrano 28, T421305, F421303. With breakfast. C *Palmar*, Ferrari 285, T421952. Good. C *Vieja Calera*, Bolívar 344, T421139. With breakfast, a/c. Many **families** rent rooms – the Boujon family, Maipú 430, D, good breakfast and other meals extra. Recommended. Several **campsites** along river bank (municipal site, excellent facilities, cheapest; also *Piedras Coloradas*, T421451). Eating places include *Hostería Restaurante del Puerto*, Alejo Peyrat 158, near tourist office, T422698. Well-restored colonial building. *El Viejo Almacén*, Gral Urquiza y Paso. Good fish.

Transport Buses Terminal at Paysandú y Sourigues. To **Buenos Aires**, 4 a day, US$13, 5 hrs; to **Concepción del Uruguay**, *Copay* and *Paccot*, 4 a day, 2 on Sun, US$2; to **Concordia**, 6 a day, US$4 (2½ hrs) and **Paraná** daily. To **Córdoba** 4 a week. **To Uruguay:** via the Artigas Bridge (US$2 toll) all formalities are dealt with on the Uruguayan side. Passports are collected on the bus. Easy crossing. Bus to **Paysandú**, US$2, 45 mins, 4 daily Mon-Fri, 2 at weekends.

This park of 8,500 ha is on the Río Uruguay, off Route 14. The park contains varied scenery with a mature palm forest, sandy beaches on the Uruguay river, Indian tombs and the remains of an 18th-century quarry and port, a good museum and many rheas and other birds. The Yatay palms grow up to 12 m and some are hundreds of years old. It is best to stay overnight as wildlife is more easily seen in the early morning or at sunset. Very popular at weekends in summer. ■ *US$2.50. Buses from Colón, 40 mins, US$1.75, will drop you at the entrance and it is easy to hitch the last 6 km to the park administration. There are camping facilities (electricity, hot water), a small hotel 8 km north of the park, with restaurant opposite, and a small shop.*

**Parque
Nacional
El Palmar**
51 km N of Colón

Just downriver from Salto, Uruguay, Concordia is a prosperous city. The Río Uruguay is impassable for large vessels beyond the rapids of Salto Chico near the city, and Salto Grande 32 km up-river, where there is a large international hydro-electric dam, providing a crossing to Uruguay. Above Salto Grande the river is generally known as the Alto Uruguay. In the streets around the main **Plaza 25 de Mayo** there are some fine public buildings. The **Museo Regional**, Plaza Urquiza, in the Palacio Arruabarrena, has local and natural history collections. ■ *Daily 0800-2100, free.* 5 km northeast is **Parque Rivadavia**, in which is the **Palacio San Carlos**, briefly inhabited by Antoine de Saint-Exupéry. ■ *Take colectivo No 2, one block from Plaza 25 de Mayo, to corner of Av Justo and Av Salto Uruguay, from where the entrance is one block north.* Tourist office on Plaza 25 de Mayo, open daily 0700-2400.

Concordia
Colour map 8, grid A5
Population: 93,800
104 km N of Colón

Sleeping and eating A *Salto Grande*, Urquiza 581, T/F421 0034. With breakfast, comfortable. A *Palmar*, Urquiza 521, T421 6050, F421 5020. Bright, comfortable, also C in older part, with breakfast. C *Centro*, La Rioja y Buenos Aires, T421 7776, F421 7746. A/c, comfortable, *comedor*. D *Argentino*, Pellegrini 560, T421 5767. With bath, old fashioned, nice patio. D *Colonial*, Pellegrini 443, T422 1448. Without breakfast, fan, pleasant. D *Concordia*, La Rioja 518, T421 6869. With fan, good. D *Embajador*, San Lorenzo 75, T4213018, near bus station. Neat. **Camping** *La Posada de Suárez – Club Viajantes* on Av Costanera near the park, warmly recommended, with good *parrillada* alongside, but beware the cats. For eating, try *La Estancia*, Plaza 25 de Mayo. Good value. *Comedor Las Dos Naciones*, Plaza 25 de Mayo y Av 1° de Mayo. Good, moderate prices, large portions. *De La Plata*, Av 1° de Mayo 59. Excellent. *Mafalda*, Plaza Urquiza y Entre Ríos. Very good home made ice cream and cakes.

Transport Buses Terminal at Justo y Yrigoyen, 13 blocks northwest of the Plaza 25 de Mayo (reached by No 2 bus). To **Buenos Aires**, 6 daily, US$14, 6½ hrs. To **Córdoba**, US$15,

Expreso Singer, 9 hrs. To **Paraná** 5 a day, to **Posadas** at 1800 and 2300, *Expreso Singer* (8½ hrs, US$20). To **Iguazú** at 1810, 13½ hrs, US$20. To **Corrientes** US$6.50. To **Paso de los Libres** direct, *El Recreo* 1500 Mon, Sat and several at 0300, US$6.50, 3½ hrs.

About 153 km upstream from Concordia lies the small port of Monte Caseros, with the Uruguayan town of Bella Unión, on the Brazilian border, almost opposite

To Uruguay Ferry: take No 4 bus from terminal marked 'Puerto', for ferry crossing to Salto US$2, tickets obtainable at a small kiosk, which shuts 15 mins before departure, outside migration in building marked 'Resguardo', 5 departures Mon-Fri, 4 departures Sat, 2 departures (0800 1800) Sun, 20 mins, passengers only. **Bus**: service via Salto Grande dam, *Flecha Bus* and *Chadre*, 2 a day each, not Sun, US$2, all formalities on Argentine side, passports checked on bus. **Bicycles** are not allowed to cross the international bridge but officials will help cyclists find a lift. The **Uruguayan consulate** is at Pellegrini 709, of 1 C, T421 0380.

Directory **Communications** Internet: *Dampermic*, Sarmiento 55. **Post Office:** La Rioja y Buenos Aires. **Telephone:** 700 block of San Luis (24 hrs).

Paso de los Libres
Colour map 8, grid A5
Population: 25,000
336 km N of Concordia

Linked to the larger Brazilian town of Uruguaiana by a bridge over the Alto Uruguay, Paso de los Libres was founded in 1843 by General Madariaga. It was here that he crossed the river from Brazil with his 100 men and annexed Corrientes province for Argentina. **B** *Alejandro I*, Col López 502, T424100, pool, cable TV, best. **D** *Uruguay*, Uruguay 1252, T425672, not clean but friendly, good *comedor*. Opposite is **D** *26 de Febrero*. Near terminal are **D** *Capri*, T424126, and several others. **Yapeyú**, 58 km north, is the site of a Jesuit mission, famous as the birthplace of the liberator, José de San Martín. Part of the house where he was born is well preserved, and there is an interesting Jesuit Museum.

Transport Buses: Terminal is 1 km from town centre, near border. To **Buenos Aires** US$15. **To Brazil**: taxi or bus US$2.50. No bus service on Sun.

Rosario

Phone code: 0341
Colour map 8, grid B5
Population: 1 million
320 km N of Buenos Aires

The largest city in the province of Santa Fe and the third largest city in Argentina, Rosario is a great industrial and export centre on the Río Paraná. It has a lively cultural scene and is the home of many popular rock musicians and artists. There are good discothèques and theatres. Swimming is possible at the sandy **Florida beach**, about 8 km north of Rosario. On 7 October the Foundation of the City is celebrated.

From Oct to early Mar it is warm, and from Dec to the end of Feb uncomfortably hot

Worth seeing is the **Monument of the Flag**, a memorial on the river bank in honour of Gen Belgrano, designer of the Argentine flag, who raised it on this spot for the first time in 1812 (lifts go to the top). **Parque Independencia**, in the centre of the city, 126 ha, has lakes and monumental gardens. The **Cathedral**, 25 de Mayo, contains the Virgen del Rosario. A recommended pedestrian tour Called **'Paseo Centenario'** around C Córdoba touches on the interesting buildings and monuments of the 'Golden Days of Rosario' (1880-1950). **Museo de Bellas Artes J B Castagnino**, Av Pellegrini 2202, has 1,600 paintings, including works by El Greco, Goya and Titian. ■ *Tue-Sat 1200-2000, Sun 1000-2000.* **Museo de Arte Decorativo Firma y Odilio Estévez**, Santa Fe 748, has some Caravaggios, Goyas and Murillos. ■ *Thu-Sun 1500-2000.*

Che Guevara was born here in 1928. The large white house at Urquiza y Entre Ríos where he lived for the first two years of his life before his family moved to Alta Gracia, near Córdoba (see page 121), is now an insurance company. The tourist office is at Belgrano y Buenos Aires, T4495140, English spoken, very helpful, lots of information. ■ *Mon-Fri 0800-2000, Sat-Sun 0900-2000.*

Sleeping **A** *La Paz*, Barón de Mauá 36, T421 0905. Quiet. Recommended. **B** *Presidente*, Av Corrientes 919, T424 2854. Good. **C** *Rosario*, Corrientes 900, T424 2170. With breakfast, parking, large rooms, good beds. **C** *Savoy*, San Lorenzo 1022 near San Martín, T448 0071. Built 1900 and retaining original bathrooms, with breakfast, **E** without bath, large rooms, cheap restaurant, good value. **D** *Normandie*, Mitre 1030, T421 2694. Helpful, central. **Around terminal On Santa Fe** (all **C-D**, and recommended): *América*, No 3746, T438 6584, without breakfast, best value on this street. *Casas*, No 3600, T430 4717, without breakfast, a/c, pleasant. *Embajador*, No 3554, T438 4188, with breakfast, a/c extra. *Le Nid*, Iriondo 660, T438 8762. Without breakfast, a/c, modern, pleasant. **Camping** In La Florida, near the river.

Don Rodrigo, Sante Fe 968, and *Fénix*, Santa Fe next to Citibank, are both very good. *La China*, Santa Fe 1882. *Tenedor libre*. *La Máquina*, Urquiza y Entre Ríos. Bar with some food, popular with young people and artists. *El Nuevo Mejor*, Santa Fe 1166. *Parrilla*, stays open till after midnight.Along the river are good cheap restaurants and fishing club barbecues, good atmosphere. **Eating**

Café de la Opera, Laprida y Mendoza. Bar with cabaret, live music. Highly recommended. **Entertainment**

Air Airport at Fisherton, 8 km from centre. *Transportes Ayolas* minibus (Deán Funes 1525, T483 9863) connects with flights, US$2, to and from hotels and AR office. Taxi or *remise* US$6.50. Several flights daily to **Buenos Aires** with *AR/Austral*, *AIRG* and *Southern Winds*. *Southern Winds* has services to many major cities, from Salta in the north to Neuquén in the south. *Varig* flies to **São Paulo** and **Rio de Janeiro. Buses** To **Buenos Aires**, via San Nicolás on Route 9, 4 hrs, or via Pergamino, less frequent, on Route 8 (*Chevallier* bus every hour, US$12; also *Ablo, Gen Urquiza, La Unión*). Northwest to **Córdoba** and **Tucumán**. To **Santa Fe**, US$6.50. To **Mendoza**, US$24. To **Puerto Iguazú**, US$30. **Trains** The Buenos Aires-Tucumán service stops in Rosario; to **Tucumán**, 13 hrs. **Transport**

Airline offices *Aerolíneas Argentinas*, Santa Fe 1410, T424 9332/0810-2228 6527. *Southern Winds*, Santa Fe 1412, T425 3808. **Banks** *Lloyds TSB Bank* (BLSA), La Rioja 1205. *Citibank*, Santa Fe 1101. *Amex*, Grupo 3 de Turismo, Córdoba 1015, T447 0006. **Communications** Post Office: Córdoba y Buenos Aires. **Telephone:** San Luis, between San Martín and Maipú. **Directory**

The capital of Entre Ríos was founded in 1588 and from 1853-62 was the capital of the Republic. The centre is situated on a hill offering fine views over the Río Paraná and beyond to Santa Fe. There are many fine buildings. In the centre is the **Plaza Primero de Mayo**, where there are fountains and a statue of San Martín. Around the Plaza are the **Municipalidad**, the **Cathedral**, notable for its portico and its interior, and the **Colegio del Huerto**, seat of the Senate of the Argentine Confederation between 1853 and 1861. The **Casa de Gobierno** at Santa Fe y Laprida has a grand façade. The city's glory is **Parque Urquiza**, to the northwest. It has an enormous statue to Gen Urquiza, and a bas-relief showing the battle of Caseros, at which he finally defeated Rosas; also an open-air theatre. There are pleasant walks along the river bank and around the fishing *barrio* of **Puerto Sánchez**. There is a **Museo de Bellas Artes**, Buenos Aires 355 and a **Museo Histórico**, Buenos Aires y Laprida. ■ *Tue-Fri 0700-1300, 1500-2000, Sat 0900-1200, 1600-1900 (winter), 1700-2000 (summer), Sun 0900-1200.* The tourist office is at 25 de Mayo 44.

Paraná
Phone code: 0343
Colour map 8, grid A5
Population: 210,000
180 km above Rosario

Sleeping A *Mayorazgo*, Etchevehere y Córdoba, on Costanera Alta, T423 0333. 5-star, with fine view of park and river, has casino and swimming pool. **B** *Paraná*, 9 de Julio 60, T423 1700. With breakfast, pleasant. **D** *Bristol*, Alsina 221, T431 3961. Close to the bus terminal, basic. **D** *Roma*, Urquiza 1069. With bath, basic, central. **Camping** Balneario Thompson, just west of the tunnel.

Accommodation may be scarce at peak times (Semana Santa, Jul); tourist office arranges rooms with families

Transport Buses Terminal on Av Ramírez, 1 km southeast of centre. East across Entre Ríos to **Concordia** on Río Uruguay, 5 a day, 5 hrs. To **Buenos Aires**, US$13. **Travelling between Santa Fe and Paraná** The two cities do not face one another, but are 25 km apart and are separated by several islands. From Paraná the Hernandarias tunnel, toll US$1 per car, passes under the Río Paraná to connect with the west bank; from here a road runs 23 km west to Santa Fe across two islands and bridges. Trucks with dangerous loads cross the river by a

Argentina

launch which also carries pedestrians and operates Mon-Sat, 0600-2100, 20 mins journey, frequency depending on demand from trucks. Frequent bus service between the two cities by *Etacer* and *Fluviales del Litoral*, US$1.40, 1 hr.

Santa Fe

Phone code: 0342
Colour map 8, grid A4
Population: 400,000
165 km from Rosario

Santa Fe, a larger city, is the capital of its province and the centre of a very fertile region. It was founded by settlers from Asunción in 1573, though its present site was not occupied until 1660. You can swim in the river at Guadalupe beach, reached by local bus. The San Jerónimo festival is on 30 September and the Foundation of City is celebrated on 15 November.

The south part of the city, around the **Plaza 25 de Mayo** is the historic centre. On the Plaza itself is the majestic **Casa de Gobierno**, built in 1908 in French-style on the site of the historic Cabildo, in which the 1853 constitution was drafted. Opposite is the **Cathedral**, with its twin towers capped by blue cupolas. On the east side is the **Colegio de la Inmaculada Concepción**, established by the Jesuits and including the Iglesia de **Nuestra Señora de los Milagros**, dating from 1694, more richly decorated with an ornate dome. One block south of the plaza is the Iglesia y Convento de **San Francisco** built in 1680. The church has fine wooden ceilings, made from timber floated down the river from Paraguay, carved by indigenous craftsmen and fitted without the use of nails. The **Museo de San Francisco** includes a reconstruction with wax figures of the Constituent Congress of 1852-1853. ■ *Daily 1000-1200, 1500-1800*. The Convent of **Santo Domingo**, a block west of the Plaza at 3 de Febrero y 9 de Julio, has a fine patio and museum. North of the centre at Javier de la Rosa 623, is the modern neo-gothic style Iglesia de **Nuestra Señora de Guadalupe**, with attractive stained glass windows. ■ *Daily 0730-2000. Bus 4 from the centre, 20 mins.*

Museo Histórico Provincial, 3 de Febrero y San Martín, in a building dating from 1680 (one of the oldest surviving civil buildings in the country), includes pieces from the former Jesuit mission of San Javier and artefacts associated with the dictator Rosas and with Urquiza, who overthrew him. ■ *Tue-Fri 0830-1230, 1430-1900, Sat-Sun 1500-1800.* **Museo Etnográfico**, 3 de Febrero y Av Costanera, includes a large collection of artefacts from Santa Fe La Vieja (the original site of the city) and items from indigenous cultures. ■ *Mon-Fri 0900-1200, 1530-1900, Sat 1530-1830, Sun 1000-1200, 1530-1830.* Tourist offices at San Martín 2836 and at the bus terminal: maps, friendly.

Sleeping
There is a greater selection of hotels at lower prices than in Paraná

A *Corrientes*, Corrientes 2520, T459 2126. With breakfast, garage, restaurant, comfortable. **A** *Hostal de Santa Fe de la Vera Cruz*, San Martín 2954, T455 1740. Best, well-kept and run. **A** *Río Grande*, San Gerónimo 2586, T455 1025. Modern. Recommended. **B** *Suipacha*, Suipacha 2375, T452 1135. Safe, a/c, garage, pleasant. Recommended. **C** *Imperatriz*, Irigoyen Freire 2440, T453 0061. Pleasant, good value. **C** *Niza*, Rivadavia 2755, T452 2047. Very nice, without breakfast, a/c. **Near the terminal** **B** *Bertaina*, H Irigoyen 2255, T/F455 3068. Parking, a/c, good beds, well maintained. **C** *Brigadier*, San Luis 3148, T453 7387, 2 blocks from bus station. Good, a/c, some English spoken, parking. **C** *Colón*, San Luis 2862, T454 5167. **E** without bath, pleasant, large rooms.

Camping Several sites on the lakes and rivers outside town including: *Luz y Fuerza*, 7 km north near Lago Guadalupe. *Cámara del Hogar*, 4 km east on Route 168.

Eating
Many good eating places, with excellent meals with good wine

El Quincho de Chiquito, Obispo Príncipe y Almte Brown. Excellent and good value, classic fish restaurant, huge helpings. Excellent grills including *surubí* (local fish) at *Gran Parrillada Rivadavia*, Rivadavia 3299. *Surubí* also at *España*, San Martín 2644. *Baviera San Martín*, San Martín 2941. Good salads. *Café de la Paix*, San Martín y Santiago del Estero.

Transport

Air Airport at Sauce Viejo, 17 km south. Daily *Austral, AIRG, LAER* and *Southern Winds* to and from Buenos Aires; *LAER* also to Paraná. **Buses** Terminal near the centre, Gen M Belgrano 2910. To **Córdoba**, US$13, 5 hrs. Many buses to **Buenos Aires** US$12-17; to

Paraná frequent service US$1.40, 45 mins; to **Rosario** very frequent, 2½ hrs by autopista, US$6.50; daily to **Mendoza** (2100), **Posadas**, 12 hrs, US$18, several companies, and **Santiago del Estero**. To **Concordia** 4½ hrs, US$11.

Banks *Lloyds TSB Bank*, 25 de Mayo 2501, open 0715-1315. *Citibank*, San Martín 2609. *Amex* representative, *Vacaciones Felices*, San Martín 2632, T455 6786. Also *Casas de Cambio.Tourfé*, San Martín 2901, Sat 0830-1230, changes TCs.

Directory

The **Esteros del Iberá** (**Iberá marshes**) are a 1.3 million ha nature reserve covering an environment similar to the Pantanal in Brazil. Among the species are the endangered aguará-guazú (maned wolf), the marsh deer and the broad-snouted caiman. Other interesting species include capybaras, brocket deer, curiyús or yellow anaconda and tegú lizards. About 300 species of birds have been identified, among them the Yabirú (or Juan Grande) stork – the largest stork in the western hemispere, southern screamers and several species of ducks. Trips can be organized through Marcus Moncada, of *Turismo Aventura 4WD*, Junín 1062, Loc 4, Corrientes T/F433269, advance booking essential. **B** *Ñande-Reta Inn*, T420155, pnoailles@usa.net Day trips organized, beautiful setting.

Iberá Marshes

Mercedes (*Population*: 20,750), south east of Corrientes, on the road to Uruguay, is a good base for visiting the marshes. 27 km south of Mercedes are the strange Ita Pucú rock formations, remnants of a mountain massif long disappeared. **C** *Rancho Ypa Sapukai*, Sarmiento 212, T03773-420155, T15-629536 (mob), ypasapukai@ibera.net Full board or bed and breakfast, photo safaris, trekking, riding. Hotels in town: *Turismo*, Caaguazú y Sarmiento. *Plaza*, San Martín 699, cheapest.

At **Carlos Pellegrini**, 110 km northeast of Mercedes, a new visitors' centre to the marshes has been opened (take food, sleeping bag, light, binoculars). Workers at the visitors centre take boat trips in small punts, a recommended way of discovering the wildlife quietly. Bottled water is sold at the main store in the village. **A**, T/F076-929827/076-929532, iberalaguna@starmedia.com Elsa Güiraldes runs a full pension, English spoken, tours arranged. **B** *Hostería Ñandé Retá*, T03773-499411, www.nandereta.com Full or half board, safaris and expeditions, pool, transfers not included. **F** pp private house of Pera Roque, basic. Daily bus from Mercedes, times differ.

Corrientes

Corrientes, founded in 1588 is some 40 km below the confluence of the Ríos Paraguay and Alto Paraná. The 2¾ km Gen Belgrano bridge across the Río Paraná (toll US$1 per car) links the city with Resistencia (25 km), from where Route 11 goes north to Formosa and Asunción. East of Corrientes, Route 12 follows the Alto Paraná to Posadas and Iguazú. The river can make the air heavy, moist and oppressive, but in winter the climate is pleasant. The city is capital of Corrientes province and the setting for Graham Greene's novel, *The Honorary Consul*.

Phone code: 03783
Colour map 6, grid C6
Population: 258,000

The main **Plaza 25 de Mayo** is one of the best-preserved in Argentina. On the north side is the police station built in 19th-century French style. On the east side is the Italianate **Casa de Gobierno** and on the north is the church of **La Merced**. Two blocks east at Quintana y Mendoza is the **Convent of San Francisco**, rebuilt in 1861 (the original dated from the early 17th century). The **Cathedral**, built in 1874 is on Plaza Cabral where there is a statue to the sergeant who saved San Martín's life at the battle of San Lorenzo. The church of **La Cruz de los Milagros** (1897) houses a miraculous cross placed there by the founder of the city, Alonzo de Vera – Indians who tried to burn it were killed by lightning from a cloudless sky. A beautiful walk eastwards, along the Av Costanera, beside the Paraná river leads to **Parque Mitre**, from where there are good views of sunsets over the river. Calle Junín is pedestrianized, with restaurants and shops, crowded at night. Tourist office on Plaza Cabral.

Sights
Museums include:
Histórico Regional,
9 de Julio 1044.
Bellas Artes, San Juan
643. Artesanía, Buenos
Aires y Quintana

Argentina

Argentina

Two teas

Yerba mate (ílex paraguayensis) is made into a tea which is widely drunk in Argentina, Paraguay, Brazil and Uruguay. Traditionally associated with the gauchos, the modern mate paraphernalia is a common sight anywhere: the gourd (un mate) in which the tea leaves are steeped, the straw (usually silver) and a thermos of hot water to top up the gourd. It was the Jesuits who first grew yerba mate in plantations, inspiring one of the drink's names: té de jesuitas. Also used has been té de Paraguay, but now just mate or yerba will do. In southern Brazil it is called ximarão; in

Paraguay tereré, when drunk cold with digestive herbs.

In Northeast Corrientes and in Misiones more Indian tea is now grown than can be absorbed by the internal market. The Indian-tea industry was started by Sir Herbert Gibson, who sent for seed from Assam in 1929; it was sown in Playadito, Corrientes province. Six seeds developed into sturdy bushes. Year after year their seed was given to anyone interested. All Argentina's tea plantations today have their origin in Sir Herbert Gibson's enterprise. Good Indian tea is also grown and sold in Brazil.

Sleeping
More expensive than Resistencia

A *Gran Hotel Guaraní*, Mendoza 970, T423663, F424620. With breakfast, very good, a/c, restaurant. **B** *Corrientes*, Junín 1549, T465019, F465025. With breakfast, a/c, parking, good value, good restaurant. **B** *Hostal de Pinar*, Martínez y Italia, T469060. Modern, breakfast, parking, sauna. **B** *San Martín*, Santa Fe 955, T465004, F432326. With breakfast, good beds, restaurant, parking. **B** *Turismo*, Entre Ríos 650, T/F433173, one block from river. Breakfast, restaurant, pool, laundry service, parking. In the centre **D** *Robert*, La Rioja 437. Basic, without bath. Several near the terminal including **D** *Caribe*, Av Maipú Km 3, T469045. **Camping** Near bus terminal is *Camping-club Teléfono*, Av Maipú, hot showers or bath. There is another campsite on the riverbank, go up through Parque Mitre and continue along the road closest to the river; the site is just past the water works.

Eating *El Nuevo Balcón*, Pelligrini 962. Good food, clean, reasonable prices. Many others, and various *pizzerías*. Several tea rooms on San Juan, and on Junín. Try local baked delicacy called *chipa*.

Transport **Air** Camba Punta Airport, 10 km from city. (Bus No 8 from urban bus terminal at river end of La Rioja.) *AR/Austral* (T427442), *AIRG* (T431625) and *LAER* from Buenos Aires and Formosa. **Buses** To **Resistencia** US$0.70, *Cota*, every 15 mins, 40 mins journey, labelled 'Chaco', leaving from harbour; terminal 5 km south of centre (bus No 6 or 11), US$0.25. To **Posadas** US$11, 5½ hrs, road paved. To **Buenos Aires**, US$18, but there are more services from Resistencia to Buenos Aires, Rosario and Santa Fe. To **Paso de los Libres**, 5 hrs, US$6.50. To **Concordia** US$6.50, *Empresa Gualeguaychú*, 2 a day.

Directory **Communications** Internet: *Cybermate*, Jujuy 1087. Open 24 hrs. **Post Office:** San Juan y San Martín. **Telephone:** Pelligrini y Mendoza.

The Chaco

Between the northwest highlands and the Río Paraná to the east lies the Argentine Chaco, comprising the entire provinces of Formosa and Chaco, parts of Salta, Santiago del Estero and Santa Fe, and a tiny corner of the province of Córdoba. Its south limit is the Río Dulce valley. It is a sprawling alluvial lowland, rising gradually toward the west, covered by palm savanna and sometimes impenetrable thorn scrub; the birdlife is abundant and interesting. Numerous **indigenous peoples**, who call themselves Wichi, inhabit the Chaco, including the Toba, Mataco, Mocoví and Pilagá.

Climate There are two climatic zones: the Dry Chaco and the Humid Chaco, each with distinct flora and fauna. South America's highest temperatures, exceeding 45°C, have been recorded here, but winters are mild, with an occasional touch of frost in the south. Rain falls mostly in summer, decreasing from east to west.

The Chaco is mostly cattle country, consisting of large *estancias* with low stocking rates. Tannin and cotton are the traditional industries together with sunflowers, maize and sorghum. The iron-hard *quebracho* (axe-breaker) tree, which grows only in the Argentine and Paraguayan Chaco, is the purest known source of tannin. The industry is struggling against competition from synthetic tannin and the huge mimosa plantations in South Africa. The more accessible eastern forests have nearly disappeared; deforestation of all species is proceeding rapidly in the north and west of the province, which produces charcoal for a military steel foundry in Jujuy. Small roadside factories also produce custom furniture.

Economy

The hot and energetic capital of the Province of Chaco, Resistencia is situated 6½ km up the Barranqueras stream on the west bank of the Paraná. On the Paraná itself is the little port of Barranqueras. Resistencia is known as the 'city of the statues', there being over 200 of these in the streets. The **Fogón de los Arrieros**, Brown 350, entre López y French, is a famous club frequented by local artists and full of local art and '*objets*' from abroad. It promotes the city's statues. ■ *Open to non-members Mon-Sat 0800-1200, Tue, Wed, Thu only, 2130-0100, US$2.* **Museo Histórico Regional**, Donovan 425, in the Escuela Normal Sarmiento, traces the development of the city. ■ *Mon-Fri 0800-1200, 1600-1800.* **Museo de Bellas Artes**, Mitre 175, collection of 19th- and 20th-century local works. ■ *Tue-Sat, 0730-1200, 1500-1900.* **Museo Del Hombre Chaqueño**, Illia 655, sections on indigenous peoples, European immigration and the fauna of the Chaco. **Museo Policial**, Roca 233, sections on marijuana and other drugs. ■ *Mon-Fri 0800-1200, 1800-2000, Sat 0800-1200.* The tourist office is at Santa Fe 178, T/F423547. There are banks and *cambios* in the centre for exchange.

Resistencia
Phone code: 03722
Colour map 6, grid C6
Population: 218,000
544 km N of Santa Fe

Argentina

Excursions To the Isla del Cerrito, an island forming a provincial nature reserve, 63 km northwest. Tour operator : *Puerto Aventura*, Saavedra 557, T/F432932, is very helpful.

Sleeping and eating B *Colón*, Sta María de Oro 143, T422862. Old fashioned, comfortable. B *Covadonga*, Güemes 182, T444444, F443444. Small rooms, a/c, *Tabaré* snack bar. C *Sahara*, Güemes 160. A/c. Recommended. D *Alfil*, Santa Maria de Oro 495, T420882. A/c extra, English spoken. D *Celta*, Alberdi 210, T422986. With bath, basic. D *Res Alberdi*, Av Alberdi 317. F without bath, basic but clean, restaurant. Recommended. **Camping** *Parque Dos de Febrero*, Av Avalos. Very pretty, near artificial lake. *Restaurant Sociedad Italiana*, Yrigoyen 204. Excellent cuisine, smart, pricey. *Charly*, Güemes 213. Excellent food and service, good value.

Transport Air Airport 8 km from town (no bus). *Austral* (T445550), *ARG* (T430201) and *Southern Winds* (T443300) to/from Buenos Aires; *Southern Winds* also to Córdoba, Formosa, Rosario, Salta and Tucumán. **Buses** Modern terminal on south outskirts (bus 3 or 8 to centre, 20 mins, US$0.35; remise US$2). To **Corrientes** over the Río Paraná bridge, every 15 mins from Av Alberdi near Plaza 25 de Mayo, 40 mins, US$0.70. To **Buenos Aires** 14 hrs, US$21 several companies, most services overnight. To **Santa Fe**, 8 hrs, US$15. To **Formosa** 2½ hrs, US$6.50. To **Iguazú** US$21. To **Posadas**, 5½ hrs, US$11. To **Santiago del Estero**, several companies daily, 9 hrs, US$17-20. To **Salta** (for connections to Bolivia), *Veloz del Norte*, *Burbuja* and *Central Sáenz Peña*, daily 1830 and 1900, 15 hrs, US$18. To **Bolivian border at Aguas Blancas/Bermejo**, take bus for Salta, change at Güemes, for direct connection to Orán. To **Clorinda** and Paraguayan border US$10, 5 hrs. To **Asunción** daily, via Formosa, *La Internacional*, 6½ hrs, US$12.

Roque Sáenz Peña

Phone code: 03714
Population: 75,000
160 km N of Resistencia

Route 16, the main road across the Chaco, runs northwest from Resistencia to connect with Route 9, the main northern highway, north of Metán and provides the quickest route between Paraguay and northwest Argentina. It is mostly paved, several tolls. **Presidencia Roque Sáenz Peña** offers almost no shade for relief from the overpowering summer heat. The Parque Zoológico, 3 km from the centre, is one of the best in the country, containing a wide variety of animals native to the Chaco, as well as a botanical reserve of local species. **A** *Gualok*, San Martín 1198, T420521, including use of thermal baths (also available to non-residents for a small charge), safe car park. **B** *Augustus*, Belgrano 483, T422809, a/c. Res Asturias, Belgrano 402, T420210, fair. Res Sáenz Peña, Sub Palmira 464, T420320, near bus station, cheap. ■ *Buses to Buenos Aires, daily 2000, US$24 (from Buenos Aires also daily 2000),* La Estrella *and* La Internacional *alternate days; to Santiago del Estero and Tucumán, daily; to Resistencia (connection for Salta 1700 daily), 2 hrs, US$2.75.*

Parque Nacional Chaco

An ecological island, preserving some of the last remaining eastern Chaco forest and savanna

Between Resistencia and Sáenz Peña, this 15,000 ha park is a good place to see the region's abundant bird life. Flora includes three species of *quebracho* as well as the palo borracho. The park keeper offers a 1-2 hours' walk, explaining the region's plants and animals. Recommended. Entry US$2.50. There are camping facilities, good, free, cold showers, but the nearest supplies are in Capitán Solari, 6 km from the park entrance. ■ *Buses from Resistencia 4 daily, 2½ hrs, US$2.75, as far as Capitán Solari, where transport is available, US$1.40 pp, ask around.*

At 31 km northwest of Roque Sáenz Peña is **Avia Terai**, where the road forks. Provincial Route 94 goes southwest to General Pinedo, then continues paved as national Route 89 to Quimilí and Santiago del Estero. Federico Kirbus tells us that on the border of Chaco and Santiago del Estero provinces on this road is **Campo del Cielo**, a meteorite impact field about 15 km by 4 km where approximately 5,000 years ago a planetoid broke before landing into 30 main pieces. Some of the meteorites are on display in Buenos Aires (the Rivadavia Museum and the Planetarium), but the largest, 'El Chaco' (33.4 tonnes), is on display at the Campo. ■ *Access at Gancedo, where you travel 15 km south to Las Víboras.*

From Avia Terai, Route 16, heading northwest passes through **Pampa del Infierno** on its route to Route 9 in Salta province. There are service stations at Roque Sáenz Peña, Pampa del Infierno, Pampa de los Guanacos (good hot, clean and free showers at the YPF station, and good value set dinner at the *comedor* next door), **Taco Pozo** (basic *Hospedaje* half block from ACA station), **El Quebrachal** (gaucho festival in late Nov) and **Joaquín V González** (last fuel before Güemes en route to Salta). Fuel cannot be pumped during frequent power cuts. In general, Chaco roads are poor.

Formosa

Phone code: 03717
Colour map 6, grid C6
Population: 95,000
240 km above Corrientes

The capital of Formosa Province is the only Argentine port of any note on the Río Paraguay. The surroundings, still in the Chaco, are flat and swampy, the climate and vegetation subtropical. **Museo Histórico Regional**, 25 de Mayo y Belgrano, has a large collection of artefacts with no particular logic. ■ *Mon-Fri 0730-1200, 1500-1930, free.* Tourist offices at Brandzen 117, T426502, and at bus terminal, very helpful.

Sleeping and eating **B** *Turismo*, San Martín 759, T426004. Best, parking, a/c. **B** *Colón*, Belgrano 1068, T426547. Noisy, a/c, colour TV, spacious, **C** without a/c, good, includes breakfast. **D** *Colonial*, San Martín 879, T426345. Basic, a/c, parking. **D** *Casa de Familia*, Belgrano 1056. Good. Opposite bus terminal is **E** *Hosp El Extranjero*, Gutnisky 2660, T428676. Modern, a/c, with bath, also short stay. **Camping** *Camping Banco Provincial*, 4 km south on Ruta 11, good facilities including pool, T429877. *Las Arianas*, 10 km south (turn off Route 11 at El Pucu, Km 6), T427640. **Eating:** *Ser San*, 25 de Mayo y Moreno. Good. *Pizzería Italia*, 25 de Mayo y Rivadavia. Also on 25 de Mayo: *El Tono María*, No 55. Good Italian food, nice atmosphere, expensive. *Parrillada La Cascada*, No 335.

Transport **Air** El Pucu airport, 7 km north; *Austral*, **ARG** (T435713) and *Southern Winds* to Buenos Aires. **Buses** Terminal on west outskirts (bus 4 or 11 to/from centre). To **Asunción**,

0400, 0800 and 1730, 3 hrs, US$6.50; easier to go to Clorinda on the border (US$4.50) and then take a micro to Asunción. To **Resistencia**, 6 a day, US$6.50; to **Buenos Aires** US$24, *La Internacional*.

Clorinda lies almost opposite Asunción (Paraguay). The Puente Loyola crosses to Puerto Falcón, Paraguay (easy border crossing). From Puerto Pilcomayo, close to Clorinda (bus US$0.25) there is a vehicle ferry service to Itá Enramada (Paraguay), a US$0.50, 20 minutes journey every 20 minutes. Clorinda has a banana festival in early October. There are various hotels (**B-C**). ■ *Buses from Argentine end of Puente Loyola: to Formosa (10 a day), Resistencia (4) and Santa Fe/ Rosario/Bs As (3).*

Clorinda
Phone code: 03718
Colour map 6, grid C6
Population: 40,000
137 km N of Formosa

Some 50,000 ha, 65 km northwest of Clorinda is this national park with its flora including quebrachos, caranday palms and palo boracho trees. Among the protected species are aguará-guazú, giant anteaters and tapirs. Caimans, tegú lizards, black howler monkeys, rheas and a variety of birds can also be seen. You must be accompanied by *guardaparques*. ■ *Buses run to Laguna Blanca, 4 km from the Park Entrance; 3 km further is the guardaparque office, near which camping is permitted.*

Parque Nacional Río Pilcomayo

Argentina

Posadas

This is the main Argentine port on the south bank of the Alto Paraná and the capital of the province of Misiones. It is very hot in summer. Yerba mate, tea and tobacco are grown in the area. On the opposite bank of the river lies the Paraguayan town of Encarnación, reached by the San Roque bridge. The city's centre is **Plaza 9 de Julio**, on which stand the **Cathedral** and the **Gobernación**, in imitation French style. There is a good **Museo Regional** at Alberdi 600 in the Parque Río del Paraguay, 11 blocks north of Plaza 9 de Julio, by the river. ■ *Mon-Fri 0800-1200.* A good way of seeing the city is to take the No 7 bus ('Circunvalación') from C Junín. **Museo Andrés Guacurarí**, Gen Paz 1865, houses archaeological pieces from the areas to be flooded by the Yacyretá hydroelectric project, and a section on the Jesuit missionary era. ■ *Mon-Fri 0700-1300, 1400-1900.* **Museo de Ciencias Naturales**, San Luis (47)1968, includes sections on the Guaraní, Jesuit missions, especially San Ignacio Miní, European colonization and endangered species. ■ *Mon-Fri 0800-1200, 1500-1900, Sat-Sun (summer) 0900-1200, US$0.50.*

Phone code: 03752
Population: 141,000
377 km above Corrientes

The bus terminal which used to be at Uruguay (45) y Mitre (54) has now been converted into the *Paseo Cultural La Terminal* and a new terminal built on the southern outskirts. The tourist office is at Colón (39) 1985 y La Rioja (42), T424360, helpful, maps and brochures in English of Posadas, Formosa and Iguazú Falls. Municipal kiosk on Plaza 9 de Julio, open 0800-1200, 1400-2000 daily, hotel listings for Misiones province.

All streets are numbered instead of named: the central plaza is bounded by C 36, 38, 37 and 39. Numbers shown in brackets in text

A *Libertador*, San Lorenzo (41) 2208, T437601, F439448. With breakfast, also cheaper rooms for travellers. **B** *Continental*, Bolívar (38) 1814, T438966, F435302. Comfortable but noisy, restaurant, safe, parking, breakfast. **B** *Posadas*, Bolívar (38) 1949, T440888, F430294. Garage, a/c, TV, comfortable, good service, snack bar, laundry. Highly recommended. **C** *City*, Colón (39) 1780, T433901. A/c, central, small rooms and beds, good restaurant. **C** *Res Marlis*, Corrientes (50) 1734, T425764. German spoken. Highly recommended. **C** *Le Petit*, Santiago del Estero (52) 1630, T436031. Parking. Recommended. **D** *Res Andresito*, Salta (48) 1743, T423850. Youth hostel style, noisy. **D** *Colonial*, Barrufaldi (56) 2419, near *Paseo Cultural La Terminal*. Recommended. **D** *Res Nagel*, Calle 58 No 2146 (formerly Pedro Méndez 211), 2 blocks from *Paseo Cultural La Terminal*. Small rooms, shared shower, no hot water, shady patio, no breakfast. **Camping** Municipal campsite on the river, off the road to San Ignacio Miní, electric showers, dirty, shop, reached by buses 4 or 21 from centre.

Sleeping
After street number changes, all buildings have old and new numbers

Eating

Several cheap places on Mitre near the Paseo Cultural La Terminal, near the market and on the road to the port

La Ventana, Bolívar (38) 1725. Excellent. *Restaurant de la Sociedad Española*, La Rioja (42) 1848. Good food, popular lunches. *El Estribo*, Tucumán (50) y Ayacucho (43). Good cooking in attractive atmosphere. Recommended. *La Querencia*, Bolívar (38) 322, on Plaza 9 de Julio. Good value. Recommended. *Pizzería Los Pinos*, Sarmiento (34) y Rivadavia (33). Excellent and cheap. *Pizzería La Grata Alegría*, Bolívar (38) y Junín (45). Good. *Sukimo*, Azara (37) near San Martín (36). Good for breakfast. The restaurant at San Martín (36) 1788 serves excellent meals, good value.

Tour operators

Express Travel, Félix de Azara (37) 2097, T437687, Amex. *Guaraní*, Buenos Aires (35) 1405. Good programmes, skilled guides, ask for Marcía Diaz. *Viajes Turismo*, Colón (39) 1901. Ask for Kenneth Nairn, speaks English, most helpful, good tours to Iguazú and local sights.

Transport

Air Gen San Martín Airport, 12 km west, reached by Bus No 8 or 28 in 20 mins, US$0.45, taxi US$13. To **Buenos Aires**, *AIRG* (Catamarca (46) 1899, T426700 – also to Iguazú), *AR/Austral* (Ayacucho (43) 264, T432889) and *Southern Winds*.

Buses New terminal about 3 km out of the city on Av Quaranta (126), the road to Corrientes. To **Buenos Aires**, 15 hrs, shop around off season for best deal; *Singer* and *Tigre-Iguazú* each have several buses a day: *común* US$28, *diferencial* US$35, *ejecutivo* (with hot meal) US$55; some go via Resistencia, some via Concordia. From the Argentine side of the international bridge bus tickets to Buenos Aires are sold which include taxi to bus terminal and breakfast. Frequent services to San Ignacio Miní, 1 hr, US$2.50, and Puerto Iguazú, *servicio común* US$10, 7 hrs, *expreso*, US$12, 5 hrs. To **Corrientes** US$11. To **Formosa**, US$5.50. To **Resistencia**, 6-7 hrs, US$11. To **Concordia**, *Singer*, US$19, 2100 daily, 10 hrs. To **Concepción del Uruguay**, *Singer*, US$18, 11 hrs. To **Córdoba** with *Singer* and *Litoral* on alternate days at 1200, 15 hrs, US$21. To **Tucumán**, *La Estrella*, *Vosa*, *Brown*, daily, 17 hrs, US$28. **International** To Asunción, *Nuestra Señora de la Asunción*, daily except Sun at 1130, US$11, 7 hrs.

Directory

Banks *Banco de Iberá*, Bolívar (38) 1821 (main plaza), changes Amex TCs. *Banco Nacional del Lavoro*, Plaza 9 de Julio, ATM accepts MasterCard and Visa. *Cambio Mazza*, Bolívar (38) 1932 and Buenos Aires (35) 1442, open Sat 0800-1200, TCs accepted. If stuck when banks and *cambios* are closed, cross the river to Encarnación and use the street changers. **Communications** Post Office: Bolívar (38) y Ayacucho (43). **Consulates** Brazil, Mitre (54) 2131, T424830, 0800-1200, visas issued free, photo required, 90 days given. **Paraguay**, San Lorenzo (41) 179.

Border with Paraguay

For Paraguayan immigration, see page 1069

Argentine immigration and customs are on the Argentine side of the bridge to Encarnación. Buses across the bridge (from opposite bus terminal every 15 minutes, *servicio común* US$1, *servicio diferencial* US$2) do not stop for formalities; you must get exit stamps. Get off the bus, keep your ticket and luggage, and catch a later bus. Pedestrians and cyclists are not allowed to cross; cyclists must ask officials for assistance. The ferry across the river is for locals only.

San Ignacio Miní

Phone code: 03752 Colour map 7, grid C1 63 km E of Posadas

The site of the most impressive Jesuit ruins in the Misiones region is a good base for visiting the other Jesuit ruins and for walking. The local festival is 30-31 July. San Ignacio was founded on its present site in 1696. The 100 sq-m, grass-covered plaza is flanked north, east and west by 30 parallel blocks of stone buildings with 10 small, one-room dwellings in each block. The roofs have gone, but the massive metre-thick walls are still standing except where they have been torn down by the *ibapoi* trees. The public buildings, some of them still 10 m high, are on the south side of the plaza. In the centre are the ruins of a large church finished about 1724. The masonry, sandstone from the Río Paraná, was held together by a sandy mud.

Inside the entrance 200 m to the ruins is the **Centro de Interpretación Jesuítico-Guaraní**, or 'Museo Vivo', with representations of the lives of the Guaraníes before the arrival of the Spanish, the work of the Jesuits and the

The Real Mission

The Jesuits set up their first missions among the Guaraní Indians about 1609, in the region of Guaíra, now in Brazil. The missions flourished: cotton was introduced, the Indians wove their own clothes, dressed like Europeans, raised cattle, and built and sculpted and painted their own churches. But in 1627 they were violently attacked by the slave-hunting Bandeirantes from São Paulo, and by 1632 the position of the missions had become impossible: 12,000 converts, led by the priests, floated on 700 rafts down the Paranapanema into the Paraná, only to find their route made impassable by the Guaíra Falls. They pushed for 8 days through dense virgin forests on both sides of the river, then built new boats and continued their journey. 725 kilometres from their old homes they founded new missions in what is now Paraguay, Argentine Misiones, and Brazilian Rio Grande do Sul. By the early 18th century there were, on both sides of the river, 30 mission villages with a combined population of over 100,000 souls. Only four of these show any

signs of their former splendour: San Ignacio Miní, São Miguel (Brazil), and Jesús and Trinidad (Paraguay). (Note Trinidad can also be visited by bus from Posadas. See Paraguay section for details.) At the height of its prosperity in 1731 San Ignacio contained 4,356 people. In 1767, Charles III of Spain expelled the Jesuits from Spanish territory; the Franciscans and Dominicans then took over. After the Jesuits had gone, there was a rapid decline in prosperity. By 1784 there were only 176 Indians at San Ignacio Miní; by 1810, none remained. By order of the Paraguayan dictator Francia, all the settlements were evacuated in 1817, and San Ignacio was set on fire. The village was lost in the jungle until it was discovered again in 1897. In 1943 an agency of the Argentine Government took control. Some of the craft work produced at the settlement can be seen at two museums in Buenos Aires: the Museo Colonial Isaac Fernández Blanco and the municipal Museo de Arte Colonial.

consequences of their expulsion, as well as a fine model of the mission in its heyday. **Museo Provincial** contains a small collection of artefacts from Jesuit reducciones. The site is maintained by UNESCO as a National Monument. There are heavy rains in February. Mosquitoes can be a problem. ■ *0700-1900, US$1.25, US$5 with guide, tip appreciated if the guards look after your luggage. Allow about 1½ hrs for a leisurely visit. Go early to avoid crowds; good birdwatching. Son et-lumière show at the ruins, 2000 (not Mon or Tue), weekends only out of season, cancelled in wet weather, Spanish only, tickets from museum.*

The ruins of another Jesuit mission, **Loreto**, can be reached by a 3 km dirt road (signposted) which turns off the main road 6 km west of San Ignacio. Little remains other than a few walls, though excavations are in progress. *Colonial* hotel, at entrance, secluded. A second ruined mission, **Santa Ana**, 16 km west, is much less well preserved but more extensive in area than San Ignacio. Santa Ana was the site of the Jesuit iron foundry. The ruins are 1½ km along a path from the main road (signposted), entry US$0.50.

The house of writer Horacio Quiroga, beautifully secluded with a fine view, is 2 km outside town, entry US$1, recommended. From here the path leads to Puerto Nuevo on the Río Paraná, from where, during summer, boats cross to Paraguay.

D *Hosp El Descanso*, Pellegrini 270, T470207, a long way from ruins. Modern, quiet, owner speaks German, **E** without bath, excellent camping. Recommended (but breakfast not so good). **D** *Hosp Alemán Los Salpeterer*, Sarmiento y Centenario, T470362, 100 m from bus terminal. **E** without bath, kitchen, nice garden, Argentine run, pleasant, 'pool', camping. Recommended, book in advance. *Hosp Los Lagartos*, Pellegrini y Quiroga, between Quiroga's house and the ruins. English and French spoken, kitchen regional meals and sweets, riding, excursions, new in 2001. **Camping** 2 pleasant sites by small lake about 5 km south of San Ignacio, on Route 12, cold showers only. There are *comedores* near the entrance to the ruins, eg *El Coco*, large choice, good food; *Santa Clara*, cheap, tasty, simple. A shop opposite the entrance sells huge homemade ice creams.

Sleeping & eating

Argentina

Argentina

Transport Some buses leave from terminal but many services stop only at the entrance to **San Ignacio**. Buses to/from **Posadas** every 30 mins-1 hr, US$2.50, last return bus at 2100. To **Puerto Iguazú**, US$10. To **Buenos Aires**, US$21 including dinner, 24 hrs, depart 1800 or 1900.

San Ignacio to Puerto Iguazú

North of San Ignacio is **Eldorado**, a prosperous town (*Population*: 14,440. *Phone code*: 03751) surrounded by flourishing *mate*, tung, citrus, eucalyptus and tobacco plantations. The *ACA* office, Av San Martín 1905, T422284, is very helpful and has a large illuminated map of Eldorado and its surroundings. For information on the **Misiones Rainforest Reserve**, contact Daphne Colcombet, T421351. **A** *Hostería ACA*, Esperanza y Ruta 17, Km 9, T421370, pool, good facilities. **C** *Atlántida*, San Martín 3087, T421441. A/c, pool, parking, good restaurants. Recommended. *Estancia Las Mercedes*, Av San Martín Km 4, T076960921/075131512, www.estancialasmercedes.com.ar An old yerba mate farm, period furnishings, all meals, transfers, riding, canoeing, pool, excursions. *Gran Riojano*, Av San Martín 314, T422217, five minutes walk from main road crossing, with restaurant. **Camping** Municipal site in Parque Schweim, Av San Martín, Km 1, T42154, free, good.

Near **Wanda**, 42 km further north, at Km 1,593, there are two open-cast amethyst and quartz mines which sell gems. There are free guided tours to one of them, Tierra Colorada, daily. Regular buses from Posadas and Puerto Iguazú, then walk 1½ km. Nearby at **Puerto Esperanza** is the **C** *Hotel Las Brisas*, Swiss-owned, English and German spoken, discount for Swiss nationals. (Buses between Posadas and Puerto Iguazú stop near the mines and the hotel.)

The Iguazú Falls

Colour map 7, grid C1
The main falls are 20 m higher than Niagara and about half as wide again

The mighty Igazú Falls are the most overwhelmingly magnificent in all of South America. So impressive are they that Eleanor Roosevelt remarked "poor Niagara" on witnessing them.

The Iguazú Falls, on the Argentina-Brazil border, are 19 km upstream from the confluence of the Río Iguazú with the Río Alto Paraná. The Río Iguazú (*guazú* is Guaraní for big and *I* is Guaraní for water), which rises in the Brazilian hills near Curitiba, receives the waters of some 30 rivers as it crosses the plateau. Above the main falls, the river, sown with wooded islets, opens out to a width of 4 km. There are rapids for 3½ km above the 60 m precipice over which the water plunges in 275 falls over a frontage of 2,470 m, at a rate of 1,750 cu m a second.

Viewed from below, the tumbling water is majestically beautiful in its setting of begonias, orchids, ferns and palms. Toucans, flocks of parrots and cacique birds and great dusky swifts dodge in and out along with myriad butterflies (there are at least 500 different species). Above the impact of the water, upon basalt rock, hovers a perpetual 30 m high cloud of mist in which the sun creates blazing rainbows.

The first European visitor to the falls was the Spaniard Alvar Núñez Cabeza de Vaca in 1541, on his search for a connection between the Brazilian coast and the Río de la Plata.

Between Oct and Feb (daylight saving dates change each year) Brazil is 1 hr ahead of Argentina

On both sides of the falls there are National Parks. Transport between the two parks is via the Ponte Tancredo Neves as there is no crossing at the falls themselves. The Brazilian park offers a superb panoramic view of the whole falls and is best visited in the morning when the light is better for photography (entry fee payable in reais only). The Argentine park (which requires a day to explore properly) offers closer views of the individual falls in their forest setting with its wildlife and butterflies, though to appreciate these properly you need to go early and get well away from the visitors areas. Busiest times are holiday periods and on Sunday. Both parks have visitors' centres and tourist facilities on both sides are constantly being improved.

Parque Nacional Iguazú The park covers an area of 67,620 ha. The fauna includes jaguars, tapirs, brown capuchin monkeys, collared anteaters and coatimundi, but these are rarely seen around the falls. There is a huge variety of birds; among the butterflies are shiny blue morphos and red/black heliconius. The **Circuito Inferior**, Lower Trail, leads down very steep steps to the lower falls and the start of the boat trip to **Isla San Martín**. Ferry leaves on demand, free, three minutes. A path on the island leads to the top of the hill, where there are trails to some of the less visited falls and rocky pools (take bathing gear in summer). The **Circuito Superior**, or Upper Trail, follows the top of the falls, giving panoramic views. A second train route takes visitors to the **Garganta del Diablo** (Devil's Throat). A visit here is particularly recommended in the evening when the light is best and the swifts are returning to roost on the cliffs, some behind the water. The catwalks and platform get very crowded in mid-morning after tour buses arrive. A path, the **Sendero Verde**, taking about 20 minutes from near the Visitors' Centre, leads to the start of the Upper and Lower trails.

■ *US$4, payable in pesos, reais or dollars (guests at Hotel Sheraton should pay and get tickets stamped at the hotel to avoid paying again). Open daily 0800-1900. Visitors' Centre includes a museum of local fauna and an auditorium for periodic slide shows (on request, minimum 8 people), no commentary, only music; it also sells a good guide book on Argentine birds. Access: A free train service completed in 2001 leaves every 20 mins from the Visitors' Centre, departing for the start of 2 sets of walkways, both taking about an hour. In the rainy season, when water levels are high, waterproof coats or swimming costumes are advisable for some of the lower catwalks and for boat trips. Cameras should be carried in a plastic bag. Wear shoes with good soles, as the rocks can be very slippery in places.*

Activities A number of activities are offered, both from the Visitors' Centre and through agencies in Puerto Iguazú and the *Sheraton*. *Aventura Náutica* is a journey by launch along the lower Río Iguazú, US$15. *Safari Náutico*, a 4-km journey by boat above the falls, US$15. *Gran Aventura*, an 8-km ride through the jungle, followed by a

Argentina

Puerto Iguazú

■ Sleeping	6 Hostería Casa Blanca	11 Res San Fernando	2 El Criollito
1 Alexander	7 Hostería Los	12 Saint George	3 Fechoría
2 Ana	Helechos	13 Tierra Colorada	Jardín de Iguazú
3 Bompland	8 Noelia		5 La Rueda
4 El Libertador	9 Res Gastón	● Eating	6 Panificadora Real
5 Hospedaje Uno	10 Res Paquita	1 El Charro	

N
Not to scale

Argentina

boat trip on the rapids to the Devil's Throat, US$33. *Full Day* combines *safari náutico* with *aventura náutica*, US$30 (five hours), or US$45 with *gran aventura* (seven hours), lunch extra. There are sometimes night-time walking tours between the *Hotel Sheraton* and the falls when the moon is full; on clear nights the moon casts a blue halo over the falls. Mountain bikes and boats can also be hired, US$3 an hour. For serious birdwatching and nature walks with an English speaking guide contact Daniel Samay (*Explorador* agency) or Miguel Castelino, Apartado Postal 22, Puerto Iguazú (3370), Misiones, T420157, FocusTours@aol.com   Highly recommended.

Sleeping & eating

See under Puerto Iguazú or Foz do Iguaçu (Brazil). Puerto Iguazú is the safer of the two towns, but after the collapse of the Argentine economy, many hotels have closed. Food and drinks are available in the park, either cheap snacks or more expensive fare (no vegetarian options).

Transport

For transport between the Argentine and Brazilian sides see below under Puerto Iguazú

Transportes El Práctico buses run every hour from Puerto Iguazú bus terminal, stopping at the National Park entrance for the purchase of entry tickets, continuing to the Visitors' Centre, US$5 return. First bus 0740, last 1940, last return 2000, journey time 30 mins. These buses are sometimes erratic, especially when it is wet, even though the times are clearly indicated. Cars are not allowed beyond Visitors' Centre (car entry US$3).

Puerto Iguazú

Phone code: 03757
Colour map 7, grid C1
Population: 19,000

This modern town is situated 18 km northwest of the falls high above the river on the Argentine side near the confluence of the Ríos Iguazú and Alto Paraná. It serves mainly as a centre for visitors to the falls. The port lies to the north of the town centre at the foot of a hill: from the port you can follow the Río Iguazú downstream towards Hito Argentino, a *mirador* with views over the point where the Ríos Iguazú and Alto Paraná meet and over neighbouring Brazil and Paraguay. There are souvenir shops,

Around the Iguazú Falls

	2	Sheraton Internacional
Sleeping		Iguazú Resort
1	Das Cataratas	

toilets and *La Barranca* pub here; bus US$0.25. **Museums**: **Museo Mbororé**, San Martín 231, exhibition on Guaraní culture, also sells Guaraní-made handicrafts, cheaper than shops. ■ *Mon-Sat 1700-2100, US$0.50*. **Museo Imágenes de la Selva**, Calle Los Cedros y Guatambú, one block west of Av Victoria Aguirre, displays the sculptures in wood of Rodolfo Allou, mostly from materials found in the forest. He was related to Jules Verne. ■ *0800-1200, 1500-1800, US$1*. **Other sites**: **La Aripuca** is a large wooden structure housing a centre for the appreciation of the native species and their environment. Turn off Ruta 12 just after *Hotel Cataratas*; T423488, English and German spoken. At **Güira Oga** (Casa de los Pájaros) birds that have been injured are cured and reintroduced to the wild. There is also a trail in the forest and a breeding centre for endangered species. Turn off Ruta 12 at *Hotel Orquídeas Palace*; T156-70684 (mob). A Zona Franca (free trade zone) is being built between Argentine immigration post and the bridge to Brazil. It will be open to tourists. **Tourist information** Aguirre 311, T420800, helpful, can arrange good value taxi tours. ■ *Mon-Fri 0800-1300, 1400-2000, Sat-Sun 0800-1200, 1630-2000*.

Sleeping

L *Sheraton Internacional Iguazú Resort*, T421600, F491810, or 0800-8889180, in Buenos Aires 011-4318 9390, www.sheraton.com Fine position overlooking the falls, completely remodelled, rooms with garden views cost less, excellent, check-out can take ages. **B** *Saint George*, Córdoba 148, T420633, www.hotelsaintgeorge.com With breakfast, comfortable, pool and garden, good, expensive restaurant, close to bus station. Recommended. **C** *Alexander*, Córdoba 685, opposite bus station, T420249, T420566. With breakfast, a/c, pool. **C** *Hostería Casa Blanca*, Guaraní 121, two blocks from bus station, T421320. **D** in low season, with breakfast, fan, large rooms with phone. **C-D** *Hostería Los Helechos*, Amarante 76, off Córdoba, behind *Saint George*, T/F420338. With breakfast, cheaper rooms have no TV, owner speaks German, pleasant, a/c or fan, pool. **C** *El Libertador*, Bompland 110, T/F420984. Modern, central, helpful, large bedrooms and public rooms, rooms at back have balconies overlooking garden and swimming pool. **D** *La Cabaña*, Av Tres Fronteras 434, T420564. Breakfast extra, very helpful, bus to falls stops outside. **D** *Res Paquita*, Córdoba 158, opposite terminal, T420434. Some rooms with terrace, a/c extra, nice setting. **D** *Res Rioselva*, San Lorenzo 140, at end of street, T421555. Laundry facilities, large garden, pool, communal barbecue. Recommended. **D** *Res San Fernando*, Córdoba, near terminal, T421429. With breakfast, popular. **D** *Tierra Colorada*, Córdoba y El Urú 28, T420649, F420572. Fan or a/c, cheaper without breakfast, pool, trips arranged, very good. **E** *Bompland*, Av Bompland 33, T420965. More with a/c, barbecue, central, family run. **E** *Res Gastón*, Félix de Azara 590, T423184. With breakfast, a/c, youth hostel style, by river. **F** pp *Ana*, San Lorenzo 70. With breakfast, kitchen, German spoken, quiet, good. **F** *Noelia*, Fray Luis Beltrán 119, T420729. Not far from bus terminal, good value, with bath. **Youth hostel D** *Hospedaje Uno*, Beltrán 116, T420529, iguazu@hostels.org.ar With breakfast, **E** in dormitory accommodation, HI. Recommended, tour to Itaipú, Foz de Iguaçu and Brazilian side of the falls. The **Tourist Office** has a list of family accommodation (**E**).

Parque Nacional
Foz do Iguaçu

Río Iguazú Superior

Circuito Inferior
Brazilian Visitors' Centre
Garganta del Diablo

Argentine Visitors' Centre

Circuito Superior & Saltos Bossetti, Mbigua, Adán y Eva, San Martín

Isla San Martín

Iguazu Falls

Floriano Falls

Bañado

To Puerto Canoas

To Bernardo de Yrigoyen

Parque Nacional Iguazú

To Airport

Argentina

Camping Municipal site, Corrientes y Entre Ríos, reported as 'grim'. *Camping El Pindo*, Av Aguirre, Km 3 at the southern edge of town, US$1.50 pp, plus charge for tent and for use of pool, friendly, but very run down. There are also facilities at *Camping El Yaguarete*, Route 12, Km 5, T420168.

Eating *La Rueda*, Córdoba 28. Good food at reasonable prices. *El Charro*, Córdoba 106. Good food, *pizzería* and *parrilla*, popular with locals, good value, no credit cards. *El Criollito*, Tres Fronteras 62. Good range of vegetarian options. Recommended. *Jardín de Iguazú*, Córdoba y Misiones, at bus terminal. Good. *Fechoría*, Ingeniero Eppens 294. Good *empanadas*. *Panificadora Real*, Córdoba y Guaraní. Good bread, open Sun evening; another branch at Victoria y Brasil in the centre.

Tour operators *Turismo Dick*, Aguirre 226, T420778, turismodick@interiguazu.com.ar Open Mon-Sat 0830-1300, 1630-2000. *Turismo Cuenca del Plata*, Amarante 76, T421330, F421458, cuencadelplata@fnn.net *IGRTur*, Terminal de Omnibus, local 5, T/F422983 (also at *Sheraton* and airport). All tours sold, mountain bike hire, 2-hr circuit in forest on quadbikes, information on hostels and other accommodation. *Aguas Grandes*, Mariano Moreno 58, T421140, F423096 Tours to both sides of the falls and further afield: Saltos de Mocona, 5,000 m wide; Puerto Península, using old logging trails, rope ladders in trees and abseiling down; Sendero de los Saltos, giant ferns, abseiling down waterfalls, swimming; Raices Guaraníes to an indigenous community; bilingual and local guides, flexible. *Cabalgatas por la Selva*, Ruta 12, just after the Rotonda for the road to the international bridge, T155-42180 (mob). For horse riding. *Explorador Expediciones*, Perito Moreno 217, 1 B, T/F421632. Photographic safaris.Recommended taxi-guides, *Juan Villalba*, T420973 (radiotaxi 044), good value, speaks basic English; *Orlando Kalbermatter*, T420983, T0700-20288 (mob). Agencies arrange day tours to the Brazilian side (lunch in Foz), Itaipú and Ciudad del Este, though more time is spent shopping than at the Falls, and to a gem mine at Wanda, the Jesuit ruins at San Ignacio Miní and a local zoo (10 hrs driving time, entry fees not included).

Transport **Radio taxis** T420973/421707, fares: to airport US$10, to Argentine falls US$10, to Brazilian falls US$12, to centre of Foz US$10, to Ciudad del Este US$10, to Itaipu US$18 return, to Wanda gem mines with wait US$21.

Air Airport is south of Puerto Iguazú near the Falls. *Expreso del Valle* buses (T420348) between airport and bus terminal connect with plane arrivals and departures, US$2. Check times at AR office. Taxis charge US$6.50 to *Hotel Sheraton*, at least US$11 to Puerto Iguazú, US$10 to Foz do Iguaçu and US$15 to the Brazilian airport. *AR/Austral* and *AIRG* fly direct to **Buenos Aires**, 1 hr 40 mins. For the best view on landing, sit on the right side of the aircraft.

From Brazil T55-74-227229 to compare onward bus prices with those offered in Foz rodoviária

Buses The bus terminal, at Av Córdoba y Av Misiones, has a phone office, a Municipalidad office, various tour company desks (see above) and bus offices. To **Buenos Aires**, 21 hrs, most at 1130 and 1830, *Expreso Singer*, *Tigre Iguazú*, *Crucero del Norte*, *ViaBariloche*, daily, US$20-24 *semi cama*, US$30 *cama* (some offer student discounts). It is cheaper to take a local bus to Posadas and then rebook. To **Posadas**, stopping at San Ignacio Miní, frequent, 5 hrs, US$12, *expreso*, 7 hrs US$10 *común*; to **San Ignacio Miní**, US$10 *común*. *Agencia de Pasajes Noelia*, local 3, T422722, can book tickets beyond Posadas for other destinations in Argentina, ISIC discounts available.

Directory **Airline offices** *Aerolíneas Argentinas*, Brasil y Aguirre, T420194/0810-2228 6527. *AIRG*, Perito Moreno 184, loc 2-3, T420390. **Banks** *Banco de la Nación*, Av Aguirre 179. Has ATM for many cards. Several *cambios* on Aguirre near the outskirts of town towards the Falls. *Turismo Dick* (address above), changes TCs at high commission (up to 10%). **Communications** Internet: *Intercom Iguazú*, Victoria Aguirre 240, p 2, T/F423180. *Telecentro*, Victoria Aguirre y Horacio Quiroga, T420177, phone, fax, post office and *Banelco* ATM. **Embassies and consulates** Brazil, Av Guaraní 70, T/F420131.

Border with Brazil Crossing via the Puente Tancredo Neves. When leaving Argentina, Argentine immigration is at the Brazilian end of the bridge.

Transport Buses leave Puerto Iguazú terminal for Foz do Iguaçu every 20 mins, US$1. The bus goes straight through the Argentine side and stops at the Brazilian end of the bridge for both Argentine and Brazilian formalities. The bus waits for those who need stamps. Taxis: between the border and Puerto Iguazú US$10; between the border and *Hotel Sheraton Iguazú* US$21.

Crossing to Paraguay is via Puente Tancredo Neves to Brazil and then via the Puente de la Amistad to Ciudad del Este. Brazilian entry and exit stamps are not required unless you are stopping in Brazil. The Paraguayan consulate is at Bompland 355.
■ *Direct buses (non-stop in Brazil), leave Puerto Iguazú terminal every 30 mins, US$2.50, 45 mins, liable to delays especially in crossing the bridge to Ciudad del Este.*

Border with Paraguay

The Lake District

The Lake District contains a series of great lakes strung along the foot of the Andes from above 40°S to below 50°S in the Parque Nacional Los Glaciares area. This section covers the northern lakes; for convenience the southern lakes, including those in the Los Glaciares park area, are described under Patagonia. The area is good for fishing, watersports, walking, climbing and skiing. The most important centre is the city of Bariloche.

See the Chilean chapter, The Lake District, for map and details of the system of lakes on the far side of the Andes. These can be visited through various passes. **NB** Off season, from mid-August to mid-November, many excursions, boat trips, etc, run on a limited schedule, if at all. Public transport is also limited. For Fishing, see page 78. For information on the web for Argentine and Chilean Lakes and Patagonia: www.interpatagonia.com/loslagos/, www.cpatagonia.com, and www.hotelesenpatagonia.com.ar, on Argentina, in Spanish

Neuquén

Founded in 1904 on the west side of the confluence of the Ríos Limay and Neuquén, Neuquén is a pleasant provincial capital and a major stop en route from the east coast to the northern lakes and Bariloche. It serves both the oilfields to the west and the surrounding fruit orchards. There are also many wine *bodegas* nearby. At the Parque Centenario (be sure *not* to take the bus to Centenario industrial suburb), is a *mirador* with good views of the city and the confluence of the rivers, where they become the Negro. Visit **Museo Provincial Carlos Ameghino**, Yrigoyen 1047, modest but interesting. Facing Neuquén and connected by bridge is Cipolletti, in Río Negro province (*Population*: 43,600) a prosperous centre of the fruit-growing region. All the towns in the valley celebrate the Fiesta Nacional de la Manzana (apples are the main local crop) in the second half of March. The tourist office is at Félix San Martín 182, T4424089, turismo@neuquen.gov.ar ■ *Mon-Fri 0700-2030, Sat-Sun 0800-1500.*

Phone code: 0299
Colour map 8, grid C2
Population: 200,000
223 km from Choele
Choel by Route 22

A *del Comahue*, Av Argentina 387, T442 2440, reservas@hoteldelcomahue.com.ar 4-star, very good. **D** *Res Inglés*, Félix San Martín 534, T442 2252. Convenient, without breakfast, good. **D** *Alcorta* , Alcorta 84, T442 2652. **E** with shared bath, good value new section. **F** *Hospedaje Pani*, Félix San Martín 238. Some rooms with bath, run down but convenient for bus station. 13 km south on Zapala road is **A** *Hostal del Caminante*, T444 0118. With pool and garden, popular. Municipal **camping** site near river, free, packed with locals on weekend afternoons. Eating places include *Tutto al Dente*, Alberdi 49, pasta. *Barracuda*, Rivadavia 265, for basic, quick meals.

Sleeping & eating
Do not confuse the streets Félix San Martín and Gral San Martín

Transport **Air** Airport 7 km west of centre. Bus US$1.50, taxi US$8. To **Buenos Aires**, *Austral, Dinar, Southern Winds* and *AIRG*. *Southern Winds* and *LADE* fly to many destinations, the latter in the Lake District and Patagonia. Schedules change frequently. **Buses** Terminal at Mitre 147. About a dozen companies to **Buenos Aires** daily, US$25-35, 18½ hrs. To **Zapala** daily, 2-3 hrs, US$6.50. To **San Martín de los Andes** (US$13, 4 hrs). To **Bariloche**, 7 companies, US$12-18, 5-6 hrs, sit on left. To **Mendoza**, *Andesmar* and 3 others, daily, US$24-28. **To Chile**: services to **Temuco** stop for a couple of hrs at the border, 12-14 hrs, US$27, some companies offer discount for return, departures Mon-Thu and Sat; 7 companies, some continuing to destinations en route to Puerto Montt.

Directory **Airline offices** *AR/Austral*, Santa Fe 52, T442 2409/0810-2228 6527. *LADE*, Brown 163, T443 1153. *AIRG*, Av Argentina 30, T443 8555. *Southern Winds*, Av Argentina 327, T442 0124. **Banks** *HSBC*, Justo 75, and *Lloyds*, Justo e Yrigoyen. **Communications** Internet: Paseo del Sol, p 1, Perito Moreno y Río Negro, closed Sun and Sat afternoon. *Telecom*, 25 de Mayo 20, open daily till 0030, and Olascoaga 222, open till 2345. **Post Office**: Rivadavia y Santa Fe.

Driving from **Neuquén to Bariloche**, the most direct road (426 km) is by Route 237, then Route 40, missing Junín and San Martín (both 'de los Andes'). The road is fast, skirting the entire length of the Ezequiel Ramos Mexía reservoir, formed by El Chocón dam. Then it drops over an escarpment to cross the Collón Curá river before following the Río Limay valley to Confluencia (see page 183). A more attractive route turns west after the reservoir to go via Junín and San Martín), taking Routes 237, 40 and 234.

The **El Chocón** is an area rich in dinosaur fossils. Red sedimentary rocks have preserved, in relatively good condition, bones and footprints of the animals which lived in this region during the Cretaceous period about 100 million years ago. The **Museo Paleontológico Ernesto Bachmann** (open daily 0900-1900) displays the fossils of a giant carnivor (Giganotosaurus carolinii), bigger than the famous T-rex. *Aventura Jurásica*, in El Chocón (Alejandro París, T4901243) offers guided visits to the museum and the surroundings from US$3 pp not including transfers, 2-3 hours. A *La Posada del Dinosaurio*, T0299-490 1118, F490 1161, posadadino@ infovia.com.ar With breakfast, good.

Plaza Huincul (*Population*: 11,000), 107 km west of Neuquén, is at the heart of the Neuquén oil-fields. In the **Carmen Funes** municipal museum, there are the vertebrae of a dinosaur, Argentinosaurus huinculensis, one of the largest that ever lived on Earth; its vertebrae are estimated to have weighed 70 kg each; a recovered tibia is 1.60 m in length. There is also a nest with fossilized dinosaur eggs.

Zapala
Phone code: 02942
Colour map 8, grid C2
Population: 35,000
185 km W of Neuquén

There is an excellent geology museum here, **Museo Mineralógico Professor Olsacher**, Etcheluz 52. Among the collections of minerals, fossils, shells and rocks, is a complete crocodile jaw, believed to be 80 million-years-old. ■ *Daily 1000-1400, 1800-2000, weekends and holidays 1800-2100, free.* There is an airport, an *ACA* service station, Km 1399 Ruta 22. B *Hue Melén*, Brown 929, T422391, good, restaurant. C *Coliqueo*, Etcheluz 159, T421308, opposite bus terminal, good. C *Nuevo Pehuén*, Vidal y Etcheluz, 1 block from bus terminal, T421308, recommended. E *Odetto's Grill*, Ejército Argentino 455, T422176, near bus terminal, OK. There is a municipal camping site.

Transport **Buses** 4 companies to **San Martín de los Andes**, US$12 (3-4 hrs) via Junín de los Andes. To **Bariloche** 3 direct buses daily, *Albus, TAC, ViaBariloche*. To **Temuco** (Chile) all year, *Centenario* Mon, Wed, Fri, US$25. Buy Chilean currency before leaving.

North of Zapala on the Chilean border is the **Reserva Nacional Copahue**, best-known for its thermal baths and volcano of the same name. The **Termas de Copahue** (*Altitude*: 1,980 m) are enclosed in a gigantic amphitheatre formed by mountain walls, with an opening to the east. Accommodation in the town of

Copahue (*Valle del Volcán*, T02948-495048, *Termas*, T495045, *Pino Azul*, T495071, *Hualcupén* T495049) 15 km from the Termas. Buses connect Copahue with the winter sports resort of Caviahue which offers excellent cross-country skiing in winter, and horseriding, trekking and birdwatching in summer. **A-B** *La Cabaña de Tito*, T495093, open December-April, July-September, warm atmosphere, excellent meals on request. Recommended. **C** *Lago Caviahue*, T495110, restaurant, great views, kitchen facilities. **D** *El Refugio de Caniche*, T495060, shared rooms with kitchen facilities, campsite (summer only), breakfast and dinner, helpful. ■ *There are buses from Neuquén (6½ hrs, US$15).*

Junín de los Andes

Phone code: 02972
Colour map 8, grid B4
Population: 9,000

Known as the trout capital of Argentina, Junín de los Andes is 38 km west of Route 40, between Zapala and Bariloche. A short detour from Junín leads to the very beautiful lakes of Huechulafquen and Paimún (bus, *Airén*, US$5 one way, summer only, check return journey with driver). **A** *Estancia Huechahue* (reached from the Junín-Bariloche bus), T491303, English run, comfortable, farmhouse accommodation, horseriding, fishing, river trips. **B** *Hostería Chimehuín*, Suárez y 25 de Mayo, T491132, fishing hostelry. **C** *Posada Pehuén*, Col Suárez 560, T491569, good value, charming owners, Rosi and Eduardo, recommended. **E** *Marita y Aldo*, 25 de Mayo y Olavarría, T491042, **G** for floorspace, summer only, fun atmosphere, kitchen facilities, popular, good meals on request. **Camping**: *Mallín Beata Laura Vicuña*, T491149, and *La Isla*, both on the river and good. Several campsites in beautiful surroundings on Lagos Huechulafquen and Paimún. Good restaurants include *Ruca Hueney*, Col Suárez y Milanesio, trout and pasta dishes and *Pizzaría Fitzroya*, Rivadavia 1048. Tourist office at Milanesio y Col Suárez, T/F491160, www.mercotour.com/junindelosandes ■ *Between Junín and San Martín is Chapelco civil airport, served by* Austral *and* Southern Winds *from Buenos Aires and* LADE *(Gen Roca 636, San Martín de los Andes, F427672) from Bahía Blanca, Esquel, Mar del Plata, Neuquén, Bariloche and Viedma.*

Border with Chile – The Tromen Pass

Formalities are carried out at the Argentine side of the Tromen Pass (Chileans call it Mamuil Malal). This route runs through glorious scenery to Pucón (135 km) on Lago Villarrica (Chile). It is less developed than the Huahum and Samoré (Puyehue) routes further south, and definitely not usable during heavy rain or snow (Jun to mid-Nov). Parts are narrow and steep; it is unsuitable for bicycles. (Details of the Chilean side are given under **Puesco**, the Chilean customs post, **The Lake District**, page 700.) There is a campsite at Puesto Tromen (though very windy), but take food as there are no shops at the pass. ■ *The international bus will officially only pick up people at Tromen but at the discretion of the driver can pick up passengers at Puesco (no hotel) at 0900 and Currarehue stops. Buses San Martín (Tue, Thu, Sat) and Igi-Llaima (on other days) Junín de los Andes-Pucón, Temuco, Villarrica, Valdivia, US$15.*

Parque Nacional Lanín

This beautiful, large park has sparkling lakes, wooded mountain valleys and the snow capped Lanín Volcano

Geologically, Lanín Volcano (3,776 m) is one of the youngest of the Andes; it is extinct and one of the world's most beautiful mountains. Two routes (4-5 hours, or 6-7 hours) lead from the Argentine customs post at Tromen pass to two *refugios* at 2,400 m; from here it is 6-7 hours to the summit across ice and rock fields. Crampons and ice-axe are essential, as is protection against strong, cold winds (park wardens check all climbers' equipment and experience). Limited *refugio* space. The best base for exploring the park is San Martín de los Andes. ■ *Entry US$2.50. Lanín National Park office, Frey 749, San Martín, on main plaza, helpful but maps poor; Assistance also from* Club Andino *in Junín.*

San Martín de los Andes

Phone code: 02972
Colour map 8, grid A3
Population: 20,000
40 km SW of Junín

This lovely but expensive little town is at the east end of Lago Lacar. Mirador Bandurrias, 6 km from the centre offers good views. There is excellent skiing on Cerro Chapelco, and facilities for water skiing, windsurfing and sailing on Lago Lacar. Tourist office at Rosas 790, on main plaza, corner of San Martín, T/F427347. Open 0800-2200 (2100 in winter), very helpful.

The most popular trips by car are to Lagos Lolog, Aluminé, Huechulafquen and Paimún, to a campsite in the shadow of Lanín Volcano (bus from San Martín via Huechulafquen to Paimún, 0800, US$1.40, *Empresa San Martín*). Shorter excursions can be made on horseback or by launch. A small road runs west from San Martín along the south edge of Lago Lacar for 10 km to Quila Quina, where there are Indian engravings and a waterfall. Boat trip from San Martín to Quila Quina, 45 minutes one way, US$6.50 return. A good route for cyclists is Route 234 to Cerro Chapelco, where you can take your bike up the hill in the funicular railway, then cycle back down the paths.

Sleeping

Single accommodation is scarce. Rates are much lower off season

AL-A range All recommended: *Alihuen Lodge*, Ruta 62, Km 5 (road to Lake Lolog), T426588, F426045. Includes breakfast, other meals available (very good), lovely location and grounds, very comfortable. *La Cheminée*, Gral Roca y Mariano Moreno, T427617, lacheminee@smandes.com.ar Very good, breakfast included, but no restaurant. *La Masia*, Obeid 811, T427879. Very good. **A-B** *La Raclette*, Pérez 1170, T427664. 3-star, charming, warm, excellent restaurant. **A-B** *Posta del Cazador*, San Martín 175, T427501, laposta@satlink.com Very good. **B** *Hostería Los Pinos*, Brown 420, T427207. German-run, with a/c, breakfast, lovely garden. **B** *Hostería Anay*, Cap Drury 841, T427514, anay@smandes.com.ar Central, good value. **B** *Hostería Las Lucarnas*, Pérez 632, T427085/427985. English and French spoken. **B** *Colonos del Sur*, Rivadavia 686, T427224 Good value. **B-C** *Intermonti*, Villegas 717, T/F427454, www.mercotour.com/hotelintermonti In old wing, good rooms (**A**) in new wing. **C** *Casa Alta*, Obeid 659, T427456. Chalet in rose garden, 'beyond comparison and fantastic' (closed in low season). **C** *Crismalu* Rudecindo Roca 975, T427283, F427583. With breakfast, good value. **C** *Hostería Cumelén*, Elordi 931, T427304. Hot water, breakfast. **E** Elordi 176, T442775. Sleeping bag essential, kitchen facilities. **D** *Hosteria Bärenhaus*, Los Alamos 156, Barrio Chapelco (8370), T/F422775, www.baerenhaus.com Outside town, free pick-up from bus terminal and airport, rooms with bath and heating, tours and transport arranged, English and German spoken.

Consult Tourist Office for other private addresses, but these are only supplied in high season. **Youth hostel: E** *Puma*, A Fosbery 535, T422443, puma@smandes.com.ar Discount for HI and ISIC members, shared and double rooms (**C**), laundry, kitchen facilities, internet access, bikes for hire, very good.

Camping *ACA Camping*, Av Koessler 2176, T429430, with hot water and laundering facilities. **F**, "gorgeous" site by the lake at *Quila Quina*, 27 km from San Martín, with beaches, immaculate toilet blocks, well-stocked shop.

Pionieri, General Roca 1108. Excellent Italian meals in a cosy house, also regional specialities, good service, English and Italian spoken. Recommended. Same owners run *Los Patos* (next door) for take-away food, T428459. *La Chacha*, Rivadavia y San Martín. Regional meals (trout and venison), good food. *El Amanecer de Carlitos*, San Martín 1374. Pancakes, sandwiches and omelettes, quite cheap, popular. *Ku*, San Martín 1053. Regional meals. *Piscis*, Villegas 598. Regional meals, also pasta and *parrilla*. *La Tasca*, Moreno 866. Excellent *picadas regionales*. Recommended. *Pura Vida*, Villegas 745. The only vegetarian in town, small, warm, also fish and chicken dishes. *La Iguana Azul*, San Martín y Mariano Moreno. Nice atmosphere, garden, also bikes for hire (US$2.50 per hr). *Dely*, Villegas y MA Camino (on the shore). *Confitería* with beautiful views of the lake.

Eating

Cycling Many places rent mountain and normal bikes in the centre, reasonable prices, maps provided. **Skiing** There are several chair-lifts of varying capacity on Cerro Chapelco and a ski-tow higher up. Bus from San Martín to slopes, US$5 return. Very good slopes and snow conditions. Details from www.chapelco.com.ar At the foot of the mountain are a restaurant and base lodge. There are 3 more restaurants on the mountain and a small café at the top. For information on trout **fishing** guides, contact the tourist office or the National Park office. *Jorge Cardillo* fly shop, General Roca 626, T/F428372, cardillo@smandes.com.ar, sells fishing equipment, offering also guided fishing excursions.

Sports

Tiempo Patagónico, San Martín 950, T427113. Excursions and adventure tourism. *Chapelco Aventura*, Elordi y San Martín, T/F427845, chapelco@interar.com.ar Activities on Cerro Chapelco.

Tour operators

Air See under Junín de los Andes above. **Buses** Terminal at Villegas 251, good toilet facilities. To **Buenos Aires**, US$42-60, daily, 6 companies. To **Bariloche**, 4 hrs, US$10.50, *Ko Ko* daily via La Rinconada, or via the Seven Lakes in summer only, also *Albus*. **To Chile**: Temuco with *Empresa San Martín*, Mon, Wed, Fri, *Igi-Llaima*, Tue, Thu, Sat, US$15, 6-8 hrs (rough journey via Paso Hua Hum – see below, sit on the left).

Transport

Banks *Banco de la Nación*, San Martín 687. *Banco de la Provincia de Neuquén*, Obeid y Belgrano. *American Express (Grupo 3)*, San Martín 1141, T428453. **Police station** Belgrano 611.

Directory

A road along the north shore of Lago Lacar through the Lanín National Park crosses the border to Puerto Pirehueico. Buses daily at 0600, US$4. Daily bus to Pirehueico 0900, US$5.50, two hours. Hua Hum at the west end of the lake has camping and a shop; a boat leaves San Martín at 0930, returns 1800, US$12 (T427380). For connections from Puerto Pirehueico to Panguipulli and beyond, see Chile chapter, page 702.

Border with Chile – the Hua Hum Pass
This route is theoretically open all year round

San Martín de los Andes to Bariloche

There are two routes south to Bariloche: one, via Lago Hermoso and Villa La Angostura, known as the '**Seven Lakes Drive**', is very beautiful. (National Park permit holders may camp freely along this route.) From a bridge 7 km south of San Martín, you can see the Arroyo Partido: at this very point the rivulet splits, one stream flowing to the Pacific, the other to the Atlantic. Further south the road passes **Lago Villarino** (*Hostería Lago Villarino*, good food, beautiful setting, camping). The other route, more direct but less scenic is via **Confluencia** on the paved Bariloche highway (ACA station and a hotel, also motel *El Rancho* just before Confluencia). See under San Martín for buses on the Seven Lakes route. Round trip excursions along the Seven Lakes route, five hours, are operated by several companies.

Argentina

Parque Nacional Nahuel Huapi
This park contains lakes, rivers, glaciers, waterfalls, torrents, rapids, valleys, forest, bare mountains and snow-clad peaks

Covering 750,000 ha and stretching along the Chilean border, this is the oldest National Park in Argentina. Many kinds of wild animals live in the region, including the pudú, the endangered huemul (both deer) as well as river otters, cougars and guanacos. Bird life, particularly swans, geese and ducks, is abundant. The outstanding feature is the splendour of the lakes. The largest is **Lago Nahuel Huapi** (*Altitude*: 767 m), 531 sq km and 460 m deep in places. Some 96 km long, and not more than 12 km wide, the lake is very irregular in shape; long arms of water, or *brazos*, stretch far into the land. There are many islands: the largest is **Isla Victoria**, on which stands the forest research station. Trout and salmon have been introduced.

A glacial moraine in one of the northern *brazos* separates Lago Nahuel Huapi from Lago Correntoso, which is quite close to Lago Espejo. Lago Traful, a short distance to the northeast, can be reached by a road which follows the Río Limay through the Valle Encantado, with its fantastic rock formations. **Villa Traful** is 'a camper's paradise'. There are also hotels on the lake. Marvellous views, fishing excellent. South of Nahuel Huapi there are other lakes: the three main ones are Mascardi, Guillelmo, and Gutiérrez. **A** pp *Hotel Tronador* is on Lake Mascardi, beautiful setting, many activities, good hikes, price is full board, highly recommended (T02944-441062/468127) also camping *La Querencia*. On the shore of Lago Gutiérrez, in a grotto, is the Virgen de las Nieves (Virgin of the Snows). Towering over the whole scene is Tronador (3,478 m). **AL** *El Retorno*, Villa Los Coihues, on the shore of the lake, T467333, hretorno@bariloche.com.ar **A** in low season, with breakfast, beautiful hotel, quiet, recommended in every way. Take Bus 50 from Bariloche.

Villa La Angostura
Population: 3,000
90 km NW of Bariloche on Lago Nahuel Huapi

This is a picturesque town with a port, 3 km from town, which is spectacular in summer. At 12 km south of the port, at the south end of the Quetrihue Peninsula, is **Parque Nacional Los Arrayanes**, containing 300 year old specimens of the rare Arrayan tree. Tour boats from Villa La Angostura daily 1500 and 1600, US$10 return (*Huemul II*, reservations at **B** *Hotel Angostura*, T/F494224, www.laangostura.com – hotel has other sports facilities). See below for tours by boat from Bariloche. To visit on foot or by bike, it's a 24 km round trip, or you can take the boat one way. Tourist office opposite bus terminal at Av Sete Lagos 93, T/F494124, www.villalaangostura.net.ar

Sleeping A *Hostal Las Nieves*, Av Siete Lagos 980, T494573. Small, good location, top quality, English spoken, helpful. **A** *Verena's Haus*, Los Taiques 268, T 494467. Adults and non-smokers only, German and English spoken, cosy, garden, offers light dinners. Recommended. **B** *Las Piedritas*, Huemul y Route 231, T/F494222, einstein@cybernet.com.ar Run by Adán and Eva, small, pleasant, good value off season, English spoken, excursions, restaurant. **C** *Nahuel*, Route 231 y Huiliches, T 494737. Good rooms, restaurant. **C** *Río Bonito*, Topa Topa 260 (2 blocks from bus station), T 494110. Warm, English spoken, discounts for long stays. **G** *Sra Isolina*, Las Mutisias 59, T494282. Breakfast and dinner extra, converted family home. **Camping** *El Cruce*, 500 m from terminal, US$2 pp, dirty toilets.

Transport To/from **Bariloche**, 1¼ hrs, US$3.50-5, several companies. If going on to Osorno (Chile), you can arrange for the bus company to pick you up at La Angostura, US$10 to Osorno, road paved. Daily buses to **San Martín de los Andes** with *Ko Ko* and *Albus*.

Bariloche

Phone code: 02944
Colour map 8, grid C1
Population: 77,750

On the south shore of Lago Nahuel Huapi, founded 1903, San Carlos de Bariloche is the best centre for exploring the National Park. Renowned for its chocolate industry, it is a beautifully-situated town, perched upon a glacial moraine at the foot of Cerro Otto. The forests are particularly glorious around March-April.

Getting there The airport is 15 km east of town, the bus and train stations 3 km east. Taxis charge US$8 to the former, US$2 to the latter. *Aerolíneas Argentinas* run a bus service for flight passengers (US$2) and the hourly public bus fare to the station is US$0.50. If staying on the road to Llao-Llao, west of town, expect to pay more for transport to your hotel.

Ins & outs
For more detailed information see Transport, page 189

Getting around At peak holiday times (Jul and Dec-Jan), Bariloche is very busy with holidaymakers and secondary school students. The best times to visit are in the spring (Sep-Nov), Feb for camping and walking and Aug for skiing. Obtain maps and information about the district in Buenos Aires at the National Park Tourist Office at Santa Fe 690, or at the provincial offices (see page 107). It is hard to obtain these in the provinces themselves. Park wardens are also useful sources of information

Tourist offices Oficina Municipal de Turismo, in Centro Cívico, open daily 0900-2100, Sat 0900-1900, securturismo@ bariloche.com.ar Has full list of city buses, and details of hikes and campsites in the area and is helpful in finding accommodation. Web addresses: www.bariloche.com.ar, or www.bariloche.org Nahuel Huapi National Park information at San Martín 24, T423111, open 0900-1400.

The **cathedral**, built in 1946, dominates the town. There is a **belvedere** at the top of Cerro Otto with wide views over the town and the lake and mountain. The **Lido swimming pool** on the lake shore is beautifully sited. The clock in the **Centro Cívico** has four figures which rotate at noon. **Museo de La Patagonia** in the Centro Cívico, displays of patagonian fossils, good section on indigenous peoples, engravings of early-19th-century Buenos Aires. ■ *Tue-Fri 1000-1200, 1400-1900, Mon and Sat 1000-1300, US$1.25.*

Sights

The resort of **Llao Llao** (bus No 20, 45 minutes, US$1) lies 24 km west along Av Bustillo. Hotels on this road and in the resort are given below. At Km 17.7 there is a chairlift to **Cerro Campanario** (daily 0900-1200, 1400-1800 , US$6.50), from the top of which there are fine views of Isla Victoria and Puerto Pañuelo. At Km 18.3 begins the **Circuito Chico**, a 60-km circular route around Lago Moreno Oeste, past Punto Panorámico and through Puerto Pañuelo and Llao Llao itself. Tour companies do the circuit and it can be driven in half a day (it can also be cycled). It can be extended to a full day: Bariloche-Llao Llao-Bahía López-Colonia Suiza (on Lago Moreno Este)-Cerro Catedral-Bariloche; the reverse direction misses the sunsets and afternoon views from the higher roads, which are negotiable in winter (even snow-covered). The surrounding countryside offers beautiful walking, eg to Lago Escondido on a 3½ km trail off the Circuito Chico. A longer walk is to Cerro López (three hours, with a *refugio* after two); take Colonia Suiza bus (No 10 from the monument at the corner of Salta and Av San Martin) and alight at Picada. From the same bus, alight at the stop in Colonia Suiza and follow the red dots for a day's hike to Laguna Negra (4 hours there). Longer still is the hike to *refugio Italia* (same bus, but alight at SAC); details of this and three to five day continuations from Club Andino.

Excursions

A half-day excursion (1300-1830) may be taken from Puerto Pañuelo, to **Isla Victoria**. The full-day excursion (0900-1830, or 1300 till 2000 in season) at US$15 includes the Arrayanes forest on the Quetrihue peninsula further north, and three hours on Isla Victoria, picnic lunch advised. It is best to book this trip through an agency, as the boat fare alone is US$11. Some boats call first at Isla Victoria, early enough to avoid boat-loads of tourists. All boats are very crowded in season, but operators have to provide seating for all passengers. See also Villa La Angostura.

Out of season, tour boats only sail if demand is sufficient

A less well-known excursion is to **Puerto Blest**, where native forest can be seen. Take 0700 bus to Puerto Pañuelo and 0800 boat to Puerto Blest, check return journey time in advance. For climbing and skiing on Cerros Catedral and Otto, see Sports below. A half-day excursion is possible taking a bus to Virgen de las Nieves on Cerro Catedral, walking 2 km to arrive at beautiful Lago Gutiérrez; walk along lake shore to the road from El Bolsón and walk back to Bariloche (about 4 hours). Alternatively take Bus 50 direct to Lago Gutiérrez.

Argentina

Argentina

Tours Most travel agencies charge the same price. Tours get very booked up in season. Whole-day trip to Lagos Gutiérrez, Mascardi, Hess, the Cascada Los Alerces and Cerro Tronador (3,478 m) leaves at 0800, US$18, and visits the Black Glacier, interesting. *Catedral* and *Turisur* have a nine-hour excursion, leaving at 0900 (afternoon depart also December-March), to Puerto Pañuelo, sailing down to Puerto Blest and continuing by bus to Puerto Alegre and again by launch to Puerto Frías (US$12). A visit to the Cascada de los Cántaros is made (stay off the boat at the Cascada and walk around to Puerto Blest through beautiful forest, one hour, recommended). Several companies run 12-hour minibus excursions to San Martín de los Andes along the Seven Lakes Drive, returning via Paso de Córdoba and the Valle Encantado, but these involve few stops.

Sleeping

Most hotels outside the town include half-board, and those in the town include breakfast. Hotels with lake views normally charge extra per room per day, for the view in high season; the following selection gives lake-view high-season prices where applicable

If you arrive in the high season without a reservation, consult the listing with map published by the *Oficina Municipal de Turismo*, which also has a booking service at Florida 520 (Galería), room 116, Buenos Aires. **On the road to Llao Llao (Av Bustillo) LL-L** *Hotel Llao-Llao*, Km 25.5, T448530/0800-666 5555, www.llaollao.com Deservedly famous and recommended, superbly situated in 'chocolate box' surroundings, fine views (reservations: Paraguay 577, p 9, Bs As, T/F4311 3434). **C** *Hostería Katy*, Km 24, T448023. Recommended. **C** *Piccolo Paradiso*, Km 12.5, C Calquin norte/Panque 12521, T/F462009, piccoloparadiso@bariloche.com.ar Large garden, private beach, good, breakfast and meals available. **A** *La Cascada*, Km 6, T441046, lacascada@infovia.com.ar Recommended. **C** *La Caleta*, Km 1.9, T441837. Bungalows sleeping 4, shower, open fire, excellent value, self-catering. Recommended.

In Bariloche L *Edelweiss*, San Martín 202, 5-star, T430462, www.edelweiss.com.ar Modern, excellent food, indoor pool with a view. Highly recommended. **A** *Tres Reyes*, Av 12 de Octubre 135, T426121, h3reyes@bariloche.com.ar Lakeside, splendid views, English spoken. Highly recommended. **A** *Res Tirol*, Pasaje Libertad 175, T426152, host_tirol@bariloche.com.ar Good, German spoken. **B** *Aguas del Sur*, Moreno 353, T424329. Includes excellent 4-course meal, helpful. Recommended. **B** *Hostería El Radal*, 24 de Septiembre 46, T422551. Comfortable, warm, English spoken. **B** *La Pastorella*, Belgrano 127, T424656, pastorel@satlink.com English and French-spoken, central. Recommended. **C** *Res Piuké*, Beschtedt 136, T423044. German, Italian spoken. Recommended. **C** *Hostería El Ñire*, J

Bariloche

Lake Nahuel Huapi

Puerto San Carlos

N Not to scale

■ **Sleeping**
1 Aguas del Sur
2 Albergue Patagonia Andina
3 Albergue Rucalhué
4 Edelweiss
5 El 1004
6 El Ciervo Rojo
7 Hostería El Ñire
8 Hostería El Radal
9 Hostería Güemes
10 La Bolsa del Deporte
11 La Pastorella
12 Mochilero's
13 Nogarre
14 Periko's
15 Res Piuké
16 Res Premier
17 Res Puyehue
18 Res Rosán Arko
19 Res Tirol
20 Tres Reyes

● **Eating**
1 Ahumadero
2 El Viejo Maitén
3 El Viejo Munich
4 Familia Weiss
5 La Jirafa
6 La Marmite
7 Parrilla 1816 & El Boliche de Alberto
8 Pavarotti

O'Connor 94, T423041. Very pleasant, heated, German, English spoken, prefers longer-stay visitors, also apartments. Recommended. **C** *Res Puyehue* Elordi 243, T422196. Discount for *SAH* users, **E** pp in low season. **D** *Res Premier*, Rolando 263, T426168. Hot showers, English and German spoken, small rooms. Recommended. **D** *Hostería Güemes*, Güemes 715, T424785. Helpful. Recommended. **E** *El Ciervo Rojo*, Elflein 115, T/F435541, www.elciervorojo.com Showers, TV, information about treks. **E** *Res No Me Olvides*, Av Los Pioneros Km 1, T429140, 30 mins walk' from centre or Bus 50/51 to corner of C Videla then follow signs. Nice house in quiet surroundings, use of kitchen, camping. Highly recommended. **E** *Res Rosán Arko*, Güemes 691, T423109. English and German spoken, cooking facilities, helpful, good trekking information, beautiful garden, camping. Repeatedly recommended.

Family accommodation Among those recommended are: **F** *Familia Posaz*, Frey 635. Dormitory, cooking and laundry facilities, motorcycle parking. **F** *Eloisa Lamunière*, Paso 145, T422514. With breakfast, homely, helpful, cooking facilities. **E** *Casa Nelly*, Beschtedt 658, T422295. Hot showers, kitchen, camping. **E** *Nogarre*, Elflein 58, T422438. Comfortable, warm, eccentric owner. **F** *Mariana Pirker*, 24 de Septiembre 230, T424873. 2 3-bed apartments with kitchen. **E** *pensión* of Sra Carlota Baumann, Los Pioneros 86 (T429689, ingridb@arnet.com.ar), follow 20 de Febrero uphill for 10-15 mins. Kitchen, good breakfast, laundry service, English and German spoken.

The tourist office keeps a list of family accommodation

Youth hostels **E** *Albergue Patagonia Andina*, Morales 564, T422783, www.bariloche.com.ar/patagoniaandina Small dormitories, kitchen facilities, information. Recommended. **E** *Alaska*, Lilinquen 328 (buses 10, 20, 21, get off at La Florida), T/F461564, www.visitbariloche.com/alaska HI-affiliated, good atmosphere, cooking and washing facilities, internet access, mountain bikes, pleasant location, English spoken, good information on local treks, book in advance in summer. Under same ownership: *Periko's*, Morales 555, T522326, perikos@bariloche.com.ar Pleasant, kitchen, laundry, internet, dormitories, helpful, English and some German spoken. **F** *Albergue Rucalhué*, Güemes 762, T430888. Cheaper in loft and in low season, luggage store. **F** *La Bolsa del Deporte*, Palacios y Elflein, T/F423529, bolsadep@bariloche.com.ar Dormitories, English, German spoken, popular, use of kitchen, book exchange, internet, cycle hire. Repeatedly recommended (but annex not so good). All offer 10% discount to ISYC and youth card holders. **E** *Mochilero's*, San Martín 82, p 1, T423187, cecilia@bariloche.com.ar Dormitory. Recommended. **E** *El 1004*, San Martín 127, T432228, elalfabeta@cybersnet.com.ar Kitchen, laundry, **F** sleeping bag on carpeted floor. **G** *Refugio Cordillera*, Av Bustillo 18600, T/F448261. Heating, drinking water, dormitories in log cabins, helpful, convenient for hikes. Also **B** *Albergue Buenos Aires*, Buenos Aires 296, 200 m from terminal, T491147, buenosaires@cotecal.com.ar

Camping List of sites from Tourist Office. Two sites on Bustillo: *Selva Negra*, Km 2.5, T444013. US$4 pp. *El Yeti*, Km 5.6. Recommended. *Petunia*, Km 13.5. Well protected from winds by trees, hot showers, shop. Recommended. Shops and restaurants on most sites closed outside Jan-Mar. *Fraca*, Moreno 371 (Pasillo al Fondo), repairs tents and equipment.

La Marmite, Mitre 329. Small, cosy, excellent mixed fondues, expensive. Recommended. *El Viejo Munich*, Mitre 102. Good meat and fish. Recommended. *Caza Mayor*, Quaglia y Elflein. Game and fish, good but expensive. *El Viejo Maitén*, Elflein 49. Very good value. *Kandahar*, 20 de Febrero 698. Excellent. *Parrilla 1816*, Elflein 167. Good meat. Recommended. Similar at *El Boliche de Alberto* at Elflein 163. *Pavarotti*, Morales 362, very good *parrillada*, reasonably priced. *Ahumadero*, Palacios 167, excellent food and service. *El Boliche de Alberto*, Villegas 360. Very good value *parrillada*. *Lennon*, Moreno 48. Small, good food, reasonably priced, English spoken. *La Jirafa*, Palacios 288. Good food, good value. *Familia Weiss*, Palacios 170 (with good delicatessen round corner on Mitre). Excellent local specialities. *La Rondine*, San Martín 536. Italian, luxurious, good. *Jauja*, Quaglia 366. Good local dishes. *La Andinita*, Mitre 56. Recommended, pizzas, good value. *Cocodrilo*, Mitre y Urquiza. Big choice of good pizzas, good value, take-away service. *Vegetariano*, Av 20 de Febrero 730. Excellent fixed menu, good value. Recommended. *La Alpina Confitería*, Moreno 98. Open fire, reasonably priced, cheese fondue recommended, very popular. Good pastries and hot chocolate at *Hola Nicolás*, Moreno y Urquiza (see the graffiti-graven tables). *Del Turista*, Mitre 231. Chocolates, ice cream. *Algunas Frases*, Mitre 211. Bar, open 24 hrs.

Eating
Many good delicatessens with takeaway food, including chicken, pizzas and cheeses, for picnics. Guía Sabores, available at large hotels, lists restaurants and offers discounts

Argentina

For ice cream, branches of **Bari**, eg on Mitre. **Cervecería Blest**, Av Bustillo Km 11.6, T4610026. Brews own beer, good food, cosy.

Shopping

The main commercial centre is on Mitre between the Centro Cívico and Beschtedt; there are lots of galerías here

The local chocolate is excellent: several shops on Mitre. You can watch chocolates being made at **El Turista**, Mitre 252. 1 block away is **Mamushka**, excellent. Very good chocolate at **Estrella Alpina**, Villegas 216 and **Benroth**, Beschtedt 569. Local wines, from the Alto Río Negro, are also good. Woollen goods are recommended. Handicraft shops along San Martín. **Feria Artesanal Municipal**, Moreno y Rolando. Recommended. **Feria Naturista**, Elflein 73, vegetarian and health foods. **Todo** supermarket, Moreno 319, good selection, cheap.

Sport

Apart from sailing and boating, there are golf, mountaineering, walking, birdwatching, skiing, and fishing (permit needed). Excellent trout fishing Nov-Mar; arrange boat hire with tackle shops

Bicycles: may be hired beside the lake in high season (eg A Carlucci, Mitre 723, US$10 per day). **Dirty Bikes**, V O'Connor 681, dirtybike@bariloche.com.ar US$7.50 per day. Also *La Bolsa del Deporte* hostel. **Hiking and trekking**: Club Andino (see below) has sketch maps of hikes. Horseflies (*tábanos*) frequent the lake shores and lower areas in summer; lemon juice is good for keeping them away, but can cause skin irritation. For **horse trekking** trips contact *Carol Jones*, Casilla 1436 (or through Hans Schulz – see under Tour operators), highly recommended. Also *Cumbres y Lagos Patagonia*, see Tour operators. Or **Tom Wesley**, Mitre 385, T435040.

Note that at higher levels, winter snow storms can begin as early as Apr, making climbing dangerous

Mountain climbing: best information from **Club Andino Bariloche**, 20 de Febrero 30, T422266, www.clubandino.com.ar Open Mon-Fri 0900-1200, 1500-2000, Sat 0900-1200. The club arranges guides; ask for Sr Ricardo, the secretary, who organizes easy weekend climbs and walks. Its booklet '*Guía de Sendas y Picadas*' gives details of climbs and it provides maps (1:150,000) and details of all campsites, hotels and mountain lodges. There is something for every kind of mountaineer. National Park mountain guides are available but can be expensive. Book: *Excursiones, Andinismo y Refugios de Montaña en Bariloche*, by Tonchek Arko, available in local shops, US$2, or from the author at Güemes 691. In treks to *refugios* remember to add costs of ski lifts, buses, food at *refugios* and lodging (in *Club Andino refugios*: US$3 per night, plus US$1.50 for cooking, or US$2.50 for breakfast, US$4 for dinner). Take a sleeping bag. There are convenient rest lodges from 1,000 to 2,000 m on the mountains. Firing, light and food are provided at these points. The only disadvantage at Bariloche is that the snow is unreliable except at the top

Skiing: there is good skiing during the winter season (Jul to early Oct), supervised by the *Club Andino Bariloche*. It is best organized with a tour company. The favourite slopes are on Cerro Catedral. **Codao**, Moreno 470, T432830, runs daily buses to Villa Catedral. There is a cable car from the foot of Cerro Catedral to points high on the ridge (US$5 single, US$8 return) and a chair lift (US$60 full week, US$13-16 high season, US$9-11 low – full day). Red and yellow markers painted on the rock mark a trail from the top, which leads to Refugio Frey (well equipped, blankets, meals, US$3-4, bed US$2.50 pp) on the edge of a small mountain lake (allow 6 hrs; you can return through the forest to the ski complex the next day and take a bus back to Bariloche). The seasonal cable car, with a chair lift from its upper terminal, takes you higher than the main (2-stage) chair lift. Check at tourist office if cable car is running, as everything closes in Mar. Bus tours from Bariloche to the foot of Cerro Catedral give time for less than 2 hrs on top of the mountain. There are other skiing slopes 5 km out of Bariloche, on **Cerro Otto** (cable car, US$7.50-10 pp; open 0930-1800 Jan, Feb, Jul, Aug, and 1000-1800 rest of year; free connecting bus service to cable car from Mitre y Villegas; revolving restaurant at top, opens 1000, nice *confitería* belonging to *Club Andino* on Cerro Otto, 20 mins walk from main *confitería* on summit). Guided walks, mountain bikes and paragliding at the top in summer. Cerro Otto can be reached in 2-3 hrs walk from the town; take the paved Av de los Pioneros, then switch to the signed dirt track 1 km out of Bariloche, or in a minibus which goes every 30 mins from a car park near the national park headquarters between 1400 and 1600, US$2.50 round trip (local bus US$1.20 return). Also at Piedras Blancas (bus US$3.50 return); López (US$7 for a tour, 1400-1830), Dormilón and La Ventana. Ski hire US$4.50-8 a day, depending on quality, dearer at Cerro Catedral than in town. Ski clothes can also be rented by the day, at US$0.50-1 per item, from *Kiwanis* sport stores, Mitre 210, or *El Iglú*, Galería Arrayanes II, Rolando 244.

Tour buses pick you up from your hotel. Agencies charge same prices: Circuito Chico US$5-6.50, Cerro Catedral US$6.50, Cerro Tronador US$14.50, El Bolsón US$14.50. Most agencies now sell excursions which include ride on 'la Trochita' from El Maitén. *Catedral Turismo*, Mitre 360 and Palacios 167, T425443/5, cattur@bariloche.com.ar Runs boats to Chile for Peulla-Puerto Montt trip, see below. Recommended. *Cumbres y Lagos Patagonia*, Villegas 222, T423283, cumbrs@bariloche.com.ar For rafting, horseriding, trekking, fishing. Recommended. *Del Lago Turismo*, Quaglia 156, T/F430056. Helpful, English spoken. *Pueblo Blanco*, San Martín 127, loc 7, T421314. Specializes in tours for younger travellers, camping trips, flight tickets. *San Carlos Travel*, Mitre 213, p 2, T/F432999, sancartrav@bariloche.com.ar Birdwatching and other specialist tours. Recommended. *Hans Schulz*, Casilla 1017, T423835/426508. Speaks Spanish, German and English, arranges tours and guides. Highly recommended. *Tacul Viajes*, San Martín 430, T426321, tacul@bariloche.com.ar English spoken. Recommended. *Turisur*, Villegas 310, T426109, turisur@bariloche.com.ar Organizes trips on lake and on land. Arrange trekking with recommended guide *Daniel Feinstein*, T/F442259, speaks fluent English, naturalist and mountaineer, very experienced in both Argentina and Chile.

Tour operators
Check what your tour includes; funicular rides and chair lifts are usually charged as extras

Local Car hire: *A1 International*, at airport and in town (San Martín 235, T422582, F427494); no flat rates, unless reservation made outside Argentina. *Open*, Mitre 382, T/F426325, much cheaper. To enter Chile a permit is necessary, US$25, allow 48 hrs. **Taxis**: *Remise Bariloche*, T430222. *Auto Jet*, España 11, T422408. Some drivers speak English or German. **Long distance Air**: Taxi to airport US$7; bus US$2 from *AR* office (timetable posted in office window). Many flights to **Buenos Aires**, with *AR/Austral, Dinar, Southern Winds* and *AIRG*. *Southern Winds* to **Calafate, Córdoba** and **Ushuaia**. *LADE* to **Bahía Blanca,Comodoro Rivadavia, Esquel, Mar del Plata, Neuquén, Puerto Madryn, San Martín de los Andes, Trelew** and **Viedma**.

Transport
Airport is 15 km E of town. Train station is 3 km E of centre. Bus terminal is next to railway station. For international car rental agencies, see Essentials, page 48

  Buses: Same buses to terminal as to train station. Left luggage at bus terminal US$0.50 per day. Bus company offices: *Andesmar/Albus*, Palacios 240, T430211; *Chevallier/La Estrella/Ko Ko*, T425914; *TAC*, Villegas 147, T432521; *Tas Choapa*, Moreno 138, T432521; *Cruz del Sur*, San Martín 453, T422818; *Don Otto/Río de La Plata*, T421699. To **Buenos Aires**, 6 companies daily, 22½ hrs, US$39-43 *coche cama*, *Andesmar coche cama* 21 hrs, US$50 (prices rise in Dec). To **Bahía Blanca**, 3 companies, US$24. To **Mendoza**, US$35, *TAC* and *Andesmar*, 19 hrs, via Piedra de Aguila, Neuquén, Cipolleti and San Rafael. To **Esquel**, *Don Otto*, *Mar y Valle*, *Vía Bariloche*, *Andesmar*, US$7-11. To **Puerto Madryn**, 14 hrs, US$27, 14 hrs with *Mar y Vale* and *Don Otto*. To **San Martín de los Andes**, *Ko Ko*, Mon-Sat 1430, US$11, 4 hrs. No direct bus to **Río Gallegos**; you have to spend a night in **Comodoro Rivadavia** en route: *Don Otto* daily, US$40, 14½ hrs. To **Puerto Montt**, see the route to Chile from Bariloche, page 190.

  To **Calafate**, ask at youth hostel *Alaska*, or *Periko's* about *Safari Route 40*, a 4-day trip down Ruta 40 to Calafate via the Perito Moreno national park, Cueva de Las Manos and Ftiz Roy, staying at *Estancia Melike* and Río Mayo en route. US$95 plus accommodation at US$5 per day. www.visitbariloche.com/alaska

  Trains: Booking office at station (T423172) closed 1200-1500 weekdays, Sat afternoon and all Sun, station reached by local buses 10, 20, 21, 70, 71, 80 (US$1), taxi US$2.50. Information from the Tourist Office. The only trains to run are special steam services for tourists to **Perito Moreno** halt, 30 km east.

Airline offices *Aerolíneas Argentinas/Austral*, Quaglia 238, T422144/423161. *LADE*, Gal Vía Firenze, Quaglia 242, T423562. *AIRG*, Palacios 266, T437000. *Southern Winds*, Villegas 147, T423704. **Banks** Banks and exchange shops, buy and sell virtually all European and South American currencies, besides US dollars; Sat is a bad day. **Communications** Internet: Several cybercafés in the centre, all with similar rates. Post Office: Moreno 175, closed Sat afternoon and Sun. Telephone: Many *locutorios* in the centre. *Telecom*, Mitre y Rolando, has internet. **Consulates** Austria, 24 de Septiembre 230, T424873. **Chile**, JM de Rosas 180, T422842, helpful. **Germany**, Ruiz Moreno 45, T425695. **Switzerland**, Quaglia 342, T426111. **Medical facilities** Clinic: Cruz Azul, Capraro 1216.

Directory
Immigration office, Libertad 175

Argentina

Argentina

Border with Chile

The Samoré, formerly Puyehue Pass A good broad paved highway, goes around the east end of Lago Nahuel Huapi, then follows the north side of the lake through Villa La Angostura. It passes the junction with 'Ruta de Los Siete Lagos' for San Martín at Km 94, Argentine customs at Km 109 and the pass at Km 125 at an elevation of about 1,280 m. Chilean customs is at Km 146 in the middle of a forest. The border is open from the second Saturday of October to 1 May, 0900-1900. It is a six-hour drive, but liable to be closed after snow-falls.

Via Lake Todos Los Santos The route is Bariloche to Llao-Llao by road, Puerto Pañueto to Puerto Blest by boat (1½ hours), Puerto Blest to Puerto Alegre on Lago Frías by bus, cross the lake to Puerto Frías by boat (20 minutes), then 1½ hours by road to Peulla. Leave for Petrohué in the afternoon by boat (2½ hours), cross Lago Todos Los Santos, passing the Osorno volcano, then by bus to Puerto Montt. This route is beautiful, but not recommended in wet or foggy weather as it is tiring.

The Argentine and Chilean border posts are open every day. The launches (and hence the connecting buses) on the lakes serving the direct route via Puerto Blest to Puerto Montt generally do not operate at weekends; check. There is an absolute ban in Chile on importing any fresh food – meat, cheese, fruit – from Argentina. Further information on border crossings in the Lake District will be found in the Chile chapter. You are strongly advised to get rid of all your Argentine pesos before leaving Argentina; it is useful to have some Chilean pesos before you cross into Chile from Bariloche. Chilean currency can be bought at Puyehue customs at a reasonable rate.

Transport Five bus companies run daily services from Bariloche to *Osorno* (4-6 hrs, US$9-10) and **Puerto Montt** (7-8 hrs, same fare) via the Samore pass: buses usually leave 0730-0800. Companies include *Río de La Plata*, *Cruz del Sur*, and *Andesmar* (addresses under Bariloche). Sit on left side for best views. You can buy a ticket to the Chilean border, then another to Puerto Montt, or pay in stages in Chile, but there is little advantage in doing this.

Turismo Catedral sells 1 and 2-day crossings to Puerto Montt via roads and lakes (route as stated above). The 1-day crossing costs US$120 plus cost of lunch at Peulla (US$20), credit cards accepted; this excursion does not permit return to Bariloche next day. (1 Sep-30 Apr, take own food, buy ticket day in advance, departs 0700). For a 2-day crossing (operates all year round), there is an overnight stop in Peulla. Details about accommodation under Peulla, in Chile. Several tour companies sell this tour, including transport, board and lodging. Book in advance during the high season. The other agencies sell excursions to Puerto Frías with a bus to Puerto Pañuelo, a *Turisur* boat to Puerto Blest and share a bus and boat to Puerto Frías with excursion groups going on to Chile. Information from *Turismo Catedral* which owns the exclusive rights to the excursion via the lakes, using their own boats and bus from Puerto Pañuelo to Puerto Frías (*Andina del Sud* operates with them on the Chilean side).

El Bolsón

Phone code: 02944
Colour map 8, grid C1
Population: 8,000

The road from Bariloche to El Bolsón is entirely paved. It passes the beautiful lakes Gutiérrez, Mascardi and Guillelmo. **Río Villegas**, about 80 km south of Bariloche on the road to El Bolsón, is very beautiful (**E** *Hostería Río Villegas*, pleasant, restaurant, just outside the gates of the national park, by the river).

El Bolsón, at Km 130, is an attractive town in beautiful country, with many mountain walks and waterfalls (dry in summer) nearby. As it lies in a hollow at about 300 m, it can be very hot in summer. It has good fishing and Lagos Puelo (see below) and Epuyén (shops and petrol available) are within easy access. Famous local fruit preserves can be bought at the factories in town. The handicraft and local produce market on Tuesday, Thursday, Saturday (biggest) and Sunday is worth a visit. The Balneario Municipal is 300 m from the town centre, pleasant river swimming. The tourist office is on the main plaza, open 0900-2000, helpful, English spoken, has information on farms that can be visited.

To Lago Puelo, about 20 km south in the Parque Nacional Lago Puelo. Regular buses, US$1.40, from Av San Martín y Dorrego in El Bolsón go to the lake via Villa Lago Puelo (*Hostería Enebros*, T155-57331 (mob); *Hostal del Lago*, T499199, both **D**; also *cabañas*) where there are shops and fuel. Good information on the park is available from the wardens at the entrance. Boats can be taken across the lake. Canoes can be rented for US$1.50 per hour to appreciate the beauty of the lake.

B *Cordillera*, San Martín 3210, T492235, cordillerahotel@elbolson.com With breakfast, warm, good. **C** *Valle Nuevo*, 25 de Mayo y Belgrano, T156-02325 (mob). Small, quiet, good value. **D** *Hostería Steiner*, San Martín 300, T492224. Pleasant, wood fire, lovely garden. **D** *Salinas*, Rocas 641, T492396. Recommended. **D** *La Posada de Hamelin*, Int Granollers 2179, T492030, gcapece@elbolson.com Hot water, German spoken. Recommended. **E** *Sol del Valle*, 25 de Mayo y Pellegrini, T156 02325 (mob). Recommended. **F** *Campamento Ecológico*, Pagano y Costa del Río, T491293. Bunks, US$2.50 camping, hot water, cooking facilities.

Youth hostel E *El Pueblito*, 3 km north in Luján, 1 km off Route 258, T/F493560, elpueblitobolson@hotmail.com Cooking and laundry facilities, shop, open fire; 6 km from town is *La Casona de Odile*, small farm, home cooking, reservations only (Apdo 83, 8430 El Bolsón, Pca Río Negro, T/F492753, odile@red42.com.ar). 20 km north of El Bolsón, at Rinconada del Mallín Ahogado (daily bus from El Bolsón) is **B** *Hostería María y Pancho Kramer*, warmly recommended, wholefood meals, hot shower, sauna, swimming pool, chess, volleyball, horseback and trekking excursions to lakes and mountains. At Lago Epuyén, 40 km south of El Bolsón, **D** *Refugio del Lago*, with breakfast, also full and half pension, meals with fresh food, tours, trekking, riding, camping. Recommended. French owned, Sophie and Jacques Dupont, Correo Epuyén, 9211 Chubut, or leave a message, T02944-499025.

Camping *La Chacra*, to the south at Belgrano 1128, T492111, 15 mins walk from town, US$2.50 pp, hot showers, kiosk, restaurant. *Aldea Suiza*, 4 km north on Route 258, T492736, tennis courts, hot showers, good restaurant. Recommended. *El Bolsón*, 1 km north of town, clean, small brewery. Recommended. The paying campsite (US$2.50) at Lago Puelo has beautiful views across the lake to Tres Picos, but the walking is limited, expensive shop and café. Frequent public transport from El Bolsón.

Sleeping
Very difficult to find
accommodation in
the high season

La Calabaza, San Martín y Hube. Good food including vegetarian, English owner, nice atmosphere. *Don Diego*, San Martín 3217, Good. *El Viejo Maitén*, Roca 359. Good. *Parrilla Las Brasas*, Sarmiento y P Hube. Good. *Jauja*, San Martín 2867. Pasta, delicious natural ice cream, English spoken. *La Posada del Alquimista*, Belgrano y Berutti. Lively bar with pool tables and internet access. *La Tosca*, San Martín y Roca. Café, restaurant in summer, warm atmosphere. *La Posada de Olaf*, at Las Golondrinas, Route 258, 6 km south, T471550. Very good *parrilla*, Scandinavian specialities, excellent smoked trout, also has *cabañas*. Recommended.

Quen Quen Turismo, Belgrano y Berutti, T493522, quenquen@red42.com.ar Horse riding, rafting and parachuting. *Transitando Lo Natural*, Dorrego y San Martín, T492495, transitando@elbolson.com Birdwatching tours from US$15 pp, canyoning, flights.

Buses Full-day tours from Bariloche are run by *Don Otto*, 11 hrs, very crowded in high season. Also local bus by 5 companies from **Bariloche**, US$5-6.50, 2 hrs.

This town offers superb views of Lago Cholila, crowned by the Matterhorn-like mountains of Cerros Dos and Tres Picos. The ranch where Butch Cassidy, the Sundance Kid and Etta Place lived between 1901 and 1905 is 13 km north along Ruta 71 ■ *entry US$5*. Behind the ranch is *Casa de Té Galés*, which is most hospitable. Fiesta del Asado is in the third week in January.

A *La Rinconada*, T498091, larinconada@interlink.com.ar Offers tours, horse riding, kayaking, American-owned. **C** *El Trébol*, T/F498055. With breakfast, comfortable rooms with stoves, meals and half board also available, popular with fishing expeditions, reservations advised, bus stops in village 4 km away. **Camping F** *Autocamping Carlos Pelligrini*, next to El Trébol. Free camping in El Morro park. *Camping El Abuelo*, 13 km south. *Butch Cassidy Teahouse* has photos about Butch and co and the proprietress is well-informed about local history.

Esquel

Phone code: 02945
Colour map 9, grid A1
Population: 18,800
260 km S of Bariloche

Esquel was originally an offshoot of the Welsh colony at Chubut, 650 km to the east. A modern town in a fertile valley, Esquel is known for its tulips, chocolate, and jams. A centre for visiting the Parque Nacional Los Alerces, it is also famous for La Trochita. Good walks from the town to Laguna La Zeta, 5 km, and to Cerro La Cruz, two hours. **Cascada Yrigoyen** is a double waterfall with superb views over Lago Futalaufquen; a bus goes there every day at 0830 from the bus terminal, returning at 1930 from Villa Futalaufquen. **Museo Indígena**, Belgrano near San Martín, Indian artefacts; **Museo de Arte Naif y Capilla Seion**, Rivadavia near 25 de Mayo, Welsh museum. The tourist office is at Alvear y Sarmiento, T451927, www.esquelonline.com.ar Very friendly. Closed Saturday and Sunday off-season.

Sleeping
Ask at tourist office for lodgings in private houses. Hotels are often full in Feb. All hotels in this list are recommended

A *Cumbres Blancas*, Ameghino 1683, T/F455100, cumbres@teletel.com.ar Small, luxurious, sauna and massages, restaurant with local specialities. **A** *Tehuelche*, 9 de Julio 825, T452420, tehuelche@teletel.com.ar Heating, breakfast, restaurant, some staff speak English. **B** *Angelina*, Alvear 758, T452763. Good food, warm, Italian spoken. **B** *Canela*, C Los Notros, Villa Ayelén, on road to Trevelin, T/F453890, www.canela-patagonia.com Bed and breakfast and tearoom, English spoken, knowledgeable about Patagonia, skiing at La Hoya. **C** *La Chacra*, Km 4 on Ruta 259 towards Trevelin, T452471. Tranquil, huge breakfast, laundry, Welsh/English/Spanish spoken. **C** *La Tour D'Argent*, San Martín 1063, T454612, www.cpatagonia.com/esq/latour With breakfast, good value, nice. **D** *Esquel*, San Martín 1044, T452534. Helpful, heating. **D** *Huentru Niyeu* (no sign), Chacabuco 606, T452576. Quiet, modern, garage. **D** *Res Huemul*, Alvear y 25 de Mayo, T450817. Without breakfast, good *confitería*. **D** *Lihuen*, San Martín 820, T/F452589, ejarque@teletel.com.ar Without breakfast, English spoken, good value, **F** in youth hostel. **D** *Hostería Los Tulipanes*, Fontana 365, T452748. Good rooms and service. **E** *Res El Cisne*, Chacabuco 778, T452256. With cooking facilities, good. **F** Mrs Elena Rowlands' guesthouse at Rivadavia 330, T452578. Welsh spoken, with breakfast, shared bath. **F** *Casa Emma Cleri*, Alvear 1021, T452083, T156-87128 (mob). Helpful and hospitable.

Youth hostel E *Lago Verde*, Volta 1081, T454396, F452251, esquel@hostels.org.ar Doubles only, breakfast extra, modern, comfortable, no kitchen. Recommended. Those with sleeping bags can go to the Salesian school and sleep in the school classrooms, Dec to Mar. Get recommendation from tourist office.

Camping *El Hogar del Mochilero*, Roca 1028, T452166, US$1.50 pp, 400 m from bus terminal, laundry facilities, 24-hr hot water, friendly owner, internet, free firewood. Recommended. *Millalen*, Ameghino 2063, T456164, good services. Campsite at Laguna Zeta La Colina, Darwin 1400, T454962, US$1.75 pp, hot showers, kitchen facilities, lounge, log fire. Recommended. *EG3* service station has free camping northeast of town.

Eating
Cassis, Sarmiento 120. Cosy, German and English spoken, try lamb or trout. *Don Chiquino*, 9 de Julio 970. Good, Italian. *Vascongada*, 9 de Julio y Mitre. Trout specialities. *La Trochita*, 25 de Mayo 633. Basic meals, good value. *Parrilla de María*, Rivadavia 1024. Popular. *Pizzería Don Pipo*, Fontana 649. Good pizzas and *empanadas*. *El Viejo Obelisco*, Rivadavia 920, T4350839. Good pizzeria, satellite TV. Recommended. *La Española*, Rivadavia 740. Excellent beef, salad bar, some Arab dishes. *Tango Gourmet*, Alvear 949, tangogourmet@hotmail.com Restaurant/bar with tango shows and lessons, open 1100-2400. *Vestry*, Rivadavia 1065. Welsh tea room owned by Marta Luisa Hughes de Hughes, opens 1600. Home made chocolate and the famous local mazard berry liquor is sold at the *Braese Store*, 9 de Julio 1059.

Shopping
Casa de Esquel (Robert Müller), 25 de Mayo 415, T452544, F453901. Wide range of new and second hand books on Patagonia, also local crafts.

La Trochita (The Old Patagonian Express)

Esquel is the terminus of a 402-km branch-line from Ingeniero Jacobacci, a junction on the old Buenos Aires-Bariloche mainline, 194 km east of Bariloche. This narrow-gauge line (0.75 m wide) took 23 years to build, being finally opened in 1945. It was made famous outside Argentina by Paul Theroux who described it in his book The Old Patagonian Express. *The 1922 Henschel and Baldwin steam locomotives (from Germany and USA respectively) are powered by fuel oil and use 100 litres of water every km. Water has to be taken on at least every 40 km along the route. Most of the coaches are Belgian and also date from 1922. If you want to see the engines you need to go to El Maitén where the workshops are.*

Until the Argentine government handed responsibility for railways over to the provincial governments in 1994, regular services ran the length of the line. Since then, services have been maintained between Esquel and El Maitén by the provincial government of Chubut. For timetable see under **Esquel**.

In El Maitén there are two hotels, same owner, both overpriced: Accomazzo, with good restaurant; **C** *La Vasconia, near station, basic. On Thursday a bus for Esquel meets the train in El Maitén, check details first in Esquel.*

Argentina

Sport

Fishing: tourist office has advice. **Skiing**: La Hoya, 15 km north, has 7 ski-lifts. For skiing information ask at **Club Andino Esquel**, Volta 649, T453248; bus to La Hoya from Esquel, 3 a day, US$4.75 return, ski pass US$6-10 depending on season, equipment hire US$3.50 a day.

Tour operators

Esquel Tours, Fontana 754, T452704, and at airport. Good local tours, to Lagos Menéndez and Cisnes, good car hire. *Trekways*, Roca 687, T/F453380, trekways@cybersnet.com.ar Trekking, canoeing, *estancias*, horseriding, knowledgeable guides. Recommended.

Transport

Mechanic: Claudio Peinados, Brown 660, T453462, highly recommended

Long distance Air Airport, 20 km east of Esquel, by paved road, US$9 by taxi, US$1.50 by bus, US$2.75 by *Esquel Tours* bus 1 hr before each *LADE* flight. To **Buenos Aires** with *Austral* via San Martín de los Andes. *LADE* (Alvear 1085, F452124) to **Bahía Blanca, Bariloche, Comodoro Rivadavia, El Bolsón, El Maitén, Mar del Plata, Neuquén** and **Viedma**,

Trains There is one public service of La Trochita (see box above) – the Viejo Expreso Patagónico, Old Patagonian Express – from El Maitén on Sat, 6 hrs, US$12.50, with pullman car and dining car. Tourist services: Esquel to Nahuel Pan (19 km) up to twice a day (less frequent in winter), 2½ hrs, US$7.50. Information in El Maitén, T02945-495190, in Esquel T451403. www.esquelonline.com.ar has information in Spanish, but not schedules.

Buses Terminal at Alvear y Fontana, T452233, also for taxis. From Buenos Aires travel via **Bariloche**: *Andesmar* (T450143) can be booked Esquel-Buenos Aires, including change in Bariloche, US$60. To **Comodoro Rivadavia** (paved), *Don Otto* (T453012), 4 times a week (but usually arrives from Bariloche full in season) or *Angel Giobbi*, Tue, and Fri 0600, US$18, via Río Mayo. *Don Otto, Andesmar, Mar y Valle* (T453712), *Vía Bariloche* (T453528) to **Bariloche**, US$7-11, direct. To **El Bolsón**, 5 hrs, US$3.50-5.50. To **Trelew**, US$15-18, 8 hrs, *Mar y Valle, Emp Chubut – Don Otto* daily. To **Trevelin**, *Codao* (T455222), every hour 0700-2100, every 2 hrs weekends, US$1.05.

Directory

Banks *Banco de la Nación* Alvear y Roca, accepts MasterCard, open 0730-1300. *Banco de Chubut*, Alvear 1131, ATM. **Communications Internet**: Café in Shell station, Alvear y 25 de Mayo, has internet access, open 24 hrs. **Post office** and **telephones** opposite the bus terminal at Fontana y Alvear (open 0800-2000).

Trevelin

Colour map 9, grid A1
Population: 5,000
23 km SW of Esquel

An offshoot of the Welsh Chubut colony (see box in Patagonia section), Trevelin has a Welsh chapel (built 1910, closed), tea rooms and a good tourist office in the central plaza. The **Museo Regional**, in the old mill (1918) includes artefacts from the Welsh colony and a model of the Futaleufú hydro electric dam which is at the southern end of Parque Nacional Los Alerces. ■ *US$1.* The **Hogar de Mi Abuelo** is a private park and museum (*El Malacara*, named after Evans' horse), dedicated to John Evans, one

Argentina

of the first settlers, whose granddaughter acts as a guide. ■ *US$1*. The Nant-y-fall Falls lie 17 km southwest on the road to the border. ■ *US$0.25 pp including guide to all seven falls (1½-hr walk)*.

Sleeping & eating **D** *Hostería Estefanía*, Perito Moreno s/n, T480148. Good value. **D** *Pezzi*, Sarmiento 351, T480146, marianapezzi@hotmail.com Dec-Mar, English spoken, garden. Recommended. **D-E** *Albergue Casa Verde*, Los Alerces s/n, T/F480091, trevelin@hostels.org.ar HI member, all meals available, kitchen, log-cabin style. Recommended. Large meals (particularly breakfast) at *Oregon*, Av San Martín y Laprida. *El Rancho de Mario*, main plaza. *Parrilla* and home-made pasta. Several others and tea rooms offering *té galés* and *torta negra*: eg *Nairn Maggie*, P Moreno 179. Recommended. Municipal **campsite** near centre. On the road to Esquel 3 km from Trevelin, signposted on the righthand side, is **C** *La Granja Trevelin*, T480096. Owned by Domingo Giacci, macrobiotic meals and good Italian cooking, sells milk, cheese and onions; camping, hot water and toilet, bungalows; excellent horses for hire.

Parque Nacional Los Alerces
Colour map 9, grid A1
60 km W of Esquel

This national park includes larch trees over 1,000 years old and several lakes including **Lago Futalaufquen**, entry US$2.50 (even if just passing through on Route 258). The east side of Los Alerces has much the same natural attractions as the Nahuel Huapi and Lanín parks, but is much less developed for tourism. Lago Futalaufquen has some of the best fishing in the area (season 15 November-Easter). The park administration and Visitors' Centre are at Villa Futalaufquen, at the southern end of the lake. Nearby is a service station, a kiosk selling fishing licences and two expensive supermarkets.

Trekking and tours The west side of Lago Futalaufquen is untouched by tourism, by law. There is good walking, eg to El Dedal, a six-hour hike from *Hotel Futalaufquen* up and back. A leaflet describing the flora and fauna along the trail up to Cerro Dedal is available at the park headquarters. Regular full day launch trip from Puerto Limonao (reached by early morning minibus) on Lago Futalaufquen (a sheer delight) through Río Arrayanes to windless Lago Verde. From here you can walk out to Lago Rivadavia (8 km). There is also a daily boat service in high season at 1200 from Puerto Chucao (reached after a 30-minute walk across the bridge over Río Arrayanes), across Lago Menéndez to its western side (90 minutes) to visit the 1,000-year-old *alerce* forest (guided tours only). Also access to remote Lago Cisne is possible. Recommendable to book in advance through travel agents in Esquel or Trevelin, and to arrive early to claim your space (boat departures daily in high season from Puerto Limonao, nine hours round trip, about US$20-25 pp; low season, few services, US$14 pp). Ask for boat excursions to Lago Krüger.

Sleeping On the east side of Lago Futalaufquen: **A** *Hostería Los Tepúes*, T471013, simple, rustic, open all year, family bungalow for rent. **A** *Pucón Pai*, T451425, good restaurant, recommended for fishing (holds a fishing festival to open the season); open out of season for large groups only; has campsite. Next door **D** *Cabañas Tejas Negras*, T471046 good facilities for camping. *Cume Hué*, T453639, also recommended for fishing.

   On the west side **L** *Hostería Futalaufquen* just north of Puerto Limonao, T471008, cleona@teletel.com.ar Recommended, especially rooms 2/3 and 4/5 which have balconies overlooking the lake, open all year (no heating in rooms); good walking around the hotel. **Camping**: *Los Maitenes*, Villa Futalaufquen, excellent, US$1.50 pp plus US$2 per tent. Several campsites at Lagos Rivadavia, Verde and Río Arrayanes, from free to US$3 depending on facilities.

Transport **From Esquel** Bus (*Transportes Esquel*, T453529) to **Lago Verde**, US$6, passing along the east side of Lago Futalaufquen at 0800, daily – and others – in season (it passes 3 hotels and drives into 2 camp sites). In Jan-Feb and on Sat and Sun it continues to **El Bolsón** and **Lago Puelo**.

There is a campsite (Camping Río Grande) on the Argentine side of river. Cross the border river by the bridge after passing Argentine customs; Chilean customs is 1 km on the other side of river (one hour for all formalities, see page 731). ■ *From Esquel to Paso Futaleufú, Codao bus Mon, Fri, 0800, 1700, US$3.15, 2 hrs, return departures 1100, 1900. Minibus from Paso Futaleufú to Futaleufú (10 km) US$2. Very little traffic for hitching. (For transport from Futaleufú to Chaitén, Chile see Chile chapter.) From Esquel to the Palena border crossing, bus Sun, Mon, Wed 1700, Fri 0900, return departures Mon, Tue, Thu 0700, Fri 1700.*

Border with Chile – Paso Futaleufú
Colour map 9, grid A1
70 km SW of Esquel via Trevelin

South of Esquel, Route 40 is paved through the towns of Tecka and **Gobernador Costa** (E *Hotels Jair*, good value, and *Vega*; municipal campsite with all services, US$1) in Chubut province. At 34 km south of Gobernador Costa, gravelled Route 40 forks southwest through the town of Alto Río Senguer, while provincial Route 20 heads almost directly south for 81 km, before turning east towards Sarmiento and Comodoro Rivadavia. At La Puerta del Diablo, in the valley of the lower Río Senguer, Route 20 intersects provincial Route 22, which joins with Route 40 at the town of Río Mayo (see page 205). This latter route is completely paved and preferable to Route 40 for long-distance motorists; good informal campsites on the west side of the bridge across the Río Senguer.

Argentina

Patagonia

Patagonia is the vast, windy, treeless plateau south of the Río Colorado bordered by the Atlantic coast which is rich in marine life, most easily seen around Puerto Madryn. In the south of the region is the Parque Nacional de los Glaciares, with journeys on lakes full of ice floes and to the Moreno glacier. In the Chubut Valley is Argentina's Welsh community. Large parts of this area have less than one person to the sq km, and there are virtually no trees except in the north and the Andean foothills.

Buenos Aires

Over the whole land there blows a boisterous, cloud-laden wind which raises a haze of dust in summer, but in winter the dust can turn into thick mud. Temperatures are moderated by the proximity of the sea and are singularly mild, neither rising high during the summer nor falling low during the winter. In the foothills of the Andes rainfall is high, supporting a line of beech forests which run from Neuquén to Tierra del Fuego. Amounts of rain decline rapidly as you go east and Eastern Patagonia is more or less desert. Deep crevices or canyons intersect the land from east to west. Few of them contain permanent water, but ground water is easily pumped to the surface. The great sheep *estancias* are along these canyons, sheltered from the wind, and in the depression running north from the Strait of Magellan to Lagos Argentino and Buenos Aires and beyond. During a brief period in spring, after the melting of the snows, there is grass on the plateau. Most of the land is devoted to sheep raising. Over-grazing leads to much erosion. Wild dogs, pumas and red foxes are the sole predators of the sheep. Because of the high winds and insufficient rainfall there is little agriculture except in the north, in the valleys of the Colorado and Negro rivers. Some cattle are raised in both valleys where irrigation permits the growing of alfalfa.

In all Patagonia there is only one town – Comodoro Rivadavia – with a population over 100,000. Most of the towns are small ports, which used only to work during the wool-shipping season but have livened up since the local economy began to diversify.

Background
Although geographically Patagonia consists of the provinces of Neuquén, Río Negro, Chubut and Santa Cruz, this section covers only the latter two provinces and eastern parts of Río Negro

Guanacos and rheas are a common sight: there are also *maras* (Patagonian hares). Along the coast there are sea lion and penguin colonies; some protected waters are breeding grounds for the Commerson's dolphin and the grey dolphin. Elephant seals and Southern right whales breed along the coast of Valdés peninsula and the

Wildlife

nearby gulfs. The best viewing season is between October and April (for full details, see page 200). Further south, the Magellan goose (*caiquén*) is one of the most commonly seen of the 152 species of birds (recommended reading, *Aves de Argentina y Uruguay*, available, in English, from main bookshops in Buenos Aires as well as major tourist centres in Patagonia).

Colonization The first European to visit the coast of Patagonia was the Portuguese Fernão Magalhães (Ferdinand Magellan), then in the service of Spain, in 1519. Later European attempts to settle along the coast were deterred by isolation, lack of food and water and the harsh climate as well as the dour and obdurate local Indians, but these were almost entirely wiped out in the wars of 1879-83, generally known as the 'Campaign of the Desert'. Before this there had been a long established colony at Carmen de Patagones; it shipped salt to Buenos Aires during the colonial period. There had also been a settlement of Welsh people in the Chubut Valley since 1865 (see box below). After the Indian wars colonization was rapid, the Welsh, Scots and English taking a great part. Chilean sheep farmers from Punta Arenas moved north along the depression at the foot of the Andes, eastwards into Tierra del Fuego, and north to Santa Cruz.

Transport **Air** Main air services are given in the text below. Check for discounts on flights. Prepare for delays in bad weather. Many air force **LADE** flights in the region south of Bariloche must be booked in advance from the flight's departure point. The baggage allowance is 15 kg. Flights are often heavily booked ahead, but always check again on the day of the flight if you are told beforehand that it is sold out. *LADE* tickets are much cheaper for a long flight with stops than buying separate segments. *LADE*'s computer reservation system is linked to *Aerolíneas Argentinas*, so flight connections are possible between these airlines.

Road The main road, Route 3, which is paved, runs near the coast from Buenos Aires to Río Gallegos. South of this town it is paved as far as Tolhuin, from where it is all weather to Ushuaia. Sometimes bus passengers going south have to pay for baggage by weight. Many buses do not operate between early Apr and late Oct.

The principal roads in Patagonia roughly form an inverted triangle. Route 3 has regular traffic and adequate services. At the southern end, this route enters Chile and crosses the Magellan Straits to Tierra del Fuego by the car ferry at Primera Angostura. The western route (Route 40) zigzags across the moors, is lonely and is good in parts, poor in others (more details given below); there is hardly any traffic except in December, January and February, the tourist season. However, it is by far the more interesting road, with fine views of the Andes and plenty of wildlife as well as the Alerces and Glaciares National Parks. Camping is no problem, and there are good hotels at Esquel, Perito Moreno and Calafate, with third class accommodation also at Gobernador Gregores and Río Mayo. The road across Patagonia, from Esquel in the Lake District to Comodoro Rivadavia, is paved. The northern part of the triangle is formed by the paved highway running from Bariloche through Neuquén to San Antonio Oeste.

Many of the roads in southern Argentina are gravelled. Drivers should look out for cattle grids (*guardaganados*), even on main highways. They are signed; cross them very slowly. Carry warm clothing and make sure your car has anti-freeze. Always carry plenty of fuel, as service stations may be as much as 300 km apart. Fuel prices throughout Patagonia are about half the price of the rest of the country.

Sleeping In summer hotel prices are very high, especially in Calafate; in some places there may not be enough hotel beds to meet the demand. Camping is increasingly popular and *estancias* seem hospitable to travellers who are stuck for a bed. Many *estancias*, especially in Santa Cruz province, offer transport, excursions and food as well as accommodation. *ACA* establishments, which charge the same prices all over Argentina, are a bargain in Patagonia. As very few hotels and restaurants have a/c or even fans, it can get uncomfortably hot in Jan.

These two towns lie on opposite banks of the Río Negro, about 27 km from its mouth and 250 km south of Bahía Blanca. Most services are in **Viedma** (*Population*: 26,000. *Phone code*: 02920), on the south bank, the capital of Río Negro Province. **C** *Austral*, Villarino 292, T422019, modern. Recommended. **D** *Peumayen*, Buenos Aires 334, T425243. *Restaurant Munich*, Buenos Aires 150, open late. There is a good municipal campsite near the river, US$2 per person, all facilities including hot showers. The tourist office is at Belgrano 544, p 9.

Viedma & Carmen de Patagones
Colour map 8, grid C4

Excursions Beautiful beach, El Cóndor, 30 km south of Viedma, three buses a day from Viedma in summer, hotel open January-February, restaurants and shops, free camping on beach 2 km south. Lobería Punta Bermeja is a sealion colony 30 km south from El Cóndor; daily bus in summer from Viedma; hitching easy in summer.

On a hill behind **Carmen de Patagones** (*Population:* 16,000) a monument commemorates an attack on the twin towns by a Brazilian squadron in 1827. There are three museums, one in Patagones, two in Viedma. The swimming is recommended on the Viedma side of the river, where there is a nice shady shore. The two towns are linked by two bridges and a ferry.

Transport Air *LADE* (Saavedra 403, T/F424420) fly to **Buenos Aires**, **Mar del Plata**, **Bahía Blanca**, **Neuquén**, **San Martín de Los Andes**, **San Antonio Oeste**, **Puerto Madryn**, **Trelew** and **Comodoro Rivadavia**. **Buses** Terminal at C A Zatti y Lavalle about 6 blocks from main plaza. To/from **Buenos Aires** US$27, *La Estrella/Cóndor*. To **San Antonio Oeste**, US$5.25.

Almost due west and 180 km along the coast, on the Gulf of San Matías, is **San Antonio Oeste**. 17 km south is a popular seaside resort, **Las Grutas**, developed in the 1960s with a good safe beach (the caves themselves are not really worth visiting); bus from San Antonio hourly US$1. Las Grutas closes down in mid-March.

San Antonio Oeste
Phone code: 02934
Colour map 8, grid C3
Population: 10,000

Sleeping At San Antonio C *Kandava*, Sarmiento 240, T421430. Hot water, good. **D** *Iberia*, Sarmiento 241. Without breakfast, small rooms, but recommended. **E** *Betty*, Islas Malvinas 1410, T422370. There are also many good camping sites (eg *La Entrada*, US$2.50 per tent, on edge of town above beach). Seafood restaurants. *Olaff*, Sarmiento y Costanera. *Parrilla*, good value.

Transport Buses North to **Bahía Blanca** and south to **Río Gallegos** and **Punta Arenas** by *Transportes Patagónicos*. To **Puerto Madryn** and **Trelew**, *Don Otto*, 0200 and 1530, 4 hrs, US$12. To **Buenos Aires**, US$27 via Bahía Blanca, frequent.

Puerto Madryn and Península Valdés

A port on a wide bay, Golfo Nuevo, Puerto Madryn was the site of the first Welsh landing in 1865. The town was founded in 1886 and named after the Welsh home of the colonist, Jones Parry. It has a giant alumina plant (visits, Monday 1430, arranged at the tourist office) and fish processing plants. The town is a popular tourist centre, with a casino, skin-diving and nature reserves, both close to town and on the nearby Valdés peninsula. **Museo de Ciencias Naturales y Oceanográfico**, Domecq García y J Menéndez, is informative and worth a visit. ■ *Tue-Sat 0900-1200, 1630-2030, Sun evening only, US$1, ask to see video.* The tourist office is at Roca 223, T473029, sectur@madryn.gov.ar and www.madryn.com Helpful, has notice board for messages, list of current hotel rates and interesting video on the region. ■ *Mon-Fri 0700-1300, 1500-2100, Sat/Sun 0800-1300, 1700-2100 but only Mon-Fri in winter.*

Puerto Madryn
Phone code: 02965
Colour map 9, grid A3
Population: 50,000
250 km S of San Antonio Oeste

Argentina

Argentina

Sleeping

Often full in summer, when prices rise; make bookings early. Many smaller places close out of season

A *Península Valdés*, Roca 155, T471292, info@hotel-peninsula-valdes.com With breakfast, sea view, suites available, sauna, comfortable. Recommended. **A** *Bahía Nueva*, Roca 67, T/F451677, hotel@bahianueva.com.ar With breakfast, bar, very comfortable. **A** *La Posada de Madryn*, Matthews 2951, T474087, www.la-posada.com.ar Quiet, English spoken. Recommended. **A** *Villa Pirén*, Roca 439, T/F456272, piren@ internet.sisccotel.com Sea view, suites, good beds, excellent accommodation. **B** *Fantili*, Mitre 619, T455124, hotelfantili@ arnet.com.ar Very helpful, breakfast on 4th floor, good views. **B** *Tolosa*, Sáenz Peña 250, T471850, tolosa@hoteltolosa.com.ar 3-star, good breakfast. **B** *Hostal del Rey*, Brown 681, T471156. On beach, 2-star, breakfast extra, restaurant with fixed price menu. Recommended. **C** *Marina*, Roca 7, T474044. Showers, warm, kitchen facilities. **C** *Muelle Viejo*, Yrigoyen 38, T471284. Opposite pier, good, restaurant, quiet. **D** *Res Petit*, Alvear 845, T451460, respetit@infovia.com.ar Quiet, good. **D** *Res La Posta*, Roca 33, T472422. Good, heating, fan, cooking and laundry facilities. **D** *Yanco*, Av Roca 626, T456411, jacd39@infovia.com.ar Central, good, **F** in room with bunks, cheap restaurant. **D** *Anclamar*, 25 de Mayo 875, T451509. Quiet. Recommended. **D** *Del Centro*, 28 de Julio 149, T473742. Good, basic, hot water. **D** *Costanera*, Brown 759, T452800. Good value. **D** *Res Manolo's*, Roca 763, T472390. Breakfast extra, small, quiet, kitchen facilities, homely. **D** *Vaskonia*, 25 de Mayo 43, T472581. Central, good value. **D** *Hosp Santa Rita*, Gob Maiz 370, T471050. Shared bath, use of kitchen, heating, helpful.

Youth hostels 25 de Mayo 1136, T/F474426, madrynhi@hostels.org.ar **F** pp dormitory, **D** double room, laundry and kitchen facilities, bike rental, English and French spoken (in theory), tours, safe deposit (not free), no luggage store, uncooperative. **F** pp *Huefur*, Mitre 798,

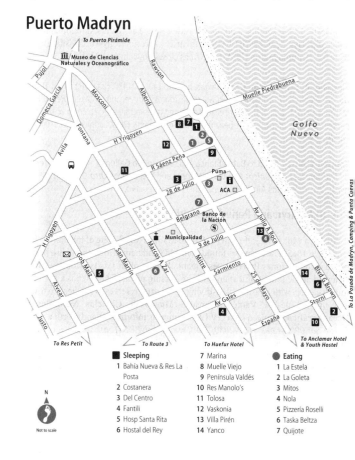

Puerto Madryn

Sleeping ■
1 Bahía Nueva & Res La Posta
2 Costanera
3 Del Centro
4 Fantili
5 Hosp Santa Rita
6 Hostal del Rey
7 Marina
8 Muelle Viejo
9 Península Valdés
10 Res Manolo's
11 Tolosa
12 Vaskonia
13 Villa Pirén
14 Yanco

Eating ●
1 La Estela
2 La Goleta
3 Mitos
4 Nola
5 Pizzería Roselli
6 Taska Beltza
7 Quijote

N

Not to scale

T453224, huefur@ssdnet.com.ar Dormitories or private rooms, laundry and kitchen facilities, English spoken, internet.

Camping All closed out of season. At Punta Cuevas, Blvd Brown, 4 km south of town, is *ACA* site with evening hot showers, shop, café, good facilities and shady trees, T452952, US$6 per tent, but many people camp on beach; nearby is a swimming pool in the rocks which gets its water at high tide, very pleasant, and free. Municipal site at Ribera Sur, 500 m before *ACA* site, bus 2 from centre, T455460 (gives student discount). All facilities, busy, US$1.50 pp, US$1 per tent, room with bunkbeds, **F** pp. Camping also at El Golfito, road to Lobería Punta Loma, T454544. Camping out can be interesting as one can watch foxes, armadillos, skunks and rheas roaming around in the evening.

Las Aguilas, M A Zar y Sáenz Peña. Recommended, large portions, good for seafood. **Eating** *La Estela*, Sáenz Peña 70. Very good, moderately priced. *Mitos*, 28 de Julio 64. Snacks, pizzas, pasta, sandwiches, good. *Cantina El Náutico*, Roca y Lugones. Very good food, especially fish. *Nola*, Roca 485. Not cheap but good French-style food, attentive service. *París*, Muella Piedrabuena. Good and reasonably priced. *Pizzería Roselli*, Sáenz Peña y Roca. Good, with vegetarian selections. *Quijote*, Belgrano 138. Reasonable prices, very good. *Pequeño*, Roca 820. Good value. *Barbarians*, 25 de Mayo y 28 de Julio. Good coffee. *Taska Beltza*, 9 de Julio 345. Good food and service.

For excellent Welsh afternoon teas, *La Goleta*, Roca 87, 1700-1900. Several local chocolate makers; try *Península* on Roca; *Café de la Ciudad*, 25 de Mayo y 28 de Julio. Very popular.

Diving Puerto Madryn is a diving centre. Tours, including for novices, are organized by: **Sport** *Ocean Divers*, Brown entre 1 y 2 Rotundas, T452648. *Hydrosport*, Balneario Rayentray, T457014. Specialists in diving and swimming with dolphins. Courses on video, photography and underwater communication. The underwater environment: clear waters, sunlight penetrates to a depth of 70 m, ideal for underwater photography. There's a Parque Submarino with guided tour. A ship, the *Albatros*, was sunk on purpose so that divers can see various life forms growing on it.

Several agencies do tours to the Valdés Peninsula, all are for 12 hrs, see below. Note that **Tour operators** return distances of some tour destinations are high: Península Valdés 430 km, Punta Tombo 400 km, Ameghino Dam 400 km (last 2 better from Trelew). The following are all recommended: *Argentina Visión*, Roca 536, T451427, F451108, arvision@arvision.com.ar Also arranges nature walks and 4WD circuits. *Puma*, 28 de Julio 46, T/F471482, pumatrvl@satlink.com Small groups. *Mar y Valle*, Roca 297, T450872. *South Patagonia*, Roca 295, T471545. Small groups, ask for English-speaking guide, good service. *Coyun Co*, Roca 165, T451845. Good service. *Factor Patagonia*, 25 de Mayo 186, local 3, T454990. Small groups, Spanish only, good value.

Local Car hire: expensive. *Coyun-Co*, Roca 171. *Puerto Madryn Turismo*, Roca 624. **Transport** *Renta Car Patagonia*, Roca 295. And international agencies. **Cycle Hire**: *XT*, Roca 700 block. *Pablo Neme*, Humphreys 85, T471475, also rents sandboards. Many others.

Long distance Air: Airport 10 km west; *Dinar* and *LADE* to *Buenos Aires*; *LADE* also to *Mar del Plata, Bahía Blanca, Viedma, San Antonio Oeste, Trelew* and *Comodoro Rivadavia*. Other flights from Trelew (see below). Direct bus to Trelew airport, *Puma*, US$3.50, leaves 1½ hrs before flight and takes arriving passengers back to Puerto Madryn (taxi US$27).

Buses: Terminal at Yrigoyen y San Martín in old railway station. To **Buenos Aires**, 18-19 hrs, daily, 6 companies, US$24-35. To **Río Gallegos**, US$27.50, about 20 hrs, 4 companies, including *Don Otto* and *Pingüino* (connections to El Calafate, Río Turbio, Punta Arenas and Puerto Natales). To **Comodoro Rivadavia**, 6 companies, US$10-12. To **Bariloche**, *Mar y Valle* daily except Wed, US$27, 15 hrs. To **Trelew**, by *28 de Julio* and *Mar y Valle*, hourly, US$2.50, 1 hr. Take own food and drink on long trips, regardless of what refreshments you are promised when booking. **Taxis**: outside bus terminal and on main plaza.

Argentina

Argentina

Directory **Airline offices** *Dinar*, Roca 165, T451845. *LADE*, Roca 119, T451909. **Banks** Banks open Mon-Fri 0830-1330 (0800-1300 in summer). *Banco de la Nación*, 25 de Mayo y 9 de Julio. *Banco del Sud*, Sáenz Peña, ATM for Visa. *Banco Provincia Chubut*, 25 de Mayo, MasterCard and Amex ATM. There are no *casas de cambio*, but fair rates from travel agents. **Communications** Internet: *Madryn Computación*, Roca 31, closed Sun. *Telecom*, 28 de Julio 293 (US$3 1300-1700). *Arnet*, Marcos Zar 125. 0900-2100, closed Sun. *Re Creo*, R Sáenz Peña 101. **Post Office**: Belgrano y A Maiz. **Telephone:** Many *locutorios* in the centre.

Patagonian wildlife and nature reserves

See also Puerto Deseado, page 207 and Punta Tombo, page 203

The natural history of the region is very interesting, with **elephant seal** and **sea lion** colonies, breeding grounds for **Southern right whales** in the Golfo Nuevo and the Golfo San José, fossils in the cliffs, and **guanacos**, **rheas** and **armadillos** in the countryside. Whales can be seen from perhaps as early as May to, at the very latest, end-December. The sea lion breeding season runs from late December to late January, but visiting is good up to end-April. Bull elephant seals begin to claim their territory in the first half of August and the breeding season is late September/early October. The seals leave in March. Orcas tend to attack the seals at Punta Norte in February/March. Conservation officials can be found at the main viewpoints, informative but only Spanish spoken. The *EcoCentro Puerto Madryn*, Julio Verne 3784, T/F457470-73, www.ecocentro.org.ar, studies the marine ecosystems.

The **Punta Loma** sea lion reserve is 15 km southeast of Puerto Madryn. Sea lions can even be seen in Puerto Madryn harbour. ■ *0900-1200, 1430-1730; Dec and Jan are the best months, US$2.50 (free with Península Valdés ticket). Information and video. Getting there: taxis US$10.*

Península Valdés The Golfos Nuevo and San José are separated by the Istmo Carlos Ameghino, which leads to Península Valdés. In depressions in the heart of the peninsula are large salt flats; Salina Grande is 42 m below sea level. At the entrance to the peninsula, on the isthmus, there is an interesting Visitors' Centre and a conservation officer is stationed here. ■ *Entry US$3.50.* Near the entrance, Isla de los Pájaros can be seen in Golfo San José. Its seabirds can only be viewed through fixed telescopes (at 400 m distance), except for recognized ornithologists who can get permission to visit. Best time to see birds: September-April. The centre for visits to the Peninsula is **Puerto Pirámide** (*Population*: 100), 90 km east of Puerto Madryn. It is from here that whale-watching boat trips depart; sailings are controlled by the Prefectura, according to weather and sea conditions. There is a small tourist office on the edge of town, useful information for hikes and driving tours.

At Punta Norte (176 km) at the north end of the Valdés Peninsula, there are high, white cliffs and elephant seals (best seen at low tide); reasonably priced restaurant for meals and snacks. At Caleta Valdés, 45 km south of Punta Norte you can see elephant seals at close quarters. At Punta Delgada (at the south of the peninsula) elephant seals and other wildlife can be seen. The beach on the entire coast is out of bounds; this is strictly enforced.

■ *The best way to see the wildlife is by car. See Puerto Madryn for car hire (a day's fuel will cost about US$10); a taxi costs US$70 per vehicle for the day. Roads are all gravel except the road from Puerto Madryn to Puerto Pirámide. In summer there are several well-stocked shops, but if staying take sun and wind protection and drinking water. Getting there:* Mar y Valle *bus company from Puerto Madryn to Puerto Pirámide, Thu, Sun at 1000 returns 1800, US$4.50 each way.*

Sleeping and eating **At Puerto Pirámide**: **B** *ACA Motel*, T495004. Poor restaurant, camping. There is also an *ACA* service station (open daily) with good café and shop. **B** *Estancia El Sol* , T495007, with restaurant. **B** *Paradise Pub*, T495030. Helpful, good value food and beer, good atmosphere. Recommended. **C** *Cabañas El Cristal*, T495033, 4 bed cabañas. Recommended. **D** *Español*, T495031. Basic but pleasant. Municipal campsite by the black sand beach, T495000, US$2.50 pp (free out of season), hot showers

The Welsh Settlement

On 28 July 1865, 153 Welsh immigrants landed at Puerto Madryn, then a deserted beach deep in Indian country. After three weeks they pushed, on foot, across the parched pampa and into the Chubut river valley, where there is flat cultivable land along the riverside for a distance of 80 kilometres upstream. Here, maintained in part by the Argentine Government, they settled, but it was three years before they realized the land was barren unless watered. They drew water from the river, which is higher than the surrounding flats, and later built a fine system of irrigation canals. The colony, reinforced later by immigrants from Wales and from the United States, prospered, but in 1899 a great flood drowned the valley and some of the immigrants left for Canada. The last Welsh contingent arrived in 1911. The object of the colony had been to create a `Little Wales beyond Wales', and for four generations they kept the Welsh language alive. The language is, however, dying out in the fifth generation. There is an offshoot of the colony of Chubut at Trevelin, at the foot of the Andes nearly 650 km to the west, settled in 1888 (see page 193). It is interesting that this distant land gave to the Welsh language one of its most endearing classics: Dringo'r Andes (Climbing the Andes), written by one of the early women settlers.

Argentina

US$0.50, good, get there early to secure a place. Do not camp on the beach: people have been swept away by the incoming tide.

Punta Delgada **A** *Faro*, T471910. Full board, comfortable, excellent food. Reservations at *Hotel Península Valdés*, Puerto Madryn. There is a separate restaurant.

Tour operators Full-day tours take in Puerto Pirámide (with whale-watching in season), plus some, but not necessarily all, of the other wildlife viewing points. Prices are US$17.50-30 pp, in some cases including the entry to the national park; boat trip to see whales US$10 if not included in tour price. On all excursions take drink, food if you don't want to eat in the expensive restaurants, and binoculars. Most tour companies (addresses above) stay 50-60 mins on location. *Hydro Sports*, T495065, rents scuba equipment and boats, has a small restaurant, and organizes land and sea wildlife tours (ask for Mariano). Off season tours run when demand is sufficient, usually on Thu and Sun, departing at 0955 and returning at 1730. Check all excursion dates and opening times in advance. Tours do not run after heavy rain in the low season.

Trelew

Pronounced 'Trel-A-Yoo', Trelew is a prosperous town which has lost its Welsh look. The Founding of Chubut festival is on 28 July and Petroleum Day is 13 December. The **Capilla Tabernacle** on Belgrano between San Martín and 25 de Mayo is a red brick chapel dating from 1889. Nearby is another brick building from the same period, the Asociación San David. On the road to Rawson, 3 km south is **Chapel Moriah**, the oldest standing Welsh chapel. Built in 1880, it has a simple interior and the graves of many original settlers. The **Museo Paleontológico Egidio Feruglio**, in a new building at Av Fontana 140 y 9 de Julio, organizes excursions to the Parque Paleontológico Bryn-Gwyn, traces the history of dinosaurs with models made from moulds of dinosaur bones (not all from Patagonia). ■ *Mon-Fri 1000-1800, closes 2 hrs later weekends, holidays and in summer, US$3, students US$2, guided tours in English, German and Italian, T432100, info@mef.org.ar* **Museo Regional**, Fontana y 9 de Julio, has displays on indigenous societies, on failed Spanish attempts at settlement and on Welsh colonization; interesting. ■ *0700-1300, 1400-2000, US$1.* **Museo del Chacarero**, Treorcky, museum of the earliest settlers in the region, *Feria de Productores del Valle Inferior del Río Chubut* each Saturday and Sunday, with produce for sale, meals, 30-minute horse-drawn trips (US$2.50). Tourist offices at the airport and at San Martin y Mitre, T/F420139, eturismotw@arnet.com.ar Free maps, hotel prices and self-guided city tour.

Phone code: 02965
Colour map 9, grid A3
Population: 61,000

Argentina

Sleeping **A** *Rayentray*, San Martín y Belgrano, T434702, rcvtw@internet.siscotel.com Pool, expensive but excellent restaurant, helpful, comfortable. **B** *Libertador*, Rivadavia 31, T435132, T420220, hlibertador@infovia.com.ar With breakfast, good rooms, good restaurant, quiet, good value. **C** *Touring Club*, Av Fontana 240, T/F425790, htouring@internet.siscotel.com Excellent, with breakfast. **C** *Res San Carlos*, Sarmiento 758, T421038. Recommended. **C** *Res Rivadavia*, Rivadavia 55, T434472, hotelriv@infovia.com.ar Helpful, also cheaper rooms **D**. Recommended. **D** *Res Argentino*, Abraham Matthews 186, T436134. Welcoming quiet, good, garage, near bus terminal. **D** *Galicia*, 9 de Julio y Rivadavia, T433802, castroab@infovia.com.ar Very warm, without bath.

Eating *El Quijote*, 25 de Mayo 90. Seafood, not cheap. *Sugar*, 25 de Mayo 247. Good *menú del día*. *Napoli*, Rivadavia y 9 de Julio. Old fashioned *confitería*. *La Casa de Juan*, Moreno 360. Cosy, good pizzas. *Café Vittorio*, Belgrano 341. Good service. Opposite is *Pizzería Girifalco*. Good pizzas and pasta, mid-price. Café at *Hotel Touring Club*, popular, good coffee. Fast food and *minutas* at *Hipertía* supermarket, Soberanía Nacional y Belgrano, and *La Anónima* supermarket, Av Yrigoyen, or Colombia. For ice cream: *Rottofer*, 25 de Mayo y Ameghino, and *Vía Roca*, opposite the Casino.

Shopping *Chocolates Patagónicos*, Belgrano y Pasaje Mendoza, for local chocolate. *Camping Sur*, Pellegrini 389 for camping equipment.

Tour operators Agencies run tours to Punta Tombo, US$15, Chubut Valley (half-day), US$7.50, Florentino Ameghino, US$15. Tours to Península Valdés are best done from Puerto Madryn. *Sur Turismo*, Belgrano 326-330, T434550. Organizes good excursions. *Estrella del Sur Turismo*, San Martín 129, T431282. English spoken. Recommended. And others.

Transport **Car hire**: expensive. Airport desks are staffed only at flight arrival times and cars are snapped up quickly. All have offices in town. **Air** Airport 5 km north of centre; taxis about US$4. Local buses to/from Puerto Madryn stop at the airport entrance if asked, turning is 10 mins walk, US$3.50; *AR* runs special bus service to connect with its flights. *AIRG* and *AR* have flights to/from **Buenos Aires** and **Comodoro Rivadavia**. *LADE* flies to Patagonian airports from

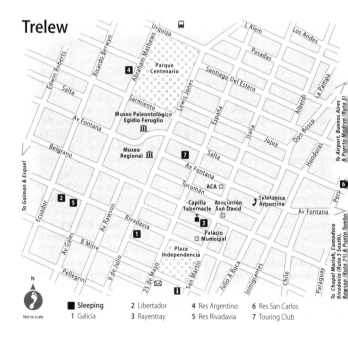

Viedma to Comodoro Rivadavia, as well as **Bariloche**. **Buses** Terminal on northeast side of Plaza Centenario. To **Buenos Aires**, 5 companies daily, 19-21 hrs, US$25-42. To **Bahía Blanca**, US$20 daily with *Don Otto*, 0730. To **Esquel**, US$15-18, 8-12 hrs, *Mar y Valle*. Frequent buses to **Gaiman**, US$1; hourly to **Puerto Madryn**, US$2.50 with *28 de Julio* and *Mar y Valle*. To **Comodoro Rivadavia** 7 companies, US$10, 4-5 hrs. To **Río Gallegos**, daily, several companies, 15-17 hrs, US$20.

Airline offices *AR/Austral*. *LADE*, Sarmiento 282, T435740. *AIRG*, Belgrano 206, T423438. **Banks** *Banco de la Nación*, 25 de Mayo y Fontana. *Banco del Sud*, 9 de Julio 370, cash advance on Visa. **Communications** Internet: *Telefónica*, 25 de Mayo 219, 0730-0100; San Martín y Rivadavia. **Post Office**: 25 de Mayo and Mitre. **Telephone**: *Telefónica Fontana*, Fontana 418. *Telefónica Argentina*, Roca near Fontana.

Directory

Argentina

A pretty town of well-built brick houses, Gaiman hosts the annual Eisteddfod (Welsh festival of arts) in October. **Museum** in the old railway station. ■ *Open in summer, Mon-Sat 1600-2000, in winter, Tue-Sat 1500-1900, US$0.50. Curator Mrs Roberts is 'full of stories'.* **El Desafío**, two blocks west of the plaza, is a private theme-park, 16 years work by Sr Joaquín Alonso. It is constructed entirely of rubbish (drinks cans, bottles, piping and wire), a labyrinth of coloured plastic, glass and aluminium with mottos at every turn. ■ *US$2.50, tickets valid 2 months.*

Gaiman
Colour map 9, grid A3
Population: 4,400
18 km W of Trelew

Sleeping and eating A *Plas y Coed*, Miguel D Jones 123, T491133. Also 3 cheaper rooms for backpackers, Welsh-owned, also tea house (oldest, excellent tea 'and enough food for a week', Marta Rees speaks English and is very knowledgeable about the area), includes breakfast. Highly recommended, frequently. **D** pp *Gwesty Tywi*, MD Jones 342, T/F2965-491292, gwestywi@infovia.com.ar Rooms with or without bath, also cheaper dormitories, internet access, bus transfer, tours arranged, very helpful. Small municipal **campsite** beyond Casa de Té Gaiman (poor, no facilities).

Becws, MD Jones 418. Same owners as *Gwesty Tywi*, excellent food, vegetarian options, reasonable prices. Welsh teas are served from about 1500 (US$10-12) by several **Tea Rooms**, including *Casa de Té Gaiman*, Yrigoyen 738, excellent. *Ty Gwyn*, 9 de Julio 111. Recommended. *Ty Nain*, Yrigoyen 283. Frequented by tour buses, display of historical items. *Ty Te Caerdydd*, Finca 202, T491610, 2 km from town. Very good. And *Eima*, Tello 571.

Most facilities are closed out of season

Dolavon, is a small town 20 km further west. The main street runs parallel to the irrigation canal built by the settlers; there is a chapel over the canal. The old flour mill at Maipú 61, dates from 1930 and can be visited: key kept in the Municipalidad, Roca 188 (next to Banco Provincial del Chubut). Municipal campsite near the service station on the way into town, good facilities, free. ■ *Some Trelew-Gaiman buses continue to Dolavan; check at Trelew bus terminal. For Esquel, buses pass 1 km from Gaiman at the roundabout on Trelew-Esquel road, Mon, Wed, Fri, 0830, US$17.50.*

The paved Route 25 runs from Dolavon west to the upper Chubut Valley. It passes near the **Florentino Ameghino** dam, 110 km inland on the Río Chubut. The dam covers 7,000 ha with water and irrigates 28,000 ha in the lower Chubut valley, as well as producing electric power. An oasis of cool green trees, recommended for a change of landscape, it's a popular excursion from Trelew (**F** *El Lago* hotel and restaurant, recommended). From Ameghino to Tecka on Route 40 (south of Trevelin) is one of the most beautiful routes across Patagonia from the coast to the Andes, lots of wildlife to be seen. It goes through Las Plumas (mind the bridge if driving), Los Altares, which has camping, fuel and some shops, and Paso de Los Indios.

This nature reserve is 107 km south of Trelew. Its wildlife includes guanacos and rheas on the way to the penguin colony, where scavenger birds like chimangos, skuas and kelp gulls can be seen. Season for penguins, September-March (January-February is the time when the young are taking to the water). The reserve closes after March

Punta Tombo
The largest breeding ground for Magellenic penguins in Patagonia

(check date at the Tourist Office). When visits are permitted it is a fantastic experience. ■ *Park entrance US$5. Trelew and Puerto Madryn travel agencies run tours, spending 30 mins at the site. There are 2 routes to the reserve: one is by a well-marked road which branches off Route 3, west of Dos Pozos, driving time 1¾ hrs. The other is by a turning which branches off Route 1, a ripio road between Trelew and Camarones.*

Another large **penguin colony** at Cabo Dos Bahías is 35 km along a dirt road from **Camarones**(*Population*: 800; 275 km south of Comodoro Rivadavia. ■ *Open all year, US$5.* In Camarones ask the Guardia Fauna on Monday or Friday for transport, or the owner of Kau-i-Keuken hotel (**C**, good food), private car will charge US$25-30, ask at Busca Vida. ■ *There are 2 buses a week, US$6.50, on Mon and Fri from Trelew to Camarones* (Don Otto), *0800, 2½ hrs, returns same day 1600.*

Argentina

Comodoro Rivadavia

Phone code: 0297
Colour map 9, grid A2
Population: 158,000
387 km S of Trelew

The largest city in the province of Chubut, oil was discovered here in 1907 and about 30% of all Argentina's production comes from wells to the south and west. **Museo del Petroleo**, 3 km north in Gral Mosconi (bus No 6 from San Martín y Abasolo). From here southward, prices begin to rise very rapidly, so stock up before reaching Río Gallegos. Good beach at Rada Tilly, 12 km south (buses every 30 minutes); walk along beach at low tide to see sea lions. Local holidays are on 28 July (Founding of Chubut) and 13 December (Petroleum Day). Tourist office at Rivadavia y Pellegrini.

Sleeping & eating

B *Austral*, Rivadavia 190, T472200, F472444. Noise from traffic but otherwise comfortable, reasonable restaurant. **B** *Res Azul*, Sarmiento 724, T467539. Comfortable, spotless. Recommended. **D** *Hosp Belgrano*, Belgrano 546, T478439. Hot water. **Camping** Municipal site in Rada Tilly, reached by Expreso Rada Tilly bus from town, hot and cold water. Eating places include *La Rastra*, Rivadavia 384. Very good for *churrasco*, but not much else. *Pizzería El Nazareño*, San Martín y España. Good. *Posta del Cangrejo*, on waterfront. Good seafood. *Bom-Bife*, España 832. Good food, inexpensive. Several *rotiserías*, much cheaper, on 400 block of Rivadavia, in municipal market.

Transport

Air Airport, 9 km north. Bus No 6 to airport from bus terminal, hourly (45 mins), US$0.25. Taxi to airport, US$4.50. To **Buenos Aires**, *AIRG*, *Dinar* and *AR*. **Córdoba**, **Mendoza**, **Neuquén**, **Salta**, **Tucumán** and **Ushuaia** are served by *Southern Winds*. *LADE* flies to all Patagonian destinations once or twice a week, plus Bariloche, El Bolsón and Esquel.

Buses Terminal conveniently located in centre; has luggage store, good *confitería* upstairs, lousy toilets, *remise* taxi booth, some kiosks. Services to **Buenos Aires** daily at 1200 and 2115, 32 hrs, US$70. To **Coyhaique** (Chile), *Angel Giobbi*, US$18, 12 hrs, twice a week (Mon and Thu) 0100, Jun-Sep and 3 a week (Mon, Wed, Fri), 0100, Oct-May (weather permitting), also *Turibus*, Tue and Sat 0800. To **Bariloche**, US$27 (*Don Otto*, 14 hrs). To **Esquel** (paved road) 8 hrs direct with *ETAP* and *Don Otto*, US$18. In summer buses heading south usually arrive full. To **Río Gallegos**, *Don Otto*, *Pingüino* and *TAC* daily, 11 hrs, US$13. To **Puerto Madryn**, US$10-12, and **Trelew**, US$10, several companies. *La Unión* to **Caleta Olivia**, hourly, US$2.50. To **Sarmiento**, US$5, 2½ hrs at 0700, 1300, 1900.

Directory

Airline offices *AR*, 9 de Julio 870, T444 0050/0810-2228 6527. *Dinar*, T444 1111. *AIRG*, Rivadavia 396, T447 2400. *LADE*, Rivadavia 360, T447 0585. *Southern Winds*, T447 1111. **Banks** *Banco de la Nación*, San Martín 108, has the best rates on US$. Amex agent is *Orbe Turismo Show*, San Martín 488, T429699. Several travel agencies change money. **Communications** Post Office: San Martín y Moreno. **Consulates** **Belgium**, Rivadavia 283. **Chile**, Sarmiento 936. **Italy**, Belgrano 1053.

From Comodoro Rivadavia to Chile

Sarmiento
Colour map 9, grid A2
Population: 7,000

The road to Chile runs inland from Comodoro Rivadavia to (156 km) Colonia Sarmiento (commonly called Sarmiento), which is situated south of two large lakes, Lago Musters and Lago Colhué Huapi. On the north side of the Plaza is the **Museo**

Desiderio Torres, with displays of indigenous artefacts. In the area there are two **petrified forests**, 70,000,000 years old, of fallen araucaria trees, nearly 3 m round and 15-20 m long: a remarkable sight: the **Bosque Petrificado José Ormachea**, 32 km south of Sarmiento on a gravel road, entry US$2.50, and the **Víctor Szlapelis** park, some 40 km further southwest along the same road (follow signposts, road from Sarmiento in good condition). ■ *Getting there: Taxi, Sarmiento to forests, US$24 (three passengers), including 1 hr wait, for each extra hr US$4.50. Contact Sr Juan José Valero, the park ranger, for guided tours, Uruguay 43, T097-489 8407 (see also the Monumento Natural Bosques Petrificados, page 207). Buses to Comodoro Rivadavia, 0700, 1300, 1900. To Chile via Río Mayo, Giobbi, 0200. Mon, Wed, Fri (Mon and Thu, Jun-Sep); seats are scarce in Río Mayo.*

From Sarmiento you can reach Esquel (448 km north along Routes 20 and 40); overnight buses on Sunday stop at Río Mayo, take food for journey.

The tourist office is on Avenida San Martín, almost at Alberdi, T489 8220, friendly, has map of town.

Sleeping

C *Hostería Los Lagos*, Roca y Alberdi, T493046. Good, heating, restaurant. 10 km from Sarmiento is **C** *Chacra Labrador*, T0297-489 3329, agna@coopsar.com.ar An excellent place to stay on a small *estancia*, breakfast included, other meals extra and available for non-residents (US$6), English and Dutch spoken, run tours to petrified forests at good prices, will collect guests from Sarmiento (same price as taxi). **E** *Musters*, Ing Coronel 215, T493097. In Dec-Mar you may be permitted to sleep in the Agricultural School (take sleeping bag) on the road to petrified forest, opposite the ACA petrol station. **Camping** Municipal site 2 km north of centre on Route 24, basic, no shower, US$1.50 for tent, US$0.50 pp, beside river.

Tourist information
T420400

Río Mayo (*Population*: 2,260; fuel and hotels **D-E**) is reached by Route 22 (paved) which branches southwest 84 km west of Sarmiento. From Río Mayo, a road continues west 114 km to the Chilean border at Coyhaique Alto for Coyhaique and Puerto Aisén in Chile. ■ *Mon-Fri at 0300 Giobbi bus takes Route 40 north from Río Mayo direct to Esquel; other connections (eg for Sarmiento or Coyhaique, Chile) from bus office in the centre. LADE flights to Comodoro Rivadavia once a week, T420060.*

South of Río Mayo Route 40 is unpaved as far as Perito Moreno (124 km) but there is no public transport and very few other vehicles even in mid-summer. At Km 31 on this road a turning leads west to Lago Blanco, to Chile via Paso Huemules and Balmaceda.

Perito Moreno
Population: 1,700
Altitude: 400 m

Perito Moreno is close to Lago Buenos Aires, which extends into Chile as Lago Gen Carrera. Do not confuse it with the famous glacier of the same name on Lago Argentino near El Calafate, nor with nearby Parque Nacional Perito Moreno, see below. Tourist office in the new bus terminal, at roundabout at north end of town.

Sleeping and eating **C** *Belgrano*, San Martín 1001, T42019. With shower, no heating, restaurant. Recommended. **E** *Santa Cruz*, on Belgrano. Heating, shared bath and hot water, good bakery opposite. 25 km south on Route 40, **C** pp *Telken*, sheep station of the Nauta family, T02963-432079, F432303 (in BsAs T4797 7216). Offers accommodation Oct-Apr, discounts for families with 2 children, camping, breakfast included, other communal meals extra, English and Dutch spoken, horse treks and excursions. Highly recommended. **Camping** Municipal site 2 km east of centre, clean, hot showers. Parque Laguna in town, opposite Laguna Cisnes, well shielded, but dirty, US$1 pp, showers extra, also cabins **D**, basic, no sheets.

Transport Air: Airport 7 km east of town; *LADE* (Av San Martín 1207, T432055) flies to Perito Moreno from **Río Gallegos, Río Grande, Ushuaia, Calafate** and **Gob Gregores** on Wed and to those destinations on Tue; from **Comodoro Rivadavia** on Tue, check in well in advance. **Bus**: If crossing from Chile at Los Antiguos you can take *Transportes Padilla*, Av San Martín 1494, T432839, for El Chaltén and El Calafate. There are buses to **Río Gallegos**.

Border with From Perito Moreno Route 43 (paved) runs south of Lago Buenos Aires to
Chile – Los **Los Antiguos**, 67 km west, 2 km from the Chilean border. (Service station;
Antiguos salmon fishing; annual cherry festival in early January.) **C** *Argentino*, comfortable,
restaurant, outstanding municipal campsite, hot showers, 2 km from centre,
US$1.25 pp. Also *Antigua Patagonia*, Ruta 43, T02963-491038/491055,
www.antiguapatagonia.com.ar Very good hotel on the lake, trips to Estancia El
Bagual, sauna, gym, restaurant. At Km 29 **A** *Hostería La Serena* offers accommodation in *cabinas*, 10% reduction to *South American Handbook* users, good restaurant and organizes trips in both the Chilean and Argentine Lake Districts, open
October-June; further details from Geraldine des Cressonières, Estancia La
Serena, Casilla 11, 9040 Perito Moreno, Santa Cruz, T02963-432340/0297-15-624
6549. Nearby is Los Chilcas where Indian remains can be found (trout fishing).

It is nearly impossible **Transport Buses**: To **Comodoro Rivadavia**, US$12, *Co-op Sportsman*, from near *Hotel*
to hitchhike between *Argentino*, 1400 daily, 7½ hrs, via **Perito Moreno** and **Caleta Olivia** (also to Río Gallegos,
Perito Moreno US$27.50), and *Empresa La Unión*, 0700, 1300 from bar *El Triunfo*. *Transportes Padilla*, San
and Calafate Martín 44 Sur, T491140, for **El Calafate** via Perito Moreno, Tue Thu, Sat in high season, 13 hrs,
US$42.50. Also *Chaltén Travel* every other day to **El Chaltén** and **Calafate** via Perito
Moreno, US$41.50. To **Chile**, *VH* buses to **Chile Chico**, 8 km west, US$1.40, 45 mins (for
routes from Chile Chico to Coyhaique and Puerto Aisén see Chile, page 738).

Cueva de Route 40 is unpaved and rough south of Perito Moreno; at Km 118, a marked road
las Manos goes directly to the famous **Cueva de las Manos** (44 km). The series of galleries with
No public transport 10,000-year-old paintings of human hands and animals in red, orange, black, white
goes anywhere and green, are interesting even for those not interested in rock art. The canyon in
near the caves. For which the caves are situated is very beautiful, especially in the evening light.
tours see below ■ *US$1.50. A ranger lives at the site; he is helpful with information. Camping is permit-*
ted but very windy. If it is not busy the ranger may let you sleep inside the park building.

Sleeping B *Hostería Cueva de Las Manos*, 20 km from the cave, T02963-432856/839
(Buenos Aires 4901 0436, F4903 7161). Open 1 Nov-5 Apr, with hostel (**D**) from 10 Dec,
closed Christmas and New Year, includes breakfast, other meals US$10, runs tours to the
caves, US$10 with guide (7.50 without), horseriding, transport to Perito Moreno US$18.
Estancia Turística Casa de Piedra, 75 km south of Perito Moreno on Ruta 40. Camping **G**,
also has rooms **E**, hot showers, breakfast extra, homemade bread, use of kitchen, excursions
to Cueva de las Manos, 10 km by vehicle then 1½-2 hrs' walk, and volcanoes by car or horse,
in Perito Moreno ask for Sr Sabella, Av Perón 941, T432199.
    Tours from Perito Moreno, US$100 for groups up to 10; ask at tourist office.
Hector Yerio, T432127, takes up to 7 people in a pick-up, US$50, 2 hrs journey, 5 hrs at site.

Bajo Caracoles (*Population*: 100) is a tiny forlorn pit stop, with a very expensive grocery store and very expensive fuel. (**D** *Hotel Bajo Caracoles*, hospitable, meals.) 92 km
south of Bajo Caracoles is the turning off west to Lago Belgrano and Parque Nacional
Perito Moreno. 7 km east, along Route 521 is *Hotel Las Horquetas* (very basic) with a
café/bar, and 15 km beyond this is the Tamel Aike village (police station, water).
'Super' grade fuel is available in most places; carry extra, since the only other available
source of fuel before Tres Lagos involves a 72 km detour to Gobernador Gregores.
From the Parque Moreno junction to Tres Lagos, Route 40 improves considerably.
    At **Tres Lagos** (accommodation at *Restaurant Ahoniken*, Av San Martín, **E**;
camping at *Estancia La Lucia*, US$2.50, water, barbecue, 'a little, green paradise';
supermarket, fuel) a road turns off northwest to Lago San Martín; nearby is the
Estancia La Maipú, T422613, where the Leyenda family offer accommodation,
meals, horse riding, trekking and boat excursions on the lake, 'real atmosphere of a
sheep farming *estancia*' (Santiago de la Vega), reasonable prices.
    From Tres Lagos Route 40 deteriorates rapidly and remains very rugged until
after the turnoff to the Fitz Roy sector of Parque Nacional Los Glaciares. 21 km

beyond is the bridge over Río La Leona, with a hotel which has a bar/café. The remainder of the highway to Calafate, while slow, holds no major problems.

Midway between Perito Moreno and Gobernador Gregores, at the end of a 90 km spur is **Parque Nacional Perito Moreno**. The largest of the lakes here is Lago Belgrano, where the mountains are streaked with a mass of differing colours and ammonite fossils can be found. On the way to Cerro León is *Estancia La Oriental*, T0966-42445/42196, guest house and camping site, **D, B** full board, horses for hire. Good chance of spotting condors here. There are few visitors and no formal facilities, apart from a free campsite. The park is situated south of Cerro San Lorenzo, highest peak of the Patagonian Andes. ■ *Entrance and camping are free, park ranger has maps and information. There is no public transport into the park but it may be possible to arrange a lift with estancia workers from Hotel Las Horquetas.*

Parque Nacional Perito Moreno
This is excellent hiking country, where guanaco and other wildlife roam among a large, interconnected system of lakes below glaciated peaks

Argentina

Comodoro Rivadavia to Río Gallegos

Caleta Olivia lies on the Bahía San Jorge, 74 km south of Comodoro Rivadávia (*Population*: 13,000. Hotels; municipal campsite near beach). It is the urban centre for important oilfields. On the central roundabout in front of the bus station is a huge granite monument of an oil driller with the tools of his trade. Local holiday 20 November (founding of the city). ■ *Buses to Río Gallegos, Pingüino, US$12.50 overnight. Many buses to Comodoro Rivadavia, 1 hr, US$2.50. To Calafate, depart 1400, 5 hrs; to Perito Moreno and Los Antiguos, 5 hrs, 2 daily.*

A good starting point for hitching south

The **Monumento Natural Bosques Petrificados**, in a bizarre landscape surrounding the Laguna Grande, has the largest examples of petrified trees. There is a small museum and a 1 km, well-documented nature walk. ■ *1000-2000, no charge but donations accepted; please do not remove 'souvenirs'. There are 2 unpaved access roads from Route 3: 82 km along provincial route 93 which branches off 22 km south of Fitz Roy (73 km south of Caleta Oliva; fuel); 48 km along provincial route 49 which branches off 86 km south of Fitz Roy. Nearest campsite at Estancia la Paloma, 25 km before the entrance.*

Puerto Deseado lies at the mouth of the Río Deseado which drains Lago Buenos Aires, far to the west. It is reached by Route 281, which branches off Route 3, 10 km south of Fitz Roy. Founded in 1884, it is the second largest fishing port in Patagonia. Local holidays are 31 January, San Juan Bosco, and 9 October, Coat of Arms day. The estuary of the Río Deseado is a nature reserve with a colony of Magellanic penguins, the nesting areas of four species of cormorants including the unique red-legged cormorant, and breeding grounds of Commerson's dolphin, which, with its black and white pattern, is considered one of the most beautiful in the world. Cabo Blanco, 72 km north of Puerto Deseado, is the site of the largest fur seal colony in Patagonia, breeding season December-January. The tourist office is in the *vagón histórico* (San Martín y Almte Brown, T470220), a railway carriage with a grim history associated with the breaking of a strike by shepherds in 1921.

Puerto Deseado
Phone code: 02967
Colour map 9, grid B3
Population: 4,100

Sleeping and eating B *Los Acantilados*, Pueyrredón y España, T470167. Beautifully located, good breakfast. **B** *Isla Schaffers*, San Martín y Moreno, T472246. Modern, central. *Estancia La Madrugada*, accommodation, excursions to sea lion colony and cormorant nesting area, English spoken, T434963 or in Puerto Deseado: Almte Zar 570, T470204, F472298. Highly recommended. Eating places include *El Viejo Marino*, Pueyrredón 224. Considered best by locals. *La Casa de Don Ernesto*, San Martín 1245. Seafood and *parrilla*. *El Pingüino*, Piedrabuena 958. *Parrilla*.

Tour operators *Gipsy Tours*, T472155, F472142. Run by Ricardo Pérez, excursions by boat to Río Deseado reserve, 2 hrs, US$12.50, knowledgeable, honest. *Los Vikingos*, T424 5141. Tours to Reserva Natural Ría Deseado, Reserva Provincial Isla Pingüino.

Puerto San Julián
Colour map 9, grid B2
Phone code: 02962
Population: 4,480

Puerto San Julián, founded in 1901 and 268 km south of Fitz Roy, is the best place for breaking the 834 km run from Comodoro Rivadavia to Río Gallegos. There is much wildlife in the area: red and grey foxes, guanacos, wildcats in the mountains, rheas and marine birds in the coastal Reserva San Julián. Ceramics are made at the Escuela de Cerámica; good handicraft centre at Moreno y San Martín. There is a regional museum at the end of San Martín on the waterfront. The first mass in Argentina was held here after Magellan had executed a member of his crew. Francis Drake also put in here to behead Thomas Doughty, after amiably dining with him. *Estancia La María*, 150 km west, offers transport, accommodation and meals and covers one of the main archeological areas of Patagonia, including a huge canyon with 25 caves with paintings of human hands, guanacos etc 4,000-12,000 years old, less visited than the Cueva de las Manos. Contact Fernando Behm, Saavedra 1168, T42328, F42269. The tourist office is at San Martín 581, T42871.

Sleeping and eating **B** *Municipal*, 25 de Mayo 917, T42300/1. Very nice, well-run, good value, no restaurant. **B** *Bahía*, San Martín 1075, T43144. Modern, comfortable, good value. Recommended. **B** *Res Sada*, San Martín 1112, T42013. Nice, hot water, but on busy main road, poor breakfast. Good municipal campsite Av Costanera entre Rivadavia y Roca, US$2.50 per site plus US$1.50 pp, repeatedly recommended, all facilities. Restaurants include *Sportsman*, Mitre y 25 de Mayo. Excellent value. *Rural*, Ameghino y Vieytes. Good, but not before 2100. A number of others. Also bars and tearooms.

Transport Air: *LADE* (Berutti 985, T452137) flies weekly to **Comodoro Rivadavia**, **Gobernador Gregores**, **Puerto Deseado** and **Río Gallegos**. **Buses**: To/from Río Gallegos, *Pingüino* 6 hrs. US$10.

Piedrabuena (*Population*: 2,600; hotels, restaurants) on Route 3 is 146 km south of San Julián on the Río Santa Cruz. On Isla Pavón, south of town on Route 3 at the bridge over Río Santa Cruz, is a popular campsite with wildlife park, liable to get crowded in good weather. 36 km further south, a dirt road branches 22 km to **Monte León**, a provincial nature reserve which includes the Isla Monte León, an important breeding area for cormorants and terns, where there is also a penguin colony and sea lions. There are impressive rock formations and wide isolated beaches at low tide. Campsite with basic facilities. Provincial Route 9 (1603 on some maps, unpaved, no petrol) from 43 km south of Piedrabuena runs to Calafate, but most traffic to Calafate goes from Río Gallegos.

Río Gallegos

Phone code: 02966
Colour map 9, grid C2
Population: 75,000
232 km S of Piedrabuena

The capital of Santa Cruz Province, on the estuary of the Río Gallegos, was founded in 1885 as a centre for the trade in wool and sheepskins. Local holidays are 31 January (Don Juan Bosco) and 19 December (Foundation Day). The small Plaza San Martín, one block from the post office is well tended, with a fascinating collection of trees, many planted by the early pioneers. Opposite the plaza is the tiny cathedral, built of corrugated iron, but with a wood-panelled ceiling in the chancel and stained glass windows. At Maipú 13, south side of the plaza is the **Museo de Arte Eduardo Minichelli**, with work by local artists. ■ *Tue-Fri 0800-1900, Sat-Sun and holidays 1500-1900 (closed Jan)*. **Museo Regional Provincial Manuel José Molinas**, in the Complejo Cultural Santa Cruz, Av San Martín y Ramón y Cajal 51, has collections of local history, flora, fauna, rock samples, also PREPAP local crafts centre. ■ *Mon-Fri 1000-1800 (English speaking guide available in morning), weekends 1100-1900*. **Museo de los Pioneros**, Alberdi y Elcano in the former house of Dr Arthur Fenton, a British physician who was one of the early pioneers (see Estancia Monte Dinero, below). ■ *1300-2000, free*. Another historic building is the old Customs House, a timber 'kit' house shipped from Germany at the turn of the 20th century. It has been restored as the Casa de Cultura, Fundacruz. Provincial tourist office at Roca 863, T/F422702, T438725, www.scruz.gov.com.ar/turismo Helpful, English spoken, has list of *estancias*. They will phone round hotels for you. ■ *Mon-Fri 0900-2000 (2100 summer) Sat 1000-1700/Sun 1700-2000 (summer only)*. Also at airport ■ *Limited opening hours*. Municipal tourist office has a small desk at bus terminal, T442159. ■ *Mon-Fri 0700-1300, 1400-2100, Sat-Sun 1000-1300, 1600-2000, helpful but limited English*.

Excursions

To **Cabo Vírgenes**, 134 km south of Río Gallegos, where a nature reserve protects the second largest colony of Magellanic penguins in Patagonia. ■ *US$2.50*. The Navy allows visitors to climb up Cabo Vírgenes lighthouse for a superb view. *Confitería* close by with snacks and souvenirs, run by Estancia Monte Dinero. To get there, follow Route 3 then branch off on Route 1 for 3½ hrs (unpaved). 13 km north of Cabo Vírgenes is **Estancia Monte Dinero**, 426900/428922/3, where the English speaking family Fenton offers accommodation (**L**), food and excursions, excellent. Transport or a day trip to the *estancia*, lighthouse and Pingüinera can be arranged with Eric Fraser, T423292. ■ *US$15 if minimum 4 passengers, Fri, Sat, Sun, or by special arrangement*.

Sleeping

A *Río Gallegos Apart Hotel*, San Martín 1237 (before centre), T/F427260, riogallegosapart@ciudad.com.ar, apts New, top quality, English spoken. **B** *Punta Arenas*, F Sphur 55, T422743. In new wing, also **C** in old part, no bathroom, breakfast/discounts if you ask. **B** *Santa Cruz*, Roca 701, T420601. Central, with breakfast, **A** in new wing. **C** *Croacia*, Urquiza 431, T421218. With breakfast, comfortable, quiet, English spoken. **C** *París*, Roca 1040 (central), T420111. 'Historic' building, modernised, English spoken. **C** *La Posada*, Ameghino 331, T436445. New, small, popular with estancia workers, kitchen facilities. **C** *Sehuen*, Rawson 160, T425683. New, good quality. **D** *Residencial Círculo Gendarmería Nacional*, L de la Torre esq French y Lavalle, T422363/422677. Owned by NCO's club, easy access from bus terminal, breakfast/evening meal extra, quiet, excellent value. Recommended. **E** Private house of *Elvira*, Pasaje Zuccarino 431, between Ruta 3 and Santa Fe (not far from bus station), T429856/423789. Shared bath, kitchen, homely. **Camping** *Camping ATSA* Route 3, en route to bus terminal, US$2.50 pp plus US$0.50 for tent.

Do not confuse streets Comodoro Rivadavia with (nearby) Bernardino Rivadavia, nor Mariano Moreno and Perito Moreno. Accommodation may be hard to find because of transient workers in town. Many places will include a simple breakfast in the price and up to 25% discounts may be negotiated for cash

Argentina

Río Gallegos

■ Sleeping
1 La Posada
2 París
3 Punta Arenas
4 Santa Cruz
5 Sehuen

Not to scale

Eating

Plenty of good restaurants. Evening meals are hard to find before 2000

Bifería La Vasca, Roca 1084. Snack bar, good value, young crowd, rock music, open till 0300. **Don Bartolo**, Sarmiento124. Fresh pasta, pizzas, excellent *parrilla*. **El Dragón**, 9 de Julio 27. Chinese run, *tenedor libre*, US$5, pseudo-Chinese food, good for veggies, very popular with locals, especially families, very good value. **Club Británico**, Roca 935. Good, reasonably priced. **Monaco**, Roca y San Martín. Good café, expensive, go 'to be seen'. **Super Quick**, España y Alberdi. 'Fast-food' (not junk food) style, including salad bar and *parilla*, all fresh ingredients, good value, annexe to *La Anónima* supermarket.

Shopping

Most places close 1200-1400, but stay open until 2000

Souvenirs and crafts: **Artesanías Keóken**, San Martín 336. Woollen goods and other local crafts **Rincón Gaucho**, Roca 69. Traditional leather and gaucho handicrafts. Supermarkets open 0930-2100, daily, good *rotisería* (freshly made take-away meals, hot and cold) and *panadería* sections for breads, cakes, filled rolls etc: **La Anónima**, Roca y España, larger branch on Lisandro de la Torre, near bus terminal. **Alas**, Zapiola y Corrientes.

Tour operators

Interlagos and *Taqsa* at bus terminal and airport offer tours to Calafate and Perito Moreno glacier, US$35, without accommodation.

Transport

Local Car rental: *Eduardo Riestra*, San Martín 1504, T421321T/F 421588, rentacar@ ar.inter.net, www.riestrarentacar.com Essential to book rental in advance in season with US$100 deposit. **Motorcycle mechanic**: *Juan Carlos Topcic*, Costa Rica 25, Casa 48, T423572, friendly and helpful. **Taxis**: Taxi ranks plentiful, rates controlled, *remise* slightly cheaper. Hiring a *remise* for group excursions may be no more expensive than taking a tour bus.

Flights may leave early, sometimes up to 40 mins

    Long distance Air: Airport 10 km from centre. Taxi (*remise*) to/from town US$3; hitching from car park is possible, but can't be relied upon. To/from **Buenos Aires**: **AR/Austral, AIRG, Southern Winds**. Several flights to **Ushuaia** and **Río Grande** direct, *AR/Austral, LADE* or *AIRG. Southern Winds* also to Ushuaia, and to Córdoba, Calafate (Sat only), Comodoro Rivadavia, Mendoza, Neuquén, Salta and Tucumán. *LADE* to Comodoro Rivadavia, Gob Gregores and Ushuaia twice a week, to Calafate, Perito Moreno, Puerto Deseado, Río Grande, Río Turbio, San Julián and Puerto Santa Cruz once a week. *LADE* flights should be booked as far in advance as possible.

    Buses Terminal at corner of Route 3 and Av Parque, 3 km from centre (crowded, no left luggage, *confitería*, few toilets, kiosks); taxi to centre US$1.50, bus US$0.60 (flat rate for any distance around town), Nos 1 and 12 from posted stops around town to/from terminal. To **Calafate** via airport and coinciding with flight arrivals, 4-5 hrs, US$10-12.50, *Taqsa* and *Interlagos*, turn up with ticket 30 mins before departure. To **Los Antiguos**, *Sportsman* (T442595) daily at 2100, US$27.50. *Pingüino* daily at 2000 to **Caleta Olivia**, US$12.50, 11 hrs. To **Trelew**, US$20, and **Puerto Madryn**, US$27.50, daily (18 hrs). To **Comodoro Rivadavia**, *Pingüino, Don Otto* and *TAC*, 10 hrs, US$13. For **Bariloche**, take bus to Com Rivadavia, then the 2150 *Don Otto* bus to Bariloche (fare to Bariloche US$40). To **Buenos Aires**, 33 hrs, *Pingüino, Don Otto, TAC*, US$42.50. To **Río Turbio**, 4 hrs *Pingüino*, US$7.50 (hitching practically impossible). To **Río Grande** and **Ushuaia** *Tecnic (TAC)*, Tue, Fri, Sat, at 1000, US$20-27.50, 6 – 8 hrs **To Chile Buses**: to **Puerto Natales**, *Pingüino*, Tue-Sat, 7 hrs, US$8.50. *Bus-Sur* Tue and Thu 1700. To **Punta Arenas**, *Pingüino* and others, US$11 daily. **By car**: make sure your car papers are in order (go first to Tourist Office for necessary documents, then to the customs office at the port, at the end of San Martín, very uncomplicated). For road details, see Tierra del Fuego sections in Argentina and Chile.

    Hitchhiking: appearance important. To Buenos Aires is possible in about 5-7 days, with trucks from service station in front of bus terminal, be there at 0600. To Tierra del Fuego from police control at Chimen Aike on Route 3 going south. To Calafate, from police control (30km) out of town on Route 3.

Directory

Airline offices *AR/Austral*, San Martín 545, T422020/0810-222-86527. *AIRG*, Estrada 71, T428382. *LADE*, Fagnano 53, T422316. **Banks** 24-hr ATMs for all major international credit and debit cards proliferate all over centre, far better than over-the-counter transactions. *Banco Tierra del Fuego*, Roca 831, changes TCs 3% commission. Change TCs here if going to Calafate, where it is even more difficult. *Cambio El Pingüino*, Zapiola 469. Will change Chilean pesos as well as US$ and pesos,

Communications **Internet:** J@va *cybercafe* (next to British Club on Roca); also various *locutorios* offer internet services US$1 per hr. **Post Office:** Roca 893. **Telephone:** *Locutorios* all over town, international dial-direct for most places world-wide. **Consulates** **Chile**, Mariano Moreno 136, Mon-Fri, 0900-1300; tourist cards issued at border.

El Calafate

Situated on the south shore of **Lago Argentino**, El Calafate is a modern town which has grown rapidly as a tourist centre for the **Parque Nacional los Glaciares**, 50 km away. People flock to the rural show on 15 February (Lago Argentino Day) and camp out with much revelry; dances and *asados* (barbecued sides of sheep). There are also *asados* and *gineteadas* (rodeos) etc on El Día de la Tradición, 10 November.

Phone code: 02902
Colour map 9, grid B1
Population: 4,000
312 km NW of
Río Gallegos

From the Centro Cívico, visit Capilla Santa Teresita in Plaza San Martín. Behind it is Cerro Perito Moreno; walk to the top for views of the southern end of the Andes, Bahía Redonda and Isla Solitaria on Lago Argentino. Bahía Redonda is a shallow part of the lake just west of the town centre: it is good for birdwatching in the evenings, but has been fenced off. There is good hill-walking to the south of the town, while Elephant Hill, west of Calafate on the road to the Moreno glacier, is good for rock climbing. The **tourist office** is in the bus terminal, info@calafate.com Hotel prices are shown on a large chart; also has a list of taxis but undertakes no arrangements. Helpful staff. ■ *Oct-Apr daily 0700-2200.* For information on the Parque Nacional los Glaciares, park office (*Intendencia*) is at Libertador 1302, T491005. ■ *Mon-Fri 0800-1600.*

For the main excursion to the Moreno glacier, see below. Travel by road to the most interesting spots is limited and may require expensive taxis, or excursions laid on by hotels. At **Punta Gualicho**, on the shores of Lago Argentino 15 km east of town, there are cave paintings (badly deteriorated). A recommended walk is from the Intendencia del Parque, following the new road among cultivated fields and orchards to **Laguna Nimes**, a bird reserve (fenced in), with flamingos, ducks, and

Excursions

Around El Calafate

abundant birdlife (Cecilia Scarafoni, T493196, ecowalks@cotecal.com.ar, leads birdwatching walks, 2 km from town, two hours, US$3.50). **El Galpón**, 21 km west of Calafate, is an *estancia* offering evening visits (from 1730) featuring walks through a bird sanctuary, horse riding, displays of sheep shearing and an *asado* (visits at other times on request), transport arranged, English spoken; in Calafate T/F491793; BsAs, Av Paseo Colón 221, p 7, T4343 8185, F4334 2669.

Sleeping

Calafate is very popular in Jan-Feb, so book all transport and accommodation in advance. Best months to visit are Oct, Nov and Mar. Credit cards are widely accepted. Discounts may be given for cash. Many hotels open only from Oct to Apr/May

L *Los Alamos*, Moyano y Bustillo, T491145, posadalosalamos@cotecal.com.ar Comfortable, very good food and service, extensive gardens. Recommended. **AL** *Frai Toluca*, Perón 1016, T/F491773 (Buenos Aires T/F4523 3232), fraitolucahotel@cotecal.com.ar Good views, comfortable, restaurant. **AL** *Hostería Kau-Yatún*, 25 de Mayo (10 blocks from town centre), T491259, F491260, kauyatun@cotecal.com.ar Many facilities, old *estancia* house, comfortable, restaurant and *asados*, horse-riding tours with guides. **A** *Kalken*, V Feilberg 119, T491073, F491036, hotelkalken@cotecal.com.ar With breakfast, spacious. **A** *La Loma*, Roca 849, T491016 (Bs As: Av Callao 433, p 8, T/F4371 9123), lalomahotel@cotecal.com.ar With breakfast, modern, multilingual, restaurant, tea room, spacious rooms, attractive gardens. **A** *Michelangelo*, Espora y Gob Moyano, T491045, michelangelohotel@cotecal.com.ar With breakfast, modern, reasonable, good restaurant. **A** *El Quijote*, Gob Gregores 1191, T491017, elquijote@cotecal.com/ar Good. **B** *ACA Hostería El Calafate*, Av del Libertador 1353, T491004, F491027. Modern, good view, open all year. **B** *Hostería Schilling*, Paradelo 141, T491453. With breakfast, nice rooms. **C** *Amado*, Libertador 1072, T491134, familiagomez@cotecal.com.ar Without breakfast, restaurant, good. **C** *Cabañas Nevis*, Libertador 1696, T493180, F491193. For 4 or 8, self-catering, lake view. **C** *Las Cabañitas*, V Feilberg 218, T491118, lascabanitas@cotecal.com.ar Cabins, hot water, kitchen and laundry facilities, helpful. **C** *Cerro Cristal*, Gob Gregores 989, T491088. Helpful. **C** *del Norte*, Los

El Calafate

Sleeping		
1 ACA Hostería El Calafate	8 El Quijote	16 La Loma
2 Albergue Lago Argentino	9 Frai Toluca	17 Las Cabañitas
3 Amado	10 Hospedaje Alejandra	18 Los Alamos
4 Cabañas Nevis	11 Hospedaje Buenos Aires	19 Los Lagos
5 Calafate Hostel	12 Hospedaje Los Dos Pinos	20 Michelangelo
6 Cerro Cristal	13 Hostería Schilling	21 Paso Verlika
7 del Norte	14 Kalken	22 Upsala
	15 Kápenke	23 Youth Hostel Albergue del Glaciar

Eating	
1 El Rancho	
2 Family House	
3 La Cocina	
4 Pizzería Onelli, Heladería Aquarela & Mi Viejo	
5 Rick's Café	

Gauchos 813, T491117. Open all year, kitchen facilities, comfortable, owner organizes tours. **C** *Kápenke*, 9 de Julio 112, T491093. Includes breakfast, good beds. **C** *Los Lagos*, 25 de Mayo 220, T491170, loslagos@cotecal.com.ar Very comfortable, good value. **C** *Paso Verlika*, Libertador 1108, T491009, F491279. With breakfast, good value restaurant. **C** *Upsala*, Espora 139, T491166, F491075. Includes breakfast, good beds.

D *Youth Hostel Albergue del Glaciar*, Los Pioneros 251, T/F491243 (reservations in Bs As T/F03488-469416, off season only), www.glaciar.com Discount for ISIC or IYHA members, open mid-Sep to end-May, kitchen facilities, English, French, Dutch, German, Italian spoken, internet access, also rooms with bath (**C**) and sleeping bag space (**E**), *Punto de Encuentro* restaurant with good value fixed menu and vegetarian options, booking service for hotels and transport throughout Patagonia. Recommended. Tour agency *Patagonia Backpackers*, runs tours to Moreno glacier (US$17.50 pp, good value) and elsewhere, free shuttle service from bus terminal, Navimag agents, book in advance in summer. **E** *Hosp Buenos Aires*, Buenos Aires 296, 200 m from terminal, T491147, hospbuenosaires@cotecal.com.ar Comfortable, kitchen facilities, helpful, good hot showers, luggage store. **E** *Hosp Alejandra*, Espora 60, T491328. Without bath, hot water, warm, good value. **E** *Calafate Hostel*, Gob Moyano 1226, 300 m from bus terminal, T492450, www.hostelspatagonia.com Hostel with bunks, also private rooms, hot water, heating, kitchen, internet, baggage store, *Chaltén Travel* and *El Témpano Errante* restaurant (25 de Mayo 201). **E** *Hosp Los Dos Pinos*, 9 de Julio 358, T491271. **C** in double with bath, triple and dormitory accommodation, cooking and laundry facilities, also cabins, and camping **F**, arranges tours to glacier, popular, internet access. **E** pp *Albergue Lago Argentino*, Campaña del Desierto 1050, T491423, F491139. Near bus terminal, dormitory accommodation, **F** with sleeping bag, limited bathrooms facilites, helpful.

In the Parque Nacional los Glaciares 80 km west of Calafate on the road to the Moreno glacier: **L** *Los Notros*, T/F499510, www.lastland.com With breakfast and transfers to the *mirador*, spacious, rooms with glacier views, recommended, transport from airport and other meals extra (in Bs As: Arenales 1457, p 7, T4814 3934, F4815 7645). On the southern shore of Lago Viedma: **L** *Estancia Helsingfors*, T/F02966-420719, San Martín 516, Río Gallegos, or BsAs T/F4824 46623/3634. With breakfast, all other meals available, many treks and boat trips available, also riding, sheep-shearing, daily sailing across Lago Viedma, via Glaciar Viedma, at 0930 in summer.

Camping Municipal campsite behind YPF service station, T491344/491440, campingmuniciapl@cotecal.com.ar (reservations off season 491829). US$2 pp, hot water, security, restaurant, open 1 Oct-30 Apr. 3 campsites in the Park en route to the glacier: *Río Mitre*, near the park entrance, 52 km from Calafate, 26 km east of the glacier, US$1.50 pp. *Bahía Escondida*, 7 km east of the glacier, crowded in summer, US$1.50 pp, off season free but no water. Unmarked site at Arroyo Correntoso, 10 km east of the glacier, no facilities but nice location and lots of firewood. Take food to all 3. *Lago Roca*, T499500, US$3 pp, restaurant/confitería. *Ferretería Chuar*, Libertador 1242, sells white gas for camping.

Eating

El Rancho, 9 de Julio y Gob Moyano. Large, cheap pizzas, popular. Recommended. On Libertador: *Pizzería Onelli*, No 1177. Reasonable, open out of season. *La Tablita*, at Rosales, just east of bridge. Good *parrillada*. *Mi Viejo*, No 1111. *Parrilla*. *La Cocina*, No 1245. *Pizzería*, pancakes, pasta. *Heladería Aquarela*, No 1177. Good ice cream. *Family House*, at Espora. Good value local food. Recommended. *Rick's Café*, No 1105. *Tenedor libre*, popular, US$5.50. *Bar Don Diego de la Noche*, No 1603. Local specialities, lamb and seafood, live music (traditional Argentine folk dancing and tango show), good atmosphere.

Tour operators

Chaltén Travel, see *Calafate Hostel*, above. *Los Glaciares*, Libertador 920, T491159. Good value. *Hielo y Aventura*, Av Libertador 965, T491053. Minitrekking includes walk through forests and 2-hr trek on glacier with crampons, US$37.50. Recommended. *Interlagos*, Libertador 1175. Tours to Moreno glacier, plenty of time allowed, provide cheapest transport to El Chaltén (but double check return!), English and Spanish speaking guide. Recommended. *Leutz*, 25 de Mayo 43, T492316. Daily excursion to Lago Roca 1000-1800, US$20 pp, plus US$11 for lunch at *Estancia Nibepo Aike*. *Mil Outdoor Adventure*, Av Libertador 1029, T491437. Excursions in 4WD, 4-6 hrs, US$20-40. *Santa Cruz*, Campo del Desierto 1695,

T493166. Helpful. *Sólo Patagonia*, Av Libertador 963. Efficient, Brenda is a good English-speaking guide. Most agencies charge the same rates for excursions: to the Perito Moreno Glacier US$17.50-20; to Lago Roca, at 0930 return 1700, US$17.50; El Chaltén, at 0600 return 1900, US$25, Gualichó caves, 2 hrs, US$8. **Mountain bikes** can be hired from *Bike Way*, Espora 20, T492180, US$3 per hr, US$12.50 per day.

Transport **Air** El Calafate International airport, T491220, 22 km east of town, *Aerobus*, T492492, from airport to hotels US$2.50, stand at airport. *AR* and *ARG* (Av Libertador 1015, T491171) fly from Buenos Aires. To Ushuaia, *AR* and *ARG*. *LADE* (Av Libertador 1080, T491262) to **Río Turbio**, **Ushuaia**, **Perito Moreno**, **Gob Gregores**, **Río Gallegos**, and **Comodoro Rivadavia** once a week. Many more flights in summer. To **Puerto Natales** *Aerovías Dap* daily, summer only (Oct – Mar).

Buses Terminal on Roca, 1 block from Libertador. To **Ushuaia** via Río Gallegos, Tierra del Fuego ferry and Río Grande, total cost US$22. *Interlagos* daily at 0900 (summer) or 0915 Tue, Thu, Sat (winter) to **Río Gallegos** and its airport; also *Taqsa*, 0300 and 0915 daily, and 1600 Mon, Fri, Sat, 4½ hrs, US$10-12.50. To **Río Turbio** with *Taqsa*, 2 a day, US$12, 4 hrs. Taxi (*remise*) to Río Gallegos, 4 hrs, US$100 irrespective of number of passengers, up to 5 people. *Padilla*, Albergue del Glaciar, T491243, to Perito Moreno and Los Antiguos, sometimes with a stop at Cueva de las Manos, US$42.50, Wed, Fri, Sun, 13 hrs, minimum 3 passengers, book a week in advance. *Safari Route 40* to Bariloche (see under Bariloche, Buses) can be booked at *Albergue del Glaciar* and *Calafate Hostel*. **Direct services to Chile**: *Cootra* to **Puerto Natales** via Río Turbio, daily, US$12.50, 6 hrs (advance booking recommended, tedious border crossing). *Bus Sur* (Tue, Sat 0800) and *Zaahj* (Wed, Fri, Sun 0800) run to Puerto Natales via Cerro Castillo (a simpler crossing at Cancha Carrera), 4½-5 hrs, US$12.50. Travel agencies including *Albergue del Glaciar* run regular services in summer, on demand in winter, up to US$30, 5 hrs. These connect at Cancha Carrera/Cerro Castillo with buses from Puerto Natales to Torres del Paine (**NB** Argentine pesos cannot be exchanged in Torres del Paine).

Directory **Banks** Best to take cash as high commission is charged on exchange, but there are ATMs at *Banco de la Provincia de Santa Cruz*, Libertador, and at *Banco de Tierra del Fuego*, 25 de Mayo. Travel agencies such as *Interlagos* change notes. **Communications** Post Office: on Libertador; postal rates much lower from Puerto Natales (Chile) and delivery times much quicker. **Telephone: Cooperativa Telefónica de Calafate** (Cotecal), Espora y Gob Moyano, 0700-0100, also has internet (US$5 per hr) and fax facilities, all services expensive, collect calls impossible. **Laundry** *El Lavadero*, Libertador 1118, US$3.50 a load, also has internet access.

Parque Nacional Los Glaciares

This park, the second-largest in Argentina, extends over 660,000 ha. Some 40% of the park is covered by ice fields (*hielos continentales*) off which break 13 glaciers which descend into the park to feed two great lakes: Lago Argentino and, further north, Lago Viedma, linked by the Río La Leona, flowing south from Lago Viedma. The park consists of the southern area around Lago Argentino, the central area between Lago Argentino and Lago Viedma, and the northern area around Cerro El Chaltén (Fitz Roy). ■ *Access to the central area is difficult and there are no tourist facilities. Access to the southern part of the park is from Calafate, entry US$2.50.*

Ventisquero Moreno

The vivid blue hues of the ice floes, with the dull roar as pieces break off and float away as icebergs from the snout, are spectacular, especially at sunset

At the western end of Lago Argentino (80 km from Calafate) the major attraction is the Ventisquero Perito Moreno, until recently one of the few glaciers in the world that was advancing. It descends to the surface of the water over a 5 km frontage and a height of about 60 m. It used to advance across the lake, cutting the Brazo Rico off from the Canal de los Témpanos; then the pressure of water in the Brazo Rico would break through the ice and reopen the channel. Since February 1988 this spectacular rupture has not occurred, possibly because of global warming and increased water consumption with the demands of local services. Wooden walkways with handrails permit viewing; there is a fine of up to US$250 for leaving the walkways.

From Calafate there are buses by *Interlagos*. Many agencies also run minibus tours (park entry not included) leaving 0800 returning 1800, giving three hours at glacier, book through any agency in Calafate, return ticket valid if you come back next day (student discount available). *Albergue del Glaciar* trips go out by different route passing the *Estancia Anita* and have been recommended. They also do walking tours on the glacier, book ahead. Taxis, US$40 for four passengers round trip. It is possible to visit from Puerto Natales (Chile). Take food, drink and warm clothes. Ask rangers where you can camp out of season, no facilities, but at the carpark facing the glacier there is a new café/restaurant/shop with toilets for day-trippers. Boat trips on the lake are organized by *Hielo y Aventura*, T491053, with large boats for up to 60 passengers: 'Safari Náutico', US$10 per person, one hour offering the best views of the glacier; or 'Minitrekking', US$47.50, day trip including 2½ hours walk on the glacier (with crampons provided), recommended, but not for the faint-hearted, take your own lunch.

Out of season, trips to the glacier are difficult to arrange, but you can gather a party and hire a taxi (remise taxis T491745/491044)

At the northwest end of Lago Argentino, 60 km long and 4 km wide, Upsala Glacier is considered the largest in South America. It can be reached by motor-boat from Punta Bandera, 50 km west of Calafate (check before going that access to the glacier face is possible). The trip also goes to Lago Onelli and glacier and Spegazzini glacier. From the dock on Bahía Onelli to Lago Onelli is an easy 2 km trail done with a guide (in English, German or Spanish) through a lovely southern forest wreathed in bearded moss, with a stop at the secluded restaurant en route. Small **Lago Onelli** is quiet and very beautiful, beech trees on one side, and ice-covered mountains on the other. The lake is full of icebergs of every size and sculpted shape.

The Upsala Glacier
Out of season it is extremely difficult to get to the glacier

Tour boats usually operate a daily trip to the glacier, the catamaran *Serac*, US$45, or the *Nunatak* (slightly cheaper); operated by *Fernández Campbell*, Av Libertador 867, T491155, F491154. The price includes bus fares and park entry fees – take food. Bus departs 0730 from Calafate for Punta Bandera. One hour is allowed for a meal at the restaurant (price not included) near the Lago Onelli track. Return bus to Calafate at 1930; a tiring day, it is often cold and wet, but memorable. *Upsala Explorer* organize tours for US$64, including food, 4WD trip, guided hikes around Estancia Cristina with amazing views of the glacier. Many travel agencies make reservations.

El Chaltén lies 230 km northwest of Calafate in the north of the park, at the foot of the peak of the same name. It is reached by a *ripio* road which branches off Route 40. Even in late summer transport can be unreliable, as the climate is unpredictable and the road rough with a very precarious bridge over the river. The Chaltén massif towers above the nearby peaks, its sides normally too steep for snow to stick. The town of El Chaltén, founded in 1985, is the rapidly growing National Centre for Trekking (information from national park office). In winter, though there is no transport, cross-country skiing is possible. There are stupendous views and anyone within 500 miles would be a fool to miss them. Trekking here is an absolute must. Occasionally at sunrise the mountains are briefly lit up bright red for a few seconds: this phenomenon is known as the 'sunrise of fire', or 'amanecer de fuego'. **Día de la Tradición** (10 November) is celebrated with gaucho events, riding and *asados* (US$2.50).

El Chaltén
*Phone code 02962
Local Tehuelche name meaning the 'smoking mountain'. Early explorers renamed it Fitz Roy*

The **Lago del Desierto**, 37 km north of El Chaltén, is surrounded by forests. Excursions from El Chaltén by *Chaltén Travel* daily in summer; daily boat trips on the lake on *La Mariana II*, 1030, 1330, 1630, two hours, US$15 (details and booking, *Hotel El Quijote*, Calafate).

Sleeping and eating AL *Hostería El Puma*, T493017, fitzroyexpediciones@infovia.com.ar With breakfast, comfortable, lounge with log fire. Recommended. **A** *Casa de Piedra*, Lago de Desierto s/n, T/F493015. Single, double, triple rooms including breakfast, and **AL** 4 bed cabins, all with bath, new restaurant, trekking guides (English, French and Italian spoken). **B** *Estancia La Quinta*, 3 km from Chaltén, T493012. Half-board, no heating, prepares lunch for trekkers. Recommended. **B** *Lago del Desierto*, T493010, alessandra@arnet.com.ar Good

In high season places are likely to be full and expensive

Argentina

beds, *comedor*, English and Italian spoken, camping US$2.50 pp. **C** *La Base*, Av del Desierto, T493031. Nice atmosphere, kitchen facilities, video room, hot water, heating, helpful. **C** *Fitz Roy Inn*, T493062 or Calafate 491368, caltur@cotecal.com.ar With breakfast, restaurant, also **E** in shared cabins. Opposite is **E** *Albergue Patagonia*, T/F493019, alpatagonia@ infovia.com.ar IYHA-affiliated, dormitory accommodation **F**, kitchen and laundry facilities, TV and video, book exchange, mountain bike rental US$10 per day, reservations for local excursions. Highly recommended. Next door is their restaurant *Bar de Ahumados*, regional specialities, homemade pastas, local ice cream. **D-E** *Albergue Rancho Grande*, San Martín s/n, T493005, rancho@cotecal.com.ar HI-affiliated, small dormitories, good bathrooms, hot water, laundry and kitchen facilities, small shop, bar, English, Italian, French, German spoken. Highly recommended but reconfirm bookings. Reservations in *Calafate Hostel/Chaltén Travel*, Calafate. **E** *Albergue Los Ñires*, T493009. Small dormitories, also camping US$2.50 pp. **E** *Despensa 2 de Abril*, 1 room, cheapest. **Camping** *Camping Madsen* (free). A stove is essential for camping as firewood is scarce and, because of fire risk, lighting fires is prohibited in campsites in the higher parts of the National Park. Take plenty of warm clothes and a good sleeping bag. It is possible to rent equipment in El Chaltén, ask at park entrance or *Rancho Grande*. Restaurants: *La Senyera del Torre*, excellent bread, use of shower US$1. Recommended. *Josh Aike*, excellent *confitería*, homemade food, beautiful building. Recommended. *Cervecería*, near *Rancho Grande*, brews its own beer.

Southern Santa Cruz & Parque Nacional Los Glaciares

○	Parque Nacional Los Glaciares		
1 Ventisquero Perito Moreno	2 Canal de los Témpanos	4 Lago Onelli	6 Spegazzini Glacier
	3 Brazo Rico	5 Upsala Glacier	

Sport Hiking: trails from Chaltén around the base of the Fitzroy massif are: 1) northwest via a good campsite at Lago Capri, wonderful views, to Campamento Río Blanco, and, nearby Campamento Poinecnot, 2-3 hrs, from where a path leads up to Lago de los Tres and Lago Sucia, 2-3 hrs return from the camps. From the camps a trail also runs north along the Río Blanco and west along the Río Eléctrico to Lago Eléctrico. 2) west along the Río Fitz Roy to Laguna Torre, beautifully situated at Cerro Torre and fed by Glaciar Torre, 3 hrs (on the return take the path signed 'El Chaltén Norte'). A map is essential, even on short walks: the park information centre has good information and provides photocopied maps of treks, but the best is one published by *Zagier and Urruty*, 1992, US$10 (Casilla 94, Sucursal 19, 1419 Buenos Aires, F45725766) and is available in shops in Calafate and Chaltén. For trekking on horseback with guides: *Rodolfo Guerra*, T493020; *El Relincho*, T493007; *Albergue Los Ñires*, T493009; prices: Laguna Capri US$10; Laguna Torre, US$12.50, Río Blanco US$15, Piedra del Fraile US$15, Laguna Toro US$15. **Climbing**: base camp for Fitz Roy (3,375 m) is Campamento Río Blanco (see above). Other peaks include Cerro Torre (3,102 m), Torre Egger (2,900 m), Cerro Solo (2,121 m), Poincenot (3,002 m), Guillaumet (2,579 m), Saint-Exupery (2,558 m), Aguja Bífida (2,394 m) and Cordón Adela (2,938 m): most of these are for very experienced climbers. The best time is mid-Feb to end-Mar; Nov-Dec is very windy; Jan is fair; winter is extremely cold. Permits for climbing are available at the national park information office. Guides are availabe in Chaltén: ask Sr Guerra about hiring animals to carry equipment. *Fitz Roy Expeditions*, in Chaltén, T493017, F491364, owned by experienced guide Alberto del Castillo, organize adventure excursions including on the *Campo de Hielo Continental* (US$35 with equipment, 8½ hrs), highly recommended, English and Italian spoken.

The weather changes hourly, so don't wait for a sunny day to go hiking. Just be prepared for sudden deterioration in the weather. Don't stray from the paths

Shopping *Viento Oeste*, T493021, rents and sells mountain equipment. There are several small shops selling food, gas and batteries (*Despensa 2 de Abril* is said to be cheapest) but buy supplies in Calafate (cheaper and more choice). Many places bake good bread. Fuel is available.

Transport Mechanic: ask for Julio Bahamonde or Hugo Masias. **Bus**: daily buses from Calafate, 4 hrs, US$12.50 one way: run by *Chaltén Travel* and *Caltur*. 0830, 1900 high season, returning from El Chaltén 0700, 1900 (*El Chaltén*), reduced service in winter (ask at information centre). Best to book return before departure during high season. Day trips from Calafate involve too much travelling and too little time to see the area. Some agencies offer excursions, for example return travel by regular bus and 1 night accommodation.

Off season, travel is difficult: little transport for hitching

El Calafate to Chile

About 40 km before reaching the border there are small lagoons and salt flats with flamingoes. From Calafate take the almost completely paved combination of provincial Route 11, national Route 40 and provincial Route 5 to La Esperanza (165 km), where there is a service station, campsite and a large but expensive *confitería* (accommodation **D** with bath). From La Esperanza, gravelled Route 7 heads west along the valley of the Río Coyle. 90 km southeast of Calafate, at El Cerrito, Route 40 takes a rough shortcut (closed in winter) which avoids the circuitous La Esperanza route and joins Route 7 at Estancia Tapi Aike. Route 7 continues to the border crossing at Cancha Carrera (see below) and then meets the unpaved but good road between Torres del Paine and Puerto Natales (63 km). For bus services along this route see under Calafate.

Between Calafate to Punta Arenas it is possible to see guanacos and condors at frequent intervals

The site of Argentina's largest coalfield has a railway, the most southerly regular line in the world (no passengers) connecting it with Punta Loyola. Tourist information in the municipality on San Martín. Visitors can see Mina 1, where the first mine was opened; the present mining and industrial area, with the school museum, can also be visited. The area is good for trekking and horse riding. Skiing: Valdelén has 6 pistes and is ideal for beginners. There is also scope for cross-country skiing nearby. Season from early June to late September.

Río Turbio
Colour map 9, grid C2
Population: 8,000
257 km W of
Río Gallegos
30 km from Puerto
Natales (Chile)

Argentina

Sleeping Hotels almost always full: **B** *Hostería Capipe*, Dufour (9 km from town, T482935, F482930). **B** *Gato Negro*, T491226, also dormitory accommodation **E**. **E** *Albergue Municipal*, at Valdelén. *Restaurant El Ringo*, near bus terminal, will shelter you from the wind.

Transport **Buses**: To **Puerto Natales**, 2 companies, US$2.75, regular. To **Calafate**, *Cootra* daily, 6 hrs, US$12. *Expreso Pingüino* daily at 0200 and *Taqsa* at 0100 to **Río Gallegos**, 4 hrs, US$7.50. *LADE* flight to **Río Gallegos** once a week (airport 15 km from town, taxi US$5 pp).

Border with Chile
1) **Paso Mina Uno/Dorotea** is 5 km south of Río Turbio. Open all year, 24 hours 31 November – 31 March, daytime only rest of year. On the Chilean side this runs south to join the main Puerto Natales-Punta Arenas road.

2) **Paso Casas Viejas** is 33 km south of Río Turbio via 28 de Noviembre. Open all year, daytime only. On the Chilean side this runs east to join the main Puerto Natales-Punta Arenas road.

3) **Paso Cancha Carrera** is 55 km north of Río Turbio, this is the most convenient crossing for Parque Nacional Torres del Paine. Open November-April only. Argentine customs are fast and friendly. On the Chilean side the road continues 14 km to the Chilean border post at Cerro Castillo, where it joins the road from Puerto Natales to Torres del Paine. Chilean immigration open 0830-1200, 1400-2000, November-March or April only.

Tierra del Fuego

The island at the extreme south of South America is divided between Argentina (east) and Chile (west). The south has beautiful lakes, woods and mountain scenery, and there is much birdlife. Boat trips can be made on the Beagle Channel; there is skiing in winter.

Background
Colour map 9, grid C3 Accommodation is sparse and the island is becoming popular among Argentines in summer. Hotel beds and seats on aircraft may run short as early as Nov. Fruit and meat may not be taken onto the island

Tierra del Fuego is bounded by the Magellan Strait to the north, the Atlantic Ocean to the east, the Beagle Channel to the south – which separates it from the southern islands – and by the Whiteside, Gabriel, Magdalena and Cockburn Channels etc, which divide it from the islands to the west. Although the island was inhabited by four indigenous groups, all are now extinct. Throughout Tierra del Fuego the main roads are narrow and gravelled. The exceptions are San Sebastián (Argentina)-**Tolhuin** (fuel; **G** pp *Hain del Lago*, on Lago Khami, T02964-425951, *refugio* and camping, good), the last 30 km to Ushuaia, both of which are paved, and the road for about 50 km out of Porvenir (Chile), which is being widened. Part of the south is a national park: trout and salmon in nearly all the lakes and rivers, and in summer wild geese, ducks, 152 other species of birds, and imported musk rats and beaver. March-April is a good time to visit because of the beautiful autumn colours.

Routes to Tierra del Fuego
For details of all transport and hotels on Chilean territory, see the Chile chapter. It is not always possible to cross the Chilean part in one day because of the irregularity of the ferry

There are no road/ferry crossings between the Argentine mainland and Argentine Tierra del Fuego. You have to go through Chilean territory. From Río Gallegos, Route 3 reaches the Chilean border at Monte Aymond (about 55 km; open 0800-1900), passing Laguna Azul (3 km off main road in an old crater; an ibis breeding ground, beautiful colours). For bus passengers the border crossing is very easy; similarly for car drivers if papers are in order. 41 km into Chile is **Punta Delgada**, from where a 16 km road (half paved) goes to the dock for the 30-minute ferry-crossing over the Primera Angostura (First Narrows) to **Punta Espora**. Some 40 km south, on Chilean Tierra del Fuego, is Cerro Sombrero, from where the road continues 85 km to Chilean San Sebastián. 14 km east, across the border, is Argentine San Sebastián, from where the road is paved to Río Grande (see below).

The alternative ferry crossing is **Punta Arenas-Porvenir**. The road from Punta Delgada goes on 103 km to the intersection with the Punta Arenas-Puerto Natales road, 54 km before Punta Arenas. 5 km east of Punta Arenas, at Tres Puentes, there is a daily ferry crossing to Porvenir, from where a 225 km road runs east to Río Grande (six hours) via San Sebastián. (**B** ACA motel, T02964-425542; service station open 0700-2300.) Border police at San Sebastián will sometimes arrange lifts to Ushuaia or Río Grande. Hitching after San Sebastián is easy. The best way to hitch from Río Gallegos to Punta Arenas is to take any lorry as far as the turn-off for Punta Delgada ferry. Then there is plenty of Chilean traffic from Punta Delgada to Punta Arenas. *Hotel San Gregorio* will put you up if you get stuck near the turn-off.

Entering Argentina from Chile, be firm about getting an entry stamp for as long as you require. Going in the other direction, don't stock up with food in Argentina, as border guards will confiscate fruit, vegetable, dairy and meat products entering Chile

Río Grande

Argentina

The largest settlement in Tierra del Fuego, Río Grande is a sprawling modern town in windy, dust-laden sheep-grazing and oil-bearing plains. (The oil is refined at San Sebastián in the smallest and most southerly refinery in the world.) The *frigorífico* (frozen meat) plant and sheep-shearing shed are among the largest in South America. Government tax incentives to companies in the 1970s led to a rapid growth in population; the subsequent withdrawal of incentives has produced increasing unemployment and emigration. The gymnasium has free hot showers for men. *La Nueva Piedmontesa*, Belgrano y Laserre, 24-hour food store. *Tia* supermarket, San Martín y Piedrabuena, good selection; also *La Anónima* on San Martín, cheaper. Food is cheaper than in Ushuaia. Tourist office at the Municipalidad, on Elcano, Monday-Friday. Tour operator *Yaganes*, San Martín 641, is helpful.

*Phone code: 02964
Colour map 9, grid C2
Population: 35,000*

La Candelaria, the Salesian Mission 11 km north, houses a museum, with displays of Indian artefacts and natural history. ■ *Mon-Sat 1000-1230,1500-1900, Sun 1500-1900, US$1.50. Afternoon teas, US$3.* Local festivals are the Trout Festival, third Sunday in February; Snow Festival, third Sunday in July; Woodsman Festival, first week of December.

A *Posada de los Sauces*, Elcano 839, T/F430868. With breakfast, good beds, comfortable, good restaurant, bar. Recommended. **B** *Los Yaganes ACA*, Belgrano 319, T430823, F423897. With breakfast, comfortable, good expensive restaurant. **B** *Federico Ibarra*, Rosales y Fagnano, T432485. With breakfast, good beds, large rooms, excellent restaurant. **D** *Villa*, San Martín 277, T422312.Without breakfast, very warm. **D** *Hosp Noal*, Rafael Obligado 557. Cosy. Recommended. **Camping**: *Club Naútico Ioshlelk-Oten*, Montilla 1047, 2 km from town on river. Clean, cooking facilities, camping inside heating building in cold weather. YPF petrol station has hot showers. Eating places include *Don Rico*, Belgrano y Perito Moreno, in ultra-modern building in centre. Interesting, closed Mon. *La Nueva Colonial*, Rosales 640. *Pizzería*, friendly. *Rotisería CAI*, on Moreno. Cheap, fixed price, popular with locals.

Sleeping & eating
Accommodation can be difficult to find if arriving at night

L *Estancia Viamonte*, some 40 km southeast of Río Grande on the coast, T430861, www.EstanciaViamonte.com Founded in 1902 by the sons of pioneer Rev Thomas Bridges, this working *estancia* has fully equipped cottages to let, rates reduced for 4-6 day stay, activities (riding, trekking, fishing – at extra cost), meals extra.

Car hire: *Rent-a-Car*, Belgrano y Ameghino, T422657. Others at airport. **Air** Airport 4 km west of town. Bus US$0.30. Taxi US$3.50. To **Buenos Aires**, *AR* and *ARG* daily, 3½ hrs direct. To **Ushuaia**, *ARG* 3 a week, and *LADE*, which also flies to **Río Gallegos**, 1 hr (book early in summer, 1 a week) and other Patagonian airports. **Buses** All buses leave from terminal, Elcano y Güemes. To **Porvenir**, Chile, 5 hrs, US$12, *Gesell*, Wed, Sun, 0800, meticulous passport and luggage control at San Sebastián. To **Punta Arenas**, Chile, via Punta Delgada, 10 hrs, *Pacheco*, Tue, Thu, Sat 0730, US$18, *Los Carlos*, Mon, Fri, 0700, same price. To **Río Gallegos**, Mon, Wed, Fri, US$20. To **Ushuaia**, *Tecni Austral*, 3-4 hrs, 2 daily, US$15 and *Lider*, 4 daily, US$8. Also *Tolkeyen*, US$10, 4 daily including at 1900 (which is supposed to connect with service from Punta Arenas, but there are earlier services).

Transport
*Very difficult to hitch to Porvenir or north into Argentina
Try the truck stop opposite the bus terminal or the police post 7 km out of town
Hitching to Ushuaia is relatively easy in summer*

Directory **Airline offices** *AR/Austral*, San Martín 607, T422711/0810-2228 6527. *ARG*, Av San Martín 641, T432620. *LADE*, Laserre 425, T422968. **Banks** Exchange is difficult: if coming from Chile, buy Argentine pesos there. **Communications** Post Office: Piedrabuena y Ameghino.

Ushuaia

Phone code: 02901
Colour map 9, grid C2
Population: 44,976
234 km SW of Río Grande on new road via Paso Garibaldi

The most southerly town in Argentina and one of the most expensive. Situated on the northern shore of the Beagle Channel, named after the ship in which Darwin sailed the Channel in 1832, its streets climb steeply towards snow covered Cerro Martial to the north. There are fine views over the green waters of the Beagle Channel and the snow-clad peaks. The mainstays of the local economy are fishing and tourism. The local festival is on 12 October: Founding of Ushuaia. The old prison, **Presidio**, Yaganes y Gob Paz, at the back of the Naval Base, houses the **Museo Marítimo**, with models and artefacts from seafaring days, the **Museo Antártico** and, in the cells, the **Museo Penitenciario**, which details the history of the prison. ■ *Mon-Sun 1000-2000, US$4.50 for foreigners.* **Museo del Fin del Mundo**, Maipú y Rivadavia, small displays on indigenous peoples, missionaries and first settlers, as well as natural history section (you can get an 'end of the world museum' stamp in your passport), recommended. ■ *Mon-Sun 1000-1300, 1500-1930,US$2.50, students US$1, T421863.* The building also contains an excellent library with helpful staff and a post office. ■ *Open afternoons when the main one is closed.* **Mundo Yámana**, Rivadavia 56, fascinating scale models showing scenes of everyday life of indigenous peoples, English-speaking owner, grew up on the island, highly recommended. ■ *Daily 1000-2000, high season, otherwise closed lunchtime, US$2, T422874.*

Tourist offices San Martín 674, T432000/1, F424550, freephone 0800-333 1476, www.tierradelfuego.org.ar 'Best in Argentina', literature in English, German and Dutch, helpful, English spoken. Large chart of hotels and prices and information on travel and staying at Estancia Harberton. Has noticeboard for messages. ■ *Mon-Fri 0800-2200, Sat, Sun and holidays 0900-2000.* **National Park Office**, on San Martín between Patagonia y Sarmiento, has a small map but not much information. The *ACA* office, Malvinas Argentinas y Onachaga, T421121, also has maps and information.

Ushuaia

N
Not to scale

■ Sleeping	3 Albergue Turístico	6 Canal Beagle
1 Albergue Refugio	Torre al Sur & Kaisken	7 César
de Mochilero	4 Alojamiento	8 Familia Cárdenas
2 Albergue Saint	Internacional	9 Hostería Alakaluf
Christopher	5 Cabo de Hornos	10 Hostería América

Tren del Fin del Mundo, the world's southernmost steam train, run by *Tranex* **Excursions**
Turismo, with new locomotives and carriages, uses track first laid by prisoners to
carry wood to Ushuaia. A Decauville 600 mm gauge train runs a tourist excursion
with English-speaking guide, from the Fin del Mundo station, west of Ushuaia, to
the boundary of the Tierra del Fuego National Park, 5.6 km, and back. Three
departures daily (two end-April to end-September), US$16 (tourist), US$25 (first
class) return, plus US$2.50 park entrance and US$2 for bus to the station. It is
planned to extend the line to city centre. Tickets at station, or from *Tranex* kiosk in
the port, T430709, www.trendelfindelmundo.com.ar Sit on left outbound for
superb views.

To **Cerro Martial**, offering fine views down the Beagle Channel and to the north,
about 7 km behind the town; to reach the chairlift (*Aerosilla*, US$3) follow
Magallanes out of town, allow 1½ hours; last ascent 1815. *Pasarela* and *Kaupen* run
minibus services, several departures daily in summer, US$2.50 return. The Munici-
pality runs a cheap combi service (*Línea Regular*) to Glaciar Martial, Lapataia and
other sites, stop on Maipú opposite ACA station. Excursions can also be made to the
Río Olivia falls and to **Lagos Fagnano** and **Escondido**.

The **Estancia Harberton**, the oldest on the island, now run by descendents of a
British missionary, Thomas Bridges, is 85 km from Ushuaia on Route J. It offers
guided walks through protected forest (not Monday) and tea, in *Manacatush*
confitería (T422742). The Museo Akatushún has skeletons of South American birds
and sea mammals, the result of 23 years' scientific investigation in Tierra del Fuego.
You can camp free, with permission from the owners. ■ *Museum entrance US$2,*
T422742, T/F422743, ernestopasman@hotmail.com (estancia), ngoodall@
tierradelfuego.org.ar (museum). Getting there:Access is from a dirt road which
branches off Route 3, 40 km east of Ushuaia and runs 25 km through forest before the
open country around Harberton. Parts of the road are bad; tiring driving, about two
hours. Agency tours by land cost US$15 plus US$3.50 entrance; take your own food if
not wishing to buy meals at the Estancia.

Argentina

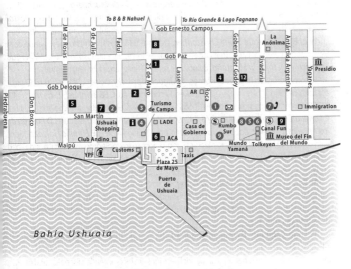

11 Maitén	● **Eating**	**5** Helados Masera
12 Miguel Zaprucsky	**1** Bar Ideal	**6** La Casa de los Mariscos
13 Posada de	**2** Barcleit 1912	**7** La Rueda
los Angeles	**3** Café de la Esquina	**8** Moustacchio
	4 El Galeón	**9** Tía Elvira

Sea Trips

Note that the Beagle Channel can be very rough. Food and drink on all boats is expensive

Excursions can be booked through most agencies. The main trips are: Isla Alicia ■ *Mon, Wed, Fri, Sun, 1800, 1 hr, US$7.50*. To the sea lion colony at Isla de los Lobos, Isla de los Pájaros, Les Eclaireurs lighthouse ■ *2½ hrs on catamaran, US$16, 4½-5 hrs on the Tres Marías, US$23 including 1 hr trekking on Bridges island and hot drink*. To Isla de los Lobos, Isla de los Pájaros, Les Eclaireurs lighthouse, and the Isla Martillo penguin colony ■ *4½ hrs on catamaran, US$27*. To Isla de los Lobos, Isla de los Pájaros, Isla Martillo penguin colony, Les Eclaireurs lighthouse and Estancia Harberton, ■ *8 hrs round trip on catamaran, US$33, includes packed lunch but not US$3.50 entrance at Estancia, Tue, Thu, Sat*.

Sleeping

The tourist office has comprehensive lists of all officially registered accommodation and will help with rooms in private homes, campsites etc

L *Cabo de Hornos*, San Martín y Rosas, T422187, F422313, cabodehornos@arnet.com.ar Comfortable, with breakfast, often full, good value, restaurant (residents only). **L** *Las Lengas*, Florencia 1722, T423366, laslengas@tierradelfuego.org.ar Superb setting, heating, good dining room. **L** *Tolkeyen*, Del Tolkeyen 2145, 5 km from town, T445315, info@tolkeyenhotel.com.ar Includes transfer from town centre, recommended restaurant (see below). **AL** *Canal Beagle*, Maipú y 25 de Mayo, T421117, hotelcanalb@impsat1.com.ar Discounts for *ACA* members, breakfast included, restaurant. **A** *César*, San Martín 753, T421460, F432721, cesarhostal@infovia.com.ar Comfortable, includes breakfast. Recommended. **B** *Hostería Alakaluf*, San Martín 146, T436705, alakalufes@arnet.com.ar With breakfast, quiet. Recommended. **B** *Hostería Posada Fin del Mundo*, Valdez 281, T437345, posadafindelmundo@infovia.com.ar Family atmosphere, good value. Recommended. **C** *Maitén*, Av 12 de Octubre 140, T422745, F422733. Good value, 1 km from centre, no singles, 10% discount for ISIC and youth card holders. **C** *Hostería América*, Gob Paz 1665, T423358, www.alfinal.com/hosteriaamerica With breakfast, modern. **D** pp *Albergue Turístico Torre al Sur*, Gob Paz 1437, T430745, torrealsur@impsat1.com.ar HI-affiliated, heating, good atmosphere, kitchen facilities, some long-term residents. **D** *Alojamiento Internacional*, Deloqui 395, T423483/423622. Very basic, scruffy, dormitory, take sleeping bag, no security, good meeting place, changes money. **D** *Kaisken*, Gob Paz 1437, T436756, kaisken@infovia.com.ar Central, breakfast extra, helpful, dicount for large groups, shared bath and kitchen, laundry service, internet. **F** pp *Casa de Alba*, Belakamain 247, T430473, www.lacasadealba.freeservers.com Good beds, hot water, cash only, airport pick-up, kitchen, internet. Recommended. **D** pp *Albergue Refugio de Mochilero*, 25 de Mayo 241, T436129, refmoch@infovia.com.ar Small dormitories with kitchen facilities. **F** pp *Hostal Home*, Kayén 438, T432581, zerofun@impsat1.com.ar Helpful, luggage store, internet, kitchen. **F** pp *Albergue Saint Christopher*, Deloqui 636, hostel_christopher@yahoo.com Hot water, kitchen facilities, free coffee and tea, cakle TV, nice atmosphere. **F** pp *Albergue Turístico Violeta de la Montaña*, Belgrano 236, T421884. Large kitchen, helpful.

Many people offer rooms in private houses at the airport

Accommodation in private homes B *Miguel Zapruscky*, Deloqui 271, T421316. **C** without bath, parking, TV, kitchen, English spoken. Recommended. **C** *B&B Nahuel*, 25 de Mayo 440, T423068. Without bath or breakfast (US$3 extra), hot water, laundry and cooking facilities. **C** *Familia Cárdenas*, 25 de Mayo 345, T421954. Without bath or breakfast, quiet. **D** *Posada de los Angeles*, Paz 1410, opposite *Torre al Sur*. Dorms, good kitchen. **E** *Familia Galeazzi*, Gdor Valdez 323, T423213, F432605, in pleasant suburb close to town. Bedrooms in house and 5-bed cabin in garden, excellent food. Highly recommended. **F** pp *Silvia Casalaga*, Gob Paz 1380 (Yellow Tower), T423202. Without bath, heating, breakfast extra, no sign. Recommended.

At Lago Escondido A *Hostería Petrel*, 60 km from Ushuaia after a spectacular climb through Garibaldi Pass, on the road to Río Grande (various buses daily, Take Río Grande bus, US$4), T433569. Also has self-catering cabins with maid service, trout fishing possible, boat rides, friendly staff.

At Lago Fagnano B *Hostería El Kaiken*, 100 km north of Ushuaia on a promontory, T492208. Self-catering apartments with maid service. Also **D** cheaper rooms, nice site. Facilities at *Kaiken* and *Petrel* are open all year round. These inns are recommended for peace and quiet.

Camping On eastern edge of town is: *Camping Río Pipo*, Ushuaia Rugby Club (Km 4) US$2.50 pp, friendly owners, all facilities. On Route 3 heading for Río Grande: *Camping del Solar del Bosque* (Km 18) US$2.50 pp, hot showers. *Camping Haruwen*, in the Haruwen Winter Sports complex (Km 33), T/F424058, US$2.50 per tent, electricity, shop, bar, restaurant. Inside the Parque Nacional Tierra del Fuego (entry fee US$2.50) is *Camping Lago Roca*, 21 km from Ushuaia, at Lapataia, by forested shore of Lago Roca, with good facilities, dirty, showers (US$2), noisy, reached by bus Jan-Feb, expensive small shop, cafetería. **F** *Hain*, Tolhuin 3 km west on Lago Fagnano, T425951, hot water, clean, bar, restaurant, recommended. There are also various sites with no facilities, eg: *Ensenada Camping* 16 km from Ushuaia; *Camping Las Bandurrias* and *Camping Laguna Verde*, both 20 km from Ushuaia.

These are some of the longer established places: *Barcleit 1912*, Fadul 148. Cordon bleu cooking at reasonable prices. *Kaupé*, Roca 470. English spoken, excellent food and wine. Recommended, expensive. *Tía Elvira*, Maipú 349. For king crab in season. Best place to eat lamb *asado* is at *Quincho Tolkeyen*, Del Tolkeyen 2145, 5 km from town, taxi US$7. *Bar Ideal*, San Martín 393. Good, cheap, very popular. *La Rueda*, San Martín 193. Good *parrilla*. *Volver*, Maipú 37. Interesting decor, sea view, not cheap. *La Casa de los Mariscos*, San Martín 234. Fish and seafood. *Moustacchio*, San Martín 298. Good fish, good value *tenedor libre*, expensive à la carte. *Café de la Esquina*, San Martín y 25 de Mayo. Nice view, pleasant, not cheap. Opposite is *El Galeón*. *La Vieja Casona* Rivadavia and Gob Campos, T436945. Recommended. Good value set lunches at restaurant in *Ushuaia Shopping*, San Martín 788. *Helados Massera*, San Martín 270-72. Good. For an excellent evening's entertainment, live Argentine folk music and dance, with full *parrilla*: *Rancho Argentino* San Martín 237 T430100. US$5-7, popular. Popular on Sat night are the discos.

Shopping in general is very expensive, especially imported gear and touristy souvenirs etc. But there are some cheap imported goods, eg electrical equipment and cigarettes. *La Boutique del Libro*, San Martín entre Piedrabuena y Belgrano. Recommended for books about the area, some in English. **Supermarkets** *La Anónima*, Rivadavia y Gob Paz. Good for take-away freshly made food, has a fast-food diner.

Sports Centre on Malvinas Argentinas on west side of town (close to seafront). **Fishing**: trout. Season 1 Nov-31 Mar, licences US$10 per week, US$5 per day. Contact **Asociación de Caza y Pesca** at Maipú y 9 de Julio, which has a small museum. **Skiing**, **hiking**, **climbing**: contact **Club Andino**, Fadul 50. Plenty of information available at Municipal Tourist Office. **Skiing**: various centres offer a variety of winter and snow sports facilities, rentals, cafetería, bar, restaurants, trips in a sledge pulled by Huskies etc. Glaciar Martial Winter Sports Centre is 7km from town, has double chairlifts, 1,130 m of pistes and equipment hire. From Jun to Oct the Cerro Castor complex is the best alpine skiing centre, 27 km from the town. The Haruwen Winter Sports complex is the furthest, 36 km east on Route 3. The area is also excellent for cross country skiing, with various new centres at 19-22 km east of Ushuaia, with high standard facilities for cross country skiing, snow shoeing and snowmobiling.

All agencies charge the same fees for excursions: Tierra del Fuego National Park, 4 hrs, US$13 (entry fee extra); Lagos Escondido and Fagnano, 8 hrs, US$20. With 3 or 4 people it is often little more expensive to hire a *remise* taxi (*Carlitos*, San Martín 989, T422222, *Bahía Hermosa*, Belakamain 334, T422233). The 2 largest agencies are: *Rumbo Sur*, San Martín 342, T422441/423085, F430499, rumbosur@satlink.com.ar Runs a range of tours, offers a 2-day package to Calafate, US$75, good value, also organizes bus to ski slope, very helpful but little English; and *Tolkeyen*, Maipú 237, T437073, pretour@arnet.com.ar Recommended. *All Patagonia*, Juana Fadul 26, T430725, F430707, allpat@satlink.com Amex agent, packages to *Cabañas del Martial*. *Canal Fun*, Rivadavia 82, T437395, www.canalfun.com Offer a range of activities, riding, 4x4 excursions. Recommended. *Turismo de Campo*, 25 de Mayo 76, T437351, F432419, info@turcampo.com Estancia tourism, horse riding and trekking.

Car hire: various firms, some offer free mileage, prices range from US$35-72 per day. *Tagle (Avis)*, San Martín y Belgrano, T422744. *Cardos Rent A Car (Patagonia y Aventura SRL)*, San Martín 845, T436388, 24-hr T1551-3500 (mob), free mileage US$35 per day economical, up to US$75 4WD fully equipped.

Eating
Many new places springing up, also many closing. Ask around for currently available seafood, especially centolla (king crab) and cholga (giant mussels)

Shopping
Beachcombing can produce whale bones

Sport

Tour operators
Information also available at Municipal Tourist Info office

Transport

Argentina

Services are more frequent in high season; in winter weather often impedes flights. In the summer tourist season it is sometimes difficult to get a flight out

Air Taxi to airport US$2.50 (no bus). *AR/Austral, Southern Winds* and *AIRG* to Buenos Aires via Río Gallegos, all year round, 3½ hrs direct. *LADE* to Comodoro Rivadavia, Gob Gregores, Puerto Deseado, Río Grande, San Julián and Santa Cruz once a week, and Río Gallegos. At the airport ask around for a pilot willing to take you on a 30 mins flight around Ushuaia, US$20 pp (best to go in evening when wind has dropped). Alternatively ask about flights at the tourist office in town. Aerial excursions over the Beagle Channel with local flying club, hangar at airport, 3-5 seater planes, 30 mins: Lago Fagnano, Lapataia and Ushuaia Bay.

Buses To **Río Grande** 3 hrs, *Tecni Austral (Tolkar*, Roca 157, T423396/423304), and *Líder* (Gob Paz 921, T436421), both US$8, 2 a day, and *Tolkeyen* (Maipú 237, T/F437073, pretour@tierradelfuego.org.ar), 4 a day US$10. To **Punta Arenas**, *Tecni Austral*, Mon, Wed, Fri 0700, US$23, and *Tolkeyen/Pacheco*, Tue, Thu, Sat, 0800, 12 hrs, US$25, a comfortable ride via Punta Delgada ferry (30 mins' crossing). Both also have services through **Porvenir** with 2½-hr ferry. No through services to Río Gallegos (change at Río Grande but book connection in Ushuaia).

Hitching Trucks leave Ushuaia for the refinery at San Sebastián Mon-Fri. It's easy to hitch to Río Grande. A good place to hitch from is the police control 5 km from town on Route 3 (take a bus). **Boats To Puerto Williams** (**Chile**) No regular sailings. Yachts carry charter passengers in summer, returning the same day, fares US$25-35 one way. Enquire at *AIASN* agency for cruise through Beagle Channel. Most possibilities are in Dec because boats visit Antarctica in Jan. Luxury cruises around Cape Horn via Puerto Williams are operated by the Chilean company, *Tierra Austral*, 7/8 days, US$1,260. **To Antarctica**: most tourist vessels to Antarctica call at Ushuaia and, space permitting, take on passengers. Enquire at *Rumbo Sur, All Patagonia* or other agencies. All agencies charge similar price, US$1,100 pp for 8-9 day trip, though prices may be lower for late availability, which are posted in window of *Rumbo Sur*. Try at *Turismo del Campo* for other possibilities Nov-Mar.

Directory **Airline offices** *LADE*, San Martín 542, shop 5, T/F421123, airport T421700. *Aerolíneas Argentinas*, Roca 116, T421218/436444, F431291, airport 437265. *ARG*, 25 de Mayo 64, T432112/3, or 0800-777 2743. *Tapsa*, agent is *Rumbo Sur*, San Martín 342, T421139. **Banks** Banks open 1000-1500 (in summer). Useful to have credit cards here as difficult to change TCs and very high commission (up to 10% – may be changed at *Casa Thaler* cambio). *Banco de la Nación*, Rivadavia y San Martín, only bank which accepts Chilean pesos. Cash advance on MasterCard and Visa at *Banco de Tierra del Fuego*, San Martín 396, accepts Amex TCs, 5% commission. **Communications** Internet: Places and services are constantly changing and increasingly popular. **Post Office**: San Martín y Godoy, Mon-Fri 0900-1300 and 1700-2000, Sat 0830-1200. **Telephone**: San Martín 1541, also internet service at same address, US$2.50 per hour. **Embassies and consulates** Consulates: Chile, Malvinas Argentinas y Jainen, Casilla 21, T421279. Finland, Paz y Deloqui. Germany, Rosas 516. Italy, Yaganes 75.

Parque Nacional Tierra del Fuego
In winter the temperature drops to as low as -12°C, in summer it goes up to 25°C. Even in the summer the climate can often be cold, damp and unpredictable

Covering 63,000 ha of mountains, lakes, rivers and deep valleys, the park stretches west to the Chilean border and north to Lago Fagnano, though large areas have been closed to tourists to protect the environment. The lower parts are forested. Fauna include several species of geese including kelp geese, ducks including the beautiful torrent duck, Magellanic woodpeckers and austral parakeets. Introduced species like beavers and muskrats, have done serious environmental damage. The Patagonian grey fox is becoming more common with the increase of human settlement and tourism. It can be a pest scavenging around campsites and on edges of town. Near the Chilean border beaver dams can be seen and with much luck and patience the beavers themselves. Stand still and down-wind of them: their sense of smell and hearing are good, but not their eye sight. There are several beautiful walks; the most popular ones are a trail along Lapataia Bay, good for birdwatching, a 4-5 km walk along Lago Roca to the Chilean border at Hito XXIV, and a 3 km climb to Cerro Pampa Alta which offers fine views. Good climbing on Cerro Cóndor, recommended. There are no legal crossing points to Chile. ■ *The park entrance is 12 km west of Ushuaia. Park administration is in Ushuaia (see above). Entry US$2.50. In summer buses and minibuses, US$5, to the park are run by several companies leaving from stops at frequent intervals around town. Timetables vary with demand, tourist office has details. Ask at the tourist office about cycling tours in the park, US$32.50 full day, also 'Eco Treks' available and cultural events. It is possible to hitchhike as far* *as Lapataia.* Club Andino *has a booklet explaining routes in the park (in Spanish) with poor maps. Topographical maps are sold at* Oficina Antártica, *Maipú and Laserre, or consult the Municipal Tourist Office. See above for Camping possibilities.*

Background

History

For some 270 years after its foundation in 1535, Buenos Aires was of little importance. From 1543 all the Spanish territories in South America were governed from Lima, the Vice-Regal capital. Spanish trade was via Lima, Panama and the Caribbean and Spain did not allow Buenos Aires to take part in any overseas trade until 1778; its population then was only 24,203. It was merely a military outpost for Spain to confront the Portuguese settlement at Colonia, across the estuary; the main trade was smuggling. Even when in 1776 the Viceroyalty of Río de la Plata was formed, it made little difference to Buenos Aires as a capital, for its control of the *cabildos* (town councils) in distant towns was very tenuous. When the British, following Spain's alliance with Napoleon, attacked Buenos Aires in 1806 and again in 1807 before being repulsed by local levies, there was no inkling of its future potential. But the defeat of these attacks, known as the Reconquista, had one important result: a great increase in the confidence of the *porteños* (the name given to those born in Buenos Aires) to deal with all comers, including the mother-country, whose restrictions on trade were increasingly unpopular. On 25 May 1810, the *cabildo* of Buenos Aires deposed the viceroy and announced that it was now governing on behalf of King Ferdinand VII, then a captive of Napoleon. Six years later, in July 1816, when Buenos Aires was threatened by invasion from Peru and blockaded by a Spanish fleet in the Río de la Plata, a national congress held at Tucumán declared independence. The declaration was given reality by José de San Martín, who marched an Argentine army across the Andes to free Chile and embarked his forces for Peru, where he captured Lima, the first step in the liberation of Peru.

Independence from Spain

When San Martín returned home, it was to find the country rent by conflict between the central government and the provinces. On the one hand stood the Unitarist party, bent on central control; on the other the Federalist party, insisting on local autonomy. The latter had for members the great *caudillos* (the large landowners backed by the *gauchos*) suspicious of the cities. One of their leaders, Juan Manuel de Rosas, took control in 1829. During his second term as Governor of Buenos Aires he asked for and was given extraordinary powers. The result was a 17-year reign of terror which became an international scandal. When he began a blockade of Asunción in 1845, Britain and France promptly countered with a three-year blockade of Buenos Aires. In 1851 Justo José de Urquiza, Governor of Entre Ríos, one of his old henchmen, organized a triple alliance of Brazil, Uruguay, and the Argentine opposition to overthrow him. He was defeated in 1852 at Caseros, a few kilometres from Buenos Aires, and fled to England, where he farmed quietly for 25 years, dying at Southampton. Rosas had started his career as a Federalist; once in power he was a Unitarist. His downfall meant the triumph of federalism. In 1853 a federal system was finally incorporated in the constitution, but Buenos Aires refused to join the new federation, which had its capital at Paraná. In 1859 Buenos Aires, under Bartolomé Mitre, was defeated by the federal forces under Urquiza, but two years later Buenos Aires defeated the federal forces. Once again it became the seat of the federal government, with Mitre as its first constitutional president. (It was during his term that the Triple Alliance of Argentina, Brazil, and Uruguay defeated Francisco Solano López of Paraguay.) There was another political flare-up of the old quarrel in 1880, ending in the humiliation of the city of Buenos Aires, which was separated from its province and made into a special federal territory; a new provincial capital was founded at La Plata, 56 km to the southeast. The conquest at about the same time of all the Indian tribes of the pampas and the south by a young colonel, Julio A Roca, was to make possible the final supremacy of Buenos Aires over all rivals.

The formation of the republic

Argentina

20th century Politically Argentina was a constitutional republic with a very restricted right to vote up to the passage in 1912 of the Sáenz Peña law, which established universal manhood voting rights. From 1916 to 1930 the Unión Cívica Radical (founded in 1890) held power, under the leadership of Hipólito Yrigoyen and Marcelo T de Alvear, but lost it to the military uprising of 1930. Though seriously affected by the world depression of the 1930s, Argentina's rich soil and educated population had made it one of the 10 wealthiest countries in the world, but this wealth was unevenly distributed, and the political methods followed by the conservatives and their military associates in the 1930s denied the middle and working classes any effective share in their own country's wealth and government.

Peronism & A series of military coups in 1943-44 led to the rise of Col Juan Domingo Perón, basing his power
its legacy on an alliance between the army and labour; his contacts with labour were greatly assisted by his charismatic wife Eva (since commemorated in the rock-opera and film *Evita*). In 1946 Perón was elected President. His government is chiefly remembered by many Argentines for improving the living conditions of the workers. Especially in its early years the government was strongly nationalistic, taking control over the British-owned railways in 1948. Opposition parties were harassed and independent newspapers taken over. Although Perón was re-elected in 1951, his government soon ran into trouble: economic problems led to the introduction of a wage freeze, upsetting the labour unions, which were the heart of Peronist support; the death of Evita in 1952 was another blow. In September 1955 a military coup unseated Perón, who went into exile. Perón's legacy dominated the period 1955-1973: society was bitterly divided between Peronists and anti-Peronists; the economy struggled; the armed forces, constantly involved in politics, were also divided. The military group which seized power in 1966 was discredited by a deteriorating economy and the emergence of several guerrilla groups, in a climate of tension and violence. When it bowed out in 1973, elections were won by the Peronist candidate, Hector Campora. Perón returned from exile in Madrid to resume as President in October 1973, but died on 1 July 1974, leaving the Presidency to his widow, Vice-President María Estela Martínez de Perón (his third wife). The subsequent chaotic political situation, including guerrilla warfare, led to her deposition by a military junta, led by Gen Jorge Videla in March 1976.

The Dirty War Under the military, guerrilla warfare and the other features of dissidence were repressed with great brutality: about 9,000 people (according to official statistics; human rights organizations believe the total is at least double this) disappeared without trace during the so-called 'dirty war'. Gen Videla was appointed President in 1978 by the military; his nominated successor, Gen Roberto Viola took over for three years in March 1981 but was replaced by Gen Leopoldo Galtieri in December 1981. The latter was in turn replaced in June 1982 by Gen (ret) Reynaldo Bignone.

Return to Confidence in the military ebbed when their economic policies began to go sour in 1980.
democracy In 1982-83 pressure for a democratic restoration grew particularly after the Falklands (Islas Malvinas) War with Great Britain in 1982, when Argentina invaded the South Atlantic islands run by the British, in an attempt to reclaim them. General elections on 30 October 1983 were won by the Unión Cívica Radical (UCR) with Dr Raúl Alfonsín as president. During 1985 Generals Videla, Viola and Galtieri were sentenced to long terms of imprisonment for their parts in the 'dirty war'. President Alfonsín's popularity gradually waned as his Government failed to solve economic problems.

Menem & after When Alfonsín was defeated by Dr Carlos Saúl Menem of the Partido Justicialista (Peronists) in May 1989, Alfonsín stepped down early because of economic instability. Strained relations between the Peronist Government and the military led to several rebellions, which President Menem attempted to appease by pardoning the imprisoned Generals. His popularity among civilians declined, but in 1991-92 the Economy Minister Domingo Cavallo succeeded in restoring confidence in the economy and the Government as a whole. The key was a Convertibility Law, passed in 1991, fixing the peso at par with the US dollar, and permitting the Central Bank to print local currency only when fully backed by gold or hard currency. This achieved price stability; the annual average growth of consumer prices fell from 3,080% in

1989 to 3.9% in 1994 and remained in single figures until 2001. Before the 1995 elections, President Menem, with the support of Alfonsín, had succeeded in changing the constitution to permit the re-election of the president for a second term of four years. The majority of the electorate, favouring stability, returned him to office. Menem's renewed popularity was short-lived: joblessness remained high, corruption unrestrained and new labour legislation was regarded as in contravention of some of Peronism's founding tenets. In the run-up to the October 1999 presidential elections, Menem tried for a while to force another change to the constitution to allow him to stand for a third term. His bid failed, but his rivalry with the Peronists' eventual candidate, Eduardo Duhalde, governor of Buenos Aires province, was one of the factors behind the victory of Fernando de la Rúa of the Alliance for Work, Justice and Education (Alianza). De la Rúa pledged to reduce joblessness from its end-1999 level of 14%, provide better healthcare and end corruption. Among his first challenges was labour reform, not just to stamp his own authority on the unions, but also to boost competitiveness with Brazil and to calm investors worried by the minority government and Peronists clinging to power in major provinces, many of which were heavily in debt.

Within a year, de la Rúa was facing scandals and a series of economic crises. The peso became increasingly overvalued, but the government refused to modify the Convertibility Law. By the end of 2001, the country was in deep recession, unemployment was 20% and the government had practically run out of money to service its US$132 bn debt. As faith in the banking system and the government plummeted, Argentines started to take back their savings from banks; on 30 November 2001 alone, US$2 bn were withdrawn. The government imposed a US$250 weekly limit on cash withdrawals, leading to rioting, looting and 27 deaths which eventually forced de la Rúa out of office. Three subsequent presidents resigned. On 2 January 2002, Eduardo Duhalde was sworn in as Argentina's fifth president in two weeks. Duhalde and his economic advisers faced a mammoth task in dragging the economy out of recession and restoring confidence. Half the population was living in poverty, desperate for work and food. Those with savings saw their value plummet as the peso, floated against the dollar in January, fell from 1 peso to 2.50 pesos = US$1 by April 2002. Meanwhile, the IMF refused to release emergency funds pending a new austerity programme.

Government

The country's official name is La República Argentina, the Argentine Republic. The form of government has traditionally been a representative, republican federal system. Of the two legislative houses, the Senate has 72 seats, and the Chamber of Deputies 257. By the 1853 Constitution (amended most recently in 1994) the country is divided into a Federal Capital (the city of Buenos Aires) and 23 Provinces. Each Province has its own Governor, Senate and Chamber of Deputies. The municipal government of the Federal Capital is exercised by a Mayor who is directly elected. The Constitution grants the city autonomous rule.

Culture

People

Total population in 2001 was 37.5 million. The average annual growth rate between 1995 and 2000 was 1.3%. In the Federal Capital and Province of Buenos Aires, where about 45% of the population lives, the people are almost exclusively of European origin. In the far northern provinces, colonized from neighbouring countries, at least half the people are *mestizos* though they form about 15% of the population of the whole country. It is estimated that 12.8% are foreign born and generally of European origin, though there are also important communities of Syrians, Lebanese, Armenians, Japanese and Koreans.

Forecast population growth 2000-2005: 1.2%
Urban population in 2000: 90%
Infant mortality: 20 per 1,000 live births

Not surprisingly, the traditional image of the Argentine is that of the *gaucho*; *gauchismo* has been a powerful influence in literature, sociology and folklore, and is celebrated each year in the week before the 'Day of Tradition', 10 November. In the highlands of the northwest, in the Chaco, Misiones and in the southwest, there are still some indigenous groups. The total of the Indian population is unknown; estimates vary from 300,000 to 500,000. As was noted above, the pampas Indians were virtually exterminated in the 19th century; the Indians of Tierra del Fuego are extinct. Surviving peoples include the Wichi and others in Salta and Jujuy provinces (see page 130), various Chaco Indians (see page 168) and tribes related to the Mapuche and Tehuelche nations in the southwest. A number

Argentina

of organizations represent indigenous interests, but any legislation, under federal law, has to be enacted separately by each province.

Books

Federico B Kirbus has written the highly informative *Guía de Aventuras y Turismo de la Argentina* (with comprehensive English index – 1989), obtainable at *Librería La Rayuela,* Buenos Aires 96, Salta and El Ateneo, Florida 340, basement, Buenos Aires. *Kirbus* has also written the *Guía Ilustrada de las Regiones Turísticas Argentinas,* four volumes, with about 300 black and white photos, colour pictures and colour plates on flora and fauna (published by El Ateneo, US$18-21 each); also *La Argentina, país de maravillas,* Manrique Zago ediciones (1993), a beautiful book of photographs with text in Spanish and English, *Patagonia* (with Jorge Schulte) and *Ruta Cuarenta,* both fine photographic records with text (both Capuz Varela). *Pirelli Guide,* edited by Diego Bigongiari, including map for cultural, historical and nature information, highly recommended. *Nuestros Paisanos Los Indios* by Carlos Martínez Sarasola is an excellent compendium on the history and present of Argentine Indian communities, recommended. A 19th-century classic text on the same subject is *A Visit to the Ranquel Indians* by Lucio V Mansilla, translated by Eva Gillies (Nebraska University Press). The Fundación Vida Silvestre, Defensa 245/251, has information and books on Argentine flora and fauna; *Patagonia. Las leyes del bosque,* 1999, English translation 2000. *Patagonia. Las leyes entre las costas y el mar,* and *Antártida. Las leyes entre las costa y el mar.* Field guide to Argentine birds: *Guía para la identificación de las aves de Argentina y Uruguay* by T Narosky and D Yzurieta, with drawings and colour illustrations. *The High Andes,* by John Biggar (Castle Doublas: Andes, 1999), is a guide for climbers.

For Patagonia, *In Patagonia* by Bruce Chatwin. *Patagonia,* by Metzeltin and Buscaini (Dall' Oglio, Milan). *At Home with the Patagonians,* by George Musters (history of 19th-century life of Patagonian Indians), ed John Murray, London 1871/1973. *Argentine Trout Fishing. A Fly Fisherman's Guide to Patagonia* by William C Leitch (ISBN 1-87817-5-06-8). *Cuentan los Chonkes,* narrated by Mario Echeverría Baleta, translated by Christine A Fox as *Tales of the Tehuelche Tell – Patagonian Legends* (Río Gallegos, 2001, US$12 in local shops, contact SADE, Vélez Sarsfield 777, 9400 Río Gallegos, or C A Fox, book@traduzcaike.plus.com

For Tierra del Fuego, *Tierra del Fuego: The Fatal Lodestone,* by Eric Shipton; *Uttermost Part of the Earth,* by E Lucas Bridges. Available in USA: *Birds of Isla Grande* (Tierra del Fuego) by Philip S Humphrey, and *A Guide to the Birds of South America,* by Rodolphe Meyer de Schauensee. *Map of Tierra del Fuego,* published by Zagier & Urruty, obtainable in Ushuaia and Buenos Aires.

In 1872, José Hernández (1834-86) published *El gaucho Martín Fierro,* an epic poem about the disruption of local communities by the march of progress; the eponymous hero and dispossessed outlaw came to symbolize Argentine nationhood. A second great gaucho work, *Don Segundo Sombra,* written by Ricardo Güiraldes (1886-1927), further cemented the figure of the gaucho as national hero. In the 20th century, traditional symbols were rejected in favour of urban and experimental themes. Argentina's most famous writer, Jorge Luis Borges (1899-1986) was at the forefront of the avant-garde. He is best known for his teasing, revolutionary and poetic short stories, best seen in *Ficciones* (*Fictions,* 1944) and *El Aleph* (1949). Julio Cortázar (1914-84) was the leading Argentine representative of the 1960s 'boom'. His novel *Rayuela* (*Hopscotch,* 1963) typifies the experimentation, philosophy and freedom of the period. Also important at this time was Ernesto Sábato (1911-), whose most famous novel is *Sobre héroes y tumbas* (*On Heroes and Tombs,* 1961) and who also wrote the preface to *Nunca más* (*Never again,* 1984), the report of the commission into the disappearances in the 1970s 'dirty war'. Manuel Puig (1932-90) was fascinated by mass culture, gender roles and the banal as art and expressed these ideas in novels such as *El beso de la Mujer Araña* (*The Kiss of the Spider Woman,* 1976 – made into a renowned film). Many writers dealt with dictatorship and the 'dirty war', such as Osvaldo Soriano (1943-98) in *No habrá más penas ni olvido* (*A Funny, Dirty Little War,* 1982) and Luisa Valenzuela (1938 -) in *Cola de lagartija* (*The Lizard's Tail,* 1983). Tomás Eloy Martínez (1934 -) has written novels on two of Argentina's enduring 20th-century figures, *Santa Evita* (1995) and *La novela de Perón* (*The Perón Novel,* 1985), both highly acclaimed.

Bolivia

The highest capital city in the world, sunk in a canyon at a breathless 4,000 m, and the largest salt flat on earth, a vast blinding-white expanse on which sits a hotel made of the stuff. In Bolivia, you learn to expect the unexpected. This is where flamingoes feed from red and green lakes rimmed by volcanoes, where Dali-esque rock structures dot the Altiplano like so many giant baby's building blocks, and waterfalls crash down on vehicles on one of the most dangerous roads in the world. Turn the corner and you can swim with pink river dolphins in jungle waters, fish for piranhas in the pampas and fill your bags with everything from the beautiful autumnal colours of the textiles, to packs of dried llama foetuses, which protect homes from evil spirits.

4

230

Bolivia

Essentials

Planning your trip

La Paz This is the best place to start as many international flights end there and it is closest to the well-travelled overland routes from Peru and Chile. The capital is easy to explore, but you do need to adjust to the altitude which will leave you breathless. There are some good museums and churches and an Indian market area of overwhelming proportions. Daytrips include the pre-Inca city of Tiahuanaco, which is close to the beautiful Lake Titicaca; to appreciate the lake fully a night or more on its shores is recommended. Northeast of La Paz, over the cordillera, are the Yungas, deep subtropical valleys, rich in vegetation, where a town like Coroico can provide welcome relief from the rigours of the altiplano. Equally pleasant and lower than La Paz is Sorata, a good base for trekking and climbing.

South of La Paz Oruro, a route centre and mining city, has one of the most famous of Latin American carnival celebrations, *La Diablada*, usually in mid-Feb. Southeast of here are the colonial cities of Potosí, where Spain garnered much of its imperial wealth from abundant silver deposits and present-day miners scour the mountain for more meagre pickings, and Sucre, Bolivia's official capital, with an array of fine buildings. Uyuni, further south again, is the jumping off place for trips into stunning salt flats to see coloured lakes, flamingoes and horizons of volcanoes: bitterly cold at night, blindingly unsurpassed by day. Tarija, south of Potosí and not as high above sea level, is best known for its fruits and wine and for the remains of dinosaurs. Continuing beyond here you come to the Argentine border.

East of La Paz Cochabamba, Bolivia's third city, conveniently placed between the altiplano and the lowlands, has a lovely climate and is the centre of one of the country's main agricultural zones. The Parque Nacional Toro Toro, with its dinosaur tracks, rock paintings, canyons and waterfalls, is a tough but stunning excursion. Further east is Santa Cruz, also economically important, from where you can visit the Parque Nacional Amboró, Samaipata archaeological site, the beautiful Jesuit missions of the Chiquitanía, or take the long rail journey to Corumbá in Brazil. Like its eastern neighbour, Bolivia has a Pantanal wetland, just opening up to tourism, with opportunities to see a magnificent range of wildlife.

Northern lowlands From either La Paz or Santa Cruz there are tiring overland routes into Bolivia's Amazonian territory. From the capital, Rurrenabaque is the chief destination and starting point for the fantastic *Chalalán Ecolodge* in the Parque Nacional Madidi which claims a greater bio-diversity than anywhere else on earth. Trinidad is where to head for from Santa Cruz (like Rurrenabaque, it can be reached by air). The further north you go the fewer tourists you will meet. Apr to Oct are the months to visit.

The most popular season for visitors is Jun-Aug, while some of the best festivals, eg Carnival and Holy Week, are in the wet season which is considered to be from Dec to Mar. The country has four distinct climatic zones: (1) The Puna and Altiplano; average temperature, 10° C, but above 4,000 m may get down to -25° C at night in Jun-Aug. By day the tropical sun raises temperatures over 20° C. Rainfall on the northern Altiplano is 400 to 700 mm, much less further south. Little rain falls upon the western plateaux between May and Nov, but the rest of the year can be wet. (2) The Yungas north of La Paz and Cochabamba, among the spurs of the Cordillera; altitude, 750-1,500 m; average temperature, 24° C. (3) The Valles, or high valleys and basins gouged out by the rivers of the Puna; average temperature, 19° C. Rainfall in the Yungas valleys is from 700 to 800 mm a year (heaviest Dec-Feb), with high humidity. (4) The tropical lowlands; altitude between 150 m and 750 m; rainfall is high but seasonal (heaviest Nov-Mar, but can fall at any season); large areas suffer from alternate flooding and drought.

Bolivia

The climate is hot, ranging from 23° to 25° C in the south and to 27° C in the north. Occasional cold dust-laden winds from the south, the *surazos*, lower the temperature considerably.

Finding out more

Tourism is under the control of the **Dirección Nacional De Turismo**, Edificio Ballivián, piso 18, Calle Mercado, La Paz, T236 7463/4, F237 4630. The **Viceministerio de Turismo** is at Av Mcal Santa Cruz, Palacio de Cominicaciones, p 16, La Paz, www.mcei.gov.bo/web_mcei/Turismo/turismo.htm   See under each city for addresses of tourist offices. For more websites, see below. For national parks information: **Sistema Nacional de Areas Protegidas**, Edif El Cóndor, p13-15, Batallón Coloradas 24, La Paz, T231 6077, F231 6230.

Websites   **www.bolivia.com** (in Spanish), for news, entertainment, tourism and information on regions. Tourism sites include: **www.bolivian.com**, **www.bolivianet.com/turismo/** (both in Spanish) **www.boliviaweb.com** (in English); **www.poorbuthappy.com/bolivia/new/** **www.bolivia-tourism.com/** in Spanish, English and German. www.wtgonline.com/data/bol/bol.asp Information on travel in Bolivia, cities, precolumbian cultures, folk dances, festivals, traditional medicine and more.
www.gorp.com/gorp/location/latamer/bolivia/basic_b.htm Has an overview of the country, with more detailed info on Amboró, Las Yungas, Choro Trail and jungle trips.
www.boliviangeographic.com is an on-line magazine with good articles.
www.geocities.com/yosemite/gorge/1177/Information on climbing, mountaineering and parapenting, from **Club de Montañismo Halcones** of Oruro
www.enlacesbolivia.net and **www.megalink.com** For links to other Bolivian sites.
www.boliviabiz.com on doing business in Bolivia.
www.andes.org/ Quechua language lessons, music, songs, poems, stories and resources.
www.megalink.com/fobomade/ Website of the **Foro Boliviano sobre Medio Ambiente y Desarrollo**. For environmental issues, in Spanish.
www.bolivianstudies.org Site of the **Bolivian Studies Association** with a journal, newsletter, database and travellers' notes.

Before you travel

Visas &   A passport only is needed for citizens of almost all Western European countries, Israel, Japan,
immigration   North and South American countries (except Venezuela), South Africa, Australia and New Zealand. Irish citizens are advised to check with a Bolivian Embassy before leaving home on latest requirements. All are granted 30 days on entry, but are entitled to 90. Extensions can be easily arranged at immigration. Among those countries whose nationals require a visa and must gain authorization from the Bolivian Ministry of Foreign Affairs (can take 3-5 weeks) are: Bangladesh, China, Egypt, Haiti, India, Indonesia, Iran, Iraq, Jordan, Kuwait, Laos, Lebanon, Libya, Malaysia, North Korea, Oman, Pakistan, Palestine, Saudi Arabia, Singapore, Syria, Taiwan,

Bolivia

Bolivian embassies and consulates

Australia and New Zealand, 74 Pitt Street Level 6, Sydney NSW 2000, T02-923 51858

Austria, Waaggasse 10/4 A-1040 Wien (Vienna), T43-1-587 4675/586 6800, 106211.3207@compuserve.com

Belgium, Av enue Louise N 176 Boite 6, 1050 Brussels, T2-647 2718, embolbrus@arcadis.be

Canada, 130 Albert Street, Suite 416, Ottowa, ON K1P 5G4, T613-236 5730, www.iosphere.net/~bolcan/

France, 12 avenue Du President Kennedy, 75016 Paris 16, T01-4224 9344, consubol@club-internet.fr

Germany, Wichmannstrasse 6, 10787 Berlin, T263 9150, embolberlin@t-online.de/ or Konstantinstrasse 16, D5300, Bonn 2 – Germany T0228-362038

Israel, Rehor Carmel 5, apt 9, 90805 Mevasseret Zion, CPZ823, T2- 533 5195, totora@netvision.net.il

Italy, Via Brenta 2/A, int18, 00198 Rome, T6-884 1001, embabolivia@cdc.it

Japan, No 38 Kowa Building, room804, Nishi Azabu 4-12-24, Minato-Hu, Tokyo 106-0031, T3-3499 5441, embolivia-tokio@rree.gov.bo

Netherlands, Nassaulaan 5 2514 JS La Haya (The Hague), T70-361 6707, emboltk@interlink.or.jp

Spain, Velázquez 26, 3° piso, 28001 Madrid, T91-578 0835, www.boliviano.com/EMBAJADA.HTM

Sweden, Södra Kungsvägen 60,18132 Lidingö, Stockholm, T8-731 5830, emb.bolivia@lidingo.mail.Phoneia.com

Switzerland, Gartenstrasse 33, 8023 Zurich, T201 2833, F201 2825, mission.bolivia@itu.ch

UK, 106 Eaton Square, London SW1 9AD, T0207-235 4248, F0207-235 1286, 100746.1347@compuserve.com

USA, 3014 Massachusetts Avenue NW, Washington DC 20008, T202-483 4410, or 211 East 43 Road Street, Suite 702 New York, NY 10017, T212-499 7401, www.bolivia-usa.org

Thailand, Tunisia, Vietnam and Yemen. Those countries which require a visa but not authorisation are: Croatia, the Czech Republic, Cuba, Hungary, South Korea, Malta, Mexico, Panama, Romania, Slovenia and Venezuela. This takes 1-2 working days. Nationals of African countries, the rest of Asia, former Yugoslavia and former Soviet Union countries should make special enquiries as the Bolivian government had yet to decide if they needed visas at the time of going to press. The cost of a visa varies from nationality to nationality. Visas (or permit to stay) can be renewed at any Migración office up to 90 days at no cost. After this time renewal is at the discretion of the immigration officer. If refused, leave the country and return. There should be a statutory 72 hours period outside Bolivia before renewing a visa but 24 hours is usually acceptable. On arrival ensure that visas and passports are stamped with the same, correct date of entry or this can lead to 'fines' later. If you outstay your visa the current fine is US$1.50 per day. Business visitors (unless passing through as tourists) are required to obtain a visa from a Bolivian consulate. This costs £35 (or equivalent); applicants should check all requirements and regulations on length of stay and extensions in advance.

200 cigarettes, 50 cigars and one pound tobacco.   **Duty-free**

Inoculate against typhoid. Visitors should have yellow-fever vaccination when visiting Santa   **Vaccinations**
Cruz or the Oriente. A yellow fever vaccination certificate, at least 10 days old, is officially required for leaving and entering the country. Hepatitis is widespread.

Clothing Visitors to the Altiplano and the Puna should not underestimate the cold at night.   **What to take**
The climate in the Eastern Lowlands is tropical. Oruro and Potosí are colder than La Paz; Cochabamba can be very warm. **Contact lens solution** is hard to find.

Money

The unit of currency is the boliviano (Bs), divided into 100 centavos. There are notes for 200,   **Currency**
100, 50, 20, 10 and 5 bolivianos, and coins of 2 and 1 boliviano and 50, 20 and 10 centavos.   *boliviano exchange*
Bolivianos are often referred to as pesos; expensive items, including hotel rooms, are often   *rate with US$: 7.42*

Bolivia

Bolivia

quoted in dollars. When changing money, try to get notes in as small denominations as possible. Bs 100 notes are very difficult to change in La Paz and impossible elsewhere; keep small denominations. Change is often given in forms other than money: eg cigarette, sweet, or razor blade. Watch out for forged currency, especially dollars (US$100 notes in particular) and Chilean pesos. It is almost impossible to buy dollars at points of exit when leaving or to change bolivianos in other countries. Establishments which change travellers' cheques are given in the text; outside major cities it can be impossible. Changing US$ cash presents no problems anywhere. It is not worth trying to change other currencies. All the larger, recognized *casas de cambio* will give US$ cash in exchange for travellers' cheques, usually with a commission. If arriving on Fri night, bring bolivianos or US dollars cash as it is difficult to change travellers' cheques at the weekend (in La Paz, try *El Lobo* restaurant, usually changes TCs at any time, good rates, or *Hotel Gloria*, good rates for most western currencies).

Credit cards Credit cards are commonly used in most cities to obtain cash and for purchases; an extra charge, up to 10%, may be made. American Express is not as useful as Visa, or, to a lesser extent, MasterCard. In all cities and large towns there are plenty of 24-hour cash machines. Those displaying the *Enlace* sign are the best, accepting both Visa, Visa Electron and MasterCard (and therefore pretty much every foreign card). You can draw US dollars or bolivianos. Enlace has a toll-free number for information about ATMs, 0800 3060. RedBank ATMs allow Visa holders to take out bolivianos or dollars, but MasterCard holders only bolivianos.

Cost of travelling Bolivia is cheaper than most neighbouring countries. Rents, appliances, some clothing, and especially toilet goods and medicines, are high priced. Food, accommodation and transport are not expensive. Budget travellers can get by on US$25-30 pp a day for two travelling together. For a basic hotel: US$3 pp; breakfast US$1-2; *almuerzos* cost from US$1.05-2.50.

Getting there

Air **From Europe** Either fly to Lima, Rio de Janeiro, São Paulo or Buenos Aires for connections, or via Miami.
From North America *American Airlines* and *LAB* from Miami daily to La Paz and Santa Cruz. From other North American cities, connect in Miami.
Within South America There are flights to Santa Cruz from the capitals of all Hispanic South American republics except Ecuador and Uruguay, as well as Rio de Janeiro and São Paulo, Brazil. There are also two Cusco-La Paz flights a week (*LAB*) and daily flights from Arica and Iquique, Chile, besides those from Santiago. Many international flights call at Cochabamba as well as Santa Cruz.

Road There are three routes from Puno (Peru): see Crossing the Peruvian frontier, page 269.
From Salta-Jujuy-La Quiaca (**Argentina**) to Potosí or Tarija. Alternative routes lead from the Argentine province of Salta via Bermejo or Yacuiba to Tarija or Santa Cruz. Dry weather only. From Ollagüe (**Chile**) to Uyuni, see page 280. From Arica (**Chile**) via Tambo Quemado or via Visviri (see By Road from La Paz to the Pacific Coast, page 260).
Travel to Paraguay Apart from the journey described on page 324 (also taken by Santa Cruz-Asunción buses), an alternative way of getting to Paraguay is to travel by bus to Salta or Orán (**Argentina**), then on to Asunción via Resistencia (**Argentina**).

Touching down

Airport taxes **Departure taxes** Tax of US$25, payable in dollars or bolivianos, cash only, is levied on leaving by air. On internal flights a tax of US$2.25 is paid. Tax on airline tickets 14.9%.

Tipping Up to 10% in restaurants; in all other cases a tip is given in recognition of a service provided, eg to a taxi driver who has been helpful (an extra Bs 0.50-1), to someone who has looked after a car or carried bags. Usual tip Bs 0.50-1.

Touching down

Business hours 0900-1200 (sometimes 1230 in La Paz), and 1400-1800 (sometimes 1900 in La Paz). Saturday is a half day. Opening and closing in the afternoon are several hours later in the provinces.
Banks 0900-1200, 1400-1630, but closed on Saturday.
Official time Four hours behind GMT.
IDD 591. Equal tones with long pauses means it is ringing. Equal tones with equal pauses indicate it is engaged.
Voltage Varies considerably. Generally 110 volts, 50 cycles AC in La Paz, 220 volts 50 cycles AC elsewhere, but check before using any appliance. (You may even find 110 and 220 in the same room.) US-type plugs can be used in most hotels.
Weights and measures Metric.

The procedure for reporting a robbery is to go to the **Departamento de Criminalística**, or the office for stolen property, in the town where the theft took place. Purchase official paper from the police for them to write the report, then, with patience and politeness, you may get a report costing between US$1.30 and US$5.25.

Safety

Throughout 2001 and into 2002, civil disturbance in Bolivia included strikes and demonstrations in major cities and many road blocks throughout the country, some lasting a few hours, others weeks. Try to be flexible in your travel plans if you encounter such disruptions and make the most of the attractions where you are staying if overland transport is not running.

Where to stay

Throughout Bolivia some hotels impose their own curfews. In La Paz it tends to be midnight (check) but it can be as early as 2130 in Copacabana. These locking up times are strictly adhered to by hotel keepers. Ask for the hot water schedule, it changes with the season, water pressure, etc, although now even the cheapest hotels tend to have electric showers which offer hot/warm water all day. Clothes washing is generally not allowed in bathrooms but many of the cheaper hotels have a hand-washing area. Many mid-range hotels will keep money and valuables in the safe if there are no safety-deposit boxes. Cheaper hotels rarely have heating in the rooms. Youth Hostels are not necessarily cheaper: many middle range *residenciales* are affiliated to the **IYHA**.

Hotels
See inside front cover of the book for our hotel grade price guide. Hotels must display prices by law

One can camp almost anywhere in safety, except near settlements (unless unavoidable). Warm sleeping gear essential, even in the lowlands in the winter. Sleeping bags are also useful for getting some sleep on the buses or long distance trains, especially those crossing the Andes. Mosquito nets can be purchased in La Paz, but they are not cheap. Beware sandstorms south of Oruro. Camping gas-style and Epigas cannisters are available in La Paz and all large cities; white gas for Coleman stoves is difficult to find. Kerosene is much easier to find outside La Paz, even in small towns. *Alcohol potable* (meths) is widely available.

Camping

Getting around

Internal air services are run by *Lloyd Aéreo Boliviano* (LAB www.labairlines.com), *Aero Sur* (www.angelfire.com/on/aerosur) and *TAM* between the main cities and towns. *LAB* and *Aero Sur* are generally reliable but *TAM* much less so. Boarding passes are issued only at airports; after obtaining one, pay airport tax (see above). *LAB* offers a 30-day domestic airpass for US$296 for international travellers using *LAB* (or a foreign carrier with whom *LAB* may have a pooling arrangement) for a maximum of five flights between the main cities; note that many flights radiate from La Paz, Santa Cruz or Cochabamba. *LAB* have 5% discounts for family members if they travel together (take passport); *LAB* and *Aero Sur* also offer discounts of 5% to students under 26 and *Aero Sur* offer 20% discounts to passengers over 65. Note that a 'through' flight may require a change of plane, or be delayed waiting for a connecting flight coming from elsewhere. Only on international flights is overnight lodging provided during delays. Insure your bags heavily as they tend to get left around and *LAB* is reluctant to give compensation.

Air

Bolivia

NB If your internal flight is delayed keep your baggage with you and do not check it in until the flight is definitely announced. There have been robberies of prematurely checked-in baggage.

Road The national highway system at the end of 1995 totalled 55,487 km, of which only 5 were paved and under 25 gravel-surfaced. Nearly all Bolivian road surfaces, even the paved sections, are bad, and after flooding or rough weather they are even worse. Even main roads may be closed in the rainy season. **NB** On election day no public transport runs whatsoever; only cars with a special permit may be on the road.

Bus Buses ply most of the roads (interurban buses are called *flotas*, urban ones *micros*, also minibuses and *trufis* (shared taxis)). Reporting time is half an hour before the bus leaves. You should always try to reserve, and pay for, a seat as far as possible in advance and arrive in good time, but substantial savings can be made by buying tickets just before departure as there is fierce competition to fill seats. In the wet season, bus travel is subject to long delays and detours at extra cost. In the dry season journeys can be very dusty. On all journeys, take food and toilet wipes. It is best to travel by day, not just so you can see the scenery and avoid arriving at your destination at night, but also because drivers work very long hours and there is less chance of them falling asleep in daylight. Bus companies are responsible for any luggage packed on the roof. A small charge is made for use of major bus terminals; payment is before departure. **NB** The problem of drivers falling asleep applies equally to trucks. Think twice before hitching a ride with them; fatal accidents do occur.

Car **Motorists** (including motor-cyclists) To bring a private car into Bolivia temporary admission must be sought, but is not easily obtainable. A *carnet de passages* is recommended. You must have an International Driving Permit. When hiring a car the rental company may only require your national licence but police controls may ask for an international licence. A hire company can arrange a 'blanket' driving permit for tourists which is valid for several days and destinations. Two authorization certificates are required in La Paz: the first from the **Automóvil Club Boliviano**, corner of 6 de Agosto and Arce, T/F237 2139, and the second from the traffic police at the **Comando Departamental, Organismo Operativo de Tránsito**, corner of Mcal Santa Cruz and Plaza San Francisco.

For taking a vehicle across the border from Bolivia, check with *Automovil Club Boliviano*, La Paz for any special documents which may be required, depending on the registration of your vehicle.

Take great care when driving at night (it is best not to): cyclists do not usually have lights; truck drivers almost never dip their headlights (keep your own on full beam to make the truck dip his); some truck drivers are drunk, or fall asleep at the wheel. At the slightest sign of danger, pull out of the way. Day or night, watch out for people asleep at the roadside in lowland areas; they tend to lie with head and torso in the road where there are fewer mosquitoes. Tolls vary from US$0.50 to US$2.50 for journeys up to 100 km.

Trucks congregate at all town markets, with destinations chalked on the sides. They charge what they think the market will bear, but are normally much cheaper when there's competition.

Petrol is sold from the drum in every small village **Petrol** (gasoline) two grades: 85 and 92 octane. 85 octane costs US$0.44, super US$0.56; diesel costs US$0.50 per litre. Costs are higher in Guayaramerín, Riberalta and Puerto Suárez. Around Lake Titicaca, there are no petrol stations; the only two that exist frequently run out.

Train Bolivia has 3,774 km of railway. *Empresa Nacional de Ferrocarriles* (ENFE), was privatized in 1996. La Paz railway station was closed in 1997. Trains to the Argentine border start at Oruro. The only other public railways of significance run from Santa Cruz. For train information in La Paz T241 6545/6. Always check departure times in advance.

Tickets can be bought in advance

Maps **Instituto Geográfico Militar** head office is at Estado Mayor General, Av Saavedra Final, Miraflores, La Paz, open Mon-Thu 0900-1100, 1500-1700, Fri 0900-1100, take passport to purchase maps immediately. Or go to Oficina 5, Juan XXIII 100 (mud track between Rodríguez y Linares), Mon-Thu 0800-1200 and 1430-1800, Fri 0800-1400. *IGM* map prices: 1:50,000

Bolivia

topographical sheet US$6.25 (photocopy US$4.70); 1:250,000 sheet US$7.00 (copy US$5.50); national communications map (roads and towns) US$7.80; 4-sheet Bolivia physical 1:1,000,000, US$14; 4 sheet political 1:1,500,000 US$14. *Liam P O'Brien* has produced a 1:135,000, full colour, shaded relief topographic map of the Cordillera Real, US$10 per copy, also a 1:2,200,000 full colour travel map of Bolivia highlighting the National Parks, from 28 Turner Terrace, Newtonville, MA02160, USA, or from map distributors (*Bradt, Stanfords*, etc). *Walter Guzmán Córdova* colour maps, 1:150,000, of Choro-Takesi-Yunga Cruz, Mururata-Illimani, Huayna Potosí Oruro-Potosi-Salar de Uyuni, Illampu-Ancohuma, Titicaca-Tiwanaku-Yungas, Nigruni-Condoriri, La Paz department, Santa Cruz department, Sajama and Mapa Físico-Político-Vial (1:2,250,000, up-to-date road map), available from bookshops (US$6.70-7.50). The German Alpine Club (**Deutscher Alpenverien**) produces 2 good maps of Sorata-Ancohuma-Illampu and Illimani, often available from IGM (US$6.50). A map and guide of La Paz, in English, is published by *Editorial Quipus*, Casilla 1696, Calle Jáuregui 2248, T234 0062. Also Tiwanaku, Sucre and Cochabamba guides. Quipus is also the Poste Restante for **South American Explorers** members.

Keeping in touch

Internet

Internet access is extensive and often easier and more reliable than the phone. Every major town has at least one internet café, with more springing up daily. Outside La Paz connections can be slow and frustrating, but persevere and you'll get through (see main text for details).

Post

Post offices use the post box (casilla) system. Items sent by post should therefore bear, not the street address, but the casilla number and town. Hours are Mon-Sat 0800-2000, Sun 0800-1200. For security, send mail 'certificado'. There is a national and international express post system; special counters and envelopes provided. Air-mail letters to and from Europe should take between five and 10 days. Letter/postcard up to 20 g to Europe US$0.90, to North America US$0.75; rest of the world US$1; letter over 30 g to Europe US$2.20, to North America US$1.50, rest of the world US$2.30. Packages up to 2 kg can be posted from the ground floor of the main post office in La Paz between 1200-1430 when the main parcels department, downstairs, is taking lunch: to Europe a 2 kg parcel costs US$30, to North America US$20.30, to the rest of the world US$42. Surface mail parcels up to 2 kg cost US$16 to North America, US$19 to Europe and US$21 to the rest of the world. Parcels are checked by customs officers before being sealed. We have received reports of customs officers trying to charge for inspecting parcels: politely refuse to pay. After inspection and repacking parcels are wrapped in cloth and sewn up for security reasons, there is a small fee for this service.

Telephone
In 2001, digital exchange was introduced and the system was deregulated. Phone numbers have been changed

All phone numbers have seven digits. To dial long distance you must prefix each seven-digit number with a regional code: towns and cities in the departments of La Paz, Oruro and Potosí (the Occidente) carry the prefix 02; those in Santa Cruz, Beni and Pando (the Oriente) take 03; those in Cochabamba, Chuquisaca and Tarija (the Centro) take 04. Dialling from private phones requires an additional prefix, that of the telephone company you wish to use, between the zero and number of the regional code: 0 + access number + 2 + local 7-digit number for Occidente, 0 + access number + 3 + local 7-digit number for Oriente and 0 + access number + 4 + local 7-digit number for Centro. The telephone company access numbers are: 10 for *Entel* (www.10.com.bo – be patient), 11 for *AES*, 12 for *Teledata* and 13 for *Boliviatel*. So, choosing *Entel* to call the British Embassy in La Paz from a private phone in Santa Cruz you would dial 0102-243 1073; using *Teledata* you would dial 0122 243 1073. Calling Bolivia from abroad conforms to systems elsewhere in the world. Dial the access code for Bolivia, 00-591, then add the full long-distance 9-digit number minus its initial zero. Thus, to call the British Embassy in La Paz from Europe or the USA, dial 00-591-2-243 1073. Dialling mobile phones: all mobile numbers are now eight digit, starting with 7. If the person is local then dial their eight-digit number; if they are out of town you must dial a 0 first.

Direct calls are possible from major cities to Europe, USA, Australia and elsewhere, clear lines, delays minimal; US$2.10 per minute to Europe and Mexico, US$1.79 to USA and South America, US$2.25 to Australia. This is peak rate; 2100-2300 and all day Sun calls are US$0.31

cheaper. From 2300-0730 weekdays and Sat they are US$0.62 cheaper. Fax to Europe costs US$5 per page, to the USA US$3.80, to Australia, New Zealand US$6. Phone calls within city limits are free for private calls from a private phone. For public phones, coins/fichas or phone cards are necessary. Direct collect-call numbers: US *AT&T* 0800 1111, *MCI* 0800 2222, *Sprint* 0800 3333, *IDB* (*TRT*) 0800 4444; UK *BT* 0800 0044; Spain *Telefónica* 0800 0034; Brazil 0800 0055; Chile *Entel* 0800 0056; Canada *Teleglobe* 0800 0101; Japan *KDD* 0800 0081.

Media In La Paz: morning papers – *Presencia*, daily, largely Catholic; *La Razón*, www.la-razon.com *El Diario* (sensationalist), www.eldiario.net *Ultima Hora*, and *Jornada* (evenings). In Cochabamba – *Los Tiempos*, www.lostiempos.com and *Extra*. In Oruro – *La Patria*, mornings (except Monday). *El Día*, *La Estrella del Oriente*, *El Mundo* and *El Deber* are the Santa Cruz daily papers. *Deber* also appears in La Paz and Trinidad. In Sucre, *El Correo*. *Presencia*, *El Diario*, *El Mundo*, *La Razón* all have good foreign coverage. Weekly: *Nueva Economía*. La Paz papers are on sale in other cities. English language weekly *The Bolivian Times*, published Friday, US$1.50, available in major cities, many local reports (Jauregui 2248, Sopocachi, La Paz, casilla 1696. International papers are available in La Paz. Also, there are about 85 radio stations, a commercial government TV station and a university TV service.

Food and drink

Food
The normal international cuisine is found at most good hotels and restaurants

Salteñas are meat or chicken pasties (originating from Salta, Argentina, but popular throughout the Andean countries), eaten regularly by Bolivians, mostly in the morning. Some are *muy picante* (very hot) with red chili peppers, but *medio picante* and *poco picante* ones can normally be obtained. *Marraqueta* is bread from La Paz, crusty, with a soft centre; *pan de Batallas* is a sandwich loaf.

In the north lowlands, many types of wild meat are served in tourist restaurants and on jungle tours. Bear in mind the turtles whose eggs are eaten are endangered and that other species not endangered soon will be if they stay on the tourist menu.

Bolivian highland cooking is usually very tasty and often *picante*. Local specialities, which visitors should try, include *empanadas* (cheese pasties) and *humitas* (maize pies); *pukacapas* are *picante* cheese pies. Recommended main dishes including *sajta de pollo*, hot spicy chicken with onion, fresh potatoes and *chuño* (dehydrated potatoes), *parrillada* (a Bolivian kind of mixed grill), *fricase* (juicy pork dish served with *chuño*), *silpancho* (fried breaded meat with eggs, rice and bananas), *saice*, a dish of minced meat with picante sauce, served with rice, potatoes, onions and tomatoes, *pique macho*, roast meat with chips, onion and pepper, and *ají de lengua*, ox-tongue with chilis, potatoes and *chuño* or *tunta* (another kind of dehydrated potato). The soups are also good, especially a *chairo* soup made of meat, vegetables, *chuño* and *ají* (hot pepper) to which the locals like to add *llajua* or *halpahuayca* (hot sauces always set on restaurant tables) to make it even more *picante*. Fried vizcacha is eaten in some places, mostly outside the main towns and cities.

In the lowland Oriente region, the food usually comes with cooked banana and yuca; eg *Pollo Broaster* is chicken with rice, chips, yuca and fried banana. The bread in this region is often sweet with cheese on top, and the rice bread is also unusual.

In the *pensiones* and cheaper restaurants a basic lunch (*almuerzo* – usually finished by 1300) and dinner (*cena*) are normally available. The *comida del día* is the best value, in any class of restaurant. Good cheap and clean breakfasts are served in the markets in most towns (most restaurants do not open very early in the morning). Lunch can also be obtained in many of the modern market buildings in the main towns; eat only what is cooked in front of you. Dishes cooked in the street are not safe. Llama meat contains parasites (similar to those in pork), so make sure it has been cooked for a long time and is hot when you eat it. Be very careful of salads; they may carry a multitude of amoebic life as well as vile green bacteria.

Drink The several makes of local beer, lager-type, are recommendable; El Inca is a dark beer, sweet, like a stout; the local hot maize drink, *api* (with cloves, cinnamon, lemon and sugar), should be tried (usually US$0.12), as well as *singani*, distilled from grapes, good, cheap and bracing. *Chuflay* is *singani* and 7 Up or Canada Dry (or whatever carbonated drink is available). Good wines are produced by La Concepción vineyard, near Tarija. *Chicha* is a fermented maize drink, popular around Cochabamba. It is not always alcoholic. In the countryside, look for the white flag outside the houses selling *chicha*. Bottled water, *Naragua* and *Viscachani*, is easily available but make sure the seal is unbroken (rain water is sometimes offered as an alternative). There are also several brands of flavoured mineral water, Cayacayani, La Cabaña, Mineragua. The local tap water should not be drunk without first being sterilized. Local water purifier is 'Lugol Fuerte Solución', an iodine-based product, US$1.75 per small bottle; also *iodo* from *farmacias*, US$0.50. For milk, try sachets of Leche Pil (plain, chocolate or strawberry-flavoured), at US$0.25 each.

Shopping

Best Buys Llama-and alpaca-wool knitted and woven items are at least as good as those from Peru and much cheaper. Ponchos, *mantas*, bags, *chullos* (bonnets). Gold and silverware. Musical instruments such as the *charango* (mandolin traditionally with armadillo-shell sound-box, now usually of wood) and the *quena* (Inca flute), and other wooden items.

Holidays and festivals

1 January, New Year's Day; Carnival Week, Monday, Shrove Tuesday, Ash Wednesday; Holy Week: Thursday, Friday and Saturday; 1 May, Labour Day; Corpus Christi (movable); 16 July, La Paz Municipal Holiday; 5-7 August, Independence; 2 November, Day of the Dead; Christmas Day.

Public holidays & festivals

   In Andean regions, *Carnaval Campesino* begins on **Ash Wednesday** and lasts for five days, ending with *Domingo de Tentación* in many small towns. Two weeks before Carnaval is *Jueves de Compadres* and one week before Jueves de Compadres, **Shrove Tuesday** is celebrated as *Martes de Challa*, when house owners make offerings to Pachamama and give drinks to passers-by. **2 February**: *Virgen de la Candelaria*, in rural communities, Copacabana, Santa Cruz. **Palm Sunday** (Domingo de Ramos) is the occasion for parades to the church throughout Bolivia; the devout carry woven palm fronds, then hang them outside their houses. *Corpus Christi* is also a colourful festival. **3 May**: *Fiesta de la Invención de la Santa Cruz*, various parts. **2 June**: *Santísima Trinidad* in Beni Department. **24 June**: *San Juan*, all Bolivia. **29 June**: *San Pedro y San Pablo*, at Tiquina and Tihuanaco. **28 July**: *Fiesta de Santiago* (St James), Altiplano and lake region; Achocalla a convenient place to go to. **16 August**: *San Roque*, patron saint of dogs, the animals are adorned with ribbons and other decorations. **1** and **2 November**: *All Saints and All Souls*, any local cemetery. **18 November**: *Beni's Departmental anniversary*, especially in Trinidad. For other festivals on the Altiplano enquire at hotels or tourist office in La Paz. Remember cities are very quiet on national holidays, but colourful celebrations will be going on in the villages. Beware of water-filled balloons thrown during carnival in even the coldest. Hotels are often full at the most popular places, for instance Copacabana on Good Friday, worth booking in advance.

Sport and special interest travel

Climbing Bolivia has some of the best **mountaineering** in the world, but infrastructure is not well-developed. With a dozen peaks at or above 6,000 m and almost a thousand over 5,000 m, most levels of skill can find something to tempt them. The season is May to Sep, with usually stable conditions Jun to Aug. Proper technical equipment, experience and/or a competent guide are essential to cross glaciers and climb snow and ice safely. The four ranges in which to climb are: the **Cordillera Real**, which has 600 5,000 m plus mountains, including six at 6,000 m or above: Illimani 6,439 m, Ancohuma 6,427 m, Illampu 6,368 m, Chearoco 6,104 m, Huayna Potosí 6,088 m (the most popular) and Chachacomani 6,000 m. A week's acclimatization at the height of La Paz or equivalent is necessary before attempting to climb above 5,000 m. Access is easy from the flat Altiplano, but public transport is not always possible. **Quimza Cruz**, southeast of La Paz, is hard to get to but offers some excellent possibilities. The volcanic **Cordillera Occidental** contains Bolivia's highest peak, Sajama (6,542 m), plus Parinacota and Pomerape, see under Sajama, page 278. The **Apolobamba** range, northwest of La Paz, has many 5,000-m-plus peaks.

Do not expect rescue

Bolivia

Bolivia

Mountain biking Bolivia is blessed with some of the most dramatic terrain in the world and seven months of almost daily crystal clear skies and perfect weather for the sport. Nevertheless, mountain biking is relatively new to Bolivia. Generally speaking, many areas have yet to be explored properly and as of now there is no mountain biking guidebook. Hard-core, experienced, fit and acclimatized riders can choose from a huge range of possibilities. Either take a gamble and figure it out from a map, or find a guide and tackle the real adventure rides. Some popular rides in the La Paz region, achievable by all levels of riders, are **La Cumbre to Coroico**, down the so-called 'world's most dangerous road'; the **Zongo Valley** descent into the Yungas; **Chacaltaya to La Paz**, down from the world's highest ski-slope; **Hasta Sorata**, to the trekking paradise of Sorata. If you are planning on bringing your own mountain bike and doing some hard riding, be prepared for incredibly abusive conditions (and that's in the dry season. In the Dec-Feb wet season, the conditions are often so bad as to be unsafe). There is an almost complete absence of spare parts and very few good bike mechanics. Alternatively, there are now a number of operations offering guided mountain biking tours, but few agencies rent good quality, safe machines. Furthermore, the wealth of good downhill rides has encouraged a number of companies to opt for the 'quick buck' approach, using inappropriate and potentially dangerous bicycles, inexperienced guides, insufficient guide-to-client ratios, and little or no instruction during the ride. Choose a reputable company, guides who speak your language and only opt for the best, US-made bikes.

Trekking There are many opportunities for trekking in Bolivia, from gentle one-day hikes in foothills and valleys to challenging walks of several days from highlands to lowlands on Inca or gold-diggers trails. The best known are: the **Choro**, **Takesi** and **Yunga Cruz** hikes, all of whose starting points can be reached from La Paz; the Mapiri Trail and the Illampu Circuit, both approached from Sorata; and the Apolobamba treks in the northwest. None of these should be attempted without full planning and equipment.

Various treks are outlined in the text, especially near La Paz and from Sorata. Note that all these trails are remote in parts and that robbery and violent attacks have been made on tourists and Bolivians alike. It is advisable to hike these trails in large, organized groups. The local tourist office also produces leaflets with sketch maps on walks in the vicinity of La Paz. There are also some excellent guides available through local clubs. See also Books, in Background.

Nature tourism With more than 40 well-defined ecological regions and the transition zones between them, there is ample scope for enjoying the wildlife of this remarkable country. One of the most popular tours is the four-day trip to the **Salar de Uyuni** (salt flats), which includes the **Lagunas Colorada** and **Verde**. Not only will you see Andean birdlife, but also landscapes of unmatched, stark beauty and you will experience the bitter cold of the high altitudes. For seeing lowland birds and animals, the main options are **Rurrenabaque in the lowlands of the river Beni**, which is a centre for tours to the jungle and to the subtropical pampas, and the **Parque Nacional Amboró**, three hours west of Santa Cruz, containing ecosystems of the Amazon basin, Andean foothills and the savannahs of the Chaco plain. Other opportunities include protected areas, wildlife refuges and rehabilitation centres, the sight of llamas and alpacas on any highland bus journey and even the tracks of dinosaurs.

Health

See Health in the Essentials chapter

For vaccinations, see page 233. Whatever their age, travellers arriving in La Paz by air (too quickly, that is, for a progressive adaptation to the altitude) should rest for half a day, taking very little food and alcoholic drink (drink plenty of non-alcoholic beverages). In Bolivia, do as the Bolivians do: above 3,000 m, walk slowly, very slowly uphill. Local remedies are *maté de coca*, *Sorojchi* and *Micoren* capsules (neither is medically proven). Medical services are sketchy outside the towns and mining camps. Public hospitals charge five bolivianos for consultation, compared with up to and over US$100 in private hospitals. Epidemics are comparatively rare on the Altiplano, but cholera is a problem in times of drought. Malaria, cholera and yellow fever are still problems in the Oriente and Santa Cruz, and hepatitis and Chagas disease are endemic in the warmer parts of the country. Take anti-malaria tablets if visiting the lowlands. A good remedy for stomach amoebas is *Tinidazol*.

La Paz

The minute you arrive in La Paz, the highest capital city in the world, you realise this is no ordinary place. La Paz's airport is at a staggering 4,000 m above sea level. The sight of the city, lying 500 m below, at the bottom of a steep canyon and ringed by snow-peaked mountains, takes your breath away – literally. For at this altitude breathing can be a problem.

The Spaniards chose this odd place for a city on 20 October 1548, to avoid the chill winds of the plateau, and because they had found gold in the Río Choqueyapu, which runs through the canyon.The centre of the city, Plaza Murillo, is at 3,636 m, about 400 m below the level of the Altiplano and the new city of El Alto,perched dramatically on the rim of the canyon.

Phone code: 02
Colour map 6, grid A2
Population: 1.2 million

Bolivia

Getting there Air: El Alto, above La Paz, the highest commercial **airport** in the world (4,058 m) connected to the city by motorway, T281 0122/3. A taxi from the airport takes about 30 mins, US$7 to centre; current prices, including luggage, should be on display at the airport exit (enquire at the tourist office in town, or at the airport). There are 3 main **bus terminals**; the bus station at Plaza Antofagasta, the cemetery district for Sorata, Copacabana and Tiahuanaco, and Villa Fátima for Coroico and the Yungas. Details under Bus, below.

Ins & outs
For more detailed information see Transport, page 256

    Getting around   There are 3 types of city bus: large Fiat buses run by the city corporation, on fairly limited routes; *micros* (Bluebird-type buses), which charge US$0.18 in the centre, US$0.24 from outside centre; and minibuses, US$0.20/0.34, quicker than *micros*. *Trufis* are fixed route collective taxis which charge US$0.30-0.40 pp within city limits. Both taxis and colectivos are white, but recognize colectivos by red number plates.

    Climate   The mean average temperature is 10°C, but this varies greatly during each day; nights are cold. It rains almost every day from Dec to Feb, but the sun usually shines for several hours. The rest of the year is mostly clear and sunny. Snow is rare. Beware of *soroche* (altitude sickness), especially if arriving from much lower altitudes by air.

    Tourist offices   Information office at the bottom end of Av 16 de Julio (Prado) on Plaza del Estudiante on corner with C México. Helpful, English and French spoken, free leaflets, map of La Paz US$2.25. Open Mon-Fri 0830-1200, 1430-1900, Sat 0900-1200. There are smaller offices at Linares 932, which has a good selection of guide books for reference, purchase or exchange, and outside the main bus terminal.

The city's main street runs from Plaza San Francisco as Av Mcal Santa Cruz, then changes to Av 16 de Julio (more commonly known as the Prado) and ends at Plaza del Estudiante. The business quarter, government offices, central university (UMSA) and many of the main hotels and restaurants are situated in this area. The Prado is closed to vehicles every Sunday from 0800 to 1700, when it is lined with handicraft sellers and bookstalls. On the hills above Plaza Mendoza are the poorer parts of the city. From the Plaza del Estudiante, Av Villazón and its extensions lead further southeast towards the wealthier residential districts, which run from Sopocachi to the bed of the valley at Obrajes, 5 km from the centre and 500 m lower than Plaza Murillo. Sopocachi, through which runs Av 6 de Agosto, has many restaurants, discos, bars, etc. Beyond Obrajes are the upper-class districts of Calacoto and La Florida.

Orientation

    El Alto is now a city in its own right, reputedly the fastest growing city in South America. Apart from the district known as Ciudad Satélite, it is almost 100% indigenous; almost everyone is an immigrant from the countryside. Costs are much lower than in La Paz, but construction, etc is more basic. There is a market on Thursday and Sunday in Av Alfonso Ugarte, more interesting for its size than the items for sale. El Alto is connected to La Paz by motorway (toll US$0.50, cycles free). Buses from Plaza Eguino and Pérez Velasco leave regularly for Plaza 16 de Julio, El Alto.

Bolivia

Sights

There are few colonial buildings left in La Paz; probably the best examples are in **Calle Jaén**. Late 19th/early 20th century architecture, often displaying heavy European influence, can be found in the streets around Plaza Murillo, but much of La Paz is modern. **The Plaza del Estudiante** (Plaza Franz Tamayo), or a bit above it, marks a contrast between old and new styles, between the commercial and the more elegant. The **Prado** itself is lined with high-rise blocks dating from the 1960s and 1970s. **Plaza Murillo**, three blocks north of the Prado, is the traditional centre. Facing its formal gardens are the huge, graceful **Cathedral**, the **Palacio Presidencial** in Italian renaissance style, usually known as the Palacio Quemado (burnt palace) twice gutted by fire in its stormy 130-year history, and, on the east side, the **Congreso Nacional**. In front of the Palacio Quemado is a statue of former President Gualberto Villarroel who was dragged into the plaza by an angry mob and hanged in 1946. Across from the Cathedral on C Socabaya is the **Palacio de los Condes de Arana**, see the Museo Nacional del Arte, below. Calle Comercio, running east-west across the Plaza, has most of the

La Paz

N

| 0 | metres | 100 |
| 0 | yards | 100 |

■ **Sleeping**
1 Andes *B1*
2 Continental *B2*
3 Copacabana *D5*
4 El Dorado *D5*
5 España *D5*

6 Estrella Andina *C2*
7 Europa *C5*
8 Galeria *B3*
9 Hostal Claudia *D5*
10 Hostal
  Copacabana *C2*

11 Hostal La Estancia *C4*
12 Hostal República *B4*
13 Ingavi *A3*
14 Italia *B2*
15 La Joya *C1*
16 La Paz City *D4*

stores and shops. On Av Libertador Simón Bolívar (to which Mt Illimani provides a backdrop), is the interesting indigenous **Central Market** (called **Mercado Camacho**), selling food. Further east is the residential district of Miraflores.

At the upper end of Av Mcal Santa Cruz is the **Plaza San Francisco** with the church and monastery of San Francisco, dating from 1549. This is one of the finest examples of colonial religious architecture in South America and well worth seeing. ■ *It opens at 1530. Indigenous weddings can be seen on Sat 1000-1200 otherwise the church opens for Mass at 0700, 0900, 1100 and 1900, Mon-Sat and also at 0800, 1000 and 1200 on Sun.* Behind the San Francisco church a network of narrow cobbled streets rise steeply. Much of this area is a permanent street market. Handicraft shops line the lower part of **Calle Sagárnaga**. The **Mercado de Hechicería**, 'witchcraft market', on Calles Melchor Jiménez and Linares, which cross Santa Cruz above San Francisco, sells fascinating charms, herbs and more gruesome items like llama foetuses. Further up, from Illampu to Rodríguez and in neighbouring streets, is the **Rodríguez market**, for fruit, vegetables and meat (daily, but main days are Saturday and Sunday morning).

Bolivia

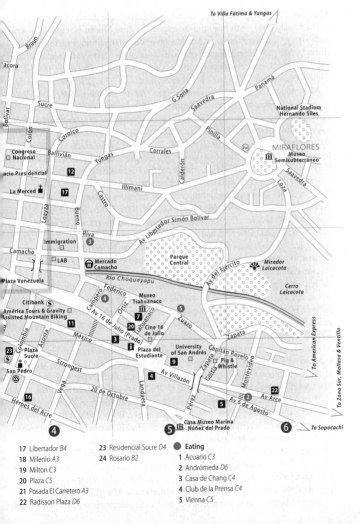

17 Libertador *B4*	**23** Residencial Sucre *D4*	● **Eating**	
18 Milenio *A3*	**24** Rosario *B2*	**1** Acuario *C3*	
19 Milton *C3*		**2** Andrómeda *D6*	
20 Plaza *C5*		**3** Casa de Chang *C4*	
21 Posada El Carretero *A3*		**4** Club de la Prensa *C4*	
22 Radisson Plaza *D6*		**5** Vienna *C5*	

Turning right on Max Paredes, heading west, is **Av Buenos Aires**, one of the liveliest streets in the Indian quarter, where small workshops turn out the costumes and masks for the Gran Poder festival. Continuing west along Max Paredes towards the **cemetery district**, the streets are crammed with stalls selling every imaginable item. Transport converges on the cemetery district (for more information see Transport). Do not expect to go anywhere in a hurry in this part of the city. There are good views of Illimani from these heights.

Other churches include **Santo Domingo** (originally the cathedral), Calles Ingavi y Yanacocha, with its decorative 18th-century façade; **La Merced**, on a plazuela at Calles Colón and Comercio; **San Juan de Dios**, on Loayza between Merced and Camacho, with a carved portico; and **San Sebastián**, the first church to be built in La Paz, in Plaza Alonso de Mendoza (named after the church's builder). On **Plaza Sucre** is **San Pedro** church, Av 20 de Octubre y Colombia, built 1720.

A worthwhile walk is to **Mirador Laicacota** on Av del Ejército, for a great view of La Paz changing from day to night. There are also good views from the delightful **Parque Montículo**, at the eastern end of Av Ecuador, in Sopocachi district.

Museums **Museo de Arte Religioso**, C Socabaya 432, in the baroque palace of the Condes de Arana (built 1775), with beautiful exterior and patio. **Museo Nacional de Arte**, Socabaya y Comercio, has a fine collection of colonial paintings including many works by Melchor Pérez Holguín, considered one of the masters of Andean colonial art, and also exhibits the works of contemporary local artists. ■ *Tue-Fri 0900-1230, 1500-1900, Sat-Sun 1000-1300, US$0.45, students US$0.25, T237 1177.*

Museo de Arte Contemporáneo Plaza, Av 16 de Julio 1698, T233 5905, www.museoplaza.com A new museum in a 19th-century house which has been declared a national monument. There is a good selection of contemporary art from national and international artists. Rotating exhibits, some work for sale. Frequently recommended. ■ *Daily 0900-2100, US$1.50.* **Museo Tiahuanaco** (Tiwanaku), or Museo Nacional de Arqueología: go down the flight of stairs by the Hotel Plaza on the Prado. This modern building, simulating the Tiwanaku style, contains good collections of the arts and crafts of ancient Tiwanaku and items from the eastern jungles. It also has a two room exhibition of gold statuettes and objects found in Lake Titicaca. ■ *Tue-Fri 0900-1230, 1500-1900, Sat 1000-1200, 1500-1830, US$0.75, students US$0.10 (including video show).* **Museo Semisubterráneo**, or Templete del Estadio, is in front of the National Stadium, with restored statues and other artefacts from Tiahuanaco. It's in a sunken garden and much can be seen from street level. No explanations are given and the statues are being badly eroded by pollution. **Museo Nacional de Etnografía y Folklore**, in the palace of the Marqueses de Villaverde, exhibits on the Chipaya, Tarabuceño and Ayoreo Indians, quite good library adjoining. ■ *Tue-Fri 0900-1230, 1500-1900, Sat-Sun 0900-1300, C Ingavi 916, T235 8559.* **Museo de la Coca**, devoted to the coca plant, its history, cultural significance, medical values, political implications. Recommended. ■ *Daily 1000-1800, US$1.05, shop with interesting items for sale, Linares 906.*

The following four museums with well-displayed items in colonial buildings are included on a single ticket, which costs US$0.60, students US$0.15 (free on Sat), from Museo Costumbrista. All are on C Jaén, a picturesque colonial street with many craft shops, worth seeing for itself. ■ *Tue-Fri 0930-1230, 1500-1900, Sat and Sun 1000-1230.*

Museo Costumbrista Miniature displays depict incidents in the history of La Paz and well-known Paceños. Also has miniature replicas of reed rafts used by the Norwegian Thor Heyerdahl, and the Spaniard Kitin Muñoz, to prove their theories of ancient migrations. ■ *T237 8478, Plaza Riosinio, at top of Jaén.*

Museo del Litoral Boliviano, with artefacts of the War of the Pacific, and interesting selection of old maps. ■ *T237 8478, Jaén 789.* **Museo de Metales Preciosos**, well set out with Inca gold artefacts in basement vaults, also ceramics and archaeological exhibits. ■ *Jaén 777, T237 1470.* **Museo Casa Murillo**, the home of Pedro Domingo Murillo, one of the martyrs of the La Paz independence movement of 16

July 1809: a good collection of paintings, furniture and national costumes in a restored colonial house; also two rooms of paintings. ■ *Jaén 790, T237 5273.*

Museo de Instrumentos Musicales de Bolivia, run by Ernesto Cavour, based on 30 years' of research, lessons available, international charango association is based here. Recommended. ■ *Daily except Mon 0930-1230, 1430-1830, US$0.75, students US$0.15, Jaén 711, T233 1075.* **Casa Museo Marina Núñez del Prado**, excellent collection of her sculptures housed in the family mansion. ■ *Tue-Fri 0930-1300, 1500-1900, Sat-Mon 0930-1300, US$0.75, students US$0.30, T/F232 4906, Ecuador 2034.* **Museo Tambo Quirquincho**, in a restored colonial building, modern painting and sculpture, carnival masks, silver, early 20th century photography and city plans. Recommended. ■ *Tue-Fri, 0930-1230, 1500-1900, Sat-Sun, 1000-1230, US$0.15 (Sat and students free), C Evaristo Valle, near Plaza Mendoza.* **Museo de Textiles Andinos Bolivianos** Good displays of textiles from around the country, with detailed explanations and a knowledgeable owner. ■ *Mon-Sat 0800-1200, 1400-1830, Sun 1000-1300, T224 3601, Plaza Benito Juárez 488, Miraflores.*

Excursions

A worthwhile nearby excursion is to Río Abajo. Through the suburbs of Calacoto and La Florida follow the river road past picnic spots and through some weird rock formations, known as the Valle de la Luna, or 'Moon Valley'. About 3 km from the bridge at Calacoto the road forks. Get out of the minibus (see below) at the turning and walk a few minutes east to the Valle entrance, or get out at the football field which is by the entrance. Take good shoes and water. Just past the Valle de la Luna is **Mallasa** where several small roadside restaurants and cafés have opened; also **B** *Oberland*, T274 5040, www.h-oberland.com, a Swiss-owned, chalet-style restaurant (excellent) and hotel resort, gardens, cabañas, sauna, pool (open to public (US$2), beach volley, tennis, permits camping with vehicle. **The zoo** is on the road to Río Abajo, entrance just past Mallasa after Valle de la Luna, in beautiful, wide open park-like setting. Conditions for the animals and birds are not uniformly good. The climate in this valley is always much warmer than in the city. ■ *Daily 0900-1700, US$0.50 adults, US$0.25 children.*

■ *Getting there: Minibus A can be caught on the Prado. If you do not want to walk in the valley, stay on the bus to the end of the line and take a return bus, 2 hrs in all. Alternatively take Micro 11 ('Aranjuez'-large, not small bus) from C Sagárnaga, near Plaza San Francisco, US$0.65, and ask driver where to get off. Most of the local travel agents organize tours to the Valle de la Luna. These are very brief, 5 mins stop for photos in a US$15 tour of La Paz and surroundings; taxis cost US$6.*

Valle de la Luna

Bolivia

Essentials

Sleeping
Try to arrive early in the day as hotels, especially cheaper ones, can be hard to find. Prices include 20% tax and service charge

LL *Europa*, Tiahuanacu 64, T231 5656 (0800-5656), PO Box 1800, behind *Plaza, unico@hotel-europa-bolivia.com* Difficult access but excellent facilities (*Summit Group*). Recommended. **LL** *Presidente*, Potosí 920 y Sanjines, T240 6666, F240 7240. Includes breakfast, 'the highest 5-star in the world', pool, gym and sauna all open to non-residents, bar, disco, excellent service, comfortable, good food. Recommended. **LL** *Radisson Plaza*, Av Arce 2177, T244 1111, radissonbolivia@usa.net 5-star hotel with all facilities, excellent buffet in restaurant (see Eating below). **L** *Plaza*, Av 16 de Julio 1789, T237 8311, plazabolivia@usa.net Good value restaurant (see below), peña show on Fri. **AL** *El Rey Palace*, Av 20 de Octubre 1947, T239 3016, hotelrey@caoba.intelnet.bo Includes breakfast, large suites, excellent restaurant, stylish, modern. **AL** *Gran Hotel París*, Plaza Murillo esq Bolívar, T220 3030, hparis@caoba.intelnet.bo Includes breakfast, English spoken, elegant restaurant. **A** *Gloria*, Potosí 909, T240 7070, www.gloria-tours-bolivia.com 2 restaurants, 1 on top floor with good view, 1 vegetarian, excellent food and service (see below). Recommended. **A** *Libertador*, Obispo Cárdenas 1421, T231 3434, libertad@ceibo.entelnet.bo Good cheap restaurant, helpful, baggage stored. Highly recommended.

B *El Dorado*, Av Villazón, T236 3403, F239 1438. With breakfast, digital phones, safe luggage deposit, secure parking nearby. **B** *Galería*, C Santa Cruz 583, T246 1015, F246 1253. **C** without bath, lots of daylight, includes breakfast, quiet, good value. **B** *Hostal Naira*, Sagárnaga 161, T235 5645, F231 1214. Hot water, comfortable, cafeteria for breakfast, above *Peña Naira*. **B** *Rosario*, Illampu 704, Casilla 442, T245 1658, www.hotelrosario.com *Turisbus* travel agency downstairs (see Tour operators), 3-star, includes excellent buffet breakfast, very popular with foreigners, cable TV, modem connection, sauna, laundry, internet café *Jiwhaki* (free for guests, great view), good restaurant, stores luggage, very helpful staff.

La Paz centre

Sleeping
1 Arcabucero
2 Austria
3 El Alem
4 El Lobo
5 Gloria
6 Gran Hotel París
7 Hostal Happy Days
8 Hostal Naira
9 Hostería Blanquita
10 Julia Rojo Briseño
11 Majestic
12 Presidente
13 Residencial Plaza
14 Sagárnaga
15 Señorial
16 Torino

Eating
1 100% Natural
2 Alexander Coffee Shop
3 Anglo Colonial
4 Café Confitería de la Paz
5 Casa del Corregidor
6 Dos Laureles
7 Jackie Chan
8 Jiskáuta & Le Pot-Pourri des Gourmets
9 La Diligencia Churrascaría
10 Laksmi
11 Los Escudos
12 Wall St Bistro-Café

Highly recommended. Next door is **C** *Estrella Andina*, Illampu 716 esq Aroma, T456421, F451401. With breakfast, cheaper without bath, family run, tidy, helpful, internet access. **C** *Copacabana*, Av 16 de Julio 1802, T235 2244, F232 7390. Restaurant and grill room (lunch only at latter), good service, safe deposit, rooms a bit small. Recommended. **C** *Hostería Blanquita*, Santa Cruz 242, T/F245 7495. Includes breakfast, hot showers, comfortable, 'baroque'. **C** *Sagárnaga*, Sagárnaga 326, T235 0252, F236 0831. **D** without bath, including basic restaurant, laundry, English spoken, lift, *peña*, ATM. **C-D** *Hostal República*, Comercio 1455, T220 2742, F220 2782. **D** without bath, old house of former president, hot water, inadequate shared bathrooms, luggage stored, helpful, laundry service, café, very popular with cyclists, usually full; separate house also available, **AL** sleeps 6, all facilities. **C-D** *La Joya*, Max Paredes 541, T245 3841, www.hoteljoya.com.bo Phone, **E** without bath or TV, **E-F** pp in low season, modern and comfy, lift, laundry, includes breakfast, popular area with free pickup from town centre, close to bus and train station.

D *Arcabucero*, C Viluyo 307, Linares (close to Museo de Coca), T/F 231 3473. Pleasant new rooms in converted colonial house, excellent value, breakfast extra. **D** *Condeza*, Diagonal Juan XXII 190, entre Illampu y Linares, T231 1317. Hot water, TV, good. **D** *Continental*, Illampu 626, T/F245 1176. **E** without bath, nice rooms, stores luggage. **D** *Hostal Copacabana*, Illampu 734, T245 1626, combicop@ceibo.intelnet.bo Hot water, **E** without bath, includes breakfast, changes TCs. **D** *El Alem*, Sagárnaga 334, T236 7400. Hot water, **E** pp without bath, helpful, secure, laundry service, includes breakfast, has travel agency. **D** *El Valle*, Evaristo Valle 153, T245 6085. **E** with shared bath, central, large rooms, good beds, helpful, quiet. Recommended. **D** *España*, Av 6 de Agosto 2074, T244 2643, F244 1329. Hot water, cheaper without bath, very nice, quiet, restaurant. **D** *Hostal Claudia*, Av Villazón 1965, T237 2917. **E** without bath, secure. Recommended. **D** *Hostal La Estancia*, México 1559, T231 0336, F236 9242. With breakfast, TV, helpful, good restaurant. **D** *Latino*, Junín near Sucre, T228 2828, F228 0340. Hot water, TV, luggage stored, helpful. **D** *Majestic*, Santa Cruz 359 esq Ilampu T245 1628. Comfortable, laundry, safe. Recommended. **D** *Milton*, Illampu y Calderón No 1124, T236 8003, F236 5849, PO Box 5118. Hot water, includes breakfast, laundry, safe parking around corner, popular, will store luggage, excellent views from roof, good restaurant. **D** *Res Sucre*, Colombia 340, on Plaza San Pedro, T249 2038, F248 6723. Cheaper without bath, quiet area, hot water, big rooms, luggage stored, helpful. Recommended. **D** *Señorial*, Yanacocha 540, Casilla 5081, T240 6042. Rooms with or without bath (also TV), hot water, kitchen, laundry, café, helpful, pleasant, good. **D** *Tambo de Oro*, Armentia 367, T228 1565, F228 2181. Near bus station, hot showers, TV, helpful, good value, safe for luggage.

E *Hostal Happy Days*, Sagárnaga 229, T231 4759, happydays@zuper.net Hot water, TV, popular, internet café next door. **E** *Ingavi*, Ingavi 727, T232 3645. Nice rooms with hot water, good value. **E** *Julia Rojo Briseño*, Murillo 1060, p 10, press 1001 on bellpush outside, T231 0236, juliarojo@hotmail.com Family house, 1 block from central post office, use of phone, fax and washing machine, includes breakfast (US$60 for a week for 2). **E** *Torino*, Socabaya 457, T240 6003. Ask for rooms in new section, **F** without bath, dingy, run-down rooms in old

Bolivia

Bolivia

section, free book exchange, good (if pricey) internet café and breakfast spot next door (delicious bread!), 0100 cyrfew. **E-F** *El Lobo*, Santa Cruz 441 – see Eating. **F** *Alojamiento Illimani*, Av Illimani 1817. Hot water, quiet and safe, uncomfortable beds, laundry facilities, often full. **F** *Andes*, Av Manco Kapac 364, T245 5327. Cheaper without bath, hot water, includes breakfast, stores luggage, good restaurant. Recommended. **F** *Austria*, Yanacocha 531, T240 8540. Without bath, **G** pp in shared room, hot water but long queues for showers, safe deposit, laundry, TV, helpful daytime staff, mainly dingy rooms, book in advance, overpriced. **F** *Italia*, Av Manco Kapac 303, T245 6710. Hot water, luggage store, off-street motorcycle parking. Recommended, but noisy disco Fri and Sat night. **F** *La Paz City*, Acosta 487, T249 4565. Quiet, stores luggage, secure, basic, shared hot showers. **F** *Posada El Carretero*, Catacora 1056, entre Junín y Yanacocha, T228 5271. Double, single and dormitory rooms, safe deposit, laundry service, kitchen, reports book, information, backpackers' place, Spanish lessons with William Ortiz, internet café. **F** *Res Plaza*, Plaza Pérez Velasco 785, T240 6099. Nice old building, hot water, cheaper without bath, laundry and luggage storage facilities, helpful. **F** *El Solario*, Murillo 776, T236 7963. Central, luggage store, good bathrooms, good value. **G** *Res Imperial*, Pando, esq Incachaca. Hot water 24 hrs, stores luggage, cheap laundry. Recommended. **G** *Milenio*, Jiménez 818 (no sign), T245 1421. Large family house, helpful owner, quiet, kitchen, limited hot showers.

Youth Hostel *Asociación Boliviana de Albergues Juveniles*, ABAJ, has hostels around the country, which are given in the text. To use hostels you must have a Bolivian YHA card, US$2, 2 photos needed, available from ABAJ, which also sells international cards, US$20. **G** *Ciudad Satélite*, Plan 561, Calle 3-1073, T812341/015-76896, sugarsplash@usa.net Unaffiliated, hot showers, use of kitchen, internet access, Spanish taught (*Fastalk*), take minibus 'Satélite' from Prado and get off at Mercado Satélite, then phone.

Camping No organized site, but Mallasa (Municipal Park, unmarked, turn left at Aldeas Infantiles SOS), Valencia and Palca below the suburb of La Florida have been recommended. For camping equipment and camping gas: *Andean Summits*, Comercio Doryan, Sagárnaga y Murillo, T/F242 2106, www.andeansummits.com, sells white gas, *bencina blanca*, US$5 per litre. *Caza y Pesca*, Edif Handal Center, no 9, Av Mcal Santa Cruz y Socabaya, T240 9209. Other camping shops on Granjero, entre Murillo e Illampu. Kerosene for pressure stoves is available from a pump in Plaza Alexander, Pando e Inca. Public showers at Duchas La Paz, 20 de Octubre 1677.

Restaurants with international cuisine are mainly on Av 16 de Julio (the Prado), Av 6 de Agosto and Av 20 de Octubre. Service charges and tax of up to 23% are usually included on bill but it's customary to leave tip of 10% anyway.

Eating

Av 16 de Julio There are many snack bars, including **Confitería Elis** (1497 and 1800), good lunches, excellent soups, breakfasts and pastries, not cheap. Also *Eli's Pizza Express* in same block. English spoken, open daily including holidays (also at Comercio 914). *Alexander Coffee Shop*, No 1832, also Potosí 1091. Excellent coffee, muffins, cakes and good, cheap salads and sandwiches, open Mon-Fri 0800-2230, Sat and Sun 0900-2230. Recommended. Opposite *Eli's* is *Unicornio* (1940). Great ice cream, lunch buffet upstairs. *Utama*, in *Plaza* hotel (1789). Excellent salad bar, great value lunch, excellent view. Highly recommended.

Street numbers given in brackets

    Av Mcal Santa Cruz *Los Escudos* (1223, Edif Club de La Paz, T232 2028). Munich-type bierkeller with fixed 4-course lunch, good *peña* on Fri and Sat nights (2100-0100), US$5 cover charge. *La Fiesta* (1066). Excellent, good lunches. *Jackie Chan*, Cochabamba 100 (just south of Av Mcal Santa Cruz). Good value Chinese, popular with locals. *Restaurant Verona*, esq Colón. Economical *plato del día*, popular in the evenings.

    South of the Prado *Angelo Colonial*, Linares 922. Excellent food and ambience, candlelight, antiques, internet access too, open early for breakfast. *Casa del Corregidor*, Murillo 1040, T236 3633. Centrally heated, Spanish colonial restaurant with Bolivian and European dishes, excellent food, bar. *Dos Laureles*, Evaristo Valle 120. Good cheap 4-course lunch. Recommended. *Jiskáuta*, Linares 906, Museo de la Coca. Just six tables, graffiti over walls and ceiling from past customers, great cheap Mexican and vegetarian food. Recommended.

El Lobo, Santa Cruz 441. Huge portions, Israeli dishes, good meeting place, noticeboard, very popular (rooms to rent next door, **E**, **F** without bath). *Pizzería Romana*, Santa Cruz 260. Good pizzas and pastas, good value. *Le Pot-Pourri des Gourmets*, Linares 888, close to Sagárnaga. Bolivian and a variety of main courses including vegetarian, *almuerzo* US$2, pastries, snacks, hot and cold drinks, quiet, homely, music. *Tambo Colonial*, in *Res Rosario* (see above). Excellent local and international cuisine, good salad bar, huge buffet breakfast, *peña* at weekend. Recommended.

Numerous cheap places to eat

North of the Prado *Club de la Prensa*, C Campero. In a pleasant garden, limited menu is typical Bolivian – meat only, in copious quantities – lively company. *Café Confitería de la Paz*, Camacho 1202, on the corner where Ayacucho joins Av Mcal Santa Cruz. Good tea room, traditional, meeting place for businessmen and politicians, great coffee and cakes. *Café Maxim*, restaurant in *Gran Hotel París*, Plaza Murillo esq Bolívar. Good food. *Tranquera*, Potosí 1008, Centro Comercial Cristal, planta 3. Good set lunches US$3. **Also on Potosí:** *La Kantuta*, in *Hotel Presidente*, No 920. Excellent food, good service. *La Fregata*, Yanacocha 525. Good value. *Wall Street Bistro-Café*, Camacho 1363 entre Loayza y Colón. Good, not cheap (discount for ISIC card holders), owner speaks English and French (opens 0900 on Sun). *Casa de Chang*, Juan de la Riva 1522. Good, set Chinese meals. *Chifa Estrella*, opposite Plaza San Francisco between Comercio y Potosí. Good Chinese, large portions. *El Calicanto*, Sanjines 467. Good food including regional specialities, renovated colonial house, live music at weekends, US$5. *La Casa de los Paceños*, Sucre 856. Excellent Bolivian food. There are many other eating places on C Comercio: for example *La Diligencia Churrascaría*, No 803, good grill and set meals, open 1200-2400 daily. Recommended.

Near Plaza del Estudiante *Luigi's Pizzería*, Villazón 2048. Good. *Andrómeda*, Arce 2116, T354723. European-style including a few vegetarian dishes, excellent US$3 lunch. *Jalapeños*, Arce 2549. Excellent Mexican dishes for US$5-6.50. Just behind it, Pasaje Pinilla 2557, is *Wagamama* (Tue-Sat 1200-1430, 1900-2000, Sun 1200-1500, closed Mon) which serves huge plates of amazing sushi for under US$10. Recommended. *Radisson Plaza Hotel*, Av Arce 2177, T244 1111, radissonbolivia@usa.net Excellent buffet in 5-star setting, Mon and Wed, 2000-2300, US$5.50, delicious, friendly to backpackers. *Mongo's*, Hnos Manchego 2444, near Plaza Isabela la Católica. Open Mon-Thu 1000-0130, Fri-Sun 1800-0300, set lunch US$3-4, burgers and great fish and chips, 3 large wood fires, very Western, very popular. *Chifa Emy*, Capitán Ravelo 2351, esq Belizario Salinas. Daily 1100-1500, 1830-2300 (Thu-Sat until 0200), best Chinese in town, shows Wed-Fri 2130. *Vienna*, Federico Zuazo 1905, Casilla 56, T244 1660, www.restaurantvienna.com German, Austrian and local food, excellent food and service, very popular with Bolivians and foreigners, open Mon-Fri 1200-1400, 1830-2200, Sun 1200-1430. On Plaza del Estudiante, *Café Ciudad*. 24 hr coffee shop, full menu, good but expensive, internet service.

See also under Entertainment, below

In the Sopocachi district Up-market Italian cuisine at *Pronto*, Jáuregui 2248, T244 1369, in basement, Mon-Sat 1830-2230. Beautiful decor, around US$7 pp, popular, good service. Opposite is **Reineke Fuchs**, Jáuregui 2241. Mon-Sat 1800-0100, many European beers and food. **La Bohème**, Guachalla 448, and adjacent *Confitería Creperie*, both French, good. For curry, **Restaurant Indio**, in front of Mercado Sopacachi, near the corner of Sánchez Lima. Owners Bob and Sonya also have gourmet coffees and imported Earl Grey tea. **On Av 6 de Agosto**: *El Arriero* (No 2535, Casa Argentina). Best barbecue with large portions, US$11.50 pp. **Kuchen Stube**, Rosendo Gutiérrez 461. Excellent cakes, coffee and German specialities, Mon 1200-1900, Tue-Fri 0900-2000, Sat-Sun 1000-1230, 1430-1900. **On Av 20 de Octubre:** *El Gaucho*, No 2041. Steakhouse, good. **Gringo Limón**, esq Salazar. Food by weight, also take-away. **La Quebecoise**, near Plaza Abaroa (No 2355). French Canadian, good value, pleasant atmosphere.

Cevicherías *Acuario*, Rodríguez 203. **Cevichería El Pulpo** at Galería Los Cántaros, Av Montenegro 1337, local 3, next to *Automanía*. On Av Saavedra, Miraflores Sur: **Y se Llama Perú**, No 1911, and **Contigo Perú**, No 1983, both with seafood and fish menu, good.

Vegetarian restaurants *Hotel Gloria*, Potosí 909. Very popular for *almuerzo*, US$3, be there by 1200 for a table, also buffet breakfast and dinner after 1900 for US$2.20, Sun 0700-1000 only. **Laksmi**, Sagárnaga 213, p 2. Vegetarian and vegan menu, set lunch US$1, closed Sun. Recommended. **100% Natural**, Sagárnaga 345. Full range of healthy, tasty fast foods, good breakfasts, closed Sun. **El Vegetariano**, Loayza 400 block, next to *Hotel Viena*. Good, breakfast, lunch (*almuerzo* US$1.25) and dinner.

For strictly limited budgets and strong stomachs is **Comedor Popular**, often referred to as **Comedor Familiar**, cheap but filling local meals around US$0.80-1.50, available at San Francisco, Camacho, Rodríguez and Lanza markets. Stalls in the markets sell cheap burgers; don't have *ají*, mayo or mustard and watch it being cooked. Bread from street vendors and Cochabamba wholemeal bread (*pan integral*), sold at the main markets, is recommended.

Calacoto This area begins after the bridge at La Florida beside the attractive Plaza Humboldt. The main road, Av Ballivián, begins at C 8 and continues up the hill to the shopping district of San Miguel on C 21 (about a 20 min walk). **On Av Ballivián:** on the left side between C 9 y 10 is **Rumors**, American/Mexican bar, restaurant, excellent music, popular late night place. **Puerto del Sol**, on the left, esq C 11, good Chinese. Opposite is an excellent arts and handicrafts shop, weavings, ceramics, silver etc. Between C 15 y 16 on the left is **The Britannia**, open daily from 1700, closed Sun, cosy, popular, bar snacks. Next door No 969 is **Abracadabra**, open 7 days for lunch and dinner, great ribs and best hamburgers and pizza in town, American owner. The **Ronería** next door is a very popular bar. 5-min walk further up the hill on the right is C 21 (the church of San Miguel is on the corner) which has a huge variety of shops, fast-food cafés, banks and a post office. On Muñoz Reyes *are* **Chalet la Suisse**, No 1710, excellent fondue, steaks, expensive. **Sabores Peruanos**, No 1714, Peruvian. *El Nuevo Galeon*, No 1210, for excellent seafood. On Av Mcal de Montenegro is **Alexander Coffee Shop**, good coffee and sandwiches, and others.

Situated in The Valley 15 mins south of the centre, 'La Zona Sur' (US$0.40 by trufi, US$0.30 by minibus) is home to the resident foreign community. It has international shopping centres, supermarkets with imported items and some of the best restaurants and bars in La Paz

Best entertainment for visitors are the folk shows (*peñas*), which present the wide variety of local musical instruments. Enquire at the *Rumillajta* shop (in the *galería* close to San Francisco church) about future performances by the famous folk group of that name. Good *peña* at **Casa del Corregidor**, see under Eating above, dinner show Mon-Thu, no cover charge, Fri and Sat *peña* US$4, both 2100, colonial atmosphere, traditional music and dance). See under Eating for **Los Escudos** and **El Calicanto**. **Marko Tambo**, Jaén 710. US$7 all inclusive, repeatedly recommended (also sells woven goods). **El Parnaso**, Sagárnaga 189, T231 6827. Purely for tourists but a good way to see local costumes and dancing. **Bocaisapo**, Indaburo 654 y Jaén. Live music and no cover charge. If you wish to lean a local instrument, contact **Academia 'Walisuma'**, Av Apumalla 512, old Cemetery District between José M Asin and José M Aliaga, Pedro Mar teaches bi-lingual courses, English/Spanish, for *quena*, *zampoña* and *charango*. Also **Eddy Lima**, Sagárnaga 177, Edif Galacentro, eddylima@hotmail.com "Master of the Bolivian flute".

Entertainment
For up-to-the-minute information, check Quéhacer, free magazine with Saturday's La Razón, or visit www.la-razon.com There's also a free magazine called Happening found in pubs and cafés in Spanish but easy to understand www.hpng.net

Salsa At **La Salsa del Loro**, Rosendo Gutiérrez y Av 6 de Agosto. Open Thu, Fri and Sat evening (salsa lessons at *Gym Cec*, Illampu 868, p 1, T231 0158, US$4 per hour). **Equinoccio**, Sánchez Lima 2191. Top venue for live music and bar. **Café Montmartre**, Fernando

Bolivia

Bolivia

 The Alacitas Fair

One of the most intriguing items for sale in Andean markets is Ekeko, the god of good fortune and plenty and one of the most endearing of the Aymara folk legends. He is a cheery, avuncular little chap, with a happy face, a pot belly and short legs. His image, usually in plaster of Paris, is laden with various household items, as well as sweets, confetti and streamers, food, and with a cigarette dangling cheekily from his lower lip. Believers say that these statues only bring luck if they are received as gifts. The Ekeko occupies a central role in the fesitval of Alacitas, the Feast of Plenty, which takes place in La Paz at the end of January. Everything under the sun can be bought in miniature: houses, trucks, buses, suitcases, university diplomas; you name it, you'll find it here. The idea is to have your mini-purchase blessed by a Yatiri, an Aymara priest, and the real thing will be yours within the year.

Guachalla 399 y 20 de Octubre, next to *Alliance Française*, T244 2801. Good French menu, set lunch US$3.50, fashionable bar with live music some weekends, open 1200-1500, 1700-0200, closed Sun. *Pig and Whistle*, Goitia 155, T239 0429. Serves a selection of beers and whiskies. *Deadstroke*, Av 6 de Agosto 2460. Pub, café and billiards bar, food, drinks, billiards, pool and other games, opens 1700. *La Luna*, Oruro 197 esq Murillo. Best bar in the centre of town, opens 2200, good cocktails. *Theolonius Jazz Bar*, 20 de Octubre 2172, T233 7806. Tue-Sat from 1700. *Café en Azul*, 20 de Octubre 2371. Great bohemian atmosphere. *Forum Disco*, Sanjinez 2908, a few blocks beyond Plaza España. Very popular, good variety of music, US$5 cover charge including couple of drinks. *Underground*, Pasaje Medinacelli 2234, Sopocachi. Very popular nightclub with *paceños* and foreigners on Thu and Fri night.

Teatro Municipal Alberto Saavedra Pérez has a regular schedule of plays, opera, ballet and classical concerts, at Sanjines y Indaburo. The National Symphony Orchestra is very good and gives inexpensive concerts. Next door is the *Teatro Municipal de Cámara*, a small studio-theatre which shows dance, drama, music and poetry. *Casa Municipal de la Cultura 'Franz Tamayo'*, almost opposite Plaza San Francisco, hosts a variety of exhibitions, paintings, sculpture, photography, videos, etc, most of which are free. It publishes a monthly guide to cultural events, free from the information desk at the entrance. The *Palacio Chico*, Ayacucho y Potosí, in old Correo, operated by the *Secretaría Nacional de Cultura*, also has exhibitions (good for modern art), concerts and ballet, Mon-Fri 0900-1230, 1500-1900, closed at weekends, free. It is also in charge of many regional museums. Listings available in Palacio Chico. **Cinemas** show films mainly in English with Spanish subtitles. Best are *16 de Julio* (T244 1099) and *Monje Campero* (T233 0192; both on Av 16 de Julio) and *6 de Agosto* (Av 6 de Agosto, T244 2629). Expect to pay around US$2.50. The *Cinemateca Boliviana*, Capitán Ravelo y Rosendo Gutiérrez, 2 blocks from Puente de las Américas, is La Paz's art film centre with festivals, courses, etc, US$1.20, students US$0.60.

Festivals Jan/Feb: the *Alacitas Fair*, from 24 Jan to first week of Feb, in Parque Central up from Av del Ejército, also in Plaza Sucre/San Pedro (see box). **End May/early Jun** *Festividad del Señor de Gran Poder*, the most important festival of the year, with a huge procession of costumed and masked dancers on the third Sat after Trinity. **Jul** *Fiestas de Julio*, a month of concerts and performances at the Teatro Municipal, offers a wide variety of music, including the University Folkloric Festival. **8 Dec**, festival around Plaza España, not very large, but colourful and noisy. On **New Year's Eve** fireworks are let off and make a spectacular sight; view from higher up. See also page 238 for national holidays and festivals outside La Paz.

Shopping
Look around and bargain first. In the low season many shops close Sat afternoon and Sun

There are good jewellery stores throughout the city: for example *Joyería Cosmos*, Handal Center, Loc 13, Socabaya y Av Mcal Santa Cruz. Inca and Bolivian designs in gold and silver, colonial objects. Visit the gold factories for lower prices and special orders. There is inexpensive silver and jewellery in the little cabinets outside Lanza market on Av Santa Cruz. Up Sagárnaga, by the side of San Francisco church (behind which are many handicraft stalls in the Mercado Artesanal), are booths and small stores with interesting local items of all sorts, best value on Sun morning when prices are reduced. The lower end of Sagárnaga is best for antiques. At Sagárnaga 177 is an entire gallery of handicraft shops. *Millma*, Sagárnaga 225, and in *Hotel Plaza*. For alpaca sweaters (made in their own factory) and antique and rare textiles. *Wari*, unit 12, Comercio Doryan, Sagárnaga y Murillo, always closes Sat afternoon. Will make to measure very quickly, English spoken, prices reasonable. Also *Toshy* on Sagárnaga for top quality knitwear (closed Sat afternoon). *Mother Earth*, Linares 870. High-quality alpaca sweaters with natural dyes. Good quality alpaca goods also at *LAM* shops on Sagárnaga. *Artesanía Sorata*, Linares 862, and Sagárnaga 311. Mon-Sat 0930-1900 (and Sun 1000-1800 high season), specializes in dolls, sweaters and weavings. On Linares, between Sagárnaga and Santa Cruz, high quality alpaca goods priced in US$, also in *Comercio Doryan*, Sagárnaga y Murillo. *Comart Tukuypai*, Linares 958, T/F231 2686, www.terranova.nu/comart High-quality textiles from an artisan community association. At *Kunturi*, Nicolás Acosta 783, T249 4350, you will find wonderful handicrafts produced by the Institute for the Handicapped, including embroidered cards.

Bookshops *Los Amigos del Libro*, Mercado 1315, T220 4321, also Edif Alameda, Av 16 de Julio (1 block from *Plaza Hotel*), Av Montenegro y C 18 (San Miguel) and El Alto airport. They sell a few tourist maps of the region from Puno to the Yungas, and walking-tour guides, and will also ship books. *Gisbert*, Comercio 1270, libgis@ceibo.entelnet.bo Books, maps, stationery, will ship overseas. *Multi-Libro*, Loayza 233, T239 1996. Small, good for maps, politics, religion, psychology etc. *Librería Plural*, Pedro Salazar 489, Plaza Abaroa. Recommended. *Librería e Importaciones*, Av Mcal Santa Cruz y Colón. Has an excellent stock of Aymara books. *Yachaywasi*, just below Plaza del Estudinate, opposite *Hotel Eldorado*. Large selection, popular with students. Historian Antonio Paredes-Candia has a kiosk selling rare historical works on a walkway below street level on Colón near Ayacucho (also on the Prado on Sun). Other bookstalls here and on a small street off Av Ismael Montes, overlooking Plaza San Francisco.

Cycle spares See *Gravity Assisted Mountain Biking* under *América Tours* in Tour operators, below, very knowledgeable, www.gravitybolivia.com In Calacoto: *Bicicar* (Trek Bikes), Av Montenegro y C 18, local 2. *Nosiglia Sport* (Cannondale), Av Costanera 28, T274 9904, nossport@ceibo.entelnet.bo *Massa* (Raleigh and Nishiki), C 21 No 8341, T/F279 7820.

Markets In addition to those mentioned in Sights, above, the 5-km square El Alto market is on Thu and Sun (the latter is bigger). Take a Ceja bus from along the Prado to Desvío. At the toll plaza on the autopista, change buses for one marked 16 de Julio; most other passengers will be doing the same, follow them. Arrive around 1000 and stay to 1600. Goods are very cheap. Don't take anything of value, just a black bin liner to carry your purchases. The Mercado Sopocachi is a well-stocked covered market selling foodstuffs, kitchen supplies, etc. *The Tourist Office has a full list of all markets*

Musical instruments *Rumillajta*, 1 of the Galería shops adjacent to the San Francisco church entrance. Many shops on Sagárnaga/Linares, for example *El Guitarrón*, Sagárnaga 303 esq Linares, *Marka 'Wi*, No 851.

Shopping malls *Shopping Norte*, Potosí y Socabaya, modern mall with restaurants and expensive merchandise. *Supermercado Ketal*, Ballivián esq C 15, Calacoto, is huge, also on C 21, San Miguel, and Av Arce, opposite *Jalapeños*. *Hipermaxi* in Miraflores, Cuba y Brazil, much cheaper and good for trekking food.

Football: is popular and played on Wed and Sun at the Siles Stadium in Miraflores (Micro A) and at Cañada Strongest. There are reserved seats. **Golf**: *Mallasilla*, the world's highest course, 3,318 m. Non-members can play at Mallasilla on weekdays: green fee US$90 on Sun, US$50 weekdays, when it is empty, no need to book. Club hire is US$10 and a caddy (compulsory) also costs US$10. The course is in good condition and beautiful (take water). **Snooker/pool**: *San Luis*, Edif México, 2do Sótano, C México 1411. *Picco's*, Edif 16 de Julio, Av 16 de Julio 1566. Both have good tables and friendly atmosphere. **YMCA sportsground** **Sport**

and **gymnasium**: opposite the University of San Andrés, Av Villazón, and clubhouse open to the public, Av 20 de Octubre 1839 (table tennis, billiards, etc). Regular meetings Tue and Thu 1930 of a mountaineering group which runs weekend trips. See also Trekking, Climbing and Skiing below.

Tour operators *Akhamani Trek*, Illampu 707, T237 5680, tourtrek@ceibo.entelnet.bo Trekking in Sorata *Those listed are all* and Coroico, also day trips, English spoken, safe, good porters, well-organized. *recommended.* *América Tours*, Av 16 de Julio 1490, T237 4204, F231 0023, Casilla 2568, jmiranda@ *Flight tickets are the* ceibo.entelnet.bo and *Gravity Assisted Mountain Biking*, www.gravitybolivia.com Cul- *same price at airlines* tural and ecotourism trips to many parts of the country (including the renowned *Chalalan* *and agencies* *Lodge* near Rurrenabaque and Parque Nacional Noel Kempf Mercado), trekking, horse riding and mountain biking (including to Coroico, US$49), English spoken. Both companies are highly professional. *Turismo Balsa*, Capitán Ravelo 2104, T244 0817, turismo_balsa@megalink.com and Av 16 de Julio 1650, T235 4049, F237 1898. City and local tours (recommended), see also under Puerto Pérez, page 263. *Camel Travel*, Murillo 904, T231 0070, www.boliviatrek.com Gravity assisted mountain biking, climbing, trekking, English and German spoken. *Carmoar Tours*, C Bueno 159, headed by Günther Ruttger T231 7202, carmoar@zuper.net Has information and maps for the Inca Trail to Coroico, rents trekking gear. *Crillon Tours*, PO Box 4785, Av Camacho 1223, Casilla 4785, T233 7533, www.titicaca.com With 24-hr ATM for cash on credit cards. In USA, 1450 South Bayshore Dr, suite 815, Miami, FL 33131, T305-358 5353, F305-372 0054, darius@titicaca.com Joint scheduled tours with Lima arranged. Full details of their Lake Titicaca services will be found on page 263. *Detour*, Av Mariscal Santa Cruz, Edif Camara Nacional de Comercio, T236 1626. Good for flight tickets. *Diana Tours*, Sagárnaga 326, T235 1158, F236 0831. Some English spoken, tours to Coroico and Tiwanaku, bus to Puno US$12. *Explore Bolivia*, Sagárnaga 339, Galería Sagárnaga of 1, T/F239 1810, explobol@ceibo.entelnet.bo Adventure sports, good bikes (Trek). *Exprinter*, Av 6 de Agosto 2455 Edif Hilda p1, T244 2442, explpb@caoba.entlenet.bo Exchange facilities (helpful), trips to Cusco via Desaguadero with a stop in Puno. *Fremen*, C Pedro Salazar 537, Plaza Avaroa, T241 7062, F241 7327, Casilla 9682, www.amazoncharters.com (3530 Piedmont Rd, Suite 5-B, Atlanta GA 3035, USA T404-266 2180). Own *Flotel* in Trinidad for jungle cruises in the Beni and *Hotel El Puente* in the Chapare, run tours throughout country, English and French spoken.

Magri Turismo, Capitán Ravelo 2101, PO Box 4469, T244 2727, magri_emete@megalink.com Amex representative, gives TCs against American Express card but doesn't change TCs, offers Amex emergency services and clients' mail. Recommended for tours in Bolivia, travel services. *Nuevo Continente*, at *Hotel Alem*. Recommended for trip to Zongo, Clemente is a good driver, cheap service to airport, very helpful. *Pachamama Tours*, Sagárnaga 189 y Murillo Shopping Doryan p2, of35, T/F231 9740, www.megalink.com/pachamama Cheap air fares within South America, very knowledgeable and professional, English spoken, also arranges cultural tours to indigenous groups. *Paititi*, Juan de la Riva, of106 (off Capitán Ravelo 2123), T244 0586, www.paitititravel.com Adventure travel, helpful, several

Bolivia

languages spoken. *Sky Bolivia*, Sagárnaga 368, T/F231 0272, skyinter@kolla.net Mountain biking, trekking and jungle tours, owner Alejandro speaks good English. *Tauro Tours*, Mercado 1362, Galería Paladium Mezz, local 'M', T220 1846, F220 1881. Top end adventure tours, jeep trips everywhere, run by the highly experienced and trained Carlos Aguilar. *Tawa Tours*, Sagárnaga 161, T233 4290, vernay@ceibo.entelnet.bo French-run, run jungle tours to their own camp as well as the Salar de Uyuni, good guides. *Toñito Tours*, Sagárnaga 189, Comercio Doryan, T233 6250, www.bolivianexpeditions.com Tours of the Salar, also book bus and train tickets. *Transturin*, C Alfredo Ascarrunz 2518, Sopocachi, PO Box 5311, T242 2222, F241 1922, emergency 715-61630, www.travelbolivia.com Full travel services, with tours ranging from La Paz to the whole country. Details of their Lake Titicaca services will be found on page 264. *Turisbus*, Illampu 704, Casilla 442, T245 1341, www.travelperubolivia.com Helpful, trekking equipment rented, agent for Peruvian railways, *ENAFER*, tickets to Puno and Cusco, also local and Bolivian tours. Recommended. Many agencies arrange excursions or travel to Peru (Puno, Cusco, Arequipa), as well as local tours. See also names and addresses under 'Exchange Houses', page 257. *Bracha*, T232 7472, has details of and sells tickets for trains from Santa Cruz.

Transport *For local buses,* *see page 241.* *See page 48 in* *Essentials for* *multinational* *car hire websites*	**Local Car hire**: cars may be hired direct from *Imbex*, Av Montes 522, T245 5432, F245 5433, info@imbex.com Well-maintained Suzuki jeeps from US$60 per day, including 200 km free for 4-person 4WD. Highly recommended. *Kolla Motors*, Av Sánchez Lima 2321, T241 9141. Well-maintained 6-seater 4WD Toyota jeeps, insurance and gasoline extra. *Petita Rent-a-car*, Cañada Strongest 1837, T237 9182, T772-26481 (mob). www.rentacarpetita.com Swiss owners Ernesto Hug and Aldo Rezzonico. Recommended for well-maintained 4WD jeeps, etc, also offer adventure tours, German, French, English spoken. Recommended. Also arranges fishing trips. Ernesto also has garage for VW and other makes, Av Jaimes Freyre 2326, T241 5264. Highly recommended. **Car Park** on corner of Ingavi and Sanjines, US$1.35 for 24 hrs, safe and central.

Taxi: normal taxis charge US$0.75 pp for short trips within city limits. Taxi drivers are not tipped. Don't let the driver turn the lights out at night. Radio taxis (eg *Alfa* T232 2427, *La Rápida* 239 2323) charge US$1.45 in centre and US$2.80 to suburbs. Also good value for tours for 3 people, negotiate price. *Eduardo Figueroa*, T278 6281, taxi driver and travel agent. Recommended. *Adolfo Monje Palacios*, in front of *Hotel El Dorado* or T235 4384. Highly recommended for short or long trips. *Oscar Vera*, Simón Aguirre 2158, Villa Copacabana, La Paz, T223 0453, specializes in trips to the Salar de Uyuni and the Western Cordillera, speaks English. Recommended.

Long distance Air: *Cotranstur* minibuses, white with 'Cotranstur' and 'Aeropuerto' written on the side and back, go from Plaza Isabel La Católica, anywhere on the Prado and Av Mcal Santa Cruz to the airport between 0800-0830 to 1900-2000, US$0.55 (allow about 1 hr), best to have little luggage, departures from the airport every 5 mins or so. Colectivos from Plaza Isabel La Católica charge US$3.45 pp, carrying 4 passengers. Taxi is US$7 to airport. There is an *Enlace* ATM for Cirrus, Plus, Visa and MasterCard credit/debit cards in the international departures hall for taking out local cash and a bank which changes cash, OK rates. To change money when bank is closed, ask at the departure tax window near information. The international departures hall is the main concourse, with all check-in desks, and is the hall for all domestic arrivals and departures. Small tourist office at the Airport, some maps available, English spoken, helpful (when staffed). Bar/restaurant and café (cheaper) upstairs. For details of **services**, see under destinations. Note that *TAM* uses the nearby military airport.

Bus: For information, T228 0551. Buses to: **Oruro**, **Potosí**, **Sucre**, **Cochabamba**, **Santa Cruz**, **Tarija** and **Villazón**, leave from the main terminal at Plaza Antofagasta (micros 2, M, CH or 130), see under each destination for details. Taxi to central hotels, US$0.90. The terminal (open 0700-2300) has a tourist booth outside, internet, a post office, *Entel*, restaurant, luggage store (0530-2200) and agencies, such as *Turisbus*, *Diana*, *Vicuña* (cheaper than their offices in town). Touts find passengers the most convenient bus and are paid commission by the bus company. Buses to **Chokilla** and **Yanachi** leave from a street just off Plaza 24 de Septiembre at 0800 and 1500, 3-4 hrs, US$2.75.

Buses to **Sorata**, **Copacabana** and **Tiahuanaco** leave only from the Cemetery district. Companies include *Flota Copacabana*, *Manco Kapac*, *2 de Febrero*, *Ingavi*, *Trans Perla Andina*. To get to the Cemetery district, take any bus or minibus marked 'Cementerio' going up C Santa Cruz (US$0.17); the route is Santa Cruz, Max Paredes, Garita de Lima, Mariano Bautista, Plaza Félix Reyes Ortiz/Tomás Katari (look out for the cemetery arch on your left). On Plaza Reyes Ortiz are *Manco Kapac*, recommended (T235 0033) and *2 de Febrero* (T237 7181) for Copacabana and Tiquina. From the Plaza go up Av Kollasuyo and at the 2nd street on the right (Manuel Bustillos) is the terminal for minibuses to Achacachi, Huatajata and Huarina, and buses for Sorata (*Trans Unificada*, T301693). Several micros (20, J, 10) and minibuses (223, 252, 270, 7) go up Kollasuyo; look for 'Kollasuyo' on the windscreen in most, but not all cases.

Buses to **Coroico and the Yungas** leave from Villa Fátima (25 mins by micros B,V,X,K, 131, 135, or 136, or *trufis* 2 or 9, which pass Pérez Velasco coming down from Plaza Mendoza, and get off at the service station, C Yanacachi 1434).

International buses from Plaza Antofagasta terminal: to **Buenos Aires**, US$110,daily at 1630, *San Roque*, T228 1959, via Yacuiba, or 1700, San Lorenzo, T228 2292, both take 2½ days. *Expresso Sur* (T228 1921) leaves at 1630 and charges U$10 more. Alternatively, go to Villazón and change buses in Argentina. To **Santiago, Chile**, *ChileBus* (T228 2168) leaves daily at 0630, arriving at Arica (1400) and Santiago 1700 1½ days later, US$43. To **Arica** via the frontier at Tambo Quemado and Chungará at 1300 Mon-Thu, with *Litoral*, T228 1920, 9 hrs on paved road, US$12. Also with *ChileBus* daily 0630, US$12 (good service), *Trans Salvador* daily, and *Transportes Cali*, 3 a week. To **Iquique**, take *Litoral's* Arica service, arriving 2200-2230, and continue to Iquique arriving 0400, US$15 including breakfast and lunch. To **Cusco**, *Litoral*, We, Fri, Sun, 0800, US$17, 12 hrs. Colectivos and agencies to **Puno** daily with different companies most easily booked through travel agencies, US$12, 10 hrs. **NB** Of the various La Paz-Puno services, only *Transturin* does not make you change to a Peruvian bus once over the border. *Exprinter/Cruz del Sur*, T236 2708, go via Desaguadero Tue, Thu, Sat 0800, US$7.20. For luxury and other services to Peru see under Lake Titicaca below.

Airline offices *Aerolíneas Argentinas*, Edif Gundlach, of 201, Reyes Ortiz 73, esq Federico Suárez, T235 1711, F239 1059. *Aero Sur*, Av 16 de Julio 616, T243 0430, F231 3957. *American Airlines*, Av 16 de Julio 1440, Edif Herman, T235 1316, www.aa.com *British Airways* and *Iberia*, Ayacucho 378, Edif Credinform p 5, T220 3885, F220 3950. *Ecuatoriana*, T0800-3001. *LanChile*, Av 16 de Julio 1566, p 1, T235 8377, www.lanchile.com *Lloyd Aéreo Boliviano (LAB)*, Camacho 1460, T0800-3001. *KLM, TAM* and *SAETA*, Plaza del Estudiante 1931, T244 1595, F244 3487. *Lufthansa*, Av 6 de Agosto 2512 y P Salazar, T243 1717, F243 1267. *Swissair*, Edif Gundlach Torre Oeste, of 502, Reyes Ortiz 73, esq Federico Suárez, T235 0730, F239 1740. *Transportes Aéreo Militar (TAM)*, Av Montes 738 esq Serrano, T237 9286, Mon-Fri 0830-1200 and 1430-1830. *Varig*, Av Mcal Santa Cruz 1392, Edif Cámara de Comercio, T231 4040, F239 1131.

Banks *Citibank*, Av 16 de Julio 1434, T279 1414. Open Mon-Fri 0900-1600, cashes its own TCs, no commission, but will not advance cash against Citibank MasterCard. *Bisa*, Av Gral Camacho 1333, open 0830-1200, 1430-1800, Sat 1000-1300, good service, changes cash and Amex TCs. Cash advance (in bolivianos) on Visa at *Banco Santa Cruz de la Sierra* (branch in Shopping Norte is open Sat afternoon), *Banco Mercantil*, Mercado 1190 (good, quick service), *Banco Popular*, *Banco Nacional* and *Banco Boliviano Americano*, Camacho (good, quick service). *Visa*, Av Camacho 1448, p 11 y 12, T231 8585 (24 hrs), F281 6525, for cancelling lost or stolen credit cards. *Enlace* ATMs at many sites in the city. *Amex*, see *Magri Turismo* under Tour operators. **Exchange houses:** *Sudamer*, Colón 256 y Camacho, good rates also for currencies other than US$, 3% commission on TCs into dollars, no commission into bolivianos, frequently recommended. Very few deal in Argentine and Chilean pesos. Street changers on corners around Plaza del Estudiante, Camacho, Colón and Prado, OK rates.

Communications Internet: There are many internet cafés in the centre of La Paz, opening and shutting all the time. Cost US$0.75-1 per hr. Internet connections are normally faster in the mornings and at weekends. Most open at 0900 and close anytime between 2100 and 2300; few open on Sun.

Directory

Bolivia

Post Office: Correo Central, Av Mcal Santa Cruz y Oruro, Mon-Fri 0800-2000, Sat 0830-1800, Sun 0900-1200. Another on Linares next to Museo de Coca, 0830-2000. Stamps are sold only at the post offices. Good philately section/museum on 1st floor of Correo Central. There are a number of shops selling good postcards, etc, and one selling Walter Guzmán Córdova maps. *Poste Restante* keeps letters for 2 months, good service, no charge. Check the letters filed under all parts of your name. For the procedure for sending parcels and for mailing prices, see page 236. Don't forget moth balls (difficult to buy – try C Sagárnaga) for textile items. To collect parcels costs US$0.15. Express postal service (top floor) is expensive. All firms pick up packets. *DHL*, Av Mcal Santa Cruz 1297, T0800-4020, also *Western Union* office. *FedEx*, Rosendo Gutiérrez 113 esq Capitán Ravelo, T244 3537. *UPS*, Av 16 de Julio 1479, p 10. **Telephone:** *Entel* (T236 7474) office for telephone calls and fax is at Ayacucho 267 (the only one open on Sun), and in Edif Libertad, C Potosí. Long wait for incoming calls. Many small *Entel* offices throughout the city, with quicker service. For international and national calls, rather than wait for a booth, buy a phonecard (Bs 5, 10, 20 or 100) and use it in the phones to the left in the main *Entel* office, also throughout the city. For local calls buy a *ficha* (US$0.10) from the person sitting next to red *Entel* phone booths; or use a phone in any shop or stall with 'teléfono' sign (US$0.20).

Cultural centres British Council, Av Arce 2730, T431240, F431377, bcouncil@ceibo.entelnet.bo Café serves English breakfasts, open 0645-2100, 1600-2030, Mon-Fri, library with British newspapers and magazines, films every Wed 2000, also English classes. **Centro Boliviano Americano** (CBA), Parque Zenón Iturralde 121, T235 1627/234 2582 (10 mins walk from Plaza Estudiante down Av Arce). Has public library and recent US papers (Mon-Wed 0900-1230, 1500-1930, till 2000 Thu and Fri). **Goethe-Institut**, Av 6 de Agosto 2118, T244 2453, www.goethe.de Library open Mon, Tue, Thu 1600-2000, Wed, Fri 1000-1300, 1600-2000; institute open Mon-Thu 0900-1300, 1500-1900, Fri 0900-1300. Excellent library, recent papers in German, CDs, cassettes and videos free on loan, German books for sale.

Embassies and consulates Argentine Consulate, Sánchez Lima 497, T241 7737, 24 hrs for visa, 0900-1330. **Austrian Consulate**, Edif Petrolero, p 1, of 11, Av 16 de Julio 1616, T231 3953, 1430-1600. **Belgium**, Calle 9, No 6, Achumani, T277 0081, 0830-1700. **Brazil**, Av Arce, Edif Multicentro, T244 0202, 0900-1300, Mon-Fri (visas take 2 days). **Britain**, Av Arce 2732, T243 3424, F243 1073, Casilla 694, Mon-Fri 0900-1200, Mon, Tue, Thu also 1330-1630, visa section open 0900-1200 has a list of travel hints for Bolivia, doctors, etc. **Canadian Consulate**, Edif Barcelona p 2, Victor Sanjinez 2678, Plaza España, T241 4453, 0900-1200. **Chilean Consulate**, H Siles 5873, esq C 13, Obrajes district, T278 5275, open Mon-Fri 0900-1200, 1500-1700, visa same day if requested in the morning (take microbus N, A or L from Av 16 de Julio). **Danish Consulate**, Av Arce 2799 and Cordero, Edif Fortaleza, p 9, T243 2070, Mon-Fri, 0800-1600. **Finnish Consulate**, Av Sánchez Lima 2560, esq L Gutiérrez, T243 0170, Mon-Fri 0830-1200, 1400-1830. **French Consulate**, Av Hernando Siles 5390, esq C 08 Obrajes, T278 6189 (take microbus N, A or L down Av 16 de Julio), Mon-Fri 0830-1230, 1400-1600. **German**, Av Arce 2395, T244 0606, F244 1441, Mon-Fri 0900-1200. **Israel**, Av Mcal Santa Cruz, Edif Esperanza, p 10, T237 4239, Casilla 1309/1320, Mon-Fri 0900-1600. *El Lobo* restaurant deals with mail for Israeli travellers. **Italy**, Av 6 de Agosto 2575, PO Box 626, T243 4955, F243 4975, Mon-Fri 1030-1230. **Japan**, Rosendo Gutiérrez 497, esq Sánchez Lima, PO Box 2725, T237 3151, Mon-Fri 0830-1145. **Netherlands Consulate**, Av 6 de Agosto 2455, Edif Hilda, p 7, T244 4040, F244 3804, Casilla 10509, nlgovlap@unete.com 0830-1700. **Norwegian Consulate**, C René Moreno

1096 in San Miguel, T/F277 0009, Mon-Fri 0900-1230, 1430-1700. **Paraguayan Consulate**, Edif Illimani, p 1, Av 6 de Agosto y P Salazar, good visa service, T243 2201, F243 3176, Mon-Fri 0800-1600. **Peru**, Edif Alianza office 110, Av 6 de Agosto 2190 y C F Guachalla, T244 0631, F244 4199, Mon-Fri 0900-1300, 1500-1700, visa US$10 in US$, issued same day if you go early. **Spanish Consulate**, Av 6 de Agosto 2827 and Cordero, T243 0118, Mon-Fri 0900-1330. **Swedish Consulate**, Av 14 de Septiembre 5080 y C5 Obrajes, T/F278 7903, Casilla 852, open 0900-1200. **Switzerland**, Edif Petrolero p 6, Av 16 de Julio 1616, T231 5617, F239 1462, Casilla 9356, Mon-Fri 0900-1200. **USA**, Av Arce 2780 y Cordero, T243 3520, F243 3854, Casilla 425, Mon-Fri 0800-1700.

Language schools *Alliance Française* (see also above). *Casa de Lenguas*, T/F++34-91 591 2393, www.casadelenguas.com (Also see Sucre, page 295). *Centro Boliviano Americano* (address under Cultural centres above), US$140 for 2 months, 1½ hrs tuition each afternoon. *Instituto de La Lengua Española*, María TeresaTejada, C Aviador esq final 14, No 180, Achumani, T279 6074, T715-56735 (mob), sicbol@caoba.entelnet.bo 1-to-1 lessons US$7 per hr. Recommended. *Speak Easy Institute*, Av Arce 2047, between Goitia and Montevideo, just down from Plaza del Estudiante, T/F244 1779, speakeasyinstitute@yahoo.com US$5 for private lessons, cheaper for groups and couples, Spanish and English taught. *The Spanish Language Learning Process*, C Murillo 1046 (3 p), T/F2311471, T706 28016 (mob), Maria_daza@hotmail.com **Private Spanish lessons** from: *Cecilia Corrales*, José María Camacho 1664, San Pedro, T248 7458, besteaching75@hotmail.com *Isabel Daza Vivado*, Murillo 1046, p 3, T231 1471, T706-28016 (mob), maria_daza@hotmail.com US$3 per hr. *William Ortiz (ABC)*, Pisagua 634, T228 1175, T712-62657 (mob), williamor@hotmail.com US$5.50 per hr. *Enrique Eduardo Patzy*, Mendez Arcos 1060, Sopocachi, T241 5501 or 776-22210, epatzy@hotmail.com US$6 an hr one-to-one tuition, speaks English and Japanese. Recommended.

Medical services Ambulance service: T222 4452. Health and hygiene: Unidad Sanitaria La Paz, on Ravelo behind *Hotel Radisson Plaza*, yellow fever shot and certificate for US$12. **Ministerio de Desarollo Humano, Secretaría Nacional de Salud**, Av Arce, near *Radisson Plaza*, yellow fever shot and certificate, rabies and cholera shots, malaria pills, bring own syringe (US$0.20 from any pharmacy). **Centro Piloto de Salva**, Av Montes y Basces, T236 9141, 10 mins walk from Plaza San Francisco, for malaria pills, helpful. **Laboratorios Illanani**, Edif Alborada p3, of 304, Loayza y Juan de la Riva, T231 7290, open 0900-1230, 1430-1700, fast, efficient, hygienic, blood test US$4.75, stool test US$9.50. Tampons may be bought at most *farmacias* and supermarkets. The daily paper, *Presencia*, lists chemists/pharmacies on duty (*de turno*). For contact lenses, **Optaluis**, Comercio 1089, well-stocked.

For hospitals, doctors and dentists, contact your consulate or the tourist office for recommendations

Useful addresses Immigration: to renew a visa go to **Migración Bolivia** (don't wait in the queue on the stairs – go straight up), Av Camacho 1433, p 2 (opposite *Banco de Santa Cruz*), T0800-3007 (toll free). Mon-Fri 0830-1600, go early. **Tourist Police:** Plaza del Estadio, Miraflores, next to *Love City* disco, T222 5016. Open 24 hrs, for insurance claims after theft, English spoken, helpful.

Trekking near La Paz

Start at Ventilla (see Transport below), walk up the valley for about three hours passing the village of Choquekhota until the track crosses the river and to the right of the road, there is a falling down brick wall with a map painted on it. The Takesi and Alto Takesi trails start here, following the path to the right of the wall. The road continues to Mina San Francisco. In the first hour's climb from the wall is excellent stone paving which is Inca or pre-Inca depending on who you believe either side of the pass at 4,630 m. There are camping possibilities at *Estancia Takesi* and, in the village of **Kakapi**, you can sleep at the **G** *Kakapi Tourist Lodge*, 10 beds with good matresses, solar shower and toilet. It is run by the local community and sponsored by Fundación Pueblo. It is also possible to camp. You also have to pass the unpleasant mining settlement of Chojlla, between which and Yanakachi is a gate where it is necessary to register and often pay a small 'fee'. Yanakachi has a number of good places to stay, several good hikes and an orphanage you help at. The Fundación Pueblo office on the plaza has information. Buy a minibus ticket on arrival in Yanakachi or walk 45 minutes down to the La Paz-Chulumani road for transport. The trek can be done in one long day, especially if you organize a jeep to the start of the trail, but is more relaxing in two or three if you take it slowly though

Takesi (Mina San Franciscoto Yanacachi)

Bolivia

you'll have to carry camping kit. Hire mules in Choquekhota for US$8 per day plus up to US$8 for the mulateer.

A 2-3 day alternative is from Mina San Francisco to El Castillo and the village of Chaco on the La Paz-Chulumani road. This trek is called **La Reconquistada** and has the distinction of including a 200 m disused mining tunnel.

Transport Take a Palca bus from C Venacio Burgoa esq C Boquerón, San Pedro, 0600 during the week, more often at weekends, and get off at Ventilla; or catch a Palca/Ventilla bus from outside *comedor popular* in C Max Paredes above junction with C Rodríguez, daily at 0530, US$1; or take any bus going to Bolsa Negra, Tres Ríos or Pariguaya (see Yunga Cruz below). Alternatively, take any micro or minibus to Chasquipampa or Ovejuyo and try hitching a lift with anything heading out of La Paz. If there isn't any transport, haggle with drivers of empty minibuses in Ovejuyo; you should be able to get one to go to Ventilla for about US$10. To Mina San Francisco: hire a jeep from La Paz; US$70, takes about 2 hrs. *Veloz del Norte* (T02-221 8279) leaves from Ocabaya and Av Las Américas in Villa Fátima, 0900 and 1400; 3½ hrs, continuing to Chojlla. Buses to La Paz (US$1.65) leave from Yanakachi at 0545 and 1245-1300 or 1400 daily.

Choro
(La Cumbre to
Coroico)

Immediately before the road drops down from La Cumbre to start the descent to Los Yungas, there is a collapsing plastered brick wall on the left which marks the start of the trail. However, there is nothing to help you get across the featureless moonscape to the *apacheta* where the trail starts properly. Cloud and bad weather are normal at La Cumbre (4,700 m): follow the left hand of the statue of Christ, take a map and compass or guide to get you to the start of the trail which is then well-signposted. The trail passes Chucura, Challapampa (camping possible, US$0.40, wood and beer for sale), the Choro bridge and the Río Jacun-Manini (fill up with water at both river crossings). At Sandillani it is possible to camp in the carefully-tended garden of a Japanese man who keeps a book with the names of every passing traveller. He likes to see postcards and pictures from other countries. There is good paving down to Villa Esmeralda, after which is Chairo, then to Yolosa. It takes three days to trek from La Cumbre to Chairo and a further long day on foot to Coroico, unless you take a truck from Chairo to Yolosa (allegedly at 0600, or hire one if enough people: US$2.25 each). From Yolosa it is 8 km uphill to Coroico with regular transport for US$1 per person. ■ *To La Cumbre: take a bus or camión from Villa Fátima (US$1, about 1 hr); make sure the driver knows you want to get off at La Cumbre. Alternatively, get a radio taxi from central La Paz for about US$12, or hire a jeep for US$40.*

Yunga Cruz
(Lambate or
Chuñavi to
Chulumani)
Best but hardest
of the 4 'Inca' trails
and therefore less
popular, so less
litter and begging

From Chuñavi follow path left (east) and contour gently up. Camping possible after two hours. Continue along the path staying on left hand side of the ridge to reach Cerro Khala Ciudad (literally, Stone City Mountain, you'll see why). Good paving brings you round the hill to join the path from Lambate (this heads uphill for two days through Quircoma and then to Cerro Khala Ciudad after which you descend to join the path from Chuñavi). Head north to Cerro Cuchillatuca and then Cerro Yunga Cruz, where there is water and camping is possible. After this point water and camping are difficult and normally impossible until you get down to Chulumani. The last water and camping possibilities are all within the next hour, take advantage of them. Each person should have at least two litres of water bottles. For water purification, only use iodine-based preparations (iodine tincture, *iodo* in *farmacias* costs US$0.50: use 5 drops per litre.) There are some clearances on the way down but no water. Starting in Chuñavi saves two days' walking and makes the trek possible in three days but misses the best bits. Starting in Lambate the trek normally takes five days.

Transport Take the bus to Pariguaya at 0900 Mon-Sat 0900, from C Gral Luis Lara esq Venacio Burgoa near Plaza Líbano, San Pedro, US$2, 6 hrs to Chuñavi, US$2.25; 6½ hrs to Lambate (3 km further on). Buses to Tres Ríos and Bolsa Negra depart at same time but stop well before Chuñavi or Lambate. It's not possible to buy tickets in advance, be there between 0700 and 0800 on the day to ensure ticket.

Guides must be hired through a tour company. *Club Andino Boliviano*, C México 1638, T232 4682, Casilla 5879 (closed Sat) can provide a list of guides and now works with the Bolivian association of mountain guides. Also recommended: *Ricardo Albert* at *Inca Travel*, Av Arce 2116, Edif Santa Teresa. *Dr Juan Pablo Ando*, Casillo 6210, T278 3495, trained in Chamonix, for mountaineering, rock climbing, trekking and ecological tours. *Iván Blanco Alba*, *Asociación de Guías de Montaña y Trekking*, C Chaco 1063, Casilla 1579, T235 0334. *Trek Bolivia*, C Sagárnaga 392, T/F231 7106. *Azimut Explorer*, Sagárnaga 173, Galery Gala Centro of 1, T/F329464/366155, PO Box 14907, azimexbo@wara.bolnet.bo Guide Juan Villarroel is one of the best. *Alaya Aventura*, Linares 880, of 13, T235 6787, recommended for Huayna Potosí, good meals. The *Club de Excursionismo, Andinismo y Camping*, helps people find the cheapest way to go climbing, trekking, etc; foreigners may join local groups, T278 3795, Casilla 8365, La Paz, or ask at the University. Each week there is a meeting and slide show.

Maps All treks in the Cordillera Real are covered by the map of the Cordillera Real, 1:135,000, Liam O'Brien. Takesi, La Reconquistada, Choro and Yunga Cruz are covered by the Walter Guzmán Córdova 1:150,000 map; see Maps in **Essentials**. There are also the *IGM* 1:50,000 sheets: Takesi Chojlla 6044 IV; Choro Milluni 5945 II, Unduavi 6045 III and Coroico; Yunga Cruz Lambate 6044 II and 6044. **Guidebooks** For guidebooks on trekking and climbing, see page 239.

Bolivia

Climbing
See Climbing in Essentials, page 50, and above for details of guides

Huayna Potosí is normally climbed in two days, with one night camped on a glacier at 5,600 m. There is a refugio *Huayna Potosí*, which costs US$10 per night, plus food, US$160 for three-day tour. Contact through office at *Hotel Continental*, Illampu 626, Casilla 731, T/F02-245 6717, bolclimb@mail.megalink.com or La Paz agencies for further information. The starting point for the normal route is at **Zongo**, whose valley used to have a famous ice cave (now destroyed by global warming). ■ *It can be reached by transport arranged through tourist agencies (US$70) or the refugio. Camión from Plaza Ballivián in El Alto early morning or midday Mon, Wed, Fri (return next day), taxi (US$30), or minibus in the high season. If camping in the Zongo Pass area, stay at the site maintained by Miguel and family near the white house above the cross.*

Chacaltaya
90 mins by car from La Paz (40 km) Altitude: 5,345 m

Chacaltaya was the highest ski run in the world. In 1999 skiing was discontinued as there was not enough snow, but it's now becoming popular for downhill mountain biking. Check at the Club Andino Boliviano (address above) if they still run excursions to their refuge on the mountain. You can walk to the summit of Chacaltaya for views of Titicaca on one side, La Paz on the other, and Huayna Potosí. Tiring, because of the altitude, but you have most of the day to do the climb and other peaks. Laguna Milluni, near Chacaltaya, is a beautiful lake to visit, but do not drink its heavily contaminated water. Take plenty of mineral water and protection against sun and ultra-violet light.

For the really hardy, accommodation at the Chacaltaya ski station is free, but take very warm clothes, sleeping bag and bed roll, food and water, as there is no heating, or bedding. Meals are available at the hut at weekends. ■ *Taxi or minibus US$30 (whole car) for a ½-day trip, or similar to the top by rented car costs about US$70, and really only at weekends. However, the trip can be hair-raising, buses carry no chains. Often the buses and tours only go half way. Many agencies do day trips, US$12.50, often combined with Valle de la Luna.*

Tiahuanaco

This remarkable archaeological site takes its name from one of the most important precolumbian civilizations in South America. It is now the most popular excursion fom La Paz. Many archaeologists believe that Tiahuanaco existed as early as 1600 BC, while the complex visible today probably dates from the eight to the 10th centuries AD. The site may have been a ceremonial complex at the centre of an empire which covered almost half Bolivia, south Peru, north Chile and northwest Argentina. It was also a hub of trans-Andean trade. The Tiahuanaco civilization's demise,

Towards Tiahuanaco
72 km W of La Paz, near the S end of Lake Titicaca

Bolivia

according to studies by Alan Kolata of the University of Illinois, could have been precipitated by the flooding of the area's extensive system of raised fields (*Sukakollu*), which were capable of sustaining a population of 20,000. The Pumapunka section, 1 km south of the main complex may have been a port, as the waters of the lake used to be much higher than they are today. The raised field system is being successfully re-utilized in the Titicaca area.

The site There is a small museum at the ticket office, the **Museo Regional Arqueológico de**
For the best light **Tiahuanaco**, containing a well-illustrated explanation of the raised field system of
for photos, go agriculture. The main structures are: Kalasasaya, meaning 'standing stones', refer-
before midday ring to the statues found in that part. Two of them, the Ponce monolith (centre of inner patio) and the Fraile monolith (southwest corner), have been re-erected. In the northwest corner is the Puerta del Sol, originally at Pumapunku. The split in the top probably occurred in the move. Its carvings, interrupted by being out of context, are thought to be either a depiction of the creator God, or a calendar. The motifs are exactly the same as those around the Ponce monolith. The Templo Semisubterráneo is a sunken temple whose walls are lined with faces, all different, according to some theories depicting states of health, the temple being a house of healing. The Akapana, originally a pyramid, still has some ruins on it. At Pumapunku, some of whose blocks weigh up to 132 tonnes, a natural disaster may have put a sudden end to the construction before it was finished. Most of the best statues are in the *Museo Tiahuanaco* or the *Museo Semisubterráneo* in La Paz.

■ *The site opens at 0900, US$2 for foreigners, including entry to museum. Allow 4 hrs to see the ruins and village. Guidebooks in English:* Tiwanaku, *by Mariano Baptista, Plata Publishing Ltd, Chur, Switzerland, or* Discovering Tiwanaku *by Hugo Boero Rojo.* Guía Especial de Arqueología Tiwanaku, *by Edgar Hernández Leonardini, a guide on the site, recommended. Written guide material is difficult to come by; hiring a good guide costs US$10. Map of site with historical explanation in English (published by Quipus) for sale at ticket office, US$2.50. Adjacent to the museum is* La Cabaña del Puma *restaurant where you can have lunch for US$1.80. Locals sell copies of Tiahuanaco figures; cheaper here than La Paz.*

Tiahuanaco Tiahuanaco, the present-day village, has arches at the four corners of its plaza, dat-
village ing from the time of independence. The church, built 1580-1612, used precolumbian masonry. In fact, Tiahuanaco for a long while was the 'quarry' for the altiplano. For the festival on **21 June**, before sunrise, there are colourful dances and llama sacrifices. On the 8th day of carnival (Sun), there is a local colourful, carnival. Souvenirs for sale, bargain hard, do not take photographs. Market day in Tiahuanaco is Sunday; do not take photos then either. There is a hotel (**E** *Tiahuancao*, with bath, restaurant), the restaurant/*residencial Kala-Huahua* (southeast corner of the plaza, T241 2769) and 2 restaurants.

Transport Take any Micro marked 'Cementerio', get out at Plaza Félix Reyes Ortiz, on Mariano Bautista (north side of cemetery), go north up Aliaga, 1 block east of Azin to find Tiahuanaco micros, US$1, 1½ hrs, every 30 mins, 0600 to 1700. Tickets can be bought in advance. Taxi for 2 costs about US$20-25 (can be shared), return, with unlimited time at site (US$30-40 including El Valle de la Luna). Some buses go on from Tiahuanaco to Desaguadero; virtually all Desaguadero buses stop at Tiahuanaco, US$0.65. Return buses (last back 1730-1800) leave from south side of the Plaza in village. Most tours from La Paz cost US$60 stopping at Laja and the highest point on the road before Tiahuanaco. Some tours include El Valle de la Luna.

Lake Titicaca

La Paz

Lake Titicaca is two lakes joined by the Straits of Tiquina: the larger, northern lake (Lago Mayor, or Chucuito) contains the Islas del Sol and de la Luna at its southern end; the smaller lake (Lago Menor, or Huiñamarca) has several small islands. The waters are a beautiful blue, reflecting the hills and the distant cordillera in the shallows of Huiñamarca, mirroring the sky in the rarified air and changing colour when it is cloudy or raining. A trip on the lake is a must if you're in the area; boat services are given below.

See page 328 for recommended reading on the region

La Paz to Copacabana

A paved road runs from La Paz to the Straits of Tiquina (114 km El Alto-San Pablo). The closest point to the capital on Lake Titicaca, the port was the original harbour for La Paz. It was founded in the 19th century by British navigators as a harbour for the first steam boat on the lake (the vessel was assembled piece-by-piece in Puno). Colourful fiestas are held on New Year's Day, Carnival (days may change each year), 3 May and 16 July. ■ *Regular minibus service from La Paz Cementerio district: across from the cemetery, above the flower market, ask for buses to Batallas, price US$0.75.*

Puerto Pérez
72 km from La Paz Superb views of lake and mountains. Spectacular sunsets

Sleeping and eating L *Hotel Las Balsas*, owned and operated by *Turismo Balsa* (see La Paz, Tour Operators), locally T/F02-2813226. In a beautiful lakeside setting, with views of the cordillera, all rooms have balcony over the lake. Advertised as 5-star; willing to negotiate out of season; fitness facilities including pool, massage, jacuzzi, sauna, racket ball. Excellent restaurant with fixed price lunch or dinner good value at US$12. Nearby on the Plaza is **C** *Hostería Las Islas*, same owners, shared bath, hot water, heated rooms, comfortable but can get crowded, *Blue Note* jazz bar next door. *Turismo Balsa* operate boat trips to Suriqui and Kalahuta (see below), and services to Puno and Cusco.

Further north along the east shore of the lake is Huatajata, with *Yacht Club Boliviano* (restaurant open to non-members, open Saturday, Sunday lunch only, sailing for members only) and *Crillon Tours International Hydroharbour* and *Inca Utama Hotel* (see below). Next to *Inca Utama*, is *Restaurant Huatajata Utama*, highly recommended. Then *Inti Raymi*, with fresh fish and boat trips (US$22 per boat); and others. The restaurants are of varying standard, most lively at weekends and in the high season. Máximo Catari's *Inti Karka* restaurant is on the road (full menu, open 7 days, average prices, good fish), also a hotel (**F**) on the waterfront, T0811 5058. Between Huatajata and Huarina (at Km 80 from La Paz) is the **B** *Hotel Titicaca*, T02-237 4877, F239 1225. Beautiful views, sauna, pool, good restaurant, very quiet during the week (address in La Paz, Potosí y Ayacucho 1220, p 2). ■ *Bus: La Paz-Huatajata/Tiquina, US$0.85, Transportes Titikaka, Av Kollasuyo 16, daily from 0400, returning between 0700 and 1800.*

Huatajata

Beyond here is **Chúa**, where there is fishing, sailing and Transturin's catamaran dock (see below). The public telephone office, *Cotel*, is on the plaza just off the main road. About 2 km before Chúa is a turning to the right to *La Posada del Inca*. Open Saturday, Sunday and holidays for lunch only, in a beautiful colonial *hacienda*, good trout, average prices.

Crillon Tours (address under La Paz, Tour Operators) run a hydrofoil service on Lake Titicaca with excellent bilingual guides. *Crillon's* tours stop at the **Andean Roots cultural complex** at *Inca Utama*: the **Bolivian History Museum** includes a recorded commentary; a 15 min video precedes the evening visit to the Kallawaya (Native Medicine) museum, where you meet a Kallawaya fortune teller, very interesting. In all 7 cultures are represented. The *Inca Utama*

Lake Titicaca tours

Bolivia

hotel has a **health spa** based on natural remedies; the rooms are comfortable, with heating, electric blankets, good service, bar, good food in restaurant (5-star accommodation, **AL**, reservations through *Crillon Tours*, T La Paz 02-233 7533, www.titicaca.com). Also at *Inca Utama* is an **observatory** (*Alajpacha*) with two telescopes and retractable thatched roof for viewing the night sky, a floating restaurant and bar on the lake (*La Choza Náutica*), a 252-sq m floating island, a new colonial-style tower with 15 de-luxe suites, panoramic elevator and 2 conference rooms. Health, astronomical, mystic and ecological programmes are offered. The hydrofoil trips include visits to Andean Roots complex, Copacabana, Islas del Sol and de la Luna, Straits of Tiquina and past reed fishing boats. See Isla del Sol below for *La Posada del Inca*. Trips can be arranged to/from Puno (bus and hydrofoil excursion to Isla del Sol) and from Copacabana via Isla del Sol to Cusco and Machu Picchu. Other combinations of hydrofoil and land-based excursions can be arranged (also jungle and adventure tours). Cost is US$173 from La Paz to Puno, US$145 for day excursion from La Paz; fascinating, not least for the magnificent views of the Cordillera on a clear day. All facilities and modes of transport connected by radio. In Puno, *Crillon*'s office is at *Arcobaleno Tours*, Lambayeque 175, T/F351052, arcobaleno@ titicacalake.com where all documentation for crossing the border can be done.

Transturin (see also La Paz, Tour operators) run catamarans on Lake Titicaca, either for sightseeing or on the La Paz-Puno route. The catamarans are more leisurely than the hydrofoils of *Crillon* so there is more room and time for on-board entertainment, with bar, video and sun deck. From their dock at Chúa, catamarans run day and day/night cruises starting either in La Paz or Copacabana. Puno may also be the starting point for trips. Overnight cruises involve staying in a cabin on the catamaran, moored at the Isla del Sol, with lots of activities. On the island, *Transturin* has the **Inti Wata cultural complex** (Paulino Esteban, formerly of Suriqui island, works here – he helped in the construction, out of totora reeds, of Heyerdahl's craft). The complex has restored Inca terraces, an Aymara house and the **underground Ekako museum**. There is also a 70-passenger totora reed boat for trips to the

La Paz, Lake Titicaca & the Yungas

Polkokaina Inca palace. Prices range from US$108-213; all island-based activities are for catamaran clients only. *Transturin* runs through services to Puno without a change of bus, and without many of the usual formalities at the border. *Transturin* has an office in Puno, Jr Libertad 176, T352771, F351316, www.travelbolivia.com *Transturin* offers last minute, half-price deals for drop-in travellers (24-48 hrs in advance, take passport): sold in Copacabana only, half-day tour on the lake, continuing to Puno by bus, or La Paz; overnight Copacabana-Isla del Sol-Copacabana with possible extension to La Paz. Sold in La Paz only: La Paz-Isla del Sol-La Paz, or with overnight stay (extension to Puno is possible on request).

Turisbus (see La Paz, Tour operators and *Hoteles Rosario*, La Paz, and *Rosario del Lago*, Copacabana) offer guided tours in the fast launches *Titicaca Explorer I* (28 passengers) and *II* (8 passengers) to the Isla del Sol, returning to Copacabana via the Bahía de Sicuani for trips on traditional reed boats (half-day US$29). Also La Paz-Puno, with boat excursion to Isla del Sol, boxed lunch and road transport (one day US$49), or with additional overnight at *Hotel Rosario del Lago* (US$79.50).

On **Suriqui** (1½ hours from Huatajata) in Lake Huiñamarca, a southeasterly extension of Lake Titicaca, you can visit the museum/craft shops of the Limachi brothers (now living at the *Inca Utama* cultural complex). The late Thor Heyerdahl's *Ra II*, which sailed from Morocco to Barbados in 1970, his *Tigris* reed boat, and the balloon gondola for the Nasca (Peru) flight experiment (see page 1190), were also constructed by the craftsmen of Suriqui. Reed boats are still made on Suriqui, probably the last place where the art survives. On **Kalahuta** there are *chullpas* (burial towers), old buildings and the uninhabited town of Kewaya. On **Pariti** there is Inca terracing and very good examples of weaving. Máximo Catari (see above) arranges boats to the islands in Lago Huiñamarca, Pariti, Kalahuta and Suriqui: prices, to Suriqui US$22 for 4-5 people, to all three islands US$40, one hour boat trip US$7.50, sailing

Islands of Lake Huiñamarca

Bolivia

boat for three US$16 for a day (boat trips recommended). Boats can also be hired in Tiquina for trips to Suriqui, US$3 per person in a group.

From Chúa the main road reaches the east side of the Straits at San Pablo (clean restaurant in blue building, with good toilets). On the west side is San Pedro, the main Bolivian naval base, from where a paved road goes to Copacabana. Vehicles are transported across on barges, US$4. Passengers cross separately, US$0.35 (not included in bus fares) and passports are checked. Expect delays during rough weather, when it can get very cold.

To Yucumo, Rurrenabaque, San Borja & Trinidad ▲

o Koka

Santa
Puerto Ana
Linares o

o Palos Blancos
Sapecho o San Miguel
de Huachi

o Covendo

o Alcoche

aranavi o

Nor Yungas

Río Boopi

o San Pedro

o Challa

roico
losa

o Coripata

Sud Yungas

o Chulumani

Puente
Villa o Irupana
Chicaloma
rurata o
Yunga
Cruz Trail

o Chuñavi

o Lambate

To Inquisivi ▲

Río La Paz

Copacabana

An attractive little town on Lake Titicaca, Copacabana has a heavily restored, Moorish-style cathedral containing a famous 16th century miracle-working Dark Virgin of the Lake, also known as the Virgin of Candelaria, the patron saint of Bolivia. **The cathedral** itself is notable for its spacious atrium with four small chapels; the main chapel has one of the finest gilt altars in Bolivia. The basilica is clean, white, with

Phone code: 02
Colour map 6, grid A2
158 km from La Paz by paved road

Beware of sunburn especially on the lake, even when it does not feel hot

Bolivia

coloured tiles decorating the exterior arches, cupolas and chapels. Vehicles are blessed in front of the church daily, especially on Sunday. An *hospicio* (serving now as an almshouse) with its two arcaded patios is worth a visit; ask permission before entering. There are 17th and 18th century paintings and statues in the sanctuary. Entrance at side of Basilica opposite *Entel*. ■ *Mon-Fri 1100-1200, 1400-1800, Sat-Sun, 0800-1200, 1400-1800, only groups of 8 or more, US$0.60. The tourist information kiosk is on Plaza 2 de Febrero, helpful when open.*

On the headland which overlooks the town and port, **Cerro Calvario**, are the Stations of the Cross. On the hill behind the town (Cerro Sancollani) overlooking the lake, roughly southeast of the Basilica, is the **Horca del Inca**, two pillars of rock with another laid across them (probably a sun clock rather than a gallows, now covered in graffiti). ■ *US$3.* There is a path marked by arrows. Boys will offer to guide you: fix price in advance if you want their help.

There is a lovely walk along the lakeside north to Yampupata, 15 km (allow 3½ hours), through unspoilt countryside. At the village of Sicuani ask for a rowing boat to Isla del Sol (US$1-3.50), or José Quispe Mamani who provides a motor launch, plus meals and accommodation.

Sleeping   **A** *Rosario del Lago*, Rigoberto Paredes between Av Costanera and Av 16 de Julio, T862 2141, reservaslago@hotelrosario.com Same ownership as *Rosario*, La Paz, includes breakfast, hot water, *Turisbus* office (see above), small rooms with lake view, colonial style, beautifully furnished, internet café, handicrafts display, restaurant. Recommended. **B** *Gloria*, 16 de Julio, T/F862 2094, same group as *Gloria* in La Paz, www.gloria-tours-bolivia.com With hot water, bar, café and restaurant with international and vegetarian food, gardens, money exchange. **B-C** *Chasqui de Oro*, Av Costanera 55, T862 2343. Includes breakfast, lakeside hotel, café/breakfast room has great views, trips organized, video room. **C-D** *La Cúpula*, C Michel Pérez 1-3, T862 2029, www.hotelcupula.com 5 mins' walk from centre, price depends on room (most expensive have kitchen and bath), sitting room with TV and video, fully-equipped kitchen, library, hot water, book exchange, vegetarian restaurant (plus trout and some meat dishes, pricier than others in town), great breakfast, offer local tours, run by Amanda and Martin Strätker whose *Centro Cultural Arco y Hamaca* offers painting and sculpting classes and courses in Spanish and English. Very warmly recommended. **D** *Utama*,

Copacabana

Lake Titicaca

To Cerro Calvario
To El Baño del Inca (2.5km)
To Yunguyo, Peru
To Cerro Sancollani & Horca del Inca
To La Paz

■ **Sleeping**	6 Gloria	11 Residencial Porteñita	2 Kala Uta
1 Ambassador	7 Hostal La Luna	12 Residencial Sucre	3 La Leyenda
2 Boston	8 La Cúpula	13 Rosario del Lago	4 La Orilla
3 Chasqui de Oro	9 Playa Azul		5 Snack 6 de Agosto
4 Colonial del Lago	10 Residencial Pacha	● **Eating**	6 Sol y Luna
5 Emperador	Aransaya & Café	1 Bar Chirimoski	7 Sujna Wasi

0 metres 100
0 yards 100

Michel Pérez, T862 2013. With breakfast, hot water, good showers, comfortable. **E** *Boston*, Conde de Lemos, near Basilica, T862 2231. **F** without bath, good, quiet. **E** *Colonial del Lago*, Av 6 de Agosto y Av 16 de Julio, T862 2270, titicacabolivia@yahoo.com Bright rooms, some with lake view, **F** without bath, breakfast included, garden, restaurant and *peña*. **E** *Playa Azul*, 6 de Agosto, T862 2228, F862 2227. Rooms OK, but chilly, includes breakfast, tepid electric showers, water supply and toilets poor, good food. **E** *Res Sucre*, Murillo 228, T862 2080. Hot water, parking, quiet, good cheap breakfast, laundry US$1.20, offers tours of lake. **E-F** *Ambassador*, Bolívar y Jáuregui. Balcony, heater US$2 per day, hot water, rooftop restaurant, reduction for more than 1 night or with YHA card, 10% with student card, luggage store, parking. Recommended. **G** *Res Pacha Aransaya*, Av 6 de Agosto 121, T862 2229. Being refurbished, basic, hot shower but water problems, good trout in restaurant. **G** *Alojamiento Aroma*, Av Jáuregui, towards beach. Hot showers, good views, day trips can be booked, helpful and informative owner. **G** *Emperador*, C Murillo 235, behind the Cathedral, T862 2083. Breakfast served in room for US$2, popular, laundry service and facilities, shared hot showers, helpful for trips to Isla del Sol. Repeatedly recommended. **G** *Kota Kahuaña*, Av Busch 15. Hot showers, quiet, kitchen facilities, some rooms with lake view. Recommended. **G** *Hostal La Luna*, José P Mejía 260, T862 2051. Warm showers, laundry, breakfast in room on request (US$1), can arrange discounts on trips to Isla del Sol. **G** *Res Porteñita*, by market on Jáuregui. Safe. Recommended. **G** *Alojamiento Punata*, José P Mejía. Hot shower, nice beds, basic. Many other *residenciales* in **G** range.

Eating
Very few places open before 0800

On Plaza 2 de Febrero *Napolés*. Reasonable prices, does vegetarian tortilla, changes money. **On 6 de Agosto** *Colonial*, corner of 16 de Julio. Decent lunch, good trout. *Snack 6 de Agosto*, 2 branches, good trout, big portions, some vegetarian dishes, serves breakfast. Also has good rooms for rent, **D** with bath, **E** without, breakfast extra, laundry facilities. *Kala Uta*, nice atmosphere, good vegetarian food. *La Orilla*, tasty Mexican food, stir fries, vegetarian options, cosy atmosphere, usually open 0700-2200. Recommended. *Pacha Café*, No 121, good. *Sujna Wasi*, Jáuregui 127, open 0730-2300, excellent, good breakfasts and other meals, especially fish, in the market on C Abaroa. *La Leyenda*, on beach between 6 de Agosto and Busch. Vegetarian dishes, *menú* US$1.50, good. *Bar Chirimoski*, Murillo, next to *Entel* (due to move to lakeside in 2002). Run by Argentine guitarist, good food, barbecues at weekends, books, video room, comfy, rock and funk music, opens 1930 till whenever. *Sol y Luna*, Av 16 de Julio. Well-decorated bar with good music, internet, book exchange, guide books and CD library

Festivals
At these times hotel prices quadruple

1-3 Feb *Virgen de la Candelaria*, massive procession, dancing, fireworks, bullfights. **Easter**, with candlelight procession on Good Friday. **2-5 May**, very colourful. **23 Jun**, San Juan, also on Isla del Sol. **4-6 Aug**, *La Virgen de Copacabana*.

Transport

Road By car from La Paz to Copacabana (direct), 4 hrs, take exit to 'Río Seco' in El Alto. **Agency buses**: several agencies go from La Paz to Puno, stopping at Copacabana for lunch, or with an open ticket for continuing to Puno later. They charge US$12 and depart La Paz 0800; La Paz-Copacabana takes 4 hrs, US$4-6. Companies include: *Diana Tours*, Hotel Ambassador, Plaza Sucre. *Vicuña Tours*, 6 de Agosto, T862 2155. *Turisbus*, Rigoberto Paredes in *Hotel Rosario del Lago*. They continue to Peruvian border at Yunguyo and on to Puno, stopping for immigration formalities and changing money. 3½ hrs to Puno, US$3.30-4.25 depending on season, depart Copacabana around 1200-1400. It's also possible to catch a tour bus to Cusco, usually depart around 1400, tickets US$17-20, change bus in Puno, tour company arranges connection. **Motorcycle and bicycle hire** Ask boys at the beach, but bargain. **Public transport** To/from La Paz, US$2.05 plus US$0.35 for Tiquina crossing (also need to show passport), several departures daily between 0700-1800 with *Manco Capac*, T862 2234, or 245 3035 in La Paz. *2 de Febrero*, T862 2233, or 237 7181, La Paz. Both have offices on Copacabana's main plaza and in La Paz at Plaza Reyes Ortiz, opposite entrance to cemetery. Buses also from main terminal, US$3. Buy bus tickets as soon as possible as all buses are usually full by day of travel, especially Sun. 1-day trips from La Paz are not recommended as they allow only 1½-2 hrs in Copacabana. (See also Frontier via

Copacabana page 269.) Bus to **Huatajata**, US$2.10 and to **Huarina**, US$2.50. *Tour Perú* leaves Copacabana daily at 1330, arrives **Cusco** 0200 with no change of bus at the border, can sleep on the bus till 0600.

Directory **Banks** *Banco Unión*, 6 de Agosto opposite Oruro, reasonable rates of exchange, TCs at US$5 commission, cash advance on Visa and MasterCard 3% commission. Several *artesanías* on Av 6 de Agosto buy and sell US$ and Peruvian soles. **Communications** Internet: *Alf@Net*, Av 6 de Agosto, next to *Hostal Colonial*, 0830-2200, US$2.95, very fast connection In Municipal building, Plaza 2 de Febrero, US$2.95 per hr. *Ifa-Internet*, Av 16 de Julio y Jáuregui, Plaza Sucre. US$3.50 per hr. **Post Office:** Plaza 2 de Febrero, open (in theory) Tue-Sat 0900-1200, 1300-1800, Sun 0900-1500, *poste restante*. **Telephone:** *Entel*, open 0800-1230, 1330-2000, international phone and fax, accept US$.

Isla del Sol The site of the main Inca creation myth (there are other versions) is a short distance by boat from Copacabana. Legend has it that Viracocha, the creator god, had his children, Manco Kapac and Mama Ocllo, spring from the waters of the lake to found Cusco and the Inca dynasty. A sacred rock at the island's northwest end is worshipped as their birthplace. On the east shore near the jetty for *Crillon Tours'* hydrofoils and other craft is the Fuente del Inca, a pure spring, and Inca steps leading up from the water. A 2 km walk from the landing stage takes one to the main ruins of Pilcocaina, a two storey building with false domes and superb views. ■ *US$1*. Southeast of the Isla del Sol is the **Isla de la Luna** (or Coati), which also may be visited – the best ruins are an Inca temple and nunnery, both sadly neglected. The **Museo Comunitario de Etnografía** was opened on the Isla del Sol in 2001 by the Challa community after four years' work. It celebrates costumes used in sacred dances. Director Esteban Quelima, an anthropolgist (museo_templodelsol@latinmail.com), hopes in the future to expand the museum to include natural history. He also hopes to provide accommodation in local homes. ■ *Daily 0900-1200, 1300-1800, entry by voluntary contribution.*

It is worthwhile staying overnight for the many beautiful walks through villages and Inca terraces, some still in use

Children beg persistently for money

Sleeping It is not possible to see all the sites on the Isla del Sol and return to Copacabana in 1 day; it's 3 hrs on foot from one end of the island to the other. Take camping equipment, all food and water (or water sterilizers), stay in one of the dozen *posadas* on the island, or accept a room with one of the many families who offer accommodation. Most of these are at Yumani, on the south side near the Inca steps: *La Posada del Inca* is a restored colonial hacienda, owned by *Crillon Tours*, solar-powered electricity and hot water, with bath, dining room, rustic but very comfortable, can only stay here as part of a tour with *Crillon*. There are 20 rooms with private bathroom, electric blanckets and individual heating. **D** *Casa de Don Ricardo*, with bath, heating and breakfast, good beds, nice atmosphere, small, Argentine-owned. At the peak of the hill above the village s **D** (**G** without bath) *Puerta del* Sol. Nearby is the owner's father's hostel, **G** *Templo del Sol*, with clean rooms, electric showers and a restaurant. There are several others, all **G**, basic but clean, few have hot water (although the island now has electricity), meals provided US$1-2. *El Imperio del Sol*, peach-coloured house, comfortable, no running water. Recommended. Also **G** *Albergue Inca Sama*, next to Pilcocaina ruins, sleep on mattresses on floor, good food, also camping in typical tents (contact via *Hotel Playa Azul*, Copacabana, or La Paz T235 6566), Sr Pusari, offers boat service from Copacabana and trips to the north of island. Accommodation also at Challa, on the northeast coast, **G** *Posada del Inca*, right on the beach. 8 double rooms, very basic outside toilets, no showers, contact Juan Mamani Ramos through *Entel* office (T013-5006), food is provided and beer or *refrescos* are for sale. Several places to stay around the Plaza in Challapampa, at the north end of the island. Ask for Lucio Arias or his father, Francisco, who have opened 2 basic hostels. **G** *Posada Manco Kapac* has rooms for 35 people and a garden for camping, hot showers and views of Illampu. The second hostel has the same name but is further up the beach. See also *Transturin's* overnight options under Lake Titicaca, Tours, above.

Transport *Inca Tours* and *Titicaca Tours* run motor boats to the island; both have offices on Av 6 de Agosto in Copacabana, as do other companies. Boats leave Copacabana at 0815, arrive at the south end at 1000. They leave the north end of the island at 1600, arriving back at 1730-1800. This gives you enough time to walk the length of the island (take food and water). With the same ticket you can stay on the island and return another day. Other options are: half-day tours and tours which include north and south of Isla del Sol and Isla de La Luna in one day (not recommended, too short). Full-day tour US$3 pp (US$4.50 if you stay overnight). Other boats to the jetty by the Fuente del Inca leave at 0830 and 1330, returning punctually at 1600. Boats also departs to Isla del Sol from Yampupata, cost US$8 (see Copacabana excursions).

Border with Peru

The road goes from La Paz 91 km west to **Guaqui**, formerly the port for the Titicaca passenger boats (*Res Guaqui*, near port, good value, basic, friendly; tiny restaurant on the Plaza de Armas has been recommended). The road crosses the border at **Desaguadero** 22 km further west and runs along the shore of the lake to Puno. Bolivian immigration is just before the bridge, is open 0830-1230 and 1400-2030. Get exit stamp, walk a few hundred metres across the bridge then get entrance stamp on the other side. Get Peruvian visas in La Paz. There are a few basic hotels on both sides of the bridge, as well as restaurants. Money changers just over the bridge on Peruvian side give reasonable rates. ■ *Road paved all the way to Peru. Buses from La Paz to Guaqui and Desaguadero depart from same location as micros for Tiahuanaco (see above) every 30 mins, US$1.55, 1½-2 hrs. From Desaguadero to La Paz last bus departs 1700, buses may leave later if enough passengers, but charge a lot more.*

The west side of Lake Titicaca
There are three La Paz-Puno routes (see also page 1208)

From Copacabana an unpaved road leads south to the Bolivian frontier at Kasani, then to Yunguyo. Do not photograph the border area. For La Paz tourist agency services on this route see under **International Buses** (page 257) and under Lake Titicaca above. The border is open 0830-1930 (Bolivian time). Buses/colectivos stop here and at the Peruvian side; or you can walk, 500 m, between the 2 posts. If crossing into Bolivia with a motorcycle, do not be fooled into paying any unnecessary charges to police or immigration. For Peruvian Immigration, see page 1217. Going to Peru, money can be changed in Yunguyo at better rates than at the border. Coming into Bolivia, the best rates are at the border, on the Bolivian side. Soles can be changed in Copacabana (see above).

Via Copacabana

Transport In Peru, this starts at Yunguyo. Colectivo Copacabana-Kasani US$0.50 pp, Kasani-Yunguyo US$0.60 pp. Make sure, if arranging a through ticket La Paz-Puno, that you get all the necessary stamps en route, and find out if your journey involves a change of bus. Note the common complaint that through services La Paz-Puno (or vice versa) deteriorate once the border has been crossed, eg smaller buses are used, extra passengers taken on, passengers left stranded if the onward bus is already full, drivers won't drop you where the company says they will.

From Huarina, a road heads northwest to **Achacachi** (market Sunday; fiesta 14 September). Here, one road goes north across a tremendous marsh to Warisata, then crosses the altiplano to Sorata.

Along the east side of Lake Titicaca

Sorata

A beautiful place, set in a valley at the foot of Illampu east of Lake Titicaca, Sorata has lovely views and is ideal country for hiking and climbing. There is a delightful plaza, with views of the snow-capped summit of Illampu on a clear day. The market area is near the plaza, half block down Muñecas on the right. Market day is Sunday; fiesta 14 September.

Phone code: 02
Colour map 6, grid A2
Altitude: 2,578 m
163 km from La Paz
Bring insect repellent

Sleeping & eating

D-E *Landhaus Copacabana*, 20 mins downhill from the centre (look for the signs), T/F813 5042, www.khainata.com/sorata **F** pp with shared bathroom, breakfast included, good restaurant, nice views, internet access US$3.60 per hr. **E** *Res Sorata*, just off plaza, T/F813 5218, resorata@ceibo.entelnet.bo Cheaper with shared bath at the back, rambling old place (a bit neglected) with original fittings, huge rooms, some with private bath, saggy beds, also has modern section, restaurant, lunch/dinner US$2.75, breakfast US$2, big garden, washing machine US$1.80, owner Louis Demers from Quebec, internet access US$3.60 per hr, slow. Recommended. **F** *Gran Hotel Sorata* (Ex-*Prefectural*), on the outskirts immediately above the police checkpoint, T2817378, call from Plaza for free pick-up. Spacious although bathrooms (electric showers) a bit tired, free filtered water, large garden with great views, swimming pool (open to non-residents for US$0.50), games room, good restaurant, internet café, accepts credit cards. **F** pp *Paraíso*, Villavicencio 117, T813 5043. Pleasant, American breakfast US$1.80, hot water, restaurant. **G** *Alojamiento Chura*, Ingavi, 2 doors up from *Altai* restaurant, 1st and 2nd floors (no sign). Bright, hot showers (US$0.45). **G** pp *Hostal Mirador*, on Muñecas, same road and under same ownership as *Restaurant Terraza*, T813 5052. Good rooms, comfortable, clean showers and toilets, sun terrace. **G** *Hostal Panchita*, on plaza, T813 5038. Shared bath, large rooms, hot water, basic, good restaurant. At the road junction below *Café Illampu*, María Angela Sangines, T813 5055, mas1@ceibo.entelnet.bo has 3 self-catering bungalows (US$15 per night) for 4, minimum 1 week's stay, also has a deli with wines and cheeses from around the world.

There are several small **restaurants** around the plaza (*Pizzería Napolés* and 2 other Italian), also *Altai*, Ingavi y Muñecas, mainly vegetarian, gringo-run, very good, set meal US$2, closed Mon (has *Oasis* restaurant, with **camping** and self-catering cabins 30 min walk from town, by river US$1.50), open 0830-2200. *Café Illampu*, on the way to San Pedro cave. Swiss-run, excellent sandwiches, bread and cakes, **camping** US$1 (an extra US$0.50 to hire tent), bikes for hire, closed Tue and Feb-Mar. *El Nuevo Ceibo*, on Muñecas. Good for fish and set meals. *La Terraza*, just below market. Cheap, good breakfast and lunch, some vegetarian dishes. *The Spider Bar*, 250 m west of plaza, near *Hostal Mirador*, www.geocities.com/r_h_bryant The most popular alcoholic and non-alcoholic drinking hole with snacks, English owner, book exchange, musical instruments.

Shopping

For handicrafts, *Artesanía Sorata* on plaza, open Mon-Sat 0900-2000, Sun 0900-1600, also cashes TCs and accepts them as payment.

Transport

Bus From La Paz with *Trans Unificada* (from C Manuel Bustillos, esq Av Kollasuyo, 2 blocks up from Cementerio in La Paz), 0430-1500, 4½ hrs, US$1.65; from Sorata every hour daily 0400-1400 (till 1700 Fri and Sun). To, or from Peru, change buses at Huarina for Copacabana.

Directory

Banks Bank on the plaza changes US$ cash only, no ATM. Try *Artesanía Sorata, Res Sorata* or *Hotel Landhaus Copacabana*. **Communications Internet:** Various hotels as above. María Angela Sangines, road junction nr *Café Illampu*, US$3 per hr. **Post Office:** on north side of plaza, 0830-1230, 1500-1800. *Cotel*, next door, same hours, for local calls only. **Telephone:** *Entel*, on plaza at entrance to *Hostal Panchita*, for national and international calls, open daily 0700-2130. **Medical services Hospital:** Villamil de Rada e Illampu. Has oxygen and X-ray.

Hiking & climbing

Climbing season: late Apr to early Sep

Armed robbery reported on the Illampu Circuit

Sorata is the starting point for climbing **Illampu** and Ancohuma (experience and full equipment necessary). All routes out of Sorata are difficult, owing to the number of paths in the area and the very steep ascent. It is best to hire mules; Louis at *Residencial Sorata* can arrange guides and mules. *Club Sorata* (at *Hotel Landhaus Copacabana*) rents equipment and can arrange long and short treks, guides and mules, US$20 per person per day all inclusive, also quad bikes. Sorata guides association, President Eduardo Chura, office opposite side entrance of *Res Sorata* (T813 5044, guiasorata@hotmail.com), for trekking guides only (very good, but not experienced for glacier climbing), porters, mules and equipment hire. Daily prices: guide US$15, porters and mules extra, remember you have to feed your guide/porter. When trekking avoid sedimented glacier melt water for drinking and treat with iodine all other water. For more information on trekking and walking in this area, see Guidebooks, page 328.

There are lots of walking possibilities, including day hikes. The most popular is to **San Pedro cave**, beyond the village of San Pedro. The cave is lit, but not up to much but you can swim in the underground 'lake'. ■ *0800-1700, US$1. Toilets at entrance; best not to go alone. It is reached either by road, a 12 km walk (2½ hrs) each way, or by a path along the Río San Cristóbal (about 3½ hrs one way). Get clear directions before setting out. Take water, at least 1 litre pp, or else take sterilizing tablets and fill up at the tap in San Pedro. Ask for the house selling refrescos in San Pedro.*

A highly recommended hike is to Laguna Chillata and Inca Marka, a strenuous full-day walk, climbing from Sorata to 4,207 m (either take plenty of water, or a water filter). Go with a guide because this is a sensitive area and the path is very hard to find; the lake is sacred and Inca Marka is a burial place, dating back to the precolumbian Mollu culture. Camping is forbidden; do not touch anything, not even bits of paper, bottles, etc, which may be offerings. This can be extended to a 3-day trek up to a glacier.

The '**Circuito Illampu**', a 4-7 day high-altitude trek (five passes over 4,500 m) around Illampu, is excellent. It can get very cold and it is a hard walk, though very beautiful with nice campsites on the way. Some food can be bought in Cocoyo on the third day. You must be acclimatized before setting out.

It is also possible to hike from Sorata to Lake Titicaca. It is much cheaper to go to Sorata and ask about trekking there than to book up a trek with an agency in La Paz. See warning in Hiking, page 240.

Sorata is the starting point for an extended trek into the Yungas. The **Mapiri Trail** is very tough, seven to eight days, starting at Ingenio, four hours from Sorata by pick-up, US$6, and ending at Mapiri, an ugly mining town on the river of the same name. From Mapiri, you can continue to **Guanay** another mining town with several cheap hotels and places to eat (eg *Der Auslander Club*). Boats can be hired to go to Rurrenabaque, US$300 for up to 25 passengers. Alternatively, you can make an adventurous journey by road back to Sorata.

To Peru At Achacachi, another road runs roughly parallel to the shore of Lake Titicaca, through Ancoraimes (small Sunday market), Carabuco (with colonial church), **Escoma**, which has a large Aymara market every Sunday morning, to **Kasiri Puerto Acosta** on the Peruvian border. The area around Puerto Acosta is good walking country and the locals are friendly. From La Paz to Puerto Acosta the road is paved as far as Escoma, then good thereafter (best in the dry season, approximately May to October). North of Puerto Acosta towards Peru the road deteriorates rapidly and should not be attempted except in the dry season.

There is an immigration office in Puerto Acosta, but it is advisable to get an exit stamp in La Paz first. There is one hotel (**G**) but no restaurants. There is a Peruvian immigration office 30 minutes' walk from the border, before Tilali. ■ *Buses: La Paz (Cementerio district)-Puerto Acosta, 5 hrs, US$2.50, Fri 1130, Sat/Sun 0630. Many trucks travel La Paz-Puerto Acosta on Tue and Fri evening. The only transport beyond Acosta is early on Wed and Sat morning when a couple of trucks go to the markets, some 25 km from Puerto Acosta on the border.*

The Cordillera Apolobamba, the north extension of the Cordillera Real, with many 5,000 m-plus peaks, can be reached by public transport from La Paz, the main starting out points being **Charazani**; bus from C Reyes Cardona, Cemetery district, Wednesday 1100, US$6, 18-24 hours, and Pelechuco, bus three days a week, also trucks with no specific schedule. Transport passes through the Parque Nacional Ulla Ulla. Guides are available in Charazani and Pelechuco. For further information on hiking in this area see the *Bolivia Handbook*.

Bolivia

La Paz

The Yungas

The lush forested slopes behind the mountains to the north of La Paz are the main production area of citrus, bananas, coffee and coca leaves for the capital. It is also a favourite retreat for those escaping the Andean chill.

Bolivia

La Paz to The most commonly-used route to the Yungas is via La Cumbre, northeast of La
the Yungas Paz. The road out of La Paz circles cloudwards over La Cumbre pass at 4,725 m; the highest point is reached in an hour; all around are towering snowcapped peaks. Soon after Unduavi the paving ends, the road becomes 'all-weather' and drops over 3,400 m to the green semi-tropical forest in 80 km. The roads to Chulumani and Coroico divide just after Unduavi, where there is a *garita* (check point), the only petrol station, and lots of roadside stalls. From Unduavi leading to Yolosa, the junction 8 km from Coroico, is steep, twisting, clinging to the side of sheer cliffs, and it is very slippery in the wet. It is a breathtaking descent (best not to look over the edge if you don't like heights) and its reputation for danger is more than matched by the beauty of the scenery. A new road from La Paz, including a 2½-km tunnel, is being built to Coroico via Chuspipata and Yolosa. It is creating a lot of damage and is unlikely to be completed until 2004. For the La Cumbre-Coroico hike (Choro), see page 260. *Gravity Assisted Mountain Biking* (address under La Paz, Tour operators, *América Tours*) run La Cumbre-Coroico with top quality bikes, guide, helmet, gloves and minibus to La Cumbre, US$49; four hours La Cumbre-Yolosa, then transport to Coroico. Highly recommended. Other companies do this trip, too, and taking a reputable organized tour is the only sensible option. Cheap rented bikes may have inadequate (or no) brakes.

Chulumani

Phone code: 02
Colour map 6, grid A3
Altitude: 1,640 m
124 km from La Paz

Lively market
on Sat/Sun

The capital of Sud Yungas is an attractive, relaxed little town with beautiful views and many hikes. The road from Unduavi goes through Puente Villa (**C** *Hotel Tamapaya*, T02-270 6099, just outside town, beautiful setting, with shower, good rooms, pool, recommended), where a road branches north to Coroico through Coripata. Fiesta 24 August (lasts ten days). **Apa Apa Ecological Park**, 8 km away, is the last area of original Yungas forest with lots of interesting wildlife. US$25 for up to five people park fee including transport and hiking guide (no reduction for fewer people); accommodation and campsite with bathrooms (US$5 per tent). The road to Irupana, a colonial village 1½ hours from Chulumani, passes the turn-off to the park; ask to get off and walk 15 minutes up to the *hacienda* of Ramiro Portugal and his wife, Tildi (both speak English); you can use their pool after trek. Or T813 6106 to arrange transport from town; or T (La Paz) 279 0381, or write to Casilla 10109, Miraflores, La Paz. The tourist office is in the centre of the main plaza, sells locally-grown coffee, teas, jams and honey. ■ *Allegedly Mon-Fri 0900-1330, 1500-2200, Sat, Sun 0700-2200.*

Sleeping **B** *San Bartolomé Plaza Resort*, 2 km from *tránsito* down Irupana road, arrange hotel trans-
& eating port beforehand if arriving by bus, no taxis, www.sanbartolome@usa.net Pleasant, superb setting with fabulous views of mountains, swimming pool, can be booked through the *Hotel Plaza*, La Paz, T237 8311, ext 1221. **B** pp *San Antonio*, 3 km out of town on La Paz road, T234 1809, F237 7896. Pleasant cabins and pool. **D** *Huayrani*, just off Junín, T813 6351. Lovely views, fine garden, more expensive in winter season. **E** *Country House*, 400 m out of town. Bed and breakfast, beautifully furnished, pool, good value, restaurant with tasty home cooking, owner Xavier Sarabia has information on all hikes. Recommended. **E** *Hostal Familiar*

Dion, Alianza, just off the plaza, T813 6070. Modern, roof terrace, includes breakfast, laundry facilities and use of kitchen, **F** without bathroom and breakfast, very good. **E** *Panorama*, at top of hill on Murillo, T813 6109. Some rooms with view, basic, garden, breakfast, pool. **G** *El Mirador*, on Plaza Libertad, T813 6117. Cheaper without bath, good beds, restaurant, noisy at weekends from disco. **G** *Alojamiento Danielito*, Bolívar. Hot water extra, laundry facilities, good view. *El Mesón*, on Plaza. Open 1200-1330 only, good cheap lunches, great views. Also on Plaza, **Chulumani**, pleasant, good *almuerzo*. **La Hostería** on Junín close to the *tranca*, good pizzas and hamburgers.

Buses from La Paz: *Trans San Bartolomé*, Virgen del Carmen 1750, Villa Fátima, T221 1674, daily at 0800-1600 or when full, 4 hrs, US$2.50. *Trans Arenas*, daily at 0730-1800, US$2.25. *Trans 24 de Agosto* micros, 15 de Abril 408 y San Borja, T221 0607, 0600-1600 when full. Buses return to La Paz from the plaza, micros from the *tranca*. **Transport**

Banks On Plaza Libertad, *Banco Unión*, changes US$100 or more only in cash and TCs (5% commission), Mon-Fri 0830-1200, 1430-1800. *Cooperativa San Bartolomé*, changes cash Mon-Fri 0800-1200, 1400-1700, Sat-Sun 0700-1200. **Communications** Internet: in tourist office, US$1.05 per hr. **Directory**

Bolivia

Coroico

The little town of Coroico is perched on a hill at 1,760 m amid beautiful scenery. The hillside is covered with orange and banana groves; coffee is also grown and condors circle overhead. It is a first-class place to relax with several good walks. There is horse riding with *El Relincho* (Reynaldo, mob T7192 3814) 100 m past *Hotel Esmeralda* (see below for location). A colourful 4-day festival is held on 19-22 October. It is great fun. On 2 November, All Souls' Day, the local cemetery is festooned with black ribbons. A tourist office called *Vagantes* provides information, guides and taxis to surrounding places of interest. On the main plaza are the agencies *Eco Adventuras* and *Inca Land Tours*.

Phone code: 02
Colour map 6, grid A3

There have been several incidents of young women being raped or attacked on the trails around Coroico; on no account hike alone in this area

B *El Viejo Molino*, T/F813 6004, valmar@waranet.com 2 km on road to Caranavi, 5-star, pool, jacuzzi, games room etc. **C** *Gloria*, C Kennedy 1, T/F813 6020, www.gloria-tours-bolivia.com Spacious, large pool, breakfast extra, restaurant, internet, free transport from plaza. **C** *Esmeralda*, T010 221 36017, www.hotelesmeralda.com 10 mins uphill from plaza (Casilla 9225, La Paz), cheaper without private bathroom and view, free pick-up service (ring from *Totai Tours*), German owned, English spoken, restaurant, hikes arranged, Visa, MasterCard accepted (no commission), credit card phones, great views, fantastic hot showers, videos, restaurant, garden, pool, laundry service, free internet access, 2 hrs a night, some rooms noisy, best to book ahead. **D** *Bella Vista*, C Héroes del Chaco (2 blocks from main plaza), T7156 9237 (mob). Beautiful rooms, beautiful views, **E** without bath but much smaller, 2 racquetball courts, terrace, bikes for rent, restaurant, covered pool being built 2001. Recommended. **D** *Don Quijote*, 500 m out of

Sleeping & eating
Hotel rooms can be difficult to find at holiday weekends and as the area is a popular retreat for the rich from La Paz, prices are higher. The Cámara Hotelera on the plaza also functions as a tourist information centre

town, on road to Coripata, T813 6007, quijote@mpoint.com.bo With bath, pool, quiet, English spoken. **D** *Hostal Kory*, at top of steps leading down from the plaza. Pool, **E** without bath, hot showers, kitchen, restaurant, laundry. Recommended. **D** *Moderno*, C Guachalla (1 block from main plaza), T240 7864 (La Paz – for reservations). Large rooms, good views, pool. **E** *Cevra Verde*, Ayacucho 5037. With bath, new in 2001, pool, pick-up service. **E-F** pp *Sol y Luna*, 15-20 mins beyond *Hotel Esmeralda*, T813 6126. 5 *cabañas* with bath and kitchen, splendid views, 5 rooms with shared bath for 1-4 people **G** pp, meals available, vegetarian specialities and Indonesian banquet, camping US$2 pp (not suitable for cars), lovely garden, pool, laundry service, massages, meditation, ceramics classes, TCs accepted, good value, Sigrid, the owner, speaks English, French, German and Spanish. Reserve through *Chuquiago Turismo*, Planta Baja, Edif La Primera, Av Santa Cruz 1364, Casilla 4443, La Paz, T236 2099. **F** pp *La Casa Colonial*, on Pando. Shared bath, comfortable, good value. **F** *Las Hamacas*, Andrés Muñoz, esq P Salazar (1 block from main plaza), T241 7818. Basic, without bath, music and films at night, restaurant downstairs for pasta and vegetarian. **F** *Lluvia de Oro*, F Reyes Ortiz, T813 6005, 1 block from church. Good value, good food, pool. **G** *El Cafetal*, beside hospital, T7193 3979 (mob). French-run, very nice, restaurant with excellent French/Indian/ vegetarian cuisine, good value. Highly recommended. **G** *La Residencial Coroico*, F Reyes Ortiz. Without bath, basic, hot shower extra. **Campsite** by the small chapel on the hill overlooking the town.

Restaurants: *La Casa*, downhill from *Kory*, T813 6024. German-run, good food and setting, also hotel (**E**), vegetarian dishes, fondue and raclette for dinner (reserve in advance), wonderful views, pool, slow internet connection (US$3.50). Recommended. The convent opposite sells biscuits, peanut butter, wine and coffee liqueurs. *Deutsche Backstube*, next to *Hostal Kory*. German pastries, set lunch, good breakfast, expensive (has house for rent for 3 or more days, T7193 5594 (mob)). *La Taberna*, north side of plaza. Owner Luis Torres is very friendly, juices, American breakfast and banana pancakes recommended, shows videos.

Transport From La Paz all companies are on C Yanacachi, beside YPFB station in Villa Fátima: *Turbus Totai* (T221 8385), US$2.25, 3 hrs, several daily from 0730-1630 each way, as does *Flota Yungueña* (T221 3275); worth booking in advance. Best views on left hand side on the descent to Yungas. Extra services run on Sun. It can be difficult to book journeys to La Paz on holidays and on Sun evenings/Mon morning (though these are good times for hitching). Trucks and pick-ups from La Paz may drop you at Yolosa, 7 km from Coroico; there is usually transport Yolosa-Coroico, US$1, or you can walk, uphill all the way, 2 hrs. In Coroico trucks leave from the market. Buses, trucks and pick-ups run from Yolosa to **Rurrenabaque** via Caranavi, daily at 1500 with *Yungueña*, except Sun at 1730, with *Turbus Totai*, US$8.75, 13-15 hrs, the company will take you down to Yolosa to catch the bus from La Paz. *13 de Mayo* (on Virgen del Carmen, Villa Fátima) run 4-6 day jeep tours of the Yungas.

Directory **Banks** *Banco Mercantil*, on central plaza. Mon-Fri 0830-1230, 1430-1830, Sat 0900-1230, cash advances (no commission) on MasterCard and Visa. **Communications** Internet: Carlos, who lives on C Caja de Agua, T/F813 6041, has an internet café, will exchange Spanish for English lessons. **Post Office** on plaza. **Telephone**: *Entel*, on Sagárnaga next to Flota Yungueña, for international and local calls. *Cotel*, next to church, phones, public TV. **Medical services** **Hospital**: T813 6002, the best in the Yungas, good malaria advice. **Police** East side of main plaza.

La Paz

Southwest Bolivia

The mining town of Oruro with its famous carnival of the devil, vast salt-flats, multi-coloured lakes, flamingoes and volcanoes are all found in this remote, starkly beautiful corner of Bolivia which borders Chile and Argentina.

Oruro

Although **Oruro** became famous as a mining town, there are no longer any working mines. It is, however, an important railway junction and the commercial centre for the mining communities of the altiplano, as well as hosting the country's best-known carnival (see box La Diablada). Several fine buildings in the centre hint at the city's former importance, notably the **baroque concert hall** (now a cinema) on Plaza 10 de Febrero and the **Casa de la Cultura** (see under **Museums**) built as a mansion by the tin baron Simón Patiño. There is a good view from the **Cerro Corazón de Jesús**, near the church of the **Virgen del Socavón**, five blocks west of Plaza 10 de Febrero at the end of C Mier.

Phone code: 02
Colour map 6, grid A2
Population: 183,422
Altitude: 3,706 m

Phone companies Coteor and Entel operate in Oruro; Coteor uses prefix 52, Entel 51 before final 5 digits 30 km SE of La Paz

Museo Etnográfico Minero is inside the Church of the Virgen del Socavón, west end of C Mier, it contains mining equipment and other artefacts from the beginning of the century as well as a representation of El Tío (the devil.) ■ *Entry via the church 0900-1200, 1400-1800,US$0.50.* **Casa de la Cultura**, Soria Galvarro 5755, run by the Universidad Técnica de Oruro, contains European furniture and a carriage imported from France, also houses temporary exhibitions. ■ *Mon-Fri 0900-1200, 1400-1830, US$0.30.* **Museo Antropológico**, south of centre on Av España (take micro A heading south or any trufi going south) has a unique collection of stone llama heads as well as impressive carnival masks. ■ *Mon-Fri 0900-1200, 1400-1800, Sat-Sun 1000-2000, 1500-1800, US$0.75.* **Museo Mineralógico**, part of the University (take micro A south to the Ciudad Universitaria), with over 3,000 mineral specimens. ■ *Mon-Fri 0800-1200, 1430-1700, US$0.60.*

A very helpful and informative tourist office is at Montes 6072, Plaza 10 de Febrero, T/F525 0144. ■ *Mon-Fri 0800-1200 and 1400-1800 .* Another kiosk is outside *Entel* on C Bolívar. Colour map and guide (Spanish only), US$1. ■ *Same hours.*

Sleeping

In the centre B *Gran Sucre*, Sucre 510 esq 6 de Octubre, T527 6800, F525 4110. **D-E** without bath, includes breakfast, heaters on request. Recommended. **D** *Repostero*, Sucre 370 y Pagador, T525 8001. **E** without bath, hot water, includes breakfast, ageing but clean, parking. **E** *América*, Bolívar 347, T527 4707. Ring bell, cheaper without bath, TV, restaurant. **E** *Gloria*, Potosí 6059, T527 6250. 19th century building, basic but OK, hot water, open 24 hrs. **F** *Res San Miguel*, Sucre 331. Nice rooms, some with bath, hot water, restaurant. Recommended. **G** *Alojamiento 15 de Octubre*, 6 de Agosto 890, T527 6012. Without bath, hot showers, safe, good value.

Near the bus terminal B *International Park*, above bus terminal, T527 6227, F525 3187. Best in town, includes breakfast, with bath, parking. **E** *Bernal*, Brasil 701, opposite terminal, T527 9468. Modern, good value, excellent hot showers, heaters on request, restaurant, tours arranged. **E** *Gutiérrez*, Bakovic 580, T525 6675, F527 6515. Open 24 hrs, cable TV, heaters on request, internet access US$0.90 per hr, good restaurant. **E** *Lipton*, Av 6 de Agosto 225, T527 6538. **G** pp without bath, secure, parking extra, open 24 hrs, good value.

Near the railway station G *Res San Salvador*, V Galvarro 6325, T527 6771. Hot water, best in this area. **G** *Alojamiento San Gerardo* V Galvarro 1886, T525 6064. Cheapest and largest on this street, shared bath, renovations and internet café under way.

Eating

La Cabaña, Junín 609. Comfortable, smart, good international food, bar, reasonable prices, Sun and Mon 1200-1530 only. *Club Social Arabe*, Junín 729 y Pres Montes. Good value

Bolivia

Bolivia

lunches from US$1. *Govinda*, 6 de Octubre 6071. Excellent vegetarian, lunch US$1.40, Mon-Sat 0900-2130. *El Huerto*, Bolívar 359. Good and cheap, vegetarian options, open Sun. *Chifa Rosa*, A Mier, north side of main plaza. Good value Chinese with large portions. A good *pizzería* is *La Casona*, Pres Montes 5970, opposite Post Office. *Libertador*, Bolívar 347. Excellent set lunch for US$1.50. *SUM Confitería*, Bolívar esq S Galvarro. Good coffee and cakes, popular at lunch, 0800-2300, Sun till 1600. *Mateos*, Bolívar y 6 de Octubre. *Confitería*, good, reasonable prices, also ice cream. *Nayjama*, Aldana esq Pagador. Best in town, huge portions, main dishes from US$6. For good coffee, *El Nochero*, Av 6 de Octubre 1454, open 1700-2400. *Caramello*, Junín y 6 de Octubre. Café, bar, good *almuerzos*, open till early hours for snacks, live music every 3 weeks, good atmosphere. Recommended. *Café Sur*, Arce 163, near train station. Live entertainment, seminars, films, Tue-Sat.

Oruro

N

0 metres 200
0 yards 200

■ Sleeping
1 Alojamiento
   15 de Octubre *B3*
2 Alojamiento
   San Gerardo *D3*
3 América *D3*
4 Bernal *A3*
5 Gloria *C2*
6 Gran Sucre *D2*
7 Gutiérrez *A3*
8 International Park *A3*
9 Lipton *A3*
10 Repostero *D3*
11 Residencial
   San Miguel *D3*
12 Residencial
   San Salvador *D3*

● Eating
1 Caramello *C2*
2 Chifa Rosa *C2*
3 Club Social Arabe *C2*
4 El Nochero *C2*
5 Govinda *D2*
6 La Casona *C2*
7 Libertador &
   El Huerto *D2*
8 Mateos *D2*
9 Nayjama *D3*
10 SUM Confitería *D2*

Festivals: La Diablada

On the **Saturday before Ash Wednesday**, Oruro Carnival stages the **Diablada** ceremony in homage to the miraculous Virgen del Socavón, patroness of miners, and in gratitude to Pachamama, the Earth Mother. The entire procession starts its 5 km route through the town at 0700, reaching the Sanctuary of the Virgen del Socavón at 0400 on Sunday. There the dancers invoke her blessing and ask for pardon. The company then proceeds to the Av Cívica amphitheatre, where the dancers perform two masques. Afterwards, the dancers all enter the sanctuary, chant a hymn in Quechua and pray for pardon. The **Diablada** was traditionally performed by Indian miners, but several other guilds have taken up the custom. The Carnival is particularly notable for its fantastically imaginative costumes. The working-class Oruro district known as La Ranchería is particularly famous for the excellence of its costumes.

The **Gran Corso del Carnaval** takes place on the Sunday, a very spectacular display. Monday is **El Día del Diablo y del Moreno** in which the Diablos and Morenos, with their bands, compete against each other on Av Cívica in demonstrations of dancing. Every group seems to join in, in 'total marvellous chaos'. The action usually parades out of the amphitheatre, ending up at the Plaza de Armas. At dusk dancers and musicians go their separate ways, serenading until the early hours. By Tuesday the main touristic events have ended; **Carnaval del Sur** takes place, with ch'alla rituals to invoke ancestors, unite with Pachamama and bless personal possessions. This is also the día del agua on which everyone throws water and sprays foam at everyone else (though this goes on throughout carnival; plastic tunics are sold for US$0.20 by street vendors).

The Friday before carnival, traditional miners' ceremonies are held at mines, including the sacrifice of a llama. Visitors may only attend with a guide and permission from Comibol, via the tourist office. The Sunday before carnival the groups practise and make their final pledges. In honour of its syncretism of Andean, precolumbian tradition and Catholic faith, La Diablada has been included on UNESCO's Heritage of Humanity list.
NB A more detailed description is given in the Bolivia Handbook.

Seating Around the Plaza de Armas, along Avenida 6 de Agosto and on Avenida Cívica, seats cost US$5-10 a day, bought from the Alcaldía in the plaza, or whichever business has erected stands outside its building. Seats on Avenida Bolívar, etc, cost US$5 a day from the shops who built stands. To wander among the dancers you are officially supposed to purchase a professional photographer's ticket for US$15, but amateurs can pay only US$1.50 by showing a small camera and insisting.

Sleeping Must be booked in advance for carnival; prices range from US$10 per person without bath, to US$20 per person with, to US$100 per person per day in the better places. The tourist office has list of all householders willing to let rooms; host and guest arrange the price, at least US$10 per person. Most hotels sell only three-night packages.

Transport Prices from La Paz triple. Organized day trips from La Paz cost US$30-45, including transport departing 0430, food and a seat in the main plaza, returning at 1600-1700 (missing the last 8-9 hours).

Bolivia

Shopping
Mercado Campero, V Galvarro esq Bolívar. Sells everything, cheap food in *comedor popular*, also *brujería* section for magical concoctions. *Mercado Fermín López*, C Ayacucho y Montes. Food and hardware, big *comedor popular*. C Bolívar is the main shopping street. *Micro Market Delicia*, A Meier y Soria Galvarro (off Plaza 10 de Febrero). Small supermarket well stocked with good quality produce. *Reguerín*, 6 de Octubre 6001 esq Mier. Good Diablada dolls and masks. On Av La Paz the 4 blocks between León and Belzu, 48-51, are largely given over to workshops producing masks and costumes for Carnival.

Tour operators
Viajeros del Tiempo, Soria Galvarro 1220, T5271166, www.contactoenoruro.com They offer trips to the nearby mines, hot pools and other attractions, open Mon-Fri 0900-1230, 1500-1930, Sat 0900-1200.

Bolivia

Transport
To check train times,
call T5274605

Train Two companies run services from Oruro to Uyuni and on to Villazón via Tupiza: *Nuevo Expreso del Sur* Mon and Fri at 1530, arriving in **Uyuni** at 2156 (*Premier* US$7.75, *Salón* US$5.40); *Wara Wara del Sur* Sun and Wed at 1900, arriving in Uyuni at 0200 (*Salón* US$4.20). For details of trains from Uyuni to **Villazón** and for trains from Uyuni to Oruro, see Uyuni. For return times from Villazón, see page 284. Passengers with tickets Villazón-La Paz are transferred to a bus at Oruro.

Bus Bus terminal 10 blocks north of centre at Bakovic and Aroma, T525 3535, US$0.20 terminal tax to get on bus. Micro No 2 to centre, or any saying 'Plaza 10 de Febrero'. Daily services to: **La Paz** at least every hour 0400-2200, US$2, 3 hrs;. **Cochabamba** 0430-2230, US$2.25, 4½ hrs. **Potosí** 0800-1900, US$4.50, 8 hrs. **Sucre** 0845 and 2100, US$6, 12 hrs. **Uyuni** 2000, US$3, 9 hrs (longer in rainy season), several companies. **Santa Cruz** 0600-1530, US$10.45, 12 hrs. **Pisiga** (Chilean border) 1200, US$4.50, 5 hrs. **International buses** (US$2 to cross border): to Iquique via Pisiga, *Trans Salvador*, T527 0280, *semi-cama*, US$12, 14 hrs, Sun-Fri 1230, Wed also 2330. *Trans Paraíso*, T527 0765, *bus cama*, toilet, video, US$12.75, 10hrs, Mon-Sun 1230 and 2230. **Arica** via Tambo Quemado, *Trans Paraíso*, US$12.75, 14 hrs, Mon-Sun 1330.

Directory

Banks *Enlace* ATM opposite *Banco Nacional de Bolivia*, La Plata 6153. TCs can be changed at *Banco Boliviano Americano*, 5% commission, or *Banco de Santa Cruz*, Bolívar 670 (also at Pagador y Caro, Sat 0900-1200). It is quite easy to change dollars (cash) on the street, or at shops in centre and around Mercado Campero displaying 'compro dolares' signs. **NB** Exchange rates are the worst in Bolivia; up to 5% below the official rate. **Communications** Internet: *ICP*, Bolívar 469. *Ultranet*, 6 de Octubre 5864. **Post Office:** Presidente Montes 1456, half block from plaza. **Telephone:** *Entel*, Bolívar, esq S Galvarro.

Lago Poopó
About 65 km south is the **Santuario de Aves Lago Poopó**, an excellent bird reserve on the lake of the same name. The lake dries up completely in winter. It can be visited from Challapata, 120 km south of Oruro on a paved road; buses from Oruro 0800 and 1430, 2½ hours, US$1. In Challapata is a gas station, basic lodging at main crossing opposite *Hotel Potosí* (**F**, good beds, basic restaurant); *fiesta* 15-17 July.

Parque Nacional Sajama

A one day drive to the west of Oruro is the **Parque Nacional Sajama**, established in 1942 and covering 100,000 ha. The park contains the world's highest forest, consisting mainly of the rare Kenua tree (Polylepis Tarapana) which grows up to 5,200 m. The scenery is wonderful and includes views of three volcanoes (**Sajama** – Bolivia's highest peak at 6,549 m – Parinacota and Pomerape). The road is now paved. There are restaurants in the park but no fresh food, so take plenty. Once you move away from the Río Sajama or its major tributaries, lack of water is a serious problem.

Sajama
village
Population: 500
Altitude: 4,200 m

In Sajama village, Telmo Nina has a book with descriptions of the various routes to the summit. Park entry fee US$2; basic accommodation available with families and there are four *comedores*. It can be very windy and cold at night (good sleeping bag, gloves, hat essential; crampons, ice axe and rope are needed for climbing the volcanoes and can be hired in Sajama village). Horses can be hired, US$8 per day. Good bathing in hot springs 7 km northwest of village, interesting geothermic area 5 km west of village (jeeps can be rented to visit either, US$5-6). The Sajama area is a major centre of alpaca wool production and Telmo Nina works on a natural dye project (outlet in La Paz at Sagárnaga 177, local 4, founders Peter and Juana Brunhart).

■ *Getting there: Take a La Paz-Oruro bus and change at Patacamayo, in front of Restaurant Capitol, for Tambo Quemado, buses leave when full between 1000-1600, US$2.25. Or take a La Paz-Arica bus, ask for Sajama, pay the full fare. Either way you have to walk 10 km from the road to Sajama village unless enough passengers on the Patacamayo-Tambo Quemado bus want to go into the village, US$0.75 extra.*

There are two routes from La Paz to Chile: the shortest and most widely used is the road to **Arica via the border at Tambo Quemado (Bolivia) and Chungará (Chile)**. From La Paz take the highway south towards Oruro. Immediately before Patacamaya, turn right at green road sign to Puerto Japonés on the Río Desaguadero, then on to Tambo Quemado. Take extra petrol (none available after Chilean border until Arica), food and water. The journey is worthwhile for the breathtaking views.

By road to Chile

Bolivian customs is at Lagunas, 12 km on from Sajama, a popular 'truck-stop'. Petrol available. Restaurant/bar *Lagunas* offers cheap set menu, helpful, friendly. Owner can usually find accommodation somewhere in the village, US$1, take your own sleeping bag, extra blankets, warm clothing. Facilities are at best very basic; you may well be sleeping on a straw mattress on a dirt floor. No water or electricity, gas lamps or candles are usual. It may be possible for men to sleep at the Puesto Militar, beside the new road, 100 m from village. Nights can be bitterly cold and very windy. In the daytime there are spectacular views of nearby snowcapped Mt Sajama. The Bolivian border control is at Tambo Quemado, 10 km on from Lagunas. Best to change a small amount of currency into Chilean pesos in La Paz. From Tambo Quemado there is a stretch of about 7 km of 'no-man's land' before you reach the Chilean frontier at Chungará. Here the border crossing, which is set against the most spectacular scenic backdrop of Lago Chungará and Volcán Parinacota is strictly controlled; open 0800-2100. Expect a long wait behind lines of lorries. Avoid Sunday; best to travel midweek. Drivers must fill in *'Relaciones de Pasajeros'*, US$0.25 from kiosk at border, giving details of driver, vehicle and passengers. Do not take any fruit, vegetables, or dairy products into Chile.

An alternative route, on which there are no trucks, is to go by good road from **La Paz via Viacha to Santiago de Machaco** (130 km, petrol); **then 120 km to the border at Charaña** (F *Alojamiento Aranda*; immigration behind railway station), very bad road. In Visviri (Chile) there is no fuel, accommodation, electricity, ask for restaurant and bargain price. From Visviri a regular road runs to Putre, see Chile chapter.

Uyuni

Uyuni lies near the eastern edge of the Salar de Uyuni. Still a commercial and communication centre, Uyuni was, for much of this century, important as a major railway junction. A giant statue of an armed railway worker, erected after the 1952 Revolution, dominates Av Ferroviaria. Most services are near the station. Market on Av Potosí between the clock and Avaroa sells everything almost every day. Fiesta 11 July. Train buffs should visit the **Railway Cemetery**: engines from 1907-1950s. The tourist office is in the public clocktower on Av Potosí with Plaza Arce. ■ *Mon-Fri 0900-1230, 1500-1930.* The head office (go here if you want to complain about a tour) is nearby, at Av Potosí 13, ■ *Mon-Fri 0830-1200, 1400-1830, Sat-Sun 0830-1200. T693 2060 and ask for the tourist information office.*

Phone code: 02
Colour map 6, grid B3
Population: 11,320
Altitude: 3,665 m

Uyuni is the jumping off point for trips to the salt flat, volcanoes and mulit-coloured lakes of SW Bolivia

A road and railway line run south from Oruro, through Río Mulato, the junction for trains to Potosí, to Uyuni (323 km). The road is sandy and, after rain, very bad, especially south of Río Mulato. The train journey is quicker in the wet and, anyway, more scenic (see Transport below).

C *Kory Wasy*, Av Potosí, entre Arce y Sucre. **D** low season, rather basic for the price but good fun, sunny lobby, restaurant planned, tour agency. **D** *Mágia de Uyuni*, Av Colón entre Sucre y Camacho, T693 2541 F693 2121, magia_uyuni@latinmail.com Includes breakfast. Recommended. **D** *Kutimuy*, Avaroa esq Av Potosí, near market, T693 2391. Includes continental breakfast, fair, electric showers, **F** without bath. **D** *Hostal Marith*, Av Potosí 61, T693 2174. **F** without bath, good budget option, hot showers, sunny patio with laundry sinks. Recommended. **E** *Avenida*, Av Ferroviaria 11, opposite the train station, T693 2078. Cheaper with shared bath, popular, good hot showers, laundry facilities, parking. **G** *Hostal Europa*, Ferroviaria opposite train station. Good gas-powered showers, good beds, noisy in the early hours from people arriving off the train, basic kitchen facilities, storage, secure, English spoken. **G** *Residencial Sucre*, Sucre 132,

Sleeping & eating
Water is frequently cut off and may only be available between 0600 and midday

Bolivia

T693 2047. Very welcoming and warm though the 3 stars on the sign is optimistic.
G *Residencial Urkupiña*, Plaza Arce. Small, basic, quite clean, hot shower US$0.50.

Eating, on Plaza Arce: *Arco Iris*, good Italian food and atmosphere, occasional live music.
16 de Julio, opens 0700, not cheap, fair, meeting place. *Kactus*, good pancakes, omelettes,
plus Bolivian dishes, heating, popular. *Urkupiña*, Plaza Arce, open for breakfast, good standard stuff. **NB** Avoid eating in market. This is not a good place to get ill.

Transport

Bus tickets include a small 'bus station construction' charge

Bus Bus offices are on Av Arce, in the same block as the post office. To **La Paz**, change in
Oruro, 2000 (also 1930 every day with *Belgrano* except 2100 on Thu), US$7.45, 11-13 hrs.
Panasur direct Wed and Sun 1800, US$9, 13 hrs (*Panasur* from La Paz bus terminal daily 1730
via Oruro, direct Tue and Fri). Same schedule to **Oruro**, US$3, 8 hrs (bitterly cold trip; take
blanket or sleeping bag). To **Potosí** 1000, 1900, US$4.50, 5-7 hrs, spectacular scenery. To
Sucre 1000, 1900, US$5.20, 9½ hrs. To **Tupiza** Wed and Sun 0900, US$5.25, 10 hrs. To
Camargo 1000, US$6.70, 11-12 hrs, via Potosí. Likewise to **Tarija** 1000, US$9, 14 hrs.

Train Check services on arrival, T693 2153. *Nuevo Expreso del Sur* leaves for **Oruro** on
Tue and Sat at 2352, arriving 0625 (*Premier* US$7.75; *Salón* US$5.40). *Wara Wara del Sur* ser-
vice leaves on Mon and Thu at 0122, arriving 0825 (*Salón* US$4.20). To **Atocha**, **Tupiza** and
Villazón *Expreso del Sur* leaves Uyuni on Mon and Fri at 2216, arriving, respectively, at 0015,
0315 and 0620 (*Premier* US$4.95, US$9.70, US$14.65; *Salón* US$1.95, US$4.17, US$6.40).
Wara Wara leaves on Sun and Wed at 0235, arriving 0430, 0800 and 1135 (*Salón* US$1.65,
US$3,45, US$5.10). The ticket office opens at 0830 and 1430 each day and one hour before
the trains leave. It closes once tickets are sold – get there early or buy through a tour agent.

Do not attempt to take coca leaves across the border; it is an arrestable offence

To Chile: The easiest way is to go via San Pedro de Atacama as part of your jeep trip to the Salar
and *lagunas*. See below. Otherwise, there is a train service to Calama leaving between 0500 and
0800 Thu, US$13.45. It takes 1 hr to change trains at Avaroa, then it's 40 mins to Ollagüe, where
Chilean customs take 2-4 hrs. All passports are collected and stamped in the rear carriage and
should be ready for collection after 1-2 hrs; queue for your passport, no names are called out. After
that it is an uncomfortable 6 hrs to Calama. On Mon an 0800 service runs only as far as Avaroa and
you must organize your own change of trains; there is a service from there to Calama. *Predilecto*
and *Trans 11 de Julio* each has a **bus** to Calama which leaves from its office Mon and Thu 0400,
US$10.50, 15 hrs (depending on border crossing). *Colque Tours*, Av Potosí 54, T/F639 2199,
www.colquetours.terra.cl, as well as running Salar and Lagunas tours that take you to San Pedro
de Atacama, has a **jeep** direct there leaving their office every day at 1900, US$25 pp, 16 hours.
Whichever route you take, no exit stamp is needed in advance; the Bolivian border post charges
US$2.50 on exit. If you take your own food, eat fresh things first as the Chileans do not allow dairy
produce, teabags (of any description), fruit or vegetables to be brought in.

Chile is 1 hr ahead of Bolivia from mid-Oct to Mar

By road to Chile From Colchani it is about 60 km across to the west shore of the salar. There
are 2 or 3 parallel tracks about 100 m apart and every few kilometres stones mark the way;
the salt is soft and wet for about 2 km around the edges. There is no real danger of getting
lost, especially in the high season, but it is a hard trip and the road is impassable after rain.
There is no gasoline between Uyuni and Calama (Chile). It is 20 km from the west shore to
'Colcha K', the military checkpoint. From there, a poor gravel road leads 28 km to San Juan,
where tour groups spend the night (very cold, no heating), then the road enters the Salar de
Chiguana, a mix of salt and mud which is often wet and soft with deep tracks which are easy
to follow. 35 km away is Chiguana, another military post, then 45 km to the end of the salar, a
few kilometres before border at Ollagüe. This latter part is the most dangerous; very slippery
with little traffic. Alterantively, *Toñito Tours* of Uyuni will let you follow one of their groups
and even promise help in the event of a break-down.

Directory **Banks** *Banco de Crédito*, Av Potosí, entre Bolívar y Arce, does not change money. Instead, go to the
exchange shop to its left, which changes dollars, Chilean pesos and TCs, as does a *cambio* almost
opposite *M@c Internet Café* on Av Potosí. *Hotel Avenida* changes dollars cash. *Colque Tours*, Av Potosí
54, changes TCs. Tour agencies and some shops accept payment in TCs. **Communications** Internet:
M@cNet, Av Potosí near Arce, open daily 0900-2300 or later if you ask, fast satellite connection.

Bolivia

Servinet, Potosí y Bolívar, 0800-1300, 1400-2200 daily. Both US$1.50 per hr. **Post office:** Av Arce esq C Cabrera. **Telephone:** *Entel*, Av Arce above Av Potosí, 0830-2200. **Useful addresses Immigration:** Av Sucre 94, corner of Av Potosí, open daily 0800-2000 daily for visa extensions.

Salar de Uyuni

Driving across the salt lake is a fantastic experience, especially during June and July when the bright blue skies contrast with the blinding-white salt crust (sunglasses essential). At the otherside are the volcanoes and multi-coloured lakes that make up some of weirdest landscapses in South America.

The largest and highest salt lake in the world.

On its west side, five hours from Uyuni, is **Llica**, capital of Daniel Campos province. Good for llama and wool handicrafts, but there are no shops or electricity, only a basic hotel, meals in private houses. Bus from Uyuni 1200 daily, truck 1100.

The best map of the area is by Walter Guzmán Córdova (see page 237)

Tours to Lagunas Colorada & Verde
346 km SW of Uyuni

10 hours straight driving over unmarked, rugged truck tracks from Uyuni is one of Bolivia's most spectacular and most isolated marvels. The shores and shallows of the lake are crusted with gypsum and salt, an arctic-white counterpoint to the flaming red, algae-coloured waters (from midday) in which the rare James flamingoes, along with the more common Chilean and Andean flamingoes, breed and live (see *Aves de la Reserva Nacional de Fauna Andina Eduardo Avaroa*, by Omar Rocha and Carmen Quiroga – Museo Nacional de Historia Natural, La Paz 1996 – in Spanish). The **Reserva Eduardo Avaroa (REA** – 714,000 ha), which includes both lakes, has an office at Potosí 23 in Uyuni, excellent map for sale, US$5 entry (not included in tour price; pay in bolívares, write your name on the back of the ticket and do not surrender it on departure).

The standard outing (see below for operators) lasts four days. **Day 1**: Uyuni to Colchani, from there to the Salar, including a salt-mine visit, lunch on the cactus-studded Isla Pescado, and overnight at a village, eg San Juan, south of the Salar (simple lodging, eg **G** *Alojamiento Licancábur*, Teófilo Yucra, hot showers extra, helpful, electricity 1900-2100, running water). **Day 2**: to Laguna Colorada, passing active Volcán Ollagüe and a chain of small, flamingo-specked lagoons. Overnight at Laguna Colorada; demand to stay at *Reserva Eduardo Avaroa* headquarters US$4.50 per person, clean, comfortable, modern, quite warm – it's far better than Eustaquio Berna's hut which is also US$3 per person and favoured by the Uyuni agencies. There are two other places to stay, one good, one bad. Camping is not permitted here. **Day 3**: drive past belching geysers at Sol de Mañana (take care not to fall through the crust) and through the barren, surreal landscape of the Pampa de Chalviri at 4,800 m, via a pass at 5,000 m, to the wind-lashed jade waters of the **Laguna Verde** (4,400 m) at the foot of Volcán Licancábur (for best views arrive before 1100), and back to Laguna Colorada or further. At Aguas Termales Chalviri, between the two lakes, hot springs feed the salty water at about 30° C (hottest early morning). *Refugio* at Laguna Verde, US$2 per person, small, mattresses, running water, view of lake. **Day 4**: Return to Uyuni. A three day version eliminates the Salar de Uyuni or Laguna Verde, while an extension will permit ascent of Licancábur (not a difficult climb, guide compulsory, US$30).

Organization of tours from Uyuni is only reasonable, but even good companies have their off days. The staggering scenery makes up for any discomfort. Ask for a written contract which states a full day by day itinerary, a full meal by meal menu (vegetarians should be prepared for an egg-based diet), what is included in the price and what is not (accommodation is normally not included – add US$3 pp per night). If the tour doesn't match the contract, go back to the operator and demand a refund (unless you have been able to persuade them not to take the full price at the beginning). This seldom yields positive results, in which case complain to **Sr Ciprián Nina** in the tourism office in Uyuni (see above) and then to the **Director Regional de Turismo**, La Prefectura del Departamento de Potosí, Calle La Paz, Potosí (T02-622 7477). Trip prices are based on a 6-person group – it is easy to find other people in Uyuni. If there are fewer

Tour operators
Take a good sleeping bag, sunglasses, sun hat, sun protection, lots of warm clothing (record low measured in 1996 at Laguna Colorada: -30° C), water bottle, water purification tablets/iodine tincture, lots of film

Bolivia

Bolivia

than 6 you each pay more. The standard 4-day trip (Salar de Uyuni, Lagunas Colorada and Verde) costs US$65-220 pp depending on agency, departure point and season. There is no refund for leaving to Chile after Laguna Verde. Shorter (including one day to the Salar) and longer trips are possible but 4 days in a jeep is as much as most people's bottoms will stand.

For the latest recommendations, speak to travellers who have just returned from a tour and try the following: *As Tours*, Av Ferroviaria 304, T/F693 2772. Also owns a hotel at the lakes. *Esmeralda*, Av Ferroviaria esq Arce, T693 2130. Good tours at the cheaper end of the market. *Licancábur*, Sucre (no street number), T693 2667. Incorporates the usual trip with a journey to Tupiza, passing several reportedly beautiful and seldom-visited lagoons on the way. *Paula*, Av Arce 27, T690 2678. Good value. *Toñito Tours*, Av Ferroviaria 152, T693 2819, F693 2094, tonitotours@yahoo.com Offers a variety of tours (also in La Paz, see page 256). *Transandino*, Av Arce 27, T693 2132. *Uyuni Andes Travel Office*, Ayacucho 222, T693 2227. Good reports, run by Belgian Isabelle and Iver. *Wilson Tours*, Av Potosí 305, T693 2217. English-speaking guides, helpful, enthusiastic. Agencies in Potosí and La Paz also organize tours, but in some cases this may involve putting you on a bus to Uyuni where you meet up with one of the Uyuni agencies and get the same quality tour for a higher price.

Border with Chile If you wish to continue from here into Chile, all agencies now offer the option of crossing at **Hito Cajón**. Here there is a Bolivian immigration post which will charge you US$2.65 for an exit stamp. Agencies will organize a bus (US$10 – your jeep driver should ensure you are safely on before leaving) both to the immigration post and on to San Pedro de Atacama in Chile, where the bus will wait for your lengthy immigration formalities to be completed. As with the train crossing, do not take any fresh fruit or coca leaves. Buy Chilean pesos in Uyuni, but don't change all your money as you'll need bolivianos for national park entry and the exit tax.

To **San Pedro de Atacama (Chile)** From Laguna Verde it is 7 km to Hito Cajón, the frontier post with Chile. A further 8 km is La Cruz, the junction with the east-west road between the borax and sulphur mines and San Pedro. The meteorological station at Laguna Verde will radio for a pick-up from San Pedro. This service costs US$10 per person Hito Cajón-San Pedro. Transport Laguna Verde to Chile via Hito Cajón is becoming more plentiful and the crossing is getting much easier and popular. **Do not underestimate the dangers of getting stuck without transport or lodging at this altitude**. Do not travel alone.

Tupiza

Phone code: 02
Colour map 6, grid B3
Population: 20,000
Altitude: 2,990 m
200 km S of Uyuni

This is the place from where to take Butch Cassidy and the Sundance kid tours. The statue in the main plaza is to Victor Carlos Aramayo, the founding member of the Aramayo mining dynasty, pre-eminent in the late 19th, early 20th centuries. Chajra Huasi, a palazzo-style, abandoned home of the Aramayo family across the Río Tupiza, may be visited. Beautiful sunsets over the fertile Tupiza valley can be seen from the foot of a statue of Christ on a hill behind the plaza. Hikes, horse and jeep tours in the eroded landscape of the surroundings are the highlight of Tupiza, eg the Quebrada Palala with the nearby 'Stone Forest', the Valle de los Machos and the Quebrada Seca (tour operators have details). *IGM* office, for maps, is in the Municipal building to the right of the church, second floor.

Sleeping & eating **E** *Mitru*, Av Chichas, T694 3001, tpztours@latinmail.com Spacious, best in town, tourist information, excellent showers, TV, pool, kitchen, laundry facilities and service (US$1.20 per kg), book exchange, parking and free showing of *Butch Cassidy and the Sundance Kid* and documentary. Enjoying the same facilities is **F** *Refugio* (no double beds). Excellent value. Visa, MasterCard or TCs (4% extra) accepted at both. Under same ownership, **E** *Mitru Anexo*, Abaroa, T694 3002. Hot shower, snack shop and restaurant. **E** *Roca Colorada*, Av Chichas 220, T694 2633. **F** with shared bath, pleasant, good rooms, cable TV, electric showers. **E** *Hostal Valle Hermoso*, Av Pedro Arraya 478, T694 2592, hostalvh@hotmail.com Good hot showers, pleasant TV/breakfast room, book exchange, tourist advice, expensive laundry, internet US$3 per hr, *Butch Cassidy* video, firm beds, cheaper with shared bath, motorbikes can be parked in restaurant, accepts credit cards and TCs (5% extra). **F** *Res Centro*, Av Santa Cruz 287, 2 blocks from station, T694 2705. Warm water, nice patio, motorbike and car parking. **F** *El Rancho*, Av Pedro Araya 86, T694 3116. **G** without bath, spacious, hot water, laundry facilities. Recommended. Tupiza is famous for its *tamales*, a delicious scrap of spicy dried llama meat encased in a ball of corn mash and cooked in the leaves of the plant. *Los Helechos*, next door to *Mitru Anexo* on Abaroa. Burgers and main courses, good salad bar, closed alternate Suns. *Il Bambino*, Florida y Santa Cruz. Recommended, especially for *salteñas*, closed Sat and Sun evenings. *La Casa de Irma*, in supermarket *Frial Castro*, Florida. Home-cooked lasagnes, chicken, meat and vegetarian dishes with an hour's notice, for US$2.25. *Picantería Las Brisas*, on the opposite side of the river. Open only Nov-Mar, large helpings. *El Atajo*, Florida 157. Sandwiches and, at night, *chicharrón de pollo*, open Mon-Sat 0800-1200, 1500-2200, internet US$2.10 per hr.

Tour operators

Tupiza Tours, in *Hotel Mitru*, Av Chichas 187, Casilla 67, T694 3513. Offer 2-day tours which follow Butch and Sundance's movements in 1908 (see below), US$140 pp, includes transport, guide, meals and lodging, also tours to the Salar de Uyuni, horse riding, US$3 per hr/US$20 per day, jeep tours to local sites. Similar services from *Valle Hermoso Tours*, opposite its parent hotel, T/F694 2592. Also *Explore Andina Tours*, Av Chichas 220, T694 3016. Hires out jeeps.

Transport
Train station in the centre.
Bus station 5 blocks further south

Bus To **Villazón** 2½ hrs, US$1.50, 3 a day. To **Potosí**, US$4.50, 8 hrs, daily 1000, 1030, 2030. Same schedule to Oruro and Sucre, both US$7.45. To **Uyuni**, Mon, Thu 1100, US$5.25, 10 hrs, poor road on a river bed which floods in the wet. *Expreso Tupiza* has a direct bus to La Paz at 1030, otherwise via Potosí, 14-17 hrs, US$8.95. A 2-way dirt road has been built from Uyuni to Atocha, winding through beautiful scenery. Road from Potosí which goes on south to Villazón is also 2-way, dirt, with a new bridge over the Río Suipacha. Book transport in advance.

Train To Villazón: *Nuevo Expreso del Sur* Mon and Fri 0325, arriving 0620; *Wara Wara* Sun and Wed at 0835, arriving 1135. To Atocha, Uyuni and Oruro, *Expresso del Sur* Tue and Sat at 1820; *Wara Wara* Mon and Thu at 1900. The ticket office is open in theory on Mon from 0730 for that afternoon's train; Mon from 1800 for that leaving on Tue; Wed 0800 for the Thu service; Fri 1500 for the Sat train.

Directory

Banks *Banco Mercantil*, south side of the plaza, open Mon-Fri 0830-1200, 1430-1700, and *Banco Crédito*, opposite side, Mon-Fri 0830-1230, 1430-1830, will change US$ cash. Many shops will change dollars at better rates than in Villazón. **Communications** Internet: *Full Internet*, Plaza Independencia 477, US$2.25 per hr. Post office: on Abaroa, northwest of plaza, Mon-Fri 0830-1800, Sat 0900-1700, Sun 0900-1200. Telephone: *Entel*, is at end of same street, Mon-Sat 0800-2300, Sun 0800-1300, 1500-2200.

San Vicente
Population: 400
Altitude: 4,500 m
103 km NW of Tupiza
(4-6 hrs on good dirt road)

Tupiza is the centre of Butch Cassidy and the Sundance Kid country. On 4 November 1908, they held up an Aramayo company payroll north of Salo. (Aramayo *hacienda* in Salo, one hour north of Tupiza, still stands. Roadside kiosks serve excellent roast goat, *choclo*, *papas*, soup.) Two days later they encountered and were killed by a four-man military-police patrol in **San Vicente**. Shootout site off main street – ask locals. Butch and Sundance are buried in the cemetery, but the grave has yet to be identified. Tours from Tupiza. An investigation of the supposed grave, by the Nova project in 1991, proved negative, but see *Digging Up Butch and Sundance*, by Anne Meadows (Bison Books, 1996). Basic *alojamiento* on main street marked 'Hotel'. Restaurant *El Rancho* next door. Several *tiendas* sell beer, soda, canned goods, etc. Trucks from Tupiza on Thursday early morning from Av Chichas near *Hotel Mitru*. Alternatively hire a vehicle: Fermín Ortega at Taller Nardini, Barrio Lourdes, recommended; Don Manuel at *Hotel Mitru* can suggest others, US$30 to US$80 one-way. (Also accessible and a bit closer from Atocha, but fewer vehicles for hire.)

Bolivia

South to Argentina

Villazón
Phone code: 02;
Cotevi phone company
prefix 596, Entel 597
Population: 13,000
Altitude: 3,443 m
81 km S of Tupiza

The Argentine border is here. There is not much to see (two cinemas and good indoor market). The border area must not be photographed. *Banco de Crédito*, Oruro 111, changes cash only; try the *casas de cambio* on Av República de Argentina, near border. Travellers' cheques can be exchanged at *Restaurante Repostero*, Av 20 de Mayo 190, 5% commission. Several internet cafés charge US$1.50 per hour. Post office and *Entel* are on Av Independencia, opposite side to bus station. The tourist office on the plaza is not very useful. *Diamante Tours*, Edificio de Turismo, Plaza 6 de Agosto, T/F596 2315, are helpful (also in Potosí and Uyuni.)

Sleeping & eating

E *Res El Cortijo*, 20 de Mayo 338, behind post office, T596 2093. Breakfast included, intermittent hot water, restaurant. **E** *Grand Palace*, 25 de Mayo 52, 1 block southwest of bus terminal, T596 4693. Safe, **F** without bath. Recommended. **E** *Hostal Plaza*, Plaza 6 de Agosto 138, T596 3535. Modern, **F** without bath, TV, comfortable, good restaurant. **F** *Hostal Buena Vista*, Av Antofagasta 508, T596 3055. Good rooms, shared bath, hot showers US$1.05, close to the train and bus stations, above reasonable restaurant. **G** *Res Martínez*, 25 de Mayo 13, T596 3353, 1 block southwest of bus station. Well signed, shared bath, hot water. **G** *Res Panamericano*, C 20 de Mayo 384, T596 2612. Shared bath, risky electric showers, sagging beds, laundry facilities, parking. *Charke Kan*, J M Deheza 'the only bona fide restaurant'. Beside it is *Snack Pizzería Don Vicco*. *Chifa Jardín*, on the Plaza. Expensive but huge helpings. *Snack El Turista*, Edificio de Turismo, is open at 0900 for breakfast. Better to cross the border to La Quiaca to eat.

Transport

Road An unpaved road goes to Tarija, improved for the last 16 km. The road linking Potosí with Villazón via Camargo is in poor condition and about 100 km longer than the better road via Tupiza. **Bus** Bus terminal is near plaza, 5 blocks from the border. Taxi to border, US$0.35 or hire porter, US$1, and walk across. From **La Paz**, several companies, 25 hrs, US$7.50 (even though buses are called 'direct', you may have to change in Potosí, perhaps to another company), depart La Paz 1800, 1900, depart Villazón 0800, 0830. To **Potosí** several between 0800-0830 and 1800-1900, 10 hrs by day, 12 hrs at night, US$3-4.50 (terrible in the wet, can take 24 hrs; freezing at night). To **Tupiza**, 3 a day, US$1.50. To **Tarija**, beautiful journey but most buses overnight only, daily at 2000-2030, US$4.50, 6 hrs, very cold on arrival but passengers can sleep on bus until daybreak. **Train** Station about 1 km north of frontier on main road, taxi US$2.35. To **Tupiza**, **Atocha**, **Uyuni** and **Oruro**: *Nuevo Expreso del Sur* Tue, Sat, 1530, *Wara Wara del Sur* Mon, Thu 1530. Ticket office opens 0800, long queues.

Border with Argentina
Bolivian time is 1 hr
behind Argentina

Bolivian immigration office is on Av República de Argentina just before bridge; open daily 0600-2000. They will issue an exit stamp. Officials are efficient, but be on your guard at all times. For Argentine immigration see page 143. Change all your Bolivianos into dollars or pesos, because it is impossible to change them in Argentina. The Argentine consulate is at Av Saavedra 311; open Monday-Thursday 1000-1300.

La Paz

Potosí, Sucre and the Southern Highlands

This is a region which boasts the World Cultural Heritage sites of Potosí, with its rich mining past and current mining misery, and Sucre, the white city. In the south, Tarija is known for its fruit and wines and its traditions which set it apart from the rest of the country.

Potosí

Bolivia

Potosí is the highest city of its size in the world. It was founded by the Spaniards on 10 April 1545, after they had discovered Indian mine workings at Cerro Rico, which dominates the city. Immense amounts of silver were once extracted. In Spain 'es un Potosí' (it's a Potosí) is still used for anything superlatively rich. By the early 17th century Potosí was the largest city in the Americas, but over the next two centuries, as its lodes began to deteriorate and silver was found elsewhere, Potosí became little more than a ghost town. It was the demand for tin – a metal the Spaniards ignored – that saved the city from absolute poverty in the early 20th century, until the price slumped because of over supply. Mining continues in Cerro Rico – mainly tin, zinc, lead, antimony and wolfram.

Phone code: 02
Colour map 6, grid B3
Population: 112,000
Altitude: 4,070 m

There is a tourist office on Plaza 6 de Agosto, T622 7405, gobmupoi@cedro.pts.entelnet.bo Town maps US$0.40 (English, French, German and Spanish), better than glossy US$0.60 map (Spanish only), helpful. ■ *Mon-Fri 0800-1200, 1400-1800 (allegedly).*

Sights

Large parts of Potosí are colonial, with twisting streets and an occasional great mansion with its coat of arms over the doorway. UNESCO has declared the city to be 'Patrimonio de la Humanidad'. Some of the best buildings are grouped round the Plaza 10 de Noviembre. The old Cabildo and the Royal Treasury – Las Cajas Reales – are both here, converted to other uses. **The Cathedral** faces Plaza 10 de Noviembre. ■ *Mon-Fri 0930-1000, 1500-1730, Sat 0930-1000.*

The Casa Nacional de Moneda, or Mint, is nearby, on C Ayacucho . Founded in 1572, rebuilt 1759-73, it is one of the chief monuments of civil building in Hispanic America. In 30 of its 160 rooms are a museum with sections on on mineralogy, and an art gallery in a splendid salon on the first floor. One section is dedicated to the works of the acclaimed 17th-18th century religious painter Melchor Pérez de Holguín. Elsewhere are coin dies and huge wooden presses which made the silver strip from which coins were cut. The smelting houses have carved altar pieces from Potosí's ruined churches. You cannot fail to notice the huge, grinning mask of Bacchus over an archway between two principal courtyards. Erected in 1865, its smile is said to be ironic and aimed at the departing Spanish. Wear warm clothes, as it is cold inside. ■ *Tue-Fri 0900-1200, 1400-1830, Sat-Sun 0900-1300, US$3, US$1.50 to take photos, US$3 for video. Entry by regular, 2 hr guided tour only (in English at 0900, usually for 10 or more people), T622 2777.*

The **Convento y Museo de Santa Teresa** at Chicas y Ayacucho, T622 3847, has an interesting collection of colonial and religious art, obligatory guide. ■ *0900-1100, 1500-1700, only by guided tour in Spanish or English, US$3.15, US$1.50 to take photos, US$25(!) for video.* Among Potosí's baroque churches, typical of 18th-century Andean or 'mestizo' architecture, are the Jesuit **Compañía** church, on Ayacucho, with an impressive bell-gable. ■ *0800-1200, 1400-1800.* **San Francisco** (Tarija y Nogales,

Bolivia

T622 2539) with a fine organ, worthwhile for the views from the tower and roof, museum of ecclesiastical art, underground tunnel system. ■ *Mon-Fri 0900-1200, 1430-1700, Sat 0900-1200, US$1.50, US$1.50 to take photos, US$3 for video.* Also **San Lorenzo** (1728-44) with a rich portal, on Héroes del Chaco, fine views from the tower. **San Martín** on Hoyos, with an uninviting exterior, is beautiful inside, but is normally closed for fear of theft. Ask the German Redemptorist Fathers to show you around; their office is just to the left of their church. Other churches to visit include **Jerusalén**, close to the *Hotel Centenario*, with **Museo Sacro** displaying gold work and painting. ■ *Mon-Sat 1430-1830, US$0.75,* and **San Agustín** (only by prior arrangement with tourist office) on Bolívar y Quijarro, with crypts and catacombs (the whole city was interconnected by tunnels in colonial times). ■ *Tour starts at 1700, US$0.10*

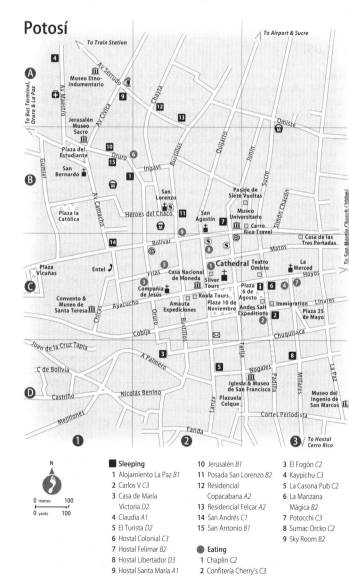

Potosí

■ Sleeping	10 Jerusalén *B1*	3 El Fogón *C2*
1 Alojamiento La Paz *B1*	11 Posada San Lorenzo *B2*	4 Kaypichu *C3*
2 Carlos V *C3*	12 Residencial	5 La Casona Pub *C2*
3 Casa de María	Copacabana *A2*	6 La Manzana
Victoria *D2*	13 Residencial Felcar *A2*	Mágica *B2*
4 Claudia *A1*	14 San Andrés *C1*	7 Potocchi *C3*
5 El Turista *D2*	15 San Antonio *B1*	8 Sumac Orcko *C2*
6 Hostal Colonial *C3*		9 Sky Room *B2*
7 Hostal Felimar *B2*	**● Eating**	
8 Hostal Libertador *D3*	1 Chaplin *C2*	
9 Hostal Santa María *A1*	2 Confitería Cherry's *C3*	

Opposite Jerusalén is 24, **San Bernardo**, which houses the Escuela Taller Potosí where you can see a display of restoration work. ■ *T22467.* **Teatro Omiste** (1753) on Plaza 6 de Agosto has a fine façade. The **Museo Universitario**, C Bolívar 698, displays archaeology and some good modern Bolivian painting. ■ *Mon-Fri, 0800-1200, 1400-1800, US$0.75.* **Museo del Ingenio de San Marcos**, Betanzos y La Paz, is a well-preserved example of the city's industrial past, with machinery used in grinding down the silver ore. It also has a good restaurant, cultural activities and an exhibition of Calcha textiles. ■ *1000-2300; restaurant open 1200-2300, information office 1130-1230, 1430-1530, exhibition Mon-Sat 1300-2000, T622 2781.* **Museo Etno-indumentario** (also known as **Fletes**), Av Serrudo 152, and has a thorough display of the different dress and customs and their histories of Potosí department's 16 provinces. ■ *Mon-Fri 0900-1200, 1400-1800, Sat 0900-1200, US$1.10, includes tour in Spanish and basic German, very interesting, T622 3258.*

In Potosí, 2,000 colonial buildings have been catalogued. At Quijarro and Omiste is the Esquina de las Cuatro Portadas (two houses with double doors), or Balcón de Llamacancha. There is a fine stone doorway (house of the Marqués de Otavi, now a bank) in Junín between Matos and Bolívar. Off Junín, see the Pasaje de Siete Vueltas (the passage of the seven turns). At Lanza 8 was the house of José de Quiroz and of Antonio López de Quiroga (now a school). Turn up Chuquisaca from Lanza and after three blocks right into Millares; here on the left is a sculpted stone doorway and on the right a doorway with two rampant lions in low relief on the lintel. Turning left up Nogales you come to an old mansion in a little plaza. Turn left along La Paz and one block along there is another stone doorway with suns in relief. At La Paz y Bolívar is the Casa del Balcón de la Horca. Turn left for the Casa de las Tres Portadas.

B *Claudia*, Av Maestro 322, out of centre, T622 2242, F622 5677. Helpful, modern. Recommended. **B** *Hostal Colonial*, Hoyos 8, T622 4265, F622 7146. A pretty colonial house near the main plaza, with heating, has names and telephone numbers of guides, very helpful, even if you're not staying there, very expensive for long-distance phone calls, best hotel in centre. Book in advance. **B** *Hostal Libertador*, Millares 58, T622 7877, hostalib@cedro.pts.entelnet.bo Central heating, quiet, helpful, comfortable, parking. Recommended. **C** *Hostal Cerro Rico*, Ramos 123 entrre La Paz y Millares, T/F622 3539, www.hostalcerrorico.8k.com Very good rooms upstairs, heating, hot water, **D** without bath, cable TV, internet, helpful, parking. **C** *Jerusalén*, Oruro 143, T/F622 2600, hoteljer@cedro.pts.entelnet.bo Pleasant, with breakfast, **F** without bath, helpful, *comedor*, parking, laundry, internet US$2 per hour, good value. **D** *Hostal Compañía de Jesús*, Chuquisaca 445, T622 3173. Central, attractive, good value, includes breakfast. **D** *Hostal Felimar*, Junín 14, T622 4357. Hot water, includes breakfast, 2 roof-top suites, solar-powered (some rooms with electric showers), 1st floor rooms have no exterior windows but warm, quiet. **D** *Hostal Santa María*, Av Serrudo 244, T622 3255. Hot water, cold rooms, good cafeteria, popular. **E** *Gran*, Av Universitario 1002, T624 3483, opposite bus terminal. With bath, hot water, breakfast, TV, helpful. Recommended for early departures. **E** *El Turista*, Lanza 19, T622 2492, F622 2517. Also LAB office, helpful, hot showers, breakfast (US$1), great view from top rooms, good value. Recommended but poor beds. **E** *San Antonio*, Oruro 136, T622 3566. **G** without bath, 10% discount with valid IYHA card if sharing room, noisy. **F** *Res Felcar*, Serrudo 345 y Bustillos, T622 4966. Shared bath, hot water 0800-1600, popular, nice patio garden. **F** *Carlos V*, Linares 42 on Plaza 6 de Agosto, T622 5121. With breakfast, **F** without bath, occasional hot water 0700-1200, luggage store, 2400 curfew. **F** *Casa de María Victoria*, Chuquisaca 148, T22132. All rooms open onto colonial courtyard, **G** without bath, lukewarm water, stores luggage, popular with backpackers, arranges mine tours, owner speaks English, good breakfast, leave nothing unattended. **F** *San Andrés*, Camacho 283, T622 9025. Helpful, shared bath, good. **G** *Res Copacabana*, Av Serrudo 319, T622 2712. Single or shared rooms, restaurant, separate hot showers, will change $ cash, safe car park (owner's son, Dr Hugo Linares Fuentes will give medical assistance). **G** *Alojamiento La Paz*, Oruro 262, T622 2632. Central, basic, 1 shower for the whole hotel, lukewarm water. **G** *Posada San Lorenzo*, C Bustillos 967, opposite market. Colonial building, nice courtyard, no showers.

Sleeping

Unless otherwise stated hotels have no heating in rooms

Bolivia

Eating

Some places charge 13% for credit cards; check

La Casona Pub, Frías 34. Good food (meat fondue and trout recommended) and beer, open Mon-Sat 1000-1230, 1800-2400. *Chaplin*, Quijarro y Matos 10. Pleasant, good breakfasts, best *tucumanos* before 1200, closed Sun. *Confitería Cherry's*, Padilla 8. Good cakes, very popular, good breakfast, cheap, open 0800. *Da Tong*, Oruro 526. Authentic Chinese, large portions, inexpensive. *El Fogón*, Oruro y Frías. Upmarket pub-restaurant, good food and atmosphere, open 1200-1500, 1800-2400. *Potocchi*, Millares 24, T22467. Great traditional food, opens 0800, *peña* most nights. Recommended. *The Sky Room*, Bolívar 701. Good views of the town and the Cerro, OK, slow service, opens 0800-2230 (1700 Sun). *Sumac Orcko*, Quijarro 46. Large portions, cheap set lunch, reasonably priced, very popular with travellers, heating. **Vegetarian**: *Kaypichu*, Millares 24. Stylish, open 0700-1300 and 1600-2100, closed Mon. *La Manzana Mágica*, Oruro 239. Good food and value, open 0700-2200, lunch US$2. Good value food in Mercado Central, between Oruro, Bustillos, Héroes del Chaco and Bolívar, breakfast from 0700, fresh bread from 0600.

Festivals

8-10 Mar is *San Juan de Dios*, with music, dancing, parades etc. In **May** there is a market on C Gumiel every Sun, with lotteries and lots of fun things for sale. *Fiesta de Manquiri*: on **3 consecutive Sat at the end of May/beginning of Jun** llama sacrifices are made at the cooperative mines in honour of *Pachamama*; the same occurs on **1 Aug**, the *Ritual del Espíritu*. *Carnaval Minero*, 2 weeks before carnival in Oruro, includes Tata Ckascho, when miners dance down Cerro Rico and El Tío (the Dios Minero) is paraded. *San Bartolomé*, or the Fiesta de Chutillos, is held **from the middle of Aug**, with the main event being processions of dancers on the weekend closest to the 24th-26th; Sat features Potosino, and Sun national, groups. Costumes can be hired in *artesanía* market on C Sucre. Hotel and transport prices go up by 30% for the whole of that weekend. In **Oct**, *Festival Internacional de la Cultura*, in Potosí and Sucre. **10 Nov**, *Fiesta Aniversiario de Potosí*. Potosí is sometimes called the 'Ciudad de las Costumbres', especially at Corpus Cristi, Todos Santos and Carnaval, when special cakes are baked, families go visiting friends, etc.

Shopping

Mercado Central (see address above), sells mainly food and produce but silver is sold near the C Oruro entrance. *Mercado Artesanal*, at Sucre y Omiste, sells handwoven cloth and regional handicrafts. Some Fri the merchants organize music, food and drink (*ponche*), not to be missed. *La Feria*, Indian market, at weekends between centre and bus terminal. The best bookshop is at the University, open Mon-Fri, 1000-1200, 1500-1700.

Tour operators

Trips to the Salar de Uyuni, Laguna Colorada and Laguna Verde are expensive here. See page 281 for practical advice on booking a trip

The following have been recommended (see also Guides to the mines): *Amauta Expediciones*, Ayacucho 17, T6225515. For trips to Uyuni, the lagoons and the mines (hands 15% of its income to the miners). *Cerro Rico Travel*, Bolívar 853, T6227044, T71835083, jacky_gc@yahoo.com Jaqueline knows the mines well and speaks good English. Also English and French guides for trips to village *artesanía* markets north of the city and to colonial *haciendas*, horse and mountain bike hire, treks, trips to Toro Toro including cave visits. *Hidalgo Tours*, Junín y Bolívar 19, T6225186, F6229212, www.salaruyuni.com Upmarket and specialized services within the city and to Salar de Uyuni. *Koala Tours*, Ayacucho 5, T6224708, F6222092. Excellent mine tours, guides are former miners, speak English, frequently recommended. *Silver Tours*, Quijarro 12, Edif Minero, T6223600, F6223600, www.silvertours.8m.com One of the cheaper firms, guide Fredi recommended.

Transport

533 km SE of La Paz

New road to La Paz under construction will reduce journey time to 6 hrs

Local Bus: US$0.12. **Taxi**: US$1.

Long distance Air: Airport is 5 km out of town on the Sucre road. *Aero Sur* (C Hoyos 10, T622 2088), to **La Paz** 0800 Mon-Sat; *TAM* to/from **La Paz**, Mon. Flights frequently cancelled. **Bus**: The bus terminal is 20 mins downhill walk or a short taxi or micro ride from the centre of town on Av Universitaria below rail station, T624 3361, *Entel*, post office, police, US$0.10 terminal tax. When you buy your ticket you check your luggage into the operator's office and it is then loaded directly onto your bus. Daily services: to **La Paz** 1830-1930, US$4.50, 11 hrs, *buscama* with *Flota Copacabana* US$7.50. To travel by day, go to **Oruro**, 5 a day from 0700, US$4.50, 7 hrs. To **Cochabamba** 1830 and 1900, US$4.50, 12 hrs. To **Sucre** 4 daily 0700-1800, US$3, 3 hrs. To **Santa Cruz** 1900 (change in Sucre or Cochabamba), US$12, 18 hrs. To **Villazón** 0800, 1900,

US$3-4.50, 11 hrs. To **Tarija** 1600, 1900, US$9.35, 12 hrs. Buses to **Uyuni** leave from either side of the railway line (uphill the road is called Av Antofagasta or 9 de Abril, downhill it is Av Universitaria), daily 1100, 1830, US$4.50, 6 hrs, superb scenery; book in advance.

Banks There are ATMs around the centre. *Banco Nacional*, Junín 4-6. Exchange for US$ TCs and cash. *Banco Mercantil*, Sucre y Ayacucho. 1% commision on US$ TCs, no commission on Visa cash withdrawals. Almost opposite is *Casa Fernández* for cash exchange. *Banco de Crédito*, Bolívar y Sucre. Cash withdrawals on Visa. Many shops on Plaza Alonso de Ibáñez and on Bolívar, Sucre and Padilla display 'compro dólares' signs. **Communications** Internet: All US$0.75 per hr. *Café Candelaria*, Ayacucho 5, T622 8050, also crafts, postcards, book exchange. *Tuko's Café*, Junín 9, p 3, T622 5489/7, tuco25@hotmail.com Open 0800-2300, information, English spoken, popular music, videos, good food. *Vistu Net*, Comercio San Francisco, p 2, Bolívar y Oruro, T22853. Another opposite bus terminal. **Post Office**: Lanza 3, Mon-Fri 0800-2000, Sat till 1930, Sun 0900-1200. **Telephone**: *Entel*, on Plaza Arce at end of Av Camacho, T43496 (use of internet US$2.75 per hour). Also at Av Universitaria near bus terminal, and on Padilla, opposite *Confitería Cherys*. **Cultural centres** *Alianza Francesa*, Junín e Ingavi, French and Spanish lessons, *Le Boulevard* restaurant, Bolívar 853, with good set lunches (arrive early), 'impressive' toilets. **Useful addresses** Migración: Linares esq Padilla, T622 5989. Mon-Fri 0830-1630, closed lunchtime, beware unnecessary charges for extensions. **Police station**: on Plaza 10 de Noviembre.

Directory

The state mines in Cerro Rico were closed in the 1980s and are now worked as cooperatives by small groups of miners. A 4½-hour morning tour to the mines and ore-processing plant involves meeting miners and seeing them at work in medieval conditions. Visitors need to be reasonably fit and acclimatized as parts are very hard going; not recommended for claustrophobics, those afraid of heights or asthmatics. There are many explosions in the afternoon, better to visit in the morning. Sunday is the quietest day as it's the miners' day off. Guided tours are offered by former miners, who provide essential equipment – helmet, lamp and usually protective clothing (but check when booking). Wear old clothes and take torch and a handkerchief to filter the dusty air. The smaller the group the better. The price of tours is US$10 per person and includes transport. A contribution to the miners' cooperative is appreciated as are medicines for the new health centre (*Posta Sanitaria*) on Cerro Rico. New projects include a radio and drinking water.

Visits to the mines
Take presents for the miners – dynamite, coca leaves, cigarettes, Coca-cola, or water

Recommended guides are: *Juan Mamani Choque* and *Pedro Montes Caria* of **Koala Tours** (run by Eduardo Garnica Fajardo, who rarely guides now. He speaks English, French and some Hebrew). *Koala's* guides are good and the company offers lunch of 'plato típico' with llama meat, they also donate 15% of their fee to support on-site health-care facilities. *Raul Braulio*, Millares 96, T/F622 5175, turismo_potosi@hotmail.com (or at his agency, **Andes Salt Expediciones**, Plaza Alonso de Ibáñez 3). Experienced, speaks English. *Santos Mamani*, Quintanilla s/n (**Carola Tours**), T622 8212. *Gerónimo Fuentes* (**Amauta**). Speaks English, small groups. *Juan Carlos González*, Bustillos 1092, T622 4058 (**Sin Fronteras**). Spanish spoken only. *Efraín Huanca*, T622 5186 (**Hidalgo Tours**). Very informative. *Roberto Méndez*, Campamento Pailaviri 4, T622 6900. The size of tour groups varies – some are as large as 20 people, which is excessive.

By law all guides have to work with a travel agency and carry an ID card issued by the Prefectura

A good place to freshen up after visiting the mines (or to spend a day relaxing) is Tarapaya, where there are thermal baths, Tarapaya itself (in poor condition) and Miraflores (public, US$0.30, private, US$0.60). On the other side of the river from Tarapaya is a 50 m diameter crater lake, whose temperature is 30° C; take sun protection. Below the crater lake are boiling ponds **but on no account swim in the lake**. Several people have drowned in the boiling waters of the lake; agencies do not warn of the dangers. ■ *Buses, micros and colectivos from the bus terminal, outside Chuquimia market on Av Universitaria, every 30 minutes, 0700-1700, US$0.55. Taxi US$7.50 for a group. Last colectivo back to Potosí at 1800. Camping by the lake is possible and there is accommodation at Balneario Tarapaya.*

Tarapaya

Sucre

Bolivia

Phone code: 04
Colour map 6, grid B3
Population: 131,769
Altitude: 2,790 m

Climate: 24°C
Nov-Dec, 7°C Jun
Mean temperature
12°C, mild

Founded in 1538 as the city of La Plata, it became capital of the audiencia of Charcas in 1559. Its name was later changed to Chuquisaca. The present name, Sucre, was adopted in 1825 in honour of the first president of the new republic. In 1992 UNESCO declared the city a 'Patrimonio Histórico y Cultural de la Humanidad'. There are two universities, the older dating from 1624. Long isolation has helped it to preserve its courtly charm; by tradition all buildings in the centre are painted in their original colonial white. It is sometimes referred to as La Ciudad Blanca. The city, the official capital of Bolivia, has grown rapidly since the mid-1980s following severe drought which drove campesinos from the countryside and the collapse of tin mining in 1985.

Ins & outs
For more detailed information see Transport, page 294

Juana Azurduy de Padilla **Airport** is 5 km northwest of town (T645 4445). **Bus terminal** is on north outskirts of town, 2 km from centre on Ostria Gutiérrez, T645 2029; taxi US$0.75; Micro A or trufi No 8. Taxis cost US$0.45 pp within city limits.

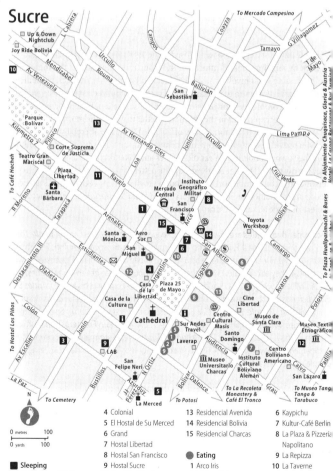

Sucre

■ Sleeping
1 Alojamiento El Turista
2 Alojamiento La Plata
3 Casa de Huéspedes Colón 220
4 Colonial
5 El Hostal de Su Merced
6 Grand
7 Hostal Libertad
8 Hostal San Francisco
9 Hostal Sucre
10 Municipal Simón Bolívar
11 Potosí
12 Real Audiencia
13 Residencial Avenida
14 Residencial Bolivia
15 Residencial Charcas

● Eating
1 Arco Iris
2 Bibliocafé Sureña
3 El Germen
4 Eli's Pizza Express
5 Joy Ride Café
6 Kaypichu
7 Kultur-Café Berlin
8 La Plaza & Pizzería Napolitano
9 La Repizza
10 La Taverne
11 Penco Penquito
12 Salon de Té Las Delicias
13 Shanghai

0 metres 100
0 yards 100

Tourist offices At the bus station, allegedly open Mon-Fri 0800-1600, Sat 0800-1200; the airport, to coincide with incoming flights; in town, at the municipal tourist booth, Argentina y Olañeta, Mon-Fri 0800-1200, 1400-1600, free pocket guide. More detailed information, at the *Casa de la Cultura*, Argentina 65, T642 7102 (same hours). Another office on Plaza 25 de Mayo 22, Mon-Fri 0830-1230, 1430-1830. For country maps try **Instituto Geográfico Militar**, Arce 172, 1st floor, T645 5514. Open Mon-Fri 0830-1200, 1430-1800.

Sights

Plaza 25 de Mayo is large, spacious, full of trees and surrounded by elegant buildings. Among these are the **Casa de la Libertad**, formerly the Assembly Hall of the Jesuit University, where the country's Declaration of Independence was signed. It contains a famous portrait of Simón Bolívar by the Peruvian artist Gil de Castro, admired for its likeness. ■ *Mon-Fri 0900-1115, 1430-1745, Sat 0930-1115, US$1.50 with guided tour; US$1.50 to take photographs, US$3 to use video.,T645 4200.* Also on the Plaza is the beautiful 17th century **Cathedral**, entrance through the museum in C Ortiz. Worth seeing are the famous jewel-encrusted Virgin of Guadalupe, 1601, and works by Viti, the first great painter of the New World, who studied under Raphael. ■ *Mon-Fri 1000-1200, 1500-1700, Sat 1000-1200, US$1.50. If door is locked wait for the guide.* Four blocks northwest of Plaza 25 de Mayo is the **Corte Suprema de Justicia**, one of the seats of Bolivia's judiciary. ■ *Free but must be smartly dressed, leave passport with guard, guide can be found in library.* The nearby **Parque Bolívar** contains a monument and a miniature of the Eiffel tower in honour of one of Bolivia's richest 20th century tin barons, Francisco Argandoña, who created much of Sucre's latter-day splendour. The obelisk opposite the **Teatro Gran Mariscal**, in **Plaza Libertad**, was erected with money raised by fining bakers who cheated on the size and weight of their bread. Also on this plaza is the **Hospital Santa Bárbara** (1574).

Southeast of the city, at the top of Dalence, lies the Franciscan monastery of **La Recoleta** (see **Museums**) with good views over the city. Behind the monastery a road flanked by Stations of the Cross ascends an attractive hill, **Cerro Churuquella**, with large eucalyptus trees on its flank, to a statue of Christ at the top. In the cemetery are mausoleums of presidents and other famous people, boys give guided tours; take C Junín south to its end, 7 to 8 blocks from main plaza.

Church opening times seem to change frequently, or are simply not observed

San Miguel, completed in 1628, has been restored and is very beautiful with Moorish-style carved and painted ceilings, *alfarjes* (early 17th century), pure-white walls and gold and silver altar. In the Sacristy some early sculpture can be seen. It was from San Miguel that Jesuit missionaries went south to convert Argentina, Uruguay and Paraguay. ■ *1130-1200. No shorts, short skirts or short sleeves.* **San Felipe Neri**, church and monastery, neoclassical, attractive courtyard with cloisters. The monastery is used as a school. The church is closed but ask the guide nicely to gain access. The roof (note the penitents' benches), which offers fine views over the city, is only open for an hour between 1630 and 1800 (times change). ■ *US$1 (extra charge for photos) with a free guide from Universidad de Turismo office on Plaza 25 de Mayo, T645 4333.* Across the corner is **La Merced** (Azurduy y J J Pérez), which is notable for its gilded central and side altars. **Santa Mónica** (Arenales y Junín) is perhaps one of the finest gems of Spanish architecture in the Americas, but has been converted into a *salón multiuso* (multipurpose space). **San Francisco** (1581) in C Ravelo has altars coated in gold leaf and 17th century ceilings; the bell is the one that summoned the people of Sucre to struggle for independence. ■ *0700-1200, 1500-1900.* **San Lázaro**, Calvo y Padilla (1538), is regarded as the first cathedral of La Plata (Sucre). On the nave walls are six paintings attributed to Zurbarán; it has fine silverwork and alabaster in the Baptistery. ■ *Daily for mass 0630-0730, 1830-1930.*

Museums

These include the **Museo Universitario Charcas**, Bolívar 698, anthropological, archaeological, folkloric, and colonial collections and presidential and modern-art galleries. ■ *Mon-Fri 0800-2000, Sat 0900-1200, 1500-1800, Sun 0900-1200, US$2.60, photos US$1.50.* **Museo Textil-Etnográfico** The textile museum run by Antropológicas del Surandino (ASUR), excellent displays of regional textiles and

Bolivia

Bolivia

traditional techniques, craft shop sells local textiles. Highly recommended. ■ *Mon-Fri 0830-1200, 1430-1800, Sat 0930-1200 (and Sat afternoon Jul/Aug/Sep), US$2, English, German and French-speaking guide; San Alberto 413 (Caserón de la Capellanía), T645 3841, www.bolivianet.com/asur* The **Museo de Santa Clara**, Calvo 212, displays paintings, books, vestments, some silver and musical instruments (including a 1664 organ); there is a window to view the church; small items made by the nuns on sale. ■ *Mon-Fri 0900-1200, 1500-1800, Sat 0900-1200, US$0.75.* The **Museo de la Recoleta**, Pedro de Anzúrez, at the Recoleta monastery, notable for the beauty of its cloisters and gardens; the carved wooden choirstalls above the nave of the church see the martyrs transfixed by lances). In the grounds is the Cedro Milenario, a 1,400-year-old cedar. ■ *Mon-Fri 0900-1130, 1430-1630, US$1.20 for entrance to all collections, guided tours only.* **Tanga Tanga**, is an interactive children's museum with art, music, theatre, dance and books. It also has the excellent *Café Mirador* in the garden.Good coffee, snacks, sandwiches, proceeds to the museum. ■ *Tue-Sun1000-1800, Iturricha 297, La Recoleta, T644 0299.*

Castillo de la Glorieta
5 km S on the Potosí road

The former mansion of the Argandoña family was built in a mixture of contrasting European styles with beautiful painted ceilings and stands in gardens which must once have been delightful. Ask to see the paintings of the visit of the pope, in a locked room. ■ *Daily 0830-1200, 1400-1800. It is in the military compound, US$1.05. Take any bus marked 'Liceo Militar' from the Plaza, or bus or trufi 4 or E.*

Cal Orcko
7 km N of Sucre

An extensive area of dinosaur footprints found in the Fanesca cement works. A company employee will show you around for a tip. ■ *Tours in English are available for US$2. Recommended. Tour agencies charge US$10 pp as do taxi drivers who have trained as guides (untrained drivers charge US$7); ask tourist office for approved drivers.* Dino Truck *leaves daily 0930, 1200, 1430 from main plaza, US$3, good explanations in English.*

Sleeping

A *Real Audiencia*, Potosí 142, T/F646 0823, realaudiencia2000@hotmail.com Modern, large rooms, excellent restaurant, heated pool. Recommended. **B** *El Hostal de Su Merced*, Azurduy 16, T644 2706, sumerced@mara.scr.entelnet.bo Beautifully-restored colonial building, more character than any other hotel in the city, owner speaks fluent French and English, good breakfast buffet. Recommended. **C** *Colonial*, Plaza 25 de Mayo 3, T645 4079, colonial@mara.scr.entelnet.bo Some rooms noisy, but generally recommended, good breakfast. **C** *Hostal Libertad*, Arce y San Alberto, p 1, T645 3101, F646 0128. Spacious comfortable rooms, hot water and heating, TV. Highly recommended. **C** *Hostal Sucre*, Bustillos 113, T645 1411, hosucre@mara.scr.entelnet.bo Rooms on patio noisy, breakfast for US$2.25. Recommended. **C-D** *Municipal Simón Bolívar*, Av Venezuela 1052, T645 5508, F645 1216. Including breakfast in patio, helpful, restaurant. Recommended. **D** *Grand*, Arce 61, T645 2104, F645 2461, www.statusprd.com/grandhotel Comfortable (ask for room 18), hot showers, includes breakfast in room, good value lunch in *Arcos* restaurant, laundry, safe. Recommended. **D** *Hostal los Piños*, Colón 502, T645 4403, H-Pinos@ mara.scr.entelnet.bo Comfortable, hot showers, nice garden, quiet, peaceful, includes breakfast, laundry, kitchen, parking.

E *Res Bolivia*, San Alberto 42, T645 4346, F645 3239. **F** without bath, spacious rooms, hot water, includes breakfast, clothes washing not allowed. **E** *Casa de Huéspedes Colón 220*, Colón 220, T645 5823, colon220@bolivia.com Family-run colonial house, quiet, basic but clean, laundry, helpful owner speaks English and German and has tourist information. **E** *Res Charcas*, Ravelo 62, T53972, F2496, hcharcas@mara.scr.entelnet.bo **F** without bath, good value, breakfast, hot showers, helpful, runs bus to Tarabuco on Sun. **E** *Hostal San Francisco*, Av Arce 191 y Camargo, T645 2117, hostalsf@cotes.net.bo Pleasant, meals available, includes breakfast, quiet, comfortable, large patio, laundry. Recommended. **F** *Res Avenida*, Av H Siles 942, T645 2387. Hot showers, breakfast US$1, laundry, helpful, use of kitchen. **G** *Alojamiento El Turista*, Ravelo 118, T645 3172. Hot showers 0700-1200 only, basic, meeting place, cheap meals, use of kitchen, central rooms noisy, doors closed at 2300.

G *Alojamiento La Plata*, Ravelo 32, T645 2102. Without bath, limited shower facilities, basic, noisy, nice courtyard, good beds, popular with backpackers (lock rooms at all times). **G** *Potosí*, Ravelo 262, T/F645 1975. Basic, popular, helpful, internet, good value.

On Av Ostria Gutiérrez (near bus station) **D** *Austria*, No 506, T645 4202. Hot showers, redecorated, great beds and carpeted rooms, some with cable TV, cafeteria, parking, **F** rooms available and, next door, **G** in the *Alojamiento* (parking extra). **E** *Alojamiento Chuquisaca*, No 33, T645 4459. **G** shared bath, safe car parking (US$0.75 per day). **G** *Gloria*, No 438, T645 2847, opposite bus station. Pleasant, great value.

Outside Sucre **B** *Refugio Andino Bramadero*, 30 km from the city, details from Raul y Mabel Cagigao, Avaroa 472, Casilla 387, T645 5592, bramader@yahoo.com Cabins or rooms, well-furnished, full board, drinks and transport included, excellent value, owner Raul is an astronomer and advises on hikes, book in advance. Recommended. **C** *Kantu Nucchu*, 21 km southwest of Sucre, details from Augusto Marion, San Alberto 237, T438 0312, tursucre@mara.scr.entelnet.bo With bath, kitchen, full board, **G** pp without meals, peaceful, colonial hacienda, hiking, swimming. Recommended.

Bolivian/Latin American *El Asador*, Plaza Cumaná 485. Very good steak and best fries. *El Chaqueño*, Av R Barrientos 749, Barrio Petrolero. Excellent steaks, best *charqui*, US$8 for a great meal (taxi US$1 each way). Recommended. *El Huerto*, Ladislao Cabrera 86 (take a taxi at night). In beautiful garden, dishes from US$5.20, good *almuerzo*. Highly recommended. *La Plaza*, Plaza 25 de Mayo 33. With balcony, good food and pisco sours, good live music on Fri nights, popular with locals, set lunch US$2.10. Good for *salteñas*, *El Patio*, Ravelo y San Alberto and other branches. *La Casona*, Ostria Guitiérrez 401, near bus terminal. Stylish, *platos típicos*, good value. Good chicken and chips cafés on Av H Siles between Arce and Loa, eg *Pollos Claudia*.

European *Arco Iris*, N Ortiz 42. Good service, expensive but good, *peña* on Sat, excellent *roesti*, live music some nights. *Bibliocafé Sureña*, N Ortiz 50, near plaza. Good pasta and light meals, *almuerzo* US$3 1100-1600, closes 2000 (opens 1800 on Sun), music. *Eli's Pizza Express*, España 130. Good. *Kultur-Café Berlin*, Avaroa 326, open 0800-2400 (except Sun). Good breakfasts, German newspapers, *peña* every other Fri (in same building as *Instituto Cultural Boliviano Alemán* – ICBA), popular meeting place. *La Repizza*, N Ortiz 78. Good value lunches, small but good pizzas in evening. Recommended. *La Taverne* of the *Alliance Française*, Aniceto Arce 35, ½ block from plaza. Closed Sun evening, *peñas* Thu-Sat in Jul and Aug, good French food, also regular films and cultural events, good meeting place. *La Vieja Bodega*, N Ortiz 38. Good value, excellent meat fondue, cheapish wine. *Café Monterosso*, Bolívar 426. Open after 1900, delicious, cheap set dinner. *Pizzería Napolitano*, Plaza 25 de Mayo 30. Excellent pizzas and pastas, good home-made ice cream, not cheap.

Oriental *Shanghai*, Calvo 70. Good, popular. *New Hong Kong*, San Alberto 242. Not as good as *Chifa Dragón, Hong Kong III*, Plaza 25 de Mayo 46; and at Ravelo 74.

Vegetarian *El Germen*, San Alberto 231. Very good, includes set lunches (US1.80), attractive, elegant, excellent breakfast, US$1.05-2.10, open Mon-Sat 0800-2200, book exchange, German magazines. Warmly recommended. *Kaypichu*, San Alberto 168 y Bolívar. Good, breakfast US$1.35-2.55, closed Mon and 1400-1700.

Cafés *Amanecer*, Junín 855, German *pastelería*, run by social project supporting disabled children, excellent, opens 1530. *La Luna*, Argentina 65, back of Casa de la Cultura. Video pub with occasional live music, popular. *Salon de Té Las Delicias*, Estudiantes 50. Great cakes and snacks, favourite student hangout, open 1600-1900. *Café Hacheh*, Pastor Sainz 233. Coffee bar, open 1100-2400 (opens at 1700 on Sun), art gallery, tasty lunch and fresh fruit juices. Highly recommended. *Joy Ride Café*, N Ortiz 14, same Dutch owner as Joy Ride Bolivia (see **Tour operators**). Good vibes and popular at night, great food and drink, safe salads, open 0800-0200. Highly recommended. *Julyo's Chop*, Junín esq Colón. Popular bar, open late. *Penco Penquito*, Arenales 108. Excellent coffee and cakes. *Tertulias*, Plaza 25 de Mayo 59. Good meeting place, Italian and other dishes, poor service. *Café Al Tronco*, Topater 57, 100 m behind La Recoleta. Bolivian-German owned café with wide choice of meals and drinks, homely, open daily 1500-2400, tourist information, books and magazines.

Eating
Many fruit juice and snack stalls in the central market; clean stalls also sell cheap meals (US$0.75-1.40). The local sausages and chocolate are recommended

Bolivia

Bolivia

Entertainment **Disco** *Mitsubanía*, Av del Maestro y Av Venzuela. Popular with local, younger, fashionable crowd, mixture of music with lots of *cumbia*, US$3 for men, women do not pay. *Up and Down*, opposite Mendizábal 222. **Folklore** Look out for the **Ballet Folclórico** of the Universidad San Francisco Xavier in the *Teatro Gran Mariscal*, Plaza Libertad.

Festivals **24-26 May:** *Independence* celebrations, most services, museums and restaurants closed on 25. **8 Sep:** *Virgen de Guadalupe*, 2-day fiesta. **Sep:** *Festival Internacional de la Cultura*, second week, shared with Potosí. **21 Sep:** *Día del Estudiante*, music and dancing around main plaza.

Shopping The central market is clean and colourful, wide variety of goods, many stalls selling *artesanía*.
Famed chocolate shops can be found on Arce and Arenales Beware theft. A bus from the central market will take you to the *Mercado Campesino* near football stadium. *Antropológicos del Surandino*, *ASUR*, San Alberto 413, T642 3841 (see Museums). Weavings from around Tarabuco and from the Jalq'a. Weavings are more expensive, but of higher quality than elsewhere. *Artesanía Bolivia*, Argentina 31. Has a variety of arts and crafts from Tarabuco. *Artesanías Calcha*, Arce 103, opposite San Francisco church. Recommended, very knowledgeable proprietor. *Charcas*, Camargo 481 y España. High quality hats. *Fundación Aprecia*, Raul F de Córdova 49, just off Colón, T642 4718. A workshop for blind weavers making beautiful rugs (they can make to order with advance notice). Camping equipment can be bought at *Alfher*, San Alberto y Arce, and at *Sport Camping*, same entrance as *Hostal Libertad* (see above), but no gas.

Tour operators *Candelaria Tours*, Audiencia No 1, C 322, T646 1661, F646 0289. Organizes excursions and also organizes Bolivian textile fashion shows, English spoken. *Joy Ride Bolivia*, Mendizábal 229, T642 5544, www.joyridebol.com Top quality quad and dirt bike trips, European standards of safety and bike-to-bike radio, Dutch owner Gert van der Meijden, insurance, take motorcycle licence for dirt bikes, car licence for quads. *Seatur*, Plaza 25 de Mayo 24, T/F646 2425, seatur@latinmail.com Local tours, English, German, French spoken. *Sur Andes*, N Ortiz 6, T645 3212, F644 2561. Organizes trekking from half a day to 5 days, eg to precolumbian sites such as Pumamachay and the Camino Prehispánico (must take sleeping bag and good shoes, all else provided, but no porters).

Transport **Long distance Air**: Aero Sur and *LAB* fly to La Paz and Santa Cruz, *LAB* also flies to
164 km from Potosí (fully paved) 366 km to Cochabamba (for first hr from Sucre road is OK, terrible to Epizana, then paved) Cochabamba and Tarija. Few flights are daily. *Aero Sur*, Arenales 31, T646 2141 (Toll free 0800 3030). *LAB*, Bustillos 127, T645 4994 (Toll free 0800 3001). Airport minibus goes from entrance and will drop you off on Siles y Junín, and returns from here, 1½ hrs before flight (not always), US$0.70, 20-30 mins. Taxi US$4-5. *Trufis* No 1 and F go from entrance to H Siles y Loa, 1 block from main plaza, US$0.55, 25 mins. **Bus**: Daily to/from **La Paz** at 1430 (*10 de Noviembre*, 16 hrs via Potosí, US$6), 1730 (*Flota Copacabana*, bus-cama, 15hrs, US$7.50), 1730 (*Trans Copacabana*, bus-cama, 15hrs, US$10.45). To **Cochabamba**: several companies daily at 1830, arriving 0630, US$4.50-5.25 (*bus-cama*, US$8.90). To **Potosí**: 3 hrs on a good paved road, frequent departures between 0630 and 1800, US$3. *Silito Lindo* taxis take 4 people to Potosí with door-to-door service for US$5; T644 1014. To **Tarija**: several companies, 16hrs, US$8.95. To **Uyuni**: 0700 (*Emperador*), 0800 (*Trans Capital*), 10 hrs, US$5.20. Alternatively catch a bus to Potosí and change; if possible book the connecting bus in advance as these fill up quickly – see *Trans Real Audencia* below. To **Oruro**: 1700 with *Emperador* via Potosí, arrives 0300, US$6 (*bus-cama*, US$8.95). To **Santa Cruz**: many companies go between 1600 and 1730, 15 hrs, US$6-7.50. To **Villazón**: at 1300 (*Transtin Dilrey*, direct) and 1400 (*Villa Imperial*, via Potosí) both 15 hrs, US$8.20. *Trans Real Audencia*, Arce 99 y San Alberto (same entrance as Hostal Libertad), T644 3119, for hassle-free bus tickets reservations to: Potosí (US$3), Uyuni (US$6.70), Villazón and Tupiza (US$7.45), Tarabuco (Sun 0700 from outside office, US$3 return).

Banks *Banco Nacional*, España esq San Alberto. Cash given on Visa and MasterCard US$3 commission, good rates for dollars, TCs changed, 5% commission. Diagonally opposite is *Banco Santa Cruz*. Good rates for cash, advances on Visa, MasterCard and Amex, US$10 fee.There is many *Enlace* 24hr ATMs around town. Travel agencies' rates are good and at *El Arca*, España 134, T646 0189. Good rates for TCs, 3% commission into US $, free into bolivianos. *Casa de Cambio Ambar*, San Alberto 7, T645 1339. Good rates for TCs. Stalls at corner of Camargo and Arce buy and sell cash $ as well as Argentine, Chilean and Brazilian currency at good rates. Many shops and street changers on Hernando Siles/Camargo buy and sell $ cash. **Communications** Internet: Many around town, generally slow connections, average US$0.60 per hr. Also at *Alianza Francesa*, 0900-1200, 1500-1930, closed Sat pm and Sun. **Post Office:** Ayacucho 100 y Junín, open till 2000 (1600 Sat, 1200 Sun), good service. *Poste Restante* is organized separately for men and women. **Telephone:** *Entel*, España 252. Open 0730-2300. **Cultural centres** The *Instituto Cultural Boliviano-Alemán* (Goethe Institute), Avaroa 326, Casilla 304, T645 2091. Shows films, has German newspapers and books to lend (0930-1230 and 1500-2100), runs Spanish, German, Portuguese and Quechua courses and it has the *Kulturcafé Berlín* (see above). Spanish lessons cost from US$6 for 45 mins for 1 person, with reductions the more students there are in the class. The ICBA also runs a folk music *peña* on Fri. *Centro Cultural Masis*, Bolívar 561, T645 3403, Casilla 463. Promotes the Yampara culture through textiles, ceramics, figurines and music. Instruction in Quechua, traditional Bolivian music (3 hrs a week for US$15 a month, recommended) and handicrafts; stages musical events and exhibitions; items for sale. Open Mon-Sat 1430-2000 (knock if door closed); contact the director, Roberto Sahonero Gutierres at the centre Mon, Wed and Fri. *Alianza Francesa*, Aniceto Arce 35, T645 3599. Offers Spanish classes. *Centro Boliviano Americano*, Calvo 301, T644 1608, cba@mara.scr.entelnet.bo Library open Mon-Fri 0900-1200, 1500-2000 (recommended for reference works). Recommended for language courses. The *Centro Cultural Hacheh* (see address for *Café Hacheh* above), run by Felix Arciénega, Bolivian artist who organizes folk and jazz concerts, conferences, exhibitions and discussions, and is the editor of an art and poetry journal 'Hacheh'. *Casa de la Cultura*, Argentina 65, in beautiful colonial building, presents art exhibitions, concerts, folk dancing etc, good breakfast in café, open Mon-Fri 0830-1230, 1400-2200. **Embassies and consulates** *France*, Bustillos 206, T645 3018. *German consul*, Eva Kasewitz de Vilar, Rosendo Villa 54, T645 1369. *Spain*, Pasaje Argandoña, T645 1435. *Italy*, Vice Consul, Dalence 19, T645 4280. *Paraguay*, Plaza 25 de Mayo 28, T645 2573. *Perú*, Avaroa 472, T642 0356. **Language schools** *Academia Latinoamericana de Español*, Dalence 109, T646 0537, latino@sucre.bo.net Professional, well-structured classes, good extracurricular activities. *Casa de Lenguas*, T/F5912393, www.casadelenguas.com (see also La Paz). *Sofia Sauma*, Loa 779, T645 1687, sadra@mara.scr.entelnet.bo US$5 per hr. **Useful addresses** Immigration: Pastor Sáenz 117, T645 3647, Mon-Fri 0830-1630. **Police radio patrol:** T110 if in doubt about police or security matters.

Directory

For hospitals, doctors and dentists, contact your consulate or the tourist office for recommendations

Bolivia

There is a very colourful Indian market on Sunday, with local people in traditional dress. It starts around 0930-1000 and is very popular with tourists, but still an enjoyable experience. Those in search of a bargain should have an idea about the quality on offer. **NB** The market is not held at Carnival (when all Tarabuco is dancing in Sucre), Easter Sunday or on a holiday weekend in November. The *Phujllay* independence celebration in mid-March is very colourful and lively. No one sleeps during this fiesta. There are at least 2 budget hotels. Try the Plaza (*Snack Kuky*) or food stalls in market offering tasty local dishes. **Guide to Tarabuco**: *Alberto* from Sucre tourist office, US$45 for a full day in a car for 4 people.

Tarabuco

Colour map 6, grid B4 Altitude: 3,295 m 64 km SE from Sucre (good road)

■ *Getting there: Buses (US$1.25) and trucks (very crowded) leave from 0630 or when full from Plaza Huallparimachi, Av Manco Capac, or across the railway (take micro B or C from opposite Mercado), 2½ hrs (or taxi, US$45). On Sun only, at least 1 bus will wait on Ravelo by the market for travellers, charging US$3 return to Tarabuco. Shared trufi taxis can be arranged by hotels, with pick-up service, starting at 0700, US$3.25 return. First bus back 1300. Andes Bus run tourist service, depart 0800 (or when full), return 1530, US$6, book at office (address above), take food and drink. Transport more difficult on weekdays; take an early bus and return by truck.*

Bolivia

East and south of Sucre

On to Paraguay   A main road runs southeast from Sucre through Tarabuco and Monteagudo, then joins the road south from Santa Cruz to Camiri and Boyuibe (see page 324). From here a road heads east to the frontier with Paraguay at Hito Villazón (not to be confused with Villazón on the frontier with Argentina, see page 284), but most public transport now goes south through Villamontes and a new road east to Paraguay, or continues south to Yacuiba on the border with Argentina (see page 325). The journey is beautiful through wild mountains. At **Monteagudo** (Km 323, Altitude: 1,138 m; phone code: 04) there are daily buses to Santa Cruz, two companies (book early), US$8, 14 hours. **Sleeping** Several hotels including **E** *Fortín*, Plaza 20 de Agosto 1-2, T647 2135, with bath, TV, includes breakfast. **F** *Alojamiento los Naranjos*, on road to bus terminal, hot showers. A few restaurants, including *Res Monteaguado*, Sucre 126, T647 2091.

■ *Getting there: Sucre to Paraguay: either take a bus Sucre-Santa Cruz, then international bus to Asunción, or take the* **Emperador** *bus Sucre-Camiri, 1730, or* **Andes Bus**, *1800 on alternate days, 18 hrs, US$4.30. Then take a colectivo to Villamontes, 3 hrs, US$5, but stop in Boyuibe to get an exit stamp. In Villamontes, catch the bus at about 0600 the day after it leaves Santa Cruz. Bargain hard not to pay the full Santa Cruz-Asunción fare. (See also page 324.)*

Tarija

Phone code: 04
Colour map 6, grid B4
Population: 109,000
Altitude: 1,840 m
Best time to visit: Jan onwards, when the fruit is in season

Tarija was founded 4 July 1574, in the rich valley of the Río Guadalquivir. The city declared itself independent of Spain in 1807, and has a strong cultural heritage. The Indian strain is less evident here than elsewhere in Bolivia. Tarija is a pleasant, small city, with a delightful climate and streets and plazas planted with flowering trees. In **Plaza Luis de Fuentes** there is a statue to the city's founder, Capitán Luis de Fuentes Vargas. The Av Las Américas, or **Costanera**, flanks the river.

Sights   The **Cathedral**, on La Madrid, is open in the morning and from 1700. **San Francisco** church (La Madrid y Daniel Campos), is beautifully painted inside, with praying angels depicted on the ceiling; note the four evangelists at the four corners below the dome. The library is divided into old and new sections, the old containing some 15,000 volumes, the new a further 5,000. The oldest book is a 1501 *Iliad* incorporating other works. There are also old manuscripts and 19th century photograph albums. To see the library, go to the door at Ingavi 0137. ■ *The Basilica is open 0700-1000, 1800-2000, Sun 0630-1200, 1800-2000.* Tarija's **university museum**, Trigo y Lema, contains a palaeontological collection (dinosaur bones, fossils, remains of an Andean elephant), as well as smaller mineralogical, ethnographic and anthropological collections. ■ *Mon-Fri 0800-1200, 1500-1800 (Sat opens at 0900).* The **Casa Dorada**, Trigo y Ingavi (entrance on Ingavi), or Maison d'Or, is now the Casa de Cultura. ■ *Mon-Fri 0900-1200, 1500-1800, Sat 0900-1200, guided tours only; voluntary donation (minimum US$0.30).* It belonged to importer/exporter Moisés Narvajas and his wife Esperanza Morales, begun in 1886, and has been beautifully restored inside and out, the photography room contains pictures of Tarijan history and the restoration of the house. Near Parque Bolívar (shady, pleasant) is another of Narvajas' houses, the **Castillo de Beatriz**, Bolívar entre Junín y O'Connor; ask the owner if it is possible to visit.

Excursions   The outskirts of the city can be a good place to look for fossils: take a micro or taxi in the direction of the airport. 5 km out of town, before the police control (*garita*), you see lovely structures of sand looking like a small canyon (*barrancos*). Here have been found bones, teeth, parts of saurian spines, etc; things come to the surface each year after the rains. You may have to go a long way from the city.

The road passes Tomatitas river bathing (5 km) and a popular picnic area before reaching **San Lorenzo**. San Lorenzo's plaza is very pleasant, with a huge church. Just off the plaza is the Museo Méndez, the house of the independence hero Eustaquio Méndez, El Moto (he lost his right hand, many stories as to how it happened). The small museum exhibits his weapons, his bed, his 'testimonio'. ■ *0900-1230, 1500-1830, minimum US$0.30 entry. At lunchtime on Sun, many courtyards serve very cheap meals. Take a trufi from Barrio del Carmen, at the roundabout just north of San Juan Church. They return from San Lorenzo plaza; 45 mins, US$0.45.*

15 km, trufis from La Loma, top of D Paz, return from San Lorenzo plaza, 45 mins, US$0.40

Aranjuez **bodega** is a short walk across the river at Av Los Sauces 1976 (shop at 15 de Abril O-0241): ask Sr Milton Castellanos at the Agrochemical shop at Trigo 789 (Monday-Friday 1000-1200, 1500-1730, Saturday 0900-1200); he can also arrange visits to *Campos de Solana* (shop 15 de Abril E-0259). To the *Rugero Singani* bodega at **El Valle de Concepción**, an appointment must be made with Ing Sergio Prudencio Navarro, Bodegas y Viñedos de la Concepción at La Madrid y Suipacha s/n, T664 3763. Ing Prudencio will show visitors round the vineyards and the bodega. To Concepción, 36 km south of Tarija, *trufis* go from Parada del Chaco every 20-30 minutes, US$0.75, return from plaza. There are also vineyard tours, see Tour operators.

All bodegas are closed Sat afternoon and Sun

Bolivia

A *Gran Hotel Tarija*, Sucre N-0770, T664 2684, F664 4777. Modernized, comfortable, parking, central. **A** *Los Ceibos*, Av Víctor Paz Estenssoro y La Madrid, T663 4430, F664 2461. Including excellent buffet breakfast, large rooms, mini-bar, good restaurant, outdoor pool and cocktail bar. Recommended. **A** *Victoria Plaza*, on Plaza Luis de Fuentes, T664 2600, F664 2700. 4-star, includes buffet breakfast in *Café-Bar La Bella Epoca*, laundry service. Recommended. **B** *Hostal Loma de San Juan*, Bolívar s/n (opposite Capela Loma de San Juan), T664 4522, F664 4206. Comfortable, pool, sumptuous buffet breakfast included. **C** *Gran Hostal Baldiviezo*, La Madrid O-0443, T/F663 7711. New, good beds and bathrooms, very central. **D** *Hostal Carmen*, Ingavi O-0784 y R Rojas, T664 3372, vtb@olivo.tja.entelnet.bo Shower, good value, **E** without cable TV, some ground floor rooms without exterior windows, good breakfast, transfer stand at airport, tour agency, book in advance. Well recommended. **D** *Hostal Libertador*, Bolívar O-0649, T664 4231, F663 1016. Electric showers, excellent breakfast extra, family-run, near cathedral. Recommended. **E** *Hostería España*, Alejandro Corrado O-0546, T664 1790. Hot showers, **F** without bath, pleasant. **E** *Zeballos*, Sucre O966, T664 2068. Nice atmosphere, **F** without bath, with breakfast, cable TV, quiet, safe, helpful, laundry, 5 mins from plaza. **E** *Res Rosario*, Ingavi O-0777, T42942, residen_rosario@latinmail.com **F** without bath, great showers, cable TV, quiet, laundry, good value. Recommended. **G** *Alojamiento Familiar*, Rana S 0231 y Navajas, T664 0832. Shared hot shower, no breakfast, modern, helpful, close to bus terminal, traffic noise.

Sleeping
Blocks west of C Colón have a small O before number (oeste), and all blocks east have an E (este); blocks are numbered from Colón outwards. All streets north of Av Las Américas are preceded by N

A, B and C hotels have cable TV

La Taberna Gattopardo, on main plaza. Pizza, *parrillada* with Argentine beef, local wines, hot dogs, snacks, excellent salads, good value, lively atmosphere, opens 0700-0200 daily. *Pizzería Europa*, main plaza west side. Also has internet (US$0.90 per hr), good *salteñas* in the morning. *Club Social Tarija*, east side of the plaza. Pleasant, old-fashioned, haunt of Tarija's business community, excellent *almuerzo* for US$1.80. Recommended. *Mateo's*, Trigo N-0610. Excellent a*lmuerzo* US$3 (includes salad bar), good value evening meals with a wide selection of local and international dishes, pasta a speciality, closed 1530-1900 and Sun. *Gringo Limón*, Trigo N-0345. Pay by weight, nothing special. *Chingo's*, Plaza Sucre. Popular, and many more places serving cheap local food, including *Bagdad Café* for beer and a game of dice, often has live music at night. *Cabaña Don Pedro*, Padilla y Av Las Américas. Good typical, moderately-priced food, close to the river. *Cabaña Don Pepe*, D Campos N-0138, near Av Las Américas, some way from the centre. Excellent steaks at moderate prices, *peña* at weekends with local folk music. *Chifa Wang Fu*, D Campos N-0179, closed 1430-1800. Good Chinese. Also *Chifa New Hong Kong*, Sucre O-0235. Smart, good service, moderate prices. *El Solar,* Campero y V Lema. Vegetarian, set lunch, Mon-Sat 0800-1400 only. *La Fontana*, La Madrid y Campos, is good for ice cream, snacks and coffee; also *Gloria*, Trigo 670. For a cheap breakfast try the market. Try the local wines, eg *Aranjuez, La Concepción, Santa Ana de Casa*

Eating
Many restaurants (and much else in town) close between 1400 and 1600

Real or *Kohlberg*, the *singani* (a clear brandy, *San Pedro de Oro* and *Rugero* are recommended labels), also local beer, *Astra*.

Festivals The city is famous for its colourful *niño* (child) processions. In the 3-day **San Roque** festival from the **first Sun in Sep** the richly dressed saint's statue is paraded through the streets, wearing lively colours, cloth turbans and cloth veils, the people dance before it and women throw flowers from the balconies. Dogs are decorated with ribbons for the day. On **2nd Sun in Oct** the flower festival commemorates the **Virgen del Rosario** (celebrations in the surrounding towns are recommended, eg San Lorenzo and Padcaya). Another flower festival takes place in **Easter** week. Also in **Oct**, on 2 weekends mid-month, there is a **beer festival** on Av de las Américas. Colourful processions take place on **15 Mar**, *Día de Tarija*.

Santuario Chaguaya, south of El Valle, beyond Padcaya by road, is 60 km south of Tarija. At the fiesta for **La Virgen de Chaguaya**, **15 Aug**, people walk all 45 km from the city. Línea P *trufi* from Plaza Sucre, Tarija, to Padcaya, US$1; bus to Chaguaya and Padcaya from terminal, daily, 0700, returns 1700, US$1.35.

Tour operators *Internacional Tarija*, Sucre 721, T664 4446, F664 5017. Flights and tours, helpful. *Mara Tours*, Gral Trigo N-739, T664 3490, marvin@olivo.tja.entelnet.bo Helpful. *Viva Tours*, Sucre 0615, T663 8325, vivatour@cosett.com.bo Vineyard tours US$30 with lunch. *VTB*, at *Hostal Carmen* (see Sleeping above). All tours include a free city tour; 4-6 hr trips including singani bodegas, US$19 pp; comprehensive 10 hr "Tarija and surroundings in 1 Day", US$27; can also try your hand on an excavation with their palaeontology specialist!

Transport **Air** *LAB* flies to La Paz, Santa Cruz, Cochabamba and Sucre; also once a week to Salta (Argentina). *Aero Sur* flies 3 times a week to La Paz. Schedules change frequently; also flights are frequently cancelled and/or delayed. *TAM* fly to/from Tarija. *LAB* office: Trigo N-0327, T644 2195. *TAM* office: La Madrid O-0470, T664 5899. *Aero Sur* office: Ingavi entre Sucre y Daniel Campos, T663 0894. Taxi to airport, US$3.75, or *micro* A from Mercado Central which drops you 1 block away. Some hotels have free transport to town, you may have to call them. On arrival at Tarija, reconfirm you return flight immediately. Airport information T664 3135. **Bus** The bus station is in the outskirts on Av de Las Américas (30 min walk from centre, 7-8 mins from airport), T663 6508. Daily on the 935 km route **Potosí-Oruro-La Paz**, depart 0700 and 1700 (24 hrs, US$15; check which company operates the best buses, eg *San Lorenzo* has heating). To **Potosí** (386 km), daily at 1630, 12 hrs, US$9.35 with *San Lorenzo*, *San Jorge* and *Emperador*, at 0700 with *Trans Yacuiba*. To **Sucre**, direct with *Andesbus* (recommended), *Emperador* and *Villa Imperial*, depart 1600-1630, 17-18 hrs, US$8.95, check if you have to change buses in Potosí. To **Villazón**, several companies daily, departs morning and afternoon, 7 hrs, US$4.50, unpaved road. To **Santa Cruz**, several companies, US$10.45-12, 24 hrs over rough roads, last 140 km from Abapó is paved; via Entre Ríos, Villamontes (see page 325), Boyuibe and Camiri, between Entre Ríos and Villamontes is spectacular. Trucks to all destinations depart from Barrio La Loma, 10 blocks west of market.

Directory **Banks** *Banco Mercantil*, Sucre y 15 de Abril. Exchanges cash and gives cash against Visa and MasterCard (US$5 authorization charge). *Banco de Crédito*, Trigo N-0784, *Bisa*, Plaza de Armas, *Banco Nacional*, Av Trigo, all change TCs. Many ATMs accepting foreign cards. Dollars and Argentine pesos can be changed at a number of casas de cambio on Bolívar between Campos and Sucre. **Communications** Internet: *Café Internet Tarija On-Line*, Campos N-0488, US$0.75 per hr. *Pizzería Europa* (see above), US$0.90 per hr. 2 on Plaza Sucre. **Post Office:** V Lema y Sucre. Also at bus terminal. **Telephone:** *Entel*, on main plaza, at V Lema y D Campos and at terminal. **Embassies and consulates** *German*, Sucre 665, T664 2062, helpful. *Argentine*, Ballivián N-0699 y Bolívar, T664 4273, Mon-Fri, 0830-1230. **Langauge classes** *Julia Gutiérrez Márquez*, T663 2857, garaysergio@latinmail.com Recommended for language classes and information. **Tourist offices** On the main plaza in the Prefectura. Mon-Fri 0800-1200, 1430-1830, helpful, city map and guide for US$0.20 each, T663 1000. Also at Sucre y Bolívar.

To Argentina
Bolivia is 1 hr behind Argentina

The road to Villazón, 189 km, is the shortest route to Argentina, but only the first 15 km is paved, a tiring 6 hours in all. The alternative route to Argentina via Bermejo is the most easily reached from Tarija, 210 km, the views are spectacular (sit on right); not recommended in the rainy season or a month or so after. The first 50 km out of Tarija, and the last 20 km to Bermejo are paved. Do not try to cycle. Many buses daily, usually at night, some early morning, 4-5 hours, US$7.75, truck US$4.50. At **Bermejo** (*Population*: 13,000. *Altitude*: 415 m. At least three hotels, two *casas de cambio* on main street, thorough customs searches) cross river by ferry to Aguas Blancas, Argentina. From Tarija to Yacuiba/Pocitos border is 290 km (see page 143). Daily buses to Yacuiba 0700-1800, 12 hours, US$5-8, mostly old buses, Expresos Tarija and Narváez are better. **NB** Crossing to Argentina, expect up to four hours to pass through customs and immigration. Electronic goods must be entered in your passport for later checks.

Cochabamba and around

The fertile foothills surrounding the city of Cochabamba provide much of the country's grain, fruit and coca. Colonial villages and precolumbian sites are also within reach. With its wonderful climate Cochabamba is an ideal half-way house between the cold of the altiplano and the tropical heat of the lowlands. It is 394 km from La Paz to Cochabamba by road, now completely paved.

Bolivia

Cochabamba

Cochabamba deserves its unofficial title of 'City of Eternal Spring'. Set in a bowl of rolling hills at a comfortable altitude, its inhabitants enjoy a wonderfully warm, dry and sunny climate. Its parks and plazas are a riot of colour - from the striking purple of the bougainvilleaea to the subtler tones of jasmin, magnolia and jacaranda. Bolivia's fourth largest city was founded in 1571. Today it is an important commercial and communications centre with many modern features, but it retains a small-town, rural feel.

Phone code: 04
Colour map 6, grid A3
Population: 594,790
Altitude: 2,570 m

Neither **airport**, nor **bus station** are far from the centre. Buses and taxis serve both. The central **tourist office** booth is at General Achá, next to *Entel*, helpful, photocopied city map and free guide. ■ *Mon-Fri 0830-1230, 1430-1815, Sat 0830-1230*. Administration offices are at Colombia E-0340, between 25 de Mayo y España, T422 1793. ■ *Mon-Fri 0830-1630*. The tourist police are here for complaints. Also at Jorge Wilstermann airport.

Ins & outs
For more detailed information see Transport, page 303

At the heart of the old city is the arcaded **Plaza 14 de Septiembre** with the **Cathedral** dating from 1571, but much added to. Nearby are several colonial churches: **Santo Domingo** (Santiváñez y Ayacucho) begun in 1778 and still unfinished; **San Francisco** (25 de Mayo y Bolívar) 1581, but heavily modernized in 1926; the **Convent of Santa Teresa** (Baptista y Ecuador) original construction 1760-90; and **La Compañía** (Baptista y Achá), whose whitewashed interior is completely devoid of the usual riot of late Baroque decoration. From **Plaza Colón**, at the north end of the old town, the wide Av Ballivián (known as **El Prado**) runs northwest to the wealthy modern residential areas. To the south of the old town lie the bus and train stations and some of the best produce markets in Bolivia. Overlooking the bus station is the **San Sebastián hill**, offering grand views of the city. From here you can walk to the adjoining **La Coronilla hill**, topped by an imposing monument commemorating the defence of Cochabamba by its womenfolk from Spanish troops in 1812 (beware of robbery). At the east end of Av Heroínas is another hill, the **Cerro de San Pedro**, with a statue to Cristo de la Concordia. ■ *Sun 0800-2000, closed Mon, cable car 1000-1830, US$0.45; US$0.15 to climb inside the statue for viewpoint.*

Sights

To the north of Plaza Colón at Av Potosí 1450 (T243137) lies **Palacio de Portales**, the Patiño mansion, now the *Centro Cultural Pedagócico Simón J Patiño*, reached by micro G from Av San Martín. Built in French renaissance style, furnished from Europe and set in 10 ha of gardens inspired by Versailles, the house was finished in 1927 but never occupied. ■ *Guided tours Mon-Fri 1700, 1730, 1800, Sat 1100 in Spanish and English, US$1.50, don't be late, T424 3137, useful library. There is an excellent art gallery in the basement. The gallery and gardens are open Mon-Fri 1700-1800, Sat-Sun 1000-1200.*

Museo Arqueológico, Jordán between Aguirre and Ayacucho, part of the Universidad de San Simón, small but interesting display of artefacts including amerindian hieroglyphic scripts and pre-Inca textiles, good 1½ hours tour. ■ *Tue-Sun 0900-1800,US$2.25, free student guide (Spanish, French or English).* **Casa de la Cultura**, 25 de Mayo y Av Las Heroínas, has a library and first editions of local newspapers. Its museum with exhibitions of paintings colonial and modern, is now at **Casona Santiváñez**, Santiváñez O-0156. ■ *Mon-Fri 0800-1200, 1430-1830, free, T425 9788.*

Essentials

Sleeping

Street numbering: the city is divided into 4 quadrants based on the intersection of Av Las Heroínas running west to east, and Av Ayacucho running north to south. In all longitudinal streets north of Heroínas the letter N precedes the 4 numbers. South of Heroínas the numbers are preceded by S. In all transversal streets west of Ayacucho the letter O (Oeste) precedes the numbers and all streets running east are preceded by E (Este). The first 2 numbers refer to the block, 01 being closest to Ayacucho or Heroínas; the last 2 refer to the building's number

L *Portales*, Av Pando 1271, T428 5444, F424 2071. 5-star, swimming pool open to non-residents (US$4 a day, US$8 on Sun with buffet), a long way from centre. **AL** *Aranjuez*, Av Buenos Aires E-0563, T428 0076, F424 0158, Casilla 3056. 4-star, 2 blocks from Los Portales, small, colonial style, good restaurant, jazz in the bar Fri and Sat night, small pool opoen to public (US$1). Recommended. **A** *Gran Hotel Cochabamba*, Plaza Ubaldo Anze, T428 2551, F428 2558. Beautifully set in the north part of the city (2 blocks from Los Portales at La Recoleta), with garden, swimming pool (US$3 for non-guests) and tennis courts, popular with tour groups. Recommended. **In the city: A** *Ambassador*, C España N-0349, T425 9001, ambass@comteco.entelnet.bo Modern, central and reasonable, includes breakfast, good restaurant. **B** *Americana*, Esteban Arce S-788, T425 0554, americana@ mail.infornetcbba.com.bo Fan, helpful, lift, laundry, parking, *Rodizio* grill next door, good service. **C** *Boston*, C 25 de Mayo 0167, T422 8530. Restaurant, luggage deposit, quiet rooms at back, safe parking. Recommended. **C** *Ideal*, España N-0329, T425 9430, F425 7930. Includes breakfast, restaurant, comfortable, good value. **C** *Regina*, Reza 0359, T425 7382, F411 7231. Spacious, efficient, breakfast extra, restaurant. **C-D** *City*, Jordán E-0341, T422 2993. Central, includes breakfast, cheaper rooms on upper floors, noisy but modern. **E** *Res Buenos Aires*, 25 de Mayo N-0329, T425 3911. **F** without bath, pleasant, clean communal baths, breakfast US$1.35. **E** *Hostal Elisa*, Agustín López S-0834, T423 5102. **F** without bath, good showers, hot water, good breakfast US$2.25, modern, garden, 2 blocks from bus station, laundry service, very popular with travellers. Recommended. **E** *Hostal Florida*, 25 de Mayo S-0583, T425 7911, floridah@elsito.com **F** without bath or cable TV, hot water, noisy, popular, laundry service, safe deposit box, internet, breakfast. **E** *Hostería Jardín*, Hamiraya N-0248, T424 7844. **F** without bath, garden, safe car-park, breakfast US$1 extra **E** *Versalles*, Av Ayacucho N-0714, T422 1096, 5 mins walk from terminal. Excellent, entrance through shopping arcade. **F** *Colonial*, Junín N-0134, T422 1791. With garden and terrace, rooms with big balcony but run down, peaceful, secure, laundry service, breakfast served on terrace. **F** *Res Familiar*, Sucre E-0554, T422 7988, with annex at 25 de Mayo S-0234, T422 7986. Pleasant, secure, good showers. **F** *Maracaibo*, Agustín López S-0925, T422 7110. Close to bus terminal, popular, safe. **G** *Res Agustín López*, Agustín López S-0859, T425 6926. Basic, hot water. **G** *Alojamiento Escobar*, Aguirre S-0749, T422 5812. Shared bath, good value (not to be confused with *Residencial* at Uruguay E-0213). **G** *Virgen de Copacabana*, Av Arce S-0875 y Brasil, T422 7929, near bus station. Hot showers, shared bath, good breakfast US$0.75, motorcycle parking, stores luggage. Recommended. Many cheap and basic places to stay near the bus station, most are short-stay and the area is unsafe.

Youth hostel *ABAJ* affiliate, **E** *Res Jordán*, C Antesana S-0671, T422 9294. Modern, basic, with cable TV and small pool. Annex (**D**) at 25 de Mayo S-0651, T422 5010.

Cochabamba

Bolivia

Fiesta de la Virgen de Urkupiña, Quillacollo

The festival lasts four days with much dancing and religious ceremony, its date varies each year between June and August. Plenty of transport from Cochabamba, hotels all full. Be there before 0900 to be sure of a seat, as you are not allowed to stand in the street. The first day is the most colourful with all the groups in costumes and masks, parading and dancing in the streets till late at night. Many groups have left by the second day and dancing stops earlier. The third day is dedicated to the pilgrimage. (Many buses, micros and trufis from Heroínas y Ayacucho, 20 minutes, US$0.30.)

Eating

The restaurant and nightlife district centres around España, Ecuador and Colombia Plaza Colón and Av Ballivián and north of Río Rocha near Av Santa Cruz

Local and Latin American Mid-range: *El Asador*, Junín O-0942. Good meat, huge portions, stylish. *Bufalo*, Torres Sofer, p 2, Av Oquendo N-0654. Brazilian *rodizio* grill, all-you-can-eat buffet for US$7.50, great service. Highly recommended. *La Estancia*, Av Uyuni E-0718 (Pando). Best steak in town, also grilled fish and chicken (in side street off Plaza Recoleta), also has a salad bar. Recommended. *Habana Café*, M Rocha E-0348. Genuine Cuban food and drinks, can get lively at night, open 1200-last person leaves. *Jacaranda*, Arce S-0628. Pleasant patio, excellent food including duck with salad and vegetables. *Marco's*, Av Oquenda entre Cabrera y Uruguay. Good Peruvian ceviche, Sat-Sun 1200-1500. **Cheap**: Excellent food in Incallacta market for under US$1. A few kilometres north of the city, in the village of **Tiquipaya**, are many *comida criolla* restaurants, eg *El Diente*, recommended.

International and European styles Expensive: *La Cantonata*, España N-0409. Italian. Highly recommended. *La Cuisine*, España N-0384, T228614. French, elegant, excellent. *Suiza*, Av Ballivián 820. Popular, recommended for international cuisine, good value. **Mid-range**: *BJ*, Av Libertador Bolívar 1580. International cuisine. Recommended. *Metrópolis*, España N-0299. Good pasta dishes, huge portions, good vegetarian options, noisy; *Metrópolis Pizza*, next door, good value. *Picasso's*, España 327, entre Ecuador y Mayor Rocha. Good value Italian and Mexican. **Cheap**: *Eli's Pizza Express*, 25 de Mayo N-0254. Son of the famous La Paz branch, great pizzas and serves Mexican fast food.

Chinese *José*, Plaza 14 de Setiembre 0209. Popular, not expensive, not entirely Chinese. *Lai-Lai*, Recoleta E-0729. Also takeaway service. Recommended.

Vegetarian *Bohemia*, España casi Mayor Rocha. Lots of choice, set lunch US$2, excellent desserts, reading room, left luggage service, book exchange, relaxing. *Comida Vegetariana*, M Rocha E-0375. Vegetarian food using soya milk and meat. *Gopal*, C España 250, Galería Olimpia. Hare-krishna, vegetarian lunch 1200-1500, US$1.50, vegetarian restaurant in evening, pleasant garden, English spoken, closed Sat and Sun night. *Snack Uno*, Av Heroínas E-0562. Good lunches and dinners including vegetarian. *Tulasi*, Av Heroínas E-0262. Open 0800-2200, till 1500 weekends, good, buffet lunch, US$1.50.

General *Café Clap*, Arce y Jordán. Good coffee and tea, pleasant. *Café Express Bolívar*, Bolívar ente San Martín y 25 de Mayo. Great coffee. *Café París*, España entre Las Heroínas y Colombia. Good for juices, nice setting. *Fragmento's Café*, Ecuador E-0325. Good coffee, snacks, nice atmosphere, popular with students, artists, occasional live music, cultural information. *Les Temps Modernes*, España N-0140. Fine coffee, French-style snacks, patisserie, Mon-Sat 1500-late. Recommended. Good **ice-cream** parlours on Av Heroínas: *Dumbo*, 0440, popular eating and meeting spot, also does cheap meals. *Cristal*, 3 doors away, similar but smaller and quieter. Recommended. *Unicornio*, Heroínas y Baptista. Large, attractive, popular gringo hangout, pricey.

Bars & nightlife

Discos Many, including *Lujos*, Beni E-0330. Nice atmosphere. *D'Mons*, Tarija y América. Mix of Latin, contemporary and classic American music. Both open 2300, US$4 including first drink. **Nightlife** *Panchos*, M Rocha E-0311, just off España. A lively dancing and drinking place. *Chilimania*, M Rocha E-0333. Also good for drinking and dancing. *Wunderbar*, Venezuela E-0635. Cable TV Sports Mon, music, darts upstairs, ribs, wings, subs, opens 1930.

Entertainment

Frequent **concerts** and **plays** at the elegant *Teatro Achá*, España y Las Heroínas, T422 1166. More popular stage productions (stand-up comedy, music and dance) at *Tra La La*, Plazuela

4 de Noviembre, T428 5030. **Peña**: *Totos*, M Rocha y Ayacucho, T452 2460. Fri night only, 2000-0300; may decide to have on Sat too. A real locals' place, free entry.

Carnival is celebrated 15 days before **Lent**. Rival groups (*comparsas*) compete in music, dancing, and fancy dress, culminating in El Corso on the last Sat of the Carnival. *Mascaritas* balls also take place in the carnival season, when the young women wear long hooded satin masks. **14 Sep**: *Day of Cochabamba*.

Festivals

Artesanías Casa Fisher, C Ramón Rivero E-0204, opposite the *Tennis Club*, PO Box 3782, T/F424 9846. Beautiful woollen goods, prices about US$85 locally, US$225-265 in USA. *Fotrama*, factory at Av Circunvalación 0413, T422 5468, outlet at Bolívar 0439. Cooperative for alpaca sweaters, stoles, rugs, alpaca wool, etc (expensive), run by *Maryknoll Mission*. *Arizona*, Juan Capriles E-0133. Recommended. Lots of antique shops on Calle España, near Plaza 14 de Septiembre. **Markets** are very good for tourist items and souvenirs (beware pickpockets). La Cancha market (San Martín, Punata, República y Pulacoyo) is packed on Wed and Sat with campesinos, 'huge and well worth a visit'; woollen items are expensive but high quality, US$35-50 for an alpaca sweater. There is a Sat market at Av América y Libertador, best before 0900. Mercado Incallacta is for fruit and vegetables; also sells tourist souvenirs. A very good **bookshop** is *Los Amigos del Libro*, Ayacucho S-0156, T450 4150, in *Hotel Portales* and *Gran Hotel Cochabamba*, in the new Torres Sofer shopping centre and at Jorge Wilsterman airport. Stocks US and English magazines as well as *South American Handbook*. Good city map and guide in colour for US$2.50. **Camping equipment** *Ans Em Ex*, Heroínas O-0225, T422 9711. Limited range. Camping gas available at several shops on Av San Martín.

Shopping

Turismo Balsa, Av Heroínas O-0184, T422 7610, F422 5795. Daily city tours, excursions to Quillacollo, Inca-Rakay, Samaipata, Torotoro, etc, airline reservations (see also under La Paz Tour Operators). *Carve*, Heroínas E-0637, T425 8627, and *Caxia Tours*, Arce 0563, T422 6148, caxiasrl@supernet.com.bo Both recommended. *Fremen*, Tumusla N-0245, T425 9392, F411 7790. City and local tours, specializes in travel in Bolivian Amazonia, using the *Reina de Enin* floating hotel out of Puerto Varador near Trinidad, also run *Hotel El Puente* in Villa Tunari (see below).

Tour operators

Local Micros and colectivos, US$0.20; *trufis*, US$0.30. Anything marked 'San Antonio' goes to the market. *Trufis* C and 10 go from bus terminal to the city centre. **Taxi**: about US$0.50 from anywhere to the Plaza, more expensive to cross the river; double after dark.

Transport
Be careful in Plaza San Antonio Boys spit in your face then either grab or slash your bag

  Long distance Air: Jorge Wilstermann airport, T459 1820. Airport bus is Micro B from Plaza 14 de Septiembre, US$0.40; taxis from airport to centre US$3.60. Reconfirm all flights (and obtain reconfirmation number), and arrive early for international flights. Several flights daily to/from **La Paz** (30 mins) and **Santa Cruz** (45 mins) with *LAB* and *Aero Sur* (book early for morning flights). *LAB* also to **Guayaramerín**, **Riberalta**, **Sucre**, **Trinidad** and **Tarija**. International flights to **Asunción**, **Buenos Aires**, **Cusco**, **Lima** and **São Paulo**. *LAB*, Heroínas, entre Sánchez y Baptista, open 0800, T0800-30011. *Aero Sur*, Av Villarroel 105, esq Av Oblitos (Pando), T440 0909/459 0077 (airport). **Bus**: the main bus terminal is on Av Ayacucho on opposite side from Montes and Punata (T155). To **Santa Cruz**, 10 hrs, from 0530-2200, US$4-5 (*buscama* US$7.50); only minibuses take the old mountain road via Epizana, from Av 9 de Abril y Av Oquendo, all day. See page 306, below. To/from **La Paz** many companies, shop around for best times, services and prices (about US$2.25-3.75, *buscama* US$4.50-6), by night or day, 7 hrs on paved road. Bus to **Oruro**, US$2.25-3, 4½ hrs, buses hourly. To **Potosí**, US$4.50-5.25 via Oruro, several companies 1830-2000. Daily to **Sucre**, US$4.50-5.25, 10 hrs, several companies between 1930 and 2030 (*Flota Copacabana* and *Trans Copacabana* recommended; latter *buscama* US$8.90). To **Sucre** by day; take a bus to Aiquile (see below), then a bus at midnight-0100 passing en route to Sucre (if you want to take a truck in daylight, wait till next day). Local buses leave from Av Barrientos y Av 6 de Agosto, near La Coronilla for **Tarata**, **Punata** and **Cliza**. Av República y Av 6 de Agosto to **Epizana** and **Totora**. Av Oquendo y 9 de Abril (be careful around this area), to **Villa Tunari**, US$2.70, 4-5 hrs, several daily; **Chimoré**, US$5.75; **Eterazama**, US$5.75; **Puerto Villarroel**, US$4, 6-8 hrs (from 0800 when full, daily); **Puerto San Francisco**, US$6.50.

Bolivia

Directory

For hospitals, doctors and dentists, contact your consulate or the tourist office for recommendations

Banks Cash on Visa or MasterCard from many banks; no commission on bolivianos. Visa and MasterCard at *Enlace* cash dispensers all over the town (especially on Av Ballivián) and next to the bus terminal. *Exprint-Bol*, Plaza 14 de Septiembre S-0252, will change TCs into dollars at 2% commission. *Ultramar*, 25 de Mayo N-0167, changes TCs and cash. Money changers congregate at most major intersections, especially outside *Entel*, good rates. **Communications** Internet: Many cybercafés all over town, charging US$0.60 per hr. Post Office: Av Heroínas y Ayacucho, next to *LAB* office (main entrance on Ayacucho), Mon-Fri 0800-2000, Sat 0800-1800, Sun 0800-1200. **Telephone:** *Entel*, Gral Achá y Ayacucho, international phone, fax (not possible to make AT&T credit card calls), open till 2300. **Cultural centres** Centro Boliviano Americano, 25 de Mayo N-0365, T221288. Library of English-language books, open 0900-1200 and 1430-1900; also offers language classes. **Alianza Francesa**, Santiváñez O-0187. **Instituto Cultural Boliviano-Alemán**, Sucre 693, Casilla 1700, T228431, F228890. Spanish classes offered. Highly recommended repeatedly. **Embassies and consulates** Argentina, F Blanco E-0929, T425 5859. Visa applications 0830-1300. **Brazil**, Edif Los Tiempos Dos, Av Oquendo, p 9, T425 5860. Open 0830-1130, 1430-1730. **Germany**, Edif La Promotora, p 6, of 602, T425 4024, F425 4023. **Italy**, Ayacucho Gal Cochabamba p 1, T423 8650. 1800-1930 Mon-Fri. **Netherlands**, Av Oquendo 654, Torres Sofer p 7, T425 7362. 0830-1200, 1400-1630 Mon-Fri. **Norway**, Av Guillermo Urquidi E-2279, T/F423 1951. Mon-Wed and Fri 0800-0900. **Paraguay**, Edif El Solar, 16 de Julio 211, T425 0183. 0830-1230, 1430-1830 Mon-Fri. **Peru**, Av Pando 1325, T424 0296. 0800-1200, 1400-1800 Mon-Fri. **Spain**, Los Molles y Paraíso, Urb Irlandés, T425 5733. 1100-1200 Mon-Fri. **Sweden**, Barquisimeto, Villa La Glorieta, T/F424 5358. 0900-1200 Mon-Fri. **USA**, Av Oquendo, Torres Sofer p 6, T425 6714. 0900-1200 (will also attend to Britons and Canadians). **Language classes** *Sra Blanca de La Rosa Villareal*, Av Libertador Simón Bolívar 1108, esq Oblitas, Casilla 2707 (T424 4298). US$5 per hr. *Runawasi*, J Hinojosa, Barrio Juan XXIII s/n, Casilla 4034, T/F424 8923. Spanish and Quechua, also arranges accommodation. *Sra Alicia Ferrufino*, JQ Mendoza N-0349, T428 1006. US$10 per hour, *Elizabeth Siles Salas*, Casilla 4659, T423 2278, silessalas@latinmail.com *Reginaldo Rojo*, T424 2322, frojo@supernet.com.bo US$5 per hr. *María Pardo*, Pasaje El Rosal 20, Zona Queru Queru behind Burger King on Av América, T428 4615. US$5 per hr, also teaches Quechua. *Carmen Galinda Benavides*, Parque Lincoln N-0272, Casilla 222, T424 7072. *Maricruz Almanzal*, Av San Martín 456, T422 7923, maricruz_almanza@hotmail.com US$5 for 50 mins, special offers for extended tuition. See also Cultural centres, above. **Useful addresses** Immigration Office: Jordán y Arce, p 2, T422 5556, Mon-Fri 0830-1630.

Around Cochabamba

Quillacollo, 13 km west of the city, has a good Sunday market but no tourist items; the *campesinos* do not like being photographed. 2 to 3 km beyond Quillacollo is a turn-off to the beautiful Pairumani *hacienda*, centre of the Patiño agricultural foundation, eight from Quillacollo. Known also as Villa Albina, it was built in 1925-32, furnished from Europe and inhabited by Patiño's wife, Albina. ■ *Mon-Fri 1500-1600, Sat 0900-1130. T426 0083 to check if it is open. Getting there: bus 7 or 38, or trufi 211 from Cochabamba.*

Some 27 km west of Cochabamba, near Sipe-Sipe, are **Inka-Rakay** ruins. The main attraction is the view from the site of the Cochabamba valley and the mountains around the ruins. **Tarata**, 33 km southeast of Cochambamba, is a colonial town with a traditional arcaded plaza on which stand the church, containing an 18th-century organ and other colonial artefacts (open 0800-1300 daily), the Casa Consistorial, and the Municipalidad. Inside the Franciscan Convent overlooking the town are the remains of the martyr, San Severino, patron saint of the town, more commonly known as the 'Saint of Rain'; festival, on the last Sunday of November, attracts thousands of people. Large procession on 3 May, day of La Santa Cruz, with fireworks and brass band. Market day Thursday (bus US$0.65, one hour, last return 1800).

Punata, 48 km to the east, has a very lively and colourful market on Tuesday. It is famous for its Señor de los Milagros festival on 24 September. Behind the main church, which has many baroque/mestizo works of art, new vehicles are lined up to be blessed by the priest. The local speciality is *garapiña*, a mixture of *chicha* and ice-cream. Beyond Punata, at Villa Rivera, woven wall hangings are produce.

In the province of Potosí, but best reached from Cochabamba (135 km), is **Torotoro**, a small village, set amid beautiful rocky landscape (*Tinku* festival 25 June; *Santiago* 24-27 July). The village is in the centre of the **Parque Nacional Torotoro**. Attractions include caves, a canyon, waterfalls, pictographs, ruins; fossilized dinosaur tracks and rock paintings can be seen by the Río Toro Toro just outside the village. ■ *Entry to the park is US$3; local guide US$5 per day, plus his food for trips of over a day. Despite the difficulties of getting there, this trip is highly recommended. Tourist information is available at the national park office in Torotoro (open daily).* Umajalanta cave, which has many stalagtites and a lake with blind fish, is about 8 km northwest of Torotoro; a guide is necessary, US$5 per person in a group of 2 to 5. Mario Jaldín (Spanish speaking only) is highly knowledgeable and will take you to the best places. He lives two doors to the right of *Alojamiento Charcas*. He also leads a four-day trek to see canyons, condors, orchids, many birds and, if lucky, the Andean Bear and pumas. Cost: US$80-100 per person, depending on the size of the group. Includes camping gear and food. Bring your own sleeping bag.

Parque
Nacional
Torotoro
Torotoro covers an area of 16,570 ha and was declared a National Park in 1989

Sleeping and eating There are 3 *tiendas* in the village. *Alojamientos*, all **G**: *Charcas* near bus terminal, with restaurant; *Trinidad*. The Becerra family is building a hotel and cabins are being built. Lydia García's *Salón de Té* bakes cakes, etc. 2 *pensiones* provide 3 meals a day.

The village has no electricity, only a generator which runs in the evening until the village's 1 video cinema ends its screening, around 2130-2200

Transport Travel to Torotoro is impossible overland in the wet season (end Nov-Mar), as flooded rivers wash out roads, but it is possible to fly quite cheaply as a group. Swiss pilot Eugenio Arbinsona charges US$120 for up to 5 passengers in his Cessna. It takes only 25 mins, but he may be persuaded to lengthen the journey by flying you through a canyon or two on the way! T424 6289 (home), T422 7042 (hangar) or T 0717-23779 (mob). Check bus schedules at all times of year with Gonzalo Milán, *Comercial El Dorado*, Honduras 646, Cochabamba, T422 0207. Transport to Torotoro goes in convoy from Av República y 6 de Agosto at 0600 Sun and Thu, US$4 in a bus or the cab of a truck, US$3 in the back, 10 hrs. Transport returns to Cochabamba every Mon and Fri, 0600. Groups can arrange with Gonzalo Milán to be picked up at a hotel. Alternatively, pay in advance and arrange to be picked up in Cliza where buses and trucks stop at 0800.

Bolivia

Cochabamba to Santa Cruz

The lowland road from Cochabamba to Santa Cruz runs through Villa Tunari, Sinahota and Chimoré (a centre for DEA operations; three hotels). The road is paved Villa Tunari-Santa Cruz. **Villa Tunari** (Phone code: 04; see Cochabamba, Transport, Buses, above) is a relaxing place and holds an annual Fish Fair 5 and 6 August, music and dancing, delicious meals. *Parque Ecoturístico Machía* is just outside town and offers good trails through semi-tropical forest. ■ *Free, but donations welcome.* Beside the park is the animal refuge *Inti Wara Yassi*, where rescued animals are nursed back to health. Travellers can stay in **G** accommodation as volunteers (must be self-supporting), or just visit for the day. ■ *Daily 0900-1700, free, but donations welcome. There is a charge to take photos, US$2.25 and videos US$3.75. Contact Nena Baltazar in Villa Tunari, T04-413 4621. Also Casilla 9519, La Paz, or ciwy99@yahoo.com*

To Santa Cruz via Chapare
On this descent to the lowlands, the birdwatching is superb as many types of habitat are traversed

Sleeping and eating **A** *Country Club Los Tucanes*, opposite turn-off for *El Puente*, T413 4108. Includes breakfast, a/c, 2 swimming pools. **B** *El Puente*, Av de la Integración, 3 km from town, T425 0302 (Cochabamba). With breakfast and bath, cabins from 2 people to family-size (book in advance at *Fremen* Travel Agency in Cochabamba or La Paz), pool, tours to Carrasco national park, the hotel has a beautiful stream and 14 natural pools. **B** *Las Palmas*, T4103, 1 km out of town. With breakfast, pool and good restaurant, changes US$ cash. Recommended. **B** *Los Araras*, across bridge on main road to Santa Cruz. **C** midweek, large rooms, nice gardens, good breakfast. **F** *Las Palmas 2*, corner of plaza. With bath, breakfast, fan, swimming pool (not very clean). **G** *La Querencia*, pleasant terrace on river front, avoid noisy rooms at front, good cheap food, clothes washing facilities. Several other hotels; also two internet cafés, *Entel* office (T4101/2) and post office. Best restaurant is **Cuqui**, 1 km west of town, fish specialities, also has tents for camping. **Cristiana's**, on plaza opposite police station. Good value at US$1.25.

The mountain road

The 500 km road via the mountains and Epizana to Santa Cruz (page 313) is not paved and the new lowland route is preferred by most transport

Before the Siberia pass, 5 km beyond Montepunco (Km 119), the 23 km road to Pocona and **Inkallajta** turns off. The Inca ruins (1463-72, rebuilt 1525), on a flat spur of land at the mouth of a steep valley, are extensive and the main building of the fortress is said to have been the largest roofed Inca building. There are several good camping sites. The Cochabamba Archaeological Museum has some huts where visitors can stay, free, but take sleeping bag and food. Water available at nearby waterfall. ■ *Getting there: Take a micro to the checkpoint 10 km from Cochabamba, then a truck to Km 119, walk towards Pocona or take a truck for 15 km, to where a large yellow sign indicates the trail. After approximately 10 km the trail divides, take the downhill path and the ruins are a further 2 km.*

Totora, on the Sucre road, is a beautiful, unspoiled colonial village. There is **G** *Residencial Colonial*, behind the church. Hot water in mornings, restaurant also. Daily buses from Cochabamba, República y 6 de Agosto at 1600, also at 1430 on Saturday; return 0500 Monday-Saturday, 1100 Sunday. Daily bus to Aiquile at 1600 and to Sucre. **Aiquile**, south of Totora and 217 km from Cochabamba, is famous for its wooden *charangos* (guitar made from armadillo shell): *charango* festival in late October/early November, ask tourist office. Sunday market, for which the town fills up on Saturday. ■ *Getting there: Daily buses from Cochabamba with* Flotas Aiquile *(Av Barrientos S-2365, 100 m past Av 6 de Agosto junction, trufis 1, 10, 14, 16, 20 pass in front) and 3 a week with* Trans Campero *(Av Barrientos S-2291), 5 hrs; 1300, return at 1700. All nightly buses from Sucre to Cochabamba and Santa Cruz pass Aiquile between 2300 and 0130; few sell tickets only to Aiquile.* Unificado *has an office on the main road in Aiquile beneath the shabby Aloj Turista with buses leaving every day for Sucre (0100), Cochabamba (1100) and Santa Cruz (2130).*

The Northern Lowlands

Bolivia's Northern lowlands, the Cuenca Amazónica, account for about 70% of national territory. Beni department has 53% of the country's birds and 50% of its mammals, but destruction of forest and habitat is proceeding at an alarming rate. From scrubby east lowlands to dense tropical jungle in the north, this is pioneer country; home to missionaries, rubber tappers and cocaine refiners. Improved roads to Rurrenabaque and Trinidad are opening up the area and wildlife expeditions are becoming increasingly popular.

Caranavi to San Borja

From Caranavi, a road runs north to **Sapecho**. Beyond Sapecho, the road passes through Palos Blancos 7 km from the bridge (Saturday market day, several cheap lodgings). The road between Sapecho and Yucumo is now a very good all-weather gravel surface, three hours from Sapecho *tránsito*. There are *hospedajes* (**F**) and restaurants in **Yucumo** where a road branches northwest, fording rivers 13 times on its way to Rurrenabaque. ■ *Yucumo is on the La Paz-Caranavi-Rurrenabaque or San Borja bus routes. Rurrenabaque-La Paz bus passes through about 1800. If travelling to Rurrenabaque by bus or truck take extra food in case there is a delay for river levels to fall.*

From Yucumo it is 50 km (1-2 hours, truck at 0730) to **San Borja**, a small, wealthy-looking cattle-raising centre with hotels (**D-F**) and restaurants clustered near the plaza.

Transport *Flota Yungueña* daily except Thu at 1300 to **La Paz** (19 hrs); also to **Rurrenabaque** (*Buses 1 de Mayo*, T03-895 3467, US$4.40), **Santa Rosa**, **Riberalta**, **Guayaramerín** Thu, Sat, Sun. From San Borja the road goes east to **Trinidad** via **San Ignacio de Moxos**. There are 5-6 river crossings and, in the wetlands, flamingoes, blue heron and a multitude of waterfowl. The road surface Caranavi-San Borja is good; San Borja-San Ignacio poor, long stretches are rutted and pot-holed; San Ignacio-Trinidad is good. Gasoline available at Yolosa, Caranavi, Yucumo, San Borja and San Ignacio. Minibuses and camionetas run daily between San Borja and Trinidad throughout the year, US$15, about 7 hrs including 20 mins crossing of Río Mamoré on ferry barge (up to 14 hrs in wet season); *1 de Mayo* to **San Ignacio** (US$8), **Trinidad** and **Santa Cruz** at 0850; or hitch on a timber truck.

Parque Nacional Madidi is quite possibly the most bio-diverse of all protected areas on the planet. It is the variety of habitats, from the freezing Andean peaks of the Cordillera Apolobamba in the southwest (reaching nearly 6,000 m), through cloud, elfin and dry forest at mid elevations to steaming tropical jungle and pampas (neo-tropical savannah) in the north and east, that account for the array of flora and fauna within the park's boundaries. In an area roughly the size of Wales or El Salvador are an estimated 1,000 bird species, 10 species of primates, five species of cat (with healthy populations of jaguar and puma), giant anteaters and many reptiles. Madidi is at the centre of a bi-national system of parks. The Heath river on the park's northwestern border forms the Bolivia/Peru frontier and links with the Parque Nacional Tambopata-Candamo/Bahuaja Sonene in Peru. To the southwest the Ulla Ulla National Fauna and Biosphere Reserve protects extensive mountain ecosystems. Beyond the Beni River in the southeast runs the Pilón Lajas Biosphere and Indigenous Territory, home to several native groups. Together these areas constitute approximately 40,000 sq km, one of the largest systems of protected land in the Neotropics.

Parque Nacional Madidi & Pilón Lajas
Visit www.ecobolivia.org/ for information on Madidi

At San José de Uchupiamonas, in Madidi, 5 hrs upriver from Rurrenabaque, is Bolivia's top ecotourism project – *Chalalán Ecolodge*, C Comercio, T892 2519, chalalan@cibol.rds.org.bo In La Paz, contact Jazmín Caballero (fluent English) at *América Tours* (address under La Paz Tour operators). It was founded by the local community, Conservation International and the Interamerican Development Bank. Accommodation is in thatched cabins, and activities include fantastic wildlife spotting and birdwatching, guided and self-guided trails, river and lake activities, and relaxing in pristine jungle surroundings. A 5-day trip includes travel time from La Paz, but not air fares, US$260 in low season, US$350 in high season.

Tours
On tours, insect repellent and sun protection are essential

Rurrenabaque (see below) provides the easiest access for tours in Madidi. Jungle tours normally last four days and three nights (US$25 per day). The jungle is very hot and humid in the rainy season with many more biting insects and far fewer animals to be seen. You see a lot of wildlife on a three-day Pampas tour (US$30 per day), which involves a 3½-hour jeep ride to the Río Yacuma, then a series of boat trips. You see howler, squirrel and capuchin monkeys, caiman, capybara, pink dolphins, possibly anacondas and a huge variety of birds. The weather and general conditions are more pleasant than the jungle; season July to October. For pampas and jungle tours, one-day trips are reportedly a waste of time as it takes three hours to reach the jungle.

The **Pilón Lajas Biosphere and Indigenous Territory** in the Beni, under the auspices of UNESCO, has been set up. A biological reserach station at El Porvenir, half way between San Borja and San Ignacio de Moxos, caters for visitors, US$12 per person including three meals. From Rurrenabaque, there is a **Day for the community** tour, called *Ecological and Social Project*. It demonstrates how four different communities of economic refugees from different areas of Bolivia live and work in the buffer zone of Pilon Lajas. NGOs have been working with the people of La Unión, Playa Ancha, Nuevos Horizontes and El Cebó to develop sustainable forestry, fish farming, beekeeping, cattle ranching, *artesanía* and even fruit wines. Book with Rurrenabaque tour operators, US$22.

Rurrenabaque

Phone code: 03
Population: 10,000

This is a charming, picturesque jungle town, on the Río Beni, with San Buenaventura on the opposite bank offering cheap tours with the chance to fish for piranha and swim with pink river dolphins. There is a public swimming pool in town, US$1.

Sleeping & eating

Most hotels are noisy owing to all-night discos. Electricity 1800-0300

C-E *Beni*, by river, T892 2408, F892 2273. Best rooms have a/c and TV, hot showers extra for cheaper without bath or a/c (but with fan). spacious, pleasant, good service. **C** *Hotel Safari*, on the outskirts by the river (a hot walk), T892 2410. Beautiful garden, pool, terrace. Recommended. **C** *Taquara*, on plaza. Generally better than others, pool, accepts credit cards. **D** *Asaí*, C Vaca Díez, T892 2439. Electric showers, laundry area, courtyard and hammocks, luggage store. **E** *El Porteño*, C Vaca Díez. Cheaper without bath, quite good. **E** *Oriental*, on plaza. Cheaper without bath, breakfast available, quiet. Recommended. **F** *Rurrenabaque*, 1 block east of plaza. Safe, cooking and laundry facilities, good. **F** *Santa Ana*, 1 block north of plaza on Avaroa, T892 2399. Cheaper without bath in hammock area, basic, hot showers extra, laundry, luggage store, pretty courtyard, car park. Recommended. **F** *Tuichi*, C Avaroa y Santa Cruz. **G** without bath, cold showers, luggage storage, laundry facilities, fan, good value, accepts TCs. **G** *Hostal Eden*, southern end of C Bolívar, T892 2452. With or without bath, has hammocks and kitchen, new, good value. **G** pp *Jislene*, C Comercio, T892 2526. Erlan Caldera and family very hospitable, hot water, fan, basic, good breakfast if booked in advance, information, helpful. Restaurants: *Club Social Rurrenabaque*, on Comercio 1 block north of Santa Cruz. Vegetarian dishes on request, good juices, fishburgers. *Café Motacu*, Av Santa Cruz beside TAM. Excellent meals, book exchange, closed Tue and Sun and 1200-1830. *Camila's*, Santa Cruz. Good Mexican and Italian food, fast food. *Bambi*, opposite *Flota Yungueña* office. Good meeting place; *heladería* which also does meals. *El Tacuara*, opposite *Camila's*. Good, also for breakfast. Just downriver from *El Porteño* is *Moskkito Bar*, good for ½-price cocktails 1900-2100; next door is a tasty Italian restaurant. Good *almuerzos* and fruit juices in the market.

Tour operators

Mosquito nets can be bought here much more cheaply than in La Paz. It is cheaper to book tours in Rurrenabaque than La Paz

As in many other places, make enquiries about services and personnel. We continue to receive reports of **drugging and rape**; use only established tour operators and always go in company. Please be aware of **Israel Janco Cáceres** who has a conviction for rape and a history of raping foreign women around Rurrenabaque. As rape is not considered a serious crime in Bolivia he has not been sent to jail and continues to operate as a tour guide. *Agencia Fluvial*, at *Hotel Tuichi*, T892 2372, runs jungle tours on the Río Tuichi, normally 4 days, but shorter by arrangement, US$25 pp per day (payable in dollars) including food, transport and mosquito nets (write to Tico Tudela, *Agencia Fluvial*, Rurrenabaque). Take swimming costume and insect repellent. Also 3-day 'Pampas Tours' on a boat to Río Yacuma, US$30 pp per day. Tico Tudela has opened *Hotel de la Pampa* near Lago Bravo, 2½ hrs from Rurrenabaque, as a base for visiting Lago Rogagua (birds) and Río Yacuma. Fully inclusive tours (including meals and accommodation) US$40 pp per day. *Aguila Tours*, Av Avaroa, T892 2478 (associated with *Flecha Tours*, Avaroa y Santa Cruz, who are also recommended), excellent jungle and pampas tours, very knowledgeable guides, well-organized (can be booked through *Eco Jungle Tours*, C Sagárnaga, La Paz). Recommended. *Bala Tours*, C Comercio, T892 2527. Arranges 'Pampas' and 'Jungle' tours, good base camp. Recommended. *Donato Tours*, C A Arce, T7179 5722/7779 5722 (mob). For regular tours and A Day for the Community – see Tours page 307.

Transport

Air **TAM** (C Santa Cruz, T892 2398), 4 a week, US$65 one way from La Paz (also has charter for 8 people). Book all flights as early as possible and buy return to La Paz on arrival. Check flight times in advance; they change frequently. Expect delays and cancellations in wet season. Airport tax US$2. Motorcycle taxi from town, US$1. **Road** To/from La Paz via Caranavi daily at 1100 with *Flota Yungueña* and *Totai*; 18-20 hrs, US$8.20. Returns at 1100. *Flota Unificada* leaves La Paz (also from Villa Fátima) on Tue, Thu, Fri, Sat at 1030, same price. Continues to Riberalta and Guayaramerín; return departure time depends on road conditions. *Flota Yungueña* also has a 1030 bus which leaves Villa Fátima and continues to Riberalta and Guayaramerín. Rurrenebaque-Riberalta should take 12-18 hrs, but can take 6 days or more in the wet. Take lots of food, torch and be prepared to work. To **Trinidad**, Tue, Thu, Sat, Sun at 2230 with *Trans Guaya* via Yucumo and San Borja. **River** Boats to **Guanay**, US$16 pp; ask at any tour agency; take your own food.

Banks No banks or *casas de cambio*. *Bala Tours* will give cash advance against credit cards at 7.5% commission.Try hotels or agencies for small amounts of cash. TCs are difficult (agencies will accept them as payment for tours), but try *Agencia Fluvial*, 5% commission. **Communications** **Internet:** Two next door to each other on C Santa Cruz, next to *Camila's*, US$3 per hr. Another on the same road, near the ferry. **Post office:** on C Bolívar. Both open Sat and at lunchtimes. **Telephone:** *Entel*, on C Comercio, 2 blocks north of plaza; also at Santa Cruz y Bolívar.

Directory

This town, at the confluence of the Madre de Dios and Beni rivers, is off the beaten track and a centre for brazil nut production. Change cash in shops and on street. Recent reports indicate an increase in theft and rape, worth knowing when the bus drops you in the middle of the night and everything is closed. Some 25 km away is **Tumi-Chucua** situated on a lovely lake. Nearby are the Nature Gardens. Here you can fish in the lake, good for birdwatching. They also have lots of information on the rainforest, the rubber boom and brazil nut production. Contact *Dr Willy Noack*, T/F0352-2497 for further information.

Riberalta
Phone code: 03
Colour map 3, grid B6
Population: 60,000
Altitude: 175 m

Bolivia

Sleeping and eating Ask for a fan and check the water supply. **C-D** *Hostal Tahuamanu*, M Hanicke 75, T852 8006. Modern, smart, very comfortable, a/c, including excellent breakfast. Recommended. **E** *Colonial*, Plácido Méndez 1. Charming colonial casona, large, well-furnished rooms, nice gardens and courtyard, comfortable, good beds, helpful owners. Recommended. **F** *Res Los Reyes*, near airport, T852 8018. With fan, safe, pleasant but noisy disco nearby on Sat and Sun. **F** *Comercial Lazo*, NG Salvatierra, T852 8326. **D** with a/c, comfortable, laundry facilities, good value. **F** *El Campo*, Av Moreno s/n, T852 3691. With fan, well-kept, good view from roof. Recommended. **G** *Res El Pauro*, Salvatierra 157. Basic, shared baths, good café. For eating, try, *Club Social Progreso*, on plaza. Good value *almuerzo*, excellent fish. *Club Social Riberalta*, on Maldonado. Good *almuerzo* US$3.50, smart dress only. *Quatro Ases*, Arce. Good. *Tucunare*, M Chávez/Martínez. Recommended. Good lunch at *comedor popular* in market, US$1.50.

Transport **Air** *Aero Sur*, on plaza (T852 2798), flies 5 times weekly to **Trinidad** and **Santa Cruz**. Expect delays in the wet season. *LAB* fly to **Guayaramerín, Trinidad** and **Cobija** ; office at M Chávez 77, T852 2239 (0800-3001). *TAM* flies to **Cochabamba**, **Santa Cruz** and **La Paz,** Fri (US$100 to La Paz); office Av Suárez/Chuquisaca, T852 3924. Check all flight details in advance. **Road** Several companies (including *Yungueña*) to **La Paz**, via Rurrenabaque and Caranavi Tue-Sat at 1100, also Tue, Thu, Sat at 1000; US$22.40 (same price to Rurrenebaque, 18 hrs). To **Trinidad** with *8 de Diciembre* Mon, Wed, Thu, Sat, Sun at 0830, also *Trans Guaya* daily at 0930, via Rurrenabaque; **Guayaramerín** daily, US$3, 3 hrs. To **Cobija** on Wed, Fri, Sat at 0900 with *8 de Diciembre*, Mon, Thu at 1000 with *TransAmazonas*. Buses stop in Santa Rosa for meals. **River** Cargo boats carry passengers along the **Río Madre de Dios**, but they are infrequent. There are not many boats to Rurrenabaque.

Guayaramerín is a cheerful, prosperous little town on the bank of the Río Mamoré, opposite the Brazilian town of Guajará-Mirim. It has an important *Zona Libre*. Passage between the two towns is unrestricted; boat trip US$1.65 (more at night).

Guayaramerín
Phone code: 03
Colour map 4, grid C1
Population: 35,000

Sleeping and eating **B** *Esperanza* out of town in nearby Cachuela Esperanza, Casilla 171, reserve through *Aero Sur*, T855 3594, or in La Paz, *American Tours*, T02-237 4204, F02-231 0023, www.america-ecoturs.com Eco-friendly. **C** *San Carlos*, 6 de Agosto, 4 blocks from port, T855 2152/3. With a/c (**D** without), hot showers, changes dollars cash, TCs and reais, swimming pool, reasonable restaurant. The following eating places are all on the plaza:

Made in Brazil, good coffee. *Gipsy*, good *almuerzo*. *Los Bibosis*, popular with visiting Brazilians. *Only*, 25 de Mayo/Beni, good *almuerzo* for US$2.50, plus Chinese. On road to airport *Heladería Tutti-Frutti*, excellent.

Transport Air *Aero Sur*, on plaza (T855 3594) to **Trinidad**. *LAB* flies to **Trinidad, Riberalta**,and **Cobija**; office at 25 de Mayo 652, T855 3540 (0800-3001). *TAM* flies to **Cochabamba, Santa Cruz** and **La Paz**; office at 16 de Julio (road to airport). **Bus** To/from **La Paz**, *Flota Yungueña*, daily 0830 (1030 from La Paz), 36 hrs, US$22.40. Also *Flota Unificada*, leaving La Paz Tue, Thu, Fri, Sat 1030, US$26.90.To **Riberalta** 3 hrs, US$3, daily 0700-1730. To **Trinidad** Fri, 30 hrs, US$23. To **Rurrenabaque**, US$16. To **Cobija** 4 a week. To **Santa Cruz** via Trinidad, 1-2 a week, 2½ days. Buses depart from Gral Federico Román. Roads are very difficult in wet season. **River** Check the notice of boats leaving port on the Port Captain's board, prominently displayed near the immigration post on the river's bank. Boats up the Mamoré to Trinidad are fairly frequent – a 3-day wait at the most.

Border with Brazil Bolivian immigration is on Av Costanera near port; open 0800-1100, 1400-1800. Passports must be stamped here when leaving, or entering Bolivia. On entering Bolivia, passports must be stamped at the Bolivian consulate in Guajará-Mirim. For Brazilian immigration, see page 560. The Brazilian consulate is on 24 de Septiembre, Guayaramerín, open 1100-1300; visas for entering Brazil are given here. Exchange money here (but not travellers' cheques) as this is very difficult in the State of Rondônia in Brazil.

Cobija
Phone code: 03
Colour map 6, grid B2
Population: 7,000
Altitude: 252 m

The capital of the lowland Department of Pando lies on the Río Acre which forms the frontier with Brazil. As a duty-free zone, shops in centre have a huge selection of imported consumer goods at bargain prices. Brazilians and Peruvians flock here to stock up. **NB** In this border area, watch out for scams and con.s

Sleeping and eating E *Prefectural Pando*, Av 9 de Febrero, T842 2230. Includes breakfast, *comedor* does good lunch, manager Sr Angel Gil, helpful. **F** *Res Crocodilo*, Av Molina, T842 2215. Comfortable, good atmosphere, rooms with fan. **G** *Res Frontera*, 9 de Febrero, T842 2740. Good location, basic but clean, fan. *La Esquina de la Abuela*, opposite *Res Crocodilo*, good food, not cheap. Good cheap meals in *comedor popular* in central market.

Transport Local Taxi: are very expensive, charging according to time and distance, eg US$10 to the outskirts, US$12 over the international bridge to Brasileia. Besides taxis there are motorbike taxis (much cheaper). Brasileia can also be reached by canoe, US$0.35.
     Long distance Air: *Aero Sur*, Av Fernández Molina, T842 3132, flies 2 days a week to **La Paz** and **Trinidad**. *LAB*, R Barrientos 343, T842 2170, twice a week to **Riberalta, Guayaramerín, Trinidad** and **Santa Cruz**. *TAM* office on 2 de Febrero, T842 2267 (check schedule). **Bus**: *Flota Yungueña* to **La Paz** via Riberalta and Rurrenabaque Sat at 0700 (check times first, T842 2318). To **Riberalta** with several bus companies and trucks, depart from 2 de Febrero, most on Wed, Fri, Sun at 0600; good all-weather surface; 5 river crossings on pontoon rafts, takes 10-11 hrs.

Directory Banks Lots of money changers along Av 2 de Febrero. Most shops will accept dollars or reais, or exchange money. **Communications Internet:** Internet place near the university, 100 m from the plaza. **Post Office:** on plaza. **Telephone:** *Entel*, on C Sucre, for telephone calls internal and abroad and fax, much cheaper than from Brazil.

Another route into Beni Department is via the lowland road between Cochabamba and Santa Cruz. At Ivirgazama, east of Villa Tunari, the road passes the turn-off to **Puerto Villarroel**, 27 km further north, from where cargo boats ply irregularly to Trinidad in about four to 10 days. You can get information from the Capitanía del Puerto notice board, or ask at docks. **E-G** *Amazonas Eco-hotel* with restaurant, T/F04-423 5105, boat trips arranged. *Alojamiento El Jazmín*, small, helpful, pleasant, meals served. Also **F-G** *Alojamiento Petrolero*. There are very few stores in Villarroel. Sr Arturo Linares at the Cede office organizes boat trips to the jungle – not cheap.

Villa Tunari to the Lowlands
As this is coca-growing territory the police advise not to stray from the main road, don't talk to strangers and don't guard or carry other people's luggage

Transport **F-G** *Camionetas* go from the junction on the main road to Puerto Villarroel a few times a day, 1 hr, US$1.20. From Cochabamba you can get a bus to Puerto Villarroel (see Cochabamba Transport, Bus), Puerto San Francisco, or Todos Santos on the Río Chapare.

Trinidad

The hot and humid capital of the lowland Beni Department, founded 1686, is a dusty city in the dry season, with many streets unpaved. There are two ports, Almacén and Varador, check which one your boat is docking at. Puerto Varador is 13 km from town on the Río Mamoré on the road between Trinidad and San Borja; cross the river by the main bridge by the market, walk down to the service station by the police checkpoint and take a truck, US$1.70. Almacén is 8 km from the city. The main mode of transport in Trinidad (even for taxis, US$0.40 in city) is the motorbike; rental on plaza from US$2 per hour, US$8 per half day.

Phone code: 03
Colour map 6, grid A3
Population: 80,000
Altitude: 237 m

Hire a motorbike or jeep to go to the river; good swimming on the opposite bank; boat hire US$5. 8 km from town is the Laguna Suárez, with plenty of wildlife; the water is very warm, the bathing safe where the locals swim, near the café with the jetty (elsewhere there are stingrays and alligators). See under Eating, below. Motorbike taxi from Trinidad, US$1.30.

About 17 km north is **Chuchini** with the Madriguera del Tigre, an ecological and archaeological centre, accessible by road in dry season and by canoe in wet season. Contact Efrem Hinojoso at Av 18 de Noviembre 543, T462 4744/1811. Three days and two nights US$210 per person, including accommodation and meals; plenty of wildlife to be seen; also including **Museo Arqueológico del Beni**, containing human remains, ceramics and stone objects from precolumbian Beni culture, said to be over 5,000 years old.

A *Gran Moxos*, Av 6 de Agosto y Santa Cruz, T462 2240, F462 0002. Includes breakfast, a/c, fridge bar, cable TV, phone, good restaurant, accepts Visa and MasterCard. **C-D** *Hostal Aguahi*, Bolívar y Santa Cruz, opposite *TAM*, T462 5569. A/c, fridge, comfortable, swimming pool in pleasant garden. **C-D** *Monte Verde*, 6 de Agosto 76, T462 2738. With or without a/c, fridge bar, includes breakfast, owner speaks English. Recommended. **D** *Copacabana*, Tomás Villavicencio 627, 3 blocks from plaza, T462 2811. Good value, **F** pp without bath. **D-E** *Res Castedo*, Céspedes 42, T462 0937, 200 m from bus terminal. A/c or fan, cheaper without bath, breakfast. **D-E** *Hostal Jarajorechi*, Av 6 de Agosto y 27 de Mayo, Casilla 299, T462 1716. With bath and breakfast, comfortable, ecotourism centre offering jungle expeditions, equipment and transport hire. **F** *Paulista*, Av 6 de Agosto 36, T462 0018. Cheaper without bath, comfortable, good restaurant. **F** *Res Oriental*, 18 de Noviembre near Vaca Díez, T462 2534. Good value. **G** *Res 18 de Noviembre*, Av 6 de Agosto 135, T462 1272. Laundry facilities, OK but noisy.

Sleeping

Carlitos, on Plaza Ballivián. Recommended. *La Casona*, Plaza Ballivián. For good pizzas and set lunch, closed Tue. *La Clave*, López 124, off Bolívar. *Parrillada*, good *almuerzo*, open-air seating. *Club Social 18 de Noviembre*, N Suárez y Vaca Díez on plaza. Good lunch for US$1.35. *Chifa El Dragón de China*, Joaquín de Sierra 177. Good Chinese, not cheap. *La Estancia*, Barrio Pompeya, on Ibare entre Muibe y Velarde. Excellent steaks. *Pakumutu*, Av 18 de Noviembre near Féliz Pinto, near airport, excellent beef. *Pescadería El Moro* , Bolívar 707 y Natusch.

Eating
Cheap meals, includes breakfast, served at the fruit and vegetable market. Try delicious sugar cane juice with lemon

Bolívia

Excellent fish. Also several good fish restaurants in Barrio Pompeya, south of plaza across the river. Burgers, ice cream and snacks at *Kivón* cafeteria on main plaza. Also on plaza, *Heladería Oriental*, good coffee, ice-cream, cakes, popular with locals, and *Snack Kentucky* (north side), good value. *Balneario Topacare* is a restaurant and bathing resort with swimming pool 10 mins out of town on Laguna Suárez, delicious local specialities, lunch or dinner, beautiful location, excellent bird watching, favourite spot for locals at weekends.

Tour operators *Fremen*, Cipriano Berace 332, T462 1834. Run speed boat trips along the Mamoré and Iboré rivers and to Parque Nacional Isiboro, US$80 per day; their *Flotel Reina de Enin* offers tours of more than 1 day, US$80 pp per day, good food. Others on 6 de Agosto: *Tarope Tours*, No 57, T/F462 1468. For flights. *Moxos*, No 114, T462 1141. Recommended. *Paraíso Travel*, No 138, T/F462 0692, paraiso@sauce.ben.entelnet.bo Does 'Conozca Trinidad' packages. *Amazonia Holiday*, No 680, T462 5732, F462 2806. Good service. Most agents offer excursions to local *estancias* and jungle tours down river to Amazonia. Most *estancias* can also be reached independently in 1 hr by hiring a motorbike.

Transport **Air** *Aero Sur*, Av Barace 51, T462 0765; daily except Sun to Santa Cruz; less frequently to Guayaramerín and Cobija. *LAB*, Santa Cruz 234, T462 0595; to La Paz, Cochabamba, Cobija, Guayaramerín and Riberalta (check schedules). *TAM*, Bolívar s/n entre 18 de Noviembre y Santa Cruz, T462 2363, at airport, T462 0355, to Baures, Bella Vista, Magdalena and Huacaraje, Riberalta, Guayaramerín, Santa Cruz and La Paz (do not leave any valuables in baggage that you check in). Airport authority, **AASANA**, T462 0678. Taxi to airport US$1.20.

Bus Bus station is on Mendoza, between Beni and Pinto, 9 blocks east of main plaza. Motorbike taxis will take people with backpacks from bus station to centre for US$0.45.

Several *flotas* daily to/from La Paz via San Borja and Caranavi, 20-21 hrs, depart 1730, US$17.50 (see also under San Borja, Transport). To Santa Cruz (12 hrs in dry season, US$5.80) and Cochabamba (US$11.60), with *Copacabana*, *Mopar* and *Bolívar* at 1700, 1730 and 1800; Trinidad to Casarabe is paved and Santa Cruz to El Puente; otherwise gravel surface on all sections of unpaved road. To **Rurrenabaque** (US$15.40), **Riberalta** (US$21.15) and **Guayaramerín** (US$23), connecting with bus to Cobija; *Guaya Tours* daily at 1000; road often impassable in wet season, at least 24 hrs to **Rurrenabaque**.

River Cargo boats down the Río Mamoré to **Guayaramerín** take passengers, 3-4 days, assuming no breakdowns, best organized from Puerto Varador (speak to the Port Captain). *Argos* is recommended as friendly, US$22 pp, take water, fresh fruit and toilet paper. Ear-plugs are also recommended as hammocks are strung over the engine on small boats; only for the hardy traveller.

Directory **Banks** *Banco Mercantil*, J de Sierra, near plaza. Changes cash and TCs, cash on Visa. *Banco Ganadero*, Plaza Ballivián. Visa agent. Street changers on 6 de Agosto. **Communications** Post: and telephone (open daily till 1930) in same building at Av Barace, just off plaza. **Tourist office** In the Prefectural building at Joaquín de Sierra y La Paz, ground floor, T462 1305, ext 116, very helpful, sells guide and city map, US$2. Transport can be arranged from the airport.

San Ignacio de Moxos
90 km W of Trinidad

Electricity is supplied in town from 1200 to 2400

This is known as the folklore capital of the Beni Department. The traditions of the Jesuit missions are still maintained with big *fiestas*, especially during Holy Week; 31 July is the town's patron saint's day, one of the country's most famous and colourful celebrations. *Macheteros*, who speak their own language, comprise 60 of the population. There are a few cheapish *residencias* (**E-F**) on the main plaza, several other basic *alojamientos* on and around plaza. Restaurants do not stay open late. *Isireri*, on plaza, good and cheap set lunches and delicious fruit juices. *Casa Suiza*, good European food. *Donchanta*, recommended for tasty meat dishes. ■ *Bus Trinidad to San Borja stops at* Restaurant Donchanta *for lunch, otherwise difficult to find transport to San Borja. Minibus to Trinidad daily at 0730 from plaza, also* camionetas, *check times beforehand.*

Bolivia

This charming town northeast of Trinidad stands on the banks of the Río Itonama. There is an abundance of wildlife and birds in the surrounding area. The city's main festival is on 22 July, Santa María Magdalena, attracting many groups and visitors from all over Beni and beyond. There are some restaurants and basic hotels. Also **B** *Internacional*, T03-886 2210, info@hwz-inc.com 3-star, with breakfast, 2 pools, beautiful setting. Drinking water is available and electricity runs from 1800-2400. There is a bank (changes travellers' cheques), an *Entel* office and PO on the plaza. *LAB* flies from Trinidad (T886 3020). An unpaved road goes to Trinidad via San Ramón (pick-up US$10.50), passable only in the dry season. Traffic is sparse: San Ramón to Magdalena takes six hours on motorbike taxi, US$16.

East of Magdalena, **Bella Vista** on the Río Blanco is considered by many to be one of the prettiest spots in northeast Bolivia. Lovely white sandbanks line the Río San Martín, 10 minutes paddling by canoe from the boat moorings below town (boat-men will take you, returning later by arrangement; also accessible by motorcycle). Check that the sand is not covered by water after heavy rain. Other activities are swimming in the Río San Martín, canoeing, hunting, good country for cycling. **F** *Hotel Pescador*, owner Guillermo Esero Gómez very helpful and knowledgeable about the area, shared bath, provides meals for guests, offers excursions. 3 well-stocked shops on plaza, but none sells mosquito repellent or spray/coils: many mosquitoes at the beginning of the wet season (apply repellent before leaving the plane). No bank or *Entel* office. There are *TAM* flights; ask at the office on the road nearest the river, 2-3 blocks east of plaza.

Magdalena & Bella Vista
Population: 5,000

Bolivia

Eastern Bolivia

The vast and rapidly developing plains to the west of the Eastern Cordillera are Bolivia's richest area in natural resources. For the visitor, the pre-Inca ruins of Samaipata and the beautiful churches of former Jesuit missions west of Santa Cruz are worth a visit.

La Paz

Santa Cruz de la Sierra

Bolivia's second city, capital of the Department of Santa Cruz, was founded in 1561 by the Spaniard Ñuflo de Chávez, who had come from Paraguay. Until the 1950s Santa Cruz was fairly cut off, but rail and road links ended this isolation. Now there is an ever-increasing flow of immigrants from the highlands as well as Mennonites mostly from USA and Canada, and Japanese settlers, such as the Okinawan colonies 50 km from Montero, who grow soya, maize, sugar, rice, coffee and other crops, which yield profusely. Cattle breeding and timber projects are also important. The exploitation of oil and gas in the Department of Santa Cruz has greatly contributed to the city's rapid development and relative wealth.

Phone code: 03
Colour map 6, grid A4
Population: 950,000
Altitude: 437 m
851 km from La Paz

The **Plaza 24 de Septiembre** is the city's main square with the huge **Cathedral**, the Casa de Cultura and the Palacio Prefectural set around it. ■ *The Cathedral museum is open Tue, Thu 1000-1200, 1600-1800, Sun 1000-1200, 1800-2000, US$0.75.* **Casa de la Cultura** has occasional exhibitions and also an archaeological display; also plays, recitals, concerts and folk dancing. The heart of the city, with its arcaded streets, retains a colonial air, despite the variety of modern shops and the new building that surrounds it. Five blocks north of the Plaza is **Parque El Arenal** in which is a mural by the celebrated painter, Lorgio Vaca, and depicts the city's history. Nearby is the **Museo Etno-Folklórico**, Beni y Caballero, which houses a collection of artefacts from lowland cultures. ■ *Mon-Fri 0830-1200, 1430-1830, US$0.75, T335 2078.* The **Museo de Historia Natural, Noel Kempff Mercado**, Av Irala s/n entre

Sights
The city has four ring roads, Anillos 1, 2, 3 and 4. Equipetrol suburb, where many hotels and bars are situated, is NW of the heart of the city between Anillos 2 and 3

Velasco e Independencia, has a video library. Contact them for trips and information to Parque Nacional Noel Kempff Mercado. ■ *Mon-Fri 0800-1200, also Mon-Tue 1500-1830. US$0.15, T/F336 6574/337 1216, www.museo.sczbo.org* 5 km out of town on the road to Cotoca are the **Botanical Gardens** (micro or colectivo from C Suárez Arana, 15 mins).

Sleeping

Accommodation is relatively expensive. It's hard to find good value mid and lower-range hotels

L *House Inn*, Colón 643, T336 2323, Casilla 387, www.houseinn.com.bo 5-star suites with computer in each room, unlimited internet use, price includes taxes and breakfast, 2 pools, sauna, restaurant, a/c, parking, modern. Recommended. **L** *Los Tajibos*, Av San Martín 455 in Barrio Equipetrol out of town in 15 acres of lush vegetation, 5-star, T342 1000, lostajib@bibosi.scz.entelnet.bo A/c, *El Papagayo* restaurant good (*ceviche* is recommended), business centre, *Viva Club Spa* has sauna etc, swimming pool for residents only.

Santa Cruz

■ Sleeping
1 Alojamiento Santa Bárbara *B1*
2 Bibosi *B1*
3 Colonial *B2*
4 Copacabana *B1*
5 Excelsior *B2*
6 Gran Hotel Santa Cruz *C2*
7 House Inn *D1*
8 Las Américas *B2*
9 Posada El Turista *B1*
10 Residencial Ballivián *B2*
11 Residencial Bolívar *B2*
12 Residencial Sands *B3*
13 Residencial 26 de Enero *C1*
14 Roma *A2*
15 Viru-Viru *B1*

● Eating
1 Capri *D1*
2 El Patito Pekín *B2*
3 Hawaii *B2*
4 Il Gatto *B2*
5 La Esquina del Pescado *B1*
6 Leonardo *C3*
7 Michelangelo *D2*
8 Pizzería Marguerita *B2*
9 Sabor Brasil *B1*
10 Tía Lía *B2*
11 Vegetariano *B1*

N

0 metres 200
0 yards 200

AL *Gran Hotel Santa Cruz*, René Moreno 269, T334 8811, www.boliviant.scz.com Fully restored to its 1930s glory, a/c, spacious, pool, open to non-residents. Recommended. **A** *Las Américas*, 21 de Mayo esq Seoane, T336 8778, americas@mail.zuper.net A/c, discount for longer stay, parking, arranges tours and car rental, restaurant, bar, 5-star service. Recommended. **B** *Colonial*, Buenos Aires 57, T333 3156, F333 9223. A/c, breakfast included, restaurant, comfortable. Recommended. **B** *Viru-Viru* Junín 338, T333 5298, F336 7500. Includes breakfast, a/c, cheaper with fan, pleasant. Recommended.

C *Bibosi*, Junín 218, T334 8548, F334 8887. **D** with shared bath, breakfast included, internet. Recommended. **C** *Copacabana*, Junín 217, T332 1843, F333 0757. **B** with a/c, **E** without bath, cheap laundry service, includes breakfast, restaurant. **C** *Excelsior*, René Moreno 70, T332 5924, excelsior@cotas.net Includes breakfast, good rooms, good lunches. **C** *Roma*, 24 de Septiembre 530, T332 3299, F333 8388. Pleasant, a/c, good value, helpful.

E *Res 26 de Enero*, Camiri 32, T332 1818, F333 7518. **F** without bath, very clean. **E** *Res Sands*, Arenales 749, 7 blocks east of the main plaza, T337 7776. Unbelievable value, better than many in much higher price brackets, cable TV, fan, very comfortable beds, pool. **E** *Res Bolívar*, Sucre 131, T334 2500. Hot showers, some rooms with bath, lovely courtyard with hammocks, alcohol prohibited, excellent breakfast US$1.20. Repeatedly recommended.

F *Res Ballivián*, Ballivián 71, T332 1960. Basic, shared hot showers, nice patio. Recommended. **F-G** *Res Cañada*, Cañada 145, near local bus terminal, T334 5541. Cheaper without bath. Recommended. **G** *Alojamiento Santa Bárbara*, Santa Bárbara 151, T332 1817. Hot showers, shared bath, helpful, will store luggage, good value. Recommended. **G** *Posada El Turista*, Junín 455, T336 2870. Small basic room, central, quiet.

Eating

Barrio Equipetrol is the area for the poshest restaurants and nightlife. Most restaurants close Mon. Try local speciality arroz con leche in markets, only available before 1100

Expensive: *Michelangelo*, Chuquisaca 502. Excellent Italian. Mon-Fri 1200-1400, 1900-2330, Sat evenings only. *Leonardo*, Warnes 366. Italian, also recommended. Mon-Sat 1900-2330. *Il Boliche*, Arenales 135. Open 1930 onwards, serves good crêpes. *Il Gatto*, 24 de Septiembre 285. Bright and clean, good pizzas, US$2.25 buffet 1200-1500. *Capri*, Irala 634, "The best pizzas in town". *Mid-range*: For truly superb filet mignon, go to *Pizzería Marguerita*, northwest corner of the plaza. A/c, good service, coffee, bar, also recommended for, Mon-Fri 0900-2400, Sat-Sun 1600-2400. *El Fogón*, Av Viedma 434. Tue-Sun 1200-1400, 1900-2330, Mon only evening. *La Buena Mesa*, Av Cristóbal de Mendoza 538, and *Churrasquería El Palenque*, Av El Trompillo y Santos Dumont,1200-1400,1830-2330, closed Tue, are all excellent for barbecued steak. There are many other barbecue restaurants around the Segundo Anillo, including *La Casa Típica de Camba*, Cristóbal de Mendoza 539. "A must for the total camba experience." *Escuela Gastronómica Tatapy*, Av Santa Cruz 832, 2nd anillo. Gastronomy school restaurant with quality food at reasonable prices, tourist information. Two excellent Chinese restaurants are *Shanghai*, Av 26 de Febrero 27, and *Mandarin 2*, Av Potosí 793. *Cheap*: *Tía Lía*, Murillo 40. US$1.50 (US$2.25 weekends) for all the beef, chorizos, pork and chicken you want from a *parrillada*, huge selection of salads, pasta and bean dishes, Mon-Fri 1100-1500, Sat-Sun 1100-1600. Brazilian-style *por kilo* places are popular: eg *Rincón Brasil*, Libertad 358, every day 1130-1500, also (à la carte only) Tue-Sat from 1800, or *Sabor Brasil*, off Buenos Aires, entre Santa Bárbara y España, No 20. For fish, La Esquina del Pescado, Sara y Florida. US$1.60 a plate. *El Patito Pekín*, 24 de Septiembre 307. Basic Chinese food, Mon-Sun 1100-1400, 1800-2000.

Vegetarian: *Vegetariano*, Ayacucho 444. Breakfast, lunch and dinner, good. *Vegetariano Cuerpomente*, Pari 228. Wide choice, good. **Snacks and ice cream**: There are lots of very pleasant a/c cafés and ice cream parlours, where you can get coffee, ice cream, drinks, snacks and reasonably-priced meals. Among the best are: *Hawaii*, Sucre 100 y Beni, open at 0730-2400 every day; *Dumbos*, Ayacucho 247; *Heladería Pastelería Manolo*, 24 de Septiembre 170; and *Kívón*, Ayacucho 267. Highly recommended for ice cream; also at Quijarro 409 in Mercado Los Pozos. For good coffee, go to *Alexander Coffee* at Av Monseñor Rivero 400 in Zona El Cristo. Many cheap restaurants near the old bus terminal on Av Cañoto serving fried chicken. Also on the extension of C 6 de Agosto behind Los Pozos market (daytime). Excellent *empanadas* are sold in the food section of Los Pozos market. The bakeries on Junín, Los Manzanos and España sell the local specialities: *empanadas de queso* (cheese pies), *cuñapés* (yuca buns), rice bread and *humintas* (maize pies).

Bolivia

Bolivia

Festivals

Cruceños are famous as fun-lovers and their music, the carnavalitos, can be heard all over South America

Of the various festivals, the brightest is *Carnival*, celebrated for the **15 days before Lent**: music in the streets, dancing, fancy dress and the coronation of a queen. Beware the following day when youths run wild with buckets and balloons filled with water – no one is exempt. The *mascaritas* balls also take place during the pre-Lent season at *Caballo Blanco*: girls wear satin masks covering their heads completely, thus ensuring anonymity. *International Trade Fair* held each **Sep** (entry US$2.50 – worth a visit); **24 Sep** is a holiday. *Misiones de Chiquitos* is an international music festival held every even year, concerts in Santa Cruz, San Javier, Concepción, among other places, including Renaissance and Baroque recitals.

Shopping

Artesanía shops on Libertad and on Plaza 24 de Septiembre y Bolívar. *Artecampo*, Salvatierra 407 esq Vallegrande, T334 1843. Run by a local NGO, sells handicrafts made in rural communities in department, high quality, excellent value. *RC Joyas*, Bolívar 262, T333 2725. Jewellery and Bolivian gems, the manager also produces and sells good maps of Santa Cruz City and department. *Los Pozos market*, taking up the whole block between 6 de Agosto, Suárez Arana, Quijarro and Campero, is clean, good for midday meals, food aisles serve local and Chinese food, and worth visiting in summer for its exotic fruits. The market is open daily, beware of bag-snatching. There are plenty of smuggled Brazilian goods on sale, exchanged for Bolivian coca. *Bazar Siete Calles*, mainly for clothing, but food and fruit is sold outside, main entrance is in 100 block of Isabel La Católica, also on Camiri and Vallegrande, past Ingavi. There is a fruit and vegetable market at Sucre y Cochabamba, and a large Indian market on Sun near the bus terminal. *El Aventurero Caza y Pesca*, Florida 126-130, has some equipment for fishing, climbing, trekking. Also *Safari Camping*, 21 de Mayo and Seoane, T337 0185; *Jara Caza y Pesca*, Bolívar 458. **Books** *Los Amigos del Libro*, Ingavi 14, T332 7937. Sells foreign language books and magazines. *El Ateno*, Cañoto y 21 de Mayo, T333 3338. Books in English, access to internet. International magazines and newspapers often on sale in kiosks on main Plaza, eg *Miami Herald*, after arrival of Miami flight.

Tour operators

Taking a taxi can work out much cheaper than using a tour, and some taxi drivers speak English

Exprinter, 21 de Mayo 327, T333 5133, xprintur@bibosi.scz.entelnet.bo *Magri Turismo*, Warnes esq Potosí, T334 5663. American Express agent. Recommended. *Fremen*, Beni 79, T333 8535, F336 0265. Local tours, also jungle river cruises. *Bracha*, in one of the hotels by the train/bus station, T346 7795. Open Mon, Wed, Fri 0800-1800, otherwise 0830-1230, 1430-1830, closed Sun, for rail tickets to Quijarro and *Empresa Yacyretá* buses to Asunción. *Mario Berndt*, Casilla 3132, T342 0340, tauk@em.daitec-bo.com Does large-scale tailored tours off the beaten track, mostly to the Altiplano, requires approx 3 months notice, speaks English, German and Spanish and is very knowledgeable about the area. *Jean Paul Ayala*, jpdakidd@roble.scz.entelnet.bo Recommended for birwatching trips, speaks English.

Transport

Local Taxi: about US$1 inside first Anillo, US$1.20 inside 3rd Anillo, fix fare in advance. **Car hire**: *Aby's*, 3rd Anillo, esq Pasaje Muralto 1038 (opposite zoo), T345 1560, www.abys@khainata.com *Across*, 4th Anillo, esq Radial 27 (400 m from Av Banzer Oeste), T344 1617. US$70 per day for basic Suzuki 4x4 (200 km per day) with insurance *Barron's*, Av Alemana 50 y Tajibos, T342 0160, www.rentacarbolivia.com

Long distance Air: The international airport is at Viru-Viru, about 16 km north of the city. Information T181; has Emigration/Immigration office, *Entel* office, luggage lockers, duty free shop, restaurant (expensive), bank open 0830-1830, changes cash and travellers' cheques, withdrawal on Visa and MasterCard (when closed try **AASANA** desk, where you pay airport tax). Airport bus every 20 mins from the bus terminal, 25 mins (US$0.70), also *colectivos*. Taxi, US$7.50. From airport take bus to bus terminal then taxi to centre. *LAB* flies at least twice daily to **La Paz** and **Cochabamba**, and to **Sucre**, **Tarija**, **Trinidad**, **Cobija** and **Guayaramerín**. *Aero Sur* flies to **La Paz** (several daily) and **Puerto Suárez**. International destinations include most South American capitals (2 a week each to **Asunción** with *LAB* and *Mercosur*), Rio de Janeiro, São Paulo, Santiago (Chile), **Panama City**, **Mexico City** and **Miami**. From Trompillo airport in the south part of the city, flights in small planes to local destinations.

Train: The combined bus and train station, Terminal Bimodal, is on the southeastern edge of the city between Av Brasil and Tres Pasos, between the second and third *anillos* (3 hotels nearby **D-E**); No 12 bus to/from the centre, taxi US$1.50. Ferroviaria Oriental, T346 3900 ext 307/303. To **Quijarro, for Brazil**, and **Yacuiba, for Argentina**, see below. **Bus**: Long distance buses leave from the new bus/train terminal, T336 0320. Local buses for the time being leave from terminal at Av Cañoto y Av Irala, T333 8391. Daily buses to **Cochabamba** (from US$4-5, 10 hrs), many *flotas* leave between 0600-0900 and 1630-2100. Direct to **Sucre** daily between 1700 and 1800, 14 hrs, US$6-7.50. **Oruro** and **La Paz** 16 hrs, US$10.45, between 1700-1930 (some are *buscama*). To **San Ignacio**, see under **The Chiquitano Jesuit Missions**. To **Yacuiba** and **Tarija**, daily, several companies; 26-32 hrs to Tarija. To **Camiri, Cotoca, Montero**, many colectivos and micros from outside *Hotel España* (US$3.75 to Camiri). To **Trinidad**, several daily, 12 hrs, US$4.50, all depart 1700 or 1900. **NB** Many companies have offices in streets around terminal; eg *Expreso del Sur, San Lorenzo* and *Expresos Tarija*. **Bus**: **International**: *Empresa Yacyretá*, daily **Santa Cruz-Asunción**, US$65, 30 hrs in the dry, no upper limit in the wet. For information T334 9315. Also *Trans Suárez*, T333 7532, for Asunción, Buenos Aires, Montevideo, Iguazú and São Paulo. *Bolpar* 4 a week to Asunción at 1900 with connection to Buenos Aires, Av Monsignor Salvatierra 559, T/F366800, but poor service.

Airline offices *Aerolíneas Argentinas*, Edif Banco de la Nación Argentina, on main Plaza, T333 9776. *Aero Sur*, Irala 616, T336 7400. *American Airlines*, Beni 167, T334 1314. *LAB*, Warnes y Chuquisaca, T334 4159. *TAM*, 21 de Mayo, T337 1999. **Banks** *Banco Mercantil*, René Moreno y Suárez de Figueroa. Cash advance on Visa, changes cash and TCs. *Banco de Santa Cruz*, Junín 154. TCs, bolivianos on Visa and MasterCard, no commission. *Banco Boliviano-Americano*, René Moreno 366 and Colón y Camiri (Siete Calles). *Enlace* cash dispenser for Visa and MasterCard. *Casas de cambio*: *Medicambio* on Plaza 24 de Septiembre will change TCs into dollars at 3% commission. Also on main plaza, *Alemán* (changes TCs at 2% commission for $ or bolivianos). *Menno Credit Union*, 10 de Agosto 15, T332 8800, small office in Mennonite area of town, open 0900-1600, changes TCs, 1% commission, English, German and Dutch spoken. Street money changers on Plaza 24 de Septiembre and around bus terminal. ATM in airport departure lounge. **Communications Internet:** cybercafés everywhere, US$0.60-0.90 per hr. **Post Office:** C Junín 146. **Telephone:** *Entel*, Warnes 36 (entre Moreno y Chuquisaca), T332 5526, local and international calls and fax, open Mon-Fri 0730-2330, Sat, Sun and holidays 0730-2200. Also small *Entel* office at Quijarro 267. **Cultural centres** Centro Boliviano Americano, Cochabamba 66, T334 2299. Library with US papers and magazines, English classes, some cultural events. **Instituto Cultural Boliviano Alemán** and **Alianza Francesa**, 24 de Septiembre 266 (Boliviano Alemán T/F332 9906; Alianza Francesa T333 3392, afscz@roble.scz.entelnet.bo) Joint cultural institute with language courses, cultural events, library (internet access), both open Mon-Fri 0900-1200, 1530 (1600 Alemán)-2000, Francesa Sat 0900-1200. **Centro Iberoamericano de Formación**, Arenales 583, Casilla 875, T335 1322, F332 2217 (concerts, films, art exhibitions, lectures, etc), very good. **Embassies and consulates** Argentina, in Edif Banco de la Nación Argentina, Plaza 24 de Septiembre, Junín 22, T334 7133, Mon-Fri 0800-1300. Austria, Pilcomayo 242, T352 5333, Mon-Fri 1430-1730. Belgium, Av Cristo Redentor, T342 0662. Brazil, Av Busch 330, near Plaza Estudiantes, T333 44400, Mon-Fri 0900-1500. It takes 24 hrs to process visa applications, reported as unhelpful. Canada, contact Centro Menno, C Puerto Suárez 28, T334 3773. Denmark, Landívar 401, T352 5200, Mon-Fri, 0830-1200, 1430-1830. France, Alemania y Mutualista, off the 3rd ring, T343 3434, Mon-Fri 1630-1800. Germany, C Ñuflo de Chávez 241, T333 2485, Mon-Fri 0830-1200. Israel, Bailón Mercado 171, T342 4777, Mon-Fri 1000-1200, 1600-1830. Italy, Av El Trompillo 476, Edif Honnen p 1, T353 1796, Mon-Fri 0830-1230. Netherlands, Av Roque Aguilera 300, 3rd ring, T333 2000, Mon-Fri 0900-1230. Paraguay, Manuel Ignacio Salvatierra 99, Edif Victoria, of 1A T336 6113. Colour photo required for visa, Mon-Fri 0730-1400. Spain, Monseñor Santiesteban 237, T332 8921, Mon-Fri 0900-1200. Switzerland, Cristo Redentor 470, T342 4000, Mon-Fri 0830-1200, 1430-1900. UK, Parapetí 28, 2nd floor, T334 5682. USA, Güemes Este 6, Equipetrol, T333 3072, Mon-Fri 0900-1130. **Tourist office** In *Prefectura del Departamento* (Direcciones), on the north side of the main plaza, T333 2770 ext 14. *Guía de Santa Cruz*, published by Rede, is available in bookshops. It gives all details on the city. **Useful addresses Immigration:** 3er Anillo Interno esq Av Cronenbold, opposite the zoo, T333 6442/2136, Mon-Fri 0830-1200, 1430-1800.

Directory
For hospitals, doctors and dentists, contact your consulate or the tourist office for recommendations

Bolivia

Samaipata
Phone code: 03
Colour map M6,
grid A4
Altitude: 1,650 m
Average temp: 24°C
120 km from
Santa Cruz

The drive along the Piray gorge and up into the highlands on the old road to Cochabamba is worthwhile. On this road is the town of Samaipata, a great place to relax mid-week, with good lodging, restaurants, hikes and riding, and a helpful ex-pat community. Local *artesanías* include ceramics. The **Centro de Investigaciones Arqueológicas y Antropológicas Samaipata** has a collection of pots and vases with anthropomorphic designs, dating from 200 BC to 200 AD and, most importantly, provides information on the nearby pre-Inca ceremonial site commonly called **El Fuerte**.
■ *Centro open daily 0930-1230, 1430-1830; El Fuerte 0900-1700, US$3 including El Fuerte, US$0.75 for Centro de Investigaciones only.* This sacred structure (1,970 m) consists of a complex system of channels, basins, high-relief sculptures, etc, carved out of one vast slab of rock. Latest research on dates is conflicting. Some suggests that Amazonian people created it around 1500 BC, but it could be later. There is evidence of subsequent occupations and that it was the eastern outpost of the Incas' Kollasuyo (their Bolivian Empire). It is no longer permitted to walk on the rock, so visit the museum first to see the excellent model. El Fuerte is 9 km from the town; 3 km along the highway, then 6 km up a rough, signposted road (taxi US$1.20); two hours' walk one way, or drive to the entrance. Pleasant bathing is possible in a river on the way to El Fuerte.

Rooms may be hard to find at weekends in high season. Most cabins listed have kitchen, bathroom, barbecue and hammocks

Sleeping and eating C *La Víspera*, 1.2 km south of town, T944 6082, vispera@entelnet.bo Dutch-owned organic farm with accommodation in 4 cosy cabins, camping US$3 (US$4 to hire tent), delicious local produce for breakfast, US$3 pp. Very peaceful; Margarita and Pieter know pretty much everything about the local area and can arrange all excursions. Highly recommmended. Across the road is C *Cabañas de Traudi*, T944 6094, traudiar@cotas.com.bo Cabins for 2-8, also **E** lovely rooms (**F** with shared bathroom), heated pool US$1.50 for non residents, sitting area with open fire, TV and music system, ceramics shop, great place. Most central of all the *cabañas* is C *Landhaus*, T944 6033. Beautiful place with a small pool, sun loungers, garden, hammocks, parking, internet and sauna (US$20 for up to 8 people), also rooms only with shared bathroom **F**; excellent restaurant and café. Several other *cabañas* west of town. Hotels in town include **E** *Hostería Mi Casa*, Bolívar, T944 6292. Pretty flower patio, snack bar, **F** with shared bath, 1 cabaña (**D**). **F** *Don Jorge*, Bolívar, T944 6086. Cheaper with shared bath, hot showers, good beds, large shaded patio, good set lunch. **F** *Aranjuez*, on the main road at the entrance to town, T944 6223. Upstairs terrace, clothes washing area, food available, includes breakfast, good value. **F** *Residencial Kim*, near the plaza, T944 6161. Use of kitchen, **G** with shared bath, good value. **G** *Alojamiento Vargas*, around corner from museum. Clothes washing facilities, use of kitchen, includes breakfast, owner Teresa, kind. Recommended.

Café Hamburg, Bolívar. Laid back, bar, food (including vegetarian), well stocked book exchange, internet US$2.25 per hr (only after 1900), see *Roadrunners* tour agency below. *El Descanso en Los Alturas*. Wide choice including excellent steaks and pizzas. There are several restaurants on and around the plaza, most of which are cheap. Good *almuerzo* (US$1.05) at *Media Vuelta*. Dutch-owned *Chakana* bar/restaurant/café open every day 0900-late, relaxing, *almuerzos* for US$2.25, good snacks and salads, seats outside, a book exchange, cakes and ice cream. *Café Baden*, 1 km towards Santa Cruz, good for ice cream and torts as well as steak and *schweizer würstsalat*. For superb biscuits, bread, home-made pastas, herbs, cheese, yoghurts and cold meats, try Swiss-run *Panadería Gerlinde*, open daily 0700-2200, which also has a weekend stall in the market.

All those in this list are recommended and offer trips to similar destinations. Expect to pay US$15-20 pp in a group of 4

Tour operators *Gilberto Aguilera*, T944 6050, considered the most knowledgeable local guide, good value tours. *Amboró Tours*, T/F944 6293, erickamboro@cotas.com.bo Run by Erick Prado who speaks only Spanish. *Michael Blendinger*, T944 6186, mblendinger@cotas.com.bo German guide who speaks English and Spanish, runs fully-equipped in 4WD vehicle, short and long treks, horse rides, specialist in nature and archaeology. Accommodation in cabins available, also inclusive packages. *Roadrunners*, Olaf and Frank, T944 6193, speak English, enthusiastic, lots of inforamtion and advice, recommended tour of El Fuerte. See *La Víspera*, above, Margarita and Pieter. All lead trips to Amboró and other interesting places.

Bolivia

Transport Buses leave Santa Cruz from the provincial bus station (may move to the new bus/train terminal) Mon-Sat 1600. Colectivo taxis run from Tundi 70 near the old terminal), 2 hrs, US$15 per taxi for 4 people. Departures are more frequent early in the day. Colectivos will pick you up from your hotel, or else take one from the petrol station. Buses and micros leaving Santa Cruz for **Sucre** pass through Samaipata between 1800 and 2000; tickets can be booked with 2 days' notice through *Roadrunners*. There's also a bus to Santa Cruz at 0430, 0445 and 0545 Mon-Sat from the plaza outside *El Tambo* store, US$2.25 (ask at *Roadrunners*), and sometimes an afternoon bus. Sun is much easier: buses leave 1100-1530. You can get to Samaipata by bus from Sucre; these leave at night and arrive soon after dawn, stopping in Mairana or Mataral for breakfast, about ½ hr before Samaipata.

Some 115 km south of the Santa Cruz-Cochabamba road is La Higuera, where Che **La Higuera** Guevara was killed. On 8 October each year, people gather there to celebrate his memory. At *Hospital Nuestro Señor de Malta* you can see the old laundry building where Che's body was shown to the international press on 9 Ocotober 1967. Near the air strip you can see the results of excavations carried out in 1997 which finally unearthed his physical remains (now in Cuba)– ask an airport attendant to see the site. Pedro Calzadillo, headmaster of the school at La Higuera, will guide visitors to the ravine of El Churo, where Che was captured on 8 October 1967. ■ *No fee, but voluntary contribution to the health station, built on the site of the school where Che was held captive till his execution. Sr Calzadillo only speaks Spanish.* Flota Bolívar has *4 daily buses from Santa Cruz to Vallegrandevia Samaipata, 5 hrs, return most days at 0730 and/or 1300. Several pleasant, basic places to stay, all F-G, on or around the plaza. Good restaurant on corner of plaza, also several cheap places to eat near market. From Vallegrande market, a daily bus departs 0800 to Pucara (45 km), from where there is transport (12 km) to La Higuera. Taxi Vallegrande-La Higuera US$20-30.*

Regular buses leave from beside Santa Cruz terminal hourly from 0500-1500 (also **Parque** minibuses from Montero, US$1, and buses from Villa Tunari, US$5) to **Buena Vista** **Nacional** (100 km from Santa Cruz; phone code: 03), near the **Parque Nacional Amboró** **Amboró** (637,000 ha). The park is home to butterflies, humming birds, macaws, hoatzin and other native fauna (many of them endangered species). Many biting insects; much wading is required to get around the park. All entrances to the park involve crossing the Río Surutú, which is usually in flood in the wet season. 28 km is the access from Espejitos to Río Isama and Cerro Amboró. 35 km is the access from Las Cruzes to Macañucu and the Villa de Amboró in the buffer zone. Macañucu has the best services in the park, with horse riding, hiking trails, guides, camping, kitchen area and showers (US$20 per person per day), radio contact with the park office. ■ *There is a national park office just over a block from the plaza in Buena Vista, T932 2032 (permit free). Office is closed Sun and siesta time. They can help with guides and suggestions. Two agencies,* Amboró Tours, *near the park office, T932 2093,* amborotours@yahoo.com *and* Amboró Adventures, *on the plaza, T932 2090, run excursions, US$27-33 pp per day for guide and transportation, not including food. For getting there, see Transport, below.*

Sleeping **L** *Flora y Fauna*, known as 'Doble F', T7194-3706 (mob), Casilla 2097, Santa Cruz. Hilltop cabins, viewing platforms for birdwatchers, specialist guiding (Robin Clark has written the definitive guide book to birds in Amboró). **B** *Pozoazul*, on the bypass, T932 2091. A/c, kitchen, pool, good restaurant, helpful, also camping US$14 inclusing showers and pool. **D** *Sumuqué*, Av 6 de Agosto 250, T932 2080. Cabins in pleasant gardens, marked trails. **F** *Nadia*, T932 2049. Central, small, family run. There are other hotels, cabins and restaurants. **In the park**: CARE has funded cabins on the far bank of the Río Surutú just past Villa Aguiles on the road from Buena Vista to the river. Well-located in the multiple-use area with lots of flora and fauna; good trails.

Transport **From Buena Vista** the most popular entrance to the park is Las Cruces, 35 km away, reached by a daily morning bus whose route runs alongside the Río Surutú for several km. From Las Cruces, the trail leads directly to the settlement of Villa Amboró, in the park's buffer zone. **From Samaipata** the park can be approached from the old Santa Cruz-Cochabamba road. The going is rough, so a guide is highly recommended. If going on your own, first contact the *Fundación Amigos de la Naturaleza* (FAN), Sucrey Murillo (T03-944 6017) in Samaipata, who can offer up-to-date information and will allow trekkers to use their radio telephone to contact the few park rangers in the area.

The Chiquitano Jesuit Missions

Six Jesuit churches survive east of Santa Cruz: San Javier, Concepción, Santa Ana, San Rafael, San Miguel and San José de Chiquitos. All are UNESCO World Heritage Sites. The first four were built by the Swiss Jesuit, Padre Martin Schmidt, the other two (plus the one at San Ignacio de Velasco, demolished in 1948, see below) were built by other priests. Besides organizing *reducciones* and constructing churches, for each of which he built an organ, Padre Schmidt wrote music (some is still played today on traditional instruments) and he published a Spanish-Idioma Chiquitano dictionary based on his knowledge of all the dialects of the region. He worked in this part of the then Viceroyalty of Peru until the expulsion of the Jesuits in 1767 by order of Charles III of Spain.

Access to the mission area is by bus or train from Santa Cruz: a paved highway runs north to San Ramón (139 km), then north on a good, all-weather gravel road through San Javier (45 km), turning east here to Concepción (68 km) and San Ignacio. One road continues east to San Matías and the Brazilian border; others head south either through San Miguel, or Santa Ana to meet at San Rafael for the continuation south to San José de Chiquitos. By rail, leave the Santa Cruz-Quijarro train at San José and from there travel north. The most comfortable way to visit is by jeep, in four days. The route is straightforward and fuel is available. **Jeep hire**: see under Santa Cruz, **Transport Car hire**. (Check kilometre allowance; 1,385 km driving in total to see missions.)

San Javier The first Jesuit mission in Chiquitos (1691), its church completed by Padre Schmidt in 1750. The original wooden structure has survived more or less intact and restoration was undertaken between 1987 and 1993 by the Swiss Hans Roth. Subtle designs and floral patterns cover the ceiling, walls and carved columns. One of the bas-relief paintings on the high altar depicts Martin Schmidt playing the piano for his Indian choir. The modern town prospers from extensive cattle ranching. Many fine walks in the surrounding countryside; also good for cycling with an all-terrain bike. Local *fiesta*, 3 December. ■ *Micros to Santa Cruz, 4-5 hrs, US$3.75, several between 0800 and 1730.*

Sleeping and eating C *Gran Hotel El Reposo del Guerrero*, T03-963 5022, or Santa Cruz 332 7830. More expensive Sat-Sun, cheaper with shared bath, includes breakfast, comfortable, restaurant, bar. Several hotels in **F-G** range in town and a few kilometres out of town is *Hotel Cabañas Totaitú*, T337 0880, totaitu@e,.daitec-bo.com With pool, hot springs, tennis court etc, all included packages. Best restaurant is *Ganadero*, in *Asociación de Ganaderos* on plaza. Excellent steaks. Others on plaza.

Concepción The magnificent cathedral was completed by Padre Schmidt in 1756; it was totally restored by Hans Roth 1975-82, whose team of European experts had to recreate the building from the crumbling original. The interior of this beautiful church has an altar of laminated silver. In front of the church is a bell-cum-clock tower housing the original bells and behind it are well-restored cloisters. The town boasts one of the region's most beautiful plazas; *Entel* office on the corner; private Centro Médico one block away. **Sleeping B** *Gran Hotel Concepción*, on plaza, T964 3031, very comfortable, excellent service, including buffet breakfast, pool, bar. Highly recommended. One block from the church is **D** *Apart Hotel Los Misiones*, T964 3021, pleasant rooms around a courtyard, good value. **D-F** *Colonial*, ½ block from plaza, T964 3050, also good value. **F** *Residencial Westfalia*, 2 blocks from plaza, T9643040, cheaper without bath, German-owned, nice patio. Various restaurants. ■ *Many buses between Santa Cruz and San Ignacio pass through about midnight, but drop you at main road, several blocks from plaza; ask around for transport to centre.* Flota La Veloz del Norte *and* 31 del Este *micros to San Javier (1½ hrs, US$1.50) and Santa Cruz (US$4.50) at 0730, 1400 and 1800, from opposite* Alojamiento Tarija. *Electricity in town is turned off at 0130, just as buses from Santa Cruz arrive in the wet season; take a torch.*

A lack of funds for restoration led to the demolition of San Ignacio's Jesuit church in 1948. A modern replacement contains the elaborate high altar, pulpit and paintings and statues of saints. A museum in the Casa de la Cultura on the plaza has a few musical instruments from the old church. Laguna Guapomó on the outskirts of town is good for swimming, boating and fishing. *Entel* two blocks from plaza.

San Ignacio de Velasco

Bolivia

Sleeping and eating A-AL *La Misión*, Plaza 31 de Julio, T962 2333, hotel-lamision@unete.com Luxurious, colonial style with a/c, cable TV and pool, rooms of various standards and prices, includes buffet breakfast, tours arranged. **E** *Casa Suiza*, at the end of C Sucre, 5 blocks west of plaza (taxi US$0.75). Small guesthouse run by Horst and Cristina, German and French spoken, full board, excellent food, very comfortable, family atmosphere, hires horses. Highly recommended. **E** *Plaza*, on the plaza. Cheaper without bath, hot water, includes breakfast, comfortable, good value. There are other hotels (**C-F**) and places to eat near the plaza.

Transport Bus: from Santa Cruz, *Flota Chiquitana*, from new terminal 1900 daily, 10 hrs, US$6.70; also *Expreso Misiones del Oriente* daily at 1930, T337 8782. From San Ignacio: *Flota Chiquitano* and *Trans Velasco* at 1900; both from near market; *Trans Joá* at 2030 (office on plaza). These companies and several others go to **San Matías** for Brazil (see below), 9 hrs, US$7.50; the final 92 km of road is very poor. Some continue to **Cáceres**, 20½ hrs, US$28. To **San José de Chiquitos**, *Trans Carretón*, Tue, Thu, Sun at 0800, US$4.50, 5 hrs. Micros to Santa Ana, San Rafael and San Miguel from market area; also *Trans Bolivia* bus at 0730 to San Miguel, 30 mins, US$0.75, returns 1730.

The church in **Santa Ana** (founded 1755, constructed after the expulsion of the Jesuits), is a lovely wooden building, currently being restored. Sr Luis Rocha will show you inside; ask for his house at the shop on the plaza where the bus stops. Two *alojamientos* in town and meals at Sra Silva's *Pensión El Tacú*, next to church. **San Rafael's** church was completed by Padre Schmidt in 1748. It is perhaps the best, beautifully restored with frescoes in beige paint over the exterior (*Hotel Paradita*, **F**, and two restaurants on plaza). The Austrian nuns are friendly and informative. The frescoes on the façade of the church (1766) at **San Miguel** depict St Peter and St Paul; designs in brown and yellow cover all the interior and the exterior side walls. The mission runs three schools and workshop; the sisters are very welcoming and will gladly show tourists around. 4 km away is the Santuario de Cotoca, beside a lake where you can swim; ask at *La Pascana* for transport. (*Alojamiento y Restaurant La Pascana*, on plaza, basic, cheap meals; just up the hill are two other *alojamientos* and *Entel*.)

Santa Ana, San Rafael & San Miguel
A day trip by taxi from San Ignacio to these villages costs US$35-40 (negotiate)

The whole of one side of the plaza of this dusty little town is occupied by the superb frontage of the Jesuit mission. The stone buildings, in Baroque style, are connected by a wall. They are the restored chapel (1750); the church, unfinished at the expulsion of the Jesuits, with a triangular façade and side walls standing (restoration work in progress); the four-storey bell-tower (1748); the mortuary (*la bóveda* – 1754), with one central window but no entrance in its severe frontage. Behind is a long colonnaded hall. There is an *Entel* office and a hospital. Various hotels (**E-F**, *Raquelita* is good, T972 2037) and restaurants are on the plaza and near the train station. Electricity is cut from 0200-0600; the town is lighted when trains arrive. On Monday,

San José de Chiquitos

Bolivia

Mennonites bring their produce to sell to shops and to buy provisions. The colonies are 50 km west and the Mennonites, who speak English, German, plattdeutsch and Spanish, are happy to talk about their way of life.

About 4 km from San José is the **Parque Nacional Histórico Santa Cruz la Vieja**, which includes the ruins of the original site of Santa Cruz (about 1540), a *mirador* giving views over the jungle and, 5 km into the park, a sanctuary. The park's heavily-forested hills contain much animal and bird life; various trails; guides available from the small village in the park (take insect repellent). 2 km past the entrance, at the end of the road at the foot of high hills, is a large swimming pool fed by a mountain stream (open daily, free, no facilities other than changing rooms; take refreshments). The park and pool are best visited by car or taxi because it is a very hot, dusty walk there (allow over one hour on foot). ■ *Entry to park US$2, to pool US$0.75.*

Transport Train: schedule from Santa Cruz as for Quijarro (see **Travel to Brazil**), 8 hrs to San José, standard: Pullman US$7.20, 1st class US$3.15, 2nd class US$2.70; luxury: *cama* US$27.80, *semi-cama* US$23.75. To Quijarro daily except Sun at 2130; Pullman US$13.15, 1st class US$4.20, 2nd class US$3.30. *Ferrobus* Sun, Tue, Thu at 2340; *cama* US$21.35, *semi-cama* US$18.20. It is possible to reserve seats on either service at the train station up to a week in advance. **Bus**: to **San Ignacio**, *Flota Universal*, Mon, Wed, Fri and Sat at 0700, leaving from close to the railway track, a few yards west of the station building, next to *Pollos Curichi*. They also leave from their office opposite the petrol station where you can reserve a seat (best to take a taxi there in this heat). *Trans Carretón* leaves Tue, Thu, Sun at 1300 from their office at 24 de Septiembre, southeast of the plaza. Both go via **San Rafael** and **San Miguel**; 4 hrs.

Travel to Brazil

There are three routes: two via Puerto Suárez and/or Quijarro, one via San Matías. Puerto Suárez, reached by air, is near Quijarro which is the terminus of the railway from Santa Cruz. On the Brazilian side of the border is Corumbá and the southern Pantanal. San Matías is reached by road from Santa Cruz, with road links to Cáceres, Cuiabá and the northern Pantanal in Brazil.

Puerto Suárez

Phone code: 03
Colour map 6, grid B6
Population: 15,000

On the shore of Laguna Cáceres, is a friendly, quiet, small town, with a shady main plaza. There is a nice view of the lake from the park at the north end of Av Bolívar. The area around the train station is known as *Paradero*. Fishing and photo tours to the Pantanal can be arranged more cheaply than on the Brazilian side. **AL pp** *Centro Ecológico El Tumbador*, T03-762 8699 or T7106 7712 (mob), eltumbador@ yahoo.com A non-profit-making organization working for sustainable development in the Bolivian Lowlands runs ½-day to 4-day river, trekking and 4WD tours from its research station and lodge on the lake; prices from US$82 per person all-inclusive.

Sleeping and eating C *Bamby*, Santa Cruz 31 y 6 de Agosto, T976 2015. A/c, **D** with fan, cheaper with shared bath, comfortable. **C** *Frontera Verde*, Vanguardia 24 y Simón Bolívar, T976 2468, F62470. Best in town, a/c, **D** with fan, breakfast included, parking, helpful, English spoken. **C-D** *Sucre*, Bolívar 63 on main plaza, T976 2069. A/c, with bath, pleasant, good restaurant. **D** *Beby*, Av Bolívar 111, T976 2270. A/c, **E** with shared bath and fan. **D** *Ejecutivo*, at south end of Bolívar, T976 2267. A/c, parking, cheaper with fan, comfortable. **D** *Roboré*, 6 de Agosto 78, T976 2170. Fan, **E** with shared bath, basic, restaurant next door. **E** *Progreso*, Bolívar 21. Shared bath, basic. **E** *Res Puerto Suárez*, Bolívar 105. Shared bath, fans, showers, basic. Beware the water, it is straight from the river. *Parillada Jenecherú*, Bolívar near plaza. Grilled meats. Opposite is *Al Paso*, Bolívar 43. Very good value set meals and à la carte, popular. *El Taxista*, Bolívar 100 block. Several other small inexpensive restaurants nearby.

Tour operators *R B Travel*, Bolívar 65 by Plaza, T976 2014, for airline tickets, helpful.

Transport Taxi: to Paradero US$1.65; to airport US$2; to Quijarro or the border, US$5 (day), US$6 (night) or US$0.80 pp in a colectivo. **Air**: airport is 6 km north of town, T62347; airport tax US$2. Daily except Tue and Sat to/from Santa Cruz with *Aero Sur* and *LAB*. *TAM* to **Santa Cruz**, continues to Trinidad and La Paz. **NB** Do not buy tickets for flights originating in Puerto Suárez in Corumbá, you will have to pay more. **Train**: the station for Puerto Suárez is about 3 km from town. It is the first station west of Quijarro. Bracha agent, Bolívar 86, T/F976 2577.

Immigration office at airport issues Bolivian exit/entry stamps

Directory Airline offices: *LAB*, La Paz 33, T976 2241. *Aero Sur*, Bolívar near plaza, T976 2581. *TAM*, C del Chaco s/n, T976 2205. **Banks**: *Supermercado Tocale* changes Bolivianos, reais and US$, cash only. **Embassies and consulates**: Brazilian Consulate, Santa Cruz entre Bolívar y 6 de Agosto.

The eastern terminus of the Bolivian railway is at **Quijarro**, the gateway to Brazil, an unappealing town created around the railway station. There have been reports of drug trafficking and related problems in this border area and caution is recommended.

Quijarro
Colour map 6, grid B6
Population: 15,000

Sleeping and eating C *Santa Cruz*, Av Brazil 2 blocks east of station, T978 2113, F978 2044. A/c, cheaper with fan, **D** with shared bath, good rooms, nice courtyard, good restaurant, parking. Highly recommended. **D** *Gran Hotel Colonial*, Av Brazil y Panamá, T/F978 2037. A/c, cheaper with fan, **E** with shared bath, good restaurant. **D** *Oasis*, Av Argentina 20, T978 2159. A/c, fridge, cheaper with shared bath and a/c, **E** with fan, OK. **D** *Yoni*, Av Brazil opposite the station, T978 2109. A/c, fridge, **E** with shared bath and fan, comfortable, mosquito netting on windows. **F** *Res Paratí*, Guatemala s/n. Shared bath, fan, laundry facilities.

Water supply is often unreliable, try tap before checking in. Most people prefer to go on to Corumbá where hotels are better. The food stalls by the station and market are best avoided

Tour operators *Santa Cruz*, in hotel of same name, sells Bracha and airline tickets.

Transport Taxi to the border (Arroyo Concepción) US$0.40 pp; to Puerto Suárez US$0.80 pp, more at night. **Train** See Transport, Border with Brazil, below.

Directory Banks: Bolivianos, reais and US$ cash traded along Av Brazil opposite the station by changers with large purses sitting in lawn chairs; good rates, but beware of tricks. **Communications**: Telephone: *Entel*, at the south end of Av Naval, national and international calls, Mon-Sat 0700-2300, Sun 0700-2000. Also small office at Guatemala y Brazil near the station.

The municipality by the border is known as **Arroyo Concepción**. You need not have your passport stamped if you visit Corumbá for the day. Otherwise get your exit stamp at Bolivian immigration (see below), formalities are straightforward. There are no formalities on the Brazilian side, you must get your entry stamp in Corumbá (see page 580); there is also an office at the bus station which is usually closed. Yellow Fever vaccination is compulsory to enter Bolivia and Brazil, have your certificate at hand when you go for your entry stamp, otherwise you will be sent to get revaccinated. Bolivian immigration is at the border at Arroyo Concepción, blue building on right just before bridge, opens 0700, closed for lunch 1130-1400; at Puerto Suárez airport; in San Matías. Passports may be stamped at Santa Cruz station if leaving by train, which may avoid spurious exit charges at Quijarro. Money can be exchanged at the Quijarro border. You will probably only be able to sell bolivianos in Bolivia. Embassies and consulates **Brazilian consulate**, in Santa Cruz, or in Puerto Suárez, a yellow fever certificate is required.

Border with Brazil
You can leave Bolivia at Quijarro when the border post is closed, but you have to return from Brazil for a Bolivian exit stamp within 8 days

Transport Air The simplest way to Brazil is to fly to Puerto Suárez then share a taxi to the border, US$7.50 per car. See Puerto Suárez Transport above.
    Train All trains from Santa Cruz go via San José de Chiquitos to Quijarro, from where travellers must go by colectivo to the border post (beware overcharging, fare should be US$0.40 pp), then by bus to Corumbá. Standard service, 20 hrs, leaves at daily except Sun at 1530; Pullman US$16.25, 1st class US$7.20, 2nd class US$6, also has *Bracha* coach, US$23.50; returns at 1500 Mon-Sat. A *ferrobus* runs Tue, Thu, Sun at 1900, returning Mon, Wed, Fri 1900, 13 hrs, US$31.55 *semi-cama*, 36.55 *cama* (not as luxurious as it claims). Take food, drinking water, insect repellent and a torch, whichever class you are travelling. From Mar-Aug take a sleeping bag for the cold; be

Bolivia

prepared for delays. Tickets may be purchased the day prior to travel, counter opens at 0800, go early because queues form hours before and tickets sell fast. Take passport. Tickets for *Bracha* (see Santa Cruz Tour operators), can be bought in advance at travel agencies; *Bracha* staff are very friendly and honest, 10% fee, highly recommended to avoid queues at the station, also advises on transporting vehicles by rail. Office in Quijarro, T03-976 2325; in La Paz T02-232 7472. At Quijarro station Willy Solís Cruz, T978 2204, runs a left-luggage room, speaks English, very helpful, assists with ticket purchases for US$3 (has been known to let people sleep in the luggage room). The Quijarro ticket office sells tickets only on day of departure, open 0700-1600, queuing starts much earlier, it gets crowded, much pushing and shoving, touts resell tickets at hugely inflated prices. For a couple of dollars more you can buy tickets at agencies near the border without the queues. To buy tickets you must take your passport showing all relevant entry and exit stamps. Note that times of departure from Quijarro are approximate as they depend on when trains arrive. 500 m from station is a modern a/c shopping complex with banks, restaurants and pool. If tickets are sold out, guards will sell you a ticket on the train with a 15% surcharge.

Road The road route from Santa Cruz is via San Ignacio de Velasco to San Matías, then on to Cáceres and Cuiabá. See under San Ignacio for bus information. Get your passport stamped in San Ignacio as there is no passport control in San Matías, but plenty of military checks en route. Once in Brazil go to immigration in Cáceres or, on Sun, to Polícia Federal in Cuiabá. **San Matías** is a busy little town with hotels and restaurants. *Servicio Aéreo Pantanal* flies daily from Santa Cruz (office at El Trompillo airport, T03-353 1066).

Travel to Paraguay

South of Santa Cruz the road passes through Abapó and Camiri. A paved road heads south from Camiri, through Boyuibe, Villamontes and Yacuiba to Argentina (see below). At Boyuibe another road heads east to Paraguay, used less now than a new road from Villamontes (see below) to Mariscal Estigarribia in the Paraguayan Chaco. It is possible to drive from Boyuibe into Paraguay direct on the old road in a truck or four-wheel drive, high clearance vehicle, carrying insect repellent, food and water for a week. No help can be relied on in case of a breakdown; a winch is advisable, especially after rain. There are some rivers to ford and although they are dry in the dry season they can be impassable if there is rain in the area. The new route, once you leave the paved road at Villamontes, should be treated with the same respect. **Boyuibe**, Km 519, *Altitude*: 817 m, is the last town in Bolivia where exit stamps can be obtained if going to Paraguay (*Alojamiento Boyuibe*, has hot showers, restaurant, and two others, all **G**). All buses stop at *Parador-Restaurante Yacyretá*, on main road, owners are helpful, sell bus tickets to Asunción and have rooms to rent; change cash here (poor rates) or at immigration. Fuel and water are available. Passports are stamped at military checkpoint. If travelling by bus, passports are collected by driver and returned on arrival at Mcal Estigarribia, Paraguay, with Bolivian exit stamp. Paraguayan entry stamps are given in Pozo Colorado. As entry stamps are not given at Mcal Estigarribia, to visit the Chaco legally, you must stay on the bus to Pozo Colorado, then return to the Chaco. Enquire locally for alternatives. (For Mcal Estigarribia and the continuation of this route see **Paraguay**: **The Paraguayan Chaco**. See Santa Cruz **Transport Bus**: for international bus services.)

Villamontes
Phone code: 04
Colour map 6, grid B4
280 km E of Tarija

South of Boyuibe is **Villamontes,** renowned for fishing. It holds a Fiesta del Pescado in August. It is a friendly town, and very hot, on the edge of the Gran Chaco and is on the road and rail route from Santa Cruz to the Argentine border at Yacuiba. You can change buses here to/from Paraguay on the Santa Cruz-Yacuiba bus route, or to/from Tarija (Monday and Thursday), or if coming from Sucre. There are two banks (no ATM, exchange limited), *TAM* office (T672 2135) and internet café (next to *El Arriero* restaurant) on Plaza 15 de Abril. *Entel* is one block northeast of this plaza.

Sleeping and eating C pp *El Rancho*, 3 km from centre opposite station (taxi US$0.45) T672 2059, F672 2985. Lovely rooms, a/c, TV, excellent restaurant, also annexe **F** pp.

Recommended. **C** *Gran Hotel Avenida*, 3 blocks east of Plaza 15 de Abril, T672 2297, F672 2412. A/c, includes breakfast, helpful owner, parking. **F** *Res Raldes*, 1 block from Plaza 15 de Abril, T672 2088. **G** pp without bath, neat rooms, poor showers. **E** *Res Miraflores*, 500 block of Avenida. **F** without bath, basic, not very clean, owner Rolando Rueda arranges fishing trips. Good, cheap meals at *Parillada El Arriero*, Plaza 15 de Abril. For pizzas and grilled meat, *Churrasquería Argentina*, ½ block from same plaza. Locals favour *Bar Cherenta*, Plaza 15 de Abril, and for ice cream *Heladería Noelia*, halfway from the plaza to bus station.

Transport Air: *TAM* flies to La Paz, Sucre and Tarija on Sun and Santa Cruz on Sat. **Bus**: to **Tarija** via Entre Ríos (unpaved road, 10 hrs) Thu 0500 and 0600, Sun 0600, US$7.50; via Yacuiba 3 daily, 10 hrs. To **Santa Cruz** at 1030, 12 hrs, US$4.50, **Sucre** at 1930, US$7.50, and **La Paz** at 2000, US$9. Also to **Camiri**, **Tupiza**, **Villazón**. **Train**: for **Yacuiba** on Mon, Wed and Fri at 0400, US$1.20 and for **Santa Cruz** on Tue, Thu and Sat at 1930, US$11.35 (Pullman), US$5.25 (1st class), US$4.20 (2nd class).

The road to Paraguay runs east to **Ibibobo**. The first 80 km is an all-weather gravel surface. From Ibibobo to the frontier at Picada Sucre is 75 km, then it's 15 km to the border and another 8 km to the Paraguayan frontier post at **Fortín Infante Rivarola**. If you want to go by truck to Paraguay, it is cheaper than the bus, but you may have to wait a long time in Villamontes. Moreover, the bus provides food, stops at the right immigration posts, protects you from dust (more-or-less) and rain and, if you get stuck, 30-odd passengers have more chance of pushing a bus out of the mud than 4-5 passengers on a heavily-laden truck.

Travel to Argentina

From Santa Cruz the route goes Boyuibe, Villamontes and Yacuiba, a prosperous city at the crossing to Pocitos in Argentina. From Villamontes to Yacuiba road is paved, but no bridges; river crossings tricky in wet season. In Yacuiba, there is **C** *Hotel París*, Comercio y Campero, T682 2182, the best. **C** *Monumental*, Comercio 1270, T682 2088, includes breakfast. **D** *Valentín*, Av San Martín 1462, opposite rail station, T682 2645, F682 2317, **E** without bath, excellent value. Also *Entel* and Correos. Argentine consul at Comercio y Sucre. The border crossing is straightforward. Passengers leaving Bolivia must disembark at Yacuiba, take a taxi to Pocitos on the border (US$0.40, beware unscrupulous drivers) and walk across to Argentina.

Yacuiba
Colour map 6, grid B4
Population: 11,000

Train Santa Cruz-Yacuiba trains on Mon, Wed, Fri 1700, arrive 0600-0700, Pullman US$14, 1st class US$6.70, 2nd class US$5.40; return to Santa Cruz Tue, Thu, Sat 1700. **Bus** Good connections in all directions. To **Santa Cruz**, about 20 companies run daily services, mostly at night, 14 hrs, US$13. To **Tarija**, daily morning and evening. To **Potosí-Oruro-La Paz**, with *Trans Yacuiba* and *Expreso Tarija*. Daily to **Sucre** with *Flota Copacabana*.

Transport

Background

Post independence history

Two main features dominated this period: the importance of mining and chronic political instability. Although silver had been of paramount importance in the colonial period, the Bolivian economy depended for much of the 20th century on exports of tin. The construction of railways and the demand for tin in Europe and the USA (particularly in wartime) led to a mining boom after 1900. By the 1920s the industry was dominated by three entrepreneurs, Simón Patiño, Mauricio Hochschild and the Aramayo family, who exercised great influence over national politics. The importance of mining and the harsh conditions in the isolated mining camps of the Altiplano led to the rise of a militant miners movement.

Bolivia

Bolivia

Bolivian politics have been even more turbulent than elsewhere in Latin America. Although in the 19th century the army was very small, officers were key figures in power-struggles, often backing different factions of the landowning elite. Between 1840 and 1849 there were 65 attempted *coups d'état*. The longest lasting government of the 19th century was that of Andrés Santa Cruz (1829-39), but when he tried to unite Bolivia with Peru in 1836, Chile and Argentina intervened to overthrow him. After the War of the Pacific (1879-83) there was greater stability, but opposition to the political dominance of the city of Sucre culminated in a revolt in 1899 led by business groups from La Paz and the tin-mining areas, as a result of which La Paz became the centre of government.

Since independence Bolivia has suffered continual losses of territory, partly because of communications difficulties and the central government's inability to control distant provinces. The dispute between Chile and Peru over the nitrate-rich Atacama desert in 1879 soon dragged in Bolivia, which had signed a secret alliance with Peru in 1873. Following its rapid defeat in the War of the Pacific Bolivia lost her coastal provinces. As compensation Chile later agreed to build the railway between Arica and La Paz. When Brazil annexed the rich Acre Territory in 1903, Bolivia was compensated by another railway, but this Madeira-Mamoré line never reached its destination, Riberalta, and proved of little use; it was closed in 1972. There was not even an unbuilt railway to compensate Bolivia for its next loss. A long-running dispute with Paraguay over the Chaco erupted into war in 1932. Defeat in the so-called Chaco War (1932-35) resulted in the loss of three quarters of the Chaco (see Paraguay chapter, page 1075).

Modern Bolivia The Chaco War was a turning point in Bolivian history, increasing the political influence of the army which in 1936 seized power for the first time since the War of the Pacific. Defeat bred nationalist resentment among junior army officers who had served in the Chaco and also led to the creation of a nationalist party, the Movimiento Nacionalista Revolucionario (MNR) led by Víctor Paz Estenssoro. Their anger was directed against the mine owners and the leaders who had controlled Bolivian politics. Between 1936 and 1946 a series of unstable military governments followed. This decade witnessed the apparent suicide in 1939 of one president (Germán Busch) and the public hanging in 1946 of another (Gualberto Villarroel). After a period of civilian government, the 1951 elections were won by the MNR but a coup prevented the party from taking office.

The 1952 revolution In April 1952 the military government was overthrown by a popular revolution in which armed miners and peasants played a major role. Paz Estenssoro became president and his MNR government nationalized the mines, introduced universal suffrage and began the break-up and redistribution of large estates. The economy, however, deteriorated, partly because of the hostility of the US government. Paz's successor, Hernán Siles Zuazo (president 1956-64), a hero of the 1952 revolution, was forced to take unpopular measures to stabilize the economy. Paz was re-elected president in 1960 and 1964, but shortly afterwards in November 1964 he was overthrown by his vice president, Gral René Barrientos, who relied on the support of the army and the peasants to defeat the miners.

Military rule in the 1970s The death of Barrientos in an air crash in 1969 was followed by three brief military governments. The third, led by Gral Torres, pursued left-wing policies which alarmed many army officers and business leaders. In August 1971 Torres was overthrown by Hugo Banzer, a right-wing colonel who outlawed political parties and trade unions. After Banzer was forced to call elections in 1978, a series of short-lived military governments overruled elections in 1978 and 1979 giving victories to Siles Zuazo. One of these, led by Gral García Meza (1980-81) was notable for its brutal treatment of opponents and its links to the cocaine trade, which led to its isolation by the international community.

Return to democracy In August 1982 the military returned to barracks and Dr Siles Zuazo assumed the Presidency in a leftist coalition government with support from the communists and trade unions. Under this regime inflation spiralled out of control. The elections of 1985 were won again by Víctor Paz Estenssoro, who imposed a rigorous programme to stabilize the economy. A new currency was created, the boliviano, linked to the US dollar in a controlled float. As international financial aid began to flow again, inflation came down to 10-20% a year, although unemployment continued to rise and living standards to fall. In the elections of 1989, Gonzalo Sánchez de Lozada of the MNR (chief architect of the stabilization programme) failed to win enough votes to prevent Congress choosing Jaime Paz Zamora of the Movimiento de la Izquierda Revolucionaria (MIR), who came third in the elections, as president in August 1989. Paz had made an unlikely alliance with the former military dictator, Hugo Banzer (Acción Democrática Nacionalista).

Although Gonzalo Sánchez de Lozada just failed to gain the required 51% majority to win the presidency in the 1993 elections, the other candidates recognized his victory. The main element in his policies was the capitalization of state assets, in which investors agreed to inject fresh capital into a chosen state-owned company in return for a 50% controlling stake. The other 50% of the shares were distributed to all Bolivians over 18 via a private pension fund scheme, an ambitious proposal in a country where only 5% of the population had bank accounts and savings were negligible. State companies included in this scheme were electricity, telecommunications, air transport, railways and the oil and gas company, YPFB. As the programme gained pace, so did opposition to it. In the elections of 1 June 1997, Banzer and the ADN secured 22% of the vote and ADN became the dominant party in a new coalition with MIR, Unidad Cívica de Solidaridad (UCS) and Conciencia de Patria (Condepa), giving the government a large majority in the Senate and lower house of Congress. In his first two years in office, Banzer pursued economic austerity and the US-backed policy of eradicating coca production. In 2000, however, economic hardship in rural areas, which had not benefited from the previous decade's reforms, together with unemployment and anger at both the coca eradication and a plan to raise water rates led to violent protests and road blocks in many parts of the country. Through 2001 and into 2002, the situation had hardly improved and demonstrations large and small against social conditions were held throughout the country. In early 2001 the Ministry of the Economy highlighted the acute hardship in a report that stated that five out of eight Bolivians live in poverty with inadequate basic food supplies, high illiteracy, and no access to transportation, irrigation or means of financial betterment.

With the country's economic and social problems still severe, President Banzer was forced to resign in August 2001 because of cancer. His replacement, Vice-President Jorge Quiroga, had just a year left of Banzer's term to serve before new elections would be held.

The Constitution of 1967 vests executive power in the President, elected by popular vote for a term of five years, who cannot be immediately re-elected. Congress consists of two chambers: the Senate, with 27 seats, and the Chamber of Deputies, with 130 seats. There are nine departments; each is controlled by a Prefecto appointed by the President.

Government
Sucre is the legal capital, La Paz is the seat of government

Culture

Of the total population, 8,500,000 in 2001, some two thirds are **Indians**, the remainder being *mestizos* (people of mixed Spanish and indigenous origin), **Europeans** and **others**. The racial composition varies from place to place: Indian around Lake Titicaca; more than half Indian in La Paz; three-quarters *mestizo* or European in the Yungas, Cochabamba, Santa Cruz and Tarija, the most European of all. Since the 1980s, regional tensions between the 'collas' (*altiplano* dwellers) and the 'cambas' (lowlanders) have become more marked. About two-thirds of the population lives in adobe huts. Under 40% of children of school age attend school even though it is theoretically compulsory between 7 and 14.

The most obdurate of Bolivian problems has always been that the main mass of population is, from a strictly economic viewpoint, in the wrong place, the poor Altiplano and not the potentially rich Oriente; and that the Indians live largely outside the monetary system on a self-sufficient basis. Since the land reform of 1952 isolated communities continue the old life but in the agricultural area around Lake Titicaca, the valleys of Cochabamba, the Yungas and the irrigated areas of the south, most peasants now own their land, however small the plot may be. Migration to the warmer and more fertile lands of the east region has been officially encouraged. At the same time roads are now integrating the food-producing eastern zones, with the bulk of the population living in the towns of the Altiplano or the west-facing slopes of the Eastern Cordillera.

People
Forecast population growth 2000-2005: 2.2%
Urban population in 2000: 63%
Infant mortality: 56 per 1,000 live births

Bolivia

Bolivia

The highland Indians are composed of two groups: those in La Paz and in the north of the Altiplano who speak the guttural Aymara (an estimated one million), and those elsewhere, who speak Quechua, the Inca tongue (three million – this includes the Indians in the northern Apolobamba region). Outside the big cities many of them speak no Spanish, but knowledge of Spanish is increasing. In the lowlands are some 150,000 people in 30 groups, including the Ayoreo, Chiquitano, Chiriguano, Garavo, Chimane and Mojo. The lowland Indians are, in the main, Guaraní. About 70 of Bolivians are Aymara, Quechua or Tupi-Guaraní speakers. The first two are regarded as national languages, but were not, until very recently, taught in schools, a source of some resentment. There are also about 17,000 blacks, descendents of slaves brought from Peru and Buenos Aires in 16th century, who now live in the Yungas.

The Indian women retain their traditional costume, with bright petticoats (*polleras*), and in the highlands around La Paz wear, apparently from birth, a brown or grey bowler (locally called a *bombín*). Indians traditionally chew the coca leaf, which deadens hunger pains and gives a measure of oblivion. Efforts to control the cultivation of coca is one of many sources of friction between the indigenous population and the authorities; others include landlessness, and exploitation of labour. On feast days they drink with considerable application, wear the most sensational masks and dance till they drop.

Books

An Insider's Guide to Bolivia, by **Peter McFarren** (Fundación Cultural Quipus, Casilla 1696, La Paz, 3rd edition, 1992, US$25) has been recommended, especially for its section on culture. *Descubriendo Bolivia*, **Hugo Boero Rojo** (1989), is a tour through the departments of present-day Bolivia, with photographs and road routes (also available in English). *Bolivia in Focus*, by **Paul Van Lindent** and **Otto Verkaren** (Latin American Bureau, London 1994) is a concise study of Bolivian politics, economy, culture and people. *Guía Boliviana de Transporte y Turismo* (GBT) published monthly at Plaza del Estudiante 1920, T02-232 1027, F02-239 1641, US$6 a month, US$65 a year, gives information on transport, accommodation, restaurants, useful data etc, with town plans, for the whole country.

Trekking For more detail on treks and climbs see the *Bolivia Handbook* (Footprint); *Backpacking and Trekking in Peru and Bolivia* (7th edition) by **Hilary Bradt** (published by Bradt, 1999); *Trekking in Bolivia* by **Yossi Brain**, **Andrew North** and **Isobel Stoddart** (The Mountaineers, Seattle, 1997) and *Bolivia – a climbing guide* also by **Yossi Brain** (The Mountaineers, Seattle, 1999); a paperback reprint of *La Cordillera Real de los Andes, Bolivia*, by **Alain Mesili** (Los Amigos del Libro, La Paz, 1984) is available in Spanish. *The High Andes* by **John Biggar** (Castle Douglas: Andes 1999); a climbing guide.

Lake Titicaca **Tristan Jones**, who crossed South America in his sailing cutter *Sea Dart*, spent over eight months cruising Lake Titicaca, see his book *The Incredible Voyage*, Futura Publications. *An Insider's Guide to Bolivia* (see above) gives a good historical background, including an interesting article about archaeological discoveries in Lake Titicaca, by **Johann Reinhard**.

Mining *We Eat the Mines and the Mines Eat Us* by **June Nash**, New York, 1979. *The Potosí Mita* 1573-1700 by **Jeffery Cole**, Stanford University Press, 1985. *The Great Tin Crash – Bolivia and the world tin market* by **John Crabtree** (Latin America Bureau, London, 1987).

History and culture Herbert S Klein, *Bolivia: The Evolution of a Multi-Ethnic Society* (Oxford University Press). *Rebellion in the Veins – political struggle in Bolivia 1952 to 1982*, James Dunkerley (Verso, London, 1984).

20th-century fiction and poetry A selection: the works of the modernist poet Adela Zamudio (1854-1928); *El las tierras de Potosí* (1911) by **Jamie Mendoza** and *Raza de Bronce* (1919) by **Alcides Arguedas** both examine the life of the campesino in a society dominated by whites; *Sangre de mestizos* (1936) by **Augusto Céspedes** is a collection of short stories about the Chaco War; *Los fundadores del alba* (1969) by **Renato Prado de Oropeza** was inspired by Che Guevara's campaigns in the 1960s; *Antología del terror político* (1979) deals with Bolivia under dictatorship.

Brazil

Described as the sexiest people on earth, Brazilians know how to flirt, flaunt and have fun. The Rio Carnival, with its heady atmosphere and costumes to die for, is the most exuberant of a calendar of festivals. In this, the world's fifth largest country, football, looking good and dancing are the national pastimes. Everyone is seduced by the sounds of samba and the lure of the beach. But Brazilians also have a spiritual side. Many religions flourish, most obviously the African-based candomblé, which lives happily alongside Catholicism. For a change from cosmopolitan life, sling a hammock on a river boat up the Amazon, or take a walk with wildlife in the Pantanal, a vast wetland, where caiman, piranhas and jaguars rub shoulders with herds of cattle.

5

Brazil

Essentials

Planning your trip

The Southeast: Rio de Janeiro was for a long time THE image of Brazil, with its beautiful setting – the Sugar Loaf and Corcovado overlooking the bay and beaches, its world renowned carnival, the nightlife and its *favelas* (slums – which are now being incorporated into tourism). It is still a must on many itineraries, but Rio de Janeiro state has plenty of other beaches, national parks and colonial towns (especially **Paraty**) and the imperial cities of **Petrópolis** and **Teresópolis**. **São Paulo** is the country's industrial and financial powerhouse; with some fine museums and its cultural life and restaurants are very good. All the São Paulo coast is worth visiting and inland there are hill resorts and colonial towns. The **state of Minas Gerais** contains some of the best colonial architecture in South America in cities such as Ouro Preto, Mariana, São João del Rei and Diamantina. All are within easy reach of the state capital, Belo Horizonte. Other options in Minas include national parks with good hill scenery and bird-watching and hydrothermal resorts.

The atmosphere of the **South** is dominated by its German and Italian immigrants. The three states, Paraná, Santa Catarina and Rio Grande do Sul have their coastal resorts, especially near Florianópolis, capital of Santa Catarina. **Rio Grande do Sul** is the land of Brazil's *gaúchos* (cowboys) and of its vineyards, but the main focus of the region is the magnificent **Iguaçu Falls** in the far west of Paraná, on the borders of Argentina and Paraguay.

The **Northeast** is famous for beaches and colonial history. Combining both these elements, with the addition of Brazil's liveliest African culture, is **Salvador de Bahia**, one of the country's most famous cities and a premier tourist destination. Huge sums of money have been lavished on the restoration of its colonial centre and its carnival is something special. Inland, Bahia is mostly arid *sertão*, in which a popular town is **Lençóis**, a historical monument with a nearby national park. The highlight of the southern coast of Bahia is the beach and party zone around **Porto Seguro**, while in the north the beaches stretch up to the states of Sergipe and Alagoas and on into Pernambuco. **Recife**, capital of Pernambuco, and its neighbour, the colonial capital **Olinda**; also mix the sea, history and culture, while inland is the major handicraft centre of Caruaru. Travelling around to the north-facing coast, there are hundreds of beaches to choose from, some highly developed, others less so. You can swim, surf or ride the dunes in buggies. Last stop before the mouth of the Amazon is **São Luís**, in whose centre most of the old houses are covered in colonial tiles.

Through the **North** flows the **Amazon**, along which river boats ply between the cities of Belém, Santarém and Manaus. From **Manaus** particularly there are opportunities for exploring the jungle on adventurous expeditions or staying in lodges. North of Manaus is the overland route through Boa Vista to Venezuela. The forest stretches south to the central tableland which falls to the **Pantanal** in the far west. This seasonal wetland, the highlight of the **Centre West**, is one of the prime areas for seeing bird and animal life in the continent. At the eastern end of the Centre West is **Brasília**, built in the 1960s and now a World Heritage Site in recognition of its superb examples of modern architecture. Also in this region are the old mining towns of **Goiás**, one of the largest river islands in the world (Bananal – a mecca for fishing) and the delightful hill and river landscapes of **Bonito** in Mato Grosso do Sul.

Brazil is a tropical country, but the further south you go the more temperate the winters become and there are places in the coastal mountains which have gained a reputation for their cool climate and low humidity. The heaviest rains fall at different times in the different regions: Nov to Mar in the southeast, Dec to Mar in the centre west and Apr to Aug on the northeast coast around Pernambuco (irregular rainfall causes severe draughts). The rainy season in the north and Amazônia can begin in Dec and is heaviest Mar-May, but it is getting steadily shorter, possibly as a result of deforestation. It is only in rare cases that the rainfall can

Brazil

be described as either excessive or deficient: few places get more than 2,000 mm – the coast north of Belém, some of the Amazon Basin, and a small area of the Serra do Mar between Santos and São Paulo, where the downpour has been harnessed to generate electricity.

May to Sep is usually referred to as winter, but this is not to suggest that this is a bad time to visit. On the contrary, Apr to Jun and Aug to Oct are recommended times to go to most parts of the country. One major consideration is that carnival falls within the hottest, wettest time of year (in Feb), so if you are incorporating carnival into a longer holiday, it may be wet wherever you go. Also bear in mind that mid-Dec to Feb is the national holiday season, which means that hotels, planes and buses may be full and many establishments away from the holiday areas may be shut.

The average annual temperature increases steadily from south to north, but even on the Equator, in the Amazon Basin, the average temperature is not more than 27°C. The highest recorded was 42°C, in the dry northeastern states. From the latitude of Recife south to Rio, the mean temperature is from 23° to 27°C along the coast, and from 18° to 21°C in the Highlands. From a few degrees south of Rio to the boundary with Uruguay the mean temperature is from 17° to 19°C. Humidity is relatively high in Brazil, particularly along the coast.

Finding out more

Tourist information The national tourist board is **Embratur**. Its head office is at Setor Comercial Norte, Quadra 02, Bloco G, 70710-500, Brasília, BF, Brazil; T0xx61-429 7777, F0xx61-429 7910, www.embratur.gov.br For information abroad, contact Brazil's representation overseas, see box below. Tourist information bureaux in cities and towns are not usually too helpful regarding information on cheap hotels. It is also difficult to get information on neighbouring states. Many of the more expensive hotels provide locally-produced tourist information magazines for their guests. Note that telephone yellow pages in most cities (but not Rio) contain good street maps.

National parks are run by **Ibama**, the Instituto Brasileiro do Meio Ambiente e dos Recursos Naturais Renováveis (Brazilian Institute of Environmental Protection): SAIN, Avenida L-4, bloco B, Térreo, Edifiço Sede de Ibama, CEP 70800-200, Brasília, DF, T0xx61-226 8221/9014, F0xx61-322 1058, www.ibama.gov.br The Institute is underfunded, often understaffed and visitors may find it difficult to obtain information. National parks are open to visitors, usually with a permit from Ibama. For further details, see individual parks.

Brazil on the web

www.ipanema.com www.copacabana.com Two websites for the English-speaking community in Rio: **www.umbrellaonline.com.br** and **www.expats.co.br** São Paulo: **www.spguia.com.br** Bahia: **www.bahiatursa.ba.gov.br/** and **www.uol.com.br/agendasalvador** The Paraná site, **www.pr.gov.br/turismo** has lots of information and access to all states in the country, just click on Conheça o Brasil. **www.cidadeshistoricas.terra.com.br** information on colonial cities. **www.brazil.org.au www.brasilemb.org www.brazil.org.uk www.brazilinfo.net www.brazil-brasil.com www.vivabrazil.com www.brazilweb.com** (in Portuguese and English). **www.ecosolidaridade.com.br** (in Portuguese, English, Spanish, French, Italian and German, with links to many other sites). **www.wwf.org.br**

Language

For the low-budget traveller, Portuguese is essential

The language is Portuguese. Efforts to speak it are greatly appreciated. If you cannot speak Portuguese, apologize and try Spanish, but note that the differences in the spoken languages are very much greater than appears likely from the printed page and you may well not be understood: you will certainly have difficulty in understanding the answers. One important point of spelling is that words ending in 'i' and 'u' are accented on the last syllable, though (unlike Spanish) no accent is used there. This is especially important in place names: Parati, Iguaçu. Note also that 'meia' (half) is frequently used for number six (ie half-dozen). There are Brazilian tutors in most cities (in London, see *Time Out* and *Leros*, the Brazilian magazine, for advertisements).

Volunteering

In addition to suggestions in Essentials at the front of the Handbook, contact **RioVoluntário**, which supports 450 voluntary organizations, from environmental to healthcare. T+55-21-2262 1110, ask for Isadora or Fábio, www.riovoluntario.org.br

Before you travel

Nationalities which do not need a visa Consular visas are not required for stays of up to 90 days by tourists from Andorra, Argentina, Austria, Bahamas, Barbados, Belgium, Bolivia, Chile, Colombia, Costa Rica, Denmark, Ecuador, Finland, France, Germany, Greece, Iceland, Ireland, Israel, Italy, Liechtenstein, Luxembourg, Malaysia, Monaco, Morocco, Namibia, Netherlands, Norway, Paraguay, Peru, Philippines, Portugal, San Marino, South Africa, Spain, Suriname, Sweden, Switzerland, Thailand, Trinidad and Tobago, United Kingdom, Uruguay, the Vatican and Venezuela. For them, only the following documents are required at the port of disembarkation: a passport valid for at least six months (or *cédula de identidad* for nationals of Argentina, Chile, Paraguay and Uruguay); and a return or onward ticket, or adequate proof that you can purchase your return fare, subject to no remuneration being received in Brazil and no legally binding or contractual documents being signed. Venezuelan passport holders can stay in Brazil for 60 days on filling in a form at the border.

Visas & immigration

Visas US and Canadian citizens, Australians and New Zealanders and people of other nationalities, and those who cannot meet the requirements above, *must* get a visa before arrival, which may, if you ask, be granted for multiple entry. Visas are valid form date of issue. Visa fees vary from country to country, so apply to the Brazilian consulate, in the country of residence of the applicant. The consular fee in the USA is US$55. Do not lose the emigration permit they give you when you enter Brazil. Leaving the country without it, you may have to pay up to US$100 pp.

Renewals Foreign tourists may stay a maximum of 180 days in any one year. 90-day renewals are easily obtainable, but only at least 15 days before the expiry of your 90-day permit, from the Polícia Federal. The procedure varies, but generally you have to fill out three copies of the tax form at the Polícia Federal, take them to a branch of Banco do Brasil, pay US$15 and bring two copies back. You will then be given the extension form to fill in and be asked for your passport to stamp in the extension. According to regulations (which should be on display) you should be able to show a return ticket, cash, cheques or a credit card, a personal reference and proof of an address of a person living in the same city as the office (in practice you simply write this in the space on the form). Some offices will only give you an extension within 10 days of the expiry of your permit. Some points of entry, such as the Colombian border refuse entry for longer than 30 days, renewals are then for the same period, insist if you want 90 days. For longer stays you must leave the country and return (not the same day) to get a new 90-day permit. If your visa has expired, getting a new visa can be costly (US$35 for a consultation, US$30 for the visa itself) and may take anything up to 45 days, depending on where you apply. If you overstay your visa, or extension, you will be fined US$7 per day, with no upper limit. After paying the fine to Polícia Federal, you will be issued with an exit visa and must leave within eight days. If you cannot pay the fine you must pay when you next return to Brazil. **NB** Officially, if you leave Brazil within the 90-day permission to stay and then re-enter the country, you should only be allowed to stay until the 90-day permit expires. If, however, you are given another 90-day permit, this may lead to charges of overstaying if you apply for an extension. For UK citizens a joint agreement allows visits for business or tourism of up to six months a year from the date of first entry.

Identification You must always carry identification when in Brazil; it is a good idea to take a photocopy of the personal details in your passport, plus that with your Brazilian immigration stamp, and leave your passport in the hotel safe deposit. Always keep an independent record of your passport details. It is a good idea to register with your consulate to expedite document replacement if yours gets lost or stolen.

Duty free allowance Clothing and personal articles are free of import duty. Cameras, movie cameras, portable radios, tape-recorders, typewriters and binoculars are also admitted free if there is not more than one of each. Tourists may also bring in, duty-free, 24 alcoholic drinks (no more than 12 of any one type), 400 cigarettes, 25 cigars, 280 g of perfume, up to 10 units of cosmetics, up to three each of any electronic item or watch, up to a total value of US$500 monthly. There is a limit of US$150 at land borders and a written declaration must be made to this effect. Duty free goods may only be purchased in foreign currency.

Customs

Brazil

Vaccinations   Proof of vaccination against yellow fever is necessary if you are visiting Amazônia and the Centre-West, or are coming from countries with Amazonian territories, such as Bolivia, Colombia, Ecuador and Peru. It is strongly recommended to have an inoculation before visiting northern Brazil since those without a certificate will be inoculated on entering any of the northern and centre-western states. Although the vaccination is free it might be administered in unsanitary conditions. Yellow fever (see page 56) and some other vaccinations can be obtained from the Ministério da Saúde, R Cais de Pharoux, Rio de Janeiro. Less common ones can be obtained at Saúde de Portos, Praça 15 de Novembro, Rio de Janeiro. If visiting the Amazon basin, get vaccinations against hepatitis and typhoid. Poliomyelitis vaccination is required for children from three months to six years.

Money

real exchange rate with US$: 2.83   **Currency**   The unit of currency is the *real*, R$ (plural *reais*) introduced on 1 July 1994 on a par with the US dollar. It was floated against the dollar in early 1999. Any amount of foreign currency and 'a reasonable sum' in *reais* can be taken in; residents may only take out the equivalent of US$4,000. Notes in circulation are: 100, 50, 10, 5 and 1 *real*; coins 1 *real*, 50, 25, 10 and 5 centavos.

Banks open between 1000-1600 or 1630 Mon-Fri   **Banks**   In major cities banks will change cash and travellers' cheques. If you keep the exchange slips, you may convert back into foreign currency up to 50% of the amount you exchanged. This applies to the official markets only; there is no right of reconversion unless you have an official exchange slip. The black market, found in travel agencies, exchange houses and among hotel staff, was of marginal benefit compared with bank rates in 2001. Travellers' cheques are usually lower than for cash and they are less easy to change; commission may be charged. Many banks may only change US$300 minimum in cash, US$500 in travellers' cheques. Dollars cash are becoming more frequently used for tourist transactions and are also useful for those places where travellers' cheques cannot be changed and for when the banks go on strike: damaged dollars may be rejected. Parallel market and official rates are quoted in the papers and on TV news programmes. Tourists cannot change US$ travellers' cheques into US$ notes, but US$ travellers' cheques can be obtained on an American Express card (against official policy).

MasterCard emergency phone number 000811-887 0553 Visa emergency number 000811-933 5589   **Credit cards**   Credit cards are widely used; Diners Club, MasterCard, Visa and American Express are useful. MasterCard/Access is accepted by Banco Real. Overseas credit cards need authorization from São Paulo, this can take up to two hrs, allow plenty of time if buying air tickets. MasterCard and Diners are equivalent to Credicard, and Eurocheques can be cashed at Banco Alemão (major cities only). Banco Bradesco, subtitled Dia e Noite, handles the international Visa cash machine (ATM) network, Visa cash advances also at Banco do Brasil. Some of Banco Itaú's ATMs give cash withdrawals on MasterCard/Cirrus as do those at Bamerindus, but they are not as common as Visa ATMs. Both Bradesco and Itaú have machines at airports, shopping centres and major thoroughfares. Banco 24 Horas machines, at similar locations, operate with MasterCard, Amex, Diners, Boston and Citibank among others. Credit card transactions are charged at the tourist official rate. Cash advances on credit cards will only be paid in *reais* at the tourist rate, incurring a 1½% commission. ATMs are common in Brazil: it's worth remembering your PIN number since queues can be extremely long. Note however, that you may have to try many machines before being able to use your card. *Banco 24 Horas* kiosks advertise that they take a long list of credit cards in their ATMs. In fact, the likelihood of being able to use an international credit card is remote.

Cost of living   Accommodation in all but the 5-star hotels is good value. Budget hotels may have few frills, but you should have no difficulty finding a room costing US$10 pp, or less outside the cities and holiday centres. Eating in smart restaurants is costly, but *comida a kilo* (pay by weight) restaurants offer good value, with a wide range of food. They are ideal if you are not good at Portuguese as you help yourself. Shopping prices are equivalent to Europe. Prices are higher in Amazônia than elsewhere.

Brazilian embassies and consulates

Australia, *19 Forster Crescent, Yarralumla, Canberra ACT 2600, T00612-6273 2372, brazil@connect.net.au* **Consulate**, *St Martins Tower L 17, 31 Market Street, Sydney NSW 2000, T00612-9267 4414, F9267 4419.*
Austria, *Am Lugeck 1/5/15, A-1010 Wien, T00431-512 0631, F513 8374, ausbrem@utanet.at*
Belgium, *350 Avenue Louise, 6eme Étage, Boite 5-1050 Bruxelles, T00322-640 2015/ 640 2111, F640 8134, brasbruxelas@beon.be*
Canada, *450 Wilbrod Street, Sandyhill, Ottawa, ON K1N 6M8, T001613-237 1090, F237 6144, mailbox@brasembottawa.org*
Denmark, *Ryvangs Alle, 24-2100 Kobenhavn, T00453-920 6478, F927 3607, dinbrem@inet.uni-c.dk*
Finland, *Itainen Puisotie 4B 1/2-00140 Helsinki, Suomi, T003589-177922, F650084, brasemb.helsinki@kolumbus.fi*
France, *34 Cours Albert I, 75008 Paris, T00331-4561 6300, F4289 0345, www.bresil.org*
Germany, *Wallstrasse 54, 10179 Berlin, T30-726280, brasil@brasemberlim.de*
Ireland, *Harcourt Centre, Europa House, 5th Floor, 41-54 Harcourt Street, Dublin 2, T003531-475 6000/475 1338, F475 1341, irlbra@iol.ie*
Israel, *Beit Yachin, 2 Kaplan Street, 8th Floor, Tel Aviv, T009723-696 3934, F691 6060, embrisra@netvision.net.il*
Italy, *14 Piazza Navona, 00186 Roma, T003906-683981, F686 7858, brasital@tin.it*
Japan, *11-12 Kita-Aoyama 2-Chome, Minato-Ku, Tokyo 107, T00813-3404 5211, brasemb@brasemb.or.jp*
Netherlands, *Mauritskade 19-2514 HD, The Hague, T003170-302 3959, F302 3950, brasemb@dataweb.nl*

Norway, *Sigurd Syrs Gate 4, 1st floor, 0244 Oslo, T0047-2254 0741, F2254 0730, noruega@online.no*
Portugal, *Estrada das Laranjeiras, 144-1600 Lisboa, T003511-726 7777, F726 7623, embrasilport@mail.telepac.pt*
Spain, *C Fernando El Santo, 6 DP 28010 Madrid, T00341-700 4650, F700 4660, chanceleria@embajadadebrasil.es* **Consulate**, *Carrer Consell de Cent, 357/1a Ed Brasilia, 08007 Barcelona, T0034-934-882288, F934-872645.*
Sweden, *Odengatan 3, S114 24 Stockholm, T5451 6300, stockholm@brasemb.se*
Switzerland, *Monbijouster 68-3007 Berne, T004131-371 8515, F371 0525, brasbern@iprolink.ch*
UK, *32 Green Street, London WIY 4AT, T004420-7399 9000, F7399 9100, info@brazil.org.uk* **Consulate**, *6 St Albans Street, London SW1Y 4SQ, T004420-7930 9055, F7839 8958. For tourism information, T020-7629 6909, F7399 9102, tourism@brazil.org.uk*
USA, *3006 Massachusetts Avenue NW, Washington DC 20008-3699, T001202-238 2700/2805, F238 2827, webmaster@brasilemb.org* and *consular@brasilemb.org* **Consulates**: *2601 South Bay Shore Drive, Suite 800, Miami, Florida 33133, T001305-285 6200, F285 6232, consbras@brazilmiami.org 1185 Avenue of the Americas, 24th floor, New York City, 10036, T001-917-777 7777, F001-212-827 0225, consulado@brazilny.org Montgomery St, Suite 900, San Francisco, CA 94104-1913, T001-415-981 8170, F981 3628, brazilsf@brasilsf.org*

Brazil

Getting there

From Europe Rio de Janeiro and São Paulo are connected with the capitals of Europe by many major airlines, including *Varig*. TAP flies from Lisbon to Salvador, Recife and Fortaleza, while *Varig* flies from Milan to Fortaleza and Recife.

From USA Rio de Janeiro and São Paulo are connected to the USA direct by *Varig, Vasp, TAM, American Airlines, Continental, Delta* and *United Airlines* from a number of US gateways. *Varig* flies Miami-Manaus once a week respectively. There are daily flights from the USA to Belo Horizonte with *Varig* (Miami via São Paulo), and *American Airlines* (New York). *Air Canada* flies Toronto-São Paulo.

From Latin America Most capitals are connected to São Paulo and Rio. If buying a ticket to another country but with a stopover in Brazil, check if two tickets are cheaper than one.

Air
Regulations state that you cannot buy an air ticket in Brazil for use abroad unless you first have a ticket out of Brazil

Touching down

Business hours 0900-1800 Monday to Friday for most businesses, which close for lunch some time between 1130 and 1400. **Shops** open on Saturday till 1230 or 1300. **Government offices** 1100-1800 Monday to Friday. **Banks** 1000-1600, but closed on Saturday.
IDD: 55 Equal tones with long pauses means it is ringing; equal tones with equal pauses indicates engaged.
Official time Brazilian standard time is three hrs behind GMT; of the major cities, only the

Amazon time zone, Manaus, Cuiabá, Campo Grande and Corumbá are different, with time five hrs behind GMT. The State of Acre is four hrs behind GMT. Clocks move forward one hr in summer for approximately five months (usually between October and February or March) but times of change vary. This does not apply to Acre.
Voltage This varies, see directory under individual towns.
Weights and measures The metric system is used by all.

From elsewhere *South African Airways* fly between São Paulo and Johannesburg three times a week. There are regular flights between Tokyo and São Paulo (*Varig/All Nippon* and *Japan Airlines*). A consortium of Latin American airlines including *Varig* and *Aerolíneas Argentinas* operate the **Mercosur Airpass**, see page 38.

Road   To drive in Brazil you need an international licence. A national driving licence is acceptable as long as your home country is a signatory to the Vienna and Geneva conventions. (See Motoring, Essentials.) There are agreements between Brazil and all South American countries (but check in the case of Bolivia) whereby a car can be taken into Brazil (or a Brazilian car out of Brazil) for a period of 90 days without any special documents; an extension of up to 90 days is granted by the customs authorities on presentation of the paper received at the border, this must be retained. This may be done at most customs posts and at the **Serviço de Controle Aduaneiro**, Ministério da Fazenda, Av Pres A Carlos, Sala 1129, Rio de Janeiro.

For cars registered in other countries, the requirements are proof of ownership and/or registration in the home country and valid driving licence (as above). A 90-day permit is given by customs and procedure is very straightforward. Nevertheless, it is better to cross the border into Brazil when it is officially open because an official who knows all about the entry of cars is then present. You must specify which border station you intend to leave by, but application can be made to the Customs to change this.

Touching down

Airport tax   The amount of tax depends on the class of airport. All airports charge US\$36 for international departure tax. First class airports charge R\$9.50 domestic tax; second class airports R\$7; domestic rates are lower still in third and fourth class airports. Tax must be paid on checking in, in *reais* or US dollars. Tax is waived if you stay in Brazil less than 24 hrs.

Rules, customs & etiquette   **Clothing** Fashions are provocative, and while women are advised to dress in the local style, this can have unnerving effects. It is normal to stare and comment on women's appearance, and if you happen to look different or to be travelling alone, you will undoubtedly attract attention. You are very unlikely to be groped or otherwise molested: this is disrespectful, and merits a suitable reaction. Be aware that Brazilian men can be extraordinarily persistent, and very easily encouraged. In general, clothing requirements in Brazil are less formal than in the Hispanic countries. It is, however, advisable for men visiting restaurants to wear long trousers (women in shorts may also be refused entry), trousers and jackets or pullovers in São Paulo (also for cinemas). As a general rule, it is better not to wear shorts in official buildings, cinemas, inter-state buses and on flights.

Conduct Men should avoid arguments or insults (care is needed even when overtaking on the road); pride may be defended with a gun. Gay men, while still enjoying greater freedom than in many countries, should exercise reasonable discretion.

Brazil

Colour The people of Brazil represent a unique racial mix: it is not uncommon for the children of one family to be of several different colours. Individuals are often described by the colour of their skin (ranging through several shades of brown), and 'white' can refer to people who would not necessarily be thought white in Europe or North America. Generally speaking, the emphasis is on colour rather than racial origins. Racial discrimination is illegal in Brazil. There is, however, a complex class system which is informed both by heritage and by economic status. This effectively discriminates against the poor, who are chiefly (but by no means exclusively) black due to the lack of inherited wealth among those whose ancestors were servants and slaves. Some Brazilians might assume a black person is poor, therefore of low status. Black visitors to the country may encounter racial prejudice. We have also received a report from a black North American woman who was the subject of sexual advances by non-Brazilian, white tourists. Black women travelling with a white man may experience some problems, which should disappear with the realization that your partnership is not a commercial arrangement. A surprising number of Brazilians are unaware that black Europeans exist, so you could become the focus of some curiosity.

Tipping Tipping is usual, but less costly than in most other countries, except for porters. Restaurants, 10% of bill if no service charge but small tip if there is; taxi drivers, none; cloakroom attendants, small tip; cinema usherettes, none; hairdressers, 10-15%; porters, fixed charges but tips as well; airport porters, about US$0.50 per item.

Safety Personal safety in Brazil has deteriorated in recent years, largely because of economic recession, and crime is increasing. Some recommend avoiding all large cities, but efforts are being made to improve the situation in major tourist centres like Rio de Janeiro and Salvador. The situation is much more secure in smaller towns and in the country. The police are reported to be charging for documents reporting crimes if these are required quickly. See the Safety section in Essentials at the beginning of the book for general advice.

Police There are three types of police: **Polícia Federal**, civilian dressed, who handle all federal law duties, including immigration. A subdivision is the **Polícia Federal Rodoviária**, uniformed, who are the traffic police. **Polícia Militar** is the uniformed, street police force, under the control of the state governor, handling all state laws. They are not the same as the Armed Forces' internal police. **Polícia Civil**, also state-controlled, handle local laws; usually in civilian dress, unless in the traffic division.

Where to stay

Hotels
See inside front cover for our hotel grade price guide.

The best guide to hotels in Brazil is the *Guia Brasil Quatro Rodas*, with good maps of towns. Motels are specifically intended for very short-stay couples: there is no stigma attached and they usually offer good value (the rate for a full night is called the *pernoite*), though the decor can be a little unsettling. The type known as *hotel familia*, to be found in the interior – large meals, communal washing, hammocks for children – is much cheaper, but only for the enterprising. *Pousadas* are the equivalent of bed-and-breakfast, often small and family run, although some are very sophisticated and correspondingly priced. Usually hotel prices include breakfast; there is no reduction if you don't eat it. In the better hotels (category **B** and upwards) the breakfast is well worth eating: rolls, ham, eggs, cheese, cakes, fruit. Normally the *apartamento* is a room with bath; a *quarto* is a room without bath. The service stations (*postos*) and hostels (*dormitórios*) along the main roads provide excellent value in room and food, akin to truck-driver type accommodation in Europe, for those on a tight budget. The star rating system for hotels (five-star hotels are not price-controlled) is not the standard used in North America or Europe. Business visitors are strongly recommended to book in advance, and this can be easily done for Rio or São Paulo hotels with representation abroad. If staying more than three nights in a place in low season, ask for a discount.

NB Taxi drivers will try to take you to expensive hotels, who pay them commission for bringing in custom. Beware! Leave rooms in good time so frigobar bills can be checked; we have received reports of overcharging in otherwise good hotels

Roteiros de Charme In 31 locations in the Southeast and Northeast, this is a private association of hotels and *pousadas* which aims to give a high standard of accommodation in establishments which represent the town they are in. If you are travelling in the appropriate budget range (our **A** price range upwards), you can plan an itinerary which takes in these

Brazil

hotels, with a reputation for comfort and good food, and some fine places of historical and leisure interest. Roteiros de Charme hotels are listed in the text and any one of them can provide information on the group. Alternatively, contact office in *Caesar Park Hotel* in Rio de Janeiro Av Vieira Souto 460, Ipanema, T0xx21-2525 2525, F2522 1102, www.roteirosdecharme.com.br

Youth hostels For information about youth hostels contact **Federação Brasileira de Albergues da Juventude**, R Gen Dionísio 63, Botafogo, Rio de Janeiro, RJ 2222271-050, T0xx21-2286 0303, F2286 5652, www.albergues.com.br Its brochure provides a full list of good value accommodation. Also see the **Internet Guide to Hostelling** which has list of Brazilian youth hostels: www.hostels.com/br.html Low-budget travellers with student cards (photograph needed) can use the Casa dos Estudantes network.

Camping Members of the *Camping Clube do Brasil* or those with an international campers' card pay only half the rate of a non-member, which is US$10-15 pp. The Club has 43 sites in 13 states and 80,000 members. For enquiries, **Camping Clube do Brasil**, Divisão de Campings, R Senador Dantas 75, 29th floor T210 3171, Rio de Janeiro, ccb@ax.ibase.org.br It may be difficult to get into some Clube campsites during the high season (Jan-Feb). Private campsites charge about US$8 pp. For those on a very low budget and in isolated areas where there is no camp site, service stations can be used as camping sites (Shell stations recommended); they have shower facilities, watchmen and food; some have dormitories; truck drivers are a mine of information. There are also various municipal sites; both types are mentioned in the text. Campsites often tend to be some distance from public transport routes and are better suited to those with their own transport. Never camp at the side of a road; wild camping is generally not possible. Good camping equipment may be purchased in Brazil and there are several rental companies. Camping gas cartridges are easy to buy in sizeable towns in the south, eg in HM shops. *Guia de Camping* is produced by Artpress, R Araçatuba 487, São Paulo 05058; it lists most sites and is available in bookshops in most cities. Quatro Rodas' *Guia Brasil* lists main campsites, see page 332. Most sizeable towns have laundromats with self service. *Lavanderias* do the washing for you but are expensive.

Getting around

Air
External tickets must be paid for in dollars

Because of the great distances, flying is often the most practical option. Internal air services are highly developed and the larger cities are linked several times a day. All national airlines offer excellent service on their internal flights. The largest airlines are *TAM, Varig,* and *Vasp*. Rio-Sul and Nordeste (both allied to *Varig*) and *Transportes Aéreos Regionais* have extensive networks.

Deregulation has reduced prices by about a third, so flying is more affordable than of late. In addition, no-frills airlines are starting up: *Gol* (T0300-789 2121, with English-speaking operators, or www.voegol.com.br, but website is in Portuguese), *BRA, Trip* and *ATA*. Double check all bookings (reconfirm frequently) and information given by ground staff. Economic cutbacks have led to pressure on ground service, including baggage handling (but not to flight service).

Internal flights often have many stops and are therefore quite slow. Most airports have left-luggage lockers (US$2 for 24 hrs). Seats are often unallocated on internal flights: board in good time. Available in all airports is the Protecto-Bag, US$8, a plastic wrapping which helps prevent opportunistic thieving.

Varig and *TAM* offer 21-day air passes, but since deregulation these are not as good value as they used to be. The **Varig** and **TAM** airpasses cover all Brazil and each costs US$530 for five coupons. Additional coupons, up to a maximum of nine, cost US$100 each. All sectors must be booked before the start of the journey. Two flights forming one connection count as one coupon. The same sector may not be flown more than once in the same direction. Date or route changes are charged at US$30. There is no child discount, but infants pay 10%. For the *TAM* airpass, passengers may arrive in Brazil on any carrier. *Varig* passengers must arrive on *Varig* or, if coming from the UK, *British Airways*. Routes must be specified before arrival.

All airpasses must be purchased outside Brazil, no journey may be repeated and none may be used on the Rio-São Paulo shuttle. Remember domestic airport tax has to be paid at each departure. Hotels in the *Tropical* and *Othon* chains, and others, offer discounts of 10% to Varig airpass travellers. Promotions on certain destinations offer a free flight, hotel room, etc; enquire when buying the airpass. Converting the voucher can take some hours, do not plan an onward flight immediately, check at terminals that the airpass is still registered, faulty cancellations have been reported. Cost and restrictions on the airpass are subject to change.

Small scheduled domestic airlines operate Brazilian-built *Bandeirante* 16-seater prop-jets into virtually every city and town with any semblance of an airstrip.

Road

Though the best paved highways are heavily concentrated in the southeast, those serving the interior are being improved to all-weather status and many are paved. Brazil has over 1.65 million km of highways, of which 150,000 km are paved, and several thousand more all-weather. Most main roads between principal cities are paved. Some are narrow and therefore dangerous. Many are in poor condition.

Bus

Many town buses have turnstiles which can be inconvenient if you are carrying a large pack. Urban buses normally serve local airports

There are three standards of bus: *comum* (conventional), which are quite slow, not very comfortable and fill up quickly; *executivo* (executive), which are a few reais more expensive, comfortable (many have reclining seats), but don't stop to pick up passengers en route and are therefore safer; and *leito* (literally, bed), which run at night between the main centres, offering reclining seats with foot and leg rests, toilets, and sometimes refreshments, at double the normal fare. For journeys over 100 km, most buses have chemical toilets. A/c can make *leito* buses cold at night, so take a blanket or sweater (and plenty of toilet paper); on some services blankets are supplied. Some companies have hostess service. Ask for window seats (*janela*), or odd numbers if you want the view.

Brazilian bus services have a top speed limit of 80 kph (buses are supposed to have governors fitted). They stop fairly frequently (every 2-4 hrs) for snacks. The cleanliness of these *postos* is generally good, though may be less so in the poorer regions. Standards of comfort on buses and in *postos* vary from line to line, which can be important on long journeys. Take a drink on buses in the north.

Bus stations for interstate services and other long-distance routes are usually called *rodoviárias*. They are normally outside the city centres and offer snack bars, lavatories, left-luggage stores ('guarda volume'), local bus services and information centres. Buy bus tickets at rodoviárias (most now take credit cards), not from travel agents who add on surcharges. Reliable bus information is hard to come by, other than from companies themselves. Some companies allow passengers to purchase return tickets at the point of departure, rather than individual tickets for each leg. Buses usually arrive and depart in very good time; you cannot assume departure will be delayed. *Itapemirim* coaches have a toll-free booking line at T0800-992627, www.itapemirim.com.br

Car & car hire

Driving laws impose severe fines for many infringements of traffic regulations. Driving licences will be endorsed with points for infringements; 20 points = loss of licence

Any foreigner with a passport can purchase a Brazilian car and travel outside Brazil if it is fully paid for or if permission is obtained from the financing body in Brazil. Foreigners do not need the CPF tax document (needed by Brazilians – you only have to say you are a tourist) to purchase a car, and the official purchase receipt is accepted as proof of ownership. Sun papers carry car advertisements and there are second-hand car markets on Sun mornings in most cities – but don't buy an alcohol-driven car if you propose to drive outside Brazil. It is essential to have an external intake filter fitted, or dust can rapidly destroy an engine. VW Combi vans are cheapest in Brazil where they are made, they are equivalent to the pre-1979 model in Europe. Be sure to travel with a car manual and good quality tools, a VW dealer will advise. There are VW garages throughout the continent, but parts (German or Latin American) are not always interchangeable. In the main, though, there should be no problems with large components (eg gears). If a lot of time is to be spent on dirt roads, the Ford Chevrolet pickup is more robust. A letter in Spanish from your consul explaining your aims and that you will return the vehicle to Brazil can make life much easier at borders and checkpoints. Brazilian cars may not meet safety regulations in North America and Europe, but they can be easily resold in Brazil.

Car hire It is essential to have a credit card in order to hire in Brazil; very few agencies accept travellers' cheques, dollars cash may not be accepted, but *reais* cash may qualify for a discount. Renting a car in Brazil is expensive: the cheapest rate for unlimited mileage for a

Brazil

small car is about US$50 per day. Minimum age for renting a car is 21. Companies operate under the terms *aluguel de automóveis* or *autolocadores*. Compare prices of renting from abroad and in Brazil. If you intend to hire a car for a long time, buying and reselling a vehicle within Brazil may be a reasonable alternative.

Fuel prices vary from week to week and region to region *Alcool comun* US$0.65 per litre; *alcool maxi* US$0.67 per litre; *gasolina comun* US$0.70-.80 per litre; *gasolina maxi* US$0.80-0.90 per litre; *maxigold* US$0.89 per litre. There is no unleaded fuel. Diesel is sold for commercial and public service vehicles and costs US$0.40-0.70 per litre, the same price as oil. **NB** It is virtually impossible to buy premium grades of petrol/gasoline anywhere. With alcohol fuel you need about 50% more alcohol than regular gasoline. Larger cars have a small extra tank for 'gasolina' to get the engine started; remember to keep this topped up. Fuel is only 85 octane (owing to high methanol content), so be prepared for bad consumption and poor performance and starting difficulties in non-Brazilian cars in winter. Diesel fuel is cheap and a diesel engine may provide fewer maintenance problems. Service stations are free to open when they like. Very few open during Carnival week.

Taxi
Beware of new Moto Taxis. Many are unlicensed and a number of robberies have been reported

Taxi meters measure distance/cost in *reais*. At the outset, make sure the meter is cleared and shows tariff '1', except 2300-0600, Sun, and in Dec when '2' is permitted. Check the meter works, if not, fix price in advance. Radio taxi service costs about 50% more but cheating is less likely. Taxi services offered by smartly-dressed individuals outside larger hotels usually cost twice as much as ordinary taxis. If you are seriously cheated, note the taxi number and insist on a signed bill, threatening to go to the police; it can work.

Hitchhiking
Information on hitchhiking (*carona* in Portuguese) suggests that it is difficult everywhere; drivers are reluctant to give lifts because passengers are their responsibility. Try at the highway-police check points on the main roads (but make sure your documents are in order) or at the service stations (*postos*).

Boat
The main areas where boat travel is practical (and often necessary) are the Amazon region, along the São Francisco River and along the Atlantic coast. There are also some limited transport services through the Pantanal.

Train
Most passenger services have been withdrawn

There are 30,379 km of railways which are not combined into a unified system. Brazil has two gauges and there is little transfer between them. Two more gauges exist for the isolated Amapá Railway and the tourist-only São João del Rei line. There are passenger services in the state of São Paulo.

Maps & guides
Quatro Rodas, a motoring magazine, publishes an excellent series of maps and guides in Portuguese and English from about US$10. Its *Guia Brasil* is a type of Michelin Guide to hotels, restaurants (not the cheapest), sights, facilities and general information on hundreds of cities and towns in the country, including good street maps (we acknowledge here our debt to this publication). It also publishes a *Guia das Praias*, with descriptions of all Brazil's beaches. Quatro Rodas Guides may be bought in Europe from: 33, rue de Miromesnil, 75008 Paris, T00331-4266 3118, F00331-4266 1399; and *Deltapress-Sociedade Distribuidora de Publicações*, Capa Rota, Tapada Nova, Linhó, 2710 Sintra, Portugal, T003511-924 9940, F003511-924 0429. In USA: Lincoln Building, 60 E 42nd St, Suite 3403, New York, NY 10165/3403, T001212-557 5990/3, F983 0972.

Keeping in touch

Internet
Email is becoming more common and public access to the internet is growing, with cybercafés in all large towns. Head for the nearest shopping mall, or computer school (*escola de informâtica*).

Post
To send a standard letter or postcard to the USA costs US$0.45, to Europe US$0.53, to Australia or South Africa US$0.60. Air mail takes four to seven days to or from Britain or the US;

Brazil

surface mail takes four weeks. 'Caixa Postal' addresses should be used when possible. All places in Brazil have a post code, *CEP*; these are given in the text. Postes restantes usually only hold letters for 30 days. You can buy charge collected stamps, Compraventa de Francamento (CF) for letters only, to be paid on delivery. The Post office sells cardboard boxes for sending packages internally and abroad (they must be submitted open); pay by the kg; you must fill in a list of contents; string, official sellotape is provided in all post offices. Franked and registered (insured) letters are normally secure, but check the amount franked is what you have paid, or the item will not arrive. Aerogrammes are most reliable. It may be easier to avoid queues and obtain higher denomination stamps by buying at the philatelic desk at the main post office. Courier services such as *DHL*, *Federal Express* and *UPS* (recommended) are useful, but note that they may not necessarily operate under those names.

Telephone

Important changes: All ordinary phone numbers in Brazil are changing from seven to eight figure numbers. The process will last until 2005. Enquire locally for the new numbers as in many cases whole numbers will change while others will simply add an extra digit. Where confirmed, 8-digit numbers have been included in the text. Where numbers have changed an electronic message should redirect callers. In addition, privatization of the phone system has led to increased competition. The consumer must now choose a phone company for long distance and international calls by inserting a two-digit code between the zero and the area code. **Phone numbers are now as follows: 0xx21 2540 5212.** 0 for a national call, followed by xx for the company code chosen, eg 21 for *Embratel*, followed by the two digit area code, eg 21 for Rio, followed by the seven, or eight digits of the number you are dialling. Thus the number for the Marina Palace Hotel in Rio would be: 021 21 2294 1644. For international calls: 00, 21 (*Embratel*), 44 (eg UK), then the city code and number.

Embratel (21) has national and international coverage. You can also choose a local operator for long distance calls but only if the call is made to a phone code within their area. For calls made within and between Rio de Janeiro, Minas Gerais, Espírito Santo, Bahia, Sergipe, Alagoas, Pernambuco, Paraíba, Rio Grande do Norte, Ceará, Piauí, Maranhão, Pará, Amapá, Amazonas and Roraima you can choose *Telemar* (31). For calls made within and between Rio Grande do Sul, Santa Catarina, Paraná, Distrito Federal, Goiás, Tocantins, Mato Grosso do Sul, Mato Grosso, Rondônia and Acre use *Tele Centro-Sul* (14). For calls made within São Paulo you can choose either *Telefônica* (15) or *Vésper, São Paulo* (89). *Vésper* also has coverage in 16 other states, using the code 85. From 2002 the operators will be able to make international calls. *Embratel*: www.embratel.com.br *Telemar*: T0800 568888, or www.telemar.com.br *Vésper*: www.vesper.com.br *Telefonica*: www.telefonica.net.br

There are telephone boxes at airports, post offices, railway stations, hotels, most bars, restaurants and cafés, and in the main cities there are telephone kiosks *for local calls only* in the shape of large orange shells, for which *fichas* can be bought from bars, cafés and newsvendors; in Rio they are known as *orelhões* (big ears).

If you need to find a telephone number, you can dial 102 in any city (*auxílio à lista*) and the operator will connect you to a pre-recorded voice which will give the number. To find the number in a different city, dial the DDD code, followed by 121 (so, if you are in Salvador and want to know a Rio number, dial 0xx21 121). If your Portuguese is not up to deciphering spoken numbers, ask a hotel receptionist, for example, to assist you.

Phone cards are available from telephone offices, newstands, post offices and some chemists. Public boxes for intercity calls are blue; there are boxes within main telephone offices for international calls, make sure you buy a card worth at least 100 international units. To use the telephone office, tell the operator which city or country you wish to call, go to the booth whose number you are given; make your call and you will be billed on exit. Not all offices accept credit cards. Collect calls within Brazil can be made from any telephone – dial 9, followed by the number, and announce your name and city. Local calls from a private phone are normally free.

At the moment it is possible to call abroad from public phones only in areas with large numbers of foreign tourists such as Rio. There are, however, boxes within most phone offices for international calls. Make sure you buy at least one 90-unit card or pay at the desk after

Brazil

making your call from a booth. Calls are priced on normal and cheaper rates, depending on time of day. Check with local phone company. Peak rate to Europe is US$4 per min, to USA US$3. There is a 40% tax added to the cost of all communications, which makes international service extremely expensive. Local phone calls and telegrams, though, are quite cheap.

NB Brazil is now linked to North America, Japan and most of Europe by direct dialling. Codes are listed in the telephone directories. *Embratel* operates Home Country Direct, available from hotels, private phones or blue public phones to the following countries (prefix all numbers with 00080); Argentina 54, Australia 61, Belgium 03211, Bolivia 13, Canada 14, Chile 56 (*Entel*), 36 (*Chile Saturday*), 37 (*CTC Mundo*), Colombia 57, Costa Rica 50, Denmark 45, France 33, Germany 49, Holland 31, Hong Kong 85212, Israel 97, Italy 39, Japan 81 (*KDD*), 83 (*ITJ*), 89 (*Super Japan*), Norway 47, Paraguay 18, Peru 51, Portugal 35, Singapore 65, Spain 34, Sweden 46, Switzerland 04112, UK 44 (*BT Direct*), USA 10 (*AT&T*), 12 (*MCI*), 16 (*Sprint*), 11 (*Worldcom*), Uruguay 59, Venezuela 58. For collect calls from phone boxes (in Portuguese: 'a cobrar'), dial 107 and ask for the *telefonista internacional*.

Fax services operate in main post offices in major cities, at telephone offices, or from private lines. In the last case the international fax rates are as for phone calls; from the post office the rates are US$3-4 per page within Brazil, US$10.50 to Europe and US$9 to the USA. To receive a fax costs US$1.40.

Media **Newspapers** The main **Rio** papers are *Jornal do Brasil*, www.jb.com.br *O Globo*, www.oglobo.com.br *O Dia*, www.uol.com.br/odia and *Jornal do Commércio*, www.jornaldocommercio.com.br **São Paulo** Morning: *O Estado de São Paulo*, www.estado.com.br *Folha de São Paulo*, www.uol.com.br/fsp *Gazeta Mercantil*, www.gazeta.com.br and *Diário de São Paulo*. Evening: *Jornal da Tarde, A Gazeta, Diário da Noite, Ultima Hora*. Around the country, the major cities have their own local press: *Diário de Pernambuco* in Recife, www.dpnet.com.br and the *Estado de Minas* in Belo Horizonte, www.em.com.br Foreign language newspapers include *The Brazilian Post* and *Sunday News* in English, and *Deutsche Zeitung* in German. In **Europe**, the *Euro-Brasil Press* is available in most capitals; it prints Brazilian and some international news in Portuguese. London office 23 Kings Exchange, Tileyard Rd, London N7 9AH, T020-7700 4033, F7700 3540, eurobrasilpress@compuserve.com **Magazines** There are a number of good, informative weekly news magazines: *Veja*: www.vejaonline.uol.com.br *Istoé*: www.uol.com.br/istoe *Exame*: www2.uol.com.br/exame/index.shl **Radio** English-language radio broadcasts daily at 15290 kHz, 19 m Short Wave (Rádio Bras, Caixa Postal 04/0340, DF-70 323 Brasília).

Food and drink

Food
The main meal is usually taken in the middle of the day; cheap restaurants tend not to be open in the evening

The most common dish is *bife (ou frango) com arroz e feijão*, steak (or chicken) with rice and the excellent Brazilian black beans. The most famous dish with beans is the *feijoada completa*: several meat ingredients (jerked beef, smoked sausage, smoked tongue, salt pork, along with spices, herbs and vegetables) are cooked with the beans. Manioc flour is sprinkled over it, and it is eaten with kale (*couve*) and slices of orange, and accompanied by glasses of *aguardente* (unmatured rum), usually known as *cachaça* (booze), though *pinga* (drop) is a politer term. Almost all restaurants serve the *feijoada completa* for Saturday lunch (that means up to about 1630).

Throughout Brazil, a mixed grill, including excellent steak, served with roasted manioc flour (farofa; raw manioc flour is known as farinha goes under the name of churrasco (it came originally from the cattlemen of Rio Grande do Sul), normally served in specialized restaurants known as churrascarias or rodízios; good places for large appetites

Bahia has some excellent fish dishes (see note on page 471); some restaurants in most of the big cities specialize in them. *Vatapá* is a good dish in the north; it contains shrimp or fish sauced with palm oil, or coconut milk. *Empadinhas de camarão* are worth trying; they are shrimp patties, with olives and heart of palm.

Minas Gerais has two splendid special dishes involving pork, black beans, *farofa* and kale; they are *tutu á mineira* and *feijão tropeiro*. A white hard cheese (*queijo prata*) or a slightly softer one (*queijo Minas*) is often served for dessert with bananas, or guava or quince paste. *Comida mineira* is quite distinctive and very wholesome and you can often find restaurants serving this type of food in other parts of Brazil.

Meals are extremely large by European standards; portions are usually for two and come with two plates. Likewise beer is brought with two glasses. If you are on your own and in a position to do so tactfully, you may choose to offer what you can't eat to a person with no food (observe the correct etiquette). Alternatively you could ask for an *embalagem* (doggy bag) or get a take away called a *marmita* or *quentinha*, most restaurants have this service but it is not always on the menu. Many restaurants now serve *comida por kilo* where you serve yourself and pay for the weight of food on your plate. Unless you specify to the contrary many restaurants will lay a *coberto opcional*, olives, carrots, etc, costing US$0.50-0.75. **Warning** Avoid mussels, marsh crabs and other shellfish caught near large cities: they are likely to have lived in a highly polluted environment. In a restaurant, always ask the price of a dish before ordering.

For vegetarians, there is a growing network of restaurants in the main cities. In smaller places where food may be monotonous try vegetarian for greater variety. Most also serve fish. Alternatives in smaller towns are the Arab and Chinese restaurants.

There is fruit all the year round, ranging from banana and orange to mango, pawpaw, custard-apple (*fruta do conde*) and guava. One should try the *manga de Ubá*, a non-fibrous small mango. Also good are *mora* (a raspberry that looks like a strawberry), *jaboticaba*, a small black damson-like fruit, and *jaca* (jackfruit), a large yellow/green fruit.

The exotic flavours of Brazilian ice creams should be experienced. Try *açaí*, *bacuri*, *biribá*, *buruti*, *cupuaçu* (not eveyone's favourite), *mari-mari*, *mucajá*, *murici*, *pajurá*, *pariri*, *patuá*, *piquiá*, *pupunha*, *sorva*, *tucumá*, *uxi* and others mentioned below under 'drinks'.

If travelling on a tight budget, remember to ask in restaurants for the *prato feito* or *sortido*, a money-saving, excellent value *table-d'hôte* meal. The *prato comercial* is similar but rather better and a bit more expensive. *Lanchonetes* are cheap eating places where you generally pay before eating. *Salgados* (savoury pastries), *coxinha* (a pyramid of manioc filled with meat or fish and deep fried), *esfiha* (spicey hamburger inside an onion-bread envelope), *empadão* (a filling – eg chicken – in sauce in a pastry case), *empadas* and *empadinhas* (smaller fritters of the same type), are the usual fare. In Minas Gerais, *pão de queijo* is a hot roll made with cheese. A *bauru* is a toasted sandwich which, in Porto Alegre, is filled with steak, while further north it has tomato, ham and cheese filling. *Cocada* is a coconut and sugar biscuit.

Drink

Imported drinks are expensive, but there are some fair local wines. Chilean and Portuguese wines are sometimes available at little more than the cost of local wines. The beers are good and there are plenty of local soft drinks. *Guaraná* is a very popular carbonated fruit drink. There is an excellent range of non-alcoholic fruit juices, known as *sucos*: *caju* (cashew), *pitanga*, *goiaba* (guava), *genipapo*, *graviola* (= *chirimoya*), *maracujá* (passion-fruit), *sapoti* and *tamarindo* are recommended. *Vitaminas* are thick fruit or vegetable drinks with milk. *Caldo de cana* is sugar-cane juice, sometimes mixed with ice. Remember that *água mineral*, available in many varieties at bars and restaurants, is a cheap, safe thirst-quencher (cheaper still in supermarkets). Apart from the ubiquitous coffee, good tea is grown and sold. **NB** If you don't want sugar in your coffee or *suco*, you must ask when you order it. *Água de côco* or *côco verde* (coconut water from fresh green coconut) cannot be missed in the Northeast.

Among the better wines are Château d'Argent, Château Duvalier, Almadén, Dreher, Preciosa and Bernard Taillan. The red Marjolet from Cabernet grapes and the Moselle-type white Zahringer have been well spoken of. It has often been noticed that a new *adega* starts off well, but the quality gradually deteriorates with time; many vintners have switched to American Concorde grapes, producing a rougher wine. Greville Brut champagne-type is inexpensive and very drinkable. A white-wine *Sangria*, containing tropical fruits such as pineapple and papaya, is worth looking out for. The Brahma, Cerpa and Antártica beers are really excellent, of the lager type, and are cheaper by the bottle than on draught. Buying bottled drinks in supermarkets, you may be asked for empties in return.

The local firewater, *aguardente* (known as *cachaça* or *pinga*), made from sugar-cane, is cheap and wholesome, but visitors should seek local advice on the best brands; São Francisco,

Praianinha, Maria Fulô, '51' and Pitu are recommended makes. Mixed with fruit juices of various sorts, sugar and crushed ice, *cachaça* becomes the principal element in a *batida*, a delicious and powerful drink; the commonest is a lime batida or *batida de limão*; a variant of this is the *caipirinha*, a *cachaça* with several slices of lime in it, a *caipiroska* is made with vodka. *Cachaça* with Coca-Cola is a *cuba*, while rum with Coca-Cola is a *cuba libre*. Some genuine Scotch whisky brands are bottled in Brazil; they are very popular because of the high price of Scotch imported in bottle; Teacher's is the most highly regarded brand. Locally made gin vermouth and campari are very good.

Shopping

As a rule, shopping is easier, quality more reliable and prices higher in the shopping centres (mostly excellent) and in the wealthier suburbs. Better prices at the small shops and street traders; most entertaining at markets and on the beach. Bargaining (with good humour) is expected in the latter

Gold, diamonds and gemstones throughout Brazil. Innovative designs in jewellery: buy 'real' at reputable dealers (best value in Minas Gerais); cheap, fun pieces from street traders. Interesting furnishings made with gemstones, marble; clay figurines from the northeast; lace from Ceará; leatherwork; strange pottery from Amazônia; carvings in soapstone and in bone; tiles and other ceramic work, African-type pottery and basketwork from Bahia. Many large hotel gift shops stock a good selection of handicrafts at reasonable prices. Brazilian cigars are excellent for those who like the mild flavours popular in Germany, the Netherlands and Switzerland. Recommended purchases are musical instruments, eg guitars, other stringed, and percussion instruments. Excellent textiles: good hammocks from the northeast; other fabrics; design in clothing is impressive, though not equalled by manufacturing quality. Buy your beachwear in Brazil: it is matchless. For those who know how to use them, medicinal herbs, barks and spices from street markets; coconut oil and local skin and haircare products (fantastic conditioners) are better and cheaper than in Europe, but known brands of toiletries are exorbitant. Other bad buys are film (including processing), cameras and electrical goods (including batteries). Sunscreen, sold in department stores and large supermarkets, is expensive.

Holidays and festivals

Carnival freephone number for tourists for all Carnival destinations 0800-701 1250, 24 hrs, English, Spanish, Portuguese

National holidays are 1 January (New Year); three days up to and including Ash Wednesday (Carnival); 21 April (Tiradentes); 1 May (Labour Day); Corpus Christi (June); 7 September (Independence Day); 12 October, Nossa Senhora Aparecida; 2 November (All Souls' Day); 15 November (Day of the Republic); and 25 December (Christmas). The local holidays in the main cities are given in the text. Four religious or traditional holidays (Good Friday must be one; other usual days: 1 November, All Saints Day; 24 December, Christmas Eve) must be fixed by the municipalities. Other holidays are usually celebrated on the Monday prior to the date.

Sport and special interest travel

Birdwatching and nature tourism Birdwatching can be very rewarding and the possibilities are too numerous to cover in this brief introduction. Habitats include Amazonian rainforest, the Pantanal wetlands, the subtropical forest at Iguaçu, the *cerrado* of the central plateau, the arid northeast, the Lagoa dos Patos of Rio Grande do Sul and the few remaining pockets of *Mata Atlântica* of the east coast. None is difficult to get to, but it would be impossible to visit every type of environment in one trip to the country. A huge variety of birds can be seen, including many endemics, but it is worth remembering that flora and mammals and reptiles in many of the different regions are of as much interest as the birds. The system of national parks and protected areas, including those offshore (Abrolhos, Fernando de Noronha), is designed to allow access to Brazil's areas of outstanding beauty for education and recreation as well as scientific research. **Ibama**, address on page 332, can provide information. A tour operator specializing in bird-watching and environmentally responsible travel is *Focus Tours*, 103 Moya Rd, Santa Fe, MN 87508, T505-466 4688, F505-466 4689, www.focustours.com The Focus Conservation Fund is a private, non-profit organization concerned with projects in the Pantanal (the Jaguar Ecological Reserve), the Amazon and the Caratinga region in Minas Gerais.

Brazil

Canoeing: This is supervised by the **Confederação Brasileira de Canoagem** (CBCa). It covers all aspects of the sport, speed racing, slalom, downriver, surfing and ocean kayaking. For downriver canoeing, go to **Visconde de Mauá** (Rio de Janeiro state) where the Rio Preto is famous for the sport; also the Rio Formoso at **Bonito** (Mato Grosso do Sul). A recommended river for slalom is the Pranhana, **Três Coroas**, Rio Grande do Sul. For kayak surfing the best places are Rio, the Ilha de Santa Catarina and Ubatuba, while ocean kayaking is popular in Rio, Búzios and Santos (São Paulo).

Caving There are some wonderful cave systems in Brazil and Ibama, the National Parks institute, has a programme for the protection of the national speleological heritage. National parks such as Ubajara (Ceará) and Chapada Diamantina (Bahia) and the state park of PETAR (São Paulo) have easy access for the casual visitor, but there are also many options for the keen potholer in the states of São Paulo, Paraná, Minas Gerais and the Federal District.

Climbing As Brazil has no mountain ranges of Andean proportions, the most popular form of climbing (*escalada*) is rock-face climbing. In the heart of Rio, you can see, or join, climbers scaling the rocks at the base of Pão de Açúcar and on the Sugar Loaf itself. Not too far away, the Serra dos Órgões provides plenty of challenges, not least the Dedo de Deus (God's Finger). Rio de Janeiro is the state where the sport is most fully developed, but not far behind are Paraná, Minas Gerais, São Paulo and Rio Grande do Sul.

Cycling Brazil is well-suited to cycling, both on and off-road. On main roads it is important to obey the general advice of being on the look out for motor vehicles as cyclists are very much second-class citizens. Also note that when cycling on the coast you may encounter strong winds which will hamper your progress. There are endless roads and tracks suitable for **mountain biking**, and there are many clubs in major cities which organize group rides, activities and competitions.

Diving: The Atlantic coast offers many possibilities for scuba diving (*mergulho* in Portuguese). Offshore, the marine park of Abrolhos (Bahia) is a good site, but the prize above all others is **Fernando de Noronha** (Pernambuco) in the open Atlantic. The underwater landscape is volcanic, with cliffs, caverns and some corals, but the marine life that shelters here is magnificent. There are sharks, a protected breeding ground of hawksbill and green turtles and, the greatest draw for divers, a bay which is the home for a pod of several hundred spinner dolphin. In the archipelago there are a number of dive sites. Also in Pernambuco, **Recife** (where planes for Fernando de Noronha leave) is a diving centre, particularly for wrecks. The reef that protects the shore up to Recife provides sheltered swimming, natural pools and many rewarding diving spots. Full of marine life, this warm, clear, greenish-blue sea attracts global visitors as well as holidaymaking Brazilians, but, fortunately, is extensive enough to accommodate everyone without becoming overcrowded. Local fishermen still use hand-trawled nets and *jangadas* (sail-powered rafts which skim just below the water's surface). Visiting sea anglers are urged to respect local traditions: many species are in danger of extinction, as is the coral which is threatened by any disturbance and all forms of pollution. Moving south, Bahia's most popular dive sites are **Abrolhos** (already mentioned) and **Porto Seguro**. In the Southeast, **Búzios, Arraial do Cabo, Cabo Frio** to the north of Rio, and, south of the state capital, the island-filled bay of **Angra dos Reis**, together with **Ilha Grande**, and **Paraty** are all recommended. **Ilhabela/São Sebastião** in São Paulo state offers good opportunities for wreck diving and other places in the state include **Ubatuba, Laje de Santos** and **Ilha de Alcatrazes**. At Fernando de Noronha and Recife you can dive all year, although Recife (like anywhere on the coast) may be subject to strong currents. The further south you go, the lower the water temperatures become in winter (15-20°C). Currents and weather can affect visibility. In some areas in Brazil, diving includes underwater sport fishing; if you like this sort of thing, contact a company which specializes in fishing.

Ecotourism To some extent there is a mingling of ecotourism and adventure tourism in Brazil. This is partly because the adventurous activities nearly always take place in unspoilt parts of the country, but also because the term 'ecotourism' is applied to almost any outdoor activity. There is a Brazilian institute of ecotourism, **Instituo Brasileiro de Ecoturismo** (IEB), Rua Minerva 156, Perdizes, São Paulo, T0xx11-3672 7571, F3673 5156, www.ecoturismo.org.br In Minas Gerais, **Amo-Te**, the Associação Mineira dos Organizadores do Turismo Ecológico, R Prof Morais 624, Apto 302, Savassi, Belo Horizonte, T0xx31-3281 5094, is helpful.

Brazil

Fishing: Brazil has enormous potential for angling given the number and variety of its rivers, lakes and reservoirs. Add to this the scope for sea-angling along the Atlantic coast and it is not difficult to see why the sport is gaining in popularity. Officially, the country's fish stocks are under the control of Ibama (see above) and a licence is required for fishing in any waters. The states of Mato Grosso and Mato Grosso do Sul require people fishing in their rivers to get the states' own fishing permit, which is not the same as an Ibama licence. All details on prices, duration and regulations concerning catches can be obtained from Ibama; the paperwork can be found at Ibama offices, some branches of the Banco do Brasil and some agencies which specialize in fishing. In Mato Grosso and Mato Grosso do Sul information is provided by *Sema*, the Special Environment Secretariat, and documents may be obtained at fishing agencies or HSBC in Mato Grosso do Sul. Freshwater fishing can be practised in so many places that the best bet is to make local enquiries on arrival. You can then find out about the rivers, lakes and reservoirs, which fish you are likely to find and what types of angling are most suited to the conditions. Favoured rivers include tributaries of the Amazon, those in the Pantanal and the Rio Araguaia, but there are many others. Agencies can arrange fishing trips and there are local magazines on the subject.

Hang gliding and paragliding Hang gliding and paragliding are both covered by the **Associação Brasileira de Vôo Livre** (ABVL – Brazilian Hangliding Association, Rio de Janeiro, T0xx21-3322 0266). There are state associations affiliated with ABVL and there are a number of operators who offer tandem flights for those without experience. Launch sites (called *rampas*) are growing in number. Among the best-known is Pedra Bonita at Gávea in Rio de Janeiro, but there are others in the state. Popular *rampas* can also be found in São Paulo, Espírito Santo, Minas Gerais, Paraná, Santa Catarina, Rio Grande do Sul, Ceará, Mato Grosso do Sul and Brasília.

Trekking This is very popular, especially in Rio de Janeiro, São Paulo, Minas Gerais, Paraná and Rio Grande do Sul. There are plenty of hiking agencies which handle hiking tours. Trails are frequently graded according to difficulty; this is noticeably so in areas where *trilhas ecológicas* have been laid out in forests or other sites close to busy tourist areas. Many national parks and protected areas provide good opportunities for trekking (eg the Chapada Diamantina in Bahia) and local information can easily be found to get you on the right track.

Some of the best trails for **horse riding** are the routes that used to be taken by the mule trains that transported goods between the coast and the interior. A company like *Tropa Serrana* in Belo Horizonte (T0xx31-3344 8986/9983 2356, tropaserrana@hotmail.com) is an excellent place to start because their tours, including overnight horse treks, explore many aspects of the Minas Gerais countryside that visitors do not normally see.

Water sports Surfing: This can be enjoyed in just about every coastal state. It does not require permits; all you need is a board and the right type of wave. Brazilians took up surfing in the 1930s and have been practising ever since: in this beach-obsessed country, with 8,000 km of coastline, all shore and water sports are taken seriously. A favourite locale is **Fernando de Noronha**, the archipelago, 345 km out in the Atlantic, but the best waves are found in the south, where long stretches of the Atlantic, often facing the swell head-on, give some excellent and varied breaks. Many Brazilian surf spots are firmly on the international championship circuit: best known is **Saquarema**, in Rio de Janeiro state.

White water rafting: This started in Brazil in 1992. Companies offer trips in São Paulo state (eg on the Rios Juquiá, Jaguarí, do Peixe, Paraibuna), in Rio de Janeiro (also on the Paraibuna, at Três Rios in the Serra dos Órgãos), Paraná (Rio Ribeira), Santa Catarina (Rio Itajaí) and Rio Grande do Sul (Três Coroas).

Health

If you are going to Amazônia, or to other low-lying forested areas, malaria prophylaxis is necessary (this can be difficult to obtain in some areas – the local name for *Paludrine* is *Doroprim*) and water purification tablets are essential. Dengue fever is now endemic in Brazil, and Rio de Janeiro is one of the worst places. Sporadic outbreaks of cholera have occurred in the Amazon region and on the northeast coast (eg Recife), but numbers have been in the tens, rather than the hundreds. Also, in the Amazon basin, sandflies abound. Be very careful about bathing in lakes or slow rivers anywhere in Brazil: harmful parasites abound (including the snails that carry schistosomiasis – this disease is rampant in Minas Gerais and most of central Brazil). South of the Amazon beware of *borrachudos*, small flies with a sharp bite that attack ankles and calves; coconut oil deters them.

See also the Health section, Essentials at the beginning of the book, page 56 For information on vaccinations, see pages 56 and 334

Water should not be drunk from taps unless there is a porcelain filter attached or unless you have water sterilizing tablets (*Hydrosteril* is a popular local brand); there is mineral water in plenty and excellent light beer, known as 'chopp' (pronounced 'shoppi'), and soft drinks. For those who have been in Brazil for a while, *água gelada* (chilled water) is usually safe to drink, being filtered water kept in a refrigerator in most hotels, restaurants and stores. Avoid ice in cheap hotels and restaurants; it is likely to be made from unfiltered water. *Colestase* is the recommended local treatment for upset stomachs.

Brazilians are famous for their open sexuality: appearances can be deceptive, however, and attitudes vary widely. To generalize, the coastal cities are very easy-going, while in smaller towns and the interior, traditional morals are strictly enforced. HIV is widespread, primarily transmitted by heterosexual sex, and tolerance of male homosexuality is diminishing. You should take reliable condoms with you, even if you are sure you won't be needing them. Local condoms are reported not to be reliable.

Tampons are available, as are *Hydrocare* contact lens products (expensive).

If staying in Brazil for any length of time, it is recommended to take out Brazilian health insurance; *Banco Econômico* and *Citibank* are reported to provide good advice.

Brazil

Brasília

Rio de Janeiro

Phone code: 0xx21
Colour map 4, grid C3
Population: 8 million

Brazilians say: God made the world in six days; the seventh he devoted to Rio. (Pronounced Heeoo by locals). Rio has a glorious theatrical backdrop of tumbling wooded mountains, stark expanses of bare rock and a deep blue sea studded with rocky islands. From the statue of Christ on the hunchbacked peak of Corcovado, or from the conical Pão de Açúcar (Sugar Loaf), you can experience the beauty of a bird's-eye view over the city which sweeps 220 km along a narrow alluvial strip on the southwestern shore of the Baía de Guanabara. Although best known for the curving Copacabana beach, for Ipanema – home to the Girl and beautiful sunsets, and for its swirling, reverberating, joyous Carnival, Rio also has a fine artistic, architectural and cultural heritage from its time as capital of both imperial and republican Brazil. But this is first and foremost a city dedicated to leisure: sport and music rule and a day spent hang-gliding or surfing is easily followed by an evening of jazz or samba.

Ins & outs
See also Transport, page 374

Getting there Most international flights stop at the **Aeroporto Internacional** Antônio Carlos Jobim on the Ilha do Governador. Left luggage only in Terminal 1. The air bridge from São Paulo ends at Santos Dumont airport in the town centre. Taxis from here are much cheaper than from the international airport. There are also frequent buses.

International and buses from other parts of Brazil arrive at the **Rodoviária Novo Rio** (main bus station) near the docks.

Getting around Because the city is a series of separate districts connected by urban highways and tunnels, you will need to take public transport. Walking is only an option once you are in the district you want to explore. An underground railway, the **Metrô**, runs under some of the centre and the south and is being extended. Buses run to all parts, but should be treated with caution at night when taxis are a better bet.

Climate Rio has one of the healthiest climates in the tropics. Trade winds cool the air. Jun, Jul and Aug are the coolest months with temperatures ranging from 22°C (18° in a cold spell) to 32°C on a sunny day at noon. Dec to Mar is hotter, from 32°C to 42°C. Humidity is high. It is important, especially for children, to guard against dehydration in summer by drinking as much liquid as possible. Oct to Mar is the rainy season. Annual rainfall is about 1,120 mm.

Tourist offices Riotur, R da Assembléia 10, 9th floor, T2217 7575, F2531 1872, www.rio.rj.gov.br/riotur Main information office: Av Princesa Isabel 183, Copacabana, T2541 7522, Mon-Fri 0900-1800, helpful with English and German spoken by some staff, has good city maps and a very useful free brochure *RIO*, in Portuguese and English. More information stands can be found at the international airport (0600-2400) and at Rodoviária Novo Rio (0800-2000), both very friendly and helpful in finding accommodation. *Alô Rio* is an information service in English and Portuguese, T2542 8080/0800-707 1808, daily from 0900-1800. **TurisRio**, R da Ajuda 5, 8th floor, T2215 0011, www.turisrio.rj.gov.br Information on the state of Rio de Janeiro. **Embratur**, R Uruguaiana 174, 8th floor, Centro, T2509 6017, www.embratur.gov.br Information on the whole of Brazil. The best guide to Rio, with excellent maps, is *Guia Quatro Rodas do Rio* in Portuguese and English (the *Guia Quatro Rodas do Brasil*, published annually in Nov, also has a good Rio section). *Trilhas do Rio*, by Pedro da Cunha e Meneses (Editora Salamandra, 2nd edition), US$22.50, describes walking trips around Rio. The guide *Restaurantes do Rio*, by Danusia Bárbara, published annually by Senac at around US$10.00 (in Portuguese only), is worth looking at for the latest ideas on where to eat in both the city and state of Rio. *Rio Botequim*, an annual guide to the best, most traditional bars and bistros, is published by the Prefeitura, US$12. Many hotels provide guests with the weekly *Rio This Month*. There is an online Favela news agency with news, comment and links, aimed at helping people understand better this aspect of the city: www.anf.org.br See also Tour operators.

Brazil

Safety The majority of visitors enjoy Rio's glamour and the rich variety of experience it has to offer without any problems. It is worth remembering that, despite its beach culture, carefree atmosphere and friendly people, Rio is one of the world's most densely populated cities. If you live in London, Paris, New York or Los Angeles and behave with the same caution in Rio that you do at home, you will be unlucky to encounter any crime. The **Tourist Police**, Av Afrânio de Melo Franco, Leblon (in front of the Casa Grande theatre), T2511 5112, publish a sensible advice leaflet (available from hotels and consulates: consulates also issue safety guidelines). Tourist police officers are helpful, efficient and multilingual. All the main tourist areas are patrolled. If you have any problems, contact the tourist police first.

History The Portuguese navigator, Gonçalo Coelho, arrived at what is now Rio de Janeiro on 1 January 1502. Thinking that the Baía de Guanabara (the name the local Indians used) was the mouth of a great river, they called the place the January River. Although the bay was almost as large and as safe a harbour as the Baía de Todos Os Santos to the north, the Portuguese did not take of advantage of it. In fact, it was first settled by the French, who, under the Huguenot Admiral Nicholas Durand de Villegagnon, occupied Lage Island on 10 November 1555, but later transferred to Seregipe Island (now Villegagnon), where they built the fort of Coligny.

In early 1559-60, Mem de Sá, third governor of Brazil, mounted an expedition from Salvador to attack the French. The Portuguese finally took control in 1567. Though constantly attacked by Indians, the new city grew rapidly and when King Sebastião divided Brazil into two provinces, Rio was chosen capital of the southern captaincies. Salvador became sole capital again in 1576, but Rio again became the southern capital in 1608 and the seat of a bishopric.

Rio de Janeiro was by the 18th century becoming the leading city in Brazil. Not only was it the port out of which gold was shipped, but it was also the focus of the

Brazil

Rio de Janeiro orientation & Metrô

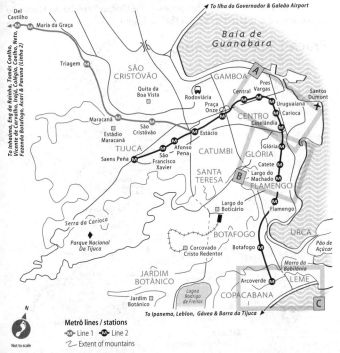

Metrô lines / stations
–Ⓜ– Line 1   –Ⓜ– Line 2
〰 Extent of mountains
Not to scale

Related maps
A Rio de Janeiro centre,
 page 352
B Glória, Santa Teresa, Catete, Flamengo,
 page 356
C Copacabana,
 page 360
Praça 15 de Novembro,
 page 350

export/import trade of the surrounding agricultural lands. On 27 January 1763, it became the seat of the Viceroy. After independence, in 1834, it was declared capital of the Empire and remained the capital for 125 years.

Sights: central Rio

The city is usually divided into north and south zones, Zona Norte and Zona Sul, with the historical and business centre, O Centro, in between. The parts that most interest visitors are the centre itself and the Zona Sul, which has the famous districts of Flamengo, Botafogo, Urca, Copacabana, Ipanema, Leblon and then out to the newer suburb of Barra de Tijuca.

The city's main artery is the Avenida Presidente Vargas, 4½ km long and over 90 m wide. It starts at the waterfront, divides to embrace the famous Candelária church, then crosses the Avenida Rio Branco in a magnificent straight stretch past the Central do Brasil railway station, with its imposing clock tower, until finally it incorporates a palm-lined, canal-divided avenue. The second principal street in the centre is the Avenida Rio Branco, nearly 2 km long, on which only a few ornate buildings remain, by Cinelândia and the Biblioteca Nacional. Some of the finest modern architecture is to be found along the Avenida República do Chile, such as the Petrobrás, the Banco Nacional de Desenvolvimento Econômico and the former Banco Nacional de Habitação buildings and the new Cathedral.

Around Praça 15 de Novembro
At weekends an antiques, crafts, stamp and coin fair is held from 0900-1900

Praça 15 de Novembro (often called Praça XV) has always been one of the focal points in Rio. Today it has one of the greatest concentrations of historic buildings in the city. The last vestiges of the original harbour, at the seaward end of the Praça, have been restored. The steps no longer lead to the water, but a new open space leads from the Praça to the seafront, beneath the Av Pres Kubitschek flyover. This space now gives easy access to the ferry dock for Niterói.

On Rua 1 de Março, across from Praça 15 de Novembro, there are three buildings related to the Carmelite order. The convent of the **Ordem Terceira do Monte do Carmo**, started in 1611, is now used as the Faculdade Cândido Mendes. The order's

Praça 15 de Novembro

```
0 metres        100
0 yards         100
```

● **Eating**
1 Confeitaria Colombo

present church, the **Igreja da Ordem Terceira do Carmo**, also in R Primeiro de Março, the other side of the old cathedral (see below) from the convent, was built in 1754, consecrated in 1770 and rebuilt between 1797 and 1826. It has strikingly beautiful portals by Mestre Valentim, the son of a Portuguese nobleman and a slave girl. He also created the main altar of fine moulded silver, the throne and its chair and much else. ■ *Mon-Fri 0800-1400, Sat 0800-1200.*

Between the former convent and the Igreja da Ordem Terceira do Carmo is the old cathedral, the **Igreja de Nossa Senhora do Carmo da Antiga Sé**, separated from the Carmo Church by a passageway. It was the chapel of the Convento do Carmo from 1590 until 1754. A new church was built in 1761, which became the city's cathedral. In the crypt are the alleged remains of Pedro Alvares Cabral, the Portuguese explorer (though Santarém, Portugal, also claims to be his last resting place).

The **Paço Imperial** (former Royal Palace) is on the southeast corner of the Praça 15 de Novembro. This beautiful colonial building was built in 1743 as the residence of the governor of the Capitania. It later became the Paço Real when the Portuguese court moved to Brazil. After Independence it became the Imperial Palace. It has the *Bistro* and *Atrium* restaurants. Recommended. ■ *Tue-Sun 1100-1830, T2232 8333*

Igreja de São José (R São José e Av Pres Antônio Carlos), is considerably altered since its 17th century construction.The current building dates from 1824. ■ *Mon-Fri 0900-1200, 1400-1700, Sun 0900-1100.*

On the northwest side of Praça 15 de Novembro, you go through the Arco do Teles and the Travessa do Comércio to Rua do Ouvidor. The **Igreja Nossa Senhora da Lapa dos Mercadores** (R do Ouvidor 35) was consecrated in 1750, remodelled 1869-72 and has been fully restored. ■ *Mon-Fri 0800-1400.* Across the street, with its entrance at R 1 de Março 36, is the church of **Santa Cruz dos Militares**, built 1780-1811. It is large, stately and beautiful and has been well renovated in a 'light' baroque style.

The Church of **Nossa Senhora da Candelária** (1775-1810), on Praça Pio X (Dez), at the city end of Av Pres Vargas where it meets R 1 de Março, has beautiful ceiling decorations and romantic paintings. ■ *Mon-Fri 0730-1200, 1300-1630, Sat 0800-1200, Sun 0900-1300.*

With entrances on Av Pres Vargas and R 1 de Março 66, the **Centro Cultural Banco do Brasil (CCBB)** is highly recommended for good exhibitions. It has a library, multimedia facilities, a cinema, concerts (US$6 at lunchtime) and a restaurant ■ *Tue-Sun 1230-1900, T3808 2000.* Opposite is the **Espaço Cultural dos Correios**, R Visconde de Itaboraí 20, which holds temporary exhibitions and a postage stamp fair on Saturdays. ■ *Tue-Sun 1300-1900, T2503 8770.* **Casa França-Brasil**, R Viscone de Itaboraí 253 and Av Pres Vargas, dates from the first French Artistic Mission to Brazil and it was the first neoclassical building in Rio. ■ *Tue-Sun 1200-2000, T2253 5366.* **Espaço Cultural da Marinha**, on Av Alfredo Agache at Av Pres Kubitschek. This former naval establishment now contains museums of underwater archaeology and navigation and the *Galeota*, the boat used by the Portuguese royal family for sailing around the Baía de Guanabara. Moored outside is the warship, *Bauru* and boats give access to the beautiful **Ilha Fiscal**. ■ *Tue-Sun 1200-1700. Boats to Ilha Fiscal, Fri, Sat, Sun, 1300, 1430, 1600, T3870 6879.*

Just north of Candelária, on a promontory overlooking the bay, is the **Mosteiro** (monastery) **de São Bento**, containing much of what is best in the 17th and 18th century art of Brazil. São Bento is reached either by a narrow road from R Dom Gerardo 68, or by a lift whose entrance is at R Dom Gerardo 40 (taxi to the monastery from centre US$5). The main body of the church is adorned in gold and red. The carving and gilding is remarkable, much of it by Frei Domingos da Conceição. The paintings, too, should be seen. The Chapels of the Immaculate Conception (Nossa Senhora da Conceição) and of the Most Holy Sacrament (Santíssimo Sacramento) are masterpieces of colonial art. The organ, dating from the end of the 18th century, is very interesting. ■ *Daily 0800-1230, 1400-1730, shorts not allowed. Every Sun at 1000, mass is sung with Gregorian chant and music, which is free, but you should arrive an hour early to get a seat. On other days, mass is at 0715.*

Brazil

Around Largo da Carioca The second oldest convent in the city is the **Convento de Santo Antônio**, on a hill off the Largo da Carioca, built between 1608 and 1615. Santo Antônio is a particular object of devotion for women looking for a husband and you will see them in the precincts. The church has a marvellous sacristy adorned with blue tiles and paintings illustrating the life of St Anthony. In the church itself, the baroque decoration is concentrated in the chancel, the main altar and the two lateral altars.

Separated from this church only by some iron railings is the charming church of the Ordem Terceira de **São Francisco da Penitência**, built in 1773. Its Baroque carving and gilding of walls and altar, much more than in its neighbour, is considered among the finest in Rio. There is also a Museu de Arte Sacra. Strongly recommended. ■ *Wed-Fri 1000-1600*.

Across Ruas da Carioca and 7 de Setembro is the Church of **São Francisco de Paula**, at the upper end of the R do Ouvidor. It contains some of Mestre Valentim's work. ■ *Mon-Fri 0900-1300*. One long block behind the Largo da Carioca and São Francisco de Paula is the **Praça Tiradentes**, old and shady, with a statue to Dom Pedro I. At the northeast corner of the praça is the **Teatro João Caetano** (T2221 0305). Shops nearby specialize in selling goods for *umbanda*, the Afro-Brazilian religion. South of the Largo da Carioca are the modern buildings on Avenida República do Chile including the new Cathedral, the **Catedral Metropolitana**, dedicated in

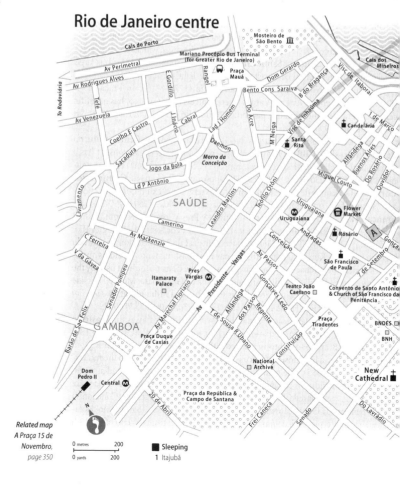

Rio de Janeiro centre

Related map A Praça 15 de Novembro, page 350

0 metres 200
0 yards 200

■ **Sleeping**
1 Itajubá

Brazil

November 1976. It is a cone-shaped building with capacity of 5,000 seated, 20,000 standing. The most striking feature is four enormous 60 m-high stained-glass windows. It is still incomplete. ■ *0800-1800.* Crossing Av República do Paraguai from the cathedral, is the Petrobrás building and the station, with museum, for the tram to Santa Teresa (entrance on R Senador Dantas – see below).

Facing Praça Marechal Floriano is the **Teatro Municipal**, one of the most magnificent buildings in Brazil in the eclectic style. It was built in 1905-09, in imitation of the Opéra in Paris. The decorative features inside and out represent many styles, all lavishly executed. Opera and orchestral performances are given here (T2544 2900). To book a tour of the theatre, ask for extension – *ramal* – 935 in advance. ■ *Mon-Fri 0900-1700, US$2. The box office is at the right hand side of the building; ticket prices start at about US$15.* The **Biblioteca Nacional**, at Av Rio Branco 219 also dates from the first decade of the 20th century. The monumental staircase leads to a hall, off which lead the fine internal staircases of Carrara marble. It houses over nine million volumes and documents. ■ *Mon-Fri 0900, US$1, T2262 8255.* The **Museu Nacional de Belas Artes**, Av Rio Branco 199, was built between 1906 and 1908, in eclectic style. It has about 800 original paintings and sculptures and some thousand direct reproductions. One gallery, dedicated to works by Brazilian artists from the 17th century onwards, includes paintings by Frans Janszoon Post (Dutch 1612-80),

Avenida Rio Branco

Brazil

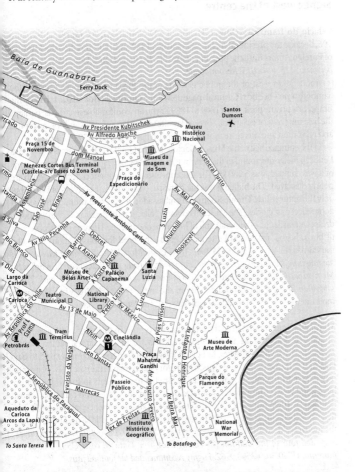

To Santa Teresa   B   To Botafogo

who painted Brazilian landscapes in classical Dutch style, and the Frenchmen Debret and Taunay. Another gallery charts the development of Brazilian art in 20th century. ■ *Tue-Fri 1000-1800, Sat, Sun and holidays 1400-1800, US$1, T2240 0068.*

Praça Mahatma Gandhi, at the end of Av Rio Branco, is flanked on one side by the old cinema and amusement centre of the city, known as Cinelândia. Next to the praça is the **Passeio Público**, a garden planted in 1779-83 by the artist Mestre Valentim, whose bust is near the old former gateway. ■ *Daily 0900-1700.*

Museu do Instituto Histórico e Geográfico, Av Augusto Severo 8 (10th floor), just off Av Beira Mar, is across the street from the Passeio Público. It has an interesting collection of historical objects, Brazilian products and the artefacts of its peoples. ■ *Mon-Fri 1200-1700.*

Praça Marechal Âncora/Praça Rui Barbosa

The **Museu Histórico Nacional**, which contains a collection of historical treasures, colonial sculpture and furniture, maps, paintings, arms and armour, silver and porcelain. ■ *Tue-Fri 1000-1730, Sat, Sun and holidays 1400-1800, US$1, T2550 9224, www.visualnet.com.br/mhr* **Museu da Imagem e do Som**, also on Praça Rui Barbosa, has many photographs of Brazil and modern Brazilian paintings; also collections and recordings of Brazilian classical and popular music and a non-commercial cinema Friday-Sunday. ■ *Mon-Fri 1300-1800.*

Sights: west of the centre

Palácio do Itamaraty (Museu Histórico e Diplomático), Av Marechal Floriano 196, became the president's residence between 1889 and 1897 and then the Ministry of Foreign Affairs until the opening of Brasília. ■ *Guided tours Mon, Wed, Fri hourly between 1315 and 1615. Recommended.*

Quinta da Boa Vista has had the problem of thieves operating by the park entrance and in the park itself

About 3 km west of the public gardens of the Praça da República (beyond the Sambódromo – see box, Carnival, page 362) is the **Quinta da Boa Vista**, formerly the Emperor's private park, from 1809 to 1889. If you are comfortable in crowds, perhaps the best time to visit is Saturday or Sunday afternoon. It is full of locals looking for fun and relaxation and therefore more police are on hand. ■ *Daily 0700-1800.*

In the entrance hall of the **Museu Nacional** in the Quinta da Boa Vista is the famous Bendegó meteorite, found in the State of Bahia in 1888; its original weight, before some of it was chipped, was 5,360 kg. The museum also has important collections which are poorly displayed. The building was the principal palace of the Emperors of Brazil, but only the unfurnished Throne Room and ambassadorial reception room on the second floor reflect past glories. The Museum contains collections of Brazilian Indian weapons, dresses, utensils etc, of minerals and of historical documents. There are also collections of birds, beasts, fishes and butterflies. Despite the need for conservation work, the museum is still worth visiting. ■ *1000-1600, closed Mon, US$2. The safest way to reach the museum is by taking a taxi to the main door. Having said that, it can be reached by Metrô to São Cristóvão, then cross the railway line and walk a few metres to the park. This is safer than taking a bus.* **Museu de Fauna**, also in the Quinta da Boa Vista, contains a most interesting collection of Brazilian fauna. ■ *Tue-Sun 1200-1700.*

Maracanã Stadium is one of the largest sports centres in the world, with a capacity of 200,000. Matches are worth going to if only for the spectators' samba bands. There are three types of ticket, but prices vary according to the game (expect to pay US$7.50-10). Agencies charge much more for tickets than at the gate. It is cheaper to buy tickets from club sites on the day before the match. Seats in the white section have good views. Maracanã is now used only for major games; Rio teams play most matches at their home grounds (still a memorable experience, about US$2 per ticket). Hotels can arrange visits to football matches: a good idea on Sunday when the metrô is closed and buses are very full. ■ *0900-1700 (0800-1100 on match days). A guided tour of the stadium (in Portuguese) from Gate 16 costs US$2 and of the museum, US$0.50, T2568 9962. Highly recommended for football fans.*

Sights: south of the centre

The commercial district ends where the Av Rio Branco meets the Av Beira Mar. This avenue, with its royal palms, bougainvilleas and handsome buildings, coasting the Botafogo and Flamengo beaches, makes a splendid drive; its scenery is shared by the urban motorway, Av Infante Dom Henrique, along the beach over reclaimed land (the *Aterro*), which leads to Botafogo and through two tunnels to Copacabana.

On the Glória and Flamengo waterfront, with a view of the Pão de Açúcar and Corcovado, is the **Parque do Flamengo**, designed by Burle Marx, opened in 1965 during the 400th anniversary of the city's founding and landscaped on 100 ha reclaimed from the bay. Security in the park is in the hands of vigilante policemen and it is a popular recreation area. At the city end of Parque Flamengo is the **Museu de Arte Moderna**, a spectacular building at Av Infante Dom Henrique 85, near the National War Memorial. It suffered a disastrous fire in 1978; the collection is now being rebuilt and several countries have donated works of art. ■ *Tue-Sun 1200-1700 (last entry 1630), US$2, T2240 4944, www.mamrio.com.br*

Beware armed robbery in Parque do Flamengo

The **Monumento aos Mortos da Segunda Guerra Mundial/National War Memorial** to Brazil's dead in the Second World War is at Av Infante Dom Henrique 75, opposite Praça Paris. The Memorial takes the form of two slender columns supporting a slightly curved slab, representing two palms uplifted to heaven. In the crypt are the remains of Brazilian soldiers killed in Italy in 1944-45. ■ *Crypt and museum open Tue-Sun 1000-1700, but beach clothes and rubber-thonged sandals are not permitted.* The beautiful little church on the Glória Hill, overlooking the Parque do Flamengo, is **Nossa Senhora da Glória do Outeiro**. It was the favourite church of the imperial family; Dom Pedro II was baptized here. The building is polygonal, with a single tower. It contains some excellent examples of blue-faced Brazilian tiling. Its main altar, of wood, was carved by Mestre Valentim. ■ *The church, 0800-1200 (only Sat-Sun) and 1300-1700 weekdays, is reached by bus 119 from the centre and 571 from Copacabana. The adjacent museum of religious art keeps the same hours, but is closed Mon, T2557 4600.*

Parque do Catete is a charming small park with birds and monkeys between Praia do Flamengo and the Palácio do Catete, which contains the **Museu da República**, R do Catete 153. The palace was built in 1858-66. In 1887 it was converted into the presidential seat, until the move to Brasília. The first floor is devoted to the history of the Brazilian republic. The museum is highly recommended. ■ *Tue-Sun 1200-1700, US$2.50, T2556 6434. Take bus 571 from Copacabana, or the Metrô to Catete station.*

Catete and north to the centre – Laranjeiras, Cosme Velho and Lapa – are being renovated 2001

Museu do Folclore Edison Carneiro, on R do Catete 181, houses a collection not to be missed. There is a collection of small ceramic figures representing everyday life in Brazil, some very funny, some scenes animated by electric motors. There are fine Candomblé and Umbanda costumes, religious objects, ex-votos and sections on many of Brazil's festivals. It has a small, but excellent library, with helpful, friendly staff for finding books on Brazilian culture, history and anthropology. ■ *Tue-Fri 1100-1800, Sat-Sun 1500-1800, free, T2285 0441. Photography is allowed, but without flash. Take bus 571 from Copacabana, or the Metrô to Catete station.*

Known as the coolest part of Rio, this hilly inner suburb southwest of the centre, boasts many colonial and 19th century buildings, set in narrow, curving, tree-lined streets. Today the old houses are lived in by artists, intellectuals and makers of handicrafts. Most visitors in the daytime will arrive by tram. If you stay to the end of the line, Largo das Neves, you will be able to appreciate the small-town feel of the place. There are several bars here, including *Goiabeira*, simple and charming with a nice view of the praça. The essential stop is the Largo do Guimarães, which has some not to be missed eating places (see Eating.) The **Chácara do Céu**, or Fundação Raymundo Ottoni de Castro Maia, Rua Murtinho Nobre 93, has a wide range of art objects and modern painters, including Brazilian; exhibitions change through the year. ■ *Tue-Sun 1200-1700, US$1, T2285 0891, www.visualnet.com.br/cmaya   Take the Santa Teresa tram to Curvelo station, walk along Rua Dias de Barros, following the signposts to Parque das*

Santa Teresa
A haven for artists and intellectuals

Ruínas. The **Chalé Murtinho,** Rua Murtinho 41, was in ruins until it was partially restored and turned into a cultural centre called **Parque das Ruínas** in 1998. There are exhibitions, a snack bar and superb views. ■ *Daily 1000-1700.*

■ *Getting there: Santa Teresa is best visited on the traditional open-sided **tram**, the bondinho: take the Metrô to Cinelândia, go to R Senador Dantas then walk along to R Profesor Lélio Gama (look for Banco do Brasil on the corner). The station is up this street. Take the Paula Mattos line (a second line is Dois Irmãos) and enjoy the trip as it passes over the **Arcos da Lapa** aqueduct, winding its way up to the district's historic streets. At Largo das Neves, the tram turns round for the journey back to R Prof L Gama. Fare US$0.40 one way. **Bus:** Nos 206 and 214 run from Av Rio Branco in the centre to Santa Teresa. At night, only take a **taxi**.*

Glória, Santa Teresa, Catete, Flamengo

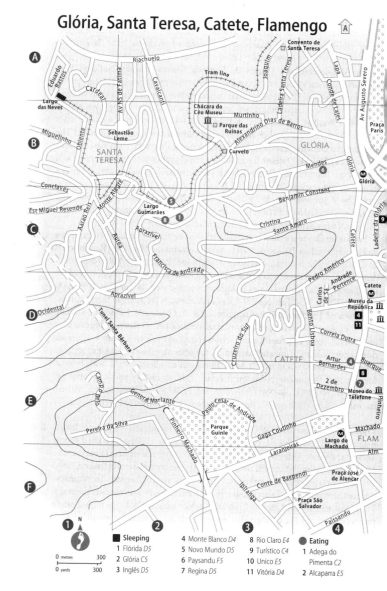

Sleeping		
1 Flórida *D5*	4 Monte Blanco *D4*	8 Rio Claro *E4*
2 Glória *C5*	5 Novo Mundo *D5*	9 Turístico *C4*
3 Inglês *D5*	6 Paysandu *F5*	10 Unico *E5*
	7 Regina *D5*	11 Vitória *D4*

● Eating
1 Adega do Pimenta *C2*
2 Alcaparra *E5*

0 metres 300
0 yards 300

Security In recent years, visitors have been put off going to Santa Teresa because of a reputation for crime which has spilled over from neighbouring *favelas*. It would, however, be a great shame to miss this unique town-within-a-city. The crime rate has been reduced and normally a policeman rides each *bondinho*, but you are advised not to take valuables. A T-shirt, shorts and enough money for a meal should be sufficient. Avoid long walks far from the main centres of Largo das Neves and Largo do Guimarães. The area around *Hotel das Paineiras* is well-patrolled.

The Pão de Açúcar, or Sugar Loaf, is a massive granite cone at the entrance to Guanabara Bay that soars to 396 m. There is a restaurant (mixed reports on food, closes 1900) and a playground for children on the Morro da Urca, half way up,

Pão de Açúcar (Sugar Loaf mountain)

The bird's eye view of the city and beaches is very beautiful

Brazil

where there are also shows at night (consult the cultural sections in the newspapers). You can get refreshments at the top. The sea level cable car station is in a military area, so it is safe to visit. At Praia Vermelha, the beach to the south of the rock, is the *Círculo Militar da Praia Vermelha* restaurant, which is open to the public (no sign). It has wonderful views, but is not so good for food or service; stop there for a drink anyway. From Praia Vermelha, the Pista Cláudio Coutinho runs around the foot of the rock. It is a paved path for walking, jogging and access to various climbing places. It is open until 1800, but you can stay on the path after that. Here you have mountain, forest and sea side-by-side, right in the heart of the city. You can also use the Pista Coutinho as a way of getting up the Pão de Açúcar more cheaply than the US$12.50 cable-car ride. About 350 m from the path entrance is a track to the left which leads though the forest to Morro de Urca, from where the cable car can be taken for US$10 (you can come down this way, too, but if you take the cable car from sea level you must pay full fare). You can save even more money, but use more energy, by climbing the Caminho da Costa, a path to the summit of the Pão de Açúcar. Only one stretch, of 10 m, requires climbing gear (even then, some say it is not necessary), but if you wait at the bottom of the path for a group going up, they will let you tag along. This way you can descend to Morro de Urca by cable car for free and walk down from there. There are 35 rock routes up the mountain, with various degrees of difficulty. The best months for climbing are April to August. See Sport, page 372, for climbing clubs; there is also a book on climbing routes.

Map labels:
National War Memorial
Marina de Glória
Parque do Flamengo
Av Beira Mar
Nossa Senhora da Glória
Trad De Nossa Senhora
Silveira Martins
Parque do Catete
useu do Folclore
lison Carneiro
Ferreira Viana
Macedo
e Assis
ENGO
amandaré
Barão do Flamengo
Praia do Flamengo
Aterro do Flamengo
Senador gueiro

3 Alho e Óleo *E5*
4 Amazônia *D4*
5 Bar do Arnaudo *C2*
6 Casa da Suiça *B4*
7 Galícia Grill *E4*
8 Sobrenatural *C2*

■ *Getting there: Bus: Bus 107 (from the centre, Catete or Flamengo) and 511 from Copacabana (512 to return) take you to the cable-car station, Avenida Pasteur 520, at the foot.* **Cable car***: Praia Vermelha to Morro de Urca: first car goes up at 0800, then every 30 mins (or when full), until the last comes down at 2200 (quietest before 1000). From Urca to Sugar Loaf, the first connecting cable car goes up at 0815 then every 30 mins (or when full), until the last leaves the summit at 2200; the return trip costs US$8 (US$6 to Morro da Urca, half-way up). The old cableway has been completely rebuilt. Termini are ample and efficient and the present Italian cable cars carry 75 passengers. Even on the most crowded days there is little queuing.*

Botafogo The **Museu do Índio**, R das Palmeiras 55, houses 12,000 objects from many Brazilian Indian groups. There is also a small, well-displayed handicraft shop (shop closes for lunch 1200-1400). ■ *Tue-Fri 1000-1730, Sat-Sun 1300-1700, US$1.75, T2286 8899, www.museudoindio.org.br From Botafogo Metrô it's a 10-min walk; from Catete, bus 571 (Glória-Leblon) passes Ruas Bento Lisboa and São Clemente.*

Corcovado Corcovado is a hunch-backed peak, 710 m high, surmounted by a 38 m high statue of Christ the Redeemer, O Cristo Redentor, which was completed on 12 October 1931. There is a superb view from the top (sometimes obscured by mist), to which there are a cog railway and road; both car and train put down their passengers behind the statue. The 3.8 km railway itself offers fine views. Average speed is 15 kph on the way up and 12 kph on the way down. There is a new exhibition of the history of the railway. From the upper terminus there is a climb of 220 steps to the top, near which there is a café. To see the city by day and night ascend at 1500 or 1600 and descend on the last train, approximately 1815. Mass is held on Sunday in a small chapel in the statue pedestal. ■ *To reach the vast statue of Cristo Redentor at the summit of Corcovado, you have to go through Laranjeiras and Cosme Velho. The road through these districts heads west out of Catete.*

The **Museu Internacional de Arte Naïf do Brasil** (MIAN), R Cosme Velho 561, T205 8612, F205 8884, is one of the most comprehensive museums of Naive and folk paintings in the world. It is only 30 m uphill, on the same street as the station for Corcovado. There is a permanent collection of some 8,000 works by Naive artists from about 130 countries. ■ *Tue-Fri 1000-1800, Sat, Sun and holidays 1200-1800; closed Mon, T2205 8612. US$2.50; discounts for groups, students and senior citizens. Has a good shop at Av Atlântica 1998.*

Those who want to see what Rio was like early in the 19th century should go to the **Largo do Boticário**, R Cosme Velho 822, a charming small square in neo-colonial style. Much of the material used in creating the effect of the square came from old buildings demolished in the city centre. The square is close to the terminus for the Corcovado cog railway.

■ *Getting there: Take a Cosme Velho bus to the cog railway station at Rua Cosme Velho 513: from the centre or Glória/Flamengo No 180; from Copacabana take No 583, from Botafogo or Ipanema/Leblon No 583 or 584; from Santa Teresa Microônibus Santa Teresa. The train runs every 20-30 mins according to demand between 0800 and 1830, journey time 10 mins (cost: US$9 return; single tickets available). Also, a 206 bus does the very attractive run from Praça Tiradentes (or a 407 from Largo do Machado) to Silvestre (the railway has no stop here now). An active walk of 9 km will take you to the top and the road is shady. For safety reasons go in company, or at weekends when more people are about. If going by car to Corcovado, the entrance fee is US$4 for the vehicle, plus US$4 pp. Coach trips tend to be rather brief and taxis, which wait in front of the station, offer tours of Corcovado and Mirante Dona Marta.*

Copacabana, Ipanema and Leblon

The world-famous beach is divided into numbered *postos*, where the lifeguards are based. Different sections attract different types of people, for example young people, artists and gays. The safest places are in front of the major hotels which have their own security, for instance the *Meridien* on Copacabana beach or the *Caesar Park* on Ipanema. The *Caesar Park* also has 24-hr video surveillance during the summer season, which makes it probably the safest patch of sand in Rio.

Built on a narrow strip of land (only a little over four sq km) between mountain and sea, Copacabana has one of the highest population densities in the world: 62,000 per sq km, or 250,000 in all. Copacabana began to develop when the Túnel Velho (Old Tunnel) was built in 1891 and an electric tram service reached it. Weekend villas and bungalows sprang up; all have now gone. In the 1930s the Copacabana Palace Hotel was the only tall building; it is now one of the lowest on the beach. The opening of the Túnel Novo (New Tunnel) in the 1940s led to an explosion of population which shows no sign of having spent its force. Unspoilt Art Deco blocks towards the Leme (city) end of Copacabana are now under preservation order.

> **Copacabana**
> *This celebrated curved beach backed by skyscraper apartments is a must for visitors*
>
> *Tourist police patrol Copacabana beach until 1700*

There is almost everything in this 'city within a city'. The shops, mostly in Avenida Nossa Senhora de Copacabana and the Rua Barata Ribeiro, are excellent. Even more stylish shops are to be found in Ipanema, Leblon and in the various large shopping centres in the city. The city's glamorous nightlife is beginning to move elsewhere and, after dark, Copacabana has lost some of its former allure. A fort at the far end of the beach, Forte de Copacabana, was an important part of Rio's defences and prevents a seashore connection with the Ipanema and Leblon beaches. Parts of the military area are now being handed over to civilian use, the first being the Parque Garota de Ipanema at Arpoador, the fashionable Copacabana end of the Ipanema beach.

■ *Getting there: Buses to and from the city centre are plentiful and cost US$0.40. The buses to take are Nos 119, 154, 413, 415, 455, 474 from Av Nossa Senhora de Copacabana. If you are going to the centre from Copacabana, look for 'Castelo', 'Praça 15', 'E Ferro' or 'Praça Mauá' on the sign by the front door. 'Aterro' means the expressway between Botafogo and downtown Rio (not open on Sun). From the centre to Copacabana is easier as all buses in that direction are clearly marked. The 'Aterro' bus does the journey in 15 mins.*

Beyond Copacabana are the beautiful seaside suburbs of Ipanema (a good place from which to watch the sunset) and Leblon. The two districts are divided by a canal from the Lagoa Rodrigo de Freitas to the sea, beside which is the Jardim de Alá. Ipanema and Leblon are a little less built-up than Copacabana and their beaches tend to be cleaner. Praia de Arpoadar at the Copacabana end of Ipanema is a peaceful spot to watch surfers, with the beautiful backdrop of Morro Dois Irmãos; excellent for photography, walk on the rocks. There is now night-time illumination on these beaches. The seaward lane of the road running beside the beach is closed to traffic until 1800 on Sundays and holidays; this makes it popular for rollerskating and cycling (bicycles can be hired).

> **Ipanema & Leblon**
> *In Ipanema are the headquarters of two stores, Amsterdam Sauer and H Stern. Both have exhibitions you can visit without any pressurized selling attached*

Backing Ipanema and Leblon is the middle-class residential area of **Lagoa Rodrigo de Freitas**, by a saltwater lagoon on which Rio's rowing and small-boat sailing clubs are active. The lake is too polluted for bathing, but the road which runs around its shores has pleasant views. The avenue on the eastern shore, Avenida Epitácio Pessoa, leads to the Túnel Rebouças which runs beneath Corcovado and Cosme Velho.

Well worth a visit are the **Jardim Botânico** (Botanical Gardens). These were founded in 1808. The most striking features are the transverse avenues of 30 m high royal palms. Among the more than 7,000 varieties of plants from around the world are examples of the *pau-brasil* tree, now endangered, and many other threatened species. There is a herbarium, an aquarium and a library (some labels are unclear). A

Brazil

new pavilion contains sculptures by Mestre Valentim transferred from the centre. Many improvements were carried out before the 1992 Earth Summit, including a new Orquidário and an enlarged bookshop. ■ *The gardens are open 0800-1700, US$2. They are 8 km from the centre; take bus No 170 from the centre, or any bus to Leblon, Gávea or São Conrado marked 'via Jóquei'; from Glória, Flamengo or Botafogo take No 571, or 172 from Flamengo; from Copacabana, Ipanema or Leblon take No 572 (584 back to Copacabana).*

The **Planetário** (Planetarium), on Padre Leonel Franco 240, Gávea, was inaugurated in 1979, with a sculpture of the Earth and Moon by Mario Agostinelli. ■ *Tours are given at 1400 and observations on Fri at 2000, Sat and Sun at 1630, 1800 and 1930. There are occasional* chorinho *concerts on Thu or Fri; check the press for details. T2274 0096, www.rio.rj.gov.br/planetario Getting there: Buses 176 and 178 from the centre and Flamengo; 591 and 592 from Copacabana.*

■ *Getting there: Buses run from Botafogo Metrô terminal to Ipanema: some take integrated Metrô-Bus tickets; look for the blue signs on the windscreen. Many buses from Copacabana run to Ipanema and Leblon.*

Leblon to Barra da Tijuca The Pedra Dois Irmãos overlooks Leblon. On the slopes is Vidigal *favela*. From Leblon, two inland roads take traffic west to the outer seaside suburb of Barra da Tijuca: the Auto Estrada Lagoa-Barra, which tunnels under Dois Irmãos, and the Estrada da Gávea, which goes through Gávea.

Parque da Cidade, a pleasant park a short walk beyond the Gávea bus terminus, has a great many trees and lawns, the *Museu Histórico da Cidade*, with views over the

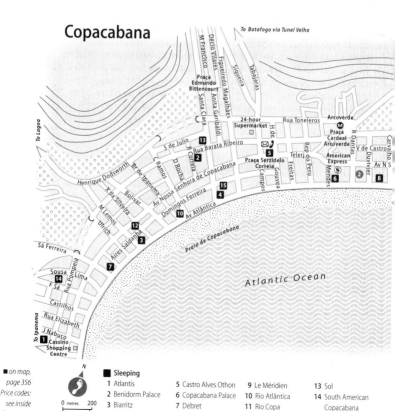

ocean. The proximity of the Rocinha favela (see below) means the park is not very safe. It is advisable to carry a copy of your passport here because of frequent police checks. ■ *Daily 0700-1700, free. Buses, Nos 593, 592, 174, 170, 546, leave you just short of the entrance, but it should be OK to walk the last part if in a group. Similarly, do not walk the trails in the park alone.* Beyond Leblon the coast is rocky. A third route to Barra da Tijuca is the Avenida Niemeyer, which skirts the cliffs on the journey past Vidigal, a small beach where the *Sheraton* is situated. Avenida Niemeyer carries on round the coast to São Conrado. On the slopes of the Pedra da Gávea, through which the Avenida Niemeyer has two tunnels, is the Rocinha favela.

The flat-topped **Pedra da Gávea** can be climbed or scrambled up for magnificent views, but beware of snakes. Behind the Pedra da Gávea is the Pedra Bonita. A road, the Estrada das Canoas, climbs up past these two rocks on its way to the Parque Nacional Tijuca. There is a spot on this road which is one of the chief hang-glider launch sites in the area (see Sport, page 372).

This rapidly developing residential area is also one of the principal recreation areas of Rio, with its 20-km sandy beach and good waves for surfing. At the westernmost end is the small beach of Recreio dos Bandeirantes, where the ocean can be very rough. The channels behind the Barra are popular with jetskiers. It gets very busy on Sundays. There are innumerable bars and restaurants, clustered at both ends, campsites (see page 367), motels and hotels: budget accommodation tends to be self-catering. A bit further out is the **Museu Casa do Pontal**, Estrada do Pontal 3295, Recreio dos Bandeirantes, a collection of Brazilian folk art. Recommended. ■ *Sat and Sun only, 1400-1800.*

Barra da Tijuca
Although buses do run as far as Barra, getting to and around here is best by car. A cycle way links Barra da Tijuca with the centre of the city

■ *Getting there: Buses from the city centre to Barra, 1 hr, are Nos 175, 176; from Botafogo, Glória or Flamengo take No 179; Nos 591 or 592 from Leme; and from Copacabana via Leblon No 523 (45 mins-1 hr). A taxi to Zona Sul costs US$15 (US$22.50 after 2400). A comfortable bus, Pegasus, goes along the coast from the Castelo bus terminal to Barra da Tijuca and continues to Campo Grande or Santa Cruz, or take the free 'Barra Shopping' bus. Bus 700 from Praça São Conrado (terminal of bus 553 from Copacabana) goes the full length of the beach to Recreio dos Bandeirantes.*

The Pico da Tijuca (1,022 m) gives a good idea of the tropical vegetation of the interior and a fine view of the bay and its shipping. A two to three hr walk leads to the summit: on entering the park at Alto da Boa Vista (0600-2100), follow the signposts (maps are displayed) to Bom Retiro, a good picnic place (1½ hours' walk). At Bom Retiro the road ends and there is another hour's walk up a fair footpath to the summit (take the path from the right of the Bom Retiro drinking fountain; not the more obvious steps from the left). The last part consists of steps carved out of the solid rock; look after children at the summit as there are

Parque Nacional Tijuca
National park information, T208 4194

● **Eating**
1 Cervantes
2 Churrascaria Palace

Carnival

Carnival in Rio is spectacular. On the Friday before Shrove Tuesday, the mayor of Rio hands the keys of the city to Rei Momo, the Lord of Misrule, signifying the start of a five-day party. Imagination runs riot, social barriers are broken and the main avenues, full of people and children wearing fancy dress, are colourfully lit. Areas throughout the city such as the Terreirão de Samba in Praça Onze are used for shows, music and dancing. Bandas and blocos (organized carnival groups) seem to be everywhere, dancing, drumming and singing.

There are numerous samba schools in Rio divided into two leagues, both of which parade in the Sambódromo. The 14 schools of the Grupo Especial parade on Sunday and Monday whilst the Grupos de Acesso A and B parade on Saturday and Friday respectively. There is also a mirins parade (younger members of the established schools) on Tuesday. The judging takes place on Wednesday afternoon and the winners of the various groups parade again on the following Saturday.

The Carnival parades are the culmination of months of intense activity by community groups, mostly in the city's poorest districts. Every school presents 2,500-6,000 participants divided into alas (wings) each with a different costume and 5-9 carros alegóricos, beautifully designed floats. Each school chooses an enredo (theme) and composes a samba (song) that is a poetic, rhythmic and catchy expression of the theme. The enredo is further developed through the design of the floats and costumes. A bateria (percussion wing) maintains a reverberating beat that must keep the entire school, and the audience, dancing throughout the parade. Each procession follows a set order with the first to appear being the comissão de frente, a choreographed group that presents the school and the theme to the public. Next comes the abre alas, a magnificent float usually bearing the name or symbol of the school. The alas and other floats follow as well as porta bandeiras and mestre salas, couples dressed in 18th century costumes bearing the school's flag, and passistas, groups traditionally of mulata dancers. An

ala of bahianas, elderly women with circular skirts that swirl as they dance is always included as is the velha guarda, distinguished members of the school who close the parade. Schools are given between 65 and 80 minutes and lose points for failing to keep within this time. Judges award points to each school for components of their procession, such as costume, music and design, and make deductions for lack of energy, enthusiasm or discipline. The winners of the Grupos de Acesso are promoted to the next higher group while the losers, including those of the Grupo Especial, are relegated to the next lowest group. Competition is intense and the winners gain a monetary prize funded by the entrance fees.

The **Sambódromo**, a permanent site at R Marquês de Sapucai, Cidade Nova, is 600 m long with seating for 43,000 people. Designed by Oscar Niemeyer and built in 1983-84, it handles sporting events, conferences and concerts during the rest of the year.

Rio´s bailes (fancy-dress balls) range from the sophisticated to the wild. The majority of clubs and hotels host at least one. The Copacabana Palace hotel´s is elegant and expensive whilst the Scala club has licentious parties. It is not necessary to wear fancy dress; just join in, although you will feel more comfortable if you wear a minimum of clothing to the clubs (crowded, hot and rowdy). The most famous are the Red & Black Ball (Friday) and the Gay Ball (Tuesday) which are both televised.

Bandas and blocos can be found in all neighbourhoods and some of the most popular and entertaining are Cordão do Bola Preta (meets at 0900 on Saturday in Rua 13 de Maio 13, Centro), Simpatia é Quase Amor (meets at 1600 Sunday in Praça General Osório, Ipanema) and the transvestite Banda da Ipanema (meets at 1600 on Saturday and Tuesday in Praça General Osorio, Ipanema). It is necessary to join a bloco in advance to receive their distinctive T-shirts, but anyone can join in with the bandas.

The expensive hotels offer special Carnival breakfasts from 0530. Caesar Park is highly recommended for a wonderful meal and a top-floor view of the sunrise over the beach.

Brazil

Tickets The Sambódromo parades start at 1900 and last about 12 hrs. Gates (which are not clearly marked) open at 1800. There are cadeiras (seats) at ground level, arquibancadas (terraces) and camarotes (boxes). The best boxes are reserved for tourists and VIPs and are very expensive or by invitation only. Seats are closest to the parade, but you may have to fight your way to the front. Seats and boxes reserved for tourists have the best view, sectors 3, 5, 7, 9 and 11 all have good views (4, 7 and 11 house the judging points). 6 and 13 are least favoured, being at the end when dancers might be tired, but have more space. The terraces, while uncomfortable, house the most fervent fans, tightly packed; this is where to soak up the atmosphere but not take pictures (too crowded). Tickets start at US$40 for arquibancadas, rising to US$160 for prime tourist seats, and are sold at banks and travel agencies as well as the Maracanã Stadium box office. Tickets are usually sold out before Carnaval weekend but touts outside can generally sell you tickets at inflated prices. Samba schools have an allocation of tickets which members sometimes sell, if you are offered one of these check its date. Tickets with no seat allocation cost about US$25 (2001). Tickets for the champions' parade on the Saturday following Carnival are much cheaper. Taxis to the Sambódromo are negotiable and will find your gate, the nearest metrô is Praça Onze and this can be an enjoyable ride in the company of costumed samba school members. You can follow the participants to the concentração, the assembly and formation on Avenida Presidente Vargas, and mingle with them while the queue to enter the Sambódromo. Ask if you can take photos.

Sleeping and security Visitors wishing to attend the Carnival are advised to reserve accommodation well in advance. Virtually all hotels raise their prices during Carnival, although it is usually possible to find a room. Your property should be safe inside the Sambódromo, but the crowds outside can attract pickpockets; as ever, don't brandish your camera, and only take the money you need for fares and food which is sold in the Sambódromo.) It gets hot so wear little.

Taking part Most samba schools will accept a number of foreigners and you will be charged upwards of US$125 for your costume as your money helps to fund poorer members of the school. You should be in Rio for at least two weeks before carnival. It is essential to attend fittings and rehearsals on time, to show respect for your section leaders and to enter into the competitive spirit of the event. For those with the energy and the dedication, it will be an unforgettable experience.

Rehearsals Ensaios are held at the schools' quadras from Oct onwards and are well worth seeing. It is wise to go by taxi, as most schools are based in poorer districts. Tour agents sell tickets for glitzy samba shows, which are nothing like the real thing. When buying a Carnival video, make sure the format is compatible (Brazilian format matches the USA; VHS PAL for most of Europe).

Samba Schools Acadêmicos de Salgueiro, R Silva Teles 104, Andaraí, T238 5564, www.salgueiro.com.br Beija Flor de Nilópolis, Pracinha Wallace Paes Leme 1025, Nilópolis, T791 2866, www.beija-flor.com.br Imperatriz Leopoldinense, R Prof. Lacê 235, Ramos, T270 8037, www.love-rio.com/ imperatriz/ Mocidade Independente de Padre Miguel, R Coronel Tamarindo 38, Padre Miguel, T3332 5823, www.mocidade.com Portela, R Clara Nunes 81, Madureira, T3390 0471, www.gresportela.com.br Primeira Estação de Mangueira, R Visconde de Niterói 1072, Mangueira, T567 4637, www.mangueira.com.br Unidos da Viradouro, Av do Contorno 16, Niterói, T717 7540, www.databrasil.com/viradouro/

Useful information Riotur's guide booklet gives concise information on official and unofficial events in English. The entertainment sections of newspapers and magazines such as O Globo, Jornal do Brasil, Manchete and Veja Rio are worth checking. Liga Independente das Escolas de Samba do Rio de Janeiro, www.liesa.com.br The book, Rio Carnival Guide, by Felipe Ferreira, has good explanations of the competition, rules, the schools, a map and other practical details. 9-12 Feb 2002 (1-4 Feb 2003) are the big parade days.

Brazil

several sheer drops, invisible because of bushes. The route is shady for almost its entire length. The main path to Bom Retiro passes the Cascatinha Taunay (a 30 m waterfall) and the Mayrink Chapel (built 1860). Beyond the Chapel is the restaurant *A Floresta*. Other places of interest not passed on the walk to the peak are the Paulo e Virginia Grotto, the Vista do Almirante and the Mesa do Imperador (viewpoints). Allow at least five to six hours for the excursion. Maps of the park are available. If hiking in the national park other than on the main paths, a guide may be useful if you do not want to get lost: *Sindicato de Guías*, T22674582.

■ *Getting there: Take bus No 221 from Praça 15 de Novembro, No 233 (which continues to Barra da Tijuca) or 234 from the rodoviária or from Praça Sáens Pena, Tijuca (the city suburb, not Barra – reached by Metrô), or No 454 from Copacabana to Alto da Boa Vista, for the park entrance.* **Jeep tours** *are run by* Atlantic Forest Jeep Tour, *daily; T2495 9827, T9974 0218 (mob), or contact through travel agencies.*

Ilha de Paquetá
A paradise of giant pebbles, and home to butterflies and flowers

The island, the second largest in Guanabara Bay, is noted for its gigantic pebble shaped rocks, butterflies and orchids. At the southwest tip is the interesting Parque Darke de Mattos, with beautiful trees, lots of birds and a lookout on the Morro da Cruz. The island has several beaches, but ask about the state of the water before bathing. The only means of transport are bicycles and horse-drawn carriages (US$15 per hr, many have harnesses which cut into the horse's flesh). Neither is allowed into the Parque Darke de Mattos. A tour by *trenzinho*, a tractor pulling trailers, costs US$1.25, or just wander around on foot, quieter and free. Bicycles can be hired. The island is very crowded at weekends and on public holidays, but is usually quiet during the week. The prices of food and drink are reasonable. ■ *Getting there: Ferry services that leave more or less every two hrs from Praça 15 de Novembro, where there is a general boat terminal; there are boats from 0515 (0710 on Sun and holidays) to 2300, T2533 7524, or hydrofoils between 1000 and 1600, Sat and Sun 0800-1630 hourly, T2533 4343 or Paquetá 3397 0656 (fare US$0.85 by boat, 1 hr, US$2.50 by hydrofoil, 20 mins' journey, which more than doubles its price Sat, Sun and holidays). Buses to Praça 15 de Novembro: No 119 from Glória, Flamengo or Botafogo; Nos 154, 413, 455, 474 from Copacabana, or No 415 passing from Leblon via Ipanema. Other boat trips: Several agencies offer trips to Paquetá. Some also offer a day cruise, including lunch, to Jaguanum Island (see under Itacuruçá) and a sundown cruise around Guanabara Bay.* Saveiros Tour, *Rua Conde de Lages 44, Glória, T2224 6990, www.saveiros.com.br, offers tours in sailing schooners around the bay and down the coast, also 'Baía da Guanabara Histórica' historical tours.*

Essentials

Sleeping
See Telephone, page 341 for important phone changes Price codes: see inside front cover

All hotels A-B and above in the following list are a/c. A 10% service charge is usually added to the bill and tax of 5% or 10% may be added (if not already included). Note that not all higher-class hotels include breakfast in their room rates. Economy hotels are found mainly in the 3 districts of Rio: Flamengo/Botafogo (best), Lapa/Fátima and Saúde/Maúá. The city is noisy. An inside room is cheaper and much quieter. Always ask for the actual room price: it usually differs from that quoted, frequently much lower.

Copacabana
■ *on map, page 360 See Essentials for new telephone number changes*

LL to L: *Copacabana Palace*, Av Atlântica 1702, T2548 7070, www.copacabanapalace.orient-express.com World famous hotel with distinguished guest list, tennis courts, popular pool. *Le Méridien*, Av Atlântica 1020, T3873 8888, sales@meridien.com.br World-renowned hotel chain but rooms quite small and better on upper floors, pool, huge breakfast. *Rio Atlântica*, Av Atlântica 2964, T2548 6332, rioatlan@netgate.com.br Excellent suites hotel, pool, 2 restaurants and other facilities. Recommended. *Rio Othon Palace*, Av Atlantica 3264, T2525 2500, F2525 1500, www.hoteis-othon.com.br

L-A: *Califórnia Othon*, Av Atlântica 2616, T/F2257 1900, gevenrio@othon.com.br good. *Lancaster Othon*, Av Atlântica 1470, T/F2543 8300, lancaster@othon.com.br Easy to change travellers' cheques, non-smoking rooms, balconies overlook the beach, helpful management, airline discount can cut price. Recommended. *Benidorm Palace*, R Barata Ribeiro 547, T2548 8880, hotelbenidorm@zipmail.com.br Suites and double rooms, sauna. Recommended. *Rio Roiss*, R Aires Saldanha 48, T2522 1142, rioroiss@tropicalbr.com.br Very good, restaurant. *South American Copacabana*, R Francisco de Sá 90, T2522 0040, southamerican@uol.com.br Good location 2 blocks from the beach, safe area, front rooms noisy, helpful front desk staff, highly rated.

A: *Castro Alves Othon*, Av Nossa Senhora de Copacabana 552, T/F2548 8815, srorio@othon.com.br Central, very comfortable and elegant. Recommended. *Debret*, Av Atlântica 3564, T2522 0132, sales@debret.com Good, helpful staff, some inner rooms dark. *Rio Copa*, Av Princesa Isabel 370, T2275 6644, riocopa@mtec.com.br Good value, English spoken. Recommended.

A-B: *Atlantis*, Av Bulhões de Carvalho 61, T2521 1142, atlantishotel@uol.com.br Very good, swimming pool, turkish bath, good breakfast, close to Ipanema and Copacabana beaches. *Biarritz*, R Ayres Saldanha 54, T2522 1087, biarritz@hoteisgandara.com.br Very reasonable considering good position close to beach. *Sol*, R Santa Clara 141, T2257 1840, www.copacabanasolhotel.com.br A/c, modern, safe, quiet, good breakfast, helpful. *Toledo*, R Domingos Ferreira 71, 1 block from beach, T2257 1995, F2257 1931. Good breakfast, single rooms are gloomy, but excellent value.

LL *Caesar Park*, Av Vieira Souto 460, T2525 2525, hotel@caesarpark-rio.com One of Rio's finest hotels, excellent service, beach patrol. **L** *Mar Ipanema*, R Visconde de Pirajá 539, Ipanema, 1 block from the beach, T2512 9898, maripa@domain.com.br Helpful, good buffet breakfast. **L** *Marina Palace*, Av Delfim Moreira 630, T22941794, F22941644, hotelmarina@callnet.com.br All rooms have sea view. Sauna, massage, pool.**L** *Sol Ipanema*, Av Vieira Souto 320, T2625 2020, www.solipanema.com.br Best Western. Recommended. **A** *Arpoador Inn*, Francisco Otaviano 177, T2523 0060, arpoador@unisys.com.br Recommended. **A** *Ipanema Inn*, Maria Quitéria 27, behind *Caesar Park*, T25233092, F25115094. Good value and location. **B** *San Marco*, R Visconde de Pirajá 524, T/F2540 5032. 2-star, simple breakfast. Recommended. **D** *Harmonia*, R Barão da Torre 175, casa 18, T2523 4905, T9817 1331 (mob), hostelharmonia@hotmail.com 3 blocks from beach, doubles or dormitories, kitchen facilities, English, Spanish, German and Swedish spoken, good internet, very welcoming and helpful.

LL *Sheraton*, Av Niemeyer 121 (Vidigal), T2274 1122, res255sheraton@sheraton.com Several pricey restaurants located directly on beach front, 3 pools and full sports facilities, Gray Line travel agency and other services associated with 5-star hotel. Near the *Sheraton* is **D** *The White House*, Estrada de Vidigal 605, T2249 4421. Clean hostel accommodation.

L *Glória*, R do Russel 632, T2555 7272, www.hotelgloriario.com.br Stylish and elegant old building, 2 swimming pools. Highly recommended. **L** *Novo Mundo*, Praia Flamengo 20, T2557 6226, www.hotelnovomundo-rio.com.br Well recommended but noisy. **AL** *Flórida*, Ferriera Viana 71/81, T2556 5242, eventos.excelsior@windsorhoteis.com.br Sauna, pool, safe, quiet, good views, great breakfast. Recommended. **A** *Regina*, Ferreira Viana 29, T2556 1647, hotelregina@hotelregina.com.br Very safe, good breakfast. **B** *Paysandu*, Paissandu 23, T/F2558 7270. Comfortable and good value, helpful staff, good location, organized tours available. **B** *Turístico*, Ladeira da Glória 30, T2557 7698, F2558 9388. With breakfast, a/c, tourist information provided, mixed reports, some highly favourable. **C** *Caxambu*, Correia Dutra 22, T2265 9496. With bath, TV, popular cheap hotel. **C** *Inglês*, Silveira Martins 20, T2558 3052, F2558 3447. A/c, TV, reasonable breakfast. **C** *Único*, Buarque de Macedo 54, T/F2205 9932. TV, a/c, fridge. Recommended. On R do Catete: **D** *Monte Blanco*, No 160, T2225 0121, F2558 5042. Breakfast, a/c, helpful. **D** *Rio Claro*, No 233, T2558 5180. Small rooms, poor breakfast, a/c, safe. **D** *Vitória*, No 172, T2205 5397, F2557 0159. With breakfast, hot water, a/c, mixed reports.

Ipanema & Leblon
Outer seaside residential and commercial area

São Conrado
Spectacular settings, but isolated and far from centre

Flamengo & Catete
■ *on map, page 356*
Residential area between centre and Copacabana, with good bus and Metrô connections

Brazil

Lapa & Fátima

Between Lapa and Praça Tiradentes is an inner residential area, less desirable than Flamengo. Parts of this area are deserted from 2200 onwards

Near Cinelândia Metrô station are a lot of cheap hotels, but many are hourly rentals. This area is not really recommended as it is not very safe and the nearby sites of interest should only be visited in daylight. In Cinelândia is **B** *Itajubá*, R Álvaro Alvim 23, T2210 3163, itahotel@Openlink.com.br Helpful staff, a little shabby, convenient for the centre. **D** *Marialva*, Gomes Freire 430, near New Cathedral, convenient for Av Rio Branco, buses etc, T2509 3187, F2509 4953. 2-star, a/c, breakfast in room. Recommended. **E** *Love's House*, Joaquim Silva, 87, T2509 5655. Ask for room with window, safe, respectable, good value.

Youth hostels

If intending to stay between Christmas and Carnival, reserve youth hostels well in advance

D *Chave do Rio de Janeiro*, R Gen Dionísio 63, Botafogo, T2286 0303, F2286 5652. HI, cheaper for members, clean showers, hot water, laundry and cooking facilities, but insufficient toilets. Superb breakfast. Noisy but frequently recommended. **D** *Novo Copa Chalet*, R Henrique Oswald 103, T2236 0047, www.copachalet.com.br **E** pp. Recommended. **E** pp *Copacabana Praia*, R Tte Marones de Gusmão 85, Bairro Peixoto, T2353817, www.wcenter.com.br/cop_apraia Dormitory, apartments also available. Associations: **ALBERJ** (for Rio), R da Assembléia 10, l 61, T2531 2234, F2531 1943. **Federação Brasileira** (Brazil), at *Chave do Rio de Janeiro* hostel.

Self-catering apartments

A popular form of accommodation in Rio, available at all price levels: eg furnished apartments for short-term let, accommodating up to 6, cost US$300 per month in Maracanã, about US$400 in Saúde, Cinelândia, Flamengo. Copacabana, Ipanema and Leblon prices range from about US$25 a day for a simple studio, starting at US$500-600 a month up to US$2,000 a month for a luxurious residence sleeping 4-6. Heading south past Barra da Tijuca, virtually all the accommodation available is self-catering. Renting a small flat, or sharing a larger one, can be much better value than a hotel room. Blocks consisting entirely of short-let apartments can attract thieves, so check the (usually excellent) security arrangements; residential buildings are called *prédio familiar*. Higher floors (*alto andar*) are considered quieter.

Brazil

Apart-Hotels are listed in the *Guia 4 Rodas* and *Riotur*'s booklet. Agents and private owners advertise in *Balcão* (like the UK's *Exchange and Mart*), twice weekly, *O Globo* or *Jornal do Brasil* (daily); under 'Apartamentos – Temporada'; advertisements are classified by district and size of apartment: 'vagas e quartos' means shared accommodation; 'conjugado' (or 'conj') is a studio with limited cooking facilities; '3 Quartos' is a 3-bedroom flat. There should always be a written agreement when renting.

The following rent apartments in residential blocks: ***Copacabana Holiday***, R Barata Ribeiro 90A, Copacabana, T2542 1525, www.copacabanaholiday.com.br Recommended, well-equipped small apartments from US$500 per month, minumum 30 days let. ***Fantastic Rio***, Av Atlântica 974, Suite 501, Copacabana, BR-22020-000, T/F2543 2667, hpcorr@hotmail.com All types of furnished accommodation from US$20 per day, owned by Peter Corr. Recommended. ***Fernando***, R Catete 214, casa 31/201, T9818 0396 (mob). Apartments in Flamengo and Catete, any length of stay, good value, Fernando speaks English and acts as a guide. ***Paulo de Tarso***, Av Princesa Isabel, 236, Apto 102, T2542 5635, pauldetarso@ig.com.br Apartments near Copacabana beach from US$25 pp, very helpful. ***Yvonne Reimann***, Av Atlântica 4066, Apto 605, T2227 0281. Rents apartments, all with phone, near beach, a/c, maid service, English, French, German spoken, all apartments owned by agency, from US$50 per flat. ***Rio Residences***, Av Prado Júnior 44, apto 508, T2541 4568, F2541 6462. Swiss run, includes airport transfer. Also ***RIOFLATRENTAL***, Av Fleming 212, Barra da Tijuca, CEP 226110040, T2495 3562, www.rioflatrental.com

Camping

Camping Clube do Brasil, Av Sen Dantas 75, 29th floor, Centro, CEP 20037-900, T2210 3171, has 2 beach sites at Barra da Tijuca: Av Sernambetiba 3200, T2493 0628 (bus 233 from centre, 702 or 703 from the airport via Zona Sul, US$5 – a long way from the centre), sauna, pool, bar, café, US$12 (half price for members), during Jan and Feb this site is often full and sometimes restricted to members of the *Camping Clube do Brasil*; a simpler site at Estrada do Pontal 5900, T2437 8400, lighting, café, good surfing, US$6. Both have trailer plots. *Ostal*, Av Sernambetiba 18790, T2437 8350; and *Novo Rio*, at Km 17 on the Rio-Santos road, T2437 6518. If travelling by trailer, you can park at the Marina Glória car park, where there are showers and toilets, a small shop and snack bar. Pay the guards to look after your vehicle.

Eating

Cariocas usually have dinner at 1900 or 2000, occasionally later at weekends after going out to the cinema, theatre or a concert or show

You can eat well for an average US$10-20 pp, less if you choose the *prato feito* at lunchtime (US$1.50-6), or eat in a place that serves food by weight (starting at about US$0.65 per gm). You can expect to pay US$20-40 pp in first-class places, more in the very best restaurants. While many of Rio's quality hotels offer world-class food and service, they may lack atmosphere and close at midnight. There are much livelier and cheaper places to eat if going out for an evening meal. In Rio, avoid mussels! There are many juice bars with a wide selection (eg the *Rei dos Sucos* chain). Most restaurants are closed on 24 and 25 Dec.

Centre

Many restaurants in this business district are open only for weekday lunch

Expensive: *Republique*, Praça da República 63 (2nd floor). Chic, designed by the architect Chicô Gouveia, good food. **Mid-range**: *Café do Teatro*, Rio Branco, Teatro Municipal. Traditional cuisine served in the grand manner, no shorts or scruffy clothes allowed, weekday lunch only. **Cheap**: *Albamar*, Praça Marechal Âncora 184-6. Good, reasonably priced fish and seafood, with lovely views of the bay, 1130-1600 Mon, 1130-2200 Tue-Sat. *Al-kuwait*, Av Treze de Maio, T2240 1114. Charming Middle Eastern restaurant in unprepossessing alley off Treze de Maio, no English menu but helpful staff, closed Sat and Sun. *Bistro do Paço*, Praça 15 de Novembro 48 (Paço Imperial), T2262 3613. Excellent, good value food in attractive surroundings, Swiss-run. Recommended. *Fiorino*, Av Heitor Beltrão 126, Tijuca, T25674476. Delicious, home-cooked Italian food with indulgent deserts. Recommended. *Mala e Cuia*, R Candelária 92. For *comida mineira*. Recommended. *Rio Minho*, R do Ouvidor 10, T2509 2338. For excellent seafood in historic building. **Seriously cheap**: Many *lanchonetes* offer good meals in the business sector. R Miguel Couto (opposite Santa Rita church) is called the *Beco das Sardinhas* because on Wed and Fri in particular it's full of people eating sardines and drinking beer. There are several Arab restaurants on Av Senhor dos Passos, which are also open Sat and Sun. *Luciano*, R das Marrecas 44. This functional all-you-can-eat buffet is one of several on this street.

Brazil

Santa Teresa **Mid-range**: One of the best restaurants in Rio is the *Bar do Arnaudo*, in the Largo do Guimarães, R Almte Alexandrino 316, T2252 7246. Tue-Sat 1200-2200, Sun 1200-1600, it is decorated with handicrafts; the cuisine is northeastern, prices are reasonable and portions huge; try the *caipirinhas*, the *carne do sol* (sun-dried beef, or jerky) with *feijão de corda* (brown beans and herbs), or the *queijo coalho* (a country cheese, grilled). Also in the Largo do Guimarães is *Adega do Pimenta*, R Almte Alexandrino 296. Mon, Wed-Fri 1130-2200, Sun 1100-1800. A very small German restaurant with excellent sausages, sauerkraut and cold beer. On the same praça, *Sobrenatural*, R Almirante Alexandrino 432, T22241003. Daily 1200-2400, a charming rustic restaurant serving fish caught daily on the owner's boat, with a menu in English. For a light lunch, order a mix of excellent appetizers. Recommended.

Lapa & Glória **Mid-range**: *Adega Flor de Coimbra*, R Teotônio Regadas 34, Lapa. Founded 1938, serving Portuguese food and wines, speciality *bacalhau*. Very good. *Café Glória*, R do Russel 734, T2205 9647. Daily for lunch and dinner, beautiful Art Nouveau building, helpful staff, excellent food.*Casa da Suíça*, R Cândido Mendes 157, T2252 5182. Bar/restaurant, good atmosphere; several others on this street.

Flamengo **Mid-range/cheap**: There are a lot of eating places on R do Catete: *Estação República*, No
& Catete 104, good self-service. *Restaurante e Pizzaria Guanabara*, No 150, excellent value and selection. *Catelandia*, No 204, excellent and cheap, pay by weight. *Amazônia*, No 234B, downstairs, 1-price counter service, upstairs for good, reasonably priced evening meals. Recommended. *Catete Grill*, No 239, good. *Galícia Grill*, No 265, very good pizza, good service. At Largo do Machado, *O Bom Galeto*, R do Catete 282, for chicken and meats. Next door is *Trattoria Gambino*, recommended for pasta, pleasant on summer evenings. In the gallery at Largo de Machado 29 is *Rotisseria Sirio Libaneza*, ljs 32 e 33, very good value Arabic food. *Alcaparra*, Praia do Flamengo 144, elegant traditional Italian, reasonable. *Alho E Óleo*, R Buarque de Macedo 13. Fashionable, pleasant. Recommended. *Lamas*, Marquês de Abrantes 18A. Excellent value, good food, great atmosphere, opens late, popular with Brazilian arts/media people. Recommended.

Botafogo **Mid-range**: *Raajmahal*, R Gen Polidoro 29. Authentic Indian food. In Baixo Botafogo R Visconde de Caravelas has several interesting bars and restaurants, eg *Aurora*, corner of R Capitão Salomão 43 (cheap), and *Botequim*, No 184, varied menu, good food and value. Also here is *Cobal Humaitá*, a fruit market with many popular restaurants (Mexican *tacos*, pizzería, etc). Rio Sul Shopping has a lot of choice for food, including *Chez Michou*, crêpes and chopp, 4th floor, *Habib's*, Arabic fast-food, 2 branches of *Kotobuki* sushi bar (another branch on the road to Praia Vermelha, recommended) and *Chaika* for milkshakes, ice creams and sandwiches (4th floor, original branch on Praça Nossa Senhora da Paz, Ipanema).

Copacabana **Expensive**: *Shirley*, R Gustavo Sampaio 610, T2275 1398. Spanish, small, seafood, book
& Leme in advance. *Churrascaria Marius*, Av Atlântica 290, also at R F Otaviano 96, Ipanema. Recommended. **Mid-range**:*Chon Kou*, Av Atlântica 3880, T2287 3956. Traditional Chinese restaurant also offering an extensive sushi menu, a/c, sit upstairs for good views over Copacabana beach. *Churrascaria Palace*, R Rodolfo Dantas 16B, Long-established, 20 different kinds of meat, good food and value. *Nino*, Domingos Ferreira 242. Italian cuisine, Argentine beef, excellent dinner with wine for US$25 pp. **Cheap**: *Aipo and Aipim*, Av NS de Copacabana 391. Excellent food by weight at this popular chain with other branches on this road. *Al Capo*, Av NS de Copacabana e J Nabuco. Excellent fresh pasta. *Cervantes*, Barata Ribeiro 07-B e Prado Júnior 335B. Stand-up bar or sit-down, a/c restaurant, open all night, queues after 2200, said to serve the best sandwiches in town, a local institution. *A Marisquera*, Barata Ribeiro 232. Good seafood. *Maximix*, R Siqueira Campos 12, loja A. Buffet by weight, opens late, very popular. Recommended. *Ponto de Encontro*, Barata Ribeairo 750. Portuguese, try baked *bacalhau*. *Siri Mole & Cia*, R Francisco Otaviano 90. Brazilian cuisine, don't miss coffee after the meal from an

old-fashioned coffee machine. *Taberna do Leme* , Princesa Isabel e Av NS Copacabana. Bar/restaurant with helpful waiters, comprehensive menu in English includes delicious crab pancakes. Warmly recommended for eating as well as drinking. **Seriously cheap**: There are stand-up bars selling snacks all around this area. *Marakesh*, Av NS de Copacabana 599. Good quality and value, pay by weight.

Expensive: *Amarcord*, R Maria Quitéria 136. Recommended. *Il Capo*, Visconde de Pirajá 276. Recommended. *Alho e Óleo*, next door. Fashionable, friendly. Recommended. *Pax Delícia*, Praça NS da Paz. Excellent light foods and salads, vegetarian options, lively crowd. Mon from 2000 and Tue-Sun from 1200. Recommended. **Mid-range**: *Grottamare*, R Gomes Carneiro 132. Good seafood. *Mostarda*, Av Epitácio Pessoa 980. Excellent food (often seasoned with mustard sauce), nightclub upstairs, entry fee can be avoided if you eat in the 1st floor restaurant before 2200-2300. Recommended. *Porção*, Barão de Torre 218, a very good *churrascaria*, US$25 pp (another branch at Av NS de Copacabana 1144). *Satyricon*, R Barão da Torre 192, T2521 0627. Upmarket establishment specialising in Mediterranean cuisine.*Yemenjá*, R Visconde de Pirajá 128. Brazilian food from the Bahia region. **Cheap**: *Casa da Feijoada*, Prudente de Morais 10. Serves an excellent *feijoada* all week. *Del Mare*, at corner of Prudente de Morais and Vinícius de Morais. Recommended. *La Frasca*, R Garcia d'Ávila 129. Good Italian, pleasant atmosphere. **Seriously cheap**: *Amarelinho*, R Farme de Amoedo 62. Great corner lanchonete with tables outside, fresh food, good value, friendly, open until 0300. Recommended. *Delicats*, Av Henrique Dumont 68. Good Jewish deli.

Ipanema

Ipanema is quieter than Copacabana, many nice places round Praça Gen Osório

Expensive: *Antiquarius*, R Aristides Espínola 19. Restaurant-cum-antique shop, seafood and international cuisine. **Mid-range**: *Ettore*, Av Ataulfo de Paiva 1321, loja A. Excellent Italian. *Mediterráneo*, R Prudente de Morais 1810. Excellent fish. *Un, Deux, Trois*, R Bartolomeu Mitre 123. Very fashionable, restaurant, nightclub. **Cheap**: *Celeiro*, R Dias Ferreira 199. Some of the best salads in the city, and light food, pay by weight.

Leblon

Expensive: *Claude Troisgros*, R Custódio Serrão 62. Elegant French restaurant. Recommended. *Enotria*, R Frei Leandro 20. Excellent Italian food, service, atmosphere and prices. Recommended. **Mid-range**: *Mistura Fina*, Av Borges de Medeiros 3207, T2537 2844. Classy, popular, friendly nightclub upstairs.

Jardim Botânico & Lagoa

Grill or barbecue houses (*churrascarias*) are relatively cheap, especially by European standards. There are many at São Conrado and Joá, on the road out to Barra da Tijuca (see page 361). *Galetos* are lunch counters specializing in chicken and grilled meat, very reasonable. In the shopping centres there is usually a variety of restaurants and snack bars grouped around a central plaza where you can shop around for a good meal. Most less-expensive restaurants in Rio have basically the same type of food (based on steak, fried potatoes and rice) and serve large portions. *La Mole*, at 11 locations, serves good, cheap Italian food, very popular.

Fast food

There are plentiful hamburger stands and lunch counters all over the city

For those who like their teas served English style, the sedate *Confeitaria Colombo*, R Gonçalves Dias 32, near Carioca Metrô station, is highly recommended for atmosphere, being the only one of its kind in Rio. Over 100 years old, it has the original Belle Epoque décor, 0900-1800, lunch available, no service charge so tip the excellent waiters. More modern but similar establishments in some of the main hotels, eg *Pergula*, *Copacabana Palace Hotel*, Av Atlântica 1702, Mon-Fri 1400-1700. Recommended. Also *Casarão*, Souza Lima 37A, Copacabana. *Traiteurs de France*, Av NS de Copacabana 386. Delicious tarts and pastries, not expensive.

Cafés

Brazil

Brazil

Bars

A beer costs around US$1.50, but up to US$5 in expensive hotel bars. A cover charge of US$3-7 may be made for live music, or there might be a minimum consumption charge of around US$3; sometimes both. Snack food is always available

Copacabana, Ipanema and Leblon have many beach *barracas*, several open all night. The seafront bars on Av Atlántica are great for people-watching. The big hotels have good cocktail bars (*Copacabana Palace*, poolside, recommended). Seafront restaurant/bars in Ipanema: **Barril 1800**, Av Vieira Souto 110, T2523 0085. Good Brazilian menu, fish and meat, nice place to watch the sunset. **A Garota de Ipanema**, R Vinícius de Morais 49, is where the song 'Girl from Ipanema' was written, very lively. On the same street, No 39, 2nd floor, is **Vinícius**, live music and international cuisine from 1900. In Leblon is the **Academia da Cachaça**, R Conde de Bernadotte 26-G, with another branch at Av Armando Lombardi 800, Barra da Tijuca. Lots more bars are opening in districts to the south. **Bar Lagoa**, Av Epitácio Pessoa 1674, Lagoa. Recommended ('arty crowd', evenings only). On weekday evenings, Cariocas congregate at the bars around Praça Santos Dumont, Gávea. British ex-pats meet at **Porão**, under the Anglican church hall, R Real Grandeza 99, Botafogo, Fri only.

Lapa, once run-down and to be avoided at night, is now one of the trendiest districts to go for drinking and music: **Carioca da Gema**, Av Mem de Sá 79, Centro, T2221 0043. 1800 Mon-Fri and 2100 Sat, a 'musical café ' with a varied programme, cover charge US$3.20 and minimum consumption US$3.20. Next door at No 81 is **Sacrilégio**, a 'cultural café' open from 1900 every night for cutting-edge theatre and other events, T2507 3898 for more information. **Semente**, R Joaquim Silva 138, T2242 5165. Popular for samba, choro and salsa from 2200 Mon-Sat, US$2.50 cover, minimum consumption US$2, book at weekends, great atmosphere inside and in the street outside. Recommended.

Nightclubs

Rio nightlife is rich and infinitely varied, one of the main attractions for most visitors. If you are not in Rio for Carnival, it's worth seeing a samba show; entry is cheaper if you pay at the door

The usual system in nightclubs is to pay an entrance fee (about US$10) and then you are given a card onto which your drinks are entered. There is often a minimum consumption of US$10-15 on top of the entry charge. Do not lose your card or they may charge you more than you could possibly drink. Most places will serve reasonable snack food. Trendiest clubs playing contemporary dance music are **El Turf** (aka *Jockey Club*) , opposite the Jardim Botânico, Praça Santos Dumont 31. Opens 2100, gets going at 2300, you may have to wait to get in at the weekend if you arrive after midnight, no T-shirts allowed, very much a singles and birthday party place; another branch in Rio Sul Shopping Centre. **Fun Club**, also in Shopping Centre Rio Sul, 4th floor. **Le Boy**, Raul Pompéia 94, Copacabana, gay. **Papillon Club**, Inter Continental Hotel, Av Prefeito Mendes de Moraes 222, São Conrado, T3322 2200. **The Basement**, Av Nossa Senhora de Copacabana 1241, alternative. **W**, Visconde de Piraja, Ipanema, fashionable, good crowd. In Barra da Tijuca, **Rock 'n' Rio Café**, Barra Shopping. Good food, young crowd, a long way from the centre (taxis hard to find in the early morning). **Greenwich Village**, at Posto 6 on the beach front. Good reputation. There are dozens of other good clubs, most open Wed-Sun, action starts around midnight, lone women and male-only groups may have trouble getting in.

Gafieiras, for Samba dancing, including **Elite Club**, R Frei Caneca 4, 1st floor, Centro, also reggae. **Estudantina**, Praça Tiradentes 79, Thu-Sat. There are many cheaper *gafieiras*. All types of music and entertainment are represented: **Copa Show**, Av Nossa Senhora de Copacabana 435, has been recommended for forró and disco music (safe). **Reggae Rock Cafe**, Largo de São Conrado 20, T3322 4197. **Raizes**, Av Sernambetiba 1120, T3389 6240, for Afro-Brazilian beats. For samba, choro, forró, **Severyna**, R Ipiranga 54, Laranjeiras (also serves northeastern food), cover US$3. **Discoteca Fundição do Progresso**, downtown, near Lapa/Centro. Very trendy disco. Copacabana is full of discos where the girls are prostitutes. Sleazier shows are concentrated around Leme, as are gay clubs; many gay clubs also around Lapa (Cinelândia), but good ones exist all over the city.

Entertainment **Cinemas** New American releases (with original soundtrack), plus Brazilian and worldwide films and classics are all shown. See the local press. The normal seat price is US$4, discounts on Wed and Thu (students pay half price any day of the week).

Music Free concerts throughout the summer on Copacabana and Ipanema beaches, in Botafogo and at the parks: mostly samba, reggae, rock and MPB (Brazilian pop): no advance schedule, check the local press (see below). **Canecão** is a big, inexpensive venue for live concerts, most nights, see press for listings: R Venceslau Brás 215, Botafogo, T2543 1241. Rio's famous jazz, in all its forms, is performed in lots of enjoyable venues, see the press, which also lists who is playing at *Teatro Rival*, R Alvaro Alvim 33, Cinelândia, T2532 4192. *Centro Cultural Carioca*, R do Teatro, 37, T2242 9642, www.centroculturalcarioca.com 1830-the early hours, an exciting new venue, combining music (mostly samba) and dance, restored old house attracting a lovely mix of people. Professional dancers perform with musicians; after a few tunes the audience joins in. Thu is impossibly crowded; Sat calmer, bar food available, US$3 cover. Highly recommended. For purely local entertainment on Mon night, *Praia do Vermelha* at Urca. Residents bring musical instruments and chairs onto the beach for an informal night of samba from around 2100-midnight. Free. Bus no 511 from Copacabana.

There are about 40 theatres in Rio, presenting a variety of classical and modern performances in Portuguese. Seat prices start at about US$15; some children's theatre is free. **Theatre**

Less hectic than Carnival, but very atmospheric, is the festival of *Iemanjá* on the night of **31 Dec**, when devotees of the *orixá* of the sea dress in white and gather on Copacabana, Ipanema and Leblon beaches, singing and dancing around open fires and making offerings. The elected Queen of the Sea is rowed along the seashore. At midnight small boats are launched as offerings to Iemanjá. The religious event is dwarfed, however, by a massive New Year's Eve party, called *Reveillon* at Copacabana. The beach is packed as thousands of revellers enjoy free outdoor concerts by big-name pop stars, topped with a lavish midnight firework display. It is most crowded in front of *Copacabana Palace Hotel*. Another good place to see fireworks is in front of *Le Meridien*, famous for its fireworks waterfall at about 10 mins past midnight. **NB** Many followers of *Iemanjá* are now making their offerings on 29 or 30 Dec and at Barra da Tijuca or Recreio dos Bandeirantes to avoid the crowds and noise of Reveillon. The festival of *São Sebastião*, patron saint of Rio, is celebrated by an evening procession on **20 Jan**, leaving Capuchinhos Church, Tijuca, and arriving at the cathedral of São Sebastião. On the same evening, an *umbanda festival* is celebrated at the Caboclo Monument in Santa Teresa. **Festas Juninas**: *Santo Antônio* on **13 Jun**, whose main event is a mass, followed by celebrations at the Convento do Santo Antônio and the Largo da Carioca. Throughout the state of Rio, the festival of *São João* is a major event, marked by huge bonfires on the night of **23-24 Jun**. It is traditional to dance the *quadrilha* and drink *quentão*, cachaça and sugar, spiced with ginger and cinnamon, served hot. The *Festas Juninas* close with the festival of *São Pedro* on **29 Jun**. Being the patron saint of fishermen, his feast is normally accompanied by processions of boats. **Oct** is the month of the feast of *Nossa Senhora da Penha*. **Festivals other than Carnival**

Jewellery *H Stern*, R Visconde de Pirajá 490/R Garcia Dávila 113, Ipanema, have 10 outlets, plus branches in major hotels. Next door is *Amsterdam Sauer*, R Garcia D'Ávila 105, with10 shops in Rio and others throughout Brazil. They offer free taxi rides to their main shop. There are several good jewellery shops at the Leme end of Av NS de Copacabana. For mineral specimens as against cut stones, try *Mineraux*, Av NS de Copacabana 195, Belgian owner. **Shopping** *Buy precious and semi-precious stones from reputable dealers*

Bookshops *Argumento*, R Dias Ferreira 417, Leblon, sells imported English books, including *Footprint*. *Da Vinci*, Av Rio Branco 185 lojas 2, 3 and 9, all types of foreign books, *Footprint* available. *Dazibão*, Praça 15 de Novembro and in Botafogo, Ipanema and Catete, www.dazibao.com.br Art, culture and history of Brazil. *FNAC* has a megastore at Barra Shopping, with French, English and other imported titles, including *Footprint*, CDs, etc. *Kosmos*, R do Rosário 155, good shop (in the centre and Av Atlântica 1702, loja 5). *Letras e Expressões*, R Visconde de Pirajá 276, Ipanema and Av Ataulfo 1292, Leblon, www.letras.com Wide selection of books and magazines (Brazilian and foreign), CDs, café, internet access, 24 hrs. *Saraiva* has a megastore at R do Ouvidor 98, T507 9500, also with a music and video shop and a café; other branches in Shopping Iguatemi and Shopping Tijuca. *Siciliano*, Av Rio Branco 156, loja 26. European books, also at Nossa Senhora de Copacabana 830 (stocks *Footprint*) and branches; French books at No 298. Branches of *Sodiler* at both airports (sell *Footprint*) and Barra Shopping, Rio Sul, other shopping centres and at R São José 35, loja V. *Livraria da Travessa*, Travessa do Ouvidor 11-A, superb new branch at Av Rio Branco 44 and R Visconde de Pirajá 572, Ipanema (stocks *Footprint*). Excellent.

Brazil

Brazil

Markets Northeastern market at Campo de São Cristóvão, with music and magic, on Sun 0800-2200 (bus 472 or 474 from Copacabana or centre). A recommended shop for northeastern handicrafts is *Pé de Boi*, R Ipiranga 55, Laranjeiras, www.pedeboi.com.br Sat antiques market on the waterfront near Praça 15 de Novembro, 1000-1700. Also in Praça 15 de Novembro is *Feirarte II*, Thu-Fri 0800-1800. *Feirarte I* is a Sun open-air handicrafts market (everyone calls it the *Feira Hippy*) at Praça Gen Osório, Ipanema, 0800-1800, touristy but fun: items from all over Brazil. A stamp, coin and postcard market is held in the Passeio Público on Sun, 0800-1300. Markets on Wed 0700-1300 on R Domingos Ferreira and on Thu, same hrs, on Praça do Lido, both Copacabana (Praça do Lido also has a *Feirarte* on Sat-Sun 0800-1800). Sun market on R da Glória, colourful, cheap fruit, vegetables and flowers; early-morning food market, 0600-1100, R Min Viveiros de Castro, Ipanema. Excellent food and household-goods markets at various places in the city and suburbs (see newspapers for times and places).

Saara is a multitude of little shops along R Alfândega and R Senhor dos Passos (between city centre and Campo Santana), where clothes bargains can be found (especially jeans and bikinis); it is known popularly as 'Shopping a Céu Aberto'. Little shops on Aires Saldanha, Copacabana (1 block back from beach), are good for bikinis and cheaper than in shopping centres.

Music For a large selection of Brazilian Music, jazz and classical, *Modern Sound Música Equipamentos*, R Barata Ribeiro 502D, Copacabana. *Toca do Vinícius*, R Vinícius de Moraes 129C, Ipanema. Specializes in Bossa Nova books, CDs, doubles as a performance space.

Shopping Centres The *Rio Sul*, at the Botafogo end of Túnel Novo, has almost everything the visitor may need. Some of the services in Rio Sul are: *Telemar* (phone office) for international calls at A10-A, Mon-Sat 1000-2200; next door is *Belle Tours Câmbio*, A10. There is a post office at G2. A good branch of *Livraria Sodiler* is at A03. For Eating and Entertainment, see above; live music at the *Terraço*; the *Ibeas Top Club* gym; and a cinema. A US$5 bus service runs as far as the *Sheraton* passing the main hotels, every 2 hrs between 1000 and 1800, then 2130. Other shopping centres, which include a wide variety of services, include: *Cassino* (Copacabana), *Norte Shopping* (Todos os Santos), *Plaza Shopping* (Niterói), *Barra* in Barra da Tijuca (see page 361). At São Conrado, *The Fashion Mall* is smaller and more stylish.

Sport There are hundreds of excellent gyms and sports clubs; most will not grant temporary (less than 1 month) membership. Big hotels may allow use of their facilities for a small deposit. **Cycling** Tours (hire available) with *Rio Bikers*, R Domingos Ferreira 81, room 201, T2274 5872. **Diving** *Squalo*, Av Armando Lombardi 949-D, Barra de Tijuca, T/F2493 3022, squalo1@hotmail.com Offers courses at all levels, NAUI and PDIC training facilities, also snorkelling and equipment rental. **Football** See under Maracanã stadium, above. **Hang-gliding** *Just Fly*, T/F2268 0565, T9985 7540 (mob), www.justfly.lookscool.com US$80 for tandem flights with Paulo Celani (licensed by Brazilian Hang Gliding Association), pick-up and drop-off at hotel included, in-flight pictures US$15 extra, flights all year, best time of day 1000-1500 (5% discount for *South American* and *Brazil Handbook* readers on presentation of book at time of reservation). Recommended. *Ultra Força Ltda*, Av Sernambetiba 8100, Barra da Tijuca, T3399 3114; 15 mins. **Horse racing and riding** *Jockey Club Racecourse*, by Jardím Botânico and Gávea, meetings on Mon and Thu evenings and Sat and Sun 1400, entrance US$1-2, long trousers required, a table may be booked. Take any bus marked 'via Jóquei'. *Sociedade Hípico Brasileiro*, Av Borges de Medeiros 2448, T527 8090, Jardim Botânico – riding. **Parapenting** Tandem jumping (*Vôo duplo*); *Barra Jumping*, Aeroporto de Jacarepaguá, Av Ayrton Senna 2541, T3325 2494/9988 1566. Several other people offer tandem jumping; check that they are accredited with the Associação Brasileira de Vôo Livre. Ask for the *Parapente Rio Clube* at São Conrado launch site, tandem flight US$80. **Rock climbing and hill walking** *ECA*, Av Erasmo Braga 217, room 305, T2242 6857/2571 0484, personal guide US$100 per day, owner Ralph speaks English; *Clube Excursionista Carioca*, also recommended for enthusiasts, R Hilário Gouveia 71, room 206, T2255 1348, meets Wed and Fri. *Paulo Miranda*, R Campos Sales 64/801, RJ20270-210, T/F2264 4501.

Turismo Clássico, Av NS de Copacabana 1059/805, T2523 3390, classico@infolink.com.br **Tour operators**
Warmly recommended. *Metropol Viagens e Turismo*, R São José 46, T2533 5010, F2533
7160, metropol@metropolturismo.com.br Eco, adventure and culture tours to all parts of
Brazil. *Marlin Tours*, Av NS de Copacabana office 1204, T2548 4433, bbm.robin@
openlink.com.br Recommended for hotel, flights and tours, Robin and Audrey speak English. *Hanseatic*, R 7 de Setembro 111/20, T2224 6672. German-run (English, French, Portuguese spoken). Recommended. *Rio Hiking*, T9874 3698, www.riohiking.com.br Hiking
tours to the top of Rio's mountains. Organized trips to Samba shows cost US$50 including
dinner, good, but it's cheaper to go independently. *Fenician Tours*, Av NS de Copacabana
335, T2235 3843, offers a cheaper tour than some at US$30 including transport from/to
hotel. Regular sightseeing tours are operated by *American Sightseeing*, T2236 3551,
Sul América, T2257 4235, *Passamar Turismo*, Av Rio Branco 25, T2233 8883.
Atlantic Forest Jeep Tour, T2495 9827, T9974 0218 (mob). As well as running jeep tours to
the Parque Nacional Tijuca (see above), run trips to coffee *fazendas* in the Paraíba Valley, trips
to Angra dos Reis and offshore islands and the Serra dos Órgãos. *Dantur*, Largo do Machado
29 (Galeria Condor) loja 47, T2557 7144. Helena speaks English and is friendly and helpful.

Favela Tour, Estr das Canoas 722, Bl 2, apt 125, CEP 22610-210, T3322 2727, T9989
0074/9772 1133, www.favelatour.com.br Guided tours of Rio's favelas, safe, different and
interesting, US$20, 3 hrs. Also ask Marcelo Armstrong, the owner, about eco tours, river raft-
ing and other excursions. He speaks English, French, Spanish, Italian and can provide guides
in German and Swedish. For the best attention and price call Marcelo direct rather than
through a hotel desk. *Jeep Tours* also offer favela tours, T3890 9336, T9977 9610 (mob),
www.jeeptour.com.br *Cultural Rio*, tours escorted personally by Professor Carlos Roquette,
R Santa Clara 110/904, Copacabana, T3322 4872, T9911 3829 (mob),
www.culturalrio.com English and French spoken, almost 200 options available.
Fábio Sombra offers private and tailor-made guided tours focusing on the cultural aspects
of Rio and Brazil, T2295 9220, T9729 5455 (mob), fabiosombra@hotmail.com *Rio Life*, R Visc

Brazil

de Pirajá 550, office 215, Ipanema, T2259 5532, T9637 2522 (mob), www.travelrio.com Good company offering personalised tours run by Luiz Felipe Amaral who speaks good English.

Helicopter sightseeing tours: *Helisight*, R Visconde de Pirajá 580, loja 107, Térreo, Ipanema, T2511 2141, www.helisight.com.br Prices from US$43 pp for 6-7 mins from Morro de Urca over Sugar Loaf and Corcovado, to US$148 pp for 30 mins over the city.

Transport

There are good services, but buses are very crowded and not for the aged and infirm during rush hours; buses have turnstiles which are awkward if you are carrying luggage. Hang on tight, drivers live out Grand Prix fantasies

Bus At busy times allow about 45 mins to get from Copacabana to the centre by bus. The fare on standard buses is R$1.10 (US$0.45) and suburban bus fares are US$0.75. Bus stops are often not marked. The route is written on the side of the bus, which is hard to see until the bus has actually pulled up at the stop. Private companies operate air-conditioned *frescão* buses which can be flagged down practically anywhere: *Real, Pegaso, Anatur*. They run from all points in Rio Sul to the city centre, Rodoviária and the airports. Fares are US$1.50 (US$1.80 to the international airport). *City Rio* is an a/c tourist bus service with security guards which runs between all the major parts of the city. Good maps show what sites of interest are close to each bus stop, marked by grey poles and found where there are concentrations of hotels. T0800 258060. Distances in km to some major cities with approximate journey time in brackets: Juiz de Fora, 184 (2¾ hrs); Belo Horizonte, 434 (7 hrs); São Paulo, 429 (6 hrs); Vitória, 521 (8 hrs); Curitiba, 852 (12 hrs); Brasília, 1,148 (20 hrs); Florianópolis, 1,144 (20 hrs); Foz do Iguaçu, 1,500 (21 hrs); Porto Alegre, 1,553 (26 hrs); Salvador, 1,649 (28 hrs); Recife, 2,338 (38 hrs); Fortaleza, 2,805 (48 hrs); São Luís, 3,015 (50 hrs); Belém, 3,250 (52 hrs).

For international car rental websites, see Car hire, Essentials, page 48

Car hire *Golden Car*, R Ronald de Carvalho 154C, Copacabana, T2275 4748; *Interlocadora*, international airport T3398 3181; *Nobre*, Av Princesa Isabel 7, Copacabana, T2541 4646; *Telecar*, R Figueiredo Magalhães 701, Copacabana, T2235 6778. Many agencies on Av Princesa Isabel, Copacabana. A credit card is virtually essential for hiring a car. Recent reports suggest it is cheaper to hire outside Brazil. You may also obtain fuller insurance this way.

Motoring Service stations are closed in many places Sat and Sun. Road signs are notoriously misleading in Rio and you can end up in a *favela*. Take care if driving along the Estr da Gávea to São Conrado as it is possible to enter unwittingly Rocinha, Rio's biggest slum.

Metro The Metrô provides good service, clean, air conditioned and fast. Line 1: between the inner suburb of Tijuca (station Saens Peña) and Arcoverde (Copacabana), via the railway station (Central), Glória and Botafogo. Line 2: from Pavuna, passing Engenho da Rainha and the Maracanã stadium, to Estácio. It operates 0600-2300, Sun 1400-2000; closed holidays. The fare is R$1.30 (US$0.55) single; multi-tickets and integrated bus/Metrô tickets are available. Substantial changes in bus operations are taking place because of the extended Metrô system; buses connecting with the Metrô have a blue-and-white symbol in the windscreen.

Taxi The fare between Copacabana and the centre is US$7. Between 2300 and 0600 and on Sun and holidays, 'tariff 2' is used. Taxis have red number plates with white digits (yellow for private cars, with black digits) and have meters. Smaller ones (mostly Volkswagen) are marked TAXI on the windscreen or roof. Make sure meters are cleared and on tariff 1, except at those times mentioned above. Only use taxis with an official identification sticker on

Brazil

the windscreen. Don't hesitate to argue if the route is too long or the fare too much. Radio Taxis are safer but more expensive, eg *Cootramo*, T2560 5442, *Coopertramo*, T2260 2022, *Centro de Táxi*, T2593 2598, *Transcoopass*, T2560 4888. Luxury cabs are allowed to charge higher rates. Inácio de Oliveira, T2225 4110, is a reliable taxi driver for excursions, he only speaks Portuguese. Recommended. *Grimalde*, T2267 9812, has been recommended for talkative daytime and evening tours, English and Italian spoken, negotiate a price.

Air Rio has 2 airports: **Antônio Carlos Jobim International Airport**, previously called Galeão, and the **Santos Dumont** airport on Guanabara Bay for domestic flights. Jobim international airport is situated on Governador Island some 16 km from the centre of Rio. It is in 2 sections: international and domestic. There is a *Pousada Galeão* (**A**), comfortable, good value if you need an early start, follow signs in airport.

Long distance
See also Ins and outs, page 348

There are a/c taxis; *Cootramo* and *Transcopass* have fixed rates (US$18.75 Copacabana). Buy a ticket at the counter near the arrivals gate before getting into the car. Fixed rate taxi fares from Terminal 2 are US$8.50 to Centro, US$10 to Copacabana/Ipanema, US$15.50 to Barra da Tijuca. Credit cards accepted by some companies. The hire is for the taxi, irrespective of the number of passengers. Make sure you keep the ticket, which carries the number to phone in case of difficulty. Ordinary taxis also operate with the normal meter reading (about US$12.50, but some may offer cheaper rates from Copacabana to the airport, US$7-8.50). Do not negotiate with a driver on arrival, unless you are a frequent visitor. Beware pirate taxis which are unlicensed. It is better to pay extra for an official vehicle than run the risk of robbery.

The a/c *'Real'* bus runs very frequently from the first floor of the airport to Recreio dos Bandeirantes via the municipal rodoviária and city centre, Santos Dumont Airport, Flamengo, Copacabana, Ipanema and Leblon. Fares are collected during the journey; to Zona Sul US$1.75, to Santos Dumont US$1.50. The driver will stop at requested points (the bus runs along the seafront from Leme to Leblon), so it's worth checking a map beforehand so that you can specify your required junction. The bus returns by the same route. Town buses M94 and M95, *Bancários/Castelo*, take a circular route passing through the centre and the interstate bus station. They leave from the 2nd floor of the airport.

There are *câmbios* in the airport departure hall. There is also a *câmbio* on the first floor of the international arrivals area, but it gives worse rates than the Banco do Brasil, 24-hr bank, third floor, which has Visa ATMs and will give cash advances against Visa. Duty-free shops are well-stocked, but not especially cheap. Duty free is open to arrivals as well as departures. Only US dollars or credit cards are accepted on the air-side of the departure lounge. There is a wider choice of restaurants outside passport control.

The **Santos Dumont airport** on Guanabara Bay, right in the city, is used for Rio-São Paulo shuttle flights (US$150 single, US$300 return), other domestic routes, air taxis and private planes. The shuttle services operate every 30 mins from 0630 to 2230. Sit on the right-hand side for views to São Paulo, the other side coming back, book in advance for particular flights. The main airport, on Governador Island, some 16 km from the centre of Rio, is in 2 sections, international and domestic (including Vasp's jet shuttle from Rio to São Paulo).

Bus Rodoviária Novo Rio, Av Rodrigues Alves, corner with Av Francisco Bicalho, just past the docks, T2291 5151. Some travel agents sell interstate tickets, or will direct you to a bus ticket office in the centre. Agencies include: *Dantur Passagens e Turismo*, Av Rio Branco 156, subsolo loja 134, T2262 3424/3624; *Itapemirim Turismo*, R Uruguaiana 10, loja 24, T2509 8543, both in the centre; *Guanatur*, R Dias da Rocha 16A, Copacabana, T2235 3275, F2235 3664; and an agency at R Visconde de Pirajá 303, loja 114, Ipanema. They charge about US$1 for bookings. Buses run from Rio to all parts of the country. It is advisable to book tickets in advance. The rodoviária has a *Riotur* information centre, which is very helpful. Left luggage costs US$3. There are *câmbios* for cash only. The local bus terminal is just outside the rodoviária: turn right as you leave and run the gauntlet of taxi drivers – best ignored. The air conditioned *Real* bus (opposite the exit) goes along the beach to São Conrado and will secure luggage. If you need a taxi collect a ticket, which ensures against overcharging, from the office inside the entrance (to Flamengo US$7.50). On no account give the ticket to the taxi driver.

The rodoviária attracts thieves be careful
The main bus station is reached by buses M94 and M95, Bancários/Castelo, from the centre and the airport; 136, 172, Rodoviária/Glória/Flamengo/Botafogo; 127, 128, 136, Rodoviária/Copacabana; 170, Rodoviária/Gávea/São Conrado; 128, 172, Rodoviária/Ipanema/Leblon.

Brazil

International bus Asunción, 1,511 km via Foz do Iguaçu, 30 hrs (*Pluma*), US$70; **Buenos Aires** (*Pluma*), via Porto Alegre and Santa Fe, 48 hrs, US$100 (book 2 days in advance); to **Uruguaiana**, US$90, cheaper and quicker to get a through ticket; **Santiago de Chile**, with *Pluma* US$135, or *Gen Urquiza*, about 70 hrs.

Hitchhiking To hitch to **Belo Horizonte** or **Brasília**, take a C-3 bus from Av Pres Antônio Carlos to the railway station, cross through the station to a bus station and catch the Nova Iguaçu bus. Ask to be let off at the Belo Horizonte turn off. For the motorway entrance north and south, take bus 392 or 393 from Praça São Francisco.

Directory **Airline offices** *Aerolíneas Argentinas*, R São José 70, 8th floor, Centro, T2292 4131, airport T3398 3520. *Air France*, Av Pres Antônio Carlos 58, 9th floor, T2532 3642, airport T3398 3488. *Alitalia*, Av Pres Wilson 231, 21st floor, T2292 4424, airport T3398 3143. *American*, Av Pres Wilson 165, 5th floor, T0800-703 4000. *Avianca*, Av Pres Wilson 165, offices 801-03, T2240 4413, airport T3398 3778. *British Airways*, airport T3398 3889. *Iberia*, Av Pres Antônio Carlos 51, 8th and 9th floors, T2282 1336, airport T3398 3168. *Japan Airlines*, Av Rio Branco 156, office 2014, T2220 6414. *KLM*, Av Rio Branco 311A, T2542 7744, airport T3398 3700. *Lan Chile*, R da Assembléia 92, office 1301, T2220 9722/0800-554 9000, airport T3398 3797. *LAB*, Av Calógeras 30A, T2220 9548. *Lufthansa*, Av Rio Branco 156D, T2217 6111, airport T3398 5855. *RioSul/Nordeste*, Av Rio Branco 85, 10th floor, T2507 4488 (has an advance check-in desk in Rio Sul Shopping). *Swissair*, Av Rio Branco 108, 10th floor, T2297 5177, airport T3398 4330. *TAP*, Av Rio Branco 311-B, T2210 1287, airport, T3398 3455. *United*, Av Pres Antônio Carlos 51, 5th floor, T0800-245532. *Varig*, Av Rio Branco 277G, T2220 3821, information, T0800 997000 bookings; airport T3398 2122. *Vasp*, R Santa Luzia 735, T0800-998277

Banks *Banco Internacional* (Bank of America and Royal Bank of Canada), R do Ouvidor 90. *Banco Holandês Unido*, R do Ouvidor 101. *Citibank*, R Assembléia 100, changes large US$ TCs into smaller ones, no commission, advances cash on Eurocard/MasterCard. Many others. *Banco do Brasil*, there are only 2 branches in Rio which will change US$ TCs, Praia de Botafogo, 384A, 3rd floor (minimium US$200) and the central branch at R Sen Dantas 105, 4th floor (minimum US$500 – good rates). *Banco do Brasil* at the International Airport is open 24 hrs a day. The international airport is probably the only place to change TCs at weekends. Visa cash withdrawals at *Banco do Brasil* (many ATMs at the R Sen Dantas branch, no queues) and *Bradesco* (personal service or machines). MasterCard and Cirrus cash machines at most *Bamerindus* branches in Centro, Copacabana, Ipanema and other locations. Some *BBV* branches have Visa and MasterCard ATMs. Also at Santos Dumont airport. *Lloyds TSB Bank*, R da Alfândega 332, 7th floor.

Money changers: *American Express*, Av Atlântica 1702, loja 1, T2548 2148 Mon-Fri 0900-1600, Av Pres Wilson 231, 18th floor, Centro, and at Galeão airport, T3398 3671 (VIP room 1st floor), good rates (toll-free number 0800-785050). Most large hotels and reputable travel agencies will change currency and TCs. Copacabana (where rates are generally worse than in the centre) abounds with *câmbios* and there are many also on Av Rio Branco. *Câmbio Belle Tours*, Rio Sul Shopping, ground floor, loja 101, parte A-10, Mon-Fri 1000-1800, Sat 1000-1700, changes cash. In the gallery at Largo do Machado 29 are *Câmbio Nick* at loja 22 and, next door but one, *Casa Franca*.

Communications **Internet:** *@point*, Barra Shopping, Av das Americas 4666, Barra da Tijuca. Several places in Rio Sul Shopping, Botafogo. Many on Av NS de Copacabana and others on R Visconde de Pirajá, Ipanema. *Tudo é Fácil*, 3 branches in Copacabana: R Xavier da Silveira, 19; Av Prado Júnior 78 and R Barata Ribeiro 396. Well-organized, with identification cards so once registered you can bypass the front desk, telephone booths and scanners, US$2 per hr, discounts for extended use. **Post :** The central Post Office is on R 1 de Março 64, at the corner of R do Rosário. Av NS de Copacabana 540 and many other locations. All handle international post. There is a post office at Galeão airport. Poste Restante: Correios, Av NS de Copacabana 540 and all large post offices (letters held for a month, recommended, US$0.10 per letter). *Federal Express*, Av Calógeras 23 (near Santa Luzia church) T2262 8565, is reliable. **Telephone:** International calls can be made at Av NS de Copacabana 540, 2nd floor; Jobim international airport; Santos Dumont airport, mezzanine (0530-2300); Novo Rio rodoviária; R Dias da Cruz 192, Méier-4, 24 hrs, 7 days a week; Urca, near the Pão de Açúcar cable car; Praça Tiradentes 41, a few mins' walk from Metrô Carioca; R Visconde de Pirajá 111, Ipanema; R do Ouvidor 60, Centro. International telephone booths are blue. Larger *Embratel* offices have telex and fax, as do many larger Correios, eg Av NS de Copacabana 540, fax number for receiving messages F2547 4774.

Brazil

Cultural centres British Council, R Elmano Cardim 10, Urca, T2295 7782, F2541 3693. **Sociedade Brasileira de Cultura Inglesa**, Av Graça Aranha 327 and in Copacabana, T2267 4048 (central information). **German Cultur-Institut** (Goethe), Av Graça Aranha 416, 9th floor. Mon-Thu 1200-1900, Wed-Thu 1000-1100.

Embassies and consulates **Argentina**, Praia de Botafogo 228,T2553 1646. Very helpful over visas, 1130-1600. **Australia** , Av Presidente Wilson, T3824 4624. Mon-Fri 9000-1300, 1430-1800. **Austria**, Av Atlântica 3804, T2522 2286. **Canada**, R Lauro Müller 116, T2543 3004. **Denmark**, Praia do Flamengo 66, T2558 6050. **France**, Av Pres Antônio Carlos 58, T2210 1272. **Germany**, R Pres Carlos de Campos 417, T2553 6777. *Israel*, Av NS de Copacabana 680, T2548 5432. **Netherlands**, Praia de Botafogo 242, 10th floor, T2552 9028. **Paraguay**, same address, 2nd floor, T2553 2294. **Sweden, Finland** and **Norway**, Praia do Flamengo 344, 9th floor, T2553 5505. **Switzerland**, R Cândido Mendes 157, 11th floor, T2252 4119. **UK**, Praia do Flamengo 284, 2nd floor. T2555 3223 (consular section direct line)/5976, F2553 6850, consular section is open Mon-Fri 0900-1230 (the consulate's hrs are 0830-1700), Metrô Flamengo, or bus 170, issues a useful 'Guidance for Tourists' pamphlet. **Uruguay**, Praia de Botafogo 242, 6th floor,T2553 6030. **USA**, Av Pres Wilson 147, T2292 7117. Mon-Fri 0800-1100.

Language courses *Instituto Brasil-Estados Unidos*, Av Copacabana 690, 5th floor, 8-week course, 3 classes a week, US$200, 5-week intensive course US$260. Good English library at same address. *IVM Português Prático*, R do Catete 310, sala 302, US$18 per hr for individual lessons, cheaper for groups. Helpful staff. Recommended. *Cursos da UNE* (União Nacional de Estudantes), R Catete 243, include cultural studies and Portuguese classes for foreigners.

Laundry *Fénix*, R do Catete 214, loja 20. *Laundromat* at Av NS de Copacabana 1216. In Rio Sul are self-service laundrettes such as *Lavelev*, about US$7 for a machine, including detergent and drying, 1 hr. Also at R Buarque de Macedo 43B, Catete; R Voluntários da Patria 248, Botafogo; Av Prado Júnior 63B, Copacabana. *Lavlev Flamengo*, RC de Baependi 78, or R das Laranjeiras 43, L28.

Medical services Vaccinations at **Saúde de Portos**, Praça Mcal Âncora, T2240 8628/8678, Mon-Fri 1000-1100, 1500-1800 (international vaccination book and ID required). *Policlínica*, Av Nilo Peçanha 38. Recommended for diagnosis and investigation. A good public hospital for minor injuries and ailments is **Hospital Municipal Rocha Maia**, R Gen Severiano 91, Botafogo, T2295 2295/2121, near Rio Sul Shopping Centre. Free, but there may be queues. **Hospital Miguel Couto**, Mário Ribeiro 117, Gávea, T274 6050. Has a free casualty ward. **Health:** Dentist: English-speaking, *Amílcar Werneck de Carvalho Vianna*, Av Pres Wilson 165, suite 811. *Dr Mauro Suartz*, R Visconde de Pirajá 414, room 509, T2287 6745. Speaks English and Hebrew, helpful.

Take note of local advice on water pollution. Air pollution also occurs

Useful addresses Immigration: Federal Police, Praça Mauá (passport section), entrance in Av Venezuela, T2291 2142. To renew a 90-day visa, US$12.50. The web site www.addresses.com.br/ is a comprehensive guide to addresses in the city. **Ibama**, Praça 15 de Novembro 42, 8th floor, T2506 1737, F2221 4911. *Student Travel Bureau*, Av Nilo Peçanha 50, SL 2417, Centro, T/F544 2627, and R Visconde de Pirajá 550, lj 201, Ipanema, T512 8577, F51 1437, www.stb.com.br (with offices throughout the country) has details of travel, discounts and cultural exchanges for ISIC holders.

Rio de Janeiro State: East and Inland from Rio

This city is reached across Guanabara Bay by ferries which carry some 200,000 commuters a day. Founded in 1573, Niterói has various churches and forts, plus buildings associated with the city's period as state capital (until 1960). Many of these are grouped around the Praça da República. The **Capela da Boa Viagem** (1663) stands on a fortified island, attached by a causeway to the mainland. The most important historical monument is the **Fortaleza Santa Cruz** (16th century, still a military establishment), on a promontory which commands a fine view of the entrance to the bay. It is about 13 km from the centre of Niterói, on the Estrada Gen Eurico Gaspar Dutra, by Adão e Eva beach. ■ *Daily 0900-1600, US$1.50. Go with compulsory guide. T2710 7840.*

The **Museu de Arqueologia de Itaipu** is in the ruins of the 18th century Santa Teresa Convent and also covers the archaeological site of Duna Grande on Itaipu beach. It is 20 km from the city. ■ *Wed-Sun 1300-1800, T2709 4079.* **Museu de Arte**

Niterói
Phone code: 0xx21
Colour map 7, grid B5
Population: 459,451

Brazil

Contemporânea-Niterói, Mirante da Praia da Boa Viagem, is an Oscar Niemeyer project and worth visiting. It is best seen at night, especially when the pond beneath the spaceship design is full of water. The exhibition inside changes. ■ *Tue-Sun 1100-1900, US$1, Sat 1300-1900, free, T2620 2400, www.macnit.com.br* The **Tourist office** is *Neltur*, Estrada Leopoldo Fróes 773, T2710 2727, in the São Francisco district, 5 km from ferry dock.

Transport Crossing from Rio: **Ferry**: from the 'barcas' at Praça 15 de Novembro (ferry museum at the terminal), ferry boats and launches cross every 10 mins to Niterói (15-20 mins, US$0.50). There are also catamarans ('aerobarcas') every 10 mins (about 3 mins, US$2.45). Of the frequent ferry and catamaran services from Praça 15 de Novembro, Rio, the slow, cheaper ferry gives the best views. **Bus/car**: the toll on the the Rio-Niterói bridge for cars is US$0.65. Bus 996 Gávea-Jurujuba, 998 Galeão-Charitas, 740-D and 741 Copocabana-Charitas, 730-D Castelo Jurujba, US$0.60-0.75.

Local beaches Take bus no 33 from the boat dock, passing Icaraí and São Francisco, both with polluted water but good nightlife, to the fishing village of Jurujuba. About 2 km further along a narrow road are the attractive twin beaches of Adão and Eva beneath the Fortaleza da Santa Cruz (see above). To get to the ocean beaches, take a 38 or 52 bus from Praça Gen Gomes Carneiro to Piratininga, Camboinhas, Itaipu (see the archaeology museum, above) and Itacoatiara. These are fabulous stretches of sand and the best in the area, about 40 minutes' ride through picturesque countryside.

Lagos Fluminenses To the east of Niterói lie a series of salt-water lagoons, the Lagos Fluminenses. The first major lakes, Maricá and Saquarema are muddy, but the waters are relatively unpolluted and wildlife abounds in the surrounding scrub and bush. An unmade road goes along the coast between Itacoatiara and Cabo Frio, giving access to the many long, open beaches of Brazil's **Costa do Sol**.

In the holiday village of **Saquarema**, the little white church of Nossa Senhora de Nazaré (1675) is on a green promontory jutting into the ocean. Saquarema is a fishing town and the centre for surfing in Brazil. Beware of strong currents, though. ■ Mil e Um *(1001) bus Rio-Saquarema, every 2 hrs 0730-1800, 2 hrs, US$3.40.*

The almost constant breeze makes the lake perfect for windsurfing and sailing

The largest lake is **Araruama** (220 sq km), famous for its medicinal mud. The salinity is extremely high, the waters calm, and almost the entire lake is surrounded by sandy beaches, making it popular with families looking for safe, unpolluted bathing. All around are saltpans and the wind pumps used to carry water into the pans. At the eastern end of the lake is **São Pedro de Aldeia**, which, despite intensive development, still retains much of its colonial charm.

There are many hotels, youth hostels and campsites in the towns by the lakes and by the beaches.

Cabo Frio Cabo Frio is a popular holiday and weekend haunt of Cariocas because of its cool weather, white sand beaches and dunes, scenery, sailing and good under-water swimming (but mosquitoes are a problem). Forte São Mateus, 1616, is now a ruin at the mouth of the Canal de Itajuru, which connects the Lagoa Araruama and the ocean. A small headland at its mouth protects the nearest beach to the town, Praia do Forte, which stretches south for about 7½ km to Arraial do Cabo. Tourist information is in a large orange building, Av do Contorno 200, Praia do Forte, T2647 1689, www.cabofrio.tur.br ■ *A new airport has opened linking the area with Belo Horizonte, Brasília, Rio de Janeiro and São Paulo. The rodoviária is 2 km from the centre. Bus from Rio every 30 mins, 2½ hrs, US$8. To Búzios, from the local bus terminus in the town centre, every hr, US$1.*

Phone code: 0xx24
Colour map 7, grid B5
Population: 126,828
156 km from Rio

Sleeping A wide selection of hotels including: **L** *La Plage*, R dos Badejos 40, Praia do Peró, T/F26435690. Close to the beach, with restaurant and pool. **B** *Pousada Suzy*, Av Júlia

Brazil

Kubitschek 48, T2643 1742. Conveniently located 100 m from the rodoviária. **D** *Praia das Palmeiras*, Praia das Palmeiras 1, T/F2643 2866. **E** pp *Remmar Residence*, Av Teixeiroa e Souza 1203 (main route into town), close to beach and bus station, T2643 2313, F2645 5976. Short stay apartments with kitchen, bath and laundry. **Youth hostels** *São Lucas*, R Goiás 266, Jardim Excelsior, T2645 3037, 3 mins from the rodoviária; reservations are necessary in Dec-Feb. **Camping** Clube do Brasil site at Estrada dos Passageiros 700, 2 km from town, T2643 3124. On the same road, at No 370 is *Camping da Estação*, T2643 1786. **Eating Mid-range**: *Picolino*, R Mcal Floriano 319. Good, local seafood with some international dishes in a pleasant setting. **Cheap**: *Do Zé*, on the canal quayside. Brazilian food, reliable. **Very cheap**: Fast food outlets can be found along the seafront (Av do Contorno) at Praia do Forte.

Búzios

Known as a lost paradise in the tropics, this village found fame in the 1964 when Brigite Bardot was photographed sauntering barefoot along the beach. The world's press descended on the sophisticated, yet informal resort, following the publicity. Originally a small fishing community, founded in 1740, Búzios remained virtually unknown until the 1950s when its natural beauty started to attract the Brazilian jet-set who turned the village into a fashionable summer resort. The city gets crowded at all main holidays, the price of food, accommodation and other services rises substantially and the traffic jams are long and stressful.

During the daytime, the best option is to head for one of the 25 beaches. The most visited are Geribá (many bars and restaurants; popular with surfers), Ferradura (deep blue sea and calm waters), Ossos (the most famous and close to the centre), Tartaruga and João Fernandes. To help you to decide two to three hr schooner trips pass many of the beaches: US$10-15. *Escuna Buziana*, T2623 6760, or *Escuna Queen Lory*, T2623 1179.

Phone code: 0xx24
Colour map 7, grid B5
Population: 18,208
192 km to Rio
37 km to Arraial do Cabo
For information
www.buzioschannel.com.br

Brazil

AL *Colonna Park*, Praia de João Fernandes, T2623 2245, colonna@colonna.com.br Top quality, fantastic view of the sea. **AL** *La Mandrágora*, Av J B Ribeiro Dantas 1010, Portal da Ferradura, T2623 1348, mandragora@uol.com.br One of the most famous in Búzios. **A** *Pousada Hibiscus Beach*, R 1, No 22, Quadra C, Praia de João Fernandes, T2623 6221, www.hibiscusbeach.com.br Run by its British owners, garden, pool, light meals available, help with car/buggy rentals and local excursions. **A-B** *Saint Germain*, Altos do Humaitá 5, Praia da Armação, T2623 1044, www.buzioschannel.com.br/saintgermain Includes breakfast, fully-equipped, 150 m from beach, family run, English, Italian, Spanish and Scandinavian languages spoken, discount for Handbook owners. **B** *Pousada dos Tangarás*, R dos Namorados 6, lote 4, Geribá, T2623 1275, tangaras@mar.com.br Good. **B** *Pousada La Coloniale*, R das Pedras 52, T2623 1434, lacoloniale@uol.com.br Ideally located for nightlife, but noisy until the early hrs. **D** *Pousada Axé*, R do Sossego 200, T2623 2008. Includes

Sleeping
Even though there are more than 150 pousadas, prior reservations are needed in summer, at holidays such as Carnival and the New Year's Eve, and weekends. For cheaper options and better availability, try Cabo Frio

breakfast, a/c, TV, fridge, helpful, good value, pool. **D** *Brigitta's Guest House*, Rua das Pedras 131, T/F2623 6157, brigittas@mar.com.br Beautifully decorated little *pousada* with a nice restaurant, bar and tea house. **D** *Casa da Ruth*, R dos Gravatás, Geribá, T2623 2242, www.buziosturismo.com **Youth hostel E** *Praia dos Amores*, Av José Bento Ribeiro Dantas 92, T2623 2422. IYHA, not far from the bus station. Recommended. Several private houses rent rooms, especially in summer and holidays. Look for the signs: 'Alugo Quartos'.

Eating

Restaurants on R das Pedras tend to be expensive. Cheaper options can be found in the surrounding streets

Expensive: *Estância Don Juan*, R das Pedras, 178. Grill and restaurant. *Moqueca Capixaba*, R Manoel de Carvalho 116, Centro. Brazilian seafood. *Kassai*, R das Pedras 275. Japanese. **Cheap**: *Bob's*, in front of *Shopping One*, R das Pedras. Hamburgers and chips to take away. *Chez Michou*, R das Pedras 90. Open-air bar with videos and music, pancakes accompanied by ice cold beer. *Skipper*, Av J B Ribeiro Dantas 392, Praia do Canto. Pizza. **Cheap** A few places on Praça Santos Dumont off R das Pedras offer sandwiches and self-service food, including *La Prima* on Av Manuel Turibo de Farias which doubles as a bakery.

Nightlife

A must in Búzios. R das Pedras has the best choice of restaurants, cafés, art galleries and bars. Crowded at weekends and holidays, especially after 2300. Good options are: *Zapata Mexican Bar*, R das Pedras. A Mexican theme bar and restaurant that serves as the only disco in town. *Ta-ka-ta ka-ta*, R das Pedras 256. One of the craziest bars in Búzios: owned by a foreigner who speaks fluent Portuguese, Spanish, English, German, Dutch, worth a visit.

Transport By car via BR-106 takes about 2½ hrs from Rio. **Bus:** *Mil e Um* from Novo Rio, go to T0xx21-2516 1001,US$ 8, 2½ hrs (be at the bus terminal 20 mins before departure). 4 departures daily 0815 from Rio a/c, 1300 from Búzios a/c. You can also take any bus to Cabo Frio (many more during the day), from where it's 30 mins to Búzios. Buy the ticket in advance on major holidays. Búzios' rodoviária is a few blocks' walk from the centre. Some pousadas are within 10 mins on foot, eg La Coloniale, Brigitta's, while others need a local bus (US$0.50) or taxi. Buses from Cabo Frio run the length of the peninsula and pass several pousadas.

Directory **Communications** Internet: *buzios@internet*, Av J B Ribeiro Dantas, 97, close to *Shopping One* US$1.20 for 30 mins.

Petrópolis

Phone code: 0xx24
Post code: 25600
Colour map 7, grid B5
Population: 286,537
Altitude: 809 m
68 km N of Rio

A steep scenic mountain road from Rio leads to this summer resort, known for its floral beauty and hill scenery, coupled with adventure sports. Until 1962 Petrópolis was the 'summer capital' of Brazil. Now it combines manufacturing industry (particularly textiles) and tourism. There are possibilities for whitewater rafting, hiking, climbing, riding and cycling in the vicinity. Petrópolis celebrates its foundation on 16 March. Patron saint's day, *São Pedro de Alcântara*, 29 June.

The **Museu Imperial** (Imperial Palace) is Brazil's most visited museum. It is an elegant building, neoclassical in style, fully furnished and equipped. It is so well-kept you might think the imperial family had left the day before, rather than in 1889. It's worth a visit just to see the Crown Jewels of both Pedro I and Pedro II. In the palace gardens is a pretty French-style tearoom, the *Petit Palais*. ■ *Tue-Sun 1100-1700, US$2, R da Imperatriz 220, T2237 8000*. The Gothic-style **Catedral de São Pedro de Alcântara**, completed in 1925, contains the tombs of the Emperor and Empress. The Imperial Chapel is to the right of the entrance; ■ *Tue-Sat 0800-1200, 1400-1800*. The summer home of air pioneer **Alberto Santos Dumont**, known as 'A Encantada', R do Encanto 22. ■ *Tue-Sun 0900-1700. US$1*. The interior of the **Casa de Petrópolis**, R Ipiranga 716, T2237 2133, is completely original and over-the-top, but has been lovingly restored. It holds art exhibitions and classical concerts. A charming restaurant in the old stables is worth a stop for coffee, if not for lunch. ■ *Tue-Sun 1100-1900, Sat 1100-1300, US$2*. **Orquidário Binot**, R Fernandes Vieira 390 (take bus to Vila Isabel), a huge collection of orchids from all over Brazil (plants may be purchased). ■ *Mon-Fri 0800-1100, 1315-1630, Sat 0700-1100*.

Brazil

L *Pousada da Alcobaça*, R Agostinho Goulão 298, Correas, T2221 1240, F222 3162. Delight- **Sleeping**
ful, family-run country house in flower-filled gardens, pool and sauna. Worth stopping by for
tea on the terrace, or dinner at the restaurant. Recommended. **A** *Margaridas*, R Bispo Pereira
Alves 235, T2242 4686, near Trono de Fátima. Chalet-style in lovely gardens with a swimming pool, charming proprietors. **A** *Casablanca*, R da Imperatriz 286, T2242 6662, F2242
5946. Most atmospheric of the 3 in this chain, pool. **B** *Casablanca Center*, Gen Osório 28,
T2242 2612, F2242 6298; and **B** *Casablanca Palace*, R 16 de Março 123, T2242 0162, F2242
5946. **B** *York*, R do Imperador 78, T2243 2662, F2242 8220. A short walk from the Rodoviária,
convenient, helpful, the fruit and milk at breakfast come from the owners' own farm. Recommended. **C** *Comércio*, R Dr Porciúncula 55, T2242 3500, opposite the Rodoviária. Shared
bath, very basic.

Mid-range: *Falconi*, R do Imperador 757. Traditional Italian. Recommended. **Cheap**: **Eating**
Cantina Bom Giovanni, R do Imperador 729 upstairs. Popular, Italian, lunch and dinner.
Casa d'Ángelo, R do Imperador 700, by Praça Dom Pedro II. Traditional tea house with self
service food that doubles as a bar at night.

Bus From Rio every 15 mins throughout the day (US$3) with *Única Fácil*, Sun every hr, 1½ **Transport**
hrs, sit on the left hand side for best views. Return tickets are not available, so buy tickets for
the return on arrival in Petrópolis. The ordinary buses leave from the rodoviária in Rio; a/c
buses, hourly from 1100, from Av Nilo Peçanha, US$4. To **Teresópolis**, *Viação Teresópolis*, 8
a day, US$3. *Salutário* to **São Paulo**, daily at 2330.

Banks *Banco do Brasil*, R Paulo Barbosa 81. A Banco 24 Horas ATM is located by the *Varig* office at R **Directory**
Marechal Deodoro 98. Travel agencies with exchange: *BKR*, R Gen Osório 12, *Goldman*, R Barão de
Amazonas 46, and *Vert Tur*, R 16 de Março 244, from 1000-1630. **Communications** Internet:
Compuland, R do Imperador opposite Praça Dr Sá Earp. US$1.50 per hr. **Post Office:** R do Imperador
350. **Telephone:** *Telerj*, R Marechal Deodoro, just above Praça Dr Sá Earp. **Tourist offices**: Petrotur, in
the Prefeitura de Petrópolis, at the rear of the Casa do Barão de Mauá, Praça da Confluência 03, T2243
3561/0800-241516, has a list of tourist sites and hotels and a good, free coloured map of the city.
Mon-Fri 0900-1830, closed Sat and Sun. There is a tourist kiosk on Praça Dom Pedro II.

Brazil

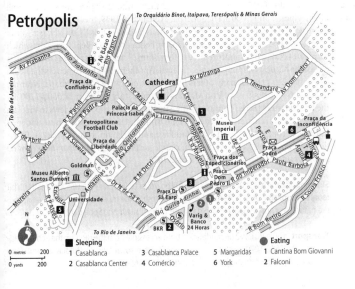

Petrópolis

To Orquidário Binot, Itaipava, Teresópolis & Minas Gerais

■ Sleeping		● Eating
1 Casablanca	3 Casablanca Palace	5 Margaridas	1 Cantina Bom Giovanni
2 Casablanca Center	4 Comércio	6 York	2 Falconi

0 metres 200
0 yards 200

Teresópolis

Phone code: 0xx21
Post code: 25950
Colour map 7, grid B5
Population: 138,081
Altitude: 910 m

Near the Serra dos Órgãos, 91 km northeast of Rio, this is the highest city in the state of Rio de Janeiro. Its name is a homage to the Empress Teresa Cristina, of whom it was the favourite summer residence. See the **Colina dos Mirantes** hill, a 30-min steep climb from R Jaguaribe (2 km from the centre), which has sweeping views of the area (a taxi up is not expensive). Around the town are the Sloper and Iaci lakes, the Imbui and Amores waterfalls, and the Fonte Judith (which has mineral-rich water, access from Av Oliveira Botelho, 4 km southwest). Just off the road to Petrópolis is the **Orquidário Aranda**, Alameda Francisco Smolka, T2742 0628 (5 km from the centre).

Sleeping **A** *Fazenda Montebello*, at Km 17 on the Nova Friburgo road, T/F2644 6313. A modern hotel with pool, price including 3 meals. Recommended. **C** *Várzea Palace*, R Sebastião Teixeira 41, T2742 0878. Highly recommended. Many cheap hotels in R Delfim Moreira, near the Praça. **Youth hostel** *Retiro da Inglesa*, 20 km on road to Nova Friburgo, Fazenda Boa Esperança, T2742 3109. Book in advance in Jan-Feb, dorm and family rooms, in the beautiful Vale dos Frades; camping beside the hostel. **Camping** *Quinta de Barra*, R Antônio Maria 100, Km 3 on Petrópolis road, T2643 1050.

Festivals **13 Jun**, patron saint's day, *Santo Antônio*; *São Pedro*, **29 Jun**, is celebrated with fireworks. **7 Jul** is the anniversary of the city's foundation. A second saint's day is *Santa Terezinha*, **15 Oct**. In **May** there is *Festa das Colônias*.

Transport **Rio-Teresópolis**: buses leave every 30 mins from the Novo Rio rodoviária. Book the return journey as soon as you arrive at Teresópolis; rodoviária at R 1 de Maio 100. Fare US$3.60. From Teresópolis to **Petrópolis**, 8 a day, US$3.

Directory **Tourist offices: Secretaria de Turismo**, Praça Olímpica, T2742 3352, ext 2082, and **Terminal Turístico Tancredo Neves**, Av Rotariana at entrance to town from Rio, T2742 3352, ext 2106.

Serra dos Órgãos The Serra dos Órgãos, so called because their strange shapes are said to recall organ-pipes, is an 11,000-ha national park (created in 1939, the second oldest in the country). The main attraction is the precipitous Dedo de Deus ('God's Finger') Peak (1,692 m). The highest point is the 2,263 m Pedra do Sino ('Bell Rock'), up which winds a 14-km path, a climb of three to four hours. The west face of this mountain is one of the hardest climbing pitches in Brazil. Another well-known peak is the Pedra do Açu (2,245 m) and many others have names evocative of their shape. Near the Sub-Sede (see below) is the **Von Martius** natural history museum. ■ *0800-1700*. By the headquarters (Sede) entrance is the Mirante do Soberbo, with views to the Baía de Guanabara. To climb the Pedra do Sino, you must sign a register (those under 18 must be accompanied by an adult and have authorization from the park authorities). ■ *Entrance US$1, with an extra charge for the path to the top of the Pedra do Sino. For information from Ibama, T2642 1070.*

Sleeping *Ibama* has some hostels, US$5 full board, or US$3 first night, US$2 thereafter, a bit rough. **Camping** 2 sites in the Sub-Sede part, 1 close to the museum, the other not far from the natural swimming pool at Poço da Ponte Velha; 1 site in the Sede part.

Transport The park has 2 dependencies, both accessible from the BR-116: the Sede (headquarters, T/F2642 1070) is closer to Teresópolis (from town take Av Rotariana), while the Sub-Sede is just outside the park proper, off the BR-116.

Brazil

Situated in a beautiful valley with excellent walking and riding, this is a popular resort during summer months.It was founded by Swiss settlers from Fribourg, the first families arriving in 1820. A cable car from Praça dos Suspiros goes 650 m up the **Morro da Cruz**, for a magnificent view of the rugged country (US$5). Most of the interesting sites are in the surrounding countryside, so a car may be necessary to see everything. ■ *Buses from Rio (every hr), 2 hrs, US$3.*

Nova Friburgo
Phone code: 0xx24
Post code: 28600
Colour map 7, grid B5
Population: 173,418
Altitude: 846 m

Sleeping A *Garlipp*, German-run, in chalets, with meals, at Muri, 8 km south, Km 70.5 from Rio, T/F2542 1173. Under the same ownership as *Garlipp* is **A** *Fazenda São João*, T2542 1304, 11 km from *Garlipp* up a side road. Riding, swimming, sauna, tennis, hummingbirds and orchids; the owner will meet guests in Nova Friburgo or even in Rio. **B** *Mount Everest*, R Manoel António Ventura 75, T2522 7350. Comfortable, good breakfasts. **B** *Fabris*, Av Alberto Browne 148, T2522 2852. Central, TV, hot showers, plentiful breakfast buffet, **D** without bath, good breakfast. Recommended. **Camping** *Camping Clube do Brasil* has sites on the Niterói road, at Caledônia (7 km out, T2522 0169) and Muri (10 km out).

North of Rio de Janeiro: the Coffee Zone

Miguel Pereira, 113 km north of Rio, has an excellent mountain climate. In the mid-19th century the area was entirely given over to coffee. There are several hotels and places to eat. The **Miguel Pereira-Conrado** railway: a tourist train, also known as the *Trem Azul*, affords beautiful views of mountains, rivers and waterfalls. The round trip of 56 km takes 4½ hours, costs US$25, and leaves Miguel Pereira at 0930 on Saturday, Sunday and public holidays. Museum at the railway station. ■ *Tue-Fri 1200-1700, Sat-Sun 0900-1400, T0xx24-2484 4877.*

Brazil

Northwest of Miguel Periera are the old coffee towns of Vassouras, Valença and Conservatória, all in the mountains, all with some fine 19th century buildings. During the 19th-century coffee boom, Vassouras was surrounded by coffee farms whose owners became immensely rich. The majority of their opulent town houses are still there, surrounding the beautiful main Praça Barão de Campo Belo. One example is at R Custódio Guimarães 65, the **Casa da Cultura**. Tourist information is available here. At the top of the praça is the church of **Nossa Senhora da Conceição** (1853). Behind the church is the Praça Sebastião Lacerda, surrounded by huge fig trees. A visit to the cemetery is recommended. At R Dr Fernandes Junior 160 is the fascinating **Casa da Hera** museum, an old country house covered with ivy. All the furniture, decoration and architecture is original. ■ *Wed-Sun 1100-1700, T2471 2342.*

Vassouras
Phone code: 0xx24
Post code: 27700
Colour map 7, grid B5
Population: 31,451

■ *Getting there: Several buses every day from Rodoviária Novo Rio with Normandy: first at 0615, last at 2030; first bus returns at 0430, last at 1900; 2 hrs; US$6.50.*

Sleeping and eating **B** *Mara Palace*, R Chanceler Dr Raul Fernandes 121, T2471 1993. Built in 1870, fully preserved, pool, bar, sauna, sports, nice atmosphere and good service, accepts major credit cards, owner (Gerson) can arrange visits to *fazendas*. The best restaurants are located on 'The Broadway' (R Expedicionário Oswaldo de Almeida Ramos), for example *Sputnik* and *Mafioso*; they have similar prices for pizza, pasta, steak etc, plus 'by weight' for weekday lunch.

Directory Banks Change all the money you will need in Rio before departing. As a last resort, try the local *Banco do Brasil* at R Caetano Furquim. **Communications** Telephone: *Telerj* between RR Caetano Furquim and Expedicionário Oswaldo de Almeida Ramos.

West from Rio

The Dutra Highway, BR-116, heads west from Rio towards the border with São Paulo. It passes the steel town of **Volta Redonda** and some 30 km further west, the town of **Resende**. In this region, 175 km from Rio, is **Penedo**, (five buses a day from

Resende) which in the 1930s attracted Finnish settlers who brought the first saunas to Brazil. There is a Finnish museum, a cultural centre and Finnish dancing on Saturday. This popular weekend resort also provides horse riding, and swimming in the Portinho River. For tourist information, T0xx24-3352 1660, ext 305. (**B** *Bertell*, R Harry Bertell 47, T3351 1288, with meals. **B** *Pousada Penedo*, Av Finlândia, T3351 1309, safe, pool, recommended, and many others. There are two campsites.)

Parque Nacional Itatiaia
This is a good area for climbing, trekking and birdwatching

Founded 1937 on the Serra de Itatiaia in the Mantiqueira chain of mountains, the park was the first to be created in Brazil. Its entrance is a few km north of the Via Dutra (Rio-São Paulo highway). The town of Itatiaia is surrounded by picturesque mountain peaks and lovely waterfalls. Worth seeing are the curious rock formations of Pedra de Taruga and Pedra de Maçã, and the waterfalls Poranga and Véu de Noiva (many birds). There is a **Museu de História Natural**, ■ *1000-1600, closed Mon*, and a wildlife trail, **Três Picos**, which starts near the *Hotel Simon*.

For tourist information in the town of Itatiaia, T024-3352 1660

Ins and outs Information and maps can be obtained at the park office. The **Administração do Parque Nacional de Itatiaia** operates a refuge in the park which acts as a starting point for climbs and treks. Information from **Ibama**, T0xx24-3352 1461 for the local headquarters, or T0xx21-224 6463 for Rio de Janeiro state. Information on treks can be obtained from **Clube Excursionista Brasileira**, Av Almte Barroso 2, 8th floor, T220 3695, Rio. It is very difficult to visit the park without a car and some parts are only possible in a 4WD vehicle.

Sleeping Cabins and dorms available in the park; you will need to book in season by writing to **Administração do Parque Nacional de Itatiaia**, Caixa Postal 83657, Itatiaia 27580-000, RJ, telephone as above. **A** *Simon*, Km 13 on the road in the park, T3352 1122. With meals, lovely views, helpful with advice on getting around the park. Recommended. **A** *Hotel do Ypê*, on the road in the park, Km 14, T3352 1453, with meals. Recommended. **B** *Pousada do Elefante*, 15 mins walk back down hill from *Hotel Simon*. Good food, swimming pool, lovely views, may allow camping. Cheap lodging at R Maricá 255, T3352 1699, possibility of pitching a tent close to the national park. **D** *Hotel Alsene*, at 2,100 m, 2 km from the side entrance to the Park, take a bus to São Lourenço and Caxambu, get off at Registro, walk or hitchhike from there (12 km), very popular with climbing and trekking clubs, dormitory or camping, chalets available, hot showers, fireplace, evening meal after everyone returns, drinks but no snacks. **Camping** *Clube do Brasil* site is entered at Km 148 on the Via Dutra.

Transport Bus: a bus from Itatiaia, marked *Hotel Simon*, goes to the Park, 1200, returns 1700; coming from Resende this may be caught at the crossroads before Itatiaia. Through tickets to São Paulo are sold at a booth in the large bar in the middle of Itatiaia main street.

The Costa Verde or Emerald Coast

The Rio de Janeiro-Santos section of the BR101 is one of the world's most beautiful highways, hugging the forested and hilly Costa Verde southwest of Rio. It is complete through to Bertioga (see page 404), which has good links with Santos and São Paulo. Buses run from Rio to Angra dos Reis, Paraty, Ubatuba, Caraguatatuba, and São Sebastião, where it may be necessary to change for Santos or São Paulo. The coast is littered with islands, beaches, colonial settlements and mountain *fazendas*.

Itacuruçá, 91 km from Rio, is a delightful place to visit. Separated from the town by a channel is the Ilha de Itacuruçá, the largest of a string of islands stretching into the bay. Further offshore is Ilha de Jaguanum, around which there are lovely walks. *Saveiros* (schooners) sail around the bay and to the islands from Itacuruçá: *Passamar*, T9979 2420; *Rio Sightseeing*, T2680 7339. Ilha de Itacuruçá can also be reached from **Muriqui**, a popular beach resort 9 km from Itacuruçá. There are hotels on the island. **Mangaratiba**, 22 km down the coast, is half-way from Rio to

Angra dos Reis. Its beaches are muddy, but the surroundings are pleasant and better beaches can be found outside town.

Transport Bus From Rio Rodoviária with *Costa Verde*, several daily, US$4.25. **Ferry** Daily boats to **Ilha Grande** (see below) at 0800, return 1730, US$30 return. This is a highly recommended trip. Check at the ferry station at Praça 15 de Novembro, Rio (see page 350).

Angra dos Reis

Said to have been founded on 6 January 1502 (O Dia dos Reis – The Day of Kings), this is a small port with an important fishing and shipbuilding industry. It has several small coves with good bathing within easy reach and is situated on an enormous bay full of islands. Of particular note are the church and convent of **Nossa Senhora do Carmo**, built in 1593 (Praça Gen Osório), the **Igreja Matriz de Nossa Senhora da Conceição** (1626) in the centre of town, and the church and convent of **São Bernardino de Sena** (1758-63) on the Morro do Santo Antônio. On the Largo da Lapa is the church of **Nossa Senhora da Lapa da Boa Morte** (1752), with a sacred art museum. Tourist information is opposite the bus station on the Largo da Lapa, very good, T3336 51175, ext 2186.

Phone code: 0xx24
Post code: 23900
Colour map 7, grid B4
Population: 119,247
151 km SW of Rio

Brazil

Excursions On the Península de Angra, just west of the town, is the **Praia do Bonfim**, a popular beach, and a little way offshore the island of the same name, on which is the hermitage of Senhor do Bonfim (1780). **Boat trips** around the bay are available, some with a stop for lunch on the island of Gipóia (five hours). Several boats run tours from the Cais de Santa Luzia and there are agencies for *saveiros* in town, boats depart between 1030-1130 daily, U$10-12 (during January and February best to reserve in advance. T3365 1097). For **Diving**, *Aquamaster*, Praia da Enseada, T3365 2416, US$60 for two dives with drinks and food, take a 'Retiro' bus from the port in Angra.

Sleeping & eating **L** *Frade*, on the road to Ubatuba (Km 123 on BR-101, 33 km from Angra), T3369 9500, F3369 2254. Luxury hotel on the Praia do Frade with restaurants, bar, sauna, sports facilities on land and sea. **A** *Pousada Marina Bracuhy*, at Km 115 on BR-101, 23 km from Angra, T3365 1485, F3363 1122. Lots of facilities for watersports, nightly shows and dancing during summer season or sailing events, restaurant. **C** *Pousada Tropicália*, R Silva Travassos 356, Frade, T3369 2424. With a/c, **D** without, **F** pp in dormitory, lovely building, helpful staff, also has restaurant/pizzeria, good. **E** pp *Rio Bracuí*, Estr Santa Rita 4, Bracuí, on the road to Santos at Km 115 (take bus to Paraty and ask driver to get off one stop after Marina Bracuhy, just past the bridge), T3363 1234, ajriobracui@quick.com.br Youth hostel open all year. **In town** is: **B** *Caribe*, R de Conceição 255, T3365 0033, F3365 3450. Central. Recommended. *Taberna 33*, R Dr Moacir de Paula Lobo 25, Centro. Popular Italian restaurant with moderate prices.

Festivals In **Jan**: at New Year there is a *Festa do Mar*, with boat processions; on the 5th is the *Folia dos Reis*, the culmination of a religious festival that begins at **Christmas**; the 6th is the anniversary of the founding of the city. In **May** is the *Festa do Divino* and, on the second Sun, the *Senhor do Bonfim* maritime procession. As elsewhere in the state, the *Festas Juninas* are celebrated in **Jun**. **8 Dec**: the festival of *Nossa Senhora da Conceição*.

Transport **Bus** To **Angra** at least hourly from Rio's rodoviária with *Costa Verde*, several direct, T516 2437, accepts credit cards, comfortable buses take the 'via litoral', sit on the left, US$5.75, 2½ hrs. From Angra to **São Paulo**, 5 buses daily (3 on Sat), US$12;. To **Paraty**, many buses leave from bus station or just flag the bus down at bus stops on the highway, US$3. To **Bracuí**, take Divisa Paraty, Frade and Residencial US$1.00, 35 minutes ride to the youth hostel. **Ferry** To Ilha Grande, 1½ hrs, daily at 1530, returns 1000, US$6.75. For day trips, go from Mangaratiba, see above. Fishing boats take passengers from Angra for about US$5. Also try the pier where the ferry leaves as there are often boats to Abraão carrying building material, US$3.

Ilha Grande

Phone code 0xx21
The island is covered
in Atlantic forest,
surrounded by
transparent green
waters

A two-hr ferry ride makes a most attractive trip through the bay to **Vila do Abraão**, the main village on Ilha Grande. There are about 100 beaches around the island, three dozen of which are regular tourist spots. The weather is best from March to June, it is best to avoid the peak summer months from December to February. There is a very helpful **tourist office** as you get off the boat, 0800-1100 and 1700-2100. It was once an infamous lair for European pirates, then a landing stage for slaves. In the 19th century, it was a leper colony and in the 20th century had one of Brazil's larger high security prisons (closed in 1994 and later destroyed). Most of it is now a state park, including the **Reserva Biológica da Praia do Sul**. Cars are not allowed on the island, so transport is either by boat, or on foot.

Sleeping and eating Many *pousadas* in **Abraão**: for example on R da Praia, none is large but all have a/c. **A** *Pousada do Canto*, 2 blocks from downtown, T3361 5115. Very good value, quiet location. Highly recommended. **B** *Tropicana*, R da Praia 28, T3361 5047, www.pousadatropicana.com **A** in high season, beachfront, French run, good open-air restaurant with great breakfast. **B** *Solar da Praia*, R da Praia 32, T3361 5368. Raphael speaks English and will act as a trekking guide. Others in this range. **C** *Estalagem Costa Verde*, nice place in green surroundings, near beach, T0xx11-3104 7940 (São Paulo), speak to Marcia or Marly. **C** *Pousada Cachoeira*, at the end of the village, T3361 5083. Run by German-Brazilian couple, English spoken, bungalows in green surroundings, pleasant. **C** *Pousada Beija Flor*, R da Assambléia 70, Vila do Abraão, T9648 8177. Good breakfast, fridge, book exchange, laundry service. **Youth hostel D** pp *Ilha Grande*, R Pres Vargas 13 (past Igreja Evangélica and turn left), T3361 5217. With breakfast, cheaper in low season. Alternatively you can rent a room in Abraão. For eating, try *Casa da Sogra*, Travessa do Beto. Recommended. *Mar da Tranquilidade*, reasonably priced, vegetarian options. *Minha Deusa*, R Professor Alice Coury 7, next to church. Brazilian, excellent food, reasonable prices.

Transport Ferry: see above under Angra dos Reis and Mangaratiba. **Boat**: boat trips cost US$10 without food or drinks, but including fruit. Recommended boats are *Victória Régia* (owned by Carlos, contact at *Pousada Tropicana*), *Papyk* or *André Maru* (owned by André). There is some good scuba diving around the coast; instructor Alexandre at Bougainville shop No 5. **Bicycle**: can be hired and tours arranged; ask at *pousadas*.

Paraty

Phone code: 0xx24
Post code: 23970
Colour map 7, grid B4
Population: 29,544

The town centre is out
of bounds for motor
vehicles; heavy chains
are strung across the
entrance to the streets.
In spring the roads are
flooded, while the
houses are above the
water level

Paraty is a charming colonial town whose centre has been declared a national historic monument in its entirety. It was the chief port for the export of gold in the 17th century and a coffee-exporting port in the 19th century. It is reached by taking the road beyond Angra dos Reis, which continues 98 km along the coast past the nuclear-power plant at Itaorna. Much of the accommodation available is in colonial buildings, some sumptuously decorated, with flourishing gardens or courtyards.

There are four churches: **Santa Rita** (1722), built by the 'freed coloured men' in elegant Brazilian baroque, faces the bay and the port. It houses an interesting **Museum of Sacred Art**. ■ *Wed-Sun 0900-1200, 1300-1800, US$1*. **Nossa Senhora do Rosário e São Benedito** (1725, rebuilt 1757), R do Comércio, built by black slaves, is small and simple. ■ *Tue 0900-1200*. **Nossa Senhora dos Remédios** (1787-1873), is the town's parish church, the biggest in Paraty. ■ *Mon, Wed, Fri, Sat 0900-1200, Sun 0900-1500*. **Capela de Nossa Senhora das Dores** (1800) is a small chapel facing the sea that was used mainly by the wealthy whites in the 19th century (Ms Grassa will open it for visitors if requested in advance). There is a great deal of distinguished Portuguese colonial architecture in delightful settings. **R do Comércio** is the main street in the historical centre. The **Casa da Cadeia**, close to Santa Rita church, is the former jail and is being converted into a historical museum. On the northern headland is a small fort, **Forte do Defensor Perpétuo**, built in 1822. The town has plenty of souvenir and handicraft shops. Nearby beaches **Praia do Forte** and **Praia do Jabaquara**, are worth visiting.

At **Fazenda Murycana**, an old sugar estate and 17th century *cachaça* distillery, you can taste and buy the different types of *cachaça*. It has an excellent restaurant. Mosquitoes can be a problem, take repellent and don't wear shorts. ■ *Getting there: Take a Penha/Ponte Branca bus from the rodoviária, four a day; alight where it crosses a small white bridge and then walk 10 mins along a signed, unpaved road.*

Excursions
There is a good chance of hitching a lift on the way back to Paraty

AL *Pousada do Sandi*, Largo do Rosário 1, T3371 2100, F3371 1236. 18th century building, charming, spacious rooms. **A** *Pousada Pardieiro*, R do Comércio 74, T3371 1370, F3371 1139. Attractive colonial building with lovely gardens, delightful rooms facing internal patios, extremely pleasant, swimming pool, calm, sophisticated atmosphere, but always full at weekends, does not take children under 15. **A** *Pousada Porto Parati*, R do Comércio, T3371 1205, F3371 2111. Good value. Highly recommended. **A** *Pousada do Príncipe*, Roberto Silveira 289, T3371 2266, F3371 2120. Belongs to descendants of the former Imperial family, lovely atmosphere with genuine works of art from the Brazilian Empire, all facilities, pool. Highly recommended (a Roteiro de Charme hotel, see page 337). **A** *Pousada Mercado do Pouso*, Largo de Santa Rita 43, T/F3371 1114, close to the port and Santa Rita. Recommended. **A** *das Canoas*, R Silveira 279, T3371 1133, F3371 2005. Recommended, swimming pool, a/c. **B** *Pousada Capitão*, R Luiz do Rosário 18, T3371 1416, www.paraty.com.br/capitao.htm Charming, close to the the historical centre, pool, English and Japanese spoken. **A** *Morro do Forte*, R Orlando Carpinelli, T/F3371 1211. Lovely garden, good breakfast, pool, German owner Peter Kallert offers trips on his yacht. Recommended. **B** *Pousada Villaggio*, R José Vieira Ramos 280, T3371 1870. Pleasant, between historical centre and rodoviária, pool, garden, good. **C** *Pouso Familiar*, R José Vieira Ramos 262, T3371 1475. Run by Belgian (Joseph Yserbyt) and his Brazilian wife (Lucia), near bus station, laundry facilities, English, French, German and Flemish spoken. Recommended. **C** *Solar dos Gerânios*, Praça da Matriz, T/F3371 1550. Beautiful colonial building, hard beds, but recommended.

D *Marendaz*, R Patitiba 9, T3371 1369. With breakfast, family run, simple, charming, close to the historical centre. **D** *Pousada da Matriz*, R da Cadeia, close to corner with R do Comércio, in historic centre. Basic but clean rooms, with bath, without breakfast, friendly if a little noisy. **D** *Pousada Lua Nova*, R Marechal Deodoro, T3371 2345. Cheap, pleasant, central. **Youth hostel** at R Antonio Vidal 120, Chacara (walking distance from bus station), T3371 2223/9914 5506. **Camping** There is a small Camping Club site on the Praia do Pontal, good, very crowded in Jan and Feb, US$8 pp, T3371 1877. Also at Praia Jabaquara, T3371 2180. *Camping Beira-Rio*, just across the bridge, before the road to the fort.

Sleeping
Many pousadas; in midweek look around and find a place that suits you best

Hiltinho, R Marechal Deodoro 233, T/F3371 1432, historical centre. Local dishes, excellent seafood, good service, expensive but worth it. *Corto Maltese*, R do Comércio 130. Italian, pasta. *Punto Divino*, R Marechal Deodoro 129. Excellent Italian. *Dona Ondina*, R do Comércio 2, by the river. Family restaurant, well-prepared simple food, good value (closed on Mon between Mar and Nov). *Café Parati*, R da Lapa e Comércio. Sandwiches, appetizers, light meals, also bar at weekends with live music. *Candeeiro*, R da Lapa 335. Good local food. *Umoya*, R Comendador José Luiz. Video bar and café, live music at weekends. *Bar Dinho*, Praça da Matriz at R da Matriz. Good bar with live music at weekends, sometimes mid-week. The less expensive restaurants, those offering *comida a quilo* (pay by weight) and the fast food outlets are outside the historical centre, mainly on Av Roberto Silveira. *Bar do Turquinho*, on the side street off Av Roberto Silveira opposite the petrol station. Tasty, cheap *prato do dia*.

Eating

Teatro Espaço, The Puppet Show, R Dona Geralda 327, T3371 1575, ecparaty@ax.apc.org Wed, Sat 2100, US$10: this world-famous puppet show should not be missed.

Entertainment

Feb/Mar: *Carnival*, excellent; Mar/Apr: *Semana Santa*, with religious processions and folk songs. Jul: *Semana de Santa Rita*, traditional foods, shows, exhibitions and dances (different days each year). Aug: *Festival da Pinga*, the *cachaça* fair, plenty of opportunities to over-indulge. Sep (around the 8th): *Semana da Nossa Senhora dos Remédios*, processions and religious events. Sep/Oct: *Spring Festival of Music*. 31 Dec: *Reveillon*, a huge party with open-air concerts and fireworks (reserve accommodation in advance).

Festivals

Brazil

Tour operators *Antígona*, Praça da Bandeira 2, Centro Histórico, T/F3371 1165, daily schooner tours, 5 hrs, bar and lunch on board. Recommended. *Paraty Tours*, Av Roberto Silveira 11, T/F3371 1327. English and Spanish spoken. All can arrange schooner trips, city tours, trekking in the rain forest and on the old gold trail, visits to Trindade beach, mountain biking, sugar estate visits and transfers. *Sol Nascente*, Praça da Bandeira 1, loja 3, T/F33711536. Diving specialist. *Narwhal*, T3371 1399, and *Cavalho Marinho*, R da Lapa, T/F3371 2148, also offer diving. *Soberana da Costa*, T3371 1114, and others offer schooner trips, US$10-US$20, 6 hrs, meals sometimes included. Recommended.

Transport **Bus** Rodoviária at the corner of R Jango Padua and R da Floresta. 9 buses a day go to **Rio** (241 km, 3¾ hrs, US$8.10, *Costa Verde* – see under Angra dos Reis for details; to **Angra dos Reis** (98 km, 1½ hrs, every 1 hr 40 mins, US$4). 3 a day to **Ubatuba** (75 km, just over 1 hr, São José company, US$4). To **São Paulo**, 1100 and 2335 (304 km via São José dos Campos, 5½ hrs, US$8.50, *Reunidas*, booked up quickly, very busy at weekends) and São Sebastião. On holidays and in high season, the frequency of bus services usually increases.

Directory **Banks** *Banco do Brasil*, Av Roberto Silveira, not too far from the bus station, exchange 1100-1430, ask for the manager. Exchange also at *Atrium Turismo*, R do Comércio 26, 1000-1900. **Communications** **Post Office:** R da Cadeia e Beco do Propósito, 0800-1700, Sun 0800-1200. **Telephone:** *Telerj* for international calls, Praça Macedo Soares, opposite the tourist office. Local and long distance calls can be made from public phones. **Tourist office** Centro de Informações Turísticas, Av Roberto Silveira, near the entrance to the historical centre, T3371 2148.

Brasília

The state of São Paulo

Population:
37 million
Area: 247,898 sq km

The state of São Paulo is the industrial heart of Brazil. São Paulo city is the financial centre of Brazil and has much of cultural interest in the way of museums and the famous Butantã Snake Farm. On the coast there are fine beaches, although pollution is sometimes a problem. Inland there are hill resorts and an important area of caves.

Background A narrow zone of wet tropical lowland along the coast rises in an unbroken slope to
There is ample rainfall; the ridge of the Great Escarpment – the Serra do Mar – at from 800 m to 900 m above
indeed, the highest sea level. The upland beyond the Great Escarpment is drained westwards by the trib-
rainfall in Brazil (3,810 utaries of the Rio Paraná. The broad valleys of the uplands are surmounted by ranges
mm) is over a small of low mountains; one such range lies between the São Paulo basin and the hinter-
area between Santos land of the state. West of the low mountains between the basin and the rest of the
and São Paulo; at São state lie the uplands of the Paraná Plateau, at about 600 m above the sea. One of the
Paulo itself it is no soils in this area is the *terra roxa*, the red earth in which coffee flourishes. When dry it
more than 1,194 mm gives off a red dust which colours everything; when wet it is sticky and slippery.

History The first colonial settlement in the area was São Vicente on the coast, near today's port of Santos, founded in 1532. In 1554 two Jesuit priests from São Vicente, Blessed José Anchieta and Padre Manuel Nóbrega, founded São Paulo as a *colégio*, a combined mission and school. They chose to settle inland because they wished to distance themselves from the civil authority, based in Bahia, and on the plateau there was much easier access to Indians to convert to Catholicism. The Paulistas embarked on a long period of expeditions into the interior searching for precious metals and gemstones. They pushed the frontiers of Portuguese territory further and further into Brazil in the era of the *bandeirantes*.

Between 1885 and the end of the century the boom in coffee and the arrival of large numbers of Europeans transformed the state out of all recognition. By the end of the 1930s São Paulo state had one million Italians, 500,000 each of Portuguese and immigrants from the rest of Brazil, nearly 400,000 Spaniards and nearly 200,000 Japanese. It is the world's largest Japanese community outside Japan. In the early 20th century, significant numbers of Syrian-Lebanese came to São Paulo.

Brazil

São Paulo

The overall aspect of the most populous city in South America is one of skyscrapers, long avenues, traffic and crowds. Most of its citizens are proud of São Paulo's high-rise architecture, of its well-lit streets and of the Metrô, but they also mourn the loss of innumerable historical buildings and green areas through short-sighted planning policies in the 1980s. The inhabitants of the city are called Paulistanos, to differentiate them from the inhabitants of the state, who are called Paulistas. Characteristic sharp changes of temperature cause people to catch cold often. In dry weather eyes and nose are continually troubled. The amount of air pollution can be exasperating and thermal inversions, in which a blanket of warm air prevents the dispersal of the industrial and automobile pollutants, are common

Phone code: 0xx11
Post code: 01000
Colour map 7, grid B4
Population: 18 million
Altitude: 760 m
429 km from Rio

Brazil

São Paulo orientation

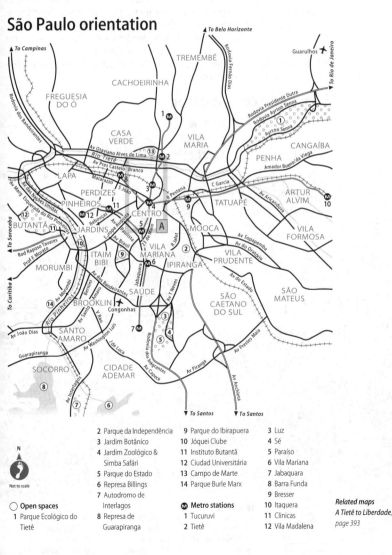

Open spaces
1 Parque Ecológico do Tietê

2 Parque da Independência
3 Jardim Botânico
4 Jardim Zoológico & Simba Safári
5 Parque do Estado
6 Represa Billings
7 Autodromo de Interlagos
8 Represa de Guarapiranga

9 Parque do Ibirapuera
10 Jóquei Clube
11 Instituto Butantã
12 Ciudad Universitária
13 Campo de Marte
14 Parque Burle Marx

Ⓜ Metro stations
1 Tucuruvi
2 Tietê

3 Luz
4 Sé
5 Paraíso
6 Vila Mariana
7 Jabaquara
8 Barra Funda
9 Bresser
10 Itaquera
11 Clinicas
12 Vila Madalena

*Related maps
A Tietê to Liberdade,
page 393*

Not to scale

History Until the 1870s São Paulo was a sleepy, shabby little town known as 'a cidade de barro' (the mud city), as most of its buildings were made of clay and packed mud. The city was transformed architecturally at the end of the 19th century when wealthy landowners and the merchants of Santos began to invest. One of the main reasons for the city's development lay in its position at the focus of so much agricultural wealth, and the availability of plentiful hydroelectric power. Nowadays, it covers more than 1,500 sq km – three times the size of Paris.

Ins & outs **Getting there** There are air services from all parts of Brazil, Europe, North and South Amer-
For more detailed ica to the international **airport** at Guarulhos, also known as Cumbica, Av Monteiro Lobato
information, see 1985, T6445 2945 (30 km from the city). *Varig* has its own, new terminal for international
Transport, page 400 flights, adjoining the old terminal which all other airlines use (*Infraero Sala VIP*, Mon-Fri 0800-1800, US$5 for comfort, coffee, cable TV). The local airport of Congonhas, 14 km from the city centre on Av Washington Luiz, is used for the Rio-São Paulo shuttle, some flights to Belo Horizonte and Vitória and private flights only, T5090 9195. The **main rodoviária** is Tietê (T235 0322), which is very convenient and has its own Metrô station. But the rodoviária has to cope with millions of people and the only way to the platforms is by stairs. This is very difficult for people with heavy luggage and, for the disabled, almost impossible. There are three other bus stations for inter-state bus services.

São Paulo centre detail

N

0 metres (approx) 200
0 yards (approx) 200

■ **Sleeping**
1 Bourbon
2 Central
3 Eldorado Boulevard
4 Gran Corona
5 Grand Cã d'Oro
6 Hilton
7 Itamarati
8 Othon Palace
9 Plaza Marabá & Términus
10 San Juan
11 São Sebastião

Brazil

Getting around and orientation Much of the centre is pedestrianized, so there is no option other than to walk if you wish to explore it. All the rodoviárias (bus stations) are on the Metrô (underground railway), but if travelling with luggage, take a taxi. The shopping, hotel and restaurant centre embraces the districts of Av São Luis, the Praça da República, and R Barão de Itapetininga. The central commercial district, containing banks, offices and shops, is known as the Triângulo, bounded by R Direita, 15 (Quinze) de Novembro, São Bento and Praça Antônio Prado, but it is rapidly spreading towards the Praça da República.

R Augusta begins close to Avenida São Luis, extends as far as **Avenida Paulista**, and continues beyond into one of the most affluent areas, Jardins. Both sides of R Augusta have a variety of shops, snackbars and restaurants, but the Jardins side contains the more exclusive boutiques and fashion houses, while the part which leads to the centre is a rather curious but colourful mix of seedy bars, saunas and five-star hotels. Avenida Paulista is now Brazil's largest financial centre housing most banking head offices (most consulates as well), and the Museu de Arte de São Paulo (see below). It has become a new downtown area, more dynamic, but considerably less colourful than the old centre. Set to replace Avenida Paulista as the main centre is Avenida Faria Lima, at the southwest edge of Jardins 8 km from Praça da República. Newer still is the movement of offices to Avenida Luis Carlos Berrini, which is yet further southwest, parallel to the Avenida das Nações Unidas and the Rio Pinheiros. Other popular residential areas are Vila Madalena and Pinheiros, both west of the centre.

Beware of assaults and pickpocketing in São Paulo. Thieves often use the mustard-on-the-back trick to distract your attention while someone else robs you. The areas around Luz station, Praça da República and Centro are not safe at night, and visitors should not enter favelas

Brazil

- - ▶ - - Historic buildings
walk

Tourist offices Information kiosks: **Praça da República**, very helpful, 0900-1800 daily, T231 2922. **Largo de São Bento**, 0900-1800. **Praça Dom José Gaspar** (corner Av São Luís), Mon-Fri 0900-1800, T257 3422. **Av Paulista** at Parque Trianon, 0900-1800 except Sat, T251 0970. **Av Brigadeiro Faria Lima** opposite the *Iguatemi Shopping Centre*, Mon-Fri 0900-1800, T211 1277. Shopping centres *Morumbi* and *Paulista*, 1000-2200 (Sat till 2000). An excellent free map is given at all these offices. Head office: Av Olavo Fontoura 1209, Parque Anhembi, T6971 5000/5423. **Tours of the city** three types of tour leave the kiosk on Praça da República each Sun, costing US$2: 3 to places of `green' interest, also historical and cultural, T6971 5000. Other tours leave R 15 de Novembro 347 Tue-Sun at 1000 and 1400, free. There are 2 different itineraries (2 hrs each). Tourist offices have free magazines in Portuguese and English: *Where* and *São Paulo This Month* (also available from most travel agencies and better hotels). Also recommended is Quatro Rodas' *Guia de São Paulo*. News stands sell a wide range of magazines and books which deal with tourism in the city and the state. Information on the web: *SPGUIA: O Guia Interativo Oficial da Cidade de São Paulo*, has a lot of information, www.spguia.com.br There are also offices at Guarulhos and Congonhas airports, helpful (0800-2200, Sat, Sun and holidays 0900-2100). **National parks**: Ibama, Alameda Tietê 637, Jardim Cerqueira, T3083 1300.

Sights

An historic buildings walk is indicated on the city map

A focal point of the centre is the **Parque Anhangabaú**, an open space between the Triângulo and the streets which lead to Praça da República (Metrô Anhangabaú is at its southern end). Beneath Anhangabaú, north-south traffic is carried by a tunnel. Crossing it are two viaducts: **Viaduto do Chá**, which is open to traffic and links R Direita and R Barão de Itapetininga. Along its length sellers of potions, cures, fortunes and trinkets set up their booths. The **Viaduto Santa Ifigênia**, an iron bridge for pedestrians only, connects Largo de São Bento with Largo de Santa Ifigênia.

On **Largo de São Bento** is the **Igreja e Mosteiro de São Bento**, an early 20th-century building (1910-22) on the site of a 1598 chapel. Due south of São Bento on R Líbero Badaró at Av São João is the **Martinelli building**, the city's first skyscraper. ■ *Mon-Sat 0900-1600, entry to 26th floor, free.* On Praça Antônio Prado stands the **Antigo Prédio do Banco do São Paulo**, the ground floor used for fairs and exhibitions. ■ *Mon-Fri 0900-1800.* The **Pátio do Colégio** is just east of Praça Padre Manuel da Nóbrega. This is the site of the founding of São Paulo and the present building is a reconstruction. It houses the **Capela de Anchieta** and the **Museu Casa de Anchieta**, which houses items from the Jesuit era, including paintings and relics. ■ *The chapel is open Mon-Fri 0730-1700; the museum Tue-Sun 1300-1630, US$1.*

A short distance southeast of the Pátio do Colégio is the **Solar da Marquesa de Santos**, an 18th-century residential building, which now contains the **Museu da Cidade**, R Roberto Simonsen 136. ■ *Tue-Sun, 0900-1700, T239 4238.* The **Praça da Sé** is a huge open area south of the Pátio do Colégio, dominated by the **Catedral Metropolitana**, a massive, peaceful space. The cathedral's foundations were laid over 40 years before its inauguration during the 1954 festivities commemorating the fourth centenary of the city. It was fully completed in 1970. This enormous building in neo-Gothic style has a capacity for 8,000 worshippers in its five naves. The interior is mostly unadorned, except for the two gilt mosaic pictures in the transepts: on the north side is the Virgin Mary and on the south Saint Paul. ■ *Closed in 2002.*

West of the Praça da Sé, along R Benjamin Constant, is the Largo de São Francisco. Here is the **Igreja da Ordem Terceira de São Francisco**. The convent was inaugurated in 1647 and reformed in 1744. To the right is the Igreja das Chagas do Seráphico Pai São Francisco (1787), painted like its neighbour in blue and gold. Across the Viaduto do Chá is the **Teatro Municipal**, one of the few distinguished early 20th-century survivors that São Paulo can boast (T223 3022). Viewing the interior may only be possible during a performance; as well as the full evening performances, look out for midday, string quartet and 'vesperais líricas' concerts.

Praça da República

It is easy to walk from Parque Anhangabaú to the Praça da República. Either go along Av São João (which is rather seedy in this part, with cinemas and sex shops) or, preferably, take the pedestrian streets from Viaduto do Chá. These streets tend to be crowded, but they have a wide variety of shops, places to eat and some hotels. In Praça da República the trees are tall and shady. There are also lots of police. Near the Praça is the city's tallest building, the **Edifício Itália** on the corner of Av Ipiranga and Av São Luís. There is a restaurant on top and a sightseeing balcony. Two blocks northwest of the Praça is the **Largo do Arouche**, by which is a large flower market. If you walk up Av São Luís, which has many airline offices and travel agencies (especially in the Galeria Metrópole), you come to Praça Dom José Gaspar, in which is the **Biblioteca Municipal Mário de Andrade**, surrounded by a pleasant shady garden.

North of the centre

About 10 minutes' walk from the centre of the city is the old **Mercado Municipal** covering 27,000 sq m at R Cantareira 306. ■ *Mon-Sat 0400-1600.* **Parque da Luz** on Av Tiradentes (110,000 sq m) was formerly a botanical garden. It is next to the Luz railway station. There are two museums on Av Tiradentes, near the park: the **Museu de Arte Sacra** in the Convento da Luz, No 676, ■ *Tue-Sun 1300-1800, T227 7694* and the **Pinacoteca do Estado** (State Art Collection) at No 141. ■ *Tue-Sun 1000-1800, free, T229 9844.* The **Igreja e Convento Nossa Senhora da Luz**, which

Brazil

houses the Sacred Art Museum, was built in 1774, one of the few colonial buildings left in São Paulo; the chapel dates from 1579.

Directly south of the Praça da Sé, and only one stop on the Metrô, is Liberdade, the **Liberdade** central Japanese district. The Metrô station is in Praça da Liberdade, in which there

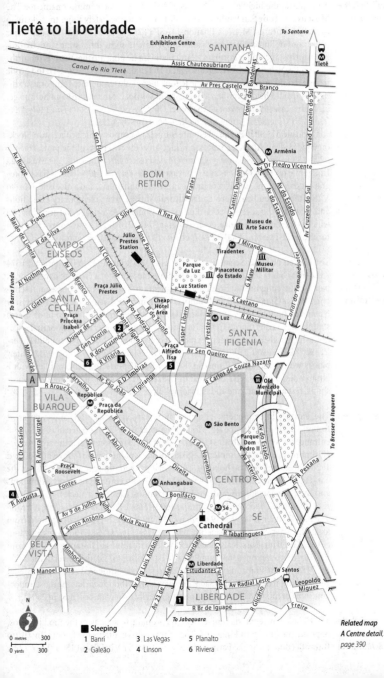

Tietê to Liberdade

Anhembi
Exhibition Centre

To Santana

SANTANA

Tietê

Canal do Rio Tietê

Assis Chateaubriand

Av Pres Castelo Branco

Ponte das Bandeiras

Viad Cruzeiro do Sul

Armênia

Av Dr Piedro Vicente

Av Rudge

Gen Flores

Sójon

BOM
RETIRO

R Prates

Av Santos Dumont

Av do Estado

Av Cruzeiro do Sul

Barão de Limeira

E Prado

R da Silva

R Silva

R Tres Rios

J Miranda

Museu de
Arte Sacra

CAMPOS
ELISEOS

Al Cleveland

R José Paulino

Júlio
Prestes
Station

Parque
da Luz

Tiradentes

Pinacoteca
do Estado

Museu
Militar

G Maia

To Barra Funda

Al Nothman

Av Rio Branco

Praça Júlio
Prestes

Luz Station

S Caetano

Canal do Tamanduatei

Al Glette

SANTA
CECÍLIA

Praça
Princesa
Isabel

Duque de Caxias

R dos Andradas

R do Triunfo

Cheap
Hotel
Area

Gaspar Libero

Luz

R Mauá

SANTA
IFIGÊNIA

R Gen Osorio

R Santa Ifigênia

R dos Gusmões

R Vitoria

Praça
Alfredo
Issa

Av Prestes Maia

Av Sen Queiroz

R D Timbiras

Av São João

R Ipiranga

R Carlos de Souza Nazaré

Old
Mercado
Municipal

A

R Arouche

Carvalho

República

VILA
BUARQUE

Praça da
República

São Bento

Parque
Dom
Pedro II

Av do Estado

To Bresser & Itaquera

R Dr Cesário

Av Amaral Gurgel

São Luís

7 de Abril

R Br de Itapetininga

15 de Novembro

Av do Exterior

R Pestana

CENTRO

Praça
Roosevelt

Fontes

Direita

Av 9 de Julho

Viad 9 de Julho

Anhangabau

J Bonifácio

SÉ

R Augusta

Santo Antônio

Maria Paula

Sé

Cathedral

R Tabatinguera

BELA
VISTA

Minhocão

R Manoel Dutra

Liberdade

R Cons

Liberdade
Estudantes

To Santos

Av Radial Leste

Leopoldo
Miguez

Av Brig Luís Antônio

Av 23 de Maio

Furtado

1

LIBERDADE

R Br de Iguape

R Glicério

I Freire

To Jabaquara

N

0 metres   300
0 yards   300

■ **Sleeping**		
1 Banri	**3** Las Vegas	**5** Planalto
2 Galeão	**4** Linson	**6** Riviera

Related map
A Centre detail,
page 390

Brazil

is an oriental market every Sunday (see Shopping). **Museu da Imigração Japonesa**, R São Joaquim 381, Liberdade (T279 5465), is excellent, with a nice roof garden; ask at the desk for an English translation of the exhibits. ■ *Tue-Sun 1330-1730, free.*

Avenida Paulista & the Jardins district Either Metrô station Vergueiro or Paraíso is convenient for the southeastern end of Av Paulista, the highlight of which is **MASP**. This is the common name for The **Museu de Arte de São Paulo**, at Av Paulista 1578 (immediately above the 9 de Julho tunnel); the nearest Metrô is Trianon-MASP (T251 5644). The museum has major collections of European painters and sculptors, and some interesting work by Brazilian artists, including Portinari. Particularly interesting are the pictures of northeastern Brazil by Dutch artists during the Dutch occupation (1630-54): the exotic tropical landscapes have been made to look incredibly temperate. Temporary exhibitions are also held and when a popular show is on, it can take up to an hour to get in. In this case, the later you go the better. ■ *Tue-Sun 1100-1800 (Thu 1100-2000, free), US$8; bus 805A from Praça da República goes by MASP.*

Opposite MASP is **Parque Tenente Siqueira Campos**, which covers two blocks on either side of Alameda Santos; a bridge links the two parts of the park. ■ *Daily 0700-1830 and is a welcome green area in the busiest part of the city.* The **Museu da Imagem e do Som** (MIS) is at Av Europa 158. ■ *Tue-Fri 1400-1800.* It has photographic exhibitions, archives of Brazilian cinema and music, and a nice café. Next to MIS is the **Museu Brasileiro da Escultura** (MuBE); free to temporary exhibitions and recitals in the afternoons. Av Europa continues to Av Brigadeiro Faria Lima, on which is the **Casa Brasileira**, Av Faria Lima 774, T210 3727, a museum of Brazilian furniture. ■ *Tue-Sun 1300-1800. It also holds temporary exhibitions.*

Other museums & sights in the central area The **Museu de Lasar Segall**, R Alfonso Celso 388/R Berta 111, Vila Mariana, T574 7322 (near Santa Cruz Metrô station), shows the works of a German expressionist painter who emigrated to Brazil. It has a cinema and library. Free courses and seminars. ■ *Tue-Sun 1400-1830.* **Memorial da América Latina**, designed by Oscar Niemeyer, built in 1989, at Av Mário de Andrade 664, next to Barra Funda Metrô station. Has a relief map of Central and South America under a glass floor in the section which houses a permanent exhibition of handicrafts from all over Latin America. ■ *Tue-Fri 0900-2100, Sat 0900-1800, Sun 1000-1800, free, T3823 9611.* A few blocks west is the **SESC Pompeia**, R Clélia 93, a sports and arts complex with a library, designed by Lina Bo Bardi in 1982-86. It has theatre, exhibitions, workshops, restaurant and café and is a vibrant place.

Ibirapuera The Parque do Ibirapuera, designed by Oscar Niemeyer and landscape artist Roberto Burle Marx for the city's fourth centenary in 1954, is open daily 0600-1730; entrance on Av Pedro Álvares Cabral. Within its 1.6 million sq m is the architecturally impressive new **Assembléia Legislativa** and a **planetarium** (shows at 1530 and 1730 at weekends and on holidays, US$5, half price for those under 18). Also in the park is the **Museu de Arte Moderna** (MAM), with contemporary art exhibitions and an exciting sculpture garden (see Nuno Ramos' *Craca* – Barnacle). ■ *Tue, Wed, Fri 1200-1800, Thu 1200-2200, Sat-Sun 1000-1800, US$2, students half price, free all Tue and Fri after 1700, T5549 6688, www.mam.org.br* Bicycles can be hired from local character Maizena beside the city hall, *Prodam*, US$1.25 for a bike wthout gears, US$2 with gears, leave document as security. Buses to Ibirapuera, 574R from Paraíso Metrô station; 6364 from Praça da Bandeira. ; to Cidade Universitária 702U or 7181 from Praça da República. Every even-numbered year the **Bienal Internacional de São Paulo** (São Paulo Biennial) at Ibirapuera has the most important show of modern art in Latin America, usually in September (next in 2004).

Cidade Universitária & Morumbi The Cidade Universitária (university city) is on the west bank of the Rio Pinheiros, opposite the district of Pinheiros. The campus also contains the famous **Instituto Butantã** (Butantã Snake Farm and Museum), Av Dr Vital Brasil 1500, T813 7222.

The snakes are milked for their poison six times a day but you may not witness this. It also deals with spider and scorpion venom, has a small hospital and is a biomedical research institute. What visitors see is the museum of poisonous animals and public health, with explanations in Portuguese and English. ■ *Tue-Sun 0900-1700, US$1(children and students half price). From Praça da República take bus marked 'Butantã' or 'Cidade Universitária' (Nos 701U or 792U) along Av Paulista, and ask to be let out at Instituto Butantã.* The **Museu de Arte Contemporâneo** (MAC), with an important collection of Brazilian and European modern art, is in the Prédio Novo da Reitoria, T3818 3039. ■ *Tue-Sat 1200-1800, Sun 1000-1800, free.* Also the **Museu de Arqueologia e Etnologia** (MAE), R Reitoria 1466, T3812 4001, with a collection of Amazonian and ancient Mediterranean material. Not far from the Butantã Institute, just inside Cidade Universitária, is the **Casa do Bandeirante** at Praça Monteiro Lobato, the reconstructed home of a pioneer of 400 years ago (T211 0920).

On the west bank of the Rio Pinheiros, just southeast of the Cidade Universitária, is the palatial **Jóquei Clube/Jockey Club** racecourse in the Cidade Jardim area (Av Lineu de Paula Machado 1263, T3816 4011.) Take Butantã bus from República, among others). Race meetings are held on Monday and Thursday at 1930 and Saturday and Sunday at 1430. It has a **Museu do Turfe**. ■ *Tue-Sun, but closed Sat and Sun mornings.*

Morumbi is a smart residential district due south of the Cidade Universitária. In the area are the state government building, **Palácio dos Bandeirantes** (Av Morumbi 4500), the small, simple **Capela de Morumbi** (Av Morumbi 5387), and the Morumbi stadium of São Paulo Football Club, which holds 100,000 people. Motor racing fans might like to visit the Morumbi cemetery, last resting place of Ayrton Senna; take 6291 bus to R Profesor Benedito Montenegro.

Museu da Fundação Maria Luisa e Oscar Americano, Av Morumbi 3700, Morumbi, T842 0077, is a private collection of Brazilian and Portuguese art and furniture. The garden has fascinating paths, patios and native plants. ■ *Tue-Fri 1100-1830, Sat-Sun 1000-1830.* It is close to the Palácio dos Bandeirantes.

Burle Marx Park, Av Dona Helena Pereira de Moraes 200, Morumbi. Designed by famous landscape designer Burle Marx, it is the only place in the city where you can walk in trails in the Mata Atlântica (Atlantic Rain forest). ■ *Daily 0700-1900.*

Parque da Independência

In the suburb of Ipiranga, 5½ km southeast of the city centre, the Parque da Independência contains the **Monumento à Independência**; beneath the monument is the Imperial Chapel, with the tomb of the first emperor, Dom Pedro I, and Empress Leopoldina ■ *Tue-Sun 1300-1700.* **Casa do Grito**, the little house in which Dom Pedro I spent the night before his famous cry of Ipiranga – 'Independence or Death' – is preserved in the park ■ *Tue-Sun 0930-1700.* The **Museu Paulista** contains old maps, traditional furniture, collections of old coins and of religious art and rare documents, and a department of Indian ethnology; ■ *Tue-Sun 0900-1645, US$1.* Behind the Museum is the **Horto Botânico/Ipiranga Botanical Garden** and the **Jardim Francês** ■ *Tue-Sun 0900-1700. Take bus 478-P (Ipiranga-Pompéia for return) from Ana Rosa, or take bus 4612 from Praça da República.*

Parque do Estado (Jardim Botânico)

This large park, a long way south of the centre, at Água Funda (Av Miguel Estefano 3031-3687), contains the Jardim Botânico, with lakes and trees and places for picnics, and a very fine orchid farm worth seeing during November-December (orchid exhibitions in April and November). ■ *Wed-Sun 0900-1700, T5584 6300. Take Metrô to São Judas on the Jabaquara line, then take a bus.*

Excursions

In Tremembé, a little beyond Cantareira, 30 minutes north of downtown, is the **Horto Florestal** (R do Horto 931, in Parque Estadual Alberto Löfgren, T952 8555), which contains examples of nearly every species of Brazilian woodland flora, 15 km of natural trails, a museum, a view of São Paulo from Pedra Grande on the right of the entrance to the park. ■ *Daily 0600-1800.* **Embu** (*M'Boy* – Big Snake),

Brazil

www.prefeituradeembu.com.br, 28 km from São Paulo, is a colonial town which has become a centre for artists and craftsmen. The town itself, on a hill, is surrounded by industry and modern developments and the colonial centre is quite small. Many of the old houses are painted in bright colours and most contain arts, furniture, souvenir or antiques shops. There are many good restaurants (eg *Orixas* and *Garimpo* on R NS do Rosario). On Sunday afternoons there is a large and popular arts and crafts fair (0900-1800). On Monday almost everything is closed. In the Largo dos Jesuítas is the church of **Nossa Senhora do Rosário** (1690) and the **Museu de Arte Sacra** ■ *Sat-Sun 1200-1700*. Tourist office on R Capelinha, on the Largo 21 de Abril.

Transport From São Paulo, *Soamin* bus number 179 leaves from Av Cruzeiro do Sul between Tietê rodoviária and Metrô station (it is marked 'Embu-Engenho Velho'); departures between 0610 and 2310, US\$2, 1 hr 45 mins. The route passes Clínicas Metrô, goes down Av Francisco Morato, then through Taboão da Serra: you see a lot of southwest São Paulo, but it is a long ride. A quicker alternative is to take a 'SP-Pinheiros' bus from Clínicas, which takes the main highway to Embu.

Essentials

Brazil

Sleeping

See Essentials for new telephone number changes ■ *on maps, pages 393 & 390* *Price codes: see inside front cover*

The best hotels are around Av Paulista and in Jardins. Around Praça da República there are some slightly cheaper, but still very good hotels and cheaper hotels can still be found on the pedestrian streets between Praça da República and Anhangabaú. In the daytime, this area is OK, but at night you should be careful. Ask your hotel which streets should be avoided. The Japanese district of Liberdade, south of Praça da Sé, has some pleasant hotels and is quite a good place to stay. Again, ask your hotel which directions are safest. The area between Av São João and Estação da Luz is where the cheapest hotels are. Some, but not all, are very seedy and the neighbourhood can be alarming at night.

Between Av Paulista and Praça Dom José Gaspar: The **LL** *Mofarrej Sheraton*, Al Santos 1437, T253 5544, F289 8670, on the south side of Av Paulista. Recommended. There are other international chain hotels. **L** *Della Volpe Garden*, R Frei Caneca 1199, T285 5388, F288 8710. Recommended. **L-A** *Grand Hotel Cà d'Oro*, R Augusta 129, T3236 4300, www.cadoro.com.br Extensive parking, good food, well decorated.

The following hotels are also good and are less expensive than the top flight establishments. They tend to be located closer to the downtown area. **AL** *Eldorado Boulevard*, Av São Luís 234, T214 1833, www.hoteiseldorado.com.br/hbouleva.htm Excellent. **AL** *Bourbon*, Av Vieira de Carvalho 99, T3337 2000, F221 4076, hbnsao@uol.com.br Very smart, pleasant. **AL** *Linson* R Augusta 440, Consolação, T256 6700, www.linson.com.br All apartments with double bed, kitchenette, sitting room, bath, TV, security system, restaurant, pool. **LL** *São Paulo Othon Classic*, R Líbero Badaró 190, T3291 5000, F3107 7203, www.hoteis-othon.com.br The only high-class hotel in the Triângulo, good. **AL** *Planalto*, Cásper Líbero 117, Santa Ifigênia, T230 7311, F227 7916. Secure, helpful, good service, good dining room. **A** *Gran Corona*, Basílio da Gama 95/101, T214 0043, F214 4503, in a small street just off Praça da República, www.spguia.com.br/grancorona/index.html Comfortable, good services, good restaurant. Warmly recommended. **A** *San Juan*, R Aurora 909, also near Praça da República, just behind Emtu airport bus terminal, T/F3225 9100. Recommended. There are many other Aparthotels which are recommended for longer stays.

In **Liberdade**: **B** *Banri*, R Galvão Bueno 209, T270 8877, F278 9225, near Metrô station Liberdade, good, Chinese owners. Recommended. Also **E** *Ikeda*, Rua dos Estudantes. With breakfast, shared bath, quiet.

There are scores of hotels with prices below the luxury ranges, of which we include a selection. **In the vicinity of Praça da República** On Av Ipiranga are **B** *Plaza Marabá*, No 757, T220 7811, F220 7227, recommended, and **B** *Términus*, No 741, T222 2226, F220 6162, also OK. **C-D** *Itamarati*, Av Vieira de Carvalho 150, T222 4133, 1½ blocks from Praça da República, www.hotelitamarati.com.br Good location, safe. Highly recommended and very popular. **C** *São Sebastião*, R 7 de Abril 364, T257 4988/255 1594. TV, fridge, phone, laundry service. Recommended.

Most of the cheaper hotels are in the area between Av São João and Estação Luz. The area can be approached either from Metrô República or Luz, but the red light district is in the blocks bounded by RR Santa Ifigênia, dos Andradas, dos Gusmões and Av Ipiranga, and is not recommended for women travelling alone. The area around Av Rio Branco is rather seedy and not entirely safe late at night. **C** *Riviera*, Av Barão de Limeira 117, T221 8077. Excellent value. Highly recommended. **D** *Central*, Av São João 288, T222 3044. Cheaper without shower, good, helpful, central. **D** *Center Plaza*, R Maestro Cardim 418, Paraíso, near São Joaquim metro station, T/F 289 3633, centerplaza@uol.com.br TV, fan, phone, accepts credit cards. **D** *Galeão*, R dos Gusmões 394, T220 8211. Safe, helpful, hot showers. **D** *Las Vegas*, R Vitória 390 (corner Av Rio Branco). Also recommended. **E** *Aliança*, R Gen Osório 235, corner of Santa Ifigênia. Nice. **E** *Joamar*, R José de Barros 187. With bath and breakfast; many others in the district.

Youth hostels Associação Paulista de Albergues da Juventude, R 7 de Abril 286, 2nd floor, Centro, T258 0388, www.alberguesp.com.br Membership is US$15 per year. Hostel at *Magdalena Tagliaferro*, Estrada Turística do Jaguará 651, Km 18, via Anhangüera, 05161-000 São Paulo, T258 0388. Open all year, reservations necessary, IYHF affiliated, take a Jaguará 8696 bus from Anhangabaú Metrô station to the Parque Estadual Jaguará, the hostel is 100 m from the entrance. **E** *Praça da Árvore*, Pageú 266, T/F5071 5148, www.spalbergue.com.br Member of Hostelling Internacional, kitchen, laundry, includes breakfast but not sheets, towels or luggage store, internet service (US$4.15), overpriced. An unaffiliated hostel is *Primavera* at R Mariz e Barros 350, Vila Santa Eulália, T215 3144 (bus 4491 from Parque Dom Pedro in the centre). US$10-15, cooking and washing facilities.

Camping A list of sites can be obtained from **Camping Clube do Brasil**, R Minerva 156, Perdizes, T3861 7133.

Apart from the international cuisine in the first-class hotels, here are a few recommendations out of many. The average price of a meal in 2002 was US$10-15 in trattorias, US$25-30 in first class places, but more in the very best restaurants; remember that costs can be cut by sharing the large portions served.

Eating

Brazilian *Bassi*, R 13 de Maio 666, T3104 2375, Bela Vista, for meat. *Paulista Grill*, R João Moura 257, Pinheiros, T853 5426. Top quality meat, excellent value, popular. *Vento Haragano*, Av Rebouças 1001, Jardim Paulista, T3085 6039. *Churrascaria rodizio*, very good. *Moraes*, Al Santos 1105, Cerqueira César, T289 3347, and Praça Júlio de Mesquita 175, Vila Buarque (Centro), T221 8066. Traditional meat dishes. *Sujinho*, R da Consolação 2078, T231 5207. Very popular *churrascaria*, with other branches on the same street. *Boi na Brasa*, R Bento Freitas by Praça da República. Very good, reasonable prices. *Dinho's Place*, Al Santos 45, Paraíso, T3284 5333. Fri seafood buffet, also meat, has daily bargains, also Av Morumbi 7976, T536 4299. *Paddock*, R da Consolação 222, sobreloja, T257 4768, and R Campo Verde 88, Jardim Paulistano, T814 3582. Traditional fare, excellent *feijoada*. *Dom Place*, Largo do Arouche 246. Good food and very good value (US$7 plus drinks). *Bolinha*, Av Cidade Jardim 53, Jardim Paulistano, T3061 2010. For *feijoadas* daily, and other dishes. *Oxalá*, Tr Maria Antônia 72, just off Consolação. Bahian specialities at modest prices.

French *La Casserole*, Largo do Arouche 346, Centro, T220 6283. Best known bistro in São Paulo, closed Mon. *Marcel*, R da Consolação 3555, T3064 3089. Sensational soufflés.

German *Arnold's Naschbar*, R Pereira Leite 98, Sumarezinho, T3672 5648. *Eisbein peruruca*. Recommended. *Bismarck*, Av Ibirapuera 3178, T240 0313. Good food and excellent draught beer.

Italian *Il Sogno di Anarello*, R Il Sogno di Anarello 58, Vila Mariana, T5575 4266. Mon-Fri 1900-0100 only, excellent, typical *cantina paulistana*. *Lellis*, R Bela Cintra 1849, T3083 3588. Very good but pricey, *salada Lellis* is a must, and fresh squid in batter. *Massimo*, Al Santos 1826, Cerqueira César, T3284 0311, Italian and international cuisine. *L'Osteria do Piero*, Al Franca 1509, Cerqueira César, T3085 1082. Excellent. *Famiglia Mancini*, R Avanhandava 81, Bela Vista, T256 4320. Excellent, salads and cold dishes, always queues between 2000-2400. *Gigetto*, Avanhandava 63, T256 9804. For pasta, reasonable prices. *La Trattoria*, R Antônio Bicudo 50, Pinheiros, T3088 3572. Closed Mon, midweek until 1900, Fri, Sat till 0100, reasonably priced food, *strozzapreti* a must. *Cantina D'Amico Piolin*, R Augusta 311, T255 4587.

Many restaurants now serve food by weight, even some of the better class places (but these are naturally more expensive per kg). You should compare prices carefully because an expensive per kg restaurant can work out more expensive than a normal one

Brazil

US$20pp including wine, good food. There are many Italian restaurants in the Bela Vista/Bixiga area, especially on R 13 de Maio; recommended pizzerias are *Capuano*, R Conselheiro Carrão 416, T288 1460, *Margherita*, Al Tietê 255, T3086 2556.

Portuguese *Antiquarius*, Al Lorena 1884, Cerqueira César, T3082 3015. Excellent.

Swiss *Chamonix*, R Pamplona 1446, Jardins, T3884 3025, and *Le Jardin Suisse*, Al Franca 1467, T5505 3110, both in Jardim Paulista. Expensive, very good.

Arabic *Almanara*, a chain of reasonably priced restaurants serving Middle Eastern/Lebanese food, Oscar Freire 523 (Cerqueiro César), R Basilio da Gama 70 and Av Vieira de Carvalho 109/123 (either side of Praça da República) and in Shoppings Iguatemi, Morumbi amd Paulista. *Bambi*, Al Santos 59, Paraíso, T284 4944. Mostly Arabic food. *Rubayat*, Al Santos 86, T289 6366. Excellent meat, fixed price meals.

Oriental (Japanese tends to be expensive) *Iti Fuji*, Al Jaú 487, Cerquera César, T285 1286. Typical Japanese. *Komazushi*, R São Carlos do Pinhal 241, loja 5, Bela Vista, T287 1820. Renowned for its *sushi*, closed weekends. *Kar Wua* Chinese restaurant, at R Mourato Coelho 30, Vila Beatriz, T881 1581. Highly praised. Many other Chinese and Japanese restaurants in Liberdade, where there is a Japanese food market in the square by the Metrô station.

General *Terraço Itália*, on top of Edifício Itália (Ipiranga 344 e São Luis), 41 floors up, 1130-0100, fixed price lunch and other meals, dancing with excellent band and superb view (minimum consumption charge of US$10 to be allowed to see the view), US$85 pp including wine in dancing part, US$65-70 otherwise, dress smartly. *Mexilhão*, R 13 de Maio 626/8, Bela Vista, T3263 6135, seafood. *Charlô*, R Barã de Capanema 440, Jardim Paulista, mostly French but also Brazilian. *Restaurante do MASP*, Av Paulista 1578, in the basement of the museum, reasonably priced, often has live music.

Vegetarian Almost always the cheapest option in São Paulo. *Sattva*, R da Consolação 3140, Cerqueira César. *O Arroz de Ouro*, Largo do Arouche 88. Shop as well, central. *Cheiro Verde*, Peixoto Gomilde 1413, Cerqueira César. More expensive than most. *Intergrão*, R Joaquim Antunes 377, Jardins. Macrobiotic. *Delícia Natural*, Av Rio Branco 211 (4th floor), corner of Av Ipiranga. Lunch only. *Sabor Natural*, same building, 1st floor, lunch only. *Folhas e Raizes*, Líbero Bádaro 370, Centro. Good value buffet lunch. *Saúde Sabor*, São Bento 500, Centro. Lunch only. *Sansão*, Av 7 de Abril. Good choice, including vegetarian, cheap. 'Vida Integral' monthly newspaper gives details of some health food restaurants and stores in São Paulo.

Comida por kilo restaurants can be found all over the city; there are many on R Augusta: very popular at lunchtime. One recommended local chain is *Viena*. In most Shopping Centres there is a *Praça da Alimentação*, where various food counters are gathered together, fast and simple. *Frevinho Lanches*, R Augusta 1563, famous for its *beirute* (speciality of São Paulo), as well as many other toasted sandwiches with pitta bread. *Baguette*, Consolação 2418, near Av Paulista, opposite Belas Artes cinema. For sandwiches, especially lively around midnight, also at R 13 de Maio 68. *Absolute*, Al Santos 843. Among the best hamburgers in town. *Rock Dreams*, Av Brigadeiro Faria Lima 743. For hamburgers and sandwiches. *Casa da Fogazza*, R Xavier de Toledo 328 and R 7 de Abril 60 (both close to Praça da República). *Calzone*, with different fillings, juices. Recommended.

There are several chains of bars selling mate and other teas and beverages, plus snacks and sandwiches

Bars and cafés *Fran's Café*, 24 hrs, Av Paulista 358; R Heitor Penteado 1326 (Sumaré); R Haddock Lobo 586; Alameda Lorena 1271 (Jardim Paulista); R Tamandaré 744 (Liberdade), and others. A recommended chain for a meal, day or night. *Café Paris*, Av Waldemar Ferreira 55, Butantã. Open 365 days. *Café do Bexiga*, 13 de Maio 76 and lots of others in Bixiga/Bela Vista area with live music, eg *Café Piu Piu* (closed Mon) and *Café Pedaço*, at 13 de Maio 134 and 140. Bixiga is traditionally known as the 'Bohemian' area and bars here are usually cheaper than Jardins and Pinheiros areas. *Finnegan's Pub*, R Cristiano Viana 358, Pinheiros, on an Irish theme, specializes in hamburgers and whiskey (not necessarily together). *Pé pra Fora*, Av Pompéia 2517, Sumarezinho, closed Sun, open-air. Recommended.

Entertainment See the *Guia da Folha* section of *Folha de São Paulo* and *Veja São Paulo* of the weekly news magazine *Veja* for listings. **Cinema** In cinemas entrance is usually half price on Wed; normal seat price is US$5 in the centre, US$7-8 in R Augusta, Av Paulista and Jardins. Cine clubs: *Cine SESC*, R Augusta 2075, and cinemas at the Museu da Imagem e do Som, Centro Cultural Itaú and Centro Cultural São Paulo.

Brazil

Nightclubs Clubs: Entrance US$5-20 which may include a drink: *Columbia* upstairs, R Estados Unidos 1570. Lively. *Hell's Club* downstairs, opens 0400. Techno, wild. *Cha-Cha-Cha*, R Tabapuã 1236. Closed Mon, no Brazilian music, art on walls, candles, gay and straight. *Balafon*, R Sergipe 160. Wed-Sun, small, Afro-Brazilian. *Reggae Night*, Av Robert Kennedy 3880, Interlagos. Thu-Sun, outdoors on lakeside. *Limelight Industry*, R Franz Schubert 93. Pop hits, Japanese restaurant upstairs. 5 other nightspots on this street. *Plataforma 1*, Av Paulista 424. Dinner and folkloric show, very touristy but extremely popular. *B.A.S.E*, Av Brig Luís Antônio 1137, Bela Vista. Techno and dance music. *Love Club & Lounge*, R Pequetita 189, Vila Olímpa. Trance, house, drum 'n' bass.

São Paulo is teeming with clubs catering to most preferences

Disco bars: *Banana-Banana Café*, Av 9 de Júlio 5872 (Jardim Paulista). Closed Mon. *HB Club*, R Cardeal Arcoverde 2958 (Pinheiros). Closed Sun, bar, snooker, and informal dance lessons. Test your new skills at *Blen-Blen*, same address at weekends, live Latin bands. *Cervejaria Continental*, R dos Pinheiros 1275 and R Haddock Lobo 1573. Packed, mixed music. *DaDo Bier*, Av Juscelino Kubitschek 1203, Itaim. Beer made on the premises, live music or disco.

Entrance/cover charges US$10-20

Theatre The *Teatro Municipal* (see Sights) is used by visiting theatrical and operatic groups, as well as the City Ballet Company and the Municipal Symphony Orchestra who give regular performances. There are several first-class theatres: *Aliança Francesa*, R Gen Jardim 182, Vila Buarque, T259 0086; *Itália*, Av Ipiranga 344, T257 9092; *Paiol*, R Amaral Gurgel 164, Santa Cecília, T221 2462; among others. Free concerts at *Teatro Popular do Sesi*, Av Paulista 1313, T284 9787, at midday, under MASP (Mon-Sat); see also Museums.

The most popular sport, for spectators and for players, is association **football**. The most important matches are played at Morumbi and Pacaembu stadia. **Horse racing** (Jockey Club) is mentioned above. For **hiking excursions**, etc, *Free Way*, R Leôncio de Carvalho 267, Paraíso, T285 4767/283 5983.

Sport

Foundation of the City 25 Jan. *Carnival* in **Feb** (most attractions are closed).This includes the parades of the escolas de samba in the Anhembi sambódromo – the São Paulo special group parades on the Fri and Sat and the Rio group on the Sun and Mon to maximise TV coverage. In Jun there are the *Festas Juninas* and the *Festa de São Vito*, the patron saint of the Italian immigrants. *Festa da Primavera* in **Sep**. In Dec there are various Christmas and New Year festivities. Throughout the year, there are countless anniversaries, religious feasts, international fairs and exhibitions, look in the press or the monthly tourist magazines to see what is on while you are in town. See Sights for the São Paulo Biennial.

Local holidays

Handicrafts Souvenirs from *Casa dos Amazonas*, Al Jurupis 460. *Galeria Arte Brasileira*, Al Lorena 2163, galeria@dialdata.com.br Good value. *Ceará Meu Amor*, R Pamplona 1551, loja 7. Good quality lace from the northeast. There is a *Sutaco* handicrafts shop at República Metrô station; this promotes items from the State of São Paulo, Tue-Fri 1000-1900, Sat 1000-1500; there is a showroom at R Augusta 435, 6th floor.

Shopping

   Jewellery There are many other shops selling Brazilian stones, including branches of *H Stern* and *Amsterdam Sauer*.

   Typical of modern development are the huge Iguatemi, Ibirapuera and Morumbi **shopping centres**. They include luxurious cinemas, snack bars and most of the best shops in São Paulo. Other malls include Paulista and Butantã. On a humbler level are the big supermarkets of *El Dorado* (Av Pamplona 1704) and *Pão de Açúcar* (Praça Roosevelt, near the *Hilton*); the latter is open 24 hrs a day (except Sun).

   Open-air markets 'Oriental' fair, Praça de Liberdade Sun 1000-1900, good for Japanese snacks, plants and some handicrafts, very picturesque, with remedies on sale, tightrope walking, gypsy fortune tellers, etc. Below the Museu de Arte de São Paulo, an **antiques market** takes place on Sun, 1000-1700. **Arts and handicrafts** are also sold in Parque Tenente Siqueira Campos/Trianon on Sun from 0900-1700. There are **flea markets** on Sun in the main square of the Bixiga district (Praça Don Orione) and in Praça Benedito Calixto in Pinheiros. The **Ceasa flower market** should not be missed, Av Doutor Gastão Vidigal 1946, Jaguaré, Tue and Fri 0700-1200.

São Paulo is relatively cheap for film and clothes (especially shoes)

Brazil

Bookshops *FNAC*, Av Pedroso de Morais 858, Pinheiros. Excellent range of foreign books, including Footprint. *Livraria Cultura*, Av Paulista 2073, loja 153, also at Shopping Villa-Lobos, Avdas Nações Unidas 4777, Jardim Universale. New books in English, stocks Footprint and other guidebooks. *Livraria Freebook*, R da Consolação 1924, ring bell for entry, wide collection of art books and imported books in English. *Livraria Triângulo*, R Barão de Itapetininga 255, loja 23, Centro, sells books in English. *Livraria Kosmos*, Av São Luís 258, loja 6, international stock. In various shopping malls *Livrarias Saraiva*, and *Laselva* (also at airports) sell books in English; *Siciliano*, at Shoppings Eldorado and Iguatemi, sells Footprint. *Sodiler*, Shopping Market Place, Av Nações Unidas 13947, Brooklin, loja 121A, floor T. *Librairie Française*, R Barão de Itapetininga 275, ground floor, wide selection, also at R Professor Atilio Innocenti 920, Jardins. *Letraviva*, Av Rebouças 1986, Mon-Fri 0900-1830, Sat 0900-1400, specializes in books and music in Spanish. *Duas Cidades*, R Bento Freitas 158, near República, good selection of Brazilian and Spanish American literature.

Maps *Quatro Rodas*, *Mapograf*, *Cartoplam*, and the map given out by the tourist kiosks; *RGN Public Ltda* produces a map which is given out free in various places and which is adapted to show its sponsors' locations. A variety of maps and timetables are sold in news stands. Map shops: *Mapolândia*, 7 de Abril 125, 1st floor. There are 2 private map publishers: *Geo Mapas*, R Gen Jardim 645, 3rd floor, Consolação (40% discount for volume purchases, excellent 1988 1:5,000,000 map of Brazil, town maps), and *Editorial Abril*, R do Cartume 585, Bl C, 3rd floor, Lapa, CEP 05065-001.

Transport **Local Bus**: these are normally crowded and rather slow, but clean. Maps of the bus and metro system are available at depots, for example Anhangabaú. Some city bus routes are run by trolley buses.

Car hire: See Car hire, Essentials for international car rental agencies, page 48. *Interlocadora*, several branches, São Luís T255 5604, Guarulhos T6445 3838, Congonhas T240 9287. **Driving**: the *rodízio*, which curbs traffic pollution by restricting car use according to number plate, may be extended beyond the winter months. Check.

Metrô: 2 main lines intersecting at Praça de Sé: north-south from Tucuruvi to Jabaquara; east-west from Corinthians Itaquera to Barra Funda (the interchange with *Fepasa* and *RFFSA* railways and site of the São Paulo and Paraná rodoviária); an extension east to Guaianases is under construction. A 3rd line runs from Vila Madalena in the west, along Av Paulista, to Ana Rosa in the south, joining the Jabaquara line at Paraíso and Ana Rosa. The system is clean, safe, cheap and efficient; the 2 main lines operate from 0500-2400, Ana Madalena to Ana Rosa 0600-2030. Fare US$0.80, US$1.35 for a double ticket, US$6.50 for a book of 10 tickets; backpacks are allowed. Combined bus and Metrô ticket are available, US$1, for example to Congonhas airport.

Taxi: display cards of actual tariffs in the window (starting price US$3). There are ordinary taxis, which are hailed on the street, or at taxi stations such as Praça da República, radio taxis and deluxe taxis. For **Radio Taxis**, which are more expensive but involve fewer hassles, T974 0182 (*Central de Táxi*), 5061 6630 (*Central Rádio Táxi*), 251 1733 (*Vermelho e Branco*), 233 1977 (*TeleTáxi*), or look in the phone book; calls are not accepted from public phones.

Guarulhos International Airport, T6445 2945. Congonhas local airport, T5090 9195

Long distance **Air**: from the international airport Guarulhos (also known as Cumbica) there are airport **taxis** which charge US$35-40 on a ticket system (go to the 2nd booth on leaving the terminal and book a *Co-op* taxi at the Taxi Comum counter, the best value). Fares from the city to the airport are US$35-40 and vary from cab to cab. *Emtu* bus service every 30 mins from Guarulhos to Praça da República 343 (northwest side, corner of R Arouche), US$6.50, 30-45 mins, very comfortable (in the airport buy ticket at the booth in Domestic Arrivals); the same company runs services from Guarulhos to the main bus terminal, Tietê (hourly). Buses run to Bresser bus station from Guarulhos and there are other buses to Jabaquara bus terminal, without luggage space, usually crowded. Inter-airport bus US$12. From Congonhas airport, there are about 400 flights a week to Rio (US$100 one way). **Airport information** Money exchanges, in the arrivals hall, Guarulhos, 0800-2200 daily. Post office on the 3rd floor of *Asa A*. The Infraero Sala VIP has been recommended for coffee, cable TV for US$5. Mon-Fri 0800 to 1800. See Ins and outs above for the tourist office.

Brazil

Trains: São Paulo has 4 stations: 1) **Estação da Luz**, for commuter trains between the northwest and southeast of São Paulo state. There is also a Metrô stop here. A train runs from Luz 8 times a day to connect with the **tourist train** from Paranapiaçaba to Rio Grande da Serra, US$0.50. 2) **Barra Funda**, services go to São José do Rio Preto (overnight), Barretos, Londrina, Maringá, Sorocaba and Ponta Grossa. There is a Metrô station and a rodoviária at Barra Funda; 3) **Júlio Prestes** station, for commuter services to the west; T0800 550121 for these three. 4) **Roosevelt**, T6942 1199, for commuter trains to the east.

Bus: the main rodoviária is **Tietê**, which handles buses to the interior of São Paulo state, all state capitals (but see also under Barra Funda and Bresser below) and international buses. The **left luggage** charges US$0.80 per day per item. You can sleep in the bus station after 2200 when the guards have gone; tepid showers cost US$2.

Buses from Tietê: To **Rio**, 6 hrs, every 30 mins, US$12.50 (*leito*, 25), special section for this route in the rodoviária, request the coastal route via Santos ('via litoral') unless you wish to go the direct route. To **Florianópolis**, 11 hrs (US$23.75, *leito* 36.75). To **Porto Alegre**, 18 hrs, US$36.50 (*leito*, 60). **Curitiba**, 6 hrs, US$10.25-12.50. **Salvador**, 30 hrs, US$51 (executive, 64). **Recife**, 40 hrs, US$60-70. **Cuiabá**, 24 hrs, US$42. **Porto Velho**, 60 hrs (or more), US$75. **Brasília**, 16 hrs, US$30 (*leito*, 60). **Foz do Iguaçu**, 16 hrs, US$24. **São Sebastião**, 4 hrs US$8.85 (say 'via Bertioga' if you want to go by the coast road, beautiful journey but few buses take this route).

International buses from Tietê: to **Montevideo**, via Porto Alegre, with *TTL*, departs Mon, Thu, Sat 2200, 31 hrs, US$100, cold a/c at night, plenty of meal stops, bus stops for border formalities, passengers disembark only to collect passport and tourist card on the Uruguayan side (also *EGA*, same price, US$67 to **Chuy**, Tue, Fri, Sun). To **Buenos Aires**, *Pluma*, 36 hrs, US$145. To **Santiago**, *Pluma* or *Chilebus*, 56 hrs, US$130, *Chilebus*, poor meals, but otherwise good, beware overbooking. To **Asunción** (1,044 km), 18 hrs with *Pluma* (US$57, *leito* 112), *Brújula* (US$64) or *RYSA* (US$110), all stop at Ciudad del Este (US$43, 50 and 84 respectively, *Pluma leito* US$84). *Cometa del Amambay* runs to **Pedro Juan Caballero** and **Concepción**.

There are 3 other bus stations: **Barra Funda**, T3666 4682, with Metrô station, for buses from cities in southern São Paulo state, **Campo Grande**, 14 hrs, US$33, and many places in Paraná. **Bresser**, T6692 5191, on the Metrô, is for destinations in Minas Gerais. Buses from Santos arrive at **Jabaquara**, at the southern end of the Metrô. To **Santos**, US$3.60, and destinations on the southern coast of São Paulo state, use Jabaquara station. Buses from here for Santos leave every 15 mins, taking about 50 mins, last bus at 0100, US$3.60. Buses at Bresser, *Cometa* (6967 7255) or *Transul* (T6693 8061) go to Minas Gerais: **Belo Horizonte**, 10 hrs, US$15.60, 11 a day (*leito* 31.20); 9 a day with *Gontijo*. *Translavras* and *Útil* also operate out of this station. Prices are given under destinations.

Airline offices *Aerolíneas Argentinas*, Araújo 216, 6th floor, T214 6022 (Guarulhos airport 6445 3806). *Alitalia*, Av São Luís 50, cj 291, T257 1922 (6445 3791). *American Airlines*, Araújo 216, 9th floor, T256 8010/258 3385. *Avianca*, R da Consolação 293, 10th floor, T257 6511 (6445 3798). *British Airways*, Av São Luís 50, 32nd floor, T259 6144 (6445 2462). *Continental*, R da Consolação 247, 13th floor, T0800-554777 (6445 4187). *Delta*, R Marquês de Itu 61, T258 5866. *Iberia*, Araújo 216, 3rd floor, T257 6711 (6445 2060). *JAL*, Av Paulista 542, 2nd floor, T251 5222 (6445 2040). *KLM*, Al Santos 1787, 10th floor, T34573234, (Guarulhos 6445 2011). *LanChile*, R da Consolação 247, 12th floor,, T259 2900 (6445 2824). *Lufthansa*, R Gomes de Carvalho 1356, 2nd floor, T3048 5868 (6445 2220). *Rio-Sul*, R Bráulio Gomes 151, T5561 2161. *TAM*, R da Consolação 247, 3rd floor, T5582 8631 (6445 2220). *TAP*, Av São Luís 187, T255 5366 (6445 2400). *United*, Av Paulista 777, 9-10th floor, T253 2323 (6445 3283). *Varig*, R da Consolação 362/372, Av Paulista 1765, T5091 7000 (Guarulhos 6445 2825, Congonhas 535 0216). *Vasp*, Praça L Gomes/Aurora 974, Av São Luís 72, T0800-998277.

Directory

Banks There are many national and international banks; most can be found either in the Triângulo, downtown, or on Av Paulista, or Av Brigadeiro Faria Lima. *Banco do Brasil* will change cash and TCs and will advance cash against Visa. All transactions are done in the foreign exchange department of any main branch (eg Av São João 32, Centro), but queues are long. *Citibank*, Av Ipiranga 855, or Av Paulista 1111 (1100-1500), cash on MasterCard. *Banespa*, for example at R Duque de Caxias 200, Centro, or Praça da República 295, accepts Visa, TCs and cash. *MasterCard*, cash against card, R Campo Verde 61,

1000-1600; but some vary. All have different times for foreign exchange transactions (check at individual branches)

Brazil

4th floor, Jardim Paulistano. *MasterCard* ATMs at branches of *HSBC Bank*. *American Express*, Al Santos 1437 (*Hotel Mofarrej Sheraton*) T251 3383, Av Maria Coelho Aguiar 215, Bloco F, 8th floor, T3741 8478 and Guarulhos international airport, terminal 1, 1st floor of Asa A, T6412 3515. *Western Union* at Banco Itamarati, T0800-119837. **Money changers:** there are many *câmbios* on or near Praça da República. There are none near the rodoviária or Tietê hotels. *Interpax*, Praça da República 177, loja 13, changes cash (many currencies) and TCs, 0930-1800, Sat 0930-1300. *Amoretur*, Praça da República 203, will change TCs. *Coraltur*, Praça da República 95. Most travel agents on Av São Luís change TCs and cash at good rates, but very few are open on Sat. *Avencatur*, Av Nações Unidas 1394, Morumbi, changes TCs, Deutschmarks, good rates.

Communications Internet: at Av Paulista 1499, conj 1001 (Mêtro Trianon), 1100-2200, English spoken, secondhand books; *Saraiva Megastore*, Shopping El Dorado, US$3; *Kiosknet*, Shopping Light, 4th floor, R Cel Xavier de Toledo 23, opposite Teatro Municipal, T3151 3645, US$2.50 per hr; *O Porão*, R Tamandaré 1066, near Vergueiro metro station. **Post Office:** Correio Central, Praça do Correio, corner Av São João and Prestes Máia. Booth adjoining tourist office on Praça da República, weekdays only 1000-1200, 1300-1600, for letters and small packages only. *UPS*, Brasinco, Alameda Jaú 1, 1725, 01420 São Paulo. *Federal Express*, Av São Luís 187, Galeria Metropole, loja 45, is reliable, also at Av das Nações Unidas 17891; *DHL*, Av Vereador José Diniz 2421. **Telephone:** *Telefônica*, R 7 de Abril 295, near Praça da República; many other offices. *Embratel*, Av São Luís 50, and Av Ipiranga 344. For the international operator dial 000111; for international collect calls dial 000107. Red phone boxes are for national calls, blue ones for international phone calls.

Cultural centres Centro Brasileiro Britânico, R Ferriera de Araújo 741, Pinheiros, T3039 0567. **American Library**, União Cultural Brasil-Estados Unidos, R Col Oscar Porto 208. **Goethe-Instituto**, R Lisboa 974 (Mon-Thu 1400-2030). **Centro Cultural Fiesp**, Av Paulista 1313, 0900-1900 Tue-Sun, has foreign newspapers and magazines. See under Entertainment for Alliance Française Theatre.

Embassies and consulates Consulates: **Argentina**, Av Paulista 1106, T2841355 (0900-1300, very easy to get a visa here). **Australia**, R Tenente Negrão 140, T3849 6281. **Austria**, R Augusta 2516, 10th floor, T282 6223, Mon-Thu 0930-1130. **Bolivia**, R Honduras 1447, T3081 1688 (0900-1300). **Canada**, Av Nações Unidas 12901, T5509 4343, 0900-1200, 1400-1700. **Denmark**, R Oscar Freire 379, T3061 3625, 0900-1700, Fri until 1400 only. **France**, Av Paulista 1842, 14th floor, T287 9522, 0830-1200. **Germany**, Av Brigadeiro Faria Lima 2092, T3814 6644, 0800-1130. **Ireland**, Av Paulista 2006, 5th floor, T287 6362, 1400-1700. T284 2044. **Israel**, Av Brig Faria Lima 1713, T3815 7788. **Netherlands**, Av Brigadeiro Faria Lima 1779, T3813 0522, 0900-1200. **New Zealand**, Av Campinas 579, T288 0700. **Norway and Sweden**, R Oscar Freire 379, 3rd floor, T883 3322 (Norway), 3061 1700 (Sweden) (Caixa Postal 51626), 0900-1300. **Paraguay**, R Bandeira Paulista 600, 15th floor, T3849 0455, 0830-1600. **Peru**, R Votuverava 350, T3819 1793, 0900-1300. **South Africa**, Av Paulista 1754, T285 0433. **Switzerland**, Av Paulista 1754, 4th floor, Caixa Postal 30588, T253 4951. **UK**, Av Paulista 37, 17th floor, T287 7722, consulad@ uol.com.br **Uruguay**, Al Santos 905, T284 0998, 1000-1600. **US**, R Padre João Manuel 933, T3081 6511, 0800-1700. **Venezuela**, R Veneza 878, T3887 4583, 0900-1130.

Language courses *Universidade de São Paulo (USP)* in the Cidade Universitária has courses available to foreigners, including a popular Portuguese course, registry is through the **Comissão de Cooperação Internacional**, R do Anfiteatro 181, Bloco das Colméias 05508, Cidade Universitária.

Medical services Hospital Samaritano, R Conselheiro Brotero 1486, Higienópolis, T824 0022. Recommended. **Emergency and ambulance** T192, no charge. **Fire:** T193.

Useful addresses Police: Deatur, special tourist police, Av São Luís 91, T214 0209, R 15 de Novembro 347, T3107 8332. **Cepol**, civil police, T147. **Radio Patrol**, T190. **Federal Police**, Av Prestes Maia 700, 1000-1600 for visa extensions.

Santos

Phone code: 0xx13
Post code: 11000
Colour map 7, grid C4
Population: 417,983
72 km SE of São Paulo

Santos is a holiday resort with magnificent beaches and views. It is about 5 km from the open sea and the most important Brazilian port, best known for its commerce. Over 40% by value of all Brazilian imports and about half the total exports pass through it. The scenery on the routes crossing the Serra do Mar is superb. The roadway includes many bridges and tunnels. From Rio the direct highway, the Linha Verde (see pages 384 and 404) is also wonderful for scenery. The port is approached by the winding Santos Channel; at its mouth is an old fort (1709). The island upon which the city stands can be circumnavigated by small boats. The centre of the city is on the north side of the island. Due south, on the Baía de Santos, is **Gonzaga**, where hotels and bars line the beachfront. Between these two areas, the eastern end of the island curves round within the Santos Channel. At the eastern tip, a ferry crosses the estuary to give access to the beaches of the sophisticated resort of Guarujá.

Sights

The streets around **Praça Mauá** are very busy in the daytime, with plenty of cheap shops. In the centre is the **Bolsa Oficial de Café**, the coffee exchange, at R 15 de Novembro 95. Two churches in the centre are **Santo Antônio do Valongo** (17th century, but restored), which is by the railway station on Largo Monte Alegre, and the **Capela da Ordem Terceira de Nossa Senhora do Carmo** (1760, also later restored), Praça Barão do Rio Branco. **Monte Serrat**, just south of the city centre, has at its summit a semaphore station and look-out post which reports the arrival of all ships in Santos harbour. There is also a quaint old church, dedicated to Nossa Senhora da Monte Serrat. ■ *The top can be reached on foot or by funicular, which leaves every 30 mins, US$6.* **Museu do Mar**, R República do Equador 81, is in the eastern part of the city; with a collection that includes several thousand shells. In the western district of José Menino is the **Orquidário Municipal**, municipal orchid gardens, in the **Praça Washington** (flowering October-February, orchid show in November). ■ *Daily 0800-1745, the bird enclosure 0800-1100, 1400-1700, US$1 (children and senior citizens, free).*

The **Ilha Porchat**, a small island reached by a bridge at the far end of Santos/São Vicente bay, has beautiful views over rocky precipices, of the high seas on one side and of the city and bay on the other. At the summit is *Terraço Chopp*, a restaurant which has live music most evenings. On summer evenings the queues to get in can last up to 4 hours, but in winter, even if it may be a little chilly at night, the queues are non-existent (Al Ary Barroso 274, Ilha Porchat, São Vicente).

Itatinga, 30 km from Santos in the Serra do Mar, has remnants of Atlantic forest, mangrove and sandbanks. The area is full of wildlife. There are trails graded according to difficulty. ■ *Access is with one of the travel agencies officially permitted to lead groups: contact* Sictur *(the tourism department – see below). Access is either via the village of Itatinga by boat, 3 hours, then by street car. Or take the BR-101 (Santos-Rio) road, a 3-min crossing by boat and then 7.5 km by street car.*

Sleeping & eating

Many beach front hotels on Av Pres Wilson, eg: **A** *Atlântico*, No 1, T3289 4500. Good. There are many cheap hotels near the Orquidário Municipal (Praça Washington), 1-2 blocks from the beach. **D** *Hotel Natal*, Av Marechal Floriano Peixoto 104, T3284 2732. Restaurants: *Hong Kong Palace*, Av Conselheiro Nébias 288 (Chinese). First class *Pizzaria Zi Tereza*, Av Ana Costa 449. *Bar Heinz*, R Dr Lincoln Feliciano 104. Good German food, reasonable prices. *Zum Fass*, Av Marechal Deodoro 31, Gonzaga. German food, nice place.

Local festivals

26 Jan, *Foundation of Santos; Good Friday; Corpus Christi; Festejos Juninos*. Throughout the summer there are many cultural, educational and sporting events. 8 Sep, *Nossa Senhora de Monte Serrat*.

Transport

Local Bus: in Santos US$0.60; to São Vicente, US$0.90. **Taxi**: all taxis have meters. The fare from Gonzaga to the bus station is about US$5.

Long distance Bus: to São Paulo (50 mins, US$3.60) every 15 mins, from the rodoviária near the city centre, José Menino or Ponta da Praia (opposite the ferry to Guarujá). (The 2 highways between São Paulo and Santos are sometimes seriously crowded, especially at rush hours and weekends.) To Guarulhos/Cumbica airport, *Expresso* Brasileiro 3-4 daily, US$5, allow plenty of time as the bus goes through Guarulhos, 3 hrs. *TransLitoral* from Santos to Congonhas airport then to Guarulhos/Cumbica, 4 daily, US$7.25, 2 hrs. To **Rio**

Brazil

(*Normandy* company), several daily, 7½ hrs, US$22.50; to Rio along the coast road is via São Sebastião (US$7.25, change buses if necessary), Caraguatatuba and Ubatuba.

Directory **Banks** *Banco do Brasil*, difficult to get cash on MasterCard or Diners, but Visa OK. Banks open: 1000-1630. Many **Money changers**. **Communications** Internet: *Viva Shop*, in Shopping Parque Balneario, Av Ana Costa, US$3 per hr. Main **post office** at R Cidale de Toledo 41, Centro, also at R Tolentino Filgueiras 70, Gonzaga. **Telephone: International calls:** can be made at R Galeão Carvalhal 45, Gonzaga. **Embassies and consulates** Britain, R Tuiuti 58, 2nd floor, Caixa Postal 204, T3219 6622, daw@wilson.com.br Denmark, R Frei Gaspar 22, 10th floor, 106, CP 726, T3219 6455, 1000-1100, 1500-1700. **Tourist office** at the rodoviária, Praça da Bandeira and Orquidário Municipal. Sictur, Praça dos Expedicionários, 10, 8th floor, T3222 4166. *Livraria Siciliano* in Praiamar Shopping sells *Footprint Handbooks*. **Voltage** 220 AC, 60 cycles.

Beaches east of Santos
Population: 226,500

A vehicle ferry (free for pedestrians) crosses from Ponta da Praia to **Guarujá**, which becomes very crowded in summer. There are good seafood restaurants on the road (SP-061) between Guarujá and **Bertioga**, the next major beach centre up the coast (1 hr by bus). It, too, can be overcrowded in summer. A ferry crosses the mouth of the Canal de Bertioga. The town is on the north bank of the canal and beyond is a long sweeping bay with seven beaches divided by a promontory, the Ponta da Selada. The hills behind Bertioga are covered in forest which is now being used for walking in the Mata Atlântica by local agencies. **Sleeping A** *Marazul*, Av Tomé de Souza 825, Enseada, T3317 1109, good seafood restaurant; many others. There are several **tourist offices**: *Suinã Turismo*, T3317 3667, offers 'eco-tours', including to Itatinga (see under Santos). *Departamento de Esportes e Turismo Municipal*, R Luiz Pereira de Campos 901, Vila Itapanhaú, T3317 1213, ext 2075.

The coastal road beyond Bertioga is paved, and the Rio-Santos highway, 1 or 2 km inland, provides a good link to São Sebastião. Beyond Praia Boracéia are a number of beaches, including **Camburi**, surrounded by the Mata Atlântica, into which you can walk on the Estrada do Piavu (bathing in the streams is permitted, but use of shampoo is forbidden). There are a number of good hotels and restaurants in Camburi and at Praia de Boracéia, **B-C** *Chalés do Brasa*, Rua E No 99, T4330 3149/9331 4702, family chalets, garden setting, close to beach. ■ *Daily buses from São Paulo to Camburi, 160 km, en route to São Sebastião/Ilhabela, US$3.60*. The road carries on from Camburi, past clean beach **Maresias**, a fashionable place for surfers.

São Sebastião
Phone code: 0xx12
Post code: 11600
Colour map 7, grid B4
Population: 58,038

From Maresias it is 21 km to São Sebastião. In all there are 21 good beaches and an adequate, but not overdeveloped tourist infrastructure. The natural attractions of the area include many small islands offshore and a large portion of the **Parque Estadual da Serra do Mar** on the mainland, with other areas under protection for their different ecosystems. Trails can be walked through the forests. There are also old sugar plantations. In the colonial centre is a **Museu de Arte Sacra**, in the 17th century chapel of São Gonçalo (R Sebastião Neves 90). The town's parish church on Praça Major João Fernandes was built in the early 17th century and rebuilt in 1819. There is a **Museu do Naufrágio** near the church (entrance free) exhibiting shipwrecks and natural history of the local area.

The beaches within 2-3 km of São Sebastião harbour are polluted; others to the south and north are clean and inviting. Ilhabela tends to be expensive in season, when it is cheaper to stay in São Sebastião.

Sleeping B *Hotel Roma*, on the main Praça, T452 1016. Excellent. Warmly recommended. **C** *Bariloche*, R Três Bandeirantes 133. Basic but clean. 6 km south of São Sebastião is *Camping do Barraqueçaba Bar de Mar de Lucas*, hot showers, English spoken, cabins available. Recommended.

Transport Bus: 2 buses a day from **Rio** with *Normandy*, 0830 and 2300 (plus 1630 on Fri and Sun), to Rio 0600 and 2330, heavily booked in advance, US$12.60 (US$5 from Paraty); 4 a day from **Santos**, 4 hrs, US$7.60; 4 *Litorânea* buses a day also from **São Paulo**, US$8.85, which run inland via São José dos Campos, unless you ask for the service via Bertioga, only 2 a day. Free **ferry** across the narrow strait to Ilhabela for foot passengers, see below.

The island of São Sebastião, known popularly as Ilhabela, is of volcanic origin, roughly 390 sq km in area. The four highest peaks are Morro de São Sebastião, 1,379 m, Morro do Papagaio, 1,309 m, Ramalho, 1,28 m, and Pico Baepi, 1,025 m. All are often obscured by mist. Rainfall on the island is heavy, about 3,000 mm a year. The slopes are densely wooded and 80% of the forest is protected by the Parque Estadual de Ilhabela. The only settled district lies on the coastal strip facing the mainland, the Atlantic side being practically uninhabited except by a few fisherfolk. The terraced **Cachoeira da Toca** waterfalls amid dense jungle close to the foot of the Baepi peak give cool freshwater bathing; lots of butterflies (US$4, includes insect repellent). You can walk on a signed path, or go by car; it's a few kilometres from the ferry dock. The locals claim there are over 300 waterfalls on the island, but only a few of them can be reached on foot. In all shady places, especially away from the sea, there thrives a species of midge known locally as *borrachudo*. A locally sold repellent (*Autan*) keeps them off for some time, but those allergic to insect bites should remain on the inhabited coastal strip. There is a small hospital (helpful) by the church in town.

No alterations are allowed to the frontage of the main township, **Ilhabela.** It is very popular during summer weekends, when it is difficult to find space for a car on the ferry. It is, however, a nice place to relax on the beach, with good food and some good value accommodation. The **tourist office** *Secretaria Municipal de Turismo* is at R Bartolomeu de Gusmão 140, Pequeá, T472 1091.

Visit the old **Feiticeira** plantation, with underground dungeons. The road is along the coast, sometimes high above the sea, towards the south of the island (11 km from the town). You can go by bus, taxi, or horse and buggy. A trail leads down from the *fazenda* to the beautiful beach of the same name. Another old *fazenda* is **Engenho d'Água**, which is nearer to the town, which gives its name to one of the busiest beaches (the *fazenda* is not open to the public).

Beaches and watersports On the mainland side the beaches 3-4 km either side of the town are polluted: look out for oil, sandflies and jellyfish on the sand and in the water. There are some three dozen beaches around Ilhabela, only about 12 of them away from the coast facing the mainland. **Praia dos Castelhanos**, reached by the rough road over the island to the Atlantic side (no buses), is recommended. Several of the ocean beaches can only be reached by boat. The island is considered the **Capital da Vela** (of sailing) because its 150 km of coastline offers all types of conditions. There is also plenty of adventure for divers.

Sleeping and eating A *Ilhabela*, Av Pedro Paulo de Morais 151, T/F472 1083, hoibela@mandic.com.br Good breakfast. Recommended. Next door is **AL** *Itapemar*, No 341, T472 1329, F472 2409. Windsurfing equipment rented. **B** *Pousada dos Hibiscos*, same avenue No 714, T472 1375. Good atmosphere, swimming pool. Recommended. Others in this price range and some other less expensive hotels in the **A-B** range, mostly on the road to the left of the ferry. **E** pp, *Ilhabela*, IYHA youth hostel, Av Col José Vicente Faria Lima 1243, Perequê, T472 8468, hostelling@iconet.com.br IYHA. **Camping** in addition to Pedras do Sino, there are campsites at Perequê, near the ferry dock, and at Praia Grande, a further 11 km south. A reasonable eating place is *Perequê*, Av Princesa Isabel 337. *Farol*, Av Princesa Isabel 1634, Perequê. Good, especially seafood. Recommended.

Transport Bus A bus runs along the coast facing the mainland. *Litorânea* from São Paulo connects with a service right through to Ilhabela; office in Ilhabela at R Dr Carvalho 136. **Ferry** At weekends and holidays the 15-20 min ferry between São Sebastião and Perequê runs non-stop day and night. During the week it does not sail between 0130 and 0430 in the morning. Passengers pay nothing; the fare for cars is US$7 weekdays, US$10 at weekends.

Ilha de São Sebastião
The island abounds in tropical plants and flowers, and many fruits grow wild, whose juice mixed with cachaça (firewater) and sugar makes as delicious a cocktail as can be imagined

Phone code: 0xx12
Population: 20,836; the island's population rises to 100,000 in high season

Brazil

North of São Sebastião On the Santos-Rio road is São Francisco da Praia, opposite the northern end of Ilhabela, beyond which begin the beaches of **Caraguatatuba** (*Phone code*: 0xx12). In all there are 17 good beaches to the northeast and southwest, most divided between two sweeping bays. As well as watersports, Caraguatatuba is known for hang-gliding. It is a popular place at weekends and in the summer, with good hotels, restaurants, bars and campsites. For tourist information visit the *Secretaria Municipal de Turismo*, R Luiz Passos 50, T420 8142.There are several youth hostels: *Recanto das Andorinhas*, R Engenheiro João Fonseca 112, Centro, 11660-000, T422 6181, one street from the central bus terminal, 50 m from the beach. ■ *Direct buses to Caraguatatuba from Rio (US$12, same schedule as for São Sebastião), São Paulo and Santos; direct buses from São Paulo go via São José dos Campos.*

Ubatuba

Phone code: 0xx12
Post code: 11680
Colour map 7, grid B4
Population: 66,861

This is one of the most beautiful stretches of the São Paulo coast with a whole range of watersports on offer. In all, there are 72 beaches, some large, some small, some in coves, some on islands. They are spread out over a wide area, so if you are staying in Ubatuba town, you need to use the buses which go to most of them. The commercial centre of Ubatuba is at the northern end of the bay. Here are shops, banks, services, lots of restaurants (most serving pizza and fish), but few hotels. These are on the beaches north and south and can be reached from the Costamar bus terminal.

Saco da Ribeira, 13 km south, is a natural harbour which has been made into a yacht marina. Schooners leave from here for excursions to **Ilha Anchieta** (or dos Porcos), a popular 4-hr trip. On the island are beaches, trails and a prison, which was in commission from 1908-52. Agencies run schooner trips to Ilha Anchieta and elsewhere. Trips leave Saco da Ribeira at 1000, returning 1500, 4-hr journey, US$20 per person. A 6-hr trip can be made from Praia Itaguá, but in winter there is a cold wind off the sea in the afternoon, same price. The *Costamar* bus from Ubatuba to Saco da Ribeira (every 20 mins, 30 mins, US$0.85) drops you at the turn-off by the *Restaurante Pizzaria Malibu*.

Sleeping
At all holiday times it is expensive, with no hotel less than US$30

Beach hotels On many of the beaches there are hotels and *pousadas*, ranging from luxury resorts to more humble establishments. **AL** *Saveiros*, R Laranjeira 227, Praia do Lázaro, 14 km from town, T442 0172, F442 1327. Pool, restaurant, English spoken.

In town The main hotels in the centre are **A** *São Charbel*, Praça Nóbrega 280, T432 1090, F432 1080. Very helpful and comfortable, a/c, TV, restaurant, bar, swimming pool, etc. **A** *São Nicolau*, R Conceição 213, T432 5007, F432 3310. Good, TV, fridge, good breakfast. **A** *Xaréu*, R Jordão Homem da Costa 413, T432 1525, F432 3060. Pleasant, quiet. Recommended. These three are all convenient for the town beach, restaurants and services, and their prices fall to **B** in the low season. **D** *Pousada Taiwan*, R Felix Guisard Filho 60, T432 6448. Fan or a/c, with breakfast, TV, refrigerator.

Youth hostels *Cora Coralina*, Rodovia Oswaldo Cruz, Km 89, CEP 11680-000, T011-258 0388. 0800-2300, near the Horto Florestal. *J S Brandão*, R Nestor Fonseca 173, Jardim Sumaré, CEP 11880-000, T432 2337. 0700-2300, near the Tropic of Capricorn sign south of town. **Camping** 2 *Camping Clube do Brasil* sites at Lagoinha (25 km from town), T443 1536, and Praia Perequê-Açu, 2 km north, T432 1682. There are about 8 other sites in the vicinity.

Tour operators Companies offer trekking tours graded according to difficulty lasting from 2 hrs to 2 days.

Transport **Bus** There are 3 bus terminals: 1) Rodoviária Costamar, at R Hans Staden e R Conceição, which serves all local destinations; 2) Rodoviária at R Profesor Thomaz Galhardo 513 for São José buses to Paraty, US$2.25, some *Normandy* services (to Rio, US$9) and some *Itapemirim* buses; 3) Rodoviária Litorânea, the main bus station: go up Conceição for 8 blocks from Praça 13 de Maio, turn right on R Rio Grande do Sul, then left into R Dra Maria V Jean. Buses from here go to **São Paulo**, 3½ hrs, frequent, US$8, **Caraguatatuba**, US$2.

Taxi in town are a rip-off, for example US$6 from the centre to the main bus terminal.

Communications Internet: *Due Punti Café*, R Tamoios 05, T432 5206, duepunti@iconet.com.br
Post Office: is on R Dona Maria Alves between Hans Staden and R Col Dominicano. **Telephone:** *Telesp*, is on Galhardo, close to *Sérgio* restaurant. **Tourist office** Comtur, Praça 13 de Maio and on Av Iperoig opposite R Profesor Thomaz Galhardo, is very helpful.

Straddling the border of São Paulo and Rio de Janeiro states is the **Parque Nacional Serra da Bocaina**, which rises from the coast to its highest point at Pico do Tira (or Chapéu) at 2,200 m, encompassing three strata of vegetation. ■ *Permission to visit must be obtained in advance from Ibama, T0xx12-3117 2183/88 in São José do Barreiro, the nearest town.*

Southwest from Santos

It is 8 km from São Vicente to **Praia Grande**, the beach most used by Paulistanos. Next comes Mongaguá then, 61 km from Santos, **Itanhaém** (*Phone code:* 0xx13), with its pretty colonial church of Sant'Ana (1761), Praça Narciso de Andrade, and the Convento da Nossa Senhora da Conceição (1699-1713, originally founded 1554), on a small hill. There are several good seafood restaurants along the beach, hotels and camping. There are more beaches 31 km south of Itanhaém at **Peruíbe**, where the climate is said to be unusually healthy owing to a high concentration of ozone in the air. Local rivers have water and black mud which has been proven to contain medicinal properties. There are plenty of places to stay in Peruíbe (none close to the bus station), including **C** Vila Real, Av Anchieta 6625, T458 2797 breakfast, shower. Also, there are places to eat. The *tourist office* is at R Nilo Soares Ferreira 50, T455 2070. Peruíbe marks the northernmost point of the **Estação Ecológico Juréia-Itatins**, 820 sq km of protected Mata Atlântica, "as it was when the Portuguese arrived in Brazil". The station was founded in 1986. The four main ecosystems are *restinga*, mangrove, Mata Atlântica and the vegetation at 900 m on the Juréia mountain range. ■ *Contact the Instituto Florestal, R do Horto 931, CEP 02377-000, São Paulo, T0xx11-6997 5000, for permission to visit the ecological station.*

At the southern end of Juréia-Itatins is the town of Iguape founded in 1538. Typical of Portuguese architecture, the small **Museu Histórico e Arqueológico** is housed in the 17th-century Casa da Oficina Real de Fundição, R das Neves 45. ■ *Tue-Sun 0900-1730.* There is also a **Museu de Arte Sacra** in the former Igreja do Rosário, Praça Rotary. ■ *Sat-Sun 0900-1200, 1330-1700.* For tourist information, visit the *Prefeitura Municipal*, R 15 de Novembro 272, T841 1626, F841 1620.

Iguape
Phone code: 0xx13
Colour map 7, grid C3
Population: 27,427

Opposite Iguape is the northern end of the **Ilha Comprida** with 86 km of beaches (some dirty and disappointing). This Área de Proteção Ambiental is not much higher than sea level and is divided from the mainland by the Canal do Mar Pequeno. The northern end is the busiest and on the island there are good restaurants, hotels, supermarkets – fresh fish is excellent. There is also accommodation.

Sleeping B-C *Silvi*, R Ana Cândida Sandoval Trigo 515, T841 1421, silvihotel@virtualway.com.br With bath and breakfast, good. There is a **campsite** at Praia da Barra da Ribeira, 20 km north, and wild camping is possible at Praia de Juréia, the gateway to the ecological station.

Transport Bus To **Iguape**: from São Paulo, Santos, or Curitiba, changing at Registro. **Sea** A continuous ferry service runs from Iguape to Ilha Comprida (free but small charge for cars); buses run until 1900 from the ferry stop to the beaches. From Iguape it is possible to take a boat trip down the coast to Cananéia and Ariri (see below). Tickets and information from **Dpto Hidroviário do Estado**, R Major Moutinho 198, Iguape, T841 1122. It is a beautiful trip, passing between the island and the mainland.

Brazil

Cananéia &
Ilha do
Cardoso
Colour map 7, grid C3
Population: 12,298
270 km from
São Paulo

There are lots of idyllic
beaches; best for
surfing is Moretinho

At the southern end of Ilha Comprida, across the channel, is Cananéia. The colonial centre, around Praça Martim Afonso de Souza and neighbouring streets, contains the 17th-century church of **São João Batista** and the **Museu Municipal**. To the south are a number of good beaches and the waterways are popular with fisherfolk. For tourist information, visit the *Departamento de Esportes e Turismo*, Av Beira Mar 247, Cananéia, T851 1473, ext 342. For guides, contact *Manoel Barroso*, Avenue Independencia 65, T013-851 1273, Portuguese only. Recommended. Or try the *Secretaria do Parque Estadual da Ilha do Cardoso*, Av Profesor Besnard s/n, near the port. Cananéia has several hotels, starting in price range **B**.

To reach the densely wooded Ilha do Cardoso, which is a Reserva Florestal e Biológica, take a ferry from the dock at Cananéia, 4 hours, three services daily (*R Princesa Isabel*, T841 1122). Alternatively, drive 70 km along an unpaved road, impassable when wet, to **Ariri**, from where the island is 10 mins by boat. The tiny village of Marujá, which has no electricity, has some very rustic *pousadas* and restaurants. Camping is allowed at designated places.

Caves

Southwest of the state capital, west of the BR-116, are the caves of the Vale of Ribeiro, one of the largest concentrations of caverns in the world. The 8-km **Caverna do Diabo** (Devil's Cave), or **Gruta da Tapagem**, is well-lit. It is 40 km from **Eldorado Paulista**; ■ *Mon-Fri 0800-1100, 1200-1700, Sat, Sun and holidays 0800-1700, US$2; bar and toilets*. 43 km from Caverna do Diabo is **Petar**, the Parque Estadual Turístico do Alto Ribeira, with the caves **Núcleo Santana** and the Núcleo Ouro Grosso. This section of the park is 4 km from the town of **Iporanga**. The third Núcleo is Caboclos, near the town of Apiaí. ■ *Guided tours of Petar cost US$50 a day from the Associação Serrana Ambientalista, T015-556 1188*.

Iporanga is the most convenient town for visiting all the caves; it is 64 km west of Eldorado Paulista, 42 km east of Apiaí, on the SP-165, 257 km southwest of São Paulo. ■ *Bus São Paulo-Apiaí, from Barra Funda rodoviária, US$22. If coming from Curitiba, change at Jacupiranga on the BR-116 for Eldorado Paulista*.

Campinas
Phone code: 0xx19
Post code: 13000
Colour map 7, grid B3
Population: 969,396
88 km from São Paulo

Bus to São Paulo, US$3

An industrial centre linked with São Paulo by the fine Via Anhangüera highway, Campinas is important as a clearing point for coffee. Visits can be made to the **Instituto Agronômico** to see all the aspects of coffee; Av Barão de Itapura 1481, Guanabara. ■ *Mon-Fri 0800-1100, 1300-1700, T3231 5330*. The Viracopos international airport is 11 km from Campinas, which also has its own airport. See the fine **Catedral Metropolitana Nossa Senhora da Conceição**, built in 1883 in neoclassical style with baroque elements (Praça José Bonifácio), and the **Mercado Municipal** (old market, 1908) on Av Benjamin Constant. There are several museums: **Carlos Gomes**, R Bernardino de Campos 989, T3231 2567, of arts and sciences. In the Bosque de Jequitibás are the **Museus de História Naturaldo e Folclore**. The arts centre in the **Centro de Convivência Cultural**, Praça Tom Jobim, T3252 5857, has a noted symphony orchestra.

Tourist trains 25 km from Campinas, at **Jaguariúna**, is a railway preservation group with steam engines and wagons. ■ *Every weekend and public holiday two trains (three on Sun) run between Jaguariúna and Campinas on a 2-hr trip. You can either take an hourly bus from Campinas to Jaguariúna, or take the steam train itself from Campinas (station behind Carrefour, Anhumas, reached by town bus). For schedules and information, T3253 6067*.

Sleeping
& eating

C *Parati Palácio*, R Bernardino de Campos 426, T3232 0395. German spoken. Recommended. **C** *Hotel IPE*, R Bernardino de Campos 1050, T3231 7746. Recommended. *Bar Restaurante Barão*, Barão de Jaguará 1381. Chinese food. *Nutrir*, R Dr Quirino 1620. Vegetarian, very good value. *Sucão*, R Benjamin Constant 1108. Good variety of juices. *Pastelaria do Sr Júlio*, R de 13 Maio 143. Helpful, cheap. Recommended.

Four towns some 80-100 km northeast of Campinas are well-known for the quality of their mineral waters. Hotels and parks have been established around the springs and the spas have become popular for conferences and conventions. **Serra Negra** (*Phone code*: 0xx19) is at 925 m, 152 km from São Paulo. There are two hotels and a youth hostel. 13 km from Serra Negra is the even better-known spa of **Lindóia**, whose still waters are bottled and sent all over Brazil. 7 km away is a separate spa, **Águas de Lindóia**. The fourth town, **Socorro**, is 22 km southeast of Lindóia.

Americana (one hotel) is 42 km from Campinas in an area settled by Confederate refugees from the south of the United States after the Civil War. There is a museum at Santa Bárbara d'Oeste, 12 km west, and a visit to the confederados' cemetery nearby reveals an unusual number of English surnames. The town is now a centre for the textile industry and there are various factory outlets.

Colour map 7, grid C3

 The Via Anhangüera continues northwest from Campinas to **Ribeirão Preto,** 319 km from São Paulo (4-5 hours by bus, US$20). The **Museu do Café**, in the former Fazenda Monte Alegre on the campus of the Universidade de São Paulo, tells the history of coffee in the area. ■ *On the road to Sertãozinho, T633 1986*. Some 115 km northwest of Ribeirão Preto, **Barretos** is where, in the third week in August, the **Festa do Peão Boiadeiro** is held. This is the biggest annual rodeo in the world. The town is taken over as up to a million fans come to watch the horsemanship, enjoy the concerts, eat, drink and shop in what has become the epitome of Brazilian cowboy culture. Tours from the UK are run by *Last Frontiers*, see page 24.

Brazil

Minas Gerais

Brasília

This state has a wealth of attractions: fine colonial cities; national parks; and a number of spas and hill resorts. It also has its fair share of festivals and a famous cuisine, the comida mineira. The capital is Belo Horizonte, now a major industrial centre, but also culturally very active.

Minas Gerais was once described as having a heart of gold and a breast of iron. Half the mineral production of Brazil comes from the state, including most of the iron ore. Diamonds and gold are still found. Minas Gerais also produces 95% of all Brazil's gemstones. The 19th century coffee boom was the first stage in Minas' diversification into large-scale agricultural production. Being frost-free, the state is also a major producer of coffee. The easy availability of power and the local agricultural and mineral production has created a large number of metal-working, textile, mineral water, food processing and timber industries.

Background
State population:
17.9 million

 The State of Minas Gerais is somewhat larger than France, is mountainous in the south, rising to the 2,787 m peak of Agulhas Negras in the Mantiqueira range, and in the east, where there is the Parque Nacional ParCaparaó containing the Pico da Bandeira (2,890 m). From Belo Horizonte north are undulating grazing lands, the richest of which are in the extreme west: a broad wedge of country between Goiás in the north and São Paulo in the south, known as the Triângulo Mineiro.

Belo Horizonte

Belo Horzonte is surrounded by mountains and enjoys an excellent climate (16°-30°C) except for the rainy season (December-March). It was founded on 12 December 1897 and is one of Brazil's fastest growing cities, now suffering from atmospheric pollution. The city celebrates *Maundy Thursday*; *Corpus Christi*; 15 August, *Assunção* (Assumption); 8 December, *Conceição* (Immaculate Conception). The third largest city in Brazil is a hilly city with streets that rise and fall and trees lining many of the central avenues.

Phone code: 0xx31
Post code: 30000
Colour map 7, grid B5
Population: 4.8 million
Altitude: 800 m

The large **Parque Municipal** is an oasis of green in the heart of downtown; closed at night and on Monday, except for a small section in the southwest corner. The main commercial district is around Av Afonso Pena and during the day is the best area for eating at lunch time; at night the *movimento* shifts to Savassi, southwest of the centre.

Sights

As in any large city watch out for sneak thieves in the centre and at the bus station. The Parque Municipal is not too safe, so it is best not to go alone

The principal building in the Parque Municipal is the **Palácio das Artes**, Afonso Pena 1537, T3237 7234, which contains the **Centro de Artesanato Mineiro** (with craft shop), an exhibition of painting in Minas Gerais, a cinema, three theatres and temporary exhibitions. ■ *Mon 1300-1800, Tue-Fri 0900-2100, Sat 0900-1300, Sun 1000-1400*. On the stretch of Av Afonso Pena outside the Parque Municipal an open-air market operates each Sunday morning (0800-1400). The avenue is transformed by thousands of coloured awnings covering stalls selling every conceivable type of local handicraft. Six blocks up Av João Pinheiro from Av Afonso Pena is the **Praça da Liberdade**, which is surrounded by fine public buildings, some in eclectic, *fin-de-siècle*-style, others more recent. At the end of the Praça is the **Palácio da Liberdade**. ■ *Sun 0900-1800 only*. The Praça itself is very attractive, with trees, flowers, fountains which are lit at night and joggers and walkers making the most of the paths. The **railway station**, with a museum on the 2nd floor showing a model railway, is part of a complex which includes a number of buildings dating from the 1920s around the **Praça da Estação** (also called Praça Rui Barbosa).

Belo Horizonte orientation & Pampulha

Related map
A Belo Horizonte centre, page 412

0 km   2
0 miles   2

■ Sleeping
1 Ouro Minas

Museu Mineiro, Av João Pinheiro 342, houses religious and other art in the old Senate building. ■ *Tue-Fri 1230-1830, Sat-Sun 1000-1600, T3269 1168.* **Museu Histórico Abílio Barreto**, R Bernardo Mascarenhas, Cidade Jardim, T3296 3896, in an old *fazenda* which is the last reminder of Belo Horizonte's predecessor, the village of **Arraial do Curral d'el Rey**, houses most interesting historical exhibits (take bus 2902 from Av Afonso Pena).**Museu de História Natural**, Instituto Agronómico, R Gustavo da Silveira 1035, Santa Inês, has geological, palaeontological and archaeological displays (take bus 8001). ■ *Mon-Thu 0800-1130, 1300-1630, Sat-Sun 0900-1600.* Also here is the **Jardim Botânico**.

About 8 km northwest from the centre is the picturesque suburb of **Pampulha**, famous for its modern buildings and the artificial lake, created in the 1930s by Brasilia architect Oscar Niemeyer and landscaped by Roberto Burle Marx. The **Igreja São Francisco de Assis**, Av Otacílio Negrão de Lima Km 12, T3491 2319, was inaugurated in 1943. The painter Cândido Portinari installed beautiful blue and white tiles depicting Saint Francis' life on the exterior. On the wall behind the altar is a powerful composition also by Portinari. On the opposite shore is the glass and marble **Museu de Arte de Pampulha** (MAP), at Av Octacílio Negrão de Lima 16585 ■ *Tue-Sun 0800-1800, free, T3277 7946.* It has a fine collection of modern art from Minas Gerais. The **Casa do Baile** is a perfect example of Niemeyer's fascination with the curved line. Just south of the lake is the **Mineirão** stadium, about 750 m away. This is the second largest stadium in Brazil after the Maracanã stadium in Rio. Seats cost between US$5 and US$10. Nearby is the 25,000-seater Mineirinho stadium and multi-sport facility.

In the southern zone of the city, just 3 km from the central area, the **Parque de Mangabeiras** is on the Serra do Curral at between 1,000 m and 1,400 m above sea level. There are good views of the city, especially from the Mirante da Mata. Three forest trails have been laid out. ■ *Thu-Sun 0800-1800.* The natural amphitheatre, Praça do Papa, where the Pope spoke in 1980, is on the way up to Parque Mangabeiras; there is an iron monument marking the occasion.

Suburbs

Sleeping

You may spend the night in the rodoviária only if you have an onward ticket (police check at midnight)

See Essentials for new telephone number changes

LL *Othon Palace*, Av Afonso Pena 1050, T3247 0000, F3247 0001, www.hoteis-othon.com.br Deluxe, modern, glass-fronted, excellent, safe deposit boxes, good restaurant, pool on roof, helpful staff, rooms on lower floors can be noisy. **AL** *Sol Meliá*, R da Bahia 1040, T/F3274 1344, www.solmeliabh.com.br Comfortable, all facilities, pool and sauna. **AL** *Boulevard Plaza*, Av Getúlio Vargas 1640, Savassi district (chic shopping area), T3269 7000, www.boulevardhoteis.com.br Very nice. **L** *Grandville*, R Espírito Santo 901, T0800-311188, F3248 1100. Well-appointed, convenient for city centre. **L-AL** *Normandy*, R dos Tamóios 212, T3201 6166, normandyhotel@ig.com.br Excellent grill. **A** *Wembley Palace*, R Espírito Santo 201, T3273 6866, www.hotelwembley.co.br Excellent, central. **B** *Esplanada*, Av Santos Dumont 304, T3273 5311, F3222 7725 **D** without bath, good restaurant, own garage, good value. **C** *Magnata*, R Guarani 124, T3201 5368. With breakfast, near rodoviária, good hot shower, safe deposit. Recommended. **C** *Continental*, Av Paraná 241, T3201 7944, F3201 7336. Central, quieter interior rooms recommended. **D** *São Cristovão*, Av Oiapoque 284, T3201 4860. Quiet, breakfast. **D** *Madrid*, R Guarani 12, T3201 1088/6330. Recommended, but in a noisy location. Near the rodoviária and in R Curitiba many hotels are for very-short-stay couples. **E** *São Salvador*, R Espírito Santo 227, T3222 7731. Recommended. **E** *Gontijo*, R dos Tupinambás 731, T3272 1177. With bath and breakfast, TV, safe.

Youth hostels *Pousadinha Mineira*, R Araxá 514, Floresta, T3446 2911, pipe@gold.com.br 15 mins from the rodoviária, very helpful, popular with Brazilians, HI, bedding and towels can be hired, breakfast extra on request. Recommended. *Chalé Mineiro*, R Santa Luzia 288, Santa Efigênia, T3467 1576. Attractive, splash pool, recommended. **Federação Brasileira de Albergues Juveniles**, R Sergipe 1449, Savassi, T3284 9958.

Brazil

Eating

Comida mineira is the local speciality; good, wholesome food, served in big black pots and earthenware dishes from which you help yourself

Chico Mineiro, R Alagoas 626, corner of Av Brasil, T3261 3237. Local chicken specialities, good, closed Sun. *Dona Lucinha*, R Sergipe 811, T3261 5930. Recommended, also at R Padre Odorico 38, Savassi, T3227 0562. *Interior de Minas*, R Rio de Janeiro 1191. Central, good for lunch, good value, also at Av Olegário Maciel 1781, Lourdes. *Mala e Cuia*, a chain of restaurants serving good *comida mineira*, for example at R Gonçalves Dias 874, Savassi, Av Antônio Carlos 8305, Pampulha, Av Raja Gabaglia 1617, São Bento. **Other Brazilian** *La Greppia*, R da Bahia 1204 (Centro). Lunch only, good. Cheap local food is served in the restaurants around the rodoviária, *prato feito* US$1. There are many bars and restaurants around Praça Raúl Soares; more on R Rio de Janeiro. *Flor de Líbano*, R Espírito Santo 234. Cheap and good. *Tampa*, R Tupis between Av Curitiba and R São Paulo. Cheap, pizza, dish of the day, open evenings. *Aquarius*, Av Curitiba between R dos Carijós and R dos Tamoios. Cheap, simple food, open Sun evenings.

International *Santa Felicidade*, R Profesor Morais 659 (Savassi). Pastas, fish, grill, buffet, open for lunch and in the evening. **Italian** *Buona Távola*, R Santa Rita Durão 309 (Savassi), T3227 6155. Excellent. *Dona Derna*, R Tomé de Souza 1380 (Savassi), T3223 6954. Highly recommended. *Pizzarela*, Av Olegário Maciel 2280, Lourdes, T3222 3000. Good for pizzas. *Vecchio Sogno*, R Martim de Carvalho 75/R Dias Adorno, Santo Agostinho, T3292 5251, under the Assembléia Legislativo. Good food, top wine list, closed Sun. **French** *Taste Vin*, R Curitiba 2105, Lourdes. Recommended. **German** *Alpino*, Av Contorno 5761 (Savassi). Good value and popular. **Oriental** *Yun Ton*, Chinese, R Santa Catarina 946, T3337 2171. Recommended. *Kyoto*, Japanese, R Montes Claros 323, Anchieta. Recommended. **Vegetarian** *Mandala*, R Cláudio Manoel 875, Savassi, T3261 7056.

Belo Horizonte centre

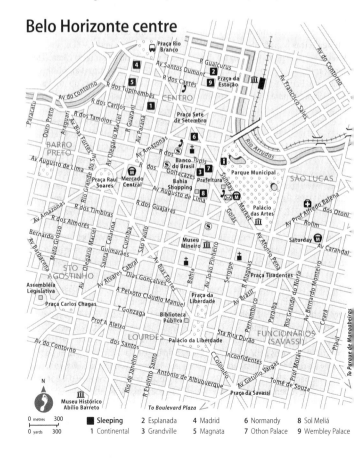

■ **Sleeping**	2 Esplanade	4 Madrid	6 Normandy	8 Sol Meliá
1 Continental	3 Grandville	5 Magnata	7 Othon Palace	9 Wembley Palace

Cafés *Café Belas Artes*, R Gonçalves Dias 1581, Lourdes, in the foyer at Unibanco Belas Artes Liberdade. Popular. *Café Belas Artes Nazaré*, R Guajajaras 37, near Av Afonso Pena, in the Unibanco Nazaré Liberdade cinema. *Café Três Corações*, Praça Diego de Vasconcelos, Savassi. Coffees and snacks. *Koyote Street Bar*, R Tomé de Souza 912. Street café.

Bars Recommended bars are *Alambique*, Av Raja Gabaglia 3200, Chalé 1D, Estoril, T3296 7188. Specializes in *cachaça*, with *mineira* appetizers, designed like a country house. *Amoricana*, R Pernambuco 1025. *Entre Folhas*, R Floralia 40. Outdoor café bar with live music, US$1.50, open until midnight Tue-Sun. Recommended. *Bar Nacional*, Av Contorno 1076, Barro Preto. Good value. *Heaven*, Av Getúlio Vargas 809.

Entertainment

Theatres The city prides itself on its theatre and dance companies (look out for the *Grupo Galpão*) and has at least a dozen theatres. The local press and tourist literature give details of shows and events.

Shopping

Mercado Central, Av Augusto de Lima 744, is large and clean, open every day. See above for the Sun *handicraft fair* on Av Afonso Pena. A **flower market** is held at Av Bernardo Monteiro, near Av Brasil, every Fri from 1200 to 2000. For **gemstones**, try *Manoel Bernardes*, Av Contorno 5417, Savassi, very reasonable. For **music**, *Cogumelo*, Av Augusto de Lima 399. **Bookshops** *Daniel Vaitsman*, R Espírito Santo 466, 17th floor, for English language books. Foreign language books at *Livraria Van Damme*, R das Guajajaras 505, also good local and Portuguese selection. *Siciliano* in BH Shopping sells *Footprint Handbooks*. Used foreign-language books at *Livraria Alfarrábio*, R Tamóios 320.

Tour operators

Master Turismo (Amex representative), R da Bahia 2140, T3330 3655, www.masterturismo.com.br At Sala VIP, Aeroporto de Confins, and Av Afonso Pena 1967, T3330 3603 (very helpful). *Ouro Preto Turismo*, Av Afonso Pena 4133, T3287 0505, F3287 0103, www.ouropretotour.com and *Revetur*, R Espírito Santo 1892, 1st floor, Lourdes, T3337 2500, www.revetour.com.br Both have been recommended. *Ametur*, R Alvarengo Peixoto 295, loja 102, Lourdes, T/F3275 2139, 0900-1200, 1400-1900, has information on *fazendas* which welcome visitors and overnight guests. **Ecotourism and adventure sports:** *Amo-Te*, *Associação Mineira dos Organizadores do Turismo Ecológico*, R Prof Morais 624, Apto 302, Savassi, T3281 5094, oversees ecotourism in Minas Gerais. For companies which arrange trekking, riding, cycling, rafting, jeep tours, canyoning, visiting national parks, or *fazendas*, speak to *Amo-Te* in the first instance. For recommended **horse riding** tours, contact *Tropa Serrana*, Tullio Marques Lopes Filho, T3344 8986, T9983 2356 (mob).

Transport

Local Bus: the city has a good public transport system: red buses run on express routes and charge US$0.75; yellow buses have circular routes around the Contorno, US$0.50; blue buses run on diagonal routes charging US$0.65. There are also buses which integrate with the regional, overground Metrô. A new system is being introduced, in which all routes will feed into an *estação*, or route station; passengers will purchase tickets before boarding the bus.

Taxi: are plentiful, although hard to find at peak hrs.

Long distance Air: the international airport is near Lagoa Santa, at Confins, 39 km from Belo Horizonte, T3689 2700. Taxi to centre, US$50, cooperative taxis have fixed rates to different parts of the city. Airport bus, either *executivo* from the exit, US$11, or comfortable normal bus (*Unir*) from the far end of the car park hourly, US$2.20, both go to/from the rodoviária.

Closer to the city is the national airport at Pampulha, which has shuttle services from several cities, including Rio and São Paulo, T3490 2001. Urban transportation to/from this airport is cheaper than from Confins. From Pampulha airport to town, take blue bus 1202, 25 mins, US$0.65, passing the rodoviária and the cheaper hotel district.

Train: to **Vitória**, daily 0700, tickets sold at 0530, US$17.50 *executivo*, US$11.50 1st class, US$7.80 2nd, 12 hrs.

Bus: the rodoviária is by Praça Rio Branco at the northwest end of Av Afonso Pena, T3271 3000/8933. The bus station has toilets, post office, phones, left-luggage lockers (attended service 0700-2200), shops and is clean and well-organized. Buses leave from the rather gloomy platforms beneath the ticket hall. Do not leave belongings unattended.

To **Rio** with *Cometa* (T3201 5611) and *Útil* (T3201 7744), 6½ hrs, US$12.75 (ordinary), *leito*, US$25.50. To **Vitória** with *São Geraldo* (T3271 1911), US$14.50 and *leito* US$29. To **Brasília** with *Itapemirim* (T3291 9991) and *Penha* (T3271 1027), 10 hrs, 6 a day including 2 *leitos*, only one leaves in daylight (0800), US$19.25, *leito* US$38.50. To **São Paulo** with *Cometa* and *Gontijo* (T3201 6130), 10 hrs, US$15.60. To **Foz do Iguaçu**, US$42, 22 hrs. To **Salvador** with *Gontijo*, US$40, 24 hrs, at 1900 daily, and *São Geraldo* at 1800. *São Geraldo* also goes to **Porto Seguro**, 17 hrs, direct, via Nanuque and Eunápolis, US$33. To **Recife** with *Gontijo*, 2000, US$41. To **Fortaleza**, US$63. To **Natal**, US$66. To **Belém** with *Itapemirim* at 2030, US$72. To **Campo Grande** with *Gontijo* (at 1930) and *Motta* (3 a day), US$31-36, a good route to Bolivia, avoiding São Paulo. All major destinations served. For buses within Minas Gerais, see under each destination.

Hitchhiking To Rio or Ouro Preto, take a bus marked 'Shopping', to the *BH* shopping centre above Belo Horizonte on the Rio road.

Directory **Airline offices** *American*, Av Bernardo Monteiro 1539,, Funcionários, T3274 3166.*TAM*, Av Cristóvão Colombo 485, 7th floor, T3228 5500, Pampulha T3441 8100. *United*, Av Getúlio Vargas 840, T3339 6060, Confins T3689 2736. *Varig/Rio Sul/Nordeste*, Av Getúlio Vargas 840T3339 6000/0800-997000, Confins airport T3689 2350. *Vasp*, Av Getúlio Vargas 1492, T0800-998277, Confins T3689 2394. **Banks** *Banco do Brasil*, R Rio de Janeiro 750, Av Amazonas 303; cash is given against credit cards at *Banco Itaú*, Av João Pinheiro 195. *Citibank*, R Espírito Santo 871. Visa ATM at *Bradesco*, R da Bahia 947. *Master Turismo*, see Tour operators, above. American Express representative. Changing TCs is difficult, but hotels will change them for guests at a poor rate. **Communications** Internet: *Internet Café Club*; R Fernandes Tourinho 385, Plaza Savassi, US$5 per hr. Post Office: Av Afonso Pena 1270, with fax, philatelic department and small museum, service is slow (unless the quick counter is open), closes 1800; poste restante is behind the main office at R de Goiás 77 (unhelpful). The branch office on R da Bahia is less busy. **Telephone:** *Telemig*, Av Afonso Pena 1180, by the Correios, daily 0700-2200; also at the rodoviária, Confins airport, R Caetés 487 and R Tamóios 311 in the centre; R Paraíba 1441, Savassi. **Embassies and consulates** Austria, R José Américo Cançado Bahia 199, T3333 5363, F3333 1046. Denmark, R Paraíba 1122, 5th floor, T3286 8626, F3269 8785. Finland, Av Contorno 6283, salas 602/4, T3281 1052, F3281 9514. France, R Bernardo Guimarães 1020, lj 3, Funcionários, T3261 7805, F3261 7806. Germany, R Timbiras 1200, 5th floor, T3213 1568. Italy, Av Afonso Pena 3130, 12th floor, T3281 4211. Netherlands, R Sergipe 1167, loja 5, T3227 5275. Spain, R Curitiba 778, sl 701, T/F3212 3759. UK, R dos Inconfidentes 1075, sala 1302, Savassi, T3261 2072, F3261 0226, britcon.bhe@terra.com.br **Medical services** *Mater Dei*, R Gonçalves Dias 2700, T3339 9000. Recommended. **Tourist offices** Belotur, the municipal information office, is at R Pernambuco 284, Funciários, T3277 9797, F3277 9730, www.pbh.gov.br/belotur/index.htm Very helpful, with lots of useful information and maps. The monthly *Guia Turístico* for events, opening times etc, is freely available. Belotur has offices also at the southwest corner of Parque Municipal, at Confins and Pampulha airports, and at the rodoviária (particularly polyglot). **Turminas**, Praça Rio Branco 56, T3272 8573, F3272 5605, www.turminas.mg.gov.br/intminas.html The tourism authority for the state of Minas Gerais. It, too, is very helpful and its *Gerais Common Ways* booklet has a useful facts section. The daily newspaper, *Estado de Minas*, www.em.com.br, has interesting articles and information on the city and the state. Ibama, Av do Contorno 8121, Cidade Jardim, CEP 30110-120, Belo Horizonte, T3337 2624, F3335 9955. **Voltage** 120-220 AC, 60 cycles.

Nature reserves near Belo Horizonte The **Parque Natural de Caraça** is a remarkable reserve about 120 km east of Belo Horizonte. It has been preserved so well because the land belongs to a seminary, part of which has been converted into a hotel. The rarest mammal in the park is the maned wolf; the monks feed them on the seminary steps in the evening. Also endangered is the southern masked titi monkey. Other primates include the common marmoset and the brown capuchin monkey. Some of the bird species at Caraça are endemic, others rare and endangered. The trails for viewing the different landscapes and the wildlife are marked at their beginning and are quite easy to follow. ■ *0700-2100; if staying overnight you cannot leave after 2100. US$5 per vehicle.*

Sleeping and eating The seminary hotel, *Hospedaria do Caraça*, has pleasant rooms; room rates vary, **AL-B**, full board. For reservations write to Santuário do Caraça, Caixa Postal 12, 35960-000 – Santa Bárbara, MG, T0xx31-837 2698, or phone 101 and ask the operator to connect you to PS1 do Caraça. There is a restaurant serving good food which comes from farms within the seminary's lands. Lunch is served 1200-1330.

Transport Turn off the BR-262 (towards Vitória) at Km 73 and go via Barão de Cocais to Caraça (120 km). There is no public transport to the seminary. Buses go as far as Barão de Cocais, from where you have to take a taxi, US$12 one way. You must book the taxi to return for you, or else hitch (which may not be easy). The park entrance is 10 km before the seminary. The alternatives are either to hire a car, or take a guide from Belo Horizonte, which will cost about US$75 (including guiding, transport and meals). It is possible to stay in **Santa Bárbara** (**D** *Hotel Karaibe*. **D** *Santa Inés*), 25 km away on the road to Mariana and hitchhike to Caraça. 11 buses a day from Belo Horizonte – Santa Bárbara (fewer on Sat and Sun).

About 105 km northeast of Belo Horizonte, **Parque Nacional da Serra do Cipó**, 33,400 sq km of the Serra do Espinhaço, has scenic beauty and several endemic plants, insects and birds. In the last category, the Cipó Canestero is only found in one small area in the south of the park. The predominant habitat is high mountain grassland, with rocky outcroppings. Full details from *Ibama*, T0xx31 651 2456. ■ *The park can be reached via road MG-010. This road continues unpaved to Serro (see page 425); buses run on this route. Agencies offer excursions from the city to the park. It is recommended to take a guide because the trails are unmarked; ask locally.*

Colonial cities around Belo Horizonte

East of the state capital by 23 km is the colonial gold-mining (and steel-making) town of Sabará, strung along the narrow steep valleys of the Rio das Velhas and Rio Sabará. For tourist information, visit the *Secretaria de Turismo*, R Pedro II 200, T671 1522. www.sabara.mg.gov.br ■ *Viação Cisne bus, from Belo Horizonte, US$0.75, 30 mins, from separate part of Belo Rodoviária from main departure hall.*

Sabará
Colour map 7, grid B5
Population: 115,352

Worth seeing is R Dom Pedro II, which is lined with beautiful 18th-century buildings. Among them is the **Solar do Padre Correa** (1773) at No 200, now the **Prefeitura**; the **Casa Azul** (also 1773), No 215; and the **Teatro Municipal**, former Opera House (1770 – the second oldest in Brazil). At the top of R Dom Pedro II is the Praça Melo Viana, in the middle of which is **Nossa Senhora do Rosário dos Pretos** (left unfinished at the time of the slaves' emancipation). There is a museum of religious art in the church. ■ *Church and museum: Tue-Sun 0800-1100, 1300-1700.* To the right of the church as you face it is the **Chafariz do Rosário** (the Rosário fountain). In R da Intendência is the museum of 18th century gold mining in the **Museu do Ouro**. It contains exhibits on gold extraction, plus religious items and colonial furniture. The building itself is a fine example of colonial architecture. ■ *Tue-Sun 1200-1730, US$1.* Another fine example is the **Casa Borba Gato**, R Borba Gato 71; the building currently belongs to the Museu do Ouro.

The church of **Nossa Senhora do Carmo** (1763-74), with doorway, pulpits and choirloft by Aleijadinho (see below) and paintings by Athayde, is on R do Carmo ■ *US$1; includes a leaflet about the town.* **Nossa Senhora da Conceição** (begun 1701, construction lasting until 1720), on Praça Getúlio Vargas, has much visible woodwork and a beautiful floor. The carvings have much gilding, there are painted panels and paintings by 23 Chinese artists brought from Macau. The clearest Chinese work is on the two red doors to the right and left of the chancel. ■ *Free.* **Nossa Senhora do Ó**, built in 1717 and showing unmistakable Chinese influence (paintings much in need of restoration), is 2 km from the centre of the town at the Largo Nossa Senhora do Ó (take local bus marked 'Esplanada' or 'Boca Grande').

If you walk up the Morra da Cruz hill from the *Hotel do Ouro* to a small chapel, the Capela da Cruz or Senhor Bom Jesus, you can get a wonderful view of the whole area.

Brazil

Sleeping B *Pousada Solar das Sepúlvedas*, R da Intendência 371, behind the Museu do Ouro, T671 2708. Grand, rooms with TV, pool. **D** *Hotel do Ouro*, R Santa Cruz 237, Morro da Cruz, T671 5622. With bath, hot water, with breakfast, marvellous view, best value.

Caeté
Colour map 7, grid B5
Population: 36,299
60 km from
Belo Horizonte

A further 25 km is Caeté, which has several historical buildings and churches. On the Praça João Pinheiro are the **Prefeitura** and **Pelourinho** (both 1722), the **Igreja Matriz Nossa Senhora do Bom Sucesso** (1756 rebuilt 1790) ■ *Daily 1300-1800*, and the **Chafariz da Matriz**. Also on the Praça is the tourist information office in the Casa da Cultura (T6511855). Other churches are **Nossa Senhora do Rosário** (1750-68), with a ceiling attributed to Mestre Athayde, and **São Francisco de Assis**. The **Museu Regional**, in the house of the Barão de Catas Altas, or Casa Setecentista, R Israel Pinheiro 176, contains 18th and 19th century religious art and furniture. ■ *Tue-Sun 1200-1700*.

Ouro Preto

Phone code: 0xx31
Post code: 35400
Colour map 7, grid B5
Population: 66,277
Altitude: 1,000 m

Founded in 1711, this famous former capital of the state has cobbled streets that wind up and down steep hills which are crowned with 13 churches. Mansions, fountains, churches, vistas of terraced gardens, ruins, towers shining with coloured tiles, all blend together to maintain a delightful 18th century atmosphere. From October-February the climate is wet, but the warmest month of the year is February (30°C on average). The coldest months are June, July and August, with lowest temperatures being in July (10°C).

Sights
Photography is
prohibited in all
the churches
and museums

In the central **Praça Tiradentes** is a statue of the leader of the **Inconfidentes**, Joaquim José da Silva Xavier. Another Inconfidente, the poet Tomás Antônio Gonzaga lived at R Cláudio Manoel 61, close to São Francisco de Assis church. On the north side of the praça (at No 20) is a famous **Escola de Minas** (School of Mining), founded in 1876, in the fortress-like **Palácio dos Governadores** (1741-48); it has the interesting **Museu de Mineralogia e das Pedras**, with 23,000 stones from around the world. ■ *Tue-Sun 1200-1700*. On the south side of the Praça, No 139, is the **Museu da Inconfidência**, a fine historical and art museum in the former **Casa de Câmara e Cadeia**, which has some drawings by Aleijadinho and the Sala Manoel da Costa Athayde, in an annex. ■ *Mon-Fri 0800-1800, US$1.50*. **Casa das Contas**, R São José 12, built between 1782-87, is the Centro de Estudos do Ciclo de Ouro (Centre for Gold Cycle Studies) and a museum of money and finance. ■ *Tue-Sat 1230-1730, Sun and holidays 0830-1330, US$0.50*. The **Casa Guignard**, R Conde de Bobadela 110, displays the paintings of Alberto da Veiga Guignard. ■ *Tue-Sat 1230-1730, Sun 0830-1330, free*. The **Teatro Municipal** in R Brigadeiro Musqueiro, is the oldest functioning theatre in Latin America. It was built in 1769. ■ *Daily 1230-1800*.

The **Mina do Chico Rei**, R Dom Silvério is not as impressive as some other mines in the area, but is 'fun to crawl about in'; restaurant attached. ■ *0800-1700, US$1.50*. Near the Padre Faria Church (NS do Rosário dos Brancos) is another small mine, **Mina Bem Querer**, with a swimming pool with crystal clear water that runs through the mine. ■ *US$1*. (Between Ouro Preto and Mariana is the **Minas de Passagem** gold mine, dating from 1719. ■ *A guided tour visits the old mine workings and underground lake (take bathing suit), entrance US$7.50, visiting hours 0900-1730, last admissions at 1645.*)

Churches
These churches are all
closed Mon, but are
open at the times
given on other days

São Francisco de Assis (1766-96), Largo de Coimbra, is considered to be one of the masterpieces of Brazilian baroque. Aleijadinho worked on the general design and the sculpture of the façade, the pulpits and many other features. Mestre Athayde (1732-1827) was responsible for the painted ceiling. ■ *0830-1145, 1330-1640, US$1; the ticket also permits entry to NS da Conceição (keep your ticket for admission to the museum).*

O Aleijadinho

Antônio Francisco Lisboa (1738-1814), the son of a Portuguese architect and a black slave woman, was known as O Aleijadinho (the little cripple) because in later life he developed a maiming disease (possibly leprosy) which compelled him to work in a kneeling (and ultimately a recumbent) position with his hammer and chisel strapped to his wrists. His finest work, which shows a strength not usually associated with the plastic arts in the 18th century, is probably the set of statues in the gardens and sanctuary of the great Bom Jesus church in Congonhas do Campo, but the main body of his work is in Ouro Preto, with some important pieces in Sabará, São João del Rei and Mariana.

Nossa Senhora da Conceição (1722) is heavily gilded and contains Aleijadinho's tomb. It has a museum devoted to him. ■ *0830-1130, 1330-1645, Sun 1200-1645.* **Nossa Senhora das Mercês e Perdões** (1740-72), R das Mercês, was rebuilt in the 19th century. Some sculpture by Aleijadinho can be seen in the main chapel. ■ *1000-1400.* **Santa Efigênia** (1720-85), Ladeira Santa Efigênia e Padre Faria; Manuel Francisco Lisboa (Aleijadinho's father) oversaw the construction and much of the carving is by Francisco Xavier de Brito (Aleijadinho's mentor). ■ *0800-1200; has wonderful panoramic views of the city.* **Nossa Senhora do Carmo**, R Brigadeiro Mosqueira (1766-72); museum of sacred art with Aleijadinho sculptures. ■ *1330-1700, and entry is shared with Nossa Senhora do Pilar.* **Nossa Senhora do Pilar** (1733); which also contains a religious art museum. ■ *1200-1700.* **Nossa Senhora do Rosário**, Largo do Rosário, dated from 1785, has a curved façade. The interior is much simpler than the exterior, but there are interesting side altars.

Ask at the tourist office for accommodation in *casas de família*, reasonably priced. Avoid touts who greet you off buses and charge higher prices than those advertised in hotels; it is difficult to get hotel rooms at weekends and holiday periods.

    AL *Pousada Solar de NS do Rosário*, Av Getúlio Vargas 270, T3551 5200, rosario@bis.com.br Fully restored historic building with a highly recommended restaurant, bar, sauna, all facilities in rooms. **AL-A** *Pousada do Mondego*, Largo de Coimbra 38, T3551 2040, F3551 3094. Beautifully kept colonial house in a fine location by São Francisco church, room rates vary according to view, small restaurant, Scotch bar, popular with groups (a Roteiro de Charme hotel, see page 337), the hotel runs a *jardineira* bus tour of the city, 2 hrs, minimum 10 passengers, US$10 for non-guests. Recommended. **B** *Pousada Casa Grande*, R Conselheiro Quintiliano, 96, T/F3551 4314. TV, fridge, including breakfast, safe, good views. Recommended. **B** *Grande*, R Senador Rocha Lagoa 164, T/F3551 1488, www.hotelouropreto.com.br Largest hotel in town and the only modern structure, designed by Oscar Niemeyer, the feel of the place is somehow more dated than the colonial buildings that surround it, but that is no reflection on the service. **C** *Pouso Chico Rei*, R Brigadeiro Mosqueira 90, T3551 1274. A fascinating old house with Portuguese colonial furnishings, very small and utterly delightful, book in advance (room No 6 has been described as a 'dream'). **C** *Solar das Lajes*, R Conselheiro Quintiliano 604, T/F3551 3388, www.solardaslajes.com.br A little way from centre, excellent view, swimming pool, well run. **C** *Colonial*, Travessa Cônego Camilo Veloso 26, T3551 3133, colonial@ouropreto.feop.com.br Close to Praça Tiradentes, with new rooms and older rooms refurbished, pleasant. **C** *Pousada Itacolomi*, R Antônio Pereira 43, T3551 2891. Small, TV in rooms. Recommended. **C** *Pousada Nello Nuno*, R Camilo de Brito 59, T3551 3375. Cheaper without bath, charming owner Annamélia speaks some French. Highly recommended. **C** *Hospedária de Ouro Preto*, R Xavier da Veiga 1, T3551 2203. A restored colonial house. Recommended. **C** *Pousada Ouro Preto*, Largo Musicista José dos Anjos Costa 72, T3551 3081, www.asminasgerais.com.br Small, laundry facilities, English spoken by owner, Gérson Luís Cotta (most helpful), good views. Recommended. **C** *Pousada Tiradentes*, Praça Tiradentes 70, T3551 2619. Comfortable, TV, fridge, rooms a bit spartan and small, very convenient. **D** *Pousada dos Bandeirantes*, R das Mercês 167, T551 1996, F551 1962, behind São

Sleeping
Prices indicated here are for high season; many hotels offer, or will negotiate lower prices outside holiday times or when things are quiet

Brazil

Francisco de Assis. Beautiful views, TV, fridge, very pleasant. **D** *Pousada São Francisco de Paula*, Padre JM Pena 202 (next to the São Francisco de Paula church), T3551 3456, pousadas@hotmail.com In a garden, panoramic view, veranda with hammock, multilingual staff, trips organized to nearby villages, mountains, mines, waterfalls, 8 rooms including a dormitory, with or without a simple breakfast, private or communal bathroom, full breakfast and snacks available. Recommended. **Youth hostel**: R Costa Sena 30-A, Largo de Coimbra, T/F3551 6705, www.users.task.com.br/albergue **F** pp *Brumas*, Ladeira São Francisco de Paula 68, 150 m downhill from rodoviária, just below São Francisco de Paula church, T3335 7809, brumasonline@hotmail.com Dormitory, kitchen, superb views. Don't walk down from bus station after dark.

Students May be able to stay, during holidays and weekends, at the self-governing student hostels, known as *repúblicas* (very welcoming, "best if you like heavy metal music" and "are prepared to enter into the spirit of the places"). The Prefeitura has a list of over 50 *repúblicas* with phone numbers, available at the *Secretaria de Turismo*. Many are closed between Christmas and Carnival.

Camping Camping Clube do Brasil, 2 km north of the city at Rodovia dos Inconfidentes Km 91, T551 1799, is quite expensive but very nice.

Eating *Casa Grande* and *Forno de Barro*, both on Praça Tiradentes (Nos 84 and 54 respectively). Good local dishes. *Pasteleria Lampião*, Praça Tiradentes. Good views at the back (better at lunchtime than in the evening). *Tacho de Ouro*, Conde de Bobadela 76. Good lunch buffet, popular. *Casa do Ouvidor*, Conde de Bobadela 42, above Manoel Bernardis jewellery shop. Good. *Satélite*, R Conde de Bobadela 97. Restaurant and pizzeria, bar next door, good value. *Pizzaria Zebão*, R Paraná 43. *Ouro Grill*, R Senador Rocha Lagoa 61. Self-service at lunchtime, US$5, good value, restaurant after 1600. *Vide Gula*, R Senador Rocha Lagoa 79A. Food by weight, good, friendly atmosphere. Recommended. *Taverna do Chafariz*, R São José 167. Good local food. *Café & Cia*, R São José 187. Closes 2300, very popular, *comida por kilo* at lunchtime, good salads, juices. Recommended. *Chale dos Caldos*, R Pandia Calogera between *Pousada Circolo de Ouro* and *Pousada Ouro Preto*. Good soups, pleasant setting. *Adega*, R Teixeira Amaral 24. 1130-1530, vegetarian smorgasbord, US$5, all you can eat. Highly recommended. *Beijinho*, Direita 134A. Recommended for pastries and cakes. Try the local *licor de jaboticaba*.

Festivals Ouro Preto is famous for its **Holy Week** processions, which in fact begin on the Thu before Palm Sunday and continue (but not every day) until Easter Sunday. The most famous is that commemorating Christ's removal from the Cross, late on Good Friday. Many shops close during this holiday, and on winter weekends. Attracting many Brazilians, *Carnival* here is also memorable. In Jun, *Corpus Christi* and the *Festas Juninas* are celebrated. Every **Jul** the city holds the *Festival do Inverno da Universidade Federal de Minas Gerais (UFMG)*, the Winter Festival, about 3 weeks of arts, courses, shows, concerts and exhibitions. Also in **Jul**, on the 8th, is the *anniversary of the city*. **15 Aug**: *Nossa Senhora do Pilar*, patron saint of Ouro Preto. **12-18 Nov**: *Semana de Aleijadinho*, a week-long arts festival.

Shopping Gems are not much cheaper from freelance sellers in Praça Tiradentes than from the shops, and in the shops, the same quality of stone is offered at the same price – *Gemas de Minas* and *Manoel Bernardis*, Conde de Bobadela 63 and 48 respectively, are recommended. If buying on the street, ask for the seller's credentials. Buy soapstone carvings at roadside stalls and bus stops rather than in cities; they are much cheaper. Many artisans sell carvings, jewellery and semi-precious stones in Largo de Coimbra in front of São Francisco de Assis church.

Transport **Bus** The rodoviária is at R Padre Rolim 661, near São Francisco de Paula chruch, T3551 1081.
Don't walk from the rodoviária to town at night; robberies have occurred A 'Circular' bus runs from the rodoviária to Praça Tiradentes, US$0.40. Taxis charge exorbitant rates. 11 buses a day from Belo Horizonte (2 hrs, *Pássaro Verde*), US$3.50, taxi US$30. Day trips are run. Book your return journey to **Belo Horizonte** early if returning in the evening; buses get crowded. Bus from **Rio**, *Útil* or 0830 or 2330 (US$15, 7.5 hrs), return bus to Rio at 2330 (book in advance). There are also *Útil* buses to **Conselheiro Lafaiete**, 3-4 a day via

Itabirito and Ouro Branco (see below), US$3.75, 2¾ hrs, for connections to **Congonhas do Campo**. Other *Útil* services to Rio, Barbacena, Conselheiro Lafaiete and Congonhas go via Belo Horizonte. Direct buses to **São Paulo**, 3 a day with *Cristo Rei*, 11 hrs, US$19.25. *Gontijo* go to Salvador via Belo Horizonte.

Banks *Banco do Brasil*, R São José 189, high commission, changes TCs. *Bradesco*, corner of Senador Rocha Lagoa and Padre Rolim, opposite the Escola de Minas. *Banco 24 Horas*, Praça Alves de Brito, next to Correios. **Communications** Internet: *Point* Language School, Xavier da Veiga 501. **Post Office:** Praça Alves de Brito. **Tourist offices** Praça Tiradentes 41 (opens 0800, Portuguese only spoken), very helpful, T3551 2655. The *Secretaria de Turismo* is in the Casa de Gonzaga, R Cláudio Manoel 61, T3559 3282, F3559 3251. It has lists of hotels, restaurants and local sites and a map. **Guidebooks**: Bandeira's *Guia de Ouro Preto* in Portuguese and English, normally available at tourist office. Also available is Lucia Machado de Almeida's *Passeio a Ouro Preto*, US$6 (in Portuguese, English and French). The tourist office sells a guide with maps to Ouro Preto and Mariana, *Guia Prático*, for US$5. A local guide for a day, **Associação de Guias de Turismo** *(AGTOP)*, can be obtained through the tourist office (a recommended guide is *Cássio Antunes*), T3551 2655 at the tourist office, or T3551 1544 ext 269. The **Guiding Association** (T3551 2504, or T3551 1544 ext 205) offers group tours of US$30 for 1 to 10 people, US$45 for more than 10. If taking a guide, check their accreditation. **Voltage** 110 volts AC.

Directory

Mariana

Brazil

Streets are lined with beautiful, two-storey 18th century houses in this old mining city, which is much less hilly than Ouro Preto. Twelve kilometres east of Ouro Preto, on a road which goes on to join the Rio-Salvador highway, Mariana's historical centre slopes gently uphill from the river and the Praça Tancredo Neves, where buses from Ouro Preto stop. The first street parallel with the Praça Tancredo Neves is R Direita, and is home to the 300-year-old houses. At No 54 is the **Casa do Barão de Pontal**, whose balconies are carved from soapstone, unique in Minas Gerais. The ground floor of the building is a museum of furniture. ■ *Tue 1400-1700*. At No 35 is the **Museu-Casa Afonso Guimarães** (or Alphonsus de Guimaraens), the former home of a symbolist poet: photographs and letters. ■ *Free*. No 7 is the **Casa Setecentista**, which now belongs to the Patrimônio Histórico e Artístico Nacional.

Phone code: 0xx31
Post code: 35420
Colour map 7, grid B5
Population: 46,710
Altitude: 697 m

R Direita leads to the Praça da Sé, on which stands the **Cathedral**, Basílica de Nossa Senhora da Assunção. The portal and the lavabo in the sacristy are by Aleijadinho. The painting in the beautiful interior and side altars is by Manoel Rabello de Sousa. Also in the cathedral is a wooden German organ (1701), a gift to the first diocese of the Capitania de Minas do Ouro in 1747. ■ *Organ concerts are given on Fri at 1100 and Suns at 1200, US$7.50*. On R Frei Durão is the **Museu Arquidiocesano**, which has fine church furniture, a gold and silver collection, Aleijadinho statues and an ivory cross ■ *0900-1200, 1300-1700, closed Mon, US$1.50*. Opposite is the **Casa da Intendência/Casa de Cultura**, No 84, which holds exhibitions and has a museum of music. ■ *0800-1130, 1330-1700*. On the south side of Praça Gomes Freire is the **Palácio Arquiepiscopal**, while on the north side is the **Casa do Conde de Assumar**, who was governor of the Capitania from 1717 to 1720.

From Praça Gomes Freire, Travessa São Francisco leads to Praça Minas Gerais and one of the finest groups of colonial buildings in Brazil. In the middle of the Praça is the **Pelourinho**, the stone monument to Justice, at which slaves used to be beaten. On one side of the square is the fine **São Francisco** church (1762-94), with pulpits designed by Aleijadinho, paintings by Mestre Athayde, who is buried in tomb No 94, a fine sacristy and one side-altar by Aleijadinho. ■ *Daily 0800-1700*. At right angles to São Francisco is **Nossa Senhora do Carmo** (1784), with steatite carvings, Athayde paintings, and chinoiserie panelling. ■ *Daily 1400-1700*. Across R Dom Silvério is the **Casa da Cámara e Cadéia** (1768), at one time the Prefeitura Municipal. On Largo de São Pedro is **São Pedro dos Clérigos** (begun in 1753), one of the few elliptical churches in Minas Gerais. Restoration is under way.

Capela de Santo Antônio, wonderfully simple and the oldest in town, is on R Rosário Velho. It is some distance from the centre. Overlooking the city from the north, with a good viewpoint, is the church of **Nossa Senhora do Rosário**, R do Rosário (1752), with work by Athayde and showing Moorish influence.

Sleeping & eating **B** *Pousada Solar dos Corrêa*, R Josefá Macedo 70 and R Direita, T/F3557 2080. Central, with breakfast, TV, fridge in room, parking. **C** *Pousada do Chafariz*, R Cônego Rego 149, T3557 1492. TV, fridge, parking, breakfast included, family atmosphere. Recommended. **C** *Providência*, R Dom Silvério 233, T3557 1444. Run by nuns, small rooms, pool, quiet. **C** *Central*, R Frei Durão 8, T/F3557 1630. **C** without bath, on the attractive Praça Gomes Freire, pleasant, quiet. Recommended but avoid downstairs rooms. The modern service station (*Posto Mariana*) on the highway above the town offers good clean rooms (**D**) with hot showers. **D** pp *Müller*, Av Getúlio Vargas 34, T3557 1188. Across the river from the Terminal Turístico. Recommended. Restaurants: *Mangiare della Mamma*, D Viçoso 27, Italian. Recommended. *Tambaú*, R João Pinheiro 26. typical meals. *Engenho Nôvo*, Praça da Sé 26. Bar at night, English spoken by the owners and clients. Recommended by English travellers. *Panela de Pedra* in the Terminal Turístico serves food by weight at lunchtime.

Transport **Bus** From Escola de Minas, Ouro Preto, for Mariana, every 30 mins, US$0.60, all passing Minas de Passagem. Buses stop at the new rodoviária, out of town on the main road, then at the Posto Mariana, before heading back to centre of Mariana at Praça Tancredo Neves. Buses from Mariana to Ouro Preto can be caught by the bridge at the end of R do Catete.

Directory **Tourist offices** In the *Terminal Turístico Manoel Costa Athayde*, Praça Tancredo Neves, is the local guides' association (**AGTURB**, T3557 1158), who run tours for US$40. There is also a small tourist office; map US$1.50. A free monthly booklet, *Mariana Agenda Cultural*, has details of the historical sites, accommodation, restaurants, shopping, transport etc, plus articles, poems and a calendar of events.

Congonhas do Campo
Phone code: 0xx31
Post code: 36404
Colour map 7, grid B5
Population: 41,256
Altitude: 866 m

This hill town is connected by a paved 3½ km road with the Rio-Belo Horizonte highway. Most visitors spend little time in the town, but go straight to **O Santuário de Bom Jesus de Matosinhos**, which dominates Congonhas. The great pilgrimage church was finished in 1771; below it are six linked chapels, or *pasos* (1802-18), showing scenes with life-size Passion figures carved by Aleijadinho and his pupils in cedar wood. These lead up to a terrace and courtyard. On this terrace (designed in 1777) stand 12 prophets, sculpted by Aleijadinho between 1800 and 1805. Carved in soapstone with dramatic sense of movement, they constitute one of the finest works of art of their period in the world. Inside the church, there are paintings by Athayde and the heads of four sainted popes (Gregory, Jerome, Ambrose and Augustine) sculpted by Aleijadinho for the reliquaries on the high altar. To the left of the church, as you face it, the third door in the building alongside the church is the Room of Miracles, which contains photographs and thanks for miracles performed. ■ *Tue-Sun 0700-1900. There are public toilets on the Alameda das Palmeiras. The information desk at the bus station will guard luggage.*

On the hill are a tourist kiosk, souvenir shops, the *Colonial Hotel* and *Cova do Daniel* restaurant. From the hotel the Alameda das Palmeiras sweeps round to the **Romarias**, which contains the Espaço Cultural, the headquarters of the local tourist office (*Fumcult*, T3731 1300 ext 114 or 3731 3133), workshops, the museums of mineralogy and religious art and the Memória da Cidade.

■ *Getting there: A bus marked 'Basílica' runs every 30 mins from the centre of the rodoviária to Bom Jesus, 5 km, US$0.45. A taxi from the rodoviária costs US$5, US$10 return including the wait while you visit the sanctuary. In town, the bus stops in Praça JK. You can walk up from Praça JK via Praça Dr Mário Rodrigues Pereira, cross the little bridge, then go up Ruas Bom Jesus and Aleijadinho to the Praça da Basílica.*

Sleeping and eating **D** *Colonial*, Praça da Basílica 76, opposite Bom Jesus, T3731 1834. Comfortable but noisy, breakfast extra, cheaper without bath, fascinating restaurant (*Cova do Daniel*) downstairs is full of colonial handicrafts and local food. **E** *Freitas*, R Marechal Floriano 69, T3731 1543. Basic, with breakfast, cheaper without bath. *Estalagem Romaria*, 2 mins from *Hotel Colonial* in the Romarias, good restaurant and pizzeria, reasonable prices.

Congonhas is famous for its **Holy Week** processions, which have as their focus the Bom **Festivals**
Jesus church. The most celebrated ceremonies are the meeting of Christ and the Virgin Mary
on the Tue, and the dramatized Deposition from the Cross late on Good Friday. The pilgrimage season, first half of **Sep**, draws many thousands. **8 Dec**, *Nossa Senhora da Conceição*.

Bus The Rodoviária is 1½ km outside town; bus to town centre US$0.40; for 'Basílica', see **Transport**
above. To/from **Belo Horizonte**, 1½ hrs, US$3, 8 times a day. To **São João del Rei**, 2 hrs,
US$3.60, tickets are not sold until the bus comes in. Bus to **Ouro Preto**: go via Belo Horizonte
or Conselheiro Lafaiete. Whether going from Ouro Preto or Rio to Congonhas do Campo,
there is no direct bus; you have to change at **Conselheiro Lafaiete.** Frequent service
Conselheiro Lafaiete-Congonhas do Campo, US$1.

São João del Rei

This colonial city is at the foot of the Serra do Lenheiro. A good view of the town and   *Phone code: 0xx32*
surroundings is from Alto da Boa Vista, where there is a Statue of Christ (Senhor dos   *Post code: 36300*
Montes). São João del Rei is very lively at weekends. Through the centre of town   *Colour map 7, grid B5*
runs the Corrego do Lenheiro; across it are two fine stone bridges, A Ponte da Cadeia   *Population: 78,616*
(1798) and A Ponte do Rosário (1800).

There are five 18th century churches in the town, three of which are splendid
examples of Brazilian colonial building. **São Francisco de Assis** (1774), Praça Frei
Orlando: the façade, with circular towers, the doorway intricately carved and the
greenish stone framing the white paint to beautiful effect was designed by
Aleijadinho. Inside are two sculptures by Aleijadinho, and others of his school. The
six side altars are in wood; restoration has removed the plaster from the altars,
revealing fine carving in sucupira wood. ■ *0830-1200 and some afternoons, US$1.*

Basílica de Nossa Senhora do Pilar (the Cathedral, R Getúlio Vargas – formerly
R Direita), built 1721, has a 19th century façade which replaced the 18th century
original. It has rich altars and a brightly painted ceiling. In the sacristy are portraits of
the Evangelists. ■ *Open afternoons.* **Nossa Senhora do Carmo**, Praça Dr Augusto
Viegas (Largo do Carmo), very well restored, is all in white and gold. Construction
commenced in 1733. ■ *Open afternoons.*

Almost opposite São Francisco is the house of **Bárbara Heliodora** (1759-1819), R   **Museums**
Padre José Maria Xavier, which also contains the **Museu Municipal Tomé Portes
del Rei**, with historical objects and curios. In the same building is the Instituto
Histórico e Geográfico. Downstairs is the tourist office: *Secretaria de Turismo*,
T3371 7833, 0900-1700, free map. **Museu de Arte Sacra**, Praça Gastão da Cunha 8,
by Nossa Senhora do Pilar, is small but recommended; it has sculptures, vestments
and a room full of silver. ■ *Tue-Sun 1100-1700, US$1.* The **Memorial Tancredo
Neves**, R Padre José Maria Xavier 7, is a homage to the man and his life. ■ *Wed-Fri
1300-1800, weekends and holidays 0900-1700, US$1.* The **Museu de Arte Regional
do Patrimônio Histórico**, in Praça Severiano de Resende, in a fine three-storey
building (1859), has 18th and 19th century furniture and pictures and a city archive.
■ *Tue-Sun 0800-1200, 1330-1730, US$1.*

The **Museu Ferroviário** (railway museum), Av Hermílio Alves 366, T371 8004, (see
below for the train to Tiradentes) is well worth exploring. The museum traces the history
of railways in general and in Brazil in brief. You can walk along the tracks to the round
house, in which are several working engines in superb condition, an engine shed and a
steam-operated machine shop, still working. It is here that the engines get up steam
before going to couple with the coaches for the run to Tiradentes. On days when the
trains are running, you can get a good, close-up view of operations even if not taking the
trip; highly recommended. ■ *Tue-Sun 0900-1130, 1300-1700, US$0.50.*

Worth a visit is the **pewter factory** (with exhibition and shop), Av Leite de Castro
1150, run by the Englishman John Somers and his son Gregory. ■ *10 mins' walk
from the rodoviária, 0900-1800, T3371 8000, F3371 7653.*

Sleeping & eating **A** *Lenheiro Palace*, Av Pres Tancredo Neves 257, T/F3371 8155, www.mgconecta.com.br/lenheiros/index.html A modern hotel with good facilities, parking, *Lenheiros Casa de Chá* tea house, breakfast, no restaurant. **B** *Porto Real*, Av Eduardo Magalhães 254, T/F3371 7000. Also modern, comfortable, sizeable rooms, good restaurant. **C** *Pousada Casarão*, opposite São Francisco church, in a converted mansion, Ribeiro Bastos 94, T3371 7447, F3371 2866. Firm beds, TV, fridge, swimming pool, games room, delightful. **C** *Aparecida*, Praça Dr Antônio Viegas 13, T3371 2540. Central, by the bus and taxi stop, has a restaurant and *lanchonete*. **D** *do Hespanhol*, R Mcal Deodoro 131, T3371 4677. Also central, price varies according to room. **E** *Brasil*, Av Presidente Tancredo Neves 395, T3371 2804. In an old house full of character and staircases, on the opposite side of the river from the railway station, cheap. Recommended but basic and early morning alarm call from neighbouring rooster, no breakfast. **E** *Pousada São Benedito*, R Marechal Deodoro 254, T371 7381. Shared rooms only, shared bath. *Quinto do Ouro*, address as *pousada* above, good regional food, reasonable prices; also on Praça Severiano de Resende is *Churrascaria Ramón*, No 52, good.

Festivals Apr, *Semana Santa*; 15-21 Apr, *Semana da Inconfidência*. May or Jun, *Corpus Christi*. First 2 weeks of Aug, *Nossa Senhora da Boa Morte*, with baroque music (*novena barroca*). Similarly, **12 Oct**, *Nossa Senhora do Pilar*, patron saint of the city. **8 Dec**, *founding of the city*. FUNREI, the university (R Padre José Maria Xavier), holds *Inverno Cultural* in Jul.

Transport **Bus** Buses to **Rio**, 5 daily with *Paraibuna* (3 on Sat and Sun), 5 hrs, US$10-12. *Cristo Rei* to
Rodoviária is 2 km **São Paulo**, 8 hrs, 5 a day (also to Santos), and *Translavras*, 4 a day (also to Campinas),
west of centre US$12.50. **Belo Horizonte**, 3½ hrs, US$6.60. To **Juiz de Fora**, US$5.40, at least 8 a day with
of São João *Transur*. To **Tiradentes** with *Meier*, 8 a day, 7 on Sat, Sun and holidays, US$0.65.

Directory **Banks** *Bemge*, Av Pres Tancredo Neves 213, has exchange, 1100-1600. **Communications** Telephone: *Telemig* at Av Pres Tancredo Neves 119, 0700-2200.

Tiradentes

Phone code: 0xx32 This charming little town, 15 km from São João, with its nine streets and eight
Post code: 36325 churches, is at the foot of the green Serra São José. It is very busy during Holy Week,
Population: 5,759 when there are numerous religious processions. It was founded as São José del Rei on 14 January 1718. After the ousting of the emperor in 1889 the town was renamed in honour of the martyr of the Inconfidência.

Sights The **Igreja Matriz de Santo Antônio** (1710-36) contains some of the finest gilded
The tourist office is wood carvings in the country. The church has a small but fine organ brought from
in the Prefeitura, Porto in the 1790s. The upper part of the reconstructed façade is said to follow a
R Resende Costa 71 design by Aleijadinho. In front of the church are also a cross and a sundial by him. ■ *Daily 0900-1700.* **Santuário da Santíssima Trindade**, on the road which leads up behind the Igreja Matriz de Santo Antônio, is 18th century, while the room of miracles associated with the annual Trinity Sunday pilgrimage is modern.

The charming **Nossa Senhora do Rosário** church (1727), on a small square on R Direita, has fine statuary and ornate gilded altars. ■ *Thu-Mon 1200-1600, US$0.50.* **São João Evangelista** is on the Largo do Sol, a lovely open space. It is a simple church, built by the Irmandade dos Homens Pardos (mulattos). ■ *Thu-Mon 0900-1700.* Beside Igreja São João Evangelista is the **Museu Padre Toledo**, the house of one of the leaders of the Inconfidência Mineira. It exhibits some good pieces of furniture. At the junction of R da Câmara and R Direita is the **Sobrado Ramalho**, said to be the oldest building in Tiradentes. It has been beautifully restored as a cultural centre. **Nossa Senhora das Mercês** (18th century), Largo das Mercês, has an interesting painted ceiling and a notable statue of the Virgin (Sunday 0900-1700). The magnificent **Chafariz de São José** (the public fountain, 1749) is still used for drinking, clothes washing and watering animals. You can follow the watercourse into the forest of the Serra de São José (monkeys and birds can be seen).

Brazil

The **train** on the line between São João del Rei and Tiradentes (13 km) has been in continuous operation since 1881, using the same locomotives and rolling stock, running on 76 cm gauge track, all lovingly cared for. The maximum speed is 20 km per hr. ■ *Tickets cost US$13 return interior, US$6.50 return meia. The train runs on Fri, Sat, Sun and holidays, 1000 and 1415 from São João del Rei, returning from Tiradentes at 1300 and 1700.*

AL-A *Solar da Ponte*, Praça das Mercês (proprietors John and Anna Maria Parsons), T3355 1255, www.roteirosdecharme/sol.htm Has the atmosphere of a country house, the price includes breakfast and afternoon tea, only 12 rooms, fresh flowers in rooms, bar, sauna, lovely gardens, swimming pool, light meals for residents only, for larger meals, the hotel recommends 5 local restaurants (it is in the Roteiros de Charme group, see page 337). Recommended. **A** *Pousada Três Portas*, R Direita 280A, T3355 1444, F3355 1184. There are more expensive suites, has sauna, thermal pool, hydromassage, heating. **A** *Pousada Mãe D'Água*, Largo das Forras 50, T3355 1206, F3355 1221. Including breakfast but not tax, very nice. **B** *Pousada Maria Barbosa*, R Antônio Teixeira Carvalho 144, T/F3355 1227, www.idasbrasil.com.br Near bridge that leads out of town, pool, very pleasant, price includes breakfast, lunch and evening snack, during the week it is **C** (breakfast only). **B** *Hotel Ponto do Morro*, Largo das Forras 88, T3355 1342, F3355 1141. With pool, sauna, fridge, TV, phone, also has 2 chalets, the hotel has a nice entry. There are lots of other *pousadas*.

Quartier Latin, R São Francisco de Paula 46, Praça da Rodoviária. French, cordon bleu chef, excellent but expensive. *Quinto de Ouro*, R Direita 159. Recommended. *Virados do Largo*, Largo do Ó. Good food and service. *Estalagem*, R Ministro G Passos 280. *Padre Toledo*, R Direita 202. *Pasta & Cia*, R Frederico Ozanan 327. Beautiful restaurant with excellent freshly cooked meals served in glazed tile earthenware. Recommended. *Aluarte*, Largo do Ó 1, is a bar with live music in the evening, nice atmosphere, US$4 cover charge, garden, sells handicrafts. Recommended. There are other restaurants, snack bars and *lanchonetes* in town.

Bus Last bus back to São João del Rei is 1815, 2230 on Sun; fares are given above. **Taxi** To São João del Rei costs US$10. Around town there are pony-drawn taxis; ponies can be hired for US$5. For horse-riding treks, contact John Parsons at the *Solar da Ponte*.

Sleeping

Eating

Transport

The most remote of the colonial cities to the north of the State capital is reached from Belo Horizonte by taking the paved road to Brasília (BR-040). Turn northeast to **Curvelo**, beyond which the road passes through the impressive rocky country of the Serra do Espinhaço.

Diamantina

This centre of a once active diamond industry Diamantina has excellent colonial buildings. Its churches (difficult to get into, except for the modern Cathedral) are not as grand as those of Ouro Preto, but it is possibly the least spoiled of all the colonial mining cities, with carved overhanging roofs and brackets. This very friendly, beautiful town is in the deep interior, amid barren mountains. It is lively at weekends. President Juscelino Kubitschek, the founder of Brasília, was born here. His house, R São Francisco 241, has been converted into a museum. ■ *Tue-Thu 0900-1700, Fri-Sat 0900-1800, Sun 0900-1400.* Local festivals are *Carnival.* 12 September is *O Dia das Serestas*, the Day of the Serenades, for which the town is famous; this is also the anniversary of Kubitschek's birth.

Phone code: 0xx38
Post code: 39100
Colour map 7, grid A5
Population: 44,259
Altitude: 1,120 m

The oldest church in Diamantina is **Nossa Senhora do Rosário**, Largo Dom Joaquim, built by slaves in 1728. **Nossa Senhora do Carmo**, R do Carmo, dates from 1760-65 and was built for the Carmelite Third Order. It is the richest church in the town, with fine decorations and paintings and a pipe organ, covered in gold leaf, made locally.

Sights
The office will arrange a free tour of churches with guide who has keys (tip guide)

Brazil

São Francisco de Assis, R São Francisco, just off Praça JK, was built between 1766 and the turn of the 19th century. It is notable for its paintings. Other colonial churches are the **Capela Imperial do Amparo** (1758-76), **Nossa Senhora das Mercês** (1778-84) and **Nossa Senhora da Luz** (early 19th century). The **Catedral Metropolitana de Santo Antônio**, on Praça Correia Rabelo, was built in the 1930s in neo-colonial style to replace the original cathedral.

After repeated thefts, the diamonds of the **Museu do Diamante** (Diamond Museum), R Direita 14 (US$1), have been removed to the Banco do Brasil. The museum does house an important collection of the materials used in the diamond industry, plus other items from the 18th and 19th centuries. The **Casa de Chica da Silva** is at Praça Lobo Mesquita 266, ■ *Free*. Chica da Silva was a slave in the house of the father of Padre Rolim (one of the Inconfidentes). She became the mistress of João Fernandes de Oliveira, a diamond contractor. Chica, who died on 15 February 1796, has become a folk-heroine among Brazilian blacks.

Behind the 18th century building which now houses the **Prefeitura Municipal** (originally the diamonds administration building, Praça Conselheiro Matta 11) is the **Mercado Municipal** or **dos Tropeiros** (muleteers), Praça Barão de Guaicuí. The **Casa da Glória**, R da Glória 297, is two houses on either side of the street connected by an enclosed bridge. It contains the Instituto Eschwege de Geologia.

Excursions Walk along the **Caminho dos Escravos**, the old paved road built by slaves between the mining area on Rio Jequitinhonha and Diamantina. A guide is essential (ask at the Casa de Cultura – cheap), and beware of snakes and thunderstorms.

Along the river bank it is 12 km on a dirt road to **Biribiri**, a pretty village with a well-preserved church and an abandoned textile factory. It also has a few bars and at weekends it is a popular, noisy place. About half-way, there are swimming pools in the river; opposite them, on a cliff face, are animal paintings in red. The age and origin are unknown. The plant life along the river is interesting and there are beautiful mountain views.

Sleeping **C** *Dália*, Praça JK (Jota-Ka) 25, T3531 1477. Fairly good. **C** *Tijuco*, Macau do Melo 211,
& eating T/F3531 1022. The best, with good food. **D** *JK*, opposite the rodoviária, with good breakfast, hot showers. **E** *Pensão Comercial*, Praça M Neves 30. Basic. Wild camping is possible near the waterfall just outside town. A recommended eating place is *Capistrana*, R Campos Carvalho 36, near Cathedral square. *Santo Antônio* in the centre has a good self-service *churrasco* and salad for US$3 during the week.

Entertainment *Serestas* (serenades) are sung on Fri and Sat nights. Many young people hang out in the bars in Beco da Mota. *Taverna de Gilmar* is recommended for a good mix of music, although it gets packed quickly. *Cavernas Bar*, Av Sílvio Felício dos Santos, is good for *pagode* on Sat and Sun from late afternoon.

Transport 6 buses a day to **Belo Horizonte**, via Curvelo, with *Pássaro Verde*: 2½ hrs to **Curvelo**, US$3, to **Belo Horizonte**, US$10, 5½ hrs. To Bahia, take the *Gontijo* Belo Horizonte-Salvador bus to **Araçuaí** (**D** *Pousada Tropical*, opposite rodoviária behind the policlínica, T3731 1765, with bath, good) and change there, US$11.50 but you have to check an hr or so beforehand to see if there is space in the bus. The bus passes Diamantina at about 1330-1400, or 0200. It's a very bumpy ride through Couto de Magalhães de Minas and Virgem da Lapa. From Araçuaí take a bus to Itaobim (US$2.65, 2 hrs) then connect to Vitória da Conquista (US$5.50, 4 hrs).

Directory **Useful information Tourist office** Departamento de Turismo, is in the Casa de Cultura, Praça Antônio Eulálio 53, 3rd floor, T3531 1636, F3531 1857; pamphlets and a reliable map are available, information about churches, opening times, friendly and helpful. **Voltage** 110 AC.

From Diamantina, 92 km by paved road and reached by bus from there or from Belo Horizonte, is this unspoiled colonial town on the Rio Jequitinhonha. It has six fine baroque churches, a museum and many beautiful squares. It makes *queijo serrano*, one of Brazil's best cheeses, being in the centre of a prosperous cattle region. The most conspicuous church is **Santa Rita** on a hill in the centre of town, reached by a long line of steps. On the main Praça João Pinheiro, by the bottom of the steps, is **Nossa Senhora do Carmo**, arcaded, with original paintings on the ceiling and in the choir. The town has two large mansions: those of the **Barão de Diamantina**, Praça Presidente Vargas, now in ruins, and of the **Barão do Serro** across the river on R da Fundição, beautifully restored and used as the town hall and Casa de Cultura. ■ *Tue-Sat 1200-1700, Sun 0900-1200*. The **Museu Regional Casa dos Ottoni**, Praça Cristiano Ottoni 72, is an 18th century house now containing furniture and everyday objects from the region.

Just by the Serro turnoff is the town of **Datas**, whose spacious church (1832) decorated in red and blue contains a striking wooden image of Christ with the crown of thorns. **A** *Pousada Vila do Príncipe*, T3541 1485, very clean, in an old mansion at R Antônio Honório Pires 38, contains its own museum, the artist Mestre Valentim is said to have been born in the slave quarters; other cheap hotels.

Serro
Phone code: 0xx38
Post code: 39150
Colour map 7, grid B5
Population: 21,012

Eastern Minas

In this park are the Pico da Bandeira (2,890 m), Pico do Cruzeiro (2,861 m) and the Pico do Cristal (2,798 m). From the park entrance (where a small fee has to be paid) it is 6 km on a poorly maintained road to the car park at the base of the waterfall. From the hotel (see below) jeeps (US$20 per jeep) run to the car park at 1,970 m (2½ hours' walk), then it's a three to four hr walk to the summit of the Pico da Bandeira, marked by yellow arrows; plenty of camping possibilities all the way up, the highest being at Terreirão (2,370 m). This is good walking country. It is best to visit during the dry season (April-October). It can be quite crowded in July and during Carnival. ■ *Contact via Caixa Postal 17, Alto Jequitibá, MG, CEP 36976-000, T0xx32-747 2555, Alto do Caparaó.*

Parque Nacional Caparaó
The park features rare Atlantic rainforest in its lower altitudes and Brazilian alpine on top

Sleeping B *Caparaó Parque*, T(PS-101)741 2559, 2 km from the park entrance, 15 mins' walk from the town of Caparaó, nice. Ask where **camping** is permitted in the park. In **Manhumirim D** *São Luiz*, good value, but *Cids Bar*, next door, Travessa 16 do Março, has better food.

Transport Parque Nacional Caparaó is 49 km by paved road from Manhuaçu (about 190 km south of Governador Valadares) on the Belo Horizonte-Vitória road (BR-262). There are buses from Belo Horizonte (twice daily with *Pássaro Verde*), Ouro Preto or Vitória to **Manhumirim** (*Population*: 20,025), 15 km south of Manhuaçu. From Manhumirim, take a bus direct to Caparaó, 0930, 1630 US$1, or to Presidente Soares (several, 7 km), then hitch 11 km to Caparaó. By car from the BR-262, go through Manhumirim, Presidente Soares and Caparaó village, then 1 km further to the *Hotel Caparaó Parque*.

A modern planned city, Governador Valadares is a good place to break the Belo Horizonte-Salvador journey. It is a centre of gemstone mines and lapidation, as well as for the cut-crystal animals one finds in tourist shops all around Brazil. It is also one of the world's top cross-country paragliding/hang-gliding sites; hitch a ride up to the launch site at 1000, but take a blue Rio Doce bus from the road near the landing site back to town. Several **A-B** hotels and many cheap hotels near the bus station. *JB restaurant*, R Israel Pinheiro 1970. Recommended. On same street, *Dom de Minas*, No 2309, *churrascaria*, pay by weight. ■ *The airport is on the BR-381, 6 km from the city centre with flights to Belo Horizonte and Ipatinga. Bus: 5½ hrs from Belo Horizonte with* Gontijo, *US$11.50, US$21 leito.*

Governor Valadares
Phone code: 0xx33
Post code: 35100
Colour map 7, grid B5
Population: 247,131
Altitude: 170 m
324 km from
Belo Horizonte

Brazil

Phone code: 0xx33
Post code: 39800
Colour map 7, grid A6
Population: 129,424
Altitude: 335 m

Teófilo Otoni, 138 km from Governador Valadares, is a popular buying spot for dealers of crystals and gemstones, with the best prices in the state. **C** *Pousada Tio Miro*, R Dr Manoel Esteves 389, T3521 4343, relaxed atmosphere. Recommended.
■ *Buses from Belo Horizonte with Gontijo, US$15.50, leito US$29; to Porto Seguro via Nanuque (can break Belo Horizonte-Salvador journey here.* **D** Hotel Minas, *at the rodoviária, adequate, and others nearby).*

Southern Minas Gerais

Tres Corações is the birthplace of Pelé, the legendary football star, to whom there is a statue in Praça Col José Martins. It is eight kilometres east of BR-381 (*Phone code:* 0xx35. *Post code:* 37410) in southern Minas, but not a spa. Sleeping: **B** *Hotel Cantina Calabreza*, R Joaquim Bento de Carvalho 65, T/F3231 1183, TV, fridge, swimming pool, sauna, has a reasonable restaurant (Italo-Brasileira), and take-away service. **D** *Capri*, Av Getúlio Vargas 111, T3231 1427, not far from bridge across the river, with or without bath or TV, simple but OK.

Transport Bus: there are 3 daily buses (2 on Sun) to **São Tomé das Letras**, US$1.65, 1½ hrs (the first 30 mins is on a paved road). To **Belo Horizonte**, *Gardénia*, 4 a day (3 on Sun), US$10.50, 5½ hrs, roadworks permitting. To **São Paulo**, *Transul*, 7 a day, US$8.10. *Beltour* runs buses to Rio; *Cristo Rei* to Santos.

São Tomé das Letras

Phone code: 0xx35
Colour map 7, grid B4
Population: 6,204
The average maximum
temperature is 26°C,
the minimum is 14°C.
Rainy season: Oct-Mar

A beautiful hilltop town, one of the five highest places in Brazil, São Tomé has attracted many new age visitors and its hotels are graded in UFOs instead of stars. It is said to be a good vantage point for seeing UFOs, which draw crowds at weekends. Nearby are caves with inscriptions, which some say are extraterrestrial in orgin. It is believed that there are many places with special energies. Behind the town are rocky outcrops on which are the Pyramid House, the Cruzeiro (Cross, 1,430 m, with good 360° views), the Pedra da Bruxa and paths for walking or, in some parts, scrambling. A quarry town since the beginning of the 20th century, there is evidence of the industry everywhere you look.

The bus stops at the main Praça, on which is the frescoed 18th-century **Igreja Matriz** beside the fenced cave in which are the faded red rock paintings ('letras') of the town's name. A second church, the **Igreja das Pedras** (Nossa Senhora do Rosário – 18th century) is on a Praça to the left as you enter town (R Ernestina Maria de Jesus Peixoto). It is constructed in the same style as many of the charming old-style buildings, with slabs of the local stone laid on top of each other without mortar. The post office and *Bemge Bank* are in the group of buildings at the top right of the Praça, facing the Gruta São Tomé. Tourist office R José Cristiano Alves 4.

Tours In the surrounding hills are many caves, waterfalls and rapids. Some of these places make a good hike from the town, but you can also visit several in a day on an organized tour. T3237 1283 or enquire at *Néctar* shop on R José Cristiano Alves. Tours run on weekends and holidays from the Praça at 1000 and 1400 to waterfalls, caves, etc, T3237 1353 and ask for Jaime or Iraci. The Carimbado cave is especially rich in myths and legends. Shangri-lá, which is a beautiful spot, is also called the Vale do Maytréia. And so on.

Note that streets
are hard to follow
because their names
seem to change almost
from one block to
the next; numbering
is also chaotic

Sleeping There are lots of *pousadas* and rooms to let all over town: **C** *Pousada Arco-Iris*, R João Batista Neves 19, T/F3237 1212. Rooms and chalets, sauna, swimming pool. **D** *dos Sonhos II* (do Gê), Trav Nhá Chica 8, T3237 1235. Very nice, restaurant, swimming pool, sauna. Recommended. **E** *Hospedaria dos Sonhos I*, R Gabriel Luiz Alves. With bath, restaurant, shop, groups accommodated. On the main Praça is the shop of the **Fundação Harmonia**, whose headquarters are downhill, on the road to Sobradinho (4 km). The community emphasizes several disciplines for a healthy lifestyle, for mind and body, 'new age', workshops, massage, excursions, vegetarian food, clean accommodation (**D** pp). Address Estrada para Sobradinho s/n, Bairro do Canta Galo, São Tomé das Letras, CEP 37418-000, T3237 1280. There are many restaurants and bars.

Brazil

Espírito Santo

The coastal state of Espírito Santo is where mineiros head to for their seaside holidays. Five bridges connect the island on which Vitória stands with the mainland. The state capital is beautifully set, its entrance second only to Rio's, its beaches quite as attractive, but smaller, and the climate is less humid. Port installations at Vitória and nearby Ponta do Tubarão have led to some beach and air pollution at places nearby. It is largely a modern city: The upper, older part of town, reached by steep streets and steps, is much less hectic than the lower harbour area which suffers dreadful traffic problems.

On Av República is the huge **Parque Moscoso**, an oasis of quiet, with a lake and playground. Colonial buildings still to be seen in the upper city are the **Capela de Santa Luzia**, R José Marcelino (1551), now an art gallery; the church of **São Gonçalo**, R Francisco Araújo (1766) and the ruins of the **Convento São Francisco** (1591). In the **Palácio do Governo**, or **Anchieta**, Praça João Climaco (upper city) is the tomb of Padre Anchieta, one of the founders of São Paulo. The **Teatro Carlos Gomes**, on Praça Costa Pereira, often presents plays, also jazz and folk festivals. **Vila Velha**, reached by a bridge across the bay, has an excellent beach, but it is built up and noisy: take a bus from Vitória marked Vilha Velha. See the mostly ruined, fortified monastery of **Nossa Senhora da Penha**, on a high hill above Vila Velha; the views are superb. There is also a pleasant ferry service to Vila Velha. Urban beaches such as **Camburi** can be affected by pollution, but it is quite pleasant, with a fair surf. 10 km south of Vila Velha is **Barra do Jucu**, which has bigger waves.

Excursions Visit **Santa Leopoldina** or **Domingos Martins**, both around 45 km from Vitória, less than an hr by bus (two companies run to the former, approximately every three hours). Both villages preserve the architecture and customs of the first German and Swiss settlers who arrived in the 1840s. Domingos Martins (also known as Campinho) has a Casa de Cultura with some items of German settlement. Santa Leopoldina has an interesting museum covering the settlers' first years in the area. ■ *Tue-Sun 0900-1100, 1300-1800*.

To **Santa Teresa**, a charming hill town 2½ hours, 90 km by bus from Vitória (US$6 a beautiful journey). There is a unique hummingbird sanctuary at the **Museu Mello Leitâo**, Av José Ruschi 4, which is a library including the works of the hummingbird and orchid scientist, Augusto Ruschi. Hummingbird feeders are hung outside the library. ■ *0800-1200, 1300-1700, T259 1182*.

Sleeping C *Avenida*, Av Florentino Avidos 350, T3223 4317. With breakfast. Recommended. C *Vitória*, Cais de São Francisco 85, near Parque Moscoso. Excellent restaurant, changes money. Recommended. D *Europa*, 7 de Setembro, corner Praça Costa Pereira. Noisy but cheap, good value restaurant (nearby is a good value vegetarian restaurant and a money changer, ask at hotel). Adequate hotels can be found opposite the rodoviária. Other hotels are located in beach areas, Camburi to the north, Vila Velha to the south, both 15 mins from city centre. **Youth hostel** *Jardim da Penha*, R Hugo Viola 135, T3324 0738, F3325 6010, take 'Universitário' bus, get off at first University stop. There is another youth hostel in Vila Velha, *Praia da Costa*, R São Paulo 1163, Praia da Costa, CEP 29101-300, T3329 3227.

Transport Trains Daily passenger service to **Belo Horizonte**, 14 hrs, US$17.50 executivo (very comfortable), US$11.50 1st class, US$7.80 2nd. **Bus** Rio, 8 hrs, US$15 (*leito* 25). **Belo Horizonte**, US$14.50 (*leito* 29). **Salvador**, 18 hrs, US$27; **Porto Seguro** direct 11 hrs with lots of stops, US$18 (also *leito* service); alternatively, take a bus to Eunápolis, then change to buses which run every hr.

Tourist offices Cetur, Av Princesa Isabel 54, T3322 8888, at airport and at rodoviária (friendly, good free map). Also *Instituto Jones dos Santos Neves*, Av Marechal Campos 310, 3rd floor, Ed Vitória Centre, CEP 29040-090, T3322 2033, ext 2215, F3322 2033, ext 225.

Vitória
Phone code: 0xx27
Post code: 29000
Colour map 7, grid B6
Population: 292,304

Brazil

Eurico Salles airport at Goiaberas, 11 km from city. The rodoviária is a 15-min walk west of the centre

Directory
www.sebes.com.br/ turismo

Guarapari
Colour map 7, grid B6
Population: 88,400

South of Vitória (54 km) is Guarapari, whose beaches are the closest to Minas Gerais, so they get very crowded at holiday times. The beaches also attract many people seeking cures for rheumatism, neuritis and other complaints, from the radio-active monazitic sands. Information about the sands can be found at *Setuc*, in the Casa de Cultura, Praça Jerônimo Monteiro, T3261 3058, and at the Antiga Matriz church on the hill in the town centre, built in 1585.

A little further south (20 km) is the fishing village of **Ubu**, then, 8 km down the coast, **Anchieta**. Near here are Praia de Castelhanos (5 km east, on a peninsula) and **Iriri**, a small village with two beaches, Santa Helena and Inhaúma. There is accommodation in these places.

The next spot down the coast, 5 km, is **Piúma**, a calm, little-visited place, renowned for its craftwork in shells. About 3 km north of the village is Pau Grande beach, where you can surf. The resort town of **Marataízes**, with good beaches, hotels and camping, is 30 km south of Piúma. It is just north of the Rio state border.

Turtle beaches

The **Reserva Biológica Comboios**, 104 km north of Vitória via Santa Cruz, is designed to protect the marine turtles which frequent this coast (for information, contact *Ibama* in Vitória, Av Marechal Mascarenhas 2487, CP 762, CEP 29000, T3324 1811, or T0xx27-264 1452). **Regência**, at the mouth of the Rio Doce, 65 km north of Santa Cruz, is part of the reserve and has a regional base for *Tamar*, the national marine turtle protection project.

Linhares, 143 km north of Vitória on the Rio Doce, has good hotels (**E** *Modenezi*, opposite bus terminal, with bath) and restaurants. It is a convenient starting place for the turtle beaches. Besides those at the mouth of the Rio Doce, there is another *Tamar* site at **Ipiranga**, 40 km east of Linhares by an unmade road.■ *For information, also contact* Tamar *at Caixa Postal 105, CEP 29900-970, Linhares, ES.*

Conceição da Barra
Colour map 7, grid B6
Population: 26,494
261 km N of Vitória

The most attractive beaches in the state are around this town. Corpus Christi (early June) is celebrated with an evening procession for which the road is decorated with coloured wood chips. Viewed from its small port, the sunsets are always spectacular. Conceição da Barra has pleasant beach hotels, also **D** *Caravelas*, Avenue Dr Mário Vello Silvares 83, T762 1188, one block from the beach, basic, shared bathroom, light breakfast. Recommended. **E** *Pousada Pirámide*, next to rodoviária, T762 1970, good value, 100 m from beach. *Camping Clube do Brasil* site with full facilities, Rodovia Adolfo Serra, Km 16, T762 1346.

Itaúnas, 27 km north by road, or 14 km up the coast, has been swamped by sand dunes, 30 m high. From time to time, winds shift the sand dunes enough to reveal the buried church tower. Itaúnas has been moved to the opposite river bank. The coast here, too, is a protected turtle breeding ground (*Tamar*, Caixa Postal 53, Conceição da Barra, T0xx27-762 1124). There are a few *pousadas* and a small campsite at Itaúnas. At Guaxindiba, 3 km north, is **A** *Praia da Barra*, Av Atlântica 350, T0xx27-762 1100; and others. ■ *Bus from the bakery in Conceição da Barra at 0700, returns 1700.*

Brazil

Southern Brazil: Paraná

Paraná has one of the premier tourist sites in South America, the Iguaçu Falls. The state has a short coastline and its main port, Paranaguá, is connected with the capital, Curitiba, by one of the best railways in South America. The culture of Paraná has been heavily influenced by its large immigrant communities including Japan, Poland, Italy, Syria and the Ukraine.

Population: 9.5 million

Curitiba

One of the three cleanest cities in Latin America, the capital of Paraná state has extensive open spaces and some exceptionally attractive modern architecture. Curitiba was founded on 29 March 1693. Local holidays: *Ash Wednesday* (half-day); *Maundy Thursday* (half-day); 8 September (Our Lady of Light).

Phone code: 0xx41
Post code: 80000
Colour map 7, grid C2
Population: 1,587,315
Altitude: 908 m

The commercial centre is the busy R 15 de Novembro, part of which is a pedestrian area called **Rua das Flores**. The **Boca Maldita** is a particularly lively part where local artists exhibit. Another pedestrian area is behind the cathedral, near Largo da Ordem, with a flower clock and old buildings, very beautiful in the evening when the old lamps are lit – nightlife is concentrated here. There is a small fish fair on Saturday mornings at **Praça Generosa Marques**, and an art market in **Praça Garibáldi** on Sunday mornings. The **Centro Cívico** is at the end of Av Dr Cândido de Abreu, 2 km from the centre: a monumental group of buildings dominated by the **Palácio Iguaçu**, headquarters of the state and municipal governments. In a patio behind it is a relief map to scale of Paraná. The **Bosque de João Paulo II** behind the Civic Centre on R Mateus Leme, was created in December 1980 after the Pope's visit to Curitiba. It also contains the **Memorial da Imigração Polonesa no Paraná** (Polish immigrants memorial). All that remains of the magnificent old **Palácio Avenida**, Travessa Oliveira Belo 11, is the façade, which was retained during remodelling works in 1991. Nowadays it has banks, offices, an auditorium for 250 people and various cultural activities. The **Solar do Barão**, built in 1880-83, is used for concerts in the auditorium and exhibitions, R Presidente Carlos Cavalcanti 53. ■ *T322 1525.*

A fine example of the use of tubular steel and glass is **Rua 24 Horas**, where the whole street is protected by an arched roof. The street's shops, bars and restaurants never close. The popular **Passeio Público**, in the heart of the city (closed Monday), inaugurated in 1886. It has three lakes, each with an island, and a playground.

About 4 km east of the rodoferroviário, the **Jardim Botânico Fanchette Rischbieter** has a fine glass house, inspired by Crystal Palace in London. The gardens are in the French style and there is also a **Museu Botánico**, R Ostoja Roguski (Primeira Perimetral dos Bairros), T321 8646, 362 1800 (museum). ■ *Take the orange Expreso buses from Praça Rui Barbosa.*

On Praça Tiradentes is the **Cathedral**, R Barão do Serro Azul 31, T222 1131, built in neo-gothic style and inaugurated in 1893 (restored in 1993). The oldest church in Curitiba is the **Igreja de Ordem Terceira da São Francisco das Chagas**, built in 1737 in Largo da Ordem. Its most recent renovation was in 1978-80. In its annex is the **Museu de Arte Sacra** (T223 7545). The **Igreja de Nossa Senhora do Rosário de São Benedito** was built in the Praça Garibáldi in 1737 by slaves and was the Igreja dos Pretos de São Benedito. It was demolished in 1931 and a new church was inaugurated in 1946. A mass for tourists, Missa do Turista, is held on Sunday at 0800.

Churches

Museu Paranaense, Praça Generoso Marques, includes documents, manuscripts, ethnological and historical material, stamps, works of art, photographs and

Museums

Brazil

archaeological pieces. ■ *Tue-Fri 1000-1800, other days 1300-1800, closed first Mon of each month, T323 1411.* **Museu de Arte Contemporânea**, R Desembargador Westphalen 16, Praça Zacarias, displays Brazilian contemporary art in its many forms, with an emphasis on artists from Paraná. ■ *Tue-Fri 0900-1900, Sat-Sun 1400-1900, T222 5172.* **Museu de Arte do Paraná**, in the Palácio São Francisco, exhibits the work of many of Paraná's artists. ■ *T2343172.* **Museu de História Natural**, R Benedito Conceição 407, natural history with lots of zoology and scientific collections, also details on endangered species in the State. ■ *T366 3133.*

Sleeping

There are some incredibly good value hotels in the city in the C and B categories

L *Bourbon & Tower*, Cândido Lopes 102, T322 4001, www.bourbon.com.br Most luxurious in centre. **A** *Lancaster*, R Voluntários da Pátria 91, T/F322 8953. Wood-panelled, very comfortable, caters to business clients as well as tourists. **B** *Costa Brava Palace*, R Francisco Torres 386, T262 7172. Good restaurant. Recommended. **B** *Curitiba Palace*, R Ermelino de Leão 45, T322 8081, curitibapalace@cwb.palm.com.br Central, polished and cosy with vast rooms, 24-hr restaurant, pool, good value. **B** *Del Rey*, R Ermelino de Leão 18, T/F322 3242. On Rua das Flores, upmarket yet relaxed, large rooms, good restaurant, fantastic value. Recommended. **C** *King's*, Av Silva Jardim 264, T322 8444. Good apartment hotel, secure. Highly recommended. **C** *Nova Lisboa*, Av 7 de Setembro 1948, T264 1944. With breakfast, bargain for cheaper rates without breakfast. Recommended. **C** *O'Hara*, R 15 de Novembro 770, T232 6044. Good location, fan, excellent breakfast, parking. **C** *Paraty*, R Riachueto 30, T223 1355. Central, apartments with kitchen, with breakfast, spacious, good. **C** *Tourist Universo*, Praça Gen Osório 63, T322 0099, F223 5420. On one of the city's most attractive squares, very smart for price, with sauna and pool, intimate and excellent value. Recommended. **D** *Cervantes*, R Alfredo Bufrem 66, T222 9593. Central, small, but cosy. **D** *Estação Palace*, R Des Westphalen 126, T322 9840, F324 5307. Excellent for price, 24-hr room service and internet. Recommended. **B** *Itamarati*, Tibagi 950, T222 9063. Fan, garage, good breakfast, showers can be dangerous, rather run down.

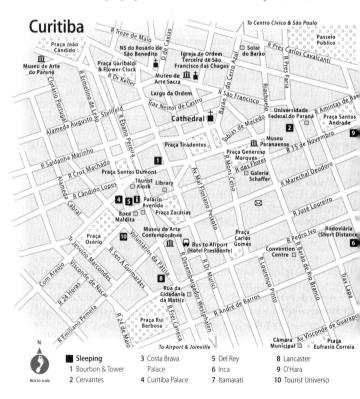

Curitiba

Not to scale

■ Sleeping
1 Bourbon & Tower
2 Cervantes

3 Costa Brava Palace
4 Curitiba Palace

5 Del Rey
6 Inca
7 Itamarati

8 Lancaster
9 O'Hara
10 Tourist Universo

E pp *Inca*, R João Negrão 370, T223 8563. Breakfast OK, safe, good. **E** pp *Nova Lisboa*, Av 7 de Setembro 1948, T264 1944. With breakfast, cheaper without breakfast. Recommended. **E** pp *Palace*, one block from R de Novembro, T222 2554. With breakfast, secure parking, TV, a little noisy but friendly. Recommended. **F** pp *Maia*, Av Presidente Afonso Camargo 360 block, opposite Rodoferroviária, T264 1684. Quiet, with breakfast, cheapest. **F** *Pensão PP*, Rua Gen Carneiro 657, T263 1169. Basic, no breakfast. Recommended.

Youth hostels E pp *AJ de Curitiba*, Av Padre Agostinho 645, Mercês, Curitiba PR, T233 2746, ajcwb@uol.com.br IYHA. **E** *Casa dos Estudantes*, Parque Passeio Público, north side, with student card, 4 nights or more. **F** *Casa do Estudante Luterano Universitario*, R Pr Carlos Cavalcanti 239, T324 3313. Good. This hostel is fully booked Jan and the week before Christmas. **Associação Paranaense de Albergues de Juventude**, Av Padre Agostinho 645, Curitiba PR, CEP 80.410, T233 2746. **Camping** Camping Clube do Brasil, 16 km, BR-116, Km 84.5, direction São Paulo, T358 6634.

Expensive *Ile de France*, Praça 19 de Dezembro 538, T223 9962. French, closed Sun. *Boulevard*, R Voluntários da Pátria 539, T224 8244. French, closed Sun. Also good. **Eating**
Mid range *Baviera*, Alameda Augusto Stellfield, corner with Al Dr Murici. Intimate and atmospheric in style of beer cellar, cantina, pizzeria and delivery service established over 30 years, open 1800-2300. *Jangil*, Praça Osório 45, upper floor. Quirky place at top of stairwell, with balcony overlooking lovely main praça. Go for a drink, tapas or dinner (pizza, pasta, fish and churasco) served by fatherly figures in white dinner jackets. *Saccy*, R São Franscisco 350, corner with Mateus Leme 12. Pizza, tapas and lively bar with live music. *Salmão* , R Emiliano Perneta 924. In historic house, delicious fish and pizza, often special promotions, live music every night, open till 0100. Short taxi ride from centre. **Churrascarias** all recommended: *Badida*, Av Batel 1486, Batel, T243 0473. *Churrascão Colônia*, Av Manoel Ribas 3250, Vista Alegre, T335 8686. *Devon's* , R Lysimaco Ferreira da Costa 436, Centro Cívico, T254 7073.

A Sacristia, R João Manuel 197. Restaurant, pizzeria, bar, very good. *Salão Italiano*, R Padre G Mayer 1095, Cristo Rei. Good Brazilian and Italian food. *Scavollo*, R Emiliano Perneta 924, Batel, T225 2244. Recommended for pizza. Local and Italian food and local red wine in nearby Santa Felicidade northeast of the centre, for example *Madalosso*, Av Manoel Ribas 5875, T372 2121. Enormous Italian *rodizio*, allegedly the 2nd largest in the world, cheap. Recommended. *Dom Antônio*, same street No 6121, T273 3131. Excellent; and others. *Mikado*, R São Francisco 126. Good, Japanese, vegetarian, lunch only. *Nakaba*, R Nunes Machado 56. Japanese. Huge set meal. *Cantina do Eisbein*, Av dos Estados 863, Água Verde. Owner Egon is friendly, duck specialities highly recommended. Closed Mon. *Oriente Arabe*, R Ebano Pereira 26 (1st floor), T223 2708. Excellent, huge Arab lunch. **Cheap** *Kisco*, 7 de Setembro near Tibagi. Good, huge *prato do dia*, friendly. Cheap food also near the old railway station and good meals in the bus station. Close to the Rodoferroviária is the market, where there are a couple of *lanchonetes*. Hot sweet wine sold on the streets in winter helps keep out the cold. For addicts, there are *McDonald's*, and takeaway Chinese and pizzas. *Happy Rango*, Av Visconde de Nacar 1350, near R 24 horas. Brightly lit, basic corner joint selling fast food and pizzas, open 24 hrs. *Mister Sheik*, Av Vicente Machado 534. Arabic fast food in pitta with salad, popular for deliveries. Recommended. Cheap food near old railway station and a good meal in the bus station. Close to the Rodoferroviária is the market, where there are a couple of *lanchonetes*. Hot sweet wine sold on the streets in winter helps keep out the cold. Restaurants offering buffets are usually good value at around US$12.

Vegetarian Most closed at night. *Vherde Jante*, R Pres Faria 481, Centro, T225 1627. Very good (open in evening). *Super Vegetariano*, R Presidente Faria 121, T223 6277, Cruz Machado 217, R Dr Murici 315, lunch and dinner Mon-Fri, very good and cheap buffet. *Greenland*, R 15 de Novembro 540, T232 3813. Recommended. *Panini*, R da Glória 307. Recommended for buffet lunches (US$4 with meat; US$2.50 vegetarian) in a charming house.

Bars A cluster of bars at the Largo da Ordem have tables and chairs on the pavement, music which tends to be rock, and bar food: *Fire Fox*, Av Jaime Reis 46, flanked by *Tuba's* and *The Farm*. *London Pub*, São Francisco 350 and, one block away, *Bar do Alemão*, interesting and popular bar also serving lunch and dinner.

Entertainment There are several modern **theatres**: the *Teatro Guaíra*, R 15 de Novembro, T322 2628, for plays and revues (also has free events – get tickets early in the day), the *Teatro Paiol* in the old arsenal, R Col Zacarias, T322 1525, the *Ópera de Arame* opera house on R João Gava, T252 9637, and others. A theatre festival takes place in Mar. There are **cinemas** in several shopping centres, and other places showing international films. Tickets are usually US$4-5 Mon-Thu, and US$6-8 at weekends. Best to look in the newspaper for music and what's on in the bars, clubs and theatres; *Gazeta do Povo* has a what's on section called *Caderno G*.

Shopping For souvenirs and handicrafts, try *Lojas Leve Curitiba*, at several locations, R 24 Horas, Afonso Pena airport, Ópera de Arame, Jardim Botânico, Memorial de Curitiba. *Lojas de Artesanato*, Casa de Artesanato Centro, R Mateus Leme 22, T352 4021. *Lojas de Artesanato 'Feito Aqui'*, Dr Muricy 950, International Airport and Shopping Mueller. *Feira de Arte e Artesanato*, Praça Garibáldi, Sun 0900-1400. Curitiba is a good place to buy clothes and shoes. *H Stern* jewellers at Mueller Shopping Centre. **Bookshops** *Livraria Saraiva*, in Shopping Crystal, has a large selection of books and music as well as a cyber café. Branch in Shopping Curitiba sells *Footprint*. Also *Ginghone* and *Curitiba* on Rua 15 and at Shoppings Curitiba and Crystal. *Figaro*, R Lamenha Lins 62, buys and sells second hand paperbacks in English and German. *Trovutare*, R de São Francisco 48. Good choice of books in English, Dutch, Spanish and French.

Tour operators *BMP Turismo*, R Brigadeiro Franco, 1845, T322 8566, American Express representative, emergency cash available with Amex.

Transport **Local** There are several route types on the integrated transport system and you are advised to pick up a map with details. **Express** are red and connect the transfer terminals to the city centre, pre-paid access, they use the silver 'tubo' bus stops; **Feeder** orange conventional buses connect the terminals to the surrounding neighbourhoods; **Interdistrict** green buses run on circular routes connecting transfer terminals and city districts without passing through the centre; **Direct or speedy** silver grey buses use the 'tubo' stations to link the main districts and connect the surrounding municipalities with Curitiba; **Conventional** yellow buses operate on the normal road network between the surrounding municipalities, the Integration Terminals and the city centre; **City circular** white mini buses, *Linha Turismo,* circle the major transport terminals and points of interest in the traditional city centre area. US$3.50 (multi-ticket booklets available), every 30 mins from 0900-1700, except on Mon. First leaves from R das Flores, narrow street in front of McDonalds. Three stops allowed.

Long distance **Air**: Afonso Pena (21 km away) for international and national flights, T381 1515. Silver Ligeirinho bus 'Aeroporto' leaves from 'tubo' stop near Circulo Militar to airport, stopping at rodoferroviária every 30 mins, US$0.60, 50 mins.

Bus: Short-distance bus services within the metropolitan region (up to 40 km) begin at Terminal Guadalupe at R João Negrão s/n, T321 8611. The Terminal Rodoviário/Estação Rodoferroviária is on Av Afonso Camargo s/n, T320 3000, for other cities in Paraná and other states. Restaurants, banks, bookshops, shops, phones, post office, pharmacy, tourist agency, tourist office and public services are all here. Frequent buses to **São Paulo** (6 hrs, US$10-12.50) and **Rio** (12 hrs, US$25). To **Foz do Iguaçu**, 10 a day, 10 hrs, US$15. **Porto Alegre**, 10 hrs. **Florianópolis**, 4½ hrs; **Blumenau** 4 hrs, US$6.50, 3 daily with **Penha/Catarinense**. Good service to most destinations in Brazil. *Pluma* bus to **Buenos Aires** (change buses at Foz de Iguaçu) and to **Asunción**. *TTL* runs to **Montevideo**, 26 hrs, 0340 departure (*semi-cama*).

Train: Rodoferroviária, Av Afonso Camargo s/n, T323 4007 (Serra Verde Express). Passenger trains to Paranaguá, see below.

Airline offices *Lufthansa*, Barão do Cerro Azul 325, T322 8227. *TAM*, Ermelino de Leão 75, 1st floor, T234 1234/323 5201. *Varig*, T0800-997000. *Vasp*, R 15 de Novembro 537, T221 7422/0800-998227. **Banks** *Bradesco*, R 15 de Novembro 155, Visa ATM. Plus or Cirrus associated credit cards can cash money at *Citibank*, R Marechal Deodoro 711 or at Buenos Aires 305 near Shopping Curitiba. *Sigla Turismo*, R Marechal Deodoro 427, Centro, popular for exchange. *Diplomata*, R Presidente Faria 145 in the arcade. *Câmbio*, 15 de Novembro 467, Edif Carvalho Lorreiro. **Communications** Internet: at *Livraria Saraiva* in Shopping Crystal, *Livraria Curitiba*, R das Flores (US$2 per hr), and Estação Plaza Shopping (four blocks from Rodoferroviária) after 1100. *Arena Network*, R Lopez 331. US$4 per hr. Also in R 24 Horas at *Digitando o Futuro*, free access but you need to book in advance T350 6366, and *Internet 24 Horas*, in the bookshop, open 24 hrs, US$3 per hr. *Monkey*, Av Vicente Machado 534, corner with R Brigadeiro. Cool, modern with lots of computers and internet games, open daily till 2400. **Post Office:** main post office is at Mcal Deodoro 298; post offices also at R 15 de Novembro and R Pres Faria. *UPS*, T2626180. **Telephone:** *Tele Centro-Sul* information, T102. *Embratel*, Galeria Minerva, R 15 de Novembro. **Cultural centres** Sociedade Brasileira de Cultura Inglesa (British Council), R Gen Carneiro 679 (Caixa Postal 505). *Instituto Goethe*, R Schaffenberg, near Military Museum, Mon-Thu 1500-1900, Library, Mon-Tue till 2130. **Embassies and consulates** Austria, R Cândido Hartmann 570, Ed Champagnat, 28th floor, T336 1166, Mon-Fri 1000-1300. Britain, R Pres Faria 51, 2nd floor, T322 1202, F322 3537, consulado.britanico@mais.sul.com.br Mon-Fri 0830-1200, 1400-1730. Denmark, R Prof Francisco Ribeiro 683, Caixa Postal 321, T843 2211, F843 1443. Germany, R Emiliano Perneta 297, 2nd floor, T222 6920, Mon-Fri 0800-1200. Netherlands, Av Candido de Abreu 469, conj 1606, T254 7846, consul Tony Bruinjé, open 1400-1700, except emergencies. Uruguay, R Voluntários da Pátria 475, 18th floor. **Medical services** Emergency: T190 for Police and T193 for ambulance or fire. The *Cajuru Hospital* is at Av São José 300, T362 1100, and the *Evangélico* is at Al Augusto Stellfeld 1908, T322 4141, both of which deal with emergencies. **Tourist offices**: Secretaria de Turismo, R da Glória 362, 3rd floor, T352 8000 (free map, good information, English spoken). **Paranatur**, R Deputado Mário de Barros 1290, 3rd floor, Centro Cívico, Edif Caetano Munhoz da Rocha, T254 7273/6933, F254 6109; www.pr.gov.br/turismo **Disque Turismo** T1516 (for the state), T352 8000 (for the city); there are also booths at the airport (T381 1153), railway ticket counter at Rodoferroviária (0700-1300), inside an old tram in front of the main cathedral in Praça Tiradentes (0900-1800 daily, German spoken), and in R 24 Horas (T352 8000, 0800-2200). *Guía Turística de Curitiba e Paraná*, annual, US$4, on sale at all kiosks; free weekly leaflet, *Bom Programa*, available in shops, cinemas, paper stands. **Voltage** 110 V, 60 cycles.

Directory
Visa extensions: Federal police, Dr Muricy 814, 1000-1600

This route can be done by paved road or rail to Paranaguá. The railway journey is the most spectacular in Brazil. There are numerous tunnels with sudden views of deep gorges and high peaks and waterfalls as the train rumbles over dizzy bridges and viaducts. Near Banhado station (Km 66) is the waterfall of Véu da Noiva; from the station at Km 59, the mountain range of **Marumbi** can be reached, see below.

Curitiba to Paranaguá

There are 2 trains running on the line from Curitiba to Paranaguá: the **Litorina**, a modern a/c railcar with on-board service with bilingual staff, which stops at the viewpoint at the Santuário da Nossa Senhora do Cadeado and Morretes; hand luggage only; tickets can be bought 2 days in advance; departs Sat-Sun and holidays 0900, returns 1500, US$28 one way tourist class, 3½ hours (advanced booking is very bureaucratic, allow 2 hours). Also the **Trem Classe Convencional**, which stops at Marumbi and Morretes, buy tickets 2 days in advance, departs Tue-Sun

Return by bus (see below), if you do not want to stay 4½ hrs in Paranaguá

0800, returns 1600, *turístico*, US$10, 4 hours. The train also leaves on Mon from Jan until Carnival. Schedules change frequently; check times in advance. For information and reservations, *Serra Verde Express*, T323 4007, tickets sold at the Rodoferroviária, Portão 8, Curitiba, open Mon-Sat 0800-1800, Sun 0700-1000. Sit on the left-hand side on journey from Curitiba. On cloudy days there's little to see on the higher parts. The train is usually crowded on Sat and Sun. *Serra Verde Express* also gives information about trips by car on the Estrada de Graciosa.

Parque Nacional Marumbi Marumbi Park is one of the largest remaining preserved Atlantic rainforests in Brazil and is a UNESCO World Heritage site and Biosphere Reserve. The forest in the 2,343 ha park is covered in banana trees, palmito and orchids. There are rivers and waterfalls and among the fauna are monkeys, snakes, toucans and jaguars. A climbing trail reaches 625 m to Rochedinho (2 hours). Hands need to be free to grasp trees, especially during the rainy season (December-March), when trails are muddy. The last 5 minutes of the trail is a dangerous walk along a narrow rock trail. ■ *At the park entrance, notify administration of your arrival and departure. There is a small museum, video, left luggage and the base for a search and rescue unit at weekends. Volunteer guides are available at weekends. Call Marumbi T432 2072. In Curitiba ask for Harvey T262 6488. Wooden houses can be rented for US$55 a night. Arrange with Harvey; take torch. Camping is free. To get there take the Paranaguá train from Curitiba at 0800, arriving Marumbi at 1000. Return at 1800 to Curitiba. If continuing the next day to Paranaguá your Curitiba-Marumbi ticket is valid for the onward journey. NB Inform conductor you want to stop at Marumbi and notify him of your return time as the train does not stop unless there are passengers.*

You can also visit **Antonina** (a port, not on the main route) and **Morretes** (on the main route), two sleepy colonial towns which can be reached by bus on the old Graciosa road, which is almost as scenic as the railway. In Morretes,try *barreado*, beef cooked for 24 hours, especially good in the two restaurants on the river bank, highly recommended. ■ *Buses from Paranaguá to Antonina stop en route at Morretes, 6 a day (US$1.50). 12 buses daily Morretes-Curitiba US$2; 11 buses a day Curitiba-Antonina.*

About 14 km north of Morretes is the beautiful village of **São João de Graciosa**, 2 km beyond which is a flower reserve. The Graciosa road traverses the **Marumbi** range for 12 km, with six rest stops with fire grills, shelters and camping. You can also hike the original trail which follows the road and passes the rest-stops. Take food, water and plenty of insect repellent. (See above.)

Paranaguá

Phone code: 0xx41
Post code: 83200
Colour map 7, grid B3
Population: 127,339
268 km S of Santos

Chief port of the state of Paraná and one of the main coffee-exporting ports, Paranaguá was founded in 1585. It is on a lagoon 29 km from the open sea and is approached via the Baia de Paranaguá, dotted with picturesque islands. Paranaguá is a free port for Paraguay. *Banco do Brasil* is at Largo C Alcindino 27. *Câmbio*, R Faria Sobrinho, for cash. Tourist offices are outside the railway station (1100-1700, free maps), also at the docks in front of the pier where boats to IIha do Mel leave, T422 6882, 0800-1900: boat schedules, toilet, and left luggage.

The **fort of Nossa Senhora dos Prazeres** was built in 1767 on a nearby island; one hr's boat trip. The former Colêgio dos Jesuitas, a fine baroque building, has been converted into a **Museu de Arqueologia e Artes Populares**. ■ *Tue-Sun 1200-1700, US$1.* Other attractions are a 17th century fountain, the church of **São Benedito**, and the shrine of **Nossa Senhora do Rocio**, 2 km from town. There are cruises on Paranaguá Bay by launch, daily between 0900-1300, minimum 15 people, US$5 from Cais do Mercado.

Matinhos, 40 km south, is invaded by surfers in October for the Paraná surf competition; several hotels, including **B** *Praia e Sol*, R União 35, T452 1922, recommended. There are four camp sites in the vicinity. ■ *8 buses a day from Paranaguá.*

AL *Hotel Camboa*, R Jõao Estevao, T423 2121. Large colonial building, near bus station. **A** *Portofino*, Av Atlântica s/n, T/F458 1488, Balneário Portofino, 35 km from Paranagu. Very nice. **D** *Palacio*, R Correia de Freitas 66, T422 5655, F423 2518. Good value. Recommended. **D** *Karibe*, F Simas 86, T422 1177. Good value. **E** *Litoral*, R Correia de Freitas 68. Without breakfast, comfortable. **Camping** *Arco Iris* at Praia de Leste, on the beach, 29 km south of Paranaguá, 30 mins. T458 2001. For eating, try *Bobby's*, Faria Sobrinho 750. *Danúbio Azul*, 15 de Novembro 91, good, open 24 hrs, view of river, *prato do mar* US$8.50 for 1 person, US$12 for 2. *Dirienzo Cucina*, Praça Leoncio Corrreia 16, good *comida por kilo*, nice setting at harbour, Italian owner with Beverly Hills background. *Tres Irmãos*, Av Gabriel de Lara 40, good but not cheap seafood, rodizio style.

Sleeping & eating
There are cheap restaurants in the old market building, and plenty of cheap ones near the markets on the waterfront

Bus All buses operated by *Graciosa*. To **Curitiba**, US$4, many, 1½ hrs (only the 1500 to Curitiba takes the old Graciosa road). Also direct buses to **Rio** and **Joinville**.

Transport

Ilha do Mel

Ilha do Mel is at the mouth of the Baía de Paranaguá and was of strategic use in the 18th century. The Fortaleza da Barra was built in 1767 on the orders of King José I of Portugal, to defend what was one of the principal ports in the country. The island is now an ecological reserve (no cars permitted and visitors limited to 5,000 per day), but is well-developed for tourism. Its four villages, **Nova Brasília**, **Praia das Encantadas**, **Praia da Fortaleza** and **Farol** are linked by pathways. The beaches, caves, bays and hill walks are beautiful. The hike to the fort is very rewarding. December-March are very rainy months here and there are very persistent *mutucas* (biting insects) in November, so April-October is the best time to visit. There is electricity on the island 1000-0200. In summer and at holiday times the island is very crowded with an active nightlife and *Forró* dancing; at other times it is very quiet.

Brazil

Sleeping and eating There are 18 *pousadas* at Praia do Farol, 12 at Praia das Encantadas and a few others at Nova Brasília, and Praia da Fortaleza. There are mini **campsites** with facilities at Encantadas, Farol and Brasília. Camping is possible on the more deserted beaches. At Praia das Encantadas, you can rent a fisherman's house – ask for *Valentim's Bar*, or for Luchiano. Also **E** *Coração da Ilha*, Praia das Encantadas, T457 9601. With good breakfast. At Praia do Farol, **B** *Pousadinha*, on the road to Praia do Farol, T978 3366, excellent breakfast, delightful rooms, good beds, fan, bath, mosquito nets, owner Marcos speaks English. **B** *Pousada Praia do Farol*, T978 3433, or **C** *Estalagem Ancoradouro*, T978 3333, both with breakfast. If camping, watch out for the tide, watch possessions and beware of the *bicho de pé* which burrows into feet (put foot in hot water to soften skin, remove with a needle and alcohol) and of the *borrachudos* (discourage with *Autan* repellent). *Lanchonete Paraíso*, nice meeting place, good food and music; more expensive restaurant next door to *Forró Zorro*, Praia das Encantadas. Restaurant *Toca do Abutre*, 1 km from Nova Brasília, Praia do Farol das Conhas, and bar *Barranco*.

Transport By ferry from Paranaguá, Sat at 1000, Mon and Fri at 1500, Sat and Sun at 0900 from Dec until Carnival, US$3,1 hr 40 mins, boats leave from R Gen Carneiro (R da Praia) in front of the Tourist Information kiosk; by ferry from Pontal do Paraná (Pontal do Sul), daily from 0800 to 1800, every 40 mins, 30 mins. From Paranaguá, take the bus to Pontal do Sul (many daily, 1½ hrs, US$0.60), then wait for the ferry, US$3.25. The last bus back to Paranaguá leaves at 2200. Alternatively, go the small harbour in Paranaguá and ask for a boat to Ilha do Mel, US$5 one way (no shade). Make sure the ferry goes to your chosen destination (Nova Brasília or Encantadas are the most developed areas).

The island of Superagui is a national park and a UNESCO World Heritage Site. With its neighbour Peças it is one of the principal research stations investigating Atlantic forest. Wildlife includes the rare yellow-fronted alligator and the black-faced monkey, and many species of threatened and migratory birds.

Parque Nacional Superagui

There is also an Indian village at the top of the island's hill; other inhabitants are mostly of European descent, living off fishing. There is a certain amount of resentment that the wildlife receives more help than the community (*Population*: 1,200). There are some 10 *pousadas* on Superagui: most popular with foreigners is **E** pp *Carioca*, T9978 4213, cheaper without bath, breakfast, lots of information. Booking necessary at holiday times, January-February; can arrange rooms elsewhere if full. **E** pp *Bella Ilha*, T9998 2953, with breakfast. **F** pp *Golfinhos*, T9959 8852, with breakfast. Camping US$1.50. Take torch and mosquito repellent. The *Restaurante dos Golfinhos* (blue, on beach) can arrange boat trips for the Indian village, ask for Lurdinho or Nagibe, US$12 slow boat, US$15 motor boat, arrange pick-up time. Another restaurant is *Crepúsculo*. In both cases book lunch or dinner in advance. No dollars or credit cards accepted on the island. ■ *Getting there: Boat from Paranaguá on Sat 1000 arriving 1400, return Sun 1530 (2 stops en route), US$6 one way. Private boats from Ilha do Mel run if the weather is good.*

Parque Nacional Vila Velha
Colour map 7, grid C2
Allow all day if visiting all 3 sites (unless you hitch, or can time the buses well, it's a lot of walking)

West of Curitiba on the road to Ponta Grossa is the **Museu Histórico do Mate**, an old water-driven mill where mate was prepared. ■ *Free, 20 km, at Km 119.* On the same road is Vila Velha, 91 km from Curitiba: the sandstone rocks have been weathered into most fantastic shapes. 4 km away are the Furnas, three water holes, the deepest of which has a lift (US$1 – not always working) which descends almost to water level. ■ *US$0.20.* Also in the park is the Lagoa Dourada (surrounded by forest) whose water level is the same as that in the Furnas. ■ *The park office (phone, toilets, lanchonete, tourist information) is 300 m from the highway and the park a further 1½ km (entrance – also to Furnas, keep the ticket – US$2 – opens 0800).*

Transport Take a bus from Curitiba to the park, not to the town of Ponta Grossa 26 km away. *Princesa dos Campos* bus from Curitiba 0730 and 1400, 1½ hrs, US$5.65 (the last bus leaves the park at 1600). One bus from Vila Velha between 1530-1600, US$0.65, 4½ km to turn-off to Furnas (another 15 mins' walk) and Lagoa Dourada. Bus Mon-Sat 1330 to Furnas – Ponta Grossa that passes the car park at the top of the park. On Sun, 1200,1620,1800. It may be advisable to go to Ponta Grossa and return to Curitiba from there (114 km, 6 buses a day, US$4.25, *Princesa dos Campos*, also with buses to Foz do Iguaçu, 9 hrs).

Iguaçu Falls

The Iguaçu Falls are the most stunning waterfalls in South America. Their magnitude, and the volume of water that thunders over the edge, is incredible. They are 32 km from the city of Foz do Iguaçu. For a description of the falls, together with maps and an account of road links between Argentina, Brazil and Paraguay, see the Argentina chapter, page174.

Parque Nacional Foz do Iguaçu
Colour map 7, grid C1

The Brazilian national park was founded in 1939 and the area was designated a World Heritage Site by UNESCO in 1986. Fauna most frequently encountered are little and red brocket deer, South American coati, white-eared opossum, and a sub-species of the brown capuchin monkey. The endangered tegu lizard is common. Over 100 species of butterflies have been identified, among them the electric blue Morpho, the poisonous red and black heliconius and species of Papilionidae and Pieridae. The bird life is especially rewarding for birdwatchers. Five members of the toucan family can be seen.

Visitor's Centre and information All cars and public buses stop here (open daily 0800-1700) where the park fee is paid, US$3 (payable only in reais). You transfer to a free park shuttle bus. There are souvenir shops, a *Banco do Brasil* ATM and *câmbio* (1300-1700), a small café and car park here. If possible, visit on a weekday when the walks are less crowded. **NB** The Brazilian side of the falls is closed on Mon until 1300 for maintenance. Whichever side you decide to stay on, most establishments will accept reais, pesos or dollars. While the

Argentine economy is in chaos (2002), the real/peso exchange rate is very poor; best to pay in the currency of the country you are in. Cross-border transport usually accepts guaraníes.

First stop with the shuttle bus is **Macuco Safari**, US$33 (bookable through most agencies, which may charge a premium for transfers), which takes 1¾ hrs, leaving every 15 mins from near the falls. Electric vehicles take visitors to the start of a short, steep trail (those with walking difficulties can be driven the whole way) to the river. From here motorboats run right up to the falls, soaking passengers. Guides speak Portuguese, English and Spanish; take insect repellent. *Macuco Safari*, Rodovia das Cataratas Km 22, T529 6263, macucosafari@foznet.com.br

Second stop with the bus is the *Cataratas Trail* (starting from the hotel of the same name, non-residents can eat at the hotel, mid-day and evening buffets). This 1½-km paved walk runs part of the way down the cliff near the rim of the falls, giving a stupendous view of the whole Argentine side of the falls. It ends up almost under the powerful Floriano Falls: from here an elevator carries visitors to the top of the Floriano Falls (from 0800; US$0.50) and to a path leading to Porto Canoa (if there is a queue, it is easy and quick to walk up). A catwalk at the foot of the Floriano Falls gives a good view of the Garganta do Diabo. There are toilets and a *lanchonete* on the path down and more toilets at the top of the elevator.

Helicopter tours over the falls leave from *Hotel das Cataratas*, US$60 pp, 10 mins. Book through any travel agency or direct with *Helisul*, T523 1190. Apart from disturbing visitors, the helicopters are also reported to present a threat to some bird species which are laying thinner-shelled eggs: the altitude has been increased, making the flight less attractive.

The **Porto Canoas** complex, with its snack bar, souvenir shops and terraces with views of the falls, was completed in 2000 after some controversy. Its restaurant serves a delicious US$12 buffet, and is highly recommended for a memorable lunch.

Tours Many hotels organize tours to the falls: these have been recommended in preference to taxi rides. If visiting the Brazilian side from Puerto Iguazú by bus, ask the driver to let you off shortly after the border at the roundabout for the road to the falls (BR-469), where you can get another bus.

Transport Bus: these leave Foz do Iguaçu, from Terminal Urbana, Av Juscelino Kubitschek, one block from Infantry Barracks (new terminal under construction in 2002). The grey or red buses go to the falls every 30 mins, 0530-2330, along Av Juscelino Kubitschek, Jorge Schimmelpfeng, Av das Cataratas, to the airport and and Parque das Aves, terminating at the Visitor Centre. 40 mins, US$0.80 one-way, payable in *reais* only. Return buses 0800-1900. Private cars must be left in visitor centre car park. **Taxi**: US$7 or US$30 for return trip, including waiting (negotiate in advance).

Foz do Iguaçu

A rapidly developing and improving town 28 km from the falls, with a wide range of accommodation and good communications by air and road with the main cities of southern Brazil and Asunción in Paraguay.

Phone code 0xx45
Population 258,543
For tourist information, see Directory

Excursions

The **Parque das Aves** bird park, at Rodovia das Cataratas Km 16, 100 m before the entrance to the park, has received frequent good reports. It contains Brazilian and foreign birds, many species of parrot and beautiful toucans, in huge aviaries through which you can walk, with the birds flying and hopping around you. There is also a butterfly house. ■ *0830-1700, US$8, for a guided tour T529 8282. The park is within walking distance of the* Hotel San Martin; *the* Paudimar *youth hostel (see below) offers a discount for its guests.*

The **Itaipu dam**, on the Río Paraná 12 km north, is the site of the largest single power station in the world built jointly by Brazil and Paraguay. Construction of this massive scheme began in 1975 and it became operational in 1984. The main dam is 8 km long, creating a lake which covers 1,400 sq km. The 18 turbines have an installed capacity of 12,600,000 Kw and produce about 75 billion Kwh a year, providing 80% of Paraguay's electricity and 25% of Brazil's. The Paraguayan side may be visited from Ciudad del Este. (There is also the **Ecomuseu de Itaipu**, Av Tancredo Neves, Km 11, ■ *Mon 1400-1700, Tue-Sat 0900-1100, 1400-1700, T520 5813/6034* and Iguaçu Environmental Education Centre are geared to educate about the preservation of the local culture and environment, or that part which isn't underwater. ■ *Free with guide, recommended*).

Tours of Itaipu The 'executive' bus and agency tours are an unnecessary expense. No 110 or 120 from Terminal Urbana (stand 50 Batalhão) go every 13 mins to the Public Relations office at the main entrance (US$0.40), 110, Conjunto C Porto Meira, 120 via Sul goes within 500 m. Visits are free, but in groups only. The Visitors' Centre (T520 6999, www.itaipu.gov.br) presents a short video presentation (ask for the English version) with stunning photography and amazing technical information, apparently available in English but usually only in Portuguese. After the film and a brief visit to the souvenir shop where an English guidebook is available, a coach will take you to the dam itself. As it crosses the top you get a stomach-churning view of the spillways and really begin to appreciate the scale of the project. There are several tours Mon-Sat at 0800, 0900, 1000, 1400 and 1530 (closed between 1100 and 1400). If it's sunny, go in the morning as the sun is behind the dam in the afternoon and you will get poor photographs.

Sleeping

Av Juscelino Kubitschek and the streets south of it, towards the river, have a reputation as being unsafe at night as a favela is nearby. Take care if walking after dark. Many prostitutes around R Rebouças and Almirante Barroso. Taxis are only good value for short distances when you are carrying all your luggage

Hotels outside Foz do Iguaçu: **L-AL** *Hotel das Cataratas (Tropical)*, directly overlooking the Falls, 28 km from Foz, T521 7000, F574 1688; 20% discount for holders of the Brazil Air Pass. Generally recommended but caters for lots of groups, attractive colonial-style building with pleasant gardens (where a lot of wildlife can be seen at night and early morning) and pool. Receipt of email for guests only. Check the exchange rate if paying in dollars. Non-residents can eat here, midday and evening buffets (mixed reports); also à-la-carte dishes and dinner with show. On the road to the Falls (Rodovia das Cataratas) are **L** *San Martin*, Km 17, T523 2323, F574 3207, www.fnn.net/hoteis/sanmartin/new 4-star, a/c, TV, pool, sports, nightclub, several eating options, luxury, comfortable (any problems ask for Miguel Allou). Recommended. **AL** *Carimã*, Km 10, T523 1818, F574 3531. 4-star, pool, restaurant, bars, very good value. Recommended. **AL** *Colonial*, Km 16, T529 1777, F529 7732. 1 km from the airport, spacious, fine location, price includes breakfast and mediocre dinner, no English.

Hotels in Foz do Iguaçu: **A** *Rafain Centro*, Mcal Deodoro 984, T/F523 1213. Smart, communal areas and attractive pool area, although rooms rather worn. **B** *Baviera*, Av Jorge Schimmelpfeng 697, T523 5995, hotelbavieraiguassu@foznet.com.br Chalet-style exterior, on main road, central for bars and restaurants, comfortable, if rather gloomy rooms. **B** *Suiça*, Av Felipe Wandscheer 3580, T525 3232, F525 3044. Swiss manager, helpful, pool. **C** *Bogarí*, Av Brasil 106, T/F523 2243, www.bogarihotel.com.br Restful atmosphere, large pool with pleasant walled terrace, central. Opposite is **C** *Foz do Iguaçu*, Av Brasil 97, T523 4455, hotelfoz@purenet.com.br Newly decorated, good value, attractive, quiet pool area, smart breakfast room, English spoken. Recommended. **C** *Foz Plaza Hotel*, R Marechal Deodoro 1819, T/F523 1448, fozplaza@uol.com.br Serene and very nice. **C** *Foz Presidente*, R Xavier da Silva 1000, T/F572 4450. Restaurant, pool, with breakfast, convenient for buses. Recommended. **C** *Foz Presidente II*, R Mcal Floriano Peixoto 1851, T523 2318. Smaller, but a little more expensive, also with pool, bar and restaurant. **C** *San Remo*, Kubitschek e Xavier da Silva 563, T572 2956. A/c, good breakfast. Recommended. **D** *King*, Av Brasil 267, T523 5057. With breakfast. **D** *Luz*, Av Costa e Silva Km 5, near Rodoviária, T522 3535, F522 2474. Recommended. **D** *Tarobá*, R Tarobá 1048, T523 9722. Helpful, a/c, small indoor pool, good value. Recommended. **E** *Pousada da Laura*, R Naipi 671, T/F572 3374. Good breakfast, hot water, bathroom, central, secure, kitchen, laundry facilities, good place to meet other travellers, Spanish, English, Italian and French spoken, excellent. **E** *15 de Julho*, Almte Barroso 1794, T574 2664. A/c, TV, hot water, pool, German and some English spoken, excellent value. Recommended. **F** *Athenas*, R Almte Barroso 2215 on corner with Rebouças, T574 2563. Good value, special rates for backpackers, some rooms with shared bath, fan, breakfast extra, beers sold. **F** *Minas*, R Rebouças 809, T574 5208. Basic, but fine for price and central position, a/c, hot water, safe, no breakfast, cheaper with fan. **F** *Pousada Evelina Navarrete*, R Irlan

Kalichewski 171, Vila Yolanda, T/F574 3817. Lots of tourist information, English, French, Italian, Polish and Spanish spoken, helpful, lots of information, good breakfast and location, near Chemin Supermarket, near Av Cataratas on the way to the falls. Warmly recommended. **F** *Trento*, R Rebouças 829, T574 5111. Fan, without breakfast, noisy, but recommended.

Youth hostel There are 2 branches of *Paudimar youth hostel*, both **E** pp (in high season IYHA members only): *Paudimar Campestre*, Av das Cataratas Km 12.5, Remanso Grande, near airport, T/F529 6061, paudimarcampestre@paudimar.com.br From airport or town take Parque Nacional bus (0525-0040)and get out at Remanso Grande bus stop, by *Hotel San Juan*, then take the free shuttle (0700-1900) to the hostel, or 1.2 km walk from main road. Camping as well, pool, soccer pitch, quiet, kitchen and communal meals, breakfast. Highly recommended. For assistance, ask for owner, Gladis. *Paudimar Centro*, R Rui Barbosa 634, T/F574 5503, paudimarcentro@paudimar.com.br Safe, laundry, kitchen, TV, central, convenient for buses to falls, also very friendly. Recommended. For assistance, ask for Lourdes. English, Spanish and Portuguese spoken. Hostel will pay half taxi fare from rodoviária or airport if staying more than 2 days. Both hostels have telephone, fax and internet for guests' use. You can stay at 1 hostel and use the facilities of the other; tours run to either side of the falls, US$8 to Argentine side 0830-1700 (good value). *Paudimar* desk at rodoviária.

Camping E Pousada Internacional, R Manêncio Martins, 600 m from turnoff, T523 3053. For vehicles and tents, helpful staff, English, German and Spanish spoken, pool, restaurant. Recommended. *Camping Clube do Brasil*, by the national park entrance 17 km from Foz, T523 8599, US$10 pp (half with International Camping Card), pool, clean. Park vehicle or put tent away from trees in winter in case of heavy rain storms, no restaurants, food there is not very good, closes at 2300. Camping is not permitted by the Hotel das Cataratas and falls.

Camping
Camping is not permitted by the Hotel das Cataratas and falls

Brazil

Foz do Iguaçu

Sleeping ■
1 Athenas
2 Bogari
3 Foz do Iguaçu
4 Pousada de Laura
5 Paudimar Centro IYHA
6 Rafain Centro
7 Trento

Eating ●
1 Bar Capitão
2 Brasil & Brasil
3 Bufalo Branco
4 Marias e Maria

0 metres 100
0 yards 100

Eating **Expensive** *Búfalo Branco*, R Rebouças 530. Superb all you can eat churrasco, includes filet mignon, bull's testicles, salad bar and desert. Sophisticated surroundings and attentive service. Highly recommended. *Cabeça de Boi*, Av Brasil 1325. Live music, buffet, churrasco, but coffee and pastries also. *Rafain*, Av das Cataratas, Km 6.5, T523 1177, closed Sun. Out of town, take a taxi or arrange with travel agency. Set price for excellent buffet with folkloric music and dancing (2100-2300) from throughout South America, touristy but very entertaining. Recommended. *Zaragoza*, R Quintino Bocaiúva 882. Large and upmarket, for Spanish dishes and seafood. Recommended. **Mid range** *Boulevard*, Av das Cataratas 1118. Food court open daily from 1700, and all day Sun. *Brasil & Brazil*, Brasil 157. A handful of food stalls, with live music and dancing 2000 to 0200, bingo. *Tropicana*, Av Juscelino Kubitschek 228. All-you-can-eat pizza or *churrascaria* with salad bar, good value. **Cheap** *Barbarela's*, Av Brasil 1119B. Excellent juice and sandwich bar. *City Caffé*, Av Jorge Schimmelpfeng 898. Stylish café open daily 0800-2330 for sandwiches, Arabic snacks and pastries. *Marias e Maria*, Av Brasil 50. Good *confeitaria*. *Oficina do Sorvete*, Av Jorge Schimmelpfeng 244, open daily 1100-0100. Excellent ice-creams, a popular local hang-out.

Bars & nightclubs Bars, all doubling as restaurants, concentrated on Av Jorge Schimmelpfeng for two blocks from Av Brasil to R Mal Floriano Peixoto. Wed to Sun are best nights; crowd tends to be young. *Alquimia*, No 334, T5723154. Popular, nightclub, *Dancing*, attached, open 2400-0500, US$3. *Bier Garten*, No 550. Pizzaria and choparia; beer garden in name only but some trees. *BR3*, corner with Av Brasil. Modern, open til 2400. *Capitão Bar*, No 288 and Almte Barroso, large, loud and popular, nightclub attached. *Armazém*, R Edmundo de Barros 446. Intimate and sophisticated, attracts discerning locals, good atmosphere, mellow live music, US$1 cover. Recommended. *Oba! Oba!*, Av das Cataratas 3700, T529 6596 (Antigo Castelinho). Live samba show Mon-Sat 2315-0015, very popular, US$9 for show and 1 drink.

Shopping *Kunda Livraria Universitária*, R Almte Barroso 1473, T523 4606. Guides and maps of the area, books on the local wildlife, novels etc in several languages.

Tour operators There are many travel agents on Av Brasil. *Caribe Tur* at the airport and *Hotel das Cataratas*, *Beware of* T523 1612, runs tours from the airport to the Argentine side and *Hotel das Cataratas* (book *overcharging for* hotel direct, not at the airport desk). *Jaha Iguassu Explorer*, T523 1484, T9106 6985 (mob), *tours by touts at* 24 hrs, chilelindo7@hotmail.com Provides useful bus information for all sights, visits to rural *the bus terminal* Paraguay (full day, US$25), Argentinian falls (in mini-van, US$10, includes lunch but not guide or entrance fee), bike tours to Argentina, horse riding and overnight stays in national park. Ruth Campo Silva, *STTC Turismo*, Hotel Bourbon, Rodovia das Cataratas, T/F529 8580 American Express).

Transport **Air** Iguaçu international airport, 18 km south of town near the falls, T521 4200. In Arrivals is *Banco do Brasil* and *Caribe Tours e Câmbio*, car rental offices, tourist office and an official taxi stand, US$10 to town centre (US$11 from town to airport). All buses marked Parque Nacional pass the airport in each direction, US$0.50, 0525-0040, does not permit large amounts of luggage but backpacks OK. Many hotels run minibus services for a small charge. Daily flights to **Rio, São Paulo, Curitiba** and other Brazilian cities.

Bus For transport to the falls see above under Parque Nacional Foz do Iguaçu. Long distance terminal (Rodoviária), Av Costa e Silva, 4 km from centre on road to Curitiba, T522 2590; bus to centre, any bus that says 'Rodoviária', US$0.65. Taxi US$4. Book departures as soon as possible. As well as the tourist office (see below), there is a *Cetreme* desk for tourists who have lost their documents, Guarda Municipal (police) and luggage store. To **Curitiba**, *Pluma, Sulamericana*, 9-10 hrs, paved road, US$15. To **Guaíra** via Cascavel only, 5 hrs, US$10. To **Florianópolis**, *Catarinense* and **Reunidas**, US$28, 14 hrs. *Reunidas* to **Porto Alegre**, US$30. To **São Paulo**, 16 hrs, *Pluma* US$30, executivo 6 a day, plus one *leito*. To **Rio** 22 hrs, several daily, US$38. *Cambio Corimeira*, Almte Barroso 2037, T523 3550, sells national bus tickets in the centre.

Airline offices *Rio Sul*, J Sanways 779, T574 6080. *TAM*, R Rio Branco 640, T523 8500 (offers free transport to Ciudad del Este for its flights, all cross-border documentation dealt with). *Varig*, Av Juscelino Kubitschek 463, T523 2111. *Vasp*, Av Brasil 845, T523 2212 (airport 529 7161). **Banks** It is difficult to exchange on Sun but quite possible in Paraguay where US dollars can be obtained on credit cards. There are plenty of banks and travel agents on Av Brasil. *Banco do Brasil*, Av Brasil 1377. Has ATM, high commission for TCs. *Bradesco*, Av Brasil 1202. Cash advance on Visa. *HSBC*, Av Brasil 1151, for MasterCard ATM. *Banco 24 Horas* at Oklahoma petrol station. *Itaú*, Av Kubitschek e Bocaiúva. Câmbio at *Vento Sul*, Av Brasil 1162, no TCs, good rates for cash. Also *Corimeira*, see Bus, above. **Communications** Internet: *Boulevard* cinema complex, Av das Cataratas 1118, T5234245. Open from 1700 and all day Sun. *Cafe Internet*, R Rebouças 950, T/F523 2122, 0900-2300, US$1.50 per hr, open 0900-2300 and Sun pm. *Café Pizzanet*, R Rio Branco 412, corner with Av Juscelino Kubitschek, US$2 per hr. Pizzaria too. *Zipfoz.com*, R Barão do Rio Branco 412, corner with Av Juscelino Kubitschek. Smart, a/c, US$1.50 per hr. **Post Office:** Praça Getúlio Vargas 72. **Telephone:** *Tele Centro Sul* on Edmundo de Barros. **Embassies and consulates** Argentina, Travessa Eduardo Bianchi 26, T574 2969. Open Mon-Fri 1000-1430. **France**, R Federico Engels 48, Villa Yolanda, T574 3693, 0900-1200, 1400-1700. **Paraguay**, Bartolomeu de Gusmão 738, T523 2898. **Medical services** Free 24-hr clinic, Av Paraná 1525, opposite Lions Club, T573 1134. Few buses: take taxi or walk (about 25 mins). **Tourist offices** Secretaria Municipal de Turismo, Praça Getúlio Vargas 69, T521 1455, 0700-2300, very helpful, English spoken. There is a 24-hr tourist help line number, T0800-451516. Very helpful. Airport tourist information is also good, open for all arriving flights, gives map and bus information, English spoken. Helpful office, free map, at the rodoviária, English spoken. **Delegacia do Turista e da Mulher** (police station for tourists and women), Av Brasil 1374, opposite Banco do Brasil, T523 3036. A newspaper, *Triplice Fronteira*, carries street plans and other tourist information. **Voltage** 110 volts a/c.

Directory

Brazil

This crossing via the Puente Tancredo Neves is straightforward. Even if crossing on a day visit, you must have your passport stamped. Between October-February Brazil is 1 hr ahead of Argentina. It takes about 2 hours to get from Foz to the Argentine falls, very tiring when the weather is hot. *Paudimar*'s tours are much better.

Border with Argentina

Transport Buses marked 'Puerto Iguazú' run every 20 mins from the Terminal Urbana, crossing the border bridge; 30 mins' journey, no stops for border formalities, 3 companies: *Pluma* and *Três Fronteiras*, US$1.50 or 2 reais. When you get out of the bus to get your passport stamped at immigration, the bus waits. **NB** Be sure you know when the last bus departs from Puerto Iguazú for Foz (usually 1900). Combined tickets to Puerto Iguazú and the falls cost more than paying separately. To **Buenos Aires**, *Pluma* daily 1200, 18 hrs, US$46 (see Puerto Iguazú, Transport for alternatives from there). It is cheaper to go to **Posadas** via Paraguay. **Taxi** Foz-Argentina US$35, US$45 to *Hotel Sheraton Iguazú*.

The *Ponte de Amizade/Puente de Amistad* (Friendship Bridge) over the Río Paraná, 6 km north of Foz, leads straight into the heart of Ciudad del Este. Paraguayan and Brazilian immigration formalities are dealt with at opposite ends of the bridge. Ask for relevant stamps if you need them.

Border with Paraguay
Brazil is 1 hr ahead of Paraguay

Transport Bus: (marked Cidade-Ponte) leave from the Terminal Urbana, Av Juscelino Kubitschek, for the Ponte de Amizade (Friendship Bridge), US$0.40. To **Asunción**, *Pluma* (0700), *RYSA* (direct at 1430), from Rodoviária, US$11 (cheaper if bought in Ciudad del Este). **Motoring**: If crossing by private vehicle and only intending to visit the national parks, this presents no problems. Another crossing to Paraguay is at **Guaíra**, at the northern end of the Itaipu lake. It is 5 hrs north of Iguaçu by road and can be reached by bus from Campo Grande and São Paulo. Ferries cross to Saltos del Guaira on the Paraguayan side (see page 1063).

Brasília

Santa Catarina

Population: 5.4 million

Famous for its beaches and popular with Argentine and Paraguayan holidaymakers in high summer, this is one of the best stretches of Brazilian coast for surfing, attracting 1½ million visitors to the 170 beaches just in the summer months of January and February. For the rest of the year they are pleasant and uncrowded. Immigrant communities, such as the German, give a unique personality to many towns and districts with the familiar European pattern of mixed farming. Rural tourism is important and the highlands, 100 km from the coast, are among the coldest in Brazil, giving winter landscapes reminiscent of Europe, or Brazil's southern neighbours

Florianópolis

Phone code: 0xx48
Colour map 5, grid B5
Population: 342,315

Half way along the coast of Santa Catarina is the state capital Florianópolis, founded in 1726 on the Ilha de Santa Catarina. The natural beauty of the island, beaches and bays make Florianópolis a magnet for holidaymakers in summer.

The island is joined to the mainland by two bridges, one of which is Ponte Hercílio Luz, the longest steel suspension bridge in Brazil (closed for repairs). The newer Colombo Machado Salles bridge has a pedestrian and cycle way beneath the roadway. It is a port of call for coastal shipping, 725 km from Rio and 420 km from Santos. The southern beaches are usually good for swimming, the east for surfing, but be careful of the undertow.

Boat trips can be made in the bay with Scuna Sul, T225 1806, www.scunasul.com.br From US$7.50

In the 1960s Florianópolis port was closed and the aspect of the city's southern shoreline was fundamentally changed, with land reclaimed from the bay. The two main remnants of the old port area are the late 19th-century **Alfândega** and **Mercado Público**, both on Rua Conselheiro Mafra, fully restored and painted ochre. In the Alfândega is a handicraft market. ■ *Mon-Fri 0900-1900, Sat 0900-1200, T224 6082.* The market is divided into *boxes*, some are bars and restaurants, others shops. ■ *Mon-Fri 0600-1830, Sat 0600-1300, a few fish stalls open on Sun, T225 3200.* The **Cathedral** on Praça 15 de Novembro was completed in 1773. **Forte Santana** (1763), beneath the Ponte Hercílio Luz, houses a **Museu de Armas Major Lara Ribas**, with a collection of guns and other items, mostly post Second World War. ■ *Tue-Sun 0830-1200, 1400-1800 (Mon 1400-1800), free, T229 6263.* **Museu Histórico**, in the 18th-century Palácio Cruz e Souza, on Praça 15 de Novembre, contains furniture, documents and objects belonging to governors of the state. ■ *Tue-Fri 0800-1900, Sat 1300-1900, Sun 1530-1900, T221 3504.* **Museu de Antropologia**, at the Trindade University Campus, has a collection of stone and other archaeological remains from the cultures of the coastal Indians. ■ *Mon-Fri 0900-1200, 1300-1700, T331 8821.* **Museu do Homem Sambaqui**, at the Colégio Catarinense, R Esteves Júnior 711, exhibits pieces from the *sambaqui* culture and fossils. ■ *Mon-Fri 1330-1630, T224 9190.* There is a look-out point at **Morro da Cruz** (take *Empresa Trindadense* bus, US$0.60, waits 15 mins, or walk).

Sleeping   **A** *Castelmar*, R Felipe Schmidt 1260, T225 3228, F225 3126 www.iaccess.com.br/castelmar Pool, a/c, TV, laundry, restaurant. **A** *Faial*, R Felipe Schmidt 603, T225 2766, F225 0435, faial@interspace.com.br Good restaurant. **A** *Florianópolis Palace*, R Artista Bittencourt 14, T224 9633, F223 0300. Recommended. **A** *Mercure Diplomata*, Av Paulo Fontes 1210, T224 4455, F225 5082. Very good views, 4-star hotel but prices sometimes negotiable. **A-B** *Valerim Plaza*, R Felipe Schmidt 705, T/F225 3388, valerim@iaccess.com.br Three-star, more modern than *Valerim Center*, buffet restaurant open till 2300. **B** *Oscar*, Av Hercílio Luz 760, T222 0099, F222 0978, oscarhotel@oscarhotel.com.br A/c, TV, safe, central. **B** *Porto da Ilha*, R Dom Jaime Câmara 43, T322 0007, F322 0144, hotelpi@matrix.com.br Central, comfortable. Recommended. **B** *Valerim Center*, R Felipe Schmidt 554, T225 1100. Large rooms, hot water, hard beds. **C** *Pousada Recanto da Costa*, R 13 de Maio 41. With breakfast, hot water, laundry facilities, parking, 15 mins' walk from centre. **D** *Cacique*, R Felipe Schmidt 423, same owners as *Valerim*, T222 5359. No breakfast but good value, rooms vary. **D-E** *Felippe*, R João Pinto 132, 1 block from 15 de Novembro, by Terminal Urbano, T222 4122. Small rooms, some with no windows, breakfast is just a cup of coffee, dirty bathrooms.

Youth hostels E pp *Ilha de Santa Catarina*, R Duarte Schutel 227, T225 3781, F225 1692. IYHA. Recommended, breakfast included, cooking facilities, clean, some traffic noise, very friendly, will store luggage. Prices rise in Dec-Feb; more expensive for non-members.

Camping *Camping Clube do Brasil*, São João do Rio Vermelho, north of Lagoa da Conceição, 21 km out of town; also at Lagoa da Conceição, Praia da Armação, Praia dos Ingleses, Praia Canasvieiras. 'Wild' camping allowed at Ponta de Sambaqui and Praias Brava, Aranhas, Galheta, Mole, Campeche, Campanhas and Naufragados; 4 km south of

Florianópolis

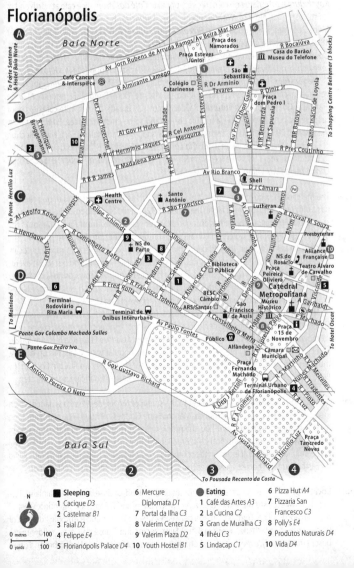

Brazil

N

0 metres 100
0 yards 100

■ **Sleeping**
1 Cacique *D3*
2 Castelmar *B1*
3 Faial *D2*
4 Felippe *E4*
5 Florianópolis Palace *D4*

6 Mercure
  Diplomata *D1*
7 Portal da Ilha *C3*
8 Valerim Center *D2*
9 Valerim Plaza *D2*
10 Youth Hostel *B1*

● **Eating**
1 Café das Artes *A3*
2 La Cucina *C2*
3 Gran de Muralha *C3*
4 Ilhéu *C3*
5 Lindacap *C1*

6 Pizza Hut *A4*
7 Pizzaria San
  Francesco *C3*
8 Polly's *E4*
9 Produtos Naturais *D4*
10 Vida *D4*

Florianópolis, camping site with bar at Praia do Sonho on the mainland, beautiful, deserted beach with an island fort nearby. 'Camping Gaz' cartridges from *Riachuelo Supermercado*, on R Alvim and R São Jorge.

Eating Take a walk along Rua Bocaiúva, east of R Almte Lamego, to find the whole street filled with Italian restaurants, barbecue places and an exclusive fish restaurant, *Toca da Garoupa* (turn on to R Alves de Brito 178). *Don Pepé Forno a Lenha* is a great place to go for a quiet romantic meal with a *serenador* (cover charge added to bill for singer). *Papparella*, Almte Lamego 1416. Excellent giant pizzas. Shrimp dishes are good everywhere. A popular place to start a night out (after 2100) is the *Nouvelle Vague*, more commonly known as *A Creperia*, buzzing every weekend, wide selection of sweet and savoury pancakes. *Macarronada Italiana*, Av Beira Mar Norte 2458. Good. Next door is *Pizza da Piedra*. *Casa de Coimbra*, Av Beira Mar Norte 2568. Specializes in chicken with polenta and salad, Portuguese, good. Next door is *Kayskidum* lanchonete and crêperie, very popular. *Café das Artes*, nice café at north end of R Esteves Junior, No 734. With excellent cakes. *Lindacap*, R Felipe Schmidt 1132 (closed Mon). Recommended, good views. *Pizzaria San Francesco*, R São Francisco 2000, opens at 1800. Good service, popular, quite expensive. *Polly's*, Praça 15 de Novembro 151, 1st floor. Good food and service, reasonable prices. *Mirantes*, R Alvaro de Carvalho 246, Centro. Buffet self-service, good value. Recommended; also on R Vidal Ramos opposite *Produtos Naturais*.

Vegetarian *La Cucina*, R Padre Roma 291. Buffet lunch, Mon-Sat, pay by weight, good, vegetarian choices. Recommended. *Vida*, R Visc de Ouro Preto 298, next to Alliance Française. Good. *Produtos Naturais*, R Vidal Ramos 127. Breads, cereals, nuts, café next door sells pizzas, *pasteis*, vegetable and fruit dishes (and some chicken), juices. *Panino in Due*, Vidal Ramos 79, near Trajano, also sells vegetarian snacks, breads, salads. For a wide selection of juices and snacks (not vegetarian): *Cía Lanches*, Ten Silveira e R Trajano, downstairs, and, in Edif Dias Velho al R Felipe Schmidt 303, *Laranja Madura*, *Sabor e Sucos* and *Lanchonete Dias Velho*.

Bars & nightclubs
Free open air concert every Sat morning at the market place near the bus terminal

The Mercado Público in the centre, which is alive with fish sellers and stalls during the day, has a different atmosphere at night; the stall, *Box 32*, is good for seafood and becomes a bar specializing in *cachaça* for hard working locals to unwind. *Restaurant Pirão* overlooks the market square with a quieter view and live Brazilian music on Tue, Thu and Fri. The *Alfândega* bar is right in the middle of the market and a good place to mix with locals. *Empórium*, Bocaiúva 79, is a shop by day and popular bar at night. To find out about events and theme nights check the Beiramar centre for notices in shop windows, ask in surf shops or take a trip to the University of Santa Catarina in Trindade and check out the noticeboards. The news-paper *Diário Catarinense* gives details of bigger events, eg Oktoberfest.

Nightclubs *Baccarat*, R Bocaiúva. Opens its doors around 2300 at the weekend, Greek-style building with 2 dance floors, 1 for live bands, 1 for popular music, crème de la crème of clubs in town with prices to match. *Ilhéu*, Av Prof Gama d'Eça e R Jaime Câmara. Bar and club open until early hrs, tables spill outside, very popular with locals, fills up quickly, music a mixture of 1980s and 1990s hits but dance floor shamefully small. *Café Cancun*, Av Beira Mar Norte, T225 1029. Wed-Sat from 2000, bars, restaurant, dancing, sophisticated.

Festivals In **Dec** and **Jan** the whole island dances to the sound of the *Boi-de-Mamão*, a dance which incorporates the puppets of Bernunça, Maricota (the Goddess of Love, a puppet with long arms to embrace everyone) and Tião, the monkey. The Portuguese brought the tradition of the bull, which has great significance in Brazilian celebrations. Around **Easter** is the Festival of the Bull, *Farra de Boi*. It is only in the south that, controversially nowadays, the bull is killed on Easter Sunday. The festival arouses fierce local pride and there is much celebration.

Transport **Local Bus**: there are 3 bus stations for routes on the island, or close by on the mainland: Terminal de Ônibus Interurbano between Av Paulo Fontes and R Francisco Tolentino, west of the Mercado Público; Terminal Urbano between Av Paulo Fontes and R Antônio Luz, east of Praça Fernando Machado; a terminal at R Silva Jardim and R José da Costa. Yellow micro buses (*Transporte Ejecutivo*), starting from the south end of Praça 15 de Novembro and other stops, charge US$0.75-US$1.45 depending on destination. Similarly, normal bus fares vary according to destination, from US$0.65.

Car hire: *Auto Locadora Coelho*, Felipe Schmidt 81, vehicles in good condition. *Interlocadora*, T236 0179 at the airport, F236 1370, rates from US$40 a day before supplements.

Long distance Air: international and domestic flights arrive at Hercílio Luz airport, Av Deomício Freitas, 12 km from town, T331 4000. Take *Ribeiroense* bus 'Corredor Sudoeste' from Terminal Urbano.

Bus: international and buses from other Brazilian cities arrive at the rodoviária Rita Maia on the island, at the east (island) end of the Ponte Colombo Machado Salles, T224 2777.

Regular daily buses to **Porto Alegre** (US$16, 7 hrs), **São Paulo**, 9 hrs (US$23.75, *leito* US$36.25), **Rio**, 20 hrs (US$31 *convencional*, US$42 *executive*, US$55 *leito*); to **Foz do Iguaçu** (US$28, continuing to **Asunción** US$30), to most other Brazilian cities. To **Blumenau** US$7, 3 hrs. To **São Joaquim** at 1145, 1945 with *Reunidos*, 1815 with *Nevatur*, 5-6 hrs, US$9.30; to **Laguna** US$5.25.

International buses: Montevideo, US$52, daily, by *TTL*. Buenos Aires, US$55, *Pluma*, buses very full in summer, book 1 week in advance.

Directory

Airline offices *Aerolíneas Argentinas*, R Tte Silveira 200, 8th floor, T224 7835. *Nordeste/Rio Sul*, Av Rio Branco 883, T0800-492004. *TAM*, at airport, T236 0003. *Varig*, Av Rio Branco 796, T224 7266/0800-997000. *Vasp*, Av Osmar Cunha 105, T224 7824/0800-998277. **Banks** *Banco do Brasil*, Praça 15 de Novembro, exchange upstairs, 1000-1500, huge commission on cash or TCs. Lots of ATMs downstairs, some say Visa/Plus. *Banco Estado de Santa Catarina*, (BESC) câmbio, R Felipe Schmidt e Jerônimo Coelho, 1000-1600, no commission on TCs. *Lovetur*, Av Osmar Cunha 15, Ed Ceisa and *Centauro Turismo* at same address. *Açoriano Turismo*, Jaime Câmara 106, T2243939, takes Amex. Money changers on R Felipe Schmidt outside BESC. ATM for MasterCard/Cirrus at *Banco Itaú*, Shopping Centre Beiramar (not in the centre, bus Expresso). **Communications** Internet:Internet café on R Felipe Schmidt 700 block, opposite *Lav Lev* laundry, US$1.55 per hr. **Post Office:** Praça 15 de Novembro 5. **Telephone:** Praça Pereira Oliveira 20. **Embassies and consulates** Argentina, Av Rio Branco 387, 5th floor, T224 6441. **France**, R Durval Melquíades de Souza 645, 3rd floor, T324 1180. **Uruguay**, Av Rio Branco 387, 5th floor, T222 3718. **Tourist offices** Setur, head office at Portal Turístico de Florianópolis, mainland end of the bridge, Av Eng Max de Souza 236, Coqueiros, T244 5822 or 224 1516 information line, open 0800-2000 (Sat/Sun 1800). Also near the Cathedral, Praça 15 de Novembro, Centro, T222 9200, reliable for leaving messages, open 0800-1800 (2200 in high season). At Rodoviária, Av Paulo Fontes, T223 2777, and airport, maps available, free, 0700-1800 (0800 Sat/Sun). www.guiafloripa.com.br *Santur*, Edif ARS, R Felipe Schmidt 249, 9th floor, T224 6300, F222 1145, helpful, www.ciasc.gov.br and www.sc.gov.br/santur **Voltage** 220 volts AC.

Ilha de Santa Catarina

There are 42 beaches around the island. The most popular are the surfers' beaches such as Praia Moçambique; for peace and quiet try Campeche or the southern beaches; for sport, the Lagoa de Conceição has jet skis and windsurfing. You can walk in the forest reserves, hang glide or paraglide from the Morro da Lagoa, sandboard in the dunes of Joaquina. Surfing is prohibited 30 April-30 July because of the migration of the island's largest fish, the *tainha*.

Colour map 7, grid C3

Lagoa da Conceição has beaches, sand dunes, fishing, church of NS da Conceição (1730), market every Wednesday and Saturday, post office. Tandem hang gliding, *Lift Sul Vôo Livre*, T232 0543. From the Centro da Lagoa on the bridge there are daily boat trips to Costa da Lagoa which run until about 1830, check when you buy your ticket, US$4 return, the service is used mostly by the local people who live around the lake and have no other form of public transport.

Across the island at **Barra da Lagoa** is a pleasant fishing village and beach, surfing, lively in the summer season, with plenty of good restaurants, which can be reached by 'Barra da Lagoa' bus (Transol No 403, every 15 mins from Terminal Urbano, 55 mins, US$0.75). The same bus goes to beaches at **Mole** (good for walking, soft sand beach, surfing) and at **Joaquina** (surfing championships in January).

There is a pleasant fishing village at **Ponta das Canas**, walk 1 km to Praia Brava for good surfing, and the beach at **Canasvieiras** is good. Also in the north of the island, is **Praia dos Ingleses** (bus 602). **Forte São José da Ponta Grossa** is beautifully restored with a small museum. ■ *US$1.50. Buses to Jureré and Daniela beaches go there, 1 hr.*

In the south of the island are **Praia do Campeche**, 30 mins by bus (Pantano do Sul or Costa de Dentro) from Florianópolis, **Praia da Armação** with, just inland, **Lagoa do Peri** (a protected area). Further south is **Pântano do Sul**, an unspoilt fishing village with a long, curved beach, lovely views, several *pousadas*, bars and restaurants, though not much nightlife. From here it's a good 4-km walk over rocks and a headland to beautiful **Lagoinha do Leste**. **Praia dos Naufragados**: take bus to Caieira da Barra do Sul and then a one hr walk through fine forests. **Forte Nossa Senhora da Conceição** is on a small island just offshore. It can be seen from the lighthouse near Praia dos Naufragados or take a boat trip with Scuna Sul from Florianópolis.

Sleeping & eating

Lagoa da Conceição D *Pousada Zilma*, R Geral da Praia da Joaquina 279, T232 0161. Quiet, safe. Recommended. Ricardo, R Manoel S de Oliveira 8, CEP 88062, T232 0107, rents self-contained apartments, can arrange houses also. Recommended. Restaurant: *Oliveira*, R Henrique Veras, excellent seafood dishes.

Barra da Lagoa C *Pousada Floripaz*, Estrada Geral (across hanging bridge at bus station, take bus 403 from terminal municipal), T232 3193. Book in advance, safe, family run, helpful owners, will organize tours by boat and car on island. Highly recommended. **D** *Pousada-Lanchonete Sem Nome*, Praia do Moçambique. In 4-bunk rooms, bathrooms separate, kitchen, laundry. Recommended. **D** *Albergue do Mar*. Basic, good for lone travellers. *Camping da Barra*, T232 3199. Beautiful clean site, helpful owner. Restaurant: *Meu Cantinha*, R Orlando Shaplin 89, excellent seafood.

Joaquina AL *Hotel Cris*, T232 0380, F232 0075. Luxurious. Recommended. **Ponta das Canas A** *Hotel Moçambique*, T/F266 1172. In centre of village, noisy at weekends. Houses to let from Frederico Barthe, T266 0897. **Canasvieiras Praia dos Ingleses A** *Sol e Mar*, T262 1271. Excellent. Recommended. **Praia de Campeche AL** *Hotel São Sebastião da Praia*, Av Campeche 1373, T/F237 4247. Resort hotel on splendid beach, offers special monthly rate Apr to Oct, excellent value. **Near Pântano do Sul B** *Pousada dos Tucanos*, Estrada Geral da Costa de Dentro 2776, T237 5084, Caixa Postal 5016. English, French, Spanish spoken, spacious bungalows in garden setting, excellent organic food. Very highly recommended. Take bus to Pântano do Sul, walk 6 km or telephone and arrange to be picked up by German owner. Hostelling International **F** *Albergue do Pirata*, Pântano do Sul, www.megasites.com.br/pirata With breakfast, natural surroundings, lots of trails.

Entertainment

Throughout the summer the beaches open their bars day and night. The beach huts of Praia Mole invite people to party all night (bring a blanket). Any bars are worth visiting in the Lagoa area (around the Boulevard and Barra da Lagoa).

Porto Belo Beaches

Phone code: 0xx47
Population: 10,704

On the coast north of Florianópolis there are many resorts. They include Porto Belo, a fishing village on the north side of a peninsula settled in 1750 by Azores islanders, with a calm beach and a number of hotels and restaurants. Around the peninsula are wilder beaches reached by rough roads: Bombas, Bombinhas, Quatro Ilhas (quieter, 15 mins' walk from Bombinhas), Mariscal, and, on the southern side, Zimbros (or Cantinho). Many of the stunning beaches around **Bombinhas** are untouched, accessible only on foot or by boat. Its clear waters are marvellous for diving.

Sleeping Porto Belo: **D** *Pousada Trapiche*, no breakfast. Lots of apartments, mostly sleep 4-6, in **B** range, good value for a group. **Zimbros**: **B** *Pousada Zimbros*, R da Praia 527, T369 3225/1225. Cheaper off season, on beach, sumptuous breakfast, restaurant, spear fishing guide. Highly recommended. **Camping**: There are lots of camp sites around the peninsula.

Transport Bus Florianópolis to Porto Belo, several daily with *Rainha*, fewer at weekends, more frequent buses to Tijuca, Itapema and Itajaí, all on the BR-101 with connections. Buses from Porto Belo to the beaches on the peninsula.

This is now the most concentrated development on Brazil's southern coast. From 15 December to end-February it is very crowded and expensive; the rest of the year it is easy to rent furnished apartments by the day or week. A few kilometres south, at Lojas Apple, there is Parque Cyro Gevaerd, a museum (archaeology, oceanography, fishing, arts and crafts) and aquarium; and Meia Praia, which is quieter and cleaner than Camboriú. A *teleférico* has been built to Praia Laraneiras, previously deserted; US$5 return from Barra Sul shopping centre to Laranjeiras via Mata Atlântica station. Between Camboriú and Itajaí is the beautiful, deserted (and rough) beach of Praia Brava. ■ *Buses from Florianópolis, Joinville and Blumenau. TTL buses Montevideo-São Paulo stop here at about 1800, a good place to break the journey.*

Camboriú
Phone code: 0xx47
Colour map 7, grid C3
Population: 41,445
80 km N of
Florianópolis

Blumenau

Some 47 km up the Rio Itajaí-Açu is this prosperous city, where hightech and electronics industries are replacing textiles as the economic mainstay. The surrounding district was settled mostly by Germans. It is clean and orderly with almost caricatured Germanic architecture. See the **Museu da Família Colonial**, German immigrant museum, Av Duque de Caxias 78. ■ *Mon-Fri 0800-1130, 1330-1730, Sat morning only, US$0.15.* Also worth a visit is the **German Evangelical Church**, and the houses, now **museums** (open 0800-1800), of **Dr Bruno Otto Blumenau** and of **Fritz Müller** (a collaborator of Darwin), who bought the Blumenau estate in 1897 and founded the town.

Phone code: 0xx47
Post code: 89100
Colour map 7, grid C3
Population: 261,808
61 km by paved
road from Itajaí
Voltage: 220 AC

Brazil

Oktoberfest, the second largest street party in Brazil, after Carnival is usually held in the first half of October. During the day the narrow streets are packed around the Molemann Centre, which contains a mixture of bars, live music and of course, Chopp beer. At 1900 the doors of the Oktoberfest pavilion open for different events, including drinking competitions, the 'sausage Olympics', traditional dress and cake making competitions. There is also a fun fair and folk dancing shows. Visitors report it is worth attending on weekday evenings but weekends are too crowded. It is repeated, but called a 'summer festival', in the three weeks preceding Carnival.

At **Pomerode**, 33 km west of Blumenau, the north German dialect of Plattdeutsch is still spoken and there are several folkloric groups keeping alive the music and dance of their ancestors. The Museu Pomerano, Rodovia SC 418, Km 3, T387 0477, tells the story of the colonial family. Museu Ervin Kurt Theichmann, R 15 de Novembro 791, T387 0282, has sculptures. The *Confeitaria Torten Paradies*, R 15 de Novembro 211, serves excellent German cakes. *Festa do Pomerania* in January. ■ *Coletivos Volkmann (T387 1321) Blumenau-Pomerode daily US$0.75, 1 hr; check schedule at tourist offices.*

C *Blumenau Turist Hotel*, R Francisco Margarida 67, T323 3554, 200 m from bus station. Helpful. **C** *Glória*, R 7 de Setembro 954, T326 1988, F326 5370. German-run, excellent coffee shop, best deal is 'meal of soups', US$2.30 for salad bar, 4 soups, dessert and wine. **D** *Herrmann*, Floriano Peixoto 213, T322 4370, F326 0670. One of the oldest houses in Blumenau, rooms with or without bath, excellent big breakfast, German spoken. Many cheap hotels do not include breakfast. Youth hostel *Grün Garten Pousada*, R São Paulo 2457, T323 4332, 15 mins' walk from rodoviária. **Camping** Municipal campsite, 3 km out on R Pastor Osvaldo Hesse; Paraíso dos Poneis, 9 km out on the Itajaí road, also Motel; Refúgio Gaspar Alto, 12 km out on R da Glória.

Sleeping
Reservations are
essential during
Oktoberfest

Good German food at *Frohsinn*, Morro Aipim (panoramic view) and *Cavalinho Branco*, Av Rio Branco 165, huge meals. International eating at *Moinho do Vale*, Paraguai 66. *Amigo*, Peixoto 213, huge cheap meals. *Deutsches Eck*, R 7 de Septembro 432. Recommended,

Eating

especially *carne pizzaiola*. **Gruta Azul**, Rodolfo Freygang 8. Good, popular, not cheap. *Internacional*, Nereu Ramos 61. Chinese, very good, moderate prices. **Chinês**, R 15 de Novembro 346, near Tourist office. Good. **Tunga**, R 15 de Novembro. Patio, live music. **Patisseria Bavaria**, Av 7 Septembro y Zimmerman. Very good cakes and fruit juices, friendly and caring staff.

Transport   **Bus**   Rodoviária is 7 km from town (get out of bus at the big bridge over the river and walk 1 km to centre). Bus to the rodoviária from Av Presidente Castelo-Branco (Beira Rio). There are good bus connections in all directions from Blumenau. To **Curitiba**, US$6.50, 4 hrs, 3 daily (*Penha* and *Catarinense*).

Directory   **Banks** *Câmbios*/travel agencies: *Vale do Itajaí Turismo e Cambio*, Av Beira Rio 167, very helpful, German spoken. **Tourist office** T387 2627. *Tilotur Turismo*, Alameda Rio Branco e 15 de Novembro, 2nd floor, T326 7999.

São Francisco do Sul
Phone code: 0xx47
Colour map 7, grid C3
Population: 32300

80 km up the coast at the mouth of the Baia de Babitonga, São Francisco do Sul is the port for the town of Joinville, 45 km inland at the head of the Rio Cachoeira. There is an interesting **Museu Nacional do Mar** reflecting Brazil's seafaring history. The centre has over 150 historical sites and has been protected since 1987. The **cathedral** was built between 1699 and 1719 and still has its original walls made with sand, shells and whale oil. There are some excellent **beaches** nearby. **AL-A** *Zibamba*, R Fernandes Dias 27, T/F444 2020, central, good restaurant. ■ *Bus terminal is 1½ km from centre. Direct bus (*Penha*) daily to Curitiba at 0730, US$6, 3½ hrs.*

Joinville itself (*Phone code*: 0xx47) is the state's largest city. It lies 2 km from the main coastal highway, BR-101, by which Curitiba and Florianópolis are less than two hours away. The industry does not spoil the considerable charm of the city. The **Alameda Brustlein**, better known as the **R das Palmeiras**, is an impressive avenue of palm trees leading to the **Palácio dos Príncipes**. The trees have been protected since 1982. The **Cathedral** on Av Juscelino Kubitscheck with R do Príncipe (T433 3459), is futuristic with spectacular windows recounting the story of man. The **Casa da Cultura** (Galeria Municipal de Artes 'Victor Kursansew'), R Dona Fransisca 800, also contains the School of Art 'Fritz Alt', the School of Music 'Vila Lobos' and the School of Ballet. ■ *Mon-Fri 0900-1800, Sat 0900-1300*. A number of museums and exhibition centres reflect the history of, and immigration to the area and the city's artistic achievements. In July, Joinville hosts the largest dance festival in the world, which attracts around 4,000 dancers who stay for 12 days and put on shows and displays ranging from jazz, folklore, classical ballet and other styles. There is also an annual beer festival, *Fenachopp*, in October. There are many good restaurants and good air and road links to other parts of Brazil. **Tourist offices** Corner Praça Nereu Ramos with R do Príncipe, T433 1511/1437, F433 1491. *Promotur*, in Centreventos Cau Hansen, A José Vieira 315, sala 20, T423 2633, www.promotur.com.br Also www.joinville.sc.gov.br

Sleeping   **A** *Tannenhof*, Visconde de Taunay 340, T/F433 8011, www.tannenhof.com.br 4-star, pool, gym, traffic noise, excellent breakfast, restaurant. **A** *Anthurium Parque*, São José 226, T/F433 6299, www.anthurium.com.br Colonial building, once home to a bishop, good value, English spoken, pool, sauna. **D** *Mattes*, 15 de Novembro 801, T422 3582, www.hotelmattes.com.br Good facilities, big breakfast. **E** *Novo Horizonte*, at bus station, basic, clean.

Southern Santa Catarina

At **Praia do Rosa**, 101 km south of Florianópolis, is the headquarters of the Right Whale Project (*Projeto Baleia-franca*) and one of Brazil's prime **whale-watching** sites. The right whales come to the bay to calve from May to November and trips can be arranged to see them. The project's base is the *Pousada Vida, Sol e Mar*, T354

0041/355 6111, which has cabins, pool, restaurant and surf school. For packages contact *Rentamar Turismo*, 338 Milton Rd, Cambridge, CB4 1LW, UK, T/F+44-1223 424244, Glauce.UK@tesco.net There are other lodgings at Praia do Rosa and other fine beaches in the area. The nearest major town is Imbituba.

Some 15 km from Tubarão is the small fishing port of **Laguna**. The town, founded in 1676, was the capital of the Juliana Republic in 1839, a short-lived separatist movement led by Italian idealist Guiseppe Garibáldi. At Laguna is the **Anita Garibáldi Museum**, containing documents, furniture, and personal effects of Garibáldi's devoted lover. ■ *Buses to/from Porto Alegre, 5½ hrs, with Santo Anjo Da Guarda; same company goes to Florianópolis, 2 hrs, US$5.25, 6 daily.*

Laguna
Phone code: 0xx48
Colour map 7, grid C3
Population: 47,568
124 km S of
Florianópolis

About 16 km away (by ferry and road) are beaches and dunes at **Cavo de Santa Marta**. Also from Laguna, take a *Lagunatur* or *Auto Viação São José* bus to **Farol** (four buses a day Monday-Friday, one on Saturday, US$1.50, beautiful ride). You have to cross the mouth of the Lagoa Santo Antônio by ferry (10 mins) to get to Farol; look out for fishermen aided by dolphins (*botos*). Here is a fishing village with a lighthouse (Farol de Santa Marta), built by the French in 1890 of stone, sand and whale oil. It is the largest lighthouse in South America and has the third largest view in the world. ■ *Guided tours available (taxi, US$10, not including ferry toll). It may be possible to bargain with fishermen for a bed, or there are campsites at Santa Marta Pequena by the lighthouse, popular with surfers.*

Sleeping C *Turismar*, Av Beira Mar 207, T647 0024, F647 0279. 2-star, view over Mar Grosso beach, TV. D *Recanto*, Av Colombo 17, close to bus terminal. With breakfast, modern but basic. D *Beiramar*, T644 0260, 100 m from *Recanto*, opposite Angeloni Supermarket. No breakfast, TV, rooms with view over lagoon.

Buses from the coalfield town of Tubarão (27 km from Laguna) go inland to Lauro Müller, then over the Serra do Rio do Rastro (beautiful views of the coast in clear weather) to **Bom Jardim da Serra** which has an apple festival every April. The road continues to **São Joaquim**. The highest town in southern Brazil, it regularly has snowfalls in winter; a very pleasant town with an excellent climate. 11 km outside the town on the way to Bom Jardim da Serra is the **Parque Ecológico Vale da Neve** (Snow Valley). It is an easy hike and very beautiful, the entrance is on the main road, US$3, and there is a restaurant. The owner is American and an English speaking guide will take you for a 1½ hr walk through the forest. The **Parque Nacional de São Joaquim** (33,500 ha) in the Serra Geral has canyons containing sub-tropical vegetation, and araucaria forest at higher levels. There is no bus (local *Ibama* office, T048-222 6202, *Secretaria de Turismo de São Joaquim*, T049-233 0258).

São Joaquim
Colour map 7, grid C2
Population: 22,836
Altitude: 1,360 m

Sleeping In São Joaquim: D *Nevada*, T/F233 0259. Expensive meals. D *Maristela*, T233 007, French spoken, no heating so can be cold, helpful, good breakfast; both on R Manoel Joaquim Pinto, 190 and 220 respectively (5 mins' walk from rodoviária). In **Bom Jardim da Serra**, E *Moretti*, family atmosphere, owner very helpful. **Camping** *Clube do Brasil* site.

Transport Bus to **Florianópolis** 0700 and 1700 via Bom Retiro (*Reunidos*) and 0800 via Tubarão (*Nevatur*), 5½ hrs, US$9. Florianópolis-Bom Jardim da Serra, US$10.

West of Florianópolis, 212 km by paved road (BR 282), is **Lages**, a convenient stopping place on BR-116 between Caxias do Sul and Curitiba (*Phone code*: 0xx49). The area around Lages is particularly good for 'rural tourism' with lots of opportunities for hiking, horse riding, river bathing, working on a farm and other activities. The weather can get really cold in winter. Many of the local *fazendas* are open for visitors and offer accommodation. A *Grande*, R João de Castro 23, T/F222 3522, good. One of the three hotels near the rodoviária is D *Rodeio*, T223 2011, with or without bath, good breakfast. In the same building is a good *churrascaria*, open in the evening

Colour map 7, grid C2

Brazil

Brazil

US$7.50. Voltage 220 AC. ■ *Bus station is 30 mins' walk southeast of the centre. Bus to the centre (Terminal Municipal), 'Rodoviária' runs Mon-Fri only, or 'Dom Pedro II' every 40 mins at weekends. To Florianópolis 6-8 buses daily on the direct road (BR282), 5 hrs, US$10; to Caxias do Sul, 3¾ hrs, US$5.60.*

The route can also be done on poorer roads via São Joaquim (see above), which is perhaps the most interesting journey in the state, with scenery changing as the road climbs out of coastal forest.

Brasília

Rio Grande do Sul

Population:
10.2 million

Rio Grande do Sul is gaúcho country; it is also Brazil's chief wine producer. The capital, Porto Alegre, is the most industrialized city in the south, but in the surroundings are good beaches, interesting coastal national parks and the fine scenery of the Serra Gaúcha. On the border with Santa Catarina is the remarkable Aparados da Serra National Park. In the far west are the remains of Jesuit missions. Look out for local specialities such as comida campeira, te colonial and quentão.

Background The Great Escarpment runs down the coastal area as far as Porto Alegre. South of Tubarão to the borders of Uruguay the hills of southern Rio Grande do Sul, which never rise higher than 900-1,000 m, are fringed along the coast by sand bars and lagoons. In southern Rio Grande do Sul, south and west of the Rio Jacuí (draining into the Lagoa dos Patos) there are great grasslands stretching as far as Uruguay to the south and Argentina to the west. This is the distinctive land of the *gaúcho*, or cowboy (pronounced ga-oo-shoo in Brazil), of the flat black hat, of *bombachas* (the baggy trousers worn by the *gaúcho*), of the poncho and *ximarão* (also spelt *chimarrão*, it is *mate* without sugar), the indispensable drink of southern cattlemen. The *gaúcho* culture is increasingly developing a sense of distance from the African-influenced culture of further north. This separatist strain was most marked in the 1820s and 1830s when the Farroupilha movement, led by Bento Gonçalves, proclaimed the República Riograndense in 1835.

Porto Alegre

Phone code: 0xx51
Colour map 7, inset
Population: 1,360,590
The market area in
Praça 15 de Novembro
and the bus terminal
are dangerous at
night. Thefts have
been reported in
Voluntários da Pátria
and Praça Parcão

The capital of Rio Grande do Sul lies at the confluence of five rivers (called Rio Guaíba, although it is not a river in its own right) and thence into the great freshwater lagoon, the Lagoa dos Patos, which runs into the sea. The freshwater port, one of the most up-to-date in the country, handles ocean-going vessels and. Porto Alegre is one of the most heavily industrialized cities in Brazil. Standing on a series of hills and valleys on the banks of the Guaíba, it has a temperate climate through most of the year, though the temperature at the height of summer can often exceed 40°C and drop below 10°C in winter. Mosquitoes are plentiful.

Sights
On Sun there are
guided walks from
Praça da Alfândega
and on Sat from Praça
da Matriz, 1500 or
1600, free, contact
Central de Informações
Turísticas, R Vasco da
Gama 253, Bom Fim,
T311 5289, or in the
Mercado Público.

The older residential part of the town is on a promontory, dominated previously by the **Palácio Piratini** (Governor's Palace) and the imposing modern **cathedral** on the **Praça Marechal Deodoro** (or da Matriz). Also on, or near this square, are the neoclassical **Theatro São Pedro** (1858), the **Solar dos Câmara** (1818, now a historical and cultural centre) and the **Biblioteca Pública**, but all are dwarfed by the skyscraper of the **Assembléia Legislativa**. Down Rua General Câmara from Praça Marechal Deodoro is the **Praça da Alfândega**, with the old customs house and the Museu de Arte de Rio Grande do Sul (see below). A short walk east of this group, up Rua 7 de Setembro, is Praça 15 de Novembro, on which is the neoclassical **Mercado Público**, next to the Prefeitura. A large part of **Rua dos Andradas** (Rua da Praia) is permanently closed to traffic and by around 1600 it is jammed full of people. Going west along Rua dos Andradas, you pass the wide stairway that leads up to the two high white towers of the church of **Nossa Senhora das Dores**. At the end of the promontory, the **Usina do Gasômetro** has been converted from a thermoelectric station into a cultural centre. Its enormous chimney has become a symbol for the city. In the **Cidade Baixa** quarter are the colonial **Travessa dos Venezianos** (between Ruas Lopo Gonçalves and Joaquim Nabuco) and the **house of Lopo Gonçalves**, Rua João Alfredo 582, which houses the **Museu de Porto Alegre Joaquim José Felizardo**, a collection on the history of the city. ■ *Tue-Sun 0900-1700, free.*

The central **Parque Farroupilha** (called Parque Redenção) which has many attractions and on Sundays there is a *feira* of antiques, handicrafts and all sorts at the José Bonifácio end. The **Jardim Botânico** (Bairro Jardim Botânico, bus 40 from Praça 15 de Novembro), is on Rua Salvador França 1427, *zona leste.*

Museu Júlio de Castilhos, Duque de Caxias 1231, has an interesting historical collection about the state of Rio Grande do Sul. ■ *Tue-Sun 0900-1700.* For art from the state, visit the **Museu de Arte do Rio Grande do Sul**, Praça Senador Florêncio (Praça da Alfândega). ■ *Tue 1000-2100, Wed-Sun 1000-1700, free.* **Museu de Comunicação Social**, Rua dos Andradas 959, in the former *A Federação* newspaper building, deals with the development of the press in Brazil since the 1920s. ■ *Mon-Fri 1200-1900, T224 4252.*

Museums

Brazil

The 5-km wide **Rio Guaíba** lends itself to every form of boating and there are several sailing clubs. Two boats run trips around the islands in the estuary: *Cisne Branco*, from Cais do Porto, near Museu de Arte de Rio Grande do Sul, T224 2802, several sailings on Sunday, fewer mid-week, one hr, US$5; and *Noiva do Caí*, from the Usina do Gasômetro, T211 7662, several on Sunday, fewer mid-week, one hr, US$3.50 (check winter schedules). You can see a good view of the city, with glorious sunsets, from the **Morro de Santa Teresa** (take bus 95 from the top end of Rua Salgado Filho, marked 'Morro de Santa Teresa TV' or just 'TV'). Another good sunset-viewing spot is the Usina do Gasômetro.

A *Continental*, Lg Vespasiano Júlio Veppo 77, T211 2344, F228 5024, www.hoteiscontinental.com.br High standards, pool, gym. Recommended. **A-B** *Ritter*, Lg Vespasiano Júlio Veppo 55, opposite rodoviária, T228 4044, F228 1610. Four-star and 3-star wings, English, French, German spoken, bar, small pool, sauna. Fine restaurant, good service. Recommended. **B** *Açores*, R dos Andradas 885, T221 7588, F225 1007. Central, cramped but friendly. **B** *Lancaster*, Trav Acelino de Carvalho 67, T224 4737, F224 4630. Central, quiet, a/c, restaurant. **B** *São Luiz*, Av Farrapos 45, T228 1722, Spotless, good service, but near rodoviária so a bit noisy. **C** *Terminaltur*, Lg Vespasiano Júlio Veppo 125, opposite rodoviária, T227 1656, F225 8447. A/c, breakfast, heating, small rooms and tiny bathrooms, not too comfortable. **C** *Palácio*, Av Vigário José Inácio 644, T225 3467. Central, hot water. Recommended. **C** *Savoy*, Av Borges Medeiros 688, T224 0843, F224 0511. Good value. **E** pp *Erechim*, Av Júlio de Castilhos 341, near rodoviária, T228 7044, F225 1090. With or without bath, good value. **E** *Hotel Ritz Youth Hostel*, R Des André da Rocha, T255 3423. Shared bathroom, hot water, clean but basic. **Camping** Praia do Guarujá, 16 km out on Av Guaíba.

Sleeping
■ *on map*
Price codes:
see inside front cover
Hotels in the area
around R Garibáldi
and Voluntários da
Patria between Av
Farrapos and
rodoviária are
overpriced and used
for short stays

Eating

There are many good restaurants. Gaúcho cooking features large quantities of meat, while German cuisine is also a strong influence. Regional farm (campeiro) food, now a dying art, uses plenty of rice, vegetables, and interesting sauces. Vegetarians might try some of the campeiro soups and casseroles, otherwise stick to Italian restaurants or churrascaria salad bars

Churrasco *Capitão Rodrigo*, Av Albert Bins 514 (in *Plaza São Rafael* hotel), T221 6100. Self service, open 1200-1430, 1900-2300, closed Mon. *Gauchão*, at Rodoviária. Inexpensive, live entertainment nightly. *Moinhos de Vento*, R Dona Laura 424, T331 1847. Closed Sun afternoon. **General** *Chalé da Praça 15*, Praça 15 de Novembro. Average food but recommended for early evening drinks and snacks. *Komka*, Av Bahia 1275, San Geraldo, T222 1881. Recommended. **German** *Chopp Stübel*, R Quintino Bocaiúva 940, Moinhos de Vento, T332 8895. Open 1800-0030, closed Sun, Recommended. *Hannover*, Av C Colombo 2140, Floresta, T222 7902. Closed Mon. Recommended. *Sociedade Germânia*, Av Independência 1269, 6th floor, T222 9094. Sat night dinner dance, closed Mon, Sat lunch, Sun evenings. Recommended. *Wunderbar*, R Marquês do Herval 5981, Moinhos de Vento, T222 4967. Very busy 1900-0100. Recommended. **Italian** *Al Dente*, R Mata Bacelar 210, Auxiliadora, T343 1841. Expensive northern Italian cuisine. *Atelier de Massas*, R Riachuelo 1482, Excellent, not cheap. *Spaguetti Express*, Centro Comercial Nova Olária, Lima e Silva 776. Good. **Regional** *Recanto do Tio Flor*, Av Getúlio Vargas 1700, Menino Deus, T233 6512. *Comida campeira, gaúcho* music. Recommended, 1130-1400, 1900-0100. *Pulperia*, Trav do Carmo 76, Cidade Baixa, T227 1172. Inexpensive, music, opens till 0400, closed Sun lunch. *Porky's*, Av Cristóvão Colombo 1971, Floresta, T222 7552. Serves wild boar and buffalo, closed Sun. Recommended. *Farroupilha*, Fernando Machado 973 (corner of Borges de Medeiros). Delicious *prato feito*. **Vegetarian** *Associação Macrobiotica*, R Mcal Floriano 72, T225 4784. Weekdays only. *Ilha Natural*, R Gen Câmara 60. Self-service, cheap, lunch only Mon-Fri.

Bars & nightclubs

Cía Sandwiches, Getúlio Vargas 1430. Beer, sandwiches and music. *João de Barro*, R da República 546, Cidade Baixa. Good jazz. *Bar do Goethe*, R 24 de Outubro 112, Moinhos de Vento, T222 2043, www.compuserv.com.br/bardogoethe/ Reunion each Tue, 2030, for

Porto Alegre

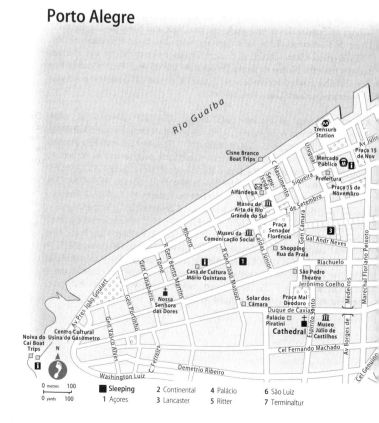

		Sleeping	2 Continental	4 Palácio	6 São Luiz
			1 Açores	3 Lancaster	5 Ritter	7 Terminaltur

foreign language speakers. *Crocodillo's*, 24 de Outubro, Auxiliadora. Recommended disco. *Best Bier*, Av C Colombo 3000, corner R Germano Petersen Júnior, Higienópolis. Mon-Fri 1800-0100, weekends 2000-0200, mixed crowd, live music, choice of ambiences. *Barong*, R Mostadeiro 517, T222 1663. Balinese style, Indian snack food, music, closed Sun. Gay bars include *Fly*, R Gonçalvo de Carvalho 189. Predominantly male, attractive bar with art exhibition, sophisticated, open 2100-0200, closed Tue. *Descretu's*, Venâncio Aires 59. Gay club, shows at 0230. *Doce Vício*, R Vieira de Castro 32. Three floors with games room, bar, restaurant, 1830-0230, closed Mon. *We Cia*, R Mostadeiro 462. Predominantly female, bar and club, 1200-0300, closed Mon-Tue.

Art galleries *Casa de Cultura Mário Quintana*, R dos Andradas 736. A lively centre for the arts, with exhibitions, theatre, pleasant bar etc, open 0900-2100, 1200-2100 Sat-Sun. Bookshop sells English books. **Theatre** *São Pedro*, Praça Mcal Deodoro. Free noon and late afternoon concerts Sat, Sun, art gallery, café. **Entertainment**

The main event is on **2 Feb** (a local holiday), with the festival of *Nossa Senhora dos Navegantes* (Iemanjá), whose image is taken by boat from the central quay in the port to the industrial district of Navegantes. *Semana Farroupilha* celebrates *gaúcho* traditions with parades in traditional style, its main day being on **20 Sep**. The Carnival parade takes place in Av A do Carvalho, renamed Av Carlos Alberto Barcelos (or Roxo) for these 3 days only, after a famous carnival designer. **Festivals**

The Praia de Belas shopping centre, claimed to be the largest in Latin America, is a US$1.50 taxi ride from town. There is a street market (leather goods, basketware etc) in the streets around the central Post Office. Good leather goods are sold on the streets. Sun morning handicraft and bric-a-brac market (plus sideshows) Av José Bonifácio (next to Parque Farroupilha). There is a very good food market. **Bookshops** *Livraria Kosmos*, R dos Andradas 1644 (international stock). *Livraria Londres*, Av Osvaldo Aranha 1182. Used books in English, French and Spanish and old *Life* magazines. *Saraiva Megastore*, in Shopping Praia de Belas. *Siciliano*, R dos Andradas 1273 (stocks Footprint) and other branches. Each year a *Feira do Livro* is held in Praça da Alfândega, Oct-Nov. **Shopping**

To Guaíba Bridge

Garibaldi

To Airport

Farrapos

Av Alberto Bins

Av Independência

R dos Andradas

Osvaldo Aranha

University

Paulo Gama

Luis Englert

Parque Farroupilha

To Museu de Porto Alegre Joaquim José Felizardo

Mercatur, Av Dom Pedro II 1240 cj 402, T337 8055, F225 6954. AmEx representative. See Turismo section in 'Zero Hora' classifieds (Thu, Sat, Sun) for tour companies' advertisements. **Tour operators**

Local Bus 1st-class minibuses (*Lotação*), painted in a distinctive orange, blue and white pattern, stop on request, fares about US$1. Safer and more pleasant than normal buses (US$0.35). **Air** The international airport is on Av dos Estados, 8 km from the city, T371 4110. There are regular buses to the rodoviária and a metrô service, *Trensurb*, to the Mercado Público, via the rodoviária, US$0.30. **Transport**

Brazil

Long Distance Bus International and interstate buses arrive at the rodoviária at Largo Vespasiano Júlio Veppo, on Av Mauá with Garibáldi, T145, www.rodoviaria-poa.com.br Facilities include a post office and long-distance telephone service until 2100. There are 2 sections to the terminal; the ticket offices for interstate and international destinations are together in 1 block, beside the municipal tourist office (very helpful). The intermunicipal (state) ticket offices are in another block; for travel information within the state, ask at the very helpful booth on the station concourse.

To **Rio**, US$48.50 (*leito* US$85), 24 hrs; **São Paulo**, US$66.50 (*leito* US$60), 18 hrs; **Florianópolis**, US$16, 7 hrs with *Santo Anjo* or *Eucatur* (take an *executivo* rather than a *convencional*, which is a much slower service); **Curitiba**, from US$21 *convencional* to US$37 *leito*, coastal and *serra* routes, 11 hrs; **Rio Grande**, US$10, every 2 hrs from 0600, 4½ hrs. **Foz do Iguaçu**, US$30, 15 hrs. To **Jaguarão** on Uruguayan border at 2400, 6 hrs, US$10. **Uruguaiana**, US$13, 8 hrs. Many other destinations.

Take your passport and tourist card when purchasing international bus tickets

International buses To Montevideo, with *TTL* (daily 1700 and 2000, US$39, US$56 *leito*), alternatively take bus to border town of Chuí at 1200 daily, 7½ hrs, US$13, then bus to Montevideo (US$13). To **Asunción** with *Unesul* at 1900, Tue, Fri, 18 hrs via **Foz do Iguaçu**, US$35. There are bus services to **Buenos Aires**, US$45, 19 hrs (depending on border) with *Pluma*, 1805 daily, route is Uruguaiana, Paso de los Libres, Entre Ríos and Zárate. For **Misiones** (Argentina), take 2100 bus (not Sat) to Porto Xavier on the Río Uruguay, 11 hrs, US$15, get exit stamp at police station, take a boat across to San Javier, US$2, go to Argentine immigration at the port, then take a bus to Posadas (may have to change in Leandro N Além).

Road Good roads radiate from Porto Alegre, and Highway BR-116 is paved to Curitiba (746 km). To the south it is paved (mostly in good condition), to Chuí on the Uruguayan border, 512 km. In summer visibility can be very poor at night owing to mist, unfenced cows are a further hazard. The paved coastal road to Curitiba via Itajaí (BR-101), of which the first 100 km is the 4-lane Estrada General Osório highway, is much better than the BR-116 via Caxias and Lajes. The road to Uruguaiana is entirely paved but bumpy.

Directory

Banks *Banco do Brasil*, Av dos Estados 1515, T371 1955 (also has Visa/Plus ATM), and Av Assis Brasil 2487, T341 2466. 1000-1500, good rates for TCs. Branch at Uruguai 185 has Visa/Plus ATM. Many branches of *Bradesco* have Visa ATMs; also branches of *Banco Bilbao Vizcaya Argentaria Brasil*. *Citibank*, R7 de Setembro 722, T220 8619. *MasterCard* ATMs at any *HSBC* branch or *Banco 24 Horas*. *MasterCard*, cash against card, R 7 de Setembro 722, 8th floor, Centro. *Exprinter*, R Hilário Ribeiro 292 (best for cash). For other addresses consult tourist bureau brochure. **Communications** Internet:Cyber cafés in shopping malls. **Post office:** R Siqueira Campos 1100, Centro, Mon-Fri 0900-1800, Sat 0900-1230. *UPS*, T434 972 (Alvaro). **Telephone:** R Borges de Medeiros 475. **Cultural centres** Sociedade Brasileira da Cultura Inglesa, Praça Mauricio Cardoso 49, Moinhos de Vento. **Instituto Goethe**, 24 de Outubro 122. Mon-Fri, 0930-1230, 1430-2100, occasional concerts, bar recommended for German *Apfelkuchen*. **Embassies and consulates** Argentina, R Prof Annes Dias 112, 1st floor, T224 6799. **Germany**, R Prof Annes Dias 112, 11th floor, T224 9255, F2264909. **Italy**, Praça Marechal Deodoro 134, T228 2055. 0900-1200. **Japan**, Av João Obino 467, Alto Petrópolis, T334 1299, F334 1742. 0900-1230, 1500-1700. **Portugal**, R Prof Annes Dias 112, 10th floor, T224 5767. 0900-1530. **Spain**, R Ildefonso Simões Lopes 85, T338 1300, F338 1444. **Sweden**, Av Sen Salgado Filho 327, Apdo 1303, T227 1289. 0900-1100. **UK**, R Itapeva 110, Sala 505, Edif Montreal, Bairro Passo D'Areia, T/F341 0720, 0900-1200, 1430-1800. **Uruguay**, R Siquera Campos 1171, 5th and 6th floors, T224 3499, F224 2644. **Language courses** Portuguese and Spanish, *Matilde Dias*, R Pedro Chaves Barcelos 37, Apdo 104, T331 8235, intermm@pro.via-rs.com.br US$15 per hr. **Tourist offices** Escritório Municipal de Turismo, R dos Andradas 680, 3rd floor, T212 1734, F212 2432, www.portoalegre.rs.gov.br Excellent. Another site: www.uol.com.br/guiapoa Also at Salgado Filho airport, friendly; interstate bus station, very helpful (free city maps); **Casa de Cultura Mário Quintana**, open 0900-2100; Mercado Público, Mon-Sat 0900-1800.

Porto Alegre beach resorts The main beach resorts of the area are to the east and north of the city. Heading east along the BR-290, 112 km from Porto Alegre is **Osório**, a pleasant lakeside town with a few hotels. From here it is 18 km southeast to the rather polluted and crowded beach resort of **Tramandaí** (5 buses daily from Porto Alegre, US$3.50). The beaches

Brazil

here are very popular, with lots of hotels, bars, restaurants, and other standard seaside amenities. Extensive dunes and lakes in the region provide an interesting variety of wildlife and sporting opportunities. The beach resorts become less polluted the further north you travel, and the water is clean by the time you reach Torres (see below). Among the resorts between the two towns is **Capão da Canoa**, with surfing at Atlântida beach. The Lagoa dos Quadros, inland, is used for windsurfing, sailing, water-skiing and jet-skiing.

Torres
Phone code: 0xx51
Colour map 7, inset
Population: 30,880

Torres is a well developed resort, with a number of beaches, several high class, expensive hotels, a wide range of restaurants, professional surfing competitions and entertainment. Torres holds a ballooning festival in April. There is an annual independence day celebration, when a cavalcade of horses arrives in town on 16 September from Uruguay. Torres gets its name from the three huge rocks, or towers, on the town beach, Praia Grande. Fishing boats can be hired for a trip to **Ilha dos Lobos**, a rocky island 2 km out to sea, where sea lions spend the winter months. During May, dolphins visit Praia dos Molhes, north of the town. The tourist office is at R Rio Branco 315, T664 1219. ■ *Bus Porto Alegre-Torres, 6 a day, US$6.60.*

There is a paved road running south from Tramandaí along the coast to Quintão, giving access to many beaches. Of note is **Cidreira**, with *Hotel Farol* on the main street (**D** with bath). Bus from Porto Alegre US$3.40. A track continues to **Mostardas**, thence along the peninsula on the seaward side of the Lagoa dos Patos to São José do Norte, opposite Rio Grande (see below, Rio Grande Excursions). South of Mostardas is **Tavares**, on the **Lagoa do Peixe**, a national park, which is a resting place for migrating birds (details from Praça Luís Martins 30, Mostardas, CEP 96270-000, T673 1464).

São Lourenço do Sul
Phone code: 0xx53
Population: 43,691

40 km to the south (towards Rio Grande) begins the Costa Doce of the Lagoa dos Patos. São Lourenço is a good place to enjoy the lake, the beaches, fish restaurants and watersports. The town hosts a popular four-day festival in March. **C** *Vilela*, R Almte Abreu 428, family hotel. ■ *Bus from Porto Alegre US$6.50, six a day.*

Serra Gaúcha

Population:
Canela, 33,625;
Gramado, 29,593

Inland is the pleasant Serra Gaúcha, the most beautiful scenery being around the towns of **Canela** and **Gramado**, about 130 km from Porto Alegre to the north. There is a distinctly Bavarian flavour to many of the buildings in both towns. In spring and summer the flowers are a delight, and in winter there are frequently snow showers. This is excellent walking and climbing country among hills, woods, lakes and waterfalls. In both towns it is difficult to get rooms in the summer/Christmas. Local crafts include knitted woollens, leather, wickerwork, and chocolate.

Nine kilometres from Canela is the **Parque Estadual do Caracol**, which has a 130 m-high waterfall. There is an excellent view from the *teleférico* at the nearby Parque Floresta Encantada. ■ *A local bus goes to the park at 0800.* From the high point at Ferradura, 7 km from the park (well-marked trail with several viewpoints), there is a good view into the canyon of the Rio Cai. On the other side of town is Parque das Sequoias, with a walk through araucaria pines. Beyond are good views also from Morro Pelado (*Altitude*: 600 m) and Morro Queimado. Follow signs from behind the town (not recommended when wet). ■ *There is a tourist office on Canela's main praça, with good maps and hotel lists. Voltage is 220 V AC.*

Gramado holds a festival of Latin American cinema each August. There is a tourist office at Av das Hortênsias (Pórtico) Praça Major Nicoletti/Av Borges de Medeiros 1674, T286 1418. Plenty of hotels and places to eat (mostly expensive). The local speciality is *café colonial*, a meal at 1700 of various dishes, including meats, recommended at *Café da Torre*, das Hortênsias 2174, open 1300-2200. Visitors should also sample hot *pinhões* (nuts from the Paraná pine) and *quentão* (hot red wine, cachaça, ginger, cloves, sugar and cinnamon, often topped with *gemada* –

Brazil

beaten egg yolks and sugar). Internet at *Parador do Ibiza*, opposite *Hotel Serra Azul* (R Garibáldi 152), free is f you buy a drink; Ramiro is helpful and has lots of information. ■ *Frequent bus service to Canela, 10 mins.*

Sleeping Canela: **A** *Vila Suzana Parque*, R Col Theoboldo Fleck 15, T282 2020, F282 1793. Chalets, heated pool, attractive. On R Oswaldo Aranha: **B** *Bela Vista*, No 160, T/F282 1327, near rodoviária. Good breakfasts. **D** *Turis Café*, No 223, T282 2774. Breakfast, English speaking staff. Recommended. **D** *Central*, Av Júlio de Castilhos 146. Recommended, safe. **D** pp*Pousada do Viajante*, R Ernesto Urbani 132, T2822017. Kitchen facilities. Recommended. **Camping** *Camping Clube do Brasil*, 1 km from waterfall in Parque do Caracol, 1 km off main road, signposted (8 km from Canela), T282 4321; excellent honey and chocolate for sale here. Highly recommended. *Sesi*, camping or cabins, R Francisco Bertolucci 504, 2½ km outside Canela, T/F282 1311. Clean, restaurant. Recommended.

Parque Nacional de Aparados da Serra
Colour map 7, inset

The major attraction at the Parque Nacional de Aparados da Serra is a canyon, 7.8 km long, known locally as the Itaimbezinho. Here, two waterfalls cascade 350 m into a stone circle at the bottom. There is a free campsite and a restaurant, which has a few rooms, in the park. For experienced hikers (and with a guide) there is a difficult path to the bottom of Itaimbezinho. One can then hike 20 km to Praia Grande in Santa Catarina state. As well as the canyon, the park, its neighbour, the **Parque Nacional da Serra Geral**, and the surrounding region have several bird specialities. The park is 80 km from São Francisco de Paula (18 km east of Canela, 117 km north of Porto Alegre). ■ *Wed-Sat 0900-1700, US$3, plus US$2.50 for car, T251 1262. Further information from Porto Alegre tourist office or* Ibama, *R Miguel Teixeira 126, Cidade Baixa, Caixa Postal 280, Porto Alegre, CEP 90050-250, T225 2144.*

Tourist excursions, mostly at weekends, from **São Francisco de Paula** (hotel: **A** *Veraneio Hampal*, RS-235 road to Canela, Km 1, T644 1363). At other times, take a bus to Cambará do Sul: several *pousadas* including **C** *Mirão*, R Benjamin Constant, breakfast, rooms and apartments, recommended; **E** *Pousada Paradiso*. Sign up at the tourist office and a truck will pick you up to go the park if there are enough passengers, US$17.50 per truck.

Caxias do Sul

Phone code: 0xx54
Post code: 95000
Colour map 7, inset
Population: 360,419
122 km from Porto Alegre

This city's population is principally of Italian descent and it is an expanding and modern city, the centre of the Brazilian wine industry. Vines were first brought to the region in 1840 but not until the end of the century and Italian immigration did the industry develop. The church of **São Pelegrino** has paintings by Aldo Locatelli and 5 m-high bronze doors sculptured by Augusto Murer. There is a good **Museu Municipal** at R Visconde de Pelotas 586, with displays of artefacts of the Italian immigration. ■ *Tue-Sat 0830-1130, 1330-1700, Sun 1400-1700, T221 2423.* Italian roots are again on display in the **Parque de Exposições Centenário**, 5 km out on R Ludovico Cavinato. January-February is the best time to visit. There is a tourist information kiosk in Praça Rui Barbosa. ■ *Rodoviária, R Ernesto Alves 1341, T222 3000, is a 15-min walk from the main praça, but many buses pass through the centre.*

Excursions

Caxias do Sul's festival of grapes is held in February-March. Many *adegas* accept visitors (but do not always give free tasting). Good tour and tasting (six wines) at *Adega Granja União*, R Os 18 de Forte 2346. Visit also the neighbouring towns and sample their wines: **Farroupilha** 20 km from Caxias do Sul. **Nova Milano**, 6 km away (bus to Farroupilha, then change – day trip). **Bento Gonçalves**, 40 km from Caxias do Sul. **Garibáldi**, which has a dry ski slope and toboggan slope – equipment hire, US$5 per hr.

A restored steam train leaves Bento Gonçalves Wednesday and Saturday at 1400 for **Carlos Barbosa**; called '*a rota do vinho*' (the wine run), it goes through vineyards in the hills. US$25 round trip, including wines, with live band; reserve in advance through *Giodani Turismo*, R Emy H Dreher 197, T451 2788. For information on the local *Vinícolas* which can be visited in the **Vale dos Vinhedos**, contact Aprovale, Travessa Guaiba 75, T452 4901, English spoken.

Another nice excursion is to **Antônio Prado**, 1½ hours by *Caxiense Bus*. The town is now a World Heritage Site because of the large number of original buildings built by immigrants in the Italian style.

Caxias do Sul D *Peccini*, R Pinheiro Machado 1939. Shared bath, good breakfast. **D** *Pérola*, Marquês de Herval 237, T223 6080. Good value. **D** *Hotel Praça*, R Cândido Mendes 330, T521 3782. Good. Hotels fill up early in the afternoon. **Farroupilha D** *Grande*, R Independência, T/F261 1025, 2 blocks from the church where the buses from Caxias do Sul stop, no breakfast, clean. And others. **Bento Gonçalves E** *Pousada Somensi*, R Siba Paes 367, T453 1254, near the Pipa Pórtico and Cristo Rei church in the upper town. Bath, without breakfast, good rooms. 6 km out of town in Vale dos Vinhados is **B** *Pousada Casa Valduga*, at the *adega*, T452 4338, F452 6204. Beautiful, pool. Youth hostel *Pousada Casa Mia*, Trav Niterói 71, T451 1215. HI. **Camping** *Palermo*, 5 km out on BR-116 at Km 118, T222 7255. *Recanto dos Pinhais*, on BR-453 towards Lajeado Grande at Km 23, T283 1144. At Garibáldi, Camping Clube do Brasil, estrada Gen Buarque de Macedo 4 km.

Sleeping

South of Porto Alegre

On the BR-116, **Pelotas** is the second largest city in the State of Rio Grande do Sul, 271 km S of Porto Alegre. It is a river port on the Rio São Gonçalo which connects the shallow Lagoa dos Patos with the Lagoa Mirim. For tourist information, contact *Integrasul*, Praça Col Pedro Osório 6, T225 8355, which has information on Pelotas and the southern region. There are many good hotels and transport links to all of the state and the Uruguay border at Chuí and Jaguarão.

Colour map 7, inset

South of Pelotas on the BR-471, is the **Taim** water reserve on the Lagoa Mirim. Many protected species, including black swans and the *quero-quero* (the Brazilian lapwing), migrate to the Taim for the breeding season. Information from Ibama in Porto Alegre.

Some 59 km south of Pelotas, at the entrance to the Lagoa dos Patos, is this city, lying on a low, sandy peninsula 16 km from the Atlantic Ocean. Founded in 1737, today it is the distribution centre for the southern part of Rio Grande do Sul, with significant cattle and meat industries. During the latter half of the 19th century Rio Grande was an important centre, but today it is a rather poor town, notable for the charm of its old buildings. The **Catedral de São Pedro** dates from 1755-75. **Museu Oceanográfico**, has an interesting collection of 125,000 molluscs, 2 km from centre on Av Perimetral, bus 59 or walk along waterfront. ■ *Daily 0900-1100, 1400-1700, T231 3496*. The tourist office is on R Riachuelo, on the waterfront, behind the Câmara de Comércio and beneath the Hidroviária; good map and information.

Rio Grande
Phone code: 0xx53
Colour map 7, inset
Population: 186,544
274 km S of Porto Alegre

Excursions To **Cassino**, a popular seaside town on the ocean, 24 km, over a good road. Travelling south, beaches are Querência (5 km), Stela Maris (9 km), Netuno (10 km), all with surf. The breakwater (the Barra), 5 km south of Cassino, no bus connection, through which all vessels entering and leaving Rio Grande must pass, is a tourist attraction. Barra-Rio Grande buses, from the east side of Praça Ferreira pass the Superporto. Across the inlet from Rio Grande is the little-visited settlement of **São José do Norte**, founded in 1725. ■ *There are frequent ferries (2 hrs approximately), São José to Rio Grande; there are also 3 car ferries daily, T232 1500. Tourist information from R Gen Osório 127. Buses run north to Tavares (see page 455).*

Sleeping and eating Rio Grande A *Charrua Rio Grande*, R Duque de Caxias 55, T231 3833. Recommended, good value. **D** *Paris*, R Marechal Floriano 112,. Old, charming. For eating, try *Recanto Doce*, Silva Paes 370, cheap. *China Brasil*, R Luís Loréa 389. Good but not cheap. *Pescal*, Marechal Andréa 389. For fish, fairly expensive. *Caumo's*, Dr Nascimento 389.

Brazil

Good *churrascaria*. *Jensen*, Al Abreu 650, near rodoviária. Good and cheap. *Bar Brejeiro*, Andrades 193, jazz upstairs. *Tia Laura*, 29 km from town on BR-392 north to Pelotas. Excellent, specializes in home cooking and *café colonial*.

Transport Bus: Frequent daily buses to and from **Pelotas** (56 km), **Bagé** (280 km), **Santa Vitória** (220 km), and **Porto Alegre** (US$10, 4½ hrs). All buses to these destinations go through Pelotas. Road to Uruguayan border at **Chuí** is paved, but the surface is poor (5 hrs by bus, at 0700 and 1430). Bus tickets to Punta del Este or Montevideo at *Bentica Turismo*, Av Silva Paes 373, T232 1321/232 1807.

Western Rio Grande do Sul

Jesuit Missions
Colour map 7, grid C1
Colour map 8, grid A6

West of **Passo Fundo**, 'the most *gaúcho* city in Rio Grande do Sul', are the **Sete Povos das Missões Orientais**. The only considerable Jesuit remains in Brazilian territory (very dramatic) are at **São Miguel das Missões**, some 50 km from **Santo Ângelo**. At São Miguel, now a World Heritage Site, there is a church, 1735-45, and small museum. ■ *0900-1800*. A *son et lumière* show in Portuguese is held daily, in winter at 1900, and a different time in summer, although all times rather depend on how many people there are. The show ends too late to return to Santo Ângelo. *Gaúcho* festivals are often held on Sunday afternoons, in a field near the Mission.

Sleeping Santo Ângelo: **A** *Maerkli*, Av Brasil 1000, T/F312 2127. Recommended. **D** *Hotel Nova Esperança*, behind bus station, without breakfast. Other cheap central hotels on or near Praça Rio Branco, fairly near old railway station, including **D** *Brasil*, Av Vernáncio Aires and **E** *Comércio*, Av Brasil, good for the price, a bit run down, hotel next door also **E** is more than basic. **São Miguel**: **C** *Hotel Barichello*, the only place to stay, nice, quiet, restaurant for *churrasco* lunch. In the evening it is difficult to find a place to eat, try one of the 2 snack bars for hamburgers.

Border with Argentina
Colour map 8, grid A6

Exchange rates are better in the town than at the border

In the extreme west are **Uruguaiana**, a cattle centre 772 km from Porto Alegre, and its twin Argentine town of Paso de los Libres, also with a casino. A 1,400 m bridge over the Rio Uruguai links the cities. Brazilian immigration and customs are at the end of the bridge, five blocks from the main praça; exchange and information in the same building. If you arrive in Uruguaiana from Porto Alegre in the early hours of the morning and need money, cross the border with *Pluma* bus, wait in Paso de los Libres until opening time (0730) and then go to the Visa ATM in *Banco Francés*.

Sleeping A *Glória*, R Domingos de Almeida 1951, T412 4422, F412 4804. Good. **A** *Fares Turis Hotel*, Pres Vargas 2939, T/F412 3358. May let you leave your bags while you look around town. **D** *Palace*, Praça Rio Branco. Without breakfast.

Transport Taxi or bus across the bridge about US$3.50. Buses connect the bus stations and centres of each city every 30 mins; if you have to disembark for visa formalities, a following bus will pick you up without extra charge. There are buses to Porto Alegre. *Planalto* buses run from Uruguaiana via Barra do Quaraí/Bella Unión to Salto and Paysandú in Uruguay.

Border with Uruguay: inland routes
Colour map 8, grid A6

At **Aceguá**, 60 km south of Bagé, there is a crossing to the Uruguayan town of Melo, and further east, **Jaguarão** with the Uruguayan town of **Rio Branco**, linked by the 1½ km long Mauá bridge across the Rio Jaguarão. Police post for passport checks is 3 km before the bridge; customs are at the bridge. For road traffic, the border at Chuy (see below) is better than Río Branco or Aceguá.

    Entering Uruguay Before crossing into Uruguay, you must visit Brazilian *Polícia Federal* to get an exit stamp; if not, the Uruguayan authorities will send you back. The crossing furthest west is **Barra do Quaraí** to Bella Unión, via the Barra del Cuaraim bridge. This is near the confluence of the Rios Uruguai and Quaraí. Thirty kilometres east is another crossing from **Quaraí** to **Artigas** in a cattle raising and agricultural area.

The southern interior of the state is the region of the real *gaúcho*. Principal towns of this area include **Santana do Livramento**. Its twin Uruguayan city is Rivera. All one need do is cross the main street to Rivera, but by public transport this is not a straightforward route between Brazil and Uruguay. For motorists there are three customs offices in Santana do Livramento, about 30 mins needed for formalities. There is a *Banco do Brasil* on Av Sarandí. *Val de Marne* has the best rates for Amex TCs. ■ *Bus to Porto Alegre, 2 daily, 7 hrs, US$20; 3 daily to Uruagaiana (4 hrs, US$10), services also to São Paulo and other destinations. Rodoviária is at Gen Salgado Filho e Gen Vasco Alves.*

Santana **A** *Jandaia* R Uruguai 1452, T242 2288. Recommended. **A** *Portal*, Av Tamandaré 2076, T242 3244, F242 3443. Parking, clean. Recommended. **C** *Uruguaiana*, close to bus station. **Youth hostel** **E** pp *Hotel Palace*, R Manduca Rodrigues 615, T/F242 3340. With breakfast, single rooms available, old and grimy.

The Brazilian border town is Chuí; its Uruguayan counterpart is called Chuy. The BR-471 from Porto Alegre and Pelotas skirts the town and carries straight through to Uruguay, where it becomes Ruta 9. The main street crossing west to east, Av Internacional (Av Uruguaí on the Brazilian side, Av Brasil in Uruguay) is lined with clothes and household shops in Brazil, duty free shops and a casino in Uruguay. Chuí is a tranquil town with about half a dozen hotels. São Miguel fort, built by the Portuguese in 1737, now reconstructed with period artefacts, is worth a visit. A lighthouse 10 km west marks the Barro do Chuí inlet, which has uncrowded beaches and is visited by sea lions. Brazilian immigration is about 2½ km from the border, on BR-471, road to Pelotas. All buses, except those originating in Pelotas, stop at customs on both sides of the border; if coming from Pelotas, you must ask the bus to stop for exit formalities. International buses, for example *TTL* from Porto Alegre, make the crossing straightforward: the company holds passports; hand over your visitor's card on leaving Brazil and get a Uruguayan one on entry. Have luggage available for inspection. Make sure you get your stamp, or you will have trouble leaving Brazil.

Entering Brazil From Uruguay, on the Uruguayan side, the bus will stop if asked, and wait while you get your exit stamp (with bus conductor's help); on the Brazilian side, the appropriate form is completed by the rodoviária staff when you purchase your ticket into Brazil. The bus stops at Polícia Federal (BR-471) and the conductor completes formalities while you sit on the bus. Also, if entering by car, fill up with petrol in Brazil, where fuel is cheaper.

Border with Uruguay: coastal route
Colour map 7, inset
Population: 5,167

Brazil

Sleeping **A** *Bertelli Chuí*, BR-471, Km 648, 2 km from town, T053-265 1266, F265 1207. Comfortable, with pool. **D** *Rivero*, Colômbia 163-A, T265 1271. With bath, without breakfast. **E** *San Francisco*, Av Colombia e R Chile. Shower, restaurant.

Transport **Bus**: Rodoviária on R Venezuela. Buses run from Chuí to **Pelotas** (6-7 daily, US$6.60, 4 hrs), **Rio Grande** (0700, 1400, 5 hrs, US$6.10) and **Porto Alegre** (1200, 2400, 7¾ hrs, US$13); also from Chuí to **Santa Vitória do Palmar** nearby (US$1, 35 mins), where there are a few hotels and regular bus services to the main cities eg *Embaixador* to Pelotas US$7.50, 3¾hrs.

Bahia

Salvador, the capital of Bahia, is one of Brazil's most historic cities, with a wealth of colonial architecture. The state is also dubbed 'Africa in exile': the mixture of African and European finds its most powerful expression in Carnival. The state's coast has many fine beaches, particularly in the south around Porto Seguro. Inland is the harsh sertão, traversed by the Rio São Francisco.

Background Bahia is the southernmost of the nine states of the northeastern bulge of Brazil. The other eight are Sergipe, Alagoas, Pernambuco, Paraíba, Rio Grande do Norte, Ceará, Piauí, and Maranhão. They cover 2.6 million sq km and contain a third of Brazil's people. The birth rate is the highest in Brazil, but so is the infant mortality rate. The average annual income from subsistence farming is deplorably low. Despite the misery, both regional and state loyalty remain ineradicable.

The nine states may be roughly divided into three contrasting parts. One is the sugar lands of the *Zona da Mata* along the coast between Salvador and Natal, where the rainfall can be depended upon. This was the first part of Brazil to be intensively colonized; hence the wealth of 16th century buildings and the density of old settlements. Inland from the Zona da Mata is the *Zona do Agreste*, with less rainfall, but generally enough for cattle raising. Inland again is the true interior, the *sertão*, where rainfall cannot be depended upon; there is a little agriculture where water allows it but the herding of goats, and occasionally cattle, is more important. There are few black people here; the inhabitants are mostly of Portuguese-Indian stock, making up one of the most distinctive peoples in Brazil. They are known as *sertanejos* until drought forces them to emigrate, when they become *flagelados*, the scourged ones.

When there is rain, food in the zone is plentiful and varied. But in the years of drought, when the hot dry winds from Africa scorch the earth, the effects can be tragic. Migration towards the coast and the southern towns begins, and the people are exposed to castigation of yet another sort: exploitation by grasping labour contractors. But at the first news that there is rain, the *flagelado* heads for home.

The main export crops of the northeast are sugar, cotton and cacao. Sugar and cotton have long been in decline, and now the southern states grow more than half of the Brazilian total. But cacao is grown almost entirely in southern Bahia, inland from the port of Ilhéus. Some of Brazil's main oilfields are in the State of Bahia; there are also offshore wells in the waters off Alagoas, Sergipe and Rio Grande do Norte.

Salvador

Phone code: 0xx71
Post code: 40000
Colour map 5, grid C5
Population:
3.02 million

The third largest city in Brazil it is often referred to as Bahia, rather than Salvador. It is home to a heady mix of colonial buildings, beautiful beaches, African culture and pulsating musical rhythms. It stands on the magnificent Bahia de Todos os Santos, a sparkling bay dotted with 38 islands. The bay is the largest on the Brazilian coast covering an area of 1,100 sq km. Rising above the bay on its eastern side is a cliff which dominates the landscape and, perched on top, 71 m above sea level, are the older districts with buildings dating back to the 17th and 18th centuries.

Ins & outs
For more detailed
information, see
Transport, page 476

Getting there Luis Eduardo Magalhães **Airport** is 32 km from city centre. The **Rodoviária** is 5 km from the city with regular bus services to the centre and Campo Grande; the journey can take up to 1 hr especially at peak periods.

Getting around The broad peninsula on which the city of Salvador is built is at the mouth of the Bahia de Todos Os Santos. On the opposite side of the bay's entrance is the Ilha de Itaparica. The commercial district of the city and its port are on the sheltered, western side of the peninsula; residential districts and beaches are on the open Atlantic side. The point of the peninsula is called Barra, which is itself an important area. The centre of the city is divided into 2 levels, the Upper City (or Cidade Alta) where the Historical Centre lies, and the Lower City (Cidade Baixa) which is the commercial and docks district. The 2 levels are connected by a series of steep hills called *ladeiras*. The easiest way to go from one level to the other is by the *Lacerda* lift which connects Praça Cairu and the famous Mercado Modelo. There is also the Plano Inclinado Gonçalves, a funicular railway which leaves from behind the Cathedral going down to Comércio, the commercial district. Most visitors limit themselves to the Pelourinho and historical centre, Barra, the Atlantic suburbs and the Itapagipe peninsula, which is north of the centre. The roads and avenues between these areas are straightforward to follow and are well-served by public transport. Other parts of the city are not as easy to get around, but have less of a tourist interest. If going to these areas a taxi may be advisable until you know your way around.

Climate Temperatures range from 25°C to 32°C, never falling below 19°C in winter. Humidity can be high, which may make the heat oppressive. It rains somewhat all the year but the main rainy season is between May and Sep. Nevertheless, the sun is never far away.

Tourist offices Bahiatursa, R das Laranjeiras 12, Historical Centre, T321 2133, open daily 0830-2200, English and German spoken. Rodoviária, T4503871, good, English spoken; airport, T2041244, open daily 0800-2245, friendly; in the Mercado Modelo, T2410242, Mon-Sat 0900-1800; Sac Shopping Centre, Av Centenario 2992, T2644566. Useful information (often only available in Portuguese) includes *BahiaCultural*, the month's programme of events with maps of themed points of interest. *Bahiatursa* has lists of hotels and accommodation in private homes. Map, US$1.20, not all streets marked; also a free map, clear map of the historic centre. Offices have noticeboards for messages. The offices also have details of travel throughout the State of Bahia. T131-06000030 for tourist information in English. **Emtursa**, at airport, T377 2262, Mon-Sat 0800-2200, is helpful and has good maps. www.emtursa.com.br **Maps:** from **Departamento de Geografia e Estadística**, Av Estados Unidos (opposite Banco do Brasil, Lower City): also from news stands including the airport bookshop, US$1.50. See also www.uol.com.br/agendasalvador, for what's on.

Security Be very careful of your money and valuables at all times and in all districts. Avoid the more distant beaches out of season, when they are empty (eg Itapoã, Piatã, Placafor); on Sun they are more crowded and safer. There have been reports of armed muggings on the sand dunes surrounding Lagoa do Abaeté. Do not visit them alone. At night, the areas around and in the lifts and buses are unsafe. Leave valuables securely in your hotel, particularly at night (including wristwatch and cameras if possible: disposable cameras are widely available). Carry a small amount of money that you can hand over if you are threatened. Do not walk down any of the links between the old and new city, especially the Ladeira de Misericôrdia, which links the Belvedere, near the Lacerda Lifts, with the lower city. Should a local join you at your table for a chat, leave at once if drugs are mentioned. The civil police are reported to be very sympathetic and helpful and more resources have been put into policing the old part of the city and Barra, which are now well-lit at night. Police are little in evidence after 2300, however.

History On 1 November 1501, All Saints' Day, the navigator Amérigo Vespucci sailed into the bay. As the first European to see it, he named it after the day of his arrival. The first Governor General, Tomé de Sousa, arrived on 23 March 1549 to build a fortified city to protect Portugal's interest from constant threats of Dutch and French invasion. Salvador was formally founded on 1 November 1549 and remained the capital of Brazil until 1763. By the 18th century, it was the most important city in the Portuguese Empire after Lisbon, ideally situated in a safe, sheltered harbour along the trade routes of the 'New World'.

The city's first wealth came from the cultivation of sugar cane and tobacco, the plantations' workforce coming from the West coast of Africa. For three centuries Salvador was the site of a thriving slave trade. Even today, Salvador is described as the most African city in the Western Hemisphere and the University of Bahia boasts the only chair in the Yoruba language in the Americas. The influence permeates the city: food sold on the street is the same as in Senegal and Nigeria, Bahian music is fused with pulsating African polyrhythms, men and women nonchalantly carry enormous loads on their heads, fishermen paddle dug-out canoes in the bay, the pace of life is a little slower than elsewhere. The pulse of the city is *candomblé*, an Afro-Brazilian religion in which the African deities of Nature, the Goddess of the sea and the God of creation are worshipped. These deities (or *orixás*) are worshipped in temples (*terreiros*) which can be elaborate, decorated halls, or simply someone's front room with tiny altars to the *orixá*. *Candomblé* ceremonies may be seen by tourists – but not photographed – on Sunday and religious holidays. Contact the tourist office, *Bahiatursa*, or see their twice monthly calendar of events. Salvador today is a city of 15 forts, 166 Catholic churches, 1,000 *candomblé* temples and a fascinating mixture of old and modern, rich and poor, African and European, religious and profane. It is still a major port exporting tropical fruit, cocoa, sisal, soya beans and petrochemical products. Its most important industry, though, is tourism. Local government has done much to improve the fortunes of this once rundown, poor and dirty city and most visitors feel that the richness of its culture is compensation enough for any problems they may encounter.

Culture The Bahianas – black women who dress in traditional 18th century costumes – are street vendors who sit behind their trays of delicacies, savoury and seasoned, made from the great variety of local fish, vegetables and fruits. Their street food is one of the musts for visitors.

Salvador orientation

Related map
A Centro
Histórico,
page 465

Capoeira, a sport developed from the traditional foot-fighting technique introduced from Angola by African slaves. The music is by drum, tambourine and *berimbau*; there are several different kinds of the sport. If you want to attempt Capoeira, the best school is *Mestre Bimba*, R das Laranjeiras, T322 0639, open 0900-1200, 1500-2100, basic course US$25 for 20 hours. Other schools are *Filhos de Bimba*, R Durval Fraga, 6, Nordeste, T345 7329 and *Escola de Mestre Pastinha*, R Castro Rabelo, T321 6251. Classes on Monday, Wednesday and Friday 1900-2100, Saturday-Sunday 1500-1700 (if you want to get the most out of it, knowledge of Portuguese is essential). There are two more schools in Forte de Santo Antônio behind Pelourinho, but check addresses at the tourist office. Exhibitions take place in the Largo do Pelourinho, very picturesque, in the upper city. ■ *US$2*. You can also see the experts outside the Mercado Modelo on most days, around 1100-1300, and at Campo Grande and Forte de Santo Antônio on Sunday afternoons; they often expect a contribution. Negotiate a price before taking pictures or demands may be exorbitant. At the Casa da Cultura at Forte de Santo Antônio there is also free live music on Saturday night.

Every Tuesday night *Banda Olodum*, a drumming troupe made famous by their innovative powerhouse percussion and involvement with Paul Simon, Michael Jackson and Branford Marsalis, rehearse in the Largo Teresa Batista ■ *starts 1930, US$10* in front of packed crowds. They also rehearse free of charge in the Largo do Pelourinho on Sunday; T321 5010.

Music in Bahia

Brazil

Established in Liberdade, the largest suburb of the city, *Ilê Aiyê* is a thriving cultural group dedicated to preserving African traditions which under the guidance of its president Vovô is deeply committed to the fight against racism. Rehearsals take place mid week at Boca do Rio and on Saturday nights in front of their headquarters at Ladeira do Curuzu in Liberdade.

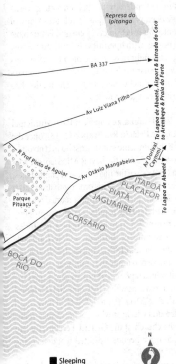

Araketu hails from the sprawling Periperi suburb in the Lower City. Once a purely percussion band *Araketu* has travelled widely and borrowed on various musical forms (samba, candomblé, soukous etc) to become a major carnival attraction and one of the most successful bands in Bahia. Rehearsals take place on Wednesday nights on Avenida Contorno.■ *As these get very full, buy tickets in advance from Av Oceânica 683, Barra Centro Comercial, Sal 06, T247 6784.*

Neguinho do Samba was the musical director of *Olodum* until he founded *Didá*, an all-woman drumming group based along similar lines to *Olodum*. They rehearse on Friday nights in the Praça Teresa Batista, Pelourinho. ■ *Starts 2000, US$10.*

Filhos de Gandhi, the original African drumming group and the largest, was formed by striking stevedores during the 1949 carnival. The hypnotic shuffling cadence of *Filhos de Gandhi*'s *afoxé* rhythm is one of the most emotive of Bahia's carnival.

■ **Sleeping**
1 Bahía Othon Palace

N
Not to scale

Carlinhos Brown is a local hero. He has become one of the most influential musical composers in Brazil today, mixing great lyrics, innovative rhythms and a powerful stage presence. He played percussion with many Bahian musicians, until he formed his own percussion group, *Timbalada*. He has invested heavily in his native Candeal neighbourhood: the Candy All Square, a centre for popular culture, is where the *Timbalada* rehearsals take place every Sunday night. ■ *1830, US$10 from Sep to Mar. Not to be missed.* During the winter (July-September) ring the *blocos* to confirm that free rehearsals will take place.

Artistes and bands using electronic instruments and who tend to play in the *trios eléctricos* draw heavily on the rich rhythms of the drumming groups creating a new musical genre known as *Axé*. The most popular of such acts is Daniela Mercury, following the steps to international stardom of Caetano Veloso, Maria Bethânia, João Gilberto, Gilberto Gil. Other newer, interesting acts are Margareth Menezes who has travelled extensively with David Byrne. Gerónimo was one of the first singer/songwriters to use the wealth of rhythms of the Candomblé in his music and his song 'E d'Oxum' is something of an anthem for the city. All the above have albums released and you can find their records easily in most record stores. See Shopping in the Pelourinho. Also try *Billbox* in Shopping Barra on the third floor.

Sights

Centro Histórico
There is much more of interest in the Upper than in the Lower City. From Praça Municipal to the Carmo area 2 km north along the cliff is the Centro Histórico (Historical Centre), now a national monument and also protected by UNESCO. It was in this area that the Portuguese built their fortified city and where today stand some of the most important examples of colonial architecture in the Americas. This area is undergoing a massive restoration programme funded by the Bahian state government and UNESCO. Colonial houses have been painted in pastel colours. Many of the bars have live music which spills out onto the street on every corner. Patios have been created in the open areas behind the houses with open air cafés and bars. Artist ateliers, antique and handicraft stores have brought new artistic blood to what was once the bohemian part of the city. Many popular traditional restaurants and bars from other parts of Salvador have opened new branches here. Its transformation has also attracted many tourist shops and the area can get crowded.

Praça Municipal, Praça de Sé & Terreiro de Jesus
Dominating the Praça Municipal is the old Casa de Câmara e Cadeia or **Paço Municipal** (Council Chamber – 1660), while alongside is the **Palácio Rio Branco** (1918), once the Governor's Palace now the headquarters of Bahiatursa, the state tourist board (no office open to the public). Leaving it with its panoramic view of the bay, R Misericórdia goes north passing the **Santa Casa Misericórdia** (1695 – see the high altar and painted tiles, open by arrangement 0800-1700, T322 7666) to Praça da Sé. This praça with its mimosa and flamboyant trees leads into Terreiro de Jesus, a picturesque praça named after the church which dominates it. Built in 1692, the **church of the Jesuits** became the property of the Holy See in 1759 when the Jesuits were expelled from all Portuguese territories. The façade is one of the earliest examples of baroque in Brazil, an architectural style which was to dominate the churches built in the 17th and 18th centuries. Inside, the vast vaulted ceiling and 12 side altars in baroque and rococo frame the main altar completely leafed in gold. The tiles in blue, white and yellow in a tapestry pattern are also from Portugal. It houses the tomb of Mem de Sá. The church is now the city Cathedral (**Catedral Basílica**); parts are currently being renovated. ■ *0900-1100, 1400-1700.* On the eastern side of the square is the church of **São Pedro dos Clérigos** which is beautifully renovated, while close by, on the south-side, is the church of the **Ordem Terceira de São Domingos** (Dominican Third Order), which has a beautiful painted wooden ceiling and fine tiles. ■ *Mon-Fri 0800-1200, 1400-1700, US$0.25.*

Facing Terreiro de Jesus is Praça Anchieta and the church of **São Francisco**. Its simple façade belies the treasure inside. The entrance leads to a sanctuary with a spectacular painting on the wooden ceiling, by local artist José Joaquim da Rocha (1777). The main body of the church is the most exuberant example of baroque in the country. The cedar wood carving and later gold leaf was completed after 28 years in 1748. The cloisters of the monastery are surrounded by a series of blue and white tiles from Portugal. ■ *0830-1700, entry to cloisters US$0.20, church free.* Next door is the church of the **Ordem Terceira de São Francisco** (Franciscan Third Order – 1703) with its façade intricately carved in sandstone. Inside is a quite remarkable Chapter House with striking images of the Order's most celebrated saints. ■ *0800-1200, 1300-1700, US$0.20.*

Leading off the Terreiro de Jesus is R Alfredo Brito, a charming, narrow cobbled street lined with fine colonial houses painted in different pastel shades. This street leads into the Largo do Pelourinho (Praça José Alencar), which was completely renovated in 1993. Considered the finest complex of colonial architecture in Latin America, it was once the site of a pillory where slaves were publicly punished and ridiculed. It was also the site of the slave market. After the cleaning of the area, new galleries, boutiques and restaurants are opening, and at night the Largo is lively, especially on Tuesday (see Nightlife below). **Nosso Senhor Do Rosário Dos Pretos** church, the so-called Slave Church, dominates the square. It was built by former slaves over a period of 100 years. The side altars honour black saints. The painted ceiling is very impressive, the overall effect being one of tranquillity in contrast to the complexity of the Cathedral and São Francisco. ■ *Small entry fee.*

Largo do Pelourinho

Brazil

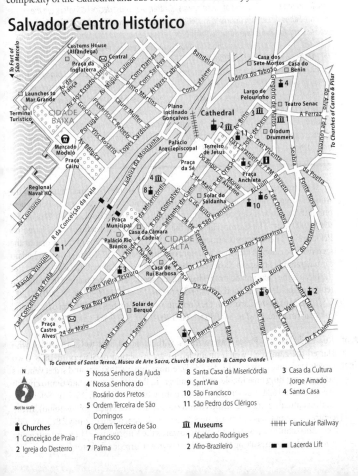

Salvador Centro Histórico

To Convent of Santa Teresa, Museu de Arte Sacra, Church of São Bento & Campo Grande

N

Not to scale

✚ **Churches**
1 Conceição de Praia
2 Igreja do Desterro
3 Nossa Senhora da Ajuda
4 Nossa Senhora do Rosário dos Pretos
5 Ordem Terceira de São Domingos
6 Ordem Terceira de São Francisco
7 Palma
8 Santa Casa da Misericórdia
9 Sant'Ana
10 São Francisco
11 São Pedro dos Clérigos

🏛 **Museums**
1 Abelardo Rodrigues
2 Afro-Brazileiro
3 Casa da Cultura Jorge Amado
4 Santa Casa

╫╫╫╫ Funicular Railway

■ ■ Lacerda Lift

Brazil

☞ **Carnival in Bahia**

Carnival officially starts on Thursday night at 2000 when the keys of the city are given to the Carnival King 'Rei Momo'. The unofficial opening though is on Wednesday with the Lavagem do Porto da Barra, when throngs of people dance on the beach. Later on in the evening is the Baile dos Atrizes, starting at around 2300 and going on until dawn, very bohemian, good fun. Check with Bahiatursa for details on venue, time etc (see under Rio for carnival dates).

Carnival in Bahia is the largest in the world and it encourages active participation. It is said that there are 1½ million people dancing on the streets at any one time.

There are two distinct musical formats. The **Afro Blocos** are large drum-based troupes (some with up to 200 drummers) who play on the streets accompanied by singers atop mobile sound trucks. The first of these groups was the Filhos de Gandhi (founded in 1949), whose participation is one of the highlights of Carnival. Their 6,000 members dance through the streets on the Sunday and Tuesday of Carnival dressed in their traditional costumes, a river of white and blue in an ocean of multicoloured carnival revellers. The best known of the recent **Afro Blocos** are Ilê Aiye, Olodum, Muzenza and Malê Debalê. They all operate throughout the year in cultural, social and political areas. Not all of them are

receptive to foreigners among their numbers for Carnival. The basis of the rhythm is the enormous surdo (deaf) drum with its bumbum bumbum bum anchorbeat, while the smaller repique, played with light twigs, provides a crack-like overlay. Ilê Aiye take to the streets around 2100 on Saturday night and their departure from their headquarters at Ladeira do Curuzu in the Liberdade district is not to be missed. The best way to get there is to take a taxi to Curuzu via Largo do Tanque thereby avoiding traffic jams. The ride is a little longer in distance but much quicker in time. A good landmark is the Paes Mendonça supermarket on the corner of the street from where the bloco leaves. From there it's a short walk to the departure point.

The enormous **trios eléctricos** 12 m sound trucks, with powerful sound systems that defy most decibel counters, are the second format. These trucks, each with its own band of up to 10 musicians, play songs influenced by the **afro blocos** and move at a snail's pace through the streets, drawing huge crowds. Each **Afro Bloco** and **bloco de trio** has its own costume and its own security personnel who cordon off the area around the sound truck. The **bloco** members can thus dance in comfort and safety.

The traditional Carnival route is from Campo Grande (by the Tropical Hotel da

At the corner of Alfredo Brito and Largo do Pelourinho is a small museum to the work of Jorge Amado, **Casa da Cultura Jorge Amado**. Information is in Portuguese only, but the café walls are covered with colourful copies of his book jackets. ■ *Mon-Sat 0900-1900, free.* The Carmo Hill is at the top of the street leading out of Largo do Pelourinho. The **Carmo** (Carmelite Third Order) church (1709) houses one of the sacred art treasures of the city, a sculpture of Christ made in 1730 by a slave who had no formal training, Francisco Xavier das Chagas, known as O Cabra. One of the features of the piece is the blood made from whale oil, ox blood, banana resin and 2,000 rubies to represent the drops of blood. ■ *Mon-Sat 0800-1130 and 1400-1730, Sun 1000-1200, US$0.30.* **Museu do Carmo**, in the Convento do Carmo, has a collection of icons and colonial furniture. ■ *Mon-Sat 0800-1200, 1400-1800, Sun 0800-1200, US$0.10.*

South of the Praça Municipal   Rua Chile leads to **Praça Castro Alves**, with its monument to Castro Alves, who started the campaign which finally led to the Abolition of Slavery in 1888. Two streets lead out of this square, Av 7 de Setembro, busy with shops and street vendors selling everything imaginable, and, parallel to it, R Carlos Gomes. **São Bento** church (rebuilt after 1624, but with fine 17th century furniture) is on Av 7 de Setembro. Both eventually come to **Campo Grande** (also known as Praça Dois de Julho). In the centre of the praça is the monument to Bahian Independence, 2 July 1823. Av 7 de Setembro continues out of the square towards the Vitória area. There are some fine 19th century homes along this stretch, known as Corredor da Vitória.

Bahia) to Praça Castro Alves near the old town. The **blocos** go along Avenue 7 de Setembro and return to Campo Grande via the parallel R Carlos Gomes. Many of the trios no longer go through the Praça Castro Alves, once the epicentre of Carnival. The best night at Praça Castro Alves is Tuesday (the last night of Carnival) when the famous 'Encontro dos trios' (Meeting of the Trios) takes place. Trios jostle for position in the square and play in rotation until dawn (or later!) on Ash Wednesday. It is not uncommon for major stars from the Bahian (and Brazilian) music world to make surprise appearances.

There are grandstand seats at Campo Grande throughout the event. Day tickets for these are available the week leading up to Carnival. Check with Bahiatursa for information on where the tickets are sold. **Tickets** are US$10 (or up to US$30 on the black market on the day). The blocos are judged as they pass the grandstand and are at their most frenetic at this point. There is little or no shade from the sun so bring a hat and lots of water. Best days are Sunday to Tuesday. For those wishing to go it alone, just find a friendly barraca in the shade and watch the blocos go by. Avoid the Largo da Piedade and Relogio de São Pedro on Avenue 7 de Setembro: the street narrows here, creating human traffic jams.

The other major centre for Carnival is Barra to Ondina. The **blocos alternativos** ply this route. These are nearly always **trios eléctricos** connected with the more traditional blocos who have expanded to this now very popular district. Not to be missed here is Timbalada (see **Music** in Bahia).

Recommended Blocos Traditional Route (Campo Grande): Mel, T245 4333, Sunday, Monday, Tuesday; Cameleão, T336 6100 (www.cameleao.com.br), Sunday, Monday, Tuesday; Pinel, T336 0489, Sunday, Monday, Tuesday; Internacionais, T245 0800, Sunday, Monday, Tuesday; Cheiro de Amor, T336 6060, Sunday, Monday, Tuesday. **Afro Blocos** Araketu: T237 0151, Sunday, Monday, Tuesday; Ilê Aiye, T388 4969, Saturday, Monday; Olodum, T321 5010, Friday, Sunday. **Blocos Alternativos** Timbalada, T245 6999, Thursday, Friday, Saturday; Nana Banana, T245 1000, Friday, Saturday; Melomania, T245 4570, Friday, Saturday.

Prices range from US$180 to US$450 (including costume). The quality of the **bloco** often depends on the act that plays on the **trio**. A related website is www.meucarnaval.com.br

---

Barra

From Praça Vitória, the avenue continues down Ladeira da Barra (Barra Hill) to Porto da Barra. The best city beaches are in this area. Also in this district are the best bars, restaurants and nightlife. The Barra section of town has received a major facelift with the installation of a new lighting system. The pavements fill with people day and night and many sidewalk restaurants and bars are open along the strip from Porto da Barra as far as the Cristo at the end of the Farol da Barra beach. Great attention to security is now given. A little further along is the **Forte de Santo Antônio da Barra** and **lighthouse**, 1580, built on the spot where Amérigo Vespucci landed in 1501. It is right at the mouth of the bay where Bahia de Todos Os Santos and the South Atlantic Ocean meet and is the site of the first lighthouse built in the Americas. The interesting **Museu Hidrográfico** is housed in the upper section of the Forte de Santo Antônio, fine views of the bay and coast, recommended. ■ *Tue-Sat 1300-1800, US$1. It has a good café for watching the sunset.*

Atlantic beach suburbs

The promenade leading away from the fort and its famous lighthouse is called Av Oceânica, which follows the coast to the beach suburbs of Ondina, Amaralina and Pituba. The road is also called Av Presidente Vargas, but the numbering is different. Beyond Pituba are the **best ocean beaches** at Jaguaripe, Piatã and Itapoã En route the bus passes small fishing colonies at Amaralina and Pituba where *jangadas* can be seen. A *jangada* is a small raft peculiar to the northeastern region of Brazil used extensively as well as dug-out canoes. Near Itapoã is the **Lagoa do Abaeté**, surrounded by brilliant, white sands. This is a deep, freshwater lake where local women traditionally come to wash their clothes and then lay them out to dry in the sun. The road leading up from the lake offers a panoramic view of the city in the distance, the coast, and the contrast of the white sands and fresh water less than 1 km from the sea and its golden beaches. **NB** See Security, below. Near the lighthouse at **Itapoã** there are two campsites on the beach. A little beyond the campsites are the magnificent ocean beaches of Stella Maris and Flamengo, both quiet during the week but very busy at the weekends. Beware of strong undertow at these beaches.

Bonfim & See also the famous church of **Nosso Senhor do Bonfim** on the Itapagipe peninsula
Itapagipe in the suburbs north of the centre, whose construction began in 1745. It draws endless supplicants (particularly on Friday and Sunday) offering favours to the image of the Crucified Lord set over the high altar; the number and variety of ex-voto offerings is extraordinary. The processions over the water to the church on the third Sunday in January are particularly interesting. Also on the Itapagipe peninsula is a colonial fort on **Monte Serrat** point, and at Ribeira the church of **Nossa Senhora da Penha** (1743). The beach here has many restaurants, but the sea is polluted (bus from Praça da Sé or Av França).

Museums The **Museu de Arte Moderna**, converted from an old sugar estate house and out-
Many guides offer buildings off Av Contorno, is only open for special exhibitions. The good restaurant
their services in (*Solar do Unhão*) is still there, and the buildings are worth seeing for themselves
museums, but their (take a taxi there as access is dangerous). ■ *Tue-Fri 1300-2100, Sat 1500-2100 and*
English is poor and *Sun 1400-1900, T329 0660.* **Museu de Arte Sacra** is in the 17th century monastery
their expectations and church of Santa Teresa, at the bottom of the steep Ladeira de Santa Teresa, at R
of a tip high do Sodré 276 (off R Carlos Gomes). Many of the 400 carvings are from Europe, but a number are local. Among the reliquaries of silver and gold is one of gilded wood by Aleijadinho (see page 417). ■ *Mon-Fri 1130-1730, US$1.50.* **Museu Abelardo Rodrigues**, Solar Ferrão, Pelourinho (R Gregório de Mattos 45), is a religious art museum, with objects from the 17th, 18th and 19th centuries, mainly from Bahia, Pernambuco and Maranhão. ■ *1300-1900 except Mon, US$0.40.*

Museu Afro-Brasileiro, in the former Faculty of Medicine building, Terreiro de Jesus, compares African and Bahian Orixás (deities) celebrations, beautiful murals and carvings, all in Portuguese. ■ *Mon-Fri 0900-1700, US$1.* **Museu Arqueológico e Etnográfico**, in the basement of the same building, houses archaeological discoveries from Bahia (stone tools, clay urns etc), an exhibition on Indians from the Alto Rio Xingu area (artefacts, tools, photos), recommended. There is a museum of medicine in the same complex. ■ *Mon-Fri 0900-1700, US$0.40.* **Casa do Benin**, below NS do Rosario dos Pretos, shows African crafts, photos, a video show on Benin and Angola. ■ *Mon-Fri 1000-1800.* **Museu da Cidade**, Largo do Pelourinho, has exhibitions of arts and crafts and old photographs. From the higher floors of the museum you can get a good view of the Pelourinho. ■ *Weekdays except Tue 0930-1800, Sat 1300-1700, Sun 0930-1300, free.* **Museu Costa Pinto**, Av 7 de Setembro 2490, is a modern house with collections of crystal, porcelain, silver, furniture etc. It also has the only collection of *balangandãs* (slave charms and jewellery), highly recommended. ■ *Weekdays 1430-1900, but closed Tue, Sat-Sun 1500-1800, US$2.* **Museu de Arte da Bahia**, Av 7 de Setembro 2340, Vitória, has interesting paintings of Brazilian artists from the 18th to the early 20th century. ■ *Tue-Fri 1400-1900, Sat-Sun 1430-1900, US$1.20.*

36 km from the city is the **Museu do Recôncavo** (Museu do Vanderlei do Pinho) in the old Freguesia mill – 1552, in which one can find artefacts and pictures of three centuries of the economic and social life of this region. The Casa Grande e Senzala (the home of the landowner and the combined dwelling and working area of the slaves) is still intact. It is a peaceful way to spend an afternoon, but difficult to get to by public transport; the museum is near the town of São Francisco do Conde, 7 km from the main highway. ■ *Tue, Thu and Sun 0900-1700.*

Brazil

Essentials

City centre B *Palace*, R Chile 20, T322 1155, palace@e-net.com.br Traditional, a little past its best, good breakfast. **C** *Imperial*, Av 7 de Setembro 751, Rosário, T/F329 3127. A/c, helpful, breakfast. Recommended. **C** *Pousada da Praça*, Rui Barbosa, 5, T321 0642, gifc@zaz.com.br Simple, pretty old colonial house, quiet, secure, big breakfast, rooms with and without bath. Recommended. **D** *Internacional*, R Sen Costa Pinto 88, T321 3514. Convenient, good value. **D** *Paris*, R Rui Barbosa 13, T321 3922. A/c rooms more expensive, shared showers, breakfast, restaurant in same building. Recommended. **D** *São Bento*, Largo de São Bento 3, T243 7511. Good cheap restaurant. Cheaper hotels on Av 7 de Setembro: **E** *São José*, No 847. Safe. Recommended. **F** pp *Pousada*, No 2349. Warmly recommended. Near the Praça da Sé the following have been recommended: **C** *Pelourinho*, R Alfredo Brito 20, T243 2324. Run down but charismatic. **D** *Solara*, R José Alencar 25, Largo do Pelourinho, T326 4583. With shower, breakfast, laundry facilities. **D** *Themis*, Praça da Sé 398, Edif Themis, 7th floor, T329 6955. Fan, wonderful views over bay and old city. Recommended restaurant with French chef. **E** *Ilhéus*, Ladeira da Praça 4, 1st floor, T322 7240. Breakfast.

This includes the old city of Pelhouring and the main shopping area

A 10% service charge is often added to the bill. Check which credit cards are accepted. All luxury hotels have swimming pools

Santo Antônio A *Pousada Redfish*, R Direita do Santo Antônio, T/F243 8473, www.hotelredfish.com Incredibly stylish, modern design. English-owned, some rooms with terraces and open-air showers, very special. **B** *Pousada das Flores*, R Direita de Santo Antônio 442, near Santo Antônio fort, T/F243 1836. Brazilian/French owners, excellent breakfast, beautiful old house. **B** *Pousada do Boqueirão*, R Direita do Santo Antônio 48, T241 2262, www.pousadaboqueirao.com.br Family-run, beautiful house overlooking the bay, relaxed atmosphere, most European languages spoken, great food. **B** *Pousada Villa Carmo*, R do Carmo 58, T/F241 3924. Italian/Brazilian owned, many European languages spoken, very comfortable, rooms with fan or a/c. **B-C** *Pousada Baluarte*, R Baluarte, 13, T327 0367. Bohemian household, lovely owners, 5 rooms, cheaper without bath. **D** *Pensão Von Sandt Platz*, R Direita de Santônio 351, T/F326 6551. Relaxing family house of Nazaré Schubeler, sumptuous breakfasts, legendary caipirinhas, email and fax facilities, laundry, "prepare to be mothered".

This quiet district just 5 mins walk NE of Pelourinho has attracted Europeans who have set up pousadas in beautifully restored buildings. Without exception, they are imaginatively designed and full of character; all are recommended. This is now undoubtedly the ideal, if not the cheapest, area to stay

Campo Grande/Vitória L *Tropical Hotel da Bahia*, Praça 2 de Julho 2, Campo Grande, T255 2000, F336 9725. Well-run, owned by *Varig*, convenient for city centre, very much a business hotel. **A** *Bahia do Sol*, Av 7 de Setembro 2009, T338 8800, F336 7776. Comfortable, safe and frigobar in room, family run, good breakfast and restaurant, bureau de change. Highly recommended (no pool). **D** *Caramuru*, Av 7 de Setembro 2125, Vitória, T336 9951. Cosy, with lounge and terrace, safe parking. Recommended.

Upmarket residential area, between Barra and city centre, convenient for museums

Barra All recommended: On Av 7 de Setembro: **B** *Barra Turismo*, No 3691, Porto da Barra, T245 7433. Breakfast, a/c, fridge, on beach. **C-E** *Pousada Santa Maria*, No 3835, T264 4076, pousadasmaria@hotmail.com Excellent breakfast, English and German spoken, TV, laundry service, internet, restaurant/bar, exchange, car rental. **C** *Pousada Ambar*, R Afonso Celso 485, T264 6956, www.ambarpousada.com.br Good service, nicely decorated, excellent breakfast, convenient, run by Paulo and Christine (French, also speaks English). **C** *Pousada Malu*, No 3801, T264 4461. Small and homely, with breakfast, cooking facilities and laundry service. **C** *Villa Romana*, R Lemos Brito 14, T336 6522, F247 6748. Good location, pool, a/c. **C** *Enseada Praia da Barra*, R Barão de Itapoã 60, Porto da Barra, T235 9213. Breakfast, safe, money exchanged, accepts credit cards, laundry bills high, otherwise good value, near beach. **D** *Bella Barra*, R Afonso Celso 439, T237 8401, F235 4131. A/c. **E** Rooms to let in private apartments: *Carmen Simões*, R 8 de Dezembro 326. Safe, helpful. *Gorett*, R 8 de Dezembro 522, Apt 002, Edif Ricardo das Neves, Graça, T264 3584/3016, gorettmagalhaes@hotmail.com Convenient, use of kitchen, patio, internet, safe.

Barra has fallen a little from favour in recent years, so unless you are desperate to be by the beach, stay in Pelhourino to enjoy its unique nightlife and travel here by bus during the day. Taxis are recommended after dark. Care should be taken on Sun when the beaches are extremely busy

Brazil

This modern suburban area runs along the coast from Ondina to Itapoã for 20 km towards the airport. The best beaches are after Pituba. All hotels recommended

Atlantic Suburbs **LL** *Bahia Othon Palace*, Av Presidente Vargas, 2456, Ondina, T203 2000, T0800 7010098, F2454877, www.hoteis-othon.com.br **A** *Catharina Paraguaçu*, R João Gomes 128, Rio Vermelho, T247 1488. Charming, small, colonial-style, tastefully decorated. **A** *Ondina Plaza*, Av Pres Vargas 3033, Ondina, T245 8158, F247 7266. A/c, pool, good value, on beach. **C** *Mar*, R da Paciência 106, Rio Vermelho, T331 2044, F245 4440. Good nightlife in the area. In **Patamares**, 17 km from the city: **A** *Sol Bahia Atlântico*, R Manoel Antônio Galvão 100, T370 9000, F370 9001, near one of the best beaches in Salvador, set high on the hill with great views of the coastline.

In **Itapoã**: **L** *Catussaba*, R Alameida da Praia, Itapoã, T374 0555, www.catussaba.com.br Elegant, colonial-style interior, beautiful gardens leading to beach, but beware of ocean currents when swimming, convenient for airport. **A** *Villa do Farol*, Praia do Pedra do Sol, T374 2618, F374 0006. Small Swiss-run *pousada*, pool, homely, great restaurant, 1 block from beach. First class. **B** *Grão de Areia*, R Arnaldo Santana 7, Piatã, T375 4818. A/c, pool, near good beach. **D** *Pousada Glória*, R do Retiro 46, T/F375 1503. No breakfast, near beach.

Self-contained apartments with fully equipped kitchen and a/c, with all the facilities of hotels, rented by the day. Standards are generally high

Apart hotels **L** *Ondina Apart Hotel*, Av Oceânica 2400, Ondina, T203 8000. Five-star, self-contained apartments, on beach. Highly recommended. In **A** range: *Bahia Flat*, Av Oceânica 235, Barra, T3394140, dflat@terra.com.br English spoken. On beach, pool, sauna. *Flat Jardim de Alá*, Av Otávio Mangabeira 3471, Armação, T343 6014, beautiful location by beach. Pool, sauna. Recommended. *Porto Farol*, R Milton de Oliveira 134, Barra, T247 5566, F247 6555. Recommended. *Pituba Apart Hotel*, R Paraíba 250, Pituba, T240 7077, F345 8111. Pool, sauna. Recommended. *Lucia Arleo*, R Miguel Bournier 59, Apto 203, T237 2424. Specially furnished apartments near the beach. Recommended.

Youth hostels Albergues de Juventude, **D**-**E** pp including breakfast, but sometimes cheaper if you have a IYHA membership card. Prices are higher and hostels very full at carnival. **Pelourinho**: *Albergue das Laranjeiras*, R Inácio Accioli 13, T/F321 1366, www.alaranj.com.br In a beautiful colonial building in the heart of the historical district, can be noisy, café downstairs, English spoken. Good for meeting other travellers. Warmly recommended. *Albergue Solar*, R Ribeiro dos Santos 45-47, T/F241 0055. *Albergue do Peló*, same street No 5, T/F242 8061. IYHA, laundry facilities. *Albergue do Passo*, No 3, T326 1951, F351 3285. Safe, group rates available, English, French and Spanish spoken. Highly recommended. *Pousada Gloju*, R das Laranjeiras 34, T321 8249. No breakfast but stunning views of Pelourinho, en suite bathrooms, warm showers. *Vagaus*, R Alfredo Brito 25, Pelourinho, T321 6398, vagaus@elitenet.com.br Independent youth hostel, all rooms collective with breakfast, internet access available. Recommended. **Carmo**: *Albergue do Carmo*, R do Carmo 06, www.albergue@bol.com.br Dormitories, safe, sea view, good staff, computers with free internet access. Recommended.

On the beaches: *Albergue do Porto*, R Barão de Sergy 197, T264 6600, albergue@e-net.com.br One block from beach, short bus ride or 20 minutes on foot from historical centre. IYHA hostel in beautiful turn-of-the-century house, breakfast, convenient, English spoken, double room with a/c and bath available, kitchen, laundry facilities, safe, TV lounge, games room, internet, courtyard. Highly recommended. *Casa Grande*, R Minas Gerais, 122, Pituba, T248 0527, F240 0074. IYHA, laundry and cooking facilities. *Pousada Azul*, R Praguer Fróis 97, Barra, T264 9798, pousada@provider.com.br Youth hostel-style, near beach, airport transfers. *Pousada Marcos*, Av Oceânica 281, T235 5117. Youth hostel-style, great location near the lighthouse, very busy, notices in Hebrew for potential travelling companions, efficient.

Pensionatos are places to stay in shared rooms (up to 4 per room); part or full board available. Houses or rooms can be rented for US$5-35 a day from *Pierre Marbacher*, R Carlos Coqueijo 68A, Itapoã, T249 5754 (Caixa Postal 7458, 41600 Salvador), he is Swiss, owns a beach bar at Rua K and speaks English. At Carnival it's a good idea to rent a flat; the tourist office has a list of estate agents (eg *José Mendez*, T237 1394/6). They can also arrange rooms in private houses; however, caution is advised as not all householders are honest.

Camping *Camping Clube do Brasil*, R Visconde do Rosario 409, Rosario, T242 0482. *Ecológica*, R Alameida da Praia, near the lighthouse at Itapoã, take bus from Praça da Sé direct to Itapoã, or to Campo Grande or Barra, change there for Itapoã, about 1 hr, then 30 mins walk, T3743506. Bar, restaurant, hot showers. Highly recommended.

Sea bathing is dangerous off shore near the campsites

Local specialities The main dish is *moqueca*, seafood cooked in a sauce made from coconut milk, tomatoes, red and green peppers, fresh coriander and *dendê* (palm oil). It is traditionally cooked in a wok-like earthenware dish and served piping hot at the table. Served with *moqueca* is *farofa* (manioc flour) and a hot pepper sauce which you add at your discretion, it's usually extremely hot so try a few drops before venturing further. The *dendê* is somewhat heavy and those with delicate stomachs are advised to try the *ensopado*, a sauce with the same ingredients as the *moqueca*, but without the palm oil.

Eating

Nearly every street corner has a Bahiana selling a wide variety of local snacks, the most famous of which is the *acarajé*, a kidney bean dumpling fried in palm oil which has its origins in West Africa. To this the Bahiana adds *vatapá*, a dried shrimp and coconut milk paté (also delicious on its own), fresh salad and hot sauce (*pimenta*). For those who prefer not to eat the palm oil, the *abará* is a good substitute. *Abará* is steamed, wrapped in banana leaves. Seek local advice on which are most hygienic stalls to eat from. Two good Bahianas are *Chica*, at Ondina beach (on the street at the left side of *Mar A Vista Hotel*) and *Dinha* at Largo da Santana (very lively in the late afternoon), who serves *acarajé* until midnight, extremely popular. Bahians usually eat *acarajé* or *abará* with a chilled beer on the way home from work or on the beach at sunset. Another popular dish with African origins is *Xin-Xin de Galinha*, chicken on the bone cooked in *dendê*, with dried shrimp, garlic and squash.

Pelourinho (Historical Centre) Expensive: *Bargaço*, R das Laranjeiras 26, T242 6546. Traditional seafood restaurant, Bahian cuisine, open daily except Tue. *Casa do Benin*, Praça José Alencar 29. Afro-Bahian, great surroundings, try the shrimp in the cashew nut sauce, closed Mon and 1600-1900. *Maria Mata Mouro*, R Inácio Accioli 8, T321 3929. International menu, excellent service, relaxing atmosphere, closed Sun night. *Pizzeria Micheluccio*, R Alfredo Brito 31, T323 0078. Best pizzas in Pelourinho, open daily 1200 till late. *Uauá*, R Gregório de Matos 36, T321 3089. Elegant, colonial restaurant and bar, typical Bahian cuisine. **Mid-range**: *Jardim das Delicias*, R João de Deus, 12, T321 1449. Elegant restaurant and antiques shop with tropical garden, very reasonable for its setting, classical or live music. *Senac*, Praça José Alencar 8, Largo do Pelourinho. State-run catering school, a selection of 40 local dishes, buffet, lunch 1130-1530, dinner 1830-2130, all you can eat for US$16, inconsistent quality but very popular, folkloric show Thu-Sat 2030, US$5. *Quilombo do Pelô*, R Alfredo Brito 13, T322 4371. Rustic Jamaican restaurant, open daily from 1100, good food with relaxed, if erratic service, vegetarian options. *Mamabahia*, R Alfredo Brito 21. Good open-air steak house. Near the Carmo church: *Casa da Roça*, R Luis Viana 27. Pizzas, caipirinhas and live music at weekend. **Cheap**: *Bahiacafe.com*, Praça da Sé 20. Funky, Belgian-run internet café, good breakfasts, excellent food, English spoken. *Coffee Shop* , Praça da Sé. Cuban-style café serving sandwiches; main attraction is excellent coffee, and tea served in china cups, doubles as cigar shop. *Gramado*, Praça da Sé. One of few food-by-weight restaurants in area, basic, lunch only.

Recommended places to eat

Atelier Maria Adair, R J Castro Rabelo 2. Specializing in coffees and cocktails, owner Maria is a well known artist whose highly original work is on display. Good wholemeal snacks and juices at *Bar da Tereza*, No 16, open daily 0900-2330. *Dona Chika-Ka*, No 10, 1100-1500 and 1900-0200. Good local dishes. Open gates beside *Dona Chika-Ka* lead to an open square, Largo de Quincas Berro d'Água (known locally as Quadra 2M) with many bars and restaurants. On the next block down is *Tempero da Dadá*, R Frei Vicente 5. Open daily 1130 till late, closed Tue, Bahian cuisine, owners Dadá and Paulo are genial hosts, extremely popular. Across the street is *Quereres*, a restaurant and bar with good live music. *Kilinho*, Ribeiro dos Santos 1. Fresh salads, popular with locals. *Restaurante e lanchonete Xango*, Praça Cruzeiro de São Francisco. Good for fruit juices. *Carvalho*, R Conselheiro Cunha Lopez 33, Centro. *Comida a kilo*, tasty, excellent fish, clean, cheap. *Casa da Gamboa*, R João de Deus 32, 1st floor. 1200-1500 and 1900-2400, closed Mon. Also at R Newton Prado 51 (Gamboa de Cima),

Brazil

beautifully located in old colonial house overlooking the bay, good reputation, open Mon-Sat 1200-1500, 1900-2300, not cheap. Good *feijoada* at *Alaíde do Feijão*, R Fransisco Muniz Barreto 26, daily 1100-2400. Also at *da Dinha* on Praça José Alencar 5, Mon-Sat 0800-2000. *Encontro dos Artistas*, R das Laranjeiras 15, T321 1721, Ribeiro do Santos 10, Passo – Pelourinho, cheap. *Galeria Villa Manhattan e Bistro*, Rua das Laranjeiras 52. Good pasta.

Between the Historical Centre and Barra Expensive: *Chez Bernard*, R Gamboa de Cima, 11. French cuisine, open daily except Sun. **Mid-Range** The best *churrascaria* in Salvador is *Baby Beef*, Av AC Magalhães, Iguatemi. Top class restaurant, excellent service, extremely popular, open daily 1200-1500 and 1900-2300. An excellent Japanese restaurant is *Beni-Gan*, Praça A Fernandes 29, Garcia, intimate atmosphere, Tue-Sun 1900 till midnight. *Casa D'Italia*, corner of Av 7 and Visconde de São Lourenço. Reasonable prices, good service. *Recanto das Coroas*, underneath the *Hotel Themis* (see above), looks uninviting but the food is excellent. *Ristorante d'Italia*, Av 7 de Setembro, 1238, Campo Grande has won awards. Very reasonable, with large portions, closed Sun night, music some evenings. **Cheap**: There are some good snack bars on Av 7 de Setembro: *Nosso Cantinho*, near *Hotel Madrid*, good value. *Kentefrio*, No 379, the best, clean, counter service only, closed Sun. *Grão de Bico*, No 737, very good vegetarian.

At the bottom of the Lacerda Lift is Praça Cairu and the famous *Mercado Modelo*: on the upper floor of the market are 2 very good restaurants, *Camafeu De Oxossi* and *Maria De São Pedro*, both specializing in Bahian dishes, great atmosphere, good view of the port, daily 1130 till 2000, Sat lunchtime is particularly busy. Opposite the Mercado Modelo, the Paes Mendonça supermarket self-service counter is good value, 1100-1500, 1st floor. *Divino Gula*, Av Francia 414, 400 m from the *Mercado Modelo* is good and frequented by locals. On Av Contorno, *Solar Do Unhão*, in a beautiful 18th century sugar estate on the edge of the bay, lunch and dinner with the best folklore show in town, expensive. *Juárez*, Mercado de Ouro, Comércio, good steaks, cheap.

There are a number of restaurants specializing in crab, along the sea front promenade

Barra Expensive: *Caranguejo do Farol*, Av Oceânica 231, raised above the road. Specializing in crab, extremely busy. A little further along is *Restaurante do Sergipe*, also very busy. **Mid-range**: *Ban Zai*, Av 7 de Setembro 3244, Ladeira da Barra, T336 4338, by the yacht club. Sushi bar, always busy, open daily except Mon. *Oceânia*, Av Oceânica. Street café, noisy, good people watching, open every day until late. Almost next door is *Don Vitalone Pizzaria*, No 115, excellent pizzas. *Don Vitalone Trattoria*, T235 7274, is a block away, part of the same chain. Great Italian food, open daily for lunch and evening meal. *Pizzaria Il Forno*, R Marques de Leão 77 (parallel to the promenade), T247 7287. Italian food at a good price, good service, open daily for lunch and evening meal. *Yan Ping*, on R Airova Galvão, T245 6393. Good Chinese, open daily 1100 until midnight, reasonably priced, generous portions. **Cheap**: *Mediterrânio*, R Marques de Leão 262. Pay by weight, open daily. *A Porteira*, R Afonso Celso 287, T235 5656. Open for lunch only, pay by weight northeastern Brazilian food. *Nan Hai*, Av 7 de Setembro 3671. Good Chinese, lunch and dinner (Porto da Barra). *Unimar* supermarket, good cheap meals on 2nd floor. *Califa's* on the first floor of Shopping Barra is a basic Arabian place. Other places in this mall: *Pizza e Cia* on the ground floor. Good selection of fresh salads, also good pizzas, good value. Opposite is *Perini*, great ice cream, chocolate, savouries and cakes. *Saúde Brasil*, on the top floor (L3), for very good wholefood snacks, cakes and a wide variety of juices.

Near the lighthouse at the mouth of the bay (Farol Da Barra) there are a number of good fast food places: *Micheluccio*, Av Oceânica 10, good pizza, always busy. Next door is *Baitakão*, good hamburgers and sandwiches. *Mon Filet*, R Afonso Celso 152. Good steaks, pastas, open 1830-2400. On the same street, *Pastaxuta*, pizza, pasta, reasonable prices, and a number of other good cheap restaurants, for example *Maná*, opens 1100 till food runs out, different menu each day, closed Sun, popular, owner Frank speaks a little English. The best Bahian restaurant in the area is *Frutos Do Mar*, R Marquês de Leão 415. A very good vegetarian restaurant is *Rama*, R Lord Cochrane, great value. *Don Vitalone*, D M Teixeira 27, near the lighthouse, off the seafront. Excellent Italian, open daily for lunch and evening meal.

In Ondina *Double Gula* in *Mar A Vista Hotel*, R H Carneiro Ribeiro 1. Excellent meat. Further along Av Oceânica towards the Rio Vermelho district is *Sukiyaki*, No 3562. Excellent Japanese, open 1200-1500, 1900 till midnight, US$20-25. *Extudo*, Largo Mesquita 4, T237 4669. Good varied menu, lively bar at night, attracts interesting clientèle, open 1200-0200, closed Mon, not expensive. *Manjericão*, R Fonte do Boi (the street leading to *Meridien Hotel*). Excellent wholefood menu, Mon-Sat 1100-1600. *Marisco*, at Paciência Beach nearby. Good seafood, 1100-1500, 1800-2100, good value. *Margarida*, R Feira de Santana, Parque Cruz Aguiar. Open daily for lunch 1130-1500, original dishes, pasta, seafood, meat, imaginative salads, pay by weight, great desserts, very friendly owners, attracts interesting clientèle. *Postudo*, R João Gomes 87, T245 5030. Over a small shopping mall called *Free Shop*, open daily except Sun, reasonably priced good food in an interesting setting, always busy. Across the street at the base of the hill in Largo da Santana is *Santana Sushi Bar*, T237 5107. Open Tue-Sat, authentic. There is an interesting fish market at Largo da Mariquita with a number of stalls serving food from noon until the small hrs, clean, good atmosphere, popular with locals. A good kiosk is *Riso e Nega* (kiosk with green tables), friendly, good basic food. Nearby is *Brisa*, R Augusto Severo 4. Mon-Sat, 1100-1500, excellent wholefood restaurant, small, simple, cheap, owner Nadia is very friendly. *Cantina Famiglia-Salvatore*, Largo da Mariquita 45. Delicious, authentic Italian pasta, 2 other branches.

Further along Av Oceânica at Jardim Armação *Yemanjá*, Av Octavio Mangabeira 4655, T461 9010, a 20-minute taxi ride from the centre. Excellent Bahian seafood, open daily from 1130 till late, very typical, always busy, reasonably priced, good atmosphere. *Deutsches Haus*, Av Otávio Mangabeira 1221. Good German cooking. *Rodeio*, Jardim dos Namorados, Pituba, T240 1762. Always busy, good value 'all you can eat' *churrascaria*, open daily from 1130-midnight. Also nearby is *Rincão Gaúcho*, R Pedro Silva Ribeiro s/n, Jardim Armação, T231 3800. Excellent *churrascaria*, huge selection of salads, many different cuts of meat, very popular with locals.

A Porteira at Boca do Rio. Specializes in northeastern dishes, 1200-1600 and 1800-2300, seafood dishes also served. Nearby on the same street is *Bar Caribe* (more commonly known as *Pimentinha*). Zany décor, little comfort, hard to believe that it could be so busy, extremely busy on Mon (its best night), tables on the street, blessings given by the owner, a *pai de santo*, no other bar like this anywhere, food served, healthy portions, expect delays though. In Itapoã near the lighthouse, 2 good restaurants are *Mistura Fina*, R Professor Souza Brito 41, T249 2623, seafood, pasta dishes, open daily 1000-midnight and *O Lagostão*, R Agnaldo Cruz 12, T375 3646, Bahian cuisine, open daily 1100 till midnight. *Casquinha De Siri* at Piatã beach. Daily from 0900, live music every night, cover charge US$2, very popular. The beaches from Patamares to Itapoã are lined by *barracas*, thatched huts serving chilled drinks and freshly cooked seafood dishes, ideal for lunch and usually very cheap. Try *Ki-Muqueca*, Av Otávio Mangabeira 36 (Av Oceânica), for large helpings of excellent Bahian food in attractive surroundings. *Restaurant Uauá*, Av Dorival Caymmi 46. Open Thu to Sun. Fri and Sat are very busy with forró dancing till 0400.

Cinema The main shopping malls at Barra, Iguatemi, Itaigara and Brotas, and *Cineart* in Politeama (Centro), run more mainstream movies. The impressive Casa do Comércio building near Iguatemi houses the *Teatro do SESC* with a mixed programme of theatre, cinema and music Wed-Sun. The **Fundação Cultural do Estado da Bahia** edits *Bahia Cultural*, a monthly brochure listing the main cultural events for the month. These can be found in most hotels and Bahiatursa information centres. Local newspapers *A Tarde* and *Correio da Bahia* have good cultural sections listing all events in the city.

Entertainment

Brazil

Much of the nightlife is concentrated in the historical centre. The compact network of cobbled streets around R João de Deus is dotted with small, basic bars with plastic tables and chairs on the pavement. Busy nights in the Pelourinho are Tue and weekends

Brazil

Nightlife See Music in Bahia for times and venues of the *bloco* rehearsals. The best time to hear and see artists and groups is during carnival but they are also to be seen outside the carnival period. Busy nights in the Pelourinho are Tue and weekends. There is free live music every night throughout the summer in the other squares of Pelourinho (Quincas Berro d'Água and Pedro Arcanjo). Sat nights are very busy, the most popular band being the *Fred Dantas Orchestra*, which plays a fusion of big band music and Latin rhythms. Reggae hangs in the air of Pelourinho with many reggae bars such as *Bar do Reggae*, *Casa do Olodum* and *Bar do Olodum*, all within a short walk of each other. *Casa do Olodum*, R Gregório de Matos, is a bar and dance floor where the band *Olodum* performs on Tue to packed crowds (hang out on the pavement outside if you don't want to pay the entrance fee); the rest of the week it's open to all. Almost directly opposite at No 15 is: *NR*, a great after-hours bar with live music (which is not always so great). There's a US$0.50 charge if you sit down. A good jam session takes place every Sat night (Aug-Mar) in the grounds of the *Solar do Unhão*, Av Contorno. Guest musicians are welcome. It is best to go by taxi as bus connections are difficult.

Pelourinho *Cantina da Lua*, Terreiro De Jesus. Open daily, popular and a good spot on the square with outdoor seating, but gets crowded and the food isn't good. Many bars on the Largo de Quincas Berro d'Água (see above), Good café and great chocolate at *Cailleur*, R Gregório de Matos 17, open daily 0930-2100, bar service continues till 0100.

Barra *Mordomia Drinks*, Ladeira Da Barra. Enter through a narrow entrance to an open air bar with a spectacular view of the bay, very popular. Most Barra nightlife happens at the Farol da Barra (lighthouse). R Marquês de Leão is very busy, with lots of bars with tables on the pavement: *Habeas Copos*, R Marquês de Leão 172. Famous and traditional street side bar, very popular.. *Barra Vento 600* is a popular open air bar on the beachfront. Bar in the ICBA (Goethe Institute), has good light snacks, attracts a young bohemian clientèle, closes 2300, very pleasant courtyard setting. Further along the coast at Ondina is the *Bahia Othon Palace Hotel* with a disco called *Kasullo Dancing Hall*, busy at weekends. **Rio Vermelho** This district was once the bohemian section of town and where Jorge Amado and Caetano Veloso still have houses. The nightlife in this region rivals Pelourinho. *Alambique* is a good dance bar (especially on Sat night US$10). *Chico* and *Rocco* are along the same strip. *Porto Seguro* at *Salvador Praia Hotel*, T245 5033. *New Fred's*, Av Visconde de Itaboraí 125, T248 4399 (middle-aged market, singles bar). *Bell's Beach* disco at Boca Do Rio. Open Tue-Sat 2200-0400, up-market, expensive

Theatres *Castro Alves*, at Campo Grande (Largo 2 de Julho), T339 8000, seats 1400 and is considered one of the best in Latin America. It also has its own repertory theatre, the *Sala de Coro*, for more experimental productions. The theatre's *Concha Acústica* is an open-air venue used frequently in the summer, attracting the big names in Brazilian music. *Teatro Vila Velha*, Passéio Público, T336 1384, Márcio Meirelles, the theatre's director works extensively with Grupo Teatro Olodum; although performed in Portuguese productions here are very visual and worth investigating. *Instituto Cultural Brasil-Alemanha* (ICBA) and the *Associação Cultural Brasil Estados Unidos* (ACBEU), both on Corredor de Vitória have a varied programme, the former with a cinema. In the Pelourinho is the *Teatro XVIII*, R Frei Vicente, T 332 0018, an experimental theatre. *Teatro Gregório de Matos* in Praça Castro Alves offers space to new productions and writers. *Balé Folclórico da Bahia*, R Inácio Aciolli 11, T322 1962. Good selection of dances, 2000 daily, US$2.50.

Festivals 6 Jan (*Epiphany*); *Ash Wednesday* and *Maundy Thursday*, half-days; 2 Jul (*Independence of Bahia*); 30 Oct; *Christmas Eve*, half-day. An important local holiday is *Festa do Nosso Senhor do Bonfim*; it takes place on the second Sun after Epiphany, but the washing or *lavagem* of the Bonfim church, with its colourful parade, takes place on the preceding Thu (usually **mid-Jan**). The *Festa da Ribeira* is on the following Mon. Another colourful festival is that of the fishermen of Rio Vermelho on **2 Feb**; gifts for Yemanjá, Goddess of the Sea, are taken to sea in a procession of sailing boats to an accompaniment of *candomblé* instruments. The Holy Week processions among the old churches of the upper city are also interesting.

Shopping **Shopping in Pelourinho** The major carnival *afro blocos* have boutiques selling T-shirts etc. *Boutique Olodum*, on Praça José Alencar, *Ilê Aiyê*, on R Francisco Muniz Barreto 16

and *Muzenza* next door. On the same street is *Modaxé*, a retail outlet for clothes manufactured by street children under the auspices of the Projeto Axé, expensive but these are the trendiest T-shirts in town. Also on this street at No 18 is *Brazilian Sound*, for the latest in Brazilian and Bahia music, CDs mainly. Good music shops in nearby Praça da Sé are *Mini Som* and an unnamed shop between R da Misericórdia and R José Gonçalves, helpful, CDs only with discounts for multiple purchases. The record shop at the Rodoviária is also good for regional Bahian music.

Instituto Mauá, R Gregório de Matos 27. Open Tue-Sat 0900-1800, Sun 1000-1600, good quality Bahian handicrafts at fair prices, better value and better quality for traditional crafts than the Mercado Modelo. A similar store is *Loja de Artesanato do SESC*, Largo Pelourinho (T321 5502). Mon-Fri 0900-1800 (closed for lunch), Sat 0900-1300. *Rosa do Prado* , R Inacio Aciolly, 5. Cigar shop packed with every kind of Brazilian *'charuto'* imaginable. *Scala* , Praça da Sé, T/F321 8891. Handmade jewellery using locally mined gems (eg. acquamarine, amythyst and emerald), workshop at back. Other jewellery stores are *Lasbonfim* (T242 9854) and *Simon* (T242 5218), both in the Terreiro de Jesus. They both have branches in the nearby Carmo district. *Casa Moreira* , Ladeira da Praça, just south of Praça da Sé. Exquisite jewellery and antiques, most very expensive, but some affordable charms. Excellent hand-made lace products at *Artesanato Santa Bárbara*, R Alfredo Brito 7. For local art the best stores are *Atelier Portal da Cor*, Ladeira do Carmo 31 (T242 9466), run by a co-operative of local artists, Totonho, Calixto, Raimundo Santos, Jô, good prices. Recommended. Also across the street at *Casa do Índio*, Indian artefacts and art, restaurant and bar open here till late, good surroundings. Good wood carvings on R Alfredo Brito, next to *Koisa Nossa* (No 45), by a co-operative of sculptors, Palito and Negão Barão being the most famous. Hand-made traditional percussion instruments (and percussion lessons) at *Oficina de Investigação Musical*, Alfredo Brito 24 (T322 2386), Mon-Fri 0800-1200 and 1300-1600, US$15 per hr.

Bookshops *Livraria Brandão*, R Ruy Barbosa 104, Centre, T243 5383. Secondhand English, French, Spanish and German books. *Livraria Civilização Brasileira*, Av 7 de Setembro 912, Mercês, and in the Barra, Iguatemi and *Ondina Apart Hotel* shopping centres have some English books. Also *Graúna*, Av 7 de Setembro 1448, and R Barão de Itapoã 175, Porto da Barra, many English titles. *Siciliano* in Shopping Barra sells Footprint Handbooks. *Livraria Planeta*, Carlos Gomes 42, loja 1, sells used English books. The bookshop at the airport has English books and magazines.

Markets The *Mercado Modelo*, at Praça Cairu, lower city, offers many tourist items such as wood carvings, silver-plated fruit, leather goods, local musical instruments. Lace items for sale are often not handmade (despite labels), are heavily marked up, and are much better bought at their place of origin (for example Ilha de Maré, Pontal da Barra and Marechal Deodoro). Cosme e Damião, musical instrument sellers on 1st floor, has been recommended, especially if you want to play the instruments. Bands and dancing, especially Sat (but very much for money from tourists taking photographs), closed at 1200 Sun. There is a photograph exhibition of the old market in the basement. (Many items are often cheaper on the Praça da Sé.) The largest and most authentic market is the *Feira de São Joaquim*, 5 km from Mercado Modelo along the sea front: barkers, trucks, *burros*, horses, boats, people, mud, all very smelly, every day (Sun till 1200 only), busiest on Sat morning; interesting African-style pottery and basketwork; very cheap. (The car ferry terminal for Itaparica is nearby.) *Iguatemi Shopping Centre* sells good handicraft items, it is run by the government so prices are fixed and reasonable. Similarly at *Instituto Mauá*, Porto da Barra. Every Wed from 1700-2100 there is a **handicrafts fair** in the 17th century fort of Santa Maria at the opposite end of Porto da Barra beach. On Fri from 1700-2100, there is an open air market of handicrafts and Bahian food in *Porto da Barra*, a popular event among the local young people. Mosquito nets from *Casa dos Mosquiteros*, R Pedro Sá 6F, Calçada, T226 0715.

Football: Esporte Clube Bahia play at the Otávio Mangabeira Stadium, Travessa Joaquim Maurício s/n, Nazaré, T/F242 3322.

Sport

Bus tours are available from several companies: *LR Turismo*, T264 0999, also offers boat trips, *Itaparica Turismo*, T2483433, *Tours Bahia*, Praça Jose Anchieta 4, T322 3676 (Austrian

Tour operators

Brazil

guide Victor Runa has been recommended), and *Alameda Turismo*, T248 2977, city tour US$15 pp. *Bahiatours'* *Bahia by Night* including transport to the *Senac* restaurant, a show, dinner and a night-time walk around Pelourinho (US$15 pp). All-day boat trip on Bahia de Todos Os Santos last from 0800-1700 including a visit to Ilha dos Frades, lunch on Itaparica (US$10 extra), US$15 pp. *Tatur Turismo*, Av Tancredo Neves 274, Centro Empresarial Iguatemi, Sala 228, Bloco B, Salvador 41820-020, Bahia Brasil. T450 7216, F450 7215, tatur@svn.com.br Run by Irishman, Conor O'Sullivan. English spoken. Specializes in Bahia, arranges private guided tours and can make any necessary travel, hotel and accommodation arrangements. Highly recommended. *Kontik*, Av Tancredo Neves 969, sala 1004, T341 2121, F341 2071. A recommended guide who speaks German, English and Portuguese is *Dieter Herzberg*, T334 1200.

Transport **Local** **Bus**: local buses US$0.70, *executivos*, a/c, US$1.40, US$1.50 or US$3 depending on the route. On buses and at the ticket-sellers' booths, watch your change and beware pickpockets (one scam used by thieves is to descend from the bus while you are climbing aboard). To get from the old city to the ocean beaches, take a 'Barra' bus from Praça da Sé to the Barra point and walk to the nearer ones; the Aeroporto *executivo* leaves Praça da Sé, passing Barra, Ondina, Rio Vermelho, Amaralina, Pituba, Costa Azul, Armação, Boca do Rio, Jaguaripe, Patamares, Piatã and Itapoã, before turning inland to the airport. The glass-sided Jardineira bus goes to Flamengo beach (30 km from the city) following the coastal route; it passes all the best beaches; sit on the right hand side for best views. It leaves from the Praça da Sé daily 0730-1930, every 40 mins, US$1.50. For beaches beyond Itapoã, take the *executivo* to Stella Maris and Flamengo beaches. These follow the same route as the Jardineira. During Carnival, when most streets are closed, buses leave from Vale do Canela (O Vale), near Campo Grande.

If renting a car check **Car hire**: *Interlocadora*, at airport, T377 2550/204 1019, in the centre T377 4144. *Unidas*,
whether credit card Av Oceânica 2456, Ondina, T336 0717.
or cash is cheapest.
See page 48, for **Taxi**: taxi meters start at US$0.50 for the 'flagdown' and US$0.10 per 100 m. They charge
multinational car US$15 per hr within city limits, and 'agreed' rates outside. Taxi Barra-Centro US$3 daytime;
rental agencies US$4 at night. Watch the meter, especially at night; the night-time charge should be 30 higher than daytime charges. *Chame Táxi* (24-hr service), 241 2266, and many others.

Long distance **Air**: an a/c bus service every 30-40 mins between the new Luis Eduardo Magalhães Airport (T 204 1244) and the centre, a distance of 32 km, costs US$1.20. It takes the coast road to the city, stopping at hotels en route. Service starts from the airport at 0500 (last bus 2200, 0600-2200 at weekends) and from Praça da Sé at 0630 (last bus 2100). Also ordinary buses, US$0.50. 'Special' taxis to both Barra and centre (buy ticket at the airport desk next to tourist information booth), US$23; normal taxis (from outside airport), US$18, bus-taxi service, US$10. Allow plenty of time for travel to the airport and for check-in. ATMs are hidden around the corner on ground floor to right as you arrive. Tourist information booth open 24 hrs, English spoken, has list of hotels and useful map.

Daily flights to all the main cities. *Nordeste* have daily flights to Porto Seguro and several flights a week to destinations in the interior of Bahia. *Tam* and *VASP* also fly to Porto Seguro.

Bus: bus from the Rodoviária (T450 4500); bus RI or RII, 'Centro-Rodoviária-Circular'; in the centre, get on in the Lower City at the foot of the Lacerda lift; buses also go to Campo Grande (US$0.70). A quicker executive bus from Praça da Sé or Praça da Inglaterra (in front of McDonalds), Comércio, run to Iguatemi Shopping Centre, US$1.50, weekdays only, from where there is a walkway to the rodoviária (take care in the dark, or a taxi, US$10). To **Belém** US$48 *comercial* with Itapemirim. To **Recife**, US$18-25, 13 hrs, 2 a day and 1 *leito*, *Itapemirim*, T358 0037. To **Rio** (28 hrs, US$45.50, *leito* US$91, *Itapemirim*, good stops, clean toilets, recommended). **São Paulo** (30 hrs), US$51, *leito* US$64 (0815 with *Viação Nacional*, 2 in afternoon with São Geraldo, T358 0188). To **Fortaleza**, 19 hrs, US$33 at 0900 with *Itapemirim*. **Ilhéus**, 7 hrs, *Aguia Branca*, T358 7044, *comercial* US$14.50, *leito* US$29, several. To **Lençóis** 0700, 1200, 2330, 8 hrs, US$12 with *Real Expresso*, T358 1591. **Belo Horizonte**, *Gontijo*, T358 7448, at 1700, US$40 *comercial*, US$50 *executivo*, São Geraldo at 1800. There are daily bus services to **Brasília** along the fully paved BR-242, via Barreiras, 3 daily, 23 hrs,

Paraíso, T358 1591, US$40. Frequent services to the majority of destinations; a large panel in the main hall lists destinations and the relevant ticket office.

Hitchhiking: out of Salvador, take a 'Cidade Industrial' bus from the rodoviária at the port; it goes on to the highway.

Airline offices *Nordeste/Rio Sul*, R Almte das Espadtodias 100, Camino das Arvores, T0800-992004. *TAM*, Praça Gago Coutinho, T0800-123100. *TAP*, Edif Ilheus, sala 401, Av Estados Unidos 137, T243 6122. *Varig*, R Carlos Gomes 6, T0800-997000. *Vasp*, R Chile 27, T0800-998277.

Directory

Banks Don't change money on the street especially in the Upper City where higher rates are usually offered. Changing at banks can be bureaucratic and time-consuming. Selected branches of major banks have ATMs (which accept Visa and Cirrus cards) and exchange facilities. *Citibank*, R Miguel Calmon 555, Comércio, centre, changes TCs. Branch at R Almte Marquês de Leão 71, Barra, has ATM. Visa ATM at *Banco do Brasil*, Av Estados Unidos 561, Comércio, in the shopping centre opposite the Rodoviária (also a *câmbio* here) very high commission on TCs, at the airport (1st floor, open 0830-1530 and 1600-2100 Mon-Fri and 0900-1600 Sat, Sun and holidays); branches in Barra, R Miguel Bournier 4, in Shopping Barra and in Ondina. MasterCard at *Credicard*, 1st floor, Citibank building, R Miguel Calmon 555, Comércio. MasterCard ATMs at branches of *HSBC*, eg Av 7 de Setembro 136, and any *Banco 24 Horas*. *Iguatemi Cambio e Turismo*, Shopping Iguatemi, 2nd floor. Changes all brands of TCs at good rates. *Figueiredo*, opposite *Grande Hotel da Barra* on Ladeira da Barra will exchange cash at good rates. *Shopping Tour* in Barra Shopping centre changes dollars, as will other tour agencies. If stuck, all the big hotels will exchange, but at poor rates.

Banks are open 1000-1600

Communications Internet: *Bahiacafe.com*, Praça da Sé (see Eating, above). US$1.20 for 30 mins. *Internetcafe.com*, Av 7 de Setembro 3713, Porto da Barra and R João de Deus 2, historical centre. US$2 per hr, closed Sun. *Internet Access*, R Alfonso Celso 447, Barra. US$1.20 per hr. *Novo Tempo*, Ladeira do Carmo 16, Centro Histórico. **Post Office:** main post office and poste restante is in Praça Inglaterra, in the Lower City, open Mon-Fri 0800-1700, Sat 0800-1200, F243 9383 (US$1 to receive fax). Several other offices, including R Alfredo Brito 43, Mon-Sat 0800-1700, Sun 0800-1200, has a philatelic section; rodoviária, ; airport; Barra and Iguatemi Shopping Malls. **Telephone:** *Embratel*, R do Carro 120. *Telemar* has branches at Campo da Pólvora, Trav Joaquim Maurício 81, open 0630-2400, on R Hugo Baltazar Silva (open 0700-2200 daily), airport (daily 0700-2200) and rodoviária (Mon-Sat 24 hrs and Sun 0700-2200).

Cultural centres Cultura Inglesa, R Plínio Moscoso 357, Jardim Apipema. *Associação Cultural Brasil-Estados Unidos*, Av 7 de Setembro 1883, has a library and reading room with recent US magazines, open to all, free use of internet for 30 mins, and at No 1809 on the same avenue is the German **Goethe Institut**, also with a library and reading room; both have cafés.

Embassies and consulates Austria, R Jardim Armacao, T371 4611. **Belgium**, Av Trancredo Neves 274A, sala 301, Iguatemi, T623 2454. **Denmark**, Av 7 de Setembro 3959, Barra, T336 9861. Mon-Fri 0900-1200, 1400-1700. **Finland**, Jardim Ipiranga 19, T247 3312, Mon-Fri 0800-1000 and after 1900. **France**, R Francisco Gonçalves 1, sala 805, Comércio, T241 0168, Mon, Tue, Thu 1430-1700. **Germany**, R Lucaia 281, 2nd floor, Rio Vermelho, T334 7106, Mon-Fri 0900-1200. **Holland**, Av Santa Luzia, 1136 Ed

Brazil

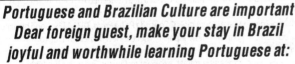

Porto Empresarial, Sala 302, T341 0410, Mon-Fri 0800-1200. **Italy**, Av 7 de Setembro 1238, Centro, T329 5338, Mon, Wed, Fri 1500-1800. **Norway**, Av Estados Unidos, 14, 8th floor, T326 8500 , Mon-Fri 0900-1200, 1400-1600. **Portugal**, Largo Carmo 4, Sto Antônio, T241 1633. **Spain**, R Mcal Floriano 21, Canela, T336 1937, Mon-Fri 0900-1400. **Sweden**, Av Estados Unidos 357, Ed Joaquim Barreto, sala 501, Comércio, T242 4833. **Switzerland**, Av Tancredo Neves 3343, 5th floor, sala 506b, T341 5827. **UK**, Av Estados Unidos 4, 18B, Comércio, T243 7399, Mon-Thu, 0900-1100, 1400-1600, Fri 0900-1100. **USA**, R Pernambuco 51, Pituba, T345 1545, Mon-Fri, 0900-1130, 1430-1630.

Language classes *Casa do Brasil*, R Milton de Oliveira 231, Barra, T264 5866, www.casa-do-brasil.net *Superlearning Idiomas*, Av Sete de Setembro 3402, Ladeira da Barra, T337 2824, www.allways.com.br/spl Uses music and relaxation as learning techniques.

Medical services Clinic: Barão de Loreto 21, Graça. *Dr Argemiro Júnior* speaks English and Spanish. First consultation US$40, 2nd free. **Medical:** yellow fever vaccinations free at **Delegação Federal de Saúde**, R Padre Feijó, Canela. Israeli travellers needing medical (or other) advice should contact *Sr Marcus* (T247 5769), who speaks Hebrew.

Useful addresses **Immigration:** (for extensions of entry permits), Policia Federal, Av O Pontes 339, Aterro de Água de Meninos, Lower City, T319 6082, open 1000-1600. Show an outward ticket or sufficient funds for your stay, visa extension US$17.50. **Tourist Police:** R Gregório de Matos 16, T320 4103. **Delegacia de Proteção ao Turista**, R Gregório de Matos 1, T242 3504.

Itaparica

Phone code: 071
Colour map 5, grid C5

Across the bay from Salvador lies the island of Itaparica, 29 km long and 12 km wide. The town of Itaparica is very picturesque, with a fair beach in the town, and well worth a visit. Take a bus or kombi by the coast road (Beira Mar) which passes through the villages of Manguinhos, Amoureiras and Ponta de Areia. The beach at Ponta de Areia is one of the best on the island and is very popular. There are many *barracas* on the beach, the best and busiest is *Barraca Pai Xango*, always very lively.

In Itaparica there are many fine residential buildings from the 19th century, plus the church of **São Lourenço**, one of the oldest in Brazil, and there are delightful walks through the old town. During the summer months the streets are ablaze with the blossoms of the beautiful flamboyant trees. The beaches at Mar Grande are fair but can be dirty at times. There are many *pousadas* in Mar Grande and at the nearby beaches of Ilhota and Gamboa (both to the left as you disembark from the ferry).

From Bom Despacho there are many buses, kombis and taxis to all parts of the island, inlcuding beaches at Ponta de Areia, Mar Grande, Berlinque, Aratuba and Cacha Pregos. Kombi and taxis can be rented for trips but be prepared to bargain. There are also buses to other towns such as Nazaré das Farinhas, Valença (see below) and also **Jaguaribe**, a small, picturesque colonial port. Both of these towns are on the mainland connected by a bridge on the southwest side of the island, turn off between Mar Grande and Cacha Pregos (bus company, *Viazul*). There are good beaches across the bay on the mainland, but a boat is needed to reach these (US$12).

Sleeping A good simple *pousada* at Amoureiras is **C** *Pousada Pé na Praia*, T831 1389. Good breakfast, good sized rooms, English and French spoken. There are few *pousadas* in the town. The best is **A** *Quinta Pitanga*, T831 1554. Beautifully decorated by the owner Jim Valkus, 3 suites and 2 singles, beachfront property, a retreat, excellent restaurant. Expensive but highly recommended, accepts day visitors. **D** *Pousada Icarai*, Praça da Piedade, T831 3119. Charming, good location.

Mar Grande The following are all recommended: **A** *Pousada Arco Iris*, Estrada da Gamboa 102, T833 1130. Magnificent building and setting in mango orchard, expensive, good if slow restaurant, *Manga Rosa*. They have camping facilities next door, shady, not always clean. **C** *Pousada Estrela do Mar*, Av NS das Candeias 170, T833 1108. Good rooms, fan or a/c. **D** *Lagoa e Mar*, R Parque das Dunas, 01-40, T/F8231573. Very good breakfast, spacious bungalows, swimming pool, 200 m to beach, restaurant, helpful. **D** *Pousada Scórpio*,

Brazil

R Aquários, T823 1036. Breakfast, beach, swimming pool, simple rooms, weekend restaurant. **D** *Pousada Sonho do Verão*, R São Bento 2, opposite *Pousada Arco Iris*, T833 1616. Chalets and apartments, cooking facilities, French and English spoken. Like other *pousadas* they rent bicycles (US$3 per hr); they also rent horses (US$5 per hr). Near the church in the main praça is the **D** *Pousada Casarão da Ilha*, T833 1106. Spacious rooms with a great view of Salvador across the bay, swimming pool, a/c. **E** *Pousada Samambaia*, AV NS das Candeias 61. Good breakfast, French spoken.

Aratuba D *Pousada Zimbo Tropical*, Estrada de Cacha Pregos, Km 3, Rua Yemanjá, T/F8381148. French/Brazilian-run, good breakfast, evening meals available. Recommended.

Cacha Pregos *Club Sonho Nosso*, T837 1040 or T226 1933. Very clean huts on clean beach, good service, collect you from anywhere on the island – also Bom Despacho. Kombis stop in front of entrance, a 5-min walk. Recommended. **C** *Pousada Babalú*, T837 1193. Spacious bungalows, frigobar, fan, good breakfast. Recommended. **D** *Pousada Cacha Pregos*, next to the supermarket, T837 1013. With fan, bath, no breakfast, good.

Good restaurants in Mar Grande are *Philippe's Bar and Restaurant*, Largo de São Bento, **Eating** French and local cuisine, information in English and French. *O Pacífico* is peaceful. *Restaurant Rafael* in the main praça for pizzas and snacks. Also pizzas at *Bem Me Quer*, opposite *Pousada Samambaia*, down an alley. There are many Bahianas selling acarajé in the late afternoon and early evening in the main praça by the pier.

Ferry The island is reached from the mainland by several ferries. The main passenger ferry **Transport** leaves for Bom Despacho from São Joaquim (buses for Calçada, Ribeira stop across the road from the ferry terminal; the 'Sabino Silva – Ribeira' bus passes in front of the Shopping Barra). The first ferry from Salvador leaves at 0540 and, depending on demand, the ferries leave at intervals of 45 mins. The last ferry from Salvador is at 2230. Returning to Salvador the 1st ferry is at 0515 and the last at 2300. During the summer months the ferries are much more frequent. Enquiries at the **Companhia de Navegação Bahiana** (CNB), T321 7100 from 0800 to 1700. A one way ticket for foot passengers Mon-Fri is US$1, Sat-Sun US$1.20. There is also a catamaran departing for Bom Despacho twice daily, US$3. **Mar Grande** can be reached by a smaller ferry (*Lancha*) from the Terminal Marítimo in front of the Mercado Modelo in Salvador. The ferries leave every 45 mins and the crossing takes 50 mins, US$1.80 return.

Small boats for trips around the bay can be hired privately at the small port by the **Tours of** Mercado Modelo called Rampa do Mercado. A pleasant trip out to the mouth of the **Todos os** bay should take 1½ hours as you sail along the bottom of the cliff. When arranging to **Santos bay** hire any boat ensure that the boat is licensed by the Port Authority (Capitânia dos Portos) and that life-jackets are on board. There are also sailings from the Base Naval/São Tomé to the Ilhas da Maré and dos Frades. American yachtsman Steve Lafferty is highly recommended for enjoyable sailing trips, for up to four people: R do Sodré 45, apt 301, T241 0994.

Nazaré das Farinhas, 60 km inland from Itaparica, is reached over a bridge by bus **Nazaré das** from **Bom Despacho**. This 18th-century town is celebrated for its market, which **Farinhas** specializes in the local ceramic figures, or *caxixis*. There is a large market in Holy *Colour map 5, grid C5* Week, particularly on Holy Thursday and Good Friday. 12 km from Nazaré (taxi *Population: 26,365* US$4.25, also buses) is the village of **Maragojipinha**, which specializes in making the ceramic figures. Bus from Salvador, 1530, takes five hours.

The area around Salvador, known as the Recôncavo Baiano, was one of the chief **The Recôncavo** centres of sugar and tobacco cultivation in the 16th century. Some 73 km from Salvador is **Santo Amaro da Purificação**, an old sugar centre sadly decaying, noted for its churches (often closed because of robberies), municipal palace (1769), fine main praça, birthplace of the singers Caetano Veloso and his sister Maria Bethania and ruined mansions including Araújo Pinto, former residence of the Barão de Cotegipe. Other attractions include the splendid beaches of the bay, the falls of

Vitória and the grotto of Bom Jesus dos Pobres. The festivals of **Santo Amaro**, 24 January-2 February, and **Nossa Senhora da Purificação** on 2 February itself are interesting. There is also the **Bembé do Mercado** festival on 13 May. Craftwork is sold on the town's main bridge. There are no good hotels or restaurants.

Cachoeira & São Félix
At 116 km from Salvador and only 4 km from the BR-101 coastal road are the towns of Cachoeira (Bahia's 'Ouro Preto', *Population*: 30,416) and São Félix (*Population*: 13,699), on either side of the Rio Paraguaçu below the Cachoeira dam. Cachoeira was twice capital of Bahia: once in 1624-25 during the Dutch invasion, and once in 1822-23 while Salvador was still held by the Portuguese. There are beautiful views from above São Félix.

Cachoeira's main buildings are the **Casa da Câmara e Cadeia** (1698-1712), the **Santa Casa de Misericórdia** (1734 – the hospital, someone may let you see the church), the 16th-century **Ajuda** chapel (now containing a fine collection of vestments), and the Convent of the **Ordem Terceira do Carmo**, whose church has a heavily gilded interior. Other churches are the **Matriz** with 5 m-high *azulejos*, and **Nossa Senhora da Conceição do Monte**. There are beautiful lace cloths on the church altars. All churches are either restored or in the process of restoration. The **Museu Hansen Bahia,** R Ana Néri, houses fine engravings by the German artist who made the Recôncavo his home in the 1950s, recommended. There is a great wood-carving tradition in Cachoeira. The artists can be seen at work in their studios. Best are Louco Filho, Fory, both in R Ana Néri, Doidão, in front of the Igreja Matriz and J Gonçalves on the main praça. A 300 m railway bridge built by the British in the 19th century spans the Rio Paraguaçu to São Felix where the Danneman cigar factory can be visited to see hand-rolling. Tourist office: Casa de Ana Néri, Cachoeira. ■ *Buses from Salvador* (Camurjipe) *every hr or so from 0530;* Feira Santana, *2 hrs, US$3.*

Sleeping and eating **Cachoeira** **A** *Pousada do Convento de Cachoeira*, T725 1716. In a restored 16th-century convent, good restaurant. **D** *Santo Antônio*, near the rodoviária. Basic, safe, laundry facilities. Recommended. **E** *Pousada Tia Rosa*, near Casa Ana Neri, T725 1692. With breakfast, very basic. **Youth hostel** Av Parnamirim 417, T268 4844/3390. *Cabana do Pai Thomaz*, 25 de Junho 12, excellent Bahian food, good value, also an hotel, **C** with private bath and breakfast. *Gruta Azul*, Praça Manoel Vitorino. Lunch only. *Do Nair*, R 13 de Maio. Delicious food and sometimes Seresta music. *Casa do Licor*, R 13 Maio 25. Interesting bar, try the banana-flavoured spirit. **São Félix** *Xang-hai*, good, cheap food. Warmly recommended. Try the local dish, *maniçoba* (meat, manioc and peppers).

Festivals *São João* (**24 Jun**), 'Carnival of the Interior' celebrations include dangerous games with fireworks. *Nossa Sehora da Boa Morte* (**early Aug**) is also a major festival. A famous *candomblé* ceremony at the Fonte de Santa Bárbara is held on **4 Dec**.

Lençóis

Phone code: 0xx75
Colour map 5, grid C4
Population: 8,910
400 km W of Salvador
on BR-242

This historical monument and colonial gem was founded in 1844 to exploit the diamonds in the region. While there are still some *garimpeiros* (gold prospectors), it is not precious metals that draw most visitors, but the climate, which is cooler than the coast, the relaxed atmosphere and the wonderful trekking and horseriding in the hills of the Chapada Diamantina. A few of the options are given below under Excursions, and *pousadas* and tour operators offer guiding services to point you in the right direction. This is also a good place for buying handicrafts.

Sleeping **A** *Recanto das Águas*, Av Senhor dos Passos s/n, T/F334 1154. Comfortable, good location, swimming pool, a/c or fan. Recommended. **A** *Hotel de Lençóis*, R Altinha Alves 747, T/F334 1102. With breakfast, swimming pool. Recommended. **C** *Pousalegre*, R Boa Vista 95, T334 1124/1245. With good regional breakfast, dormitories only, safe, hot showers, good

Brazil

vegetarian restaurant. **C** *Estalagem de Alcino*, R Gen Vieira de Morais 139, T334 1171. **D** pp shared bath, beautiful, restored 19th-century house, superb breakfast. Highly recommended. **D** *Pousada Casa da Geleia*, R Gen Viveiros 187, T334 1151. 2 excellent chalets set in a huge garden at the entrance to the town, and 4 very nice rooms, English spoken, good breakfast (Ze Carlos is a keen birdwatcher and an authority on the region, Lia makes excellent jams). **D** *Casa de Hélia*, R das Muritiba 102, T334 1143. Attractive and homely, English and some Hebrew spoken, good facilities, renowned breakfast. Recommended. **D** *Tradição*, R José Florêncio, T334 1137. Breakfast, fridge, mosquito net, pleasant. **D** *Pousada Violeiro*, R Prof Assis 70, T334 1259. Nice rooms with fan, some with bath, good view and breakfast. **E** *Pousada dos Duendes*, R do Pires s/n, T/F334 1229, oliviadosduendes@zaz.com.br Welcoming, very comfortable, run by the ever helpful Olivia Taylor who will sort out all trekking and walking activities for visitors, rooms with bath, fan, some with veranda, hot showers, small campsite, excellent food, vegetarian and vegan options, basically a home from home for all road-weary travellers. Olivia's travel agency, *H2O*, organizes day trips, hikes and kayaking. Highly recommended. **E** *Pousada Diangela*, R dos Mineiros 60, T334 1192. With good breakfast and vegetarian dinner. Juanita on R do Rosário rents rooms with access to washing and cooking facilities, US$3.50 pp. Cláudia and Isabel, R da Baderna 95, T334 1229, rent a house on the main praça in front of the Correios, US$4 pp without breakfast; they also have an agency with sort and long-term rents. **Camping**: *Alquimia*, 2 km before Lençóis, T334 1241, and *Camping Lumiar*, near Rosário church in centre, friendly. Recommended.

Picanha na Praça, opposite the bandstand on the square just above the main praça. Best **Eating** steak in town. *Artistas da Massa*, R Miguel Calmon. Italian. *O Xente Minina*, 100 m past the *Recanto das Águas* on the road out of town. Excellent pizzas and ambience. *Goody*, R da Rodaviária s/n. Good simple cooking. *Grisante*, on main praça. Good local food.The best night spots are *Veneno Café Bar*, on main praça. For drinks and sandwiches, plays good music. At weekends there is a local nightclub called *Inferninho* on R das Pedras. Not up to much but can be amusing, R$1 for men, free for girls. *Dom Oba*, at the top of town. Bar with good music and *churrasco*.

Artesanato Areias Coloridas, R das Pedras, owned by Taurino, is the best place for local sand **Shopping** paintings made in bottles. These are inexpensive and fascinating to see being done. They will *The Monday morning* make one as you wait. For ceramic work, the most original is *Jota*, who has a workshop *market is* which can be visited. Take the steps to the left of the school near the *Pousada Lençóis*. There *recommended* is a local craft market just off the main praça every night.

H2O, see Sleeping. *Lentur*, Av 7 de Setembro 10, T/F334 1271. Organizes day trips to nearby **Tour operators** caves and to see the sunset at Morro do Pai Inácio. Recommended. *Pé de Trilha Turismo Aventura*, Praça dos Nagos opposite the market building, T334 1124. Guiding, trekking, rents camping equipment, etc, can make reservations for most of the *pousadas* in the Chapada Diamantina (see below), represented in Salvador by *Tatur Turismo* (see above). Guides: *Edmilson* (known locally as Mil), R Domingos B Souza 70, T334 1319; he knows the region extremely well and is very knowledgeable. *Roy Funch*, T334 1305, royfunch@gd.com.br, the ex-director of the Parque Nacional Chapada Diamantina, is an excellent guide and can be found at his craft shop, *Funkart*, in the main praça (he and his wife also offer quiet and comfortable accommodation with a good breakfast at their home at Rua Pé da Ladeira 212). *Índio*, recommended, T334 1348, or ask around. Each *pousada* generally has a guide attached to it to take residents on tours, about US$20-30.

Real Expresso bus from Salvador; buses also from Recife, Ibotirama, Barreiras or Brasília, **Transport** 16 hrs, US$33.

Banks *Banco do Brasil*, 0900-1300 Mon-Fri, Visa ATM and changes TCs and US$ cash. No MasterCard. **Directory** **Communications** Post Office: main square, 0900-1700, Mon-Fri. **Tourist office** Sectur, is on Praça Oscar Maciel, next to the church across the river from town, T334 1327.

Brazil

Parque Nacional da Chapada Diamantina
Colour map 5, grid C4

Palmeiras, 50 km from Lençóis, is the headquarters of the Parque Nacional da Chapada Diamantina (founded 1985), which contains 1,500 sq km of mountainous country. There is an abundance of endemic plants, waterfalls, large caves (take care, and a strong torch, there are no signs and caves can be difficult to find without a guide), rivers with natural swimming pools and good walking tours. ■ *Information, T0xx75-332 2175, or Ibama, Av Juracy Magalhães Júnior 608, CEP 40295-140, Salvador, T0xx71-240 7322.*

Excursions near Lençóis and in the Chapada Diamantina Near the town, visit the **Serrano** with its wonderful natural pools in the river bed, which give a great hydro massage. A little further away is the **Salão de Areia**, where the coloured sands for the bottle paintings come from. **Ribeirão do Meio** is a 45-min walk from town; here locals slide down a long natural water chute into a big pool (it is best to be shown the way it is done and to take something to slide in). **Gruta do Lapão**, 3 hours from Lençóis, guide essential, is in quartz rock and therefore has no stalagmites. Some light rock climbing is required. **Cachoeira da Primavera**, two very pretty waterfalls close to town, recommended. **Cachoeira Sossego**, 45 mins from town, a 'picture postcard' waterfall, swimming pool, recommended. **Morro de Pai Inácio**, 30 km from Lençóis, has the best view of the Chapada, recommended at sunset (bus from Lençóis at 0815, 30 mins, US$1). In the park is the **Cachoeira da Fumaça** (Smoke Waterfall, also called **Glass**), 384 m, the second highest in Brazil. To see it, go by car to the village of **Capão** and walk 2½ hours. The view is astonishing; the updraft of the air currents often makes the water flow back up creating the 'smoke' effect. Olivia Taylor at the *Pousada dos Duendes* offers a three-day trek, the village of Capão and Capivara and Palmital falls from US$45. ■ *Local guides can often arrange transport to the more remote excursions, certainly this is possible when groups are involved.*

Sleeping Capão: **C** *Candombá*, F0xx75-332 2176, or through *Tatur Turismo* in Salvador. Good breakfast, excellent food, home-grown vegetables, run by Claude and Suzana (Claude speaks French and English and guides in the region). **D** *Pousada Verde*, at entrance to town. Very good breakfast. Recommended. **E** *Pouso Riacho do Ouro*. Recommended. **E** *Tatu Feliz*. No breakfast. **Mucugê**: **A** *Alpina Resort*, on a hill above the town, T0xx75-338 2150, www.alpinamucuge.com.br Panoramic views, log fires, helpful staff. Recommended.

South of Salvador

Valença
Phone code: 0xx75
Colour map 7, grid A6
Population: 77,509
271 km from Salvador via paved road

This small, attractive town stands at the mouth of the Rio Una. Two old churches stand on rising ground; the views from Nossa Senhora do Amparo are recommended. The town is in the middle of an area producing black pepper, cloves and piaçava (used in making brushes and mats). Other industries include the building and repair of fishing boats (saveiros). The Rio Una enters an enormous region of mangrove swamps. The main attraction of Valença is the beaches on the mainland (Guabim, 14 km north) and on the island of Tinharé. Avoid touts at the rodoviária. Better to visit the friendly tourist office opposite (T741 3311).

Sleeping **B** *do Porto*, Av Maçônica 50, T741 3066. Helpful, safe, good breakfast, good restaurant. **C** *Rafa*, Praça da Independência, T741 1816. Large rooms. Recommended. Next door is **D** *Guabim*, Praça da Independência, T741 3804. Modest with bath and buffet breakast. good *Akuarius* restaurant. **D** *Valença*, R Dr H Guedes Melo 15, T741 1807. Comfortable, good breakfast. Recommended.

Long-distance buses from new rodoviária, Av Maçônica, T741 1280.
Local buses from the old rodoviaria

Transport Many buses a day to/from **Salvador**, 5 hrs, US$6, several companies including *Aguia Branca* (T450 4400). For the shortest route to Valença, take the ferry from São Joaquim to Bom Despacho on Itaparica island, from where it is 130 km to Valença via Nazaré das Farinhas. To/from Bom Despacho on Itaparica, *Camarujipe* and *Águia Branca*, 16 a day, 1 hr 45 mins, US$3.60.

Tinharé and Morro de São Paulo

Tinharé is a large island separated from the mainland by the estuary of the Rio Una and mangrove swamps, so that it is hard to tell which is land and which is water. The most popular beaches and *pousadas* are at Morro de São Paulo. Immediately south is the island of **Boipeba**, separated from Tinharé by the Rio do Inferno. On this island, too, there are lovely beaches and a small fishing village, also called Boipeba.

1½ hrs south of Valença by boat

Morro de São Paulo is situated on the headland at the northernmost tip of Tinharé, lush with ferns, palms and birds of paradise. The village is dominated by the lighthouse and the ruins of a colonial fort (1630), built as a defence against European raiders. It has a landing place on the sheltered landward side, dominated by the old gateway of the fortress. From the lighthouse a path leads to a ruined look out with cannon, which has panoramic views. The fort is a good point to watch the sunset from. Dolphins can be seen in August. Fonte de Ceu waterfall is reached by walking along the beach to **Gamboa** then inland. Watch the tide; it's best to take a guide, or take a boat back to Morro (US$0.50-1). No motor vehicles are allowed on the island. On 7 September there's a big festival with live music on the beach.

There is a port tax of US$1 payable at the prefeitura on leaving the island; this is resented by many

Morro de São Paulo There are many cheap *pousadas* and rooms to rent near the fountain (Fonte Grande) but this part of town is very hot at night. **C** *Pousada Gaúcho*. Huge breakfast, shared bath. A little further along and up some steep steps to the left is **B** *Pousada Colibri*. Cool, always a breeze blowing, excellent views, only 6 apartments, Helmut, the owner, speaks English and German.

Sleeping
Expensive Dec-Mar, cheaper and more tranquil during the rest of the year. Very crowded during public holidays

Beach hotels The beaches on Morro de São Paulo are at the bottom of the main street where one turns right on to the first beach (Primeira Praia). **A** *Pousada Vistabella*, T0xx73-783 1001. Owner Petruska is extremely welcoming, good rooms, those to the front have good views and are cooler, all have fans, hammocks. **B** *Pousada Farol do Morro*, T483 1036, F243 4207. All rooms with sea view, cool. **C** *Pousada Ilha da Saudade*. Good breakfast, simple. **C** *Pousada Ilha do Sol*. Good views. On third beach (Terceira Praia) is **A** *Pousada Fazenda Caeira*, T0xx75-4411272. Large grounds, private, well stocked library with snooker and other games. **D** *Pousada Aradhia*. Balconies with ocean view. **E** *Pousada Govinda*. Simple, good breakfast, other meals available, English and Spanish spoken.

In **Boipeba** **A** *Pousada Tassimirim*, T9981 2378 (R Com Madureira 40, 45400-000 Valença), www.ilhaboipeba.org.br Bungalows, bar, restaurant, including breakfast and dinner, secluded. **D** *Pousada Luar das Águas* (T9981 1012). Simple, good.

Mid-range *Bahiana*, on the main square, good food. Recommended. *Belladonna* on the main street is a very good Italian restaurant with great music, a good meeting point, owner Guido speaks Italian, English and French, and is a willing source of information on the Morro, open daily from 1800 till the small hours. *Morena Bela*, good for *moqueca*. *Restaurant Gaúcho* for good, reasonably priced, typical regional cooking. **Cheap** *Casablanca* is a good simple restaurant, open daily till late, good breakfasts at *Comida Natural*, on the main street, *comida a kilo*, good juices. Good pasta dishes at *Club do Balango* on the second beach, where many beach huts offer cool drinks and meals. *Barraca Caita* opens till late with good music at weekends. They have snorkelling equipment for hire, popular meeting point, potent cocktail parties every night! Another *barraca* is **Ponto da Ilha** alongside. There are many other *barracas* on the third beach.

Eating

From Salvador, several companies operate a ferry (1 hr 30 mins) and catamaran (30 mins) service from the Terminal Marítimo in front of the Mercado Modelo to Morro de São Paulo. Times vary according to the weather and season. Lancha Farol do Morro, T241 7858 and *Catamara Gamboa do Morro*, T9975 6395.

Transport
Part of the trip is on the open sea, which can be rough

Boats leave every day from Valença for Gamboa (1½ hrs) and Morro de São Paulo (1½ hrs) from the main bridge in Valença 5 times a day (signalled by a loud whistle). The fare is US$2.50. A *lancha rápida* taking 25 mins travels the route between Valença and Morro, US$8. Only buses between 0530-1100 from Salvador to Valença connect with ferries. If not

Brazil

stopping in Valença, get out of the bus by the main bridge in town, don't wait till you get to the rodoviária, which is a long way from the ferry. Private boat hire can be arranged if you miss the ferry schedule. A responsible local boatman is *Jario*, T0xx75-741 1681. He also offers excursions to other islands, especially Boipeba. There is a regular boat from Valença to Boipeba on weekdays 1000-1230 depending on tide, return 1500-1700, 3-4 hrs.

Ilhéus

Phone code: 0xx73
Post code: 45650
Colour map 7, grid A6
Population: 222,127
462 km S of Salvador

At the mouth of the Rio Cachoeira, the port serves a district which produces 65% of all Brazilian cocoa. Shipping lines call regularly. A bridge links the north bank of the river with Pontal, where the airport is located. The local beaches are splendid, but the central beach is polluted. It is the birthplace of Jorge Amado (1912) and the setting of one of his most famous novels, *Gabriela, cravo e canela* (*Gabriela, Clove and Cinnamon*). There is a tourist office on the beach opposite Praça Castro Alves (a few minutes from the cathedral), T634 3510, friendly, maps US$2, recommended. *Festa de São Sebastião* (17-20 January), *Carnival, Festa de São Jorge* (23 April), *Foundation day*, 28 June, and *Festa do Cacau* throughout October. The church of **São Jorge** (1556), the city's oldest, is on the Praça Rui Barbosa; it has a small museum. The cathedral of **São Sebastião**, on the Praça Dom Eduardo, near the seashore, is a huge, early 20th-century building. In Alto da Vitória is the 17th century **Nossa Senhora da Vitória**, built to celebrate a victory over the Dutch. Ask in travel agencies for trips to Rio de Engenho to visit **Santana** church (1537).

North of Ilhéus, two good beaches are Marciano, with reefs offshore and good surfing, and Barra, 1 km further north at the mouth of the Rio Almada. South of the river, Pontal beaches can be reached by 'Barreira' bus; alight just after *Hotel Jardim Atlântico (AL)*. Between Ilhéus and **Olivença** are fine beaches, such as Cururupe, Batuba (good surfing) and Cai n'Água in Olivença itself (also good surfing).

Local drink, coquinho, coconut filled with cachaça, only for the strongest heads! Also try suco de cacau at juice stands

Sleeping and eating **A** *Hotel Barravento* on Malhado beach, R NS das Graças 276, T/F634 3223. Ask for the penthouse – usually no extra charge, including breakfast and refrigerator. **A** *Ilhéus Praia*, Praça Dom Eduardo (on beach), T634 2533. Pool, helpful. Recommended. **B** *Pousada Sol Atlântico*, Av Lomanto Júnior 1450, Pontal T231 8059. Good view over bay, fan, TV, balcony. Plenty of cheap hotels near the municipal rodoviária in centre, also **D** *Hotel Atlântico Sul*, R Bento Berilo 224, Centro, T231 4668. Good bar/restaurant. Recommended. **D** *Cacau D'Ouro*, R Vieiro 33, T231 3713. With bath and breakfast, restaurant with good views of the town. **Campsite** *Estância das Fontes*, 19 km on road south to Olivença, T212 2505. Cheap, shady. Recommended. A recommended eating place is *Os Velhos Marinheiros*, Av 2 de Julho, on the waterfront. *Vesúvio*, Praça Dom Eduardo, next to the cathedral, made famous by Amado's novel (see above), now Swiss-owned. Very good but pricey. *Nogar*, Av Bahia 377, close to the sea. Good pizzas and pasta.

Transport **Bus**: Rodoviária is 4 km from the centre on Itabuna road. Several daily to **Salvador**, 7 hrs, US$14.40 (*leito* US$29, *Expresso São Jorge*); 0620 bus goes via Itaparica, leaving passengers at Bom Despacho ferry station on the island – thence 50-mins ferry to Salvador. To **Eunápolis**, 5 hrs, US$5.40, this bus also leaves from the central bus terminal. Other destinations also served; local buses leave from Praça Cairu. Insist that taxi drivers have meters and price charts.

Porto Seguro

About 400 km south of Ilhéus on the coast is the old town of Porto Seguro. Building is subject to controls on height and materials, in keeping with traditional Bahian styles (colonial or Indian). In the area are remains of original Atlantic coastal forest, with parrots, monkeys, marmosets and snakes.

Pedro Álvares Cabral sighted land at Monte Pascoal south of Porto Seguro. As the sea here was too open, he sailed north in search of a secure protected harbour, entering the mouth of the Rio Burnahém to find the harbour he later called Porto Seguro (safe port). Where the first mass was celebrated, a cross marks the spot on the road between Porto Seguro and Santa Cruz Cabrália. A tourist village, Coroa Vermelha, has sprouted at the site of Cabral's first landfall, 20 mins by bus to the north of Porto Seguro. It has souvenir shops selling Pataxó-Tupi Indian items, beach bars, hotels and rental houses, all rather uncoordinated.

Phone code: 0xx73
Post code: 45810
Colour map 7, grid A6
Population: 95,721

Town beaches are not recommended. The best beaches are north of town along the Santa Cruz de Cabrália road (known as Av Beira Mar – BR-367). For beaches south of the Rio Buranhém, see below under Arraial d'Ajuda and further south

Brazil

From the roundabout at the entrance to Porto Seguro take a wide, steep, unmarked path uphill to the historical city, **Cidade Histórica**, three churches (Nossa Senhora da Misericórdia-1530, Nossa Senhora do Rosário-1534, and Nossa Senhora da Pena-1718), the former jail and the monument marking the landfall of Gonçalo Coelho; a small, peaceful place with lovely gardens and panoramic views. There are *borrachudos*, little flies that bite feet and ankles in the heat of the day; coconut oil keeps them off; at night mosquitoes can be a problem (but there is no malaria, dengue or yellow fever).

Guided tours of the area can be arranged with *BPS*, at the Shopping Centre, T288 2373. *Companhia do Mar* (Praça dos Pataxós, T288 2981) does daily trips by schooner to coral reefs. The most popular is to Recife de Fora, with good snorkelling; it leaves daily at 1000, returns 1630, about US$10, US$2.50 extra for snorkelling gear.

Porto Seguro

The town is a popular holiday resort with many charter companies flying in directly from Rio and São Paulo. Room capacity of the local hotel industry is greater than that of Salvador.

A *Pousada Imperador*, Estrada do Aeroporto, T288 2759, F288 2900. 4-star, all facilities, interesting architecture, above the city, great views from pool deck. **A** *Estalagem Porto Seguro*, R Marechal Deodoro 66, T288 2095, F288 3692. In an old colonial house, relaxing atmosphere, a/c, TV, pool, good breakfast. Highly recommended. **A** *Pousada Casa Azul*, 15 de Novembro 11, T/F288 2180. TV, a/c, good pool and garden, quiet part of town. **A** *Pousada Alegrete*, Av

Sleeping

Prices rise steeply Dec-Feb and Jul. Off-season rates can drop by 50%, for stays of more than 3 nights: negotiate. Outside Dec-Feb rooms with bath and hot water can be rented for US$150 per month

■ **Sleeping**
1 Pousada Aquarius
2 Pousada dos Navegantes

dos Navegantes 567, T/F288 1738. All facilities. Recommended. **B** *Pousada Las Palmas*, Praça Antônio Carlos Magalhães 102, T/F288 2643. A/c, TV, no pool. Highly recommended. **B** *Pousada Jandaias*, R das Jandaias 112, T288 2611, F288 2738. Fan, great breakfast, tranquil. Recommended. **B** *Pousada dos Raizes* (**C** without breakfast), Praça dos Pataxós 196, T/F288 4717. Recommended. **C** *Pousada Coral*, R Assis Chateaubriand 74, T/F288 2630. A/c, TV, good location. **C** *Pousada Da Orla*, Av Portugal 404, T/F288 1131. Fan, good breakfast, great location. Highly recommended. **C** *Pousada do Francês*, Av 22 de Abril 180, T/F288 2469. A/c, TV, breakfast. Recommended. **C** *Pousada Mar e Sol*, Av Getúlio Vargas 223, T/F288 2137. Fan in most apartments, a/c in a few, family run. **C** *Pousada dos Navegantes*, Av 22 de Abril 212, T288 2390, F288 2486, www.portonet.com.br/navegantes Family-run, a/c, TV, pool, conveniently located for all services. Recommended. **D** *Pousada da Praia*, Av Getúlio Vargas 153, T/F288 2908. A/c, TV, pool, breakfast, comfortable. **D** *Pousada Aquárius*, R Pedro Álvares Cabral 174, T/F288 2738. No breakfast, family run, central. **D** *Estalagem da Yvonne*, R Marechal Deodoro 298, T/F288 1515. Some rooms with a/c. **E** *Porto Brasília*, Praça Antônio Carlos Magalhães 234. Fans, mosquito nets, with breakfast, **E** without. **F** *Pousada Alto Mar*, R Bela Vista, behind the cathedral. Cheaper without breakfast, hot water, safe, good views of the port. **F** *Pousada Casa Grande*, Av dos Navegantes 107, Centro, T288 2003. Comfortable, multilingual, hearty breakfast. **Youth hostels** *Porto Seguro*, R Cova da Moça 720, T/F288 1742. *Coroa Vermelha*, on road to Santa Cruz Cabrália, T872 1155. Both IYHA. **Camping** *Camping dos Marajas*, Av Getúlio Vargas, central. *Camping da Gringa*, Praia do Cruzeiro, T288 2076. Laundry, café, pool, excellent, US$5 per night. *Camping Mundaí Praia*, US$8 per night, T879 2287. *Tabapiri Country*, BR-367, Km 61.5, next to the rodoviária on the road leading to the *Cidade Histórica*, T288 2269.

Eating   **Expensive** *Cruz de Malta*, R Getúlio Vargas 358. Good seafood. **Mid-range** *Anti-Caro*, R Assis Chateaubriand 26. Good. Recommended. Also antique shop, good atmosphere. *Les Agapornis*, Av dos Navegantes 180. Wide selection of crêpes and pizzas. *Prima Dona*, No 247. Italian, good. *Tres Vintens*, Av Portugal 246. Good imaginative seafood dishes. Recommended. *Vida Verde*, R Dois de Julho 92, T2882766. Vegetarian food, open 1100-2100 except Sunday. **Cheap** Good breakfast at *Pau Brasil*, Praça dos Pataxós. *Preto Velho*, on Praça da Bandeira. Good value à la carte or self-service. On Praça Pataxós: *da Japonêsa*, No 38. Excellent value with varied menu, open 0800-2300. Recommended. *Ponto do Encontro*, No 106. Good simple food, owners rent rooms, open 0800-2400.

Entertainment   Porto Seguro is famous for the *lambada*. A good bar for live music is *Porto Prego* on R Pedro Álvares Cabral, small cover charge. *Sotton Bar*, Praça de Bandeira, is lively as are *Pronto Socorro do Choppe*, *Doce Letal 50* and *Studio Video Bar*. There are lots of bars and street cafés on Av Portugal.

Tour operators   *Brazil travel*, Av 22 de Abril 200, T/F288 1824/679 1276 braziltravel@braziltravel.tur.br Dutch-run travel agency, all types of trips organized, English, German, Dutch, French and Spanish spoken. Several agencies at the airport. **Diving**: *Portomar Ltda*, R Dois de Julho 178. Arranges diving and snorkelling trips to the coral reefs offshore, professional instructors, equipment hire.

Transport   **Rentals**   **Car hire:** Several companies at the airport. **Bicycles**, *Oficina de Bicicleta*, Av Getúlio Vargas e R São Pedro, about US$10 for 24 hrs. Also at Praça de Bandeira and at 2 de Julho 242.

Airport T288 *1877/2010*   **Air**   Daily from Rio, with *Nordeste*, via São Paulo; *Nordeste* also twice daily from Salvador; *TAM* daily from Salvador, Belo Horizonte (except Mon) and São Paulo (except Thu); *Vasp* twice a week to Belo Horizonte and Salvador. Taxi airport-Porto Seguro, US$7. Also buses.

At Brazilian holiday times, all transport north or south should be booked well in advance   **Bus**   From Porto Seguro: **Salvador** (*Águia Branca*), daily, 12 hrs, US$22.25. **Vitória**, daily, 11 hrs, US$18. **Ilhéus**, daily 0730, 5½ hrs, US$11. **Eunápolis**, 1 hr, US$2. For **Rio** direct buses (*São Geraldo*), leaving at 1745, US$35 (*leito* 70), 18 hrs, from Rio direct at 1600 (very cold a/c), take warm clothes), or take 1800 for Ilhéus and change at Eunápolis. To **Belo Horizonte** daily, direct, US$33 (*São Geraldo*). To **São Paulo** direct, 1045, 25 hrs, not advisable, very slow, much better to go to Rio then take Rio-São Paulo express. Other services via Eunápolis (those going north avoid Salvador) or Itabuna (5 hrs, US$9).

There is a new rodoviária, with reliable luggage store and lounge on the 3rd floor, on the road to Eunápolis, 2 km from the centre, regular bus service (30 mins) through the city to the old rodoviária near the port. Local buses US$0.30. Taxis charge US$5 from the rodoviária to the town or ferry (negotiate at quiet times). For local trips a taxi is an economic proposition for 2 or more passengers wishing to visit various places in 1 day.

Banks *Banco do Brasil*, Av Beira Mar, open 1000-1500, changes TCs and US$ cash, also Visa ATM. Also at airport. *Bradesco*, Av Getúlio Vargas, Visa ATM. *Adeltur*, in Shopping Avenida, near Banco do Brasil. *Agência do Descobrimento*, Av Getúlio Vargas, also arranges flight tickets and house rental. **Communications** Internet: *Ellisnet*. Post Office: In the mini-shopping centre on the corner of R das Jandaias and Av dos Navegantes **Telephone:** *Telemar* service, post, Praça dos Pataxós beside ferry terminal, open daily 0700-2200, cheap rates after 2000, receives and holds faxes, 288 3915. **Tourist office** Secretaria de Turismo de Porto Seguro, T288 4124, turismo@portonet.com.br A website is www.portonet.com.br/guia/default.htm

Directory

Only 10 mins north of Coroa Vermelha, **Santa Cruz Cabrália** is a delightful small town at the mouth of the Rio João de Tiba, with a splendid beach, river port, and a 450-year-old church with a fine view. A good trip from here is to Coroa Alta, a reef 50 minutes away by boat, passing along the tranquil river to the reef and its crystal waters and good snorkelling. Daily departure at 1000. A recommended boatman is Zezé (T/F282 1152) on the square by the river's edge, helpful, knowledgeable. The trip costs around US$15 without lunch. *Secretaria de Turismo*, T282 1122. A 15-minute river crossing by ferry to a new road on the opposite bank gives easy access to the deserted beaches of **Santo André** and **Santo Antônio**. There are two *pousadas*: *Victor Hugo*, T9985 5292 (mob) and *Tribo da Praia*, T282 1002, helpful American owner. Hourly buses from Santa Cruz to Porto Seguro (23 km).

Sleeping C *Pousada do Mineiro*, T282 1042. A/c, pool, sauna, good *churrascaria*. Recommended. On the hill overlooking the town: **C** *Pousada Atobá*, T/F282 1131. A/c, pool, sauna.

Arraial da Ajuda

Across the Rio Buranhém south from Porto Seguro is the village of Arraial da Ajuda, the gateway to the idyllic beaches of the south coast. Set high on a cliff, there are great views of the coastline from behind the church of Nossa Senhora da Ajuda in the main praça. Ajuda has become very popular with younger tourists (especially Israelis; many restaurant menus in Hebrew) and there are many *pousadas*, from the very simple to the very sophisticated, restaurants, bars and small shops. Parties are held almost every night, on the beach or in the main street, called the *Broadway*. Drugs are said to be widely available, but easily avoided. At Brazilian holiday times (especially New Year and Carnival) it is very crowded.

The beaches, several protected by a coral reef, are splendid. The nearest is 15 mins' walk away. During daylight hours those closest to town (take 'R da Praia' out of town to the south) are extremely busy; excellent *barracas* sell good seafood, drinks, and play music. The best beaches are Mucugê, Pitinga (*'bronzeamento irrestrito'* or nude sunbathing!), Lagoa Azul (with medicinal white mud) and Taipé.

Colour map 7, grid A6

Each August there is a pilgrimage to the shrine of Nossa Senhora da Ajuda (1549). In the church is an interesting room full of ex-voto offerings. There are fine views from behind the church

Brazil

Sleeping

At busy times, don't expect to find anything under US$15 pp in a shared room for a minimum stay of 5-7 days. Camping is best at these times. All hotels in the list are recommended

A *Pousada Pitinga*, Praia Pitinga, T575 1067, F575 1035. Bold architecture amid Atlantic forest, a hideaway, great food and pool, a Roteiros de Charme hotel. **A** *Pousada Canto d'Alvorada*, on road to Ajuda, T575 1218. **C** out of season, Swiss run, 7 cabins, restaurant, laundry facilities. **B** *Pousada Caminho do Mar*, Estrada do Mucugê 246, T/F575 1099. Owners helpful. **B** *Pousada do Robalo*, T575 1053, F575 1078. Good grounds, welcoming, good pool. **B** *Pousada Arquipélago*, T/F575 1123. Every room decorated differently, reading library, relaxed atmosphere. **B** *Ivy Marey*, near centre on road to beach, T575 1106. 4 rooms and 2 bungalows, showers, nice décor, good bar, French/Brazilian owned. Nearby is **B** *Le Grand Bleu*, T575 7272. Same owner, good *pizzaria*. **B** *Sole Mio*, T575 1115, just off the beach road leading from the ferry to Arraial. French owners, English spoken, laid back, 4 chalets, excellent *pizzaria*.

C *Pousada Erva Doce*, Estrada do Mucugê 200, T575 1113. Good restaurant, well appointed chalets. **C** *Pousada Natur*, T288 2738. Run by a German environmentalist, English spoken. **C** *Pousada Tubarão*, R Bela Vista, beyond the church on the right, T575 1086. Good view of the coastline, cool, good restaurant. **C** *Pousada Mar Aberto*, Estrada do Mucugê 554, T/F575 1153, very near Mucugê beach, 400 m from centre of village. Set in lush gardens.

D *Pousada Flamboyant*, Estrada do Mucugê 89, T575 1025. Pleasant, good breakfast. **D** *Pousada Flor*, on praça, T575 1143. Owner Florisbela Valiense takes good care of female guests. **D** *Pousada Gabriela*, Travessa dos Pescadores, T575 1237. With breakfast. **D** *Pousada do Mel*, Praça São Bras, T575 1309. Simple, good breakfast. **D** *Pousada Porto do Meio*, on the road between the ferry and the village, T/F575 1017, portodomeio@ uol.com.br Close to beach, a/c, good breakfast, small pool, laundry facilities, Swiss run, English, French, German and Spanish spoken. **D** *Pousada Corujão*, on the way to the beach, T/F575 1508. Bungalows, cooking facilities, laundry, restaurant and book exchange.

Camping *Praia*, on Mucugê Beach, good position and facilities. *Chão do Arraial*, 5 mins from Mucugê beach, shady, good snack bar, also hire tents. Recommended. Also *Camping do Gordo*, on the left shortly after leaving the ferry, on a beach which is not as good as Mucugê. Generally, Arraial da Ajuda is better for camping than Porto Seguro.

Eating

Mid-range: *São João*, near the church, is the best typical restaurant. *Mão na Massa*, an excellent Italian restaurant, behind the church. Recommended. *Fatta em Casa*, 5 mins by taxi or 15-min walk from centre. Delicious homemade pastas, sauces and desserts, good atmosphere and value. *Los Corales*, Travessa dos Pescadores 167, Spanish, *paella* a speciality. **Cheap**: *Paulinho Pescador*, open 1200-2200, excellent seafood, also chicken and meat, US$5, English spoken, good service, very popular.*Café das Cores*, on way to the beach, good cakes and snacks, expresso coffee. *Manda Brasa*, on Broadway, good snack bar. Recommended *barracas* are *Tem Q Dá* and *Agito* on Mucugê beach and *Barraca de Pitinga* and *Barraca do Genésio* on Pitinga.

Entertainment

At the *Jatobar* bar the *lambada* is danced, on the main praça, by the church (opens 2300 – *pensão* at the back is cheap, clean and friendly). There is also a *capoeira* institute; ask for directions. *Gringo Louco* is a good bar as is *Duere*, great dance bar. Many top Brazilian bands play at the beach clubs at Praia do Parracho during the summer.

Transport

Ferries across the Rio Buranhém from Porto Seguro take 15 mins to the south bank, US$0.60 for foot passengers, US$3.60 for cars, every 30 mins day and night. It is then a further 5 km to Arraial da Ajuda, US$0.50 by bus; kombis charge US$0.75 pp; taxis US$5.

Directory

Banks Mobile *Banco do Brazil* in the main square during high season. **Communications** Internet: *Ellisnet*, Shopping Ajuda, Caminho da Praia. Also long distance calls. **Telephone:** *Telemar* on main praça, 0800-2200; faxes number is 575 1309, US$1.50 to receive.

Trancoso

25 km S of Porto Seguro
Phone code 0xx73

Some 15 km from Ajuda is Trancoso. It is a 3-hr walk along the beach, but watch out for the tides. This pretty, peaceful village, with its beautiful beaches (Praia dos Nativos is recommended, Pedra Grande is nudist), is popular with Brazilian tourists and many Europeans have built or bought houses there. There are good restaurants around the main praça. From the end of Praça São João there is a fine coastal panorama. Trancoso has an historic church, São João Batista (1656). Between Ajuda and Trancoso is the village of Rio da Barra. ■ *Trancoso can be reached by bus (1 every hr, from 0800, last returns 1800, US$1.25, 1 hr, more buses and colectivos in summer), colectivo, or by hitchhiking. Colectivos run hourly from Trancoso to Ajuda, US$1.15. Arriving from the south, change buses at Eunápolis from where the newly paved Linha Verde road runs.*

Sleeping **A** *Caipim Santo*, T668 1122, to the left of the main praça. With breakfast, the best restaurant in Trancoso. Recommended. **B** *Pousada Calypso*, Parque Municipal, T668 1113. Good apartments, comfortable, rooms at lower price also available, good library, German and English spoken. Recommended. **B** *Pousada Terra do Sol*, main praça, T668 1036. Without breakfast, good. Recommended. **C** *Pousada Canto Verde*, T0xx24-243 7823. With breakfast, restaurant only in high season. Recommended. Also on the main praça, **C** *Gulab Mahal*, oriental style, lovely garden, vast breakfast, good restaurant. Recommended. **D-E** *Pousada do Bosque*, on the way to the beach. English, German and Spanish spoken, cabins with hammocks and showers, hot water, with breakfast, camping facilities also available, good value. **E** *Pousada Beira Mar*. With bath, restaurant serving *prato feito*.

About 500 m inland away from main praça (known as the 'quadrado') lies the newer part of Trancoso (known as the 'invasão') with 2 good value *pousadas*: **D** *Pousada Quarto Crescente*, about 25 mins from beach. English, German, Dutch and Spanish spoken, cooking facilities, laundry, helpful owners, library. **D** *Luna Pousa*, further along on the left. With breakfast, well ventilated, only 4 rooms. There are many houses to rent, very good ones are rented by Clea who can be contacted at *Restaurant Abacaxi*.

Eating *Urano*, just before the main praça. Good portions. *Rama* has also been recommended, also *Silvana e Cia* in the historical centre. *Abacaxi* on the main praça does good breakfasts, light snacks and very good crêpes. Good breakfast at *Pé das Frutas*, *Maré Cheia* next door for good simple dishes, great *moqueca*. *Pacha* on the seafront does a good *prato feito*. Good ice cream at *Tão Vez*.

Apart from restaurants which serve breakfast most open at 1500 until 2200 or so

This atmospheric, peaceful fishing village on the banks of the Rio Caraíva and near the Pataxó Indian Reserve has no wheeled vehicles, no electricity nor hot water, but has marvellous beaches and is a real escape from the more developed Trancoso and Porto Seguro. Despite the difficulty of getting there, it is becoming increasingly popular. Good walks are north to Praia do Satu (Sr Satu provides an endless supply of coconut milk), or 6 km south to a rather sad Pataxó Indian village (watch the tides as you may get cut off). Horses can be hired from *Pousada Lagoa* or *Pizzaria Barra Velha*. Boats can be hired for US$40 per day from Zé Pará to Caruípe beach, snorkelling at Pedra de Tatuaçu reef and Corombau (take your own mask and fins) or for diving (best December to February). Prainha river beach, about 30 minutes away, and mangrove swamps can also be visited by canoe or launch. The high season is December-February and July; the wettest months are April-June and November. Use flip-flops for walking the sand streets and take a torch. There are no medical facilities and only rudimentary policing.

Caraíva
65 km S of Porto Seguro

Sleeping and eating **D** *Pousada Lagoa*, T/F0xx73-9965 6662. Chalets and bungalows under cashew trees, good restaurant, popular bar, own generator. The owner, Hermínia, speaks English and is very helpful and can arrange local trips and excursions. **D** *Pousada da Terra*, far end of village near Indian reserve. With breakfast. Recommended. Similar is *Pousada da Barra*. Simpler lodging: *Pousada da Canoa*, attached to *Bar do Pará*, by the river, which serves the best fish in the village, US$7-8 (try *sashimi* or *moqueca*). *Santuzzi*, 100 m from *Canaã* grocery store. *Oasis*, run by taxi driver Batista. Other good restaurants are *Natal* by *Bar do Pará*, and *Pizzaria Barra Velha*, by the canoe crossing. There is forró dancing 0100-0600 at *Pelé* and *Ouriços* on alternate nights in season.

Low season prices

Brazil

Transport Caraíva can only be reached by canoe across the river. Access roads are poor and almost impossible after heavy rain. From Porto Seguro either go to Arraial da Ajuda and take the Rio Buranhém ferry crossing, or take the detour to the Eunápolis road then on to Trancoso, after which the road is bad, especially after the turn-off to Oteiro das Brisas, 13 km before Caraíva. *Aguia Azul* bus company takes this route from Porto Seguro at 1500. Taxis are unwilling to go from Porto Seguro or Arraial, so call Batista in Caraíva, who charges US$60. If arriving by bus from the south, change to *Aguia Azul* bus in Itabela, departs at 1500, or take a taxi, about 50 km. Drivers should leave the BR-101 at Monte Pascal (Km 769, 800 m past the Texaco station) and drive 41 km to Caraíva.

Parque Nacional de Monte Pascoal
Colour map 7, grid A6

South of Porto Seguro, reached by a 14 km paved access road at Km 796 of the BR-101, the Parque Nacional de Monte Pascoal set up in 1961 to preserve the flora, fauna and birdlife of the coastal area in which Europeans made landfall in Brazil (Caixa Postal 076, CEP 45830-000 Itamaraju, T0xx73-281 2419). The Pataxó Indian reservation is located at Corombau village, on the ocean shore of the park. Corombau can be reached by schooner from Porto Seguro. A small luxury resort has been built at Corombau. ■ *From Caraíva there is a river crossing by boats which are always on hand. Buses run from Itamaraju 16 km to the south, at 0600 on Fri-Mon.*

Caravelas
Colour map 7, grid A6
Population: 20,103

Further south still, 107 km from Itamaruju (93 km south of Eunápolis), is this charming little town, rapidly developing for tourism, but a major trading town in 17th and 18th centuries. Caravelas is in the mangroves; the beaches are about 10 km away at Barra de Caravelas (hourly buses), a fishing village. Teresa and Ernesto (from Austria) organize boat trips (US$40 per day), jeep and horse hire (turn left between the bridge and the small supermarket). 'Alternative' beach holidays (organic vegetarian food, yoga, meditation, other activities) with Beky and Eno on the unspoilt island of Coçumba. Recommended. Contact *Abrolhos Turismo*, Praça Dr Imbassahi 8, T297 1149, rents diving gear and arranges boat trips. Helpful tourist information at *Ibama Centro de Visitantes*, Barão do Rio Branco 281. ■ *Buses to Texeira de Freitas (4 a day), Salvador, Nanuque and Prado. Flights from Belo Horizonte, São Paulo and Salvador to Caravelas; otherwise fly to Porto Seguro.*

Sleeping **C** *Pousada Caravelense*, 50 m from the rodoviária, T297 1182. TV, fridge, good breakfast, excellent restaurant. Recommended. **D** *Shangri-la*, Barão do Rio Branco 216. Bath, breakfast. **Barra de Caravelas C** *Pousada das Sereias*. French-owned. **E** *Pousada Jaquita*. Use of kitchen, big breakfast, bath, airy rooms, the owner is Secka who speaks English. There are some food shops, restaurants and bars.

The warm current and shallow waters (8-15 m deep) make a rich undersea life (about 160 species of fish) and good snorkelling

The **Parque Nacional Marinho dos Abrolhos** is 70 km east of Caravelas. Abrolhos is an abbreviation of Abre os olhos: 'Open your eyes' from Amérigo Vespucci's exclamation when he first sighted the reef in 1503. Established in 1983, the park consists of five small islands (Redonda, Siriba, Guarita, Sueste, Santa Bárbara), which are volcanic in origin, and several coral reefs. The park is best visited in October-March. Humpback whales breed and give birth from July to December. Diving is best December-February. The archipelago is administered by *Ibama* and a navy detachment mans a lighthouse on Santa Bárbara, which is the only island that may be visited. Permission from *Parque Nacional Marinho dos Abrolhos*, Praia do Kitombo s/n, Caravelas, Bahia 45900, T0xx73-297 1111, or Ibama, Av Juracy Magalhães Junior 608, CEP 40295-140, Salvador, T0xx71-240 7322. Visitors are not allowed to spend the night on the islands, but may stay overnight on schooners.

Transport The journey to the islands takes between 1 and 6 hrs depending on the boat. Mestre Onofrio Frio in Alcobaça, Bahia, T0xx73-293 2195 is authorized by the Navy to take tourists. Tours also available from *Abrolhos Turismo*, see above, Caravelas (about US$170 for a slow 2½ day tour by *saveiro*). 1-day tours can be made in a faster boat (US$100) from Abrolhos or the Marina Porto Abrolhos.

Brazil

North from Salvador

The paved BA-099 coast road from near Salvador airport is known as the Estrada do Coco (Coconut Highway, because of the many plantations) and for 50 km passes some beautiful beaches. The best known from south to north are Ipitanga (with its reefs), Buraquinho, Jauá, Arembepe, Guarajuba, Itacimirim, Castelo Garcia D'Ávila (with its 16th century fort) and Forte. Buses serve most of these destinations.

The fishing village, 80 km north of Salvador, takes its name from the castle built by a Portuguese settler, Garcia D'Ávila, in 1556 to warn the city to the south of enemy invasion. Praia do Forte is now a charming, tranquil fishing village with sand streets and lovely beaches. There is a strong emphasis on preservation of the local flora and fauna. Inland from the coast is a *restinga* forest, which grows on sandy soil with a very delicate ecosystem. Near the village is a small *pantanal* (marshy area), which is host to a large number of birds, caymans and other animals. Birdwatching trips on the *pantanal* are rewarding. The Tamar Project preserves the sea turtles which lay their eggs in the area. Praia do Forte is now the headquarters of the national turtle preservation programme and is funded by the Worldwide Fund for Nature. There is a visitors' centre at the project; its address is Caixa Postal 2219, Rio Vermelho, CEP 40210-990, Rio Vermelho, Salvador, Bahia, T0xx71-876 1045/1113, F876 1067. ■ *Buses to Praia do Forte from Salvador (US$2): Santa Maria/Catuense leave 5 times daily from rodoviária, 1½ hrs.*

Praia do Forte

Sleeping and eating LL *Praia do Forte EcoResort*, Av do Farol, T676 4000, reservas@ pfr.com.br Polynesian-inspired and deserving of its name, spacious, beautiful beachfront grounds and full programme of activities (including humpback whale and turtle watching), 5 pools. Recommended. **A** *Pousada Praia do Forte*, Al do Sol, T676 1116, F876 1033. Chalets in peaceful setting, on beach. Recommended. **A** *Pousada Solar da Lagoa*, R do Forte, T676 1029. Good location, spacious rooms. **A** *Pousada Sobrado da Vila*, Al do Sol, T/F676 1152. Pleasant, good value restaurant. **B** *Pousada Tatuapara*, Praça dos Artistas, T676 1015. Friendly. **B** *Pousada João Sol*, R da Corvina, T676 1054. Owner speaks English, Spanish and German, good, only 6 apartments, great breakfast. Recommended. **B** *Pousada da Sereia*, R da Corvina, T676 1032. With fan, good breakfast. **B** *Pousada Sol Nascente*, on the street parallel to the main street. Good, bath, frigobar, fan, breakfast. **C** *Tia Helena*, Helena being the motherly proprietor who provides an excellent meal and enormous breakfast, nice rooms. Highly recommended. 2-bedroom apartments at *Solar dos Arcos* on the beach, US$90, with pool, gardens, lawns. Warmly recommended. **Youth Hostel D** *Albergue da Juventude Praia do Forte*, R da Aurora 3, T676 1094, praiadoforte@albergue.com.br With bathroom, fan, breakfast, kitchen and shop, more expensive for non-IYHA members. *Bar Da Souza*, on the right as you enter the village. Best seafood in town, open daily, live music at weekends, reasonably priced. Recommended. *Brasa Na Praia*. Specializes in grilled seafood and meat, open daily, peaceful setting. Recommended. *La Crêperie*. Excellent crêpes, Tue to Sun, good music, popular, owner Klever very friendly. *Pizzaria Le Gaston*. Good pizza and pasta, also good home-made ice-creams, open daily.

Prices rise steeply in the summer season. Most hotels are in the AL price range. It may prove difficult to find cheaper accommodation

Tour operators *Odara Turismo*, in the *EcoResort Hotel*, T676 1080, F676 1018. Imaginative tours to surrounding areas and outlying villages and beaches using 4WD vehicles. They are very friendly and informative. Recommended. The owners, Norbert and Papy, speak English and German. *Bahia Adventure*, T676 1262, baadventure@svn.com.br Ecotourism, abseiling and Land Rover trips. *Rentamar UK*, 338 Milton Rd, Cambridge, CB4 1LW, T/F+44-1223-424244, Glauce.UK@tesco.net For whale and turtle watching packages. Praia do Forte is ideal for windsurfing and sailing owing to constant fresh Atlantic breezes.

The Linha Verde (the extension of the Estrada do Coco) runs for 142 km to the bordern of Sergipe, the next state north; the road is more scenic than the BR-101, especially near Conde. There are very few hotels or *pousadas* in the more remote villages. The most picturesque are **Imbassaí**, **Subaúma**, **Baixio** (very beautiful, where the Rio Inhambupe meets the sea) and **Conde**. Sítio do Conde on the coast, 6 km

The coast road north

from Conde, has many *pousadas*, but the beaches are not very good. Sítio do Conde is an ideal base to explore other beaches at Barra do Itariri, 12 km south, at the mouth of a river (fine sunsets). The road passes unspoilt beaches (the best are Corre Nu and Jacaré). You can also go to Seribinha, 13 km north of Sítio do Conde (the road goes along the beach through coconut groves and mangroves; at Seribinha are beach huts serving cool drinks or food, one *pousada* on beach). The last stop on the Linha Verde is **Mangue Seco**. Access from Sergipe is by boat or canoe on the Rio Real from Pontal (10 min crossing). A steep hill rising behind the village to tall white sand dunes offers a superb view of the coastline.■ *Bus Salvador-Conde (São Luis, T0xx71-358 4582), three a day, four on Friday, US$7.25.*

Sleeping and eating Imbassaí: **A** *Pousada Caminho do Mar*, T/F0xx71- 832 2499. 12 bungalows with a/c, restaurant, German run. **C** *Pousada Lagoa da Pedra*, T0xx71-248 5914. Large grounds, a little English spoken friendly. **D** *Pousada Anzol de Ouro*, T0xx71-322 4422. 12 chalets, ventilation, swimming pool. **Mangue Seco**: On the left from the boat landing, 15 mins' walk, **B** *Pousada Village Mangue Seco*, T0xx79-224 2965. Swimming pool, fan. Seafood restaurants can be found at the boat landing.

Inland, north from Salvador

Monte Santo & Canudos The famous hill shrine of Monte Santo, in the Sertão, is reached by 3½ km of steps cut into the rocks of the Serra do Picaraça (about 45 minutes' walk each way – set out early). This is the scene of pilgrimages and great religious devotion during Holy Week. The shrine was built by an Italian who had a vision of the cross on the mountain in 1765. One block north of the bottom of the stairs is the **Museu do Sertão**, with pictures from the 1897 Canudos rebellion. The shrine is about 270 km north of Feira da Santana, and 38 km west of the town of Euclides da Cunha on the direct BR-116 road to Fortaleza.

Canudos itself is 100 km away at the junction of the BR-116 and BR-235 (direct buses from Salvador); religious rebels led by the Antônio Conselheiro defeated three expeditions sent against them in 1897 before being overwhelmed. The events at Canudos inspired one of the most famous books written in Brazil, *Os Sertões* by Euclides da Cunha. It also spawned a more recent, fictionalized account, *La guerra del fin del mundo*, by the Peruvian novelist Mario Vargas Llosa. The Rio Vaza Barris, which runs through Canudos has been dammed, and the town has been moved to Nova Canudos by the dam. Part of the old town is still located 10 km west.

Sleeping C *Grapiuna*, Praça Monsenhor Berenguer 401, T275 1157. Cheaper without bath, downstairs. Recommended. At **Euclides da Cunha**, on the BR-116 39 km from Monte Santo, are *Hotel Lua*, simple and **B** *Hotel do Conselheiro*, Av Mal Juárez Távora 187.

Brasília

The Northeast

The eight states north of Bahia are historically and culturally rich, but generally poor economically. Steeped in history are, for instance, Recife, Olinda, or São Luís and cultural heritage abounds (eg 'Forró' and other musical styles, many good museums, lacework, ceramics). There is a multitude of beaches: those in established resorts tend to be polluted, but you don't have to travel far for good ones, while off the beaten track are some which have hardly been discovered.

Climate South of Cabo São Roque (Rio Grande do Norte) there is abundant rainfall, but in Pernambuco the zone of ample rain streches only 80 km inland, though it deepens southwards. São Luís in Maranhão also gets plenty of rain, but between eastern Maranhão and Pernambuco lies a triangle, with its apex deep inland, where the rainfall is sporadic, and occasionally non-existent for a year. Here the tropical forest gives way to the *caatinga*, or scrub forest bushes, which shed their leaves during drought.

On the BR-101, 247 km north of Salvador and almost midway between the Sergipe-Bahia border and Aracaju, is **Estância**, one of the oldest towns in Brazil. Its colonial buildings are decorated with Portuguese tiles. The month-long festival of **São João** in June is a major event. There are pleasant hotels, but most buses stop at the Rodoviária, which is on the main road (four hours from Salvador).

Sergipe & Alagoas

Aracaju

Capital of Sergipe founded 1855, it stands on the south bank of the Rio Sergipe, about 10 km from its mouth. In the centre is a group of linked, beautiful parks: **Praça Olímpio Campos**, in which stands the cathedral, **Praça Almirante Barroso**, with the Palácio do Governo, and **Praças Fausto Cardoso** and **Camerino**. Across Av Rio Branco from these two is the river. There is a handicraft centre, the **Centro do Turismo** in the restored Escola Normal, on Praça Olímpio Campos, Rua 24 Horas; the stalls are arranged by type (wood, leather, etc). ■ *0900-1300, 1400-1900.*

Phone code: 0xx79
Post code: 49000
Colour map 5, grid C5
Population: 461,534
327 km N of Salvador

A 16-km road leads to the fine **Atalaia** beach: there are oil-drilling rigs offshore. Beaches continue south down the coast. There is a better, 30 km long beach, **Nova Atalaia**, on Ilha de Santa Luzia across the river. It is easily reached by boat from the Hidroviária (ferry station), which is across Av Rio Branco from Praça Gen Valadão. Boats cross the river to **Barra dos Coqueiros** every 15 mins. Services are more frequent at weekends, when it is very lively.

Excursions

São Cristóvão is the old state capital, 17 km southwest of Aracaju on the road to Salvador. It was founded in 1590 by Cristóvão de Barros. It is the fourth oldest town in Brazil. Built on top of a hill, its colonial centre is unspoiled: the **Museu de Arte Sacra e Histórico de Sergipe** contains religious and other objects from the 17th to the 19th centuries; it is in the **Convento de São Francisco**. ■ *Tue-Fri 1000-1700, Sat-Sun 1300-1700.* Also worth visiting (and keeping the same hours) is the **Museu de Sergipe** in the former **Palácio do Governo**; both are on Praça de São Francisco. Also on this square are the churches of **Misericórdia** (1627) and the **Orfanato Imaculada Conceição** (1646, permission to visit required from the Sisters), and the **Convento de São Francisco**. On Praça Senhor dos Passos are the churches **Senhor dos Passos** and

Brazil

Aracaju

Av Coelho Campos
Av Carlos Burlemarque
Av 7 de Setembro
Old Rodoviária
Av Divina Pastora
Av Baltazar Gois
Av São Cristóvão
Av Laranjeiras
Av Propria
Av Itaporanga
Av Coelho Campos
Av José P Franco
Av Otoniel Dorea
Capela
Santo Amaro
Av A Mota
Terminal Hidroviário
Praça General Valadão
Santo Amaro
Av Itabaiana
Av J Pessoa
Av Rio Branco
Rio Sergipe
Barra dos Coqueiros
Centro do Turismo
Praça Olímpio Campos & Cacique Chá Restaurant
Palácio do Governo
Ponte do Imperador
Praça Fausto Cardoso
Cathedral
Assembléia
To Rodoviária, Maceió, BR 101 & Salvador
Av Simão Dias
Av Siriri
N
Not to scale
To Praia Atalaia & Southern Beaches
To Praia Atalaia Nova

■ **Sleeping**
1 Amado
2 Aperipê & Serigy
3 Brasília
4 Grande
5 Oásis
6 Pálace de Aracaju

Terceira Ordem do Carmo (both 1739), while on the Praça Getúlio Vargas (formerly Praça Matriz) is the 17th century **Igreja Matriz Nossa Senhora da Vitória**. ■ *Tue-Fri 1000-1700, Sat-Sun 1500-1700.* Local festivals include *Senhor dos Passos*, 15 days after Carnival. In November the town holds a *Festival de Arte*, but check the date as it sometimes falls in October. A tourist train runs between Aracaju and São Cristóvão at weekends, 0900, 3½ hours, T211 3003 to check that it is running – a minimum of 15 passengers is needed.

Sleeping & eating

Centre A *Pálace de Aracaju*, Praça Gen Valadão, T224 5000. A/c, TV, fridge, central, restaurant, pool, parking. **A** *Grande*, R Itabaianinha 371, T/F211 1383. A/c, TV, fridge, central, *Quartier Latin* restaurant. **A** *Aperipê*, R São Cristóvão 418, T211 1880. Central, a/c, phone, fridge, restaurant. **A** *Serigy*, R Santo Amaro 269, T211 1088. Same management and facilities, comfortable. **B** *Brasília*, R Laranjeiras 580, T224 8022. Good value, good breakfasts. Recommended. **B** *Oásis*, R São Cristóvão 466, T224 2125. With good breakfast, hot water, fair, a bit tatty. **C** *Amado*, R Laranjeiras 532. A/c (less with fan), laundry facilities. In town, good bar and restaurant: *Cacique Chá*, in the cathedral square, lively at weekends. *Gonzaga*, Rua Santo Amaro 181, T224 7278. Lunch only, good value, popular, excellent traditional dishes.

Festivals

On **8 Dec** there are both Catholic (***Nossa Senhora da Conceição***) and *Umbanda* (Iemenjá) religious festivals. Other festivals are: the procession on the river on **1 Jan**, *Bom de Jesus dos Navegantes*; **Santos Reis**, on the 1st weekend in **Jan**; the *Festas Juninas*.

Transport

Interstate rodoviária is 4 km from centre, linked by local buses from adjacent terminal (buy a ticket before going on the platform). Bus 004 'T Rod/L Batista' goes to the centre, US$0.50. Buses from the old terminal in town, Santo Amaro e Divina Pastora, Praça João XXIII, go to the new rodoviária and São Cristóvão (45 mins, US$1.25). Buses to the rodoviária also at the terminal near Hidroviária and from Capela at the top of Praça Olímpio Campos. To **Salvador**, 6-7 hrs, 11 a day with *Bonfim*, US$11, executive service at 1245, US$14, saves 1 hr. To **Maceió**, US$9 with *Bonfim*. To **Estância**, US$2, 1½ hrs. To **Recife**, 7 hrs, US$12-14, 1200 and 2400.

Directory

Tourist offices Secretaria de Indústria, Comércio e Turismo, Av Heríclito Rollemberg s/n, T231 1413, F217 3050. For tourist information, go to **Emsetur**, Largo Esperanto s/n, 11-13th floors, T222 8373, F224 3403, www.emsetur.com.br See also www.infonet.com.br/sergipe

The Rio São Francisco marks the boundary between Sergipe and Alagoas. The BR-101 between Aracaju and Maceió – the next port to the north – is paved, crossing the São Francisco by bridge between Propriá and Porto Real do Colégio.

Penedo

Phone code: 0xx82
Post code: 57200
Colour map 5, grid C6
Population: 56,993

A more interesting crossing into Alagoas can be made by frequent ferry (car and foot passengers) from **Neópolis** in Sergipe, to Penedo some 35 km from the mouth of the Rio São Francisco.

Penedo is a charming town, with a nice waterfront park, Praça 12 de Abril. Originally the site of the Dutch Fort Maurits (built 1637, razed to the ground by the Portuguese), the colonial town stands on a promontory above the river. Among the colonial architecture, modern buildings on Av Floriano Peixoto do not sit easily. On the Praça Barão de Penedo is the neoclassical **Igreja Matriz** (closed to visitors) and the 18th century **Casa da Aposentadoria** (1782 – the tourist office is here, T551 2827, ext 23). East and a little below this square is the Praça Rui Barbosa, on which are the **Convento de São Francisco** (1783 and later) and the church of **Santa Maria dos Anjos** (1660). As you enter, the altar on the right depicts God's eyes on the world, surrounded by the three races, one Indian, two negroes and the whites at the bottom. The church has fine *trompe-l'oeil* ceilings (1784). The convent is still in use. Guided tours are free. The church of **Rosário dos Pretos** (1775-1816), on Praça Marechal Deodoro, is open to visitors. **Nossa Senhora da Corrente** (1764), on Praça 12 de Abril, and **São Gonçalo Garcia** (1758-70) are on Av Floriano Peixoto. ■ *Mon-Fri 0800-1200, 1400-1700.* Also on Av Floriano Peixoto is the pink **Teatro 7**

de Setembro (No 81) of 1884. The **Casa de Penedo**, at R João Pessoa 126 (signs point the way up the hill from F Peixoto), displays photographs and books on, or by, local figures. ■ *Tue-Sun 0800-1800, T551 2516.*

Sleeping A *São Francisco*, Av Floriano Peixoto, T551 2273, F551 2274. Standard rooms have no a/c, TV, fridge. Recommended except for poor restaurant. **B** *Pousada Colonial*, Praça 12 de Abril 21, T551 2355, F551 3099. *Luxo* and suite have phone, TV and fridge, suites have a/c, spacious, good cheap restaurant, front rooms with view of Rio São Francisco. **D** *Turista*, R Siqueira Campos 143, T551 2237. With bath, fan, hot water. Recommended.

Transport Bus: 451 km from **Salvador** (US$12-14, 6 hrs, daily bus 0600, book in advance), at same time for **Aracaju** (US$6). Buses south are more frequent from Neópolis, 6 a day (0630-1800) to Aracaju, 2 hrs, US$3.60. 115 km from **Maceió**, 5 buses a day in either direction, US$5.40-6.60, 3-4 hrs. Rodoviária: Av Duque de Caxias, behind Bompreço supermarket.

Maceió

The capital of Alagoas state is mainly a sugar port. Two of its old buildings, the **Palácio do Governo**, which also houses the **Fundação Pierre Chalita** (Alagoan painting and religious art) and the church of **Bom Jesus dos Mártires** (1870 – covered in tiles), are particularly interesting. Both are on the Praça dos Martírios (or Floriano Peixoto). The **cathedral**, Nossa Senhora dos Prazeres (1840), is on Praça Dom Pedro II.

Phone code: 0xx82
Post code: 57000
Colour map 5, grid C6
Population: 797,759
294 km NE of Aracaju
285 km S of Recife
Voltage: 220 volts AC, 60 cycles

Brazil

Lagoa do Mundaú, a lagoon whose entrance is 2 km south at **Pontal da Barra**, limits the city to the south and west: excellent shrimp and fish are sold at its small restaurants and handicraft stalls; a nice place for a drink at sundown. Boats make excursions in the lagoon's channels.

Beyond the city's main dock the beachfront districts begin; within the city, the beaches are smarter the further from the centre you go. The first, going north, is Pajuçara where there is a nightly craft market. At weekends there are wandering musicians and entertainers. Further out, Jatiúca, Cruz das Almas and Jacarecica (9 km from centre) are all good for surfing. The beaches, some of the finest and most popular in Brazil, have a protecting coral reef a kilometre or so out. Bathing is much better three days before and after full or new moon, because tides are higher and the water is more spectacular. For beaches beyond the city, see Excursions below.

Beaches

Jangadas take passengers to a natural swimming pool 2 km off Pajuçara beach (**Piscina Natural de Pajuçara**), at low tide you can stand on the sand and rock reef (beware of sunburn). You must check the tides, there is no point going at high tide. *Jangadas* cost US$5 per person per day (or about US$20 to have a *jangada* to yourself). On Sunday or local holidays in the high season it is overcrowded (at weekends lots of *jangadas* anchor at the reef selling food and drink).

By bus (22 km south) past Praia do Francês to the attractive colonial town and former capital of Alagoas, **Marechal Deodoro**, which overlooks the Lagoa Manguaba. The 17th century **Convento de São Francisco**, Praça João XXIII, has a fine church (Santa Maria Magdalena) with a superb baroque wooden altarpiece, badly damaged by termites. You can climb the church's tower for views. Adjoining it is the **Museu de Arte Sacra**. ■ *Mon-Fri 0900-1300, US$0.30, guided tours available, payment at your discretion.* Also open to visitors is the **Igreja Matriz de Nossa Senhora da Conceição** (1783). The town is the birthplace of Marechal Deodoro da Fonseca, founder of the Republic; the modest house where he was born is on the R Marechal Deodoro, close to the waterfront. ■ *Mon-Sat 0800-1700, Sun 0800-1200, free.*

Excursions
Schistosomiasis is present in the lagoon

On a day's excursion, it is easy to visit the town, then spend some time at beautiful **Praia do Francês**. The northern half of the beach is protected by a reef, the southern half is open to the surf. Along the beach there are many *barracas* and bars selling drinks and seafood; also several *pousadas*.

Sleeping

Many hotels on Praia Pajuçara, mostly along Av Dr António Gouveia and R Jangadeiros Alagoanos. It can be hard to find a room during the Dec-Mar holiday season, when prices go up

L *Pajuçara Othon Travel*, R Jangadeiros Alagoanos 1292, T217 6400, F231 5499, www.hoteis-othon.com.br **AL** *Sete Coqueiros*, Av A Gouveia 1335, T231 8583, F231 7467. 3-star, a/c, TV, phone, popular restaurant, pool. **AL** *Enseada*, Av A Gouveia 171, T231 4726, enseada@ vircom.com.br Recommended. **A** *Velamar*, Av A Gouveia 1359, T327 5488, velamar@threenet.com.br A/c, TV, fridge, safes in rooms. **A** *Laguna Praia*, No 1231, T231 6180. Highly recommended. **A** *Maceió Praia*, No 3, T231 6391. Highly recommended. **A** *Pousada Sete Coqueteiros*, No 123, T231 5677. Recommended. **B** *Buongiorno*, No 1437, T231 7577, F231 7577. A/c, fridge, English-speaking owner, helpful. **C** *Casa Grande da Praia*, No 1528, T231 3332. A/c and TV, cheaper without. Recommended. **C** *Costa Verde*, No 429, T231 4745. Bath, fan, good family atmosphere, English, German spoken. Further from the centre, **C** *Pousada Cavalo Marinho*, R da Praia 55, Riacho Doce (15 km from the centre), facing the sea, T/F235 1247, cavmar@dialnet.com.br Use of bicycle, canoes and body boards including, hot showers, German and English spoken, tropical breakfasts, Swiss owner. Very highly recommended (nearby is *Lua Cheia*, good food and live music at night).

Youth hostels *Nossa Casa*, R Prefeito Abdon Arroxelas 327, T231 2246. *Pajuçara*, R Quintino Bocaiúva 63, Pajuçara, T231 0631. *Stella Maris*, Av Desembargador Valente de Lima 209, Mangabeiras, T325 2217. All IH affiliated, all require reservations Dec-Feb, Jul and Aug. **Camping** There is a *Camping Clube do Brasil* site on Jacarecica beach, T235 3600, a 15-min taxi drive from the town centre. *Camping Pajuçara* at Largo da Vitória 211, T231 7561, clean, safe, food for sale, recommended.

Eating

Local specialities include oysters, pitu, a crayfish (now becoming scarce), and sururu, a kind of cockle. Local ice cream, Shups, recommended

Ao Lagostão, Av Duque de Caxias 1348. Seafood, fixed price (expensive) menu. *Pizzeria Sorrisa*, Praça Visconde Sinimbu 207. Very cheap, good food, popular with Brazilians. **Vegetarian** *O Natural*, R Libertadora Alagoana (R da Praia) 112. *Nativa*, Osvaldo Sarmento 56, good views. Many good bars and restaurants in Pajuçara, eg on Av António Gouveia. The beaches for 5 km from the beginning of Pajuçara to Cruz das Almas in the north are lined with *barracas* (thatched bars), providing music, snacks and meals until midnight (later at weekends). Vendors on the beach sell beer and food

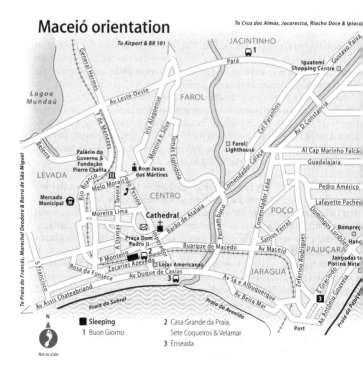

Maceió orientation

To Cruz das Almas, Jacarecica, Riacho Doce & Ipioca

To Airport & BR 101

JACINTINHO

Pará

Iguatemi Shopping Centre

Lagoa Mundaú

Av Leste-Oeste

FAROL

Farol/Lighthouse

Al Cap Marinho Falcão

Guadalajara

Palácio do Governo & Fundação Pierre Chalita

Bom Jesus dos Mártires

Pedro Américo

LEVADA

Lafayette Pacheo

Mercado Municipal

CENTRO

POÇO

Moreira Lima

Cathedral

Bompreço

Barão de Atalaia

Santos Ferraz

PAJUÇARA

Jangadas to Piscina Natu

Praça Dom Pedro II

Buarque de Macedo

Av Maceió

P Montero

JARAGUÁ

Rosa da Fonseca

Zacarias Azevedo

Lojas Americanas

Av Duque de Caxias

Av Sá e Albuquerque

Av Assis Chateaubriand

Praia do Sobral

Praia da Avenida

Av Beira Mar

Port

To Praia do Francês, Marechal Deodoro & Barra de São Miguel

N

Not to scale

■ **Sleeping**
1 Buon Giorno

2 Casa Grande da Praia, Sete Coqueiros & Velamar
3 Enseada

Brazil

during the day: clean and safe. There are many other bars and *barracas* at Ponto da Barra, on the lagoon side of the city.

27 Aug: *Nossa Senhora dos Prazeres*; **16 Sep:** *Freedom of Alagoas*; **8 Dec:** *Nossa Senhora da Conceição*; **15 Dec:** *Maceiofest*, 'a great street party with *trios elêctricos*'; *Christmas Eve; New Year's Eve*, half-day.
Local holidays & festivals

Local Bus: Frequent buses, confusingly marked, serve all parts of the city. Bus stops are not marked: it is best to ask where people look as if they are waiting. The 'Ponte Verde/Jacintinho' bus runs via Pajuçara from the centre to the rodoviária, also take 'Circular' bus (25 mins Pajuçara to rodoviária); Taxis from town go to all the northern beaches, but buses run as far as Ipioca (23 km). The Jangadeiras bus marked 'Jacarecica-Center, via Praias' runs past all the beaches as far as Jacarecica. From there you can change to 'Riacho Doce-Trapiche', 'Ipioca' or 'Mirante' buses for Riacho Doce and Ipioca. To return take any of these options, or take a bus marked 'Shopping Center' and change there for 'Jardim Vaticana' bus, which goes through Pajuçara. Buses and kombis to Marechal Deodoro, Praia do Francês and Barra de São Miguel leave from R Barão de Anádia, outside the ferroviária, opposite *Lojas Americanas*: bus US$0.75, kombi US$1 to Marechal Deodoro, 30 mins, calling at Praia do Francês in each direction. Last bus back from Praia do Francês to Maceió at 1800.
Transport

Long distance Air: 20 km from centre, taxi about US$25. Buses to airport from near *Hotel Beiriz*, R João Pessoa 290 or in front of the Ferroviária, signed 'Rio Largo'; alight at Tabuleiro dos Martins, then 7-8 mins walk to the airport, bus fare US$0.75.

Buses: The rodoviária is 5 km from centre, on a hill with good views and cool breezes. Taxi, US$7 to Pajuçara. Bus to **Recife**, 10 a day, 3½ hrs express (more scenic coastal route, 5 hrs) US$9. To **Aracaju**, US$9, 5 hrs (potholed road). To **Salvador**, 10 hrs, 4 a day, US$20 (*rápido* costs more).

Tourist offices Ematur (Empresa Alagoana de Turismo), Av da Paz 2014, Centro, T221 9465, F221 8987. Also at the airport and rodoviária . Helpful. The municipal tourist authority is **Emturma**, R Saldanha da Gama 71, Farol, T223 4016; information post on Pajuçara beach, opposite *Hotel Solara*, www.maceio.com.br
Directory

Buses
1 Rodoviária
2 To Marechal Deodoro & Praia do Francês
3 To Riacho Doce

There are many interesting stopping points along the coast between Maceió and Recife. **Barra de Santo Antônio**, 45 km north, is a busy fishing village, with a palm fringed beach on a narrow peninsula, a canoe-ride away. The beaches nearby are beautiful: to the south, near the village of Santa Luzia, are Tabuba and Sonho Verde. To the north is Carro Quebrado, from which you can take a buggy to Pedra do Cebola, or further to Praia do Morro, just before the mouth of the Rio Camaragibe.
North to Pernambuco

Beyond Barra do Camaragibe, a coastal road, unpaved in parts, runs to the Pernambuco border and São José da Coroa Grande. The main highway, BR-101, heads a little inland from Maceió before crossing the state border to Palmares.

Brazil

Pernambuco

Recife

Phone code: 0xx81
Post code: 50000
Colour map 5, grid B6
Population:
1.42 million
285 km N of Maceió
839 km N of Salvador

The capital of Pernambuco State was founded on reclaimed land by the Dutch prince Maurice of Nassau in 1637 after his troops had burnt Olinda, the original capital. The city centre consists of three portions, Recife proper, Santo Antônio and São José, and Boa Vista and Santo Amaro. The first two are on islands formed by the rivers Capibaribe, Beberibe and Pina, while the third is made into an island by the Canal Tacaruna, which separates it from the mainland. The centre is always very busy by day; the crowds and the narrow streets, especially in the Santo Antônio district, can make it a confusing city to walk around. Recife has the main dock area, with commercial buildings associated with it. South of the centre is the residential and beach district of Boa Viagem, reached by bridge across the Bacia do Pina. Olinda, the old capital, is only 7 km to the north (see page 506).

Churches
Many churches close to visitors on Sun because of services. Many are in need of repair

The best sights are the churches of **Santo Antônio do Convento de São Francisco** (1606), which has beautiful Portuguese tiles, in the R do Imperador, and adjoining it the finest sight of all, the **Capela Dourada** (Golden Chapel, 1697). ■ *Mon-Fri 0800-1130, 1400-1700, Sat morning only, US$1, no flash photography; it is through the Museu Franciscano de Arte Sacra.* **São Pedro dos Clérigos** in São José district (1782), should be seen for its façade, its fine wood sculpture and a splendid *trompe-l'oeil* ceiling. ■ *Daily 0800-1130, 1400-1600.* **Nossa Senhora da Conceição dos Militares**, R Nova 309 (1771), has a grand ceiling and a large 18th century primitive mural of the battle of Guararapes (museum next door). ■ *Mon-Fri 0800-1700.*

Other important churches are **Santo Antônio** (1753-91), in Praça da Independência, rebuilt in 1864. ■ *Mon-Fri 0800-1200, 1400-1800, Sun 1700-1900.* **Nossa Senhora do Carmo**, Praça do Carmo (1663). ■ *Mon-Fri 0800-1200, 1400-1900, Sat-Sun 0700-1200.* **Madre de Deus** (1715), in the street of that name in the district of Recife, with a splendid high altar, and sacristy. ■ *Tue-Fri 0800-1200, 1400-1600.* The **Divino Espírito Santo** (1689), the original church of the Jesuits, Praça 17 in Santo Antônio district. ■ *Mon-Fri 0800-1630, Sat 0800-1400, Sun 1000-1200.* There are many others.

14 km south of the city, a little beyond Boa Viagem and the airport, on Guararapes hill, is the historic church of **Nossa Senhora dos Prazeres**. It was here, in 1648-49, that two Brazilian victories led to the end of the 30-year Dutch occupation of the northeast in 1654. The church was built by the Brazilian commander in 1656 to fulfil a vow. ■ *Tue-Fri 0800-1200, 1400-1700, Sat 0800-1200, closed to tourists on Sun.* Boa Viagem's own fine church dates from 1707.

Sights
Forte do Brum (built by the Dutch in 1629) is an army museum. ■ *Tue-Fri 0900-1600, Sat-Sun 1400-1600.* **Forte das Cinco Pontas** (with **Museu da Cidade do Recife**), with a cartographic history of the settlement of Recife, was built by the Dutch in 1630 and altered by the Portuguese in 1677. The two forts jointly controlled access to the port at the northern and southern entrances respectively. ■ *Mon-Fri 0900-1800, Sat-Sun 1300-1700, US$0.50 donation advised.*

The first Brazilian printing press was installed in 1706 and Recife claims to publish the oldest daily newspaper in South America, *Diário de Pernambuco*, founded 1825 (but now accessible on www.dpnet.com.br/). The distinctive lilac building is on the Praça da Independência.

The artists' and intellectuals' quarter is based on the **Pátio de São Pedro**, the square round São Pedro dos Clérigos. Sporadic folk music and poetry shows are

Recife orientation

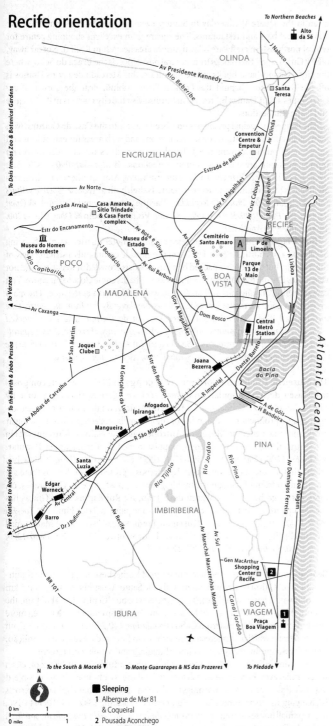

To Northern Beaches

Alto da Sé

OLINDA

Av Presidente Kennedy

Rio Beberibe

J Nabuco

Santa Teresa

Av Olinda

Convention Centre & Empetur

ENCRUZILHADA

Estrada de Belém

Gov A Magalhães

Av Cruz Cabugá

Rio Beberibe

RECIFE

To Dois Irmãos Zoo & Botanical Gardens

Av Norte

Estrada Arraial

Casa Amarela, Sítio Trindade & Casa Forte complex

Av Rosa e Silva

Estr do Encantamento

Museu do Homen do Nordeste

POÇO

Rio Capibaribe

J Bonifácio

Museu do Estado

Av Rui Barbosa

Cemitério Santo Amaro

A P de Limoeiro

A Lisboa

Av João de Barros

BOA VISTA

Parque 13 de Maio

To Várzea

MADALENA

Gov A Magalhães

Dom Bosco

Central Metrô Station

Dantas Barreto

Av Caxanga

Av San Martim

Joquei Clube

M Gonçalves da Luz

Estr dos Remédios

Joana Bezerra

R Imperial

Bacia do Pina

To the North & João Pessoa

Av Abdias de Carvalho

Afogados Ipiranga

Mangueira

R São Miguel

Rio Tijipio

Rio Jordão

Rio Pina

PINA

Atlantic Ocean

Brazil

Five Stations to Rodoviária

Santa Luzia

Edgar Werneck

Barro

Av Central

Dr J Rufino

IMBIRIBEIRA

Av Recife

Av Sul

Av Marechal Mascarenhas Morais

Av Domingos Ferreira

Av Boa Viagem

BR 101

IBURA

Gen MacArthur

Shopping Center Recife

2

BOA VIAGEM

Canal Jordão

1 Praça Boa Viagem

N

To the South & Maceió ▼

To Monte Guararapes & NS das Prazeres ▼

To Piedade ▼

■ **Sleeping**
1 Albergue de Mar 81 & Coqueiral
2 Pousada Aconchego

0 km   1
0 miles   1

Related map
A Recife, page 502

given in the square Wednesday to Sunday evenings (T3426 2728) and there are atmospheric bars and restaurants. The square is an excellent shopping centre for typical northeastern craftware (clay figurines are cheapest in Recife). Not far away, off Av Guararapes, two blocks from central post office, is the **Praça do Sebo**, where the city's second-hand booksellers concentrate; this Mercado de Livros Usados is off the R da Roda, behind the Edifício Santo Albino, near the corner of Av Guararapes and R Dantas Barreto. You can also visit the city markets in the São José and Santa Rita sections.

The former municipal prison has now been made into the **Casa da Cultura**, with many cells converted into art or souvenir shops and with areas for exhibitions and shows (also public conveniences). Local dances such as the ciranda, forró and bumba-meu-boi are held as tourist attractions. ■ *Mon-Sat 0900-1900, Sun 0900-1400. T3284 2850 to check what's on in advance.* Among other cultural centres are Recife's three traditional **theatres**, **Santa Isabel**, built in 1850. ■ *Open to visitors Mon-Fri 1300-1700, Praça da República.* **Parque.** Restored and beautiful. ■ *Open 0800-1200, 1400-1800, R do Hospício 81, Boa Vista;* and **Apolo** ■ *Open 0800-1200, 1400-1700, R do Apolo 121.*

Boa Viagem This is the main residential and hotel quarter, currently being developed at its northern end. The 8-km promenade commands a striking view of the Atlantic, but the beach is backed by a busy road, is crowded at weekends and not very clean. During the January breeding season, sharks come close to the shore. You can go fishing on *jangadas* at Boa Viagem with a fisherman at low tide. The main praça has a good market at weekends. ■ *Getting there: By bus from the centre, take any marked 'Boa Viagem'; from Nossa Senhora do Carmo, take buses marked 'Piedade', 'Candeias' or 'Aeroporto' – they go on Av Domingos Ferreira, 2 blocks parallel to the beach, all the way to Praça Boa Viagem (at Av Boa Viagem 500). Back to the centre take buses marked 'CDU' or 'Setubal' from Av Domingos Ferreira.*

Museums The **Museu do Homem do Nordeste**, Av 17 de Agosto 2223, Casa Forte comprises the **Museu de Arte Popular**, containing ceramic figurines (including some by Mestre Alino and Zé Caboclo); the **Museu do Açúcar**, on the history and technology of sugar production, with models of colonial mills, collecions of antique sugar bowls and much else; the **Museu de Antropologia**, the **Nabuco Museum** (at No 1865) and the modern museum of popular remedies, **Farmacopéia Popular**. ■ *Tue-Fri 1100-1700, Sat-Sun 1300-1700, US$1.* Either take the 'Dois Irmãos' bus (check that it's the correct one, with 'Rui Barbosa' posted in window, as there are two) from in front of the Banorte building near the post office on Guararapes, or, more easily, go by taxi. The **Museu do Estado**, Av Rui Barbosa 960, Graças has excellent paintings by the 19th-century landscape painter, Teles Júnior. ■ *Tue-Fri 0900-1700, Sat-Sun 1400-1700.* **Museu do Trem**, Praça Visconde de Mauá, small but interesting, especially the Henschel locomotive. ■ *Tue-Fri 0800-1200, 1400-1700, Sat 0900-1200, Sun 1400-1700.*

Excursions **Beaches south of Recife** About 30 km south of Recife, beyond Cabo, is the beautiful and quiet **Gaibu** beach, with scenic Cabo de Santo Agostinho on the point 5 km east of town. It has a ruined fort. To get there, take bus 'Centro do Cabo' from the airport, then frequent buses – 20 mins – from Cabo. **Itapuama** beach is even more empty, both reached by bus from **Cabo** (*Population*: 140,765), Pernambuco's main industrial city, which has interesting churches and forts and a **Museu da Abolição.** At nearby **Suape** are many 17th-century buildings and a biological reserve.

Porto de Galinhas, further south still, is a beautiful beach. It has cool, clean water, and waves. Because of a reef close to the shore, swimming is only possible at high tide (take heed of local warnings) and a rash of recently built upmarket resorts is changing its rustic atmosphere. Humberto Cavalcanti, T3426 7471/9944 0196, has two small houses for rent. ■ *Porto de Galinhas is reached by bus from the southern end of Av Dantas Barreto, 8 a day, 7 on Sun, 0700-1700, US$1.25.*

Brazil

Boa Viagem is the main tourist district and the best area to stay. All hotels listed in this area are within a block or two of the beach. There is not much reason to be in the city centre and accommodation here is of a pretty low standard.

Centre A *Recife Plaza*, R da Aurora 225, T3231 1200, Boa Vista. Overlooking the Rio Capibaribe, every comfort, fine restaurant (very popular at lunchtime). **B** *4 de Outubro*, R Floriano Peixoto 141, Santo Antônio, T3224 4900, F3424 2598. 4 standards of room, hot water, TV, phone, a/c. **C** *Hotel Park 13 de Mayo*, Rua do Hospício, T3231 7627. Safe, OK. **D** *América*, Praça Maciel Pinheiro 48, Boa Vista, T221 1300. Cheaper without a/c, front rooms pleasanter, quiet.

Boa Viagem A *Recife Monte*, R Petrolina e R dos Navegantes 363, T3465 7422, F3465 8406. Very smart and good value for category, caters to business travellers. **B** *Aconchego*, Félix de Brito 382, T3326 2989, aconchego@novaera.com.br Motel style rooms around pleasant pool area, a/c, sitting room, English-speaking owner, will collect you from the airport. **B** *Setúbal*, R Setúbal 932, T3341 4116. Helpful, good breakfast, comfortable. **C** *Coqueiral*, R Petrolina, 43, T3326 5881. Dutch-owned (Dutch, English, French spoken), a/c, small and homely with pretty breakfast room. Recommended. **C** *Praia Mar*, Av Boa Viagem 1660, T3465 3759. Intimate and safe. Recommended. **C** *Uzi Praia*, Av Conselheiro Aguiar 942, T/F3466 9662. A/c, cosy, sister hotel across the road. **D** *Navegantes Praia* , R dos Navegantes 1997, T3326 9609, F3326 2710. One block from beach, basic but a/c, TV and room service. Good value **D** *Pousada da Julieta*, R Prof Jose Brandão 135, T3326 7860, hjulieta@elogica.com.br One block from beach, very good value. Recommended. **D** *Pousada da Praia*, Alcides Carneiro Leal 66, T3326 7085. A/c, TV, safe, a/c, rooms vary (some tiny), very helpful, popular with Israelis. Roof-top breakfast room.

Praia de Piedade C *Casa da Praia*, Av Beira Mar, 1168, T461 1414. On a quiet street, with garden, good breakfast, owner speaks French. Recommended.

Youth hostels D *Albergue do Mar 81*, R dos Navegantes 81, T3326 2196. Cheaper for IYHA members, good breakfast and atmosphere. **D** *Albergue Mandacaru*, R Maria Carolina 75, T3326 1964. Stores luggage, English and German spoken, good breakfast. Recommended. **E** *Maracatus do Recife*, R Maria Carolina 185, T3326 1221, alberguemaracatus@yahoo.com Good breakfast, no hot water, simple, cooking facilities, pool, safe, membership not needed, mosquitoes can be a problem. Membership information from Associação Pernambucano de Albergues da Juventude (APEAJ), from Empetur (see below – take 2 photos). **Camping** There is no camping within the city. For information on camping throughout Pernambuco state, call **Paraíso Camping Clube**, Av Dantas Barreto 512, loja 503, T3224 3094.

Private accommodation During Carnival and for longer stays at other times, private individuals rent rooms and houses in Recife and Olinda; listings can be found in the classified ads in *Diário de Pernambuco*, or ask around the streets of Olinda. This accommodation is generally cheaper, safer and quieter than hotels.

City Expensive: *Leite* (lunches only), Praça Joaquim Nabuco 147/53 near Casa de Cultura. Old and famous, good service, smart (another branch in Boa Viagem, at Prof José Brandão 409). *Lisboa á Noite*, R Geraldo Pires 503. Good, reasonable, open Sun evenings (unlike many). **Mid-range**: *Galo D'Ouro*, Gamboa do Carmo 83. Well-established, international food. At No 136, *Casa de Tia*, lunch only, must arrive by 1215, try *cosido*, a meat and vegetable stew, enough for 2. *Tivoli*, R Matias de Albuquerque, Santo Antônio. Lunches downstairs, a/c restaurant upstairs, good value. *O Vegetal*, R Cleto Campelo e Av Guararapes (2nd floor) behind Central Post Office, lunch only, closed Sat-Sun. **Cheap**: *Casa dos Frios*, da Palma 57, loja 5. Delicatessen/sandwich bar, salads, pastries etc. *Buraquinho*, Pátio de Sao Pedro. Lunch only, all dishes good, generous servings of *caipirinha*, friendly. *Savoy Bar*, Av Guararapes. The haunt of Pernambucan intellectuals since 1944, with poetry all over the walls and the legend that Sartre and De Beauvoir once ate there, buffet Mon-Sat 1100-1500, US$2, also lunch by weight. *Lanchonetes* abound in the city, catering to office workers, but tend to close in evening. *Gelattos*, Av Dantas Barreto, 230. Great *sucos* (try the delicious *guarana do amazonas* with nuts), hamburgers and sandwiches.

Boa Viagem Restaurants on the main beach road of Av Boa Viagem are pricey; venture a block or two inland for cheaper deals. **Expensive**: *Bargaço*, Av Boa Viagem 670. Typical

Sleeping
For Olinda hotels, see page 507

Opportunistic theft is unfortunately common in the streets of Recife and Olinda (especially on the streets up to Alto da Sé). Keep hold of bags and cameras, and do not wear a watch. Prostitution is reportedly common in Boa Viagem, so choose nightclubs with care

Brazil

Eating
There are many good restaurants, at all prices, in the city, and along beach at Boa Viagem

northeastern menu specialising in seafood, sophisticated with small bar. *La Maison*, Av Boa Viagem, 618, T3325 1158. Fondue restaurant in low-lit basement, appropriately cheesey and good fun, with rosé wine and peach melba on menu. **Mid-range**: *Chica Pitanga*, R Petrolina, 19, T3465 2224. Upmarket, excellent food by weight, be prepared to queue. *Churrascaria Porcão*, Av Eng Domingos Ferreira 4215. Good for meat and salad eaters alike, very popular. *Ilha da Kosta*, R Pe Bernardino Pessoa, 50, T3466 2222. Self-service seafood, sushi, pizza and Brazilian cuisine, open 1100 to last client and all afternoon. *La Capannina*,

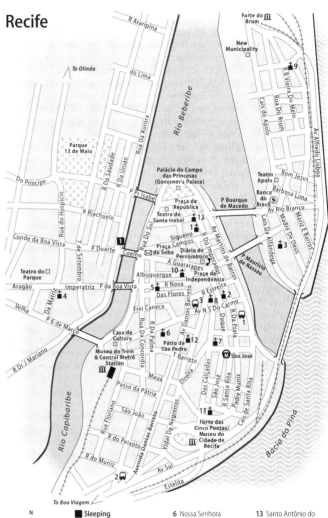

Recife

■ **Sleeping**	6 Nossa Senhora do Carmo	13 Santo Antônio do Convento de São Francisco
1 Recife Plaza	7 Nossa Senhora do Livramento	
✚ **Churches**	8 Nossa Senhora do Rosário dos Pretos	🚍 **Buses**
1 Capela Dourada	9 Pilar	1 To Itamaracá & Igarassu
2 Espírito Santo	10 Santo Antônio	2 To Porto da Galinhas
3 Madre de Deus	11 São José do Ribamar	3 To Boa Viagem
4 Matriz de Boa Vista	12 São Pedro dos Clérigos	
5 Nossa Senhora da Conceição dos Militares		

N

0 metres 200
0 yards 200

Av Cons Aguiar 538, T3465 9420. Italian, pizzas, salad, pasta and sweet and savoury crêpes, delivery service. *Parraxaxa*, R Baltazar Pereira, 32, T9108 0242. Rustic-style, award-winning, northeastern buffet, including breakfast. Recommended. *Pizza Hut*, Av Eng. Domingos Ferreira 3742 and Shopping Centre Recife, T3267 1515 for deliveries, open 1200-2400. Shopping Center Recife (open 1000-2200, T3464 6000) in Boa Viagem has a range of options, eg. *Sushimi*, T3463 6500. Classic, Japanese fast-food in suitably sterile surroundings. **Cheap**: *Dunkin' Donuts*, Av Cons Aguiar, on corner with R Atlântico. Good coffee, a/c, try Brazil-ian-style mini doughnuts with goiaba or canela filling. *Peng* , Av Domingos Ferreira, 1957. Self-service, some Chinese dishes, bargain, rather than gourmet food, in area with few other restaurants. *TioDadá*, R Baltazar Pereira 100. Loud, TV screens, good value portions of beef. *Gibi*, Av Cons Aguiar, 542. Basic but popular hamburger joint. *Realeza*, Av Boa Viagem, on corner with Av Atlântico. Beachfront location, hamburgers, snacks and pizza. *Romana*, R Setubal 225. Deli/bakery with a few tables and chairs, pastries, coffee, yoghurt for breakfast or snack. *Tempero Verde*, R S H Cardim, opposite *Chica Pitanga*. Where the locals go for a bargain meal of beans, meat and salad, US$1.50, simple, self-service, pavement tables.

Be careful of eating the local small crabs, known as *guaiamum*; they live in the mangrove swamps which take the drainage from Recife's *mocambos* (shanty towns).

Entertainment

Agenda Cultural details the cultural events for the month, free booklet from tourist offices, some shops and theatres

Most bars (often called 'pubs', but nothing like the English version) stay open until dawn. The historic centre of *Recife Antigo* has been restored and is now an excellent spot for nightlife,. Bars around R do Bom Jesus such as **London Pub**, No 207, are the result of a scheme to reno-vate the dock area. *Calypso Club*, R do Bom Jesus, US$5, has live local bands playing any-thing from traditional music to rock. The two most popular nightclubs (both enormous, 2300 to dawn) are **Downtown Pub**, R Vigário Tenório, disco, live music, US$5, and **Fashion Club**, Av Fernando Simões Barbosa 266, Boa Viagem in front of *Shopping Centre Recife*, T3327 4040, US$8. Techno and rock bands. The Graças district, west of Boa Vista, on the Rio Capibaribe, is popular for bars and evening entertainment. Discos tend to be expensive and sophisticated. Best times are around 2400 on Fri or Sat, take a taxi. The Pina zone, north of the beginning of Boa Viagem, is one of the city's major hang-out areas with lively bars, music and dancing. In Boa Viagem, *Baltazar*, R Baltazar Pereira 130, T3327 0475. Live music nightly, bar snacks, large and popular. Open 1600 to early hours. Try to visit a northeastern *Forró* where couples dance to typical music, very lively especially Fri and Sat, several good ones at Candeias. *Papillon Bar*, Av Beira Mar 20, Piedade, T3341 7298. *Forró* Wed-Sat. **Theatre** Shows in the Recife/Olinda Convention Center, US$10, traditional dances in full costume.

Festivals

1 Jan, *Universal Brotherhood*. **12-15 Mar,** parades to mark the city's foundation. **Mid-Apr,** *Pro-Rock Festival*, a week-long celebration of rock, hip-hop and manguebeat at Centro de Convenções, Complexo de Salgadinho and other venues. Check *Diário de Pernambuco* or *Jornal do Comércio* for details. **Jun**, *Festejos Juninos*. The days of Santo Antônio (13 Jun), São João (24 Jun), São Pedro and São Paulo (29 Jun), form the nuclei of a month-long celebration whose roots go back to the Portuguese colony. Intermingled with the Catholic tradition are Indian and African elements. The annual cycle begins in fact on São José's day, **19 Mar**, his-torically the first day of planting maize; the harvest in June then forms a central part of the festejos juninos. During the festivals the *forró* is danced. This dance, now popular throughout the Northeast, is believed to have originated when the British builders of the local railways held parties that were 'for all'. **11-16 Jul**, *Nossa Senhora do Carmo*, patron saint of the city. Aug is the **Mes do Folclore**. Oct, *Recifolia*, a repetition of carnival over a whole weekend; dates differ each year. **1-8 Dec** is the festival of *Iemanjá*, with typical foods and drinks, cele-brations and offerings to the goddess; also **8 Dec**, *Nossa Senhora da Conceição*.

Shopping

Markets The permanent craft market is in the *Casa da Cultura*; prices for ceramic figurines are lower than Caruaru. *Mercado São José* (1875) for local products and handicrafts. *Hippy fair* at Praça Boa Viagem, on the sea front, life-sized wooden statues of saints, week-ends only. Sat craft fair at *Sítio Trindade*, Casa Amarela. On 23 Apr, here and in the Pátio de São Pedro, one can see the *xangô* dance. Herbal remedies, barks and spices at Afogados mar-ket. *Cais de alfandega*, Recife Barrio, market of local artesans' work, 1st weekend of every

Carnival in Pernambuco

There is a pre-carnavalesca *week which starts with the 'Bloco da Parceria' in Boa Viagem bringing top Axé music acts from Bahia and the 'Virgens de Bairro Novo' in Olinda which features men in drag. These are followed by Carnival balls such as Baile dos Artistas (popular with the gay community) and the Bal Masque held at the Portuguese club,* Rua Governador Agamenon Magalhães, T2315400. *On the following Saturday morning the bloco Galo da Madrugada with close on a million participants officially opens carnival (wild and lively), see the local press for routes and times. The groups taking part are* maracatu, caboclinhos, troças, tribos de índios, blocos, ursos, caboclos de lança, escolas de samba *and* frevo. *Usually they start from Rua Conde da Boa Vista and progress along Rua do Hospício, Rua da Imperatriz, Ponte da Boa Vista, Praça da Independência, Rua 1° de Março and Rua do Imperador. This is followed by the main days Sunday to Tuesday.*

During Carnival (and on a smaller scale throughout the year) the Casa de Cultura has frevo *demonstrations where visitors can learn some steps of this unique dance of Pernambuco (check press for details of Frevioca truck and* frevo *orchestras during Carnival in the Pátio de São Pedro). The best place to see the groups is from the balconies of* Hotel do Parque *or* Recife Palace Hotel.

Seats in the stands and boxes can be booked up to a fortnight in advance at the central post office in Avenida Guararapes.

The Maracatu groups dance at the doors of all the churches they pass; they usually go to the Church of Nossa Senhora do Rosário dos Pretos, patron saint of the slaves (Rua Estreita do Rosário, Santo Antônio), before proceeding into the downtown areas. A small car at the head bears the figure of some animal and is followed by the king and queen under a large, showy umbrella. The bahianas, *who wear snowy-white embroidered skirts, dance in single file on either side of the king and queen. Next comes the* dama do passo *carrying a small doll, or* calunga. *After the* dama *comes the* tirador de loas *who chants to the group which replies in chorus, and last comes a band of local percussion instruments.*

Still flourishing is the dance performance of the caboclinhos. *The groups wear traditional Indian garb: bright feathers round their waists and ankles, colourful cockades, bead and animal teeth necklaces, a dazzle of medals on their red tunics. The dancers beat out the rhythm with bows and arrows; others of the group play primitive musical instruments, but the dance is the thing: spinning, leaping, and stooping with almost mathematical precision.*

Further information from Casa da Carnaval, *office of Fundação da Cultura de Recife, Pátio de São Pedro, lojas 10-11.* Galo da Madrugada, *Rua da Concórdia, Santo Antônio, T2242899.*

---

month. ***Domingo na Rua***, Sun market in Recife Barrio, with stalls of local artesanato and performances. **Bookshops** *Livraria Brandão*, R da Matriz 22 (used English books and some French and German), and bookstalls on the R do Infante Dom Henrique. *Livro 7*, R do Riachuelo 267. A huge emporium with a very impressive stock. *Sodiler* at Guararapes airport has books in English (including *Footprint*), newspapers, magazines; also in the *Shopping Center Recife*. *Livraria Saraiva*, Rua 7 de Setembro 280. The best selection of Brazilian literature in the city. *Almanque Livros*, Largo do Varadouro 418, loja 58. Bohemian atmosphere, sells food and drink. A great local character, ***Melquísidec Pastor de Nascimento***, has a second-hand stall at Praça do Sebo. Shopping malls ***Shopping Center Recife*** between Boa Viagem and the airport. ***Shopping Tacaruna***, in Santo Amaro, buses to/from Olinda pass it.

Sport **Diving** Offshore are some 20 wrecks, including the remains of Portuguese galleons; the fauna is very rich. *Mergulhe Coma*, T3552 2355, T9102 6809 (mob), atlanticdivingasr@ hotmail.com English speaking instructors for PADI courses. *Seagate*, T3426 1657/9972 9662, www.seagaterecife.com.br Daily departures and night dives.

Transport **Local Bus**: city buses cost US$0.30-60; they are clearly marked and run frequently until about 2300 weekdays, 0100 weekends. Many central bus stops have boards showing routes.

CID/SUB or SUB/CID signs on the front tell you whether buses are going to or from the suburbs from/to the city centre (cidade). On buses, especially at night, look out for landmarks as street names are written small and are hard to see. Integrated bus-**metrô** (see Train below) routes and tickets (US$1) are available. Urban transport information, T158. See below for buses to Olinda and other destinations outside the city. Taxis are plentiful; fares double on Sun, after 2100 and on holidays; number shown on meter is the fare; don't take the taxi if a driver tells you it is km.

Long distance Air: the principal international and national airlines fly to Guararapes airport, 12 km from the city in Boa Viagem. T3464 4188. Internal flights to all major cities. Bus to airport, No 52, US$0.40. Airport taxis cost US$5 to the seafront. There is a bank desk before customs which gives much the same rate for dollars as the moneychangers in the lobby.

  Train: commuter services, known as the **Metrô** but not underground, leave from the central station; they serve the rodoviária (frequent trains, 0500-2300, US$0.40 single). To reach the airport, get off the Metrô at Central station (not Joana Bezerra, which is unsafe) and take a bus or taxi (US$8) to Boa Viagem.

  Bus: the rodoviária, mainly for long-distance buses, is 12 km outside the city at São Lourenço da Mata (it is called Terminal Integrado dos Passageiros, or TIP, pronounced 'chippy'). T3452 1999. There is a 30-min metrô connection to the central railway station, entrance through Museu do Trem, opposite the Casa da Cultura, 2 lines leave the city, take train marked 'Rodoviária'. From Boa Viagem a taxi all the way costs US$20, or go to Central Metrô station and change there. Bus US$1, 1 hr, from the centre or from Boa Viagem. The train to the centre is much quicker than the bus. Bus tickets are sold at Cais de Santa Rita (opposite EMTU) and *Fruir Tur*, at Praça do Carmo, Olinda.

  To **Salvador**, daily 1930, 12 hrs, US$18-25. To **Rio**, daily 2100, 44 hrs, US$58-65. To **São Paulo**, 1630 daily, 50 hrs, US$60-70. To **Santos**, daily 1430, 52 hrs, US$60. To **Foz do Iguaçu**, Fri and Sun 1030, 55 hrs, US$90. To **Curitiba**, Fri and Sun, 52 hrs, US$76. To **Brasília**, daily 2130, 39 hrs, US$49-60. To **Belo Horizonte**, daily 2115, 34 hrs, US$41. To **João Pessoa**, every 20-30 mins, 2 hrs, US$2.50. To **Carauru**, every hr, 3 hrs, US$3. Buses to Olinda, see below; those to the beaches beyond Olinda from Av Dantas behind the post office. To **Cabo** (every 20 mins) and beaches south of Recife from Cais de Santa Rita.

Airline offices. *BRA*, T3421 7060, *Gol*, T3464 4793. *RioSul/Nordeste*, Av Domingos Ferreira 801, loja 103-5, T(Nordeste) 3465 6799, T(Rio Sul) 3465 8535. *TAM*, airport T3462 6799/0800-123100. *TAP*, Praça Min Salgado Filho, Imbiribeira, T3465 0300. *Trip*, T3464 4610. *Varig*, R Conselheiro Aguiar 456, T3464 4440. Vasp, Av Manoel Borba 488, Boca Viagem, T32126 2000.

  Banks *Banco do Brasil*, Shopping Centre Boa Viagem (Visa), helpful. *MasterCard*, cash against card, Av Conselheiro Aguiar 3924, Boa Viagem. *Citibank*, Av Marques de Olinda 126 and Av Cons Aguiar 2024, MasterCard with ATM. Also at branches of *HSBC*, eg Av Conde de Boa Vista 454 and Av Cons Aguiar 4452, Boa Viagem, and at *Banco 24 Horas. Lloyds TSB Bank*, Rua A.L. Monte 96/1002. *Bradesco*, at: Av Cons Aguiar 3236, Boa Viagem; Av Conde de Boa Vista; Rua da Concórdia 148; Getúlio Vargas 729; all have credit card facility, 24-hr ATMs but no exchange. **Exchange:** *Anacor*, Shopping Center Recife, loja 52, also at Shopping Tacaruna, loja 173. *Norte Câmbio Turismo*, Av Boa Viagem 5000, and at Shopping Guararapes, Av Barreto de Menezes.

  Communications Internet: Internet access in bookshop (signposted) in Shopping Centre Recife in Boa Viagem. Also, *lidernet* , Shopping Boa Vista, city centre. *popul@r.net*, R Barão de Souza Leão, near junction with Av Boa Viagem. Open daily 0900-2100. **Post Office**: including poste restante, Central Correios, 50001, Av Guararapes 250. In Boa Viagem, Av Cons Aguiar e R Col Sérgio Cardim. **Telephone**: *Embratel*, Av Agamenon Magalhães, 1114, Parque Amorim district; also Praça da Independência. **International telephones**: *Telemar*, Av Conselheiro Aguiar, Av Herculano Bandeira 231, and Av Conde da Boa Vista, all open 0800-1800.

  Cultural centres British Council, Domingos Ferreira 4150, Boa Viagem, T3465 7744, F3465 7271, www.britcoun.org/br 0800-1500, supplied with current English newspapers, very helpful. Alliance Française, R Amaro Bezerra 466, Derby, T/F3222 0918.

  Embassies and consulates Denmark, Av M de Olinda 85, Ed Alberto Fonseca 2°, T3224 0311, F3224 0997. Open 0800-1200, 1400-1800. Finland, R Ernesto de Paula Santos 1327, T3465 2940, F3465 2859. France, Av Conselheiro Aguiar 2333, 6th floor, T3465 3290. Japan, R Padre Carapuceiro 733, 14th

Directory

*Banks open
1000-1600, hours
for exchange vary
between 1000 and
1400, sometimes later*

Brazil

floor, Boa Viagem, T3327 7264. **Netherlands**, Av Conselheiro Aguiar 1313/3, Boa Viagem, T3465 6764. **Sweden**, R Ernesto de Paula Santos, Boa Viagem, T3465 2940. **Switzerland**, Av Conselheiro Aguiar 4880, loja 32, Boa Viagem, T3326 3144. **UK**, Av Cons Aguiar 2941, 3rd floor, Boa Viagem, T3465 0230, F3465 0247, recife@britishconsulate.org.br 0800-1130. **US**, Gonçalves Maia 163, Boa Vista, T3421 2441, F3231 1906.

Dengue fever has been resurgent in Recife

Medical services *Unimed*, Av Bernardo Vieira de Melo 1496, Guararapes, T3462 1955/3461 1530, general medical treatment. *Unicordis*, Av Conselheiro Aguiar 1980, Boa Viagem, T3326 5237, equipped for cardiac emergencies; also at Av Conselheiro Roas e Silva 258, Aflitos, T421 1000. **Tourist offices Empetur** (for the State of Pernambuco), main office, Centro de Convenções, Complexo Rodoviário de Salgadinho, T3427 8000, F3241 9601, between Recife and Olinda, www.empetur.gov.br Branches at airport – 24 hrs, T3224 2361 (helpful but few leaflets, English spoken), and Praça of Boa Viagem, T3463 3621 (English spoken, helpful). Maps are available, or can be bought at newspaper stands in city; also sketch maps in monthly guides *Itinerário Pernambuco* and *Guia do Turista*. For the **Secretaria de Turismo da Prefeitura do Recife**, T3425 8605/8070. **Secretaria de Indústria, Comércio e Turismo**, Av Rui Barbosa 458, Graças, T3231 4500, F3231 4537, www.pernambuco.gov.br Hours of opening of museums, art galleries, churches etc are published in the *Diário de Pernambuco* and *Jornal do Comércio*. The former's website has lots of tourist information, www.dpnet.com.br/turismo/ **Useful addresses** Tourist Police, T3326 9603/3464 4088. **Voltage** 220 volts AC, 60 cycles.

Olinda

Phone code: 0xx81
Post code: 53000
Colour map 5, grid B6
Population: 367,902

The old capital of Brazil founded in 1537 and named a World Heritage Site by UNESCO in 1982 is about 7 km north of Recife. A programme of restoration, partly financed by the Netherlands government, was initiated in order to comply with the recently conferred title of National Monument, but many of the buildings are still in desperate need of repair. The compact network of cobbled streets is steeped in history and invites wandering. This is a charming spot to spend a few relaxing days and a much more appealing base than Recife.

Sights

Many of the historic buildings have irregular opening hours, but can be viewed from the outside. The Tourist Office provides a complete list of all historic sites with a useful map, Sitio Histórico Guides with identification cards wait in Praça do Carmo. They are former street children and half the fee for a full tour of the city (about US$12) goes to a home for street children. If you take a guide you will be safe from mugging which, unfortunately, occurs

The **Basílica e Mosterio de São Bento**, R São Bento, was founded 1582 by the Benedictine monks, burnt by the Dutch in 1631 and restored in 1761. This is the site of Brazil's first law school and the first abolition of slavery. The magnificent gold altar was on loan to New York's Guggenheim Museum at the time of writing. ■ *Mon-Fri 0830-1130, 1430-1700. Mass Sat 0630 and 1800; Sun 1000, with Gregorian chant. Monastery closed except with written permission.* Despite its weathered exterior, the **Convento de São Francisco** (1585), Ladeira de São Francisco, has splendid woodcarving and paintings, superb gilded stucco, and azulejos in the Capela de São Roque within the church of **Nossa Senhora das Neves** in the same building. ■ *Tue-Fri 0700-1130, 1400-1700, Sat 0700-1200, US$0.40. Mass Tue 1900, Sat 1700 and Sun 0800.* Make the short, but very steep, climb up to the **Alto da Sé** for memorable views of the city and the coastline stretching all the way to Recife. Here, the simple **Igreja da Sé** (1537), a cathedral since 1677, was the first church to be built in the city, ■ *Mon-Fri 0800-1200, 1400-1700.* Nearby, the **Igreja da Misericórdia** (1540), R Bispo Coutinho, has fine tiling and gold work. ■ *Daily 1145-1230, 1800-1830.* On a small hill overlooking Praça do Carmo, the **Igreja do Carmo** church (1581) has been closed for several years, with restoration planned.

There are some houses of the 17th century with latticed balconies, heavy doors and brightly-painted stucco walls, including a house in Moorish style at **Praça João Alfredo 7**, housing the *Mourisco* restaurant and a handicrafts shop, *Sobrado 7*. The local colony of artists means excellent examples of regional art, mainly woodcarving and terracotta figurines, may be bought in the Alto da Sé, or in the handicraft shops at the **Mercado da Ribeira**, R Bernardo Vieira de Melo (Vieira de Melo gave the first recorded call for independence from Portugal, in Olinda in 1710). Handicrafts are also sold at good prices in the Mercado Eufrásio Barbosa, by the junction of Av Segismundo Gonçalves and Santos Dumont, Varadouro. There is a **Museo de Arte Sacra** in the former Palacío Episcopal (1696), R Bispo Coutínho. ■ *Tue-Fri*

Brazil (vertical side text)

0900-1300. At R 13 de Maio 157, in the 18th century jail of the Inquisition, is the **Museu de Arte Contemporânea** (same hours as Museu Regional). The **Museu Regional**, R do Amparo 128, is excellent. ■ *Tue-Fri, 0900-1700, Sat and Sun 1400-1700*. **Museu do Mamulengo**, Amparo 59, has Pernambucan folk puppetry. ■ *0900-1800, Sat-Sun 1100-1800*.

Beaches

The beaches close to Olinda are reported to be seriously polluted. Those further north from Olinda, beyond Casa Caiada, are beautiful, usually deserted, palm-fringed; at **Janga**, and **Pau Amarelo**, the latter can be dirty at low tide (take either a 'Janga' or 'Pau Amarela' bus, Varodouro bus to return). At many simple cafés you can eat *sururu* (clam stew in coconut sauce), *agulha frita* (fried needle-fish), *miúdo de galinha* (chicken giblets in gravy) and *casquinha de carangueijo* (seasoned crabmeat and *farinha de dendê* served in crabshells). Visit the Dutch fort on Pau Amarelo beach; small craft fair here on Saturday nights.

Sleeping

Historic city Accommodation is mostly in converted mansions that are full of character. If you can afford it, staying in one of these *pousadas* is the ideal way to absorb Olinda's colonial charm. **AL** *Pousada do Amparo*, R do Amparo 199, T3439 1749, www.pousadoamparo.com.br Olinda's best hotel, 18th century house full of atmosphere, distinctive rooms with a/c and fridge, some with jacuzzi, flower-filled garden, sauna, good view, very helpful, English spoken, romantic restaurant, in *Roteiros de Charme* group (see page 337). Highly recommended. **AL** *7 Colinas*, Ladeira de Sao Francisco 307, T/F3439 6055, 7colinas@hotel7 colinas.com.br Spacious, new hotel in beautiful grounds with large swimming pool, an oasis with full facilities. **B-C** *Pousada dos Quatro Cantos*, R Prudente de Morais 441, T3429 0220, www.pousada4cantos.com.br Converted mansion with original furniture; full of character, yet homely, garden, terraces and simple restaurant open till 2100. Highly recommended. **C** *Pousada d'Olinda*, P João Alfredo 178, T/F3494 2559. Nice pool area, sociable, 10% discount for *Footprint Handbooks* owners, 2 communal rooms with good view (**E**), restaurant, English, French, German and Spanish spoken. Warmly recommended. **C-D** *Pousada Peter*, R do Amparo 215, T/F3439 2171, www.pousadapeter.com.br A/c, small pool, German owner, family atmosphere, good value.

Prices at least triple during Carnival when 5-night packages are sold. Rooms at regular prices can often be found in Boa Viagem during this time. All of the following, and even most of the cheaper hotels outside the old city, have a pool

Brazil

Olinda

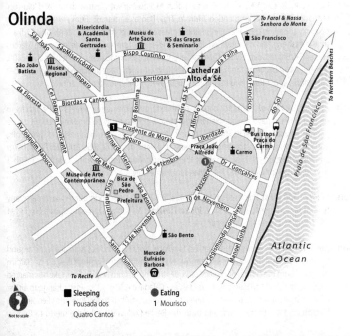

Sleeping ■
1 Pousada dos Quatro Cantos

Eating ●
1 Mourisco

Not to scale

Outside the historic centre   Hotels on R do Sol and in Bairro Novo are below the old city and on the roads heading north. **B** *Oh! Linda Pousada*, Av Ministro Marcos Freire 349, Bairro Novo, T3439 2116. Recommended. **C** *Cinco Sóis*, Av Ministro Marcos Freire 633, Bairro Novo, T/F3429 1347. A/c, fridge, hot shower, parking. **C** *Hospedaria do Turista*, Av Marcos Freire 989, T3429 1847. Excellent. **C** *Pousada São Francisco*, R do Sol 127, T3429 2109, F3429 4057. Comfortable, pool. Recommended, modest restaurant. **D** *São Pedro*, Praça Cons João Alfredo 168, T3429 2935. Cosy, helpful, laundry, Danish run, English spoken. Recommended.

Several **youth hostels** **D** *Cheiro do Mar*, Av Ministro Marcos Freire 95, T3429 0101. Very good small hostel with some double rooms (room No 1 is noisy from the disco), cooking facilities, ask driver of 'Rio Doce/Piedade' or 'Bairra de Jangada/Casa Caiada' bus (see below) to drop you at Albergue de Juventude on the sea front. **E** *Albergue da Olinda*, R do Sol 233, T3429 1592. Popular, suites with bath (**C**) and communal bunk rooms, laundry facilities, discounts for IYHA members. Highly recommended.

Camping   *Olinda Camping*, R Bom Sucesso 262, Amparo, T3429 1365. US$5 pp, space for 30 tents, 5 trailers, small huts for rent, quiet, well-shaded, on bus route, recommended.

Eating   **Expensive**   *Oficina do Sabor*, R do Amparo, 355. Consistently wins awards, pleasant terrace overlooking city, food served in hollowed-out pumpkins and lots of vegetarian options. *Goya*, R do Amparo, 157. Regional food, particularly seafood, beautifully presented. **Mid-range**   *Maison do Bomfim*, R do Bonfim, 115. Serene, fan-cooled, rustic-style restaurant, French cuisine, as well as Brazilian and Italian. *Samburá*, Av Min Marcos Freire 1551. With terrace, try *caldeirada* and *pitu* (crayfish), also lobster in coconut sauce or daily fish dishes, very good. **Cheap**   *Grande Pequim*, Av Min Marcos Freire 1463, Bairro Novo. Good Chinese food. *Mourisco*, Praça João Alfredo 7. Excellent, good value food by weight in lovely, part-covered, garden, delicious deserts. Warmly recommended. Several *lanchonetes* and fast-food options along the seafront, such as *Mama Luise* and *Gibi*, on Av Min Marcos Freire, and Av Sigismundo Gonçalves, eg *Leque Moleque* at No 537. The traditional Olinda drinks, *Pau do Índio* (which contains 32 herbs) and *Retetel*, are both manufactured on the R do Amparo. Also try *tapioca*, a local dish made of manioc with coconut or cheese.

Entertainment   *Cantinho da Sé*, Ladeira da Sé 305. Lively, good view of Recife, food served. *Farandola*, R Dom Pedro Roeser 190, behind Carmo church. Mellow bar with festival theme and 'big-top' style roof. Warmly recommended. *Marola*, Trav. Dantas Barreto 66. Funky wooden *barraca* on rocky shoreline specializing in seafood, great *caiprifrutas* (frozen fruit drink with vodka – try the cashew), can get crowded. Recommended. *Pernambucanamente*, Av Min Marcos Freire 734, Bairro Novo. Live, local music every night. Beginning at dusk, but best after 2100, the Alto da Sé becomes the scene of a street fair, with arts, crafts, makeshift bars and barbecue stands, and impromptu traditional music; even more animated at Carnival.

Every Fri night bands of wandering musicians walk the streets serenading passers-by. Each Sun from 1 Jan to Carnival there is a mini Carnival in the streets

Festivals   At Olinda's *carnival* thousands of people dance through the narrow streets of the old city to the sound of the *frevo*, the brash energetic music which normally accompanies a lively dance performed with umbrellas. The local people decorate them with streamers and straw dolls, and form themselves into costumed groups to parade down the R do Amparo; *Pitombeira* and *Elefantes* are the best known of these groups. *Foundation Day* is celebrated with 3 days of music and dancing, **12-15 Mar**, night time only.

Tour operators   *Viagens Sob O Sol*, Prudente de Moraes 424, T3429 3303, transport offered to all parts, any type of trip arranged, also car hire. *Victor Turismo*, Av Santos Domont 20, Loja 06, T3494 1467. Day and night trips to Recife.

Transport   **Bus**   **From Recife**: take any bus marked 'Rio Doce', No 981 which has a circular route around the city and beaches, or No 33 from Av Nossa Senhora do Carmo, US$0.60 or 'Jardim Atlântico' from the central post office at Siqueira Campos; from Boa Viagem, take bus marked 'Piedade/Rio Doce' or 'Bairra de Jangada/Casa Caiada' (US$0.60, 30 mins). Change to either of these buses from the airport to Olinda: take 'Aeroporto' bus to Av Domingos Ferreira, Boa Viagem, and ask to be let off; and from the Recife Rodoviária: take the metrô to Central station and then change. In all cases, alight in Praça do Carmo. Taxi drivers between Olinda and Recife try to put meters onto rate 2 at the Convention Centre (between the 2 cities), but should change it back to 1 when queried (taxi to Recife US$8, US$12 to Boa Viagem at night).

Banks *Banco do Brasil,* R Getúlio Vargas 1470. *Bradesco,* R Getúlio Vargas 729, Visa ATM. **Communications** Internet: *Studyo Web,* Praça do Carmo, US$1.20, 30 mins, a/c. *Olind@com,* Av Beira Mar 15, US$1.50, 30 mins. **Post Office:** Praça do Carmo, open 0900-1700. **Telephone:** International calls can be made at *Telemar* office on Praça do Carmo, Mon-Sat 0900-1800. **Tourist offices** Secretaria de Turismo, Praça do Carmo, T3429 9279, open daily 0900-2100.

Directory
There are no facilities to change TCs, or ATMs in the old city

North of Recife

North of Recife by 39 km on the road to João Pessoa, Igarassu has the first church built in Brazil (SS Cosme e Damião, built in 1535), the Livramento church nearby, and the convent of Santo Antônio with a small museum next door. The church of Sagrado Coração is said to have housed Brazil's first orphanage. Much of the town (founded in 1535) has been declared a National Monument; it is an attractive place, with a number of colonial houses and Brazil's first Masonic hall. ■ *Igarassu buses leave from Av Martins de Barros, infront of Grande Hotel, Recife, 45 mins, US$1.*

Igarassu
Colour map 5, grid B6
Population: 82,277

North of Igarassu you pass through coconut plantations to Itapissuma, where there is a bridge to Itamaracá island, where, the locals say Adam and Eve spent their holidays (so does everyone else on Sunday, now). It has the old Dutch **Forte Orange**, built in 1631; an interesting penal settlement with gift shops, built round the 1747 sugar estate buildings of Engenho São João, which still have much of the old machinery; charming villages and colonial churches, and fine, wide beaches. At one of them, **Praia do Forte Orange**, Ibama has a centre for the study and preservation of manatees (*Centro Nacional de Conservação e Manejo de Sirênios* or *Peixe-boi*). ■ *Tue-Sat 1000-1600, US$1.* **Excursions** Pleasant trips by *jangada* from Praia do Forte Orange to **Ilha Coroa do Avião**, a recently-formed sandy island (developing wildlife, migratory birds) with rustic beach bars.

Itamaracá

Transport Bus From Recife (*Cais de Santa Rita* opposite *Grande Hotel,* US$1.10) and *Igarassu.* From Olinda, Praça do Carmo, take bus marked 'Caetes', change at Paulista for bus or kombi to Itamaracá (ask driver to drop you off for Forte Orange, 4-km walk or kombi).

West of Recife

The paved road from Recife passes through rolling hills, with sugar cane and large cattle *fazendas,* before climbing an escarpment. As the road gets higher, the countryside becomes drier, browner and rockier. Caruaru is a busy, modern town, one of the most prosperous in the *agreste* in Pernambuco. It is also culturally very lively, with excellent local and theatre and folklore groups.

Caruaru
Colour map 5, grid C6
Population: 253,634
Altitude: 554 m
134 km W of Recife

Caruaru is most famous for its markets. The *Feira da Sulanca* is basically a clothes market supplied mostly by local manufacture, but also on sale are jewellery, souvenirs, food, flowers and anything else that can go for a good price. The most important day is Monday. There is also the *Feira Livre* or *do Troca-Troca* (free, or barter market). On the same site, Parque 18 de Maio, is the *Feira do Artesanato,* leather goods, ceramics, hammocks and basketware, all the popular crafts of the region. It is tourist-oriented but it is on a grand scale and is open daily 0800-1800.

The little clay figures (*figurinhas* or *bonecas de barro*) originated by Mestre Vitalino (1909-63), and very typical of the *Nordeste,* are the local speciality; most of the local potters live at Alto da Moura 6 km away, where a house once owned by Vitalino is open (the **Casa Museu Mestre Vitalino**), with personal objects and photographs, but no examples of his work. ■ *Bus, 30 mins, bumpy, US$0.50.*

Brazil

Sleeping and eating A *Grande Hotel São Vicente de Paulo*, Av Rio Branco 365, T3721 5011, F3721 5290. Good, central, a/c, laundry, garage, bar, restaurant, pool, TV. **C** *Central*, R Vigário Freire 71, T3721 5880. Suites or rooms, all with a/c, TV, good breakfast, in the centre. Recommended. **C** *Centenário*, 7 de Setembro 84, T3722 4011, F3721 1033. Also has more expensive suites, good breakfast, pool, in the town centre so not very quiet, otherwise recommended. A large number of cheap *hospedarias* are around the central Praça Getúlio Vargas. Lots of cheap lunch restaurants in the centre near *Banco do Brasil*.

Festivals 17 Dec-2 Jan, *Festas Natalinas*; Semana Santa, Holy Week, with lots of folklore and handicraft events; **18-22 May**, city's anniversary. **13 Jun** *Santo Antônio* and **24 Jun** *São João*, the latter a particularly huge forró festival, are part of Caruaru's Festas Juninas. **Sep**, *Micaru*, a street carnival; also in **Sep**, *Vaquejada* (a Brazilian cross between rodeo and bull fighting), biggest in the northeast.

Transport The rodoviária is 4 km from the town; buses from Recife stop in the centre. Bus from centre, at the same place as Recife bus stop, to rodoviária, US$0.40. Many buses from TIP in **Recife**, 2 hrs, US$3. Bus to **Fazenda Nova** 1030, 1 hr, US$2, returns for Caruaru 1330.

Directory Useful information The *Cultura Inglesa Caruaru*, Av Agamenon Magalhães 634, Maurício de Nassau, CEP 55000-000, T3721 4749 (cultura@netstage.co.br) will help any visitors with information.

Fernando de Noronha

Many unspoilt beaches and interesting wildlife. Excellent scuba-diving and snorkelling. The rains are from Feb-Jul; the island turns green and the sea water becomes lovely and clear. The dry season is Aug- Mar, but the sun shines all year round

One hr behind Brazilian Standard Time. No repellent available for the many mosquitoes

This small archipelago 345 km off the northeast coast was declared a Marine National Park in 1988. Only one island is inhabited and is dominated by a 321 m peak. It is part of the state of Pernambuco administered from Recife. The islands were discovered in 1503 by Amérigo Vespucci and were for a time a pirate lair. In 1738 the Portuguese built the Forte dos Remédios (begun by the Dutch), later used as a prison in this century, and a church to strengthen their claim to the islands. Remains of the early fortifications still exist.

Vila dos Remédios, near the north coast, is where most people live and socialize. At Baía dos Golfinhos is a lookout point for watching the spinner dolphins in the bay. On the south side there are fewer beaches, higher cliffs and the whole coastline and offshore islands are part of the marine park.

■ *Ibama has imposed rigorous rules to prevent damage to the nature reserve and everything, from development to cultivation of food crops to fishing, is strictly administered, if not forbidden. Many locals are now dependent on tourism and most food is brought from the mainland; prices are about double. Entry to the island has been limited to 100 tourists per day because of the serious problems of energy and water supply. A maximum of 420 tourists is allowed on the island at any one time. Moreover, there is a tax of US$13, payable per day for the first week of your stay. In the second week the tax increases each day. Take sufficient reais as dollars are heavily discounted. For information, contact the park office, Paranamar-FN, T0xx81-3619 1210.*

Sleeping & eating B *Estrela do Mar*, T3619 1366, with breakfast, excursions arranged. Also *Pousada Verde Riviere*, T3619 1312. Owner Sra Helena Maria, good food, especially fresh tuna. Independent travellers can go much cheaper as many local families rent out rooms with full board, from about US$50 pp per day. The home owners have an association, **Associação das Hospedarias Domiciliares de Fernando de Noronha**, T0xx81-3619 1142. There are 3 restaurants, *Anatalício*, *Ecológico* and *Miramar*. The speciality of the island is shark (*tubarão*), which is served in bars and at the port (Noronha Pesca Oceânica). There aren't many bars, but a good one is *Mirante Bar*, near the hotel, with a spectacular view over Boldró beach; it has loud music and at night is an open-air disco.

Sport **Scuba-diving** Diving is organized by *Atlantis Divers*, T0xx81-3619 1371, *Águas Claras*,

T3619 1225, in the hotel grounds, and **Noronha Divers**, T3619 1112. Diving costs between US$50-75 and equipment rental from US$50. This is the diving mecca for Brazilian divers with a great variety of sites to explore and fish to see.

Boat trips and jeep tours are available; it is also possible to hire a beach buggy (US$100 a day without a driver, US$30 with driver). Motorbikes can be rented for US$80 a day. You can hitch everywhere as everyone stops. There are good hiking, horse riding and mountain biking possibilities, but you must either go with a guide or ranger in many parts. **Tours**

Air Daily flights from Recife and São Paulo-Campinas-Fortaleza—Natal, with *Nordeste*, 1 hr 20 mins from Recife, 1 hr from Natal, US$400 and US$300 return respectively. Also daily flights from Recife and Natal with *Transporte Regional do Interior Paulista*. **Transport**

Paraíba

João Pessoa

It is a bus ride of two hours through sugar plantations over a good road from Recife (126 km) to João Pessoa, capital of the State of Paraíba on the Rio Paraíba. It is a capital that retains a small town atmosphere. In the **Centro Histórico** is the São Francisco Cultural Centre (Praça São Francisco 221), one of the most important baroque structures in Brazil, with the beautiful church of **São Francisco** which houses the Museu Sacro e de Arte Popular. ■ *Tue-Sat 0800-1100, Tue-Sun 1400-1700, T221 2840*. Other tourist points include the **Casa da Pólvora**, now the **Museu Fotográfico Walfredo Rodríguez** (Ladeira de São Francisco). ■ *Mon-Fri 0800-1200, 1330-1700*. Also the **Teatro Santa Roza** (1886), Praça Pedro Américo, Varadouro, T241 1230. ■ *Mon-Fri 1400-1800*. João Pessoa's parks include the 17-ha **Parque Arruda Câmara**, north of the centre, and **Parque Solon de Lucena** or **Lagoa**, a lake surrounded by impressive palms in the centre of town, the city's main avenues and bus lines go around it.

The beachfront stretches for some 30 km from Ponta do Seixas (south) to the port of **Cabedelo** (north), on a peninsula between the Rio Paraíba and the Atlantic Ocean. This is Km 0 of the Transamazônica highway. The ocean is turquoise green and there is a backdrop of lush coastal vegetation. 7 km from the city centre, following Av Presidente Epitáceo Pessoa is the beach of **Tambaú**, which has many hotels and restaurants. ■ *Bus No 510 'Tambaú' from outside the rodoviária or the city centre, alight at* Hotel Tropical Tambaú. Regional crafts, including lace-work, embroidery and ceramics are available at *Mercado de Artesanato*, Centro de Turismo, Almte Tamandaré 100. About 14 km south of the centre is the Cabo Branco lighthouse at Ponta do Seixas, the most easterly point of continental Brazil and South America; there is a panoramic view from the cliff top. **Cabo Branco** is much better for swimming than **Tambaú**. Take bus 507 'Cabo Branco' from outside the rodoviária to the end of the line; hike up to the lighthouse.

Phone code: 0xx83
Post code: 58000
Colour map 5, grid B6
Population: 597,934

Brasília

Brazil

Centre C *Guarany*, R Almeida Barreto 181 and 13 de Maio, T/F241 5005, guarany@ bomguia.com.br Cheaper without a/c and TV, cheaper still in low season, pleasant, safe, extremely good value, own self service restaurant. Recommended. **D** *Aurora*, Praça João Pessoa 51, T241 3238. A/c, cheaper with fan, on attractive square, pleasant enough. **D** *Ouro Preto*, Idaleto 162, T221 5882, Varadouro near rodoviária. With bath, fan. Cheaper hotels can be found near the rodoviária. **G** *Pousada Fênix*, R 13 de Maio, 588, T222 1193. 'Love hotel', rents rooms by hr, but spotless and real bargain.

Tambaú AL *Tropical Tambaú*, Av Alm Tamandaré 229, T2473660, F2471070, reservas.tambau@tropicalhotel.com.br Enormous round building, looks like a rocket

Sleeping
The town's main attractions are its beaches, where most tourists stay. Hotels in the centre tend to cater to business clients

launching station and a local landmark, comfortable, good service. Recommended. **A** *Sol-Mar*, Rui Carneiro 500, T226 1350, F226 3242. Pool, superb restaurant (**C** in low season). **B** *Tambia Praia*, R Carlos Alverga 36, T247 4101. Central, 1 block from beach, intimate, balconies with sea view. Recommended. **E** *Pousada Mar Azul*, Av João Maurício 315, T226 2660. Beachfront, a real bargain.

All are across from the beach, along Av Cabo Branco unless otherwise noted

Cabo Branco B *Pouso das Águas*, No 2348, T/F2265103. Homely atmosphere, landscaped areas, pool. **B** *Pousada Casa Rosada*, No 1710, T2472470. With fan, **C** with shared bath, family run. Accommodation can also be found in the outer beaches such as Camboinha and Seixas, and in Cabedelo.

Camping *Camping Clube do Brasil*, Praia de Seixas, 13 km from the centre, T247 2181.

Eating There are few options in the centre, other than the stalls in Parque Solon de Lucena next to the lake. **Tambaú Expensive**: *Adega do Alfredo*, Coração de Jesus. Excellent, popular, Portuguese. *Sagaranda*, Av Tamandaré near *Hotel Tambaú*. Very good *cozinha criativa* (similar to *nouvelle cuisine*). **Mid-range**: *Apetito Tratoria*, Osório Paes 35. Very good Italian, charming atmosphere. *Cheiro Verde*, R Carlos Alverga 43. Self-service, well-established, regional food. **Cheap**: Every evening on the beachfront, stalls are set up selling all kinds of snacks and barbecued meats.

Local holidays Pre-carnival celebrations are renowned: the bloco *Acorde Miramar* opens the celebrations the Tue before Carnival and on Wed, known as *Quarta Feira de Fogo*, thousands join the *Muriçocas de Miramar*. Celebrations for the patroness of the city, *Nossa Senhora das Neves*, take place for 10 days around **5 Aug**.

Tour operators Half-day city tours (US$6), day trips to Tambaba (US$8) and Recife/Olinda (US$12) organized by *Vida Mansa*, T226 1141. *Roger Turismo*, Av Tamandaré 229, T247 1856. A range of tours, some English-speaking guides. *Preocupação Zero Turismo*, Av Cabo Branco 2566, T226 4859, F226 4599. Local and regional tours, floating bars. *Navegar*, Artur Monteiro de Paiva 97, Bessa, T/F246 2191. Buggy tours (US$25 to Jacumã).

Transport **Local Bus**: Most city buses stop at the rodoviária and go by the Lagoa (Parque Solon de Lucena). Take No 510 for Tambaú, No 507 for Cabo Branco.

João Pessoa centre

N
Not to scale

■ Sleeping
1 Aurora 2 Guarany

Brazil

Long distance   Air: Aeroporto Presidente Castro Pinto, Bayeux, 11 km from centre, T232 1200; national flights. Taxi to centre costs US$8, to Tambaú US$12.

Bus: Rodoviária is at R Francisco Londres, Varadouro, 10 mins from the centre, T221 9611; luggage store; PBTUR information booth is helpful. Taxi to the centre US$1.50, to Tambaú US$5. To **Recife** with *Boa Vista* or *Bonfim*, every 30 mins, US$2.50, 2 hrs. To **Natal** with *Nordeste*, every 2 hrs, US$6 *convencional*, US$7.50 *executivo*, 3 hrs. To **Fortaleza** with *Nordeste*, 2 daily, 10 hrs, US$18. To **Juazeiro do Norte** with *Transparaíba*, 2 daily, US$14, 10 hrs. To **Salvador** with *Progresso*, 4 weekly, US$30, 14 hrs. To **Belém** with *Guanabara*, daily at 1000, US$46, 36-39 hrs.

Airline Offices   *BRA* , Av Almte Barroso 651, T222 6222. *TAM*, Av Senador Rui Carneiro 512, T247 2400 (airport T232 2747). *Varig*, Av Getúlio Vargas 183, Centro, T221 1140, 0800-997000. *Vasp*, Parque Solon de Lucena 530, Centro, T221 1140 (airport 247 2400). **Banks** *Banco do Brasil*, Praça 1817, 3rd floor, Centro, helpful, or Isidro Gomes 14, Tambaú, behind Centro de Turismo, poor rates. MasterCard Cirrus and Amex cashpoints at *Banco 24 Horas* kiosk in front of Centro de Turismo, Tambaú, and *HSBC*, R Peregrino de Carvalho 162, Centro. *PB Câmbio Turismo*, Visconde de Pelotas 54C, Centro, T241 4676, open Mon-Fri 1030-1630, cash and TCs. **Communications** Internet: Many cybercafés in Tambaú: at telephone office in Centro de Turismo, Almte Tamandaré 100. **Post Office:** main office is at Praça Pedro Américo, Varadouro; central office is at Parque Solon de Lucena 375; also by the beach at Av Rui Carneiro, behind the Centro de Turismo. **Telephone:** Calling stations at: Centro de Turismo, Tambaú; Av Epitácio Pessoa 1487, Bairro dos Estados; rodoviária and airport. **Tourist offices**   PBTUR, at the Centro de Turismo, Tambaú, T247 0505, pbtur@pbtur.pb.gov.br   Branches at rodoviária and airport, all open 0800-2000. Little English spoken, basic maps. **Voltage**   220 volts AC, 60 cycles.

Directory

The best known beach of the state is **Tambaba**, the only official nudist beach of the Northeast, 49 km south of João Pessoa in a lovely setting. Two coves make up this famous beach: in the first bathing-suits are optional, while the second one is only for nudists. Strict rules of conduct are enforced. Between Jacumã (many hotels, restaurants) and Tambaba are several nice beaches such as **Tabatinga** which has summer homes on the cliffs and **Coqueirinho**, surrounded by coconut palms, good for bathing, surfing and exploring caves.

Rio Grande do Norte

Brasília

In Rio Grande do Norte the coastline is famous for its towering sand dunes. It changes, becoming gradually drier and less green as it shifts from running north/south to east/west. The people are called 'Potiguares' after an Indian tribe that now resides in neighbouring Paraíba state.

Natal

Natal sits on a peninsula between the Rio Potengi and the Atlantic Ocean, and is one of the most attractive cities of Brazil's northeast coast. The oldest part of the city is the **Ribeira** along the riverfront where a process of renovation has been started. The **Cidade Alta**, or Centro, is the main commercial centre and Av Rio Branco its principal artery. The main square is made up of **Praças João Maria**, **André de Albuquerque, João Tibúrcio** and **7 de Setembro**. At Praça André de Albuquerque is the old cathedral (inaugurated 1599, restored 1996). The modern cathedral is on Av Deodoro s/n, Cidade Alta. The church of **Santo Antônio**, R Santo Antônio 683, Cidade Alta, dates from 1766, and has a fine, carved wooden altar and a sacred art museum. ■ *Tue-Fri 0800-1700, Sat 0800-1400.*

The **Museu Câmara Cascudo**, Av Hermes de Fonseca 1440, Tirol (T212 2795), has exhibits on archaeological digs, Umbanda rituals and the sugar, leather and

Phone code: 0xx84
Post code: 59000
Colour map 5, grid B6
Population: 712,317
185 km N of
João Pessoa

Brazil

petroleum industries. ■ *Mon 1400-1700, Tue-Fri 0800-1100, 1400-1700, Sat 1000-1600, US$1.50.* The **Forte dos Reis Magos** (16th century) at Praia do Forte, the tip of Natal's peninsula, is open daily 0800-1630; between it and the city is a military installation. It is possible to walk along the beach to the fort, or to go in a tour, or by taxi; it is worth it for the views. ■ *US$1.50.* **Museu do Mar**, Av Dinarte Mariz (Via Costeira), Praia de Mãe Luiza, has aquariums with regional sea life and exhibits

Brazil

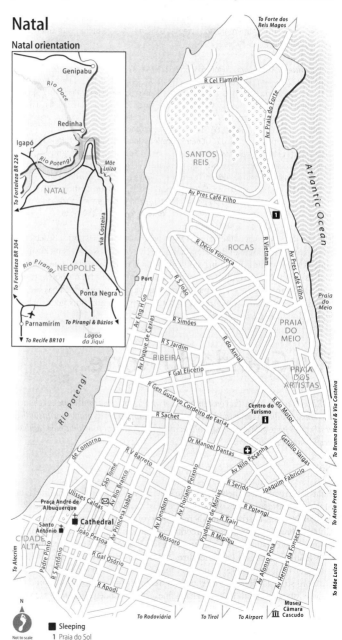

Natal

Natal orientation

Sleeping
1 Praia do Sol

with preserved specimens. ■ *Mon-Fri 0800-1700, Sat 0800-1400, T215 4433.* At Mãe Luiza is a lighthouse with beautiful views of Natal and surrounding beaches (take a city bus marked Mãe Luiza; get the key from the house next door).

Natal has excellent beaches some of which are also the scene of the city's night life. The urban beaches of Praia do Meio, Praia dos Artistas and Praia de Areia Preta have recently been cleaned up and a beachside promenade built. The **Via Costeira** runs south along the ocean beneath the towering sand dunes of **Parque das Dunas** (access restricted to protect the 9 km of dunes), joining the city to **Ponta Negra**, 12 km from the centre, the most popular beach. It is 20 mins by bus from centre; pleasant and 'quaint' atmosphere; the northern end of the beach is good for surfing, while the southern end is calmer and good for bathing. At the south end of the beach is **Morro do Careca**, a 120 m high dune with a sand skiing slope surrounded by vegetation (crowded on weekends and holidays, but not safe to wander alone when deserted, as there are robberies).

Beaches

Centre B *Casa Grande*, R Princesa Isabel 529, Centro, T211 0555. With a/c, cheaper without bath (also low season discounts), good breakfast, pleasant, excellent value. Recommended. **B** *Oassis Swiss*, R Joaquim Fabrício 291, Casa 08, Petrópolis, T/F202 2455. Swiss-owned, a/c, cheaper with fan (cheaper still in low season), pool, massive breakfasts, exceptional value. **D** *Fenícia*, Av Rio Branco 586, Centro, T211 4378. More expensive with a/c, with breakfast and shower, English spoken, low season discount. **E** *Pousada Marina*, at No 860, T202 1677, www.pousadamarina.com.br Simple, a/c, TV, fridge. Several near **rodoviária**: **B** *Pousada Esperança*, Av Capt Mor Gouveia 418, T205 1955. Cheaper with fan and without bath. **D** *Cidade do Sol*, Piancó 31, T205 1893. Cheaper with fan. **E** *Pousada Beth Shalom*, R Patos 45, T205 1141. Fan. **Praia do Meio, Praia dos Artistas and Praia de Areia Preta** Unless stated hotels are on the beachfront Av Pres Café Filho (the numbering of which is illogical); all recommended: **A** *Praia do Sol*, No 750, Praia do Meio, T211 4562, F222 6571. Opposite beach, quiet, a/c, TV. **B** *Bruma*, No 1176, T/F211 4308, www.hotelbruma@zaz.com.br Slick, intimate, beachfront balconies, pool, terrace. **D** *Beira Mar*, Av Pres Café Filho, Praia do Meio, T202 1470. With breakfast, a/c, small pool, good value, popular. **F** *Pousada do Paxá*, No 11, T2022848, www.paxaturismo.hpg.com.br Beachfront, breakfast extra, real bargain. **D** *Parque das Dunas*, R João XXIII 601 (take Bus 40, alight at Farol, 40 mins from the centre), T202 1820. Excellent breakfast (good value dinner on request), safe, **E** in low season.

   At Ponta Negra LL *Manary Praia*, R Francisco Gurgel 9067, T/F219 2900, manary@ digi.com.br Stylish, beachfront rooms and pool/terrace, a Roteiro de Charme hotel. **A** *Hotel e Pousada O Tempo e o Vento*, R Elias Barros 66, T/F219 2526. A/c (**B** in low season), fridge, cheaper with fan, pool, camping in area with trees, US$5 pp. **B** *Pousada Castanheira*, R da Praia 221, T/F236 2918, www.pousadacastanheira.com.br Small, comfortable, safe, most hospitable, English owned, pool. Recommended. **B** *Ingá Praia*, Av Erivan França 17, T219 3436, www.ingapraiahotel.com.br Very comfortable, cosy. Recommended. **B** *Miramar*, Av da Praia 3398, T2362079. Family-run, very clean, English spoken. **C** *Pousada Porta do Sol*, R Francisco Gurgel 9057, T236 2555, F205 2208. Room with bar, TV, excellent breakfast, pool, steps down onto beach, good value. Recommended. **D** *Pousada Maravista*, R da Praia, 223, T236 4677, marilymar@hotmail.com Good breakfast, English spoken, TV, fridge. **D** *Maria Bonita 2*, Estrela do Mar 2143, T236 2941, F219 2726. With a/c, **E** with fan. Recommended. **E** *Pousada Porto Seguro*, Av Pres Café Filho 1174, T9412 1039. Very sociable, beachfront terrace, good rooms and good value. Recommended.

   Youth hostels D pp: *Lua Cheia*, R Dr Manoel Augusto Bezerra de Araújo 500, Ponta Negra, T236 3696, www.luacheia.com.br Includes breakfast, IYHA. Outstanding. **E** *Albergue do Sol*, Av Duque de Caxias 190, Ribeira, T211 3233. Good breakfast, **F** in low season. **E** *Ladeira do Sol*, R Valentin de Almeida 10, Praia dos Artistas, T202 2647. *Meu Canto*, R Manoel Dantas 424, Petrópolis, T211 3954. Highly recommended.

Sleeping

The Via Costeira is a strip of enormous, upmarket beachfront hotels, which are very isolated. Ponta Negra is the ideal place to stay, with its attractive beach and concentration of restaurants. Economical hotels are easier to find in the city proper but otherwise there is not much reason to stay here

Brazil

Eating

As the largest exporter of prawns in Brazil, Natal's restaurants feature them heavily on menus

Centre and central beaches Expensive: *Doux France*, R Otâvio Lamartine, Petrópolis. Authentic French cuisine, outdoor seating. *Raro Sabor*, R Seridó 722, Petrópolis. Exclusive bistro. *Chaplin*, Av Pres Café Filho 27, Praia dos Artistas. Traditional, seaviews, good seafood, part of leisure complex with bar, English pub and nightclub. *Estação Trem de Minas*, Av Pres Café Filho 197, Praia dos Artistas. Charming rustic style, 40 brands of cachaça, live music nightly, self-service lunch and dinner. **Mid-range** *Bella Napoli*, Av Hermes da Fonseca 960, Tirol. Good Italian food. *Camarões Express*, Av Sen Salgado Filho 2234, Natal Shopping. Literally, fast-food prawns in 15 styles. Open for lunch only at weekends. *Carne de Sol Benigna Lira*, R Dr José Augusto Bezerra de Medeiros 09, Praia do Meio. Traditional, regional cuisine. *Fiorentina*, 529, delivery T202 0020. Pizzeria, huge range of seafood, try the lobster with spaghetti. Warmly recommended. *Peixada da Comadre*, R Dr José Augusto Bezerra de Medeiros 4, Praia dos Artistas. Seafood, popular with visitors. **Cheap** *Bob's*, Av Sen Salgado Filho, 2234, Natal Shopping. Hamburger chain open daily 1000-2200. *A Macrobiótica*, Princesa Isabel 524, vegetarian, shop, lunch only. *Saint Antoine*, R Santo Antônio 651, Cidade Alta. Self-service by kg. For snacks, try the stalls along the beaches.

Street numbering is not logical, but all restaurants are on Av Erivan França, the short beach road

Ponta Negra Expensive: *Tereré*, Estr de Pirangi 2316. All-you-can-eat barbecue, including Argentine beef, ribs, as well as fish and salad. **Mid-range**: *Atlântico*, No 27. Relaxed, semi-open air, beachfront, Italian and Portugese dishes, fish and carne do sol. Recommended. *Barraca do Caranguejo*, No 1180. Live music nightly from 2100, 8 prawn dishes for US$8. *Camarões*, Av Eng Roberto Freire 2610, also at Natal Shopping Centre. Touristy, but very good seafood. *Cipó Brasil*, jungle theme, 4 levels, sand floors, lantern-lit, very atmospheric, average food (pizzas and crêpes), good for cocktails, live music nightly after 2100. *Ponta Negra Grill*, No 20. Large, several terraces, popular, lively, steaks, seafood and cocktails. **Cheap**: Beach *baracas* for snacks and fast food. *Ponta Negra Mall*, stalls sell sandwiches and snacks.

Bars & nightclubs

Ponta Negra beach is lively at night and the venue for a full-moon party, when there is live music all night

Baraonda, Av Erivan França, 44, Ponta Negra, T9481 3748. Live music nightly (closed Tue), including swing and ambiente from 2300 to last customer. *Taverna Pub*, R Dr Maneol A B de Araújo 500, Ponta Negra, T236 3696. Medieval-style pub in youth hostel basement, eclectic (rock, Brazilian pop, Jazz, etc), live music Tue-Sun from 2200, best night Wed. Daily shows at *Zás-Trás*, R Apodi 500, Tirol, T211 1444, closed Sun. The *Centro de Turismo* (see Shopping) has *Forró com Turista*, a chance for visitors to learn this fun dance, Thu 2200; many other enjoyable venues where visitors are encouraged to join in. In Ribeira, Centro, there are two popular bar/nightclubs in restored historic buildings on Rua Chile: *Blackout B52*, No 25, T221 1282, '40s theme, best night is 'Black Monday', and *Downtown Pub*, No 11, 4 bars, dancefloor, games area, cybercafé, live bands Thu-Sat. *Novakapital*, Av Pres Café Filho 872, Praia dos Artistas, T202 7111. *Forró*, live music, especially rock, foam parties, US$4, from 2400.

Festivals

In **Jan** is the *Festa de Nossa Senhora dos Navegantes* when numerous vessels go to sea from Praia da Redinha, north of town. In **mid-Oct** there is a country show, *Festa do Boi*, bus marked Parnamirim to the exhibition centre, it gives a good insight into rural life. **Mid-Dec**: *Carnatal*, a lively 4-day music festival with dancing in the streets.

Shopping

Centro de Turismo, R Aderbal de Figueiredo s/n, off R Gen Cordeiro, Petrópolis, T211 6149; a converted prison with a wide variety of handicraft shops, art gallery, antique shop and tourist information booth; good views; open daily 0900-1900; bus No 46 from Ponta Negra or No 40 from rodoviária. *Centro Municipal de Artesanato*, Av Presidente Café Filho s/n, Praia dos Artistas, daily 1000-2200. *Livraria Sodiler* at the airport stocks *Footprint*. *Natal Shopping*, Av Sen Salgado Filho 2234, between Ponta Negra and Via Costeira. Large mall with restaurants, ATMs, cinemas and 140 shops, free shuttle bus service to major hotels.

Tour operators

A city tour costs US$15; if it includes the northern beaches US$20-25, including southern beaches US$30-34; buggy tours are most popular US$35-90, depending on the destination.

Brazil

Local Bus: The old rodoviária on Av Junqueira Aires, by Praça Augusto Severo, Ribeira, is a central point where many bus lines converge. Buses to some of the beaches near Natal also leave from here.

Transport

Unlike most Brazilian cities, in Natal you get on the bus in the front and get off at the back

Long distance Air: Aeroporto Augusto Severo, in Parnamirim, 15 km south from centre, T644 1000. "Parnamirim-A" minibus every 30 mins from the old rodoviária near the centre US$0.65, taxi US$25 to centre, US$20 to Ponta Negra.

Bus: Rodoviária, Av Capitão Mor Gouveia 1237, Cidade da Esperança, T205 4377, about 6 km southwest of the centre. Buses from the south pass Ponta Negra first, where you can ask to be let off. Luggage store. Regional tickets are sold on street level, interstate on the 2nd floor. City bus 'Cidade de Esperança Av 9', 'Areia Preta via Petrópolis' or 'Via Tirol' to centre. Taxi US$6 to centre, US$9 to Ponta Negra.

To **Recife** with *Napoles*, 5 daily, US$6.60 *convencional*, US$9 *executivo*, 4 hrs. To **Fortaleza**, US$15 *convencional*, US$18 *executivo*, US$29 *leito*, 8 hrs. To **João Pessoa**, every 2 hrs, US$6 *convencional*, US$7.50 *executivo*, 3 hrs. To **Salvador**, US$32.50 *executivo*, 20 hrs. To **Belém**, US$45, 32 hrs.

Airline Offices *BRA*, Av Prudente de Morais 507, Centro, T221 1155 (airport 643 2068). *FLY*, Av Prudente de Morais 3857, T206 9070 (airport 643 2124). *Nordeste*, at airport, T272 6814. *TAM*, Av Campos Sales, 500, Tirol, T201 2020 (airport 643 1624) 0800-123100. *Trip*, T234 1717/0800 2747. *Varig*, R Mossoró 598, Centro, T201 9339 (airport 743 1100), 0800-997000. *Vasp*, R João Pessoa 220, Centro, T221 4453 (airport 643 1441). **Banks** *Banco do Brasil*, seafront ATM, Ponta Negra for Cirrus/MasterCard and Visa/Plus. Also Av Rio Branco 510, Cidade Alta, US$ cash and TCs at poor rates, cash advances against Visa, Mon-Fri 1000-1600. MasterCard ATM at *HSBC*, Av Deodoro 745, and *Banco 24 Horas* ATMs (eg *Natal Shopping*). *Sunset Câmbio*, Av Hermes da Fonseca 628, Tirol, T212 2552, cash and TCs, 0900-1700. *Dunas Câmbio*, Av Roberto Freire 1776, Loja B-11, Capim Macio (east of *Parque das Dunas*), T219 3840, cash and TCs, 0900-1700. **Communications** Internet: *Sobre Ondas*, Av Erivan França 14, Ponta Negra, 0900-2400, 10 centavos/1 min. Cybercafés in *Praia Shopping*, Av Eng Roberto Freire 8790, Ponta Negra and *Natal Shopping*, see above. **Post Office:** R Princesa Isabel 711, Centro; Av Rio Branco 538, Centro; Av Praia de Ponta Negra 8920, Ponta Negra. **Poste restante:** is in Ribeira, near the old rodoviária, at Av Rio Branco and Av Gen Gustavo Cordeiro de Farias, hard to find. **Telephone:** international phone calls, *Telemar*, R Princesa Isabel 687 e R João Pessoa, Centro; Av Roberto Freire 3100, Ponta Negra, Shopping Cidade Jardim, Av Roberto Freire, Ponta Negra; and rodoviária. **Tourist office** Secretaria Estadual de Turismo (Setur): main office, Av Afonso Pena 1155, Tirol, T232 2500, www.turismorn.com.br Information booths at Centro de Turismo, T211 6149 (see Shopping below), Av Presidente Café Filho s/n, Praia dos Artistas (0800-2100 daily), Cajueiro de Pirangi (see Rota do Sul below), rodoviária (T205 4377) and airport (T643 1811). For information dial 1516. *Setur* publishes a list of prices for tourist services such as tours, taxi fares, food and drinks. **Useful address** Tourist Police: Delegacia do Turista, T232 2851, 24 hrs. **Voltage** 220 volts AC, 60 cycles.

Directory

Brazil

The *Rota do Sol/Litoral Sul* (RN-063) follows the coastline south of Natal for some 55 km and is the access to beaches south of Ponta Negra: **Pirangi do Norte**, 28 km (30 mins from new rodoviária, US$0.60) is near the world's largest cashew nut tree (*cajueiro*); branches springing from a single trunk cover an area of some 7,300 sq m. The snack bar by the tree has schedules of buses back to Natal. There are calm waters and it is popular for water sports. Land or boat tours of the Litoral Sul usually include a stop at Pirangi.

Rota do Sul

Beyond **Barreta**, 55 km, is the long, pristine beach of **Malenbar** or **Guaraíra**, access walking or by 10-min boat ride across the Rio Tibau to the south end. One of the most visited areas of the southern coast, because of its great natural beauty, is that surrounding **Tibau do Sul** (*Population*: 7,749). Lovely beaches circled by high cliffs, lagoons, Atlantic forest and dolphins are among its attractions. Access is via the BR-101 south from Natal or north from João Pessoa, as far as **Goianinha**, then east 18 km to Tibau do Sul. **Praia da Pipa**, 3 km further south (85 km from Natal), is a popular resort with many *pousadas* and charming restaurants. Just north of town, on a 70 m-high dune, is the **Santuário Ecológico de Pipa**, a 60 ha park conserving the *mata atlântica* forest; there are several trails and lookouts over the cliffs which afford an excellent view of the ocean and dolphins. ■ *0800-1600, US$3.*

The coast north of Natal is known for its many impressive, light-coloured sand dunes. A 25-min ferry crossing on the Rio Potengi or a 16 km drive along the *Rota do Sol/Litoral Norte* goes to **Redinha**, the nearest beach on the north coast. The best known beach in the state is **Genipabu**, 30 km north of the city; access from Redinha via RN-304. Its major attractions are very scenic dunes, the Lagoa de Genipabu (a lake surrounded by cashew trees and dunes) and many bars and restaurants on the sea shore. ■ *Buggy tours of the Litoral Norte cost US$100 per buggy split between four and are a good way to see many of the beaches and sights in one day. Buggy rental from* Associação dos Bugueiros, *T225 2077, US$25.*

Ceará

Fortaleza

Phone code: 0xx85
(0xx88 outside metropolitan Fortaleza)
Post code: 60000
Colour map 5, grid B5
Population: 2.1 million

Fortaleza, the fifth largest city in Brazil, is a busy metropolis with many high-rise buildings. It has an important clothes manufacturing industry with many hotels and restaurants and a lively nightlife. Fishermen's *jangadas* still dot the turquoise ocean across from the beach and transatlantic cruise ships call in for refuelling. The mid-day sun is oppressive, tempered somewhat by a constant breeze; evening temperatures can be more pleasant, especially by the sea.

Sights

Tourists should avoid the Serviluz favela between the old lighthouse (Av Vicente de Castro), the favela behind the railway station, the Passeio Público at night. Av Abolição at its eastern (Nossa Senhora da Saúde church) and western ends. Also be careful at Mucuripe and Praia do Futuro. Generally, though, the city is safe for visitors

Praça do Ferreira, from which pedestrian walkways radiate, is the heart of the commercial centre. The whole area is dotted with shady squares. **Fortaleza Nossa Senhora da Assunção**, Av Alberto Nepomuceno, originally built in 1649 by the Dutch, gave the city its name. ■ *Daily 0800-1100, 1400-1700, T251 1660.* Near the fort, on R Dr João Moreira, is the 19th century **Passeio Público** or Praça dos Mártires, a park with old trees and statues of Greek deities. West of here, a neoclassical former prison (1866) houses the **Centro de Turismo do Estado** (Emcetur), with museums, theatre and craft shops. ■ *Av Senador Pompeu 350, near the waterfront, T0800-991516, closed Sun.* Further west along R Dr João Moreira, at **Praça Castro Carreira**, is the nicely refurbished train station **Estação João Felipe** (1880).

The **Teatro José de Alencar**, on the praça of the same name, was inaugurated in 1910; this magnificent iron structure was imported from Scotland and is decorated in neo-classical and art nouveau styles. It also houses a library and art gallery. ■ *Mon-Fri 0800-1700, hourly tours, some English speaking guides, US$1, Wed free, T2291989.* The mausoleum of President Castelo Branco (1964-67) is in the **Palácio da Abolição**, Av Barão de Studart 505, former state government building. ■ *Daily 0800-1800.* The new **cathedral**, completed in 1978, in gothic style but built in concrete, stands beside the new **Mercado Central** with beautiful stained glass windows (Praça da Sé, Av Alberto Nepomuceno).

At the Centro de Turismo are the **Museu de Arte e Cultura Populares** and the **Museu de Minerais**. ■ *Mon-Fri 0800-1700, Sat 0800-1400, US$0.50, T212 3566.* **Museu do Maracatu**, Rufino de Alencar 231, at Teatro São José, houses costumes of this ritual dance of African origin. The new and exciting **Centro Dragão do Mar de Arte e Cultura** at R Dragão do Mar 81, Praia de Iracema hosts music concerts, dance, and art and photography exhibitions. ■ *Tue-Thu 100-1730, Fri-Sun 1400-2130. T488 8600, dragao@dragaodomar.org.br Free on Sun.*

Brazil

Fortaleza has 25 km of beaches, many of which are the scene of the city's nightlife; those between Barra do Ceará (west) and Ponta do Mucuripe (east) are polluted. **Eastern beaches** **Praia de Iracema** is one of the older beach suburbs with some original turn-of-the-century houses. East of Iracema, the **Av Beira Mar** (Av Presidente Kennedy) connects Praia do Meireles with Volta da Jurema and **Praia do Mucuripe**, 5 km from the centre. Fortaleza's main fishing centre, *jangadas*, bring in the catch here. **Praia do Futuro**, 8 km southeast of the centre, is the most popular bathing beach, 8 km long, with strong waves, sand dunes and fresh-water showers, but no natural shade; there are many vendors and straw shacks serving local dishes. A *Jardineira* or city bus marked 'P Futuro' from Praça Castro Carreira, 'Praia Circular', does a circular route to Praia do Futuro; a bus marked 'Caça e Pesca' passes all southeast beaches on its route. About 29 km southeast of the centre is **Praia Porto das Dunas**, popular for watersports including surfing; the main attraction is **Beach Park**, a water park (admission US$20; *jardineira* bus from centre or Av Beira Mar).

Western beaches Northwest of the centre is **Praia Barra do Ceará**, 8 km, where the Rio Ceará flows into the sea. Here are the ruins of the 1603 Forte de Nossa Senhora dos Prazeres, the first Portuguese settlement in the area. The beaches west of the Rio Ceará are cleaner, lined with palms and have strong waves. A new bridge across this river gives better access to this area, for example, **Praia de Icaraí**, 22 km, and **Tabuba**, 5 km further north. Beyond Tabuba, 37 km from Fortaleza, is **Cumbuco**, a lively beach, dirty in high season, bars, horse riding, dunes which you can sandboard down into a rainwater lake, palm trees. ■ Jardineira *minibus, US$1.15, leaves from beside the* Ideal Clube *at west corner of Av Rui Barbosa and Av Raimundo Girão.*

Urban beaches
Various minibus day tours to beaches, $US4; they gather along seafront. Also agency CPVTUR, Av Mons Tabosa 1001

Sleeping
Most hotels offer reduced prices in the low season

LL *Imperial Othon Palace*, Av Beira Mar 2500, Meireles, T242 9177, F242 7777, www.hoteis-othon.com.br, beach front location (recommended *feijoada* on Sat). **A** *Colonial Praia*, R Barão de Aracati 145, Iracema, T455 9600, F219 3501. 4-star, pleasant grounds and big pool, laundry service (10 mins walk from Av Beira Mar). **A** *Pousada Jardim*, Idelfonso Albano 950, Aldeota, T226 9711, www.hoteljardim.com.br No sign outside, by Iracema beach, nice garden, excursions arranged, many languages spoken. Warmly recommended, 20% discount for Handbook users. **A** *Zen Praia*, Av Abolição 1894, Meireles, T244 3213, F261 2196. A/c, pool, restaurant. Recommended.

B *Chevalier*, Av Duque de Caxias 465, T231 4611. Fan, pleasant. **D** *Caxambu*, Gen Bezerril 22, T/F226 2301. A/c, with breakfast, central (opposite Cathedral), good value. **B** *Nordeste Palace*, R Assunção 99 in centre, T/F221 1999. Large rooms, good value. **B** *Ondas Verdes*, Av Beira Mar 934, Iracema, T219 0871. Fan, TV. Recommended. **C** *Abril em Portugal*, Av Almte Barroso 1006. With breakfast, fan, good value. Recommended. **C** *Abrolhos Praia*, Av Abolição 2030, Meireles, T/F2481217, abrolhos@rotaceara.com.br Pleasant, one block from beach, internet access. **C** *Big*, Av Gen Sampaio 485, in centre by train station, T212 2066. With bath, fan, **D** with shared bath, good value, caution recommended at night. **C** *Iracema Mar*, DR das Tabajaras 532, Praia de Iracema, T219 1424, F252 3600. Hot shower, a/c, TV, 50 m from beach, convenient for restaurants and nightlife, good views from breakfast area. **C** *Pousada Jambo*, R Antônia Augusto 141, T219 3873, T9929481 (mob). Very private, no sign, quiet street, variety of rooms, some with kitchens at no extra cost, small pool, a/c, cheaper with fan, Swiss run, changes cash and TCs. Warmly recommended. **C** *Pousada da Praia*, Av Monsenhor Tabosa 1315, Iracema, 2 blocks from beach, T248 5935, F261 1104. With a/c, fridge, OK. **C** *Pousada Santa Maria*, Almte Barroso 617, T244 4019. Laundry, kitchen, English-run. Recommended. **C** *Villamaris*, Av Abolição 2026, Meireles, T248 3834, villamaris@fortalnet.com.br Cosy, security guard, TV, fridge, small rooftop pool, one block from beach. **D** *Dom Luis*, R Ildefonso Albano 245, T/F219 1321. Quiet street, small terrace/garden and bar, TV, a/c, fridge, laundry, good value. Recommended. **D** *Passeio*, R Dr João Moreira 221, Centro, T226 9640, F253 6165. Opposite lovely park and Centro Turismo, homely, rooms with high ceilings, a/c or fan, good value. Recommended. **F** *Pousada Cariri Oriental*, R Dr Mederinhos, Meireles. Breakfast, TV, pool, helpful.

Youth hostel *Albergue de Fortaleza*, R Rocha Lima 1186, Aldeota, T244 1850. Separate men and women dormitories, 1 room for couples, cheaper for members. *Coqueiro Verde*, R Frei Monsueto 531, Meireles, T267 1998. Dormitories, kitchen, laundry facilities.

Brazil

Camping *Fortaleza Camping Club*, R Pedro Paulo Moreira 505, Parque Manibura, Água Fria, 12 km, T273 2544, many trees for shade, US$5 pp. *Barra Encantada*, Praia do Barro Preto, Iguape, 42 km southeast (reservations in Fortaleza, T370 1173), US$9 pp, Camping Club members US$4 pp, see East Coast below. *Fazenda Lagoa das Dunas*, Uruaú (115 km southeast), T244 2929, US$4 pp Camping Club members, US$9 pp others; also rents rooms. See Beberibe, East Coast below.

Eating

At Praia de Iracema, good outdoor nightlife and a collection of cafés on the beach serve good fast food and great coffee

Expensive Several good fish restaurants at Praia de Mucuripe, where the boats come ashore between 1300 and 1500. Recommended on Av Beira Mar, Meireles are: *Alfredo*, No 4616, and, next door, No 4632, *Peixada do Meio*. *Francés-Italiano*, Av Des Moreira 155. Good lobster. Good view of Fortaleza from *Restaurant Panorámico*, R Mirante, in Mucuripe district, near the lighthouse. **Mid-range** *Amici's*, R Dragão do Mar 80. Pasta, pizza and lively atmosphere in music-filled street, evenings only. *Carneiro de Ordones*, R Azevedo Bolão 571, Parquelândia, near North Shopping. Crowded with locals at weekends for every kind of lamb dish. **Cheap** *Churrascaria Picanha de Veras*, R Carlos Vasconcelos 660, Aldeota. Good for chicken. *Dom Pastel*, R Carlos Vasconcelos 996, Aldeota. Pay-by-weight. *R Julo Ibiapina*, this street in Meireles, one block behind beach, has pizzerias, fast food restaurants and sushi bars. *Casa Nossa*, Barão de Aracati, adjacent to *Holiday Inn*, self-service (lunch only), part-covered courtyard, where the locals eat, excellent value. Recommended. *Habib*, Antônio Justa Abolição, corner with Av Barão de Studart. Modern middle-eastern fast-food restaurant, excellent service, set menus are a bargain, good deserts. Highly recommended. **Praia do Futuro** *Sandras*, Av Engenheiro Luis Vieirra 555. Lobster has been recommended. **Centre Expensive** Emcetur restaurant, *Xadrez*, in the old prison, good atmosphere, overpriced, open to 2400, reported safe to 2100. **Cheap** Several options around and in the railway station. *Alivita*, Barão do Rio Branco 1486. Good for fish and vegetarian, lunch only, Mon-Fri. *Fonte de Saúde*, R Pedro 339. Excellent vegetarian food, sold by weight, and a wide range of fruit juices.

Fortaleza

Sleeping

1 Caxambu
2 Chevalier
3 Imperial Othon Palace
4 Nordeste Palace
5 Ondas Verdes
6 Pousada de Praia
7 Zen Praia

To Rodoviária & Airport

BR 116 to the South & to East Coast

Not to scale

Some of the best areas for entertainment, with many bars and restaurants are: the Av Beira Mar, Praia de Iracema, the hill above Praia de Mucuripe and Av Dom Luís. The streets around Centro Cultural Dragão do Mar on R Dragão do Mar are lively every night of the week. Brightly painted, historic buildings house restaurants where musicians play to customers and the pavements are dotted with cocktail carts. The cultural centre hosts free concerts some nights. *Caros Amigos*, R Dragão do Mar, 22. Live music at 2030: Tue, Brazilian instrumental; Wed, jazz; Thu, samba; Sun, Beatles covers, $US1. *Chopp do Bixiga* , lively outdoor corner bar. Some recommended bars: *Espaço Cultural Diogo Fontenelle*, R Gustavo Sampaio 151, art gallery and bar with live music. *Forró* is the most popular dance and there is a tradition to visit certain establishments on specific nights. **Theatre** In the centre are *Teatro José de Alencar*, Praça José de Alencar and *Teatro São José*, R Rufino de Alencar 363, T231 5447; both with shows all year. For information about **cinema** programming dial T139.

Entertainment
Fortaleza is renowned for its night life and prides itself with having the liveliest Mon night in the country

6 Jan, *Epiphany*; *Ash Wednesday*. **19 Mar**, *São José*; *Christmas Eve*; *New Year's Eve*, half-day. The *Festas Juninas* in Ceará are much livelier than carnival. A festival, the *Regata Dragão do Mar*, takes place at Praia de Mucuripe on the last Sun in Jul, during which the traditional *jangada* (raft) races take place. Also during the last week of Jul, the out-of-season Salvador-style carnival, *Fortal*, takes place along Avs Almte Barroso, Raimundo Giro and Beira Mar. On **15 Aug**, the local Umbanda *terreiros* (churches) celebrate the *Festival of Iemanjá* on Praia do Futuro, taking over the entire beach from noon till dusk, when offerings are cast into the surf. Well worth attending (members of the public may 'pegar um passo' – enter into an inspired religious trance – at the hands of a *pai-de-santo*).

Local holidays

Diving *ASPA (Atividades Subaquáticas e Pesquisas Ambientais)*, R Eduardo Garcia 23, s 13, Aldeota, T268 2966. Or *Projeto Netuno*, R do Mirante 165, Mucuripe, T/F263 3009. **Surfing** Surfing is popular on a number of Ceará beaches. *Projeto Salva Surf*, a surfers rescue service operated by the fire department, may be reached by dialing 193. **Trekking** The Fortaleza chapter of the *Trekking Club do Brasil* has walks once a month to different natural

Sport

Brazil

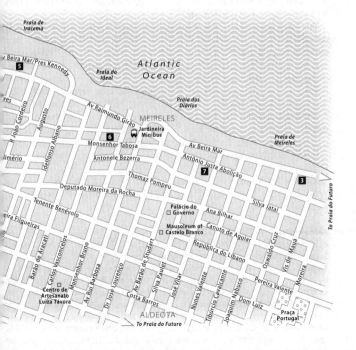

areas; visitors welcome, US$20 for transport and T-shirt, T212 2456. **Windsurfing** A number of Ceará beaches are excellent for windsurfing; equipment can be rented in some of the more popular beaches such as Porto das Dunas and in the city from *Windclub*, Av Beira Mar 2120, Praia dos Diários, T982 5449, lessons also available.

Shopping Fortaleza has an excellent selection of locally manufactured textiles, which are among the cheapest in Brazil, and a wide selection of regional handicrafts. The local craft specialities are lace and embroidered textile goods; also hammocks (US$15 to over US$100), fine alto-relie-vo wood carvings of northeast scenes, basket ware, leatherwork and clay figures (*bonecas de barro*). Bargaining is OK at the *Mercado Central*, Av Alberto Nepomuceno (closed Sun), and the *Emcetur Centro de Turismo* in the old prison (more expensive). Crafts also available in shops near the market. The *Sine* shop, at R Dr João Moreira 429, is part of a state government initiative to promote small independent producers. Every night (1800-2300) there are stalls along the beach at Praia Meireiles, lively, fair prices. Crafts also available in the commercial area along Av Monsenhor Tabosa as it approaches the beach.

Tour City and beach tours (US$20): *Lavila*, Rui Barbosa 1055, T261 4777. Recommended.
operators *Lafuente Turismo*, Av Senador Virgílio Távora 496, T242 1010. Tours to Jericoacoara: *Pousada Ondas Verdes*. Recommended. *Duplatour*, Eduardo Garcia 23, loja 2, T264 2810, F261 2656. Boat tours: *Ceará Saveiro*, Av Beira Mar 4294, T263 1085. Sailboat and yacht trips, daily 1000-1200 and 1600-1800 from Praia de Mucuripe. *Martur*, Av Beira Mar 4260, T263 1203. Sailing boat and schooner trips, from Mucuripe, same schedule as above. Tours to the interior by rail and bus: *Turistar*, Praça Castro Carreira at the railway station, T212 3090/982 4675, F212 2456. Helpful with general information. *BIC*, R Sen Virgílio Távora 480, T242 4599. American Express representative.

Transport **Air** Aeroporto Pinto Martins, Praça Eduardo Gomes, 6 km south of centre, T477 1200. Direct flights to major cities. Bus 404 from airport to Praça José de Alencar in the centre, US$0.65, also 066 Papicu to Parangaba and 027 Papicu to Siqueira, or luxury Guanabara service from Beira Mar via Iracema, a/c, US$0.75; taxis US$10.

Bus Rodoviária at Av Borges de Melo 1630, Fátima, 6 km south from centre, T186, ATM outisde left luggage. Many city buses (US$0.65) including 'Aguanambi' 1 or 2 which go from Av Gen Sampaio, 'Barra de Fátima-Rodoviária' from Praça Coração de Jesus, 'Circular' for Av Beira Mar and the beaches. Taxi to Praia de Iracema, US$5. No luggage store, only lockers.

Nordeste: To **Natal**, 7 daily, US$15 *convencional*, US$18 *executivo*, US$29 *leito*, 8 hrs. **João Pessoa**, 3 daily, US$18 *convencional*, 10 hrs. *Guanabara*, to **Recife**, 5 daily, US$27 convencional, US$33 executivo, US$40 *leito*, 12 hrs, book early for weekend travel. *Itapemirim* to **Salvador**, US$33, 21 hrs. *Timbira* and *Boa Esperança*: to **Teresina**, several daily, US$13.50, 10 hrs. To **Belém**, 2 daily, US$35 *convencional*, US$40.25 *executivo*, 23 hrs (Expresso Timbira also sells Belém-Manaus boat tickets). *Piripiri*, for Parque Nacional de Sete Cidades, US$11, 9 hrs, a good stop en route to Belém. *Guanabara* to **São Luís**, 3 daily, US$27, 18 hrs.

Car hire *HM*, R Vicente Leite 650, Aldeota, T261 7799, cars and buggies. *Loc Car*, Av Virgílio Távora 206, Aldeota, T224 8594, cars and buggies. *Loca Buggy*, Av Beira Mar 2500, Meireles, T/F242 6945.

Directory **Airline offices** On Av Santos Dumont, Aldeota are: *Varig*, No 2727, T266 8000. *Vasp*, No 3060, sala 803, T244 6222/0800-998277. *TAM*, Av Santos Dumont 2849, T261 0916. *TAF*, T272 7474, flights to Juazeiro do Norte and other places in the interior. **Banks** *Banco do Nordeste*, R Major Facundo 372, a/c, helpful, open 0900-1630. Recommended. TCs exchanged and cash with Visa at *Banco do Brasil*, R Barão do Rio Branco 1500, also on Av Abolição. *Banco Mercantil do Brasil*, Rua Major Facundo 484, Centro, Praca do Ferreira: cash against MasterCard. Cirrus/MasterCard ATM at international airport; others at *HSBC* and *Banco 24 Horas* throughout the city. ATM for Cirrus/MasterCard and Visa outside cinema at Centro Cultural Dragão do Mar. Also at Av Antonio Sales and *Iguatemi Shopping*. Exchange at *Tropical Viagens*, R Barão do Rio Branco 1233, T221 3344, English spoken, *Libratur*, Av Abolição 2794. Recommended. *ACCtur*, has exchange booths for dollars (cash and TCs) throughout the city, main office Av Dom Luís 176, Aldeota, T261 9955. **Communications** Internet: Cybercafés at Av Beira-Mar

2120, Aldeota, open 0800-2230, US$3.50 per hr, and outside Avenida Shopping, Av Dom Luís 300, US$2.50 per hr. *Abrolhos Praia*, Av Abolição 2030, Meireles, part of hotel of same name, US$2.50 per hr, open daily, closes 1400 Sun. **Post Office:** main branch at R Senador Alencar 38, Centro; Av Monsenhor Tabosa 1109, Iracema; at train station. Parcels must be taken to Receita Federal office at Barão de Aracati 909, Aldeota (take 'Dom Luiz' bus). **Telephone:** international calls from *Emcetur* hut on Iracema beach and from offices of *Telemar*; at rodoviária and airport. **Embassies and consulates Belgium**, R Eduardo Garcia 609, Aldeota, T264 1500. **Denmark**, R Inácio Capelo 50, Colônia, T228 5055, open 0800-1800. **France**, R Bóris 90, Centro, T254 2822. **Germany**, R Dr Lourenço 2244, Meireles, T246 2833. **Sweden** and **Norway**, R Leonardo Mota 501, Aldeota, T242 0888. **Switzerland**, R Dona Leopoldina 697, Centro, T226 9444. **UK**, c/o Grupo Edson Queiroz, Praça da Imprensa s/n, Aldeota, T466 8580, F261 8763, annette@edsonqueiroz.com.br **US**, Nogueira Acioli 891, Centro, T252 1539. **Medical services Instituto Dr José Frota** (IJF), R Barão do Rio Branco 1618, T255 5000. Recommended public hospital. Tourist police, R Silva Paulet 505, Aldeota, T261 3769/445 8112. **Tourist offices Setur**, state tourism agency; Centro Administrativo Virgílio Távora, Cambeba, T488 3858/0800-991516, www.turismo.ce.gov.br Information booths at Centro de Turismo, T488 7411, helpful, has maps (sometimes), information about beach tours (0700-1800, Sun 0700-1200); rodoviária, T256 4080 (0600-1800 daily), airport, T477 1667 (24 hrs) and Museu de Fortaleza, old lighthouse, Mucuripe, T263 1115 (0700-1730). **Fortur** municipal agency, Av Santos Dumont 5335, Papicu, T265 1177, F265 3430; for information T252 1444. Information booths at Praça do Ferreira, Av Beira Mar (walkway at Praia do Meireles, very informative and friendly, several languages spoken) and at the airport. www.ceara.com **Voltage** 220 volts AC, 60 cycles.

Brazil

Eastern coast

For bus information in Fortaleza, T272 1999

Aquiraz, 31 km east of Fortaleza, first capital of Ceará which conserves several colonial buildings and has a religious art museum, is the access point for the following beaches: **Prainha**, 6 km east, a fishing village and 10 km long beach with dunes, clean and largely empty. You can see *jangadas* coming in daily in the late afternoon. The village is known for its lacework: you can see the women using the *bilro* and *labirinto* techniques at the **Centro de Rendeiras**. 18 km southeast of Aquiraz is **Praia Iguape**, another fishing and lacework village, 3 km south of which is **Praia Barro Preto**, wide, tranquil, with sand dunes, palms and lagoons. All these beaches have accommodation. ■ *Daily bus service to all these beaches from Fortaleza rodoviária; Prainha, 11 daily, US$1; Iguape, hourly between 0600 and 1900, US$1.10.*

Cascavel (Colour map 5, grid B5), 62 km southeast of Fortaleza (Saturday crafts fair by the market), is the access point for the beaches of **Caponga and Águas Belas**, where traditional fishing villages coexist with fancy weekend homes and hotels. ■ *Direct bus from Fortaleza rodoviária (4 a day, US$1.30) or take a bus from Fortaleza to Cascavel (80 mins) then a bus from Cascavel (20 mins); bus information in Caponga T334 1485.*

Some 4 km from **Beberibe**, 78 km from Fortaleza, is **Morro Branco**, with a spectacular beach, coloured craggy cliffs and beautiful views. *Jangadas* leave the beach at 0500, returning at 1400-1500, lobster is the main catch in this area. The coloured sands of the dunes are bottled into beautiful designs and sold along with other crafts such as lacework, embroidery and straw goods. *Jangadas* may be hired for sailing (one hr for up to six people US$30). Beach buggies (full day US$100) and taxis are also for hire. The beach can get very crowded at holiday times. Recommended hotels: **B** *Recanto Praiano*, T224 7118, and **C** *Pousada Sereia*, T330 1144. You can rent fishermen's houses. Meals can also be arranged at beach-front bars. South of Morro Branco and 6 km from Beberibe is **Praia das Fontes**, which also has coloured cliffs with sweet-water springs; there is a fishing village and a lagoon. South of Praia das Fontes are several less developed beaches including **Praia Uruaú** or **Marambaia**. The beach is at the base of coloured dunes, there is a fishing village with some accommodation. Just inland is Lagoa do Uruaú, the largest in the state and a popular place for watersports. Buggy from Morro Branco US$45 for four.

Transport *São Benedito* bus from Fortaleza to Morro Branco, US$2.15; 2½ hrs, 5 a day. To Natal, take 0600 bus to Beberibe, then 0800 bus (only 1) to Aracati, US$0.60, then on to Natal.

Canoa Quebrada

Colour map 5, grid B5
The town's telephone numbers are 421 1401 and 421 1761, 3-digit numbers below are extension numbers

On the shores of the Rio Jaguaribe, **Aracati** is the access point to the southeast-ern-most beaches of Ceará; it is along the main BR-304. The city is best known for its Carnival and for its colonial architecture. **B** *Pousada Litorânea*, R Col Alexandrino 1251, T421 1001, a/c, **D** with fan, near rodoviária. ■ *Natal-Aracati bus via Mossoró, 6 hrs, US$7.50; from Mossoró (90 km) US$2.50, 2 hrs; Fortaleza-Aracati (142 km), São Benedito, Guanabara or Nordeste many daily, US$4, 2 hrs; Aracati-Canoa Quebrada from Gen Pompeu e João Paulo, US$0.60; taxi US$3.60.*

About 10 km from Aracati is Canoa Quebrada on a sand dune, famous for its *labirinto* lacework and coloured sand sculpture, for sand-skiing on the dunes, for the sunsets, and for the beaches. There are many bars, restaurants and *forró* establishments. To avoid biting insects (*bicho do pé*), wear shoes. There is nowhere to change money except *Banco do Brasil* in Aracati. In the second half of July the *Canoarte Festival* takes place, it includes a *jangada* regatta and music festival. ■ *Fortaleza-Canoa Quebrada, São Benedito, 3 daily, US$4.25. Fortaleza-Majorlândia, São Benedito, 4 daily, US$4.25.*

The town's telephone number is 421 1748, 3-digit numbers are extensions

South of Canoa Quebrada and 13 km from Aracati is **Majorlândia**, an attractive village, with many-coloured sand dunes and a wide beach with strong waves, good for surfing; the arrival of the fishing fleet in the evening is an important daily event; lobster is the main catch. It is a popular weekend destination with beach homes for rent and Carnaval here is quite lively. (**C** *Pousada Esquina das Flores*, T188. **D** *Pousada do Gaúcho*, R do Jangadeiro 323, T195, with restaurant. **D** *Pousada e Restaurante Requinte*, 100 m before beach on main road, airy rooms with or without bath, use of kitchen.)

Sleeping Canoa Quebrada: **B** *Pousada Latitude*, R Dragão do Mar, T323. A/c, fridge, cheaper with fan, restaurant. **C** *Pousada do Rei*, R Nascer do Sol 112, T316. Fan, fridge. Highly recommended. **C** *Pousada Maria Alice*, R Dragão do Mar, T421 1852. Fan, restaurant, safe. **C** *Pousada Alternativa*, R Francisco Caraço, T335. With or without bath, central. Recommended. **C** *Pousada Via Láctea*, off the main street (so quieter). Beautiful view of beach which is 50 m away, some rooms with hot shower, fridge, fan, good breakfast, safe parking, horse and buggy tours, English spoken. Highly recommended. **C** *Tenda do Cumbe*, at end of the road on cliff, T421 1761. Thatched huts, restaurant. Warmly recommended. **D** *Pousada do Holandês*, R Nascer do Sol. Rooms without bath (**E**), no breakfast, kitchen use. **E** *Pousada California*, R Nascer do Sol 136, T/F416 1039, california@secrel.com.br A/c, TV, pool, bar, jeep tours, horse riding available. **F** *Pousada Quebramar*, on the beach front, T416 1044. With breakfast, safe, hot water. Villagers will let you sling your hammock or put you up cheaply (Verónica is recommended, European books exchanged; Sr Miguel rents good clean houses for US$10 a day).

Western coast **Paracuru**, a fishing port which has the most important Carnaval on the northwest coast, is 2 hours by bus from Fortaleza and . West of Paracuru, about 120 km from Fortaleza and 12 km from the town of Paraipaba, is **Lagoinha**, a very scenic beach, with hills, dunes and palms by the shore; a fishing village is on one of the hills. ■ *Bus from Fortaleza, 3 daily, US$3.15, T272 4483.* Some 7 hours by bus and 230 km from Fortaleza is the sleepy fishing village of **Almofala**, home of the Tremembés Indians who live off the sea and some agriculture. There is electricity, but no hotels or restaurants, although locals rent hammock space and cook meals. Bathing is better elsewhere, but the area is surrounded by dunes and is excellent for hiking along the coast to explore beaches and lobster-fishing communities. In Almofala, the church with much of the town was covered by shifting sands and remained covered for 50 years, reappearing in the 1940s; it has since been restored. There is also a highly praised turtle project. ■ *From Fortaleza 0700 and 1530 daily, US$6, T272 2728.*

Jijoca de Jericoacoara (Gijoca) near the south shore of scenic Lagoa Paraíso (or Lagoa Jijoca) is the access point for **Jericoacoara**, or Jeri as the locals call it. One of the most famous beaches of Ceará and all Brazil, it has towering sand dunes, deserted beaches with little shade, cactus-covered cliffs rising from the sea and interesting rock formations. Its atmosphere has made it popular with Brazilian and international travellers, with crowds at weekends mid-December to mid-February, in July and during Brazilian holidays. Electricity depends on generators until it is fully installed. Jericoacoara is part of an environmental protection area which includes a large coconut grove, lakes, dunes and hills covered in *caatinga* vegetation.

Watching the sunset from the top of the large dune just west of town, followed by a display of capoeira on the beach, has become a tradition among visitors

Sleeping

A *Avalon*, R Principal, T224 5677 (Fortaleza). With fan, pleasant, restaurant. **A** *Hippopotamus*, R do Forró, T0xx85-244 9191(Fortaleza). With pool, light, fan, restaurant, tours. **B** *Capitão Tomáz*, on east end of beach, T669 1185. Good. Recommended apart from breakfast. **C** *Casa Nostra*, R das Dunas. Nice rooms, good breakfast, can pay with US$ or German marks, money exchange, Italian spoken. Recommended. **C** *Casa do Turismo*, R das Dunas, T0xx88-621 0211, jericoacoara@secrel.com.br Cabins, information, tours, horse rental, bus tickets, telephone calls, post office, exchange. **C** *Isabel*, R do Forró by beach. Light and shower. Recommended. **C** *Papagaio*, Beco do Forró, T/F268 2722 (Fortaleza). Recommended, runs tours. **C** *Pousada Renata*, T621 0554. Patio with hammocks, breakfast, English, Italian and German spoken. **D** *Calanda*, R das Dunas, T621 1144. With solar energy, Swiss run, good rooms, good breakfast, good views, helpful, German, English and Spanish spoken, full moon party every month. Warmly recommended. **D** *Pousada do Véio*, R Principal. With and without bath (**E**), **camping** in shady area US$3 per tent, tours. **E** *Por do Sol*, Bairro Novo Jeri, 1 street west of R das Dunas, behind main dune. Basic, good value. **F** *Pousada Tirol*, R São Francisco, T964 8840. With breakfast, hot water, safe. Recommended.

Many establishments operate during high season, only about half close at other times when hotel prices go down some 30%. The town's calling centre telephone number is (0xx88) 621 0544; you can leave a message for most hotels through this number

Eating

There are several restaurants serving vegetarian and fish dishes: *Alexandre* (R Oceano Atlântico), *Isabel* (R do Forró), both on the beach, good seafood, pricey. *Acoara do Jerico*, R Principal by the beach, reasonable. Home cooking, all on R Principal: *Samambaia*, good value. *Catavento*, good. *Espaço Aberto*, delicious seafood, pleasant atmosphere. Recommended. *Naturalmente*, on the beach, nice atmosphere, wonderful crêpes. Recommended. *Sorrisa de Natureza* cheap, tasty food. Recommended. Italian food and pizza at: *Pizza Banana*, R Principal, good. *Senzala*, same street, nice, pleasant atmosphere (allows **camping** in its grounds). *Taverna*, opposite *Planeta Jeri*, lovely pasta and pizza. *Cantinho da Masa*, R do Forró, good. Several shops sell basic provisions, so camping is possible.

Entertainment

Forró nightly in high season at R do Forró, Wed and Sat in low season, 2200. Action moves to bars when *forró* has stopped about 0200. There are also frequent parties to which visitors are welcome. Once a week in high season there is a folk dance show which includes *capoeira*.

Transport

A *jardineira* (open-sided 4WD truck) meets *Redenção* bus from/to Fortaleza, at Jijoca: 1½ hrs, US$1.05, from Jijoca at 1400, 0200, from Jericoacoara at 0600, 2200, from R das Dunas by Casa do Turismo. At other times pick-ups can be hired in Jijoca, US$6 pp. For a direct connection take the *Redenção* bus leaving Fortaleza 0900 (arrive Jeri 1600) or 2100 (arrive Jeri 0330, US$7.50); the 0600 bus from Jeri arrives in Fortaleza 1430, the 2200 bus arrives between 0430 and 0600, from the rodoviária it goes to Praia Iracema; night buses are direct, while daytime ones make many stops; Fortaleza-Jericoacoara US$8.50. 2 or 3-day tours from Fortaleza are available, book through travel agencies. If coming from Belém or other points north and west, go via Sobral (from Belém US$28.25, 20 hrs), where you change for Cruz, 40 km east of Jijoca, a small pleasant town with basic hotels (Sobral-Cruz: Mon-Sat at 1200; Cruz-Sobral: Mon/Wed/Fri at 0400, Tue/Thu/Sat at 0330; US$7.25; 3-4 hrs). Continue to Jijoca the next day (Cruz-Jijoca, daily about 1400, US$1.25, meets *jardineira* for Jeri, Cruz-Jericoacoara, US$2.20).

If on a motorcycle, it is not possible to ride from Jijoca to Jericoacoara (unless you are an expert in desert conditions). Safe parking for bikes in Jijoca is not a problem

Western Ceará

At 348 km from Fortaleza is **Ubajara** with an interesting Sunday morning market selling produce of the *sertão*; and 3 km from town is **Parque Nacional Ubajara**, with 563 ha of native highland and *caatinga* brush. The park's main attraction is the

Brazil

Ubajara cave on the side of an escarpment. Fifteen chambers totalling 1,120 m have been mapped, of which 400 m are open to visitors. Access is along a footpath and steps (2-3 hours, take water) or with a cablecar which descends the cliff to the cave entrance. ■ *0830-1630, US$4.* Lighting has been installed in nine caverns of the complex, but a torch and spare batteries may be useful. An *Ibama* guide leads visitors in the cave; the *Ibama* office at the park entrance, 5 km from the caves, is not always helpful and not always open, T0xx85-634 1388. The views of the *sertão* from the upper cablecar platform are superb; beautiful walks among forest and waterfalls and old sugar-mills scattered around the plateau.

Camping is not allowed in the park

Sleeping and eating Near the park B *Pousada da Neblina*, Estrada do Teleférico, 2 km from town, T/F634 1270. In beautiful cloud forest, swimming pool, with breakfast and private shower (**C** without breakfast) restaurant open 1100-2000. Meals recommended. Campground (US$15 per tent). Opposite is **C** *Pousada Gruta da Ubajara*, rustic, restaurant. Recommended. **D** *Sítio do Alemão*, take Estrada do Teleférico 2 km from town, after the Pousada da Neblina turn right, 1 km to Sítio Santana, in the coffee plantation of **Herbert Klein**, on which there are 3 small chalets, with full facilities, excursions, bicycle hire offered, if chalets are full the Kleins accommodate visitors at their house (Caixa Postal 33, Ubajara, CE, CEP 62350-000). Warmly recommended. **Ubajara** town **C** *Le Village*, on Ibiapina road 4 km south from town, T634 1364. Restaurant, pool, sauna, good value. **D** *Pousada da Neuza*, R Juvêncio Luís Pereira 370, T634 1261. Small restaurant.

Piauí

Parnaíba
Phone code: 0xx86
Post code: 64200
Colour map 5, grid A4
Population: 132,282

Between the states of Maranhão and Piauí runs the Rio Parnaíba. Near the river mouth is the anchorage of Luís Correia, where ships unload for final delivery by tugs and lighters at Parnaíba 15 km up river, the collecting and distributing centre for the Piauí's tropical products and cattle trade. It is partly encircled by shifting sands in white dunes up to 30 m high. There are beaches at Luís Correia, which with Parnaíba has radioactive sands. The town is a relaxed, friendly place. There is a regular connection here to Tutóia, for boats across the Parnaíba delta (see page 528). A tour in the delta costs US$20 per person. There is a tourist office, *Peimtur* T321 1532, at Porto das Barcas, a pleasant shopping and entertainment complex with several good restaurants and a large open-air bar on the riverside. **Sleeping L** *Cívico*, Av Gov Chagas Rodrigues, T322 2470, F322 2028. With a/c, good breakfast. Recommended. **A** *Pusada dos Ventos*, Av São Sebastião 2586, Universidade, T/F322 2177/4880. Pool. Recommended. **D** *Rodoviária*, and other basic hotels in the centre.

Teresina

Phone code: 0xx86
Post code: 64000
Colour map 5, grid B3
Population: 715,360

About 435 km up the Rio Parnaíba is the state capital. The city is reputed to be the hottest after Manaus (temperatures rise to 42°C). The **Palácio de Karnak** (the old governor's palace), just west of Praça Frei Serafim, contains lithographs of the Middle East in 1839 by David Roberts RA. Also see the Museu do Piauí, Praça Marechal Deodoro. ■ *Tue-Fri 0800-1730, Sat-Sun 0800-1200, US$0.60.* There is an interesting **open market** by the Praça Marechal Deodoro and the river is picturesque, with washing laid out to dry along its banks. The market is a good place to buy hammocks, but bargain hard. Every morning along the river bank there is the **troca-troca** where people buy, sell and swap. An undercover complex (**Mercado Central do Artesanato**) has been built at R Paissandu 1276 (Praça Dom Pedro II). ■ *Mon-Fri 0800-2200.* Most of the year the river is low, leaving sandbanks known as *coroas* (crowns). There is a good, clean supermarket on Praça Marechal Deodoro 937 with fresh food. Local handicrafts include leather and clothes.

L *Rio Poty*, Av Marechal Castelo Branco 555, Ilhota, T223 1500, F222 6671, 5-star. Recommended. **B** *Sambaíba*, R Gabriel Ferreira 230-N, 2-star, T222 6711. Central, good. **D** *Fortaleza*, Felix Pacheco 1101, Praça Saraiva, T222 2984. Fan, basic. Recommended. **D** *Santa Terezinha*, Av Getúlio Vargas 2885, opposite rodoviária, T219 5918. With a/c, cheaper with fan. Many other cheap hotels and *dormitórios* around Praça Saraiva. **D** *Grande*, Firmino Pires 73, very friendly and clean. Many cheap ones in R São Pedro and in R Alvaro Mendes. For fish dishes, *Pesqueirinho*, R Domingos Jorge Velho 6889, in Poty Velho district. *Camarão do Elias*, Av Pedro Almeida 457, T232 5025. Good seafood. *Sabores Rotisserie*, R Simplício Mendes 78, Centro. By kg, good quality and variety. Many eating places for all pockets in Praça Dom Pedro II.

Sleeping & eating

Teresina is proud of its *Carnival*, which is then followed by *Micarina*, a local carnival in Mar. There is much music and dancing in Jul and Aug, when there is a *Bumba-meu-Boi*, the Teresina dance festival, *Festidanças*, and a convention of itinerant guitarists.

Festivals

Air Flights to Fortaleza, Brasília, Rio, São Paulo, Goiânia, São Luís, Belém, Manaus, Salvador, Cuiabá, Salvador. Buses from outside the airport run straight into town and to the rodoviária. **Bus** The bus trip from **Fortaleza** is scenic and takes 9 hrs (US$13.50). There are direct buses to **Belém** (13 hrs, US$23.40), **Recife** (16 hrs, US$27) and to **São Luís** (7 hrs, US$12).

Transport

Banks Banks with ATMs: *Banco do Brasil*, Av Nossa Senhora de Fátima 754, Visa. *Bradesco*, Av Frei Serafim 2277, Visa (and other branches). MasterCard ATMs at *Banco 24 Horas – TecBan*, Av João XXIII 2220, *Droga Center*, and Av Pres Kennedy 02, *Droga Iguatemi*, and 2 others. *Mirante Câmbio*, Av Frei Serafim 2150, T223 3633. *Alda Tur*, R A de Abreu 1226. **Tourist offices** Piemtur, R Acre s/n, Centro de Convenções, Cabral, T222 6202, F2224377, information office at R Magalhães Filho s/n (next to 55 N, English spoken); kiosks at rodoviária and airport. **Singtur** (Sindicato dos Guías de Turismo de Piauí), R Paissandu 1276, T221 2175, has information booths at the Centro de Artesanato (helpful), the Encontro das Águas, Poty Velho and on the shores of the Rio Poty.

Directory

Unusual eroded rock formations decorated with mysterious inscriptions are to be found in the **Parque Nacional de Sete Cidades**, 12 km from Piracuruca. The rock structures are just off the Fortaleza-Teresina road. From the ground it looks like a medley of weird monuments. The inscriptions on some of the rocks have never been deciphered; one theory suggests links with the Phoenicians, and the Argentine Professor Jacques de Mahieu considers them to be Nordic runes left by the Vikings. There is plenty of birdlife, and iguanas, descending from their trees in the afternoon. If hiking in the park, beware of rattlesnakes. *Ibama* provides a free bus (see below). ■ *For park information, contact* Ibama, *Av Homero Castelo Branco 2240, Teresina, CEP 64048-400, T232 1142. Small booklet with sketch map (not really good enough for walking), entrance US$3. Ibama hostel in the park, T343 1342, **E** pp, pleasant, good restaurant, natural pool nearby, camping (US$5). Local food is limited and monotonous: bring a few delicacies, and especially fruit. Free Ibama bus service leaves the Praça da Bandeira in Piripiri (26 km away), at 0700, passing Hotel Sete Cidades at 0800 (at Km 63 on BR-222, T0xx86-276 2222; also has a free pick-up to the park), reaching the park 10 minutes later. Return at 1630, or hitchhike (to walk takes all day, very hot, start early). Piripiri is a cheap place to break the Belém-Fortaleza journey; several good hotels.*

National parks
Colour map 5, grid B4
190 km NE of Teresina

Transport Taxi from Piripiri, US$15, or from Piracuruca, US$21. Bus Teresina-Piripiri and return, throughout the day 2½ hrs, US$4. Bus São Luís-Piripiri, 1200, 1630, 2130, 10 hrs, US$15. Several daily buses Piripiri-Fortaleza, 9 hrs, US$11. Bus Piripiri-Ubajara (see above), marked 'São Benedito', or 'Crateús', 2½ hrs; US$4, first at 0700 (a beautiful trip).

The fossilized extinct remains of sabre-toothed tigers, giant sloths larger than elephants, and armadillos bigger than a compact car, have been discovered by Brazilian and French archaeologists in the **Parque Nacional Serra da Capivara**. This 130,000

Colour map 5, grid B3

ha park is also renowned for some 30,000 prehistoric rock paintings on limestone dating from between 6,000 and 12,000 years ago. The paintings are of daily life, festivities and celebrations, as well as hunting and sex scenes. The park is about 500 km south of Teresina. Specially trained guides are available. The area is good for hiking in the *caatinga* with its canyons and wildlife, in particular birds. The main organization is the **Fundação do Homem Americano** (Fumdham), R Abdias Neves 551, CEP: 64770-000, São Raimundo Nonato, Piauí, T0xx86-582 1612/1389, F582 1656, which has a museum for scientists. For further information and reservations in local hotels, contact Dr Niéde Guidonn at the address above.

Transport Access is from São Raimundo Nonato on the BR-324, or from Petrolina in Pernambuco (the nearest airport, 290 km away). Taxi from Petrolina airport will cost about US$200 one way, or there are buses.

Brasília

Maranhão

Maranhão state is flat and low-lying, with highlands to the south. The Atlantic coastline – a mass of sandbanks, creeks and sandy islands on one of which stands São Luís – is 480 km long. A quarter of Maranhão is covered with babaçu palms, the nuts and oil of which are the state's most important products. Rice comes a poor second. There are salt pans along the coast.

Parque Nacional Lençóis Maranhenses
Colour map 5, grid A3

Crossing the Parnaíba delta, which separates Piauí from Maranhão, is possible by boat arriving in Tutóia: an interesting trip through swamps sheltering many birds. This park has 155,000 ha of beaches, lakes and dunes, with very little vegetation and largely unstudied wildlife. It is a strange landscape of shifting white dunes, stretching about 140 km along the coast between **Tutóia** and Primeira Cruz, west of **Barreirinhas**. The best time to visit is during the rainy season (June-September), when the dune valleys fill with water. Reflections of the sky make the water appear vivid blue, a spectacular contrast against brilliant white sand. ■ *Ribamar at Ibama, Av Jaime Tavares 25, São Luís, T222 3066, is helpful on walks and horse rides; other Ibama address, Av Alexandre Mowa 25, Centro, T231 3010, F231 4332.*

Sleeping Tutóia: **D** *Pousada Em-Bar-Cação*, R Magalhães de Almeida 1064, T479 1219. On the beach, breakfast US$3. Recommended for good food and *tiquira*, a drink made of manioc. **Barreirinhas D** *Pousada Lins*, central praça, T0xx98-349 1203. Shared bath, good but shop around before taking their tours. **D** *Pousada do Baiano*, T0xx98-349 1130. *Pousadas* at Praia Cabure, 5 hrs by boat from Barreirinhas (or truck from Tutóia), friendly, fresh seafood daily.

Transport Parnaíba-Tutóia: bus, 4 hrs, US$6; river boat up the Parnaíba delta, 8 hrs, US$6. Recommended. Private boat hire is also possible. São Luis-Barreirinhas: bus, 8 hrs on an awful road, US$12. Private tour buses, US$24, are more comfortable but cannot improve the road, organized bus tours cost US$72.50. Plane (single propeller), 1 hr, US$75. Recommended. A fabulous experience giving panoramic views of the dunes, pilot *Amirton*, T225 2882. Agencies charge about US$200 for a tour with flight. **Boat** Excursions from/to Barreirinhas: regular boat service between Barreirinhas and Atins (7 hrs return, US$5): boat along Rio Preguiça, 4 hrs then 1 hr walk to the dunes, US$12. Highly recommended. **Speedboats**, about US$100 for 5 people, from *Cláudio*, T549 1183, or *Sr Carlos*, T349 1203. They also have a Kombi, US$150 for up to 15 people. The only forms of transport that can get across the dunes right into the park are a **jeep** or a **horse**, both about US$15. It is a 2-3 hr walk from Barreirinhas to the park; you will need at least another 2 hrs in the dunes. At Mandacaru, a popular stop on tours of the area, the lighthouse gives a very impressive view.

Brazil

São Luís

The capital of Maranhão state, founded in 1612 by the French and named for St Louis of France, is in a region of heavy tropical rains, but the surrounding deep forest has been cut down to be replaced by *babaçu* palms. It stands upon São Luís island between the bays of São Marcos and São José. The urban area extends to São Francisco island, connected with São Luís by three bridges. An old slaving port, the city has a large black population, and has retained much African culture.

Phone code: 0xx98
Post code: 65000
Colour map 5, grid A3
Population: 870,028
1,070 km W
of Fortaleza
806 km SE of Belém

The old part, on very hilly ground with many steep streets, is still almost pure colonial. The historical centre is being restored with UNESCO support and the splendid results (eg the part known as Reviver) rival the Pelourinho of Salvador. The damp climate stimulated the use of ceramic tiles for exterior walls, and São Luís shows a greater variety of such tiles than anywhere else in Brazil, in Portuguese, French and Dutch styles. The commercial quarter (R Portugal, also called R Trapiche) is still much as it was in the 17th century. The best shopping area is R de Santana near Praça João Lisboa. There is a *Funai* shop at R do Sol 371 and a *Centro do Artesanato* in the main street of the São Francisco suburb, over the bridge from the city.

Sights

The **Palácio dos Leões** (Governor's Palace), Av Dom Pedro II, has beautiful floors of dark wood (*jacarandá*) and light (*cerejeira*), great views from terrace. ■ *Mon, Wed and Fri 1500-1800.* The restored **Fortaleza de Santo Antônio**, built originally by the French in 1614, is on the bank of the Rio Anil at Ponta d'Areia. The **Fábrica Canhamo**, a restored factory, houses an arts and crafts centre, R São Pantaleão 1232, Madre de Deus, near Praia Grande. ■ *Mon-Fri 0900-1900, T232 2187.* The **Centro da Creatividade Odylo Costa Filho**, R da Alfândego 200, Praia

Brazil

São Luís historical centre

Sleeping
1 Vila Rica
2 Pousada Colonial

N
Not to scale

Grande, is an arts centre with theatre, cinema, exhibitions, music, a bar and café; a good meeting place. ■ *Mon-Fri 0800-2200, T231 4058.*

The best colonial churches are the **Cathedral** (1629) on Praça Dom Pedro II, and the churches of **Carmo** (1627), Praça João Lisboa, **São João Batista** (1665), Largo São João, **Nossa Senhora do Rosário** (1717 on R do Egito), and the 18th century **Santana**, R de Santana. On Largo do Desterro is the church of **São José do Desterro**, finished in 1863, but with some much older parts.

The **Cafua das Mercês**, R Jacinto Maia 43, is a museum housed in the old slave market, worth the effort to find: a building opposite the Quartel Militar. ■ *Mon-Fri 1330-1700.* Also visit the Casa dos Negros, next door. **Museu de Artes Visuais**, Av Portugal 289, shows ceramics and post war art. ■ *Mon-Fri 0800-1300, 1600-1800.*

Sleeping **A-B** *Vila Rica*, Praça D Pedro II 299, T232 3535, F232 7245, www.hotelvilarica.com.br Central, many amenities. Recommended. **B** *Deodoro*, R de Santaninha 535, T23 15811. Good. **B** *Pousada Colonial*, R Afonso Pena 112, T232 2834. In a beautiful restored, tiled house. Recommended. **B** *São Marcos*, Saúde 178, T232 3768. Restored colonial house, a/c, family-run. Recommended. **C** *Lord*, R Nazaré 258, T/F221 4655, facing Praça Benedito Leite. Comfortable, good breakfast. Recommended. **D** *Pousada Solar dos Nobres*, R 13 de Maio 82, Centro, T232 5705. Bright, welcoming, superb breakfast, very good. **E** *Hotel Casa Grande*, Rua Isaac Martins 94, Centro, T232 2432. Basic, single, double, triple rooms. Recommended. Many cheap hotels can be found in R da Palma, very central (eg **G** *Pousada Ilha Bela*, safe), and R Formosa. **Youth hostels** (**E-F**): *Dois Continentes*, R 28 de Julho 129, Praia Grande, T/F222 6286, family run, and *Solar das Pedras*, R da Palma 127, T/F232 6694.

Eating **Local food and seafood** *Base de Edilson*, R Alencar Campos 31. Shrimp only, excellent. *Tia Maria*, Av Nina Rodrigues 1 (Ponta d'Areia). Seafood. Recommended. *Base da Lenoca*, R Don Pedro II 181. Good view, seafood, big portions. *La Bohème*, R Isaac Martins 48. Very good food, live music, expensive, popular. *Beiruth 2*, Av Castelo Branco 751-B, T227 8447. Recommended. *Naturalista Alimentos*, R do Sol 517. Very good, natural foods shop and restaurant, open till 1900. *Cia Paulista*, R Portugal e R da Estrela. Good, simple food, cheap. R da Estrela has many eating places with good food and outdoor terraces. There is further choice in the São Francisco district, just across bridge.

Festivals On **24 Jun** (São João) is the *Bumba-Meu-Boi*. For several days before the festival street bands parade, particularly in front of the São João and São Benedito churches. There are dances somewhere in the city almost every night in Jun. In **Aug**, *São Benedito*, at the Rosário church.

Transport **Air** Internal flights only, 15 km from centre; buses ('São Cristovão') to city until midnight, US$0.75. **Bus** Rodoviária is 12 km from the centre on the airport road, 'Rodoviária via Alemanha' bus to centre (Praça João Lisboa), US$0.50. Bus to **Fortaleza**, US$27, 4 a day, 18 hrs. To **Belém**, 13 hrs, US$20, *Transbrasiliana*. Also to **Recife**, US$45, 25 hrs, all other major cities and local towns.

Directory **Banks** TCs at *Banco do Brasil*, Praça Deodoro. *HSBC*, off Praça João Lisboa. Accepts MasterCard/Maestro. *Agetur*, R do Sol 33-A, T231 2377. **Communications** Telecommunications: Embratel, Av Dom Pedro II 190. **Language courses** Portuguese lessons: Sra Amin Castro, T227 1527. Recommended. **Medical services** Clínica São Marcelo, R do Passeio 546, English speaking doctor. **Tourist office** Maratur, R Djalma Dutra 61-A, Centro, T221 1231, F221 5277, maratur@ geplan.ma.gov.br, T231 2000 for tourist information.

Alcântara Some 22 km away by boat is Alcântara the former state capital, on the mainland bay
Colour map 5, grid A3 of São Marcos. Construction of the city began at the beginning of the 17th century
Population: 21,291 and it is now a historical monument. There are many old churches, such as the ruined **Matriz de São Matias** – 1648, and colonial mansions (see the **Casa**, and **Segunda Casa, do Imperador**, also the old cotton barons' mansions with their blue,

Portuguese tiled façades). In the Praça Gomes de Castro is the pillory, the **Pelourinho** (1648), also a small museum (0900-1300, US$0.20) and the **Forte de São Sebastião** (1663) now in ruins. See also the **Fonte de Mirititiua** (1747). Canoe trips go to **Ilha do Livramento**, good beaches, good walking around the coast (can be muddy after rain), mosquitoes after dark. A rocket-launching site has been built nearby. Principal festivals: **Festa do Divino**, at Pentecost (Whitsun); 29 June, **São Pedro**; early August, **São Benedito**.

Sleeping and eating **C** *Pousada do Mordomo Régio*, R Grande 134, T337 1197. TV, refrigerator, good restaurant. **D** *Pousada do Pelourinho*, Praça de Matriz 55, T337 1257. Breakfast, good restaurant, shared bath. Recommended. Ask for hammock space or rooms in private houses, friendly but no great comfort; provide your own mineral water. *Bar do Lobato*, on the praça, is pleasant, with good, simple food, fried shrimps highly recommended.

Transport Ferries cross the bay daily, leaving São Luís dock or from São Francisco district at about 0700 and 0930, returning from Alcântara about 0815 and 1600: check time and buy the ticket at the *hidroviária* (west end of R Portugal, T232 0692) the day before as departure depends on the tides. The journey takes 90 mins, return US$15, worth paying extra for 'panorámica' seat. The sea can be very rough between Sep and Dec. Old wooden boats the *Newton Bello* and *Mensageiro da Fé* leave São Luís at 0630 and 1600 returning at 0730 (1½ hrs, US$5 return). There are sometimes catamaran tours bookable through tour operators in São Luís, meals not included.

Brasília

Northern Brazil

The area is drained by the mighty Amazon, which in size, volume of water – 12 times that of the Mississippi – and number of tributaries has no equal in the world. At the base of the Andes, far to the west, the Amazonian plain is 1,300 km in width, but east of the confluences of the Madeira and Negro rivers with the Amazon, the highlands close in upon it until there is no more than 80 km of floodplain between them. Towards the river's mouth – about 320 km wide – the plain widens once more and extends along the coast southeastwards into the state of Maranhão and northwards into the Guianas.

Brazilian Amazônia, much of it still covered with tropical forest, is 56% of the national area. Its jungle is the world's largest and densest rain forest, with more diverse plants and animals than any other jungle in the world. It has only 8% of Brazil's population, and most of this is concentrated around Belém (in Pará), and in Manaus, 1,600 km up the river. The population is sparse because other areas are easier to develop.

Successive modern Brazilian governments have made strenuous efforts to develop Amazônia. Roads have been built parallel to the Amazon to the south (the Transamazônica), from Cuiabá (Mato Grosso) northwards to Santarém (Pará), and northeast from Porto Velho through Humaitá to the river bank opposite Manaus. Unsuccessful attempts were made to establish agricultural settlements along these roads; major energy and mining projects for bauxite and iron ore are bringing rapid change. More environmental damage has been caused to the region by gold prospectors (*garimpeiros*), especially by their indiscriminate use of mercury, than by organized mining carried out by large state and private companies using modern extraction methods. The most important cause of destruction, however, has been large scale deforestation to make way for cattle ranching, with logging for hardwoods for the Asian markets coming a close second.

There is a gradually growing awareness among many Brazilians that their northern hinterland is a unique treasure and requires some form of protection and recently some encouraging moves have been made. On the other hand, government

Background
Northern Brazil consists of the states of Pará, Amazonas, Amapá and Roraima. The states of Rondônia and Acre are dealt with under Southern Amazônia

Brazil

is still intent upon some form of development in the region, as its seven-year Avança Brasil programme demonstrated. Scientists argued in 2001 that if the plan went ahead, its road improvement and other elements would lead to a loss of between 28% and 42% of Amazon rainforest by 2020, with only about 5% of the region untouched. This report led to a reassessment of the plan.

Climate The rainfall is heavy, but varies throughout the region; close to the Andes, up to 4,000 mm annually, under 2,000 at Manaus. Rains occur throughout the year but the wettest season is between Dec and May, the driest month is Oct. The humidity can be extremely high and the temperature averages 26°C. There can be cold snaps in Dec in the western reaches of the Amazon basin. The soil, as in all tropical forest, is poor.

Up the Amazon River

The Amazon system is 6,577 km long, of which 3,165 km are in Brazilian territory. Ships of up to 4-5,000 tonnes regularly negotiate the Amazon for a distance of about 3,646 km up to Iquitos, Peru

Rivers are the arteries of Amazônia for the transport of both passengers and merchandise. The two great ports of the region are Belém, at the mouth of the Amazon, and Manaus at the confluence of the Rio Negro and Rio Solimões. Manaus is the hub of river transport, with regular shipping services east to Santarém and Belém along the lower Amazon, south to Porto Velho along the Rio Madeira, west to Tabatinga (the border with Colombia and Peru) along the Rio Solimões and northwest to São Gabriel da Cachoeira along the Rio Negro. There is also a regular service connecting Belém and Macapá, on the northern shore of the Amazon Delta, and Santarém and Macapá.

The size and quality of vessels varies greatly, with the largest and most comfortable ships generally operating on the Manaus-Belém route. Hygiene, food and service are reasonable on most vessels but **overcrowding** is a common problem. Many of the larger ships offer air-conditioned berths with bunkbeds and, for a higher price, 'suites', with a private bathroom (in some cases, this may also mean a double bed instead of the standard bunkbed). The cheapest way to travel is 'hammock class'; on some routes first class (upper deck) and second class (lower deck) hammock space is available, but on many routes this distinction does not apply. Although the idea of swinging in a hammock may sound romantic, the reality is you will probably be squeezed in with other passengers, possibly next to the toilets, and have difficulty sleeping because of **noise** and an aching back. Most boats have some sort of rooftop bar serving expensive drinks and snacks.

Riverboat travel is no substitute for visiting the jungle. Except for a few birds and the occasional dolphin, little wildlife is seen. However, it does offer an insight into the vastness of Amazônia and a chance to meet some of its people, making a very pleasant experience.

Extensive local inquiry and some flexibility in one's schedule are indispensable for river travel. **Agencies** on shore can inform you of the arrival and departure dates for several different ships, as well as the official (highest) prices for each, and they are sometimes amenable to bargaining. Whenever possible, **see the vessel** yourself (it may mean a journey out of town) and have a chat with the captain or business manager to confirm departure time, length of voyage, ports of call, price, etc. Inspect cleanliness in the kitchen, toilets and showers. All boats are cleaned up when in port, but if a vessel is reasonably clean upon arrival then chances are that it has been kept that way throughout the voyage. You can generally arrange to sleep on board a day or two before departure and after arrival, but be sure to secure carefully your belongings when in port. If you take a berth, lock it and keep the key even if you will not be moving in right away. If you are travelling hammock class, board ship at least 6-8 hrs before sailing in order to secure a good spot (away from the toilets and the engine and check for leaks in the deck above you). Be firm but considerate of your neighbours as they will be your intimate companions for the duration of the voyage. Always keep your gear locked. Take some light warm clothing, it can get very chilly at night.

Compare fares for different ships and remember that prices may fluctuate with supply and demand. As a general rule of thumb they will be about one third of the prevailing one-way airfare, including all meals, but not drinks. Most ships sail in the evening and the first night's supper is not provided. Empty cabins are sometimes offered to foreigners at reduced rates once boats have embarked. **Payment** is usually in advance. Insist on a signed ticket indicating date, vessel, class of passage, and berth number if applicable.

All ships carry cargo as well as passengers and the amount of cargo will affect the length of the voyage because of weight (especially when travelling upstream) and loading/unloading at intermediate ports. All but the smallest boats will transport vehicles, but these are often damaged by rough handling. Insist on the use of proper ramps and check for adequate clearance. Vehicles can also be transported aboard cargo barges. These are usually cheaper and passengers may be allowed to accompany their car, but check about food, sanitation, where you will sleep (usually in a hammock slung beneath a truck), and adequate shade.

The following are the **major shipping routes** in Amazônia giving a selection of vessels and indicating intermediate ports, average trip durations, and fares. Facilities in the main ports are described in the appropriate city sections below. Not all ships stop at all intermediate ports. There are many other routes and vessels providing extensive local service. All **fares shown are one-way only** and include all meals unless otherwise stated; berth and suite fares are for two people, hammocks per person. Information is generally identical for the respective return voyages (except Belém-Manaus, Manaus-Belém).

Prices vary according to the vessel; generally it is not a good idea to go with the cheapest fare you are quoted

Belém-Manaus via Breves, Almeirim, Prainha, Monte Alegre, Curua-Uná, Santarém, Alenquer, Óbidos, Juruti, and Parintins on the lower Amazon. 5-6 days upriver, 4 days downriver, including 18-hr stop in Santarém, suite US$350 upriver, 250 down, double berth US$180 upriver, 150 down, hammock space US$75 upriver, US$65 down. Vehicles: small car US$250, combi US$320 usually including driver, other passengers extra, 4WD US$450 with 2 passengers; motorcycle US$80. *Nélio Correa* is best on this route. *Defard Vieira*, very good and clean, US$75. *São Francisco* is largest, modern but toilets smelly. *Cisne Branco* of similar quality. *Cidade de Bairreirinha* is also new, a/c berths. *Lider II* has good food and pleasant atmosphere. *João Pessoa Lopes* is also recommended. *Santarém* is clean, well-organized and recommended. The Belém-Manaus route is very busy. Try to get a cabin.

Boat services

Belém-Santarém, same intermediate stops as above. 2½ days upriver, 1½ days downriver, fares suite US$150, berth US$135, hammock US$45 up river, US$38 down. All vessels sailing Belém-Manaus will call in Santarém.

Santarém-Manaus, same intermediate stops as above. 2 days upriver, 1½ days downriver, fares berth US$85, hammock US$30. All vessels sailing Belém-Manaus will call in Santarém and there are others operating the Santarém-Manaus route, including: *Cidade de Terezinha III* and *IV*, good. *Miranda Dias*, family run and friendly. Speedboats (*lanchas*) are sometimes available on this route, 16 hrs sitting, no hammock space, US$35.

Belém-Macapá (Porto Santana) non-stop, 24 hrs on large ships, double berth US$110, hammock space US$30 pp, meals not included but can be purchased onboard (expensive), vehicle US$90, driver not included. Same voyage via Breves, 36 to 48 hrs on smaller riverboats, hammock space US$25 pp including meals. See page 538.

Macapá (Porto Santana)-Santarém via Vida Nova, Boca do Jari, Almeirim, Prainha, and Monte Alegre on the lower Amazon (does not call in Belém), 2 days upriver, 1½ days downriver, berth US$130, hammock US$40. Boats include *Viageiro V* (nice), *São Francisco de Paula*.

Manaus-Porto Velho via Borba, Manicoré, and Humaitá on the Rio Madeira. 4 days upriver, 3½ days downriver (up to 7 days when the river is low), double berth US$180, hammock space US$65 pp, vehicle US$225. Recommended boats are *Almirante Moreira II*, clean, friendly owner. *Lord Scania*, friendly. *Ana Maria VIII*, modern. *San Antônio da Borda*, clean, friendly, good meals. The *Eclipse II* is a very nice boat which sails Manaus-Manicoré (2 days, US$80 double berth, US$20 hammock). Many passengers go only as far as Humaitá and take a bus from there to Porto Velho, much faster.

To ship a vehicle ask truck drivers at the dock if they can carry the car and share the cost (similarly to Belém)

Manaus-Tefé via Codajás and Coari, 24 to 36 hrs, double berth US$70, hammock space US$20 pp. *Capitão Nunes* is good. *Jean Filho* also OK. Boats every other day to Tabatinga (also Varig flights Manaus-Tefé-Tabatinga).

Manaus-Tabatinga via Fonte Boa (3 days), Foz do Jutaí, Tonantins (4 days), Santo Antônio do Iça, Amaturá, Monte Cristo, São Paulo de Olivença (5 days) and Benjamin Constant along the Rio Solimões. Up to 8 days upriver (depending on cargo), 3 days downriver, double berth US$220, hammock space US$65 pp upriver, cheaper down. *Voyagers*, *Voyagers II* and *Voyagers III* (T236 3782) recommended. *Almirante Monteiro* (boat is good, but beware overcharging), *Avelino Leal*, and *Capitão Nunes VIII* all acceptable, *Dom Manoel*, cheaper, acceptable but overcrowded.

Brazil

Manaus-São Gabriel da Cachoeira via Novo Airão, Moura, Carvoeiro, Barcelos, and Santa Isabel do Rio Negro along the Rio Negro. Berth US$180, hammock US$60, most locals prefer to travel by road. Boats on this route: *Almirante Martins I* and *II*, *Capricho de Deus*, *Manoel Rodrigues*, *Tanaka Netto* departing from São Raimundo dock, north of main port. For more details, see Footprint's *Brazil Handbook*.

What to take A hammock is essential on all but the most expensive boats; it is often too hot to lie down in a cabin during day. Light cotton hammocks seem to be the best solution. Buy a wide one on which you can lie diagonally; lying straight along it leaves you hump-backed. A climbing carabiner clip is useful for fastening hammocks to runner bars of boats. It is also useful for securing baggage, making it harder to steal.

Health There is a danger of malaria in Amazônia. Mosquito nets are not required when in motion as
See also Health, boats travel away from the banks and too fast for mosquitoes to settle, though repellent is a
Essentials, page 63 boon for night stops. From Apr to Oct, when the river is high, the mosquitoes can be repelled by *Super Repelex* spray or *K13*. A yellow-fever inoculation is strongly advised; it is compulsory in some areas and may be administered on the spot with a pressurized needle gun. The larger ships must have an infirmary and carry a health officer. Drinking water is generally taken on in port (ie city tap water), but taking your own mineral water is a good idea.

Food Ample but monotonous, better food is sometimes available to cabin passengers. Meal times can be chaotic. Fresh fruit is a welcome addition; also take plain biscuits, tea bags, seasonings, sauces and jam. Fresh coffee is available; most boats have a bar of sorts. Plates and cutlery may not be provided. Bring your own plastic mug as drinks are served in plastic beakers which are jettisoned into the river. A strong fishing line and a variety of hooks can be an asset for supplementing one's diet; with some meat for bait, *piranhas* are the easiest fish to catch. Negotiate with the cook over cooking your fish. The sight of you fishing will bring a small crowd of new friends, assistants, and lots of advice – some of it useful.

In Amazônia Inevitably fish dishes are very common, including many fish with Indian names, eg *pirarucu, tucunaré*, and *tambaqui*, which are worth trying. Also shrimp and crab dishes (more expensive). Specialities of Pará include duck, often served in a yellow soup made from the juice of the root of the manioc (*tucupi*) with a green vegetable (*jambu*); this dish is the famous *pato no tucupi*, highly recommended. Also *tacaca* (shrimps served in *tucupi*), *vatapá* (shrimps served in a thick sauce, highly filling, simpler than the variety found in Salvador), *maniçoba* (made with the poisonous leaves of the bitter cassava, simmered for 8 days to render it safe – tasty). *Caldeirada*, a fish and vegetable soup, served with *pirão* (manioc puree) is a speciality of Amazonas. There is also an enormous variety of tropical and jungle fruits, many unique to the region. Try them fresh, or in ice creams or juices. Avoid food from street vendors.

Belém

Phone code: 0xx91 Belém (do Pará) is the great port of the Amazon. It is hot (mean temperature, 26°C),
Post code: 66000 but frequent showers freshen the streets. There are some fine squares and restored
Colour map 5, grid A1 historic buildings set along broad avenues. Belém used to be called the 'City of
Population: Mango Trees' and there are many such trees remaining.
city 1.3 million,
state 6.2 million   The largest square is the **Praça da República** where there are free afternoon concerts; the main business and shopping area is along the wide Av Presidente Vargas leading to
Belém has its share of the river and the narrow streets which parallel it. The neoclassical **Teatro da Paz**
crime and is prone to (1868-74) is one of the largest theatres in the country. It stages performances by
gang violence. Take national and international stars and also gives free concert and theatre shows; worth
sensible precautions visiting, recently restored. ■ *Tue-Fri 0900-1800, tours US$1.50.* Visit the **Cathedral**
especially at night. (1748), another neoclassical building which contains several remarkable paintings.
Police for reporting ■ *Mon 1500-1800, Tue-Fri 0800-1100, 1530-1800.* It stands on Praça Frei Caetano
crimes, R Santo Brandão, opposite the 18th-century **Santo Aleixandre** church which is noted for its
Antônio e Trav Frei wood carving. The 17th-century **Mercês** church (1640), near the market, is the oldest
Gil de Vila Nova

church in Belém; it forms part of an architectural group known as the Mercedário, the rest of which was heavily damaged by fire in 1978 and is being restored.

The **Basílica of Nossa Senhora de Nazaré** (1909), built from rubber wealth in romanesque style, is an absolute must for its stained glass windows and beautiful marble. ■ *Mon-Sat 0500-1130, 1400-2000, Sun 0545-1130, 1430-2000.* It is on Praça Julho Chermont on Av Magalhães Barata. A museum at the basilica describes the Círio de Nazaré religious festival. The **Palácio Lauro Sodré** or **Museu do Estado do Pará**, on Praça Dom Pedro II, a gracious 18th-century Italianate building, contains Brazil's largest framed painting, 'The Conquest of Amazônia', by Domenico de Angelis. ■ *Mon-Fri 0900-1800, Sat-Sun 1900-1200, T225 3853.* The **Palácio Antônio Lemos**, **Museu da Cidade**, which houses the **Museu de Arte de Belém** and is now the **Prefeitura**, was originally built as the Palácio Municipal between 1868 and 1883. In the downstairs rooms there are old views of Belém; upstairs the historic rooms, beautifully renovated, contain furniture, paintings etc, all well explained. ■ *Palácio: Tue-Fri 0900-1200, 1400-1800, Sat-Sun 0900-1300.*

The Belém market, known as '**Ver-o-Peso**' was the Portuguese Posto Fiscal, where goods were weighed to gauge taxes due (hence the name: 'see the weight'). It now has lots of gift shops selling charms for the local African-derived religion, *umbanda*; the medicinal herb and natural perfume stalls are also interesting. It is one of the most varied and colourful markets in South America; you can see giant river fish being unloaded around 0530, with frenzied wholesale buying for the next hour; a new dock for the fishing boats was built just upriver from the market in 1997. The area around the market swarms with people, including many armed thieves and pickpockets.

In the old town, too, is the **Forte do Castelo**, Praça Frei Caetano Brandão 117. ■ *Daily 0800-2300, T223 0041.* The fort overlooks the confluence of the Rio Guamá and the Baía do Guajara and was where the Portuguese first set up their defences. It was rebuilt in 1878. The site also contains the *Círculo Militar* restaurant (entry US$1; drinks and *salgadinhos* served on the ramparts from 1800 to watch the sunset; the

Belém orientation

Sleeping
1 Novotel

Related map
A Belém, page 537

Brazil

Brazil

restaurant serves Belém's best Brazilian food). At the square on the waterfront below the fort the *açaí* berries are landed nightly at 2300, after picking in the jungle (*açaí* berries ground up with sugar and mixed with manioc are a staple food in the region).

At the **Estação das Docas**, the abandoned warehouses of the port have been restored into a complex with an air-conditioned interior and restaurants outside. The Terminal Marítimo has an office of *Valverde Tours*, which offers sunset and nighttime boat trips. The Boulevard das Artes contains the *Cervejaria Amazon* brewery, with good beer and simple meals, an archaeological museum and arts and crafts shops. The Boulevard de Gastronomia has smart restaurants and the 5-star *Cairu* ice cream parlour (try *açaí* or the *Pavê de Capuaçu*). Also in the complex are ATMs, internet café, phones and good toilets.

The **Bosque Rodrigues Alves**, Av Almte Barroso 2305, is a 16-ha public garden (really a preserved area of original flora), with a small animal collection; yellow bus marked 'Souza' or 'Cidade Nova' – any number – 30 minutes from 'Ver-o-Peso' market, also bus from Cathedral. ■ *0900-1700, closed Mon, T226 2308*. The **Museu Emílio Goeldi**, Av Magalhães Barata 376, takes up a city block and consists of the museum proper (with a fine collection of Marajó Indian pottery, an excellent exhibition of Mebengokre Indian lifestyle) and botanical exhibits including Victoria Régia lilies. ■ *Tue-Thu 0900-1200, 1400-1700, Fri 0900-1200, Sat-Sun 0900-1700, US$1, additional charges for specialist areas. Take a bus from the Cathedral.*

Excursions A return trip on the ferry from Ver-o-Peso to **Icaoraci** provides a good view of the river. Several restaurants here serve excellent seafood; you can eat shrimp and drink coconut water and appreciate the breeze coming off the river. Icaoraci is 20 km east of the city and is well-known as a centre of ceramic production. The pottery is in Marajoara and Tapajonica style. Take the bus from Av Presidente Vargas to Icoaraci (one hr). Open all week but best on Tuesday-Friday. Artisans are friendly and helpful, will accept commissions and send purchases overseas.

The nearest beach is at **Outeiro** (35 km) on an island near Icoaraci, about an hour by bus and ferry (the bus may be caught near the Maloca, an Indian-style hut near the docks which serves as a nightclub). A bus from Icoaraci to Outeiro takes 30 mins. Further north is the island of **Mosqueiro** (86 km) accessible by an excellent highway, with many beautiful sandy beaches and jungle inland. It is popular at weekends when traffic can be heavy (also July) and the beaches can get crowded and polluted. ■ *Buses Belém-Mosqueiro every hr from rodoviária, US$1.45, 80 mins.* Many hotels and weekend villas are at the villages of Mosqueiro and Vila; recommended (may be full weekends and July). Camping is easy and there are plenty of good places to eat.

Sleeping

International chain hotels: Hilton and Novotel. Many cheap hotels close to waterfront, none too safe. Several others near the rodoviária which are generally OK

A *Itaoca*, Av Pres Vargas 132, T241 3434, F241 0891. Charming, a/c, ask for a quiet room. **A** *Regente*, Av Governador José Malcher 485, T241 1222, F241 1333, hregente@zaz.com.br 3-star, modest, comfortable, good breakfast. **B** *Le Massilia*, R Henrique Gurjão 236, T224 7147. Also has French restaurant. **C** *Novo Avenida*, Av Pres Vargas 404,T/F223 8893, avenida@hotelnovoavenida.com.br Central, on busy street, a/c, fridge, cheaper with fan, very well looked after. Recommended. **C** *Vidonho's*, R Ó de Almeida 476, T/F224 7499. A/c, fridge, good breakfast, in a side street. **C** *Zoghbi Park*, R Padre Prudêncio 220, T/F241 1800, zoghbi@zoghbi.com.br Smart if dated, spacious, good value, small pool, restaurant, caters to business clients. Recommended. **D** *Central*, Av Pres Vargas 290, T242 4800. With a/c (**E** without bath), on busy street, some rooms noisy, but comfortable, good meals, a must for art-deco fans. **D** *Sete-Sete*, Trav 1 de Março 673, T222 7730, F224 2346. Clomfortable, safe, in quiet street, with breakfast. Recommended. **D** *Ver-o-Peso*, Av Castilho França 308, T241 2022. Functional, rooftop restaurant, TV and fridge, not too clean, but good position near port and Ver-o-Peso market. **D** *Vitória Rêgia*, Trav Frutuoso Guimarães 260, T/F212 2077. With breakfast, more with a/c, fridge (**E** without), safe. **E** *Fortaleza*, Trav Frutuoso Guimarães 276, T212 1055. Very basic but OK for price. **E** *Palacio das Musas*, Trav Frutuoso Guimarães 275, T212 8422. Big rooms, shared bath.

Eating

Expensive: All the major hotels have upamrket restaurants; the *Açaí* at the *Hilton* is recommended for regional dishes and others, Sun brunch or daily lunch, dinner with live music. *Lá em Casa*, Av Governador José Malcher 247 (also in Estação das Docas). Try *menu paraense*, good cooking, fashionable. **Mid-range**: *Cantina Italiana*, Trav Benjamin Constant 1401. Very good Italian, also delivers. *Casa Portuguesa*, R Sen Manoel Barata 897. Good, Portuguese dishes. *Churrascaria Rodeio*, Rodovia Augusto Montenegro Km 4. Excellent meat, salad bar, reasonable prices. *Churrascaria Tucuruvi*, Trav Benjamin Constant 1843, Nazaré. Good value, generous portions.*Germania*, R Aristides Lobo 604. Munich-style. *Miako*, Trav 1 de Março 766, behind Praça de República. Very good Japanese, oriental and international food. *Okada*, R Boaventura da Silva 1522, past R Alcindo Cacela. Japanese, excellent, try 'Steak House', various types of meat, rice and sauces, vegetables, all you can eat, also try *camarão à milanesa com salada*. *Pizzaria Napolitano*, Praça Justo Chermont 12. Pizzas and Italian dishes. **Cheap**: *Nectar*, Av Gentil Bittencourt, Travessa P Eutíquio 248, pedestrian zone. Good vegetarian, lunch only. *Tempero*, R Ò de Almeida, 348. Self-service, some Middle-Eastern dishes, real bargain. Warmly recommended. Specially recommended are some very good snack-bars, mostly outdoors, where you can buy anything up to a full meal, much cheaper than restaurants: *Charlotte*, Av Gentil Bittencourt 730, at Travessa Quintino Bocaiúva, for best *salgadinhos* in the city, also good desserts, very popular. Many buffet-style restaurants along R Santo Antônio pedestrian mall and elsewhere in the *Comércio* district including *Doce Vida Salgado*, 1 de Março 217, good food and prices; generally lunch only, good variety, pay by weight. *Sabor Paranse*, R 13 de Maio, 450. food by weight, lunch only.

Bars & nightclubs

Many venues around Av Doca de Souza Franco, often just called 'Doca', especially popular Thu. *African Bar*, Praça Waldemar Henrique 2. Rock or Samba, weekends only. *Baixo Reduto*, R Quintino Bocaiúva, Reduto. Blues on Wed; Brazilian pop, Thu; rock, Fri and jazz, Sa. The Reduto district has recently become the place to go at night. *Cachaçaria Água Doce*, R Diogo Móia 283 esq Wandenkolk. Specializes in fine cachaças, good appetizers, live music, informal atmosphere. *Bar Teatro Bora Bora*, R Bernal do Couto 38, restaurant, bar and nightclub. MPB and Pagode open from 2100 until late Thu-Sun. *Colarinho Branco Chopperia*, Av Visconde de Souza Franco 80, near the river. Open Tue-Sun 1800 to last customer, nightly performers of Brazilian popular music. *Escapóle*, Rodovia Augusto Montenegro 400. Huge dance hall with various types of music, live and recorded, frequented by all age groups, open Wed-Sat from 2200 (take a radio taxi for safety), no a/c, dress

Brazil

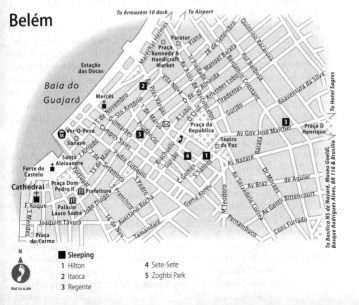

Belém

To Armazém 10 dock   To Airport

Baía do Guajará

Estação das Docas

To Hotel Sagres

To Basílica NS de Nazaré, Museu Goeldi,
Bosque Rodrigues Alves, BR 116 & Brasília

N
Not to scale

■ **Sleeping**
1 Hilton   4 Sete-Sete
2 Itaoca   5 Zoghbi Park
3 Regente

informally. *Olê Olá*, Av Tavares Bastos 1234. Disco, live music and dance floor. Thu-Sun, 2230 to last customer.

Local holidays *Maundy Thursday*, half-day; *9 Jun*, *Corpus Christi*; *15 Aug*, accession of Pará to independent Brazil; *7 Sep*, *Independence Day*, commemorated on the day with a military parade, and with a students' parade on the preceding Sun (morning); *30 Oct*, half-day; *2 Nov*, *All Souls Day*; *8 Dec*, *Immaculate Conception*; *Christmas Eve*, half-day. *Círio*, the Festival of Candles in **Oct**, is based on the legend of the Nossa Senhora de Nazaré, whose image was found on the site of her Basílica around 1700. On the second Sun in Oct, a procession carries a copy of the Virgin's image from the Basílica to the cathedral. On the Mon, 2 weeks later, the image is returned to its usual resting-place. There is a Círio museum in the crypt of the Basílica, enter at the right side of the church; free. (All hotels are fully booked during Círio.)

Shopping *Parfumaria Orion*, Trav Frutuoso Guimarães 268, has a wide variety of perfumes and essences from Amazonian plants, much cheaper than tourist shops. The *Complexo São Brás* on Praça Lauro Sodré has a handicraft market and folkloric shows in a building dating from 1911. Belém is a good place to buy hammocks, look in the street parallel to the river, 1 block inland from Ver-o-Peso. Bookshop on Av Presidente Vargas with English titles in arcade next to *Excelsior Hotel*.

Tour operators *Amazon Star*, R Henrique Gurjão 236, T/F212 6244, amazonstar@amazonstar.com.br City and river tours, Ilha de Marajó, very professional, good guides, jungle tours. Recommended. *Amaz*ônia *Sport & Ação*, Av 25 de Setembro, 2345, T226 8442. Extreme sports, diving, rock-climbing. *Angel*, in *Hilton*, T224 2111, angel@datanetbbs.com.br Tours, events, issues ISIC and IH cards.

Transport **Air** Bus 'Perpétuo Socorro-Telégrafo' or 'Icoaraci', every 15 mins from the Prefeitura, Praça Felipe Patroni, to the airport, 40 mins, US$0.50. Taxi to airport, US$10 (ordinary taxis are cheaper than Co-op taxis, buy ticket in advance in Departures side of airport). ATMs for credit cards in the terminal. T257 0626.

Daily flights south to **Brasília** and other Brazilian cities, and west to **Santarém** and **Manaus**. To **Paramaribo** and **Cayenne**, 3 a week with *Surinam Airways*, while *Pena* flies daily except Sun to Cayenne. Travellers entering Brazil from Guyane may need a 60-day visa (takes 2 days) before airlines will confirm their tickets. Internal flights also offered by *Vasp*, *Nordeste*, *TAM*, *Pena* and *Tavaj* (Amazonian destinations).

Bus The rodoviária is at the end of Av Governador José Malcher 5 km from the centre (T246 8178). Take Aeroclube, Cidade Novo, No 20 bus, or Arsenal or Canudos buses, US$0.50, or taxi, US$5 (day), US$7 (night) (at rodoviária you are given a ticket with the taxi's number on it, threaten to go to the authorities if the driver tries to overcharge). It has a good snack bar and showers (US$0.10) and 2 agencies with information and tickets for riverboats. Regular bus services to all major cities. To **Santarém**, via Marabá (on the Transamazônica) once a week (US$45, more expensive than by boat and can take longer, goes only in dry season). *Transbrasiliana* go direct to Marabá, 16 hrs, US$20. To **São Luís**, 2 a day, US$20, 13 hrs, interesting journey through marshlands. To **Fortaleza**, US$35-40 (24 hrs), several companies. To **Recife**, US$52, 34 hrs.

River services To **Santarém, Manaus**, and intermediate ports (see River Transport, Amazônia, page 533). All larger ships berth at Portobrás/Docas do Pará (the main commercial port) at Armazém (warehouse) No 10 (entrance on Av Marechal Hermes, corner of Av Visconde de Souza Franco). The guards will sometimes ask to see your ticket before letting you into the port area, but tell them you are going to speak with a ship's captain. Ignore the touts who approach you. *Macamazónia*, R Castilho Franca, sells tickets for most boats, open Sun. There are 2 desks selling tickets for private boats in the rodoviária; some hotels (eg *Fortaleza*) recommend agents for tickets. Purchase tickets from offices 2 days in advance. Smaller vessels (sometimes cheaper, usually not as clean, comfortable or safe) sail from small docks along Estrada Nova (not a safe part of town). Take the Cremação bus from Ver-o-Peso.

To **Macapá (Porto Santana)**, the quickest (12 hrs) are the catamaran *Atlântico I* or the launches *Lívia Marília* and *Atlântico II* (slightly slower), all US$30-45 and leaving at 0700 on alternate days. Other boats take 24 hrs: *Silja e Souza* (Wed) of Souzamar, Trav Dom Romualdo Seixas corner R Jerônimo Pimentel, T222 0719, and *Almirante Solon* (Sat) of Sanave (Serviço Amapaense de Navegação, Castilho Franca 234, opposite Ver-o-Peso, T222 7810), slightly cheaper, crowded, not as nice. Via Breves, ENAL, T224 5210; *Bartolomeu I* of Enavi, OK. *Rodrigues Alves* has been recommended (see River Transport in Amazônia, page 533). Smaller boats to Macapá also sail from Estrada Nova.

Hitchhiking Going south, take bus to Capanema, 3½ hrs, US$2.30, walk 500 m from the rodoviária to BR-316 where trucks stop at the gas station.

Airline offices *Varig*, Av Pres Vargas 768, T224 3344, airport T257 0481. *Vasp*, T0800-998277, airport 257 0944. *Surinam Airways*, R Gaspar Viana 488, T212 7144, airport 211 6038, English spoken, helpful with information and documentation. **Banks** *Banco do Brasil*, Av Pres Vargas (near *Hotel Central*), good rates, Visa ATMs, and other Brazilian banks (open 0900-1630, but foreign exchange only until 1300). *HSBC*, Av Pres Vargas near Praça da República has MasterCard Cirrus and Amex ATMs. *Banco de Amazônia* (Basa), on Pres Vargas, gives good rates for TCs (Amex or Citicorp only), but does not change cash. *Itaú*, R Boaventura 580, good TCs and cash rates. In early 2002 the local authorities closed all **Casas de câmbio**, so money could only be changed at banks during the week. At weekends hotels will only exchange for their guests, while restaurants may change money, but at poor rates. Exchange rates are generally the best in the north of the country. **Communications** Internet: *Amazon*, 2nd floor of Estação das Docas. *InterBelém*, Av Jose Malcher 189, US$1 per hr, helpful South African owner, English spoken. In *Shopping Iguatemi*, US$1.40 per hr. Post Office: Av Pres Vargas 498, but international parcels are only accepted at the Post Office on the praça at the corner of Trav Frutuoso Guimarães e R 15 de Novembro, next door to NS das Mercês (hard to find). **Telephone:** telegrams and fax at the Post Office, Av Pres Vargas. For phone calls: *Telemar*, Av Presidente Vargas. **Embassies and consulates** Denmark (Consul Arne Hvidbo), R Senador Barata 704, sala 1503, T241 1588 (PO Box 826). Finland, Av Sen Lemos 529, T222 0148. France, R Pres Pernambucio 269, T224 6818, also for Guyane. Germany, Campos Sales 63, sala 404, T222 5666. Netherlands, R José Marcelino de Oliveira 399, T255 0088. Suriname, R Gaspar Viana 490, T212 7144. Sweden, Av Sen Lemos 529, mailing address Caixa Postal 111, T241 1104, open 1600-1800. UK, Robin Burnett, Ed Palladium Centre, room 410/411, Av Governador José Malcher 815, T222 5074, F212 0274, open at 1130. USA, Av Osvaldo Cruz 156, T223 0800. Venezuela, opposite French Consulate, Av Pres Pernambuco 270, T222 6396 (Venezuelan visa for those entering overland takes 3 hrs, costs US$30 for most nationalities, but we are told that it is better to get a visa at Manaus, Boa Vista or before you leave home. **Medical services** Health: a yellow fever certificate or inoculation is mandatory. It is best to get a yellow fever vaccination at home (always have your certificate handy) and avoid the risk of recycled needles. Medications for malaria prophylaxis are not sold in Belém pharmacies. You can theoretically get them through the public health service, but this is hopelessly complicated. Such drugs are sometimes available at pharmacies in smaller centres, eg Santarém and Macapá. Bring an adequate supply from home. **Clínica de Medicina Preventativa**, Av Bras de Aguiar 410 (T222 1434), will give injections, English spoken, open 0730-1200, 1430-1900 (Sat 0800-1100). **Hospital Ordem Terceira**, Trav Frei Gil de Vila Nova 2, doctors speak some English, free consultation but it's a bit primitive. Surgery open Mon 1300-1900, Tue-Thu 0700-1100, 24 hrs for emergencies. The British consul has a list of English-speaking doctors. **Tourist offices** Belemtur, Av José Malcher 592, T242 0900, F241 3194, belemtur@cinbesa.com.br Also at airport, T211 6151. **Paratur**, Praça Kennedy on the waterfront, T223 2939/212 6601, F223 6198. By the handicraft shop, helpful, many languages spoken; has a good map of Belém in many languages (but some references are incorrect). Town guidebook, US$2.75. **Ibama**, Av Conselheiro Furtado 1303, Batista Campos, CEP 66035-350, T241 2621/224 5899, F223 1299. **Voltage** 110 AC, 60 cycles.

Directory

Brazil

Ilha do Marajó

At almost 50,000 sq km, the world's largest island formed by fluvial processes is flooded in rainy December-June and provides a suitable habitat for water buffalo, introduced from India in the late 19th century. They are now farmed in large numbers (try the cheese and milk). It is also home to many birds, crocodiles and other wildlife, and has several good beaches. It is crowded at weekends and in the July holiday season. The island was the site of the precolumbian Marajoaras culture.

Colour map 5, grid A1

Ponta de Pedras Boats leave Belém (near Porto do Sal, seat US$3.60, cabin US$38 for two, five hours) most days for Ponta de Pedras (**D** *Hotel Ponta de Pedras*, good meals, buses for Soure or Salvaterra meet the boat). Bicycles for hire (US$1 per hr) to explore beaches and the interior of the island. Fishing boats make the eight-hr trip to Cachoeira do Arari (one pousada, **D**) where there is a Marajó museum. A 10-hr boat trip from Ponta de Pedras goes to the Arari lake where there are two villages, Jenipapo built on stilts, forró dancing at weekends, and Santa Cruz which is less primitive, but less interesting (a hammock and a mosquito net are essential). There is a direct boat service to Belém twice a week.

Soure The 'capital' of the island has fine beaches: Araruna (2 km – take supplies and supplement with coconuts and crabs, beautiful walks along the shore), do Pesqueiro (bus from Praça da Matriz, 1030, returns 1600, eat at *Maloca*, good, cheap, big, deserted beach, 13 km away) and Caju-Una (15 km). Small craft await passengers from the Enasa boats, for Salvaterra village (good beaches and bars: seafood), US$7.50, 10 minutes, or trips are bookable in Belém from *Mururé*, T241 0891. There are also 17th-century Jesuit ruins at Joanes as well as a virgin beach.

Colour map 5, grid A1
Population: 19,958

Changing money is only possible at very poor rates. Take plenty of insect repellent

Sleeping Soure B *Ilha do Marajó*, 15 mins' walk from centre, T/F741 1315. A/c, bath, pool. **C** *Soure*, R 3, Centro. A/c, basic. **D** *Pousada Asa Branca*, Rua 4, T741 1414. A/c, **E** with fan, breakfast, dirty, good food. **D** *Pousada Búfalo*, Trav 17, T741 1113. A/c, cheaper with fan, breakfast, bar, restaurant. **F** *Casa Alemão*, 8a Rua, T741 1234. German/Brazilian owned, hospitable, tourist information. *Canecão*, Praça da Matriz, sandwiches, meals. Recommended. **Salvaterra A** *Pousada das Guarãs*, Av Beira Mar, Salvaterra, T/F765 1133, www.pousadadosguaras.com.br Well-equipped, tour programme, on beach. **Joanes D** *Pousada Ventania do Rio-Mar*, take bus, US$1.20 from Foz do Cámara, T9992 5716, pousadas@hotmail.com Near the beach, with bath and breakfast, arranges tours on horseback or canoe, Belgian and Brazilian owners.

Transport Ferry: From Belém docks the Enasa ferry sails to Soure on Fri at 2000 (4 hrs, US$5). There are daily boats to Foz do Cámara at 0630, 0700 and 1300 (1½-3 hrs US$4). Then take a bus to Salvaterra and a ferry to Soure. Boats return from Foz do Cámara at 0800 and 1100. There is a 'taxi-plane' service to Soure leaving Belém at 0630 returning 1600, US$30.

Macapá

Phone code: 0xx96
Post code: 68900
Colour map 2, grid C6
Population: 283,308

The capital of Amapá State is situated on the northern channel of the Amazon Delta and is linked to Belém by boat and daily flights. Along with Porto Santana it was declared a Zona Franca in 1993 and visitors flock to buy cheap imported electrical and other goods. Each brick of the **Fortaleza de São José do Macapá**, built between 1764 and 1782, was brought from Portugal as ballast; 50 iron cannons remain. Today it is used for concerts, exhibits, and colourful festivities on the anniversary of the city's founding, 4 February. In the handicraft complex (**Casa do Artesão**), Av Azárias Neto, craftsmen produce their wares onsite. A feature is pottery decorated with local manganese ore, also woodcarvings, leatherwork and Indian crafts. ■ *Mon-Sat 0800-1900.* **São José Cathedral**, inaugurated by the Jesuits in 1761, is the city's oldest landmark.

The riverfront is a very pleasant place for an evening stroll. The **Complexo Beira-Rio** has food and drink kiosks, and a nice lively atmosphere. The pier (*trapiche*) has been rebuilt and is a lovely spot for savouring the cool of the evening breeze, or watching sunrise over the Amazon. There is a monument to the equator, **Marco Zero** (take Fazendinha bus). The equator also divides the nearby enormous football stadium in half, aptly named O Zerão. South of here, at Km 12 on Rodovia Juscelinho Kubitschek, are the **botanical gardens**. **Fazendinha** (16 km from the centre) is a popular local beach, very busy on Sunday. **Curiarú**, 8 km from Macapá, was founded by escaped slaves, and is popular at weekends for dancing and swimming.

LL-AL *Centro Equatorial de Turismo Ambiental Amazônico (Ceta)*, R do Matodouro 640, Fazendinha, T227 3396, F227 3355, turismoambiental@zaz.com.br All furniture made on site, a/c, sports facilities, gardens with sloths and monkeys, ecological trails. Highly recommended. **A** *Ekinox*, R Jovino Dinoá 1693, T222 4378, F223 7554, j-f@uol.com.br Nice atmosphere, a/c, book and video library, excellent meals and service, riverboat tours available. Recommended. **B** *Mara*, R São José 2390, T222 0859. With bath, a/c, TV, fridge, good, breakfast. **C** *Glória*, Leopoldo Machado 2085, T222 0984. A/c, minibar, TV. **C** *Mercúrio*, R Cândido Mendes 1300, 2nd floor, T223 1699. With breakfast, cheaper without a/c. Recommended. **D** *Santo Antônio*, Av Coriolano Jucá 485, T222 0226, near main praça. Cheaper with fan, **E** with shared bath, good breakfast extra; **F** in dormitory. *Cantinho Bahiano*, Av Beira-Rio 1, Santa Inês. Good seafood. Many other good fish restaurants on the same road, eg *Martinho's Peixaria*, No 810. *Chalé*, Av Pres Vargas 499. Nice atmosphere. *Bom Paladar Kilo's*, Av Pres Vargas 456. Good pay-by-weight buffet. *Sorveteria Macapá*, R São José 1676, close to centre. Excellent ice cream made from local fruit. *Rithimus*, R Odilardo Silva e Av Pres Vargas. Thu night popular with local rhythm *Brega*.

Marabaixo is the traditional music and dance of the state of Amapá; a festival held 40 days after Easter. The *sambódromo*, near Marco Zero, is used by Escolas de Samba during Carnaval and by Quadrilhas during the São João festivities.

Awara, Av Presidente Vargas 2396-B, T/F222 0970, www.awara.com.br Recommended for city and river tours, English and French spoken. *Marco Zero*, R São José 2048, T223 1922, F222 3086. Recommended for flights.

Air *Varig* (R Cândido Mendes 1039, T223 4612), *TAM* (T223 2688), and *Vasp* (R Independência 146, T224 1016), all fly to Belém and other Brazilian cities. *Penta* (Av Mendonça Júnior 13D, T223 5226), fly to Belém, Cayenne, Oiapoque and Santarém. *Gol* fly to Belém, Brasília and São Paulo.

Boat Ships dock at Porto Santana, 30 km from Macapá (frequent buses US$1.30, or share a taxi US$15). To Belém, *Silja e Souza* of Souzamar, Cláudio Lúcio Monteiro 1375, Santana T281 1946, and *Almirante Solon* of Sanave, Av Mendonça Furtado 1766, T223 0244. See under Belém, River Services, for other boats. Purchase tickets from offices 2 days in advance. Also smaller and cheaper boats. The faster (12 hr) catamaran *Atlântico I* or launches leave for Belém most days. *São Francisco de Paula I* sails to **Santarém** and **Manaus**, not going via Belém.

Bus New rodoviária on BR-156, north of Macapá. To **Amapá** (US$15) and **Calçoene** (US$20) daily at 1500. To **Oiapoque** (US$25) daily at 0630, another at 2000 except Sun. Oiapoque buses stop in Calçoene, but not Amapá.

Banks *Banco do Brasil*, R Independência 250, cash, Visa, ATM and TCs. Visa ATM also at *Bradesco*, Cândido Mendes 1316. MasterCard and Amex ATM at *HSBC*, Av Pres Vargas. *Casa Francesa*, Independência 232, changes French francs (francs can be bought in Macapá and Belém). **Communications** Post Office: Av Coriolano Jucá. International calls can be made at São José 2050, 0730-1000. **Embassies and consulates** For the French honorary consul, ask at *Pousada Ekinox*, visas for Guyane have to be obtained from Brasília which can take a while. **Tourist offices** Detur, R Independência 29, T212 5335, F212 5337, detur@prodap.org.br Offices at the airport and rodoviária. **Useful addresses** Ibama, R Hamilton Silva 1570, Santa Rita, CEP 68.906-440, Macapá, T/F214 1100.

The main road crosses the Rio Caciporé and continues to the border with Guyane at **Oiapoque**, on the river of the same name. It is 90 km inland from the Parque Nacional Cabo Orange, Brazil's northernmost point on the Atlantic coast. About 7 km to the west is Clevelândia do Norte, a military outpost and the end of the road in Brazil. Oiapoque is remote, with its share of contraband, illegal migration, and drug trafficking. It is also the gateway to gold fields in the interior of both Brazil and Guyane. As it is quite a rough place, the visitor should be cautious, especially late at night. Prices here are high, but lower than in neighbouring Guyane. The **Cachoeira Grande Roche** rapids can be visited, upstream along the Oiapoque River, where it is

Sleeping & eating

Festivals

Tour operators

Transport

Directory

Border with Guyane
Colour map 2, grid B6

Brazil

Brazil

possible to swim, US$25 per motor boat. The road north to the Guyane border (BR-156) is unpaved from Tatarugalzinho and is difficult in parts, especially during the wet season (but open throughout the year). It is advisable to carry extra fuel, food and water from Macapá onwards.

Sleeping and eating C *Oiapoque*, on the waterfront opposite the petrol station. With breakfast, fridge, restaurant. **D** *Amapá*, R Lélio Silva 298, near the Praça (1 block from the bus stop), T521 1768. A/c, bath, no breakfast. Recommended. **D** *Pousada Central*, Av Coracy Nunes 209, one block from the river, T521 1466. A/c, bath, **F** with fan and shared bath. **E** *Mini Hotel*, Av Coaracy Nunes, near bus stop, T521 1241. Fan, bath. Other cheap hotels along the waterfront are mainly used by Brazilians waiting to cross to Guyane. *Pantanal Bar*, next to the monument at riverfront, has dancing at weekends.

Transport Air: Flights to Macapá Mon-Fri with *Penta*, office on the waterfront, T/F521 1117. While waiting for flights to Cayenne from St-Georges, it is much cheaper to stay on the Brazilian side. **Bus**: leave for Macapá at 1400 and 1800 Mon-Sat, 12 hrs (dry season), 14-24 hrs (wet season), US$25. You may be asked to show your Polícia Federal entry stamp and Yellow Fever vaccination certificate either when buying a ticket from the offices on the waterfront or at the bus station when boarding for Macapá. **Crossing to Guyane**: motorized canoes cross to St-Georges de L'Oyapock, 10 mins downstream, US$4 pp, bargain for return fare. A vehicle ferry will operate until a bridge is eventually built.

Directory Banks Exchange: It is possible to exchange US$ and reais to francs, but dollar rates are low and TCs are not accepted anywhere. *Banco do Brasil*, Av Barão do Rio Branco, open 1000-1500, and *Bradesco*, have Visa facilities to withdraw reais which can be changed into francs. *Casa Francesa*, on the riverfront, and one *câmbio* in the market sell reais for US$ or French francs. Rates are worse in St-Georges. Best to buy francs in Belém, or abroad. **Communications** Post Office: Av Barão do Rio Branco, open 0900-1200, 1400-1700. **Useful addresses** Immigration: Polícia Federal, for Brazilian exit and entry stamps, is on the road behind the church about 500 m from the river.

Belém to Manaus A few hours up the broad river from Belém, the region of the thousand islands is entered. The passage through this maze of islets is known as 'The Narrows' and is perhaps the nicest part of the journey. The ship winds through 150 km of lanes of yellow flood with equatorial forest within 20 m or 30 m on both sides. On one of the curious flat-topped hills after the Narrows stands the little stucco town of **Monte Alegre**, an oasis in mid-forest (airport; some simple hotels, **E**). There are lagoon cruises to see lilies, birds, pink dolphins; also village visits (US$25-40 per day).

Santarém

Phone code: 0xx91
Post code: 68000
Colour map 4, grid A5
Population: 262,538

The third largest city on the Brazilian Amazon is small enough to walk around. It was founded in 1661 as the Jesuit mission of Tapajós; the name was changed to Santarém in 1758. There was once a fort here and attractive colonial squares overlooking the waterfront remain. Standing at the confluence of the Rio Tapajós with the Amazon, on the southern bank, Santarém is half-way (two or three days by boat) between Belém and Manaus. Most visitors breeze in and out on a stopover by boat or air.

The yellow Amazon water swirls alongside the green-blue Tapajós; the **meeting of the waters**, in front of the market square, is nearly as impressive as that of the Negro and Solimões near Manaus. A small **Museu dos Tapajós** in the old city hall on the waterfront, now the **Centro Cultural João Fora**, downriver from where the boats dock, has a collection of ancient Tapajós ceramics, as well as various 19th-century artefacts. The unloading of the fish catch between 0500 and 0700 on the waterfront is interesting. There are good beaches nearby on the Rio Tapajós.

Excursions To **Alter do Chão**, a friendly village on the Rio Tapajós, at the outlet of Lago Verde, 34 km west. Of particular interest is the **Centro do Preservação de Arte Indígena**,

R Dom Macedo Costa, T527 1110, which has a substantial collection of artefacts from tribes of Amazônia and Mato Grosso. ■ *0800-1200, 1300-1700*. Good swimming in the Tapajós from the beautiful, clean beach. **B** *Pousada Tupaiulândia*, Pedro Teixeira 300, T0xx91-527 1157. A/c, unimpressive but OK, very helpful, good breakfast for US$5, next to telephone office opposite bus stop. **E** *Pousada Villa Praia*, first on the right as you enter the village. Large rooms, a/c, very helpful staff, good value. *Lago Verde*, Praça 7 de Setembro, good fresh fish, try *caldeirada de tucunaré*, huge portions. ■ *Bus tickets and information from the bus company kiosk opposite Pousada Tupaiulândia. From Santarém: bus stop on Av São Sebastião, in front of Colégio Santa Clara, US$1, about 1 hr.*

A *Amazon Park I*, Av Mendonça Furtado 4120, T523 2800, amazon@stm.interconect.com.br Swimming pool, 4 km from centre, taxi US$4. **C** *Brasil Grande Hotel*, Trav 15 de Agosto 213, T522 5660. Family-run, with restaurant. **C** *New City*, Trav Francisco Correia 200, T523 3149. A/c, frigobar, good, will collect from airport. **C** *Santarém Palace*, Rui Barbosa 726, T523 2820. A/c, TV, fridge, comfortable. **D** *Mirante*, Trav Francisco Correa, 115, T523 3054/08007073054, www.mirantehotel.com Homely, a/c, fridge, TV, some rooms with balcony, individual safes, internet, good value. Recommended. **D** *Brasil*, Trav dos Mártires 30, T523 5177. Nice, family-run, includes breakfast, communal bath, good food, good service. **D** *Horizonte*, Trav Senador Lemos 737, T522 5437, horizontehotel@bol.com.br With a/c, **F** with fan, modern. **D** *Rios*, R Floriano Peixoto 720, T522 5701. Large rooms, comfortable, a/c, fridge and TV. Recommended. *Mascote*, Praça do Pescador 10. Open 1000-2330, restaurant, bar and ice cream parlour. *Santa Antonio*, Av Tapajós 2061. Churrasco and fish. *Mascotinho*, Praça Manoel de Jesus Moraes, on riverfront. Bar/pizzeria, popular, outside seating, good view. *Lucy*, Praça do Pescador. Good juices and pastries. Recommended.

Sleeping & eating

Santarém 29 Jun, *São Pedro*, with processions of boats on the river and boi-bumbá dance dramas. **Alter do Chão** 2nd week in Jul, *Festa do Sairé*, religious processions and folkloric events. Recommended.

Festivals

Amazon Tours, Trav Turiano Meira, 1084, T522 1928, amazontours@amazonriver.com The owner Steve Alexander is a very friendly, helpful man who can give you lots of hints on what to do. He also organizes excursions for groups to remote areas which are quite expensive. Recommended. *Coruá-Una Turismo*, R Dr Hugo Mendonça 600, T518 1014. Offers various tours, Pierre d'Arcy speaks French. Recommended. *Santarém Tur*, in *Amazon Park*, and at R Adriano Pimental 44, T522 4847, F522 3141. Owned by Perpétua and Jean-Pierre Schwarz (speaks French), friendly, helpful, also group tours (for a group of 5 US$50 per day pp). Recommended. *Gil Serique*, Praça do Pescador 131, T522 5174. English-speaking guide. Recommended. *Tapam Turismo*, Trav 15 de Agosto, 127 A, T523 2422. Recommended.

Tour operators

Air 15 km from town, T523 1021. Internal flights only. Buses run to the centre or waterfront. From the centre the bus leaves in front of the cinema in Rui Barbosa every 80 mins from 0550 to 1910, or taxis (US$8 to waterfront). The hotels *Amazon Park* and *New City* have free buses for guests; you may be able to take these.

    Bus Rodoviária is on the outskirts (T522 3392), take 'Rodagem' bus from the waterfront near the market, US$0.25. Santarém to **Marabá** on the Rio Tocantins with *Transbrasiliana*. From Marabá there are buses east and west on the Transamazônica. Enquire at the rodoviária for other destinations. Road travel during rainy season is always difficult, often impossible.

    Shipping services To Manaus, Belém, Macapá, Itaituba, and intermediate ports (see River transport, page 533). Boats to Belém and Manaus dock at the Cais do Porto, 1 km west, take 'Floresta-Prainha', 'Circular' or 'Circular Externo' bus; taxi US$4. Boats to other destinations, including Macapá, dock by the waterfront by the centre of town. Local service to **Óbidos**, US$10, 4 hrs, Oriximiná US$12.50, Alenquer, and **Monte Alegre** (US$10, 5-8 hrs).

Transport

Airline offices *Fly*, Av Monsenhor Tabosa 1069, T219 7171. *Penta*, Trav 15 de Novembro 183, T523 2532. *TAVAJ*, R Floriano Peixoto 95, T523 7666. *Varig/Nordeste*, Av Rui Barbosa, 790, T523 2488.

Directory

Brazil

Banks Cash withdrawals on Visa at *Banco do Brasil*, Av Rui Barbosa 794. It is very difficult to change dollars (impossible to change TCs anywhere), try travel agencies. **Communications** Internet: *Tapajós On Line*, Mendonça Furtado 2454, US$3.50 per hr. **Post Office**: Praça da Bandeira 81. **Telephone**: *Posto Trin*, R Siquiera Campos 511. 0700-1900 Mon-Sat, 0700-2100 Sun. **Tourist office**: COMTUR, R Floriano Peixoto 343, T/F523 2434, good information available in English.

Óbidos
Population: 46,490

At 110 km up-river from Santarém (5 hours by boat), Óbidos is located at the narrowest and deepest point on the river. It is a picturesque and clean city with many beautiful, tiled buildings and some nice parks. Worth seeing are the **Prefeitura Municipal** (T547 1194), the cuartel and the **Museu Integrado de Óbidus**, R Justo Chermont 607. ■ *Mon-Fri 0700-1100, 1330-1730*. There is also a **Museu Contextual**, a system of plaques with detailed explanations of historical buildings throughout town. The airport has flights to Manaus, Santarém and Parintins. **C** *Braz Bello*, R Corrêia Pinto, on top of the hill, shared bath, full board available. **C** *Pousada Brasil*, R Correia Pinto, basic with bath, cheaper without and others in same price range.

Just across the Pará-Amazonas border, between Santarém and Manaus, is **Parintins** (*Phone code: 0xx92. Post code: 69150-000*), 15 hours by boat upriver from Óbidos. Here, on the last three days of June each year, the **Festa do Boi** draws over 50,000 visitors. Since the town has only two small hotels, everyone sleeps in hammocks on the boats that bring them to the festival from Manaus and Santarém. The festival consists of lots of folkloric dancing, but its main element is the competition between two rival groups, the Caprichoso and the Garantido, in the *bumbódromo*, built in 1988 to hold 35,000 spectators. ■ *Apart from boats that call on the Belém-Manaus route, there are irregular sailings from Óbidos (ask at the port). Journey times are about 12-15 hrs from Manaus and 20 from Santarém. There is also a small airport with flights to Manaus, Óbidos and Santarém.*

Manaus

Phone code: 0xx92
Post code: 69000
Average temp: 27°C
Colour map 4, grid A3
Population: 1.4 million

The next city upriver is Manaus, capital of Amazonas State – the largest in Brazil – and once an isolated urban island in the jungle. The city sprawls over a series of eroded and gently sloping hills divided by numerous creeks (igarapés).

Background

Manaus is the collecting-point for the produce of a vast area which includes parts of Peru, Bolivia and Colombia. Manaus is an excellent port of entry for visiting the Amazon. Less than a day away are river islands and tranquil waterways. The opportunities for canoeing, trekking in the forest and meeting local people should not be missed and, once you are out of reach of the urban influence, there are plenty of animals to see. There is superb swimming in the natural pools and under falls of clear water in the little streams which rush through the woods, but take locals' advice on swimming in the river. Electric eels and various other kinds of unpleasant fish, apart from the notorious piranhas, abound and industrial pollution of the river is growing.

Manaus time is 1 hr behind Brazilian standard time (2 hours behind Oct-Feb, Brazil's summer time)

Manaus is building fast; 20-storey modern buildings are rising above the traditional flat, red-tiled roofs. Under recent municipal administrations (1997) the city, including the Zona Franca, old commercial district, port area and nearby markets, has been kept relatively clean and orderly and new markets have been built. An impressive initiative in 2001 saw the start of a significant restoration programme in which historic buildings have been given a new lease of life and theatres, cultural spaces and libraries created.

Ins & outs
See Transport, page 550 for further details

Getting there Boats sock at different locations depending on where they have come from. The **docks** are quite central. The **airport** is 18 km from the centre, the **bus terminal** 9 km. Both are served by local buses and taxis.

Brazil

Getting around All city bus routes start below the cathedral in front of the port entrance; just ask someone for the destination you want. The city centre is easily explored on foot.

Tourist office Av Eduardo Ribeiro, 666, near *Teatro Amazonas*, T231 1998. Open Mon-Fri 0800-1800, Sat 0800-1300. Limited English and information. **Secretaria de Estado da Cultura e Turismo**, Av 7 de Setembro 1546, Vila Ninita, behind *Centro Cultural Pálacio Rio Negro*, T633 2850, F233 9973. Open Mon-Fri 0730-1700. At the airport, open daily 0700-2300, T652 1120. Also in Amazonas Shopping Center and in a trailer opposite Palácio da Policia. Town map from *Amazon Explorers*, or news kiosks. Weekend editions of *A Crítica*, newspaper, list local entertainments and events. *Mananara Guia*, a very detailed Manaus street index and guide, is available from news kiosks, US$18. A site with lots on information in Portuguese is www.amazonsite.com Also see www.terra.com.br/cidades/mns

Security Manaus is a friendly, if busy city and a good deal safer than the big cities of southern Brazil. As in any city, the usual precautions against opportunist crime should be taken, especially when arriving at night (see River transport in Amazônia on staying on boats in port). Bars along R Joaquim Nabuco are reported particularly unsafe. This and the port area are not places to hang around after dark. A tourist police force, **Politur**, has been created in an effort to assist visitors. See below for advice on choosing a jungle tour.

Sights

Dominating the centre is a **Cathedral** built in simple Jesuit style on a hillock; very plain inside or out. Nearby is the main shopping and business area, the tree-lined Av Eduardo Ribeiro; crossing it is Av 7 de Setembro, bordered by ficus trees. The opulent **Teatro Amazonas**, on the Praça São Sebastião, was completed in 1896 during the great rubber boom following 15 years of construction. It has been restored four times and should not be missed. There are ballet, theatre and opera performances several times a week and free popular Brazilian music on Monday nights, June-December. ■ *Mon-Sat 0900-1600, 20-min tour US$7. Recommended. About same price for a concert, for information on programmes T622 2420.* **Igreja São Sebastião**, on the same praça, has an unusual altar of two giant ivory hands holding a water lily of Brazil wood.

On the waterfront, the **Mercado Adolfo Lisboa**, R dos Barés 46, was built in 1902 as a miniature copy of the now demolished Parisian Les Halles. The wrought iron-work which forms much of the structure was imported from Europe and is said to have been designed by Eiffel. The remarkable **harbour installations**, completed in 1902, were designed and built by a Scottish engineer to cope with the up to 14 m annual rise and fall of the Rio Negro. The large passenger ship floating dock is connected to street level by a 150 m-long floating ramp, at the end of which, on the harbour wall, can be seen the high water mark for each year since it was built. When the water is high, the roadway floats on a series of large iron tanks measuring 2½m in diameter. The large yellow **Alfândega** (Customs House) on R Marquês de Santa Cruz stands at the entrance to the city when arriving by boat. It was entirely prefabricated in England, and the tower once acted as lighthouse. ■ *Mon-Fri 0800-1300.*

The **Biblioteca Pública Estadual** (Public Library) at R Barroso 57, inaugurated in 1871, features an ornate European cast iron staircase. It is well stocked with 19th century newspapers, rare books and old photographs, and worth a visit. ■ *Mon-Fri 0730-1730, T234 0588.* The **Centro Cultural Pálacio Rio Negro**, Av 7 de Setembro was the residence of a German rubber merchant until 1917 and later the state government palace. It now holds various cultural events, including exhibitions, shows and films; there is also a café. ■ *Tue-Fri 1000-1700, Sat-Sun 1600-2100, T232 4450.*

There is a curious little church, **Igreja do Pobre Diabo**, at the corner of Avenidas Borba and Ipixuna in the suburb of Cachoeirinha; it is only 4 m wide by 5 m long, and was built by a tradesman, the 'poor devil' of the name. Take Circular 7 Cachoeirinha bus from the cathedral to Hospital Militar.

Museums

Instituto Geográfico e Histórico do Amazonas, located in a fascinating older district of central Manaus, houses a museum and library of over 10,000 books which thoroughly document Amazonian life through the ages, R Bernardo Ramos 117

Brazil

(near Prefeitura). ■ *Mon-Fri 0800-1200, US$0.20, T232 7077.* **Museu do Índio,** kept by the Salesian missionaries: this interesting, if rather run down, museum's collection includes handicrafts, ceramics, clothing, utensils and ritual objects from the various Indian tribes of the upper Rio Negro, R Duque de Caxias (near Av 7 Setembro); excellent craft shop. ■ *Mon-Fri 0800-1200, 1400-1700, Sat 0830-1130, T234 1422, US$3.* **Museu do Homem do Norte,** Av 7 de Setembro 1385 (near Av J Nabuco), reviews the way of life of the Amazonian population; social, cultural and economic aspects are displayed with photographs, models and other pieces. ■ *Mon-Thu 0900-1200, 1300-1700, Fri 1300-1700, T232 5373, US$1.* The very small **Museu Tiradentes**, on Praça da Polícia, is run by the military police and holds selected historical items and old photographs. ■ *Mon 1400-1800, Tue-Fri 0800-1200, 1400-1800, T234 7422.*

Botanic Gardens, **Instituto Nacional de Pesquisas Amazonas** (INPA), Estrada do Aleixo, at Km 3, not far from the Museu de Ciências Naturais da Amazônia, is the centre for scientific research in the Amazon; labs here (not open to the public) investigate farming, medicines and tropical diseases in the area. There is a small museum and restaurant, lots of birds, named trees and manatees (best seen Wednesday and Friday mornings when the water is changed), caimans and giant otters; worth a visit. ■ *Mon-Fri 0900-1100, 1400-1630, Sat-Sun 0900-1600, T643 3377/643 3192, US$2, take any bus to Aleixo.* The **Museu de Ciências Naturais da**

Brazil

Manaus centre

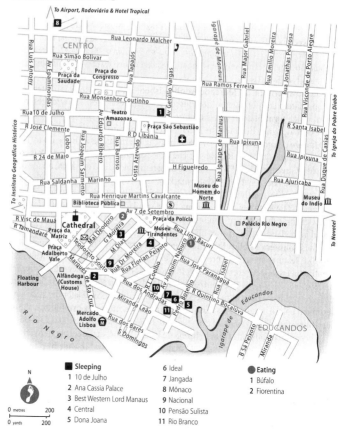

Sleeping ■
1 10 de Julho
2 Ana Cassia Palace
3 Best Western Lord Manaus
4 Central
5 Dona Joana

6 Ideal
7 Jangada
8 Mônaco
9 Nacional
10 Pensão Sulista
11 Rio Branco

Eating ●
1 Búfalo
2 Fiorentina

0 metres 200
0 yards 200

Amazônia has a pavilion with insects and fish of the region and is located at Al Cosme Ferreira, Colonia Cachoeira Grande, 15 km from the city. ■ *Mon-Sat 0900-1700, US$4, T644 2799, difficult to get to, take 'São José-Acoariquarape/ Tropolis' bus 519 to Conjunto Petro, then 2 km walk. Best to combine with a visit to INPA, and take a taxi from there.* **Jardim Botânico 'Chico Mendes'** (Horto Municipal). The botanical gardens contain a collection of plants from the Amazon region. Av André Araujo s/n. ■ *Daily 0800-1200, 1400-1700, buses 'Aleixo', 'Coroado'.*

Meeting of the waters About 15 km from Manaus is the confluence of the yellow-brown Solimões (Amazon) and the blue-black Rio Negro, which is itself some 8 km wide. The two rivers run side by side for about 18 km (says one traveller) without their waters mingling. Tourist agencies run boat trips to this spot (US$60-160). The simplest route is to take a taxi or No 713 'Vila Buriti' bus to the Careiro ferry dock, and take the car ferry across. The ferry (very basic, with no shelter on deck and no cabins) goes at 0700 returning 1000, and 1500 returning 1800 (approximately). Small private launches cross, 40 mins journey, US$10-15 per seat, ask for the engine to be shut off at the confluence, you should see dolphins especially in the early morning. Alternatively, hire a motorized canoe from near the market (US$15 approximately; allow 3-4 hours to experience the meeting properly). A 2-km walk along the Porto Velho road from the Careiro ferry terminal will lead to a point from which Victoria Regia water lilies can be seen in April/May-September in ponds, some way from the road. Agencies can arrange tours.

Arquipélago de Anavilhanas The largest archipelago in a river in the world is in the Rio Negro, some 100 km upstream from Manaus, near the town of Novo Airão. There are hundreds of islands, covered in thick vegetation. When the river is low, white sand beaches are revealed, as well as the roots and trunks of the trees. Tour companies arrange visits to the archipelago (US$195-285, one day).

Excursions

Essentials

L *Tropical*, Praia de Ponta Negra, T658 5000, F658 5026, ghathm@tropicalhotel.com.br A lavish, 5-star Varig hotel 20 km outside the city (taxi to centre, US$20). Parkland setting, wave pools, beach with new dock, departure point for many river cruises, tennis courts, churrascaria, pool, 24-hr coffee shop, open to well-dressed non-residents. Take minibus from R José Paranaguá in front of Petrobras building at the corner of Dr Moreira, US$5 return, 0830, 0930, 1130 to hotel, 1200, 1400, 1500, 1800 to town, or take Ponta Negra bus, US$0.70, then walk. It is rarely full, except in Jan-Feb. **Central hotels L** *Holiday Inn Taj Mahal*, Av Getúlio Vargas 741, T633 1010, tajmahal@internext.com.br Large, impressive, one of best hotels in city, popular, tour agency, revolving restaurant, massage and high level of service. Recommended. **A** *Ana Cassia Palace*, R dos Andradas 14, T622 3637, F234 4163. Gloriously faded, large rooms, some with great views of port, restaurant, pool. **A** *Best Western Lord Manaus*, R Marcílio Dias 217, T622 7700, bwmanaus@internext.com.br Conveniently located in heart of Zona Franca, comfortable, bar. **A** *Manaós*, Av Eduardo Ribeiro 881, T6335744, manaos@argo.com.br Good option near Teatro Amazonas. **A** *Mônaco*, R Silva Ramos 20, T622 3446, F622 3637. Rooms have good view, pleasant (some rooms noisy), rooftop restaurant/bar, delicious breakfast. **B** *Brasil*, Av Getúlio Vargas 657, T233 6575, hotel-brasil@internext.com.br Mid-market option close to centre. **B** *Central*, R Dr Moreira 202, T622 2600, hcentral@zaz.com.br Dated, high ceilings, quiet. **D** *Nacional*, R Dr Moreira 59, T232 9206. Fine for price. **D** *Palace*, Av 7 de Septembro 593, T622 4522, palace@argo.com.br Recently restored, simple, traditional rooms with high ceilings, some with wrought iron balconies, excellent location on praça overlooking cathedral. Highly recommended. **D** *Rey Salomão*, R Dr Moreira 119, T234 7374. In commercial centre, modern, quiet, a/c, restaurant, excellent value. Recommended. **E** *Ideal*, R dos Andradas 491, T/F233 9423. A/c, **F** with fan. **E** *Pensão Sulista*, Av Joaquim Nabuco 347, T234 5814. Run down, a/c, **F** with fan and shared bathroom. **E** *Rio Branco*, R dos Andradas 484, T/F233 4019. Basic,

Sleeping
10% tax and service must be added to bills. Hotel booking service at airport. When taking a taxi from the airport, insist on being taken to the hotel of your choice, not to the one which pays the driver commission

Although the area around Av Joaquim Nabuco and R dos Andradas has lots of cheap (pretty grubby) hotels, this is a low-key red light district and not particularly safe at night. A much better option is the nearby Zona Franca, which is convenient for shops, banks restaurants and the port area

Brazil

uncooperative, laundry facilities, a/c. **E** *10 de Julho*, R Dez de Julio 679, T232 6280. Near opera house, a/c, good value and breakfast. Recommended. **F** *Dona Joana*, R dos Andradas 553, T233 7553. A/c, fridge, TV, newly decorated, homely, good value, the hotel is safe although the area is not. **F** *Jangada*, R dos Andradas 473,T622 0264. Basic, a bargain, a/c and TV. Recommended.

Camping There are no campsites in or near Manaus; it is difficult to find a good, safe place to camp wild.

<table>
<tr>
<td>

Eating

Many restaurants close on Sun nights and Mon. City authorities grade restaurants for cleanliness: look for A and B

</td>
<td>

Expensive *La Barca*, R Recife 684. Wide variety of fish dishes, very swanky, popular, often has live music. *Himawari*, R 10 de Julho 618. Swish, sushi and Japanese food, attentive service, opposite *Teatro Amazonas*, open Sun night, when many restaurants close. Recommended. Japanese at *Miako*, R São Luís 230. *Restaurant Tarumã* in Tropical Hotel (see above). Dinner only. **Mid-range** *Búfalo*, churrascaria, Av Joaquim Nabuco 628. Best in town, US$7, all you can eat Brazilian barbecue. *Canto da Peixada*, R Emílio Moreira 1677 (Praça 14 de Janeiro). Superb fish dishes, lively atmosphere, unpretentious, close to centre, take a taxi. *Fiorentina*, R José Paranaguá 44, Praça da Polícia. Fan-cooled, traditional Italian, including vegetarian dishes, average food but one of best options in centre, watch out for the mugs of wine! Great *feijoada* on Sat, half-price on Sun. *Pizzaria Scarola*, R 10 de Julho, corner with Av Getúlio Vargas. Standard Brazilian menu, pizza delivery, popular. *São Francisco*, Blvd Rio Negro 195, 30 mins walk from centre (or bus 705), in Educandos suburb. Good fish, huge portions. *Suzuran*, R Teresina, 155, Adrianópolis, Japanese cuisine, closed Tue, take taxi. **Cheap** *Alemã*, R José Paranaguá, Praça da Polícia. Food by weight, great pastries, hamburgers, juices, sandwiches. *Brasil*, next to hotel of same name, see above. Food by weight, juice and sandwich kiosk outside hotel. *Casa do Guaraná*, R Marcílio Dias. Marvellous juices mixed with *guaraná*. *Gruta do Peixe*, R Saldanha Marinho 609. Self-service and *pratos* in attractive basement, lunch only. Recommended. *La Veneza*, Av Getúlio Vargas 257. Food by weight, lunch only. *Senac*, R Saldanha Marinho, 644. Cookery school, self-service, open daily, lunch only. Highly recommended. *Sorveteria Glacial*, Av Getúlio Vargas 161 and other locations. Recommended for ice cream. *Skina dos Sucos*, Eduardo Ribeiro e 24 de Maio. Juices and snacks. *Super Guaraná*, R Guilherme Moreira 395. Guaraná with juice, hamburgers, pies. *Xamêgo*, Av Getúlio Vargas, corner with R Dez de Julio. Basic self-service, popular with locals.

</td>
</tr>
<tr>
<td>

Entertainment

</td>
<td>

Boiart's, R José Clemente 500, next to *Teatro Amazonas*. Touristy, popular disco with jungle theme and shows. Cachoeirinha has a number of bars offering music and dancing, liveliest at weekends. *Tucano* nightclub in the *Tropical Hotel* attracts Manaus's wealthy citizens on Thu-Sat, as does its bingo club. Nearby Ponta Negra beach becomes extremely lively late on weekend nights and during holidays, with outdoor concerts and samba in the summer season. *Studio 5*, R Contorno, Distrito Industrial, T2378333, disco, part of leisure complex with several cinema screens. **Performing Arts** For *Teatro Amazonas* and *Centro Cultural Pálacio Rio Negro*, see above. *Teatro da Instalação*, R Frei José dos Inocentes, T/F2344096. Performance space in recently restored historic buildings with free music and dance (everything from ballet to jazz), Mon-Fri May-Dec at 1800. Charge for performances Sat and Sun. Recommended. In Praça da Saudade, R Ramos Ferreira, there is a Sunday **funfair** from 1700; try prawns and calaloo dipped in *tacaca* sauce.

</td>
</tr>
<tr>
<td>

Local holidays

</td>
<td>

6 Jan: *Epiphany*; *Ash Wednesday*, half-day; *Maundy Thursday*; 24 Jun: *São João*; 14 Jul; 5 Sep; 30 Oct; 1 Nov, *All Saints Day*, half-day; *Christmas Eve*; *New Year's Eve*, half-day. **Feb:** *Carnival* dates vary – 5 days of Carnival, culminating in the parade of the Samba Schools. 3rd week in **Apr:** *Week of the Indians*, Indian handicraft. In **Jun:** *Festival do Amazonas*; a celebration of all the cultural aspects of Amazonas life, indigenous, Portuguese and from the northeast, especially dancing; **29 Jun:** *São Pedro*, boat processions on the Rio Negro. In **Sep:** *Festival da Bondade*, last week, stalls from neighbouring states and countries offering food, handicrafts, music and dancing, SESI, Estrada do Aleixo Km 5. **Oct:** *Festival Universitário de Música – FUM,* the most traditional festival of music in Amazonas, organized by the university students, on the University Campus. **8 Dec:** *Processão de Nossa Senhora da Conceição*, from the Igreja Matriz through the city centre and returning to Igreja Matriz for a solemn mass.

</td>
</tr>
</table>

Brazil

Bookshops *Livraria Nacional*, R 24 de Maio 415, stocks some French books. *Usados CDs e Livros*, Av Getúlio Vargas 766. Selection of used books, English, German, French and Spanish. *Valer*, R Ramos Ferreira 1195. A few English classics stocked, best bookshop in city. Maps from *Paper Comunicação*, Av J Nabuco 2074-2. **Markets and souvenirs** Go to the *Mercado Adolfo Lisboa* (see above) early in the morning when it is full of good quality regional produce, food and handicrafts, look out for *guaraná* powder or sticks, scales of *pirarucu* fish (used for manicure), and its tongue used for rasping *guaraná* (open Mon-Sat 0500-1800, Sun and holidays 0155-1200). In the Praça do Congresso, Av E Ribeiro, there is a very good Sun craftmarket. There is a good supermarket at the corner of Av Joaquin Nabuco and Av Sete de Setembro. *Shopping Amazonas*, outside the city, is a mall with cinema, super-market, fast food. *Artesanato da Amazônia*, R José Clemente 500, loja A, opposite *Teatro Amazonas*. Good, reasonably priced, selection of regional products. The **Central Artesanato**, R Recife s/n, near Detran, has local craft work. The souvenir shop at the INPA has some inter-esting Amazonian products on sale. *Selva Amazônica*, Mercado Municipal, for wood carv-ings and bark fabric. For hammocks go to R dos Andradas, many shops.

Shopping
Since Manaus is a free port, the whole area a few blocks off the river front is full of electronics shops. All shops close at 1400 on Sat and all day Sun

Swimming: for swimming, go to Ponta Negra beach by *Soltur* bus for US$0.70, though the beach virtually disappears beneath the water in Apr-Aug; popular by day and at night with outdoor concerts and samba in the summer season. Every Sun, boats leave from the port in front of the market to beaches along Rio Negro, US$2, leaving when full and returning at end of the day. This is a real locals' day out, with loud music and food stalls on the sand. Good swimming at waterfalls on the Rio Tarumã, where lunch is available, shade, crowded at weekends. Take Tarumã bus from R Tamandaré or R Frei J dos Inocentes, 30 mins, US$0.80 (very few on weekdays), getting off at the police checkpoint on the road to Itacoatiara.

Sport

Brazil

Amazon Clipper Cruises, R Sucupira 249, Conj Kissia, Planalto, T656 1246. Informed guides, well-planned activities, comfortable cabins and good food. *Amazon Explorers*, R Nhamundá 21, Praça NS Auxiliadora, T633 3319, www.amazonexplorers.com.br Day tour including 'meeting of the waters', Lago do Janauari, rubber collecting and lunch. *Espaço Verde Turismo*, R Costa Azevedo 240, T6334522, rogerio-evtur@internext.com.br Opposite *Teatro Amazonas*, river boat tours, one day US$30, including lunch; flights; trips to lodges, English spoken, helpful. *Heliconia*, R Col Salgado 63, Aparecida, T2345915, alternatur@internext.com.br Run by French researcher Thérèse Aubreton. *Jaguar Adventure Tours* R Marciano Armond, Vila Operária 23A, Cachoeirinha T/F663 2998, T9982 7285 (mob), www.objetivonet.com.br/jaguartours Carlos Jorge Damasceno, multi-lingual, deep jungle exploration with an ecological slant and visits to remote historical and Indian settlements. *Swallows and Amazons*, R Quintino Bocaiúva 189, Suite 13, T/F622 1246, www.swallowsandamazonstours.com Mark and Tania Aitchison offer a wide range of riverboat tours and accommodation (up to 14 days), prices start at US$95 per day; they have their own houseboat, covered motorized canoe and 8-room private jungle lodge, *The Over Look Lodge*, just before the Anavilhanas islands. Very comprehensive service, with full

Tour operators

assistance for travellers (reservations, email, transfers, medical, etc), English, French and Spanish speaking guides. *The Global Heritage Expeditions*, R Floriano Peixoto 182, T233 3010, T9965 2327 (mob), www.amazonpda.hpg.com.br Sandro Gama speaks English, small group tours in the Amazon basin. **Guides** sometimes work individually as well as for various tour agencies and the best ones will normally be booked up well in advance. Some will only accompany longer expeditions and often subcontract shorter trips. It is generally safer to book guides through agencies.

Transport

Local flights leave from airport terminal 2: make sure in advance of your terminal

Airport T652 1120

Air **International flights**: *Varig* to Miami, once a week. *Aeropostal* flies daily to Caracas. To the Guyanas, connection must be made in Belém. Make reservations as early as possible, flights may be full. **Internal flights**: there are frequent internal flights with *Varig, Vasp, Penta, TAM* and *Tavaj*. Domestic airport tax US$7.

The taxi fare to or from the airport is US$7.50, fixed rate, buy ticket at airport and in most hotels; or take bus 306 marked 'Aeroporto Internacional' from R Tamandaré near the cathedral, US$0.50, or 1107 from Ed Garagem on Av Getúlio Vargas every 30 mins. No buses 2300-0700. (Taxi drivers often tell arrivals that no bus to town is available, be warned!) It is sometimes possible to use the more regular, faster service run by the *Tropical Hotel*; many tour agencies offer free transfers without obligation. Check all connections on arrival. **NB** Check in time is 2 hrs in advance. Allow plenty of time at Manaus airport, formalities are very slow especiallly if you have purchased duty-free goods. The restaurant serves good à la carte and buffet food through the day. Many flights depart in the middle of the night and while there are many snack bars there is nowhere to rest.

Bus Manaus rodoviária is 9 km out of town at the intersection of Av Constantino Nery and R Recife. Take a local bus from centre, US$0.50, marked 'Aeroporto Internacional' or 'Cidade Nova' (or taxi, US$5). Local buses to Praça 14 or the airport leave from Praça Adalberto Vale (take airport bus and alight just after Antárctica factory) or take local bus to Ajuricaba.

Road Hitchhiking with truckers is common, but not recommended for women travelling alone. To hitch, take a Tarumã bus to the customs building and hitch from there, or try at 'posta 5', 2 km beyond the rodoviária. The Catire Highway (BR 319) from Manaus to Porto Velho (868 km), has been officially closed since 1990. However, we have received reports that the road is passable for light vehicles, but some bridges are flimsy. The alternative for drivers is to ship a car down river on a barge, others have to travel by boat (see below).

Shipping To **Santarém, Belém, Porto Velho, Tefé, Tabatinga** (for Colombia and Peru), **São Gabriel da Cachoeira**, and intermediate ports (see River Transport, page 533). Almost all vessels now berth at the first (downstream) of the floating docks which is open to the public 24 hrs a day. Bookings can be made up to 2 weeks in advance at the ticket sales area by the port's pedestrian entrance (bear left on entry). The names and itineraries of departing vessels are displayed here as well as on the docked boats themselves; travellers still recommend buying tickets from the captain on the boat itself. The port is relatively clean, well organized, and has a pleasant atmosphere.

ENASA (the state shipping company) sells tickets for private boats at its office in town (prices tend to be high here), T633 3280. Local boats and some cargo barges still berth by the concrete retaining wall between the market and Montecristi. Boats for São Gabriel da Cachoeira and Novo Airão go from São Raimundo, up river from the main port. Take bus 101 'São Raimundo', 112 'Santo Antônio' or 110, 40 mins; there are 2 docking areas separated by a hill, the São Raimundo *balsa*, where the ferry to Novo Airão, on the Rio Negro, leaves every afternoon (US$10); and the Porto Beira Mar de São Raimundo, where the São Gabriel da Cachoeira boats dock (most departures Fri). **NB** Departures to the less important destinations are not always known at the **Capitânia do Porto**, Av Santa Cruz 265, Manaus. Be careful of people who wander around boats after they've arrived at a port: they are almost certainly looking for something to steal.

Immigration For those arriving by boat who have not already had their passports stamped (eg from Leticia), the immigration office is on the first of the floating docks. Take the dock entrance opposite the cathedral, bear right, after 50 m left, pass through a warehouse to a group of buildings on a T section.

Airline offices *Aeropostal*, Av Marcílio Dias 292, T233 8547. *Penta*, R Barroso 352, T234 1046. *TAM*, Av Tarumã, 433, T233 1828. *Tavaj*, R Rui Barbosa 200B, T0800-927070. *Varig*, Marcílio Dias 284, T622 4500, English spoken, helpful. *Vasp*, Av 7 de Setembro 993, T622 3470/633 2213.

Banks *Banco do Brasil*, Guia Moreira, and airport changes US$ cash, 8% commission, both with ATMs for Visa/Plus, Cirrus/MasterCard. Most offices shut at 1500; foreign exchange operations 0900-1200 only, or even as early as 1100. *Bradesco*, Av 7 de Setembro 895/293, for Visa ATM. *HSBC*, R Dr Moreira, 226. ATM for Visa, Cirrus, MasterCard and Plus. *Credicard*, Av Getúlio Vargas 222 for Diner's cash advances. Cash at main hotels; *Câmbio Cortez*, 7 de Setembro 1199, converts TCs into US$ cash, good rates, no commission. Do not change money on the streets.

Communications Internet: Free internet access available from all public libraries in city, eg *Biblioteca Arthur Reis*, Av 7 de Setembro 444, open 0800-1200, 1400-1700, with virtual Amazon library and English books. *Amazon Cyber Cafe*, Av Getúlio Vargas 626, corner with R 10 de Julho, US$1.50 per hr. Another at No 188, 0800-2300, US$2 per hr. *Discover Internet*, R Marcílio Dias 304, next to Praça da Polícia, cabins in back of shop with Internet phones and scanners, US$1.50 per hr. *Internext*, R 24 de Maio 220, US$3 per hr. Post Office: main office including poste restante on Marechal Deodoro. On the 1st floor is the philatelic counter where stamps are sold, avoiding the long queues downstairs. Staff don't speak English but are used to dealing with tourists. For airfreight and shipping, Alfândega, Av Marquês Santa Cruz (corner of Marechal Deodoro), Sala 106. For airfreight and seamail, Correio Internacional, R Monsenhor Coutinho e Av Eduardo Ribeiro (bring your own packaging). UPS office, T232 9849 (Custódio). Telephone: International calls can be made from local call boxes with an international card. Also *Telemar*, Av Getúlio Vargas 950 e R Leo Malcher.

Embassies and consulates Austria, Rua 5, 4 Qde Jardim Primavera T642 1939/236 6089. Belgium, 13 qd D conj Murici, T236 1452. Colombia, R 24 de Maio 220, Rio Negro Center, T234 6777, double check whether a Colombian tourist card can be obtained at the border. Denmark, R Miranda Leão 45, T622 1365, also handles Norway. Finland, R Marcílio Dias 131, T234 5084. France, R Joaquim Nabuco 1846, Bl A sala 2, T233 6583. Germany, Av 24 Maio 220, Ed Rio Negro Centre, sala 812, T234 9045, 1000-1200. Italy, R Belo Horizonte 240, T611 4877. Japan, R Fortaleza 460, T234 8825. Netherlands, R M Leão 41, T622 1366. Peru, R KL c/6, Morada do Sol, Aleixo, T642 1646. Portugal, R Terezina 193, T633 1577. Spain, R Mons Coutinho 941, T234 4144. Sweden, R M Leão 45, T633 1371. UK, Swedish Match de Amazônia, R Poraquê 240, Distrito Industrial, T237 7869/613 1819, F613 1420, vincent@internext.com.br US, R Recife 1010, T234 4546; will supply letters of introduction for US citizens. Venezuela, R Rio Jetau 868, T233 6004, F233 0481, 0800-1200. Everyone entering Venezuela overland needs a visa. The requirements are: 1 passport photo, an onward ticket and a yellow fever certificate, US$30 (check with a Venezuelan consulate in advance for changes to these regulations).

Medical services *Clínica São Lucas*, R Alexandre Amorin 470, T622 3678, reasonably priced, some English spoken, good service, take a taxi. *Hospital Tropical*, Av Pedro Teixeira (D Pedro I) 25, T656 1441. Centre for tropical medicine, not for general complaints, treatment free, some doctors speak a little English. Take buses 201 or 214 from Av Sete de Setembro in the city centre. *Pronto Soccoro 28 de Agosto*, R Recife, free for emergencies. **Useful addresses** Police: to extend or replace a Brazilian visa, take bus from Praça Adalberto Vale to Kissia Dom Pedro for Polícia Federal post, people in shorts not admitted. Ibama: R Ministro João Gonçalves de Souza s/n, BR-319, Km 01, Distrito Industrial, Caixa Postal 185, CEP 69900-000, T237 3718, F237 5177. **Voltage** 110 volts AC. Some hotels 220 volts AC, 60 cycles.

Tours from Manaus

There are **two types** of tours: those based at jungle lodges and river boat trips. Most tours, whether luxury or budget, combine river outings on motorised canoes with piranha fishing, caiman spotting, visiting local families and short treks in the jungle. Specialist tours include fishing trips and those aimed specifically at seeing how the people in the jungle, *caboclos*, live. Booking in advance on the internet is likely to secure you a good guide (who usually works for several companies and may get booked up). Be sure to ascertain in advance the exact itinerary of the tour, that the price includes everything (even drink and tips), that guides are knowledgeable and will accompany you themselves and that there will be no killing of anything rare. Ensure that others in your party share your expectations and are going for the same length of time. Choose a guide who speaks a language you can understand. A shorter tour may be better than a long, poor one. Packaged tours, booked overseas, are usually of the same price and quality as those negotiated locally.

NB There are many hustlers at the airport and on the street (particularly around the hotels and bars on Joaquim Nabuco and Miranda Leão), and even at the hotels. It is not wise to go on a tour with the first friendly face you meet; all go-betweens earn a commission so recommendations cannot be taken at face value. Employing freelance guides not attached to a company is potentially dangerous. Make enquiries and check credentials personally. *Secretaria de Estado da Cultura e Turismo* is not allowed by law to recommend guides, but can provide you with a list of legally registered companies. Unfortunately, disreputable operations are rarely dealt with in any satisfactory manner and most continue to operate. When you are satisfied that you have found a reputable company, book direct with the company itself and ask for a detailed, written contract if you have any doubts.

Flights over the jungle give a spectacular impression of the extent of the forest. Bill Potter, resident in Manaus, writes: "opposite Manaus, near the junction of the Rio Negro and the Rio Solimões, lies the **Lago de Janauri**, a small nature reserve. This is where all the day or half-day trippers are taken, usually combined with a visit to the 'meeting of the waters'. Although many people express disappointment with this area because so little is seen and/or there are so many 'tourist-trash' shops, for those with only a short time it is worth a visit. You will see some birds and with luck dolphins. In the shops and bars there are often captive parrots and snakes. The area is set up to receive large numbers of tourists, which ecologists agree relieves pressure on other parts of the river. Boats for day trippers leave the harbour constantly throughout the day, but are best booked at one of the larger operators. Remember that in the dry season, one-day tours may not offer much to see if the river is low."

Those with more time can take the longer cruises and will see various ecological environments. To see virgin rainforest, a five-day trip by boat is needed. Most tour operators operate on both the Rio Solimões and the Rio Negro. The Rio Negro is considered easier to navigate, more pristine, generally calmer and with fewer biting insects. This area has more visible upland rainforest and it is easier to see animals such as sloths because there are fewer people. The Solimões, which is flooded for six months of the year, has more birds, piranha and alligators, but you're likely to be constantly fighting the mosquitoes and sandflies. Another alternative is to go upriver to one of the jungle hotels. From the base, you can then take short trips into the forest or along the river channels.

Generally, between Apr and Sep excursions are only by boat; in the period Oct-Mar the Victoria Regia lilies virtually disappear. Fishing is best between Sep and Mar (no flooding). If using a camera, do remember to bring a fast film as light is dim.

Prices vary, but usually include lodging, guide, transport, meals and activities. The recommended companies charge within the following ranges (pp): one day, US$60-95; three days, eg to Anavilhanas Archipelago, US$195-285. Longer, specialized, or more luxurious excursions will cost significantly more. Most river trips incorporate the meeting of the waters on the first day, so there is no need to make a separate excursion.

What to take Leave luggage with your tour operator or hotel in Manaus and only take what is necessary for your trip. Long sleeves, long trousers, shoes and insect repellent are advisable for treks where insects are voracious. A hat offers protection from the sun on boat trips. Bottled water and other drinks are expensive in the jungle, so you may want to take your own supplies.

Lodges There are several lodges within a few hrs boat or car journey from Manaus. Most emphasize comfort (although electricity and hot water is limited) rather than a real jungle experience and you are more likely to enjoy a nice buffet in pleasant company than come face to face with rare fauna. Nevertheless, the lodges are good if your time is limited and you want to have a brief taste of the Amazon rainforest. Agencies for reservations are also listed.

L *Amazon Ecopark Lodge*, Igarapé do Tarumã, 20 km from Manaus, 15 mins by boat, jungle trails; 60 apartments with shower, bar, restaurant, T/F23s 2559, www.amazonecopark.com.br Nearby is the **Amazon Monkey Jungle**, an ecological park where many monkey species are treated and rehabilitated in natural surroundings. The Living Rainforest Foundation, which administers the *Ecopark*, also offers educational jungle trips and overnight camps (bring your own food). Entrance US$15. **L** *Acajatuba Jungle Lodge*, Lago Acajatuba 4 hrs up the Rio Negro from Manaus, 30 apartments with shower, bar, restaurant, contact T233 7642, www.acajatuba.com.br **L** *Amazon Village*, Lago do Puraquequara, 60 km, 2 hrs by boat from Manaus, a comfortable lodge on dry land, with nice cabins, 32 apartments with cold shower, restaurant. Recommended. Contact T633 1444, www.internext.com.br/avillage **A** *Amazon Lodge*, a floating lodge on Lago do Juma, 80 km from Manaus, 30 mins by Careiro ferry, then 1½ hrs by bus, then 2 hrs by boat, 12 basic apartments with cold shower, restaurant, good excursions. Highly recommended. Contact T656 3357, www.naturesafaris.com **L** *Ariaú Amazon Towers*, Rio Ariaú, 2 km from Archipélago de Anavilhanas, 60 km and 2 hrs by boat from Manaus on a side channel of the Rio Negro. Complex of towers connected by walkways, beach (Sep-Mar), trips to the Anavilhanas islands in groups of 10-20. Rates pp: US$280 for 2-days/1-night, US$400, 3 nights/4 days. Highly recommended. Manaus office at R Leonardo Malcher 699, Centro, T622 5000/0800-925000, www.ariau.tur.br **A** *Boa Vida Jungle Resort*, 53 km from Manaus by route AM-10, direction Itacoatiara, 7 apartments and 6 chalets, shower, fridge, bar, restaurant, fishing, boating; contact T234 5722, F232 2482. *Pousada dos Guanavenas*, on Ilha de Silves, 300 km from Manaus on the road to Itacoatiara then by boat along the Rio Urubu, views of Lago Canacari, 33 rooms, a/c, fridge, electric showers, T656 1500, www.guanavenas.com.br **A** *Rainforest Lodge*, on the banks of Lago Januacá, 4 hrs from Manaus, 14 bungalows with fans, pool, restaurant, snack bar, contact **MS Empreendimentos**, T233 9182, rflodge@n3.com.br **A** *Lago Salvador Lodge*, Lago Salvador, 30 km from Manaus, 40 mins by boat from the *Hotel Tropical*, 12 apartments, cold shower, bar, restaurant; contact T659 5119, www.lagosalvador.com.br

Amazon Youth Hostel, near the town of Maués, southeast of Manaus. US$75 per week in dormitory, US$150 per week in cabin, 5-day backpacking tours US$250, kitchen, lounge, hiking, canoeing. Contact Doña Nailê or Joe Maldonado, www.amazon-hostal.com **Rico Airlines**, T652 1553, fly Manaus-Maués US$75, 1 hr, or boat at 1600, arrive 1100 next day, US$25 (take own hammock) or US$65 in cabin. In Maués go to *Casa Quixada* store and take a water taxi to the hostel, US$30 per group.

Manaus to Colombia and Peru

Benjamin Constant is on the border with Peru, with Colombian territory on the opposite bank of the river. ■ *Boat services from Manaus, 7 days, or more; to Manaus, 4 days, or more.* **Sleeping** Recommended hotels: **B** *Benjamin Constant*, beside ferry. A/c, some rooms with hot water and TV, good restaurant, arranges tours, postal address Apto Aéreo 219, Leticia, Colombia. **D** *Márcia Maria*. With bath, a/c, fridge. **E** *Hotel São Jorge*. Meals available. **E** *Hotel Lanchonete Peruana*, good food. Eat at *Pensão Cecília*, or *Bar-21 de Abril*, cheaper.

Colour map 3, grid A5

Tabatinga is 4 km from Leticia (Colombia). The Port Captain in Tabatinga is reported as very helpful and speaks good English. **NB** The port area of Tabatinga is called Marco. A good hammock will cost US$15 in Tabatinga (try Esplanada Teocides) or Benjamin Constant. A mosquito net for a hammock is essential if sailing upstream from Tabatinga; much less so downstream. ■ *Airport to Tabatinga by*

Brazil

minibus, US$1. Varig *to Manaus 3 times a week. See also under Leticia (Colombia) page 878. Regular minibus to Leticia, US$0.60.*

Sleeping and eating D *Residencial Aluguel Pajé*. With bath, fan. D *Solimões*. Military-run, close to airport, with breakfast, other meals available if ordered in advance, excellent value. VW colectivo from barracks to centre, harbour and Leticia. There are decent places to stay near the boat companies for Peru. Excellent *Canto do Peixado*, on main street. Highly recommended. *Lanchonete e Sorveteria Mallet*, fresh juices, ice creams, burgers, popular.

Directory Banks: no exchange facilities at Tabatinga port. Best to change money in Leticia. Dollars are accepted everywhere; Colombian pesos are accepted in Tabatinga, Peruvian soles rarely accepted.

Border with Brazil, Colombia & Peru

In this area, carry your passport at all times

It is advisable to check all requirements and procedures before arriving at this multiple border. Travellers should enquire carefully about embarkation/disembarkation points and where to go through immigration formalities. If waiting for transport, Tabatinga has convenient hotels for early morning departures. **NB** When crossing these borders, check if there is a time difference (for example, Brazilian summer time, usually mid-October to mid-February). **Consulates** Brazilian, C 11, No 10-70, Leticia, T27531, 1000-1600, Monday-Friday, efficient, helpful; onward ticket and 2 black-and-white photos needed for visa (photographer nearby); allow 36 hours. Peruvian, Cra 11, No 6-80, Leticia, T27204, F27825, open 0830-1430; no entry or exit permits are given here.

If coming from Peru, you must have a Peruvian exit stamp and a yellow fever certificate

Brazilian immigration Entry and exit stamps are given at the *Polícia Federal*, 10 mins walk from the Tabatinga docks, opposite *Café dos Navegantes* (walk through the docks and follow the road to its end, turn right at this T-junction for 1 block to a white building), open 24 hours; also at the airport, open Wed and Sat only. Proof of US$500 or an onward ticket may be asked for. There are no facilities in Benjamin Constant. One-week transit in Tabatinga is permitted. The Colombian consulate is near the border on the road from Tabatinga to Leticia, opposite *Restaurant El Canto de las Peixadas*. Open 0800-1400. Tourist cards are issued on presentation of 2 passport photos.

Transport Travel between Tabatinga and Leticia is very informal; taxis between the two towns charge US$5 (more if you want to stop at immigration offices, exchange houses, etc; beware of taxi drivers who want to rush you expensively over the border before it 'closes'), or US$0.80 in a colectivo (more after 1800). **Boat** From Manaus to Benjamin Constant boats normally go on to Tabatinga, and start from there when going to Manaus. They usually wait 1-2 days in both Tabatinga and Benjamin Constant before returning to Manaus; you can stay on board. Tabatinga and Leticia are 1½-2 hrs from Benjamin Constant (ferry/*recreio* US$2.50; much quicker by speedboat, US$13. For information on boats to/from Manaus, see Manaus Shipping and River Transport in Amazônia.

There are no customs formalities for everyday travel between Leticia and Tabatinga

Colombian immigration *DAS*, C 9, No 8-32, T27189, Leticia, and at the airport. Exit stamps to leave Colombia by air or overland are given by DAS no more than 1 day before you leave. If flying into Leticia prior to leaving for Brazil or Peru, get an exit stamp while at the airport. Check both offices for entry stamps before flying into Colombia. To enter Colombia you must have a tourist card to obtain an entry stamp, even if you are passing through Leticia en route between Brazil and Peru (the Colombian consul in Manaus may tell you otherwise; try to get a tourist card elsewhere). The Colombian Consular Office in Tabatinga issues tourist cards; 24-hr transit stamps can be obtained at the DAS office. If visiting Leticia without intending to go anywhere else in Colombia, you may be allowed to enter without immigration or customs formalities (but travellers' cheques cannot be changed without an entry stamp). ■ *Travel between Colombia and Brazil and Peru is given above and below respectively. Travel from/into Colombia is given under Leticia.*

Peruvian immigration Entry/exit formalities take place at Santa Rosa. Every boat leaving and entering Peru stops here. There is also an immigration office in Iquitos (Napo 447), where procedures for leaving can be checked. There is no Brazilian consulate in Iquitos No exchange facilites in Santa Rosa; reais and dollars are accepted.

Transport Between Tabatinga and Iquitos in Peru there are 4 companies with speedboats, US$50 one way, buy ticket 1 day in advance. They take 11-12 hrs. Departure from Tabatinga is 0600. There are also cheaper, slower *lanchas*, which 2 days (US$15-17.50 hammock, US$25-30 cabin). Boat services are given under **Iquitos** in the Peru chapter. Passengers leaving and entering Peru must visit immigration at Santa Rosa when the boat stops there. For entry into Brazil, formalities are done in Tabatinga; for Colombia, in Leticia.

A paved road connects Manaus with **Caracaraí**, a busy port with modern installations on the Rio Branco. A new bridge crosses the river for traffic on the the Manaus-Boa Vista road. *Silas* in the Drogaria on the south side of town will change dollars. **D** *Maroca*, opposite fuel tanks, one street back from the river. **E** *Caracaraí*, down the street from the rodoviária, friendly but dirty. *Sorveteria Pizzaria Lidiany*. Recommended. ■ *Buses from Caracaraí to Boa Vista costs US$9, 3 hrs.*

The Rio Branco
Colour map 2, grid B2
Population: 14,286

The road which connects Manaus and Boa Vista (BR-174 to Novo Paraíso, then the Perimetral, BR-210, rejoining the BR174 after crossing the Rio Branco at Caracaraí) can get badly potholed. There are service stations with toilets, camping, etc, every 150-180 km, but all petrol is low octane. Drivers should take a tow cable and spares, and bus passengers should prepare for delays in the rainy season. At Km 100 is Presidente Figueiredo, with many waterfalls and a famous cave with bats, shops and a restaurant. About 100 km further on is a service station at the entrance to the **Uaimiri Atroari Indian Reserve**, which straddles the road for about 120 km. Private cars and trucks are not allowed to enter the Indian Reserve between sunset and sunrise, but buses are exempt from this regulation. Nobody is allowed to stop within the reserve at any time. At the northern entrance to the reserve there are toilets and a spot to hang your hammock (usually crowded with truckers overnight). At Km 327 is the village of Vila Colina with *Restaurante Paulista*, good food, clean, you can use the shower and hang your hammock. At Km 359 there is a monument to mark the equator. At Km 434 is the clean and pleasant *Restaurant Goaio*. Just south of Km 500 is *Bar Restaurante D'Jonas*, a clean, pleasant place to eat, you can also camp or sling a hammock. Beyond here, large tracts of forest have been destroyed for settlement, but already many homes have been abandoned.

Manaus to Venezuela & Guyana

Boa Vista has road connections with the Venezuelan frontier at Santa Elena de Uairén (237 km, paved, the only gasoline 110 km south of Santa Elena) and Bonfim for the Guyanese border at Lethem. Both roads are open all year.

Boa Vista

The capital of the extreme northern State of Roraima has a modern functional plan, which often necessitates long hot treks from one function to another. It has an interesting modern cathedral; also a museum of local Indian culture (poorly kept). There is swimming in the Rio Branco, 15 mins from the town centre (too polluted in Boa Vista), reachable by bus only when the river is low.

Phone code: 0xx95
Post code: 69300
Colour map 2, grid B2
Population: 200,568
785 km N of Manaus

B *Aipana Plaza*, Praça Centro Cívico 53, T224 4800, aipana@technet.com.br Modern, a/c, good service, best food in town, buffet US$7.20-8. **C** *Eusêbio's*, R Cecília Brasil 1107, T224 0300, F623 8690 Run down in 2001, a/c, good restaurant, swimming pool, free transport to rodoviária or airport. **C** *Itamaraty*, Av NS da Consolata 1957, T/F224 9757, itamaraty@osite.com.br A/c, parking, good. **C** *Roraima*, Av Cecília Brasil e Benjamin Constant, T224 9843. Recommended. The restaurant opposite is also recommended. **C** *Uiramutam Palace*, Av Capt Ene Garcez 427, T/F2249912. Good service, a/c, restaurant, pool. **D** *Três Nações*, Av

Sleeping
Accommodation is generally expensive. Economic hardship has caused an increase in crime, sometimes violent

Brazil

Ville Roy 1885, T/F224 3439. Close to the rodoviária, some rooms a/c, refurbished, basic. Often recommended. **E** *Imperial*, Av Benjamin Constant 433, T224 5592. A/c, cheaper with fan, welcoming, safe motorcycle parking. Recommended. **D** *Brasil*, Benjamin Constant 331, near Drogafarma. Good meals (do not confuse with dirty, overpriced *Hotel Brasa* in the same street). At Av Ville Roy 1906-24 Carlos Alberto Soares lets a room, warm shower. Recommended. **E** *Terraço*, Av Cecília Brasil 1141. Without bath, noisy, friendly. **Camping** Rio Caaumé, 3 km north of town (unofficial site, small bar, clean river, pleasant).

Eating *Ver O Rio*, R Floriano Peixoto 116. For best fish dishes. In smae area are *Makuchic*, also for
Most restaurants fish, and *Black and White*, fixed price lunch and more expensive by weight. *Café Pigalle*, R
close at night, Cecília Brasil, just off central praça, next to *Eusêbio's*. Good food, drinks and atmosphere,
except for pizza, open till all hrs. *Churrascaria La Carreta*, R Pedro Rodrigues 185, 500 m from *Eusêbio's*.
including delivery Good, US$3 buffet, nice atmosphere. Recommended. *La Góndola*, Benjamin Constant e Av
Amazonas. Good. *Vila Rica*, R Ville Roy, near the rodoviária. Good cheap lunch. *Catequeiro*,
Araújo Filho e Benjamin Constant. Recommended *prato feito*. *Café com Leite Suiço*, at Santa
Cecilia, 15 mins by car on road to Bom Fim. Open 0630-1300 for regional food, US$4, good.

Transport **Air** *Varig* daily to and from Rio, Brasília and Manaus (also Penta to Manaus). Confirm flights before reaching Boa Vista as they are fully booked. Aircraft maintenance, baggage checking and handling are unreliable. No left luggage, information or exchange facilities at the airport, which is 4 km from the centre. Bus 'Aeroporto' from the centre is US$0.40. Taxi to rodoviária, US$5, to centre US$7, 45 mins walk.

Bus (See also Border Crossings below.) Rodoviária is on the town outskirts, 3 km at the end of Av Ville Roy; taxi to centre, US$5, bus US$0.45, 10 mins (marked '13 de Setembro' or 'Joquey Clube' to centre). The local bus terminal is on Av Amazonas, by R Cecília Brasil, near the central praça. Note that it is difficult to get a taxi or bus to the rodoviária in time for early morning departures; as it's a 25-min walk, book a taxi the previous evening. To **Manaus**, US$26-32.50, several companies including *Eucatur/União Cascavel* (T224 0505), 12 hrs, at least 6 daily, *executivo* service at 1800/1900 with meal stop. Advisable to book. Boa Vista-Caracaraí US$9, 3 hrs.

Hitchhiking To Santa Elena, Venezuela, is not easy; either wait at the bridge and police checkpoint on the road to the border, or try to find a Venezuelan driver on the praça. Hitching from Boa Vista to Manaus is fairly easy on the many trucks travelling south; try from the Trevo service station near the rodoviária. Truck drivers ask for approximately half the bus fare to take passengers in the cab (bargain), much cheaper or free in the back. The view from the truck is usually better than from the bus and you can see the virgin forest of the Indian Reserve in daylight. Take some food and water.

Directory **Airline offices** *Penta*, Av Sebastião Diniz 122, T224 6853. *META*, Praça Santos Dumont 100, T224 7677. *Varig*, R Araújo Filho 91, T224 2269. *Tavaj*, Av B Constant 64, T224 1103. **Banks** US$ and Guyanese notes can be changed in Boa Vista. TCs and cash in *Banco do Brasil*, Av Glaycon de Paiva 56, 1000-1300 (minimum US$200), has Visa/Plus ATM. There is no official exchange agency and the local rates for bolívares are low: the Banco do Brasil will not change bolívares. *HSBC*, Av Ville Roy 392, MasterCard ATM. *Bradesco*, Av Jaime Brasil 441, Visa ATM. Best rate for dollars, *Casa Pedro José*, R Araújo Filho 287, T224 9797, also changes TCs and bolívares; *Timbo's* (gold and jewellery shop), Av B Constant 170, T224 4077, will change money. **Embassies and consulates** Venezuela, Av Benjamin Constant 525E, T224 2182, Mon-Fri 0830-1300, but may close earlier. **Medical services** Yellow fever inoculations are free at a clinic near the hospital. **Tourist offices** Information is available at the rodoviária; also R Col Pinto 241, Centro, T623 1230, F623 1831. At the rodoviária, Leyla King at *Maikan Turismo* is very helpful; she speaks English and can arrange tours. Travellers can seek information and free hammock space from Klaus, T9963 7915/9111 3339/623 9960, or ask for Lula at *Guri Auto Elétrica*, R das Mil Flores 738, near rodoviária. **Tour Guide** boat trips on Rio Branco and surrounding waterways (jungle, beaches, Indian reservations), *Acqua*, R Floriano Peixoto 505, T224 6576. Guide Elieser Rufino is recommended.

Border with Border searches are thorough and frequent at this border crossing. If entering Brazil,
Venezuela ensure in advance that you have the right papers, including yellow fever certificate, before arriving at this border. Officials may give only two months' stay and car

drivers may be asked to purchase an unnecessary permit. Ask to see the legal documentation. Everyone who crosses this border must have a visa for Venezuela. Check beforehand. Current procedure is to take filled out visa form, two photos and deposit slip from *Banco do Brasil* (US$30) to the Venezuelan consulate (address above), be prepared to wait an hour, but it may be possible to get a visa at the border; check requirements in advance. There is another Venezuelan consulate in Manaus which issues one-year, multiple entry visas.

On the Brazilian side there is a basic hotel, *Pacaraima Palace*, a guest house, camping possibilities and a bank. ■ *Buses leave Boa Vista rodoviária at 0700, 0830, 1300, 1700 for Santa Elena de Uairén, stopping at all checkpoints, US$15, 4 hrs, take water. It is possible to share a taxi. There are through buses to Ciudad Guayana, Ciudad Bolívar (eg Caribe), US$33.*

The main border crossing between Brazil and Guyana is from **Bonfim**, 125 km (all paved) northeast of Boa Vista, to Lethem. The towns are separated by the Rio Tacutu, which is crossed by small boats for foot passengers; vehicles cross by ferry on demand, US$4 return. The river crossing is 2.5 km from Bonfim, 1.6 km north of Lethem. A bridge is under construction. Formalities are generally lax on both sides of the border, but it is important to observe them as people not having the correct papers may have problems further into either country.

Border with Guyana
Colour map 2, grid B3
Population: 9,326

Brazilian immigration is at Polícia Federal (closed for lunch): from the rodoviária in Bonfim take a taxi, obtain exit stamp, then walk to the river. Once across, do not go to the Guyanese police for immigration, but to the airport. Brazilian customs is at Ministério da Fazenda checkpoint, before entering Bonfim; jeeps from here charge US$1 to immigration. There is no Guyanese consul in Boa Vista, so if you need a visa for Guyana, you must get it in São Paulo or Brasília (see Guyana Documents in Essentials). *Reais* can be changed into Guyanese dollars in Boa Vista. There are no exchange facilities in Lethem, but *reais* are accepted in town.

Sleeping and eating D *Bonfim*, owned by Mr Myers, who speaks English and is very helpful, fan, shower. *Domaia*. There is a café at the rodoviária, opposite the church, whose owner speaks English and gives information. *Restaurante Internacional*, opposite the rodoviária, on other side from church; another restaurant a bit further from the rodoviária serves good food. Local speciality, fried cashew nuts. English-speaking teacher, Tricia Watson, has been helpful to bewildered travellers.

Transport Bus: Boa Vista-Bonfim 6 a day US$6, 2½ hrs; colectivos charge US$18. **Ferry**: to cross the river, take a canoe (see above), US$0.25 (no boats at night).

Southern Amazônia

Brasília

Rondônia and Acre, lands which mark not just the political boundaries between Brazil and Peru and Bolivia, but also developmental frontiers between the forest and colonization. Much of Rondônia has been deforested. Acre is still frontier country with great expanses of forest in danger of destruction.

Rondônia, with a population of 1.4 million, is the focus of experimental agriculture, with attendant colonization. At the same time, much of the state is reserved for Indians and national forests. The Rio Madeira, on which Porto Velho, the state capital stands, is one of the Amazon's major tributaries. The four main rivers which form it are the Madre de Dios, rising a short distance from Cusco (Peru); the Beni, coming from the southern Cordillera bordering Lake Titicaca; the Mamoré, rising near Sucre, Bolivia; and the Guaporé, coming out of Mato Grosso, in Brazil.

Background

Porto Velho

Phone code: 0xx69
Post code: 78900
Colour map 4, grid B1
Population: 334,661

NB Malaria is
common; the drinking
water is contaminated
with mercury (from
gold panning).

The city is relatively
safe for tourists, but
take care in the
evenings and even
during the day near
the railway station
and port

This city stands on a high bluff overlooking a curve of the Rio Madeira. It prospered during the local gold and timber rush but this has slowed. At the top of the hill, in Praça João Nicoletti, is the **Cathedral**, built in 1930, with beautiful stained glass windows; the **Prefeitura** is across the street. The principal commercial street is Av 7 de Setembro, which runs from the railway station and market hall to the upper level of the city, near the rodoviária. The centre is hot and noisy, but not without its charm, and the port and old railway installations are interesting. In the old railway yards known as Praça Madeira-Mamoré are the **Museus Ferroviário** and **Geológico** (both 0800-1800), the **Casa do Artesão** (see Shopping) and a promenade with bars by the river, a wonderful place to watch the sunset. A neoclassical **Casa do Governo** faces Praça Getúlio Vargas, while Praça Marechal Rondon is spacious and modern. There are several viewpoints overlooking the river and railway yards: **Mirante I** (with restaurant) is at the end of R Carlos Gomes; **Mirante II** (with a bar and ice cream parlour), at the end of R Dom Pedro II. There is a clean fruit and vegetable market at the corner of R Henrique Dias and Av Farquhar and a dry goods market three blocks to the south, near the port.

Excursions Five km northeast of the city is the **Parque Nacional Municipal**, a small collection of flora in a preserved area of jungle and one of very few parks in the city. The **Cachoeira de Santo Antônio**, rapids on the Rio Madeira, seven km upriver from Porto Velho, is a popular destination for a swim during the dry season; in the rainy season the rapids may be underwater and swimming is dangerous. ■ *Access is by boat, taking a tour from Porto Cai N'Água, one hr; or by train on Sun (see Madeira-Mamoré Railway, below); or by city bus No 102, Triângulo, which runs every 50 mins from the city bus terminus or from the bus stop on R Rogério Weber, across from Praça Marechal Rondon.* Gold dredges may be seen working near Porto Velho, ask around.

Sleeping **A** *Rondon Palace*, Av Gov Jorge Teixeira corner Jacy Paraná, away from the centre, T/F223 3420/3422. A/c, fridge, restaurant, pool, travel agency. **C** *Central*, Tenreiro Aranha 2472, T224 2066, F224 5114. A/c, TV, fridge. Recommended. **D** *Líder*, Av Carlos Gomes, near rodoviária. Honest, welcoming, reasonably clean, fan, coffee. Recommended. **E** *Tía Carmen*, Av Campos Sales 2995, T221 7910. Very good, honest, good cakes in *lanche* in front of hotel. Highly recommended. From the rodoviária, take bus No 301 'Presidente Roosevelt' (outside *Hotel Pontes*), which goes to railway station at riverside, then along Av 7 de Setembro as far as Av Marechal Deodoro, passing: **C** *Pousada da Sete*, No 894, T221 8344. A/c, cheaper with fan, **D** with shared bath. **D** *Guaporé Palace*, Av G Vargas 1553, T221 2495. A/c, restaurant. **D** *Missionero*, No 1180, T221 4080. Good, a/c, cheaper with fan, **E** with shared bath, fan. Recommended. **E** *Laira*, Joaquim Nabuco, just off 7 de Setembro. Good, cheap. **F** *Yara*, Av 7 do Septembre y R Gonçalves Dias. Shared room with breakfast, safe, helpful staff.

Eating *Churrascaria Natal*, Av Carlos Gomes 2783. Good meat and chicken. *Assados na Brasa*, Carlos Gomes 2208. Similar. *Mister Pizza II*, Carlos Gomes e José de Alencar. Good. *Almanara*, R José de Alencar 2624. Good authentic Lebanese food, popular, not cheap. Recommended. *Chá*, Av Presidente Dutra 3024. By kilo buffet, pricey. A number of good restaurants around the intersection of Dom Pedro II and Av Joaquim Nabuco: *Champagne*, recommended for pizzas, and a good Chinese, Joaquim Nabuco 2264. *Bella Italia*, Joaquim Nabuco 2205. Italian, pizza and *comida caseira*. Many *lanches* in town: recommended are *Petiskão*, Av 7 de Setembro e Joaquim Nabuco. Excellent juices. *Panificadora Popular*, Av Marechal Deodoro between 7 de Setembro e Dom Pedro II. Good juices and soups. *Xalezinho*, opposite, for an even bigger bowl of soup. *Banana Split*, Av 7 de Setembro. Popular, good by the kg meals; also *Sorvette Pinguim* for ice creams.

Avoid eating much fish because of mercury contamination

Shopping **Indian handicrafts** *Casa do Índio*, R Rui Barbosa 1407 and *Casa do Artesão*, Praça Madeira-Mamoré, behind the railway station, Thu-Sun 0800-1800. **Bookshop** *Livraria da Rose*,

Av Rogério Weber 1967, opposite Praça Marechal Rondon, exchanges English paperbacks; Rose, the proprietor, speaks English, friendly. Other bookshops nearby. **Supermercado Maru**, 7 de Setembro e Joaquim Nabuco.

Ecoporé, R Rafael Vaz e Silva 3335, Bairro Liberdade, T221 5021, carol@ronet.com.br For ecotourism projects in rubber tappers' communities on the Brazil/Bolivia border, US$50 pp per day, full details from Carol Doria, who speaks English. **Tour operators**

Air Airport 8 km west of town, T225 1339. Take bus marked 'Aeroporto' (last one between **Transport** 2400-0100). Daily flights to many Brazilian cities. *Road journeys are best*
Bus Rodoviária is on Jorge Teixeira between Carlos Gomes and Dom Pedro II. From town *done in the dry season,* take 'President Roosevelt' bus No 301 (if on Av 7 de Setembro, the bus turns at Av Marechal *the 2nd half of the year* Deodoro); 'Aeroporto' and 'Hospital Base' (No 400) also go to rodoviária. Health and other controls at the Rondônia-Mato Grosso border are strict. To break up a long trip is much more expensive than doing it all in one stretch.

Bus to **Humaitá**, US$5, 3 hrs. To **São Paulo**, 60-plus hrs, US$75. To **Cuiabá**, 23 hrs, US$45, expensive food and drink is available en route. To **Guajará-Mirim**, see below. To **Rio Branco**, **Viação Rondônia**, 5 daily, 8 hrs, US$12.50. Daily bus with **Eucatur** from Cascavel (Paraná, connections for Foz do Iguaçu) via Maringá, Campo Grande and Cuiabá to Porto Velho (Porto Velho-Campo Grande 36 hrs, US$60). To **Cáceres** for the Pantanal, 18 hrs, US$30. Hitching is difficult, try the gasoline stations on the edge of town.

River services See River Transport, page 533. Passenger service from **Porto Cai N'Água** (which means 'fall in the water', watch out or you might!), for best prices buy directly at the boat, avoid touts on the shore. Boat tickets for Manaus are also sold in the rodoviária. The Rio Madeira is fairly narrow so the banks can be seen and there are several 'meetings of waters'. Shipping a car: São Matheus Ltda, Av Terminal dos Milagros 400, Balsa, takes vehicles on pontoons, meals, showers, toilets, cooking and sleeping in your car is permitted.

Car hire **Silva Car**, R Almte Barroso 1528, Porto Velho, T221 1423/6040, US$50 per day.

Airline offices *TAM*, RJ Castilho 530, T221 6666. *Tavaj*, T225 5908. *Varig*, Av Campos Sales 2666, T224 **Directory** 2262/225 1675, F224 2278, English spoken. *Vasp*, R Tenheiro Aranha 2326, T224 4566/225 3226. **Banks** Banks are open in the morning only; *Banco do Brasil*, Dom Pedro II 607 e Av José de Alencar, cash and TCs with 2% commission, minimum commission US$15, minimum amount exchanged US$200. *Marco Aurélio Câmbio*, R José de Alencar 3353, T221 4922, T984 0025 (mob), quick, efficient, good rates, Mon-Fri 0900-1500. *Parmetal* (gold merchants), R Joaquim Nabuco 2265, T221 1566, cash only, good rates, open Mon-Fri 0730-1800, Sat 0730-1300. Exchange is difficult elsewhere in Rondônia. **Communications** Post Office: Av Presidente Dutra 2701, corner of Av 7 de Setembro. **Telephone:** *Tele Centro Sul*, Av Presidente Dutra 3023 e Dom Pedro II, 0600-2300 daily. **Medical services** Hospital Central, R Júlio de Castilho 149, T/F224 4389, 24 hr emergencies. **Dentist:** at Carlos Gomes 2577; 24-hr clinic opposite. **Tourist office** Departamento de Turismo, R Padre Chiquinho 670, Esplanada das Secretarias, CEP 78904-060, T221 1499, F225 2827. **Fundação Cultural do Estado de Rondônia** (*Funcer*) is at same address. Also www.terra.com.br/cidades/pvh/ **Voltage** 110 volts AC, Guajará-Mirim also, elsewhere in Rondônia 220 volts.

The BR-364

The Marechal Rondon Highway, BR-364, is fully paved to Cuiabá, 1,550 km. A *Colour map 4, grid C2* result of the paving of BR-364 is the development of farms and towns along it; least *At the Mato Grosso* population density is in the south between Pimenta Bueno and Vilhena. From *state border, proof* Porto Velho south, the towns include **Ariquemes** (202 km from Porto Velho. *of yellow-fever* (*Phone code* 0xx69. *Post code*: 78930; buses hourly from 0600, 3-4 hours, hotels, *if no proof is presented,* bank); **Ji Paraná** (376 km.*Post code*: 78960. *Phone code*: 0xx69; bus to Porto *a new shot is given* Velho, US$16.25, 16 hours; to Cuiabá, 15 hours, US$28), on the shores of the Rio Machado, a pleasant town with a small riverside promenade, which has several bars, lively at night; several hotels.

Brazil

Parque Nacional Pacaás Novos
765,800 ha

The Parque Nacional Pacaás Novos, lies west of the BR-364; it is a transitional zone between open plain and Amazonian forest. The majority of its surface is covered with *cerrado* vegetation and the fauna includes jaguar, brocket deer, puma, tapir and peccary. The average annual temperature is 23°C, but this can fall as low as 5°C when the cold front known as the *friagem* blows up from the South Pole. Details from *Ibama*, Av Jorge Teixeira 3477, CEP 78.904-320, T0xx69-223 2599/3597, Porto Velho, T0xx69-223 3607/3598, F221 8021, or R João Batista Rios s/n, CEP 78958-000 Pacaás Novas-RO.

The Madeira-Mamoré Railway

Porto Velho was the terminus of the Madeira-Mamoré railway. It was supposed to go as far as Riberalta, on the Rio Beni, above that river's rapids, but stopped short at Guajará Mirim. The BR-364 took over many of the railway bridges, leaving what remained of the track to enthusiasts to salvage what they could. The line works all week but tourist excursions to Santo Antônio are on Sunday only, departures at 0800, 1115 and 1430, returning at 0915, 1500 and 1600, US$3 return, crowded with people going to bathe at the falls during the dry season – good fun; there are dolphins at Santo Antônio. The roundhouse, recently restored, has two antique locomotives on display. Mr Johnson at the station speaks English.

Guajará Mirim
Phone code: 0xx69
Colour map 4, grid B1
Population: 38,045

From Porto Velho, the paved BR-364 continues 220 km southwest to Abunã (hotels **E**), where the BR-425 branches south to Guajará Mirim. The BR-425 is a fair road, partly paved, which uses the former rail bridges (in poor condition). It is sometimes closed March-May. Across the Mamoré from Guajará Mirim is the Bolivian town of Guayaramerín, which is connected by road to Riberalta, from where there are air services to other Bolivian cities. Guajará Mirim is a charming town. The **Museu Municipal** is at the old Guajará Mirim railway station beside the ferry landing; interesting and diverse. Highly recommended. ■ *0500-1200, 1400-1800, T541 3362. Banco do Brasil only changes money in the morning.*

Sleeping and eating **C** *Jamaica*, Av Leopoldo de Matos 755, T/F541 3721. A/c, fridge, parking. **C** *Lima Palace*, Av 15 de Novembro 1613, T541 3421, F541 2122. A/c, fridge, parking. **C** *Mini-Estrela*, Av 15 de Novembro 460, T541 2399. A/c, parking. **D** *Chile*, Av Q Bocaiúva. Good value, includes breakfast. Recommended. **D** *Fénix Palace*, Av 15 de Novembro 459, T541 2326. Highly recommended. **D** *Mamoré*, R M Moraes, T541 3753. Clean, friendly. **Youth hostel** *Centro Deportivo Afonso Rodrigues*, Av 15 de Novembro, T541 3732. There is a basic dorm, **E**, opposite the rodoviária. Best to eat is *Oasis*, Av 15 de Novembro 460. Recommended (closed Mon). *Lanchonates*, self-service, good value. Recommended.

Transport **Bus** From Porto Velho to Guajará Mirim, 5½ hrs or more depending on season, 8 a day with *Viação Rondônia*, US$18. Taxi from Porto Velho rodoviária, US$25 pp for 4-5, 3 hrs, leaves when full.

Border with Bolivia

Get Brazilian exit and entry stamps from Polícia Federal, Av Presidente Dutra 70, corner of Av Quintino Bocaiúva, T541 4021. The Bolivian consulate is at Av C Marquês 495, T541 2862, Guajará Mirim; visas are given here. ■ *Speedboat across the Rio Mamoré (border), US$1.65, 5-min crossing, operates all day, tickets at the waterside; ferry crossing for vehicles, T541 3811, Mon-Sat 0800-1200, Mon-Fri 1400-1600, 20-min crossing.*

Rio Branco

The BR-364 runs west from Porto Velho to Abunã (239 km), then in excellent condition, 315 km to Rio Branco the capital of the State of Acre. This intriguing state, rich in natural beauty, history and the *seringueiro* culture, is still very much off the beaten track. During the rubber boom of the late 19th century, many *Nordestinos* migrated to the western frontier in search of fortune. As a result, the unpopulated Bolivian territory of Acre was gradually taken over by Brazil and formally annexed in the first decade of the 20th century. In compensation, Bolivia received the Madeira-Mamoré railroad, as described above. In 1913, Rio Branco became capital of the new Território Federal do Acre, which attained statehood in 1962. The chief industries remain rubber and *castanho-de-pará* (Brazil nut) extraction, but timber and ranching are becoming increasingly important and improved road access is putting the state's tropical forests at considerable risk.Despite improved air and road links, Rio Branco remains at the 'end of the line', a frontier outpost whose depressed economy, high unemployment and prevalent drug-running make the city unsafe at night.

The Rio Acre is navigable upstream as far as the Peru and Bolivia borders. It divides the city into two districts called Primeiro (west) and Segundo (east), on either side of the river. In the central, Primeiro district are **Praça Plácido de Castro**, the shady main square; the **Cathedral**, Nossa Senhora de Nazaré, along Av Brasil; the neo-classical **Palácio Rio Branco** on R Benjamin Constant, across from Praça Eurico Gaspar Dutra. There is a market off R Epaminondas Jácome. Two bridges link the districts. In the Segundo district is the **Calçadão da Gameleira**, a pleasant promenade along the shore, with plaques and an old tree marking the location of the original settlement. There are several large parks in the city; the **Horto Forestal**, popular with joggers, in Vila Ivonete (1° distrito), 3 km north of the centre ('Conjunto Procon' or 'Vila Ivonete' city-buses), has native Amazonian trees, a small lake, paths and picnic areas.

Museu da Borracha (Rubber Museum), Av Ceará 1177, in a lovely old house with a tiled façade, has information about the rubber boom, archaeological artefacts, a section about Acreano Indians, documents and memorabilia from the annexation and a display about the Santo Daime doctrine (see excursions below). Recommended. ■ *Mon-Sat 0730-1900*. **Casa do Seringueiro**, Av Brasil 216, corner of Av Getúlio Vargas, has a good exhibit on rubber tappers and on **Chico Mendes** in particular; the Sala Hélio Melo has a display of Melo's paintings, mainly on the theme of the forest.

Post code: 69900
Phone code: 0xx68
Colour map 3, grid B6
Population: 253,059

NB Rio Branco time is one hour behind Porto Velho and Manaus time; this means two hours behind Brazilian Standard Time

Brazil

Excursions

About 8 km southeast of town, upriver along the Rio Acre, is **Lago do Amapá**, a U-shaped lake good for boating and watersports; access is by river or by land via route AC-40. 2 km beyond along the AC-40 is **Praia do Amapá**, a bathing beach on the Rio Acre; there is an annual arts festival here in September. Excursions can be made to **rubber plantations** and rubber extraction areas in native forest (*seringais nativos*). Some 13 km from Rio Branco is **Colônia Cinco Mil** (access along AC-10), a religious centre of the followers of the Santo Daime doctrine: its members (many originally from outside Acre and Brazil) live a communal life, working in agriculture and producing crafts made of latex. The religion is based around the use of *Ayahuasca*, a hallucinogenic potion adopted from local Indians. Visitors are usually welcome, but enquire beforehand.

Sleeping

Few economical hotels in the centre, but a reasonable selection of these by the rodoviária

In 1° distrito (west bank) A *Pinheiro Palace*, Rui Barbosa 91, T224 7191, pinheiro@mdnet.com.br A/c, pool. Recommended. C *Inácio Palace*, R Rui Barbosa 72, T224 6397, F224 5726. Fridge, TV, overpriced, fair restaurant. B *Rio Branco*, R Rui Barbosa 193, T224 1785, F224 2681, by Praça Plácido de Castro. A/c, fridge, TV, nice but simple. C *Triângulo*, R Floriano Peixoto 727, T224 9265, F224 4117. A/c, TV, fridge, restaurant. C *Albemar*, R Franco Ribeiro 99, T224 1938. A/c, fridge, TV, good breakfast, good value. Recommended. D *Xapuri*, Nações Unidas 187, T225 7268. Shared bath, fan, basic, 15 mins' walk from the centre. **In 2° distrito (east bank), in Cidade Nova by the rodoviária B** *Rodoviária*, R Palmeiral 268, T224 4434. A/c, fridge TV, **D** with shared bath, fan, good value. **C** *Skina*, Uirapuru 533, T224 0087. A/c, fridge, TV, fan. **D** *Nacional*, R Palmeiral 496, T224 4822. Fan, both cheaper with shared bath. **Youth hostel** *Fronteira Verde*, Travessa Natanael de Albuquerque, 2° distrito, T225 7128.

Eating *Kaxinawa*, Av Brasil at Praça Plácido de Castro. The best in town for Acreano regional food. *Pizzaria Tutti Frutti*, Av Ceará 1132, across from the Museu da Borracha. Pizzas, ice cream, not cheap. *Casarão*, Av Brasil 310, next to the telephone office. Good food and drink. *Churrascaria Triângulo*, R Floriano Peixoto 727. As much charcoal-grilled meat as you can eat. Recommended. *Remanso do Tucunaré*, R José de Melo 481, Bairro Bosque. Fish specialties. *Anexos*, R Franco Ribeiro 99, next to *Albemar Hotel*. Popular for meals and drinks. For ice cream *Sorveteria Arte Sabor*, Travessa Santa Inés 28, corner Aviarsio, 1° distrito, 15 mins' walk from the centre. Excellent home made ice cream, many jungle fruit flavours. Recommended. **Local specialities** *Tacacá*; a soup served piping hot in a gourd (*cuia*) combines manioc starch (*goma*), cooked *jambu* leaves which numb the mouth and tongue, shrimp, spices and hot pepper sauce; recommendation from Sra Diamor, Boulevar Augusto Monteiro 1046, Bairro 15 in the 2° distrito (bus Norte-Sul from the centre), other kiosks in town, ask around.

Transport
Prices for car rentals with the nationwide agencies are higher in Acre than in other states

Air The airport is on AC-40, Km 1.2, in the 2° distrito. Taxi from the airport to the centre US$20 flat rate, but going to the airport the meter is used, which usually comes to less. By bus, take 'Norte-Sul' or 'Vila Acre'. Flights with *Varig* and *Vasp* daily to **Porto Velho**, Manaus, Brasília and São Paulo. Local flights, including Cruzeiro do Sul, with *Tavaj*, who also fly to Manaus and Porto Velho.

Bus Rodoviária on Av Uirapuru, Cidade Nova, 2° distrito (east bank); city bus 'Norte-Sul' to the centre. To **Porto Velho**, *Viação Rondônia*, 5 daily, 8 hrs, US$12.50. To **Guajará Mirim**, daily with *Rondônia* at 1130 and 2200, 5-6 hrs, US$10; or take *Inácio's Tur* shopping trip, 3 per week. From Rio Branco the BR-364 continues west (in principle) to Cruzeiro do Sul and Japim, with a view to reaching the Peruvian frontier further west when completed.

Directory **Airline offices** *Varig*, T224 1182/0800-997000. **Communications** Post Office: on the corner of R Epaminondas Jácome and Av Getúlio Vargas. **Telephone:** on Av Brasil between Marechal Deodoro and Av Getúlio Vargas, long delays for international calls. **Tourist offices** SIC/AC, Secretaria de Indústria e Comércio, Av Getúlio Vargas 659, Centro, or Dpto de Turismo, BR-364, Km 05, Distrito Industrial, for either T224 1032/223 1901, F224 6333 (SIC) or 223 1210 (Dpto).

Border with Bolivia & Peru The BR-317 from Rio Branco heads south and later southwest, parallel to the Rio Acre; it is paved as far as **Xapuri** (the location of the Fundação Chico Mendes); one very basic lodging and two restaurants. The road continues to **Brasiléia** (three buses daily to/from Rio Branco, five hours in the wet, faster in the dry, US$10; three hotels, two basic lodgings, several restaurants – *La Felicitá* is good, Polícia Federal give entry/exit stamps), opposite the Bolivian town of Cobija on the Rio Acre. It is possible to stay in Epitaciolândia (**D** *Hotel Kanda*, 5 minutes' walk from the police post) and cross into Bolivia early in the morning.

The road ends at Assis Brasil where the Peruvian, Bolivian and Brazilian frontiers meet. Across the Rio Acre are Iñapari (Peru), border crossing difficult, even out of the wet season, and Bolpebra, Bolivia. A bus service operates only in the dry season beyond Brasiléia to Assis Brasil, access in the wet season is by river. In **Assis Brasil**, there are two hotels (one basic but clean, friendly, **E**), two restaurants, some shops, a bank which does not change US dollars (the hotel owner may be persuaded to oblige). You get between Iñapari and Assis Brasil by canoe, or by wading across the river. **NB** There is no Polícia Federal in the village, get entry/exit stamps in Brasília. Take small denomination dollar bills or Peruvian soles as there is nowhere to change money on the Peruvian side.

Brazil

Brasília

The Centre West

The Centre West is the frontier where the Amazon meets the central plateau. It is also Brazil's frontier with its Spanish American neighbours. Lastly, it contains the border between the expansion of agriculture and the untouched forests and savannahs. On this region's eastern edge is Brasília, the symbol of the nation's commitment to its empty centre. Not far away are the historic mining towns of Goiás.

Brasília

The purpose-built federal capital of Brazil succeeded Rio de Janeiro (as required by the Constitution) on 21 April 1960. Only light industry is allowed in the city and its population was limited to 500,000; this has been exceeded and more people live in a number of shanty towns, with minimal services, located well away from the main city, which is now a UNESCO World Heritage Site. Brasília is on undulating ground in the unpopulated uplands of Goiás, in the heart of the undeveloped Sertão. The official name for central Brasília is the Plano Piloto.

Phone code: 0xx61
Post code: 7000
Colour map 7, grid A3
Population: 2.1 million (2000)
Altitude: 1,171 m
960 km from Rio

Brazil

The climate is mild and the humidity refreshingly low, but overpowering in dry weather. The noonday sun beats hard, but summer brings heavy rains and the air is usually cool by night.

Background The creation of an inland capital had been urged since the beginning of the 19th century, but it was finally brought into being after President Kubitschek came to power in 1956, when a competition for the best general plan was won by Professor Lúcio Costa, who laid out the city in the shape of a bent bow and arrow. (It is also described as a bird, or aeroplane in flight.)

The Eixo Monumental divides the city into Asa Sul and Asa Norte (north and south wings) and the Eixo Rodoviário divides it east and west. Buildings are numbered according to their relation to them. For example, 116 Sul and 116 Norte are at the extreme opposite ends of the city. The 100s and 300s lie west of the Eixo and the 200s and 400s to the east; Quadras 302, 102, 202 and 402 are nearest the centre and 316, 116, 216 and 416 mark the end of the Plano Piloto. Residential areas made up of large six-storey apartment blocks, called the 'Super-Quadras'. All Quadras are separated by feeder roads, along which are the local shops. There are also a number of schools, parks and cinemas in the spaces between the Quadras (especially in Asa Sul), though not as systematically as was originally envisaged.

The main shopping areas, with more cinemas, restaurants and so on, are situated on either side of the city bus station (rodoviária). There are now several parks, or at least green areas. The private residential areas are west of the Super-Quadras, and on the other side of the lake.

At right angles to these residential areas is the 'arrow', the 8-km long, 250 m wide **Eixo Monumental**. The main north-south road (Eixo Rodoviário), in which fast-moving traffic is segregated, follows the curve of the bow; the radial road is along the line of the arrow – intersections are avoided by means of underpasses and cloverleaves. Motor and pedestrian traffic is segregated in the residential areas.

Sights At the tip of the arrow is the **Praça dos Três Poderes**, with the Congress buildings, the Palácio do Planalto (the President's office), the Palácio da Justiça and the Panteão Tancredo Neves. Nineteen tall Ministry buildings line the Esplanada dos Ministérios, west of the Praça, culminating in two towers linked by a walkway to form the letter H, representing Humanity. They are 28 storeys high: no taller buildings are allowed in Brasília. Where the bow and arrow intersect is the city bus terminal (rodoviária), with the cultural and recreational centres and commercial and financial areas on either side. There is a sequence of zones westward along the shaft of the arrow; a hotel centre, a radio city, an area for fairs and circuses, a centre for sports, the **Praça Municipal** (with the municipal offices in the Palácio do Buriti) and, lastly (where the nock of the arrow would be), the combined bus and railway station (rodoferroviária) with the industrial area nearby. The most impressive buildings are all by Oscar Niemeyer, Brazil's leading architect.

The **Palácio da Alvorada**, the President's official residence (not open to visitors), is on the lakeshore. The 80-km drive along the road round the lake to the dam is attractive. There are spectacular falls below the dam in the rainy season. Between the Praça dos Três Poderes and the lake are sites for various recreations, including golf, fishing and yacht clubs, and an acoustic shell for shows in the open air. The airport is at the eastern end of the lake. Some 395 ha between the lake and the northern residential area (Asa Norte) are reserved for the Universidade de Brasília, founded in 1961. South of the university area, the Av das Nações runs from the Palácio da Alvorada along the lake to join the road from the airport to the centre. Along it are found all the principal embassies. Also in this area is the attractive vice-presidential residence, the **Palácio do Jaburu** (not open to visitors). This area is very scenic.

A fine initial view of the city may be had from the **television tower**, which has a free observation platform at 75 m up; also bar and souvenir shop. ■ *Mon 1400-2000, Tue-Sun 0800-2000, West Eixo Monumental.* If the TV tower is closed, the nearby *Alvorada* hotel has a panoramic terrace on the 12th floor (lift to 11th only): ask at reception. A good and cheap way of seeing Brasília is by taking bus rides from the municipal rodoviária at the centre: the destinations are clearly marked. The circular bus routes 106, 108 and 131 go round the city's perimeter. If you go around the lake by bus, you must change at the Paranoá dam; to or from Paranoá Norte take bus 101, 'Rodoviária', and to and from Sul, bus 100, bypassing the airport. Tours from 1300-1700, start from the downtown hotel area and municipal rodoviária (US$12-20). Many hotels arrange city tours (see also Tour operators). ■ *Some buildings are open 1000-1400 Sat-Sun with guided tours in English, well worth going.*

It is worth telephoning addresses away from the centre to ask how to get there. An urban railway, Metrô, runs to the southwest suburbs

Brazil

Brasília: Plano Piloto

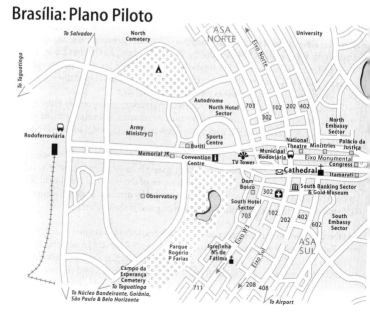

Praça dos Três Poderes: **Congress** is open to visitors, who may attend debates when Congress is in session (Friday morning). Excellent city views from the 10th floor in Annex 3. ■ *Mon-Fri 0930-1200, 1430-1630 (take your passport), guides free of charge (in English 1400-1700).* The **Palácio do Planalto** may also be visited. ■ *Sun 0930-1330, 30-min tours. The guard is changed ceremonially at the Palácio do Planalto on Friday at 1730.* The President attends if he is available. Opposite the Planalto is the Supreme Court building, **Supremo Tribunal Federal**. **Museu Histórico de Brasília** is really a hollow monument, with tablets, photos and videos telling the story of the city. ■ *Tue-Sun and holidays 0900-1800.* The sculpture 'Os Candangos' in front of the Planalto is a symbol of the city. By Bruno Giorgi, it pays homage to the *candangos*, or pioneer workers who built Brasília on empty ground. The marvellous building of the Ministry of Foreign Affairs, the **Itamarati**, has modern paintings and furniture and beautiful water gardens. ■ *Guided visits Mon, Wed, Fri 1500-1700, free.* Opposite the Itamarati is the **Palácio da Justiça**, with artificial cascades between its concrete columns. ■ *Mon-Fri, 0900-1200, 1500-1700.* The **Panteão Tancredo Neves** is a 'temple of freedom and democracy', built 1985-86 by Niemeyer. It includes an impressive homage to Tiradentes, the precursor of Brazilian independence. **Espaço Lúcio Costa** contains a model of Plano Piloto, sketches and autographs of the designer's concepts and gives the ideological background to the planning of Brasília.

Town clothes (not shorts or minis) should be worn when visiting all these buildings

The **Catedral Metropolitana**, on the Esplanada dos Ministérios, is a spectacular circular building in the shape of the crown of thorns. Three aluminium angels, suspended from the airy, domed, stained-glass ceiling, are by the sculptor Alfredo Ceschiatti, who also made the five life-sized bronze apostles outside. The baptistery, a concrete representation of the Host beside the cathedral, is connected to the main building by a tunnel (open Sundays only). The outdoor carillon was a gift from the Spanish government: the bells are named after Columbus's ships. ■ *0800-1930, T224 4073.*

South of the TV tower on Av W3 Sul, at Quadra 702, is the Sanctuary of **Dom Bosco**, a gothic-style building with narrow windows filled with blue glass mosaics, purple at the four corners; the light inside is most beautiful. ■ *0800-1800, T223 6542.*

The **Templo da Boa Vontade**, Setor Garagem Sul 915, lotes 75/76, is a seven-faced pyramid topped by one of the world's largest crystals, a peaceful place dedicated to all philosophies and religions. ■ *T245 1070, open 24 hrs. Take bus 151 from outside the Centro do Convenções or on Eixo Sul to Centro Médico.*

Lago Do Paranoá

Palácio da Alvorada

Palácio do Jaburu

Palácio do Planalto

Praça dos Três Poderes

Avenida das Nações

N

Not to scale

A permanent memorial to Juscelino Kubitschek, the '**Memorial JK**', contains his tomb and his car, together with a lecture hall and exhibits. ■ *Daily 0900-1745, US$0.50, has toilets and lanchonete.* Some 15 km out along the Belo Horizonte road is the small wooden house, known as '**O Catetinho**', in which President Kubitschek stayed in the late 1950s during his visits to the city when it was under construction; it is open to visitors and most interesting. The **Monumental Parade Stand** has unique and mysterious acoustic characteristics (the complex is north of the Eixo Monumental, between the 'Memorial JK' and the rodoferroviária). There are remarkable stained glass panels, each representing a state of the Federation, on the ground floor of the Caixa Econômica Federal.

Excursions

Brazil

Northwest of Brasília, but only 15 minutes by car from the centre, is the **Parque Nacional de Brasília** (about 28,000 ha), founded in 1961 to conserve the flora and fauna of the Federal Capital. Only a portion of the park is open to the public without a permit. There is a swimming pool fed by clear river water, a snack bar and a series of trails through gallery forest (popular with joggers in the early morning and at weekends). The rest of the park is rolling grassland, gallery forest and *cerrado* vegetation. Large mammals include tapir, maned wolf and pampas deer; birdwatching is good. ■ *Contact* Ibama, *SAIN, Av L/4 Lote 04/08, Ed Sede do Ibama, T316 1080, or the park's office, Via Epia SMU, T233 3251, F233 5543.*

Sleeping

Prices include breakfast, but 10% must be added. Weekend discounts of 30% are often available, but must be asked for. It is not advisable to walk around at night

See Essentials for new telephone number changes

In the Southern Hotel Sector L *Nacional*, Quadra 1 bloco A, T321 7575, hotelnacional@hotelnacional.com.br Cavernous, old-fashioned and a city landmark with many tour agencies located outside. **A** *Alvorada*, Quadra 4 bloco A, T332 1122, alvoradahotel@zaz.com.br Comfortable high rise with good view from roof terrace. **A** *Bristol*, Qd 4 bloco F, T321 6162, bristolh@tba.com.br Very traditional, piano bar, 24 hr room service. **D** *Pousada da Nilza*, W3 Sul, quadra 703, bloco A, casa 54, T226 5786, F225 5902. Family-run, range of rooms, functional, but one of few cheaper options in area.

In the Northern Hotel Sector AL *Aracoara*, Qd 5 bloco C, T3289222, F3289067, www.aracoara.com.br Four-star, 24-hr room service and international restaurant. One road gives access to: **A** *Aristus*, Quadra 2 bloco O, T328 8675, F326 5415. Good, a/c, TV, phone, money exchange, small restaurant. **A** *Casablanca*, Qd 3 bloco A, T3288586, casablanca@brasilia.com.br More intimate than most of hotels in this area. **B** *El Pilar*, Quadra 3 bloco F, T328 5915, F328 9088. A/c or fan, TV. **C** *Mirage*, Quadra 2 lote N, T225 7150. Fan, good value. And others. Moderately-priced hotels can be found in the Northern Hotel Sector only. **D** *Cury's Solar*, HIGS 707, Bloco I, Casa 15, T11362 52/244 1899, www.conectanet.com.br/curyssolar Cramped but helpful, safe, around 30 mins from the centre (Eixo Monumental) along W3 Sul. Recommended. **D** *Pensão da Zenilda*, W3 Sul Quadra 704, Bloco Q, Casa 29, T224 7532. Safe.

Teresa Tasso, SQN312-'K'-505, T273 4844 or 272 4243, offers accommodation in an apartment in the Asa Sul at US$20 pp (sleeps 5, kitchen, bath, laundry facilities), excellent value, Teresa gives city tours for US$15-20 pp for 3-4 hrs, and will collect you at the airport if you phone in advance (bus to flat from centre, 5 mins). Rooms to let (**D-C**) from: *Getúlio Valente*, warmly recommended, Av W3 Sul, HIGS 703, Bl N casas 10, 34, near the TV tower, good, cheap meals available, Portuguese speakers T226 8507/225 5021 and Getúlio will pick you up; otherwise, turn right off Av W3 Sul between 703 and 702, then take first left (an unpaved driveway). The tourist office has a list of *pensões*.

Camping The city's main site is 2 km out of the centre, by the Centro Esportivo, near the motor-racing track, with room for 3,100 campers, mixed reports. Take bus 109 (infrequent) from municipal rodoviária. Água Mineral Parque, 6 km northwest of city, direct buses only at weekend, mineral pool, showers. **Associação Brasileira de Camping** (Edif Márcia, 12th floor, Setor Comercial Sul, T225 8768) has two sites: one at Km 19 on the Belo Horizonte road and one 25 km northeast of Brasília at Sobradinho. *Camping Clube do Brasil* has a site at Itiquira waterfall, 100 km northeast of the city, near Formosa; information from Edif Maristela, room 1214, Setor Comercial Sul, T223 6561.

Eating

Southern Hotel Sector tends to have more restaurants than the Northern. At weekends few restaurants in central Brasília open

Asa Norte Expensive: All the large hotels in this area have upmarket restaurants, most catering to business visitors. **Mid range**: *Boa Saúde*, Av W3 Norte Quadra 702, Edif Brasília Rádio Center. Vegetarian open Sun-Fri 0800-2000. *Bom Demais*, Av W3 Norte, Qd 706. Comfortable, serving fish, beef and rice etc, live music at weekends (cover charge US$0.50). *Churrascaria do Lago*, SHTN, Conj 1-A, by Palácio da Alvorada, a number of Brazilian restaurants and some serving Amazonian food. *El Hadj*, in Hotel Torre Palace, Setor Hoteleiro Norte, Qd 4 bloco A. Very good Arabic food. **Cheap**: *Conjunto Nacional*, SDN, Cj A, enormous mall and food court with 50 restaurants. *Habib's*, SCN Quadra 4. Arabic food and pizzas at bargain prices at this upmarket chain restaurant. Recommended. The municipal rodoviária provides the best coffee and *pasteis* in town (bottom departure level).

Brazil

Asa Sul Expensive: *Gaf*, Centro Gilberto Salomão, Lago Sul, excellent international food, especially meat dishes. *Le Français*, Av W3 Sul, Qd 404, bloco B. French food served in bistro atmosphere, classic and modern dishes. *La Chaumière*, Av W3 Sul, quadra 408, bloco A. Traditional French cuisine in suitable surroundings, established 1966, no smoking. *Porcão*, Sector de Clubes Sul, Trecho 2, cj 35, lt 2B. Upmarket chain restaurant specialising in *churrasco*, piano bar, large veranda. **Mid range**: *China in Box*, Comércio local Sul 402, bloco C, loja 13. Reliable Chinese, delivery service. *Kazebre 13*, Av W3 Sul, Qd 504, loja 2. Traditional Italian. *O Espanhol*, Av W3 Sul, Qd 404, bloco C, loja 07. Spanish paella and seafood, open daily. *Roma*, Av W3 Sul, Qds 501 and 511. Good value Italian. **Cheap**: *Cedro do Líbano*, SCS, Qd 6, bloco A, loja 218. Self-service, some Arabic dishes, friendly, closes 2200. Recommended. *Centro Venâncio 2000* at the beginning of Av W3 Sul, has several budget options, including *Salada Mista*, lunch only. *Coisas da Terra*, SCS, Qd 5, bloco B, loja 41. Comfortable self-service, lunch only. Recommended. There are many cheap places on Avenida W3 Sul, eg at Blocos 502 and 506.

Snack bars: (ie those serving *prato feito* or *comercial*, cheap set meals) can be found all over the city, especially on Av W3 and in the Setor Comercial Sul. Other good bets are the Conjunto Nacional and the Conjunto Venâncio, 2 shopping/office complexes on either side of the municipal rodoviária. Tropical fruit flavour ice cream can be found in various parlours, eg Av W3 Norte 302. Freshly made fruit juices in all bars.

Bars/pubs *Gates Pub*, Av W3 Sul 403, T2254576, with disco; and *London Tavern*, Av W3 Sul 409. The *Grenada* bar near the *Hotel Nacional* has good pavement atmosphere in early evening. Nightclubs in Conjunto Venâncio, Centro Gilberto Salomão and in the main hotels. *Bier Fass*, SHS Q 5, bloco E, loja 52/53, cavernous restaurant/bar with wine cellar, live music Tue-Sun, open to 0200. *Dom Quichopp Choparia*, SLCS 110, bloco A, loja 17, open Tue-Sun 1630-0300, sports theme bar.

Nightlife & entertainment

Information about entertainment etc is available in 2 daily papers, *Jornal de Brasília* and *Correio Brasiliense*. Any student card (provided it has a photograph) will get you into the cinema/theatre/concert hall for half price. Ask for 'uma meia' at the box office. **Cinema Pier 21**, SCSS, Trecho 2, Cj 32/33, is an enormous complex with 13 cinema screens, nightclubs, restaurants, video bars and children's theme park. **Theatre** There are 3 auditoria of the *Teatro Nacional*, Setor Cultural Norte, Via N 2, next to the bus station, T325 6109, foyer open 0900-2000, box office open at 1400; the building is in the shape of an Aztec pyramid. The Federal District authorities have 2 theatres, the *Galpão* and *Galpãozinho*, between Quadra 308 Sul and Av W3 Sul. There are several other concert halls. *Planetarium*, Setor de Divulgação Cultural, T325 6245. West Eixo Monumental next to the TV tower, being restored in 2002.

Ash Wednesday; *Holy Thursday*, half-day; **8 Dec** (Immaculate Conception); *Christmas Eve*.

Local holidays

Shopping complexes include the vast **Conjunto Nacional** on the north side of the rodoviária, the **Conjunto Venâncio** on the south side, the **Centro Venâncio 2000** at the beginning of Av W3 Sul, the **Centro Venâncio 3000** in the Setor Comercial Norte, **Parkshopping** and the **Carrefour** hypermarket just off the exit to Guará, 12 km from centre. For handicrafts from all the Brazilian states try *Galeria dos Estados* (which runs underneath the *eixo* from Setor Comercial Sul to Setor Bancário Sul, 10 mins' walk from municipal rodoviária, south along Eixo Rodoviário Sul). For Amerindian handicrafts, *Artíndia*, SRTVS, Qd 702, also in the rodoviária and at the airport. There is a *feira hippy* at the base of the TV tower Sat, Sun and holidays: leather goods, wood carvings, jewellery, bronzes. English books (good selection) at *Livraria Sodiler* in Conjunto Nacional and at the airport (stocks *Footprint*).

Shopping

Buriti Turismo, SCLS 402, bloco A, lojas 27/33, Asa Sul, T225 2686, American Express representative. *Presmic Turismo*, SHS Q 1 Bloco A, loja, 35, T225 5515. Full, half-day and night-time city tours (0845, 1400 and 1930 respectively). *Toscana* SCLS 413, Bloco D, loja 22/24, T242 9233. Recommended as cheap and good. 3-4 hr city tours with English commentary can also be booked at the airport by arriving air passengers – a convenient way of

Tour operators
Many tour operators have their offices in the shopping arcade of the Hotel Nacional

Brazil

getting to your hotel if you have heavy baggage. Some tours have been criticized as too short, others that the guides speak poor English, and for night-time tours, the flood lighting is inadequate on many buildings.

Transport **Air** Airport, 12 km from centre, T354 9000. Frequent daily flights to **Rio** and **São Paulo** (1½ hrs in both cases) and to main cities. Bus 102 or 118 to airport, regular, US$0.65, 30 mins. Taxi is US$10 (meter rate 2 used to airport), worth it. Left luggage facilities at airport (tokens for lockers, US$0.50).

Bus The bus terminal (rodoferroviária, T363 2281) beside the railway station, from which long-distance buses leave, has post office (0800-1700, Sat 0800-1200) and telephone facilities. Bus 131 between rodoviária, the municipal terminal, and rodoferroviária, US$1.25; taxi rodoferroviária to Setor Hoteleiro Norte, US$9. There are showers (US$0.50). Both bus stations have large luggage lockers. To **Rio**: 17 hrs, 6 *comuns* (US$32) and 3 *leitos* (about US$64) daily. To **São Paulo**: 16 hrs, 7 *comuns* (about US$30) and 2 *leitos* (about US$60) daily (*Rápido Federal* recommended). To **Belo Horizonte**: 12 hrs, 9 *comuns* (US$20) and 2 *leitos* (US$40) daily. To **Belém**: 36 hrs, 4 daily (US$55, *Trans Brasília* T233 7589). To **Recife**: 40 hrs, US$49-60. To **Salvador**: 24 hrs, 3 daily (US$40). To **Cuiabá**: 17½ hrs (US$30) daily at 1200 with *São Luis*. **Mato Grosso**: generally *Goiânia* seems to be the better place for Mato Grosso destinations. **Barra do Garças**: 0830 and 2000, takes 9 hrs with *Araguarina*, T233 7598, US$13.20 return. All major destinations served. Bus tickets for major companies are sold in a subsidiary office in Taguatinga, Centro Oeste, C8, Lotes 1 and 2, Loja 1; and at the city rodoviária.

Car hire: all large companies are represented at the airport and the Car Rental Sector. Multinational agencies and *Interlocadora*, airport, T365 2511. *Unidas*, T365 3343, and at airport, T365 1412.

Directory **Airline offices** *BRA*, SHS Quadra 1, bloco A, loja 71/72, in front of *Nacional Hotel*, T321 7070. *GOL*, airport, T364 9370, premium rate number, T0300-7892121. *Rio-Sul/Nordeste*, SCLN 306, bloco B, loja 24, T242 2590; airport T365 9020. *TAM/Brasil Central*, SHN Hotel Nacional, Gallery Store, 36/37, T325 1300; airport, T365 1000. *Varig*, SCN Qd 4, bloco B, T329 1240; airport, T364 9219. *Vasp*, SCLN 304, bloco E, lojas 80/100, T329 0404; airport, T365 3037.

Banks Foreign currency (but not always Amex cheques) can be exchanged at branches of: *Banco Regional de Brasília*, SBS Q 1, Bl E, T412 8282 and *Banco do Brasil*, Setor Bancário Sul, latter also at airport (ATM, bank open weekends and holidays), charges US$20 commission for TCs. *American Express*, SCS Q 6, Edif Federação do Comércio, 1st floor, T321 6570. *MasterCard* office, SCRN 502, Bl B, loja 31-32, T225 5550, for cash against card; ATMs at *Citibank*, SCS Quadra 06, bloco A, loja 186, T215 8000, *HSBC*, SCRS 502, bloco A, lojas 7/12, and *Banco 24 Horas* at airport, and all over the city, including the Rodoferroviária. Good exchange rates at *Hotel Nacional* and hotels with 'exchange-turismo' sign.

Communications Internet: *Café.Com.Tato*, CLS 505, bloco C, loja 17, Asa Sul, open daily. *Liverpool Coffee Shop*, CLS 108, R da Igreijinha. **Post Office:** Poste restante, Central Correio, 70001; SBN-Cj 03, BL-A, Ed Sede da ECT, the central office is in the Setor Hoteleiro Sul, between *Hotels Nacional* and *St Paul*. Another post office is in Ed Brasília Rádio, Av 3 Norte

Cultural centres British Council, Setor C Sul, quadra 01, Bloco H, 8th floor, Morro Vermelho Building, T323 6080. **Cultura Inglesa**, SEPS 709/908 Conj B, T243 3065. **American Library**, Casa Thomas Jefferson, Av W4 Sul, quadra 706, T243 6588. **Aliança Francesa**, Sul Entrequadra 707-907, Bloco A, T242 7500. **Instituto Cultural Goethe**, Edifício Dom Bosco, Setor Garagem Sul 902, Lote 73, Bloco C, T224 6773, Mon-Fri, 0800-1200, also 1600-2000, Mon, Wed, Thu.

Embassies and consulates Australia: Caixa Postal 11-1256, SHIS QI-09, Conj 16, Casa 1, T248 5569. **Austria**: SES, Av das Nações 40, T243 3111. **Canada**: SES, Av das Nações 16, T321 2171. **Denmark**: Av das Nações 26, T443 8188, 0900-1200, 1400-1700. **Finland**: SES, Av das Nações, lote 27, T443 7151. Germany: SES, Av das Nações 25, T443 7330. **Greece**: SES, Av das Nações, T443 6573. **Guyana**: SDS, Edifício Venâncio III, 4th floor, sala 410/404, T224 9229. **Netherlands**: SES, Av das Nações 5, T321 4769. New Zealand, SHIS Q1 09, conj 16, casa 01, Lgo Sul, T248 9900, F248 9916, zelandia@terra.com.br **South Africa**: SES, Av das Nações, lote 06, T312 9503. **Sweden**: Av das Nações 29, Caixa Postal 07-0419, T243 1444. **Switzerland**: SES, Av das Nações 41, T443 5500. **UK**: SES, Quadra 801, Conjunto K (with British Commonwealth Chamber of Commerce), Av das Nações, T225 2710, F225 1777, www.reinounido.org.br **US**: SES, Av das Nações 3, T321 7272. **Venezuela**: SES, Av das Nações 13, T223 9325.

Tourist offices At the Centro de Convenções, 3rd floor, **Adetur**, helpful, good map of Brasília, open to public 0800-1200, 1300-1800, some English spoken, T325 5700, F225 5706; small stand at rodoferroviária (open daily 0800-2000), friendly but not very knowledgeable. Airport tourist office, T325 5730, open daily 0800-2000, will book hotels, limited English and information, no maps of the city. **Embratur** head office, Setor Comercial Norte, Quadra 02, bloco G, CEP 70710-500, T224 9100, F323 8936, webmaster@embratur.gov.br The information office in the centre of Praça dos Tres Poderes has a colourful map and lots of useful text information. The staff are friendly and have interesting information about Brasília and other places in Goiás – only Portuguese spoken. **Maps** 'Comapa', Venâncio 200 business complex, 2nd floor, have expensive maps.

Voltage 220 volts, 60 cycles.

From Saída Sul (the southern end of the Eixo) the BR-040/050 goes to **Cristalina** where it divides; the BR-040 continues to Belo Horizonte and Rio, the BR-050 to Uberlândia and São Paulo (both paved). Also from Saída Sul, the BR-060 goes to Anápolis, Goiânia and Cuiabá; from Anápolis the BR-153 (Belém-Brasília) heads north to Belém (paved – for a description of this road, see page 573) and from Goiânia the BR-153 goes south through the interior of the states of São Paulo and Paraná (also paved).

Leaving Brasília

From Saída Norte (the northern end of the Eixo) the BR-020 goes northeast to **Formosa** (1½ hours by frequent buses from Brasília, **D** *Hotel Mineiro* and one other, cheaper, clean and friendly; cheap restaurants), Barreiras (*colour map 5, grid C2*), and after Barreiras on the BR-242 (all paved) to Salvador and Fortaleza. The BR-020 is in good condition for 120 km. At Alvorada do Norte (130 km) there are cheap but very basic hotels. **Posse** (295 km, *colour map 5, grid C2*) is picturesque (accommodation on Av Padre Trajeiro, including *Hoki Mundial*, friendly).

Goiânia

Just off the BR-060, 209 km southwest of Brasília: the second (after Belo Horizonte) of Brazil's planned state capitals, Goiânia was founded in 1933 and replaced Goiás Velho as capital four years later. It is a spacious city, with many green spaces and well-lit main avenues, ornamented with plants, radiating out from the central **Praça Cívica**, on which stand the Government Palace and main Post Office. Just off the Praça Cívica is the **Museu Estadual 'Zoroastro Artiaga'**, Praça Dr P L Teixeira 13, has a collection of local handicrafts, religious objects, animals and Indian artefacts. **Museu Antropológico do UFG** on the Praça Universitária (1 km east of Praça Cívica) has wide-ranging ethnographic displays on the Indians of the Centre West. ■ *Mon-Fri 0900-1700.*

Phone code: 0xx62
Post code: 74000
Colour map 7, grid A3
Population: 1.1 million city; state of Goiás 5.0 million

L *Castro's Park*, Av República do Líbano 1520, Setor Oeste, T223 7766, F225 7070. Warmly recommended. **A** *Karajás*, Av Goiás e R 3 No 860, T224 9666, F229 1153, 3 blocks north of Praça. Convenient and comfortable. **A** *Vila Rica*, Av Anhangüera 5308, T223 2733, F223 2625. 2-star Embratur hotel, a/c, convenient. **C** *Príncipe*, Anhangüera 2936 e Av Araguaia, T224 0085. Fans, good value. Several cheap hotels (**C-D**) near the rodoviária. Northwest of the rodoviária are many cheap *dormitórios*.

Sleeping
Av Anhangüera, on which many hotels are located, runs east-west 4 blocks north of the Centro Cívico; it is busy and noisy

Camping At *Itanhangá* municipal site, Av Princesa Carolina, 13 km, T292 1145, attractive wooded location, reasonable facilities.

There are many *churrascarias*. Goiânia is famous for its street bars, some with live music. Av Ricardo Paranhos, Setor Sul, is full of bars and crowds of young people after 2000. For **regional specialities** try the *Centro de Tradições Goiánas*, R 4 No 515 (above the Parthenon Centre), rice and fish cuisine. *Piquiras*, Av República do Líbano 1758 (near *Castro's Hotel*) and R 139/R 146 No 464, T2814344, Setor Marista. Try the appetizer *pastelzinho de piquí* (a regional fruit used in many traditional Goiás dishes). Street stands (*pamonharias*) sell *pamonha* snacks, tasty pastries made with green corn, sweet, savoury, or *picante*/spicy; all are served hot and have cheese in the middle, some include sausage. Recommended are: *Pomonharia 100*, R 101 esq R Dr Olinto Manso Pereira, behind the Forum, Setor Sul.

Eating
Goiânia is much cheaper for eating than Brasília

Brazil

Frutos da Terra, Av Perimetral 669, for home delivery T233 1507/281 4049. *Pura*, Av 83 No 193, Setor Sul. Local meat pies (*empadões de Goiás*) are also delicious.

Shopping Ceramic, sisal and wooden handicrafts from *Centro Estadual do Artesanato*, Praça do Trabalhador (0800-1800). Sun handicrafts markets at the Praça Cívica (morning) and Praça do Sol (afternoon). The latter starts after 1530, until 2100, known as the Honey Fair as all types of honey are sold. Also good for a Sun snack, with many sweets sold along the street.

Transport **Air** Santa Genoveva, 6 km northeast off R 57 (T207 1288). Daily flights to main cities and many provincial centres. Several car hire firms at the airport. Taxi from centre US$6. *Varig*, Av Goiás 285, T224 5059; *Vasp*, R 3 No 569, T224 6389.

Bus Rodoviária on R 44 No 399 in the Norte Ferroviário sector, about a 40-min walk to downtown (T224 8466). Buses 'Rodoviária-Centro' (No 404) and 'Vila União-Centro' (No 163) leave from stop on city side of terminal, US$0.80; No 163 goes on to the Praça Tamandaré.

To **Brasília**, 207 km, at least 15 departures a day, 2½ hrs, US$5, and **São Paulo**, 900 km via Barretos, US$25, 14½ hrs. To **Goiás Velho**, hourly from 0500, 2½ hrs, US$5. **Pirenópolis** 0700 and 1700, 2 hrs, US$5. **Campo Grande**, 935 km, 4 services daily, 18 hrs, US$32.

To **Cuiabá** (Mato Grosso) for the Pantanal, most buses take the BR-060/364 via Jataí, 928 km (paved), 4 buses a day, US$25.20, 15-16 hrs. Another route is 916 km on BR-158/070 via Aragarças (on the Goiás side) and **Barra do Garças** (on the Mato Grosso side of the Rio Araguaia). Barra (*population*: 52,092) is the pleasanter of the two and has the better facilities, including several banks and hotels. At Iporá, 200 km west of Goiânia on BR-158, there is a good hotel. From Barra there is a bus to São Félix do Araguaia (for Ilha do Bananal, see below) at 2000, US$21, arrives early afternoon, wildlife may be seen in the early morning.

Directory **Tourist offices** Sictur, Centro Administrativo, Praça Cívica s/n, 7th floor, CEP 74319-000, T223 0669, F223 3911, and **Dirtur**, R 30 corner of R 4, Centro de Convenções, CEP 74025-020, T217 1121, F217 2256. Extensive information, maps and bus routes in *Novo Guia Turístico de Goiás*, readily available at news stands, US$2.25.

Anápolis
Phone code: 0xx62
Post code: 75000
Colour map 7, grid A3
Population: 288,085

A busy trading centre 57 km nearer Brasília, Anápolis has the **Centro de Gemologia de Goiás**, Quadra 2, Módulo 13, Daia, about 10 km out on the Brasília highway (near the Embratel tower). It has a fine collection of gemstones, library, sales and lapidary courses, and will show visitors how real and synthetic gemstones are distinguished. ■ *Mon-Fri 0730-1630*.

Accommodation is cheaper than the capital and more convenient than Goiânia

At Anápolis the BR-153 (Brasília-Belém) turns north and begins the long haul (1,964 km) through Tocantins, Maranhão and Pará to Belém, a bumpy, monotonous trip of 35 hours or more, US$55. There are regular bus services to Pirenópolis (66 km north).

Goiás Velho
Colour map 7, grid A2
Population: 27,120
144 km NW of Goiânia

NB Most churches and museums are closed on Mon

The former state capital is a picturesque old gold-mining town (founded 1727 as Vila Boa) with narrow streets, seven baroque churches and many well-preserved 18th-century colonial mansions and government buildings. The oldest church, **São Francisco de Paula** (1761), Praça Alves de Castro, faces the Market. There is a good view of the town from **Santa Bárbara** church (1780) on the R Passo da Pátria. Also worth visiting are: the **Museu da Boa Morte**, in the colonial church of the same name (a small, but interesting collection of old images, paintings, etc). The old **Government Palace** is next to the red-brick Cathedral in the main praça. The **Palácio Conde dos Arcos**, Praça Castelo Branco (across from the Cathedral), still has its original 1755 furniture on display. ■ *Tue-Sat 0800-1700, Sun 0800-1200*. **The 18th century Mercado Municipal** is next to the rodoviária, 500 m west of the central Praça do Coreto. Visit the *Centro de Tradições Goianas*, in *Hotel Vila Boa*, and (cheaper) *Associação dos Artesãos de Goiás*, at the Rosário Church and in the Municipal Market, for local crafts. Many types of sugary sweets can be purchased direct from the bakeries. The streets of Goiás Velho blaze with torches during the solemn *Fogaréu* processions of Holy Week, when hooded figures re-enact Christ's descent

Brazil

from the cross and burial. ■ *The rodoviária is 2 km out of town. Regular bus services to Goiânia (2½ hrs), Aruanã, Barra do Garças and Jussara.*

Sleeping and eating AL *Vila Boa*, Av Dr Deusdete Ferreira de Moura, 1 km southeast on the Morro do Chapéu do Padre, T371 1000. Pool, bar, restaurant, a/c, good views. Recommended. **D** *Araguaia*, Av Ferreira de Moura (the road into town from the south), T371 1462. Best budget place, fans, comfortable. Recommended. **D** *Pousada do Ipê*, R Boa Vista 32. Breakfast included, great lunch, garden. **Camping** Attractive, well-run *Cachoeira Grande* campground, 7 km along the BR-070 to Jussara (near the tiny airport), with bathing place and snack bar. More basic site (*Chafariz da Carioca*) in town by the river.

This lovely colonial silver-mining town in the red hills of Goiás was founded in 1727 and declared a National Heritage Site in 1989. As the nation's unofficial silver capital, shopping for jewellery and related items here is unsurpassed. Pirenópolis was the birthplace of José Joaquim da Veiga Valle, the 'Aleijadinho of Goiás', many of whose works are in the Boa Morte museum in Goiás Velho. *Festa do Divino Espírito Santo*, 45 days after Easter (Pentecost), is one of Brazil's most famous and extraordinary folkloric/religious celebrations, lasting three days, with medieval costumes, tournaments, dances and mock battles between Moors and Christians, a tradition held annually since 1819.

The **Igreja Matriz Nossa Senhora do Rosário** is the oldest church in the state (1728), but that of **Nosso Senhor de Bonfim** (1750-54), with three impressive altars and an image of the Virgin brought from Portugal, is the most beautiful. A museum of religious art is housed in the church of **Nossa Senhora do Carmo** (open daily 1300-1700), and another displays regional historical items, the **Museu Família Pompeu**, R Nova 33. ■ *Tue-Fri 1300-1700, Sat 1300-1500, Sun 0900-1200.*

Pirenópolis
Colour map 7, grid A3
Population: 21,245
Altitude: 770 m
165 km due west of Brasília

Sleeping A *Hotel Fazenda Quinta da Santa Bárbara*, in garden setting at R do Bonfim 1, T/F331 1304. All facilities including *Restaurante Brasília*. **C** *Pousada das Cavalhadas*, Praça da Matriz, T331 1261. Central, fans, fridges in rooms, best of the budget choices. All accommodation is filled during the Festa (see above) and even the downtown municipal camping site beside the Rio das Alvas overflows; better to visit from Brasília at this time.

In the elevated region 200 km north of Brasília is the popular **Chapada dos Veadeiros**. The main attractions are a number of high waterfalls complete with palm-shaded oases and natural swimming pools, and the varied wildlife: capybara, rhea, tapir, wolf, toucan, etc. ■ *US$0.50, Ibama R 219 No 95, Setor Universitário, 74605-800 Goiânia, T0xx62-224 2488, or T0xx61-646 1109.* There is a small hotel (**D**) by the rodoviária in Alto Paraíso and a very basic *dormitório* in São Jorge (take sleeping bag or hammock). The best season to visit is May-October. ■ *Getting there: The park is reached by paved state highway 118 to Alto Paraíso de Goiás, then gravel road west towards Colinas for 30 km where a sign marks the turnoff (just before São Jorge village). Buses Brasília-Alto Paraíso 1000 and 2200, US$3.60; occasional local buses Alto Paraíso-São Jorge, includes 1600 departure, then 5-km walk to entrance.*

Parque Nacional Chapada dos Veadeiros & Emas

In the far southwest of the state, covering the watershed of the Araguaia, Taquari and Formoso rivers, is the small **Parque Nacional Emas**, 98 km south of Mineiros just off the main BR-364 route between Brasília and Cuiabá (112 km beyond Jataí). Almost 132,868 ha of undulating grasslands and *cerrado* contain the **world's largest concentration of termite mounds**. Pampas deer, giant anteater, greater rhea, or 'ema' in Portuguese, and maned wolf are frequently seen roaming the grasses. The park holds the greatest concentration of blue-and-yellow macaws outside Amazônia, and blue-winged, red-shouldered and red-bellied macaws can also be seen. (There are many other animals and birds.) Along with the grasslands, the park supports a vast marsh on one side and rich gallery forests on the other. As many of the interesting mammals are nocturnal, a spotlight is a must.

Brazil

Sleeping Mineiros A *Pilões Palace*, Praça Alves de Assis, T661 1547. Restaurant, comfortable. **C** *Boi na Brasa*, R Onze 11, T661 1532. No a/c, good *churrasco* restaurant attached. Next door **D** *Mineiros Hotel*, with bath and huge breakfast, good lunch. Recommended. Dorm accommodation at the park headquarters; kitchen and cook available but bring own food.

Transport The park is 6 hrs by car from Campo Grande, about 20 hrs from Goiânia, paved road poor. The road to the park is paved; twice weekly bus from Mineiros. The São José monastery, Mineiros, can arrange the necessary permission to visit, turn left out of the rodoviária and walk 500 m along dirt road (or from *Ibama*, as above, also from *Secretaria de Turismo*, Praça Col Carrijo 1, T661 1551). Day trips are not recommended, but 4-day, 3-night visits to the Park can be arranged through agencies (eg *Focus Tours*, see Special Interest Travel).

The Rio Araguaia: north of Goiânia

Yellow-fever vaccination is recommended for the region. Borrachudas, tiny biting insects, are an unavoidable fact of life in Central Brazil in June and July; repellent helps a little

Brazilians are firmly convinced that the 2,630-km-long Rio Araguaia is richer in fish than any other in the world. A visit to the 220-km stretch between **Aruanã** (a port 180 km northwest of Goiás Velho by paved road), and the Ilha do Bananal during the fishing season is quite an experience. As the receding waters in May reveal sparkling white beaches, thousands of Brazilian and international enthusiasts pour into the area. As many as 400 tent 'cities' spring up, and vast quantities of fish are hauled in before the phenomenon winds down in September, when the rivers begin to rise again and flood the surrounding plains.

Ilha do Bananal
Colour map 5, grid C1 Home to a variety of rare wildlife

Bananal is the **world's largest river island**, located in the state of Tocantins. The island is formed by a division in the south of the Rio Araguaia and is approximately 320 km long. The entire island was originally a national park (**Parque Nacional Araguaia**), but it has been reduced from two million ha to its current size of 562,312 ha. The island, and especially the park, form one of the more spectacular wildlife areas on the continent, in many ways similar to the Pantanal. The vegetation is a transition zone between the *cerrado* (woody savanna) and Amazon forests, with gallery forests along the many waterways. There are several marshlands throughout the island. The fauna is also transitional. More than 300 bird species are found here, including the hoatzin, hyacinthine macaw, harpy eagle and black-fronted piping guan. The giant anteater, maned wolf, bush dog, giant otter, jaguar, puma, marsh deer, pampas deer, American tapir, yellow anaconda and South American river turtle also occur here. The island is flooded most of the year, with the prime visiting (dry) season being from June to early October, when the beaches are exposed. Unfortunately, the infrastructure for tourism aside from fishing expeditions is very limited. ■ *Permission to visit the park should be obtained in advance from Ibama, R 219, No 95, Setor Universitário, 74605-800 Goiânia.*

São Félix do Araguaia
Colour map 5, grid C1 Mosquito nets are highly recommended: high incidence of malaria

Bananal can be visited from São Félix do Araguaia . Many Carajás indians are found in town; a depot of their handicrafts is between the *Pizzaria* and *Mini Hotel* on Av Araguaia. With permission from Funai in the town, you cross the river to the Carajá village of **Santa Isabela de Morra** and ask to see the chief, who can tell you the history of the tribe. **Tours** Many river trips are available for fishing or to see wildlife. Juracy Lopes, a very experienced guide, can be contacted through *Hotel Xavante*; he has many friends, including the chief and council, in Santa Isabela. *Icuryala* is recommended, T0xx62-223 9518 (Goiânia), excellent food, drink, and service, US$100 per day, independent visitors also welcomed. Another access to Bananal is through the small but pleasant town of **Santa Teresinha** which is north of São Felix. A charming hotel is the **A** *Bananal*, Praça Tarcila Braga 106, CEP 78395 (Mato Grosso), with full board.

Sleeping and eating A very simple hotel with the best view in São Félix is the **C** *Mini Hotel Araguaia*, Av Araguaia 344, T0xx65-522 1154. Includes breakfast. They have a/c rooms, not recommended, electricity is turned off at night and the closed-in room gets very hot. Recommended is **C** *Xavante*, Av Severiano Neves 391, T522 1305. A/c, shower, frigobar, excellent breakfast, delicious *cajá* juice, Sr e Sra Carvalho very hospitable. A good restaurant is the **Pizzaria Cantinho da Peixada** on Av Araguaia, next to the Texaco station, overlooking the river: the owner, Klaus, rents rooms, **E**, better than hotels, T522 1320, he also arranges fishing trips. Recommended.

Transport Air Access to both Santa Teresinha and São Félix is by *Brasil Central/TAM* flights, unreliable and, as the planes hold just 15 passengers, it is common to get held over for a day or two. **Bus** to São Félix from Barra do Garças, see above. Rodoviária is 3 km from the centre and waterfront, taxi US$5; buses to Barra do Garças at 0500, arrive 2300, or 1730, arrive 1100 next day.

The Brasília-Belém highway runs through the new state of Tocantins (277,322 sq km). **Palmas** is the state capital and the newest city in Brazil. It is not really on the tourist trail yet. There are hotels and restaurants and waterfalls in the surrounding mountains and beaches on the River Tocantins. For tourist information *ACSE*, 01-conjunto 04, lote 10, Ed Jamir Resende, 2nd floor, CEP 77100-100, Palmas, TO, T0xx63- 215 1156, F0xx63-215 1494. At Fátima, on the BR-153, a paved road heads east 52 km to a new bridge over the Rio Tocantins to **Porto Nacional** (*Post code*: 77500-000. *Phone code*: 0xx63). From here a road runs north to Palmas, 55 km. Porto Nacional has hotels, restaurants and a regional airport.

At **Guaraí** the road forks, one branch goes to **Araguaína**, whereafter the BR-226 goes to Estreito in Maranhão, from where the BR-010 runs north through Imperatriz to Belém. The other continues west into Pará, then turns north to Xinguara and on to Marabá on the Transamazônica. For a real adventure, the unpaved PA 279 heads west from Xinguara 250 km to **São Félix do Xingú**, at the confluence of the Xingú and Fresco rivers. Christopher W M Read (Hove, UK) writes: "The Xingú is truly beautiful, with the green wall of the forest on either side and the most spectacular sunsets." An American, Russ Clement, runs *Adventure Xingú Camp*, two hours upriver, for birdwatching, fishing, jungle safaris. He is an authority on local tribes and has endless stories. He and his wife, Sonia, have the *Xingú Lodge Restaurant* in town (**E**, good food, T0xx91-435 1246, www.xingusafaris.com; in USA T304-728 3884). ■ *Bus Goiânia- São Félix do Xingú 1900, 36 hrs minimum, US$40* (Monte Belo).

Mato Grosso do Sul and Mato Grosso

The Pantanal is a mecca for wildlife tourism or fishing. Whether land or river-based, seasonal variations make a great difference to the practicalities of getting there and what you will experience. Other worthwhile places to go are the ancient landscapes of the Chapada dos Guimarães and the lovely area around Bonito.

To the west of Goiás are the states of Mato Grosso and Mato Grosso do Sul, with a **Background** combined area of 1,231,549 sq km and a population of only about 4.6 million, or about three people to the sq km. The two states are half covered with forest, with the large wetland area (230,000 sq km) called the Pantanal (roughly west of a line between Campo Grande and Cuiabá, between which there is a direct road), partly flooded in the rainy season (see page 581). Cattle ranching is very important, with over 21 million head of beef cattle on 16 million ha of free range pasture in Mato Grosso do Sul alone. A road runs across Mato Grosso do Sul via Campo Grande to Porto Esperança and Corumbá, both on the Rio Paraguai; much of the road is across the wetland, offering many sights of birds and other wildlife.

Brazil

Campo Grande

Phone code: 0xx67
Post code: 79000
Colour map 7, grid B1
Population: 663,621

Capital of the State of Mato Grosso do Sul. It was founded in 1899. It is a pleasant, modern city. Because of the *terra roxa* (red earth), it is called the 'Cidade Morena'. In the centre is a shady park, the **Praça República**, commonly called the Praça do Rádio after the Rádio Clube on one of its corners. Three blocks west is **Praça Ari Coelho**. Linking the two squares, and running through the city east to west, is Av Afonso Pena; much of its central reservation is planted with yellow ypé trees. Their blossom covers the avenue, and much of the city besides, in spring.

Museu Dom Bosco (Indian Museum), R Barão do Rio Branco 1843, is superb. Its exhibits from the five Indian groups with which the Salesian missionaries have had contact in the 20th century all have explanatory texts. There are also collections of shells, stuffed birds, butterflies and mammals from the Pantanal, as well as a two-headed calf. Each collection is highly recommended. ■ *Mon-Sat 0800-1700, Sun 1200-1700, US$0.50, T383 3994.* **Museu do Arte Contemporâneo**, Marechal Rondón e Calógeras, has modern art from the region. ■ *Mon-Fri 1300-1800, free.*

Sleeping

Large, mid-range hotels, many with small pools and restaurants, and all very traditional, are found along Av Calógeras, away from the bus station and its budget options

A *Exceler Plaza*, Av Afonso Pena 444, T321 0102, F321 5666. Very comfortable, traditional hotel that caters to tourists and business visitors, small pool, tennis. **A** *Vale Verde*, Av Afonso Pena 106, T321 3355. Pleasant and well-maintained, small pool. Recommended. **B** *Paris*, Av Costa e Silva 4175, T387 1795, F325 7744. A/c, mini bar, **C** with fan. **C** *Central*, R 15 de Novembro 472, T384 6442. Fan, basic, cheaper with shared bath. **C** *Concord*, Av Calógeras 1624, T384 3081, F382 4987. Very good, pool, mini bar. **E** *Americano*, R 14 de Julho 2311 and Mcal Rondón, T321 1454. A/c, fridge, cheaper with fan, a bit run down, in main shopping area. **E** *Pousada LM*, R 15 de Novembro 201, T321 5207, lmhotel@enersulnet.com.br Nice rooms motel-style around courtyard, TV, fridge, terrace, on busy road, **F** with fan, **G** single room, also rents by the month. Good value. Recommended.

This area is not safe at night

Near the rodoviária There is a wide variety of hotels in the streets around the rodoviária so it is easy to leave bags in the *guarda volumes* and shop around. **A** *Internacional*, Allan Kardec 223, T384 4677, F321 2729, **B** with fan. Modern, comfortable, small pool. **B** *Palace*, R Dom Aquino 1501, T384 4741. A/c, fridge, **C** with fan, some rooms small. **B** *Saigali*, Barão do Rio Branco 356, T384 5775. A/c, mini bar, parking, cheaper with fan, comfortable. Recommended. **D** *Iguaçu*, R Dom Aquino 761, T384 4621, F321 3215. A/c, bar **E** with fan, modern, pleasant, internet for guests US$4 per hr. Recommended. **D** *Nacional*, R Dom Aquino, 610,

Campo Grande

T383 2461. A/c, **E** with fan, shared bath, or single, busy, includes breakfast, real bargain. **F** *Cosmos*, R Dom Aquino 771, T384 4270. Nice, quieter than others in area, good value. Recommended. **Youth hostel**: **E** Large block opposite rodoviária. Laundry, kitchen, reception open 24 hrs. Recommended.

Mid range *Cantina Romana*, R da Paz 237. Established over 20 years, Italian and traditional cuisine, good atmosphere. *Casa Colonial*, Av Afonso Pena 3997, on corner with R Paraíba. Traditional, regional and Italian cuisine, with large dessert menu. *Dom Leon*, Av Afonso Pena 1907. Large *churrascaria*, pizzeria and restaurant, self-service lunch, live music evenings. *Largo de Ouro*, R 14 de Julho, 1345. No-frills, large pizzeria and restaurant that does brisk trade. *Morada dos Bais*, Av Noroeste 5140, corner with Afonso Pena, behind tourist office. Pretty courtyard, Brazilian and Italian dishes, US$2 lunch Tue-Sat. **Cheap** *Shopping Campo Grande*, Av Afonso Pena, has a wide selection of restaurants in this category, including *Pão de Queijo Express*. There are also lots of good, cheap options around the bus station and Praça Ari Coelho, and several self-service restaurants on R Cândido Mariano, Nos 1660 to 2512. **Local specialities** *Caldo de piranha* (soup), *chipa* (Paraguayan cheese bread), sold on streets, delicious when hot, and the local liqueur, *pequi com caju*, which contains *cachaça*.

Eating

Local native crafts, including ceramics, tapestry and jewellery, are good quality. A local speciality is Os Bugres da Conceição, squat wooden statues covered in moulded wax. Very good selections are found at *Casa do Artesão*, Av Calógeras 2050, on corner with Av Afonso Pena, housed in an historic building, Mon-Fri 0800-2000, Sat 0800-1200 (also has maps and information), and *Barroarte*, Av Afonso Pena 4329. Also *Arte do Pantanal*, Av Afonso Pena 1743.

Shopping
There is a market (Feira Livre) on Wed and Sat

Asteco Turismo, R 13 de Maio, 3192, T321 0077, www.ecotur-ms.com.br/com/as Two-day (1-night) trips from US$60-US$75, depending on activities and hotel. *Ecological Expeditions*, R Joaquim Nabuco 185, T321 0505, www.pantanaltrekking.com Attached to youth hostel at bus station, see above. Budget camping trips (sleeping bag needed) for 3/4/5 days ending in Corumbá. Recommended. *Impacto*, R Padre João Crippa 1065, sala 101, T325 1333. Helpful, Pantanal and Bonito tour operators, prices vary according to standard of accommodation; a wide range is offered. Two-day packages for 2 people from US$190-600. Transfers and insurance included. *Time Tour*, R Joaquim Murtinho 386, T312 2500, American Express representative.

Tour operators

Air Daily flights to most major cities. Airport T368 6000. City bus No 158, 'Popular' stops outside airport. Taxi to airport, US$6. *Banco do Brasil* at airport exchanges dollars. Post office, fax and phones in same office. It is safe to spend the night at the airport. *Varig*, R Barão do Rio Branco 1356, Centro, T0800-997000, airport 763 1213.

Transport
Car hire agencies on Av Afonso Pena and at airport

    Bus Rodoviária is in the block bounded by Ruas Barão do Rio Branco, Vasconcelos Fernandes, Dom Aquino and Joaquim Nabuco, T383 1678, all offices on 2nd floor. At the V Fernandes end are town buses, at the J Nabuco end state and interstate buses. In between are shops and *lanchonetes*, 8 blocks' walk from Praça República. Cinema in rodoviária, US$1.20. (Taxi to rodoviária, US$3.60.)

    São Paulo, US$33, 14 hrs, 4 buses daily, 1st at 1030, last at 2200, *leito* US$40. **Cuiabá**, US$21, 10 hrs, 12 buses daily, *leito* at 2100 and 2200 US$50. To **Brasília**, US$32, 23 hrs at 1000 and 2000. To **Goiânia**, São Luís company 1100, 2000, 15 hrs on 1900 service, US$32, others 24 hrs, US$1 cheaper. **Corumbá**, with *Andorinha* (T782 3420), 8 daily from 0600, 6 hrs, US$12. Campo Grande-Corumbá buses connect with those from Rio and São Paulo, similarly those from Corumbá through to Rio and São Paulo. Twice daily direct service to **Foz do Iguaçu** (17 hrs) with *Integração*, US$27. To **Pedro Juan Caballero** (Paraguay), *del Amambay* company, 0600, US$8.50. *Amambay* goes every Sun morning to **Asunción**.

Good connections throughout the country

Banks ATMs at *Banco do Brasil*, 13 de Maio e Av Afonso Pena, open 1000-1500, commission US$10 for cash, US$20 for TCs, regardless of amount exchanged. And *Bradesco*, 13 de Maio e Av Afonso Pena. *HSBC*, R 13 de Maio 2837, ATM. *Banco 24 horas*, R Maracaju, on corner with 13 de Junho. Also at R Dom Aquino e Joaquim Nabuco. *Overcash Câmbio*, RRui Barbosa 2750, open Mon-Fri 1000-1600.

Directory

Brazil

Communications Internet: *Cyber Café Iris*, Av Alfonso Pena 1975. **Post Office:** on corner of R Dom Aquino e Calógeras 2309 and Barão do Rio Branco corner Ernesto Geisel, both locations offer fax service, US$2.10 per page within Brazil. **Telephone:** *Tele Centro Sul*, R Dom Aquino 1805, between P Celestino and Rui Barbosa, open 0600-2200. **Embassies and consulates** Bolivia, R João Pedro de Souza 798, T382 2190. **Paraguay**, R 26 Agosto 384, T324 4934. **Medical services** Yellow and Dengue fevers are both present in Mato Grosso do Sul. Get your immunizations at home. **Tourist offices** Maps and books for sale at the municipal **Centro de Informação Turística e Cultural**, Av Noroeste 5140 corner Afonso Pena, T/F324 5830, pensao@ms.sebrae.com.br Housed in Pensão Pimentel, a beautiful mansion built in 1913, also has a database about services in the city and cultural information. Open Tue-Sat 0800-1900, Sun 0900-1200. Kiosk at airport, open 24 hrs, T363 3116. A useful website in Portuguese is www.campogrande.net

Ponta Porã

Voltage is 220 volts AC

There is a paved road from Campo Grande to the Paraguayan border to Ponta Porã (*Post code*: 79900. *Phone code*: 0xx67), separated from Pedro Juan Caballero in Paraguay only by a broad avenue. With paved streets, good public transport and smart shops, Ponta Porã is more prosperous than its neighbour, although Brazilians cross the border to play the casino. *Banco do Brasil* changes travellers' cheques. Many banks in the centre of town (but on Sundays change money in hotels).

Sleeping **B** *Porta do Sol Palace*, R Paraguai 2688, T431 3341, F431 1193. A/c, pool, very nice. **B** *Guarujá*, R Guia Lopes 63, T431 1619. Recommended. Opposite is **C** *Barcelona*, No 45, T/F431 3061. Maze-like building, a/c, restaurant, pool. **C** *Alvorada*, Av Brasil 2977, T431 5866. Good café, close to post office, good value but often full. **C** *Internacional*, R Internacional 1267, T431 1243. **D** without a/c, hot water, good breakfast. Recommended. Brazilian hotels include breakfast, Paraguayan ones do not.

Transport **Bus**: To **Campo Grande**, 9 a day from 0100-2130, 5 hrs, US$10; the rodoviária is 3 km out on the Dourados road ('São Domingos' bus, taxi US$3).

Border with Paraguay

Colour map 7, grid B2

There are no border posts between the two towns and people pass freely for local visits. The Brazilian general police office for entry and exit visas is on the second floor of the white engineering supply company building at R Marechal Floriano 1483, T431 1428. ■ *Weekdays 0730-1130, 1400-1700*. The two nations' consulates face each other on R Internacional (border street), a block west of **Ponta Porã**'s local bus terminal; some nationalities require a visa from the Paraguayan consul (next to *Hotel Internacional*), open only 0800-1200 Monday-Friday. **Check requirements carefully**, and ensure your documents are in order: without the proper stamps you will inevitably be sent back somewhere later on in your travels. ■ *Taking a taxi between offices can speed things up if pressed for time; drivers know border crossing requirements; US$4.25.*

Bonito

Phone code: 0xx67
Post code: 79290
Colour map 6, grid B6
Population: 16,956
248 km from Campo Grande

The municipality of Bonito in the Serra do Bodoquena yields granite and marble and is clad in forest. The area's main attractions are in its rivers, waterfalls and caves. There are spectacular walks through mountains and forest, rafting and snorkelling in clear rivers and wildlife such as birds, rheas, monkeys, alligators and anaconda. Bonito has become very popular with Brazilian vacationers, especially during December-January, Carnival, Easter, and July (at these times advance booking is essential). Prices are high. The wet season is January-February; December-February is hottest, July-August coolest.

Caves **Lagoa Azul**, 26 km from Bonito, has a lake 50 m long and 110 m wide, 75 m below ground level. The water, 20°C, is a jewel-like blue as light from the opening is refracted through limestone and magnesium. Prehistoric animal bones have been found in the lake. The light is at its best January-February, 0700-0900, but is fine at other times. A 25-ha park surrounds the cave. ■ *You must pay a municipal tax, US$5; if not using your own transport, a car for 4 costs US$20.* Also open is **Nossa Senhora Aparecida cave**, which has superb stalactites and stalagmites; no tourism infrastructure.

The **Balneário Municipal** on the Rio Formoso (7 km on road to Jardim), with changing rooms, toilets, camping, swimming in clear water, plenty of fish to see (strenuous
efforts are made to keep the water and shore clean), US$5. **Hormínio** waterfalls, 13
km, eight falls on the Rio Formoso, suitable for swimming; bar and camping, entry
US$0.15. **Rafting** on the Rio Formoso: 2½ hours, minimum four people, US$15 per
person, a mixture of floating peacefully downriver, swimming and shooting four
waterfalls, lifejackets available; arranged by many agencies. The **Aquário Natural** is
one of the springs of the Rio Formoso; to visit you must have authorization from the
owners; you can swim and snorkel with five types of fish (US$25). Do not swim with
suntan oil on. Other tours are: from the **springs of the Rio Sucuri** to its meeting with
the Formoso (permission required to visit), about 2 km of crystal-clear water, with
swimming or snorkelling, birdwatching, very peaceful; **Aquidaban**, a series of lime-
stone/marble waterfalls in dense forest; **Rio da Prata** a spring with underground snorkelling for 2 km, stalactites, bats, very beautiful, also parrots and other animals can be
seen on the trip, US$24. The **fishing** season is from 1 March-31 October. In late Octo-
ber, early November is the *piracema* (fish run), when the fish return to their spawning
grounds. Hundreds can be seen jumping the falls. **NB** Bonito's attractions are nearly
all on private land and must by visited with a guide. Owners also enforce limits on the
number of daily visitors so, at busy times, pre-booking is essential.

River excursions

Brazil

A-B *Pousada Olho d'Água*, just outside Bonito, Km 1 on road to Três Morros, T255 1430,
F255 1741, bonito@pousadaolhodagua.com.br 3 km from town, accommodation in cabins,
including breakfast, fan, showers with solar-heated water, fruit trees, fresh vegetables, small
lake, own water supply, horse riding, bicycles. Recommended. **A** *Tapera*, Estrada Ilha do
Padre, Km 10, on hill above Shell station on road to Jardim, T255 1700, F255 1470,
taperahotel@bonitonline.com.br Fine views, cool breezes, peaceful, a/c, very comfortable,
own transport an advantage. **A** *Canaã*, Pilad Rebuá 1293, T255 1255, F255 1282, hcanaa@
bonitonline.com.br Parking, TV, a/c, fridge, phone, restaurant and *churrascaria*. **B** *Bonanza*,
R Col Pilad Rebuá (main street) 1876, T/F255 1162, hbonanza@bonitonline.com.br Suites
and family rooms available, a/c. Frequently recommended. **C** *Alvorada*, Pilad Rebuá 2097,
T255 1707. 2-4 bedded rooms (latter cramped), fan, hot water. **D** pp *Pousada Muito Bonito*,
Pilad Rebuá 1448, T/F255 1645, muitobonito@uol.com.br With bath, or rooms with
bunkbeds, nice patio, excellent, helpful owners, including breakfast, also with tour company
(Mario Doblack speaks English, French and Spanish). Warmly recommended. Also on Rebuá
at 1800 is a hostal **E**, owned by the Paraíso tour agency, T255 1477, shared bath. Recommended. **E** *Pousada São Jorge*, Av Col Pilad Rebuá 1605, T255 1956, saojorge@
bonitonline.com.br Hot water, tropical breakfast, a/c, cheaper with fan, car parking, internet
access, international telephone, laundry. Recommended. **Youth hostel** *Bonito Hostelling
International*, R Lúcio Borralho 716, T/F255 1022, www.ajbonito.com.br Pool, kitchen and
laundry facilities, English spoken. Recommended.

Sleeping

    Camping At *Ilha do Padre*, 12 km north of Bonito, T/F255 1430. Very pleasant, no regu-
lar transport. 4 rustic cabins with either 4 bunks, or 2 bunks and a double, US$10 pp, youth
hostel with dorms, US$6 pp, same price for camping, toilets, showers, clothes' washing,
meals available, bar, electricity, can swim anywhere, to enter the island for a day US$3.
Camping also at *Poliana* on Rio Formosa, 100 m past Ilha do Padre, T255 1267. Very pleasant.

Tapera, Pilad Rebuá 1961, T255 1110, good, home-grown vegetables, breakfast, lunch, pizzas, meat and fish dishes, opens 1900 for evening meal. *Comida Caseira*, Luís da Costa Leite
e Santana do Paraíso, good local food, lunch and dinner, not open Sun afternoon.
Verdo-Frutos e Sucos Naturais, Pilad Rebuá 1853, good juices and fruits.

Eating

Sérgio Ferreira Gonzales, R Col Pilad Rebuá 628, T255 1315, is an authority on the caves. Recommended. *Hapakany Tour*, Pilad Rebuá 628, T/F255 1315. Jason and Murilo, for all local
tours. Diving trips US$40 per day. *Tapera Tour*, R Col Pilad Rebuá 1961, T255 1757. Guides,
information, tours, clothes shop. Recommended. For information in English and French, contact Henrique Ruas, T/F255 1430, see *Ilha do Padre* or *Pousada Olho d'Água* above.

Tour operators
*The Associação dos
Guias de Turismo
can be reached
on T255 1837*

Transport **Bus** Rodoviária is on the edge of town, T255 1606. From **Campo Grande**, US$11, 5½-6 hrs, 1500, returns at 0530. Bus uses MS-345, with a stop at Autoposto Santa Cruz, Km 60, all types of fuel, food and drinks available. For Aquidauana, take Campo Grande bus. Bus Corumbá-Miranda-Bonito-Jardim-Ponta Porã, Mon-Sat, leaves either end at 0600, arriving Bonito 1230 for Ponta Porã, 1300 for Miranda; can change in Jardim (1400 for 1700 bus) or Miranda (better connections) for Campo Grande; fare **Corumbá**-Bonito US$12.50. Also connections on 1230 route in Bela Vista at 2000 for Asunción and Col Oviedo.

Directory **Banks** *Banco do Brasil*, R Luiz da Costa Leite 2279, for Visa. Hoteliers and taxi drivers may change money. **Communications** Post Office: R Col Pilad Rebuá. **Telephone:** Santana do Paraíso. **Tourist office** Comtur, R Col Pilad Rebuá 1780, T255 1850. On the web see www.portalbonito.com.br

Campo Grande to Corumbá and Bolivia

BR-262 is paved most of the way from Campo Grande to Corumbá and the Bolivian border. The scenery is marvellous.

Aquidauana
Colour map 7, grid B1
Population: 43,440
131 km W of
Campo Grande

There are several daily buses from Campo Grande. Turn south here to Jardim, with connections to Paraguay, and for one route to Bonito. Aquidauana is a gateway to the Pantanal. Excursions in fishing boats negotiable around US$50 per person a day, or via *Chalanatur*, T241 3396.

Sleeping and eating **D** *Fluminense*, R Teodoro Rondon 865, T241 2038. With fan and breakfast, a/c more expensive. **D** *Lord*, R Manoel Paes de Barros 739, T241 1857. Shared bathroom in single room, private bath in double room. Recommended. *O Casarão (grill)*, R Manoel Paes de Barros 533, T241 2219. Recommended.

All recommended **Tour operators** *Buriti Viagens e Turismo Ltda*, R Manoel Paes de Barros 720, T241 2718, F241 2719. *Lucarelli Turismo Ltda*, R Manoel Paes de Barros 552, T241 3410. *Cordon Turismo*, R Búzios, T384 1483. Organizes fishing trips into the Pantanal. *Panbratur*, R Estevão Alves Correa 586, T/F241 3494. Tour operator in southern Pantanal.

Further west by 77 km is **Miranda** another entrance to the Pantanal. There is a *jacaré* farm, *Granja Caimã*, which is open to visitors. ■ US$1. A road heads south to Bodoquena and on to Bonito. ■ *Bus Campo Grande-Miranda, seven a day with Expresso Mato Grosso, US$5.10, and others.* The Campo Grande-Corumbá road crosses the Rio Miranda bridge (two service stations before it) then carries on, mostly paved to cross the Rio Paraguai.

Corumbá

Phone code: 0xx67
Post code: 79300
Colour map 6, grid B6
Population: 95,701

Situated on the south bank by a broad bend in the Rio Paraguai, 15 minutes from the Bolivian border, the city offers beautiful views of the river, especially at sunset. It is hot and humid (70%); cooler in June-July, very hot from September to January. It has millions of mosquitoes in December-February.

There is a spacious shady **Praça da Independência** and the port area is worth a visit. Av Gen Rondon between Frei Mariano and 7 de September has a pleasant palm lined promenade which comes to life in the evenings. The **Forte Junqueira**, the city's most historic building, which may be visited, was built in 1772. In the hills to the south is the world's greatest reserve of manganese, now being worked. Corumbá is the best starting point for the southern part of the Pantanal, with boat and jeep trips and access to the major hotel/farms.

Brazil

B *Internacional Palace*, R Dom Aquino Correia 1457, T/F231 6247. A/c, fridge, pool, sauna, parking, cafe. **B** *Nacional Palace*, R América 936, T231 6868, F231 0202. A/c, fridge, good pool, parking. **B** *Carandá*, R Dom Aquino Corrêa 47, T/F231 2023. A/c, fridge, pool, good, helpful, restaurant. **B** *Laura Vicunha*, R Cuiabá 775, T231 5874, F231 2663. A/c, fridge, **C** for simpler room, parking, modern. Recommended. **D** *Beira Rio*, R Manoel Cavassa 109, T231 2554. A/c, cheaper with fan, by the port, popular with fishermen. **D** *Pensâo do Tato*, R 13 de Junho 720, T231 7727. A/c, cheaper with fan, small rooms. **D** *Timoneiro*, R Cabral 879, T231 5530, between rodoviária and centre. A/c, **E** with fan, cheaper with shared bath. **E** *Angola*, R Antônio Maria 124, T231 7233. A/c, **F** with fan, restaurant. **E** *Campus*, R Antônio João 1333. Fan, cheaper with shared bath, good value. **E-F** *City*, R Cabral 1031, T231 6373, between rodoviária and centre. A/c, **C** with fan, cheaper with shared bath, parking. **E** *Roboré*, R Dom Aquino Correia 587. Shared bath, small rooms, basic. **Near the rodoviária are** **D** *Internacional*, R Porto Carreiro 714, T231 4654. Shared bath, fan, basic, simple breakfast, owner organizes fishing trips. **E** *Beatriz*, R Porto Carreiro 896, T231 7441. Fan, cheaper with shared bath, small rooms, simple. **E** *Esplanada*, opposite railway station. Cold shower, basic. **E** *Irure*, R 13 de Junho 776. Small and clean.

Sleeping
The combination of economic hard times since 1994 and drug-running make the city unsafe late at night

There are several good restaurants in R Frei Mariano. *Churrascaria do Gaúcho*, No 879. Good value. *Peixaria do Lulú*, R Dom Aquino Correia 700. Good fish. *Churrascaria Rodéio*, 13 de Junho 760. Very good, lunchtime buffet. Recommended. *Viva Bella*, R Arthur Mangabeira 1 (behind Clube Corumbaense 1 block from Gen Rondon). Fish, meat, pizza, home made pastas, drinks, magnificent views over the river especially at sunset, live music Wed-Sat, opens at 1700, good food and atmosphere. Recommended. *Almanara*, R America 964 next to *Hotel Nacional*. Good Arabic food. On the waterfront you can eat good fish at *Portal do Pantanal*. Lots of open-air bars on the river front. Many good ice cream parlours: *Cristal*, R 7 de Setembro e Delamaré. Recommended.

Eating

Local specialities These include *peixadas corumbaenses*, a variety of fish dishes prepared with the catch of the day; as well as ice cream, liquor and sweets made of *bocaiúva*, a small yellow palm fruit, in season Sep-Feb.

2 Feb, *Festa de Nossa Senhora da Candelária*, Corumbá's patron saint, all offices and shops are closed. **24 Jun**, *Festa do Arraial do Banho de São João*, fireworks, parades, traditional food stands, processions and the main event, the bathing of the image of the saint in the Rio Paraguai. **21 Sep**, Corumbá's anniversary, includes a Pantanal fishing festival held on the eve.

Festivals

Casa do Artesão, R Dom Aquino Correia 405. Open Mon-Fri 0800-1200, 1400-1800, Sat 0800-1200, good selection of handicrafts, small bookshop, friendly staff but high prices. *CorumbArte*, Av Gen Rondon 1011. For good silk-screen T-shirts with Pantanal motifs. *Livraria Corumbaense*, R Delamaré 1080. For state maps. **Supermarkets** *Ohara*, Dom Aquino 621. *Frutal*, R 13 de Junho 538, open 0800-2000.

Shopping
Shops tend to open early and close by 1700

Corumbá has many travel agencies selling tours to the Pantanal. For more information see page 583: *Pantur*, R Frei Mariano 1013, T231 2000, F231 6006. Tours, agents for *Hotel Fazenda Xaraés* in Nhecolândia, sells train tickets to Santa Cruz. *Taimã*, R Antônio M Coelho 786, T/F231 2179. River trips, flights over Pantanal, airline tickets.

Tour operators

Air Airport, R Santos Dumont, 3 km, T231 3322. Daily flights to Campo Grande, Londrina and São Paulo with TAM. No public transport from airport to town, you have to take a taxi.
 Buses The rodoviária is on R Porto Carreiro at the south end of R Tiradentes, next to the railway station. City bus to rodoviária from Praça da República.
 Car hire: *Unidas*, R Frei Mariano 633, T/F231 3124.
 Taxi: are extortionate, but moto-taxis only charge US$0.65. *Andorinha* services to all points east. To **Campo Grande**, 7 hrs, US$22, 13 buses daily, between 0630 and midnight, interesting journey ('an excursion in itself') – take an early bus to see plentiful wildlife, connections from Campo Grande to all parts of Brazil. To **São Paulo** direct, 22 hrs, US$50, 2 a day,

Transport

confirm bus times in advance (T231 2033). To **Ponta Porã**, 12 hrs, US$20, via Bonito (6 hrs, US$12.50) and Jardim (9 hrs, US$15), Mon-Sat at 0600; ticket office open 0500-0600 only, at other times call T231 2383.

Directory **Banks** *Banco do Brasil*, R 13 de Junho 914, ATM, 15% commission on exchange. *HSBC*, R Delamare 1068, ATM. **Communications** Internet: *Caffe.com*, R Frei Mariano 635, T231 7730. *PantanalNET*, Rua América 403,Centro, US$2.50 per hr. **Post Office:** main at R Delamaré 708 (has fax service); branch at R 15 de Novembro 229. **Telephone:** *Tele Centro Sul*, R Dom Aquino 951, near Praça da Independência, open 0700-2200 daily. To phone Quijarro/Puerto Suárez, Bolivia, it costs slightly more than a local call, dial 214 + the Bolivian number.

Border with Over the border from Corumbá are Arroyo Concepción, Puerto Quijarro and
Bolivia Puerto Suárez. From Puerto Quijaro a 650-km railway runs to Santa Cruz de la
If you arrive in Brazil Sierra. There is a road of sorts. There are flights into Bolivia from Puerto Suárez.
without a yellow **Brazilian immigration** Formalities are constantly changing so check proce-
fever vaccination dures in advance. You need not have your passport stamped to visit Quijarro or
certificate, you may Puerto Suárez only for the day. Otherwise, get your passport stamped by Brazilian
have to go to R 7 de Polícia Federal at Praça da Republica 37, next to NS da Candelária, 0800-1130,
Setembro, Corumbá, 1400-1730. The visa must be obtained on the day of departure. If leaving Brazil
for an inoculation merely to obtain a new visa, remember that exit and entry must not be on the same
day. Money changers at the border and in Quijarro offer the same rates as in Corumbá. The Bolivian consulate is at R Antônio Maria Coelho 881, Corumbá, T231 5605. ■ *Mon-Fri, 0700-1100, 1500-1730, Sat and Sun closed.* A fee is charged to citizens of those countries which require a visa. A yellow fever vaccination certificate is required.

Transport Leaving Brazil, take Canarinho city bus marked Fronteira from the port end of R Antônio Maria Coelho to the Bolivian border (15 mins, US$0.35), walk over the bridge to Bolivian immigration (blue building), then take a colectivo to Quijarro or Puerto Suárez. When travelling from Quijarro, take a taxi or walk to the Bolivian border to go through formalities. Just past the bridge, on a small side street to the right, is the bus stop for Corumbá, take bus marked Fronteira or Tamengo to Praça da República, US$0.50, every 45 mins between 0630 and 1915, don't believe taxi drivers who say there is no bus. Taxi to centre US$6. Find a hotel then take care of Brazilian formalities at Polícia Federal, address above.

The schedules of **trains** from Puerto Quijarro to Santa Cruz are given on page 323. Timetables change frequently, so check on arrival in Corumbá. It may be best to stay in Quijarro to get a good place in the queue for tickets.

Pantanal

This vast wetland, measuring 230,000 sq km between Cuiabá, Campo Grande and the Bolivian frontier, is one of the **world's great wildlife preserves**. Parts spill over into neighbouring Bolivia and Paraguay, and the entire area has been opened up to tourism.

Wildlife Similar in many ways to the Amazon basin, though because of the more veldt-like
For the Pantanal on open land, the wildlife can be viewed more easily than in the dense jungle growth.
the web see Principal life seen in this area is about 650 species of birds, including the hyacinth
www.geocities.com/ macaw, jabiru stork (the *tuiuíu*, almost 1.2 m tall), plumbeous ibis, both
RainForest/1820/ blue-throated and red-throated piping guans, rhea, curasow and roseate spoonbill.
(Portuguese Easy to see on the river-banks are the ubiquitous capybara, a kind of giant aquatic
and English) guinea-pig, and caiman (*jacaré*). You may also come across otters, anteaters, opossums, armadillos, bare-eared marmosets, black-and-gold howler monkeys and marsh deer. Harder to spot are maned wolf, South American coati, ocelot, margay, jaguarundi and even pumas, jaguars and yellow anacondas. There are some 230 varieties of fish, from the giant *pintado*, weighing up to 80 kg, to the tiny, voracious *piranha*. Fishing here is exceptionally good (best May-October). The extraordinary

thing is that man and his domesticated cattle thrive together with the wildlife with seemingly little friction. Local farmers protect the area jealously.

Only one area is officially a national park, the **Parque Nacional do Pantanal Matogrossense** in the municipality of Poconé, 135,000 ha of land and water, only accessible by air or river. Hunting in any form is strictly forbidden throughout the Pantanal and is punishable by four years imprisonment. Fishing is allowed with a licence (enquire at travel agents for latest details); it is not permitted in the spawning season or *piracema* (1 October to 1 February in Mato Grosso do Sul, 1 November to 1 March in Mato Grosso). Like other wilderness areas, the Pantanal faces important threats to its integrity. Agro-chemicals and *garimpo* mercury washed down from the neighbouring *planalto* are a hazard to wildlife. Visitors must share the responsibility of protecting the Pantanal and you can make an important contribution by acting responsibly and choosing your guides accordingly: take out your rubbish, don't fish out of season, don't let guides kill or disturb fauna, don't buy products made from endangered species, don't buy live birds or monkeys, and report any violation of these norms to the authorities.

The International Union for the Conservation of Nature is concerned at the amount of poaching, particularly of jacaré skins, birds and capybaras. The Forestry Police have built control points on all major access roads to the Pantanal. Biologists interested in research projects in the area should contact the *Coordenador de Estudos do Pantanal*, Dpto de Biologia, Universidade Federal do Mato Grosso do Sul, Caixa Postal 649, Campo Grande, CEP 79070-900, T0xx67-387 3311 ext 2113, F387 5317.

Permission to visit the park needs to be obtained at Ibama, R Rubens de Mendonça, Cuiabá, CEP 78008-000, T644 1511/1581

Brazil

When to go

The Pantanal is good for seeing wildlife year-round. However, the dry season between Jul and Oct is the ideal time as animals and birds congregate at the few remaining areas of water. During these months you are very likely to see jaguars. This is the nesting and breeding season, when birds form vast nesting areas, with thousands crowding the trees, creating an almost insupportable cacophony of sounds. The white sand river beaches are exposed, caiman bask in the sun, and capybaras frolic amid the grass. Jul sees lots of Brazilian visitors who tend to be noisy, decreasing the chances of sightings. From the end of Nov to the end of Mar (wettest in Feb), most of the area, which is crossed by many rivers, floods. At this time mosquitoes abound and cattle crowd on to the few islands remaining above water. In the southern part, many wild animals leave the area, but in the north, which is slightly higher, the animals do not leave.

What to take

Most tours arrange for you to leave your baggage in town, so you need only bring what is necessary for the duration of the tour with you. In winter (Jun-Aug), temperatures fall to 10°, warm clothing and covers or sleeping bag are needed at night. It's very hot and humid during summer and a hat and sun protection is vital. Wear long sleeves and long trousers and spray clothes as well as skin with insect repellent. Insects are less of a problem Jul-Aug. Take insect repellent from home as mosquitoes, especially in the North Pantanal, are becoming immune to local brands. Drinks are not included in the price of packages and tend to be over-priced, so if you are on a tight budget bring your own. Mosty importantly, try to get hold of a pair of binoculars.

Getting there

The Pantanal is not easy or cheap to visit. The best starting points are Corumbá, Cuiabá, and to a lesser extent Campo Grande, from where one finds public transport all around the perimeter, but none at all within. Wild camping is possible if you have some experience and your own transport. Remember that the longer you stay and the further you go from the edges (where most of the hotels are located), the more likely you are to see rare wildlife.

From Corumbá there is access to the Pantanal by both road and river, offering a variety of day trips, luxury house boat excursions, and connections to many surrounding *fazendas*. Along the road from Corumbá to Campo Grande (BR-262) are Miranda and Aquidauana, both important gateways to various fishing and tourist lodges. The BR-163 which connects Campo Grande and Cuiabá skirts the east edge of the Pantanal. Coxim, 242 km north of

Campo Grande, offers access via the Rio Taquari but few facilities. From Cuiabá there is year-round road access to Barão de Melgaço and Poconé, both of which can be starting points for excursions. The Transpantaneira Highway runs south from Poconé to Porto Jofre, through the heart of the Pantanal, providing access to many different lodges, but does not have any bus service. During the rainy season, access is restricted between Pixaim and Porto Jofre. Finally Cáceres, 215 km west of Cuiabá at the northwest corner of the Pantanal, offers access along the Rio Paraguai to one of the least developed parts of the region.

Types of tour Tourist facilities in the Pantanal currently cater to four main categories of visitors. **Sport fish-**
Whatever your budget, **ermen** usually stay at one of the numerous speciality lodges scattered throughout the
take binoculars region, which provide guides, boats, bait, ice and other related amenities. Bookings can be made locally or in any of Brazil's major cities. **All-inclusive tours** combining air and ground transportation, accommodation at the most elaborate *fazendas*, meals, guided river and land tours, can be arranged from abroad or through Brazilian travel agencies. This is the most expensive option. **Moderately priced tours** using private guides, camping or staying at more modest *fazendas* can be arranged locally in Cuiabá (where guides await arrivals at the airport) or through the more reputable agencies in Corumbá. **The lowest priced tours** are offered by independent guides in Corumbá, some of whom are unreliable and travellers have reported at times serious problems here (see below). For those with the barest mini-mum of funds, a glimpse of the Pantanal and its wildlife can be had on the bus ride from Campo Grande to Corumbá, by lodging or camping near the ferry crossing over the Rio Paraguai (Porto Esperança), and by staying in Poconé and day-walking or hitching south along the Transpantaneira.

Choosing Most tours combine 'safari' jeep trips, river-boat trips, piranha fishing and horse riding with
a tour accommodation in lodges. As sunset and sunrise are the best times for spotting bird and wildlife, excursions often take place at these times. A two-day trip, with a full day taken up with travel each way, allows you to experience most of what is on offer. Longer tours tend to have the same activities spread out over a longer period of time.

Many budget travellers en route to or from Bolivia make Corumbá their base for visiting the Pantanal. Such tourists are often approached, in the streets and at the cheaper hotels, by salesmen who speak foreign languages and promise complete tours for low prices. They then hand their clients over to agencies and/or guides, who often speak only Portuguese, and may deliver something quite different. Some travellers have reported very unpleasant experiences and it is important to select a guide with great care anywhere. By far the best way is to speak with other travellers who have just returned from a Pantanal tour. Most guides also have a book containing comments from their former clients. Do not rush to sign up when first approached, always compare several available alternatives. Discuss the planned itinerary carefully and try to get it in writing (although this is seldom possible – threaten to go to someone else if necessary). Try to deal directly with agencies or guides, not salesmen (it can be difficult to tell who is who). Always get an itemized receipt. Bear in mind that a well-organized three-day tour can be more rewarding than four days with an ill-prepared guide. There is fierce competition between guides who provide similar services, but with very different styles. Although we list a few of the most reputable guides below, there are other good ones and most economy travellers enjoy a pleasant if spartan experi-ence. Remember that travellers must shoulder part of the responsibility for the current cha-otic guiding situation in Corumbá. Act responsibly and don't expect to get something for nothing. (See also Corumbá guides section.)

It appears to be the case that once a guide is recommended by a guidebook, he ceases to guide and sets up his own business working in promoting and public relations, using other guides to work under his name. Guides at the airport give the impression that they will lead the tour, but they won't. Always ask who will lead the party and how big it will be. Less than four is not economic and he will make cuts in boats or guides.

Brazil

From Campo Grande **LL** full board *Pousada São Francisco*, 135 km from Aquidauana in the Rio Negro area of Nhecolândia, T241 3494, accessible only by air during the wet, with bath, fan, screening, horse riding, price including transport, meals, tours, bookings through *Impacto Turismo*, Campo Grande, T/F0xx67-725 1333 (full address above). **LL** full board *Refúgio Ecológico Caiman*, 36 km from Miranda, 236 km from Campo Grande, first class, full board, excursions, T0xx67-687 2102, T/F687 2103, or São Paulo 3079 6622, F3079 6037, www.caiman.com.br A Roteiro de Charme hotel. **L** full board *Pousada Aguapé*, Fazenda São José, 59 km north of Aquidauana, 202 km from Campo Grande, T686 1036, farmhouse hotel, screened rooms, some with a/c, pool, horse riding, boat trips, trekking, meals and tours included, bookings through *Impacto Turismo*, as above, or T241 2889, F241 3494. **AL** *Fazenda Salobra*, T0xx67-242 1162, 6 km from Miranda, 209 km from Corumbá, 198 km from Campo Grande, is recommended, with bath, including all meals, tours, boat rentals and horses are extra; it is by the Rio Salobra (clear water) and Rio Miranda, with birds and animals easily seen. Take bus from Campo Grande to Miranda, and alight 50 m from the bridge over Rio Miranda, turn left for 1,200 m to the *Fazenda*. *Fazenda Rio Negro*, 13,000 ha farm on the shores of the Rio Negro, farm house dating to 1920, tours, horses, fishing, T725 7853, F724 9345, or São Paulo 214 2777. *Pousada Mangabal*, in Nhecolândia, T241 3494, farm setting, horses, tours, walks, bookings through *Panbratur*, Aquidauana, T/F241 3494. **B** *Fazenda Toca da Onça*, 10 km from Aquidauana on the shores of the Rio Aquidauana, cabins, a/c, restaurant, boats, bookings through *Panbratur*, Aquidauana, as above, or T986 0189. **B** *Pousada Águas do Pantanal*, Av Afonso Pena 367, Miranda, T/F0xx67-241 4241/1702, contact Fátima or Luis Cordelli. Very good, good food, restaurant serves *jacaré* legally. There is a good campsite 30 km past Miranda. Alternatively, hire a car in Corumbá and drive to Miranda, but note that the dirt road is bad after rain (consequently not much traffic and more wildlife can be seen). Car with driver can be hired at Salobra for US$25. There are several camping possibilities along the shores of the Rio Aquidauana including *Camping Baía*, 50 km from Aquidauana, T241 3634, on a bay on the river, trees for shade, boats. *Pequi Camping*, 48 km from Aquidauana, with toilets, electricity. *Camping Itajú*, 18 km from Aquidauana, sandy beach, cabins, lanchonete, shower, electricity, boat rental. **Camping allows you to see the wildlife at its greatest period of activity** – dawn and dusk, but protection against mosquitoes is essential. Care should also be taken to avoid dangerous animals: snakes (especially in the rainy season), piranhas (especially in the dry season), killer bees and the larger jacarés.

Some of Corumbá's many agencies are listed on page 579. Tours out of Corumbá are of 3-4 days, costing up to US$100 (includes all food, accommodation and transport).1 day river trips are also available on river boats with a capacity of 80 passengers, US$25 half-day; US$50 full day, including transfers and hot fish meal. Smaller boats US$15 pp for 3 hrs. Tickets at travel agents and by port. Boats may be hired, with fishing tackle and guide, at the port (US$100 per day, up to 3 people, in season only). Cattle boats will on occasion take passengers on their round trips to farms in the Pantanal, but take your own food – it is not always possible to disembark. Ask at Bacia da Prata, 10 mins out of Corumbá on the Ladário bus. The going rate for a 3-day camping photo safari by jeep is US$100 pp for 4-6 people; US$110-120 pp for 4 days. Fishing trips in luxurious floating hotels for 8, US$1,200-2,000 per day, minimum 5 days. There are also hotels specializing in fishing, all reached from Corumbá by road.

Lodges **LL** full board *Pousada do Pantanal*, T0xx67-725 5267/231 5212, or 0xx11-214 2777, 125 km from Corumbá near the Campo Grande road at *Fazenda Santa Clara*. A working cattle ranch, very comfortable, easy access by bus, reservations from all agencies in Corumbá; US$190 pp for 3 days/2 nights, minimum 2 persons, good food (drinks not included), with excursions on horseback (US$8), car (US$20) and boat (US$20), guides included, canoes, simple fishing gear, motor boats for rent (try bargaining in the off-season for reduced rates). **LL** full board *Hotel Fazenda Xaraés*, T0xx67-231 4094, T0xx11-870 4600, Rio Abobral, 130 km from Corumbá, luxurious, a/c, pool, restaurant, horses, boats. **A** *Fazenda Santa Blanca*, on the Rio Paraguai, 15 mins by boat south of Porto Esperança (where the BR-262 crosses the Rio Paraguai), full board, good kayak excursions, horse riding,

Sleeping
The inexperienced should not strike out on their own. Many lodges with fair to good accommodation, some only approachable by air or river; most are relatively expensive. One option is to hire a car and check for yourself: in Jun-Sep, especially Jul, book in advance.
An ordinary vehicle should be able to manage the Transpantaneira out of Cuiabd throughout most of the year, but in the wet season you should be prepared to get stuck, and muddy, pushing your car from time to time

Trips from Corumbá

Brazil

information from R 15 de Novembro 659, 79300 Corumbá, T231 1460, or *Flins Travel* (Walter Zoss), R do Acre 92, 6th floor, 602, CEP 20081, Rio, T0xx21-253 8588/0195 or *Safári Fotográfico*, R Frei Mariano 502, Corumbá, T231 5797.

Tour operators Travel is in the back of a pick-up (good for seeing animals), up to a maximum of 6. Accommodation is in a hammock under a palm thatch on a *fazenda*. Food can be good. If you want flushing toilets, showers or luxury cabins, approach an agency. Guides provide bottled mineral water (make sure enough is carried), but you must take a hat, sun screen and mosquito repellent. Some guides go to *fazendas* without permission, have unreliable vehicles, or are inadequately equipped, so try to check their credentials. Agencies sometimes subcontract to guides over whom they have no control. If you are asked to pay half the money directly to the guide check him out as if he were independent and ask to see his equipment. Guides will generally not make the trip with fewer than 5 people, so if you have not already formed a group, stay in touch with several guides. This is most important during Mar-Oct, when very few tourists are around and many agencies shut up shop for the low season. Decide on your priorities: try to ensure that your guide and other group members share your ideas. We list below those guides who have received positive reports from travellers: *Katu*, R Dom Aquino 220, T231 1987. Recommended. *Tucan Tours*, R Delamaré 576, T231 3569, guide William Chaparro speaks English, Hebrew and Spanish, contact him via email at w_chaparro@ hotmail.com *Saldanha Tour*, R Porto Carreiro 896B, T231 16891, saldanha_v@hotmail.com Owner Eliane is very helpful to travellers. *Carola Alice Reimann*, creimann@hotmail.com Speaks English, knowledgeable. There are many other guides not listed here; lots have received criticisms (some repeatedly) from travellers. There may be others on whom we have received no feedback.

Another access to the Pantanal from the east is **Coxim** (*Phone code: 0xx67; CEP: 79400*; 242 km north of Campo Grande) on the BR-163, half way between Campo Grande and Rondonópolis; it sits in a green bowl, on the shores of the Rio Taquari; the area has great potential for tourism, but there are no official tours to the Pantanal, a great place if you have your own boat. **Sleeping A** *Coxim*, 4 km south of town, T/F291 1479. A/c, fridge, TV, restaurant. **A** *Santa Ana*, R Miranda Reis on the river bank, T291 1602. Cabins for 4, pool. **C** *Santa Teresa*, 5 km south of town, T291 2215, F291 1289. With bath, fan. There are several simpler hotels in town.

Cuiabá to Pantanal

Colour map 6, grid A6 A paved road turns south off the main Cuiabá-Cáceres road to **Poconé** (102 km from Cuiabá, hotels, 24-hr gas station – closed Sunday). From here, the Transpantaneira runs 146 km south to Porto Jofre (just a gas station, gasoline and diesel, but no alcohol available). At the entrance to the Pantanal, there is a gate across the road where drivers are given a list of rules of conduct. The road is of earth, in poor condition, with ruts, holes and many bridges that need care in crossing. Easiest access is in the dry season (July-September), which is also the best time for seeing birds and, in September, the trees are in bloom. In the wet, especially January-February, there is no guarantee that the Transpantaneira will be passable. The wet season, however, is a good time to see many of the shyer animals because more fruit, new growth and other high calorie foods are available, and there are fewer people.

Campos de Jofre, about 20 km north of Porto Jofre, is said to be magnificent between August and October, with very large concentrations of birds and animals. In Poconé one can hitch (not much traffic, bumpy, especially in a truck) to Porto Jofre, or hire a vehicle in Cuiabá. You will get more out of this part of the Pantanal by going with a guide; a lot can be seen from the Transpantaneira in a hired car, but guides can take you into *fazendas* some 7 km from the Transpantaneira and will point out wildlife. Recommended guides in Cuiabá are under Tour operators. Although there are gas stations in **Pixaim** (a bridge across the Rio Pixaim, two hotels and a tyre repair shop) and Porto Jofre, they are not always well stocked, best to carry extra fuel.

In Pixaim and The Transpantaneira L *Pantanal Mato Grosso*, T/F0xx65-321 9445. Modern cabins, 35 rooms for 3-6 people, with full board, fan, hot water (also family-size apartments with a/c), pool, good home-grown food, in radio contact with office on R Barão de Melgaço in Cuiabá, camping possible, boat rental with driver US$30 per hr. **AL** *Hotel-Fazenda Cabanas do Pantanal*, 142 km from Cuiabá, 50 km from Poconé by the Rio Pixaim, on the northern edge of the Pantanal. 10 chalet bedrooms with bath, restaurant, boat trips (few in dry season), horse-riding, fishing, helpful proprietor and staff, everything except boat trips and bar drinks included in price (booking: *Confiança*, Cuiabá). **A** *Araras EcoLodge*, Km 32 on Transpantaneira, T682 2800, F682 1260, 14 rooms with bath, pool, good food, home-made *cachaça*, well-informed guides, can book through *Expeditours* in Cuiabá. Recommended. **A** *Pousada Pantaneira*, full board, 7 rooms with 2-3 bunk beds each, bath, simple, owned and operated by *pantaneiros* (reservations through *Faunatur* in Cuiabá), about 45 km from Pixaim. Next to *Pousada Pantaneira* is the private Jaguar Ecological Reserve, owned by *pantaneiros*, funded by donation; all further details through *Focus Tours* (see Bridwatching & nature tourism, in Essentials). **A** *Pousada Pixaim*, built on stilts, T721 1899. Full board (meals also available separately), 10 rooms with a/c or fan, mosquito-netted windows, hot water, electricity 24 hrs, pleasant setting, boat trips – US$30 per hr with driver, camping possible US$10 per tent or free if you eat in the restaurant. **E** *Pousada Piuval*, at Fazenda Ipiranga, Matogrossense, Rod Transpantaneira Km 10, T983 7425, www.vehiculum.com/piuval A/c, with bath, **G** for camping with outside shower, horse riding, boat trips available.

On Rio Cuiabá, 130 km from Cuiabá (*TUT* bus at 0730 and 1500, US$6.50), Barão de Melgaço is reached by two roads: the shorter, via Santo Antônio de Leverger, unpaved from Santo Antônio to Barão (closed in the wet season), or via São Vicente, longer, but more pavement. The way to see the Pantanal from here is by boat down the Rio Cuiabá. Boat hire, for example from *Restaurant Peixe Vivo* on waterfront, up to US$85 for a full day; or enquire with travel agencies in Cuiabá. The best time of day would be sunset, but it would need some organizing to be in the best part at the best time, without too much boating in the dark. Protect against the sun when on the water. Initially the river banks are farms and small habitations, but they become more forested, with lovely combinations of flowering trees (best seen September-October). After a while, a small river to the left leads to the Baia and Lakes Chacororé and Sia Mariana, which join each other. Boats can continue beyond the lakes to the Rio Mutum, but a guide is essential because there are many dead ends. The area is rich in birdlife and the waterscapes are beautiful.

Barão de Melgaço
Colour map 7, grid A1

Sleeping L *Pousada Passárgada*, programmes from 3 days up, full board, boat, car and trekking expeditions, transport from Barão de Melgaço, owner speaks English, French and German, food excellent, closed Dec to Feb; reservations T713 1128, in Barão de Melgaço on riverside, through *Nature Safaris*, Av Marechal Rondon, Barão de Melgaço, or São Paulo T0xx11-284 5434, or Rio 0xx21-287 3390. Much cheaper if booked direct with the owner, Maré Sigaud, Mato Grosso, CEP 786807, *Pousada Passárgada*, Barão de Melgaço. Highly recommended. **L** *Sapé Pantanal Lodge*, Caixa Postal 2241 – CEP 78020.970, Cuiabá, T0xx65-391 1442, www.sapehotel.com.br Basic, self-contained accommodation, meals buffet-style, 4-day, 3-night all-inclusive programme US$800, sport fishing, wildlife observation and photography excursions. A complete programme includes road transport from Cuiabá airport to Barão de Melgaço (wet season), or Porto Cercado (dry season) with onward river transportation (about 1½ hrs); outboard powered boats with experienced guides at guests' disposal; optional trekking and horse riding in dry season, paddling in wet; English, French, Spanish spoken. *Sapé*, which is highly recommended, is closed 20 Dec-31 Jan. Reservations can be made through agencies at favourable rates.

Cuiabá

Phone code: 0xx65
Post code: 78000
Colour map 7, grid A1
Population: 483,346
Altitude: 176 m

The capital of Mato Grosso state on the Rio Cuiabá, an upper tributary of the Rio Paraguai, is in fact two cities: Cuiabá on the east bank of the river and Várzea Grande, where the airport is, on the west. It is very hot; coolest months for a visit are June, July and August, in the dry season.

Cuiabá has an imposing government palace and other fine buildings round the green **Praça da República**. On the square is the **Cathedral**, with a plain, imposing exterior, two clock-towers and, inside, coloured-glass mosaic windows and doors. Behind the altar is a huge mosaic of Christ in majesty, with smaller mosaics in side chapels. Beside the Cathedral is the leafy **Praça Alencastro**. On **Praça Ipiranga**, at the junction of Avs Isaac Póvoas and Tenente Col Duarte, a few blocks west of the central squares, there are market stalls and an iron bandstand from Huddersfield, UK. On a hill beyond the praça is the church of **Bom Despacho**, built in the style of Notre Dame de Paris (in poor condition, closed to visitors). In front of the Assembléia Legislativa, Praça Moreira Cabral, is a point marking the **Geogedesic Centre of South America** (see also under Chapada dos Guimarães). **Museus de Antropologia, História Natural e Cultura Popular**, in the Fundação Cultural de Mato Grosso, Praça da República 151, has historical photos, a contemporary art gallery, stuffed Pantanal fauna, Indian, archaeological finds and pottery. ■ *Mon-Fri 0800-1730, US$0.50.* At the entrance to Universidade de Mato Grosso, 10 minutes by bus from the centre, is the small **Museu do Índio/Museu Rondon** (by swimming pool), with well-displayed exhibits.

Sleeping
The port area is best avoided day and night

AL *Áurea Palace*, Gen Mello 63, T623 1826, F623 7390, aureaph@zaz.com.br Pleasant rooms, restaurant, swimming pool, good. **AL** *Best Western Mato Grosso Pálace*, Joaquim Murtinho 170, T614 7000, F321 2386, pwmt@zaz.com.br A/c, fridge, central, very popular, restaurant. **A** *Abudi Palace*, No 259, T322 7399. A/c, good. **B** *Jaguar Palace*, Av Getúlio Vargas 600, T624 4404, jaguarph@zaz.com.br New extension with rooms around large pool, older rooms are large with sofas and wonderfully old-fashioned (once used by prospectors who paid for their room in gold nuggets), comfortable and good value. Recommended. **B** *Real Pálace*, 13 de Junho 102, Praça Ipiranga, T321 5375, F611 1141. Large rooms, some with a/c, good breakfast. **C** *Samara*, R Joaquim Murtinho 270, T322 6001. Central, with bath, hot shower, fan, basic but good, cheaper with shared bath. **C** *Mato Grosso*, R Comandante Costa 2522, T614 7777, bwmt@zaz.com.br Excellent value, with breakfast, a/c, **D** with fan, good restaurant, English spoken, luggage stored whilst guests tour Chapada or Pantanal. **E** *Pousada Ecoverde*, R Pedro Celestino 391, T624 1386. 5 rooms with shared bath around a courtyard in colonial family house, kitchen, laundry facilities and lovely walled garden with hammocks. Highly recommended. **E** *Presidente*, Barão de Melgaço e Av G

Cuiabá

To Rodoviária & Chapada dos Guimarães

Sleeping
1 Áurea Palace
2 Best Western Mato Grosso Pálace
3 Mato Grosso
4 Presidente

Not to scale

Vargas, T624 1386. On a busy central corner, convenient but lots of traffic outside and run down, a/c, **F** with fan, fridge, cheaper with shared bath. By the rodoviária, on Jules Rimet are: **A** *Skala Pálace*, at No 26, T322 4347. With a/c, fridge, restaurant, smart lobby, front rooms noisy. **B** *Brazil*, No 20, T621 2703. A/c, fridge, parking, **D** with fan, cheaper with shared bath, ground floor rooms are best. **C** *Ipanema*, s/n, T621 3069. A/c, **D** with fan, cheaper with shared bath, good value, good breakfast. Recommended. **D** *Grande*, No 30, T621 3852. A/c, **E** with fan, cheaper with shared bath, basic. Others in same area.

Youth hostel E *Portal do Pantanal*, Av Isaac Povoas 655, T/F624 8999, www.portaldopantanal.com.br IYHA, with breakfast, cheaper with fan, internet access US$2.50 per hr, laundry, kitchen.

Expensive *Getúlio*, Av Getúlio Vargas 1147. Somewhat pretentious a/c restaurant with pavement tables, dance floor and sushi bar, excellent food, with meat specialties and pizza. **Mid range** *Cedros*, Praça 8 de Abril 750, Goiabeiras. Fan-cooled, friendly and very popular place offering wide selection of Arabic food, including *tabule* salad and 'pizza' made with pitta bread. Delivery service, T624 9134. Recommended. *China in Box*, Av Lavapés,70, T623 8400. Chinese food with a Brazilian twist, also fish dishes and desserts. Open daily for lunch and dinner; delivery service. *Choppão*, Praça 8 de Abril. This local institution buzzes at any time of the day or night. Go for huge portions of delicious food or just for beer. The house dish of chicken soup promises to give diners drinking strength in the early hours and is a meal in itself. Warmly recommended. *Lig-China*, R Presidente Marques 960. Sophisticated, a/c restaurant with standard Chinese and Japanese menu, open daily for lunch and dinner till 2400, also delivers. **Cheap** There are several restaurants and *lanchonetes* on R Jules Rimet across from the rodoviária. *Hong Kong*, Av G Vargas 647, opposite *Jaguar Hotel*. Self-service Chinese, good quality for price. *Lanchonete Presidente*, Hamburgers and sandwiches, next to hotel of same name, open late for eating, drinking and TV watching.

Eating
City centre restaurants only open for lunch. On Av CPA are many good restaurants and small snack bars

Cuiabá is quite lively at night, bars with live music and dance on Av CPA. *Bierhaus*, Isaac Póvoas 1200. Large, sophisticated, semi open-air bar/restaurant with music. *Tucano* bar/restaurant, Av CPA, beautiful view, specializes in pizza. Recommended. Av Mato Grosso also has many bars and restaurants. 4 cinemas in town.

Entertainment

Handicrafts in wood, straw, netting, leather, skins, Pequi liquor, crystallized *caju* fruit, compressed *guaraná* fruit (for making the drink), Indian objects on sale at the airport, rodoviária, craft shops in centre, and daily market, Praça da República, interesting. The *Casa de Artesão*, Praça do Expedicionário 315, T321 0603, sells all types of local crafts in a restored building. Recommended. Fish and vegetable market, picturesque, at the riverside.

Shopping

Confiança, R Cândido Mariano 434, T623 4141. Very helpful travel agency, tours to Pantanal US$75 per day. Also recommended *Pantanal Explorers*, Av Governador Ponce de Arruda 670, T682 2800. Sightseeing, fishing trips for 4-5 days by boat. *Anaconda*, R Mal Deodoro 2142, T624 4142, anaconda@anacondapantanal.com.br Upmarket agency providing airport transfers, all meals and high standard of accommodation both in Cuiabá before departure and on trips (guide Fábio Mendes, multilingual, has been recommended).1-3 day tours to Pantanal, day tour to Chapada dos Guimarães or Águas Quentes, Amazon trips to Alta Floresta/Rio Cristalino region (price does not include airfare). Recommended. *Ametur*, R Joaquim Murtinho 242, T/F624 1000. Very helpful, good for air tickets. Adriana Coningham of *Ararauna Turismo Ecológica*, Av Lavapes 500, loja 07, T/F626 1067. Highly recommended.

Tour operators
All these agencies arrange trips to the Pantanal; for longer or special programmes, book in advance

Brazil

All guides work freelance for other companies as well as employing other guides for trips when busy. Most guides await incoming flights at the airport; compare prices and services in town if you don't wish to commit yourself at the airport

Recommended guides (in alphabetical order): *Sérgio Alves*, F623 5258. Speaks English, birdwatching and other tours. *Paulo Boute*, R Getúlio Vargas 64, Várzea Grande, near airport, T686 2231. Speaks Portuguese, English, French, also sells Pantanal publications. *Marcus W Kramm*, R Franklin Cassiano da Silva 63, Cuiabá, T/F321 8982. Speaks Portuguese, English, German. *Djalma dos Santos Moraes*, R Arnaldo Addor 15, Coophamil, 78080 Cuiabá, T/F625 1457. US$100 pp per day. *Laércio Sá, Fauna Tour*, T682 0101, T9983 7475 (mob 24 hrs), faunatur@zaz.com.br Very well-informed, helpful and knowledgeable about environmental issues. Speaks English, Spanish and Italian, 2 and 3-day Pantanal tours (including transport, accommodation in farmhouses rather than hotels, meals, all activities). Has own car, can arrange longer tours and camping (Aug-Oct) on request, also excursions to Chapada dos Guimarães. *Gregório de Silva*, T9975 3347 (mob). 20 years experience of guiding in the Pantanal, multilingual. *Joel Souza*, owner of *Pousada Ecoverde*, see below. Can be contacted at Av Getúlio Vargas 155A, next to *Hotel Presidente*, T646 1852, T9956 7229 (mob), joelsouza@zaz.com.br Speaks English, German and Italian, knowledgeable, checklists for flora and fauna provided, will arrange all transport, accommodation and activities, tends to employ guides rather than guiding himself.

Transport

Local Bus: many bus routes have stops in the vicinity of Praça Ipiranga. To/from airport, see below; bus 501 or 505 (Universidade) to University museums (ask for 'Teatro') from Av Tenente Col Duarte by Praça Bispo Dom José, a triangular park just east of Praça Ipiranga. To rodoviária, No 202 from R Joaquim Murtinho behind the cathedral, 20 mins.

Long distance Air Airport in Várzea Grande, T682 2213. By air to most major cities. ATMs outside include Banco do Brasil for Visa, MasterCard/Cirrus; there is a post office. Taxi to centre US$8, bus US$0.40 (take any white Tuiuiú bus, name written on the side, in front of the airport to Av Tenente Col Duarte; to return take 'Aeroporto' bus from Praça Ipiranga). *Varig*, R 15 de Novembro 230, Bairro Porto, T624 6498, airport T682 1140/3672.

Bus: Rodoviária is on R Jules Rimet, Bairro Alvorada, north of the centre; town buses stop at the entrance. Comfortable buses (toilets) to **Campo Grande**, 10 hrs, US$20, 12 buses daily, *leito* at 2000 and 2100, US$50. **Goiânia**, 14 hrs, US$25; direct to **Brasília**, 24 hrs, US$30, *leito* US$60. To **Porto Velho**, 6 *União Cascavel* buses a day (T621 2551), US$45, 21 hrs. *Andorinha* (T621 3416) 1700 bus São Paulo-Cuiabá connects with Porto Velho service. Several to **São Paulo**, eg *Motta* (T621 1159), US$42. To **Barra do Garças**, *Xavante* (T621 2755) 0800, 1300 and 2030, US$15, also *Barattur*, T621 1300. Connections to all major cities.

Directory

Banks *Banco do Brasil*, Av Getúlio Vargas e R Barão de Melgaço, commission US$10 for cash, US$20 per transaction for TCs, very slow for TCs, but best rates, also has ATM; *Incomep Câmbio*, R Gen Neves 155, good rates. It is difficult to get cash advances on credit cards especially MasterCard, for Visa try *Banco do Brasil*. **Communications** Internet: *Copy Grafic*, Praça Alencastro 32, fax and email, English spoken, friendly. *Netnave*, in Três Américas shopping centre, Av Brasília 200, 2nd floor. Not central but fast access, multimedia machines, US$2.50 per hr. Free short-term access at the tourist office. **Post Office**: main branch at Praça da República, fax service. **Telephone**: *Tele Centro Sul*, R Barão de Melgaço 3209, 0700-2200, also at rodoviária, 0600-2130, international service. **Embassies and consulates** Bolivia: Av Isaac Póvoas 117, T623 5094, open Mon-Fri.e **Tourist offices** Secretaria de Desenvolvimento do Turismo, *Sedtur*, Praça da República 131, next to the post office building, T/F624 9060, Mon-Fri, 0700-1800. Good maps, helpful, contact them if you have any problems with travel agencies; also book hotels and car hire, some English and Spanish spoken. Also at the airport, T682 2213, ext 2252. *Ramis Bucair*, R Pedro Celestino 280, is good for detailed maps of the region. **Voltage** 110 volts AC, 60 cycles.

Chapada dos Guimarães

Phone code: 065
Post code: 78195
Colour map 7, grid A1
Population: 15,755

Some 68 km northeast of Cuiabá lies one of the oldest plateaux on earth. It is one of the most scenic areas of Brazil and visitors describe it as a mystical, energising place. The pleasant town of Chapada dos Guimarães, the main population centre, is a base for many beautiful excursions in this area; it has the oldest church in the Mato Grosso, **Nossa Senhora de Santana** (1779), a bizarre blending of Portuguese and

French baroque styles, and a huge spring-water public swimming pool (on R Dr Pem Gomes, behind the town). Formerly the centre of an important diamond prospecting region, today Chapada is a very popular destination for Cuiabanos to escape the heat of the city at weekends and on holidays. It is a full day excursion from Cuiabá through lovely scenery with many birds, butterflies and flora. There is a post office at R Fernando Corrêa 848. The *Festival de Inverno* is held in last week of July, and Carnival is very busy. Accommodation is scarce and expensive at these times.

The Chapada is an immense geological formation rising to 700 m, with rich forests, curiously-eroded rocks and many lovely grottoes, peaks and waterfalls. A **national park** has been established in the area just west of the town, where the **Salgadeira** tourist centre offers bathing, camping and a restaurant close to the Salgadeira waterfall. The beautiful 85 m **Véu da Noiva** waterfall (Bridal Veil), 12 km before the town near Buriti (well-signposted, ask bus from Cuiabá to let you off), is reached by a short route, or a long route through forest. Other sights include the **Mutuca** beauty spot, **Rio Claro**, the viewpoint over the breathtaking 80 m-deep **Portão do Inferno** (Hell's Gate), and the falls of **Cachoeirinha** (small restaurant) and **Andorinhas**.

About 8 km east of town is the **Mirante do Ponto Geodésico**, a monument officially marking the Geodesic Centre of South America, which overlooks a great canyon with views of the surrounding plains, the Pantanal and Cuiabá's skyline on the horizon; to reach it take R Fernando Corrêa east, drive 8 km then turn right (there is no sign anymore). Continuing east, the road goes through agricultural land and later by interesting rock formations including a stone bridge and stone cross. 45 km from Chapada you reach the access for **Caverna do Francês** or Caverna Aroe Jari ('the dwelling of the souls' in the Bororo language), a sandstone cave over 1 km long, the second largest in Brazil; it is a 1-km walk to the cave, in it is Lagoa Azul, a lake with crystalline blue water. Take your own torch/flashlight (guides' lamps are sometimes weak). A guide is necessary to get through *fazenda* property to the cave, but not really needed thereafter.

Other excursions are to the **Cidade de Pedra** rock formations, 25 km from town along the road to the diamond prospecting town of Água Fria. Nearby is a 300 m wall formed by the Rio Claro and 60 km from town are the **Pingador** and **Bom Jardim** archaeological sites, caverns with petroglyphs dating back some 4,000 years.

Tours The **Secretaria de Turismo e Meio Ambiente** office, R Quinco Caldas 100, near the praça, provides a useful map of the region and organizes tours. José Paulino dos Santos is a guide working with this office (weekdays 0800-1100, 1300-1800, T791 1245). Recommended tours with Jorge Belfort Mattos from Ecoturismo Cultural, Praça Dom Wunibaldo 464, T/F301 1393; he speaks English and knows the area well (however not all of the other guides speak English); several 4-6 hr itineraries from US$20-50 pp (minimum 4 people or prices increase). Cássio Martins of *AC Tour*, R Tiradentes 28, T791 1122, often waits at the rodoviária. 4-hr tours are about US$20 pp, minimum 5 persons; 7- 8 hr tours, US$25 pp, minimum 5; horseback day tour, US$25 pp, minimum 2; an 8-10 km hike with a guide, US$20 pp, minimum 2; bicycle tour with guide, US$20 pp, minimum 2. Tours from Cuiabá cost US$35-40 pp, but a one-day tour is insufficient for a full appreciation of what the area has to offer.

Sleeping **A** *Pousada Pequizeiro*, 1 km from centre on unmarked road, T301 3333, www.terra.com.br/ chapadadosguimaraes/pequizeiro A/c, fridge, TV, small pool, breakfast, new and good. **B** *Hotel da Chapada*, R Fernando Correia 1065, 2 km out on Cuiabá road (MT 251, Km 63), T791 1171, F791 1299. A/c, fridge, cheaper with fan, very comfortable, restaurant, bar, pool, sports facilities, parking. **B** *Estância San Francisco*, at the entrance to town from Cuiabá (MT 251, Km 62), T791 1102, F791 1537. On 42-ha farm with 2 lakes, a/c, fridge, breakfast fresh from the farm. **B** *Rio's Hotel*, R Tiradentes 333, T791 1126. A/c, fridge, **C** with fan, cheaper with shared bath, good breakfast. Recommended. **B** *Chapadense*, R Vereador José de Souza 535, T/F791 1410. A/c, fridge, **C** with fan, restaurant serves *comida caseira*. **C** *Turismo*, R Fernando Corrêa 1065, a block from rodoviária, T791 1176, F791 1383, hotelturismo@

chapadadosguimaraes.com A/c, fridge, cheaper with fan, restaurant, breakfast and lunch excellent, very popular, German-run, Ralf Goebel, the owner, is very helpful in arranging excursions. **C** *Pousada Bom Jardim*, Praça Bispo Dom Wunibaldo s/n, T791 1244. Fan, comfortable, parking, good breakfast. Recommended. **D** *São José*, R Vereador José de Souza 50, T791 1152. Fan, cheaper with shared bath and no fan, hot showers, basic, good, owner Mário sometimes runs excursions. **E** *Dormitório*, R Tiradentes s/n. Basic, no fan, cheaper with shared bath. **Camping E** pp *Aldeia Velha*, in the Aldeia Velha neighbourhood at the entrance to town from Cuiabá, T322 7178 (Cuiabá). Fenced area with bath, hot shower, some shade, guard.

Eating *Nivios*, Praça Dom Wunibaldo 631. Good regional food, closed Mon. *Fogão da Roça*, Praça Dom Wunibaldo 488. *Comida mineira*, generous portions, good quality. Recommended. *O Mestrinho*, R Quinco Caldas 119. Meat, regional dishes, *rodízio* at weekends. *Choppada* (*O Chopp da Chapada*), R Cipriano Curvo s/n near praça. Drinks and meals, regional dishes, live music at weekends. *Trapiche*, R Cipriano Curvo 580. Pizza, drinks, regional dishes. *O Mestrinho*, *Peixaria Serrano*, R Dr Pem Gomes 505 (near pool). Fish specialities and *comida caseira*, cheaper than those near the praça. *Veu da Noiva*, R Dr Pem Gomes 524. Regional dishes, fish in season (*piracema* fishing ban 1 Oct-1 Mar). *Pequi* is a regional palm fruit used to season many foods; *arroz com pequi* is a rice and chicken dish.

Shopping Crafts, indigenous artefacts, sweets and locally-made honey from *Casa de Artes e Artesanato Mato Grossense* (Praça Dom Wunibaldo). Regional sweets from *Doceria Olho de Sogra*, Praça Dom Wunibaldo 21.

Transport Seven bus departures daily to and from **Cuiabá** (*Rubi* 0700-1900, last back to Cuiabá 1800), 1½ hrs, US$2.75. Hiring a car in Cuiabá is the most convenient way to see many of the scattered attractions, although access to several of them is via rough dirt roads which may deteriorate in the rainy season; drive carefully as the area is prone to dense fog. Hitchhiking from Chapada town to the national park is feasible on weekends and holidays.

Cáceres

Phone code: 065
Post code: 78200
Colour map 6, grid A6
Population: 85,857
200 km W of Cuiabá

Situated on the banks of the Rio Paraguai, Cáceres is very hot but clean and hospitable. The city has many well mantained 19th century buildings, painted in pastel colours.

The **Museu Histórico de Cáceres** (R Antônio Maria by Praça Major João Carlos) is a small local history museum. The main square, Praça Barão de Rio Branco, has one of the original border markers from the Treaty of Tordesillas, which divided South America between Spain and Portugal; it is pleasant and shady during the day. In the evenings, between November and March, the trees are packed with thousands of chirping swallows (*andorinhas*). The praça is surrounded by bars, restaurants and ice cream parlours and comes to life at night. The city is known for its many bicycles as most people seem to get around on two wheels. Until 1960, Cáceres had regular boat traffic, today it is limited to a few tour boats and pleasure craft. The town is at the edge of the Pantanal. Vitória Regia lilies can be seen north of town, just across the bridge over the Rio Paraguai along the BR-174. Local festivals are *Piranha Festival*, mid-March; *International Fishing Festival* in mid-September; annual cattle fair.

Sleeping **A** *Ipanema*, R Gen Osório 540, T223 1177, F223 1743. With a/c, fridge, garage, good restaurant. **A** *Caiçaras*, R dos Operários 745, corner R Gen Osório, T223 3187, F223 2692. A/c, **B** without fridge and TV, pleasant, modern, parking. **B** *Fênix*, R dos Operários 600, T223 1027, F221 2243. Fridge, a/c, comfortable. **B** *Rio*, Praça Major João Carlos 61, T223 3387, F223 3084. A/c, **C** without fridge, TV, **D** with shared bath, fan. **C** *Charm*, Col José Dulce 405, T/F223 4949. A/c, **D** with shared bath, friendly. Near the rodoviária: **C** *Capri*, R Getúlio Vargas 99, T223 1711. A/c, comfortable. **C** *Gasparin*, Av Sangradouro 162, T223 4579. A/c, fridge, cheaper with fan. **D** *União*, R 7 de Setembro 340. Fan, **E** with shared bath, basic, good value. **D** *Rio Doce*, R 7 de Setembro. A/c, cheaper with shared bath, good value. Many other cheap hotels.

Brazil

Corimbá, R 15 de Novembro s/n, on riverfront. Fish specialities, good, not cheap. *Bistecão*, R Costa Marques 997. Meat, opens erratically. *Kaskata*, floating restaurant at the end of R Col José Dulce, by the port. Nice setting, fish and *jacaré* specialties, fanciest in town, expensive. *Gulla's*, R Cel José Dulce 250. Buffet by kilo, good quality and variety. Recommended. *Hispano*, Praça Barão de Rio Branco 64. Buffet by kilo. *Panela de Barro*, R Frei Ambrósio 34, near rodoviária. *Comida caseira*.

Eating

Traditional folkloric dance groups *Chalana*, T2233317 and *Tradição*, T2234505 perform shows at different locations.

Entertainment

Náutica Turismo, R Bom Jardim 119A, by the waterfront, for fishing and camping supplies and boat repairs.

Shopping

Bus Rodoviária, T224 1261. *Colibri/União Cascavel* buses Cuiabá-Cáceres, US$9, many daily between 0630-2400 (book in advance, very crowded), 3½ hrs. Cáceres-Porto Velho, US$32. **River** For information on sailings, ask at the **Capitânia dos Portos**, on the corner of the main square at the waterfront. In the dry season there are practically no boats. At the waterfront you can hire a boat for a day trip, US$5 per hr pp, minimum 3.

Transport

Banks *Banco do Brasil*, R Cel José Dulce 234. *HSBC*, R Cel José Dulce 145. *Casa de Câmbio Mattos*, Comandante Bauduino 180, next to main praça, changes cash and TCs at good rates. **Communications** Telephone: Praça Barão de Rio Branco s/n.

Directory

An unpaved road runs from Cáceres to the Bolivian border at San Matías. Brazilian immigration is at R Col Farías, Cáceres, for exit and entry formalities; when closed (for example, Sunday), go to *Polícia Federal*, Av Rubens de Medarca 909. Leaving Bolivia, get your passport stamped at Bolivian immigration (1000-1200, 1500-1700), then get your passport stamped at Cáceres, nowhere in between, but there are three luggage checks for drugs.

Border with Bolivia

Transport Bus: the bus fare Cáceres-San Matías is US$9 with *Transical-Velásquez*, Mon-Sat at 0630 and 1500, Sun 1500 only (return at same times), 3 hrs. Some buses run Cáceres-San Ignacio de Velasco, US$28, 20½ hrs.

Brazil

Brazil

Background

History

Struggle for independence Three centuries under the paternal eye of Portugal had ill-prepared the colonists for independent existence, except for the experience of Dutch invasion (1624 in Salvador, and 1630-54 in Recife). The colonists ejected the Dutch from Brazil with little help from Portugal, and Brazilians date the birth of their national sentiment from these events. Resentment against Portuguese government and trade intervention led to the **Inconfidência**, the first revolution, masterminded by **Tiradentes** with 11 other citizens of Minas Gerais. They were unsuccessful (Tiradentes was executed), but when France invaded Portugal in 1807, King João VI was shipped to safety in Brazil, escorted by the British navy. Rio was temporarily declared the capital of the Portuguese Empire. The British, as a price for their assistance in the Portuguese war, forced the opening of Brazil's ports to non-Portuguese trade. King João VI returned to the mother country in 1821, leaving his son, the handsome young Pedro, as Regent. Pedro refused to return control of Brazil to the Portuguese Côrtes (parliament), and on 13 May 1822, by popular request, he agreed to stay and assumed the title of 'Perpetual Defender and Protector of Brazil'. On 7 September he declared Brazil's independence with the cry 'Independence or Death' by the Rio Ipiranga; on 12 October he was proclaimed constitutional emperor of Brazil, and on 1 December he was crowned in Rio.

Imperial Brazil Dom Pedro the First had the misfortune to be faced by a secession movement in the north, to lose the Banda Oriental (today Uruguay) and to get too involved in his complicated love life. Finally, he abdicated as the result of a military revolt in 1831, leaving his five-year-old son, Dom Pedro the Second, in the hands of a regent, as ruler. On 23 July 1840, the lad, though only 15, was proclaimed of age. Dom Pedro the Second, a strong liberal at heart, promoted education, increased communications, developed agriculture, stamped on corruption and encouraged immigration from Europe. Under his rule the war with the dictator López of Paraguay ended in Brazilian victory. Finally, he declared that he would rather lose his crown than allow slavery to continue, and on 13 May 1888, it was finally abolished by his daughter, Princess Isabel, who was acting as Regent during his temporary absence.

There is little doubt that it was this measure that cost him his throne. Many plantation owners, who had been given no compensation, turned against the Emperor; they were supported by elements in the army and navy, who felt that the Emperor had not given due heed to their interests since the Paraguayan War. On 15 November 1889, the Republic was proclaimed and the Emperor sailed for Europe. Two years later he died in a second-rate hotel in Paris, after steadfastly refusing a pension from the conscience-stricken revolutionaries. At the time of the first centenary of independence in 1922 the imperial family was allowed to return to Brazil, and the body of Dom Pedro was brought back and buried in the cathedral at Petrópolis.

From Republic to dictatorship The history of the 'Old Republic' (1889-1930), apart from the first 10 years which saw several monarchist rebellions, was comparatively uneventful, a time of expansion and increasing prosperity. Brazil declared war on Germany during both wars and Brazilian troops fought in the Italian campaign in 1944-45. In 1930 a revolution headed by Getúlio Vargas, Governor of Rio Grande do Sul, who was to become known as 'the Father of the Poor' for the social measures he introduced, deposed President Wáshington Luís. Vargas assumed executive power first as provisional president and then as dictator. He was forced to resign in October 1945. In 1946 a liberal republic was restored and the following 18 years saw considerable economic development and social advance.

An increase in government instability and corruption prompted the military to intervene in civil affairs. From March 1964 until March 1985, the military governed Brazil using political repression and torture, yet achieving great economic success (up to 1980). Between 1964-74 average growth was 10% a year, but the divide between rich and poor widened. Labour leaders were oppressed, dissenters were jailed and *favelas* mushroomed. Political reform did not occur until 1980 and free elections were not held until 1989.

In January 1985 a civilian, Tancredo Neves, representing a broad opposition to the military régime, was elected President by the electoral college introduced under the military's 1967 constitution. He was unable, because of illness, to take office: the vice-president elect, Sr José Sarney, was sworn in as acting President in March 1985, and in April became President on Sr Neves' death. After complete revision by a Constituent Assembly in 1987-88, Brazil's new constitution of 1988 permitted direct presidential elections in November 1989. The elections, held in two rounds, gave Fernando Collor de Melo, of the small Partido da Reconstrução Nacional, 53% of the vote, narrowly defeating his left-wing rival, Luis Inácio da Silva (Lula), of the Workers Party (PT). Just over half-way through his five-year term, Collor was suspended from office after a landslide congressional vote to impeach him over his involvement in corruption. He avoided impeachment by resigning on 29 December 1992. Vice-president Itamar Franco took over, but had scant success in tackling poverty and inflation until the introduction of an anti-inflation package which introduced the real as the new currency.

Return to democracy

The success of the **real** plan was the principal reason for its architect, finance minister Fernando Henrique Cardoso, defeating Lula (see above) in the presidential elections of October 1994. Cardoso's alliance of the Brazilian Social Democrat Party (PSDB), the Liberal Front (PFL) and the Labour Party (PTB) failed to gain a majority in either house of congress, which prevented swift progress of any reform.

Recent developments

Throughout 1997 and 1998, the financial crisis in Asia threatened Brazil's currency and economic stability. The failure to push through the necessary measures to cut public spending emphasized the scale of the budget deficit and the vulnerability of the real to speculation. Cardoso was therefore obliged to introduce policies which, at the cost of slowing down economic growth, would prevent an upsurge in inflation and a devaluation of the currency. At the same time, the President was still faced with the social imbalances which his government had failed to redress: rising unemployment, unequal income distribution, crime, the low level of police pay, lamentable prison conditions, poor services in the state-run health and education services, land reform and the violence associated with landlessness. These issues notwithstanding, Cardoso again defeated Lula in presidential elections in October 1998 without recourse to a second ballot. The five-party coalition that he led won a majority in Congress, but that did not guarantee support for every policy initiative. As Cardoso battled to enforce greater budgetary discipline, the economy finally succumbed to internal and external pressures in early 1999. The final straw was the decision by Itamar Franco, governor of Minas Gerais, to declare a moratorium on interest payments on debt due to Brasília. Brazil's decision in mid-January to devalue the real by 9% sent shockwaves through world financial markets as it implied that an IMF rescue package of November 1998 had failed. As capital continued to leave the country, the Government was soon forced to let the real float freely. In March 1999 the IMF resumed lending to Brazil, with support from the USA, and as early as May 1999 the economy showed signs of having confounded all the worst expectations. Despite further external shocks in 2001, such as 11 September and the economic crisis in Argentina, the economy remained stable thanks largely to the external sector. Growth was positive and inflation low, but domestic demand was sluggish. This as not helped by prolonged energy shortages in mid-year.

The recession had lowered Cardoso's popularity and thus his influence over his coalition partners. His one-time allies turned their attention away from governing the country towards fighting for political advantage and popular support. Meanwhile the opposition parties were also divided, presenting no serious challenge to the government. Additional

Brazil

pressure was put on the ruling coalition in 2001 when the PFL, led by outgoing Senate president Antônio Carlos Magalhães, failed to win either presidency of the Senate or Congress. This weakened the PFL's resolve to support Cardoso, even if the party did not withdraw fully from the alliance. In March 2001, São Paulo state governor Mário Covas, co-founder of Cardoso's PSDB and close friend of the president, died of cancer. With presidential elections due in 2002, this was a serious blow as it was hoped that Covas would have been instrumental in fashioning the PSDB's strategy in the election campaign.

Government

Constitution The 1988 constitution provides for an executive president elected by direct popular vote, balanced by a bicameral legislature (81 seats in the Federal Senate, 513 seats in the Chamber of Deputies) and an independent judiciary. The vote has been extended to 16-year-olds and illiterates. Presidential elections are held every five years, with a second round one month after the first if no candidate wins an outright majority. Congressional elections are held every four years, the deputies being chosen by proportional representation.

Culture

People

Forecast population growth 2000-2005: 1.2%
Urban population in 2000: 81%
Infant mortality: 38 per 1,000 live births

At first the Portuguese colony grew slowly. From 1580 to 1640 the population was only about 50,000 apart from the million or so indigenous Indians. In 1700 there were some 750,000 non-indigenous people in Brazil. Early in the 19th century Humboldt computed there were about 920,000 whites, 1,960,000 Africans, and 1,120,000 Indians and *mestiços*: after three centuries of occupation a total of only four million, and over twice as many Africans as there were whites.

Modern immigration did not begin effectively until after 1850. Of the 4.6 million immigrants from Europe between 1884 and 1954, 32% were Italians, 30% Portuguese, 14% Spanish, 4% German, and the rest of various nationalities. Since 1954 immigrants have averaged 50,000 a year. There are some one million Japanese-descended Brazilians; they grow a fifth of the coffee, 30% of the cotton, all the tea, and are very active in market gardening. The total population according to the 2000 census was 169,799,170 (all population figures in the text are taken from the 2000 census).

Today the whites and near-whites are about 54% of the population, people of mixed race about 40%, and Afro Brazilians 5%; the rest are either Indians or Asians. There are large regional variations in the distribution of the races: the whites predominate greatly in the south, which received the largest flood of European immigrants, and decrease more or less progressively towards the north.

Most of the German immigrants settled in the three southern states: Santa Catarina, Rio Grande do Sul, and Paraná. The Germans (and the Italians and Poles and other Slavs who followed them) did not in the main go as wage earners on the big estates, but as cultivators of their own small farms.

The arid wastes of the Sertão remain largely uncultivated. Its inhabitants are people of mixed Portuguese and Indian origin (*mestiço*); most live off the 'slash and burn' method of cultivation, which involves cutting down and burning the brushwood for a small patch of ground which is cultivated for a few years and then allowed to grow back.

Brazilian culture is rich in African influences. Those interested in the development of Afro-Brazilian music, dance, religion, arts and cuisine will find the whole country north of São Paulo fascinating, and especially the cities of Bahia and São Luís which retain the greatest African influences. Though there is no legal discrimination against black people, the economic and educational disparity – by default rather than intent of the Government – is such that successful Afro Brazilians are active almost exclusively in the worlds of sport, entertainment and arts. Black Pride movements are particularly strong in Bahia. Further reading: *Towards the Abolition of Whiteness* by **David Roediger**, Verso, (a sociological study of how 'colour' is determined by economic status, mostly in the USA and UK).

Indigenous peoples It is estimated that, when the Portuguese arrived in Brazil, there were between three and five million Indians living in the area. Today there are only about

Brazil

350,000. Tribal groups number 210; each has a unique dialect, but most languages belong to four main linguistic families, Tupi-Guarani, Ge, Carib and Arawak. A few tribes remain uncontacted, others are exclusively nomadic, others are semi-nomadic hunter-gatherers and farmers, while some are settled groups in close contact with non-Indian society. The struggle of groups such as the Yanomami to have their land demarcated in order to secure title is well-documented. The goal of the Statute of the Indian (Law 6.001/73), for demarcation of all Indian land by 1978, is largely unmet. It was feared that a new law introduced in January 1996 would slow the process even more. Funai, the National Foundation for the Support of the Indian, a part of the Interior Ministry, is charged with representing the Indians' interests, but lacks resources and support. There is no nationwide, representative body for indigenous people. Most of Brazil's indigenous people live in the Amazon region; they are affected by deforestation, encroachment from colonizers, small- and large-scale mining, and the construction of hydroelectric dams. Besides the Yanomami, other groups include the Xavante, Tukano, Kreen-Akrore, Kaiapó, Arawete and Arara.

Rural and urban population The population has historically been heavily concentrated along the coastal strip where the original Portuguese settlers exploited the agricultural wealth, and further inland in the states of Minas Gerais and São Paulo where more recent development has followed the original search for gold, precious stones and slaves. Much of the interior of Pará, Amazonas, Goiás and the Mato Grosso has densities of one person per sq km or less. Internal migration has brought to the cities problems of unemployment, housing shortage, and extreme pressure on services; shanty towns – or *favelas, mocambos, alagados*, according to the region – are an integral part of the urban landscape. But while the northeast, because of its poverty, has lost many workers to the industries of the southeast, many rural workers from southern Brazil have moved north, drawn by the rapid development of Amazônia, creating unprecedented pressures on the environment.

Books

Historical travellers: Jean Baptiste Debret, *Viagem Pitoresca e Histórica ao Brasil* (São Paulo: Livraria Martins, 1954) translated by Sérgio Milliet; text and black and white reproductions of Debret's wonderful illustrations. Lt-Col P H Fawcett, *Exploration Fawcett*, arranged from his records by Brian Fawcett (Hutchinson, 1953). **Charles Waterton**, *Wanderings in South America*. Introduction by David Bellamy (Century, 1983).
Modern travellers: Richard Gott, *Land without Evil. Utopian Journeys across the South American Watershed* (Verso, 1993). Redmond O'Hanlon, *In Trouble Again* (Penguin). **Alex Shoumatoff**, *The Rivers Amazon* (Hutchinson, 1987). **Mark J Plotkin**, *Tales of a Shaman's Apprentice* (1993). *Travelers' Tales, Brazil*, ed by **Annette Haddad and Scott Doggett** (San Francisco, CA: Traveler's Tales, 1997).
Culture: Alma Guillermoprieto, *Samba* (Bloomsbury, 1991). David J Hess and Roberto A Damatta (eds), *The Brazilian Puzzle. Culture on the Borderlands of the Western World* (Columbia University Press, 1995). **Roberto Schwartz**, *Misplaced Ideas* (Verso, 1992).
History and politics: Leslie Bethel, ed, *Colonial Brazil* (Cambridge University Press, 1987). **C R Boxer**, *The Dutch in Brazil, 1624-54* (Clarendon Press, 1957) and *The Golden Age of Brazil, 1695-1750* (University of California Press, 1962). **Gilberto Freyre**, *New World in the Tropics. The Culture of Modern Brazil* (Alfred A Knopf, 1959); see also Freyre's major work, *Casa-Grande e Senzala (The Masters & The Slaves)*. **Márcio Moreira Alves**, *A Grain of Mustard Seed. The Awakening of the Brazilian Revolution* (Doubleday, 1973); on the Marxist guerrillas' campaign in the 1960s. *The Discovery of the Amazon*, translated by **Bertram T Lee**, (Dover, 1988). Alain Gheerbrant, *The Amazon, Past and Present* (Thames & Hudson, 1992). **Michael Goulding, Nigel J H Smith, Dennis J Mahar**, *Floods of Fortune. Ecology & Economy of the Amazon* (Columbia University Press, 1996). **John Hemming**, *Amazon Frontier. The Defeat of the Brazilian Indians* and *Red Gold. The Conquest of the Brazilian Indians* (Papermac 1987/1995 and 1995).
Brazilian Literature: Joaquim Maria Machado de Assis (1839-1908) was the classical satirical novelist of the Brazilian 19th century, one of the most original writers to have

emerged from Latin America. **Euclides da Cunha** (1866-1909) *Os sertões* (1902): *Rebellion in the Backlands* (University of Chicago Press, 1944, often reprinted, including Picador, 1995): the 'epic' story of the military campaign to crush the rebellion centred in Canudos in the interior of the State of Bahia. One of the great books about the Brazilian national make-up. Manuel Bandeira (1886-1968) was a member of the Modernist movement and one of Brazil's greatest poets, master of the short, intense lyric. For a collection in English, see *This Earth, that Sky: Poems by Manuel Bandeira* (University of California Press, 1988). **Graciliano Ramos** (1892-1953) was the greatest of the novelists of the 1930s and 1940s: a harsh realist. **Carlos Drummond de Andrade** (1902-87), perhaps Brazil's greatest poet, with a varied, lyrical, somewhat downbeat style. See, in English, *Travelling in the Family: Selected Poems* (Random House, 1986). Over a long career **Jorge Amado** (1912-) has published many best-sellers: he is sometimes criticized for producing an overly optimistic, sexily tropical view of the country. **Clarice Lispector** (1920-77), Brazil's greatest woman writer, now has a considerable following outside Brazil. Many of her stories and novels have been translated into English. **Ivan Ângelo** (1936-) has written much the best novel about the political, social and economic crisis at the end of the 1960s, the worst period of the military regime: *A festa* (1976): *The Celebration* (Avon Books, 1992). **Caio Fernando Abreu** (1948-96) was one of the writers most effective in dealing with life in the Latin American megalopolis.

Brazil

chile

Chile is a ribbon of land squashed between the Pacific and the Andes. Its landscape embraces glacial wilderness and moonscapes, lakes and volcanoes, beaches and salt flats and the burnt colours of the driest desert in the world. In one day it is possible to scale a mountain with ice axe and crampons, soak off the exhaustion in a thermal bath and rest beneath the stars of the Southern Cross. Real stargazers will want to visit the astronomical observatories, while lovers of mystery will head for the folklore of Chiloé, Land of Seagulls. Chile is famous for its wines and seafood, both among the most celebrated in the world, and for the legacy of its recent turbulent politics, which inspired headlines around the globe, but also some of the continent's most committed singers and writers.

Chile

PERU

Arica

Iquique

Calama

Antofagasta

Salta

ARGENTINA

La Serena

Viña del Mar
Valparaíso SANTIAGO

Rancagua
Talca

Concepción Chillán

Valdivia Osorno
Puerto Montt Bariloche

Chaitén

Puerto Aysén Coyhaique
Puerto Ibáñez

Pacific
Ocean

Puerto Atlantic
Natales Ocean

Punta Arenas Ushuaia

Essentials

Planning your trip

Santiago and the heartland A great many of Chile's attractions are out of doors, in the national parks, adventure sports, etc, but the capital, Santiago, has a rich cultural life and is a good base for visiting nearby areas. These include the port of Valparaíso and the beach resorts to north and south, principally Viña del Mar; the vineyards of the Central Valley; the Andean foothills; the ski resorts.

North of Santiago La Serena is a popular seaside resort, from which can be reached the Elqui Valley, where Chilean *pisco* is made, and three major astronomical observatories. Heading north, the land becomes more barren, but after rain, usually September-October, the flowers that have lain dormant in the desert burst into bloom; if you are in the area, a sight not to be missed. Inland from Antofagasta, the next main city, a road goes to Calama, the huge copper mine at Chuquicamata and the isolated Andean town and popular tourist resort of San Pedro de Atacama. Its attractions are lunar landscapes, hot geysers, salt flats and the way of life at high altitude. Alternatively, from Antofagasta you can take the spectacular coast road to the **Far North** and the ports of Iquique, near which are several archaeological sites, thermal springs and abandoned nitrate mines, and Arica, the last main town before Peru. The road route into Bolivia from Arica passes through the magnificent Parque Nacional Lauca, with its wealth of Andean bird and animal life, high lakes and remote volcanoes.

South of Santiago The longitudinal highway runs south through the Central Valley passing a number of cities which are worth a stop: Rancagua, Talca, Chillán, Concepción (the country's second city), and others. There are national parks which deserve a visit in both the Andean foothills and in the coastal range of mountains.

The Lake District Here, the most popular lakes are Villarrica and Llanquihue, but there are many others with much less development. Protected areas of great beauty and first-class opportunities for adventure sports and fishing abound. Temuco, at the northern end of this region, is also the centre of the Mapuche culture. Valdivia, near the coast, is worth a detour for the trip to the mouth of the river to see the ruined Spanish forts that protected this outpost of the empire. The southern gateway to the Lake District is Puerto Montt, also the starting point for the long haul south. From Puerto Montt you can cross to Argentina by road and ferries on Lago Todos los Santos and neighbouring Lagos Frías and Nahuel Huapi on the way to Bariloche.

South of Puerto Montt The island of Chiloé, a short bus and ferry ride from Puerto Montt, has a distinctive culture and a green landscape which is the result of more than enough rain. On the mainland, running south from Puerto Montt, the Camino Austral has opened up an area of forests, lakes and rivers, linking small communities of settlers. The biggest town is Coyhaique and there is a regular excursion by sea to the stunning glacier at the Laguna San Rafael. A four-day sea voyage takes you to Puerto Natales in **Chilean Patagonia**, near Chile's most dramatic national park, the Torres del Paine. Hiking around the vertical mountains with their forested slopes, past lakes and glaciers, in the presence of a multitude of southern Andean wildlife is an unforgettable experience (but do allow for the unpredictability of the weather). If you prefer not to venture this far south by ship, there are regular flights to the main city of Chilean Patagonia, Punta Arenas, and there is no problem crossing from Argentina by road or by ferry from **Tierra del Fuego**. The contrast between this southernmost part of the country with the dry, desert north could not be greater.

The best times to visit vary according to geographical location. For Santiago and the heartland, any time between Oct and Apr is good, but the most pleasant seasons are spring (Sep-Nov) and autumn (Mar-April). The heat of the north is less intense from Jun to Sep. In the south Dec to Mar, summer, is the best time. In the far south this is the only realistic time to travel because at other times ferry schedules are restricted and in mid-winter many transport

Chile

services do not run at all. Also bear in mind that the summer in the Lake District and further south is the busiest season, with hotels and buses full, lots of backpackers on the road and advance booking often essential. In this holiday season business visitors may find making appointments difficult, but otherwise any time of year is good for working in Santiago.

Finding out more

The national secretariat of tourism, **Sernatur**, has offices throughout the country (addresses given in the text), www.sernatur.cl City offices provide town maps and other useful information. A recommended book is *Turistel*, published annually in three parts, *Norte*, *Centro*, and *Sur*, sponsored by the CTC phone company, with information and a wealth of maps covering the whole country and neighbouring tourist centres in Argentina (eg Mendoza, San Martín de los Andes, Bariloche), in Spanish only. Each volume costs between US$11-15, depending where you buy it, but buying the whole set is better value; they can be found in CTC offices, bookshops, but best of all in the news stands in the centre of Santiago. *Turistel* also publishes a *Mapa rutero* annually, US$4 from news stands and a guide to camping US$9. See www.turistel.cl (in Spanish). *Matassi* maps (*JLM Mapas*), usually with a red cover, are good value, US$5.50-6.50, F02-236 4808, jmatassi@interactiva.cl **Conaf** (the Corporacíon Nacional Forestal), Presidente Bulnes 291, p 1, Santiago, T390 0126, publishes a number of leaflets and has documents and maps about the national park system that can be consulted or photocopied (not very useful for walking). **CODEFF** (Comité Nacional Pro-Defensa de la Fauna y Flora), Bilbao 691, Providencia, T251 0262, can also provide information on environmental questions.

Websites www.chile.cl (Spanish); www.gochile.cl (English and Spanish); www.prochile.cl – Spanish, and www.chileinfo.com – English (both principally trade information), www.visitchile.org (English, Spanish); www.chilelindo.com (Spanish)

Chile

The government's site is **www.gobiernodechile.cl www.tnet.cl** is Chilean version of Terra, which covers much of Latin America in Spanish. Its tourism page is **www.tnet.cl/turismo/**

www.hotelschile.com For hotel information, reservations, advice and tours.

See also **www.chip.cl**, the site of *Chile Information Project*, Av Santa María 227, of 12, Recoleta, Santiago, T777 5376, which gives access to *The Santiago Times* English-language daily, travel information, hotels, economics, history, wine and LOM books.

For information and loads of links in Patagonia, visit **www.chileaustral.com**

For Valparaíso, visit **www.valparaisochile.cl**

For the outdoors, **www.chile-outdoors.cl**

www.ancientforests.org *Ancient Forest International*, Box 1850, Redway, CA 95560, T/F707-923 4475, USA, can be contacted regarding Chilean forests. See also **www.greenpeace.cl** for environmental issues (in Spanish).

The local pronunciation of Spanish, very quick and lilting, with final syllables cut off, can present difficulties to the foreigner. **Language**

Before you travel

Passport (valid for at least six months) and tourist card only are required for entry by all foreigners except citizens of Guyana, Haiti, Dominica, Kuwait, Egypt, Saudi Arabia and United Arab Emirates, most African countries, Cuba and some former Eastern bloc countries (excluding Croatia, the Czech Republic, Estonia, Hungary, Poland, Slovak Republic, Slovenia and Yugoslavia), who require visas. It is imperative to check tourist card and visa requirements before travel. National identity cards are sufficient for entry by citizens of Argentina, Brazil, Paraguay, and Uruguay. Tourist cards are valid for 90 days. For nationals of Greece, Indonesia and Peru validity is 60 days; Belize, Costa Rica, Malaysia and Singapore 30 days. Tourist cards can be obtained from immigration offices at major land borders and Chilean airports; you must surrender your tourist card on departure and it is essential that you keep it safe. If you wish to stay longer than 90 days (as a tourist), you must buy a 90-day extension from the Departamento de Extranjería (address under Santiago Useful addresses), or any local *gobernación* office. It costs US$100. To avoid this, make a day-trip to Argentina and return with a new tourist card. An onward ticket is officially required but is seldom asked for. Tourist card holders are not allowed to change their status to enable them to stay on in employment or as students: to do this you need a visa, obtained from a Chilean consulate. On arrival you will be asked where you are staying in Chile. **NB** On arrival, US citizens will be charged an administration fee of US$61, Canadians US$55, Australians US$30 and Mexicans US$15. This must be paid in cash. For some nationalities a visa will be granted within 24 hours upon production of an onward ticket, for others (eg Guyana), authorization must be obtained from Chile. For other nationalities who need a visa, a charge is made, but it varies from country to country. Note that to travel overland to or from Tierra del Fuego a multiple entry visa is essential since the Argentine-Chilean border is crossed more than once (it is advisable to get a multiple entry visa before arriving, rather than trying to change a single entry visa once in Chile). A student card is sometimes useful for obtaining discounts on buses, etc. They can be obtained from Hernando de Aguirre 201, of 602, Providencia and cost US$8, photo and proof of status required; www.isic.cl

Visas & immigration

Duty free allowance 500 cigarettes, 100 cigars, 500 gms of tobacco, three bottles of liquor, camera, and all articles of personal use. Unlike neighbouring countries, Chile's agricultural sector is free of many diseases, so fruit, vegetables, meat, flowers and milk products may not be imported. These will be confiscated at all land borders, where there are thorough searches. This applies even to those who have had to travel through Argentina in the far south to get from one part of Chile to another. **NB** There are internal customs checks for all travellers going south from Region I in the far north. This is mainly to inspect for duty-free goods from Iquique, but fruit, vegetables, meat, flowers and milk products will also be confiscated.

Customs

Chile

Chile

 Chilean embassies and consulates

Australia, 10 Culgoa Circuit, O'Malley 2606, ACT, PO Box 69, Monaro Crescent, ACT2603, T61-6-6286 2430, F6286 1289, www.embachile-australia.com

Belgium, *40 rue Montoyer, 1000 Brussels, T32-2-280 1620, F280 1481, embachile.belgica@skynet.be*

Canada, *50 O'Conner Street, suite 1413, Ottawa, K1 P6L2, T1-613-235 4402, F235 1176, www.chile.ca*

Denmark, *Kastelsvej 15, 3, 2100 Copenhagen, T45-3526 1535, F3538 4201, www.chiledk.dk*

France, *2 ave de la Motte Picquoet, 75007 Paris, T33-1-4418 5960, F4418 5961, echile@amb-chili.fr*

Germany, *Lepziger Strasse 63, 10117 Berlin*

Israel, *Havkook N 7, Tel Aviv, T972-3-602 0131, F602 0133, www.embachile-israel.org.il*

Japan, *Nihon Seimei Akabanebashi Bldg, 8F 3-1-14 Shiba, Minato-Ku, Tokyo 105, T81-3-3452 7561, F3452 4457, embajada@chile.or.jp*

Netherlands, *Mauritskade 51, 2514 HG, The Hague, T31-70-312 3640, F361 6227, echilenl@euronet.nl*

New Zealand, *1-3 Willeston Street, Willis Coroon House 7th floor, PO Box 3861, Wellington, T64-4-471 6270, F472 5324, www.prochinz.co.nz*

Norway, *Meltzers Gate 5, 0257 Oslo, T47-2244 8955, F2244 2421, www.home.online.no/~embachile*

Spain, *Lagasca 88, p 6, Madrid 28001, T34-1-431 9160, F455 4833, echilees@tsai.es*

Sweden, *Sturegatan 8, 3rd floor, 11435 Stockholm, T46-8-679 8280, F679 8540, www.chileemb.se*

Switzerland, *Eigerplatz 5, 12th floor, 3007 Bern, T41-31-371 0745, F372 0025, echilech@swissonline.ch*

UK, *12 Devonshire Street, London, W1N 2DS, T020-7580 6392, F020-7436 5204, www.echileuk.demon.co.uk*

USA, *1140 Connecticut Avenue NW, Washington, suite 703, DC 20036, T1-202-785 1746, F1-202-887 5579, www.chile-usa.org*

Vaccinations Inoculation against hepatitis and typhoid is a wise precaution. Hepatitis type B inoculation is unavailable.

What to take Warm sunny days and cool nights are usual during most of the year, but the two main exceptions are at altitude in the far north, where nights can be bitterly cold, and in the far south where the climate is wet, windy and very changeable. Be prepared for cold and rain in this region. In the central area ordinary European medium-weight clothing can be worn during the winter (Jun to mid-Sep). Light clothing is best for summer (Dec to Mar). Chileans are very fashion-conscious. Dress well, though conservatively: practical travel clothing makes you stick out as a foreigner. If camping, trekking, cycling or skiing, consider taking all your own equipment because, although it may be available in Chile, it will be expensive. Also note that in the Lake District, between mid-Dec and mid-Jan, huge horseflies (*tavanos*) can be a real problem when camping, hiking and fishing: do not wear dark clothing. Tampons are available but expensive.

Money

Currency
peso exchange rate with US$: 695.7
MasterCard emergency T1230-020-2012;
Visa emergency T1230-020-2136;
Amex emergency T02-695 2422

The unit is the peso, its sign is $. Notes are for 500, 1,000, 5,000, 10,000 and 20,000 pesos and coins for 1, 5, 10, 50, 100 and 500 pesos. There is a shortage of change so keep a supply of small denomination coins. **Banks** The easiest way to obtain cash is by using ATMs (in major cities) which operate under the sign Redbanc (www.redbanc.cl, for a full list); they take Cirrus (MasterCard) and Plus (Visa) and permit transactions up to US$400 per day. Diners' Club, Visa and MasterCard are common in Chile (Bancard, the local card, is affiliated to the last two). American Express is less useful. Travellers' cheques are most easily exchanged in Santiago. It has become more difficult to change TCs in most towns apart from Arica, Antofagasta and Puerto Montt. Even slightly damaged US dollar notes may be rejected for exchange. Exchange shops (*casas de cambio*) are open longer hours and often give slightly better rates than banks. It is always worth shopping around. Rates tend to get worse as you go north from Santiago. Official rates are quoted in *El Economista* and *El Mercurio*.

Prices may be quoted in US dollars; check if something seems ridiculously cheap. Remember that foreigners who pay with US dollars cash or travellers' cheques are not liable for VAT.

Shops throughout Chile are well stocked and there is a seasonal supply of all the usual fruits and vegetables. Milk in pasteurized, evaporated, or dried form is obtainable. Chilean tinned food is expensive. Food is reasonable, but food prices vary tremendously. Santiago tends to be more expensive for food and accommodation than other parts of Chile.

The average cost for a traveller on an economical budget is about US$40 per day. Cheap accommodation in Santiago costs US$8-10 pp while north and south of the capital rates are US$7-12 pp. Breakfast in hotels, if not included in price, is about US$2 (instant coffee, roll with ham or cheese, and jam). *Alojamiento* in private houses (bed, breakfast and often use of kitchen) costs US$7-10 pp (bargaining may be possible). Southern Chile is more expensive between 15 Dec and 15 Mar. **Cost of travelling**

Getting there

From Europe There are regular flights to Santiago from Paris, Barcelona and Madrid, and Frankfurt with *LanChile* and/or European carriers. Connections from London and other European cities can be made in the above, New York, Bogotá, Brazil or Buenos Aires. **Air**

From North America Several airlines have flights from Miami, New York, Atlanta, Chicago, Dallas and Los Angeles to Santiago. From other US cities make connections in Miami, New York or Los Angeles. From Toronto or Vancouver, Canada, make onward connections in New York, Miami or Los Angeles.

Transpacific routes *LanChile* flies two to four times a week, depending on season, between Tahiti and Santiago; they stop over at Easter Island. For flights from Japan, make connections in the USA. From Australia and New Zealand change planes in Buenos Aires.

Within Latin America All the South American capitals, plus Córdoba and Mendoza (Argentina), Guayaquil (Ecuador), Santa Cruz (Bolivia) and Rio de Janeiro and São Paulo (Brazil), have regular flights to Santiago. In addition, *LanChile* fly to Arica and Iquique from La Paz and and Mercosur to Iquique from Asunción.

Overland from Neighbouring Countries By land: Roads connect Santiago with Mendoza, and Osorno and Puerto Montt with Bariloche, in Argentina. Less good road connections north and south of Santiago are described in the main text. The main route connecting northern Chile with Bolivia (Arica-La Paz) is paved. Similarly, the road route Arica-Tacna (Peru) is paved. Other routes are poor. Note that any of the passes across the Andes to Argentina can be blocked by snow from April onwards. **Road**

Four international railways link Chile with its neighbours: two to Bolivia: between Arica and La Paz (448 km), and from Calama to Oruro; one to Peru: Arica-Tacna; and one to Argentina, between Antofagasta and Salta. There are usually passenger services only on Calama-Oruro and Arica-Tacna. **Train**

Touching down

Airport tax is 7,500 pesos, or US$18.25 for international flights; US$9 for domestic flights. There is a tourist tax on single air fares of 2%, and 1% on return fares beginning or ending in Chile; also a sales tax of 5% on all transport within Chile. **Airport & other taxes**

In restaurants, if service is not included in the bill, tip 10%; tip a few pesos in bars and soda fountains. Railway and airport porters: US$0.10 a piece of luggage. Cloakroom attendants and cinema usherettes: US$0.05. Taxi-drivers are not tipped. **Tipping**

Chile is generally one of the safest countries in South America for the visitor. **Law enforcement** officers are *Carabineros* (brown military uniforms), who handle all tasks **Safety**

Chile

Touching down

Business hours Banks: 0900-1400, closed on Saturday. **Government offices:** 1000-1230 (the public is admitted for a few hours only). **Business hours:** 0830-1230, 1400-1800 (Monday to Friday). **Shops (Santiago):** 1030-1930, 0930-1330 Saturday. **IDD** 56. A double ring repeated regularly means it is ringing; equal tones with equal pauses means it is engaged.

Official time GMT minus four hours; minus three hours in summer. Clocks change from mid-September or October to early March.
VAT 18%
Voltage 220 volts AC, 50 cycles.
Weights and measures The **metric** system is obligatory but the quintal of 46 kg (101.4 lbs) is used.

except immigration. Investigaciones, in civilian dress, are the detective police who deal with everything except traffic. **Policia Internacional**, a division of Investigaciones, handle immigration (head office Gral Borgoña 1052, Santiago, T737 2443/1292).

Where to stay

Sleeping
In expensive hotels, if you pay in US$ cash or TCs, you may not have to pay IVA, but unless the establishment has an agreement with the government, hotels are not obliged to exclude IVA for dollar payments

On hotel bills service charges are usually 10%, and IVA(VAT) on bills is 18%. Check on arrival whether hotel rates include VAT. When booking in make certain whether meals are included in the price or only breakfast or nothing at all, and don't rely on the posted sheet in the bedroom for any prices. It is often worth asking for a discount, especially out of season. Particularly in North and Central Chile breakfast is likely to be coffee and bread or toast. In popular tourist destinations, especially in the south, large numbers of families offer accommodation: these are usually advertised by a sign in the window. People often meet buses to offer accommodation. In summer especially, single rooms can be hard to find. If you are looking for a motel, ask for a *motel turístico*; most motels are short stay.

Camping
Camping is easy but not always cheap at official sites. A common practice is to charge US$10 for up to five people, with no reductions for fewer than five. 'Camping Gaz International' stoves are recommended, since green replaceable cylinders are available in Santiago (white gas – *benzina blanca* – is available in hardware shops; for good value try the *Sodimac* chain of DIY stores). *Copec* run a network of 33 'Rutacentros' along Ruta 5 which have showers, cafeterias and offer free camping. Free camping is also available at many filling stations.

Youth hostels
There are youth hostels throughout Chile; average cost about US$5-8 pp. Although some hostels are open only from Jan to the end of Feb, many operate all year round. The IYHA card is usually readily accepted. In summer they are usually crowded and noisy, with only floor space available. Chilean YHA card costs US$5. A Hostelling International card costs US$15. These can be obtained from the **Asociación Chilena de Albergues Turísticos Juveniles**, Hernando de Aguirre 201, of 602, Providencia, Santiago, T233 3220/234 3233, www.hostelling.cl, together with a useful guidebook of all Youth Hostels in Chile, *Guía Turística de los Albergues Juveniles*. In summer there are makeshift hostels in many Chilean towns, usually in the main schools; they charge US$3-4 pp.

Getting around

Air
You have to confirm domestic flights at least 24 hrs before departure

Most flights of *LanChile* and its subsidiary, Lan Express, between Santiago and major towns and cities, are given in the text. Try to sit on the left flying south, on the right flying north to get the best views of the Andes. *LanChile* offers a 30-day 'Visit Chile' ticket. It must be purchased abroad in conjunction with an international ticket and reservations made well ahead since many flights are fully booked in advance. If arriving in Chile on *LanChile* or *Iberia*, three coupons cost US$250, if on another carrier US$350. Extra coupons cost US$60, or US$80 respectively. The maximum number of coupons is six. Rerouting charge US$30. Travel must commence within 14 days of arriving in Chile. There is a special sector fare of US$525 if using

LanChile translatlantic for Santiago-Easter Island-Santiago. **NB** Book well in advance (several months) for flights to Easter Island in Jan-Feb. If arriving in Chile on *LanChile*, ask about discounts on individual sector, domestic flights. Check with the airlines for matrimonial, student and other discounts.

Road

About one-half of the 79,293 km of roads can be used the year round, though a large proportion of them are unimproved and about 12,685 km are paved. The region round the capital and the Central Valley are the best served. The main road is the Panamericana (Ruta 5), which is now dual carriageway from La Calera to Los Angeles; the plan is eventually to make the dual carriageway run from La Serena to Puerto Montt. A paved coastal route running the length of Chile is also being constructed, which should be ready by 2007.

Bus

Buses are frequent and on the whole good. Apart from holiday times, there is little problem getting a seat on a long-distance bus. *Salón-cama* services run between main cities (*TurBus* and *Pullman* highly recommended). Generally avoid back seats near toilet due to smell and disruption of passing passengers. *Salón-cama* means 25 seats, *semi-cama* means 34 and *Salón-ejecutivo* means 44. Stops are infrequent. Prices are highest between Dec-Mar and fares from Santiago double during the Independence celebrations in Sep. Students and holders of HI cards may get discounts, amount varies, but not usually in high season. Most bus companies will carry bicycles, but may ask for payment (on *TurBus* payment is mandatory).

Since there is lots of competition between bus companies, fares may be bargained lower, particularly just before departure

Car

For drivers of private vehicles entering Chile, customs will type out a *título de importación temporal de vehículos* (temporary admission), valid for three months, or in accordance with the length of stay granted by immigration. Your immigration entry/exit card is stamped 'entrada con vehículo' so you must leave the country with your vehicle (so you cannot make an excursion to Bariloche, for example, without your car). There are very strict controls for fresh fruit, vegetables, meat, fish, etc. Insurance is obligatory and can be bought at borders.
Fuel and spares Gasoline (sold in litres) costs the equivalent of US$2.85 a US gallon; it becomes more expensive the further north and further south you go. Unleaded fuel, 93 octane, is available in all main cities; unleaded 95 and 97 octane is less common. Diesel fuel is widely available. Esso service stations usually accept credit cards. Other companies may not; always ask beforehand. When driving in the south (on the Camino Austral particularly), and in the desert north, always top up your fuel tank and carry spare petrol/gasoline. Car hire companies may not have fuel cans. These are obtainable from some supermarkets but not from service stations. Tyres need to be hard-wearing (avoid steel belt); it is recommended to carry more than one spare and additional tubes.

Carabineros are strict about speed limits; Turistel maps mark police posts, make sure you are not speeding when you pass them. Car drivers should have all their papers in order and to hand since there are frequent checks, but fewer in the south

Car hire

Many agencies, both local and international, operate in Chile. Vehicles may be rented by the day, the week or the month, with or without unlimited mileage. Rates quoted do not normally include insurance or 18% VAT. Make sure you know what the insurance covers, in particular third-party insurance. Often this is only likely to cover small bumps and scratches. Ask about extra cover for a further premium. If you are in a major accident and your insurance is inadequate, your stay in Chile may well be prolonged beyond its intended end. A small car, with unlimited mileage costs about US$500 a week in high season, a pick-up much more. In some areas rates are much lower off-season. (At peak holiday times, eg Independence celebrations, car hire is very difficult.) Shop around, there is much competition. Note that the *Automóvil Club de Chile* has a car hire agency (with discounts for members or affiliates) and that the office may not be at the same place as the Club's regional delegation. **NB** If intending to leave the country in a hired car, you must obtain an authorization from the hire company, otherwise you will be turned back at the border. When leaving Chile this is exchanged for a quadruple form, one part of which is surrendered at each border control. (If you plan to leave more than once you will need to photocopy the authorization.)

Hitchhiking

Hitchhiking is easy and safe, but in some regions traffic is sparse.

Chile

Motorcycling Most major towns have motorcycle mechanics. Enduro sports bikes are very popular. A *carnet de passages* is not officially required for foreign-owned motorcycles: a temporary import paper is given at the border.

Taxis Taxis have meters, but agree beforehand on fares for long journeys out of city centres or special excursions. A 50% surcharge is applied after 2100 and on Sun. Taxi drivers rarely know the location of any streets away from the centre. There is no need to tip unless some extra service, like the carrying of luggage, is given. Colectivos (collective taxis) operate on fixed routes identified by numbers and destinations. They have fixed charges, which increase at night and weekends and which are usually advertised in the front windscreen. They are flagged down on the street corner (in some cities such as Puerto Montt there are signs). It is best to take small change as the driver takes money and offers change while driving. Colectivos also operate on some interurban routes (especially in the north), leaving from a set point when full. Collective taxis (colectivos) are often little more expensive than buses.

Boat Shipping information is given in the text under Santiago and all the relevant southern ports. Local newspapers are useful for all transport schedules.

Train There are 6,560 km of line, of which most are state owned. Most of the privately owned 2,130 km of line are in the desert north, where the northern terminal is Iquique. Passenger services in the south go as far as Temuco. Passenger services north of the Valparaíso area have ceased. Trains in Chile are moderately priced, and not as slow as in other Andean countries, but dining car food is expensive. See Santiago, Transport, Long Distance, Trains for rail company offices.

Maps The **Instituto Geográfico Militar**, Dieciocho 369, Santiago, T698 7278, has published a *Guía Caminera*, with roads and city plans (available only at IGM offices, not 100% accurate). Reasonable road maps may also be obtained from the **Automóvil Club de Chile**, Av Vitacura 8620, Santiago; or other regional offices. You will find several individual maps provide much greater detail than the Club's road atlas. Members of foreign motoring organizations may join the *Automóvil Club de Chile* (US$58 for three months), and obtain discounts at hotels. The *Turistel* Guides are very useful for roads and town plans, but note that not all distances are exact and that the description 'ripio' (gravel) usually requires high clearance; 'buen ripio' should be OK for ordinary cars.

Keeping in touch

Internet Internet access is becoming widely available; in cyber cafés expect to pay US$0.80-3 per hour. *Entel* phone offices often have internet access.

Post Airmail takes three to four days from the UK. Seamail takes eight to 12 weeks. There is a daily airmail service to Europe with connections to the UK. Poste restante only holds mail for 30 days, then returns it to sender. *Lista de Correos* in Santiago, Central Post Office, is good and efficiently organized. Rates: letters to Europe/North America US$0.60, aerogrammes US$0.55. To register a letter costs US$0.75.

Telephone National and international calls have been opened up for competition. There are eight main companies (*portadores*, carriers) offering competing rates (widely advertised). Callers choose companies by dialling an access code before the city code. Access codes: *Entel* 123; *CTC Mundo* 188, *CNT* (*Telefónica del Sur* – in Regions X and XI) 121; *VTR* 120; *Chilesat* 171; *Bell South Chile* 181; *Iusatel Chile* 155; *Transam Comunicaciones* 113. For international calls you dial the company code, then 0, then the country code. International calls are cheap. Ask which carrier has the best links with the country you wish to call (eg for making collect calls); for instance CTC is good for phoning Germany.

Telephone boxes can be used to make local and long-distance calls, for making collect calls and receiving calls. Although it is cheaper to make international calls from these phones, in practice it may be easier to go to a company office. Telephone boxes have been

Chile

programmed to direct calls via one carrier: to make a local call, simply dial the number you require and pay the rate charged by the carrier who owns the booth, US$0.10 per minute. To call mobiles, use phone boxes, US$0.25-30 per minute. To make an inter-urban call, dial '0' plus the area code (DDD) and the number; if you wish to select a carrier, dial its code, then the area code (leaving out '0'), then the number. The area codes given in the text include '0'; omit this if selecting a carrier. To make an international call from a carrier's booth without choosing a different company, dial '00' before the country code. Blue phones accept pre-paid phone cards costing 5,000 pesos (*tarjeta telefónica* – CTC are the most common); available from kiosks. On phone cards, only the time of the call is charged rather than the normal three-minute minimum. There are special phones for long-distance domestic calls which accept credit cards (MasterCard and Visa). Entel phone cards available in Entel offices for sending faxes and making calls abroad (but the recorded instructions are in Spanish). Entel has strategically placed, self-dialling phones, which are white. Users press a button and are instantly connected with the operator from their own country.

Newspapers Santiago daily papers *El Mercurio* (centre-right) www.emol.com *La Nación* **Media** (liberal-left), *La Segunda*, *La Tercera* www.tercera.cl, and *La Quarta*. *Las Ultimas Noticias*. *La Hora*. Online is *El Mostrador*, www1.elmostrador.cl In English is *The News Review*, published weekly on Friday, sold at selected kiosks; Casilla 151/9, Santiago, T236 1423, F236 2293. There is a German-language magazine, *Cóndor*, www.condor.cl Weekly magazines; *Hoy*, *Qué Pasa*, *Ercilla*, www.ercilla.cl

Television TV channels include TVUC (Universidad Católica) on Channel 13, the leading station; TVN (government operated) on Channel 7; on the web www.tvn.cl/24horas; Megavisión (private) on Channel 9 and La Red (private) on Channel 4.

Food and drink

A very typical Chilean dish is *cazuela de ave*, a nutritious stew containing large pieces of **Food** chicken, potatoes, rice, and maybe onions, and green peppers; best if served on the second day. *Valdiviano* is another stew, common in the south, consisting of beef, onion, sliced potatoes and eggs. Another popular Chilean dish is *empanadas de pino*, which are turnovers filled with a mixture of raisins, olives, meat, onions and peppers chopped up together. *Pastel de choclo* is a casserole of meat and onions with olives, topped with a maize-meal mash, baked in an earthenware bowl. *Humitas* are mashed sweetcorn mixed with butter and spices and baked in sweetcorn leaves. *Prieta* is a blood sausage stuffed with cabbage leaves. A normal *parrillada* or *asado* is a giant mixed grill served from a charcoal brazier. The *pichanga* is similar but smaller and without the brazier. *Bistek a lo pobre* (a poor man's steak) can be just the opposite: it is a steak topped by a fried egg, mashed potatoes, onions and salad.

What gives Chilean food its personality is the seafood. The delicious *congrio* fish is a national dish, and *caldillo de congrio* (a soup served with a massive piece of conger, onions and potato balls) is excellent. A *paila* can take many forms (the *paila* is simply a kind of dish), but the commonest are made of eggs or seafood. *Paila Chonchi* is a kind of bouillabaisse, but has more flavour, more body, more ingredients. *Parrillada de mariscos* is a dish of grilled mixed seafood, brought to the table piping hot on a charcoal brazier. Other excellent local fish are the *cojinoa*, the *albacora* (swordfish) and the *corvina*. Some shellfish, such as *loco* (known to Australians as abalone) and mussels may be periodically banned because they carry the disease *marea roja* (which is fatal in humans). *Cochayuyo* is seaweed, bound into bundles, described as 'hard, leathery thongs'. The *erizo*, or sea-urchin, is also commonly eaten. *Luche* is dried seaweed, sold as a black cake, like 'flakey bread pudding' to be added to soups and stews.

Avocado pears, or *paltas*, are excellent, and play an important role in recipes. Make sure that vegetables are included in the price for the main dish; menus often don't make this clear. Always best, if being economical, to stick to fixed-price *table d'hôte* meals or try the local markets. A *barros jarpa* is a grilled cheese and ham sandwich and a *barras luco* is a grilled cheese and beef sandwich. *Sopaipillas* are cakes made of a mixture which includes pumpkin, served in syrup (traditionally made in wet weather). Ice cream is very good; *lúcuma* and *chirimoya* are highly recommended flavours.

Chile

Breakfast is poor: instant coffee or tea with bread and jam are common. Lunch is about 1300 and dinner not before 2030. *Onces* (Elevenses) is tea taken at 1700, often accompanied by a snack. The cocktail hour starts at 1900. Waiters are known as *garzón* – never as *mozo*. Good, cheap meals can usually be found in Centros Españoles or Casinos de Bomberos. By law restaurants have to serve a cheaper set meal at lunchtime; it is called *colación* and may not be included on the menu.

Coffee is generally instant except in expresso bars including popular chains of cafés such as **Café Haiti, Café Brasil** and **Dino**, found in major cities. Elsewhere specify *café-café*, *expresso*. The soluble tea should be avoided, but tea-bags are widely available. If you order '*café*, or *té, con leche*', it will come with all milk; to have just a little milk in either, you must specify that. After a meal, instead of coffee, try an *agüita* (infusion) – hot water in which herbs such as mint, or aromatics such as lemon peel, have been steeped. There is a wide variety, available in sachets, and they are very refreshing.

Drink

Tap water is fairly safe to drink in the main cities but bottled water is safer away from the larger centres. Police will provide water in villages

The local wines are very good; the best are from the central areas. The bottled wines are graded, in increasing excellence, as *gran vino, vino especial* and *vino reservado*. Champagne-style wines are also cheap and acceptable. A small deposit, US$0.30, is charged on most wine bottles. Beer is quite good and cheap (about US$0.75, plus US$0.75 deposit in shops); the draught lager known as *Schop* is good; also try *Cristal Pilsener* or *Royal Guard* in the central regions and *Escudo* and *Polar* in the south. *Malta*, a brown ale, is recommended for those wanting a British-type beer.

Pisco, made from grapes, is the most famous spirit. It is best drunk as a 'Pisco Sour' with lime or lemon juice. Good gin is made in Chile. *Manzanilla* is a local liqueur, made from *licor de oro* (like Galliano); *crema de cacao*, especially Mitjans, has been recommended. Two popular drinks are *vaina*, a mixture of brandy, egg and sugar and *cola de mono*, a mixture of *aguardiente*, coffee, milk and vanilla served very cold at Christmas. *Chicha* is any form of alcoholic drink made from fruit; *chicha cocida* is 3-day-old fermented grape juice boiled to reduce its volume and bottled with a tablespoonful of honey. Cider (*chicha de manzana*) is popular in the south. *Chicha fresca* is plain apple juice. *Mote con huesillo*, made from wheat hominy and dried peaches, is refreshing in summer.

Holidays and festivals

1 January, New Year's Day; Holy Week (two days); 1 May, Labour Day; 21 May, Navy Day; 15 August, Assumption; 18, 19 September, Independence Days; 12 October, Columbus' arrival in America; 1 November, All Saints Day; 8 December, Immaculate Conception; 25 December.

Sport and special interest travel

The Federación de Andinismo de Chile and the Escuela Nacional de Montaña are both at Almirante Simpson 77A in Santiago (full address under Sports)

Climbing   There are four different terrains: rock climbing; high mountains; ice climbing; and volcanoes. Some volcanoes and high mountains are difficult to get to and, being in border areas, need permission to climb. Other volcanoes, like Villarrica and Osorno are popular excursions, although access is controlled by *Conaf* (see Finding out more).

Fishing   The lakes and rivers of Araucania, Los Lagos and Aisén offer great opportunities for trout and salmon fishing. The season runs from mid-Nov to the first Sun in May (or from mid-Sep on Lago Llanquihue). A permit must be obtained, usually from the local Municipalidad, police or angling associations. The price of a permit varies from town to town, but is usually about US$11.50 for foreigners. Some of the world's best fishing is in the Lake District, but this is a very popular region. Better still, as they are less-heavily fished, are the lakes and rivers south of Puerto Montt. Sea fishing is popular between Puerto Saavedra (Araucania) and Maullín (Los Lagos). The mountain resort of Río Blanco is where residents of Santiago and Valparaíso go to fish.

Horseriding   Treks on horseback in the mountains can be organized in Santiago, but south of Concepción there are more opportunities and a number of companies organize riding holidays. A popular national pastime in the centre and south is rodeo and events are held throughout the summer in stadia known as *media lunas* (half moons). There is also horse racing.

Mountain biking This is a popular sport locally as there are lots of opportunities in the mountains and the Lake District. The Camino Austral is also a great ride. Bikes are manufactured locally, but quality is variable.

Nature tourism Birdwatching can be extremely rewarding with opportunities which vary from the flamingoes and wildfowl of the altiplano, as found in the Parque Nacional Lauca in the far north, to the birds of the forests in the south, to the condors, geese and other species in the Torres del Paine. Mammals include those of the camel family, the llama, alpaca, vicuña and guanaco, and some rare deer, the miniature pudú and the huemul. The trees of Chile are another attraction: many deciduous varieties, the araucaria, or monkey-puzzle tree, and areas of very ancient forest, more and more of which are being protected. Also, as mentioned above, the flowering of the desert is a sight to look out for.

Rafting and kayaking Over 20 rivers between Santiago and Tierra del Fuego are excellent for white water rafting. Some run through spectacular mountain scenery, such as the Río Petrohué, which flows through temperate rainforest beneath the Osorno and Calbuco volcanoes. Rafting is generally well organized and equipment is usually of a high standard. Access to headwaters of most rivers is easy. For beginners, many agencies in Santiago, Puerto Varas and Pucón offer half-day trips on Grade 3 rivers. Sea kayaking is best enjoyed in the waters between Chiloé and the mainland and in the sheltered fjords off the northernmost section of the Camino Austral. Kayaking and other watersports such as windsurfing take place in many lakes in the Lake District, notably Lagos Villarrica and Llanquihue, which holds an annual kayaking regatta.

Sailing Apart from sailing on the lakes, ocean sailing is best, again, in the sheltered waters south of Puerto Montt. There is ample scope for yachting in the waters east of Chiloé. Things get more adventurous is you sail down the coast to Cape Horn and expertise is needed for such a trip. Most coastal towns on the entire Chilean coast have yacht clubs.

Skiing The season is from Jun to Sep/Oct, weather permitting. The major international ski resorts are in the Andes near Santiago, Farellones, El Colorado, La Parva, Valle Nevado, Portillo and Lagunillas. South of Santiago, skiing is mostly on the slopes of volcanoes. The larger resorts are Termas de Chillán, Villarrica/Pucón and Antillanca, but there are a great many smaller places with limited facilities which are worth the effort to get to for some adventurous fun.

Details of the major resorts and some smaller ones are given in the text. Addresses of ski federations, clubs and operators are given under Santiago, Sports, page 625

Trekking Trekking possibilities are endless, ranging from short, sign-posted trails in national parks to hikes of several days, such as the circuit of the Parque Nacional Torres del Paine.

Other popular sports are **football** and **basketball**. Viña del Mar has a **cricket** ground; on Sat there are **polo** matches at Santiago. *Sernatur* will give all the necessary information about sport.

Chile

Santiago

Santiago and the heartland

Dramatically situated in the Central Valley, Santiago is within easy reach of vineyards, beaches and Andean ski resorts. With its parks, museums, high-rises, nightlife and boutiques, the city bursts with possibilities. It is the political, economic and financial capital of Chile and now the fifth largest city in South America.

Background From a third to half of the width of the area is taken up by the Andes, which are formidably high in the northern sector; at the head of the Río Aconcagua the peak of Aconcagua (in Argentina), the highest in the Americas, rises to 6,964 m. The region suffers from earthquakes. There is a mantle of snow on the mountains, beginning at around 4,000 m. The lower slopes are covered with dense forests. Between the forest and the snowline there are alpine pastures; during the summer cattle are driven up to these pastures to graze.

The coastal range, over 2,000 m in places, takes up another third of the width. It is lower here than in the northern desert, but the shoreline is unbroken; only Valparaíso and San Antonio have good harbours. Between the coastal range and the Andes lies the Central Valley; rivers cross it at right angles, cutting their way to the sea through narrow canyons in the coastal highland.

Nearly 70% of the people of Chile live in the comparatively small heartland. The population density in the area around the capital is over 300 per sq km.

Climate There is rain during the winter, but the summers are dry. The rain increases to the south. On the coast at Viña del Mar it is 483 mm a year, but is less inland. Temperatures, on the other hand, are higher inland than on the coast. There is frost now and then, but very little snow falls. Temperatures can reach 33° C in January, but fall to 13° C (3° C at night) in July. Days are usually hot, the nights cool.

Santiago

Phone code: 02
Colour map 8, grid B1
Population:
almost 5 million
Altitude: 600 m

Santiago, founded by Pedro de Valdivia in 1541, is one of the most beautifully set of any South American city, standing in a wide plain. The city is crossed from east to west by the Río Mapocho, which passes through an artificial stone channel, 40 m wide, spanned by several bridges. Public gardens are filled with flowers and kept in good order. The magnificent chain of the Andes, with its snow-capped heights, is in full view for much of the year, rain and pollution permitting; there are peaks of 6,000 m about 100 km away. More than half the country's manufacturing is done here; it is essentially a modern capital, full of skyscrapers, bustle, noise and traffic. Smog is a problem especially between April and September: tables for air pollution are published in the daily papers, as are the registration numbers of those cars which are not allowed into the city each day.

Ins & outs **Orientation and getting there** Santiago's central district is roughly at the mid-point of an

For more detailed information, see Transport on page 627

axis running from southwest to northeast. This axis runs on the broad Alameda, Avenida O'Higgins, meeting the Río Mapocho just east of the centre, then running through Providencia and Las Condes to the wealthy northeastern suburbs. The **airport** is 26 km northwest of the centre. Regular bus services run to the centre, *Tur Bus* and *Centropuerto*, both US$2.50. There are also services to/from hotels and private addresses (US$5-7) and taxis (US$17).

Chile

The **railway station**, Escacíon Central, which only serves the south of the country, is 7 blocks east of 3 of the 4 main **bus terminals** on the Alameda. The 4th bus terminal, also on the Alameda, is nearer to the centre. All can be reached by city buses, taxi or the Metro. The bus terminals are Alameda, for *Pullman-Bus* and *TurBus* services; Santiago, for the whole country and some international destinations; San Borja, for central and some national destinations; Los Héroes (nearest the centre) for some southern, northern and international routes.

Getting around The **Metro** (underground railway) has 3 lines, 1 east-west, 2 and 5 north-south. Fares range from US$0.50 to US$0.75 depending on time of day. The east-west line follows the main axis, linking the bus and train stations, the centre, Providencia and beyond. Metrobus services connect the subway with outlying districts. **City buses**: other than the blue metrobuses, yellow buses serve the whole city. Fares are US$0.50. **Taxis** are abundant and not expensive (minimum charge US$0.60, plus US$0.12 per 200 m). **Colectivos** (collective taxis) run on fixed routes to the suburbs, US$0.75-1.50.

Tourist offices Servicio Nacional de Turismo (*Sernatur* – the national tourist board), Av Providencia 1550 (Casilla 14082), between metros Manuel Montt and Pedro de Valdivia, next to Providencia Municipal Library, T731 8300, F251 8469. English and German spoken and maps (road map US$1.50), brochures and posters are available. Good notice board. ■ *Mon-Fri 0845-1900, Sat 0900-1800, Sun 1000-1500.* Kiosk on Ahumada near Agustinas (erratic opening times). Information office also at the airport, open 0900-2100 daily. **Municipal Tourist Board**, Casa Colorada, Merced 860, T336700/330723. Has a good free booklet, *Historical Heritage of Santiago: A Guide for Tourists* in English and Spanish, on historic buildings.

Security Like all large cities, Santiago has problems of theft. Pickpockets and bagsnatchers, who are often well-dressed, operate especially on the Metro and around the Plaza de Armas. Many tourist offices outside Santiago are closed in winter, so stock up on information here.

Sights

The centre of the old city lies between the Mapocho and the Av O'Higgins, which is usually known as the **Alameda**. From the **Plaza Baquedano** (usually called **Plaza Italia**), in the east of the city's central area, the Mapocho flows to the northwest and the Alameda runs to the southwest. From Plaza Italia the Calle Merced runs due west to the **Plaza de Armas**, the heart of the city, five blocks south of the Mapocho.

Santiago orientation

N

To La Serena & the north

To Los Andes, Portillo & Mendoza

0 km 2
0 miles 2

CONCHALI

Parque Metropolitano

Pan-American Highway

Río Mapocho

Arturo Merino Benítez

A B C D

68

NUÑOA

MACUL

Aeropuerto Los Cerillos

Pan-American Highway

LA FLORIDA

LA CISTERNA

Av Américo Vespucio

5

To Rancagua & the south

To Farellones, El Colorado, La Parva & Valle Nevado

Pedro de Valdivia

To Valparaíso & Viña del Mar

Around the Plaza de Armas

On the eastern and southern sides of the Plaza de Armas there are arcades with shops; on the northern side is the Post Office and the Municipalidad; and on the western side the Cathedral and the archbishop's palace. The **Cathedral**, much rebuilt, contains a recumbent statue in wood of San Francisco Javier, and the chandelier which lit the first meetings of Congress after independence; it also houses an interesting museum of religious art and historical pieces (0930-1230, 1530-1830, free). In the **Palacio de la Real Audiencia** on the Plaza de Armas is the **Museo Histórico Nacional**, covering the period from the Conquest until 1925. ■ *Tue-Sat 1000-1745, Sun 1000-1600, US$1.70, No 951.* A block west of the Cathedral is the **former Congress** building now occupied by the Ministry of Foreign Affairs (the new Congress building is in

Related maps
A West of Centre, page 618
B Santiago Centre, page 612
C Bellavista, page 620
D Providencia Detail, page 616

Chile

Valparaíso). At C Merced 864, close to the Plaza de Armas, is the **Casa Colorada**, built in 1769, the home of the Governor in colonial days and then of Mateo de Toro, first President of Chile. It is now the **Museo de Santiago** (history of Santiago from the Conquest to modern times), with excellent displays and models, guided tours. ■ *Tue-Sat1000-1900, Sun and holidays, 1000-1400, US$1.* From the Plaza de Armas Paseo Ahumada, a pedestrianized street lined with cafés runs south to the Alameda four blocks away, crossing Huérfanos, which is also pedestrianized.

Four blocks north of the Plaza de Armas is the interesting **Mercado Central**, at 21 de Mayo y San Pablo. The building faces the Parque Venezuela, on which is the Cal y Canto metro station, the northern terminus of Line 2, and, at its western end, the former **Mapocho Railway Station**, now a cultural centre. If you head east from Mapocho station, along the river, you pass through the Parque Forestal (see below), before coming back to Plaza Italia.

Along the Alameda The Alameda runs through the heart of the city for over 3 km. It is 100 m wide, and ornamented with gardens and statuary: the most notable are the equestrian statues of Generals O'Higgins and San Martín; the statue of the Chilean historian Benjamín

Chile

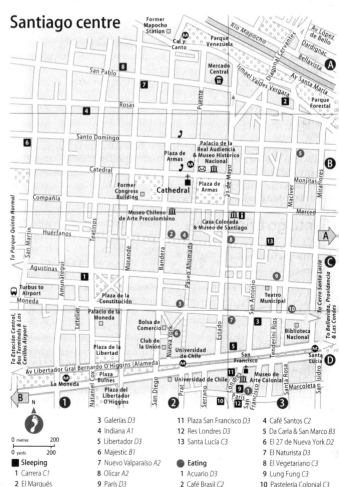

Santiago centre

Sleeping	
1 Carrera *C1*	
2 El Marqués del Forestal *A3*	
3 Galerías *D3*	11 Plaza San Francisco *D3*
4 Indiana *A1*	12 Res Londres *D3*
5 Libertador *D3*	13 Santa Lucía *C3*
6 Majestic *B1*	
7 Nuevo Valparaíso *A2*	**Eating**
8 Olicar *A2*	1 Acuario *D3*
9 París *D3*	2 Café Brasil *C2*
10 Plaza Londres *D2*	3 Café Caribe *C2*
	4 Café Santos *C2*
	5 Da Carla & San Marco *B3*
	6 El 27 de Nueva York *D2*
	7 El Naturista *D3*
	8 El Vegetariano *C3*
	9 Lung Fung *C3*
	10 Pastelería Colonial *C3*

0 metres 200
0 yards 200

Vicuña MacKenna who, as mayor of Santiago, beautified Cerro Santa Lucía (see Parks and Gardens below); and the great monument in honour of the battle of Concepción in 1879.

From the Plaza Italia, where there is a statue of Gen Baquedano and the Tomb of the Unknown Soldier, the Alameda skirts, on the right, Cerro Santa Lucía, and on the left, the Catholic University. Beyond the hill the Alameda goes past the neo-classical **Biblioteca Nacional** on the right, Moneda 650 (good concerts, temporary exhibitions). Beyond, on the left, between C San Francisco and C Londres, is the oldest church in Santiago: the red-walled church and monastery of **San Francisco** (entry US$1). Inside is the small statue of the Virgin which Valdivia carried on his saddlebow when he rode from Peru to Chile. South of San Francisco is the Barrio París-Londres, built in 1923-1929, now restored and pedestrianized. Two blocks north of the Alameda on C Agustinas is the **Teatro Municipal**. ■ *Guided tours Tue 1300-1500, Sun 1100-1400, US$3.* A little further west along the Alameda, is the **Universidad de Chile**; the **Club de la Unión** is almost opposite. Nearby, on C Nueva York is the **Bolsa de Comercio**. One block further west is the Plaza de la Libertad. To the north of the Plaza, hemmed in by the skyscrapers of the Centro Cívico, is the **Palacio de la Moneda** (1805), the Presidential Palace containing historic relics, paintings and sculpture, and the elaborate 'Salón Rojo' used for official receptions. Although the Moneda was damaged by air attacks during the military coup of 11 September 1973 it has been fully restored. (Ceremonial changing of the guard every other day, 1000, never on Sunday; Sunday ceremony is performed Monday. The courtyards, with sculptures and carabineros in dress uniform, are open to all – entry from the north.)

West of the centre is **Barrio Brasil**, with Plaza Brasil at its heart and the Basílica del Salvador two blocks from the plaza. One of the earliest parts of the city, it has some old buildings, but also modern amenities (Metro República). The Alameda continues westwards to the **Planetarium**. ■ *US$2.50, shows Tue-Sun 1800, 2000, Alameda 3349, T776 2624.* Opposite it on the southern side, the railway station (Estación Central or Alameda). On Av Matucana, running north from here, is the very popular **Parque Quinta Normal** (see below).

Between the Parque Forestal, Plaza ItaliaItalia and the Alameda is the **Lastarria** neighbourhood (Universidad Católica Metro). For those interested in antique furniture, objets d'art and old books, the area is worth a visit, especially the **Plaza Mulato Gil de Castro** (C José V Lastarria 305). Occasional shows are put on in the square. Nearby, on Lastarria, are the **Jardín Lastarria**, a cul-de-sac of craft and antique shops. **Lastarria & Bellavista**

The **Bellavista** district, on the north bank of the Mapocho from Plaza Italia at the foot of Cerro San Cristóbal (see below), is the main focus of nightlife in the old city. Around C Pío Nono are restaurants and cafés, theatres, entertainments, art galleries and craft shops (especially those selling lapis lazuli).

East of Plaza Italia, the main east-west axis of the city becomes **Avenida Providencia** which heads out towards the residential areas, such as Las Condes, at the eastern and upper levels of the city. It passes through the neighbourhood of Providencia, a modern area of shops, offices and restaurants around Pedro de Valdivia and Los Leones metro stations, which also contains the offices of Sernatur, the national tourist board. At Metro Tobalaba it becomes Avenida Apoquindo. **Providencia**

Cerro Santa Lucía, bounded by C Merced to the north, Alameda to the south, Calles Santa Lucía and Subercaseaux, is a cone of rock rising steeply to a height of 70 m. It can be climbed from the Caupolicán esplanade, on which, high on a rock, stands a statue of that Mapuche leader, but the ascent from the northern side of the hill, where there is an equestrian statue of Diego de Almagro, is easier. There are striking views of the city from the top (reached by a series of stairs), where there is a **Parks & gardens**

Chile

fortress, the Batería Hidalgo (closed to the public). ■ *The Cerro closes at 2100; visitors must register at the entrance, giving ID card number.* It is best to descend the eastern side, to see the small Plaza Pedro Valdivia with its waterfalls and statue of Valdivia. The area is famous, at night, for its gay community.

Parque O'Higgins lies about 10 blocks south of Alameda. It has a small lake, playing fields, tennis courts, swimming pool (open from 5 December), an open-air stage, a discothèque, the racecourse of the Club Hípico, an amusement park, *Fantasilandia* (admission US$7-9, unlimited rides, open at weekends until 2000 only in winter, and not when raining), kite-flying contests on Sunday, good 'typical' restaurants, craft shops, an aquarium, an insect and shellfish museum and the **Museo del Huaso**, a collection of criollo clothing and tools. ■ *Museum: Tue-Fri 1000-1300, 1430-1715, Sat, Sun and holidays 1000-1800, free.To the park, take Metro Line 2 to Parque O'Higgins station. Bus from Parque Baquedano via Avs MacKenna and Matta.*

North of the Estación Central on Av Matucana y D Portales is the **Quinta Normal**, founded as a botanical garden in 1830. In or near the park are: **Museo de la Solidaridad Salvador Allende**, Herrera 360, T681 4954, www.mssa.cl A well-presented collection of works donated to Chile by Latin American and European artists (including Matta, Miró and Saura) between 1970 and 1973 to demonstrate solidarity with Allende's government. Recommended. ■ *Tue-Sun 1000-1900, US$1, good café with set lunch, US$3. Information sheet in English.* **Museo Nacional de Historia Natural**, founded in 1830, housed in an impressive neoclassical building, has exhibitions on Chile's flora and fauna. ■ *Tue-Sat 1000-1730, Sun and holidays 1100-1830, US$0.80, free on Sun.* **Museo Ferroviario** containing 13 steam engines built between 1884 and 1953 and a presidential stage coach. ■ *Tue-Fri 1000-1800, Sat, Sun and holidays, 1100-1900, US$1, free to those over 60, photography permit, US$2.50.* **Museo Ciencia y Tecnología**, US$1, same hours as **Ferroviario**. **Museo Artequín**, nearby at Av Portales 3530, in the Chilean pavilion built for the 1889 Paris International Exhibition, containing prints of famous paintings and activities and explanations of the techniques of the great masters, recommended. ■ *Tue-Fri 0900-1700, Sat, Sun and holidays 1100-1800, US$2.50.*

Parque Forestal lies due north of Santa Lucía hill and immediately south of the Mapocho. **Museo Nacional de Bellas Artes**, in an extraordinary example of neo-classical architecture, has a large display of Chilean and foreign painting and sculpture; contemporary art exhibitions are held several times a year. ■ *Tue-Sat 1000-1800, Sun and holidays 1100-1800,US$0.80.* In the west wing of the building is the **Museo de Arte Contemporáneo**. **Parque Balmaceda** (Parque Gran Bretaña), east of Plaza Italia, is perhaps the most beautiful in Santiago (the Museo de los Tajamares, which holds monthly exhibitions, is here).

The sharp, conical hill of **San Cristóbal**, forming the **Parque Metropolitano**, to the northeast of the city, is the largest and most interesting of the city's parks. There are two entrances: from Pío Nono in Bellavista and further east from Pedro de Valdivia Norte. On the summit (300 m) stands a colossal statue of the Virgin, which is floodlit at night; beside it is the astronomical observatory of the Catholic University which can be visited on application to the observatory's director. Further east in the Tupahue sector there are terraces, gardens, and paths; in one building there is a good, expensive restaurant (*Camino Real*, T232 1758) with a splendid view from the terrace, and an Enoteca (exhibition of Chilean wines: you can taste one of the three 'wines of the day', US$1.50 per glass, and buy if you like, though prices are higher than in shops). Nearby is the Casa de la Cultura which has art exhibitions and free concerts at midday on Sunday. There are two good swimming pools (see **Sports** below). East of Tupahue are the Botanical Gardens, with a collection of Chilean native plants, guided tours available. ■ *Getting there: by funicular: every few mins from Plaza Caupolicán at the northern end of C Pío Nono (it stops on its way at the Jardín Zoológico near the Bellavista entrance), US$2 in week, US$2.25 weekends 1000-1900 Mon-Fri, 1000-2000 Sat and Sun (closed for lunch 1330-1430). Fares:*

from Plaza to zoo, US$2.40 (easily walked); from zoo to San Cristóbal, US$3.20. By teleférico from Estación Oasis, Av Pedro de Valdivia Norte via Tupahue to San Cristóbal, the funicular's upper station, 1030-1900 at weekends, 1500-1830 weekdays except Tue (in summer only), US$2.80. A combined funicular/teleférico ticket is US$6. An open bus operated by the teleférico company runs to San Cristóbal and Tupahue from the Bellavista entrance with the same schedule as the teleférico itself. To get to Tupahue at other times you must take the funicular or a taxi (or walk to/from Pedro de Valdivia Metro station, about 1 km). By taxi either from the Bellavista entrance (much cheaper from inside the park as taxis entering the park have to pay entrance fee), or from Metro Pedro de Valdivia.

Situated in the barrio of Recoleta, just north of the city centre, this cemetery contains the mausoleums of most of the great figures in Chilean history and the arts, including Violeta Para, Víctor Jara and Salvador Allende. There is also an impressive monument to the victims, known as "desaparecidos" (disappeared) of the 1973-90 military government. ■ *Take any Recoleta bus from Calle Miraflores to get there.*

Cementerio General

Museo Chileno de Arte Precolombino, Bandera 361, in the former Real Aduana, representative exhibition of objects from the precolumbian cultures of Central America and the Andean region, highly recommended for the quality of the objects and their presentation. ■ *Tue-Sat 1000-1800, Sun and holidays 1000-1400, US$3, T688 7348.*

 Museo de Arte Colonial, Londres 4, beside Iglesia San Francisco, T639 8737. Religious art, includes one room with 54 paintings of the life of St Francis; in the cloisters is a room containing Gabriela Mistral's Nobel medal; also a collection of locks. ■ *Tue-Sat 1000-1300,1500-1800, Sun and holidays 1000-1400, US$1.50, some information in English.*

 Palacio Cousiño, C Dieciocho 438, five blocks south of the Alameda, a large mansion in French rococo style with a superb Italian marble staircase and other opulent items. ■ *Tue-Fri 0930-1330, 1430-1700, Sat, Sun and holidays 0930-1330, US$3. Guided tours only, in Spanish, English and Portuguese, visitors have to wear cloth bootees to protect the floors. Recommended.*

 La Chascona, F Márquez de la Plata 0192, T777 8741, the house of the poet Pablo Neruda and now headquarters of the Fundación Pablo Neruda. ■ *Daily except Mon, 1000-1300, 1500-1800, US$3 guided visits only (see page 644).*

 In Lastarria and Bellavista is the **Museo Arqueológico de Santiago**, in Plaza Mulato Gil de Castro, Lastarria 307, Chilean archaeology, anthropology and precolumbian art. ■ *Mon-Fri 1000-1400, 1500-1800, Sat 1000-1400, free.*

 Museo Ralli, Sotomayor 4110, Vitacura, an excellent collection of works by modern European and Latin American artists, including Dali, Chagall, Bacon and Miró. ■ *Tue-Sun 1030-1600, closed in summer, free.*

Museums
Almost all museums are closed on Mon and on 1 Nov

Essentials

In the **Providencia area** L *Park Plaza*, Ricardo Lyon 207, T233 6363, bookings@ parkplaza.cl Good. L *Sheraton San Cristóbal*, Santa María 1742, T233 5000, guest@ stgusheraton.cl Best in town, good restaurant, good buffet lunch, and all facilities. **AL** *Aloha*, Francisco Noguera 146, T233 2230/7, resaloha@panamericanahoteles.cl Helpful, good restaurant. **AL** *Orly*, Pedro de Valdivia 027, Metro Pedro de Valdivia, T231 8947, www.orlyhotel.com Fully renovated, comfortable, *Cafetto* café attached with cheap food.

 In **Las Condes LL** *Hyatt Regency Santiago*, Av Kennedy N 4601, T218 1234, info@hyatt.cl Superb, beautifully decorated, large outdoor pool, gym, Thai restaurant. Highly recommended. **L** *Santa Magdalena Apart Hotel*, Helvecia 244, Las Condes, T374 6875, www.santamagdalena.cl

 In **Santiago Centre LL** *Carrera*, Teatinos 180, T698 2011, hotel.carrera@chilnet.cl Art-deco lobby, pool, rooftop restaurant (good buffet lunch), helpful staff and great atmosphere. **L** *Galerías*, San Antonio 65, T638 4011, galerias@entelchile.net Excellent,

Sleeping
■ *on maps*
Check if breakfast and 18% tax are included in the price quoted. If you pay by credit card, there is usually a 10% surcharge). Cheap places do not charge the 18% tax

Chile

welcoming. **L** *Plaza San Francisco*, O'Higgins 816, T639 3832, F639 7826. *Lufthansa*-affiliated, excellent breakfast, good, LanChile office. **A** *Conde Ansúrez*, Av República 25, T696 0807, F671 8376, Metro República. Convenient for central station and bus terminals, helpful, safe, luggage stored. **A** *Da Carlo*, Manuel Thompson 3940, 2 blocks from Universidad de Santiago Metro, T776 4523, F778 7329. Very good suites, tasteful, helpful. **A** *Foresta*, Subercaseaux 353, T639 6261, F632 2996. Heating, laundry service, restaurant, bar. **A** *Libertador*, O'Higgins 853, T639 4212, info@hotellibertador.cl Helpful, stores luggage, good restaurant. **A** *Majestic*, Santo Domingo 1526, T695 8366, hotelmajestic@entelchile.net With breakfast, good Indian/vegetarian restaurant open to non-residents, pool, English spoken. **A** *El Márques del Forestal*, Ismael Valdés Vergara 740, opposite Parque Forestal, T633 3462. Good value, several rooms with cooker and sink, all have TV, phone. **A** *Monte Carlo*, Subercaseaux 209, T633 9905, info@hotelmontecarlo.cl At foot of Santa Lucía, modern, restaurant, with heating, stores luggage, good.

   B *Plaza Londres*, Londres 75-77, T633 3320, F664 0086. Cable TV, breakfast, quiet. **B** *Hostal Río Amazonas*, Rosas 2234, T698 4092, F671 9013, www.hostalrioamazonas.cl Convenient centre, good, internet access. **B** *Santa Lucía*, San Antonio 327 y Huérfanos, p 4, T639 8201, santalucia@terra.cl Garage 2 blocks away, comfortable, small, quiet restaurant. **B** *Tokio*, Almte Barroso 160, T671 4516, F698 4500. Lovely garden, convenient location, good breakfast, Japanese and English spoken, no credit cards. **B** *Hostal Vía Real*, Marín 066, T635 4676, F635 4678. Charming, helpful, small, TV, laundry. Recommended. **C** *Res Alemana*, República 220 (no sign), T671 3668, residencial.alemana@usa.net Metro República, pleasant patio, heating on request, good cheap meals available. Recommended. **C** *Hostal Americano*, Compañía 1906, T/F698 1025, hostal@mi.terra.cl Breakfast extra, bath shared between 2 bedrooms, convenient. **C** *Res Londres*, Londres 54, T/F638 2215, unico54@ctcinternet.cl Old mansion with original features, without breakfast, cheaper without bath, pleasant common rooms, good, safe, laundry service, often full. **C** *París*, París 813, T/F639 4037, www.hotelparis.cl Old fashioned, good meeting place, but cold, luggage store.

Sleeping
1 Aloha
2 Orly
3 Park Plaza
4 Santa Magdalena
5 Sheraton San Cristóbal

Eating
1 A Pinch of Panch
2 Brannigan Pub
3 Carousel
4 Cafetto
5 Centre Catalá
6 Coco Loco
7 Coppellia

Chile

D *Indiana*, Rosas 1339, T688 0008, hostal_indiana@hotmail.com Kitchen facilities, popular with Israelis, internet US$2-3 per hr, convenient but noisy, basic. **D** *Nuevo Valparaíso*, Morandé 791, T671 5698. Basic gringo meeting place, central, erratic hot water, safe, poor beds, use of kitchen (no utensils), cable TV, popular. **D** *Olicar*, San Pablo 1265, T698 3683. Laundry, kitchen, quiet, a bit run down. **D** *Res Gloria*, Latorre 449, T698 8315, Metro Toesca. Including breakfast. Recommended. **D** *Res del Norte*, Catedral 2207, T696 9251. Includes breakfast, safe, large rooms, credit cards accepted.

E *La Casa Roja*, Agustinas 2113, Barrio Brasil, T696 4241, info@lacasaroja.tie.cl **F** pp in dormitory, converted historic house, meals extra, internet, convenient for metro and lots of amenities, new in 2001. **E** pp *San Patricio*, Catedral 2235, T695 4800.Cheaper without bath, hot shower, with breakfast, "rough and ready" but safe and quiet, good value, parking. **F** pp *Caribe*, San Martín 851, T696 6681. Double rooms or dormitories, kitchen, hot showers in day, quiet, helpful, internet US$1.10 per 30 mins, luggage store, laundry.

Near bus terminals and Estación Central C *Res Mery*, Pasaje República 36, off 0-100 block of República, T696 8883, m.mardones@entelchile,net Big green building down an alley, without bath, quiet. Recommended. **D** *Alojamiento Diario*, Salvador Sanfuentes 2258 (no sign), T699 2938. Safe, kitchen facilities. **E** pp *Hostal Internacional Letelier*, Cumming 77, 3 blocks from Alameda, T965 6861. Very helpful, no meals, internet, Spanish lessons arranged. **E-F** pp *Scott SCS Habitat*, San Vicente 1798, T683 3732. Kitchen, hot showers, laundry facilities, helpful, huge breakfast, popular, English spoken, maps and camping equipment sold/rented, cycles for hire, safe bike parking. Recommended. **F** *Res Vicky*, Sazié 2105, T698 4057. Laundry, kitchen, discount for weekly/monthly stay. Recommended. Another **F** family *hostal* at Sazie 2048, casa 1, T695 3570, large rooms, big breakfafst. **F** *Res Sur*, Ruiz Tagle 055, T776 5533. Pleasant, helpful, meals available. On north side of Alameda opposite bus terminals: **F** pp *Federico Scoto* 130, T779 9364. Use of phone and fax, good meals, cooking facilities, often full. Highly recommended.

Accommodation near airport B pp *Hacienda del Sol y La Luna*, 4 Hijuela 9978, Pudahuel, T/F601 9254. English, German, French spoken. Recommended.

Family accommodation C pp *Marilu's Bed & Breakfast*, Rafael Cañas 246-c, Providencia T235 5302, tradesic@ intermedia.cl French and English spoken, good breakfast, comfortable. **C** pp *Antonio y Ana Saldivia*, Guillermo Tell 5809, La Reina, T226 6267. Very hospitable elderly couple, with breakfast, dinner extra, quiet, take bus 244 from Alameda. **C** pp *Urania's B&B*, Bocaccio 60, Las Condes, T537 1596, F201 2922, uraniae@hotmail.com Comfortable, good breakfast. **D** pp *Rodrigo Sauvageot*, Gorbea 1992, dept 113, T672 2119. Includes breakfast, phone first. **E** pp *Sra Lucía*, Catedral 1029, p 10, dept 1001, T696 3832. Central, safe, cooking facilities, wonderful views. **E** pp *Señora Marta*, Catedral 1029, dept 401, T672 6090, half a block from main plaza. Basic, safe, good breakfast. Warmly recommended. **E** pp *Sra Fidela*, San Isidro 261, Apt H, T222 1246. Shared bathroom, breakfast. Recommended. **D** *Cecilia Parada*, Llico 968, T522 9947, F521 6328.1 block from Metro

Recommended accommodation in comfortable family guest houses through Amigos de Todo el Mundo, Libertad 371 (Metro U Latinoamericana), Casilla 52861, Correo Central Sgto, T681 7638, F698 1474, Sr Arturo Navarrete

8 El Huerto
9 Gatsby
10 La Pizza Nostra
11 Louisiana River Pub
12 Mr Ed
13 Phone Box Pub
14 Red Pub

Chile

Departamental, washing machine, gardens, quiet. **D** *Sra Marta*, Amengual 035, Alameda Alt 4.400, T779 7592 (Metro Ecuador). Good, hospitable, kitchen facilities, motorcycle parking.

You cannot install a phone line unless you have permanent Chilean residence; you may need a friend to put the line in

Longer stay accommodation See the classified ads in *El Mercurio*; flats, homes and family *pensiones* are listed by district, or in *El Rastro* (weekly), or try the notice board at the tourist office. Estate agents handle apartments, but often charge ½ of the first month's rent as commission, while a month's rent in advance and 1 month's deposit are required. Recommended apartments are *Santa Magdalena*, see Sleeping, Las Condes. Also *Edificio San Rafael*, Miraflores 264, T633 0289, F222 5629. US$30 a day double, minimum 3 days, very central.

Youth hostels E pp *Hostelling Internacional Santiago*, Cienfuegos 151, T671 8532, F672 8880, histgoch@ entelchile.net (5 mins from Metro Los Héroes). Modern, satellite TV, no cooking facilities, cafeteria, parking. Information from Youth Hostel Association, Hernando de Aguirre 201, of 602, Providencia, T233 3220/234 3233, hostelling@hostelling.cl (worth getting a list of YH addresses around the country as these change). Supplies student cards (2 photos required and proof of student status, though tourist card accepted), US$16.

Camping Excellent facilities about 70 km southwest from Santiago at Laguna de Aculeo, called *Club Camping Maki*: including electricity, cold water, swimming pool, boat mooring,

Santiago west of centre

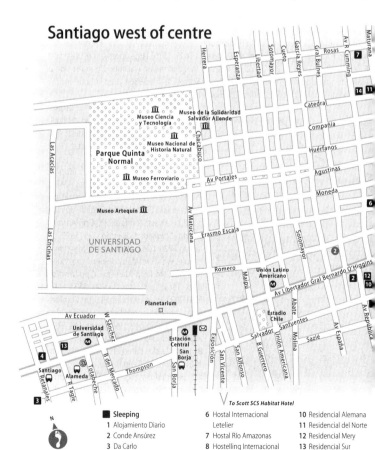

N

0 metres 200
0 yards 200

■ Sleeping	
1 Alojamiento Diario	
2 Conde Ansúrez	
3 Da Carlo	
4 Federico Scoto 130	
5 Hostal Americano	

6 Hostal Internacional Letelier	10 Residencial Alemana
7 Hostal Río Amazonas	11 Residencial del Norte
8 Hostelling Internacional Santiago	12 Residencial Mery
9 La Casa Roja	13 Residencial Sur
	14 San Patricio

To Scott SCS Habitat Hotel

restaurant, but only available to members of certain organizations. An alternative site is *El Castaño* camping (with casino), 1 km away, on edge of lake, very friendly, café sells fruit, eggs, milk, bread and kerosene, good fishing, no showers, water from handpump.

In the centre Mid-range: *Acuario*, París 817. Excellent seafood, attentive service, good value set lunch. *Los Adobes de Argomedo*, Argomedo 411 y Lira, T222 2104 for reservations. Hacienda-style, good Chilean food and floor show including cueca dancing, salsa and folk, Mon-Sat, only place in winter which has this type of entertainment on a Mon. *Les Assassins*, Merced 297. French, very good. Highly recommended. *Da Carla*, MacIver 577. Italian food, good; and *San Marco*, 2 doors away, better still. *El 27 de Nueva York*, Nueva York 27. Central, good, live music. *Faisán d'Or*, Plaza de Armas. Good *pastel de choclo*, pleasant place to have a drink and watch the world go by. *Fra Diavolo*, París 836. Lunches only, excellent food and service, popular. *Guimas*, Huérfanos y Teatinos. Good value *almuerzo*. *El Lagar de Don Quijote*, Morandé y Catedral. Bar, restaurant, *parrillada*, good, popular. *Lung Fung*, Agustinas 715. Delicious oriental food, large cage in the centre with noisy parrots. *Ostras Azócar*, Gral Bulnes 37. Excellent quality, reasonable prices for oysters. *Las Vacas Gordas*, Cienfuegos 280, Barrio Brasil. Good value grilled steaks.

   Cheap *Bar Central*, San Pablo 1063. Cheap, typical food. Recommended. *Bar Nacional No 1*, Huérfanos 1151 and *Bar Nacional No 2*, Bandera 317. Good restaurants, popular, local specialities. *El Rápido*, next to *No 2*, specializes in *empanadas*, good food, good fun, "happening locals' joint". *Círculo de Periodistas*, Amunátegui 31, p 2. Unwelcoming entrance, good value lunches. Recommended. *Mermoz*, Huérfanos 1048. Good for lunches. *Nuria*, MacIver 208. Wide selection. *Torres*, Alameda 1570. Traditional bar/restaurant, good atmosphere, live music at weekends.

   Seriously cheap On C San Diego, south of the Alameda: *La Caleta de Done Beno*, No 397, *parrilladas*, seafood, popular, a bit pricier than other places. *Masticón*, No 152, good service, excellent value. *Sena*, No 145, wide choice, good cocktails. *Las Tejas*, No 234, for typical dishes and drinks, rowdy. *Tercera Compañía de Bomberos*, Vicuña Mackenna 097. Recommended.

On López de Bello: *Le Coq au Vin*, No 0110. French, excellent, good value. *La Divina Comida*, No 93. Italian with 3 rooms – Heaven, Hell and Purgatory, good seafood. Highly recommended. *El Otro Sitio*, No 53. Peruvian, excellent food, elegant. *R*, Plaza Mulato Gil de Castro. Fine food. *San Fruttuoso*, Mallinckrodt 180. Italian, recommended. **Mid-range**: *Calamar,* Pío Nono 241. Recommended. *Como Agua para Chocolate*, Constitución 88. Good food and value. *Eladio*, Pío Nono 251. Good steaks, Argentine cuisine, excellent value. *Gatopardo*, Lastarria 192. Good value. Highly recommended. *Off the Wall*, López de Bello 155. Recommended for fish. *La Pergola de la Plaza* in Plaza Mulato Gil de

Eating
● *on maps*
Some of the best seafood restaurants are to be found in the Mercado Central (by Cal y Canto Metro, lunches only), or at the Vega Central market on the opposite bank of the Mapocho

Chile

Visit El Mercurio online, www.emol.com, and go to "tiempo libre", to search for types of restaurants and areas of the city

● **Eating**
1 Las Vacas Gordas
2 Ostras Azócar

Castro. Cosy. *El Rincón Español*, just off C Rosal. Spanish, good *paella*. Next door is *El Bar Escondido*, small and pleasant. *La Tasca Mediterránea*, Purísima 165. Good food. Recommended. Next door is *Libro Café Mediterráneo*, popular with students, lively, cheap.*Tragaluz*, Constitución 124. Good Chilean food, not cheap. *Venezia*, Pío Nono, corner of López de Bello, huge servings, good value. **Cheap**: *Café Universitario*, Alameda 395 y Subercaseaux (near Santa Lucía). Good *almuerzos*, lively at night, rock videos, very pleasant.

It is difficult to eat cheaply in the evening apart from fast food, so budget travellers should make the almuerzo their main meal. In the centre cheap lunches and evening meals from several fuentes de soda and schoperías

In Providencia Expensive: *Centre Catalá*, Av Suecia 428 near Lota. Good food and décor, reasonably-priced set lunch. *Coco Loco*, La Concepción 236. Good seafood, reservation advised. *Lomit's*, Av Providencia 1980. Good food and service. *Oriental*, Manuel Montt 584. Excellent Chinese. Highly recommended. *Salvaje*, Av Providencia 1177. Good international menu, open-air seating, good value. Warmly recommended. **Mid-range**: *A Pinch of Pancho*, Gral del Canto 45. Very good seafood. On Av Providencia: *Gatsby*, No 1984. American food, as-much-as-you-can-eat buffet and lunch/dinner, snack bar open till 2400, tables outside in warm weather, good (also has a good branch at the airport). *Mare Nostrum*, La Concepción 281. Good for seafood. *La Pez Era*, No 1421. Seafood, smart but not too expensive. **Italian** all expensive: *La Pizza Nostra*, Av Providencia 1975. Pizzas and good Italian food, real coffee, also at Av Las Condes 6757 and Luis Thayer Ojeda 019. *da Renato*, Mardoqueo Fernández 138 (Metro Los Leones). Good. **French**: all expensive: *Au Bon Pain*,

Chile

Bellavista

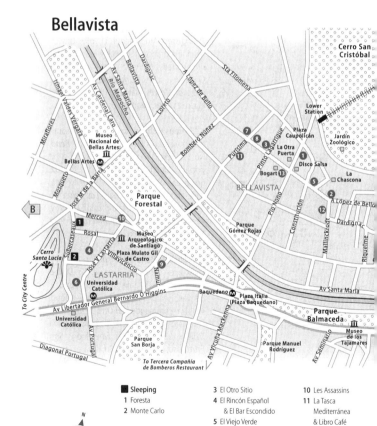

Sleeping	3 El Otro Sitio	10 Les Assassins
1 Foresta	4 El Rincón Español	11 La Tasca
2 Monte Carlo	& El Bar Escondido	Mediterránea
	5 El Viejo Verde	& Libro Café
Eating	6 Gatopardo	Mediterráneo
1 Calamar & Eladio	7 HBH Bar	12 San Fruttuoso
2 Café de la Dulcería	8 La Divina Comida	13 Venezia
Las Palmas	9 La Pergola de la Plaza & R	

N

0 metres	200
0 yards	200

11 de Septiembre 2263. "French bakery café", very good, has other branches. *Carousel*, Los Conquistadores 1972. Very good, nice garden. *El Giratorio*, 11 de Septiembre 2250, p16. Revolving restaurant with good food.

In Las Condes *Cuerovaca*, El Mañío 1659. Fantastic tender steaks, Argentine and Chilean cuts, expensive. **On Vitacura Expensive**: *El Madroñal*, No 2911, T233 6312. Spanish, excellent, booking essential. *Sakura*, No 4111. Japanese, sushi, very good. **Mid-range**: *Delmónico*, No 3379. Excellent, reasonably priced. *Le Fournil*, No 3841. Excellent French bakery and restaurant, popular a lunchtime. *Praga*, No 3917. Czech. *The Wok House*, No 4355. Chinese, take-away available. **On Isadora Goyenechea** *La Cascade*, No 2930. French, excellent. *Pinpilinpausha*, No 2900. Good. *Puerto Marisco*, No 2928. Seafood, good. *Taj Mahal*, No 3215 (Metro El Golf). Indian, expensive but excellent. **On El Bosque Norte** there are many good restaurants, eg *El Mesón del Calvo*, corner with Roger de Flor, expensive seafood. *Diego Pizza*, corner with Don Carlos. Good cocktails, popular. *You*, No 036. Good sushi.

Many 1st-class restaurants, including grills, Chilean cuisine (often with music), French cuisine and Chinese This area tends to be more expensive than central restaurants

Vegetarian *El Huerto*, Orrego Luco 054, Providencia, T233 2690. Open daily, live music Fri and Sat evenings, varied menu, very good but not cheap, popular. Recommended. Its sister café, *La Huerta*, next door, is cheaper. *El Naturista*, Moneda 846. Excellent, closes 2100. Repeatedly recommended. *Natural Green*, Huérfanos 1188, and Puente 689, loc 314. *Unicornio*, Plaza Lyon, Loc 49. *El Vegetariano*, Huérfanos 827, local 18. *El Viejo Verde*, López de Bello 94, Bellavista.

Statue of the Virgin
Cumbre Station (Teleférico)
Upper Station (Funicular)
Parque Metropolitano
Sofía Concha
Arz Casanova
M Concha
Bellavista
A
To Providencia & Las Condes
Av Andrés Bello
Salvador
Av Providencia
Av Salvador
Gral Salvo
Av Eliodoro Yañez
Av José M Infante

HHHH Funicular railway

In the centre *Café Paula*, several branches, eg Estado at entrance to Galería España. Excellent coffee, cakes and ice cream, good breakfast, also on San Antonio opposite the Teatro Municipal. *Pastelería Colonial*, MacIver 133. Recommended. *Café Santos*, Huérfanos 830. Popular for 'onces' (afternoon tea), many branches. *New York*, Moneda y Tenderini. Good coffee, helpful. *Bombón Oriental*, Merced 345. Superb Turkish, specialities, coffee, Falafel and cakes. *Tip-Top Galetas*, recommended for freshly baked biscuits, branches throughout the city, eg Merced 867. **In Bellavista and Lastarrria** *Café de la Dulcería Las Palmas*, López de Bello 190. Good pastries and lunches. *La Chimenea*, Pasaje Príncipe de Gales 90. Hidden away upstairs in a small street, atmospheric, meals during the day, unpretentious, lively. Bavarian-style beer brewed to traditional recipes in Temuco at *HBH Bars*, Pío Nono 129 and Purísima y López de Bello, also at Irarrázaval 3176, near Plaza Ñuñoa, and Gral Holley 124, Providencia. **In Providencia** *Flannery's Irish Geo Pub*, Encomenderos 83. With beer and food, live music Wed and Fri, internet. *Le Flaubert*, Orrego Luco 125. Good *salón de té* and restaurant. **Many on Av Providencia including**: *Phone Box Pub*, No 1652. Serves imported British beers, popular with locals

Cafés & bars
For good coffee try Café Haití, Café Brasil and Café Caribe, all on Paseo Ahumada and elsewhere in centre and Providencia, mainly for men – look at the waitresses to see why – women advised to go escorted. Almost all hotel bars are closed on Sun

Chile

and gringos. *Salón de Té Tavelli*, drugstore precinct, No 2124. Recommended. *Golden Bell Inn*, Hernando Aguirre 27. Popular with expatriates. Many other good bars nearby on Av Suecia including *Mr Ed*, No 1552; *Morena Pizza*, No 0120 (see also **Discotheques**, below) *Brannigan Pub*, No 35, good beer, live jazz; *Red Pub*, No 29; *Louisiana River Pub*, Suecia y Gral Holly, live music. **For snacks and ice cream** Several good places on Av Providencia including *Coppellia*, No 2211, *Bravissimo*, No 1406, and *El Toldo Azul*, No 1936. **In Las Condes** *Country Village*, Av Las Condes y Estoril. Further east on Av Las Condes at Paseo San Damián are several popular bar-restaurants including *T'quila* (annex of *Santa Fe*, No 10690, a colourful, popular Mexican restaurant).

Entertainment
Some of the restaurants and cafés which have shows are given above

Nightclubs For all entertainments, nightclubs, cinemas, restaurants, concerts, *El Mercurio Online* website has all listings and a good search feature. Look under *Tiempo libre*: www.emol.com Listings in weekend newspapers, particularly *El Mercurio* and *La Tercera*. Also *Santiago What's On*. Lively areas to head for are: Bellavista, good selection of varied restaurants, bars, discotheques and salsotheques. Reasonable prices (Metro Baquedano). Avs Suecia and Gral Holley, much of it pedestrianized. Lots of bars and some restaurants, disco- and salsotheques (Metro Los Leones). El Bosque Norte, chic bars and expensive restaurants for the Chilean jetset (Metro Tobalaba). Barrio Brasil, a number of bars and restaurants dotted around the Plaza Brasil and on Avs Brasil and Cumming. Popular with Chilean students (Metro República). Plaza Ñuñoa. A number of good bars dotted around the Plaza in the middle-class suburb of Ñuñoa.

Peña Nano Parra, San Isidro 57. Good folk club, cheap. *Club de Jazz de Santiago*, Av Pedro Alessandri 85, Ñuñoa, www.clubdejazz.cl Regular live jazz in candle-lit bar, pleasant. *Morena*, Av Suecia 0120. Good dance floor and sound system, techno, open till 0200, live music weekends. *Ilé Habana*, Bucaré, just off Suecia. Bar with salsa, often live, and a good dance floor. *Heaven*, Recoleta 345. Expensive. *Enigma*, Av Las Condes 9179. *Club Tucán Salsoteca*, Av Pedro de Valdivia 1783. **On López de Bello, Bellavista**: *Caribbean*, No 40, reggae pub-disco. *Bogart*, No 34, disco-rock bar. **On**

Pío Nono: *Disco Salsa*, No 223 (salsa and classes); *La Otra Puerta*, No 348 (lively *salsoteca*); *Tu Tu Tango*, No 127 (good value).

Cinemas 'Ciné Arte' (quality foreign films) is very popular and 7 small cinemas specialize in this type of film: *El Biógrafo*, Lastarria 181, T633 4435. *Casa de Extensión UC*, Alameda 390, T635 1994. *Normandie*, Tarapacá 1181, T697 2979. *AIEP*, Miguel Claro 177, T264 9698. *Espaciocal* and *Lo Castillo*, Candelaría Goyenechea 3820, T246 1562/244 5856. *Tobalaba*, Av Providencia 2563, T231 6630. Try also Goethe-Institut (address below). Many multiplex cinemas across the city show mainstream releases, nearly always in the original English with subtitles. Seats cost US$4-6 with reductions on Wed (elsewhere in the country the day varies).

Good guide to daily cinema in the free newspapers, La Hora and tmg, given out at metro stations on weekday mornings

Theatres *Teatro Municipal*, Agustinas y San Antonio. Stages international opera, concerts by the Orquesta Filarmónica de Santiago, and the Ballet de Santiago, throughout the year. On Tue at 2100 there are free operatic concerts in the Salón Claudio Arrau; tickets range from US$7 for a very large choral group with a symphony orchestra, and US$8 for the cheapest seats at the ballet, to US$70 for the most expensive opera seats. Some cheap seats are often sold on the day of concerts. *Teatro Universidad de Chile*, Plaza Italia, is the home of the Orquesta y Coro Sinfónica de Chile and the Ballet Nacional de Chile. There are a great number of theatres which stage plays in Spanish, either in the original language or translations. *Santiago Stage* is an English-speaking amateur drama group. Outdoor rock concerts are held at the *Estadio Nacional*, Av Grecia y Pedro de Valdivia, at the *Teatro Teletón*, Rosas 325 (excellent sound system), and elsewhere.

Free classical concerts are sometimes given in San Francisco church in summer. Arrive early for a seat. Theatres and events are listed in El Mercurio and La Tercera

During **Nov** there is a free art fair in the Parque Forestal on the banks of the Río Mapocho, lasting a fortnight. In **Oct** or **Nov** there are a sumptuous flower show and an annual agricultural and industrial show (known as Fisa) in Parque Cerrillos. Religious festivals and ceremonies continue throughout Holy Week, when a priest ritually washes

Festivals

the feet of 12 men. The image of the *Virgen del Carmen* (patron of the Armed Forces) is carried through the streets by cadets on **16 Jul**.

Shopping

Book prices are high compared with neighbouring countries and Europe

Bookshops *Librería Albers*, Vitacura 5648, Las Condes, T218 5371, F218 1458. Spanish, English and German, good selection, cheaper than most, helpful, stocks Footprint Handbooks, also German and Swiss newspapers. *Apostrophes*, Merced 324, T/F632 3569, apos@cybercenter.cl Specializes in French books, book exchange, internet service. Second-hand English books from *Books*, Av Providencia 1652, Metro Pedro de Valdivia, T235 1205, exchange for best deal (the artist's shop in same precinct sells attractive cards). Next to *Books* is *Chile Ilustrado*, No 1652, T235 8145, chileil@tnet.cl Specializes in books relating to Chile, flora, fauna, history and anthropology (mostly in Spanish). *Feria Chilena del Libro*, Huérfanos 623, T639 6758, and in Drugstore precinct, Providencia 2124. Good for travel books and some maps. *Librería Inglesa*, Huérfanos 669, local 11, Pedro de Valdivia 47, Providencia 2653, Vitacura 5950, www.libreriainglesa.cl Good selection of English books. *LOM Ediciones*, Estación Mapocho. Very good, large stock from its own publishing house (literature, history, sociology, art, politics), also bar and reading room with recent Chilean papers and magazines, Mon-Fri 1000-2000, Sat 1000-1400. *South American Way*, Apoquindo 6856, Las Condes, T211 8078. Sells books in English. *Librería Universitaria*, Alameda 1050, T687 4216, in unmistakable yellow building next to Universidad de Chile metro. Good selection of books in Spanish. *Librairie Française*, books and newspapers, Estado 337. For cheap English books, try the second-hand book kiosks on San Diego between Eleuterio Ramírez and Cóndor, 4 blocks south of Plaza Bulnes, or *Drago*, Rosas 3260, near Parque Quinta Normal.

Camping equipment Standard camping gas cartridges can be bought at *Fabri Gas*, Bandera y Santo Domingo. *Mountain Service* (see under skiing equipment). Imported camping goods from *Club Andino* and *Federación de Andinismo* (see below): *Outdoors & Travel*, Encomenderos 206, Las Condes, T/F335 7104. German/Chilean owned, clothing, equipment, maps. *Industria Yarur*, Rosas 1289 y Teatinos, T672 3696 (metro Cal y Canto). Sells wide range of *Doite* products (Chilean, good value). *La Cumbre*, Apoquindo 5258, Las Condes, T678 4285/220 9907, la_cumbre@email.com Dutch-owned, very helpful. *Reinaldo Lippi*, Av Italia 1586, Ñuñoa, T344452. Makes tents, sleeping bags, packs, etc, sells secondhand kit, repairs, helpful. Repair of camping stoves at *Casa Italiana*, Tarapacá 1120. For second-hand equipment look for adverts in cheaper hotels or try Luz Emperatriz Sanhuela Quiroz, Portal Lyon, Loc 14, Providencia 2198 (Metro Los Leones), expensive for new equipment, as is *Patagonia Retail Store*, Helvecia 210 e Ebro, near Metro Tobalaba, T335 1716. Try also the arcades around the Central railway station.

Crafts *Cooperativa Almacén Campesino*, Purísima 303, Bellavista, T737 2127. A cooperative association in an attractive colonial building, selling handicrafts from all over Chile, including attractive Mapuche weavings, wood carvings, pottery and beautiful wrought copper and bronze. Highly recommended for variety, quality and value. Prices are similar to those in similar shops in Temuco. Ask about shipping. The gemstone lapis lazuli can be found in a few expensive shops in Bellavista but is cheaper in the arcades on south side of the Plaza de Armas and in the *Centro Artesanal Santa Lucía* (Santa Lucía Metro, south exit) which also has a wide variety of woollen goods, jewellery, some folk music and other miscellanea. *Amitié*, Ricardo León y Av Providencia (Metro Los Leones) and *Dauvin Artesanía Fina*, Providencia 2169, Local 69 (Metro Los Leones) have also been recommended. *Cema-Chile* (Centro de Madres), Portugal 351 and at Universidad de Chile Metro stop, *Manos Chilensis*, Portugal 373, *Artesanías de Chile*, Varas 475, *Artesanía Popular Chilena*, Av Providencia 2322 (near Metro Los Leones), and *Artesanía Chilena*, Estado 337, all have a good selection of handicrafts. *Chile Vivo*, Dardignac 15, Bellavista, T735 0227, chilevivo@latinmail.com Typical handicrafts, jewellery making, art gallery, internet café, owner Doris Berdichevsky is very helpful. *Prisma de los Andes*, Santo Domingo 1690 T673 0540, Metro Santa Ana. Textiles, crafts, tapestries, rucksacks, bags, kids clothes etc. Antique stores in Plaza Mulato Gil de Castro and elsewhere on Lastarria (Merced end).

Beside and behind the Iglesia de los Dominicos, on Av Apoquindo 9085, is *Los Graneros del Alba*, or *El Pueblo de Artesanos*. Open 1030-2100 in summer, 1000-1900 in winter. All types of ware on sale, classes given in some shops, interesting. To get there, take a No 326 or 327 bus from Av Providencia, marked 'Camino del Alba'; get out at the children's playground at the junction of Apoquindo y Camino del Alba, at the foot of the hill leading up to the church, and walk up. *Plaza Artesanos de Manquehue*, Av Manquehue Sur, block 300-600, just off Apoquindo. Good range of modern Chilean crafts from ceramics to textiles. Take any bus east from Providencia or Escuela Militar which goes via Apoquindo.

Maps *Automóvil Club de Chile*, Vitacura 8620. Route maps of Chile, 7 maps in total, US$6 each or US$3 each if affiliated to motor organization. *Instituto Geográfico Militar*, Dieciocho 369, T460 8222. Has detailed geophysical and topographical maps of the whole of Chile, very useful for climbing. Expensive (US$11 each), but the Biblioteca Nacional, Alameda 651 (T360 5200) has copies and will allow you to photocopy parts of each map. *Mapas*, Gral del Canto 105, of 1506, Providencia, T236 4808, jmattassi@interactiva.cl Sells good comprehensive maps available for the whole of Chile. Some specialize in marking trekking routes, especially in national parks where maps are produced in conjunction with *Conaf*. Maps are US$6 each. Purchase direct from small office on 15th floor of highrise just off Providencia. Mon-Fri 1000 –1330 and 1430-1700. Basic plans of central Santiago can be obtained free from tourist info centres in Vitacura, Paseo Ahumada and airport. More detailed and extensive ones can be bought at same places. *Atlas de Chile* street map, from bookshops and news stands, has been recommended, US$6.50. Telefónica Plano de Santiago in booklet format recommended, US$6.See also Finding our more in Essentials.

Markets *Mercado Central*, between Puente y 21 de Mayo by the Río Mapocho (Cal y Canto Metro) is excellent but quite expensive. There is a cheaper market, the *Vega Central*, on the opposite bank of the river. There are other craft markets in an alleyway, 1 block south of the Alameda between A Prat and San Diego, on the 600 to 800 blocks of Santo Domingo (including pieces from neighbouring countries) and at Pío Nono y Santa María, Bellavista. The shopping arcade at the Central Station is good value, likewise the street market outside. The *Bío Bío* flea market on C Bío Bío, Metro Franklin (follow the crowds) on Sat and Sun morning and a good outside fruit market at Puente 815, by *Frutería Martínez*.

Music *Feria de Disco*, Paseo Ahumada and in numerous malls. The biggest chain, often sell tickets for rock concerts. *Musimundo*, Huérfanos 930 (complete with listening stations) and Providencia 2266, megastores.

Shopping malls Numerous: most central is *Mall del Centro*, Rosas 900 block, just north of the Plaza de Armas. *Alto Las Condes*, Av Kennedy 9001; *Apumanque*, Manquehue y Apoquindo; *Parque Arauco*, Av Kennedy 5413, north of Metro Escuela Militar; *Plaza Vespucio* at terminus of Línea 5, Bellavista de La Florida. Generally open daily 1000-2100.

Wine *El Mundo del Vino*, Isidora Goyenechea 2931, T244 8888, for all types of Chilean wines, good selection across the price range. Similar at *Vinopolis*, El Bosque Norte 038 and Pedro de Valdivia 036. Mon-Fri 0900-2300, Sat 1000-2300, Sun 1000-2200. Also at airport. *The Wine House*, Vitacura 2904, Mall Parque Arauco, loc 333.

Bicycles: for new models, parts and repairs at best prices go to San Diego, 800 and 900 blocks, south of the Alameda. **Cricket**: Sat in summer at **Club Príncipe de Gales**, Las Arañas 1901 (bus from Tobalaba Metro), US$5, membership not required. **Football**: main teams including Colo Colo who play at the Estadio Monumental, T688 3244 (reached by any bus to Puente Alto; tickets from Cienfuegos 41), Universidad de Chile, Campo de Deportes, Ñuñoa, T239 2793 (Estadio Nacional, Grecia 2001, T238 8102) and Universidad Católica who play at San Carlos de Apoquindo, reached by bus from Metro Escuela Militar, tickets from Andrés Bello 2782, Providencia, T231 2777. **Racecourses**: **Club Hípico**, Blanco Encalada 2540, highly recommended "if only to watch dusk over the Andes" (Steve Collins), entry to main

Sport

Chile

stand US$6, every Sun and every other Wed; Hipódromo Chile every Sat. **Skiing and climbing**: ClubAndino de Chile, Enrique Foster 29, ski club (open 1900-2100 on Mon and Fri). **Federación de Andinismo de Chile**, Almte Simpson 77A (T222 0888, F222 6285). Open daily (frequently closed Jan/Feb), has a small museum, library (weekdays except Wed 1930-2100), shop selling guides and equipment. **Escuela Nacional de Montaña** (ENAM), at same address, T222 0799, holds seminars and courses and has the addresses of all the mountaineering clubs in the country. It has a mountaineering school. **Club Alemán Andino**, El Arrayán 2735, T242 5453. Open Tue and Fri, 1800-2000, May-Jun. Also try **Skitotal**, Apoquindo 4900, of 32,33,43, T246 0156, for 1-day excursions and good value ski hire. Equipment hire is much cheaper in Santiago than in ski resorts. Sunglasses are essential. For ski resorts in the Santiago area see below page 633. **Skiing and climbing equipment**: Mountain **Service**, Santa Magdalena 75, of 306, Providencia, T234 3439, F234 3438, www.mountainservice.cl Metro Los Leones. English spoken, tents, stoves, clothing, equipment rental, recommended. **Swimming Pools**: *Tupahue* (large pool with cafés, entry US$10 but worth it) and *Antilen*, both on Cerro San Cristóbal. Open daily in summer except Mon 1000-1500 (check if they are open in winter, one usually is). In Parque O'Higgins, 1330-1830 summer only, US$3. Olympic pool in Parque Araucano (near Parque Arauco Shopping Centre, Metro Escuela Militar), open Nov-Mar Tue-Sat 0900-1900. **Tennis**: Municipal courts in Parque O'Higgins. Estadio Nacional, Av Grecia y Av Marathon, has a tennis club which offers classes.

Tour operators   *Asatej Student Flight Centre*, H de Aguirre 201, Oficina 401, T335 0395, www.sertur.cl For cheap flights and youth travel. Recommended. *Turismo Cocha* (American Express representatives with mail service), El Bosque Norte 0430, PO Box 191035, Providencia, Metro Tobalaba, T230 1000, www.cocha.com *Eurotur*, Huérfanos 1160, local 13, www.eurotur.com For cheap air tickets to Europe. *Turismo Joven*, 11 de Septiembre 2305, local 11, Providencia, T232 3174, turjoven@mailnet.rdc.cl Youth travel services for young people and students for travel, studies, leisure with links in Latin America and worldwide. *Ladatco*, USA T800-327-6162, www.ladactco.com Runs South-American wide tours. *Passtours*, Huérfanos 886, of 1110, T639 3232, F633 1498. Helpful. *Tajamar*, Orrego Luco 023, Providencia, T336 8000. Good for flights. *Wagons-Lits* , Carmencita, Providencia, T233 0820. Recommended. *Hotelschile.com*, and *experiencechile.org*, T313 3389, hotels and tours. **For adventure tours and trekking**: *Altue Expediciones*, Encomenderos 83, p 2, Las Condes (above *Geo Pub*), T232 1103, altue@entelchile.net For wilderness trips including tour of Patagonia. Recommended. *Andina del Sud*, Bombero Ossa 1010, p 3, of 301, T697 1010, F696 5121. For tours in the Lake District. *Antu Aventuras*, Casilla 24, Santiago, T271 2767. Climbing and adventure tours in the Lake District and elsewhere. *Azimut 360*, Arzobispo Casanova 3, Providencia, T735 8034, www.azimut.cl Adventure and ecotourism including mountaineering all over Chile, low prices. Highly recommended. *Turismo Cabo de Hornos*, Av Vitacura 2898, Las Condes, T335 0550, hornos@chilesat.net For DAP flights and Tierra del Fuego/Antarctica tours. *Mountain Service* (see under skiing and climbing). *Nicole Aventuras*, Nicole Schoenholzer, Mar del Plata 1957-42, Providencia, T/F225 6155, www.fis.puc.cl/~gtarrach/avenic 1 and 3-day trips to national parks, trekking and adventure tours in precordillera and coastal mountain range, English, French, German spoken. *Patagonia Connection* SA, Fidel Oteíza 1921, of 1006, Providencia (Metro Pedro de Valdivia), T225 6489, www.patagoniaconnex.cl For excursion by boat Puerto Montt-Coyhaique/Puerto Chacabuco-Laguna San Rafael. *Racies*, Plaza Corregidor Zañartu 761, T/F638 2904. Cultural tours, including Robinson Crusoe Island and Antarctica. *Southern Cross Adventure*, J M de la Barra 521, 4E, T/F639 6591, www.scadventure.com Climbing, riding, trekking, overland expeditions, fishing in Patagonia, many languages spoken. *Sportstours*, Moneda 970, p 14, T549 5200, www.sportstour.cl German-run, helpful, 5-day trips to Antarctica (offices also at Hotels *Carrera*, and *San Cristóbal*), only for tours organized from abroad. *Valle Nevado*, T206 0027, www.vallenevado.com Skiing, trekking and mountain biking. *Catamaranes del Sur*, Isidora Goyenechea 3250, of 802, the Counts, T333 7127, F232 9736, offers tours of Chilean Patagonia. At Puerto Montt: Km 13, Chinquihue, T48 2308 and Avda Diego 510 Vestibules, T26 7533; at Chaitén: Avda Father Juan Todesco 180,

T73 11 99; at Chacabuco Port: Jose Miguel Race 50, T35 1112, www.catamaranesdelsur.cl
Lime Light Tour, Av 11 September 1945, of 1213, Providence, T3811510, F3811509, www.limelighttour.cl, offers tours of Chilean Patagonia.

A number of agencies offer day trips from Santiago. Typical excursions are to the Wine Valleys, Valparaíso and Viña del Mar, Isla Negra (Pablo Neruda's seaside villa), visits to nearby haciendas and adventure tours such as whitewater rafting, rock climbing or trekking in the Cajón del Maipo, southeast of the city. Many agencies advertise in the **Sernatur** tourist office (see above).

Local Buses are called *micros*. Destinations are marked clearly on the front. In theory passengers put the exact change in a ticket machine to get a printed ticket. In practice this is only one of three options, the other two being that you give the money to the driver who will arrange a printed ticket, or the driver will give you an old-style paper ticket. There are also **colectivos** (collective taxis) on fixed routes to the suburbs, US$0.75-1.50. Routes are displayed with route numbers. **Taxis** (black with yellow roofs) are abundant, and not expensive, with a minimum charge of US$0.60, plus US$0.12 per 200 m. Taxi drivers are permitted to charge more at night, but in the daytime check that the meter is set to day rates. At bus terminals, drivers will charge more – best to walk a block and flag down a cruising taxi. Avoid taxis with more than one person in them especially at night. For journeys outside the city arrange the charge beforehand. The private taxi service which operates from the bottom level of *Hotel Carrera* has been recommended (same rates as city taxis), as has **Radio Taxis** Andes Pacífico, T225 3064/2888; similarly **Rigoberto Contreras**, T638 1042, ext 4215, but rates above those of city taxis.

Car hire: prices vary a lot so shop around first. Main international agencies and others are available at the airport (see Essentials, page 48 for agency web addresses). **Seelmann**, Las Encinas 3057, Ñuñoa, T09-331 0591. English and German spoken. **Just Rent a Car**, Helvecia 228, Las Condes, T232 0900. English and Portuguese spoken. **Costanera**, Av Andrés Bello 1255, T235 7835. **Automóvil Club de Chile** car rental from head office (see Maps), discount for members and members of associated motoring organizations. A credit card is usually asked for when renting a vehicle. Remember that in the capital driving is restricted according to licence plate numbers; look for notices in the street and newspapers.

Metro: (www.metro-chile.cl) There are 3 lines: Line 1 which runs west-east between San Pablo and Escuela Militar, under the Alameda; Line 2 which runs north-south from Cal y Canto to Callejón Ovalle; Line 5, from Santa Ana via Baquedano south to La Florida (an extension to Quinta Normal is due for completion by 2003). The trains are fast, quiet, and very full. The first train is at 0630 (Mon-Sat), 0800 (Sun and holidays), the last about 2230. Fares vary according to time of journey; there are 2 charging periods: high 0715-0900, 1800-1900, US$0.75; economic, at all other times, US$0.50. The simplest solution is to buy a *boleto valor/carnet*, US$5 for 10 journeys. Blue *metrobus* services connect with the metro at Lo Ovalle, Las Rejas, Pila de Ganso, Caly Canto, Salvador, Escuela Militar and La Florida for outlying districts, fare US$0.50.

Motorcycles: *Colvin & Colvin,* Av Las Condes 8038, T224 3434, colvinycolvin@ entelchile.net Run by Winston Colvin, friendly, helpful, speaks English, knows about necessary paperwork for buying bikes, Honda and Yamaha parts and service. **Solomoto**, Vitacura 7510, T218 3152. English spoken, service and parts for Honda and Yamaha. **Moto Service**, Tabancura 1332, T215 4570. New and second-hand Honda and Yamaha dealer. Authorized BMW service, **Williamson Balfour**, Av Portugal 441, T634 4499, F222 7722. Good mechanics.

Long distance Air: International and domestic flights leave from Arturo Merino Benítez Airport at Pudahuel, 26 km northwest of Santiago. There are two terminals: domestic and international. The international terminal is more modern and has most facilities, including *Afex cambio* (poor rates, change only what you need), ATMs, *Sernatur* office which will book accommodation and a fast-food plaza. The domestic terminal has a few shops, but they are very expensive, as are the bar and restaurant. **Left luggage** US$2.50 per bag per day.

Airport taxi, about US$17-20 but bargain hard and agree fare beforehand: more expensive with meter. Taxi to airport is much cheaper if flagged down in the street rather than booked by phone. Frequent bus services to/from city centre by 2 companies: *Tur Bus* (buses

Margin notes

Transport
Hang on to your bus ticket, inspectors occasionally ask for them

Chile

Tax of 18% is charged but usually not included in price quoted. If possible book a car in advance. Information boards full of flyers from companies at airport and tourist office

See next page for Metro map

Airport information T601 9709

from Moneda y San Martín in the centre) US$2.50, every 30 mins; and *Centropuerto* (T601 9883, from Metro Los Héroes), US$2.50, first from centre 0600, last from airport 2330. Buses leave from outside airport terminal and, in Santiago, call at Plazoleta Los Héroes (near the yellow 'Línea 2' sign), Estación Central, the Terminal Santiago and most other regular bus stops. (Beware the bus marked *Aeropuerto* which stops 2 km short of the Airport). *Delfos* runs shuttle bus for larger groups and cars for 1 or 2 people, fare from centre US$13, book in advance, T601 1111. *Transfer* runs minibuses from your house or hotel to airport (or vice-versa), any time day or night, US$6 to centre, US$7 Providencia, US$8 Las Condes, T777 7707 for reservation (cheaper than taxi). Recommended. *Navett*, Av Ejército Libertador 21 (nearest Metro Los Héroes), T695 6868 has a round-the-clock service, US$7. For domestic flights from Santiago, see under destinations.

Check if student rates are available (even for non-students), or reductions for travelling same day as purchase of ticket; it is worth bargaining over prices, especially shortly before departure and out of summer season

Buses: There are frequent, and good, interurban buses to all parts of Chile. Take a look at the buses before buying the tickets (there are big differences in quality among bus companies); ask about the on-board services, many companies offer drinks for sale, or free, and luxury buses have meals and wine, colour videos, headphones. Reclining seats are common and there are also *salón cama* sleeper buses. Fares from/to the capital are given in the text. On Fri evening, when night departures are getting ready to go, the terminals can be chaotic. There are 4 bus terminals: 1) **Terminal de Buses Alameda**, which has a modern extension called Mall Parque Estación, O'Higgins 3712, Metro Universidad de Santiago, T270 7150. All *Pullman-Bus* and *TurBus* services go from here, they serve almost every destination in Chile, good quality but prices a little higher than others. 2) **Terminal de Buses Santiago**, O'Higgins 3878, 1 block west of Terminal Alameda, T376 1755, Metro Universidad de Santiago. Services to Valparaíso, Viña del Mar and all parts of Chile, including Punta Arenas with *Turibus.* Also international departures. The best place to start shopping around for prices. 3) **Terminal San Borja**, O'Higgins y San Borja, 1 block west of Estación Central, 3 blocks east of Terminal Alameda, Metro Estación Central (entrance is, inconveniently, via a busy shopping centre), T776 0645. Some national departures and buses to outlying parts of Región Metropolitana and Region 5. Booking offices and departures organized according to

Santiago Metro

Transport
- ▬▬ Metro line 1
- ▬▬ Metro line 2
- ▬▬ Metro line 5
- ▪ ▪ ▪ Under construction
- ⊙ Transfer station
- 1 🚌 Bus terminal
- 2 🚌 Metrobus terminal
- ▬ Train station

N

Not to scale

destination. Left luggage US$1.50 per piece per day. 4) **Terminal Los Héroes** on Tucapel Jiménez, just north of the Alameda, Metro Los Héroes, T420 0099. Booking offices of 8 companies, to the north, the south and Lake District and some international services (Lima, Asunción, Montevideo, Buenos Aires, Bariloche, Mendoza). Some long-distance buses call at Las Torres de Tajamar, Providencia 1108, which is more convenient if you are planning to stay in Providencia. *TurBus* has an office on Av Apoquindo, just west of junction with Av Las Condes; *Cruz del Sur*, *Varmontt* and *Pullman Express* have offices on Paseo Los Leones.

See the note under Taxis about not taking expensive taxis parked outside bus terminals.

International buses   Short distance: there are frequent services from Terminal Santiago and less frequent services from the Alameda terminal through the Cristo Redentor tunnel to **Mendoza** in Argentina, 6-7 hrs, US$12, many companies, departures around 0800, 1200 and 1600, touts approach you in Terminal Santiago. There are also collective taxis from the Terminal Los Héroes and from the 800/900 blocks of Morandé (*Chi-Ar* taxi company, Terminal Santiago of 62, T776 0048, recommended; *Chilebus*, Morandé 838; *Cordillera Nevada*, Morandé 870, T698 4716), US$15, 5 hrs, shorter waiting time at customs.

Most services leave from Terminal Santiago, though there are also departures from Terminal Los Héroes

   Long distance: to **Buenos Aires**, US$40, 22 hrs (eg *Tas Choapa* and *Ahumada* from Los Héroes terminal); to **Montevideo**, involving a change in Mendoza, *El Rápido*, 27 hrs; to **Córdoba** direct, US$28, 18 hrs, several companies including *TurBus*, *Tas Choapa* and *TAC* (El Rápido not recommended); to **San Juan**, *TAC*, *Tas Choapa*, US$20; To **Lima**, *Ormeño* (Terminal Santiago Sur of 83, T779 3443), 51 hrs, US$70, it is cheaper to take a bus to Arica, a colectivo to Tacna, then bus to Lima.

Trains: All trains leave from Estación Central at O'Higgins 3170. The line runs south to Rancagua, San Fernando, Curicó, Talca, Linares, Parral, Chillán, Concepción and Temuco. Trains are still fairly cheap and generally very punctual, although 1st class is generally more expensive than bus; meals are good though expensive. Trains can be cold and draughty in winter and spring. There are also frequent local *Metrotren* services to Rancagua. For reservations T376 8500, efereservas@entelchile.net, www.efe.cl Booking offices: for *State Railways*, at Universidad de Chile Metro station, local 10, T688 3284, Mon-Fri 0830-1900, Sat 0900-1300; Estación San Bernardo, Baquedano 590, T859 1977; or *Agencia Traveller Zone*, Paseo Las Palmas 2229, local 18, Providencia, T946 1835 *Dormitorio* carriages were built in Breslau (now Wroclaw, Poland) in 1929, with sleeping compartments (*departamento*), bunks (comfortable) lie parallel to rails, US-Pullman-style (washrooms at each end, one with shower-bath – often cold water only); an attendant for each car. Also a car-transporter service to Chillán and Temuco. **Left luggage** office at Estación Central.

Schedules change with the seasons, so check timetables before planning a journey. See under destinations for fares and notes on schedules. In summer services are booked up a week in advance

Shipping companies: *Navimag*, Av El Bosque Norte 0440, p 11, Las Condes, T442 3120, F203 5025, www.navimag.com, for services from **Puerto Montt** to **Puerto Natales** and vice versa. *Transmarchilay*, Av Providencia 2653, loc 24, T600-600 8687/88, www.tmc.cl For services between **Chiloé** and the mainland and ferry routes on the Camino Austral. M/n *Skorpios*: Augusto Leguía Norte 118, Las Condes, T231 1030, F232 2269, www.skorpios.cl For luxury cruise out of Puerto Montt to **Laguna San Rafael**. *Transmarchilay* also sail to the Laguna San Rafael in summer.

Check shipping schedules with shipping lines rather than Sernatur

Directory

Airline offices *Aerolíneas Argentinas*, Moneda 756, T639 5001. *Aerovías DAP*, Luis Thayer Ojeda 0180, of 1304, Providencia, T334 9658, F334 5843. *American Airlines*, Huérfanos 1199, and Bosque Norte 0107, T679 0000. *Avianca*, Santa Magdalena 116, Providencia, T695 4105. *British Airways*, Isidora Goyenechea 2934, Oficina 302, T601 8571/2, 232 9560 (for confirmation). *Continental*, Nueva Tajamar 481, T204 4000. *Ecuatoriana*, T334 1606. *Iberia*, Bandera 206, p 8, T870 1070. *KLM*, San Sebastián 2839, of 202, T233 0011 (233 0991 reservations). *LAB*, Moneda 1170, T688 8678. *Lacsa*, Dr Barros Borgoño 105, T235 5500. *LanChile*, sales office: Huérfanos 926, T526 2000, Mon-Fri 0900-1900, Sat 0900-1230 (to avoid queues, buy tickets at the office in the airport). *Lufthansa*, Moneda 970, p 16, T630 1655. *Swissair*, Barros Errázuriz 1954, of 1104, T244 2888. *United*, El Bosque 0177, T337 0000. *Varig*, El Bosque Norte 0177, T707 8000.

Chile

Banks, open 0900-1400, closed on Sat. Exchange rates are published in El Mercurio

Banks For Cirrus/MasterCard, Visa ATMs go to any bank or *Copec* petrol station with Redbanc sign. Visa at *Corp Banca*, Huérfanos y Bandera, but beware hidden costs in 'conversion rate', and *Banco Santander*, Av Providencia y Pedro de Valdivia, no commission. For stolen or lost Visa cards go to *Transbank*, Huérfanos 770, p 10. *Banco de Chile*, Ahumada 251 and other branches, minimum of formalities. *Citibank*, Av Providencia 2653. *Banco American Express*, Av Andrés Bello 2711, p 9 T350 6700 (Metro Tobalaba), for representative office, see *Turismo Cocha*, above. *Casas de Cambio* (exchange houses) in the centre are mainly situated on Agustinas and Huérfanos. Use them, not banks, for changing TCs. *Exprinter*, Bombero Ossa 1053, good rates, low commission. *Transafex*, Moneda 1140, good rates for TCs. In Providencia several on Av Pedro de Valdivia Some *casas de cambio* in the centre open Sat morning (but check first). Dollars can only be bought for Chilean pesos in *casas de cambio*. Most *cambios* charge 3% commission to change US$ TCs into US$ cash; check beforehand. Only residents can buy dollars against credit cards. Always avoid street money changers (particularly common on Ahumada and Agustinas): they pull any number of tricks, or will usually ask you to accompany them to somewhere obscure. The passing of forged notes and muggings are reported.

Communications Internet: **In centre** *Dazoca*, Monjitas 448, 1000-2400 daily. *Sonnets*, Londres 43, of 11, T664 4725, www.2central.com 1000-2100 daily, helpful, many languages spoken, book exchange. *Sicosis*, José M de la Barra 544. *La Araña*, San Isidro 171, Casa 2, in Mall del Centro (Santo Domingo with Puente). Also at Ramón de Corvalán 119, just south of Alameda near Plaza Italia. Agustinas 869, p2. 60 flat-screen computers, US$1.50 per hr, open 0700-2300 daily, popular. **In and near Barrio Brasil** *463@café*, Av Brasil 463, 1000-2200 daily. *Cyber Station*, Brasil 167, Mon-Fri 0900-2200, Sat-Sun 1000-2200. *Banda Ancha*, República 16, also in Cienfuegos 161 next to Youth Hostel, Mon-Sat 0930-2300, Sun 1730-2300, and at Salvador Sanfuentes 2150, Mon-Sat 1000-2300, Sun 1730-2300. *ES Computación*, S Sanfuentes 2352, T688 7395, metro República, nine@ctc.internet.cl Helpful. **In Bellavista** *Chileinternet*, López de Bello 45, T732 0699. Email, scanning service, chat lines, phones and café. *Connections*, López de Bello entre Pío Nono y Constitución. **In Providencia** *Dazoca*, Providencia 1370 y Almte Pastene, p 2, 1000-2400 daily. *Café Phonet*, Gral Holley 2312 and San Sebastián 2815, 0900-2300 daily. *Cafeaquí*, Providencia y E Yáñez, 0800-2000. **Bus terminal** Small access point in Terminal Alameda in *CTC Telefónica* office, lower floor of attached shopping gallery. **Post Office:** Plaza de Armas and Moneda between Morandé and Bandera. Also sub offices in Providencia at Av 11 de Septiembre 2092, Manuel Montt 1517, Pedro de Valdivia 1781, Providencia 1466, and in Estación Central shopping mall. These open Mon-Fri 0900-1800, Sat 0900-1230. Poste restante well organized (though only kept for 30 days), US$0.20, passport essential, list of letters and parcels received in the hall of central Post Office (one list for men, another for women, indicate Sr or Sra/Srta on envelope); Plaza de Armas office also has philatelic section, 0900-1630, and small stamp museum (ask to see it). If sending a parcel, the contents must first be checked at the Post Office. Paper, tape etc on sale. **Telephone:** *CTC*, Moneda 1151, closed Sun. International phone calls also from: *Entel*, Huérfanos 1133. Mon-Fri 0830-2200, Sat 0900-2030, Sun 0900-1400, calls cheaper 1400-2200. Fax upstairs, fax also available at *CTC* offices, eg Mall Panorámico, 11 de Septiembre, 3rd level (phone booths are on level 1). There are also *CTC* phone offices at some metro stations, La Moneda, Escuela Militar, Tobalaba, Universidad de Chile and Pedro de Valdivia for local, long-distance and international calls. There are also phone boxes in the street from which overseas calls can be made.

Cultural centres Instituto Chileno Británico de Cultura, Santa Lucía 124, T638 2156. 0930-1900, except 1330-1900 Mon, and 0930-1600 Fri, has British papers and library (also in Providencia, Darío Urzúa 1933, and Las Condes, Renato Sánchez 4369), runs language courses. **British Council**, Eliodoro Yáñez 832, near Providencia, T223 4622, www.britcoun.cl/index.htm **Instituto Chileno Francés de Cultura**, Merced 298, T639 8433. In a beautiful house. **Instituto Chileno Alemán de Cultura**, Goethe-Institut, Esmeralda 650, T638 3185. **Instituto Chileno Italiano de Cultura**, Triana 843, T236 0712. **Instituto Chileno Israeli de Cultura**, E Yáñez 2342, T209 4624. **Instituto Chileno Japonés de Cultura**, Alcántara 772, T207 1896. **Instituto Chileno Norteamericano de Cultura**, Moneda 1467, T696 3215. Good for US periodicals, cheap films on Fri. Also runs language courses and free Spanish/English language exchange hours (known as Happy Hours) which are a good way of meeting people. (Ask also about Mundo Club which organizes excursions and social events.) **Instituto Cultural del Banco del Estado de Chile**, Alameda 123. Regular exhibitions of paintings, concerts, theatrical performances. **Instituto Cultural de Providencia**, 11 de Septiembre 1995 (Metro Pedro de Valdivia). Art exhibitions, concerts, theatre. **Instituto Cultural Las Condes**, Apoquindo 6570, near beginning of Av Las Condes. Also with art exhibitions, concerts, lectures, etc.

Embassies and consulates Argentina, Miraflores 285, T633 1076. Consulate Vicuña MacKenna 41, T222 6853. Australians need letter from their embassy to get visa here, open 0900-1400 (visa US$25, free for US citizens), if you need a visa for Argentina, get it here or in the consulates in Concepción, Puerto Montt or Punta Arenas, there are no facilities at the borders. **Australia**, Gertrudis Echeñique 420, T228 5065, 0900-1200. **Austria**, Barros Errázuriz 1968, p 3, T223 4774. **Belgium**, Av Providencia 2653, depto 1104, T232 1070. **Bolivia**, Santa María 2796, T232 8180 (Metro Los Leones). 0930-1400. **Brazil**, Alonso Ovalle 1665, p 15, T698 2496. Visas issued by Consulate, MacIver 225, p 15, Mon-Fri 1000-1300, US$10 (visa takes 2 days); take: passport, 2 photos, ticket into and out of Brazil, photocopy of first 2 pages of passport, tickets, credit card and Chilean tourist card. **Canada**, Nueva Tajamar 481, p 12, T362 9660, www.dfait-maeci.gc.ca/santiago (prints a good information book). **Denmark**, Jaques Cazotte 5531, T218 5949. **Finland**, Av 11 de Septiembre 1480 of 73, T263 4947. **France**, Condell 65, T225 1030. **Germany**, Agustinas 785, p 7 y 8, T633 5031. **Israel**, San Sebastián 2812, T750 0500. **Italy**, Román Díaz 1270, T225 9439. **Japan**, Av Ricardo Lyon 520, T232 1807. **Netherlands**, C Las Violetas 2368, T223 6825. 0900-1200. **New Zealand**, Av El Golf 99, of 703, Las Condes, T290 9802, nzembassychile@adsl.tie.cl **Norway**, San Sebastián 2839, T234 2888. **Peru**, Andrés Bello 1751, T235 6451 (Metro Pedro de Valdivia). **South Africa**, Av 11 de Septiembre 2353, Edif San Román, p 16, T231 2862. **Spain**, Av Andrés Bello 1895, T235 2755. **Sweden**, 11 de Septiembre 2353, Torre San Ramón, p 4, Providencia, T231 2733, F232 4188. **Switzerland**, Av Americo Vespucio Sur 100, p 14, T263 4211, F263 4094, metro Escuela Militar. Open 1000-1200. **United Kingdom**, El Bosque Norte 0125 (Metro Tobalaba), Casilla 72-D, T370 4100, F335 5988, www.britemb.cl Will hold letters, consular section (F370 4170) open 0930-1230. **United States**, Andrés Bello 2800, T232 2600, F330 3710. Consulate, T710133, Merced 230 (visa obtainable here).

Language schools *Instituto Chileno-Suizo de Idiomas y Cultura*, San Isidro 171, casa 2, T638 5414, chilenosuizo@tie.cl Coordinates stays in Chile for foreign-language students, courses in several languages, *La Araña* cybercafé (see above), *La Cafetería* meeting place, *El Rincón del Libro* study area and art gallery. *Escuela de Idiomas Violeta Parra*, Ernesto Pinto Lagarrigue 362A, Recoleta-Barrio Bellavista, T735 8240, vioparra@chilessat.net Courses aimed at budget travellers, information programme on social issues, arranges accommodation and visits to local organizations and national parks. *Centro de Idiomas Bellavista*, Crucero Exeter 0325, T737 5102, www.cib.in.cl Group and individual courses, accommodation with families, free activities. *Natalis English Centre*, Vicuña Mackenna 6, p 7, T222 8721, natalislang@hotmail.com Many **private teachers**, including *Carolina Carvajal*, Av El Bosque Sur 151, dpto Q, Las Condes, T734 7646, ccarvajal@interactiva.cl Exchange library, internet access. Highly recommended. *Patricia Vargas Vives*, JM Infante 100, of 308, T/F244 2283. Qualified and experienced (US$12.50 per hr). *Lucía Araya Arévalo*, Puerto Chico 8062, Villa Los Puertos, Pudahuel, T236 0531. Speaks German and English. *Patricio Ríos*, Tobalaba 7505, La Reina, T226 6926. Speaks English. Recommended.

Medical facilities Hospitals Emergency hospital at Marcoleta 377 costs US$60. For yellow fever vaccination and others (but not cholera). **Hospital San Salvador**, J M Infante 551, T225 6441, Mon-Thu 0800-1300, 1330-1645, Fri 0800-1300, 1330-1545. Also **Vaccinatoria Internacional**, Hospital Luis Calvo, MacKenna, Antonio Varas 360. **Clínica Central**, San Isidro 231, T222 1953, open 24 hrs.

If you need to get to a hospital, it is better to take a taxi than wait for an ambulance

Useful addresses Immigration For extension of tourist visa, or any enquiries regarding legal status, go to **Departamento de Extranjería**, Teatinos 950 (near Estación Mapocho), T674 4000. Mon-Fri 0900-1200. They will give you the information you need. Then, to get the paperwork done, you will have to go round the back of the building and queue. Office open 0900-1300. Make sure you are in the queue before 0800 and take a good book. **Policia Internacional**: For lost tourist cards, etc, Gral Borgoño 1052, T737 2443/1292.

Around Santiago

In this little town, pottery can be bought and the artists can be seen at work. The area is rich in clay and the town is famous for its cider in the apple season, for its *chicha de uva* and for its Chilean dishes, highly recommended. ■ *From Santiago take the Melipilla bus from outside the San Borja terminal, every few minutes, US$1 each way, Rutabus 78 goes on the motorway, 1 hr, other buses via Talagante take 1 hr 25 mins (alight at side road to Pomaire, 2-3 km from town, colectivos every 10-15 mins – these buses are easier to take than the infrequent, direct buses).*

Pomaire
65 W of Santiago

Chile

Visits to vineyards

The Maipo Valley is considered by many experts to be the best wine producing area of Chile

Several vineyards in the Santiago area can be visited. *Cousiño-Macul*, Av Quilin 7100 on east outskirts of the city, offers tours Monday-Friday, phone first T248 1011, vtaparticular@cousinomacul.cl Take bus 390 from Alameda, or 391 from Merced, both marked Peñalolén. *Concha y Toro* at Pirque, near Puente Alto, 40 km south of Santiago, T821 7069, rpublicas@conchaytoro.cl Short tour (Spanish, English, French, German, Portuguese), Monday-Saturday and Sunday afternoon. Entry US$6, includes free wine glass and 3 tastings. Recommended. Take Metro to Bellavista de La Florida (end of Línea 5), then blue Metrobus to Pirque. The *Undurraga* vineyard at Santa Ana, southwest of Santiago, T372 2800, sproduccion@undurraga.cl Permits visits with prior reservation only, 1000-1600 on weekdays (tours given by the owner-manager, Pedro Undurraga). Take a Melipilla bus (but not Rutabus 78) to the entrance. *Viña Santa Rita*, Padre Hurtado 0695, Alto Jahuel, Buín, 45 km south, T362 2520, rrivas@santarita.cl Good tour in English and spanish, US$6, reserve 3 days in advance, daily except Monday at specific times. Take a bus from Terminal San Borja to Alto Jahuel.

Upper Maipo Valley

If visiting this area or continuing further up the mountain, be prepared for military checks

Southeast of Santiago is the rugged, green valley of the Cajón del Maipo. A road runs through the villages of San José de Maipo, Melocotón and San Alfonso, near which is the Cascada de Animas waterfall. At **El Volcán** (1,400 m), 21 km beyond San Alfonso, there are astounding views, but little else (the village was wiped away in a landslide). From El Volcán the road (very poor condition) runs east to the warm natural baths at **Baños Morales**. ■ *Open from Oct, entry to baths US$2.* 12 km further east up the mountain are **Baños Colina** (not to be confused with Termas de Colina, a popular thermal resort north of Santiago); hot thermal springs. ■ *Horses for hire.* This area is popular at weekends and holiday times, but is otherwise deserted.

Chile

Santiago region

Sleeping and eating At **Baños Morales D** pp *Hostería Baños Morales*, full board, hot water. **D** pp *Res Los Chicos Malos*, T288 5380, comfortable, fresh bread, good meals; free campsite. **E** *Pensión Díaz*, T861 1496, basic, good food. Excellent café in the village, serving homemade jam, it closes at Easter for the winter. 14 km east of El Volcán, just after Baños Morales, **B** pp *Refugio Alemán Lo Valdés*, T220 7610, stone-built chalet accommodation, full board, own generator, good food, a good place to stay for mountain excursions, open all year, recommended. A splendid region which deserves the journey required to get there. At **Baños Colina: D** pp *Res El Tambo*, full board, restaurant, also camping. No shops so take food (try local goats cheese).

Transport Buses from Metro Parque O'Higgins to **El Volcán** daily at 1200 (US$2) and on to **Baños Morales**, US$4, 3 hrs, returns at 1745; buy return on arrival to ensure seat back.

There are six main ski resorts near Santiago, four of them around the mountain village of Farellones, 51 km east of the capital. **Farellones**, situated on the slopes of Cerro Colorado at 2,470 m and reached by road in under 90 minutes, was the first ski resort built in Chile. Now it is more of a service centre for the three other resorts, but it provides affordable accommodation, has a good beginners area with fairly basic equipment for hire and is connected by lift to El Colorado. Popular at weekends, it has several large restaurants. It offers beautiful views for 30 km across 10 Andean peaks and incredible sunsets. Daily ski-lift ticket, US$30; a combined ticket for all four resorts is also available, US$40-50 depending on season. 1-day excursions are available from Santiago, US$5; enquire Ski Club Chile, Goyenechea Candelaria 4750, Vitacura (north of Los Leones Golf Club), T211 7341.

El Colorado is 8 km further up Cerro Colorado and has a large but expensive ski lodge at the base, offering all facilities, and a mountain restaurant higher up. There are nine lifts giving access to a large intermediate ski area with some steeper slopes. Lift ticket US$37. **La Parva**, nearby at 2,816 m, is the upper class Santiago weekend resort with 12 lifts, 0900-1730. Accommodation is in a chalet village and there are some good bars in high season. Good intermediate to advanced skiing, not suitable for beginners. Lift ticket, US$40; equipment rental, US$10-15 depending on quality. In summer, this is a good walking area.

Valle Nevado is 16 km from Farellones and owned by Spie Batignolles of France. It offers the most modern ski facilities in Chile. There are 25 runs accessed by eight lifts. The runs are well prepared and are suitable for intermediate level and beginners. There is a good ski school and excellent heli skiing. Lift ticket US$30 weekdays, US$42 weekends. ■ *Buses from Santiago to Farellones, El Colorado, La Parva and Valle Nevado leave from in front of Omnium building, Av Apoquindo, 4 blocks from Escuela Militar Metro, daily at 0800, essential to book in advance, T246 6881, US$9. It is easy to hitch from the junction of Av Las Condes/El Camino Farellones (petrol station in the middle), reached by a Barnechea bus.*

Portillo, 2,855 m, is 145 km north of Santiago and 62 east of Los Andes near the customs post on the route to Argentina. One of Chile's best-known resorts, Portillo is on the Laguna del Inca, 5½ km long and 1½ km wide; this lake, at an altitude of 2,835 m, has no outlet, is frozen over in winter, and its depth is not known. It is surrounded on three sides by accessible mountain slopes. The runs are varied and well prepared, connected by 12 lifts, two of which open up the off-piste areas. This is an excellent family resort, with a highly regarded ski school. Cheap packages can be arranged at the beginning of and out of season. Lift ticket US$35, equipment hire US$22. There are boats for fishing in the lake (afternoon winds can make the homeward pull much longer than the outward pull). Out of season this is another good area for walking, but get detailed maps before setting out. ■ *Except in bad weather, Portillo is easily reached by taking any bus from Santiago or Los Andes to Mendoza; you may have to hitch back.*

Lagunillas is 67 km southeast of Santiago in the Cajón del Maipo. Accommodation is in the lodges of the Club Andino de Chile (see **Skiing** above). Lift ticket

Skiing

The season runs from Jun-Sep/Oct, weather permitting, although some resorts have equipment for making artificial snow. Altitude sickness can be a problem, especially at Valle Nevado and Portillo. Manzur Expediciones, T777 4284, run buses to all ski resorts from metro Baquedano, Wed, Sat, Sun 0830

Chile

US$25; long T-bar and poma lifts; easy field. Being lower than the other resorts, its season is shorter, but it is also cheaper. ■ *Public transport goes as far as San José de Maipo, 17 km west of the resort. Bus from Metro Parque O' Higgins, Av Norte-Sur, or west side of Plaza Ercilla, every 15 mins, US$1, 2 hrs.*

Sleeping and eating Farellones B pp *Refugio Club Alemán Andino* (address under **Skiing and Climbing**, above), hospitable, good food. **AL** *Posada Farellones*, T Santiago 201 3704, highly recommended. And others. **El Colorado L** *Edificio Los Ciervos* and *Edificio Monteblanco*, in Santiago, San Antonio 486, of 151, T233 5501, F231 6965. **La Parva L** *Condominio Nueva Parva*, good hotel and restaurant, reservations in Santiago: Roger de Flor 2911, T212 1363, F220 8510. Three other restaurants. **Valle Nevado** Several hotels and restaurants. *Casa Valle Nevado*, Gertrudis Echeñique 441, T206 0027, F228 8888. **Portillo L** *Hotel Portillo*, cinema, nightclub, swimming pool, sauna and medical service, on the shore of Laguna del Inca. Lakefront suites, family apartments and bunk rooms without or with bath (from **C** up), parking charges even if you go for a meal, jacket and tie obligatory in the dining room, self-service lunch, open all year. Reservations, Roger de Flor 2911, T231 3411, F231 7164, Santiago. **AL** *Hostería Alborada*, includes all meals, tax and service. Reservations, Agencia Tour Avión, Agustinas 1062, Santiago, T726184, or C Navarro 264, San Felipe, T 101-R. Cheaper accommodation can be found in Los Andes but the road is liable to closure due to snow. **Eating at El Portillo** Cheaper than the hotels are *Restaurant La Posada* opposite *Hotel Portillo*, open evenings and weekends only. *Restaurant Los Libertadores* at the customs station 1 km away.

Santiago to Argentina

The route across the Andes via the Redentor tunnel is one of the major crossings to Argentina. Before travelling check on weather and road conditions beyond Los Andes. See under Santiago, International Buses.

Los Andes
Phone code: 034
Colour map 8, grid B1
Population: 30,500
Altitude: 730 m
77 km N of Santiago

Situated in a wealthy agricultural, fruit-farming and wine-producing area, Los Andes is also the site of a large car assembly plant. There are monuments to José de San Martín and Bernardo O'Higgins in the Plaza de Armas, and a monument to the Clark brothers, who built the Transandine Railway to Mendoza (now disused). There are several workshops where hand-painted ceramics are made: the largest is *Cala*, Rancagua y Gen Freire. Good views from El Cerro de la Virgen, reached by a trail from the municipal picnic ground on Independencia (one hour). Tourist office is on the main plaza, opposite the post office. *Automóvil Club de Chile*, Chacabuco 33, T422790. ■ *Bus terminal 1 block from the plaza. To Santiago US$2.50, also to Mendoza (Argentina); any Mendoza bus will drop you off at Portillo ski resort, US$6.*

Sleeping A *Baños El Corazón*, at San Esteban, 2 km north, T421371. With full board, use of swimming pool but thermal baths extra, take bus San Esteban/El Cariño (US$0.50). **A** *Plaza*, Esmeralda 367, T421929. Good but restaurant expensive. **E** *Estación*, Rodríguez 389, T421026. Cheap restaurant. There are various other hotels (**C-F**).

Directory Banks ATMs on the plaza. *Cambio Inter* at *Plaza Hotel*, good rates, changes TCs. **Communications Telephone:** *CTC*, O'Higgins 405.

The road to Argentina follows the Aconcagua valley for 34 km until it reaches the village of **Río Blanco** (1,370 m). East of Río Blanco the road climbs until Juncal where it zig-zags steeply through a series of 29 hairpin bends at the top of which is Portillo. ■ *Reached by hourly buses to Saladillo.*

The old pass, with the statue of Christ the Redeemer (**Cristo Redentor**), is above the tunnel on the Argentine side. On the far side of the Andes the road descends 203 km to Mendoza. The Chilean border post of Los Libertadores is at Portillo, 2 km from the tunnel. Bus and car passengers are dealt with separately. Bicycles must be taken through on a pick-up. There may be long delays during searches for fruit, meat and vegetables, which may not be imported into Chile. For Argentine formalities, see page 152. A Casa de Cambio is in the customs building in Portillo.

Border with Argentina: Los Libertadores
The 4 km long tunnel is open 24 hrs Sep-May, 0700-2300 Chilean time Jun-Aug, toll US$3

Valparaíso and Viña del Mar

○Santiago

Pacific beaches close to the capital include the international resort of Viña del Mar and others. On the same stretch of coast are the ports of Valparaíso and San Antonio.

This coastline enjoys a Mediterranean-style climate; the cold sea currents and coastal winds produce much more moderate temperatures than in Santiago and the central valley. Rainfall is moderate in winter and the summers are dry.

Climate

Chile

Valparaíso

Sprawling over a crescent of forty-two hills (*cerros*) that rear up from the sea, Valparaíso, the capital of Región V, is unlike any other Chilean city. The main residential areas obey little order in their layout and the *cerros* have a bohemian, slightly anarchic atmosphere. Here you will find mansions mingling with some of Chile's worst slums and many legends of ghosts and spirits. It is an important naval base and, with the new Congress building, it is also the seat of the Chilean parliament.

Founded in 1542, Valparaíso became, in the colonial period, a small port used for trade with Peru. It was raided by pirates at least seven times in the colonial period. The city prospered from independence more than any other Chilean town. It was used in the 19th century by commercial agents from Europe and the United States as their trading base in the southern Pacific and became a major international banking centre as well as the key port for US shipping between the East Coast and California and European ships that had rounded Cape Horn. Its decline was the result of the development of steam ships which stopped instead at the coal mines around Concepción and the opening of the trans-continental railway in the United States and then the Panama Canal in 1914. Since then it has declined further owing to the development of a container port in San Antonio, the shift of banks to Santiago and the move of the middle-classes to nearby Viña del Mar.

Little of the city's colonial past survived the pirates, tempests, fires and earthquakes of the period, but a remnant of the old colonial city can be found in the hollow known as El Puerto, grouped round the low-built stucco church of La Matriz. Most of the principal buildings date from after the devastating earthquake of 1906 (further serious earthquakes occurred in July 1971 and in March 1985) though some impression of its 19th century glory can be gained from the banking area of the lower town and from the mansions of wealthy merchants. President Ricardo Lagos is intent upon turning Valparaíso into the Cultural Capital of Chile, renovating the historical centre and museums and building new galleries.

Phone code: 032
Colour map 8, grid B1
Population: 345,000
116 km W of Santiago

Robbery is common in El Puerto and around the ascensores, especially on Cerro Santo Domingo. Beware packs of dogs

Sights

Bus No 9 'Central Placeres' gives fine views over the hills to port; also bus 'Mar Verde' (O) from Av Argentina near the bus terminal to Plaza Aduana

There are two completely different cities. The lower part, known as **El Plan**, is the business centre, with fine office buildings on narrow streets strung along the edge of the bay. Above, covering the hills ('cerros'), is a fantastic agglomeration of fine mansions, tattered houses and shacks, scrambled in oriental confusion along the narrow back streets. Superb views over the bay are offered from most of the 'cerros'. The lower and upper cities are connected by steep winding roads, flights of steps and 15 *ascensores* or funicular railways dating from the period 1880-1914. The most unusual of these is **Ascensor Polanco** (entrance from C Simpson, off Av Argentina a few blocks southeast of the bus station), which is in two parts, the first of which is a 160 m horizontal tunnel through the rock, the second a vertical lift to the summit on which there is a *mirador*. Note that the lower entrance is in an area which can be unsafe: do not go alone and do not take valuables. UNESCO is considering declaring **Cerros Concepción** and **Alegre** a World Heritage Site. Both have fine architecture and scenic beauty and are becoming very popular with tourists. A well-marked, two-km walk starts at the top of Ascensor Turri (Cerro Concepción), leading to Paseo Mirador Gervasoni and Calle Pupudo through a labyrinth of narrow streets and stairs. The Camino Cintura/Av Alemania is the only road which connects all hills above Valparaíso; it affords constantly changing views, perhaps the best being from Plaza Bismark.

The old heart of the city is the **Plaza Sotomayor**, dominated by the former **Intendencia** (Government House), now used as the seat of the admiralty. Opposite is a fine monument to the 'Heroes of Iquique' (see page 667). Bronze plaques on the Plaza illustrate the movement of the shoreline over the centuries and an opening, protected by a glass panel, shows parts of the original quay, uncovered when a car park was being excavated. The modern passenger quay is one block away (with poor, expensive handicraft shops) and nearby is the railway station. The streets of El Puerto run on either side from Plaza Sotomayor. C Serrano runs northwest for two blocks to the Plaza Echaurren, near which stands the church of **La Matriz**, built in 1842 on the site of the first church in the city. Further northwest, along Bustamante lies the Plaza Aduana from where Ascensor Artillería rises to the bold hill of **Cerro Artillería**, crowned by a park, the huge Naval Academy and the **Museo Naval** (naval history 1810-1880, exhibitions on Chile's two naval heroes, Lord Cochrane and Arturo Prat). ■ *Tue-Sun 1000-1800, US$0.35.*

Southeast of Plaza Sotomayor Calles Prat, Cochrane and Esmeralda run through the old banking and commercial centre to Plaza Aníbal Pinto, around which are several of the city's oldest bars. On Esmeralda, just past the Turri Clock Tower and Ascensor is the building of **El Mercurio de Valparaíso**, among the oldest newspapers in Latin America, first published in 1827. Further east is the Plaza Victoria with the Cathedral. South of the Plaza on Cerro Bellavista is the **Museo al Cielo Abierto**, a collection of 20 murals on the exteriors of buildings, designed by 17 of Chile's most distinguished contemporary artists. It is reached by a steep flight of steps leading up from Calle Aldunate, opposite Calle Huito. East of Plaza Victoria, reached by following Calle Pedro Montt is Plaza O'Higgins (flea market on Sunday mornings), which is dominated by the imposing new **Congreso Nacional**. It has been decreed that Congress should return to Santiago, date unspecified. What the fate of the new congress building will be is unknown. One of the best ways to see the lower city is on the historic trolley bus, which takes a circular route from the Congress to the port (US$0.20). Some of the cars, imported from Switzerland and the US, date from the 1930s.

To the west of **Cerro Artillería** the Av **Playa Ancha** runs to a stadium, seating 20,000 people, on Cerro Playa Ancha. Avenida Altamirano runs along the coast at the foot of Cerro Playa Ancha to **Las Torpederas**, a picturesque bathing beach. The **Faro de Punta Angeles**, on a promontory just beyond Las Torpederas, was the first lighthouse on the West Coast; you can get a permit to go up. On another high point on the other side of the city is the **Mirador de O'Higgins**, the spot where the Supreme Dictator exclaimed, on seeing Cochrane's liberating squadron: 'On those four craft depends the destiny of America'. The New Year is celebrated by a firework display launched from the harbour and naval ships, which is best seen from the Cerros. The display is televised nationally and about a million visitors come to the city at this time (make reservations well in advance). Small boats make 30-minute tours of the harbour. No fixed fee (about US$2), bargain hard.

Laguna Verde, 18 km south of Valparaíso, is a picturesque bay for picnics, reached by a dusty walk over the hills. There is **E** pp *Posada Cruz del Sur*, while *Casa Gener* (**F**) offers bed, breakfast and hot showers, but is owned by the electricity generating company whose staff have first claim to rooms. *Camping Los Olivos* has good facilities. ■ *Buses from Pedro Montt via Playa Ancha.*

Museo Municipal de Bellas Artes, with Chilean landscapes and seascapes and some modern paintings, housed in Palacio Baburizza, Paseo Yugoslavo. www.museobaburriza.cl ■ *To reopen after refurbishment end 2002. Take Ascensor El Peral from Plaza Justicia, off Plaza Sotomayor.*

Museo del Mar Almirante Cochrane, housing collection of naval models built by local Naval Modelling Club, good views over the port. ■ *Tue-Sun 1000-1800, free. Take Ascensor Cordillera from C Serrano, off Plaza Sotomayor, to Cerro Cordillera; at the top, Plazuela Eleuterio Ramírez, take Calle Merlet to the left, No 195.*

Museo de Historia Natural and **Galería Municipal de Arte**, both in 19th century Palacio Lyon, Condell 1546. ■ *Tue-Fri 1000-1300, 1400-1800, Sat 1000-1800, Sun 1000-1400.*

Casa "La Sebastiana", former house of Pablo Neruda (see also his house at Isla Negra, below). It has an art gallery and a small café. ■ *Tue-Fri 1030-1410, 1530-1800. Sat, Sun, holidays, 1030-1800. In summer, Tue-Sun 1030-1850,US$2.50, Tue-Fri students half-price. Ferrari 692, Av Alemania, Altura 6900 on Cerro Florida, T256606. Bus O from Av Argentina, US$0.30, or colectivo from Plazuela Ecuador, US$0.60.*

Casa Mistral, Av Gran Bretaña y Amunátegui, Playa Ancha, exhibition dedicated to life and work of Gabriela Mistral. ■ *Tue-Sun 1000-1330, 1530-1930.*

Casa de Lukas, Paseo Mirador Gervasoni 448, Cerro Concepción, is a beautiful villa dedicated to the work of Chile's most famous caricaturist. ■ *Tue-Sun, summer 1100-2200, winter 1030-1400, 1530-1830.*

Museums

Chile

Hotels in **El Plan A** *Puerta de Alcalá*, Piramide 524, T227478, www.chileinfo.cl/ puertadealcalahotel High standard of facilities, good if expensive restaurant. **C** *Prat*, Condell 1443, T253081, F213368. Comfortable, good restaurant with good value *almuerzo*. **C** *Hostal Kolping*, Valdés Vergara 622, T216306, F230352. Without bath, pleasant, quiet, good value, near bus terminal. **E** pp *Castillo family*,12 de Febrero 315, T220290, T09-6347239 (mob). Hot showers, good local knowledge. **E** pp *María Pizarro*, Chacabuco 2340, Casa No 2, T230791. Lovely rooms, central, quiet, kitchen. Frequently recommended. Also her neighbour, *Elena Escobar*, Chacabuco 2340, Casa No 7, T214193, same price. Recommended. **E** pp *Res Eliana*, Av Brasil 2146, T250954. Large old house, without breakfast. Recommended, slightly rough area. **E** pp *Res El Rincón Universal*, Argentina 825, T/F235184. With breakfast, laundry, study, cable TV, internet, good, the area can be intimidating at night. **E** pp *Sra Mónica Venegas*, Av Argentina 322, Casa B, T215673, 2 blocks from bus terminal. Often booked up. Recommended. **E** pp *Sra Silvia*, Pje La Quinta 70, Av Argentina, 3 blocks from Congress, T216592. Quiet, kitchen facilities. Recommended, not safest area at night.

Cerro Bellavista A *Robinson Crusoe*, Héctor Calvo Jofre 389, T495499, robinsoncrusoeinn@hotmail.com Beautiful rooms and spectacular views, new 2002. **Cerro Alegre E** pp *Arcoiris*, Cirilo Armstrong, Pasaje 6, Casa 2, T09-4304394 (mob), arcoirischile@ yahoo.com Near the police station, safe, one room only, good breakfast, balcony with great views, English spoken. Recommended. **E** pp *Casa Aventura*, Pasaje Galvez 11, off Calle Urriola, Cerro Alegre, T/F755963, casatur@ctcinternet.cl In restored traditional house, good breakfast, German and English spoken, Spanish classes offered, good value tours, informative, kitchen facilities. Highly recommended. **Cerro Concepción B** *Brighton*, Paseo Atkinson 151, T223513, brighton-valpo@entelchile.net New building in traditional style, good views, good rooms and service, live tango and bolero music in the bar at weekends.

Sleeping
Don't seek accommodation around La Matriz; it's a dangerous area at night

B *Templemann Apartments*, Pierre Loti 65, T257067, chantalderementeria@hotmail.com Stylish self-contained apartments, peaceful. Recommended. **E** pp *Sr Juan Carrasco*, Abtao 668, T210737. **Playa Ancha E** pp *Villa Kunterbunt*, Av Quebrada Verde 192, T288873. Lovely building, fine views, with breakfast, garden, English and German spoken. Highly recommended. Bus 1, 2, 5, 6, 17, 111, N, *colectivo* 150, 151, 3b all pass by.

Eating **Expensive**: *Club Español*, Brasil 1589. Fine Spanish cuisine, elegant surroundings. *Club Valparaíso*, Condell 1190, piso 10. International cuisine, exclusive. *Coco Loco*, Blanco 1781 pisos 21 y 22, T227614. Plush revolving restaurant 70 m above the bay. *La Colombina*, Paseo Yugoslavo 15, Cerro Alegre, T236254. Fish and seafood, good wines, fine views, reasonable food but a bit of a tourist trap. Also owns *Apolo 77* tour agency. *Turri*, Templemann 147, Cerro Concepción, T259198. Good food and service, wonderful views, lovely place. **Mid-range**: *Bar Inglés*, Cochrane 851 (entrance also on Blanco Encalada). Historic bar dating from the early 1900s, a chart shows the ships due in port. Good food and drink. Recommended. *Cinzano*, Plaza Aníbal Pinto 1182. The oldest bar in Valparaíso, also serving food. Flamboyant live music at weekends, noted for tango (no dancing by guests allowed). Service can be awful. *Club Alemán*, O'Higgins y Bellavista. Good German food. *La Costeñita*, Blanco 86, good seafood. *Los Porteños*, Valdivia 169 and Cochrane 102, perennial favourite for fish and shellfish, terse service but good food. *Pekin*, Pudeto 422, one of the best Chinese restaurants. *Pizzería Napoletana*, Pedro Montt 2935, in front of Congress. Excellent, try the vegetarian pizza. *Sancho Panza*, Yungay 2250. Parrillada, popular. At Caleta Membrillo, 2 km northwest of Plaza Sotomayor, there are several good fish restaurants including *Club Social de Pescadores*, Altamirano 1480, good, and *El Membrillo*. **Cheap**: *Ave Cesár*, P Montt 1776. Fast food, good. *Bambú*, Pudeto 450, Mon-Sat 1000-1800, vegetarian. *El Dómino*, Cumming 67. Traditional, serves *empanadas*, *chorillanas* etc. Recommended. *Gioco*, Molina 586-B. Vegetarian set lunches with fruit juices. *La Puerta del Sol*, Montt 2033. Traditional

Chile

Valparaíso

Sleeping	Eating	
1 Casa Aventura	1 Bar Inglés & Westfalia	7 Coco Loco
2 Brighton	2 Bogarín	8 El Dómino
3 Prat	3 Cinzano	9 Gioco
4 Puerta de Alcalá	4 Club Alemán	10 La Colombina
5 Robinson Crusoe	5 Club Español	11 La Costeñita
6 Templemann Apartments	6 Club Valparaíso	12 Le Filou Montpellier

Chilean dishes, great chips served outside. ***Le Filou Montpellier***, Almte Montt 382. French-run, Sat menu deservedly popular. ***Marco Polo***, Pedro Montt 2199. Delicious cakes, good Italian, good value *almuerzo*. There are many supercheap restaurants on Pedro Montt (eg ***La Vertiente***, No 2729) and behind the bus station. Also on the second floor of the market (off Plaza Echaurren), where the portions are large (closed in the evenings). ***Empanadas Famosas's de Adali***, S Donoso 1379-81. Best *empanadas* in Valparaíso.

Cafés ***Bogarín***, Plaza Victoria. Great juices, sandwiches. ***Café do Brasil***, Condell 1342. Excellent coffee, juices, sandwiches. ***Color Café***, Papudo 526, Cerro Concepción. Cosy arty café with a wide selection of teas and real coffee, fresh juice, good cakes, snacks and all-day breakfasts, regular live music, art exhibits, local art and craft for sale. ***Hespería***, Victoria 2250. Classic old-time coffee emporium, the internet annex makes a strange contrast. ***Pan de Magia***, Almte Montt 738 y Templemann, Cerro Alegre. Cakes, cookies, and by far the best wholemeal bread in town. ***Riquet***, Plaza Aníbal Pinto. Comfortable, expensive, good coffee and breakfast. Recommended. ***Westfalia***, Cochrane 847. Coffee, breakfasts, vegetarian lunches. **Bars and music**: ***La Piedra Feliz***, Errázuriz 1054. Every type of music depending on the evening, large pub, live music area, and dance floor, entrance US$8. ***Proa Al Cañaveral***, Errázuriz 304. Good seafood restaurant downstairs, pleasant bar upstairs with dancing from 0100 Fri and Sat, poetry reading on Thu. ***Valparaíso Eterno***, Almte Señoret 150, entre Blanco y Cochrane, 1 block from port. The most famous venue in the city, live music on 3 floors at weekends 2300-0400, Chilean and other Latin American musicians and singers, cover US$2, drinks cheap. Highly recommended.

Shopping

Chile

Bookshop: *CHAOS*, on Pedro Montt by the bus terminal. Excellent new and second-hand bookshop. ***Librería Universitaria***, Esmeralda 1132. Good selection of regional history. Many others. **Market**: Huge antiques market on Plaza O'Higgins every Sun. Very good selection, especially old shipping items. **Department stores**: ***Ripley*** and ***Falabella***, both on Plaza Victoria.

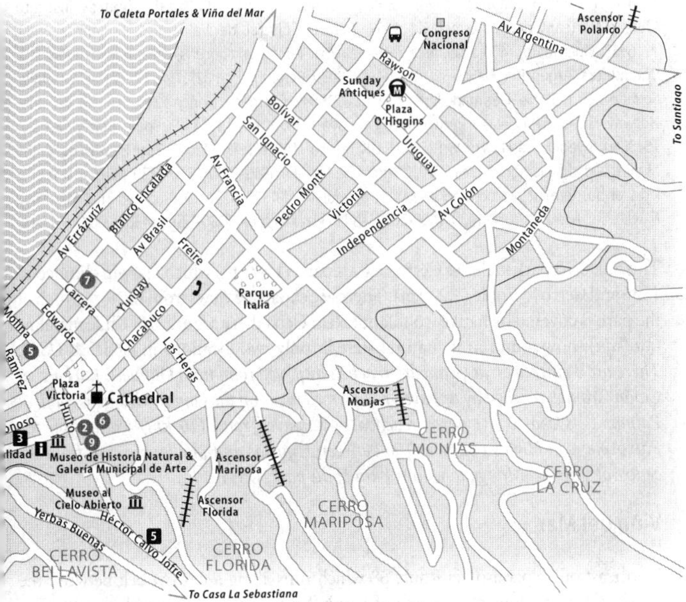

13 Los Porteños
14 Pekin & Bambú
15 Proa al Cañaveral
16 Riquet
17 Turri
18 Valparaíso Eterno

Funicular railways (Ascensores)

Transport **Local Buses**: US$0.45 within city limits. **Ascensores**: US$0.20 going up, US$0.10 coming down. **Taxis**: are more expensive than Santiago: a short run under 1 km costs US$1. Taxi colectivos, same rates as buses, carry sign on roof indicating route, very convenient.

Long distance Buses: Terminal is on Pedro Montt 2800 block, corner of Rawson, 1 block from Av Argentina; plenty of buses between terminal and Plaza Sotomayor. Excellent and frequent service to **Viña del Mar**, 15 mins, US$0.40 from Plaza Aduana, passing along Av Errázuriz; colectivos to Viña US$0.60. To **Santiago**, 1¾ hrs, US$4.15-2.75, shop around, frequent (book on Sat to return to the capital on Sun). To **Concepción**, 11 hrs, US$12. To **Puerto Montt**, 17 hrs, US$18. To **La Serena**, 7 hrs, US$10. To **Calama**, US$35. To **Arica**, US$40, *Fénix salón cama* service, US$50. To Argentina: to **Mendoza** 4 companies, 6-7 hrs, US$15-30.

Trains: Regular service on Merval, the Valparaíso metropolitan line between Valparaíso, **Viña del Mar** (US$0.35-0.40), **Quilpué** and **Limache** (US$0.60-0.75 – continuation to Los Andes under reconstruction); to Viña del Mar every 15-30 mins. Trains are 70 years old, made by FIAT.

Directory **Airline offices** *LanChile*, Esmeralda 1048, T251441. **Banks** Banks open 0900 to 1400, but closed on Sat. Many *Redbanc* ATMs on Blanco and Prat, and also one in the bus terminal. Good rates at *Banco de Crédito e Inversiones*, Cochrane 820 and *Banco de Santiago*, Prat 816. *Casas de Cambio*: Many on Esemralda; also *Exprinter*, Prat 887 (the building with the clocktower at junction with Cochrane). Good rates, no commission on TCs, open Mon-Fri 0930-1400, 1500-1800. *Inter Cambios*, Errázuriz esq Plaza Sotomayor. Good rates. *New York*, Prat 659. Best rates for cash. When *cambios* are closed, street changers operate outside *Inter Cambios*. **Communications** Internet: average price US$1.40 per hr. *@rob' Art Café*, Edwards 625, cheaper for students. *Café Bell@vista*, Bellavista 463, loc 201. *Color Café*, Calle Papudo 526 (see above). *Cybervalparaíso*, Condell 1217, loc 215 (Galería O'Higgins). *Internet*, Carampangue y Blanco. *Prat*, Condell 1443, of 24. **Post office:** Pedro Montt entre San Ignacio y Bolívar. **Telephone:** The cheapest call centres are all around the bus terminal, eg on Rawson. *CTC*, Esmeralda 1054 or Pedro Montt 2023. *Entel*, Condell 1491. **Cultural centres** Instituto Chileno-Norteamericano, Esmeralda 1069. **Centro Cultural de Valparaíso**, Esmeralda 1083, T216953. Open daily 1400-2200, with restaurant/bar *Winnipeg*, concerts, theatre, exhibitions etc. **Consulates** Argentina, Blanco 890, of 204, T250039. Belgium, Prat 827, Piso 12, T213494. Bolivia, Serrano 579, T259906. Denmark, Errázuriz 940, T213942. Germany, Blanco 1215, of 1102, T250039. Norway, Freire 657, T252219. Peru, Blanco Encalada 1215, of 1402, T253403. Spain, Brasil 1589, p 2, T685860. Sweden, Casilla 416-V, T256507. UK, Blanco 1190, p 5, T/F213063. **Tourist offices** In the Municipalidad building, Condell 1490, Oficina 102. Mon-Fri 0830-1400, 1530-1730. Municipal Tourist kiosk at bus terminal (good map available), helpful. 0900-1300, 1530-1930 (closed Thu, Mar-Nov); Muelle Prat, Nov-Mar 1030-1430, 1600-2000, and in Plaza Victoria, 1030-1300, 1430-2000 Nov-Mar.

Parque This 8,000-ha park includes Cerro La Campana (1,828 m) which Darwin climbed in
Nacional La 1836 and Cerro El Roble (2,200 m). There are extensive views from the top. Much of
Campana the park is covered by native woodland. Near Ocoa there are areas of Chilean palms (*kankán*), now found in its natural state in only two locations in Chile. ■ *US$2. There are 3 entrances: at Granizos, reached by paved road from Olmué, 5 km east; at Cajón Grande, reached by unpaved road which turns off the Olmué-Granizos road; at Palmar de Ocoa to the north reached by unpaved road (10 km) leading off the Pan-American Highway at Km 100 between Hijuelas and Llaillay. Micros from the centre of Viña del Mar go to within 1 km of the park, US$1, 1 hr.*

Viña del Mar

Phone code: 032
Colour map 8, grid B1
Population: 304,203

Northeast of Valparaíso via Route 68 which runs along a narrow belt between the shore and precipitous cliffs is one of South America's leading seaside resorts. The older part is situated on the banks of a lagoon, the Marga Marga, which is crossed by bridges. Around Plaza Vergara and the smaller Plaza Sucre to its south are the **Teatro Municipal** (1930) and the exclusive **Club de Viña**, built in 1910. The municipally owned **Quinta Vergara**, formerly the residence of the shipping entrepreneur Francisco Alvarez, lies two blocks south. The grounds are superb and include a double avenue of palm trees. The **Palacio Vergara**, in the gardens, houses the **Museo de Bellas Artes** and the Academia de Bellas Artes ■ *Museum hours Tue-Sun 1000-1400, 1500-1800, US$0.50, T680618*. Part of the grounds is a children's playground, and there is an outdoor auditorium where concerts and ballet are performed in the summer months, and in February/March an international song festival, one of the premier music events in Latin America, is held. (Tickets from the Municipalidad.) El Roto festival is on 20 January, in homage to the workers and peasants of Chile.

On a headland overlooking the sea is **Cerro Castillo**, the summer palace of the Presidents of the Republic; its gardens can be visited. Just north, on the other side of the lagoon is the **Casino**, built in the 1930s and set in beautiful gardens, US$5 to enter, jacket and tie for men required (open all year).

The main beaches, Acapulco and Mirasol are located to the north, but south of Cerro Castillo is Caleta Abarca, also popular. Beaches may be closed because of pollution. One of the most popular places in town is **La Grúa**, a converted cargo crane on the beach (you can't miss it), now full of bars and discotheques. At sunset it gives beautiful views of Valparaíso. The coastal route north to Reñaca provides lovely views over the sea. East of the centre is the **Valparaíso Sporting Club** with a racecourse and playing fields. North of here in the hills are the Granadilla Golf Club and a large artificial lake, the **Laguna Sausalito**, adjacent to which is the Estadio Sausalito (home to Everton soccer team, among many other sporting facilities). It possesses an excellent tourist complex with swimming pools, boating, tennis courts, sandy beaches, water skiing, restaurants, etc. ■ *US$2.50, children under 11, US$1.75. Take colectivo No 19 from C Viana.*

Museo de la Cultura del Mar, in the Castillo Wolff, on the coast near Cerro Castillo, contains a collection on the life and work of the novelist and maritime historian, Salvador Reyes. ■ *Tue-Sat 1000-1300, 1430-1800, Sun 1000-1400, T625427.* **Palacio Rioja**, Quillota 214, was built in 1906 by a prominent local family and now used for official municipal receptions, ground floor preserved in its original state.

Chile

Viña del Mar

■ Sleeping
1 Alcázar
2 Andalué & Restaurant Flavia
3 Cap Ducal
4 El Escorial
5 Gala
6 Offenbacher Hof
7 Quinta Vergara
8 Residencial Blanchart
9 Residencial Capric
10 Residencial Remanso
11 Residencial Tajamar
12 Residencial Villarica

● Eating
1 Africa
2 Alster
3 Armandita
4 Casino Chico
5 El Encuentro
6 Machitún Ruca
7 Pizzería Mama Mía
8 Raul
9 Samoiedo

N

Not to scale

■ *Tue-Sun, open to visitors 1000-1400, 1500-1730, US$0.40. Recommended.* **Museo Sociedad Fonk**, C 4 Norte 784, is an archaeological museum, with objects from Easter Island and the Chilean mainland, including Mapuche silver. ■ *Tue-Fri 1000-1800, Sat-Sun 1000-1400, US$1.*

The tourist office is *Sernatur*, Valparaíso 507, Oficina 303, T882285. Municipal office on Plaza Vergara. *Automóvil Club de Chile*, 1 Norte 901, T689509.

Excursions The **Jardín Botánico Nacional**, formerly the estate of the nitrate baron Pascual Baburizza, now administered by Conaf, lies 8 km southeast of the city. Covering 405 ha, it contains over 3,000 species from all over the world and a collection of Chilean cacti, but the species are not labelled. ■ *US$1. Take bus 20 from Plaza Vergara.*

Sleeping Many in **L-A** range, some with beach. **LL-L** *Gala*, Arlegui 273, loc 10, T686688, galahotel@webhost.cl Excellent, all mod-cons. **AL** *Alcázar*, Alvarez 646, T685112, hotelalcazar@chile.ia.cl 4-star, good restaurant. **AL** *Cap Ducal*, Marina 51, T626655, F665471. Old mansion charm, good restaurant. **A** *Genross*, Paseo Monterrey 18, T661711, genrosshotel@hotmail.com Beautiful old mansion, airy rooms, garden patio and sitting room, very informative, English spoken. Recommended. **A** *Quinta Vergara*, Errázuriz 690, T685073, hotelquinta@hotmail.com Large rooms, beautiful gardens. Recommended. **B** *Andalué*, 6 Poniente 124, T684147, F684148. With breakfast, central. Recommended. **B** *Offenbacher Hof*, Balmaceda 102, T621483, F662432. Recommended. **B** *Petit Palace*, Paseo Valle 387, T/F663134. Small rooms, good, central, quiet. **C** *El Escorial*, 5 Poniente 114 and 441, T975266. With breakfast, shared bath, central. **C** *Res Remanso*, Av Valparaíso 217, esq Ecuador, T689057. Shared bath, comfortable, good breakfast, safe, spotless. **C** *Res Victoria*, Valparaíso 40, T977370. Without bath, with breakfast, central. **C** *Res Villarica*, Arlegui 172, T881484, F942807. Shared bath, good. **D** *Res Capric*, von Schroeders 39, T978295. Dark rooms, with breakfast (special rates for IYHA card holders). **D** *Res Tajamar*, Alvarez 884, T882134, opposite railway station. Old-fashioned, central, full of character, atmospheric. **D** *Res de Casia*, von Schroeders 151, T971861. Safe, helpful. **D** pp *Julia Toro Córtez*, Toro Herrera 273, T621083, T09-885 8307 (mob), julia_toro_cortez@hotmail.com Family house, breakfast included, steps to beach. **E** pp *Res Blanchart*, Valparaíso 82, T974949. With breakfast, good service.

Youth hostels E pp *Asturias*, Valparaíso 299. Has double rooms with bath, internet. See also *Res Capric* above.

There are many more places to stay including private accommodation (E-F pp; ask at tourist office). Out of season agencies rent furnished apartments. In season it's cheaper to stay in Valparaíso and visit Viña beaches. During the music festival in Feb, accommodation is almost impossible to find

Eating **Expensive**: *Alster*, Valparaíso 225. Smart. *Casino Chico*, Valparaíso y von Schroeders. Fish, seafood. *Flavia*, 6 Poniente 121, good Italian food, service, desserts and wine selection. **Mid-range**: *Africa*, Valparaíso 324. Extraordinary façade, very good, has vegetarian. *Armandita*, San Martín 501. *Parrilla*, large portions, good service. *El Encuentro*, San Martín y 6 Norte. Fish, very good. *Kumei*, Valparaíso entre Von Schroeders y Ecuador. Best set lunches in town, wide selection. *Machitún Ruca*, San Martín 529. Excellent. *Pizzería Mama Mía*, San Martín 435. Good. *Raul*, Valparaíso 533. Live music. *Samoiedo*, Valparaíso 637, *Confitería*, grill and restaurant. **Cafés**: *Café Big Ben*, Valparaíso 469. Good coffee, good food. **Bars**: *Barlovento*, 2 Norte y 5 Poniente. The designer bar in Viña, on 3 floors with a lovely roof terrace, serves great pizzas.

Transport **Buses** Terminal at Av Valparaíso y Quilpué. To **Santiago**, US$2.75, 2 hrs, frequent, many companies, heavily booked in advance for travel on Sun afternoons, at other times some buses pick up passengers opposite the train station. To **La Serena**, 6 daily, 8 hrs, US$10. To **Antofagasta**, 20 hrs, US$35. **Trains** Services on the Valparaíso Metropolitan line (Merval) stop at Viña (details under Valparaíso).

Beware pickpockets around shops in the terminal

Directory **Banks** Many *Redbanc* ATMs on Libertad near 7 y 8 Norte; also on Valparaíso (but this is not a safe area at night). Many *casas de cambio* on Arlegui. Also in the tourist office. **Communications** Internet: *Etnia Com*, Valparaíso 323, T711841. Inexpensive. *Rue Valparaiso*, Valparaíso 286, T/F710140, www.multimania.com/ruevalparaiso Cybercafé with net phone. **Telephone**: *CTC*, Valparaíso 628. *Global Telecommunications/Entel*, 15 Norte 961. **Cultural centres** Centro Cultural, Libertad 250, holds regular exhibitions.

North of Viña del Mar the coast road runs through Las Salinas, a popular beach between two towering crags, Reñaca (good restaurants) and Cochoa, where there is a sealion colony 100 m offshore, to Concón (18 km). There is a much faster inland road, between Viña del Mar and **Concón**, on the southern shore of a bay at the mouth of the Río Aconcagua. It has six beaches and is famous for its seafood restaurants. **Quintero** (*Population*: 16,000) 23 km north of Concón, is a fishing town situated on a rocky peninsula with lots of small beaches (hotels and *residenciales*).

Resorts north of Viña del Mar

    Horcón (also known locally as Horcones) is set back in a cove surrounded by cliffs, a pleasant small village, mainly of wooden houses. On the beach young travellers sell cheap and unusual jewellery and trinkets. Vegetation is tropical with many cacti on the cliff tops. Packed out in January-February, the rest of the year it is a charming place, populated by fishermen and artists. A new condominium is set to change the atmosphere of the town.

Beware if cycling from Valparaíso, the road is very bad with lots of traffic

    Further north is well-to-do **Maitencillo** (*Population*: 1,200), with a wonderful long beach. 14 km beyond is **Zapallar** (*Population*: 2,200) a fashionable resort. A hint of its former glory is given by a number of fine mansions along Av Zapallar. At Cachagua, 3 km south, a colony of penguins may be viewed from the northern end of the beach.

    Papudo (*Phone code*: 033 *Population*: 2,500), 10 km further north, was the site of a naval battle in November 1865 in which the Chilean vessel *Esmeralda* captured the Spanish ship *Covadonga*. Following the arrival of the railway Papudo rivalled Viña del Mar as a fashionable resort in the 1920s but it has long since declined. With its lovely beach and fishing port, it is an idyllic spot.

Sleeping and eating **Concón** L *Hostería Edelweiss*, Borgoño 19200, T814043, F903666. Modern cabins, comfortable, sea views, includes breakfast, excellent food in attached restaurant, German spoken. Highly recommended. Several other *cabañas* and motels. Good seafood *empanadas* at bars. Excellent seafood restaurants at Caleta Higuerilla, Av Borgoño, and at La Boca; cheaper *picadas* in Alto Higuerillas.

    Horcón B-C *Arancibia*, D without bath, T796169, pleasant gardens, good food. Recommended. D *Juan Esteban*, Pasaje Miramar, Casa 2, T796056, www.geocities.com/jestebanc Also F pp, English, Portuguese, Italian spoken, nice terrace with view, fully equipped cabañas, B for 4 people. Recommended. *El Ancla*, *cabañas* and restaurant. Recommended.

    Papudo A *Carande*, Chorrillos 89, T791105. Best, quiet. B *Moderno*, Concha 150, T711496. B *De Peppino*, Concha 609, T791108. Many more.

Transport Buses from Valparaíso and Viña del Mar: To **Concón** bus 9 or 10 (from Av Libertad between 2 and 3 Norte in Viña), US$0.50; to **Quintero** and **Horcón**, *Sol del Pacífico*, every 30 mins, US$1, 2 hrs; to **Zapallar** and **Papudo**, *Sol del Pacífico*, 4 a day (2 before 0800, 2 after 1600), US$3.

San Antonio is a commercial centre for this part of the coast. It is a container and fishing port and is the terminal for the export of copper brought by rail from El Teniente mine, near Rancagua. To the south are the resorts of Llolleo and Rocas de Santo Domingo. **Sleeping A** *Rocas de Santo Domingo*, La Ronda 130, T444356, F444494. Restaurant, cable TV, good breakfast included, 20 minutes to sea. ■ *From San Antonio: buses to Valparaíso, Pullman Bus, every 45 mins until 2000, US$2; to Santiago, Pullman Bus, every 10 mins, 0600-2200, US$2.*

Resorts south near the mouth of the Río Maipo

    Cartagena, 8 km north of San Antonio, is the biggest resort on this part of the coast. The centre is around the hilltop Plaza de Armas. To the south is the picturesque Playa Chica, overlooked by many of the older hotels and restaurants; to the north is the Playa Larga. Between the two a promenade runs below the cliffs; high above hang old houses, some in disrepair but offering spectacular views. Cartagena is very popular in summer, but out of season it is a good centre for visiting nearby resorts of Las Cruces, El Tabo and El Quisco. There are many hotels and bus connections are good. For more information on Cartagena, look at www.cartagena-chile.cl **Sleeping D** *Violeta*,

Chile

Condell 140, T234093. Swimming pool, good views. **E** pp *Res Carmona*, Playa Chica, T450485. Small rooms, basic, good value. **E** pp *Residencial Patye*, Alacalde Cartagena 295, T450569. Nice spot, good value.

North of Cartagena in the village of **Isla Negra** is the beautifully-restored **Museo-Casa Pablo Neruda**. Bought by Neruda in 1939, this house, overlooking the sea, was his writing retreat in his later years. It contains artefacts gathered by Neruda from all over the world. Neruda and his last wife, Mathilde, are buried here; the touching gravestone is beside the house. ■ *T035-461284 for opening hrs or to book English guide (see also his house, La Chascona, under Santiago Museums, and La Sebastiana, under Valparaíso Museums), US$4. It is open for guided tours in Spanish, English or French (last 2 only after 1500), Tue-Sun 1000-2000 in summer, rest of year Tue-Fri 1000-1400, 1500-1800. It has a good café specializing in Neruda's own recipes. Tours from Santiago, departing at 0900 from Plaza de Armas (Compañía y Ahumada),US$20 and include seaside resorts, T232 2574.* In **Isla Negra** is **F** pp *Hostal Casa Azul*, Av Santa Luisa s/n, T035-461154. Shared bath, hot showers, garden, kitchen and laundry facilities, breakfast included, helpful. Highly recommended. ■ *Pullman or Bahía Azul bus from Santiago, 1½ hrs, US$2.80, from Valparaíso 1 hr, US$2.50.*

Santiago

North of Santiago

See page 674 for a list of service stations between Santiago and the Peruvian border

The chief interest lies along the coast; the land becomes less fertile as you go further north. The largest resort is La Serena, from where access can be made to the pisco-producing Elqui Valley and to one of the world's major astronomical centres.

From the Río Aconcagua to the Río Elqui is a transitional zone between the fertile heartland and the northern deserts. The first stretch of the Pan-American Highway from Santiago is inland through green valleys with rich blue clover and wild artichokes. North of La Ligua, the Highway mainly follows the coastline, passing many beautiful coves, alternately rocky and sandy, with good surf, though the water is very cold. The valleys of the main rivers, the Choapa, Limarí and Elqui, are intensively farmed using irrigation to produce fruit and vegetables. Elsewhere the vegetation is characteristic of semidesert (dry scrub and cactus), except in those areas where condensation off the sea provides sufficient moisture for woods to grow.

Climate Rainfall is rare and occurs only in winter. On the coast the average temperature is 14° C; the interior is dry, with temperatures averaging 16-17°.

Ovalle

Phone code: 053
Colour map 8, grid A1
Population: 53,000
Altitude: 200 m
412 km N of Santiago

This town lies inland in the valley of the Río Limarí, a fruit-growing and mining district. Market days are Monday, Wednesday, Friday and Saturday, till 1600; the market (*feria modelo*) is on Benavente. The town is famous for its *talabarterías* (saddleries) and for its products made of locally mined lapis lazuli. **Museo del Limarí**, in the old railway station, Covarrubias y Antofagasta, has displays of petroglyphs and a good collection of Diaguita ceramics and other artefacts. ■ *Tue-Fri 0900-1300, 1500-1900, Sat-Sun 1000-1300, US$1.* Tourist information kiosk on the Plaza de Armas. *Automóvil Club de Chile*, Libertad 144, T620011 is very helpful and has overnight parking. ■ *Buses to Santiago, several, 6½ hrs, US$7; to La Serena, 20 a day, 1¼ hrs, US$2.50; to Antofagasta, US$18.*

Excursions The **Monumento Nacional Valle del Encanto**, about 22 km southwest of Ovalle, is a most important archaeological site. Artefacts from hunting peoples from over 2,000 years ago have been found but the most visible remains date from the Molle culture (AD 700). There are over 30 petroglyphs as well as great boulders, distributed in six sites. Camping facilities. ■ *0800-1800, US$0.50. Getting there: no local bus service; you must take a southbound long distance bus and ask to be dropped off – 5 km walk to the valley; flag down a bus to return.*

Termas de Socos, 35 km southwest of Ovalle on the Pan-American Highway, has fine thermal springs (entrance US$5, very popular), a good hotel (**L**, T 02-681692, Casilla 323) and a campsite (**F** per tent, but bargain) nearby. ■ *Bus US$2.*

Parque Nacional Fray Jorge, 90 km west of Ovalle and 110 km south of La Serena at the mouth of the Río Limarí, the Park is reached by a dirt road leading off the Pan-American Highway. It contains original forests which contrast with the otherwise barren surroundings. Receiving no more than 113 mm of rain a year, the forests survive because of the almost constant covering of fog. ■ *Sat, Sun and public holidays only, entry 0900-1600, last departure 1800, US$2.50. Visits closely controlled owing to risk of fire.* Two campsites, one in the desert and one at the admin area, both with hot showers; also rooms available at an old hacienda, **F** pp, and a *cabaña*, **B**. Camping costs US$16 pp including park entry. Waterproof clothing essential. ■ *Round trip in taxi from Ovalle, US$30, Abel Olivares Rivera, T Ovalle 620352, recommended.*

Monumento Nacional Pichasca, 47 km northeast of Ovalle at an altitude of 1,350, reached by an unpaved and largely winding road. It contains petrified tree trunks, archaeological remains, including a vast cave with vestiges of ancient roof paintings, and views of gigantic rock formations on the surrounding mountains. ■ *0800-1800, US$2.20. Daily buses from Ovalle to San Pedro pass the turn off about 42 km from the city. From here it is 3 km to the park and about 2 km more to sites of interest.*

A *Hotel Turismo*, Victorio 295, T623258, F623536. Parking, modern. **B** *Gran Hotel*, Vicuña Mackenna 210 (entrance through Galería Yagnam), T621084, yagnam@terra.cl Decent rooms, negotiate. **D** *Roxy*, Libertad 155, T620080. Constant hot water, big rooms, patio, *comedor*. Highly recommended. **E** pp *Hotel Venecia*, Libertad 261, T09-7635928 (mob). Safe. Recommended. **E** pp *Res Socos*, Socos 22, T629856. Quiet, family run, breakfast extra. Recommended. *Bavaria*, V MacKenna 161. Maindishes and sandwiches. *Club Social Arabe*, Arauco 255. Spacious glass-domed premises, limited selection of Arab dishes, good but not cheap. *La Bocca*, Benavente 110. Specializes in shellfish. *Club Comercial*, Aguirre 244 (on plaza), open Sun. *El Quijote*, Arauco 294. Intimate atmosphere, good seafood, inexpensive. Good value *almuerzos* at *Casino La Bomba*, Aguirre 364, run by fire brigade. *Yum Yum*, V MacKenna 21. Good, cheap, lively.

Sleeping & eating

The good inland road between Ovalle and La Serena makes an interesting contrast to Ruta 5 (Panamericana), with a fine pass and occasional views of snowcapped Andes across cacti-covered plains and semi-desert mountain ranges. North of Ovalle 61 km a side road runs 44 km southeast (last 20 km very bad) to **Andacollo** (*Population*: 10,216. *Altitude*: 1,050 m). This old town, in an area of alluvial gold washing and manganese and copper mining, is one of the great pilgrimage sites in Chile. In the enormous **Basilica** (1893), 45 m high and with a capacity of 10,000, is the miraculous Virgen del Rosario de Andacollo. The Fiesta Grande from 23-27 December (most important day December 26) attracts 150,000 pilgrims. The ritual dances date from a pre-Spanish past. Colectivos run to the festival from C Benavente, near Colocolo, in La Serena, but 'purists' walk (torch and good walking shoes essential). There is also a smaller festival, the Fiesta Chica on the first Sunday of October. ■ *Colectivo to Ovalle, US$2; bus, US$1.40. The tourist office on the Plaza arranges tours to the Basilica and to mining operations.*

There are no hotels, but some pensiones. During the festival private houses rent beds and some let you pay for a shower

Chile

Coquimbo

Phone code: 051
Colour map 8, grid A1
Population: 106,000
84 km N of Ovalle
A tourist kiosk in Plaza de Armas is open in the summer only

On the same bay as La Serena is this important port, with one of the best harbours on the coast and major fish-processing plants. The city is strung along the north shore of a peninsula. On the south shore lies the suburb of Guayacán, with an iron-ore loading port, a steel church designed by Eiffel, an English cemetery and a 83-m high cross to mark the Millennium (US$1.50 to climb it). In 1981 heavy rain uncovered 39 ancient burials of humans and llamas which had been sacrificed; they are exhibited in a small museum in the Plaza Gabriela Mistral. Tours of nearby islands with sealions go from beside the fish market, can be cold and rough but boats have blankets and life vests (US$2). Nearby is **La Herradura**, 2½ km from Coquimbo, which has the best beaches. Resorts further south, Totoralillo (12 km), Guanaqueros (37 km) and Tongoy (50 km), have good beaches and can be reached by Ruta Costera buses or colectivos.

The seafood is better at Coquimbo than La Serena, especially cheap in the market, Melgarejo entre Bilbao y Borgoño

Sleeping and eating Generally accommodation is much cheaper than in La Serena. **D** *Iberia*, Bandera 206, p 8, T312141. Recommended. **D** *Prat*, Bilbao y Aldunate, T311845. Comfortable, pleasant. Several hotels in La Herradura. **Camping** *Camping La Herradura*, T263867, mac-food@ctcinternet.cl **F** for up to 5 people. Recommended restaurants: *Sal y Pimienta del Capitán Denny*, Aldunate 769, one of the best, pleasant, old fashioned. *La Picada*, Costanera near statue of O'Higgins. Good *pebre*. *Mai Lai Fan*, Av Ossandón 1. Excellent Chinese. *La Bahía*, Pinto 1465. Good value. *La Barca*, Ríos y Varela. Modest but good. *La Bahía*, Pinto 1465. Good value.

Festivals Coquimbo hosts *La Pampilla*, by far the biggest independence day celebrations in Chile. Between 200-300,000 people come from all over the country for the fiesta, which lasts for a week from **14-21 Sep**. It costs a nominal US$1.50 to enter the main dancing area (*peñas* cost extra); plenty of typical Chilean food and drink.

Transport Bus terminal at Varela y Garriga. To **La Serena**, US$0.30.

La Serena

Phone code: 051
Colour map 8, grid A1
Population: 120,000
473 km N of Santiago

La Serena, built on a hillside 2 km inland from Bahía de Coquimbo, is an attractive city and tourist centre. It is 12 km north of Coquimbo and is the capital of IV Región (Coquimbo).

La Serena was founded by Juan de Bohón, aide to Pedro de Valdivia, in 1544, destroyed by Diaguita Indians in 1546 and rebuilt by Francisco de Aguirre in 1549. The city was sacked by the English pirate Sharpe in 1680. In the colonial period the city was the main staging-post on the route north to Peru. In the 19th century the city grew prosperous from copper-mining. The present-day layout and architectural style have their origins in the 'Plan Serena' drawn up in 1948 on the orders of Gabriel González Videla, a native of the city.

Sights

There are 29 other churches, several of which have unusual towers

Around the attractive Plaza de Armas are most of the official buildings, including the Post Office, the **Cathedral** (built in 1844 and featuring a carillon which plays every hour) and the **Museo Histórico Casa González Videla**, which includes several rooms on the man's life. ■ *Tue-Sat 0900-1300, 1600-1900, Sun 1000-1300, US$0.80*. Ticket also valid for **Museo Arqueológico**, Cordovez y Cienfuegos, outstanding collection of Diaguita and Molle Indian exhibits, especially of attractively decorated pottery, also Easter Island exhibits. ■ *Tue-Sat 0900-1300, 1600-1900, Sun 1000-1300, US$0.80*.

La Recova, the new market, at Cienfuegos y Cantournet, includes a large display of handicrafts and, upstairs, several good restaurants. One block west of the Plaza de Armas is the **Parque Pedro de Valdivia**, near which is the delightful Parque Japonés, "El Jardín del Corazón". ■ *Daily 1000-2000, US$1.25*.

Av Francisco de Aguirre, a pleasant boulevard lined with statues and known as the **Alameda**, runs from the centre to the coast, terminating at the **Faro**

Monumental, a neo-colonial mock-castle. ■ *US$0.45.* A series of beaches stretch from here to Peñuelas, 6 km south, linked by the Av del Mar. Many apartment blocks, hotels, *cabañas* and restaurants have been built along this part of the bay.

Tourist offices Main *Sernatur* office in Edificio de Servicios Públicos (next to the Post Office on the Plaza de Armas), T225199. ■ *Mon-Fri 0845-1830 (2030 in summer), Sat-Sun 1000-1400 (1000-1400, 1600-2000 in summer).* Kiosks at bus terminal (summer only) and Balmaceda y Prat, helpful. ■ *Open in theory Mon-Sat 1100-1400, 1600-1900.* Automóvil Club de Chile, *de la Barra 435, T225279.*

Sleeping

Accommodation in the centre of town is expensive; prices are much higher in Jan-Feb. Route 5 from La Serena to Coquimbo is lined with cheaper accommodation, from hotels to cabañas, and restaurants

There are no buses along Av del Mar, but it is only ½ km off Route 5. The tourist office in the bus terminal has accommodation information, helpful. Do not be pressurized at the bus station into choosing rooms. There is much more choice than touts would have you believe. **AL** *Pucará*, Balmaceda 319, T211966, F211933. With breakfast, modern, helpful, quiet. **A** *Francisco de Aguirre*, Córdovez 210, T222991, www.chile-hotels.com/faguirre With breakfast, good rooms, reasonable restaurant. **A** *Mediterráneo*, Cienfuegos 509, Casilla 212, T/F225837. Includes good breakfast. Recommended. **A-B** *Berlín*, Córdovez 535, T222927, F223575. Safe, efficient, good value. Recommended. **C** *Hostal Santo Domingo*, Andrés Bello 1067, T212718. With breakfast. Highly recommended. **C** *Lido*, Matta 547, T213073. Hot water, good. **D** *Edith González*, Los Carrera 889, T221941/224978. **E** without bath, cooking and laundry facilities, meets passengers at bus terminal. Recommended. **D** *Hostal Croata* Cienfuegos

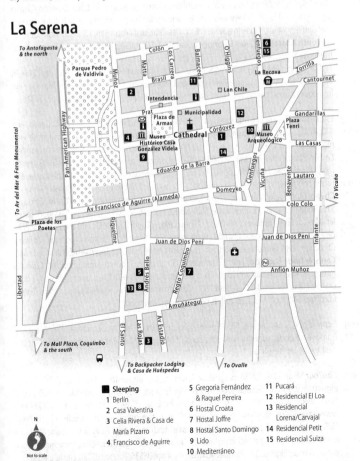

La Serena

To Antofagasta & the north

To Av del Mar & Faro Monumental

Plaza de los Poetas

Libertad

To Mall Plaza, Coquimbo & the south

To Backpacker Lodging & Casa de Huéspedes

To Ovalle

To Vicuña

N
Not to scale

■ **Sleeping**
1 Berlín
2 Casa Valentina
3 Celia Rivera & Casa de María Pizarro
4 Francisco de Aguirre

5 Gregoria Fernández & Raquel Pereira
6 Hostal Croata
7 Hostal Joffre
8 Hostal Santo Domingo
9 Lido
10 Mediterráneo

11 Pucará
12 Residencial El Loa
13 Residencial Lorena/Carvajal
14 Residencial Petit
15 Residencial Suiza

Chile

Chile

248, T/F224997. **E** without bath, with breakfast, laundry facilities, cable TV, patio, hospitable, excellent value. Recommended. **D** *Res Suiza*, Cienfuegos 250, T216092. With breakfast, good beds, excellent value. Highly recommended. **D** *Rosa Canto*, Cantournet 976, T213954. Kitchen, comfortable, family run, good value. Recommended.

E pp *Amunátegui 315*. Kitchen facilities, patio, good beds. Recommended. **E** pp *Backpacker Lodging*, El Santo 1058, T227580. Kitchen facilities, central, camping. **E** pp *Casa de Huéspedes*, El Santo 1410, T213557. Convenient for bus terminal, including breakfast, hot water, cable TV. Recommended. **E** pp *Casa Valentina*, Brasil 271, T2213142, fampintz@hotmail.com Good information, hot showers, kitchen facilities, patio, laundry service, English and German spoken. **E** pp *Celia Rivera*, Las Rojas 21, T215838. Near terminal, use of kitchen. **E** pp *Gabriela Matus*, Juan de Dios Peni 636, T211407. Helpful. **E** pp *Gregoria Fernández*, Andrés Bello 979A, T224400. Very helpful, good beds, 3 blocks from terminal, excellent breakfast, book ahead, good local information; if full she will divert you to her mother's house, also good but less convenient for the bus station. Highly recommended. Next door is **E** pp *Raquel Pereira*, Andrés Bello 979B, T222419. Dormitory accommodation, with breakfast. **E** pp *Hostal Joffre*, Rgto Coquimbo 964 (entre Pení y Amunátegui), T222335, hostaljofre@hotmail.com With breakfast, good beds, garden, near bus terminal, tours of Elqui arranged, Héctor is best guide. Recommended. **E** pp *Res El Loa*, O'Higgins 362, T210304. Without bath, with breakfast, good inexpensive home cooking, good value. **E** pp *Res Lorena*, Cantournet 850, T223330. Quiet, pleasant. **E** pp *Res Lorena/Carvajal*, Av Santo 1056, T/F224059. Family home, kitchen facilities, central camping. **F** pp *Casa de María Pizarro*, Las Rojas 18, T229282. Very welcoming, laundry facilities, camping, very helpful. Recommended repeatedly, book in advance. **E** pp *Res Petit*, de la Barra 586, T212536. Hot water.

Youth hostel **E** pp *Res Limmat*, Lautaro 914, T/F211373. With breakfast, central, patio, tours offered.

Camping *Maki Payi*, 153 Vegas Norte, about 5 km north of La Serena, near sea, T213628. Self-contained cabins available. Recommended. *Hipocampo*, 4 km south on Av del Mar (take bus for Coquimbo and get off at Colegio Adventista, US$7.50 site by Playa El Pescador), T214316.

Eating

Most restaurants close off season on Sun. For good fish lunches (middle range/cheap) try the restaurants on the upper floor of the Recova market, where as soon as you enter you will be assailed by numerous waiters

Expensive: *Donde El Guatón*, Brasil 750. *Parrillada*, paradise for meat eaters. *El Cedro*, Prat 572. Arab cuisine. **Mid-range**: *Bavaria*, E de la Barra 489. International menu, excellent service, nice place. *Ciro's*, Av de Aguirre 431, T213482. Old-fashioned, good lunch. Recommended. *La Mía Pizza*, O'Higgins 360, T215063. Italian, good value (branch on Av del Mar 2100 in summer). *Pastissima Limitado*, O'Higgins 663. Wide variety of pizzas, delicious pancakes, live music and dancing at weekends. *La Tabla*, Av del Mar 3200. For seafood, extensive wine list. **Cheap**: *Club Social*, Córdovez 516, p 1. Unpretentious but excellent value. *D'Carlo*, Córdovez 516. Good fish, seafood, good value. *Diavoletto*, Prat 565 and O'Higgins 531. Fast food, popular. *Mai Lai Fan*, Córdovez 740. Good Chinese. *Plaza Royal*, Prat 465. Light meals and snacks, pleasant. Recommended. *Qahlúa*, Balmaceda 655. Good fish, seafood, popular. *Taiwan*, Cantournet 844. Cantonese, good quality. For ice cream, make for *Bravissimo*, Balmaceda 545. **Cafés & bars** *Bocaccio*, Prat y Balmaceda. Good cakes, modern, smart, popular. *Café del Patio*, Prat 470. Café, bar with pub (*Tijuana Blues*) from 2100 with live music to the early hours. On Sat, offers *The Beatles Club* from 2300. *Café do Brasil*, Balmaceda 461. Good coffee. *Tahiti*, Córdovez 540, local 113. Real coffee, pastries. Recommended.

Shopping

Many shops close Thu afternoon

Cema-Chile, Los Carrera 562. For handicrafts. *Las Brisas* supermarket, Cienfuegos y Cordovez. *Rendic* supermarket, Balmaceda 561, good. *Mall Plaza*, on the Panamericana next to the bus terminal.

Tour operators

GiraTour, Prat 689, T223535, giratour@ctcinternet.cl *Ingservitur*, Matta 611, T/F220165, ingsvtur@ctcreuna.cl Guided tours to Valle del Encanto, Fray Jorge, Andacollo, Isla Chañaral, Valle del Elqui and to observatories. *Intijalsu Tours*, Matta 621, T/F217945, www.intijalsu.cv.cl Specially trained guides and telescopes in a mobile observatory. *Talinay Adventure Expeditions* and *Inca Travel*, both at Café del Patio (address above), both offer a range of local tours including Valle del Elqui, also trekking and climbing. Approximate tour prices: Valle del Elqui US$30, Parque Nacional Fray Jorge US$35, Tongoy US$28, city tour US$11.

Local Bicycle repairs: *Mike's Bikes*, Av F de Aguirre 004, T224454. North American run, **Transport**
good parts, rental, information on local cycle routes. **Buses**: City buses US$0.25. **Car hire**:
Daire, Balmaceda 3812, T293140, recommended, good service; **La Florida** at airport,
T271947. Cheapest is *Gala*, Balmaceda 1785, T221400. **Taxis**: US$0.75 + US$0.20 per every
200 m. Colectivos with fixed rates, destination on roof; also to Coquimbo from Aguirre y
Balmaceda, and Ovalle and Vicuña from Domeyko y Balmaceda.

Long distance Air Aeropuerto Gabriela Mistral, 5 km east of the city. To **Santiago**,
LanChile/Lan Express; also to destinations in northern Chile. **Buses** Bus terminal, El Santo y
Amunátegui (about 8 blocks south of the centre). Buses daily to **Santiago**, several compa-
nies, 7-8 hrs, US$9-12 (*salón-cama*)-20 (*pullman*). To **Valparaíso**, 7 hrs, US$10. To **Caldera**, 7
hrs, US$10. To **Calama**, US$17, 16 hrs. To **Antofagasta**, 12-13 hrs, several companies,
US$13, and to **Iquique**, 17 hrs, US$20. To **Arica**, US$20. To **Vicuña** and **Pisco Elqui**, see
below. To **Coquimbo**, bus No 8 from Av Aguirre y Cienfuegos, US$0.30, every few minutes.
TurBus office, Balmaceda entre Prat y Cordovez.

Airline offices *LanChile*, Melgarejo 1086, T315099, also an office in the Mall Plaza. **Banks** ATMs at **Directory**
most banks and outside *Las Brisas* supermarket. **Corp Banca**, O'Higgins 529, Visa. *Casas de cambio*:
Cambio Intercam, De la Barra 435B. *Cambio Caracol*, Balmaceda 460, in the basement, building closed
1400-1600. *La Portada*, Prat 515, open all day Sat. If heading north note that La Serena is the last place
to change TCs before Antofagasta. **Communications** Internet: Cyber Cafe at *Ingservtur*, Matta 611,
ingsvtur@ctcreuna.cl *Cyber-Bazaar 2000*, Av F de Aguirre 343-A. *Net Café*, Cordovez 285, T212187,
also bar. *Shalom*, Av F de Aguirre 343. **Telephone:** *CTC*, Cordovez 446. *Entel*, Balmaceda 896 and Prat
571. **Cultural centres** Instituto Chileno Francés de Cultura, Cienfuegos 632, T224993. Library, films,
etc. **Centro Latino-Americano de Arte y Cultura**, Balmaceda 824, T229344. Dance workshops, art
gallery, *artesanía*.

El Tololo at 2,200 m, 89 km southeast of La Serena in the Elqui Valley, 51 km south **Observatories**
of Vicuña, belongs to Aura, an association of US and Chilean universities. It pos- *The La Serena area is*
sesses one of the largest telescopes in the southern hemisphere (4-m diameter), *one of the main*
seven others and a radio telescope. ■ *It is open to visitors by permit only every Sat* *astronomical centres*
0900-1200, 1300-1600; for permits (free) write to Casilla 603, La Serena, *of the world, with 3*
observatories. It is
T051-205200, F205212, then pick your permit up before 1200 on the day before (the *imperative to book*
office is at Colina Los Pinos, on a hill behind the new University – personal applications *tours to all in advance*
can be made here for all three observatories). They will insist that you have private *up to 3-4 months*
transport; you can hire a taxi, US$35 for the whole day, but you will require the regis- *ahead in holiday times*
tration number when you book.

See VLT under Tour
operators, Antofagasta

La Silla at 2,240 m, 150 km northeast of La Serena, belongs to ESO (European
Southern Observatory), financed by eight EU countries, and comprises 14 telescopes. ■ *Every Sat, 1430-1730; registration in advance in Santiago essential (Alonso*
de Córdoba 3107, Santiago, T228 5006/698 8757) or write to Casilla 567, La Serena,
T224527, www.eso.org Getting there: from La Serena it is 114 km north along Route 5
to the turn-off (D Posada La Frontera, cabañas), then another 36 km.

Las Campanas at 2,510 m, 156 km northeast of La Serena, 30 km north of La Silla,
belongs to the Carnegie Institute, has four telescopes and is altogether a smaller facility than the other two. ■ *It is open with permission every Sat 1430-1730, T224680, or*
write to Casilla 601, La Serena. Getting there: follow Route 5 to the same junction as for
La Silla, take the turning for La Silla and then turn north after 14 km. La Silla and Las
Campanas can be reached without private transport by taking any bus towards
Vallenar 2 hrs, US$3.25) getting out at the junction (desvío) and hitch from there.

Tours Travel agents in La Serena and Coquimbo including *Ingservtur* and *GiraTour*, receive
tickets from the observatories and arrange tours to Tololo and La Silla (to Tololo US$22 pp).

The Elqui Valley

The valley of the Río Elqui is one of the most attractive oases in this part of northern Chile. There are orchards, orange groves, vineyards and mines. The road up the valley is paved as far as Varillar, 24 km beyond Vicuña, the valley's capital. Except for Vicuña, most of the tiny towns have but a single street. The Elqui Valley is the centre of *pisco* production with nine distilleries, the largest being Capel in Vicuña. Huancara, a delicious liqueur introduced by the Jesuits, is also produced in the valley.

Vicuña
Phone code: 051
Colour map 8, grid A1
Population: 7,716
66 km east of
La Serena

This small, clean, friendly, picturesque town was founded in 1821. On the west side of the plaza are the municipal chambers, built in 1826 and topped in 1905 by a medieval-German-style tower – the Torre Bauer – imported by the German-born mayor of the time. Also on the plaza is the Iglesia Parroquial, dating from 1860. Tourist office on Plaza de Armas. There are good views from Cerro La Virgen, north of town. The Capel Pisco distillery is 1½ km east of Vicuña, to the right of the main road. ■ *Guided tours (in Spanish) are offered Dec-Feb, daily 1000-1800, free. No booking required.* **Museo Gabriela Mistral**, Gabriela Mistral 759, containing manuscripts, books, awards and many other details of the poet's life. ■ *Mon-Sat 1000-1900, Sun 1000-1800, US$1.* Next door is the house where the poet was born. **Museo Entomológico**, C Chacabuco has over 3,000 insect species. ■ *In summer Mon-Sun 1000-2100; in winter, Mon-Fri 1030-1330, 1530-1930, Sat-Sun 1030-1900, US$0.50.* **Museo Histórico**, C Prat, has sections on Hispanic and Diaguita cultures. ■ *Mon-Sun 0900-2000 in Jan and Feb, 1000-1800 the rest of the year, US$0.50.* **Observatorio Astronómico Comunal de Vicuña**, on Cerro Mamalluca, 10 km from Vicuña, 1500 m above sea level, offers tours to the public at 2030, 2230, 2430 in summer, 1800, 2000, 2200 in winter. ■ *Gabriela Mistral 260,*

Chile

T411352, F411255, www.mamalluca.org Price is US$6.50 for tour, plus US$2 for transport, guides in English and Spanish.

Sleeping and eating AL *Hostería Vicuña*, Sgto Aldea 101, T411301, F411144. Swimming pool, tennis court, excellent restaurant. **C** *La Elquina*, O' Higgins 65, T411317. Lovely garden, laundry and kitchen facilities. **On Gabriela Mistral D** *Valle Hermoso*, No 706, T411206. Comfortable, parking. Recommended. **E** *Sol del Valle*, No 743. Including breakfast, swimming pool, vineyard, restaurant. **Camping** *Camping y Piscina Las Tinajas*, east end of Chacabuco. Swimming pool, restaurant. Eating places are mainly on G Mistral *Club Social de Elqui*, No 435. Very good, attractive patio, good value *almuerzo*. *Mistral*, No 180. Very good, popular with locals, good value *almuerzo*. *Halley*, at No 404. Good meat dishes, also *chopería*, swimming pool (US$5 pp). *Yo Y Soledad*, No 364. Inexpensive, good value.

From Vicuña a 46-km road runs south through the Andes to the village of Río Hurtado, a secluded, picturesque place. Beyond the village the old trading route from Argentina, known as the Inka Trail, leads to Vado Morrillas, 3 km west of Hurtado. Along the trail are rock paintings, old Indian campsites and aqueducts. **C** pp *Hacienda Los Andes*, Vado Morillas, T053-1982106, www.haciendalosandes.com German-Austian management, bed & breakfast, colonial-style, English spoken, horse riding and outdoor activities. Access from Vicuña or Ovalle via Monumento Nacional Pichasca.

Transport Buses to **La Serena**, about 10 a day, most by *Vía Elqui/Megal Bus*, first 0800, last 1930, 1 hr, US$1.75, colectivo from Plaza de Armas US$2.50. To **Pisco Elqui**, 4 a day, *Vía Elqui*, 1 hr, US$2.

From Vicuña the road runs through Paihuano (camping) to Monte Grande, where the schoolhouse where Gabriela Mistral lived and was educated by her sister is now a museum. ■ *US$0.50*. The poet's tomb is situated 1 km out of town. (Buses from the plaza in Vicuña.) Here the road forks, one branch leading to El Colorado. Along this road are several Ashram places. The other branch leads to **Pisco Elqui**, an attractive town with a shady plaza. Here there are two *pisco* plants with another outside town. Horses can be hired, with or without guide. ■ *Buses to La Serena, US$2.50, via Vicuña.*

Pisco Elqui

Sleeping C *El Elqui*, O'Higgins s/n. Hot shower, good restaurant, not always open. Recommended. **C** *El Tesoro del Elqui*, T/F451958. *Cabañas*, café, pool, German spoken. **E** pp *Hostería de Don Juan*, with breakfast, fine views, noisy. **F** pp *Sol de Barbosa*, T451102. Also camping, open all year. **F** *Camping El Olivo*, small restaurant, pool, excellent facilities, closed in winter. Well-stocked supermarket 1 block from the plaza.

Paso Agua Negra (4,775 m) is reached by unpaved road from Rivadavia. Chilean immigration and customs at Juntas, 84 km west of the border, 88 km east of Vicuña. Basic accommodation at Huanta (Guanta on many maps) Km 46 from Vicuña, F, clean, ask for Guillermo Aliaga. Huanta is the last chance to buy food. Border open 0800-1700; Jan-Apr only, check rest of year. No public transport beyond Rivadavia.

Border with Argentina: Paso Agua Negra

Chile

Santiago

North of La Serena

North of the Río Elqui, the transitional zone continues to the mining and agro-indus-trial centre of Copiapó. Thereafter begins the desert, which is of little interest, except after rain. Then it is covered with a succession of flowers, insects and frogs, in one of the world's most spectacular wildlife events. Rain, however, is rare: there is none in sum-mer; in winter it is light and lasts only a short time. Annual precipitation at Copiapó is about 115 mm. Drivers must beware of high winds and blowing sand north of Copiapó.

The Huasco valley is an oasis of olive groves and vineyards. It is rugged and spectac-ular, dividing at Alto del Carmen, 30 km east of Vallenar, into the Carmen and Tránsito valleys. There are pisco distilleries at Alto del Carmen and San Félix. A sweet wine known as Pajarete is also produced.

Vallenar

Phone code: 051
Colour map 8, grid A1
Population: 42,725
Altitude: 380 m
194 km N of La Serena

This is the chief town of the Huasco valley. **Museo del Huasco** Sgto Aldea 742, con-tains historic photos and artefacts from the valley ■ *Tue-Fri 1500-1800, US$0.70.* For tourist information, the staff at the Municipalidad on Plaza de Armas are help-ful. At the mouth of the river, 56 km west, is the pleasant port of **Huasco** (cheap sea-food restaurants near the harbour). The **Humboldt Penguin Natural Reserve** is on Islas Chañaral, Choros and Damas, where, besides penguins, there are seals, sea lions, a great variety of seabirds and, offshore, a colony of grey dolphin. ■ *Permis-sion to land on Isla Damas (US$2.50) from* Conaf *in Punta de Choros, T051-272798. No public transport to Punta de Choros (42 km from Panamericana;* **C** *Cabañas Los Delfines, T09-639 6678* (mob)*); tours from La Serena.*

Listed hotels and restaurants all recommended Cheap eating places along south end of Av Brasil

Sleeping and eating **A** *Hostería Vallenar*, Ercilla 848, T614379, hotval@ctc.cl Excellent, pool, restaurant. **B** *Cecil*, Prat 1059, T614071. Hot water, pool, modern. **C** *Hostal Camino del Rey*, Merced 943, T/F613184. Cheaper without bath, good value. **D** *Vall*, Aconcagua 455, T613380. With breakfast, good value. **E** *Viña del Mar*, Serrano 611, T611478. Nice rooms, *comedor*. For eating, try *Bavaria*, Serrano 802. Good all round. *Pizza Il Boccato*, Plaza O'Higgins y Prat. Good coffee, good food, popular. *La Pica*, Brasil y Faez. Good for cheap meals, seafood, cocktails. *Shanghai*, Ramírez 1267. Chinese.

Tour operators and Transport *Agencia de Viajes Irazu*, Prat 1121A, T/F619807. They do not organize excursions, but will organize flights. If it rains (usually Sep-Oct) a guided tour of the desert in flower can be done with *Roberto Alegría*, T613865. **Bus offices** Each bus company has its own terminal: *TurBus*, Merced 561; *Pullman*, opposite (the most frequent buses going north); *Tas Choapa*, next door.

Directory Banks *Corp Banca*, Prat 1070, with ATM. *Banco de Chile*, Prat 1010, with ATM. **Communications** Telephone: *Entel*, Colchagua 550.

Copiapó

Phone code: 052
Colour map 6, grid C2
Population: 100,000
Altitude: 400 m
144 km N of Vallenar

The valley of the Río Copiapó, generally regarded as the southern limit of the Atacama desert, is an oasis of farms, vineyards and orchards about 150 km long. **Copiapó** is an important mining centre. Founded in 1744, Copiapó became a prosperous town after the discovery in 1832 of the third largest silver deposits in South America at Chañarcillo (the mine was closed in 1875). The discoverer, Juan Godoy, a mule-driver, is commem-orated at Matta y O'Higgins. Fiesta de la Candelaria, first Sunday in February.

The **Cathedral**, on Plaza Prat, dates from 1851. **San Francisco**, five blocks west of the Plaza, built in 1872 (the nearby convent is from 1662) is a good example of a 19th cen-tury construction using Oregon Pine and Guayaquil cane. **Belén**, Infante near Yerbas

Buenas, a colonial Jesuit church, was remodelled in 1856. The **Santuario de la Candelaria**, 3 km southeast of the centre, is the site of two churches, the older built in 1800, the other in 1922; inside the latter is the Virgen de la Candelaria, discovered in the Salar de Maricunga in 1788. **Museo Mineralógico**, Colipí y Rodríguez, one block east from Plaza Prat, is the best of its type in Chile. Many ores shown are found only in the Atacama desert. ■ *Mon-Fri 1000-1300, 1530-1900, Sat 1000-1300, US$0.80.* **Museo Regional del Atacama**, Atacama y Rancagua, entrance US$1 (free on Sunday), deals with local history; interesting. ■ *Mon 1400-1745, Tue-Fri 0900-1745, Sat 1000-1245, 1500-1745, Sun 1000-1245.* The museum at the **railway station** opens irregularly, but the Norris Brothers steam locomotive and carriages used in the inaugural journey between Copiapó and Caldera in 1851 (the first railway in South America) can be seen at the Universidad de Atacama about 2 km north of the centre on Avenida R Freire. The helpful tourist office is at Los Carrera 691, north side of Plaza Prat, T212838.

Sleeping

AL *Diego de Almeida*, O'Higgins 656, Plaza Prat, T/F212075, dalmeida@tnet.cl TV, fridge, good restaurant, bar pool. **AL** *Hostería Las Pircas*, Av Copayapu 095, T213220, hosteria.laspirca@chilnet.cl Bungalows, pool, good restaurant. **B** *San Francisco de la Selva*, Los Carrera 525, T217013, hosanco@entelchile.net TV, café-bar, garage, modern. **B-C** *Montecatini*, Atacama 374, T211516. Good, modern, quiet, breakfast. **B-C** *Palace*, Atacama 741, T212852. Comfortable, good breakfast, nice patio. **D** *Res Chacabuco*, O'Higgins 921, T213428. **F** shared bath, quiet, near bus terminal. **D** *Res Rocío*, Yerbas Buenas 581, T215360. **E** without bath, good value, attractive patio. **E** *Res Nuevo Chañarcillo*, Rodríguez 540, T212368. Without bath (more with), comfortable. Recommended. **E** *Res Torres*, Atacama 230, T240727. Shared bath, hot water, quiet. **F** *Res Casagrande*, Infante 525, T244450. With breakfast, in beautiful old house, excellent value.

Eating

Mid-range: *Bavaria*, Chacabuco 487 (Plaza Prat) and round corner on Los Carrera. Good variety on offer. *El Corsario*, Atacama 245. Good food, value and atmosphere. **Cheap**: *Benbow*, Rodríguez 543. Good value *almuerzo*, extensive menu. *Don Elias*, Los Carrera e Yerbas Buenas. Excellent seafood. *Chifa Hao Hwa*, Colipi 340 and Yerbas Buenas 334. Good Chinese. *La Pizza de Tito*, Infante y Chacabuco. Pizzas, sandwiches and *almuerzos*.

Copiapó

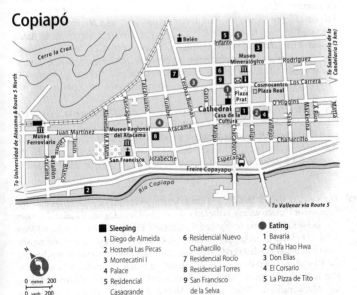

Sleeping
1 Diego de Almeida
2 Hostería Las Pircas
3 Montecatini I
4 Palace
5 Residencial Casagrande
6 Residencial Nuevo Chañarcillo
7 Residencial Rocío
8 Residencial Torres
9 San Francisco de la Selva

Eating
1 Bavaria
2 Chifa Hao Hwa
3 Don Elias
4 El Corsario
5 La Pizza de Tito

0 metres 200
0 yards 200

Shopping *Cosmocentro Plaza Real*, Plaza Prat, shops, eating places and *Andrés Bello* bookshop (loc H109).

Transport **Cycle repairs**: *Biman*, Los Carrera 998A, T/F217391, excellent. **Air** Airport 12 km north of town. *LanChile/Lan Express*, Colipi 484, T213512, daily to/from Santiago, also to northern destinations. **Buses** Terminal 3 blocks from centre on Freire y Chacabuco. To **Santiago** US$15, 12 hrs. To **La Serena** US$7.50, 5 hrs. To **Caldera**, US$1-2, 1 hr.

Directory **Banks** *Redbanc* ATMs at central banks and in *Plaza Real* shopping mall. **Communications** Internet: *Zona Virtual*, Rodríguez y Colipi, T240308, www.zonavirtual.cl *Terra*, Chacabuco 3280, US$1.80 per hr. **Post Office**: O'Higgins 531. **Telephone**: *CTC*, O'Higgins 531; *Entel*, Colipi 484. **Cultural centres** *Casa de la Cultura*, O'Higgins 610, Plaza Prat. Wide range of arts, workshops, *artesanía* shops, good café *El Bramador*.

Border with Argentina: Paso San Francisco

Officially open all year, this crossing is liable to closure in winter T052-238032 for road reports

Paso San Francisco is reached either by poor unpaved road northeast from Copiapó, via the Salar de Maricunga and Laguna Verde or by an unpaved road southeast from El Salvador: the two roads join near the Salar de Maricunga, 96 km west of Paso San Francisco. On the Argentine side a paved road continues to Tinogasta. Chilean immigration and customs are near the Salar de Maricunga, 100 km west of the border, open 0900-1900; US$2 per vehicle charge for crossing Saturday, Sunday and holidays. Always take spare fuel.

Caldera

Phone code: 052
Colour map 6, grid C2
Population: 12,000
73 km W of Copiapó

This is a port and terminal for the loading of iron ore. **Iglesia de San Vicente** (1862) on the Plaza de Armas was built by English carpenters working for the railway company. **Bahía Inglesa**, 6 km south of Caldera, 6 km west of the Highway, is popular for its beautiful white sandy beaches and unpolluted sea (very expensive and can get crowded January-February and at weekends). It was originally known as Puerto del Inglés after the visit in 1687 of the English 'corsario', Edward Davis.

Cheaper to stay in Caldera than Bahía Inglesa in summer

Sleeping and eating In Caldera B *Hostería Puerta del Sol*, Wheelwright 750, T315205. Includes tax, cabins with kitchen, view over bay. **B** *Portal del Inca*, Carvallo 945, T315252. Cabins with kitchen, English spoken, restaurant not bad, order breakfast on previous night. **C** *Costanera*, Wheelwright 543, T316007. Takes credit cards, simple rooms. **E** pp *Res Millaray*, Cousiño 331, Plaza de Armas. Good value, basic. *Miramar*, Gana 090. At pier, good seafood. *El Pirón de Oro*, Cousiño 218. Good but not cheap. **In Bahía Inglesa B** *Los Jardines de Bahía Inglesa*, Av Copiapó, *cabañas*, T315359. Open all year, good beds, comfortable. *Camping Bahía Inglesa*, Playa Las Machas, T315424. **C** tent site, fully equipped *cabañas* for up to 5 persons, **B**. *El Coral* restaurant has some cabins **C**, T315331, Av El Morro, overlooking sea, good seafood, groups welcome, open all year.

Transport Buses to **Copiapó** and **Santiago**, several daily. To **Antofagasta**, US$11, 7 hrs. Buses on the Panamericana do not go into Caldera, but stop at Cruce Caldera, outside town (*Restaurante Hospedaje Mastique*, Km 880, is a good place to eat and stay, **D**). To travel north, it may be better to take a bus to **Chañaral** (Inca-bus US$2), then change. Between Bahía Inglesa and Caldera colectivos charge US$1 all year; frequent bus service Jan-Feb US$0.30.

Chañaral

Phone code: 052
Colour map 6, grid C2
Population: 12,000
968 km N of Santiago

The valley of the Río Salado, 130 km in length, less fertile or prosperous than the Copiapó or Huasco valleys, is the last oasis south of Antofagasta. **Chañaral**, a town with old wooden houses perched on the hillside at the mouth of the Salado, is 93 km north of Caldera. In its heyday it was the processing centre for ore from the nearby copper mines of El Salado and Las Animas. Now it is a base for visits to beaches and the Parque Nacional Pan de Azúcar. There is a tourist information kiosk on the Pan-American Highway at the south end of town (closed winter). If it is closed, go to the Municipalidad. ■ *Bus terminal Merino Jarpa 854. Frequent services to Antofagasta US$10, 5 hrs, and Santiago.*

Sleeping and eating B *Hostería Chañaral*, Miller 268, T480055. Excellent restaurant. **C** *Nuria*, Costanera 302, T480903. Good. **E** *Jiménez*, Merino Jarpa 551, T480328. Without bath, patio with lots of birds, restaurant good value. Recommended. **F** *La Marina*, Merino Jarpa 562. Basic, pleasant patio, good value. Eating: *Rincón Porteño*, Merino Jarpa 567. Good and inexpensive.

The park, north of Chañaral, consists of the Isla Pan de Azúcar on which Humboldt penguins and other sea-birds live, and some 43,754 ha of coastal hills rising to 800 m. There are fine beaches (popular at weekends in summer). Fishermen near the *Conaf* office offer boat trips round Isla Pan de Azúcar to see the penguins, US$5 pp. Vegetation is mainly cacti, of which there are 26 species, nourished by frequent sea mists (*camanchaca*). After rain in some of the gullies there are tall alstroemerias of many colours. The park is home to 103 species of birds as well as guanaco and foxes.

There are two entrances: north by good secondary road from Chañaral, 28 km to Caleta Pan de Azúcar; from the Pan-American Highway 45 km north of Chañaral, along a side road 20 km (road in parts deep sand and very rough, 4WD essential). A taxi costs US$25 from Chañaral, or hitch a lift from fishermen at sunrise. There is a *Conaf* office in Caleta Pan de Azúcar, 0830-1800 daily, maps available. Park entry is US$4. **Camping E** per site, no showers, take all food and drinking water; also 2 *cabañas*, T213404.

Parque Nacional Pan de Azúcar
There are heavy fines for driving in 'restricted areas' of the park

This is the only town between Chañaral and Antofagasta, a distance of 420 km. Along Av Prat are several wooden buildings dating from the late 19th century, when Taltal prospered as a mineral port of 20,000 people. It is now a fishing port with a mineral processing plant. North 72 km is the Quebrada El Médano, a gorge with ancient rock-paintings along the upper valley walls. ■ *Buses to Santiago 2 a day; to Antofagasta, TurBus and Ramos, US$5. Many buses bypass Taltal: to reach the Panamericana take a taxi, US$8.*

Taltal
Phone code: 055
Colour map 6, grid C2
Population: 9,000
146 km N of Chañaral

Sleeping and eating C *Hostal de Mar*, Carrera 250, T611612. Comfortable, modern. **C** *Hostería Taltal*, Esmeralda 671, T611625. Excellent restaurant, good value *almuerzo*. **C** *Verdy*, Ramírez 345, T611105. **E** pp without bath, spacious, restaurant. Recommended. Opposite is **E** *Taltal City*, without bath. **E** *San Martín*, Martínez 279, T611088. Without bath, good *almuerzo*. *Caverna*, Martínez 247. Good seafood. *Club Social Taltal*, Torreblanca 162. The old British club (see the ballroom and poker room), excellent, good value.

Antofagasta

The largest city in Northern Chile, Antofagasta is the capital of the Second Region and is a major port for the export of copper from La Escondida and Chuquicamata. It is also a major commercial centre and home of two universities. While not especially attractive in itself, its setting beside the ocean and in view of tall mountains is dramatic. The climate is delightful (apart from the lack of rain); the temperature varies from 16° C in June/July to 24° C January/February, never falling below 10° C at night.

Phone code: 055
Colour map 6, grid C2
Population: 225,316
1,367 km N of Santiago

In the main square, **Plaza Colón**, is a clock tower donated by the British community in 1910 to commemorate 100 years of Chilean independence. It is a replica of Big Ben in London. **Calle A Prat**, which runs southeast from Plaza Colón, is the main shopping street. Two blocks north of Plaza Colón, at the old port, is the **former Aduana**, built as the Bolivian customs house in Mejillones and moved to its current site after the War of the Pacific. It houses the **Museo Histórico Regional**, which has fascinating visual displays (explanations in Spanish only) on life on land and in the oceans, development of civilization in South America, minerals, human artefacts, recommended. ■ *Tue-Sat 1000-1300, 1530-1830, Sun 1100-1400, US$1, children half-price; museoanto@terra.cl* Opposite are the former **Capitanía del Puerto** (now the administrative offices and library of the Museo Regional) and the **former**

Sights

Chile

Resguardo Marítimo (now housing Digader, the regional coordinating centre for sport and recreation).

East of the port are the buildings of the **Antofagasta and Bolivia Railway Company** (FCAB) dating from the 1890s and beautifully restored, but still in use. **Museo del Ferrocarril a Bolivia** at Bolívar 255 has an interesting museum of the history of the Antofagasta-Bolivia railway, with photographs, maps, instruments and furniture. Reservations must be made 48 hours in advance, T206311, jlyons@fcab.cl **Museo Geológico** of the Universidad Católica del Norte, Av Angamos 0610, inside the university campus. ■ *Mon-Fri, 0900-1200, 1500-1800, free, Gchong@socompa.ucn Colectivo 3 or 33 from town centre.*

Tours of the port by boat leave from *La Cabaña de Mario*, C Aníbal Pinto s/n between the Museo Regional and the Terminal de Pescadores. ■ *30 mins, US$3.50.*

The Tourist Office is at Prat 384, T451818, Mon-Fri 0830-1300, Mon-Thu 1500-1930, Fri 1500-1930, very helpful. There is also a kiosk on Balmaceda, Mon-Fri 0930-1300, 1530-1930, Sat-Sun 0930-1300; kiosk at airport (open summer only). *Automóvil Club de Chile*, Condell 2330, T225332. *Conaf*, Argentina y Baquedano.

Excursions The fantastic cliff formations and symbol of the Second Region at **La Portada** are 16 km north, reached by any bus for Mejillones from the Terminal Centro (or ask at a travel agency). Taxis charge US$11 (for a small extra fee, taxis from the airport will drive past La Portada). Hitching is easy. From the main road it is 2 km to the beach which, though beautiful, is too dangerous for swimming; there is an excellent seafood restaurant (*La Portada*) and café (open lunch-time only). A number of bathing beaches are also within easy reach.

Juan López, 38 km north of Antofagasta, is a windsurfers' paradise (**A** *Hotel La Rinconada*, T261139; **C** *Hostería Sandokan*, T692031). Buses at weekends in summer only, also minibuses daily in summer from Latorre y Sucre. For those with their own transport, follow the road out of Juan López to the beautiful cove at Conchilla. Keep on the track to the end at Bolsico. The sea is alive with birds, especially opposite Isla Santa María.

Mejillones (*Population:* 5,500), a little fishing port 60 km north of Antofagasta, stands on a good natural harbour protected from westerly gales by high hills. Until 1948 it was a major terminal for the export of tin and other metals from Bolivia: remnants of that past include a number of fine wooden buildings: the Intendencia Municipal, the Casa Cultural (built in 1866) and the church (1906), as well as the Capitanía del Puerto.

Sleeping **AL** *Antofagasta*, Balmaceda 2575, T/F228811. Garage, pool, lovely view of port and city, good but expensive restaurant (bar serves cheaper snacks), with breakfast (discount for Automóvil Club members), beach, but rooms facing the city are noisy due to all night copper trains. **A** *Plaza*, Baquedano 461, T269046, F266803, hplaza@chilesat.net TV, salon de té, pool and sports, parking. Recommended, also has apartments. **B** *Ancla Inn*, Baquedano 508, T224814, www.ancla.inn@entelchile.net Salón de té, also has 4 self-contained apartments. Recommended. **B** *Colón*, San Martín 2434, T261851, F260872. With breakfast, local phone calls free, quiet. **B** *Marsal*, Prat 867, T268063, F221733, marsalhotel@terra.cl Modern, very comfortable, Catalan owner. Recommended. **B** *Parina*, Maipú, T223354, F266396. Modern, comfortable, restaurant, conference centre, good value. **B** *Sol del Horizonte*, Latorre 2450, T/F221886, hotelsoldelhorizonte@123click.cl Cable TV, bar, pleasant, good value. Recommended. **C** *Dakota*, Latorre 2425, T251649. With breakfast and cable TV, popular, good value. Recommended. **C** *San Martín*, San Martín 2781, T263503, F268159. TV, parking, safe.

D *Ciudad de Avila*, Condell 2840, T/F221040. TV, restaurant, excellent value. Warmly recommended. **D** *Maykin*, Condell 3130, T/F259400. Modern, helpful, good value. Recommended. **D** *Hostal del Norte*, Latorre 3162, T251265, F267161. Without bath, comfortable, quiet. **D** *Valdivia*, Ossa 2642, T265911. Recommended. **E** pp *Res El Cobre*, Prat 749, T225162. Without bath, clean, but unattractive. **E** pp *Res La Riojanita*, Baquedano 464, T226313. Basic, very helpful, noisy but recommended.

Camping To the south on the road to Coloso are: *Las Garumas*, Km 6, T247763 ext 42, **E** per site (bargain for lower price out of season), **C** for cabins, cold showers and beach (reservations Av Angamos 601, casilla 606). *Rucamóvil*, Km 11, T223929 and 7 *cabañas*. Both open year-round, expensive.

Expensive: *Club de la Unión*, Prat 474, p 2. Open to non-members, excellent *almuerzo*, good service. **Mid-range**: *Bavaria*, Ossa 2428. Excellent meat and German specialities, cheaper cafetería downstairs, real coffee. *Chifa Pekín*, Ossa 2135. Chinese, smart. *D'Alfredo*, Condell 2539. Pizzas, good. *El Arriero*, Condell 2644. Good service, cheaper set lunch, popular, live music. *Panda*, Condell y Baguedano. Self-service, eat all you can for US$8. *Pizzante*, Carrera 1857. Good pasta and seafood. *Tío Jacinto*, Uribe 922. Good seafood. **Cheap**: *Casa Vecchia*, O'Higgins 1456. Good value. *Chicken's House Center*, Latorre 2660. Chicken, beef and daily specials, open till 2400. *Oliver Café Plaza*, Plaza Colón. Self-service, modern. Recommended. Good fish restaurants in *Terminal Pesquero Centro* and at *Caleta Coloso*, 8 km south.

Cafés It is difficult to find coffee or breakfast before 0900. For real coffee: *Café Bahía*, Prat 474, and *Café Caribe*, Prat 482. Open 0900. *Café Haiti*, in Galería at Prat 482. *Cafetería* of *Hotel Nadine*, Baquedano 519, real coffee, pastries, ice cream. Recommended. Good

Eating

Above the market are several good places selling cheap seafood almuerzos and supercheap set lunches Many bars and restaurants are closed on Sun

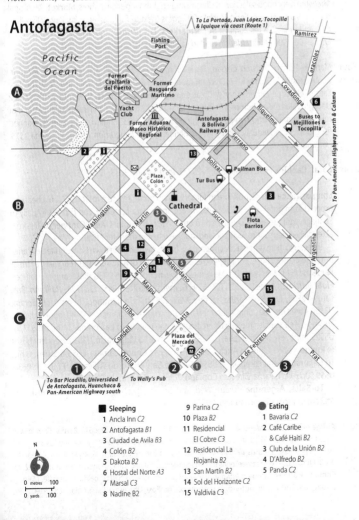

Antofagasta

To La Portada, Juan López, Tocopilla
& Iquique via coast (Route 1)

Pacific Ocean

To Bar Picadillo, Universidad de Antofagasta, Huanchaca & Pan-American Highway south

To Wally's Pub

0 metres 100
0 yards 100

N

■ **Sleeping**
1 Ancla Inn *C2*
2 Antofagasta *B1*
3 Ciudad de Avila *B3*
4 Colón *B2*
5 Dakota *B2*
6 Hostal del Norte *A3*
7 Marsal *C3*
8 Nadine *B2*
9 Parina *C2*
10 Plaza *B2*
11 Residencial El Cobre *C3*
12 Residencial La Riojanita *B2*
13 San Martín *B2*
14 Sol del Horizonte *C2*
15 Valdivia *C3*

● **Eating**
1 Bavaria *C2*
2 Café Caribe & Café Haiti *B2*
3 Club de la Unión *B2*
4 D'Alfredo *B2*
5 Panda *C2*

Chile

panaderías: *Chez Niko's*, Ossa 1951. *La Palmera*, Ossa 2297. *Panadería El Sol*, Baquedano 785. Ice cream at *Heladería Latorre*, Baquedano y Latorre.

Entertainment

Because of Antofagasta's high student population, there is thriving nightlife

Bars: *Bar Picadillo*, Av Grecia 1000. Lively atmosphere, also good food. *Castillo Pub*, Pasaje Carrera 884. Live music, good food with good value *almuerzo*, good fun. *Wally's Pub*, Toro 982. British expat-style with darts and beer, closed Sun. **Discos**: The most popular discotheques are south of the town in Balneario El Huascar. Take Micro 2 on Calle Matta to get there. **Theatre**: *Teatro Municipal*, Sucre y San Martín, T264919. Modern, state-of-the art. *Teatro Pedro de la Barra*, Condell 2495. Run by University of Antofagasta, regular programme of plays, reviews, concerts etc, high standard, details in press.

Festivals

29 Jun, *San Pedro*, patron saint of the fishermen: the saint's image is taken out by launch to the breakwater to bless the first catch of the day. On the **last weekend of Oct**, the foreign communities put on a joint festival on the seafront, with national foods, dancing and music.

Shopping

Bookshops *Librería Andrés Bello*, Condell 2421. Good selection. *Librería Universitaria*, Latorre 2515. Owner Germana Fernández knowledgeable on local history. Opposite is *Multilibro*, very good selection of Chilean and English-language authors. **Market** Municipal market, Matta y Uribe. *Feria Modelo O'Higgins* (next to fish market on Av Pinto). Excellent fruit and veg, also restaurants. **Supermarkets** *Las Brisas*, Baquedano 750. *Korlaert*, on Ossa 2400-2500 block. *Líder* on road to La Portada.

Tour operators

Many including *Turismo Corssa*, San Martín 2769, T/F227675. Recommended. *Intitour*, Baquedano 460, T266185, F260882, intitour@entelchile.net Ask here about visiting the Very Large Telescope Observatory (VLT) at Cerro Paranal, last 2 Sats of every month. *Maerz* (Joseph Valenzuela Thompson), PO Box 55, T243322, F259132, maerz@entelchile.net For tours in German. *Tatio Travel*, Washington 2513, T/F263532.English spoken, tours arranged for groups or individuals. Highly recommended. *Terra Expedition Tour*, Balmaceda 2575, *Hotel Antofagasta*, T/F223324. To Salar de Atacama, etc.

Transport

Local Car hire: *First*, Bolívar 623, T225777. *Iqsa*, Latorre 3033, T264675.

Long distance Air: Cerro Moreno Airport, 22 km north. Taxi to airport US$7, but cheaper if ordered from hotel. Bus US$3 or less, *Tur Bus* and others. *LanChile, Lan Express* fly daily to Santiago, Iquique and Calama; also to other northern airports. *Aero Continente* (less reliable) daily except Sat to Santiago and Iquique (change there for Arica).

Buses: No main terminal; each company has its own office in town (some quite a distance from the centre). Buses for **Mejillones** and **Tocopilla** depart from the Terminal Centro at Riquelme 513. Minibuses to Mejillones leave from Latorre 2730. Bus company offices: *Flota Barrios*, Condell 2682, T268559; *Géminis*, Latorre 3055, T251796; *Pullman Bus*, Latorre 2805, T262591; *TurBus*, Latorre 2751, T264487. To **Santiago**, 20 hrs (*Flota Barrios*, US$50, *cama* includes drinks and meals); many companies: fares US$35-40, book 2 days in advance. If all seats to the capital are booked, catch a bus to **La Serena** (11 hrs, US$13, or US$25 *cama* service), or **Ovalle**, US$18, and re-book. To **Valparaíso**, US$30. Frequent buses to **Iquique**, US$9, 8 hrs. To **Arica**, US$10, 13½ hrs. To **Chuquicamata**, US$5, frequent, 3 hrs. To **Calama**, several companies, US$4, 3 hrs; to **San Pedro de Atacama**, *TurBus* at 0630, US$9.50, or via Calama. Direct to **Copiapó**, *TurBus* daily, 7 hrs, US$14.

To Salta, Argentina *TurBus*, Wed, and *Gemini*, Tue, Fri, via Calama, San Pedro de Atacama, Paso de Jama and Jujuy, US$43, 18 hrs.

Directory

Impossible to change TCs south of Antofagasta until you reach La Serena

Airline offices *LanChile*, Paseo Prat, T265151. *LAB*, San Martín 2395, T260618. **Banks** *Corp Banca*, Plaza Colón for Visa. ATMs at major banks around Plaza Colón, *Hotel Antofagasta*, and *Las Brisas* and *Tricot* supermarkets. *Casas de Cambio* are mainly on Baquedano, such as Ancla, No 524, Mon-Fri 0900-1400, 1600-1900 (at weekends try ice cream shop next door) and shopping centre at No 482-98. **Communications** Internet: *Intitour*, see tour operator above, US$0.60 per hr. Cybercafé, Maipú y Latorre, US$1.30 per hr. Sucre 671, US$0.80 per hr. Post Office: on Plaza Colón. 0830-1900, Sat

0900-1300. Also at Washington 2613. **Telephone:** *CTC*, Condell 2529 and 2750 (open Sun). *Entel Chile*, Condell 2451. **Cultural centres** Instituto Chileno Norteamericano, Carrera 1445, T263520. Instituto Chileno Alemán, Bolívar 769, T225946. **Centro Cultural Nueva Acrópolis**, Condell 2679, T222144, lots of activities, talks, discussions. **Consulates** Argentina, Blanco Encalada 1933, T220440. **Bolivia**, Washington 2675, p 13, T225010. **France and Belgium**, Baquedano 299, T268669. **Germany**, Pérez Zujovic 4940, T251691. **Italy**, Matta 1945, of 808, T227791. **Netherlands**, Washington 2679, of 902, T266252. **Spain**, Rendic 4946, T269596.

Tocopilla is 187 km north of Antofagasta via the coastal road and 365 km via the Pan-American Highway. It has one of the most dramatic settings of any Chilean town, sheltering at the foot of 500-m high mountains that loom inland. There are some interesting early 20th century buildings with wooden balustrades and façades. The port facilities are used to unload coal and to export nitrates and iodine from María Elena and Pedro de Valdivia. There are two good beaches: Punta Blanca (12 km south) and Balneario Covadonga, with a swimming pool.

Tocopilla
Phone code: 055
Colour map 6, grid B2
Population: 24,600

Sleeping **C** *Bolívar*, Bolívar 1332, T812783. **F** pp without bath, modern, helpful. Opposite is *Sucre*, same ownership, same price. **C** *Vucina*, 21 de Mayo 2069, T/F813088. Modern, good restaurant. **D** *Hotel Colonial*, 21 de Mayo 1717, T811621, F811940. With breakfast, TV, helpful. **E** pp *Casablanca*, 21 de Mayo 2054, T813187. Helpful, good restaurant, good value. **F** pp *Res Royal*, T/F 811488, 21 de Mayo 1988. Helpful, basic, without breakfast or bath. Several others.

There is a good range of eating places in town

Transport Buses to **Antofagasta** many daily, US$3, 2½ hrs. To **Iquique**, along coastal road, 3 hrs, US$4, frequent. To **Chuquicamata** and **Calama**, 2 a day, 3 hrs, US$5.

Bus company offices are on 21 de Mayo

East of Tocopilla a good paved road runs up the narrow valley 72 km to the Pan-American Highway. From here the paved road continues east to Chuquicamata.

North of the crossroads 81 km is **Quillagua** (customs post, all vehicles and buses are searched) and 111 km further is the first of three sections of the **Reserva Nacional del Tamarugal**. In this part are the **Geoglyphs of Cerro Pintados**, some 400 figures (humans, animals, geometric shapes) on the hillside (3 km west of the highway). The second part of Tamarugal is near La Tirana (see page 669), the third 60 km north of Pozo Almonte.

The coastal road from Tocopilla north to Iquique is now a very good paved road, 244 km, offering fantastic views of the rugged coastline and tiny fishing communities. The customs post at Chipana-Río Loa (90 km north) searches all southbound vehicles for duty-free goods; 30 minutes delay. Basic accommodation is available at San Marcos, a fishing village, 131 km north. At Chanaballita, 184 km north there is a hotel, *cabañas*, camping, restaurant, shops. There are also campsites at Guanillos, Km 126, Playa Peruana, Km 129 and Playa El Aguila, Km 160.

Calama

Calama lies in the oasis of the Río Loa. Initially a staging post on the silver route between Potosí and Cobija, it is now an expensive, unprepossessing modern city, serving the nearby mines of Chuquicamata and Radomiro Tomic. Calama can be reached from the north by Route 24 via Chuquicamata, or, from the south, by a paved road leaving the Pan-American Highway 98 km north of Antofagasta at Carmen Alto (petrol and food). This road passes many abandoned nitrate mines (*oficinas*).

Phone code: 055
Colour map 6, grid B2
Population: 106,970
Altitude: 2,265 m
202 km N of Antofagasta

Two kilometres from the centre on Av B O'Higgins is the **Parque El Loa**, which contains a reconstruction of a typical colonial village built around a reduced-scale reproduction of Chiu Chiu church. ■ *Daily 1000-1800*. Nearby in the park is the **Museo Arqueológico y Etnológico**, with an exhibition of pre-hispanic cultural history. ■ *Tue-Sun 1000-1300, 1540-1930*. Also the new **Museo de Historia Natural**, with an interesting collection on the *oficinas* and on the region's ecology and

Chile

The slow train to Oruro

The line between Calama and Oruro in Bolivia is the only section of the old Antofagasta and Bolivia Railway line still open to passenger trains. It is a long, slow journey but well worthwhile for the scenery. The journey is very cold, both during the day and at night (-15°C). From Calama the line climbs to reach its highest point at Ascotán (3,960 m); it then descends to 3,735 m at Cebollar, skirting the Salar de Ascotán.

Chilean customs are at Ollagüe and the train is searched at Bolivian customs at Avaroa. From the border the line runs northeast to Uyuni, 204 km (six hours), crossing the Salar de Chiguana and running at an almost uniform height of 3,660 m. Uyuni is the junction with the line south to the Argentine frontier at Villazón. Río Mulato is the junction for Potosí, but it is much quicker to travel by bus from Uyuni.

palaeontology. ■ *Wed-Sun, 1000-1300, 1430-2000, US$0.65.* The tourist office is at Latorre 1689, T345345, map, city tours, helpful. ■ *Mon-Fri 0900-1300, 1430-1900. Automóvil Club de Chile,* Av Ecuador 1901, T/F342770.

Sleeping **L** *Lican Antai,* Ramírez 1937, T341621, hotellicanantai@terra.cl With breakfast, central, good service and good restaurant, TV. Recommended. **L-AL** *Hostería Calama,* Latorre 1521, T341511, hcalama@directo.cl Comfortable, good food and service. **AL** *Park,* Camino Aeropuerto 1392, T319900, F319901 (Santiago T233-8509). First class, pool, bar and restaurant. Recommended. **A** *El Mirador,* Sotomayor 2064, T/F340329, hotelelmirador@hotmail.com With bath, good atmosphere, clean, helpful. Recommended. **C** *Casablanca,* Sotomayor 2160, on plaza. Quiet, safe, with breakfast. **C** *Génesis,* Granaderos 2148, T342841. Cheaper double rooms, **D**, near Geminis bus terminal. Recommended. **D** *Hostal Splendid,* Ramírez 1960, T341841. Central, clean, friendly, hot water, often full, good. **E** pp *San Sebastián,* Pinto 1902, T343810. Good beds, meals available, decent choice, family run. **F** pp *Casa de Huéspedes,* Sotomayor 2079. Poor beds, basic but reasonable, pleasant courtyard, hot shower. **F** pp *Cavour,* Sotomayor 1841, T317392. Simple, basic, hospitable. **F** pp *Claris Loa,* Granaderos 1631, T319079. Quiet, good value, central.

Eating **Mid-range**: *Bavaria,* Sotomayor 2095. Good restaurant with cafetería downstairs, real coffee, open 0800, very popular, also at Latorre 1935. *Los Adobes de Balmaceda,* Balmaceda 1504. Excellent meat. *Los Braseros de Hans Tur,* Sotomayor 2030. Good ambience, good food. *Mariscal JP,* Félix Hoyos 2127. Best seafood. *México,* Latorre 1986. Genuine Mexican cuisine, live music at weekends. **Cheap**: Best Chinese is *Nueva Chong Hua,* Abaroa 2006. Several places on Abaroa on Plaza 23 de Marzo: *Club Croata,* excellent value 4-course *almuerzo,* good service; *D'Alfredo Pizzería* and *Di Giorgio* for pizzas, etc; *Plaza,* good *almuerzos,* opens early, good service. *Lascar,* Ramírez 1917. Good value *almuerzo.* *Nueva Victoria,* Vargas y Abaroa. Good *almuerzos* and à la carte, popular. *Pukará,* Abaroa 2054B. Typical local food, excellent, very cheap.

Shopping **Market** on Antofagasta between Latorre and Vivar, selling fruit juices and crafts. Craft stalls on Latorre 1600 block. **Supermarkets** *Economico,* Grecia 2314, *El Cobre,* Vargas 2148.

Tour operators Several agencies run 1-day and longer tours to the Atacama region, including San Pedro; these are usually more expensive than tours from San Pedro and require a minimum number for the tour to go ahead. Operators with positive recommendations include: *Azimut 360,* T/F333040, www.azimut.cl Tours to the Atacama desert, mountaineering expeditions. *Turismo Buenaventura,* T/F341882, buenventur@entelchile.net *Colque Tours,* C Caracoles, T851109, colquetours@terra.cl 4WD tours of Andes and salt plains into Bolivia. *Turismo El Sol,* V. Mackenna 1812, T340152. Main office in San Pedro de Atacama. Turismo Tujina, Ramirez 2222, T/F342261.

Local Car hire A 4WD jeep (necessary for the desert) costs US$80 a day, a car US$63. All offices close Sat 1300 till Mon morning. Airport offices only open when flights arrive. *IQSA*, O'Higgins 877, T310281. See Essentials, page 48 for agency web addresses.

Long distance Air *LanChile/Lan Express* (T341394), daily, to **Santiago**, via Antofagasta. Taxi to town US$6 (courtesy vans from Hotels *Calama*, *Alfa* and *Lican Antai*). Also buses into town. Recommended service with ***Alberto Molina***, T324834; he'll pick you up at your hotel, US$3.

Trains To **Uyuni** (Bolivia), weekly service, Wed 2300, though often doesn't leave till early next morning. If on time the train arrives in **Ollagüe** at 0830. The Chilean engine returns to Calama and you have to wait up to 7 hrs for the Bolivian engine. You have to disembark at the border for customs and immigration. Interpol is in a modern building 400 m east of the station. Through fare to Uyuni is US$13.45. Book seats (passport essential) after 1500 on day of travel from the *Ferrocarril* office in Calama (closed 1300-1500 for lunch) or a local travel agency. Catch the train as early as possible: although seats are assigned, the designated carriages may not arrive; passengers try to occupy several seats to sleep on, but will move if you show your ticket. Sleeping bag and/or blanket essential. Restaurant car operates to the border, cheap. There is no food or water at Ollagüe. If you haven't brought any with you, you'll suffer as you wait for the Bolivian engine to turn up. Money can be changed on the train once in Bolivia, but beware forged notes.

Buses No main terminal, buses leave from company offices: *Frontera*, Antofagasta 2041, T318543; *Kenny Bus*, Vivar 1954; *Flota Barrios*, Ramírez 2298. To **Santiago** 23 hrs, US$25 (*salón cama*, US$40). To **Valparaíso/Viña del Mar**, US$25. To **La Serena**, usually with delay in Antofagasta, 15 hrs, US$17. To **Antofagasta**, 3 hrs, several companies, US$4. To **Iquique**, 8 hrs, via Chuquicamata and Tocopilla, US$7, most overnight, but *Tur Bus* have one early morning and one mid-afternoon service. To **Arica**, usually overnight, US$9, 8 hrs, or change in Antofagasta. To **Chuquicamata** (see below). For services to **San Pedro de Atacama** and Toconao, see below. **To Argentina** *Tur Bus* leave for **Salta** at 0915 on Wed, US$30, *Géminis* on Tue and Fri, US$32 (leaving from *Pullman* terminal), 22 hrs. **To Bolivia** *Buses Manchego* leave for Uyuni at midnight, Wed and Sun, US$10.50, also serving Ollagüe, US$5.25, T318466.

Banks Exchange rates are generally poor especially for TCs. Many *Redbanc* ATMs on Latorre and Sotomayor. *Casas de Cambio*: **Moon Valley**, Sotomayor 1960. Another at No 1837. **Communications** Internet: At Calle Vargas 2014, p 2, And 2054, both US$1.50 per hr. *Cybercafé Machi*, Vivar 1944. **Post Office**: Granaderos y V Mackenna. 0830-1300, 1530-1830, Sat 0900-1230, will not send parcels over 1 kg. **Telephone**: *CTC*, Sotomayor 1825. *Entel*, Sotomayor 2027. **Consulates** *Bolivia*, Sr Reynaldo Urquizo Sosa, Bañados Espinoza 2232, Apdo Postal 85, T341976. Open (in theory only) Mon-Fri 0900-1230, 1530-1830, helpful.

North of Calama 16 km is the site of the world's largest open-cast copper mine, employing 8,000 workers and operated by Codelco (the state copper corporation). Everything about Chuquicamata is huge: the pit from which the ore is extracted is four km long, two km wide and 730 m deep; the giant trucks, with wheels over 3½m high, carry 310 ton loads and work 24 hours a day; in other parts of the plant 60,000 tons of ore are processed a day. ■ *Guided tours, by bus, in Spanish (also in English if enough people) leave from the office of Chuqui Ayuda (a local children's charity) near the entrance at the top end of the plaza, Mon-Fri 0945 (less frequently in low season – tourist office in Calama has details), 1 hr, US$2.50 requested as a donation to the charity; register at the office 30 mins in advance; passport essential. No filming permitted. In order to get on the tour, the tourist office in Calama recommends that you catch a colectivo from Calama at 0800. From Calama: yellow colectivo taxis (marked 'Chuqui') from the corner of the main plaza, US$0.75.*

Transport
Remember that between Oct and Mar, Chilean time is 1 hr later than Bolivian. A hired car shared between several people is an economic alternative for visiting the Atacama region.

A very uncomfortable journey with many delays, and no heating or toilets (improvise in the space between the carriage and the dining car)

Thieves operate at the bus stations

Directory

Chuquicamata
Phone code: 055
Colour map 6, grid B2

Altitude: 2,800 m
The town surrounding the mine will close in 2003 and the families will be moved to Calama

Chile

The desert to the eastern side of the road is extensively covered by minefields. There is no petrol between Calama and Uyuni in Bolivia If really short try buying from the carabineros at Ollagüe or Ascotán, the military at Conchi or the mining camp at Buenaventura (5 km from Ollagüe)

From Calama it is 273 km north to Ollagüe, on the Bolivian border. The road follows the Río Loa, passing **Chiu Chiu** (33 km), one of the earliest Spanish settlements in the area. Just beyond this oasis, a small turning branches off the main road to the hamlet of **Lasana**, 8 km north of Chiu Chiu. Petroglyphs are clearly visible on the right-hand side of the road. There are striking ruins of a pre-Inca *pukará*, a national monument; drinks are on sale. If arranged in advance, Línea 80 *colectivos* will continue to Lasana for an extra charge – pre-book the return trip, or walk back to Chiu Chiu. At **Conchi**, 25 km north of Lasana, the road crosses the Río Loa via a bridge dating from 1890 (it's a military zone, so no photographs of the view are allowed). Beyond Chiu Chiu the road deteriorates, with deep potholes, and, north of Ascotán (*carabinero* checkpoint at 3,900 m), it becomes even worse(ask about the conditions on the Salares at Ascotán or Ollagüe before setting out, especially in December/January or August). There are many llama flocks along this road and flamingoes on the salares.

Ollagüe

Colour map 6, grid B2 Altitude: 3,690 m The border with Bolivia is open 0800-2100; US$2 per vehicle charge for crossings 1300-1500, 1850-2100. A bad unmade road from Ollagüe runs into Bolivia (see Bolivia, page 280)

This village, on the dry floor of the Salar de Ollagüe, is surrounded by a dozen volcanic peaks of over 5,000 m. Police and border officials will help find lodging. There are few services and no public toilets. At this altitude the days are warm and sunny, nights cold (minimum temperature -20° C). There are only 50 mm of rain a year, and water is very scarce. Ollagüe can be reached by taking the Calama-Uyuni train or by *Manchego* bus (see above). If you stop off, hitching is the only way out.

Between Chiu Chiu and El Tatio (see below), **Caspana** (*Population*: 400; *altitude* 3,305 m) is beautifully set among hills with a tiny church dating from 1641 and a museum with interesting displays on Atacameño culture. Basic accommodation is available. A poor road runs north and east through valleys of pampas grass with llama herds to **Toconce**, which has extensive prehispanic terraces set among interesting rock formations. A community tourism project has been set up, designed to help stem the flow of people moving to Calama. Three rooms are available, accommodation for up to 12 people, with full board, **B**. There are archaeological sites nearby and the area is ideal for hiking. Further information from the tourist office in Calama, who may also help with arranging transport, or T321828, toconce@mixmail.com

San Pedro de Atacama

Phone code: 055 Colour map 6, grid B2 Population: 2,824 Altitude: 2,436 m 103 km SE of Calama (paved; no fuel, food or water)

At Paso Barros Arana (Km 58) en route to San Pedro de Atacama from Calama look out for vicuñas and guanacos. The main road skirts the Cordillera de la Sal about 15 km from San Pedro. There are spectacular views of sunset over to the Western Cordilleras. San Pedro de Atacama is a small town, more Spanish-Indian looking than is usual in Chile. While it is now famous among visitors as the centre for excursions in this part of the Atacama, it was important as the centre of the Atacameño culture long before the arrival of the Spanish. There is a definite sense of history in the shady streets and the crumbling ancient walls which drift away from the town into the fields, and then into the dust. Owing to the clear atmosphere and isolation, there are wonderful views of the night sky after the electricity supply is switched off. Lunar landscapes, blistering geysers and flamingos strutting on salt flats are all close by. The **Iglesia de San Pedro**, dating from the 17th century, has been heavily restored (the tower was added in 1964). The roof is made of cactus. Nearby, on the Plaza, is the **Casa Incaica**, the oldest building in San Pedro.

Museo Arqueológico, the collection of Padre Gustave Paige, a Belgian missionary who lived in San Pedro between 1955 and 1980, is now under the care of the Universidad Católica del Norte. It is a fascinating repository of artefacts, well organized to trace the development of prehispanic Atacameño society. Labels on displays in Spanish are good, and there is a comprehensive booklet in Spanish and English. ■ *Mon-Fri, 0900-1300, 1500-1900; Sat-Sun, 1000-1200, 1500-1800, US$1.50, museospa@entelchile.net* The tourist office is on the plaza, with little information and rarely open, www.sanpedroatacama.com

The **Valle de la Luna** with fantastic landscapes caused by the erosion of salt mountains, is a nature reserve 12 km west of San Pedro. It is crossed by the old San Pedro-Calama road. Although buses on the new Calama-San Pedro road will stop to let you off where the old road branches off 13 km northwest of San Pedro (signposted to Peine), it is far better to travel from San Pedro on the old road, either on foot (allow three hours there, three hours back; no lifts), by bicycle (only for the fit) or by car (a 20-km round trip is possible). The Valle is best seen at sunset (provided the sky is clear). Take water, hat, camera and torch.

Excursions
Although sunset is the best time to visit, it is also the most crowded with visitors

North of San Pedro along the river is the **Pukará de Quitor**, a pre-Inca fortress restored in 1981. The fortress, which stands on the west bank of the river, was stormed by the Spanish under Pedro de Valdivia (the path involves fording the river several times). A further 4 km up the river there are Inca ruins at Catarpe. At **Tulor**, 12 km southwest of San Pedro, there is an archaeological site where parts of a stone-age village (dated 500-800 BC) have been excavated; worth a visit on foot (you can sleep in two reconstructed huts), or take a tour, US$5 pp. Nearby are the ruins of a 17th century village, abandoned in the 18th century because of lack of water.

El Tatio, the site of geysers, is a popular attraction. From San Pedro it is reached by a maintained road which runs northeast. The geysers are at their best 0630-0830, though the spectacle varies: locals say the performance is best when weather conditions are stable. A swimming pool has been built nearby (take costume and towel). There is a workers' camp which is empty apart from one guard, who will let you sleep in a bed in one of the huts, **F**, take food and sleeping bag. From here you can hike to surrounding volcanoes if acclimatized to altitude. There is no public transport and hitching is impossible. If going in a hired car, make sure the engine is suitable for very high altitudes and is protected with antifreeze; four-wheel drive vehicle is advisable. If driving in the dark it is almost impossible to find your way: the sign for El Tatio is north of the turn off (follow a tour bus). Tours arranged by agencies in San Pedro and Calama.

El Tatio
*Warning: People have been killed or seriously injured by falling into the geysers, or through the thin crust of the mud. Do not stand too close as the geysers can erupt unexpectedly
Altitude: 4,500 m*

Toconao is on the eastern shore of the Salar de Atacama. All houses are built of bricks of white volcanic stone, which gives the village a very characteristic appearance totally different from San Pedro. The 18th century church and bell tower are also built of volcanic stone. East of the village is a beautifully green gorge called the Quebrada de Jérez, filled with fruit trees and grazing cattle (entry US$0.80). The quarry where the stone (*sillar*) is worked can be visited, about 1½ km east (the stones sound like bells when struck). Worth visiting also are the vineyards which produce a unique sweet wine. There are basic *residenciales* (**F** pp) – ask around in the village. Camping is possible along the Quebrada de Jérez. ■ Frontera *bus from San Pedro, 4 a day, US$0.80.*

Toconao
*Colour map 6, grid B2
Population: 500
37 km S of San Pedro de Atacama*

South of Toconao is one of the main entrances to the Salar de Atacama, 300,000 ha. Rich in minerals including borax, potassium and an estimated 40% of world lithium reserves, the Salar is home to the pink flamingo and other birds (though these can only be seen when lakes form in winter). The air is so dry that you can usually see right across the Salar. ■ *Entry is controlled by* Conaf *in Toconao, US$3.* Three areas of the Salar form part of the **Reserva Nacional de los Flamencos**, which is in seven sectors totalling 73,986 ha and administered by *Conaf* in San Pedro.

The 3rd largest expanse of salt flats in the world

From Toconao the road heads south through scenic villages to the mine at Laco (one poor stretch below the mine), before proceeding to Laguna Sico (4,079 m), and Paso Sico to Argentina.

Chile

Sleeping

There is electricity, but take a torch (flashlight) for walking at night. Residenciales supply candles, but better to buy them in Calama beforehand. Accommodation is scarce in Jan/Feb and expensive

L *Explora*. Luxury full-board and excursion programme, advance booking only (Av Américo Vespucio Sur 80, p 5, Santiago, T206 6060, F228 4655, explora@entelchile.net). Recommended. **L** *Hostería San Pedro*, Solcor, T851011, hsanpedro@chilesat.net Pool (residents only), petrol station, tents for hire, cabins, hot water, has own generator, restaurant (good *almuerzo*), bar, takes Amex but no TCs. **L** *Terrantai*, Tocopilla, T851140, terrantai@adex.cl All-inclusive packages only, 24-hr hot water, heating, comfortable, breakfast, lovely garden. **L** *Tulor*, Atienza, T/F851248, tulor@chilesat.net Good service, pool, heating, laundry, excellent restaurant. Recommended. **AL** *Kimal*, Atienza y Caracoles, T851159, kimal@entelchile.net Comfortable, excellent restaurant. **A** *El Tatio*, Caracoles, T851263, hoteleltatio@usa.net Comfortable, small rooms, bargain off season, English spoken. **AL** *La Casa de Don Tomás*, Tocopilla, T851055, dontomas@rdc.cl Very pleasant, quiet, pool, good restaurant. Recommended. **B** *Casa Corvatsch*, Le Paige, T/F851101, corvatsch@ entelchile.net Cheaper rooms **F** pp, pleasant views, English/German spoken, usually recommended, but some mixed reports. **B** *Hostal Takha-Takha*, Caracoles, T851038. **F** pp for cheaper rooms, lovely garden, nice rooms, camping **G** pp, laundry facilities. **B** *Tambillo*, Le Paige, T/F851078. Pretty, 24-hr electricity and hot water, good value. **B** *Res Licancábur*, Toconao, T851007, **C** off-season, cheaper rooms **E-F** pp, nicely furnished. **C** *Katarpe*, Atienza, T851033, katarpe@galeon.com Comfortable, quiet, nice patio, good value. Recommended. **C** *Res Juanita*, on the plaza, T851039. **E** without bath, hot water, run-down, decent value, restaurant. **D** *La Quinta Adela*, Toconao, T851272, qtadela@cvmail.cl Hot water, no breakfast, good. **D** pp *Res Sonchek*, Calama 370, T851112. Pleasant but strict, shared bath, also dormitory, no towels, laundry facilities, use of kitchen, garden, restaurant, French and English spoken, mixed reports. **E** pp *Hostal Casa Adobe*, Atienza 582, T851249. Shared hot shower, laundry facilities, hospitable. **E** pp *Casa de Nora*, Tocopilla, T851114. Family accommodation, simple rooms, lovely patio. Recommended. **E** pp *Hostal Edén Atacameño*, Toconao, T851154. No singles, basic, hot showers, also camping with laundry and cooking facilities, **F**. **E** pp *Res Chiloé*, Atienza, T851017. Hot water, sunny veranda, good beds and bathrooms, good meals, laundry facilities, luggage store, good value. **F** pp *Res Florida*, Tocopilla, T851021. Without bath, basic, quiet patio, hot water evenings only, laundry facilities, no singles.

Camping *Kunza*, Antofagasta y Atienza, T851183, **F** pp, but disco next door at weekends.

San Pedro de Atacama

Not to scale

Sleeping		
1 Casa Corvatsch	8 Residencial Chiloé	**Eating**
2 El Tatio	9 Residencial Florida	1 Adobe & Casa Piedra
3 Hostal Takha-Takha	10 Residencial Juanita	2 Café El Viaje
4 Hostería San Pedro	11 Residencial Licancábur	3 Café Export
5 Katarpe	12 Residencial Sonchek	4 Café Tierra Todo Natural
6 Kimal	13 Tambillo	5 La Casona
7 Kunza Camping	14 Terrantai	6 La Estaka

Mid-range: *Adobe*, Caracoles. Open fire, good atmosphere and meeting place, loud music, small portions. *Café Export*, Toconao y Caracoles. Nice décor, vegetarian options, real coffee, English spoken, loud music. *Casa Piedra*, Caracoles. Open fire, also has a cheap menu, many of the waiters are musicians, good food and cocktails. Recommended. *La Casona*, Caracoles. Good food, vegetarian options, cheap *almuerzo*, large portions, popular. Recommended. **Cheap**: *Café Tierra Todo Natural*, Caracoles. Excellent fruit juices, "the best bread in the Atacama", real coffee, yoghurt, best for breakfast, opens earliest. *Café El Viaje*, Tocopilla in the Casa de la Arte. Nice patio, good for vegetarians. *Quitor*, Licancábur y Domingo Atienza. Good, basic food. *Tahira*, Tocopilla. Excellent value *almuerzo*, local dishes. **Bar**: *La Estaka*, Caracoles. Lively after 2300, also good cuisine and service. Recommended.

Eating
● *on maps*
Price codes:
see inside front cover
Few places are open
before 1000

Mountain biking: bicycles for hire all over town, by the hour or full day. *Pangea*, Tocopilla, T851111. English spoken, US$2 per hr, US$15 per day. Recommended. **Mountaineering**: *Campamento Base*, Toconao 544, T851451, basecamp@mail.com A bit more expensive than others (US$80-100 a day), but offers full insurance, for all levels of ability, good break-fast, good guides, English and German spoken (Stephan will give 5% discount to *Footprint* owners). Also offers rock climbing and has a good vegetarian café. Highly recommended. **Sand boarding**: *Desert Sports*, Toconao 447A/B, T851373, cabanasports@hotmail.com Good value, tuition, pizzería, also rents mountain bikes. Recommended. **Swimming Pool**: *Piscina Oasis*, at Pozo Tres, only 3 km southeast but walking there is tough and not recommended. Open all year daily (except Mon) 0500-1730, US$1.50 to swim, sometimes empty. Camping US$3 and picnic facilities, very popular at weekends.

Sport

Usual tour rates (may rise in high season): to Valle de la Luna, US$4-6. To Toconao and the Salar de Atacama, US$25-30 including breakfast and lunch. To El Tatio (begin at 0400) US$12-14 (take swimming costume and warm clothing). *Cosmo Andino Expediciones*, Caracoles s/n, T/F851069, cosmoandina@ entelchile.net Very professional and experienced. English, German, French and Dutch spoken, book exchange in the above languages, wide selection, owner Martin Beeris (Martín El Holandés). Recommended. Opposite are *Desert Adventure*, Caracoles s/n, T/F851067, desertsp@ctcinternet.cl Recommended. *Atacama Inca Tour*, Toconao s/n, Frente a la Plaza, T581034, F851062. Private and group tours. Recommended. *Labra*, Caracoles s/n, T851137. Expert guide Mario Banchon, English and German spoken. Recommended. *Pachamama*, Toconao, T851064. Not open all year. *Rancho Cactus*, Toconao, T851108, F851052. Offers horseriding with good guides to Valle de la Luna and other sites (Farolo and Valerie – speaks French and English). *Expediciones Corvatsch/Florida*, Tocopilla s/n, T851087, F851052. Group discounts. *Turismo El Sol*, Tocopilla 432-A, T851230, turismoelsol@hotmail.com Internet access as well as tours. *Southern Cross Adventure*, Toconao 544 (see under Santiago, Tour operators). *Turismo Colque*, Caracoles, T851109, run tours to Laguna Verde, Laguna Colorada, Uyuni and other sites in Bolivia. 3 days, changing vehicles at the border as the Bolivian authorities refuse permits for Chilean tour vehicles, US$65 pp, basic accommodation, take own sleeping

Tour operators
Beware of tours to
Valle de la Luna
leaving too late to
catch sunset – leave
before 1530

Before taking a tour,
check that the agency
has dependable
vehicles, suitable
equipment (eg oxygen
for El Tatio), a guide
who speaks English if
so advertised, and that
the company is
well-established
Report any complaints
to the municipality
or Sernatur

Chile

bag, food and especially water (1-day tour to Laguna Verde possible). Recommended. Obtain passport stamps before departure. Beware of altitude sickness. *SanPedroAtacama.com*, contacto@sanpedroatacama.com offers tours, maps, and transport tickets. Bolivian company **Andean Summits** also has a local office here for cross-border expeditions, www.andeansummits.com

Transport **Buses From Calama**: *Tur Bus* daily 0950, *Atacama 2000* 3 a day from Abaroa y Antofagasta, *Frontera* 9 a day from Antofagasta 2142, last bus 2030, US$1.50, 1½ hrs. To Calama, *Tur Bus*, 1800 (continues to Antofagasta); *Frontera* first 0900, last 1900. Frequencies vary with more departures in Jan-Feb and some weekends. Book in advance to return from San Pedro on Sun afternoon. **To Argentina**: *Géminis*, Tue and Fri, and *Tur Bus*, Wed, stop in San Pedro en route from Antofagasta/Calama to **Salta**, reserve in advance and book Salta hotel as bus arrives 0100-0200 (schedules change often).

Directory **Banks** There is no bank or ATM, so take plenty of pesos: only place that changes TCs is *cambio* on Toconao, 1030-1800 daily, poor rates. Some agencies and hotels change dollars. **Communications** Internet: *in Café Adobe , Caracoles, and Café Étnico, Tocopilla. Post Office: G Paige s/n, opposite museum. Mon-Fri 0830-1230, 1400-1800, Sat morning only. Telephone: CTC, Caracoles y Toconao, 0900-1300, 1800-2000, public fax 851052. Entel on the plaza, Mon-Fri 0900-2200, Sat 0930-2200, Sun 0930-2100.*

Border with Bolivia & Argentina
At all border crossings, incoming vehicles and passengers are searched for fruit, vegetables and dairy produce, which may not be brought into Chile

Hito Cajón for the border with Bolivia is reached by a poor road 45 km east from San Pedro. From the border it is 7 km north to Laguna Verde. Chilean immigration and customs are in San Pedro, open 0900-1200, 1400-1600. For the Bolivian consulate, see under Calama. ■ *The only transport to Bolivia is that arranged in advance with tour companies in Uyuni (see Turismo Colque, above).*

For Argentina, the **Paso de Jama** (4,200 m) is reached by a poor road, which continues on the Argentine side to Susques and Jujuy. This is more popular than the **Paso Sico** route. (see below) Chilean immigration and customs are in San Pedro. When crossing by private vehicle, check the road conditions before setting out as Paso de Jama can be closed by heavy rain in summer and blocked by snow in winter.

Border with Argentina: Socompa
The Chilean side is open 0800-2200. On the Argentine side the road carries on to San Antonio de los Cobres and Salta. Argentine immigration is at San Antonio de los Cobres. See page 137. When crossing with a private vehicle, US$2 is charged between 1300-1500 and 1860-2100.

Santiago

The Far North

The Atacama Desert extends over most of the Far North to the Peruvian border. The main cities are Iquique and Arica; between them are old mineral workings and even older geoglyphs. Large areas of the Andean highland have been set aside as national parks.

The Cordillera de la Costa slowly loses height north of Iquique, terminating at the Morro at Arica: from Iquique north it drops directly to the sea and as a result there are few beaches along this coast. Inland the central depression (pampa) 1,000-1,200 m is arid and punctuated by salt-flats south of Iquique. Between Iquique and Arica it is crossed from east to west by four gorges. East of this depression lies the sierra, the western branch of the Andes, beyond which is a high plateau, the altiplano (3,500-4,500 m) from which rise volcanic peaks. In the altiplano there are a number of lakes, the largest of which, Lago Chungará, is one of the highest in the world.

Climate The coastal strip and the pampa are rainless; on the coast temperatures are moderated by the Pacific, but in the pampa variations of temperature between day and night are extreme, ranging from 30° C to 0° C. In the *sierra* temperatures are lower, averaging 20° C in summer and 9° C in winter. The *altiplano* is much colder, temperatures averaging 10° C in summer and -5° C in winter. Both the *sierra* and the *altiplano* receive rain in summer. Around Iquique the rainy season is mainly in Jan.

Iquique

The name of the capital of I Región (Tarapacá) and one of the main northern ports, is derived from the Aymara word *ique-ique*, meaning place of 'rest and tranquillity'. The city is situated on a rocky peninsula at the foot of the high Atacama pampa, sheltered by the headlands of Punta Gruesa and Cavancha. The city, which was partly destroyed by earthquake in 1877, became the centre of the nitrate trade after its transfer from Peru to Chile at the end of the War of the Pacific. A short distance north of town along Amunátegui is the Free Zone (Zofri), a giant shopping centre selling all manner of imported items, including electronic goods: it is worth a visit (much better value than Punta Arenas), good for cheap camera film (Fuji slide film available). ■ *Mon-Sat 0800-2100. Limit on tax free purchases US$650 for foreigners, US$500 for Chileans. Colectivo from the centre US$0.50.*

Phone code: 057
Colour map 6, grid B2
Population: 145,139
492 km N of
Antofagasta
47 km W of the
Pan-American
Highway

   The beaches at Cavancha just south of the town centre are good; those at Huaiquique are reasonable, November-March. There are restaurants at Cavancha. Piscina Godoy is a fresh water swimming pool on Av Costanera at Aníbal Pinto and Riquelme, open in the afternoon, US$1.

Iquique has some of
the best surfing in
Chile, not for beginners

In the centre of the old town is **Plaza Prat** with a clock tower and bell dating from 1877. On the northeast corner of the Plaza is the **Centro Español**, built in Moorish style by the local Spanish community in 1904; the ground floor is a restaurant, on the upper floors are paintings of scenes from Don Quijote and from Spanish history. On the south side of the Plaza is the **Teatro Municipal** built in 1890; the façade features four women representing the seasons. Three blocks north of the Plaza is the old **Aduana** (customs house) built in 1871; in 1891 it was the scene of an important battle in the Civil War between supporters of President Balmaceda and congressional forces. Part of it is now the **Museo Naval**, focusing on the Battle of Iquique, 1879. Along C Baquedano, which runs south from Plaza Prat, are the attractive former mansions of the 'nitrate barons', dating from between 1880 and 1903. The finest of these is the **Palacio Astoreca**, Baquedano y O'Higgins, built in 1903, subsequently the Intendencia and now a museum of fine late 19th century furniture and shells. ■ *Tue-Fri 1000-1400, 1500-1900, Sat-Sun 1000-1300, US$1.* **Museo Regional**, Baquedano 951, contains an archaeological section tracing the development of prehispanic civilizations in the region; an ethnographical collection of the Isluga culture of the Altiplano (AD 400), and of contemporary Aymara culture; also a section devoted to the nitrate era which includes a model of a nitrate office and the collection of the nitrate entrepreneur, Santiago Humberstone. ■ *Mon-Fri 0800-1300, 1500-1850, Sat 1030-1300, Sun (in summer) 1000-1300, 1600-2000.*

Sights

   Sea lions and pelicans can be seen from the harbour. There are cruises from the passenger pier. ■ *US$2.50, 45 mins, minimum 10-15 people.*

   The tourist office is at Serrano 145, of 303, T427686, sernatur_iquiq@entelchile.net Masses of information, helpful. ■ *Mon-Fri, 0830-1630. Automóvil Club de Chile, Serrano 154, T426772.*

To **Humberstone**, a large nitrate town, now abandoned, at the junction of the Pan-American Highway and the road to Iquique. Though closed since 1961, you can see the church, theatre, *pulpería* (company stores) and the swimming pool (built of metal plating from ships' hulls). ■ *Entry by 'donation', US$1.50, guided tours Sat-Sun, leaflets available. Colectivo from Iquique US$2; phone near site for booking return.* Nearby are the ruins of other mining towns including Santa Laura. Local tour companies run trips to the area, including Humberstone, Santa Laura, Pisagua and

Excursions
Many other sites
around Iquique,
including the Giant
of the Atacama
(see page 659),
are difficult to visit
without a vehicle

Pozo Almonte, 52 km east (population about 5,400). This town was the chief service provider of the nitrate companies until their closure in 1960. The **Museo Histórico Salitrero**, on the tree-shaded plaza, displays artefacts and photographs of the nitrate era. ■ *Mon-Fri 0830-1300 and 1600-1900.*

To Cerro Pintados (see page 659) take any bus south, US$2.50, and walk from the Pan-American Highway then hitch back or flag down a bus.

Sleeping

Accommodation is scarce in the weeks before Christmas as many Chileans visit Iquique to shop in the Zofri. All hotels in list recommended

AL-A *Arturo Prat*, Plaza Prat, T411067, hap@entelchile.net 4-star, pool, health suite, expensive restaurant, tours arranged. **A-B** *Barros Arana*, Barros Arana 1330, T412840, hba@ctcreuna.cl Modern, pool, good value. **B** *Atenas*, Los Rieles 738, T431075. Pleasant, personal, good value, good service and food. **B** *Cano*, Ramírez 996, T416597, hotelcano@hotmail.com Big rooms, nice atmosphere, good value. **C** *Caiti*, Gorostiaga 483, T/F423038. Pleasant, with breakfast and all mod cons. **C** *Inti-Llanka*, Obispo Labbé 825, T311104, F311105. Nice rooms, helpful, good value. **D** *Hostal América*, Rodríguez 550, near beach, T427524. Shared bath, no breakfast, motorcycle parking, good value. **D** *Danino*, Serrano 897, T417301, F443079. With breakfast, free local phone calls, modern, good value. **E** pp *Durana*, San Martín 294, T410959. Central, hot water, breakfast included. **E** pp *Hostal Cuneo*, Baquedano 1175, T428654. Modern, nice rooms, helpful, pleasant, good value. **D** pp *Hostal Jean IV*, Esmeralda 938, T/F510855, mespina@entelchile.net With breakfast, nice lounge and patio, convenient for buses to Bolivia, excellent value. **E** pp *Res Nan-King*, Thompson 752, T423311. Small but nice rooms. **F** pp *Casa de Huéspedes Profesores*, Ramirez 839, T314692, inostrozaflores@entelchile.net With breakfast, helpful, old building with lots of character. **F** pp *Hostal Li Ming*, Barros Arana 705, T421912, F422707. Simple, good value, small rooms.

Eating

Beware of the expensive and poor value tourist restaurants on the wharf on the opposite side of Av Costanera from the bus terminal. Several good, cheap seafood restaurants on the 2nd floor of the central market, Barros Arana y Latorre

Expensive: *Bavaria*, Pinto 926. Expensive restaurant, reasonably priced café serving real coffee, snacks and *almuerzo*. *Casino Español*, good meals well served in beautiful building, and *Club de la Unión*, roof terrace with panoramic views, open lunchtimes only, both on Plaza Prat. *Otelo*, Valenzuela 775. Italian specialities, seafood. **Mid-range**: *El Barril del Fraile*, Ramírez 1181. Good seafood, nice atmosphere. *Colonial*, Plaza Prat. Fish and seafood, popular, good value. *Sciaraffia*, Sgto Aldea 803 (Mercado Centenario). Open 24 hrs, good value, large choice. **Cheap**: *Bolivia*, Serrano 751. *Humitas* and *salteñas*. Recommended. *Compañía Italiana de Bomberos*, Serrano 520. Authentic Italian cuisine, excellent value *almuerzo*, otherwise more expensive. *La Picada Curicana*, Pinto y Zegers. Good local cuisine, good value *menu de la casa*. Many *chifas* including *Win Li*, San Martin 439, and *Sol Oriental*, Martínez 2030 and 6 cheaper ones on Tarapacá 800/900 blocks. **Cafés** *Cioccolata*, Pinto 487 (another branch in the Zofri). Very good. *Splendid*, Vivar 795. Good *onces*, inexpensive. *Salon de Té Ricotta*, Vivar y Latorre. Very popular for *onces*, quite expensive. For juices, snacks: *Tropical*, Baquedano y Thompson; *Via Pontony*, Baquedano y Zegers; *Jugos Tarapacá*, Tarapacá 380. **Bars** *Santa Fé*, Mall Las Américas, locales 10-11-193. Mexican, live music, great atmosphere, very popular. *Taberna Barracuda*, Gorostiaga 601. For late night food, drink, video entertainment, dancing, nice décor, nice atmosphere.

Tour operators

The tourist office maintains a full list

Empresas Turísticas, Baquedano 958, T/F416600. Good tours, student discount, ask for guide Jaime Vega González. *Iquitour*, Lynch 563, T/F412415. Tour to Pintados, La Tirana, Humberstone, Pica, etc, day tours start at US$20. *Viatours*, Baquedano 736, T/F417197, viatours@entelchile.net

Transport

Local **Car hire**: *Iqsa*, Labbé 1089, T/F417068. *Procar*, Serrano 796, T/F413470.

Long distance **Air**: Diego Aracena international airport, 35 km south at Chucumata. Taxi US$9.50; airport transfer, T310800, US$3.20 for 3 or more passengers, unreliable. *LanChile*, *Lan Express* and *Aerocontinente* fly to **Arica**, **Antofagasta** and **Santiago**. *Lan Chiledeco* flies to **La Serena**. See Getting there, Essentials, for international flights.

Buses: Terminal at north end of Patricio Lynch (not all buses leave from here); bus company offices are near the market on Sgto Aldea and B Arana. *Tur Bus*, Ramírez y Esmeralda, with *Redbanc* ATM and luggage store. Southbound buses are searched for duty-free goods, at Quillagua on the Pan-American Highway and at Chipana on the coastal Route 1. To **Arica**, buses and colectivos, frequent, US$5, 4½ hrs. To **Antofagasta**, US$9, 8 hrs. To **Calama**, 8 hrs, US$7. To **Tocopilla** along the coastal road, buses and minibuses, several companies, 4 hrs, US$4. To **La Serena**, 17 hrs, US$20. To **Santiago**, 28 hrs, several companies, US$30 (US$50 *salón cama*).

International buses: to Bolivia *Litoral*, T423670, daily to **Oruro**, US$8, and **La Paz**, US$12. *Bernal, Paraíso, Salvador*, and others from Esmeralda near Juan Martínez around 2100-2300, US$8-13 (may have a cold wait for customs to open at 0800).

Airline offices *LanChile*, Tarapacá 465, T427600, and in Mall Las Américas. **Banks** Numerous *Redbanc* ATMs in the centre and the Zofri. *Cambios: Afex*, Serrano 396, for TCs. *Money Exchange*, Lynch 548, loc 1-2. Best rates for TCs and cash at *casas de cambio* in the Zofri, eg *Wall Street* (sells and cashes Amex TCs). **Communications** Internet: *Fassher Internet*, Vivar 1497, p 2. US$0.80 per hr. Same price is *PC@NET Computación*, Vivar 1373. More central is *Obispo Labbé y Serrano*, US$1.50 per hr. **Post Office:** *Correo Central*, Bolívar 485. **Telephone:** *CTC*, Serrano 620. *Entel*, Tarapacá 476. **NB** Correos and phone companies all have offices in the Plaza de Servicios in the Zofri. **Consulates** Bolivia, Gorostiaga 215, Departamento E, T421777. Mon-Fri 0930-1200. Italy, Serrano 447, T421588. **Netherlands**, Manzana 11, Galpón 2, Zofri, T426074. **Peru**, Zegers 570, T411466. **Spain**, Manzana 2, Sitio 5 y 9, Zofri, T422330. **Language schools** *Academia de Idiomas del Norte*, Ramírez 1345, T411827, F429343, idiomas@chilesat.net Swiss run, Spanish classes and accommodation for students.

Directory

From Pozo Almonte 74 km (paved), **Mamiña** (*Population*: about 600. *Altitude*: 2,750 m) has abundant thermal springs and a mud spring (Baño Los Chinos; open 0930-1300). The therapeutic properties of the waters and mud are Mamiña's main claim to fame. Mineral water from the spring is sold throughout northern Chile. There are ruins of a pre-hispanic *pukará* (fortress) and a church, built in 1632, the only colonial Andean church in Chile with two towers. An Aymara cultural centre, *Kaspi-kala*, has an *artesanía* workshop and outlet. **Sleeping** There are several hotels and *residenciales* offering rooms with bath fed by the springs and full board. They include **B** pp *Los Cardenales*, T438182, T09-545 1091 (mob). Beautifully designed, comfortable, superb food, English and German spoken, pool. **B** pp *Refugio del Salitre*, T751203, T420330. Secluded, nice rooms, pool. **C** pp *Termal La Coruña*, T09-543 0360. Good, Spanish cuisine, horse riding, nice views. **C** pp *Llama Inn*, T Iquique 419893. Room only, good meals extra (including vegetarian on request), comfortable, pool, English spoken. ■ *Getting there:* Transportes Tamarugal, *Barros Arana 897, Iquique, daily 0800, 1600, return 1800, 0800, 2½ hrs, US$4, good service. Also Mamiña, Latorre 779, daily.*

Around Iquique

Chile

La Tirana (*Population*: 550. *Altitude*: 995 m) is famous for a religious festival to the Virgen del Carmen, held from 10 to 16 July, which attracts some 80,000 pilgrims. Over 100 groups dance night and day, starting on 12 July. All the dances take place in the main plaza in front of the church; no alcohol is served. Accommodation is impossible to find, other than in organized camp sites (take tent) which have basic toilets and showers. It is 10 km east of the Pan-American Highway (70 km east of Iquique), turn-off 9 km south of Pozo Almonte.

Pica (*Population*: 1,767. *Altitude*: 1,325 m), 42 km from La Tirana, was the most important centre of early Spanish settlement in the area. Most older buildings date from the nitrate period when it became a popular resort. The town is famous for its pleasant climate, citrus groves and two natural springs, the best of which is Cocha Resbaladero. ■ *0700-2000 all year, US$2, snack bar, changing rooms, beautiful pool. Tourist office.* **Sleeping and eating C** *Suizo*, Ibáñez 210, T741551. Austrian-Danish owners, with shower, TV, modem, comfortable, parking, excellent food in café. **D** *Los Emilios*, Cochrane 213, T741126. Pool, with breakfast. **D** *San Andrés*, Balmaceda 197, T741319. With breakfast, basic, good restaurant. **D** *El Tambo*, Ibáñez 68, T741041. House dates from nitrate era, shared bath, hot water, good value, *cabañas* for rent. Under same ownership is **D** *O'Higgins*, Balmaceda 6.

Try the local alfajores, delicious cakes filled with cream and mango honey

Modern, well furnished. Campsite at *Camping Miraflores*, near terminal, T741338, also rents *cabañas* as do 3 other places. *El Edén*, Riquelme 12. 1st class local food in delightful surroundings. On Balmaceda, *La Palmera*, No 115, and *La Mía Pappa*, both good. *La Viña*, Ibáñez 70. Good cheap *almuerzo*. ■ *Getting there: Minibus Iquique-Pica: San Andrés, Sgto Aldea y B Arana, Iquique, daily 0930, return 1800;* Pullman Chacón, *Barros Arana y Latorre, many daily;* Santa Rosa, *Barros Arana 777, daily 0830, 0930, return 1700, 1800. US$2.50 one-way, 2 hrs.*

From Iquique to the Bolivian Border

At **Huara** (population 450), 33 km north of Pozo Almonte, a road turns off the Pan-American Highway to **Colchane**. At 13 km east of Huara are the huge geoglyphs of **Cerro Unitas**, with the giant humanoid figure of the Gigante del Atacama and a sun with 24 rays, on the sides of two hills (best seen from a distance). This road is in a terrible state, with long-term roadworks and a diversion heavily damaged by lorries. ■ *Some buses from Iquique to La Paz and Oruro pass through, or* La Paloma *at 2300 from Esmeralda y Juan Martínez.*

173 km northeast is the Bolivian border at Pisiga. ■ *Daily 0800-1300, 1500-1800.*

Some of the best volcanic scenery in northern Chile

Northwest of Colchane, the **Parque Nacional Volcán Isluga** covers 174,744 ha at altitudes above 2,100 m. The village of **Isluga**, near the park entrance, 6 km north-west of Colchane, has an 18th century Andean walled church and bell tower. Wild-life varies according to altitude but includes guanacos, vicuñas, llamas, alpacas, vizcachas, condors and flamingoes. ■ *Park Administration at Enquelga, 10 km north of the entrance, but guardaparques are seldom there. Phone Arica 58-250570 for details of* hospedaje *at the* guardería *(D pp).*

North towards Arica

The Pan-American Highway runs across the Atacama desert at an altitude of around 1,000 m, with several steep hills which are best tackled in daylight (at night, sea mist, camanchaca, can reduce visibility)

At Zapiga, 80 km north of Pozo Almonte, there is a crossroads: east through **Camiña** (*Population*: 500. *Altitude*: 2,400 m), a picturesque village in an oasis, 67 km east of Zapiga along a poor road. Thence mountain roads lead across the Parque Nacional Volcán Isluga to Colchane. The westerly branch runs 41 km to **Pisagua** (*Population*: 200), formerly an important nitrate port, now a fishing village. Several old wooden buildings are National Monuments. The fish restaurants make a pleasant stop for a meal. Mass graves dating from just after the 1973 military coup were discovered near here in 1990. At Km 57 north of Huara there is a British cemetery at Tiliviche dating from 1825. The **Geoglyphs of Tiliviche** representing a group of llamas (signposted, to left, and easily accessible), Km 127, can be seen from the highway.

Arica

Phone code: 058
Colour map 6, grid A1
Population: 174,064

Chile's most northerly city, 20 km south of the Peruvian border, is built at the foot of the Morro headland, fringed by sand dunes. The Andes can be clearly seen from the anchorage. Arica used to be the principal route for travellers going overland to Bolivia, via the Parque Nacional Lauca. Now there is competition from the San Pedro de Atacama-Uyuni route, so new routes are being considered to link this part of the coast with San Pedro, via the high altitude national parks.

This is an important port and route-centre. The road route to La Paz via Tambo Colorado is now paved and Arica is frequented for sea-bathing by Bolivians, as well as the locals. A 63-km railway runs north to Tacna in Peru. Regrettably, Arica is also becoming a key link in the international drugs trade.

Sights

The **Morro**, with a good view from the park on top (10 minutes' walk by footpath from the southern end of Colón), was the scene of a great victory by Chile over Peru in the War of the Pacific on 7 June 1880. **Museo Histórico y de Armas**, on the sum-mit of the Morro, contains weapons and uniforms from the War of the Pacific. ■ *Daily 0830-2000 (2200 Jan-Feb), US$0.60.*

At the foot of the Morro is the Plaza Colón with the cathedral of **San Marcos**, built in iron by Eiffel. Though small it is beautifully proportioned and attractively painted. It was brought to Arica from Ilo (Peru) in the 19th century, before Peru lost Arica to Chile, as an emergency measure after a tidal wave swept over Arica and destroyed all its churches. Eiffel also designed the nearby **Aduana** (customs house) which is now the Casa de la Cultura. ■ *Mon-Fri 0830-2100.* Just north of the Aduana is the La Paz railway station; outside is an old steam locomotive (made in Germany in 1924) once used on this line. In the station is a memorial to John Roberts Jones, builder of the Arica portion of the railway. The **Casa Bolognesi**, Colón y Yungay, is a fine old building painted blue and white. It holds temporary exhibitions.

The tourist office, *Sernatur*, is at San Marcos 101, T252054, a kiosk next to the Casa de la Cultura. Very helpful, English spoken, good map, list of tour companies. ■ *Mon-Fri 0830-1330, 1500-1900.* Head office is at Prat 305, p 2,T232101, sernatur_arica@entelchile.net A municipal kiosk is also on San Marcos, opposite Sernatur, opens at 0830.

Excursions

To the Azapa valley, east of Arica, by yellow colectivo from P Lynch y Chacabuco and 600 block of P Lynch, US$1. At Km 13 is the **Museo Arqueológico de San Miguel** of the University of Tarapacá, built around an olive press. It contains a fine collection of precolumbian weaving, pottery, wood carving and basketwork from the coast and valleys, and also seven mummified humans from the Chinchorro culture (8000-1000 BC), the most ancient mummies yet discovered. Explanations in several languages are loaned free at the entrance. ■ *Daily Jan-Feb 0900-2000, Mar-Dec 1000-1800, US$2. Worth a visit. T224248, www.uta.cl/masma/* In the forecourt of the museum are several boulders with precolumbian petroglyphs. In San Miguel itself is an old cemetery and several typical restaurants. On the road between Arica and San Miguel there are several groups of geoglyphs of humans and llamas ('stone mosaics') south of the road (signed to Cerro Sagrado, Cerro Sombrero – an Azapa Archaeological Circuit is advertised).

To the **Lluta valley**, north of Arica along Route 11, bus from Mackenna y Chacabuco. Between Km 14 and Km 16 can be seen along the hillsides four groups of geoglyphs, representing llamas, and eagle and human giants. The road continues through the Parque Nacional Lauca and on to Bolivia.

Sleeping

In Jan-Feb the municipality supplies cheap basic accommodation, ask at the tourist office. Cheap residenciales on Prat 500 block, Velázquez 700 block, P Lynch 600 block. Others opposite bus terminal

L *Arica*, San Martín 599, T254540, F231133, about 2 km along shore (frequent micros and colectivos). Best, price depends on season, good value, good and reasonable restaurant, tennis court, pool, lava beach (not safe for swimming), American breakfast. **L** *El Paso*, Gen Velásquez 1109, T231965. Bungalow style, pleasant gardens, swimming pool, with breakfast, good restaurant *Araksaya*. **A** *Savona*, Yungay 380, T232319, F231606. Comfortable, quiet. Highly recommended. **A** *Volapuk*, 21 de Mayo 425, T252575, volapuk@ctcreuna.cl Good service, nicely decorated, with breakfast, hot water, TV, a/c. **B** *Diego de Almagro*, Sotomayor 490, T224444, F221248. Helpful, comfortable, parking, stores luggage. Recommended (but ask for a room without a balcony as these are not secure). **B** *Plaza Colón*, San Marcos 261, T/F231244, hotel_plaza_colon@entelchile.net With breakfast, comfortable, convenient. **C** *Hotel D'Marie-Jeanne y David*, Velásquez 792, T/F258231. With breakfast, TV, laundry, parking, snacks in café, French spoken. **C** *Sotomayor*, Sotomayor 367, T232149, reservas@hotelsotomayor.cl Comfortable, helpful, restaurant, parking, cheaper if paying in dollars. **D** *Res América*, Sotomayor 430, T254148. **F** pp without bath, hot water, hospitable, breakfast included if staying more than 1 day. **D** *Hostal Jardín del Sol*, Sotomayor 848, T232795, F231462. With breakfast, quiet, safe, laundry. Recommended. **D** *Res Las Condes*, Vicuña Mackenna 628, T251583. Helpful, hot showers, kitchen, motorcycle parking. Recommended. **D** *Res Nilda*, Raúl del Canto 947, T222743. Very nice *casa de familia*, kitchen facilities, laundry, near bus terminal and Playa Chinchorro. **D** *Hostal Venecia*, Baquedano 741, T255937, F252877. Spotless, small rooms. Recommended.

E *Hostal Chez Charlie*, Paseo Thompson 236, T/F250007, latinor@entelchile.net Central, comfortable, shared bath, hot water, good value, French and English spoken (same owner as *La Ciboulette* and *Latinorizons*). **E** *Hostal Ecuador*, Juan Noé 989, T/F251934. With breakfast, very helpful, kitchen, laundry. **E** *Res Las Vegas*, Baquedano 120, T231355. Basic, dark rooms,

Chile

Chile

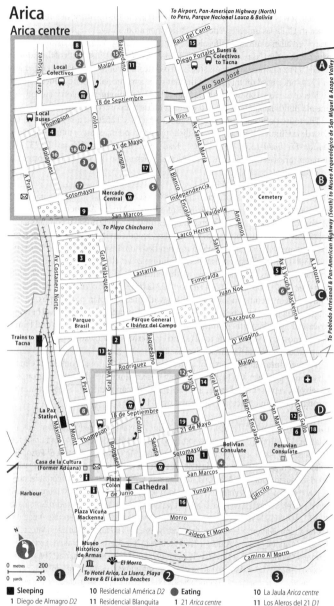

Arica
Arica centre

Sleeping
1 Diego de Almagro *D2*
2 D'Marie-Jeanne
   y David *C1*
3 El Paso *C1*
4 Hostal Chez Charlie
   & La Ciboulette
   Restaurant *Arica centre*
5 Hostal Ecuador *C3*
6 Hostal Jardín del Sol *C3*
7 Hostal Venecia *D2*
8 Mar Azul *Arica centre*
9 Plaza Colón *Arica centre*

10 Residencial América *D2*
11 Residencial Blanquita
   Arica centre
12 Residencial Caracas *D3*
13 Residencial Chillán *D1*
14 Residencial El Sur *D2*
15 Residencial Nilda *A2*
16 Savona *E2*
17 Sotomayor *Arica centre*
18 Stagnaro *D3*
19 Volapuk *D2*

Eating
1 21 *Arica centre*
2 Bavaria *Arica centre*
3 Caffelatte, Helados Di
   Mango & Altillo
   Arica centre
4 Chin Huang Tao *D2*
5 D'Aurelio *Arica centre*
6 Don Floro *C3*
7 El Rey del Marisco
   Arica centre
8 Kau Chea *D1*
9 La Bomba *Arica centre*

10 La Jaula *Arica centre*
11 Los Aleros del 21 *D1*
12 Panadería Belo Ortiz *D2*
13 Panadería/Pastelería
   Loredo *D2*
14 Papagallo *Arica centre*
15 San Fernando *Arica centre*
16 Scala & Schop 21
   Arica centre
17 Shaolin *Arica centre*
18 Tortas y Tartas
   Arica centre
19 Yuri *D2*

safe, central. **E** pp *Mar Azul*, Colón 665, T256272, www.hotelmarazul.cl Small rooms and family rooms, fan, TV, restaurant, small pool, sauna. **E** *Stagnaro*, Arturo Gallo 294, T231254. With breakfast, good value. Recommended. **F** pp *Res Blanquita*, Maipú 472, T232064. Breakfast extra, laundry and kitchen facilities. **F** pp *Res Caracas*, Sotomayor 867, T253688. Breakfast included. **F** *Res Chillán*, Velásquez 747, T251677. Hot shower, laundry, nice garden. **F** pp *Res El Sur*, Maipú 516, T252457. Small rooms, shared bath, basic. **F** *Sunny Days*, Tomás Aravena 161 (lane off P de Valdivia, 800 m from bus terminal), T241058, sunnydaysarica@ hotmail.com Run by a New Zealander, nice atmosphere, lots of information. Recommended.

    Camping *Gallinazos*, at Villa Frontera, 15 km north, T232373. Full facilities, pool. *El Refugio de Azapa*, Valle de Azapa, Km 1.5, T227545.

Mid-range: *Bavaria*, Colón 613, upstairs. Good restaurant, coffee and cakes. *D'Aurelio*, Baquedano 369. Italian specialities, good pasta, seafood. *Don Floro*, V MacKenna 847. Good seafood and steaks, good service. Highly recommended. *El Rey del Marisco*, Maipú y Colón, upstairs. Excellent seafood. *Los Aleros del 21*, 21 de Mayo 736. Recommended for seafood and service. *Maracuyá*, San Martín 0321. Seafood, splendid location on the coast. *Chin Huang Tao*, Lynch 224. Excellent Chinese. **Cheap**: *Acuario*, Muelle Turístico. Good food in fishy environment, good value *menu de casa*. *La Bomba*, Colón 357, at fire station. Good value *almuerzo*, friendly service. *La Ciboulette*, Paseo Thompson 238. Good food, pleasant atmosphere. Recommended. *La Jaula*, 21 de Mayo 293. Snacks, meals, good. *Papagallo*, Colón 639. Lunches, juices, extensive menu. *Yuri*, Maipú y Lynch. Good service, cheap lunches. Recommended. Cheaper Chinese restaurants include *Kau Chea*, 18 de Septiembre y Prat, good value, and *Shaolin*, Sotomayor 275. There are many cheap restaurants on Baquedano 600/700 blocks including *San Fernando*, corner with Maipú. Simple breakfast, good value *almuerzo*. **Cafés** Many good places on 21 de Mayo and offering meals, drinks, real coffee, juices and outdoor seating: *Caffelatte*, No 248; *Helados Di Mango*, No 244; *Scala*, No 201; *Schop 21*; *Tortas y Tartas*, No 233; *21*, No 301, also restaurant and residencial. At No 260 (above *Globo Tour*) is *Altillo* pub. *Panadería/pastelería Loredo*, No 481, smart. Bread also at *Panadería Belo Ortiz*, P Lynch 651.

Eating
The centre is full of eating places, mainly chicken or fast food types, beer and sandwiches

Theatre *Teatro Municipal de Arica*, Baquedano 234. Wide variety of theatrical and musical events, exhibitions. Recommended.

Entertainment

Poblado Artesanal, Plaza Las Gredas, Hualles 2825 (take bus 2, 3 or 7). Expensive but especially good for musical instruments, open Tue-Sun 0930-1300, 1530-1930, *peña* Fri and Sat 2130. *Mercado Central*, Sotomayor y Sangra, between Colón and Baquedano. Mostly fruit and vegetables. Smaller fruit and veg market, with food stalls, on Colón between 18 de Septiembre and Maipú. *Feria Turística Dominical*, Sun market, along Chacabuco between Valásquez and Mackenna. Good prices for llama sweaters. **Bookshop** *Andrés Bello*, Sotomayor 363, wide selection.

Shopping
Many shopping galerías in the centre, also pharmacies, electrical appliances and clothes shops Ferias for clothes on Velázquez

Swimming: Olympic pool in Parque Centenario, Tue-Sun, US$0.50. Take No 5A bus from 18 de Septiembre. The best beach for swimming is Playa Chinchorro, north of town. Buses 7 and 8 run to beaches south of town – the first two beaches, La Lisera and El Laucho, are both small and mainly for sunbathing. Playa Brava is popular for sunbathing but not swimming (dangerous currents). Strong currents also at Playa Las Machas which is popular with surfers. Good surfing on La Isleta near Club de Yates and on Playa Chinchorro.

Sport

Globo Tour, 21 de Mayo 260, T/F231085. Very helpful for international flights. *Latinorizons*, Bolognesi 439, T/F250007, latinor@entelchile.net Specializes in tours to Parque Nacional Lauca, small groups in four-wheel drive Landcruiser; also bike rental. Recommended. Several others. Agencies charge similar prices for tours: Valle de Azapa US$12; city tour US$10; Parque Nacional Lauca, see page 675.

Tour operators

Local Bus: buses run from 18 de Septiembre at Bolognesi, US$0.25. Colectivos on fixed routes within city limit line up on Maipú entre Velásquez y Colón (all are numbered), US$0.50

Transport

Chile

pp (more after 2000). Taxis are black and yellow and are scarce; hire a colectivo instead, US$1.20-1.50. **Car hire**: *American*, Gen Lagos 559, T252234, servturi@entelchile.net *Cactus*, Baquedano 635, T257430, cactusrent@latinmail.com *Ghama*, Diego Portaqles 840, of 161, T225158. Several others and at Chacalluta airport. Rates start at US$26 per day, up to US$50-60 for 4WD. Antifreeze is essential for Parque Nacional Lauca, 4WD if going off paved roads. **Motoring Automóvil Club de Chile**: Chacabuco 460, T252878, F232780. **Car insurance**: at **Dirección de Tránsito**; may insist on car inspection.

Long distance Air: Airport 18 km north of city at Chacalluta, T222831. Taxi to town US$9, colectivo US$4-5 pp. Flights: to **La Paz**, *LanChile*; to **Santiago**, *LanChile*, *Lan Express* and *Aerocontinente* via Iquique and, less frequently, Antofagasta. To **Lima**, from Tacna (Peru), enquire at travel agencies in Arica.

Buses: Bus terminal at Av Portales y Santa María, T241390, many buses and colectivos (eg No 8) pass (US$0.25, or US$0.50); terminal tax US$0.15. All luggage is carefully searched for fruit prior to boarding. Bus company offices at bus terminal. Local services: *Flota Paco (La Paloma)*, Germán Riesco 2071 (bus U from centre).

To **Iquique**, frequent, US$5, 4½ hrs, also collective taxis, several companies, all in the terminal. To **Antofagasta**, US$10, 10 hrs. To **Calama** and **Chuquicamata**, 12 hrs, US$9, several companies, all between 2000 and 2200. To **La Serena**, 18 hrs, US$14-20. To **Santiago**, 28 hrs, a number of companies, eg *Carmelita*, *Ramos Cholele*, *Fénix* and *Flota Barrios* US$22-26, also *salón cama* services, run by *Fichtur*, *Flota Barrios*, *Fénix* and others, US$34 (most serve meals of a kind, somewhat better on the more expensive services; student discounts available). To **Viña del Mar** and **Valparaíso**, US$26, also *salón cama* services.

International buses: to La Paz, Bolivia, at least 6 companies from terminal, US$10-12, most via **Putre** and **Chungará** (some daily); for Visviri/Charaña route, see below. *Géminis*, T241647, to **Jujuy** and **Salta**, Argentina, Tue and Sat.

Motorists: It is illegal to take fruit and dairy products south of Arica: all vehicles are searched at Cuya, 105 km south, and at Huara, 234 km south. **Service stations** between the Peruvian border and Santiago can be found at: Arica, Huara, Iquique, Pozo Almonte, Oficina Victoria, Tocopilla, Oficina María Elena, Chuquicamata, Calama, Carmen Alto, Antofagasta, La Negra, Agua Verde (also fruit inspection post), Taltal, Chañaral, Caldera, Copiapó, Vallenar, La Serena, Termas de Soco, Los Vilos, and then every 30 km to capital.
By road to Bolivia: There are 2 routes:
1) Via **Chungará** (Chile) and **Tambo Quemado** (Bolivia). This, the most widely used route, begins by heading north from Arica on the Pan-American Highway (Route 5) for 12 km before turning right (east towards the cordillera) on Route 11 towards Chungará via Putre and Parque Nacional Lauca. This road is now paved to La Paz, estimated driving time 6 hrs.
2) Via **Visviri** (Chile) and **Charaña** (Bolivia), following the La Paz-Arica railway line. This route should not be attempted in wet weather.

Directory **Airline offices** *LanChile*, 21 de Mayo 345, T255941 (closes 1330 on Sat). *Aero Continente*, 21 de Mayo 421. **Banks** Many *Redbanc* ATMs on 21 de Mayo and by Plaza Colón. Money changers on 21 de Mayo and its junction with Colón, some accept TCs. *Cambio*, in Cosmo Center, Colón 600, cash and TCs, reasonable rates. **Communications** Internet: Plenty of *locutorios* with internet and cyber cafés in the centre, eg on 21 de Mayo or Bolognesi, average price US$0.75-1 per hr. *Virtual Home*, Velázquez 650, p 1, lots of machines, quick. Post Office: Prat 375, down pedestrian walkway. Mon-Fri 0830-1330, 1500-1900, Sat 0900-1230. To send parcels abroad, contents must be shown to Aduana (first floor of post office) on Mon-Fri 0800-1200. Your parcel will be wrapped, cheaply, but take your own carton. *DHL*, Colón 351. Telephone: *Entel-Chile*, 21 de Mayo 345. Open 0900-2200. *CTC*, Colón 430 and at 21 de Mayo 211. Many other phone offices. **Consulates** Bolivia, P Lynch 298, T231030. **Peru**, San Martín 235, T231020. **Cultural institutes**: Instituto Chileno-Británico de Cultura (library open Mon-Fri 0900-1200, 1600-2100), Baquedano 351, T232399, Casilla 653. **Useful addresses** Conaf, Av Vicuña MacKenna 820, T250570. Mon-Fri 0830-1300, 1430-1630 (take Colectivo 1). Aug-Nov is best season for mountain climbing; permits needed for summits near borders. Write, fax or visit **Dirección Nacional de Fronteras y Límites del Estado** (DIFROL) Bandera 52, p 5, Santiago, F56-2-697 1909.

Immigration is open 0800-2400; a fairly uncomplicated crossing. For Peruvian immigration, see page 1208. When crossing by private vehicle, US$2 per vehicle is charged between 1300-1500, 1850-2400 and on Saturday, Sunday, holidays. Drivers entering Chile are required to file a form, *Relaciones de Pasajeros*, giving details of passengers, obtained from a stationery store in Tacna, or at the border in a booth near Customs. You must also present the original registration document for your car from its country of registration. The first checkpoints outside Arica on the road to Santiago also require the *Relaciones de Pasajeros* form. If you can't buy the form, details on a piece of paper will suffice or you can get them at service stations. The form is *not* required when travelling south of Antofagasta. There are exchange facilities at the border.

Border with Peru: Chacalluta-Tacna
Between Oct-Mar Chilean time is 1 hr later than Peruvian, 2 hrs later Oct-Feb/Mar, varies annually

Transport Colectivos: run from the international bus terminal on Diego Portales to **Tacna**, US$3 pp, 1½ hrs. There are many companies and you will be besieged by drivers. For quickest service take a Peruvian colectivo heading back to Peru. Give your passport to the colectivo office where your papers will be filled. After that, drivers take care of all the paperwork.*Chile Lintur*,T225038; *San Andrés*, T260167; *San Remo*, T260509; *El Morro*, T262477; *Perú Express*, T249970. Colectivos will pick you up from hotel. Also buses from the same terminal, US$1.50, 2½ hrs. For Arequipa it is best to go to Tacna and catch an onward bus there. **Train**: Station is at the end of Chacabuco, Arica-Tacna and vice versa 0500 and 1600, US$1 (no trains in late 2001).

Immigration is open 0800-2400. Chilean formalities at Visviri, Bolivian formalities at Charaña, 10 km east. See page 261. When crossing with a private vehicle, US$2 per vehicle is charged between 1300-1500, 1850-2100 and Saturday, Sunday and holidays.

Border with Bolivia: Visviri

Transport Buses from Arica to Visviri, *Humire*, T220198/260164, Tue and Fri, 1030, US$7, also Sun 0830 en route to La Paz; *Martínez*, Tue and Fri 2230 en route to La Paz, both from terminal. Colectivos from Arica US$10. In Visviri take a jeep across the border to Charaña. Buses from Charaña to La Paz, leave before 1000, US$11, 7 hrs. Trucks leave afternoon.

Parque Nacional Lauca

The Parque Nacional Lauca, stretching to the border with Bolivia, is one of the most spectacular national parks in Chile. On the way is a zone of giant candelabra cactus, between 2,300-2,800 m. At Km 90 there is a pre-Inca *pukará* (fortress) above the village of Copaquilla and, a few kilometres further, there is an Inca *tambo* (inn) at Zapahuira. Situated at elevations from 3,200 m to 6,340 m (beware of soroche unless you are coming from Bolivia), the park covers 137,883 ha and includes numerous snowy volcanoes including three peaks of over 6,000 m. At the foot of Volcán Parinacota and its twin, Pomerape (in Bolivia – they are known collectively as Payachatas), is a series of lakes among a jumble of rocks, called Cotacotani. Black lava flows can be seen above Cotacotani. **Lago Chungará** (4,517 m, 7 km by 3 km) is southeast of Payachatas, a must for its views of the Parinacota, Sajama and Guallatire volcanoes and for its varied wildlife. At the far end of the lake is the Chile/Bolivia border. The park contains over 140 species of bird, resident or migrant, as well as cameloids, vizcacha and puma. A good base for exploring the park and for acclimatization is **Putre** (*population*: 4,400; *altitude*: 3,500 m), a scenic village, 15 km before the entrance with a church dating from 1670 and surrounded by terracing dating from pre-Inca times, now used for cultivating alfalfa and oregano. From here paths provide easy walking and great views.

176 km E of Arica. Access is easy as the main Arica-La Paz road runs through the park and is paved. During the rainy season (Jan-Feb) roads in the park may be impassable; check in advance with Conaf in Arica. It can be foggy as well as wet in Jan-Mar

At **Parinacota** (4,392 m), at the foot of Payachatas, there is an interesting 17th century church – rebuilt 1789 – with 18th-century frescoes and the skulls of past priests (ask for the man with the key). Local residents knit alpaca sweaters, US$26 approximately; weavings of wildlife scenes also available. Weavings are sold from stalls outside the church. From here an unpaved road runs north to the Bolivian

Chile

Chile

border at Visviri (see above). You can climb Guane Guane, 5,097 m, in two to three hours, ask at the *Conaf refugio*. Lago Chungará is 20 km southeast of Parinacota.

Sleeping **At Putre AL** *Hostería Las Vicuñas*, T/F228564. Bungalow-style, helpful, heating, restaurant, does not accept TCs or credit cards. **B** *Casa Birding Alto Andino*, see below. 2 bedroom house, heating, cooking facilities, naturalist library. On Baquedano: **E** pp *Res Cali*. Pleasant, no heating, hot water, good restaurant, supermarket. **E** pp *Res La Paloma*. Hot showers, no heating but lots of blankets, being extended, good food in warm restaurant, indoor parking; supermarket opposite. **E** pp *Res Rosamel*, T300051. Hot water, pleasant, good restaurant. **Camping** Sra Clementina Cáceres, blue door on C Lynch, allows camping in her garden. Several eating places.

If arriving from Bolivia, remember that no fresh produce may be brought across the border into Chile, so plan accordingly if using a Conaf refugio

In **Parinacota** Accommodation with various families, ask at the food and *artesanía* stands. There are 3 *Conaf* refuges **in the park**, but check in advance with Conaf in Arica that they are open: at **Parinacota** (also camping US$6 per tent), at **Lago Chungará**, and at **Las Cuevas** (emergencies only, no tourist facilities). The first two have cooking facilities, hot showers, **E** pp, sleeping bag essential, take your own food, candles and matches. Advance booking recommended. A map of the park is available from *Sernatur* in Arica. Maps are also available from the *Instituto Geográfico Militar*.

Shopping Food is available in Putre, which has several stores, 2 bakeries and several private houses selling fresh produce. Petrol is more expensive than in Arica but available in cans in Putre from the *Cali* and *Paloma* supermarkets and from *ECA*, a government subsidized market on the plaza (cheapest). Other than a small shop with limited supplies in Parinacota, no food is available outside Putre. Take drinking water with you as water in the park is not safe.

Tour operators *Alto Andino Nature Tours*, Baquedano 299 (Correo Putre) T058-300013 (voice mail), F058-222735 (put "para Alto Andino"), www.birdingaltoandino.com Allow a week for reply to email. Run general tours and specialist bird-watching tours to remote areas of the park, to the Salar de Surire and Parque Nacional Isluga and to low-level parts of Atacama; English spoken, owner is an Alaskan biologist. *Freddy Torrejón and Eva Mamami*, Valle de Surunche, Putre, T058-253361, F225685, www2.gratisweb.com/losandeschileno/ Run tours to local sites and offer accommodation and meals. *Turismo Taki*, is located in Copaquila, about 45 km west of Putre, 100 km east of Arica. Restaurant, camping site and excursions to nearby *pucarás*, Inca *tambo* and cemetery, good local food, English and Italian spoken. 1-day tours are offered by most travel agencies and some hotels in Arica (addresses above), daily in season, according to demand at other times, US$17-20 pp with breakfast and light lunch; but some find the minibuses cramped and dusty. You spend all day in the bus (0730-2030) and you will almost certainly suffer from soroche ("the advantage of a one-day tour is that, in the evening, you are OK again", Ann Sleebus, Antwerp). You can leave the tour and continue on another day as long as you ensure that the company will collect you when you want (tour companies try to charge double for this). Much better are 1½-day tours, 1400-1800 next day (eg *Latinorizons*), which include overnight in Putre and a stop on the ascent at the Aymara village of Socorama, US$56. For 5 or more, the most economical proposition is to hire a vehicle.

Transport **Buses** *Flota Paco* buses (known as *La Paloma*) leave Arica for **Putre** daily at 0645, 4 hrs, US$4, returning 1300; *Jurasi* collective taxi leaves Arica daily at 0700, picks up at hotels, T222813, US$6.50. If you take an Arica-La Paz bus for Putre, it is about 4 km from the crossroads to the town at some 4,000 m, tough if you've come straight up from sea level. *Martínez* and *Humire* buses run to **Parinacota** Tue and Fri. Bus to La Paz from Putre crossroads or Lago Chungará can be arranged in Arica (same fare as from Arica).

Hitchhiking Hitching back to Arica is not difficult; you may be able to bargain on one of the tour buses. Trucks from Arica to La Paz sometimes give lifts, a good place to try is at the Poconchile control point, 37 km from Arica.

Directory **Banks** Bank in Putre changes dollars but commission on TCs is very high.

South of Lauca is the beautiful **Reserva Nacional Las Vicuñas**, at an average altitude of 4,300 m, covering 209,131 ha of altiplano. Many camelids can be seen as well as, with luck, condors, rheas and other birds. A high clearance vehicle is essential and, in the summer wet season, four-wheel drive vehicle: take extra fuel. Administration is at **Guallatiri**, reached by turning off the Arica-La Paz road onto the A147 2 km after Las Cuevas, where there is also a *Conaf* office. ■ *Mar-Nov*. The same road leads into the **Monumento Natural Salar de Surire**, which is open for the same months and for which the same conditions apply. The Salar, also at 4,300 m, is a drying salt lake of 17,500 ha. It has a year-round population of 12,000-15,000 flamingos (Chiliean, Andean and James). Administration is in **Surire**, 45 km south of Guallatiri and 129 km south of Putre. At Surire there is a *Conaf refugio*, four beds, very clean, prior application to Conaf in Arica essential. There is also a campsite at Polloquere, 16 km south of Surire, no facilities. There is no public transport to these wildlife reserves, but tours can be arranged in Putre or Arica. Operators such as *Latinorizons* are developing routes through these parks from Arica to San Pedro de Atacama.

Altitude: 4,300-6,060 m Be prepared for cold, skin burns from sun and wind

Immigration is open 0800-2100; US$2 per vehicle crossing 1300-1500, 1850-2100 and Saturday, Sunday and holidays. ■ *For details of through buses between Arica and La Paz see above under Arica.*

Border with Bolivia: Chungará

South of Santiago

Chile

Santiago

One of the world's most fecund and beautiful landscapes, with snowclad peaks of the Andes to the east and the Cordillera de la Costa to the west, the Central Valley contains most of Chile's population. A region of small towns, farms and vineyards, it has several protected areas of natural beauty. To the south are the major city of Concepción, the port of Talcahuano and the main coal-mining area. Five major rivers cross the Central Valley, cutting through the Coastal Range to the Pacific: from north to south these are the Rapel, Mataquito, Maule, Itata and Biobío, one of the three longest rivers in Chile.

Road and railway run south through the Central Valley; the railway has been electrified from Santiago to just south of Temuco. Along the road from Santiago to Temuco there are several modern motels. From Santiago to San Javier (south of Talca), the highway is dual carriageway, with 2 tolls of US$3 to pay.

Cyclists: Watch out for inattentive truck drivers on the highway to Rancagua

The capital of VI Región (Libertador Gen Bernardo O'Higgins) lies on the Río Cachapoal. Founded in 1743, it is a service and market centre. At the heart of the city is an attractive tree-lined plaza, the **Plaza de los Héroes**, and several streets of single-storey colonial-style houses. In the centre of the plaza is an equestrian statue of O'Higgins. The **Merced** church, one block north, several times restored, dates from 1758. The **Museo Histórico**, Estado y Ibieta, housed in a colonial mansion, contains collections of religious art and late 19th century furniture. The main commercial area lies along Av Independencia, which runs west from the plaza towards the bus and rail terminals. The National Rodeo Championships are held at the end of March, with plenty of opportunities for purchasing cowboy items. The tourist office is at Germán Riesco 277, T230413, F232297, helpful, English spoken. Kiosk in Plaza de los Héroes. *Automóvil Club de Chile*, Ibieta 09, T239930, F239907.

Rancagua
Phone code: 072 Colour map 8, grid B1 Population: 167,000 82 km S of Santiago

Sleeping and eating AL *Camino del Rey*, Estado 275, T239765, F232314. 4-star, best. **A-B** *Rancagua*, San Martín 85, T232663, F241155. Quiet, secure parking. Recommended. **C** *España*, San Martín 367, T230141. Cheaper without bath, central, pleasant. *Bravissimo*, Astorga 307, for ice cream. *Lasagna*, west end of Plaza, for bread and *empanadas*.

Train station, T230361 **Transport Trains** Main line services between Santiago and Concepción and Chillán stop here. Also regular services to/from **Santiago** on Metrotren, 1¼ hrs, 10-13 a day, US$2.65. **Buses** Main terminal at Doctor Salinas y Calvo; local and Santaigo buses leave from the Terminal de Buses Regionales on Ocarrol, just north of the market. Frequent services to **Santiago**, US$3, 1¼ hrs.

Directory Banks *Afex*, Av Campos 363, for US$ cash.

Curicó

Phone code: 075
Colour map 8, grid B1
Population: 103,919
Altitude: 200 m
192 km from Santiago

Situated between the Ríos Lontué and Teno, Curicó is the only town of any size in the Mataquito Valley. It was founded in 1744. In mid-March is the Fiesta de la Vendimia with displays on traditional wine-making. In the **Plaza de Armas** there are fountains and a monument to the Mapuche warrior, Lautaro, carved from the trunk of an ancient beech tree. There is a steel bandstand, built in New Orleans in 1904, which is a national monument. The church of **San Francisco** (1732), also a national monument, partly ruined, contains the 17th century Virgen de Velilla, brought from Spain. Overlooking the city, the surrounding countryside and with views to the distant Andean peaks is **Cerro Condell** (100 m); it is an easy climb to the summit from where there are a number of walks. 5 km south of the city is the **Torres wine bodega** take a bus for Molina from the local terminal or outside the railway station and get off at Km 195 on the Pan-American Highway. ■ *0900-1230, 1500-1730, no organized tour, Spanish only, worthwhile, T310455.*

Tourist information is available from the mayor's secretary in the Gobernación Provincial, Plaza de Armas. ■ *Mon-Fri 0900-1300, 1600-1800, helpful, has street map.* Conaf *is in the same building, 1st floor, 0900-1430 Mon-Fri.* Automóvil Club de Chile, *Chacabuco 759, T311156.*

Sleeping and eating AL *Comercio*, Yungay 730, T310014, F317001. Cheaper without bath. Recommended. **D** *Res Rahue*, Peña 410, T312194. Basic, meals, annex rooms have no ventilation. **E** *Prat*, Peña 427, T311069. Pleasant patio, laundry facilities. **E** *Res Colonial*, Rodríguez 461, T314103. Good, **F** without bath. *Club de la Unión*, Plaza de Armas. Good. *American Bar*, Yungay 647. Real coffee, small pizzas, good sandwiches, pleasant atmosphere, open early morning to late afternoon including weekends. Recommended. *El Fogón Chileno*, M Montt 399. Good for meat and wines. *Café-Bar Maxim*, Prat 617. Light meals, beer and wine. *Centro Italiano Club Social*, Estado 531. Good, cheap meals.

Transport Trains Station is at the end of Prat, 4 blocks west of Plaza de Armas, T310028. To/from **Santiago**, 4 a day, 2½ hrs, US$5 *salon*, US$4.15 *turista*, US$3.25 *económico*. To/from **Chillán**, 4 a day, 3 hrs, US$7 *salon*, US$5 *turista*. **Buses** Long distance terminal at Prat y Maipú. Local buses, including to coastal towns, as well as some long distance services, from Terminal Rural, Prat y Maipú. *Pullman del Sur* terminal, Henríquez y Carmen. Many southbound buses bypass Curicó, but can be caught by waiting outside town. To **Santiago** US$5, 2½ hrs, *Pullman del Sur*, frequent. To **Temuco**, *LIT* and *TurBus*, US$7.

Directory Banks Major banks around the Plaza de Armas. *Casa de Cambio*, Merced 255, Local 106. No TCs. **Communications Internet**: Several places in the centre. **Telephone**: *CTC*, Peña 650-A.

Área de Protección Radal Siete Tazas

The park is in two parts, one at Radal, 65 km east of Curicó, the other at Parque Inglés, 9 km further on. At Radal, the Río Claro flows through a series of seven rock bowls (*siete tazas*) each with a pool emptying into the next by a waterfall. The river goes through a canyon, 15 m deep but only 1½m wide, ending abruptly in a cliff and a beautiful waterfall. ■ *Oct-Mar. Administration is in Parque Inglés. Dirty campsites near entrance. Getting there: buses from Molina, 26 km south of Curicó to within 7 km of Park, on Tue and Thu 1700, returning Wed and Fri 0800; impossible to hitch the rest of the way. Daily bus from Curicó in summer, 1545, 4½ hrs, returns 0745 (Sun 0700, returns 1900). Access by car is best as the road through the park is paved.*

Talca

At 56 km south of Curicó, this is the most important city between Santiago and Concepción. It is a major manufacturing centre and the capital of VII Región (Maule). Founded in 1692, Talca was destroyed by earthquakes in 1742 and 1928. Just off the Plaza de Armas at 1 Norte y 2 Oriente is the **Museo O'Higginiano** in a colonial mansion in which Bernardo O'Higgins lived as a child. The house was later the headquarters of O'Higgins' Patriot Government in 1813-14 (before his defeat at Rancagua). In 1818 O'Higgins signed the declaration of Chilean independence here: the room (Sala Independencia) is decorated and furnished in period style. The museum also has a collection of regional art. ■ *Tue-Fri 1030-1300, 1430-1845, Sat-Sun 1000-1300.* The tourist office is at 1 Poniente 1281, T233669. ■ *Mon-Fri 0830-1930 (1730 winter). Automóvil Club de Chile,* 1 Poniente 1267, T223274.

About 8 km southeast is **Villa Huilquilemu,** a 19th century hacienda, now part of the Universidad Católica del Maule, housing museums of religious art, handicrafts, agricultural machinery and wine. ■ *Tue-Fri 1500-1830, Sat 1600-1830, Sun 1100-1400, US$1, T242474. Take San Clemente bus.*

Phone code: 071
Colour map 8, grid B1
Population: 160,000
258 km from Santiago via dual carriageway

Sleeping

A *Cabañas Entre Ríos*, Panamericana Sur Km 250, 8 km north, T223336, F220477 (Santiago: San Antonio 486, of 132, T633 3750, F632 4791). Very good value, excellent breakfast, pool, very helpful owner. Highly recommended. **B** *Cordillera*, 2 Sur 1360, T22187, F233028. **C** without bath, good breakfast. **B** *Hostal del Puente*, 1 sur 407, T220930, F225448. Large breakfast extra, family-owned, parking in central courtyard. Recommended for atmosphere, price and surroundings. **B-D** *Amalfi*, 2 Sur 1265, T225703. With breakfast, old-fashioned, central. **D** pp *Hostal Victoria*, 1 Sur 1737, T212074. Good. Cheap hotels between Nos 1740 and 1790 of 3 Sur, near 11 Oriente. **E** pp *Casa Chueca*, 5 mins from Talca by the Río Lircay, Casilla 143, T197 0096, T09-419 0625 (mob), F197 0097, casachueca@hotmail.com, or www.trekkingchile.com Free pick up from Taxutal terminal (phone hostal from bus terminal then take Taxutal A micro in direction of San Valentín; get off at last stop where hostal will pick you up), or taxi US$5.20. With breakfast, very good vegetarian food (US$6), Austrian and German owners, many languages spoken, lovely setting, swimming pool, good tours (including climbing) arranged. Enthusiastically recommended. At **Pelarco**, 18 km northwest, **E** *Hosp Santa Margarita*, T/F09-335 9051, www.backpackersbest.cl Swiss run, with breakfast, reservations advised (Casilla 1104, Talca). Recommended.

Eating

Bavaria, 1 Sur 1370. *Casino de Bomberos*, 2 Sur y 5 Oriente. Good value. Cheap lunches at *Casino Sociedad de Empleados*, 1 Norte 1025, and *Casino Club Deportivo*, 2 Sur 1313. *Mi Sandwich*, Plaza de Armas, and *Café Brasil*, nearby, real coffee.

Transport

Trains Station at 2 Sur y 11 Oriente, T226254. To **Santiago**, 5 a day, US$3.855. **Buses** Terminal at 12 Oriente y 2 Sur. To **Chillán**, frequent, US$2. To **Puerto Montt**, US$15, 12 hrs.

Directory

Banks *Edificio Caracol*, Oficina 15, 1 Sur 898, for US$ cash. **Communications Internet**: at 1 Poniente 1282 and 2 Sur 1661 (free, reserve in advance). **Post Office:** 1 Oriente s/n. **Telephone:** *CTC*, 1 Sur 1156 and 1 Sur 835.

Vilches
63 km E of Talca

This is the starting point for the climb to the volcanoes Quizapu (3,050 m) and Descabezado (3,850 m). For walks on Descabezado Grande and Cerro Azul (ice axe and crampons needed) contact recommended guide Carlos Verdugo Bravo, Probación Brilla El Sol, Pasaje El Nickel 257, Talca (Spanish only). ■ *5 buses a day, US$1.50, 2-2½ hrs.*

The **Reserva Nacional Altos del Lircay** 2 km from Vilches, covers 12,163 ha and includes three peaks, several small lakes and the Piedras Tacitas, a stone construction supposedly made by the aboriginal inhabitants of the region. There are two good hikes: Laguna del Alto, 8 hours, and El Enladrillado, 12 hours. A visitors' centre and administration are near the entrance.

Chile

To the border with Argentina: Paso Pehuenche

A road from Talca runs 175 km southeast along **Lago Colbún** and up the valley of the Río Maule, passing through some of the finest mountain scenery in Chile to reach the Argentine border at Paso Pehuenche. At the western end of the lake is the town of Colbún, from where a road goes to Linares on the Panamericana. Thermal springs 5 km south of Colbún at Panimávida, and 12 km, Quinamávida. Campsites on south shore. **C** pp *Ecological Reserve Posada Campesina*, at Rabones on the road Linares/Panimávida, T09-752 0510, full board, *estancia* offering forest trails, trekking and horseback expeditions, English spoken, highly recommended.

Paso Pehuenche (2,553 m) is reached by unpaved road southeast from Lago Colbún. On the Argentine side the road continues to Malargüe and San Rafael. The border is open December-March 0800-2100, April-November 0800-1900.

Chillán

Phone code: 042
Colour map 8, grid B1
Population: 146,000
Altitude: 118 m
150 km S of Talca

Chillán is capital of Ñuble province and a service centre for this agricultural area. Following an earthquake in 1833, the site was moved slightly to the northwest, though the older site, Chillán Viejo, is still occupied. Further earthquakes in 1939 and 1960 ensured that few old buildings have survived. Chillán was the birthplace of Bernardo O'Higgins (Arturo Prat, Chile's naval hero, was born 50 km away at Ninhue). The Fiesta de la Vendimia is an annual wine festival held in the third week in March.

Sights

The centre of the city is Plaza O'Higgins, on which stands the modern **Cathedral** designed to resist earthquakes. The **San Francisco** church, three blocks northeast of the Plaza, contains a **museum** of religious and historical artefacts. ■ *US$1.* Northwest of the Plaza O'Higgins, on the Plaza Héroes de Iquique, is the **Escuela México**, donated to the city after the 1939 earthquake. In its library are murals by the great Mexican artists David Alvaro Siqueiros and Xavier Guerrero which present allegories of Chilean and Mexican history. ■ *Daily 1000-1300, 1500-1830.* The **Mercado y Feria Municipal** (covered and open markets at Riquelme y Maipón) sell regional arts and crafts and have many cheap, good restaurants, serving regional dishes; open daily, Sunday until 1300. Three blocks further south is the **Museo Naval El Chinchorro**, Collin y I Riquelme, contains naval artefacts and models of Chilean vessels. ■ *Tue-Fri 0930-1200, 1500-1730.* In **Chillán Viejo** (southwest of the centre) there is a monument and park at O'Higgins' birthplace; it has a 60 m long mural depicting his life (an impressive, but sadly faded, mosaic of various native stones), and a **Centro Histórico y Cultural**, with a gallery of contemporary paintings by regional artists. ■ *The park is open 0830-2000.* The tourist office is at 18 de Septiembre 455, at the side of Gobernación, T223272; street map of city, leaflets on skiing, Termas de Chillán, etc. *Automóvil Club de Chile*, O'Higgins 677, T212550.

Quinchamalí is 27 km southwest of Chillán, a little village famous for the origiality of its craftsmen in textiles, basketwork, black ceramics, guitars and primitive paintings (all on sale in Chillán market). Handicraft fair, second week of February. ■ *Bus from Chillán local terminal (see below), 30 mins, US$1.*

Sleeping
Lots of cheap hospedajes on Constitución 1-300

A *Cordillera*, Arauco 619, on Plaza de Armas, T215211, F211198. 3-star, small, all rooms with heating, good. **A** *Rucamanqui*, Herminda Martín 590 (off Plaza de Armas), T222704. Spartan, but OK. **B** *Quinchamalí*, El Roble 634, T223381, F227365. Central, quiet, hot water. **C** *Floresta*, 18 de Septiembre 278, T222253. Quiet, old fashioned. **C** *Libertador*, Libertad 85, T223255. Large rooms, without breakfast, parking, good, a few minutes' walk from the railway station and better than the closer hotels. **D** *Claris*, 18 de Septiembre 357, T221980. Welcoming, hot water, but run down, **E** pp without bath. **D** *Cañada*, Libertad 269, T234515. Without bath or breakfast, good beds. **F** pp *Hosp Sonia Segui*, Itata 288, T214879. Generally good, especially breakfast, helpful, but bathroom dirty.

Mid-range: *Arcoiris*, El Roble 525. Vegetarian. *Café París*, Arauco 666. Fine restaurant upstairs. Also *Café Europa*, Libertad 475. *La Cosa Nostra*, Libertad 398. Mainly Italian home-made food, top quality, excellent wine and cocktails, nice atmosphere, German and Italian spoken. *Fuente Alemana*, Arauco 661. For real coffee. In Chillán Viejo, **Los Adobes**, on Parque O'Higgins. Good food and service. **Cheap**: *Club Comercial*, Arauco 745. Popular at lunchtime, good value *almuerzo*, popular bar at night. *Jai Yang*, Libertad 250. Good Chinese. *La Copucha*, 18 de Septiembre y Constitución. Inexpensive meals and sandwiches. *La Masc'a*, 5 de Abril 544. Excellent meals, *empanadas de queso*, drinks.

Eating
The Chillán area is well-known for its pipeño wine (very young) and its longanizas (sausages)

Trains Station, T222424. To **Santiago**, 2 daily, 5½ hrs, *salón* US$7.40-10.50 depending on the service, *económico* US$4.75-6.50. **Buses** 2 long-distance terminals: Central, Brasil y Constitución (*TurBus, Línea Azul, Tas Choapa, LIT*); Northern, Ecuador y O'Higgins for other companies. Local buses leave from Maipón y Sgto Aldea. To **Santiago**, 5½ hrs, US$7-11. To **Concepción**, every 30 mins, 1¼ hrs, US$3. To **Curicó** or 2 a day, US$5. To **Temuco**, 4½ hrs, US$6.

Transport

Chillán

Chile

Sleeping	5 Hospedaje	Eating	5 Jai Yang
1 Cañada	Sonia Segui	1 Arcoiris	6 La Casa Nostra
2 Claris	6 Libertador	2 Café Europa	7 La Masc'a
3 Cordillera	7 Quinchamalí	3 Café París	
4 Floresta	8 Rucamanqui	4 Fuente Alemana	

0 metres 200
0 yards 200

Directory **Banks** Better rates than banks at *Casa de Cambio*, Constitución 550, or *Café de París* (ask for Enrique Schuler). **Communications** Internet: *Gateway*, Libertad 360. *Planet*, Arauco 683, p 2. **Post office:** in Gobernación on Plaza de Armas. **Telephone:** *Entel*, 18 de Septiembre 746. *CTC*, Arauco 625.

Termas de Chillán East of Chillán 82 km by good road (paved for the first 50 km), 1,850 m up in the Cordillera, are thermal baths and, above, the largest ski resort in southern Chile. There are two open-air thermal pools (officially for hotel guests only) and a health spa with jacuzzis, sauna, mud baths etc. Suitable for families and beginners and cheaper than centres nearer Santiago, the ski resort has 28 runs, nine lifts, snowboarding and other activities. It also has two hotels (the 5-star *Gran Hotel*, and the 3-star *Pirigallo*) and condominium apartments. Season: middle December to the end of March. Lift pass US$30 per day, US$20 per half-day. Information and reservations from Termas de Chillán, Av Libertad 1042, Chillán, T223887, F223576, or Santiago, Av Providencia 2237, oficina P 41, T02-233 1313, F02-231 5963, www.termaschillan.com Equipment hire also from Chillán Ski Centre (about US$25 pp).

Sleeping At Termas de Chillán, see above. At Las Trancas on the road to the Termas, Km 70-76 from Chillán are **AL** *Parador Jamón*, *Pan y Vino*, Casilla 618, Chillán, T373872, F220018, arranges recommended horse riding expeditions, and **B** pp *Hotel Los Pirineos*, T293839. There are many other *cabañas* in the village and *Galería de Arte de Luis Guzmán Molina*, a painter from Chillán, Entrada por Los Pretiles Km 68.5. **Camping** 2 km from the slopes.

Transport Ski buses run from **Libertador** 1042 at 0800 and from Chillán Ski Centre, subject to demand, US$30 (includes lift pass). Summer bus service (Jan-mid-Mar), from Anja, 5 de Abril 594, Thu, Sat, Sun only, 0730, US$5 return, book in advance. Taxi US$30 one way, 1½ hrs. At busy periods hitching may be possible from Chillán Ski Centre.

Concepción

Phone code: 041
Colour map 8, grid B1
Population: 210,000
516 km from Santiago

The third biggest city in Chile, and the most important city in southern Chile, is also one of the country's major industrial centres. Capital of VIII Región (Biobío), Concepción is 15 km up the Biobío River. Founded in 1550, Concepción became a frontier stronghold in the war against the Mapuche after 1600. Destroyed by an earthquake in 1751, it was moved to its present site in 1764. The climate is very agreeable in summer, but from April to September the rains are heavy; the annual average rainfall, nearly all of which falls in those six months, is from 1,250 mm to 1,500 mm.

Sights In the attractive Plaza de Armas at the centre are the **Intendencia** and the **Cathedral**. It was here that Bernardo O'Higgins proclaimed the independence of Chile on 1 January 1818.

Cerro Caracol can easily be reached on foot starting from the statue of Don Juan Martínez de Rozas in the Parque Ecuador, arriving at the Mirador Chileno after 15 minutes. From here it is another 20 minutes' climb to **Cerro Alemán**. The Biobío and its valley running down to the sea lie below. On the far side of the river you see lagoons, the largest of which, **San Pedro**, is a watersport centre.

The **Galería de la Historia**, Lincoyán y V Lamas by Parque Ecuador, is an audiovisual depiction of the history of Concepción and the region; upstairs is a collection of Chilean painting. ■ *Mon 1500-1830, Tue-Fri 1000-1330, 1500-1830, Sat-Sun 1000-1400, 1500-1930, free.* The **Casa del Arte**, Roosevelt y Larenas, contains the University art collection; the entrance hall is dominated by *La Presencia de América Latina*, by the Mexican Jorge González Camerena (1965), an impressive allegorical mural depicting Latin American history. ■ *Tue-Fri 1000-1800, Sat 1000-1600, Sun 1000-1300, free. Explanations are given free by University Art students.*

The **Museo y Parque Hualpen**, a house built around 1885 (now a national monument) and its gardens; contains beautiful pieces from all over the world, two hour visit, recommended. ■ *Tue-Sun 1000-1300, 1400-1900, free.* The park also contains

Chile

Playa Rocoto, which is at the mouth of the Río Biobío. Take a city bus to Hualpencillo from Freire, ask the driver to let you out then walk 40 minutes, or hitch. You have to go along Av Las Golondrinas to the Enap oil refinery, turn left, then right (it is signed).

Tourist office at Aníbal Pinto 460 on Plaza, T227976, has information on the more expensive hotels and *residenciales. Automóvil Club de Chile*, O'Higgins 630, Of

Concepción

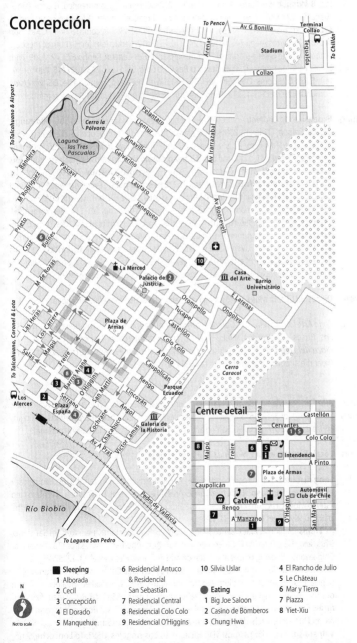

Sleeping	6 Residencial Antuco	10 Silvia Uslar	4 El Rancho de Julio
1 Alborada	& Residencial		5 Le Château
2 Cecil	San Sebastián	**Eating**	6 Mar y Tierra
3 Concepción	7 Residencial Central	1 Big Joe Saloon	7 Piazza
4 El Dorado	8 Residencial Colo Colo	2 Casino de Bomberos	8 Yiet-Xiu
5 Manquehue	9 Residencial O'Higgins	3 Chung Hwa	

303, T245884, for information and car hire (T222070). *Codeff* (Comité Nacional pro Defensa de la Fauna y Flora), Caupolicán 346, oficina E, p 4, T226649.

Sleeping
Good budget accommodation is hard to find

A *Alborada*, Barros Arana 457, Casilla 176, T/F242144. Good. **A** *Concepción*, Serrano 512, T228851, F230948. Central, comfortable, heating, English spoken. Recommended. **A-B** *El Dorado*, Barros Arana 348, T229400, T231018. Comfortable, central, cafeteria, parking. **B** *Manquehue*, Barros Arana 790, p 8, T238350. Highly recommended. **C** *Cecil*, Barros Arana 9, T230667, near railway station. With breakfast, quiet. Highly recommended. **C-D** *Res Antuco*, Barros Arana 741, flats 31-33, T235485. Recommended. **C** *Res San Sebastián*, Barros Arana 741, flat 35, T242710, F243412. Reductions for HI (both of these are entered via the Galería Martínez). Recommended. **D** *Res Central*, Rengo 673, T227309. With breakfast, large rooms, a bit run down. **D** *Res Colo Colo*, Colo Colo 743, T227118. With breakfast. **E** *Res O'Higgins*, O'Higgins 457, T228303. With breakfast, comfortable. **E** *Silvia Uslar*, Edmundo Larenas 202, T227449 (not signed). Excellent, good breakfast, quiet, comfortable.

Eating

Expensive: *Le Château* Colo Colo 340. French, seafood and meat, closed Sun. **Mid-range**: *Big Joe Saloon*, O'Higgins 808, just off plaza. Popular at lunchtime, open Sun evening, good breakfasts, vegetarian meals, snacks and pizzas. *El Rancho de Julio*, O'Higgins 36. Argentine *parrillada*. *Piazza*, 631, p 2r. Good pizzas. **Cheap**: *Casino de Bomberos*, O'Higgins y Orompello. Good value lunches. *Mar y Tierra*, Colo Colo 1182, Seafood. **Oriental** *Yiet-Xiu*, Angol 515. Good, cheap. *Chung Hwa*, Barros Arana 262. **Cafés and bars** Several *fuentes de soda* and cafés on Caupolicán near the Plaza de Armas including: *Café El Dom*, No 415, *Café Haiti*, No 515, both open Sun morning, good coffee; *Fuente Alemana*, No 654. Recommended. *Treinta y Tantos*, Prat 356. Nice bar, good music, wide selection of *empanadas*, good breakfasts and lunches. Recommended. *La Capilla*, Vicuña MacKenna 769, good *ponches*, popular. *Nuria*, Barros Arana 736. Very good breakfasts and lunches, good value. *QuickBiss*, O'Higgins between Tuscapel and Castellón. Salads, real coffee, good service, good lunches. *Saaya 1*, Barros Arana 899. Excellent *panadería/pastelería/rotisería*. Highly recommended.

Entertainment

Discos *El Cariño Malo*, Barros Arana esq Salas. Live music, popular, not cheap.

Shopping
Main shopping area is N of Plaza de Armas. The market has excellent seafood, fruit and vegetables

Feria Artesanal, Freire 757. *Galería Internacional*, Caupolicán y Barros Arana is worth a visit. *Las Brisas* supermarket, Freire y Lincoyán. *Supermercado Unimarc*, Chacabuco 70. *Plaza del Trébol* mall with multiscreen cinemas north of the city off the road to Talcahuano (near the airport). Take any bus for Talcahuano.

Tour operators

Alta Luz, San Martín 586, p 2, T217727. Tours to national parks. *Chile Indomito Adventure*, Serrano 551, of 3, T221618, Trekking in Reserva Nacional Ralco. *South Expeditions*, O'Higgins 680, p 2, of 218D, T/F232290. Rafting and trekking expeditions, 1 and 2-day programmes.

Transport

Local Bicycle repairs: *Martínez*, Maipú y Lincoyán, very helpful.

Long distance Air Airport north of the city, off the main road to Talcahuano. Flights daily to and from **Santiago** (*LanChile/Lan Express*); less frequent to **Valdivia, Temuco** and **Puerto Montt**. *Lan* run bus services to the airport from their office, leaving 1 hr before flight, US$2.50, also meet flights. Taxi US$8.

Trains Station at Prat y Barros Arana, T226925. Regular nightly train to/from **Santiago**, 9 hrs; *salón* US$10, *turista* US$8, *económico* US$6. Also suburban services from Talcahuano to Chiguayante. Booking offices at the station and at Galería Plaza, local 13, T225286.

Buses Main long distance terminal, known as Terminal Collao, is 2 km east, on Av Gen Bonilla, next to athletics stadium. (To the city centre take a bus marked 'Hualpencillo' from outside the terminal and get off in Freire, US$0.40, taxi US$4.) *TurBus*, *Línea Azul* and *Buses Bío Bío* services leave from Terminal Camilo Henríquez 2 km northeast of main terminal on J M García, reached by buses from Av Maipú in centre. To **Santiago**, 8½ hrs, US$12. To **Valparaíso**, 9 hrs, US$12 (most via Santiago). To **Los Angeles**, US$3. To **Loncoche**, 7 hrs,

Chile

US$6.50. To **Pucón**, 8 hrs, US$8. To **Valdivia**, US$10. To **Puerto Montt** several companies, US$15, about 12 hrs. Best direct bus to **Chillán** is *Línea Azul*, 2 hrs, US$2. For a longer and more scenic route, take the *Costa Azul* bus which follows the old railway line, through Tomé, Coelemu and Ñipas on to Chillán (part dirt-track, takes 5½ hrs). Services to **Lota**, **Lebu**, **Cañete** and **Contulmo** are run by *J Ewert* (terminal at Carrera y Tucapel) and *Los Alerces* (terminal at Prat y Maipú). To **Talcahuano** frequent service from Plaza de Armas (bus marked 'Base Naval'), US$0.30, 1 hr, express US$0.50, 30 mins.

Airline offices *LanChile*, Barros Arana 560, T248824. **Banks** ATMs at banks, most of which are on O'Higgins. Several *cambios* in Galería Internacional, entrances at Barros Arana 565 and Caupolicán 521. **Communications** Internet: *Barros Arana 541* and *Caupolicán 567*. **Post Office:** O'Higgins y Colo Colo. **Telephone:** *CTC*, Colo Colo 487, Angol 483. *Entel*, Barros Arana 541, Caupolicán 567, p 2. **Cultural centres** Alliance Française, Colo Colo y Lamas. Library, concerts, films, cultural events. **Chilean-British Cultural Institute**, San Martín 531. British newspapers, library. **Chilean-North American Institute**, Caupolicán 301 y San Martín. Library. **Consulates** Argentina, San Martín 472, of 52, T230257.

Directory

Situated at the neck of a peninsula, **Talcahuano** has the best harbour in Chile. It is Chile's main naval station and an important commercial and fishing port. Two good roads run from Concepción. The **Huáscar**, a relic of the War of the Pacific, is in the naval base and can be visited. ■ *Tue-Sun 0900-1230, 1330-1730, US$1.50; surrender passport at main gate.* On Península Tumbes is **Parque Tumbes**, owned by Codeff: paths lead along the coast, no services, no admission charge (details from Codeff office in Concepción). *Benotecas*, on the seafront, has a row of four restaurants sharing one window facing the harbour, superb fish and seafood in each one, reasonable prices, recommended. *La Aguada*, Colón 912, shellfish dishes. *Domingo Lara*, Aníbal Pinto 450, seafood specialities, excellent.

Talcahuano
Population: 244,000
Fine seafood at low prices in the market

South of Concepción

South of the Biobío is the Costa del Carbón, the main coal producing area of Chile, linked with Concepción by road and two bridges over the Biobío. **Lota** (*Population*: 52,000; 42 km south of Concepción) was, until its closure in 1997, the site of the most important coalmine in Chile. ■ *Guided tours by former miners, 1000-1700, US$5, T870682.* In the church on the main plaza you can see a virgin made of coal. The **Parque de Lota**, covering 14 ha on a promontory to the west of the town, was the life's work of Isadora Cousiño, whose family owned the mine. Laid out by English landscape architects in the last century, it contains plants from all over the world, ornaments imported from Europe, romantic paths and shady nooks offering views over the sea, and peafowl and pheasants roaming freely. ■ *Daily 1000-1800, till 2000 in summer, US$2.50, no picnicking.* **South of Lota** the road runs past the seaside resort of **Laraquete** where there are miles of golden sands. ■ *Buses Concepción-Lota, 1½ hrs, US$0.50. Many buses by-pass the centre: catch them from the main road.*

Costa del Carbón

Some 149 km south of Concepción, Lebu is a fishing port and coal washing centre. It lies at the mouth of the Río Lebu and is the capital of Arauco province. There are enormous beaches to both north and south, popular on summer weekends: 3 km north at Playa Millaneco are caves with steep hills offering good walks and majestic views.

Lebu
Phone code: 041
Population: 20,000

Sleeping A *Hostería Millaneco*, at Playa Millaneco, T/F511540. *Cabañas* sleep 7, good restaurant. Recommended. **D** pp *Central*, Pérez 183, T/F511904. **E** without bath, parking. Recommended. **D** *Gran*, Pérez 309, T511939. **E** without bath, old fashioned, *comedor*. **E** *Res Alcázar*, Alcázar 144. With breakfast, cold water.

Chile

Cañete

Phone code: 041
Colour map 8, grid C1
Population: 15,642
There is nowhere to change dollars in town

A small town on the site of Fort Tucapel where Pedro de Valdivia and 52 of his men were killed by Mapuche warriors in 1553. **Museo Mapuche**, 1 km south on the road to Contulmo, is housed in a modern building inspired by the traditional Mapuche *ruca*; includes Mapuche ceramics and textiles. ■ *0930-1230, 1400-1830, daily in summer, closed Mon in winter, US$1.50.*

Sleeping and eating C *Nahuelbuta*, Villagrán 644, T611073. Cheaper without bath, pleasant. D *Derby*, Mariñán y Condell, T611960. Without bath, basic, restaurant. E *Comercio*, 7° de la Línea, T611218. Very pleasant. Recommended. E *Gajardo*, 7° de la Línea 817 (1 block from plaza). Without bath, old fashioned, pleasant. A very good eating place recommended by the locals is *Don Juanito*, Riquelme 151. Real coffee at *Café Nahuel*, off the plaza.

Transport Buses leave from 2 diifferent terminals: J Ewert, *Inter Sur* and *Thiele* from Riquelme y 7° de la Línea, *Jeldres*, *Erbuc* and other companies from the Terminal Municipal, Serrano y Villagrán. To **Santiago**, *Inter Sur*, daily, 12 hrs. To **Concepción**, 3 hrs, US$3.50. To **Lebu** US$1.50. To **Angol** US$3.50.

Contulmo

Population: 2,000

A road runs south from Cañete along the north side of Lago Lanalhue to **Contulmo**, a sleepy village at the foot of the Cordillera. It hosts a Semana Musical (music week) in January. The wooden **Grollmus House and Mill** are 3 km northwest along the south side of the lake. The house, dating from 1918, has a fine collection of every colour of *copihue* (the national flower) in a splendid garden. The mill, built in 1928, contains the original wooden machinery. From here the track runs a further 9 km north to the *Posada Campesina Alemana*, an old German-style hotel in a fantastic spot at the water's edge (open December – March, details from Millaray 135, Contulmo). The **Monumento Natural Contulmo**, 8 km south and administered by *Conaf*, covers 82 ha of native forest. ■ *Buses to Concepción, Thiele, US$4.50, 4 hrs; to Temuco, Thiele and Erbuc, US$4; to Cañete, frequent, US$1.*

Sleeping In Contulmo C *Contulmo*, Millaray 116, T894903. E pp without bath, hospitable. Recommended. D *Central*, Millaray 131, T618089. Without bath, no sign, very hospitable. **On the lake**: B pp *Hostal Licahue*, 4 km north towards Cañete (Casilla 644, Correo Contulmo) T09-870 2822 (mob). With breakfast, also full board, attractively set overlooking lake, pool. Highly recommended. **Camping at Playa Blanca, 10 km north of Contulmo** *Elicura*, clean, US$6. Recommended. *Playa Blanca*, clean. *Camping Huilquehue*, 15 km south of Cañete on lakeside.

Los Angeles

Phone code: 043
Colour map 8, grid C1
Population: 114,000

Situated on the Pan-American Highway, Los Angeles is 110 km south of Chillán. It is the capital of Biobío province. Founded in 1739 as a fort, it was destroyed several times by the Mapuche. It has a large Plaza de Armas and a good daily market. The tourist office is on Caupolicán, close to the Post Office. *Conaf*, Ercilla 936, 0900-1300. *Automóvil Club de Chile*, Villagrán y Caupolicán, T322149.

Sleeping A *Gran Hotel Müso*, Valdivia 230 (Plaza de Armas), T313183, F312768. Good restaurant open to non-residents. C *Res Santa María*, Plaza de Armas, and C *Winser*, Rengo 138, are both overpriced but otherwise OK. Private house at Caupolicán 651, E, large breakfast, good value. Opposite, also No 651, cheaper. E pp *Res Winser*, Colo Colo 335, T323782. Small rooms. **Outside town**: recommended are: D pp *El Rincón*, Panamericana Sur Km 494 (20 km north of LA), exit El Olivo (Cruce La Mona) 2 km east/south, T09-441 5019, F043-317168, elrincon@cvmail.cl Beautiful property beside a small river, restful, South American and European cuisine, includes vegetarian (B pp full board), Spanish classes, tours arranged, English, French, German and Spanish spoken. D pp *Antukelen*, Camino Los Angeles-Santa Bárbara-Ralco, 62.7 km southeast on the Alto Biobío, reservations Siegfried Haberl, Casilla 1278, Los Angeles, T09-450 0210. Camping US$15 per site, *cabañas*, showers, German, English and French spoken, vegetarian food, Spanish classes, natural therapy centre and excursions.

El Arriero, Colo Colo 235. Good *parrillas* and international dishes. *Bavaria*, Colón 357. Good. **Eating**
Rancho de Julio, Colón 720. Excellent *parrilla*. *D'Leone*, Av Alemania 686. Good lasagne.
Julio's Pizzas, Colón 542. Cheap, good.

Long distance bus terminal on NE outskirts of town, local terminal at Villagrán y Rengo in centre. **Transport**
To **Santiago**, 9 hrs, US$12. To **Viña del Mar** and **Valparaíso**, 10 hrs, US$14. Every 30 mins to
Concepción, US$3, 2¼ hrs. To **Temuco**, US$5, hourly. To **Curacautín**, daily at 0600, 3 hrs, US$4.

Banks ATMs at banks and at supermarket at Av Alemania 686. *Agencia Interbruna*, Caupolicán 350, **Directory**
T313812, F325925, best rates. **Tour operators** , *Agencia Interbruna*, address above, interbruna@
hotmail.com, offers local and national tours. *Los Angeles*, Lautaro 267, T321700, www.ccla.cl

Chile

Chile

Salto El Laja At 25 km north of Los Angeles is this spectacular waterfall where the Río Laja plunges 47 m over the rocks. Free entry out of season – swimming in some of the cool natural pools, popular with local teenagers. **A-B** *Hostería Salto del Laja* (Casilla 562, Los Angeles, T321706, F313996), with fine restaurant, two swimming pools and chalet-type rooms on an island overlooking the falls. Nearby is **B** *Complejo Turístico Los Manantiales*, T/F314275, with camping. Several motels. ■ *Buses (Bío-Bío) from Los Angeles, US$1, 30 mins; to Chillán, US$2.*

Parque Nacional Laguna de Laja East of Los Angeles by 93 km via a road which runs past the impressive rapids of the Río Laja, this park is dominated by the Antuco volcano (2,985 m), which is still active, and the glacier-covered Sierra Velluda. The Laguna is surrounded by stark scenery of scrub and lava. There are 46 species of birds including condors and the rare Andean gull. ■ *ERS Bus from Los Angeles (Villagrán 507) to Abanico, 20 km past Antuco (US$1.50), then 4 km to park entrance. Or bus to Antuco, 2 hrs, weekdays 5 daily, 2 on Sun and festivals, last return 1730, then hitch last 24 km. Details from Conaf in Los Angeles (see above).*

Sleeping *Cabañas y Camping Lagunillas*, T321086 (or Caupolicán 332, of 2, Los Angeles T231066) 50 m from the river, 2 km from park entrance. Open all year, restaurant, poor campsite US$2.50 pp. Camping not permitted on lake shore. 21 km from the lake is the *Refugio Chacay* offering food, drink and bed (**B**, T Los Angeles 222651, closed in summer). 2 other *refugíos*: *Digeder*, **E**, and *Universidad de Concepción*, both on slopes of Volcán Antuco, for both T Concepción 229054, office O'Higgins 740. Nearby is the Club de Esquí de los Angeles with 2 ski-lifts, giving a combined run of 4 km on the Antuco volcano (season, May-Aug). **Abanico**: **E** pp *Hostería del Bosque*, restaurant, also good campsite.

Angol
Phone code: 045
Colour map 8, grid C1
Population: 39,000

Capital of the Province of Malleco, **Angol** is reached by paved roads from Collipulli and Los Angeles. Founded by Valdivia in 1552, it was seven times destroyed by the Indians and rebuilt. The church and convent of **San Beneventura**, northwest of the attractive Plaza de Armas, built in 1863, became the centre for missionary work among the Mapuche. **El Vergel**, founded in 1880 as an experimental fruit-growing nursery, now includes an attractive park and the **Museo Dillman Bullock** with precolumbian Indian artefacts. ■ *Mon-Fri 0900-1900, Sat-Sun 1000-1900, US$1. 5 km from town, colectivo No 2.* There is an excellent tourist office on O'Higgins s/n, across bridge from bus terminal, T711255. *Conaf*, Prat 191, p 2, T711870.

Sleeping Several in town. **D** pp *La Posada*, at El Vergel, T712103. Full board. **D** *Res Olimpia*, Caupolicán 625, T711162. Good. **E** *Casa de Huéspedes*, Dieciocho 465. With breakfast.

Transport Bus to Santiago US$6.50, **Los Angeles**, US$1.20. To **Temuco**, *Trans Bío-Bío*, frequent, US$2.50.

Parque Nacional Nahuelbuta
Rough maps are
available at the park
entrance for US$0.25

Situated in the coastal mountain range at an altitude of 800-1,550 m, the park covers 6,832 ha of forest and offers views over both the sea and the Andes. Although the forest includes many species of trees, the araucaria is most striking; some are over 2,000 years old, 50 m high and 3 min diameter. There are also 16 species of orchids. Fauna include pudu deer, Chiloé foxes, pumas, black woodpeckers and parrots. There is a Visitors' Centre at Pehuenco, 5 km from the entrance, open summer only 0800-1300, 1400-2000. Camping is near the Visitors' Centre, US$9 – there are many free campsites along the road from *El Cruce* to the entrance. ■ *Open all year (snow Jun-Sep).*

Transport Bus to **Vegas Blancas** (27 km from Angol) 0700 and 1600 daily, return 0900 and 1600, 1½ hrs, US$1.20, get off at *El Cruce*, from where it is a pleasant 7 km walk to park entrance (entry US$4.50).

The Lake District

Santiago

This region has beautiful scenery: a variety of lakes, often with snow-capped volcanoes as a backdrop, stretch southwards to the salt water fjords which begin at Puerto Montt. There are a number of good bases for exploring (Valdivia has the added attraction of colonial forts a river trip away) and many national parks.

South from the Río Biobío to the Gulf of Reloncaví the same land formation holds as **Background** for the rest of Chile to the north: the Andes to the east, the coastal range to the west, and in between the central valley. The Andes and the passes over them are less high here, and the snowline lower; the coastal range also loses altitude, and the central valley is not as continuous as from Santiago to Concepción. The climate is cooler; the summer is no longer dry, for rain falls all the year round, and more heavily than further north. The rain decreases as you go inland: some 2,500 mm on the coast and 1,350 mm inland. This is enough to maintain heavy forests, mostly beech, but agriculture is also important; irrigation is not necessary. The farms are mostly medium sized, and no longer the huge *haciendas* of the north. The characteristic thatched or red tiled houses of the rural north disappear; they are replaced by the shingle-roofed frame houses typical of a frontier land rich in timber.

Between parallels 39° and 42° south is found one of the most picturesque lake regions in the world. There are some 12 great lakes of varying sizes, some set high on the Cordillera slopes, others in the central valley southwards from Temuco to Puerto Montt. Here, too, are imposing waterfalls and snowcapped volcanoes. Out of season many facilities are closed, in season (from mid-December to mid-March), prices are higher and it is best to book well in advance, particularly for transport.

About 20,000 **Mapuches** live in the area, more particularly around Temuco. There are possibly 150,000 more of mixed descent who speak the Indian tongue, though most of them are bilingual.

Chile

Temuco

Founded in 1881 after the final treaty with the Mapuches, this city is the capital of IX Region (Araucanía) and one of the fastest growing commercial centres in the south. The city centre is the Plaza Aníbal Pinto, around which are the main public buildings including the cathedral and the Municipalidad. The **cattle auctions** in the stockyards behind the railway station on A Malvoa, Thursday mornings, are interesting; you can see the *huasos*, or Chilean cowboys, at work. Temuco is the Mapuches' market town and you may see some, particularly women, in their typical costumes in the produce market (Lautaro y Pinto). Mapuche textiles, pottery, woodcarving, jewellery etc are also sold inside and around the **municipal market**, Aldunate y Diego Portales (it also sells fish, meat and dairy produce), but these are increasingly touristy and poor quality. The **Casa de la Mujer Mapuche**, Prat 285, sells textiles made by a Mapuche weavers' co-operative; all items are 100% wool with traditional designs (Monday-Friday 0900-1300, 1500-1900). **Museo de la Araucanía**, Alemania 84, is devoted to the history and traditions of the Mapuche nation, with a section on German settlement. ■ *Mon-Fri 0900-1700, Sat 1100-1645, Sun 1100-1300, US$1 (free Sun). Take bus 1 from the centre.* There are views of Temuco from **Cerro Ñielol** (entry US$1), a park with a fine collection of native plants in the natural state, including the national flower, the *copihue rojo*. There is also a restaurant (open 1200-2400). On Cerro Ñielol is also La Patagua, the tree under which the final peace was signed with the Mapuches in 1881.

Phone code: 045
Colour map 8, grid C1
Population: 225,000
Altitude: 107 m
679 km S of Santiago

The Lake District

Chile

♦ National parks

1 Conguillío	4 Puyehue	8 Lanín
2 Huerquehue	5 Vicente Pérez Rosales	9 Mocho Choshuenco
3 Villarrica	6 Alerce Andino	10 Nalcas Malalcahuello
	7 Nahuel Huapi	

Not to scale

AL *Nuevo Hotel de la Frontera*, Bulnes 726, T200400, F200401. With breakfast, excellent.
AL-A *Bayern*, Prat 146, T276000, F212291. 3-star. Small rooms, clean, helpful. **A** *C'est Bayonne*, Vicuña MacKenna 361, T234119, netchile@entelchile.net With breakfast, small, modern, German and Italian spoken. **A** *Don Eduardo*, Bello 755, T214133, deduardo@ctcinternet.cl Parking, suites with kitchen. Recommended. **B-C** *Continental*, Varas 708, T238973, continental@ifrance.com Popular with business travellers, old fashioned building, large rooms, excellent restaurant, popular bar, cheaper rooms without bath. Recommended. **C** *Espelette*, Claro Solar 492, T/F234805. Helpful, quiet. **C** *La Casa de Juanita*, Carrera 735, T213203, www.lacasadejuanita.co.cl Cheaper without bath, breakfast, hot water, laundry, heating, parking, very helpful. Recommended.

D *Bulnes 1006 y O'Higgins*. Good double rooms, hot water, above drugstore, ask for house key otherwise access limited to shop hours. **D** *Flor Acoca*, Lautaro 591. Hot water, breakfast. **D** *Hostal Argentina*, Aldunate 864. With breakfast, hot water. **D** *Rupangue*, Barros Arana 182. Hot shower, helpful, good value. **D** *Casa Blanca*, Montt 1306 y Zenteno, T272667, F212740. Good breakfast, but dirty bathrooms and a little overpriced. **D** *Hosp Aldunate*, Aldunate 187, T213548. Cooking facilities, also **E** dormitory accommodation. **D** *Hospedaje 525*, Zenteno 525, T233982. Without breakfast, new section has small rooms with bath, good value, older part has poor beds but also good value. **D** *Oriente*, M Rodríguez 1146, T/F233232. Recommended. **E** pp *Hosp Millaray*, Claro Solar 471. T645720. Simple, basic. Other private houses on this street. **E** pp *Blanco 1078*, T272926, T09-566 7542 (mob). Use of kitchen, good breakfast.

    Camping *Camping Metrenco*, on Pan-American Highway, Km 12.

Mid-range: *Caletas*, Bello y V MacKenna. Fish/seafood. *Centro Español*, Bulnes 483. *D'Angelo*, San Martín 1199. Good food, pleasant. *La Parrilla de Miguel*, Montt 1095, good for meat and wine. **Cheap**: *Ñam-Ñam*, Portales 802. Sandwiches etc, good. *Pront Rapa*, Aldunate 421. For take-away lunches and snacks. *Quick Biss*, Varas 765. Fast food. *Restaurante del Sur*, Portales 921. Open 24hrs. *Temedors*, San Martín 827. Good value lunch. **Cafés**: for real coffee: *Marriet*, Prat 451, loc 21, *Ripley*, Prat y Varas, and *Della Maggio*, Bulnes 536 (light meals).

Bookshops *Librería Alemana*, M Montt 850, No 104. Books in English, German and Spanish (English-speaking German proprietor). **Crafts** Best choice in the indoor municipal market at Aldunate y Portales. **Supermarket** Modern shopping mall north of city; buses 2 or 7. *Frutería Las Vegas*, Matta 274, dried fruit (useful for climbing/trekking).

Turismo Ñielol, Claro Solar 633, T/F239497. To Parque Nacional Conguillio US$34; to Villarrica volcano US$60.

Local Car hire: Automóvil Club de Chile, Varas 687, T248903 for car hire and at airport. *Euro*, MacKenna 426, T210311, helpful, good value. *Christopher Car*, Varas 522, T215988, recommended. *Full Famas*, at airport and in centre T215420, highly recommended. **Motor mechanic**: *ServiTren*, Edgardo Schneider Reinike and Peter Fischer (peocito@yahoo.de),Matta 0545 y Ruta 5, T/F212775, for cars and motorcycles, German spoken **Bicycle repairs:** on Balmaceda, *Don Cheyo*, No 1266, another at No 1294, *Monsalves*, No 1448, opposite rural bus terminal. Several others on Portales eg *Oxford, Bianchi*.

Long distance Air: Manquehue Airport 6 km southwest of the city. *LanChile, Lan Express* to **Santiago, Osorno, Valdivia** and **Puerto Montt**. There is an airport transfer service to hotels in Villarrica and Pucón, US$12 (may not run out of season).

    Trains: Station at Barros Arana y Lautaro Navarro, T233416. To **Santiago**: at 2030, 11-12 hrs: fares *económico* US$10.25, *turista* US$12.45, *salón* US$17, restaurant car expensive (take your own food). Ticket office at Bulnes 582, T233522, open Mon-Fri 0900-1300, 1430-1800, Sun 0900-1300 as well as at station. No train service south of Temuco. Special bus services take rail passengers to Valdivia, Osorno, Frutillar and Puerto Montt.

Sleeping
Do not confuse the streets Vicuña MacKenna and Gen MacKenna. Accommodation in private houses, category D-E, can be arranged by tourist office. Cheap residenciales and pensiones can be found in the market area

Eating
For those on a budget, make for the market or the rural bus terminal, where there are countless restaurants serving very cheap set meals at lunch

Shopping

Tour operators

Transport

Chile

Buses: New long-distance bus terminal north of city at Pérez Rosales y Caupolicán, taxi US$2.50. *JAC* has its own efficient terminal at Balmaceda y Aldunate, 7 blocks north of the Plaza. *NarBus* and *Igi-Llaima* are opposite. Buses to **Santiago**, overnight, 9 hrs, US$18. To **Concepción**, *Bío Bío* (Lautaro entre Prat y Bulnes), US$5, 4½ hrs. To **Chillán**, 4 hrs, US$6. *Cruz del Sur*, 3 a day to **Castro**, 10 a day to **Puerto Montt** (US$6-9, 6 hrs), to **Valdivia** US$4. To **Osorno** US$6. To **Villarrica** and **Pucón** many between 0705 and 2045, 1½ hrs, US$3, and 2 hrs, US$4. Buses to neighbouring towns leave from Terminal Rural, Pinto y Balmaceda. To **Coñaripe**, 3 hrs, and **Lican Ray**, 2 hrs. To **Panguipulli**, *Power* and *Pangui Sur* 3 hrs, US$3. *Pangui Sur* to **Loncoche**, **Los Lagos**, US$4, **Mehuin** in summer only. To **Curacautín**, *Erbuc*, US$2, 6 daily, 2½ hrs. To **Lonquimay**, *Erbuc*, 4 daily, 5½ hrs, US$3. To **Laguna Captrén**, *Erbuc*, Mon and Fri 1645, 4 hrs, US$3. To **Contulmo**, US$4, 2 hrs, **Cañete**, US$4 and **Lebu**, *Erbuc* and *Thiele*.

Buses to Argentina: *Igi Llaima* 4 days a week and *San Martín* 3 a week to **Junín de los Andes**, US$15. *Ruta Sur* (Miraflores 1151) to **Zapala**, 10-12 hrs (US$25), 3 a week. To

Temuco

N
Not to Scale

Sleeping		Eating
1 Bayern	9 Hospedaje 525	1 Centro Español
2 Bulnes 1006 y	10 Hospedaje Aldunate	2 La Parrilla de Miguel
O'Higgins	11 Hospedaje Millaray	3 Ñam-Ñam
3 C'est Bayonne	12 Hostal Argentina	4 Pizzería Madonna
4 Casa Blanca	13 La Casa de Juanita	5 Pront Rapa
5 Continental	14 Nuevo Hotel de	6 Quick Biss
6 Don Eduardo	la Frontera	7 Restaurante del Sur
7 Espelette	15 Oriente	8 Ripley
8 Flor Acoca		9 Temedors

Neuquén, 7 companies, 16 hrs (US$27), via Paso Pino Hachado. To **Bariloche** you have to change bus in Osorno, US$23.

Airline offices *LanChile*, Bulnes 699, T272138. **Banks** Many ATMs at banks on Plaza Aníbal Pinto. Also at the *JAC* bus terminal (Visa). Many *cambios* around the plaza, all deal in dollars and Argentine pesos. **Communications** Internet: *Araucanet*, A Varas 924, Plaza de Armas, below street level, T406090. Email, fax, photocopying and other telecommunications services. Others at M Montt 334, near Las Heras, T402680, open until 2030, and MacKenna 445. **Post Office:** Portales 839. **Telephone:** *CTC*, A Prat just off Claro Solar and plaza. *Entel*, Bulnes 303. **Consulates Netherlands**, España 494, Honorary Consul, Germán Nicklas, is friendly and helpful. **Tourist offices** Bulnes 586, T211969. Daily in summer 0830-2030, Mon-Fri 0900-1200, 1500-1700 in winter. Also at Balmaceda y Prat. *Conaf* is at Bilbao 931, T234420.

Directory

East of Temuco

Curacautín is a small town situated 84 km northeast of Temuco (road paved) and 56 km southeast of Victoria by paved road. Its main industry is forestry (there are several sawmills); it is a useful centre for visiting the nearby national parks and hot springs. ■ *Bus terminal in the old railway station on the main road, west of plaza. Buses to/from Temuco and Los Angeles.*

Curacautín
Population: 12,737
Altitude: 400 m

Sleeping C *Plaza*, Yungay 157 (main plaza), T881256. Restaurant good but pricey. **E** *Hostal Las Espigas*, Miraflores 315, T881138, rivaseugenia@hotmail.com Good rooms, kitchen, breakfast, dinner available on request. **E** *Turismo*, Tarapacá 140, T881116. Good food, comfortable, good value. **E** Rodríguez 705 (corner of plaza), with breakfast, kitchen facilities.

Termas de Manzanar, are indoor hot springs, 17 km east of Curacautín (US$5, open all year) are reached by bus from Temuco and Victoria. The road passes the Salto del Indio (Km 71 from Victoria), and Salto de la Princesa, 3 km beyond Manzanar. **L-A** *Termas de Manzanar*, T/F045-881200, termasmanzanar@ indecom.cl Also simple rooms with bath. **C** *Hostería Abarzúa*, T045-870011, simple, **E** without bath.

The beautiful pine-surrounded **Termas de Tolhuaca** (open 1 November-30 April) are 35 km to the northeast of Curacautín by unpaved road, or 57 km by unpaved road from just north of Victoria (high clearance four-wheel drive vehicle essential). ■ *Daily Nov-Apr, otherwise weekends only.* And 2 km north of the Termas is the **Parque Nacional Tolhuaca**, including waterfalls, two lakes, superb scenery and good views of volcanoes from Cerro Amarillo. Park administration is near Laguna Malleco, with a campsite nearby. ■ *Dec-Apr.* **AL** *Termas de Tolhuaca*, with full board, including use of baths and horse riding, very good, T045-881164, F045-881211. **E** pp *Res Roja*, food, camping near the river, good.

Situated northeast of Curacautín, this 31,305 ha park is on the slopes of the **Lonquimay volcano**. It is much less crowded than nearby Parque Nacional Conguillio. The volcano began erupting on Christmas Day 1988; the new crater is called Navidad. To see it, access is made from Malalcahuello, 15 km south and half-way between Curacautín and Lonquimay town. Conaf has opened three marked trails in the park, which is one of the best areas for seeing unspoilt araucaria forest. The teacher at Malalcahuello school, José Córdoba, organizes tours and horse riding for groups. Sra Naomi Saavedra at *Res Los Sauces* arranges transport. The Reserve is also a popular centre for fly-fishing. ■ *Bus Erbuc from Temuco, US$2 to Malalcahuello, 4 a day, 3 hrs, 4½ to Lonquimay town, US$3. Conaf office on main road in Malalcahuello gives information, as does La Suizandina, which gives good access to treks and the ascent of the volcano, see below.*

Reserva Nacional Nalcas Malalcahuello

Los Arenales ski resort is at Las Raices Pass on the road from Malalcahuello to Lonquimay town. Four lifts go up to 2,500 m with great views. It is a good, small resort with a nice restaurant. ■ *Season Jun-Sep.*

Chile

Sleeping *Res Los Sauces*, in Malalcahuello, **D** pp full board, or **E** pp with use of kitchen, hot water, good value. There is also a *Conaf* lodge in the Reserva Nacional. Accommodation is also available at the Centro de Ski Lonquimay, 10 km from the bus stop, **B** pp with breakfast, full board also available, free camping, open only in season, ski pass US$17. **E-G** pp *La Suizandina*, Km 83 Carretera Internacional a Argentina, T09-884 9541, www.suizandina.com Hostel 3 km before Malalcahuello (*Erbuc* bus from Temuco 2½ hrs), with a range of rooms (**A** in private room with heating and breakfast), laundry, book exchange, bike and ski rental, horse riding, travel and trekking information, good meals available. Recommended.

Parque Nacional Conguillio

East of Temuco by 80 km, this is one of the most popular parks in Chile, but is deserted outside January/February and weekends. In the centre is the 3,050 m **Llaima volcano**, which is active. There are two large lakes, Laguna Verde and Laguna Conguillio, and two smaller ones, Laguna Arco Iris and Laguna Captrén. North of Laguna Conguillio rises the snow covered Sierra Nevada, the highest peak of which reaches 2,554 m. This is the best place in Chile to see araucaria forest, which used to cover an extensive area in this part of the country. Other trees include cypresses, lenga and cinammon. Birdlife includes the condor and the black woodpecker.

Crampons and ice-axe are essential for climbing Llaima. Climb south from *Guardería Captrén*. Allow five hours to ascend, two hours to descend. Information on the climb is available from *Guardería Captrén*. There is a range of walking trails, from 1 km to 22 km in length. Details are available from park administration or *Conaf* in Temuco.

Llaima ski resort, one of the prettiest in Chile, is reached by poor road from Cherquenco, 30 km west (high clearance vehicle essential).

There are three entrances: From Curacautín, north of the park: see Transport below; from **Melipeuco**, 13 km south of the southern entrance at Truful-Truful; and from Cherquenco to the west entrance near the Llaima ski resort. It is then a two or three day hike around Volcán Llaima to Laguna Conguillio, which is dusty, but with beautiful views of Laguna Quepe, then on to the Laguna Captrén *guardería*. ■ *Dec-Mar, US$4. Administration and information, open Nov-Jun, at Laguna Arco Iris, Laguna Captrén and at Truful-Truful. Out of season administration is at the western entrance. There is a Visitors' Centre at Laguna Captrén.*

Sleeping & eating
Buy supplies in Temuco or Melipeuco: much cheaper than the shop in the park. All camping in the park is administered by Conaf

At **Laguna Conguillio** campsite (US$15 per tent, hot water, showers, firewood), cheaper campsite (*camping de mochileros*, US$5 pp, plus US$1 pp for shower, US$2 for firewood), *cabañas* (**A** summer only, sleep 6, no sheets or blankets, gas stove, and café/shop). In **Melipeuco E** *Germania*, Aguirre 399. Basic, good food. **E** *Pensión Hospedaje*, Aguirre 729. More spacious. Recommended. **C** *Hostería Hue-Telén*, Aguirre 15, Casilla 40, T693032 to leave message. Good restaurant, free municipal campsite. Also **Camping Los Pioneros**, 1 km out of town on road to the park, hot water. *Restaurant Los Troncos*, Aguirre 352. Recommended. 2 km off the road from Melipeuco to Paso Icalma is *La Baita*, cabins (**AL-A**) with electricity, hot water, kitchen and wood stoves, T730138, www.labaitaconguillio.cl Charming, Italian/Chilean owned.

Transport
For touring, hire a 4WD vehicle in Temuco. Private transport is the best way to see the area

To the northern entrance: Bus from Temuco Terminal Rural, *Nar Bus*, 5 daily, 0900-1830, 4 hrs, US$1.30, ask driver to drop you at the road fork, 10 km from park entrance, last back to Temuco at 1630. Taxi from Curacautín to Laguna Captrén, US$30 one way. To the western entrance: Daily buses from Temuco to Cherquenco, from where there is no public transport to the park. Transport can be arranged from Melipeuco into the park (ask in grocery stores and *hospedajes*, US$25 one way).

Border with Argentina

Paso Pino Hachado (1,884 m) can be reached either by newly paved road, 77 km southeast from Lonquimay, or by unpaved road 103 east from Melipeuco. On the Argentine side this road continues to Zapala. Chilean immigration and customs are in Liucura, 22 km west of the border, open December-March 0800-2100, April-November 0800-1900. Very thorough searches and 2-3 hour delays reported. ■ *Buses from Temuco to Zapala and Neuquén use this crossing: see under Temuco.*

   Paso de Icalma (1,298 m) is reached by unpaved road, 53 km from Melipeuco, a good crossing for those with their own transport. On the Argentine side this road continues to Zapala. Chilean immigration is open December-March 0800-2100, April-November 0800-1900.

Villarrica

Wooded Lago Villarrica, 21 km long and about 7 km wide, is one of the most beautiful in the region, with snow-capped Villarrica volcano (2,840 m) to the southeast. The town of Villarrica, pleasantly set at the extreme southwest corner of the lake, can be reached by a 63-km paved road southeast from Freire (24 km south of Temuco on the Pan-American Highway), or from Loncoche, 54 km south of Freire, also paved. Founded in 1552, the town was besieged by the Mapuche in the uprising of 1599: after three years the surviving Spanish settlers, 11 men and 13 women, surrendered. The town was refounded in 1882. Next to the **Museo Histórico** at Pedro de Valdivia y Zegers is the **Muestra Cultural Mapuche** featuring a Mapuche *ruca* and handicraft stalls. Festival Cultural Mapuche, with a market, is held usually in the second week of February. Enquire at the Santiago or Temuco tourist office. Villarrica's tourist office is at Valdivia 1070, T411162, F414261, information and maps. ■ *Open all day all week in summer.*

Phone code: 045
Colour map 8, grid C1
Population: 36,000
Altitude: 227 m

Sleeping

Private homes in D range on Muñoz 400 and 500 blocks, Koerner 300 block and O'Higgins 700 and 800 blocks

A *El Ciervo*, Koerner 241, T411215, elciervo@villaricanet.com German spoken, beautiful location, pool. Recommended. **A** *Hostería la Colina*, Ríos 1177, overlooking town, T411503, aldrich@entelchile.net With breakfast, large gardens, good service, good restaurant. Recommended. **A** *Hotel y Cabañas El Parque*, 3 km east on Pucón road, T411120, hotelparque@entelchile.net Lakeside with beach, tennis courts, with breakfast, good restaurant set meals. Recommended. **A** *Hostería Kiel*, Koerner 153, T411631. **D** off season, lakeside, good. **A** *Hostería Bilbao*, Henríquez 43, T411452. Small rooms, pretty patio, good restaurant. **B** *Bungalowlandia*, Prat 749, T/F411635, bungalowlandia@villarica.net. *Cabañas*, dining room, good facilities. **C** *Kolping*, Riquelme 399, T/F411388. Good breakfast. Recommended. **C** *Rayhuen*, Pedro Montt 668, T411571. Lovely garden. Recommended. **D** *Yandaly*, Henríquez 401, T411452. Small rooms, good, also restaurant. Recommended. **D** *La Torre Suiza*, Bilbao 969, T/F411213, www.torresuiza.com Kitchen facilities, camping, cycle rental, book exchange, small breakfast. Recommended. **D** Vicente Reyes 854, T414457. Good breakfast, good bathrooms but only one for 4-5 rooms, use of kitchen, camping in garden. **E** *Maravillas del Sur*, Bilbao 821, T411444. With bath and breakfast, good value, parking. Several private homes on Bilbao, eg *Eliana Castillo*, No 537. **F** *Hostería Las Rosas del Lago*, Julio Zegers 897, T411463. Helpful and clean. Urrutia 407, large breakfast, kitchen. Matta 469, cooking facilities. **Youth hostel E** pp *Res San Francisco*, Julio Zegers 646. Shared rooms. **Camping** Many sites east of town on Pucón road: nearest are *Los Castaños*, T412330, and *du Lac*, T210466, F214495, quiet, not much cheaper than a *pensión*, but buy supplies at *Los Castaños* which is cheaper.

Eating

El Tabor, S Epulef 1187. Excellent but pricey. **Mid-range**: *Rapa Nui*, V Reyes 678. Good, closed Sun. *El Rey de Mariscos*, Letelier 1030. Good seafood. *Treffpunkt*, P de Valdivia 640. *The Travellers*, Letelier 753. Varied menu, Asian food, good bar, English spoken. **Cheap**: *El Viejo Bucanero*, Henríquez 552. Good set lunch, live music at weekends. *Café 2001*, Henríquez 379. Coffee and ice cream, good.

Transport

Bicycles *Mora Bicicletas*, G Korner 760, helpful. **Bus** terminal at Pedro de Valdivia y Muñoz. *JAC* at Bilbao 610, T411447, and opposite for Pucón and Lican-Ray. Terminal Rural for other local services at Matta y Vicente Reyes. To **Santiago**, 10 hrs, US$20, several companies. To **Pucón**, with *Vipu-Ray* (main terminal) and *JAC*, in summer every 30 mins, 40 mins' journey,

Chile

US$1; same companies to **Lican-Ray**, US$1. To **Valdivia**, *JAC*, US$3.50, 3 a day, 2½ hrs. To **Coñaripe** (US$1.60) and **Liquiñe** at 1600 Mon-Sat, 1000 Sun. To **Temuco**, *JAC*, US$3. To **Loncoche** (Ruta 5 junction for hitching), US$1.50. To **Panguipulli**, go via Lancoche, no direct bus. To **Junín de los Andes (Argentina)** *San Martín* (Muñoz 604) a week and *Igi-Llaima*, Valdivia 611, T412733, 4 a week, US$25, 6 hrs, but if the Tromén pass is blocked by snow buses go via Panguipulli instead of Pucón.

Directory **Banks** ATMs at banks on Pedro de Valdivia between Montt and Alderete. *Carlos Huerta*, A Muñoz 417, *Turcamb*, Henríquez 576, and *Cristopher Exchange*, Valdivia 1061, all change TCs and cash. **Communications** Internet: *Cybercafé Salmon*, Letelier y Henríquez. *New Yandaly*, Henríquez 401. **Post Office:** A Muñoz 315. Open 0900-1300, 1430-1800 (Mon-Fri), 0900-1300 (Sat). **Telephone:** *Entel*, Henríquez 440 and 575. *CTC*, Henríquez 544. *Chilesat*, Henríquez 473, best rates.

Pucón

Phone code: 045
Colour map 8, grid C1
Population: 8,000
Altitude: 280 m

Pucón, on the southeastern shore of Lago Villarrica, 26 km east of Villarrica, is the major tourist centre on the lake. It has a good climate. The black sand beach is very popular for swimming and watersports. Between New Year to end-February it is very crowded and expensive; off season it is very pleasant but many places are closed. Apart from the lake, other attractions nearby include whitewater rafting and winter sports (see Skiing below). There is a pleasant walk to **La Península** for fine views of the lake and volcano, pony rides, golf, etc (private land owned by an Apart-Hotel, ask permission first). There is another pleasant *paseo*, the **Otto Gudenschwager**, which starts at the lake end of Ansorena (beside *Gran Hotel Pucón*, Holzapfel 190, T441001) and goes along the shore. Launch excursions from the landing stage at La Poza at the end of O'Higgins at 1500 and 1900, US$4 for two hours. There is a large handicraft centre where you can see spinning and weaving in progress. The Municipal Tourist Office is at O'Higgins y Palguín, T441125/443238, sells fishing licences (US$1 per month), www.pucon.com *Conaf*, O'Higgins 669, very helpful.

Excursions Walk 2 km north along the beach to the mouth of the Río Pucón, with views of the volcanoes Villarrica, Quetrupillán and Lanín. To cross the Río Pucón: head east out of Pucón along the main road, then turn north on an unmade road leading to a new bridge; from here there are pleasant walks along the north shore of the lake to Quelhue and Trarilelfú, or northeast towards Caburga (see page 699), or up into the hills through farms and agricultural land, with views of three volcanoes and, higher up, of the lake.

Sleeping
In summer (Dec-Feb)
rooms may be hard
to find. Plenty of
alternatives (usually
cheaper) in Villarrica

Prices below are Jan-Feb. Off-season rates are 20-40% lower and it is often possible to negotiate. **LL** *Antumalal*, luxury class, 2 km west, T441011, www.antumalal.com Very small, picturesque chalet-type, magnificent views of the lake (breakfast and lunch on terrace), lovely gardens, with meals, open year round, pool. **L** *Interlaken*, Colombia y Caupolicán, T441276, F441242. Chalets, open Nov-Apr, water skiing, pool, TCs changed, no restaurant. Recommended. **AL** *Gudenschwager*, Pedro de Valdivia 12, T441156, gudens@cepri.cl Classic Bavarian type, views over lake, volcano and mountains, attentive staff, comfortable, excellent restaurant (open in summer only). **AL** *Munich*, Alderete 275, T/F442293. Modern, spacious, German and English spoken. **AL** *Hostería El Principito*, Urrutia 291, T441200. Good breakfast. Recommended. **A** *La Posada*, Valdivia 191, T441088, laposada@unete.com Cheaper without bath, full board available, also spacious cabins (**C** low season), small breakfast. **A** *Los Maitenes*, Fresia 354, T441820. Light and airy, comfortable, homely, breakfast, TV, very helpful. **B** *Hostería Millarrahue*, O'Higgins 460, T411610. Good, inexpensive restaurant. **C-D** *Hosp La Casita*, Palguín 555, T441712, lacasita@entelchile.net Laundry and kitchen facilities, English and German spoken, large breakfast, garden, motorcycle parking, ski trips, Spanish classes, **D** off season. Recommended. **C** *La Tetera*, Urrutia 580, T/F441462, www.tetera.cl 6 rooms, some with bath, with breakfast, German and English spoken, book swap, meeting place, information centre, agency for *Navimag* ferries. Warmly recommended. **C** *Hosp El Montañés*, O'Higgins 472, T441267. Good value, TV, central, restaurant, next to JAC buses. **D** *Res Lincoyán*, Av Lincoyán, T441144, www.lincoyan.cl Cheaper without bath, comfortable. **D** pp *Hostería ¡école!*, Urrutia 592, T/F441675, trek@ecole.cl With breakfast, no singles, also dormitory accommodation, **E** pp (sleeping bag essential), good vegetarian and fish restaurant, ecological shop, forest treks, rafting, biking, information, language classes, massage, youth hostelling discount. **E** pp *Raíces*, O'Higgins 865, T444159, raices@volkanix.com New, good facilities, relaxed, helpful. **E** pp *Casa de Campo Kila-Luefe*, about 20 km east on road to Curarrahue, T09-711 8064, margotex@yahoo.com Rooms on the Martínez family farm, contact daughter Margot in advance, price includes breakfast and dinner, home-grown food, horseriding, boat tours, treks. Recommended. **E** pp *Donde Germán*, Brasil 640, T442444. Fun, organizes tours, internet, good view.

Recommended accommodation in private houses, all **D** or **E** pp unless stated: **On Palguín** *Familia Acuña*, No 223 (ask at *peluquería* next door). Without breakfast, kitchen and laundry facilities, good meeting place. *María del Pilar García*, No 361, no sign, above saddlery. English spoken, quiet, use of kitchen. **On Lincoyán** **C** *Hosp El Refugio*, No 348, T441347. With breakfast, good. *Hosp Sonia*, No 485, T441269. Use of kitchen, meals. *Hosp Irma Torres*, No 545. Cooking facilities. *Hosp Lucía*, No 565, T441721, luciahostal@hotmail.com Safe, quiet, cooking facilities. *Casa Eliana*, Pasaje Chile 225, T441851. Kitchen facilities. **E** Adriana Molina, No 312. With breakfast, helpful. **F** pp, No 630, T441043. Kitchen facilities, good value. **F** *Casa de María*, Urrutia 560, T443264. Use of kitchen, good location, helpful. *Hosp Graciela*, Pasaje Rolando Matus 521 (off Av Brasil). Comfortable, good food. Irma Villena, Arauco 460. Use of kitchen, very hospitable. **F** pp *Roberto y Alicia Abreque*, Perú 170. Basic, noisy, popular, kitchen and laundry facilities, information on excursions. **F** pp *Casa Richard*, Paraguay 140. Cooking facilities.

Camping There are many camping and cabin establishments: those close to Pucón include *La Poza*, Costanera Geis 769, T441435, **F** pp, hot showers, good kitchen. Recommended. West along Lago Villarrica: **A-B** *Huimpalay-Tray*, Km 12, T450079 (Santiago 231 4248). "Gorgeous", fine location on lake, well-equipped. Recommended all round. *Saint John*, Km 7, T441165/92, Casilla 154, open Dec-Mar, also *hostería*. Several sites en route to the volcano, including *L'Etoile*, Km 2, T442188, in attractive forest, **C** per site; *Mahuida*, Km 6. Cheaper sites en route to Caburga. **Camping equipment** *Eltit supermarket*, O'Higgins y Fresia. *Outdoors & Travel*, Lincoyán 361, clothing, equipment, maps.

Expensive: *En Alta Mar*, Urrutia y Fresia. For seafood and fish. *Puerto Pucón*, Fresia 251. Spanish, stylish. **Mid-range**: *El Fogón*, O'Higgins 480. Very good. *El Palet*, Fresia 295. Genuine local food, good value. Recommended. *El Refugio*, Lincoyán 348. Some vegetarian dishes, expensive wine. *La Buonatesta*, Fresia 243. Good pizzería. **Cheap**: *Trabun*, Palguín 348. Good value lunches. **Cafés** *Brasil*, Fresia 477. *Fresia Strasse*, Fresia 161. Good coffee and cakes. *Holzapfel Backerei*, Holzapfel 524. German cafe. Recommended. *La Tetera*, Urrutia 580, wide selection of teas, good coffee, snacks. **Bars** *Pub La For You*, Ansorena 370, English-style pub, runs minibuses in high season to its disco 1 km from town. *Bar Riga*, Fresia 135. Good, also serves good value meals.

Fishing: Local tourist office will supply details on licences and open seasons etc. **Horse riding**: enquire at *La Tetera* for Hans Bacher (Austrian), or *Rancho de Caballos* (German run). Day excursions US$55, also half-day US$35. *Centro de Turismo Ecuestre Huepil Malal*, T09-643 2673/643 3204, Rodolfo Coombs and Carolina Pumpin, PO Box 16, Pucón, 40 mins from town. Highly recommended. **Mountain biking**: Bike hire from US$5 per hr to US$20 per day. **Taller el Pollo**, Palguín 500 block. Try also travel agencies on O'Higgins. **Parapenting and Paragliding**: Fabrice Pini, Colo Colo 830, US$55 for 30 mins. **Watersports**: water-skiing, sailing, windsurfing at Playa Grande beach by *Gran Hotel* and La Poza beach end of O'Higgins (more expensive than Playa Grande, not recommended). Playa Grande: waterskiing US$10 for 15 mins, Laser sailing US$11 per hr, sailboards US$10 per hr, rowing boats US$4 per hr. **Whitewater rafting**: is very popular on the Río Trancura. Many agencies offer trips (see below), Trancura Bajo (grade 3), US$10-15; Trancura Alto (grade 4), US$25. 3-day trips to the Biobío are also offered.

Many families offer rooms, look for the signs or ask in bars/restaurants

Chile

Buy supplies in Villarrica (cheaper)

Eating
See Sleeping for recommendations

Sport
Pucón and Villarrica are celebrated as centres for fishing on Lake Villarrica and in the beautiful Lincura, Trancura and Toltén rivers. In high season, sports shops open, especially for biking and watersports

Tour operators

All arrange trips to thermal baths, trekking to volcanoes, whitewater rafting, etc. For falls, lakes and termas it is cheaper, if in a group, to flag down a taxi and bargain

Many agencies, so shop around: prices vary at times, quality of guides and equipment variable. In high season, when lots of groups are going up together, individual attention may be lacking. Prices for climbing Villarrica are given below. Tours to Termas de Huife, US$20 including entry. On O'Higgins: *Florencia*, No 480, T443026. *Politur*, No 635, T/F441373, turismo@politur.com *Rayenco* No 524, T449506, F442040, aventur_ rayenco@latinmail.com Excellent tours, fishing, accommodation (**E**), internet, quad bikes. *Servitour*, No 447, T441959. *Sol y Nieve* (esq Lincoyán), T/F441070, solnieve@entelchile.net Generally recommended. *Off Limits*, Fresia 273, T441210. Specialize in biking and fishing, helpful. *Klaus Thiele*, O'Higgins 535, T441048, F441236. Agency specializing in rafting, trips to springs, hiking tours. Good contact for travellers.

Transport

Local Car hire: Prices start at US$33 for a car. *Christopher Car*, O'Higgins 335, T/F449013. *Pucón Rent A Car*, Camino Internacional 1395, T441922, kernayel@cepri.cl **Taxis**: *Co-operative*, T441009.

Long distance Buses No municipal terminal: each company has its own terminal: *JAC*, Uruguay y Palguín; *TurBus*, O'Higgins, 1180, east of town; *Igi Llaima* and *Cóndor*, Colo Colo y O'Higgins; *LIT*, O'Higgins y Palguín. *JAC* to **Villarrica** (US$1), **Temuco** (frequent, US$3, 2 hrs, *rápido* US$3.50, 1 hr) and **Valdivia** (US$5). *TurBus* at 1115 direct to **Valdivia, Osorno** and **Puerto Montt**, 6 hrs, US$8. To **Santiago**, 10 hrs, US$18-25, many companies, overnight only; daytime go via Temuco; *cama* service by *TurBus* and *JAC*, US$40. Colectivos to **Villarrica** from O'Higgins y Palguín. **Buses to Argentina**: Buses from Temuco to **Junín** pass through Pucón, fares are the same as from Temuco.

Directory

Airline offices *LanChile*, Fresia 275. **Banks** ATMs in *Banco Santander*, Fresia y O'Higgins, *Eltit*, supermarket, O'Higgins, *Banco BCI*, Fresia y Alderete, and in casino. Several *casas de cambio* on O'Higgins. *Eltit*, also changes TCs, but rates for TCs in Pucón are poor. **Communications** Internet: Several sites on O'Higgins, US$2 per hr. Also at Palguín y O'Higgins. **Post Office**: Fresia 183. **Telephone**: CTC, Gen Urrutia 472. *Entel*, Ansorena 299.

Parque Nacional Villarrica

The park has three sectors: **Volcán Villarrica**, **Volcán Quetrupillán** and the **Puesco sector** which includes the slopes of the Volcán Lanín on the Argentine border. Each sector has its own entrance and ranger station. A campsite with drinking water and toilets is below the refuge, 4 km inside the park.

The **Villarrica** volcano, 2,840 m, 8 km south of Pucón (entry US$6) can be climbed up and down in eight to nine hours (go in summer when days are longer), good boots, ice axe and crampons, sunglasses, plenty of water and sun block essential. Beware of sulphur fumes at the top – take a cloth mask moistened with lemon juice.

Entry to Volcán Villarrica is permitted only to groups with a guide and to individuals who can show proof of membership of a mountaineering club in their own country. Several agencies take excursions, US$40-50 (plus park entry, US$3.50) including guide, transport to park entrance and hire of equipment (no reduction for those with their own equipment); at the park entrance equipment is checked. Entry is refused if the weather is poor. Note that travel agencies will not start out if the weather is bad: establish in advance what terms apply in the event of cancellation and be prepared to wait a few days. **Guides**: *Alvaro Martínez*, Cristóbal Colón 430; *Juan Carlos*, at Oliva's *pensión*, or his pool room on main street, recommended. Many others, all with equipment; ask for recommendations at the tourist office. Crampons, ice axe, sunglasses can be rented for US$4 per day from the *Taller El Pollo* bicycle shop (see Sport, above).

Skiing trips to the summit are very tough going and only for the fit

Skiing The Pucón resort, owned by the *Gran Hotel Pucón*, is on the eastern slopes of the volcano, reached by a track, 35 minutes. The lodge offers equipment rental (US$15 per day, US$82 per week), ski instruction, first aid, restaurant and bar as well as wonderful views from the terrace. Lift ticket US$15-25 full day; high season is July to November. Information on snow and ski-lifts (and, perhaps, transport) from *Gran Hotel Pucón*. Good for beginners; more advanced skiers can try the steeper areas.

Lago Caburga (spelt locally Caburgua), a very pretty lake in a wild setting 25 km northeast of Pucón, is unusual for its beautiful white sand beach (other beaches in the area are of black volcanic sand). The east and west shores of the lake are inaccessible to vehicles. The north shore can be reached by a road from Cunco via the north shore of **Lago Colico**, a more remote lake north of Lago Villarrica. The village of Caburga, at the southern end is reached by a turning off the main road 8 km east of Pucón. **B** *Hostería Los Robles*, 3 km from village, T236989, lovely views, good restaurant, campsite, closed out of season. The southern end of the lake and around Caburga is lined with campsites. There are no shops, so take your own food. Rowing boats may be hired US$2 per hour. Just off the road from Pucón, Km 15, are the **Ojos de Caburga**, beautiful pools fed from underground, particularly attractive after rain (entry US$0.30; ask bus driver to let you off). East of the lake is **D** pp *Landhaus San Sebastián*, F443057, with bath and breakfast, good meals, laundry facilities.

Lagos Caburga & Colico

Transport To **Caburga**: taxi day trips from Pucón, US$25 return. *JAC* bus departs regularly for Caburga (US$1 single), and there are colectivos from Ansorena y Uruguay or you can try hitching. If walking or cycling, turn left 3 km east of Pucón (sign to Puente Quelhue) and follow the track (very rough) for 18 km through beautiful scenery. Recommended.

East of Lago Caburga, the park includes steep hills and at least 20 lakes, some of them very small. Entrance and administration are near **Lago Tinguilco**, the largest lake, on the western edge. From the entrance there is a well-signed track north to three beautiful lakes, Lagos Verde, Chico and Toro (private car park, US$1.50, 1½ km along the track). The track zig-zags up (sign says 5 km, but worth it) to Lago Chico, then splits left to Verde, right to Toro. From Toro you can continue to Lago Huerquehue and Lago de los Palos (camping). ■ *The park entrance is 7 km (3 km uphill, 3 km down, one along Lago Tinquilco) from Paillaco, which is reached by an all-weather road which turns off 3 km before Caburga, US$3.25. The park is open officially only Dec-Mar, but you can get in at other times. The warden is very helpful; people in the park rent horses and boats. Take your own food.*

Parque Nacional Huerquehue

Chile

Sleeping *Refugio Tinquilco*, 3½ km from park entrance, where forest trail leads to lakes Verde and Toro, T02-777 7673, T09-822 7153 (mob), patriciolanfranco@entelchile.net **B** with bath to **E** for bed and no sheets, meals extra, heating, hot water, electricity sunset to midnight, cooking facilities, very good. Recommended. **D** *Hospedaje Carlos Alfredo Richard*, southwest shore of the lake, 2 km from park entrance, parque_huerquehue@hotmail.com Large rooms with bath, hot water, breakfast included, restaurant, rowing boats for hire (also at Arauco 171 in Pucón, shared rooms, use of kitchen, internet access). Camping only at the park entrance, 2 sites, US$8. 1½ km before the park entrance, 2 German speaking families, the Braatz and Soldans, offer accommodation, **E** pp, no electricity, food and camping (US$6); they also rent rowing boats on the lake. **E** pp Nidia Carrasco Godoy runs a *hospedaje* in the park, T09-443 2725 (mob). With breakfast, hot water, camping.

Transport *JAC* bus from Pucón to Paillaco, 1½ hrs, US$1, Mon-Fri 0700, 1230, 1700, Sat-Sun 0700, 1600, returns immediately – last at 1800.

South of the Huerquehue Park on a turning from the Pucón-Caburga road there are **Termas de Quimey-Co**, about 29 km from Pucón, campsite, two cabins and hotel (*Termas de Quimey-Co*, T045-441903), new, less ostentatious or expensive than **Termas de Huife** (*Hostería Termas de Huife*, T441222, PO Box 18, Pucón), Km 33, US$12 high season (US$9 low), including use of one pool, modern, pleasant (taxi from Pucón, US$23 return with taxi waiting, US$16 one way). Beyond Huife are the hot springs of **Los Pozones**, Km 35, beautiful, US$4.50.

Reserva Forestal Cañi, south of Parque Nacional Huerquehue and covering 500 ha, is a private nature reserve. It contains 17 small lakes and is covered by ancient native forests of coihue, lenga and some of the oldest araucaria trees in Chile. From its highest peak, El Mirador, five volcanoes can be seen. There is a self-guided trail; for tours with guide, contact *Fundación Lahuén*, Urrutia 477, T/F441660, Pucón, lahuen@interaccess.cl US$17 pp plus transport, or *Hostería ¡école!*

The route to Argentina From Pucón a road runs southeast via Curarrehue to the Argentine border. At Km 18 there is a turning south to the **Termas de Palguín**. There are many beautiful waterfalls within hiking distance: for example, Salto China (entry US$0.60, restaurant, camping); Salto del Puma (US$0.60) and Salto del León (US$1.25), both 800 m from the Termas. **D** *Rancho de Caballos* (Casilla 142, Pucón), T441575, restaurant with vegetarian dishes, laundry and kitchen facilities; also, *cabañas* and camping, horse riding, English and German spoken. ■ *From Pucón take* Bus Regional Villarica *from Palguín y O'Higgins at 1100 to the junction (10 km from Termas); last bus from junction to the Termas at 1500, so you may have to hitch back. Taxi from Pucón, US$17.*

Near Palguín is the entrance to the **Quetrupillán** section of the Parque Nacional Villarrica (high clearance vehicle necessary, horses best), free camping, wonderful views over Villarrica Volcano and six other peaks. Ask rangers for the route to the other entrance.

The road from Pucón to Argentina passes turnings north at Km 23 to **Termas de San Luis** and Km 35 to **Termas de Pangui**, both with hotels (T045-411388 and 045-442039 respectively). It continues to Curarrehue, from where it turns south to Puesco and climbs via **Lago Quellehue**, a tiny gem set between mountains at 1,196 m to reach the border at the Mamuil Malal or Tromén Pass. To the south of the pass rises the graceful cone of Lanín volcano. On the Argentine side the road runs south to Junín de los Andes, San Martín de los Andes and Bariloche.

Chilean immigration and customs is at **Puesco**, open December-March 0800-2100, April-November 0800-1900, US$2 per vehicle at other times. There are free Conaf campsites with no facilities at Puesco and 5 km from the border near Lago Tromén. ■ *Daily bus from Pucón, 1800, 2 hrs, US$2.*

Lago Calafquén

Colour map 8, grid C1
Population: 1,700
Altitude: 207 m

Dotted with small islands, Lago Calafquén is a popular tourist destination. **Lican-Ray** 25 km south of Villarrica on a peninsula on the north shore, is the major resort on the lake. There are two fine beaches each side of the rocky peninsula. Boats can be hired (US$2 per hour) and there are catamaran trips (US$3; trips to islands US$11 per hour). Although very crowded in season, most facilities close by the end of March. The tourist office on the plaza is open daily in summer, Monday to Friday off season. 6 km to the east is the river of lava formed when the Villarrica volcano erupted in 1971.

Sleeping & eating **On Playa Grande** **B** *Hostería Inaltulafquen*, Casilla 681, T431115, F410028. With breakfast, English spoken, comfortable. **On Playa Chica** **C** *Hosp Los Nietos*, Manquel 125, T431078. Without breakfast. **D** *Res Temuco*, G Mistral 515, T431130. Without bath, with breakfast, good. **Camping** *Floresta*, T211954, **B** for 6 people, ½ mile east of town. 6 sites to west and many along north shore towards Coñaripe. *Café Ñaños*, Urrutia 105. Very good, reasonable prices, helpful owner. *Restaurant-Bar Guido's*, Urrutia 405. Good value.

Transport Buses leave from offices around plaza. To **Villarrica**, 1 hr, US$1, *JAC* frequent in summer. In Jan-Feb, there are direct buses from **Santiago** (*TurBus* US$20, 10 hrs) and **Temuco** (US$3). To **Panguipulli**, Mon-Sat 0730.

Coñaripe (*Population: 1,253*), 21 km southeast of Lican-Ray at the eastern end of Lago Calafquén, is another popular tourist spot. Its setting, with a black sand beach surrounded by mountains, is very beautiful. From here a road around the lake's southern shore leads to Lago Panguipulli (see below) and offers superb views over

Villarrica volcano. **D** *Antulafquen*, T317298, homely. **E** pp *Hospedaje House*, with breakfast. Campsites on beach charge US$20, but if you walk ½-¾ km from town you can camp on the beach free. Cold municipal showers on beach, US$0.35. ■ *Buses to Panguipulli, 7 a day (4 on Sat), US$1.80 and Villarrica, US$1.60.*

From Coñaripe a road runs southeast over the steep Cuesta Los Añiques offering views of tiny **Lago Pellaifa**. The **Termas de Coñaripe** (T411407), excellent hotel (**A** pp) with four pools, good restaurant, cycles and horses for hire, are at Km 16. Further south at Km 32 are the **Termas de Liquiñe** (hotel, T063-317377, **A** pp full board, cabins, restaurant, hot pool, small native forest; accommodation in private houses, **E**; **F** *Hosp La Casona*, T045-412085, Camino Internacional, hot shower, good food, comfortable; tours from Lican-Ray in summer, US$17, 0830-1830 with lunch). Opposite Liquiñe are the new *Termas Río de Liquiñe*, good heated *cabañas*, good food, personal spa bath, large outdoor thermal pool, highly recommended. From there you can walk up to the thermal source, US$0.25 to cross river by boat, one hour excursion.

The border with Argentina, **Paso Carirriñe**, is reached by unpaved road from Termas de Liquiñe. It is open 15 October-31 August. On the Argentine side the road continues to San Martín de los Andes.

Lago Panguipulli

The lake is reached by paved road from Lanco on the Pan-American Highway or unpaved roads from Lago Calafquén. A road leads along the beautiful north shore, wooded with sandy beaches and cliffs. Most of the south shore is inaccessible by road. **Panguipulli**, at the northwest corner of the lake in a beautiful setting, is the largest town in the area. The streets are planted with roses: it is claimed that there are over 14,000. The **Iglesia San Sebastián**, is in Swiss style, with twin towers; its bell-tower contains three bells from Germany. Fishing excursions on the lake are recommended. Boat hire US$3. There are also good rafting opportunities on river in the area. In the last week of January is Semana de Rosas, with dancing and sports competitions. The tourist office is on the plaza. ■ *Dec-Feb only.*

Phone code: 063
Colour map 8, grid C1
Population: 8,326
Altitude: 136 m

Rates of exchange
poor for cash, TCs not
accepted anywhere

Sleeping & eating

B *Hostería Quetropillán*, Etchegaray 381, T311348. Comfortable. **D** *Central*, Valdivia 115, T311331. Good breakfast. Recommended. **D** *Res La Bomba*, JM Carrera y R Freire. Quiet. **D** private house opposite *Quetropillán*, beautiful garden. **D** *Olga Berrocal*, JM Carrera 834. Small rooms. **D** *Eva Halabi*, Los Ulmos 62, T311483. Good breakfast. **E** *Albergue Juvenil*, opposite bus terminal. **Camping** *El Bosque*, P Sigifredo 241, T311489, US$7.50 per site. "Small but perfect", hot water. Also 3 sites at Chauquén, 6 km southeast on lakeside. *Café Central*, M de Rozas 750. Fixed menu all day. Several cheap restaurants in O'Higgins 700 block.

Transport

Bus terminal at Gabriela Mistral y Portales. To **Santiago** daily, US$20. To **Valdivia**, frequent (Sun only 4), several lines, 2 hrs, US$3. To **Temuco** frequent, *Power* and *Pangui Sur*, US$2, 3 hrs. To **Puerto Montt**, US$7. To **Choshuenco**, Neltume and Puerto Fuy, *La Fit* at 1000, 1500 (not every day), 1630 Mon-Sat/1800 Sun, or *Huahum* 1130, 1530 Mon-Sat and 1900 Mon-Fri to Neltume, US$3, 2½ hrs. To **Coñaripe** (with connections for Lican-Ray and Villarrica), 7 daily Mon-Fri, 4 Sat, 1½ hrs, US$2.

Choshuenco (*Population*: 622) lies 23 km east of Panguipulli at the eastern tip of the lake. Various *hosterías*, including **D** *Hostería Rayen Trai* (former yacht club), María Alvarado y O'Higgins. Good food, open all year. Recommended. *Restaurant Rucapillán* lets out rooms. To the south is the **Reserva Nacional Mocho Choshuenco** (7,536 ha) which includes two volcanoes: Choshuenco (2,415 m) and Mocho (2,422 m). On the slopes of Choshuenco the Club Andino de Valdivia has ski-slopes and three *refugios*. This can be reached by a turning from the road which goes south from Choshuenco to Enco at the east end of Lago Riñihue (see page 702). East of Choshuenco a road leads to Lago Pirehueico, via the impressive waterfalls of **Huilo Huilo**, where the river channels its way through volcanic rock before thundering down into a natural basin. The falls are three hours' walk from Choshuenco, or take the Puerto Fuy bus and get off at *Alojamiento Huilo Huilo*, Km 9 (1 km before Neltume) from where it is a five-minute walk to the falls. **E** pp *Alojamiento Huilo Huilo*, basic but comfortable and well situated for walks, good food. Highly recommended.

East of Choshuenco is **Lago Pirehueico**, a long, narrow and deep lake, surrounded by virgin *lingue* forest. It is totally unspoilt except for some logging activity. There are no roads along the shores of the lake, but two ports. **Puerto Fuy** (*Population*: 300) is at the north end 21 km from Choshuenco, 7 from Neltume, with **F** pp at *Restaurant Puerto Fuy*, hot water, good food. Accommodation is also in private houses. A campsite is on the beach (take your own food). **Puerto Pirehueico** is at the south end, with **E** pp in *Hospedaje Pirehueico*. There is also accommodation in private houses. A ferry runs from Puerto Fuy to Puerto Pirehueico, then a road to the Argentine border crossing at Paso Huahum.

Transport Buses Daily *Puerto Fuy* to Panguipulli, 3 daily, 3 hrs, US$3. **Ferries** The *Mariela* sails from Puerto Fuy to Puerto Pirehueico, 2-3 hrs, US$1, cars US$21. A beautiful crossing (to take vehicles reserve in advance at the *Hotel Quetropillán* in Panguipulli). Schedule: beginning Dec–end Feb 3 times daily each way; rest of the year once a day, leaving Puerto Fuy at 0700.

The border with Argentina, **Paso Huahum** (659 m), is a four hour walk from Puerto Pirehueico. On the Argentine side the road leads to San Martín de los Andes and Junín de los Andes. Chilean immigration is open summer 0800-2100, winter 0800-2000.

Valdivia

Phone code: 063
Colour map 8, grid C1
Population: 110,000
839 km S of Santiago

Valdivia was one of the most important centres of Spanish colonial control over Chile. Founded in 1552 by Pedro de Valdivia, it was abandoned as a result of the Mapuche insurrection of 1599 and the area was briefly occupied by Dutch pirates. In 1645 it was refounded as a walled city, the only Spanish mainland settlement south of the Río Biobío. The coastal fortifications at the mouth of the river also date from the 17th century. They were greatly strengthened after 1760 owing to fears that Valdivia might be seized by the British, but were of little avail during the Wars of Independence: overnight on 2 February 1820 the Chilean naval squadron under Lord Cochrane seized San Carlos, Amargos and Corral and turned their guns on Niebla and Mancera, which surrendered the following morning. From independence until the 1880s Valdivia was an outpost of Chilean rule, reached only by sea or by a coastal route through Mapuche territory. From 1849 to 1875 Valdivia was a centre for German colonization of the Lake District.

Situated at the confluence of two rivers, the Calle Calle and Cruces which form the Río Valdivia, the capital of Valdivia province is set in rich agricultural land receiving some 2,300 mm of rain a year. To the north of the city is a large island, Isla Teja, where the Universidad Austral de Chile is situated.

Sights The city centre is the tree-lined, shady **Plaza de la República**. A pleasant walk is along **Avenida Prat** (or **Costanera**), which follows the bend in the river, from the bus station to the bridge to Isla Teja, the **Muelle Fluvial** (boat dock) and the riverside market. On **Isla Teja**, near the library in the University, are a **botanic garden** and **arboretum** with trees from all over the world. **Lago de los Lotos** in Parque Saval on the island has beautiful blooms in November, entry US$0.50. Also on Isla Teja is the **Museo Histórico y Antropológico**, run by the University, which contains archaeology, ethnography and history of German settlement. ■ *Tue-Sun, 1000-1300, 1400-1800, US$1.50.* Next door is the **Museo de Arte Moderno**. ■ *Tue-Fri 1000-1300, 1400-1800, Sat-Sun 1000-1300, 1500-1900, US$0.60.*

The tourist office is at Av Prat 555, by the dock, T215396. Good map of region and local rivers, list of hotel prices and examples of local crafts with artisans' addresses. There is a helpful kiosk in the bus terminal, mainly bus information. *Conaf*, Ismael Váldez 431, T218822. *Automóvil Club de Chile*, García Reyes 49075, T250376, also for car hire.

The district has lovely countryside of woods, beaches, lakes and rivers. The various rivers are navigable and there are pleasant journeys by rented motor boat on the Ríos Futa and Tornagaleanes around the Isla del Rey. Boat tours go to the **Santuario de la Naturaleza Río Cruces**, flooded as result of the 1960 earthquake, where lots of bird species are visible. ■ Isla del Río, *daily 1415, 6 hrs, US$15 pp.*

Excursions

AL *Pedro de Valdivia*, Carampangue 190, T/F212931. Good. **A** *Melillanca*, Alemania 675, T212509, F222740. Recommended. **A** *Palace*, Chacabuco y Henríquez, T213319, F219133. Good, comfortable. **C** *Hostal Centro Torreón*, P Rosales 783, T212622. With breakfast, without bath, old German villa, nice atmosphere, car parking. **C** *Hostal Esmeralda*, Esmeralda 651, T215659. **C** without bath, a bit rundown, big rooms, breakfast, also *cabañas*, parking. **B** *Prat*, Prat 595, T222020. With good breakfast, TV. **C** *Hosp Turístico*, Henríquez 745, T250086. **E** pp without bath, lovely villa in large gardens, large rooms, kitchen and laundry facilities, highly recommended especially food. **D** *Donde Marcelo*, Janequero 355, T/F205295. Quiet, fresh bread for breakfast, helpful. Recommended. **D** *Hosp Elsa Martínez*, Picarte 737, T212587. Highly recommended. **E** Henríquez 749, Casa 6, T222574, F204313. Charming old house, large rooms, kitchen, laundry, English spoken. Highly recommended.

Around the bus terminal **D** *Res Germania*, Picarte 873, T212405. With breakfast, poor beds, German spoken, HI reductions. **On A Muñoz, outside terminal** **E** pp No 345. With breakfast. **E** pp No 353. Breakfast. Recommended. **On C Anwandter** **D** *Hostal Casa Grande*,

Sleeping

Chile

Valdivia

Universidad
Austral de Chile
Botanic Garden

Av Prat (Costanera)

Main Bus Terminal

ISLA TEJA

Encinas

Los Robles

Municipalidad

Plaza de la República

Cathedral

Museo Histórico y Antropológico & Museo de Arte Moderno

Muelle Fluvial (Dock)

Río Valdivia

Los Laureles

San Carlos

Yungay Gral Lagos

Perez Rosales

Franciscan

Cochrane

Carrillo

To the south

N

Not to Scale

■ Sleeping	5 Hospedaje	12 Pedro de Valdivia	3 Cats Club
1 Ana María Vera	Internacional	13 Prat	4 Dino
2 Hospedaje	6 Hostal Arauco	14 Residencial	5 Entrelagos
Andwandter	7 Hostal Casa Grande	Germania	6 New Orleans
3 Hospedaje Aredi &	8 Hostal Centro Torreón		7 Palace
Hostal La Terraza	9 Hostal Esmeralda	● Eating	8 Tragobar
4 Hospedaje	10 Melillanca	1 Bar Olimpia	
Elsa Martínez	11 Palace	2 Café Haussmann	

No 880, T202035. With bath, TV, no singles, attractive old house, laundry facilities. Highly recommended. **E** *Hosp Aredi*, No 624, Casa 2, T214162. With breakfast, good value, *comedor*. **B** *Hostal La Terraza*, No 624, Casa 4, T212664. With breakfast, very comfortable, lovely views, parking. **E** pp *Hosp Andwandter*, No 482. With bath, breakfast, hot water. **D** *Hospedaje Ana María*, José Martí 11, 3 mins from terminal, T222468. With breakfast, shared bath, use of kitchen, good value. **E** pp *Hostal Arauco*, Arauco 869, T206013/225251. Hot water, kitchen, laundry, excellent breakfast. Highly recommended.

Other, cheaper accommodation E pp, Gen Lagos 874, T215946. With breakfast, old German house, pleasant family atmosphere. Recommended. **E** pp Riquelme 15, T218909. With breakfast, good value. **E** pp *Ana María Vera*, Beauchef 669, T218542. Good breakfast, hot water. **D** *Hosp Internacional*, García Reyes 658, T212015. With breakfast, helpful, English and German spoken, use of kitchen. Recommended. **D** Sra Paredes, García Reyes 244. With breakfast. Recommended. **F** *Albergue Juvenil*, García Reyes s/n, off Picarte, Jan/Feb only.

Campsite *Camping Centenario*, in Rowing Club on España. **E** per tent, overlooking river. *Isla Teja*, T213584, lovely views over river.

Eating

Several restaurants on the Costanera facing the boat dock, good food and atmosphere. Others upstairs in the municipal market

Mid-range: *La Calesa*, Yungay 735. Peruvian and international, music, art gallery, pier. Highly recommended. *La Cava del Buho*, Av Alemania 660. Very good food, service and interesting décor. *Palace*, Arauco y P Rosales. Popular, good atmosphere. *Selecta*, Picarte 1093. Pleasant, excellent fish and meat. *Shanghai*, Andwandter y Muñoz. Pleasant Chinese. **Cheap**: *Bar Olimpia*, Libertad 28. Always full, 24 hrs, good meeting point. *Cats Club*, Esmeralda 657. Good food, salad bar, pleasant atmosphere. *Chester's*, Henríquez 314. Good, popular. *New Orleans*, Esmeralda 652. Large portions. **Cafés**: *Café Haussmann*, O'Higgins 394. Good tea and cakes. *Café Express*, Picarte 764. Real coffee. *Dino*, Maipú y Rosales. Good coffee. *Entrelagos*, Pérez Rosales 622. Ice cream and chocolates. *Tragobar*, Beauchef 620. Great drinks, good music and ambience. **Bakery** *La Baguette*, Libertad y Yungay. French-style cakes, brown bread. Repeatedly recommended. *Cervecería Kunstmann*, Ruta T350, No 950, Casilla 1441, on road to Niebla. Restaurant serving German/Chilean food, brewery with 3 types of beer, beautiful interior. Recommended.

Festivals

Accommodation scarce during festival

Semana Valdiviana, in **mid-Feb**, culminates in Noche Valdiviana on the Sat with a procession of elaborately decorated boats which sail past the Muelle Fluvial.

Shopping

Bookshop/Cultural centre: *Librería/Centro Cultural 787*, Pérez Rosales 787. Old mansion, with café and art exhibitions. **Supermarket**: *Hiper-Unico*, Arauco 697. There's a colourful riverside market with livestock, fish etc

Tour operators

To Corral and Niebla, try the kiosks along the Muelle Fluvial

Turismo Koller, José Martí 83, T/F255335, turismokoller@koller.cl *Paraty Club*, Independencia 640, T215585. *OutDoorsChile*, Quineo 636, T253377, www.OutDoorsChile.com Has information on the web in English and German.

Transport

Air *LanChile/Lan Express* to/from **Santiago** every day via Temuco, or Concepción. **Buses** Terminal at Muñoz y Prat, by the river. To **Santiago**: several companies, 13 hrs, most services overnight, US$12-17 (*TurBus* good) *salón cama* US$45. Half-hourly buses to **Osorno**, 3 hrs, several companies, US$3-5. To **Panguipulli**, US$3, *Empresa Pirehueico*, about every 30 mins, US$3. Many daily to **Puerto Montt**, US$6, 3 hrs. To **Puerto Varas**, 2 hrs, US$6. To **Frutillar**, US$4, 3 hrs. To **Villarrica**, by *JAC*, 6 a day, 2½ hrs, US$3.50, continuing to **Pucón**, US$4.50, 3 hrs. Frequent daily service to Riñihue via Paillaco and Los Lagos. **To Argentina**: to Bariloche via Osorno, 7 hrs, *Bus Norte*, US$20; to **Junín de los Andes**, *Igi-Llaima*, 4 times a week, *San Martín*, 3, US$25.

Directory

Airline offices *LanChile*, Maipú 271, T218841/258840. **Banks** *Redbanc* ATM at *Supermercado Hiper-Unico* (see above). Good rates for cash at *Banco Santander*, P Rosales 585, *Corp Banca* (Visa), Picarte 370, will change cash and TCs. *Banco Santiago*, Arauco e Independencia, MasterCard. *Casa de Cambio* at Carampangue 325, T213305. *Turismo Austral*, Arauco y Henríquez, Galería Arauco, accepts

Chile

TCs. **Communications** Internet: *Café Phonet*, Libertad 127. *Centro Internet Libertad*, Libertad 7. **Post Office:** O'Higgins y Maipú.

At the mouth of the Río Valdivia there are attractive villages which can be visited **Coastal resorts** by land or river boat. The two main centres are Niebla on the north bank and Cor- **near Valdivia** ral opposite on the south bank. **Niebla**, 18 km from Valdivia, is a resort with seafood restaurants and accommodation. To the west of the resort is the Fuerte de la Pura y Limpia Concepción de Monfort de Lemus, on a promontory. Partially restored in 1992, it has an interesting museum on Chilean naval history. ■ *Daily in summer 1000-1900, closed Mon in winter, US$1, Wed free. Tourist information and telephone office nearby.*

Sleeping *Cabañas Fischers*, T282007. **C** per cabin, 2 campsites. **D** pp *Villa Santa Clara*, T282018 (Casilla 52, Valdivia). With breakfast, kitchen and laundry, also *cabañas*. *Las Delicias*, T213566. With restaurant with 'a view that would be worth the money even if the food wasn't good'. Also *cabañas* and camping.

Corral, a fishing port with several good restaurants is 62 km from Valdivia by road (unsuitable for cars without four-wheel drive or high clearance). The Castillo de San Sebastián, with 3 m wide walls was defended by a battery of 21 guns. It has a museum and offers a view upriver. In summer 18th-century battles are re-enacted.Entry US$4 January-February, US$1 rest of the year. North along the coast are the remains of Castillo San Luis de Alba de Amargos (three km) Castillo de San Carlos (4 km). The coastal walks west and south of Corral are splendid.

In midstream, between Niebla and Corral is **Isla Mancera** a small island, fortified by the Castillo de San Pedro de Alcántara, which has the most standing buildings. The island is a pleasant place to stopover on the boat trips, but it can get crowded when an excursion boat arrives. (**C** *Hostería Mancera*, T/F216296, open December-March, depending on weather, no singles, phone first: water not drinkable.)

Sleeping **D** *Hostería Los Alamos*. A delightful hideout for those seeking a quiet life. **E** *Residencial Mariel*, Tarapacá 36, T471290. Modern, good value.

Transport The tourist boats to **Isla Mancera** and **Corral** offer a guided half-day tour (US$20 with meals – cheaper without) from the Muelle Fluvial, Valdivia (behind the tourist office on Av Prat 555), 1330 daily. The river trip is beautiful, but you can also take a bus to Niebla from the north end of the wharf, next to the bridge in Valdivia, roughly every 20 mins between 0730 and 2100, 30 mins, US$0.75 (bus continues to Los Molinos), then cross to Corral by boat, frequent, US$1. There are occasional buses from Valdivia to Corral.

Osorno

Founded in 1553, abandoned in 1604 and refounded by Ambrosio O'Higgins and Juan MacKenna O'Reilly in 1796, Osorno later became one of the centres of German immigration. On the large **Plaza de Armas** stands the modern, concrete and glass cathedral, with many arches. West of the centre on a bend overlooking the river is the **Fuerte María Luisa**, named after the Spanish queen much painted by Goya, built in 1793, restored 1977, with only the river front walls and end turrets standing. East of the main plaza along MacKenna are a number of late 19th century mansions built by German immigrants, now preserved as National Monuments. **Museo Histórico Municipal**, Matta 809, includes displays on natural history, Mapuche culture, refounding of the city and German colonization. ■ *Mon-Sun 1100-1900 in summer; winter Mon-Fri 0930-1730, Sat 1500-1800, US$1, entrance in Casa de Cultura.* Sernatur tourist office is in the provincial government office, on Plaza de Armas, O'Higgins s/n, p 1, T234104. Municipal office in the bus terminal and kiosk on the Plaza de Armas. ■ *Both open Dec-Feb. Free city tours Jan-Feb, Mon-Fri*

Phone code: 064
Colour map 8, grid C1
Population: 114,000
921 km from Santiago
105 km N of
Puerto Montt

Chile

1500-1700. Automóvil Club de Chile, *Bulnes 463, T232269, has information and car hire. Contact* Club Andino, *O'Higgins 1073, for advice on skiing possibilities.*

Sleeping **L** *Del Prado*, Cochrane 1162, T235020. Pool, garden, good meals, well-located, charming. **AL** *Waeger*, Cochrane 816, T233721, PO Box 802, F237080. 4-star, restaurant, comfortable. Recommended. **A** *Pumalal*, Bulnes 630, T243520, F242477. With breakfast, modern, airy. **A** *Res Riga*, Amthauer 1058, T232945. Pleasant. Highly recommended but heavily booked in season. **A-B** *Eduviges*, Eduviges 856, T/F235023. Spacious, quiet, attractive, gardens, also *cabañas*. Recommended. **B** *Res Bilbao*, Bilbao 1019, T236755, F321111 and *Res Bilbao II*, MacKenna 1205, T242244. With breakfast, parking, restaurant. **C** *Res Hein*, Cochrane 843, T234116. **C** without bath, old-fashioned, spacious, family atmosphere.

   Near bus terminal **D** Amunátegui 520. Good. **D** *Res Ortega*, Colón y Errázuriz. Parking, basic, toilet facilities limited.

   E pp *Res San Diego*, Los Carrera 1575. With breakfast. **E** pp Colón 844. With breakfast. **F** pp *Res Carillo*, Angulo 454. Basic. Private houses at Germán Hube, pasaje 1, casa 22, población Villa Dama, **E** pp, use of kitchen. Recommended. **Camping** Municipal site off Ruta 5 near south entrance to city, open Jan-Feb only, good facilities, US$5 per site, swimming pool.

Eating **Mid-range**: *Dino's*, Ramírez 898, on the plaza. Restaurant upstairs, bar/cafeteria downstairs, good. *La Paisana*, Freire 530. Arab specialities. *Peter's Kneipe*, M Rodríguez 1039. Excellent German restaurant. *Shangri-La*, Ramón Freire 542, local 16. Chilean and Nepalese cuisine, French, English spoken. Recommended. **Cheap**: *Waldis*, on Plaza de Armas. Real coffee. *Travels* in bus terminal for cheap snacks. Bakery at Ramírez 977 has good wholemeal bread.

Shopping *Ekono*, supermarket, Colón y Errázuriz. For good fishing gear: *Climet*, Angulo 603, and *The Lodge*, Los Carrera 1291, local 5. *Alta Artesanía*, MacKenna 1069, Chilean crafts, not cheap. *CM Books*, Freire 542. Some English books, owner Claudia Montiel speaks English.

Transport **Air** *Lan Express*, Matta 862, T314900, operate daily flights Osorno-Santiago, via Temuco.
   Buses Main terminal 4 blocks from Plaza de Armas at Errázuriz 1400. Left luggage open 0730-2030. Bus from centre, US$0.30. To **Santiago**, frequent, US$17, *salón cama* US$25, 16 hrs. To **Valparaíso** and **Viña del Mar**, *Tas Choapa*, US$21. To **Concepción**, US$10. To **Temuco**, US$6. To **Pucón** and **Villarrica**, *TurBus*, frequent, US$6. To **Panguipulli**, *Buses Pirehueico*, 4 a day. To **Valdivia**, frequent, 3 hrs, several companies, US$3-5. To **Frutillar**, US$1.50, **Llanquihue**, **Puerto Varas** and **Puerto Montt** (US$3) services by *Varmontt* every 30 mins. to **Puerto Octay**, US$2, *Vía Octay* 6 daily between 0815-1930 (return 0800-1930) Mon-Sat, 5 on Sun between 0800 and 2000 (4 return buses). To **Bariloche**, 5 hrs, US$12-18. Local buses to **Entre Lagos**, **Puyehue** and **Aguas Calientes** leave from the Mercado Municipal terminal, 1 block west of the main terminal. To **Entre Lagos** frequent services in summer, *Expreso Lago Puyehue* and *Buses Puyehue*, 1 hr, US$1.20, reduced service off-season. Some buses by both companies also continue to **Aguas Calientes** (off-season according to demand) 2 hrs, US$2.

Directory **Banks** ATMs at *Bancos BCI*, MacKenna 801, and *Santiago*, MacKenna 787 (Visa). For good rates try *Cambio Tur*, MacKenna 1010, T234846. *Turismo Frontera*, Ramírez 949, local 11 (Galería Catedral). If stuck try *Travels* bar in bus terminal. **Communications** Internet: 3 internet places in the mall at Freire 542. *Chat-Mail-MP3*, P Lynch 1334, near Colón. Post Office: O'Higgins 645. **Telephone**: Ramírez at central plaza and Juan MacKenna y Cochrane.

Lago Puyehue
Colour map 8, grid C1
Altitude: 207 m

Lago Puyehue is about 47 km east of Osorno, surrounded by relatively flat country-side. At the western end is **Entre Lagos** (*Population*: 3,358) and the **Termas de Puyehue** is at the eastern end. ■ *Entry US$15 pp, 0900-2000.*

Sleeping and eating **D** *Hospedaje Miraflores*, E Ramirez 480, T371275. Quiet. Recommended. **D** pp *Hosp Millarey*. Ramírez 333, T371251. With breakfast, excellent. *Restaurant Jardín del Turista*. Very good. *Pub del Campo*, reasonable prices. Highly recommended. **On the south lakeshore** *Chalet Suisse*, Ruta 215, Km 55 (Casilla 910, Osorno, T Puyehue 647208, Osorno 064-234073). *Hostería*, restaurant with excellent food. **B** *Hostería Isla Fresia*, located on own island, T236951, Casilla 49, Entre Lagos, transport provided. **At the Termas L-AL** pp *Gran Hotel Termas de Puyehue*, T232157/371272 (cheaper May to mid-Dec). 2 thermal swimming pools (one indoors, very clean), well maintained, meals expensive, in beautiful scenery, heavily booked Jan-Feb (postal address Casilla 27-0, Puyehue, or T Santiago 231 3417, F283 1010), reception can be inexperienced. Accommodation also in private house nearby, **E** pp full board. **Camping** *Camping No Me Olvides*, Km 56, US$10, also *cabañas*. *Playa Los Copihues*, Km 56.5 (hot showers, good), all on south shore of Lake Puyehue.

Transport Bus 2½ hrs, schedule under Osorno. **Buses**. Buses do not stop at the lake (unless you want to get off at *Gran Hotel Termas de Puyehue* and clamber down), but continue to Aguas Calientes.

Parque Nacional Puyehue

The Park, east of Lago Puyehue, stretches to the Argentine border. On the east side are several lakes and two volcanic peaks: **Volcán Puyehue** (2,240 m) in the north (access via private road US$2.50) and **Volcán Casablanca** (also called Antillanca, 1,900 m). Park administration is at Aguas Calientes, 4 km south of the Termas de Puyehue. There is a ranger station at Anticura. Leaflets on attractions are available.

At **Aguas Calientes** there is an open-air pool with very hot thermal water beside the Río Chanleufú (open 0830-1900, US$2), and a very hot indoor pool (open Monday-Friday in season only, 0830-1230, 1400-1800, Saturday, Sunday and holidays all year, 0830-2030, US$6, children US$3).

From Aguas Calientes the road continues 18 km southeast to **Antillanca** on the slopes of Volcán Casablanca, past three small lakes and through forests. This is particularly beautiful, especially at sunrise, with the snow-clad cones of Osorno, Puntiagudo and Puyehue forming a semicircle. The tree-line on Casablanca is one of the few in the world made up of deciduous trees (southern beech). From Antillanca it is possible to climb Casablanca for even better views of the surrounding volcanoes and lakes, no path, seven hours return journey, information from Club Andino in Osorno. Attached to the *Hotel Antillanca* is one of the smallest ski resorts in Chile; there are three lifts, ski instruction and first aid available. Skiing quality depends on the weather: though rain is common it often does not turn to snow. ■ *See under Osorno for buses. No public transport from Aguas Calientes to Antillanca; try hitching – always difficult, but it is not a hard walk.*

Sleeping A *Hotel Antillanca*, T235114. Includes free mountainbiking and parapenting, at foot of Volcán Casablanca, excellent restaurant/café, with pool, sauna, friendly club-like atmosphere. **Camping** *Chanleufú*, in Aguas Calientes. With hot water, US$4 pp, good *cabañas* (**A** in season, **C** off season) T236988, a poorly-stocked shop – better to take your own food, and an expensive café. *Los Derrumbes*, 1 km from Aguas Calientes, no electricity, US$20 per site. *Conaf refugio* on Volcán Puyehue, but check with *Conaf* in Anticura whether it is open.

Border with Argentina: Paso Puyehue
Cyclists should know that there are no supplies between Entre Lagos and La Angostura (Argentina)

Chilean immigration is open the second Saturday in October to 1 May 0800-2100, otherwise 0800-1900. The Chilean border post is at Pajaritos, 4 km east of **Anticura**, which is 22 km west of the border (*Hostería y Cabañas Anticura*; *Camping Catrue*). For vehicles entering Chile, formalities are quick (about 15 minutes), but includes the spraying of tyres, and shoes have to be wiped on a mat. Pay US$2 to 'Sanidad' and US$1.25 at the documents counter. Passage will be much quicker if you already have Chilean pesos and don't wait to change at the border. This route is liable to closure after snow

Transport To Anticura, bus at 1620 from **Osorno**, 3 hrs. Several bus companies run daily services from **Puerto Montt** via Osorno to Bariloche along this route (see under Puerto Montt for details). Although less scenic than the ferry journey across Lake Todos Los Santos and Laguna Verde (see page 712) this crossing is cheaper, more reliable and still a beautiful trip.

Chile

Lago Llanquihue

The lake, covering 56,000 ha, is the second largest in Chile. Across the great blue sheet of water can be seen two snowcapped volcanoes: the perfect cone of Osorno (2,680 m) and the shattered cone of Calbuco (2,015 m), and, when the air is clear, the distant Tronador (3,460 m). The largest towns, Puerto Varas, Llanquihue and Frutillar are on the western shore, linked by the Pan-American Highway. There are roads around the rest of the lake: that from Puerto Octay east to Ensenada is very beautiful, but is narrow with lots of blind corners, necessitating speeds of 20-30 kph at best in places (see below).

Puerto Octay
Phone code: 064
Colour map 8, grid C1
Population: 2,000
56 km SE of Osorno

A small town at the north tip of the lake in a beautiful setting, Puerto Octay was founded by German settlers in 1851. The town enjoyed a boom in the late 19th century when it was the northern port for steamships on the lake. The church and the enormous German-style former convent survive from that period. **Museo el Colono**, Independencia 591, has displays on German colonization. Another part of the museum, housing agricultural implements and machinery for making chicha, is just outside town on the road to Centinela. ■ *Tue-Sun 1500-1900, Dec-Feb only.* 3 km south along an unpaved road is the Peninsula of **Centinela**, a beautiful spot with a launch dock and watersports. From the headland are fine views of the volcanoes and the Cordillera of the Andes; a very popular spot in good weather (taxi US$2.50 one way).

Sleeping and eating B *Haase*, Pedro Montt 344, T391193. With breakfast, attractive old building, elderly owner. C *Posada Gubernatis*, Santiago s/n. Lakeside, comfortable. D pp *Hosp Raquel Mardorf*, Germán Wulf 712. Owners have *Restaurante La Cabaña* at No 713. E pp *Hosp La Naranja*, Independencia 361. Without bath, with breakfast, restaurant. E pp *Hosp Fogón de Anita*, 1 km out of town. Good breakfast. E pp *Zapato Amarillo*, 35 mins' walk north of town, T/F391575, PO Box 87, Puerto Octay, www.zapatoamarillo.8k.com Excellent for backpackers and others, use of spotless kitchen, great breakfasts with home-made bread, German and English spoken (house has a grass roof). Recommended. *Restaurante Baviera*, Germán Wulf 582. Cheap and good. **Camping** *El Molino*, beside lake, US$5 pp. Recommended. **Centinela** *Hotel Centinela*, T 391326. Superb views, also has *cabañas*, restaurant, bar, open all year. E pp *Hostería La Baja*, Casilla 116, T391269. Beautifully situated at the neck of the peninsula, with breakfast and bath. **Camping** Municipal site on lakeside, US$15 per site.

Transport Buses to **Osorno** 7 a day, US$2; to **Frutillar** (1 hr, US$0.90), **Puerto Varas** (2 hrs) and **Puerto Montt** (3 hrs, US$2) *Thaebus*, 8 a day. Around the east shore: to **Las Cascadas** (34 km; E *Hostería Irma*, very pleasant, good food; also farmhouse accommodation and camping) Mon-Fri 1700, return next day 0600. Bus to **Ensenada** 0600, daily in season, less frequent out of season.

Frutillar
Phone code: 065
Colour map 8, grid C1
Population: 5,000
Altitude: 70 m

About half-way along the west side of the lake, **Frutillar** is divided into Alto Frutillar, just off the main highway, and Bajo Frutillar beautifully situated on the lake, 4 km away. (Colectivos run between the two towns, five minutes, US$0.50.) Bajo Frutillar is possibly the most attractive – and expensive – town on the lake. At the north end of the town is the **Reserva Forestal Edmundo Winckler**, run by the Universidad de Chile, 33 ha, with a guided trail through native woods. **Museo Colonial Alemán**, includes a watermill, replicas of two German colonial houses with furnishings and utensils of the period, a blacksmith's shop (personal engravings for US$5), and a *campanario* (circular barn with agricultural machinery and carriages inside), gardens and handicraft shop. ■ *Daily 0930-1900 summer, Tue-Sun 0930-1400, 1530-1800 winter, US$2.* In late January to early February there is a highly-regarded classical music festival (accommodation must be booked well in advance). The helpful tourist office is on lakeside opposite *Club Alemán*.

Chile

Sleeping North of Frutillar Bajo L *Salzburg*, T421589 or Santiago 206 1419. Excellent, restaurant, sauna, mountain bikes, arranges tours and fishing. **In Frutillar Bajo** A *Casona del 32*, Caupolicán 28, Casilla 101, T421369. With breakfast, comfortable old house, central heating, English and German spoken, excellent. On Av Philippi: A *Ayacara*, No 1215, T421550. Beautiful rooms with lake view, welcoming, have a *pisco sour* in the lilbrary in the evening. C *Hosp El Arroyo*, No 989, T421560. With breakfast. Highly recommended. C *Winkler*, No 1155, T421388. Cabins. Recommended. C No 451, T421204. Good breakfast. **C-D** *Hosp Costa Azul*, No 1175, T421388. Mainly for families, good breakfasts. **C-D** *Residenz/Café am See*, No 539. Good breakfast. D pp *Hosp Vivaldi*, No 851, T421382, Sra Edith Klesse. Quiet, comfortable, excellent breakfast and lodging, also family accommodation. Recommended. D *Hosp Trayén*, No 963, T421346. With bath, nice rooms, good breakfast. D Pérez Rosales 590. Excellent breakfast.

In Frutillar Alto D *Faralito*, Winkler 245. Cooking facilities (owner can be contacted at shop at Winkler 167, T421440). Cheap accommodation in the school, sleeping bag required. **Camping** *Playa Maqui*, 7 km north of Frutillar, T339139. Fancy, expensive. *Los Ciruelillos*, 2 km south, T339123. Most services.

Several along Carlos Richter (main street)

Eating *Club Alemán*, Av Philippi 747. Good but not cheap. *Casino de Bomberos*, Philippi 1060. Upstairs bar/restaurant, best value, memorable painting caricaturing the firemen in action. Many German-style cafés and tea-rooms on C Philippi (the lakefront) eg *Salón de Te* Frutillar, No 775. *Der Volkladen*, O'Higgins y Philippi. Natural products, chocolates and cakes, natural cosmetics.

Transport Buses to **Puerto Varas** (US$0.75) and **Puerto Montt** (US$1.25), frequent, *Varmontt* and **Full Express**. To **Osorno**, *Turismosur* 1½ hrs, US$1.50. To **Puerto Octay**, *Thaebus*, 6 a day, US$0.90. Most buses leave from opposite the *Copec* station in Alto Frutillar.

Directory Useful services Toilet, showers and changing cabins for beach on O'Higgins. *Banco Santander*, on the lakeside, has *Redbanc* ATM.

Puerto Varas

This beauty spot was the southern port for shipping on the lake in the 19th century. The Catholic church, built by German Jesuits in 1918, is a copy of the church in Marieenkirche in the Black Forest. North and east of the **Gran Hotel Puerto Varas** (1934) are German style mansions dating from the early 20th century. **Parque Philippi**, on top of the hill, is pleasant; walk up to *Hotel Cabañas del Lago* on Klenner, cross the railway and the gate is on the right. The tourist office is at San Francisco 441, T232402, F233315, helpful, finds cheap accommodation, also has an art gallery. ■ *0900-2100 in summer*.

Phone code: 065
Colour map 8, grid C1
Population: 16,000
20 km N of
Puerto Montt

Puerto Varas is a good base for trips around the lake. On the south shore two of the best beaches are Playa Hermosa (Km 7) and Playa Niklitschek (entry fee charged). **La Poza**, at Km 16, is a little lake to the south of Lago Llanquihue reached through narrow channels overhung with vegetation. **Isla Loreley**, an island on La Poza, is very beautiful (frequent boat trips); a concealed channel leads to yet another lake, the Laguna Encantada.

Excursions

L *Los Alerces*, Pérez Rosales 1281, T233039. 4-star hotel, with breakfast, cabin complex (price depends on season when rest of hotel is closed), attractive, helpful. L *Colonos del Sur*, Del Salvador 24, T233369, F233394. Good views, good restaurant, tea room. **AL** *Antonio Varas*, Del Salvador 322, T232375, F232352. Very comfortable. **AL** *Cabañas del Lago*, Klenner 195, T232291, calago@entelchile.net On Phiippi hill overlooking lake, good breakfast, restaurant. Also self-catering cabins sleeping 5 (good value for groups), heating, sauna. **AL** *Licarayén*, San José 114, T232305, F232955. Overlooking lake, comfortable, book in season, C out of

Sleeping
Accommodation is expensive, it is cheaper to stay in Puerto Montt

season. Enthusiastically recommended. **A** *Bellavista*, Pérez Rosales 60, T232011, F232013. Cheerful, restaurant, overlooking lake. Recommended. **A** *El Greco*, Mirador 134, T233388. Modern, good. **B** *Loreley*, Maipo 911, T232226. Homely, quiet. Recommended.

D pp *Hospedaje Amac*, San Bernardo 313, T234216. Apartment-style, comfortable, heating in lounge, TV, use of kitchen, hot water. **D** pp Andrés Bello 321. Nice atmosphere, good breakfast. **D** *María Schilling Rosas*, La Quebrada 752. Recommended. **D** pp *Outsider*, San Bernardo 318, T/F232910, outsider@telsur.cl With bath, real coffee, meals, also horse riding, rafting, sea kayaking, climbing. **D** *Res Alemana*, San Bernardo 416, T232419. With breakfast, without bath. **D** *Hosp Imperial*, Imperial 653, T232451. Includes breakfast, central. Recommended. **D** *Hosp Ellenhaus*, Martínez 239, T233577. Laundry facilities, lounge, hospitable. **E** pp *Casa Azul*, Mirador 18, T232904, www.casaazul.net Cosy rooms, good breakfast (US$4), kitchen facilities, German and English spoken. Highly recommended. **E** *Compas del Sur*, Klenner 467, T232044, mauro98@telsur.cl Chilean-Swedish run, kitcehn facilities, internet, good breakfast, German, English, Swedish spoken. **E** *Hosp Don Raúl*, Salvador 928, T234174. Laundry and cooking facilities, camping **F** pp. Recommended. **E** *Elmo & Ana Hernández Maldonado*, Itata 95. Breakfast or use of kitchen, helpful. Recommended. **F** pp *Colores del Sur*, Santa Rosa 318, T338588. Bed only in dormitory, use of kitchen, hospitable, meeting place.

Wild camping and use of barbecues is not allowed on the lake shore

Camping Sites on south shore of Lago Llanquihue east of Puerto Varas: Km 7, *Playa Hermosa*, T338283, or *Puerto Montt*, T252223, fancy, take own supplies, recommended. Km 8, *Playa Niklitschek*, T338352, full facilities; Km 20, *Playa Venado*, *Camping Municipal*; Km 49, *Conaf* site at Puerto Oscuro, beneath road to volcano, very good. *Campo Aventura* has 2 lodges with camping facilities, horse riding, fishing, birdwatching, Spanish classes and vegetarian food. Contact: San Bernardo 318, Puerto Varas, T/F232910, www.campo-aventura.com

Eating **Expensive**: *Merlín*, Imperial 0605. One of the best in the Lake District. **Mid-range**: At the Puerto Chico end of Pérez Rosales are *Dicorazzo*, No 01071, recommended and *Ibis*, No 1117, warmly recommended. *Espigas*, Martínez 417, local 3. Vegetarian. **Cheap**: *El Amigo*, San Bernardo 240. Large portions, good value. *Domino*, Del Salvador 450. Good. *Donde El Gordito*, downstairs in market. Huge portions, very popular. *Café Danés*, Del Salvador 441. Good coffee and cakes. *Giorgio Café*, San Bernardo 318. Danish-run, good food. Recommended.

Shopping Supermarkets: *Las Brisas*, Salvador 451. *Vyhmeistur*, Gramado 565. Good selection, reasonably priced.

Sport **Cycle hire**: *Thomas Held Expeditions*, Martínez 239, T/F311889, US$20 per day. *The area around Puerto Varas is popular for fishing* **Fishing** Licence US$2.50 a year, obtainable from Municipalidad. Expeditions organized by *Quiroz Hnos*, Estación 230, T233771/239693. **Horse riding**: *Cabañas Puerto Decher*, Fundo Molino Viejo, 2 km north, T338033, guided tours, minimum 2 people. See Outsider, under Sleeping.

Tour operators *Al Sur*, Del Salvador 100, T232334, F232300, alsur@telsur.cl Rafting on Río Petrohué, good camping equipment, tours, English

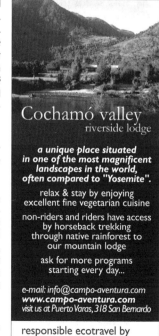

spoken. *Andina del Sud*, Del Salvador 72, T232511. Operate 'lakes' trip to Bariloche, Argentina via Lago Todos los Santos, Peulla, Cerro Tronador (see under Puerto Montt, To Argentina), plus other excursions, good. *Aqua Motion*, San Pedro 422, T/F232747, paulina@aquamotion.cl For trekking, rafting and climbing, German and English spoken, good equipment, also offers ethno-astronomical tours based in La Serena. *Tranco Expeditions*, Santa Rosa 190. Trekking on volcano, rafting, fishing and more. Recommended. *Travel Art*, Imperial 0661, T232198, F234818, www.travelart.cl Biking and hiking tours. Several others. Most tours operate in season only (1 Sep-15 Apr).

Buses Varmontt terminal, San Francisco 500 block. To **Santiago**, normal US$24, *semi cama* US$36, *cama* US$48, **TurBus**, 12 hrs. To **Puerto Montt**, 30 mins, *Varmontt*, *Thaebus* and *Full Express* every 15 mins, US$0.50. Same frequency to **Frutillar** (US$0.75, 30 mins) and **Osorno** (US$3, 1½ hrs). To **Valdivia** US$6. To **Bariloche**, *Andina del Sud*, see above. Minibuses to **Ensenada** and leave from San Bernardo y Martínez. **Transport**

Banks *Redbanc* ATMs at several banks. *Turismo Los Lagos*, Del Salvador 257 (Galería Real, local 11). Open daily 0830-1330, 1500-2100, Sun 0930-1330, accepts TCs, good rates. **Communications** Internet: *Ciber Service*, Salvador 264, loc 6-A. *George's*, San Ignacio 574. Av Gramado 560, p 2. San José 380, p 2. **Post Office:** San José y San Pedro. **Telephone:** 4 agencies in town. **Directory**

East of Puerto Varas by 47 km, Ensenada is at the southeast corner of Lake Llanquihue, which is the town's main attraction. A half-day trip is to Laguna Verde, about 10 minutes from *Hotel Ensenada*, along a beautiful circular trail, one-hour long, behind the lake (take first fork to the right behind the information board), and then down the road to a campsite at Puerto Oscuro on Lago Llanquihue. The site is quiet and secluded, a good spot for a picnic. Ludwig Godsambassis, owner of *Ruedas Viejas*, who works for *Aqua Motion* in season, works independently as a guide out of season and is very knowledgeable. ■ *Minibuses run from Puerto Varas, frequent in summer (see above). Hitching from Puerto Varas is difficult.* **Ensenada**

Sleeping and eating **AL** *Cabañas Brisas del Lago*, T212012. Chalets for 6 on beach, good restaurant nearby, supermarket next door. Highly recommended for self-catering. **AL** *Hotel Ensenada*, Casilla 659, Puerto Montt, T338888. Olde-worlde, good food (closed in winter), good view of lake and Osorno Volcano, runs tours, hires mountain bikes (guests only). Also *hostal* in the grounds, cooking facilities, cheaper. **C** *Hosp Ensenada*, T338278. Excellent breakfast. **C** *Ruedas Viejas*, T/F212050, for room, or **D** in cabin, about 1 km west from Ensenada, HI reductions. Basic, damp, restaurant. **C** *Hosp Arena*, T212037. With breakfast. Recommended. **E** pp *Hospedaje* above *Toqui* grocery. Cheapest in town, basic, quiet, hot water, use of kitchen, beach in the backyard. Recommended. **Camping** *Montaña*, central Ensenada, **E** per site. Fully equipped, nice beach sites. Also at Playa Larga, 1 km further east, US$10 and at Puerto Oscuro, 2 km north, US$8. *Trauco*, 4 km west, T212033. Large site with shops, fully equipped, US$4-9 pp. *Canta Rana* is recommended for bread and *kuchen*. *Ruedas Viejas*, the cheapest eating place.

Most eating places close off season, there are a few pricey shops. Take your own provisions

North of Ensenada, can be reached either from Ensenada, or from a road branching off the Puerto Octay-Ensenada road at Puerto Klocker, 20 km southeast of Puerto Octay. Weather permitting, *Aqua Motion* (address under Puerto Varas) organize climbing expeditions with local guide, transport from Puerto Montt or Puerto Varas, food and equipment, US$150 pp payment in advance (minimum group of two, maximum of six with three guides) all year, setting out from the *refugio* at La Burbuja. They check weather conditions the day before and offer 50% refund if climb is abandoned because of bad weather. From La Burbuja it is six hours to the summit. *Conaf* do not allow climbing without a guide and insist on one guide to every two climbers. Only experienced climbers should attempt to climb right to the top, ice climbing equipment essential. **Volcán Osorno**

Chile

Sleeping The **Club Andino Osorno** (address under Osorno) has 3 *refugios*: north of the summit at La Picada (20 km east of Puerto Klocker) at 950 m; south of the summit: *La Burbuja*, 14 km north of Ensenada at 1,250 m; and, 15 km from Ensenada at 1,200 m *Refugio Teski Club*, **D** pp, bunk accommodation, restaurant and bar, sleeping bag useful, bleak site just below snow line; a good base for walking.

Parque Nacional Vicente Pérez Rosales

Lago Todos los Santos
The most beautiful of all the lakes in southern Chile

This long, irregularly shaped sheet of emerald-green water has deeply wooded shores and several small islands rising from its surface. In the waters are reflected the slopes of Volcán Osorno. Beyond the hilly shores to the east are several graceful snow-capped mountains, with the mighty Tronador in the distance. To the north is the sharp point of Cerro Puntiagudo, and at the northeastern end Cerro Techado rises cliff-like out of the water. The ports of **Petrohué** at its western and **Peulla** at its eastern ends are connected by boat. Trout and salmon fishing are excellent in several parts including Petrohué. ■ Conaf *office in Petrohué with a visitors' centre, small museum and 3D model of the park. There is a guardaparque office in Puella. Free entry.*

There are no roads round the lake and the only scheduled vessel is the *Andino del Sud* service with connections to Bariloche (Argentina), but private launches can be hired for trips (tickets for two-hour lake tours are sold on the Petrohué-Puella ferry). Isla Margarita, the largest island on the lake, with a lagoon in the middle, can be visited (in summer only) from Petrohué, boats by *Andino del Sud* leave 1500, US$30.

The park is infested by horseflies in Dec and Jan: cover up as much as possible with light-coloured clothes which may help a bit

Petrohué, 16 km northwest of Ensenada, is a good base for walking. The **Salto de Petrohué** (entrance, US$1.50) is 6 km (unpaved) from Petrohué, 10 km (paved) from Ensenada (a much nicer walk from Petrohué). Near the falls is a snackbar; there are also two short trails, the Senderos de los Enamorados and Carileufú. **Peulla**, is a good starting point for hikes in the mountains. The Cascadas Los Novios, signposted above the *Hotel Peulla*, are stunning once you have climbed to them.

On the south shore of Lago Todos Los Santos is the little village of **Cayutué**, reached by hiring a boat from Petrohué, US$30. From Cayutué it is a three hour walk to Laguna Cayutué, a jewel set between mountains and surrounded by forest. Good camping and swimming. From here it is a five-hour hike south to Ralún on the Reloncaví Estuary (see below). This is part of the old route used by missionaries in the colonial period to travel between Nahuel Huapi in Argentina and the island of Chiloé. It is now part of a logging road and is good for mountain bikes.

Sleeping & eating
There is a small shop in Andino del Sud building but best to take your own food

At Petrohué L *Fundo El Salto*, near Salto de Petrohué. Run by New Zealanders, mainly a fishing lodge, good home cooking, fishing trips arranged, Casilla 471, Puerto Varas. **AL** *Hostería Petrohué*, T/F258042. With bath, excellent views, log fires, cosy. Owner a former climbing guide, can advise on activities around the lake. **E** pp *Familia Küschel* on other side of river (boat across). With breakfast, meals available, electricity only 3 hrs in afternoon, dirty, noisy, poor value, camping possible. Albergue in the school in summer. Conaf office can help find cheaper family accommodation. **At Peulla LL** *Hotel Peulla*, PO Box 487, Puerto Montt, T258041 (including dinner and breakfast, direct personal reservations A3, PO Box 487, Puerto Montt, cheaper out of season). Beautiful setting by the lake and mountains, restaurant and bar, expensive meals (lunch poor), cold in winter, often full of tour groups (tiny shop at back of hotel). **D** pp *Res Palomita*, 50 m west of hotel. Half board, family-run, simple, comfortable but not spacious, separate shower, book ahead in season, lunches.

Camping and picnicking is forbidden

Camping At Petrohué on far side beside the lake, US$5 per site, no services, cold showers, locals around the site sell fresh bread (local fishermen will ferry you across, US$0.50). At Peulla, opposite *Conaf* office, US$1.50. Good campsite 1½ hrs' walk east of Peulla, take food.

Minibuses: from Puerto Varas to Ensenada continue to Petrohué, frequent in summer. **Boat**: The boat between Petrohué and Peulla costs US$30 day return or one way (book in advance). It leaves Petrohué at 1030, Peulla at 1500 (not Sun, 2½ hrs – most seating indoors, no cars carried, cycles free), commentaries in Spanish, English and German. This connects with the *Andina del Sud* tour bus between Puerto Montt and Bariloche (see under Puerto Montt). Local fishermen make the trip across the lake, but charge much more than the public service.

For crossing the border with Argentina, **Paso Pérez Rosales**. Chilean immigration is in Peulla, 30 km west of the border, open summer 0800-2100, winter 0800-2000.

Transport
It is impossible to do this journey independently out of season as then there are buses only as far as Ensenada, there is little traffic for hitching and none of the ferries takes vehicles

The Reloncaví estuary, the northernmost of Chile's glacial inlets, is recommended for its local colour, its sealions, dolphins and its peace. **Ralún**, a small village at the northern end of the estuary, is 31 km southeast from Ensenada by a poorly paved road along the wooded lower Petrohué valley. Roads continue, unpaved, along the east side of the estuary to Cochamó and Puelo and on the west side to Canutillar. In Ralún there is a village shop and post office. Lodging (**E** pp) is available at restaurants *El Refugio* and *Navarrito* and *posadas Campesino* (**F** pp) and *El Encuentro* (**E** pp). *Cabañas Ralún*, T Santiago 632 1675 or Puerto Varas 278286, at south end of the village, has cabins, **A** for 6. Just outside the village there are thermal springs, reached by boat, US$2.50 pp. ■ *Bus from Puerto Montt via Ensenada, 7 a day*, Bohle *and* Fierro, *between 1000 and 1930, 6 on Sat, return 0700-1830, US$2*. Fierro *buses also go to Canutillar via Ensenada and Ralún.*

Reloncaví Estuary

Cochamó, 17 km south of Ralún on the east shore of the estuary, is a pretty village, with a fine wooden church similar to those on Chiloé, in a striking setting, with the estuary and volcano behind. **D** *Cochamó*, T216212, basic but clean, often full with salmon farm workers, good meals. Recommended. **D** *Hosp Maura*, JJ Molina 12, beautiful location overlooking the estuary, excellent food, good for kids, highly recommended. Also a large number of *pensiones* (just ask), a campsite and a few eating places. ■ *Bus* Fierro *to Ralún, Ensenada, Puerto Varas and Puerto Montt, 3 daily; to Puelo 2 daily.*

Campo Aventura (San Bernardino 318, Puerto Varas) T/F065-232910, www.campo-aventura.com In Valle Río Cochamó, offers accommodation 4 km south of Cochamó (**E** pp, kitchen, sauna, camping) and at their other base in the valley of La Junta. They specialize in horseback and trekking expeditions between the Reloncaví Estuary and the Argentine border, 2-10 days (in Europe, PO Box 111945, 86044 Augsburg, Germany).

Puelo, further south, on the south bank of the Río Puelo, is a most peaceful place (ferry crossing until bridge over Río Puelo is completed). Basic lodging is available at the restaurant or with families – try Roberto and Olivia Telles, no bath/shower, meals on request, or Ema Hernández Maldona; two restaurants. From here the road (very rough) continues to Puelche on the Camino Austral. **Transport** *Buses Bohle* from Puerto Montt, Sun 0900 and 1500 (from Puerto Varas 30 mins later). Daily buses from Cochamó Mon-Sat 0745 and 1645, Sun 1100 and 1500. In summer boats sail up the Estuary from Angelmó. Tours from Puerto Montt US$30. Off season the *Carmencita* sails once a week, leaving Puelo Sun 1000 and Angelmó Wed 0900 (advisable to take warm clothes, food and seasickness pills if it's windy).

Puerto Montt

The capital of X Región (Los Lagos) was founded in 1853 as part of the German colonization of the area. Good views over the city and bay are offered from outside the Intendencia Regional on Avenida X Region. The port is used by fishing boats and coastal vessels, and is the departure point for vessels to Puerto Chacabuco, Laguna San Rafael and for the long haul south to Puerto Natales. A paved road runs 55 km southwest to Pargua, where there is a ferry service to Chiloé.

The **Iglesia de los Jesuitas** on Gallardo, dating from 1872, has a fine blue-domed ceiling; behind it on a hill is the **campanario** (clock tower). **Museo Regional Juan**

*Phone code: 065
Colour map 8, grid C1
Population: 110, 139
1,016 km S of Santiago*

Pablo II, Portales 997 near the bus terminal, documents local history and has a fine collection of historic photos of the city; also memorabilia of the Pope's visit. ■ *Daily 1030-1800, US$1.* The little fishing port of **Angelmó**, 2 km west, has become a tourist centre with many seafood restaurants and handicraft shops (reached by Costanera bus along Portales and by collective taxi Nos 2, 3, 20 from the centre, US$0.30).

Tourist offices: *Sernatur* has two offices, in the Gobernación Provincial building on the Plaza de Armas, ■ *Daily in summer 0900-1300, 1500-1900, Mon-Fri in winter 0830-1300, 1400-1800.* Also in the Intendencia Regional, Av Décima Región 480 (p 3), Casilla 297, T/F254580. ■ *0830-1300, 1330-1730 Mon-Fri.* For more information and town maps, go to the kiosk just southeast of the Plaza de Armas run by the municipality. ■ *Open till 1800 on Sat. Telefónica del Sur* and *Sernatur* operate a phone information service (INTTUR), dial 142 (cost is the same as a local call). Dial 149 for chemist/pharmacy information, 148 for the weather, 143 for the news, etc. The service operates throughout the Tenth Region. *Conaf* is at Ochogavia 458, and Amunátegui 500 (off Gallardo) for information on national parks (in theory). *Automóvil Club de Chile*, Esmeralda 70, T252968.

Excursions The wooded **Isla Tenglo**, reached by launch from Angelmó (US$0.50 each way), is a favourite place for picnics. Magnificent view from the summit. The island is famous for its *curantos*, served by restaurants in summer. ■ *Boat trips round the island from Angelmó, 30 mins, US$8.*

Parque Provincial Lahuen Nadi contains some ancient trees in swampland, more accessible than some of the remoter forests. Take the main road to the airport, which leads off Ruta 5. After 5 km, turn right (north) and follow the signs. West of Puerto Montt the Río Maullin, which drains Lago Llanquihue, has some attractive waterfalls and good fishing (salmon). At the mouth of the river is the little fishing village of **Maullin**, founded in 1602.

Puerto Montt

■ **Sleeping**	7 Colina	14 Le Mirage
1 Albergue	8 Don Luis	15 Millahue
2 Alda González	9 El Talquino	16 Montt
3 Burg & Café Amsel	10 Hospedaje Erica	17 O'Grimm
4 Casa Gladis	11 Hospedaje Leticia	18 Residencial Central
5 Casa Perla	12 Hospedaje Polz	19 Residencial El Turista
6 Club Presidente	13 Hostal Pacifico	20 Residencial Embassy

L *Vicente Pérez Rosales*, Varas 447, T252571. With breakfast, excellent restaurant, seafood, tourist and climbing information. Recommended. **AL** *Viento Sur*, Ejército 200, T258701, F258700. Good restaurant, sauna, gym, excellent views. **AL** *Burg*, Pedro Montt y Portales, T253941. Modern, central heating, centrally located, good, interesting traditional food in restaurant. **AL** *Club Presidente*, Portales 664, T251666, F251669. 4-star, with breakfast, very comfortable, also suites. Recommended. **AL** *Don Luis*, Urmeneta y Quillota, T259001, F259005. Heating, very good. **A** *Le Mirage*, Rancagua 350, T255125, F256302. With breakfast, small rooms. **A** *Hostal Pacífico*, J J Mira 1088, T256229. **B** without bath, with breakfast, cable TV, parking, comfortable. Recommended. **A** *Res Urmeneta*, Urmeneta 290, T253262. **B** without bath, comfortable, IYHA reductions. Recommended. **B** *Colina*, Talca 81, T253502. Spacious, good restaurant, bar, car hire. Recommended. **B** *Millahue*, Copiapó 64, T253829, F253817, and apartments at Benavente 959, T/F254592. With breakfast, modern, good restaurant. **B** *Montt*, Varas y Quillota, T253651. **C** without bath, good value, good restaurant. **D** *Res Embassy*, Valdivia 130, T253533. **E** pp without bath, stores luggage. Recommended.

Near the bus terminal C *Hosp Polz*, J J Mira 1002, T252851. With breakfast, warm, good beds. Recommended. **D** *Res El Turista*, Ancud 91, T254767. With and without bath, with breakfast, comfortable, small rooms, heating. Recommended. The following are all **E** pp: *Casa Gladis*, Ancud 112 y Mira. Some double rooms, or dormitory style, kitchen and laundry facilities, crowded. *Res Central*, Lota 111, T257516. Use of kitchen. Recommended. *Hosp Godoy*, Goecke 119, T266339. With breakfast, cooking facilities, poor bathroom. **D** *Vista Hermosa*, Miramar 1486, T/F268001. Cheaper in low season, with breakfast, very good, without bath, ask for front room (10 mins' walk from terminal). *El Talquino*, Pérez Rosales 114 esq JJ Mira, T253331. Includes breakfast, hot water, family-run, cosy. Recommended. **F** pp *Hosp Leticia*, Lota 132, T256316. Hot showers, with breakfast, basic, safe, cooking facilities. Recommended. **F** pp *Hosp El Valle*, Chorrillos 1358, T258464. Hot showers, internet. **F** *Sra Victoria*, Goecke 347, T288954. Family-run, quiet. Recommended.

Other cheaper accommodation All **E** pp unless otherwise stated: *Alda González*, Gallardo 552, T253334. With or without bath, with breakfast, cooking facilities, popular. Recommended. **F** pp *Res El Tata*, Gallardo 621. Floor space, very basic, popular, packed in summer. **D** *Aníbal Pinto 328*. With breakfast, popular, laundry facilities, 10 mins' walk from centre. Recommended. *Casa Perla*, Trigal 312, T262104, casaperla@hotmail.com With breakfast, French, English spoken, helpful, meals, Spanish classes offered off season. Recommended. **D** *Casa Patricia*, Trigal 361. Family run, welcoming. *Hosp Erica*, Trigal 309, T259923. Kitchen facilities, TV, big bathroom, good views. *La Familia*, Bilbao 380, T256514. Hot water, comfortable. *Gamboa*, Pedro Montt 157, T252741. With breakfast, TV, comfortable, warm. *Sra María Oyarzo*, Subida Miramar 1184, T259957. Includes breakfast, basic (no heating, hot water next door), good beds. *Res Emita*, Miraflores 1281. Includes breakfast with homemade bread, safe. **D** pp *Hosp Suizo*, Independencia 231, T/F252640. With breakfast, painting and Spanish classes, German and Italian spoken, Spanish classes. **E** pp *Hosp Rocco*, Pudeto 233, T/F272897, hospedajerocco@hotmail.com Without bath, with breakfast, real coffee, English spoken. **On Allende** No 119, T258638. Recommended. *Hosp Montesinos*, No 121, T255353. With breakfast, recommended. *El*

Sleeping
Accommodation is expensive in season, much cheaper off season. Check Tourist Office

Several lodgings in E pp range on C Huasco, east of the Plaza de Armas

Chile

21 Residencial Urmeneta
22 Vicente Pérez Rosales
23 Viento Sur
24 Vista Hermosa

● Eating
1 Balzac
2 Café Real & Café Alemán
3 Centro Español
4 Club Alemán

To Pelluco, Chamiza & Camino Austral

Forastero, Colo Colo 1350, T263342. With good breakfast. *Albergue*, in school opposite bus station (2 Jan-15 Feb). Sleeping bag on floor (**F** pp), cold showers, kitchen and laundry facilities, no security.

Camping *Camping Municipal* at Chinquihue, 10 km west (bus service), open Oct-Apr, fully equipped with tables, seats, barbecue, toilets and showers. Small shop, no kerosene. *Camping Anderson*, 11 km west, American-run, hot showers, private beach, home-grown fruit, vegetables and milk products. *Camping Metri*, 30 km southeast on Camino Austral, T251235, *Fierro* bus, US$2 per tent.

Eating

Local specialities include picoroco al vapor, a giant barnacle whose flesh looks and tastes like crab, and curanto

Expensive: *Balzac*, Urmeneta y Quillota. Very good. *Centro Español*, O'Higgins 233. Very good. *Club Alemán*, Varas 264. Old fashioned, good food and wine. *Club de Yates*, Costanera east of centre. Excellent seafood. **Mid-range**: *Café Amsel* (in *Hotel Burg*), Pedro Montt y Portales. Superb fish. *New Harbour Café*, San Martín 185 y Urmeneta. Good coffee and atmosphere (closed Sin lunchtime) **Cheap**: *Al Passo*, Varas y O'Higgins. Simple food, warm atmosphere. *Café Real*, Rancagua 137. For *empanadas*, *pichangas*, *congrío frito*, and lunches. *Costa de Reloncaví*, Portales 736. Good. *Dino*, Varas 550. Restaurant upstairs, snacks downstairs (try the lemon juice). *Rincón Sureña*, Talca 86. Excellent lunches, popular.Excellent and cheap food at **Rodoviaria** in bus terminal (all credit cards accepted). **Cafés** *Café Alemana*, Rancagua 117. Good, real coffee. *Color Café*, Chillán 144. Small selection of good food, pleasant, good coffee, Canadian-run. *Café Plaza*, Urmeneta 326. Good location, pool table, nice atmosphere. *El Rinconcito*, Portales 1014, Galería Comercial España, a good bar.

In **Angelmó** There are many small, seafood restaurants in the old fishing port, very popular, ask for *té blanco* (white wine – they are not legally allowed to serve wine). *Asturias*, Angelmó 2448. Often recommended. Check hygiene before eating in those seafood restaurants on stilts. *Puerto Café*, Angelmó 2456 (above Travellers). Vegetarian dishes, real coffee, English spoken. Recommended.

Other seafood restaurants in **Chinquihue**, west of Angelmó. In **Pelluco** (4 km east), many seafood restaurants, including *Pazos*, T252552. Best *curanto* in Puerto Montt. *Azurro*, good Italian restaurant and, around the corner, a great pub called *Taitao*, façade like a galleon.

Shopping

Woollen goods and Mapuche-designed rugs can be bought at roadside stalls in Angelmó and on Portales opposite the bus terminal. Prices are much the same as on Chiloé, but quality is often lower.

Supermarkets *Las Brisas* and *Fullfresh*, opposite bus terminal, open 0900-2200 daily. *Fullfresh* also in the *Paseo del Mar* shopping mall, Talca y A Varas, and in the old railway station. *Santa Isabel*, Varas y Chillán. *Dimarse*, Varas y Chillán. Sells bulbs for Maglight torches/flashlights. *Libros*, Portales 580. Small selection of English novels, also maps.

Sport

Aerial Sports: Felix Oyarzo Grimm, owner of the *Hotel O'Grimm* (Gallardo 211, T252845) can advise on possibilities, especially parachuting. **Fishing**: Luis Wellman, at the *Hotel Don Luis* is very knowledgeable about fishing in the area. **Rafting and water sports**: *Alsur*, Varas 445, T/F287628.

Sailing: 2 Yacht Clubs in Chinquihue: *Marina del Sur* (MDS), T/F251958. Modern, bar and restaurant, sailing courses, notice board for crew (*tripulante*) notices, *MDS Charters* office (also Santiago T/F231 8238) specializes in cruising the Patagonian channels. Charters US$2,200-8,500 per week depending on size of boat. *Club de Desportes Náuticas*, founded by British and Americans in 1940s, more oriented towards small boat sailing, windsurfing, watersports.

There are many tour operators. We have received good reports about: *Andina del Sud*, very close to central tourist kiosk, Varas 437-445, T257797/257686. Sells a daily tour at 0830 (not Sun) to Puerto Varas, Parque Nacional V Pérez Rosales, Petrohué, Lago Todos los Santos, Peulla and back (without meals US$27, with meals US$37), and to other local sights, as well as skiing trips to the Osorno volcano (see below for trip to Bariloche). *Patagonia Verde*, Portales 514. Mountaineering, fishing, trekking, horse riding. *Petrel Tours*, San Martín 167, of 403, T/F255558. *Reloncaví*, Angelmó 2448, T288080, F288081. *Travellers*, Av Angelmó 2456, PO Box/Casilla 854, T262099, F258555, www.travellers.cl Close to 2nd port entrance and *Navimag* office, open Mon-Fri 0900-1330, 1500-1830, Sat 0900-1400 for booking for *Navimag* ferry *Puerto Edén* to Puerto Natales, money exchange, flights, bespoke incoming tours, car hire, also runs computerized tourist information service, book swap ('best book swap south of Santiago'), map display, TV, real coffee, English-run. Most offer 1-day excursions to Chiloé (US$20) and to Puerto Varas, Isla Loreley, Laguna Verde, and the Petrohué falls: both these tours are much cheaper from bus company kiosks inside the bus terminal, eg Bohle, US$15 to Chiloé, US$11 to the lakes. Some companies, eg *Reloncaví*, also offer 2-day excursions along the Camino Austral to Hornopirén, US$76 including food and accommodation.

Tour operators

Local Car hire: *Automotric Angelmó*, Talca 79. Cheap and helpful. **Automóvil Club de Chile**, Ensenada 70, T254776, and at airport (US$235 per week). *Autovald*, Portales 1330, T256355. Cheap rates. *Formula Uno*, Santa María 620, T254125. Highly recommended. *Full Famas*, Portales 506, T258060 and at airport. Helpful, good value, has vehicles that can be taken to Argentina. **Cycle repairs**: *Kiefer*, Pedro Montt 129, T253079. 3 shops on Urmeneta, none very well stocked. **Motorcycle repairs**: *Miguel Schmuch*, Urmeneta 985, T/F258877.

Transport
See Essentials, page 48 for international agencies

Chile

Long distance Air: *ETM* bus from terminal 1½ hrs before departure, US$2; also meets incoming flights. *ETM* minibus service to/from hotels, US$4 pp, T294294. Taxi US$12. To **Santiago** and **Punta Arenas** many daily flights by *LanChile*, *Lan Express* and *Aero Continente*. To **Temuco**, *LanChile/Lan Express* daily. In Jan, Feb and Mar you may well be told that flights are booked up, but cancellations may be available from the airport. To **Balmaceda**, *Lan Express* daily. *Don Carlos* flies to **Chaitén**, 1115 and 1515 Mon-Fri, Sat 1115 (fares under Chaitén), and runs regular charters for 5 passengers to Bariloche, Chaitén, and Coyhaique. To Chaitén, *Aeromet* Mon-Fri 1200, US$40; also *Aerosur* and *AeroVip*.

El Tepual Airport is 13 km NW of town

  Buses Terminal (very crowded, but well-organized) on sea front at Portales y Lota, has Telephone, restaurants, *casa de cambio* (left luggage, US$1.50 per item for 24 hrs). To **Puerto Varas** (US$0.50), **Llanquihue**, **Frutillar** (US$1.25), **Puerto Octay** (US$2) and **Osorno** (US$5) minibuses every few minutes, *Varmontt, Expreso Puerto Varas, Thaebus* and *Full Express*. To **Ensenada** and **Petrohué**, *Buses JM* at least 3 a day. To **Pucón**, US$8. To **Temuco** US$6-9, to **Valdivia**, US$7, 3½ hrs. **Concepción**, US$12. To **Santiago**, express 15 hrs, US$20, *cama* US$45, several companies including *TurBus*, very good, 14 hrs, *Tas Choapa Royal Class* US$33. To **Punta Arenas**, *Austral*, *TurBus* and *Ghisoni*, between 1 and 3 times a week, US$53-70 depending on company (bus goes through Argentina via Bariloche), 32-38 hrs. Take plenty of food for this "nightmare" trip. Book well in advance in Jan-Feb and check if you need a multiple-entry Chilean visa. Also book any return journey before setting out. For services to **Chiloé**, see page 722.

  Buses to Argentina via Osorno and the Puyehue pass Daily services to Bariloche on this route via Osorno, US$18, 6 hrs, are run by *Cruz del Sur, Río de la Plata, Tas Choapa* and *Bus Norte*. Out of season, services are reduced. Buy tickets for international buses from the bus terminal, not through an agency. If intending to return by this route, buy an open return ticket as higher fares are charged in Argentina. Book well in advance in Jan and Feb. For the route to Argentina via Lago Todos Los Santos see below.

  Shipping offices in Puerto Montt: *Catamaranes del Sur*, Av Diego Portales 510, T267533, and Km 13 Chinquihue, T482308 (Isadora Goyenechea 3250, of 802, Las Condes, Santiago, T333 7127), www.catamaranesdelsur.cl *Cruce de Lagos*, www.lakecrossing.cl, includes departures to **Puerto Varas** and **Bariloche**. *Navimag* (Naviera Magallanes SA), Terminal Transbordadores, Angelmó 2187, T432300, www.navimag.com *Skorpios Cruises*, Angelmó 1660 y Miraflores (Castilla 588), T252619, F258315, www.skorpios.cl *Transmarchilay Ltda*, Angelmó 2187, T600-600 8687/88, www.tmc.cl

Airline offices *AeroContinente*, on O'Higgins, T347777. *LanChile*, O'Higgins y Urmeneta, T253141. *Don Carlos*, Quillota 127, T253219. **Banks** For Visa *Corp Banca*, Pedro Montt y Urmeneta, good rates. For MasterCard ATM, *Banco de Santander*, A Varas 520. Many other ATMS in the city. Commission charges vary widely. *Travellers* travel agent in Angelmó (address above) has exchange facilities. *Afex*, Portales 516. *Turismo Los Lagos*, Varas 595, local 13. *La Moneda de Oro* at the bus terminal exchanges some Latin American currencies, not Argentine pesos (Mon-Sat 0930-1230, 1530-1800). Obtain Argentine pesos before leaving Chile. **Communications** Internet: *Latin Star*, Av Angelmó 1684, T310036. Interenet café, cheap phone rates, stamps, fax, English spoken, helpful. Others on Av Angelmó near *Navimag*. 3 internet cafés on San Martín (eg No 232). **Post Office:** Rancagua 126. Open 0830-1830 (Mon-Fri), 0830-1200 (Sat). **Telephone:** Pedro Montt 114 (has free internet access for 30 mins) and Chillán 98. *Entel*, Urmeneta y Pedro Montt. *Telefónica del Sur*, A Varas entre Talca y Pedro Montt. **Consulates** Argentina, Cauquenes 94, p 2, T253996, quick visa service. **Germany**, Varas y Gallardo, p 3, of 306. Tue-Wed 0930-1200. **Netherlands**, Chorillos 1582, T253003. **Spain**, Rancagua 113, T252557.

To Argentina via Lago Todos Los Santos

This popular route to Bariloche, involving ferries across Lago Todos Los Santos, Lago Frías and Lago Nahuel Huapi is outstandingly beautiful whatever the season, though the mountains are often obscured by rain and heavy cloud. The route is via Puerto Varas, Ensenada and Petrohué falls (20 minutes stop) to Petrohué, where it connects with catamaran service across Lago Todos Los Santos to Peulla. Lunch stop in Peulla two hours (lunch not included in fare: *Hotel Peulla* is expensive, see page 712 for alternatives). Chilean customs in Peulla, followed by a 1½-hour bus ride through the Paso Pérez Rosales to Argentine customs in Puerto Frías, 20 minute boat trip across Lago Frías to Puerto Alegre and bus from Puerto Alegre to Puerto Blest. From Puerto Blest it is a beautiful 1½ hour catamaran trip along Lago Nahuel Huapi to Puerto Pañuelo (Llao Llao), from where there is a 45-minute bus journey to Bariloche (bus drops passengers at hotels, camping sites or in town centre). From 1 May to 30 August this trip is done over two days with overnight stay in Peulla, add about US$89 to single fare for accommodation in *Hotel Peulla*. (Baggage is taken to *Hotel Peulla* automatically but for alternative accommodation see under Peulla.)

Transport The route is operated only by *Andino del Sud* see under Tour operators. Bus from company offices daily at 0800; the fare is US$120 one way. Note that the trip may be cancelled if the weather is poor; difficulty in obtaining a refunds or assistance have been reported. Try both Puerto Montt and Puerto Varas offices if you want to take the trip in sections.

To Puerto Natales The dramatic 1,460 km journey first goes through Seno Reloncaví and Canal Moraleda. From Bahía Anna Pink along the coast and then across the Golfo de Penas to Bahía Tarn it is a 12-17 hours sea crossing, usually rough. The journey continues through Canal Messier, Angostura Inglesa, Paso del Indio and Canal Kirke (one of the narrowest routes for large shipping). Two vessels make the journey, *Navimag's Puerto Edén* and *Magallanes*. The latter, being quicker of the two, calls at Puerto Chacabuco en route south and north, while both ships stop off Puerto Edén on Isla Wellington (1 hour south of Angostura Inglesa). This is a fishing village with one *hospedaje* (20 beds), three shops, scant provisions, one off-licence, one café, but no camping, or running water. Population is 180, plus five *carabineros* and the few remaining Alacaluf Indians. It is the drop-off point for exploring Isla Wellington, which is largely untouched, with stunning mountains. If stopping, take food; maps (not very accurate) available in Santiago.

Sea routes south of Puerto Montt
Taxi from centre to ferry terminal, US$2. All shipping services should be checked in advance; schedules change frequently

The *Puerto Edén* and *Magallanes* sail **to Puerto Natales** throughout the year on Fri and Mon respectively, taking 4 days and 3 nights. They return on Tue and Fri (board the night before). The fare, including meals, ranges from US$250 pp economy on *Puerto Edén* and US$297 cheapest cabin on *Magallanes*, to US$1,513 pp in a private cabin on either boat (there are various classes of cabin). 10% discount on international student cards in cabin class only. Cars are carried for US$280 (US$190 northbound), motorcycles US$56 and bicycles US$34. Payment by credit card or foreign currency is accepted in all *Navimag* offices. The vessels are mixed cargo/passenger ferries which include live animals in the cargo. The *Magallanes*, which started

This can be a 'real gringo experience', with lots of cards played and beer drunk. It is cheaper to fly and quicker, although tedious in the extreme, to go by bus via Argentina

Chile

service in Mar 2001, only has cabins and is more spacious than her sister ship. Economy class accommodation on *Puerto Edén* is basic, in 24-berth dormitories and there is scarce additional space for economy class passengers when weather is bad. Apart from videos, entertainment on board is limited. Economy class and cabin passengers eat the same food in separate areas. Some report good food, others terrible. Standards of service and comfort vary, depending on the number of passengers and weather conditions. Take seasickness tablets.

Booking Economy class can only be booked, with payment, through *Navimag* offices in Puerto Montt and Puerto Natales. Economy tickets are frequently sold just before departure. Cabin class can be booked in advance through *Travellers* in Puerto Montt (see Tour operators), through *Navimag* offices in Puerto Montt, Puerto Natales and Punta Arenas, or through **Cruceros Australis** (*Navimag* parent company) in Santiago, Av El Bosque Norte 0440, Las Condes, T442 3120, F203 5173. Book well in advance for departures between mid-Dec and mid-Mar especially for the voyage south (Puerto Natales to Puerto Montt is less heavily booked). It is well worth going to the port on the day of departure if you have no ticket. Departures are frequently delayed by weather conditions – or even advanced. For details and next season's fares: www.travellers.cl, or see *Navimag*'s website.

To Puerto Chacabuco Apart from the *Magallanes* (see above), *Navimag*'s roll on/roll off vehicle ferry m/n *Evangelistas* sails twice weekly to Puerto Chacabuco (80 km west of Coyhaique). The cruise to Puerto Chacabuco lasts about 24 hrs. The fares are US$26 for a reclining seat, US$66 for a bunk with shared bath, US$82 for a bunk in a cabin with private bath, US$100 pp in a double cabin with bath. There is a small canteen; long queues if the boat is full. Food is expensive so take your own. Throughout the year this same vessel goes to Laguna San Rafael, on specific dates depending on the time of year. It is a 5-day, 4-night trip, with activities, all meals and a boat trip to the glacier. Accommodation ranges from cabins costing US$465 (pp in double suite), to bunks at US$340 (with bath) and US$315 (without bath), to reclining seats at US$200 pp.

Transmarchilay's *El Colono* sails to Puerto Chacabuco on Tue, returning Wed between 1 Jan and early Mar, calling at Melinka and Puerto Aguirre, 24 hrs; passengers US$30-65 pp, suite US$93 pp, vehicles US$103, motorcycles US$30, bicycles US$15.

To Laguna San Rafael The m/n *Skorpios 1, 2* and *3* of **Skorpios Cruises** leave Puerto Montt or Puerto Chacabuco for a luxury cruises with various itineraries. The fare varies according to season, type of cabin and number of occupants: a double ranges from US$410 (low) to US$620 (high) on *Skorpios 1*, from US$890 (low) to US$1,650 (high) on *Skorpios 2* and US$1,680 (low) to US$2,500 (high) on *Skorpios 3*. It has been reported that there is little room to sit indoors if it is raining on *Skorpios 1*, but generally service is excellent, the food superb, and at the glacier, you can chip ice off the face for your whisky. (After the visit to San Rafael the ships visit Quitralco Fjord where there are thermal pools and boat trips on the fjord.)

Patagonia Connection SA, Fidel Oteíza 1921, of 1006, Providencia, Santiago, T225 6489, F274 8111, www.patagoniaconnex.cl Operates *Patagonia Express*, a catamaran which runs from Puerto Chacabuco to Laguna San Rafael via Termas de Puyuhuapi, see page 731. Tours lasting 4 to 6 days start from Puerto Montt and include the catamaran service, the hotel at Termas de Puyuhuapi and the day excursion to Laguna San Rafael. High season 20 Dec-20 Mar, low season 11 Sep-19 Dec and 21 Mar-21 Apr. High season fares for a 4-day tour from US$1430, all inclusive, highly recommended.

Raymond Weber, Av Chipana Pasaje 4 No 3435, Iquique, T09-885 8250/883 3685, www.chilecharter.com Runs charters on luxury sailing catamarans to Laguna San Rafael and Golfo de Ancud.

Other Routes See under Quellón and Chaitén for details of *Navimag*, *Transmarchilay* and other sailings between Chiloé and the mainland.

Chiloé

The culture of Chiloé has been strongly influenced by isolation from Spanish colonial currents, the mixture of early Spanish settlers and Mapuche indians and a dependence on the sea. Religious and secular architecture, customs and crafts, combined with delightful landscapes, all contribute to Chiloé's uniqueness.

Thick forests cover most of the western side of the island of Chiloé. The hillsides in summer are a patchwork quilt of wheat fields and dark green plots of potatoes. The population is 116,000 and most live on the sheltered eastern side. The west coast, exposed to strong Pacific winds, is wet for most of the year. The east coast and the offshore islands are drier, though frequently cloudy.

Colour map 9, grid A1 The island is 250 km long, 50 km wide and covers 9,613 sq km. Marea Roja, the toxin that is potentially fatal in humans, was found here in mid-2002. Seek advice before eating any shellfish here

Chile

Chiloé

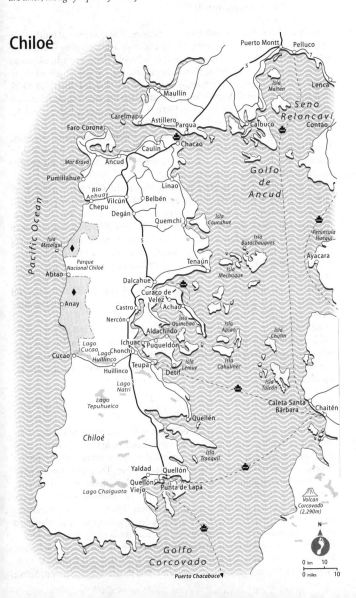

Ins & outs

Regular ferries cross the straits of Pargua between Pargua, 55 km SW of Puerto Montt on the mainland, and Chacao on Chiloé Dolpins, seals and birds can be seen

Getting there Buses Puerto Montt to Pargua, frequent, US$2, 1 hr, though most buses go through to Ancud (3½-4 hrs) and Castro. Transport to the island is dominated by *Cruz del Sur*, who also own *Trans Chiloé* and *Regional Sur* and have their own ferries. *Cruz del Sur* run frequent services from Puerto Montt to Ancud and Castro, 6 a day to Chonchi and Quellón; their fares are highest but they are faster (their buses have priority over cars on *Cruz del Sur* ferries). Fares from Puerto Montt: to Ancud, *Cruz del Sur* US$4.50, *Regional Sur* US$4.50, **Queilén Bus** (independent company), US$4; to Castro, *Cruz del Sur* US$7.50, *Trans Chiloé* US$6 and *Queilén Bus*; to Chonchi, US$7, Quellón, US$9. There are direct bus services from Santiago, Osorno, Valdivia, Temuco and Los Angeles to Chiloé. Buses drive on to the ferry (passengers leave the bus). **Ferries** About 24 crossings daily, 30 min crossing, operated by several companies including *Transmarchilay* and *Cruz del Sur*; all ferries carry buses, private vehicles (cars US$10 one way, motorcycles US$6, bicycles US$3) and foot passsengers (US$1).

History

The original inhabitants of Chiloé were the Chonos, who were pushed south by the Mapuches invading from the north. The first Spanish sighting was by Francisco de Ulloa in 1553 and in 1567 Martín Ruiz de Gamboa took possession of the islands on behalf of Spain. The small Spanish settler population divided the indigenous population and their lands between them. The rising of the Mapuche after 1598 which drove the Spanish out of the mainland south of the Río Biobío left the Spanish community on Chiloé (some 200 settlers in 1600) isolated. During the 17th century, for instance, it was served by a single annual ship from Lima.

The islanders were the last supporters of the Spanish Crown in South America. When Chile rebelled the last of the Spanish Governors fled to the island and, in despair, offered it to Britain. Canning, the British Foreign Secretary, turned the offer down. The island finally surrendered in 1826.

The availability of wood and the lack of metals have left their mark on the island. Some of the earliest churches were built entirely of wood, using wooden pegs instead of nails. These early churches often displayed some German influence as a result of the missionary work of Bavarian Jesuits. Two features of local architecture often thought to be traditional are in fact late 19th century in origin. The replacement of thatch with thin tiles (*tejuelas*) made from alerce wood, which are nailed to the frame and roof in several distinctive patterns, and *palafitos* or wooden houses built on stilts over the water.

The island is also famous for its traditional handicrafts, notably woollens and basketware, which can be bought in the main towns and on some of the off-shore islands, as well as in Puerto Montt.

Although the traditional mainstays of the economy, fishing and agriculture, are still important, salmon farming has become a major source of employment. Seaweed is harvested for export to Japan. Tourism provides a seasonal income for a growing number of people. Nevertheless, the relatively high birth rate and the shortage of employment in Chiloé have led to regular emigration.

Ancud

Phone code: 065
Colour map 9, grid A1
Population: 23,148

Ancud lies on the north coast of Chiloé 30 km west of the Straits of Chacao at the mouth of a great bay, the Golfo de Quetalmahue. Founded in 1767 to guard the shipping route around Cape Horn, it was defended by two fortresses, the Fuerte San Antonio and Fuerte Ahui on the opposite side of the bay. The port is dominated by the **Fuerte San Antonio**, built in 1770, the site of the Spanish surrender of Chiloé to Chilean troops in 1826. Close to it are the ruins of the **Polvorín del Fuerte** (a couple of cannon and a few walls). A lovely 1 km walk north of the fort leads to the secluded beach, **Arena Gruesa**. 2 km east is a **Mirador** offering good views of the island and across to the mainland, even to the Andes on a clear day. Near the Plaza de Armas is the **Museo Regional**, with an interesting collection on the early history of Chiloé. ■ *Summer daily 1100-1900, winter Tue-Fri 0900-1300, 1430-1830, Sat 1000-1330, 1430-1800, US$1, reductions for students. Has good shops and café.* Sernatur *tourist* *office, Libertad 665, T622665. Ask here about the* Agro Turismo *programme, staying with farming families.* ■ *Mon-Fri 0900-1300, 1430-1730.*

To **Faro Corona**, the lighthouse on Punta Corona, 34 km west, along the beach, which offers good views with interesting birdlife and dolphins. The duty officer may give a tour, recommended. To **Pumillahue**, 27 km southwest, where nearby there is a penguin colony (the birds are seen early morning or late afternoon): hire a fishing boat to see it, US$2.50 pp. ■ *Buses: Mon-Sat 0645, return 1730; no bus is suitable for seeing the birds.*

Chepu, on the coast southwest of Ancud (35 km) is famed for its seafishing and the drowned forest and environment of its river (a wide range of birds here). It is also the northern entry for the Parque Nacional Chiloé, see page 726.

Sleeping

In summer the school on Calle Chacabuco is used as an albergue

L *Hostería Ancud*, San Antonio 30, T622340, www.hosteriancud.com Overlooking bay, attractive, very comfortable, helpful, restaurant. **AL** *Lacuy*, Pudeto 219 near Plaza de Armas, T/F623019. With breakfast, restaurant. Recommended. **A** *Montserrat*, Baquedano 417, T/F622957. With breakfast, good views, attractive. **C** *Hostería Ahui*, Costanera 906, T622415. With breakfast, full of charm, good views. **C** *Polo Sur*, Costanera 630, T622200. Good seafood restaurant, not cheap, avoid rooms overlooking disco next door. **C** *Res Germania*, Pudeto 357, T/F622214. **C** without bath, parking, comfortable. **C** *Hosp Alto Bellavista*, Bellavista 449, T622384. Very helpful, good breakfast, with sleeping bag on floor much cheaper. **D** *Hosp Alinar*, Ramírez 348. Hospitable. **D** *Hosp Santander*, Sgto Aldea 69. **E** without bath. Recommended. **D** *Lluhay*, Cochrane 458, T622656. Meals served. Recommended. **E** pp *Elena Bergmann*, Aníbal Pinto 382. Use of kitchen, parking. **E** pp Pudeto 331, T622535. Without bath, old fashioned, very nice. **E** pp *Hosp San José*, Pudeto 619. With breakfast, good family atmosphere, hot water, shared bath, use of kitchen, internet. Recommended. **E** pp *San Bernardo*, Errázuriz 395, T622657. Good dormitory accommodation. **E** *Hosp Sra Martha*, Lautaro 988. With breakfast, TV, kitchen facilities, good beds. Recommended. **F** *Familia Vallejos*, Aníbal Pinto 738, T622243. Very friendly, basic. Recommended.

Camping *Arena Gruesa* at north end of Baquedano, T623428. *Playa Gaviotas*, 5 km north, T09-653 8096 (mob). *Playa Larga Huicha*, 9 km north, **E** per site, bath, hot water, electricity.

Eating

Excellent cheap seafood restaurants in market area

Mid-range: *Coral*, Pudeto 346. Good. *Jardín*, Pudeto 263. Good local food. **Cheap**: *Carmen*, Pudeto 159. Chilean cooking, *pasteles*. *El Cangrejo*, Dieciocho 155. Seafood. Highly recommended. *Hamburguería*, Av Prat. Much better than name suggests, good seafood. *Lydia*, Pudeto 254. Chilean and international. *La Pincoya*, Prat 61, on waterfront. Good food, service and views. *El Trauco*, Blanco y Prat. Seafood excellent. Highly recommended.

Tour operators

Austral Adventures, Pudeto 22, Casilla 432, T/F625977, www.australadventures.com Tours on land and sea. *Turismo Ancud*, Pudeto 219, Galería Yurie, T622235. *Paralelo 42*, Latorre 558, T622458. Recommended for tours to the Río Chepu area, including 2-day kayak trips, guide Carlos Oyarzun.

Transport

Buses Terminal on the east outskirts at Aníbal Pinto y Marcos Vera, reached by bus, or Pudeto colectivos. To **Castro**, US$2.50, frequent (see below), 1½ hrs. To **Puerto Montt**, frequent services by *Cruz del Sur, Regional Sur* and *Queilén Bus*. To **Quemchi** via the coast, 2 hrs, US$1.50.

Directory

Banks ATMs at *BCI*. **Communications** Internet: Phone office at Pudeto 219 has internet. **Post Office:** on corner of Plaza de Armas at Pudeto y Blanco Encalada. **Telephone:** Plaza de Armas. Mon-Sat 0700-2200.

Ancud to Castro

There are two routes: direct along Route 5, the Pan-American Highway, crossing rolling hills, forest and agricultural land, or via the east coast along unpaved roads passing through small farming and fishing communities. The two main towns along

Chile

the coastal route, **Quemchi** (*Population*: 2,000, basic accommodation) and Dalcahue, can also be reached by roads branching off Route 5.

Dalcahue (*Population*: 2,300), 74 km south of Ancud, is more easily reached from Castro, 30 km further south. It is one of the main ports for boats to the offshore islands, including Quinchao and Mechuque. The wooden church on the main plaza dates from the 19th century. The market is on Sunday, from 0700 to 1300; good quality. Tourist kiosk in season. There are various basic hotels (**D-E**) and a restaurant. ■ *Buses to Castro, hourly, 40 mins, US$1. Also collective taxis.*

Quinchao
Don't miss the oysters sold on the beach

The main settlement on this island is **Achao**, a quiet, pretty fishing village with a market. Its wooden church, built in 1730 and saved by a change of wind from a fire which destroyed much of the town in 1784, is a fine example of Chilote Jesuit architecture. The original construction was without use of nails. The tourist office at Serrano y Progreso is open between December and March only. There are various hotels (**D-E**) and restaurants. ■ *Ferry from Dalcahue, frequent, free for pedestrians and cyclists. Buses:* Arriagada, *from Ancud, 5 a day. Frequent to Castro, US$1.50,* Achao Express.

Castro

Phone code: 065
Colour map 9, grid A1
Population: 20,000
88 km S of Ancud

The capital of Chiloé lies on a fjord on the east coast. Founded in 1567, the centre is situated on a promontory, from which there is a steep drop to the port. On the Plaza de Armas is the large **Cathedral**, strikingly decorated in lilac and orange, with a splendid wood panelled interior, built by the Italian architect, Eduardo Provosoli in 1906. South of the Plaza on the waterfront is the **Feria**, or Mercado Municipal de Artesanía, where excellent local woollen articles (hats, sweaters, gloves) can be found (also imported goods). *Palafitos* can be seen on the northern side of town and by the bridge over the Río Gamboa. There are good views of the city from **Mirador La Virgen** on Millantuy hill above the cemetery. **Museo Regional** on Esmeralda, contains history, folklore, handicrafts and mythology of Chiloé and photos of the 1960 earthquake. ■ *Summer Mon-Sat 0930-2000, Sun 1030-1300; winter Mon-Sat 0930-1300, 1500-1830, Sun 1030-1300.* **Museo de Arte Moderno**, near the Río Gamboa, in the Parque Municipal, over 3 km northwest of the centre, reached by following C Galvarino Riveros up the hill west of town, take bus marked 'Al Parque'. ■ *1000-1900, T632787, F635454.* The tourist information kiosk is on the Plaza de Armas opposite Cathedral. It has a list of accommodation and prices. *Conaf* is on Gamboa behind the Gobernación building.

Sleeping

AL *Hostería Castro*, Chacabuco 202, T632301, F635668. Attractive building, wonderful views. Recommended. **AL** *Gran Alerce*, O'Higgins 808, T632267. Heating, helpful, breakfast, also has *cabañas* and restaurant 4 km south of Castro. **AL** *Unicornio Azul*, Pedro Montt 228, T632359, F632808. Good views over bay, comfortable, restaurant. **A** *Cabañas Trayen*, 5 km south of Castro, T633633. **B** off season, lovely views. **B** *Casita Española*, Los Carrera 359, T635186. Heating, TV, parking. Recommended. **B** *Chilhue*, Blanco Encalada 278, T632956. Good.

On San Martín (convenient for bus terminals) **B-C** *Hostal Quelcún*, No 581, T632396. Cheaper without bath, some rooms small, heating, helpful. **E** pp *Hosp Chiloé*, No 739. Breakfast. Recommended. **E** pp *Res Capullito*, No 747. Small rooms, pretty. **E** pp *Res Capullito*, No 709. Quiet. **F** pp No 879. With big breakfast, central. Highly recommended. **F** pp *Lidia Low*, No 890. With good breakfast, warm showers, use of kitchen.

Several lodgings on Los Carrera 500-700 blocks, E range

Other Budget accommodation D *Hilton*, Ramírez 385. Good value, restaurant. **D** *Hosp Sotomayor*, Sotomayor 452, T632464. With breakfast, quiet, small beds. **E** pp *Hosp de Jessie Toro*, Las Delicias 287. Good breakfast, helpful, spacious, good bathrooms, also cabins. Warmly recommended. **E** pp *Res La Casona*, Serrano 488, above TV shop. With breakfast. Recommended. **E** *Hosp El Molo*, O'Higgins 486, T635026. Comfortable, safe, welcoming, internet. **E** pp Eyzaguirre 469. Comfortable. Recommended. **E** pp, Freire 758. Breakfast, good value. **E** pp Chacabuco 449. Good beds, quiet, water only warm. **E** pp *Lodging El Mirador*,

Barros Arana 127, T633795. Good breakfast, **C** with bath, cosy, relaxing, kitchen. Highly recommended. **F** pp *María Zuñiga*, Barros Arana 140, T635026. Includes breakfast, comfortable, cooking facilities, secure. Recommended. **F** *Hosp América*, Chacabuco 215, T634364. With breakfast, shared bath, cable TV, very good food. **F** *Globetrotters*, Thompson 262. Kitchen, living room, cable TV, information, owner enjoys a party. **F** *Hosp Victoria*, Barros Arana 745. Warm water. Recommended. **F** pp *Hosp Polo Sur*, Barros Arana 169, T635212. Safe, cooking facilities, wonderful views. Basic accommodation Dec-Feb in the Gimnasio Fisical, Freire 610, T632766, **F** with breakfast.

Camping *Camping Pudú*, Ruta 5, 10 km north of Castro, T635109, cabins, showers with hot water, sites with light, water, children's games. Several sites on road to Chonchi.

Cheap: *Palafito* restaurants near the Feria Artesanía on the waterfront offer good food and good value, including *Rapa Nui*, *Mariela* and *La Amistad*.*Chilo's*, San Martín 459. Good lunches. *Don Camilo*, Ramírez 566. Good food. Recommended. *Maucari*, Lillo 93. Good seafood. *Sacho*, Thompson 213. Good sea views, clean. **Cafés**: *La Brújula del Cuerpo*, Plaza de Armas. Good coffee, snacks. *Stop Inn Café*, Prat y Chacabuco. Good coffee. In the market, try *milcaos*, fried potato cakes with meat stuffing. Also *licor de oro*, like Galliano.

Eating
Breakfast before 0900 is difficult to find

Cema-Chile outlet on Esmeralda. For books on Chiloé, *El Tren*, Thompson 229, *Anay*, Serrano 357, and *Libros Chiloé*, Blanco Encalada 204. Cassettes of typical Chilote music are widely available. **Supermarket** *Beckna*, O'Higgins y Aldea. Bakes good bread. The municipal market is on Yumbel, off Ulloa, uphill northwest of town: fish and vegetables.

Shopping

Turismo Isla Grande, Thompson 241, *Navimag* and *Transmarchilay* agents. *Pehuén Expediciones*, Blanco Encalada 299, T632361, pehuentr@entelchile.net *LanChile* agency, horse riding, trips to national park and islands.*Turismo Queilén*, Gamboa 502, T632776. Good tours to Chonchi and Chiloé National Park. Recommended. Local guide *Sergio Márquez*, Felipe Moniel 565, T632617, very knowledgeable, has transport. Tour prices: to Parque Nacional Chiloé US$25, to Isla Mechuque (east of Dalcahue) US$37.

Tour operators

Local buses: frequent services to Chonchi, choose between buses (*Cruz del Sur*, *Queilén Bus* and others), minibuses and colectivos (from Esmeralda y Chacabuco). *Arroyo* and *Ocean Bus* both run to Cucao, 6 a day in season, US$2.20 (1 a day off season, avoid Fri when school children are going home – much slower, lots of stops). To **Dalcahue** frequent services by *Gallardo* and *Arriagada*, also colectivos from San Martín 815. To **Achao** via Dalcahue and Curaco de Vélez, *Arriagada*, 4 daily, 3 on Sun, last return from Achao 1730, US$1.75. To **Puqueldón** on the island of Lemuy, *Gallardo*, Mon-Fri 1315, US$2. To **Quemchi**, 2 a day, 1½ hrs, US$2.50. To **Quellón**, *Regional Sur* and *Trans Chiloé*, frequent. To **Queilén**, *Queilén Bus*, 6 a day, US$2.50. **Long distance buses** Leave from 2 terminals: *Cruz del Sur*, T632389, *Trans Chiloé* and *Arriagada* from Cruz del Sur terminal on San Martín behind the cathedral. Other services leave from the Municipal Terminal, San Martín, 600 block (2 blocks further north). Frequent services to **Ancud** and **Puerto Montt** by *Cruz del Sur*, *Trans Chiloé* and *Queilén Bus*. *Cruz del Sur* also run to **Osorno**, **Valdivia**, **Temuco**, **Concepción** and **Santiago**. *Bus Norte* to Ancud, Puerto Montt, Osorno and Santiago daily. To **Punta Arenas**, *Queilén Bus*, Mon, 36 hrs, US$60. **Bicycle hire**: San Martín 581. **Ferries**: *Catamaranes del Sur* sail Castro-Chaitén, Mon, Wed, Fri 0900, US$20, returning same days at 1800.

Transport

Banks Many of the banks in the centre have ATMs for credit and bank cards (pesos only). *Banco de Chile* with ATM at Plaza de Armas, accepts TCs (at a poor rate). *BCI*, Plaza de Armas, MasterCard and Visa ATM. Better rates from *Julio Barrientos*, Chacabuco 286, cash and TCs. **Communications** Internet: *Cadesof Ltda*, Gamboa 447, p 2, entry from alley beside *Chilexpress*. O'Higgins 486, open 0900-1300, 1600-2200, US$7 per hr. *N@vegue*, San Martín 309. **Post Office**: on west side of Plaza de Armas. **Telephone**: Latorre 289. *Entel*: O'Higgins entre Gamboa y Sotomayor.

Directory

Chile

Chonchi

Phone code: 065
Colour map 9, grid A1
Population: 3,000

Chonchi is a picturesque fishing village 25 km south of Castro. From the plaza Calle Centenario, with several attractive but sadly neglected wooden mansions, drops steeply to the harbour. Fishing boats bring in the early morning catch which is carried straight into the nearby market. The wooden church, on the plaza, was built in 1754, remodelled in neo-classical style in 1859 and 1897 (key from handicraft shop next door). Sadly, its steeple fell down in a storm in early 2002. There is another 18th century church at Vilopulli, 5 km north. A tourist information kiosk is open in the main plaza in summer.

Sleeping & eating **A** *Posada El Antiguo Chalet*, Gabriela Mistral, T671221. **B** in winter, charming, beautiful location, very good. **B** *Cabañas Amankay*, Centenario 421, T671367. Homely, kitchen facilities. Recommended. **D** *Huildin*, Centenario 102, T671388. Without bath, old fashioned, good beds, also *cabañas* **A**, garden with superb views, parking. **D** *Hosp Mirador*, Alvarez 198. With breakfast. Recommended. **E** *Esmeralda By The Sea*, on waterfront 100 m south of market, T/F671328 (Casilla 79), grady@telsur.cl With breakfast, good beds, attractive, welcoming, English spoken, boat trips offered, information, use of internet, bunkhouse for 8, cooking facilities, book exchange, rents bicycles, use of bathroom. Highly recommended. **E** *Res Turismo*, Andrade 299, T671257. Without bath, with breakfast. **G** *Sra Fedima*, Aguirre Cerda 176. Own sleeping bag required, use of kitchen, good. **Camping**: *Los Manzanos*, Aguirre Cerda y Juan Guillermo, T671263. **E** per site. For eating, try *La Parada*, Centenario 133. Good selection of wines, erratic opening hours. Recommended. *El Alerce*, Aguirre Cerda 106. Good seafood, excellent value.

Shopping Handicrafts from *Opdech* (Oficina Promotora del Desarrollo Chilote), on the waterfront, and from the *parroquia*, next to the church (open Oct-Mar only).

Transport **Buses** and taxis to **Castro**, frequent, US$1, from main plaza. Services to **Quellón** (US$3) and **Queilén** from Castro and Puerto Montt also call here. **Ferry** to Chaitén via the outer islands, Tue, Wed, Fri 0800, 8 hrs (including an island stopover), US$20 Jan-Feb, US$15 Oct-Dec, Mar-May, bicycles US$10, weather permitting; tickets from *Esmeralda By The Sea* (see above), T/F671328.

Cucao From Chonchi a road leads west to **Cucao**, 40 km, one of two settlements on the west coast of Chiloé. At Km 12 is Huillinco (road paved), a charming village on Lago Huillinco (**E** pp *Residencia*, good food, or stay at the Post Office). At Cucao there is an immense 15 km beach with thundering Pacific surf and dangerous undercurrents. **E** *Hosp El Arrayan*, T633040, ask for Erice or Ojede. Friendly, good food and restaurant. **E** pp *Hosp Paraíso*, T633040 (Sra Luz Vera), ask for Sra Edvina for horse-hire. **E** pp *Posada Cucao*, T633040, with breakfast, meals. **E** pp with full board or *demi-pension* at *Provisiones Pacífico* (friendly, good, candles provided, no hot water). **E** pp *Casa Blanca*, with breakfast. **E** *Chela*, close to beach and withing walking distance of park, helpful, use of kitchen, good breakfast. There are several campsites including *Parador Darwin*, which also has rooms (**F** pp), breakfast, vegetarian and other meals, real coffee, recommended. *Las Luminarias* sells excellent *empanadas de machas* (local shellfish). ■ *For buses from Castro see above; in season as many as four buses a day, last departure 1600, reduced service off-season; hitching is very difficult.*

Parque Nacional Chiloé The Park, which is in three sections, covers 43,057 ha. Much of the park is covered by evergreen forest. The northern sector, covering 7,800 ha, is reached by a path which runs south from Chepu (see page 723). The second section is a small island, Metalqui, off the coast of the north sector. The southern sector, 35,207 ha, is entered 1 km north of Cucao, where there is an administration centre (limited information), small museum and guest bungalow for use by visiting scientists (applications to

Conaf via your embassy). Park entry US$2. No access by car. Maps of the park are available (**NB** *Refugios* are inaccurately located.)

A path runs 3 km north from the administration centre to Laguna Huelde (many camp sites) and then north a further 12 km to Cole Cole (*refugio*, free camping, dirty) offering great views, best done on horseback (return journey to/from Cucao nine hours by horse). The next *refugio* is at Anay, 9 km further north on the Río Anay. There are several other walks but signposting is limited. Many houses in Cucao rent horses at US$2.50 per hour, US$22 per day (check horses and equipment carefully). *Miguelangelo Allende* has been recommended. If you hire a guide you pay for his horse too. Horseflies are bad in summer (wear light coloured clothing).

Quellón

There are pleasant beaches nearby at Quellón Viejo (with an old wooden church), Punta de Lapa and Yaldad. The launch *Puerto Bonito* sails three times daily in summer from the pier, US$12.50 to tour the bay passing Punta de Lapa, Isla Laitec and Quellón Viejo. A trip can also be made to Chaiguao, 11 km east, where there is a small Sunday morning market. Horses can be hired US$2.50 per hour. Also kayaks with a guide, US$2.50 per hour. Camping US$3.50. **Museo de Nuestros Pasados**, Ladrilleros 255, includes reconstructions of a traditional Chilote house and mill. Tourist kiosk on the Plaza de Armas, ask about *hospedajes* not listed in their information leaflet. ■ *Mid-Dec to mid-Mar.*

Phone code: 065
Colour map 9, grid A1
Population: 18,700
92 km S of Castro
Amazing views of the mainland on a clear day

Sleeping

B *Melimoyu*, P Montt 375, T681250. Good beds, parking. **C-D** *Playa*, P Montt 427, T681278. Without breakfast or bath, not very clean. **E** pp *Hosp La Paz*, La Paz 370, T681207. With breakfast, hot water. **F** pp *Las Brisas*, P Montt 555, T681413. Without bath, basic. **F** pp *Club Deportes Turino*, La Paz 024. Floor space and camping, cold water, kitchen facilities, basic, open Dec-Feb only. *Albergue*, Ladrilleros, near Carrera Pinto, **F** pp, dormitory accommodation.

Eating

Rucantú on P Montt. Good food, good value. *El Coral*, 22 de Mayo. Good, reasonably priced, superb views. *Fogón Las Quilas*, La Paz 053, T206. Famous for lobster. Recommended. *Los Suizos*, Ladrilleros 399. Swiss cuisine, good, slow service, internet.

Transport

Buses To Castro, 2 hrs, frequent, *Cruz del Sur*, US$3; also services to **Ancud** and **Puerto Montt**.
    Ferries From Dec to early Mar, the *Navimag* vessel *Alejandrina* sails to **Chaitén** on the mainland, 3 times a week, 5 hrs crossing, US$18 reclining seat, US$15 passenger. The ship continues from Chaitén to **Puerto Montt**, US$22 reclining seat, US$18 passenger. *Transmarchilay's Pincoya* sails to **Chaitén** Sat, Sun at 1500, US$19 pp. *Navimag* sails Quellón-**Puerto Chacabuco** Tue 1900. If you take this ferry when heading south you miss a large section of the Camino Austral, even though the sea crossing is beautiful in good weather. If you wish to see the Camino's scenery, take the ferry to Chaitén (ferry sometimes arrives very late at night, book a room in advance). *Navimag*, Pedro Montt 457, Quellón, T682207, F682601, www.navimag.com

Directory

Banks *Banco del Estado*, US$12 commission on TCs, no credit cards, no commission on US$ cash.

Chile

Santiago

The Camino Austral

Construction of the Camino Austral has opened up the impressive landscapes of this wet and windy region of mountains, channels and islands. The main town is Coyhaique. A boat journey, either as a means of access, or for viewing the glacier at Laguna San Rafael gives an equally magnificent, but different perspective.

Background

Portal for the Aisén region: www.patagonia chile.cl

A third of Chile lies to the south of Puerto Montt, but its land and climate are such that, until recently, it has been put to little human use: less than 3 of the country's population lives here. South of Puerto Montt the sea has broken through and drowned the central valley between the Andes and the coastal mountain range. The higher parts of the latter form a maze of islands, stretching for over 1,000 km and separated from the coast by tortuous fjord-like channels. It is fortunate for shipping that this maze has a more or less connected route through it: see page 719.

There is no real dry season. On the offshore islands and the western side of the Andes annual rainfall is over 2,000 mm. Westerly winds are strong, especially in summer. Temperatures vary little between day and night. Inland on the steppelands the climate is drier and colder. January and February are probably the best months for a trip to this region.

Routes

This road can be divided into three major sections: Puerto Montt-Chaitén, Chaitén-Coyhaique, and Coyhaique-Villa O'Higgins. It is described on Chilean maps as a 'camino ripio' (paved with stones): some sections are difficult after rain. Paving from Puerto Montt to Cerro Castillo is expected to be complete by 2005. An access road to Tortel at the southern end is under construction. Most of the villages along the Camino are of very recent origin and consist of a few houses which offer accommodation and other services to travellers. Motorists need to carry sufficient fuel and spares, especially if intending to detour from the highway itself. Unleaded fuel is available as far south as Cochrane. Until paving is complete, protect windscreens and headlamps. Cyclists: beware stones thrown up by passing vehicles

Puerto Montt to Chaitén

This section of the Camino Austral, 242 km, includes two, sometimes three ferry crossings. Before setting out, it is imperative to check when the ferries are running and, if driving, make a reservation: do this in Puerto Montt (not Santiago), at the *Transmarchilay* office, Angelmó 2187, T600-600 8687. The alternative to this section is by ferry from Puerto Montt or Quellón to Chaitén.

Ranger posts have little information; map available from Conaf in Puerto Montt. No camping within park boundaries

The road (Ruta 7) heads east out of Puerto Montt, through Pelluco and after an initial rough stretch follows the shore of the beautiful Seno Reloncaví. It passes the southern entrance of the **Parque Nacional Alerce Andino**, which contains one of the best surviving areas of alerce trees, some over 1,000 years old (the oldest is estimated at 4,200 years old). Wildlife includes pudú, pumas, vizcachas, condors and black woodpeckers. There are two entrances: 2½ km from Correntoso (35 km east of Puerto Montt) at the northern end of the park (with ranger station and campsite) and 7 km east of Lenca (40 km south of Puerto Montt) at the southern end. There are three other ranger posts, at Río Chaicas, Lago Chapo and Sargazo. ■ *US$5. To north entrance: take* Fierro *or Río Pato bus to Correntoso (or Lago Chapo bus which passes through Correntoso), several daily except Sun, then walk. To south entrance: take any* Fierro *bus to Chaicas, La Arena, Contau and Hornopirén, US$1.50, getting off at Lenca sawmill, then walk (signposted).*

Chile

At 46 km from Puerto Montt (allow one hour), is the first ferry at **La Arena**, across the Reloncaví Estuary to Puelche. ■ *30 mins, every 1½ hrs, US$10 for a car, US$5 for motorcycle, 0715-2045 daily. Arrive at least 30 mins early to guarantee a place; buses have priority. Roll-on roll-off type operating all year.*

Río Negro is now called **Hornopirén** after the volcano above it. From here you catch the second ferry, to Caleta Gonzalo, the centre for the new Parque Nacional Pumalín, created to protect alerces and other native tree species; T250079 (Puerto Montt) or 731288 (Chaitén) for details. At the mouth of the fjord is **Isla Llancahué**, good for hiking in the forests amid beautiful scenery. *Hotel Termas de Llancahué* charges **A** full board (excellent food), hot spring at the hotel. To get there, make arrangements by phoning T09-653 8345. The hotel will send an open boat for you; the one hour crossing affords views of dolphins and fur seals.

Hornopirén
Colour map 9, grid A1
Population: 1,100
58 km S of Puelche

Sleeping and eating (Electricity 1900-0100). **A** *Holiday Country*, O'Higgins 666, T263062, hot shower, restaurant. *Hornopirén*, Carrera Pinto 388, T255243, at the water's edge. Highly recommended.

Electricity 1900-0100

Transport Buses *Fierro* run daily 0800 and 1500 from **Puerto Montt. Ferries** Río Negro – Caleta Gonzalo, *Transmarchilay*, daily 1600, 4 hrs (may be much longer if the ferry cannot dock in rough weather). Going north the ferry leaves Caleta Gonzalo at 0900, daily. Fare for cars US$80, motorcycles US$16, passengers US$13, bicycles, US$9. Ferry operates Jan-Feb only and can be very busy; there can be a 2-day wait for vehicles to get on the ferry.

South of Caleta Gonzalo there is a steep climb on a coarse gravel surface to Laguna Blanca. Caleta Santa Bárbara, a black sand beach with nice camping and swimming, is at Km 48. (**NB** Do not camp close to the water.) It is a further 12 km to Chaitén.

Parque Pumalin, created by the US billionaire Douglas Tompkins, is a private reserve of 320,000 ha which has been given Nature Sanctuary status. Covering large areas of the western Andes, most of the park is occupied by temperate rainforest and is seen by many as one of the most important conservation projects in the world. The park protects the lifestyles of its inhabitants as well as the physical environment. There is a native tree nursery and an apiculture project; in 2000, bee stations produced 30,000 kg of honey. ■ *Free. Treks range from short trails into the temperate rainforest to arduous hikes lasting for several days. Cabins from **D** pp sleep up to 4; meals extra. Camping at several sites from US$1 pp. T/F02-7358034; www.pumalin.org*

The capital of Palena province, **Chaitén** is important as a port for ferries to Puerto Montt and Quellón and is a growing centre for adventure tourism and fishing. There is excellent fishing nearby, especially to the south in the Ríos Yelcho and Futaleufú and in Lagos Espolón and Yelcho. Fishing licences are sold at the Municipalidad. There are good views over the Corcovado Bay from Avenida Corcovado. The forestry service, off the main plaza, will let you photocopy their map.

Chaitén
Phone code: 065
Colour map 9, grid A1
Population: 3,258

Sleeping and eating **A** *Mi Casa*, Av Norte, T731285, on a hill. Fine views, sauna, gym, restaurant, set meals. **B** *Schilling*, Corcovado 230, T731295. With breakfast, heating, restaurant. **D** *Hotel Restaurant El Triángulo*, Juan Todesco 8, T731312. No heating nor private bath, but good meals, very helpful. Recommended. **E** *Hosp Hogareño*, Pedro de Valdivia 129, T731413. With breakfast, meals, use of kitchen, hot water, camping. **E** pp *Hosp Lo Watson*, Ercilla 580, use of kitchen. **E** pp *Martín Ruiz*, Camino Austral 1 km north. Includes breakfast, nice views. **E** pp *Hosp Recoba*, Libertad 432 (*B y V* bus office), T731390. With breakfast, good meals. **F** pp *Ancud*, Libertad 105. With breakfast and use of kitchen, welcoming. *Los Arrayanes* campsite 4 km north, with hot showers and close to sea, good. Eating places include *Flamengo*, Corcovado, 218. Popular. *Mahurori*, Independencia 141, also has rooms. *El Quijote*, O'Higgins 42. Bar, snacks. Bakery with email facilities (US$6 per hr) on D Portales.

Chile

Tour operators *Chaitur*, Diego Portales 350, T/F731429, nchaitur@hotmail.com English, French spoken, helpful, excursions, trekking, riding, fishing. Recommended. Opposite is an office for Parque Pumalin.

Transport Air Flights to **Puerto Montt** with *Aerosur, AeroVip* and *Aeromet* (daily 1200, 35 mins, US$40). *AeroVip* also flies to **Castro**. Bookings can be made through *Chaitur*. **Buses** Several companies operate minibuses along the Camino Austral from the terminal, O'Higgins 67: in summer up to 6 a week, in winter 3 a week with overnight stop in La Junta or Puyuguapi. The agent for all services is *Chaitur*. To **La Junta** US$11, 4 hrs; to **Puyuguapi** US$13, 5 hrs; to **Coyhaique** US$25, 11 hrs (*Bus Norte*, O'Higgins 067, T731429, or Libertad 432, T731390). Minibuses usually travel full so are unable to pick up passengers en route. To **Futaleufú**, US$9, 5 hrs, *B y V*, Mon-Sat 1500. The same company also runs to **Caleta Gonzalo**. Hitching the whole route takes about a week, but you must be prepared for a day's wait if you find yourself out of luck. **Ferries** Port about 1 km north of town. From Puerto Montt, *Catamaranes del Sur*, Av J Todesco 180, T731199, Mon, Wed, Fri 0900, returning from Chaitén 1500, US$33 one way (see under Castro for service to Chiloé). *Navimag*'s *Alejandrina* sails between Chaitén and **Quellón** (Chiloé) Dec-early Mar, 3 times a week, 5 hrs (reduced service in low season). It also runs to Puerto Montt on Sat in summer, 10 hrs, US$18-22 (reduced service in low season). Office at Carrera Pinto 188, T731571. *Transmarchilay*'s *Pincoya* runs between Chaitén and Quellón, Wed, Sat, Sun 0900, 5 hrs, fares under Quellón. *Transmarchilay* also run 3 ferries a week Puerto Montt-Chaitén. Office Av Corcovado 266, T731272/3.

Directory Banks *Banco del Estado*, O'Higgins y Libertad, charges US$10 to change TCs and has an ATM. **Communications Internet:** at the *Entel* office.

Chaitén to Coyhaique

This section of the Camino Austral, 422 km, runs through small villages and passes through the Parque Nacional Queulat; roads branch off east to the Argentine border and west to Puerto Cisnes.

Puerto Cárdenas, 46 km south of Chaitén, is on the northern tip of **Lago Yelcho**, a beautiful lake on Río Futaleufú surrounded by hills and frequented by anglers. Further south at Km 60, a path leads to **Ventisquero Yelcho** (two hours' walk). Lodging includes *Cabañas Cavi*, with bath, hot water, kitchen facilities, restaurant, video room, laundry, also camping with electricity, hot showers, drinking water, barbecue area, fishing boats for hire (in Santiago *Turismo Austral*, Santa Magdalena 75, of 902, Providencia, T334 1309/232 7105, F334 1328).

The Argentine border is reached in two places, Futaleufú and Palena by a road which branches off at **Villa Santa Lucía** (Km 81). The road to the border is single track, gravel, passable in a regular car, but best with a good, strong vehicle; the scenery is beautiful. At **Puerto Ramírez** at the southern end of **Lago Yelcho** the road

divides: the north branch runs along the valley of the Río Futaleufú to **Futaleufú** and the southern one to Palena. **Lago Espolón**, west of Futaleufú, reached by a turning 41 km northeast of Villa Santa Lucía, is a beautiful lake in an area enjoying a warm microclimate: 30° C in the day in summer, 5° at night. The Río Futaleufú and Lago Espolón provide excellent fishing. ■ *Several* cabañas *and campsites. Bus Futaleufú-Chaitén Mon-Sat 0730.*

Sleeping At Villa Santa Lucía Several places on main street: at No 7 (Sra Rosalía Cuevas de Ruiz, basic, meals available), No 13 (breakfast extra) and No 16 (not bad), all **F** pp, none has hot water. **At Puerto Ramírez** *Hostería Río Malito.* Rooms, camping, fishing. Also *Hospedaje Las Casas*. **At Futaleufú** (prefix all telephone numbers with 258633 and ask for the 'anexo'): **D** pp *Hotel Continental*, Balmaceda 595, T222. Basic, cheap restaurant. Recommended. **F** *Res Carahue*, O'Higgins 322, T221. *Río Grande*, O'Higgins y Aldea, T320. Several others. **At Palena** *La Frontera*, T741240. *Res La Chilenita*, T258633.

Chilean immigration is in **Futaleufú**, 8 km west of the border. Straightforward crossing. The border is just west of the bridge over the Río Grande. For Argentina immigration, see page 195. Change money in Futaleufú (poor rates); nowhere to change at the border but you can pay the bus fare to Esquel (Argentina) in US dollars. ■ *From west side of plaza in Futaleufú a bus runs to the border, Mon and Fri 0900 and 1800, connecting with services to Trevelin and Esquel, US$3, 30 mins (leaves opposite the small grey store, Kitty, Balmaceda 419).*

> **Border with Argentina**

Alternatively, cross into Argentina further south near **Palena**, which is 8 km west of the border and has a Chilean immigration office. ■ Expreso Yelcho *bus from Chaitén Tue, Thu, 0830, US$12, 5½ hrs.*

A friendly and drab village at the confluence of Río Rosselot and Río Palena. 151 km south of Chaitén. **Lago Rosselot**, surrounded by forest in the **Reserva Nacional Lago Rosselot**, 9 km east of La Junta, can be reached by a road which continues east, 74 km, to Lago Verde and the Argentine border. *Campo Aventura* have built an outback camp with a 6-km nature trail, all visitors get a free guide book.

> **La Junta**
> *Population: 1,070*

Sleeping A *Hostal Espacio Tiempo*, T314141, F314142, www.espacio-y-tiempo.cl Restaurant, attractive gardens, fishing expeditions. **D** *Hostería Valdera*, Varas s/n, T314105. Includes breakfast, very good value. **D** *Res Copihue*, Varas 611, T314184. Without bath, includes breakfast, good meals. Recommended. **D** *Café Res Patagonia*, Lynch 331, T314120. Good meals, small rooms, limited bathrooms. Stove alcohol can be bought at the large gas station on main road, also food supplies.

> *If desperate to change money try the hotels, but bargain hard*

Transport Fuel is available. Buses to **Coyhaique**, 6 a week in summer, US$12, 7 hrs, 2 a week in winter. To **Chaitén**, 4 hrs, US$10.

The Camino Austral runs south along the west side of Lago Risopatrón, to Puyuguapi (also spelt Puyuhuapi), 45 km further south at the northern end of the Puyuguapi fjord. The village was founded by four Sudeten German families in 1935. Southwest 18 km, accessible only by boat, are **Termas de Puyuhuapi**, several springs with 40° C water filling three pools near the beach (baths cost US$15 pp, children under 12 US$10, take food and drink). 24 km south of Puyuguapi is the beautiful **Ventisquero Colgante** (Hanging Glacier) in the Parque Nacional Queulat, US$3 to visit (*Conaf* campsite with cold showers, US$4). The Camino Austral passes through the park. ■ *Bus:* Bus Norte, *O'Higgins s/n, T325130: to Coyhaique, US$14, and Chaitén, US$16, Mon, Wed, Fri.*

> **Puyuguapi**
> *Phone code: 068*
> *Population: 500*

Sleeping and eating LL-AL *Hotel Termas de Puyuhuapi* (price depends on season and type of room). Including use of baths and boat transfer to hotel, full board US$40 extra, good restaurant. Recommended. For reservations: *Patagonia Connection SA*, Fidel Oteíza 1921, of

Chile

1006, Providencia, Santiago, T225 6489, F274 8111 or directly at the *Hotel Termas de Puyuhuapi*, T/F325103/129. Boat schedule from jetty, 2 hrs' walk from town, 0930, 1000, 1200, 1230, 1830, 1900, US$3 each way, 10 mins crossing. Transport by seaplane may be arranged independently in Puerto Montt. **B** *Hostería Alemana*, Otto Uebel 450, T325118. A large wooden house on the main road, comfortable. Highly recommended. **B-C** pp *Hostería Ludwig*, Otto Uebel 850, T325220, F (Santiago) 206 4154, www.contactchile.cl/casaludwig **C-D** low season, excellent, including breakfast, good views, German spoken. **E** pp *Hostería Elizabeth*, Llantureo y Henríquez, T325106. Includes breakfast. **E** *Hospedaje* at bus stop. Use of kitchen, arranges car hire with driver. **A** *Cabañas Fiordo Queulat* (T Coyhaique 233302). Recommended. **A** *Cabañas El Pangue*, Km 240, T325128, cpangue@entelchhile.net With bath, hot water, heating, swimming pool, fishing trips, horse riding, mountain bikes. There is a dirty campsite by the fjord behind the general store. The store (good) is at the north end of town, behind the service station, which sells fuel until 1930. *Café Rossbach*. In style of a Black Forest inn, with limited menu, not cheap, excellent salmon; 2 bars.

Puerto Cisnes At 59 km south of Puyuguapi, a road branches west and follows the Río Cisnes 35 km to **Puerto Cisnes** (*Population*: 1,784), an attractive settlement at the mouth of the river. Fuel is available. The Río Cisnes, 160 km in length, is recommended for rafting or canoeing, with grand scenery and modest rapids except for the horrendous drop at Piedra del Gato. Good camping in the forest. **B** *Hostal Michay*, Mistral 112, T346462. **C** *Res El Gaucho*, Holmberg 140, T346514. With bath and breakfast, dinner available, welcoming, hot water. **D** *Hosp Bellavista*, Séptimo de Línea 112, T346408. Also various *cabañas*. ∎ *To Coyhaique, Transportes Terra Austral, T346757, daily 0630, US$14; Bus Norte, T346440, 3 a week, US$12.*

At 89 km south of Puyuguapi is **Villa Amengual** (**F** pp *Res El Encanto*, Fca Castro 33-A). At Km 92 a road branches east, 104 km to La Tapera and to the Argentine border. Chilean immigration is 12 km west of the **border**, open daylight hours only. On the Argentine side the road continues to meet up with Ruta 40, the north-south road at the foot of the Andes.

Coyhaique

Phone code: 067
Colour map 9, grid A1
Population: 36,367
420 km S of Chaitén, it is the administrative and commercial centre of the XI Region

Situated in the broad green valley of the Río Simpson, Coyhaique was founded in 1929. It provides a good base for hiking, skiing and, especially, fishing excursions. On the pentagonal plaza stand the Cathedral, the Intendencia, the Liceo San Felipe Benicio and a handicraft market. The **Museo Regional de la Patagonia Central** in the Casa de Cultura, has sections on history, minerology, zoology and archaeology, plus photos of the Camino Austral, good. ∎ *Tue-Sun 0900-2000, 0830-1730 in winter, US$1, Baquedano 310.* From the bridge over the Río Simpson look for the **Piedra del Indio**, a rock outcrop which looks like a face in profile. *Sernatur* tourist office is at Bulnes 35 (Casilla 601), T/F231752, F233949, sernatur-coyhai@ entelchile.net Helpful, English spoken, has bus timetable. ∎ *Mon-Fri 0830-2100, Sat & Sun 1100-2000.* There is a municipal kiosk on the plaza, and another at the museum, Baquedano 310. *Conaf* office, Ogana 1060. Maps (photocopies of 1:50,000 IGM maps) from Dirección de Vialidad on the plaza.

Sleeping
In summer rooms are in very short supply; the tourist office has a list, but also look out for notices in windows (several on Baquedano and Almte Simpson)

A *Los Ñires*, Baquedano 315, T232261, F233372. With breakfast, comfortable, parking. **A** *Austral*, Colón 203, T/F232522. English spoken, tours arranged. **C** *Hostal Bon*, Serrano 91, T231189. With breakfast, also *cabañas* **D** pp, good meals. Recommended. **B** *El Reloj*, Baquedano 444, T/F231108. With breakfast, restaurant, comfortable. **C** *Hostal San Cayetano*, Av Simpson 829, T/F231555. **D** without bath, cooking facilities, good. **D** *Hostal Licarayen*, Carrera 33A, T233377 (Santiago T743 1294). With breakfast, no singles. Recommended. **D** without bath, restaurant and bar, run down. **D** *Hosp Lautaro*, Lautaro 532, T231852. Comfortable, kitchen facilities, large rooms. Recommended. Another of the same name at Lautaro 269, T/F238116, franciscos@entelchile.net

D *Albergue Las Salamandras*, 2 km south in attractive forest, T/F211865. Camping, kitchen facilities, winter sports and trekking (Jun-Oct). Recommended. **E** pp *Hospedaje* at Baquedano 20, T232520, Patricio y Gedra Guzmán. Room in family home, *cabaña*, use of kitchen, breakfast, bathroom and laundry facilities, space for camping, access to river, English spoken, most hospitable. Recommended. **E** *Hosp Natti*, Av Simpson 417, T231047. Good. **E** pp *Los Cuatro Hermanos* Colón 495, T232647. Without breakfast (more with). **E** pp *Hosp Pierrot*, Baquedano 130, T221315. Hospitable, homemade bread, internet access. Recommended. **F** pp *Casa Irene*, 12 de Octubre 503. With breakfast, kitchen and laundry facilities, good. **F** pp *Hosp Ogana*, Av Ogana Pasaje 8, 185, T232353. Cooking facilities, with breakfast, helpful, also camping and *cabañas*. **F** *Los Profesores*, Errázuriz y Prat. Good beds and showers, no cooking facilities. **F** *Don Santiago*, Errázuriz 1040, T231116. With parking and kitchen, good value. Many more *hospedajes* and private houses with rooms; ask tourist office for a list.

Many places especially on Baquedano, Av Simpson and Lautaro

Cabañas AL *Los Pinos*, Camino Teniente Vidal, Parcela 5, T234898. Fishing area, near river and beach and natural park. **AL** *San Sebastián*, Baquedano 496, T/F233427. With breakfast. **B** *Río Simpson*, T/F232183, Km 3 road to Pto Aisén. Cabins for 5, fully equipped, horse hire, fishing. **B-C** *La Pasarela*, T234520, F231215, Km 1.5 Carretera a Aisén. Good atmosphere, *comedor*.

Chile

Coyhaique

To Hospedaje at Baquedano 20, Cabañas La Pasarela, Puerto Aisén & Camino Austral North

To Conaf, Airport, Albergue Las Salamandras, Puerto Ibáñez & Camino Austral South

To Don Santiago

N
Not to scale

■ Sleeping
1 Austral
2 Casa Irene
3 El Reloj
4 Hospedaje Lautaro
5 Hospedaje Pierrot
6 Hospedaje Natti
7 Hostal Bon
8 Hostal Licarayen
9 Los Cuatro Hermanos
10 Los Ñires
11 San Sebastián

● Eating
1 Café Kalu
2 Café Oriente
3 Café Ricer
4 Cafetería Alemana
5 Casino de Bomberos
6 La Olla
7 Loberías de Chacabuco

Camping There are many camping sites in Coyhaique and on the road between Coyhaique and Puerto Aisén, eg at Km 1, 2 (*Camping Alborada*, US$8.50 per site, T238868, hot shower), 24, 25, 35, 37, 41, 42 (*Camping Río Correntoso*, T232005, US$15 per site, showers, fishing, *Automobile Club* discount) and 43.

Eating **Mid-range**: *Café Ricer*, Horn 48. Good. *Loberías de Chacabuco*, Prat 386. Good seafood, slow service. *La Olla*, Prat 176. Popular, good lunches. **Cheap**: *Cafetería Alemana*, Condell 119. Nice, excellent cakes and coffee, vegetarian dishes. *Casino de Bomberos*, in the fire station, Gen Parra 365. Wide range, good value. Highly recommended. *Lito's*, Lautaro 147, next to Bus Terminal. Good food and atmosphere. *Pizzería La Fiorentina*, Prat 230. Good. **Cafés and bars**: *Café Kalu*, Prat 402. Snacks, beer. *Café Oriente*, Condell 201. Good bakery, tea. A trendy bar is *@bar*, Moraleda y Carrera. *Bar West*, Bilbao y Magallanes. Western style.

Shopping *Cema-Chile* on plaza, between Montt and Barroso. *Feria de Artesanía* on the plaza. Super-markets: *Central*, Magallanes y Bilbao, open daily till 2230 and at Lautaro y Cochrane. *Brautigam*, Horn 47. Stocks fishing and camping gear. 2 smaller ones on Prat, Nos 480 and 533, open Sun.

Tour operators *Aerohein*, Baquedano 500, T/F232772, www.aerohein.cl Air tours to Laguna San Rafael, recommended. All types of adventure tourism with *Adventure Expeditions Patagonia*, Casilla 519, T/F411330, riobaker@entelchile.net *Aventura*, Parra 220, aventuraturismo@entelchile.net Offers rafting. *Encounter Patagonia*, Colón 166, T215001, info@encounterpatagonia.com (in USA 5209 Saratoga Ave, Chevy Chase, MD 20815, T1-888-280 7036) Shannon Skaggs runs excellent tours and excursions, lots of activities. Recommended. *Exploraciones Lucas Bridges*, E Lillo 311, Casilla 5, T/F233302, lbridges@entelchile.net Small group adventure trips. Recommended. *Turismo Prado*, address in Banks below. Helpful. *Expediciones Coyhaique*, Portales y 12 de Mayo, T/F232300. Both offer tours of local lakes and other sights, arrange Laguna San Rafael trips, etc; *Prado* does historical tours, while *Expediciones* does fishing trips and excursions down the Río Baker. *El Puesto Expeditions*, Moraleda 299, T/F233785, elpuesto@entelchile.net Hiking, fishing, climbing. *Turismo Queulat*, 21 de Mayo 1231, T/F231441. Trips to Queulat glacier, adventure and nature tourism, fishing, etc. **Horse-riding** and other excursions from *Cabot*, Parra 177, T230101, www.cabot.cl (useful site) *Touraustralis*, Moraleda 589, T/F239696, touraustralis@entelchile.net Also fishing, birdwatching. *Turismo Aysén*, Lillo 194, T238036, F235294, also fishing.

Transport **Local** **Bicycle rental**: *Figón*, Simpson y Colón, T234616, check condition first, also sells spares. **Repairs**: *Tomás Madrid Urrea*, Pasaje Foitzich y Libertad, F252132. Recommended. **Car hire**: *Automóvil Club de Chile*, Bolívar 254, T/F231649, rents jeeps and other vehicles. *Automundo AVR*, Bilbao 510, T231621. *Traeger-Hertz*, Baquedano 457, T231648. **Car repairs**: *Motortech*, Baquedano 131. *Automotores Santiago*, Los Ñires 811, T238330. English spoken, can get spares quickly. **Taxis**: US$5 to airport (US$1.65 if sharing). Fares in town US$1.35. 50% extra after 2100. Colectivos congregate at Prat y Bilbao, average fare US$0.50.

Long distance **Air**: Most flights from Balmaceda (see page 736), although Coyhaique has its own airport, Tte Vidal, about 5 km southwest of town. *Don Carlos* to **Chile Chico** (daily, US$39), **Cochrane** (Mon, Fri, US$70) and **Villa O'Higgins** (Mon, Thu, US$104, recommended only for those who like flying, with strong stomachs, or in a hurry).

Buses: Terminal at Lautaro y Magallanes, but few buses use this. Most leave from bus company offices: *Bus Norte*, Gen Parra 337, T232167; *Don Carlos*, Subteniente Cruz 63, T232981; *Suray*, A Prat 265, T238387; *Turibus*, Baquedano 1171, T231333. Full list of buses from tourist information.

To/from **Puerto Montt**, via Bariloche, all year, *Turibus*, Tue and Sat 1700, US$46, with connections to Osorno, Valdivia, Temuco, Santiago and Castro, often heavily booked. To **Punta Arenas** via Coyhaique Alto, *Bus Sur*, Tue and Fri 1600, US$50. To **Puerto Aisén**, minibuses run every 45 mins, 1 hr *Suray* and *Don Carlos*, US$2, connections for **Puerto Chacabuco**. There are daily buses to **Mañihuales**, *Trapananda* and *Sao Paulo* from bus terminal (daily 1300, US$1 and US$1.85 respectively). To **Puerto Ibáñez** on Lago Gen Carrera, several colectivo companies (connect with *El Pilchero* ferry to Chile Chico) 0530-0600 from your hotel, 3 hrs, book the day before (eg *Sr Parra*, T251073, *Don Tito*, T250280), US$7.

Buses on the **Camino Austral** vary according to demand: north to **Chaitén**, *Bus Norte* and *Trans Daniela* (T231701) on alternate days, US$30; in winter these stop overnight in La Junta. To **Puerto Cisnes**, *Terra Austral* (T254475), Mon-Fri, US$14. South to **Cochrane** at 0815, *Don Carlos*, Tue, Sat 0830, *Acuario 13*, Wed, Fri, Sat 1000, and *Los Ñadis*, Tue, Thu, Sun, 1100, 10-12 hrs, US$20. *Don Carlos* also has buses on Tue and Sat to **Cerro Castillo** (US$5), **Bahía Murta** (US$10), **Puerto Tranquilo** (US$11) and **Puerto Bertrand** (US$15).

To Argentina: options are given below and under Balmaceda and Chile Chico. Many border posts close at weekends.

Shipping: *Transmarchilay*, 21 de Mayo 447, T231971, F232700. *Navimag*, Ibáñez 347, T233306, F233386.

Airline offices *LanChile*, Moraleda 401 y Parra, T231188 (Balmaceda). **Banks** *Banco Santander*, Condell 100, MasterCard and Visa ATM. *Turismo Prado*, 21 de Mayo 417, T/F231271. Accepts TCs. *Emperador*, Bilbao 222. **Communications** Internet: *Ciber Patagonia*, 21 de Mayo 525. Cheap, good. *Hechizos*, 21 de Mayo 460. Cheao. Post Office: Cochrane 202. Telephone: at Barroso 626. Open till 2200, opens on Sun about 0900. *Entel*, Prat 340, also has internet access, US$7 per hr. **Language schools** *Baquedano International Language School*, Baquedano 20, at *Hospedaje* of Sr Guzmán (see Sleeping), T232520, www.patagoniachile.cl/com/bils US$300 per week course including lodging and all meals, 4 hrs a day one-to-one tuition, other activities organized at discount rates.

Directory (margin)

Chile (margin, vertical)

A 43-km road runs east to this crossing. On the Argentine side the road leads through Río Mayo and Sarmiento to Comodoro Rivadavia. Chilean immigration is at Coyhaique Alto, 6 km west of the border, open May-August 0800-2100, September-April 0700-2300. ■ *To Comodoro Rivadavia, Empresa Giobbi, Coyhaique terminal, T232067, Thu 0930, 12-13 hrs, and Turibus, Mon, Fri, 1100, US$22.*

Border with Argentina: Coyhaique Alto (margin)

Puerto Aisén

The paved road between Coyhaique and Puerto Aisén passes through **Reserva Nacional Río Simpson**, which has beautiful waterfalls, good views of the river and very good fly-fishing. Administration is at the entrance; campsite opposite the turning to Santuario San Sebastián, US$5.

Phone code: 067 (margin)
Colour map 9, grid A1
Population: 13,050
426 km S of Chaitén

Puerto Aisén is 65 km west of Coyhaique at the meeting of the rivers Aisén and Palos. They say it rains 370 days a year here. Formerly the region's major port, it has been replaced by Puerto Chacabuco, 15 km to the west. There are few vestiges of the port left, just some boats high and dry on the river bank when the tide is out and the foundations of buildings by the river, now overgrown with fuchsias and buttercups. The local folklore festival is in the second week in November.

The longest suspension bridge in Chile and a paved road lead to **Puerto Chacabuco**; a regular bus service runs between the two. The harbour is a short way from the town.

www.portchacabuco. cl, gives information on shipping movements (margin)

In season the *Apulcheu* sails regularly to **Termas de Chiconal**, about one hour from Puerto Chacabuco, two hours by boat – book in *Sernatur* (Gobernación, Esmeralda 810, T332562, F332628, 1 December to end-February only), offering a good way to see the fjord, US$30, take own food.

Unless otherwise stated, services are in **Puerto Aisén**. D *Res Aisén*, Serrano Montaner 37, T332725. Good food, full board available. D *Res Serrano Montaner*, Montaner 471, T332574. Very pleasant and helpful. Recommended. E *Plaza*, O'Higgins 237, T332784. Without breakfast. E *Roxy*, Aldea 972, T332704. Large rooms, most without bath or toilet, meals available, helpful. E pp *Yaney Ruca*, Aldea 369, T332583. No campsite but free camping easy. A restaurant is *Gastronomía Carrera*, Cochrane 465. Large, very good, popular. In **Puerto**

Sleeping & eating (margin)
Accommodation is hard to find, most is taken up by fishing companies in both ports

Chacabuco AL *Parque Turístico Loberías de Aisén*, Km 2 Camino a Puerto Aisén, T234520. Accommodation overpriced, best food in the area, climb up steps direct from port for drink or meal before boarding ferry. **E** *Moraleda*, O'Higgins 82, T331155. No other places to buy food or other services.

Transport **Buses** To **Puerto Chacabuco**, *Don Carlos* and *Suray* every 30 mins to 1 hr, US$1. To **Coyhaique**, *Don Carlos* minibuses 8 daily, *Suray* minibuses hourly, both US$2, 1 hr journey. *Pincoya* and *Evangelistas* have been described as "floating buses", very basic, all passengers except those in cabins sleep in seats, little luggage space. **Ferries** *Transmarchilay*'s *Colono* runs from Puerto Chacabuco via the Canal Moraleda to **Puerto Montt**, Wed 2100, 26 hrs, all year service (fares under Puerto Montt); meals are available. From Jan to early Mar the ship also makes an excursion from Puerto Chacabuco to Laguna San Rafael each Fri 2100, returning Sun 0800 (fares, including food, US$200-270 pp, ranging from economy class to cabin). *Navimag* sails to **Quellón** on Chiloé Sun 2000, all year round. *Navimag*'s *Evangelistas* sails each Thu and Sun from Puerto Chacabuco to Puerto Montt, taking about 24 hrs (fares under Puerto Montt, the *pionero* seats are quite spacious and comfortable and there is a cafeteria selling burgers, sandwiches, soft drinks, beer, hot beverages, etc); it too diverts from its schedule in summer to run a 5-day trip from Puerto Montt to Laguna San Rafael, leaving Puerto Chacabuco Sat, fares under Puerto Montt (see also under Puerto Montt for the *Magallanes* on the Puerto Natales route). *Catamaranes del Sur* also have sailings to Laguna San Rafael, US$472-525 pp in double cabin, depending on season. **Shipping Offices**: *Agemar*, Tte Merino 909, T332716, Puerto Aisén. *Catamaranes del Sur*, J M Carrera 50, T351112. *Navimag*, Terminal de Transbordadores, Puerto Chacabuco, T351111, F351192. *Transmarchilay*, Av O'Higgins s/n, T351144, Puerto Chacabuco. It is best to make reservations in these companies' offices in Puerto Montt, Coyhaique or Santiago (or, for *Transmarchilay*, in Chaitén or Ancud). For trips to Laguna San Rafael, see below (page 720). Out of season, they are very difficult to arrange, but try *Edda Espinosa*, Sgto Aldea 943, or ask at *Restaurant Yaney Ruca* or *Restaurant Munich*.

Directory **Banks** *Banco de Crédito*, Prat, for Visa. *Banco de Chile*, Plaza de Armas only changes cash, not TCs. **Communications Post Office**: on south side of bridge. **Telephone**: on south side of Plaza de Armas, next to *Café Rucuray*, which posts boat information. *Entel*, Libertad 408. Has internet access.

South of Coyhaique

The southernmost section of the Camino Austral, 443 km, ends at Villa O'Higgins. Branch roads run off to Balmaceda and Puerto Ibáñez and Chile Chico on Lago General Carrera. The section around the west of Lago Gen Carrera is reckoned by some to be the most beautiful.

At Km 41 a paved road runs east to **Balmaceda** on the Argentine border at Paso Huemules (no accommodation). Chilean immigration is open May-July 0800-2000, September-April 0730-2200.

Transport **Air**: Balmaceda airport is used by *Lan Express* for flights from **Santiago** via **Puerto Montt** for Coyhaique, and once a week to Punta Arenas. *Don Carlos* flies to **Chile Chico** Tue, Thu, Sat, US$41. Airlines run connecting bus services to/from Coyhaique, US$2 (leave town 2 hrs before flight). Minibuses to/from hotels, US$4.50, several companies including *Travel*, Moraleda y Parra, T230010, *Transfer*, Lautaro 828, T233030. Taxi from airport to Coyhaique, 1 hr, US$6. **Buses** Daily to Coyhaique, 0800, US$1.70.

Lago General Carrera Straddling the border, Lago General Carrera (Lago Buenos Aires in Argentina) covers 2,240 sq km. Sheltered from the prevailing west winds by the Campo de Hielo Norte, the region prides itself in having the best climate in Southern Chile, with some 300 days of sunshine; as a result, much fruit is grown especially around Chile Chico. Rainfall is very low for this area. The main towns, Puerto Ibáñez on the north shore and Chile Chico on the south, are connected by a ferry, the *Pilchero*. There are two alternative routes to Chile Chico: through Argentina or on the Camino Austral which runs west around the lake.

Puerto Ibáñez (*Population*: 828), the principal port on the Chilean section of the lake, is reached by taking a branch road, 31 km long, from the Camino Austral 97 km south of Coyhaique. There are various hotels (**D-E** eg **E** *Vientos del Sur*, Bertrán Dixon 282, T 423208, good) and fuel (sold in 5 litre containers) is available at Luis A Bolados 461 (house with 5 laburnum trees outside). Most shops and restaurants are closed on Sunday. There are some fine waterfalls, the Salto Río Ibáñez, 6 km north.

Transport Minibus: to Coyhaique, 2½ hrs, US$7. There is a road to **Perito Moreno**, Argentina, but no public transport. **Ferries** The car ferry, *El Pilchero*, sails from Puerto Ibáñez to **Chile Chico**, Tue, Wed, Fri 0900, Sat 1000, return Tue 1730, Thu 1400, Fri 1730, Sun 1300. Fares for cars US$45, for passengers US$4.40, 2¼ hr crossing, motorbikes and bicycles US$8. Number of passengers limited to 70; reservations possible (**Sotramin**, Portales 99, Coyhaique, T233515). A cold crossing, even in summer; take warm clothes. Buses and jeeps meet the ferry in Puerto Ibáñez for Coyhaique.

From the turning to Puerto Ibáñez the Camino Austral goes through **Villa Cerro Castillo** (Km 8) which has a small supermarket and six *residenciales* (none has phone): from **D** pp *San Sebastián*, Camino Austral s/n, to **F** pp *El Castillo*, O'Higgins 241. The **Reserva Nacional Cerro Castillo** nearby, is named after the fabulous mountain (2,675 m), which looks like a fairytale castle, with pinnacles jutting out of thick snow. The park includes several other peaks in the northern wall of the Río Ibáñez valley. *Guardería* on the Senda Ibáñez, opposite Laguna Chinguay. ■ *Nov-Mar. Maps given out by the rangers are of little use. Get IGM maps in advance. Camping US$5.* The Camino climbs out of the valley, passing the aptly named Laguna Verde and the Portezuelo Cofré. It descends to the boggy Manso valley, with a good campsite at the bridge over the river, watch out for mosquitoes.

Bahía Murta, 5 km off the Camino, lies at Km 198, on the northern tip of the central 'arm' of Lago General Carrera. *Hostal Lago General Carrera*, 5 de Abril 647, T419601, *Res La Bahía*, 5 de Abril 653 and *Res Patagonia*, Pasaje España 64 (all **E**) and free camping by lake, good view of Cerro Castillo. From here the road follows the lake's western shore. **Río Tranquilo**, Km 223, is where the buses stop for lunch: fuel is available at the *ECA* store from a large drum (no sign). Take a small boat to Capilla del Marmol, US$30 per boat. **C** *Hostal Los Pinos*, 2 Oriente 41, T411576, warmly recommended; similarly **E** *Cabañas Jacricalor*, before the bridge, T419500, hot shower, good meals, god information for climbers; and various **D-E** range hotels. **El Maitén**, Km 273, is at the southwest tip of Lago Gen Carrera: here a road branches off east along the south shore of the lake towards Chile Chico, hitching possible (see below). *Cabañas Mallín Colorado*, Camino Austral Km 273, 2 km south of El Maitén, is beautifully located cabin accommodation at the edge of Lago General Carrera, with horse riding, fishing, rafting, www.patagonia-pacific.cl

The colour of the water here is an unbelievable blue-green, reflecting the mountains that surround it and the clouds above

South of El Maitén the Camino Austral becomes steeper and more bendy (in winter this stretch, all the way to Cochrane, is icy and dangerous). **Puerto Bertrand**, Km 284, is good for fishing (Jonathan, who lives beside the lake, can arrange fishing, rafting, canoeing, riding and walking). Nearby is a sign to the Nacimiento del Río Baker: the place where the Río Baker is reckoned to begin. **A** pp *Hostería Campo Baker*, T/F411447, and other lodges. *Hospedaje Doña Ester* has **E** rooms; *Casa de Huéspedes*, has dormitory accommodation. There is one small shop.

Beyond, the road climbs up to high moorland, passing the confluence of the Ríos Neff and Baker (there is a *mirador* – lookout – here), before winding into Cochrane. The scenery is splendid all the way; the road is generally rough but not treacherous. Watch out for cattle on the road and take blind corners slowly.

At **Puerto Guadal**, 10 km east of El Maitén, there are shops, a post office and petrol. **Sleeping and eating D** *Hostería Huemules*, Las Magnolias 382, T411202. With breakfast, good views. **E** pp *Res Maitén* , Las Magnolias. Campsite at east end of village. *Restaurant La Frontera*, Los Lirios y Los Pinos. *Playa Guadal Cabanas*, 2 km from Puerto Guadal, T/F067-411443, near beach. Fishing, lake views, beautiful setting. *Patagonian Lodge*, Km 1.5 Camino a Chile Chico, reservations through Azimut 360 in Santiago T735 8034, F777 2375, azimut@reuna.cl Organizes hiking and treks from here. ■ *Getting there: minibus to Chile Chico Tue, Thu 0745, and Mon, Fri 0830.*

Further east are the villages of Mallín Grande (Km 40) and **Fachinal** (locals will let you stay for free if you have a sleeping bag). Parts of this road were built into the rock face, giving superb views, but also dangerous, unprotected precipices.

Chile Chico
Population: 2,200

This is a quiet, friendly but dusty town in a fruit-growing region, 122 km east of El Maitén. It has an annual festival at end-January. There are fine views from Cerro de las Banderas. The tourist office is at O'Higgins 333, T411359, F411355. Ask here or at the Municipalidad for help in arranging tours.

Sleeping and eating **C** *Hostería de la Patagonia*, Camino Internacional s/n, Casilla 91, T411337, F411444. Full board, excellent food, English, French and Italian spoken, trekking, horse-riding and white-water rafting. Recommended. **E** pp *Casa Quinta No me Olvides/ Manor House Don't Forget Me*, Camino Internacional s/n. *Hospedaje* and camping, cooking facilities, bathrooms, hot showers, honey, eggs, fruit and vegetables for sale, tours arranged to Lago Jeinimeni and Cueva de las Manos. Recommended. **E** *Hosp Don Luis*, Balmaceda 175, T411384. Meals available. **F** *Hosp Alicia*, Ramón Freire 24. Rooms for 1, 2 or 3, clean, use of kitchen. **Camping** Free campsite at Bahía Jara, 5 km west of Chile Chico, then turn north for 12 km. Restaurants: apart from *Residenciales*: *Cafetería Loly y Elizabeth*, PA González 25, on Plaza serves coffee and delicious ice-cream and cakes. *Café Holiday*, PA González 115, has good beer and coffee. *Café Refer*, O'Higgins 416. Good, despite the exterior. Supermarket on B O'Higgins.

See above for ferry to Puerto Ibáñez and connecting minibus to Coyhaique

Transport **Air**: *Don Carlos* to **Coyhaique** daily, US$36; to **Balmaceda**, Tue, Thu, Sat, US$41. **Minibuses**: run along the south side of the lake to **Cochrane**: *Transportes Ales*, T411739 (also has a good *hospedaje*, **E**), Tue, Sat to **Cochrane**, US$20. *Seguel*, T411443 Mon, Fri 1600, *Ales*, Tue, Thu 1015, and *Sergio Haro*, T411251 to **Puerto Guadal**, US$10.

Directory **Banks**: Best to change money in Coyhaique: dollars and Argentine pesos can be changed in small amounts in shops and cafés, including *Loly y Elizabeth*, at poor rates. **Communications**: Post office on the plaza.

For the border with Argentina, Chilean immigration is 2 km east of Chile Chico. Open 0800-2000. ■ *3 companies run minibuses from Chile Chico to Los Antiguos on the Argentine side, US$3 (US$, or Argentine pesos), ½ hr including formalities: Arcotrans T411358, Jaime Acuña T411590, Padilla T411224 (at weekends once a day each). Beware pirate vehicles which don't have the correct papers for crossing to Argentina. From here buses run daily to Perito Moreno and Caleta Olivia.*

Cochrane
Population: 2,000
343 km S of Coyhaique

Sitting in a hollow on the Río Cochrane, this is a simple place, sunny in summer, good for walking and fishing. The **Reserva Nacional Lago Cochrane**, 12 km east, surrounds Lago Cochrane. Campsite at Playa Vidal. ■ *Boat hire on the lake costs US$12.* Northeast of Cochrane is the **Reserva Nacional Tamango**, with lenga forest, a few surviving huemul deer as well as guanaco, foxes and lots of birds including woodpeckers and hummingbirds. It is inaccessible in the four winter months. ■ *Ask in the Conaf office about visiting because some access is through private land and tourist facilities are rudimentary, entry US$3.* The views from the reserve are superb, over the town, the nearby lakes and to the Campo de Hielo Norte to the west. Horses can e hired for excursions in the surrounding countryside, eg *Don Pedro Muñoz*, C Los Ñadis 110, T522244, F522245 (recommended). *Samuel Smiol*, T522487, offers tours to the icefields and mountains, English spoken.

Sleeping and eating B *Hostería Wellmann*, Las Golondrinas 36, T/F522171. Comfortable, warm, good meals. Recommended. B *Res Rubio*, Tte Merino 4, T522173. Very nice, breakfast included, lunch and dinner extra. D *Residencia Cero a Cero*, Lago Brown 464, T522158. With breakfast, welcoming. In summer it is best to book rooms in advance. E *Res Cochrane*, Dr Steffens 451, T522377. Also serves dinner, US$4.25, laundry, camping, hot shower, breakfast. Recommended. Also camping. E *Res El Fogón*, San Valentín 651, T522240. Its pub is the only eating place open in low season, it's the best restaurant at any time of year. E *Res Sur Austral*, Prat 334, T522150. Breakfast included, also very nice. Eating places include *Café Rogeri*, Tte Merino 502, which also has *cabañas*, E pp including breakfast.

Transport Air *Don Carlos* to Coyhaique, Mon, Fri, US$70; also from Balmaceda. **Bus** company agencies: *Don Carlos*, Prat 344, T522150; *Los Ñadis*, Tte Merino y Río Maitén, T522196/522691; *Acuario 13*, Río Baker 349, T522143. *Don Carlos*, Wed, Sun 0830 to Coyhaique, *Los Ñadis*, Mon, Wed, Sat 0830, *Acuario 13*, Tue 0815, Fri 1300, US$20. *Ales* to Chile Chico, Wed and Sun, US$20. To Villa O'Higgins, *Los Ñadis*, Mon via Vagabundo, return Tue, US$8.50. To Vagabundo (for Tortel), *Los Ñadis*, Tue, Thu, Sun, 1000, 2½ hrs, US$7, *Acuario 13* on Tue, Thu, Sun 0930, US$7 (buses meet boats to Tortel). Petrol is available, if it hasn't run out, at the *Empresa Comercial Agrícola* (ECA) and at the *Copec* station.

The Camino Austral runs south of Cochrane. At Km 98, boats sail down the Río Baker through thick forest to **Tortel** (*Population*: 443), a village built on a hill at the mouth of the river (a road is due for completion in late 2002). It has no streets, only walkways of cypress wood (slippery when wet). Its main trade is logging, but this is declining and the town is looking towards tourism once the road is open in 2001. Located between the Northern and Southern Ice Fields, Tortel is within reach of two glaciers: **Glaciar Steffens** is to the north, a 2½-hour boat journey and 2½-hour walk, crossing a glacial river in a rowing boat. A speedboat for 9 people costs US$100 and a *lancha* US$120 for 12. **Glaciar Jorge Montt** is to the south, 5 hours by *lancha*, US$220 for 12 people, 2 hours by speedboat, US$170 for 9. Another boat trip is to the **Isla de los Muertos**, which has an interesting history. For all information and boat charters, contact the Municipality, T/F067-211876. There is a post office, open Monday-Friday 0830-1330, mail leaves on the Wednesday flight. The phone office number is T234815. The bank arrives by plane twice a month and doctors and nurses visit the medical centre monthly.

Sleeping and eating E pp *Hostal Costanera*, Sra Luisa Escobar Sanhueza, T/F234815. Cosy, warm, attractive, lovely garden, full board US$21. F pp *Hosp Casa Rural Sra Elisa Urrutia Iníquez*, full board US$18. F pp *Hosp Casa Rural Sra Brunilda Landeros Sepúlvevda*, US$16. All offer breakfast (US$2-2.50); all prices cheaper in low season. Free campsite near the beach, 15-mins' walk south of main plaza, cold showers, drinking water, long drop, fire places and cooking area. *Café Celes Salom*, bar/restaurant serving basic meals, disco on Sat, occasional live bands.

Transport *San Rafael* flies to Tortel and *Don Carlos* to Villa O'Higgins, see under Coyhaique. **Boat** (until the road is built): Vagabundo-Tortel, a public launch, *lancha*, runs Tue and Sun, 3 hrs; return, upstream, 5 hrs, US$2, primarily for residents, tourist taken only if there is space. A speedboat, *chata*, runs on Thu, 1½ hrs, also US$2. Buses from Cochrane connect with boats.

Once a month there is a boat from Tortel to **Puerto Edén** (US$3, 24 hrs, rough, cold and uncomfortable, but very interesting). For the adventurous traveller who gets the timing right (ask the Municipalidad in Tortel in advance), you can catch the *Navimag* boat in Puerto Edén and continue to Puerto Natales. By going in stages from Puerto Montt to Tortel on the Camino Austral, this works out cheaper than *Navimag* all the way.

The Camino Austral runs to Puerto Yungay (122 km from Cochrane), then another 110 km to **Villa O'Higgins**. There is one ferry crossing between Yungay (military base) and Río Bravo (1200 from Yungay, return 1300, 4-5 cars, free); the road beyond Río Bravo is very beautiful, but often closed by bad weather (take food – no shops on the entire route, few people and few vehicles for hitching). At O'Higgins there is *Hospedaje Patagonia*, Río Pascua 191, T234813, and *Hospedaje y Residencial Apocalipsis 1:3*, T216927, good value (both **D** pp), various *cabañas* and private lodgings. Information is available from the Municipalidad, Lago Christie 121, T/F067-211849.

Parque Nacional Laguna San Rafael

The glacier is disintegrating and is predicted not to last beyond 2011. Some suggest that the wake from tour boats is contributing to the erosion

Some 150 nautical miles south of Puerto Aisén is the **Laguna San Rafael**, into which flows a glacier, 30 m above sea level and 45 km in length. The glacier has a deep blue colour, shimmering and reflecting the light. It calves small icebergs, which seem an unreal, translucent blue, and which are carried out to sea by wind and tide. The glacier is very noisy; there are frequent cracking and banging sounds, resembling a mixture of gun shots and thunder. When a hunk of ice breaks loose, a huge swell is created and the icebergs start rocking in the water. The thick vegetation on the shores, with snowy peaks above, is typical of Aisén. The glacier is one of a group of four that flow in all directions from Monte San Valentín. This icefield is part of the **Parque Nacional Laguna San Rafael** (1.74 million ha), regulated by *Conaf*. ■ *Park entry US$6. At the glacier there is a small ranger station which gives information; a pier and 2 paths have been built. One path leads to the glacier.*

In the national park are puma, pudú (miniature deer), foxes, dolphins, occasional sealions and sea otters, and many species of bird. Walking trails are limited (about 10 km in all) but a lookout platform has been constructed, with fine views of the glacier.

Transport

The only access by plane or by boat. The glacier is equally spectacular from the air or the sea

Air Taxi from Coyhaique (*Aerohein*), US$200 each if party of 5. Charters are also run by *Don Carlos* and *San Rafael*. The flights, which can be very rough, give a fine view before landing, after which there is a launch trip (5 hrs in all). **Sea** The official cruises are: *Skorpios 1,2* and 3 (see under Puerto Montt); *Catmaranes del Sur*, *Navimag*'s *Evangelistas* and *Transmarchilay*'s *Colono* (see under Pto Chacabuco); *Patagonia Express* a catamaran which runs from Puerto Chacabuco to Laguna San Rafael via Termas de Puyuhuapi, in tours lasting 4-6 days, from Puerto Montt via Coyhaique including the catamaran service, the hotel stay at Termas de Puyuhuapi and the day excursion to Laguna San Rafael (see page 720). Other charters are available, such as *Cordillera Primera* or *Empresa Cordillera*, Cochrane 845 esq Condell, Puerto Aisén, T/F332929, 8 passengers, 3-day trip, US$290 pp including all food and open bar throughout. Similarly *Iceberg Expedition* from *Hostería Coyhaique* in Coyhaique, US$254 pp. Private yachts can be chartered in Puerto Montt for 6-12 passengers. Alternatively ask at *Sernatur* in Puerto Aisén about contracting a fishing boat (18-20 hrs each way).

Chilean Patagonia

Santiago

This area covers the glacial regions of southern Patagonia and Chilean Tierra del Fuego. Punta Arenas and Puerto Natales are the two main towns, the latter being the gateway to the Torres del Paine and Balmaceda national parks. In summer it is a region for climbing, hiking, boat trips and the southernmost crossings to Argentina.

Magallanes (XII Región), which includes the Chilean part of Tierra del Fuego, has 17.5% of Chile's total area, but it is inhabited by under 1% of Chile's population.

For much of this century, sheep breeding was the most important industry, before being replaced after 1945 by oil. Although oil production has ceased, large quantities of natural gas are now produced and coal is mined near Punta Arenas. Sheep farming continues to be important: about 50 of all Chilean sheep are in the Magallanes region. Tourism is growing rapidly, making an increasingly important contribution to the area's economy.

In summer the weather is most variable, with temperatures seldom rising above 15° C. In winter snow covers the country, except those parts near the sea, making many roads more or less impassable, except on horseback. Cold, piercing winds blow, particularly in spring, when they may exceed 100 km an hour. In summer, too, windproof clothing is a must. The dry winds parch the ground and prevent the growth of crops, except in sheltered spots and greenhouses.

Background & climate
When travelling in this region, protection against the sun's ultraviolet rays is essential

Chile

Punta Arenas

The most southerly city in Chile and home of La Polar, the most southerly brewery in the world, Punta Arenas lies on the eastern shore of the Brunswick Peninsula facing the Straits of Magellan at almost equal distance from the Pacific and Atlantic oceans. It is a centre for the local sheep farming and fishing industries and exports wool, skins, and frozen meat. Although it has expanded rapidly, particularly in recent years, the capital of XII Región remains tranquil and pleasant. Several new hotels have been built in response to increased tourism. From here, you can visit a spectacular colony of Magellanic penguins. Good roads connect the city with Puerto Natales, 247 km north, and with Río Gallegos in Argentina.

*Phone code: 061
Colour map 9, grid C2
Population: 110,000
2,140 km S of Santiago
it gets freezing at night
For those interested in trivia, the ATMs here are the most southerly on earth*

Sights

Around the **Plaza Muñoz Gamero** are a number of former mansions of the great sheep ranching families of the late 19th century. See the **Palacio Sara Braun**, which dates from 1895. In the centre of the plaza is a statue of Magellan with a mermaid and two Fuegian Indians at his feet. According to local wisdom those who rub the big toe of one of the Indians will return to Punta Arenas. Just north of the plaza on C Magallanes are the **Museo de Historia Regional Braun Menéndez** and the **Teatro Cervantes** (now a cinema): the interiors of both are worth a visit. The **Museo Historia Regional** at Magallanes 949 (entry at rear on Navarro), T244216, is located in the former mansion of Mauricio Braun, built in 1905, recommended. Part is set out as room-by-room regional history, the rest of the house is furnished (guided tours in Spanish only). ■ *Tue-Sat 1030-1700, Sun 1030-1400 (summer, 1100-1300 (winter), US$1.50, loan of explanatory booklet in English.* Further north, at Avenida Bulnes 929, is the **Cemetery**, with a **statue of Indiecito**, the little Indian (now also an object of reverence, bedecked with flowers, the left knee well-rubbed, northwest

Punta Arenas

Not to scale

■ **Sleeping**
1 Alojamiento Golondrina *A2*
2 Backpackers' Paradise *B2*
3 Cabo de Hornos *C2*
4 El Bosque *A2*
5 Finis Terrae *B2*
6 Hostal Carpa Manzano *A2*
7 Hostal de la Avenida *B1*
8 Hostal del Sur *B1*
9 Hostal José Menéndez *B2*
10 Hostal Martita *B3*
11 Hostal Paradiso *A2*
12 Hostal Patagonia *A2*
13 Isla Rey Jorge *C2*
14 José Nogueira *B2*
15 Mercurio *C1*
16 Monte Carlo *B2*
17 O'Higgins 879 *B2*
18 Pink House *A3*
19 Plaza *C2*
20 Residencial Sonia Kuscevic *A1*
21 Sanhueza 750 *B1*
22 Tierra del Fuego *B2*

● **Eating**
1 Asturias *B2*
2 Centro Español *C2*
3 El Estribo *B2*
4 El Mercado *B2*
5 El Mesón del Calvo *B3*
6 El Quijote *C2*
7 Golden Dragon *B1*
8 La Casa de Juan *C2*
9 Lomit's *B2*
10 Los Años 60 The Mitchel *C2*
11 Parrilla Apocalipsis *C2*
12 Quick Lunch Patagónico *C1*
13 Sotitos *C2*
14 Turismo Punta Arenas *C1*

side of the cemetery), cypress avenues, and many memorials to pioneer families and victims of shipping disasters. ■ *Daily 0800-1800.*

East of the Plaza Muñoz Gamero on C Fagnano is the **Mirador Cerro de La Cruz** offering a view over the city. Nearby on Waldo Seguel are two reminders of the British influence: the **British School** and **St James' Church** next door. The **Parque María Behety**, south of town along 21 de Mayo, features a scale model of Fuerte Bulnes and a campsite, popular for Sunday picnics.

Museo Regional Salesiano Mayorino Borgatello, in the Colegio Salesiano, Avenida Bulnes 374, entrance next to church, covers the history of the indigenous peoples, with sections on local animal and bird life, and other interesting aspects of life in Patagonia and Tierra del Fuego. ■ *Tue-Sat 1000-1200, 1500-1800, Sun 1500-1800, hours change frequently, US$2.* The **Instituto de la Patagonia**, Avenida Bulnes Km 4 north (opposite the University), has an open-air museum with artefacts used by the early settlers, pioneer homes, a naval museum and botanical gardens. ■ *Outdoor exhibits open Mon-Fri 0800-1800, indoor pavilions: 0830-1130, 1430-1815, Sat 0830-1300, US$2, T244216.*

Sernatur tourist office is at Waldo Seguel 689, Casilla 106-D, T241330, at the corner with Plaza Muñoz Gamero, helpful, English spoken. ■ *0830-1745, closed Sat and Sun.* Kiosk on Colón between Bories and Magallanes. ■ *Mon-Fri 0900-1300, 1500-1900, Sat 0900-1200, 1430-1730, Sun (in the summer only) 1000-1230. Turistel Guide* is available from the kiosk belonging to *Café Garogha* at Bories 831. *Conaf*, Menéndez 1147, p 2, T223841, is open Monday-Friday.

Chile

Excursions

At 56 km south, **Fuerte Bulnes** is a replica of the wooden fort erected in 1843 by the crew of the Chilean vessel *Ancud* to secure Chile's southernmost territories after Independence. Nearby is Puerto de Hambre. Tours by several agencies, US$12. At the intersection of the roads to Puerto de Hambre and Fuerte Bulnes, 51 km south of Punta Arenas, is a small marker with a plaque of the Centro Geográfico de Chile, ie the midway point between Arica and the South Pole.

Isla Magdalena, a small island 25 km northeast, is the location of the **Monumento Natural Los Pingüinos**, a colony of 60,000 Magellanic penguins. Deserted apart from the breeding season (November-January), the island is administered by *Conaf*. Magdalena is one of a group of three islands (the others are Marta and Isabel), visited by Drake, whose men killed 3,000 penguins for food. ■ *Boat with* Comapa *(see Tour operators): daily in high season (Dec-Feb only), less frequently otherwise, 1500, 2 hrs each way, with 2 hrs on the island, returns 2100, US$30; take your own refreshments, expensive on board. Highly recommended, cancelled if windy. Also* Melinka *of Agencia Broom (see Ferries to Tierra del Fuego, below), from Tres Puentes Tue, Thu, Sat 1530 Jan-Feb, returns 2100, US$30.*

At 70 km north of Punta Arenas, **Otway Sound** is the site of a small colony of Magellanic penguins which can be visited (November-March only). There are fences and bird-hides. The best time for viewing is in the afternoon. Rheas and skunks can also be seen. ■ *Getting there: Bus Fernández 1530, return 1930, US$4. Tours by several agencies, US$6, entry US$4; taxi US$35 return.*

Sleeping

Hotel prices are substantially lower during winter months (Apr-Sep). Most hotels include breakfast in the room price

LL *Cabo de Hornos*, Plaza Muñoz Gamero 1025, T242134, www.hch.co.cl Recommended. **LL** *Finis Terrae*, Colón 766, T228200, www.finisterctcreuna.cl Modern, some rooms small, safe in room, English spoken, rooftop café/bar with lovely views, parking. **L** *Isla Rey Jorge*, 21 de Mayo 1243, T222681, reyjorge@ctinternet.cl Modern, pleasant, pub downstairs, excursions, car hire. **LL** *José Nogueira*, Plaza de Armas, Bories 959 y P Montt, in former Palacio Sara Braun, T248840, www.hotelnogueira.com Beautiful loggia, excellent service, lovely atmosphere. Recommended. **L** *Tierra del Fuego*, Colón 716, T/F226200. Good breakfast, parking, *Café 1900* downstairs. Recommended. **AL** *Plaza*, Nogueira 1116, p 2, T241300, F248613. **B** without bath, pleasant, good breakfast. **A** *Hostal Carpa Manzano*, Lautaro Navarro 336, T/F248864. Recommended. **A** *Hostal de la Avenida*, Colón 534, T247532. Good breakfast, safe. Recommended. **A** *Mercurio*, Fagnano 595, T/F242300, mercurio@chileaustral.com Good restaurant and service. Recommended. **A** *Hostal Patagonia*, Croacia 970, T249970, ecopatagonia@entelchile.net **B** without bath, good breakfast, excellent.

B *Hostal Calafate 1*, Latuaro Navarro 850, T/F248415, and *2*, Magallanes 922, T/F241281. Both cheaper with shared bath, TV, very comfortable, good quality, internet access. **B** *Hostal del Sur*, Mejicana 151, T227249, F222282. Large rooms, TV, heating, central, excellent breakfast. Recommended. **B** *Monte Carlo*, Av Colón 605, T/F243438. Central, old building, well-kept, charming, good value restaurant. Recommended. **C** *Hostal José Menéndez*, José Menéndez 882, T/F221279. Convenient for Ushuaia bus, family-run, helpful, also dormitory. **C** *Hostal Paradiso*, Angamos 1073, T224212. With bath, breakfast, parking, use of kitchen. Recommended.**C** *Res Sonia Kuscevic*, Pasaje Darwin 175 (Angamos altura 550), T248543. Popular, HI accepted, with breakfast, heating, parking. **D** *El Bosque*, O'Higgins 424, T221764, F224637 (Santiago 321 5012), elbosque@patagonian.com Breakfast, use of kitchen, hot water, internet, video, washing machine, associated projects at Yendegaia and Caleta María, hiking. **D** *Casa Dinka*, Caupolicán 169, T226056, fueguino@entelchile.net With breakfast, use of kitchen, noisy. Good lodging next door, too. **D** *Hosp Lodging*, Sanhueza 933, T221035. Heating, cheaper without bath, modern, OK. **D** pp *Hostal O'Higgins*, O'Higgins 1205, T225205, F243438. Cheap meals, cooking facilities. **D** *Sra Carlina Ramírez*, Paraguaya 150, T247687. Hot water, safe motorcycle parking, meals. Recommended.

Accommodation in private houses, usually E pp, ask at tourist office

E pp *Hosp Gloria*, Mejicana 1174, T227678. Shared bath, good showers, quiet, use of kitchen. **E** pp *Alojamiento Golondrina*, Lautaro Navarro 182, T229708. Hot water, kitchen facilities, meals served, English spoken. Recommended. **E** *Hospedaje Independencia*, Independencia 374, T227572, independencia@chileaustral.com Breakfast, use of kitchen, laundry. Highly recommended. **E** pp *Manuel*, O'Higgins 646-8, T245441, F220567. Big dormitories, with breakfast, kitchen, laundry, hot shower. **E** pp *Hostal Martita*, Colón 1195, T223131, alojamientobetty@hotmail.com Without bath, good. **E** *Nena's*, Boliviana 366, T242411. With breakfast. Highly recommended. **E** pp *O'Higgins 879*. With breakfast, heating, cable TV, nice. **E** pp *Pink House*, Caupolicán 99, T222436, pinkhous@chileaustral.com English spoken, with breakfast. **E** Sanhueza 750. Homely. Recommended. **F** pp *Backpackers' The Blue House*, Balmaceda 545, T227006, Crigar73@yahoo.com Hot water, internet, kitchen, very helpful, regional meals. **F** pp *Backpackers' Paradise*, Carrera Pinto 1022, T222554, backpackers_paradise_chile@yahoo.com Popular, large dormitories, cooking and laundry facilities, limited bathroom facilities, internet, good meeting place, luggage store, can book *refugios* in Torres del Paine. Recommended. **F** pp *Costanera*, Rómula Correa 1221, T240175. Welcoming, warm, lots of information, kitchen facilities. Recommended. **F** *Hosp Miramar*, Errázuriz y Señoret (upstairs, enter from Señoret). Very good, enthusiastic owners, good views, ask if the suite is available.

Camping Camping gas canisters from *Danilo Jordán*, O'Higgins 1120.

Eating **Mid-range**: *Centro Español*, Plaza Muñoz Gamero 771, above Teatro Cervantes. Large helpings, limited selection. *El Estribo*, Carrera Pinto 762. Good grill, also fish. *Golden Dragon*, Colón 529. Chinese, good. *El Mercado*, Mejicana 617. Open 24 hrs, reasonably priced set lunch, expensive à la carte. *El Mesón del Calvo*, Jorge Montt 687. Excellent. *Quick Lunch Patagónico*, Sanhueza 1198. Good, Mexican, vegetarian and Chinese. Seafood at *Sotitos*, O'Higgins 1138. Good service and cuisine. Recommended. *Yaganes*, Camino Antiguo Norte Km 7.5. Beautiful setting, weekend buffet. **Cheap**: *Asturias*, Lautaro Navarro 967. Good food and atmosphere. *La Casa de Juan*, O'Higgins 1021. Spanish food. *Lomit's*, Menéndez 722. Cheap snacks and drinks, open when the others are closed. *Parrilla Apocalipsis*, Chiloé esq Balmaceda. Good lunches. *Pizzería Dino's*, Bories 557. Excellent. *El Quijote*, Lautaro Navarro 1087. Good sandwiches. Highly recommended. **For economic set lunches several along Chiloé**: *Restaurant de Turismo Punta Arenas*, No 1280. Good. *Los Años 60 The Mitchel*, No 1231. Also serves beer and 26 varieties of sandwiches, open 24 hrs. Cheap fish meals available at stalls in the *Cocinerías*, Lautaro Navarro south of the port entrance. Excellent *empanadas*, bread and pastries at *Pancal*, 21 de Mayo 1280. Also at *La Espiga*, Errázuriz 632. Excellent pastries at *Casa del Pastel*, Carrera Pinto y O'Higgins. *Centolla* (king crab) is caught illegally by some fishermen using dolphin, porpoise and penguin as live bait. There are seasonal bans on *centolla* fishing to protect dwindling stocks, do not purchase *centolla* out of

Many eating places close Sun. Some of the main hotels have good value set lunches and dinners

Chile

season. At times *centolla* fishing is banned if the crabs are infected with a disease which is fatal to humans: *marea roja* (red tide). If this occurs, bivalve shellfish must not be eaten. Mussels should not be picked along the shore owing to pollution and the *marea roja*. *Sernatur* and the *Centros de Salud* have leaflets.

Entertainment

Discos *Kamikaze*, Bories 655. Popular, recommended. *Borssalino*, Bories 587. **On the outskirts of town, to the south**: *Torreones*, Km 5.5, T261985. **To the north**: *Drive-In Los Brujos*, Km 7.5, T212600. *Salsoteca*, Km 6.

Shopping

Punta Arenas has certain free-port facilities; the Zona Franca is 3½ km north of the centre, on the right hand side of the road to the airport. Quality of goods other than leather and sheepskin is low and prices little better than elsewhere. You can buy *Maglight* bulbs there. Mon-Sat 1030-1230, 1500-2000 (bus E or A from Plaza Muñoz Gamero. Many colectivo taxis; taxi US$3). Handicrafts at *Pingüi*, Bories 404, *Casa Díez*, Bories 712 and 546, *Artesanía Ramas*, Independencia 799, *Chile Típico*, Carrera Pinto 1015 and outdoor stalls at the bottom of Independencia, by the port entrance. English book exchange at *Apenrade SA*, O'Higgins 1198. **Chocolate** Hand-made chocolate from *Chocolatería Tres Arroyos*, Bories 448, T241522 and *Chocolatería Regional Norweisser*, José Miguel Carrera 663, both good. **Leather goods and repairs** *Talabartería Araucaria*, Magallanes 775, Saddlery and repairs to leather goods including rucksacks. **Supermarkets** *Abu-Gosch*, between Magallanes and Bories, north of Carrera Pinto. *Cofrima*, Lautaro Navarro 1293 y Balmaceda. *Cofrima 2*, España 01375. *Listo*, 21 de Mayo 1133. *Marisol*, Zenteno 0164.

Sport

Skiing: Cerro Mirador, only 9 km west from Punta Arenas in the Reserva Nacional Magallanes, one of the few places where one can ski with a sea view. *Transtur* buses 0900 and 1400 from in front of *Hotel Cabo de Hornos*, US$3, return, taxi US$7. Daily lift-ticket, US$7; equipment rental, US$6 per adult. Mid-way lodge with food, drink and equipment. Season Jun-Sep, weather permitting. In summer there is a good 2-hr walk on the hill, with labelled flora. Contact the **Club Andino**, T241479, about crosscountry skiing facilities. Also skiing at Tres Morros.

Tour operators

Most organize tours to Torres del Paine, Fuerte Bulnes and pingüineras on Otway sound: shop around as prices vary

Arka Patagonia, Ignacio Carrera Pinto 946, T248167, F241504, www.arkaoperadora.com All types of tours, rafting, fishing, etc. *Turismo Aonikenk*, Magallanes 619, T228332. Recommended. *Turismo Aventour*, J Nogueira 1255, T241197, F243354. English spoken, helpful, good, specializes in fishing trips, organize tours to Tierra del Fuego. *Columbus Travel*, Sra Nadica Skármeta, T221994. Knowledgeable, helpful with travel arrangements to Patagonia and the Falklands/Malvinas, booking agent for Russian planes to Antarctica. And others. *Turismo Comapa*, Independencia 840, T241437, F247514, www.comapa.com Tours to Torres del Paine, Tierra del Fuego and Isla Magdalena, charter boats to Cape Horn. *El Conquistador*, Menéndez 556, T222896. Recommended. *Turismo Lazo*, Angamos 1366, T/F223771. Wide range of tours. Highly recommended. *Turismo Runner*, Lautaro Navarro 1065, T247050, F241042. Adventure tours. *Operatur Patagónica*, Pedro Montt 966, T240513, F241153, www.operatur.com Good for Torres del Paine, biking and trekking (combined with *Andes Patagónicos*). *Turismo Patagonia*, Bories 655 local 2, T248474, F247182. Specializes in fishing trips. *Turismo Pehoé*, J Menéndez 918, T244506, F248052, www.pehoe.cl Organizes tours and hotels, enquire here about catamaran services. *Viento Sur*, Fagnano 565, T/F228712, www.chileaustral.com/vientosur For camping equipment, fishing expeditions, tours. *Sr Mateo Quesada*, Chiloé 1375, T222662, offers local tours in his car, up to 4 passengers. *Jürgen Schulmeister*, T218358. Guide who speaks German, English.

Transport

All transport is heavily booked from Christmas to Mar: advance booking strongly advised

Local Car hire: There are many agencies, international and local. Recommended are: *Autómovil Club*, O'Higgins 931, T243675, F243097, and at airport. *Internacional*, Sarmiento 790-B, T228323, F226334. *Willemsen*, Lautaro Navarro 1038, T247787, F241083. **NB** You need a hire company's authorization to take a car into Argentina. This takes 24 hrs (not Sat or Sun) and involves mandatory international insurance at US$240. **Car repair**: *Automotores del Sur*, O'Higgins 850, T224153. **Taxis**: ordinary taxis have yellow roofs. Colectivos (all black)

Chile

run on fixed routes, US$0.50 for anywhere on route. Reliable service from *Radio Taxi Austral*, T247710/244409.

Long distance **Air**: Carlos Ibáñez de Campo Airport, 20 km north of town. Bus service by *Buses Transfer*, Pedro Montt 966, entre Navarro y O'Higgins, scheduled to meet flights, US$2.50. Buses to **Puerto Natales** also stop. *LanChile* and *DAP* have their own bus services from town, US$2.50. Taxi US$12. The airport restaurant is good. To **Santiago**, *LanChile*, *Lan Express* and *Aero Continente* daily, via **Puerto Montt** (sit on right for views). When no tickets are available, go to the airport and get on the standby waiting list. To **Porvenir**, *Aerovías DAP* daily at 0815 and 1730, return 0830 and 1750 (US$30), plus other charter flights (eg to Puerto Natales with overflight of Torres del Paine, Antarctica), with Twin-Otter and Cessna aircraft. (Heavily booked with long waiting list so make sure you have your return reservation confirmed.) **Services to Argentina**: To **Ushuaia**, Argentina, *Aerovías DAP* twice a week, daily in summer, US$120 (schedules change frequently). Reserve well in advance from mid-Dec to Feb.

Buses: **Company offices**: *Pingüino* and *Fernández*, Sanhueza 745, T242313, F225984; *Pacheco*, Colón 900, T242174; *Bus Sur*, Colón y Magallanes, T244464; *Bus Sur 2*, Menéndez 565, T224864; *Los Carlos*, Plaza Muñoz Gamero 1039, T241321; *TurBus*, Errázuriz 932, T/F225315. **Bus services**: buses leave from company offices. To **Puerto Natales**, 3½ hrs, *Fernández*, *Bus Sur*, and *Buses Transfer* several every day, last departure 2000, US$5, with pick-up at the airport, book in advance. *TurBus, Ghisoni* and *Austral* have services through Argentina to **Osorno** and **Puerto Montt**. Fares: to Puerto Montt or Osorno US$55 (cheaper off season), 36 hrs. *TurBus* continues to **Santiago**, US$95 (US$60 in winter), 46 hrs.

To **Río Gallegos**, Argentina, via Route 255 through Punta Delgada, then Argentine Route 3: *Pingüino* daily 1200, return 1300; *Ghisoni*, daily except Fri, 1000; *Magallanes Tour*, Tue 1000; also *Bus Sur*. Fares US$11, officially 5 hrs, but can take up to 8, depending on customs, 15 mins on Chilean side, up to 3 hrs on Argentine side, including 30 mins lunch at Km 160. To **Río Grande**, *Hector Pacheco*, Mon, Wed, Fri 0730 via **Punta Delgada**, return Tue, Thu and Sat, 0730, 8-9 hrs, US$18, heavily booked. To **Ushuaia** via **Punta Delgada**, 12-14 hrs, *Ghisoni/Tecni Austral*, Tue, Thu, Sat 0800, US$23; *Tolkeyen* Mon, Wed, Fri 0800, US$25. Book well in advance in Jan-Feb.

Ferries For services to **Porvenir** (Tierra del Fuego), see page 757.

Shipping Offices *Navimag*, Independencia 830, p 2, T200200, F225804, www.navimag.com *Comapa* (*Compañía Marítima de Punta Arenas*), Independencia 830, T244400, F247514. **Shipping Services** For *Navimag* services Puerto Montt–Puerto Natales, see under Puerto Montt (confirmation of reservations is advised). Visits to the beautiful fjords and glaciers of Tierra del Fuego are highly recommended. *Comapa* runs a once a fortnight 22-hr, 320-km round trip to the fjord d'Agostino, 30 km long, where many glaciers come down to the sea. The luxury cruiser, *Terra Australis*, sails from Punta Arenas on Sat via Ushuaia and Puerto Williams; details from *Comapa*. Advance booking (advisable) from *Cruceros Australis SA*, Miraflores 178, p 12, Santiago, T696 3211.

To Antarctica Other than asking in agencies for possible spare berths on cruise ships, the only possibility is with the Chilean Navy. The Navy itself does not encourage passengers, so you must approach the captain direct. Spanish is essential. Two vessels, *Galvarino* and *Lautaro*, sail regularly (no schedule); usual rate US$80 pp per day, including 4 meals.

Directory **Airline offices** *LanChile*, Lautaro Navarro 999, T241232, F222366. *Aerovías DAP*, O'Higgins 899, T223340, F221693, aeroviasdap@ctcinternet.cl Open 0900-1230, 1430-1930. **Banks** Most banks and some supermarkets have ATMs. Banks open Mon-Fri 0830-1400. *Casas de cambio* open Mon-Fri 0900-1230, 1500-1900, Sat 0900-1230. Outside business hours try *Buses Sur*, Colón y Magallanes, kiosk at *Calypso Café*, Bories 817 and the major hotels (lower rates). Good rates at *Cambio Gasic*, Roca 915, Oficina 8, T242396, German spoken. *La Hermandad*, Lautaro Navarro 1099, T243991, excellent rates, US$ cash for Amex TCs. *Sur Cambios*, Lautaro Navarro 1001, T225656, accepts TCs. *Kiosco Redondito*, Mejicana 613 in the shopping centre, T247369. **Communications** Internet: *Austral*, Croacia 690 and Bories 687, p 2, T/F229297, www.australinternet.cl US$4.75 per hr. *Ciber Room Gon-fish*, Croacia 1028, US$2.75-3.60 (cheaper before breakfast). Tourist centre at wharf end of C Independencia, US$5 per hr. *Canadian Language Institute*, B O'Higgins y Carrero Pinto, open till 0400. **Post Office:** Bories 911 y J Menéndez. Mon-Fri 0830-1930, Sat 0900-1400. **Telephone:** for international and national calls and faxes (shop around): *CTC*, Nogueira 1106, Plaza Muñoz Gamero, daily 0800-2200, and Magallanes 922, loc 23, daily 0900-2030. *Entel*, Lautaro Navarro 957, Mon-Fri 0830-2200, Sat-Sun 0900-2200, expensive. For international calls and faxes at any hour *Hotel Cabo de Hornos*, credit cards accepted, open to non-residents. **Consulates** **Argentina**, 21 de Mayo 1878, T261912, open 1000-1400, visas take 24 hrs, US$25. **Belgium**, Roca 817, Oficina 61, T241472. **Denmark**, Colón 819, Depto 301, T221488. **Finland**, Independencia 660, T247385. **Germany**, Pasaje Korner 1046, T241082, Casilla 229. **Italy**, 21 de Mayo 1569, T242497. **Netherlands**, Magallanes 435, T248100. **Norway**, Independencia 830, T242171. **Spain**, J Menéndez 910, T243566. **Sweden**, Errazúriz 891, T224107. **UK**, Roca 924, T228312, F228322. **Medical facilities** **Hospitals: Hospital Regional Lautaro Navarro**, Angamos 180, T244040. Public hospital, for emergency room ask for *La Posta*. Has good dentists. **Clínica Magallanes**, Bulnes 01448, T211527. Private clinic, minimum US$45. **Hospital Naval**, Av Bulnes 200 esq Capitán Guillermos. Open 24 hrs, good, friendly staff. Recommended.

From Punta Arenas a paved road runs north to Puerto Natales. Fuel is available in Villa Tehuelches, 100 km from Punta Arenas. Along this road are several hotels, including **AL** *Hostal Río Penitente*, Km 138, T331694, in an old *estancia*. Recommended. **C** *Hotel Rubens*, Morro Chico, roughly halfway between Punta Arenas and Puerto Natales, Km 183, T226916, there is only a police station, a few shops and the hotel, water is available. Popular for fishing. **A** *Hostería Llanuras de Diana*, Km 215, T/F212853/219401 (Punta Arenas), T411540 (Puerto Natales) hidden from road. Highly recommended. **C** *Hostería Río Verde*, Km 90, east off the highway on Seno Skyring, T311122, F241008, private bath, heating.

Puerto Natales

Standing close to the Argentine border at Río Turbio on the Ultima Esperanza gulf, Puerto Natales is surrounded by spectacular scenery and is the jumping-off place for the magnificent Balmaceda and Torres del Paine national parks. Very quiet in the winter, busy in the summer. **Museo De Agostini**, in the Colegio Salesiano at Padre Rossa 1456, one room on regional fauna. ■ *Free.* A recommended walk is up to **Cerro Dorotea**, which dominates the town, with superb views of the whole Ultima Esperanza Sound. Take any bus going east and alight at the road for summit (Km 9.5).

The **Monumento Natural Cueva Milodón** (50 m wide, 200 m deep, 30 m high), 25 km north, contains a plastic model of the prehistoric ground-sloth whose bones were found there in 1895. Evidence has also been found here of occupation by early Patagonian humans some 11,000 years ago. (Free camping once US$4 entrance fee has been paid.) ■ *Buses* J y B *regular service US$7.50; taxi US$18 return or check if you can get a ride with a tour; both* Adventur *and* Fernández *tour buses to Torres del Paine stop at the cave.* The tourist kiosk is on the waterfront, Av Pedro Montt y Phillipi, T412125. ■ *Mon-Fri 0830-1930, Sat 0930-1300, 1430-1830.* Also at Municipalidad, Bulnes 285, T411263. *Conaf*, Carrera Pinto 566.

LL *Costa Australis*, Pedro Montt 262, T412000, F411881. Modern, good views, popular cafeteria. **L** *Juan Ladrilleros*, Pedro Montt 161, T411652, F412109. Modern, good restaurant. **L** *Martín Gusinde*, Bories 278, T412770, F412820, www.chileaustral.com/grey Phone, TV, tourist information, parking, pub, restaurant. **AL** *Saltos del Paine*, Bulnes 156, T/F410261, www.hsaltodelpaine.nt.cl With breakfast and welcome drink, very pleasant, good value. **A** *Hostal Lady Florence Dixie*, Bulnes 659, T411158, F411943. Modern. **A** *Lukoviek*, Ramírez 324, T411120, F412580. Breakfast, restaurant, helpful. **B** *Blanquita*, Carrera Pinto 409. Quiet, stores luggage. **B** *Lago Sarmiento*, Bulnes 90, T411542. With bath, comfortable living room with good view, well-run.

C *Concepto Indigo*, Ladrilleros 105, T413609, www.conceptoindigo.com No singles, dormitory **D**, good base for organizing activities, restaurant (pizzas, vegetarian) with good views, breakfast, internet. **C** *Natalino*, Eberhard 371, T411968. Cheaper without bath, parking, tours to Milodón Cave arranged. **C** *Oasis*, Señoret 332, T/F411675. **E** without bath, good

Chile

Phone code: 061
Colour map 9, grid C1
Population: 15,000
247 km N of
Punta Arenas

Sleeping
In season cheaper accommodation fills up quickly after the arrival of the Puerto Edén and Magallanes from Puerto Montt. Those listed below have all been recommended

Chile

showers, safe, fine. **C-D** *Hostal Puerto Natales*, Eberhard 250, T411098, huri@ chileaustral.com Helpful, homemade jams, tours arranged.

D pp *Casa Cecilia*, Tomás Rogers 60, T/F411797, redcecilia@entelchile.net Backpackers' annexe **F** pp, cooking and laundry facilities, English, French and German spoken, rents imported camping equipment and bicycles, information on Torres del Paine, organizes tours, email access US$5.75 per hr. **D** pp *Don Bosco*, Padre Rossa 1430. Good meals, use of kitchen, helpful, motorcycle parking, luggage store. **E** pp *Casa de familia Alicia*, M Rodríguez 283. With breakfast, spacious, luggage stored, helpful. **E** pp *Almte Nieto*, Bories 206. Hostel type, use of kitchen, sleeping bag necessary, good meeting place. **E** *La Casona*, Bulnes 280, T412562. With breakfast, hot showers, heated lounge, helpful. **E** pp *Res Dickson*, Bulnes 307, T411871. Good breakfast, helpful, cooking and laundry facilities. **E** pp *Hosp Dos Lagunas*, Barros Araña 104, T422407. With good breakfast, dinner available, shared bath, warm and hospitable, use of kitchen, TV and reading room, excursions and buses booked, lots of information. **E** *Sra Elsa Millán*, Sebastián El Cano 588, T414249. With breakfast, dormitory style, hot water, popular, warm. **E** pp *Res Gabriela*, Bulnes 317, T411061. Good breakfast, helpful, luggage store. **E** pp *Los Inmigrantes*, Carrera Pinto 480. Good breakfast, kitchen facilities, luggage store. **E** pp *Hosp Laury*, Bulnes 222. With breakfast, cooking and laundry facilities, warm. **E** pp *Res El Mundial*, Bories 315, T412476. Large breakfast, good value meals, luggage stored. **F** *Niko's*, E Ramírez 669, F412810. With breakfast, very hospitable, family-run, kitchen facilities, luggage store, good meals, information, travel arrangements made. **E** *Hostal Patagonia*, Patagonia 972, T412756. Helpful, tea and biscuits at any time, tours booked, laundry service, use of kitchen. **E** pp *Patagonia Adventure*, Tomás Rogers 179, T411028. Dormitory style, and private rooms, use of kitchen, breakfast, English spoken, camping equipment for hire, book exchange. **E** pp *Path@Gone*, Eberhard 595, T413291,

Puerto Natales

Sleeping	6 Hospedaje La Chila *B2*	16 Patagonia Adventure *B2*
1 Blanquita *B2*	7 Hospedaje Laury *B1*	17 Residencial Dickson *B1*
2 Bulnes *B2*	8 Hostal Lady Florence Dixie *B2*	18 Residencial El Mundial *B1*
3 Casa Cecilia *A2*	9 Juan Ladrilleros *A1*	19 Residencial Gabriela *B2*
4 Concepto Indigo *B1*	10 Lago Sarmiento *B1*	20 Saltos del Paine *B1*
5 Costa Australis *B1*	11 Los Inmigrantes *C2*	21 Sra Teresa Ruiz *B2*
	12 Lukoviek *B3*	
	13 Martín Gusinde *B1*	**Eating**
	14 Natalino *B2*	1 Andrés *B1*
	15 Niko's *C3*	2 Café Midás *B2*
		3 Centro Español *B1*
		4 Club Deportivo Natales *B1*
		5 Cristal *B2*
		6 Edén *B2*
		7 La Frontera *B3*
		8 La Repizza *B2*
		9 La Ultima Esperanza *B2*
		10 Tierra del Fuego *B1*

www.chileaustral.com/pathgone Good beds, dormitories, includes breakfast, "heavenly" showers, very good, also tour operator. **E-F** *Bulnes*, Bulnes 407, T411307. With breakfast, good, laundry facilities, stores luggage. **E-F** pp *Sra Teresa Ruiz*, Esmeralda 463. Good value, warm, with breakfast, cheap meals, quiet, tours to Torres del Paine arranged. **F** pp *Hosp La Chila*, Carrera Pinto 442. Use of kitchen, welcoming, luggage store, bakes bread. **F** pp *Hosp Gamma*, El Roble 650, T411420. Cooking and laundry facilities, evening meals, tours. **F** *Res Lili*, Bories 153, T414063. Nice rooms, kitchen, laundry, internet, helpful. **F** pp *Hosp Marie-José*, Magallanes 646. Cooking and laundry facilities, tours organized, good showers, luggage store. **F** *Hostal Patricia*, Blanco Encalada y O'Higgins. Small, kitchen, shared bath, hot water, breakfast.

Camping *Josmar 2*, Esmeralda 517, in centre. Family-run, convenient, hot showers, parking, barbecues, electricity, café, US$2.50 per site or **F** pp in double room.

North of Puerto Natales are **L-AL** *Cisne de Cuello Negro*, a former guesthouse for meat buyers at the disused meat packing plant, T411498 (Av Colón 782, Punta Arenas, T244506, F248052). Excellent cooking, 5 km from town at Km 275 near Puerto Bories **C** *Hotel 3 Pasos*, 40 km north, T228113, simple, beautiful.

Hotels in the countryside open only in summer months: dates vary

Mid-range: *Centro Español*, Magallanes 247. Reasonable. *Don Chiclo*, Luis Cruz Martínez 206, Miraflores al 200 cruce Ladrilleros. Only 1 item on menu – grilled lamb dish, but highly recommended, all you can eat US$10. *Edén*, Blanco Encalada 345. *Parrilladas*, good lamb. *La Ultima Esperanza*, Eberhard 354. Recommended for salmon, seafood, enormous portions. **Cheap**: *Andrés*, Ladrilleros 381. Excellent, good service. *Club Deportivo Natales*, Eberhard 332. Decent meals. *Cristal*, Bulnes 439. Good sandwiches and salmon. *Don Alvarito*, Blanco Encalada 915. Good. *La Frontera*, Bulnes 819. Set meals and à la carte, good value. *El Living*, Plaza de Armas. British run, real brown bread, real coffee, good sandwiches, salads. *Café Midás*, Tomás Rogers 169. Has book exchange. *Nuria*, Bulnes 186. Good value, family-run. *La Repizza*, Blanco Encalada 294. Good value. *Tierra del Fuego*, Bulnes 29. Cheap, good. **Bar**: *El Bar de Ruperto*, Bulnes 371, T414302. English/Chilean owned, open 1100-0500 Oct-Apr, 0900-0500 May-Sep, wide range of drinks and food, live music in summer, games, internet access US$3 per hr.

Eating

Camping equipment *Casa Cecilia*, Tomás Rogers 54, imported gear, also for sale. Recommended. *Las Rosas del Campo*, Baquedano 383, T410772. Some equipment, including wet weather gear for sale. *Turismo María José*, Bulnes 386. Rents good quality equipment, also arranges tours, internet access. *Patagonia Adventures*, Tomás Rogers 179. Check all equipment and prices carefully. Average charges per day: tent US$6, sleeping bag US$3-5, mat US$1.50, raincoat US$0.60, also cooking gear, US$1-2. (**NB** Deposits required: tent US$200, sleeping bag US$100.) Camping gas is widely available in hardware stores, eg at Baquedano y O'Higgins and at Baquedano y Esmeralda. **Supermarket**: *El Favorito*, Bulnes 1085. 24 hr supermarket Bulnes 300 block. Markets good, food prices variable. Cheaper in Punta Arenas.

Shopping

Azimut 360 has a base here, T410408. Good for adventure tours. *Bigfoot*, Blanco Encalada 226-B, T414611, explore@bigfootpatagonia.com Sea kayaking and ice hiking. Recommended. *Patagonian Adventure*, Tomás Rogers 179. Highly recommended. *San Cayetano*, Eberhard 145, T411112. *Michay*, Baquedano 388, T411149/411957 (Pedro Fueyo recommended). *Andescape*, Eberhard 599, T412877, F412592, www.chileaustral.com/andescape *Onas*, Blanco Encalada y Eberhard (Casilla 78), T414349, F412707, onas@chileaustral.com *Turismo Zalej*, Bulnes 459, T412260, F411355. Recommended. Patricio Canales, Eberhard 49. Recommended as a good guide. *Viapatagonia*, www.patagonia.com, for all tours across Patagonia. Several agencies offer tours to the Perito Moreno glacier in Argentina, 1 day, US$40 without food or park entry fee. The agencies will let tourists leave the tour in Calafate to continue into Argentina.

Tour operators
Reports of the reliability of agencies, especially for their trips to Parque Nacional Torres del Paine, are very mixed. It is better to book tours direct with operators in Puerto Natales than through agents in Punta Arenas

Local Bicycle repairs: *El Rey de la Bicicleta*, Ramírez 540, Arauco 779. Good, helpful. **Car hire**: *Andes Patagónicos*, Blanco Encalada 226, T411728. *Motor Cars*, Bulnes 659, T413806. *Ultima Esperanza*, Blanco Encalada 206, T410461. Hire agents can arrange permission to drive into Argentina, but this is expensive and takes 24 hrs to arrange. **Mechanic**: *Carlos González*, Ladrilleros entre Bories y Eberhard. Recommended.

Transport

Chile

Long distance Buses: To **Punta Arenas**, several daily, 3½ hrs, US$5. *Bus Fernández*, Eberhard 555, T411111, *Bus Sur*, Baquedano 534, T411325 and *Transfer*, Baquedano 414, T421616. Book in advance. To **Coyhaique**, *Urbina*, 4 days, Nov-Mar, US$120. **To Argentina**: to **Río Gallegos** direct, *Bus Sur*, US$8.50, Tue and Thu 0630 and *El Pingüino*, Wed and Sun 1200, US8.50. Hourly to **Río Turbio**, *Lagoper*, Baquedano y Valdivia, and other companies, US$2.75, 2 hrs (depending on Customs – change bus at border). To **Calafate**, *Cootra* via Río Turbio, daily, US$20, 6 hrs, or *Bus Sur* (2 a week) and *Zaahj* (3 a week) more direct service via Cerro Castillo, 4½-5 hrs, US$25. Otherwise travel agencies run several times a week depending on demand, 5 hrs, US$30, shop around, reserve 1 day ahead.

Shipping See page 717 on services from Puerto Montt. *Navimag* office: Pedro Montt 262 Loc B, Terminal Marítimo, T414300, F414361.

Directory **Banks** *Banco O'Higgins*, Bulnes 633, MasterCard, ATM. *Banco de Chile*, Bulnes 544, accepts all cards.
Poor rates for TCs, *Casas de cambio* on Blanco Encalada, eg 266 (*Enio América*). *Cambio Stop*, Baquedano 380, good for
which cannot be cash (also arranges tours). *Cambio Sur*, Eberhard 285. Good rates. Others on Bulnes and Prat. Shop
changed into US$ cash around. **Communications** Internet: *CTC*, Baquedano 383, US$5.75 per hr; also at *Casa Cecilia*, *Concepto Indigo*, see Sleeping; *Bar de Ruperto*, see Eating; and *Turismo María José*, see Tour operators. **Post Office**: Eberhard 417, open Mon-Fri 0830-1230, 1430-1745, Sat 0900-1230. **Telephone**: *CTC*, Blanco Encalada 23 y Bulnes, phones and fax.

Border with There are three crossing points: **Villa Dorotea**, 16 km east of Puerto Natales. On the
Argentina Argentine side the road continues to a junction, with alternatives south to Río
See also Argentina, Turbio and north to La Esperanza and Río Gallegos. Chilean immigration is open all
page 218 year 0800-2200 (24 hours 31 November-31 March). **Paso Casas Viejas**, 16 km northeast of Puerto Natales. On the Argentine side this joins the Río Turbio-La Esperanza road. Chilean immigration is open all year 0800 – 2200. **Cerro Castillo**, 65 km north of Puerto Natales on the road to Torres del Paine. On the Argentine side, Paso Cancha Carrera (14 km), the road leads to La Esperanza and Río Gallegos. Chilean immigration is open 0800-2200. **B** *Hostería El Pionero*, T/F411646 or 691932 anexo 722, country house ambience, good service. Three other *hospedajes* in Cerro Castillo.

Parque Usually referred to as the **Parque Nacional Monte Balmaceda**, the park is at the
Nacional north end of Ultima Esperanza Sound and can be reached by sea only. The boats
Bernardo *Nueva Galicia* (newest), *21 de Mayo* and *Alberto de Agostini* sail daily from Puerto
O'Higgins Natales in summer and on Sunday only in winter (minimum 10 passengers), US$55 (US$50 in cash). After a three hour journey up the Sound, the boat passes the Balmaceda Glacier which drops from the eastern slopes of Monte Balmaceda (2,035 m). The glacier is retreating; in 1986 its foot was at sea level. The boat docks one hour further north at Puerto Toro, from where it is a 1 km walk to the base of Serrano Glacier on the north slope of Monte Balmaceda. On the trip dolphins, sea-lions (in season), black-necked swans, flightless steamer ducks and cormorants can be seen.

Bookings direct from *Turismo 21 de Mayo*, Ladrilleros 171, T/F411478, or other agencies, expensive lunch extra, take own food, drinks available on board. Heavily booked in high season. Take warm clothes, hat and gloves.

Parque Nacional Torres del Paine

Naturally sculpted royal blue icebergs appear to be moored in a grey lake in this national park, that is a must for its wildlife and spectacular scenery. There are constantly changing views of fantastic peaks and ice-fields, vividly coloured lakes of turquoise, ultramarine, grey and green, and quiet valleys. In the centre of the park, that covers 181,414 ha, is a granite massif from which rise the Torres (Towers) and Cuernos (Horns) of Paine, oddly shaped peaks of over 2,600 m. The valleys are filled by beautiful lakes at 50 m to 200 m above sea level. There are 15 peaks above 2,000 m, of which the highest is Cerro Paine Grande (3,050 m). On the west edge of the Park is the enormous Campo de Hielo Sur ice-cap; four main glaciers (ventisqueros), Grey, Dickson, Zapata and Tyndall, branch off this and drop to the lakes formed by their meltwater. Two other glaciers, the Francés and Los Perros descend on the west side of the central massif.

Colour map 9, grid B1
145 km NW of Puerto Natales

Allow a week to 10 days to see the park properly

Ins and outs

The park is administered by **Conaf**: the Administration Centre (T691931) is in the south of the park at the north end of Lago del Toro (open 0830-2000 in summer, 0830-1230, 1400-1830 off season). The centre provides a good slide show at 2000 on Sat and Sun and there are also exhibitions. It has summaries in English of flora and fauna, but no maps to take away. For information (in Spanish) on weather conditions, phone the Administration Centre. There are six **ranger stations** (*guarderías*) staffed by rangers (*guardaparques*) who give help and advice and will also **store luggage** (except at Laguna Amarga where they have no room). Rangers keep a check on the whereabouts of all visitors: you are required to **register** and show your **passport** when entering the park. You are also requested to register at a ranger station before setting off on any hike. There are entrances at Laguna Amarga, Lago Sarmiento and Laguna Azul. Entry for foreigners: US$14, less off-season – before 1 Oct (proceeds are shared between all Chilean national parks), climbing fees US$800.

Torres del Paine has become increasingly popular with foreigners and Chileans alike and their impact is starting to show. Litter is a problem especially around the refugios and camping areas. Please take all your rubbish out of the park and remember that toilet paper is also garbage

There are a series of *refugios*, see under Sleeping. It is recommended to book *refugios* in advance, eg at *Andescape* offices in Puerto Natales; *refugios* can only accommodate 20-30 people and may be full when you get there; ask personnel to radio ahead your booking to the next *refugio*, especially if you want an evening meal.

Refugios

Warning It is vital to be aware of the unpredictability of the weather (which can change in a few minutes), see Climate below, and the arduousness of some of the stretches on the long hikes. Rain and snowfall are heavier the further west you go, and bad weather sweeps off the *Campo de Hielo Sur* without warning. It is essential to be properly equipped against cold, wind and rain at all times of year. Also, take sunglasses and sun cream. The only means of rescue are on horseback or by boat; the nearest helicopter is in Punta Arenas and high winds usually prevent its operation in the park.

Safety

A strong, streamlined, waterproof tent is preferable to the *refugios* and is essential if doing the complete circuit. Also essential are protective clothing against wind and rain, strong waterproof footwear, compass, good sleeping bag, sleeping mat, camping stove and cooking equipment. Most *refugios* will hire camping equipment for a single night. In summer take shorts and sun-screen also. At the entrance you are asked what equipment you have. Take your own food: the small shops at the Andescape *refugios* and at the *Posada Río Serrano* are expensive and have a limited selection. Maps (US$3) are obtainable at **Conaf** offices in Punta

Equipment & maps
Note that mice have become a problem around camping sites and the free refugios; do not leave food in packs on the ground

Chile

Arenas or Puerto Natales. Most other maps are unreliable but the one produced by *Cartografía Digital*, US$5, has been recommended as the most accurate.

Climate & wildlife The Park is open all year round, although snow may prevent access in the winter: warmest time is Dec-Mar, although it can be wet and windy. It is also more crowded at this time. Oct-Nov can be very nice. In winter there can be good, stable conditions and well-equipped hikers can do some good walking, but some treks may be closed and boats may not be running.

The park enjoys a micro-climate especially favourable to wildlife and plants: there are 105 species of birds including 18 species of waterfowl and 11 birds of prey. Particularly noteworthy are condors, black-necked swans, rheas, kelp geese, ibis, flamingoes and austral

Parque Nacional Torres del Paine

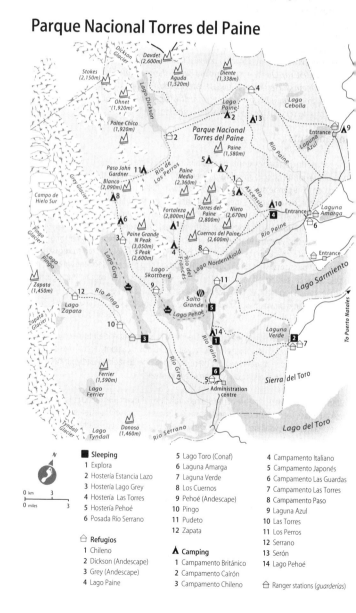

■ Sleeping	5 Lago Toro (Conaf)	4 Campamento Italiano
1 Explora	6 Laguna Amarga	5 Campamento Japonés
2 Hostería Estancia Lazo	7 Laguna Verde	6 Campamento Las Guardas
3 Hostería Lago Grey	8 Los Cuernos	7 Campamento Las Torres
4 Hostería Las Torres	9 Pehoé (Andescape)	8 Campamento Paso
5 Hostería Pehoé	10 Pingo	9 Laguna Azul
6 Posada Río Serrano	11 Pudeto	10 Las Torres
	12 Zapata	11 Los Perros
⌂ **Refugios**		12 Serón
1 Chileno	▲ **Camping**	13 Serón
2 Dickson (Andescape)	1 Campamento Británico	14 Lago Pehoé
3 Grey (Andescape)	2 Campamento Caírón	
4 Lago Paine	3 Campamento Chileno	⌂ Ranger stations (*guarderías*)

0 km 3
0 miles 3

parakeets. There are also 25 species of mammals including *guanaco*, hares, foxes, *huemules* (a species of deer), pumas and skunks. Over 200 species of plants have been identified.

Hikes

There are about 250 km of well-marked trails. Visitors must keep to the trails: cross-country trekking is not permitted.

The times indicated should be treated with caution: allow for personal fitness and weather conditions

El Circuito The main hike is a circuit round the Torres and Cuernos del Paine: it is usually done anticlockwise starting from the Laguna Amarga *guardería*. From Laguna Amarga the route is north along the west side of the Río Paine to Lago Paine, before turning west to follow the Río Paine to the south end of Lago Dickson. From here the path runs along the wooded valley of the Río de los Perros before climbing steeply to Paso John Gadner (1,241 m, the highest point on the route), then dropping to follow the Grey Glacier southeast to Lago Grey, continuing to Lago Pehoé and the administration centre. There are superb views, particularly from the top of Paso John Gadner.

It normally takes five to six days. Camping gear must be carried. The circuit is often closed in winter because of snow. The longest lap is 30 km, between *Refugio Laguna Amarga* and *Refugio Dickson* (10 hours in good weather; it has two campsites along it, *Serón* and *Cairón*), but the most difficult section is the very steep slippery slope between Paso John Gadner and *Campamento Paso*. The major rivers are crossed by footbridges, but these are occasionally washed away.

The W This route combines several of the hikes described separately below. From *Refugio Laguna Amarga* the first stage runs west via *Hostería Las Torres* and up the valley of the Río Ascensio via *Refugio Chileno* to the base of the Torres del Paine (see below). From here return to the *Hostería Las Torres* and then walk along the northern shore of Lago Nordenskjold via *Refugio Los Cuernos* to *Campamento Italiano*. From here climb the Valley of the Río del Francés (see below) before continuing to *Refugio Pehoé*. From here you can complete the third part of the 'W' by walking west along the northern shore of Lago Grey to *Refugio Grey* and Glaciar Grey before returning to *Refugio Pehoé*.

A popular alternative to El Circuito, this route can be completed without camping equipment as there is accommodation in refugios Allow 4-5 days: can be done in either direction

The Valley of the Río del Francés From *Refugio Pehoé* this route leads north across undulating country along the west edge of Lago Skottberg to *Campamento Italiano*, and then follows the valley of the Río del Francés, which climbs between (to the west) Cerro Paine Grande and the Ventisquero del Francés, and (to the east) the Cuernos del Paine to *Campamento Británico*. Allow 2½ hours from Refugio Pehoé to *Campamento Italiano*, 2½ hours further to *Campamento Británico*. The views from the *mirador* above *Campamento Británico* are superb.

Up the Río Pingo valley From *Guardería Grey* (18 km west by road from the Administration Centre) follow the Río Pingo, via *Refugio Pingo* and *Refugio Zapata* (four hours), with views south over Ventisquero Zapata (plenty of wildlife, icebergs in the lake). It is not possible to reach Lago Pingo as a bridge has been washed away. Ventisquero Pingo can be seen 3 km away over the lake.

To the base of the Torres del Paine From *Refugio Laguna Amarga* the route follows the road west to *Hostería Las Torres* before climbing along the west side of the Río Ascensio via *Campamento Chileno* to *Campamento Las Torres*, close to the base of the Torres and near a small lake. Allow 1½ hours to *Hostería Las Torres*, then two hours to *Campamento Chileno*, two hours further to *Campamento Torres* where there is a lake: the path is well-marked, but the last 30 minutes is up the moraine; to see the towers lit by sunrise (spectacular but you must have good weather), it's well worth humping camping gear up to *Campamento Torres* and spending the night. One hour beyond *Campamento Torres* is the good site at *Campamento Japonés*.

Chile

To Laguna Verde From the administration centre follow the road north 2 km before taking the path east over the Sierra del Toro and then along the south side of Laguna Verde to the *Guardería Laguna Verde*. Allow four hours. This is one of the easiest walks in the park and may be a good first hike.

To Laguna Azul and Lago Paine This route runs north from Laguna Amarga to the west tip of Laguna Azul, from where it continues across the sheltered Río Paine valley past Laguna Cebolla to the *Refugio Lago Paine* at the west end of the lake. Allow 8½ hours.

Sleeping

Hotels: **LL** *Hotel Explora*, ugly building but luxurious and comfortable, at Salto Chico on edge of Lago Pehoé, T411247. Offering spectacular views, pool, gym, tours, can arrange packages from Punta Arenas (reservations: Av Américo Vespucci 80, p 7, Santiago, 206-6060, T228 8081, F208 5479). **LL** *Hostería Pehoé*, T411390, 5 km south of Pehoé ranger station, 11 km north of park administration. On an island with spectacular view across the Lake, closed Apr-Oct, restaurant (reservations: *Turismo Pehoé* in Punta Arenas or Antonio Bellet 77, office 605, T235 0252, F236 0917, Santiago). **LL-L** *Hostería Las Torres*, head office Magallanes 960, Punta Arenas, T226054, F222641 (or Santiago 02-960 4804), www.chileaustral.com/lastorres Excellent restaurant with great evening buffet for US$25, very good service (but a bit of hard sell on the excursions etc), horse-riding, transport from Laguna Amarga ranger station. Recommended. **LL** *Hostería Lago Grey*, T/F227528, or Punta Arenas T/F241042/248167, www.chileaustral.com/grey Recommended but small rooms, good food, on edge of Lago Grey, glacier walks US$50 (reservations through *Arka Patagonia* or *Turismo Runner* in Punta Arenas). **AL** *Hostería Mirador del Payne*, beautifully situated on Laguna Verde on the east edge of the park. Comfortable, charming but inconvenient for park itself, riding, hiking, birdwatching. Recommended (reservations: *Turismo Viento Sur* in Punta Arenas). **B** *Posada Río Serrano*, an old *estancia*. Some rooms with bath, some without, near park administration, with expensive but good restaurant and a shop, may allow use of cooking facilities when quiet. (*Turismo Río Serrano*, Prat 258, Puerto Natales, T410684). *Torresdelpaine.org*, T313 3389, hotelschile@terra.cl also offers accommodation, transfers and car hire.

　Refugios **F** pp *Refugio Lago Toro*, near administration centre, run by *Conaf*, hot showers, good meeting place, sleeping bag and mattress essential, no camping, open summer only, in the winter months another more basic (free) *refugio* is open near administration centre. The following are run by *Andescape* (address under Puerto Natales): *Refugio Lago Pehoé*, on the northeast arm of Lago Pehoé (accepts Visa). *Refugio Grey*, on the eastern shore of Lago Grey. *Refugio Lago Dickson*. *Refugio Chileno*, at Campamento Chileno. All **D** pp, modern, closed in winter until 10 Sep, clean, with dormitory accommodation (sheets not provided), hot showers (US$2 for non-residents), laundry facilities,

Chile

meals served (breakfast US$5, dinner US$10), kiosk with basic food and other supplies, rental of camping equipment, campsite with cold showers (US$3 pp). **D pp** *Refugio Las Torres*, is owned by *Hostería Las Torres*, efficient, good meals served, kitchen. *Refugio Los Cuernos*, 6 hrs from *Las Torres* on the way to Campamento Italiano. In addition there are **6 free** *refugios*: Zapata, Pingo, Laguna Verde, Laguna Amarga, Lago Paine and Pudeto. Most have cooking areas (wood stove or fireplace) but Laguna Verde and Pingo do not. These are very crowded in summer (rangers know how many people are on each route and can give you an idea of how busy *refugios* will be).

Camping In addition to sites at the *Andescape refugios* there are the following sites: *Camping Serón* and *Camping Las Torres* (at *Hostería Las Torres*) both run by Estancia Cerro Paine, US$4, hot showers. *Camping Los Perros*, run by *Andescape*, US$3 pp, shop and hot showers. *Camping Lago Pehoé* and *Camping Serrano*, both run by *Turismo Río Serrano* (address above), US$20 per site at former (maximum 6 persons, hot showers) and US$15 per site at latter (maximum 6 persons, cold showers, more basic). *Camping Laguna Azul*, hot showers, US$19 per site. **Free camping** is permitted in 7 other locations in the park: these sites are known as *campamentos*. Fires may only be lit at organized *camping* sites, not at *campamentos*. The *guardaparques* expect people to have a stove if camping. (**NB** These restrictions should be observed as forest fires are a serious hazard.) The wind tends to rise in the evening so pitch tent early. Beware mice, which eat through tents. Equipment hire in Puerto Natales (see above).

Boat trips From *Refugio Lago Pehoé* to *Refugio Pudeto*, US$15 one way with 1 backpack (US$8 for extra backpacks), from Pudeto 0930, 1200, 1800, from Pehoé 1000, 1230, 1830, 1 hr, in high season reserve in advance at the *refugios* at either end or at Los Arrieros 1517, Puerto Natales, T411380, or at Magallanes 960, Punta Arenas, T220345. Off-season, radio for the boat from *Refugio Pehoé*. At all times check in advance that boats are running.

Transport **Car hire**: hiring a pick-up from *Budget* in Punta Arenas (at airport and Av O'Higgins 964) is an economical proposition for a group (up to 9 people): US$415 for 4 days. If driving there yourself, the road from Puerto Natales is being improved and, in the park, the roads are narrow, bendy with blind corners, use your horn a lot; it takes about 3½ hrs from Puerto Natales to the administration, 3 hrs to Laguna Amarga. Petrol available at Río Serrano, but fill up in case. **Horse hire**: *Baquedano Zamora*, Eberhard 565, Puerto Natales, T412911, or through *Hostería El Pionero* in Cerro Castillo.

Buses *Gómez, Servitur, Sur* and *JB Buses* run daily bus services to the park from Puerto Natales leaving between 0630 and 0800, and 1430, returning 1500 from the Admin centre, 1600 from Laguna Amarga, 2½ hrs' journey to Laguna Amarga, 3 hrs to Admin, US$10 one way, US$16 open return (return tickets are not interchangeable between different companies), from early Nov to mid Apr. Buses pass *Guardería Laguna Amarga* at 1030, *Guardería Pehoé* at 1130, arriving at Admin at 1230, leave Admin at 1400 (in high season the buses fill quickly so it is best to board at the Administration). All buses wait at *Refugio Pudeto* until the 1430 boat from *Refugio Lago Pehoé* arrives. Travel between two points within the park (eg Pudeto-Laguna Amarga) US$3. At other times services by travel agencies are dependent on demand: arrange return date with driver and try to arrange your return date to coincide with other groups to keep costs down. *Luis Díaz* has been recommended, about US$12 pp, minimum 3 persons.

In season there are minibus connections within the park: from Laguna Amarga to *Hostería Las Torres*, US$2.80, and from the administration centre to *Hostería Lago Grey*. From Torres del Paine to **Calafate** (Argentina): services from Puerto Natales (see above); alternatively take a bus from the park to Cerro Castillo (106 km south of administration centre) then catch a direct service to Calafate.

Tours Several agencies in Puerto Natales including *Scott Tours* and *Luis Díaz* offer 1-day tours by minibus, US$37.50. José Torres of *Sastrería Arbiter* in C Bulnes 731 (T411637) recommended as guide. *Enap* weekend tours in summer cost US$45 including accommodation and meals. *Buses Fernández* offer 2-day tours, US$132 and 3-day tours (which includes trip to the Balmaceda Glacier) US$177. Before booking a tour check carefully on details and get them in writing: increasingly mixed reports of tours. After mid-Mar there is little public transport and trucks are irregular.

Onas Turismo (address under Puerto Natales, Tour operators) runs trips from the Park down the Río Serrano in dinghies to the Serrano glacier and from there, on the *21 de Mayo* or *Alberto de Agostini* tour boats to Puerto Natales, US$90 pp all inclusive. Book in advance.

Tierra del Fuego

Santiago

The western side of this, the largest island off the extreme south of South America, belongs to Chile and the eastern to Argentina. The north of the island is covered by vast sheep farms. In the south are mountains, glaciers, lakes and forests. The major population centres, Ushuaia and Río Grande, are on the Argentine side, but Chile has the most southerly town in the world, Puerto Williams, on an island below Tierra del Fuego, Isla Navarino.

Ins and outs

Punta Arenas to Porvenir   The *Melinka*, sails from Tres Puentes (5 km north of Punta Arenas, bus A or E from Avenida Magallanes, or colectivo 15, US$0.40; taxi US$3) at 0900, 0930 Sun, no service Mon in season, less frequently off season, 2½-hr crossing (can be rough and cold), US$7 pp, US$10 per bike, US$44 per vehicle. Return from Porvenir 1230 Tue, Thu, Sat, 1600 Wed, Fri (1700 Sun), none on Mon. Timetable dependent on tides and subject to change: check in advance. Reservations essential especially in summer (at least 24 hrs in advance for cars), obtainable from *Agencia Broom*, Bulnes 05075, T218100, F212126, Tabsa@entelchile.net (or T580089 in Porvenir). The ferry company accepts no responsibility for damage to vehicles on the crossing.

Ferry crossings
There are two ferry crossings to Tierra del Fuego

Punta Delgada to Punta Espora (Bahía Azul)   This crossing is via the *Primera Angostura* (First Narrows), 170 km northeast of Punta Arenas. There are several crossings a day; schedules vary with the tides (information from *Agencia Broom*, as above). Foot passengers US$2.40, motorcycles US$6; US$20 per car, one way. The ferry takes about four trucks and 20 cars; before 1000 most space is taken by trucks. There is no bus service to or from this crossing. If hitching, this route is preferable as there is more traffic. In Punta Delgada there is **C** *Hostería Tehuelche*, T061-694433 at Kamiri Aike 17 km from port, with restaurant. **E** pp *Hotel El Faro*.

Porvenir is the only town in Chilean Tierra del Fuego. It's a quiet, pleasant place with many inhabitants of Croatian descent. There is a small museum, the **Museo Fernando Cordero Rusque**, Samuel Valdivieso 402, archaeological and photographic displays on the Onas; good displays on natural history and gold mining. There is exchange at *Estrella del Sur* shop, Santos Mardones.

Porvenir
Phone code: 061
Colour map 9, grid C2
Population: 4,500

Sleeping and eating   **Porvenir**   **AL** *Los Flamencos*, Tte Merino, T580049. Best. **C** *Rosas*, Phillippi 296, T580088. Heating, restaurant and bar. Recommended. **E** pp *Res Colón*, Damián Riobó 198, T580108. Also full board. **C** *España*, Croacia 698. Good restaurant with fixed price lunch. **E** pp *Miramar*, Santos Mardones 366. **D** with full board, heaters in rooms, good. *Croacia Club* does wholesome lunch (pricey). Also *Restaurante Puerto Montt*, Croacia 1169, for seafood. Recommended. Many lobster fishing camps where fishermen will prepare lobster on the spot. **Elsewhere in Chilean Tierra del Fuego**   At **Cerro Sombrero**, 46 km south of Primera Angostura: several hotels (**E-F**). *Posada Las Flores*, Km 127 on the road to San Sebastián, reservations via *Hostal de la Patagonia* in Punta Arenas. *Refugio Lago Blanco*, on Lago Blanco, T Punta Arenas 241197. For accommodation at San Sebastián see below.

Transport   **Air**: From Punta Arenas – weather and bookings permitting, *Aerovías DAP*, Oficina Foretic, T80089, Porvenir, fly daily except Sun at 0815 and 1730 to Porvenir, return at 1000 and 1930, US$20. Heavily booked so make sure you have your return reservation confirmed. **Buses**: 2 a week between Porvenir and **Río Grande** (Argentina), Tue and Sat 1400, 5 hrs, *Transportes Gessell*, Duble Almeyda 257, T580488 (Río Grande 02964-425611), US$12, heavily booked, buy ticket in advance, or phone; Río Grande-Porvenir, Wed and Sun 0800.

Chile

Ferries Terminal at Bahía Chilota, 5 km west, see above for details. From bus terminal to ferry, taxi US$6, bus US$1.50. **Motorists**: All roads are gravel. Fuel is available in Porvenir, Cerro Sombrero and Cullen. **Hitchhiking**: Police may help with lifts on trucks to Río Grande; elsewhere is difficult as there is little traffic.

Argentine time is 1 hr ahead of Chilean time, Mar-Oct The only legal border crossing between the Chilean and Argentine parts of Tierra del Fuego is 142 km east of Porvenir at San Sebastian. On the Argentine side the road continues to Río Grande. **NB** There are two settlements called San Sebastián, on each side of the border but they are 14 km apart; taxis are not allowed to cross. No fruit, vegetables, dairy produce or meat permitted on entry to Chile. For entry to Argentina, see page 218. **B** *Hostería de la Frontera*, in the annex which is 1 km away from the more expensive main building. ■ *Minibus from Porvenir to San Sebastián, US$14. For transport between Porvenir and Río Grande, see above.*

Puerto Williams

Phone code: 061 Colour map 9, grid C2 Population: 1,500 Puerto Williams is a Chilean naval base on **Isla Navarino**, south of the Beagle Channel. Situated about 50 km east of Ushuaia (Argentina) at 54° 55' 41" south, 67° 37' 58" west, it is small, friendly and remote. The island is totally unspoilt and beautiful, with a chain of rugged snowy peaks, magnificent woods and many animals, including guanacos and condors as well as large numbers of beaver, which were introduced to the island and have done a lot of damage. **Museo Martín Gusinde**, known as the *Museo del Fin del Mundo* ('End of the World Museum') is full of information about vanished Indian tribes, local wildlife, and voyages including Charles Darwin and Fitzroy of the *Beagle*, a must. ■ *Mon-Thu 1000-1300, 1500-1800, Sat &Sun1500-1800, Fri closed (subject to change), US$1.*

Excursions There is excellent trekking, including a five-day circuit of Los Dientes. Sights include beaver dams, cascades, the Villa Ukika, 2 km east of town, the place where the last descendants of the Yaganes people live, and the local *media luna* where rodeos are held. For superb views, climb Cerro Bandera (three to four hours' round trip, steep, take warm clothes). No equipment rental on island. **Tourist offices** Near the museum (closed in winter). Ask for details on hiking. Maps available.

Sleeping **D** pp *Pensión Temuco*, Piloto Pardo 224. Also half board, comfortable, hospitable, good food, hot showers. Recommended. You can also stay at private houses. **E** pp *Coiron*, owned by *Sim Ltda*, is a *refugio* with shared bath and kitchen, 4 beds per room, information, contact Jeanette Talavera, T621150, F621227, sim@ entelchile.net, or coiron@simltd.com Her husband, *Wolf Kloss* (www.simltd.com) runs sailing trips, trekking tours and many other adventure activities. Camping near the *Hostería*.

Transport **Air** From **Punta Arenas** by air, *Aerovías DAP* (details under Punta Arenas) daily 1400, return 1530, in 7-seater Cessna, US$160 return, luggage allowance 10 kg. Book well in advance; long waiting lists (be persistent). The flight is beautiful (sit on right from Punta Arenas) with superb views of Tierra del Fuego, the Cordillera Darwin, the Beagle Channel, and the islands stretching south to Cape Horn. Also army flights available (they are cheaper), but the ticket has to be bought through *DAP*.

Ferries No regular sailings from Ushuaia (Argentina). **Boats from Punta Arenas**: *Ferry Patagonia* **(Austral Broom)**, once a week, US$120 for seat, US$150 for bunk, including food, 36 hrs. The *Navarino* leaves Punta Arenas in 3rd week of every month, 12 passengers, US$150 pp one way; contact the owner, *Carlos Aguilera*, 21 de Mayo 1460, Punta Arenas, T228066, F248848 or via *Turismo Pehoé*. The *Beaulieu*, a cargo boat carrying a few passengers, sails from Punta Arenas once a month, US$300 return, 6 days. **Boat trips**: ask at the yacht club. 1 km west, on the off chance of hitching a ride on a private yacht (difficult). Luxury cruises around Cape Horn are run by *Tierra Austral* for US$800, 6 days. Captain Ben Garrett offers recommended adventure sailing in his schooner *Victory*, from special trips to Ushuaia to cruises in the canals, Cape Horn, glaciers, Puerto Montt, Antarctica in Dec and Jan. Write to *Victory Cruises*, Puerto Williams (slow mail service); Fax No 1, Cable 3, Puerto Williams; phone (call collect) asking for Punta Arenas (Annex No 1 Puerto Williams) and leave message with the Puerto Williams operator.

Airline offices *Aerovías DAP*, *LanChile* in the centre of town. **Communications** **Post Office:** closes **Directory** 1900. **Telephone:** *CTC*, Mon-Sat 0930-2230, Sun 1000-1300, 1600-2200. Telex.

The Chilean Pacific Islands

Two national park possessions in the Pacific: Juan Fernández Islands, a little easier to reach (and leave) now than in Robinson Crusoe's time, and the remarkable Easter Island.

Juan Fernández Islands

This group of small volcanic islands is a national park administered by *Conaf* and is situated 667 km west of Valparaíso. They were declared a UN World Biosphere Reserve in 1977. The islands are named after Juan Fernández, the first European to visit in 1574. There are three islands, Robinson Crusoe, the largest, which was the home (1704-09) of Alexander Selkirk (the original of Defoe's *Robinson Crusoe*), Alejandro Selkirk and Santa Clara, the smallest. Selkirk's cave on the beach of Robinson Crusoe is shown to visitors. The only settlement is San Juan Bautista on Robinson Crusoe Island, a fishing village of wooden frame houses, located on Bahía Cumberland on the north coast of the island: it has a church, schools, post office, and radio station. The islands are famous for *langosta de Juan Fernández* (a pincerless lobster) which is sent to the mainland.

Population: 500
The islands enjoy a mild climate and the vegetation is rich and varied. Fauna includes wild goats, hummingbirds and seals.
Best time for a visit: Oct-Mar.
Take insect repellent

Robinson Crusoe Island The remains of the **Fuerte Santa Bárbara**, the largest of **Sights** the Spanish fortresses, overlook San Juan Bautista. Nearby are the **Cuevas de los Patriotas**, home to the Chilean independence leaders, deported by the Spanish after the Battle of Rancagua. South of the village is the **Mirador de Selkirk**, the hill where Selkirk lit his signal fires. A plaque was set in the rock at the look-out point by British naval officers from HMS *Topaze* in 1868; nearby is a more recent plaque placed by his descendants. Selkirk, a Scot, was put ashore from HMS *Cinque Ports* and was taken off four years and four months later by a privateer, the *Duke*. The Mirador is the only easy pass between the north and south sides of the island. Further south is the anvil-shaped **El Yunque**, 915 m, the highest peak on the island, where Hugo Weber, a survivor from the *Dresden*, lived as a hermit for 12 years. (The *Dresden* was a German cruiser, cornered by two British destroyers in Bahía Cumberland in 1915; the scuttled *Dresden* still lies on the bottom and a monument on the shore commemorates the event.) The only sandy beach on Robinson Crusoe is **Playa Arenal**, in the extreme southwest corner, two hours by boat from San Juan Bautista.

Each February, a yachting regatta visits the islands; setting out from Algarrobo, the yachts sail to Isla Robinson Crusoe, then to Talcahuano and Valparaíso. At this time Bahía Cumberland is full of colourful and impressive craft, and prices in restaurants and shops double for the duration. (Thomas G Lammers, Department of Botany, University of Miami.) There are no exchange facilities. Only pesos and US$ cash accepted. No credit cards, no travellers' cheques.

A pp *Hostería Robinson Crusoe*, full board, plus 20% tax, about 1 hr walk from the village. **Sleeping** **AL** pp *Daniel Defoe Hotel*, at Aldea Daniel Defoe (Santiago T531 3772). **B** pp *Hotel Selkirk* *Lodging with* (T Santiago 531 3772). Good food, full board **A** pp. Recommended. **C** pp *Hostería Villa* *villagers is difficult* *Green*, T/F751044. Good.

Transport **Air** Air taxi daily in summer (subject to demand) from **Santiago** (Los Cerrillos airport, US$432 round trip), by *Transportes Aéreas Isla Robinson Crusoe*, Av Pajaritos 3030, of 604, Maipú, Santiago, T/F531 3772, www.tairc.cl and by *Lasa*, Av Larraín 7941, La Reina, Santiago, T273 4254, F273 4309, www.ciudadnetcom/crusoe/inicio.htm The plane lands on an airstrip in the west of the island; passengers are taken by boat to San Juan Bautista (1½ hrs, US$2 one way). **Sea** A boat service from Valparaíso, is operated by *Naviera del Sur*, Blanco Encalada 1041, of 18, T594304. It is for cargo and passengers, modest accommodation, 36-hr passage. *Agentur*, Huérfanos 757, oficina 601, T337118, Santiago. *Pesquera Chris*, Cueto 622, Santiago, T681 1543, or Cochrane 445 (near Plaza Sotomayor), Valparaíso, T216800, 2 week trips to the island (5 days cruising, a week on the island), from US$200 return. No fishing or cargo boats will take passengers.

Rapa Nui/Easter Island

Phone code: 032
Easter Island is
always two hours
behind the Chilean
mainland, summer
and winter time

Known as the navel of the world by the original inhabitants, this remote outpost is studded with giant carved statues that appear trance-like, their gaze fixed on a distant horizon on the Pacific. (Isla de Pascua Rapa Nui) is just south of the Tropic of Capricorn and 3,790 km west of Chile. Its nearest neighbour is Pitcairn Island.

Average monthly temperatures vary between 15-17° C in August and 24° C in February, the hottest month. Average annual rainfall is 1,100 mm. There is some rain throughout the year, but the rainy season is March-October (wettest in May). The tourist season is from September to April.

Anyone wishing to spend time exploring the island would be well-advised to speak to *Conaf* first (T100236); they also give good advice on special interests (biology, archaeology, handicrafts, etc).

Background
The island is triangular
in shape, 24 km
across, with an extinct
volcano at each corner

It is now generally accepted that the islanders are of Polynesian origin. The late Thor Heyerdahl's theories, as expressed in *Aku-Aku, The Art of Easter Island* (New York: Doubleday, 1975), are less widely accepted than they used to be, and South American influence is now largely discounted (see below). European contact with the island began with the visit of the Dutch admiral, Jacob Roggeven, on Easter Sunday 1722, who was followed by the British James Cook in 1774 and the French Le Perouse in 1786. The island was annexed by Chile in 1888.

The original islanders called the island Te Pito o te Henua, the navel of the world. The population was stable at 4,000 until the 1850s, when Peruvian slavers, smallpox

Rapa Nui - Easter Island

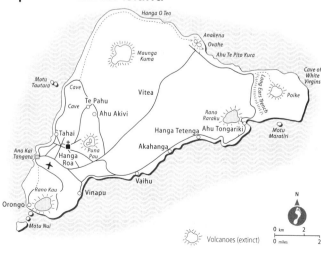

Volcanoes (extinct)

0 km 2
0 miles 2

N

and emigration to Tahiti (encouraged by plantation-owners) reduced the numbers. Now it is about 2,800, of whom about 500 are from the mainland, mostly living in the village of Hanga Roa. About half the island, of low round hills with groves of eucalyptus, is used for horses and cattle, and nearly one-half constitutes a national park (entry US$11, payable at Orongo). The islanders have preserved their indigenous songs and dances, and are extremely hospitable. Tourism has grown rapidly since the air service began in 1967. Paid work is now more common, but much carving is still done. The islanders have profited greatly from the visits of North Americans: a Canadian medical expedition left a mobile hospital on the island in 1966, and when a US missile-tracking station was abandoned in 1971, vehicles, mobile housing and an electricity generator were left behind.

The unique features of the island are the 600 (or so) *moai*, huge stone figures up to **Sights** 9 m in height and broad in proportion. One of them, on Anakena beach, was restored to its (probably) original state with a plaque commemorating Thor Heyerdahl's visit in 1955. Other *moai* have since been re-erected.

A tour of the main part of the island can be done on foot, but this would need at least two days, either camping at Anakena or returning to Hanga Roa and setting out again the next day. To see more, hire a horse or a vehicle. From Hanga Roa, take the road going southeast past the airport; at the oil tanks turn right to Vinapu, where there are two *ahu* and a wall whose stones are joined with Inca-like precision. Head back northeast along the south coast, past Vaihu (an *ahu* with eight broken *moai*; small harbour); Akahanga (*ahu* with toppled *moai*); Hanga Tetenga (one toppled *moai*, bones can be seen inside the *ahu*), Ahu Tongariki (once the largest platform, damaged by a tidal wave in 1960, being restored). Turn left to Rano Raraku (20 km), the volcano where the *moai* were carved. Many statues can be seen. In the crater is a small lake surrounded by reeds (swimming possible beyond reeds). Good views and a good place to watch the sunrise.

The road heads north past 'the trench of the long-ears' and an excursion can be made to **Poike** to see the open-mouthed statue that is particularly popular with local carvers (ask farmer for permission to cross his land). On Poike the earth is red; at the northeast end is the cave where the virgin was kept before marriage to the victor of ceremonies during the birdman cult (ask directions). The road along the north coast passes Ahu Te Pito Kura, a round stone called the navel of the world and one of the largest *moai* ever brought to a platform. It continues to Ovahe, where there is a very attractive beach with pink sand, some rather recently carved faces and a cave.

From Ovahe, one can return direct to Hanga Roa or continue to Anakena, site of **King Hotu Matua's village** and Thor Heyerdahl's landing place. From Anakena, a coastal path of variable quality passes interesting remains and beautiful cliff scenery. At Hanga o Teo there appears to be a large village complex, with several round houses, and further on there is a burial place, built like a long ramp with several ditches containing bones. From Hanga o Teo the path goes west then south, inland from the coast, to meet the road north of Hanga Roa.

A six-hour walk from Hanga Roa on the west coast passes **Ahu Tahai** (a *moai* with eyes and topknot in place, cave house, just outside town). Two caves are reached, one inland appears to be a ceremonial centre, the other (nearer the sea) has two 'windows' (take a strong flashlight and be careful near the 'windows'). Further north is Ahu Tepeu (broken *moai*, ruined houses). Beyond here you can join the path mentioned above, or turn right to Te Pahu cave and the seven *moai* at Akivi. Either return to Hanga Roa, or go to Puna Pau crater (two hours), where the topknots were carved (good views from the three crosses at the top).

Rano Kau, south of Hanga Roa, is another important site to visit; one finds the curious Orongo ruins here. The route south out of Hanga Roa passes the two caves of Ana Kai Tangata, one of which has paintings. If on foot you can take a path from the Orongo road, just past the Conaf sign, which is a much shorter route to Rano Kau crater. 200 m below is a lake with many reed islands. On the seaward side is

Chile

 The cultural development of Easter Island

Far from being the passive recipient of external influences, Easter Island shows the extent of unique development possible for a people left wholly in isolation. It is believed to have been colonized from Polynesia about AD 800: its older altars (ahu) are similar to those of (French) Polynesia, and its older statues (moai) similar to those of the Marquesas Islands in the Pacific between 8°-10° S, 140° W.

The very precise stone fitting of some of the ahu, and the tall gaunt moai with elongated faces and ears for which Easter Island is best known were later developments whose local evolution can be traced through a comparison of the remains. Indigenous Polynesian society, for all its romantic idylls, was competitive, and it seems that the five clans which originally had their own lands demonstrated their strength by erecting these complex monuments.

The moai were sculpted at the Rano Raraku quarry and transported on wooden rollers over more or less flat paths to their final locations; their red topknots were sculpted at and brought from the inland quarry of Puna Pau; and the rounded pebbles laid out checkerboard fashion at the ahu all came from the same beach at Vinapu. The sculptors and engineers were paid

out of the surplus food produced by the sponsoring family: Rano Raraku's unfinished moai mark the end of the families' ability to pay. Over several centuries from about AD 1400 this stone work slowed down and stopped, owing to the deforestation of the island caused by roller production, and damage to the soils through deforestation and heavy cropping. The birdman cult represented at Orongo is a later development after the islanders had lost their clan territoriality and were concentrated at Hanga Roa, but still needed a non-territorial way to simulate inter-clan rivalry.

The central feature of the birdman cult was an annual ceremony in which the heads of the lineages, or their representatives, raced to the islets to obtain the first egg of the sooty tern (known as the Manutara), a migratory seabird which nests on Motu Nui, Motu Iti and Motu Kao. The winning chief was named Bird Man, Tangata Manu, for the following year. It appears that the egg of the tern represented fertility to the cult, although it is less clear what the status of the Tangata Manu actually was. The petroglyphs at Orongo depict the half-man, half-bird Tangata Manu, the creator god Make Make and the symbol of fertility, Komari.

Orongo, where the birdman cult flourished, with many ruined buildings and petroglyphs. Out to sea are the 'bird islets', Motu Nui, Motu Iti and Motu Kao. It is very windy at the summit; good views at sunset, or under a full moon (it is easy to follow the road back to Hanga Roa in the dark).

In Hanga Roa is Ahu Tautira, next to a swimming area marked out with concrete walls and a breakwater (cold water). Music at the 0900 Sunday mass is 'enchanting'. Museum near Tahai, most objects are reproductions because the genuine articles were removed from the island, but it has good descriptions of island life. ■ US$6. There is a cultural centre next to the football field, with an exhibition hall and souvenir stall. Tourist information, T550055, camararapanui@entelchile.net

Recommended reading There is a very thorough illustrated book by **J Douglas Porteous**, *The Modernization of Easter Island* (1981), available from Department of Geography, University of Victoria, BC, Canada, US$6. See also **Thor Heyerdahl**'s work, details above. *Easter Island, Earth Island*, by **Paul Bahn** and **John Flenley** (Thames and Hudson, 1992) for a comprehensive appraisal of the island's archaeology. *Islas Oceánicas Chilenas*, edited by **Juan Carlos Castillo** (Ediciones Universidad Católica de Chile, 1987), contains much information on the natural history and geography of Juan Fernández and Easter Islands. **Websites** http://islandheritage.org (**Easter Island Foundation**); www.netaxs.com/~trance/rapanui.html; www.rapanui.cl

The accommodation list at the airport information desk only covers the more expensive places. Flights are met by large numbers of hotel and *residencial* representatives but it is cheaper to look for yourself. Note that room rates, especially in *residenciales* can be much cheaper out of season and if you do not take full board. **L** Hanga Roa, Av Pont, T/F100299 (Santiago 633 9130, F639 5334). Including all meals (120 beds), no credit cards. **L** Iorana, Ana Magara promontory, 5 mins from airport, T100312 (Santiago 633 2650). Excellent food, convenient for visiting Ana Kai Tangata caves. **L** O'tai, Te Pilo Te Henua, T100250. Pool, comfortable, family run. Recommended. **AL** Poike, Petero Atamu, T100283. Homely, hot water. **A** Orongo Easter Island, Policarpo Toro, Hanga Roa, T100294, or Santiago 211 6747. Breakfast and dinner (excellent restaurant), good service, nice garden. **A** Topo Ra'a, Heterki s/n, T100225, F100353, 5 mins from Hanga Roa. Very good, helpful, excellent restaurant. **A** Cabañas Taha Tai, 2 houses beyond Ana Rapu on C Apina. Fan, fridge, use of kitchen, includes breakfast and airport pick-up. **C** Vai Moana, 3 blocks from museum, 2 from Tahai, 5 mins from main street, owner Edgar Hereveri, T100626, F100105. Cabañas with shared bath, good meals, French and English spoken. Recommended.

Homes offering accommodation and tours (rates ranging from US$18 to US$35, includes meals): **AL** Res Apina Nui, Hetereki, T100292. **C** low season, but bargain, good food, helpful, English spoken. Yolanda Ika's **AL** Res Taire Ngo Oho, T100259. With breakfast, modern. Recommended. Krenia Tucki's **AL** Res Kai Poo, Av Pont, T100340. Small, hot water. **AL** Res Hanga Roa Reka, Simón Poao, T100433. Full board, good, camping. **A** Res El Tauke, Te Pito Te Henua s/n, T100253. Excellent, airport transfers, tours arranged. **A** Res Taheta One One, T100257. Motorbike rental. **B** Res Tahai, Calle-Rei-Miro, T100395. With breakfast, **AL** full board, nice garden. Recommended. **A** Res Pedro Atán Policarpo Toro, T100329, full board. **C** Anita and Martín Pate's guesthouse, Hereveri, opposite hospital in Hanga Roa, T100593, hmanita@entelchile.net   Half board in high season, less low season, good food. Recommended. **C** pp Ana Rapu, C Apina, T100540, F100318. Includes breakfast, evening meal US$7, camping US$10, family-run, hot water (except when demand is heavy), English spoken, dirty. **D** pp Res Maori, Te Pito Te Henua s/n, T100875/105, F100693. With breakfast, hot water, good. From **F** pp Mara Villa, Sara Tuki Tepano. Popular, welcoming, sometimes organizes barbecues.

Sleeping
Unless it is a particularly busy season there is no need to book in advance; mainland agencies make exorbitant booking charges

Camping Free in eucalyptus groves near the Ranger's house at Rano Raraku (with water tank), and at Anakena, no water, make sure your tent is ant-proof. Officially, camping is not allowed anywhere else, but this is not apparently strictly enforced. Many people also offer campsites in their gardens, US$5-10 pp, check availability of water first. Some families also provide food. Several habitable caves near the coast: eg between Anakena beach and Ovahe. If you must leave anything behind in a cave, leave only what may be of use to other campers, candles, oil, etc, certainly not rubbish. Camping equipment can be hired from a shop on Av Policarpo Toro, US$50 per day for everything.

Camping gas is expensive and of poor quality

Coffee is always instant. Beware of extras such as US$3 charge for hot water. *Le Pecheur*. French-run, expensive but worth it *Atamu Tekena*, at the harbour/*caleta*, T100382. Good view, good food. *Ave Rei Pua*. Limited menu, good. *Kona Koa*. Not cheap but good, live music. *Mama Sabina*, Av Policarpo Toro. Very tasty food, clean, welcoming. *Pizzería*, opposite post office. Moderately priced. *Ariki o Te Pana*, on Tuki Haka Hevari s/n. For delicious *empanadas*. Several others. Most *residenciales* offer full board.

Eating
Vegetarians will have no problems on the island

Discos There are 3 in Hanga Roa: *Maitiki* (open daily), east side of town, with pool table. *Toroko*, near harbour (open Thu-Sat), US$1.25. *Piditi*, near airport (open Thu-Sat). Action begins after 0100. Drinks are expensive: bottle of pisco US$9, canned beer US$2.

Entertainment

Tapati, or *Semana Rapa Nui*, end-Jan/beginning-Feb, lasts about 10 days. Dancing competitions, singing, sports (horse racing, swimming, modified decathlon), body-painting, typical foods (lots of small booths by the football field), necklace-making, etc. Only essential activities continue outside the festival.

Festivals

Chile

Shopping On Av Policarpo Toro, the main street, there are lots of small shops and market stalls (which may close during rain) and a couple of supermarkets, cheapest *Kai Kene* or *Tumukai*. **Handicrafts** Wood carvings, stone moais, best bought from the craftsmen themselves, such as Antonio Tepano Tucki, Juan Acka, Hipolito Tucki and his son (who are knowledgeable about the old culture). The expensive municipal market, left of church, will give you a good view of what is available – no compunction to buy. The airport shop is expensive. Good pieces cost between US$30 and 150. Souvenirs at *Hotu Matuu's Favorite Shoppe* are good, quite expensive, designs own T-shirts, fixed prices; also sells music. There is a *mercado artesanal* next to the church and people sell handicrafts at Tahai, Vaihu, Rano Raraku and Anakena. Bargaining is only possible if you pay cash. Bartering items such as shampoo, shoes, T-shirts, is common. Food, wine and beer are expensive because of freight charges, but local fish, vegetables, fruit and bread are cheap. Bring all you can from the mainland, but not fruit.

Sport **Diving**: *Mahigo Vai Kava*, Puna Apa'u s/n, T551055. Run by Mike Rapu. *Orca*, Puan Apa'u s/n, T100375, F100448, run by Michael García. Both at the harbour, all equipment provided, packages US$50 and US$60 respectively. After a check dive you will go to more interesting sights; ask for dives that suit your experience. **Hiking**: allow at least a day to walk the length of the island, one way, taking in all the sites. It is 5 easy hours from Hanga Roa to Rano Raraku (camp at ranger station); 5 hrs to Anakena (camp at ranger station, but ask first). You can hitch back to Hanga Roa, especially at weekends though there are few cars at other times. **Horseback**: the best way to see the island, provided you are fit, is on horseback: horses, US$15-20 a day. A guide is useful. Try *Emilio Arakie Tepane*, who also leads horseback tours of the island (Spanish only) T100504.

Tour operators *Hanga Roa Travel*, T551158 or 100153, hfritsch@entelchile.net English, German, Italian and Spanish spoken, good value all-inclusive tours. Recommended. *Mahinatur Ltda*, vehicle reservations in advance. Their guide, Christian Walter is recommended. Maps are sold on Av Policarpo Toro for US$15-18, or at the ranger station at Orongo for US$10. Many agencies, *residenciales* and locals arrange excursions around the island. The English of other tour guides is often poor.

Transport **Local** There are taxis and in summer a bus goes from Hanga Roa to Anakena on Sun at 0900, returning in the afternoon (unreliable). **Vehicle rental**: a high-clearance vehicle is better-suited to the roads than a normal vehicle. If you are hiring a car, do the sites from south to north since travel agencies tend to start their tours in the north. Jeep hire at *Sonoco* service station, Vaihu, T100325 or 100239, on airport road, US$10 per 1 hr, US$20 per 4 hrs, US$50 per day. *Hertz*, opposite airport, US$50 per day. Many other vehicle hire agencies on the main street. Chilean or international driving licence essential. There is no insurance available, drive at your own risk (be careful at night, many vehicles drive without lights). Check oil and water before setting out. **Motorbike rental**: about US$40 a day including gasoline (Suzuki or Honda 250 recommended because of rough roads). Rentals from Av Policarpo Toro, T100326. **Bicycles**: some in poor condition, are available for rent for US$20 on main street or from *residenciales*, or you can buy a robust one in Santiago (*LanChile* transports bikes free up to a limit of 20 kg) and sell it on the island after 4 days.

The airport runway has been improved to provide emergency landing for US space shuttles

    Long distance: *LanChile* fly 4 days a week in high season, twice a week low season, 3 hrs 40 mins. Most flights continue to Papeete, Tahiti. *LanChile* office on Av Policarpo Toro, T100279, reconfirm flights here – imperative; do not fly to Easter Island unless you have a confirmed flight out (planes are more crowded to Tahiti than back to Santiago) and reconfirm your booking on arrival on the Island. For details of *LanChile's* special sector fare to Easter Island and which must be purchased outside Chile, see Essentials. A round trip from Santiago is US$525 for those using *LanChile* transatlantic. Get to airport early and be prepared for a scramble for seats. Students studying in Chile eligible for 30% discount. If flying to or from Tahiti, check if you can stay over till another flight or even if there is time for sightseeing before the flight continues – US$10 stop-over sightseeing tours can be arranged (in either case it won't be long enough to take it all in properly). **Airport tax**: flying from Santiago to Easter Island incurs the domestic tax of US$8.

Banks Best done in Santiago. *Banco Del Estado* next to *Entel*, open 0900-1200 daily, charges US$7 commission on changing TCs, but you can change as many TCs for this fee as you like (and they can be in different names). Also gives cash against Visa, but no ATM. Cash can be exchanged in shops, hotels, etc, at about 5 less than Santiago. Good rates on Amex TCs at *Sonoco* service station. Amex TCs also changed by *Kia-Koe Land Operator*, *Hanga Roa Hotel*. Prices are often quoted in dollars, but bills can be paid in pesos or TCs (ask). Amex credit cards cannot be used to obtain cash (but enquire at *Sonoco* service station), MasterCard can be used to get cash. Cards are rarely accepted for purchases **Communications** Post Office: 0900-1700; only sends packages up to 1 kg. **Telephone:** phone calls from the Chilean mainland are subsidized, at US$0.35 per min. Calls to Europe cost US$10 for 3 mins, cheap rate after 1400. New phone and fax numbers are being introduced, with prefixes 550 and 551. If 100-numbers don't work, try one of those prefixes. **Medical facilities** There is a 20-bed hospital as well as 2 resident doctors, a trained nurse and 2 dentists on the island.

Background

History

Independence

In 1810 a group of Chilean patriots, including Bernardo O'Higgins – the illegitimate son of a Sligo-born Viceroy of Peru, Ambrosio O'Higgins, and a Chilean mother – revolted against Spain. This revolt led to seven years of war against the occupying troops of Spain – Lord Cochrane was in charge of the insurrectionist navy – and in 1817 Gen José de San Martín crossed the Andes with an army from Argentina and helped to gain a decisive victory. O'Higgins became the first head of state: under him the first constitution of 1818 was drafted. But there was one thing which was dangerous to touch in Chile: the interests of the dominant landed aristocracy, and O'Higgins's liberal policies offended them, leading to his downfall in 1823. A period of anarchy followed, but in 1830 conservative forces led by Diego Portales restored order and introduced the authoritarian constitution of 1833. Under this charter, for almost a century, the country was ruled by a small oligarchy of landowners.

The War of the Pacific

After 1879 Chilean territory was enlarged in both north and south. During the 1870s disputes arose with Boliva and Peru over the northern deserts, which were rich in nitrates. Although most of the nitrates lay in Bolivia and Peru, much of the mining was carried out by Anglo-Chilean companies. In the ensuing War of the Pacific (1879-83), Chile defeated Peru and Bolivia, mainly because her stronger navy gave her control over the sea and even allowed her to land troops in Peru and occupy Lima. Chile gained the Bolivian coastal region as well as the Peruvian provinces of Tarapacá and Arica, and for the next 40 years drew great wealth from the nitrate fields. In the south settlers began pushing across the Río Biobío in the 1860s, encouraged by government settlement schemes and helped by technological developments including repeating rifles, telegraph, railways and barbed wire. At the end of the War of the Pacific the large Chilean army was sent to subdue the Mapuches who were confined to ever-diminishing tribal lands. The territory was then settled by immigrants – particularly Germans – and by former peasants who had fought in the north.

The 20th century

The rule of the Right was challenged by the liberal regime of President Arturo Alessandri in 1920. Acute economic distress in 1924, linked to the replacement of Chilean nitrates with artificial fertilizers produced more cheaply in Europe, led to army intervention and some reforms were achieved. The inequalities in Chilean society grew ever sharper, despite the maintenance of political democracy, and gave rise to powerful socialist and communist parties. President Eduardo Frei's policy of 'revolution in freedom' (1964-70) was the first concerted attempt at overall radical reform, but it raised hopes it could not satisfy. In 1970 a marxist coalition assumed office under Dr Salvador Allende; the frantic pace of change under his regime polarized the country into Left- and Right-wing camps. Increasing social and economic chaos formed the background for Allende's deposition by the army; he died on 11 September 1973. Chile was then ruled by a military president, Gen Augusto Pinochet

Ugarte, and a four-man junta with absolute powers. In its early years particularly, the regime suppressed internal opposition by methods which were widely condemned. Despite economic prosperity and efforts to make the regime more popular, Pinochet's bid for a further eight years as president after 1989 was rejected by the electorate in a plebiscite in 1988.

Post-Pinochet As a result, presidential and congressional elections were held in 1989. A Christian Democrat, Patricio Aylwin Azócar, the candidate of the Coalition of Parties for Democracy (CPD, or Concertación), was elected President and took office in March 1990 in a peaceful transfer of power. The CPD won 71 of the 120 seats in the Chamber of Deputies, but only 22 seats in the 47-seat Senate, its majority wiped out by eight seats held by Pinochet appointees, who could block constitutional reform. Gen Pinochet remained as Army Commander although other armed forces chiefs were replaced. The new Congress set about revising many of the military's laws on civil liberties and the economy. In 1991 the National Commission for Truth and Reconciliation published a report with details of those who were killed under the military regime, but opposition by the armed forces prevented mass human rights trials. In December 1993 presidential elections were won by the Christian Democrat Eduardo Frei, son of the earlier president, but in congressional elections held at the same time the Concertación failed to achieve the required two-thirds majority in Congress to replace heads of the armed forces and end the system of designated senators. This effectively prevented any attempts by the Frei administration to reform the constitution. Oblivious to public sentiment, the military's position in the senate was strengthened when General Pinochet, who retired as army commander-in-chief in March 1998, took up a senate seat, as a former president who had held office for more than six years. Although ex-officio, Pinochet's presence, and therefore parliamentary immunity from prosecution for alleged crimes during his dictatorship, was offensive to parliamentarians who had suffered during his regime.

In October 1998, Pinochet's position came under threat from an unforeseen quarter when a Spanish magistrate filed for his extradition from London, where he was on a private visit, to face charges of torture against Spanish and Chilean citizens between 1973 and 1990. He was detained while the British judiciary deliberated and in March 1999 the Law Lords concluded that Pinochet should stand trial for criminal acts committed after 1988, the year Britain signed the international torture convention. In April, Home Secretary Jack Straw authorized the extradition, but throughout 1999 the process was subject to continuous legal disputes culminating in a health report which claimed that Pinochet was too ill to stand trial. On this evidence the Home Secretary was "minded" to allow Pinochet to return to Chile, which he did in January 2000. After arriving in Santiago apparently fully fit, Pinochet's health did decline, as did his seemingly untouchable status. Implications of his involvement in the torture and killings of the 1970s and 1980s began to surface and in June 2000 an appeals court stripped Pinochet of his immunity from trial.

Partly as a result of the Pinochet affair, but also because of economic recession, President Frei's standing suffered a sharp decline in 1999. The Concertación elected socialist Ricardo Lagos to be its December 1999 presidential candidate, in favour of the candidate from Frei's Christian Democrat party. His main opponent, Joaquín Lavín, a former economic advisor to Pinochet, gained such support that there had to be a second election in January 2000. Lagos, who won by the slimmest of majorities, thus became Chile's first socialist president since Salvador Allende. An upturn in the economy in 2000 helped to bring down the level of unemployment and reduce some of the pressures faced by Lagos' predecessor, but the main focus of attention remained the legacy of Pinochet. While the former dictator enjoyed support from the military, the erosion of his position and image continued. Documents released by the US showed that American agencies had played a significant role in "undermining Chilean democracy" before Pinochet seized power. President Lagos removed the military's right to receive extraordinary supplements from copper income under the budget, which had been customary since Pinochet's era. Most damaging were admissions by former military personnel that, under orders from above, they had committed human rights abuses in the 1970s and 1980s. The process culminated in December 2000 when Judge Juan Guzmán indicted Pinochet himself on charges of kidnapping, murder, torture and other crimes. After a series of appeals and finally submitting to health tests, he appeared in court in January 2001. In March the charges were reduced by the court from responsibility for, to covering up 75 murders by the 'Caravan of Death' army unit. A series of protests followed a subsequent appeals court decision that Pinochet's dementia was too advanced for him to stand trial.

The pre-1973 constitution was replaced, after a plebiscite, on 11 March 1981. This new constitution provided for an eight year non-renewable term for the President of the Republic (although the first elected president was to serve only four years), a bicameral Congress and an independent judiciary and central bank. In February 1994, the Congress cut the presidential term of office from eight years to six. Congress is composed of a 120-seat Chamber of Deputies and a 47-seat Senate, eight of whose members are nominated, rather than elected. In 1974 the country was divided into 13 regions, replacing the old system of 25 provinces.

Government

Culture

There is less racial diversity in Chile than in most Latin American countries. Over 90% of the population is *mestizo*. There has been much less immigration than in Argentina and Brazil. The German, French, Spanish, Italian and Swiss immigrants came mostly after 1846 as small farmers in the forest zone south of the Biobío. Between 1880 and 1900 gold-seeking Serbs and Croats settled in the far south, and the British took up sheep farming and commerce in the same region. The influence throughout Chile of the immigrants is out of proportion to their numbers: their signature on the land is seen, for instance, in the German appearance of Valdivia, Puerto Montt, Puerto Varas, Frutillar and Osorno.

There is disagreement over the number of indigenous people in Chile. The Mapuche nation, 95% of whom live in forest land around Temuco, between the Biobío and Toltén rivers, is put at one million by Survival International, but much less by others, including official, statistics. There are also 15,000-20,000 Aymara in the northern Chilean Andes and 2,000 Rapa Nui on Easter Island. A political party, the Party for Land and Identity, unites many Indian groupings, and legislation is proposed to restore indigenous people's rights. The population is far from evenly distributed: Middle Chile (from Copiapó to Concepción), 18% of the country's area, contains 77% of the total population. The Metropolitan Region of Santiago contains, about 39% of the whole population. The rate of population growth per annum, at 1.5% (1993-98), is slightly under the average for Latin America. The birth rate is highest in the cities, particularly of the forest zone. The death rate is highest in the cities. Infant mortality is highest in the rural areas. Since the 1960s heavy migration from the land has led to rapid urbanization: only about 14% of the population lives in the country. Housing in the cities has not kept pace with this increased population; many Chileans live in slum areas called *callampas* (mushrooms), or *tomas* on the outskirts of Santiago and around the factories. It is estimated that 22% of the population lives in acute poverty.

People
The total population of Chile in 2001 was 15.4 million
Forecast population growth 2000-2005: 1.2%
Urban population in 2000: 86%
Infant mortality: 12 per 1,000 live births

Chile

Books

National parks and birdwatching *Cumbres de Chile*, a book accompanied by two video tapes, part of a five-year project to cover 100 Chilean peaks. **John Biggar**, *The Andes* (Castle Douglas: Andes, 1999), a guide for climbers. *Guía de Parques Nacionales y Otras Áreas Silvestres Protegidas de Chile*, published by **Conaf. B Araya** and G Millie, *Guía de campo de las aves de Chile*.

History S Collier and W F Slater, *A History of Chile 1808-1994* (Cambridge University Press, 1996). **M H Spooner**, *Soldiers in a Narrow Land* (University of California Press, 1994) – an account of the Pinochet dictatorship by an American journalist resident in Chile at the time.

Travelogues Bruce Chatwin's *In Patagonia* has long been regarded as a travel classic, but has been criticized by **John Pilkington** in *An Englishman in Patagonia* (Century, 1991 – see also the Argentina chapter). **Toby Green**, *Saddled with Darwin* (Phoenix, 2000).

Brian Keenan and John McCarthy, *Between Extremes* (Transworld, 1999). **Rosie Swale**, *Back to Cape Horn* (Fontana, 1988) desribes her epic horse ride through Chile. **Sara Wheeler**, *Travels in a Thin Country* (Little, Brown and Co, 1994).

Literature Chile has produced some exeptional poets in the 20th century: **Gabriela Mistral** (1889-1957; Nobel Prize 1945: *Desolación* 1923, *Tala* 1938, *Lagar* 1954), **Vicente Huidobro** (1893-1948: among many books, see *Altazor*, 1931), **Nicanor Parra**, brother of the famous singer and artist **Violeta Parra** (born 1914: *Poemas y antipoemas*, 1954) and, above all, **Pablo Neruda** (1904-1973; Nobel Prize 1971). Of Neruda's many collections, see *Veinte poemas de amor y una canción deseperada* (1924), *Tercer residencia* (1947), *Canto general* (1950) and his memoirs *Confieso que he vivido* (1974). 20th-century male prose writers include **José Donoso** (1924-96, eg *El obsceno pájaro de la noche*), **Ariel Dorfman** (born 1942: eg *La muerte y la doncella/ Death and the Maiden; La última canción de Manuel Sendero/The Last Song of Manuel Sendero*) and **Antonio Skármeta** (born 1940; best known for *Ardiente paciencia*, retitled *El cartero de Neruda* and filmed as *Il Postino/The Postman*). Women novelists are represented by **Isabel Allende** (born 1942), whose novels such as *The House of the Spirits, Of Love and Shadows* and *Eva Luna* are world-famous. Also worth reading are **Marta Brunet** (1901-67: *Montaña adentro* 1923, *María Nadie* 1957), **María Luisa Bombal** (1910-80: *La última niebla* 1935) and **Damiela Eltit** (born 1949: *Vaca sagrada* 1991; *El cuarto mundo* 1988).

Wine Jan Read, *The Wines of Chile* (Mitchell Beazley, 1994).

Chile

Colombia

The adventurous will fall in love with this land of sun and emeralds, with its opportunities for trekking and diving. The Bogotá gold museum, the Lost City of the Tayrona and San Agustín all have superb examples of cultures long gone. The jewel in the country's colonial crown is the beautiful city of Cartagena, which is also one of its main beach resorts. There are mud volcanoes to bathe in, acres of flowers and a CD library's worth of music festivals. Of the country's many snow-capped mountain ranges, the Sierra Nevada de Santa Marta is the most remarkable, rising straight out of the sea. Despite the drug trade and the guerrilla violence which has scarred the minds and the landscape of this beautiful country, Colombia should not be missed.

Colombia

Essentials

Planning your trip

Bogotá. The capital stands on a plateau in the eastern cordillera of the Andes. It epitomizes the juxtaposition of the historical and the modern, with many colonial buildings of great importance. Among its attractions are La Candelaria, the old centre of the city, and the magnificent Gold Museum, which houses a remarkable collection of prehispanic items, one of the 'musts' of South America. Places to visit around Bogotá include Zipaquirá and the Chicaque Parque Natural, consisting of mainly cloud forest.

Bogotá to Cúcuta The department of **Boyacá** is full of interesting places; the colonial cities of Tunja and Villa de Leiva being the most important, and the latter being extremely beautiful. Bucaramanga in Santander department also has its major scenic and colonial attractions, including the most dramatic mountain scenery in Colombia in the Parque Nacional Cocuy. Barichara is one of the best preserved colonial towns.

The North Coast and the Islands Cartagena is the obvious centre for exploring the northern Caribbean coast and the tropical islands of San Andrés and Providencia. It is a popular, modern beach resort and also the place where Colombia's colonial past can best be seen. Here are some of the greatest examples of Spanish architecture on the continent. Santa Marta to the northeast is also a fine resort and the centre for the rocky coast to the east, including Taganga and Parque Nacional Tayrona. Week-long treks to the Ciudad Perdida (Lost City), a major archaeological site, start in Santa Marta. Northeast from Cartagena is the northern port of Barranquilla, where Carnival rivals some of those in Brazil. Going inland from this port, up the Río Magdalena, is the fascinating colonial town of Mompós.

Northwest Colombia Medellín is a modern, vibrant city with many fine new buildings, old restored architecture and friendly, outgoing people. There are many fascinating places to visit in the surrounding department of Antioquia, including the colonial towns of Rionegro and Santa Fé de Antioquia. Further west is the wettest area of the Americas, Chocó. Here, the Pacific coast is almost undeveloped for tourism, with pristine forests descending the mountain slopes to the ocean, but resorts such as Bahía Solano are beginning to open up. South of Medellín is the **Zona Cafetera**, with modern and colonial cities such as Manizales and Pereira and where coffee farms, in delightful countryside, welcome visitors.

The Southwest Further south, in the **Cauca Valley**, is Cali, with its passion for salsa. Like Medellín it has succeeded in shrugging off its poor reputation from the recent past. From Popayán, a city with a strong colonial feel, are the difficult routes to the important archaeological sites of Tierradentro and San Agustín. South of Popayán is Pasto, a pleasant town in an attractive setting, Ipiales for the border with Ecuador and Tumaco, from where you can visit the coastal national parks.

Eastern Colombia In this region are vast open plains, the Llanos, to the north, and humid Amazonian forest to the south, with the city of Leticia being the gateway to Amazonia. This is a remote area, poorly served by public transport and sparsely inhabited, but it has also been little disturbed. Ten of Colombia's national parks are here.

The best time for a visit is Dec, Jan and Feb. These are the driest months, but many local people are then on holiday. Easter is a busy holiday time, many hotels put up their rates, and transport can be overloaded. Climate is entirely a matter of altitude: there are no seasons to speak of, though some periods are wetter than others. Height in metres is given for all important towns. Generally, around 2,000 m is 'temperate', anything higher will require warm clothing for comfort in the early mornings and evenings. There is heavy rain in many places in Apr/May and Oct/Nov though intermittent heavy rain can fall at any time almost anywhere.

Colombia

Finding out more

National tourism is handled by the Tourism Vice-Ministry, part of the Ministry of Economic Development, with its offices at C 28, No 13A-15, Bogotá, T352 2120, F284 1001. Other, mainly departmental and city entities now have offices responsible for providing visitors with information. See text for local details. These offices should be visited as early as possible not only for information on accommodation and transport, but also for details on areas which are dangerous to visit. Contact Colombia's representation overseas, see box for a list of addresses. See also Useful websites. **Maps** of Colombia are obtainable at the **Instituto Geográfico Militar Agustín Codazzi**, Cra 30, No 48-51, open 0800-1530, Bogotá, or from their offices in other large cities. Drivers' route maps are included in the *AutoGuía*, by Publicación Legis, US$8 (1997). See also under Bogotá, Maps.

Websites www.uniandes.edu.co/Colombia/ History, geography, news, tourism, music, recipes, etc, in Spanish, from the **Universidad de los Andes**.
www.guiaturismo.com.co
www.conexcol.com is a Colombian search engine covering many topics.
www.ecomerz.rds.org.co Colombian handicrafts online, connected with handicraft co-operatives around the country and with the **Sustainable Development Network**.
www.natura.org.co **Fundación Natura**, excellent information on conservation projects.
www.minambiente.gov.co Ministry of the Environment, links to projects, environmental legislation, national park system, access routes and best time to visit through park's office.
www.humboldt.org.co **Instituto Von Humboldt**, excellent site on Colombia's ecosystems and ethnic communities.
www.invias.gov.co **Instituto Nacional de Vías**. Good for information on road conditions, maps, etc
www.ideam.gov.co For weather forecasts and climate information.
move.to/colombia Has reliable information on travel, jobs and safety.
www.cmi.com.co for up to date news and comment.
The government website is **www.presidencia.gov.co**

National parks Colombia has 47 reserves comprising 35 National Nature Parks (PNN), 9 Flora and Fauna Sanctuaries (SFF), 2 National Nature Reserves (RNN) and 1 Unique Natural Area (ANU). These include the tiny island of Corota in the Laguna de la Cocha near the border with Ecuador, large areas of forest in the eastern lowlands, all the significant mountain areas and 14 reserves on or near the Caribbean and Pacific coasts. All except the smallest parks have one or more centres staffed with rangers (*guardaparques*) who often offer guidance for visitors. Most, however, are remote with difficult access and few facilities. As such, they are of particular interest to those looking for unspoilt natural surroundings. Unfortunately, many have been used by guerrilla groups recently and, for the time being, are out of bounds.

The parks' service is the responsibility of the **Unidad Administrativa Especial del Sistema de Parques Nacionales Naturales** (UAESPNN) at the **Ministerio del Medio Ambiente** (Ministry of the Environment) referred to in this guide as **MA.** Their Ecotourism office for information is in the Banco Agrario building at Cra 10, No 20-30, p 4, Bogotá, T243 1634/243 3095, F241 4174. Books, souvenirs, good videos and handicrafts are available from the *Ecotienda* on the 7th floor. The national parks book, *Gran Libro de los Parques Nacionales de Colombia*, with superb photography and scientific information, costs US$50. Permits to visit the parks are obtainable here and at the many **MA** offices near the parks themselves (see text). If you intend to visit the parks, this is a good starting place. Information is also available on possibilities to work as volunteer rangers, minimum 30 days, maximum 90: Juan David Herrera, office on 4th floor, very helpful.

Other useful address: **Red de Reservas Naturales**, C23N, No 6AN-43, p 3, Cali, T661 2581, F660 6133 For private reserves around the country. **Instituto Colombiano de Antropología** (ICAN), C 12, No 2-41, T281 1051/561 9600, Bogotá, colican@col1.telecom.com.co Mon-Thu 0830-1630, Fri 0830-1230, very helpful.

Colombian embassies and consulates

Australia, *2nd floor, 101 Northbourne Avenue, Canberra, PO Box 2892, ACT 2601, T257 2027, F257 1448, www.embacol.org.au*

Austria, *Stadiongasse 6-8A, 1010 Vienna, T405 4249, F408 8303, www.embcol.or.at*

Canada, *360 Albert Street, Suite 1130, Ottawa, Ontario, K1R 7X7, T230 3760, F230 4416, www.travel-net.com/~embcolot/*

Denmark, *Kastelsvej 15, st tv 2100, Copenhagen, T263026, F262297, www.colombia.dk*

France, *22 rue de LElysée, 75008, Paris, T4265 4608, F4266 1860.*

Germany, *Tauentzienstr 15, 10789, Berlin, T2639 6110, F2655 7054.*

Holland, *Groot Hertoginelaan 14, 2517 EG The Hague, T361 4545, F361 4636.*

Irish Republic, *Calima, Brighton Road, Foxrock, Dublin 18, T/F289 3104*

Israel, *52 Pinkas St, Apt 26, floor 6, 62261 Tel Aviv, T546 1434, F546 1404.*

Japan, *310-53 Kami-Osaki, Shinagawa-ku, Tokyo 141, T3440 6451, F3440 6724, embassy.kcom.ne.jp/colombia/*

New Zealand, *10 Brandon Street, Wool House, level 11, Wellington, T472 1080, F472 1087.*

Spain, *Gen Martínez Campos 48, 28010 Madrid, T700 4770, F310 2869.*

Sweden, *Ostermlamsgatan 46, Stockholm, T218489, F218490.*

Switzerland, *Dufourstrasse 47, 3005 Bern, T351 1700, F352 7072.*

UK, *3 Hans Crescent, London SW1X 0LR, T020-7589 9177, F020-7581 1829 (consulate, T020-7637 9893), www.colombiaenlondres.com*

USA, *2118 Leroy Place, NW Washington, DC 20008, T202-387 8338, F202-332 8643, www.colombiaemb.org*

Before you travel

Visas & immigration

Tourists are normally given 90 days permission to stay on entry, though this is not automatic. If you intend to stay more than 30 days, make sure you ask for longer. If not granted at the border, extension (*salvoconducto*) can be applied for at the DAS (security police) office in any major city up to a maximum of six months. There may be delays, so apply in good time. Better, apply at the DAS office, C 100, No 11B-27, Bogotá (see under Bogotá, Useful addresses). Alternatively, if you have good reason to stay longer (eg for medical treatment), apply at the embassy in your home country before leaving. An onward ticket may be asked for at land borders or Bogotá international airport. Visitors are sometimes asked to prove that they have sufficient funds for their stay. Note that if you are going to take a Spanish course, you must have a student visa. You may not study on a tourist visa.

To visit Colombia as a tourist, nationals of Republic of Ireland, countries of former Eastern Europe and the Middle East (except Israel), Asian countries (except Japan, South Korea, Malaysia and Singapore), Dominican Republic, Haiti, Nicaragua, and all African countries need a visa. If in doubt, check regulations before leaving your home country. Visas are issued only by Colombian consulates. When a visa is required you must be prepared to present a valid passport, three photographs, the application form (in duplicate), £30 or equivalent, onward tickets, and a photocopy of all the ducuments (allow 2 weeks). Various business and temporary visas are needed for foreigners who have to reside in Colombia for a length of time. Visas must be used within three months. Supporting documentary requirements for visas change frequently. Check with the appropriate consulate in good time before your trip.

When entering the country, you will be given the copy of your DIAN (Customs) luggage declaration. Keep it; you may be asked for it when you leave. If you receive an entry card when flying in and lose it while in Colombia, apply to any DAS office who should issue one and restamp your passport for free. Normally passports are scanned by a computer and no landing card is issued, but passports still must be stamped on entry. Note that to leave Colombia you must get an exit stamp from the DAS. They often do not have offices at the small border towns, so try to get your stamp in a main city.

NB It is highly recommended that you photocopy your passport details, including entry stamps which, for added insurance, you can have witnessed by a notary. This is a valid substitute for most purposes though not, for example, for cashing travellers' cheques or

Colombia

drawing cash across a bank counter. Your passport can then be put into safe-keeping. Also, photocopy your travellers' cheques, flight ticket and any other essential documents. Generally acceptable for identification (eg to enter government buildings) is a driving licence, provided it is plastic, of credit card size and has a photograph. For more information, check with your consulate.

Duty free Duty-free allowance for portable typewriters, radios, binoculars, personal and cine cameras, but all must show use; 200 cigarettes or 50 cigars or up to 500 grams of manufactured tobacco in any form, two bottles of liquor or wine pp.

Vaccinations Hepatitis is common; get protection before your trip. Get inoculated against yellow fever if you are travelling to coastal areas and the eastern jungle or going on to other South American countries. Also see Health, in Essentials at the beginning of the book, page 56.

What to take Tropical clothing is necessary in the hot and humid climate of the coastal fringe and the eastern *llanos*. In Bogotá, Boyacá and the Zona Cafetera medium-weight clothing is needed for the cool evening and night. Medellín requires light clothing; Cali lighter still. A dual-purpose raincoat and overcoat is useful in the uplands. Higher up in the mountains it can be very cold; woollen clothing is necessary.

Money

Currency The monetary unit is the peso, divided into 100 centavos. There are coins of 50, 100, 200, 500 and
peso exchange rate 1,000 pesos; there are notes of 1,000 (rare), 2,000, 5,000, 10,000, 20,000 pesos and a 50,000 peso
with US$: 2,472 note recently issued (not often seen and very difficult to change). Change is in short supply, especially in small towns, and in the morning. There is a limit of US$25,000 on the import of foreign exchange, with export limited to the equivalent of the amount brought in.

Exchange Cash and travellers' cheques can in theory be exchanged in any bank, except the Banco de la República. Go early to banks in the smaller places to change cash or travellers' cheques: some close the service as early as 1000, though bank hours are generally getting longer. In most sizeable towns there are *casas de cambio*, which are quicker to use than banks but sometimes charge higher commission. Hotels may give very poor rates of exchange, especially if you are paying in dollars, but practice varies. It is generally dangerous to change money on the streets and you are likely to be given counterfeit pesos or bolívares. Also in circulation are counterfeit US dollar bills. Do not accept damaged bills; no one will take them off you. If you do not present your passport when changing money (a photocopy is not normally accepted), you may be liable for a 10% tax charged to residents on foreign exchange.

Travellers' When changing travellers' cheques, a photocopy of your passport may be taken, best to take
cheques a supply of photocopies with you For changing Amex Travellers' cheques, use major banks, eg
Take dollar TCs in small *Bancolombia* (the official agent for AmEx Money Gram, 1% commission for US$100, plus 15%
denominations, but, tax). You may have to provide proof of purchase. The procedure is always slow, maybe
better still, take a credit involving finger printing and photographs. Obtaining reimbursement for lost American
card (see below). Express travellers' cheques can be straightforward if you have the numbers recorded
Sterling TCs are (preferably proof of purchase), a police certificate (*diligencia de queja*) covering the
practically impossible circumstances of loss, and apply to their offices at C 85, No 20-32, T531 1919 (see Bogotá,
to change in Colombia Banks). US dollar travellers' cheques can be difficult to change in more remote areas – use local currency.

Credit cards As it is unwise to carry large quantities of cash, credit cards are widely used, especially
For credit card loss MasterCard and Visa; Diners Club is also accepted, while American Express is only accepted in
or theft, contact high-priced establishments in Bogotá. Many banks will accept **Visa** (Visaplus and ATH logos):
Visa T980-125713 *Bancolombia, Bancafé, Banco Agrario* and *Banco Popular* advance pesos against Visa, through
or MasterCard ATMs or across the counter. Similarly, for **Cirrus/MasterCard** (Maestro and Multicolor logos)
T9809-121303 go to *Bancolombia, Banco de Occidente* and many of the Savings Banks. There are ATMs for

Visa and MasterCard everywhere. You may have to try several machines, however, before you get your cash, even though they claim to accept your card. All *Carulla* supermarkets have Citibank ATMs.

Cost of living Prices are generally lower than Europe and North America for services and locally produced items, but more expensive for imported and luxury goods. For the traveller prices are among the lowest in South America. Modest accommodation will cost about US$8-10 pp per night in Bogotá and Cartagena, but a couple of dollars less elsewhere. A *comida corriente* costs about US$1.50-2 and breakfast US$1-1.75. *A la carte* meals are usually good value and fierce competition for transport keeps prices low.

Getting there

Air
Enquire when you book if there are special offers for internal flights

From Europe *British Airways* flies three times a week from London to Bogotá. *Avianca* and *Iberia* fly from Madrid daily and *Air France* has four flights a week from Paris.

From North America Frequent services to and from the US by *Avianca* and *American Airlines,* the latter from Miami, daily to Bogotá, Cali and Barranquilla. Other flights from Miami: *Avianca* to Bogotá, Cartagena, Barranquilla, Medellín, Pereira (via Bogotá) and Cali; *Aces* to Bogotá, Cali and Medellín. From New York, *Avianca* flies to Bogotá (also *Continental*), Cali and Medellín. *Continental* also flies from Houston to Bogotá while *Delta* flies daily from Atlanta. From Los Angeles, *Avianca* flies four times a week to Bogotá.

From Neighbouring Countries *Avianca* and *Lacsa* fly from San José to Bogotá. From Mexico City with *Avianca, Lacsa* and *Mexicana* to Bogotá. From Panama, *Avianca* and *Copa* daily to Bogotá; *Copa* daily to Barranquilla, Cartagena, Cali and Medellín. There are direct flights to most South American countries.

Sea The best route to ship a vehicle into Colombia from the north is Colón (Panama) – Cartagena (Colombia) in a container. For further information check with motoring organizations in your home country and see under Motoring in the Getting around section at the beginning of the book. Bureaucratic delays at either end of the passage are considerable, but can be reduced if you have a *carnet de passages* for entering Colombia.

Touching down

Airport & other taxes There is an airport tax of US$26 (in cash, dollars or pesos) that every passenger leaving has to pay. In addition, there is an exit tax of US$18 for stays of over 60 days. You will need an exit tax exemption certificate from a desk near where you check in if you have been less than 60 days in the country. (Taxes may be higher on international flights from Cartagena and Barranquilla). Travellers changing planes in Colombia and leaving the same day are exempt from both taxes. When you arrive, ensure that all necessary documentation bears a stamp for your date of arrival; without it you will have to pay the exit tax on leaving. Do not buy tickets for domestic flights outside Colombia, except for the official air passes offered by the major local airlines. There is also an airport tax on internal flights, US$3.25 (may vary), not usually included in price quotations.

Tipping Upmarket restaurants 10%. Porters, cloakroom attendants, hairdressers and barbers, US$0.05-0.25. Taxi-drivers are not normally tipped.

Safety Most travellers confirm that the vast majority of Colombians are honest and very hospitable. In addition to the general advice given in the Essentials section at the beginning of the book, the following local conditions should be noted. Colombia is part of a major drug-smuggling route. Police and customs activities have greatly intensified and smugglers increasingly try to use innocent carriers. Do not carry packages for other people. Be very polite if approached by policemen in uniform, or if your hotel room is raided by police looking for drugs. Colombians who offer you drugs could be setting you up for the police, who are very active on the north coast and San Andrés island, and other tourist resorts.

Colombia

Touching down

Business hours Monday-Friday, 0800-1200 and 1400-1730 or 1800. Certain firms in the warmer towns such as Cali start at 0700 and finish earlier. **Government offices** generally follow the same hours as businesses, but generally prefer to do business with the public in the afternoon only. **Embassy** hours for the public are 0900-1200 and 1400-1700 (Monday-Friday). **Banks** 0900-1500 Monday-Friday, except the last working day in the month when they close at 1200 or all day. However, banking hours are getting longer and some are now opening on Saturday. Outside Bogotá banks open 0800-1130, 1400-1630. Shops 0900-1230 and 1430-1830, Monday-Saturday.

IDD 57 Equal tones with long pauses means it is ringing; short tones with short pauses means engaged.

Official time Five hours behind GMT.

Voltage 120 volts AC, is general for Colombia. Transformer must be 110-150 volt AC, with flat-prong plugs (all of same size).

Weights and measures Metric: weights should always be quoted in kilograms. Litres used for liquid measures but US gallons are standard for petrol. Linear measures are usually metric. The hectare and cubic metre are officially employed but the traditional measures vara (80 cm) and fanegada (1,000 square varas) are still in common use. Food etc is often sold in libras (pounds), which are equivalent to half a kilo.

There is sporadic guerrilla activity in Colombia. At present it appears to be confined to rural areas down the eastern part of the country from Guajira through Arauca and Casanare to Putumayo, the Magdalena Medio, and from Urabá near the border with Panama into northwestern Antioquia and El Chocó. In some cases, it is related to oil production and pipeline areas and to the current destruction of drug crops by the authorities, causing local hardship and resentment. Local informed authorities agree that you should not travel between towns anywhere by road at night. Areas in which to take care are mentioned in the text, but, **to find out which areas are to be avoided**, there is no substitute for local advice. The situation changes rapidly and printed information may be out of date by the time you arrive. Decide where you want to go then ask at your embassy. It is essential to follow this up with detailed enquiries at your chosen destination. If arriving overland, go to the nearest hotel favoured by travellers (these are given in the text) and make initial enquiries there.

Where to stay

Hotels
See inside front cover for our hotel grade price guide

The more expensive hotels are not at present (2002) charging 16% VAT (IVA). This was suspended in Nov 1999 but may be reapplied. Some hotels add a small insurance charge. Between 15 Dec and 30 Apr, 15 Jun and 31 Aug, hotels in main holiday centres may increase prices by 20-30%. Some tourist offices have details of authorized prices (which may not be up to date). Although most hotels, except the very cheapest, offer private shower as a matter of course, hot water often comes only in the more expensive hotels or in colder zones. Prices are normally displayed at reception, but in quiet periods it is always worth negotiating.

Camping
Check locally very carefully before deciding to camp. You may be exposing yourself to significant danger

Sites are given in the text. Local tourist offices have lists of official sites, but they are seldom signposted on main roads, so can be hard to find. Permission to camp with tent, camper van or car is usually granted by landowners in less populated areas. Many *haciendas* have armed guards protecting their property: this can add to your safety. Do not camp on private land without permission. Those in camper vans may camp by the roadside, but it is neither particularly safe, nor easy to find a secluded spot. Vehicles may camp at truck drivers' restaurants or ask if you may overnight beside police or army posts.

Getting around

Air
Internal air services are flown principally by *Avianca/SAM* (www.avianca.com.co), *Aces* (www.aces.com.co), *Aires* and *AeroRepública*. *Avianca* offers a round ticket giving unlimited domestic travel for 21 days on *Avianca/SAM* and *Aires*, or 30 days if arriving in Colombia on

Colombia

Avianca. Conditions are that it allows up to five stops, it must be bought outside Colombia in conjunction with an international air ticket, children aged 2-11 pay 67%, infants 10%, the Air Pass is non-refundable unless the whole has been unused, one may not pass through each city more than once (except for transfers), and a proposed itinerary (not firm) must be submitted when buying the ticket. Prices are determined by high season (Jun-Aug and Dec), or low season (rest of year): Air Pass 1 is open to all nationalities including Colombians legally resident abroad, passengers must fly *Avianca* into Colombia, US$300, US$370 if including San Andrés (high), US$240, US$320 with San Andrés (low) for five stops, with the option to add three extra coupons at US$50 each. With Air Pass 2 (which is not available to Colombians), any incoming carrier may be used, US$509, US$629 with San Andrés (high), US$469, US$579 with San Andrés (low) for five stops, plus US$50 for extra coupons, maximum three. These prices and conditions change from time to time, enquire at any *Avianca* office. Similar arrangements have been made by *Aces* and *AeroRepública*. Stand-by tickets are available on busy routes. There are also good value reductions advertised in the press, eg weekend trips from Bogotá to the North coast and San Andrés. Domestic airports are good, though the tourist facilities tend to close early on weekdays, and all Sun. There is a 16% sales tax on one way tickets and an 8% tax on return trips. Local airport taxes of about US$3 are charged when you check in. Security checks tend to be thorough, watch your luggage. *Satena* fly to the remoter regions of Chocó, Amazonas and Orinoquia.

Road

The 107,377 km of roads are almost all in the western half of the country. Almost all the main routes are paved, and surfaces reasonably well maintained. In some Departments, eg Antioquia and Valle, important highways are of very good standard.

Bus

Travel in Colombia is exciting. The scenery is generally worth seeing so travel by day: it is also safer and you can keep a better eye on your valuables. On main routes you usually have choice of company and of type of bus. The cheapest (*corriente*) are basically local buses, stopping frequently, uncomfortable and slow but offering plenty of local colour. Try to keep your luggage with you. *Pullman* (each company will have a different name for the service) are long distance buses usually with a/c, toilets, hostess service, videos (almost always violent films, Spanish/Mexican or dubbed English) and limited stop. Be prepared for lack of a/c and locked windows. Sit near the back with your walkman to avoid the video and the need to keep the blinds down. Luggage is normally carried in a locked compartment against receipt. *Colectivos*, also known as *vans* or *busetas*, run by *Velotax*, *Taxis Verdes*, etc are usually 12-20 seat vehicles, maybe with a/c, rather cramped but fast, saving several hours on long journeys. You can keep your eye on luggage in the back of the van. Fares shown in the text are middle of the range where there is a choice but are no more than a guide. Note that meal stops can be few and far between, and short; bring your own food. Be prepared for climatic changes on longer routes. **If you entrust your luggage to the bus companies' luggage rooms, remember to load it on to the bus yourself; it will not be done automatically.** There are few interdepartmental bus services on holidays. If you are joining a bus at popular or holiday times, not at the starting point, you may be left behind even though you have a ticket and reservation. Always take your passport (or photocopy) with you: identity checks on buses are frequent.

Car

Motor fuel: 'premium 95' octane (only in large cities), about US$1.80 per US gallon; 'corriente' 84 octane, US$1.25 per US gallon. Diesel US$1.20. Roads are not always signposted. If driving yourself, avoid night journeys; vehicles may be unlighted and it can be dangerous. The roads may be locally in poor condition, lorry- and bus-drivers tend to be reckless, and stray animals are often encountered. **Always check safety information for your route before setting out.** Police checks are frequent in troubled areas, keep your documents handy. There are toll stations every 60-100 km on major roads: toll is about US$1.50. Motorcycles and bicycles don't have to pay. In town, try to leave your car in an attended car park (*parqueadero*), especially at night. Car parks usually charge different rates for day and night. If you are planning to sleep in your car, ask if you can stop in a *parqueadero*; you will be charged a little extra. Alternatively, find a police station and ask to sleep in your car nearby. You can also stay overnight in *balnearios campestres*, which normally have armed guards.

Spare parts are plentiful for Renault, Mazda and Chevrolet cars, which are assembled in Colombia. VW is also well represented

Colombia

International driving licences are advised, especially if you have your own car. To bring a car into Colombia, you must also have documents proving ownership of the vehicle, and a tourist card/transit visa. These are normally valid for 90 days and must be applied for at the Colombian consulate in the country which you will be leaving for Colombia. Temporary admission of a visitor's vehicle is usually given at most border controls. Procedure may take some time and patience. A *carnet de passages* is recommended when entering with a European registered vehicle. Only third-party insurance issued by a Colombian company is valid, cost around US$70; there are agencies in all ports. In Cartagena, *Aseguradora Solidaria de Colombia*, near Plaza de la Aduana is recommended. You will frequently be asked for this document while driving. Carry driving documents with you at all times.

Car hire This is relatively expensive. In addition to passport and driver's licence, a credit card may be asked for as additional proof of identity (Visa, MasterCard, American Express), and to secure a returnable deposit to cover any liability not covered by the insurance. Make sure you know what is and what is not covered by insurance. Main international car rental companies are represented at principal airports but not necessarily open all the time.

Cycling Cycling is a popular sport in Colombia. There are good shops for spares in all big cities, though
Ask about security the new standard 622/700 size touring wheel size is not very common. Take your own spare
wherever you go tyres. Recommended are: *Bike House*, C 93 B, No 15-34, of 208, T257 3107, Bogotá, and *Bicicletas de Montaña*, C 23, No 43A-104, T262 7249, Medellín.

Hitchhiking Hitchhiking (*autostop*) has become more difficult as some road routes have been under threat in 2002. Make careful enquiries before attempting long journeys. In safe areas, try enlisting the co-operation of the highway police checkpoints outside each town and toll booths. Truck drivers are often very friendly, but be careful of private cars with more than one person inside. Travelling on your own is not recommended.

Motorcycling See under Motorcycling in Essentials. If you bring a bike in by air to Bogotá, try to stay as close as possible to it while it is cleared through freight forwarders (eg Cosimex) and the Customs, to save time and damage. You can airfreight from Panama. A *carnet de passage* is strongly advised (see above). At Bogotá airport, you can have it stamped and be through in two hours. Otherwise you must go to the **Aduana Nacional** in C 65 bis, No 90A-35, T430 9670, to complete formalities. Shipping by sea, eg from Panama, will take longer and is probably no cheaper. Parking at night can be a problem, but some hotels listed have patios or their own lock up garages nearby. Otherwise use *parqueadores* (see Motoring above). Local insurance costs around US$30 for a bike over 200 cc. You may find that wearing helmets is inadvisable in trouble spots, take advice. It is illegal for two men to ride together on one motorcycle (a man and a woman is allowed). A recent law in Bogotá requires all motorcyclists to wear an outer vest showing the number of the bike. Spare parts, tyres, etc readily available in Colombia for Yamaha XT and Honda XL models (although supplies are less good for models over 500 cc), so Colombia is a suitable country for rebuilding a bike on a long trip. Medellín is good for spare parts. BMW, Triumph spares sold by *Germán Villegas Arango*, C 1 B, No 11A-43, Bogotá, T289 4399. Other recommended motorcycle repairs: *Racing Lines Ltda*, Av 30 de Agosto, No 40-51, T336 1970, Pereira; *Motoservicio Asturias*, Cra 5, No 24-35, T889 3616, Cali; *Marcus Germayer*, Av 7AN, No 56-196, Cali, T/F664 3958. English and German spoken. Recommended.

Taxi Whenever possible, take a taxi with a meter and ensure that it is switched on. If there is no meter, bargain and fix a price. All taxis are obliged to display the additional legal tariffs that may be charged after 2000, on Sun and fiestas. Don't take a taxi which is old; look for 'Servicio Público' on the side. There is a small surcharge for Radio Taxis, but they normally offer safe, reliable service. The dispatcher will give you the cab's number which should be noted in case of irregularities. Radio taxis are especially advised at night when, if possible, women should not travel alone. If the taxi 'breaks down', take your luggage out if you are asked to push, or let the driver push; it may be a trick to separate you from your luggage.

Colombia

Originally there were over 3,000 km of railways, but most lines have been closed. At present **Train**
there is only a tourist service north of Bogotá and an intermittent connection between
Medellín and Barrancabermeja.

Keeping in touch

Internet services are expanding rapidly in Colombia. You will find internet centres in all **Internet**
important towns, in business sectors and shopping malls. Typical rates are US$3-6 per hour.

There are two parallel postal systems, **Avianca**, operated by the national airline, and **Post**
Correos de Colombia, the post office proper. Both have offices in all major cities, but only *The mail service is*
Correos can be found in small towns and rural areas. **Adpostal**, part of *Correos*, will take parcels *unreliable. It is better*
for overseas. Correspondents report 10-day delivery to the UK. Prices are identical for *now to use email*
overseas airmail (which is carried by *Avianca* in any event), but *Adpostal/Correos* is much
more economical, and can be more efficient, for internal service. Anything of importance
should be registered. *Avianca* controls all airmail services and has offices in provincial cities.
Airports are often the easiest and most convenient places for posting letters. It costs US$2 to
send a letter or postcard to the US, more to Europe or elsewhere.

Inter-city calls are best made from **Telecom** offices unless you have access to a private **Telephone**
phone. Long-distance pay phones are located outside most *Telecom* offices, also at bus *For information dial*
stations and airports. They take 100 peso coins, or larger. From the larger towns it is possible *150 for Orbitel, 170*
to telephone to Canada, the USA, the UK, and to several of the Latin American republics. *for ETB and 190*
International phone charges are high (about US$7 for three mins to USA, US$8 to Europe, *for Telecom*
US$12 to Australia) but there can be substantial discounts at off-peak times, weekends and
holidays. There are now three competing local services for intercity and international calls.
NB In this chapter phone codes are all shown with the first figure 9. This will connect you
to *Telecom*. If you wish to use **Orbitel**, substitute 5; for **ETB** substitute 7. This can be
important at evenings, weekends and holiday times when cheap calls may be available. A
deposit may be required before the call is made. The best value is to purchase a phone card
and dial direct yourself. For details of international telephone company tariffs, call **AT&T** at
601 0288, or **Global One** at 621 0177, both in Bogotá. **Canada Direct** is 980-190057, AT&T
for the US dial 980-110010 and for the UK, 980-440057; **BT** Chargecards can be used for
calls within Colombia as well as country-to-country and to the UK. Other collect, or
reversed-charge, telephone calls can be made from El Dorado airport, but make sure the
operator understands what is involved or you may be billed in any case. Fax to Europe costs
US$4 per page, but is almost double this from hotels.

Newspapers Bogotá: *El Tiempo* www.eltiempo.com.co *El Espectador* **Media**
www.elespectador.com.co *La República*. **Medellín**: *El Mundo, El Colombiano*. **Cali**: *El País,*
Occidente, El Pueblo. All major cities have daily papers. Magazines are partisan, best are
probably *Semana*, www.semana.com and *Cambio*, www.cambio.com.co US and European
papers can be bought at *Librería Oma*, Cra 15, No 82-58, or at the stand outside *Tacos de la 19*,
near the corner of Cra 7/C 19 in the centre of Bogotá. *Latin American Post*, once weekly in
English, available in Bogotá and major cities. **Radio** To hear the news in English tune in to 98.5
FM daily 0500-0600; before 0500 *Voice of America* is on this wavelength and 2030-2130
French speakers can listen to *RFI*.

Food and drink

Colombia's food is very regional, but most major cities now have restaurants with non-local **Food**
Colombian food. Restaurants in smaller towns often close on Sunday, and early on weekday
evenings: if stuck, you will probably find something to eat near the bus station. If you are
economising, ask for the *plato del día* or *plato corriente* (dish of the day).
    A standard main course is *sancocho*, a filling combination of all the tuberous vegetables,
including the tropical cassava and yam, with chopped fresh fish or any kind of meat, possibly

Colombia

chicken. Colombia has its own variant of the inevitable *arroz con pollo* (chicken and rice) which is excellent. *Ajiaco de pollo* is a delicious chicken, maize, manioc, cabbage and potato stew served with cream and capers, and lumps of avocado; it is a Bogotá speciality; another Bogotá speciality is *sobrebarriga* (belly of beef). *Bandeja antioqueña* consists of meat grilled and served with rice, beans, potato, manioc and a green salad; the simpler *carne asada* is cheaper. *Mazamorra*, boiled maize in milk, is a typical *antioqueño* sweet, and so is *salpicón*, a tropical fruit salad. (In Boyacá, however, *mazamorra* is a meat and vegetable soup.) *Lechona* (sucking pig and herbs) is a speciality of Ibagué. Cartagena's rice is usually with coconut. In Nariño, guinea pig (*cuy*, *curí* or *conejillo de Indias*) is typical. *Tamales* are meat pies made by folding a maize dough round chopped pork mixed with potato, peas, onions, eggs and olives seasoned with garlic, cloves and paprika, and steaming the whole in banana leaves (which you don't eat); the best are from Tolima. From stalls in the capital and the countryside, try *mazorcas* (roast maize cobs) or *arepas* (fried maize cakes). On the Caribbean coast, eat an egg *empanada*, which consists of two layers of corn (maize) dough that open like an oyster-shell, fried with eggs in the middle, and try the *patacón*, a cake of mashed and baked plantain (green banana). *Huevos pericos*, eggs scrambled with onions and tomatoes, are a popular, cheap and nourishing snack available almost anywhere. *Pandebono*, cheese-flavoured bread is delicious.

A good local sweet is the *canastas de coco*: pastry containing coconut custard flavoured with wine and surmounted by meringue. *Arequipe* is very similar to fudge, and popular (it is called *manjarblanco* in other parts of South America). *Almojábanas*, a kind of sour-milk/cheese bread roll, are delicious if fresh. There is, indeed, quite an assortment of little fruit pasties and preserves. Then there are the usual fruits: bananas, oranges, mangoes, avocado pears, and (at least in the tropical zones) *chirimoyas*, *papayas*, and the delicious *pitahaya*, taken either as an appetizer or dessert. Other fruits such as the *guayaba* (guava), *guanábana* (soursop), *maracuyá* (passion fruit), *lulo* (naranjilla), *mora* (blackberry) and *curuba* (banana passion fruit) make delicious juices, sometimes with milk added to make a *sorbete* though *sorbetes* are best left alone unless you are satisfied the milk is fresh. There is also *feijoa*, a green fruit with white flesh, high in vitamin C. Fruit yoghurts are nourishing and cheap (try *Alpina* brand; *crema* style is best), or *kumis*, a kind of liquid yoghurt. Another drink you should try is *champús*, a corn base with lemon and other fruit.

Drink   *Tinto*, the national small cup of black coffee, is taken at all hours. Colombian coffee is always mild. (Coffee with milk is called *café perico*; *café con leche* is a mug of milk with coffee added.) *Agua de panela* is a common beverage (hot water with unrefined sugar), also made with limes, milk, or cheese. Many acceptable brands of beer are produced, almost all produced by the Bavaria group, but also popular is *Leona*. The local rum is good and cheap; ask for *ron*, not *aguardiente*, which is a 'rougher' cane-based spirit served with or without aniseed (*aguardiente anisado*). Try *canelazo* cold or hot rum with water, sugar, lime and cinnamon. Local table wines include Isabella; none is very good. Wine is very expensive, US$15 in restaurants for an average Chilean or Argentine wine, more for European and other wines.

Warning It has been reported that bottles of imported spirits bearing well-known labels have often been 'recycled' and contain a cheap and poor imitation of the original contents

Shopping

Best buys   Emeralds in Bogotá; handworked silver (excellent); Indian pottery and textiles. The state-run Artesanías de Colombia for craft work (see under Bogotá). In Antioquia buy the handbag *carriel antioqueño* traditionally made from otter skin, but nowadays from calf skin and plastic trimmed at that. Clothing and shoes are cheap in Medellín. The Colombian *ruana* (poncho) is attractive and warm in any cool climate, and comes in a wide variety of colours. Leatherwork is generally good and not expensive especially in southern Colombia.

Holidays and festivals

Public Holidays: 1 January: Circumcision of our Lord; 6 January: Epiphany*; 19 March: St Joseph*; Maundy Thursday; Good Friday; 1 May: Labour Day; Ascension Day*; Corpus Christi*; Sacred Heart*; 29 June: SS Peter and Paul*; 20 July: Independence Day; 7 August: Battle of

Boyacá; 15 August: Assumption*; 12 October: Columbus' arrival in America* (Día de la Raza); 1 November: All Saints' day*; 11 November: Independence of Cartagena*; 8 December: Immaculate Conception; 25 December: Christmas Day. When those marked with an asterisk do not fall on a Mon, or when they fall on a Sun, they will be moved to the following Mon. Public holidays are known as *puentes* (bridges).

Sport and special interest travel

Trekking Trekking is popular in many parts of the country, with walks ranging from easy one-day excursions out of Bogotá, or at San Agustín, to three to four-day hikes. Good places for longer treks include the national parks of Los Nevados (from Ibagué, Manizales or Pereira), Sierra Nevada del Cocuy in the northeast, and Puracé (between Popayán and San Agustín). Well-trodden is the path to the Ciudad Perdida in the Sierra Nevada de Santa Marta, which has as its goal one of the country's main archaeological sites. In the departments of Boyacá and Santander there are a number of colonial *caminos reales* which make for good weekend trips. Sources of information include tourist offices, **Ministerio del Medio Ambiente** (*MA* – see Tourist information and National parks, below) and organizations such as *Sal Si Puedes* (address under Bogotá, Sport).

Climbing The best possibilities for mountaineers are the national parks of Los Nevados (eg Nevado del Ruiz, Nevado de Tolima) and Sierra Nevada del Cocuy (eg Ritacuba Blanca and Ritacuba Negra). For rock and ice climbing, the Nevados and Cocuy offer some technical challenges and at Suesca, north of Bogotá near Nemocón, there is some of the best rock climbing in the country. The best source of information is Mauricio Afanador, who can be contacted at *Café y Crepes* (see Bogotá, Eating). Maps can be obtained at the **Instituto Geográfico** (see under Bogotá, Maps). If you intend to climb, bring all your own equipment. It may be hard to find easily in Colombia, eg compass. Some equipment available at *Almacén Aventura*, Cra 13, No 67-26, Bogotá, T313 3219, F248 2639, rope, boots etc; *Deportivos del Campo*, C 64, No 18-15, Bogotá, T547 9405, tents, mattresses etc, mostly imported; *Sierra Nevada* shops: Cra 7, No 55-32, T/F352 1553, Bogotá; Av 37, No 41-53, T648029, Ibagué; Cra 39, No 8-03, T268 4296, Medellín. Also at *Eco-Guías*, Cra 3, No 18-56A, Bogotá, T/F284 8991, www.ecoguias.com Light equipment, rucksacks etc of reasonable quality, can be bought in markets.

Mountain biking The possibilities are, in theory, endless for this sport and Colombians are themselves keen cyclists. Because some remote parts are unsafe, it is not wise to venture off the beaten track and you should enquire locally about the security situation before setting out. An agency like *Eco-Guías* in Bogotá (see Tour operators) can give details and information may also be available at popular travellers hotels.

Watersports Diving: There are dive sites on both the Caribbean and Pacific coasts, but the former is more developed. Caribbean diving centres are Cartagena, Santa Marta and nearby Taganga, San Andrés and Providencia, the Islas de San Bernardo off the coast of Sucre, Isla Fuerte off Córdoba department and Capurganá, near the Panamanian border. On the Pacific, Bahía Solano is the main destination. There are dive shops in most of these places (see text) and you can contact Maurice Thorin, one of the best-known divers in Colombia, T033-723 8807 (mob), colmoredive@hotmail.com Also Pedro Roa of *Aqua Sub Diving*, T613 8038, Bogotá, aquasub_dive@uole.com or aquasubdive@starmedia.com, who can put you in touch with diving instructors belonging to the *Asociación Colombiana de Instructores de Buceo* (ACIB). A five-day PADI course costs about US$140 (2002 prices). **Fishing** is particularly good at Girardot, Santa Marta and Barranquilla; marlin is fished off Barranquilla. There are regular competitions, especially on the Pacific coast, for instance at Golfo de Cupica. There is good trout fishing, in season, in the lakes in the Bogotá area, and at Lago de Tota in Boyacá. Many upmarket travel agencies in Bogotá and Medellín can arrange fishing trips.
Windsurfing: In Cartagena many of the hotels in Bocagrande hire out equipment. In Bogotá, call Erhard Martin, T249 3002, for information. **Whitewater rafting** is growing in popularity and is at present based at San Gil (Santander) and Villeta (Cundinamarca). See details in the text.

Colombia

Birdwatching The list of birds found in Colombia is claimed to be longer than any other country in South America (and the world, for that matter). There is a wide variety of habitats, from the distinct arms of the Andean cordilleras with their west and east-facing slopes, the Sierra Nevada de Santa Marta, the eastern plains, Amazonian rainforest and the dry scrub and forest of the northeast. Some of the more easily accessible areas are in the vicinity of Santa Marta (eg the Parque Nacional Tayrona, the marshes between Santa Marta and Barranquilla), several good spots around the capital, Parque Nacional Los Nevados, the Laguna de Sonso, near Buga, and the road from Cali to Buenaventura, around Popayán, Puracé and San Agustín, La Planada Reserve near Pasto, some of the routes into the eastern Llanos (eg Garzón to Florencia and Pasto to Mocoa) and around Leticia (eg the Parque Nacional Amacayacu). As with other activities that require spending time away from centres of population, birders should ask locally if the sites they want to explore are safe. *A Guide to the Birds of Colombia*, by Steven Hilty and William Brown (Princeton, 1986), is recommended (acknowledgement is also made here to *Where to watch birds in South America*, by Nigel Wheatley – London, 1994).

Spectator sports Association football is the most popular game and is of high quality, especially in Cali and Medellín. American baseball is played at Cartagena and Barranquilla. There are bullrings at Bogotá, Cali, Manizales, Medellín, Sincelejo and Cerrito. Polo is played at Medellín and Bogotá. Cockfights, cycling, boxing and basketball are also popular.

Health

See also Health in Essentials at the beginning of the book, page 63

Emergency medical treatment is given in hospitals: if injured in a bus accident, for example, you will be covered by insurance and treatment will be free. Bogotá has well-organized sanitary services, but bottled water is recommended for drinking. Outside the capital take sterilizer with you, or boil the water, or use the excellent mineral waters. Choose your food and eating places with care everywhere. *Falmonox* is recommended locally for amoebas. Mosquito nets are useful in the coastal swampy regions. There is some risk of malaria and yellow fever in the coastal areas and the eastern *llanos*/jungle regions; prophylaxis is advised. For up-to-date information, ask at the bigger clinics and hospitals. Tampons are not always available, but can easily be found in big city supermarkets.

Bogotá

Bogotá is a vast, sprawling city thick with traffic (though considerably improved since the TransMilenio rapid transit system opened in 2001) and with predictable extremes of wealth and poverty. Emerald sellers do deals on street corners, but for a safer view of all that glitters, visit the Gold Museum, one of the most stunning collections of pre-Columbian treasures in the Americas. The old centre of La Candelaria has countless fine colonial buildings while northern Bogotá is the latest in modern urban design. The capital, founded in 1538, is one of the most important cities of Latin America. It has a remarkable historic centre with a wealth of museums and colonial buildings. There are many places of interest in nearby towns for weekend excursions out of the city. The basin on which it stands, with high ranges of the Cordillera to the east, is known as La Sabana de Bogotá.

Getting there El Dorado airport has 2 terminals, 11 km northwest of the centre. The taxi fare to the city is fixed at US$6, more at night and early morning. Make sure you get a registered taxi, normally yellow, outside the main terminal or *Avianca* terminal (ask the driver to quote the fare before you get in). Unofficial taxis not advisable. There are *colectivos* (US$1 plus luggage pp) from airport to centre; also buses in the daytime, US$0.25 (not easy with bulky luggage and they may refuse to take you). Watch belongings inside and outside airport, especially at night. The long-distance bus terminal, Terminal de Transportes, is in the same direction as the airport, but not as far out. To get into town from the terminal take buses marked 'Centro' or 'Germania'; ask the driver where to get off (the 'Germania' bus goes up to the centre and La Candelaria). To get to North Bogotá from the terminal, take a bus heading in that direction on Cra 68. Taxi fares from the terminal are about US$3.50, depending on destination, surcharge at night, passengers should request a computer slip showing the exact fare (avoid unofficial taxis which tout for particular hotels).

Getting around Bus: Several types of bus cover urban routes. All stop when flagged down. There is also the TransMilenio system on dedicated lanes. **Taxi**: have meters which calculate units starting at 25. Total units for journey are converted into pesos using a table which must be displayed in the taxi. Taxis are relatively cheap, but if you are carrying valuables and especially at night, take a radio taxi rather than one on the street.

Street numbering: The Calles (abbreviated 'C', or 'Cll') run at right angles across the Carreras ('Cra' or 'K'). It is easy enough to find a place once the address system, which is used throughout Colombia, is understood. The address Calle 13, No 12-45 would be the building on Calle 13 between Carreras 12 and 13 at 45 paces from Carrera 12; however transversals (Tra) and diagonals (Diag) can complicate the system. The Avenidas, are broad and important streets. Av Jiménez de Quesada, one of Bogotá's most important streets, owes its lack of straightness to having been built over a river-bed, some of which has recently been exposed as part of a pedestrianisation scheme.

Tourist offices Instituto Distrital de Cultura y Turismo, Cra 8, No 9-83, T336 6511, turismo@idct.gov.co Also at the airport and bus terminal, operated by the city of Bogotá. Good local guide books and maps available. **Corporación La Candelaria**, C 13, No 2-58, T336 0888. Helpful, sells posters, T-shirts, booklets, etc. For information on 24-hour chemists (pharmacies), events, attractions, etc, T282 0000. A useful website for information on Bogotá is www.laciudad.com **MA**, the National Parks Office, Cra 10, No 20-30, T283 3009, F243 3091, full details in Essentials, National Parks.

Ins & outs
Phone code: 91
Colour map 1, grid B3
Population:
6.4 million (1995)
Altitude: 2,650 m
Mean temperature:
14°C

For more detailed information, see Transport, page 795

Routes through the city are changing all the time due to construction of the TransMilenio. Potholes in both roads and pavements can be very deep: avoid them, especially when it is wet

Colombia

Sights

Because of the altitude, go easy and be careful with food and alcoholic drinks for the first day or so

As in any city of this size, take care not to tempt thieves by careless display of money or valuables. Also, anyone approaching you with questions, offering to sell something or making demands, may well be a thief or a con-artist

There are three main parts of the city of interest to the visitor: La Candelaria, the historic centre; Downtown Bogotá, the old commercial centre with shops, offices and banks; and North Bogotá, where there has been great commercial expansion with the development of wealthy suburbs. **La Candelaria**, full of character, occupies the area to the south of Av Jiménez de Quesada, north of Calle 6 and east of Cra 10. There is some modern infill but many of the houses are well preserved in colonial style, of one or two storeys with tiled roofs, projecting eaves, wrought ironwork and carved balconies. The churches, museums and palaces are concentrated around and above the Plaza Bolívar. There are also many intriguing cobbled streets further out from this nucleus. Some hotels are found in this part, more along the margins, eg Av Jiménez de Quesada. The streets are relatively uncrowded and safe; care should be exercised after dark. Do not go west of Cra 10 and south of C 6.

Downtown Bogotá runs in a band northwards from Av Jiménez de Quesada. It is a thorough mix of styles including modern towers and run-down colonial and later buildings, together with a few notable ones. This commercial hub narrows to a thin band of secondary shops extending between Cra 7 and Av Caracas to around C 60. The streets are full of life; they can be paralysed by traffic at busy times. The pavements

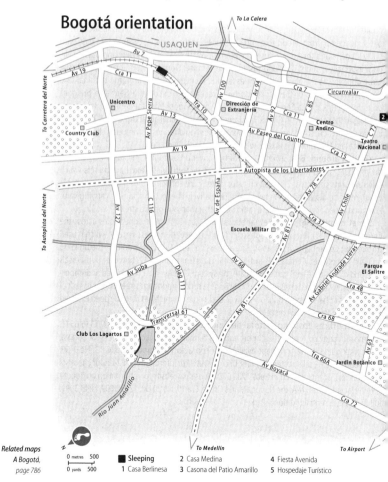

Bogotá orientation

0 metres 500	■ Sleeping	2 Casa Medina	4 Fiesta Avenida
0 yards 500	1 Casa Berlinesa	3 Casona del Patio Amarillo	5 Hospedaje Turístico

To La Calera
USAQUEN
Av 7
Cra 11
Av 19
Cra 100
Av 94
Cra 7
Circunvalar
Tra 10
Av 100
Dirección de Extranjería
Unicentro
Av Pepe Sierra
Av 15
Av 92
Cra 11
C 85
Country Club
Centro Andino
To Carretera del Norte
Teatro Nacional
C 72
Av Paseo del Country
Cra 15
Av 19
Autopista de los Libertadores
Av 13
Av de España
Av 78
Av Chile
To Autopista del Norte
Av 127
C 116
Cra 37
Av 81
Escuela Militar
Av Suba
Diag 111
Av 68
Av 81
Transversal 61
Parque El Salitre
Cra 48
Club Los Lagartos
Cra 68
Av 83
Tra 66A
Jardín Botánico
Av Boyacá
Cra 72
Río Juan Amarillo
To Medellín
To Airport

Colombia

can be very congested too, particularly Cra 7 and Av 19. Many of the budget hotels and some of the better ones are found in this area, rated as low to moderate risk.

Beyond C 60, the main city continues north to a comparatively new area, **North Bogotá**. Most of the best hotels and restaurants are in this area which is regarded as relatively safe. Away from the centre, the whole of the south and west of the city should be avoided unless there are specific reasons for a visit.

There is a very good view of the city from the top of **Monserrate** (3,210 m), the lower of the two peaks rising sharply to the east. It is reached by a funicular railway and a cable car. The new convent at the top is a popular shrine. At the summit, near the church, a platform gives a bird's-eye view of the city's tiled roofs and of the plains beyond stretching to the rim of the Sabana. Sunrise and sunset can be spectacular. Also at the top are several restaurants, including *Casa San Isidro*, French menu, seafood, fireplace, spectacular view, Monday-Saturday 1200-2400, lunch only on Sunday, expensive but good, and snack bars. The Calle del Candelero, a reconstruction of a Bogotá street of 1887, has plenty of street stalls. Behind the church are popular picnic grounds.

At the foot of Monserrate is the **Quinta de Bolívar**, C 20, No 2-91 Este, T284 6819, a fine colonial mansion, with splendid gardens and lawns. There are several cannons captured at the battle of Boyacá. The house, once Bolívar's home, is now a

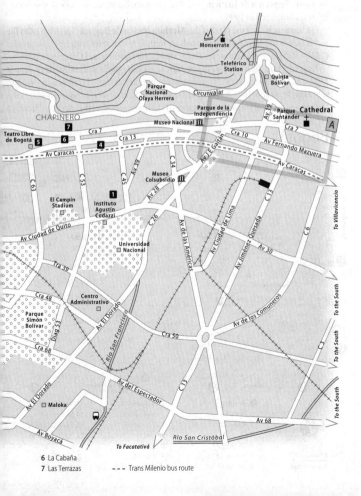

6 La Cabaña
7 Las Terrazas   - - - Trans Milenio bus route

museum showing some of his personal possessions and paintings of events in his career. ■ *Tue-Sun, 0900-1700*

■ *Getting there. The fare up to Monserrate is US$4 adult return (US$2 child). The funicular normally works only on Sun and holidays (expect to have to queue if you want to go up before about 1400, and for coming down); the cable car operates 0900-2400 daily. Times change frequently, T284 5700. A good time to walk up is Sat or Sun about 0500, before the crowds arrive. There are enough people then to make it quite safe and you will catch the sunrise. The path is dressed stone and comfortably graded all the way up with refreshment stalls at weekends every few metres. It takes about 1¼ hrs up (if you don't stop). On no account walk down in the dark. It is best not to go alone. On weekdays, it is not recommended to walk up and especially not down. You should also take a bus or taxi to the foot of the hill Mon-Fri and, at all times, from the bottom station into town. There are usually taxis waiting by the footbridge across the road. The walk up to Guadalupe, the higher peak opposite Monserrate, is not recommended at any time.*

Candelaria
Popular as a residential area, with an artists' community. All museums are closed on Mon

The **Plaza Bolívar**, contemporary with the city's foundation, is at the heart of the city. It has a statue of the Liberator at its centre. Around the Plaza are the narrow streets and mansions of the Barrio La Candelaria. On the northern side of the Plaza is the **Corte Suprema de Justicia**, wrecked in a guerrilla attack in 1985. A new building was completed in 1999.

On the west side of the plaza is the **Alcaldía Mayor de Bogotá** (City Hall). On the south side is the **Capitolio Nacional**, an imposing structure with fine colonnades (1847-1925). Several Ministries are located in the building and Congress sits here.

East of Plaza Bolívar On the eastern side of the plaza is the **Catedral**, rebuilt 1807-1823 in classical style. It has a notable choir loft of carved walnut and wrought silver on the altar of the Chapel of El Topo. Among its several treasures and relics is the banner brought by Jiménez de Quesada to Bogotá, now in the sacristy. There is a

Bogotá

	Sleeping		7	La Hostería de la	13	San Diego *B2*
1	Ambala *A4*			Candelaria *A5*	14	Sante Fe *A4*
2	Avenida Jiménez *A4*		8	La Sabana *B2*	15	Santa Mónica *A2*
3	Bacatá *A3*		9	Príncipe de Viena *C3*	16	Youth Hostel *B6*
4	Dorantes *A4*		10	Quiratama *C3*		
5	El Virrey *A3*		11	Regina *A3*	✝	**Churches**
6	Internacional *A4*		12	Residencia Aragón *A4*	1	Catedral *B5*

0 metres 200
0 yards 200

Colombia

monument to Jiménez inside the Cathedral. In one of the chapels is buried Gregorio Vásquez de Arce y Ceballos (1638-1711), the most famous painter in colonial Colombia. Many of his paintings are in the Cathedral. The beautiful **Capilla del Sagrario**, in the same block, was built at the end of the 17th century. It contains several paintings by Vásquez de Arce.

At the southeastern corner of the plaza is the **Palacio Arzobispal**, with splendid bronze doors. See the **Casa del Florero** or **Museo 20 de Julio** in a colonial house on the corner of Plaza Bolívar with C 11. It houses the famous flower vase that featured in the 1810 revolution and shows collections of the Independence War period, including documents and engravings and some fine portraits of Simón Bolívar. ■ *Tue-Sat, 0900-1615, Sun 1000-1515, US$1 (reduction with ISIC).*

In the block behind it is the colonial **Plazuela de Rufino Cuervo**. Here is the house of Manuela Sáenz, the mistress of Bolívar. Beside it is the house in which Antonio Nariño printed in 1794 his translation of Thomas Paine's 'The Rights of Man' which had a profound influence on the movement for independence. You can read an extract of the text in Spanish on the wall of the building. Across from Plazuela de Rufino Cuervo is **San Ignacio**, a Jesuit church built in 1605. Emeralds from the Muzo mines in Boyacá were used in the monstrance and it has more paintings by Gregorio Vásquez de Arce. The **Museo de Arte Colonial** (Carrera 6, No 9-77) is one of the finest colonial buildings in Colombia. It belonged originally to the Society of Jesus, and was once the seat of the oldest University in Colombia and of the National Library. It has a splendid collection of colonial art and paintings by Gregorio Vásquez de Arce, all kinds of utensils, and two charming patios. ■ *Mon-Fri 0900-1700.* Across Carrera 6 is the **Palacio de San Carlos**, C 10, No 5-51, where Bolívar lived. He is said to have planted the huge walnut tree in the courtyard. On 25 September 1828, there was an attempt on his life. His mistress, Manuela, thrust him out of the window and he was able to hide for two hours under the stone arches of the bridge across the Río San Agustín (now C 7). Santander, suspected of complicity, was arrested and banished.

2 Capilla del Sagrario
  & Palacio Arzobispal *B5*
3 La Tercera Orden *B3*
4 La Veracruz *B3*
5 Mária del Carmen *A5*
6 San Augustín *B5*
7 San Diego *B2*
8 San Francisco *B4*
9 San Ignacio *B5*
10 Santa Bárbara *B6*
11 Santa Clara *B5*
-- Trans Milenio bus route

South of the Palacio de San Carlos is the **Iglesia de María del Carmen**, Cra 5, No 8-36, the most striking church building in Bogotá, with excellent stained glass and walls in bands of red and white. Almost opposite the Palacio de San Carlos is the **Teatro Colón**, C 10, No 5-32 (operas, lectures, ballets, plays, concerts, etc), late 19th century with lavish decorations. One block northeast of here is the **Casa de la Moneda** (Mint), built in 1753, at C 11, No 4-93. The courtyard is worth seeing. ■ *Tue-Sat 1000-1800, Sun and holidays, 1000-1600, free.* Next door is the new **Donación Botero** museum, ■ *Wed-Mon 1000-2000, T343 1212.* In the same street, No 4-41, is the Banco de la República's **Biblioteca Luis Angel Arango**, one of the best endowed and arranged in South America, with three reading rooms, research rooms, art galleries and a splendid concert hall. There are exhibitions and regular concerts. The modern architecture is impressive. There is a good cafetería on the 6th floor. ■ *Library 0800-2000, Sun 0800-1600, closed Mon, free.*

Colombia

The **Palacio de Nariño** (1906), the presidential palace, occupies a large space due south of Plaza Bolívar. It has a spectacular interior and a fine collection of modern Colombian paintings. It is occasionally open to the public; enquire. The guard is ceremonially changed daily, normally at 1730. To the south is the Church of **San Agustín**, strongly ornamented (1637). It, too, has fine paintings by Vásquez Arce and the Image of Jesus, which was proclaimed Generalísimo of the army in 1812. South again is the **Santa Bárbara** church (mid-16th century), one of the most interesting colonial churches, with paintings by Gregorio Vásquez Arce. The colonial church of **Santa Clara**, west of the Palacio de Nariño, has a fine interior. It is now a religious museum and concert hall.

Close to the Palacio Nariño are: **Museo Arqueológico** (sponsored by the Banco Popular), a fine and extensive collection of precolumbian pottery, in the restored mansion of the Marqués de San Jorge, Cra 6, No 7-43. The house itself is a beautiful example of 17th century Spanish colonial architecture. ■ *Mon-Sat 0800-1200, 1300-1630, US$1.30, T282 0760.* **Museo de Artes y Tradiciones Populares**, Cra 8, No 7-21, in an old monastery, exhibits local arts and crafts. It has a shop selling handicrafts and a bar and restaurant (dishes typical of different regions of Colombia served in colonial setting, good, usually with regional traditional music). ■ *Mon-Sat 0900-1700, US$1.*

Several blocks west of Plaza Bolívar is the **Parque Mártires** (Park of the Martyrs, Cra 14 y C 10) with a monument, on the site of the Plaza in which the Spanish shot many patriots during the struggle for independence.

Downtown Bogotá Midway between Plaza Bolívar and Av Jiménez de Quesada, which marks the boundary between La Candelaria and Downtown, is the **Palacio de Comunicaciones** (Post and Telegraph building, Cra 7 y C 12A), built on the site of the colonial church of Santo Domingo. Across the Av Jiménez de Quesada, in the commercial district, is **Parque Santander**, with a bronze statue of Santander, who helped Bolívar to free Colombia and was later its President.

Next to Parque Santander is the **Banco de la República**, beside which is the wonderful **Museo del Oro** (the Gold Museum, Cra 6, No 15-82). This unique collection is a must. There are more than 35,000 pieces of precolumbian gold work in the total collection, most of which is held here. The rest are in other Museos de Oro sponsored by the Banco de la República throughout Colombia. There are tours and films in Spanish and English, enquire for times. Do not miss the Salón Dorado, a glittering display inside an inner vault, nor the ethnic collection on the 1st floor. The ancient gold objects discovered in Colombia were not made by the primitive technique of simple hammering alone, but show the use of virtually every technique known to modern goldsmiths. ■ *Tue-Sat 0900-1630, Sun and holidays, 0900-1200, US$1.50, T342 1111.*

Also around Parque Santander: **San Francisco** church (mid-16th century), with paintings of famous Franciscans, choir stalls, a famous ornate gold high altar (1622), and a fine Lady Chapel with blue and gold ornamentation. The remarkable ceiling is in Spanish-Moorish (mudéjar) style. Try to see this church when it is fully illuminated. **Palacio de San Francisco**, Av Jiménez No 7-50, built 1918-1933 in the Corinthian style on the site of the Franciscan friary, is now part of the Rosario university. Church of **La Veracruz**, first built five years after the founding of Bogotá, rebuilt in 1731, and again in 1904. In 1910 it became the Panteón Nacional e Iglesia de la República. José de Caldas, the famous scientist, was buried along with many other victims of the 'Reign of Terror' under the church. It has a bright white and red interior and a fine decorated ceiling. Fashionable weddings are held here. **La Tercera Orden**, a colonial church famous for its carved woodwork along the nave and a high balcony, massive wooden altar reredos, and confessionals, built by the Third Franciscan Order in the 17th century.

Continuing north along Cra 7, you reach **Parque de la Independencia**, at the junction with C 26. In the park is the **Planetarium**. ■ *Tue-Sun 1100-1530.* Also at

The Gilded Man

The basis of the El Dorado (Gilded Man) story is established fact. It was the custom of the Chibcha king to be coated annually with resin, on which gold dust was stuck, and then to be taken out on the lake on a ceremonial raft. He then plunged into the lake and emerged with the resin and gold dust washed off. The lake was also the repository of precious objects thrown in as offerings; there have been several attempts to drain it (the first, by the Spaniards in colonial times, was the origin of the sharp cut in the crater rim) and many items have been recovered over the years. The factual basis of the El Dorado story was confirmed by the discovery of a miniature raft with ceremonial figures on it, made from gold wire, which is now one of the most prized treasures of the Museo del Oro in Bogotá. Part of the raft is missing; the story is that the gold from it ended up in one of the finder's teeth! (Read John Hemming's The Search for El Dorado on the subject.)

this junction (Cra 7 and C 26) are the church and monastery of **San Diego**, a picturesque, restored old building. The Franciscan monastery with fine mudéjar ceiling was built in 1560 and the church in 1607 as its chapel. Local craft items are sold in part of the old monastery. Across the street is the **Tequendama Hotel**. Near the park is the **Biblioteca Nacional**, with its entrance on C 24.

Museo Nacional, on Cra 7, No 28-66, is an old prison converted into a museum, founded by Santander in 1823. There is an excellent archaeological collection. Its top floor houses a fine art section, comprising national paintings and sculptures. ■ *Tue-Sat 1000-1700, Sun 1000-1600, US$1 (pensioners free) , T334 8366. Café open 1100-1500, good salads and desserts.*

Maloka, Cra 68D, No 40A-51, is a complex of science and technology exhibits for all ages, large screen cinema. ■ *Tue-Sun 0900-1800.*

In the link between Central and North Bogotá, is the **Universidad Nacional** (about 13,000 students), which is housed in the Ciudad Universitaria shown on the orientation map. The oldest centres of learning are in Candelaria: oldest of all is the Colegio Nacional de San Bartolomé (C 10, No 6-57), across from the Chapel of El Sagrario, founded 1573, now a prestigious school. The second oldest, founded on 18 December 1653, is the Colegio Mayor de Nuestra Señora del Rosario (C 14, No 6-25); its beautiful colonial building is well worth a look (you can buy a good cheap lunch at the cafetería).

There is an interesting and well organized **Jardín Botánico**, José Celestino Mutis, Av 57, No 61-13, www.jbb.gov.co It has a collection of over 5,000 orchids, plus roses, gladioli and trees from all over the country (see map).

North Bogotá

North of C 68 is an expanding band of wealthy suburbs, shopping malls and classy restaurants. Regarded as relatively safe. The best hotels are here

Excursions

The Simón Bolívar Highway runs from Bogotá to Girardot (see page 840); this 132 km stretch is extremely picturesque, running down the mountains. About 20 km along this road from the centre of Bogotá is Soacha, now the end of the built-up area of the city. A right fork here leads past the Indumil plant to the **Chicaque Parque Natural**, a privately owned 300 ha park, principally cloud forest between 2,100 m and 2,700 m on the edge of the Sabana de Bogotá. It is a popular spot for walkers and riders at weekends with good facilities for day visitors and a Swiss-style *refugio*, about one hour down the trail from the entrance, which provides meals and accommodation for 70 or so costing US$20-25 per day including meals. ■ *Park open daily 0800-1600, US$2.50. Getting there: Take a bus to Soacha and ask for continuing transport to the Park. On Sat, Sun and public holidays, there is a minibus service from the National Stadium (Campín) in Bogotá, T368 3114/3118. If driving, there is a better route via Mosquera on the Honda road, left towards La Mesa and in 11 km left again on the road to Soacha. The park sign is 6 km along this road.*

Southwest of Bogotá

Colombia

Colombia

Northwest of Bogotá The Sabana de Bogotá is dotted with white farms and groves of eucalyptus. The road passes through two small towns, Fontibón and Madrid. **Fontibón**, 10 km from Bogotá, has a good colonial church, and about 3 km outside the town are stones with Indian pictographs. Nearby, on the road from the old Techo airport to Bogotá, there are replicas of San Agustín statues (see page 868). City buses go to Fontibón. **Facatativá** (*Population*: 67,000. *Altitude*:1,800 m) is 40 km from Bogotá (several hotels eg **E** *Sueño Dorado*, Cra 2, No 10-64, T842 4205, with bath, TV). Some 3 km from Facatativá, on the road to the west, is the park of Piedras de Tunja, a natural rock amphitheatre with enormous stones, numerous Indian pictographs and an artificial lake. A road goes southwest from Facatativá to Girardot through beautiful mountain country, a good alternative to the Simón Bolívar highway from Girardot to Bogotá.

Villeta, 71 km from Facatativá (*Population*: 13,000. *Altitude*: 950 m. *Phone code*: 91) is a popular weekend resort. The waterfalls of Quebrada Cune are nearby. Villeta has many hotels including: **A** *Mediterraneo*, C 6, No 8-68, T844 4134, best. **D** *Colonial Plaza*, Cra 4A, No 6-07, T844 4969. **F** *Gran San Diego* C 3, No 4-173, recommended. Also restaurants such as *Llamarade* near the plaza, good value; many good ice cream parlours. 15 km north of Villeta, near Tobia, is a new area of rafting on the Río Negro. Information from *Kumandai*, T255 7518/212 7478.

The road continues to Honda (see page 839), half way to which is the interesting historical town of **Guaduas** (*Population*: 23,000. *Altitude*: 1,000 m. *Phone code*: 91). In the main plaza is a statue of the liberator Policarpa Salavarrieta, the cathedral and one of several museums in the town. Sunday market. Best local dish is *quesillos*. Bus to Honda, US$2, one hour. *Hostería Colonial*, on plaza, T846 6041, a delightful restored mansion; other hotels and restaurants nearby. The surrounding countryside is beautiful, including waterfalls at Versalles (10 km). Transport for Facatativá, Villeta and Guaduas: take Bogotá-Honda buses.

North of Bogotá Interesting day trips can be made to the attractive rolling *altiplano*, leaving Bogotá on the Autopista del Norte (extension of Av 13), or on the parallel Carretera del Norte (the old road, extension of Av 7). On the latter, once out of Bogotá, there are many old fincas and good typical restaurants. The two roads join at Km 24 at La Caro where a road leaves left (west) to Chía and Zipaquirá. At this junction is the sinister looking 'castle' which belonged to the drug baron Rodríguez Gacha. By contrast, there is opposite the graceful colonial bridge over the Río Bogotá, now preserved and bypassed by the road to **Chía**, which has a typical Sunday market (bus from Av Caracas, Bogotá US$0.30).

Zipaquirá
Phone code: 91
Colour map 1, grid B3
Population: 62,000
Altitude: 2,600 m

The famous rock salt mine, 20 km beyond Chía, has been exploited for centuries. Within the mines, the **Salt Cathedral** is one of the major attractions of Colombia.The original underground cathedral was dedicated in 1954 to Nuestra Señora del Rosario (patron saint of miners). Continuing deterioration made the whole cave unsafe and it was closed. A remarkable, new salt cathedral was opened on 16 December 1995. Inside, near the entrance, are the 14 Stations of the Cross, each sculpted by a different artist. Other sections of the cathedral follow to the Nave, 180 m below the surface, with huge pillars "growing" out of the salt. All is discretely illuminated and gives a modern and austere impression. ■ *Tue-Sun 0930-1630, Sun mass at 1200, admission by ticket, US$4, half price on Wed, including 1½ hr guided tour, car park US$1. The entrance is in hills about 20 mins' walk west of the town. There is an information centre and a museum at the site.*

In the town is an interesting church and the **Museo Quevedo Zornozo**, C 3, No 7-69, which displays musical instruments and paraphenalia including the piano of General Santander. ■ *Tue-Fri 0930-1200, 1400-1600, Sat-Sun 0900-1700, US$1.*

Sleeping C-D *Hostería del Libertador*, Vía Catedral de Sal, T852 3060, F852 6851. Restored colonial mansion, near the mine, good food. **E** *Colonial*, C 3, No 6-57, T852 2690. Showers, TV in some rooms, nice. Restaurants on main plaza, *El Mesón del Zipa*, good, cheap food. *Asadero Colonial*, C 5 y Cra 7, good food, *arepas*, *bandejas*.

Transport Many buses from **Bogotá**: Cra 30 (Av Ciudad de Quito), marked 'Zipa', *Flota Alianza*, or others, US$2 each way, 1¼ hrs. The Zipaquirá bus station is 15 mins walk from the mines and cathedral. Zipaquirá can also be reached from Tunja (see page 798), by taking a Bogotá-bound bus and getting off at La Caro for connection to Zipaquirá, US$2.40.

Nemocón, 15 km northeast of Zipaquirá, has salt mines (now closed) and a church. There is a small but interesting **Museo de Sal** on the plaza, which includes history of the salt industry in the time of the Chibcha Indians, US$1. Restaurant, *El Colonial*, on main street, 100 m from the station. A side road connects with the Bogotá-Cúcuta highway. A steam-hauled *tren turístico* runs on Sunday from Bogotá to Zipaquirá and Nemocón. See under Bogotá, Train.

Some 8 km beyond Nemocón, with its own access to the main Tunja road, is **Suesca**, centre of rock climbing on sandstone cliffs overlooking the Río Bogotá. For information call Fernando Gonzalo-Rubio, 933443729 (Mob), or T856 3326.

Essentials

NB Taxi drivers at the airport or bus station occasionally say that the hotel you have chosen is "closed", "not known" etc, especially the cheaper ones. Ask them to take you to the address we quote. There are any number of small, unregistered hotels and *hostales* in other parts of the city, not listed here, many of which are cheap, some of which are clean. Such areas may be regarded as unsafe for tourists and are remote from places of interest.

In La Candelaria to Av Jiménez de Quesada AL *La Opera*, C 10, No 5-72, T336 2066, sales@hotelopera.com.co Next to Teatro Colón, only good standard colonial hotel in centre, tastefully decorated rooms, TV, phone, with breakfast, good restaurant. Recommended. **C** *La Hostería de la Candelaria*, C 9, No 3-11, T286 1479, Aptdo Aéreo 15978. Quiet, charming patio, restaurant (*Café Rosita*), suite with good view of old Bogotá, good for longer stays. **C** *Dorantes*, C 13, No 5-07, T334 6640. Cheaper without bath, hot water, high ceilings, 1950s décor, most rooms with good view of Monserrate, reasonable, safe. Recommended. **D** *Ambala*, Cra 5, No 13-46, T286 3751. Good value, central. **D** *Avenida Jiménez*, Av Jiménez, No 4-71, T243 6685. Helpful, sauna, safe. **D** *Santa Fe*, C 14, No 4-48, T342 0560, F342 1879. Good service, quiet, safe, good restaurant, popular with locals, good value. **E** *Internacional*, Cra 5, No 14-45, T341 8731. Cheaper without bath, hot water, excellent kitchen, good value, safe deposit, popular with Israelis (specify the address, there are several other hotels with similar names). **E** *Platypus*, C 16, No 2-43, T/F341 2874/3104, platypushotel@yahoo.com Pleasant, safe, kitchen facilities, hot water, free coffee, informative owner, book exchange, excellent travellers' guest house. Highly recommended. **E** *Aragón*, Cra 3, No 14-13, T342 5239/284 8325. Safe, honest, hot water, will store luggage, parking facilities. Recommended.

In Central Bogotá (Av Jiménez de Quesada up to Calle 31) A *Bacatá*, C 19, No 5-20, T283 8300, www.hbacata.com.co Downtown on busy street, cheaper at weekends, worth asking at other times, restaurant not recommended. **A** *Santa Mónica*, Cra 3, No 24-11, T336 8080. A/c, TV, comfortable, good location. **A** *San Diego*, Cra 13 y C 24, T284 2100. Large rooms, good value, accepts credit cards but not Amex TCs. **B** *El Virrey*, C 18, No 5-56, T334 1150. Modern, good value restaurant. Recommended. **B** *Quiratama*, C 17, No 12-44, T282 4515, F341 3246. Very nice rooms, good service. **C** *Principe de Viena*, C 19, No 15-35, T342 0090. Big old rooms, laundry service, bar restaurant. **C** *Regina*, Cra 5, No 15-16, T334 5137. Safe, good value. **C** *La Sabana*, C 23, No 5-23, T284 4361, F284 6552. Central, quiet, English spoken, small restaurant, Visa accepted.

Between Calles 32 and 75 **L** *Casa Medina*, Cra 7, 69A-22, T217 0288, F312 3769 (in the French 'Relais et Châteaux' chain). Nice interior, chic. **AL** *Forte Travelodge*, Av El Dorado, No 69A-51, T412 4009, F412 4412. Close to airport, modern, comfortable. **A** *Fiesta Avenida*, Av Caracas, No 47-28, T285 3407. Safe, restaurant. Recommended. **A** *Las Terrazas*, C 54A, No 3-12, T255 5777. 'Rustic charm', pleasant, nice view of city. **C** *Casa Berlinesa*, C 45A, No 21-40, T232 8504. German and English spoken, full breakfast available. **C** *La Casona del Patio Amarillo*, Cra

Sleeping
Book hotels in advance whenever possible.
■ *on map, page 786*
Price codes:
see inside front cover

Colombia

8, No 69-24, T212 8805, www.casonadelpatio.com Various room sizes, negotiate price, some with bath, quiet, pleasant patio, safe area. Recommended. **D** *La Cabaña*, C 58, No 9-55. Safe, good value. **D** *Hospedaje Turístico 61*, C 61, No 10-18, T217 0383. OK, discounts for stays over 3 days, also has short-stay section.

All recommended **Hotels in North Bogotá, Calles 76 and upwards** **LL** *La Fontana*, Av 127, No 21-10, T615 4400, www.hotellafontana.com Distinctive, very good (*Los Arcos* restaurant in hotel, superb, elegant). **LL** *Los Urapanes*, Cra 13, No 83-19, T218 1188, www.hotellosurapanes.com.co Very pleasant, smart, smaller hotel. **L** *Richmond Suites*, C 93, No 18-81, T616 7121. Convenient, quiet, excellent rooms. **L** *Windsor House*, C 95, No 9-97, T616 6417, F617 0993. Large suites, excellent. **AL** *Rincón del Chicó*, C101, No 13-32, T214 7371. Hot water, safe, family atmosphere, TV, helpful, good restaurant. **C** *Hostal Moreno*, Tra 33, No 95-28, T257 9127. Meals, house taxi driver, nearby frequent bus service to centre, safe for left luggage, quiet, comfortable, hot water, good value.

Private vehicles should **Youth Hostel Association** Colombian youth hostels are administered by the *Federación*
be parked in lockable, *Colombiana de Albergues Juveniles* (FCA), Cra 7, No 6-10, a block beyond the Palacio de
guarded parqueaderos Nariño (see map), T280 3041/3202, F280 3460. The FCA is affiliated to the IYHA. At this address is a clean, well-run hostel with 90 beds, safe area, US$4.50 pp members, US$5.50 non-members, per night, lunch available US$2 1200-1500. Ask for full information about other hostels here.

Eating If on a budget, *bandeja* (the local *plato del día*) can cost US$1.30-2 for a 2-course meal.
Many good value **In Candelaria** *Casa Vieja*, Av Jiménez 3-73. Traditional Bogotá food, live music at lunch-
comedores on C 16 time. Also at C 116, No 20-50 in North Bogotá and 2 other branches. *Eduardo*, C 13, No 8-66,
between Cras 4 y 5 T243 0118, Good business restaurant upstairs, more popular downstairs. *Cafetería Romana*,
On map, page 786. Av Jiménez, No 6-65. All meals, very clean, reasonable pasta, but excellent, expensive break-
If the menu states fast menu. Its sister restaurants are *Sorrento*, C 14, No 6-64, and *Salerno*, Cra 7, No 19-48,
that 10% IVA is good value, closes 2100. *Café L'Avenir*, C 11, No 2-98. French style, *crèpes* a speciality, pleas-
included in the price, ant atmosphere, useful notice-board, 1000-2200. Recommended. *Andante ma non*
this should not be *Troppo*, Cra 2, No 10-92. Good *comida* US$2.50, Mon-Sat 1200-1500. *Los Secretos del Mar*,
itemized as an Cra 5, No 13-20. Fish, good. *Mi Viejo*, C 11, No 5-37. Argentine steakhouse, popular at lunch-
extra on the bill. time. Recommended. *Café de Buenos Aires*, C 9, No 2-17, T561 3282. Argentine specialities,
Refuse to pay it café/bar, old colonial house and patio. Recommended. *La Puerta Falsa*, C 11, No 6-50. Good *tamales* and other dishes, open 0700-2200. *Empanadas Don Camillo*, Cra 4, No 12-15. Excellent filled *arepas*. Warmly recommended. *Cafetería Salón Fontana*, C 14, No 5-98. Excellent busy breakfast place, try their *almojábanas*,.Recommended.

Central Bogotá *Refugio Alpino*, C 23, No 7-49. An excellent international restaurant. *Pizzería El Sol de Napolés*, C 69, No 11-58, T345 3207. Small, cosy, excellent antipasto. *Chalet Suizo*, Av 22, No 39A-48. Delicious fondues and good steaks. *El Patio*, Cra 4A, No 27-86, T282 6141, and *Il Caffe*, next door. Both under same management, good Italian and international. Recommended. *Punta Roja*, Cra 7 y C 22. Good value, open 24 hrs. *Punto Rápido*, Cra 7, No 22-60. Self service, good meals, reasonable, 24 hrs service. *La Tienda de Don Zoilo*, Cra 4, No 19-56. Student pub, good food, friendly atmosphere. Rec-ommended. *Crepes y Waffeles*, restaurant chain, good value. Also *La Boliche*, C 27, No 5-64. Italian and good crepes. *Empanadas La 19*, Av 19, No 8-56. Good, cheap meals and snacks.

In North Bogotá (C 76 and above) *El Atico de los Olivos*, Tra 22, C 122-13. Rustic style, excellent cooking. *La Fragata*, C 100, No 8A-55. 12th floor of World Center, revolving. Also in *Hotel Radisson*, C 114, No 9-65, at Cra 13, No 27-98 and Diag 127A, No 30-26. Expensive, excellent fish. *La Academia de Golf*, Cra 15, No 85-42, and Cra 15, No 102-20. International, very good. *La Casa de la Paella*, C 93, No 13A-46. Superb, reasonable prices. *Le Petit Bistrot*, C 76, No 10-28. Excellent French cuisine. *Le Bilbouquet*, C 83, No 12-19. Excellent French, nice atmosphere. Recommended. *Il Pomeriggio*, Cra 11 y C 82 in Centro Andino, local 158. Popular, light meals, good atmosphere, expensive. *Il Piccolo Caffe*, Cra 15, No 96-55. Pasta etc, very good quality. *Las Tapas*, Av 19, No 114-13, Spanish bar-restaurant. *Chicanos*, Cra 11, No 88-70. Mexican, authentic, good. *Na Zdarovia*, Cra 14, No 80-71. Russian, very good. *El Mondongo y Algo Más*, Cra 11, No 97A-38. Good Colombian food. *El Buque*, C 101, No 18-18, T256 1979. Seafood, excellent. *Pesquera Jaramillo*, Cra 11, No 93B-31. Excellent seafood, branches also at Cra 8, No 20-65, and C125, No 29-23. *Fulanitos*, C 81, No 9-13. Good Valle Cauca food, friendly atmosphere. *Fridays*, C 82, No 12-18. US$10-12, Superb value. Recommended. *Welcome*, Cra 14, No 80-65, T256 4790. Japanese, good cooking supervised by perfectionist owner. *Hatsuhana*, Cra 13, No 93A-27, T236 3379, Japanese. *Tony Romas*, C 86A, No 13A-10. Good quality food and excellent service. *Café Oma*, several locations, including Cra 15, No 82-58, Av 19, No 118-78, Cra 5, No 14-71, and airport Puente Aéreo local 2-33. Good food and coffee, nice atmosphere but relatively expensive, most are open till 0100. *Café y Crepes*, Diagonal 108, No 9-11, T214 5312. Good food, good atmosphere, run by Mauricio Afanador, climbers meet here, also at Cra 16, No 82-17, T236 2688. *Houston's*, Cra 17, No 93-17. Very popular, US-style, crowded Sun. *Di Lucca*, Cra 13, No 85-32, T611 5665. Freshly made pasta, excellent cooking, open daily 1200-2400.

Vegetarian *La Berenjena*, C 19, No 34-37. Highly recommended, lunch US$2.50. *El Champiñon*, Cra 8, No 16-36, 2 other branches. Good vegetarian lunches, also fish. *Lotus Azul*, C 15, Cra 6. Good quality and good value. Vegetarian food excellent at Cra 8, No 11-19, near Plaza Bolívar. *Samovares*, Cra 11, No 69-89 (lunch only, fixed menu, nice atmosphere), also Cra 11, No 67-63 and Av Caracas No 32-64. *El Integral Natural*, Cra 11, No 95-10. Health food shop with a few tables at street level, restaurant downstairs.

Tea rooms (Pastelerías) *Panadería Florida*, Cra 7, No 20-82. Also has good pastries and is the place to try *chocolate santafereño*. *La Suiza*, Cra 25, No 9-41. Excellent pastries.

Cinema *Cinemateca Distrital*, Cra 7, No 22-79, shows foreign films. The *Museo de Arte Moderno* shows different films every day, all day. *Cine Bar Paraíso*, Cra 6, No 119B-56, T215 5361, US$5 weekends and holidays, US$2 midweek, and *Cine Bar Lumiere*, Cra 14, No 85-59, T636 0485, same prices, both have airplane-style seats, food and drink. Foreign films old and new are shown on weekend mornings in some commercial cinemas and there are many small screening rooms which run the occasional feature. Admission, US$2. There is an international film festival in Sep and a European film festival in Apr/May. **Gay bars** *Safari*, Av Caracas 73-26, T217 8262. Expensive drinks. Others on Cra 7, C 17/18. **Nightlife** There are many popular bars, discos etc in the Cra 11/13, C 80/86 region, known as the Zona Rosa. Also many popular bars and dancing places on Cra 5 with C 25, relatively safe area. Try *El Viejo Almacén*, Cra 5 y C 13-14, run by an aged Colombian lady who plays 78 tango records and sells reasonably priced beer and *aguardiente* (on Thu and Sat only). *Disco del Teatro de Candelaria*, C 15 between Cras 4 and 5. Good atmosphere especially Fri and Sat. **Theatre** Many of the theatres are in the Candelaria area. *Teatro Colón* details on page 787. *Teatro Libre de Bogotá*, C 62, No 10-65, T217 1988. *Nacional*, C 71, No 10-25, T217 4577. *La Candelaria*, C 12, No 2-59, T281 4814. *Teatro Popular de Bogotá*, C 5, No 14-71, T342 1675. Tickets usually from about US$5 up. Bogotá hosts the biennial Iberoamerican Theatre Festival (next 2002), usually in Apr: www.festivaldeteatro.com.co

Entertainment
Consult El Espectador or El Tiempo, or dial 113, for what is on; frequent programme changes

Handicrafts *Artesanías de Colombia*, Claustro de Las Aguas, next to the Iglesia de las Aguas, Cra 3A, No 18-60, has good selection of folk art and crafts. *Almacén San Diego*, in the old San Diego church, Cra 10, No 26-50. *Mercado de Pulgas* (fleamarket) on Cra 7/C 24, in car park beside *Museo de Arte Moderno*, on Sun afternoons and holidays. *Galerías Cano*, Ed Bavaria, Cra 13, No 27-98 (Torre B, Int 1-19B), also at Unicentro, and Loc 218, Airport. Sell textiles, pottery as well as gold and gold-plated replicas of some of the jewellery on display in the Gold Museum. *Galería Belarca*, No 69, No 10-81, T321 7021. Good selection of local artists, fair prices.

   Jewellery The pavements and cafés along Av Jiménez, below Cra 7, Parque de los Periodistas, and C 16 and Cra 3 are used on weekdays by emerald dealers. Great expertise is needed in buying: bargains are to be had, but synthetics and forgeries abound. *La Casa de la Esmeralda*, C 30, No 16-18. Wide range of stones. *Emerald Trade Centre*, Av Jiménez, No

Shopping
16% value-added tax on all purchases

Colombia

5-43, p1. German/English spoken. *Joyas Verdes Ltda*, Cra 15, No 39-15. *GMC Galería Minas de Colombia*, C20, No 0-86, T281 6523, at foot of Monserrate diagonal from Quinta de Bolívar. Good selection of gold and emerald jewellery at reasonable prices.

Shopping centres *Unicentro*, Cra 15, No 123-30 (take 'Unicentro' bus from centre, going north on Cra 10). *Centro Granahorrar*, Av Chile (C 72), No 10-34. *Metrópolis*, Av 68, No 75A-50 (with *Exito* supermarket opposite). *Hacienda Santa Bárbara*, Cra 7/C 116. *Bulevar Niza*, Cra 52, No 125A-59. *Centro Comercial Andino*, Cra 12,C 82/C 83. The *Carulla* supermarket chain is good for its salad and bakery counters.

Heavy duty plastic for covering rucksacks etc, is available at several shops around C 16 and Av Caracas; some have heat sealing machines to make bags to size.

Books in Colombia are **Bookshops** *Oma*, Cra 15, No 82-58 T256 5621 (and other branches including airport,
generally expensive Puente Aereo section). Good art and literature books, international newspapers, sells *Footprint Handbooks*, open late including Sun. *Librería Francesa*, Cra 8, No 63-45. Also imports English books. *Librería Lerner*, Av Jiménez, No 4-35 and C 92, No 15-23, T236 0580. Specializes in 'libros colombianos'. *Librería Buchholz*, Cra 13, No 10-18, also at Cra 13, No 52A-24. Most books in Spanish, useful advice in a number of languages. *Ateneo*, C 82, No 13-19, in the north of the city. Good selection of Colombian titles, knowledgeable staff. *Panamericana*, Cra 7, No 14-09. Disorganized, but has some guidebooks and maps. *Villegas Editores*, Av 82, No 11-50, int 3. Great coffee-table books on Colombia. *Exopotamia*, C 70, No 4-47. Good selection of books and Latin music, also branch in *Biblioteca Luis Angel Arango* in Candelaria. *Librería Central*, C 94, No 13-92. English and German books, book exchange.

Maps The best current maps of Bogotá are by *IGAC* (see below), 1:30,000 published 2000, and *Cartur*, scale 1:25,000, 1994, and of Colombia, *Mapa Vial de Colombia* by Rodríguez, scale 1:2,000,000, also 1994, about US$4 each. Hiking, topographical, town and general maps, also a good (1996) road atlas of the country (*Hojas de ruta*) from *IGAC*, Instituto Geográfico Agustín Codazzi, Av Ciudad de Quito (Cra 30), No 48-51, T368 3666, F368 0998 (www.igac.gov.co) who also have a relief map of the country: *Mapa Vial y Turístico*, 1:1,500,000, 1995, US$5.80. The topographical details of the walking maps are generally accurate, but trails and minor roads less so. They are open 0900-1500, maps are mainly from US$2.50 to US$6 and you pay at the bank next door. There is a library open to 1630 and refreshments available at lunchtime. Esso and other maps from some service stations, US$2.

Bicycle repairs *Bike House*, C 93B, No 15-34, Of 208, T257 3107.

Sport **Bullfighting**: on Sat and Sun during the season (Jan), and occasionally for the rest of the year, at the municipally-owned Plaza de Santamaría, near Parque Independencia. In season, the bulls weigh over 335 kilograms; out of season they are "comparatively small and unprofessional". (Local bullfight museum at bullring, door No 6.) **Boxing matches** are held here. **Football**: tickets for matches at El Campín stadium can be bought in advance at *Federación Colombiana de Futbol*, Av 32, No 16-22. It is not normally necessary to book in advance, except for the local Santa Fe-Millionarios derby, and of course, internationals. Take a cushion, matches Sun at 1545, Wed at 2000. **Hiking**: *Sal Si Puedes*, hiking group arranges walks every weekend and sometimes midweek on trails in Cundinamarca, and further afield at national holiday periods eg Semana Santa; very friendly, welcomes visitors. Hikes are graded for every ability, from 6 km to 4-day excursions of 70 km or more, camping overnight. The groups are often big (30-60), but it is possible to stray from the main group. Reservations should be made and paid for a week or so in advance at Cra 7, No 17-01, offices 639 to 641, T283 9086 or 341 5854, open 0800-1200 and 1400-1800. There are several other groups, good information on Thu in *El Tiempo* newspaper, *Eskape* section. **Horseriding**: *Cabalgatas San Francisco*, Cra 5, No 129-38, T615 8648. *Cabalgatas Carpasos*, Km 7 Vía La Calera, T368 7242, about US$15 per hr.

Tour operators Recommended: *Aviatur*, Av 19, No 4-62, T282 7111, www.aviatur.com.co Very good, efficient. *Bienvenidos*, Cra 62, No 127-72, T/F271 4517, biencol@cable.net.co Organizes cultural, trekking, beach and adventure tours and can advise on diving. *Eco-Guías*, Cra 3, No

18-56A, Of 202, T334 8042, ecoguias@elsitio.net.co Specialize in ecotourism, trekking, riding and tourism on coffee *fincas*. Highly recommended. *Tierra Mar Aire*, Cra 10, No 27-91, T288 2088. Has several offices around town eg Santa Bárbara: Av 15, No 118-34, T629 0277 and does city tours from *Hotel Tequendama* (T286 1111). *Viajes Chapinero*, Av 7, 124-15, T612 7716, F215 9099, with branches at C 63, No 13-37, Chapinero, and Cra 40C, No 57-08, bloque A1. Helpful with information in English.

Local Bus: Fares start at US$0.30, depending on length of route and time of day. Most buses have day/night tariff advertised in the window. *Busetas* (green) charge US$0.40, US$0.60 after 2000. There are some *ejecutivo* routes (red and white) with plush seats,and *colectivos* (small vans), cramped but faster than others, charge a bit more. Fares are also higher on holidays. The **TransMilenio,** an articulated bus system running on dedicated lanes connects North, Central and South Bogotá from C 170 (on the Autopista del Norte) to Portal de Usme (where the road to Villavicencio leaves the city). There is a spur to the west along Calle 80 and a link to Candelaria (Parque de Los Periodistas on Av Jiménez de Quesada) is due to open in 2002. *Corriente* services stop at all principal road intersections, *expresos* limited stop only. Although it was only set up in 2001, it is already working well – the journey from the centre to the north now takes less than 30 mins.More routes are planned. Journey cost US$0.40.

Transport
Urban buses are not good for sightseeing because you will be standing as likely as not

Taxi: Minimum fare US$0.70. Average fare from North Bogotá to the centre US$3.50. Check before taking your taxi if there are any additional charges above what the meter states eg: night charge. At busy times, empty taxis flagged down on the street may refuse to take you to less popular destinations. If you are going to an address out of the city centre, it is helpful to know the section you are going to as well as the street address, eg Chicó, Chapinero (ask at your hotel). Radio taxis are recommended for safety and reliability; when you call the dispatcher gives you a cab number, confirm this when it arrives, eg *Taxis Libres*, T311 1111; *Taxatelite* T222 2222 are radio taxi fleets. (The latest scam is for the driver and an accomplice to force passengers to go from ATM to ATM emptying their deposit or credit card account – *paseos milionarios*. At night it is not recommended to travel by taxi along the Av Circunvalar.) Tipping is not customary, but is appreciated.

Car hire: See Essentials, Car hire, for agencies with continent-wide distribution. *Arrencar*, Tra 17, No 121-12, Of 511, T214 1413, F620 3304, www.arrencar.com.co Good value.

Long distance Air: There are 2 terminals, the Puente Aéreo terminal (T413 8103) being 1 km before the main terminal (T413 9500) on Av El Dorado. Some *Avianca* international flights and most domestic services use Puente Aéreo, which is comfortable but there is not as much duty-free shopping. **You must check which terminal your flight will use**. (See Ins & outs for transport to the city.) The main terminal at El Dorado airport has been recently modernized. The departure areas with the usual duty-free shops are of a high standard and comfortable. Free Colombian coffee inside the customs area. Many snack bars and restaurants on 1st floor. International calls can be made from *Telecom* on 1st floor open till 2100, credit cards

Colombia

accepted; post office in main arrivals lounge. Exchange rates are marginally lower in the city, but pesos cannot be changed back into dollars at the airport without receipts. Airport bank changes travellers' cheques, but is not open at holiday times. There is a *casa de cambio*, which changes cash only. When closed, ask airport police where to change money. Allow at least 2 hrs for checking in and security. Use only uniformed porters. There is no baggage deposit. There are 2 tourist offices, one in international arrivals, the other in domestic arrivals. Both are near the respective exits for taxis.

For internal flights, which serve all parts of the country, see page 776. Sometimes, flights are overbooked, so check in well in advance. You must reconfirm all flights about 48 hrs before departure.

Long distance services were suspended in 1992

Train: there are no passenger services at present from Bogotá (La Sabana) station at C 13 y Cra 19 except a tourist steam train which runs on Sun at 0800 calling at Usaquén in the north of the city (see map), going north to Nemocón (1200), back in Bogotá, La Sabana at 1900. (All times variable) Cost: adult US$9, child up to 10, US$5.50. Information, *Turistrén Ltda*, Tra 17 A, No 98-17, T2563751. Tickets should be bought in advance here, at La Sabana station or from travel agents.

If going to towns in Boyacá or Cundinamarca for a long weekend, leave Bogotá before Fri 1200 as it can take 1½ hrs to get from Terminal to outskirts. Try to arrive back before 1300, or ask to be set down in North Bogotá and take TransMilenio bus to centre

Bus: the Terminal de Transportes is near Av Boyacá (Cra 72) between El Dorado (Av 26) and Av Centenario (C 13), T295 1100. There is also access from Cra 68. It is divided into modules serving the 4 points of the compass; each module has several bus companies serving similar destinations. If possible, buy tickets at the ticket office before travelling to avoid overcharging. **Fares and journey times are given under destinations below**. If you are travelling north, enquire if the bus company has a pick-up point on the Autopista del Norte around C 160. *Velotax busetas* are slightly quicker and more expensive than ordinary buses, as are colectivos, which go to several long-distance destinations.The terminal is well-organized and comfortable, but, as usual, watch out for thieves. We have an increasing number of reports of baggage thefts. Free self-service luggage trolleys are provided. There are shops and restaurants. There are showers at the terminal (between Nos 3 and 4), US$0.50, soap and towel provided. To get to the terminal by bus, ask at your hotel for the best route while the TransMilenio is under construction. Taxi around US$3.50.

International bus: it is better not to buy a through ticket to Caracas with *Berlinas de Fonce* as this does not guarantee a seat and is only valid for 2 Venezuelan companies; moreover no refunds are given in Cúcuta. Ideally, if you have time, make the journey to Cúcuta in 2 stages to enjoy the scenery to the full. Bus connections from San Antonio de Táchira in Venezuela to Caracas are good. *Ormeño*'s twice weekly Lima-Caracas service passes through Cúcuta (US$170 Lima-Cúcuta); there is also a Lima-Bogotá service weekly (US$150) via Cali (US$130). This is, however, a gruelling journey; better (and cheaper) to do it in stages.

Directory

Emergency numbers: Ambulance: T125 Fire: T119 Red Cross: T132

Airline offices Domestic: *Aces*, Cra 10, No 27-51, p 2, T283 0064/0240. *AeroRepública*, Cra 10, No 27-51, T342 7766. *Aires*, Aeropuerto El Dorado, T413 8500. *Avianca/SAM*, Cra 10, No 26-19, T410 1011. *Satena*, Cra 10, No 27-51, T337 5000. International: *Air France*, T254 8950. *American*, Cra 7, No 26-20, T343 2424/285 1111. *British Airways*, C 98, No 9-03, T900-331 2777. *Continental*, Cra 7, No 21-52, T312 2565. *Delta*, Cra 13 No 89-53, of 301, T980-952 0082. *Iberia*, C 85, No 20-10, T616 6111/610 9272. *Mexicana*, C 100, No 19-61, T635 3759. *Varig*, Cra 7A, No 33-24, T285 8300.

Banks Some head offices are grouped around the Avianca building and the San Francisco church, others are in North Bogotá on or near C 72. *Lloyds TSB Bank*, Cra 8, No 15-46/60, T334 5088, and 23 local agencies, will cash Thomas Cook and Amex TCs (0900-1300, with passport), will give advances against Visa, and will accept sterling, good rates. There are countless ATMs accepting Visa and MasterCard. *Banco Ganadero/BBV* is good for Visa, *Conavi* for MasterCard. The major banks, *Banco de Occidente*, *Banco Popular*, *Bancolombia*, etc, will help, but if you need counter service, go early in the day. See Hours of Business and Currency in Essentials. **Money changers:** *American Express*, Panturismo, Cra 10 No 27-51, of 206-2, T334 0640 (also at El Dorado and Puente Aéreo airports, T413 8642 and 413 8764 respectively), does not change TCs, but will direct you to those who do (eg *Bancolombia*). Other offices at C 92, No 15-63, T218 5666 and Cra 8 y C 15 are helpful. For replacing lost Amex TCs, go to *American Express* (Expreso Viajes y Turismo), C 85, No 20-32, T531 1919/621 1688, open 0800-1900, Sat 0900-1400 with full details, a police report of the loss and preferably proof of purchase. *International Money Exchange*, Cra 7, No 32-29, open Mon to Fri till 1600, check all transactions carefully. Also exchange at Av 19, No 15-35. *Cambios Country*, Western Union agents, Cra 11, No 71-40, Of 201, T346 6788. Several other city offices, good rates, speedy service. *Orotur*, Cra 10, No 26-05 (very small, below *Hotel Tequendama*) is quick and efficient, cash only. *Money Point*, Cra 10, No 27, in Centro Internacional, unit 161, good rates, take passport photocopy. *Titan*, C 19 6-19, 2nd floor, open afternoons (when all banks have ceased foreign transactions), many other branches. Other *cambios* on Av Jiménez de Quesada, between Cras 6 and 11, and in the north of the city. On Sun exchange is virtually impossible except at the airport.

Communications Internet: There are increasing numbers of internet centres all over the city, in commercial areas and in shopping centres. *Papeles La Candelaria*, C 11, No 3-89, T336 1228, F562 0705, US$2.50, open daily, also sells Latin American cultural magazines, US, European and other papers 2 days after publication. Facilities also in hotels, eg *Hotel Platypus*. Prices per hour range from US$3-5.50. **Post:** main airmail office in basement of Ed Avianca, Cra 7, No 16-36, open 0730-1900 Mon to Fri, 0730-1800 Sat, closed Sun and holidays (*poste restante* 0730-1800, Mon-Sat, letters kept for only a month, US$0.40 per letter). Also Cra 7 y C 26-27, near Planetarium; C 140 between Cra 19 y Autopista. Parcels by air, contact *Avianca*. *Adpostal*, main office, Edif Murillo Toro, Cra 7, No 12-00, 2 blocks north of Plaza de Bolívar. **International telephone calls:** from several *Telecom* offices in centre of Bogotá (eg C 12 y Cra 8, C 23, No 13-49, in the *Tequendama Hotel*/Centro Internacional complex); all close within 30 mins of 2000. Purchase of phone cards recommended if you are using call boxes.

Cultural centres British Council, C 87, No 12-79, T236 3976. Good library and British newspapers. **Centro Colombo Americano**, Av 19, No 3-05, T334 7640. English and Spanish courses. Recommended. **Alianza Colombo-Francesa**, Cra 3, No 18-45, T341 1348 and Cra 7, No 84-72, T236 8605. Films in French, newspapers, library monthly bulletin etc. **Goethe Institut**, Cra 7, No 81-57, T255 1843.

Embassies and consulates Belgium, C 26, No 4A-45, p 7, T282 8881. **Bolivia**, Cra 9C, No 114-96, T629 8252. **Brazil**, C 93, No 14-20, T218 0800. **Canada**, Cra 7, No 115-33, T657 9800, open 0800-1630 www.dfait-maeci.gc.ca/bogota/ (mailing address: Apdo Aéreo 53531, Bogotá 2, DE). **Ecuador** C 89, No 13-07, T635 0322. **French Consulate**, Cra 7, No 38-99, T285 4311, www.consutfrancebogota.com.co **France**, Cra 11, No 93-12, T618 0511. **Germany**, Cra 69, No 43B-44, T416 5743. **Israel**, Edif Caxdac, C 35, No 7-25, p 14, T232 0764. **Italy**, C 93B, No 9-92 (Apdo Aéreo 50901), T218 6680. **Japan**, Cra 7, No 71-21, p11, T317 5001. **Netherlands**, Cra 13, No 93-40, T611 5080. **New Zealand Consulate**, Diagonal 109 No 1-39, Este, T629 8524, F620 0130, Mon-Fri 0830-1730. **Panamanian Consulate**, C 92, No 7-70, T257 5067. Mon-Fri, 0900-1300. **Spain**, C 92, No 12-68, T618 1288. **Switzerland**, Cra 9, No 74-08, oficina 1101, T255 3945, open Mon-Fri 0900-1200. **UK**, Cra 9, No 76-49, T317 6690, F317 6265, www.britain.gov.co Postal address: Apdo Aéreo 4508. **USA**, C 22D bis, No 47-51 (mailing address: Apdo Aéreo 3831, Bogotá 1, DE), T315 0811, consulate/visas, T315 1566, www.usembassy.state.gov/ bogota/ **Venezuelan Consulate**, Av 13, No 103-16, T636 4011, 0830-1200. Visas (US$30) can be collected the following day 1200-1630.

Embassy and consulate opening times and rules for visas are changing continuously phone before you go

Language courses The best Spanish courses are in the *Universidad Nacional* (see map) US$180 for 2 mths, 8 hrs per week, or *Universidad de los Andes*, US$300, 6 weeks and *Pontificia Universidad Javeriana*, Centro Latino Americano de Relaciones Humanas e Interculturales, Cra 10, No 65-48, T212 3009. Accommodation with local families can be arranged. Most other schools in Yellow Pages offer one-to-one private tuition at US$10 per hour.

Medical services 24-hr emergency health service, T125. **Cruz Roja Nacional**, Av 68, No 66-31, T428 0111. Open 0830-1800, consultations/inoculations US$12.50. **Red Cross Ambulance Service**, T132 or 620 3000, 0800-1700.

Useful addresses If you have problems with theft or other forms of crime, contact a *Centro de Atención Inmediata*, CAI, for assistance: downtown, Av Jiménez/Cra 6, T286 0744, or Cra 1, No 18A-96, T336 4725/286 8972; Candelaria, Cra 7, No 4-12, T246 7203. There are many offices throughout the city, or T156. **Police:** T112 or 2224419. **DAS:** Immigration office, Cra 27, No 17-85, open 0730-1530, or T153. **Dirección de Extranjería** (for extending entry permits): C 100, No 11B-27, T6107314/7371, open Mon-Thu 0730-1600, Fri 0730-1530. DAS will not authorize photocopies of passports; look in Yellow Pages for notaries, who will.

If coming from abroad, make sure you have a student visa, preferably before you arrive, if not, from DAS, before studying. You may not study on a tourist visa

Colombia

Bogotá to Cúcuta

The main road route from Bogotá to Venezuela has some beautiful stretches. It passes through, or near, several colonial towns and gives access to the Sierra Nevada del Cocuy, excellent climbing and hiking country.

Guatavita

Phone code: 91
Colour map 1, grid B4
Population: 6,000
Altitude: 2,650 m
75 km from Bogotá

This modern town of **Guatavita Nueva** was built in colonial style when the old town of Guatavita was submerged by the reservoir. It is now a weekend haunt for Bogotanos and tourists. Cathedral, artisan workshops and small bull-ring for apprentices to practise on Sunday afternoons; two small museums, one devoted to the Muisca Indians and the other to relics of the old Guatavita church, including a delightful Debain harmonium (Paris 1867). Sunday market is best in the morning, before Bogotanos get there. The tourist information booth can find accommodation for visitors.

Laguna de Guatavita (also called Lago de Amor by locals) is where the legend of El Dorado originated. The lake is a quiet, beautiful place; you can walk right round it close to the water level, 1½ hours, or climb to the rim of the crater in several places. Opinions differ on whether the crater is volcanic or a meteorite impact, but from the rim at 3,100 m there are extensive views over the varied countryside.

Just before the road reaches Boyacá Department, it passes the Sisca reservoir where there is fishing and windsurfing. At the *Refugio de Sisca* restaurant, try the *empanadas de trucha* (cornmeal and trout snack), US$0.60, excellent.

Transport Bus Bogotá-Guatavita Nueva (*Flota Valle de Tenza*, Cra 25, No 15-72, recommended; *Flota Aguila*, Cra 15 No 14-59), US$2, 2-3 hrs, several departures morning; last return bus at 1730. You can walk (2-3 hrs) or ride (US$7 per horse) from Guatavita Nueva to the lake. An easier approach is from a point on the Sesquilé-Guatavita Nueva road (the bus driver will let you off) where there is a sign 'via Lago Guatavita'. There is a good campsite and places to eat nearby. From the main road to the lakeside the road is paved as far as a school, about half way. Follow the signs. This road and subsequent track can be driven in a good car to within 300 m of the lake where there is a car park and good restaurant, *Hostería Caminos a El Dorado*, open at weekends.

Tunja

Phone code: 98
Colour map 1, grid B4
Population: 120,000
Altitude: 2,820 m
137 km from Bogotá

The main road goes across the western slopes of the Eastern Cordillera to the capital of Boyacá Department, which stands in an dry cool mountainous area. When the Spaniards arrived in what is now Boyacá, Tunja was already an Indian city, the seat of the Zipa, one of the two Chibcha kings. It was refounded as a Spanish city by Gonzalo Suárez Rendón in 1539. The city formed an independent Junta in 1811, and Bolívar fought under its aegis during the campaign of the Magdalena in 1812. Six years later he fought the decisive battle of Boyacá, nearby (see below). Tunja has some of the finest colonial treasures of Colombia.

The **Catedral** and five other churches are all eminently worth visiting. Perhaps the most remarkable colonial building is the church of **Santo Domingo**, a masterpiece begun in 1594; the interior is covered with richly carved wood. Another is the **Santa Clara La Real chapel** (1580), also with some fine wood carving. The church of **Santa Bárbara** is noted for its treasury and colonial woodwork, and in the nearby parish house are many interesting religious objects, including silk embroidery from the 18th century.

Colombia

The **Casa de Don Juan de Vargas** is a recommended museum of colonial Tunja. ■ *US$0.50 includes guided tour in several languages.* The **Casa del Fundador Suárez Rendón**, Plaza de Bolívar, is one of the few extant mansions of a Spanish *conquistador* in Colombia (1539-43); peaceful courtyard with fine view of valley through gateway; museum open Wednesday-Sunday; see the unique series of plateresque paintings on the ceilings. ■ *US$0.50.* There are a number of other fine colonial buildings to be visited. In **Parque Bosque de la República** is the adobe wall against which three martyrs of the Independence were shot in 1816. Ask the tourist police guarding these buildings for information.

The tourist office is in Casa del Fundador, helpful. Information on Boyacá: tourist office adjacent to the *Hotel Hunza*. The market, near Plaza de Toros on the outskirts of town, is open every day (good for *ruanas* and blankets). Friday is main market day. During the week before Christmas, there is a lively festival with local music, traditional dancing and fireworks.

Excursions The battle of Boyacá was fought about 16 km south of Tunja, on the road to Bogotá. Overlooking the bridge at Boyacá is a large monument to Bolívar. He took Tunja on 6 August 1819, and next day his troops, fortified by a British Legion, the only professional soldiers among them, fought the Spaniards on the banks of the swollen Río Boyacá. With the loss of only 13 killed and 53 wounded they captured 1,600 men and 39 officers. Only 50 men escaped, and when these told their tale in Bogotá the Viceroy Samao fled in such haste that he left behind him half a million pesos of the royal funds. ■ *Daily 0800-1800. US$1.50 per car. There are several other monuments, an exhibition hall and restaurant at the site.*

Sleeping

AL *Hunza*, C 21A, No 10-66, T742 4111 (Bogotá 347 0099), F742 4119. Modern, breakfast including, good restaurant, pool, sauna. **A** *Boyacá Plaza*, C 18, No 11-22, T740 1116, F742 7635. Including breakfast, parking, good. **B** *Conquistador*, C 20, No 8-92, T743 1465, F742 3534, corner of Plaza de Bolívar. 22 traditional rooms round courtyard, nice restaurant, good. **C** *Hostería San Carlos*, Cra 11, No 20-12, T742 3716. Colonial style, interestingly furnished, good restaurant. Highly recommended. **E** *Americano*, Cra 11, No 18-70, T742 2471. Hot water, attractive lobby. **E** *Dux*, next to *Saboy*, nice creaky old hotel, good rooms, cold water, good value. **E** *Imperial*, C 19, No 7-43. Basic, cold water, some rooms with TV, use of kitchen. **E** *Saboy*, C 19, No 10-40, T742 3492. Nice covered patio, family run. **F** *Casa Colonial*, Cra 8, No 20-40. Safe. Area around bus station said not to be safe at night (eg **F** *Bolívar*; *Príncipe*).

Eating

San Ricardo, C 19, No 8-38, good. *Surtipan*, C 20, No 12-58. Good cakes and coffee. *Pollo Listo* Cra 11, No 19-30. Good. *Santo Domingo*, Cra 11, No 19-66. OK. *Americano*, Cra 11, 18-70. Light meals. *Café El Rinconcito*, C 20, No 9-14. Plaza Bolívar. Good coffee and *arepas* until late. *Doña Cecilia*, Cra 8, No 18-18. Good *comida corriente*.

Many fast food and pizza outlets in the pedestrianized streets near Plaza de Bolívar

Transport

Bus Bus station is 400 m steeply down from city centre. From **Bogotá** 2½ hrs, 4½ hrs weekends and holidays, US$5. To **Bucaramanga**, hourly, 7 hrs, US$17.

Colombia

Villa de Leiva

Phone code: 98
Colour map 1, grid B4
Population: 4,500
Altitude: 2,144 m

Some colonial houses close Mon-Fri out of season, but the trip is worth while for the views and for long, peaceful walks in the hills. Many places are closed Mon-Tue

Market day is Sat, held in the Plaza de Mercado

About 40 km west is the beautiful colonial town of **Villa de Leiva** (also spelt Leyva) which has one of the largest plazas in the Americas. It is surrounded by cobbled streets, a charming, peaceful place. A visit should be essential. The town dates back to the early days of Spanish rule (1572), but unlike Tunja, it has been declared a national monument so will not be modernized. The first president of Nueva Granada, Andrés Días Venero de Leiva, lived in the town. Many of the **colonial houses** are now hotels, others are museums eg the restored birthplace of the independence hero Antonio Ricaurte at Cra 8 y C 15. ■ *Tue-Fri 0900-1200, 1400-1700, Sat, Sun, holidays 0900-1300, 1400-1800*. Ricaurte was born in Villa de Leiva and died in 1814 at San Mateo, Venezuela, fighting with Bolívar's army. The house has a nice courtyard and garden. A **palaeontological museum**, 15 minutes' walk north of the town on Cra 9, is interesting and well displayed. ■ *US$0.75*. The **Monasterio de las Carmelitas**, C 14 y Cra 10, has one of the best museums of religious art in Colombia. ■ *Sat and Sun 1400-1700*. Part of the monastery is the **Iglesia del Carmen** and the **Convento**, all worth a visit. The shops in the plaza and the adjoining streets have an excellent selection of Colombian handicrafts and offer many bargains.

Excursions   The wide valley to the west of Villa de Leiva abounds in fossils. 5 km along the road to Santa Sofía can be seen the fossil of a dinosaur (Kronosaurus) found in 1977, now with a museum built around it. A second, smaller fossil found in 2000 nearby has been put alongside. Look for road signs to **El Fósil**. ■ *Daily 0800-1800, US$1*. 2 km from El Fósil along this road is the turning for (1 km) the archaeological site of **El Infiernito**, where there are several huge carved stones believed to be giant phalli and a solar calendar. ■ *0900-1200, 1400-1700, closed Mon, US$0.50*. 6 km after the Infiernito turning is the **Monastery of Ecce-Homo** (founded 1620); note the fossils on the floor at the entrance. There are buses from Villa de Leiva at 0645, 0930 and 1345, going to Santa Sofía, US$0.50; it is 30 minutes to the crossing, then a 2-km walk to the monastery. Beyond Santa Sofía is La Cueva de Hayal, a cave set in beautiful scenery. A tour of most of these attractions leaves the plaza at 0930, Saturday/Sunday, US$5. Recommended.

About 20 km north of Villa de Leiva is a right turn for the **Iguaque Flora and Fauna Sanctuary** (3 km) run by MA: interesting oak woods, flora, fauna and several lakes. There are guided paths and a marked trail to Lake Iguaque, a walk of 6½ hours. ■ *US$3, cars US$3; tourist centre with accommodation for 60; restaurant with good food US$1.80-2.20. Take a colectivo from Villa de Leiva-Arcabuco to the turn off to the park (1½ hrs' walk to ranger station); check for afternoon return times. (Camping is allowed, US$3 pp, safe.)*

Sleeping   **L** *Hospedería Duruelo*, C 13, No 2-88, T732 0222. Modern colonial style, beautiful views, nice
The town tends to be full of visitors at weekends and bank holidays when booking is advisable (try bargaining Mon-Thu)
gardens, also conference hotel, good food. **AL** *Plazuela de San Agustín*, C 15 entre Cra 8 y 9, T732 0842. Well appointed, nicely decorated. **AL** *El Molino la Mesopotamia*, C del Silencio (top of Cra 8), T732 0235. A beautifully restored colonial mill, 10% rebate for booking 10 days ahead, excellent home cooking, beautiful gardens, memorable. Recommended. **A** *Hostal La Candelaria*, C 18, No 8-12, T732 0534. 7 rooms, delightful, excellent breakfast. Recommended. **A** *Mesón de la Plaza Mayor*, Cra 10, No 12-31, T732 0425 (T218 7741 Bogotá). Beautifully restored. **B** *Hospedaría El Marqués de San Jorge*, C 14, No 9-20, T732 0240. Colonial mansion, beautiful courtyard, parking. **B** *Los Llanitos*, C 9, No 12-31, T732 0018. 5 mins' walk from main plaza, quiet, hot water, good food. **B** *Posada San Antonio*, Cra 8, No 11-80, T732 0538. Tastefully restored, nice patio, meals served. **D** pp *Hospedaje El Sol de la Villa*, Cra 8, No 12-28, T732 0224. Safe, hot shower, very good breakfast, cooking facilities on request, good value. Recommended. **E** *Posada San Martín*, C 14, entre Cra 9 y 10. With bath and breakfast, pleasant. **E** *Hostal El Mirador*, Tra 8, No 6-94. New, good value.

Camping *Estadero San Luis*, Av Circunvalar, T732 0617, capacity 70. *Iguaque Campestre Camping Club*, Km 1 Vía Hipódromo, T732 0889.

Nueva Granada, C 13, No 7-66. Good value, owner Jorge Rodríguez, plays classical guitar music on demand. *El Rincón Bachué*, Cra 9, No 15-17. Interesting decoration with a china factory behind. *La Misión*, Centro Verarte, Cra 9, No 13-09. Salads, light meals. 2 *pizzerias* on Plaza Mayor: *Los Arcos*, on C 13, excellent, and *Dino's*, Cra 9 next to Iglesia Parroquial (also *hospedaría* with shared bath, nice). *Casa Blanca*, C 13, No 7-16. Good juices, and *comida corriente*, open till 2100. *Tienda de Teresa*, Cra 10, 13-72. Good breakfasts. *Café y que Café*, C 12, No 8-88. Excellent *tinto*. *Panadería Francesa*, Cra 10, No 11-82. Open 0800-1900, closed Wed, excellent. *Zarina Galería Café*, C 14, No 7-67. Antique décor, good.

Eating
Restaurants tend to close early in the evening, especially during the week

Virgen del Carmen, **13-17 Jul** annually. In **Aug** (check dates) an international *kite* festival is held in the Plaza Major and a festival of *light* is held every year in **mid-Dec.**

Festivals

Guías & Travesías, C 12, No 8A-31, T732 0739/0742. Arranges trips throughout the region, guides for Parque Nacional Iguaque, Enrique Maldonado, Director, very helpful.

Tour operators

Bus Station in 8th block of Cra 9. It is recommended to book the return journey on arrival. Buses to/from **Tunja**, 1 hr, US$2 with *Flota Reina* or *Valle de Tenza*, minibuses 45 mins, US$1.40, every 20 mins. To **Bogotá** direct takes 4 hrs, US$5, several companies, and via Zipaquirá and Chiquinquirá, US$6.70. To **Ráquira** busetas at 0730, 0800, 1740, 1930 US$1, taxi, US$2.50. Bus at 1000 from Leiva to **Moniquirá** connects with bus to Bucamaranga.

Transport

Banks 2 banks and ATMs in the Plaza Mayor. **Communications** Post Office: in *Telecom* building, C 13, No 8-26. **Tourist office** Cra 9, No 13-04 just off the plaza, open daily 0800-1800 (may close lunchtime), local maps, gives advice on cheaper accommodation. Director and staff are most helpful.

Directory

Colombia

Villa de Leiva

To Museo Paleontológico & Arcabuco

To Santa Sofía, Ecce-Homo & El Fósil

To Bogotá, via Tunja or Chiquinquirá

Iglesia del Carmen

Plazuela de San Agustín

Casa de Antonio Ricaurte

Museo Luis Alberto Acuña

Alcaldía

Casa del Primer Congreso

Plaza Mayor

Iglesia Parroquial

Casa de Antonio Nariño

Parque Nariño

Plaza de Mercado

San Francisco

N

0 metres 100
0 yards 100

■ **Sleeping**
1 El Molino la Mesopotamia
2 Hospedaje El Sol de la Villa
3 Hospedaría El Marqués de San Jorge
4 Hostal El Mirador
5 Hostal La Candelaria
6 Los Llanitos
7 Mesón de la Plaza Mayor
8 Posada San Martín

Ráquira
Market day Sunday

At **Ráquira**, 25 km from Villa de Leiva, locals make mainly earthenware pottery in several workshops in and around the village. The ceramics, among the best-known in Colombia, are sold in about 10 shops on the main street. Apart from kitchen and houseware items, there are many small ornaments and toys to enjoy. The craftsmen are happy for you to watch them at work. There are two good hotels, **B** *Nequeteba*, T732 0461, converted and renovated colonial house, pool, restaurant, craft shop, helpful owner, parking, and **D** *Norteño*, nice and clean (both on plaza). At weekends it is possible to eat at the Museo de Artes y Tradiciones Populares.

About 7 km along a very rough road, which winds up above Ráquira affording spectacular views, is the beautiful 17th-century **Convento de la Candelaria**. On the altar of the fine church is the painting of the Virgen de La Candelaria, dating from 1597, by Francisco del Pozo of Tunja. The painting's anniversary is celebrated each 1 February, in addition to 28 August, the saint's day of San Agustín. Next to the church is the cloister with anonymous 17th-century paintings of the life of San Agustín ■ *Daily 0900-1200, 1300-1700, US$1 with a guided tour which includes a simple but interesting museum.* **C** Parador La Candelaria, *adjoining monastery is picturesque with good food.*

Transport Road From Villa de Leiva, take the continuation south of Cra 9 past the bus station out of town to Sáchira, turn right to Sutamarchan and Tinjaca and left at Tres Esquinas for Ráquira, a further 5 km. The road from Tres Esquinas continues to Chiquinquirá. **Bus**: Ráquira is best reached from Tunja, 1 hour, US$1.70, although there are direct buses from Bogotá (*Rápido El Carmen*, 0545, 0715, US$6, 6 hrs, returning 1300). Last bus to Tunja 1330. If stuck after 1330, walk 5 km to Tres Esquinas, where buses pass between 1530-1630, mostly going east. There are busetas from Villa de Leiva.

Chiquinquirá
Phone code: 98
Colour map 1, grid B3
Population: 38,000
Altitude: 2,550 m
134 km by road
from Bogotá,
80 km from Tunja

Situated on the west side of the valley of the Río Suárez, this is a busy market town for this large coffee and cattle region. In December thousands of pilgrims honour a painting of the Virgin whose fading colours were restored by the prayers of a woman, María Ramos. The picture is housed in the imposing **Basílica**, but the miracle took place in what is now the **Iglesia de la Renovación**, Parque Julio Flores. In 1816, when the town had enjoyed six years of independence and was besieged by the Royalists, this painting was carried through the streets by Dominican priests from the famous monastery, to rally the people. The town fell, all the same. There are special celebrations at Easter and on 26 December, the anniversary of the miracle. ■ *Buses to Villa de Leiva 1¾ hrs, US$2.70. To Tunja, 3 hrs, US$4. To Zipaquirá, US$4.30. To Bogotá, 2½ hrs, US$5 (last returns at 1730).*

Sleeping and eating B *Gran*, C 16 No 6-97, T726 3700. Comfortable, secure, good restaurant, parking. **B** *Sarabita*, C 16, 8-12, T726 2068. Business hotel, pool, sauna, restaurant, building is a national monument. **D** *Moyba*, Cra 9, No 17-53, facing plaza. Cheaper without bath, dingy. **F** *Residencias San Martín*, Cra 9, No 19-84. basic. Many others. Eating places include *El Escorial*, Parque Julio Flores, Cra 9, No 16-25, T726 2516. Good but expensive. *Plaza 17*, C 17, No 11-45, near basilica. Good. Plenty of reasonable places to eat around and near Parque Julio Flores.

Shopping The shops display the many delightful toys made locally. Along the south side of the Basilica are shops specialising in musical instruments, perhaps the best is across the plaza, *Almacén El Bambuco*, Cra 11, No 17-96.

From Tunja there are two possible routes to Cúcuta; the main road, almost entirely paved, goes via Bucaramanga, but the other heading northeast via Duitama and Málaga, rejoining the main road at Pamplona, is also interesting, though there are few filling stations north of Duitama.

Northeast of Tunja

Along the road 41 km northeast of Tunja is **Paipa**, noted for the **Aguas Termales** complex 3 km to the southeast. The baths and the neighbouring **Lago Sochagota** are very popular with Colombians and increasingly so with foreign tourists. ■ *The facilities are open daily 0600-2200, US$5, children US$3. Getting there: From Paipa there is a minibus service, US$0.50, a taxi costs US$1, or you can walk in 45 minutes. There are innumerable hotels and restaurants on the main street of Paipa (Cra 19) and on the approach road to the Aguas Termales.* A fine place to stay near the baths is **A** *Casona del Salitre*, Vía Toca, Km 3, T785 0603, a well preserved *hacienda* where Simón Bolívar stayed before the Battle of Boyacá. There is also a **Youth Hostel** in Paipa, *Cabañas El Portón*.

At Duitama, a town 15 km beyond Paipa known for basket weaving, turn right and follow the valley of the Río Chicamocha for **Sogamoso**, a large, mainly industrial town. This was an important Chibcha settlement, and a **Parque Arqueológico** has been set up on the original site. A comprehensive museum describes their arts of mummification, statuary, and crafts, including gold working ■ *Tue-Sun 0900-1300, 1400-1800, US$1.50 adults, US$0.80 children.* Cafeteria near the entrance and camping possible in the grass car park opposite, with permission. ■ *To Bogotá, 4½ hrs, US$8.50; to Yopal, US$5, 4 hrs, several daily.*

Sogamoso
Phone code: 98
Colour map 1, grid B4
Population: 70,000
Altitude: 2,569 m

Sleeping & eating **B** *Litavira*, C 12, No 10-30, T770 2585, F770 5631. Discounts at weekends, including breakfast, cable TV, private parking, good value. **D** *Bochica*, C 11, No 14-33, T770 4140. Comfortable, hot water, TV, good value. Many hotels near bus station eg **F** *Hostal Aranjuez*, basic, safe, very helpful. **F** *Residencia Embajador*, secure. Recommended. **G** *Residencia El Terminal*, basic, safe. Several reasonable restaurants near the centre, one of the best is *Susacá*, Cra 16, No 11-35, T770 2587. Open 1200-2100, specialities include trout, good *comida*, large portions, good value.

The main road south of Sogamoso climbs quite steeply to the continental divide at El Crucero at 3,100 m. At this point, the main road continues to Yopal. Turn right for Lago de Tota (3,015 m), ringed by mountains. Virtually all round the lake, onions are grown near water level, and the whole area has an intriguing 'atmosphere' of pine, eucalyptus and onion. **Aquitania** is the principal town on the lake. There are plenty of food shops and a bright, restored church with modern stained glass windows. Above the town is a hill (El Cumbre) with beautiful views. ■ *From Sogamoso, US$2, 1 hr; bus from Bogotá (Rápido Duitama), via Tunja and Sogamoso, goes round the lake to Aquitania, passing Cuitiva, Tota and the Rocas Lindas.*

Lago de Tota

Sleeping **Aquitania:** **F** *Residencia Venecia*, C 8, No 144. Clean, basic, reasonable. Numerous restaurants including *Luchos*, *Tunjo de Oro* and *Pueblito Viejo* together on corner of plaza. **Lakeside** Turn left following the lakeshore for 2 km to **A** *Camino Real*, Km 20 via Sogamoso a Aquitania, T770 0684, on the lake. Pleasant public rooms, colourful gardens, boat slipway, boats for hire. **A** *Pozo Azul*, 3 km further, in a secluded bay on the lake, T257 6586 (Bogotá), also cabins up to 6. Suitable for children, comfortable, full range of water sport facilities, good food. 3 km before Aquitania is **A** *Hotel Santa Inez*, Km 29 Sogamoso-Aquitania, T779 4199, also cabins. Good position on lake, boats for hire/fishing, good food, helpful. At Playa Blanca, southwest corner of lake, is *Las Rocas Lindas* campground, with bath and hot water, 2 cabins for 7, 1 for 8, boats for hire, dining room, bar, fireplaces. Recommended.

9 km northeast of Sogamoso is **Tópaga**, with a colonial church, unusual topiary in the plaza and the bust of Bolívar to commemorate the battle of Peñón of 11 July 1819. Turn south before Topagá to **Monguí**, which has earned the title of "most beautiful village of Boyacá province". The upper side of the plaza is dominated by

Colombia

the basilica and convent. There are interesting arts and crafts shops in all directions. Walk down Cra 3 to the Calycanto Bridge, or up C 4, to the Plaza de Toros. A recommended excursion is east to the **Páramo de Ocetá** with particularly fine *frailejones* and giant wild lupins. The tourist office is in the Municipalidad on the plaza, T778 2050, helpful Local craftwork includes leather and wool items. ■ *Bus office on plaza. To Bogotá, Libertadores daily at 0730 and 1600, US$9, 4½ hrs. To Sogamoso, every 30 mins by buseta, US$0.75, 45 mins.*

Sleeping **C** *Hostal Calycanto*, pink house next to the bridge. Lovely setting, restaurant (but give advance notice). **E** *La Cabaña*, chalet on road beyond river (cross bridge, turn left). Basic but comfortable, food if advised, information from Miriam Fernández at *Cafetería La Cabaña* next to the Municipality. Several restaurants round the plaza. *Taller de Arte Colonial*, Cra 3, coffee and snacks.

Sierra Nevada del Cocuy

The area is good for trekking and the best range in Colombia for mountaineering and rock climbers

By the bridge over the Río Chicamocha at **Capitanejo** is the turning to the attractive **Sierra Nevada del Cocuy** in the Eastern Cordillera. The Sierra consists of two parallel north-south ranges about 30 km long, offering peaks of rare beauty, lakes and waterfalls. The flora is particularly interesting. Everyone wears ruanas, rides horses and is friendly. The most beautiful peaks are Ritacuba Negro (5,300 m), Ritacuba Blanco (5,330 m) and El Castillo (5,100 m). The main towns are to the west of the Sierra. The centre for climbing the main peaks is **Guicán**, about 50 km east of Capitanejo.

Hiking and climbing Above Guicán: From *Cabinas Kanwara* (see below, Sleeping), it is a steep three hours' walk on a clear trail to the snowline on Ritacuba Blanco. Rope and crampons recommended for the final section above 4,800 m. The *Cabinas* is the best starting place for the 4-5 day walk round the north end of the Sierra, which is surrounded by snow-capped mountains. Guicán is 1-1½ hours drive by jeep from the mountains, so it is recommended to stay higher up (jeep hire about US$17 from José Riaño or 'Profe' in Guicán). Also, to get to the *Cabinas* you can take the milk truck ('el lechero') which leaves Guicán around 0500 via Cocuy for La Cruz, one hour's walk below the cabins, arriving 1100, getting back to Guicán around 1230, a rough but interesting ride. Alternatively you can take the path leading steeply east from Guicán which leads to the *Cabinas* in about 9 km.

The other main town is **Cocuy** (for information contact Pedro Moreno, Cra 5, No 8-36). Above Cocuy you can sleep at *Hacienda La Esperanza* (four hours from Guicán) US$5pp per night, meals around US$3 or you can camp and take your own food. Also camping and horses available at a nearby finca. La Esperanza is the base for climbing to the Laguna Grande de la Sierra (seven hours round trip), a large sheet of glacier-fed water surrounded by five snow-capped peaks, and also for the two-day walk to the Laguna de la Plaza on the east side of the Sierra, reached through awesome, rugged scenery. Between Cocuy and La Esperanza is Alto de la Cueva where you can stay at El Himat meterological station for US$6, basic, including three meals. There is a fine walk from here to Lagunillas, a string of lakes near the south end of the range (five hours there and back). Permission to camp can easily be obtained. Sketch maps available in Cocuy from the tourist office. It takes 6-8 days to trek from one end to the other through the gorge between the two ranges for which crampons, ice axe, rope etc are necessary if you wish to do any climbing en route. Be prepared for unstable slopes and rockfalls, few flat campsites and treacherous weather. The perpendicular rock mountains overlooking the Llanos are for professionals only. The views east towards the Llanos are stupendous. The best weather is from December to April. Check for safety before setting out.

Sleeping In **Capitanejo** are several hotels where the bus stops: *Residencias El Oasis*, *Residencia El Córdobes*, *Residencia El Dorado* and *Villa Del Mar*, all **F**, and more on the park on block below bus stop, all are basic. In **Guicán** **F** *La Sierra*, good. Owner 'Profe' has sketch maps of the region, informative visitors book for trekkers, meals available. Also, **F** *Los Andes*; **F** *Las Brisas*. In **Cocuy E** *Gutiérrez*, friendly, hot water, meals, laundry facilities. **F** *Residencia Cocuy*, cold water, meals, laundry. **E** *Colonial*, owned by Orlando Correa, a good source of information. In the **Sierra D** *Cabinas Kanwara* at 3,920 m, about 1,000 m above Guicán, 4 cabins for 4-6 people, restaurant, open fires, electrically-heated showers, or camping **F**, horse rental and guide service. Highly recommended.

Bus To **Bogotá**, from both **Guicán** and **Cocuy**, 6 buses a day, about US$15, 10-11 hrs; services by *Gacela, Paz de Río, Tricolor* and *Los Libertadores*. Between Cocuy and Guicán, several buses a day, US$1.50, 1 hour. To go north, change at **Capitanejo** from where 3 buses a day go to **Bucaramanga** and 4 to **Cúcuta**. **Transport**

From Capitanejo a picturesque road goes north to **Málaga** (population: 18,000, altitude: 2,230 m, 35 km N of Capitanejo, several hotels), Pamplona (see below) and Cúcuta.

　　To Bucaramanga is another spectacular trip through the mountains, but the road is not good and is very tortuous.

Tunja to Cúcuta

The main road goes northeast for 84 km to **Socorro**, with steep streets and single storey houses set among graceful palms. It has a singularly large stone cathedral. The **Casa de Cultura** museum (opening hours vary according to season) covers the local history and the interesting part played by Socorro in the fight for Independence. It is well worth a visit. There is a daily market. **B** *Tamacara*, C 14, No 14-15, T727 3515, swimming pool. **E** *Colonial*, Cra 15, No 12-45, T727 2842, parking, TV. **F** *Nueva Venezia*, C 13, No 14-37, shower, dining room, nice old rooms, good value.

Socorro
Phone code: 97
Colour map 1, grid B4
Population: 23,020
Altitude: 1,230 m

About 21 km beyond Socorro, northeast on the main road to Bucaramanga, is **San Gil**, a colonial town with a good climate, which has El Gallineral, a riverside park whose beautiful trees are covered with moss-like tillandsia (take insect repellent). ■ *US$0.30*. This is an important centre for adventure sports, including rafting, parapenting and caving. For information, contact the office by the entrance to El Gallineral Park, open daily, T724 0000. Good view from La Gruta, the shrine overlooking the town (look for the cross).

San Gil
Phone code: 97
Colour map 1, grid B4
Population: 28,000
Altitude: 1,140 m

Sleeping and eating A *Bella Isla*, north of town, Vía Javel San Pedro, T724 2971. Large condominium, full services, great views, beautiful gardens. **B** *Mansión Perla del Fonce*, Cra 10, No 1-44, T724 3298. Family hotel. **D** *Alcantuz*, Cra 11, No 10-15, T724 3160. Free coffee, good location, pleasant. **E** *Abril*, C 8, No 9-63, T724 3381. Secure parking, relatively quiet. **E** *Victoria*, near bus terminal, with bath. **F** *San Gil*, C 11, No 11-25, T724 2542. Cheaper without bath, upstairs rooms are preferable, basic. Plenty of restaurants, including: *Las Esteras*, Cra 9, No 3-43. *Madrigal*, C 14, No 9-70. *El Pasaje*, Cra 11, No 12-38. There are also several good restaurants near Km 2 on the road to Bucaramanga. Open air restaurant in Parque Gallineral, good in evening, music at weekends.

Transport Bus Bus station 5 mins out of town by taxi on road to Tunja. Bus to **Bogotá**, US$16. To **Bucaramanga**, US$5, 2½ hrs. To **Barichara** from C 12, US$1.50, 45 mins, hourly.

From San Gil a paved road leads 22 km to **Barichara**, a beautiful colonial town founded in 1714 and designated as a national monument. Among Barichara's places of historical interest are the Cathedral and 3 churches and the house of the former president Aquiles Parra (the woman next door has the key). An interesting excursion is to **Guane**, 9 km away by road, or 2 hours' delightful walk by *camino real* (historic trail), where there are many colonial houses and an archaeological museum in the *casa parroquial*, collection of textiles, coins and a mummified woman (admission,

Barichara
Phone code: 97
Colour map 1, grid B4
Population: 10,000
Altitude: 1,300 m

Colombia

US$0.25). The valley abounds with fossils. There are morning and afternoon buses from Baricharra. Another interesting trip is to the waterfall Salto de Mica, a 30-minute walk along a trail following the line of cliffs near Baricharra.

Sleeping and eating B *Hostal Misión Santa Bárbara*, C 5, No 9-12, T726 7163. Old colonial house, quiet, pool, all meals available. **D** *Coratá*, Cra 7, No 4-08, T726 7110. Charming courtyard, restaurant and lovely cathedral views. Recommended. **D** *Diez Desitos*, Cra 6, No 4-37, T726 7224. Simple hostal, some rooms with bath. **E** *Posada de Pablo*, Cra 7, No 3-50. Ask at the *Casa de Cultura* about staying in private homes. *La Casona*, C 6, Cras 5-6. Cheap, good food. *Bahía Chala*, C 8, No 8-62. Goat-meat speciality. Light meals around the plaza.

Between San Gil and Bucamaranga is the spectacular Río Chicamocha canyon, with the best views to the right of the road.

Bucaramanga

Phone code: 97
Colour map 1, grid B4
Population: 465,000
Altitude: 1,000 m
420 km from Bogotá

The capital of Santander was founded in 1622 but was little more than a village until the latter half of the 19th century. The city's great problem is space for expansion. Erosion in the lower, western side topples buildings over the edge after heavy rain. The fingers of erosion, deeply ravined between, are spectacular. The metropolitan area has grown rapidly because of the success of coffee, tobacco and staple crops.

The **Parque Santander** is the heart of the modern city, while the **Parque García Rovira** is the centre of the colonial area. Just off Parque García Rovira is the **Casa de Cultura**. The **Casa de Bolívar**, C 37, No 12-15, is interesting for its connections with Bolívar's campaign in 1813. ■ *Tue-Sat, 0900-1200, 1400-1700.* There is an amusement park, **Parque El Lago**, in the suburb of Lagos, southwest of the city on the way to Floridablanca. On the way out of the city northeast (towards Pamplona) is the **Parque Morrorico**, well-maintained with a fine view. There is a sculptured Saviour overlooking the park, a point of pilgrimage on Good Friday.

Excursions In **Floridablanca**, 8 km southwest, is the **Jardín Botánicao Eloy Valenzuela**, belonging to the national tobacco agency. ■ *Weekends 0800-1100, 1400-1700, US$0.25. Take a* Floridablanca *bus and walk 1 km; taxi from centre, US$1.50.*

Rionegro is a coffee town 20 km to the north with, close by, the Laguna de Gálago and waterfalls. One fine waterfall is 30 minutes by bus from Rionegro to Los Llanos de Palma followed by a two-hour walk through citrus groves towards Bocas. Complete the walk along an old railway to the Bucaramanga-Rionegro road.

Phone code: 97
Population: 75,000
Altitude: 780 m

Girón a tobacco centre 9 km southwest of Bucaramanga on the Río de Oro, is a quiet and attractive colonial town, filled with Bumangueses at weekends, with a beautiful church. The buildings are well preserved and the town unspoilt by modernization. By the river are *tejo* courts and popular open air restaurants with *cumbia* and *salsa* bands. In the plaza at weekends, sweets and *raspados* (crushed ice delights) are sold. ■ *Take the bus from Cra 15 or 22 in Bucaramanga, US$1.25.*

Sleeping and eating, Girón C *Las Nieves*, C 30, No 25-71, T646 8968. Colonial house, central courtyard, balconies overlooking central plaza, good restaurant. **F** *Río de Oro*, in centre. Make sure you get a lock for the door. Restaurants: *Mansión del Fraile* on the plaza, in a beautiful colonial house. Good food, Bolívar slept here on one occasion, ask to see the bed. *La Casona*, C 28, No 27-47. Recommended. Try their *fritanga gironesa.*

Piedecuesta is 18 km southeast of Bucaramanga. Here you can see cigars being hand-made, furniture carving and jute weaving. Cheap, hand-decorated *fique* rugs can be bought. There are frequent buses to all the city's dormitory towns; a taxi costs US$6. Corpus Christi processions in these towns in June are interesting. **Sleeping**: **F** *Piedecuesta*, good, safe. ■ *Getting there:* bus from Cra 22, US$0.45, 45 mins.

Sleeping

AL *Meliá Confort Chicamocha*, C 34, No 31-24, T634 3000, www.solarhoteles.com.co Luxury, a/c, swimming pool (non guests US$1.50). **C-D** *Aquarela*, C 35, No 30-08, T/F634 3570, aquarela@b-manga.cetcol.net.co With restaurant, pool, lake with water skiing and canoes, local excursions arranged. **D** *El Pilar*, C 34, No 24-09, T634 7207. Hot water, quiet, good service and food. Recommended. **E** *Tamaná*, Cra 18, No 30-31, T630 4726. **F** without bath. Recommended. Wide variety of hotels on C 31, between Cras 18-21. **E** *Las Bahamas*, C 55, No 17A-120, T644 9002. Good value. **E** *Residencias San Diego*, Cra 18, No 54-71, T643 4273. Quiet, good. **F** *Residencias Tonchala*, C 56, No 21-23. With bath, good. **F** *Residencias Amparo*, C 31, No 20-29, T630 4089. With bath.

Since Bucaramanga is the site for numerous national conventions, it is sometimes hard to find a room

Eating

D'Marco, C 48, No 28-76. Excellent meat. *La Casa de Spagheti*, Cra 27, No 51-18. Cheap and good. *Tropical*, C 33, No 17-81. *Los Notables*, Cra 18, C 34/35. Pleasant, good breakfast. *Zirus*, C 56, No 30-88. Friendly, owner speaks a little English. **Vegetarian** *Maranatha*, Cra 24, No 36-20. Good lunches and dinners, reasonable prices. *Govinda*, Indian vegetarian, Cra 20, No 34-65. Excellent lunch. *Fonda*, C 33, No 34-42. Good, cheap. *Berna*, C 35, No 18-30. Good pastries.

Try the hormigas culonas (large black ants), a local delicacy mainly eaten during Holy Week (sold in shops, not restaurants)

Entertainment

Discotheques Several on road to Girón and on Cra 33/35. *Barbaroja*, Cra 27/C 28, a *salsa* and *son* bar set in a renovated red and white, gothic-style mansion, happy hour 1700-1800; *Mister Barbilla*, Anillo Vial, huge, good music, also restaurant.

Festivals

The annual *international piano festival* is held here in **mid-Sep** in the Auditorio Luis A Calvo at the Universidad Industrial de Santander, one of Colombia's finest concert halls. The university is worth a visit for beautiful grounds and a lake full of exotic plants.

Shopping

Camping equipment *Acampemos*, C 48, No 26-30, last place in Colombia to get camping gas cartridges before Venezuela. **Handicrafts** in Girón and typical clothing upstairs in the food market, C 34 y Cras 15-16. Similar articles (*ruanas*, hats) in San Andresito. *Feria de artesanías* in first 2 weeks of Sep, usually near the Puerta del Sol.

Transport

Taxi Most have meters; beware of overcharging from bus terminals. **Bus** charges US$0.45.
    Air Palonegro, on three flattened hilltops south of city. Spectacular views on take-off and landing. Daily *Avianca* flights to **Bogotá** (also *Aces* and *AeroRepública*), and to principal Colombian cities. *Avianca*, T642 6117; *Aces* T634 9595; *AeroRepública* T643 3384.
    Bus: the terminal is on the Girón road, with cafés, shops and showers. Taxi to centre, US$1.50; bus US$0.35. To **Bogotá**, 8-11 hrs, US$22 (Pullman) with *Berlinas del Fonce*, Cra 18, No 31-06. *Expreso Brasilia*, C 31, Cra 18-19, T642 2152. *Copetran*, C 55, No 17B-57, recommended for advance bus reservations, has 3 classes of bus to Bogotá including Pullman, 10 hrs, and to **Cartagena**, US$29, 13 hrs, leaving at 1930 daily. **Tunja**, 7½ hrs, US$17. **Valledupar**, 8 hrs, US$20. **Barranquilla**, 13 hrs (US$27 first class with *Copetran*). **Santa Marta**, 11 hrs, maybe more according to season, US$25 with *Copetran*. To **Pamplona**, *Copetran*, 3 a day, US$5 (Pullman), US$4.50 (*corriente*), 5 hrs. To **Cúcuta**, 6 hrs, US$7 (Pullman), *Copetran* US$11 (via Berlín US$3), and colectivo US$13. The trip to Cúcuta is spectacular in the region of Berlín. **Barrancabermeja**, 3 hrs, US$5. To **El Banco** on the Río Magdalena, US$15, several companies, direct or change at Aguachica. Hourly buses to **San Gil**, US$5. Other companies with local services to nearby villages on back roads, eg the colourful folk-art buses of *Flota Cáchira* (C 32, Cra 33-34).

Directory

Banks *Bancolombia*, by Parque Santander, will cash Thomas Cook and Amex TCs. Long queues (cheques and passports have to be photocopied). Other banks, many with cash machines. *Lloyds TSB Bank*, Cra 19 No 36-43, and 2 agencies. Cash changed at *Distinguidos*, C 36, No 17-52 local 1A33. The **tourist office** is on the main plaza in *Hotel Bucarica* building, C 35 y Cra 19, friendly and knowledgeable, T633 8461 (closed 1200-1400). City maps US$2. **Useful addresses** MA: Av Quebrada Seca between Cra 30/31, T6458309.

The road (paved but narrow) runs east to Berlín, and then northeast (a very scenic run over the Eastern Cordillera) to Pamplona, about 130 km from Bucaramanga. **Berlín** is an ideal place to appreciate the grandeur of the Eastern Cordillera and the hardiness of the people who live on the *páramo*. The village lies in a valley at 3,100 m, the peaks surrounding it rise to 4,350 m and the temperature is constantly around 10°C, although on the infrequent sunny days it may seem much warmer. There is a tourist complex with cabins and there are several basic eating places. Camping (challenging but rewarding) is possible with permission. At the highest point on the road between Bucaramanga and Berlín, 3,400 m, is a café where you can camp on the covered porch.

Pamplona

Phone code: 975
Colour map 1, grid B4
Population: 43,700
Altitude: 2,200 m

Founded in the mountains in 1548, it became important as a mining town but is now better known for its university. It is renowned for its Easter celebrations. Pamplona is a good place to buy *ruanas* and has a good indoor market.

Worth a visit is the **Cathedral** in the spacious central plaza. The earthquake of 1875 played havoc with the monasteries and some of the churches: there is now a hotel on the site of the former San Agustín monastery, but it is possible to visit the ex-monasteries of San Francisco and Santo Domingo. The **Iglesia del Humilladero**, adjoining the cemetery, is very picturesque and allows a fine view of the city. The **Casa Colonial** archaeological museum is a little gem C 6, No 2-56. ■ *Tue-Sat, 0900-1200, 1400-1800; Sun, 0900-1200.* **Casa Anzoátegui**, Cra 6, No 7-48, houses a museum of the Independence period. One of Bolívar's generals, José Antonio Anzoátegui, died here in 1819, at the age of 30, after the battle of Boyacá. The state in northeast Venezuela is named after him.

Sleeping & eating

C *Cariongo*, Cra 5, C 9, T682645. Very good, excellent restaurant, US satellite TV (locked parking available). **E** *Residencia Dorán*, Cra 6, No 7-21. **F** without bath, large rooms, good meals. **E** *Imperial*, Cra 5, No 5-36, T682571, on main plaza. Large rooms, hot water, safe, restaurant. **F** *Los Llanos*, C 9, No 7-35, T683441. Shared bath, cold water. Recommended. **F** *Orsúa*, C5, No 5-67, T682470, on main plaza. Cheap, good food. Hotel accommodation may be hard to find at weekends, when Venezuelans visit the town. *El Maribel*, C 5, No 4-17. Cheap lunch. *La Casona*, C 6, No 6-57. Limited but good menu. *Las Brazas*, next door. Good, cheap. *Portal Alemán*, C 7 y Cra 6. Good meals, especially breakfasts. *Angelitas*, C 7 y Cra 7. Good coffee. *Piero's Pizza*, C 9 y Cra 5. Good.

Transport

Bus To **Bogotá**, US$26, 13-16 hrs. To **Cúcuta**, US$3, 2½ hrs. To **Bucaramanga**, US$5, 4 hrs. To **Málaga** from main plaza, 5 a day from 0800, 6 hrs, US$5. To **Tunja**, US$20, 12 hrs (leaving at 0600). To **Berlín**, US$3.

Directory

Banks *Banco de Bogotá*, on the main plaza, gives Visa cash advances or try the store at C 6, No 4-37, where 'Don Dólar' will change cash and TCs. Cash machines nearby. **Communications** Post Office: Cra 6 y C 6, in pedestrian passage. **Telecom:** C 7 y Cra 5A. **Tourist office** C 5 y Cra 6, on main plaza.

Cúcuta

Phone code: 975
Colour map 1, grid B4
Population: 526,000
Altitude: 215 m

It is 72 km from Pamplona descending to **Cúcuta**, capital of the Department of Norte de Santander, 16 km from the Venezuelan border. It was founded 1733, destroyed by earthquake 1875, and then rebuilt, with tree-lined streets offering welcome shade: the mean temperature is 29°C. Coffee is the great crop in the area, followed by tobacco. There are also large herds of cattle. The **cathedral**, Av 5 between C 10 and 11, is worth a visit. Note the oil paintings by Salvador Moreno. There is a good range of leather goods, try C 10, Av 8 for leather boots and shoes. *Cuchitril*, Av 3 No 9-89, has a selection of the better Colombian craft work. The **international bridge** between Colombia and Venezuela is southeast of the city.

Just short of the border is the small town of **Villa Rosario**, where the Congress met which agreed the constitution of Gran Colombia in the autumn of 1821, one of the high points of the the career of Simón Bolívar. The actual spot where the documents were signed is now a park beside which is the **Templo del Congreso**, in which the preliminary meetings took place. Also nearby is the **Casa de Santander**, where

General Santander, to whom Bolívar entrusted the administration of the new Gran Colombia, was born and spent his childhood. The archaeological **museum** is worth a visit ■ *Tue-Sat 0800-1200, 1400-1800, Sun 0900-1330*. The **Casa de Cultura**, C13 No 3-67 incorporates the **Museo de la Ciudad** which covers the history of the city and its part in the Independence Movement.

A *Tonchalá*, C 10, Av 0, T712005, www.tonchala.com Good restaurant, swimming pool, a/c, airline booking office in hall. **B** *Acora*, C 10, No 2-75, T712156, F731139. A/c, restaurant, safe, TV, good value. **C** *Casa Blanca*, Av 6, No 14-55, T721455, F722993. Good, reasonable meals. Recommended. **C** *Lord*, Av 7, No 10-58, T713609. A/c, nice rooms, good restaurant and service, safe. **D** *Amaruc*, Av 5, No 9-73, T717625, F721805. With fan, no hot water. **D** *Cacique*, Av 7, No 9-66, T712652, F719484. A/c, cold showers only, reasonable. **E** *Flamingo*, Av 3, No 6-38, T712190. Fan, with bath, noisy. **F** *Imperial*, Av 7, No 6-28, T712866, F726376. With bath, secure. Highly recommended. **F** *Residencia Leo*, Av 6A, No 0-24 N, Barrio La Merced. With bath, clothes washing, free coffee all day. Recommended. **F** *Residencia Los Rosales*, near bus station, C 2, 8-39. Fan, with bath, good. **F** *Residencias Nohra*, C 7, No 7-52, T725889. Shared bath, quiet. **F** *Residencia Zambrano*, C 4, No 11E-87. Breakfast, laundry facilities, family run by Cecilia Zambrano Mariño. Eating places include *La Brasa*, Av 5, C 7. Good *churrascos*, modest prices. *Don Pancho*, Av 3, No 9-21. Local menus.

Sleeping & eating

Air The airport is 5 km north of the town centre, 15 mins by taxi in normal traffic from the town and border, US$3. There are only domestic flights from Cúcuta airport. For flights to Venezuelan destinations, cross the border and fly from San Antonio airport (30 mins). To **Bogotá** 3 daily with *Aces*, *Avianca* and *SAM* and direct to other Colombian cities. It is cheaper to buy tickets in Colombia for these flights than in advance in Venezuela. *Avianca* and *SAM*, C 13, No 5-09, T717758; *Aces*, T832237.

Bus Bus station: Av 7 and C O (a really rough area). Taxi from bus station to town centre,

Transport

Do not buy airline 'tickets' from Cúcuta to Venezuelan destinations, all flights go from San Antonio

Colombia

US$2.40. Bus to **Bogotá**, hourly, 17-24 hrs, US$28, *Berlinas del Fonce* (has own terminal, 2 km beyond the main terminal along continuation of Diagonal Santander) 1000, 1400, 2 stops, including 15 mins in Bucaramanga (US$2.50 extra for *cochecama*), or *Bolivariano*, 20 hrs. There are frequent buses, even during the night (if the bus you take arrives in the dark, sit in the bus station café until it is light). To **Cartagena**, *Brasilia* 1800 and 1930, 18 hrs, US$35. To **Bucaramanga**, US$7, 6 hrs, with *Copetran* and *Berlinas del Fonce* Pullman, several departures daily.

Warning Travellers have been reporting for years that the bus station is overrun with thieves and conmen, who have tried every trick in the book. This is still true. You must take great care, there is little or no police protection. On the 1st floor there is a tourist office for help and information and a café/snack bar where you can wait in comparative safety. Alternatively, go straight to a bus going in your direction, get on it, pay the driver and don't let your belongings out of your sight. For San Cristóbal, only pay the driver of the vehicle, not at the offices upstairs in the bus station. If you are told, even by officials, that it is dangerous to go to

Cúcuta and the surrounding area is a large centre for smuggling. Be careful

Cúcuta

To Ocaña & Berlinas del Fonce Bus Terminal

To Airport

Av Bogotá

Estadio General Santander

Diagonal Santander

To Pamplona, San Antonio (Venezuela) & Ureña

Venezuelan Consulate

Parque Santander

Cathedral

Parque Colón

Casa de Cultura

Avianca

Governor's Palace

N

0 metres   200
0 yards   200

■ Sleeping	
1 Acora	6 Lord
2 Amaruc	7 Nohra
3 Cacique	8 Residencia Leo
4 Flamingo	9 Residencia Los Rosales
5 Imperial	10 Tonchalá

Cúcuta and the Road to Independence

*Cúcuta, because it is the gateway of entry from Venezuela, was a focal point in the history of Colombia during the wars for independence. Bolívar captured it after his lightning Magdalena campaign in 1813. The **Bolívar Column** stands where he addressed his troops on 28 February 1813. At **El Rosario de Cúcuta**, a small town of 8,000 inhabitants 14½ km from Cúcuta on the road to the border, the First Congress of Gran Colombia opened on 6 May 1821. It was at this Congress that the plan to unite Venezuela, Ecuador, and Colombia was ratified; Bolívar was made President, and Santander (who was against the plan) Vice-President. (Santander was born at a hacienda near El Rosario which is now being developed as a tourist centre.)*

your chosen destination, double check. Report any theft to the DAS office, who may be able to help to recover what has been stolen. **NB** The exception to the above is the *Berlinas del Fonce* terminal, which is much safer.

Directory **Banks** Good rates of exchange in Cúcuta, at the airport, or on the border. *Banco Ganadero/BBV* and *Banco de Los Andes* near the plaza will give cash against Visa cards. *Bancolombia* changes TCs. *Banco de Bogotá*, on Parque Santander, advances on Visa. There are money changers on the street all round the main plaza and many shops advertise the purchase and sale of bolívares. Change pesos into bolívares in Cúcuta or San Antonio difficult to change them further into Venezuela. **Tourist office** C 10, No 0-30, helpful, has maps, etc, at the bus station (1st floor), and at the airport.

Border with Venezuela

Venezuela is 1 hr ahead of Colombia

If you do not obtain an exit stamp, you will be turned back by Venezuelan officials and the next time you enter Colombia, you will be fined

Colombian immigration is at DAS, Av 1, No 28-55, open 0800-1200, 1400-2000 daily. Take a bus from the city centre to Barrio San Rafael, south towards the road to Pamplona. Shared taxi from border is US$1, then US$0.80 to bus station. Exit and entry formalities are also handled at the DAS office in the white house before the international border bridge. DAS has a third office at the airport, which will deal with land travellers. For Venezuelan immigration, see page 1390. No documents are needed just to visit San Antonio de Táchira.

Venezuelan consulate is on Av Camilo Daza, Cúcuta, T781034, F780876, consul@coll.telecom.com.co Open 0800-1300, Monday-Friday. Overland visitors to Venezuela need a visa and tourist card, obtainable from here or the Venezuelan Embassy in Bogotá (which may send you to Cúcuta). Check with a Venezuelan consulate in advance. Requirements: two passport photographs; proof of transportation out of Venezuela, with date (not always asked for in Cúcuta); proof of adequate funds sometimes requested. In Cúcuta, pay US$30 in pesos for visa at a bank designated by the consulate, then take receipt to consulate. Apply for visa at 0800 to get it by 1400. You may need a numbered ticket to get served. If you know when you will be arriving at the border, get your visa in your home country.

Entering Colombia You must obtain both a Venezuelan exit stamp and a Colombian entry stamp at the border. Without the former you will be sent back; without the latter you will have problems with police checks, banks and leaving the country. You can also be fined. For those arriving by air, all Colombian formalities can be undertaken at the airport. The Aduana office on the road to the airport (small sign); has a restaurant.

Leaving and entering Colombia by private vehicle Passports must be stamped at DAS in town and car papers must be stamped at Aduana on the road to the airport, about 10 km from the border or at their office 40 m before the International Bridge.

Transport **Bus**: from Cúcuta to **Caracas**; **San Cristóbal**, US$1.20 (*Bolivariano*), colectivo US$2.40; **San Antonio**, taxi US$7.20, bus and colectivo from C 7, Av 4, US$1.

On any form of transport which is crossing the border, make sure that the driver knows that you need to stop to obtain exit/entry stamps etc. You will have to alight and flag down a later colectivo.

The North Coast and the Islands

Caribbean Colombia is very different in spirit from the highlands: the coast stretches from the Darién Gap, through banana plantations, swamplands and palm plantations to the arid Guajira. Though tropically hot, the heat is moderated for much of the year by trade winds. The main resorts are Cartagena, which is also steeped in colonial history, and Santa Marta, near which is the Tayrona national park with precolombian remains and the unspoilt Sierra Nevada de Santa Marta coastal range.

Cartagena

Cartagena is one of the most vibrant, interesting and beautiful cities in South America. It combines superb weather, a sparkling stretch of the Caribbean, an abundance of tropical fruit, and a rich history. There are many fine colonial buildings along the city's central narrow streets, look inside for delightful patios. Do not miss a drink by night in the cafés next to the city's oldest church, Santo Domingo, or a stroll among the small plazas of the San Diego quarter.

Phone code: 95
Colour map 1, grid A2
Population: 746,000

The core of the city was built on an island separated from the mainland by marshes and lagoons close to a prominent hill – the perfect place for a defensive port. Cartagena de Indias was founded by Pedro de Heredia on 13 January 1533. There were then two approaches to it, Bocagrande, at the northern end of Tierrabomba island – the direct entry from the Caribbean – and Bocachica, a narrow channel at the south leading to the great bay of Cartagena, 15 km long and 5 km wide. (Bocagrande was blocked after Admiral Vernon's attack in 1741 – see below.) The old walled city lies at the north end of the Bahía de Cartagena, with the Caribbean Sea to the west.

History

Colombia

    Fortifications Cartagena was one of the storage points for merchandise sent out from Spain and for treasure collected from the Americas to be sent back to Spain. A series of forts protecting the approaches from the sea, and the formidable walls built around the city, made it almost impregnable.

    Entering Bocachica by sea, the island of Tierrabomba is to the left. At the tip of a spit of land is the fortress of **San Fernando**. Opposite, right on the tip of Barú island, is the **Fuerte San José**. The two forts were once linked by heavy chains to prevent surprise attacks by pirates. Close to the head of the bay is Manga island, now an important suburb. At its northern end a bridge, **Puente Román**, connects it with the old city. This approach was defended by three forts: **San Sebastián del Pastelillo** built between 1558 and 1567 (the Club de Pesca has it now) at the northwestern tip of Manga Island; the fortress of **San Lorenzo** near the city itself; and the very powerful **Castillo San Felipe de Barajas**, the largest Spanish fort built in the Americas. Built on San Lázaro hill, 41 m above sea-level, to the east of the city, construction began in 1639 and was finished by 1657. Under the huge structure are tunnels lined with living rooms and offices. Some are open and lit; visitors pass through these and on to the top of the fortress. Baron de Pointis, the French pirate, stormed and took it, but Admiral Vernon failed to reach it (see box). ■ *Daily 0800-1800, US$3, guides are available; few signs and little printed information. Good footwear advisable for the damp sloping tunnels.*

    Yet another fort, **La Tenaza**, protected the walled city from a direct attack from the open sea. The huge encircling walls were started early in the 17th century and finished by 1735. They were on average 12 m high and 17 m thick, with six gates. They contained, besides barracks, a water reservoir.

In order to link Cartagena with the Río Magdalena, the most importat route to the interior of the continent, the Spaniards built a 145 km canal from the Bahía de Cartagena to Calamar on the river. Called the Canal del Dique, it is still in use.

Independence Cartagena declared its independence from Spain in 1811. A year later Bolívar used the city as a jumping-off point for his Magdalena campaign. After a heroic resistance, Cartagena was retaken by the royalists under Pablo Morillo in 1815. The patriots finally freed it in 1821.

Sights

Most 'grand houses' can be visited. Churches generally open to the public at 1800

The city has two main centres of attraction, the walled colonial city and the strip of land on which is the beach resort of Bocagrande. The old city streets are narrow. Each block has a different name, a source of confusion, but don't worry: the thing to do is to wander aimlessly, savouring the street scenes, and allow the great sights to catch you by surprise.

The old walled city was in two sections, outer and inner. Much of the wall between the two has disappeared. In the *outer city*, the artisan classes lived in the one-storied houses of **Getsemaní**, where many colonial buildings survive and today the greatest concentration of budget hotels and restaurants is found. Immediately adjoining is the downtown sector, known as **La Matuna**, where vendors crowd the pavements and the alleys between the modern commercial buildings. Several middle range hotels are in this district.

In the *inner city,* the houses in **El Centro** were occupied by the high officials and nobility. **San Diego** (the northern end of the inner city) was where the middle classes lived: the clerks, merchants, priests and military. Today, the streets of the inner city are relatively uncrowded; hotels and restaurants are sprinkled thinly throughout the area.

The **Puente Román** leads from the island of Manga into Getsemaní. North of the bridge, in an interesting plaza, is the church of **Santísima Trinidad**, built 1643 but not consecrated until 1839. North of the church, at C Guerrero 10 lived Pedro Romero, who set the revolution of 1811 going with his cry of "Long Live Liberty". The chapel of **San Roque** (early 17th century), near the hospital of Espíritu Santo, is by the junction of Calles Media Luna and Espíritu Santo.

If you take Calle Larga from Puente Román, you come to the monastery and church of **San Francisco**. The church (now a cinema) was built in 1590 after the pirate Martin Côte had destroyed an earlier church built in 1559. The first Inquisitors lodged at the monastery. From its courtyard a crowd surged into the streets claiming independence from Spain on 11 November 1811. Now, handicrafts are sold in the grounds of the monastery, good prices. The **Iglesia de la Tercera Orden** is still an active church and worth a visit. Opposite is the **Centro Internacional de Convenciones**, a modern building holding up to 4,000 people. Although the severe fort-like structure is more or less in keeping with the surrounding historic walls and bastions, not everyone believes this is an improvement over the colourful market previously on the site.

Immediately to the north is **Plaza de la Independencia**, with the landscaped **Parque del Centenario** just off it. At right angles to the Plaza runs the **Paseo de los Mártires**, flanked by the busts of nine patriots executed in the square on 24 February 1816 by the royalist Morillo when he retook the city. At its western end, the **Puerta del Reloj**, is a tall clock tower. Through the tower's arches (the main entrance to the inner walled city) is the **Plaza de los Coches**. Around almost all the plazas of Cartagena arcades offer refuge from the tropical sun. On the west side of this plaza is the **Portal de los Dulces**, a favourite meeting place, where sweets are still sold.

The **Plaza de la Aduana**, with a statue of Columbus, has the **Palacio Municipal** on one side. The **Museo de Arte Moderno** exhibits modern Colombian artists and has a shop. ■ *Mon-Fri 0900-1200, 1500-1800, Sat 1000-1200, US$0.50*. The **Art Gallery and Museum**, Banco Ganadero, Plaza de la Aduana, has contemporary Latin American paintings. Continue southwest to the **Church of San Pedro Claver and Monastery**, built by Jesuits in 1603 and later dedicated to San Pedro Claver, a

The Sacking of Cartagena

Despite its daunting outer forts and encircling walls, Cartagena was challenged repeatedly by enemies. Sir Francis Drake, with 1,300 men, broke in successfully in 1586, leading to a major reconstruction of the ramparts we see today. Nevertheless the Frenchmen Baron de Pointis and Ducasse, with 10,000 men, beat down the defences and sacked the city in 1697. But the strongest attack of all, by Sir Edward Vernon with 27,000 men and 3,000 pieces of artillery, failed in 1741 after besieging the city for 56 days; it was defended by the one-eyed, one-armed and one-legged hero Blas de Lezo, whose statue is at the entrance to the San Felipe fortress.

monk in the monastery, who was canonized 235 years after his death in 1654. Known as the Slave of the Slaves (El Apóstol de los Negros), he used to beg from door to door for money to give to the black slaves brought to the city. His body is in a glass coffin on the high altar and his cell and the balcony from which he sighted slave ships are shown to visitors. ■ *Daily 0800-1700. US$1.50 (reduction with ISIC), guides US$3.70 in Spanish, US$4.50 in English.*

The church and convent of **Santa Teresa**, on the corner of C Ricaurte, was founded in 1609, but is now a hotel (opened 1997, renamed the **Charleston** in 2000; see Sleeping). Opposite is a **Naval Museum** with maps, models and display of armaments ■ *US$0.75.*

The **Plaza de Bolívar** (the old Plaza Inquisición) has a statue of Bolívar. On its west side is the **Palacio de la Inquisición**, established in 1610, but this building dates from 1706. The stone entrance with its coats of arms and ornate wooden door is well preserved. The whole building, with its balconies, cloisters and patios, is a fine example of colonial baroque. There is a modest historical museum, complete with a display of torture equipment and a library. ■ *Mon-Fri, 0800-1700, US$1.50; good historical books on sale.* On the opposite side of the Plaza de Bolívar is the **Museo del Oro y Arqueológico**. It has well displayed gold and pottery. ■ *Mon-Fri 0830-1200, 1400-1630, US$0.75.*

The **Cathedral**, in the northeast corner of Plaza de Bolívar, was begun in 1575 and partially destroyed by Francis Drake. Reconstruction was finished by 1612. Great alterations were made between 1912 and 1923. It has a severe exterior, with a fine doorway and a simply decorated interior. See the gilded 18th century altar, the Carrara marble pulpit, and the elegant arcades which sustain the central nave.

The church and monastery of **Santo Domingo**, Santo Domingo y Estribos, was built 1570 to 1579 and is now a seminary. Inside, a miracle-making image of Christ, carved towards the end of the 16th century, is set on a baroque 19th century altar. There is also a statue of the Virgin with a crown of gold and emeralds. This is an interesting neighbourhood in which little has changed since the 16th century. In C Santo Domingo, No 33-29, is one of the great patrician houses of Cartagena, the **Casa de los Condes de Pestagua**, now an annex of the *Charleston* hotel. North of Santo Domingo, at C de la Factoria 36-57, is the magnificent **Casa del Marqués de Valdehoyos**, home of some of the best woodcarving in Cartagena (under refurbishment, not officially open to visitors).

The monastery of **San Agustín** (1580) is now the Universidad de Cartagena (at Universidad y La Soledad). From its chapel, today occupied by a printing press, the pirate Baron de Pointis stole a 500-pound silver sepulchre. It was returned by the King of France, but the citizens melted it down to pay their troops during the siege by Morillo in 1815. The church and convent of **La Merced**, Merced y Chichería, was founded 1618. The convent, a prison during Morillos reign of terror, is now occupied by a private university, and its church is the Teatro Heredia, beautifully restored. Building of the church of **Santo Toribio de Mongrovejo** (Badilla y Sargento) began in 1729. In 1741, during Admiral Vernon's siege, a cannon ball fell into the church during Mass and lodged in one of the central columns; the ball is

Colombia

Cartagena historic centre

Colombia

Caribbean Sea

Av Santander

Paseo de la Muralla

Santa Clara de Assisi **13**

Curato

Hobo Torno

Unbanuero Ro

7

9

Santo Toribio de Mongrovejo

Casa del Consulado

Sargento Mayor

Parque Fernánde de Madrid

La Merced

Chichería Cuartel Tabaco

Don Sancho

Tab

Casa del Marqués de Valdehoyos

Factoria

CENTRO

Universidad

San Agustín

Badillo Segunda

Moneda Cruz

Castelbondo Mantilla Soledad

C de la Iglesia

Candileso Porvenir

C Escallón

Santo Domingo

Estribos Ayos Coliseo

Palacio de la Inquisición **8**

Badillo Primera

Cathedral

Baloco

Ricaurte S Domingo

Plaza de Bolívar

Museo del Oro y Arqueológico

Gobernador

Plaza de los Coches

Plaza de Independe

Sta Teresa Las Damas

Plaza de la Aduana

Paseo de los Mártires

Santa Teresa **2**

Naval Museum Juan de Dios

Muelle de los Pegasos

Av del Merca

11

Av Santander

San Pedro Claver

San Francisco

Blas de Lezo

Centro Internacional de Convenciones

C Larga

Playa de Barahona

Playa del A

Bahía de las Ánimas

N

0 metres 100
0 yards 100

To Bocagrande

■ Sleeping	3 Del Lago	6 Hostal Baluarte	9 Las Tres Banderas
1 Casa Viena	4 Doral	7 Hostal San Diego	10 Montecarlo
2 Charleston	5 Holiday	8 Hostal Santo Domingo	11 Monterrey

now in a recess in the west wall. The font of Carrara marble in the Sacristy is a masterpiece. There is a beautiful carved ceiling (mudéjar style) above the main altar. Opens for Mass at 0600 and 1800, closed at other times. The church and monastery of **Santa Clara de Assisi**, built 1617-21, have been converted into a fine hotel (*Santa Clara*, see below).

North of Santa Clara is the **Plaza de las Bóvedas**. The walls of Las Bóvedas, built 1799, are some 12 m high and 15 to 18 m thick. From the rampart there is a grand view. At the base of the wall are 23 dungeons, now containing tourist shops. Both a lighted underground passage and a drawbridge lead from Las Bóvedas to the fortress of La Tenaza at the water's edge (see above).

Casa de Núñez, just outside the walls of La Tenaza in El Cabrero district opposite the Ermita de El Cabrero, was the home of Rafael Núñez, president (four times) and poet (he wrote Colombia's national anthem). His grandiose marble tomb is in the adjoining church. ■ *Mon-Fri 0800-1200, 1400-1800.*

Four of the sights of Cartagena are off our map. Two of them, the Fortress of San Fernando and the Castillo San Felipe de Barajas, across the Puente Heredia, have been described above. From **La Popa** hill, nearly 150 m high, is a fine view of the harbour and the city ■ *Daily 0800-1730, US$1.50, children US$0.75.* Here are the church and monastery of **Santa Cruz** and restored ruins of the convent dating from 1608. In the church is the beautiful little image of the Virgin of La Candelaria, reputed a deliverer from plague and a protector against pirates. Her day is 2 February. For nine days before the feast thousands of people go up the hill by car, on foot, or on horseback. On the day itself people carry lighted candles as they go up the hill. The name was bestowed on the hill because of an imagined likeness to a ship's poop. It is dangerous to walk up on your own; either take a guided tour, or take a public bus to Teatro Miramar at the foot of the hill (US$0.50), then bargain for a taxi up, about US$3. If driving, take Cra 21 off Av Pedro de Heredia and follow the winding road to the top.

Colombia

A new **Museo Precolombiano** has opened on two islands in the **Ciénaga de la Virgen**, north of La Boquilla. Information at C San Pedro Claver, No 31-07, T664 2197.

Beaches Take a bus south from the Puerta del Reloj, taxi US$1.25, or walk to **Bocagrande**, a spit of land crowded with hotels and apartment blocks. Thousands of visitors flock to this beach with its resort atmosphere. Sand and sea can be dirty and you may be hassled.

Marbella beach is an alternative, just north of Las Bóvedas. This is the local's beach, and therefore quieter during the week than Bocagrande and is good for swimming, though subject at times to dangerous currents.

The **Bocachica** beach, on Tierra Bomba island, is also none too clean. Boats leave from Muelle Turístico. The round trip can take up to two hours each way and costs about US$8. *Ferry Dancing*, about half the price of the faster, luxury boats, carries dancing passengers. Boats taking in Bocachica and the San Fernando fortress include *Alcatraz*, which runs a daily trip from the Muelle Turístico. Recommended.

Boats to the Islas del Rosario (see below) may stop at the San Fernando fortress and **Playa Blanca** on the Isla Barú for one hour. You can bargain with the boatman to leave you and collect you later. Take food and water since these are expensive on the island. Playa Blanca is crowded in the morning, but peaceful after the tour boats have left. There are several restaurants on the beach, the best is *La Sirena* run by Carmen 'La Española', good food, hammocks for hire US$3.50. If going only to Playa Blanca, best and cheapest is the early boat (around 0800) from near the Bazurto market, US$4. If staying the night at Playa Blanca in *cabañas* or tents, beware of ferocious sandflies. A *cabaña* will cost around US$12 pp or ask Gilberto for hammock and net, US$3. **NB** Pay for boat trips on board if possible, and be certain that you and the operator understand what you are paying for.

Sleeping On **Bocagrande** beach, 10 mins by bus from city: **L** *Capilla del Mar*, C 8, Cra 1, T665 3866, F665 5145. Resort hotel, good French restaurant with excellent buffet breakfast, swimming pool on top floor, no connection with restaurant of same name in the old city. **L-A** *Flamingo*, Av San Martín No 5-85 (cheaper in low season), T665 0623. A/c, good breakfast included, helpful, pleasant, eat on the terrace, parking. Recommended. **C** *India Catalina*, Cra 2, No 7-115, T665 5523. With breakfast, a/c, safe, convenient for groups, good cafetería, good value. **C** *Playa*, Cra 2, No 4-87, T665 0552. A/c, open air bar, restaurant, swimming pool, noisy disco next door. **C** *Residencias Internacional*, Av San Martín 4110, T665 0675. **D** in low season, small rooms, a/c, cold water, uncomfortable beds, convenient location. **C** *San Martín*, Av San Martín, No 8-164, T665 4631. Negotiable off season, bright airy. **D** *Leonela*, Cra 3, 7-142, T665 4761. Quiet, comfortable. **D** *La Giralda*, Cra 3, No 7-166, T665 4507. Fan, a/c more expensive. **D** *Sorrento*, Av San Martín No 5.52, T665 7007. Central, good. On Cra 3, there are plenty of small, pleasant **D** *residencias*, for instance *Mary*, No 6-53, T665 2833, respectable, motorcycle parking.

Hotel prices rise for high season, 1 Nov-31 Mar, and Jun-Jul. Between 15 Dec-31 Jan they rise by as much as 50% (ie increase Bocagrande hotels by at least a letter in our range at this time. In town price rises are not so steep)

In Centro and San Diego LL *Charleston* (formerly *Santa Teresa*), Cra 3A, No 31-23, T664 9494, F664 9448. Formerly a convent, elegantly converted into a hotel, pool on roof with public bar, fine hotel. **LL** *Santa Clara*, Cra 8, No 39-29, T664 6070, F664 7010, www.hotelsantaclara.com French Sofitel group, magnificently restored 16th century convent, French, Italian and Colombian restaurants, all services. **A** *Hostal San Diego*, C de las Bóvedas, No 39-120, T660 0983. Modern rooms in nice old house. **C** *Las Tres Banderas*, C Cochera de Hobo, No 38-66, T660 0160. Very pleasant, quiet, good beds. Recommended. **D** *Hostal Santo Domingo*, C Santo Domingo, No 33-46. Basic but quiet, well located. Recommended. **D** *Veracruz*, C San Agustín, No 6-15, opposite San Agustín church. More with a/c, safe, helpful but noisy disco on ground floor.

In La Matuna and Getsemaní AL *Monterrey*, Paseo de los Martires Cra 8 B, No 25-103, T664 8560, F664 8574, htlmonterreyctg@ctgred.net.co Terrace bar, business centre, jacuzzi, a/c, good. **B** *Del Lago*, C 34, No 11-15, T664 0111. A/c, phone, no singles, reasonable restaurant, laundry, credit cards accepted, no parking. **B** *Montecarlo*, C 34, No 10-16, T664 0115. A/c, safe, quiet, good location, fair restaurant, expensive breakfast.

On **Calle Media Luna** there are several hotels, many of the cheaper ones are brothels; area not advisable for women on their own. **D** *Hostal Baluarte*, Media Luna No 10-81, T664 2208. Fan, converted colonial house, family run, helpful, will arrange day trips, well-priced restaurant. **E** *Doral*, Media Luna, No 10-46, T664 1706. Nice, fan, large rooms but avoid ground floor, safe courtyard where you can park cycles/motorbikes, English spoken. **E** *Holiday*, Media Luna, No 10-47, T664 0948. Fan, quiet, pleasant courtyard, luggage store, hot water. Recommended. **E** *Punta Arena*, opposite *Familiar*. Family run. **E** *Casa Viena*, C San Andrés, No 30-53, T664 6242, www.casaviena.com Cheaper in dormitory, run by Hans and Janeth, cooking facilities, washing machine, book exchange, internet service (US$2.60 per hour), good value. **F** *El Refugio*, C Media Luna 10-35, T664 3507. Basic but safe and quiet

On the road to the airport are several hotels and *pensiones*, particularly at Marbella beach, eg **D** *Bellavista*, Av Santander. Fans, nice patio, English-speaking, Enrique Sedó, secure, nice atmosphere. Recommended for longer stays. Right behind is **F** *Mirador del Lago*. Large rooms, fan. **F** *Turístico Margie*, Av 2A, 63-175, Crespo district. Convenient for airport, walking distance to old city (or bus), family-run, modern. Southeast of the city is **E** *Santa María de los Angeles*, Pie de La Popa, Camino Arriba No 22-109, T669 2149. Run by Anglican church next door, simple, safe, *cafetería*, parking.

Youth hostel **E** *Costa del Sol*, Cra 1 y C 9, Bocagrande, T665 0844, F665 3755. 280 beds, in tower block opposite beach.

Camping On the beach is not secure. Vehicle parking overnight possible at the Costa Norte Beach Club, 2 km northeast on coast beyond the airport, US$4 per night.

Eating

Bocagrande *Italia*, Av San Martín 7-55. Good Italian, excellent ice creams and sorbets. *Palacio de las Frutas*, Av San Martín y C 6. Good *comida corrida*. *La Fonda Antioqueña*, Cra 2, No 6-161. Traditional Colombian, nice atmosphere. *Pietros*, Cra 3, No 4-101. Italian and local dishes. *Farah Express*, Cra 2 y C 9. Arab food, good, popular, also vegetarian dishes, open late, good value. *Coffee Bean Shop*, Cra 2 y C 6. Coffee, drinks, snacks, internet US$3 per hour. Cheap, good cafetería in *Carulla* supermarket, Av San Martín. Good reasonably priced food in the chain restaurants, eg *Crepes y Waffles*.

Centro and San Diego Several good establishments on Plaza Santo Domingo: *San Bernabe*, reasonable food, open till late. *Café de la Plaza*, great atmosphere, open all day. *Dalmacia*, just off plaza, run by Croatians, good, closes 1800. *El Burlador de Sevilla*, C Santo Domingo 33-88, T660 0866. Spanish, open 1200-2400, busy at weekends. *La Tablada*, C de la Tablada 7-46. Arty, cheap meals, good music, gay bar at night. *Café del Casa Santísimo*, C Santísimo 8-19, T664 3316. Quiet, attractive, good salads and sandwiches. *Nautilus*, C 37, No 10-76, San Diego. Facing statue of La India Catalina, good seafood. *El Mar de Jean*, on plaza opposite *Santa Clara* hotel. Seafood only, fine service and décor. Recommended. *Dragón de Oro*, Av Venezuela 10-24. Chinese, good, inexpensive. *Bodegón de la Candelaria*, C de las Damas 3-64, T664 7251. Good fish menu, a/c, good value, open for lunch daily, dinner Mon-Sat. *La Vitrola*, C Baloco 2-01, T664 8243. High quality, some Caribbean dishes, popular, expensive. *Capilla del Mar*, Callejón de los Estribos 2-74, T660 1129.

Colombia

Excellent seafood. Recommended. *La Escollera de la Marina*, C Santa Teresa y Ricaurte, T664 2040. Spanish, bar and disco. *La Fogacha*, C de la Mantilla y C de la Factoría 3-37, T664 9099. Italian, cheap but good, open daily 1000-2400. *San Pedro*, Plaza de San Pedro Claver. Tables outsisde, a/c inside, Asian and fish specialities, good value. Recommended.

Getsemaní and La Matuna *Nuevo Mundo*, Media Luna near plaza. Chinese, big portions, good typical menu, cheap, good value. *Café-Galería Abaloa*, C Espíritu Santo, No 29-200, Getsemaní. Quiet, cultural ambience, books, music etc, drinks, breakfasts, vegetarian dishes, also has 3 cheap rooms. *El Koral*, next to *Hotel Doral*, Media Luna. Good, cheap. *El Ganadero*, also on Media Luna. Good value. Many restaurants around Plaza Independencia and near C San Andrés/C Magdalena have good value meals.

Outside the centre *Bucarest*, Marbella, next to *Hotel Bellavista*. For seafood and juices. *Club de Pesca*, San Sebastián de Pastelillo fort, Manga island, T660 5863. Wonderful setting, excellent fish and seafood. Warmly recommended. *La Fragata*, C Real del Cabrera 41-15, T664 8734, next to *Casa de Rafael Núñez*. Very good seafood.

Vegetarian *Tienda Naturista*, C Quero 9-09. Good, cheap. *Govinda*, Plaza de los Coches 7-15. Good set meal US$2.50. *Girasoles*, C de Quero y C de los Puntales. Good. *Panadería La Mejor*, Av Arbeláez. Good for breakfast, fine wholemeal bread, coffee, yoghurt, expensive.

Local specialities At cafés try the *patacón*, a biscuit made of green banana, mashed and baked; also in Parque del Centenario in early morning. At restaurants ask for *sancocho*, a local soup of the day of vegetables and fish or meat. Also try *obleas* for a snack, biscuits with jam, cream cheese, or *ariquipe* (caramel fudge), and *buñuelos*, deep-fried cheese dough balls.

Entertainment

Discos Good discos in Bocagrande eg *La Escollera*. Bar *La Muralla* on the city wall west of Plaza Bolívar, open at night only, live music at weekends, romantic, but drinks expensive. *Quiebra Canto*, Parque Independencia, next to *Hotel Monterrey*, 2nd floor, good salsa, nice atmosphere. Also popular for salsa, *Tu Candela*, 2nd floor bar near Portón de los Dulces and Plaza de la Aduana. Several good bars and discos along Playa del Arsenal, Getsemaní.

Festivals *La Candelaria*, see La Popa. *Independence* celebrations, second week of **Nov**: men and women in masks and fancy dress roam the streets, dancing to the sound of *maracas* and drums. There are beauty contests, battles of flowers and general mayhem. This festival tends to be wild and can be dangerous. *Caribbean Music Festival* (most years) for several days in **Mar**, groups from all over the Caribbean region and beyond perform salsa, reggae, etc; loud and fun. There is an *international film festival* 2nd week of **Mar**. www.festicinecartagena.com

Shopping A good selection of *artesanías* at *Compendium* on Plaza Bolívar, but in general (except for leather goods) shopping is much better in Bogotá. Handicraft shops in the Plaza de las Bóvedas are good and have the best selection in Cartagena. Woollen *blusas* are good value. Try the *Tropicano* in Pierino Gallo building in Bocagrande. Also in this building are reputable jewellery shops. A number of jewellery shops near Plaza de Bolívar in Centro, emeralds a speciality (cheaper in Bogotá). *Centro Comercial Getsemaní*, C Larga between San Juan and Plaza de la Independencia, a large shopping centre, has many establishments. *Magali París*, Av Venezuela y C del Boquete, is an a/c supermarket, with *cafetería*.

Bookshop *Librería Bitacura*, Av San Martín 7-187, also in San Pedro Claver in the old city. English and Spanish books, second hand exchange, run by a friendly lady. *Librería Nacional*, Cra 7, No 36-27.

Sport **Bullfights**: take place mainly in Jan and Feb in the new Plaza de Toros at the Villa Olímpica on Av Pedro de Heredia, away from the centre, T669 8225. The old, wooden Plaza de Toros (in San Diego, see map) is a fine structure, but is no longer in use. **Yachting**: *Club Náutica*, Av Miramar, Isla Manga across the Puente Román, T660 5582, good for opportunities to crew or finding a lift to other parts of the Caribbean. Windsurf rental, Bocagrande, US$6.50 per hour. **Diving**: *Eco Buzos*, Edif Alonso de Ojeda, Local 102, El Laguito, Bocagrande, T/F655 1129. 2 dives including all equipment US$75, a 5-day course plus dives about US$140, snorkelling US$35, also snacks and drinks. *La Tortuga Dive Shop*, Edif Marina del Rey, 2-23 Av del

Retorno, Bocagrande, T/F665 6995. 2 dives US$70. Faster boat, which allows trips to Isla Barú as well as Los Rosarios, same price at *Hotel Caribe Dive shop*, T665 3517, though discounts are sometimes available if you book via the hotels, enquire. Recompression chamber at the naval hospital, Bocagrande. **Motorbikes**: cycles, scooters and rollerblades rented by *S&S Aquiler de Vehículos de Sport*, Av San Martín, No 9-184, T/F665 5342. Clients who own the *South American Handbook* will get a 30% discount.

Local Bus: within the city large buses (with no glass in windows) cost US$0.20 (a/c buses US$0.50; green and white *Metrocar* to all points recommended). **Taxi**: from Bocagrande to the centre US$1.50; for airport, see below. Try to fix price before committing yourself. A horse-drawn carriage can be hired for US$12.50, opposite *Hotel El Dorado*, Av San Martín, in Bocagrande, to ride into town at night (romantic but rather short ride). Also, a trip around the walled city, up to 4 people, US$12.50, from Puerta del Reloj.

Transport

Long distance Air Crespo airport, 1½ km from the city, reached by local buses from Blas de Lezo, southwest corner of inner wall. Bus from one block from airport to Plaza San Francisco US$0.20. Taxi to Bocagrande US$4, to town US$3 (official prices). Good self-service restaurant. *Casa de cambio* open 0830-2400 cashes TCs but not *Bank of America*. Better rates in town. For information, ask at travel agents offices on upper level. Daily flights to all main cities. To San Andrés, *Avianca* T665 6102 and *AeroRepública* T665 8495. From Dec to Mar flights can be overbooked; even reconfirming and turning up 2 hrs early doesn't guarantee a seat; best not to book a seat on the last plane of the day.

Bus New bus terminal is 30 mins from town on the road to Barranquilla, taxi US$4.50, or take city buses 'Terminal de Transportes', US$0.60.

Pullman bus from Cartagena to **Medellín** 665 km, US$31 (*Brasilia*, or *Rápidos Ochoa*, slightly cheaper, recommended). Several buses a day, but book early (2 days in advance at holiday times), takes 13-16 hrs. To **Santa Marta**, US$9 (with *Brasilia*, C 32, No 20D-55), 4 hrs, also cheaper lines, US$8. To **Barranquilla** US$5 with *Transportes Cartagena*, 3 hrs, or US$6 with *Expreso Brasilia* Pullman, 2 hrs. To/from **Bogotá** via Barranquilla and Bucaramanga with *Expreso Brasilia* Pullman or *Copetran*, 8 a day, US$35-46 (shop around), minimum 19 hrs (may take up to 28), depending on number of check-points. To **Magangué** on the Magdalena US$12, 4 hrs with *Brasilia*; to **Mompós**, *Unitransco*, 0530, 12 hrs including ferry crossing from Magangué, US$17. To **Valledupar** with *Expreso Brasilia*, Pullman US$13 (with a 30 mins stop in Barranquilla), for Sierra Nevada and Pueblo Bello. To **Riohacha**, US$12. Bus to **Maicao** on Venezuelan border US$18 (with *Expreso Auto Pullman*, *Expreso Brasilia* at 2000, or *Unitrasco*), 12 hrs; the road is in good condition.

Shipping There are boats leaving most days for points south along the coast, for example to Turbo cargo boats take 24 hrs, all in cost about US$25 pp. You can also go on up the Río Sinú to Montería, and up the Atrato as far as Quibdó. For the trip to Quibdó see page 849. Get full independent advice before making direct arrangements with boat owners or captains.

Banks *Banco Unión Colombiana*, Av Venezuela (C 35), No 10-26, La Matuna, changes American Express and Thomas Cook TCs. *Bancolombia*, good rates for TCs. *Bancafé*, gives money on Visa cards, both on Av Venezuela. *Banco Sudameris*, opposite conference centre, for Visa cash advances. *Lloyds TSB Bank*, C Baloco, No 2-76, and office in Bocagrande, Cra 2, No 6-33. *Citibank*, Centro Plazoleta, Av Venezuela, for MasterCard ATM. Many other ATMs in the centre and Bocagrande including supermarkets, eg *Carulla*. Also *A Toda Hora*, for Visa and MasterCard on Av Venezuela. There are *cambios* in the arcade at Torre Reloj and adjoining streets which change Amex TCs. Also *Caja de Cambio Caldas*, Av San Martín, No 4-118, Bocagrande. Never change money on the street. TCs can be changed Sat morning (arrive early) at *Joyería Mora*, Román 5-39, and at El Portal nearby, in the old city. **Communications** Internet: *Cyber Café* at C de las Palmas 3-102. *CaribeNet*, C Santo Domingo 3-54, T664 2326 ctg.caribenet.com Good service. *The Verge*, next to the Club Náutica (see above), Mon-Fri 0900-1230, 1400-1700 and Sat morning, sailing information available. Also at Hotel *Casa Viena* (see under Sleeping). Many others around town, cost generally about US$4 per hr. **Post Office:** in Avianca office near cathedral, open Mon-Fri 0800-1830, Sat 0800-1500. **Telecom:** Av

Directory

Urdaneta Arbeláez near corner of C 34; long distance phones behind this building; long distance also in Bocagrande. **Embassies and consulates** Panamanian Consulate, C 69, No 4-97, Crespo, T666 2079. **Venezuela**, Cra 3, No 8-129, Edif Centro Ejecutivo, of 1402, Bocagrande, T665 0382, F665 0449, cvenezuela@ctgred.net.com Open to 1500, possible to get a visa the same day (US$30): you need onward ticket, 2 photos, but ensure you get a full visa not a 72-hr transit, unless that is all you need. **Security** Carry your passport, or a photocopy, at all times. Failure to present it on police request can result in imprisonment and fines. Generally, central areas are safe and friendly (although Getsemaní is less secure, especially at night), but should you require the police, there is a station in Barrio Manga. Beware of drug pushers on the beaches, pickpockets in crowded areas and bag/camera snatchers on quiet Sun mornings. At the bus station, do not be pressurized into a hotel recommendation different from your own choice. On the street, do not be tempted by offers of jobs or passages aboard ship: jobs should have full documentation from the Seamen's Union office. Passages should only be bought at a recognized shipping agency. **Tourist office** lin the *Centro Internacional de Convenciones*, Salón Pórtico, Cra 8, Getsemaní, T660 2418, F660 2415, maps and general information. **Proturismo**, Muelle Turístico, 2nd floor, limited information, map, price guide. *Avianca* office has a map and guide. **Useful addresses DAS:** just beyond Castillo San Felipe, behind the church (ask), Plaza de la Ermita (Pie de la Popa), T666 4649, helpful. DAS passport office is in C Castelbondo, near Plaza de la Artillería. Get your 1-month visa extension here; it is free. **MA** (national parks office), C4, No 3-204, Bocagrande, 0800-1200, 1400-1800.

North of Cartagena The little fishing village of **La Boquilla**, northeast of Cartagena, is near the end of a sandy promontory between the Ciénaga de Tesca and the Caribbean, about 20 minutes past the airport. There is a camping area with an attractive pool surrounded by palm trees and parrots, entrance US$2. There is a good beach nearby, busy at weekends but quiet during the week. On Saturday and Sunday nights people dance the local dances. Visit the mangrove swamps nearby to see the birds, US$10 for 3 hour trip. Golf courses are under development here. **L** *Las Americas Beach Resort*, T664 4000. **E** *Los Morros* (clean, good food) and campsite, good, clean, showers, restaurant and small market, tents rented with mattresses. Go there by taxi, US$3 (there is a reasonable bus service).

A good road continues beyond La Boquilla. On the coast, 50 km northeast, is **Galerazamba**, no accommodation but good local food. Nearby are the clay baths of **Volcán del Totumo**, in beautiful surroundings. The crater is about 20 m high and the mud lake, at a comfortable temperature, 10 m across, is reputed to be over 500 m deep. Entrance US$1; a bathe will cost you US$2, masseurs available for a small extra fee. ■ *Bus from Cartagena to Galerazamba, US$1.50, 2 hrs, ask to be dropped off at Lomo Arena and walk 2 km along the main road to a right turn signposted 'Volcán del Totumo', 1½ km along a poor road. Hitching possible. Tours from Cartagena.*

Islas del Rosario
These islands are part of a coral reef, low-lying, densely vegetated, with narrow strips of fine sand beaches

The **Parque Nacional Corales del Rosario** embraces the archipelago of Rosario (a group of 30 coral islets 45 km southwest of the Bay of Cartagena), the San Bernardo (see below) and the mangrove coast of the long island of Barú to its furthest tip. Isla Grande and some of the smaller islets are easily accessible by day trippers. Permits from *MA* in Cartagena or Bogotá are needed for the rest, US$2 entrance fee. Rosario (the best conserved) and Tesoro both have small lakes, some of which connect to the sea. There is an incredible profusion of aquatic and birdlife. An Aquarium in the sea is worth visiting, US$5, not included in boat fares (check that it's open before setting out). Many of the smaller islets are privately owned. Apart from fish and coconuts, everything is imported from the mainland, fresh water included. *Hotel Caribe* in Bocagrande has scuba lessons in its pool and diving at its resort on Isla Grande, US$230 and up. *MA* Diving permit costs US$13.

Transport Travel agencies and the hotels offer launch excursions from the Muelle Turístico, leaving 0700-0900 and returning 1600-1700, costing from US$10 to US$25, lunch included; free if staying at one of the hotels. Overnight trips can be arranged through agencies but they are overpriced. Do not buy tours from touts. Note that there is an additional 'port tax' of US$2 payable at the entrance to the *Muelle* or on the boat. Book in advance. Recommended are *Excursiones Roberto Lemaitre*, C 8, No 4-66, Bocagrande, T665 2872 (owner of *Club Isla del Pirata*). They have the best boats and are near the top end of the price range. *Yates Alcatraz* are more economical; enquire at the quay. For five or more, try hiring your own boat for the day and bargain for around US$10 pp.

Before going by road south of Cartagena, check for the latest information on security. The highway south towards Medellín goes through **Turbaco**, 24 km (Botanical Garden, 1½ km before village on the left, open Tue-Sun 0900-1600, student guides), **Malagana**, 60 km (**F** *Res Margarita*, fan, basic) and **San Jacinto**, 90 km (**F** *Hospedaje Bolívar*, no sign, at turn off by petrol station, simple, showers, parking, good food at *El Llanero* next door; bus from Cartagena US$5), where local craft work, such as hand woven hammocks are made.

The capital of Sucre Department, **Sincelejo**, is a cattle centre, a hot, dusty town, with frequent power cuts. The dangerous bull-ring game in January is similar to the San Fermín festivities in Pamplona, Spain, in which bulls and men chase each other. At Easter is the 'Fiesta del Burro' where people dress up donkeys and prizes go to the best and the funniest (a big party for three days). There are various hotels (**B-E**) and restaurants.

On the coast, 35 km northwest of Sincelejo is **Tolú**, a fast developing holiday town popular for its offshore islands and diving. From Cartagena, the best approach is south from Malagana through San Onofre. This is also an easier and safer way for cyclists. From Tolú, a good trip is by boat three hours to Múcura island in the **Islas de San Bernardo**, about US$15 (details from *MA* sub-office in Tolú, or in Cartagena). If camping, take your own supplies. Trips to the mangrove lagoons also recommended. A good agency is *Mar Adentro*, Av La Playa 11-30, T288 5481, another is *Club Náutico Los Delfines*, Av 1A, No 11-08, T288 5202, daily tours to San Bernardo Islands 0800, back 1600, including aquarium on Isla Palma. There are better beaches at **Coveñas**, 20 km further southwest (several *cabañas* on the beach and hotels). This is the terminal of the oil pipeline from the oilfields in the Venezuelan border area. Buses and *colectivos* from Tolú. ■ *Colectivo Sincelejo-Tolú, or direct from Cartagena, several morning buses, 4 hrs, US$7. Also to Medellín with* Rápido Ochoa *and* Brasilia *1100 and 1800, 10 hrs, US$24.*

Sleeping and eating in Tolú B *Alcira*, Av La Playa 21-40, T288 5334, F 288 5036. Less off-season, a/c, TV, restaurant, pleasant. **C** *Ibatama*, Av La Playa 19-45, T288 5159, T/F288 5150. Comfortable, a/c, patio, restaurant. **E** *Darimar*, C 17, No 1-60, T288 5153. With bath, fan. **F** *El Turista*, Av La Playa, No 11-68, T288 5145. With bath, basic, restaurant, best value. Many others. *El Zaguán Paisa*, on Plaza, good *comidas*, open late; other places to eat nearby eg *Cafetería* on corner of Plaza, good cakes.

The main road south from Sincelejo passes **Caucasia** (194 km from Sincelejo, *Altitude*: 50 m), a convenient stopping place between Cartagena and Medellín. Visit the Jardín Botánico (entry US$0.25). ■ *From Caucasia to Medellín US$13, 7 hrs; to Cartagena US$19, 6 hrs.*

Sleeping D *Colonial*, Cra 2, No 20-68, T/F822 7461. Pleasant, a/c, cheaper with fan, good view of river. Good value. **E** *Residencias San Francisco*, Cra 49 y C 45. With bath, good value. **F** *Del Río*, T822 6666. With bath, a/c close to bus station, free morning coffee but avoid front rooms on street. **F** *Residencia El Viajero*, Cra 2, No 23-39, near centre. Quiet, fan.

Montería the capital of Córdoba Department, on the east bank of the Río Sinú, can be reached from Cartagena by air, by river boat, or from the main highway to Medellín. It is the centre of a cattle and agricultural area. It has one fine church, picturesque street life and extremely friendly people. It is hot here, average temperature 28°C ■ *Daily flights to Bogotá, Barranquilla and Cartagena. Buses from Cartagena, US$12, 5 hrs, with* Brasilia, *has own terminal in Montería, or colectivo, US$11, 5 hrs.*

Colombia

Sleeping **A** *Sinú*, Cra 3, C 31 y 32, T782 3355, F782 3980. A/c, swimming pool, TV, restaurant. **D** *Alcázar*, Cra 2, No 32-17, T782 4900. Comfortable, restaurant. **F** *Brasilia*. Good value. Also many cheap dives around.

Colombia to Panama

Turbo

Population: 127,000
Phone code 94
Colour map 1, grid A2

On the Gulf of Urabá is the port of **Turbo**, now a centre of banana cultivation, which is booming. It is a rough border community. **Before going to Turbo, or contemplating crossing Darién by land, please see below.**

Sleeping **D** *Castillo de Oro*, T827 2185. Best, reliable water and electricity, good restaurant. **D** *Playa Mar*, T827 2205. Good, but somewhat run down. **D** *Sausa*, helpful owners, pleasant dining room, water problems. **F** *Residencia Sandra*. Good. **F** *Residencia Turbo*, Cra 78, No 20-76, T827 2693. Good. **F** *Residencia Marcela*. Quiet, secure, best value. **F** *Residencia El Golfo*. Good.

Security: In 2002 travelling by road from Turbo to Santa Fé de Antioquia was not recommended

Transport **Air**: daily flights to Medellín, local services to Caribbean and Pacific resorts. **Buses**: from Cartagena and from Medellín (6 a day, 10 hrs, US$17; to Montería, 8 hrs, US$10, bad road, checkpoints). **Boats**: available to Cartagena and up the Río Atrato to Quibdó, but services are intermittent, unreliable and dangerous.

Directory **Banks**: *Banco Ganadero* and others (ATMs available) but no banks are open for exchange of TCs on Mon or Tue; try exchanging money in stores. **Useful addresses**: *DAS*: Postadero Naval, north of town just before the airport, take transport along Cra 13, open 0800-1630. **Useful services**: MA: for information on *Parque Nacional Los Katíos*, office 1 km along the road to Medellín.

Border with Panama

Colombian pesos are impossible to change at fair rates in Panama

There are various routes involving sea and land crossings around or through the **Darién Gap**, which still lacks a road connection linking the Panamanian Isthmus and South America. Detailed descriptions of these routes are given in the *Central America and Mexico Handbook* and the *Colombia Handbook*. While maps of the region are available, there is no substitute for seeking informed local advice. In all cases, it is essential to be able to speak Spanish.

Warning

Latest information from Colombia (mid 2002) is that armed groups, hostile to travellers including tourists, are particularly active in the northwest corner of Colombia which includes the area on the Colombian and Panamanian sides of the border. If information has not improved before you set out to cross Darién by land either way, you are advised not to go. This warning includes visits to Los Katíos National Park, the road south of Turbo to Dabeiba and all of Chocó Department.

Colombian immigration **DAS Office**: see under Turbo. If going from Colombia to Panama via Turbo you should get an exit stamp from the DAS office. There is also a DAS office in Capurganá (see below), opposite *Hotel Uvita* (which is by the harbour), and a Panamanian consulate, but best not to leave it that late. If leaving Colombia, check the facts at any DAS office.
   Entering Colombia Arriving from Panama, go to the DAS in Turbo for your entry stamp. Stamps from other DAS offices are not accepted. A police stamp is no substitute, though can help.
   Entering Panama Panamanian immigration at Puerto Obaldía will check all baggage for drugs and may ask for evidence of adequate funds for your stay: US$400, travellers' cheques or credit card. A ticket out of Panama is required, although a ticket from another Central American country may do.

Transport **Colombia to Panama** The simplest way is to fly from Barranquilla, Bogotá, Cali, Cartagena, Medellín or San Andrés. **Sea**: Ask on the spot in Cartagena and in Colón if you wish to transport a vehicle between the two countries. Foot passengers may be able to travel on

Colombia

reputable cargo boats, but you must arrange with the captain the price and destination before departure. Small, irregular boats may well be contraband or arms runners and should not be used.

Boat On the Caribbean side, the starting point is Turbo from where boats sail to Acandí, Capurganá and Zapzurro (all in Colombia) and Puerto Obaldía (Panama). **Acandí** (*Population*: about 7,000. *Phone code*: 9816), has several *residencias*. Most have their own electricity generators. A little further north is **Capurganá**, now a small but growing tourist resort with several hotels ranging from **AL** to **E** in price. Across the Panamanian border, **E** *Residencial Cande*, in Puerto Obaldía is good, with meals.

Crossing Darién: Caribbean side

Transport Boats normally leave Turbo at 0900 daily, US$17, for Capurganá and/or Acandí, 3 hrs. Enquire for the best passage. There are also cargo boats from Cartagena to Capurganá which take passengers, 30-50 rough hrs, US$25-30, take hammock. From Puerto Obaldía (see above on immigration), boats go to Porvenir (San Blas Islands) or Colón, planes to Panama City (daily except Sun).

Overland from Turbo Two main alternative routes cross the central Gap to Paya, from where there is a well-trodden route to Yaviza: Paya-Púcuro, six hours on foot; Púcuro-Boca de Cupe, by dugout, US$20-50; Boca de Cupe-Pinogana, also by dugout, US$15 per person, plus a walk, two hours in all; Pinogana-Yaviza, walk and ferries/dugouts. From Yaviza (one hotel, **E** *Tres Américas*, basic) buses can be caught to Panama City, US$15, 10-14 hours, road subject to wash-outs. Alternatively you may be able to get a boat from Paya to Boca del Cupe and on to El Real, which has an airstrip for flights to Panama.

One route to Paya: take a boat from Turbo across the Gulf of Urabá into the Río Tarena to **Unguía**, which has a couple of *residenciales* and basic restaurants. From here it is three to four hours to the border, then three hours to the Río Paya. You then hike down the Río Paya through dense jungle to Paya itself (about 12 hours). Do not attempt the Unguía-Paya route without a guide.

The other main route to Paya, by motorboat from Turbo across the Bahía de Colombia, through the Great Atrato Swamp and up the Río Atrato (much birdlife to be seen), is not recommended. At Travesía, also called Puente América, and the next river port, Bijao, prices are exorbitant and there is strong anti-gringo feeling. Beyond Bijao you have to go through Los Katíos National Park, which is closed, and all MA posts have been abandoned. 7-8 hours through the Park on foot is Palo de las Letras, the frontier stone, from where it is 4-6 hours to Paya. A guide, if you can find one, is essential. Approaching this route from Quibdó down the Río Atrato should not be attempted as there is severe rebel/paramilitary violence in Chocó (2002). It can be very difficult to get an entry stamp anywhere before Panama City on this route; try at every opportunity as hikers have been detained in the capital for not having an entry stamp. It may help to prove you have adequate funds for your stay.

The park, extending in Colombia to the Panamanian border, contains several waterfalls: Tilupo, 125m high; the water cascades down a series of rock staircases, surrounded by orchids and fantastic plants, Salto de La Tigra and Salto de La Tendal. A full day's hike goes to Alto de Limón for a fine view of primary forest. Also in the park are the Alto de la Guillermina, a mountain behind which is a strange forest of palms called 'mil pesos', and the Ciénagas de Tumaradó, with red monkeys, waterfowl and alligators. ■ *To visit the park, go first to the MA office in Turbo (see above) for information and entry permits. At present (mid-2002) it is closed.*

Los Katíos National Park

On the Pacific side, crossing into Panama involves travel by both boat and on foot, the quantity of each depending on the route chosen. Any routes through Chocó are not advised in 2002 because of violence and drug-running.

Crossing Darién: Pacific side

Colombia

Transport One sea route is from Bahía Solano or Juradó in Chocó Department. Launches go from both towns to Jaqué, 50 km north of the Colombian border (Juradó-Jaqué 4 hrs, US$25, very uncomfortable, take something soft to sit on), from where you can take a banana boat (US$12, plus an arbitrary tax) or fly (US$46) to Panamá City. Transport out of Jaqué is frustrating; you must obtain a DAS stamp in either Turbo or Buenaventura, without it you will have problems in Jaqué or Panama City.

Barranquilla

Phone code: 95
Colour map 1, grid A3
Population: 1,064,000

Colombia's fourth city lies on the western bank of the Río Magdalena, about 18 km from its mouth, which, through deepening and the clearing of silted sandbars, makes it a seaport (though less busy than Cartagena or Santa Marta) as well as a river port. Carnival, lasting four days, with parades, floats, street dancing and beauty contests, is one of the best in Latin America.

Barranquilla is a modern industrial city with a colourful, but polluted central area near the river, and a good residential area in the northwest, beyond C 53. The principal boulevard is **Paseo Bolívar**. The church of **San Nicolás**, formerly the Cathedral, stands on Plaza San Nicolás, the central square, and before it is a small statue of Columbus. The new **Catedral Metropolitana** is at Cra 45, No 53-120, opposite Plaza de la Paz. There is an impressive statue of Christ inside by the Colombian sculptor, Arenas Betancur. The commercial and shopping districts are round the Paseo Bolívar, a few blocks north of the old Cathedral, and in Av Murillo. The **market** is between Paseo Bolívar and the river, the so-called Zona Negra on a side channel of the Magdalena. Good parks in the northern areas include **Parque Tomás Suri Salcedo** on C 72. Stretching back into the northwestern heights overlooking the city are the modern suburbs of El Prado, Altos del Prado, Golf and Ciudad Jardín. There are five stadia in the city, a big covered coliseum for sports, two for football and the others cater for basketball and baseball. The metropolitan stadium is on Av Murillo, outside the city. The **Museo Romántico**, Cra 54, No 59-199, covers the history of Barranquilla with an interesting section on Carnival.

Regular buses from Paseo Bolívar and the church at C 33 y Cra 41 to the attractive bathing resort of **Puerto Colombia**, 19 km (US$0.60, 30 minutes). It has a pier built around 1900. The beach is clean and sandy and the water is a bit muddy. South along the Magdalena, 5 km from the city, is **Soledad** (*Population*: 16,000); around the cathedral are narrow, colonial streets.

Sleeping & eating

Hotel prices may be much higher during Carnival. Watch for thieves in downtown hotels

LL *El Prado*, Cra 54, No 70-10, T368 0111, F345 0019. Some distance from the centre, best, the social centre, swimming pool and tennis courts, good restaurant, sauna, original 1920s building is national monument, new annex behind. **A** *Royal*, Cra 54, No 68-124, T356 5533. Good service, swimming pool, modern. **C** *Capricornio*, Cra 44B, No 70-201, T356 5045. Good service, a/c. **C** *Colonial Inn*, C 42, No 43-131, T379 0241. With bath, TV, good cheap restaurant. **D** *Canadiense*, C 45, No 36-142. Fan, noisy but convenient for bus station 2 blocks away. **D** *Las Brisas*, C 61, No 46-41, T341 4107. TV, a little noisy but recommended. **E** *El Diamante*, C 41/Cra 39, T340 2924. With fan, TV room, laundry facilities. **E** *Olímpico*, Cra 42, No 33-20, T351 8310, F340 4750. With fan, TV, restaurant. Recommended.**E** *Victoria*, C 35, No 43-140. Downtown, large, scruffy rooms with fan. **F** *California*, C 32 y Cra 44. Pleasant but about to fall down, enjoy the chickens. **F** *Horizonte*, Cra 44, No 44-35, T341 7925. With bath, quiet, fan, safe.

La Puerta de Oro, C 35, No 41-100. Central, a/c good for meals (including breakfast). *El Huerto*, Cra 52, No 70-139. Good vegetarian. *Jardines de Confucio*, Cra 54, No 75-44. Good Chinese food, nice atmosphere. *La Ollita*, Cra 53, No 55-10. Good local dishes. Various Lebanese with belly-dancers; several Chinese and *pizzerías*, including *La Pizza Loca*, Cra 53, No 70-97. Many places, for all tastes and budgets, on C 70 from *Hotel El Prado* towards Cra 42. At C 70 y 44B are several *estaderos*, bars with snacks and verandas.

Bookshop *Librería Nacional*, Cra 53, No 75-129. English, French and German books. **Market** San Andrecito, or Tourist Market, Vía 40, is where smuggled goods are sold at very competitive prices; a good place to buy film. Picturesque and reasonably safe. Any taxi driver will take you there.

Taxi within the town cost US$1.25 (eg downtown to northern suburbs).

Air Ernesto Cortissoz airport is 10 km from the city. Daily flights to **Bogotá**, **Cali**, **Cartagena**, **Cúcuta**, **Medellín** and **Bucaramanga**. Less frequent flights to San Andrés, Apartadó and Montería. International flights to **Aruba**, **Curaçao**, **Maracaibo**, **Miami** and **Panama City**. City bus from airport to town, US$0.35 (US$0.40 on Sun). Taxi to town, US$6 (taxis do not have meters, fix fare in advance). To town, take only buses marked 'centro' from 200 m to right when leaving airport; the bus to the airport (marked Malambo) leaves from Cra 44 up C 32 to Cra 38, then up C 30 to Airport. Taxi to Cartagena, US$40. *Avianca/SAM*, C 72, No 57-79, T345 4355/345 6207.

Bus The main bus terminal is south of the city near the Circunvalación. Some bus companies have offices around C 34 and Cra 45. Take a bus marked 'Terminal' along C 45. To **Santa Marta**, US$3.25, Pullman (less in non-a/c, *Coolibertador*), about 2 hrs, also direct to Santa Marta's Rodadero beach. To **Valledupar**, 6 hrs, US$10. To **Montería**, US$11, 8 hrs. To **Medellín** by Pullman, 16 hrs. To **Bucaramanga**, US$27 with *Copetran*, a/c, first class, departures at 1130 most days, 9 hrs. To **Bogotá**, 20-24 hrs, US$45 direct. To **Caucasia**, US$17, 11 hrs. To **Maicao**, US$14.50, 5 hrs (with *Brasilia*, every 30 mins from 0100-1200). To **Cartagena**, 3 grades of bus, 3 hrs (US$5 with *Transportes Cartagena*, US$6 with *Expreso Brasilia*, by Brasilia Van Tours mini-bus, from their downtown offices as well as the bus terminals), 2 hrs by colectivo US$7.

Shipping See Warning under Cartagena (page 820) regarding jobs and passages aboard ship. If shipping a car into Barranquilla allow 2 days to complete paperwork to retrieve your car from the port, unless you have a *carnet de passages*, which will make it a good deal easier.

Banks *Bancolombia*, *Banco de Bogotá*, etc, and many ATMs. *Casa de cambio El Cacique*, C 34, No 43-108, T332 6392, reliable. *Lloyds TSB Bank*, Cra 52, No 72-131, T368 6876 and 1 agency. **Communications** Post Office: in Plaza Bolívar. **Embassies and consulates** Finland, Vía 40 de las Flores, Cementos del Caribe, T335 0080. **Germany**, C 80, No 78B-251, T353 2078. **Netherlands**, Cra 42H, No 85-33, T334 1282. **Norway**, C 72, No 57-33, T358 1043. **Spain**, Cra 34, No 93-43, T357 0664. **USA**, Centro Comercial Mayorista, C 77, No 68-15, opposite zoo (Apdo Aéreo 51565), T345 7088 or 345 7181 (visas obtainable only in Bogotá). **Venezuela**, Cra 5, No 68-24, TF358 0048, 0800-1500 (take 'Caldas/Recreo' or 'Boston/Boston' bus), visa issued same day, but you must be there by 0915 with photo and US$30 cash; onward ticket may be requested. **Tourist office** Cra 54, No 75-45, T345 4458. Tourist information is available at main hotels and at C 72, No 57-43, of 401, T333 6658. Maps from Instituto Agustín Codazzi, C 36, No 45-101. **Useful addresses** DAS: C 54, No 41-133, T341 1411. **Police:** (for declarations of theft, etc), Policia F2, C 47 y Cra 43.

Santa Marta

The capital of Magdalena Department is the third biggest Caribbean port, at the mouth of the Río Manzanares. It is best reached from Barranquilla by the paved road along the coast, which passes salt pans and skirts an extensive and intriguing lagoon, the Ciénaga de Santa Marta (see below). There is a paved road south to Bucaramanga (see page 806) and Bogotá.

Phone code: 95
Colour map 1, grid A3
Population: 309,000
96 km E of Barranquilla

Santa Marta, founded in 1525 by Rodrigo de Bastidas, was the first town founded by the *conquistadores* in Colombia. Most of the famous sea-dogs – the brothers Côte, Drake and Hawkins – sacked the city in spite of the forts built on the mainland and a small island at the entrance to the bay. It was here that Simón Bolívar, his dream of Gran Colombia shattered, came to die. Almost penniless, he was given hospitality at the *hacienda* of San Pedro Alejandrino, see below. He died on 17 December 1830, at the age of 47 from tuberculosis, and was buried in the Cathedral, but his body was taken to the Pantheon at Caracas 12 years later.

Colombia

Santa Marta lies on a deep bay with high shelving cliffs to the north and south. The climate ranges seasonally from hot and trying to hot but pleasant in February and March. Occasionally one can see the snow-clad peaks of the Sierra Nevada to the east, less than 50 km away. The city's promenade offers good views of the bay and is lined with restaurants, accommodation and nightlife. The main shops and banks are on Cra 5.

Casa de la Aduana, C 14 y Cra 2, displays an excellent archaeological collection, including precolombian gold artefacts; visit recommended before going to Ciudad Perdida. ■ *Tue-Sat, 0800-1200, 1400-1800, Sun 0800-1200, during the tourist season, Mon-Fri, 0800-1200, 1400-1800, the rest of the year; US$1.*

Quinta de San Pedro Alejandrino, a 17th century villa 5 km southeast of the city, has the simple room in which Simón Bolívar died with a few of his belongings. Other paintings and memorabilia of the period are on display. The villa is set in gardens and parkland with plenty of wildlife. This is an impressive memorial to the man most revered by the Colombians. ■ *Daily 0930-1630, US$2.50; take a bus or colectivo from the waterfront, Cra 1 C, in Santa Marta to Mamatoca and ask for the Quinta, US$0.25.*

Beaches Sandy beaches and headlands stretch all along this coast, surrounded by hills, green meadows and shady trees. The largest sandy bay is that of Santa Marta, with Punta Betín, a rocky promontory protecting the harbour to the north and a headland to the south. The rugged Isla El Morro lies 3 km off Santa Marta, topped by a lighthouse. **Playa El Rodadero** is the most fashionable and tourist-oriented beach, 4 km south of the city (local bus service, taxi, US$1.80). Many of the buses coming from Barranquilla and Cartagena stop at Rodadero on the way to Santa Marta.

Launches leave Rodadero beach every hour for the Aquarium, US$3 return (includes admission), last boat back 1600. From the Aquarium, it's a 10-minute walk to Playa Blanca where swimming is less crowded than elsewhere. Food is available at the beach. At Punta Betín, behind the harbour, there is a marine eco-system research centre run by Colombian and German universities. Ask for details at the **tourist office** in the former Convent of Santo Domingo, now Casa de Cultura, Cra 2, No 16-44, T423 3597. It has a library and art exhibitions. ■ *Open office hours Mon-Fri. Turcol*, which arranges trips and provides guide services (details in text), is at Cra 1C, No 20-15, T/F421 2256.

Colombia

Santa Marta

N

0 metres 200
0 yards 200

■ Sleeping		
1 Andrea Doria No 1	5 Hospedaría Casa Familiar	10 Residencia Nueva Granada
2 Bermuz	6 Hostal Bahía	11 Residencias El Titanic
3 Casa Vieja	7 Miramar	12 Residencias Bahía Blanca
4 Costa Azul	8 Panamerican	13 Sompallón
	9 Park	14 Yuldama

To Taganga
To Isla El Morro
Terminal Marítimo
Bahía de Santa Marta
Customs
Casa de la Aduana
Convento de Santo Domingo
Parque Bolívar
Avianca
Cathedral
Parque Santander
Parque San Miguel
To Rodadero, Airport & Ciénaga
To Riohacha & Parque Nacional Tayrona
To San Pedro Alejandrino
Av del Ferrocarril

For groups of 4 or more, ask about apartments for short rent. **In town** Av Rodrigo de Bastidas (Cra 1) has several seaside holiday hotels while Cra 2 and connecting Calles have many budget *residencias*. **A** *Yuldama*, Cra 1, No 12-19, T421 0063, F421 4932. Probably best in the city, a/c, reasonable food. **B** *Panamerican*, Cra 1, No 18-23, T421 1238, F421 4751. A/c or cheaper with fan, tidy, safe, nice atmosphere, good restaurant, holiday hotel. **C** *Hostal Bahía*, C 12, No 2-70, T423 0057. A/c, cheaper without, modern, plain, safe deposit. Recommended. **D** *Park*, Cra 1, No 18-67, T421 1215, F421 1574. On sea front, with shower, fan, reasonable, phone, popular with Colombians. **D** *Bermuz*, C 13, No 5-16, T421 0004, F421 3625. Good, also good vegetarian restaurant. **D** *Casa Vieja*, C 12, No 1-58, T421 4852. A/c, less with fan, good restaurant. **D** *Sompallón*, Cra 1, No 10B-57, T421 4195. Modern, with *pizzería* and *casa de cambio*. **D** *Andrea Doria No 1*, C 18, No 1C-90, T421 4329. With bath, fan, parking. **E** *Costa Azul*, C 17, No 2-09, T421 2236. Some rooms with a/c, fan, windows into courtyard. **E** *Hospedaría Casa Familiar*, C 10 C, No 2-14, T4211697. Bath, family-run. Highly recommended. **E** *Residencias Bahía Blanca*, Cra 1, No 11-13, T421 4439. With shower, fan, safe deposit, stores luggage. Recommended. **E** *Residencia Nueva Granada*, C 12, No 3-19. Old building with rooms round a pleasant courtyard. **F** *Residencias El Titanic*, C 10C, No 1C-68, T421 1947. Fan, basic, safe. **F** *Miramar*, C 10C, No 1C-59, T423 3276,2 blocks from beach. 'Gringo hotel', tends to be crowded, pretty basic but some nicer more expensive rooms, robberies have been reported, its popularity is mainly because it is cheap, motorbike parking, restaurant, can arrange trips.

At Rodadero Bay **AL** *Irotama*, Km 14, between airport and Rodadero Bay, T432 0600, F432 0077, www.irotama.com Own beach, full service, several restaurants, convention facilities, rooms, suites and bungalows. **AL** *Tamacá*, Cra 2, No 11A-98, T422 7015. Direct access to beach, fair rooms, casino, good service, fine pool. **C** *El Rodadero*, C 11, No 1-29, T422 7262, F422 7371. Swimming pool, English-speaking manageress, very helpful. **C** *La Riviera*, Cra 2, No 5-42, Apdo Aéreo 50-69. Small, safe, a/c. **C** *Edmar*, Cra 3, No 5-188, T422 7874. A/c, cafetería, welcoming. **D** *Tucuraca*, Cra 2, No 12-53, T422 7493. Fan, will store luggage. **Youth hostels**: *Hostería Tima Uraka*, C 18, No 2-59, T422 8433. Shared rooms, nice garden, owner speaks English. *Medellín*, C 19, No 1C-30, T422 0220.

Outside Santa Marta **G** pp *Carpe Diem*, 15 km from Santa Marta at 400 m. Ecological farm run by Belgians Mathias and Elsa, guests collected from *Miramar* and *Casa Familiar* (see above) Tue and Fri. Private rooms, dormitory and hammocks, meals US$1.50-2 extra, horses riding, hiking, river bathing, tours to precolumbian sites, kitchen, book exchange, Dutch, French and English spoken. Recommended.

In town *Yarimar*, Cra 1, No 26-37. Good seafood. *El Gran Wah Yuen*, C 14, No 3-74. Chinese *à la carte* and *comida corriente*, plenty of fresh vegetables. *Terraza Marina*, Cra 1, No 26-38, T423 1992. Very good fish, try the *bandeja*. *Café del Parque*, Parque de Bolívar next to Casa de la Aduana. Great place for coffee and snacks, try *café frappé* (with ice), closed Sun. *Cafetería del Calle*, Cra 3A, No 16-26. Good *empanadas*. Restaurant opposite Telecom (C 13, Cra 5), good menu and vegetarian dishes. *Merkabar*, C 10C, No 2-11. Family-run, pastas, great pancakes, good juices, good value, tourist advice. **At Rodadero Bay** *El Pibe*, C 6, No 1-26. Steaks, Argentine run. *Pez Caribe*, Cra 4, No 11-35. Seafood. *El Banano*, Cra 2, No 8-25, also Cra 2, No 7-38. Try their *carne asada con maduro* (banana) *y queso crema*, delicious. Many fast food restaurants, good juice kiosks and toasted snacks along the seafront promenades.

Diving: at Rodadero: *Tienda de Buceo* , C 8, No 2-21, p 2, T422 8179 (see also Taganga below).

Ricardo Olarté, C 22, No 16-61, T/F420 3413, has been recommended for the remoter areas of Parque Tayrona, Guajira and the Sierra Nevada de Santa Marta. For local tours: *Aviatur*, C 23, No 4-27, T421 3848. *Tierra Mar Aire*, C 15, No 2-60, T421 5161.

Air Simón Bolívar, 20 km south of city; bus, US$0.25, taxi from Santa Marta, US$6, from Rodadero, US$3. During the tourist season, get to the airport early and book well ahead.

Bus Terminal southeast of the city, towards Rodadero, minibus US$0.30; taxi US$1.50 to centre, US$3 to Rodadero. To **Bogotá**, 22 hrs, US$45, 4 a day; if going direct, ask for *Vía La Dorada*

Sleeping

If you arrive by bus, beware taxi drivers who take you to a hotel of their choice, not yours. The north end of town, in the port area, and areas near Rodadero beach are dangerous do not go there alone. Also beware of jungle tours, or boat trips to the islands sold by street touts

Eating

Sport

Tour operators
Ask about guides in hotels and tourist offices

Transport

Colombia

buses which go by the new road US$43, 15 hrs (*Brasilia* recommended). *Copetran* to **Bucaramanga** about 9 hrs, US$25. Journey time will be affected by the number of police checks. There is a good meal stop at Los Límites. Buses to **Barranquilla**, 2 hrs, US$3.25. To **Cartagena**, 4-5 hrs US$8, or US$10, *Brasilia*. To **Riohacha** US$6, 3 hrs. To **Maicao** US$12 a/c at 0500, also cheaper non a/c, 4-5 hrs. *Brasilia* runs a through bus to **Maracaibo**, schedule varies. There are 3 buses a day (*Brasilia*) direct to **Rodadero Beach** from Barranquilla, taking 2 hrs and costing US$2. They return to Barranquilla at 1300, 1530 and 1730.

Port Without a *carnet de passages*, it can take up to 4 working days to get a car out of the port, but it is usually well guarded and it is unlikely that anything will be stolen.

Directory **Airline offices** *Avianca/SAM*, C 17, No 2-76, T421 0276. **Banks** *Bancolombia*, C 13 y Cra 5, for Amex TC exchange, but in morning only. *Banco Santander*, C 14 y Cra 3A, advance on credit cards, closed Mon, slow. Quicker is *Banco Caja Social*, opposite. *Banco Ganadero/BBV*, *Banco Occidente* (good rates for MasterCard) in Plaza Bolívar. Plenty of cash machines. *Casas de cambio* in 3rd block of C 14. **Communications** Internet: *Cafenet Tayrona*, C12 1-59, US$3 per hr, open Mon-Sat 0800-2030, Sun 0800-1300, queues in the evening, free coffee. *Cybercafé* C 23, No 6-18, Local 39. Also at C 18, No 2-72. **Telephone:** *Telecom*, C 13, No 5-17. **Useful addresses** MA office, C 12, No 16D-05, T420 4504/6. DAS Office, Cra 8, No 26A-15, T423 1691/421 5205.

Around Santa Marta All types of water birds, plants and animals may be seen in the large lagoon of Ciénaga de Santa Marta. Cutting off the egress to the sea to build the coast road caused an ecological disaster. A National Environment Programme, funded with the help of Interamerican Development Bank, is working to reopen the canals and restore the area's fish and vegetation. There are several villages built on stilts in the lake. On the east shore of the lagoon is **Ciénaga** (*Population*: 75,000. Ciénaga is famous for *cumbia* music and holds a festival in January, *La Fiesta del Caiman*).

The birthplace of Gabriel García Márquez **Aracataca**, 60 km south of Ciénaga and 7 km before Fundación, is the birthplace of Gabriel García Márquez, fictionalized as Macondo in some of his stories (notably *100 Years of Solitude*). His home, now a modest museum, may be seen in the backyard of La Familia Iriarte Ahumada; it is 1½ blocks from the plaza, ask for directions. There are *residencias* (under US$3) and a restaurant (*El Fogonazo*, Cra 4, No 6-40, good, local menu), but it is better to stay in **Fundación**. *Caroli*, Cra 8, No 5-30, best.

Around Santa Marta

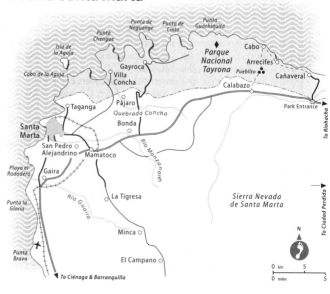

F *Fundación* (**E** with a/c). **E** *Centro del Viajero*, with a/c, good value; others at this price. ■ *Ciénaga-Fundación, US$1; Fundación-Aracataca, US$0.20; Santa Marta-Aracataca, US$2.50, 90 mins; Barranquilla via Ciénaga, US$2.50, via Río Magdalena ferry at Salamina, US$3.20.*

Close to Santa Marta (minibus US$0.30, taxi US$2.50, 15-20 minutes) is the fishing village and beach of **Taganga**. Swimming good, especially on Playa Grande, 25 minutes' walk round coast or US$2-3 by boat, but watch out for thieving. Taganga is quiet during week, but it is crowded on Sunday.

Sleeping A *La Ballena Azul*, Apdo Aéreo 799, Santa Marta, T421 9009/5, www.ballena-azul.com Most attractive, comfortable, restaurant, also run boat tours to secluded beaches, ask about tours, horses for hire. **B** *Bahía Taganga*, C 2, No 1-35, T421 7620. Overlooking bay, breakfast served on balcony, hospitable. **E** *Casa Francesa*, C 6 No 3B-05, T423 4002. 2 blocks from beach (**D** pp full board) good backpackers hostel, with bath, fan, cheap restaurant, owner Sandrine Walter. **E** *La Casa de Felipe*, 3 blocks from beach behind football field, T421 9101, F421 9022. Cheaper without bath, kitchen facilities, relaxing, hospitable, owners Jean Phillipe and Sandra Gibelin. **F** *Villa Altamar*, C 4, No 1B-12 (postal address: Apdo Aéreo 104, Santa Marta), at foot of mountains, 5 mins from beach. Excellent views over bay but not from rooms, shared bath, all meals on request. Ask on the beach for hammock space, under US$3.Food is expensive, but good fresh fish at places along the beach. There are good pancakes at the crêperie at the *Ballena Azul*.

Sport Diving: Dive shops in Taganga: *Ser Buzo*, C 2, No 1-01, T421 9007. *Centro de Buceo Tayrona*, C 18, No 1-45, T421 9195, ask for José, good reports. *Poseidon*, T421 9224, and others. Average prices: PADI course, 4 days, around US$140, 2 dives US$30. The standard of equipment ranges from "average to dangerous. Check *everything* yourself".

Parque Nacional Tayrona

The park extends from north of Taganga for some 85 km of coastline. You will see monkeys, iguanas and maybe snakes. In the wet, the paths are very slippery. The park is closed at times, check with *MA* in Santa Marta before visiting.

The wild coastal woodland is beautiful and mostly unspoilt

   The entrance is at the east end of the park, 35 km from Santa Marta.If you arrive before 0800, you may be able to pay at the car park just before **Cañaveral**, one hour walk into the park from the gate, or take a colectivo from the park entrance, US$0.50. 40 minutes west of Cañaveral on foot is **Arrecifes**, from where it is 45 minutes' walk to Cabo, then 1½ hours in a clear path up to the archaeological site of **Pueblito**. A guided tour around the site is free, every Saturday or as arranged with a park guard. Other Tayrona relics abound. At Pueblito there are Indians; do not photograph them. From Pueblito you can either return to Cañaveral, or continue for a pleasant two hours walk up to Calabazo on the Santa Marta-Riohacha road. A circuit Santa Marta, Cañaveral, Arrecifes, Pueblito, Calabazo, Santa Marta in one day needs a 0700 start at least. It is easier (more downhill) to do the circuit in reverse, ask to be dropped at Calabazo. Tours can be arranged at the *Hotel Miramar* in Santa Marta, you do no have to stay there to do this, US$10 for overnight stay and transport. Recommended.

   It is advisable to inform park guards when walking in the park. Wear hiking boots and beware of bloodsucking insects. Take food and water, but no valuables as robbery is common. You may be able to hire donkeys for the Arrecifes-Pueblito stretch, US$5 each way, but watch them as these animals eat everything. Generally, the main trails and campsites are badly littered. ■ *Opens 0800. US$2.75 pp, US$3.75 per car (more for larger vehicles).* **NB** *There is frequently conflicting information on whether or not Parque Nacional Tayrona is open. MA offices may advise it is closed, but travellers in 2002 report the facilities are open as normal. The best information is in Santa Marta. See Transport, for Getting there information.*

Colombia

Beaches Bathing near Cañaveral must take account of heavy pounding surf and treacherous tides. 40 minutes' walk left along the beach is Arrecifes. Beyond Arrecifes, walk 30 minutes to La Piscina, a beautiful, safe natural swimming pool, excellent snorkelling. Neguangue beach can be reached by colectivo from Santa Marta Market at 0700, return 1600, US$6. There are other beautiful beaches accessible by coastal path, or by boat.

Sleeping **At Cañaveral** cabins for 2-4 persons cost US$35-45 high season, US$30-40 low season, prices fixed by **MA**, great views over sea and jungle, good restaurant. Campsite US$15 per 5-person tent; has facilities, but only one restaurant with a tiny store, take all supplies; attractive site but plenty of mosquitoes. Beware of falling coconuts and omnivorous donkeys. **At Arrecifes** there are 4 campsites charging about US$3 for a tent, US$1 for hammock space and US$1.50 to hire a hammock. *Rancho Bonito* and *El Paraíso* are the best, with facilities and food. At *El Paraíso* there are cabins for US$20 and an expensive restaurant. The other 2 sites are basic. 200 m along the main road east of the park entrance is a truck stop where cyclists may be able to stay the night (US$5).

On the path to Pueblito there is a campsite at **Cabo** where the path turns inland, small restaurant and hammocks for hire; there are other camping and hammock places en route. You must obtain permission from *MA* to camp in the park if you are not staying at Cañaveral; this is normally forthcoming if you specify where you intend to stay. There is nowhere to stay at Pueblito. You can continue along the coast to deserted beaches, but the going is difficult.

Transport To get to the park entrance, take a minibus from the market in Santa Marta, Cra 11 y C 11, about US$1, 45 mins, frequent service from 0700, last back about 2000 (check on the day with the bus driver). Tourist bus from *Hotel Miramar* in Santa Marta daily at 1030, US$7 including park entrance but not food. This transport returns at 1200; visitors normally stay overnight. Other hotels help in arranging tours, but there is no need to take guides (who charge US$20 or more pp for a day trip). A boat can be hired in Taganga to go to Arrecifes, about 2 hrs along the scenic coast, US$75 for 10.

Beyond Cañaveral, east along the coast, is **Palomino**. Tours can be arranged from there to Indian villages taking up to six days, cost around US$32 per day. Enquire at *Turcol* in Santa Marta (see page 826).

Ciudad Perdida
Colour map1, grid A3

Ciudad Perdida, discovered in 1975, was founded near the Río Buritaca between AD 500 and 700 and was the most important centre of the Tayrona culture. It stands at 1,100 m on the steep slopes of Cerro Corea, which lies in the northern part of the Sierra Nevada de Santa Marta. The site covers 400 ha and consists of a complex system of buildings, paved footpaths, flights of steps and perimetrical walls, which link a series of terraces and platforms, on which were built cult centres, residences and warehouses. Juan Mayrs book, *The Sierra Nevada of Santa Marta* (Mayr y Cabal, Apdo Aéreo 5000, Bogotá), deals beautifully with the Ciudad Perdida.

Archaeologists and army guards will ask you for your permit (obtainable in Santa Marta, *MA*, *Turcol* or ask at tourist office). Ciudad Perdida is a national park: it is strictly forbidden to damage trees and collect flowers or insects. Note also that there are over 1,200 steps to climb when you get there.

Tours 1 week trips organized by the tourist office and *Turcol* in Santa Marta (addresses above) cost about US$150 pp all inclusive: price includes mules, guide and food, 3 days hike there, 1 day at site, 2 days' back. Ask at hotels in Santa Marta (eg *Hotel Miramar*) or Taganga, or at Santa Marta market (Cra 11 y C 11) for alternative tours. If you are prepared to shop around and cook and carry your supplies and belongings, a tour could cost you less. Recommended guides: *Frankie Rey*, known to German tourists as 'die graue Eminenz', very knowledgeable (contact him through *Turcol* or *Hotel Miramar*), or *Edwin Rey*, *Wilson and Edilberto Montero*, *Donaldo and Rodrigo* (ask at the tourist office about them).

Going on your own is discouraged and dangerous. Properly organized groups appear to be safe. For visiting Ciudad Perdida by helicopter, check with the tourist offices in Santa Marta, or at Sportur, Irotama Hotel (near Rodadero), T432 0600.

The **Santuario de Fauna y Flora Los Flamencos** There are several small and two large saline lagoons (Laguna Grande and Laguna de Navío Quebrado), separated from the Caribbean by sand bars. The latter is near Camarones (colectivo from Riohacha, new market) which is just off the main road. About 3 km beyond Camarones is 'La Playa', a popular beach to which some colectivos continue at week-ends. The large lagoons are fed by intermittent streams which form deltas at the south point of the lakes; flamingoes normally visit between October and December, during the wet season when some fresh water enters the lagoons, though some are there all year. The birds are believed to migrate to and from the Dutch Antilles, Venezuela and Florida. Across Laguna de Navío Quebrado is a warden's hut on the sand bar, ask to be ferried across by local fishermen or the park guards. Entry to the park is US$2.50. The locals survive, after the failure of the crustaceans in the lagoons, on tourism and ocean fishing. There are several bars, restaurants and two stores on the beach.

Santuario Los Flamencos
95 km E of Santa Marta and 25 km short of Riohacha

Riohacha

The capital of Guajira Department is a port at the mouth of the Río César, with low white houses, concrete streets, no trees or hills. It was founded in 1545 by Nicolás Federmann, and in early years its pearling industry was large enough to tempt Drake to sack it (1596). Pearling almost ceased during the 18th century and the town was all but abandoned. At the weekend, Riohacha fills up, and bars and music spring up all over the place. The sea is clean, despite the red silt stirred up by the waves. Palm trees shade the beach.

Phone code: 95
Colour map 1, grid A4
Population: 142,000
160 km E of Santa Marta

Colombia

B *Gimaura* (state-owned), Av La Playa, T727 2266. Including breakfast, helpful. Recommended. They allow camping in their grounds, with outside shower. **B** *El Castillo del Mar Suites*, C 9A, No 15-352, T727 5043. Overlooking the beach, German owner. **E** *Almirante Pedilla*, Cra 6 y C 2. Patio, laundry, restaurant with cheap *almuerzos*. **E** *Internacional*, Cra 7, No 12A-31, T727 3483. Patio, bath, fan, free iced water. Recommended. **E** *Yalconia*, Cra 7, No 11-26, T727 3487. Private bath, fan, safe, helpful, half way between beach and bus station. Many small restaurants along sea-front. *Glenppi*, Av La Marina, south end, T727 3356. Good, especially for fish.

Sleeping & eating

Good hammocks sold in the market. For mantas and other local items: *La Casa de la Manta Guajira*, Cra 6/C 12, be prepared to bargain. *Rincón Artesanal Dicaime*, C 2, No 5-61, T727 3071. *Ojo de Agua*, C 2/Cra 9.

Shopping

Administradores Costeños, C 2, No 5-06, T727 3393. *Awarraija Tours*, Av La Marina No 3-55, T727 5806. *Guajira Tours*, C 3, No 6-47, T727 3385. *Guajira Viva*, agency in *Hotel Arimaca*, T727 0607. All do tours to El Pájaro, Musichi, Manaure, Uribia and Cabo de Vela, leaving about 0600, 12-hr trip, US$40 pp, minimum 4 people.

Tour operators

Air Airport José Prudencio Padilla is south of the town towards Tomarrazón. To Bogotá, daily flights. **Bus** Main terminal is on C 15 (Av El Progreso)/Cra 11. (It is best to travel from Riohacha in a luxury bus, early morning as these buses are less likely to be stopped and searched for contraband.) Some colectivos for Uribia and the northeast leave from the new market 2 km southeast on the Valledupar road.

Transport

Banks *Banco de Bogotá*, Cra 7, between C 2/3, for Visa. **Communications** Post Office: C 2, Cra 6/7. *Avianca* for airmail, C 7, No 7-104, T727 3624, also airline ticket agency. *Telecom*, C 15/Cra 10, T727 2528. **Embassies and consulates** Venezuela, Cra 7, No 3-08, p7-B, T274076, F273967 (0900-1300, and closed from 1500 Fri to 0900 Mon). With 2 passport photographs, photocopy of passport and an

Directory

exit ticket with date most can get a visa on the same day, if you get there early, but be prepared for an interview with the consul himself; visas cost US$30 and should not be a transit visa, valid for 72 hrs only. Travellers report it is easier to get a Venezuelan visa in Barranquilla. **Tourist office** Cortguajira, Cra 7/C 1, Av La Marina, T727 2482, F727 4728, well organized. **Useful addresses** DAS Office **(immigration):** C 5, No 4-48, T727 2407, open 0800-1200, 1400-1800.

Valledupar
Phone code: 955
Colour map 1, grid A4
Population: 260,000
Altitude: 110 m

South of Riohacha on an alternative road to Maicao and the Venezuelan border is **Cuestecita** (*Hotel Turismo*; *Restaurant La Fogata*), where you can turn southwest to **Barrancas**, one of the largest coal mines in the world, El Cerrejón. Continuing on this road, which takes you either round the Sierra Nevada to Barranquilla and Santa Marta via Fundación (see above) or south to Bucaramanga, you come to **Valledupar**, capital of César Department. Valledupar claims to be the home of the *vallenato* music. Each April, *La Festival de la Leyenda Vallenata* draws thousands of visitors. Casas de cambio on C 16.

Sleeping **A** *Vajamar*, Cra 7, No 16A-30, T743939. Pool, expensive food. **F** *Residencia El Triunfo*, C 19, No 9-31. With bath, small rooms, fan, good. Next door is *Hotel/Restaurant Nutibara*. Excellent cheap meals and breakfast, excellent fruit juices. Several others on C 19.

Transport **Air**: to Bogotá, Barranquilla, Riohacha and Santa Marta. **Bus**: the bus and air terminals are 3 km southeast of the town, close to each other, taxi, US$3. From **Santa Marta**, 6 hrs, from **Cartagena**, US$13 (with *Expreso Brasilia*). To **Barranquilla**, 6 hrs, US$10. To **Bucaramanga**, 8 hrs US$20.

The Sierra Nevada de Santa Marta

The Sierra Nevada, covering a triangular area of 16,000 sq km, rises abruptly from the Caribbean to 5,800 m snow peaks in about 45 km, a gradient comparable with the south face of the Himalaya, and unequalled along the world's coasts. Pico Colón is the highest point in the country.

Unfortunately, the reluctance of the local Indians to welcome visitors, the prevalence of drug growing on the lower slopes and the presence of guerrilla and vigilante groups makes virtually the whole of the Sierra Nevada de Santa Marta a no-go area. This is a tragedy since here can be found the most spectacular scenery and most interesting indigenous communities in the country. For the latest information check with *MA* in Santa Marta and Bogotá, *ICAN* in Bogotá (see page 772), and the *Fundación Pro-Sierra Nevada*, Edif Los Bancos 502, Santa Marta, T421 4697, F421 4737, for guidance on what may be possible. Also trekking tours into the fringes of the Nevada de Santa Marta can from time to time be arranged in the Santa Marta and Valledupar areas, check with the respective tourist offices. The latest information we have is in the current edition of the *Colombia Handbook*.

Guajira Peninsula

Beyond Riohacha to the east is the arid and sparsely inhabited **Guajira Peninsula**. The Indians here collect dividivi (the curved pods of trees used in tanning and dyeing), tend goats, and fish. They are Guajiros, and of special interest are the coloured robes worn by the women. Sunsets in the Guajira are magnificent.

NB The Guajira peninsula is not a place to travel alone, parties of three or more are recommended. If going in your own transport, check on safety before setting out. Also remember it is hot, easy to get lost, and there is little cover and very little water. Locals, including police, are very helpful in giving lifts.

To visit a small part of the Peninsula take a bus from Riohacha (twice a day from the Indian market) to Manaure, US$2.40, three uncomfortable hours through fields of cactus but offering fine views of flamingoes and other brightly coloured birds. **Manaure** is known for its salt flats southwest of the town. If you walk along the beach past the salt works, there are several lagoons where flamingoes congregate. 14 km from Manaure in this direction is **Musichi**, an important haunt of the flamingoes, sometimes out of the wet season. From Manaure there are *busetas* to **Uribia** (US$1) and thence to Maicao. You can get *busetas* from Uribia to Puerto Bolívar (from where coal from El Cerrejón is exported) and from there transport to **Cabo de Vela**, where the lagoons seasonally shelter vast flocks of flamingoes, herons and sandpipers. It costs about US$3 from Uribia to Cabo de Vela. There are fine beaches.

In Manaure F *Hotel Flamingo*. At **Uribia** 1 basic *residencia*, no running water. **In Cabo de Vela** a basic but friendly, Indian-run hotel, *El Mesón* (rooms, hammock veranda, showers, good meals eg fried fish), or sling hammock at *El Caracol* where there is an expensive restaurant (better value next door at *La Tropicana* if ordered in advance). Conchita hires out a large hut, hammocks for up to 5, cooks food with prior request, along the coast, ask anyone.

Sleeping

Towards the northeast tip of the Guajira peninsula is the Serranía de Macuira, a range of hills over 500 m which create an oasis of tropical forest in the semi-desert. Moisture comes mainly from clouds that form in the evening and disperse in the early morning. Its remoteness gives it interesting flora and fauna and Indian settlements little affected by outsiders. To reach the area, you must travel northeast from Uribia either round the coast past Bahía Portete, or direct across the semi-desert, to Nazareth on the east side of the park. There are no tourist facilities anywhere nearby and no public transport, though trucks may take you from the Bahía Portete area to Nazareth, 6-8 hours (if you can find one). You may be able to arrange a trip in Riohacha, try *Guajira Tours*. *Eco-Guías* in Bogotá arrange trips here occasionally.

Parque Nacional Macuira

Maicao

The paved Caribbean coastal highway runs direct from Santa Marta to Riohacha, then paved to Maicao. **Maicao** is full of Venezuelan contraband and is still at the centre of the narcotics trade. Its streets are unmade; most commercial premises close before 1600 and after 1700 the streets are unsafe.

Phone code: 95
Colour map 1, grid A4
Population: 59,000
Altitude: 50 m

C *El Dorado*, Cra 10, No 12-45, T726 7242. A/c, TV, good water supply. **D** *Maicao Juan*, Cra 10, C 12, T726 8184. Safe.

Sleeping

Buses to **Riohacha**, US$1.50, 1 hr. **Santa Marta** (*Expreso Occidente*), US$9. **Barranquilla**, last one at 1600, US$14.50. **Cartagena**, US$18. Colectivos, known as *por puestos* in Venezuela, Maicao-Maracaibo, US$6 pp, or infrequent microbus, US$3.50, very few buses to Venezuela after midday. All buses leave from the bus terminal where you can change money; buy bus tickets and food before journey. Taxis from Maicao to Maracaibo, US$3 (plus US$0.50 road toll) will stop at both immigration posts and take you to your hotel; safe, very easy transfer.

Transport

Colombian immigration is at the border. Entering Colombia by *por puesto* make sure the driver stops at the Colombian entry post. If not you will have to return later to complete formalities. With all the right papers, the border crossing is easy.

There is now no Venezuelan consul in Maicao. If you need a visa, get it in Barranquilla, Cartagena or Riohacha. Entering Venezuela, a transit visa will only suffice if you have a confirmed ticket to a third country within three days. See **entering Venezuela**, page 1379.

Border with Venezuela

Colombia

San Andrés and Providencia

Colombia's Caribbean islands of the San Andrés and Providencia archipelago are 480 km north of the South American coast, 400 km southwest of Jamaica, and 180 km east of Nicaragua. This proximity has led Nicaragua to claim them from Colombia in the past. They are small and attractive, but very expensive by South American standards. Nevertheless, with their surrounding islets and cays, they are a popular holiday and shopping resort.

Background San Andrés is very crowded with Colombian shoppers looking for foreign-made bargains. Alcoholic drinks are cheap, but international shoppers will find few bargains, and essentials are expensive.

The original inhabitants, mostly black, speak some English, but the population has swollen with unrestricted immigration from Colombia. There are also Chinese and Middle Eastern communities.

Culture & festivals **20 Jul**: independence celebrations on San Andrés with various events. Providencia holds its *carnival* in Jun. San Andrés and Providencia are famous in Colombia for their music, whose styles include the local form of calypso, soca, reggae and church music. Concerts are held at the Old Coliseum (every Sat at 2100 in the high season). The *Green Moon Festival* is held in **May**. There is a cultural centre at Punta Hansa in San Andrés town (T25518).

San Andrés Island

San Andrés

Phone code: 985
Population: 80,000

The 11 km long **San Andrés** island is made of coral and rises at its highest to 104 m. The town, commercial centre, major hotel sector and airport are at the northern end. A picturesque road circles the island. Places to see, besides the beautiful cays and beaches on the eastern side, are the Hoyo Soplador (South End), a geyser-like hole through which the sea spouts into the air when the wind is in the right direction. The west side is less spoilt, but there are no beaches. Instead there is The Cove, the islands deepest anchorage, and Morgan's Cave (Cueva de Morgan, reputed hiding place for the pirate's treasure) which is penetrated by the sea through an underwater passage. At The Cove, a road crosses up to the centre of the island and back to town over La Loma, on which is a Baptist Church, built in 1847.

Diving off San Andrés is very good; depth varies from three to 30 m, visibility **Marine life &**
from 10 to 30 m. There are three types of site: walls of seaweed and minor coral reefs, **watersports**
large groups of different types of coral, and underwater plateaux with much marine
life. It is possible to dive in 70% of the insular platform. Diving trips to the reef: *Buzos
del Caribe*, Centro Comercial Dann, T28930, offer diving courses and equipment
hire; *Sharky Dive Shop*, T33977, on the coast 10 minutes from town, PADI advanced
certificate course, US$250.

For the less-adventurous, take a morning boat (20 minutes, none in the afternoon) to the so-called Aquarium (US$3 return), off Haynes Cay, where, using a
mask and wearing sandals as protection against sea-urchins, you can see colourful
fish. Snorkelling equipment can be hired on San Andrés for US$4-5, but it is better
and cheaper on the shore than on the island.

Pedalos can be rented for US$6 per hour. Windsurfing and sunfish sailing rental
and lessons are available from Bar Boat, on the road to San Luis (opposite the naval
base), 1000-1800 daily (also has floating bar, English and German spoken), and
Windsurf Spot, *Hotel Isleño*, T23990; water-skiing at Water Spot, *Hotel Aquarium*,
T26926, and Jet Sky. From Tominos Marina there are boat trips. Two-hour bay trips
cost US$8.75, for four hours US$17.50, including three free rum and cokes.

Boats go in the morning from San Andrés to Johnny Cay with a white beach and par- **Beaches & cays**
ties all day Sunday (US$3 return, you can go in one boat and return in another).
Apart from those already mentioned, other cays and islets in the archipelago are
Bolívar, Albuquerque, Algodón/Cotton (included in the Sunrise Park development
in San Andrés), Rocky, the Grunt, Serrana, Serranilla and Quitasueño.

On San Andrés the beaches are in town and on the east coast. Perhaps the best is at
San Luis and Bahía Sonora/Sound Bay.

AL *Aquarium*, Av Colombia 1-19, T26926, F26174. Rooms and suites, large pool, marina. **Sleeping**
AL *Casa Dorada*, Av Las Américas, T23826. Salt water washing, reasonable food. *Some hotels raise*
AL *Decamerón*, road to San Luis Km 15, T23657, www.decameron.com All-inclusive resort, *their prices by*
pool, a/c, TV, good restaurant. Recommended. **A** *Cacique Toné*, Av Colombia, No 5-02, *20-30 on 15 Dec*
T24251, www.san-andres.com/ctone/ Deluxe, a/c, pool, on sea-front. **A** *El Isleño*, Av
Colombia 3-59, T23990, F23126. 2 blocks from airport, in palm grove, good sea views.
A *Bahía Sardina*, Av Colombia No 4-24, T23793. Across the street from the beach, a/c, TV,
fridge, good service, comfortable, no swimming pool. **A** *Verde Mar*, Av 20 de Julio, T23498.
Quiet, a/c. Recommended. **A** *Viña del Mar*, Av Colombia, 3-145, T/F24791/28298. Spacious
rooms, close to beach and centre, negotiate. **B** *Capri*, Av Costa Rica No 1A-100, T24316. A/c,
good value. **C** *Nueva Aurora*, Av de las Américas No 3-46, T26077. Fan, pool, restaurant.
D *Coliseo*, Cra 5/Av Aeropuerto, T23330. Noisy, good restaurant. **D** *Olga and Federico
Archibold*, C de la Bodega Marlboro, No 91-18, T25781, have 3 self-contained apartments,
modern. **D** *Residencias Hernando Henry*, Av Las Américas 4-84, T24099. Restaurant, fan,
good value, often full, on road from airport. Also near the airport, **E** *Residencia Restrepo*, Cra
8. 'Gringo hotel', noisy ('share a room with a Boeing 727') till midnight, less for a hammock in
the porch, but you get what you pay for, the accommodation is in a poor state and the
grounds are a junkyard, not recommended. Opposite *Restrepo* is a tobacco/paper shop
whose owner rents a/c apartments with kitchen, etc, **D**. **Out of town**: **D** *Cocoplum Beach*,
Via San Luis No 43-39, T32364. Good value.

Oasis, Av Colombia No 4-09. Good. *El Zaguán de los Arrieros*, Av 20 de Julio (50 m after cin- **Eating**
ema). Good food and value. *Fonda Antioqueña Nos 1 and 2*, on Av Colombia near the main *Cheap fish meals*
beach, and Av Colombia at Av Nicaragua. Best value for fish. *Sea Food House*, Av 20 de Julio, *can be bought at*
at Parque Bolívar. Good cooking, not expensive, second floor terrace. Excellent fruit juices at *San Luis beach*
Nueva China, next to *Restrepo*, reasonable Chinese. *Fisherman's Place*, in the fishing cooperative at north end of main beach. Very good, simple.

Colombia

Transport **Local** **Bus** cover the eastern side of the island all day (15 mins intervals), US$0.30 (more at night and on holidays). **Taxi**: round the island, US$8; to airport, US$3.25; in town, US$1.25; *colectivo* to airport, US$0.50. **Train**: a 'tourist train' (suitably converted tractor and carriages) tours the island in 3 hrs for US$4.50. **Vehicle rental**: bicycles are easy to hire, usually in poor condition, choose your own bike and check all parts thoroughly (US$1.10 per hour, US$6 per day). Motorbikes also easy to hire, US$8 for minimun 2 hrs. Cars can be hired for US$15 for 2 hrs, with US$6 for every extra hour.

A cheap way to visit San Andrés is by taking a charter flight from Bogotá or other major city, accommodation and food included. See supplements in the local Colombian press

Long distance **Air** The airport is 15 mins' walk to town centre. All airline offices in town, except Aces at airport. Flights to most major Colombian cities with *Avianca* and *Aero República* (you can arrange a stop-over in Cartagena, which is good value). Sun flights are always heavily booked, similarly Jul-Aug, Dec-Jan. If wait-listed, don't give up hope. Fares are changing all the time, so for best value, shop around.

Ship Cruise ships and tours go to San Andrés; there are no other, official passenger services by sea. In Cartagena, you can enquire about possible sea crossings, ships leave from the Embarcadero San Andrés, opposite the Plaza de la Aduana. Check carefully any offers you may receive. **Boat** **Cooperativa de Lancheros**, opposite *Hotel Abacoa* for fishing and boating trips.

Directory **Banks** *Banco de Bogotá* will advance pesos on a Visa card. *Banco Occidente* for MasterCard. ATMs available in town. Many shops will change US$ cash; it is impossible to change TCs at weekends. **Communications** Internet: *Café Sol* (*Hotel Tiuna*), Av Colombia, No 3-59, US$2 per hr. **Post Office:** On Av Duarte Blum (*Avianca*). **Tourist office** Av Colombia, No 5-117, English spoken, maps.

Providencia

Phone code: 9851
Population: 5,500
80 km N-NE of San Andrés

Commonly called Old Providence, **Providencia** is 7 km long and 3 km wide and part of the east coast with the offshore reefs is a national park (**Parque Nacional Old Providence – McBean Lagoon**). Entrance US$1.50, diving with gear hire available. It is more mountainous than San Andrés, rising to 610 m. There are waterfalls, and the land drops steeply into the sea in places. Superb views can be had by climbing from Casabaja/Bottom House or Aguamansa/Smooth Water to the peak. There are

San Andrés town

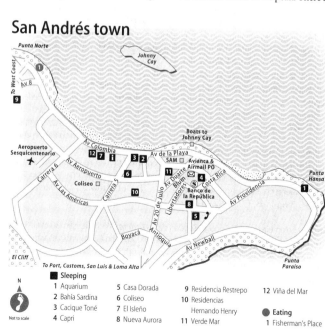

N Not to scale

■ Sleeping
1 Aquarium
2 Bahía Sardina
3 Cacique Toné
4 Capri
5 Casa Dorada
6 Coliseo
7 El Isleño
8 Nueva Aurora
9 Residencia Restrepo
10 Residencias Hernando Henry
11 Verde Mar
12 Viña del Mar

● Eating
1 Fisherman's Place

relics of the fortifications built on the island during its disputed ownership. Horse riding is available, and boat trips can be made to neighbouring islands such as **Santa Catalina** (an old pirate lair separated from Providencia by a channel cut to improve their defence), and to the northeast, Cayo Cangrejo/Crab Cay (beautiful swimming and snorkelling) and Cayos Hermanos/Brothers Cay. Trips from 1000-1500 cost about US$7 per person. Santa Catalina is joined to the main island by a wooden bridge. On the west side of Santa Catalina is a rock formation called Morgan's Head; from the side it looks like a man's profile.

The three main beaches are Bahía Manzanillo/Manchincal Bay, the largest, most attractive and least developed, Bahía del Suroeste/South West Bay and Bahía Agua Dulce/ Freshwater Bay, all in the southwest.

Like San Andrés, it is an expensive island. There is a bank in Santa Isabel that will exchange cash: exchange rates from shops and hotels are poor, but you can use credit cards. The sea food is good, water and fresh milk are generally a problem. English is widely spoken. Ask about trips around the island and day tours at your hotel. *West Caribbean Airways*, T29292 (San Andrés), flies from San Andrés, US$40 one way, 25 minutes, four times a day, bookable only in San Andrés. (Return flight has to be confirmed at the airport, where there is a tourist office.) Boat trips from San Andrés take eight hours, but are not regular.

Sleeping Most of the accommodation is at Freshwater (Playa Agua Dulce): **B** *Cabañas El Recreo* (Captain Brian's, T48010). **A** *Cabañas El Encanto*, T48131. With meals. **B** *Sol Caribe*, T48036. A/c, TV, fridge. **B** *Cabañas Aguadulce Miss Elmas*, T48160. Recommended for cheap food; also *Morgan's Bar* for fish meals and a good breakfast. **Santa Catalina**: German-owned *Cabañas Santa Catalina*. Friendly, use of kitchen. Several houses take guests. Camping possible at Freshwater Bay.

Up the Río Magdalena

The old waterway from the Caribbean, now superseded by road and air, leads from Barranquilla to the heart of Colombia at Girardot, once the river port for Bogotá. The route passes through wide plains and narrow gorges and past tierra caliente weekend resorts, before climbing to the river's upper reaches beyond Neiva.

The Lower Magdalena

The Magdalena is wide but shallow and difficult to navigate. Away to the northeast, in the morning, one can see the high snow-capped peaks of the Sierra Nevada de Santa Marta. Passenger travel by the lofty paddle boats on the river has come to an end and in general the only way of getting from one place to the other along the river is by motor launch (*chalupa*). The trip from the north coast commences with a bus to Magangué, then upriver to Puerto Berrío or Puerto Boyacá and on by bus to Bogotá; it can be completed in about four days. Insect repellent should be taken, for mosquitoes are a nuisance. **Warning**: This route is not safe (2002) because of guerrilla and paramilitary activity in the Sucre/Bolívar border area and on the Magdalena Medio. We mention only the main towns and routes, but seek local advice before travelling.

The upper reaches of the Magdalena, beyond Neiva, are dealt with on page 867

Near Pinto the river divides: the eastern branch, silted and difficult, leads to **Mompós**. It was the scene of another of Bolívar's victories: "At Mompós", he said, "my glory was born". Mompós was founded in 1537 when this was the main channel of the river. Now, thanks to its comparative isolation, its colonial character is preserved with many beautiful buildings. There are six churches and the Easter

Mompós
Phone code: 952
Colour map 1, grid A3
Population: 33,000
Altitude: 30 m

celebrations are said to be among the best in Colombia. The cemetery has considerable historical interest. The town is well known in Colombia for handworked gold jewellery.

Malaria is endemic in the surrounding countryside. If staying overnight, mosquito nets and/or coils are a must

Sleeping and eating C *Hostal Doña Manuela*, C Real del Medío (Cra 2), No 17-41, T855620, F855621. A converted colonial house, quiet and peaceful, restaurant is the best in town. **D** *Residencias Aurora*, Cra 2, No 15-65, T855930. Shower, fan, good meals, nice, bargaining possible. **E** *San Andrés*, Cra 2, No 18-23, T855886. Modern, with bath, fan, TV, central, restaurant. **E** *Residencias Villa de Mompós*, Cra 2, between C14/15, T855208. Family-run, free coffee. **E** *Posada de Virrey*, opposite *Doña Manuela*. Shared bath, modern, above medical practice. *El Galileo*, next to the Plaza. Good *comida corriente*. *Otra Parte*, Callejón de Santa Bárbara No 1-42. Good food and bar.

Most chalupas and buses run in the morning. There is little public transport after 1400

Transport Bus From **Cartagena** with *Unitransco* (0530, returns 0700), daily, 12 hrs, US$17. To **Valledupar** and **Santa Marta**, either go from El Banco (see below), or cross the river at **Talaigua** (between Mompós and Magangué, *carritos* leave Mompós early morning) to **Santa Ana**. Buses leave Santa Ana 0700 for **Santa Marta** and **Valledupar**, first 2½ hrs unpaved, then paved; US$10 to Valledupar.

River From Magangué take a *chalupa* (launch) either direct to Mompós, 2hrs, US$3.30, or to Bodega, 45 mins, and then by jeep or taxi, 1½ hrs, US$2. You can also reach Mompós in 2 hrs, US$5 by *chalupa* from El Banco to the southeast.

Magangué
Phone code: 952
Population: 65,000
Altitude: 30 m

Most vessels go by the western arm of the loop to Magangué, the port for the savannas of Bolívar. A road runs west to join the north-south Cartagena-Medellín highway. There are five hotels including **D** *Hans Burchardt*, C 17, No 4-36, T878332, a/c, fridge; **E** *Valle*, Cra 6/C15, T875806, with bath, a/c, TV. 10 *residenciales*, all **G**. There are few places to eat, *Terraza*, to the left of plaza is reasonable.

El Banco
Phone code: 95
Population: 12,000

Don't get conned into taking an expensive boat across the river. Use the bus ferry

At El Banco, 420 km from Barranquilla, the river loops join. This is an old, dirty but beautiful town known for the Festival de La Cumbia in June. Along the river front are massive stone stairways. Lots of egrets, various species of heron, ringed kingfishers.**D** *Central*, near church, modern, fan. **E** Nueva*Continental*, near jeep terminal. **E** *Casa del Viajero*, C 8, T729 2181, colour TV, fan, bath, safe. **F** *Colonial*, 1 block from harbour, with bath and fan. About a dozen others. ■ *Daily buses from El Banco to Bucaramanga, US$20, Cúcuta and Valledupar. Bus from Cartagena 0800, US$12.*

Continuing upriver are many small towns such as **Tamalameque** (basic *residencia* and restaurant), **Gamarra** (*Population*: 10,000), and **Puerto Wilches** (*Population*: 23,000). All are connected by launch.

East of the river is the main road from the coast to Bucaramanga and, eventually, Bogotá. South of Aquachica by 70 km (100 km north of Bucaramanga) at San Alberto, the new highway runs comparatively close to the Magdalena some 400 km to Honda. This is the fastest road from the capital to the Caribbean.

Barranca
Phone code: 97
Colour map 1, grid B3
Population: 181,000
Altitude: 81 m

Some 30 km above Puerto Wilches and 30 km from this new road is Barrancabermeja (or more commonly Barranca), so called because of the reddish-brown oil-stained cliffs on which it stands. It is an important oil refining centre. There is an interesting indoor market. *Banco de Bogotá* will change travellers' cheques.

Sleeping C *Bachué*, Cra 17, No 49-12, T622 2599. A/c, restaurant, safe. **F** *Hostal Real*, opposite station, T622 2239. Pleasant owner, safe (locked day and night), restaurant, good value. **F** *Residencias Ferroviario*, C 12, No 35-21, T622 4524. With bath, opposite railway station Many more around the train station and in town. A shop at C 19, Avs 18 y 19 sells good bread and muesli.

Transport Air: 10 mins by taxi from centre, daily flights to **Bogotá**, *Aces*. **Bus**: Bucaramanga, 3 hrs, US$5; **Medellín**, 1045, US$17. **River**: Boat: *Chalupa* to Puerto Boyacá, 0845, 6 hrs, US$12. Several daily to **El Banco**, 7 hrs, US$15. Launch to **Gamarra**, US$20, 4 hrs.

On the west bank is Puerto Berrío, the river port for Medellín and Antioquia Department. A railway from Medellín runs down the slopes of the Cordillera Central to Puerto Berrío. **E** *Hotel Magdalena*, pleasant, on a hilltop near river. **F** *Residencias El Ganadero*, with bath, modern, with ceiling fans. There are many others. *La Buena Mesa*, good big meals. *Heladería Joi*, good ice cream and sundaes. ■ *Train to Barrancabermeja and Medellín, check if trains are running at* **Grecia** *station, 4 km from the town (taxi only).*

Puerto Berrío
Phone code: 94
Colour map 1, grid B3
Population: 26,000
Altitude: 113 m
100 km above Barrancabermeja
756 km from Barranquilla

Puerto Boyacá, 75 km upriver from Puerto Berrío (launch US$4.10), has several *residencias* and **B** *Palagna*, a/c, large pool, good restaurant, TV, good value. *Rápido Tolima* has regular buses to Honda (three hours, US$4).

Near Puerto Boyacá is Puerto Triunfo (several *residencias*) where the new Medellín-Bogotá highway crosses the river. To the west are the Río Nus and Río Claro which go through dramatic limestone country with caves, deep gorges and waterfalls, well worth visiting.

La Dorada (*Population*: 60,000. *Altitude*: 1,767 m. *Phone code*: 968), a further 76 km along the west bank, is linked by a bridge from **Puerto Salgar**, on the east bank. The old Medellín-Bogotá highway crosses here. **F** *Rosita*, C 17, No 3-28, T572301, with bath, pleasant, recommended; others near railway station. ■ *To Bogotá by bus 5 hrs, US$11. To Medellín US$14.* The Lower Río Magdalena navigation stops at La Dorada as there are rapids above, as far as Honda. There are no passenger services south of Puerto Boyacá. The Upper Magdalena is navigable as far as Girardot.

The Upper Magdalena

On the west bank of the river, Honda is 32 km upstream from La Dorada. It is a pleasant old town with many colonial houses, an interesting indoor market and a small museum. The streets are narrow and picturesque, and the town is surrounded by hills. El Salto de Honda (the rapids which separate the Lower from the Upper Magdalena) are just below the town. Several bridges span the Ríos Magdalena and the Guali, at whose junction the town lies. In February the Magdalena rises and fishing is unusually good. People come from all over the region for the fishing and the festival of the Subienda, the fishing season. ■ *From Bogotá by* Velotax *and* Rápido Tolima, *US$8, 4 hrs.* Manizales, *US$6.* Rápido Tolima *run ½-hourly buses to La Dorada (1 hr), and beyond, to Puerto Boyacá (3 hrs), US$4.*

Honda
Phone code: 98
Colour map 1, grid B3
Population: 27,000
Altitude: 217 m
149 km from Bogotá

Sleeping and eating C *Campestre El Molino*, 5 km from Honda on Mariquita road, T251 3604. Swimming pools, fans in rooms. **C** *Ondana*, Cra 13A, No 17A-17, T251 3127. Swimming pool. **D** *Club Piscina*, Cra 12, No 19-139, T251 3273. Fan, swimming pool, arranges safe parking. Recommended. **D-E** *Dorantes*, C 14, No 12-57, T251 3423. With bath, good. There is a row of good cheap restaurants across the Río Magdalena bridge in Puerto Bogotá. *La Cascada*, overlooking river, good.

West from Honda a paved road goes to **Mariquita** (21 km), in fruit-growing country. From Mariquita the road turns south to (32 km) **Armero**, which was devastated by the eruption of the Nevado del Ruiz volcano (see page 852) in November 1985. Over 25,000 people were killed as approximately 10% of the ice core melted, causing landslides and mudflows. (Armero can be reached by colectivo from Honda; nearest lodging at **Lérida**, 12 km south.)

Colombia

Ibagué
Phone code: 98
Colour map 1, grid B2
Population: 347,000
Altitude: 1,248 m

The main road from Armero goes direct for 88 km to **Ibagué**, capital of Tolima Department. It is a large city, lying at the foot of the Quindío mountains. Parts of the town are old: see the Colegio de San Simón and the market. The Parque Centenario is pleasant. The city specializes in hand-made leather goods (there are many good, cheap shoe shops) and a local drink called *mistela*. There is an excellent Conservatory of Music. The tourist office is at Cra 3, between C 10 and 11; helpful, closed Saturday and Sunday.

Sleeping and eating **A** *Ambala*, C 11, No 2-60, T261 0982, F263 3490. TV, pool, restaurant. **D** *Farallones*, C 16, No 2-88, T261 3339. Good, fan. **E** *Bolivariano*, C 17 No 3-119, T263 3487. Good, TV. **F** *La Paz*, C 18, No 3-119. Free tinto in morning. **E** *Montserrat*, C 18, Cra 1 y 2. Quiet. Recommended. *La Vieja Enramada*, Cra 8, No 15-03. Local and international dishes. *El Espacio*, Cra 4, No 18-14. Large helpings, good value. *Govinda*, vegetarian, Cra 2 y C 13. *Punto Rojo*, shopping precinct Cra 3. 24 hrs, good.

Festivals *National Folklore Festival*, third week of **Jun**. The Departments of Tolima and Huila commemorate San Juan (**24 Jun**) and SS Pedro y Pablo (**29 Jun**) with bullfights, fireworks, and music. There are choral festivals biannually in Dec.

Transport **Air** Daily flights to Bogotá and Medellín, also to Pereira and Neiva and other cities. **Bus** Terminal is between Cras 1-2 and C 19-20. Tourist police at terminal helpful. To **Bogotá**, US$11, 4 hrs. To **Neiva**, US$9, and many other places.

Just outside, on the Armenia road, a dirt road leads up the Río Combeima to El Silencio and the slopes of the **Nevado del Tolima**, the southernmost 'nevado' in the **Parque Nacional Los Nevados**. The climb to the summit (5,221 m) takes two to three days, camping at least one night over 4,000 m, ice equipment necessary. A milk truck (*lechero*) leaves Ibagué marketplace for El Silencio between 0630 and 0730, US$2.50, two hours. ■ *US$3, car US$2.50, camping US$2.50 pp on 5 person sites. For information contact Cruz Roja Colombiana in Ibagué, Zona Industrial El Papayo, near the east entrance to the city, T264 6014, who can put you in touch with climbing groups. Helpful guides are: Claus Schlief, who speaks German and English; Manolo Barrios, who has some Himalayan experience. Fernando Reyes, C 28, No 13-27, Fenalco, Ibagué, T265 6372, can arrange accommodation, supply equipment and offers rock or ice climbing on Tolima.*

The Quindío Pass, 3,350 m (commonly called *La Línea* after the power lines that cross the mountains here) is on the road to Armenia, 105 km west of Ibagué across the Cordillera Central. On the east side of the Pass is **Cajamarca**, a friendly town in a beautiful setting at 1,900 m (**F** *Residencia Central; Nevado*, both on same street). *Bar El Globo*, on corner of the main plaza, recommended, excellent coffee. Interesting market on Sunday.

Girardot
Phone code: 98
Colour map 1, grid B3
79 km E of Ibagué on the Upper Magdalena

The former main river port for Bogotá is linked by road with the capital. Only small boats can go upriver from here. Cattle fairs are held on 5-10 June and 5-10 December. Launch rides on the river start from underneath the bridge; a 1-hour trip to Isla del Sol is recommended (US$9). ■ *Buses to Bogotá, 132 km, US$9, 3½ hrs. To Neiva, US$6, 3½ hrs.*

Sleeping **B** *Bachué*, Cra 8, No 18-04, T833 4791. Modern, large cooled pool, excellent, a/c, restaurant. **D** *Río*, Cra 10, No 16-31, T833 2858. TV, fan, restaurant, laundry, English and German spoken. **D** *Los Angeles*, on main plaza. Recommended. **E** *Miami*, Cra 7, No 13-57. Large rooms, fan, good, central location safe. Opposite new bus terminal, **F** *El Cid*, Cra 13, No 28-06, T831 1574. With fan. **F** *Rincón*, C 19, No 10-68. Balcony, fan. **Eating** *El Castillo*, Cra 11, No 19-52, T833 1742. A/c, seafood, also meat dishes. *El Fogón*, C 19, No 19-01, T832 3822. Fish – *viudo de capaz* – a speciality.

Colombia

South of Girardot, the highway and the Río Magdalena continue to Neiva. About 50 km before Neiva is a small area (300 sq km) of scrub and arid eroded red soil known as the **Tatacoa** desert, with large cacti, isolated mesas and unusual wildlife. Bus from Neiva to Villavieja, near the Río Magdalena, and the Neiva-Bogotá highway at Aipe daily 1030, 1½ hours, US$2. Contact Nelson Martínez Olaya, an official tourist guide at the *Restaurant La Tatacoa*, Villavieja, Cra 4, No 7-32, for 4 or 5 hour walks through the desert. There is also a museum showing prehistoric finds in the area. You can cross the Magdalena by motorized canoe near Villavieja for US$0.75.

Before travelling by road south to Neiva, check on safety

Neiva

The capital of Huila Department, **Neiva** was first founded in 1539, when Belalcázar came across the Cordillera Central from Popayán in quest of El Dorado. It was soon after destroyed by the Indians and refounded in 1612. It is now a pleasant, modern city on the east bank of the Río Magdalena. There is an interesting Arenas Betancur monument to the struggles for independence by the riverside. There are rich coffee plantations around Neiva. The cathedral was destroyed by earthquake in 1967. There is a large and colourful market every day. Tourist information is given at the cultural centre with museum and gallery on the main plaza. *Bancolombia*, near Parque Santander, will change US$ cash and travellers' cheques. A local festival is on 18-28 June, when the Bambuco Queen is elected: folklore, dances and feasting.

*Phone code: 98
Colour map 1, grid B2
Population: 248,000
Altitude: 442 m*

B *Tumburagua*, C 5A, No 5-40, T871 2470. Recommended. **C** *Hostería Matamundo*, in old *hacienda* 3 km from centre, on road to Garzón and San Agustín, Cra 5, No 3S-51, T873 0216. A/c, swimming pool, restaurant, disco. **D** *Central*, Cra 3, No 7-82, T871 2356. Meals, near market, good value. Recommended. **E** *Residencias Astoria*, C 6, No 1-41. Shared bath, big rooms. **F** *Residencia Magdalena*, C 1A Sur, No 8A-57, T873 3586. Close to new bus station, restaurant. *Marías*, C 8, No 7-61. Good *comida casera*. *Heladería La Pampa*, Pasaje Camacho 8. Excellent juices.

Sleeping & eating

Air La Marguita, 1½ km from city. Daily flights to/from **Bogotá** and principal cities. Taxi to bus terminal US$1. **Bus** Bus station out of town; bus from the centre leaves from the old terminal (Cra 2, Cs 5 y 6). To **Bogotá**, 5½ hrs, US$10.50. Regular bus service with *Autobuses Unidos del Sur, Cootranshuila* (0600) and *Coomotor* to **San Agustín**, US$6, 5½ hrs. To **Garzón**, US$3.60. To **Pitalito**, US$6.50. To **La Plata**, for Tierradentro, US$6.50. To **Popayán**, US$9.25, ordinary bus at 0330, 1000, 1500, 1930, 11 hrs, poor road. To **Florencia**, US$7.80. To **Ibagué** at 1200, US$9.

Transport
At the bus stations, both off and on buses, in Neiva, Garzón and especially Pitalito, theft is common

South of Neiva lie the plains of Huila Department, arid, but still capable of supporting cattle, dominated by the snow-capped Nevado del Huila to the northwest.

Colombia

□Bogotá

Antioquia and Chocó

Antioquia is the largest of the western departments and full of diversity. With its roots in the Cordilleras, it still has 100 km of Caribbean coastline. Chocó Department, almost as large, is all in the heavy rainbelt along Colombia's northwest coast, densely forested and sparsely inhabited. The Central Cordillera lies west of the Río Magdalena. In it are several of the most important cities in Colombia: Medellín, the second largest city in the country, Manizales, Pereira and Armenia. The last three are in the heart of the coffee growing area and are covered in the next section.

    The town of Santa Fé de Antioquia was founded in 1541. Then in the 17th century settlers from Spain, some of them Jewish refugees, colonised the Río Aburrá Valley and founded the city of Medellín in 1616.

Medellín

Phone code: 94
Colour map 1, grid B2
Population: 1,700,000
Altitude: 1,487 m

The city of Medellín will always be synonymous with its infamous drugs cartel, but the capital of Antioquia Department is, in reality, a fresh and prosperous city with a vibrant arts scene, shiny modern architecture and brand, spanking new Metro to shout about. Many consider this as the cultural heartland of Colombia, and though few colonial buildings remain, there are plenty of museums and public artworks on display.

    The centre of the city comprises La Candelaria, in which is Parque de Berrío, and the commercial centre of Villanueva, with Parque de Bolívar. In the south, El Poblado has become an up-market residential area and many companies have moved their headquarters there from the centre. The best hotels and restaurants are in or near El Poblado. Around Cra 70 and C 44 are busy commercial and entertainment sectors with many new hotels, shopping centres and the huge Atanasio Girardot sports stadium nearby. The climate is generally warm and pleasant though it is often cloudy and rain can come at any time.

Ins & outs
For more detailed information see Transport, page 846

Getting there International airport José María Córdoba airport (also called Rionegro), 28 km from Medellín by new highway, and 9 km from the town of Rionegro; good shops and services, no left luggage, but tourist office may oblige. Taxi to town US$12.50 (fixed, more at night), *buseta* to centre, US$1.70, frequent service, about 1 hr: sit on right going to town. There is a stop at the *Intercontinental Hotel* for passengers to El Poblado. To go to the airport catch *buseta* in small road behind *Hotel Nutibara*. To Rionegro, bus US$0.20, taxi US$8. **Metropolitan airport** Flights to nearby Colombian destinations use the Enrique Olaya Herrera airport near the centre of the city.

    The terminal for long-distance buses going north and east is **Terminal del Norte** at Cra 64 (Autopista del Norte) y Transversal 78, about 3 km north of the centre, with shops, cafeterias, left luggage (US$0.50 per day) and other facilities. Quite safe. Bus service to city centre, US$0.30, buses to station from C 50, marked: 'Terminal de Transporte', or better, by Metro to Caribe. For buses going south, **Terminal del Sur**, Cra 65, C 10, alongside the Olaya Herrera airport, for information, T285 9157. Take any bus marked 'Terminal del Sur' from C 49 along Cra 46, or the Metro to Poblado on Línea A, but you will need a taxi for the remaining 1½ km to the bus station.

Travellers should take the same safety precautions as they would in any large city particularly at night. It is nevertheless a friendly place

Getting around For your first general view of the city, take the Metro. Most of the track in the centre is elevated. There are 2 lines: A from Niquía to Itagüí, B from San Javier to San Antonio, where they intersect. One journey (anywhere on the system) US$0.28, 2 US$0.50, 10 US$2.25. **Taxi**: make sure meters are used.

    Tourist offices Fomento y Turismo de Medellín, C 57 No 45-129, T254 0800, for information on the city, helpful. There are tourist booths at both airports. Good map.

As you ride the Metro you will notice three prominent hills in the Aburrá valley: **Cerro Nutibara** (across the river from Industriales station), where there is a stage for open air concerts, sculpture park, miniature Antioquian village (known as Pueblito Paisa), souvenir shops and restaurants; **Cerro El Volador** (seen as the Metro turns between Universidad and Caribe stations), tree-covered and the site of an important Indian burial ground; and **Morro El Salvador** (to the east of Alpujarra station) with a cross and statue on top, now mostly built over and not recommended for visits. The city is based on two squares: **Parque de Berrío**, with the old **Señora de Candelaria** cathedral taking up one side, and the **Parque de Bolívar** dominated by the new **Catedral Metropolitana**, built between 1875 and 1931, one of the largest brick buildings in the world. There are three early churches near the centre, **San Benito**, **La Veracruz** and **San José**, and three early 18th century churches survive: **San Ignacio**, in Plaza San Ignacio, **San Juan de Dios**, and **San Antonio**. The commercial centre, **Villanueva**, is interesting for its blend of old and modern architecture, including many skyscrapers. There is a fine sculpture, **Monumento a la Vida**, by Rodrigo Arenas Betancur, next to the Edif Seguros Suramericana on C 50, where exhibitions of work by leading South American artists are held on the ground floor. There are many other sculptures in the city. One collection not to be missed is the works of Fernando Botero, Colombia's leading contemporary artist, in Parque San Antonio between C 44/46 and Cra 46 including the 'Torso Masculino' (which complements the female version in Parque Berrío), and the 'Bird of Peace' which was severely damaged by a guerrilla bomb in 1996. At Botero's request, it has been left unrepaired as a symbol of the futility of violence and a new one has been placed alongside to make the point yet more dramatically.

Sights
We give the Calle and Carrera numbers for easy reference. Most streets also have names. See map for both numbers and names

Colombia

Medellín

Sleeping
1 Arod
2 Lukas

Museums
1 Museo de Arte Moderno

2 Casa Museo Maestro Pedro Nel Gómez

3 Museo de Antropología at Universidad de Antioquia

Related maps
A Medellín centre, page 844

N

0 metres 500
0 yards 500

Joaquín Antonio Uribe gardens, Cra 52, C 78, are near the campus of the University of Antioquia, with 600 species of plants, orchids and trees. ■ *Daily 0800-1730, US$1.60.* There is a restaurant for lunches and snacks, pleasant.

Other interesting museums are detailed in the Colombia Handbook. Most museums close Mon

The **Museo de Antioquia**, opposite main post office, shows contemporary pictures and sculptures, including works by Fernando Botero. ■ *US$1.50, guides free, Cra 52A, No 51A-29.* The Botero collection has been augmented and displayed in the plaza nearby, officially opened 2002. **Museo de Arte Moderno**, has a small collection. ■ *Tue-Sat, 1100-1700 (foreign films shown), Cra 64B, No 51-64.* **Casa Museo Maestro Pedro Nel Gómez**, is the house of the painter and sculptor (1899-1984). ■ *Cra 51B, No 85-24, T2332633.* The **Museo Antropológico** also has exhibitions of modern art. ■ *Free, University of Antioquia, C 67, No 53-108 (new campus).* **Biblioteca Pública Piloto para América Latina** is one of the best public libraries in the country, with art and photo exhibitions, readings and films. ■ *Cra 64, No 50-32, T230 5108.* Two newer 'sights' are **Puntocero**, at the Calle 36 river bridge, an elegant steel double arch with a pendulum mounting the centre of the city (the idea of local university students) and **El Edificio Inteligente**, Calle 43/Cra 58, a highly energy-efficient building used jointly by Medellín's public services.

Sleeping
■ *on map*
Price codes:
see inside front cover

In or near Poblado LL *Intercontinental*, C 16, No 28-51, Variante Las Palmas, T266 0680, medellin@interconti.com All services, excellent. **AL** El Balcón, Cra 25, No 2-370, Transversal Superior, T 268 2511. Beautiful view of the city, good restaurant. Other up-market hotels in the area.

West of centre, near stadium L *Lukas*, Cra 70 No 44A-28, T260 1761, F260 3765. Best hotel in this area. **A** *Arod*, C 44, No 69-80, T260 1427, F260 1441. Small, secure, basement parking. Recommended.

In centre AL *Nutibara*, C 52A, No 50-46, T511 5111, F231 3713. Best in centre, casino and swimming pool. *Residencias Nutibara*, annex facing hotel of same name, slightly cheaper with the same facilities. **A** *Amaru*, Cra 50A, No 53-45, T511 2155, F231 0321. Central, quiet, good, restaurant. Recommended. **B** *Horizonte*, Cra 47 No 49A-24, T511 6188. Good, popular restaurant. **B** *Mariscal*, Cra 45, No 46-49, T251 5433. Hot shower, good service.

Medellín centre

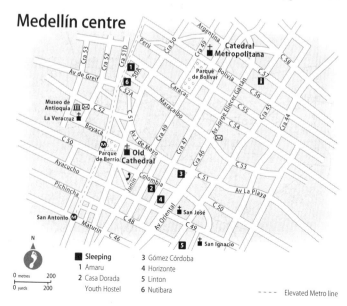

Sleeping
1 Amaru
2 Casa Dorada Youth Hostel

3 Gómez Córdoba
4 Horizonte
5 Linton
6 Nutibara

- - - - Elevated Metro line

0 metres 200
0 yards 200

Colombia

B *Villa de la Candelaria*, Cra 42, No 50-101, T239 0345. With bath, modern rooms, TV. **C** *Casa Blanca*, Cra 45, No 46-09, T251 5211. Small restaurant, safe but noisy. **D** *Linton*, Cra 45, No 47-74, T217 0847. TV, safe parking nearby US$0.50 per night, central. **D** *Comercial*, C 48, No 53-94. Hot water in some rooms, best on top floor, doors barred to all but residents after 1800, good meals. Recommended **F** *Residencias Doris*, Cra 45, No 46-23, T251 2245. Family run, hot water, clean sheets daily, laundry facilities, locked night and day, no windows but good value. **E** *Gómez Córdoba*, Cra 46, No 50-29. With bath, TV, good value, renovated, safe, central. **E** *Romania*, Av Echeverri, C 58, No 50-46. With bath, a bit noisy. **Youth Hostel** *Casa Dorada*, C 50, No47-25, T512 5300.

In or near El Poblado *Frutos del Mar*, Cra 43B, No 11-51. Good seafood. *Café Le Gris*, Centro Comercial Oviedo (Cra 43A No 6 Sur-15). Good upmarket dishes. *Aguacatala*, Cra 43A, No 7 Sur-130. An old country house with patio and wandering musical trio, *comida típica*, quiet surroundings. Similar is *La Posada de la Montaña*, Cra 43-B, No 16-22. Excellent Colombian food, very attractive setting. Recommended. *Carbón*, Variante a las Palmas, Km 1, T262 5425. Good grills, good view over city, live music at weekends. *Frutas de mi Tierra*, also Variante a las Palmas. Extraordinary fruit salads. *Hato Viejo*, opposite *International Hotel*. Good service, high quality, local dishes, free snacks with drinks, good value. Recommended. *La Grappa*, Cra 41, No 10-19, T266 2326. Good Italian.

    West of centre *Manhattan*, Cra 70, No 42-39. Good international. *Asados La 80*, Cra 81, No 30-7. Very good, large steaks. *El Palacio Chino*, Circular 4, No 74-69. Good Chinese, reasonable prices. *La Llanera*, Cra 70, Circular 1-36. Local dishes, good quality. *La Casa del Mayoral*, Cra 81, No 30A-37. Good steaks, bar. Plenty of cheap restaurants and fast food outlets around Cra 70.

    In the centre apart from the hotels, there are few of the better restaurants. Exceptions are: *Palazzetto D'Italia*, C 54, No 43-102. Excellent Italian, reasonable prices. Recommended. *El Viejo Vapor*, Cra 43, No 53-19. Café, bar, artist clientèle, good meeting place, set lunch US$3. *Hato Viejo*, Cra 49, No 50-170. Similar to the one in El Polbado. Many vegetarian restaurants, eg *Govinda*, C 51 No 52-17, excellent for lunch. *Trigo y Miel*, C 53, No 43-54. Very good vegetarian, set lunch US$3.50. Recommended. *Crepes y Waffles*, Cra 36, No 10-54. Good. *Paracelso*, C 51 y Cra 45. Big, tasty, cheap meals, open 1100-1600. There are several cheap, round-the-clock cafés on Cra Junín between Maturín and Amador. Many good, cheap restaurants on Cra 49 (eg *La Estancia*, No 54-15). Excellent pastries at *Salón de Té Astor*, Cra 49, No 52-84, a delightful traditional tea house. Also in Pasaje Junín are several upstairs bar/cafés eg *Boulevard de Junín* and *Balcones del Parque*, good for meals and refreshments while watching Medellín in action below. The best bread in Medellín is at *Pan de Abril*, Cra 51/C 44 (San Juan), near Alpujarra Metro. Ask for *pan integral* or *pan de maíz*.

Eating
● *on map*

Bars *Bar Berlín 1930*, C 10, No 41-65. Attractive, low level music, snooker table. *Bar Blue Rock*, C 10, No 40-20. Popular. *Don Edoardo*, Cra 45, No 48-57. Central, modest prices. **Cinema** Free foreign films daily at Universidad de Medellín or Universidad de Antioquia. **Discos** In central hotels, and in El Poblado. Also many discos and popular dance halls on C 50, between Cras 65 and 75, and Cra 70, between C 36 and C 44. For a dark, underground and lively young place, try *Pub* or *Bartolomé* next to each other on Autopista Palmas, Km 5, or *Templo Antonia*, nearby, large and popular. Couples only allowed in to many discos. Beyond Poblado, there are good nightspots in Envigado or try *Vinacure* in Tablaza (Caldas), cover US$5, free Thu, take transport from Itagüí Metro station.

Entertainment

Music Monthly concerts by the *Antioquia Symphony Orchestra*. Band concerts and other entertainments in the Parque Bolívar every Sun. Universidad de Medellín theatre has monthly tango shows. Tango also at *Vos ... Tango*, C 34, No 66A-13, diagonal al Super Ley de Unicentro, live music, T265 9352, US$5. *Adios Muchachos*, Cra 45 between C 53/54.

Theatre *Teatro Metropolitano*, C 41, No 57-30, T232 8584, major artistic presentations. Many other theatres of all types, check press.

Colombia

Colombia

Festivals *Flower fair* (*Feria de las Flores/Desfile de Silleteros*) is held annually in the first week of **Aug** with spectacular parades and music, one of the finest shows in Colombia. The flowers are grown at Santa Elena in the Parque Ecológico de Piedras Blancas, 14 km from Medellín.

Shopping There are *artesanía* shops on the top of Cerro Nutibara and a small handicrafts market at C 52 near Cra 46 with many stalls. *Mercado San Alejo*, Parque Bolívar, open on the first Sat of every month except Jan, and before Christmas on Sat and Sun (handicrafts on sale at good prices). Good shopping generally around Parque de Bolívar. Many textile mills have discount clothing departments where good bargains can be had; ask at your hotel. *Aluzia Correas y Cinturones*, Oviedo Shopping Center, Poblado, Unicentro Medellín, also in Bogotá, for an incredible selection of belts, US$10-30. *La Piel*, at C 53, No 49-131. An excellent selection of leather goods at very reasonable prices.

    Bicycle repairs *La Cuca Gioco*, C 60, No 52-33, T231 5409. For parts *Bike House*, Av El Poblado, No 25-41, T262 4211.

    Bookshops *Librería Científica*, C 51, No 49-52, T231 4974. Large selection, some foreign. *La Anticuaria*, C 49, No 47-46, T511 4969. Antique and secondhand books, including in English, helpful. *Centro Colombo Americano*, Cra 45, No 53-24, T513 4444. Good selection of books in English for sale (including *Footprint Handbooks*).

    Maps Local and national maps from *Instituto Geográfico Agustín Codazzi* in Fundación Ferrocarril building, Cra 52, No 14-43, office in the basement.

Sport **Bullfights**: at the bull-ring of La Macarena, C 44 and Cra 63, in February; cheapest US$12, usually fully booked. **Sports complex**: *Estadio Atanasio Girardot*, Cra 74, C 50, football, baseball, velodrome etc, next to the *Estadio* Metro station.

Tour operators *Marco Polo*, C 48, No 65-94, T230 5944. Very helpful, some English spoken. *Panturismo*, at José María Córdoba airport, local 22-10, p 2, T562 2914. AmEx representative. *Realturs*, Cra 46, No 50-28, T511 6000. Good. *Tierra Mar Aire*, C 52, No 43-124, T513 0414. Helpful.

Transport
See also Ins & outs. For international car rental agencies, see Car hire, page 48.
Local Bus: Extensive services, slightly cheaper than Metro, but slower. **Metro**: operates 0500-2300 weekdays, 0700-2200 Sun and holidays (see map). **Taxi**: Minimum charge US$0.75. Radio taxis: *Aerotaxi* for international airport, T562 2837/235 7676. *Coodetaxi*, T311 7777.

Long distance Air: Frequent services to **Bogotá**, and all major Colombian cities. Municipal airport: Olaya Herrera, non-jets only, 10 mins by taxi from the centre with flights to Quibdó, Bahía Solano, Pereira etc.

Train: no trains running at present (2002) to Barranca, Bogotá or Santa Marta, but check.

Medellín - metro

Niquía
Bello
Madera
Acevedo
Tricentenario
Railway Station
Terminal del Norte — Caribe
Universidad
(Service Link)
Hospital
San Javier — Santa Lucía — Estadio — Prado
Floresta — Suramericana — Cisneros — Parque Berrío
San Antonio
Alpujarra
Exposiciones
Industriales
Olaya Herrera Airport — Terminal del Sur — Poblado
Aguacatala
Ayurá
Envigado
Itagüí

N

Not to scale

A tourist train to and from **Cisneros** (a park and waterfalls) runs on weekends and holidays. For information call Terminales de Transportes del Norte, T267 1157, or go to the station itself, Metro to Caribe on line A.

Bus: From **Terminal del Norte**: To/from **Bogotá**, 9-12 hrs, US$14-19, every 40 mins or so, with 5 companies. To **Cartagena**, 12-15 hrs, by *Pullman* bus, US$29 (take food with you, the stops tend to be at expensive restaurants). To **Barranquilla**, 16 hrs by *Pullman*, US$31. To **Turbo**, US$15 with *Gómez* (the best), 14 hrs. From **Terminal del Sur**: Frequent buses for **Cali**, *Flota Magdalena* US$17, 10-12 hrs. Frequent buses to **Manizales**, 6 hrs US$8, by *Empresa Arauca*. To **Pereira**, 8 hrs, US$10 by *Flota Occidental Pullman*. To **Popayán**, US$22, 12 hrs, *Flota Magadalena*. To **Ipiales**, US$33, 22 hrs, *Expreso Bolivariano* (takes Visa). To **Quibdó**, 11-13 hrs, US$14. To **San Agustín**, *Rápidos Tolima*, 0600, US$34.

Directory

Banks Most banks in the 3 business zones have ATMs. Many accept international cards. Some, eg *Lloyds TSB Bank*, C 52, No 49-35 in the centre and Diagonal 47, No 15 Sur-31 in Poblado, cash Amex TCs with passport and purchase voucher, and give cash against credit and debit cards. *Bancolombia*, in El Poblada, cash against MasterCard, Amex, good rates for TCs and cash. Many banks open late and on Sat. Main hotels will cash TCs for residents when banks are closed, but at less favourable rates. **Communications** Internet: Plenty of internet cafés in El Poblado and most shopping centres. **Post Office:** Cra 46/C 51, airmail office in *Avianca* building, Cra 52, No 51A-01, Mon-Sat, 0700-2200, *poste restante*. Also, *Avianca* post office in the Colseguros building Cra 46, C 53/54. **Telecommunications:** *Telecom*, C 49, No 45-63, also Cra 49/C 49. **Cultural centres** Centro Colombo Americano, Cra 45, No 53-24, T513 4444. English classes, library, bookshop, films and exhibitions. **Alianza Francesa**, Cra 49, No 44-94. **Embassies and consulates** France, Cra 52, No 14-200, Of 204, T235 8037, F265 7291. **Germany**, Cra 43F, No 17-419, T262 1756. **UK**, Cra 49, No 46A, Sur-103, Envigado, T331 8625, F331 0046, embajadabr@geo.net.co Very helpful, take a taxi and phone for directions as its hard to find. **Medical services** *Hospital San Vicente de Paul*, C 64/Cra 51D, T263 5333, one of the best. *Clínica Soma*, C 51, No 45-93, T251 0555, good doctor and general services. There is a clinic with free consultations and basic treatment in the airport buildings. **Useful addresses** DAS, C 19, No 80A-40 in Belén La Gloria section, T341 5900. **MA** (see page 772): Cra 76, No 49-92, T422 0883. **Tourist Police** at airport, T287 2053; local police T112.

Around Medellín

On the Medellín-Bogotá highway is **Marinilla**, 46 km from Medellín. A road north goes 25 km to **El Peñol**, a precipitous, bullet-shaped rock which towers above the surrounding hills and the Embalse del Peñol reservoir. It has been eroded smooth, but a spiral staircase has been built into a crack from the base to the summit. ■ *US$1, parking US$1.* At the summit is a snack bar with fine views (meals at holiday times only). Bus to the rock and to the pretty town of **Guatapé** (*Population*: 5,000. *Altitude*: 1,900 m. *Phone code*: 94) with Cía Fco López, from Terminal del Norte, Medellín, US$2.70. One hotel (**E**), on the main plaza and several other places to stay on the lakeside, with plenty of restaurants. A popular day's outing.

Five kilometres from Medellín airport is **Rionegro** (*Phone code: 094*) in a delightful valley of gardens and orchards. The **Casa de Convención** and the **cathedral** are worth a visit. There are colourful processions in Easter Week. There are various hotels (**B**-**E**) and many places to eat in and near the plaza. ■ *Buses from Medellín, from Terminal del Norte via Santa Elena, US$1.40, 1½ hrs, every 30 mins or so. Others from Terminal del Sur. Also colectivos from C 49/Cra 42, US$2.50, 45 mins. To El Peñol from Rionegro, take a colectivo to Marinilla from near market, US$0.60.*

Around Rionegro is some very attractive country, popular at weekends with delightful places to spend the day eg **El Retiro** and nearby **Fizebad**, an old estate house, restored with original furniture and artefacts, and a display of flowering orchids ■ *US$2.50. (To Fizebad, catch a La Ceja or El Retiro bus.)*

Medellín southeast to Bogotá
Check carefully for safety before going by road anywhere in Antioquia outside Medellín

Colombia

Northwest to Turbo: Santa Fé de Antioquia
Phone code: 94
Colour map 1, grid B2
Population: 12,000
Altitude: 530 m
80 km from Medellín

The road to Turbo leads from Cra 80 northwest, winding up to Alto de Boquerón, 22 km from the city (good views). A tunnel is being built to improve this road though construction is halted at present (2002). **Santa Fé de Antioquia** (usually called Santa Fé), is 80 km from Medellín just west of the Río Cauca. It was founded as a gold mining town by the Spaniards in 1541, and became the most important town in the area. In 1813 it became the capital of the short-lived independent state of Antioquia, but by 1826 this had collapsed and even local political control was lost to Medellín. The isolation that followed has preserved this remarkable colonial town and it was given National Monument status in 1960.

The fine old Cathedral is worth seeing, as is the church of Santa Bárbara. There is a small museum next to this church. There is a wonderful suspension bridge, the **Puente de Occidente**, 300 m long, 3 km downstream from the modern steel bridge, ask for directions or take a taxi. Major local festivals at Easter and Christmas. ■ *The bus station is on the road to Turbo at the north end of Cras 9 and 10. To Medellín US$3 (Socurabá or Transporte Sierra), 2½ hrs. To Turbo, US$14, 8 hrs, every 2 hrs or so.*

Sleeping **A** *Caserón Plaza*, Plaza Mayor, T853 2040. Charming renovated colonial house, pool, restaurant, parking. Recommended. **C** *Mariscal Robledo*, Cra 12, No 9-70, T853 1111. **B** with refrigerator and TV, full during holidays and most weekends, swimming pool, good restaurant with excellent buffet lunch US$5. Recommended. **D** *Hostal del Viejo Conde*, C 9, 10-56, T853 1091. Cheaper without bath, restaurant recommended. **D** *El Mesón de la Abuela*, Cra 11, No 9-31. With breakfast, pleasant. **F** *Dally*, C 10, No 8-50. Basic. On road between centre and bridge there are 2 good family hotels. There is good food in the hotels and near the main plaza, eg *Los Faroles*, Cra 11, No 9-33.

South from Medellín

Santa Bárbara (*altitude*: 1,857 m), 57 km south of Medellín on the main road via the town of Caldas, with stunning views in every direction of coffee, banana and sugar plantations, orange-tiled roofs and folds of hills. Hotels and restaurants on main plaza; bus from Medellín, US$1.20.

A further 26 km is **La Pintada** (camping; hotels **E-F**). Here the road crosses the Río Cauca, then splits. To the left is the particularly attractive road through Aguadas, Pácora and Salamina, all perched on mountain ridges, to Manizales.

Alternatively, from La Pintada, the main road goes up the Cauca valley through **Supía**, a pleasant town 140 km south of Medellín (**F** *Hotel Mis Ninietas*, near plaza, unsigned, bath, clean) and **Riosucio**, a delightful town with fine views and a large colonial church (many restaurants and shops). At Anserma the road turns east to Manizales via Arauca. There is some beautiful country on the west side of the Río Cauca.

Shortly after Caldas, a road to the right (west) descends through Amagá to cross the Cauca at Bolombolo. From here, several attractive towns can be visited. **Jericó**, is an interesting Antioquian town with a large cathedral, several other churches, two museums and a good view from *Morro El Salvador*. **Andes** is a busy town, several places to stay and to eat, all on Cra 50/51; attractive waterfalls in the neighbourhood, and **Jardín** is 16 km southeast of Andes. This Antioquian village is surrounded by cultivated hills and the plaza is full of flowering shrubs and trees. The small museum in the Casa Cultura has paintings and local artifacts, and a bank that accepts Visa cards. **A** *Hacienda Balandú*, 5 km from town, T845 5561, comfortable rooms, pool, gardens, good restaurant, reservations T511 3133 (Medellín). Several *residencias* and restaurants on or near plaza. ■ *Buses Medellín (Terminal Sur), 4 hrs. To Riosucio, 3 hrs, US$4.40.*

If going west from Bolombolo you take the right fork at Peñalisa, you can keep to the valley of the Río San Juan for 19 km to Remolino where the road again divides, right to **Quibdó** (see below) via **Bolívar**.

Department of Chocó

Stretching between the Cordillera Occidental and the Pacific Coast, from Panamá to Valle del Cauca, Chocó is one of Colombia's least developed and most beautiful departments. It is also one of the rainiest regions on earth ('dry season': December to March). In the northern part of the department, the mountain ranges rise directly from the ocean to reach a height of about 500 m. Transport is limited to water routes along the Pacific coast from Buenaventura in the south and up the rivers Road access is via two unpaved routes across the Cordillera Occidental, one from Medellín via Bolívar, just described, the other from Pereira to the southeast via La Virginia and Pueblo Rico (see page 854).

The scenery of pristine rainforest descending the mountain slopes to the sea is spectacular

Chocó is very sparsely populated. The coastline, apart from a small number of emerging tourist spots, is dotted with fishing villages whose inhabitants are of African origin. Inland along the rivers are Indian communities, whose lifestyle is based on hunting, fishing, and subsistence farming. Along the Río San Juan, in the south, there is gold prospecting around the towns of Tadó and Istmina. The construction of a road to the mouth of the Río Tribugá, where a deep sea port is planned as an alternative to Buenaventura, is raising fears of serious threat to Chocó's unique environment. Precautions against malaria, yellow fever, and dengue are recommended.

The Department of Chocó, especially the lower Atrato, remains a very dangerous area in 2002 (guerrillas, paramilitaries, kidnappings, drug running). Much caution and detailed advance enquiry are strongly recommended. See also warning on page 822.

Quibdó is on the eastern bank of the Río Atrato. Prices are higher here than in central Colombia (higher still in the coastal villages), so it is a good place to get supplies. There is an interesting mural in the cathedral. Hordes of birds fly in to roost at dusk and there are magnificent sunsets. The San Francisco de Asís festival is held on 4 August, and the Fiesta de Los Indios at Easter.

Quibdó
Phone code: 94
Colour map 1, grid B2
Population: 131,000
Altitude: 50 m

Sleeping and eating E *Cristo Rey*, C 30, No 4-36, T671 3352. Bath, fan, safe. **E** *Del Río*. Good, with bath, safe, free coffee, its restaurant, *Club Náutico* on 2nd floor has an excellent bar, good food and views. **F** *Pacífico*. Good rooms and beds. **F** *Residencia Darién*, Cra 4, No 26-68, T671 2997. Bath, fan, space to park motorcycle. **F** *Oriental*. No private showers, quiet, charming proprietor. An excellent eating place is **El Paisa**, Cra 4, No 25-54. *Chopán* bakery, good pastries and coffee.

Transport Air Flights daily to **Bogotá** with *Aces*. **Bus** *Transportes Ochoa* to **Medellín** via **Bolívar**, 5 daily, 10-12 hrs, US$7.50 regular, US$14 luxury coach. Buses daily to **Manizales** and Pereira via Tadó, and La Virginia. Local service to Santa Cecilia and Tadó. **River** From Buenaventura up the Río San Juan to Istmina and on by road; services infrequent. Irregular cargo service down the Río Atrato to Turbo and Cartagena takes passengers. Enquire at the wharves and deal directly with boat captains.

Directory Banks *Banco de Bogotá*, cash against Visa, other banks do not change money. A few shopkeepers sometimes change US$ cash, but rates are poor. Best to buy pesos before arriving. **Useful addresses DAS Office:** C 29, Cra 4. No entry or exit stamps.

The road to Manizales and Pereira begins in a very poor state. Most is through pure jungle with colourful butterflies, waterfalls and few people. 60 km south is Las Animas where there is a turning east to cross the San Juan, reaching **Tadó** (8 km from Las Animas), with a silver-fronted church. E *Hotel Macondo*, very basic but restaurant OK; at least one other *residencia* and good places to eat. After crossing into Risaralda Department, the road improves before reaching the Cauca Valley (see page 854).

Colombia

Colombia

Towns along the Pacific Coast On the Gulf of Tribugá, surrounded by estuaries and virgin beaches, **Nuquí** is gaining popularity among Colombian sports fishermen and vacationers. A number of luxury homes have been built nearby. To the south lies the wide curve of Playa Olímpica. To the north is the even smaller hamlet of Tribugá, a splendid beach and the proposed site of a deep sea port (see above).

Sleeping and eating Along the beach at the north end of town, there are several tourist hotels usually fully booked during the holiday period, best to make arrangements through travel agents in Medellín. Smaller places include: **D** *Rosio del Mar*. Cabins with bath. **E** *Doña Jesusita*, at south end of town. Basic. Felipe and Luz Largacha will sometimes rent rooms in their home (along main street south of town centre), **F**, basic. On Playa Olímpica, the Morenos run a small hotel, **E/F** range, shared bath, pleasant. You can also pitch your tent in their coconut grove for a small fee, hammock not recommended because of heavy rains and vicious sandflies at night (mosquito net recommended, repellent a must). Meals available if arranged in advance. Several small restaurants on road to airport serving mostly fish. Shops are well stocked with basic goods, prices somewhat higher than in Quibdó. Near Nuquí are the *Cabañas Pijiba*, T260 8265 (Medellín), www.pijiba.com Award-winning ecotourism development with full board, guided trips, diving, forest walks, airport pick-up, US$200 pp for 3 days/4 nights (low season) to US$350 (high season).

Transport Overland As yet there is no access for regular vehicles. **Sea** There are launches south to **Arusi** (Mon, Wed, Fri), and north to **El Valle** (Tue, Thu, Sat), as well as occasional coastal vessels (small fuel barges) to **Buenaventura**. Sea taxis will take you to beaches along the coast.

About 50 km north of Nuquí along the coast, **El Valle** has the best bathing and surfing beaches in the area. El Almejal, north of town, is recommended. with several large but simple tourist complexes with rooms and cabins (**D/E** range). Family accommodation in El Valle, **E/F**. Between El Valle and El Almejal are **F** *Cabinas Villa Maga*, safe, family run. For more expensive accommodation, enquire in Medellín.

Transport Road A rough road runs 18 km from El Valle to Bahía Solano (passes by airport before town). Jeeps leave every morning, 1 hr ride, US$2.50, tickets can be purchased 1 day in advance. **Sea** There are launches south to **Nuquí** on Tue, Thu and Sat, and 3 times a week to **Buenaventura**.

Parue Nacional Ensenada de Utria
Colour map 1, grid B2

Between Nuquí and El Valle is **Parque Nacional Ensenada de Utria**, which is home to two varieties of whales, corals, needlefish, and many other aquatic species. The surrounding hillsides are covered with pristine rainforest and there are several magnificent white sand beaches. Unfortunately the Park was closed at the time of writing (mid-2002). It is, however, worth enquiring if it can be visited. Normally boats hired from El Valle take 1½ hrs and cost approximately US$16 return. From Nuquí, US$24. Insist on a life jacket.

Bahía Solano
Phone code: 9816

Bahía Solano lies on a large bay set against jungle covered hills. As a resort, it gets quite busy during holiday periods when prices rise. Good bathing beaches may be reached by launch or by walking about 1½ hours at low tide (for example Playa Mecana. Be sure to return before the tide rises or you will be stranded). ■ *There is daily jeep service to El Valle (see above). Launches and occasional coastal cargo vessels north to Juradó and south to Buenaventura (eg M/n Fronteras, US$45 including food, 36 hrs, cramped bunks).*

Sleeping and eating **B** *Balboa Palacio* T27074. Best in town, pool, boat service to bathing beaches. **D** *Mr Jerrys*. Hammocks cheaper, boat trips, snorkelling available. **E** *Bahía*, C3, No 2-40, T27048, in same street as Satena office. With fan and private bath, good restaurant. **F** *Hostal del Mar*, across the street. Run by Estelle and Rodrigo, good, excursions arranged. Several others. Good food at *Las Delicias* and at the restaurant run by Señora Ayde near the *Balboa* hotel.

□Bogotá

La Zona Cafetera and the Cauca Valley

Modern and colonial cities line both the fertile western slopes of the Cordillera Central which is the centre of Colombia's coffee production, and the narrow Cauca valley, whose focus is Cali, the country's southern industrial centre, served by the Pacific port of Buenaventura. The three departments of Caldas, Quindío and Riseralda are generally known as the 'Zona Cafetera'. Much of the land here is between the critical altitudes for coffee of 800 m-1,800 m, and has the right balance of rain and sunshine.

Manizales

Manizales is dominated by its enormous (still unfinished) concrete Cathedral and the Nevado del Ruiz volcano, which erupted so catastrophically in November 1985. It sits on a mountain saddle, which falls away sharply from the centre into the adjacent valleys. The climate is humid (average temperature is 17°C, and the annual rainfall is 3,560 mm), encouraging prodigious growth in the flowers that line the highways to the suburbs north and south. Frequently the city is covered in cloud. The best months of the year are from mid-December through to early March. The city looks down on the small town of Villa María, "the village of flowers", now almost a suburb. Early in January the *Fair and Coffee Festival* is held, with bullfights, beauty parades and folk dancing.

Phone code: 96
Colour map 1, grid B2
Population: 335,000
Altitude: 2,153 m
309 km from Bogotá

Colombia

The city can be reached from the capital by road through Honda and over the Páramo de Letras pass (3,700 m) or through Girardot and Ibagué, then over the La Línea pass (3,250 m) and north from Armenia.

Several earthquakes and fires have destroyed parts of the city over the years, so the architecture is predominantly modern with high-rise office and apartment blocks. Traditional architectural styles are still seen in the suburbs and the older sections of the city. The departmental **Gobernación** building, opposite the Cathedral in the Parque de Bolívar, is an imposing example of neo-colonial architecture; the **bullring** is an impressive copy of the traditional Moorish style. Along Av 12 de Octubre to the suburb of Chipre is a recreational park, providing a great view to the west (well-visited on Sunday); El Tanque, on the Avenida, is a popular landmark.

Sights

Banco de la República has a gold and anthropology museum with classical music every afternoon. ■ *Open during banking hours, Cra 23, No 23-06.* **Universidad de Caldas** has a natural history museum with good selection of butterflies, moths and birds. ■ *Daily 0800-1200, 1400-1800 (take a 'Fátima' bus to the University).* **La Galería del Arte**, Av Santander at C 55, has exhibitions of work by local artists. Pictures can be bought.

AL *Las Colinas*, Cra 22, No 20-20, T884 0255. 2 bars, good restaurant, comfortable. **B** *Europa*, Av Centenario, No 25-98, T/F897 1239. Near the bull-ring, restaurant, comfortable, very helpful. **C** *La Posada del Café*, Av Centenario No 24-12, T889 2385. Restaurant, parking, ask for room with view of Nevado del Ruiz. **C** *Tamá Internacional*, C 23, No 22-43, T884 2124, next to Cathedral. With bath, popular lunchtime restaurant, good but noisy. **D** *Rokasol*, C 21, No 19-16, T882 3307. Hot water, good restaurant, good reports. **E** *Residencias Avenida*, C 21, No 20-07, T883 5251. With bath, safe. **E** *California*, C 19, No 16-37, T884 7720. Modern, laundry facilities, safe, car parking, good. **F** *Marana*, C 18, No 17-34, T884 3872, 1 min from bus station. Bath, hot water only in the morning.

Sleeping
In Jan hotel prices are increased

F *Residencias Margarita*, C 17 No 22-14. Good but noisy, safe, private parking opposite. Several **F** range hotels around C 18, Cra 22-23.

Eating *Las Redes*, Cra 23, No 75-97. Predominantly sea food, good but pricey. *Las Brasas*, Cra 23, No 75A-65. Good grill and *comida típica*. *Fonda Paisa*, Cra 23, No 72-130. Nice local dishes with local Andean music. *Casa Kena*, Cra 23, No 72-49. Good Italian, fresh pasta daily, Caruso recordings. *La Suiza*, Cra 23, No 26-57. Good fruit juices and cakes. *El Balcón del Arriero*, Cra 23, No 26-18. Good local dishes, reasonable prices. *Caballo Loco*, Cra 61, No 23-07. Good. Another with the same name at C 21, No 23-40 is mainly a bar but serves good pizzas. *El Ruiz*, Cra 19, No 22-25. Filling 3-course meal. *Punto Rojo*, Cra 23, No 21-41. Good quality cafeteria. Plenty of fast food restaurants around the centre.

Entertainment **Theatre** *Teatro de los Fundadores* is a modern cinema-theatre auditorium. Interesting wood-carved mural by Guillermo Botero, who also has murals in the entrance hall of the *Club Manizales* and *Hotel Las Colinas*. Events held here and at other locations during **Theatre Festival** in **first 2 weeks of Sep**. Free films at the *Universidad de Caldas* on Wed at 1700. Good way to meet students.

Transport **Air** *Aces* flies to Bogotá. **Bus** New terminal with good restaurant, C 19 between Cras 15 and 17, T884 9183. Buses to **Medellín**: via Neira and Aguadas, 6 hrs, US$8; via Anserma, 10 hrs, 1st class US$8; colectivo to Medellín, US$10. Bus to **Bogotá**, *Pullman*, US$12, 7-9 hrs; *buseta*, US$13.50. To **Honda**, US$5. **Cali**, hourly, 7 hrs, US$9. **Pereira**, ½-hourly, 1½ hrs, excellent road, beautiful scenery, US$2. **Armenia**, 3 hrs, US$4. To **Quibdó**, via Pereira, 14-17 hrs, US$16.

Directory **Banks** *Lloyds TSB Bank*, Cra 22, No 17-04, and other banks. **Tourist office** Fomento y Turismo C 29, No 20-25, T884 6211/2266. Open Mon-Fri 0800-1200, 1400-1800. **Useful addresses** DAS Office: C 53, No 25A-35, T881 0600. **MA**, Cra 23, No 54-04, T881 2210.

Parque Nacional Los Nevados

This is a park with all the savage beauty associated with volcanoes. Mountains (snowcapped above 4,850 m), dormant volcanoes, hot springs and recent memories of tragic eruptions, There are hiking opportunities in the highlands.

The park comprises 58,000 ha and straddles the departments of Caldas, Quindío, Risaralda, and Tolima. To visit Nevado del Ruiz (5,400 m) with a vehicle, take the Bogotá road from Manizales, to La Esperanza (22 km). Leave the main road here to the right for excursions towards the volcano. For an alternative route, make for the Barrio La Anea (next to the airport) continuing on an unpaved road for 22 km to the hot pools at Termales del Ruiz at 3,500 m. 7 km further on, this road meets the road coming from La Esperanza. Turning right, and continuing 2 km brings you to Las Brisas (small restaurant 2 km beyond). You can walk from Las Brisas down to Manizales in a day, stopping along the way at the *Hotel Termales del Ruiz* (see Sleeping).

Past Las Brisas the road forks. To the left it continues over enormous landslides caused by the 1985 Nevado del Ruiz eruption, to the village of Ventanas (a very scenic drive) and on to Murillo in the department of Tolima. To the right it climbs steeply for 1 km to reach the **park entrance and visitors' centre** at 4,050 m. In 4 km at 4,150 m is *Chalet Arenales* (see Sleeping). The turnoff (left) to Nevado del Ruiz is 10 km beyond the park entrance and you can drive to within 2 km of the snow line. On foot from 4,050 m to the summit takes six to seven hours if you are acclimatized. At 4,800 m, there is a basic hut, no water, no beds nor any facilities, but there may be refreshments during the day. Ask at the entrance if it is open. From here, it is about three hours to the summit. An authorized guide is obligatory if you wish to climb from the snowline to the crater. Another excellent climb nearby is La Olleta (4,850 m), the ash cone of an extinct volcano. You can descend into the crater, but note your route well as fog can obliterate landmarks very quickly. The road continues (south) below the Nevados del Cisne and de Santa Isabel between which you can visit the Laguna Verde. Four-wheel drive vehicles are necessary beyond Nevado del Ruiz. 20 km further along the road and 39 km beyond the turnoff to Nevado del Ruiz is Laguna del Otún at the southern end of the park, trout fishing and camping with permission of *MA*.

Entry is US$3, vehicle US$2.50. For information in Manizales contact **MA**; or the tourist office in Manizales, which organizes day trips to Nevado del Ruiz at weekends (US$16 1 day, leave 0800, return via hot pools). A warmly recommended guide is *Javier Echavarría Carvajal*, T Manizales 874 0116. See under Pereira, page 854, for access from that city and under Ibagué, page 840, for Nevado del Tolima. Visitors to the park should come prepared for cold, damp weather, and remember to give themselves time to acclimatize to the altitude. Maps of the area are available at the **Instituto Geográfico** in Manizales, C 24, No 25-15, T884 8275.

Park information & tour operators

B *Hotel Termales del Ruiz*, T880 9832, at 3,500 m. Comfortable, with restaurant and good thermal pools on premises. You can camp at various places outside the park or inside with a permit (US$12.50 for space for 5 persons), but it is very cold, you will need a good sleeping bag, but beautiful surroundings. 4 km from the park entrance is the new *Chalet Arenales*, T880 3553, at 4,150 m run by Carlos Alberto. **D** pp including sleeping bag, food, hot showers, cooking facilities, good atmosphere, crowded at weekends. There is room for 20 people, best to book through **MA** beforehand. You can stay at the *Casa El Cisne*, a small farm at 4,200 m near Laguna Verde (see above), where a farmer allows camping (**G**) and has rooms (**F** pp), breakfast and dinner available, US$1.50-2.

Sleeping

For those without transport, it is still possible to reach Las Brisas and the park entrance with a milk truck that leaves the *Celema* dairy in Manizales, Cra 22, No 71-97, between 0500 and 0600 daily US$3, returning in the early afternoon. The *Rápido Tolima* bus daily, check time, from the Terminal in Manizales to Murillo passes near the entrance to the Park, US$3, 2 hrs.

Transport

Colombia

Pereira

Capital of Risaralda Department, Pereira stands within sight of the *Nevados* of the Cordillera Central. A severe earthquake on 5 February 1995 badly damaged several buildings and the city was also affected by the earthquake which devastated Armenia in 1999 (see below). Pereira is a pleasant modern city, founded in 1863. The central **Plaza de Bolívar**, is noted for the striking sculpture of a nude Bolívar on horseback, by Rodrigo Arenas Betancur. There are other fine works of his in the city. There are three other principal parks: the most picturesque is the Parque del Lago, with an artificial lake; a fountain is illuminated several times a week. (Good Christmas illuminations, too.) The **Cathedral** is unimpressive from the outside but has an elegant and interesting interior. The **Museo Quimbaya de Oro**, in the *Banco de la República* building, Av 30 de Agosto/C 35 is worth a short visit.

Phone code: 96
Colour map 1, grid B3
Population: 432,000
Altitude: 1,476 m
56 km SW of Manizales

A *Gran*, C 19, No 9-19, T335 9500. Including breakfast, older hotel, good restaurant, bar, travel agency, well managed. Recommended. **C** *Marandúa*, Cra 8, No 14-73, T335 7131, F333 4081. Central, restaurant. Recommended. **C** *Cataluña*, C 19, No 8-61, T335 4527, F333 0791. 2 floors up, hot water, spacious. **C** *Royal*, C 16, No 7-56, T335 8847. 2 floors up, hot water. Recommended. **D** *Residencias Minerva*, C 18, No 7-32. Central, safe, TV. **D** *Ocmara*, Cra 8, No 24-55, T335 0531. Cheaper without bath/breakfast, fan, secure, hot water, cable TV. Recommended. **F** *Los Reyes*, C 4, No 16-23. Efficient, good value.

Sleeping

El Vitral, Cra 15, No 11-55. International food, very good. *Naturista*, C 18, No 5-30. Good. *Pastelería Lucerna*, C 19, No 6-49. Large coffee shop, fountain/garden, good cakes, snacks, ice cream, clean. *El Balcón de los Arrieros*, Cra 8, No 24-65. Local and international, good food. There are good restaurants on Av 30 de Agosto (the road west to the airport), including *Kisses Parrilla*, No 46-05, good steaks. Also, past the *Hotel Meliá* on the Av Circunvalar going east, No 6-55, *Mi Ciudad*, good meat, dishes. On the same road at C 5, La Terraza, *Pizza Piccolo*, good Italian food, excellent pizzas. Recommended.

Eating

Tour operators *Eco Sueños*, C 25, No 6-57, T333 9955. Trips arranged to Ucumari Park, Los Nevados etc, manager, Soraya Quintana, very helpful and a fully qualified guide. Recommended. *Tierra Mar Aire*, Av Circunvalar No 14-60, T335 6565. General travel agency, good service.

Transport **Air** Matecaña airport is 5 km to the south, bus, US$0.25. Daily flights to **Miami**, **Bogotá**, **Cali** and **Ibagué**; less frequent to other cities. **Bus** New bus terminal, clean, with shops, 1½ km south of city centre. Bus to **Armenia**, 1 hr, US$2, a beautiful trip. To **Cali**, US$8, 4½-5 hrs, buses by night, take colectivo by day, same price. To **Medellín**, 8 hrs, US$10. **Manizales**, US$2, 1½ hrs. To/from **Bogotá**, US$12, 7 hrs (route is via Girardot, Ibagué and Armenia).

Directory **Banks** *Lloyds TSB Bank*, Cra 7, No 18-70, Suite 201, changes Amex TCs with purchase receipt, cash against most credit cards, good rates, open 0800-1130, 1400-1600. *Bancolombia*, Cra 8, No 17-50, changes Tcs. Few other banks take TCs but some have cash machines, which take foreign cards. *Casas de cambio* change cash and some exchange TCs: several around Cra 9/C 18. **Tourist offices** Compañía Regional de Turismo de Risaralda *(Corturis)*, Edif de la Gobernación, Av 30 de Agosto, C 18/19, T335 0786, F335 3994. **Oficina de Fomento al Turismo**, Cra 7, No 18-55, 2nd floor, T335 7132/7172. **Corporación Autónomo Regional de Risaralda** *(Carder)*, C 24, No 7-29, p 4-5, T335 4152, F335 5501, for information and permission to visit local national parks.

Northwest of Pereira, 30 km towards the Río Cauca, is **Marsella**, and the **Alexander von Humboldt Gardens**, a carefully maintained botanical display with cobbled paths and bamboo bridges. Just outside the town is **AL** *Ecohotel Los Lagos*, T368 5164, previously a gold mine, then a coffee *hacienda*, now restored as a hotel and nature park.

Parque Ucumari

This is one of the few places where the Andean spectacled bear survives

From Pereira, a two to four-day excursion to the beautiful **Parque Ucumari** is recommended. There is excellent camping, US$2 per person or US$30 for three good meals and dormitory for the night at the *Pastora* refuge. From *La Pastora* it is a steep, rocky 1-2 day hike to Laguna de Otún through beautiful scenery of changing vegetation (see page 853). The **Otún Quimbaya** flora and fauna sanctuary forms a biological corridor between Ucumari and Los Nevados; it protects the last remaining area of Andean tropical forest in Risaralda. There are marked paths, *cabaña* accommodation, camping and meals available. ■ *US$1. Permission to visit must be obtained from Carder* (see under Tourist offices). *Access from La Suiza, 14 km east of Pereira (bus US$2.50, 45 mins).*

Enquire also of *Carder* about hikes to the **Nevado del Ruiz** (see also page 839 and page 852).

Pereira to Armenia

A 44 km road runs through the heart of the *Zona Cafetera*. A turn off at the *Posada Alemana* goes east for 9 km to **Salento** (*Population*: 3,500. *Altitude*: 1,985 m. *Phone code*: 96), well into the foothills of the Cordillera. This small town is brightly painted with an attractive plaza. Up Cra 6 (continuation of the north side of the plaza) is a 250-step climb, 14 stations of the cross to measure your progress, to an outstanding viewpoint, overlooking the upper reaches of the Quindío and Cárdenas rivers known as the Cocora valley, one of the finest views in Colombia. It is a popular weekend resort for Colombians for walking, riding and trekking but quiet during the week. ■ *Buses to Armenia hourly, US$1.40, 40 mins. To Pereira, hourly, US$2.50, 1 hr.* For tourist information about the area, contact *Fundación Herencia Verde*, C Real (Cra 6), No 2-15, Salento, T759 3142, or in Cali, C 4 Oeste, No 3A-32, T880 8484. Trips can be arranged with guides and extended to the Parque Nacional de los Nevados and Nevado del Tolima.

Sleeping and eating **B** *La Posada del Café*, Cra 6, No 3-08, T759 3012. Breakfast, pleasant patio. **D** *El Caserón*, Cra 6, No 2-46, T759 3090. Pleasant atmosphere, cooking facilities, good restaurant with trout specialities. *La Fogata de Salento*, Cra 3, Esq Las Colinas, T759 3248. Good food. *Café Patacón y Trucha*, on Plaza. Good fish. There are other places to eat and to stay, ask around, but make arrangements early in the day.

Colombia

Staying on coffee farms

The decline of coffee prices since 1992 has had a significant effect on the Colombian coffee finca. Coffee is still by far the most important agricultural product of the area, but there has been a good deal of diversification into other crops as varied as flowers, asparagus and even bamboo. Recently, the idea caught on to open the farms to tourism. No two fincas are the same they range from beautiful historic country mansions to modest accommodation. Urban Colombian families are increasingly spending their holidays in such places and this is being broadened to include foreign visitors. For information on the possibilities, contact travel agents (Eco-Guías in Bogotá is specially recommended), or the tourist offices in Manízales, Pereira and Armenia. Turiscafe, C 19, No 5-48, Of 901, T3254157, Pereira has good information.

The centre of the Cocora valley is 12 km up from Salento along a rough track, jeeps take about 40 minutes, US$6. Three restaurants (*Las Orillas*, *Las Palmas* and *Bosque de Cocora*) serve food at weekends, check in Salento during the week. 5 km beyond Cocora at 2,770 m is the **Acaime Natural Reserve** with a visitor centre, ponies for hire, accommodation for 20 and a small restaurant. There are lots of humming birds, cloud forest and the most important area of wax palm (the national tree and one of the tallest trees of the world).

Valle de Cocora

Armenia

The capital of Quindío Department is reached from Ibagué by the Quindío pass. The city was founded in 1889. In January 1999, an earthquake flattened much of the city and parts of the surrounding department were also badly damaged. In 2002 the centre is still a major building site but Armenia is as busy as ever and the fine example of Rodrigo Arenas Betancur's work, the **Monumento al Esfuerzo**, in the Plaza de Bolívar poignantly portrays the spirit of the local people. The two main churches, the cathedral and San Francicso church are both damaged but being repaired. Few important buildings were spared and services are often in temporary accommodation. We list restored or rebuilt permanent locations. Banks are operating normally. There is no reason for leaving Armenia out of your itinerary. Indeed visitors and tourists are welcome.

Phone code: 967
Colour map 1, grid B2
Population: 220,000
Altitude: 1,838 m

Colombia

C *Maitamá*, C 21 No 16-45, T741 0488. Moved and rebuilt 1999, central. Recommended. **C** *Mariscal Sucre*, Cra 17 No 18-33, T741 0867. Hot water, discounts possible, TV. **E** *Imperial No 2*, Cra 19/C 21. Central, safe. **E** *Moderno Aristi*, C 18, No 19-67, T744 1286. With bath, TV, hot water. **F** *Los Viajeros*, Cra 18, No 17-22, T744 2039. With bath, laundry service, cooking facilities, OK.

Sleeping
Enquire in hotels for the present addresses of the tourist authorities

La Fogata, Av Bolívar No 14N-39, T749 5980. International menu, expensive but good. *Casa Verde*, Cra 14 No 11A-25, T746 6093. Seafood, meat dishes, middle/upper prices. *Mateo Madero*, Cra 14, No 35N-96, T749 3716. Steaks, good value. *Parador Los Geraníos*, Cra 14, No 53N-34, T749 3474. Typical food, very popular, good value, speciality: *frijol garra picada*. Recommended. *Pastelería Lucerna*, C 20, No 14-43. Light meals, good quality. Recommended.

Eating

Air El Edén, 13 km from city. Several daily flights to **Bogotá**. Fog often makes air services unreliable. **Bus** Terminal at Cra 19/C 35. To **Ibagué**, US$4. To **Bogotá**, hourly, 9 hrs, US$13. To **Neiva**, US$16. **Cali**, US$7, 3 hrs, frequent service.

Transport

Some 12 km northwest of Armenia is **Montenegro**, near which is the **Parque Nacional del Café**, near Pueblo Tapao. There are restaurants, a botanical garden, ecological walks, a Quimbaya Indian cemetery, a tower with a fine view and an interesting museum which covers all aspects of coffee. A cableway links to a children's theme park with many facilities (additional charges). ■ *The park is open Tue-Sun, 0900-1600, US$4, children US$2.50, parking US$1, T752 4174, F753 6095. Take a*

Parque Nacional del Café

bus (US$0.35), or colectivo (US$0.45) from Armenia to Montenegro and then a jeep marked 'Parque' (US$0.25) or taxi (US$2) to the entrance.

South to the Cauca Valley

From Pereira and Armenia roads runs west to Cartago, at the northern end of the rich Cauca Valley, which stretches south for about 240 km but is little more than 30 km wide. The road, the Panamericana, goes south along this valley to Cali and Popayán, at the southern limit of the valley proper. There it mounts the high plateau between the Western and Central Cordilleras and goes through to Ecuador.

Cartago
Phone code: 965
Colour map 1, grid B2
Population: 130,000
Altitude: 920 m
25 km SW of Pereira

Founded in 1540, Cartago still has some colonial buildings, particularly the very fine **Casa del Virrey**, C 13, No 4-29 and the **cathedral**. Cartago is noted for its fine embroidered textiles. **Sleeping**: **D** *Don Gregorio*, Cra 5, No 9-59, T627491, swimming pool, a/c. **F** *Río Pul*, Cra 2, No 2-146, fan and bath. Recommended. Many hotels in area around bus terminals (Cra 9) and railway station (Cra 9 y C 6). ■ *Buses to Cali, US$6, 3½ hrs. To Armenia, US$1.75, 2-3 hrs. To Pereira, US$1.50, 45 mins. To Medellín, US$12, 7 hrs.*

Lago Calima

If you take the road from the colonial city of Buga, south of Cartago, to Buenaventura you pass the **Laguna de Sonso** reserve, good for birdwatching, before crossing the Río Cauca. Beyond the river is the man-made **Lago Calima**. Many treasures of the Calima culture are said to have been flooded by the lake, when the dam was built. This is an important centre for watersports. The northern route round the lake goes through **Darién** at 1,500 m with an archaeological museum. ■ *Tue-Fri 0800-1700, Sat-Sun 1000-1800, with good displays of Calima and other cultures.* There is a tourist office at C 10, No 6-21, and hotels in the village, as well as cabins available at a Centro Náutico on the lakeside. Camping is possible near the village. ■ *Direct buses from Buga to Darién, 2 hrs, and Cali, 4 hrs.*

Cali

Phone code: 92
Colour map 1, grid B2
Population: 1,780,000
Altitude: 1,030 m

Cali may be second to Bogotá in terms of size, but this vibrant, prosperous city is very much número uno when it comes to partying. Cali calls itself the Salsa capital of the world, and few would dispute that claim. The sensuous, tropical rhythms are ubiquitous, seeming to seep from every port of the city's being. Cali's other major claim, and raher more contentious, is that it boasts the most beautiful girls in the country. You can judge for yourself!

This capital of Valle del Cauca Department is set in a rich agricultural area producing sugar, cotton, rice, coffee and cattle. It was founded in 1536, and until 1900 was a leisurely colonial town. Then the railway came, and Cali is now a rapidly expanding industrial complex serving the whole of southern Colombia. South of Cra 10 are many one – and a few two-storey houses, tiled and wide-eaved. Through the city runs the Río Cali, a tributary of the Cauca, with exotic trees on its banks.

Sights

The church and monastery of **San Francisco**: inside, the church has been renovated, but the 18th century monastery has a splendidly proportioned domed bell-tower. From the 18th century church of **San Antonio** on the Colina de San Antonio there are fine views. Cali's oldest church, **La Merced** (C 7, between Cras 3 and 4), has been well restored by the Banco Popular. The adjoining convent houses two museums: **Museo de Arte Colonial** (which includes the church) and the **Museo Arqueológico** with precolumbian pottery. ■ *Mon-Sat 0830-1230, 1330-1730, US$1.* Another church worth seeing is **La Ermita**, on the river between Cs 12 and 13.

The city's centre is the **Plaza de Caicedo**, with a statue of one of the independence leaders, Joaquín Caicedo y Cuero. Facing the plaza are the **Cathedral**, the **Palacio Nacional** and large offices. Across the river, which is two blocks from the Plaza de Caicedo, is the Centro Administrativo Municipal (CAM) and the main post office.

To view the city, take a taxi to the **Monumento Las Tres Cruces**, northwest of the city or to the **Monumento Cristo Rey**, 1,470 m, to the west of the city. The huge statue of Christ can be seen 50 km away across the Río Cauca. It is also worthwhile going up the skyscraper Torre de Cali for a view of the city, but you may have to buy an expensive meal as well.

Museo Calima, at C 7, No 4-69, *Banco de la República* building, has precolumbian gold work and pottery. ■ *Mon-Sat 0900-1700, US$0.50.*

There is an orchid garden, **Orchideorama**, at Av 2N, No 48-10, T6643256, annual show, November. ■ *Closed Sun, free.*

Sleeping
Although still associated with drug and anti-drug operations, the atmosphere in Cali is quite relaxed. Carry your passport (or photocopy) at all times and be prepared for police checks. At night do not walk east or south of Cra 10 and C 15

A *Aristi*, Cra 9, No 10-04, T882 2521, F883 9697, www.hotelaristi.com.co Weekend discounts, art-deco style, large and old by Cali standards, unmodernized rooms much cheaper, turkish baths, rooftop pool, restaurant. Recommended. **A** *Don Jaime*, Av 6N, No 15N-25, T667 2828. Good, restaurant recommended. **B** *Pensión Stein*, Av 4N, No 3-33, T661 4927, F667 5346. With breakfast, some cheaper rooms, very good, quiet, excellent food, French, German and English spoken, Swiss-run, swimming pool. Recommended. **B** *La Merced*, C 7, No 1-65, T882 2520. Swimming pool, pleasant staff are very helpful, good restaurant, English spoken. Recommended. **B** *Hostal Casa Republicana*, C 7 No 6-74, T896 0949. Colonial house, attractive, cable TV, restaurant, good value. **D** *Río Cali*, Av Colombia, No 9-80, T880 3156. Good, reasonably priced meals, colonial building. **D** *del Puente*, C 5, No 4-36, T882 3242. Stores luggage. Recommended. **D** *María Victoria*, C 10, No 3-38, T882 3242. 24-hr restaurant. **D** *Plaza*, Cra 6, No 10-29, T882 2560. Luggage stored, reasonably priced. **D** *Los Angeles*, Cra 6, No 13-109. Good. **E** *JJ Hotel*, Av 8 N, No 14-47, T661 8979. With bath, cheaper without, safe area, good value. **E** *Sartor*, Av 8 N, No 20-50, T668 6482. With bath, central, Italian spoken. **E** *Iguana*, C 21 N, No 9N-22, T661 3522. Some cheaper accommodation, safe area, Swiss-run, laundry, email service, luggage store, motorcycle parking, excursions and language and Salsa classes arranged, excellent travellers' guest house. **E** *Latino*,

Colombia

Cali

To Monumento Las Tres Cruces

To Buenaventura

To Museo de Arte Moderno La Tertulia & Museo de Historia Natural

To Popayán

To El Porvenir Hotel, Airport & Palmira

To Iguana Hotel

To Sartor Hotel

Av 9AN
Av 9N
Av 8N
Av 6N
Av 4N
Av 3N
C 17N
C 15N
C 8N
Av 1N
Av Colombia
Río Cali
Centro Administrativo Municipal
San Antonio
La Merced
Museo Calima
Banco de la República
Teatro Municipal
San Francisco
Plaza de Caicedo
Palacio Nacional
Cathedral
La Ermita
Cra 1
Cra 2
Cra 3
Cra 4
Cra 6
Cra 7
Cra 8
Cra 9
Cra 10
C 5
C 6
C 7
C 8
C 13
C 14
C 15
C 16
C 18

N

0 metres 100
0 yards 100

■ **Sleeping**	4 Don Jaime	7 Latino	11 Pensión Stein
1 Aristi	5 Hostal Casa	8 La Merced	12 Plaza
2 Calidad House	Republicana	9 Los Angeles	13 Residencial Chalet
3 del Puente	6 JJ	10 María Victoria	14 Río Cali

C9, No 1-34, T889 2435. Spacious rooms with bath, good view from roof. **E** *Calidad House*, C 17N, No 9AN-39, T/F661 2338. Safe location, kitchen, laundry, will store luggage, pleasant. **F** *Residencial Chalet*, Av 4N, No 15N-43, T661 2709. Safe, quiet, dark rooms. **F** *El Porvenir*, Cra 1, No 24-29,. Shared bath, cold water, no keys, no windows but quiet.

Out of town L *Pacífico Royal*, Cra 100B, No 11A-99,T330 7777, F330 6477. 5-star, 9-storey building, excellent service with a personal touch usually only found in smaller hotels. **C** *Turístico La Luna*, Autopista Sur, No 13-01, T558 2611. Safe, large pool, restaurant, good parking.

Camping On south outskirts *Balneario Campestre*, Brisas Tropicales, swimming pools, refreshments, car camping, armed guards and dogs.

Eating

Cafés and ice cream parlours abound near the university, across the river from the main part of town

Rancho Alegre, Cra 1, No 1-155, T893 0980. Colombian food. *Cali Viejo*, Cra 1, Parque El Bosque, T893 4927 (on south side of river near zoo). Colonial house, excellent local dishes. *Las Dos Parrillas*, Av 6N y C 35, T668 4646. Good steaks but expensive. *Los Girasoles*, Av 6 N y C 35, T668 4646. Excellent Colombian menu, fish, ask for day's special. Recommended. *Da Massimo*, Av 5N, No 46-10. Good Italian. *Caballo Loco*, Av 6N y Cra 16N. European food. *Don Carlos*, Cra 1, No 7-53. Excellent seafood, elegant, expensive. *Parilla de Estebán*, Cra 1, No 4-08. Good meat and fish. *El Quijote*, Cra 4, No 1-64. Atmospheric, European dishes, expensive. *Fortissimo*, Av 6N, No 14-47. Good, cheap Italian, nice atmosphere. *Balocco*, Av 6N, No 14-04. Italian and Colombian, good value. *La Terraza*, C 16, No 6N-14. Elegant, music and dance, nice atmosphere. *Aragonesa*, Av 6 N, No 13N-68. Good breakfasts. *Primos*, Av 5 B N, No 24N-95. Good meat dishes and hamburgers. At least 10 eating places in the bus station.

Vegetarian *Punto Verde*, Cra 6, No 7-40. Mon-Sat, lunch only. *Govindas*, C 14, No 4-49. Lunch at 1300, dinner 1900. *Centro Naturista Salud*, C 17N, No 6-39. Set lunch US$2. *Casona Vegetariana*, Cra 6, No 6-56. Good food, juices and bread.

There are lots of sidewalk places to eat in the centre and along and near Av 6 in the north Bread and pastries shops often have cafés or cafeterías eg **Punto Sabroso**, C 12, No 8-06; **Montecarlo**, C 10, No 8-69 in the centre. Cheaper are the **fuentes de soda**, mostly with Colombian style cooking, a decent meal costs US$2.50-3.

Entertainment

Nightclubs Locally known as Grills. The ones along Av 6 N from C 16 upwards are safest and best known. *Tropicali*, Av 6 N, No 15-66 is one of the best with food and a range of entertainments. Many others nearby, or try *Tin Tin Deo*, C 5 y Cra 22, good atmosphere, salsa at weekends. *Taberna Latina*, C 5, Cra 36. Small and friendly. *Café Libro*, C 17 N, No 8N-49. Very popular, more expensive. *Zaperoco*, Av 6/C 17N. Good salsa bar. *Caliwood*, C 16N/Av 4N. Salsa in a relaxed and alternative setting. There is a nightlife tour Fri-Sat on a *chiva* (open-sided bus) to various discos, US$14. There is a school, *Profesional Academia de Baile*, Cra 4B, No 44-24, T446 2765, director Oscar Borrero, where you can perfect your Salsa, or ask at your hotel.

Theatre *Teatro Municipal*, Cra 5, No 6-64, T883 9107, major cultural activities, including opera and concerts. *Teatro Experimental*, C 7, No 8-63, T884 3820. Films Wed nights at *Centro Colombo-Americano*, C 13N, No 8-45, T667 3539. Also films on Fri nights at the *Alianza Colombo-Francesa*, Av 6 N, No 21-34, T661 3431. *Club Imbanaco*, C 5A, No 38A-14, T558 9520, old, popular movies. Good films also shown at the *Museo La Tertulia*, Av Colombia, No5-105 Oeste.

Festivals

Fair from **25 Dec to 3 Jan**, bullfights at the Canaveralejo bull-ring, horse parades, masquerade balls, sporting contests. *National Art Festival* in **Jun** (painting, sculpture, theatre, music, etc). Also in **Jun**, *Feria Artesanal* at Parque Panamericano, C 5, handicrafts and excellent leather goods.

Shopping

Platería Ramírez, Cra 11b, No 18-64. Factory and good shop for gold, silver, brass, jewellery, table settings, etc: dubious area, best to take a taxi. *Artesanías de Colombia*, C 12, No 1-20 and for larger purchases Av 6 N, No 23-45. For boots and shoes *Chaparro* (*Botas Texanas*), Av 14N, No 6-27, T665 3805. Good, owner Edgar speaks a little English. Best shopping districts are: Av 6N, from Río Cali to C 30 Norte and on Cra 5 in the south with several new shopping malls including: *Chipichape*, at the end of Av 6N, vast, worth visiting but prices are high. **Bookshop** *Librería Nacional*, on main plaza. Has a café, as do branches elsewhere in the city. Bookstalls on the sidewalk on Cra 10 near C 10. **Maps** *Instituto Geográfico Agustín Codazzi*, Cra 6, No 13-56, T881 1351. **Bicycle repairs**: *BTT*, C5, No 57-54, T552 1579. *Bike House*, Av 20 Norte 23 AN 68, T661 5572.

Viajes Camino Real, Av 4 N, No 21-84, T661 3939. Trips locally and to Popayán, Puracé, **Tour** Leticia etc. *Panturismo*, C 18N, No 8-27, T668 2255, and other branches, including at airport, **operators** T666 3021. American Express representative. *Viajar Por Colombia*, C 10, No 29A-38, T558 3140, F558 5231, vpcol@emcali.net.co English spoken, very helpful. Recommended. *Viajes Sinisterra*, C 11 No 4-42, p 2, T889 3121. Good service especially for airline advice. *Tierra Mar Aire*, C 22N, No 5BN-53, T667 6767. Helpful. *Vela*, Cra 4, No 8-64, local 104, T889 0760. Student travel agency, cheap tickets. Recommended. **Paragliding**: *Heinz Müller*, T664 0038.

Taxi: ensure that meters are used. Prices, posted in the window, start at US$0.15. Extra **Transport** charge on holidays, Sun and at night. **Air** Palmaseca, 20 km from city, has *casa de cambio*. *Busetas (Velotax and* **B** *Hotel Aeropuerto*, T666 3229, good. Frequent services to **Bogotá**, **Medellín**, **Cartagena**, *others) charge about* **Barranquilla**, and other Colombian cities. Minibus from airport, from far end of pick-up road *50% over bus prices* outside arrivals, to bus terminal (2nd floor), every 10 mins from 0500 up to 2100, approxi- *but save time; taxi-* mately 30 mins, US$1.50. Colectivo to city about US$1.20; taxi, US$11, 30 mins. *colectivos about*

Bus Terminal is at C 30N, No 2A-29, 25 mins walk from the centre (leave terminal by the *2½ times bus prices* taxi stands, take first right, go under railway and follow river to centre). Hotel information *and save even* available, left luggage US$0.60 per item, good food at terminal. Bus information, T668 3655. *more time* *Casa de cambio*, cash only. Showers on second level (US$0.40). Buses between the bus station and the centre charge US$0.10. Taxi from centre to bus station, US$1.50. To **Popayán**, US$5, 2½-3 hrs, also colectivos, US$6.50. To **Pasto**, US$11, 9 hrs. To **Ipiales** (direct), US$14, 12 hrs; *Coomotor* and *Sotracauca* to **San Agustín**, 9 hrs, US$14-16. To **Cartago**, 3½ hrs, US$4. To **Armenia**, US$7. To **Ibagué**, US$8, 7 hrs. To **Buenaventura**, US$5, 4 hrs. To **Manizales**, US$9, 7 hrs. To **Medellín**, US$17, 10-12 hrs. To **Bogotá**, 10-15 hrs, by *Magdalena* (recommended) and *Palmira*, US$18 (sit on left of the bus).

Banks *Lloyds TSB Bank*, Av 6 N, No 25N-11, T644 0200 and several agencies. *Banco de Bogotá* on the **Directory** Plaza de Caicedo for Visa cash advances. Many other banks and *casas de cambio*. **Communications** Internet: Many in the north and centre of the city. **Post Office:** Adpostal for national service, C 10, No 6-25; Avianca for international service, C 12N, No 2A-27. **Telecom:** C 10, No 6-25. **Embassies and consulates** French, Av 3N, No 18N-24, Of 405. German, Av de las Americas No 19-08, T661 1135. Swiss, Holguines Trade Centre, Cra 100, No 11-90, Of 316, T332 0490. UK, C 25 No 1N-65, T/F896 1235, britaincali@uniweb.net.co **Tourist offices** Cortuvalle, Av 4N, No 4N-10, T661 5983, F668 0862. **Fondo Mixto de Promoción del Valle de Cauca**, C 8, No 3-14, p13, T886 1370, F886 1399. **Useful addresses** DAS office: Av 3AN, No 50N-20 T664 3809/10. For national parks, **MA**, Av 3 GN, No 37-70, T6543720. **Red de Reservas Naturales**, C 23N, No 6 AN-43, T6606133, F6612581, for information on private nature reserves.

Both the toll and (unpaved) ordinary roads from Cali to Buenaventura give beautiful **From Cali to** views of mountains and jungle, and from the old road you can reach the **Parque** **the coast** **Nacional Farallones**. Take the dirt road south from the plaza in Queremal, at 1,460 m, about one hour from Cali, 3½ hours from Buenaventura. Alternatively, take the road southwest out of Cali to Pance, where there is an entrance to the park at El Topacio (US$1 pp). Good walking and bathing in the park, and peaks to climb. Busy at weekends, camping possible at various places in the park. For information, ask in Cali **Tourist offices**, *MA*, and *Fundación Farallones*, Cra 24B, No 2A-99, Cali.

Colombia

Buenaventura

Phone code: 92
Colour map 1, grid B2
Population: 202,000
145 km from Cali

Through a pass in the Western Cordillera is **Buenaventura**, Colombia's only important port on the Pacific. It was founded in 1540, but not on its present site. It now stands on the island of Cascajal, on the Bay of Buenaventura, 20 km from the open Pacific. Beaches such as La Bocana, Juanchaco and Ladrilleros (many small hostels and restaurants) may be reached by motor launch, but they are not very safe. Trips to beaches cost between US$10-40 for 10-person launch (rate per launch).

There are still problems with malaria. The port handles the bulk of Colombia's coffee exports, and about half of total exports, including sugar and frozen shrimp.

The commercial centre is now entirely paved and has some impressive buildings, but the rest of the town is poor, with steep unpaved streets lined with wooden shacks. There is a festive atmosphere every night and the *Festival Folklórico del Litoral* is held in July. South of the town a swampy coast stretches as far as Tumaco (see page 873); to the north lies the deeply jungled Chocó Department.

Sleeping & eating

More expensive than Cali, difficult to eat cheaply or well

A *Estación*, C 2, No 1A-08, T243 4070. Good restaurant. **D** *Felipe II*, Cra 3A, No 2-44, T242 2820. A/c, restaurant. **E** *Mi Balconcito*, C 3/Cra 4. Basic, OK. **E** *Continental*, Cra 5, No 4-05. With bath. Opposite is **F** *Europa*. Without bath. **F** *Las Gaviotas*, C 3, No 3-83, T242 4652. OK. **F** *Niza*, C 6, No 5-38. With bath and fan. A very good but expensive eating place is *Los Balcones*, C 2 y Cra 3. *Mediterráneo*, C 3, No 3-92. Local and international food. Self-service restaurant on main plaza, clean, modern, open 24 hrs. *La Sazón de Merceditas*, opposite *Edif de Café*. Good seafood, soups, reasonable prices. *La Sombrita de Miguel*, near waterfront. Good seafood. Good seafood at Pueblo Nuevo market, but not very cheap.

Transport

Air Flights to **Cali** only. **Road** There are plenty of buses to Cali, US$5, 4 hrs. Colectivos run at ½-hourly intervals to Cali, US$5.75 pp. The **toll road** to Cali is fully paved; the toll is about US$1.30 for cars and US$0.30 for motorcycles. **Sea** Boats can be found going south to Tumaco and 3 times a week north to Bahía Solano.

Directory

Banks Several banks will change cash and Tcs. **Tourist office** C 1, No 1A-88, Mon-Fri, 0800-1200, 1400-1800. *Cámara de Comercio* nearby is also helpful. Maps at *CAM*, 3rd floor of office block at the far end of the seafront. **Useful addresses** DAS, near *Avianca* Post Office, T241 9592 for those arriving or departing by boat from/to Panama.

About 40 km northwest of Buenaventura on the coast, near the mouth of the Río San Juan, is **Juanchaco**, a small fishing village, the location of spectacular **dolphin and humpback whale sightings** between August and October. By launch from Buenaventura US$22, one hour, and by boat US$16.50, three hours. Whale watching tours about US$12.50 for two hours. Accommodation is basic.

Gorgona Island

Colour map 1, grid B1

150 km down the coast from Buenaventura. Many parts are unspoilt with deserted sandy beaches

The island of **Gorgona** was Colombia's high security prison (a sort of Alcatraz), until a few years ago. Convicts were dissuaded from escaping by the poisonous snakes on the island and the sharks patrolling the 30 km to the mainland (both snakes and sharks are still there). It was made a national park in 1984. From the paths you can see monkeys, iguanas, and a wealth of flora and fauna. (Rubber boots are provided and recommended.) There is an abundance of birds (pelicans, cormorants, geese, herons) that use the island as a migration stop-over. Snorkelling is rewarding, equipment can be hired (but take your own if possible), exotic fish and turtles to be seen. Killer whales visit the area from July-September. ■ *All visitors, research students and scientists must have a permit, obtainable from* MA *in Bogotá (see page 772). Entrance US$4.50 pp, US$2.60 embarcation–disembarcation fee (other* MA *offices will give advice). At holiday times application must be made 4 weeks in advance and you pay for 3 nights' accommodation at the time. Diving permit US$16. (Instructors also US$16.) If you want to volunteer your services as a park guard, contact* MA, *Bogotá. Facilities on the island are run by* MA *employees.*

Colombia

Sleeping Cabins on the island: for 4 US$50; for 8 US$90. Try to book bunk beds in advance; if you can't, prepare for a scramble. There is a restaurant with a mainly fish menu. You can take your own food but all non-biodegradable items must be taken off the island. Collect your own coconuts, but there is no other fruit on the island. Don't take alcohol, it will proba-bly be confiscated. Do take drinking water, it is in short supply and expensive on the island.

Tours and transport Organized tours: recommended are *Ecotur*, Cra 56, No 5-29, Cali, T551 7248, with a 4 day, 3 night tour from Cali for US$275 including permission from **MA**, and an offi-cial guide. *Panturismo*, C 8, No 1-38, Cali, T889 3135, offer tours to the island (see Cali, Tour operators, for other branches). To arrange on your own, find a boat at Buenaventura; they leave most days at 1600 from the El Piñal dock (Bodega Liscano) in Buenaventura. The trip, US$40 return, takes up to 10 hrs depending on conditions and can be an experience in itself.

Popayán, Tierradentro and San Agustín

°Bogotá

The Pan-American Highway climbs out of the valley to Popayán, a richly historic city which gives access to the páramo of Puracé in the Cordillera Central where four of the major rivers of Colombia rise. Nearby are the burial caves of Tierradentro and, to the south, the remarkable archaeological site of San Agustín.

Popayán

Popayán lies in the Pubenza valley, a peaceful landscape of palm, bamboo, and the sharp-leaved agave. The early settlers after setting up their sugar estates in the hot, damp Cauca valley, retreated to Popayán to live, for the city is high enough to give it a delightful climate. To the north, south, and east the broken green plain is bounded by mountains. The cone of the volcano Puracé (4,646 m) rises to the southeast.

Phone code: 92
Colour map 1, grid C2
Population: 223,000
Altitude: 1,760 m

Founded by Sebastián de Belalcázar, Francisco Pizarro's lieutenant, in 1536, it became the regional seat of government, until 1717, to the Audiencia of Quito, and later to the Audiencia of Bogotá. It is now the capital of the Department of Cauca.

Valle del Cauca and Cauca regions have had guerrilla problems recently. Enquire locally before travelling on minor roads

Popayán has given no fewer than eleven presidents to the Republic. The scientist Francisco José de Caldas was born here in 1771; it was he who discovered how to determine altitude by variation in the boiling point of water, and it was to him that Mutis (of the famous *Expedición Botánica*) entrusted the directorship of the newly founded Observatory at Bogotá. He was a passionate partisan of independence, exe-cuted in 1815 during Morillo's 'Reign of Terror'.

Having been fully restored after the March 1983 earthquake, Popayán has managed to retain its colonial character. The streets of two-storey buildings are in rococo Andalucian style, with beautiful old monasteries and cloisters of pure Spanish clas-sic architecture. During the week, the open markets are interesting – Bolívar market, C 1N, Cra 5 is best in the early morning – local foods such as *pipián*, *tamales* and *empanadas*. **The Cathedral** (C 5, Cra 6), beautifully restored, has a fine marble madonna sculpture behind the altar by Buenaventura Malagón and the unusual statue of Christ kneeling on the globe. Other churches are **San Agustín** (C 7, Cra 6), note the gilt altar piece, **Santo Domingo** (C 4, Cra 5), used by the Universidad del Cauca, **La Ermita** (C 5, Cra 2), **La Encarnación** (C 5, Cra 5), also used for religious music festivals, **San Francisco** (C 4, Cra 9 partly restored) and **El Carmen** (C 4, Cra 3). Walk to **Belén** chapel (C 4 y Cra 0), seeing the statues en route, and then continue to **El Cerro de las Tres Cruces** if you have the energy, and on to the equestrian statue

Sights
Take care if you cross any of the bridges over the river going north, especially at night

Ask the Tourist Police about which areas of the city are unsafe

There are plenty of guides offering their services: check for safety before making these walks alone

Colombia

of Belalcázar on the **Morro de Tulcán** which overlooks the city; this hill is the site of a precolumbian pyramid. It is said that Bolívar marched over the **Puente Chiquito** (C 2 y Cra 6), built in 1713.

Museums close Mon   **Museo Negret**, C 5, No 10-23, US$0.40, has works, photographs and furniture of Negret. **Museo Guillermo Valencia**, Cra 6 No 2-69, is the birthplace of the poet. **Museo de Historia Natural**, Cra 2, No 1A-25, has good displays of archaeological and geological items with sections on insects (particularly good on butterflies), reptiles, mammals and birds. US$1.

Sleeping

Prices can rise by 30% for Holy Week and festivals, eg 5-6 Jan

It is not safe walking alone at night outside the central area

AL *Monasterio*, C 4, No 10-50, T824 2191, F824 3491. In what was the monastery of San Francisco, lovely grounds, swimming pool, fully renovated, very good. **A** *Camino Real*, C 5, No 5-59, T824 1546, PO Box 248. Good service, excellent restaurant. Recommended. **A** *El Herrero*, Cra 5 No 2-08, T824 4498. Converted large colonial house, family owned, good restaurant. Highly recommended. **A** *La Plazuela*, C 5, No 8-13, T824 1071. Colonial style, courtyard, comfortable rooms, TV, restaurant. **B** *Los Balcones*, C 3, No 6-80, T824 2030, F824 1814. Hot water, Spanish-style restaurant for breakfast and lunch, good, will change TCs. Recommended. **C** *La Casona del Virrey*, C 4, No 5-78, T824 4237. Hot water, big rooms, nice colonial house. Warmly recommended. **C** *Los Olivares*, Cra 7, No 2-48, T8242186. Quiet, good local and international restaurant. **C** *La Posada del Rancho*, 5 km on road to Cali, T823 4710. Excellent restaurant. **C** *Hostal Santo Domingo*, C 4, No 5-14, T824 1607. Good value, in restored colonial building. **D** *Casa Grande*, Cra 6, No 7-11, T824 0604. Family run, attractive, hot water, stores luggage. Highly recommended. **D** *Pakandé*, Cra 6, No 7-75, T824 0846. Good beds, hot shower. Recommended. **E** *Bolívar*, Cra 5, No 7-11, T824 4844. Hot water, pleasant, good restaurant, flowery courtyard, motorcycle parking, car parking across street.

Popayán

Sleeping ◼	9 Don Blas *C2*	17 Monasterio *B1*
1 Amalia *C2*	10 El Herrero *B2*	18 Pakandé *C2*
2 Berioska *C2*	11 Hostal Santo	19 Plaza Bolívar *A2*
3 Bolívar *C2*	Domingo *B2*	20 Residencias Cataluña *C2*
4 Camino Real *B2*	12 La Casona del Virrey *B2*	21 Residencias El Viajero *C2*
5 Casa Familiar El	13 La Plazuela *B2*	22 Residencia Líder *A3*
Descanso *B2*	14 La Posada *B3*	23 Residencia Panamá *C2*
6 Casa Familiar	15 Los Balcones *B2*	24 Residencias San
Turística *B2*	16 Los Olivares *B2*	Agustín *A2*
7 Casa Grande *C2*		
8 Casa Suiza *B2*		

Colombia

E *Don Blas*, Cra 6 No 7-87, T824 0817. With bath, modern. Recommended. **E** *Casa Familiar El Descanso*, Cra 5 No 2-41, T822 4787. Good breakfast, hot water. Highly recommended. **E** *La Posada*, Cra 2, No 2-35. With bath, use of kitchen, TV room, cheaper for longer stays, Spanish lessons arranged. **E** *Casa Familiar Turística*, Cra 5, No 2-11, T824 4853. Hot water, family-run. Recommended. **F** *Casa Suiza*, C 4, No 7-79, T824 0751. Hot water, secure. **F** *Residencia Panamá*, Cra 5, No 7-33. Good, laundry service, good food. Recommended. Private accommodation at C 3, No 2-53, T824 0602, Karin and Luis Cabrera, **F**, meals, Spanish lessons arranged.

There are many hotels in the Mercado Bolívar area on Cra 6 to the north of the river, eg **F** *Residencia Líder*, Cra 6, No 4N-70, T823 0915. Good. **F** *Plaza Bolívar*, Cra 6, No 2N-12, T823 1533. With bath, good cheap restaurant, safe, good value. **F** *Residencias San Agustín*, Cra 6, No 1N-15. Family run, good beds, laundry facilities. Also, on and south of C 8: **D** *Berioska*, C 8, No 5-47, T822 3145. Well run. **F** *Amalia*, Cra 6, No 8-58. Hot water, same owners as *Berioska*, cooking and laundry facilities, good base for young travellers. Recommended. **F** *Residencias Cataluña*, Cra 5, No 8-27. Popular. **F** *Residencias El Viajero*, C 8, No 4-45, T824 3069. With bath, otherwise basic, popular, watch your belongings, modern.

Just outside town, **D** *Campobello Bed & Breakfast (Myriam and Andre)*, C 33AN, No 14A-14, T823 5545, off Pan-American Highway, 300 m down road opposite *Torremolino* restaurant. Good view, safe, meals, good value. Recommended.

For good food at reasonable prices, take a short taxi ride to the road to Cali to *Rancho Grande*, Autopista Norte 32N-50, T823 5788. 2 thatched restaurants, delicious *chuzos* (barbecued beef), credit cards accepted. *Torremolino*, Autopista Norte 33N-100, T823 4000. Similar, also evening entertainment. In the centre, the best are: *La Viña*, C 4, No 7-85. Open 24 hrs, good set lunch and dinner, also *panadería*. *Pizzería Don Sebastián*, C 3, No 2-54. Good food in a colonial mansion. *Cascada*, Cra 7, No 6-46. Good for breakfast. *La Oficina*, C 4, No 8-01. Huge servings, good value. *Los Quingos de Belén*, C 4, No 0-13. Very good Colombian food, try *empanadas* and *tamales pipianes*. *La Brasa Roja*, Cra 8 No 5-90. Set lunch and evening meal, good food and value. *Jengibre*, Cra 8, No 7-19, T824 2732. Vegetarian. *Belalcázar*, Cra 6, No 7-55, T824 1911. Good value. *Caldas*, Cra 6 y C 8. Filling 3-course set meals, their *sancocho*. Recommended. *Mey Chow*, Cra 10A, No 10-81. Good Chinese. *Chung Wah*, Cra 6, No 9-64. Huge, good Chinese, also vegetarian. *Pizzería Italiano*, C 4, No 8-83. Swiss owned, good pizzas and pastas etc, vegetarian dishes, fondues, lunch US$2.40, good meeting place. Recommended. *La Fontana*, C 6, No 7-72. Excellent bakery with café serving meals, pizzas and sandwiches. For light refreshments: *Peña Blanca*, Cra 7, No 6-73. Best bread and cakes. Recommended. *Comamos*, C 4, No 8-41, in front of cinema. Cheap, try the *arepas de queso*. *Delicias Naturales*, C 6, No 8-21. Good, cheap, vegetarian. *Olafo*, C 6, No 7-42. Good pizzas and *patacones con guacamol* and great vanilla ice cream. Good meals in the market, even cheaper with student card.

Bars *Los Balcones*, Cra 7, No 2-20. *Iguana Afro Club*, C 4, No 9-67, T824 2970, salsa and jazz. *Café Galería*, Cra 3 y C 4. Others on C 3.

Eating
The best restaurants are attached to hotels

Easter processions, every night of *Holy Week* until Good Friday, are spectacular; at the same time there is a religious music festival and the city is very crowded. In Semana Santa there is an *International Religious Music Festival*. The childrens' procession in the following week are easier to see. As at Pasto (but less violent), there are the *Día de los Negros* on **5 Jan** and *Día de los Blancos* on **6 Jan**; drenching with water is not very common. These are part of the *Fiestas de Pubensa* at which there is plenty of local music.

Festivals

At weekends people play 'sapo', see under Sport in Essentials. A good place is along the La Plata road near Belén Church. At the *Universidad del Cauca*, Cra 3, there is a good, clean swimming pool, entry US$0.50.

Sport

Taxi No meters; normal price within city is US$0.75, or US$0.90 at night. **Air** The airport is 20 mins' walk from the centre. Service to **Bogotá** with *Avianca*. **Bus** Terminal is near the airport, 15 mins walk from the centre (Ruta 2-Centro bus, terminal to centre, US$0.30, or taxi,

Transport

Colombia

US$0.75). Luggage can be stored safely (receipt given). From the bus station, turn left to statue of Bolívar, then take second right to Parque Bolívar; here are the market and cheap hotels. Beware of theft of luggage in bus station.

To **Bogotá**, *Expreso Bolivariano*, US$20, 16 hrs. To **Cali**, US$5, 2½-3 hrs, or *Velotax* microbus, US$6.50, colectivos leave from the main plaza. To **Pasto**, US$7, 5-6 hrs, spectacular scenery (sit on right). To **Ipiales**, something runs every hour but many buses arrive full from Cali, book in advance; *Supertaxis* or bus, up to US$9, 7½ hrs. To **San Agustín** via La Plata, *La Gaitana*and *Coomotor*, 13 hrs, US$13 each once a day. Via Isnos *Cootranshuila* and *Sotracauca*, US$12, 6-8 hrs. Sit on the left side for the best views. To **Tierradentro** (Cruce de Pisimbalá, also known as Cruce de San Andrés), with *Sotracauca*, 5 a day between 0500 and 1500, US$6, 4-6 hrs (see page 866) continues to La Plata. *Flota Magdalena* to **La Plata**, US$6, 5 hrs, also *Unidos del Sur* and *Sotracauca*. To **Puracé**, US$1.20, 2 hrs.

Directory **Banks** *Banco Cooperativo*, Cra 6, *Banco del Estado*, and others will change TCs. Some, eg *Banco Popular*, will give cash advances against Visa cards or *Banco del Occidente* against MasterCard. *Salvador Duque*, C 5, No 6-25, at Diana shop on the main plaza. Cash dollars can be changed at a *casa de cambio* on Cra 7 between C 6 and 7, also open on Sat. Good rates offered at *Titan*, Cra 7, No 6-40, T824 4659, who also offer an international money transfer service. There are other *cambios*, but their rates are poor. Several ATMs. **Communications** Post Office: Cra 7, No 5-77. **Telephone:** *Telecom*, Cra 4 y C 3; closes 2000. **Tourist office** Cra 5, No 4-68, T824 2251, has good maps of the city, prices of all lodgings, and bus schedules and prices. The Colegio Mayor de Cauca has details on art exhibitions and concerts. Try also the *Casa de la Cultura*, C 5, No 4-33, for information on cultural events. **Useful addresses** DAS, opposite bus terminal next to fire station, go early to extend visas. **MA:** Cra 9, No 18N-143, T8239932.

Silvia
Phone code: 92
Colour map 1, grid C2
Population: 5,000
Altitude: 2,520 m

This town lies in a high valley northeast of Popayán. The local Guambiano Indians wear their typical blue and fuchsia costumes, and are very friendly and communicative. The Tuesday market seems to be full of Otavalo Indians from Ecuador and their goods more expensive than in Otavalo. The market's at its best between 0600 and 0830, is very colourful. A typical Indian settlement, La Campana, is one hour on the *lechero* or bus; two to three hours' walk downhill back to Silvia. It is not safe to park cars in the street at night in Silvia. Tourist information 1½ blocks up from plazuela on the right hand side. *Banco Agrario* gives cash against Visa. Horse hire from Sr Marco A Mosquiro, US$3 per hour.

Silvia is reached either through Totoró on the Popayán-Tierradentro road (partly paved), or through **Piendamó** (paved), two beautiful routes.

Sleeping **In Silvia** **C** *Comfandi*, Cra 2, No 1-18, T825 1253, F825 1076, opposite church on main plaza. Safe, restaurant. **D** *Casa Turística*, Cra 2, No 14-39, T825 1034. Helpful, hot shower, good food, beautiful garden. **E** *Cali*, Cra 2, No 9-70, T825 1099. An old house, with good craft shop, including food, a little primitive, but very pleasant. **E** *Ambeima*. 3 beds per room, efficient, good simple meals. Recommended. **F** *La Parrilla*. Water supply erratic, basic, restaurant has reasonable, cheap food. **In Piendamó** **E** *Central*, behind old train station. Quiet, dubious electrics. **E** *Motel*, next to Mobil. With cold shower, TV.

Transport **Bus**: from **Popayán**, daily *Coomotorista* and *Belalcázar*, several *busetas* in the morning (US$2); additional buses on Tue; or take *Expreso Palmira* bus to **Piendamó**, every 30 mins, US$0.75; from there, colectivo to Silvia, US$0.85. On market day (Tue) you can take a bus to **Totoró**, 1200, US$1.50, 1 hr and then a bus to **Tierradentro**, 5 hrs, US$7.

Tierradentro

East of Popayán is **Inzá** which is 6 7 km beyond **Totoró**. There are several stone statues in the new plaza. 9 km beyond Inzá is the Cruce de Pisimbalá (or Cruce de San Andrés or just El Cruce), where a road turns off to **San Andrés de Pisimbalá** (4 km). The village, at the far end of the Tierradentro Park, has a unique and beautiful colonial church with a thatched roof; for the key ask behind the church. 2 km or so before

Pisimbalá is the **Tierradentro Museum** of indigenous culture: very good local information. The second floor is dedicated to the work of the Páez Indians, not to be missed. ■ *0800-1100, 1300-1700.*

The Páez Indians in the Tierradentro region can be seen on market days at Inzá (Saturday), and Belalcázar (Saturday); both start at 0600. The surroundings have spectacular natural beauty, with small Indian villages in the mountains (get exact directions before setting out).

At the archway directly opposite the museum or at Pisimbalá village you can hire horses (US$2 an hour, make sure they are in good condition) or you can walk to the **Tierradentro** man-made burial caves painted with geometric patterns. There are four cave sites – Segovia, El Duende, Alto de San Andrés and El Aguacate. The main caves are now lighted, but a torch is advisable. At Segovia (15 minutes' walk up behind the museum across the river), the guards are very informative (Spanish only) and turn lights on in the main tombs. Segovia has about 30 tombs, five of which can be lit 15 minutes up the hill beyond Segovia is El Duende (two of the four tombs are very good). From El Duende continue directly up to a rough road descending to Pisimbalá (40 minutes). El Tablón, with eight stone statues, is just off the road 20-30 minutes walk down. El Alto de San Andrés is 20 minutes from Pisimbalá From the back of El Alto it's 1½ hours up and down hill, with a final long climb to El Aguacate. Only one tomb is maintained although there may be 30 more. The views from El Aguacate are superb. Guides are available, Jaime Calderón (at Restaurante 56) is recommended. **NB** The whole area is good for birdwatching.

Parque Arqueológico Tierradentro
Entry to Park and Museum US$1.50, valid for 2 days Walking between the sites, take a hat and plenty of water. It gets crowded at Easter-time

Near the museum C *El Refugio*, T825 2904. With bath, hot water, good, restaurant and swimming pool (also available to non-residents). E *Residencias Pisimbalá*, near Telecom, T825 2921. Cheaper without bath, good, set meal and good other meals, garden, laundry facilities, mosquitos. F *Hospedaje Luzerna*. Hot showers, quiet, fresh orange juice, free coffee in morning, laundry facilities. Highly recommended, will let you camp for US$0.50.

In the village F *El Cauchito*. Pleasant, family atmosphere, meals available, will arrange horse rentals, camping. Recommended. F *Los Lagos*. Family run, good restaurant, hot water, pleasant. Recommended. F *Residencia El Bosque*. Cold showers, cheap meals, friendly owner collects coins. Recommended. F *Residencias El Viajero* (Marta Veláquez). Meals US$1. Recommended. F pp *Residencias Las Veraneras*, 2 houses, 300 m from Archaeological Park. Run by friendly young couple, restaurant, attractive garden and murals painted by locals. Ask about others who will rent rooms.

Sleeping

Colombia

Tierradentro

To Santa Rosa

El Duende (1,700m)

Quebrada Los Guazos

El Tablón (1,700m)

Quebrada Chaparquis

Segovia (1,650m)

Quebrada La Virgen

San Andrés de Pisimbalá

Quebrada San Andrés

El Alto de San Andrés (1,750m)

Museum & Administration

Quebrada El Escaño

El Aguacate (2,000m)

To El Cruce, Inzá & La Plata

N

0 metres 500
0 yards 500

Pisimbalá. Good food, cheap. Recommended. *El Diamanto*, opposite museum. Big portions, good value, order in advance. *Restaurante 56*, 50 m up from museum. Small but very good meals, has vegetarian dishes, also rents horses. Good fruit juices at the *Fuente de Soda y Artesanía* store and at *Los Alpes* (try their *mora con leche*), also good breakfasts. *La Portada*, bamboo building at jeep/bus stop in village. Excellent *comida corriente*, fresh soups, cheap. The house of *Nelli Parra de Jovar*, opposite the museum, with the long antenna, is recommended for abundance; you must book meals in advance. She can also give up-to-date information on accommodation.

Eating

The road from Popayán to **Tierradentro** is difficult and narrow, but beautiful scenery.

Transport

There is in theory a daily bus from Pisimbalá to **Popayán** at 0600, but services are very erratic. Otherwise, you must go to El Cruce. *Sotracauca* buses from Popayán, US$6, 4-6 hrs to **Cruce Pisimbalá**. Best to take early buses, as afternoon buses will leave you at the Cruce in the dark. Walk uphill (about 2 km, 30 mins) to the museum and on, 20 mins, to the village. If you want to go to **Silvia**, take this bus route and change to a colectivo (US$1.50) at Totoró. Buses from the Cruce to **La Plata** (en route to San Agustín, see below) US$3, 4-5 hrs or more frequent colectivo jeeps, US$4. If you cannot get a direct Cruce-La Plata bus, take one going to Páez (Belalcázar) (US$1.20), alight at Guadualejo, 17 km east of Inzá, from where there is a more frequent service to La Plata.

Puracé & Parque Nacional Puracé

The park is open all week, but reduced service on Mon

Some 30 km from Popayán is the small town of Puracé, at Km 12, which has several old buildings. Behind the school a 500 m path leads to Chorrera de las Monjas waterfalls on the Río Vinagre, notable for the milky white water due to concentrations of sulphur and other minerals. **F** *Residencias Cubina,* safe, cold showers, secure parking. *Restaurant Casa Grande* just above the church, meals around US$2.50. ■ *Several buses daily to Puracé from Popayán, the last returning around 1730.*

At Km 22, look for the spectacular San Francisco waterfall on the opposite side of the valley. At Km 23 is the turning right to Puracé sulphur mines (6 km) which can be visited by applying to *Industrias Puracé SA*, C 4, No 7-32 Popayán, best through the Popayán tourist office. 1 km along this road is a turning left leading in 1½ km to **Pilimbalá** in the **Parque Nacional Puracé** at 3,350 m. Here there is a park office, seven sulphur baths at 28°C. ■ *US$0.75, children half price, bring your own towels.* The national park contains Volcán Puracé (4,640 m) (for climbing see below), Pan de Azúcar (4,670 m) with its permanent snow summit, and the line of nine craters known as the Volcanes los Coconucos (a strenuous two-day hike can be made around the summits requiring high altitude camping and mountaineering equipment). The park also encompasses the sources of four of Colombia's greatest rivers: the Magdalena, Cauca, Caquetá and Patía. Virtually all the park is over 3,000 m. The Andean Condor is being reintroduced to the wild here from Californian zoos. There are many other birds to be seen and fauna includes the spectacled bear and mountain tapir. Pilimbalá is a good base from which to explore the northern end of the park. ■ *Entrance to the park US$0.60.*

Climbing Volcán Puracé On the hike to the summit, loose ash makes footholds difficult. Avoid getting down wind of the fumaroles, and do not climb down into the crater. Although the best weather is reported to be December-March and July-August, this massif makes its own climate, and high winds, rain and sub-zero temperatures can come in quickly at any time. A marked trail goes from behind the park office and eventually joins the road leading to a set of telecommunications antennae. **The area around these installations is mined, don't take shortcuts.** The summit is about 1 hour beyond the military buildings, total time from Pilimbalá at least 4 hours up and 2½ hours down. A guide is recommended.

Continuing on the main road to La Plata, at Km 31 there is a viewpoint for Laguna Rafael, at Km 35 the Cascada de Bedón (also chemically charged water) and at Km 37 the entrance to the most northerly part of the Parque Nacional Puracé. Here there is a visitors' centre, a geology/ethnology museum (entrance US$0.75), and the very interesting Termales de San Juan, 700 m from the road, entry US$0.40, where 112 hot sulphur springs combine with icy mountain creeks to produce spectacular arrays of multi-coloured mosses, algae and lichens, a must if you are in the area.

Sleeping and eating **At Pilimbalá** saloon cars will struggle up the last stretch to the centre, but it is an easy 2½ km walk from Km 23. The centre has picnic shelters, a good restaurant (rainbow trout a speciality, also has cheap *hospedaje*, very cold) and 3 *cabañas* that hold 8, US$32.50 minimum for up to 5 and US$38 for 8 people. Firewood is provided. Camping costs US$3 pp. Sleeping bags or warm clothing recommended to supplement bedding provided. **At Km 37** the visitor centre has a *cafetería* (arrange meals beforehand through Popayán Tourist Office).

Transport All these places beyond Puracé village can be reached by any bus from Popayán to La Plata or Garzón. The bus service can be erratic so check time of last daylight bus to Popayán and be prepared to spend a cold night at 3,000 m. The rangers will allow you to stay in the centre.

La Plata, whose central plaza has an enormous ceiba (planted in 1901), is 147 km from Popayán, 210 km from San Agustín.

La Plata

Sleeping and eating D *Cambis*, C 4, No 4-28, T837 0004. Modern, meals. Recommended. **E** *Berlín*, by church on plaza, 3 blocks from the bus office. **F** without bath, unappealing toilets and bugs in the beds. Next door to *Berlín* is **F** *Residencias Tunubalá*. OK. **F** *Viajero*, opposite *Sotracauca* office. Basic but convenient. **F** *Brisas de la Plata*, **F** *Hospedaje Exclusivo*, **F** *Residencia Orense* (meals available) and **F** *El Terminal*, all basic and near bus station.

Most closed by 2000. *Noche y Luna*, just off main plaza, very good. *Asadero Los Vikingos*, C 4, near *Hotel Cambis*, pizzas and all meals. Good set meals opposite Banco Cafetero. Excellent bakery on main plaza.

Bus To **Bogotá**, via Neiva, *Coomotor*, 9 hrs, at 2000 and 2100, *Cootranshuila*, 5 a day, US$18. To **Garzón**, bus or jeep 1½ hrs, US$3. To **Popayán** (*Sotracauca*) 0500 and others, US$6, 5½ hrs. To **San Agustín**, direct US$8 or take a colectivo to Garzón or Pitalito and change. For **Tierradentro** take a bus towards Popayán and alight at the Cruce US$4. Private jeep hire La Plata-Tierradentro US$32, cheaper if you agree to pick up other passengers. Ask around for best options.

Southeast of La Plata is Pital where the road forks, southeast to Garzón, and south to near Altamira. Garzón is a pleasant cathedral town set in mountains, 54 km southeast of La Plata, 92 km south of Neiva (see page 841). D *Damasco*, C 16, No 10-67, colonial building, good meals. Recommended. E *Abeyma*, state hotel, Cra 10 y C 12, it is possible to camp in the grounds. Recommended. E *Residencias Pigoanza*, on main plaza, with bath. Recommended.

Garzón
Phone code: 988
Population: 44,000
Altitude: 830 m

At Altamira, 29 km further southwest, a road heads southeast to Florencia, capital of the Department of Caquetá (see page 877). Southwest leads to **Timaná** (basic accommodation under US$3) and continues paved on to San Agustín.

Pitalito has little to offer the tourist. There are two hotels with swimming pools: **C** *Calamó*, Cra 5, No 5-41, T360600, hot water, and **D** *Timanco*, C 3 Sur, No 4-45, T360666. **E** *Los Helechos*, C 7, No 6-48, T360122, convenient for buses, family run. **F** *Residencia Pitalito*, C 5 round corner from police station, without shower, reasonable. *Crêperie*, 1 block south of main plaza, good value, excellent.

Pitalito
Phone code: 988
Population: 63,000
Altitude: 1,231 m

Transport Plenty of buses and colectivos to **San Agustín**, US$2. Bus to **La Plata**, 4 hrs, one at 1800. Buses in Pitalito go from C 3A. *Taxis Verdes* from the main plaza (US$18 to Bogotá). Bus to **Mocoa** (in the Putumayo), US$8.50, 7 hrs, also jeeps from market square, 2 in morning.

South of Pitalito is the **Parque Nacional Cueva de los Guácharos**. Between December and June swarms of oilbirds (*guácharos*) may be seen; they are nocturnal, with a unique radar-location system. The reserve also contains many of the unusual and spectacular cocks-of-the-rock and the limestone caves are among the most interesting in Colombia. The rangers are particularly friendly, providing tours and basic accommodation; permission to visit the park must be obtained from the *MA* offices in Pitalito, Cra 4, No4-21, Neiva or Bogotá. ■ *US$1.50, accommodation (when available) US$5 per night, pp. Check with MA if the park is open. Getting there: Take a bus to Palestina, US$1.20, 1 hr, and then walk for 6 hrs along an eroded, muddy path.*

Colombia

Colombia

Popayán to San Agustín direct

Avoid travelling by night between Popayán and San Agustín, the roads are dangerous. Cyclists should avoid the new direct route. Many reports of theft on the buses between these towns; do not trust 'helpfuls' and do not put bags on the luggage rack. Check carefully before taking this road

South of Puracé towards San Agustín is **Coconuco** (*Altitude*: 2,460 m). Coconuco's baths, Aguas Hirviendas, 1½ km beyond the *Hotel de Turismo* on a paved road (mostly), have one major and many individual pools with an initial temperature of at least 80°C. There is one pool where you can boil an egg in five minutes. A track from town is quicker than the road. Entry US$0.60, crowded at weekends, but during the week it is a fine area for walking and relaxing in the waters. 6 km beyond Coconuco, near the road, are Aguas Tibias, warm rather than hot, with similar facilities for visitors. **B** *Hotel de Turismo*, 500 m out of town on the way to the baths, full service, colonial style hotel run by Cali Tourist authority, restful atmosphere. There are several other modest hotels and restaurants in town. At**Aguas Hirviendas** are three cabins at US$20 per day that will hold up to six.

South of Coconuco by 24 km is **Paletará** with high grassland on a grand scale with the Puracé/Pan de Azúcar volcanoes in the background. Below the village (roadside restaurant and MA post) flows the infant Río Cauca. 10 km south of Paletará, the road enters the Parque Nacional Puracé and there is a track northeast to Laguna del Buey. The road then enters a long stretch of virgin cloud forest. This section links Paletará with Isnos and San Agustín. Heavy rain has weakened this stretch, 25 km of which are impassable to light vehicles and very tedious for buses and trucks. No efforts are being made currently to improve this road. 62 km from Paletará at the end of the cloud forest is Isnos (see page 869) followed by a steep drop to a dramatic bridge over the Río Magdalena and shortly to the main road between Pitalito and San Agustín.

San Agustín

Phone code: 988
Colour map 1, grid C3
Population: 6,000
Altitude: 1,700 m

Here, in the Valley of the Statues, are some hundreds of large rough-hewn stone figures of men, animals and gods, dating from roughly 3300 BC to just before the Spanish conquest. Nothing is known of the culture which produced them, though traces of small circular bamboo straw-thatched houses have been found. Various sculptures found here are exhibited in the National Museum at Bogotá. There are about 20 sites, described below. The area offers excellent opportunities for hiking, although some trails to remote sites are not well marked.

The rainy season is April-June/July, but it rains almost all year, hence the beautiful green landscape; the driest months are November-March. The days are warm but sweaters are needed in the evenings; average temperature 18°C.

Around San Agustín

Original Map by Joaquin Emilio Garcia

The whole site leaves an unforgettable impression, from the strength and strangeness of the statues, and the great beauty of the rolling green landscape. The nearest archaeological sites are in the **Parque Arqueológico**, which includes the **Bosque de las Estatuas**. The park is about 2½ km from San Agustín. The statues in the Parque are *in situ*, though some have been set up on end and fenced in; those in the Bosque (a little wood) have been moved and rearranged, and linked by gravel footpaths. Beyond the central area are the carved rocks in and around the stream at the **Fuente de Lavapatas** in the park, where the water runs through carved channels. The **Alto de Lavapatas**, above the Fuente, has an extensive view. ■ *Closes at 1600; refreshment stands at 'Fuente' and on the way up to Lavapatas.* There is a museum in the park which contains pottery and Indian artefacts (closes at 1700). ■ *Daily 0800-1600, entrance to both costs US$2, US$0.80 with student card, valid two days, also permits entry to the museum and the Alto de los Idolos see below. Guides: Spanish US$12.50, other languages US$20. Guidebook in Spanish/English US$3.75.* You can get a very good idea of the Parque, the Bosque and the museum in the course of three hours' walking, or add in El Tablón and La Chaquira (see below) for a full day. **Museo Arqueológico**, Cra 11, No 3-61, cultural events in the evenings, books and videos in Spanish and English, light refreshments. ■ *Mon-Sat until 2300.*

El Tablón is reached up Cra 14, over the brow of the hill and 250 m to a marked track to the right. El Tablón (five sculptures brought together under a bamboo roof) is shortly down to the left. Continue down the path, muddy in wet weather, ford a stream and follow signs to the Río Magdalena canyon. **La Chaquira** (figures carved on rocks) is dramatically set half way down to the river. Walking time round trip from San Agustín, two hours. Plenty of houses offer refreshments as far as El Tablón.

At **La Pelota**, two painted statues were found in 1984 (a three-hour return trip, six hours if you include El Tablón and La Chaquira, 15 km in all). The latest archaeological discoveries 1984/86 include some unique polychromed sculptures at **El Purutal** near La Pelota and a series of at least 30 stones carved with animals and other designs in high relief. These are known as **Los Petroglifos** and can be found on the right bank of the Río Magdalena, near the **Estrecho** (narrows) to which jeeps run.

Alto de los Idolos is about 10 km by horse or on foot (small charge, less if you have a student card), a lovely (if strenuous) walk, steep in places, via **Puente de la Chaquira**. Here on a hill overlooking San Agustín are more and different statues known as *vigilantes*, each guarding a burial mound (one is an unusual rat totem). The few excavated have disclosed large stone sarcophagi, some covered by stone slabs bearing a sculpted likeness of the inmate ■ *The site is open until 1600.* **D** *Parador de los Idolos* (three rooms, bath, hot water) is 500 m from the Alto.

Alto de los Idolos can also be reached from **San José de Isnos** (5 km northeast) 27 km by road from San Agustín. The road passes the **Salto del Mortiño**, a 300 m fall 7 km before Isnos, 500 m off the road. Isnos' market day is Saturday (bus 0500, US$1.20, return 1100, 1300, otherwise bus from Cruce on Pitalito road, or hitch). Hotels in Isnos, **E** *Casa Grande*, central, cheaper without bath. **E** *El Balcón*.

6 km north of Isnos is **Alto de las Piedras**, which has a few interesting tombs and monoliths, including the famous 'Doble Yo'. Only less remarkable than the statues are the orchids growing nearby. 8 km further is Bordones; turn left at end of the village and there is (500 m) parking for the **Salto de Bordones** falls. **D** *Parador Salto de Bordones*, hot water, restaurant.

Recommended reading The best books on the subject are *Exploraciones Arqueológicas en San Agustín*, by Luis Duque Gómez (Bogotá, 1966) or the shorter *San Agustín, Reseña Arqueológica*, by the same author (1963). The *Colombian Institute of Archaeology* has published a booklet (English/Spanish), at US$1.80, on San Agustín and Tierradentro, though it can be difficult to find.

Tour operators Sr Joaquín Emilio García, who was well known as head of the former national tourist office for many years, has now formed his own private company, *World*

Sights
Enquire about safety before walking to the more distant monuments. Beware of 'guides' and touts who approach you in the street. Have nothing to do with anyone offering drugs, precolumbian objects, gold, emeralds or other precious minerals for sale

Other archaeological sites

Colombia

Heritage Travel Office, C 3, No 10-84, T/F373940/373567, which we strongly recommend you visit on arrival. ■ *Mon-Sat 0800-2000, Sun 0800-1300*. Sr García is most helpful in all matters, he speaks English, French, Italian and a little German.

Guides Authorized guides charge US$15 for a half day, US$30 for a full day, up to 10 people per guide. You can make your own arrangements, and it may cost less, but we have received many reports of unsatisfactory experiences of unregistered guides. If you have any problems, ask at *World Heritage Travel*.

Horse hire You are strongly advised to hire horses for trips around San Agustín through hotels or *World Heritage Travel*. Charges are about US$12 per day and US$3 per hr per rider. If you require a guide, you must add the hire cost of his horse. There are fixed tariffs for 20 or so standard trips.

Vehicle tours Jeeps may be hired for between 4-5 people. Prices vary according to the number of sites to be visited, but the daily rate is about US$70. For those who like a good walk, most sites can be reached on foot, see above.

Sleeping **D** *Cabañas Los Andes*, Cra 11, No 3-70, T373461. Cabins, hot water and rooms with excellent views, basic cooking facilities. **D** *Central*, C 3, No 10-32, T373027, near bus offices. Cheaper without bath, or less still for a room just to dump your luggage in during day's visit, good meals, laundry facilities, secure motorcycle parking, will hire horses, English and French spoken. **E** *Colonial*, C 3, No 11-54, T373159. Hot shower, pleasant, good restaurant, parrots in the garden. **E** *Hospedaje D'Zuleg*, C 4, No 10-39, T373111. With bath, hot water, safe. **E** *Residencias El Imperio*, Cra 13, No 3-42. Good. **E** *Residencial Familiar*, C 3, No 11-47, T373079. Hot water, laundry, book meals in advance or eat next door at the *Colonial*, horses for hire, but noisy disco nearby at weekends. **E** *Residencias Menezu*, Cra 15, No 4-74. Shared bath, hot water, family atmosphere, safe, central. Recommended. **E** *Mi Terruño*, C 4, No 15-85. Some rooms with bath, hot water, attractive garden, motorbike parking, good, owner Carlos Arturo Muñoz also has 3 cabins, *Los Andaqui* for rent (**E**), C 5, No 23-71, with restaurant. **F** *La Casa de François*, Vereda La Antigua. New simple rooms, French-run. **F** *Copacabana*, Cra 14, via Estrecha, T373752. Good restaurant. **F** *Residencias Eduardo Motta*, C 4, No 15-71, T373031. Hot water, hard beds, morning coffee, quiet. Recommended. **F** *Residencias El Jardín*, Cra 11, No 4-10, T373455. Hot water, quiet, cooking and laundry facilities, free coffee. **F** *Residencias Náñez*, C 5, No 15-78, T373087. Hot water, good value. Recommended. **F** *Ullumbe*, Cra 13, No 3-36, T373799. Hot water, helpful, TV, family atmosphere, motorcycle parking.

There is accommodation in **private houses** for under US$3 pp. The farm of *Constantino Ortiz* is recommended, 3½ km from town, first turn on left after the Parque Arqueológico, 4 rooms, best to take a sleeping bag, meals and horses available, peaceful, inexpensive, good cooking, free morning coffee, also has camping, reservations at C 5, No 11-13 in town. Another recommended farmhouse is **F** *Posada Campesina*, Cra 14, Camino al Estrecho (on the route to El Tablón), 1 km from town, T373956, owned by Doña Silviana Patiño, who makes good pizza and cheese bread, meals with family, simple working farm, use of kitchen, camping possible, good walks nearby. **F** *Casa de Nelly*, Vía la Estrella, 1½ km west along 2 Av, T373221. Attractive peaceful finca run by Nelly Haymann (French), hot water, good food nearby, free coffee. Recommended.

Camping Next to *Yalconia* is *Camping San Agustín*, US$2 pp with own tent, US$3 pp to hire tent, clean, pleasant, toilets, lights, laundry service, horse hire (see below).

Eating *La Brasa*, opposite *Yalconia Hotel*. Good steaks. Recommended. *Brahama*, C 5, No 15-11. *Comida* including soup and drink, good fruit salads, cheap. Recommended. *Surabhi*, C 5, No 15-10. Vegetarian dishes or meat, pizzas, *menú*, juices, desserts etc. Recommended. *Superpollo*, Diagonal a la Iglesia. Good. *Acuario*, C 3. Very good, breakfasts and juices, sandwiches etc, good music. *Bambú*, C 5 No 13-34. Good food, fair prices. *La Negra*, Cra 12, No 3-40. Good *tamales*, weekends only. *The Tea Rooms*, 20 m from *Casa de Nelly*. Good food, roasts on Sun.

Tap water in San Agustín is not safe to drink

Festivals *Santa María del Carmen* in mid-Jul (not on a fixed date) in San Agustín. 2 festivals in **Jun** are *San Juan* (24th) with horse races and dances, and *San Pedro* (29th) with horse races,

Colombia

dances, fancy dress, competitions and other events. In the first week of **Oct**, the Casa de Cultura celebrates *La Semana Cultural Integrada*, with many folklore events from all parts of the country. There are cock fights on Sun, 100 m behind the church at 1900, US$1.

Bus To **Bogotá** by colectivo (*Taxis Verdes*, C 3, No 11-57) several daily, direct or change at Neiva, go early US$15, 8-9 hrs, or by bus (*Coomotor*, C 3, No 10-71), 4 a day, about US$20, 14 hrs. From **Bogotá**, *Taxis Verdes* will pick up at hotels (extra charge), T429 7504. Alternatively there are frequent services from Bogotá to **Neiva** as well as some to Pitalito (*Taxis Verdes* costs US$14). To Neiva the 1000 *Autobusco* bus arrives in time for a late flight to Bogotá. To **Popayán** and **Cali**, *Coomotor* daily via Pitalito, Garzón and La Plata, US$12 to Popayán, US$14/16 to Cali. The bus stops at La Plata, 5-6 hrs, US$5. To **Tierradentro**, check first if any of the tourist offices is running a jeep (about US$120 for minimum 4 people), otherwise, take early transport to Garzón (eg *Taxis Verdes* 0700, US$3.50) or Pitalito, then a colectivo jeep to La Plata, US$2. With luck, you will get a *chiva* to Tierradentro the same day. Alternatively, take the daily bus to **La Plata** at 1700, stay half a night at a hotel, then, next morning, take the 0500 *Sotracauca* bus to Cruce de Pisimbalá (more details and alternatives given under La Plata). Buses to **Garzón** at 1230, 1430 and 1730, US$3.25, 3 hrs, from where more buses go to La Plata for Tierradentro. Do not take a night bus to Tierradentro. There are daily buses from San Agustín to Popayán via Paletará and Coconuco with *Cootranshuila* (office on C 3, No 10-81), slow, 6 hrs, US$12; also *Sotracauca* (C 3, No 10-53), some continuing to Cali (US$14) and *Coomotor* on this route to Cali, 9 hrs. It may be advisable to book seats the day before. (For information ask at *World Heritage Travel*; the services are sometimes cut and prices vary.)

Banks Change TCs before arriving in San Agustín; the small shop opposite police station will exchange cash only, at a poor rate. *Banco Agrario* will give cash advances against Visa card.

Transport

Directory

Colombia

Southern Colombia

From Popayán to Ecuador is scenic highland country, much of it open páramo *intersected here and there by spectacular deep ravines. To the west is the long slope down to the Pacific including the mangrove swamps of much of the coast and the small port of Tumaco. To the east is the continental divide of the Cordillera Oriental and the beginning of the great Amazonian basin. The route rises still further to the border with Ecuador.*

The Pan-American Highway continues south from Popayán to Pasto (285 km, five hours driving). The road drops to 700 m in the valley of the Río Patía before climbing to Pasto with big temperature changes. 38 km before Pasto is **Chachagüí**. **E** *Hotel Imperio de los Incas*, T218054, with bath, pool, restaurant, 2 km form Pasto airport; cheaper is **F** *Casa Champagnat*, with bath and cold water, pool, helpful.

Pasto

Pasto is overlooked from the west by Volcán Galeras (when not in cloud) and to the east by green hills not yet suburbanized by the city, and is in a very attractive setting. The city, capital of the Department of Nariño, stands upon a high plateau in the southwest and retains some of its colonial character. It was founded in the early days of the conquest. During the wars of independence, it was a stronghold of the Royalists and the last town to fall into the hands of the patriots after a bitter struggle. Then the people of Nariño Department wanted to join Ecuador when that country split off from Gran Colombia in 1830, but were prevented by Colombian troops. Today Pasto is a centre for the agricultural and cattle industries of the region. Pasto varnish (*barniz*) is mixed locally, to embellish the colourful local wooden bowls.

Phone code: 927
Colour map 1, grid C2
Population: 326,000
Altitude: 2,534 m
88 km from Ecuador

The church of **Cristo Rey** (C 20, No 24-64) has a striking yellow stone west front with octagonal turrets. **La Merced**, C 18 y Cra 22, has rich decoration and gold ornaments. From the church of **Santiago** (Cra 23 y C 13) there is a good view over the city to the mountains. **San Felipe** (C 12 y Cra 27) has green tiled domes. The interior courtyard of the **municipal building** on the main plaza (corner of C 19 and Cra 24) has two tiers of colonnaded balconies.

The **Museo de Oro del Banco de la República** has a small well-displayed collection of precolumbian pieces from the cultures of southern Colombia, a library and auditorium. ■ *0830-1150, 1400-1830, US$0.30, C 19, No 21-27, T215777*. **Museo Zambrano**, C 20, No 29-78, houses indigenous and colonial period arts, especially *quiteño* (from Quito).

Sleeping **AL** *Don Saul*, C 17 No 23-52, T230618, F230622. Comfortable, good restaurant. Recommended. **A** *Cuellar's*, Cra 23, No 15-50, T232879. Roomy, well-furnished, bowling centre underneath. Recommended. **A** *Galerías*, Cra 26, No 18-71, T233069, F237069, above shopping mall. Comfortable, good restaurant. Recommended. **B** *Sindagua*, C 20, No 21B-16, T235404. Recommended. **C** *San Diego*, C 16 A No 23-27, T235050. Good. **D** *Isa*, C 18, No 22-23, T236663. Helpful, safe. **D** *Río Mayo*, Cra 20, No 17-12, T212989. Small rooms, restaurant downstairs. **D** *Metropol*, C 15, No 21-41, T214518. Restaurant, laundry facilities. **E** *Canchala*, C 17, No 20A-38, T213337. Big, safe, hot water, TV, central. **E** *Koala Inn*, C 18, No 22-37, T221101, koalainn@hotmail.com Cheaper without bath, laundry facilities, helpful, English speaking Oscar is the well-travelled owner, popular, hot water, book exchange. **F** *Embajador*, C 19, No 25-57. Quiet, bath, motorcycle parking, cold water. **F** *Nueva York*, Cra 19 bis, 18-20. Hot shower, motorcycle parking. **F** *Residencia Indi Chaya*, C 16, No 18-23 (corner of Cra 19 and C 16, up the steps), T234476. Good value, good beds, safe. Recommended. **F** *María Belén*, T230277, C 13, No 19-15. Safe, quiet, hot water. **G** *Residencia Aica*, C 17, No 20-75, T235311. Safe, shared bath, but dirty. **G** *Viena*, Cra 19B, No 18-36. Clean, restaurant downstairs, noisy.

Eating **Central** *La Merced*, Cra 22, No 17-37. Pizzas and local dishes, good. *Punto Rojo*, Cra 24, Parque Nariño. Self service, 24 hrs, good choice. *El Mundo de los Pasteles*, Cra 22, No 18-34. Cheap *comidas*. *Rancho Grande*, C 17, No 26-89. Cheap, open late. *El Vencedor*, C 18, No 20A-40. Good value, open 0600-1900. *Las Dos Parrillas*, Pasaje Dorado, No 23-22. Steaks, chicken, reasonable prices. *La Cabaña*, C 16, No 25-20. Varied menu. *Govinda*, Cra 24, No 13-91. Vegetarian, set lunch US$2. *Riko Riko*, various locations. Good fast food.

Away from centre *Sausalito*, Cra 35A, No 20-63. Seafood, good. *La Casa Vasca*, C 12A, No 29-10. Spanish. Recommended. *Cokorín*, bus terminal, T212084. Meat, chicken, local dishes.

Local specialities Try *arepas de choclo*, made with fresh ground sweet corn, at the kiosks beside the main road going north.

Bar/Disco *Honey Bar*, C 16, No 25-40, T234895. Pleasant atmosphere.

Festivals During the new year's *fiesta* there is a *Día de los Negros* on 5 Jan and a *Día de los Blancos* next day. On 'black day' people dump their hands in black grease and smear each others' faces. On 'white day' they throw talc or flour at each other. Local people wear their oldest clothes. On **28 Dec** and **5 Feb**, there is also a *Fiesta de las Aguas* when anything that moves gets drenched with water from balconies and even from fire engines' hoses. All towns in the region are involved in this legalized water war! In Pasto and Ipiales (see page 875), on **31 Dec**, is the *Concurso de Años Viejos*, when huge dolls are burnt; they represent the old year and sometimes lampoon local people.

Shopping *Casa del Barniz de Pasto*, C 13, No 24-9. *Artesanías Nariño*, C 26, No 18-91. *Artesanía-Mercado Bomboná*, C 14 y Cra 27. *Artesanías Mopa-Mopa*, Cra 25, No 13-14, for *barniz*. Leather goods shops are on C 17 and C 18. Try the municipal market for handicrafts. *Mercado Campesino*, southern end of C 16, esq Cra 7. *Supermercado Confamiliar de Nariño*, C 16B, No 30-53. Recommended. *Ley* on C 18, next to Avianca postal office. On main plaza (C 19 y Cra 25) is a shopping centre with many shops and restaurants. **Maps** Maps of Colombia and cities from **Instituto Geográfico Agustín Codazzi**, in *Banco de la República* building, C 18, No 21-20, limited selection.

Every Sun a game of paddle ball is played on the edge of the town (bus marked 'San **Sport** Lorenzo') similar to that played in Ibarra, Ecuador.

Air Daily to **Bogotá**, *Avianca*, and **Cali**, *SAM*. The airport is at Cano, 40 km from Pasto; by **Transport** colectivo (beautiful drive), 45 mins, US$2.40 or US$13.50 by taxi. There are no currency exchange facilities, but the shop will change US$ bills at a poor rate. **Bus** All interurban buses leave from the new terminal, Cra 6, C 16, 4 km from centre, taxi, US$1. **To Bogotá**, 23 hrs, US$32 (*Bolivariano Pullman*). To **Ipiales**, 2 hrs, US$3, sit on the left for the views. To **Popayán**, ordinary buses take 10-12 hrs, US$7; expresses take 5-8 hrs, cost US$9. To **Cali**, US$11, expresses, 8½ to 10 hrs. To **Tumaco**, 9 hrs by bus, 7 hrs by minibus, US$9. To **Mocoa**, 8 hrs, US$7.25.

Airline offices *Avianca*, C 18, No 25-86, T232044. **Banks** For changing TCs, *Bancolombia*, C 19, No **Directory** 24-52. *Lloyds TSB Bank*, C 17, 19-74, T213139 (best rates), Visa advances. *Banco de Bogotá* will change TCs 0930-1130. If going to Tumaco, this is the last place where TCs can be cashed. *Casas de cambio, Titan*, Cra 26, No 18-71, T729 1946, at Cra 25, No 18-97, T232294, and C 19, No 24-86, T235616, by the main plaza. **Communications** Post Office: Cra 23, 18-42 and C 18, No 24-86 (*Avianca*). **Telephone:** long distance calls, C 17 y Cra 23. **Embassies and consulates** Ecuadorean Consulate, C 17, No 26-55, p 2. 4 photos needed if you require a visa. **Tourist office** Just off the main plaza, C 18, No 25-25, T234962, friendly and helpful. Mon-Fri 0800-1200 and 1400-1800. **Useful addresses** DAS: C 16, No 28-11, T235901, will give exit stamps if you are going on to Ecuador.

The volcano, Galeras (4,276 m), quiescent since 1934, began erupting again in 1989. **Volcán** Check at the tourist office whether it is safe to climb on the mountain and whether **Galeras** you need a permit. A road climbs up the mountain to a ranger station and police post at 3,700 m. At the last report, you were not permitted beyond this point.

Colombia

On the north side of the volcano lies the village of **Sandoná** where panama hats are made; they can be seen lying in the streets in the process of being finished. Sandoná market day is Saturday. There are good walks on the lower slopes through Catambuco and Jongovito (where bricks are made). ■ *Four buses daily, US$1.50, the last back to Pasto is at 1700.*

The 250 km road west from Pasto to Tumaco on the coast is paved, but is subject to landslides – check in Pasto. It leaves the Panamericana 40 km south of Pasto at El Pedregal, passing the brick factories of the high plains of the Cordillera Occidental. In **Túquerres** (*Altitude*: 3,050 m) the market is on Thursday, good for ponchos (**F** *Residencias Santa Rita*, C 4, No 17-29; several restaurants. Bus to Pasto US$2.25, 2 hours; jeep service to Ipiales from Cra 14, C 20, US$2, 1½ hours). Ask in Túquerres about walking and climbing in the Laguna Verde/Volcán Azufral area.

About 90 km from Túquerres, at the village of **Chucunez**, a dirt road branches south to **Reserva Natural La Planada**, a private 3,200 ha nature reserve. This patch of dense cloud forest on a unique flat-topped mountain is home to a wide variety of flora and fauna, and believed to have one of the largest concentrations of native bird species in South America. ■ *Day visitors are welcome but camping is prohibited. There is accommodation, US$12.50 pp, including meals. Guides are available. For further information contact the reserve T927-753396/7, fesplan@col2.telecom.com.co*

Tumaco

Tumaco has two-storey wooden houses and a predominantly black population, and *Phone code: 927* the roads, water and electricity supplies are not good. It is in one of the world's raini- *Colour map 1, grid C2* est areas; the yearly average temperature is about 30°C. The northern part of the *Population: 115,000* town is built on stilts out over the sea (safe to visit only in daylight). A natural arch on the main beach, north of the town and port, is reputed to be the hiding place of Henry Morgan's treasure. Swimming is not recommended from the town's beaches, which are polluted; stalls provide refreshment on the beach. Swimming is safe, however, at El Morro beach, north of the town, but watch out for poisonous rays. There are many discos specializing in Afro/South American rhythms. There are no money exchange facilities, except in some shops that will buy dollars at a poor rate; change money in Cali or Pasto.

The area around is noted for the archaeological finds associated with the Tumaco culture. Ask for Pacho Cantin at El Morro Beach who will guide you through the caves.

The coastal area around Tumaco is mangrove swamp, with many rivers and inlets on which lie many villages and settlements; negotiate with boatmen for a visit to the swamps or the beautiful island tourist resort of **Boca Grande**. The trip takes 30 minutes, US$8 return; ask for Felipe Bustamante, Calle del Comercio, who rents canoes and cabins, has a good seafood restaurant on the island, where water and electricity supplies are irregular. There are several places to stay in the **F** category.

Sleeping & eating

Be very careful of food and water because there are many parasites

D *Villa del Mar*, C Sucre. Modern, with shower, toilet and fan, no hot water, good café below, also has well equipped cabins at El Morro Beach. **E** *El Dorado*, C del Comercio, near water-front and *canoa* dock. Basic. Children meet arriving buses to offer accommodation; most cheap places are in C del Comercio, many houses and restaurants without signs take guests – most have mosquito nets. The main culinary attraction of the town is the fish, in the market and restaurants, fresh from the Pacific. A number of good restaurants on the main streets, C Mosquera and C del Comercio, though the best is probably *Las Velas* on C Sucre.

Transport

Air There are daily flights to and from **Cali** with *SAM*, 35 mins. **Bus** To **Pasto**, 9 hrs, US$9, with *Supertaxis del Sur* or *Trans Ipiales* (better), 4 a day, interesting ride; minibus 7 hrs. From Ipiales go to El Espino (US$0.75, colectivo, US$1.15) and there change buses for Tumaco (US$4.80).

Border with Ecuador

It is possible to travel to Ecuador (San Lorenzo) by boat. Part of the trip is by river, which is very beautiful, and part on the open sea, which can be very rough; a plastic sheet to cover your belongings is essential. Take suncream. It is possible to go overland crossing the Río Mira to reach Ecuador, but get good advice before attempting this move.

Colombian immigration is at DAS, Alcaldía Municipal, C 11 y Cra 9, Tumaco; obtain stamp for leaving Colombia here. Office open weekdays only. Visas for Ecuador (if required) should be obtained in Cali or Pasto. Entry stamps for Ecuador must be obtained in the coastal towns.

Entering Colombia through Tumaco: you will have to go to Ipiales to obtain the entry stamp. Apparently the 24/48 hours 'unofficial' entry is not a problem, but do not obtain any Colombian stamps in your passport before presentation to DAS in Ipiales.

Transport Daily (check) service at 0800 to **San Lorenzo**, 7 hrs (but can take 14) tickets from C del Comercio (protective plastic sheeting provided). Señor Pepello, who lives in the centre of Tumaco, owns two canoes: he leaves on Sat at 0700 for San Lorenzo and Limones in Ecuador, book in advance. Also ask around the water-front at 0600, or try at the fishing centre, El Coral del Pacífico for a cheaper passage, but seek advice on safety before taking a boat (robberies en route reported). Fares: motorized canoe US$20; launch US$50.

The Putumayo

Twenty-five kilometres east of Pasto, on the road to Mocoa is **Laguna La Cocha**, the largest lake in south Colombia (sometimes called Lago Guamuez). By the lake, 3 km from the main road, is the **C** *Chalet Guamuez*, with chalets, boat and jeep trips, recommended. In the lake is the **Isla de La Corota** nature reserve with interesting trees (10 minutes by boat from the *Hotel Sindanamoy*, **B**, camping possible). There are also cheap and friendly places to stay in and near El Encano (often shown as El Encanto on maps) where there are also many restaurants serving trout.

Transport Taxi to La Cocha from Pasto, US$9, or colectivo from C 20 y Cra 20. Also you can take a bus to El Encano and walk the remaining 5 km to the chalets of *Chalet Guamuez*, or 20 mins from bus stop direct to lake shore and take a *lancha* to the chalets for US$3.

Beyond El Encano there is a steep climb over the Sierra where a large statue of the Virgin marks the entry into the Putumayo. The road then descends steeply to Sibundoy, Mocoa and Puerto Asís. For several years this has been guerrilla territory and a drug growing and processing area. Even if the authorities allow you to enter, you are advised not to do so. Should the safety situation improve, information on this area is available in the *Colombia Handbook*.

Ipiales

Passing through deep valleys and a spectacular gorge, buses on the paved Pan-American Highway cover the 84 km from Pasto to Ipiales in 1½-2 hours. The road crosses the spectacular gorge of the Río Guáitara at 1,750 m, near El Pedregal, where *choclo* (corn) is cooked in many forms by the roadside. **Ipiales**, "the city of the three volcanoes", is famous for its colourful Friday morning Indian market. The **Catedral Bodas de Plata** is worth visiting.

Phone code: 927
Colour map 1, grid C2
Population: 72,000
Altitude: 2,898 m

About 7 km east of Ipiales on a paved road is the Sanctuary of the Virgin of **Las Lajas**. Seen from the approach road, looking down into the canyon, the Sanctuary is a magnificent architectural conception, set on a bridge over the Río Guáitara: close up, it is very heavily ornamented in the gothic style. The altar is set into the rock face of the canyon, which forms one end of the sanctuary with the façade facing a wide plaza that completes the bridge over the canyon. There are walks to nearby shrines in dramatic scenery. It is a 10-15 minutes' walk down to the sanctuary from the village. There are great pilgrimages to it from Colombia and Ecuador (very crowded at Easter) and the Sanctuary must be second only to Lourdes in the number of miracles claimed for it. The Church recognizes one only. ■ *Ipiales town buses going 'near the Sanctuary' leave you 2½ km short. Take a colectivo from Cra 6 y C 4, US$1 pp, taxi, US$6 return. Several basic hotels and a small number of restaurants at Las Lajas. You may also stay at the convent. Try local guinea pig and boiled potatoes for lunch (or betting on guinea pig races in the plaza may be more to your taste).*

Excursions

B *Mayasquer*, 3 km on road to the border, T252643. Modern, nice restaurant, very good. **D** *Korpawasy*, Cra 6, No 10-47, T252246. Good food, plenty of blankets. **D** *Pasviveros*, Cra 6, No 16-90, T252622. Hot water, interesting decorations. **E** *Los Andes*, Cra 5, No 14-43. With hot water, good value. **E** *Bachué*, Cra 6, No 11-68. Safe. **E** *Belmonte*, Cra 4, No 12-111 (near *Transportes Ipiales*). Hot water, parking opposite, good value but crowded. Recommended. **E** *Rumichaca Internacional*, C 14, No 7-114, T252692. Comfortable, good restaurant. **F** *Colombia*, C 13, No 7-50. Hot water, clean except for toilets, helpful, parking for motorbikes. **F** *San Andrés*, Cra 5, No 14-75. Hot water. **G** *India Catalina*, Cra 5a, No 14-88, T254392. Hot shower, run down, 2 blocks from main plaza. **G** *Nueva York*, C 13, No 4-11, near main plaza. Run down, plenty of blankets. **G** *Oasis*, Cra 6, No 11-34, 1 block from main plaza. Shower, ask for hot water, quiet after 2100, clean, helpful. **Camping** free behind last Esso station outside town on road north.

Sleeping

Don Lucho (Los Tejados), Cra 5, No 14-13 (*antioqueño*). *Don José*, Cra 5, No 14-53. Plenty of cheap restaurants, better quality ones on Cra 7. *Panadería Galaxia*, C 15, No 7-89. Good cheap breakfast. Outside town towards the border, *La Herradura*, good food, reasonable prices, try their excellent *trucha con salsa de camarones* (rainbow trout with shrimp sauce).

Eating

Air San Luis airport is 6½ km out of town. *Aires* to **Cali**, **Neiva** and **Bogotá**. Taxi to Ipiales centre, US$4. **Bus** Bus companies have their individual departure points: *busetas/colectivos* mostly leave from the main plaza To **Popayán**, *Expreso Bolivariano*, US$9, 7½ hrs, hourly

Transport

Colombia

departures, 0430-2030; *Transportes de Ipiales*; *Super Taxis* and *Cootranar* busetas, US$12. Bus to **Cali**, US$14, 12 hrs. To **Pasto** from main plaza, colectivo US$3.25; *Flota Bolivariano* buses every hour, US$3, 3 hrs. Buses to **Bogotá** hourly from 0500, 24 hrs, US$35 (check if you have to change buses in Cali). To **Medellín**, *Expreso Bolivariano*, 22 hrs, US$33. To **Túquerres** and **Ricaurte** on the Tumaco road, *camperos* (4WD taxis) leave from in front of San Felipe Neri church; for **Tumaco** change at El Espino.

Directory   **Banks** It is not possible to cash TCs, but cash is no problem *Bancolombia*, C 14, No 5-32, cash against Visa. *Casa de Cambio* at Cra 6, No 14-09, other *cambios* on the plaza. There are money changers in street, in plaza and on border, but they may take advantage of you if the banks are closed. Coming from Ecuador, peso rates compare well in Ipiales with elsewhere in Colombia. **Communications** Telephone: International calls from Cra 6 y C 6/7.

Border with   Ipiales is 2 km from the Rumichaca bridge across the Río Carchi into Ecuador. The
Ecuador   border post stands on a concrete bridge, beside a natural bridge, where customs and passport examinations take place from 0600 to 2100.

All Colombian offices are in one complex: DAS (immigration, exit stamp given here), customs, INTRA (Dept of Transportation, car papers stamped here; if leaving Colombia you must show your vehicle entry permit) and ICA (Department of Agriculture for plant and animal quarantine). There is also a restaurant, Telecom, clean bathrooms (ask for key, US$0.10) and ample parking. See page 942 for the Ecuadorean side and see also Documents in Ecuador, Essentials, page 886. The **Ecuadorean consulate** is in the DAS complex; open weekdays 0830-1200, 1430-1800. There are many money-changers near the bridge on both sides. Better rates reported on the Colombian side but check all calculations.

Transport From Ipiales to **Tulcán**: colectivo from C 14 y Cra 11, US$0.40 to the border (buses to Ipiales arrive at the main plaza – they may take you closer to the colectivo point if you ask). Colectivo from border to **Tulcán** US$0.70, to Tulcán bus station, US$1. Ask the fare at border tourist office. To go to bus terminal, take blue bus from central plaza, US$0.05. Taxi to/from border, US$2.50. From Ipiales airport to the border by taxi, about US$6.50.

If entering Colombia by car, the vehicle is supposed to be fumigated against diseases that affect coffee trees, at the ICA office. The certificate must be presented in El Pedregal, 40 km beyond Ipiales on the road to Pasto. (This fumigation process is not always carried out.) You can buy insurance for your car in Colombia at Banco Agrario, in the plaza.

The Llanos and Leticia

The extensive cattle lands from the Cordillera Central to the Orinoco are a good place to get away from it all in the dry season. Leticia, Colombia's foothold on the Amazon, is on the southern tip of a spur of territory which gives Colombia access to the Amazon, 3,200 km upstream from the Atlantic. There is a land border with Brazil a short distance to the east beyond which are Marco and Tabatinga. Directly south across the river is another important Brazilian port, Benjamin Constant, which is close to the border with Peru. On the north side of the Amazon, Colombia has a frontage on the river of 80 km to the land border with Peru

Amazonas and to a lesser extent Los Llanos have always been difficult to visit because of their remoteness, the lack of facilities and the huge distances involved. In recent years this has been compounded by the growing of drugs in the region and guerrilla activity culminating in the declaration in 1998 of the *zona de despeje* (see below) for a significant part of Caquetá and Meta Departments. At the time of writing, the Pastrana government has launched an attack to recover this territory after the breakdown of peace negotiations. Our text has been limited to Villavicencio, Florencia and the Leticia region all of which are comparatively safe. They should only be visited by air at present (except Leticia where river routes are safe). Further information is given in the Footprint *Colombia Handbook*.

Villavicencio

A spectacular 110 km road runs southeast from Bogotá to **Villavicencio**, capital of Meta Department in the Llanos at the foot of the eastern slopes of the Eastern Cordillera. Rice is the main local crop. Villavicencio is a good centre for visiting the Llanos stretching 800 km east as far as Puerto Carreño, on the Orinoco. Cattle raising is the great industry on the plains, sparsely inhabited by *mestizos*

Population: 310,000
Altitude: 498 m
Phone code: 98
Colour map 1, grid B4

Sleeping and eating AL *Villavicencio*, Cra 30, No 35A-22, T662 6434, hotvicio@ andinet.com Suites available, a/c, hot water, very comfortable, good restaurant. **D** *Centauros*, C 38, No 31-05, T662 5106. Small rooms, reasonably clean and quiet, central. **E** *Residencias Don Juan*, Cra 28, No 37-21 (Mercado de San Isidro). Attractive family house, with bath and fan, sauna, safe. Recommended. **F** *Residencias Medina*, C 39D, 28-27. Shared shower, fair, washing facilities. **Youth Hostel**: *Granja los Girasoles*, Barrio Chapinerito, T664 2712. 160 beds, 3 km from the bus station. Several eating places sell typical food of the region, also Chinese restaurants in the centre: others, some with swimming pools, on the road to Puerto López.

Festival *Festival Nacional del Joropo*, Typical music and dances of *Los Llanos*, **Dec.**

Transport Air *Aires* to **Bogotá** most days. For flights into the Llanos, ask locally. Taxi to town, US$4, bus US$0.50. **Bus** Bus station outside town, taxi US$1. *La Macarena* and *Bolivariano* run from Bogotá about every 30 mins, US$4, 4 hrs, or colectivos *Velotax* or *Autollanos* who run every hour, US$4.20. Be prepared to queue for tickets back to Bogotá

Florencia

Florencia, capital of Caquetá Department, was originally established in 1908. The plaza contains sculptures, fountains, a large forest tree (*saba*) and flower beds. Overnight, cars are best left in the care of the fire-station (US$0.20 a night). The better hotels are located round the plaza eg *C Kamani*, C 16, No 12-27, T354101. The local saint's day is 16 July: candlelit procession in the evening. ■ *Aires flies daily to Neiva and Bogotá and most days to Cali. There are regular bus services from Neiva (US$7.80, 7 hrs), Garzón and Altamira (bus Altamira to Florencia, US$3.75). To Bogotá US$23.50.*

Phone code: 988
Colour map 1, grid C3
Population: 118,000
Altitude: 1,300 m

NB From Florencia the road runs northeast as far as San Vicente del Caguán, the centre of the demilitarized zone arranged between President Pastrana's government and the FARC guerrillas in November 1998. This **'zona de despeje'** centred on San Vicente and Cartagena del Chairá is at present (early 2002) the scene of military action by the Army and closed to tourists.

Leticia

Capital of Amazonas Department, the city is clean, modern, though run down near the river. It is rapidly merging into one town with neighbouring Marco in Brazil. There is a modern, well-equipped hospital. The best time to visit the area is in July or August, the early months of the dry season. At weekends, accommodation may be difficult to find. Leticia is a good place to buy typical products of Amazon Indians (for example *Galería Artesanal Uiraparu*, C8, No 10), and tourist services are better than in Tabatinga or Benjamin Constant. A museum set up by Banco de la República has local ethnography and archaeology, in a beautiful building at Cra 11 y C 9 with a library and a terrace overlooking the Amazon. The **tourist office** is at C 10, No 9-86. *MA*, Cra 11, No 12-45, T/F27124, will arrange tours and find guides. You may also be asked for a yellow fever inoculation certificate on arrival; if you do not have this, an inoculation will be administered on the spot (not recommended).

Phone code: 9819
Colour map 3, grid A4
Population: 23,000
Altitude: 82 m

There is an obligatory US$5 environment tax payable upon arrival in Leticia

Colombia

Sleeping **AL** *Anaconda*, Cra 11, No 7-34, T27119, www.hotelanaconda.com.co Large a/c rooms, hot water, restaurant, good terrace and swimming pool. **AL** *Parador Ticuna*, Av Libertador (Cra 11), No 6-11, T27243. Spacious apartments, hot water, a/c, sleep up to 6, swimming pool, bar and restaurant. **B** *Colonial*, C 10, No 7-08, T27164. With a/c or fans, cafetería, noisy, not including tax and insurance. **B** *Iripari*, C 8, No 7-26, T24743. A/c, TV. Recommended. **C-D** *Residencias Fernando*, Cra 9, No 8-80, T27362. Well-equipped. Recommended. **D** *Residencias La Manigua*, C 8, No 9-22, T27121. With bath, fan. **D** *Residencias Marina*, Cra 9 No 9-29 T27309. TV, some a/c, cold water, good breakfast and meals at attached restaurant.

Eating *Sancho Panza*, Cra 10, No 8-72. Good value, good meat dishes, big portions, Brazilian beer. Several small sidewalk restaurants downtown, good value *plato del día*. *Señora Mercedes*, C 8 near Cra 11. Serves good, cheap meals until 1930. Cheap food (fried banana and meat, also fish and pineapples) is sold at the market near the harbour. Also cheap fruit for sale. Many café/bars overlook the market on the river bank. Take your own drinking water.

Transport **Air** Airport is 1½ km from town, taxi US$1.60; small terminal, few facilities. Taxi direct to Brazilian immigration (Police Station) US$8. Expect to be searched before leaving Leticia airport, and on arrival in Bogotá from Leticia. *Aero República* flies to Leticia (Tabatinga airport if Leticia's is closed) from **Bogotá**, several days a week. *AeroSucre* allows passengers on its daily cargo flights Bogotá-Leticia, US$75. Go to their terminal about 3 km before the international airport in Bogotá (huge sign) and speak to the flight captain (no one else) 30 mins before take-off. Price is not negotiable and schedule changes each day, but usually at 0600. *Varig* has 3 flights a week from Manaus to Tabatinga. Regular minibus to Tabatinga, US$0.60.

Directory **Banks** There are street money changers, plenty of *cambios*, and banks for exchange. Shop around. TCs cannot be changed at weekends, and are hard to change at other times, but try *Banco de Bogotá*. **Communications** Internet: very few places, slow connections. **Post Office:** *Avianca* office, Cra 11, No 7-58. **Telecom:** Cra 11, near Parque Santander.

For the border with Brazil, Colombia and Peru all information is given in the Brazil chapter, page 554, where Colombian, Brazilian and Peruvian procedures are detailed in one section.

Jungle excursions **Monkey Island** Visits can be made to Yagua and Ticuna Indians. There are not many monkeys on the island now, those left are semi-tame. Agencies run overnight tours with full board.

Parque Nacional Amacayacu 60 km upstream, at the mouth of the Matamata Creek. There is a jungle walk to a lookout (guides will point out plants, including those to avoid) and a rope bridge over the forest canopy, with wonderful views over the surrounding jungle (US$7). Boats go to a nearby island to see Victoria Regia water lilies. The *MA* in Leticia arranges visits to its centre. Accommodation for 45 in three large, clean cabins with beds, US$10, and hammocks, US$8, mess-style meals, breakfast US$2.50, lunch/dinner US$5, friendly, efficient; lights out 2130; small handicraft shop run by the local Indian communities. Park entry US$3. Boat from Leticia US$10.50, two hours; two operators (if you buy a return check that your operator runs the day you wish to return). For park information, go to the *MA* office (see above) in Leticia.

Puerto Nariño A small, attractive settlement on the Río Loretoyacu, a tributary of the Amazon, beyond the Parque Nacional Amacayacu. Where the two rivers meet is a popular place to watch dolphins. **Sleeping**: **B** *Casa Selva*, with a/c; **E** *Brisas del Amazonas*, charming location, simple rooms; **E** *Manguare*; **E** pp *El Alto del Aguila*, 20 minutes' walk, 5 minutes by boat, owned by Hector (missionary and school-teacher) who is a good source of information, comfortable cabins, trips arranged. Tours include fishing, visits to Indians and caiman watching, four to five days (for example with *Punto Amazónico*, Cra 24, No 53-18, p 2, Bogotá, T249 3618). Two-hour trips from Leticia daily at 1400 (1200 Sat-Sun), cost US$8.50.

Tour operators Companies include *Turamazonas*, *Parador Ticuna*, Apdo Aéreo 074, T27241; *Amaturs*, in lobby of *Hotel Anaconda*; *Amazonian Adventures*, ask for Chiri Chiri. The following tours are available: to Monkey Island; to Benjamin Constant to see a rubber plantation, 8 hrs; 3 day trips to visit Indian communities with *Turamazonas*, price depends on number of people in group.

If you choose to go on an organized tour, do not accept the first price and check that the equipment and supplies are sufficient for the length of the tour

    Independent guides Many guides can be found at the riverfront. They may be cheaper and better than organized groups, but you must seek advice about reputations and fix a firm price before setting out. Recommended are **Luis Fernando Valera**, contact through *Hotel Anaconda*, and **Luis Daniel González** (Cra 8, No 9-93, Apdo Aéreo 256, Leticia), or through *Residencias Fernando*. They are often to be found at the airport, are knowledgeable, speak Spanish, Portuguese, English, and run a variety of tours. **Luis Carlos Castro**, Cra 11, No 6-81, T27163, US$30 pp day, good. **Daniel Martínez**, also knowledgeable, speaks good English. The cheaper the guide, the usually the less experienced he will be. Check that adequate first aid is taken and whether rubber boots are provided (or buy your own in Leticia, US$5-6).

    Hints On night excursions to look for caiman, the boat should have powerful halogen lamps. You can swim in the Amazon and its tributaries, but do not dive; this disturbs the fish. Do not swim at sunrise or sunset when the fish are more active, nor when the water is shallow in dry season, nor if you have a wound which may open up and bleed. Take water purification tablets since almost all the water for drinking here is taken from the river.

Background

Post-independence history

After the collapse of Simón Bolívar's Republic of Gran Colombia in 1829/30, what is now known as Colombia was called Nueva Granada until 1863. Almost from its inception the new country became the scene of strife between the centralizing pro-clerical Conservatives and the federalizing anti-clerical Liberals. From 1849 the Liberals were dominant during the next 30 years of insurrections and civil wars. In 1885 the Conservatives imposed a highly centralized constitution which was not modified for over 100 years. A Liberal revolt in 1899 turned into a civil war, 'the War of the Thousand Days'. The Liberals were finally defeated in 1902 after 100,000 people had died. It was in 1903 that Panama declared its independence from Colombia, following US pressure.

    After 40 years of comparative peace, the strife between Conservatives and Liberals was reignited in a little-publicized but dreadfully bloody civil war known as *La Violencia* from 1948 to 1957 (some 300,000 people were killed). This was ended by a unique political truce, decided by plebiscite in 1957 under which the two political parties supported a single presidential candidate, divided all political offices equally between them, and thus maintained political stability for 16 years. In 1978 the agreement was ended, though some elements of the coalition were allowed to continue until 1986. Sr Belisario Betancur, the Conservative president from 1982-86, offered a general amnesty to guerrilla movements in an attempt to end violence in the country. Following an initial general acceptance of the offer, only one of the four main guerrilla groups, the FARC, upheld the truce in 1985-87. In May 1986, when the Liberal candidate, Sr Virgilio Barco, won the presidential elections, FARC's newly-formed political party, the Unión Patriótica (UP), won 10 seats in congress; the Liberal party took the majority. Right-wing groups refused to accept the UP and by the beginning of 1990, 1,040 party members had been killed in five years. During the campaign for the 1990 presidential both the Liberal Party and the UP presidential candidates, Luis Carlos Galán and Bernardo Jaramillo, were assassinated.

In Medellín and Cali, two cartels transformed Colombia's drugs industry into a major force in worldwide business and crime. Their methods were very different: Medellín being

The narcotics trade

Colombia

ostentatious and violent, Cali much more low-key. In 1986, President Barco instigated an international effort to bring them to justice, but opposition to extradition of suspects to the USA stymied progress. Pablo Escobar, the alleged leader of the Medillín drugs cartel, who had surrendered under secret terms in 1991, escaped from custody in July 1992. Despite a multi-million dollar reward offered for his recapture and renewed conditional offers of surrender, he remained at large until he was killed in December 1993.

Modern Colombia Having won the presidential elections held on 27 May, 1990, César Gaviria Trujillo (Liberal), who took up the candidacy of the murdered Luis Carlos Galán, appointed a coalition government made up of Liberals from rival factions, Conservatives and the M-19 (Movimiento 19 de Abril).

The Gaviria government was unable to stem violence, whether perpetrated by drug traffickers, guerrillas or common criminals. Not surprisingly, this was one of the issues in the 1994 election campaign, in which Ernesto Samper (Liberal) defeated Andrés Pastrana (Conservative). The main thrust of Samper's programme was that Colombia's current economic strength should provide resources to tackle the social deprivation which causes drug use and insurgency. Most impetus was lost during 1995-97, however, in the wake of revelations that Samper's election campaign had received about US$6 mn from the Cali cartel. The debate over Samper's awareness of the funding lasted until June 1996, almost overshadowing the capture or surrender of most of the leading Cali drug lords. The USA, having decided in March 1996 to decertify (remove) Colombia from its list of countries making progress against drugs trafficking, denied Samper the right to a US visa and again decertified the country in March 1997, not least because the Cali cartel bosses were continuing their business from prison. Whatever progress was being made to eradicate drugs plantations and stocks, the denial of US aid through decertification permitted little scope for the establishment of alternative crops. Many rural communities were therefore left without means of support.

In March 1998, elections for Congress were relatively peaceful and a welcome boost to confidence was given when the US withdrew the 'decertification' restrictions the same month. The two rounds of presidential elections in May and June 1998 also passed off without excessive guerrilla disruption. The new president, Andrés Pastrana, immediately devoted his efforts to bringing the guerrillas to the negotiating table. A stop-go process began with FARC in late 1998 and the insurgents were conceded a large demilitarized zone, based on San Vicente de Caguán in Caquetá. Not everyone was in favour of Pastrana's approach, especially since FARC violence and extortion did not cease. ELN, meanwhile, angry at being excluded from talks, stepped up its campaign, demanding similar treatment. Paramilitary groups, too, showed no signs of ending their activities Pastrana also sought international aid for his Plan Colombia, aimed at combatting the drugs trade. The US$1.6 bn package was approved by the US Congress in May 2000, most of which will cover mainly military and anti-narcotics equipment, with the remainder destined for crop substitution and other sustainable agriculture projects. It has become clear that the policy of spraying drug crops has not achieved the desired result. Indeed the net area under cultivation has increased by more than 10% since 1999. Negotiatons with the guerrilla groups continued throughout 2001 but by early 2002, continued terror campaigns by the FARC and ELN increased the government's frustration and, with an eye on the approaching May 2002 elections, Pastrana abandoned his peace initative and sent in the Army. Strategic points in the demilitarized zone were quickly taken but the guerrillas melted away into the forests and countryside and the disruption and kidnapping continued. The international "war on terrorism" has facilitated Colombia's plea to the US to allow part of the Plan Colombia funds to be used for counter-insurgency equipment, but the position will certainly remain unstable for some time.

The frontrunners for the 2002 presidential elections were both Liberals: Horacio Serpa was the official party candidate, while Alvaro Uribe Vélez left the Liberals to run under his own movement, Colombia First. The main thrust of Uribe's campaigning was that the time had come to stop pandering to the left-wing guerrillas and to use a firm hand to restore order and security. This struck a chord with many Colombians, not just those who supported Pastrana's later hard line, but also the right-wing paramilitary groups who are waging their own war against FARC and ELN. Consequently, Uribe won with over 50% of the vote in the first round. He was thus the first Colombian president in modern Colombian history to achieve the post without the backing of either of the dominant political parties.

The lack of movement on the political/guerrilla front has had a negative effect on the economy and the quality of life. The economy has been in recession since 1996, compounded by the 1998 global financial crisis, the prolonged effects of El Niño on agriculture and the plunge in coffee prices. Unemployment has risen to record levels. One consequence of the increase in hardship for many Colombians is that street crime has grown. There was some economic improvement in 2001, and GDP rose 2.6% for the year. But the recession continues and new concessions to public sector workers will not help.

Government

Senators and Representatives are elected by popular vote. The Senate has 102 members, and the Chamber of Representatives has 163. The President, who appoints his 13 ministers, is elected by direct vote for a term of four years, but cannot succeed himself in the next term. Every citizen over 18 can vote. The 1886 Constitution was reformed by a Constituent Assembly in 1991. Administratively the country is divided into 32 Departments and the Capital District of Bogotá.

Culture

People

Colombia's total population in 2001 was 42,800,000. The regions vary in their racial make-up: Antioquia and Caldas are largely of European descent, Pasto is Indian, the Cauca Valley and the rural area near the Caribbean are African or *mulato*. However, continual population migrations are evening out the differences.

Forecast population growth 2000-2005: 1.6%

Urban population, percentage of total: 74%

The birth and death rates vary greatly from one area to the other, but in general infant mortality is high. Hospitals and clinics are few in relation to the population. About 66% of the doctors are in the departmental capitals, which contain about half of the population, though all doctors have to spend a year in the country before they can get their final diploma.

Infant mortality: 26 per 1,000 live births

An estimated 400,000 tribal peoples, from 60 ethnic groups, live in Colombia. Groups include the Wayuú (in the Guajira), the Kogi and Arhauco (Sierra Nevada de Santa Marta), Amazonian indians such as the Witoto, the nomadic Nukak and the Ticuna, Andean indians and groups of the Llanos and in the Pacific Coast rain forest. The diversity and importance of indigenous peoples was recognized in the 1991 constitutional reforms when indians were granted the right to two senate seats; the National Colombian Indian Organization (ONIC) won a third seat in the October 1991 ballot. State recognition and the right to bilingual education has not, however, solved major problems of land rights, training and education, and justice.

Education is free, and since 1927 theoretically compulsory, but many children, especially in rural areas, do not attend. There are high standards of secondary and university education, when it is available.

Books

A brief, introductory selection: **John Hemming**, *The Search for Eldorado*; **Alexander von Humboldt**, *Travels*. For an account of travelling in modern Colombia (specifically his adventures in the cocaine trade), **Charles Nicholl**'s *The Fruit Palace* is recommended. Also, **Stephen Smith**, *Cocaine Train* (1999). Colombian literature: **Jorge Isaacs**, *María* (1867); **José Eustacio Rivera**, *La Vorágine* (*The Vortex*, 1924); and, of course, the novels and short stories of **Gabriel García Márquez**. *Cien años de soledad* (A Hundred Years of Solitude – 1967) was the novel that brought him to prominence in Latin America and worldwide. Previously he had published many short stories and novels, for instance

Colombia

La hojarasca (*Leafstorm*, 1955) and *El coronel no tiene quien le escriba* (No-one Writes to the Colonel – 1958), but it was *Cien años de soledad* which led to his recognition as one of the major exponents of the magic realism which characterized Latin American fiction from the 1960s onwards. Later novels have included *El otoño del patriaca* (The Autumn of the Patriarch, 1975), *Crónica de una muerte anunciada* (Chronicle of a Death Foretold, 1981), *El amor en los tiempos de cólera* (Love in the Time of Cholera, 1985) and *Del amor y otros demonios* (Of Love and Other Demons, 1994). He has also continued to publish short stories and journalism and was awarded the Nobel Prize for Literature in 1982. An informative website on García Márquez is Macondo, www.themodernworld.com/gabo

Colombia

Ecuador

Tucked in between Peru and Colombia, Ecuador is small enough for you to have breakfast with scarlet macaws in the jungle and, at dinner time, be eyeballed by an iguana whose patch of Pacific beach you have just borrowed. The spectacular switchbacks of the railway that descends from the highlands, a range of volcanoes, a multitude of national parks, all emphasise the incredible variety of Ecuador. Its capital, Quito, has become one of the gringo centres of South America, bursting at the seams with language schools, travel agencies and restaurants. The exotic wildlife of the Galápagos will also keep you enthralled, whether it's playing hide-and-seek with frisky sea-lions, watching an albatross take off, or admiring the extravagant flirting techniques of the magnificent frigate bird.

8

Ecuador

Essentials

Planning your trip

The capital, **Quito**, has a colonial part, full of churches, museums and historic buildings, and a modern part, where the majority of services, including tour operators and language schools, can be found. From the city much of what you may wish to see is accessible by road in only a few hours. A variety of day trips include nature reserves, hot springs and of course the Equator. There is also good mountaineering nearby. North of Quito is **Otavalo** with its outstanding handicrafts market, a regular one-day tour, but equally popular as a base for exploring nearby villages, more nature reserves and hiking or cycling routes. Carrying on towards the Colombian border is Ibarra, another good centre for visiting the north and the starting point for the journey to San Lorenzo on the Pacific.

In the Central Sierra, south of Quito is the national park surrounding **Cotopaxi**, one of Ecuador's most frequently climbed volcanoes. Further south is the **Quilotoa circuit**, a 200 km loop through small villages and beautiful landscapes, with lots of possibilities for trekking, cycling and riding. The starting point is Latacunga on the Pan-American Highway. On one of the main routes from the Sierra to the eastern jungle is **Baños**, a very popular spa town with climbing, hiking, riding and volcano watching opportunities close at hand. The heart of the central highlands is **Riobamba**, beneath Chimborazo volcano. This is another good base for climbing and trekking, as well as the starting point for a very popular railway ride over *La Nariz del Diablo* (The Devil's Nose) – when the often-damaged line is open. The Inca ruin of **Ingapirca** is between Riobamba and **Cuenca**, a lovely colonial city in the Southern Sierra. Nearby is the Cajas Recreational Area. En route from Cuenca towards Peru are the provincial capital of **L**oja, close to the Parque Nacional Podocarpus, and **Vilcabamba**, with a delightful climate and a favourite with backpackers. Several border crossings to Peru are accessible from Loja.

Ecuador's Pacific capital is **Guayaquil**, 45 minutes by air from Quito, eight hours by bus, and 5½ hours by bus from Cuenca. It is only four hours by bus south to the Peruvian border via Machala, while to the north stretch the **Pacific Lowlands** with beaches and a growing interest in precolumbian archaeological sites. Resorts vary from the highly developed like Salinas, Bahía de Caráquez and Atacames, to smaller, but still popular places like Puerto López, Montañita, Canoa and Súa. The **Parque Nacional Machalilla** contains dry tropical forest, offshore islands and marine ecosystems. It is a good place for riding, diving, whale watching, birdwatching and relaxing on the beautiful Los Frailes beach.

The **Oriente** (eastern lowlands) offers many opportunities for nature tourism, with a number of specially designed jungle lodges, mainly in the north of the zone. A stay in one of these places is best booked in Quito or abroad, but you can head for jungle towns like Coca, Tena, Puyo or Misahuallí to arrange a tour with a local agency or guide. The southern Oriente is less developed for tourism, but interest is growing here, with Macas as the place to aim for.

Ecuador is famous for its **hot springs** and, on either side of the Andes, there is great birdwatching in a wide variety of protected areas. Other special interest activities include diving, whitewater rafting and various volunteer programmes. The nature destination par excellence, though, is the **Galápagos Islands**, 970 km west of the mainland. Tours can be arranged in Quito, Guayaquil and abroad, but if you have time and are on a more limited budget, last minute deals can sometimes be found in Puerto Ayora on Santa Cruz Island.

Ecuador's climate is highly unpredictable. As a general rule, however, in the Sierra, there is little variation by day or by season in the temperature in any particular basin: temperature depends on altitude. The range of shade temperature is from 6°C to 10°C in the morning to 19°C to 23°C in the afternoon. Temperatures can get considerably higher in the lower basins. There are two rainy seasons, from Feb to May and Oct to Nov, when the average fall in Quito is

Where to go

When to go

Ecuador

1,270 mm; the skies are mostly cloudy or overcast at this time and there are frequent rainfalls during the afternoons and nights.

In the northern coastal lowlands there are two rainy seasons, which tend to merge into one, running from Dec to Jun. Further south, the later the rains begin, the sooner they end: at Guayaquil the rains normally fall between Jan and Apr. The Santa Elena Peninsula and the southwest coast near Peru have little or no rainfall. During the dry season, May-Nov, the coast from Punta Blanca to Puerto López (provinces of Guayas and Manabí) is subject to mists (*garúa*) and cool grey days. The wettest season in the Oriente is Apr to Sep, but rain falls the year round.

The best times to visit are: in the northern and central Sierra, May to Sep; in the southern Sierra Aug to Jan; the Pacific coast Dec to Jun (even though this is the hottest, wettest time on the coastal plain, the beach is usually dry, especially the north coast). Like the coast, the Galápagos suffer from the *garúa* from Jun to Nov; from Dec to May the islands are hottest and brief but heavy showers can fall.

Ecuador's **high international tourist season** is from Jun to Aug, which is also the best time for climbing and trekking. There is also a short tourist season in Dec and Jan. In resort areas at major fiestas, such as Carnival, Semana Santa and over New Year, accommodation can be hard to find. Hotels will be full in individual towns during their particular festivals, but Ecuador as a whole is not overcrowded at any time of the year.

Finding out more

Tourism is in the hands of the **Ministerio de Turismo**, Eloy Alfaro 1214 y Carlos Tobar, Quito, T250 7560/563, F250 7564, mtur1@ec-gov.net The addresses of tourist offices are given in the **Essentials** sections of each town. Outside Ecuador, tourist information can be obtained from Ecuador's diplomatic representatives, see box. Within Ecuador, see box page 332.

Some useful websites include: The *Ecuador Handbook* site, **www.ecuadorhandbook.com** The **Ministerio de Turismo** has sites in English, **www.livecuador.com** and Spanish **www.vivecuador.com** EcuadorExplorer (**www.ecuadorexplorer.com**), a travel guide. The **Latin American Travel Advisor** (**www.amerispan.com/lata/**) offers general travel advice. **South American Explorers** (**www.samexplo.org**), with information about how to become a member and the club's services. See Quito, Tourist information for addresses and details and Essentials, page 26. **Explored** (**www.explored.com.ec**) has general information about Ecuador. Hotel bookings in Ecuador can be made through **www.bookings-americas.com/ec/** See Media for the web sites of Ecuadorean newspapers.

Language The official languages of Ecuador are Spanish and Quichua, although the latter is little used outside indigenous communities in the highlands and parts of Oriente. English and a few other European languages may be spoken in some establishments catering to tourists in Quito and the most popular tourist destinations. Away from these places, knowledge of Spanish is essential.

Before you travel

Visas & immigration All visitors to Ecuador must have a passport valid for at least six months and, in principle, an onward or return ticket. The latter is seldom asked for, but can be grounds for refusal of entry in some cases. Only citizens of the following countries require a consular **visa** to visit Ecuador as tourists: Afghanistan, Algeria, Bangladesh, China, Costa Rica, Cuba, Guatemala, Honduras, India, Iran, Iraq, Jordan, North and South Korea, Lebanon, Libya, Nicaragua, Nigeria, Pakistan, Palestinian Authority, Sri Lanka, Sudan, Syria, Tunisia, Vietnam and Yemen. Upon entry all visitors are required to complete a brief international embarkation/disembarkation card, which is then stamped along with your passport. Keep this card in your passport, losing it can cause all manner of grief when leaving the country or at a spot check.

Warning: you are required by Ecuadorean law to carry your passport at all times. Failure to do so can result in imprisonment and/or deportation. An ordinary photocopy of your passport is not an acceptable substitute and you will generally not be permitted to return to your hotel to fetch the original document. A photocopy certified by your embassy or the immigration police may be acceptable, but you should also have your original passport close at hand. Tourists are not permitted to work under any circumstances.

Length of stay. In principle, tourists are entitled to visit Ecuador for up to 90 days during any 12 month period. This may occasionally be extended, at the discretion of the **Policía Nacional de Migración** (national immigration police). In practice, those travelling by land from Peru or Colombia are seldom granted more than 30 days on arrival, but this can usually be extended. When arriving at Quito or Guayaquil airport you will be asked how long you plan to stay in the country. If you have no idea how long you will stay, ask for 90 days.

Extensions. Extensions up to 90 days total stay may only be requested at the following locations: 1) in Quito at the **Jefatura Provincial de Migración de Pichincha**, Isla Seymour 44-174 y Río Coca, T/F224 7510 (**NB** this is not the same as the *Dirección Nacional de Migración* listed below); 2) in Guayaquil at the **Jefatura Provincial de Migración del Guayas**, Av Río Daule, near the *terminal terrestre*, T229 7004; 3) in Cuenca at the **Jefatura Provincial de Migración del Azuay**, Luis Cordero 662 entre Presidente Córdova y Juan Jaramillo, T831020; 4) in Puerto Baquerizo Moreno at the **Jefatura Provincial de Migración de Galápagos**, on San Cristóbal Island, T520129. Extensions beyond 90 days and immigration problems may require a visit to immigration police headquarters in Quito: **Dirección Nacional de Migración**, Amazonas 171 y República, T245 4122. All of the above offices are normally open Mon-Fri 0800-1200 and 1500-1800, but this may vary. Immigration offices in cities other than the above cannot grant tourist visa extensions. Obtaining an extension can take less than an hour, but always leave yourself a few days slack. The above regulations are frequently subject to change, enquire well before your time expires. Polite conduct and a neat appearance are very important when dealing with the immigration authorities.

Tourists attending a course at a language school do **not** need a student visa (unless staying more than 180 days). There are many options for foreigners who wish to stay in Ecuador longer than six months a year, but if you enter as a tourist then you cannot change your status while inside the country. Additional information about immigration procedures is given in the *Ecuador Handbook* and you should always verify all details at the Consulate before departure.

NB In addition to your passport, the following documents are important for a visit to Ecuador. An **international vaccination certificate** is seldom asked for in Ecuador but must nonetheless be carried by all international travellers. A valid **drivers license** from your home country is generally sufficient to rent a car and drive in Ecuador, but an **international drivers license** may also be helpful. An **International Student Identity Card (ISIC)** may help you obtain discounts when travelling in Ecuador, but only if it is accompanied by proof of home student status. ISIC cards are sold in Quito by *Grupo Idiomas*, Roca 130 y 12 de Octubre, p 2, T250 0264, US$10.

Customs

300 cigarettes or 50 cigars or ½ lb of tobacco, one litre of spirits, a reasonable amount of perfume and gifts to the value of US$200 are admitted free of duty. If you are planning to bring any particularly voluminous, unusual, or valuable items to Ecuador (eg professional video equipment or a boat) then you should obtain permits, or be prepared to pay the prevailing duties. On departure your baggage may be inspected by security personnel and will always be sniffed by dogs searching for drugs. There are various items for which you require special permits, including wild plants and animals, original archaeological artifacts and certain works of art.

What to take

In Quito and the Sierras, take spring clothing with something warm for the cold mornings and evenings. In Guayaquil and the lowlands, wear lightweight tropical clothing. Some climbing and trekking equipment can be hired locally, but it is best to take your own. If you are going to watch birds, take your own binoculars.

Ecuador

Money

Currency

There is no substitute for cash-in-hand when travelling in Ecuador. Always bring some (but not all) of your funds as small US dollar bills

The **United States Dollar** is the only official currency of Ecuador. Only US Dollar bills circulate, in the following denominations: US$1, US$5, US$10, US$20, US$50 and US$100. US coins are used alongside the equivalent size and value Ecuadorean coins for 1, 5, 10, 25 and 50 cents. These Ecuadorean coins have no value outside the country. Many establishments are reluctant to accept bills larger than US$20 because counterfeit notes are a problem and because change may be scarce. Travellers should likewise check carefully any bills they receive as change.

There are several ways for visitors to bring their funds to Ecuador. You are strongly advised to use two or more of these, so as not to be stuck if there are problems with any one alternative. **US cash** in small denominations is by far the simplest and the only universally accepted option, but clearly a serious risk for loss or theft. **Travellers' cheques** (TCs, American Express is most widely accepted) are safe, but can only be exchanged for cash in the larger cities and up to 5% commission may be charged – although it is usually less. American Express has offices in Quito and Guayaquil, they sell TCs against an Amex card (or a cardholder's personal cheque) and replace lost or stolen TCs, but they do not give cash for TCs, nor TCs for cash. Their service is very efficient; a police report is required if TCs are stolen.

Credit cards

Establishments with credit card stickers do not necessarily take them. Some places add a hefty surcharge for credit card purchases

(Visa and Diners are most common) can be used to obtain a cash advance at some branches of some banks, and to pay at most upscale establishments, but a surcharge (at least 10%) may be applied. MasterCard holders can obtain cash advances at the company's offices in Quito, Guayaquil, Cuenca and Ambato, but no banks will provide cash advances. Those with Visa cards can obtain cash advances at the main branches of *Banco de Guayaquil* in Quito, Guayaquil and other cities; also at some branches of *Banco del Austro* and *Banco Bolivariano*, but most reliably in larger centres. Internationally linked banking machines or **ATMs** are common in Ecuador (including for MasterCard), although they cannot always be relied on and have been known to confiscate valid cards.

Funds may be rapidly wired to Ecuador by *Western Union*, but high fees and taxes apply. International bank transfers however, are not recommended. Although the Euro is gradually gaining acceptance in Ecuador, it is still best to bring US$; all other currencies are very difficult to exchange and fetch a very poor rate.

Cost of living

Prices are slowly but steadily increasing in Ecuador's dollarized economy and it is no longer the cheapest country in South America. Prices remain modest by international standards, however, and Ecuador is still affordable for even the budget traveller.

Getting there

Air

From Europe The only European cities with flights to Quito and Guayaquil which do not involve a change of plane are Barcelona/Madrid (*Iberia*) and Amsterdam (*KLM* via Curaçao). All others involve connections in Madrid, Miami, Houston, Caracas or Bogotá.

From North America Both Quito and Guayaquil can be reached by flights from New York (John F Kennedy and Newark), Miami and Houston. From other US cities make connections in Miami, Panama City, San José (Costa Rica) or Bogotá.

From Latin American cities From Bogotá, Buenos Aires, Caracas, Havana, Lima, Santiago de Chile, Mexico City, San José and Panama there are regular flights to both Quito and Guayaquil. Other destinations require a connection. *TAME*, the Ecuadorean internal airline, also has flights from Quito and Guayaquil to and from Santiago de Chile and Havana.

Road

Ecuador has international road links with Colombia and Peru. Buses from those countries run to Quito and Guayaquil. There are no cross-border trains.

Touching down

Airport tax

There is a 12% tax on air tickets for flights originating in Ecuador and a tax of US$25 on passengers departing on international flights (except those who stay under 24 hours).

Ecuadorean embassies and consulates

Australia, *11 London Circuit, 1st Floor,*
Canberra ACT 2601, T6-6262 5282,
F6-6262 5285, embecu@hotkey.net.au
Austria, *Goldschmiedgasse 10/2/24,*
A-1010 Viena, T1-535 3208, F1-535 0897,
mecaustria@chello.at
Belgium, *Av Louise 363, 9th Floor,*
1050 Brussels, T2-644 3050, F2-644 2813,
ecuador@wanadoo.be
Canada, *50 O'Connor Street No 316, Ottawa,*
ON K1P 6L2, T613-563 8206, F613-235 5776,
mecuacan@sprint.ca
France, *34 Avenue de Messine, 75008 Paris,*
T1-4561 1021, F1-4256 0664,
ambecuad@wanadoo.fr
Germany, *Kaiser-Friedrich Strasse 90, 1 OG,*
10585 Berlin, T30-238 6217, T30-3478 7126,
mecuadoral@t-online.de
Israel, *4 Rehov Weizmann (Asia House),*
4th floor, Tel Aviv 64239, T3-695 8764,
F3-691 3604, mecuaisr@netvision.net.il
Italy, *Vía Antonio Bertolini No. 8 (Paroli),*
00197 Roma, Italia, T6-807 6271, F6-807
8209, MECUROMA@FLASHNET.IT

Japan, *No 38 Kowa Building, Room 806,*
12-24 Nishi-Azabu 4 Chome, Minato-Ku,
Tokyo 1060031, T3-3499 2800,
F3-3499 4400, ecujapon@twics.com
Netherlands, *Koning innengracht 84,*
2514 AJ, The Hague, T70-346 3753,
F70-365 8910, embecua@bart.nl
New Zealand, *Ferry Bldg, 2nd Floor, Quay*
Street, Auckland, T09-309 0229, F09-303 2931.
Spain, *Calle Velásquez No.114-2º derecha,*
Madrid, T1-562 54 36, embajada@mecuador.es
Sweden, *Engelbrektsgatan 13,*
S-100 41 Stockholm, T8-679 6043,
F8-611 5593, suecia@embajada-ecuador.se
Switzerland, *Ensingerstrasse 48, 3006 Berne,*
T031-351 1755, F031-351 2771,
edesuiza@bluewin.ch
UK, *Flat 3B, 3 Hans Crescent, Knightsbridge,*
London SW1X 0LS, T7584 1367, F782 39701,
embajada@ecuador.freeserve.co.uk
USA, *2535 15th Street NW, Washington,*
DC 20009, T202-234 7200, F202-667 3482,
mecuawaa@pop.erols.com Also 1101
Brickell Avenue, Suite M-102, Miami, FL 33131,
T305-539 8214, F305-539 8313,
consecumia@aol.com

In restaurants, 10% usually included in the bill (in cheaper restaurants, tipping is uncommon – but obviously welcome!). Taxi, nil. Airport porters, US$0.50-1, according to number of suitcases.

Tipping

Urban street crime, bag snatching and slashing, and robbery along the country's highways are the most significant hazards. Secure your belongings, be wary of con tricks, avoid crowds and travel only during the daytime whenever possible. The countryside and small towns are generally safest, but theft and robbery have been reported from several places where tourists gather. It is the big cities, Guayaquil, Quito, and to a lesser extent Cuenca, which call for the greatest care. The coast is somewhat more prone to violence than the highlands, and the northern border with Colombia, including the provinces of Esmeraldas, Carchi, and especially Sucumbíos, call for additional precautions. Armed conflict in neighbouring Colombia has caused an influx of refugees, and parts of these provinces have come under the influence of insurgents. Enquire locally before travelling to and in any northern border areas, particularly Sucumbíos.

Safety
Emergency police phone number: 911 in Quito, 101 elsewhere

Occasional social unrest is part of life in Ecuador and you should not overreact. Strikes and protests are usually announced days or weeks in advance, and their most significant impact on tourists is the restriction of overland travel. Activities in towns and especially the countryside often go on as usual. Stay put at such times and make the most of visiting nearby attractions, rather than trying stick to your original itinerary or returning to Quito at all costs – the situation will soon blow over. **Drugs use or purchase in Ecuador is punishable by up to 16 years' imprisonment**.

Ecuador's active volcanoes are spectacular, but have occasionally threatened nearby communities. The following have shown visible activity in recent years: Guagua Pichincha near Quito, Tungurahua near Baños, and Sangay southeast of Riobamba. Cotopaxi is also an active volcano. The **National Geophysics Institute**, provides volcanic activity updates in Spanish at **www.epn.edu.ec**

Volcanoes

Ecuador

Touching down

Official time   Local time is five hours behind GMT (Galápagos, six hours behind).

IDD   593. If ringing expect equal tones with long pauses. Short equal tones with short pauses indicate it is engaged.

Voltage   110 volts, 60 cycles, AC throughout Ecuador. Very low wattage bulbs in many hotel rooms, keen readers are advised to carry a bright bulb.

Weights and measures   The metric system is generally used in foreign trade and must be used in legal documents. English measures are understood in the hardware and textile trades. Spanish measures are used in the retail trade.

Where to stay

Hotels
See inside front cover for our hotel price guide

Outside the provincial capitals and a few resorts, there are seldom higher-class hotels. Service of 10% and tax of 12% are added to better hotel and restaurant bills. The cheaper hotels are beginning to apply the 12% tax, but check if it is included in the price.

Larger towns and tourist centres often have more hotels than we are able to list. This is especially true of Quito. The hotels included in this chapter are among the best in each category, but were also selected to provide a variety of locations and styles.

Camping

Camping in protected natural areas can be one of the most satisfying experiences during a visit to Ecuador. For details see Trekking, page 896. Organized campsites, car or trailer camping on the other hand are virtually unheard-of. Because of the abundance of cheap hotels you should never *have to* camp in Ecuador, except for cyclists who may be stuck between towns. In this case the best strategy is to ask permission to camp on someone's private land, preferably within sight of their home for safety. It is not safe to pitch your tent at random near villages and even less so on beaches. Those travelling with their own trailer or camper-van can also ask permission to park overnight on private property, in a guarded parking lot or at a 24-hour gas station (although this may be noisy). It is not safe to sleep in your vehicle on the street or roadside.

Bluet Camping Gas is easily obtainable, but white gas, like US Coleman fuel, is hard to find. Unleaded petrol (gasoline) is available everywhere and may be an alternative for some camping stoves.

Getting around

Air

TAME is the main internal airline, flying to all major airports and the Galápagos. Routes and frequencies change constantly and up-to-date information may not be available outside Ecuador, so always enquire locally. *TAME* offices are listed under each relevant town or city; central reservations Quito T290 9900, Guayaquil T231 0305, www.tame.com.ec Smaller airlines include **Aerogal** which flies Quito-Coca, **Austro Aéreo** which flies Quito-Guayaquil, Quito-Cuenca, and Guayaquil-Cuenca, and **Icaro** which flies from Quito to Cuenca, Loja, Coca, and Lago Agrio. Make sure you confirm and reconfirm flight reservations frequently.

Road
Throughout Ecuador, intercity travel by bus or car is safest during the daytime

Bus   Bus travel is generally more convenient than in other Andean countries, with service at frequent intervals. Several companies use comfortable air-conditioned buses on their longer routes. Fares for these are higher and some companies have their own stations, away from the main bus terminals, exclusively for these better buses. A good network of paved roads runs throughout the coast and highlands. Maintenance of major highways is franchised to private firms, who charge tolls of US$0.50-1. In Oriente, most roads are dirt or gravel.

Car

Driving in Ecuador has been described as 'an experience', partly because of unexpected potholes and other obstructions and the lack of road signs, partly because of local drivers' tendency to use the middle of the road. Some roads in Oriente that appear paved, are in fact crude oil sprayed onto compacted earth. Beware the bus drivers, who often drive very fast and rather recklessly (passengers also please note). Driving at night is not recommended, see

Safety, above. The road maps published by *Ediguías* (Nelson Gómez) are probably the most useful and widely available.

There are only two grades of gasoline, 'Extra' (82 octane, US$1.12 per US gallon) and 'Super' (92 Octane, US$1.50). Both are unleaded. Extra is available everywhere, while super may not be available in more remote areas. Diesel fuel (US$0.90) is notoriously dirty and available everywhere.

Documents Obtaining temporary admission to Ecuador for a car or motorcycle can be complex and time-consuming, as is shipping in a vehicle, especially through Guayaquil; details are given in the *Ecuador Handbook*.

Car hire In order to rent a car you must be 25 (21 at a few agencies) and have an international credit card. You may pay cash, which is cheaper and may allow you to bargain, but they want a credit card for security. You may be asked to sign two blank credit card vouchers, one for the rental fee itself and the other as a security deposit, and authorization for a charge of as much as US$3,000 may be requested against your credit card account. These arrangements are all above board and the uncashed vouchers will be returned to you when you return the vehicle, but the credit authorization may persist on your account (reducing your credit limit) for up to 30 days. Be careful when dealing with some of the smaller agencies and always check the amount of deductible on insurance (up to US$4,000). Be sure also to check the car's condition and ground clearance. Always make sure the car is securely garaged at night. Rental rates vary depending on the company and vehicle, but in 2002 a small car suitable for city driving costs about US$250 per week including all taxes and insurance. A sturdier four-wheel drive (recommended for the Oriente and unpaved roads) can be twice as much.

Hitchhiking Public transport in Ecuador is so abundant that there is seldom any need to hitchhike along the major highways. On small out-of-the-way country roads however, the situation can be quite the opposite, and giving passers-by a ride is common practice and safe for drivers and passengers alike, especially in the back of a pickup or larger truck. A small fee is usually charged, best to ask in advance.

Train Sadly, the spectacular Ecuadorean railway system has all but ceased operations. In 2002, only three tourist rides were still being offered: over the Devil's Nose from **Riobamba to Sibambe** and back, a weekend excursion from **Quito to the El Boliche station** near Parque Nacional Cotopaxi, and a **45-km ride out of Ibarra**. Foreigners pay a much higher fare than Ecuadoreans on these few remaining routes.

Maps **Maps and guide books** Instituto Geográfico Militar (IGM) in Quito. Map and air photo indexes are all laid out for inspection. The map sales room (helpful staff) is open Mon-Fri 0800-1300, 1400-1600. They sell country maps and topographic maps, covering most areas of Ecuador, in various scales, US$2 each. Maps of border areas are 'reservado' (classified) and not available for sale without a military permit (requires extra time). Buy your maps here, they are rarely available outside Quito. If one is sold out you may order a photo-copy. Map and geographic reference libraries are located next to the sales room, igm2@igm.mil.ec The *IGM* is on top of the hill to the east of El Ejido park. From 12 de Octubre, opposite the *Casa de la Cultura*, take Jiménez (a small street) up the hill. After crossing Av Colombia continue uphill on Paz y Miño behind the Military Hospital and then turn right to the guarded main entrance, you have to deposit your passport or identification card. There is a beautiful view from the grounds. Some *IGM* maps also available from the *Centro de Difusión Geográfica* in the Casa de Sucre, Venezuela 573, helpful. A good series of pocket maps and city guides by Nélson Gómez, published by *Ediguías* in Quito, are available in book shops throughout the country.

Keeping in touch

Internet The internet is exceptionally accessible in Ecuador and has replaced postal and telephone services for the vast majority of travellers. Almost every place that offers internet also has *Net2Phone*. Some form of internet access may be found almost everywhere in Ecuador,

Ecuador

except for the most remote locations. Hourly internet rates range from under US$1 (in Quito) to US$7 (in Coca), *Net2Phone* rates are typically around US$0.25 per minute to North America and Europe.

Post Opening hours for post offices are generally Mon-Fri 0730-1900 and Sat 0730-1400, although there may be some variation from town to town. Postal branches in small towns may not be familiar with all rates and procedures. Your chances are better at the main branches in provincial capitals or, better yet, in Quito: at Colón corner Almagro in La Mariscal district, or at the main sorting centre on Japón near *Naciones Unidas* (behind the CCI shopping centre). **NB** Urgent or valuable items should not be entrusted to the post office since long delays and non-delivery are increasingly common. Post cards and registered mail (*correo certificado*) seem especially prone to problems. National and international courier service is available as an alternative, see below.

Ordinary airmail rates for up to 20 g are US$0.90 to the Americas, US$1.05 to the rest of the world. Registered mail costs an additional US$0.95 per item. Parcels up to 30 kg, maximum dimensions permitted are 70 by 30 by 30 cm. Air parcel rates are: to the Americas approximately US$15 for the first kg, US$4.50 for each additional kg; to the rest of the world approximately US$24 for the first kg, US$13 for each additional kg. Current rates by SAL/APR (surface air lifted) reduced priority service: to the Americas approximately US$14 for the first kg, US$4 for each additional kg; to the rest of the world approximately US$22 for the first kg, US$11 for each additional kg. There is no surface (sea) mail service from Ecuador.

Letters and parcels for Europe bearing the correct Ecuadorean postage can be dropped off at the *Lufthansa* office in Quito, 18 de Septiembre E7-05 y Reina Victoria, to be sent in the next international bag (be there by 1200 on the day before the flight).

Letters can be sent to **Poste Restante/General Delivery** (*lista de correos*, but you must specify the postal branch in larger cities), some embassies (enquire beforehand), or, for card or TC holders, American Express offices. Never send anything to Ecuador by surface (sea) mail.

Courier companies are the only safe alternative for sending or receiving valuable time-sensitive mail in Ecuador. For rapid and reliable international service, *DHL* has offices throughout the country; the most convenient locations in Quito include Colón 1333 y Foch and República 433 y Almagro, T248 5100. For courier service within Ecuador, *Servientrega* has offices throughout the country, reliable 1-2 day service is available to all areas, US$2-$3 for up to 2 kg depending on destination.

Telephone Ecuador's telephone system is currently operated by three regional state companies, whose names you should look for on telephone offices: *Andinatel* in the northern highlands and Oriente; *Pacifictel* on the coast, in the southern highlands and Oriente; and *Etapa* in Cuenca. There are also two private companies, *Bell South* and *Porta*, which provide cellular phone service, including convenient but expensive debit card operated public cell phones. Since this system is wireless, public phones have been installed in previously inaccessible locations, such as the mountain shelter on Chimborazo. Short term cell phone rentals are also available. Debit cards for public cell phones may be purchased at kiosks and many small shops; they are not interchangeable between the two companies. **NB** Changes were made to the telephone numbering system in late 2001. All cellular phones (area code 09) and phones in the provinces of Pichincha (02), (this includes Quito) and Guayas (04) currently have seven digit numbers. All other phone numbers have only six digits. There are plans eventually to change the remaining numbers to seven digits as well.

The best public places to make local, national or international calls are telephone company offices, with at least one such office in each city or town. For international calls however, you may be asked to specify how many minutes you would like to speak and pay in advance. Examples of current rates are: US$0.38 per min to the USA, US$0.46 per min to the UK, US$1.07 per min to Australia. Rates vary in small towns, and hefty surcharges may be applied to calls made from hotels, always ask in advance.

Country-direct access is available free of charge from private phones and telephone company offices throughout Ecuador (except Galápagos), although not every office knows about this nor are they familiar with the access numbers. These are: **Argentina**: 999161,

999186; **Bolivia**: 999169; **Brasil**: 999177; **Canada**: 999175; **Chile**: *Entel* 999179, *ChileSat* 999183, *Telefónica* 999188; **Dominican Republic**: 999165; **France**: 999180; **Italy**: 999164; **Mexico**: 999184; **Peru**: 999167; **Spain**: 999176; **UK**: *BT* 999178, 999181; **USA**: *ATT* 999119, *WorldPhone* 999170/2, *Sprint* 999171; **Venezuela**: 999173.

   Faxes may be sent and received at phone company offices, some post offices, hotels and many private locations. Shop around for the best rates.

Newspapers The main newspapers in Quito are *El Comercio* (www.elcomercio.com) and *Hoy* (www.hoy.com.ec); in Guayaquil *El Universo* (www.eluniverso.com). *El Mercurio* of Cuenca is also highly regarded. There are several smaller regional or local papers published in provincial capitals. Foreign newspapers are only available in some luxury hotels and a few speciality shops in Quito and Guayaquil.

Media

Food and drink

The cuisine varies extensively with region. The following are some typical dishes worth trying. **In the highlands** *Locro de papas* (potato and cheese soup), *mote* (corn burst with alkali, a staple in the region around Cuenca, but used in a variety of dishes in the Sierra), *caldo de patas* (cowheel soup with *mote*), *llapingachos* (fried potato and cheese patties), *empanadas de morocho* (fried snacks: a ground corn shell filled with meat), *sancocho de yuca* (vegetable soup with manioc root), roast *cuy* (guinea pig), *fritada* (fried pork), *hornado* (roast pork), *humitas* (tender ground corn steamed in corn leaves), and *quimbolitos* (similar to *humitas* but prepared with corn flour and steamed in banana leaves). *Humitas* and *quimbolitos* come in both sweet and savoury varieties.

   On the coast *Empanadas de verde* (fried snacks: a ground plantain shell filled with cheese, meat or shrimp), *sopa de bola de verde* (plantain dumpling soup), *ceviche* (marinaded fish or seafood, popular everywhere, see below), *encocadas* (dishes prepared with coconut milk, may be shrimp, fish, etc, very popular in the province of Esmeraldas), *cocadas* (sweets made with coconut), *viche* (fish or seafood soup made with ground peanuts), and *patacones* (thick fried plantain chips served as a side dish).

   In Oriente Dishes prepared with yuca (manioc or cassava root) and a variety of river fish.

   Throughout the country, if economizing ask for the set meal in restaurants, *almuerzo* at lunch time, *merienda* in the evening – very cheap and wholesome; it costs US$1-2. *Fanesca*, a fish soup with beans, many grains, ground peanuts and more, sold in Easter Week, is very filling (it is so popular that in Quito and main tourist spots it is sold throughout Lent). *Ceviche*, marinated fish or seafood which is usually served with popcorn and roasted maize (*tostado*), is very popular throughout Ecuador. Only *ceviche de pescado* (fish) and *ceviche de concha* (clams) which are marinated raw, potentially pose a health hazard. The other varieties of *ceviche* such as *camarón* (shrimp/prawn) and *langostino* (jumbo shrimp/king prawn) all of which are cooked before being marinated, are generally safe (check the cleanliness of the establishment). *Langosta* (lobster) is an increasingly endangered species but continues to be illegally fished; please be conscientious. Ecuadorean food is not particularly spicy. However, in most homes and restaurants, the meal is accompanied by a small bowl of *ají* (hot pepper sauce) which may vary in potency. *Colada* is a generic name which can refer to cream soups or sweet beverages. In addition to the prepared foods mentioned above, Ecuador offers large variety of delicious fruits, some of which are unique to South America.

Food
VAT/IVA of 12% is charged at restaurants and for non-essential items in food shops

Argentine and Chilean wines are available in the larger cities. The best fruit drinks are *naranjilla*, *maracuyá* (passion fruit), *tomate de árbol*, *piña* (pineapple), *taxo* (another variety of passion fruit) and *mora* (blackberry), but note that fruit juices are sometimes made with unboiled water. Main beers available are *Pilsener*, *Club* and *Biela*. Good *aguardiente* (unmatured rum, *Cristal* is recommended), also known as *paico, trago de caña*, or just *trago*. The usual soft drinks, known as *colas*, are available. Instant coffee or liquid concentrate is common, so ask for *café pasado* if you want real coffee. In tourist centres and many upscale hotels and restaurants, good cappuccino and expresso can be found.

Drink

Ecuador

Shopping

Best buys are woven items such as wall-hangings, sweaters, blankets and shawls from Otavalo or Saquisilí. Authentic Panama hats can be found at a fraction of European costs on the coast. Other handicrafts include silver jewellery, ceramics and brightly-painted carvings, usually of balsa wood. There are also beautiful carvings from *tagua*, or vegetable ivory.

Holidays and festivals

Bullfights are a part of every city's fiestas. Best known is Quito's festival, held the week preceding 6 Dec

1 January: New Year's Day; 6 January: Reyes Magos y Día de los Inocentes, a time for pranks, which closes the Christmas – New Year holiday season. 27 February: Día del Civismo, celebrating the victory over Peru at Tarqui in 1829. Carnival: Monday and Tuesday before Lent, celebrated everywhere in the Andes, except Ambato, by throwing water at passers-by: be prepared to participate. Easter: Holy Thursday, Good Friday, Holy Saturday. 1 May: Labour Day. 24 May: Battle of Pichincha, Independence. Early June: Corpus Christi. 10 August: first attempt to gain the Independence of Quito. 12 October: Columbus' arrival in America. 2 November: All Souls' Day. 25 December: Christmas Day.

Sport and special interest travel

Climbing Ecuador offers some exceptional high altitude climbing, with 10 mountains over 5,000 m – most with easy access. The four most frequently climbed are Cotopaxi (technically easy with a guide and equipment), Tungurahua (an active volcano, enquire about the level of volcanic activity before climbing), Chimborazo (a long demanding climb, with at times impassable *penitentes* – conical ice formations – near the summit) and Iliniza Norte (the only one of the 'big ten' without a glacier, but a rope is needed). The other six, Iliniza Sur, Antisana, El Altar, Sangay, Carihuairazo and Cayambe vary in degree

of difficulty and/or danger. Sangay, for instance, is technically easy, but extremely dangerous from the falling rocks being ejected from the volcano. Many other mountains can be climbed and the climbing clubs, guiding agencies and tour operators will give advice. Proper equipment and good guidance are essential. The dangers of inadequate acclimatization, snow blindness, climbing without a qualified guide or adequate equipment must be taken very seriously, especially on the 'easier' mountains which may lure the less experienced. Deglaciation continually reshapes the high altitude landscape of Ecuador and alters climbing routes. Always inform yourself of current conditions before undertaking an ascent. Information on companies which specialize in climbing, guides and clubs is given in the Quito section (page 913), Cotopaxi (page 944), Tungurahua (page 956) and Chimborazo (page 962). **Recommended climbing books are**: *Ecuador: A Climbing Guide*, by Yossi Brain (The Mountaineers, Seattle, 2000), *Climbing and Hiking in Ecuador*, by Rob Rachowiecki, Mark Thurber and Betsy Wagenhauser (Bradt Publications, 4th edition, 1997), *Montañas del Sol*, by Marcos Serrano, Iván Rojar and Freddy Landazuri, Ediciones Campo Abierto, 1994; it covers 20 main mountains and is an excellent introduction. *Cotopaxi: Mountain of Light*, by Freddy Landazuri, Ediciones Campo Abierto, 1994, in English and Spanish, is a thorough history of the mountain. *The High Andes, A Guide for Climbers*, by John Biggar (Castle Douglas, Kirkcudbrightshire, Scotland: Andes, 1999), has a chapter on Ecuador. Edward Whymper's *Travels among the Great Andes of the Equator* of 1891 (Gibbs M Smith, Salt Lake City, 1987) provides a delightful historical perspective but is now hard to find. *Die Schneeberge Ecuador* by Marco Cruz, a German translation from Spanish is excellent. **Mountaineering journals include**: *Campo Abierto* (not produced by the Travel Agency of the same name), an annual magazine on expeditions, access to mountains etc, US$1; *Montaña* is the annual magazine of the Colegio San Gabriel mountaineering club, US$1.50.

Diving Ecuador has a biologically diverse marine environment. The prime spot is the Galápagos, with more than 20 dive sites: each island has its own unique underwater environment. Off the mainland, the best place to dive is the Parque Nacional Machalilla, at Isla La Plata. Colonies of sea lions can be seen here and migrating humpback whales pass this stretch of coast between late June and October.

Fishing is possible in the lakes of the central Sierra, and in the rivers of the Oriente. For big-game fishing, bonito and marlin, the best areas are off Playas, Salinas and Manta.

Nature tourism As already noted, the Galápagos Islands are the top destination for reliably seeing wildlife close-up. They are not cheap but it is well worth paying for a good trip to the Islands. A number of the species from the Galápagos may also be seen in the Parque Nacional Machalilla and on other parts of the coast; this is a less expensive option. Ecuador's other major natural attraction is its birdlife. A huge number of species in a great variety of habitats and microclimates may be seen. There are too many **birdwatching** spots to mention here, but they fall into five general regions: western lowlands and lower foothills, western Andes, Inter-Andean forests and páramos, eastern Andes and Oriente jungle.

Rafting and kayaking Ecuador is a whitewater paradise with dozens of accessible rivers, warm waters and tropical rainforest. Regional rainy seasons differ so that, throughout the year, there is always a river to run. The majority of Ecuador's whitewater rivers share a number of characteristics. Plunging off the Andes the upper sections are very steep creeks offering, if they're runnable at all, serious technical grade V, suitable for expert kayakers only. As the creeks join on the lower slopes they form rivers navigable by both raft and kayak (ie less steep, more volume). Some of these rivers offer up to 100 km of continuous grade III-IV whitewater, before flattening out to rush towards the Pacific Ocean on one side of the ranges or deep into the Amazon Basin on the other. As a general rule the rivers running straight off the eastern and western slopes of the Andes are less subject to pollution than the highland rivers which drain some of the most densely populated regions of the country. Ask about water quality before signing up for a trip. Of the rivers descending to the Pacific coast, the Blanco and its tributaries are the most frequently run. They are within easy reach of Quito, as is the Quijos on the eastern side of the Sierra. In the Oriente, the main rafting and kayaking rivers are the Aguarico and its tributary the Dué, the Napo, Pastaza and Upano. See the relevant paragraphs under Quito Sport, Baños and Tena (page 913).

Other adventure sports include **mountain biking**, for which there are boundless opportunities in the Sierra, on coastal roads and in the upper Amazon basin. Agencies which offer tours, rent equipment and can help plan routes are listed under Quito.

Trekking Ecuador's varied landscape, diverse ecological environments and friendly villages within a compact area make travelling on foot a refreshing change from crowded buses. Hiking in the Sierra is mostly across high elevation páramo, through agricultural lands, and past indigenous communities living in traditional ways. There are outstanding views of glaciated peaks in the north and precolumbian ruins in the south. On the coast there are only a few areas developed for hiking ranging from dry forest to coastal rain forest.

In the tropical rain forests of the Oriente, local guides are often required because of the difficulty in navigation and because you will be walking on land owned by indigenous tribes. The Andean Slopes are steep and often covered by virtually impenetrable cloud forests and it rains a lot. Many ancient trading routes head down the river valleys. Some of these trails are still used. Others may be overgrown and difficult to follow but offer the reward of intact ecosystems. You may be travelling across land that is either owned outright by indigenous people or jointly managed with the Ministry of the Environment. It is important to be respectful of the people and request permission to pass through or camp. Sometimes a fee may be charged by locals but it is usually minimal. The Quito Sport section, same reference as above, lists companies which rent equipment and give advice. Recommended trekking books are: *Climbing and Hiking in Ecuador* (listed above) and *Trekking in Ecuador*, by **Robert and Daisy Kunstaetter** (The Mountaineers, Seattle, 2002); also **www.trekkinginecuador.com**

Spectator sports **Football (soccer)** is without a doubt the national sport, **ecua-volley** (three players per team) and **basketball** are also popular.

Quito

Few cities have a setting to match that of Quito, the second highest capital in Latin America after La Paz. The city is set in a hollow at the foot of the volcano Pichincha (4,794 m). The city's charm lies in its colonial centre, a UNESCO World Heritage Site, where cobbled streets are steep and narrow, dipping to deep ravines. From the top of Cerro Panecillo, 183 m above the city level, there is a fine view of the city below and the encircling cones of volcanoes and other mountains.

Modern Quito, north of the colonial city, has broad avenues, contemporary office buildings, fine private residences, parks, embassies and villas. Here you will find Quito's main tourist and business area at the district known as La Mariscal (Mcal Sucre: Av Amazonas, from Av Patria to about Av Orellana and the adjoining streets) and further north as far as Av Naciones Unidas. On Sunday La Alameda, Carolina and El Ejido parks are filled with local families. The Parque Metropolitano, above Estadio Atahualpa, is reputed to be the largest urban park in South America and is good for walking, running or biking through the forest. Despite efforts by the municipal authorities, the city has a serious air and noise pollution problem.

Phone code: 02
All Quito phone numbers have 7 digits and are prefixed with a 2.
Colour map 1a, grid A4
Population: approximately 2,000,000
Altitude: 2,850 m

Most places of historical interest are in the old city, while the majority of the hotels, restaurants, travel agencies and facilities for visitors are in the new city. In 1998, the city introduced a new street numbering system based on N (Norte), E (Este), S (Sur), O (Oeste), plus a number for each street and a number for each building. In 2002, both systems are used interchangeably.

Ins & outs
For more detailed information, see Transport, page 919

Getting there Mariscal Sucre airport is about 5 km north of the main hotel district, within the city limits. It is served by city buses, the trolley bus ('El Trole' – not designed for heavy luggage) and taxis (US$4 to the new city, recommended as the safest option). Most long distance bus services arrive at the Terminal Terrestre at the junction of Maldonado and Cumandá, south of the old city. It is safest to arrive at and leave the terminal for your hotel by taxi (US$4 to the new city), although the Cumandá stop of El Trole is nearby. Some luxury bus services run to their own offices in the new city.

The old city is closed to vehicles Sun 0900-1600, a nice time for a stroll

Getting around Both the old city and the new city can be explored on foot, but the distance between the two is best covered by some form of public transport. You should not walk at night in either part of the capital. You should also take care during the day. Public transport is easy to find and is not expensive. The trolley bus (very crowded at rush hour) runs north-south from 'La Y' to Ciudadela Quitumbe. A parallel bus artery, *La Ecovía* (mostly Av 6 de Diciembre), runs north-south from Río Coca to Plaza La Marín. Robberies can occur on city buses and trolley. Taxis are a cheap and efficient alternative, with fares starting at US$0.80; highly recommended especially at night. Authorized taxis display a unit number, driver's photograph and have a meter.

Climate Quito is within 25 km of the Equator, but it stands high enough to make its climate much like that of spring in England, the days pleasantly warm and the nights cool. Because of the height, visitors may initially feel some discomfort and should slow their pace for the first 24 hrs. Mean temperature, 13°C, rainfall, 1,473 mm. Rainy season, Oct to May with the heaviest rainfall in Apr, though heavy storms in Jul are not unknown. Rain usually falls in the afternoon. The day length (sunrise to sunset) is almost constant throughout the year.

Tourist offices *Cámara Provincial de Turismo de Pichincha* (CAPTUR) has information offices at the airport, in the new city in Parque Gabriela Mistral, Cordero y Reina Victoria, and in the old city at Venezuela y Chile. Helpful and friendly, some staff speak English. The *Ministerio de Turismo*, Eloy Alfaro 1214 y Carlos Tobar (between República and Shyris), T250 0719, F250 7565, mtur1@ec-gov.net Information counter downstairs. Some staff speak English. *Cultura Reservation Center*, *Café Cultura*, Robles 513 y Reina Victoria, T250 4078, F222 4271,

Ecuador

www.cafecultura.com Gives information and book services. *EcuadorExplorer*, reservations through www.ecuadorexplorer.com **South American Explorers** Jorge Washington 311 y Leonidas Plaza, Apartado 17-21-431, Eloy Alfaro, T/F222 5228, quitoclub@saexplorers.org Mon-Fri 0930-1700. Members may receive post and faxes, use internet and store gear. Local discounts with SAE card. Highly recommended. See also Essentials chapter.

Safety Theft and armed robbery are hazards throughout Quito, including the New City and especially the Mariscal hotel and nightlife district. The city sees many tourists and they are obvious targets. Mustard smearing and similar scams are reported on the rise. Both old and new cities are especially dangerous at night and pickpockets are active at all hours. Be careful on buses, the *Trole* and around the Terminal Terrestre. Always use taxis at night and whenever you are carrying anything of value. Do not walk through any city parks in the evening or in daylight at quiet times. Joggers are recommended to stay on the periphery. Policemen on bicycles patrol parks. **Tourist Police** HQ at Roca y Reina Victoria, T254 3983.

Panecillo: neighbourhood brigades are patrolling the area, improving public safety, visitors are charged US$0.20 to finance this operation. Taking a taxi up is safer than walking up the series of steps and paths to the Virgin which begin on García Moreno (where it meets Ambato). A taxi up and down with 30 mins' wait costs US$3. Do not carry valuables and seek local advice before going.

Sights

Guided tours in the colonial city with Empresa Centro Histórico, Palacio Arzobispal, ground floor, T258 6591, Tue-Sun 0930-1100, 1400-1430, US$10

The heart of the old city is **Plaza de la Independencia**, dominated by a somewhat grim **Cathedral**, built 1550-62, with grey stone porticos and green tile cupolas. On its outer walls are plaques listing the names of the founding fathers of Quito, and inside are the tomb of Sucre (tucked away in a corner) and a famous Descent from the Cross by the Indian painter Caspicara. There are many other 17th and 18th century paintings; the interior decoration, especially the roof, shows Moorish influence. ■ *Mon-Fri, 0600-1000.* Beside the Cathedral, round the corner, is the beautiful **El Sagrario**, originally built as the Cathedral chapel. ■ *Mon-Sat, 0700-1900, Sun 0800-1300.* Facing the Cathedral is the old **Palacio Arzobispal**, part of which now houses shops. On the northeast side is the concrete **Alcaldía Municipal** which fits in quite well. The low colonial **Palacio de Gobierno**, silhouetted against the flank of Pichincha, is on the northwest side of the Plaza; on the first floor is a gigantic mosaic mural of Orellana navigating the Amazon. The ironwork on the balconies looking over the main plaza is from the Tuilleries in Paris, sold by the French government shortly after the French Revolution. You can only see the patio. ■ *Visits with special permit only, Tue and Thu, 0930-1230. A written request must be presented several days in advance at the gate.*

Calle Morales, main street of La Ronda district (traditionally called C La Ronda and now a notorious area for pickpockets and bag slashers, avoid the area after dark), is one of the oldest streets in the city. Go past Plaza Santo Domingo to C

Ecuador

Guayaquil, the main shopping street, and on to **Parque Alameda**, which has the oldest astronomical observatory in South America. ■ *Sat 0900-1200*. There is also a splendid monument to Simón Bolívar, various lakes, and in the northwest corner a spiral lookout tower with a good view.

From Plaza de la Independencia two main streets, Venezuela and García Moreno, lead straight towards the Panecillo to the wide Av 24 de Mayo, at the top of which is a concrete building where street vendors are supposed to do their trading. Street trading still takes place daily, however, from Sucre down to 24 de Mayo and from San Francisco church west up past Cuenca.

Plaza de San Francisco (or Bolívar) is west of Plaza de la Independencia; on the northwest side of this plaza is the great church and monastery of the patron saint of Quito, **San Francisco**. The church was constructed by the Spanish in 1553 and is rich in art treasures. The two towers were felled by an earthquake in 1868 and rebuilt.

Quito Old City

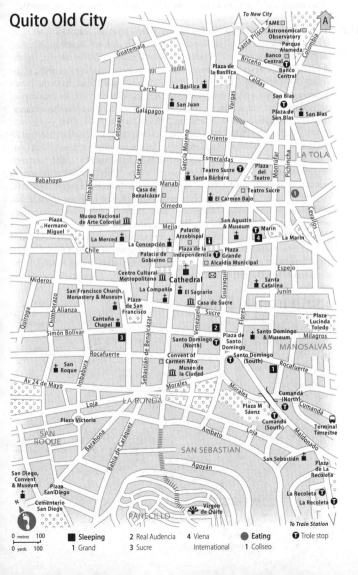

Ecuador

■ Sleeping	2 Real Audencia	4 Viena	● Eating	❶ Trole stop
1 Grand	3 Sucre	International	1 Coliseo	

0 metres 100
0 yards 100

A modest statue of the founder, Fray Jodoco Ricke, the Flemish Franciscan who sowed the first wheat in Ecuador, stands at the foot of the stairs to the church portal. See the fine wood-carvings in the choir, a high altar of gold and an exquisite carved ceiling. There are some paintings in the aisles by Miguel de Santiago, the colonial *mestizo* painter. ■ *Mon-Sat 0900-120, 1500-1700, Sun 0900-1200. Unofficial guides claim that they do not want money, then ask for it.* Adjoining San Francisco is the **Cantuña Chapel** with sculptures. ■ *0800-1200.*

Plaza de Santo Domingo (or Sucre), to the southeast of Plaza San Francisco, has to the southeast the church and monastery of **Santo Domingo**, with its rich wood-carvings and a remarkable Chapel of the Rosary to the right of the main altar. In the centre of the plaza is a statue to Sucre, pointing to the slopes of Pichincha where he won his battle against the Royalists.

On **Cerro Panecillo** there is a statue to the Virgen de Quito and a good view from the observation platform up the statue. ■ *1030-1730, US$1; also see Safety page 898.*

Churches

There are 86 churches altogether in Quito

The fine Jesuit church of **La Compañía**, in C García Moreno, one block from Plaza de la Independencia has the most ornate and richly sculptured façade and interior. See its coloured columns, its 10-sided altars and high altar plated with gold, and the gilded balconies. Several of its most precious treasures, including a painting of the Virgen Dolorosa framed in emeralds and gold, are kept in the vaults of the Banco Central and appear only at special festivals. Replicas of the impressive paintings of hell and the final judgement by Miguel de Santiago can be seen at the entrance. Extensive restoration was completed in 2002. ■ *Mass at 0700, 0800, 1800; visits Mon-Sat 1000-1200, 1500-1730, US$1.* Not far away to the north is the church of **La Merced**. In the monastery of La Merced is Quito's oldest clock, built in 1817 in London. Fine cloisters are entered through a door to the left of the altar. La Merced contains many splendidly elaborate styles; note the statue of Neptune on the main patio fountain. ■ *Mon-Sat 0600-1200, 1230-1800.* The **Basílica**, on Plaza de la Basílica (C Venezuela), is very large, has many gargoyles, stained glass windows and fine, bas relief bronze doors (under construction since 1926). A coffee shop in the clock tower gives good views over the city.Recommended. ■ *0930-1730, US$2.*

Many of the heroes of Ecuador's struggle for independence are buried in the monastery of **San Agustín** (Flores y Chile), which has beautiful cloisters on three sides where the first act of independence from Spain was signed on 10 August 1809. In the monastery of **San Diego** (by the cemetery of the same name, just west of Panecillo) are

South from El Ejido

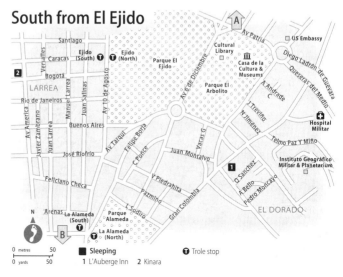

Sleeping
1 L'Auberge Inn 2 Kinara

🚏 Trole stop

some unique paintings with figures dressed in fabrics sewn to the canvas – a curious instance of present-day collage. ■ *Tue-Sun, 0930-1230, 1430-1730, US$1.50. Ring the bell to the right of the church door. All visitors are shown around by a guide.*

The **Basílica of Guápulo** (1693), perched on the edge of a ravine east of the city, is well worth seeing for its many paintings, gilded altars, stone carvings of indigenous animals and the marvellously carved pulpit. Take bus 21 (Guápulo-Dos Puentes) from Plaza de San Blas, or walk down the steep stairway behind *Hotel Quito.*

Opposite Parque El Ejido, at the junction 6 de Diciembre and Av Patria, there is a large cultural and museum complex housing the **Casa de la Cultura** and the museum of the Banco Central del Ecuador (entrance on Patria). Museums belonging to the Casa de la Cultura: **Museo de Arte Moderno**, paintings and sculpture since 1830; **Museo de Traje Indígena**, traditional dress and adornments of indigenous groups; **Museo de Instrumentos Musicales**, an impressive collection of musical instruments, said to be the second in importance in the world. ■ *T222 3392, undergoing restoration in 2002.*

Museums
Check museum opening times in advance

If you have time to visit only one museum in Quito, it should be the **Museo Nacional del Banco Central del Ecuador**, also housed in the Casa de la Cultura. It has three floors, with five different sections. The **Sala de Arqueología** is particularly impressive with beautiful precolumbian ceramics. The **Sala de Oro** has a nice collection of prehispanic gold objects. The remaining three sections house art collections. The **Sala de Arte Colonial** is rich in paintings and sculptures especially of religious themes. The **Sala de Arte Republicano** houses works of the early years of the Republic. The **Sala de Arte Contemporáneo** presents contemporary art. There are also temporary exhibits, videos on Ecuadorean culture, the various indigenous groups and other topics, a bookshop and cafeteria. Highly recommended. ■ *Tue-Fri 0900-1700, Sat-Sun 1000-1600, US$2, students with ISIC or national student card, US$1. Guided tours in English, French or German by appointment, T222 3259.*

Museo Nacional de Arte Colonial, Cuenca y Mejía, is a small collection of Ecuadorean sculpture and painting, housed in the 17th-century mansion of Marqués de Villacís. ■ *Undergoing restoration in 2002, T228 2297.*

Housed in the restored, 16th Century Hospital San Juan de Dios, is the **Museo de la Ciudad**. It takes you through Quito's history from prehispanic times to the 19th Century. ■ *Tue-Sun 0930-1730, US$4, students US$2, guide service US$6, Rocafuerte 572 y García Moreno, T228 3882.*

Museo del Convento de San Francisco in Plaza de San Francisco, has a fine collection of religious art. ■ *Tue-Sat 0900-1800, Sun 0900-1300, US$1, T228 1124.* Similar collections in: **Museo de San Agustín**, interesting exhibition of restoration work. ■ *Tue-Sun 0900-1200, 1500-1800, US$1, free on Sat, Chile y Guayaquil.*

The **Museo Jijón y Caamaño**, in the Catholic University library building has a private collection of archaeological objects, historical documents, art, portraits, uniforms, etc, very well displayed, ■ *Mon-Fri 0830-1600, US$0.60, 12 de Octubre y Roca, T256 5627 ext 1242.*

Museo de Cera, housed at the **Centro Cultural Metropolitano**, Espejo 1147 y García Moreno, depicts the execution of the revolutionaries of 1809 in the original cell. Well worth a visit, but is not for the claustrophobic. Other temporary exhibits in the same building. ■ *Tue-Fri 0800-1700, Sat 0900-1600, free, T295 0272.*

Museo de Artesanía has a good collection of Indian costume and crafts, helpful guides and a shop. ■ *Mon-Fri 0800-1600, 12 de Octubre 1738 y Madrid.*

Cima de la Libertad, museum at the site of the 1822 Battle of Pichincha, splendid view. ■ *0900-1200, 1500-1800, US$1.25. Take a taxi there as the suburbs are dangerous, or the trolley to El Recreo and a taxi from there.*

Vivarium Fundación Herpetológica Gustavo Orces, Reina Victoria y Sta María, impressive number of South American and other snakes, reptiles and amphibians. ■ *Mon-Sat, 0915-1245, 1430-1745, Sun 1100-1745, US$1, T223 0988.*

Ecuador

Museo Histórico Casa de Sucre, the beautiful house of Sucre on the corner of Venezuela y Sucre. ■ *Mon-Fri 0830-1600, Sat-Sun 1000-1600,US$1, T295 2860*.

Museo Guayasamín at Bosmediano 543, Bellavista, northeast of La Mariscal. As well as the eponymous artist's works there is a precolumbian and colonial collection,highly recommended. Works of art may be purchased and also modern jewellery, ask to see the whole collection as only a small portion is displayed in the shop. ■ *Mon-Fri 0900-1330 and 1500-1830, Sat 0900-1230, US$2, T244 6455*.

Excursions

Mitad del Mundo and Environs

23 km N of Quito

This Equatorial Line Monument is near **San Antonio de Pichincha** (C *Hostería Alemana*, 8 blocks south of monument, T239 4243, very good restaurant, highly recommended; **D** *Sol y Luna*, 2 blocks from monument, T239 4979, terrace with nice views; **E** *Residencial Mitad del Mundo*, in the village, simple.)

The location of the equatorial line here was determined by Charles-Marie de la Condamine and his French expedition in 1736, and agrees to within 150 m with modern GPS measurements. The monument forms the focal point of a park and leisure area built as a typical colonial town, with restaurants, gift shops, Post Office with philatelic sales, tourist office (0900-1600), and has a very interesting ethnographic museum inside. ■ *Mon-Fri, 0900-1800, Sat-Sun, 0900-1900, very crowded on Sun, but with a lively atmosphere (music, dance, restaurants). Admission to the monument and the museum US$3*. The museum is run by the *Banco Central*; a lift takes you to the top, then you walk down with the museum laid out all around with different Indian cultures every few steps. There is a Planetarium with hourly 30-minute shows and an attractive and interesting model of old Quito, about 10 m square, with artificial day and night, which took seven years to build. ■ *US$1*. **Museo Intiñan**, 200 m north of the monument, shows the exact location of the equator, water spinning in different directions, eggs balancing on nails and more, eclectic and very interesting. ■ *US$2, T239 5122*. Two minutes' walk before the Monument is the restaurant *Equinoccio*, about US$10 a meal, live music, open from 1200 daily, T239 4091. Available at the restaurant or at stalls outside are 'certificates' recording your visit to the Equator (free if you have a meal). Shows only take place when there are sufficient customers.

Transport A paved road runs from Quito to the Monument, which you can reach by a 'Mitad del Mundo' bus (US$0.50, 1 per hr) from Av América or the Parque Hermano Miguel (see Old City map), bus fills instantly; beware of pickpockets on the bus. Buses back to the city take a different route, so ask where to get off. An excursion to Mitad del Mundo by taxi with 1 hr wait is about US$25 per taxi.

Pululahua A few kilometres beyond the Monument, off the paved road to Calacalí, is the Pululahua crater which can be seen from a lookout on the rim. It is a geobotanical reserve, entry US$5. Try to go in the morning, there is often cloud later. Trucks will take you from the Mitad del Mundo bus stop, round trip US$5. *Calimatours*, Manzana de los Correos, Oficina 11, Mitad del Mundo, T239 4796, organizes tours to all the sites in the vicinity, US$8 per person, recommended. Restaurant *El Crater*, at the rim of the crater along a parallel access road has fantastic views, open only on weekends. Horse riding: *The Green Horse Ranch*, Astrid Muller, T252 3856, www.horseranch.de 1-10 day rides, excellent horses, US$100 pp for two-day trip, all inclusive. Recommended.

Transport Continue on the road past the Monument towards Calacalí. After a 4.7-km, 1-hr walk, the road bears left and begins to climb steeply. The paved road to the right leads to the lookout and a view of the farms on the crater floor. Buses to Calacalí (infrequent) will drop you at the fork, from where it is a 30-min walk to the rim. Plenty of traffic at weekends for hitching a lift. There is a rough track down from the rim to the crater. To get to the park and experience the rich vegetation and warm micro-climate inside, continuing past the village in the crater, turn left and follow an unimproved road up to the rim and back to the main road, a 15-20 km round trip.

Ecuador

Also in the vicinity of the Monument, 3 km from San Antonio beyond the Solar Museum, are the Inca ruins of Rumicucho. Restoration is poor, but the location is magnificent (entry US$2). Start early if you want to visit all these in one day.

A day-trip is to **Sangolquí**, about 20 minutes from Quito by bus. There is a busy Sunday market (and a lesser one on Thursday), mainly food, few tourists. **AL** *La Carriona*, Km 2½ via Sangolquí-Amaguaña, T233 1974, F233 2005, www.altesa.net Colonial country house, includes breakfast, pool, spa, horses, restaurant, lovely. **AL** *Hostería Sommergarten*, Urb Santa Rosa, Sangolquí, T233 2761, F233 0315, www.ecuador-sommerfern.com Bungalow resort, including breakfast, lots of activities available, sauna, pool.

On the opposite side of Quito, to the northwest, a worthwhile excursion can be made to **C** *Hostería San Jorge*, Km 4 Vía Antigua Cotocollao – Nono, T249 4002, www.hostsanjorge.com.ec Restaurant, pool and much else, on a traditional farm in the Bosque Protector Pichincha, quiet, peaceful, horse riding, birdwatching, sauna. Recommended.

Essentials

La Mariscal district, where most hotels are located, is not safe, especially at night. Anywhere in Quito, always take a taxi to the door of your hotel after dark. Those travelling by car may have difficulty parking in the centre of Quito and are therefore advised to choose the less central hotels.

In the New City Luxury international hotels in out **LL-L** range include: *Dan Carleton*, *Hilton*, *Holiday Inn Crown Plaza*, *Marriott*, *Radisson Royal*, *Sheraton*, and *Swissôtel*.

L *Mansión del Angel*, Wilson E5-29 y JL Mera, T255 7721, F223 7819. Includes breakfast, refurbished old building, very elegant, lovely atmosphere. **L-AL** *Alameda Real*, Roca 653 y Amazonas, T256 2345, apartec@uio.satnet.net Good breakfast buffet, restaurant, internet, can be booked through *KLM* airline, 24-hr cafeteria. **AL** *Río Amazonas*, Cordero 1342 y Amazonas, T255 6667, www.hotelrioamazonas.com Buffet breakfast, restaurant, internet, pleasant, safe, all facilities, discount for Handbook readers. **AL** *Sebastián*, Almagro N24-416 y Cordero, T222 2400, hotelsebastian@hotelsebastian.com Restaurant, internet, comfortable, safe, garage, very good. **AL-A** *Hotel Quito*, González Suárez N27-142 y 12 de Octubre, T254 4600, www.orotels.com Includes buffet breakfast, good restaurant, pool open to non-residents, internet, on a hillside above the new city, good views. **AL-A** *Sierra Madre*, Veintimilla 464 y Luis Tamayo, T250 5687, F250 5715, www.hotelsierramadre.com Restaurant, fully renovated old style villa, comfortable, sun roof.

A *Café Cultura*, Robles E6-62 y Reina Victoria, T250 4078, F224 271, www.cafecultura.com Restaurant, beautiful rooms, garden, luggage store, shop with local crafts and foods. **A** *Hostal de la Rábida*, La Rábida 227 y Santa María, T222 2169, larabida@uio.satnet.net Good

Ecuador

restaurant, Italian run, bright, comfortable. Highly recommended. **A** *La Pradera*, San Salvador 222 y Pasaje Martín Carrión, T222 6833, hpradera@uio.satnet.net Includes breakfast, restaurant, comfortable, quiet, residential area. **A** *Sol de Quito*, Alemania N30-170 y Vancouver, T254 1773. Includes breakfast, restaurant, helpful. Recommended. **A** *Villantigua*, Jorge Washington E9-48 y Tamayo, T252 8564, alariv@uio.satnet.net Furnished with antiques, suites with fireplace more expensive, quiet, multilingual staff.

B *Casa Sol*, Calama 127 y 6 de Diciembre, T223 0798, info@lacasasol.com Includes breakfast, small with courtyard, 24-hr cafeteria, very helpful, English and French spoken. Highly recommended. **B** *Chalet Suisse*, Reina Victoria N24-191 y Calama, T256 2700, F256 3966. Includes breakfast, excellent restaurant, convenient location, rooms to street noisy. **B** *La Cartuja*, Plaza 170 y Washington, T252 3662, F252 3577. Includes breakfast, restaurant, beautifully decorated, spacious comfortable rooms, safety deposit boxes, garden, very helpful and hospitable. Highly recommended. **B** *Plaza Internacional*, Plaza 150 y 18 de Septiembre, T/F250 5075, hplaza@uio.satnet.net Includes breakfast, restaurant, comfortable, multilingual staff, very helpful, good location.

C *Casa Helbling*, Veintimilla 531 y 6 de Diciembre, T222 6013, casahelbling@accessinter.net Cooking facilities, luggage store, helpful, German spoken, family atmosphere, good information, tours arranged. **C** *Hothello*, Amazonas N20-20 y 18 de Septiembre, T/F256 5835, www.cometoecuador.com Includes breakfast, restaurant, modern, heating, safety deposit, cafe with a variety of dishes, multilingual staff. **C** *Palm Garten*, 9 de Octubre 923 y Cordero, T252 3960, F256 8944. Includes breakfast, restaurant, beautiful house, luggage store. **C** *Posada del Maple*, Rodríguez E8-49 y Almagro, T254 4507, www.posadadelmaple.com Includes full breakfast, restaurant, laundry and cooking facilities, cheaper with shared bath or in dorm, warm atmosphere, free tea and coffee. **C** *Rincón Escandinavo*, Leonidas Plaza N24-306 y Baquerizo Moreno, T/F254 0794, www.escandinavohotel.com Restaurant, small, modern, well-furnished, convenient location, English spoken.

Ecuador

D *El Cafecito*, Luis Cordero 1124 y Reina Victoria, T223 4862. Cheaper in dorm, Canadian-owned, relaxed atmosphere, superb food in café including vegetarian, good information. **D** *El Centro del Mundo*, Lizardo García 569 y Reina Victoria, T222 9050. Includes breakfast, restaurant with good home-cooked food, cooking facilities, cheaper in dorm, safe, modern, bar, language school, very popular with young travellers, good meeting place. **D** *El Ciprés*, Lérida 381 y Pontevedra (La Floresta neighbourhood), T254 9558, F254 9558, elcipres@hotmail.com Includes breakfast, cheaper in dorm with shared bath, cooking facilities, parking, transport to airport/terminal if staying 3 days, very helpful. **D** *El Taxo*, Foch 909 y Cordero, T222 5593, fzalamea@yahoo.com Constant hot water, internet, cooking facilities, hostel-type, large family house, helpful, open fire, good meeting place. **D** *La Casa de Guápulo*, C Leonidas Plaza (Guápulo), T/F222 0473, F222 0473. Includes breakfast, restaurant, parking, bar, peaceful area, multilingual staff, free transfer to airport. **D** *La Casona de Mario*, Andalucía 213 y F Galicia, T/F223 0129, lacasona@punto.net.ec Kitchen and storage facilities, near Universidad Católica, sitting room, big garden, book exchange. **D** *Nassau*, J Pinto E4-340 y Amazonas, T290 6645. Hot water, English spoken, very helpful, safe, no meals but restaurant downstairs. **D** *Nuestra Casa*, Bartolomé de las Casas 435 y Versalles, T222 5470, mlo@uio.satnet.net Cooking facilities, converted family house, dinner available, camping in garden. Highly recommended. **D** *Queen's Hostal*, Reina Victoria 836 y Wilson, T255 1844, F240 6690. Cooking facilities, good, safety deposit, fireplace. **D** *Tierra Alta*, Wilson E7-79 y D de Almagro, T223 5993. Cooking facilities, parking, secure, helpful. **D-E** *Gan Eden*, Pinto 163 y 6 de Diciembre, T222 3480. Restaurant serves cheap breakfast and good Israeli food, cheaper without bath, cooking facilities, double rooms or dorm, very helpful Israeli owner, luggage store.

El Ejido north to Colón

Ecuador

0 metres 50
0 yards 50

E *Basc*, Lizardo García 537 y Reina Victoria, T250 3456, hostalbask@latinmail.com Cooking facilities, free coffee, cafeteria, nice atmosphere. **E** *Casa Paxee*, Romualdo Navarro 326 y La Gasca, T250 0441. Price includes fruit for breakfast, cooking facilities, 3 rooms only, discounts for longer stays. **E** *El Kapulí*, Robles 625 y Amazonas, T/F222 1872, sunlight87@hotmail.com 2 larger rooms with several beds and shared bath, luggage store, English spoken, very helpful. **E** *Hostal del Hoja*, Gerónimo Leyton N23-89 y Av La Gasca, T256 0832, delhoja@mixmail.com Cooking facilities, small, very helpful. **E** *La Casa de Eliza*, Isabel La Católica 1559, T222 6602, manteca@uio.satnet.net Kitchen and laundry facilities, shared rooms, safety deposit, very popular and homely, no smoking. **E** *Los Chasquis*, 12 de Octubre 338 y Tarqui, T252 6388. Hot water, breakfast US$1, laundry facilities, spacious, helpful fammily. **E** *Nueve de Octubre*, 9 de Octubre N24-171 y Colón, T255 2424. Parking, very comfortable, secure, night watchman. **E** *Rincón de Castilla*, Versalles 1127 y Carrión, T222 4312, F254 8097. Restaurant, cooking facilities, parking, safe, luggage stored, owner speaks German, French and English, also travel agency and Spanish classes.

Youth hostel *Hostelling International*, Pinto 325 y Reina Victoria, T543995, hostellingquito@hotmail.com Modern hostel with capacity for 75. **D** in private double room with bath. **E-F** pp in dormitory with lockers. Discounts for IYHF members and ISIC holders, restaurant, laundry sevice, coin operated washing machines, hot water, TV on request, safe deposit, luggage store, fax service, closed circuit TV security system.

In between the new and old cities D *L'Auberge Inn*, Av Colombia 1138 y Yaguachi, T255 2912, www.ioda.net/auberge-inn Restaurant, cheaper without bath, parking, duvets on beds, fax service, garden, lovely terrace and communal area, helpful, good atmosphere. **E** *Kinara*, Bogotá 534 y Av América, T/F222 8524, kinara@andinanet.net Including American breakfast, cooking facilities, safe deposit boxes, library, English/French spoken, free tea and coffee, spotless. Highly recommended. **E** *Margarita 1*, Elizalde 410 y Colombia (near Los Ríos), T295 2599. Cooking facilities, parking, helpful, baggage stored. Recommended. **E** *Margarita 2*, Los Ríos 1995 y Espinoza, T295 0441. Parking, good beds, sheets changed daily, great value. Highly recommended. **E** *Marsella*, Los Ríos 2035 y Espinoza, T251 5884. Cheaper without bath, parking, good rooftop terrace with views over Parque La Alameda, top floor rooms best but noisy, luggage stored, not a safe area, often full by 1700, safe deposit, notice board, good value, guard. **E** *San Blas*, Pasaje España E1-38 entre Caldas y Fermín Cevallos, T228 1434. Kitchen and laundry facilities, plaza San Blas, terrace, great value. Recommended.

In the Old City D *La Posada Colonial*, Paredes 188 y Rocafuerte, T228 2859. Cheaper without bath, parking, beautiful old building. Recommended. **D** *Plaza del Teatro*, Guayaquil 1373 y Esmeraldas, T295 9462. Restaurant, parking, carpeted rooms, stylish, good service. Recommended. **D** *Real Audiencia*, Bolívar Oe3-18 y Guayaquil at Plaza de Santo Domingo Trole stop, T295 0590, F258 0213. Includes breakfast, restaurant/bar on top floor, spacious, well furnished rooms, baggage stored, safety deposit box, great views. Highly recommended. **D** *Sucre*, Bolívar 615 and Cuenca, T295 4025. Restaurant, plaza San Francisco, a bit noisy, has terrace with great views over the old city, not for the hygienically minded but very cheap. **D** *Viena Internacional*, Flores 600 y Chile, T295 9611, F295 4633. English spoken, good value, phone, good meals, secure. **E** *Flores*, Flores 355 y Sucre, T228 0435. Ask for a room on the 1st floor, safe, convenient for bus station. **F** *Catedral Internacional*, Mejía 638 y Cuenca, T295 5438. Hot water, good rooms. **F** *Montúfar*, Sucre 160 y Montúfar, T228 4644. Private bath, hot water, safe, good value.

Near Terminal Terrestre D *Cumandá*, Morales 449 y Av.Maldonado, T295 6984, www.hotel-cumanda.com Restaurant, comfortable, garage, excellent service, safe, noisy from proximity to bus station but quieter at the back. Recommended. **E** *Grand Hotel*, Rocafuerte 1001 y Pontón, T295 9411. Good breakfast in cafeteria (0700-1200), cheaper without bath, cooking facilities, some rooms dingy but others OK. Safety deposit, luggage storage, friendly and helpful. Recommended.

Apartments AL *Apart-Hotel Antinea*, Rodríguez 175 y Diego de Almagro, T250 6839, hotelant@accessinter.net.ec Suites and apartments, from US$1,077 per month, lovely rooms. **B** *Apart-Hotel Amaranta*, Leonidas Plaza 194 y Washington, T256 0585, amaranta@impsat.net.ec Comfortable, well-equipped suites, from US$915 a month, good restaurant. **C** *Apartamentos Modernos*, Amazonas N31-75 y Mariana de Jesús, T/F223 3766, modernos@uio.satnet.net From US$450 per month, good location near La Carolina park and Mall El Jardín, English spoken, spotlessly clean.

Dining in Quito is excellent, varied, and increasingly cosmopolitan. Many restaurants throughout the city close on Sun and, in the Old City, most close early evening. In more expensive restaurants 22% tax and service is added to the bill. The following list is by type and all are in the **New City** unless otherwise stated. In all cases, assume good food, service and value. All have been recommended.

Eating
There are few restaurants in the Old City

Ecuadorean *Mama Clorinda*, Reina Victoria y Calama. Large portions, moderately priced, very good. *La Querencia*, Eloy Alfaro 2530 y Catalina Aldaz. Good views and atmosphere. *Rincón La Ronda*, Belo Horizonte 406 y Almagro. Nice atmosphere, huge Sun buffet, expensive.

    French and Swiss *Rincón de Francia*, Roca 779 y 9 de Octubre. Excellent but very expensive, reservation essential, slow service. *Amadeus Restaurant and Pub*, Coruña 1398 y Orellana, T223 0831. Very good cuisine and concerts, usually at 2300 on Fri. *Rincón de Borgoña*, Eloy Alfaro 2407. Excellent. *Chantilly*, Roca 736 y Amazonas and Whimper 394. Also bakery. *Chalet Suisse*, Reina Victoria N24-191 y Calama. Steaks and some Swiss dishes, good service, mid-range prices. *Grain de Café*, Baquedano 332 y Reina Victoria. Excellent meals desserts and coffee, vegetarian dishes, book exchange, films in English, informative owner, good meeting place. *Raclette*, Eloy Alfaro 1348 y Andrade Marín, T223 7753. Swiss specialties including raclette, fondue, some international dishes, Alpine decor, expensive.

    General *Terraza del Tártaro*, Veintimilla 1106 y Amazonas (no sign). Top floor, steaks, pleasant atmosphere. *Super Papa*, JL Mera 761 y Baquedano. Stuffed baked potatoes, some vegetarian, sandwiches and salads, cakes, takeaway service, great breakfasts, open daily, 0730-2100. *Café Tropicana*, Whimper 330 y Coruña. First class. *Sutra*, Calama 380. Good food, reasonable prices, popular meeting place, internet access. *Crêpes & Waffles*, La Rábida 461 y Orellana. Succulent savoury crêpes and salads and delicious desserts, mid-range prices. *Mango Tree Café*, Foch 721 y Amazonas. Eclectic menu, nice décor, closed Sun.

    German *Hansa Krug*, Francisco Salazar e Isabel la Católica.

    Indian *Chandani Tandoori*, JL Mera y Cordero. Simple little place, with good authentic cuisine, cheap prices. Recommended.

    International Very good Sunday buffets at *Hotel Hilton Colón* and *Swissôtel*. *La Viña*, Isabel la Católica y Cordero. Extensive and unusual menu, beautifully presented and excellent food, expensive. *Escondida*, General Roca N33-29 y José Bosmediano. Seafood, salads, pastas, tapas, expensive, closed Mon. *Cocina de Kristy*, Whymper y Orellana. Upmarket, great view from the terrace and equally great food. *El Arabe*, Reina Victoria y Carrión. Good Arabic food. *Ha Mizlala*, Reina Victoria y Pinto. Good Israeli and Middle Eastern food.

Ecuador

TGI Friday, Quicentro Shopping (Naciones Unidas y Shyris). US franchise, lively. *Zócalo*, J L Mera y Calama. Good choice on menu, live music Fri, young crowd.

Italian *La Scala*, Salazar y 12 de Octubre. Good atmosphere, expensive. *La Trattoria de Renato*, San Javier y Orellana. Nice atmosphere, expensive. *Il Grillo*, Baquerizo Moreno 533 y Almagro. Closed Mon, upmarket, great pizzas. *Il Risotto*, Pinto 209 y Diego de Almagro, T222 0400. Very popular, very good, expensive, closed Mon. *Siboney*, Atahualpa y 10 de Agosto. Homemade pasta, great huge pizzas, cheap. *La Briciola*, Toledo 1255 y Cordero, T254 7138. Extensive menu, excellent food, homely atmosphere, expensive, closed Sun. *Pavarotti*, Av 12 de Octubre 1955 y Cordero, T256 6668. Creative cuisine, good service.

Latin American and US *Adam's Rib*, Calama y Reina Victoria. For steak and pecan pie, not cheap. *La Guarida del Coyote*, Eloy Alfaro E25-94 y Portugal. Excellent Mexican food, live music. *Red Hot Chili Peppers*, Foch y J L Mera. Very good, especially the fajitas. *Churrascaría Tropeiro*, Veintimilla 564 y 6 de Diciembre. Brazilian-style, salad bar and grill. *Tex Mex*, Reina Victoria 847 y Wilson. The Tex Mex Mixta especially recommended, lively, open daily. *Los Troncos*, Los Shyris 1280 y Portugal. Argentine, excellent, expensive. *La Bodeguita de Cuba*, Reina Victoria y Pinta. Good food and music, reasonably priced. *TheMagic Bean*, Foch 681 y JL Mera. Excellent atmosphere, specializes in coffees and natural foods, mid-range prices. *The Magic Wrap*, Foch 476 y Diego de Almagro. With garden grill, food 'wraps' with a choice of fillings, pool, airhockey and other games at Cascada Mágica next door, great place.

Oriental *Casa de Asia*, Eloy Alfaro 3027 y G Alemán. Excellent Korean and Japanese. *Happy Panda*, Cordero 341 e Isabel la Católica. Excellent, mid-range prices. *Chifa China*, Carrión y Versalles. Authentic, mid-range prices.*Hong Kong*, Wilson 246 y Tamayo. Good. *Hong Tai*, La Niña 234 y Yanez Pinzón. Reasonable prices. Thai restaurants: *Thai-an*, Eloy Alfaro N34-230 y Portugal. Nice ambience, expensive. *Siam*, Calama y JL Mera. Mid-range prices, popular.

Pizza *Che Farina Pizzería*, Carrión, entre JL Mera y Amazonas also Naciones Unidas y Amazonas (open 24 hours), T244 4400. Fast service, popular, expensive, open Sun. *Pizza Le Arcate*, Baquedano 358 y JL Mera, T223 7659. Italian run, not the cheapest but worth it, home delivery, closed Mon. *El Hornero*, Veintimilla y Amazonas, T254 2518, and González Suárez. Good pizzas, try one with *choclo* (fresh corn).

Be selective when choosing a seafood restaurant, some visitors have become ill eating in less hygenic establishments

Seafood *Avalón*, Av Orellana 155 y 12 de Octubre. Excellent food, upmarket, very expensive. *Mare Nostrum*, Foch 172 y Tamayo, T254 4200. Very good, expensive, closed Sun evening. *Puerto Camarón*, Av 6 de Diciembre y Granaderos, Centro Comercial Olímpico. Varied menu, mid-range prices. *El Cebiche*, JL Mera 1232 y Calama, and Amazonas 2428 y Moreno Bellido. Delicious, "best *ceviche* in town". *Cevichería Galápagos*, Reina Victoria y García. US$2.50 for excellent *ceviche*, lunchtimes only. *Las Palmeras*, Japón y Naciones Unidas, opposite Parque la Carolina. Very good *comida Esmeraldeña*, try their *viche*, outdoor tables, good value, mid-range prices, open lunch only. *Ceviches y Banderas*, Av 12 de Octubre 1533 y Foch. Reasonably priced. *Ceviches de la Rumiñahui*, 7 branches: Real Audiencia entre Av del Maestro y Tufiño (the original branch and less clean), Quicentro Shopping Centre, Naciones Unidas y Shyris (a bit more expensive than the others): all are popular for *ceviche* and other seafood.

Spanish *La Paella Valenciana*, República y Almagro. Huge portions, superb fish and paella, expensive.

Steak *La Casa de mi Abuela*, JL Mera 1649 y la Niña. Steak and other dishes, mid-range prices. *Columbia*, Colón 1262 y Amazonas. Popular, open Sun. *Shorton Grill*, Calama 216 y Almagro. Mid-range prices.

Vegetarian *Windmill*, Versalles y Colón 2245.Reasonable. *Maranatha*, Riofrío y Larrea. Lunch Mon-Fri, vegan, clean and cheap. *El Maple*, Calama y JL Mera. Closed Sun for dinner, good selection, highly recommended, good natural yoghurt at the shop next door. *Le Champignon*, Robles 543 y JL Mera. Nice atmosphere, moderate prices. *Manantial*, 9 de Octubre 591 y Carrión and Luis Cordero 1838 y 9 de Octubre. Good, cheap set lunch. *Viejo Arribal*, JL Mera y Foch. Good, varied menu.

In the Old City *El Criollo*, Flores 731 y Olmedo. Ecuadorean food, cheap, tasty, chicken specialities, good coffee. *La Cueva del Oso*, in court of Edificio Pérez Pallares, Chile 1046 y Venezuela, across from the Plaza de la Independencia, T258 6823. Art deco interior, expensive, great atmosphere. *Las Cuevas de Luis Candela*, Benalcázar 713 y Chile. Spanish and Ecuadorean dishes, expensive, closed Sun. *Viena*, Chile y Flores. For breakfasts. *Santo Domingo*, Rocafuerte 13-47. Generous portions, cheap. *Tianguez*, Plaza de San Francisco. Ecuadorean food, cafeteria, crafts. *Girasol*, Oriente 581 y Vargas. Vegetarian, cheap, closes at 1700.

Cafés/Pastry Shops/Bakeries *Café Cultura*, Robles 513 y Reina Victoria, at the hotel. Relaxed atmosphere, tasteful décor, expensive but excellent cakes, homemade bread, good service, open daily 0800-1130 and 1500-1700. *La Cosecha*, main bakery on Los Shyris y El Comercio, several other outlets. For bread, doughnuts, oatmeal cookies, try their garlic bread. *Cyrano*, Portugal y Los Shyris. Excellent pumpernikel and whole wheat breads, outstanding pastries, French owner also runs excellent ice cream shop, *Corfú* next door. *Bangalô*, Foch y Almagro. Excellent cakes, quiches, coffees, Mon-Sat, open at lunchtime and 1600-2000, great atmosphere, good jazz at weekends. *Books & Coffee*, JL Mera 12-27 y Calama. Capuccino, espresso, sandwiches, English and German newspapers. *Café Galletti*, Amazonas 1494 y Santa María. Excellent coffee.*San Fernando*, Asunción 136. Excellent. *Delicatessen El Español* next to Libri Mundi, JL Mera y Wilson. Sandwiches, sausages, salmon, cheese, etc. **In the Old City**: *Cafetería Imperio*, Pasaje Amador B-9. Very good coffee and snacks, reasonable prices. *Café Modelo*, Sucre y García Moreno. Cheap breakfast. *Café Royal*, Portoviejo 161. Very good breakfasts, seriously cheap. *Café Condal*, Sucre 350 y García Moreno. Capuccino, snacks, also internet. *Jugos Naturales*, Oriente 449 y Guayaquil. Safe juices and extracts.

In the New City *El Pub*, San Ignacio y González Suárez. English menu, including fish and chips. *Reina Victoria Pub* , Reina Victoria 530 y Roca. Open Mon-Sat from 1700, darts, relaxed atmosphere, English beer, happy hour 1700-1800, moderately priced bar meals, both places are meeting points for British and US expats. *Bierkeller*, Muros y González Suárez. Steaks, German sausages and *parrilladas*, good salads, imported German beer, pool and darts, good atmosphere, live music on Fri. Variable schedule, T223 2435 for reservations, Austrian owner, *Taberna Austriaca* bar upstairs. *Ghoz Bar*, La Niña 425 y Reina Victoria. Swiss owned, excellent Swiss food, pool, darts, videos, games, music, German book exchange. *La Estación*, Lizardo García y JL Mera. Swiss-owned, pool and billiards, live music on Sat (US$4 cover charge), popular with locals and tourists alike. *Varadero*, Reina Victoria 1721 y La Pinta. Bar-restaurant, live Cuban music most nights, meals and snacks (US$7-9), good cocktails for around US$3, older crowd and couples. *Papillon and Tijuana Bar*, Santa María y Reina Victoria. Open every day, very popular for 'casual assignments', selective admission policy, passport needed at door. *Arribar*, JL Mera 1238 y Lizardo García. Pool table, good local beers, rap and other music, happy hour 1600-1800, Swiss-owned, more gringos than locals, fairly rough. *Alkerke*, Baquedano 340. Good bar-café, open Mon-Fri 1230-1600, Thu-Sat 1900-0200. *La Boca del Lobo*, Calama 284 y Reina Victoria. Café-bar, snacks, nice atmosphere, popular with locals and visitors, open Mon-Sat 1700-0100. *Kizomba*, Almagro y L García. Recommended for atmosphere and creative drinks, good Brazilian music. *Matices Piano Bar*, Av Isabel La Católica y Cordero. Excellent food, live piano music, owner is a well known local pianist and composer, Dr Nelson Maldonado, open 1630-0200. *No Bar*, Calama y JL Mera. Good mix of latin and rock always packed on weekends, entry US$4 on weekends.

Bars

Cinema Section C or D of *El Comercio* lists films every day. First run films at: *Multicines*, CCI, Amazonas y Naciones Unidas, US$3.60; *Multicines*, El Recreo, El Recreo 'Trole' stop in the south of the city, convenient if staying in the Old City, US$2.90; *Cinemark 7*, multiplex at Plaza de las Américas, Av América y República, www.cinemark.com.ec, US$3.70; *Universitario*, Av América y Pérez Guerrero, Plaza Indoamérica, Universidad Central; US$2. *24 de Mayo*, Granaderos y 6 de Diciembre, US$2. Discounts before 1800 and on Wed.Casa de la Cultura, Patria y 6 de Diciembre, T290 2270, often has documentaries, film festivals, and shows foreign films.

Entertainment

Dance Schools *Son Latino*, Reina Victoria 1225 y García, T223 4340, specializes in several varieties of salsa, 10 hour programmes US$40. *Ritmo Tropical*, 10 de Agosto 1792 y San Gregorio, Edif Santa Rosa, oficina 108, T222 7051, salsa, merengue, cumbia, vallenato and

One-to-one or group lessons offered for US$5-6 per hr

Ecuador

folkloric dance. *Tropical Dancing School*, Foch E4-256 y Amazonas, T222-4713, salsa, merengue, cumbia.

Music Local folk music is popular in *peñas*. Places including *Dayumac*, JL Mera y Carrión, a meeting place for local musicians, dark, bohemian, Fri-Sat 2100-0200. *Cuerdas Andinas Disco Bar*, Carrión y JL Mera, entrance only for couples. *Ñucanchi*, Av Universitaria 496 y Armero, Thu-Sat 2230-0300. Most places do not come alive until 2230. *Orquesta Sinfónica Nacional*, weekly concerts on Fri. Since the *Teatro Sucre* is being restored (see below), concerts are held at *Teatro Politécnico*, Queseras del Medio, opposite Coliseo Rumiñahui, or in one of the colonial churches. Call for information, T256 5733, US$1.50. Concerts on Tue evenings, 3 times per month, Oct-Dec and Feb-Aug, at the *Auditorio de las Cámaras* (Chamber of Commerce), Amazonas y República, T226 0265/6 ext 231. Popular concerts at the *Plaza de Toros*, Amazonas y Juan de Azcaray, in the north, or *Coliseo Rumiñahui*, Toledo y Queseras del Medio, La Floresta, tickets are sold in advance and go fast for the better known groups.

Regardless of the opening hours shown, a 2002 municipal ordinance required all establishments to close by 0100

Nightclubs *Cerebro*, 6 de Diciembre y Los Shyris, Sector El Inca. Large, with contests, and occasional well known artists perform. *La Hacienda*, Camino de Orellana near *Hotel Quito*. Varied music, young crowd, beautiful views down to Guápulo, open 2200-0200 *Macks*, Maldonado y Pujilí, in the south near El Recreo 'Trole' stop. Fine mix of music and people, huge, 5 dance halls, open Wed-Sat 2000-0200. *Mayo 68*, Lizardo García 662 y JL Mera. Salsoteca, small, an absolute must for all you authentic *salseros*. Highly recommended. *Cool-Antro*, Ponce Carrasco 282 y Almagro, T239627. Open 2100-0100 *Seseribó*, Veintimilla y 12 de Octubre, T563598. Caribbean music and salsa, open Thu-Sun 2100-0200. Recommended. *Vauzá*, Tamayo y F Salazar. Varied music, large bar in the middle of the dance floor, mature crowd, open Wed-Sat 2200-0300.

Theatre *Teatro Sucre*, Plaza del Teatro, Manabí y Guayaquil, T228 1644, built in the 1880s, small and elegant (under renovation in 2002).*Teatro Bolívar*, Flores 421 y Junín, T258 2486, another classic theatre in the Old City. It was damaged by fire in 1999, but despite restoration work, there are still performances, proceeds used for renovations. *Teatro Aeropuerto*, Juan J Pazmiño y Av de la Prensa, T250 6651, ext 121, presents the Ecuadorean folk ballet 'Jacchigua', Wed and Fri 1930, US$12 entertaining, colourful and loud, reserve ahead. *Teatro Humanizarte*, Leonidas Plaza N24-226 y Baquerizo Moreno, presents the 'Ballet Andino', US$4 (US$3 students), also folk dancing, Wed 1930. *Agora*, open-air theatre of Casa de la Cultura, 12 de Octubre y Patria, stages many concerts. *Teatro Charles Chaplin*, Cordero 1200 y J L Mera, has live theatre at weekends, check the paper for events. *Centro Cultural Afro-Ecuatoriano* (CCA), Tamayo 985 y Lizardo García, T522318, sometimes has cultural events and published material, useful contact for those interested in the black community. There are always many cultural events in Quito, many free; see the listings in *El Comercio* and other papers for details, Aug is particularly busy.

Festivals New Year, *Años Viejos*: life-size puppets satirize politicians and others. At midnight on 31 Dec a will is read, the legacy of the outgoing year, and the puppets are burnt; good along Amazonas between Patria and Colón, very entertaining and good humoured. On New Year's day everything is shut.

The solemn **Good Friday** processions are most impressive. **24 May**: is *Independence*, commemorating the Battle of Pichincha in 1822 with early morning cannonfire and parades, everything closes. **Aug**: *Mes de las Artes*, organized by the municipality, cultural events, dance and music in different places throughout the city. Fancy-dress parades for *Hallowe'en*, celebrated **last Sat in Oct**, along Av Amazonas. The city's main festival, *Día de Quito*, celebrated throughout the **week ending 6 Dec**, commemorates the foundation of the city with elaborate parades, bullfights, performances and music in the streets, very lively. Hotels charge extra, everything except a few restaurants shuts on 6 Dec. Foremost among **Christmas** celebrations is the *Misa del Gallo*, midnight mass. Over Christmas, Quito is crowded, hotels are full and the streets are packed with vendors and shoppers.

The main shopping districts are along Avenida Amazonas in the north and C Guayaquil in the Old City. In the New City much of the shopping is done in shopping centres (malls), as posh and insipid as anywhere else (see list under Foodstuffs). For **maps** see Essentials, page 52.

Bookshops *Libri Mundi*, JL Mera N23-83 y Veintimilla, and at Quicentro Shopping. Excellent selection of Spanish, English, French, German, and some Italian books, sells the *Ecuador Handbook*, *South American Handbook* and *Central America and Mexico Handbook*, knowledgeable and helpful staff, notice-board of what's on in Quito, open Mon-Sat 0800-1800 (also Sun at Quicentro). Very highly recommended. *Imágenes*, 9 de Octubre y Roca. For books on Ecuador and art, postcards. *Mr Books*, El Jardín Mall, 3rd floor. Good stock, many in English including Footprint travel guides, open daily. Recommended. *Libro Express*, Amazonas 816 y Veintimilla, also at Quicentro Shopping and El Bosque. Has a good stock of maps, guides and international magazines. *Confederate Books*, Calama 410 y JL Mera. Open 1000-1900, excellent selection of second-hand books, including travel guides, mainly English but also German and French. *Ediciones Abya-Yala*, 12 de Octubre 14-30 y Wilson. Good for books about indigenous cultures and anthropology, also has excellent library and museum. Foreign newspapers are for sale at the news stands in luxury hotels and in some shops along Amazonas. *Lufthansa* will supply German newspapers if they have spare copies.

Camping *Los Alpes*, Reina Victoria N23-45. Local and imported equipment, also rentals. *Altamontaña*, Jorge Washington 425 y 6 de Diciembre. Imported climbing equipment for sale, rentals, good advice. *The Altar*, J L Mera 615 y Carrión. Imported and local gear for sale, good prices for rentals. *Antisana*, Centro Comercial El Bosque, ground floor. Sales only. *Aventura Sport*, Quicentro Shopping, top floor. Tents, good selection of glacier sun glasses, upmarket. *Camping Sports Cotopaxi*, Colón 942 y Reina Victoria. Sales only. *Equipos Cotopaxi*, 6 de Diciembre 927 y Patria. Ecuadorean and imported gear for sale, no rentals, lockable pack covers, made to measure. *The Explorer*, Pinto E6-32 y Reina Victoria. Sales and rentals, very helpful, will buy US or European equipment. *Tatoo*, Wilson y JL Mera. Quality backpacks and outdoor clothing. For hiking boots, *Calzado Beltrán*, Cuenca 562, and other shops on the same street. Camping gas is available many of the above shops, white gas (*combusitble para lámpara Coleman*) at times from *Kywi*, Centro Comercial Olímpico, 6 de Diciembre y Granaderos.

Film processing Many labs along Amazonas and in shopping centres for rapid film processing and printing; quality varies greatly. For professional work and slide processing, *Ron Jones*, Lizardo García E9-104 y Andrés Xaura, 1 block east of 6 de Diciembre, T250 7622 is recommended.

Foodstuffs *Supermaxi* well stocked supermarket and department store with a wide range of local and imported goods, at the Centro Comercial Iñaquito (Amazonas y Naciones Unidas), *Centro Comercial El Bosque* (Av Occidental), *Centro Comercial Plaza Aeropuerto* (Av de la Prensa y Homero Salas), *Multicentro* (6 de Diciembre y La Niña), and at *Mall El Jardín* (Amazonas y Mariana de Jesús); all open Mon-Sat 1000-2000, Sun 1000-1300 (some until 1800). *Mi Comisariato*, another well stocked supermarket and department store, at Quicentro Shopping (Naciones Unidas y Shyris) and García Moreno y Mejía in the Old City. *La Feria* supermarket, Bolívar 334, entre Venezuela y García Moreno sells good wines and spirits, and Swiss, German and Dutch cheeses. *Sangre de Drago*, the Indian cure all, is sold in markets and health food shops.

Handicrafts There are carved figures, plates and other items of local woods including balsa, silver of all types, textiles, buttons, toys and other things fashioned from tagua nuts, hand-painted tiles, hand-woven rugs and a variety of antiques dating back to colonial days. Panama hats are a good buy.

A wide selection can be found at the *Mercado Artesanal La Mariscal*, on Jorge Washington, between Reina Victoria and JL Mera. This interesting and worthwhile market, built by the municipality to house street vendors, is open daily 1000-1800. There is an exhibition and sale of paintings in *Parque El Ejido*, opposite *Hotel Hilton Colón*, on Sat and Sun mornings.

Shopping
Trading generally 0900-1900 on weekdays, Sat 0900-1300, some shops close at midday, shopping centres are open at weekends

Ecuador

Indian garments (for Indians rather than tourists) can be seen and bought on the north end of the Plaza de Santo Domingo and along the nearest stretch of C Flores.

Recommended shops with a wide selection are: *Folklore*, Colón E10-53 y Caamaño, the store of the late Olga Fisch. Attractive selection of handicrafts and rugs, expensive as designer has international reputation; also at *Hotel Hilton Colón* and *Swissôtel*. *Galería Latina*, JL Mera y Baquedano. South American crafts, fine selection beautifully displayed, visiting artists sometimes demonstrate their work. *Tianguez*, run by *Fundación Sinchi Sacha*, at Plaza San Francisco, Reina Victoria 1780 y La Niña and behind *Hotel Quito* on Rafael León Larrea. Cooperative selling ceramics and other crafts from the Oriente, good display. *Artesanías Cuencanas*, Roca 626 entre Amazonas y JL Mera. Knowledgeable, wide selection. *El Aborigen*, Washington 536 y JL Mera. *Ecuafolklore*, Robles 609 entre Amazonas y JL Mera (also stocks guide books). *Los Colores de la Tierra*, JL Mera 838 y Wilson. Hand-painted wood items and unique handicrafts. *Productos Andinos*, Urbina 111 y Cordero. Artisan's coop, good selection.

Hilana, 6 de Diciembre 1921 y Baquerizo Moreno. Beautiful unique 100% wool blankets in Ecuadorean motifs, excellent quality, purchase by metre possible, inexpensive. *Marcel Creations*, Roca 766, entre Amazonas y 9 de Octubre. Panama hats.

For **T-shirts**: *Coosas*, JL Mera 838 and Quicentro Shopping. The factory outlet for Peter Mussfeldt's attractive animal designs (bags, clothes etc). *The Ethnic Collection*, Amazonas 1029 y Pinto, ethnic@pi.pro.ec Wide variety, clothing, leather, bags, jewellery, etc, English spoken. *Nomada*, La Niña y Pinzón and factory outlet at Pinzón 199 y Colón. Excellent quality T-shirts. *Amor y Café*, Foch 721 y JL Mera. Quality ethnic clothing.

Jewellery *Alquimia*, Juan Rodríguez 139. High quality silversmith. Jewelry & Design, Mall El Jardín, local 166. *Edda*, Tamayo 1256 y Cordero. Custom-made jewellery. Recommended. *Argentum*, JL Mera 614 y Amazonas. Also sells crafts and antiques, excellent selection, reasonably priced *Jeritsa*, Veintimilla E4-162 y Amazonas. Good selection, prices and service.

Watch your belongings at all markets **Markets** Main produce markets, all accesible by Trole: *Mercado Central*, Av Pichincha y Olmedo, *Mercado Santa Clara*, Versalles y Ramírez Dávalos and *Mercado Iñaquito*, Iñaquito y Villalengua. *Mercado Ipiales*, on Chile from Imbabura uphill, *Mercado Plaza Arenas* on Vargas and along 24 de Mayo y Loja, and *La Marín* are where you are most likely to find your stolen camera for sale, also try *Grau* camera shop, Plaza Santo Domingo. Not surprisingly, these are unsafe parts of town.

Sport **Football** is played at Estadio Atahualpa, 6 de Diciembre y Naciones Unidas and at Estadio Casa Blanca, in Carcelén to the north. **Bungee jumping**: Bungee Zone, Reina Victoria 24-150 y Foch, T255 1950, US$55, by appointment. **Jogging**: the **Hash House Harriers** is a club for jogging, runners and walkers, enquire at *Reina Victoria Pub*, T222 9369. **Rugby**: is played at Colegio Militar on Sunday 1000, ask for details at *El Pub* (see Bars above).

If you need to contact ASEGUIM in an emergency, call Safari Tours or Compañía de Guías (see Tour operators) **Climbing and trekking**: Aseguim, the Mountain Guide Association, C Pinto, T223 4109, ecuguide@hoy.net Open Tue and Thu 1500-1800, provides courses for their members and checks standards and equipment. They will let you know if a guide is one of their members. *Aseguim* also organizes mountain rescues, but facilities are inadequate, it can take many hours to start a rescue and lack of equipment hinders success; rescue service is expensive. Climbs and trekking tours can be arranged in Quito and several other cities, the following Quito operators have been recommended (see Tour operators below for contact information): *Safari*, uses only *Aseguim* guides, maximum 2 climbers per guide, several languages spoken, very knowledgeable, well organized and planned, has own transport and equipment; also has a glacier school, 3 and 5-day courses with bilingual guides. *Surtrek*, *Aseguim* guides, 1 guide per 2 climbers, large and small groups, German and English spoken, arranges guided climbs of most major peaks, rents and sells equipment. *Campus Trekking*, chief guide Camilo Andrade, 8 languages spoken. *Compañia de Guías*, *Aseguim* guides, several languages spoken, expensive. *Sierra Nevada*, chief guide Freddy Ramírez (fluent English, French, German), mostly *Aseguim* guides, has own equipment for rent at good rates, professional, mostly large groups. *Pamir*, chief guide Hugo Torres, very experienced, speaks

English. *Vasco Tours*, Juan Medina chief guide, professional. Several camping stores (see Shopping above) also offer climbing and trekking trips and know about guides. Independent guides do not normally provide transport or full service, ie food, equipment, insurance and, without a permit from the *Ministerio de Ambiente*, they might be refused entry to national parks. The following are all reputable. **Aseguim**: *Cosme León*, T260 3140; *Oswaldo Freire*, T226 5597; *Benno Schlauri*, T234 0709; *Gabriel Llano*, T245 0628.

Climbing clubs: Local clubs welcome new members, but they do not provide free guiding service. It is not really worth joining if you are in Ecuador for only a few weeks. The following all have climbing clubs: *Colegio San Gabriel*, *Universidad Católica* and *Nuevos Horizontes* (Colón 2038 y 10 de Agosto, T255 2154).

Mountain biking: *Bicisport*, in Quicentro Shopping, top floor and 6 de Diciembre 6327 y Tomás de Berlanga, T246 0894. Recommended. *Biciteca y Renta Bike*, Av Brasil 1612 y Edmundo Carvajal, T/F224 1687, subida al Bosque. For sales, spares, repairs, tours, rentals and information, rents high quality bikes for US$20 per day. *Bike Tech*, Andagoya 498 y Ruiz de Castilla south of Mariana de Jesús. Owners Santiago and Regis have informal 'meets' every Sun, anyone is welcome, no charge, they ride 20 or more routes around Quito, they also have a good repair shop and cheap parts. *Biking Dutchman*, Foch 714 y JL Mera, T254 2806, T099730267(Mob), www.biking-dutchman.com One and several-day tours, great fun, good food, very well organized, English, German and Dutch spoken, pioneers in mountain biking in Ecuador. *Cycloips*, Av 6 de Diciembre N36-59 y Pasaje Rutquia, T243 5220, Cyclops@bikerider.com Very helpful. *Páramo Mountain Bike Shop*, 6 de Diciembre 3925 y Checoslovaquia, T225 5403. Stocks high quality bikes. See also *Safari*, Tour operators.

For information on cycling trips and other related activities see www.lineajoven.com

Paragliding: *Da Vinci*, Vasco de Contreras 1403 y Villalengua, T227 5900, T817580 (mob), castrodiego@hotmail.com Paragliding and hang gliding around Quito and at Crucita on the Pacific coast. *Escuela Pichincha de Vuelo Libre*, Carlos Endara Oe3-60 y Amazonas, T225 6592. Complete course US$400, good.

Swimming: there is a cold spring-water pool on Maldonado beyond the Ministry of Defence building (US$1), hot shower (US$1). A public-heated, chlorinated pool is in Miraflores, at the upper end of Av Universitaria, esq Nicaragua, 10-min walk from Amazonas, open Tue-Sun, 0900-1600, US$1.50. There is another public pool at Batán Alto, on Cochapata, near 6 de Diciembre and Gaspar de Villaroelvery good, US$3.

Take a swimming cap, towel and soap to be admitted at public pools

Whitewater rafting: *Ríos Ecuador*, T255 3727, Gynner Coronel, based in Tena, T06-887438, info@riosecuador.com (see Oriente section), or book through Quito agencies. Highly recommended, very experienced. *Yacu Amu*, Foch 746 y JL Mera, T290 4054, www.yacuamu.com Australian-owned (Steve Nomchong), very professional, rafting trips of 1-8 days, also kayak courses, good equipment. Highly recommended. *Eco-Adventour*, Calama 339 entre JL Mera y Reina Victoria, T252 0647, info@adventour.com *Alfredo Meneses* runs day trips on the Ríos Blanco and Toachi, affiliated with *Small World Adventures* in the USA. *Row Expediciones*, Robles 653 y Amazonas, p 3, T223 9224, row@uio.satnet.net Contact Juan Rodríguez for 1-day trips on the Río Blanco and Toachi, depending on the water levels, very professional operation; also connected to *ROW* (River Odysseys West) of the USA, offering 6-day professionally guided trips down the Río Upano in

Ecuador

the southern Oriente (T1-800-4516034, or PO Box 579, Coeur d'Alene, ID 83816). *Sierra Nevada* (see Tour operators below), excellent trips from 1 to 3 days, chief guide Edison Ramírez (fluent English/French) is certified by *French Association*. All these outfits charge US$50-70 per day.

Tour operators

Additional information about specialized operators for climbing and trekking, mountain biking and whitewater rafting is found under Sport. For Galápagos tour operators see page 1030

When booking tours, note that national park fees are rarely included

Amerindia, Montúfar E15-14 y La Cumbre, Bellavista, T227 0550, www.quasarnautica.com Land operators for *Quasar Naútica*, full range of tours. *Andes Adventures*, Baquedano E5-27 y JL Mera, T222 2651, www.ecoandestrav.com Climbing, trekking, rafting, jungle and tourist class Galápagos tours. *Andes Explorer*, Reina Victoria 927 e/Wilson y Pinto, T290 1493, T827460 (Mob), F290 1498, www.andes-explorer.com *Andisimo*, 9 de Octubre 479 y Roca, T250 8347, www.andisimo.com Custom-made tours, adventure sports, equipment sale and rental. *Angermeyer's Enchanted Expeditions*, Foch 726 y Amazonas, T256 9960, www.angermeyer.com Operate Galápagos cruises in various categories, jungle and trekking tours. *Campus Trekking*, T/F234 0601, campus@pi.pro.ec Camilo Andrade, multilingual, trekking and climbing. *Canodros*, Portugal 448 y Catalina Aldaz, T225 6759, www.canodros.com Run luxury Galápagos cruises and jungle tours in the Kapawi Ecological Reserve, also have an office in Guayaquil. *Coltur*, Páez 370 y Robles, T222 1000, www.iconsysweb.com/coltur/index.htm Tours to Galápagos, Amazon, also travel agency. *Compañía de Guías de Montaña*, Jorge Washington 425 y 6 de Dicembre, T255 6210, guiasmontania@accessinter.net Climbing trips. *Ecuadorian Alpine Institute*, Ramírez Dávalos 136 y Amazonas, of 102, T256 5465, F2568 949, www.volcanoclimbing.com Individual or group ascents, customized itineraries, multilingual guides. *Ecuadorian Tours*, Amazonas 329 y Washington, several other locations, T256 0488, F250 1067, www.ecuadoriantours.com (Also Amex representative). Airline tickets and tours (Poste Restante can be sent to PO Box 17-01-02605, Quito). *Elinatour*, Wilson 413 y 6 de Dicembre, T290 0350, elinasp@uio.satnet.net Sells jungle, Galápagos and other tours,helpful. Recommended. *Etnotur*, Luis Cordero 1313 y J L Mera, T223 0552, F250 2682, www.etnoturecuador.com Helpful, English and German spoken, operate Galápagos cruises with first class sailboats and a catamaran. *Explorandes*, Wilson 537 y Diego de Almagro, T255 6936, F2556 938, explouio@hoy.net Trekking, rafting, climbing, jungle tours. *Explorer Tours*, Reina Victoria 1235 y L García, T250 8871, F222 2531. Good value jungle tours, owns *Sacha Lodge* and *La Casa del Suizo* on the Río Napo.

Free Biker Tours, Guipuzcoa 339, La Floresta, T256 0469, or in Switzerland, Grenzweg 48, 3645 Gwatt, T033-365128. Run by Patrick Lombriser, Enduro-Motorcycles 600cc, good tours, spectacular. *Galasam*, Amazonas 1354 y Cordero, T250 7080/81, www.galasam.com Full range of day and multiday tours in highlands, jungle trips to their own lodge on the Río Aguarico, Galápagos trips, discounts to *South American Handbook* owners. *Green Planet*, JL Mera N23-48, T252 0570, greenpla@interactive.net.ec Ecologically sensitive jungle trips, lodge on Río Aguarico, good

food. Recommended. **Kempery Tours**, Pinto 539 y Amazonas, T222 6583, www.ecuadorexplorer.com/kempery/home German, English and Dutch spoken, all kinds of tours, including Galápagos and jungle, good value. **Klein Tours**, Eloy Alfaro N34-151 y Catalina Aldaz, T226 7000, www.kleintours.com Galápagos cruises and general travel agency. **La Moneda Tours**, Eloy Alfaro N33-256 y 6 de Diciembre, T226 1616, travel@lamoneda.com.ec Specializes in coastal and archaeological tours. **Metropolitan Touring**, República de El Salvador N36-84, also Amazonas 239 y 18 de Septiembre and several other locations, T298 8232, www.metropolitan-touring.com Galápagos tours, arranges climbing, trekking expeditions led by world-known climbers, as well as tours of Quito, Parque Nacional Machalilla, rail journeys, jungle camps. Generally recommended. **Napo Tour**, JL Mera 1312 y Cordero, T254 7283. Efficient, it is better value to book Napo's *Anaconda Hotel* (near Misahuallí) in Quito than to book in

Ecuador

Misahuallí (it is also cheaper to make your own way there than to go with Napo Tour). *Native Life*, Foch E4-167 y Amazonas, T250 5158, natlife1@natlife.com.ec Tours to their Nativo Lodge in the Cuyabeno reserve. *Palmar Voyages*, Alemania N31-77 y Av Mariana de Jesús, T256 9809, www.palmarvoyages.com Small specialist company, custom made itineraries to all areas, good rates. *Pamir Travel and Adventures*, JL Mera 721 y Ventimilla, T254 2605/222 0892, pamir@travels.com.ec Galápagos cruises, climbing, trekking and jungle tours. *Quasar Nautica*, T2463 660, F2436 625, www.quasarnautica.com *Rainforestur*, Amazonas 420 y Robles, T223 9822, rainfor@interactive.net.ec Highland and jungle trips, ecologically minded.

Safari, Calama 380 y JL Mera, T255 2505, www.safari.com.ec Jean Brown and Pattie Serrano, experienced, excellent adventure travel, Galápagos booking services, customized trips, mountain climbing, free route planning, also does 1-3 day full support mountain biking trips, rafting, trekking, and jungle including Huaorani territory. Recommended. *Sierra Nevada Expeditions*, Pinto 637 y Amazonas, T255 3658, snevada@accessinter.net Climbing, rafting, jungle expeditions, experienced multi-lingual guides. *Surtrek*, Amazonas 897 y Wilson, T256 1129, T973 5448 (Mob), www.surtrek.com Climbing, trekking, expeditions, jungle and cultural tours, also flights. *Terracenter*, Reina Victoria 1343 y J Rodríguez, T/F250 7858, www.uio.telconet.net/terracenter Variety of tours, including jungle and the Galápagos. *Transturi SA*, Isla Pinzón 701 near Rio Coca, T224 5055. Part of *Metropolitan Touring*, operate a cruise ship, the *Flotel Orellana*, in 4-5 day trips along the jungle rivers. *Tropic Ecological Adventures*, República E7-320 y Diego de Almagro, Edif Taurus, dpto 1-A, T222 5907, www.tropiceco.com Run by Welshman Andy Drumm, a naturalist guide and divemaster on the Galápagos; he is also director of the *Amazon Project* run by the **Asociación Ecuatoriana de Ecoturismo** and works closely with conservation groups; a sizeable percentage of each fee is given to indigenous communities and ecological projects. *Vasco Tours*, L García 537 y Reina Victoria, T/F223 5348, vascotours@andinanet.net Climbing, trekking and jungle tours, English spoken.

Local Bus: *Popular* buses, pale blue and white (very few left), US$0.14. *Especial* buses, red and white, US$0.20. *Interparroquial* pink and white buses go to destinations within an hour of the city (fares within the city are as for *especiales*, then depend on length of journey). **Trolley bus**: 'El Trole' is an integrated transport system of trolley buses, running on exclusive lanes across the city from north to south, and feeder bus lines (*alimentadores*, painted green and white), serving suburbs from the northern and southern terminals and from El Recreo stop. It runs mainly along 10 de Agosto,the northern station is at 'La Y', the junction of 10 de Agosto, Av América and Av de la Prensa, and the southern station is at Ciudadela Quitumbe in the far south of the city. For the train station, use Chimbacalle stop if heading north, Machángara if heading south. For the main bus terminal use the Cumandá stop, at Maldonado y 24 de Mayo. In the north, some *alimentadores* run past the airport. The fare is US$0.20. **La Ecovía**, a bus-only thoroughfare, runs mostly along Av 6 de Diciembre, from Río Coca in the north to La Marín in the south, with stations like the trolley. Pending the arrival of special buses, trolley vehicles were running this route in mid-2002 **in the wrong (left) lane** – be careful when you cross! **Car rental**: all the main car rental companies are at the airport (*Avis, Ecuacars, Budget, Expo, Localiza*). For multinational rental agencies, see Essentials, page 48. City offices of local companies: *Ecuacars*, Colón 1280 y Amazonas, T252 9781. *Expo*, Av América N21-66 y Bolívia, T228688. *Santitours*, Maldonado 2441, T221 2267, also rent minibuses, buses and 4WD vehicles, chauffeur driven rental only. *Trans-Rabbit*, at the international arrivals section of the Airport, rent vans for up to 10 passengers, with driver, for trips in Quito and out of town, T256 8755. *Budget* and *Ecuacars* have been particularly recommended, helpful staff.

Taxi: Taxis are a safe, cheap and efficient way to get around the city. From the airport to the new city costs US$4; from the Terminal Terrestre to the new city is US$3; and journeys around the new city cost from US$0.80. Expect to pay around 5000% more at night. There is no increase for extra passengers. At night it is safer to use a radio taxi, there are several companies

Transport

Beware pickpockets on the trolley and city buses

Be reasonable and remember that the majority of taxi drivers are honest and helpful

Ecuador

including: *Taxi Amigo*, T222 2222/233 3333, *City Taxi*, T263 3333 and *Central de Radio Taxis*, T250 0600. Make sure they give you the taxi number so that you get the correct taxi and can trace anything you may leave behind. To hire a taxi by the hour costs from US$5. All taxis must have working meters by law, but make sure the meter is running (if it isn't, fix the fare before getting in). Also insist that the taxi drops you precisely where you want to go. All legally registered taxis have the number of their co-operative and the individual operator's number prominently painted on the side of the vehicle and on a sticker on the windshield. They are safer and cheaper than unauthorized taxis. Note the registration and the licence plate numbers if you feel you have been seriously overcharged or mistreated. You may then complain to the transit police or tourist office. For trips outside Quito, agree the fare before-hand: US$70-85 a day. Outside the luxury hotels co-operative taxi drivers have a list of agreed excursion prices and most drivers are knowledgeable. For taxi tours with a guide, try *Hugo Herrera*, T226 7891/223 6492. He speaks good English and is recommended.

If you have any luggage at all, it is much safer to take a taxi to your hotel

Long distance Air: Mariscal Sucre Airport. From the airport catch bus 'Carcelén-Congreso' or 'Pinar Alto-Hotel Quito' for the new city; 'Iñaquito-Villaflora' for the old city. A feeder line for the trolley bus service runs from outside the airport to the northern terminal at La Y. See also Local buses above. Beware of self-styled porters who grab your luggage in the hope of receiving a tip, legitimate porters wear a name tag. Left luggage facilities are just outside international arrivals. Watch bags at all times and watch out for theft by security officials when searching your bags; it has been reported that while you walk through the metal detector they remove money from your hand baggage. After checking in and before going through immigration, pay airport tax. There are duty-free shops in the international departure lounge.

Bus: The Terminal Terrestre, at Maldonado y Cumandá (south of Plaza Santo Domingo), han-dles most long-distance bus services and is really the only place to get information on sched-ules, 24-hr luggage store US$1.75 per day. It is unsafe at all hours, worst at night. Buses for destinations near Quito leave from 'La Marín', which extends the length of Av Pichincha (this is also an unsafe area); a few others leave from Cotocollao (*Trans Minas*) in the north, Villaflora in the south, or near the Patria/10 de Agosto intersection.

To or from the Terminal Terrestre, take a taxi (highly recommended), or the trolley bus (unsafe with luggage). There are company booking offices but staff shout destinations of buses leaving; you can get on board and pay later (but confirm fare in advance). For buses out of Quito it is sometimes advisable to reserve the day before (eg on holiday weekends). See under destinations for fares and schedules.

Several companies run better quality coaches on the longer routes, those with terminals in the new city are: *Flota Imbabura*, Manuel Larrea 1211 y Portoviejo, T223 6940, for Cuenca and Guayaquil; *Transportes Ecuador*, JL Mera 330 y Jorge Washington, to Guayaquil; *Panamericana Internacional*, Colón 852 y Reina Victoria, T250 1585, for Huaquillas, Machala, Cuenca, Loja, Guayaquil, Manta and Esmeraldas, they also run 'international' bus to **Bogotá** (change buses in Tulcán and Ipiales, US$76, 28 hours) and **Lima** (change buses in Aguas Verdes and Tumbes, US$60, 38 hours). *Ormeño Internacional*, from Perú, Shyris N34-432 y Portugal, T246 0027, twice a week to **Lima** (US$55, 36 hours), **Santiago** (US$130, 4 days) and **Buenos Aires** (US$190, 1 week). It is quicker and cheaper to take a bus to the border and change. The route to **Peru** via Loja and Macará takes much longer than the Huaquillas route, but is more relaxed. Do not buy Peruvian (or any other country's) bus tick-ets here, they are much cheaper outside Ecuador.

Internal flights: Details of services are given in the respective destinations. See also Air, Getting around, page 888.

Train: the railway station, 2 km south of the centre, along the continuation of C Maldonado, is reached by trolley (see above). The ticket office (T265 6142) at this beautiful but decrepit old sta-tion is supposedly open Mon-Fri 0800-1630, Sat 0800-1000, employees are not well-informed. You can also get information from railway head office, T258 2921 (Mon-Fri 0900-1700).

Ecuador

Regular passenger service has been discontinued throughout the country. A tourist train, runs from Quito to the Cotopaxi station in Area Nacional de Recreación El Boliche, Sat and Sun 0800, return 1430, US$10 each way, purchase tickets in advance as it is a popular ride. If you wish to return by bus, it is a 2 km walk from the Cotopaxi station to the Pan-American highway. *Metropolitan Touring*, T298 8232, offers various tours involving train travel.

Airline offices Local: *Aerogal*, Amazonas 7997, opposite the airport, T225 7202. *Austro Aéreo*, Amazonas 7579 y Río Curaray, T227 1536. *Icaro*, Palora Oe3-20 y Amazonas, T245 0928. *TAME*, Colón y Rábida, T290 9900, also 6 de Diciembre N26-112. Foreign: *ACES*, Naciones Unidas y Amazonas, Torre B, #411, T246 6461. *Air France*, Av 12 de Octubre N24-562 y Cordero, Torre A, #710, T252 4201. *American Airlines*, Amazonas 4545 y Pereira and in *Hotel Hilton Colón*, T226 0900. *Avensa/Servivensa*, Portugal 794 y República de El Salvador, T225 3972. *Avianca*, República de El Salvador 780 y Portugal, T226 2736. *Continental*, 12 de Octubre 1830 y Cordero, World Trade Center T255 7170. *Copa*, República de El Salvador 361 y Moscú, T227 3082. *Iberia*, Eloy Alfaro 939 y Amazonas, p 5, T256 6009. *KLM*, 12 de Octubre y Lincoln, T298 6828. *TACA*, República de El Salvador 3567 y Potugal, T292 3170. *Lan Chile*, Reina Victoria y Colón, Torres de Almagro, T256 3003 ext 2334. *Lufthansa*, 18 de Septiembre E7-05 y Reina Victoria, T254 1300. *Varig*, Portugal 794 y República de El Salvador, T225 0126.

Directory

Banks *Banco del Pacífico*, Naciones Unidas y Shyris (main branch), Amazonas y Roca, Mall El Jardín, national departures at the airport, *Swissôtel*. For Visa and MasterCard ATM, TCs (US$ only) US$5 per transaction, TCs sold at main branch. MasterCard ATMs also at branches of *Banco Popular-Ecuador*. *Banco de Guayaquil*, Colón y Reina Victoria, p 3. Visa ATM, maximum withdrawal US$100, cash advances on Visa without limit, fast and efficient. ATM also at Amazonas y Veintimilla. *Banco del Pichincha*, Amazonas y Colón. Visa cash advance. Also on Espejo 985 y Venezuela in the old town. *Citibank*, República de El Salvador y Naciones Unidas. You can only use their own cheques, money transfers from most European countries. *Produbanco*, Amazonas N35-211 y Japón, Amazonas y Robles. Change TCs various currencies, 1-2% commission, good service, no credit cards, closed Sat. The *American Express* representative is *Ecuadorean Tours*, see above, sells and replaces Amex TCs, does not change TCs or give cash advances. **Money changers:** There are few exchange houses following dollarization. These are more efficient than banks but may charge higher commission. *Multicambios*, Venezuela 689, T251 1364, Roca 720, T256 7344, and Colón 919 y Reina Victoria, T2561747, also at the airport, open Mon-Fri, 0830-1330, 1430-1730 and Sat morning, several brands of TCs. *Vazcambios*, Amazonas y Roca, *Hotel Alameda Real*, T222 5442, 1.8% commission for US$ TCs, also change TCs and cash in other currencies.

Open Mon-Fri 0900-1800, cash advance and exchange limited hours, best in the morning, Sat 0900-1400. (See also Money, page 888)

Communications Internet: Quito has very many cyber cafés. In the Mariscal tourist district it is difficult to walk two steps without bumping into one. Rates start at about US$1 per hr, net2phone around US$0.25 per min. Many are open till midnight. **Post Office:** All branches open Mon-Fri 0730-1900, Sat 0730-1400, special services until 1530 only. In principle all branches provide all services, but your best chances are at Colón y Almagro in the Mariscal district, and at the main sorting centre on Japón y Naciones Unidas, behind the CCI shopping centre. The branch on Eloy Alfaro 354 y 9 de Octubre frequently loses mail; best avoided. There is also a branch in the old city, on Espejo entre Guayaquil y Venezuela. *Poste Restante* at the post offices at Espejo and at Eloy Alfaro (less efficient). All *poste restante* letters are sent to Espejo unless marked 'Correo Central, Eloy Alfaro', but you are advised to check both *postes restantes*, whichever address you use. Letters can be sent care of American Express, Apdo 17-01-2605, Quito. *South American Explorers* hold mail for members. For more details and for parcels service and letters to Europe via Lufthansa, see page 892. **Telephone:** International and interprovincial calls from *Andinatel* at Av 10 de Agosto y Colón, in the Old City at Benalcázar y Mejía, the Terminal Terrestre, open 0800-2200; the airport, open 0800-1900. There are also debit card cell phones throughout the city.

Cultural centres *Alliance Française*, at Eloy Alfaro 1900, French courses, films and cultural events. *Casa Humboldt*, Vancouver y Polonia, T548480, German centre, including Goethe Institute, films, talks, exhibitions.

Embassies and consulates Argentina, Amazonas 477, T562292. **Austria**, Gaspar de Villaroel E9-63 y Shyris, p 3, open 0900-1300. **Belgium**, JL Mera N23-103 y Wilson, T545340. **Canada**, 6 de Diciembre 2816 y James Orton, p 4, T223 2114. **Colombia**, Atahualpa 955, T227 6542 (consulate), insists on a ticket to leave Colombia before issuing a visa. **Denmark**, República de El Salvador 733 y Portugal, Edif

Ecuador

Gabriela 3, p3 T245 8786, open 0900-1700. **Finland**, Coruña 2306 y Bejarano, T290 1501. **France**, Diego de Almagro y Pradera, Edif Kingmann, p 2, T256 9883 for the consulate, the embassy is at Gen Plaza 107 y Patria, T256 0789. **Germany**, Naciones Unidas Y República de El Salvador, Edif City Plaza, T297 0822, F297 0815, alemania@interactive.net.ec **Ireland**, Ulloa 2651 y Rumipamba, T245 1577. **Israel**, 12 de Octubre 1059 y Salazar, Edif Plaza 2000, p 9, T256 2152. **Italy**, La Isla 111 y H Albornoz, T561077. **Japan**, JL Mera N19-36 y Av Patria, Edif Corp Financiero Nacional, p 7, T561899. **Netherlands**, 12 de Octubre 1942 y Cordero, World Trade Center, p 1, T222 9229 (open 0900-1200, in evening by appointment only). **Norway and Sweden**, Pasaje Alonso Jerves 134 y Orellana, T250 9423, open 0900-1200. **Peru**, República de El Salvador 495 e Irlanda, T246 8410. **Spain**, La Pinta 455 y Amazonas, T256 4373. **Switzerland**, Sanz 120 y Amazonas, Edif Xerox, p 2, T243 4948, open 0900-1200. **UK**, Edif City Plaza, Naciones Unidas y República de El Salvador, p 14, T297 0800, F297 0809, www.britembquito.org.ec The Consulate is a few doors away, it has travel information on Peru, helpful, open Mon-Fri 0930-1230, 1430-1600. **USA**, Av 12 de Octubre y Patria, T256 2890. An official copy of a US passport, US$2.

Language schools The following schools have received favourable reports. In the New City: *Mitad del Mundo*, Gustavo Darquea Terán Oe2-58 (p 2) y Versalles, T254 6827, www.pub.ecua.net.ec/mitadmundo *Academia Latinoamericana*, José Queri 2 y Eloy Alfaro, T252 8770, www.ecua.net.ec/academia *Amazonas Education & Travel*, Jorge Washington 718 y Amazonas, Edif Rocafuerte, p 2 y 3, T/F250 4654, www.eduamazonas.com *Instituto Superior de Español*, Darquea Terán 1650 y 10 de Agosto, T222 3242, www.instituto-superior.net Also have a school in Otavalo (Sucre 1110 y Morales, T292 2414), in Galápagos (advanced booking required) and can arrange voluntary work with La Cruz Roja Ecuatoriana, at Mindo, Fundación Jatun Sacha and others. *Galápagos Spanish School*, Amazonas 258 y Washington, p 2, T/F256 5213, www.galapagos.edu.ec, also has a dance school *Son Latino*, www.galapagos.edu.ec/sonlatino (see Entertainment above.) *Estudio de Español Pichincha*, Andrés Xaura 182 y Foch, T252 8051, lvite@uio.satnet.net *South American Language Center*, Amazonas N26-59 y Santa María, T254 4715 (UK T020-8983 6724), www.southamerican.edu.ec *San Francisco*, Sucre 518 y Benalcázar (Plaza San

Ecuador

Learning the lingo

We list schools for which we have received positive recommendations each year. This does not necessarily imply that schools not mentioned are not recommended.

Quito is one of the most important centres for Spanish language study in Latin America with over 50 schools operating. There is a great variety to choose from. Identify your budget and goals for the course: rigorous grammatical and technical training, fluent conversation skills, getting to know Ecuadoreans or just enough basic Spanish to get you through your trip.

Visit a few places to get a feel for what they charge and offer. Prices vary greatly, from US$2 to US$10 per hr, but you do not always get what you pay for. There is also tremendous variation in teacher qualifications, infrastructure and resource materials. Schools usually offer courses of 4 or 7 hours tuition per day. Many correspondents suggest that 4 is enough. Some schools offer packages which combine teaching in the morning and touring in the afternoon. A great deal of emphasis has traditionally been placed on one-to-one teaching, but remember that a well-structured small classroom setting can also be very good.

The quality of homestays likewise varies, the cost including meals runs from US$10 to US$15 per day. Try to book just 1 week at first to see how a place suits you, don't be pressed into signing a long term contract right at the start. For language courses as well as homestays, deal directly with the people who will provide services to you, and avoid intermediaries. Always get a detailed receipt when you make a payment.

If you are short on time then it can be a good idea to make your arrangements from home, either directly with one of the schools or through an agency, who can offer you a wide variety of options. If you have more time and less money, then it may be more economical to organize your own studies after you arrive. South American Explorers provides a free list of recommended schools and these may give club members discounts.

Ecuador

Francisco), p3, T228 2849, sanfranciscoss_@latinmail.com *La Lengua*, Colón 1001 and J L Mera, p 8, T/F250 1271, www.la-lengua.com (Switzerland T/F851 0533, peter-baldauf@bluewin.ch). *Academia de Español Equinoccial*, Roca 533 y JL Mera, T/F252 9460, www.ecuadorspanish.com Has a second location, also arranges volunteer programmes. *Bipo & Toni's Academia de Español*, Carrión E8-183 y Plaza, T254 7090, T/F250 0732, bipo@pi.pro.ec *Academia Superior de Español Simón Bolívar*, Leonidas Plaza 353 y Roca, T/F223 6688, www.simon-bolivar.com Have their own travel agency, *Columbus Travel* also salsa lessons on Fri. *Escuela de Español Ecuador*, Lazarazo 2328 y C Zorilla, T255 7529. Provide classes at student's homes. *Cristóbal Colón*, Colón 2088 y Versalles, T250 6508, www.southtravel.com Salsa and cooking classes. *Interandina*, Foch E6-12 y Reina Victoria, F258 3086, andinadeturismo @yahoo.com *Centro de Español Siglo 21*, JL Mera 453 y Roca, T256 4128, www.espanolcentro21.com Also arrange recommended excursions to Oriente. *American Spanish School*, 9 de Octubre 564 y Carrión, T222 9166, as.school@accessinter.net *Switzerland Spanish School*, Calama E4-68 y JL Mera, p 2, T/F250 8665, www.geocities.com/switzerspanish Also arrange tours. *Universidad Católica*, 12 de Octubre y Roca, contact Carmen Sarzosa, T222 8781, csarzosa@

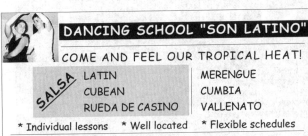

puceuio.puce.edu.ec **In the Old City**: *Beraca School*, García Moreno 858 entre Sucre y Espejo, Pasaje Amador, p3, T228 8092, beraca@interactive.net.ec Has second location in new town. *Los Andes*, 1245 García Moreno entre Mejía y Olmedo, p 2, T295 5107, quitocolonial@yupimail.com Has schools outside Quito, travel agencies, arranges voluntary work in orphanage.

Also: *Academia de Español Amistad*, Manuel Salcedo N14-56 y Montevideo, New City, T/F254 5576, www.amistad-spanish.com *Academia de Español Quito*, 130 Marchena y 10 de Agosto, T255 3647, www.academiaquito.com.ec *Ruta del Sol*, Tarqui 243 & Enrique Vacas, PO Box 17-02-5228, T2555 3914, www.rutasolacademy.com *Sintaxis*, Av 10 de Agosto 15-55 y Bolivia, Edif Andrade, p 5, T252 0006, www.sintaxis.net, *Spanish Language Institute "San Francisco"*, Amazonas N22-62 y Ramírez Dávalos, Edif Vásconez, of 202, T2521 306, www.sanfranciscospanish.com

Medical services Hospitals: **Hospital Voz Andes** Villalengua Oe 2-37 y Av 10 de Agosto, T226 2142 (reached by Trole, la Y stop). Emergency room, quick and efficient, fee based on ability to pay, run by Christian HCJB organization, has out-patient dept, T243 9343. **Hospital Metropolitano**, Mariana de Jesús y Occidental, just east of the western city bypass, T226 1520, ambulance T226 5020, catch a Quito Sur-San Gabriel bus along América, or the Trole (Mariana de Jesús stop) and walk up, or take a taxi. Very

Most embassies have the telephone numbers of doctors and dentists who speak non-Spanish languages

professional and recommended, but expensive. **Clínica Pichincha**, Veintimilla E3-30 y Páez, T256 2296, ambulance T250 1565. Another very good, expensive hospital. **Med Center Travel Clinic** (Dr John Rosenberg), Foch 476 y Almagro, T252 1104, paging service 222 7777 beeper 310. General and travel medicine with a full range of vaccines, speaks English and German, very helpful general practitioner. Laboratories: The hospitals listed above have reliable laboratories. Also good is: **Dra Johanna Grimm**, República de El Salvador 112 y los Shyris, Edif Onyx, p 3, T246 2182. Chemist: *Fybeca* is a reliable chain of 33 farmacies throughout the city. Their 24-hr branches are at Amazonas y Tomás de Berlanga near the Plaza de Toros, and at Centro Comercial El Recreo in the south. *Farmacia Colón*, 10 de Agosto 2292 y Cordero, T222 6534, also open 24 hrs.

Useful addresses Immigration Offices: see Essentials. Police: Criminal Investigations are at Cuenca y Mideros, in the Old City. To report a robbery, make a *denuncia* within 48 hrs. Thefts can also be reported at the **Policía Judicial**, Roca y JL Mera. If you wait more than 48 hrs, you will need a lawyer. **Policía de Turismo** is at Reina Victoria y Roca, T254 3983. Centralized numbers for emergency services, T101 (police), T911 (all emergencies).

Ecuador

Around Quito

Hot springs At the **Termas de Papallacta**, 65 km east from Quito, 1 km from the road to Baeza, there are eight thermal swimming pools and two cold pools. There are showers, toilets, steam room, changing rooms and a restaurant. The baths are usually quiet through the week. The view, on a clear day, of Antisana while enjoying the thermal waters is superb. There are good walking opportunities in the Termas' extensive grounds. ■ *0700-2100, US$5.* In the village of Papallacta are municipal pools, simple, clean, *US$2.* The Fundación Ecológica Rumicocha has a small office on the main street (*0800-1200, 1400-1600*). There are leaflets on the Cayambe-Coca reserve.

East of Papallacta is **L** *Guango Lodge*, including 3 good meals. Situated in temperate forest, Grey-breasted Mountain-toucans are regularly seen here along with many other birds. Reservations needed, Quito T254 7403, F222 8902, www.ecuadorexplorer.com/sanisidro

Sleeping Within the Termas complex are 6 cabins for up to 6 each, US$115 per cabin, and a restaurant (trout speciality); for reservations T250 4787 (Quito), www.papallacta.com.ec **AL** *Hostal Termas de Papallacta*, opposite the main baths with 4 pools, fireplace, heating, restaurant, reservation at same number as above. Along the access road to the Termas are: **E** *Rincón de Papallacta*, at the entrance to the valley. **E** *Hostal Antisana*, shared bath, clean, simple. **F** *Pampas de Papallacta*, T06-320624. Private bath, basic, pool, breakfast extra, very hospitable. Also several simple places to eat, trout is the local speciality. **In town F** *El Viajero*, basic, shared bath, restaurant with reasonable meals, avoid the rooms in the old building. **F** *Quito*, cheaper with shared bath, restaurant also with reasonable meals.

Transport Buses from Quito, Terminal Terrestre, 2 hrs, US$1.75: ask to be let off at the road to the springs; it's a steep 1 km walk up to the baths. On Sat and Sun there is a bus from Plaza San Blas at 0800, returning 1430.

Protected areas northwest of Quito
1,200-2,800 m
2 hrs from Quito

Despite their proximity to the capital, the western slopes of **Pichincha** and its surroundings are surprisingly wild, with fine opportunities for walking and especially birdwatching. Four roads that drop into the western lowlands from Quito each has a unique character, and each has interesting ecotourism reserves. A few are described here, complete details are found in the *Ecuador Handbook*.

The cloud forest in the 14,000-acre **Maquipucuna Biological Reserve** contains a tremendous diversity of flora and fauna, including over 325 species of birds. The reserve has five trails of varying lengths (15 minutes-full day). ■ *Foreigners US$6 pp; accommodation full board in L range; guide, US$10, for transport see below. For reservations:* Fundación Maquipucuna, *Baquerizo Moreno 238 y Tamayo, Quito, T250 7200, F250 7201, www.maqui.org The British charity,* Rainforest Concern, *can also be contacted for information (and beadsfund-raising), c/o Peter Bennett, 27 Lansdowne Crescent, London W11 2NS, T020-7229 2093, F020-7221 4094.*

At Km 68 on the old road to Mindo via Tandayapa is **Bellavista**, with **AL-L** *Hostería Bellavista* (Cabins in the Clouds), full board, hot showers, excellent birdwatching and botany, T223 2313 (Quito), or T09-949 0891, bellavista@ecuadorexplorer.com **E pp** in research station (bunk beds, meals extra, kitchen facilities), advance booking essential. ■ *For Maquipucuna and Bellavista take a bus to Nanegalito then hire a truck (US$15-20), or arrange everything with the lodges or in Quito.*

Mindo
Population: 1,700

Mindo is a small town surrounded by dairy farms and lush cloud forest climbing the western slopes of Pichincha. 19,200 ha, ranging in altitude from 1,400 to 4,780 m, have been set aside as the **Bosque Protector Mindo-Nambillo**. The reserve features beautiful flora (many orchids and bromeliads), fauna (butterflies, birds including the Cock of the rock, Golden-headed Quetzal and Toucan-Barbet) and spectacular cloud forest and waterfalls. *Amigos de la Naturaleza de Mindo* runs the *Centro de*

Educación Ambiental (CEA), 4 km from town, within the 17 ha buffer zone, capacity for 25-30 people. Guide service, lodging and food are available. Admission is US$2, lodging US$6 per person, full board including excursion US$25 per person. Take sleeping gear (none provided) and food if you wish to prepare your own (nice kitchen facilities). Arrangements have to be made in advance, contact *Amigos de la Naturaleza de Mindo*, on the main road into Mindo, 1 block from the Parque Central, T/F276 5463. If closed, enquire about Viviana Murcia. In Quito: *Ing Humberto Ochoa*, T249 0958 (best on weekends), amigosmindo@hotmail.com During the rainy season, access to the reserve can be rough. Vinicio Pérez is an excellent resident birding guide, a little English, recommended. Mindo also has an orchid garden and a butterfly farm 3 km from town. Activities include rapelling in the La Isla waterfalls, and 'inner-tubing' regattas in the rivers.

Sleeping **A** *El Carmelo de Mindo*, in 32 ha 700 m from the town, T222 4713, F254 6013. Includes breakfast, restaurant, pool, cheaper in dorm or camping, tree houses, meals available, fishing, horse rental, excursions, special rates for students. **A** *Finca Mindo Lindo*, On the main Calacalí-La Independencia road by Mindo turnoff, T245 5344, puntos_verdes@hotmail.com Includes breakfast, restaurant, day visits and overnight stays, relaxing, guided tours, meals available. Recommended. **A** *Mindo Gardens*, Next to the CEA. Luxurious, beautiful setting, good birdwatching. **B** *El Bijao*, Av Principal Km 6 Vía a Mindo, T276 5470. Good restaurant, basic but nice. **B** *Hacienda San Vicente*, 'Yellow House', 500 m south of the plaza. Including all meals, family run, nice rooms, excellent food, good walking trails nearby, great value. Recommended. **C** *El Monte*. Includes meals and guiding. Book through *Café Cultura* in Quito, T250 4078. **D** *Jardín de las Orquideas*. Nice atmosphere, beautiful gardens. **E** *Alexandras*, family-owned finca with accommodation for 8. Cooking facilities, fridge, quiet, cosy. Recommended. **E** *Gypsy*, central. 2 attractive cabins, good value, British- run.

Transport Buses from Quito at 0800 and 1545 daily, Sat-Sun also at 0900, return 0630, 1400, plus 1500 Sat-Sun, US$2, 2½ hrs, *Cooperativa Cayambe*, Larrea y Asunción, T252 7495. From **Santo Domingo de los Colorados**, daily 1200 and Sat 0800, US$3, 4 hrs. The most direct access from Quito is along the road to San Miguel de los Bancos, Puerto Quito (accommodation available in both towns) and La Independencia where it joins the Santo Domingo-Esmeraldas road. If driving go to Mitad del Mundo, continue to Calacalí and on to Nanegalito. It is a beautiful ride through native cloud forest; 24 km beyond Nanegalito, to the left, is the turnoff for Mindo. It is about 7 km down to the town.

This natural park set in humid Andean forest is run by the *Fundación Natura*, República 481 y Almagro, T250 3391. The reserve has more than 120 species of birds (unfortunately some of the fauna has been frightened away by the noise of the visitors) and 50 species of trees, situated between 2,700 m and 4,200 m. There are walks of 30 minutes to eight hours. Camping is permitted in the park (US$.75 per person). Take food and water as there are no shops and take your rubbish away with you. There is also a refuge (US$3 per person per night, with shower, has cooking facilities), but you will need a sleeping bag. ■ *Foreigners US$7, very touristy at weekends*.

Refugio de Vida Silvestre Pasochoa
45 mins SE of Quito by car

Transport From Quito buses run from La Marín to Amaguaña (ask the driver to let you off at the 'Ejido de Amaguaña'); from there follow the signs. It's about 8-km walk, with not much traffic for hitching, except at weekends. By car, take the highway to Los Chillos, at San Rafael (traffic light) continue straight towards Sangolquí and on to Amaguaña; 1.4 km past the entrance to Amaguaña turn left onto cobblestone road and follow the signs to Pasochoa, 5.4 km to the park. Tours with *Safari Tours* in Quito cost US$45 pp; a price negotiated with a taxi driver from a luxury hotel is about US$15 each way; a pick-up truck from Amaguaña is about US$6.

Ecuador

Quito

North of Quito

North of Quito to the Colombian border is an area of outstanding beauty. The land-scape is mountainous, with views of the Cotacachi, Imbabura, and Chiles volcanoes and glacier-covered Cayambe, interspersed with lakes. This is also a region renowned for its artesanía and for Otavalo's famous Saturday market.

Quito to Cayambe

Calderón, 32 km north of the centre of Quito, is the place where figurines are made of bread. You can see them being made, though not on Sunday, and prices are lower than in Quito. Especially attractive is the Nativity collection. Prices range from about US$0.10 to US$4. On 1-2 November, the graves in the cemetery are decorated with flowers, drinks and food for the dead. The Corpus Christi processions are very colourful. Many buses leave from Santa Prisca and along Av América in Quito.

The Pan-American Highway goes to Guayllabamba where two branches split, one goes through Cayambe and the second through Tabacundo before rejoining. At 8 km before Cayambe a concrete globe marks the spot where the Equator crosses the Pan-American Highway. At 10 km past Guayllabamba and 8 km before Tabacundo, just south of the toll booth, a cobbled road to the left (signed Pirámides de Cochasquí) leads to Tocachi and further on to the **Tolas de Cochasquí** archaeological site. The protected area contains 15 truncated clay pyramids, nine with long ramps, built between AD 900 and 1500 by the Cara or Cayambi-Caranqui Indians. Festivals with dancing at the equinoxes and solstices. There is a site museum. ■ *Entry only with a 1½ hr guided tour; 0830-1630. Be sure to take a bus that goes on the Tabacundo road and ask to be let off at the turnoff. From there it's a pleasant 8-km walk. If you arrive at the sign around 0815, you could get a lift from the site workers. A taxi from Cayambe costs US$8 for the round trip.*

Cayambe

Phone code: 02
Colour map 1a, grid A4
Population: 16,849

Cayambe, on the eastern (righthand) branch of the highway, 25 km northeast of Guayllabamba, is dominated by the snow-capped volcano of the same name. The surrounding countryside consists of rich dairy farms and flower plantations. The area is noted for its *bizcochos* (biscuits) served with *queso de hoja* (string cheese). On the edge of town are the pyramids of the Sun and Moon at Puntiachil, entrance at Olmedo 702, US$1 includes guided tour in Spanish. There is a *fiesta* in March for the equinox with plenty of local music; also Inti Raymi during the summer solstice blends into the San Pedro celebrations around June 29. Market day is Sunday, along C Rocafuerte.

Volcán Cayambe

Altitude: 5,790 m
The highest point in the world which lies so close to the Equator (3.25 km north)

Cayambe Ecuador's third highest peak, lies within the Reserva Ecológica Cayambe-Coca. About 1 km south of Cayambe is an unmarked cobbled road heading east via Juan Montalvo, leading in 26 km to the Ruales-Oleas-Berge refuge at about 4,800 m. **Sleeping**: The *refugio* costs US$17 per person per night, can sleep 37 in bunks, but bring a sleeping bag, it is very cold. There is a kitchen, fireplace, eating area, running water, electric light and a radio for rescue. Entry to the reserve is US$10.

The standard route, up from the west, uses the refuge as a base. The climb is heavily crevassed, especially near the summit, and is more difficult and dangerous than either Chimborazo or Cotopaxi.

■ *Getting there: You can take a camioneta from Cayambe to Hacienda Piemonte El Hato (at about 3,500 m) or a taxi for US$30. From the hacienda to the refugio it is a 3-4-hr walk minimum, the wind can be very strong but it is a beautiful walk. It is difficult to get transport back to Cayambe. A milk truck runs from Cayambe hospital to the hacienda at 0600, returning between 1700-1900. 4WD jeeps at times can go to the refugio, 1½-2 hrs.*

Ecuador

A *Jatun Huasi*, Panamericana Norte Km 1½, T236 3775, jatunhuasi@hotmail.com Includes breakfast, restaurant, indoor pool, new in 2001, north American motel style, rooms with fireplace and frigo-bar. **B** *Hacienda Guachala*, south of Cayambe on the road to Cangahua, T236 3042, guachala@uio.satnet.net Spring-fed swimming pool, a beautifully restored hacienda (1580), basic but comfortable rooms with fireplaces, delicious food, good walking, horses for rent, excursions to nearby pre-Inca ruins. Highly recommended.**C** *Shungu Huasi*, 1 km

Sleeping & eating
Hotels may be full on Fri during Jun-Sep and during the week before Valentine's Day (high season at the flower plantations)

Northern Ecuador

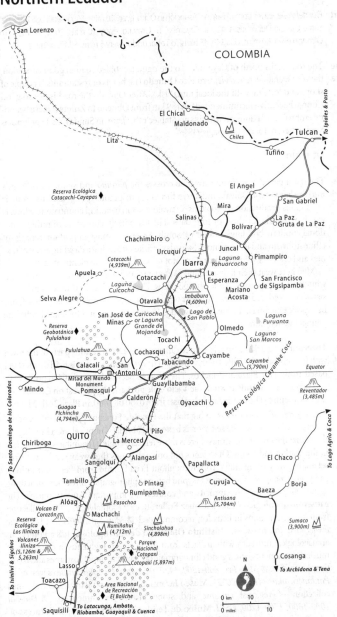

Ecuador

northwest of town, T/F236 1847, shungu@hoy.net Excellent Italian restaurant, comfortable, nice setting, offers horse riding excursions. Recommended. **D** *Cabañas de Nápoles*, Panamericana Norte Km 1, T236 0366. Good restaurant, parking, OK cabins near highway. **D** *La Gran Colombia*, Panamericana y Calderón, T236 1238, F236 2421. Restaurant, parking, OK, modern but but noisy. **E** *Mitad del Mundo*, Panamericana a little south of town, T236 0226. Restaurant, cheaper without bath, pool (open weekends), parking, good value. *Aroma*, Bolívar 404 y Ascázubi, large choice of set lunches and a la càrte, variety of desserts, very good. *El Molino*, Panamericana Norte, Km 3. Excellent breakfasts, French cuisine, cosy atmosphere.

Transport *Flor del Valle*, leaves from M Larrea y Asunción in Quito, every 10 mins, 0500-1900, US$1, 1½ hrs. Some Otavalo-Quito buses stop in Cayambe. To **Otavalo**, every 10 mins, $0.60, 40 mins. To **Olmedo** every 30 mins, US$0.40, 45 mins.To **Tabacundo**, every 5 mins, $0.17, 20 mins.

Cayambe to Ibarra The road forks north of Cayambe. To the right: a cobbled road in good condition, the very scenic *carretera vieja*, runs to **Olmedo** (no hotels or restaurants; a couple of shops and lodging with the local nuns, ask). After Olmedo the road is not so good (four-wheel drive recommended). It is 9 km from Olmedo to **Zuleta**, where beautiful embroidery is done on napkins and tablecloths; *feria* on Sunday. La Esperanza is 8½ km before Ibarra (see page 938).

Otavalo

Phone code: 06
Colour map 1a, grid A4
Population: 28,000
Altitude: 2,530 m
110 km N of Quito

The main paved road from Cayambe crosses the *páramo* and suddenly descends into the land of the Otavalo Indians, a thriving, prosperous group, famous for their prodigious production of woollens. Otavalo is set in beautiful countryside which is worth exploring for three or four days. The town itself, consisting of rather functional modern buildings is one of South America's most important centres of ethno-tourism and its enormous Saturday market, featuring a dazzling array of textiles and crafts, is second to none and not to be missed. Take plenty of cash!

Men here wear their hair long and plaited under a broad-brimmed hat; they wear white, calf-length trousers and blue ponchos. The women's colourful costumes consist of embroidered blouses, shoulder wraps and many coloured beads. Native families speak Quichua at home, although it is losing some ground to Spanish with the younger generation.

Sights
Otavalo tourist information is available at www.otavalo-web.com

The Saturday market comprises three different markets in various parts of the town with the central streets filled with vendors. The *artesanías* market is held 0700-1800, based around the Plaza de Ponchos. The livestock section begins at 0500 until 1000, and takes place outside town in the Viejo Colegio Agrícola; go west on Colón from the town centre. The produce market lasts from 0700 till 1400, in Plaza 24 de Mayo.

The *artesanías* industry is so big that the Plaza de Ponchos is filled with vendors every day of the week. The selection is better on Saturday but prices are a little higher than other days when the atmosphere is more relaxed. Polite bargaining is appropriate in the market and shops. Otavaleños not only sell goods they weave and sew themselves, but they bring crafts from throughout Ecuador and from Peru and Bolivia. Indigenous people in the market respond better to photography if you buy something first, then ask politely. Reciprocity and courtesy are important Andean norms. The **Museo Arqueológico César Vásquez Fuller**, Roca y Montalvo, excellent collection from different regions in Ecuador, recommended. ■ *Mon-Sat 1400-1800, US$1, the owner gives free tours.* The **Instituto Otavaleño de Antropología** has a library, an archaeological museum with artifacts from the northern highlands, a collection of musical instruments, and a good ethnographic display of regional costumes and traditional activities. ■ *Mon-Fri 0800-1200, 1430-1830, free, Av de los Sarances west of the Panamericana Norte, T920321.* **Museo Jaramillo**, Bolívar, off Parque Central, small collection of regional ceramic and stone pieces, recommended. ■ *Thu-Sat 1000-1300, 1500-1700, US$1.* **Museo de Tejidos El Obraje**, shows the process of traditional Otavalo weaving from shearing to final products. Traditional weaving lessons are available. ■ *Mon-Sat 0900-12, 1400-1700, Sucre 608, T920261.*

Excursions

Otavalo weavers come from dozens of communities. The easiest to visit are Ilumán (visit the Conterón-de la Torre family of *Artesanías Inti Chumbi*, on the northeast corner of the plaza; there are also many felt hatmakers in town); Agato (the Andrango-Chiza family of *Tahuantinsuyo Weaving Workshop*, gives weaving demonstrations and sells textiles); Carabuela (many homes sell crafts including wool sweaters); Peguche (the Cotacachi-Pichamba family, off the main plaza behind the church, sells beautiful tapestries). These villages are only 15-30 minutes away and all have a good bus service; buses leave from the Terminal and stop at Plaza Copacabana (Atahualpa y Montalvo). You can also take a taxi.

To reach the **Cascada de Peguche** follow the old railway track through the woods in the direction of Ibarra until the track drops away to the left and a dirt path continues up the hill towards the waterfall. From the top of the falls you can continue the walk to Lago de San Pablo (see below). Avoid the unsafe neighbourhood on the way out of town, by taking the bus to Peguche and asking to be let off where the trail to the waterfall starts. ■ *US$1.* The *Pawkar Raimi* festival is held in Peguche during carnival.

Allow 1-1½ hrs each way

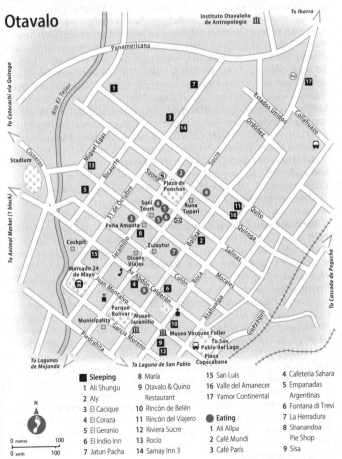

Otavalo

Ecuador

Sleeping ■
1 Ali Shungu
2 Aly
3 El Cacique
4 El Coraza
5 El Geranio
6 El Indio Inn
7 Jatun Pacha
8 María
9 Otavalo & Quino Restaurant
10 Rincón de Belén
11 Rincón del Viajero
12 Riviera Sucre
13 Rocío
14 Samay Inn 3
15 San Luis
16 Valle del Amanecer
17 Yamor Continental

Eating ●
1 Ali Allpa
2 Café Mundi
3 Café París
4 Cafetería Sahara
5 Empanadas Argentinas
6 Fontana di Trevi
7 La Herradura
8 Shanandoa Pie Shop
9 Sisa

Sleeping

Hotels may be full on Fri night before market, when prices go up

A *Ali Shungu*, Quito y Miguel Egas, T920750, www.alishungu.com Good restaurant with live music on weekends, nice rooms, lovely garden, no smoking, safe deposit boxes. US run, no credit cards, small surcharge for TCs. Recommended. **B** *Yamor Continental*, Av. Paz Ponce de León y Jacinto Collahuazo, near bus terminal, T920451, F920982. Restaurant, pool, pleasant gardens, comfortable. **C** *El Indio Inn*, Bolívar 904 y Calderón, T920325. Restaurant, also suites, spotless, attractive. **C** *Hotel Otavalo*, Roca 504 y J Montalvo, T923712, F920416. Good breakfast, expensive restaurant, refurbished colonial house, large rooms, patio, good service, helpful. **D** *Coraza*, Calderón y Sucre, T/F921225, coraza@ecuahotel.com Good restaurant, nice rooms, quiet and comfortable. Recommended. **D** *Jatun Pacha*, 31 de Octubre 19 entre Quito y Panamericana, T922223, F922871. Includes breakfast, nice, modern, a little cheaper in dorm, bicycle rentals. **D** *Samay Inn 2*, Colón y Roca, T/F922995. Modern, comfortable. **D** *Valle del Amanecer*, Roca y Quiroga, T920990, F920286. Includes breakfast, good restaurant, internet, small rooms, courtyard, popular and overpriced, mountain bike hire. **D-E** *Aly*, Salinas y Bolívar, T921831. Restaurant, nice, modern. **D-E** *Rincón del Viajero*, Roca 11-07 y Quiroga, T921741, rincondelviajero@hotmail.com Includes breakfast, cheaper without bath, rooftop hammocks, sitting room with fireplace, US-run. Recommended. **D-E** *Riviera Sucre*, García Moreno 380 y Roca, T/F920241. Good breakfasts, cafeteria, cheaper without bath, limited book exchange, nice garden, secure, good meeting place. **E** *Chukito's*, Bolívar 10-13 y Morales, chukitos@hotmail.com internet, modern. **E** *María*, Jaramillo y Colón, T/F920672. Modern, convenient, cafeteria, good value. Recommended. **E-F** *El Geranio*, Ricaurte y Colón, T920185, hgeranio@hotmail.com Restaurant, cheaper without bath, cooking facilities, quiet, family run, helpful, popular, good value. Recommended. **E-F** *Los Andes*, Sucre y Quiroga by Plaza de Ponchos, T921057. Restaurant, cheaper without bath, internet, modern. **E-F** *Rocío*, Morales y Egas, T920584. Cheaper without bath, hot showers, helpful, popular, good value. **F** *Colón*, Colón 7-13, T924245. Cheaper without bath, hot water, simple, good. **F** *El Cacique*, 31 de Octubre y Quito, T921740, F920930. Hot water, parking, spacious, nice rooftop area. **F** *Los Ponchos Inn*, Sucre y Quiroga by Plaza de Ponchos, T/F923575. Restaurant, hot water, internet, view of plaza. **F** *San Luis*, Abdón Calderón 6-02 y 31 de Octubre, T920614. Shared bath, basic, family run, secure.

Out of town In **Peguche** (see Excursions) **C-D** *Aya Huma*, on the railway line, T922663, ayahuma@imbanet.net Restaurant, cooking facilities, quiet, pleasant atmosphere, Dutch run, live folk music on Sat. Highly recommended. **D** *Peguche Tío*, near centre of the village, T/F922619. Includes breakfast, restaurant, internet, nice lounge with fireplace, decorated with works of art, interesting museum, sports fields, caters to groups.

North and west of town **L** *Hacienda Pinsaqui*, Panamericana N Km 5, T946116, info@ pinsaqui.com Includes breakfast, restaurant, 300 m north of the turn-off for Cotacachi. Beautiful antiques, lovely dining room, lounge with fireplace, colonial ambience, gardens, horse riding. **A** *Casa Mojanda*, Vía Mojanda Km 3, T09-9731737, www.casamojanda.com Includes breakfast, beautiful setting on 25 acres of farmland and forested gorge, organic garden, including all meals, comfortable, quiet, library, horse riding, mountain bikes. Highly recommended. **B** *La Casa de Hacienda*, Entrance at Panamericana Norte Km 3, then 300 m east, T946336, hosteriacasadehacienda@hotmail.com Includes breakfast, restaurant, tasteful cabins with fireplace, advance reservations required for horse riding. **C** *Las Palmeras*, outside Quichinche, 15 minutes by bus from Otavalo, T922607, palmeras@cusin.com.ec Includes breakfast, restaurant, cheaper without bath, new in 2002, rural setting, nice grounds, English owned. **C** *Troje Cotama*, 4 km north of Otavalo by Carabuela, T/F946119. Restaurant, converted grain house, very attractive, fireplace in rooms, good food, Dutch, English and German spoken. **D** *Cabañas de Miriam*, Vía a Mojanda Km 2, T920421. Good meals, library English spoken. Bus to the village of Punyaro takes you very close. **D** *La Luna de Mojanda*, Vía Mojanda Km 2, T09-973 7415, F09-737 415. Restaurant, run by young Argentine couple, organize cheap 4WD tours, games room and library, taxi service to Otavalo, English/German spoken, good restaurant. Recommended.

Eating

Café Paris, Modesto Jaramillo y Morales. Good authentic French cooking, expensive. *Fontana di Trevi*, Sucre 12-05 y Salinas, 2nd floor. Good pizza and pasta, nice juices, friendly service. *Ali Allpa*, Salinas 509 at Plaza de Ponchos, good value set meals and à la carte, trout, vegetarian, meat. Recommended. *La Herradura*, Bolívar 10-05. Good cheap set meals and à la carte, outdoor tables. *Quino*, Roca 740 y Montalvo. Good coastal cooking, good value. *Empanadas Argentinas*, Morales 502 y Sucre. Good savoury and sweet *empanadas*. *Geminis*, Moralesy Sucre. Excellent food, good atmosphere and music. Recommended. *Café Mundi*, Quiroga 608 y Jaramillo, Plaza de Ponchos. Good food and value, nice atmosphere, vegetarian available. *Cafetería Shanandoa Pie Shop*, Salinas y Jaramillo. Good pies, milk shakes and ice cream, expensive, good meeting place, recommended for breakfast, book exchange, daily movies at 1700 and 1900. *Café Sisa*, Calderón 409 entre Sucre y Bolívar. Coffee shop, cappuccino, good food (2nd floor), bookstore, art exhibitions, weekly films, live music Fri-Sun, open 0700-2200. *Cafetería Sahara*, Quiroga 4-18 y Sucre. Falafel, houmus, fruit and veg juices, water pipes, Arabic coffee and sweets, small portions. *Café San Seba's*, Quiroga entre Roca y Bolívar. Bakery with good coffee, meals, open late, *Deli* next door serves breakfast, pizza, pasta. *Oraibi Bar*, Colón y Sucre. Vegetarian dishes, salads, quiche, pleasant courtyard, snacks, live music Fri and Sat evenings, good service, book exchange. *Tabasco's*, Sucre y Salinas, Plaza de Ponchos. Mexican, attractive, good food, good views. *Chifa Long Xiang*, Quito y Roca, good.

Entertainment

Otavalo is generally safe until 2200 Avoid deserted areas. Peñas are open on Fri and Sat from 2200, entrance US$2

Peña Amauta, Jaramillo y Morales. Good local bands, welcoming, mainly foreigners. *Peña la Jampa*, Jaramillo 5-69 y Morales. Very popular. *Peña Tucano*, Morales y 31 de Octubre. *Habana Club*, Quito y 31 de Octubre. Lively disco, cover US$1. *Maracaná*, Salinas 31 de Octubre, young crowd. On Fri and Sat nights there are nightlife tours on a *chiva* (open sided bus with a musical group on board), it stops at the Plaza de Ponchos and ends its route at the *Habana Club*.

Festivals

If you wish to visit fiestas in the local villages, ask the musicians in the tourist restaurants, they may invite you

The **third week of Jun**, combines the *Inti Raymi* celebrations of the summer solstice (**21 Jun**), with the *Fiesta de San Juan* (**24 Jun**) and the *Fiesta de San Pedro y San Pablo* (**29 Jun**). These combined festivities are known as *Los San Juanes* and participants are mostly indigenous. The celebration begins with a ritual bath in the Peguche waterfall (a personal spiritual activity, best carried out without visitors and certainly without cameras). Most of the action takes place in the smaller communities surrounding Otavalo. Groups of musicians and dancers compete with each other as they make their way from one village to another over the course of the week; there is much drinking along the way. In Otavalo, indigenous families have costume parties, which at times spill over onto the streets. In the San Juan neighbourhood, near the Yanayacu baths, there is a week-long celebration with food, drink and music. *Fiesta del Yamor and Colla Raimi* first two weeks of Sep, local dishes are cooked, roulette played and bands in the plaza, as well as bullfights. *Mojandas Arriba* is an annual 2-day hike from Quito over Mojanda to reach Otavalo for the **31 Oct** foundation celebrations.

Shopping

In addition to the market, there are many shops along calles Sucre and Salinas, selling textiles and souvenirs.

Sport

Mountain bikes: for hire at *Jatun Pacha* (see Sleeping), T548068, US$10 for 5 hrs or US$12 per day. *Taller Ciclo Primaxi*, García Moreno 2-49 y Atahualpa and at the entrance to Peguche, has good bikes for rent, US$1 per hr. Recommended. *Hostal Valle del Amanecer* (see Sleeping), US$8 per day. Several travel agencies also rent bikes and offer cycling tours.

Ecuador

Tour operators

Most common tours are to native communities, Cuicocha and Mojanda, US15-30 pp

Independent travel to the Lagunas de Mojanda is not recommended because of armed robbery and chronic public safety problems. Only go with a tour

Chachimbiro Tours, Colón 412 y SucreT923633,chachim@imbanet.net Trips to Complejo de Ecoturismo Chachimbiro (thermal baths and spa, 1 hr northwest of Otavalo), US$8 pp for a day trip, US$20 pp for 2 days, including meals. **Intiexpress**, Sucre 11-10, T921436, F920737. Recommended for horse riding tours, US$20 pp, 5 hrs, $35 full day, ask them to prepare the horses before you arrive, good for those with or without experience, email service. **Intipungo**, Sucre y Calderón, T921171. For airline reservations, *DHL/Western Union* representative, horseback and vehicle tours. **Leyton's Tours**, Quito y Jaramillo, T922388, leytontour@yahoo.com Horseback and bicycle tours. **Runa Tupari**, Sucre y Quiroga, Plaza de Ponchos T/F925985, www.runatupari.com Trips to community inns in the Cotacachi area, US$15 pp per day, half board, includes transport (see Cotacachi), also the usual tours at higher-than-average prices, English and French spoken. **Suni Tours**, Morales y Sucre, T09-993 3148, www.geocities.com/sunitour Interesting itineraries, trekking and horse riding tours, trips to Intag, Piñán, Cayambe, Oyacachi, guides carry radios. English spoken, recommended. **Yuraturs**, Morales 505 y Sucre, T/F921861, www.yuratours.com Airline reservations and tours. **Zulaytur**, Sucre y Colón, p 2, T921176, F922969. Run by Rodrigo Mora, English spoken, information, map of town, slide show, horse-riding. Repeatedly recommended. **Zulay Diceny Viajes**, Sucre 1011 y Colón, T921217, zulayviajes@hotmail.com Run by Zulay Sarabino, an indigenous Otavaleña, knowledgeable native guides.

Transport

Never leave anything in your car or taxi, even if it is being watched for you

Bus Terminal at Atahualpa y Collahuazo (see map). To **Quito** 2 hrs, US$1.60, every 10 mins; all depart from the Terminal Terrestre in Quito, *Coop Otavalo* and *Coop Los Lagos* go into Otavalo, buses bound for Ibarra drop you off at the highway, this is not safe at night. From **Quito** by taxi takes 1½ hrs, US$35; shared taxis with **Supertaxis Los Lagos** (in Quito, Asunción 3-81, T256 5992; in Otavalo, Roca 8-04, T923203) who will pick you up at your hotel (in the new city only); hourly from 0830 to 1900, 2 hrs, US$6 pp, buy ticket the day before.

Around Otavalo

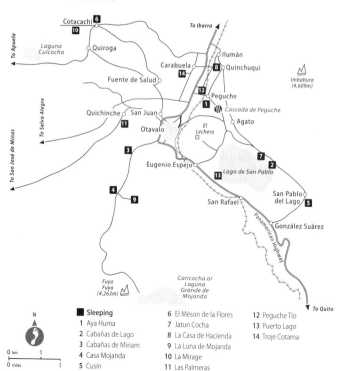

Sleeping
1 Aya Huma
2 Cabañas de Lago
3 Cabañas de Miriam
4 Casa Mojanda
5 Cusín
6 El Méson de la Flores
7 Jatun Cocha
8 La Casa de Hacienda
9 La Luna de Mojanda
10 La Mirage
11 Las Palmeras
12 Peguche Tío
13 Puerto Lago
14 Troje Cotama

Ecuador

Hotel Ali Shungu (see Sleeping) runs a shuttle bus from any hotel in Quito new city to Otavalo, US$15 pp, not restricted to *Ali Shungu* guests. To **Ibarra**, every 15 mins, US$0.32, 40 mins. To **Tulcán**, via Ibarra, frequent departures. To **Cayambe**, every 15 mins, US$0.60, 45 mins. To **Cotacachi**, every 15 mins (some via Quiroga), US$0.20, 30 mins. To **communities around Lago San Pablo**, frequent service, US$0.30, also stop at Plaza Copacabana. To **Peguche**, city bus (blue), every 15 mins, US$0.12. To the **Intag region**, 5 daily.

Banks *Vaz Cambios*, Jaramillo y Saona, Plaza de Ponchos, TCs 1.8% comission, changes Euros and Colombian Pesos. *Banco del Pichincha*, Bolívar y Piedrahita, TCs 1% comission. **Communications** Internet: Prices about US$1.60 per hr. Many in town, specially on C Sucre. **Post Office:** corner of Plaza de Ponchos, entrance on Sucre, 1st floor. **Telephone:** *Andinatel*, Calderón entre Jaramillo y Sucre. **Language schools** Spanish classes run about US$4 per hr. *Instituto Superior de Español*, Sucre 11-10 y Morales, p 2, T992414, www.instituto-superior.net (see also Quito language schools). *Academia de Español Mundo Andino*, Salinas 404 y Bolívar, T921801, español@interactive.net.ec Recommended. *Fundación Jacinto Jijón y Caamaño*, Bolívar 8-04 y Montalvo, p 2, T920725, sarance@uio.satnet.net Spanish and Quichua lessons, tours.

Directory

There is a network of old roads and trails between Otavalo and Lago de San Pablo, none of which takes more than two hours to explore. It is worth walking either to or back from the lake for the views (if you take the main road, beware traffic fumes and litter). From **San Pablo del Lago** it is possible to climb **Imbabura** volcano (4,630 m, almost always under cloud), allow at least six hours to reach the summit and four hours for the descent. Easier, and no less impressive, is the nearby Cerro Huarmi Imbabura, 3,845 m. An alternative access, is from La Esperanza (see below). Allow 10-12 hours for the round trip; take a good map, food and warm clothing. ■ *Buses from Otavalo-San Pablo del Lago every 30 mins, US$0.30, from bus terminal, with a stop at Plaza Copacabana, Atahualpa entre Calderón y Montalvo.*

Lago de San Pablo
Robberies of lone walkers have been reported, best go in a group. Take a stick to fend off dogs

Sleeping L *Hostería Cusín* in a converted 17th century *hacienda* on the east side of the lake, San Pablo del Lago, T918013, www.haciendacusin.com With fireplace, including breakfast, fine expensive restaurant, sports facilities (horses, mountain bikes, squash court, pool, games room), library, lovely grounds, book in advance, English owned, no credit cards. Recommended. **AL** *Hostería Jatun Cocha*, Panamericana Km 5½, on the west side of the lake, T/F918191. Tasteful rooms with fireplaces, restaurant, kayaks, windsurfing, bicycles. **A** *Hostería Puerto Lago Country Inn*, Panamericana Sur, Km 6, on the west side of the lake, T920920, efernand@ uio.satnet.net Includes breakfast and dinner, beautiful setting, a good place to watch the sunset, very hospitable, good expensive restaurant, motor boat trips on the lake. **B** *Cabañas del Lago*, on northeast shore of the lake, T918001 (in Quito, T243 5936), cablago@access.net.ec Nice cabins with bunk beds, restaurant, lovely garden, boats and pedalos for hire.

West of the road between Otavalo and Ibarra is Cotacachi, where leather goods are made and sold. Credit cards are widely accepted but with up to 20% surcharge. There is also access along a cobbled road directly from Otavalo through Quiroga. The **Museo de las Culturas**, García Moreno 13-41, off the main plaza, has good displays about early Ecuadorean history, regional crafts and indigenous traditions. Some English explanations. ■ *Tue-Fri 0900-1200, 1400-1700, Sat 1400-1700, Sun 1000-1300, US$1.* The local fiesta is *La Jora* during the September equinox.

Cotacachi

To promote rural/ethno-cultural tourism, the municipality has set up an interesting series of country inns in nearby villages. Visitors experience life with a native family by taking part in daily activities. The comfortable inns have space for 3, fireplace, bathroom and hot shower. US$8 per person including breakfast and dinner; more if transport is included. Arrange with *Runa Tupari* or other Otavalo agencies.

Sleeping and eating LL *La Mirage*, 500 m west of town, T915237, www.larc1.com Includes breakfast and dinner, lovely expensive restaurant, pool and gym, converted hacienda with luxurious facilities, beautiful gardens, antiques, conference facilities, and spa.

Ecuador

Recommended. **B** *El Mesón de las Flores*, García Moreno 1376 y Sucre, T916009, F915828. Restaurant, converted ex-hacienda off main plaza, meals in a beautiful patio, live music at lunch Sat-Sun. Highly recommended. **C** *Sumac Huasi*, Montalvo 11-09 y Moncayo, T915873. Includes breakfast, large modern rooms, nice but overpriced. **D** *Munaylla*, 10 de Agosto y Sucre, T916169, munailla@prodigy.net New in 2001, modern, comfortable. **D** *Plaza Bolívar*, Bolívar 12-26 y 10 de Agosto p 3, T915755, marcelmun@yahoo.com Internet, indoor parking, refurbished older building, stores luggage. Recommended. **E** *Bachita*, Sucre 16-82 y Peñaherrera, T915063. Simple, quiet.

Eating places include *El Viejo Molino*, Parque San Francisco next to Banco del Pichincha. Good value and quality, set meals and à la carte. Recommended. *Asadero La Tola*, Rocafuerte 018 y 9 de Octubre. Grill, in an old courtyard. *El Leñador*, Sucre 1012 y Montalvo. Varied menu, pricey. *Inty Huasi*, Bolívar 11-08 y 10 de Agosto. Set meals and à la carte. *Swisscoffee*, Bolívar 13-04. Snacks, sandwiches, coffee, juices; books for sale. A local specialty is *carne colorada* (spiced pork).

Transport **Bus**: terminal at 10 de Agosto y Salinas by the market. Frequent service from the Otavalo terminal, US$0.20, 20 mins. To **Ibarra**, frequent service 0500-1800, US$0.35, 45 mins. Trucks to **Cuicocha** from the market, US$5 one way.

Laguna Cuicocha
Altitude: 3,070 m
15 km from Cotacachi

The area is part of the **Reserva Ecológica Cotacachi-Cayapas**, which extends from Cotacachi volcano to the tropical lowlands on the Río Cayapas in Esmeraldas. This is a crater lake with two islands, although these are closed to the public for biological studies. There is a well-marked, 8-km path around the lake, which takes 4-5 hours and provides spectacular views of the Cotacachi, Imbabura and, occasionally, Cayambe peaks. The best views are in the early morning, when condors can sometimes be seen. There is lookout at 3 km, two hours from the start. It's best to go anticlockwise; take water and a waterproof jacket. Motor boat rides around the islands, US$1.20 per person, for minimum five persons. ■ *The US$5 park fee need not be paid if only going to the lake, but you must pay US$1 to visit the lake itself. A visitor's centre has good natural history and cultural displays, entry US$1.*

Warnings There have been armed robberies of people walking around the lake. Do not take valuables. Always enquire locally before heading out. Do not eat the berries which grow near the lake, as some are poisonous. The path around the lake is not for vertigo sufferers.

Sleeping and eating **D** *El Mirador*, above the restaurant and pier, T06-648039. Hot water, fireplace, camping possible, restaurant, hikes arranged up Cotacachi or Piñán for the fit, excellent views, return transport to Otavalo US$7. **D** *Refugio Cuicochamanta*, 2 km beyond the park entrance, on road to Intag, T06-916313, in native family's home. Breakfast and dinner included, trekking, climbing and horseback tours available, English and French spoken. Restaurant, *El Muelle*, by the pier, has a dining room overlooking the lake, expensive.

Transport **Bus**: Otavalo-Quiroga US$0.20, **Cotacachi-Quiroga** US$0.10; camioneta or taxi Quiroga-Cuicocha US$3, **Cotacachi-Cuicocha** US$5. Alternatively, hire a taxi in Otavalo, US$7 one-way. The 3-hr walk back to Cotacachi is beautiful; after 1 km on the road from the park entrance, turn left (at the first bend) on to the old road.

To the northwest of Otavalo lies the lush subtropical region of **Intag**, reached along a road that follows the southern edge of Cuicocha and continues to the town of **Apuela**. Beyond, are pleasant thermal baths at **Nangulví**. The area is rich in cloudforest and has several nature reserves.

On the southwest boundary of the Cotacachi-Cayapas reserve is **Los Cedros Research Station**, 6,400 ha of pristine cloudforest, with abundant orchids and bird life. Full board in **L** range. Contact CIBT, Quito for details: T254 0346, www.ecole-adventures.com ■ *Bus from Quito; from Plaza Cotocollao, to Saguangal, 6 hrs, then it's a 6 hr walk (basic accommodation at trailhead); or through Safari Tours in Quito. A 4WD can reach the road-end, saving 1½ hrs walk.*

Ibarra

Once a pleasant colonial town (founded in 1606), Ibarra is the main commercial centre of the northern highlands, with an increasingly big city feel. The city has an interesting ethnic mix, with blacks from the Chota valley and Esmeraldas alongside Otavaleños and other highland Indians, mestizos and Colombian immigrants. The city has two plazas with flowering trees.

Phone code: 06
Colour map 1a, grid A4
Population: 80,990
Altitude: 2,225 m

On **Parque Pedro Moncayo**, stand the Cathedral, the Municipio and Gobernación. One block away is the smaller Parque 9 de Octubre, at Flores y Olmedo, more commonly called **Parque de la Merced** after its church. Some interesting paintings are to be seen in the church of **Santo Domingo** and its museum of religious art, at the end of Simón Bolívar. ■ *Daily 0800-1800, US$0.60.* On Sucre, at the end of Av A Pérez Guerrero is the **Basílica de La Dolorosa**. A walk down Pérez Guerrero leads to the large covered **Mercado Amazonas** on Cifuentes, by the railway station. ■ *Daily, busiest Sat and Sun.* The **Museo Regional del Banco Central** at Sucre 7-21 y Oviedo, has archaeologic displays about cultures from northern Ecuador. Take care in the downtown area, especially at night. Virgen del Carmen festival is on 16 July and Fiesta de los Lagos is in the last weekend of September, Thursday-Sunday.

Tourist offices *Ministerio de Turismo*, García Moreno 744, p 2, by Parque de la Merced, T958547, very helpful, free city map and various tourist leaflets, English spoken, ■ *Mon-Fri 0830-1300, 1400-1700.*

Ibarra

Ecuador

N

0 metres   100
0 yards   100

■ Sleeping	● Eating	🚌 Buses
1 Hostal El Retorno	1 Café Floralp	1 CITA (Ambato direct)
2 Hostal Madrid	2 Casa Blanca	2 Espejo (Tulcán)
3 Imbabura	3 Heladería Rosalía Suárez	3 Expreso Turismo
4 Madrid	4 Mesón Colonial	(Quito, Tulcan)
5 Montecarlo	5 Mr Peter's	4 Trans Andina
6 Residencial Colón		(Quito, Guayaquil)
		5 Trans Otavalo
		(Otavalo)
		6 To Valle del Chota
		(San Lorenzo)

Excursions Off the main road between Otavalo and Ibarra is **San Antonio de Ibarra**, well known for its wood carvings. Bargaining is difficult. It is worth seeing the range of styles and techniques and shopping around in the galleries and workshops. Buses leave from Ibarra, 13 km, 10 minutes.

About 10 km from Ibarra is **La Esperanza**, a pretty village in beautiful surroundings. Ask in town for makers of fine clothes and embroidery. You can climb **Cubilche** volcano in three hours from La Esperanza for beautiful views. From the top you can walk down to Lago de San Pablo (see page 935), another three hours. F *Casa Aída*, with bath, hot water, Aída speaks some English and cooks good vegetarian food, recommended. Sr Orlando Guzmán is recommended for Spanish classes. Next door is F *Café María*, basic rooms, will heat water, helpful, use of kitchen, laundry facilities. ■ *The bus from Parque Germán Grijalva in Ibarra passes the hotels, US$0.30, 30 mins; taxi from Ibarra, US$6.*

Sleeping

The better class hotels tend to be fully booked during holidays and at weekends

Along the Pan-American Highway south towards Otavalo are several country inns, some in converted haciendas. **From south to north are L** *Vista del Mundo*, Panamericana at Pinsaquí toll, halfway between Otavalo and Ibarra, T946333, www.thegoldenspa.com Includes dinner, elegant expensive restaurant. Luxury hotel, spa ($85 pp), and convention centre, built around the theme of world peace. Unusual and interesting. **B** *Natabuela*, Panamericana Sur Km 8, T932032, sproano@andinanet.net Restaurant, covered pool, sauna, comfortable rooms. **B** *Chorlaví*, Panamericana S Km 4, T932222, chorlavi@imbanet.net Includes breakfast, expensive restaurant with excellent parillada, pool, in an old hacienda. Popular, busy on weekends. Folk music and crafts on Sun. **C** *San Agustín*, Panamericana Sur Km 2, T955888. Restaurant, good service, good food.

Note the 3 Madrids, they are quite different from one another

In town B *Ajaví*, Av Mariano Acosta 16-38 y Circunvalación, T955221, F952485. Restaurant, pool, along main road into town from south. **B** *El Prado*, in Barrio El Olivo, off the Pan-American at Km 1, T/F959570. Includes breakfast, restaurant, pool, luxurious, set in fruit orchards. **C** *Montecarlo*, Av Jaime Rivadeneira 5-61 y Oviedo, T958266, F958182. Restaurant, heated pool open weekends only, a better class hotel near bus stations. **D** *Hostal Madrid*, Olmedo 8-69 y Moncayo, T644918, F955301. Parking, modern and comfortable. Recommended. **D** *Hotel Madrid*, Moncayo 7-41 y Olmedo, T959017, F950796. Comfortable. **E** *El Retorno*, Pasaje Pedro Moncayo 4-32 entre Sucre y Rocafuerte, T957722. Restaurant, cheaper without bath, nice views from terrace. Recommended. **E** *Imbabura*, Oviedo 9-33 y Narváez, T950155, hotel_imbabura@hotmail.com Nice colonial building with patio, large simple rooms, stores luggage, good value, small private museum. Highly recommended. **E** *Res Madrid*, Oviedo 85-7 y Olmedo, T951760. Simple. **E** *Vaca*, Bolívar 7-53 y Moncayo, T955844. Older but well cared-for. **E-F** *Colón*, Narváez 8-62, T958695. Cheaper without bath, basic, stores luggage. Several others along Olmedo.

Eating *El Chagra*, Olmedo 7-44. *Platos típicos*, good trout, reasonable prices. Recommended. There are many restaurants on Olmedo between Flores and Oviedo: eg *El Cedrón*, No 7-45, set meals. Breakfast with good bread at *Café Pushkin*, No 7-75, opens 0730. *Chifa Nueva*, No 7-20, OK. *Chifa Muy Bueno*, No 7-23, does a good *chaulafan*. *Mr Peter's*, Sucre 5-36, opposite Parque Pedro Moncayo. Good pizza, wide choice, good service, nice atmosphere, open 1100-2200. *Casa Blanca*, Bolívar 7-83. Excellent, family-run, seating around a colonial patio with fountain, delicious food, cheap. Warmly recommended. *Mesón Colonial*, Rocafuerte 5-53, at Parque Abdón Calderón. Good food and service. Recommended. *Café Floralp*, García Moreno 4-30 y Sucre.Crêpes, fondue, good breakfast, bread, own cheese factory, yoghurt, excellent coffee, Chilean wines, open 0700-2100. Swiss-owned, warmly recommended. *Pizza El Horno*, Rocafuerte 6-38 y Flores. Good pizzas and Italian dishes, live music Sat night, closed Mon.

There are several excellent *heladerías*, including: *La Bermejita*, Olmedo 7-15. Directly opposite is *Hielo y Dulce*, Olmedo 7-08. Also *Heladería Rosalía Suárez*, Oviedo y Olmedo (over 100 years old), excellent home made *helados de paila* (fruit sherbets made in large copper basins), try *mora* or *guanábana* (soursop) flavours, an Ibarra tradition. Highly recommended.

Ecuador

Nightlife Piano bar, *El Encuentro*, Olmedo 9-59. Interesting drinks, very popular, pleasant atmosphere, unusual décor. *El Zarape*, on Circunvalacíon. *Peña* and Mexican restaurant. *Tijuana Bar*, Oviedo y Sucre. Discos include *Sambuca*, Oviedo y Olmedo and *Studio 54* at Laguna Yaguarcocha.

Entertainment

Supermarkets *Supermaxi*, south of the centre on road to Otavalo. *Supermercado Universal*, Cifuentes y Velasco. *Akí*, Bolívar y Colón.

Shopping

Paddle ball A unique form of paddle ball is played on Sat and Sun near the railway station and other parts of town; ask around for details. The players have huge spiked paddles for striking the 1 kg ball. *Balneario Primavera*, Sánchez y Cifuentes 3-33, T957425, heated pool, Turkish bath, also offers aerobics classes and remedial massage. **Paragliding** *Rainbow Tours*, T600678, courses and equipment rental.

Sport

Delgado Travel, Moncayo y Bolívar, T/F640900. Excellent service. *Metropolitan Touring*, Flores 5-76 y Sucre, see Quito.*Nevitur Cia Ltda*, Bolívar 7-35 y Oviedo, T958701, F640040. Excellent travel guides, van trips throughout the country and the Pasto region of Colombia. *Turismo Intipungo*, Rocafuerte 6-08 y Flores, T955270. Regional tours.

Tour operators

Bus Companies leave from their own terminals near the train station and obelisk: *Andina/Aerotaxi*, for **Quito** and **Guayaquil**, **Borja** and **Velasco**; *Expreso Turismo* and others, for **Quito** and **Tulcán**, **Moncayo** and **Flores**; *Trans Otavalo*, Av Vacas Galindo cuadra 3 (beside the railway track). *Valle del Chota*, Colón near the obelisk, for **San Lorenzo**. *Espejo*, Perez Guerrero y Cabezas, for **El Angel**. **CITA**, Flores y Velasco, for **Ambato** (bypassing Quito). To/from **Quito** 2½ hrs, US$2, about 50 departures a day; shared taxis (*Supertaxis Los Lagos*, Flores y Sánchez Cifuentes; in Quito, Asunción 3-81, T256 5992) for US$6. To **Tulcán**, US$2, 2½ hrs. To **Ambato**, US$4, 5 hrs. To **Otavalo**, US$0.32, 40 mins. To **Cotacachi** (US$0.35, 45 mins) some continue to **Quiroga**. For San Lorenzo, see below.

Transport
Watch your belongings in the area around the bus terminals

Banks Several banks on Olmedo have ATMs. *Banco del Pacífico*, Moncayo y Olmedo, TCs, US$5 comission. *Banco del Austro*, Colón 7-51. *Banco del Pichincha*, Bolívar y Mosquera. **Communications** Internet: prices around US$1 per hr, several places in the centre of town. Post Office: Flores opposite Parque Pedro Moncayo, 2nd floor. **Telephone:** Sucre 4-56, just past Parque Pedro Moncayo, open 0800. **Language courses** *Centro Ecuatoriano Canadiense de Idomas (CECI)*, Pérez Guerrero 6-12 y Bolívar, T951911, US$3 per hr. *CIMA*, Obelisco Casa No 2, p 2, US$1 per hr. **Medical services** Clínica Médica del Norte, Oviedo 8-24, open 24 hrs.

Directory

The spectacular train ride from Ibarra to San Lorenzo on the Pacific coast no longer operates, but an *autoferro* (motorized rail-car) runs for 1½ hours out of Ibarra to **Tulquizán**, an interesting excursion through nice scenery (US$12 return), T955050. Departures Mon-Fri 0700, Sat-Sun 0800, minimum 2 passengers. From Tulquizán (**C** *Hostería Tulquizán*), across the river. Full board, pool, Ibarra T641989.) you can continue by bus to San Lorenzo.

Twenty-four kilometres north of Ibarra is the turnoff west for Salinas and the very scenic paved road down to San Lorenzo on the Pacific coast; 15 minutes beyond Salinas is Tulquizán (see above), further ahead is **Guallupe** (**D** *Bospas Farm*, 800 m from the village, bospas22@hotmail.com full board, volunteer opportunities on experimental organic farm; **E** *Marttyzu*, pool, restaurant; **E** *El Limonal*, T648688) with an immense variety of wildlife in the surrounding tropical forest. In **Lita**, 20 km from Guallupe, there is an adequate *residencia* (**F**) and several restaurants about 1 km uphill from the train station. The remaining 93 km through a scenic area are prone to landslides during the rainy season.

Ibarra to the coast

Safety: armed holdups of vehicles travelling to San Lorenzo occurred in early 2002. Enquire locally before undertaking this journey

Bus to **Lita** 8 daily (US$2, 2 hours) with *Coop Valle de Chota*, 4 of these continue to **San Lorenzo** (US$4, 4 hours); additional departures with several other companies.

Beware of thieves on buses

Ecuador

North to Colombia

The Pan-American highway goes past Laguna Yahuarcocha (with a few hotels and restaurants) and then descends to the hot dry Chota valley. Beyond the turnoff for Salinas and San Lorenzo, 30 km from Ibarra, is a police checkpoint at Mascarilla (have your documents at hand), after which the highway divides.

The western route to the border

One branch follows an older route through Mira and El Angel to Tulcán on the Colombian border. This road is paved and in good condition as far as El Angel, but deteriorates rapidly thereafter and is impassable beyond Laguna El Voladero.

El Angel

Population: 5,700
Altitude: 3,000 m

Along the old Panamericana is El Angel, with a Monday market. The main plaza retains a few trees sculpted by José Franco (see Tulcán Cemetery, below). **B** *Hostería El Angel*, at entrance to village, T/F977584, www.ecuador-sommerfer.com Includes breakfast, meals available on request, caters to groups, reservations required, contact Quito T/F222 1480. Offers trips into reserve (see below). **E** *Asadero Los Faroles*, José Grijalva 5-96 on the plaza, T977144. Above OK restaurant, simple rooms in family home. ■ *Buses:* Trans Espejo, *hourly to Quito via Ibarra, US$3, 4 hrs (US$1.10, 1½ hrs to/from Ibarra); to Tulcán at 0730 daily, US$1.20.* Trans Mira, *hourly to Mira and Tulcán.*

The **Reserva Ecológica El Angel** nearby protects 15,715 ha of *páramo* ranging in altitude from 3,400 to 4,150 m, the reserve contains large stands of the velvet-leaved *frailejón* plant, also found in the Andes of Colombia and Venezuela. Also of interest are the spiny *achupallas* with giant compound flowers. The fauna includes *curiquingues* (birds of prey), deer, foxes, and a few condors. There are several small lakes scattered throughout the reserve. It can be very muddy during the rainy season and the best time to visit is May to August. ■ *US$10 for foreigners. The reserve's office in El Angel is at the Municipio, T/F977597, information and pamphlets are available.*

From El Angel follow the poor road north towards Tulcán for 16 km to **El Voladero** ranger station, where a self-guided trail climbs over a low ridge (30 mins' walk) to two crystal clear lakes. Camping is possible here, but you must be self-sufficient and take great care not to damage the fragile surroundings. Pickups or taxis can be hired in the main plaza of El Angel for a day trip to El Voladero, US$15 return with short wait. A longer route follows an equally poor road to Cerro Socabones, beginning in the town of **La Libertad**, 3½ km north of El Angel. This route climbs gradually to reach the high *páramo* at the centre of the reserve and, in 1 hour, the **El Salado** ranger station. Another hour ahead is **Socabones**, from where you can trek or take pack animals to the village of **Morán** (the local guide Hugo Quintanchala can take you further through the valley). There are many paths criss-crossing the *páramo* and it is easy to get lost. *Hostería El Angel* (see above) have the **AL** pp *Cotinga Lodge* in Morán, at 2,500 m, simple, comfortable rooms, meals included. Transport from El Angel to Cerro Socabones, US$25 return, a helpful driver is *Sr Calderón*, T977274. A third access to the reserve, from the north along the Tufiño-Maldonado road, is not recommended because of its proximity to the Colombian border (see Tulcán Safety, below).

The eastern route to the border

The second branch (the modern Pan-American Highway), in good repair but with many heavy lorries, runs east through the warm Chota valley to Juncal, before turning north to reach Tulcán via Bolívar and San Gabriel. West of **Juncal** are several tourist complexes with accommodations (**AL-D** ranges), restaurants, swimming, horse riding; popular with Colombian and Ecuadorean tourists. A good paved road runs between Bolívar and El Angel, connecting the two branches.

Population: 15,175

Bolívar is a neat little town where the houses and the interior of its church are painted in lively pastel colours. There is a Friday market, a basic hotel (**G**) one block north of the plaza and a restaurant by the highway.

Ecuador

Five kilometres north of Bolívar is the turnoff east for the town of **La Paz**, from which a steep but good cobbled road descends for 5 km to the **Gruta de La Paz**. Views along the road are breathtaking, including two spectacular waterfalls. The place is also called *Rumichaca* (Quichua for stone bridge) after the massive natural bridge which forms the *gruta* (grotto); not to be confused with the Rumichaca on the Colombian border. The area is a religious shrine, receiving large numbers of pilgrims during Holy Week, Christmas, and especially around 8 July, feast day of the Virgin of La Paz. There are thermal baths nearby.

Transport Excursions to La Paz from Tulcán on Sat and Sun. Also vans from San Gabriel, US$0.60 pp (20 mins) at weekends; US$6 to hire a vehicle during the week. A second access road starts 3 km south of San Gabriel along the Panamericana.

Some 10 km north of La Paz is **San Gabriel**, an important commercial centre. There are hotels (**D-F**) and restaurants. The spectacular 60 m high **Paluz** waterfall is 4 km north San Gabriel, beyond a smaller waterfall. Follow C Bolívar out of the main plaza and turn right after the bridge, or take a taxi (US$5). ■ *From San Gabriel, buses to Quito, US$3, 4 hrs; vans to Tulcán US$0.60, shared taxis US$0.80 pp. Jeeps for outlying villages leave from main plaza when full.*

Population: 19,500

East of San Gabriel by 20 km is the tiny community of **Mariscal Sucre**, also known as Colonia Huaquenia, the gateway to the **Guandera Cloudforest Reserve**, where you can see bromeliads, orchids, toucans and other wildlife in temperate forest and *frailejón páramo*. There is a lodge (Epp), take warm clothes as it gets very cold. The reserve is part of the **Fundación Jatun Sacha**. Reservations should be made at the office in Quito; Pasaje Eugenio de Santillán N34-248, T243 2246, F245 3583, www.jatunsacha.org ■ *From San Gabriel, take a taxi to Mariscal Sucre, US$15, or one of the 'blue patrols' which leave from the plaza if there are enough people, US$0.50. It is ½ hr walk to the reserve from there.*

Tulcán

A commercial centre and capital of the province of Carchi, Tulcán is always chilly. To the east of the city is a bypass road going directly to the Colombian border. There is a great deal of informal trade here with Colombia, a textile and dry goods fair takes place on Thursday and Sunday. The old and new branches of the Panamericana join at Las Juntas, 2 km south of the city.

Phone code: 06
Colour map 1a, grid A4
Population: 37,069
Altitude: 2,960 m

In the cemetery, two blocks from Parque Ayora, the art of topiary is taken to beautiful extremes. Cypress bushes are trimmed into archways, fantastic figures and geometric shapes in *haut* and *bas* relief. To see the various stages of this art form, go to the back of the cemetery where young bushes are being pruned. The artistry, started in 1936, is that of the late Sr José Franco, born in El Angel (see above), now buried among the splendour he created. The tradition is carried on by his sons.

Tourist office *Unidad de Turismo*, at the Municipio, Olmedo y Ayacucho opposite de Plaza de Independencia, helpful, Spanish only, open Mon-Fri 0800-1300, 1500-1800. **Safety** It's not a good idea to wander about after 2200. The area around the bus terminal is unsafe. Tulcán and the traditionally tranquil border province of Carchi have seen an increase in tension due to the *guerrilla* conflict in neighbouring Colombia. Do not travel outside town (except along the Panamerican highway) without advance local inquiry.

C *Machado*, Bolívar y Ayacucho, T984221, F980099. Includes breakfast, comfortable. **C** *Sara Espíndola*, Sucre y Ayacucho, on plaza, T985925, F986209. Nice restaurant, comfortable rooms, helpful staff, best in town. **D** *Lumar*, Sucre y Rocafuerte, T980402. Modern, comfortable. **D** *Park Hotel*, Across from bus station, T987325. Restaurant, parking, new in 2002, modern, small rooms, traffic noise all night. **D** *Rossy*, Sucre y Chimborazo, north of centre, T987649. Restaurant, new in 2001, simple, modern. **D** *Torres de Oro*, Sucre y Rocafuerte,

Sleeping
Many hotels are located on C Sucre

Ecuador

T980296. Includes breakfast, restaurant, parking, modern, nice. **E** *Frailejón*, Sucre y Rocafuerte, T981129. Restaurant, parking, OK. **E** *Los Alpes*, JR Arellano next to bus station, T982235. Restaurant, OK, good value. **E** *Sáenz Internacional*, Sucre y Rocafuerte, T981916, F983925. Very nice, modern, good value. Recommended. **E-F** *Florida*, Sucre y 10 de Agosto, T983849. Cheaper without bath, modern section at back, good value. **F** *Colombia*, Colón 52-017 y Ayacucho, T982761. Shared bath, hot water, parking, simple.

Eating Upscale restaurant at *Hotel Sara Esíndola*. *Mama Rosita*, Sucre y Atahualpa, typical Ecuadorean dishes. Colombian specialities at *El Patio*, on Bolívar 50-050 y 10 de Agosto and *La Fonda Paisa*, Bolívar 50-032 y Pichincha.Chinese at: *Casa China*, at the bus terminal, and several along Sucre. *Los Leños*, Olmedo y Ayacucho. Set meals and à la carte. *Café Tulcán*, Sucre 52-029 y Ayacucho. Café, snacks, desserts, juices. There are many broiled chicken places in town.

Transport **Air** *TAME* (Sucre y Ayacucho, T980675) flies Mon, Wed and Fri to **Quito** (US$32) and to **Cali** in Colombia (US$78). **Bus** The bus terminal is 1½ km uphill from centre; best to take a taxi, US$1, or a bus. To **Quito**, US$4, 5 hrs, every 15 mins. To **Ibarra**, 2½ hrs, US$2. **Otavalo**, US$2.50, 3 hrs (make sure the bus is going to Otavalo; if not get out on the Highway at the turnoff), or transfer in Ibarra. To **Guayaquil**, 20 a day, 11 hrs, US$10. To **Huaquillas**, with *Panamericana Internacional*, 1 luxury coach a day, 16-18 hrs, US$15; US$14 with *Pullman Carchi*.

Directory **Banks** *Banco del Pichincha*, at Plaza de la Independencia, Visa cash advances. *Banco del Austro*, Bolívar y Ayacucho, for Visa. Few places accept credit cards. Nowhere in Tulcán to chance TCs. Pesos Colombianos can easily be changed on Plaza de la Independencia. **Colombian Consulate**: Bolívar y Junín, visas require up to 20 days, Mon-Fri 0800-1300, 1430-1530. **Communications** Internet: prices around US$3 per hr, 1 by terminal and a couple near the Plaza de la Independencia. **Post Office**: Bolívar 53-27. **Telephone**: Olmedo y Junín and at terminal.

Border with Colombia
Money changers on both sides of the border will exchange cash Pesos for US$

The border is open 24 hrs, and is well organized. There is an *Andinatel* office for phone calls, a tourist information office with maps and general information (Mon-Fri 0830-1700) and a snack bar. Try to ask for 90 days on entering Ecuador if you need them, although you will most likely only be given 30. See page 874 for Colombian immigration.

Transport City buses run from the terminal to Parque Ayora, watch your luggage. Vans Tulcán-border leave when full from Parque Ayora (near the cemetery) US$0.60pp, shared taxi US$0.70 pp, private taxi US$3.50. **NB** These vehicles cross the international bridge and drop you off on the Colombian side, where Colombian transport waits. Remember to cross back over the bridge for Ecuadorean immigration.

The Central Sierra

South from Quito is some of the loveliest mountain scenery in Ecuador. Colourful Indian markets and colonial towns nestle among volcanic cones over 5,000 m high.

In a valley between the summits of Pasochoa, Rumiñahui and Corazón, lies the town of **Machachi,** famous for its mineral water springs and cold, crystal clear swimming pool (open 0800-1530 daily, US$0.25). The water, 'Agua Güitig', is bottled in a plant 4 km from the town and sold throughout the country (free tours 0800-1200, take identification). Machachi is in the middle of an important dairy area; annual highland 'rodeo', El Chagra, third week in July. ■ *Bus to Quito, 1 hr, US$0.45; from Quito buses leave from El Recreo, 2-3 blocks before the Trole station of that name. Taxi: to Cotopaxi, US$30 per car.*

Machachi
Phone code: 02
Altitude: 2,900 m

Sleeping and eating Out of town D *Hostal Casa Nieves*, 500 m west of the Panamericana, T231 5092. Once the home of the Marqués de Solanda, now owned by descendants of Simón Bolívar, interesting house hastily converted, somewhat overpriced. **D** *La Estación de Machachi*, 1½km west of the Panamericana, in Aloasí, T230 9246. Beautiful, family-run, fireplaces, access to Volcán Corazón. **D** *Tambo Chisinche*, 200 m east of the Panamericana, entrance 5½ km south of Machachi, T315041. Small sign, horse riding on Rumiñahui, spartan but clean, shared bath, hot water, including breakfast. *Café de la Vaca*, 4 km south of town on the Panamericana. Very good meals using produce from own farm, open Wed-Sun. **In town** E *La Estancia Real*, Luis Cordero y Panzaleo, 3 blocks east of park, T231 5760. Bath, hot water, parking, cheaper in old section. **F** *Miravalle*, Luis Cordero y Barriga, east of centre, T231 5222. Shared bath, parking, basic. *El Pedregal*, Colón 4-66, 1 block from park. Roast chicken, good. *El Chagra*, good typical food, reasonably priced, take the road that passes in front of the church, on the right-hand side, about 5 km from church.

Machachi (see map Northern Ecuador) is a good starting point for a visit to the northern section of the **Reserva Ecológica Los Ilinizas** (entry US$5). It takes 3-4 hours to walk with a full pack from 'La Virgen' to the *refugio*, a shelter below the saddle between the two peaks, at 4,750 m, with beds for 12 and cooking facilities, take a mat and sleeping bag, US$10 per night; pay at *Hacienda San José* (see below) and ask if a key is needed. Transport to refuge US$15 per truck. Iliniza Norte (5,105 m) can be climbed without technical equipment in the dry season but a few exposed, rocky sections require utmost caution, allow 2-4 hours for the ascent from the refuge, take a compass, it's easy to mistake the descent. Iliniza Sur (5,245 m) is a four-hour ice climb: full climbing gear and experience are absolutely necessary. ■ *Access to the reserve is through a turnoff west of the Panamericana 6 km south of Machachi, from where it is 7 km to the village of El Chaupi. A very badly rutted dirt road continues from here to 'La Virgen' (statue) about 9 km beyond. Nearby are woods where you can camp.*

Sleeping D *Hacienda San José del Chaupi*, 3 km southwest of El Chaupi, T09-971 3986, or T02-289 1547 (Rodrigo). Converted farm house and cabins, including breakfast, shared bath, hot water, meals available if requested in advance, kitchen facilities, horse riding. **G** pp *Hacienda Nieves*, T231 5092, 2½ km from El Chaupi on the way to los Ilinizas. Cabin for 6, kitchenette, electric shower, fireplace, horse riding. **G** pp Rooms to rent owned by the store on the main plaza in El Chaupi. New, family atmposphere, very hospitable.

Transport A pick-up truck to the 'Virgen' is about US$20. Bus from Machachi to El Chaupi every 30 mins, from Av Amazonas opposite the market, US$0.25. Horses can be hired at *Hacienda San José* or *Hacienda Nieves*.

Ecuador

Parque Nacional Cotopaxi

Colour map 1a, grid B4 Cotopaxi volcano (5,897 m) is at the heart of a much-visited national park. This scenic snow-covered perfect cone is the second highest peak in Ecuador and a very popular climbing destination. Cotopaxi is an active volcano, one of the highest in the world, and its most recent eruption took place in 1904. The National Geophysics Institute monitors this and other active volcanos, and a slight increase in activity was recorded at the end of 2001; up to date information is available at www.epn.edu.ec Volcanic material from former eruptions can be seen strewn about the páramo surrounding Cotopaxi; here is a high plateau with a small lake (Laguna Limpio Pungo), a lovely area for walking and admiring the delicate flora, and fauna including wild horses and native bird species such as the Andean Lapwing and the Chimborazo Hillstar hummingbird. The lower slopes are clad in planted pine forests, where llamas may be seen. ■ *The park administration and a small museum (0800-1200, 1400-1600) are located 10 km from the park gates, just before Limpio Pungo. The museum has a 3D model of the park and stuffed animals. Visitors to the park must register at the main entrance. Entrance fee: US$10. Park gates are open 0700-1500, although you can stay until 1800.*

Climbing Cotopaxi
A full moon is both practical and a magical experience. Check out snow conditions with the guardian of the refuge before climbing

The ascent from the refuge takes 5-8 hours, start climbing at 0100 as the snow deteriorates in the sun. Equipment and experience are required. Take a guide if you're inexperienced on ice and snow. The best season is December-April. There are strong winds and clouds in August–December but the ascent is still possible for experienced mountaineers. Climbing guides can be hired through operators in Quito, Latacunga, Riobamba and Baños. Just north of Cotopaxi are the peaks of Sincholahua (4,893 m), Rumiñahui (4,712 m) and Pasochoa (4,225 m). To the southeast is Qulindaña (4,878 m).

Sleeping
All these inns are good for acclimatization at altitudes between 3,100 and 3,800 m

There are 2 very run down *cabañas* and a couple of campsites below Limpio Pungo (US$5 per tent, no facilities). The José Ribas refuge has a kitchen, water, and 30 bunks with mattresses; US$17 pp per night, bring sleeping bag and mat, also padlock for your excess luggage when you climb, or use the lockable luggage deposit, US$2.50. New refuge under construction in 2002. **Outside the park LL** *Hacienda San Agustín de Callo*, entrance from the Panamericana 1.6 km north of the main park access, marked by a painted stone, 10 min ride from the highway, T03-719160, www.incahacienda.com Some rooms in ancient Inca structure, with fireplaces, bathtub, breakfast and dinner included, horse and bicycle hire. To the southeast of the park lies an area of rugged *páramos* and mountains dropping down to the jungle. The area has several large *haciendas* which form the Fundación Páramo, a private reserve with restricted access. Here is **L** *Hacienda Yanahurco*, Quito T224 1593, F244 5016, www.yanahurco.com Ranch-style rooms, fireplace or heater, meals, tours, yearly rodeo in Nov. **B** *Volcanoland*, between El Pedregal and the northern access to the park, www.volcanoland.com includes breakfast. Transport from Quito and complete packages available at extra cost. **B** *Albergue Cuello de Luna*, El Chasqui, Panamericana Sur Km 65, 1 km west of highway opposite national park entrance, at 3,125 m, T/F09-970 0330. Including breakfast, restored *hacienda*, restaurant, transport, tours. **B** *Tambopaxi*, Within the park at 3,750 m, 3 km south of the northern entrance (1 hour drive from Machachi) or 4 km north (left) of the turnoff for the climbing shelter, Quito T222 4241, www.tambopaxi.com Rooms with several beds, duvet blankets, shared bath with hot shower, good restaurant with set meals and Swiss specialties, llama trekking, camping US$5 pp.

Access & transport

Road There is an entrance to the Parque Nacional Cotopaxi 16 km south of Machachi, near a sign for the Clirsen satellite tracking station, which cannot be visited. This route goes past Clirsen then via **Area Nacional de Recreación El Boliche** (entry US$10) for over 30 km along a signposted dirt road, through the national park gates, past Laguna Limpio Pungo to a fork, where the right branch climbs steeply to a parking lot (4,600 m). From here it is 30 mins to 1 hr on foot to the José Ribas refuge, at 4,800 m; beware of altitude sickness. **A**

second entrance, the main one, about 9 km further south, 6 km north of Lasso, is marked by a small Parque Nacional Cotopaxi sign. It is about 36 km from here, through the main park gates, to the refuge. Nearly 1 km from the highway, turn left at a T junction and a few hundred metres later turn sharp right. Beyond this the road is either signed or you take the main fork. It is shorter and easier to follow than the 1st route which you join just at the Park gates. Walking from the highway to the refuge may exhaust you for the climb to the summit.

The third entrance, from the north, is recommended for **cyclists,** because the route from the west is too soft to climb on a bike. Access is from Machachi via Santa Ana del Pedregal. For more details, and equipment, ask Jan But, 'The Biking Dutchman' (see Quito Sport) or *South American Explorers* in Quito.

Bus Take a Quito-Latacunga bus and get off at **Lasso** (see below). Do not take an express bus as you cannot get off before Latacunga. A truck from Lasso to the parking lot below the *refugio* costs US$20 for 4 people, one-way, no bargaining. If you do not arrange a truck for the return you can sometimes get a cheaper ride down in a truck which has just dropped off another party. Alternatively, get off the bus at the main entrance where there is often a truck waiting (US$20) or hitchhike into the park from there. This is usually possible at weekends. Trucks and a jeep are available from Latacunga for about US$30 round trip.

Lasso

The railway and the Pan-American Highway cross one another at Lasso, a small town, 33 km south of Alóag, with a milk bottling plant and some simple eateries. In the surrounding countryside are several *hosterías*, converted country estates offering accommodation and meals. Along the Panamericana are *paradores* or roadside restaurants.

Sleeping and eating B *Hostería La Ciénega*, 2 km south of Lasso, west of the Panamericana, T719052, hcienega@uio.satnet.net An historic *hacienda* with nice gardens, an avenue of massive eucalyptus trees, nice rooms with heater, good expensive restaurant, horse-riding US$2 hr, camioneta from here to refuge parking area on Cotopaxi, US$35. Opposite is **C** *Posada del Rey*, T719319. Carpeted rooms, restaurant with choice of 3 set meals, covered pool, clean but a bit characterless and overpriced. **C** *San Mateo*, 4 km south of Lasso west of the Panamericana, T/F719471, san_mateo@yahoo.com Bright rooms, pricey restaurant, horse riding included, small but nice, adjoining working *hacienda* can be visited. **E** *Cabañas Los Volcanes*, at the south end of Lasso, T719524. Nice rooms with shared bath, hot water, transport to mountains, new in 2001. Along the Panamericana *Parador La Avelina*, 5 km south of Lasso, known for its cheese and ice cream. Opposite is *Parador Chalupas*, similar cafetería.

Latacunga

The capital of Cotopaxi Province is a place where the abundance of light grey pumice has been artfully employed. Volcán Cotopaxi is much in evidence, though it is 29 km away. Provided they are not hidden in the clouds, which unfortunately is all too often, as many as nine volcanic cones can be seen from Latacunga; try early in the morning. The colonial character of the town has been well preserved. The central plaza, **Parque Vicente León**, is a beautifully maintained garden (locked at night). There are several other gardens in the town including **Parque San Francisco** and **Lago Flores**.

Phone code: 03
Colour map 1a, grid B3
Population: 39,882
Altitude: 2,800 m
Street numbering system is being changed, many houses have two numbers

Casa de los Marqueses de Miraflores, Sánchez de Orellana y Abel Echeverría, in a restored colonial mansion has a modest museum, with exhibits on Mama Negra (see below), colonial art, archaeology, numismatics and a library (free).

Casa de la Cultura, Antonia Vela 3-49 y Padre Salcedo, T813247, built around the remains of a Jesuit Monastery and the old Monserrat watermill, houses an excellent museum with precolumbian ceramics, weavings, costumes and models of festival masks; also art gallery, library and theatre. ■ *Tue-Fri 0800-1200, 1400-1800, US$0.20*. It has week long festivals with exhibits and concerts for all for the local festivities. **Escuela Isidro Ayora**, Sánchez de Orellana y Tarqui, and the **Cathedral** both have museums.

Ecuador

There is a Saturday **market** on the Plaza de San Sebastián (at Juan Abel Echeverría). Goods for sale include *shigras* (fine stitched, colourful straw bags) and homespun wool and cotton yarn. The produce market, Plaza El Salto has daily trading and larger fairs on Tuesday and Saturday.

Sleeping **D** *Rodelú*, Quito 16-31, T80, rodelu@uio.telconet.net Includes breakfast, excellent restaurant, parking, comfortable. Recommended. **D** *Rosim*, Quito 16-49 y Padre Salcedo, T802172, F801517. Restaurant, parking, carpeted rooms, quiet, comfortable. **E** *Cotopaxi*, Padre Salcedo 5-61 on Parque Vicente León, T801310. Cafetería, hot water after 0700, rooms with view over plaza are noisy at weekends. **E** *Estambul*, Belisario Quevedo 6-46 y Padre Salcedo, T800354. Cheaper without bath, luggage store, tours. Recommended. **E** *Los Nevados*, Av 5 de Junio 53-19 y Eloy Alfaro, near bus terminal, T800407. Restaurant, cheaper without bath, parking, modern, spacious rooms. **E** *Santiago*, 2 de Mayo y Guayaquil, T802164. Cheaper without bath, comfortable, good value. **E** *Tilipulo*, Guayaquil y Belisario Quevedo, T810611. Restaurant, parking, cafetería, comfortable, very helpful. Recommended. **F** *El Salto*, Valencia 4-49, T803578. Restaurant, cheaper without bath, warm showers, small rooms, very basic, noisy. **F** *Jaqueline*, Antonia Vela 9-34, T801033. Hot water, basic.

Eating
Few places open on Sun

The local speciality is chugchucaras, porkskins served with corn, fried plantain, popcorn and small pieces of roast pork

Los Copihues, Quito 14-25 y Tarqui. International menu, 4 course set lunch, good generous portions, popular with businessmen, open until 2200. Recommended. *El Mashca*, Valencia 41-54. Chicken, cheap and good value, open until 2200 including Sun. Recommended. *Chifa China*, Antonia Vela 6-85 y 5 de Junio. Chinese, large portions, open daily to 2130. *Chifa Fortuna*, Antonia Vela 6-91. Chinese, open daily 1000-2230. *Pizzería Buon Giorno* Sánchez de Orellana y General Maldonado, opposite the main park. Great pizzas and lasagne, huge selection. *Pizzería Los Sabores de Italia*, Padre Salcedo, opposite the main park. Good pizza and Italian dishes, open daily 1300-2300. *Cafetería El Pasaje*, Padre Salcedo 4-50, on pedestrian mall. Snacks, burgers, coffee, closed Sun. *Valería*, Guayaquil 44-77 entre Quevedo y 2 de Mayo. Good *panadería y pastelería*. *Beer Center*, Sánchez de Orellana 74-20. Good atmosphere, bar and disco. For *chugchucaras*: *Rosita*, Panamericana 3 blocks north of main traffic lights. *La Pastorita*, Quijano y Ordoñez 1416 y Marquez de Maenza. Also try *allullas con queso de hoja*, biscuits with string cheese.

Latacunga

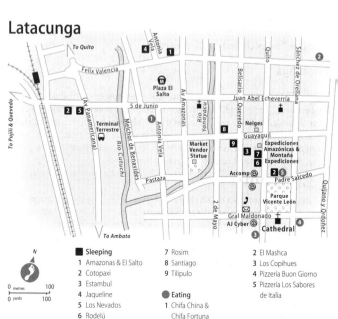

■ **Sleeping**	**7** Rosim
1 Amazonas & El Salto	**8** Santiago
2 Cotopaxi	**9** Tilipulo
3 Estambul	
4 Jaqueline	● **Eating**
5 Los Nevados	**1** Chifa China &
6 Rodelú	Chifa Fortuna
2 El Mashca	
3 Los Copihues	
4 Pizzería Buon Giorno	
5 Pizzería Los Sabores	
de Italia	

Ecuador

The *Fiesta de la Mama Negra* is held on **24 Sep**, in homage to *the Virgen de las Mercedes*. It celebrates the black slaves brought by the Spanish to work on the plantations. The civic festival of *Mama Negra* is on the **first Sun in Nov**.

Festivals

All operators and some hotels offer day trips to Cotopaxi (US$30 pp, includes park entrance fee and lunch) and Quilotoa (US$25 pp, includes lunch and a visit to a market town if on Thu or Sat); prices for 3 or more people. Climbing trips to Cotopaxi are US$125 pp for 2 days (includes equipment, park entrance fee, meals, refuge fees), minimum 2 people. Trekking trips to Cotopaxi, Ilinizas, etc US$30 pp, per day. *Estambul Tours*, at *Hotel Estambul*, T800354. Fausto Batallas, pleasant and knowledgeable. *Metropolitan Touring*, Guayaquil y Quito, T802985. Makes airline reservations. *Neiges*, Guayaquil 5-19 y Quito, T/F811199, neigestours@hotmail.com Guillermo Berrazueta, knowledgeable. *Panzaleo Tour*, Quito 1632 y Pa Salcedo, T800302, panzaleo_tour@hotmail.com *Ruta de los Volcanes*, Quito y Pa Salcedo, opposite main park, T812452, tour to Cotopaxi follows a secondary road through interesting country, instead of the Panamericana. *Tovar Expediciones*, Guayaquil 5-38 y Quito, T813080, Fernando Tovar.

Tour operators

Road Bus: Bus terminal on the Panamericana just south of 5 de Junio; has a **tourist information** office, open 0900-1800, helpful. To **Quito**, every 15 mins, 2 hrs, US$1.80. To **Ambato**, 30 mins, US$0.75. To **Guayaquil**, US$5, 6 hrs. To **Saquisilí**, every 20 mins (see below). To **Quevedo**, every 30 mins, US$3.50. Buses on the Zumbahua, Quilotoa, Chugchilán, Sigchos circuit are given below.

Transport
On Thu many buses to nearby communities leave from Saquisilí market instead of Latacunga

Banks *Banco de Guayaquil*, Maldonado, east of plaza. Nowhere to change TCs. **Communications Internet:** prices around US$1.50 per hr. Several in town, look along the Padre Salcedo pedestrian mall. **Post Office and Telephone:** both at Belisario Quevedo y Maldonado. **Medical services Hospital:** at southern end of Amazonas y Hnos Páez, good service.

Directory

The Quilotoa Circuit

The popular and recommended round trip from Latacunga to Pujilí, Zumbahua, Quilotoa crater, Chugchilán, Sigchos, Isinliví, Toacazo, Saquisilí, and back to Latacunga can be done in two to three days by bus (times given below are approximate; buses are often late owing to the rough roads). It is 200 km in total.

A fine paved road leads west to **Pujilí** (15 km, bus US$0.30), which has a beautiful church but it is closed most of the time. Good market on Sunday, and a smaller one on Wednesday. Colourful Corpus Christi celebrations. **E-F** *Res Pujilí*, Rocafuerte ½ block from highway, T723649, simple, with bath, restaurant.

Latacunga to Zumbahua

The road goes on over the Western Cordillera to Zumbahua, La Maná and Quevedo. This is a great downhill bike route. It carries very little traffic and is extremely twisty in parts but is one of the most beautiful routes connecting the highlands with the coast. Beyond Zumbahua are the pretty towns of **Pilaló** (two restaurants and petrol pumps), **El Tingo** (two restaurants and lodging at *Carmita's*) and **La Maná** (2½ km beyond La Maná towards Quevedo is **D** *Hostería Las Pirámides*, T03-688003/281, cabins and pyramids, pool, clean, restaurant; east of town is *La Herradura*; more basic hotels are in town).

Zumbahua lies ½ km from the main road, 65 km from Pujilí. It has an interesting Saturday market (starts at 0600) for local produce, not tourist items. Friday nights involve dancing and drinking. Take a windcheater, as it can be windy, cold and dusty. Many interesting crafts are practised by the Indians in the neighbouring valley of Tigua, skin paintings, hand-carved wooden masks and baskets. There is a good hospital in town.

The Saturday trip to Zumbahua market and the Quilotoa crater is one of the best excursions in Ecuador. The walk from Zumbahua to Pujilí, six hours, is also recommended.

Ecuador

Andinatel, T814603
for all enquiries

Sleeping E *Cóndor Matzi*, shared bath, hot water, best place around, reserve ahead, meals US$4. **E** *Richard's*, modern, clean, hot showers. **E** *Res Oro Verde*, first place on the left as you enter town, has small store and restaurant. **F** *Pensión Quilotoa*, grey building at the bottom of the plaza, small sign, hot shower. **F** *Pensión Zumbahua*, at the top of the plaza, many rooms. There are a couple of others in the **E-F** range. You can find a cheap meal in the market. Just below the plaza is a shop selling dairy products and cold drinks.

Transport Bus: Many daily on the Latacunga-Quevedo road (0500-1900, US$1.80). Several buses, starting at 1100, continue up to Laguna Quilotoa, if there are passengers who wish to go, which takes another hour, US$0.50. Buses on Sat are packed full; ride on roof for best views, get your ticket the day before. A pick-up truck can be hired from **Zumbahua** to **Quilotoa** for US$10-15; also to **Chugchilán** for around US$30-35. On Sat mornings there are many trucks leaving the Zumbahua market for Chugchilán which pass Quilotoa. **Taxi**: day-trip by taxi to Zumbahua, Quilotoa, return to Latacunga is US$40.

Quilotoa
Be prepared for sudden changes in the weather, it gets very cold at night

Zumbahua is the point to turn off for a visit to Quilotoa, a volcanic crater filled by a beautiful emerald lake, to which there is a steep path from the rim. From the rim of the crater several snowcapped volcanoes can be seen in the distance.

The crater is reached by a road which runs north from Zumbahua (about 12 km, three hours' walk, being paved in 2002). Go down from the village and cross the river. After a few kilometres along the road turn right and over the bridge at the fork in the road; there are no road signs. Keep climbing past Quilopungo and the Ponce turn-off to a large archway at a road to the right towards a small group of houses. The crater is just beyond; it can only be recognized when you are on top of it. Take a stick to fend off dogs. Everyone at the crater tries to sell the famous naïve Tigua pictures and carved wooden masks, so expect to be besieged. ■ *US$0.50*.

Take a good sleeping bag, it is cold

Sleeping *Zhalaló*, 40 mins walking east of village, in the Ponce area, Quito T246 7130. Restaurant with access to the lake; cabins are under construction, until they are ready temporary accommodations are offered in the **D** range, reported the best option. **D** *Cabañas Quilotoa*, T03-812044. Owned by Humberto Latacunga. Basic, very cold, wool blankets, electric shower, includes breakfast and dinner, Humberto will lead treks and provide mules, he is a good painter and has a small store. **E** *Hostal Quilotoa*, owned by José Guamangate. Very basic, giant fireplace, offers bicycle rental, food, paintings and excursions. **F** *Refugio Quilotoa*, owned by Jorge Latacunga. You sleep on mats on the floor, he will cook food and take you on a day trek round the lake if you wish, he also paints masks. Camping is possible.

Transport Bus: *Trans Vivero* takes teachers to schools in **Zumbahua** and **Quilapungo** (US$2.20), leaving Latacunga daily at 0600 arriving 0815 in Quilapungo (0750 in Zumbahua), from where it is about 1 hr walk to the crater. Alternatively, hitch a truck on Sat morning from Zumbahua market bound for Chugchilán; you will be dropped close to the volcano. Hitching a return trip should not be left till late in the afternoon. Buses bound for **Chugchilán/Sigchos** drop the traveller 5 mins from the lake. *Trans Vivero* services to **Ponce** a few times a week; from the Ponce turnoff it is about a 40 min walk north.

Chugchilán to Toacazo
Phone code: 03

Chugchilán, a poor village in one of the most scenic areas of Ecuador, is 22 km by road from the Quilotoa crater. It is a six-hour walk; or walk around part of the crater rim, then down to Huayama, and across the canyon (Río Sihui) to Chugchilán, 11 km, about five hours. Horses rented in town, Humberto Ortega has been recommended as knowledgeable.

Sleeping B-C *The Black Sheep Inn*, a few minutes below the village, T814587, www.blacksheepinn.com Run by Andy Hammerman and Michelle Kirby, 6 private rooms, cheaper in dormitory for up to 6 people, including 3 course vegetarian dinner plus breakfast or lunch and drinking water and hot drinks all day, hot showers, excellent vegetarian cooking, book exchange, organic garden, sauna, 5% discount for ISIC, seniors or SAE members, llama treks, horse riding arranged, a good base for hiking to Quilotoa, Toachi canyon and Inca ruins. Highly recommended, advance reservations advised. **D** *Hostal Mama Hilda*, 100 m from centre of Chugchilán towards Sigchos, T814814. Shared bath, hot water, cheaper in dorm, homey, including dinner and breakfast, good food, warm atmosphere, arrange horse riding and walking trips. Highly recommended. **E** *Hostal Cloud Florest*, next to Mama Hilda, T814808. Includes dinner, breakfast available, shared bath, hot water, delicious local food, helpful owners, new in 2001, tours US$25.

D *Llullu Llama*, in Isinliví, across the canyon from Chugchilán (3 hrs hike), T814790/563. Nicely refurbished house in a pleasant town, private rooms or dorm, shared bath, hot water, includes dinner and breakfast, discounts for longer stays. A good trekking centre near the village of Guantualó, which has a fascinating market on Mon.

Transport Buses depart daily from Latacunga: to **Chugchilán**, at 1130 via **Sigchos**; at 1145 via **Zumbahua**; on Thu from **Saquisilí** market via Sigchos at 1130. Either route 4 hrs, US$1.80. Buses return to Latacunga at 0300, via Sigchos, at 0400 via Zumbahua. Milk truck to Sigchos between 0930 to 1100, US$1. On Sat also pick-ups going to/from market in Zumbahua and Latacunga. To **Isinliví**, at 1100 via Sigchos and 1300 direct; on Thu both from Saquisilí market around 1100, 2½ hrs, US$1.80. One bus returns to Latacunga at 0330, the second at variable hours, enquire locally.

Continuing from Chugchilán the road runs through **Sigchos** (Sunday market). The road east to Toacazo is cobbled and from there to Saquisilí it is paved (there are gas stations at Toacazo and Yalo, below Sigchos). Sigchos is the starting point for the Toachi Valley walk, via Asache to San Francisco de las Pampas (0900 bus daily to Latacunga). **Sleeping** **E** *Res Sigchos*, basic but clean, large rooms, shared bath, hot water downstairs. **E** *Hostal Tungurahua*, shared bath, hot water, basic. Cheap accommodation at *Casa Campesina*, take sleeping bag. There are few restaurants, ask in advance for food.

Transport Bus: 6 daily to and from Latacunga (see Chugchilán above), US$1.60, 2½ hrs. On Wed to Pucayaco, via Chugchilán, Quilotoa and Zumbahua at 0400, 9 hrs (returns Thu at 0400); and to La Maná, via Chugchilán, Quilotoa and Zumbahua at 0500, 9 hrs (returns Thu at 0500 and Sat at 0400).

Some 16 km south of Lasso, and 6 km west of the Panamericana is the small but very important market town of Saquisilí. Its Thursday market (0700-1400) is famous throughout Ecuador for the way in which its seven plazas and some of its streets become jam-packed with people, the great majority of them local Indians with red ponchos and narrow-brimmed felt hats. The best time to visit the market is between 0900 and 1200 (0700 for the animal market). Be sure to bargain, as there is a lot of competition. Saquisilí has colourful Corpus Christi processions.

Saquisilí
Phone code: 03

Sleeping and eating **D** *Hostería Rancho Muller*, 5 de Junio y González Suárez, south end of town, F721103. Cabins with bath and TV, expensive restaurant, German owner organizes tours and rents vehicles. **E** *San Carlos*, Bolívar opposite the parque central, T721057. With electric shower, view of plaza, cheap breakfast, parking, good value. **G** *Pensión Chabela*, Bolívar by main park, T721114. Shared bath, water problems, very basic. **G** *Salón Pichincha*, Bolívar y Pichincha. Shared bath, warm water, cheap, restaurant-bar below, basic. *El Refugio*, ½ block from crafts market, set meals and à la carte. *El Trébol*, 24 de Mayo near craft market. Set meals, cheap. *La Abuela*, 24 de Mayo 5-60. Set meals and snacks, very cheap.

Transport Bus: Frequent service between **Latacunga** and Saquisilí, US$0.25, 20 mins; many buses daily to/from **Quito**, depart from the bus terminal, 0530 onwards, US$1.50, 2hrs. Buses and trucks to many outlying villages leave from 1000 onwards. Bus tours from Quito cost about US$45 pp, taxis charge US$50, with 2 hrs wait at market.

Ecuador

Ambato

Phone code: 03
Colour map 1a, grid B3
Population: 124,166

The city was almost completely destroyed in the great 1949 earthquake, so lacks the colonial charm of other Andean cities. Its location in the heart of fertile orchard-country has earned Ambato the nickname of 'the city of fruits and flowers' (see annual festival below). It is also the principal supply town of the central highlands and a major centre for the leather industry.

The modern cathedral faces the pleasant **Parque Montalvo**, where there is a statue of the writer Juan Montalvo (1832-89) who is buried in a neighbouring street. His house (Bolívar y Montalvo) is open to the public. ■ *Free, T821024.* In the **Colegio Nacional Bolívar**, at Sucre entre Lalama y Martínez, is the Museo de Ciencias Naturales Héctor Vásquez with stuffed birds and animals and items of local historical interest, recommended. ■ *Mon-Fri 0800-1200, 1400-1730, closed for school holidays, US$1.* The **Quinta de Mera**, an old mansion in beautiful gardens, is in Atocha suburb. ■ *0900-1200, 1400-1800. Take bus from Espejo y 12 de Noviembre.* The main **market**, one of the largest in Ecuador, is held on Monday, with smaller markets on Wednesday and Friday. They are interesting, but have few items for the tourist.

The **tourist office**, *Ministerio de Turismo*, is at Guayaquil y Rocafuerte, ■ *Mon-Fri 0800-1200, 1400-1800, T821800, helpful.*

Ecuador

Sleeping **A** *Ambato*, Guayaquil 0108 y Rocafuerte, T412006, hambato@hotmail.com Includes breakfast, good restaurant, casino, squash court, best in town. Recommended. **A** *Florida*, Av Miraflores 1131, T843040, F843074. Includes breakfast, restaurant with good set meals, pleasant setting. **B** *Miraflores*, Av Miraflores 2-27, T843224, F844395. Includes breakfast, good restaurant, heating, refurbished. **B** *Villa Hilda*, Av Miraflores 09-116 y Las Lilas, T840700, F845571. Includes breakfast, good restaurant, classic old hotel with big garden. **D** *Bellavista*, Oriente y Napo Pastaza, T851542. Recommended. **D** *Cevallos*, Montalvo y Cevallos, T824877, F820570. Includes breakfast, restaurant, parking, good. **D** *Pirámide Inn*, Cevallos y Mariano Egüez, T842092, F854358. Includes breakfast, parking, comfortable. **E** *Guayaquil*, JL Mera 7-86 y 12 de Noviembre, T823886. Renovated in 2002, good. **E** *Portugal*, Juan Cajas 01-36 y 12 de Noviembre, T822476, F828679. Near bus station, good value. **F** *Europa*, Vela 717 y JL Mera, T820591. Shared bath, hot water, basic. **F** *La Liria*, Atahualpa y Caspicara, T842314. Hot water, at south end of town. Recommended. **F** *Laurita*, JL Mera 303 y Vela, T821377. Shared bath, hot water, basic.

There are a lot of cheap *residenciales*, hotels and restaurants around Parque 12 de Noviembre, the area is not safe at night.

Eating *El Alamo Chalet*, Cevallos 1719 y Montalvo, Swiss-owned, good meals; also *Gran Alamo*, Montalvo 520 y Sucre, international food. *La Buena Mesa*, Quito 924 y Bolívar. French. Recommended. *Cafetería Marcelos*, Castillo y Rocafuerte. Good international food. *Miramar*, 12 de Noviembre y Juan Cajas, Redondel de Cumandá, near the bus terminal. Seafood, good. Several other seafood places nearby. *El Coyote Disco Club*, Bolívar y Guayaquil. Mexican-American food, disco at weekends. *Cominos*, Av Colombia. Good pizzas. *La Fornace*, Cevallos 1728 y Montalvo. Wood oven pizza. *Farid*, Bolivar 1678 y Mera. Grill. Oriental: *Chifa Nueva Hong Kong*, Bolívar 768 y Martínez. Good, cheap. *Chifa Jao Fua*, Cevallos 756. Popular. There are many good cafeterías and snackbars: eg *Mama Miche*, 13 de Abril y JL Mera, Centro Comercial Ambato, 24 hrs, cheap. *Pastelería Quito*, JL Mera y Cevallos. Good for breakfast.

Entertainment *Cuba Son*, Bolívar y Guayaquil. Bar, nice atmosphere. *Peña del Tungurahua*, Fri and Sat, in block 2 of the Centro Comercial. *Cow-Boys*, Paccha y Los Incas. *Dicotec Ilusiones*, Quis Quis y Madrid.

Festivals Ambato has a famous festival in **Feb** or **Mar**, the *Fiesta de frutas y flores*, during carnival when there are 4 days of bullfights, parades and festivities. It is impossible to get a hotel room unless you book ahead.

Supermercado, Centro Comercial Ambato, Parque 12 de Noviembre, or *Supermaxi*, Centro Comercial Caracol, Av de los Capulíes y Mirabeles, in Ficoa. Good leather hiking boots from *Calzado Piedrahita*, Bolívar 15-08 y Lalama. Leather jackets, bags, belts on Vela between Lalama and Montalvo. Many stores for leather shoes along Bolívar. **Shopping**

Coltur, Cevallos 15-57; Páez 370 y Robles, T548219, F502449. *Metropolitan Touring*, Bolívar 19-22 y Castillo, T820211, and in Centro Comercial Caracol. **Tour operators**

Bus The main bus station is on Av Colombia y Paraguay, 2 km north of the centre. Town buses go there from Plaza Cevallos in the city centre. To **Quito**, 2¾ hrs, US$2. To **Cuenca**, US$5, 7 hrs. To **Guayaquil**, 6 hrs, US$6. To **Baños**, 45 mins, US$0.70. To **Riobamba**, US$1, 1 hr. To **Guaranda**, US$1.75, 2 hrs. To **Latacunga**, 45 mins, US$0.75. To **Santo Domingo de los Colorados**, 4 hrs, US$3. To **Tena**, US$5, 6 hrs. To **Puyo**, US$2.60, 3 hrs (see below). To **Macas**, US$6.50, 6½ hrs. To **Esmeraldas**, US$5, 6 hrs. To **Loja**, US$11, 12 hrs. To **Machala**, US$6, 7 hrs. **Transport**

Airline offices *TAME*, Sucre 09-62 y Guayaquil, T826601. **Banks** *Banco de Guayaquil*, Sucre y JL Mera, TCs, cash advance on Visa. *Banco del Pacífico*, Cevallos y Lalama, and Cevallos y Unidad Nacional, TCs, Visa. *Produbanco*, Montalvo y Sucre. TCs and Euros. *Cambiato*, Bolívar 694 y JL Mera, Visa and Amex TCs, European and Latin American currencies, Mon-Fri 0900-1300 and 1430-1800, Sat 0900-1230. **Communications** Internet: rates about US$1 hr, *net2phone* US$0.25-0.50 per min. Several in the centre of town, along Castillo, also Montalvo. **Post Office:** Castillo y Bolívar, at Parque Montalvo; 0730-1930. **Telephone:** Castillo 03-31 y Rocafuerte, 0800-2130. **Directory**

To the east of Ambato, an important road leads to **Salasaca** (one hotel), where the Indians sell their weavings; they wear distinctive black ponchos with white trousers and broad white hats. Further east is Pelileo, the blue jean manufacturing capital of Ecuador with good views of Tungurahua. (**E** *Hostal Pelileo*, Eloy Alfaro 641, T871390, shared bath, hot water.) The road continues to Baños (see below) and then on along the Pastaza valley to Mera, Shell and Puyo, from where there is access to other towns in the Oriente (see page 1020). Eight kilometres northeast of Pelileo on a paved side-road is **Patate**, centre of the warm, fruit growing Patate valley. As there are excellent views of Volcán Tungurahua from town and its surroundings, it has become a tourist destination since the reactivation of this volcano (see below). The fiesta of Nuestro Señor del Terremoto is held on the weekend of **4 February**, featuring a parade with beautiful floats made with fruit and flowers, reportedly the most elaborate in Ecuador.

Sleeping and eating A *Hacienda Los Manteles*, in the Leito valley on the road to El Triunfo, T870123, T/F02-505230 (Quito). Converted farm house, restaurant, great views, horse riding, hiking. **B** *Hostería Viña del Río*, 3 km from town on the old road to Baños, T/F8780139. Cabins, restaurant, pool, good views, sport fields, horse riding. **E** *Jardín del Valle*, M Soria y A Calderón, 1 block from the main park, T870209. Nicely furnished, good breakfast, camping area. Recommended. **F** *Hospedaje Altamira*, Av Ambato y J Montalvo, on the road from Pelileo. Shared bath, hot shower, basic. *Los Arupos*, at the park, set meals. *Arepas*, sweets made of squash (unrelated to the Colombian or Venezuelan variety), are the local delicacy; sold around the park.

Baños

Baños is nestled between the Río Pastaza and the Tungurahua volcano, only 8 km from its crater. After over 80 years of inactivity, Tungurahua began venting steam and ash in 1999 and the town was evacuated because of the threat of a major eruption between October and December of that year. Volcanic activity gradually diminished during 2000, former residents and tourists returned, and the town recovered its wonderful resort atmosphere. At the time of writing volcanic activity continues at a generally low level. **Tugurahua is closed to climbers** and the road to Riobamba is

Phone code: 03
Colour map 1a, grid B4
Population: 16,000
Altitude: 1,800 m

Climate: Rainy season May-Oct, especially Jul and Aug

Ecuador

closed, but all else is normal. Since the level of volcanic activity can change, you should enquire locally before visiting Baños. The National Geophysics Institute posts reports on the web at **www.epn.edu.ec** You should also be aware of the areas of highest risk, unless volcanic activity has completely ceased. These include the Bascún Valley (where several hotels and the El Salado baths are located), the valley of the Río Ulba east of Baños and of course Tungurahua itself. The town's streets are marked with arrows which lead to safety zones.

Baños bursts at the seams with hotels, *residenciales*, restaurants and tour agencies. Ecuadoreans flock here on weekends and holidays for the hot springs, to visit the Basílica and enjoy the local *melcochas* (toffees), while escaping the Andean chill in a sub-tropical climate. Foreign visitors are also frequent, using Baños as a base for climbing Tungurahua (in quieter times), volcano watching, organizing a visit to the jungle, making local day-trips or just plain hanging out.

Tourist offices The municipal tourist office is on the 2nd floor of the bus terminal, helpful. ■ *0800-1300, 1400-1700 (1600 Sat-Sun)*. There are several private 'tourist information offices' run by travel agencies near the bus station; high-pressure tour sales, maps and pamphlets available. Local artist, J Urquizo, produces an accurate pictorial map of Baños, 12 de Noviembre y Ambato, also sold in many shops.

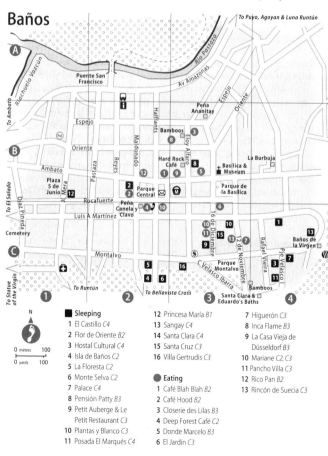

Baños

Sleeping		
1 El Castillo C4	12 Princesa María B1	7 Higuerón C3
2 Flor de Oriente B2	13 Sangay C4	8 Inca Flame B3
3 Hostal Cultural C4	14 Santa Clara C4	9 La Casa Vieja de
4 Isla de Baños C2	15 Santa Cruz C3	Düsseldorf B3
5 La Floresta C2	16 Villa Gertrudis C3	10 Mariane C2, C3
6 Monte Selva C2		11 Pancho Villa C3
7 Palace C4	**Eating**	12 Rico Pan B2
8 Pensión Patty B3	1 Café Blah Blah B2	13 Rincón de Suecia C3
9 Petit Auberge & Le	2 Café Hood B2	
Petit Restaurant C3	3 Closerie des Lilas B3	
10 Plantas y Blanco C3	4 Deep Forest Café C2	
11 Posada El Marqués C4	5 Donde Marcelo B3	
	6 El Jardín C3	

The **Manto de la Virgen** waterfall at the southeast end of town is a symbol of Baños. The **Basílica** attracts many pilgrims. The paintings of miracles performed by Nuestra Señora del Agua Santa are worth seeing; also a museum with stuffed birds and Nuestra Señora's clothing. ■ *Wed-Sun 0700-1600, US$0.40.*

Six sets of thermal baths are in the town. The **Baños de la Virgen** are by the waterfall opposite the *Hotel Sangay*. The water in the hot pools is changed three times a week, and the cold pool is chlorinated (best to visit very early morning, open 0430-1700); one small hot pool open evenings only (1800-2200), its water is changed daily. The **Piscinas Modernas** with a water slide are next door and are open weekends and holidays only. ■ *0800-1700.* **El Salado** baths (several hot pools with water changed daily, plus icy cold river water) are 1½ km out of town off the Ambato road (0430-1700). The **Santa Clara** baths, at the south end of Calle Rafael Vieira (formerly Santa Clara), are tepid, popular with children and have a gym and sauna (0800-1800). **Eduardo's** baths are next to Santa Clara, with a 25-m cold pool (the best for swimming laps) and a small warm pool (0800-1700). The **Santa Ana** baths have hot and cold pools, 1 km east of town on the road to Puyo (Fri-Sun 0800-1700). ■ *Entrance to each, US$2, except Eduardo's US$1.*

There are many interesting **walks** in the Baños area. The **San Martín shrine** is a 45-min easy walk from town and overlooks a deep rocky canyon with the Río Pastaza thundering below. Beyond the shrine, crossing to the north side of the Pastaza, is the **zoo**, 50 m beyond which is a path to the **Inés María waterfall**, cascading down, but polluted.

You can also cross the Pastaza by the **Puente San Francisco** suspension bridge, behind the kiosks across the main road from the bus station. From here a series of trails fans out into the surrounding hills, offering excellent views of Tungurahua from the ridgetops in clear weather. A total of six bridges span the Pastaza near Baños, so you can make a round trip.

On the hillside behind Baños, it is a 45-min hike to the **statue of the Virgin** (good views of the valley). Go to the south end of Calle JL Mera, before the street ends, take the last street to the right, at the end of which are stairs leading to the trail. A steep path continues along the ridge, past the statue. Another trail begins at the south end of JL Mera and leads to the *Hotel Luna Runtún*, continuing on to the village of Runtún (five to six hour round-trip). Along the same hillside, to the **Bellavista cross**, it is a steep climb from the south end of Calle Maldonado, 45 mins-1 hour. There is a café along the way. You can continue from the cross to *Hotel Luna Runtún*.

On the Puyo road 17 km from Baños is the town of **Río Verde**, at the junction of the Verde and Pastaza rivers. The Río Verde has crystalline green water with several waterfalls on its course. The most spectacular are El Pailón del Diablo (the Devil's Cauldron). In Río Verde, cross the river and take the path to the right after the church, then follow the trail down towards the suspension bridge; before the bridge take a side trail to the right (signposted) which leads you to a viewing platform above the falls (kiosk, drinks sold). Five minutes walk along a different trail are the smaller **San Miguel falls;** in town cross the bridge and take the first path to the right. It is also possible to hire bikes for the day from Baños and cycle downhill, passing El Pailón del Diablo and numerous other waterfalls on the way. Lookout for the 'shopping basket' cable car (*tarabita*) across the canyon at San Pedro, before Río Verde, driven by an old lorry engine – it is a great white knuckle ride, US$1 return.

Sleeping C pp *El Otro Lado*, on the other side of the suspension bridge, 10 minutes walk from the Pailón del Diablo Falls, reservations through *Hostal Cultural* in Baños. Cabins in a lovely setting, includes breakfast and dinner. **D** pp *Pequeño Paraíso*, 1½ km east of Río Verde, west of Machay, T09-981 9756, pequenoparaiso@gmx.net Comfortable cabins in lovely surroundings, abundant hot water, includes breakfast and dinner, tasty vegetarian meals with home-made bread, small pool, camping possible, rock climbing, canyoning,

Sights
All the baths can be very crowded at weekends and holidays; the brown colour of the water is due to its high mineral content

Excursions
Caution is advised near the San Francisco bridge as well as on the paths to Bellavista and Runtún - visitors have occasionally been robbed in these locations

Ecuador

Swiss run. Recommended. **E** pp *Indillama*, by San Miguel Falls, T09-978 5263, with breakfast, cabins, restaurant, German-run.

Transport Take any Puyo bus from Maldonado y Amazonas, opposite Baños bus station, 40 mins, US$0.50. You can cycle from Baños and take a bus back; several snack bars in Río Verde let you leave the bike while you visit the falls (eg *Paradero Amazonas*).

Sleeping

Baños is amply supplied with accommodation in all categories but can fill during holiday weekends

L *Luna Runtún*, Caserío Runtún Km 6, T740882, www.lunaruntun.com Includes dinner and breakfast, restaurant, internet, beautiful setting overlooking Baños, very comfortable rooms with balconies, gardens. Excellent service, English, French and German spoken. Hiking, horse riding and biking tours, travel agency, sports and nanny facilities. Highly recommended. **A-C** *Sangay*, Plazoleta Isidro Ayora 101, next to waterfall and thermal baths, T740490, F740056. Includes breakfast, good restaurant, pool and spa open to non-residents 1600-2000 ($3.50), tennis and squash courts, attentive service, 3 categories of rooms. Recommended. **B** *Monte Selva*, Halflants y Montalvo, T740566, F740244. Includes breakfast, restaurant, warm pool, cabins, bar, spa, excellent service. **B** *Palace*, Montalvo 20-03, T740470, hotelpalace@hotmail.com Includes breakfast, restaurant, nice garden and pool, nicely old-fashioned, front rooms with balcony. Sauna and jacuzzi. **C** *Hostal Cultural*, Pasaje Velasco Ibarra y Montalvo, T740083. Includes breakfast, restaurant, nice sitting room, more expensive rooms with fireplace. **C** *Villa Gertrudis*, Montalvo 2975, T740441, F740442. Includes breakfast, pool, classic old resort, lovely garden, reserve in advance. Recommended. **D** *Flor de Oriente*, Ambato y Maldonado on Parque Central, T740418, F740717. Parking, very good but can be noisy at weekends. **D** *Isla de Baños*, Halflants 1-31 y Montalvo, T/F740609. European breakfast, internet, some suites more expensive, German run, nice atmosphere, garden with parrots and monkeys. Recommended. **D** *La Floresta*, Halflants y Montalvo, T740457, F740717. Excellent breakfast, good restaurant, parking, comfortable rooms, nice garden. Recommended. **D** *Le Petit Auberge*, 16 de Diciembre y Montalvo, T740936. Includes breakfast, good restaurant, parking, French run, rooms with fireplace, patio, quiet. **D** *Posada El Marqués*, Pasaje Velasco Ibarra y Montalvo, T740053, posada.marques@yahoo.com Includes breakfast, good restaurant, spacious, good beds, garden. Recommended. **D** *Santa Clara*, 12 de Noviembre y Montalvo, T740349. Includes breakfast, cooking facilities, parking, simple rooms and cabins, nice garden. **D** *Santa Cruz*, 16 de Diciembre y Martínez, T740648. Includes breakfast, café, modern and comfortable. **D-E** *Plantas y Blanco*, 12 de Noviembre y Martínez, T/F740044. Excellent breakfast on roof terrace, good restaurant, French run, steam bath 0730-1100 (US$2), jeep, motorbike and mountain bike hire, luggage store. Warmly recommended. **E** *El Carruaje*, Martínez y 16 de Diciembre, T740913. Cooking facilities, comfortable. **E** *El Castillo*, Martínez y Rafael Vieira, T740285. Restaurant, parking, simple, quiet. **E** *El Oro*, Ambato y JL Mera. Includes breakfast, cooking facilities, good value. Recommended. **E** *Monik's*, Ambato y Pastaza, T740428. OK. **F** *Olguita*, Rocafuerte y Maldonado, T741065. OK. **F** *Pensión Patty*, Alfaro 556 y Oriente, T740202. Shared bath, lukewarm water, cooking facilities, basement rooms poor, otherwise OK, family-run, popular. **F** *Princesa María*, Rocafuerte y Mera, T741035, princesamaria@andinanet.net Hot water, internet, laundry and cooking facilities, good value. Recommended.

Many other cheap hotels around the two parks: Parque la Basílica and Parque Central.

Eating

There are restaurants for all tastes and budgets, many close by 2130

Ecuadorean Calle Ambato has many restaurants serving economical set meals and local fare, the *picanterías* on the outside of the market serve local delicacies such as *cuy* and *fritada*. *Donde Iván*, Halflants y Montalvo, at *Hospedaje La Floresta*. Ecuadorean and international food, excellent breakfast. *La Puerta de Alcalá*, Av Amazonas (main highway), ½ block downhill from bus terminal. Good value set meal.

French *Mariane*, Halflants y Rocafuerte opposite Andinatel, also at Martínez y 16 de Diciembre. Excellent authentic cuisine, large portions. Highly recommended. *Le Petit Restaurant*, 16 de Diciembre y Montalvo. Parisian owner, excellent food, great atmosphere. *Closerie des Lilas*, Alfaro y Oriente. Good.

International On Calle Ambato are several popular restaurants, some with sidewalk seating, among these: *La Abuela*, between Alfaro and Halflants, small, good pizzas, good

Ecuador

breakfasts. On the same block is *Pepos*, varied menu, live folkloric music. *Donde Marcelo*, near 16 de Diciembre. Good breakfasts, friendly gringo bar upstairs. *La Casa Vieja de Düsseldorf*, Ambato y Eloy Alfaro. Varied menu, good value. *Rincón de Suecia*, 12 de Noviembre y Martínez. Varied menu, good. *Higuerón*, 12 de Noviembre 270 y Martínez. Closed Wed, good European, local and vegetarian food, nice garden. *Rutas de Humboldt*, Montalvo y Alfaro. International and Ecuadorean dishes, German beer, book and video library, German run.

Italian *Bon Giorno*, Rocafuerte y 16 de Diciembre. Good, authentic dishes. *Pizzería Napolitana*, 12 de Noviembre y Martínez, good pizza and pasta, pleasant atmosphere, pool table. *Buona Pizza*, Ambato y Halflants. Good pizzas and pastas, nice atmosphere. *Il Papagallo*, Martínez y 16 de Diciembre. Pasta.

Latin American *Inca Flame*, Oriente y Alfaro. Good Mexican food, home made desserts. Also Mexican: *Pancho Villa*, 16 de Diciembre y Martínez, open 0730-2130. Good quality and service. Repeatedly recommended. *Manantial*, Martínez y 16 de Diciembre. Dishes from all over the continent, speciality is "elephant's ears", a thin piece of meat which covers your entire plate. *Quilombo*, Montalvo y 16 de Diciembre. Good *parrillada*, open 1200-1500, 1900-2300.

Vegetarian *Café Hood*, Maldonado y Ambato, at Parque Central. Excellent food, fruit juices, nice atmosphere, English spoken, always busy. *Casa Hood*, Martínez between Halflants and Alfaro. Varied menu including Indonesian and Thai dishes, some meat dishes, juices, good desserts, travel books and maps sold, book rental and exchange, repertory cinema. Recommended. *Deep Forest Café*, Rocafuerte y Halflants, at Parque Central. Middle Eastern and Greek specialities, good falafel and desserts, good breakfasts, some meat dishes. *El Paisano*, Rafael Vieira y Martínez. Variety of herbal teas and meals, fresh ingredients.

Cafeterias *Café Blah Blah*, Ambato y Halflants, good coffee, snacks, small, cosy, sidewalk seating, popular meeting place. *Rico Pan*, Ambato y Maldonado. Good breakfasts, hot bread, good fruit salads, pizzas and meals. *Pancho's*, Ambato y Pasaje Ermita de la Virgen, west of the market. Snacks, coffee, open 0800-2300.

Entertainment
Cover charge US$1-2

Peña Canela y Clavo, Rocafuerte y Maldonado, at the Parque Central. Music and drinks, nice atmosphere, open 1800-2400, closed Mon. *Peña Ananitay*, 16 de Diciembre y Espejo. Good live music and dancing. Eloy Alfaro, between Ambato and Espejo has many bars including: *Hard Rock Café*, a favourite travellers' hangout, fantastic *piña colada* and juices. *Bamboos Bar*, Alfaro y Oriente. Popular for salsa, live at weekends. *La Burbuja*, Ciudadela El Rosario, off Calle Ambato, east of the Basílica. Disco. Films are shown at *Casa Hood* (see Eating above). *Córdova Tours* has a *Chiva Mocambo*, an open sided bus, cruises town playing music, it will take you to different night spots.

Festivals

It can get very crowded and noisy on public holidays, especially Carnival and Holy Week, when hotels are fully booked and prices rise. Oct: *Nuestra Señora de Agua Santa* with daily processions, bands, fireworks, sporting events and partying through the month. Week-long celebrations ending **16 Dec**: the town's anniversary, parades, fairs, sports, cultural events. The night of **15 Dec** is the *verbenas*, when each *barrio* hires a band and there are many parties.

Shopping
Look out for jawsticking toffee (taffy, known as melcocha) made in ropes in shop doorways, or the less sticky alfeñique

Crafts stalls at Pasaje Ermita de la Vírgen, off C Ambato, by the market. For painted balsa-wood birds see *El Chaguamango* shop in the Basílica museum, open 0800-1600. *Las Orquídeas*, Ambato Y Maldonado by the Parque Central. Excellent selection of crafts, some guide books. Also *Taller Balsarte*, Ambato y Halflants, and *Pacasmayo*, Rocafuerte y Alfaro. Nice tagua (vegetable ivory made of palm nuts) crafts at several shops on Maldonado between Oriente and Espejo. Salasacan weaving from *Artesanal Salasaca*, on Halflants next to *Mariane*, and from José Masaquiza, Eloy Alfaro y Martínez, who gives demonstrations and explains the designs, materials, etc. *Galería de Arte Contemporáneo Huillac Cuna*, Rafael Vieira y Montalvo. Modern art exhibits, sells paintings and coffee-table books. Crafts and musical instruments from the Oriente at *Pusanga Women's Cooperative*, Halflants y Martínez. Leather shops on Rocafuerte entre Halflants y 16 de Diciembre. *Tucán Silver*, Ambato esq Halflants, jewellery. **Camping equipment** *Varoxi*, Maldonado 651 y Oriente. Quality packs, repairs luggage.

Ecuador

Sport **Climbing**: Due to the erratic nature of volcanic activity you may or may not be able to climb Tungurahua, check before you get there. For companies offering climbs, see Tour operators. **Cycling**: Many places rent bikes, quality varies, rates from US$4 per day; check brakes and tyres, find out who has to pay for repairs, and insist on a puncture repair kit and pump. The following have good equipment: *Hotel Isla de Baños* (cycling tours), *Hotel Charvic* (Maldonado y Oriente, also has motorcycles), *Café Ross* (Maldonado y Rocafuerte). **Horse riding**: Usual cost US$10 to 25, 3 to 5 hrs. *Christian* at *Hotel Isla de Baños* has excellent horses. *Caballos José*, Maldonado y Martínez, T740746, flexible hours; *Angel Aldaz*, Montalvo y JL Mera, on road to the Virgin; and *Jilo*, office on Ambato opposite market,good horses. Several others, but check the horses as some are not well cared for. **River rafting**: NB the Chambo, Patate and Pastaza rivers are all polluted. Fatal accidents have occurred; always pay close attention to the quality of equipment (rafts, helmets, life vests, etc) and experience of guides. *Río Loco*, Eloy Alfaro y Ambato, T/F740929. Run by Héctor Romo, experienced guide, US$30 for half day; US$50 for full day (rapids and calm water in jungle), US$120 pp 2 days with camping. See also Tour operators. **Canyoning**: An exciting new activity in the Baños area, but not without its risks. **NB** Few guides here have formal training, ask beforehand. Also check ropes and make sure you get a proper harness. Good equipment and trained guides available from *Pequeño Paraíso*, see Río Verde, page 953.

Tour operators There are very many tour agencies in town, some with several offices, as well as 'independent' guides who seek out tourists on the street (the latter are generally not recommended). Quality varies considerably; to obtain a qualified guide and avoid unscrupulous operators, it is best to seek advice from other travellers who have recently returned from a tour. We have received some critical reports of tours out of Baños, but there are also highly respected and qualified operators here. In all cases, insist on a written contract and try to pay only half the fare up-front. Check any mountaineering or other equipment carefully before heading out. Most agencies and guides offer trips to the jungle (US$25-50 per day pp) and 2 day climbing trips to Cotopaxi (approximately US$110 pp) or Chimborazo (approximately US$120 pp). There are also volcano watching, trekking and horse tours, in addition to the day-trips and sports mentioned above. Baños is a good meeting place to form a group to visit the Oriente. It is more interesting than Misahuallí, if you have to wait a few days, but the tour can be more expensive. The following agencies and guides have received positive recommendations but the list is not exclusive and there are certainly others. *Rainforestur*, Ambato y Maldonado, T/F740743, www.ecuador-paginaamarilla.com/rainforestur.htm Santiago Herrera, guides are knowledgeable and environmentally conscious. *Deep Forest Adventure*, Rocafuerte y Halflants, next to Andinatel, T741815. Eloy Torres, speaks German and Englishjungle and trekking tours. *Luna Travel*, at *Hotel Luna Runtún*, www.lunaruntun.com *Aventurandes*, Alfaro y Oriente (Pensión Patty), T740202. Experienced mountain guides Carlos Alvarez and Fausto Mayorga, also jungle tours. *Córdova Tours*, Maldonado y Espejo, T740923. Run the following tours on board their *chiva Mocambo*, an open sided bus (reserve ahead): waterfall tour, along the Puyo road to Río Verde, 0900-1400, US$5; Baños and environs, 1600-1800, US$2.50; night tour with music, 2000-2100, US$1.70 (they will drop you off at the night spot of your choice). *Geotours*, Ambato y Halflants, T741344, www.ecuadorexplorer.com/geotours Geovanny Romo, experienced agency, offer jungle, horseback, cycling, rafting and canyoning tours. *Huilla Cuna*, 3 agencies of same name, Rocafuerte y 16 de Diciembre, T741086, Byron Castillo, helpful and knowledgeable, jungle and mountain tours; at Ambato y Halflants, T741292, huilacuna@yahoo.es Marcelo Mazo organizes jungle trips; and at Rafael Vieira y Montalvo, T740187, Luis Guevara runs jungle and mountain trips. *Explorsierra*, Maldonado y Espejo, T740628/302, explorsierra@hotmail.com *Expediciones Amazónicas*, Maldonado y Rocafuerte at Parque Central, and Oriente y Halflants, T740506, expedicionesamazonicas@hotmail.com Run by Jorge and Dosto Varela, the latter is a recommended mountain guide. Mountain, jungle, trekking and rafting trips. Very professional. *Willie Navarrete*, at *Café Higuerón*, T09-932411. Recommended for climbing, *Aseguim* member.

Local Bus: City buses run between 0600 and 1830. To **El Salado** every 15 mins from Rocafuerte **Transport** behind market. To **Agoyán** every 15 mins from Alfaro y Martínez. **Long distance Bus**: the bus station is on the Ambato-Puyo road (Av Amazonas) a short way from the centre, and is the scene of vigorous volleyball games most afternoons. To/from **Quito**, via Ambato, US$2.60, 3½ hrs, frequent service; going to Quito sit on the right for views of Cotopaxi, buy tickets early for weekends and holidays. To **Ambato**, 45 mins, US$0.60. To **Riobamba**, landslides caused by Tungurahua's volcanic activity damaged the direct Baños-Riobamba road, buses go via Ambato, 2 hrs, US$1.60. To **Latacunga**, 2 hrs, US$1.60. To **Puyo**, 2 hrs, US$1.20; pack your luggage in plastic as all goes on top of the bus which drives through waterfalls; delays possible because of construction work. To **Tena**, 5½ hrs, US$3.70. To **Misahuallí**, change at Tena, or at the Río Napo crossing, see page 1018, and **Macas**, 7 hrs, US$6 (sit on right).

Banks *Banco del Pacífico*, Montalvo y Alfaro, TCs $5 per transaction, Visa and MasterCard ATM, open **Directory** Mon-Fri 0845-1630, Sat 0900-1330. *Banco del Pichincha*, Ambato y Halflants, changes TCs, open Mon-Fri, 0800-1400. The 2 hardware stores, also on Ambato y Halflants, change TCs, rates vary, open long hours. **Communications** Internet: There are many cyber cafés in town, prices US$2 per hr. **Post office:** Halflants y Ambato, across from Parque Central. **Telephone:** *Andinatel*, Halflants y Rocafuerte, by Parque Central, international calls. **Language classes** Rates for Spanish lessons in 2002 ranged from US$3.50-5 per hr. *Spanish School 16 de Diciembre*, Montalvo 5-26 y Rafael Vieira, T740232, José M Eras, English-speaking retired teacher. *Baños Spanish Center*, Julio Cañar y Oriente, T740632, elizbasc@uio.satnet.net Elizabeth Barrionuevo, English and German-speaking, flexible and recommended. *International Spanish School*, 16 de Diciembre y Espejo, T/F740612, Martha Vaca F. *Instituto de Español Alternativo IDEA*, Montalvo y Alfaro, T/F740799, idea2@idea.k12.ec *Raíces*, 16 de Diciembre near stadium, T740040 Lorena Verduga.

To the west of Ambato, a paved road climbs through tilled fields, past the páramos of Carihuairazo and Chimborazo to the great Arenal, and down through the Chimbo valley to Guaranda. This spectacular journey on the highest paved road in Ecuador takes about three hours. It reaches a height of 4,380 m and vicuñas can be seen.

Guaranda

This quaint, quiet town, capital of Bolívar province, proudly calls itself 'the Rome of *Phone code: 03* Ecuador' because it is built on seven hills. There are fine views of the mountains all *Colour map 1a, grid B3* around. Locals traditionally take an evening stroll in the palm-fringed main plaza, *Population: 15,730* **Parque Libertador Simón Bolívar**, around which are the Municipal buildings and a large stone **Cathedral**. Although not on the tourist trail, there are many sights worth visiting in the province, for which Guaranda is the ideal base. Of particular interest is the highland town of Salinas as well as the *subtrópico* region, the lowlands stretching west towards the coast.

Towering over the city, atop one of the hills, is an impressive statue of **El Indio Guaranga**, a local Indian leader after whom the city may have been named; museum (entry free), art gallery and auditorium. ■ *Take a taxi (US$0.80); or take a 'Guanujo' bus to the stadium, walk past the stadium to Av La Prensa and follow it till you reach the first turning on the right (5-10 mins walk).*

Market days are Friday and Saturday (larger), when many indigenous people in typical dress trade at the market complex at the east end of Calle Azuay, by Plaza 15 de Mayo (9 de Abril y Maldonado), and at Plaza Roja (Av Gen Enríquez). Very colourful and interesting. Carnival in Guaranda is among the best known in the country.

B *La Colina*, high up on Av Guayaquil (No 117), T/F980666. Restaurant mediocre and expen- **Sleeping** sive but good for Sun lunch, covered swimming pool, bright and attractive rooms, lovely views. **D** *Bolívar*, Sucre 704 y Rocafuerte, T980547. Good restaurant (closed Sun), parking, simple but pleasant, small courtyard. **D** *Cochabamba*, García Moreno y 7 de Mayo, T981958, vviteriv@gu.pro.ec Very good expensive restaurant (best in town), parking, hotel a bit faded but good service. **E** *Ejecutivo*, García Moreno 803 y 9 de Abril, T982044. Shared bath, hot water, OK. **F** *Rosa Elvira*, Sucre 606. Shared bath, hot water, parking, basic.

Ecuador

Eating

Most restaurants are closed on Sun

Cochabamba, see Sleeping above. *Balcón Cuencano*, Convención de 1884 entre García Moreno y Azuay. Breakfast, lunch and dinner, set meals and à la carte, good. *Pizza Buon Giorno*, Av Circunvalación 2 blocks from Plaza Roja on the way to bus terminal. Pizza and salads. *Marisquería El Conchal*, Plaza Roja. Good *ceviche de pescado, camarones* and *mixtos*, cheap, closed in the evening, open Sun. *Rumipamba*, Gen Enríquez 308, Plaza Roja. Grilled chicken, set meals and à la carte. *Juad's Pastelería*, Convención de 1884 y Azuay. Cappuccino, hot chocolate, sandwiches, fruit salad, pastries, very good, popular, best selection early in the day, closed 1300-1500 and Sun. Recommended. Many simple *comedores* around Plaza Roja serve cheap set meals.

Transport **Bus** Terminal at Eliza Mariño Carvajal, on road to Riobamba and Babahoyo; if you are staying in town get off at Plaza Roja. Many daily buses to: **Ambato**, US$1.75, 2 hrs. **Riobamba** (some along the scenic and unpaved Gallo Rumi road, others via the Arenal and Ambato), US$1.40, 2 hrs. **Babahoyo**, US$1.65, 3 hrs, beautiful ride. **Guayaquil**, US$2.30, 4 hrs. **Quito**, 3 companies run almost 30 daily services, US$3.85, 4-5 hrs.

Directory **Communications** Post Office: Azuay y Pichincha. Telephone: *Andinatel*, Rocafuerte 508 y Sucre, 0800-2200 daily; and at bus terminal.

After Ambato, the Pan-American Highway runs south to Riobamba. About half way is **Mocha**, where guinea pigs (*cuy*) are bred for the table. You can sample roast *cuy* and other typical dishes at stalls and restaurants by the roadside, *Mariadiocelina* is recommended. The highway climbs steeply south of Mocha and at the pass there are fine views in the dry season of Chimborazo and Carihuairazo. At **Urbina** (signed), 1 km west of the highway, is **E** *Posada de la Estación*, in the solitary old railway station at 3,609 m, meals available, shared bath, hot water, magnificent views, clean and comfortable but very cold at night, book through *Alta Montaña* agency in Riobamba (see below). This is a good place for acclimatization, friendly and helpful, horses, trips and equipment arranged. Recommended.

Riobamba

Phone code: 03
Colour map 1a, grid B3
Population: approx 150,000
Altitude: 2,750 m

The capital of Chimborazo Province is built in the wide **Tapi Valley** and has broad streets and many ageing but impressive buildings. Because of their central location Riobamba and the surrounding province are known as 'Corazón de la Patria' – the heartland of Ecuador – and the city boasts the nickname 'La Sultana de Los Andes' in honour of lofty Mount Chimborazo. *Fiesta del Niño Rey de Reyes*, with street parades, music and dancing, starts in December and culminates on 6 January. Around 21 April there are independence celebrations lasting several days, hotel prices rise. 11 November is the Foundation of Riobamba.

Sights The main plaza is **Parque Maldonado** around which are the **Santa Bárbara Cathedral**, the **Municipality** and several colonial buildings with arcades. The Cathedral has a beautiful colonial stone façade and an incongruously modern interior. Four blocks northeast of the railway station is the **Parque 21 de Abril**, named after the Batalla de Tapi, 21 April 1822, the city's independence from Spain. The park, better known as **La Loma de Quito**, affords an unobstructed view of Riobamba and Chimborazo, Carihuairazo, Tugurahua, El Altar and occasionally Sangay. It also has a colourfully dressed tile tableau of the history of Ecuador. **San Antonio de Padua** church, at the east corner of Parque 21 de Abril, tells Bible stories in the windows. West of the centre is **Parque Guayaquil**, the largest in the urban area, with a band-shell, playground and the *Vaca-Zebra* (zebra-cow), an unusual sculpture by well known artist Gonzalo Endara Crow.

Markets Riobamba is an important market centre where indigenous people from many communities congregate. Saturday is the main market day when the city fills with colourfully dressed Indians from many different parts of the province of Chimborazo, each wearing their distinctive costume; trading overflows the markets and buying and

Ecuador (side margin)

selling go on all over town. Wednesday is a smaller market day. The 'tourist' market is in the small **Plaza de la Concepción or Plaza Roja**, on Orozco, south of the Convento de la Concepción (see below). It is a good place to buy local handicrafts and authentic Indian clothing (Saturday and Wednesday only, 0800-1500).

The main produce markets are **San Alfonso** (Argentinos y 5 de Junio) which on Saturday spills-over into the nearby streets and also sells clothing, ceramics, baskets and hats, and **La Condamine** (Carabobo y Colombia) open daily, largest market on Fridays. Other markets in the colonial centre are **San Francisco** and **La Merced**, near the churches of the same name.

The **Convento de la Concepción**, Orozco y España, entrance at Argentinos y J Larrea. Restored by the Banco Central, it is now a religious art museum. The priceless gold monstrance, Custodia de Riobamba Antigua, is the museum's greatest treasure, one of the richest of its kind in South America. ■ *Tue-Sat 0900-1200 and 1500-1800, US$2, T965212. The guides are friendly and knowledgeable (tip expected).*

The *Ministerio de Turismo* is at Av Daniel L Borja y Brasil, next to the Municipal Library, T/F941213, very helpful and knowledgeable, English spoken. ■ *Mon-Fri 0830-1330, 1430-1700.*

Guano is a carpet-weaving town 8 km north of Riobamba. Many shops sell rugs and you can arrange to have these woven to your own design. ■ *Buses for Guano leave from the Mercado Dávalos, García Moreno y New York, every 20 mins 0600-2200, US$0.20, last bus returns to Riobamba at 1800. Taxi US$3.*

Excursions

Riobamba provides access to the central highland region of **Parque Nacional Sangay**, a beautiful wilderness area with excellent opportunities for trekking and climbing. The most popular route begins at the village of Candelaria, one bus most days around noon from Parque La Libertad, Benalcázar y Primera Constituyente, opposite Mercado San Francisco, 1½ hrs, US$1. Two km outside Candelaria, at the entrance to the national park, is D *Hostal Capac Urcu* at Hacienda Releche, T949761 (960848 Riobamba), hot water, some rooms with bath, comfortable, nice setting, meals available on request. They also operate a simpler *refugio* on the Collanes plain (book in advance) and can provide guides and pack animals. ■ *For information about Parque Nacional Sangay, Ministry of the Environment, Av 9 de Octubre y Quinta Macají, at the western edge of town, north of the roundabout at the end of Av Isabel de Godin, T963779; park people are only in the office in the early morning, be there before 0800. Park entry, US$10. Getting there: From town take city bus San Gerardo-El Batán. A new road, complete but for 1 km (Oct 2001), runs through the national park from Guamote to Macas in the Oriente. No public transport as yet, but a fabulous route through untouched wilderness. Buses go from Riobamba or Guamote to Atillo and from Macas to 9 de Octubre; between the two, hitch a ride with the road engineers. Take all supplies from Riobamba or Macas.*

Ecuador

AL *La Andaluza*, 16 km north of Riobamba along the Panamericana, T949370, www.hosteria-andaluza.com Includes breakfast, good restaurant, nice rooms in old hacienda, with heaters and roaring fireplaces, lovely views, good walking. **B** *Abraspungu*, Km 3 on the road to Guano, T940820, www.hosteria-abraspungu.com Excellent restaurant, beautiful house in country setting. Recommended. **B** *Chimborazo Internacional*, Los Cipreses y Argentinos, T963475, www.hotelchimborazo.com Restaurant overpriced, internet, attentive service, spacious rooms. **B** *El Troje*, 4½ km on the road to Chambo, T960826, gerencia@eltroje.com Good restaurant, pool and sauna, internet, nice rooms, good views, camping (US$10 pp). **B** *Zeus*, Av Daniel L Borja 41-29, T968036, hotelzeus@ecuabox.com Restaurant, jacuzzi, gym, bathtubs with views of Chimborazo. Recommended. **C** *El Cisne*, Av Daniel L Borja y Duchicela, T964573, F941982. Restaurant, modern and comfortable. **C** *Montecarlo*, Av 10 de Agosto 25-41 entre García Moreno y España, T960557, montecarlo@laserinter.net Includes breakfast, restaurant, nice house in colonial style, some mattresses are poor. **D** *Canadá*, Av de la Prensa 23-31 y Av Daniel L Borja, T/F946677, gamely20@hotmail.com Restaurant, internet, parking, near bus terminal, modern, English spoken. **D** *Los Shyris*, Rocafuerte 21-60 y 10 de Agosto, T/F960323, hshyris@

Sleeping
Riobamba suffers from chronic water shortages, make sure your hotel has a water tank

yahoo.com Cheaper without bath, hot water 0500-1100 and 1700-2300, internet, good rooms, service, and value. Rooms at the back are quieter. **D** *Majestic*, Av Daniel L Borja 43-60 y La 44, T968708. Cafeteria, electric shower, parking, near bus terminal. **D** *Riobamba Inn*, Carabobo 23-20 y Primera Constituyente, T961696, F940974. Restaurant, carpeted rooms, group discounts. **D** *Tren Dorado*, Carabobo 22-35 y 10 de Agosto, T/F964890. Restaurant, reliable hot water, modern, nice, good value. Recommended. **D** *Whymper*, Av Miguel Angel León 23-10 y Primera Constituyente, T964575, F968137. Hot water 0600-0930 and 1800-2130, safe parking, spacious rooms, friendly, but a little rundown. **D-E** *Imperial*, Rocafuerte 22-15 y 10 de Agosto, T960429. Cheaper without bath, hot water 24 hours, stores luggage, good beds, basic, good views from the roof, loud music from bar on Fri and Sat nights, good value. **D-E** *Oasis*, Veloz 15-32 y Almagro, T961210, F941499. Erratic hot water, some rooms with kitchen and fridge, small and quiet, family run, nice garden. **D-E** *Rocío*, Brasil y Av Daniel L Borja, T961848. Electric shower, nice, good value. Several cheap and basic places around the train station.

Eating

Most restaurants are closed after 2200 and on Sun

Luigi's, Condorazo y Unidad Nacional. Spanish, Italian and other international dishes, expensive and very good. *El Delirio*, Primera Constituyente 2816 y Rocafuerte (Bolívar stayed here). Closed Mon and Sun, popular with tour groups and overpriced. *Cabaña Montecarlo*, García Moreno 21-40. Good food and service, large portions, serves lunch and dinner, recommended. *Cafetería Real Montecarlo*, 10 de Agosto 25-45 y García Moreno. Excellent food and service, nice atmosphere, good breakfasts, closed at midday. Ecuadorean food at *Restaurante Montecarlo*, Primera Constituyente y Pichincha, popular. *Bonny*, Diego de Almagro y Villarroel. Regional dishes, good seafood, very popular. *Parrillada de Fausto*,

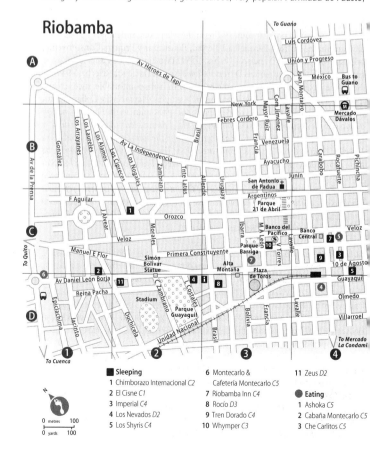

Riobamba

Sleeping	
1	Chimborazo Internacional *C2*
2	El Cisne *C1*
3	Imperial *C4*
4	Los Nevados *D2*
5	Los Shyris *C4*
6	Montecarlo & Cafetería Montecarlo *C5*
7	Riobamba Inn *C4*
8	Rocío *D3*
9	Tren Dorado *C4*
10	Whymper *C3*
11	Zeus *D2*

Eating	
1	Ashoka *C5*
2	Cabaña Montecarlo *C5*
3	Che Carlitos *C5*

0 metres 100
0 yards 100

Ecuador

Uruguay 2038 y Av Daniel L Borja. Good meat, nice atmosphere. *Che Carlitos*, Colón 22-44, entre 10 de Agosto y Primera Constituyente. Argentine owner, great *parrilladas*. *Ashoka*, Guayaquil y 5 de Junio. Vegetarian. *La Pizzería de Paolo*, Av Daniel L Borja corner Epiclachima, near the bus station. Good pizza and pasta. *Mónaco Pizzería*, Diego Ibarra y Av Daniel L Borja. Pizza and pasta, open evenings only. Excellent service, good value. *Los Sabores d'Italia*, Veloz y Carabobo. Italian, personal service, good value. Two OK Chinese are: *Chifa China*, Av Daniel L Borja 43-49, and *Chifa Joy Sing*, Guayaquil 29-27 y Carabobo.

Snacks and coffee *Caffe Johnny*, Espejo 22-45 y Primera Constituyente. Breakfast from 0730, good, closed Sun. *Helados de Paila*, Espejo entre Guayaquil y 10 de Agosto. Ice creams, café, snacks, popular, open Sun till 1930.

Bakeries *Pan Van*, Primera Constituyente y Colón. Good quality and variety.

Entertainment

Gens-Chop Bar Av Daniel L Borja 42-17 y Duchicela. Bar, good music and sport videos, open daily, popular. Recommended. The *Casa de la Cultura*, 10 de Agosto y Rocafuerte, has a good *peña* on Fri and Sat evenings. *Unicornio*, St Armand y Av Lizarzaburo, Vía Ambato Km 1. Piano Bar, Salsoteca, open Thu-Sat. *Vieja Guardia* good bar and open air disco at Av Flor 40-43 y Av Zambrano, US$1 cover. *Milenium*, Cdla Los Tulipanes, off Av de la Prensa, 3 blocks south of the bus terminal. Disco, pub, international music, popular, US$1.

Sport

Mountain biking: *Pro Bici*, at Primera Constituyente 23-51 y Larrea, T941880, F961923, run by guide and mechanic, Galo J Brito. Bike trips and rental, guided tours with support vehicle, full equipment, US$35-40 pp per day, excluding meals and overnight stays. *Julio Verne* (see Tour operators), rental US$8 per day; tours including transport, guide, meals, US$30 per day.

4 Chifa Joy Sing *D4*
5 El Delirio *C4*
6 La Pizzería de Paolo *D1*
7 Mónaco Pizzería *C3*

Shopping

Crafts Crafts are sold at the Plaza Roja on Wed and Sat (see above). Nice tagua carvings and other crafts are on sale at *Alta Montaña* (see Tour operators below). *Almacén Cacha*, Orozco next to the Plaza Roja. A co-operative of native people from the Cacha area, sells woven bags, wool sweaters and other crafts, good value (closed Sun-Mon).

Supermarkets *La Ibérica*, Av Daniel L Borja 37-62 y Allende. *Camari*, Espejo y Olmedo, opposite La Merced market.

Tour operators

Many hotels offer tours, not all are run by qualified guides

Metropolitan Touring, Av Daniel L Borja y Miguel Angel León, T969600, F969601. Railway tours, airline tickets, *DHL* and *Western Union* representatives. *Coltur*, Av Daniel L Borja y Vargas Torres,, T/F962662. Airline tickets. *Alta Montaña*, Av Daniel L Borja 35-17 y Diego Ibarra, T/F942215, aventurag@laserinter.net Trekking, climbing, cycling, bird watching, photography and horse riding tours in mountains and jungle, logistical support for expeditions, transport, equipment rental, English spoken. Recommended. *Andes Trek*, Colón 22-25 y 10 de Agosto, T940964, www.andestrek.com Climbing, trekking and mountain biking tours, transport, equipment rental, English and German spoken. *Expediciones Andinas*, Vía a Guano, Km 3, across from *Hotel*

Ecuador

Abraspungo, T964915, www.expediciones-andinas.com Climbing expeditions, operate Chimborazo Base Camp on south flank of mountain, cater to groups. *Julio Verne*, 5 de Junio 21-46 y 10 de Agosto, T/F963436, www.julioverne-travel.com Climbing, trekking, cycling, jungle and Galápagos trips, river rafting, transport to mountains, equipment rental, Ecuadorean-Dutch run, uses official guides. Recommended.

Transport

Bus Terminal Terrestre on Epiclachima y Av Daniel L Borja for buses to Quito, Guayaquil, Ambato, etc. There are smaller terminals for regional destinations. Taxi from one terminal to another, US$0.80. **Quito**, US$3, 4 hrs, about every 30 mins. To **Guaranda**, US$1.75, 2 hrs, crosses a 4,000 m pass, sit on the right, beautiful views. To **Ambato**, US$1, 1 hr, sit on the right. To **Alausí**, US$1.20, 2 hrs. To **Cuenca**, 6 a day via Alausí, 5½ hrs, US$5. This road is paved but landslides are a constant hazard and the road is often under repair. To **Santo Domingo**, hourly, US$4, 5 hrs. In early 2002 all buses to **Baños** and the Oriente were going through Ambato, leaving from the Terminal Oriental, Espejo y Cordovez, US$1.60, 2 hrs. To **Huaquillas** at 2100 with *Patria*, avoiding Guayaquil, daily except Tue and Sat, US$5.45, 9 hrs. To **Guayaquil**, about 35 a day, first one leaves at 0600, US$4, 4½ hrs, the trip is really spectacular for the first 2 hrs.

See box, page 964 **Train** Train service is very limited, but the most spectacular part of the trip – the **Devil's Nose** and **Alausí Loop** – can still be experienced. The train usually leaves **Riobamba** on Wed, Fri and Sun at 0700, arrives in **Alausí** around 1000-1030, reaches **Sibambe** about 1130-1200, and returns to Alausí by 1330-1400. From Riobamba to Sibambe and back to Alausí costs US$15 for foreigners; round trip from Alausí US$13. Tickets for the 0700 train go on sale on the eve between 1800 and 1900, or the same morning at 0600, seats are not numbered, best arrive early. Riding on the roof is fun, but hang on tight and remember that it's very chilly early in the morning. It's also a good idea to sit as far back on the roof as possible to avoid getting covered in soot from the exhaust. The train service is subject to frequent disruptions and timetables are always changing, best enquire locally about current schedules. The railway administration office is on Espejo, next to the Post Office, where information is available during office hours, T960115, or at the station itself T961909.

Metropolitan Touring operates a private *autoferro* (motorized rail-car) on the Riobamba-Sibambe route. US$35 includes train ride, snack, and bilingual guide. Contact their offices in Riobamba (see Tour Operators), Quito, or any travel agency.

Directory

Banks *Banco del Pacífico*, Av Miguel A León y Veloz, changes only Amex TCs, ; MasterCard through ATM only, open 0845-1700. *Banco de Guayaquil*, Primera Constituyente 2626 y García Moreno, cash advances on Visa, 0900-1600. *Vigo Rianxeira*, 10 de Agosto 25-37 y España, T968608, change all dollar TCs plus cash, Mon-Fri 0830-1315 and 1500-1800, Sat 0900-1700. Friendly and efficient. Recommended. **Communications** Internet: Many places, rates about US$1 per hr, *net2phone* about US$0.20 per min. Post Office: 10 de Agosto y Espejo. Telephone: *Andinatel* at Tarqui entre Primera Constituyente y Veloz, 0800-2200; also at the bus terminal.

Climbing Chimborazo
The going rate in 2002 was about US$150 pp. See Tour operators

At 6,310 m, this is a difficult climb owing to the altitude. No-one without mountaineering experience should attempt the climb, and rope, ice-axe and crampons must be used. It is essential to have at least one week's acclimatization above 3,000 m. The best seasons are December and June-September. ■ *US$10*.

Guides There is a provincial association of mountain guides, *Asociación de Andinismo de Chimborazo*, which registers approved guides. **Enrique Veloz Coronado**, technical adviser of the *Asociación de Andinismo de Chimborazo*, Chile 33-21 y Francia, T960916, best reached after 1500, very helpful, his sons are also guides and work with him. **Marcelo Puruncajas** of *Andes Trek*, member of *Aseguim*, highly recommended, speaks English, when not leading tours uses good guides, also offers trekking, four-wheel drive transport and mountain biking. **Marco Cruz** of *Expediciones Andinas*, recommended, he is a certified guide of the *German Alpine Club* and considered among the best and most expensive guides. **Rodrigo Donoso** of *Alta Montaña* (see Tour operators), for climbing and a variety of trekking and horse riding trips, speaks English.

Ecuador

□ Quito

The Southern Sierra

The colonial city of Cuenca, built on the site of an older, indigenous settlement, is the focal point of the region. A pleasant climate and magnificent mountain scenery make the Southern Sierra ideal walking country, while undisturbed páramo and cloud forest are home to many birds and other wildlife.

This is the station where many passengers join the train for the amazing descent over *La Nariz de Diablo* to Sibambe. There is a Sunday market, in the plaza by the church, just up the hill from the station; *fiesta* late June.

Alausí
Phone code: 03
Colour map 1a, grid B3
Population: 5,500

Sleeping E *Americano*, García Moreno 159, T930159. Best in the town. **E** *Panamericano*, 5 de Junio, near the bus stop, T930278. Cheap restaurant, rooms cheaper without bath, hot showers, quieter at the back. **E** *Tequendama*, 5 de Junio, T930123. Restaurant for breakfast only, parking, quieter rooms upstairs. Recommended. **F** *Alausí*, Orozco y 5 de Junio near the coliseo, T930361. Private bath, hot water, laundry facilities, small rooms, noisy. Several other basic places.

Transport Bus: From **Riobamba**, 2 hrs, US$1.20, 84 km. To **Quito**, from 0600 onwards, about 20 a day, 5½ hrs, US$3.10; often have to change in Riobamba. To **Cuenca**, 3½ hrs, US$3.20. To **Ambato** hourly, 3 hrs, US$1.35. To **Guayaquil**, 3 a day Mon-Fri, 6 hrs, US$4.25. *Coop Patria* has a small office where you can buy bus tickets. Other co-operatives have no office, but their buses pass through town, some at the highway and others outside the *Hotel Panamericano*. **Train**: The train to **Sibambe** leaves Wed, Fri and Sun around 1030-1100, 2-3 hrs return, US$13. Alausí to/from Riobamba takes 4 hrs. Tickets go on sale half an hour before departure. To check if it's running, T930126. (See box below.)

The Pan-American Highway south from Alausí runs through mountainous country and is very rough in parts. At Zhud a paved road runs to Cochancay and La Troncal in the coastal lowlands, from where there are paved roads to Guayaquil and Machala. Towards Cuenca the road loses height and the land is more intensively farmed. There are roads linking Quito-Guayaquil and Guayaquil-Cuenca, which meet at El Triunfo on the coastal plain.

A pleasant colonial town, very much the indigenous capital of the province, Cañar is in a good area for walking. Its famous double-faced weaving is now difficult to find, although prisoners in the jail (Centro de Rehabilitación Social) sell backstrap weavings to pay for food. Several shops sell Cañar hats and the Sunday market is very colourful. ■ *Buses go every 30 mins to the Terminal Terrestre in Cuenca, US$1, 2 hrs; also to Quito and El Tambo (7 km).*

Cañar
Phone code: 07
Population: 20,000
67 km N of Cuenca

Sleeping and eating D *Cinco Estrellas*, 100 m W of highway, just N of town, T236166. Restaurant, sometimes noisy. **E** *Ingapirca*, at the park. With balconies, good. **E-F** *Mónica*, main plaza, T235486. Cheaper without bath, basic, mixed reports, offers transport to Ingapirca. **G** *Cañar*, Calle Pichincha, T235682. Shared bath, hot water, laundry facilities, small. *Los Maderos Restaurant*, near the centre. *Chifa Florida*, on plaza. Good (not solely Chinese), cheap. *Café de Antaño*, Bolívar y Borrero, snacks coffee, drinks, art gallery.

Ingapirca

Ecuador's most important Inca ruin lies 5½ km east of Cañar, at 3,160 m. Access is from Cañar or El Tambo. The central structure is an *usnu* platform probably used as a solar observatory. It is faced with fine Inca masonry. Nearby is a throne cut into the

Colour map 1a, grid B3

Ecuador

The railway from the coast to the Sierra

The spectacular 464-km railway line (1.067 m gauge), which was opened in 1908, passes through 87 km of delta lands and then, in 80 km, climbs to 3,238 m. At Urbina on the summit, 3,609 m is reached; it then falls and rises before reaching the Quito plateau at 2,857 m.

Unfortunately, in 1997/98 El Niño damaged the lowland section between Durán and Sibambe, which is unlikely to be repaired owing to lack of funds. On a more positive note, the line's greatest achievements, the Alausí loop and the Devil's Nose double zigzag (including two V switchbacks), are on the part of the line open to trains, Sibambe to Riobamba. **Sibambe**, the current turning point of the train, has no hotels or bus service, so you must return by train to Alausí. Shortly after leaving Sibambe the train starts climbing the famous Nariz del Diablo (Devil's Nose), a perpendicular ridge rising in the

gorge of the Chanchán to a height of 305 m. This almost insurmountable engineering obstacle was finally conquered when a series of switchbacks was built on a 5½% grade.

Next comes **Alausí**. After crossing the 120 m long Shucos bridge, the train pulls into **Palmira**, on the crest of the first range of the Andes crossed by the railway. One by one the great snow-capped volcanoes begin to appear: Chimborazo, Carihuairazo, Altar and the burning heads of Tungurahua and Sangay, all seeming very close because of the clear air.

The best views are from the roof, but dress warmly and protect clothes from dirt. On the train, lock all luggage, even side pockets, as pilfering from luggage compartments is common. The train is popular, especially at weekends and public holidays, so you'll have to queue early.

rock, the **Sillón del Inga** (Inca's Chair) and the **Ingachugana**, a large rock with carved channels. A 10 minute walk away from the site is the **Cara del Inca**, or 'face of the Inca', an immense natural formation in the rock looking over the landscape. On Friday there is an interesting Indian market at Ingapirca. There is a good co-operative craft shop next to the church. ■ *Daily 0900-1800, US$6, including museum; bilingual guide book, US$3, an audio-visual guide in English is available and there are guides at the site; bags can be stored.*

Inca Trail to Ingapirca The three-day hike to Ingapirca on an Inca trail starts at **Achupallas**, 25 km from Alausí. The *IGM* maps (1:50,000 sheets, Alausí, Juncal and Cañar) are useful, also a compass. The name Ingapirca does not appear on the Cañar sheet and you may have to ask directions near the end. Good camping equipment is essential. Take all food and drink with you as there is nothing along the way. A shop in Achupallas sells basic foodstuffs. Some communities on the route may ask for contributions. ■*Pickups leave Alausí for Achupallas daily, at 1130 and 1230 and a bus at 1400, US$0.80, 1 hr. Many more run on Sat, which is Achupallas' market day. The ride is spectacular in its own right. In Achupallas, Gilberto Sarmiento (shop where transport stops at the entrance to town, T930657) has simple rooms for rent in F range. He is also a guide for the walk to Ingapirca. Riobamba and Quito operators also offer this walk.*

Sleeping & eating **B** *Posada Ingapirca*, 500 m above ruins (follow dirt road from parking lot up the hill, no signs)T07-832339, F832340. 8 luxurious rooms with bath, heating, including breakfast, excellent restaurant, good service. Warmly recommended. **E** *Inti Huasi*, in the village of Ingapirca. Nice rooms, quiet, hot water, restaurant.

In **El Tambo** The nearest town to Ingapirca, also provides access to the ruins. **F** *Pensión Estefanía*, on main street, T233126, near the turning for the ruins, hot water, not too clean but friendly, can leave luggage for a small fee. *Restaurant El Turista*, good and cheap food but unfriendly. Also good is *Restaurant Jesús del Gran Poder*, at the truck stop on the hill 400 m north of town. There is a small Sat food market.

Transport A direct bus from the Terminal Terrestre in **Cuenca** leaves at 0900 daily and 1300 Mon-Fri, returning at 1300 and 1600, 2 hrs, US$1.50, with *Transportes Cañar*. Organized excursions and taxi tours from Cuenca US$45 from bus terminal. Any Guayaquil, Riobamba or Quito bus

Ecuador

passes **El Tambo**, 2 hrs, US$1.30. *Coop Cañar* runs hourly buses Cañar-El Tambo from 0600, US$0.50. There is a daily 0600 bus from Cañar direct to Ingapirca (slower, rougher road than from El Tambo). *Transportes Ingapirca* run a regular service from El Tambo to the ruins, about once an hour. From the plaza on the Panamericana in El Tambo, trucks and *Transportes Juhuay* buses go to the ruins. Easy to hitch a ride there and back. **Taxi** El Tambo-Ingapirca US$5; camionetas US$1, beware of overcharging. Last colectivos leave Ingapirca at 1800 for El Tambo. It is a beautiful 2½-hr walk from Ingapirca to Cañar (take food, water and warm clothing). The start of the road is clearly signposted, along the main street.

Azogues

Phone code: 07
Colour map 1a, grid B3
Population: 21,060
36 km S of Cañar

The city is the administrative capital of the province, and a centre of the panama hat industry. The *sombrerías* are very happy to show visitors their trade, but rarely sell their hats; eg *La Sin Ribal*, C Luis Cordero y 3 de Noviembre, or *Capizhun*, E Abad y J de Olmedo, a cooperative of small communities in the area, highly recommended. The market is colourful and beautifully situated, on the hill from the Panamericana to the city's huge church and convent **San Francisco de la Virgen de las Nubes**. Some of the older buildings around the plaza still have traditional painted ceilings over the pavements.

Sleeping and eating **D** *El Paraíso*, Alberto Ochoa y Av Vintimilla, sector La Playa in the north of town, T/F244729. Comfortable rooms in modern building, restaurant, parking, quiet neighbourhood, good value. **D** *Rivera*, Av 24 de Mayo y 10 de Agosto, T248113. Modern, comfortable, on busy street. **D** *Cordillera*, C Azuay overlooking the former bus terminal, T/F240587. With restaurant, internet. **E** *Chicago*, 3 de Noviembre y 24 de Mayo, T241040. Hot water, basic. **E** *Charles*, Solano y Rivera, near plaza, T241364. Shared bath, hot water, simple. *Peleusí*, Sucre 308 y Emilio Abad, cafetería with nice atmosphere, for pizza, tamales, open 0900-1900, closed Sun. *Ochenta y siete*, 3 de Noviembre y 24 de Mayo, next to Hotel Chicago. Good. *El Cuqui*, E Abad 239, for snacks, fruit salad, juices.

Transport It is 1 hr by bus to **Cuenca** (31 km). The bus terminal is across the river from town. A paved road, which bypasses Biblián (north of Azogues), Azogues itself and Cuenca, speeds traffic heading south.

Cuenca

Founded by the Spaniard Gil Ramírez Davalos in 1557 on the site of the Inca settlement of Tomebamba. Much of its colonial air has been preserved, with many of its old buildings constructed of the marble quarried nearby and recently renovated. The climate is spring-like, but the nights are chilly. In 1999 Cuenca was designated a UNESCO World Heritage Site.

Phone code: 07
Colour map 1a, grid C3
Population: 400,000
Altitude: 2,530 m

Getting there The **Terminal Terrestre** is on Av España, 20 mins' walk northwest of the centre. The **airport** is 5 mins' walk from the Terminal Terrestre. Both can be reached by city bus. The terminal for local buses in the province is at the Feria Libre on Av Las Américas. Many city buses pass here.

Ins & outs

For more detailed information see Transport, page 971

Getting around The city is bounded by the Río Machángara to the north and the Ríos Yanuncay and Tarqui to the south. The Río Tomebamba separates the colonial heart from the newer districts to the south. Av Las Américas is a ring road around the city and the new multi-lane highway bypasses the city to the south.

The **tourist office** is on the ground floor of the Municipio, Sucre, between Benigno Malo y Cordero. It has maps of Cuenca, brochures, hotel and tour operator lists. Some staff speak English. ■ *Mon-Sat, 0800-1800, T841139*. The **Cámara de Turismo** also runs an information booth in the bus terminal. ■ *Mon-Sat 0800-1900*. A map of the city is also available from major hotels.

Ecuador

Safety Cuenca is safer than either Quito or Guayaquil, but routine precautions are nonetheless advised. The city centre is deserted and unsafe after 2200. The area around El Puente del Vado (Av 12 de Abril y Av Loja) is unsafe at night. Market areas, especially Mercado 9 de Octubre, call for caution at all hours.

Sights On the main plaza, **Parque Abdón Calderón**, are the Old Cathedral, **El Sagrario**, begun in 1557, and the immense 'New' **Catedral de la Inmaculada**, started in 1885. It contains a famous crowned image of the Virgin, a beautiful altar and an exceptional play of light and shade through modern stained glass. Sunday evening worship is recommended.

Other churches which deserve a visit are **San Blas**, **San Francisco**, **El Cenáculo** and **Santo Domingo**. Many churches are open at irregular hours only and for services. The church of **El Carmen de la Asunción**, close to the southwest corner of La Inmaculada, has a flower market in the tiny **Plazoleta El Carmen** in front. **Turi church and mirador**, south of city on Av Fray Vicente Solano, beyond the football stadium, a two hour walk or take a taxi; a tiled panorama explains the magnificent

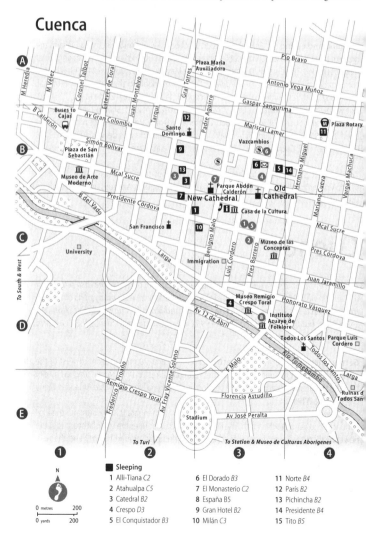

Cuenca

Sleeping
1 Alli-Tiana *C2*
2 Atahualpa *C5*
3 Catedral *B2*
4 Crespo *D3*
5 El Conquistador *B3*
6 El Dorado *B3*
7 El Monasterio *C2*
8 España *B5*
9 Gran Hotel *B2*
10 Milán *C3*
11 Norte *B4*
12 París *B2*
13 Pichincha *B2*
14 Presidente *B4*
15 Tito *B5*

Ecuador

views. There are attractive walks along country lanes further south.

There is a colourful daily market in **Plaza Rotary** where pottery, clothes, guinea pigs and local produce, especially baskets, are sold. Thursday is the busiest.

The **Banco Central 'Pumapungo'** museum complex, C Larga y Huayna Capac, on the edge of the colonial city is at the actual site of Tomebamba excavations. The **Museo Arqueológico** section contains all the Cañari and Inca remains and artifacts found at this site. There are also book and music libraries, free cultural videos and music events. ■ *Mon-Sat 0900-1700, US$1, entrance is on the far left of the building.* There are also museums of local and religious art and ethnography. About 300 m from Pumapungo, at C Larga 287, there are excavations at the Todos Los Santos site, which reveal traces of Inca and Cañari civilizations and show how the Spanish reused the stonework. ■ *Mon-Fri 0800-1600.*

The **Instituto Azuayo de Folklore**, better known as **CIDAP**, Escalinata 303 y C Larga, extension of Hermano Miguel, has an exhibition of popular art and a library.

Museums

It also supports research and promotes sales for artisan workers; recommended craft shop, good information. ■ *Mon-Fri 0930-1300, 1430-1800, Sat 100-1300, free*

Museo de las Culturas Aborígenes has a good private collection of precolumbian archaeology, in the house of Dr J Cordero López at Av 10 de Agosto 4-70, entre F Moscoso y J M Sánchez. ■ *Mon-Fri 0830-1230, 1430-1830, Sat 0830-1230, but phone in advance, T811706, US$2; guided tours in English, Spanish and French. Getting there: Taxi from centre US$1.50.*

Museo del Monasterio de las Conceptas is a well-displayed collection of religious and folk art housed in a cloistered convent founded in 1599 at Hermano Miguel 6-33 entre Pdte Córdova y Juan Jaramillo. ■ *Mon-Fri 0900-1730, Sat 1000-1300, US$2, T830625.*

Museo Municipal de Arte Moderno, Sucre 1527 y Talbot, on Plaza San Sebastián, T831027. Worth a visit for its permanent contemporary art collection and art library. It holds a biennial international painting competition and other cultural activities. ■ *Mon-Fri 0830-1830, Sat 0900-1500, Sun 0900-1300, free.* There's a small museum, art gallery and bookshop in the **Casa de la Cultura**, Luis Cordero y Sucre (second floor). In the courtyard are niches, each containing a statue of a saint. A lovely, restored colonial house is the **Casa Azul**, Gran Colombia 10-29 y Padre Aguirre, housing a travel agency, restaurant and a little museum.

● **Eating**
1 Chifa Pack How *C3*
2 El Jardín *C3*
3 El Túnel *B2*
4 La Barraca *B3*
5 Los Capulíes *C3*
6 Los Pibes *B3*
7 Raymipampa *B3*
8 Wunderbar *D3*

Ecuador

The **Casa de los Canónigos**, C Luis Cordero 888 opposite Parque Calderón, houses the **Salón del Pueblo**, T833492, with original Latin American works of art for exhibition and sale. **Museo Remigio Crespo Toral** at C Larga 7-07 y Borrero, has various collections housed in a beautifully restored colonial mansion, nice café in basement. ■ *Mon-Fri 0830-1300, 1500-1830, free.*

The **Museo de Artes de Fuego** has a display of wrought iron work and pottery. It is housed in a beautifully restored old building. ■ *Las Herrerías y 10 de Agosto, across the river from the Museo del Banco Central. Mon-Fri except for lunchtime and Sat morning.*

Excursions There are sulphur baths at **Baños**, with a domed, blue church in a delightful landscape, 5 km southwest of Cuenca. These are the hottest commercial baths in Ecuador. Above *Hostería Durán* are four separate complexes of warm baths, *Marchan, Rodas, Familiar* and *Durán*. The latter two are by far the largest and best maintained, there are numerous hot pools and tubs and steam baths. At the baths is **B** *Hostería Durán*, Km 8 Vía Baños, T892485, F892488, with a restaurant, its own well-maintained, very clean pools, US$3 for non-residents, steam bath US$3, camping is allowed. There are also four *residencias*, all **F**. ■ *Buses marked Baños, go to and from Cuenca every 5-10 mins, 0600-2330, US$0.20; buses pass the front of the Terminal Terrestre, cross the city on Vega Muñoz and Cueva, then down Todos los Santos to the river, along 12 de Abril and onto Av Loja. Taxi: cost US$4, or walk 1½ hrs.*

Sleeping **LL-L** *El Dorado*, Gran Colombia 787 y Luis Cordero, T831390, www.hoteldorado.com Excellent restaurant, cafeteria open all day, internet, good views. **L** *Oro Verde*, Ordóñez Lazo,
Prices in Cuenca T831200, ecovc@gye.satnet.net Good restaurant, small pool, internet. On the road to Cajas,
are a bit higher on a lagoon in the outskirts of town. **AL** *Crespo*, C Larga 793, T842571,
than elsewhere www.ecuadorexplorer.com/crespo Restaurant, internet, some nice rooms overlooking the river, others dark or with no windows. **A** *El Conquistador*, Gran Colombia 665, T831788, www.hotelconquistador.com Buffet breakfast, good restaurant, internet, disco, avoid back rooms Fri and Sat, good value. **A** *Patrimonio*, Bolívar 6-22 y Hno Miguel, T831126, patrimo@ etapa.com Includes breakfast, restaurant, internet, new in 2001, modern, centrally located.

B *Atahualpa*, Sucre 3-50 y Tomás Ordóñez, T831841, F842345. Includes breakfast, small restaurant and cafeteria, good. Recommended. **B** *El Molino*, Km 7.5 on road Azogues-Cuenca, T875367, F875358. Includes breakfast, restaurant, pool, pleasant location near river, rustic style. Reservations advised. Recommended. **B** *La Orquidea*, Borrero 9-31 y Bolívar, T824511, orquihos@etapa.com.ec Nicely refurbished colonial house, small patios, bright, good value. **B** *Presidente*, Gran Colombia 659, T831066, www.hotelpresidente.com Includes breakfast, good restaurant, internet, good value, comfortable, convenient. **C** *Alli Tiana*, Córdova y Padre Aguirre, T821955, F821788. Includes breakfast, restaurant, small rooms, nice view. **C** *Chordeleg*, Gran Colombia 11-15 y Gral Torres, T822536, F824611. Includes breakfast, charming, colonial style. **C** *Macondo*, Tarqui 11-64 y Lamar, T840697, macondo@cedei.org Includes breakfast, cooking facilities, restored colonial house, US run, Spanish classes. Highly recommended.

D *Caribe Inn*, Gran Colombia 10-51 y Padre Aguirre, T835175, F834157. Cheap breakfast available, restaurant, pleasant and comfortable. **D** *Casa del Barranco*, Calle Larga 8-41 entre Benigno Malo y Luis Cordero, T839763, hostalcasadelbarranc@yahoo.com Restaurant, parking, some spacious rooms, nice views over river. **D** *Catedral*, Padre Aguirre 8-17 y Sucre, T823204. Includes breakfast, good restaurant, coffee shop opens 0700, internet, cheerful, spacious, modern, but not very warm. English spoken. **D** *El Cafecito*, Honorato Vásquez 7-36 y Luis Cordero, T832337, elcafec@cue.satnet.net Good breakfast in restaurant with charming patio, noisy until midnight because of restaurant below, cheaper without bath, hot showers, colonial house, discount for longer stay. Recommended. **D** *El Monasterio*, Padre Aguirre 7-24 y Sucre, T837259, monasterio724@hotmail.com Internet, cooking facilities, nice views, secure, popular. Highly recommended. **D** *Gran Hotel*, Torres 9-70 y Bolívar, T831934, F842127. Includes breakfast, restaurant, nice patio, popular meeting place. **D** *Milán*, Pres Córdova 989 y Padre Aguirre, T831104, hotmilan@etapa.com.ec Includes breakfast, restaurant, internet, view over market, rooms variable but clean. Often full and overpriced. **D** *París*, Gral Torres 10-48 y Gran Colombia, T842656, F841468. Includes breakfast, intermittent hot water, large rooms. Recommended.

E *La Casa (Students Residence)*, Hno Miguel 4-19, T837347. Shared bath, internet, cooking facilities, simple. **E** *Norte*, Mariano Cueva 11-63 y Sangurima, T827881. Good restaurant, renovated, large rooms, comfortable. Hotel is safe but not a nice area after dark. Recommended. **E** *Pichincha*, Gral Torres 8-82 y Bolívar, T823868, karolina@etapa.com.ec Internet, parking, spacious, helpful, luggage stored. Recommended. **F** pp *Hostal Latina*, Benigno Malo 11-54 y Sangurima, T09-911 4443. New, attractive and welcoming, laundry service.

Near the bus terminal are C *España*, Sangurima 1-17 y Huayna Cápac, T831351, hespana@cue.satnet.net Includes breakfast, good restaurant, cheaper without bath, internet, spacious. Upstairs front rooms are best. **D** *Tito*, Sangurima 149 y M Vega, T/F843577. Restaurant very good value, safe. Several others of varying quality in this area.

Furnished apartments *El Jardín*, Av Pumapungo y Viracochabamba, T804103, or write to Casilla 298. Cooking facilities and parking, US$495 a month **B** *Apartamentos Otorongo*, Av 12 de Abril y Guayas, T811184, pmontezu@az.pro.ec, 10-15 mins walk from centre. With kitchenette, TV, phone, cleaning service included, very friendly owners, discount for longer stay.

El Jardín, Presidente Córdova 7-23. Lovely, very good international food, closed Sun-Mon, very expensive. *Villa Rosa*, Gran Colombia 12-22 y Tarqui. Elegant, excellent. *Molinos del Batán*, 12 de Abril y Puente El Vado. Good setting by river, good Ecuadorean food, expensive. *La Rotond*, 12 de Abril y José Peralta. Excellent French and international cooking, elegant, nice view of the river and residencial area, reservations T888111. *El Che Pibe*, Av Remigio Crespo 2-59. *Parrillada argentina* and other dishes, excellent service, open till late, expensive; also at Gran Colombia, 8-33 y Cordero, excellent pizzas, pleasant courtyard.

Los Capulíes, Córdova y Borrero. Bar-restaurant, excellent Ecuadorean food, lovely setting, reasonable prices, Andean live music Thu-Sat 2030, reservations recommended at the weekend, T832339. *Las Tres Carabelas*, part of hotel *El Conquistador*. Good value Ecuadorean food, Andean live music at weekends. *Las Campanas*, Borrero 7-69 y Sucre. Good Ecuadorean food, open untill 0200. *Casa Grande*, San Joaquín-La Cruz Verde, T839992. Local dishes, in picturesque San Joaquín district where flowers and vegetables are grown and baskets made, good food and value, popular. *New York Pizza*, Gran Colombia 10-43 y Aguirre. Very good, especially the *calzones*. *Los Pibes*, Gran Colombia 776 y Cordero, opposite *Hotel El Dorado*. Good pizzas and lasagne, moderately priced. *Los Sauces*, Bolívar 6-17. Original dishes, reasonable prices. *La Barraca*, Borrero entre Gran Colombia y Bolívar. Breakfast, dinner, quiet music, coffee, excellent, open daily 0800-2300. *La Tasca*, Pasaje 3 de Noviembre bajos del Puente Roto. Cuban and international. *El Tequila*, Gran Colombia 20-59. Local food and more, good value and service. *El Túnel*, Gral Torres 8-60, T823109. Reasonably priced, quick service, romantic atmosphere, cheap lunch menu. *Chifa Pack How*, Presidente Córdova 772 y Cordero. Not cheap. Recommended. *Chifa Asia*, Remigio Crespo 1-11 y Solano, south of Río Tomebamba. Large portions, medium price. *Sol Oriental*, Gran Colombia y Vega. Cheap.

The Zona Rosa, along Av Remigio Crespo between the stadium and the coliseum, has a variety of *pizzerías*, *heladerías*, burger and sandwich bars, steak houses, bars and discos.

Vegetarian *El Paraíso*, Tomás Ordóñez 10-45 y Gran Colombia and at Ordóñez near Juan Jaramillo. Open Mon-Sat 0800-1600, breakfast, cheap set lunch. *Govinda*, Juan Jaramillo 727 y Borrero. Good.

Snack bars and cafés *Raymipampa*, Benigno Malo 8-59, on Plaza Calderón. Open daily, very popular, local dishes, crêpes, ice cream, excellent value, also on Mcal Sucre next to Casa de la Cultura. *Wunderbar*, Hermano Miguel y C Larga, behind the Instituto Azuayo de Folklore. German-run, good atmosphere, food and coffee, also vegetarian, expensive, book exchange, German magazines, closed Sun. *Café Chordeleg*, Gran Colombia 7-87. Open late, excellent breakfast. *Café Capuchino*, Bolívar y Aguirre. Open 0930, hamburgers, real coffee and liqueur coffees. *Monte Bianco*, Bolívar 2-80 y Ordóñez, near San Blas church. Cakes, ice

Eating
Most places are closed on Sun evening. Upscale restaurants add 22% tax and service to the bill

Ecuador

cream, open Sun. *Café Austria*, Benigno Malo 5-99. Cakes, pies, sandwiches, coffee, fruit, ice cream, yoghurt, closed Mon. *Cinema Café*, Luis Cordero y Sucre, above the Casa de la Cultura cinema. Snacks, salads, popular. *Café del Centro*, Sucre 7-50. Capuccino, sandwiches and local dishes. *Heladería Holanda*, Benigno Malo 9-51. Open 0930, yoghurt for breakfast, good ice cream, fruit salads, great toilets. Across the street is *Tutto Fredo*. Pizza, sweets, ice cream, excellent. *Mi Pan*, Pres Córdova 824 between Cordero y Malo (also Bolívar y Aguirre). Opens 0930, excellent bread, cakes, tarts, doughnuts, tea, coffee and chocolate.

Bars *Chaos*, Honorato Vásquez y Hermano Miguel. Popular. *Bar del Tranquilo*, J Jaramillo y Hermano Miguel. Peña, live music, nice atmosphere. *Tapas y Canciones*, Remigio Crespo y Galápagos. Small quaint *peña*. All popular.

Entertainment **Cinemas** There are 3 cinemas, the one next to the Casa de la Cultura shows interesting films at 1430 and 2100. *Teatro Cuenca*, P Aguirre 10-50, also shows films. **Discos** *Azúcar,* Pasaje 3 de Noviembre y 12 de Abril, under the Puente Roto bridge. Latin and international music. *La Mesa Salsoteca*, Gran Colombia 3-36 y Tomás Ordoñez. Latin music, salsa, popular among travellers and locals. *Papa Galo*, Remigio Crespo y Galápagos, in the Zona Rosa. Varied music, popular with local youth. *Pop Art*, Remigio Crespo y Solano. disco-bar, popular with tourists. *Ritmo*, Benigno Malo y Lamar. International and tropical music, pizza. *Mexx*, Borrero y J Jaramillo. Live music, pleasant atmosphere. *Zoom*, Larga y M Cueva. Good mix of music, popular.

Festivals On **24 Dec** there is an outstanding parade: *Pase del Niño Viajero*, probably the largest and finest Christmas parade in all Ecuador. Children and adults from all the *barrios* and surrounding villages decorate donkeys, horses, cars and trucks with symbols of abundance. Little children in colourful Indian costumes or dressed up as Biblical figures ride through the streets accompanied by musicians. The parade starts at about 1000 at San Sebastián, proceeds along C Simón Bolívar and ends at San Blas about 5 hrs later. In the days up to, and just after Christmas, there are many smaller parades. **10-13 Apr** is the *Foundation of Cuenca*. On **Good Friday** there is a fine procession through the town to the Mirador Turi. **Jun** *Septenario*, the religious festival of Corpus Christi in Jun, lasts a week. On **3 Nov** is *Independence of Cuenca*, with street theatre, art exhibitions and night-time dances all over the city. Cuenca hosts an internationally famous art competition every 2 years, which begins in **Apr** or **May**, co-ordinated by the Museo de Arte Moderno.

Shopping Good souvenirs are carvings, leather, basketwork, painted wood, onyx, ceramics, woven stuffs, *The Cuenca region is* embroidered shirts, jewellery, etc. There are craftware shops along Gran Colombia, in *El Dorado* *noted for its artesanía* hotel (good quality), and on Benigno Malo. *Arte Artesanías y Antigüedades* at Borrero y Córdova. Textiles, jewellery and antiques. *El Tucán*, Borrero 7-35. Ecuadorean *artesanía*. Recommended. *Galería Claudio Maldonado*, Bolívar 7-75. Unique precolumbian designs in silver and precious stones. *Centro Cultural Jorge Moscoso*, Luis Cordero y Pdte Córdova, T822114. Weaving exhibitions, ethnographic museum, antiques and handicrafts. *Galería Pulla*, Jaramillo 6-90. Famous painter, sculpture and jewellery. There are several good leather shops in the arcade off Bolívar between Benigno Malo and Luis Cordero, the quality and price are comparable with Cotacachi. *Artesa*, L Cordero 10-31 y Gran Colombia, several branches. Modern Ecuadorean ceramics at good prices. *Joyería Turismo* owned by Leonardo Crespo, at Gran Colombia 9-31. Recommended. He will let wholesale buyers tour his factory. *Unicornio*, L Cordero entre Gran Colombia y Lamar. Good jewellery, ceramics and candelabra.

High quality **panama hats** are made by *Homero Ortega P e Hijos*, Av Gil Ramírez Dávalos 3-86, T823429, F834045. He will show you his factory opposite bus station, open 0900-1200, 1500-1800 for visits. Also *Kurt Dorfzaun*, Gil Ramírez Dávalos 4-34, T861707. Good prices and display of the complete hat making process. *Exportadora Cuenca*, Mcal Lamar 3-80. Jaime Ortega Ramírez and his wife, Tania, will make to order and won't apply bleach if so asked. Highly recommended.

Books *The English Café and Bookshop*, C Larga 6-69 y Hermano Miguel. Books for sale and rent, cafeteria. *Librería ASG*, B Malo y Gran Colombia. Limited supply of English books.

There's an interesting market behind the new cathedral. There is a well-stocked supermarket behind *Hotel España*; *Supermaxi*, Colombia y Av de las Américas and on Av José Peralta. Camping equipment at *Bermeo Hnos*, Borrero 8-35 y Sucre, T831522; *Créditos y Negocios*, Benigno Malo y Pdte Córdova, T829583; *Explorador Andino*, B Malo y Larga; *Recreaciones del Austro*, Bolívar 6-59 y Borreo.

Apullacta, Gran Colombia y G Torres. Rent tents. *Ecotrek*, C Larga 7-108 y Luis Cordero, T842531, F835387, contact Juan Gabriel Carrasco. Trips to Kapawi Ecological Reserve, excellent, experienced guides and great adventure travel, monthly departures, specialize in Shaman trips. *Viajes Enmotur*, Gran Colombia 10-45. Bus tours to Ingapirca US$45. *Metropolitan Touring*, Sucre 6-62 y Borrero, T831463. *Río Arriba Eco-Turismo*, Hermano Miguel 7-38 y Córdova, T840031. Recommended. *Travel Center*, Hermano Miguel 4-46 y C Larga, houses several tour operators including: *Montaruna Tours*, The Travel Center, Hermano Miguel 4-46 y Larga, T/F846395, www.montaruna.ch Horse riding, treks, German and English spoken, helpful. Recommended. Also *Terra Diversa*, T823782, F820085, info@terradiversa.com Jungle tours, well informed. **Recommended guides**: *José Rivera Baquero*, Pedro Carbo 1-48 y Guapondelig, very knowledgeable. *Eduardo Quito*, T823018, F834202, has his own 4WD, special tours for up to 10 people, speaks good English. *Luis Astudillo*, C Azuay 1-48 entre Guayas y Tungurahua, T815234, tours to Ingapirca, US$30. The **Ministerio de Turismo**, is at Presidente Córdova y Benigno Malo, T839337, and has a list of trained guides, *guías carnetizados*.

Tour operators

Local Bus: Terminal for local services is at the Feria Libre on Av Las Américas. Many city buses pass here. City buses US$0.20. **Car rental**: *Inter*, Av España, opposite the airport, T863902. **Taxi**: US$1 for short journey; US$2 to airport or bus station; US$5 per hr; US$22 per day.

    Long distance Air: Airport is 5 mins walk beyond the terminal. No ticket reservations at the airport. To **Quito** with *TAME*, 2 flights a day, US$62. To **Guayaquil** with *TAME* and

Transport

Ecuador

Austro Aéreo, US$38. To Macas with *Austro Aéreo*, 3 flights a week, US$25. Reconfirm tickets, beware extra charges at check-in, book several days in advance, flights are often full, try getting advanced boarding pass (*prechequeo*). Arrive at least 1 hr before departure.

Bus The Terminal Terrestre is on Av España, northeast of centre, 20 mins walk, or take a minibus, US$$0.20, or taxi, US$2. It is well-organized and policed. Take daytime buses to enjoy scenic routes. To/from **Quito**, 10-11 hrs, US$13, 8 hrs; *Panamericana Internacional*, Huayna Cápac y España, T840060; luxury coach service with *Sucre Express*, 8½ hrs, US$18. To **Riobamba**, 5½-6 hrs, US$5, sit on the left. To **Ambato**, US$5-9, 7 hrs (some companies take a coastal route). To **Azogues**, US$0.80, 1 per hr. To **Saraguro**, US$2.65, 4 hrs. To **Loja**, 5-6 hrs with *San Luis*, US$5, sit on the left. To **Machala**, 4-5 hrs, hourly, US$3.50, sit on the left. To **Guayaquil**, via Cajas and Molleturo, 4-5 hrs, US$7, hourly with *San Luis;* via Cañar, 4 daily with *Sucre Express*. To **Huaquillas**, 6 hrs (frequent police checks), US$4, 5 a day; to avoid a possible 2 hr wait in Machala get off at the large roundabout (well known to drivers) for the local bus to Huaquillas. *Coop Sucúa* (3 nightly, 1 at 1000) go to **Sucúa** (10 hrs, US$6). *Turismo Oriental* to **Macas** (8 hrs, US$7), the left side is best overall although the right side is good for the last part with views of approach to lowlands. To **Gualaquiza**, US$6, 10 hrs.

Directory **Airline offices** *TAME*, Benigno Malo 508 y C Larga, T843222. *Austro Aéreo*, Hermano Miguel 5-42 y Honorato Vásquez, T832677, F848659. **Banks** *Banco del Pacífico*, Benigno Malo 9-75, MasterCard ATM, good rates for TCs. *Banco del Austro*, Sucre y Borrero, T842492, changes Citicorp TCs, Visa ATM. *Banco de Guayaquil*, Sucre entre Hermano Miguel y Borrero, cash on Visa and TCs. *Banco del Pichincha*, Bolívar 9-74 y B Malo T831544, for TCs. MasterCard office at Bolívar y T Ordóñez T883577, F817290. *Banco Jaramillo Arteaga*, Bolívar y Hermano Miguel, changes US$ TCs and other currencies, cash only. *Vaz Cambios*, Gran Colombia 7-98 y Cordero, T833434, open Sat morning, efficient. **Communications** Internet: rates US$0.70-1 per hr. Many to choose from. **Post Office:** on corner of Gran Colombia and Borrero, helpful. **Telephone:** ETAPA on Benigno Malo between Córdova and Sucre, access to internet Mon-Fri 0800-2200, good value. **Embassies and consulates** British Honorary Consul, Sr Teodoro Jerves, Pasaje San Alfonso (same block as Iglesia San Alfonso), T831996.

Colombian Consulate, Cordero 9-55. **Alliance Française**, Tadeo Torres 1-92, open Mon-Fri, 0830-1230, 1430-1830. **German Honorary Consul**, Bolívar y Benigno Malo. **Language courses** Rates US$4.50-8.00 per hr. *Fundación Centro de Estudios Interamericanos*, Gran Colombia 11-02 y Gral Torres, Edif Assoc de Empleados, T839003, F833593, www.cedei.org Classes in Spanish and Quichua, accommodation at short notice, recommended, *Hostal Macondo* attached. *Centro Abraham Lincoln*, Borrero y Honorato Vásquez, T830373. Small Spanish language section. *Nexus Lenguas y Culturas*, José Peralta 1-19 y 12 de Abril, T884016, F888221. Also teach English and German, short-term basis family stays, well-run. Recommended. *Sí Centro de Español e Inglés*, Sucre 7-50, 1 p, T/F846932, T09256363 (Mob), sicentro@ecuadorexplorer.com Run by Guido and Jeaneth Abad, good teachers, pleasant atmosphere, friendly, helpful. Recommended. **Medical services** Clinics: Clínica Santa Inés, Dr Jaime Moreno Aguilar speaks English, Av Toral, T817888. Clínica Los Andes, Mariano Cueva 14-68 y Pío Bravo, T842942/832488. Excellent care, clean, 24 hr service. *Farmacia Botica Internacional*, Gran Colombia 7-20 y Borrero. Experienced staff, wide selection. **Useful addresses** Immigration: Policía Nacional de Migración, Luis Cordero 662 y J Jaramillo, T831020, tourist visa extensions.

North & east of Cuenca

Northeast of Cuenca on the new road to Méndez in the Oriente, is **Paute** on the Río Palma, the site of Ecuador's largest hydroelectric plant. Deforestation is causing the dam to silt up, so it has to be continually dredged to function. **A** *Hostería Huertos de Uzhupud*, T250339, huzhupud@cue.satnet.net, set in the beautiful Paute valley, deluxe, rooms at the back have best views, swimming pool, sports fields, gardens, lots of orchids, recommended (but has small zoo), taxi from Cuenca US$15.

Gualaceo is a thriving, modern town set in beautiful landscape, with a charming plaza and fine new church with splendid modern glass. Its Sunday market doesn't cater for tourists. Woollen goods are sold on the main street near the bus station, while embroidered goods are sold from a private home above the general store on the main plaza. Inexpensive good shoes are made locally. **B** *Parador Turístico*, T255010, outside town, chalets, rooms, modern, nice, swimming pool, good restaurant. On the same street but further down the hill are other hotels (**E-F**), including *Res Gualaceo*, Gran Colombia 302, T255006, private or shared bath, camping possible. ■ *Buses from the Terminal Terrestre in Cuenca to Gualaceo, US$0.55, 45 mins.*

South of Gualaceo is **Chordeleg**, a touristy village famous for its crafts in wood, silver and gold filigree, pottery and panama hats. Watch out for fake jewellery. *Joyería Dorita* and *Joyería Puerto del Sol*, on Juan B Cobos y Eloy Alfaro, and *Joyería Campoverde* on the main plaza, have been recommended (the latter for gold filigree). The small *Museo de la Comunidad* of local textiles, ceramics and straw work, sells some items at reasonable prices. The church is interesting with some lovely modern stained glass. It's a good uphill walk from Gualaceo to Chordeleg, and a pleasant hour downhill in the other direction. ■ *Plenty of local transport, US$0.15 from Gualaceo market, every 30 mins; direct bus from Cuenca, 1½ hrs, US$0.65.*

South of Gualaceo, 83 km from Cuenca, **Sígsig**, with a Sunday market and a few *sombrerías*, is worth a visit. ■ *Bus from Cuenca 1½ hrs, US$0.65, hourly bus also from Chordeleg.*

Parque Nacional Cajas

Northwest of Cuenca, Cajas is a 29,000 ha national park with over 230 lakes. Near the entrance is an altar and pilgrim area where a teenager saw 'Our Lady of the Faith' in 1988. The *páramo* vegetation, such as chuquiragua and lupin, is beautiful and contains interesting wildlife: Andean gull, black frogs, humming birds, even condors.

On a clear morning the views are superb, even to Chimborazo, some 300 km away

The park offers ideal but strenuous walking, at 3,500 m-4,400 m altitude, and the climate is rough. Deaths have occurred from exposure. The best time to visit is August-January, when you may expect clear days, strong winds, night-time temperatures to −8°C and occasional mist. From February-July temperatures are higher but there is much more fog, rain and snow. It is best to arrive in the early morning since it can get very cloudy, wet and cool after about 1300. Local maps are not always exact.

Ecuador

It is better to get the *IGM* maps in Quito (Chiquintad 1:50,000) and take a compass. It is easy to get lost as signs (if any) are of little help.

There is a *refugio* at Laguna Toreadora (**F** pp), cold, cooking facilities. There are also two primitive shelters by the shore of the lake, a 20 and 40-min' walk from the refuge. Take food, fuel, candles, sleeping bags, warm clothes and strong sun cream. Camping costs US$5.

■ *US$10. There is a visitors' centre and cafeteria at Laguna Toreadora (3,810 m), next to the old refuge; rarely open, so take food.*

Transport　*San Luis* buses bound for **Guayaquil** go through the park. Hourly departures starting 0615, US$2, 40 mins.

Tours　There are organized tours to the lakes from Cuenca, fishing possible, about US$35. Alternatively, hire a private truck, US$16 with driver. A group of ramblers welcomes visitors for Sun walks in Aug and Sep, look for posters in Cuenca.

The road from Cuenca to Guayaquil via Molleturo is fully paved. The road passes through Parque Nacional Cajas and continues over the mountains to the towns of Molleturo and Jesús María and on to the coast. The scenery is spectacular and there are still a few places where there is undisturbed forest. There is nowhere to stay after the *refugio* at Laguna Toreadora (see above) until you reach the lowlands between Naranjal and La Troncal.

Cuenca to Machala　From Cuenca, the Pan-American Highway runs south to La Y, about 20 km away. Here the road divides into two: one continues the Pan-American to Loja, and the other runs through sugar cane fields to Pasaje and Machala. Most buses between Cuenca and the Peruvian border at Huaquillas (see page 990) go northwest to La Troncal, then south down the coast.

One hour from Cuenca is **Girón** whose beauty is spoiled only by a modern concrete church. The road then continues through the Yungilla valley and **Santa Isabel** (**C** *La Molienda*, by Cataviña, just before Santa Isabel; **D** *Sol y Agua*, below the village) before descending through desert to the stark rocky canyon of the Río Jubones. The next town is **Casacay** (**D** *Hostería San Luis*, attractive, good, pool, pleasant climate), after which lush banana plantations are entered.

In the lowlands is **Pasaje**. **D** *San Martín*, a/c, safe; many basic *pensiones*, **G**.

South of Cuenca

Saraguro　This is a very cold town. Here the Indians, the most southerly Andean group in Ecua-
Population: 19,883　dor, dress all in black. They wear very broad flat-brimmed hard felt hats. The men are notable for their black shorts, sometimes covered by a whitish kind of divided apron, and a particular kind of saddle bag, the *alforja*, and the women for their pleated black skirts, necklaces of coloured beads and silver *topos*, ornate pins fastening their shawls. The town has a picturesque Sunday market and interesting Mass. ■ *Buses to and from Cuenca with* Coop Viajeros, *4 daily, US$2.65, 4 hrs; to Loja, US$1.40, 1½ hrs. Check if your bus is leaving from the plaza or the Panamericana.*

Sleeping and eating F *Res Armijos*, C Antonio Castro. Cold shower, quiet, good. **F** *Res Saraguro*, C Loja No 03-2 y Antonio Castro. Shared bath, nice courtyard, hot water, laundry facilities. Recommended. *Salón Cristal*, Azuay y Castro. Lunch only, simple but good food, clean. *Reina del Cisne*, at the park. Set meals.

The road between Cuenca and Loja is paved but often deteriorates after heavy rains. It undulates through several passes and is one of the most beautiful and breathtaking in Ecuador.

Ecuador

Loja

This friendly, pleasant highland city, lies near the Oriente. It was founded on its present site in 1548, having been moved from La Toma, and was rebuilt twice after earthquakes, the last of which occurred in the 1880s. The city, encircled by hills, has been a traditional gateway between the highlands and southern Amazonia. The city has two universities, with a well-known law school. The Universidad Nacional has good murals on some of its buildings. There are crude paintings on the patio walls of many of the old houses. The city has several nice parks, it is also one of the few cities in Ecuador which sorts and recycles its garbage. In 2001 it was granted third prize in the United Nations contest 'Nations in Bloom'.

Phone code:07
Colour map 1a, grid C3
Population: 117,365
Altitude: 2,063 m

The **Cathedral** and **Santo Domingo** church, Bolívar y Rocafuerte, have painted interiors. **El Valle** church, on the south edge of the city is colonial, with a lovely interior. **The Museo de la Historia y Culturas Lojanas del Banco Central** on the main plaza, 0800-1600, has exhibits of local art, archaeology, folklore and history, and the **Casa de la Cultura**, Colón entre Bolívar y B Valdivieso, sponsors cultural events. **Mercado Centro Comercial Loja** (Mercado Modelo), 10 de Agosto y 18 de Noviembre, rebuilt in 1991, is worth a visit. It is clean and efficient. ■ *Mon-Sat 0800-1800, Sun 0800-1500.* There is a market on Saturday, Sunday and Monday, attended by many Saraguro Indians. There are souvenir and craft shops on 10 de Agosto between Iberoamérica and 18 de Noviembre.

Loja is famed for its musicians and has one of the few musical academies in the country. Musical evenings and concerts are often held around the town. *El Siglo* and *Crónica* give news of events. The tourist office is at Valdivieso 08-22 y 10 de Agosto, T572964, F570485. ■ *Mon-Fri, 0800-1300, 1500-1800.* Loja tradición, cultura y turismo, *is a useful guidebook.*

Parque Educacional Ambiental y Recreacional de Argelia is superb, with trails through the forest to the *páramo*. It is 500 m before the police checkpoint on road south to Vilcabamba. ■ *0830-1700 except Tue and Wed. Take a city bus marked 'Argelia'.* Across the road and 100 m south is the **Jardín Botánico Reynaldo Espinosa**, which is nicely laid out. ■ *Mon-Fri 0900-1600, US$ 0.50.*

Excursions

C *Bombuscaro*, 10 de Agosto y Av Universitaria, T577021, F570136. Full breakfast, nice rooms and suites, good service. Recommended. **C** *Hostal del Bus*, Av 8 de Diciembre y JJ Flores, T575100, hdelgado@impsat.net.ec Restaurant, opposite the terminal, Carpeted

Sleeping

Ecuador

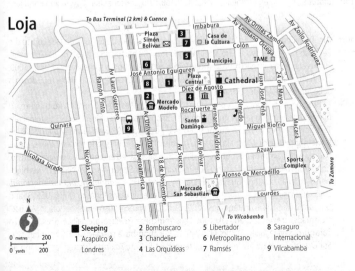

Loja

To Bus Terminal (2 km) & Cuenca

Imbabura
Av Orillas Zamora
Av Emiliano Ortega
Av Zoilo Rodríguez
Plaza Simón Bolívar
Casa de la Cultura
Colón
Municipio
TAME
José Antonio Eguiguren
Plaza Central
Cathedral
Diez de Agosto
Mercado Modelo
Rocafuerte
Santo Domingo
Ramón Pinto
Av Lauro Guerrero
Av Universitaria
Juan José Peña
24 de Mayo
Olmedo
Miguel Riofrio
Macará
Quinara
Bernardo Valdivieso
Azuay
Nicolasa Jurado
Nicolás García
18 de Noviembre
Av Sucre
Av Iberoamérica
Av Bolívar
Sports Complex
To Zamora
Av Alonso de Mercadillo
Mercado San Sebastián
Lourdes

N

0 metres 200
0 yards 200

To Vilcabamba

■ **Sleeping**
1 Acapulco & Londres
2 Bombuscaro
3 Chandelier
4 Las Orquídeas
5 Libertador
6 Metropolitano
7 Ramsés
8 Saraguro Internacional
9 Vilcabamba

rooms and suites. **C** *Libertador*, Colón 14-30 y Bolívar, T570344, F572119. Good restaurant *La Castellana*, suites available, noisy. **D** *Acapulco*, Sucre 749 y 10 de Agosto, T570651. Safe for leaving luggage, 1st floor rooms are quieter in the mornings. Recommended. **D** *Aguilera Internacional*, Sucre 01-08 y Emiliano Ortega, T/F572894. Includes breakfast, restaurant, parking, nice rooms, sauna, gym. **D** *Ramsés*, Colón 14-31 y Bolívar, T571402. Good restaurant, phone. **D** *Vilcabamba*, Iberoamérica y Pasaje la FEUE, T573393, F573645. Includes breakfast, on the river, pleasant, discount for *Handbook* users. **E** *Las Orquídeas*, Bolívar 8-59 y 10 de Agosto, T575465. **E** *Metropolitano*, 18 de Noviembre 6-41 y Colón, T570007. With bath and TV. **E** *Saraguro Internacional*, Universitaria 724 y 10 de Agosto, T570552. Restaurant closed Sun, parking. **F** *Chandelier*, Imbabura 14-82 y Sucre, T563061. With bath and TV. **F** *Londres*, Sucre 741 y 10 de Agosto. Hot water, nice big rooms, comfortable.

There are basic ***residenciales*** in our **F** range on Rocafuerte, also some along Sucre with mostly short stay customers.

Eating *Los Tayos*, Sucre 06-55. Good regional cuisine, choice of set meals, open Sun. *México*, Eguiguren 1585 y Sucre. Good set meals or à la carte, popular. Recommended. *Chalet Francia*, Valdiviezo y Eguiguren. Excellent food and value. *La Tullpa*, 18 de Noviembre y Colón. Good *churrasco*. *Parrillada Uruguaya*, Iberoamérica y J de Salinas. Opens 1700, good grilled meat, owner helpful. *Salud y Vida*, Azuay near Olmedo. Vegetarian. *Chifa El Arbol de Oro*, Bolívar y Lourdes. Good Chinese. Loja has many excellent bakeries. Good snacks, pastries and yoghurt at *Pastelería Persa*, Bolívar y Rocafuerte. *Heladería Sinai*, Plaza Central. Very popular. *Topoli*, Riofrío y Bolívar. Best coffee and yoghurt, good for breakfast (not open for lunch). *El Jugo Natural*, Eguiguren 14-18 y Bolívar. Very good fresh juices and breakfast. Closed Sun. *Café Azul*, Eguiguren entre Bolívar y Sucre. Good breakfast.

Most restaurants downtown are closed on Sun, when you have more options by the bus terminal

Festivals 16-20 Aug *Fiesta de la Virgen del Cisne*, the image of the Virgin remains in Loja until 1 Nov. The statue of the Virgin spends a month each year travelling around the province; the most important peregrination is the 3-day 70 km walk from El Cisne to Loja cathedral, beginning 17 Aug. The last 2 weeks of Aug and the 1st week of Sep are crowded.

Shopping *Cer-Art Ceramics*, precolumbian designs on ceramics, produced at the Universidad Técnica. Above the Universidad Técnica is the 'Ceramics Plaza', where you can buy directly from the crafts studio. A little higher on the same road is *Productos Lacteos*, selling cheeses and fresh butter, all produced by the university. There is a good health food shop on 10 de Agosto, behind the Cathedral.

Tour operators *Biotours*, Eguiguren y Olmedo, T578398, biotours@loja.telconet.net City, regional and jungle tours, airline tickets.

Transport **Air** The airport is at La Toma (Catamayo), 35 km west, shared taxi US$3 pp (see Loja to the Peruvian border below). There are *TAME* and *Icaro* flights to Quito direct or via Guayaquil. Flights are often cancelled due to strong winds and the airport is sometimes closed by 1000. The *TAME* office is at Prolongación 24 de Mayo y Eguiguren, T573030, 0830-1600. *Icaro* is at Eguiguren y Olmedo, T578416.

All buses leave from the Terminal Terrestre at the north of town, some companies also have ticket offices in the centre

Bus Terminal at Av Gran Colombia e Isidro Ayora, buses every 2 mins to/from centre, 10 mins journey; left luggage, information desk, shops, *Andinatel* office, US$0.15 terminal tax. Taxi from centre, US$1. To **Cuenca**, 5-6 hrs, 7 a day, US$6 with *Trans Viajeros* (18 de Noviembre y Quito). **Machala**, 10 a day, 7 hrs, US$4 (2 routes, one through Piñas, rather bumpy with hairpin bends but better views, the other paved and generally quicker). **Quito**, *Cooperativa Loja* (10 de Agosto y Guerrero), and *Trans Santa*, 4 a day, US$12, 14 (via highlands)-16 (via coast)hrs. **Guayaquil**, 5 a day, 9 hrs, US$8. *Panamericana Internacional*, office at *Grand Hotel Loja* (Iberoamérica y Rocafuerte), luxury service to Quito (US$15) and Guayaquil (US$10). To **Huaquillas** at 2030 and 2230, US$4.50, 6-8 hrs; get off at Machala crossroads, *La Avanzada*, and take a local bus from there. To **Macará**, 6 daily, 5-6 hrs, US$5. To **Saraguro**, several daily, 1½ hrs, US$1.40. To **Vilcabamba**, a spectacular 1½-hour bus ride; *Sur Oriente* leave hourly from the bus terminal, US$0.60; *Taxiruta* (shared taxis) along Av

Universitaria, US$1, 1 hr; *Vilcabaturis* vans, from the bus terminal, every 30 minutes, US$1, 1 hr. To **Zamora**, hourly, 1½ hours, US$1.90. To **Zumba** via Vilcabamba, with *Sur Oriente* and *Unión Cariamanga*, 8 daily (1st at 0530, 2nd at 0800), 7 hrs, US$5. To **Piura (Peru)**, luxury coach service with *Loja Internacional*, at 0700, 1300 and 2230 daily (Piura-Loja at 0600, 2100, 2200), 9 hrs including border formalities, US$8 (reservations can be made in Vilcabamba with *Vilcabaturis*).

Banks *Banco de Loja*, Rocafuerte y Bolívar, good rates for TCs. *Banco Mutualista Pichincha*, on plaza, cash advance on MasterCard. **Communications** Internet: Many internet cafés in town, price about US$1.20 per hr. Several around C Colón y Sucre. **Post Office:** Colón y Sucre; no good for sending parcels. **Pacifictel:** on Rocafuerte y Olmedo. **Embassies and consulates** *Peru*, Sucre y Azuay, T573600. **Useful addresses** Immigration: Bolivia y Argentina, T573600.

(margin) **Directory**

There are two sections to this park. **1**: The entrance to the upper premontane section is about 15 km south of Loja on the Vilcabamba road at Cajanuma. Take water-proofs and warm clothing. Permits (US$10) and an adequate map from the park office at C Azuay entre Valdivieso y Olmedo, Loja (T571534), open 0800; or at the entrance. There is a comfortable refuge at the information centre in Cajanuma, US$5 pp; make bookings at office in Loja before going. Camping is possible but it can be very wet. Park guardian Miguel Angel is very knowledgeable and helpful. Additional information from conservation groups: *Arco Iris*, Segundo Cueva Celi 03-15 y Clodoveo Carrión, T577-449, www.arcoiris.org.ec *Fundación Ecológica Podocarpus*, Sucre 8-47 y 10 de Agosto, PO Box 11-01-436, Loja. ■ *Take a Vilcabamba bus, the park entrance is 20 mins from Loja, US$0.80, then it's an 8-km hike uphill to the guard station. Direct transport by taxi only, US$10 round trip. You can arrange a pick up later from the guard station.*

2: The lower altitude of the Zamora side makes wet weather less threatening but waterproof hiking boots are essential, entrance fee US$10. There is a refuge at Bombuscaro, camping is possible nearby. Park guardians can suggest walks. Incredible bird life: mountain tanagers flock around the refuge.

(margin) **Parque Nacional Podocarpus** *Spectacular walking country, lush tropical cloud forest and excellent bird-watching*

Transport There are 2 possible entrances to the lower subtropical section of Podocarpus Park. Bombuscaro can be reached from **Zamora** (see below). Take a taxi US$2 to the entrance, then walk 1 km to the refuge. The other entrance is at **Romerillos**, 2 hrs south by bus. Bus departs Zamora 0630 and 1415, return to Zamora at 0815 and 1600. A 3-5 day hike is possible into this part of the park. Get permit and further information from the **Ministerio del Ambiente** in Zamora (at the entrance to town from Loja), and information from **Fundación Maquipucuna** which also has an office in Zamora and headquarters in Quito: Baquerizo Moreno E9-153 y Tamayo, T250 7200, F250 7201, www.maqui.org

The scenic road to the Oriente crosses a low pass and descends rapidly to **Zamora**, an old mission settlement about 65 km away at the confluence of the Ríos Zamora and Bombuscaro. The road is beautiful as it wanders from *páramo* down to high jungle, crossing mountain ranges of spectacular cloud forest, weaving high above narrow gorges as it runs alongside the Río Zamora. The town itself is a midway point for miners and gold prospectors heading further into the Oriente. The best month is November, but except for April-June, when it rains almost constantly, other months are comfortable. ■ *All buses leave from Terminal Terrestre. To Loja, 4 a day, 2½ hrs; to Cuenca, 1 daily via Loja, 6-7 hrs; to Yantzaza and La Paz, 6 a day.*

(margin) **East from Loja** *Population: 8,736* *This area has scarcely been affected by tourism yet colinas@verdes. ecuanex.net.ec, for information*

Sleeping and eating D *Cabañas Tzanka*, enquire at the *orquideario*. Spacious cabins with bath and kitchen. D *Orillas del Zamora*, Diego de Vaca near the car bridge. Refurbished in 2000. **E** *Gimyfa*, Diego de Vaca, 1 block from Plaza. quiet and nice. **E** *Maguna*, Diego de Vaca, T605113. Electric shower, parking, fridge, quiet, very welcoming. **F** *Venecia*, Sevilla de Oro. Shared bath, basic. **F** *Seyma*, 24 de Mayo y Amazonas, T605583. Shared bath, parking, OK. Recommended. **F** *Zamora*, Sevilla de Oro y Pío Jaramillo, T605253. Shared bath, parking, OK.

(margin, vertical) Ecuador

The restaurant in *Hotel Maguna* is good. **Comedor Don Pepe,** set meals and à la carte. *Esmeraldas*, in the market area opposite the bus terminal. Recommended. *Las Gemelitas*, opposite market. **200 Millas**, in bus terminal. Varied menu. **King Burger**, by park. Snacks.

Vilcabamba

Phone code: 07
Colour map 1a, grid C3
Population: 3,894
Altitude: 1,520 m

Once an isolated village, Vilcabamba has become increasingly popular with foreign travellers, an established stop along the gringo trail between Ecuador and Peru. The whole area is beautiful and tranquil, with an agreeable climate (17°C minimum, 26°C maximum). The local economy has benefited from the influx of tourists, but responsible tourism should not be neglected here. There are many places to stay and several good restaurants.

There are many good walks in the Río Yambala valley (maps are available at *Cabañas Río Yambala*), and on the Mandango mountain trail (exposed and slippery in parts, directions obtainable at *Madre Tierra*). Longer hikes may be made into Parque Nacional Podocarpus. There is a Tourist Office on the main plaza next to *Pacifictel*, which is helpful, with good information and maps.

Drugs Vilcabamba has become famous among travellers for its locally-produced hallucinogenic cactus juice called San Pedrillo. In addition to being illegal, it is more dangerous than it may seem because of flashbacks which can occur months or years after use. The resulting medical condition has been named the 'Vilcabamba Syndrome' and can affect sufferers for the rest of their lives. Tourist demand for San Pedrillo and other drugs is changing Vilcabamba for the worse and has angered much of the population. There has been talk of a tough crackdown. The principles of responsible tourism and common sense alike advise against involvement with the drug scene in Vilcabamba.

Sleeping
We have received reports of visitors being pressured to stay in a particular establishment. There is ample selection, so look around, make your own choice

A-C *Madre Tierra*, 2 Km N on road to Loja, follow signs, T580269, hmtierra@ecua.net.ec Includes breakfast and dinner, cheaper without bath, pool, a variety of cabins from new and very nicely decorated, to simple. Superb home cooking, vegetarian to order. Non-residents must reserve meals a day in advance. Spa (extra charge), videos, horse rental, English and French spoken, very popular. Highly recommended. **B** *Hostería Vilcabamba*, near N entrance to town, T580271, F580273. Includes breakfast, good restaurant and bar, pool and spa, comfortable, good. **C** *Las Ruinas de Quinara*, Diego Vaca de Vega E of centre, T580301, www.lasruinasdequinara.com Includes breakfast and dinner (vegetarian available), pool, internet, massage, videos, table tennis, arranges horse riding, rents bikes. **D** *Izhcayluma*, 2 km S on highway. Good restaurant with European specialties, fan, parking, new in 2001, comfortable cabins, nice grounds, lovely views, German run. **D** *La Posada Real*, Agua del Hierro s/n, T580904, laposadareal@yahoo.com Comfortable, excellent views, relaxing atmosphere. Recommended. **D** *Las Margaritas*, Sucre y Clodoveo Jaramillo, T673031. Good breakfast, pool, parking, very comfortable rooms, spacious, nice garden, family atmosphere, English and German spoken. Recommended. **E** *Hidden Garden*, Sucre y Diego Vaca de Vega, T/F580281, hiddengarden@latinmail.com Includes breakfast, shared bath, cooking facilities, quiet, nice garden, a bit run down but OK. **E** *Pole House and Rumi Huilco Ecolodge*, 10-mins' walk SE town (information at Primavera craft shop on main park), ofalcoecolodge@yahoo.com With fully furnished kitchen, a cabin for 4 built on stilts. Also other equipped, adobe cabins in a country setting. Owner Orlando Falco speaks English and runs excellent nature tours. Recommended. **F** *Mandango*, Behind bus stop. Hot water, good value. **F** *Sra Libia Toledo*, Bolívar y Clodoveo Jaramillo. Shared bath, hot water, family run. **F** *Hostal María*, Av Loja, direction hospital, T580909, mpicoita@hotmail.com Cheaper without bath, includes 2 meals, quiet, good atmosphere and food, use of kitchen, laundry, helpful, Spanish lessons. **F** *Valle Sagrado*, On main plaza. Restaurant, cheaper without bath, hot water, laundry facilities, simple but refurbished.

At the upper end of the Vilcabamba Valley, a beautiful 4 km walk from the village, are the highly recommended **D** *Cabañas Río Yambala*, office in town next to Centro Ecuestre (not always open), rio_yambala@yahoo.com Owned by Charlie and Sarah, different types of cabins for 3 to 6, or room, beautiful views in all directions, price includes breakfast and dinner, kitchen facilities if required, shopping done for you, vegetarian restaurant, hot showers, laundry service, very helpful, do not leave belongings on balcony or porch, horses for rent with or without guide, trekking arranged in the Parque Nacional Podocarpus.

There are some restaurants around the plaza, including: an unnamed, good vegetarian place. *La Terraza*, D Vaca de la Vega, opposite *Pacifictel*. Very good international food, one speciality is *fajitas*. Recommended. *La Esquina*, on Sucre y Vaca de la Vega. Ecuadorean food, set meals. Opposite is *Huilcopamba*, D Vaca de la Vega y Sucre. Very good Ecuadorean food. Recommended. *Vilcabamba Natural Yogurt*, Bolívar y F de la Vega. Open 0800-2100, for breakfasts, juices, homemade yoghurt, good value, tourist information. *Le Rendez-vous*, D Vaca de la Vega y Valle Sagrado. Crêpes speciality, French run. Recommended. El Rincón del Abuelo, Av Eterna Juventud y Clodoveo. Seafood. Along the road to Yamburara and Yambala (follow Vaca de la Vega east) are: *Manditos*, 2 blocks from the park, for snacks.*Manolo's*, 5 mins from the plaza. Excellent pizzas and pasta. Recommended. *Shanta's*, bar, pizza, snacks.

Eating

Caballos Gavilán, Sucre y D Vaca de Vega, T580281, gavilanhorse@yahoo.com New Zealander, Gavin Moore offers 3-day horse treks to the cloud forest for US$80 pp, includes food (vegetarian specialities), sleeping bags and basic lodging. Also good for beginners. Repeatedly recommended. *Centro Ecuestre*, D Vaca de Vega y Bolívar, opposite *La Terraza* restaurant, T/F673183, centroecuestre@hotmail.com A group of guides who provide horse riding excursions: day trips to Parque Recreacional Yamburara or Parque Recreacional Los Huilcos, 1-3 day trips to Podocarpus and trips to archeological ruins. About US$25 per day. Roger Toledo is a recommended guide. *Llamandina*, T/F580061, www.llamandina.com (no storefront, contact in advance) Llama trekking, friendly. *Las Palmas Reserve*, contact *Cabañas Río Yambala* (see Sleeping). Hiking and horse riding tours near Podocarpus, nice shelter with hot water, lovely scenery. *Jorge Mendieta*, Eterna Juventud y D Vaca de Vega, jorgeluis222@latinmail.com Nature guide to Vilcabamba and other areas, flexible, knowledgeable, good value. *Refugio Solomaco*, Sucre y D Vaca de Vega, T/F673183, solomaco@hotmail.com Trips to Parque Nacional Podocarpus with lodging in a private refuge at the edge of the park, also include transport, guide and French food. One day US$20, 2 days US$50, 3 days US$70 pp, discounts for groups, French-run.

Tour operators

Communications Internet: By the main park, rates US$4 per hr. **Telephone:** *Pacifictel* Bolívar near the park.

Directory

Loja to the Peruvian border

An alternative to the Huaquillas border crossing is the more scenic and tranquil route via Macará. Leaving Loja on the main paved highway going west, the airport at **La Toma** (1,200 m) is reached after 35 km. If flying to or from La Toma, it's best to stay at **Catamayo**, nearby. D *Hostería Bella Vista*, T962450, tropical gardens, pool. F *Hotel San Marcos*, on the plaza. F *Hotel El Turista*, Av Isidro Ayora, shared bath, basic, friendly, poor beds. Opposite is *Restaurant China*, good, cheap. ■ *Taxi to airport US$1, or 20 mins walk.*

At La Toma, where you can catch the Loja-Macará-Piura bus, the Pan-American Highway divides: one branch runs west, the other south. The former, which is faster, runs via Velacruz and Catacocha, with one passport check. **Catacocha** is a spectacularly placed town built on a rock; there are pre-Inca ruins around the town. From Catacocha, the paved road runs south to the border at Macará.

The south route from Catamayo to Macará is via Cariamanga. The road is paved to **Cariamanga**, via **Gonzanamá**, a pleasant, sleepy little town famed for the weaving of beautiful *alforjas* (multi-purpose saddlebags). F *Res Jiménez* (cold shower).

It's 27½ km to Cariamanga (hotels, banks), then the road twists its way westwards to **Colaisaca**, before descending steeply 2,000 m to **Utuana** (not recommended for cyclists in the other direction) to Macará.

Ecuador

Macará

Phone code: 07
Colour map 1a, grid C2
Population: 14,296
Altitude: 600 m

Macará, on the border, is in a rice-growing area. There are road connections to Sullana and Piura in Peru. **F** *Espiga de Oro*, opposite the market. Cheaper without bath, fan, TV. Recommended. **E** *Amazonas*, Rengel 418. Basic. **E** *Res Paraíso*, Veintimilla 553. Shared bath, laundry facilities, noisy, unfriendly. *Colonial Macará*, Rengel y Bolívar. Helpful, but food not too good. *Dragón Dorado*, Calderón. Seafood, popular. *Heladería Cream*, Veintimilla y Sucre. Great ice cream. *Soda Bar Manolo* for breakfast.

Transport *Coop Loja* and *Cariamanga* have frequent buses, daily from Macará to **Loja** 5-6 hrs, US$5. *Loja Internacional* buses, which have direct service Loja-**Piura**, 3 daily, can also be boarded in Macará (see Loja, Transport).

Border with Peru

Ecuadorean immigration is open 24 hrs. Formalities last about 30 minutes. It is reported as a much easier crossing than at Huaquillas. During the day there are money changers dealing in soles at the international bridge and in Macará, where there is also a *Banco de Loja* which changes Peruvian soles, 0900-1700. The international bridge over the Río Macará is 2 km from town. There is taxi and pick-up service (US$0.50 shared). On the Peruvian side, minivans run La Tina-Sullana, US$3, 3 hours (try to avoid arriving in Sullana after dark).

New border crossings

From Cariamanga (see above), a rough, unpaved road runs two hours south to **Amaluza**, a pleasant town, with a nice plaza and imposing modern church. Around the main park are: **F** *El Rocío*, basic, cheaper without bath, cold water, and **G** *Hotel Central*, dirty, very basic, shared bath, cold shower; *Restaurant Los Charros*, set meals. Several well stocked shops in town. *Unión Cariamanga* has five daily buses from Loja to Amaluza, *Cooperativa Loja* has three, US$4, 5½-6 hours. There are pickups from the plaza at Amaluza to **Jimbura** (no fixed schedule) US$1 pp or US$10 private hire, 45 minutes. Jimbura is a nice quiet town, no hotels, few places to eat. The same *camioneta* can take you to the international bridge, 4 km further on. Ecuadorean immigration is just outside Jimbura, knock on the door to get passport stamped. On the other side is the Peruvian village of Espíndola, 15 minutes walk from the bridge. Transport Jimbura to Espíndola US$4 or one hour pleasant walk. From Jimbura or Espíndola you can hire a *camioneta* to take you to Samanguilla (Peru), from where there is transport to Ayabaca, two hours.

There are eight buses a day from Loja or Vilcabamba to **Zumba** (see Loja, Transport), 112 km south of Vilcabamba; **E** *HotelOasis*, next to *Banco de Fomento*, with bath, modern, **G** *La Choza* with simple restaurant, and several others, plus eateries. It is a 3 hr rough ride by *chiva* (open-sided bus) from Zumba to La Balsa, where there is an immigration post. An oil-drum raft crosses the river to the Peruvian border post, from where there is minibus service to Namballe, 15 minutes away. Another minibus goes to **San Ignacio** (Peru) when full, 2½ hours, from where there is transport to Jaén. This opens a faster, more direct route between Vilcabamba and Chachapoyas, which can now be done in two days.

□ Quito

Guayaquil and south to Peru

Thriving and ever increasing banana plantations, with shrimp farms among the mangroves, are the economic mainstay of the coastal area bordering the east flank of the Gulf of Guayaquil. Rice, sugar, coffee and cacao are also produced. The Guayas lowlands are subject to flooding, humidity is high and biting insects are fierce. Mangroves characterize the coast leading south to Huaquillas, the main border crossing to Peru.

Guayaquil

Guayaquil is hotter, faster and brasher than the capital. It is Ecuador's largest city and the country's chief seaport, industrial and commercial centre, some 56 km from the Río Guayas' outflow into the Gulf of Guayaquil. Founded in 1535 by Sebastián de Benalcázar, then again in 1537 by Francisco Orellana, the city has always been an intense political rival to Quito. Guayaquileños are certainly more lively, colourful and open than their Quito counterparts. Since the late 1990's there have been organized movements for autonomy of Ecuador's coastal provinces, spearheaded by Guayaquil.

The Puerto Marítimo handles over 70% of the country's imports and almost 50% of its exports. Industrial expansion continually fuels the city's growth.

Getting there Simón Bolívar International **Airport** is 10 mins north of the city centre by taxi (recommended for safety, US$3-5). US$0.25 by bus; No 2 to Malecón, No 3 to Centro Cívico, No 69 to Plaza Victoria, but buses are neither safe nor practical with luggage. If going straight on to another city, get a cab directly to the **Terminal Terrestre** (bus station), which is close by; a taxi from the airport to the bus terminal is US$2. If you are arriving in Guayaquil and need a taxi from the airport, walk ½ block from the terminal out to Av Las Américas, where taxis and camionetas wait for passengers and charge about half the fare of the airport taxi cooperative, but not recommended at night. A great many local buses go from the bus terminal to the city centre. Taxi fare US$3-4.

Getting around Because of traffic congestion, it is often quicker to walk short distances in the centre, rather than take a bus or taxi (but don't walk after dark). Public transport is essential for getting to the airport and bus station and to the northern residential and restaurant districts. City buses are overcrowded and dirty, watch out for pickpockets. Fare is US$0.25; also mini-buses (*furgonetas*), US$0.20, which post up their routes in the windscreen. Buses are not allowed in the centre; almost all go along the Malecón. Bus No 15 from the centre to Urdesa, 13 to Policentro, 14 to Albanborja, 74 to La Garzota and Sauces. Taxis have no meters, so prices are very negotiable and overcharging is notorious. It should be approximately US$3 from centre to Urdesa or Policentro, short runs US$1.50 (if you are very persistent). *Taxi rutas* run a set route, charging US$0.40; they are yellow with contrasting bonnets, or stripes over the roof, eg ones with red bonnets run from the Bahía, Centro, Urdesa to Mapasingue and back.

Orientation The centre is on the west bank of the Río Guayas. **Barrio Centenario** to the south of the centre is the original residential sector, now a peaceful, tree-shaded haven. Newer residential areas are **Urdesa**, northwest of the centre, in between 2 branches of the Estero Salado (about 15 mins from downtown, traffic permitting); 5 mins by taxi from the international airport and bus terminal are the districts of **La Garzota**, **Sauces** and **Alborada**. They are cleaner, less congested and safer than the centre, but with all services, 10-15 mins by taxi.

Climate From May-Dec it is dry with often overcast days but pleasantly cool nights, whereas the hot rainy season from Jan-Apr can be oppressively humid.

Tourist offices Ministerio de Turismo, P Icaza 203 y Pichincha, 6th floor, T568764. Friendly, but only Spanish; they sell a map of Ecuador. ■ *Mon-Fri 0900-1700.* **Cámara de Turismo**, Av Delta y Simón Bolívar, Ciudadela Boliviariana (north of the centre, south of the bus terminal), T228 4514. *Mon-Fri 0900-1730.* Maps also from **INOCAR**, in the planetarium building at the naval base near the port.

Safety Since 2000, the municipal authorities have placed much emphasis on improving public safety. The Malecón, parts of Av 9 de Octubre and the Las Peñas neighbourhood are heavily patrolled and reported safer. The remainder of the city carries all the usual risks of a large seaport and metropolis. It is best not to walk anywhere with valuables and always take taxis at night. A number of tropical diseases are present.

Ins & outs
Colour map 1a, grid B2
For more detailed information see Transport, page 987

Ecuador

A website about tourism in Guayaquil is www.turismoguayas. com

Sights

The **Malecón 2000**, the tree-lined waterfront complex runs alongside the Río Guayas. It is the city's pride, with gardens, fountains, playgrounds, photo and art galleries. There are restaurants and cafés along its length and a large shopping mall and marine museum by the south end. It is attractive and definitely worth a visit. The Malecón Simón Bolívar avenue borders this complex, along it are the exclusive **Club de la Unión**, the Moorish clock tower, the imposing **Palacio Municipal** and **Government Palace** and the old Yacht Club, continuing to Las Peñas. Half way along, the Blvd 9 de Octubre, the city's main street starts in front of La Rotonda, a statue to mark the famous yet mysterious meeting between Simón Bolívar and San Martín in 1822. There are 11 piers (*muelles*) running along the Malecón; from the most northerly, near Las Peñas, ferries cross the river to Durán (not a safe place), from where trains to the Sierra and Quito used to run.

The old district of **Las Peñas** is a last picturesque vestige of colonial Guayaquil with its brightly painted wooden houses and narrow cobbled street (Numa Pompilio Llona). Gentrified in 2001, it is now an attractive place for a walk to Cerro Santa Ana, which offers great views of the city and the mighty Guayas. Security in this area is much improved. The area has a bohemian feel, with bars and restaurants. A large open-air exhibition of paintings and sculpture is held here every July.

The main plaza half way up 9 Octubre is the **Parque Centenario** with a towering monument to the liberation of the city erected in 1920. In the pleasant, shady **Parque Bolívar** stands the **Cathedral**, in Gothic style, inaugurated in the 1950s.

There are several noteworthy churches. **Santo Domingo**, the city's first church founded in 1548, stands just by Las Peñas. Also **San Francisco**, with its restored colonial interior, off 9 de Octubre and P Carbo, and the beautiful **La Merced**.

At the north end of the centre, below Cerro El Carmen, the huge, spreading **Cemetery** with its dazzling, high-rise tombs and the ostentatious mausolea of the rich is worth a visit. A flower market over the road sells the best selection of blooms in the city. It's best to go on a Sunday when there are plenty of people about.

The **Centro Cívico**, heading south, has an excellent theatre/concert hall and is home to the Guayaquil Symphony Orchestra which gives free concerts throughout the year. The new **Teatro Centro de Arte** on the road out to the coast is another first class theatre complex with a wide variety of presentations. Colourful markets are at the south end of the Malecón or along 6 de Marzo between 10 de Agosto and Ballén. The Mercado Sur, next to Club de la Unión, prefabricated by Eiffel (1905-1907), is not safe to enter because of pickpocketing.

Guayaquil is also a city of **shopping malls**, where consumerism flourishes in air-conditioned comfort. Here you will find many banks, restaurants, bars, discos, cinemas, cyber cafés and of course shops. Those who yearn for even more of a chill can visit the ice-skating rink called **Zona Fría**, at Km 2½ on the autopista La Puntilla-Samborondón. Overpasses in the city's roads are decorated with murals, replicas of Ecuador's most renowned artists.

Museums The **Museo Municipal**, in the Biblioteca Municipal, Sucre y Pedro Carbo (near the *Hotel Continental*) has paintings, gold and archaeological collections, shrunken heads, a section on the history of Guayaquil and a good newspaper library. ■ *Tue-Sat 0900–1700, free.* The Central Bank's **anthropology museum** has excellent displays of ceramics, gold objects and paintings. ■ *It is being moved to Malecón 2000, expected to reopen at the end of 2002.* **Museo del Banco del Pacífico,** Icaza 200 y Pichincha, 3rd floor, T232 8333, is a beautiful small museum mainly of archaeological exhibits. ■ *Mon-Fri 0900-1700, free.* There is an impressive collection of prehistoric gold items (but not always on display) at the museum of the **Casa de la Cultura**, together with an archaeological museum at 9 de Octubre 1200 y Moncayo. ■ *Tue-Fri 1000-1700, Sat 0900-1500, US\$1.*

Excursions

The Botanical Gardens are northwest on Av Francisco de Orellana, Ciudadela Las Orquídeas; good views and a long but pleasant walk. Over 3,000 plants, including 150 species of Ecuadorean and foreign orchids. Recommended. ■ *Daily 0800-1600. US$15, includes guiding service. Take taxi.* **Botanical Gardens**

Cerro Blanco Forest Reserve is set in tropical dry forest with an impressive variety of birds (over 190 species listed so far) and with sightings of howler monkeys, ocelot, puma, jaguar and peccaries, among others. The reserve is run by *Fundación Pro-Bosque*, Edif Promocentro, local 16, Eloy Alfaro y Cuenca, T241 6975 evonhorst@gu.pro.ec ■ *Reservations required during weekdays and for groups larger than 8 at weekends, and for birders wishing to arrive before or stay after normal opening hours (0800-1530). Guides can be hired. US$5 plus a charge depending on trails walked US$4-8, camping $7 pp. The entrance is beyond the Club Rocafuerte. Taxi from Guayaquil US$10-20. The yellow and green 'Chongonera' buses leave every 30 mins from Parque Victoria and pass the park entrance on the way to Puerto Hondo.* **Cerro Blanco Forest Reserve**

On the other side of the road is **Puerto Hondo**. Canoe trips through the mangroves can be arranged on the spot at weekends from the *Fundación Pro-Bosque* kiosk for US$7 per person with guides, or through their Guayaquil office (see above).

Heading east then south from Guayaquil, 22 km beyond the main crossroads at Km 26 on the road to Naranjal, lies the **Ecological Reserve of Manglares Churute**. Canoe trips into the mangroves with guides can see waterbirds, monkeys, dolphins and lots of other wildlife. Trips can be arranged at the Reserve information centre, or in Guayaquil through Depto Forestal, Av Quito 402 y P Solano, p 10, T239 7730, or through *Chasquitur*, Urdaneta 1418 y Av Del Ejército, T228 1085. ■ *US$10, plus US$4 for a guide (up to 10 people); a boat trip costs an extra US$40-50 (up to 15 people). Take repellent and wear long sleeves; lots of mosquitoes. Buses leave the terminalairport every 30 mins going to Naranjal or Machala. Ask to be let off at Churute information centre.* **Ecological Reserve of Manglares Churute**

The **Parque Histórico** on the way to Samborondón recreates the urban and rural environments of Guayaquil at the end of the 19th Century. ■ *Tue-Sun 0900-1700, US$2, T283 3807.* **Parque Histórico**

Essentials

Hotel prices are higher than in Quito and are set by the Tourist Board. Upmarket establishments often have one rate for nationals and a higher one for foreigners. Always check the rate and whether the 22% service and taxes are included. In the better hotels booking is advised. Most hotels are downtown, so take a taxi from the airport or bus station. The cheap hotels are pretty basic, many cater to short stay customers, and singles seem hard to find. In the following list all hotels in **LL-B** grades are recommended. **Sleeping**
Most of the downtown area is unsafe; caution is especially important at night. As an alternative you can stay in the districts of La Garzota, Sauces and Alborada, near the airport and bus terminal

In the luxury bracket are the *Hilton Colón*, which is superb, the *Oro Verde* and a new *Marriott*. **L** *Continental*, Chile y 10 de Agosto, T232 9270, F232 5454. Includes breakfast, 24 hr restaurant, a *KLM Golden Tulip* hotel, 5-star, good coffee shop, central. **L** *Hampton Inn Boulevard*, 9 de Octubre 432 y Baquerizo Moreno, T256 6700, www.hampton.com.ec Buffet breakfast, restaurant, internet, refurbished in 2000, central, very good facilities. **AL** *Gran Hotel Guayaquil*, Boyacá 1600 y 10 de Agosto, T232 9690, www.grandhotelguayaquil.com Good restaurants, pool $2 for non-residents, traditional. **AL** *Palace*, Chile 214 y Luque, T232 1080, F232 2887. Includes breakfast, 24 hr cafetería, excellent, good value for business travellers, modern, traffic noise on Av Chile side, travel agency. Recommended. **A** *Sol de Oriente*, Aguirre 603 y Escobedo, T232 5500, F232 5904. Includes breakfast, restaurant, minibar, gym, excellent value. Recommended.

Ecuador

B *Best Western Doral*, Chile 402 y Aguirre, T232 8002, www.hdoral.com Includes breakfast, restaurant, a/c, internet, good rooms and value, central. Recommended. **B** *Plaza*, Chile 414 y Clemente Ballén, T232 4006, jplamas@impsat.net.ec Includes breakfast, cafeteria, a/c, internet, cafetería, international newspapers. Recommended. **B** *Rizzo*, Clemente Ballén 319 y Chile, T232 5210, F232 6209. Includes breakfast, *Café Jambelí* downstairs for seafood, a/c, safe, central, some windowless rooms. **C** *Alexander*, Luque 1107 y Pedro Moncayo, T253 2000, F251 4161. Cafeteria, a/c, comfortable, good value, some rooms without windows, noisy. **C** *Hostal de Alborada*, Alborada IX Manzana 935 Villa 8, T223 7251. A/c, hot water, safe, near airport. A/c. **C-E** *Casa Alianza*, Av Segunda 318 y Calle 12, Los Ceibos, T235 1261, www.casaalianza.com Restaurant, cheaper with shared bath and fan, away from centre, run by a Norwegian NGO.

D *Capri*, Luque y Machala, T232 6341. Cafeteria, a/c, fridge, safe, busy at weekends. **D** *Centenario*, Vélez 726 y Santa Elena, T252 4467. Cold water, a/c. **D-E** *Ecuahogar*, Av Isidro Ayora, opposite Banco Ecuatoriano de La Vivienda, Sauces I, T224 8357, youthost@

Guayaquil

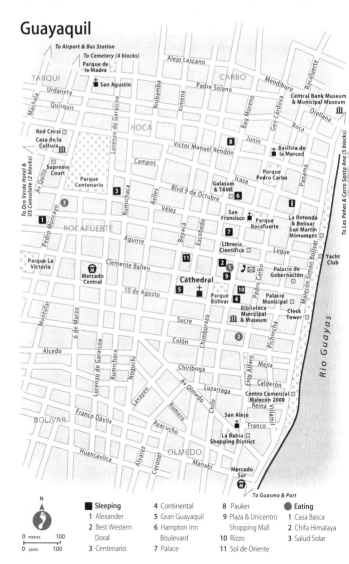

N

0 metres 100
0 yards 100

■ **Sleeping**
1 Alexander
2 Best Western Doral
3 Centenario

4 Continental
5 Gran Guayaquil
6 Hampton Inn Boulevard
7 Palace

8 Pauker
9 Plaza & Unicentro Shopping Mall
10 Rizzo
11 Sol de Oriente

● **Eating**
1 Casa Basca
2 Chifa Himalaya
3 Salud Solar

telconet.net Includes breakfast (0700-0900), cheaper in dorm with shared bath, laundry facilities, 10% discount for IYHF members. Increasingly negative reports. **D-E** *Paseo Real*, Luque 1011 y 6 de Marzo, T253 0084. A/c, cheaper with fan. **D-F** *Luque*, Luque 1214 y Quito, T252 3900. A/c, cheaper with fan. **E** *Vélez*, Vélez 1021 y Quito, T253 0356. A/c, cheaper with fan, good value. Recommended. **F** *Libertador*, Santa Elena 803 y VM Rendón, T230 4637. Private bath, fan. **F** *Pauker*, Baquerizo Moreno 902 y Junín, T256 5385. Cheaper without bath, run down and dirty, old-time haunt for travellers.

French *Decibelius*, Estrada y Cedros, Urdesa. Menu changes frequently, good steaks, crêpes and coffee.

Eating
Main areas for restaurants are the centre with many in the larger hotels, around Urdesa, or La Alborada and La Garzota, which have many good eating houses; 22% service and tax is added on in smarter places

International *Posada de las Garzas*, Urdesa Norte, Circunvalación Norte 536. Also French style dishes. *El Parque*, top floor of Unicentro, popular buffet lunches at weekends. *Juan Salvador Gaviota*, Kennedy Norte, Av Fco de Orellana. Good seafood. *La Balandra*, C 5a 504 entre Monjas y Dátiles, Urdesa. For good fish, upmarket ambience, also has a crab house at Circunvalación 506 y Ficus, Urdesa.

Italian *La Trattoria da Enrico*, Bálsamos 504. Expensive but good food and fun surroundings, good antipasto. *Trattoria de Pasquale*, Estrada y Guayacanes, Urdesa. Good atmosphere, reasonably priced. *Pizzería Cozzoli's*, Av Miraflores 115, good pizza, canelones, lasagna, resonable prices. *Riviera Urdesa*, Estrada y Ficus, Urdesa. Bright surroundings, good service, also in Mall del Sol.

Mexican *Noches Tapatías*, Primera y Dátiles, Urdesa. Fun, good live music at weekends. *Cielito Lindo*, Circunvalación 623 y Ficus. Good food and ambience, live music. *Viva México*, Datiles y Estrada, in Urdesa. The best authentic dishes.

Oriental A wide variety in the city, most do take-away, good value. *Cantonés*, Av G Pareja y C 43, La Garzota. Huge rather glaring emporium with authentic dishes and all-you-can-eat menu for US$9, karaoke. *Tsuji*, Estrada 815, Urdesa. Wonderful, authentic Japanese dishes, Teppan Yaki, expensive. *UniBar* in *UniPark Hotel* complex, C Ballén 406 y Chile. Sushi. *Chifa Himalaya*, Sucre 309 y P Carbo. Slow service but good for the price.

Seafood Crab Houses: these are almost an institution and great fun. *Manny's*, Av Miraflores 112 y Primera. Not cheap but try the excellent *arroz con cangrejo*. *Casa del Cangrejo*, Av Plaza Dañín, Kennedy. For crab dishes of every kind; several others along the same street. *Red Crab*, Estrada y Laureles, Urdesa. Interesting decor, wide variety of seafood. Very expensive. *El Cangrejo Criollo*, Av Principal, Villa 9, La Garzota. Excellent, varied seafood, reasonable price. Recommended.

Spanish *Casa Basca*, C Ballén 422. Wonderful hole-in-the-wall place, specializes in seafood and paellas, expensive food, cash only, house wine good value, great atmosphere, gets very crowded. The same owner runs *Tasca Vaska*, Chimborazo between C Ballén y Aguirre. *Caracol Azul*, 9 de Octubre 1918 y Los Ríos. Expensive and very good.

Steak Houses *Columbus*, Las Lomas 206 off Estrada, Urdesa. Good. *Donde el Ché*, F Boloña S21A. Holds competition to see who can eat the biggest steak, winner doesn't pay, music, tango and shows. *Parillada Del Ñato*, Estrada 1219. Huge variety and portions, excellent value. Recommended *La Selvita*, Av Olmos y Las Brisas, Las Lomas de Urdesa. Good atmosphere and fine panoramic views, also at Calle D y Rosa Borja, Centenario.

Typical *La Canoa* in *Hotel Continental* and in Mall del Sol. Open 24 hrs for traditional dishes rarely found these days, with different specials during the week. *Lo Nuestro*, Estrada y Higueras, Urdesa. Traditional decor, great seafood platters. *Pique Y Pase*, Lascano 16-17 y Carchi. Popular with students, lively. *El Manantial*, VE Estrada y Las Monjas. Good.

Vegetarian *Maranatá I*, Chile y Cuenca, and *II*, Quisquis y Rumichaca. *Super Nutrión I*, Chimborazo y 10 de Agosto, and *II* Chimborazo y Letamendi. *Renacer*, G Avilés y Sucre. *Hare Krishna*, 1 de Mayo y 6 de Marzo. Good food, pleasant, but in bad neighbourhood, be careful. *Salud Solar*, Pedro Moncayo y Luque. *Ollantay*, Tungurahua 508 y 9 de Octubre. Good food, cheap.

Snacks there are many places selling all sorts of snacks. Try *pan de yuca* or *empanadas*. Excellent sandwiches at *Submarine*, 9 Octubre y Chile. *Uni Deli* downstairs in the Unicentro, Aguirre y Chimborazo. Good bakery, salami and cheese. *La Chivería*, Circunvalación y Ficus. Good yoghurt and *pan de yuca*. *La Selecta*, Estrada y Laureles. Good sandwiches and sweets.

Beware of eating at street stalls

Ecuador

Good ice cream at *Top Cream*, many outlets throughout the city. **Coffee** great coffee served hot, cold, frozen in milkshakes or ices in the foodhalls of *Riocentro Los Ceibos*, *Riocentro Samborondón* and *El Bopán*, Estrada y Las Monjas, Urdesa. The latter also serves breakfast from 0700.

Entertainment
See El Universo for cinemas and other entertainments. Cinemas cost US$2-3

The **Kennedy Mall** is Guayaquil's main centre for upscale nightlife, with an ample selection of bars and discos. Prices vary from mid-range to expenive. There are also discos, bars and casinos in most of the major hotels. Also *TV Bar*, Av Rolando Pareja in La Garzota. Good drinks and music, young crowd, moderate prices. *Arthur's Café*, Numa Pompillo Lona 127, Las Peñas. Bar/restaurant, typical coastal snacks, wonderful views, live music, popular. *Jardín de la Salsa*, Av de la Américas. Largest in the city, lively, popular, free Salsa classes. There are several others.

Festivals

The *foundation of Guayaquil* is celebrated on **24-25 Jul**, and the *city's independence* on **9-12 Oct**. Both holidays are lively and there are many public events; cultural happenings are prolonged throughout Oct.

Shopping
There are lots of shopping malls – ideal for cooling off on hot days

Centro Comercial Malecón 2000 is the city's newest mall, at the south end of the Malecón. *Mall del Sol* is near the airport on Av Constitución y Juan Tanca Marengo and is the largest mall in the country. Other malls are: *Riocentro Los Ceibos*, on the coast road beyond Los Ceibos; *Unicentro*, Aguirre y Chile; *Policentro* and *Plaza Quil*, both on Av San Jorge, N Kennedy; *Albán Borja*, Av Arosemena Km 2.7; *Garzocentro 2000*, La Garzota, Av R Pareja; *La Rotonda,* entrance to La Garzota; *Plaza Mayor*, La Alborada, Av R Pareja and, nearby, *Albocentro*; *Riocentro*, Av Samborondón, across the river; and *Puntilla Mall* at La Puntilla.

Books *Librería Científica*, Luque 223 y Chile and Plaza Triángulo on the Estrada in Urdesa. English books, good for field guides to flora and fauna and travel in general. *El Librero*, in the Ríocentro. Has English books. *Nuevos Horizontes*, 6 de Marzo 924. For book exchange. *Selecciones* in Albán Borja Mall has a choice of pricey novels and lots of magazines in English.

Camping equipment Camping gas, available from *Casa Maspons*, Ballén 517 y Boyacá.

Handicrafts For variety try the *Mercado Artesanal* between Loja y Montalvo and Córdova y Chimborazo, a whole block of permanent stalls. Good prices. *Artesanías del Ecuador*, 9 Octubre 104 y Malecón are good and reliable. Good variety of *artesanías* in Albán Borja Mall at *El Telar*. *Ramayana* for good ceramics. Also several craft shops in *Centro Comercial Malecón 2000*.

The **Bahía**, or black market, on either side of Olmedo from Villamil to Chile, is the most popular place for electrical appliances, clothing, shoes, food and drink. It was traditionally where contraband was sold from boats which put into the bay and is one of the city's oldest market places. Watch your valuables and be prepared to bargain.

Tour operators
Details about agencies operating Galápagos cruises in the Galápagos section page 1029

Canodros, Luis Urdaneta 1418 T228 0164 F228 7651, www.canodros.com Run luxury Galápagos cruises and also operate the Kapawi Ecological Reserve in the southern Oriente. *Centro Viajero*, Baquerizo Moreno 1119 y 9 de Octubre, T256 2565, F256 5550, centrovi@telconet.net Airline tickets, information, English spoken. Recommended. *Ecoventura*, Av Francisco de Orellana 222, Mz 12, Solar 22, Kennedy Norte, T228 0241, F228 3148. (6303 Blue Lagoon Drive, Suite 140, Miami, FL 33126, T305-262 6264, F305-262 9609, www.ecoventura.com). See also under the Galápagos. *Ecuadorian Tours*, 9 Octubre 1900 y Esmeraldas, T228 7111. Agent for Amex, branches Chile y 10 de Agosto and in Urdesa, Estrada 117, T238 8080. *Galasam Cía Ltda*, Edif Gran Pasaje, 9 Octubre 424, 11th floor, l of 1108, T306289, see Galápagos section (page 1031). *Metropolitan Touring*, Antepara 915 y 9 de Octubre, T232 0300, also at the *Hilton Colón*. *Wanderjahr*, P Icaza 431, Edif Gran Pasaje, T256 2111, branches in Policentro, the *Hotel Oro Verde*, Albán Borja. **Whale watching** is gaining in popularity, many agencies offer this trip in addition to city tours, 2½ hrs, US$8-10 pp with English-speaking guide, eg *Royal Tours Service*, T232 6688. *Viajes Horizontes*, P Solano 1502 y Mascote, T228 1260. Arranges *chiva* rides and other tours.

Ecuador

Local For **Bus** and **Taxi**, see Ins and outs, above. **Car hire**: *Budget*, T228 8510 (airport), 232 8571 (by *Oro Verde*). *Ecuacars* T228 3247 (airport). *Avis*, T228 7906 (airport). Several more at the airport.

Transport

Long distance **Air**: Facilities at the airport include an information desk; tourist office (very helpful); *Wander Cambio*, open 7 days a week, 0900-1600 ; several bank ATMs; car hire; a modern cafetería (but none beyond customs) and a post office. To get to the baggage claim area you must leave the airport and re-enter further down the building. Show your boarding pass to enter and baggage ticket to leave. For transport, see Ins and outs, above.

Air services: many flights daily to **Quito**, US$60 one way (*TAME*). Sit on the right side for the best views. To **Cuenca** US$40, **Loja** US$36, **Machala** US$36. Daily to **Galápagos** (see page 1025).

Road: There is a 3¼-km bridge (Puente de la Unidad Nacional) in two sections across the rivers Daule and Babahoyo to Durán. A paved road from there connects with the Andean Highway at Cajabamba, near Riobamba (see page 958). Also from Durán main roads go to Babahoyo, Quevedo and Santo Domingo (the most frequently used route to Quito), to Cuenca, and to the southern lowlands around Machala. **Bus**: the Terminal Terrestre, just north of the airport, is off the road to the Guayas bridge. The company offices are on the second floor, departures on top floor. There is no left luggage depot and do not leave anything unattended. The terminal is busy at weekends. There are some expensive restaurants, use of toilet US$0.10, bus tickets include terminal tax. Several companies to/from **Quito**, 8 hrs, US$9; more expensive with *Rey Tours* non-stop, a/c service (office in *Gran Hotel*). To **Cuenca**, 5 hrs, US$7. **Riobamba**, 5 hrs, US$4. To **Santo Domingo de los Colorados**, 4 hrs, US$5. **Manta**, 3 hrs, US$4.20. **Esmeraldas**, 8 hrs, US$8. **Portoviejo**, 3 hrs, US$4.20, and to **Bahía de Caráquez**, 6hrs, US$4.50-6. To **Ambato**, 6½ hrs, US$4.80. Regular and frequent buses to **Playas**, 2 hrs, US$2; and to **Salinas**, 2½ hrs, US$2.70. For the **Peruvian border**, to **Huaquillas** direct, 5 hrs, US$4; to **Machala**, 3½ hrs, US$3.

Sea: **Shipping agent**: *Luis Arteaga*, Aguirre 324 y Chile, T253 3592/670, F253 3445, recommended, fast, US$120 for arranging car entry.

Airline offices *TAME*, 9 de Octubre 424, edif Gran Pasaje, T2310305. *American Airlines*, Gral Córdova y Av 9 de Octubre, Edificio San Francisco, p 20, T256 4111. *Continental*, Av 9 de Octubre 100 y Malecón, T256 7241, F256 7249. *Iberia*, Av 9 de Octubre 101 y Malecón, T232 0664. *KLM*, at the airport, T228 2713. **Immigration**: Río Daule, near the bus terminal, T229 7004, for visa extensions

Directory

Banks *Citibank*, 9 de Octubre 416 y Chile. Citicorp cheques only and before 1330. *Banco del Pacífico*, Icaza 200, p 4, T232 8333. TCs US$5 comission. *American Express*, 9 de Octubre 1900 y Esmeraldas. For purchase of TCs, queues are much longer in the afternoon. *Banco de Guayaquil*, Pichincha y P Ycaza, Visa ATM. MasterCard head office at P Carbo y 9 de Octubre, Edif San Francisco 300, p 7, T256 1730 for cash advances. *Casa de Cambio*: *Cambiosa*, 9 de Octubre y Pichincha. Try main hotels for TCs, but service may be only for guests.

Communications **Internet:** There are many cyber cafés in the centre and suburbs alike, the greatest number are concentrated in shopping malls. Prices around US$0.50 per hr for internet, U$0.50 per min for *Net2Phone*. **Telephone:** *Pacifictel* and the central Post office are in the same block at Pedro Carbo y Aguirre. There are branch post offices in Urdesa, Estrada y Las Lomas; by *Mi Comisariato* Supermarket; 1st floor of Policentro; at the airport and Bus Terminal. The major hotels also sell stamps. Many courier services for reliable delivery of papers and packages. *DHL*, T228 7044, is recommended for international service; *Servientrega*, offices throughout the city, for deliveries within Ecuador.

Embassies and consulates **Austria**, 9 de Octubre 1312 y Quito, p 1, T228 2303. **Belgium**, Lizardo García 301 y Vélez, T236 4429. **Canada** Edif Torre de la Merced, p 21, Córdova 808 y VM Rendón, T256 3580. **Colombia**, Edif San Francisco, p 22, 9 de Octubre y Córdova, T256 8753. **Finland**, Luis Urdaneta 206 y Córdova, T256 4268. **France**, José Mascote 909 y Hurtado, T229 4334. **Germany**, Av Carlos Julio Arosemena Km 2, Ed Berlín, T220 0500. **Netherlands**, Edif ABN-AMRO Bank, P Ycaza 454 y Baquerizo Moreno, T256 3857. **Norway**, Av 9 de Octubre 105 y Malecón, T232 9661. **Peru**, 9 de Octubre 411 y Chile, p 6, T232 2738. **Spain**, Urdesa, C Circunvalación, Solar 118 y C Unica, T288 1691. **Sweden**, Km 6.5

Ecuador

vía a Daule, T225 4111. **Switzerland**, Av 9 de Octubre 2105, T245 3607. **UK**, General Córdova 623 y Padre Solano, T256 0400. **USA**, 9 de Octubre 1571 y García Moreno, T232 3570. **Venezuela**, Chile 329 y Aguirre, T232 6566.

For doctors and dentists, contact your consulate for recommendations

Medical services Hospitals: the main hospital used by the foreign community is the **Clínica Kennedy**, Av San Jorge y la 9na, T228 4051. Also has a branch in Ciudadela La Alborada XIII, Mz-1227. It contains the consulting rooms of almost every kind of specialist doctor and diagnostic laboratory (Dr Roberto Morla speaks English and German, T229 3470); very competent emergency department. Also reliable are: **Clínica Alcívar**, Coronel 2301 y Azuay, T258 0030; **Clínica Guayaquil**, Padre Aguirre 401 y General Córdova, T256 3555 (Dr Roberto Gilbert speaks English). **Clínica Santa Marianita**, Boyacá 1915 entre Colón y Av Olmedo, T232 2500. Doctors speak English and Spanish, special rates for *SAHB* users.

Machala

Phone code: 04
Colour map 1a, grid C2
Population: 144,197

The capital of the province of El Oro is a booming agricultural town in a major banana producing and exporting region with an annual banana fair in September. It is not particularly attractive, somewhat dirty and oppressively hot, but definitely prosperous and a good stopping point on the way to Peru. The tourist office is at 9 de Mayo y Pichincha, T932106.

Puerto Bolívar, on the Estero Jambelí among mangroves, is a major export outlet for over one million tonnes of bananas annually. There is a pleasant waterfront, a few basic hotels (**F**) and from the old pier a motorized canoe service crosses to the beaches of **Jambelí**, where there are a few hotels (**D-E**), on the far side of the mangrove islands which shelter Puerto Bolívar from the Pacific. Lots of birdlife can be seen in the mangroves; rent a canoe for an hour and explore the narrow channels. Canoes depart at 0700, 1000 and 1500, returning at 0800, 1200 and 1600, US$1.35. Take insect repellent. The beach at Puerto Bolívar is pleasant but waves and currents can be dangerous, also beware of sunburn. There are lots of seafood kiosks between the old and new piers in Puerto Bolívar and good, cheap cafés at Jambelí.

Sleeping

AL *Oro Verde*, Circunvalación Norte, Urb Unioro, T07-933140, covm@ gye.satnet.net Luxury, beautiful gardens, nice pool (US$9 for non-residents), tennis courts, 2 restaurants, casino. Best in town. **B** *El Oro*, Olmedo y Juan Montalvo, T930032, F937569. A/c, includes breakfast, good, helpful, expensive restaurant but good, cheaper café downstairs. Recommended. **C** *Rizzo*, Guayas y Bolívar, T921906, F921502. A/c, TV, suites available, pool (US$2.50 for non-residents), casino, cafetería, restaurant, noisy late disco. **D** *Montecarlo*, Guayas y Olmedo, T933104, F931901. A/c, TV, hot water, modern, restaurant. **D** *Araujo*, 9 de Mayo y Boyacá, T935257. Hot water, a/c, parking, cheaper with fan, some rooms are small, parking, good value. Recommended, but noisy disco next door. **D** *San Miguel*, 9 de Mayo y Sucre, T935488. A/c, cold water, good value. **E** *Mosquera*, Olmedo entre Guayas y Ayacucho, T931752, F930390. Cheaper with fan, TV, hot water, restaurant. Recommended. **E** *Res Patty*, Boyacá 619 y Ayacucho, T931759. Cheaper with shared bathroom, fan, basic, some short stay customers. **F** *Julio César*, 9 de Mayo 1319 y Boyacá, T937978. With fan, TV. Several other basic places.

Eating

The best food is found in the better hotels

Parrillada Sabor Latina, Sucre y Guayas. Good steaks and grills. *Don Angelo*, 9 de Mayo just off main plaza. Open 24 hrs, elaborate set meals and à la carte, good for breakfast. *200 Millas*, 9 de Octubre entre Santa Rosa y Vela. Seafood specialities. *Copa Cabana*, on main plaza. Good clean snack bar. *Chifa Central*, Tarqui y 9 de Octubre. Good Chinese. *Chifa Gran Oriental*, 9 de Octubre entre Guayas y Ayacucho. Good food and service. *Mesón Hispano*, Av Las Palmeras y Sucre. Very good grill, attentive service. *Palacio Real*, 9 de Octubre y Ayacucho. Good set meal. *Las Redes*, 9 de Mayo 18-23 y Bolívar. Seafood, à la carte and choice of cheap set meals. *Aquí es Correita*, Av Arízaga y 9 de Mayo. Popular for seafood, closed Sun. *Cafetería San Francisco*, Sucre block 6. Good, filling breakfast.

Air Daily flights from **Guayaquil** with *Cedta* (light aircraft, T230 1165 Guayaquil), Mon-Fri, depart Guayaquil from the Terminal de Avionetas 4 a day, US$16 each way; also with *TAME*, Juan Montalvo y Bolívar, T930139. **Road Bus**: to **Quito**, with *Occidental* (Buenavista entre Sucre y Olmedo), 12 hrs, US$6, 8 daily 0815 to 2145, with *Panamericana* (Colón y Bolívar), 9 daily 0745 to 2130, luxury service, 9 hrs, US$10 a/c, US$8 without a/c. To **Guayaquil**, 4 hrs, US$3.80, hourly with *Ecuatoriano* Pullman (Colón y 9 de Octubre), *Cifa* and *Rutas Orenses* (9 de Octubre y Tarqui). To **Esmeraldas**, 11 hrs, US$7.40, with *Occidental* at 2200. To **Loja**, 7 hrs, US$4, several daily with *Transportes Loja* (Tarqui y Bolívar). To **Cuenca**, hourly with *Trans Azuay* (Sucre y Junín), 4-5hrs, US$3.50. To **Huaquillas**, with *Cifa* (Bolívar y Guayas) and *Ecuatoriano Pullman*, direct, 1 hr, US$1.40, every 30 mins; via Arenillas and Santa Rosa, 2 hrs, US$1.15, every 10 mins. There are passport checks on this route. **Taxi**: to **Guayaquil**, *Orotaxis* run a scheduled taxi service between the *Hotel Rizzo*, Machala, and *Hotel Rizzo*, Guayaquil, every 30 mins or so, 0600-2000, US$5 pp, T934332.

Transport
Do not take night buses into or out of Machala, there have been many holdups

Banks For Visa: *Banco del Austro*, Rocafuerte y Guayas, and *Banco de Guayaquil* , Rocafuerte y Guayas. *Banco del Pacífico*, Rocafuerte y Junín, TCs. *Banco Machala*, Rocafuerte y 9 de Mayo, Visa ATM and cash advances, friendly, efficient. **Communications Internet:** prices around US$1.50 per hr. **Post Office:** Bolívar y Montalvo. **Telephone:** *Pacifictel*, Av Las Palmeras near the stadium. **Embassies and consulates** Peruvian Consulate, at the northwest corner of Colón y Bolívar, p 1, T930680.

Directory

Southeast from Machala is the lovely old gold-mining town of Zaruma (118 km). It is reached either by paved road via the military post at Saracay and **Piñas** (two orchid growers show their collections), or via Pasaje and Paccha on a scenic, dirt road. Founded in 1549 on orders of Felipe II to try to control the gold extraction, Zaruma is a delightful town perched on a hilltop, with steep, twisting streets and painted wooden buildings. Beside the plaza is a lovely little museum showing the history of gold mining in the area. On top of the small hill beyond the market is a public swimming pool, from where there are amazing views over the hot, dry valleys. The area has virtually no tourists and is well worth a visit. ■ *Transportes Paccha departs Machala near the market, or Trans TAC, Sucre y Colón departs every every hour from 0500 to 1700 via Piñas, last bus back at 1800, US$1.70, 3 hrs to Zaruma. Also daily service to Cuenca and Loja.*

Zaruma
Altitude: 1,170 m

Sleeping D *Cerro de Oro*, Sucre 40, T/F972505. Modern, nice. Recommended. **D** *Roland*, at entrance to town on road from Portovelo, T972800. Comfortable, lovely views. **F** *Colombia*, On main plaza next to municipio, T972173. Cheaper without bath, hot water, very basic. Several good places to eat.

The petrified forest of Puyango, due south of Machala, is supposedly the most exten-sive outside Arizona. Over 120 species of birds can be seen. No accommodation in the village but ask around for floor space or try at the on-site information centre. If not, basic accommodation is available in **Alamor**, 20 km south. Campsites are also provided. For further information, contact the Dirección Provincial de Turismo, Machala, T932106. ■ *Buses for Alamor 0900 and 1330, 3 hrs, US$4, ask to be dropped off at Puyango. To return to Machala, you can catch the Loja-Machala bus which passes Puyango around 1500. Several military checkpoints between Puyango and Machala.*

Puyango

Ecuador

Huaquillas

Colour map 1a, grid C2 The most commonly used route overland to Peru is via Machala. Many buses go to Huaquillas, the Ecuadorean border town, which is something of a shopping arcade for Peruvians. It has grown into a small city with a reasonable selection of services. The climate is very hot. An information centre is just by the international bridge. It is staffed by tourism students and is friendly and helpful, but has limited information.

Sleeping & eating
A number of the cheaper hotels in Huaquillas are primarily for short stay customers

D *Lima*, Portovelo y Machala, T907794. A/c, phone, cheaper with fan, mosquito net. **D** *Vanessa*, 1 de Mayo 323, T/F907263. A/c, phone. **D** *Alameda*, Tnte Córdovez y José Mendoza. Fan, TV, mosquito net, basic. **D** *Guayaquil*, Remigio Gómez 125. Cheaper without bath, fan, mosquito net, limited water supply, noisy. **D** *Internacional*, Machala y 9 de Octubre, T907963. Fan, small rooms, basic, cheaper with shared bath. **E** *Gabeli*, Tnte Córdovez 311 y Portovelo, T907149. Fan, mosquito net, cheaper without bath, parking. **E** *Mini*, Tnte Córdovez y Rocafuerte. Fan, mosquito net, restaurant, poor water supply. **E** *Rivieras*, Tnte Córdovez y El Oro. Fan, mosquito net, OK, disco downstairs at weekends. **E** *Res San Martín*, Av la República opposite the church, 1 block from immigration, T907083. Shared bath, fan, basic, noisy, mosquito nets, convenient. For eating, try *Chic*, behind *Hotel Guayaquil*, set meal US$1. *Mini*, opposite *Transportes Loja*, good set lunch US$2. *Chesito*, Av la Repúlica y Costa Rica. Across from the police station, large portions, good. *Chifa China Norte*, Santa Rosa y Tnte Córdovez. Chinese.

Transport
If in a hurry, it can be quicker to change buses in Machala

Bus There are 3 checkpoints (Transit Police, Customs and military) along the road north from Huaquillas, keep your passport to hand. To **Machala**, with *Cifa* (Santa Rosa y Machala) and *Ecuatoriano* Pullman (Av la República y 9 de Octubre), direct, 1 hr, US$1.40, every hour between 0400 and 2000; via Arenillas and Santa Rosa, 2 hrs, US$1.15, every 10 mins. To **Quito**, with *Occidental* (Remigio Gómez 129), 3 daily, 12 hrs, US$7; with *Panamericana*, on Remigio Gómez, luxury service, 11½ hrs, 6 daily via Santo Domingo, US$10 a/c, US$8.50 without a/c; 2 daily via **Riobamba** and **Ambato**, 12 hrs, US$10. To **Guayaquil**, frequent service with *Cifa* and *Ecuatoriano Pullman*, about 5 hrs, US$3.70. To **Cuenca**, 5 daily, 6 hrs, US$4. To **Loja**, with *Transportes Loja* (Tnte Córdovez y Arenillas) daily at 1130 and 1830, 7 hrs, US$4.50. To **Tulcán** for the Colombian border, with *Panamericana*, at 1630, 16 hours, US$12.

Directory

Banks Verify rates of exchange with travellers leaving Peru. Fair rates are available for soles but you will always be offered a low rate when you first enquire. Don't be rushed into any transaction. The money changers (recognized by their black briefcases) are very clever, particularly with calculators, so be alert. Avoid those changers who chase after you. Check sol notes very carefully for forgeries: verify the watermark and that the amount written on the right side of the note appears green, blue and pink at different angles to the light. It is difficult to change TCs. **Communications** Post Office: Av la República y Portovelo. **Telephone**: *Pacifictel*, Av la República, opposite post office.

Border with Peru
Coming from Peru, there are money changers outside Peruvian immigration or in Huaquillas, but beware of sharp practices by both

The border is open 24 hrs. Passports are stamped 3 km north of Huaquillas along the road to Machala. No urban transport to immigration; inter-city buses US$0.20 from Huaquillas, taxis US$1.50. Allow up to 1-2 hours to complete formalities, although it can sometimes be much quicker. Then walk along the main street and across the international bridge into Peru. At the bridge, the police may check passports. The main Peruvian immigration and customs complex is outside Zarumilla, 3 km south of the international bridge. There is also a small Peruvian immigration office at the south end of the international bridge, which sporadically opens and closes.

Alternative border crossings

The **Huaquillas-Tumbes** crossing can be harrowing, made worse by the crowds and heat. You must always watch your belongings carefully. In addition to cheating by money changers and cab drivers, this border is known for its minor shakedowns of travellers by officials. It is best to cross in a group; women are advised not to cross alone. Those seeking a more relaxed crossing to or from Peru should consider Macará (see page 980) or the new crossings which have opened following the peace treaty between Ecuador and Peru.

Pacific Lowlands

This vast tract of Ecuador covers everything west of the Andes and north of the Guayas delta. Though popular with Quiteños and Guayaquileños, who come here for weekends and holidays, the Pacific Lowlands receive relatively few foreign visitors, which is surprising given the natural beauty, diversity and rich cultural heritage of the coast. Here you can surf, watch whales, visit archaeological sites, or just relax and enjoy the best food this country has to offer. The Parque Nacional Machalilla protects an important area of primary tropical dry forest, precolumbian ruins, coral reef and a wide variety of wildlife. Further north, in the province of Esmeraldas, there are not only well-known party beaches, but also opportunities to visit the remaining mangroves and experience two unique lifestyles: Afro-Ecuadorean on the coast and native Cayapa further inland.

The main route from Quito goes down the valley of the Ríos Naranjal/Pilatón/Blanco, turning off the Panamericana at Alóag and continuing past Tandapi. Sit on the right for views, but on the left look for El Poder Brutal, a devil's face carved in the rock face, 2½ km west of Tandapi. This road is very busy, gets much heavy truck traffic and it can be dangerous owing to careless drivers passing on the many curves, especially when foggy and at night.

Santo Domingo de los Colorados

Situated in the hills above the western lowlands, Santo Domingo became Ecuador's main transport hub in the mid-1960s when the road from Quito through Alóag was completed. Since then it has experienced very rapid growth and become an important commercial centre for surrounding palm oil and banana producing areas. The city itself is noisy and streets are prone to flooding after heavy rains. Sunday is market day, shops are closed Monday. There is a cinema.

The name 'de los Colorados' is a reference to the traditional red hair dye, made with achiote (annatto), worn by the native Tsáchila men. Today the Tsáchila only wear their native dress on special occasions and they can no longer be seen in traditional garb in the city. There are less than 2,000 Tsáchilas left, living in eight communities off the roads leading from Santo Domingo to Quevedo, Chone and Quinindé. Their lands make up a reserve of some 8,000 ha. Visitors interested in their culture are welcome at the *Complejo Turístico Huapilú*, in the Chihuilpe Commune, where there is a small but interesting museum (contributions expected) run by Augusto Calazacón. Access is via the turnoff east at Km 7 on the road to Quevedo, from where it is 4 km. Tours are available from travel agencies in town. A taxi is US$5-10, or take a city bus Centro-Vía Quevedo-Km 7 and walk.

Colour map 1a, grid A3
Population: 114,442
129 km from Quito

Ecuador

Santo Domingo is not safe late at night, caution is recommended at all times in the market areas, including the pedestrian walkway along 3 de Julio and in peripheral neighbourhoods

In town D *Diana Real*, 29 de Mayo y Loja, T275 1380, F275 4091. Modern spacious rooms, hot water, fan. **D** *Aracelly*, Vía a Quevedo y Galápagos, T275 0334, F275 4144. Large rooms, electric shower, restaurant, parking. **D** *Caleta*, Ibarra 141, T275 0277. Good restaurant, good. **E** *Genova*, 29 de Mayo e Ibarra, T275 9694. Comfortable, electric shower, parking, good value. Recommended. **E** *Jennifer*, 29 de Mayo y Latacunga, T275 0577. Some rooms with hot water, parking, restaurant, good value. **E** *San Fernando*, 2 blocks from the bus terminal, T275 3402. Cheaper with shared bath, modern, comfortable, parking. **F** *Unicornio*, 29 de Mayo y Ambato, T276 0147. Cold water, cable TV, restaurant, parking, nice.

On Av Abraham Calazacón, opposite the bus terminal are: **D** *Sheraton*, T275 1988. Modern, hot water, parking, good value. Recommended. **E** *Res España*, entrance on the side street. Basic.

Out of town 20 km from Santo Domingo, on the road to Quito, is **AL** *Tinalandia*. Pleasant and small, chalets with bathrooms, including excellent meals, own golf course

Sleeping
Many hotels are along Av 29 de Mayo, a noisy street, so request a room away from the road

overlooking the Toachi valley, many species of birds, flowers and butterflies in the woods behind (and many biting insects in the evening), entry is US$10 for non-residents (lunch extra); also self-catering bunk rooms, **E**. It is poorly signposted, take small road between Km 16 and 17 from Santo Domingo on the right; T09-949 4727, in Quito T244 9028, www.tinalandia.net **B** *Zaracay*, Av Quito 1639, T275 0316, F275 4535, 1½ km from the centre on the road to Quito. Restaurant, casino, noisy disco, gardens and a swimming pool, good rooms and service, full breakfast included, advisable to book, especially at weekend. **D** *Hostería Los Colorados*, Km 12, just west of the toll booth and police control, T/F275 3449. Nice cabins with fridge, TV, pool, artificial lake with fish, restaurants, good cafetería. **D** *Hotel del Toachi* Km 1, just west of Zaracay, T/F275 4688. Spacious rooms, good showers, TV, swimming pool, parking. **F** *Complejo Campestre Santa Rosa*, Vía Quevedo Km 16, T275 4145, F275 4144. Office in Santo Domingo at *Hotel Aracelly*, on the shores of the Río Baba, restaurant, swimming, watersports, fishing, salsoteca.

Eating *Parrilladas Argentinas*, on Quevedo road Km 5. Good barbecues. *Mocambo*, Tulcán y Machala. Good. *La Fuente*, Ibarra y 3 de Julio. Good. There are several chicken places in the Cinco Esquinas area where Avs Quito and 29 de Mayo meet, including *Rico Pollo*, Quito y Río Pove. *Tacos Mexicanos*, Quito. A super deli. Highly recommended. There are also several *marisquerías* (seafood restaurants) along Av 29 de Mayo. *Parrilladas* can be found, together with a new shopping mall, near the roundabout on Vía Quito, eg *D'Mario*, on a back street 1 block southwest of the junction. There are several restaurants on Av Abraham Calazacón across from the bus terminal, including *Sheraton*, which is popular.

Ice cream *Heladería* at Edif San Francisco, Av Quito entre Río Blanco y Río Toachi. Good, made on the premises, also sell fresh cheese. Opposite is *Pingüino*.

Tour operators *Cayapatours*, 29 de Mayo y Tulcán, T/F276 2933. Tickets and tours. *Turismo Zaracay*, 29 de Mayo y Cocaniguas, T275 0546, F275 0873. Runs tours to Tsáchila commune US$12 pp, minimum 5 persons; fishing trips US$24 pp, 8 hrs, bird/butterfly watching tours, exchanges cash.

Transport **Road** The bus terminal is on Av Abraham Calazacón, at the north end of town, along the city's bypass. Long-distance buses do not enter the city. Taxi downtown, US$1, bus US$0.20. **Bus**: as it is a very important transportation centre, you can get buses going everywhere in the country. To **Quito** via Alóag US$2, 3 hrs. To **Guayaquil** US$5, 4 hrs. To **Machala**, US$4.55, 6 hrs. To **Huaquillas** US$5.20, 7½ hrs. To **Esmeraldas** US$2.25, 3 hrs. To **Ambato** US$3, 4 hrs. To **Loja** US$9.70, 12 hrs. To **Manta** US$5.65, 6 hrs. To **Bahía de Caráquez** US$4.10, 4 hrs. To **Pedernales** US$3, 3 hrs.

Directory **Banks** *Banco Internacional*, Av Quito y Río Blanco, TCs. **Communications** **Post Office:** Av de los Tsáchilas y Río Baba. **Telephone:** *Andinatel*, Edificio San Francisco, Av Quito entre Río Blanco y Río Toachi, p 2, and at bus terminal, 0800-2200 daily.

Routes to the coast A busy paved highway connects Santo Domingo de los Colorados with Esmeraldas, 185 km to the northwest. La Concordia (**D** *Hotel Atos*, T02-272 5445, very good), just before which is the private La Perla Forest Reserve, is 40 km from Santo Domingo (you can hike in for free). La Independencia is also on this road (junction with road from San Miguel de Los Bancos and Quito) and **Quinindé** (officially called Rosa Zárate). **D** *Sanz*, on main street, T736522, TV, parking. **E** *Turista*, eight blocks south of town, on main road, T736784, quiet, parking. *Restaurant Jean*, T736831, at bottom of hill three blocks south of town on the main road, reasonable, probably the best restaurant for miles. The road deteriorates after Quinindé.

A second route from Quito to Esmeraldas avoids Santo Domingo altogether: from Quito it goes via Calacalí, Mindo (see Around Quito), San Miguel de los Bancos, Pedro Vicente Maldonado and La Independencia; 3 km from Pedro Vicente Maldonado is the **Arasha** resort, at Km 120 in the biologically rich Chocó region. It is a beautiful, top-of-the-market centre with excellent facilities, good birdwatching, trails in secondary and primary forest, spa, world-class food. Elegant and very upscale, accommodation in the **LL** range. Quito office: Los Shyris N39-41 y Río Coca, 8th floor, T253967, www.arasha1spa.com About 10 km past Pedro Vicente Maldonado, on the way to La Independencia, is the town of La Abundancia. Beyond is the hamlet of El Salazar, with **A** *Cabañas Don Gaucho*, T02-233 0315, www.ecuador-sommerfern.com **E** pp in cabin with hammock and shared bath, BBQ, camping, swim in river.

Aldea Salamandra is a beautiful nature reserve in tropical rainforest: good for birdwatching (over 200 species including toucans and hummingbirds), swimming or kayaking and rafting (US$17 for half-day), or trekking through the forest. US$17 per person per day including accommodation and all meals and excursions. For reservations and enquiries about kayaking and volunteer work (US$50 for 7 days), Calama y J L Mera, Quito, T222 8151, www.aldeasalamandra.com

140 km NW of Quito

Transport 3 hrs by bus from Quito. Take any Esmeraldas bus and ask the driver to stop 2 km before Puerto Quito. It is a 10 min walk from the main road; well signposted. From **Esmeraldas** with *Trans Esmeraldas*, 2 hrs; stop 2 km after Puerto Quito.

A paved road from Santo Domingo runs west to **El Carmen**, with a cattle market on the outskirts. From El Carmen a paved road goes to **Pedernales** (see page 1003). Continuing southwest of El Carmen is Chone where the road divides, either to Bahía de Caráquez (207 km from Santo Domingo, 340 km from Quito), or to Portoviejo and Manta (257 km from Santo Domingo, 390 km from Quito).

On the highway 1½ hours by bus south of Santo Domingo is this important route centre. It is dusty, noisy, unsafe and crowded. Set in fertile banana lands and often flooded in the rainy season, Quevedo has a fair-sized Chinese colony, with many *chifas* (Chinese restaurants). Hotels in town are noisy: **B** *Olímpico*, Bolívar y 19a, has the best restaurant. **D** *Quevedo*, Av 7 de Octubre y C 12, modern with good restaurant. **E** *Ejecutivo Internacional*, 7 de Octubre y Cuarta, large rooms, good value, is the least noisy. ■ *There are buses to Quito, US$4, 7 hrs; Guayaquil, 3 hrs, US$1.65; Portoviejo, from 7 de Octubre y C 8, 5 hrs, US$1.85, uncomfortable, watch your possessions.*

    At Km 47 from Santo Domingo on the Quevedo road is **B** *Río Palenque*, lodge with capacity for 20, cooking facilities, US$5 for day visit. Set in a biological field station, good birdwatching, T256 1646 or 223 2468 in Quito for reservations.

Quevedo
Colour map 1a, grid B3
Population: 86,910

Quevedo is connected with Guayaquil by two paved highways, one through Balzar and Daule, one through **Babahoyo**. **Sleeping: D** *Hotel Emperador*, Gral Barona, 304 y 27 de Mayo, T730535, a/c, **E** with fan, TV, restaurant. **D** *Hotel Cachari*, Bolívar 120, T734443, F731317, cheaper with fan, acceptable, restaurant nearby. There is also a very scenic road from Quevedo east through **La Maná** to Latacunga (see Quilotoa Circuit, page 947).

Phone code: 05
Capital of Los Ríos province
Population: 50,250

Playas

The beach resorts of Salinas and Playas remain as popular as ever with vacationing Guayaquileños. Both can be reached along a paved toll highway from Guayaquil. The road divides after 63 km at El Progreso (Gómez Rendón). One branch leads to General Villamil, normally known as Playas, the nearest seaside resort to Guayaquil. Look out for the bottle-shaped ceibo (kapok) trees between Guayaquil and Playas as the landscape becomes drier, turning into tropical thorn scrub where 2-5 m cacti prevail. Fishing is still important in Playas and a few single-sailed balsa rafts can still be seen among the motor launches returning laden with fish. These rafts are unique, highly ingenious and very simple. The same rafts without sails are used to spread nets close offshore, then two gangs of men take 2-3 hours to haul them in. The beach shelves gently, and is 200-400 m wide, lined with singular, square canvas tents hired out for the day.

Phone code: 04
Colour map 1a, grid B1

The road network on the coast was completely rebuilt following El Niño floods in 1997

As the closest resort to Guayaquil, Playas is prone to severe crowding, although the authorities are trying to keep the packed beaches clean and safe. Out of season (high season is December to April), when it is cloudier, or midweek the beaches are almost empty especially north towards Punta Pelado (5 km). Playas is also a popular surfing resort with six good surf points. There are showers, toilets and changing rooms along the beach, with fresh water, for a fee. **NB** Thieving is rampant during busy times – do not leave **anything** unattended on the beach.

Sleeping

Some hotels are connected to Guayaquil's mains water supply, but many have wells to take water from the sea which is slightly brackish. Downmarket places have buckets for washing, if you're lucky

Most hotels are 5 mins' walk from the *Transportes Villamil* bus station. **C** *Hostería Bellavista*, Km 2 Data Highway, T276 0600. Rooms or suites in bungalows on beach, booking necessary, Swiss-run, camping at the south end of beach. **D** *Hostería La Gaviota*, 500 m out on Data road, T276 0133. A/c, good clean restaurant. **D** *Playas*, T276 0121, on Malecón. Accepts credit cards, beach hotel, plain rooms with fans, safe, restaurant, parking. Recommended. **D** *El Delfín*, Km 1.5, T276 0125. Old fashioned, big rooms, on beach, hacienda type building, nice but sporadic water supply, electric showers, restaurant sometimes closed at night. **D** *El Galeón*, T276 0270, beside the church. Mosquito protection, cheap restaurant with seafood (closes 1800 Sun), have to wait for shower if full, good breakfast, cheaper for long stay, good value. **D** *La Terraza*, Paquisa y Guayaquil, centre of town, T276 0430. Dingy but clean rooms, substantial and good value meals. **E** *Miraglia*, T276 0154. Popular with surfers, run-down but clean, sea view, showers, fresh drinking water, parking for motorcycles, cheaper rates for longer stays.

Eating

Excellent seafood and typical dishes from over 50 beach cafés (all numbered and named). Recommended are *Cecilia's* at No 7 or *Barzola* at No 9. *Mario's*, central plaza opposite Banco de Guayaquil, big hamburgers, good yoghurt.

Transport Bus: To **Guayaquil**, with *Coop Libertad Peninsular*, Av 9 de Octubre (opposite *Hotel Turis Palm*) and *CICA* across the street, US$2, 2½ hrs, every 15 mins (the 2 companies alternate departures); taxi to Guayaquil US$30. Buses every hour, until 1715 to **Manglaralto** (US$1.25), **Puerto López** (US$2.50), **Jipijapa** (US$3.65) and **Manta** (US$4.35) from the terminal near the market. To **Quito** with *Trans Esmeraldas* (opposite *Coop Libertad Peninsular*), 2 nightly, 9½ hrs, US$11.

West of Playas is the busy port and regional market centre of **La Libertad**. The only reason for stopping here is for transport connections. **Warning** Muggings are frequent.

Salinas

Phone code: 04
Colour map 1a, grid B1
Population: 19,298

A few kilometres further on, surrounded by miles of salt flats, is Salinas, Ecuador's answer to Benidorm. There is safe swimming in the bay and high rise blocks of holiday flats and hotels line the sea front. The town is dominated by the Choclatera hill on the western point of the bay, overlooking the well-equipped and very exclusive Salinas Yacht Club. During *temporada* (December to April) it is overcrowded, with traffic jams and rubbish-strewn beaches, and its services are stretched to the limit. During off season it is quieter, but still not for 'getting away from it all'.

Sleeping & eating

Prices indicated are high season; expect lower at other times

AL *Calypsso*, Malecón, next to Capitanía de Puerto, T277 3605, calypsso@gye.satnet.net A/c, pool, gym, crafts shop, good whale watching tours. **A** *El Carruaje*, Malecón 517, T/F277 4282. A/c, TV, hot water, good restaurant, includes breakfast. **AL-A** *Hostal Francisco 1*, Gral Enríquez Gallo y Rumiñahui, T277 4106. A/c, hot water, pool, restaurant. **A** *Suites Salinas*, Gral Henríquez Gallo y 27, T/F277 2759, hotelsalinas@porta.net Modern, a/c, hot water, fridge, cable TV, good restaurant, pool, parking, internet. **B** *Yulee*, diagonal to church, near the beach, T277 2028. Cheaper without bath, hot water, cable TV, excellent food. **D** *Albita*, Av 3 y C23, Barrio Barzán, T277 3211. Good. **D** *Residencial Rachel*, C 17 y Av Quinta, T277 2526. With fans. A couple more in the **E-F** range along Av Gral Enríquez Gallo y C 22-25. Also **F** pp *Villa Venecia*, entre C 27 y 29, T277 4149. Good value, backpacker place, helpful.

Eating places: *Mar y Tierra*, Malecón y Av 7. Excellent seafood, especially lobster. Good freshly-cooked seafood in the market, 2 blocks in from the Malecón, *La Lojanita* is recommended. *La Bella Italia*, Malecón y C 19, near *Hotel El Carruaje*. Pizzería. *La Taberna de Chistorra*, near the market. Good food, nice atmosphere. *Selva del Mar*, Gral Enríquz Gallo y C 23. Good *pescado con menestra*, cheap. *Oystercatcher*, Malecón y 32, recommended, safe oysters; bird and whale watchers ask here for local expert, Ben Haase.

Tours, hire of sailing boats, water skis, fishing trips arranged through *Pesca Tours*, on the Malecón, T277 2391, or *Salitour*, T277 2800, F772789. See also *Oystercatcher* above.

Tour operators

Bus From **Guayaquil**, US$2.70, 2½ hrs; for the return journey, go to La Libertad by bus or colectivo (US$0.25, 15 mins, they pass by the market) and take a bus from there.

Transport

Banks *Banco del Pacífico* changes TCs, Visa. **Communications** Internet: *Café Planet*, Av 10 y C 25. US$2 per hr. *Salinas.Net*, C 19 y Av 2, US$1.20 per hr. **Telephone**: *Pacifictel*, at Radio Internacional.

Directory

On the south shore of the Santa Elena peninsula, 8 km south of La Libertad, is **Punta Carnero**, with a magnificent 15-km beach with wild surf and heavy undertow, virtually empty during the week. In July, August and September there is great whale watching.

The road north to Puerto López in the province of Manabí has been dubbed the 'Ruta del Sol'. It parallels the coastline and crosses the Chongón-Colonche coastal range. Most of the numerous small fishing villages along the way have good beaches and are slowly being developed for tourism, for additional details see the *Ecuador Handbook*. Beware however of rip currents and undertow. Look for the *semilleros* all along the coast trudging through waves with their red nets to collect larvae to sell to the shrimp farms.

San Pedro and Valdivia are two unattractive villages which merge together. There are many fish stalls. This is the site of the 5,000 year-old Valdivia culture. Many houses offer 'genuine' artefacts and one resident at the north end of the village will show you the skeletons and burial urns dug up in his back garden.

Valdivia

It is illegal to export precolumbian artefacts from Ecuador. The replicas are made in exactly the same manner as their predecessors, copied from genuine designs, and while sacrificing historic authenticity, their purchase prevents the trafficking of originals and provides income for the locals. Ask for Juan Orrala, who makes excellent copies, and lives up the hill from the artesans' museum, which has excellent displays (you can often see crafts people working there). Most artefacts discovered at the site are in museums in Quito and Guayaquil. Some pieces remain in the small, local **Ecomuseo Valdivia**, which also has artifacts from other coastal cultures and *in-situ* remains. There is also a handicraft section where artisans may be seen at work and lots of local information. ■ *Wed-Sun, US$0.40.*

Located 180 km north of Guayaquil, this is the main centre of the region north of Santa Elena. A tagua nursery has been started; ask to see examples of worked 'ivory' nuts. It is a nice place, with a quiet, clean beach, good surf but little shade. Pro-pueblo is an organization working with local communities, to foster family run orchards and cottage craft industry, using tagua nuts, paja toquilla (the stuff Panama hats are made from), and other local products, T901195. *Programa de Manejo de Recursos Costeros*, PMRC, is an organization promoting ecotourism in local communities. A network of community lodgings, *Red de Hospederías Comunitarias*, is being developed). Office opposite church, T290 1343, F290 1118, and a tourist information centre in Montañita (see below). ■ *Buses to La Libertad, US$1.25. Jipijapa, US$2, 3½ hrs, 100 km via Salango. Puerto López, 1 hr, US$1.50.*

Manglaralto
Colour map 1a, grid B2
Phone code: 04
Population: 18,510

Sleeping and eating **F** *Marakaya*, south of the main plaza, an orange/beige building, 1 block from the beach, T290 1294. With hot water, safe, fan, mosquito net. **F** *Alegre Calamar*, at the north end of town. Shared bath, mosquito nets, restaurant, refurbished in 2000. *La Calderada*, on the beach. Very good seafood. *Comedor Familiar* has meals weekends only. Also *Comedor Florencia*, cheap and friendly.

The best surfing in Ecuador About 3 km north of Manglaralto, **Montañita** has a good beach but watch out for the strong undertow and stingrays close to the water's edge. If stung, the small hospital in Manglaralto will treat you quickly. Windsurfing board rental US$1.50 per hour. Various windsurfing competitions are held during the year; at weekends the town is full of Guayaquileños and it's a good place to hang out, becoming increasingly popular with gringos. Major development is taking place at the northern end of the beach called **Baja Montañita**, site of the best surfing in Ecuador. ■ Transportes Manglaralto *from Montañita to La Libertad, 1 hr, US$1. CLP 3 direct buses a day to Guayaquil, 0500, 1300, 1430 (return 0600, 1300, 1430), US$3.20.*

Accommodation is impossible to find during holiday weekends **Sleeping and eating D** *Paradise South*, residential area between town and Baja Montañita, T290 1185/224 4898, paradise_south@hotmail.com Without bath, sports fields, laundry, restaurant, quiet. **D** *Hotel Montañita*, on beach just north of the village, T290 1296, hmontani@telconet.net With hot water, cheaper with cold, pool, restaurant, internet, laundry, runs a nature reserve near La Entrada, further north. **E** *La Casa Blanca*, T09-989 2281, lacasablan@hotmail.com Cheaper without bath, sporadic hot water, large, secure, helpful, internet, good fun. **E** *El Centro del Mundo II*, 4-storey timber and thatch building on beach. **F** without bath.

In Baja Montañita: **C** *Baja Montañita*, T290 1218, F290 1227. A/c, cabins and rooms, pool, jacuzzi, 2 restaurants, bars. **D** *La Casa del Sol*, T/F290 1302, www.casasol.com With cable TV, restaurant, US-run, good. **E** *Tres Palmas*, T09-975 5717. With Tex-Mex restaurant, very nice. **F** *Vito's Cabañas*, T224 1975. A bit run down, good cheap food, camping facilities. Mixed reports but generally recommended.

It's cheaper to eat in the village south of the surf beach. *La Cabaña*, at the beach. Good and cheap. *La Chifla*. Good breakfast and meals, grill. *Pizza D'Wilson*. Good, try the vegetarian thin crust. *Tiburón*. Good pizza. *Lon, Lon, Lon*, Good meals. Recommended. *Las Olas*, Baja Montañita, next to *Casa del Sol*. *Pelícano*, in Baja Montañita. Good pizzas, disco, open till 2200, later in season. *Disco Tiburón*, in town, near the plaza. There are many other restaurants, food and prices quite uniform.

At Olón, a few kilometres north with a spectacular long beach: **E** *Hostería Olón Beach*, T290 1191. Basic but clean. **F** *Hostería N & J*, on the beach. OK. **F** *Río Olón*, opposite the church. Basic. **F** *Hospedaje Rosa Mistía*, in family home, part of *Red de Hospederías Comunitarias*, see Manglaralto above. Fanny Tomalá also rents rooms. *Flor de Olón*, in the village. Simple but good food. *Verónica*, just off the beach. Scruffy, but good seafood.

Further north, by **La Entrada**, the road winds up and inland through lush forest before continuing to **Ayampe** and **Puerto Rico** back on the coast. Here is **B-C** *Hostería Alandaluz*, T278 0184, Quito T/F02-254 3042, www.alandaluz.com Bamboo cabins with thatched roofs and private bath (composting toilets). Very peaceful place, clean beach and stunning organic vegetable and flower gardens in the desert. Camping possible. Student and youth hostel discounts. Good home-made organic food, vegetarian or seafood, breakfast US$3.70, other meals US$5, and there's a bar. Expensive tours in the area. Reservations necessary, highly recommended. **C** *Hostería La Barquita*, by Las Tunas, north of Ayampe and south of Alandaluz, T05-780051. Includes breakfast, with bath, **E** with bunk beds and shared bath, by the beach, expensive restaurant, set up for partying. French run, French, English and German spoken. **D** *Piqueros Patas Azules*, North of Puerto Rico, in Piqueros, near Río Chico, T780279. Cabins overlooking beach, with bath, fan, eco-conscious. **F** pp *Cabaña*, in Puerto Rico, cabin for 6, further information at *The Whale Café* in Puerto López. **F** pp *Albergue Río Chico*, by main road at Río Chico, T05-604181. Accommodation in dormitories with restaurant. Don Julio Mero, off the main road in Puerto Rico offers meals and rents basic cabins with kitchen and bathroom for longer stays.

Transport Bus: *Trans Manglaralto* from **La Libertad**, US$2, or from **Jipijapa** if coming from the north. Ask to get off at Puerto Rico, though the centre is easily seen from the road. The last bus from the south passes at 1930, from the north at 1730; hitching is difficult. It's 20 mins from Puerto López.

Puerto López

This pleasant little fishing town is beautifully set in a horseshoe bay. The beach is cleaner at the northern end, away from the fleet of boats moored offshore; watch the fishermen arrive in the morning and evening. The town is becoming increasingly visited by foreign tourists for whale watching, Parque Nacional Machalilla and Isla de la Plata. Information centre at C Eloy Alfaro y García Moreno, open Tuesday-Saturday. Scooter rental is US$3 per hour, with daily and weekly rates available.

Phone code: 05
Colour map 1a, grid B2
Population: 10,212

The **Presley Norton archaeological museum** in the nearby village of Salango is worth visiting; entry US$1. Artefacts from the excavations in the local fish meal factory's yard are housed in a beautiful museum on the plaza. *El Delfín Mágico* (order meal before visiting museum), try the *spondilus* (spiny oyster) in fresh coriander and peanut sauce with garlic coated *patacones*. ■ *Buses to and from Puerto López every 20 mins; US$0.40, 10 mins.*

C *Manta Raya Lodge*, 3 km from town, T09-970 7954. With restaurant, pool. **D** *Hotel Cabañas Pacífico*, just off Malecón, T604147, www.hotelycabanaspacifico.com Hot showers, restaurants, breakfast, secure, a/c, cheaper with fan. **D** *La Terraza*, on hill north behind the clinic, T604235. Great views over the bay, gardens, hot water, spacious, good breakfast, evening meals available on request, run by German Peter Bernhard, free car service to/from town if called in advance. Highly recommended. **D** *Mandala*, beyond fish market at north end of the beach, T/F604181. Swiss-Italian run, helpful, good restaurant, 2-storey cabins with screened windows, hot water, garden. Recommended. **D** *Villa Colombia*, behind market, T604105. Hot water, cheaper in dorm with shared bath and kitchen facilities, nice. **D** *Los Islotes*, Malecón y Gen Córdova, T604108. Includes breakfast, private and shared bath, pleasant, popular, often booked in high season. **F** *Hostal Tuzco*, 500 m inland, uphill behind the market, T604132. Family rooms available, kitchen facilities. **F** *Cueva del Oso*, in the town centre. Above handicrafts shop, well signposted, private rooms or dormitories, hot water, kitchen facilities. Recommended. **F** *Hostal Turismar*, on Malecón Sur, 1 street back from park office, T604174. With cold water and sea view, discount for longer stays. **F** *Yubarta Guest House*, on Malecón Norte before the fish market. With kitchen and cold water, owned by guide who offers bi-lingual snorkelling and kayaking trips.

Sleeping

Carmita on the Malecón. Good for fish, also rents rooms for longer stays, **F**. Next door is *Mayflower*. Good for seafood but not cheap. *Spondylus*, on Malecón next to *Exploratur*. Good set lunch but slow service. *Viña del Mar*, on the Malecón. Good food, also basic rents rooms, friendly but not so clean. *Flipper*, next to bus stop. Cheap, best meal at best price. Recommended. *The Whale Café (La Ballena)*, Malecón Sur y Julio Izurieta. Good pizza, cakes and pies, breakfast, US-run, owners Diana and Kevin, very helpful with travel information. *Bellitalia*, on intermediate street between Malecón and the main road. Very good Italian food, Italian run. Recommended. *La Luna*, back of market near *Hostal Tuzco*, nice cafetería. The *panadería* behind the church serves excellent banana bread.

Eating
Try the local avocado licuados and chuzos, recommended

Local companies run tours to **Isla de la Plata**, **Agua Blanca**, **San Sebastián** and **Los Frailes**, (see below) as well as diving trips. Puerto López has become a major centre for whale watching trips from Jun to Sep, with many more agencies than we can list. **NB** Whales can also be seen further north. *Pacarina*, or *Whale Tours* in Guayaquil (see page 1011). *Sercapez*, T604130, arranges tours in the area, as does *Machalilla Tours*, T604206. Cheaper trips may be available in open fishing boats, which are smaller and faster and can get closer, but have no toilet. American *Kevin Gulash* (next to *Alándaluz*) runs cheaper, alternative trips.

Tour operators
There are many fly-by-night operators, so shop around and try to get a personal recommendation from other visitors

Ecuador

Transport Buses every 30 mins to **Jipijapa**, 1½ hrs, US$1.30. **La Libertad**, 2 hrs, and **Manglaralto**, 1 hr, US$1.50. To **Portoviejo**, 1 hr, good road, 68 km. To **Manta**, direct, every 2 hrs. To **Quito**, *Carlos Array* at 1900, 10 hrs, US$7.50.

Parque Nacional Machalilla

Preserves marine ecosystems as well as the dry tropical forest and archaeological sites on shore

The Park extends over 55,000 ha, including Isla de la Plata, Isla Salango, and the magnificent beach of Los Frailes. The continental portion of the park is divided into three sections which are separated by private land, including the town of Machalilla. Recommended for birdwatching, also several species of mammals and reptiles. ■ *Daily 0700-1800, US$12 for mainland portions, US$15 for Isla de la Plata, US$20 if visiting both areas (ask for 5-6 days), payable at the park office next to the market in Puerto López, or directly to the park rangers (insist on a receipt). Half price for those over 60.*

To **Los Frailes** Take a bus towards Jipijapa and alight at the turnoff just south of the town of **Machalilla** (US$0.30), then walk for 30 mins. Show your national park ticket on arrival. No transport back to Puerto López after 2000 (but check in advance).

About 5 km north of Puerto López, at Buena Vista, a dirt road to the right leads to **Agua Blanca**. Here, 5 km from the main road, in the national park, amid hot, arid scrub, is a small village and a fine, small archaeological museum containing some fascinating ceramics from the Manteño civilization. ■ *0800-1800, US$1.15. It is cheaper to find a guide for Agua Blanca in the village itself for a visit to the pre-Inca ruins; US$1.50 pp for a 2-3 hr tour for 2 people. It's a 45-min walk to the ruins, or hire horses for US$7.50 pp per day.*

San Sebastián, 9 km from Agua Blanca, is in cloud forest at 800 m; orchids can be seen and possibly howler monkeys. Although part of the national park, this area is administered by the Comuna of Agua Blanca, which charges its own fees in addition to the park entrance. ■ *A tour to the forest costs US$15 per day for the guide (fixed rate), US$1.50 pp to stay overnight at guide's house, US$5 for meals, US$15 per horse. Transport to Agua Blanca is an extra US$5 pp. Five hours on foot or by horse.*

Sleeping & eating **In Machalilla** **D** *Hotel Internacional Machalilla*, T345905. Conspicuous building, fan, overpriced, enquire about cheaper rates for longer stays. Next door is *Comedor La Gaviota*. *Bar Restaurant Cabaña Tropical* at south end of town. A few shops with basic supplies. **In Agua Blanca** Camping and 1 very basic room for rent above the museum, US$1.50 pp, minimal facilities. **In San Sebastián** Camping is possible, US$1.50.

Transport Public transport to **Agua Blanca** leaves Sat only from *Carmita's* in Puerto López at 0630 and 1200, returning 0700 and 1300.

Trips to the **Isla de la Plata**, about 24 km offshore, have become popular because of the similarities with the Galápagos. Wildlife includes nesting colonies of waved albatross, frigates and three different booby species. Whales can be seen from June to September, as well as dolphins. It is also a precolumbian site with substantial pottery finds, and there is good diving and snorkelling. There are two walks, of three and five hours; take water. ■ *US$20 in high season (Jul-Sep), US$15 rest of year.*

Transport The island can be visited on a day trip. Reservations can be arranged at most nearby hotels in Puerto López, Puerto Cayo or Machalilla and there are touts only too willing to organize a trip. Many agencies, see Puerto López above. The park wardens in Puerto López will arrange trips which don't use pirate operators. Take dry clothes, water, precautions against sun and seasickness and snorkelling equipment.

Puerto López to Manta The road turns inland for Jipijapa at **Puerto Cayo**. The beach gets cleaner as you walk away from town. Ask about whale-watching tours, June-September. ■ *Buses to Manglaralto, 2 hrs, US$2; to Puerto López, 1½ hrs, US$1.30; to Manta, 1 hr. Buses leave from the plaza. The last bus to the coast is 1800.*

Sleeping and eating C *Hostal Jipijapa Los Frailes*, T616014. A/c, cheaper without, TV, fridge, restaurant, tours. **D** *Puerto Cayo*, south end of beach, T04-230 1772, www.puertocayo.com Rooms with terrace and hammocks, good, expensive restaurant, also runs tours. **F** *Residencial Zavala*, on Malecón. With bath, meals available. **F** *Barandhua*, north end of the beach. Basic. *La Cabaña* just back from the beach for good seafood. *D'Comer*, next to *Zavala*. Good cheap seafood.

At **La Pila**, due north of Jipijapa, the road turns east for Portoviejo. The village's main industry is fake precolumbian pottery, with a thriving by-line in erotic ceramics. A few kilometres further west is **Montecristi**, below an imposing hill, high enough to be watered by low cloud which gives the region its only source of drinking water. The town is renowned as the centre of the panama hat industry. Hats can be bought at half price late afternoon; also varied straw and basketware and wooden barrels, which are strapped to donkeys for carrying water. Ask for José Chávez Franco, Rocafuerte 203, T/F606343, where you can see panama hats being made; wholesale and retail.

Manta

Ecuador's second port after Guayaquil, it is a busy town that sweeps round a bay filled with all sorts of boats. The western section comprises steep, narrow streets and the Malecón that fills in the evenings with impromptu parties and cars cruising, music blaring. The constant breeze makes it pleasant to walk along the front or stop for a drink at one of the many small bars. Playa Murciélago at the west end of the Malecón is very wide but unprotected from the wild surf. Further west towards the point, beaches are spotless and isolated. The town's fine wooden church was destroyed by a cargo plane crash in 1996. Miraculously, the statue of the Virgin survived. The *Banco Central* museum, Av 6 y C4, has a small but excellent collection of ceramics of the Huancavilca-Manteño culture (AD 800-1550). ■ *0830-1630*. A bridge joins the main town with **Tarqui** on the east side of the Río Manta. The Tarqui beach is more popular, but dirtier. Do not leave **anything** unattended anywhere (in Tarqui or Manta). The tourist office is on Pasaje José María Egas, Av 3 y C 11, T622944, helpful, Spanish only.

Phone code: 05
Colour map 1a, grid B2
Population: 156,981

Water shortages are very common. Most offices, shops and the bus station are in Manta. There is a wider selection of hotels in Tarqui. **In Manta L** *Oro Verde*, Malecon y Cirunvalación, on the beach front, T629200, ov_mta@oroverdehotels.com With all luxuries, best in town. **A** *Cabañas Balandra*, Av 8 y C20, Barrio Córdova, T620316, F620545. A/c cabins, breakfast included, secure. **B** *Manta Imperial*, Malecón by Playa Murciélago, on beach, T621955, F623016. Including taxes, a/c, pool, parking, disco and dancing, plenty of insect life. **In Tarqui B** *Las Gaviotas*, Malecón 1109 y C 106, T620140, F611840. The best in Tarqui by some length, a/c, poor restaurant, tennis court. **B-C** *Las Rocas*, C 101 y Av 105, T610856. A/c, cheaper with fan, pool, private parking, restaurant poor. **C** *El Inca*, C 105 y Malecón, T610986. Phone, fan or a/c, good value restaurant, OK. **D** *Pacífico Inn*, Av 106 y C 101, T622475. A/c, discount for longer stay. **D** *Panorama Inn*, C 103 y Av 105, T611552. A/c, pool, restaurant, parking, helpful. Recommended. Its *Suites*, opposite, are newer, a/c, TV, also **D**. **D** *Boulevard*, Av 105 y C 103, T625333. TV, garage. **D** *Hostal Miami*, Av 102 y C 107, T611743. Fan, basic but helpful, safe. **E** *Res Viña del Mar*, Av 106 y C104, T610854. With fan. **E** *Playita Mía*, Malecón y C 103. Restaurant, shared bath, very basic.

Sleeping
All streets have numbers; those above 100 are in Tarqui (those above C110 are not safe)

Club Ejecutivo, Av 2 y C 12, top of Banco del Pichincha building. First class food and service, great view. *Paraná*, C 17 y Malecón, near the port. Local seafood and grill, cheap. Highly recommended. *Shamu*, C11 No 1-12, downtown. Good set meals and à la carte. *Mima*, C 104 y Malecón, Tarqui. Good fish and seafood. *Riviera*, C 20 y Av 12. First class Italian food. *Mexicano*, Malecón y C 15. Very good Mexican food. *Guen Roku*, Malecón y C 16. Good Ecuadorean and international dishes.

Eating
Many good, cheap comedores on Tarqui beach which are open at weekends

Ecuador

Tour operators *Delgado Travel*, C12 y Av 2, T624614, F621497. *Ecuadorean Tours*, Av 2 y C 13. *Metropolitan Touring*, Av 3 No 11-49, T623090.

Transport **Air** Eloy Alfaro airport. *TAME* to **Quito** daily. **Bus** All buses leave from the terminal behind the new central bank building. To **Quito**, 9 hrs, US$6.60, hourly 0400-2300. **Guayaquil**, 4 hrs, US$6, hourly. **Esmeraldas**, 0630, 0800 and 2000, 8 hrs, US$7. **Santo Domingo**, 4½ hrs, US$5.65. **Portoviejo**, 45 mins, US$0.70, every 10 mins. **Jipijapa**, 1 hr, US$1, every 20 mins. **Bahía de Caráquez**, 3 hrs, US$2.20, hourly.

Directory **Banks** *Banco del Pichincha* and *Banco del Pacífico* change TCs. *Casa de Cambio Zanchi*, Av 2 No 11-28, T613857. *Cambicruz*, Av 2 No 11-22, T622235. **Communications** **Post Office:** above *Banco del Pichincha*. **Telephone:** *Pacifictel*, Malecón near C 11. **Useful addresses** **Immigration:** Av 4 de Noviembre y J-1 (police station).

Portoviejo
Phone code: 05
Colour map 1a, grid B2
Population: 167,956

Inland 40 km from Manta and 65 km northeast of Jipijapa is the capital of Manabí province, a major commercial centre and prone to crime. The cathedral overlooks Parque Eloy Alfaro, where sloths may be seen in the trees. Kapok mattresses and pillows are made here from the fluffy fibre of the seed capsule of the ceiba tree. *Banco del Pacífico* changes travellers' cheques. The tourist office is at Pedro Gual y J Montalvo, T630877.

Sleeping **B** *Hostería California*, Ciudadela California, T634415. A/c, very good. **C** *Cabrera Internacional*, García Moreno y Pedro Gual, T633201. A/c, noisy. **C** *New York*, Fco de P Moreira y Olmedo, T632037/051, F632044. A/c and fridge, **D** with fan, poor service, restaurant downstairs. **D** *Pacheco*, 9 de Octubre 1512 y Morales, T631788. With or without bath, fan. **D** *París*, Plaza Central, T652727. One of the oldest hotels, classic, with fan.

Eating *El Tomate*, on the road to Crucita and Bahía. Excellent traditional Manabí food. *La Fruta Prohibida*, C Chile. Fast food, Portoviejo's gringo hang-out. *El Galpón*, C Quito. Very good food and prices, local music at night, very popular. *Zavalito*, Primera Transversal entre Duarte y Alajuela. Lunch only, popular.

Transport **Air:** Flights to **Quito**. **Bus:** To **Quito**, 8 hrs; routes are either east via Quevedo (147 km), or, at Calderón, branch northeast for Calceta, Chone and on to **Santo Domingo de los Colorados**. Services also to **Guayaquil**. Bus station is on the edge of town, taxi US$0.90.

Directory **Communications** **Internet:** Prices around US$1.75 per hr. *Café Royal*, C Chile y 10 de Agosto. *Habla por Menos*, C Córdova y Morales.

Crucita
Phone code: 05
Population: 8,300
45 mins by road
from Portoviejo

A rapidly growing resort, Crucita is popular with bathers on Sunday. Other than during carnival, it is relaxed and friendly. Hang gliding and paragliding are practised from the dry cliffs south of town (see *Da Vinci*, under Quito, Sport). The beach and ocean are lovely but do not go barefoot as there are many pigs roaming loose and *nigua* (a flea which likes to nest under the skin of your feet, very painful) are common. Beaches are cleaner on either side of town. There is an abundance of sea birds in the area. *Pacifictel* for long distance phone calls (no international service), two blocks back from the beach on the main highway. ■ *Buses and open sided trucks with slatted seats, called chivas or rancheros, leave from the beach and plaza for Portoviejo, US$ 0.45, 45 mins. Regular buses to Manta.*

Sleeping and eating From south to north along the beach: **E** *Hipocampo*, the oldest in town. Basic, good value. **C** *Barandúa*, on the ocean front, T676185. Hot water, fan, restaurant, pool, disco, good service. **D** *Hostería Zucasa*, T634908 (Portoviejo). Fully equipped cabins for up to 6, the best accommodation in town. **D** *Hostería Las Cabañitas*, T931037. Cabins for 4-5 people, basic. There are many simple restaurants and kiosks serving mainly fish and seafood along the seafront. *Alas Delta 1 & 2* Good seafood, try their *conchas asadas*.

About 60 km north of Portoviejo (30 km south of Bahía de Caráquez) are **San Clemente** and, 3 km south, **San Jacinto**. The ocean is magnificent but be wary of the strong undertow. Both get crowded during the holiday season and have a selection of *cabañas* and hotels. ■ *Most Guayaquil-Portoviejo-Bahía de Caráquez buses pass San Clemente. To Jipijapa, 1 hr, US$1.50.*

North to Bahía
Do not go barefoot
because of the nigua,
especially in the towns

Sleeping In San Clemente recommended are: **C** *Hostería San Clemente*, T420076. Modern cabins for 6 to 10 persons, swimming pool, restaurant, book ahead, closed in low season. **D** *Las Acacias*, 150 m from the beach, 800 m north of San Clemente, T541706 (Quito). Nice 3-storey wooden building with huge verandas, prices go up in high season, good seafood. **D** *Cabañas Espumas del Mar*, on the beach. Good restaurant, family run.

Bahía de Caráquez

Set on the southern shore at the seaward end of the Chone estuary, Bahía has an attractive river front laid out with parks on the Malecón Alberto Santos. The beach stretches around the point and is quite clean. The town is busiest July to September, Christmas and Easter. It is also a centre of the shrimp farming industry. The archaeological museum of the Central Bank has a collection of precolumbian pottery and is housed in the Casa de la Cultura next door. ■ *1500-1700, free.*

Phone code: 05
Colour map 1a, grid B2
Population: 15,308

   Bahía has been declared an 'ecocity': all the organic waste from the market is recycled and there is a commitment to environmental education, reforestation and agroecology after El Niño and an earthquake in 1998. There is an annual celebration of the new status and Mangrove Day at the end of February. Information from *Fundación Stuarim*, T693490 or the *Planet Drum Foundation*, www.planetdrum.org The tourist office is at Malecón y Arenas. ■ *Mon-Fri 0830-1630, T691124.*

Isla de Fragatas, 15 mins by boat in the middle of the Bahía de Caráquez estuary, has a stunning number of bird species, including a higher concentration of frigate birds than on the Galápagos (excellent for photographers). The frigate birds can be seen displaying their inflated red sacks as part of the mating ritual (best August-January). The three hour trip costs US$14 for four (less for larger groups). Dolphins can also be seen in the estuary.

Excursions
Also see Tour
Operators

   The **Chirije** archaeological site can be visited. This site was a seaport of the Bahía Culture and is an important archaeological discovery; museum on site. The tour, at low tide, costs US$150 for two, including accommodation in basic huts; take mosquito repellent.

   Saiananda is a private park with extensive areas of reforestation and a large collection of mainly domestic fowl and animals, but also native animals. It has a Japanese garden, the Sai Baba Temple and Centre. Meals, principally vegetarian, are served in an exquisite dining area over the water. ■ *T398399/399399, owner Alfredo Harmsen, reserve in advance for meals, US$3 pp.*

A *La Piedra*, Circunvalación near Bolívar, T690780, F690154. Pool, good restaurant but expensive, laundry, modern, good service, access to beach, lovely views. **A** *La Herradura*, Bolívar e Hidalgo, T690446, F690265. A/c, cheaper with fan, comfortable, restaurant. **A** *Casa Grande*, T692097, F692088. In an exclusive residential area on the ocean, deluxe rooms and suites, pool and terrace. **D** *Italia*, Bolívar y Checa, T691137, F691092. Fan, hot water, TV, restaurant. **D** *Ecohostal Santiguado*, Padre Laennen y Juan de Velasco, 2 blocks from beach in 3 directions. Bed and breakfast, modern, nice terrace bar/café, helpful. **E** *Bahía*, on Malecón near Banco Central. Rooms at the back are nicer, fan, TV, occasional water shortages. **E** *Bahía Bed & Breakfast Inn*, Ascázubi 322 y Morales, T690146. With bath, fan, some rooms with hot water, restaurant, includes breakfast, good value. **F** *Hostal Querencia*, Malecón 1800 by the main road out of town, T690009. Some rooms with bath. Recommended. **F** *Pensión Miriam*, Montúfar, entre Ascázubi y Riofrío. Shared

Sleeping
Only hotels with their
own supply do not
suffer water shortages

Ecuador

bath, basic but clean, rooms at front have windows, has its own water supply. **F** *Residencial Vera*, Montúfar y Ante, T691581. Cheaper without bath. Recommended.

Eating   *Columbios*, Av Bolívar y Ante. Good à la carte and set meals, good service and value. *Brisas del Mar*, Hidalgo y Circunvalación. Good fish, cheap. *Los Helechos*, Montúfar y Muñoz Dávila, by Circunvalación. Good and clean. *La Chozita*, on the Malecón near the San Vicente ferry station. Barbecue style, good. *Donatella's*, 1 block from Reina del Camino bus terminal. Good, cheap pizza. *Chifa China*, Malecón y Ante, near the wharf. Cheap and good. *La Pepoteca*, Malecón y Ante opposite the wharf. Good food and service. *El Capitán*, Malecón opposite the *Hotel Bahía*. Cheap chicken and seafood.

Tour operators   Both companies listed here offer tours to the estuary islands, wetlands, to see environmental projects in including the Río Muchacho farm and the organic shrimp farm, to the Chirije archaeological site, to Punta Bellaca dry forest, to beaches, whale watching and to Machalilla. See excursions, above. *Bahía Dolphin Tours*, Av Bolívar 1004 y Riofrío, T692097/086, archtour@srv1.telconet.net, www.qni.com/~mj/bahia/bahia.html Involved with ecotourism projects, manage the Chirije site. *Guacamayo Bahiatours*, Av Bolívar y Arenas, T690597, ecopapel@impsat.net.ec, www.qni.com/~mj/riomuchacho Rents bikes, sells crafts and is involved in environmental work.

Transport   **Bus** *Coactur* and *Reina del Camino* offices are on the Malecón 1600 block. To **Quito**, 8 hrs, US$6.60. **Santo Domingo de los Colorados**, 4-4½ hrs, US$4.10. **Esmeraldas**, at 1515, 8 hrs, US$7. **Portoviejo**, 2 hrs, US$1.55, hourly. **Puerto López** or **Manta**, go to Portoviejo or Jipijapa and change. To **Guayaquil**, 6 hrs, US$6, hourly. To **Manta**, 3 hrs, US$2.20, hourly. Open-sided *rancheros* leave from the park on Aguilera to Chone (US$1.05) and other nearby destinations.

Directory   **Banks** *Banco de Guayaquil*, Av Bolívar y Riofrío, for TCs. **Communications** Internet: *Genesis*, Padre Leannen y Oracio Gostalle, T692400. *Systemcom*, Riofrío y Av Bolívar. **Post Office:** at Morales y Ante. **Telephone:** *Pacifictel* on Intriago.

From Bahía de Caráquez to the highlands there are two main roads. The first one is via **Chone**, 1½ hours east from Bahía. At the Santo Domingo exit is a strange sculpture of four people suspending a car on wires across a gorge. It represents the difficulty faced in the first ever trip to Quito by car (**C** *Atahualpa de Oro*, Av Atahualpa y Páez, T696627, TV, restaurant, garage, very good; several others). Between Chone and Santo Domingo is **El Carmen**. The second road is via San Clemente to Pichincha, Velasco Ibarra and on to Quevedo.

North to Esmeraldas

San Vicente & Canoa   On the north side of the Río Chone, San Vicente is reached by ferry from Bahía or by road west from Chone. It is the access point for the very impressive stretch of beach between San Vicente and Canoa. The area has great tourist potential. The Santa Rosa church, 100 m to the left of the wharf, contains excellent mosaic and glass work by José María Peli Romeratigui (better known as Peli). There is a good airport at San Vicente but no commercial flights were operating in 2002.

  On the beautiful 17-km beach between San Vicente and Canoa (a good walk or bike ride), many people harvest shrimp larvae, especially at full and new moon. Just north along the beach are nine natural caves at the cliff base; walk there at low tide but allow time to return (guide recommended). The clean beach is 800 m wide, the widest in Ecuador, relatively isolated and great for surf.

Sleeping & eating   **On the road to Canoa**: Across the road from the beach: **C** *Cabañas Alcatraz*, T674179. Cabins for 5, nice, a/c, pool. **C** *Monte Mar*, Malecón s/n, T674197. Excellent food, pool, views, various rooms for rent. **C** *El Velero*. Cabañas and suites, pool, restaurant, good. *El Cangrejo*, close to the bridge on the way out of town to Canoa. Restaurant and bar. *Restaurant La Piedra*, beyond

Alcatraz just over the bridge on the way to Canoa, T674451, also rents apartments. Many others, cheaper ones are in San Vicente town.

In Canoa C-D *Hostería Canoa*, 600 m south of town. Cabins and rooms, pool, sauna, whirlpool, good restaurant and bar. **D** *Sol y Luna*, 3 km south of town. Large rooms with and without bath, restaurant. **E** *Bambú*, on the beach, T09-975 3696. Shared bath, good restaurant, very popular, English and Dutch spoken. Recommended. **E** *Posada de Daniel*, at back of the village, T691201. Attractive renovated homestead, with or without bath. **E** *Pacific Fun Cabins*, 1 km south of town. Cabins with bath, no restaurant but next door is the *Sun Down Inn*, meals available, but not always open. **F** *Tronco Bar*, cheaper without bath, restaurant. *Comedor Jixsy* has rooms. *Costa Azul* has good food. *El Torbellino*. Good for typical dishes, cheap, large servings. *Arena Bar* 1 block from the beach, snacks, beer, T-shirts, hammocks.

Bus to San Vicente: *Coactur*, opposite *panga* dock, to **Portoviejo**, **Manta**, **Guayaquil**. **Transport** *Reina del Camino* (near *Hotel Vacaciones*), to **Portoviejo**, 4 daily, US$1.55. **Chone**, 7 daily, US$1, 45 mins. **Guayaquil**, 4 daily, 6 hrs, US$5.70. **Quito**, at 0630 and 2215, 7½ hrs, US$6.60. **Esmeraldas**, US$5.65. **Santo Domingo**, US$3.70. **Quinindé**, US$4.50. Several companies to **Pedernales**, US$4, 3 hrs, and **Cojimíes**. The road is paved to Pedernales and on to **Muisne**. **Boats** *Pangas* cross to **Bahía** continually until 2200, 10 mins, US$0.20; car ferry every 20 mins or so, free for foot passengers, very steep ramps, very difficult for low clearance cars.

The road cuts across Cabo Pasado to Jama (2½ hours; **F** *Pensión Jamaica*), then runs **Pedernales** parallel to the beach past coconut groves and shrimp hatcheries, inland across some low hills and across the Equator to Pedernales, a market town and crossroads with nice undeveloped beaches to the north; those in town are dirty and unattractive. A mosaic mural on the church overlooking the plaza is one of the best pieces of work by Peli (see above); exquisite examples of his stained glass can be seen inside the church. A poor unpaved road goes north along the shore to Cojimíes. The main coastal road, fully paved, goes south to San Vicente and north to Chamanga, El Salto, Muisne and Esmeraldas. Another important road goes inland to El Carmen and on to Santo Domingo de los Colorados: this is the most direct route to Quito. ■ *Buses to Santo Domingo, via El Carmen, 6 daily, 2½ hrs, US$3, and on to Quito, 6 hrs, US$5.70. To Chamanga, 1½ hrs, continuing to El Salto, where you can make a connection for Muisne, or continue to Esmeraldas.*

Sleeping and eating C *América*, García Moreno, on the road to the beach, T681174. Fans, balcony, very comfortable, expensive restaurant. **D** *Playas*, Juan Pereira y Manabí, near airport, T681125. Fans, mosquito nets, comfortable. **D** *Pedernales*, on Av Eloy Alfaro, 2 blocks from plaza. Basic but clean, rooms at front have windows, fans, nets, good value. *El Rocío*, on Eloy Alfaro. Good cheap food. *La Fontana*, just off main plaza. Good vegetarian food. *Habana Club*, next to *Hotel Playas*. Good seafood, cheap.

Muisne

The town, on an island, is a bit run down but lively and friendly. Fifteen minutes walk from town (or a tricycle ride for US$0.35) is a long expanse of beach, a pleasant walk at low tide but practically disappears at high tide. The area produces bananas and shrimp, and most of the surrounding mangroves have been destroyed. On the Río Sucio, inland from Muisne and Cojimíes, is an isolated group of Cayapa Indians, some of whom visit the town on Sunday. Marcelo Cotera and Nisvaldo Ortiz arrange boat trips to see the mangrove forests which are being replanted by the *Fundación Ecológica Muisne*, donations welcome, contact them through the tourist office.

Colour map 1a, grid A2 Warning: Walking in isolated areas after dark is not safe. There are no banks; change TCs at a slightly lower rate at Marco Velasco's store, near the dock

D *Hostal Mapara*, at the beach. Ample well furnished rooms, restaurant, modern, best in **Sleeping** town. Recommended. **E** *Oasis*, C Manabí, about 150 m from the beach. With fan, nets. Rec- **& eating** ommended. **E** *Cabañas San Cristóbal*, on the beach to the right coming from town, no sign. Some basic wooden cabins and newer cement rooms, fetch water from well nearby, cheaper

Ecuador

for long stay. **E** *Calade*, 150 m away at the south end of the beach, T480279. Cheaper without bath, hot water, comfortable but overpriced, negotiable for longer stays, excellent meals including vegetarian, internet US$6 per hr. **F** *Galápagos*, 200 m from the beach. Fan, mosquito nets, restaurant, modern. Recommended. **F** *Playa Paraíso*. Turn left as you face the sea, then 200 m. Basic but clean, mosquito nets. **In town** is **F** *Don José*. Good.

Eating includes *El Tiburón*. Good, cheap. Recommended. *Las Palmeiras*. Excellent seafood. Near the beach is *Restaurante Suizo-Italiano*. Good pizza and pasta, breakfast on request, good atmosphere. Swiss owner Daniel is very knowledgeable about the area. *Doña María*, on the beach. Good. *La Riviera*. Good. *Mai Tai*, Manabí by the beach. Italian food, breakfast, café and disco, internet US$7 per hr. *Habana Club*. Good rum and reggae. There are several other excellent kiosks on the beach. Try *encocada de cangrejo*, crab in coconut.

Transport Canoes ply the narrow stretch of water between the island and mainland (El Relleno); US$0.10. **Bus** to **Esmeraldas** US$1.50, 3 hrs. There is a direct bus to **Quito** once a night. For **Pedernales**, take a bus to **El Salto**, US$0.25, 30 mins, on the Esmeraldas road, from where there are buses going south to **Chamanga**, US$0.75, 1½ hrs, where you change again for Pedernales, 1½ hrs. At 0600 there is a direct bus Muisne-Chamanga. There are also **boats** going **Chamanga-Cojimíes** (alternate route to Pedernales and points south). Boats from Muisne to Cojimíes go only when there is demand, US$8 pp, 2 hrs; buy your ticket at the dock, take waterproofs and be prepared to wait until the boat is full.

Playa Escondida A few hours north of Muisne is the turn-off for Playa Escondida, at Km 14 via Tonchigüe-Punta Galera. This charming beach hideaway, run by Canadian Judith Barrett on an ecologically sound basis, is set in 100 ha stretching back to secondary tropical dry forest. Rustic cabins overlooking a lovely little bay. **E** pp, camping, **F** pp, three meals US$10-15; excellent food, safe swimming; completely isolated and wonderfully relaxing. For reservations, T06-733106/09-973 3368, judithbarett@ hotmail.com, www.intergate.ca/playaescondida ■ *Take a ranchera or bus from Esmeraldas for Punta Galera*. River Tavesao *departs at 0530, 0830 and 1200 and* La Costeñita *at 0730 and 1600, 2 hrs. From Quito take a bus to Esmeraldas or Tonchigüe and transfer there. Taxi from Atacames US$12, pickup from Tonchigüe US$5.*

Atacames

Phone code: 06
Colour map 1a, grid A2
25 km S of Esmeraldas

One of the main resorts on the Ecuadorean coast, Atacames is a real 24-hour party town during the high season (April-October), at weekends and national holiday times. Those who like to sleep at night should avoid the place, nearby Súa is a more tranquil alternative (see below).

Camping is unsafe. Walkers along the beach from Atacames to Súa regularly get assaulted at knife point where there is a small tunnel. Gangs seem to work daily. Also the sea can be very dangerous, there is a powerful undertow and many people have been drowned. **NB** The sale of black coral jewellery has led to the destruction of much of the offshore reef. Consider the environmental implications before buying.

Sleeping
Prices quoted are for the high season; discounts are available in the low season. Hotels are generally expensive for Ecuador

Most accommodation has salt water in the bathrooms; fresh water is not always available and not very good. It's best to bring a mosquito net as few hotels supply them. **AL** *Juan Sebastián*, towards the east end of the beach, T731049, hotelj.s@uio.satnet.net A/c, TV, restaurant, pool, parking, luxurious. **B** *Lé Castell*, T731542, F731442. Cabins with TV, phone, includes breakfast, pool, garage, restaurant, comfortable. **B** *Villas Arco Iris*, east end, T731069, www.VillasArcoiris.com With fridge, charming, English, German and French spoken. Recommended. **C-D** *Tahiti*. With TV, pool, fan, nets, breakfast, good restaurant, cabins are cheaper. **D** *Cabañas Caída del Sol*, Malecón del Río, 150 m from the beach, T/F731479. With fan, fridge, parking, spacious, quiet, good value, Swiss-run. Organize whale watching tours, US$25 pp. **D** *Cabañas Los Bohíos*, 1 block from the beach by the pedestrian bridge, T731089. Bungalows with fresh water showers, comfortable, quite good value. **D** *Cabañas de Rogers* , west end of the beach, T751011. Quiet, constant water supply, restaurant, bar. Beware of dogs. Recommended. **D** *Titanic*, at east end, T730093. With restaurant, parking, German and English spoken. **E** *La Casa del Manglar*, 150 m from the beach beside the footbridge, T731464. Cheaper without bath, fan, sweet water, laundry. Recommended. **E** *Galería Atacames*, on the beach, T731149. Fresh water, book exchange, safe deposit. **E** *Pirata Picaflor*, Malecón del Río, 1 block from beach, T09-928084. Italian run. **E** *Cabañas Rincón del Mar*, on the beach, T731064. Fresh water, secure, cosy, English, French and German spoken. Highly recommended. **F** *Jennifer*, ½ block from the beach on a perpendicular street. Cheaper with shared bath, **E** in cabins with cooking facilities and fridge. **Apartments** by the ocean with a/c, TV, balconies, with capacity for 8 for rent from *El Viejo Fritz Restaurant*, T09-945 1777.

The beach is packed with bars and restaurants offering seafood. The best and cheapest *ceviche* is found at the stands at the west end of the beach and at the market, but avoid *concha*. *Cocada*, a sweet made from coconut, peanut and brown sugar, is sold in the main plaza.

Eating
Many restaurants on the beach rent rooms

Buses to/from **Esmeraldas**, every 15 mins, US$0.70, 40 mins; to/from **Muisne**, hourly; to **Guayaquil**, US$7. To **Quito** at 1115.

Transport

Súa is a beach resort, a 15-minute bus ride south of Atacames. The beach is not very clean but it's a quiet and friendly little place, set in a beautiful bay. Just down the road is Playa de **Same**, with a long grey sandy beach lined with palms and, mostly, high-rise apartment blocks for wealthy Quiteños. Safe swimming; good birdwatching in the lagoon behind the beach. ■ *Buses every 30 mins to and from Atacames;* La Costeñita, *15 mins, 18 km, US$0.35. Make sure it drops you at Same and not at Club Casablanca. To Muisne, US$0.60.*

Sleeping and eating Súa: Hotels are much cheaper in low season if you bargain. **E** *Hostal Los Jardines*, 150 m from the beach, T731181. With fan, parking, very nice. **E** *Chagra Ramos*, on the beach, T731006. With fan, good restaurant, disco, good value. **E** *El Peñón de Súa*, T731013. Restaurant, parking. **F** *Las Acacias*, on the beach. Cabins with bath, fan, nice. **F** *Buganvillas*, on the beach, T731008. Very nice, room 10 has best views. **E** *Malibu*, on the beach, T731012. **G** without bath, basic. **F** *Súa*, on the beach, T731004. 6 rooms, fan, café-restaurant, comfortable. **F** *Cabañas El Triángulo*, on the street going to the beach. With fan, parking. **F** *Cabañas San Fernando*, near the road, T726441. Cabins, parking, basic. *Restaurant Bahía*, big portions. *Café-Bar*, on the beach past *Hotel Buganvillas*, Reggae. **Same**: **L** *Club Casablanca*, T225 2077 (Quito), www.ccasablanca.com Restaurant, tennis courts, swimming pool, luxurious. **B** *Seaflower*, on the beach, T733369. Nice accommodation, good expensive restaurant, German-Chilean run. **B** *El Rampiral*, at south end of the beach, T/F226 4134 (Quito), rampiral@uio.satnet.net Cabins by the sea. **C** *El Acantilado*, on the hill by the sea, south of Same, T245 3606 (Quito). 14 rooms for 2-3 people, 30 cabins up to 5 people, excellent food, pool, whale watching tours in season. **C** *Cabañas Isla del Sol*, at south end of beach, T733470. Cabins with fan, kitchenette, pool, cafetería serves breakfast. **D** *La Terraza*, on the beach, T254 4507 (Quito)/09-947 6949. 11 cabins for 3-4, with fan, hammocks, Spanish and Italian owners, good restaurant.

Booking is advisable at holiday times and weekends. In the low season good deals can be negotiated

Esmeraldas

Capital of the province of the same name, the city itself has little to offer and suffers from water shortages. Despite its wealth in natural resources (gold mining, tobacco, cacao, cattle ranching), Esmeraldas is among the poorest provinces in the country. Shrimp farm development has destroyed much mangrove and timber exports are decimating Ecuador's last Pacific rainforest. Baskets made by the Cayapa people are sold in the market across from the Post Office, behind the vegetables. Tolita artefacts and basketry are nearby.

Colour map 1a, grid A2
Population: 117,722

NB Mosquitoes and malaria are a serious problem throughout Esmeraldas province, especially in the rainy season. Most *residencias* provide mosquito nets (*toldos*

Ecuador

The Capital of Rhythm

Esmeraldeños prefer the livelier sound of Caribbean salsa to the cumbia heard in the sierra, and have retained the African-influenced marimba, usually accompanied by a bomero, who plays a deep-pitched bass drum suspended from the ceiling, and a long conga drum. Where there is a marimba school you will also find dancers, and the women who are too old to dance play percussion and chant songs handed down the generations, many with Colombian references, but the best marimba can only be seen in the backwoods of the province on Sundays and holidays.

or *mosquiteros*), or buy one in the market near the bus station. It's best to visit in the June-December dry season. Use sun tan lotion or cover up, even when it's cloudy. Take care in town, especially on arrival at bus terminal. *Ministerio de Turismo*, Bolívar 221 entre Mejía y Salinas ■ *Mon-Fri 0830-1700.*

Sleeping
Hotels in centre are poor; instead stay in the outskirts

C *Apart Hotel Casino*, Libertad 407 y Ramón Tello, T728700, F728704. Excellent, good restaurant, casino. **E** *Galeón*, Piedrahita 330 y Olmedo, T723820. With a/c, cheaper with fan. **E** *Hostal El Cisne*, 10 de Agosto y Olmedo, T723411. TV, very good. **F** *Diana*, Cañizares y Sucre, T727923. Secure. **F** *Asia*, 9 de Octubre 116, near the bus station, T711852. Cheaper without bath, basic but clean. **F** *Turismo*, Bolívar 843. TV and fan, basic but clean. **F** *Zulema 2*, Malecón y Rocafuerte, T726757. Modern, with TV, parking.

Eating
Typical restaurants and bars by the beach selling ceviches fried fish and patacones

Chifa Restaurante Asiático, Mañizares y Bolívar. Chinese, excellent. *La Marimba Internacional*, Libertad y Lavallén. Recommended. *Las Redes*, main plaza. Good fish, cheap. *Budapest*, Cañizares 214 y Bolívar. Hungarian-run, clean, pleasant. *Balcón del Pacífico*, Bolívar y 10 de Agosto. Nice atmosphere, good view overlooking city, cheap drinks. *El Guadal de Ña Mencha*, 6 de Diciembre y Quito, *peña* upstairs, marimba school at weekends; good.

Transport

Air Gen Rivadeneira Airport is on the road to La Tola. Taxi to centre, 30 km, about US$5, buses to the Terminal Terrestre from the road outside the airport pass about every 30 mins. Daily flights to Quito with *TAME*, 30 mins. Check in early, planes may leave 30 mins before scheduled time.

Bus To **Quito**, US$6, 5-6 hrs, 30 a day, good paved road (or 7 hrs via La Independencia, Mindo and San Miguel de los Bancos), with *Trans-Esmeraldas* (best buses, Av Piedrahita 200), *Occidental* and *Trans Ibarra*; also with *Panamericana* (at *Hotel Casino*) twice daily, slow but luxurious, US$10; by *Aerotaxi* (small bus), 5 hrs, 12 passengers, reserved seats, their office is near the main plaza. To **Santo Domingo**, US$2.25, 4 hrs. To **Guayaquil**, hourly, US$7, 8 hrs. To **Bahía de Caráquez**, via Santo Domingo de los Colorados, US$7. To **Portoviejo**, US$2.75; **Manta**, US$7. To **Quevedo**, 6 hrs. *La Costeñita* buses go to: **La Tola**, 7 daily, US$2.85, 4½-5 hrs; to **Muisne**, hourly, US$1.50, 3½ hrs; to **Súa**, **Same** and **Atacames**, every 15 mins from 0630 to 2030; to **Borbón**, every 2 hrs, US$3, 4 hrs. It's not necessary to go into Esmeraldas if you want to go on to San Lorenzo or other places.

Directory

Banks *Banco del Austro*, Bolívar y Cañizares, for Visa, until 1400. **Communications** Internet: *T@ipe.net*, Olmedo y 10 de Agosto, US$2.40 per hr. **Post Office:** Av Colón y 10 de Agosto. **Telephone:** *Pacifictel*, Malecón Maldonado y J Montalvo. **Useful addresses Immigration:** Av Olmedo y Rocafuerte, T720256.

La Tola is 94 km from Esmeraldas (San Mateo bridge) and is where you catch the boat for Limones and San Lorenzo. The road passes Las Palmas (a resort just north of Esmeraldas), Camarones, Río Verde and Rocafuerte. The shoreline changes from sandy beaches to mangrove swamp. The wildlife is varied and spectacular, especially the birds. Avoid staying overnight in La Tola; women especially are harassed. ■ *Boats between La Tola and San Lorenzo connect with buses to/from Esmeraldas; 2 hrs La Tola-San Lorenzo, US$4.25, via Limones and Tambillo. Boats can be rather overcrowded at times but the scenery makes it worthwhile.*

At **Olmedo**, a 20 min walk or a short boat ride from La Tola, is an ecotourism project run by the *Nueva Unión* (Women's Union) to protect the Majagual forest and the tallest mangrove tree in the world. The project is in the Cayapas Mataje Mangrove Reserve (entry US$5). Activities include board walk through the mangroves, swimming, boat rides, visit to La Tolita archaeological site, fishing, birdwatching, horse riding. **Sleeping**: F pp, consists of 5 rooms with 9 beds; meals extra. To make a reservation T06-780239, San Lorenzo, and ask for Sra Carmen Mina, or just turn up. If you book, the *Nueva Unión* boat can pick you up in San Lorenzo, Limones or Borbón (groups only). In Olmedo ask for the coordinator, Sra Luz del Alba.

Limones

This town is the focus of traffic down-river from much of northern Esmeraldas Province, where bananas from the Río Santiago are sent to Esmeraldas for export. The Chachi Indians live up the Río Cayapas and can sometimes be seen in Limones, especially during the crowded weekend market, but they are more frequently seen at Borbón. The people are mostly black and many are illegal immigrants from Colombia. Smuggling between Limones and Tumaco in Colombia is big business (hammocks, manufactured goods, drugs) and there are occasional drug searches along the north coastal road.

Limones has two good shops selling the very attractive Chachi basketry, including items from Colombia. The first is opposite *Restaurant El Bongó* and the second by the dock opposite *Banco de Fomento*. There are two hotels, both barely habitable. Limones and its neighbour Borbón dispute the title 'the mosquito and rat capital of Ecuador'. It's a much better idea to stay at San Lorenzo.

Transport A hired launch provides a fascinating trip through mangrove islands, passing hundreds of hunting pelicans; 6 people US$1.75 pp, 1½ hrs. Information on boat journeys from the Capitanía del Puerto, Las Palmas, reached by bus No 1 from the main plaza in Esmeraldas. From Limones you can also get a canoe or boat to **Borbón**.

Inland from Limones

On the Río Chachi past mangrove swamps, **Borbón** is dirty, unattractive, busy and dangerous, with the highest incidence of malaria in the country. It is developing as a centre of the timber industry. Ask for Papá Roncón, the King of Marimba, who, for a beer or two, will put on a one-man show. Across from his house are the offices of *Subir*, the NGO working in the Cotacachi-Cayapas reserve; they have information on entering the reserve and guide services. Most accommodation is full of construction workers and rats, best is E *Tolita Pampa de Oro*, T Quito 252 5753, with bath and mosquito nets. ■ *Buses to/from Esmeraldas, US$3 with El Pacífico, 4 hrs, 0600-1700, beware of theft or sit on the roof; by boat to Limones and San Lorenzo 3 hrs, US$5.20, at 0730 and 1100.*

Upstream are Chachi Indian villages. From Borbón hire a motor launch or go as a passenger on launches running daily around 1100-1200 to the mouth of the **Río Onzole**; US$5 per person, 3½ hours. **Santa María** is just beyond the confluence of the Cayapas and Onzole rivers.

Sleeping Board and lodging with Sra Pastora at the missionary station, **E**, basic, mosquito nets, meals US$2, unfriendly, her brother offers river trips; or at the **E** *Residencial*, basic, will prepare food but fix price beforehand, owner offers 5 hrs' jungle trips to visit Chachi villages (beware deadly red and black river snakes); or camp in front of school free. At the confluence of the Cayapas and Onzole rivers, there is a fine lodge built by a Hungarian (for advance bookings write to Stephan Tarjany, Casilla 187, Esmeraldas), **C** with full board, good value, clean, warm showers. Jungle walk with guide and small canoes at no extra charge. Water skiing available, US$12 per hr. Stephan organizes special tours to visit remote areas and a trip to the Cotacachi-Cayapas Ecological Reserve, US$250 for 3 days including transport and food.

Further upriver are **Zapallo Grande** and **San Miguel**. Trips from the latter into the **Cotacachi-Cayapas Ecological Reserve** (entry US$5) cost US$22.50 for a group with a guide, US$5 for boat rental, US$5 per meal. Ask for an official guide, eg Don Cristóbal; or make arrangements in Borbón. You can sleep in the rangers' hut, **E**, basic (no running water, no electricity, shared dormitory, cooking facilities), or camp alongside, but beware of chiggers in the grass; also **E** *residencial*. ■ *Borbón to San Miguel, US$8 pp, 5 hrs, none too comfortable but interesting jungle trip.*

San Lorenzo

Colour map1a, grid A3

Public safety is an important concern due to the proximity to the Colombian border. Inquire locally before travelling to or around San Lorenzo

The hot, humid town of San Lorenzo stands on the Bahía del Pailón, which is characterized by a maze of canals. The area around San Lorenzo is rich in timber and other plants, but unrestricted logging is putting the forests under threat. The prehistoric La Tolita culture thrived in the region. At the seaward end of the bay is a sandy beach at San Pedro, with fishing huts but no facilities, canoes Saturday and Sunday 0700 and 1500, one hour; contact Arturo or Doris, who will cook meals. Marimba can be seen during the local fiesta on 30 September. Groups practise Thursday-Saturday; one on C Eloy Alfaro. There are two discos near *Hotels Ecuador* and *Patricia*.

From San Lorenzo you can visit **Playa de Oro**, on the Río Santiago up in the Cotacachi-Cayapas Reserve. For information ask for Victor Grueso, who has a store in town and also works for the *Insituto Permacultura Madre Selva*, on the outskirts, near the football field (T780257; lodging **F** pp includes breakfast). Basic accommodation is available on the trip, but bring your own food and water; meals are cooked on request.

Trips can also be made upriver from Playa de Oro into unspoiled rainforest where you can see howler and spider monkeys and jaguar prints; an unforgettable experience. Contact Mauro Caicedo in San Lorenzo. For information on how to contact Mauro, T252 9727 (Quito), or contact Jean Brown at *Safari Tours* in Quito (see page 918).

Sleeping & eating

Expect to be hassled by children wanting a tip to show you to a hotel or restaurant.

Insect repellent is a must

D *Continental*, C Imbabura, T780125, F780127. With hot water, TV, mosquito nets, more expensive with a/c, family-run, breakfast on request, parking. **E** *Pampa de Oro*, C 26 de Agosto, T780214. A/c, cheaper with fan, TV. **E** *Puerto Azul*, C 26 de Agosto, near the train station, T780220. With TV, a/c, cheaper with fan. **F** *Carondelet*, on the plaza, T780202. With or without bath, some rooms are small, fans, mosquito nets. **F** *San Carlos*, C Imbabura, near the train station, T780240, F780284. Cheaper without bath, fan, nets. Recommended. **F** *Hostal Imperial*. Cheaper without bath, fan, nets. *La Red*, Imbabura y Ayora. Good seafood, not too clean. *La Conchita*, 10 de Agosto. Excellent fish. Recommended. *La Estancia*, next to *Hotel San Carlos*. Good food and service but expensive. Highly recommended.

Transport

Bus To **Ibarra**, 10 daily, 5-6 hrs, US$4. They leave from the train station or near *Hotel San Carlos*. To **Esmeraldas**, from main plaza 0500-1300, 6-7 hrs, US$5 (a good alternative to the boat); take this bus for **La Tola** and change at La Y de La Tola. **Sea** To **Limones**, frequent service, 1 hr, US$2. **Limones-La Tola**, hourly, 1 hr, US$1. For direct service to **La Tola**, you must hire the launch, US$24.

Border with Colombia

From San Lorenzo there are boats to **Tumaco** in Colombia every other day at 0700 and 1400. It's 1½ hours to the border at **Palmarreal**, US$3.20, from there take a canoe to **Monte Alto** and then a *ranchero* to **Puerto Palmas**, cross the Río Mira, then take a Land Rover taxi to Tumaco; 6-7 hours in total.

Entry stamps in Colombia must be obtained by crossing the border at Ipiales and returning again. When arriving in San Lorenzo from Tumaco, the customs office run by navy personnel is in the harbour, but you have to get your passport stamped at the immigration office in Ibarra or Esmeraldas. Problems may arise if you delay more than a day or two before getting an entry stamp, as the immigration police in Ibarra are less easy-going. For Colombian immigration, see page 773.

NB If taking an unscheduled boat from Colombia, be prepared for anti-narcotics searches (at least). This can be a dangerous trip, try to seek advice before taking a boat. Gringos are not normally welcome as passengers because contraband is being carried.

The Oriente

East of the Andes the hills fall away to tropical lowlands, sparsely populated with indigenous settlements along the tributaries of the Amazon. Agricultural colonists have cleared parts of the forest for cattle rearing, while even more isolated areas are major oil producers, leading to the gradual encroachment of towns into the jungle.

The Oriente is currently at a crossroads. Ecuador's ever increasing demand for land and resources must be weighed against the region's irreplaceable biodiversity and traditional ways of life. Yet the majority of this beautiful green wilderness, comprising the provinces of Sucumbíos, Orellana and Napo in the north, Pastaza in the centre, Morona Santiago and Zamora Chinchipe in the south, remains unspoiled and unexplored. Fortunately for the tourist, it is relatively accessible. Much of the Northern Oriente is taken up by the Parque Nacional Yasuni, the Cuyabeno Wildlife Reserve and most of the Cayambe-Coca Ecological Reserve.

There are frequent military checks in the Oriente, so always have your passport handy. You may be required to register at Shell-Mera, Coca and Lago Agrio. The Ecuadorean Amazon has traditionally been safe and tranquil and the few incidents which have taken place mostly involved foreign oil workers rather than tourists. Baeza, Tena, Misahuallí, Puyo and their surroundings, as well as jungle areas to the south, have experienced no difficulties. The northern Oriente, however, is at risk of being affected by conflict in neighbouring Colombia. Always enquire about public safety before visiting remote sites, particularly north of the Río Napo, and avoid areas immediately adjacent to the Colombian border.

Public safety
Yellow fever vaccine and anti-malaria precautions (tablets, net and effective repellent) are recommended to all visitors

Ecuador's eastern tropical lowlands can be reached by **four road routes**, from Quito, Ambato, Cuenca or Loja. These roads are narrow and tortuous and subject to landslides in the rainy season, but all have regular, if poor bus services and all can be attempted in a jeep or in an ordinary car with good ground clearance. Several of the towns and villages on the roads can be reached by air services from Quito, and places further into the immense Amazonian forests are generally accessible by river canoe or small aircraft from Shell or Macas. A fifth road, from Guamote, south of Riobamba, to Macas is nearing completion, but remains controversial due to its impact on Parque Nacional Sangay.

Ins & outs

These fall into four basic types: **lodges**; **guided tours** and **indigenous ecotourism. When staying at a jungle lodge**, you will need to take a torch, insect repellent, protection against the sun and a rain poncho that will keep you dry when walking and when sitting in a canoe. Rubber boots can be hired. See also Jungle lodges on the Lower Napo, below.

Visiting the jungle

   Guided tours of varying length are offered by tour operators, river cruise companies and independent guides. These should be licensed by the Ecuadorean **Ministerio de Turismo**. Tour operators and guides are mainly concentrated in Quito, Tena, Coca and Misahuallí.

   A number of indigenous communities and families offer **ecotourism** programmes on their properties. These are either community-controlled and operated, or organized as joint ventures between the indigenous community or family and a non-indigenous partner. These programmes usually involve guides who are licensed by the *Ministerio de Turismo* as *guías nativos* with the right to guide within their communities.

   Though economically attractive, touring without a local, knowledgable guide is not encouraged: from an ecotourist perspective, it does not contribute adequately to the local economy and to intercultural understanding and it may be environmentally damaging. Furthermore, it involves a greater risk of accident or injury.

Ecuador

Quito to the Oriente

From Quito, through Pifo, to Baeza, the road is paved to a point 9 km beyond the top of the Papallacta pass (4,064 m), 5 km before the turn to the Papallacta hotsprings. Thereafter it worsens. It crosses the Eastern Cordillera at the pass, just north of **Volcán Antisana** (5,705 m), and then descends via the small villages of Papallacta (see page 926) and Cuyuja to the old mission settlements of Baeza and Borja. The trip between the pass and Baeza has beautiful views of Antisana (clouds permitting), high waterfalls, tropical mountain jungle, *páramo* and a lake contained by an old lava flow. **Antisana** gets vast quantities of snow and has huge glaciers. It is very difficult to climb, experience is essential; information on the reserve (entry US$5, not climbing) from *Fundación Antisana*, Av Mariana de Jesús y La Isla, T433851, Quito.

Baeza

There are many hiking trails in this region which generally can be done without a guide

The mountainous landscape and high rainfall have created spectacular waterfalls and dense vegetation. Because of the climate, orchids and bromeliads abound. Baeza, in the beautiful setting of the Quijos pass, is about 1 km from the main junction of the Lago Agrio and Tena roads. Get off the Lago Agrio bus at the gas station and walk up the hill; the Tena bus goes through the town. Baeza Colonial (Old Baeza) is being replaced by Andalucía (New Baeza), where the post office and *Andinatel* are located. ■ *Many buses to Tena (2 hrs) and Coca, best caught at the crossroads in the village. Buses to Quito go from the Old Town, near Hotel Jumandí.*

Sleeping and eating E *Samay*, in the new town. Shared bath, basic. **F** pp *Hostal San Rafael*, in the new town. Shared bath, spacious, cheaper cabins at rear, parking, restaurant. Recommended. **E** *El Nogal de Jumandí*, in old town. Basic (lots of peepholes in the walls), breakfast available, good hot showers for US$0.15. The best restaurants are in the old town: eg *El Fogón* and *Gina* (open till 2200). Everything else closes by 2030.

Nature Reserves near Baeza **LL** *Cabañas San Isidro*, in the Cosanga Valley, including 3 excellent meals. This is a 1,200 ha private reserve with rich bird life, comfortable accommodation, private bath, hot water and warm hospitality. Recommended. Reservations necessary: Quito T547403, www.ecuadorexplorer.com/sanisidro Higher up in the same area is **L** *SierrAzul*, includes 3 meals. Has a slightly different set of birds from San Isidro. Nice cabins, private bath, hot water. US$22 transport from Quito and back. Contact Quito T264484 ext 501, www.sierrazul.com

At Baeza the road divides. One branch heads south to Tena, with a branch road going directly via Loreto to Coca (seven hours). The other goes northeast to Lago Agrio, following the Río Quijos past the villages of **Borja**, a few kilometres from Baeza, and **El Chaco** (good restaurant at the truck stop; cabins, **D**, 600 m from town, pool, parking) to the slopes of the still active volcano **Reventador**, 3,485 m. At the village of Reventador there is a basic hotel and a restaurant.

The road winds along the north side of the river, past the impressive 145-m **San Rafael Falls**, believed to be the highest in Ecuador. To get to the falls take a Quito-Baeza-Lago Agrio bus. About two to three hours past Baeza, look for a covered bus stop and an *Inecel* sign on the right-hand side of the road. From here, walk about 5 minutes to the guard's hut, just beyond a small bridge; US$3.75 entry. It's an easy 1½-hour round trip to the falls through cloudforest. Near the guard's hut is accommodation in some functional cabins, **D** pp, includes entry fee. Camping is possible, but take all equipment and food.

Ecuador

Lago Agrio

The capital of Sucumbíos is primarily an oil town with improving infrastructure and sanitation. The name comes from Sour Lake, the US headquarters of Texaco, the first oil company to exploit the Ecuadorean Amazon, but the town's official name is Nueva Loja. Cofan, Siona and Secoya Indians still come into town at the weekend, though you'll rarely see them in traditional dress.

Population: 20,000
Impossible to change
TCs or use credit cards
take US$ cash

Lago Agrio is among the places in Ecuador which has been most affected by the conflict in neighbouring Colombia. See Public safety, above. Although there is a border crossing to Colombia north of Lago Agrio, it is very dangerous. **You should not enter this area owing to the presence of guerrillas and paramilitaries (2002).**

A-B *Gran Hotel de Lago*, Km 1½ Vía Quito, T832415. Includes breakfast, restaurant, pool (open to non guests on weekends), internet, cabins, nice gardens, quiet. Recommended. **B** *Arazá*, Quito 610 y Narváez, T830223. Includes breakfast, restaurant, a/c, secure, best in town. Recommended. **C** *Cuyabeno*, 18 de Noviembre y Colombia, T830775. Restaurant, a/c, looks good. **C** *D'Mario*, Quito 171, T880989. Restaurant, a/c, cheaper with fan, central, a meeting place. Recommended. **D** *Gran Colombia*, Quito y Pasaje Gonzanamá, T831032. Restaurant, a/c, parking, convenient location. **D** *La Posada*, Quito y Orellana, T830302. Restaurant, fan, parking, good value. **D** *Lago Imperial*, Colombia y Quito, T830453. Fan, convenient, good value. **D** *Machala 2*, Colombia y Quito, T830037. Restaurant, sometimes water shortages, fan, parking, safe. **E** *San Carlos*, 9 de Octubre y Colombia, T830122. A/c, cheaper with fan, cooking facilities, safe. **F** *Secoya*, Quito 222, T830451. Basic.

Sleeping & eating
Virtually everything can be found on the main street, Av Quito

Comercial Calvopeña is the best place to buy groceries and supplies. *Mi Cuchita* beside *El Cofán*, cheap, good chicken.

A number of agencies offer tours to Cuyabeno, several on C Quito (eg *Rainforestur*, Amazonas y Quito, T09-920 0157, also have Quito office). Also *Magic River Tours*, 18 de Noviembre y Guayaquil, T831003; *Sionatour*, 12 de Febrero y 10 de Agosto, T830232.

Tour operators

Air *TAME* flight to Quito (not Sun), book 1-2 days in advance, US$55 one way. **Bus** To Quito, US$7.50, 10-11 hrs. **Baeza**, 7 hrs. **Coca**, 3 hrs; also many *ranchero* buses which leave when full. To **Tena**, US$8.50, 9 hrs.

Transport

Down the Aguarico from Lago Agrio is an extensive jungle river area on the Río Cuyabeno, which drains eventually into the Aguarico 150 km to the east. In the national park there are many lagoons and abundant wildlife. ■ *US$20*. Transport is mainly by canoe and motorboat, except for one road to Río Cuyabeno, three hours by truck from Lago Agrio. Tourist pressure has been heavy in Cuyabeno and it is becoming increasingly rare to see many animals close to the big lake. There are almost a dozen agencies offering trips and most take up to 12 in a group (which is too many). If your aim is to see animals, then look for a smaller tour which keeps away from the most heavily visited areas and adheres to responsible practices.

Cuyabeno Wildlife Reserve

Tour operators and lodges To visit Cuyabeno contact *Jungletur*, Amazonas 854 y Veintimilla, Quito, who have 6 day tours of the area. An experienced guide is Alejandro Quezada, T257 1098, Quito, takes trips to the Parque Nacional Cuyabeno, lodges, everything provided. Contact: *Centro de Reservaciones Cultura*, Robles y Reina Victoria, Quito, T/F255 8889, info@ecuadortravel.com *Pacarina*, in the same Quito office as *Hostería Alandaluz*, runs 5 day tours to a Secoya community down the Río Aguarico. *Native Life*, Foch E4-167 y Amazonas, T250 5158, F222 9077, PO Box 17-03-504 (Venezuela y 23 de Septiembre, 09-921 0858 in Lago Agrio), natlife1@natlife.com.ec Run tours to their Nativo Lodge in the Cuyabeno reserve. Recommended.

Neotropic Turis (Av Amazonas N24-03 y Wilson, Quito, T252 1212, F255 4902, info@neopicturis.com), operate the Grand Cuyabeno Lake Lodge; US$350 pp for 4 days and 3 nights (including meals, guides but not transport to and from Lago Agrio and park fee).

Transturi of Quito (Isla Pinzón 701 near Río Coca, T224 5055) do trips into the jungle on a floating hotel, *Flotel Orellana*, US$567 (4 nights, 3 days) pp in double cabin with fan, including all meals, guides, etc. Services and food are good. Flights extra; bus to Chiritza on the Río Aguarico, then launch to the *Flotel*. **Metropolitan Touring** run excursions (3/4, 4/5, 5 night/6 day) to the **Imuya** and **Iripari** camps. Depending on length, tours involve stops at the Aguarico Base Camp and the *Flotel*. **Imuya** (220 km from Lago Agrio) involves a speedboat trip to get there, earplugs provided; it is very unspoilt, with good birdlife. **Iripari**, on Lago Zancudo, involves a 5-km walk, plus a paddle across the largest lake in Ecuador's Oriente; the camp itself is basic but adequate. There are a great many others; shop around.

At Lago Agrio, a temporary ferry crosses the Río Aguarico (bridge washed away), then the road heads south to Coca. The route from Tena via Loreto also involves a ferry crossing a few kilometres before Coca, US$2 per car.

Coca

Phone code: 06
Colour map 1a, grid A5
Population: 15,199

Officially named **Puerto Francisco de Orellana**, Coca is a hot, dusty, noisy, sprawling oil town at the junction of the Ríos Coca and Napo. It is the capital of the province of Orellana and is a launch pad from where to visit more exciting jungle parts. All foreigners going beyond town into the jungle have to register with the police, and all guides who accompany foreigners have to be licensed. If going alone beyond the bridge at Coca into the jungle, you must get permission from the *Ministerio de Defensa*, Av Maldonado, Quito (full details from *South American Explorers*). Considering its relative isolation, food and supplies are not that expensive. There is usually no electricity after midnight.

Sleeping **C** *El Auca*, Napo entre Rocafurte y García Moreno, T880600. Cabins with bathroom, hot water, TV, comfortable, big garden with hammocks, manager speaks English, good meeting place to make up a tour party, restaurant and disco. Recommended. **C** *La Misión*, by riverfront, T880260, Quito contact T553674, F564675. A/c, very smart, English spoken, pool,

Coca

To Bus Terminal & Market
To Airport

Bolívar
Quito
Trans Baños
Zaracay
Cuenca
9 de Octubre
Napo
Trans Esmeraldas
Amazonas
Pol
Vicente Rocafuerte
6 de Diciembre
TAME
Flota Pelileo
Casa de Cambio
River Dolphin Expeditions
García Moreno
Putumayo
Safari
Eloy Alfaro
Loja
12 de Febrero
Andinatel
Espejo
Emerald Forest Expeditions
Ejarsytur
Chimborazo
Dock
Capitanía

To Tena & Lago Agrio
To La Misión Hotel (70m)

Río Napo

N
0 metres 50
0 yards 50

■ **Sleeping**
1 Amazonas
2 El Auca
3 Florida
4 Lojanita
5 Oasis

● **Eating**
1 Dragón Dorado
2 Media Noche
3 Ocaso
4 Pappa Dan's & Riverside Bar
5 Parrilladas Argentinas

Ecuador

restaurant and disco, arranges tours. Recommended. **D** *Amazonas*, 12 de Febrero y Espejo, T880444. Away from the centre, quiet, with restaurant. Recommended. **E** *Florida*, on main road from the airport, T880177. With fan, basic, dark rooms. **F** *Oasis*, near the bridge at the end of town, T880206. Hot water and fans. Mixed reports. **F** *Lojanita*, Cuenca y Napo, T880032. Cheaper without bath, new rooms, good. Other hotels and *residencias* are populated by oil workers and range from basic to barely habitable.

There are good restaurants at the larger hotels (see above). *Los Cedros*, down by the river, 2   **Eating**
blocks from the Capitanía. Good fish, *patacones*, *yuca*, fairly expensive. *Dragón Dorado*, Bolívar entre Quito y Napo. Chinese. *Ocaso*, Eloy Alfaro entre Napo y Amazonas. Set meals. *Pappa Dan's*, Napo y Chimborazo, by river. Hamburgers, chilli, tacos etc, good. Next door is *Riverside Bar*. *Media Noche*, C Napo, in front of *Hotel El Auca*. Inexpensive chicken dishes. *Parrilladas Argentinas*, Cuenca y Amazonas. Grill.

Air Flights to **Quito** with *Aerogal* (office near Quito airport), every morning except Sun,   **Transport**
reserve 48 hrs in advance, planes are small and flights can be very bumpy, flights in and out of **Coca** are heavily booked, military and oil workers have priority on standby; also flights to **Tena** and **Shell** from Coca on Mon, Wed and Fri.

    Bus The bus terminal is a 20-min walk from *Hotel Auca*, away from river, ask to be let off in town. Buses leave from company offices on Napo. To **Quito**, 10 hrs, US$10.50, several daily 1030-2200, *Trans Baños* and *Putumayo*, depart from their offices on Napo y Cuenca; To **Lago Agrio**, 3 hrs, US$3.40. To **Tena**, 6 hrs, US$6. To **Misahuallí**, 7 hrs. To **Baeza**, 8 hrs.

    River For **passenger boats** out of Coca, ask the Capitanía at the dock. There is no service to Misahuallí. To **Nueva Rocafuerte**, US$28; canoes go if there are 8 or more passengers, taking about 14 hrs, if it is not reached before nightfall, the party will camp beside the river.

Banks Banks won't change TCs. **Communications** Internet: prices around US$7 per hr and access is   **Directory**
unreliable. Try hotels *Auca* and *La Misión*. **Telephone:** *Andinatel* on Eloy Alfaro; 0800-110 and 1300-1700.

Most of the Coca region is taken up by the **Parque Nacional Yasuní** and **Reserva**   **Jungle tours**
Huaorani. This area is unsuited to tours of less than three days owing to the remote-   **from Coca**
ness of its main attractions. Shorter visits of three to four days are worthwhile in the Coca-Yuturi segment of the Río Napo, where the lodges are concentrated. Tours to the park and reserve really need a minimum of five days. Wildlife in this area is under threat: insist that guides and the party take all litter back and ban all hunting and shooting; it really can make a difference.

    A common misconception is that it is always easy to find a cheap tour in Coca. For people travelling alone in the low season (especially February to May) it is dif-ficult to find a big enough group to get a bargain rate. Most jungle tours out of Coca cost US$30-$50 per person per day. Furthermore, you should beware of cut-rate operators who may compromise on safety, quality or responsible practices. The cheaper the tour, the larger the group is likely to be. Maximum group size should not exceed 8-10; larger parties make too much noise and see less. Check what pre-cisely is being offered and that the price includes items such as rubber boots, tents, mosquito nets, cooking equipment and food, and transport. For a trip of any length take suitable footwear (rubber boots, or two pairs of light shoes – keep one pair dry), light sleeping bag, rain jacket, trousers (not shorts), binoculars, insect repellent, sunscreen, water-purifying tablets, sticking plasters. Wrap everything in several small plastic bags. *South American Explorers* provides updated informa-tion on how to arrange your trip.

    NB If a guide offers a tour to visit the Huaorani, ask to see his/her permission to do so. The only guides permitted to take tourists into Huaorani territory are those who have made agreements with the Huaorani organization *ONHAE*.

Ecuador

Jungle lodges on the lower Napo All Napo area lodges count travel days as part of their package, which means that often a "three-day tour" spends only one day actually in the forest. Also, the return trip must start before dawn if it is to connect to that day's Coca-Quito flight; if it starts later it will be necessary to spend the night in Coca. Most lodges have fixed departure days from Coca (eg Mon and Fri) and it is very expensive to get a special departure on another day.

La Selva is an upscale lodge 2½ hrs downstream from Coca, professionally run, on a picturesque lake surrounded by excellent forest (especially on the far side of Mandicocha). Bird and animal life is exceptionally diverse. Many species of monkey are seen regularly. A total of 580 bird species can be found here, one of the highest totals in the world for a site at a single elevation, and some of the local guides (eg José) are very good at finding them. There is a biological station on the grounds (the Neotropical Field Biology Institute) as well as a butterfly farm. Cabins have private bathrooms. Meals are excellent. Usually the guides are biologists, and in general the guiding is of very high quality. A new canopy tower was due to be built in 2001. Four-night packages from Quito including all transport, lodging, and food, cost US$684 pp. Quito office: 6 de Diciembre 2816, Quito, T255 0995, laselva@uio.satnet.net   Or book through most tour agencies in Quito.

Sacha is another upscale lodge close to La Selva, 2½ hrs downstream from Coca. Comfortable cabins with private bath and hot water, excellent meals. The bird list is outstanding, and they have a local bird expert, Oscar Tapuy (T06-881486), who can be requested in advance by birders. Guides are generally knowledgeable. Boardwalks through swamp habitats allow access to some species that are difficult to see at other lodges, and nearby river islands provide another distinct habitat. They also have a butterfly farm, an exciting canopy tower and a canopy walkway. Several species of monkey are commonly seen. A 5-day package costs US$656 pp, excluding flight from Quito. Julio Zaldumbide 375 y Toledo, Quito, T250 9504, F223 6521, www.casadelsuizo.com

Ecuador

Yuturi Forest Lodge is 4 hrs downstream from Coca and less expensive than *La Selva* or *Sacha*. Birdwatching is excellent, and there are some species (eg Black-necked Red Cotinga) that are difficult to find at the previous two lodges. There is a wide variety of habitats and a modest canopy tower. Wildlife is good. The guides are usually local people accompanied by translators. 4 nights cost US$340, exclusive of airfare. Quito office: Amazonas 1324 y Colón, T/F250 4037, www.yuturi.com

Cabañas Bataburo, a lodge in Parque Nacional Yasuní is on the Río Tigüino, a 3-6 hr canoe ride from the end of the Vía Auca out of Coca. Two cabins have private bathrooms, while the others share baths. There are shared shower facilities. Guides are mostly local people. The birds here have been little studied but macaws and other large species are present. The mammal population also appears to be quite good. Prices are US$295 for 5 days/4 nights; cabin with private bath US$20 extra. Quito office: *Kempery Tours*, see Quito Tour operators.

Añangucocha is being built by and for the local Añangu community, across the Napo from La Selva, 2½ hrs downstream from Coca. This area of hilly forest is rather different from the low flat forest of some other sites and the diversity is slightly higher. There are big caimans, good mammals, including Giant Otters, and the birding is excellent. The local guide, Giovanny Rivadeneyra, is one of the most knowledgeable birders in the Oriente. Facilities are basic at present, palm-thatch huts and an outhouse, but the price is low (US$27 per day); most of the money goes directly to the community. More elaborate facilities and a canopy tower are planned. For more information contact Chris Canaday, Quito T244 7463, canaday@accessinter.net Bookings through Cecilia, Coca T881486.

Hacienda Primavera is 2 hrs downstream from Coca in an area with little wildlife. There are clean, basic rooms **G**, or you can camp (US$0.50). Meals available. Excursions from here are not cheap however, and you should agree all prices carefully in advance.

Pañacocha

Pañacocha is halfway between Coca and Nuevo Rocafuerte, near the magnificent lagoon of Pañacocha on the Río Panayacu. This has been declared a protected forest region. Canadian Randy Smith (contact through *River Dolphin Expeditions*, García Moreno y Napo, T/F881563 in Coca, or Quito T256 3535, www.amazon-green-magician.com) is working on a management plan for the area in order to ensure that the local Quichua community get the best out of tourism. Several agencies and guides run tours from Coca (see Tour operators). Accommodation is available at **G** *Pensión*, in Pañacocha. Friendly, but watch out for chiggers in the mattresses.

Tour operators

The following operators and guides have been recommended, and there are many others. *Safari* offers 4-day all-inclusive trips with the Huaorani; responsible practices, contributions made to the community. See Quito, Tour operators. *Emerald Forest Expeditions*, Espejo y Napo, Coca, T881155, or Joaquín Pinto E4-244 y Amazonas, Quito, T/F254 1543, T252 6403 (ext 13), emerald@uio.satnet.net.ec Guide Luis Alberto García has many years experience, speaks English, and runs tours to the Pañacocha area. Recommended. *Tropic Ecological Adventures*, tropic@uio.satnet.net (see Quito, Tour operators). Run ecologically-sound tours with local and bilingual naturalist guides, and work closely with Cofan, Secoya and Huaorani communities. Highly recommended. *Ejarsytur*, opposite *Hotel Oasis*, T887142, in Quito at Santa Prisca 260 y 10 de Agosto, T258 3120. Run by the Jarrín family, German and English spoken, US$40 pp per day. Recommended. *Etnoturismo Amasanga Supay*, is an indigenous Quichua co-operative which offers a variety of trips and which helps local communities. They are opposite the Capitanía at the port, or contact César Andi at *Hotel Oasis*.

Recommended guides are *Klever and Braulio Llori*, T880487. Also *Wymper Torres*, T880336, or speak to his sister, Mady in Quito, T265 9311. He specializes in the Río Shiripuno and Pañacocha areas, speaks Spanish only. *Carlos Sevilla* runs tours of 5-15 days in the Huaorani Reserve and Parque Nacional Yasuní, small groups of 3-6, speaks Spanish only but recommended. Contact through *Hotel Auca* in Coca, or through family in Quito, T224 4205.

Coca to Nuevo Rocafuerte

An irregular canoe service (best to hire your own) passes Coca carrying passengers and cargo down-river. The end of the line is **Nuevo Rocafuerte**, where the missionaries and Sra Jesús let rooms; there are no restaurants (military permit required).

Ecuador

Transport is becoming more frequent as the border with Peru becomes more open. En route is **Laguna de Limoncocha**, an excellent spot for birding, now a Biological Reserve. Nearby is the **Pompeya Capuchin mission**, with a school and museum of Napo culture, about two hours down-river from Coca. Upriver from Pompeya is the small Monkey Island with free-roaming monkeys. Rent a canoe to visit it.

Archidona and Tena

Phone code: 06
Population: 13,790

Roads from both Baeza and Coca go south to Archidona, 65 km from Baeza. It has a striking, small painted church; 10 km further south, Tena is the capital of Napo Province. Like Archidona, it was founded in 1560 and both were important colonial missionary and trading posts. It is now a commercial centre with an attractive plaza overlooking the confluence of the Ríos Tena and Pano. A recommended walk is to Parque Amazónico, on the island, with an observation tower and botanical garden. Cross by the wooden footbridge. *Tourist office*: Bolívar y García Moreno, near the market, north end of town.

Tena has a large lowland Quichua Indian population living in the vicinity, some of whom are panning for gold in the rivers. These Indians are unlike the Indian groups further into the Oriente forests; they are Quijos, of Chibcha stock. The Tena area, which lacks the pristine jungle found deeper in the Oriente, has instead developed interesting opportunities for ethno-tourism.

Excursions The road leaving Archidona's plaza to the east goes to the village of San Pablo, and beyond to the Río Hollín. Along this road, 7 km from Archidona, is the **Reserva Ecológica Monteverde**, a 25 ha reserve with primary and secondary forest, and medicinal plants. There are walking trails, river bathing, fishing, cultural presentations for groups, and 5 cabins with bath and cold water (US$28 per person full board). ■ *Entry for day visits US$1.* Reservations necessary, contact *Residencial Regina* in Archidona T889144 or Quito T289 1041. Pickup from Archidona US$5. Along the same road, 15 km from Archidona, is **Reserva El Para**, an 80 ha forest reserve with many rare birds. It is owned by *Orchid Paradise* (see Archidona hotels below), who run tours to the reserve, US$40 plus transport for a group of up to 10.

Tours can be arranged to the **Izu Mangallpa Urcu (IMU) Foundation**, 3 km east of Archidona off a side turning down the road to San Pablo, set up by the Mamallacta family to protect territory on Galeras mountain. They charge US$35 per day for accommodation and day trips, taking groups of 8-10; US$65 per day, five days trekking, groups of two minimum; tough going but the forest is wonderful. Ask around or book through *Safari* in Quito, T255 2505.

Just outside Archidona, to the south, a small turning leads to the river. About 200 m along there is a large rock with many **petroglyphs** carved on its surface, the easiest to find of several within a 30 km radius.

The famous **Jumandí caves** are 5-6 km north of Archidona. Take a taxi, or bus from Archidona, 30 mins. It is advisable to go with a guide; take good boots and a strong torch. It is very muddy (sometimes full of water) so it can be useful to take spare clothes. The side ducts of the caves are extremely narrow and claustrophobic. There are several colonies of vampire bat (*Desmodus rotundus*) in the caves. A tourist complex has been built with pool, waterslide and restaurant. ■ *US$2 pp.*

Sleeping
The water supply in most cheaper hotels is poor

Archidona: **AL** *Orchid Paradise*, 2 km north of town, T889232, Quito T252 6223. Cabins in nice secondary forest with lots of birds. Meals not included, restaurant on site. **A** *Hakuna Matata*, 4 km S of Archidona, F886853, www.hakunamat.com Includes all meals, comfortable cabins in a spectacular setting by the Río Inchillaqui. Dutch/Belgian run, good food, horse riding. Recommended. **D** *Res Regina*, Rocafuerte 446, T889144. Modern, cheaper without bath, pleasant. Recommended. *Hostal Archidona*, hidden down a back street, 5 blocks south of the plaza. There are few decent places to eat, though *Restaurant Los Pinos*, near *Res Regina*, is good.

Tena: **B** *Los Yutzos*, at the south end of town overlooking the Río Pano, T886717, F886769. Includes breakfast, a/c, cheaper with fan, comfortable, beautiful grounds, quiet, family-run. Recommended. **C** *Establo de Tomás*, via a San Antonio, T886318. Good restaurant, 20 min out of town, Cabins on river. **D** *Traveler's Lodging*, 15 de Noviembre 422, T886372. A/c, basic, helpful, good food. More expensive rooms have view. **D** *Hostal Turismo Amazónico*, Amazonas y Abdón Calderón, T886487, F886015. Cheaper with cold shower, fan, parking, fridge. **D** *Indiana*, Bolívar entre Amazonas y García Moreno, T886334. Restaurant for breakfast only, parking. Has tour agency for jungle trips. **D** *Puma Rosa*, on Malecón near vehicle bridge, T/F886320. A/c, parking, nice grounds. Recommended. **D** *Villa Belén*, on Baeza road (Av Jumandy), T886228. Cold water, parking, north of town, quiet. Recommended. **E** *Laurita*, Opposite bus terminal. Shared bath, basic. **E** *Limoncocha*, Sangay 533, Sector Corazón de Jesús, 300 m from terminal, T887583, limoncocha@andinanet.net Breakfast available, shared bath, hot water, terrace with hammocks, German-Ecuadorean run, organize good tours (US$28 pp per day, rafting US$38). Pleasant atmosphere, enthusiastic owners, but noisy neighbours. **E** *Media Noche*, 15 de Noviembre 1125, T886490. Inexpensive restaurant, cold water, parking, near the bus station, good. **E** *Res Alemana*, Díaz de Pineda 210 y Av 15 de Noviembre, T886409. Cold water, OK, fairly clean. **F** *Jumandy*, Amazonas y Abdón Calderón, T886329. Breakfast from 0600, shared bath, cold water, with balcony, the Cerda family also arrange jungle tours (see Tour operators).

Eating

Cositas Ricas, 15 de Noviembre, next to *Traveler's Lodging*. Tasty meals, vegetarian available, good fruit juices, run by Patricia Corral of *Amarongachi Tours*. *Chuquitos*, García Moreno by Plaza. Popular. *Pollo Good*, 15 de Noviembre 1 block north of bus terminal. Tasty chicken. There are also *chifas* in town.

Tour operators

Amarongachi Tours (see under *Traveler's Lodging*; see also *Jungle Tours from Tena*). *Ecoindiana*, inside *Hostal Indiana* (see Sleeping). *Kanoa Tours*, 15 de Noviembre, opposite *Cositas Ricas*. *Ricancie*, Av 15 de Noviembre 772, T887953, www.ricancie.nativeweb.org Community-run group with a variety of tours emphasising cultural exchange, adventure, health and shamanism, expensive but worth it. *Ríos Ecuador*, 15 de Noviembre y 9 de Octubre, T887438, Quito T255 3727, info@riosecuador.com Gynner Coronel runs highly recommended white-water rafting and kayak trips and a 5-day kayak school. *Voyage Fantastic*, Av 15 de Noviembre, opposite bus station, T888424, F886490, voyagefantastic@hotmail.com Tours in the Tena/Misahuallí area, in Parque Nacional Sumaco, and from Coca. US$25 pp per day for nearby destinations, US$50 per day out of Coca. Prices include all meals and transport, but not park or museum fees.

Transport

Air: To Shell (see page 1021). US$15-20 for 15-min flight over the canopy in superlight plane, 1 person at a time, contact Jorge through *Ríos Ecuador*. **Bus**: Quito, via Baeza, 11 daily 0200-2345, US$4.50, 5 hrs, book in advance. **Baeza**, 2 hrs. **Ambato**, via Baños, Mon only, US$5, 5 hrs. **Baños**, US$3.70, 4 hrs. **Riobamba**, via Puyo, Baños and Ambato, 6 daily from 0200, US$4.50. **Archidona** every 20 mins, US$0.20, 15 mins. **Misahuallí**, hourly, US$0.50, 45 mins, buses leave from the local bus station not the long distance terminal. To **Coca**, 6 hrs, US$6, 8 daily 0600-2200. To **Lago Agrio**, with *Jumandy* at 1830, 9 hrs, US$8.50. **Puyo**, US$1.50, 3 hrs. To **Ahuano** hourly 0700-1800.

Jungle tours from Tena

Trips are organized to **Amarongachi**, 20 km southwest of Tena on the Río Jatunyacu, by Jesús Uribe at *Amarongachi Tours*, 15 de Noviembre 422, T/F886372. **B** pp per day full board, highly recommended. This co-operative travel agency works closely with local people, and also runs a hotel and restaurant (see Sleeping and Eating). You can stay in the *Shangri-La* cabins on the Río Anzu south of Río Jatunyacu (**B** pp per day, full board, transport and guide included, wooden cabins with tin roof in a rainforest setting, some have bath), or with an indigenous family; US$30 per person per day.

Comunidad Capirona is one hour by bus, then three hours on foot from Tena. Visits can be arranged here or to nine other communities in the area, US$30-40 per person per day. This is part of a highly regarded project which combines eco/

ethno-tourism and community development. There are also opportunities for volunteers. Contact the *Red Indígena de las Comunidades del Alto Napo para la Convivencia Intercultural y El Ecoturismo (Ricancie)*, 15 de Noviembre 722, T/F887072, ricancie@ecuanex.net.ec

The **Cerda family** provide tours of various lengths, camping or staying in *cabañas*. Tours focus on local indigenous life and cost US$25 per person per day. They also offer rafting trips on the Río Jatunyacu (US$40 per person including meal and equipment) and one day motorized canoe tours from Misahuallí to Huabano (US$30 per person). You must call from Quito to let them know when you're leaving so they can meet you at the terminal in Tena; T886250/887181. Both Olmedo and Oswaldo (son) are recommended guides and speak German as well as Spanish. You can also contact them through *Hotel Jumandy*.

Sr Delfín Pauchi, T886434/886088, Casilla 245, Tena, has built *Cabañas Pimpilala*, 45 minutes by taxi from Tena, where for two to four days you can live with a Quichua family for US$35 per person per day, including lodging, meals, transport and guide. Trails for hiking have been made on his 30 ha of undeveloped land, but emphasis is on culture rather than wildlife. Delfín speaks only Quichua and Spanish. He knows about plants and their medicinal uses, legends and music. He will meet you at the terminal in Tena if you call ahead. Also contact through *Naturgal* in Quito, Reina Victoria y Foch, T252 2681.

At **El Pano** (southwest of Tena on the Río Panu, 45 minutes by road), are *Cabañas Llakik Sacha*, accommodating up to 15 people (cabin with toilet, water, electricity, river bathing). All meals are available and programmes up to 5 days. Prices in **C** range, contact Profesor César Tapuy, T06-886046 (office), 887848 (private) or Jacob Andi Chimbo, guide, jacobandi@yahoo.com

Tena to Misahuallí From Tena the main highway (unpaved) runs south to Puyo. **Puerto Napo**, a few kilometres south of Tena, has a bridge across the Río Napo. (Pato García, a guide, has a nice room to rent; his tours cost US$22.) On the north bank a road runs east to Misahuallí, about 17 km downstream. From Puerto Napo you can catch a local bus from Tena to Misahuallí. If you're travelling north from Puyo, avoid going into Tena by getting off the bus here.

Misahuallí

Phone code: 06
Colour map 1a, grid B4
Population: 3,579

This small port, at the junction of the Napo and Misahuallí rivers, is perhaps the best place in Ecuador from which to visit the 'near Oriente', but your expectations should be realistic. The area has been colonized for many years and there is no extensive virgin forest nearby (except at *Jatun Sacha*, see page 1020). Access is very easy however, prices are reasonable, and while you will not encounter large animals in the wild, you can still see birds, butterflies and exuberant vegetation – enough to get a taste for the jungle. There is a fine, sandy beach on the Río Misahuallí, but don't camp on it as the river can rise unexpectedly.

Sleeping **A** *Misahuallí Jungle Hotel*, across the river from town. Cabins for up to 6, nice setting, pool, restaurant operates sporadically, packages available. Quito: Ramírez Dávalos 251 y Páez, T520043, F504872, www.miltour.com **D** *El Albergue Español*, on J Arteaga, T890004, www.alberguespanol.com All rooms screened with balconies overlooking the Napo. Good expensive restaurant. Recommended. Also operate *Hotel Jaguar* jungle lodge (see below). Quito: Eloy Alfaro 3147 y CJ Arosemena, T245 3703, alb-esp@uio.satnet.net **D** *France Amazonia*, on road from Tena across from high school, Tena T887499, france_amazonia@hotmail.com Small rooms, includes very good breakfast, French run, helpful. **D** *El Paisano*, on G Rivadeneyra. With hot water, small rooms. **E** *Marena Inn*, on Juan Arteaga, Tena T/F887584. Cold water, fan. **E** *Shaw*, Santander on Plaza, ecoselva@yahoo.es Simple rooms, cheaper without bath, operate their own tours, English spoken. Recommended. **E** *Granilandia*, on Santander at entrance to town, Quito T235 0256, F235 0873. Cold water, fan, operated by the military, unusual but friendly, nice views. **F** *La Casa Eduardo*, 200 m from bus terminal. Terrace, kitchen, pleasant, owner Eduardo is a guide. **F** *Sacha*, by beach. Basic but OK, nice location (take insect repellent).

Doña Gloria, Arteaga y Rivadeneyra by corner of plaza. Open 0730-2030 daily, very good set meals. Recommended. *Le Peroquet Bleu*, Santander y Napo by corner of plaza. A la carte and not cheap. *Bar Atarraya*, at the end of Santander. Nice atmosphere. Bars by the river have a frontier feel to them, as do the handful of general stores

Eating

Bus Local buses run from the plaza to **Tena** every 45 mins 0745-1800, US$0.50, 1 hr. Make all long distance connections in Tena, or get off at Puerto Napo to catch southbound buses.

Transport

  River With the increase in roads, river traffic is diminishing along the upper Napo. Scheduled passenger services from Misahuallí have been discontinued. Motorized canoes wait at the beach and can be hired for touring (but better to go with a guide) or transport to the location of your choice.

There are many guides available to take parties into the jungle for trips of one to 10 days, all involving canoeing and varying amounts of hiking. Travellers should ask to see a guide's licence. It is advisable to insist on paying part of the cost on completion of the trip (for Tour operators based in Quito, see page 914). The going rate is between US$25 and US$40 per person per day, depending on the season, size of group and length of trip. The same advice applies as elsewhere in Oriente (see Coca, page 1013) on checking equipment and supplies, and a guide's written permission to visit Indian villages. Some guides visit zoos of hotels where animals are kept in unsatisfactory conditions; make sure beforehand that zoos are not on the itinerary. Also see under Coca for what personal effects to take.

Jungle tours from Misahuallí
There are frequent reports of unlicensed guides cheating tourists

  There is a *mariposario* (butterfly farm) 2 blocks from the main square in Misahuallí. Several colourful species can be observed and photographed close up. Interesting. Make arrangements through *Ecoselva* (see Tour operators).

We list only those guides who have been recommended to us: *Cruceros y Expediciones Dayuma*, run tours to their ecological reserve, 15 mins by canoe plus a 4-hr walk from Misahuallí, with accommodation in bungalows with bathrooms, hammocks and restaurant. They can also organize longer trips. Guides include Douglas and Wilfred Clarke, who speak English. Office on J Arteaga on the plaza and in Quito: Av 10 de Agosto 3815 y Mariana de Jesús, edif Villacis Pazos, no 301, T256 4924/266 4490, dayuma@hoy.net *Ecoselva*, Santander on the plaza, ecoselva@yahoo.es Recommended guide Pepe Tapia González speaks English and has a biology background. Trips from 1-6 days, well organized and reliable. *Viajes y Aventuras Amazónicas*, Napo y Juan Arteaga opposite the plaza, T890031. Run by Carlos Santander and his brothers. Friendly, good food.

Tour operators

  Recommended guides *Héctor Fiallos*, contact via *Sacha Hotel* on the beach (see above), Quito T223 9044 or Tena T740002. *Marcos Estrada* is knowledgeable, honest and offers tours of different lengths. Contact *France Amazonia* office on plaza or enquire at the hotel (see above). *Sócrates Nevárez*, runs well-organized 1-10 day tours including trips further down the Río Napo; PO Box 239, Tena. *Carlos Herbert Licuy Licuy*, locally born, is good on history, legends and culture of the area. *Alfredo Andrade*, speaks English, T584965.

B *Anaconda*, on Anaconda Island in the Río Napo, about 1 hr down river by canoe from Misahuallí. Bamboo bungalows, no electric lights, but flush toilets and cold showers, good meals. Canoe and hiking trips arranged, guides only speak Spanish. Opposite, on the north bank at **Ahuano**, is **A** pp *Casa del Suizo*. Swiss/Ecuadorean-owned, price includes all meals, with vegetarian options, private bath, electricity 24 hrs, pool, animal sanctuary, trips arranged. Highly recommended for hospitality and location. Quito office: Julio Zaldumbide 375 y Toledo, T250 9504, www.casadelsuizo.com

Jungle lodges on the upper Napo

  The south shore of the Napo has road access from Tena, with frequent bus service. Along this road are several hotels, including *Cabañas Cotococha*, Km 10 Vía a Ahuano, T/F250 3423 in Quito, www.cotocochalodge.com US$170 pp for 2-night, 3-day package, includes

Ecuador

meals and excursions (cheaper without English-speaking guide); taxi from Tena US$8.
C *Isla Amazónica*, near **Venecia**, Baños T03-740609. Rustic cabins on riverfront, with private bath, hot water, meals available.

C pp *Hotel Jaguar*, 1½ hrs downstream from Misahuallí, congenial atmosphere, includes meals, vegetarian available, tours arranged. Operated by *El Albergue Español* in Misahuallí.

AL pp *Yachana Lodge*, is based in the indigenous village of **Mondaña**, 2 hrs downstream from Misahuallí. Proceeds support community development projects. Comfortable double rooms and family cabins, solar power. Highly recommended packages including transport from Quito, all meals, lodging and guides; US$425 for 5 days. Quito office: Francisco Andrade Marín 188 y Diego de Almagro, T223 7278, dtm@pi.pro.ec

Jatun Sacha   Eight kilometres downriver from Misahuallí, reached by road or river, is the **Jatun Sacha Biological Station** ('big forest' in Quichua). The biological station and the adjacent Aliñahui project together conserve 1,300 ha of tropical wet forest. So far, 507 birds, 2,500 plants and 765 butterfly species have been identified. Activities include environmental education, field research, ecotourism and excursions with good views and a well-developed trail system. ■ *25 mins by boat, US$2.50; or by road on the south bank of the Río Napo, 25 km from the bridge in Puerto Napo, bus to La Punta or Campacocha from Tena passes, but it has to ford the river – difficult if the level is high.*

Lodging is **A** pp *Cabañas Aliñahui*. 8 cabins with 2 bedrooms and bathroom, lush tropical garden, rainforest and nature trails, includes 3 delicious meals. US$6 for entrance only. Profits contribute to conservation. Quito office: *Fundación Jatun Sacha*, Pasaje Eugenio de Santillán N34-248 y Maurian, T243 2246, www.jatunsacha.org

Puyo

Phone code: 03
Colour map 1a, grid B4
Population: 15,563

The capital of the province of Pastaza and the largest centre in the whole Oriente. It feels more like a small lowland city anywhere, rather than a typical jungle town. Visits can nonetheless be made to nearby forest reserves and tours deeper into the jungle can also be arranged from Puyo. It is the junction for road travel into the northern and southern Oriente, and for traffic heading to or from Ambato via Baños. The Sangay and Altar volcanoes can occasionally be seen from town.

Excursions   **Omaere** is a 15.6 ha ethnobotanical reserve two km north of Puyo on the road to Tena. ■ *1½-hour guided tours with indigeneous experts, US$4 pp.* There are examples of different traditional dwellings (reported run down) and a botanical garden. You can swim nearby in the Río Puyo. It is run by the OPIP (*Organización de Pueblos Indígenas de Pastaza*), see below. There are other small private reserves of varying quality in the Puyo area and visits are arranged by local tour operators (see below). You cannot however expect to see large tracts of undisturbed primary jungle here. Sites include: **Criadero de Vida Silvestre Fátima**, 9 km north on the road to Tena, which attempts to 'rehabilitate'

captive jungle animals, US$2; **Jadín Botánico Las Orquídeas**, 3 km south on the road to Macas, orchids and other tropical plants, US$4; **Fundación Ecológica Hola Vida**, 27 km from Puyo near **Porvenir**, rustic accommodation in the forest.

A *Hostería Safari*, outside town at Km 5 on the road to Tena, T885465. Includes breakfast, **Sleeping** ample grounds, peaceful. **D** *Gran Hotel Amazónico*, Ceslao Marín y Atahualpa, T883094. Hot water, TV, fan, restaurant downstairs, nice. **D** *Hostería Turingia*, Ceslao Marín 294, T885180, turingia@punto.net.ec Comfortable, hot water, garden, small pool, restaurant. **D** *El Araucano*, Ceslao Marín 576, T883834. Hot water, TV, stores luggage, cheaper without breakfast. **D** *Los Cofanes*, 27 de Febrero 6-29 y Ceslao Marín, T885560, loscofanes@ yahoo.com Hot water, TV, fan, modern. **D** *Cristhian's*, Atahualpa entre 9 de Octubre y 27 de Febrero, T/F883081. Large modern rooms, hot water, TV. **F** *California*, 9 de Octubre 1354, T885189. Cold water, central, noisy. **F** *Hostal El Colibrí*, C Manabí entre Bolívar y Galápagos, T883054. Away from centre, cold water, parking, modern, good value. Recommended. **F** *Rizzo*, 9 de Octubre y Bolívar, T883279. Cold water, modern, good value.

La Carigüela, Mons Alberto Zambrano, near the bus station. Upscale dining. *El Jardín*, Paseo **Eating** Turístico Río Puyo. International food, trout. *Pizzería Buon Giorno*, in a small shopping arcade at 9 de Octubre y Orellana. Good pizza and salads, Popular. Recommended. *Chifa China*, 9 de Octubre y 24 de Mayo. Clean. *Sal y Pimienta*, Atahualpa y 27 de Febrero. Grilled meats, cheap and popular.

Amazonia Touring, 9 de Octubre y Atahualpa, T883219, F883064. Land-based and fly-in **Tour** trips for 1-10 people. *Entsa Tours*, PO Box 16-01-856, T885500. Recommended for tours into **operators** the jungle, Mentor Marino helpful and knowledgeable. The **Organización de Pueblos Indígenas de Pastaza** (OPIP) operates *Papangu Tours*, 9 de Octubre y Orellana, T883875. 1-6 day jungle trips, US$40-$50 pp per day.

Air 2 commercial flights a week to **Quito** (US$45) with *Servicio Aéreo Regional*, Shell-Mera **Transport** T795175, Quito T259 2032.

Bus Buses leave from the new Terminal Terrestre on the outskirts of town. To **Baños**, US$1.50, 2 hrs. To **Ambato**, US$2, 3 hrs. To **Quito**, US$2.75, 6 hrs via Ambato (9 hrs via Baeza, US$3.50). To **Tena**, US$1.50, 3 hrs on a rough road. To **Macas**, US$4, 6 hrs. To **Riobamba**, US$1.60, 5 hrs.

Banks *Cambios Puyo*, 9 de Octubre y Atahualpa, T/F883064, fair commission on TCs. **Directory** **Communications** Internet: *Centro de Cómputo Amazonas*, Atahualpa 2000 y 9 de Octubre, p 2, US$5 per hr. **Post Office** 27 de Febrero entre Atahualpa y Orellana. **Telephone**: *Andinatel*, Villamil y Orellana. Long queues.

Shell is 13 km west of Puyo, 50 km from Baños, 1½ hours. It has an airfield and an army checkpoint where foreigners may be asked to register (passport required). **E** *Los Copales*, west of Shell on the road to Baños, T795290. Comfortable cabins with electric shower, restaurant. **E** *Germany Hostal*, down a side street, T795134. Hot water, restaurant, family run. **F** *Hostal Cordillera*, on main street. Cheaper without bath, restaurant, basic. There are several cheap and simple *comedores* on the main street; *El Portón*, near the west end, is good.

Stretching south of the Río Pastaza, the southern Oriente is made up of the provinces of Morona-Santiago and part of Zamora-Chinchipe. The first leg of the Puyo-Macas bus journey goes as far as **Chuitayo**, on the Río Pastaza (3 hours). There is a bridge suitable only for cars and small *busetas*. On the opposite shore, a bus carries passengers the rest of the way (2½ hours) to a second suspension bridge over the Río Upano, just before Macas. It stops often at small settlements, mostly inhabited by Shuar. The road hard-packed dirt, full of potholes. The jungle which borders this road is rapidly being removed.

Macas

Phone code: 07
Colour map1a, grid B4
Population: 9,720
Altitude: 1,000 m

Capital of Morona-Santiago province, Macas is situated high above the broad Río Upano valley, and developing rapidly thanks to nearby oil deposits and beef production, Sangay volcano can be seen on clear mornings from the plaza, creating an amazing backdrop to the tropical jungle surrounding the town. The modern cathedral, with beautiful stained-glass windows, houses the much-venerated image of La Purísima de Macas. Several blocks north of the cathedral, in the park, which also affords great views of the Upano Valley, is an excellent orchid collection.

The climate is not too hot and the nights are even cool

Excursions To the **Salesian Sevilla-Don Bosco mission**, east of town. The modern archaeological museum, Don Bosco y Montalba, is a good place to rest and see views of the river, and there is a recreation area nearby. 3 km north is La Cascada, beside the Río Copueno, picnic area, swimming, slide, football, volleyball. **Complejo Hombre Jaguar** archaeological site, with many *tolas* (ceremonial or burial mounds made by prehispanic cultures), is north, near Santa Rosa and Guapula on the way to Parque Nacional Sangay (see page 1023). Allow two days to see everything; ask for directions if using public transport; day tours with *Winnie Sunka* US$25 per person (see Tour operators).

Sleeping **AL** *Cabañas Ecológicas Yuquipa*, a 3-km walk from Km 12 on the road to Puyo, T700071. Includes breakfast, restaurant, minimum 3 days stay. Package includes accommodation, guides, meals and transport. Contact *Pan Francesa* bakery at Soasti y Tarqui. **D** *Cabañas del Valle*, Vía Sur Km 1.5, T700300. Quiet and helpful. **D** *Esplendid*, Soasti 1518, T700120. Parking, modern. **D** *La Orquídea*, 9 de Octubre 1305 y Sucre, T700132. Cheaper with cold water, bright, quiet. **D** *Manzana Real*, Av 29 de Mayo at southern entrance to town, T700637. Pool, parking, comfortable, meals on request. Recommended. **D** *Peñón del Oriente*, Domingo Comín 837 y Amazonas, T700124, F700450. Parking, modern, secure. Recommended. **E** *Amazonas*, Guamote y 29 de Mayo, T700198. Cheaper without bath, parking, near the university. **F** *Residencial Macas*, 24 de Mayo y Sucre, T700254. Above *Restaurante Carmitas* (good simple cooking), quiet. **F** *Sangay*, Tarqui 605, T700457. Shared bath, cold water, basic.

Eating Not much to choose from: *Chifa Pagoda*, next to *Peñón del Oriente*, expensive. *Los Helechos*, Soasti entre Cuenca y Sucre. Good, popular with guides. *Café El Jardín*, Amazonas y D Comín. Expensive. Cheaper places include *Imperial*, on Domingo Comín, and *Super Pollo*, 10 de Agosto y Guamote.

Tour operators It is possible to visit the jungle from Macas and there are agencies specializing in tours to villages. However, contact the **Shuar Federation** (see below, Sucúa) before taking a tour and verify what is involved before signing any contract. *Aventura Tsunki Touring*, Amazonas y Domingo Comín, T/F700464, tsunki@cue.satnet.net Hiking tours with a Shuar guide and English interpreter, also canoe trips and cave exploration. *ETSA*, 24 de Mayo y 10 de Agosto, T700550. *Ikiaam*, 10 de Agosto, 2nd floor in house opposite bus terminal, T700457, tours to jungle and Parque Nacional Sangay. *ROW*, Amazonas y Quito, a US company from Idaho is offering whitewater rafting on the Upano (*River Odysseys West*, PO Box 579, Coeur d'Alene, Idaho, 83816-0579, T208-765 0841). Ecuador contact: Juan, Quito, T245 8339. Seasons are limited owing to the extreme unpredictability of the Upano River. *Tuntiak Tours*, in bus terminal, T700082, Carlos Arcos is half Shuar and speaks the language, very experienced. *Winnie Sunka*, Amazonas opposite *Chifa Pagoda*, T700088, Pablo Velín guide. Recommended.

Kapawi Ecological Reserve: is a top-of-the-line jungle lodge located on the Río Pastaza in the heart of Achuar (the Shuar belong to this tribe) territory. It is accessible only by small aircraft and motor canoe. The lodge was built in partnership with the indigenous organization **OINAE** and offers flexible programmes. It is also built according to the Achuar concept of architecture, using typical materials, and emphasizes environmentally friendly methods such as solar energy, biodegradable soaps and rubbish recycling. It is in a zone rich in biodiversity, with many opportunities for seeing the forest and its inhabitants. 4 nights in a double cabin costs US$700, plus US$200 for transport to and from Quito. The location, quality of service, cabin accommodation and food have all been highly recommended. Quito office: *Canodros*, Av Portugal 448 y Catalina de Aldaz, T225 6759, www.canodros.com Guayaquil: Urb Santa Leonor Mz 5, local 10, T04-228 5711, F228 7651, PO Box 09-01-8442.

Air Flight to Quito, *TAME*, Mon, Wed, Fri, sit on left for best views of Volcán Sangay (see below). **Bus** To **Cuenca**, 11 hrs, US$6.50, 4 a day with *Turismo Oriental*; *Transportes Sucúa*, 1700, spectacular views, 0530 bus to see it in daylight. Hourly to **Sucúa**, 1 hr, no regular service on Thu. 2 bus companies **Macas-Puyo**, continuing to **Baños, Ambato** and **Quito**: *Coop San Francisco* 5 a day, US$4.50, 6 hrs; *Coop Macas* almost hourly from 0600-1500.

Transport

Banks *Banco del Austro*, 24 de Mayo y 10 de Agosto, cash on Visa, changes TCs. **Communications Post Office:** 9 de Octubre y Domingo Comín, next to the park. **Telephone:** *Andinatel*: 24 de Mayo y Sucre, F700110, use this number to contact any establishment (be patient).

Directory

In clear weather, the surrounding hills give excellent views of the volcano Sangay, 5,230 m, within the Parque Nacional Sangay, information from Ministry of the Environment in Macas, Juan de la Cruz y 29 de Mayo. Sangay is an active volcano; *South American Explorers* has information on organizing a trip; equipment, helmet, etc, and guide essential. This seven-day trek is tough: expect long, hard days of walking and severe weather. Protection against falling stones is vital. *Mecánica Acosta*, Plaza Arenas, Quito (near the prominent basilica), will make shields, arm loops welded to an oil drum top, for US$2-3. December/January is a good time to climb Sangay. ■ *Entrance US$10. The park may be reached by bus 1½ hrs to village of 9 de Octubre, Wed, Fri and Sun 0730 and 1600, then walk. See also Riobamba, Excursions, also for notes on the new road to Guamote.*

Parque Nacional Sangay

Sucúa is of particular interest as the centre of a branch of the ex-head-hunting Shuar (Jívaro) Indians. Their crafts can be seen and bought but it is tactless to ask them about head-hunting and shrinking (a practice designed to punish those who bewitched others and to deter anyone wishing to cause sickness or disaster in future). Outside the schools, scenes from Shuar mythology are displayed in painted tableaux. You can contact the **Shuar Federation** at Domingo Comín 17-38 (C Tarqui 809), T/F704108, about visiting traditional villages. This is posible with an Indian guide, but allow at least 1½ days as the application must be considered by a council of seven and then you will be interviewed. There is a small craft shop across the street from the Shuar Federation. There is an interesting bookshop and, 10 mins walk from the town centre, a small museum and zoo (very few animals) run by Shuar Indians, in the Centro de Formación Kimi.

Sucúa

23 km from Macas

Nearby is the Río Upano, a 1½ hour walk, with plenty of Morpho butterflies. A cablecar crosses the river. Also close by is the Río Tutanangoza, a 15-minute walk, with rapids and good swimming, but be careful of the current after rain.

Sleeping and eating D *Karina*, southwest corner of plaza, above *farmacia*. Light. **E** *Hostería Orellana*, at the south end of town, T704193. 1 room with bath, others without. **E** *Hostal Alborada*. Cheap, restaurant. **E** *Rincón Oriental*. Shared bath, parking. Recommended. **F** *Sangay*, very basic. *Restaurant La Fuente*, Domingo Comín near the plaza. Good. Bar/restaurant *Sangay*, opposite *Rincón Oriental*. *Paolita*, Domingo Comín south of centre. *Jefralisavi*, north of the plaza. Snacks and drinks, open till midnight, changes US$ TCs.

From Sucúa, the road heads south for one hour to Logroño and then, another one hour south to (Santiago de) **Méndez**, a nice town with a modern church. Market day Sunday. **Sleeping**: **F** *Hostal Los Ceibos*, C Cuenca just off plaza, T760133. Hot water, spotless. Recommended. **F** *Hostal Los Sauces*, T760165. There are cheaper places. Places to eat include *El Reportero*, Domingo Comín y Cuenca; and *16 de Agosto*, Cuenca y Guayaquil. **Bus** To Gualaquiza 1600, 1900. Cuenca four a day. Macas 0600, 1100. There are also buses on the new raod to Paute.

Sucúa to Zamora

Ecuador

Two hours, 50 km south of Méndez is **Limón**, official name General Leónidas Plaza, a mission town founded in 1935, now a busy, unappealing place surrounded by high jungle. Three *residenciales* on C Quito, all **G**: *Limón*, T770114, modern, basic, front rooms noisy. *Domínguez*, friendly. *Santo Domingo*, basic. Several *chifas*.

Continuing south from Limón the road passes **Indanza** (very basic *residencial* and *comedor*), before reaching **Gualaquiza**, a pioneer town off the tourist track. It is surrounded by densely forested mountains, in which are interesting side trips. **E** *Amazonas*, Domingo Comín 08-65, basic. **F** pp *Wakis*, Orellana 08-52, with bath, best in town. Best restaurant is *Oro Verde*, near *Hotel Wakiz*, excellent food.

The Salesian mission at Bomboiza has a small museum. It's a six-hour walk to **Aguacate**, near which are precolumbian ruins; food and bed at Sr Jorge Guillermo Vázquez. Yumaza is a 40 minute walk, for more precolumbian ruins (two sites).

Bus to Cuenca, 1900, 2000 and 2100, 10 hours, US$6. Loja 0300 and 2200. Macas, 1800, 10 hours. *Rancheros* leave for Yantzaza in the morning, from where a bus reaches Zamora before dark (see Southern Sierra).

Sucúa to Cuenca Follow the same route to Limón. From here the road to Cuenca (132 km) passes through Gualaceo and Jadán. From Limón the road rises steeply with many breathtaking turns and the vegetation changes frequently, partly through cloud forest and then, at 4,000 m, through the *páramo*, before dropping very fast down to the valley of Gualaceo. There is a police checkpoint at Plan de Milagro, where foreigners have to register. There is nowhere to stay along the Limón-Gualaceo road.

Galápagos Islands

See first colour map, page 1565

A trip to the Galápagos Islands is an unforgettable experience. The islands are world-renowned for their fearless wildlife but no amount of hype can prepare the visitor for such a close encounter with nature. Here you can snorkel with penguins and sea-lions, and encounter the odd hammerhead shark, watch giant 200 kg tortoises lumbering through cactus forest and enjoy the courtship display of the blue-footed booby and magnificent frigate bird, all in startling close-up.

Lying on the Equator, 970 km west of the Ecuadorean coast, the Galápagos consist of six main islands (San Cristóbal, Santa Cruz, Isabela, Floreana, Santiago and Fernandina – the last two uninhabited); 12 smaller islands (Baltra and the uninhabited islands of Santa Fe, Pinzón, Española, Rábida, Daphne, Seymour, Genovesa, Marchena, Pinta, Darwin and Wolf) and over 40 islets. The islands have a total population of over 17,000 and because of immigration the annual growth rate is about 12%. The largest island, Isabela (formerly Albemarle), is 120 km long and forms half the total land area of the archipelago. Its notorious convict colony was closed in 1958; some 1,500 people live there now, mostly in and around Puerto Villamil, on the south coast. San Cristóbal (Chatham) has a population of 5,700 with the capital of the archipelago, Puerto Baquerizo Moreno. Santa Cruz (Indefatigable) has 10,000, with Puerto Ayora the main tourist centre; and Floreana (Charles) fewer than 90. The islands are widely scattered; by boat, Puerto Baquerizo Moreno and Puerto Ayora are six hours apart.

The islands are the peaks of gigantic undersea volcanoes, composed almost exclusively of basalt. Most of them rise from about 2,000 to 3,500 m above the surrounding seabed, but over 7,000 m above the deepest parts of the adjacent ocean floor to the west of Fernandina. The highest summit is Volcán Wolf on Isabela island, 1,660 m above sea level. Eruptions have taken place in historical times on Fernandina, Isabela, Pinta, Marchena and Santiago. The most active today are Fernandina, Isabela, Pinta and Marchena, and fumarolic activity may be seen intermittently on each of these islands. The islands are also very gradually drifting eastward, due to the movement of the tectonic plate on which they rest. Hence the oldest islands lie to the east, including San Cristóbal and Española which are approximately 3-3.5 million years old. The youngest islands, such as Fernandina and Isabela are in the west of the archipelago, and have been in existence for some 700,000 to 800,000 years.

Flora & fauna

The Galápagos have never been connected with the continent. Gradually, over many hundreds of thousands of years, animals and plants from over the sea somehow migrated there and as time went by they adapted themselves to Galápagos conditions and came to differ more and more from their continental ancestors. Thus many of them are unique: a quarter of the species of shore fish, half of the plants and almost all the reptiles are found nowhere else. In many cases different forms have evolved on the different islands. Charles Darwin recognized this speciation within the archipelago when he visited the Galápagos on the *Beagle* in 1835 and his observations played a substantial part in his formulation of the theory of evolution. Since no large land mammals reached the islands (until they were recently introduced by man), reptiles were dominant just as they had been all over the world in the very distant past. Another of the extraordinary features of the islands is the tameness of the animals. The islands were uninhabited when they were discovered in 1535 and the animals still have little instinctive fear of man.

The most spectacular species to be seen by the visitor are the **giant tortoise** (species still survive in six or seven of the islands, but mostly on Isabela); **marine iguana** (the only seagoing lizard in the world and found throughout most of the archipelago; it eats seaweed); **land iguana** (on Fernandina, Santa Cruz, Santa Fe, Isabela, Seymour and Plaza); **waved albatross** (which nests only on the island of Española – apart from several pairs on Isla de la Plata; it leaves in December and returns in late March-early April); **Galápagos hawk**, **red-footed**, **blue-footed** and **masked boobies**, **red-billed tropic-bird**, **frigate birds**, **swallow-tailed gulls**, **dusky lava gulls**, **flightless cormorants** (on Isabela and Fernandina), **mockingbirds**, 13 species of **Darwin's finches** (all endemic and the classic examples of speciation quoted by Darwin); the **Galápagos sea lion** (common in many areas) and the **Galápagos fur-seal** (on the more remote and rocky coasts).

The itineraries of tourist boats are strictly regulated in order to avoid crowding at the visitor sites and some sites are periodically closed by the park authorities in order to allow them to recover from the impact of tourism. Certain sites are only open to smaller boats, and additionally limited to a maximum number of visits per month. The most-visited islands from Puerto Ayora are Plaza Sur (an estimated 1,000 sea-lions living on 1 ha, land and sea iguana, many birds flying close to the cliff top), Santa Fe (land and sea iguanas, cactus forest, swimming with sea lions, Galápagos Hawk), Seymour Norte (sea lions, marine iguanas, swallow-tailed gulls, magnificent frigate birds, blue-footed boobies – the latter not close to the tourist trail), Rábida (sea lions, flamingos, pelican rookery), and Santiago (James Bay for fur seals, snorkelling with sea lions, migratory coastal birds; Sullivan Bay and Bartolomé Island for fantastic lava fields on the climb to the summit, fine views, snorkelling around Pinnacle Rock and maybe a few penguins). On a tour of these islands it may be possible to go also to Punto García on Isabela to see flightless cormorants (to climb Sierra Negra volcano to see the tortoises can be done on foot, horseback or by pickup – see page 1039). Daphne Island with very rich birdlife may be visited by some boats only once a month (a special permit is required).

More distant islands from Puerto Ayora, but visited from there or from Puerto Baquerizo Moreno, are Española (blue-footed boobies, masked boobies, waved albatross, many other birds, brightly coloured marine iguanas, sea-lions, snorkelling at Tortuga Islet), Genovesa (red-footed boobies – brown and white phase, masked boobies, swallow-tailed and lava gulls, frigate birds and many others, marine iguanas, snorkelling) and Floreana (flamingos, sea-lions, endemic plants, snorkelling at Corona del Diablo). There is a custom for visitors to Post Office Bay on the north side of Floreana since 1793 to place unstamped letters and cards in a

Ecuador

barrel, and deliver, free of charge, any addressed to their own destinations. Fernandina is best visited on longer cruises which include Isabela. For more details on Santa Cruz, San Cristóbal and Isabela, see below. Never miss the opportunity to go snorkelling, there is plenty of underwater life to see, including rays, sharks (not all dangerous) and many fish. All the other islands are closed to tourists.

Do not touch any of the animals, birds or plants. Do not transfer sand or soil from one island to another. Do not leave litter anywhere; it is highly undesirable in a national park and is a safety and health hazard for wildlife. Do not take raw food on to the islands.

Climate   The Galápagos climate can be divided into a hot season (Dec-May), when there is a possibility of heavy showers, and the cool or *garúa* (mist) season (Jun-Nov), when the days generally are more cloudy and there is often rain or drizzle. Jul and Aug can be windy, force 4 or 5. Daytime clothing should be lightweight. (Clothing generally, even on 'luxury cruises', should be casual and comfortable.) At night, however, particularly at sea and at higher altitudes, temperatures fall below 15°C and warm clothing is required. Boots and shoes soon wear out on the lava terrain. The sea is cold Jul-Oct; underwater visibility is best Jan-Mar. Ocean temperatures are usually higher to the east and lower at the western end of the archipelago. The islands climate and hence its wildlife are also influenced by the El Niño phenomenon. Despite all these variations, conditions are generally favourable for visiting Galápagos throughout the year.

Travel to   **By Air**   There are two airports which receive flights from mainland Ecuador, but no internathe islands   tional flights to Galápagos. The most frequently used airport is at Baltra (South Seymour), across a narrow strait from Santa Cruz, the other at Puerto Baquerizo Moreno, on San Cristóbal. The two islands are 96 km apart and on most days there are local flights in light aircraft between them, as well as to Puerto Villamil on Isabela. There is also irregular boat service between Puerto Ayora, Puerto Baquerizo Moreno, Puerto Villamil and Floreana.

   At present only TAME is operating flights to Galápagos (2 daily to Baltra and 2 a week to San Cristóbal), although it was hoped that additional services will be added. All flights originate in Quito and make a long stopover in Guayaquil. The return fare in high season (1 Nov to 30 Apr and 15 Jun to 14 Sep) is US$390 from Quito (US$345 from Guayaquil). The low season fare costs US$334 from Quito, and US$300 from Guayaquil. The same prices apply regardless of whether you fly to San Cristóbal or Baltra; you can arrive at one and return from the other. The ticket is valid for 21 days from the date of departure. Independent travellers must get their bording pass (*pre-chequeo*) for outward and return flights 2 days before departure. This is especially critical during high season and from San Cristóbal at all times.

   The above prices are subject to change without notice. Discount fares for Ecuadorean nationals and residents of Galápagos are not available to foreigners and these rules are strictly enforced. A 15% discount off the high season fare may be available to students with an ISIC card; details from *TAME* office at Edif Pichincha, p 4, Amazonas y Colón, Quito.

   Boat owners make block bookings with the airlines in the hope of filling their boat. Visitors may buy tickets where they like, but in the busy season will have to take the ticket to the tour operator for the reservation. Tickets are the same price everywhere, except for student discounts with *TAME* as above.

   Airport transfer   Two buses meet flights from the mainland at Baltra: one runs to the port or *muelle* (10 mins, no charge) where the cruise boats wait; the other goes to Canal de Itabaca, the narrow channel which separates Baltra from Santa Cruz. It is 15 mins to the Canal, free, then you cross on a small ferry for US$0.70, another bus waits on the Santa Cruz side to take you to Puerto Ayora in 45 mins, U$1.50. If you arrive at Baltra on one of the local inter-island flights (see below) then you have to wait until the next flight from the mainland for bus service, or you might be able to hire a taxi. The airport in Puerto Baquerizo Moreno is within walking distance of the town, but those on prearranged tours will be met.

By Sea In 2002, the small cargo vessels which sail from Guayaquil to Galápagos were not permitted to carry passengers.

Taxes Every foreign visitor has to pay a **national park Tax of US$100** on arrival, cash only. Be sure to have your passport on hand. Do not lose your park tax receipt; boat captains need to record it. A 50% reduction on the national park fee is available to children under 12, but only those foreigners who are enrolled in an Ecuadorean university are entitled to the reduced fee for students.

Travel between the islands *Emetebe Avionetas* offers inter-island flights in two light twin-engine aircraft (a 5-seater and a 9-seater). There is no firm schedule but flights usually operate Mon-Sat in the morning between Puerto Baquerizo Moreno (**San Cristóbal**), **Baltra** and Puerto Villamil (**Isabela**), depending on passenger demand. Baggage allowance 30 lbs, strictly enforced. Fares range from US$90 to US$120 one way, including taxes; charter rates from US$400 to US$500 per hr. *Emetebe* offices in Puerto Baquerizo Moreno, Puerto Ayora and Puerto Villamil are given in the corresponding sections below. In Guayaquil T229 2492, emetebe@ecua.net.ec

Fibras (fiberglass motor launches) operate most days between Pto Ayora (Santa Cruz), Pto Villamil (**Isabela**), and Pto Baquerizo Moreno (**San Cristóbal**), US$25-30 one way, check at the Capitanía de Puerto. The *Galamar*, sails from Puerto Baquerizo Moreno to **Puerto Ayora** on Mon, Wed and Fri, returning on Tue, Thu and Sat, 5 hrs, US$30 one way; this boat can also be chartered for trips to **Floreana** for US$400, and **Isabela** US$500. These schedules are subject to change. There is also irregular boat service from Puerto Ayora to **Floreana**; check at the Capitanía de Puerto. You must be flexible in your itinerary and allow plenty of time if you wish to travel between islands in this way.

Cruising around the islands There are two ways to travel around the islands: a *tour navegable*, where you sleep on the boat, or less expensive tours where you sleep ashore at night and travel during the day. On the former you travel at night, arriving at a new landing site each day, with more time ashore. On the latter you spend less time ashore and the boats are smaller with a tendency to overcrowding in high

Ecuador

Ecuador

season. Prices are no longer significantly cheaper in the low season, but you will have more options available. See Arranging a tour from the islands.

Itineraries are controlled by the national park to distribute tourism evenly throughout the islands. Boats are expected to be on certain islands on certain days. They can cut landings, but have to get special permission to add to a planned itinerary.

Choosing a tour

The less expensive boats are normally smaller and less powerful so you see less and spend more time travelling, also the guiding is likely to be in Spanish only (there are some exceptions to this). The more expensive boats will probably have 110 volts, a/c and private baths, all of which can be nice, but not critically important. All boats have to conform to certain minimum safety standards (check that there are enough liferafts) and have VHF radio, but the rules tend to be quite arbitrary. A watermaker can make quite a difference as the town water from Puerto Ayora or Puerto Baquerizo Moreno should not be drunk. **NB** Boats with over 18 passengers take quite a time to disembark and re-embark people, while the smaller boats have a more lively motion, which is important if you are prone to seasickness.

The least expensive boats (called economy class) cost about US$60 per day. For around US$80-100 per day (tourist class) you will also be on a faster small boat, leaving more time to spend ashore. US$150 per day ('superior tourist' or first class) is the price of the majority of better boats, most with English guiding. Over US$200 per day is entering the luxury bracket, with English guiding the norm, far more comfortable cabins and a superior level of service and cuisine. No boat may sail without a park-trained guide.

Booking a tour

Check the internet. There are many sites from which to book a Galápagos cruise, and prices may be lower

If wishing to plan everything ahead of time, there are many good tour operators. In Britain, David Horwell, arranges tailor-made tours to Ecuador and the Galápagos islands. For further details write to him at *Galápagos Adventure Tours*, 79 Maltings Place, 169 Tower Bridge Rd, London SE1 3LJ, T020-7407 1478, F020-7407 0397, www.galapagos.co.uk Also recommended is *Penelope Kellie*, T01962-779317, F01962-779458, pkellie@yachtors.u-net.com who is the UK agent for *Quasar Nautica* (see below). *Galápagos Classic Cruises,* 6 Keyes Rd, London NW2 3XA, T020-8933 0613, F020-8452 5248, galapagoscruises@compuserve.com Specialize in tailor-made cruises and diving holidays to the islands with additional land tours to Ecuador and Peru available on request. In the USA, *Galápagos Network*, see Ecoventura, Tour operators, Quito. *Wilderness Travel* (801 Allston Way, Berkeley, CA 94710, T1-800-368 2704) and *Inca Floats* (Bill Robertson, 1311 63rd St, Emeryville, CA 94608) have been recommended. Try also *International Expeditions*, One Environs Park, Helena, Alabama, 35080, T205-428 1700, T1-800-633 4734, www.ietravel.com In addition: *Galápagos Holidays*, 14 Prince Arthur Av, Suite 109, Toronto, Ontario M5R 1A9, T416-413 9090, T1-800-661 2512, info@galapagosholidays.com

Shopping around the agencies in Quito is a good way of securing a value-for-money cruise, but best if you can deal with the boat owner, or his/her representative, rather than someone operating on commission. It is worth asking if the owner has one to three spaces to fill on a cruise that leaves in a few days; you can often get them at a **discount**. A much simpler way is to email or fax from home to an agency which acts as a broker for the cruise ships. The broker can recommend a vessel which suits your requirements. Allow about two months for arrangements to be made. Recommended are *Safari*, and *Angermeyer's Enchanted Expeditions*. Full contact details of both under Quito, Tour operators.

Arranging a tour from the islands

If you wish to wait until you reach the islands, Puerto Ayora is the only practical place for arranging a cruise. Here you may find slightly better prices than the mainland, especially at the last minute, but bear in mind that you could be faced with a long wait. In the high season (Jul, Aug, and mid-Dec to mid-Jan) there is no space available on a last-minute basis, so at these times of the year you must purchase your cruise before arriving in Galápagos.

To arrange last-minute tours, a highly recommended contact is the *Moonrise* travel agency. There are also several others, including *Galasam*, in Puerto Ayora who offer this service (see Puerto Ayora, below). Especially on cheaper boats, check carefully about what is and is not included (eg drinking water, snorkelling equipment, etc).

Ecuador

Agencies & boats

With nearly 100 boats operating in the islands, we cannot give them all. We list those for which we have received positive recommendations. Exclusion does not imply poor service

For addresses not listed here, see Quito, Tour Operators page 914, many of the following also have offices in Guayaquil). *Angermeyer's Enchanted Expeditions* have been recommended for their professional, well-organized cruise on the *Beluga*, good English-speaking guide, lots of good food, worth the expense. They also operate the *Cachalote*, which is also recommended. *Ecoventura*, Almagro N31-80 y Whymper, T/F223 1034, www.ecoventura.com Excellent cruises and diving tours in luxury motor yachts, *Eric*, *Flamingo*, *Letty*, *Skydancer* and the 48-passenger *Corinthian*, highly recommended; USA office *GalápagosNetwork*, see above. *Etnotur*, Luis Cordero 1313 y J L Mera, T223 0552, F250 2682, www.etnoturecuador.com Helpful, English and German spoken, operate Galápagos cruises with first class sailboats and a catamaran. *Galacruises Expeditions*, Jorge Washington 748b, Av Amazonas y 9 de Octubre, T/F556036, www.galapagosseaman.com.ec Owners of the *Sea Man* Yacht, offer diving and nature cruises.

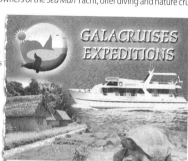

The Galápagos Boat Company, Calama 980, T222 0426, admin@safari.com.ec Broker for up to 80 boats in the islands, purchase in Quito for last minute prices. *Galasam Galapagos Tours*, Cordero 1354 y Amazonas, T250 7080, F256 7662, www.galasam.com, also 9 de Octubre 424, Gran Pasaje Building, of 9, Guayaquil, T2304488, F2311485, www.galapagos-islands.com Good value Galápagos tours in their fleet of 10-16 passenger motor yachts, ranging from the luxury *Millenium, to tourist class vessels*, discounts to *South American Handbook* owners. For representatives abroad see www.galasam.com *Galextur*, Portugal 600 y Av 6 de Diciembre, T/F226 9626, www.hotelangermeyer.com Recommended for good service, operate the *Santa Fe II*. *Metropolitan Touring* (represented in the USA by *Adventure Associates*, 13150 Coit Rd, Suite 110, Dallas, Texas 75240, T214-907 0414, F783 1286) offers 7-night cruises on the MV *Santa Cruz* (90 passengers), very professional service, with multilingual guides, also the *Isabella II*. They also use *Yate Encantada* and *Delfín II*, and have yachts for private charters (eg Ecuacruceros' *Rachel III* and *Diamante*) and can arrange tours on a number of boats of all types, from 8 to 34 passengers. Metropolitan can also arrange scuba diving trips. Bookings can also be made for the *Reina Silvia*, owned by Rolf Sievers, who also owns the *Delfín Hotel* in Puerto Ayora. This vessel makes daily sailings, returning to the hotel each night, but its speed means that the day trips are worthwhile and comfortable, recommended. *Islas Galápagos Turismo y Vapores*, República de El Salvador N36-43 y Suecia, T245 1522, F243 9888, www.ambasadorcruises.com Offers cruises aboard *Ambasador 1*. *Quasar Nautica*, Montúfar E15-14 y La Cumbre, Bellavista, T2463660, F243 6625, www.quasarnautica.com (USA T305-5999008, F305-5927060, UK representative, T01962 779317, F01962 779458), 7-10 day naturalist and diving cruises on 8-16 berth luxury sail and power yachts with multilingual guides. Also a 48-passenger vessel, the *Eclipse*. Highly recommended. *Andando Tours*, Coruña N26-311, T525727, F228519, www.andandotours.com Operate the sailing brigantine *Andando*, her sister ship, the *Sagitta*, and the motor trawler *Samba*, consistently high recommendations, personal service. *Rolf Wittmer Turismo*, Foch E7-81 y Almagro, 252 6938, F222 8520, www.rwittmer.com Rolf Wittmer, son of Margaret Wittmer of the famous 1930s Galápagos Affair, owns and runs *Tiptop II* and *III*, no snorkelling equipment. *Klein Tours* operate *Galapagos Legend*, new in 2002, excellent. *Canodros* operates the large and luxurious *Galápagos Explorer*.

In addition, *Andes Explorer*, www.galapagosislandstours.com, see Quito, Tour operators.

Other recommendations: *Georgina and Agustín Cruz*'s *Beagle III*, friendly, good cooking (book through *Metropolitan Touring*) and the motor yacht *Orca* (*Etnotours*, see Quito, Tour operators).

The sailing catamaran *Pulsar* is recommended, US$58 per day, but best when the owner Patric is on board; run by *Galaptur* (JL Mera 358 y Robles, Quito, T222 6432, F256 7622, www.galapagostour.com).

Good service on the *Golondrina* (*Golondrina Turismo*, JL Mera 689 y Carrión, Quito, T252 8570, F252 8570). *Isla Galápagos* is recommended; the guide is *Peter Freire*, good, fair English. *Lobo del Mar* (12 passengers); *Daphne* (8 – good cook); *Stella Maris* (book through *Moonrise Travel*) and *San Antonio* (12 – good food, nice crew). *Santa Fe II*, owned by *Byron Rueda*, T05-526593.

Ecuador

Ecuador

It must be stressed that a boat is only as good as its crew and when the staff change, so will these recommendations. *South American Explorers* in Quito has an extensive file of trip reports for members to consult and *Safari*, Quito, tries to keep abreast of all new developments.

Legitimate complaints may be made to any or all of the following: the **Jefe de Turismo** at the national park office in Puerto Ayora, the **Ministerio de Turismo** office or the **Capitanía de Puerto**. Any 'tour navegable' will include the days of arrival and departure as full days. Insist on a written itinerary or contract prior to departure as any effort not to provide this probably indicates problems later. *South American Explorers* has produced a useful, brief guide to the Galápagos which includes a specimen contract for itinerary and living conditions.

General advice **Tipping** A ship's crew and guides are usually tipped separately. The amount is a very personal matter; you may be guided by suggestions made onboard or in the agency's brochures, but the key factors should always be the quality of service received.

If you have problems See above for complaints regarding itineraries. If a crew member comes on strongly to a woman passenger, the matter should first be raised with the guide or captain. If this does not yield results, a formal complaint, in Spanish, giving the crew member's full name, the boat's name and the date of the cruise, should be sent to **Sr Capitán del Puerto**, Base Militar de Armada Ecuatoriana, Puerto Ayora, Santa Cruz, Galápagos. Failure to report such behaviour will mean it will continue. To avoid pilfering, never leave belongings unattended in Puerto Ayora, or on a beach when another boat is in the bay.

What to take A remedy for seasickness is recommended; the waters south of Santa Cruz are particularly choppy. A good supply of sun block and skin cream to prevent windburn and chapped lips is essential, as are a hat and sunglasses. You should be prepared for dry and wet landings, the latter involving wading ashore. Take plenty of film with you; the birds are so tame that you will use far more than you expected; a telephoto lens is not essential, but if you have one, bring it. Also take filters suitable for strong sunlight. Snorkelling equipment is particularly useful as much of the sea-life is only visible under water. Most of the cheaper boats do not provide equipment and those that do may not have good snorkelling gear. If in doubt, bring your own, rent in Puerto Ayora, or buy it in Quito. It is possible to sell it afterwards on the islands.

The cost of living The cost of living in the Galápagos is higher than the mainland, particularly in the peak season (Dec, Jul and Aug). Most food has to be imported although certain meats, fish, vegetables and fruit are available locally in the Puerto Ayora market. Bottled drinks are expensive, beer US$1-3.

Puerto Ayora

Phone code: 05
Population:
approximately 10,000

In 1959, the centenary of the publication of Darwin's *Origin of Species*, the Government of Ecuador and the International Charles Darwin Foundation established, with the support of UNESCO, the Charles Darwin Research Station at Academy Bay 1½ km from Puerto Ayora, Santa Cruz, the most central of the Galápagos islands. A visit to the station is a good introduction to the islands as it provides a lot of information. Collections of several of the rare sub-species of giant tortoise are maintained on the station as breeding nuclei, together with tortoise-rearing pens for the young. The Darwin Foundation staff will help bona fide students of the fauna to plan an itinerary, if they stay some time and hire a boat. See their website for more information, page 1040. ■ *Mon-Fri 0700-1300, 1400-1600, Sat 0700-1300.*

The *Ministerio de Turismo/CAPTURGAL* tourist office is on Av Charles Darwin by south end of Pelican Bay, T526174, cptg@pa.ga.pro.ec ■ *Mon-Fri 0800-1200, 1500-1600. Information also available at the boat owners' co-operative office nearby.*

Excursions on Santa Cruz One of the most beautiful beaches in the Galápagos islands is at **Tortuga Bay**, a one hour walk (five km) west from Puerto Ayora on a marked and cobbled path. Start at the west end of C Charles Binford; further on there is a gate where you must register, open 0600-1830 daily. The sunsets here are excellent. Take drinking water and do not go alone (occasional incidents have been reported). Also take care of the very strong undertow, the surf is calmer on the next cove to the west.

Hike to the higher parts of the island called **Media Luna, Puntudo** and **Cerro Crocker**. The trail starts at Bellavista, 7 km from Puerto Ayora. A round trip from Bellavista is 4-8 hours, depending on the distance hiked, 10-18 km (permit and guide not required, but a guide is advisable). Take water, sun block and long-sleeved shirt and long trousers to protect against razor grass. *La Choza* and *Parilladas San Luis* in Bellavista serve *parrilladas* on Sunday.

To see giant tortoises in the wild, go to the Butterfly ranch (**Hacienda Mariposa**) beyond Bellavista on the road to Santa Rosa (the bus passes the turn-off), only in the dry season; in the wet season the tortoises are breeding down in the arid zone. Vermillion flycatchers can also be seen here. ■ *Entry US$3, includes cup of hierba luisa tea, or juice; lunch can be arranged.*

There are several natural tunnels (**lava tubes**): one 3 km from Puerto Ayora on the road to Bellavista, unsigned on the left, look for the black-and-white posts (tread carefully); barn owls may be seen here. Two more are 1 km from Bellavista; on private land, US$1.50 to enter, bring torch or pay for one – it takes about 30 mins to walk through the tunnels. Ask for Bolívar at *Pensión Gloria*, his ex-wife's family have lands with lava caves, a *mirador* and other attractions.

Hike to the **Chato Tortoise Reserve**, 7 km; the trail starts at Santa Rosa, 22 km from Puerto Ayora. Horses can be hired at Santa Rosa. Again ask for Bolívar at *Pensión Gloria*, he charges $15 pp, minimum 4 persons, for a highland tour. A round trip takes one day. The Puerto Ayora-Bellavista bus stops at the turnoff for the track for the reserve (US$0.95). It's a hot walk; take food and drink. From Santa Rosa, distance to different sites within the reserve is 6-8 km (permit and guide not required). To walk to the Reserve from Santa Rosa, turn left past the school, follow the track at the edge of fields for 40 minutes, turn right at the memorial to the Israeli, 20 minutes later turn left down a track to Chato Trucha.

Two sinkholes, **Los Gemelos**, straddle the road to Baltra, beyond Santa Rosa; if you are lucky, take a *camioneta* all the way, otherwise to Santa Rosa, then walk. A good place to see the Galápagos hawk and barn owl.

The highlands and settlement area of Santa Cruz are worth seeing for the contrast of the vegetation with the arid coastal zones. Ask for Tim Grey and Anita Salcedo at *Garapata* in Puerto Ayora, they have the *Altair finca* for arranging barbecues.

To Santa Rosa and Bellavista From San Francisco school in Puerto Ayora, 3 daily buses leave for Santa Rosa and Bellavista, 30 min trip, return immediately; fare for all destinations US$0.40. There are also charters with *Coop Citeg*; also trucks (cheaper). On roads to the main sites hitching is easy but expect to pay a small fee.

Transport

L *Delfín*, On a small bay south of Puerto Ayora, accessible only by boat, T526297, F526283. Restaurant, pool, lovely beach, bar, good service, comfortable rooms. Book through Metropolitan Touring in Quito. **L** *Galápagos*, Darwin and Station entrance, T526292, jack@hotelgalapagos.com Restaurant with fixed menu, ocean-view, fruit and meat from hotel farm, day excursions, also Scuba Iguana. **AL** *Angermeyer*, Darwin y Piqueros, T526277, F526066. Includes breakfast, pool, meals available, tours, diving. **AL** *Fernandina*, 12 de Noviembre y Los Piqueros, T526499, F526122. Includes breakfast, restaurant, pool (open weekends to non guests), jacuzzi. **AL** *Red Mangrove Inn*, Darwin y las Fragatas, on the way to the research station, T527011, www.redmangrove.com Restaurant, jacuzzi, deck bar, Owner Polo Navaro offers day tours and diving. Warmly recommended. **A** *Las Ninfas*, Los Colonos y Berlanga, T526127, F526128. Includes breakfast, good restaurant, full range of services, has its own boat at reasonable price for day trips and Fernando Ortiz is helpful with arrangements. **A-B** *Sol y Mar*, Darwin y Binford, T526281, F527015. Variety of rooms in different categories. **B** *Castro*, Los Colonos y Malecón, T526113, F526508. Restaurant, cold water, fan, a/c $10 extra, owner Miguel Castro arranges tours, he is an authority on wildlife. Recommended. **B** *Palmeras*, Berlanga y Naveda, T526139, F526373. Restaurant, a/c, pool, good

Sleeping
Hotel space at the upper end of the market is limited and reservations are strongly recommended in high season

Ecuador

value. **C** *Estrella de Mar*, Darwin y 12 de Febrero, T526427, F526080. Fan, spacious rooms (more expensive with sea view), communal sitting area. **C** *Gran Hotel Fiesta*, Brito y Las Ninfas, T/F526440, fiestur@pi.pro.ec Restaurant, a/c, cheaper with fan, a 5-min walk inland from the seafront, hammocks, quiet, reasonable value but a bit remote. **D** *Flamingo*, Berlanga y Naveda, T/F526556. Fan, decent, hot. **D** *Lirio del Mar*, Naveda y Berlanga, T526212. Cafetería, pleasant, fan, good value. **D** *Lobo de Mar*, 12 de Febrero y Darwin, T526188, F526569. Modern. **D** *Los Amigos*, Darwin y 12 de Febrero, T526265. Shared bath, cool, reasonable, airy rooms (upstairs best). Recommended. **D** *New Elizabeth*, Darwin y Berlanga, T/F526178. Reasonable, owner very helpful. **D** *Salinas*, Naveda y Berlanga, T526107, F526072. Restaurant, with bath and fan, good value. **D** *Sir Francis Drake*, Herrera y Binford, T526221. Fan, good. **D-E** *Peregrina*, Darwin e Indefatigable, T526323. Including good breakfast, a/c, cheaper with fan, Highly recommended. **E** *Darwin*, Herrera y Binford, T526193. OK. Recommended but don't leave valuables in your room.

For **longer stays** there are houses for rent for US$15 pp per day. Enquire at *Moonrise Travel*.

Eating	*Salvavidas*, right on the seafront overlooking the activity at the pier. Good set lunch, good
These restaurants are on the main street unless mentioned otherwise, starting at the dock and moving north towards the Darwin Station	breakfast, seafood, hamburgers. *Santa Fe*, overlooking the bay. Bar and grill, popular. *Cucuve*. Traditional snacks like *humitas* and *tamales*. *Sabrosón*, above *Hotel Palmeras*, open air grill. OK food, nice decor. *Happy Tummy*, opposite the Capitanía de Puerto. Varied menu, good, open late even Sun. *Rincón del Alma*, north of the harbour. Good food, reasonable prices. *Limón y Café*, corner 12 de Febrero. Good snacks and drinks, lots of music, pool table, open evenings only, popular. *La Garrapata*, north of TAME, next to *La Panga* disco. Considered as the best food in town, attractive setting and good music, open morning and evening but not Sun, drinks expensive. *New Island*, by Charles Binford, near *Moonrise Travel*. Breakfast, fruit juices, seafood, ceviches. *Chocolate Galápagos*, opposite *Banco del Pacífico*. Good snacks, burgers, raclette. *Spondylus*, north of Indefatigable. Regional, Italian and international. Recommended. *Tikki Taka*, for breakfast, good bread, expensive. *Capricho*, by the tortoise roundabout. Good vegetarian food, salads and juices, breakfast. Recommended. *Media Luna*, near corner Los Piqueros. Good, pizza, also sandwiches, excellent brownies, open evenings only. *Viña del Mar*. Padre J Herrera. Popular with locals. Along Charles Binford, near Padre J Herrera are a series of kiosks selling traditional food at economic prices; *Tía Juanita* cooks well, seafood.

Bars & nightclubs *La Panga*, Av Charles Darwin y Berlanga and *Five Fingers*, Av Charles Darwin opposite the Capitanía de Puerto, are popular bar/discos. *Galapasón* is a popular salsa bar at the tortoise roundabout. *Salsa 10*, on Naveda, good latin music. *Café Bong*, above *La Panga*, popular rooftop hangout.

Shopping Most basic foodstuffs generally can be purchased on the islands, but cost more than on the mainland. The *Proinsular* supermarket opposite the pier is the best place (try their delicious locally-made yoghurt drink). The *mercado municipal* is on Padre J Herrera, beyond the telephone office, on the way out of town to Santa Rosa. Medicines, sun lotions, mosquito coils, film, and other useful items all cost more than on the mainland and at times might not be available. *Galapaguito* can meet most tourists' needs, the owners are very helpful. There is a wide variety of T-shirt and souvenir shops along the length of Av Charles Darwin. Do not buy items made of black coral as it is an endangered species

Sport	**Bicycling** Mountain bikes can be hired from travel agencies in town, US$8-16 per day; or at
Please help to maintain standards by not disturbing or touching underwater wildlife	the *Red Mangrove Inn*, US$5 per hr. *Galápagos Tour Center*, T526245, runs cycling tours in the highlands, US$16 per day.
	Diving There are several diving agencies in Puerto Ayora, they offer courses, equipment rental, dives within Academy Bay (2 dives for US$75-80), dives to other central islands (2 dives, US$110-120), daily tours for 1 week in the central islands (12 dives, US$1,260) and several day live-aboard tours (1 week tour of central islands US$1,960). There is a hyperbaric chamber in Puerto Ayora to treat divers in case of decompression sickness. Ask dive operators if they are affiliated with a plan that allows their clients to use the chamber in case of

Ecuador

emergency. Treatment is expensive, but it is much more so if the operator is not affiliated. Two agencies that offer all services and have been repeatedly recommended are: *Galápagos Sub-Aqua*, Av Charles Darwin by Pelican Bay (Quito: Pinto 439 y Amazonas, office 101, T256 5294, F290 9270; Guayaquil: Dátiles 506 y Sexta, T230 4132, F231 4510), www.galapagos-sub-aqua.com.ec Instructor Fernando Zambrano offers full certificate courses up to divemaster level (PADI or NAUI). Open 0800-1200 and 1430-1830. *Scuba Iguana*, at the *Hotel Galápagos*, T526296, T/F526330, www.scuba-iguana.com (Quito: *Scala Tours*, Foch 746 y Amazonas, T254 5856, F225 8655). Run by Jack Nelson and Mathias Espinosa, who are both experienced and knowledgeable about different sites. Mathias offers full certificate courses up to instructor level. Open 0730-1900. Divers must have their certificates and log books and can expect to be asked to do a test dive in the bay before going to more advanced sites. Making arrangements in advance, you can be met by a divemaster during a regular Galápagos cruise, you dive while your companions do a land visit.

Horse riding For horse riding at ranches in the highlands, enquire at *Moonrise Travel*.

Kayaking & Windsurfing Equipment rental and tours available from the *Red Mangrove Inn*, US$10 per hr.

Snorkelling Masks, snorkels and fins can be rented from travel agencies and dive shops, US$4-5 a day, US$60 deposit. Some bay tours include snorkelling. A full day snorkelling tour with *Scuba Iguana* is US$35 including equipment, wet suit and lunch. The closest place to snorkel is by the beaches near the Darwin Station.

Surfing There is surfing at Tortuga Bay (see Excursions) and at other more distant beaches accessed by boat. **NB** There is better surfing near Puerto Baquerizo Moreno on San Cristóbal. *Galápagos Tour Center* rents surfboards US$10 per day and organizes surfing tours, US$55 and up. Vladimir Palma is a local surfer who can be found at *Discovery* or *Galapasón* bar.

Tour operators

Moonrise Travel, Av Charles Darwin, opposite *Banco del Pacífico*, T526348, T/F526403. Last minute cruise bookings, day tours to different islands, bay tours, highland tours, airline reservations. Knowledgeable, helpful and reliable. *Galasam*, Padre J Herrera y Pelícano, near the port, T/F526126, heparton@ayora.ecua.net.ec Last minute tours, tickets for boat to Isabela. Helpful and friendly. *Sr Victor López*, at Ferretería Academy Bay, Padre J Herrera, opposite the hospital, T526136. Runs economical tours on the *Elizabeth*, very cheap. *Galápagos Tour Center*, Padre J Herrera, opposite the hospital, T526245. Bicycle rentals and tours, surfboards, snorkelling gear, motorcycle and jeep rentals. Run by Victor Vaca who speaks several languages and arranges last minute tours. There are several agencies along Av Charles Darwin on the block opposite the Capitanía de Puerto offering the full range of tours. Among them: *Enchantours*, T526657, also rents snorkeling gear; *Galápagos Cruises 2000*, T526097, in the same premises, they are agents for *DHL* courier and *Western Union*.

Directory

Banks *Banco del Pacífico*, Av Charles Darwin, open 0800-1530, US$5 for TCs, ATM for MasterCard only, cash on Visa over the counter. **Communications** Internet: US$5-6 per hr. *Galapagos.Com*, Av Charles Darwin. *Casvernet*, Pelican Bay, near the tortoise roundabout. *Shark.Net*, Av Charles Darwin y 12 de Febrero. **Post Office:** the Post Office sometimes runs out of stamps (never leave money and letters), ask in the 'red boat' (*Galería Johanna*) or *Artesanías Bambú*. **Telephone:** *Pacifictel* on Padre Herrera. No collect or country-direct calls can be made from here. **Embassies and consulates** British Consul, David Balfour, c/o Etica, Barrio Estrada, Puerto Ayora. **Language schools** *Islas Galápagos Spanish Language Center*, Roberto Schiess 22 y 12 de Noviembre, www.islas-galapagos.com **Laundry** *Lavagal*, by football stadium, machine wash and dry US$1.50 per kg, good, reliable, US$1 taxi ride from town. *Mary* opposite bank, US$1 per kg. **Medical services** Hospitals: there is a hospital on Padre Herrera; consultations US$10, medicines reasonably priced, but they cannot perform operations. **Dr Hugo A Darquea**, Barrio El Edén, T526496, speaks English. Recommended. **Useful services** Immigration: Only the immigration police in Puerto Baquerizo Moreno (San Cristóbal) can extend tourist visas.

Ecuador

Puerto Baquerizo Moreno

Population: 3,023 Puerto Baquerizo Moreno, on San Cristóbal island to the east, is the capital of the archipelago. The island is being developed as a second tourist centre. It is a pleasant place to spend a few days, with interesting excursions in the area. To the north of town, opposite Playa Mann, is the Parque Nacional Galápagos' visitor centre or **Centro de Interpretación**. It has an excellent display of the natural and human history of the islands. Highly recommended. ■ *Mon-Fri 0700-1200, 1300-1700, Sat 0730-1300, 1330-1730, Sun 0730-1200, 1300-1700, free, T520138.* In town, the cathedral, on Av Northía, has interesting mixed-media relief pictures on the walls and altar. Next door is a small museum of natural history with stuffed exhibits, old photos and a tortoise called Pepe. ■ *Mon-Sat 0930-1200, 1530-1730, US$1, ring bell.* Paintings with Galápagos motifs can be bought from the following artists: *Arni Creaciones*, Av Quito y Juan José Flores, near *Pacifictel.* Humberto Muñoz, very nice work. Recommended. *Fabo Galería de Arte*, Malecón Charles Darwin, opposite the whale statue. Paintings by the owner Fabián, silk screened T-shirts. Do not buy black coral. ■ *For transport, see Travel Between the Islands. Be warned that it can take several days to find room on a boat to Puerto Ayora.*

Excursions on San Cristóbal A good trail goes from the Centro de Interpretación (see above) to the northeast through scrub forest to **Cerro Tijeretas**, a hill overlooking town and the ocean, 30 minutes away (take water). To go back, if you take the trail which follows the coast, you will end up at **Playa Punta Carola,** a popular surfing beach, too rough for swimming. There are four buses a day inland from Puerto Baquerizo Moreno to **El Progreso** (6 km, 15 minutes, US$0.15), then it's a 2½ hour walk to El Junco lake, the largest body of fresh water in Galápagos. There are also frequent pickup trucks to El Progreso (US$1), or you can hire a pickup in Puerto Baquerizo Moreno for touring: US$15 to El Junco, US$35 continuing to the beaches at Puerto Chino on the other side of the island, past a planned tortoise reserve. Prices are return and include waiting. At El Junco there is a path to walk around the lake in 20 minutes; lovely views but it can be cold and rainy. In El Progreso is *La Casa del Ceibo*, a tree house, for rent, and there are some eating places. Another road from El Progreso continues to **La Soledad**, with a *mirador* overlooking the different types of vegetation stretching to the coast. There are two buses to La Soledad, on Sundays only. From El Progreso a trail also crosses the highlands to **Cerro Brujo** and **Hobbs Bay**, and also to **Stephens Bay**, past some lakes. **NB** Always take food and plenty of water when hiking on your own on San Cristóbal. There are many crisscrossing animal trails and it is easy to get lost. Also watch out for the large-spined opuntia cactus and the poisonwood tree (manzanillo), which can cause severe skin reactions.

Boats go to **Puerto Ochoa**, 15 minutes, for the beach; to **Punta Pitt** in the far north where you can see all three boobies (US$65 for tour). Off the northwest coast is **Kicker Rock** (León Dormido), the basalt remains of a crater; many seabirds, including masked and blue-footed boobies, can be seen around its cliffs (five hour trip, including snorkelling, recommended, US$35). Up the coast is **Cerro Brujo beach** with sea lions, birds, crabs (none in any abundance). Raul Sánchez offers short trips on his boat *Ana Mercedes*, ending in Puerto Ayora, much time spent travelling, T529163. Española (Hood) is within day trip reach.

Sleeping **B** *Islas Galápagos*, Esmeraldas y Colón, T520203, F520162. A/c, a bit run down. **B** *Northía*, Northía y 12 de Febrero, T/F520041. Includes breakfast, a/c, pleasant but pricey. **B** *Orca*, Playa de Oro, T/F520233. A/c, fridge, good food, often filled with groups, has its own boat for cruises. **C** *Cabañas Don Jorge*, above Playa Mann, T520208. Fan, simple cabins in a quiet setting overlooking the ocean, meals available. **C** *Chatham*, Northía y Av de la Armada Nacional, on the road to the airport, T520137. Includes breakfast, fan, meals on request. **C** *Mar Azul*, Northía y Esmeraldas, T520139, F520384. Fan, on the road to the airport, nice gardens, good value. Highly recommended. **D** *Flamingo*, Hernández y Av Quito, T520204.

Ecuador

Cold water, basic. **D** *Los Cactus*, Juan José Flores y Av Quito, T520078. Near Pacifictel, family run. **D** *San Francisco*, Malecón Charles Darwin y Villamil, T520304. Cold water, fan, rooms in front are nicer, simple, good.

There are several restaurants by the intersection of Ignacio de Hernández y General Villamil, including: *Rosita*. Set meals and varied à la carte menu, very good. *Barracuda*. Grilled meat, fish, and *menestras*, cheap. *Pizzería Bambú*. Good economical set meals and pricey pizza and à la carte dishes. *Sabor Latino*, Hernández y Manuel J Cobos. Good set meals, busy at lunch. *La Playa*, Av de la Armada Nacional, by the navy base. Nice location, popular. *Miconia*, Darwin e Isabela. Varied menu, meat, fish, pizza, Italian. *Albacora*, Av Northía y Española. Good set meals, cheap. *Casa Blanca*, Malecón by the whale statue. Breakfast, ceviches, snacks, grill at weekends, closed Mon. *Genoa*, Malecón Charles Darwin by Post office. A la carte, evenings only, music, good atmosphere, popular with surfers. *Galapaluz*, Malecón Charles Darwin y Manuel J Cobos. Snacks, coffee, drinks. *Panadería Fragata*, Northía y Rocafuerte. Excellent bread and pastries, good selection.

Eating

El Barquero, Hernández y Manuel J Cobos. Bar and *peña*, open daily. *Blue Bay* and *Neptuno*, both at Malecón Charles Darwin y Herman Melville, opposite the whale and opposite each other. Discos, young crowd, open Tue-Sat 2030-0300. *La Terraza*, at bottom of Manuel J Cobos, by the waterfront. Disco, large dance floor.

Bars & nightclubs

Chalo's Tours, T520953, variety of tours and, with Gustavo Hernández (T520526), operates diving, US$75 per day for 2 people but not always available; also rents surf boards, snorkelling equipment and mountain bikes.

Tour operators

Banks *Banco del Pacifico*, Malecón Charles Darwin y 12 de Febrero, by the waterfront. Same services as in Puerto Ayora. Open Mon-Fri 0800-1530, Sat 1000-1200. **Communications** **Internet:** US$5-US$6 per hr. *Cyber Jean Carlos*, Española y Malecón, Mon-Sat 0800-1230, 1430-2130, Sun 1630-1930. *Iguana Net*, Malecón Charles Darwin y Villamil, Mon-Sat 0800-1230, 1500-2000. **Post Office:** Malecón Charles Darwin y 12 de Febrero. **Telephone:** *Pacifictel* on Av Quito, 3 blocks from the Malecón, same services as in Puerto Ayora. **Medical services** There is a hospital providing only basic medical services. **Dr David Basantes**, opposite *Hotel Mar Azul*, is a helpful general practitioner. *Farmacia San Cristóbal*, Villamil y Hernández, is the best stocked pharmacy. **Laundry** *Lavandería Limpio y Seco*, Av Northía y 12 de Febrero. Wash and dry US$2. Open daily 0900-2100. **Useful services** Immigration and Police: at Police Station, Malecón Charles Darwin y Española, T/F520129.

Directory

Isabela Island

Isabela is not highly developed for tourism but if you have a few days to spare it is worthwhile spending time there. Villamil is the main town and there are villages in the highlands. The beach at Villamil is good for swimming, the one to the east for snorkelling in rocky inlets and mangroves, the one to the west for surfing. Walks and trips include to the Centro de Crianza, 30 minutes west, where tortoises are bred and reintroduced to the wild. 40 minutes beyond is the lagoon at Manzanilla, with flamingos and other water birds. The Muro de Lágrimas is 2½ hours each way (horses available for part of the way). Flamingo breeding grounds are a strenuous seven-hour walk each way to the west. Fishermen go to see white-tipped sharks at Las Grietas (US$8 per boat); other boat trips to sea lion colonies and islets. Day trips are arranged by *Isabela Tours* on the Plaza, expensive, T529207, F529201, or by Dora at *Ballena Azul* (see below). A volcano tour costs US$20, minimum two people. The climb up the volcanoes takes three days, one for the ascent, one at the top and one to come down. Horses can be hired from Modesto Tupiza, T529217, and Sr Tenelema, T529102, US$5-10. There is a national parks office one block from the plaza, open weekdays. A 3-5 day trip can be arranged in Puerto Ayora.

A *La Casa de Marita*, east end of village, T529238, F529201, hcmarita@ga.pro.ec Includes breakfast, with kitchenette, set menu for other meals, order in advance, beautiful, travel

Sleeping & eating

Ecuador

agency. **C** *Ballena Azul and Isabela del Mar*, T529220, F529125. Good meals on request, Swiss run. Recommended. **D** *Tero Real*, Tero Real y Opuntia, T529195. Cabins with bath, cold water, fan, meals on request. **E** *Antonio Gil*. Rents 2 rooms with shower. Helpful, guides tours. **E** *San Vicente*, Cormoran y Las Escalalias, T529140. Cold water, fan, meals on request, good value, popular.

The best restaurant is *El Encanto de la Pepa*, lots of character, also the most expensive. *Costa Azul*, opposite Capitanía, modern, good specials. Other smaller places.

Transport   There is regular service from Baltra and Puerto Ayora by light aircraft and boat, respectively. See Travel between the islands. **Bus** Two daily to the highlands, 48 km round trip: departs 0700 by the market, returns 0845; 2nd trip at 1200, returns around 1400. The bus passes villages of Santo Tomás, Marianitas, La Esperanza and La Cura. From La Cura it is a 20-mins' walk to where one can take horses up to the Sierra Negra volcano. Trucks can be rented to various destinations around the village or in the agricultural zone.

Floreana Island

Floreana, the island with the richest human history has 90 inhabitants, 40 in Puerto Velasco Ibarra, the rest in the highlands. There is one school in town and one telephone at the Wittmers (T05-520150, only in the evening when the generator is on). Unless you visit with one of the few boats which land at black beach for a few hours, it is difficult to get onto and off the inhabited part of the island. This is an ideal place for someone who wants peace and quiet to write or escape the world. Services are limited however; don't go unless you can be self-sufficient and very flexible about travel times. Staying with the Wittmers is delightful (**A** with full board), the pace of life is gentle and locally produced food is good, but you will not be entertained. Margret Wittmer died in 2000, however you can meet her daughter, granddaughters and great grandsons. The climate in the highlands is fresh and comfortable, good for birdwatching.

Recommended reading   The **Galápagos Guide** by **Alan White** and **Bruce White Epler**, with photographs by Charles Gilbert, is published in several languages; it can be bought in Guayaquil in *Librería Científica* and the airport, Libri Mundi (US$5) in Quito, or at the Charles Darwin station. *South American Explorers* in Quito sells a useful brief guide, *Galápagos Package*, US$4. *Galápagos: the Enchanted Isles* by **David Horwell** (London: Dryad Press, 1988, available through his agency). *The Enchanted Isles. The Galápagos Discovered*, **John Hickman** (Anthony Nelson, 1985). *Journal of the Voyage of HMS Beagle*, by **Charles Darwin**, first published in 1845. *The Galápagos Islands*, 1:500,000 map by **Kevin Healey** and **Hilary Bradt** (Bradt Publications, 1985). *Galápagos: A Natural History Guide*, **Michael H Jackson** (University of Calgary Press, 1985). *The Galápagos Islands*, by **Pierre Constant** (Odyssey, 2000). *Reef Fish Identification*, **Paul Humann** (Libri Mundi, 1993). *A Field Guide to the Fishes of Galápagos*, **Godfrey Merlen** (Libri Mundi, 1988). *Flowering Plants of the Galápagos*, **Conley K McMullen** (Cornell University Press, 1999). *A Guide to the Birds of the Galápagos Islands*, **Isabel Castro** and **Antonia Phillips** (Christopher Helm, 1996).

The **Galápagos Conservation Trust** (5 Derby Street, London W1J 7AB, T020-7629 5049, gct@gct.org) publishes a quarterly Newsletter for its members. *Noticias de Galápagos* is a twice-yearly publication about science and conservation in the islands. It is the official publication of the Charles Darwin Foundation. 'Friends of the Galápagos' (US$25 per year membership) receive the journal as a part of their membership. The **Charles Darwin Research Station** and the **Galápagos Conservation Trust** can be reached via the internet: www.galapagos.org (a site which also carries news articles). Also go to www.gct.org and www.darwinfoundation.org Or write to CDF Secretary General Office, Casilla 17-01-3891, Quito, T244803/241573, F443935, cdrs@fcdarwin.org.ec Other sites include The **Naturalist Net** (www.naturalist.net), dedicated to Galápagos ecosystems, and *GalápagosIslands* (www.galapagosislands.com), a booking service for Galápagos tours. The **Galápagos Coalition** web pages are also worth visiting: serv1.law.emory.edu/PI/GALAPAGOS

Ecuador

Background

History

Ecuador decided on complete independence from the Gran Colombia confederation in August 1830, under the presidency of Juan Flores. The country's 19th century history was a continuous struggle between pro-Church conservatives and anti-Church (but nonetheless devoutly Catholic) liberals. There were also long periods of military rule from 1895, when the liberal Gen Eloy Alfaro took power. During the late 1940s and the 1950s there was a prolonged period of prosperity (through bananas, largely) and constitutional rule, but the more typical pattern of alternating civilian and military governments was resumed in the 1960s and 1970s. Apart from the liberal-conservative struggles, there has been long-lasting rivalry between Quito and the Sierra on one hand and Guayaquil and the Costa on the other.

After independence

Following seven years of military rule, the first presidential elections under a new constitution were held in 1979. The ensuing decades of democracy saw an oscillation of power between parties of the centre-right and centre-left. Governments of both political tendencies towed the international economic line and attempted to introduce neoliberal reforms. These measures were opposed by the country's labour organizations and, more recently, by the indigenous movement, which gained considerable political power. Against a backdrop of this tug-of-war, disenchantment with the political process grew apace with bureaucratic corruption and the nation's economic woes. In 1996 the frustrated electorate swept a flamboyant populist named Abdalá Bucaram to power. His erratic administration lasted less than 6 months.

Return to democracy

Following an interim government and the drafting of the country's 18th constitution, Ecuador elected Jamil Mahuad, a former mayor of Quito, to the presidency in 1998. Mahuad began his term by signing a peace treaty to end the decades-old and very emotional border dispute with Peru. This early success was his last, as a series of fraudulent bank failures sent the country into an economic and political tailspin. A freeze on bank accounts failed to stop landslide devaluation of the Sucre (Ecuador's currency since 1883) and Mahuad decreed the adoption of the US Dollar in a desperate bid for stability.

Less than a month later, on 21 January 2000, he was forced out of office by Ecuador's indigenous people and disgruntled members of the armed forces. This was the first overt military coup in South America in over two decades, but it lasted barely three hours before power was handed to vice-president Gustavo Noboa. Significantly, all of the foregoing years of social unrest were never accompanied by serious bloodshed.

Noboa, a political outsider and academic, stepped into Mahuad's shoes with remarkable aplomb. With assistance from the US and the International Monetary Fund, his government managed to flesh out and implement the dollarization scheme, thus achieving a measure of economic stability at the cost of deepening poverty. Social unrest diminished, mainly out of weariness, as the country resigned itself to sit out another interim administration. The next presidential elections are due in October 2002.

Following the end of conflict with Peru, attention has shifted to Ecuador's northern border with Colombia. Escalating armed confrontation in that neighbouring country, and increased US involvement, threaten to produce a regional escalation of the conflict.

There are 22 provinces, including the Galápagos Islands. Provinces are divided into *cantones* which are subdivided into *parroquias* for administration.

Government

Under the 1998 constitution, all citizens over the age of 18 are both entitled and required to vote. The president and vice-president are elected for a four-year term and may be re-elected. The president appoints cabinet ministers and provincial governors. The parliament (Congreso Nacional) has 123 members who are elected for a four-year term at the same time as the president.

Ecuador

Culture

People

*Forecast population
growth 2000-2005:
1.7%
Urban population,
percentage of total:
65%
Infant mortality:
41 per 1,000 live births*

The last census was carried out in November 2001, but results were unavailable at the close of this edition. Based on projections from the previous census (1990), Ecuador's total population is approximately 12-13 million. Roughly 48% of Ecuador's people live in the coastal region west of the Andes, and 47% in the Andean Sierra. Migration is occurring from the rural zones of both the coast and the highlands to the towns and cities, particularly Guayaquil and Quito, and agricultural colonization by highlanders is occurring in parts of the coastal lowlands and the Oriente. There has also been an important flux of mostly illegal migrants out of Ecuador, seeking opportunities in the USA and Spain. Ecuador's national average population density is the highest in South America. Average income per head has risen fast in recent years like that of other oil-exporting countries, but the distribution has become increasingly skewed and a few citizens are spectacularly wealthy.

According to 1989 figures, about 40% of the population was classed as Amerindian, 40% *mestizo*, 15% white and 5% black. Different classifications state that there are 2-3 million Quichua-speaking highland Indians and about 70,000 lowland Indians. The following indigenous groups maintain their distinct cultural identity: in the Oriente, Siona-Secoya, Cofán, Huaorani (also known as Aucas, a derogatory term), Záparo, Quichua, Achuar and Shuar (formerly known as Jívaro); in the Sierra, Otavalo, Salasaca (Tungurahua province), Puruha (Chimborazo), Cañar and Saraguro (Loja province); on the coast, Chachi (also known as Cayapas, Esmeraldas province), Tsáchilas (also known as Colorados, Pichincha lowlands) and Awas (also known as Cuaiquer, Esmeraldas and Carchi provinces). Many Amazonian Indian communities are fighting for land rights in the face of oil exploration and colonization.

Books

*See also under
Climbing and
Trekking, Essentials,
as well as Galápagos
Islands for
related books*

Ecuador in Focus (Latin America Bureau, 1997). *Ecuador* (Ediciones Libri Mundi); Kevin Kling and Nadia Christianson, *Ecuador: Island of the Andes* (Thames and Hudson, 1988); Rolf Wesche, *The Ecotourist's Guide to the Ecuadorean Amazon* (1995). Moritz Thomsen, *Living Poor* (Eland), *The Saddest Pleasure* and *The Farm on the River of Emeralds*; Tom Miller, *The Panama Hat Trail* (Abacus, 1986); Henri Michaux, *Ecuador* (1929; Oxford, 1952).

Fiction: Jorge Icaza, *Huasipungo* (1934; London, 1962). The compilation *Los que se van*, by three of the writers of the **Grupo de Guayaquil** (first half of the 20th century). Jorge Enrique Adoum, *Entre Marx y una mujer desnuda* (1976). *Diez cuentistas ecuatorianos* (Libri Mundi, 1993). Alfonso Barrera Valverde, *El País de Manuelito* (Editorial El Conejo, Quito, 1991). Kurt Vonnegut, *Galapagos* (1986). William Burroughs, *Queer* (1985).

Paraguay

An air of mystery hangs over this little visited pocket of South America. Here, at one end, are the remains of the Mission settlements built by Jesuits and, at the other end of the country, is the hot, wild, impenetrable Chaco. Land-locked Paraguay has had a strange history of charismatic leaders, steadfastness and isolation. Taking mate is such a way of life here that it is not unusual to see a leather-clad biker, speeding on his machine, Thermos under one arm, mate gourd in hand, pouring as he rides. The indigenous language, Guaraní, is officially recognised, but all those odd-looking names cannot hide the warmth of Paraguayan hospitality.

Paraguay

Essentials

Planning your trip

The capital, **Asunción**, stands on a bay on the eastern bank of the Río Paraguay and is the largest city in the country, followed by three smaller cities: Encarnación to the south, Ciudad del Este to the east and Concepción to the north. There are several other large towns scattered across the country. Asunción is the political and commercial heart and much of its architecture dates from the early 19th century, when Paraguayan identity became firmly established during the rule of a number of charismatic dictators. The other clearly defining thing is the strong identification with Guaraní, the indigenous language, which is still spoken widely and is taught in schools to this day.

East and south of Asunción is the fertile agricultural part of the country. The towns and villages are quiet and traditional in their way of life. Many have unique crafts associated with them. There are also many signs of the Jesuit heritage, which is best exemplified in the ruins of the reductions at Trinidad and Jesús, which are close to the city of Encarnación. From here you can cross the Río Paraná to the Argentine city of Posadas in the province of Misiones. Paraguay's eastern border with Brazil has several frontier posts, but the principal one is Ciudad del Este, a duty-free shopper's paradise (or hell, depending on your point of view). Across the Friendship Bridge from Ciudad del Este is Foz do Iguaçu in Brazil, where you can visit Itaipú, the largest hydroelectric dam in the world, and the magnificent Iguaçu Falls.

North of Asunción is the main town of Concepción and the most direct route there is by river boat from the capital. Since the boat ride takes at least a day, the quickest way is via the Chaco, along part of the 400-km Transchaco Highway. Beyond Concepción, the Río Paraguay leads to the Brazilian Pantanal, but access is by road rather than by river these days.

The Gran Chaco takes up the western half of the country. Divided into 3 sections, the Chaco begins as a marshy palm savanna, but becomes an increasingly impenetrable and hostile thorn forest as it approaches the border with Bolivia. The Transchaco Highway crosses the Chaco and, apart from scattered military outposts, the main centres of habitation are the Mennonite communities in the Middle Chaco, based around the towns of Filadelfia, Loma Plata and Neuland. The Chaco is the best place in Paraguay to see wildlife, especially birds, but you should not venture off the beaten track in this empty area.

The climate is sub-tropical, with a marked difference between summer and winter and often between one day and the next throughout the year. The best time for a visit is May-Sep, when the heat is not too oppresive. Apr-Jun is autumn, with mild days, but cold nights. During winter (Jul-Sep) the temperature can be as low as 5°C, though it can also be much higher. Temperatures below freezing are rare, and it never snows. The heaviest rains are from Oct to Apr, but some rain falls each month. Take an umbrella if visiting at this time and be prepared for heat and humidity, especially Jan-Mar, the summer, when temperatures range from 25° to 43° C.

The **Dirección General de Turismo** has an office at Palma 468 in Asunción, T441530, F491230, www.senatur.gov.py Information about weather and roads from **Touring y Automóvil Club Paraguayo** (TACP) at Brasíl y 25 de Mayo, p 2, T/F215011 (who also produce a road map), and the office of the traffic police in Asunción, T493390.

For information on national parks: **Dirección de Parques Nacionales y Vida Silvestre**, Presidente Franco 736 y Ayolas, Edif Ayfra p 1, bloque B, Asunción, T445214, Mon-Fri 0715-1300 (a permit is required to visit the 11 National Parks and Reserves open to the public; there are 8 protected areas closed to the public). There are 2 organizations for conservation: **Fundación Moisés Bertoni para la Conservación de la Naturaleza**, Prócer Argüello 208 entre Mcal López y Boggiani, Asunción, T608740/600855, F608741, www.mbertoni.org.py/ Open Mon-Fri 0800-1700, permits must be obtained here for the Moisés Bertoni Park and

Paraguay

Museum in Alto Paraná. **Fundación Ecocultura**, whose website has a lot of interesting information in Spanish on a variety of topics, including the Amambay conservation area: www.quanta.net.py/ecocultura

Business visitors Foreign business is transacted in Asunción, Ciudad del Este and Pedro Juan Caballero (with retail outlets particularly in the last two).

Other useful websites: www.paraguay-hotel.com/py has links to tourist information as well as hotels. Paraguay portals include: **www.yagua.com**, **www.infoparaguay.com**, **www.terere.com** For more commerical links, but also links to the press **www.pla.net.py** Extensive links can be found on **www.lanic.utexas.edu/la/sa/paraguay/** On Paraguay, has a newsletter, links, marketplace, culture and information for children, **www.onparaguay.com** The official site of the presidency is **www.presidencia.gov.py/Presidencia/default.htm** (in Spanish) A tourism site in Spanish is **www.contacto.com.py**

Before you travel

Visas & immigration
Make sure you are stamped in and stamped out of the country to avoid future problems

A passport is required to enter Paraguay and tourist visas are issued at the point of entry for a stay of up to 90 days. Visitors are registered on arrival by the immigration authorities and get their documents back immediately. This procedure applies to those who do not require previously-granted visas. Citizens of the following countries do NOT need a previously-granted visa: Argentina, Austria, Belgium, Bolivia, Brazil, Chile, Colombia, Costa Rica, Ecuador, El Salvador, Finland, France, Germany, Italy, Israel, Japan, Liechtenstein, Luxembourg, Norway, Panama, Peru, South Africa, Spain, Sweden, Switzerland, UK, Uruguay, USA and Venezuela. All others (including Australia, Canada, Ireland, New Zealand) must apply for a visa before they travel, which costs £36 (US$50, or equivalent), presenting a valid passport, photograph (for a business visa, a supporting letter from one's employer should suffice). If you do not get an entrance stamp in your passport you can be turned back at the border, or have trouble when leaving Paraguay.

Duty-free allowance
'Reasonable quantities' of tobacco products, alcoholic drinks and perfume are admitted free of duty.

Vaccinations Visitors should be inoculated against hepatitis, tetanus and typhoid.

Money

Currency
guaraní exchange rate with US$: 5,979

Dirty and/or torn US$ bills are very difficult to change or spend, especially in the Chaco. Check notes carefully before accepting. A bank such as Lloyds TSB will replace all legitimate bills with acceptable ones

The Guaraní (plural Guaraníes) is the unit of currency, symbolized by the letter G (crossed). There are bank notes for 1,000, 5,000, 10,000, 50,000 and 100,000 guaraníes and coins for 10, 50, 100 and 500 guaraníes. Get rid of all your guaraníes before leaving Paraguay; there is no market for them elsewhere (except in some *cambios* in Buenos Aires or Montevideo). Asunción is a good place for obtaining US$ cash for TCs or on MasterCard or Visa especially if heading for Brazil. Many banks in Asunción (see page 1059) give US$ cash, but charge up to 5½% commission. Rates for all foreign currencies, except bolivianos, are reasonable. *Casas de cambio* may want to see customers' records of purchase before accepting TCs. Visitors are advised to check on the situation on changing travellers' cheques in advance. Visa and MasterCard cash advances are possible in Asunción, Caacupé and Encarnación. ATMs for Visa and MasterCard are common in Asunción and offer good rates of exchange. Street dealers operate from early morning until late at night, even at weekends or public holidays.

Credit cards Visa and MasterCard credit cards are widely accepted even for small purchases. Foreign-issued Visa cards may not always be accepted, though a phone call will often resolve the problem. Credit card transactions are sometimes subject to a surcharge.

Cost of travelling Allow US$50 pp per day to cover all expenses, less if staying in the cheapest hotels and not moving around much.

Paraguayan embassies and consulates

Australia, *107 Gloucester Street, The Rocks, Sydney, NSW 2000, T/F9241 1802.*

Belgium, *Avenue Louise 475, 12th floor, 1050 Brussels, T649 9055, F647 4248, emparpar@skynet.be*

Canada, *151 Slater Street, Suite 401, Ottawa, KIP 5H3, T567 1283, F567 1679, embapar@magmacom.com*

France, *113 rue de Courcelles, F-75017, Paris, T4222 8505, F4222 8357, www.univercom.fr/paraguay*

Germany, *Hardenbergstrasse 12, D-10623 Berlin, T319 9860, F319 9867, www.paraguay.spacenet.de/paraguay.html*

Israel, *Carmel ¼ Mevasseret Zion 90805, Tel Aviv, T533 4830, F533 3878, embapyil@.netvision.net.il*

Italy, *Viale Castro Pretorio 116, p 2 int 5, CAP 1-00185, Rome, T4470 4684, F446 2406, embaparoma@mclink.it*

Japan, *3-12-9, Kami-Osaki, Shinagawa-Ku, Tokyo. 141-0021, T3443 9703, F3443 9705, embapar@gol.com*

Netherlands, *Consulate, Goudsesingel 8D, 3° unit 3, NL-3011 KA, Rotterdam, T/F404 5541.*

Spain, *Eduardo Dato 21, 4 izquierda, Madrid, T308 2746, F308 4905.*

Switzerland, *Kramgasse 58, CH-3011 Bern, T312 3222, F312 3432, embapar@access.ch*

UK, *Braemar Lodge, Cornwall Gardens, London SW7 4AQ, T020-7937 6629, F020-7937 5687, 101472.230@compuserve.com*

USA, *2400 Massachusetts Avenue NW, Washington DC 20008, T483 6960, F234 4508, www.embassy.org/embassies/py.html*

Getting there

Air

From Europe There are no direct flights to Asunción from Europe. Connections must be made either in Buenos Aires or São Paulo.

From North America *American Airlines* operate daily from Los Angeles and Miami via São Paulo; flights from other US cities connect in Miami, Buenos Aires or Brazil.

Within South America From Montevideo, *TAM/Mercosur* three times and *Pluna* five times a week; from Buenos Aires by *Aerolíneas Argentinas* (joint operation with TAM/Mercosur) and *Varig* daily, direct from Ezeiza; from Santiago daily except Sun with *LanChile* (joint operation with TAM/Mercosur); from Santa Cruz, Bolivia, twice a week with *LAB*, 4 with *TAM/Mercosur*; from São Paulo, daily direct with *Varig* and *TAM/Transportes Aereos Meridionais* and *TAM/Mercosur* via Ciudad del Este. See Getting there: Air, in Brazil, Essentials, on the *Mercosur* airpass.

Road

From Argentina From Buenos Aires, the 2 main road routes to Asunción are, 1) via Santa Fe to Clorinda and then on a paved road via the border at Puerto Falcón and the Remanso Castillo suspension bridge to Asunción: 1,370 km, about 23 hrs. 2) via Posadas to Encarnación across the San Roque bridge. Good bus services on these routes.

From Brazil The main road connections are between Foz do Iguaçu and Ciudad del Este, and between Pedro Juan Caballero and Ponta Porã.

Touching down

Airport tax

Airport tax is US$18, payable in US$ or guaraníes (tends to be cheaper).

Tipping

Restaurants, 10%. Porters US$0.15 a suitcase. Taxis, 10%. Porters at docks US$0.40 a suitcase.

Safety
Ambulance T141
Police T130

Paraguay is generally safer than neighbouring countries, although there has been an increase in crime in Asunción since the 1999-2000 recession. Check prices and change. Beware police seeking bribes, especially at Asunción bus station.

Paraguay

Touching down

Hours of business *Shops,* **offices** *and* **businesses**: *open between 0630 and 0700. Siesta (generally observed all year round) is from 1200 to 1500. Commercial office hours are from 0730 to 1100 or 1130, and 1430 or 1500 to 1730 or 1900.* **Banks**: *from 0845 to 1500, closed on Saturday and Sunday.* **Government offices**: *open 0630 to 1130 in summer, 0730 to noon, in winter, open on Saturday.*

IDD *595. If ringing: equal tones with long pauses. If engaged: equal tones with equal pauses.*

Official time *Three to four hours behind GMT (clocks go on one hour in local summer time, October-February/March, dates change annually).*

Voltage *Nominally 220 volts AC and 50 cycles, but power surges and voltage drops are frequent. European round pin plugs are used.*

Weights and measures *The metric system is used except by carpenters, who use inches.*

Where to stay

There are a few hotels in our **G-F** ranges and many good ones in our **C-E** ranges, with breakfast, private shower and toilet. Most hotels have two rates – one for a room with a/c, the other without.

Getting around

Air There are scheduled services to most parts of the country by *Aerolíneas Paraguayas* (Arpa), *Líneas Aéreas de Transporte Nacional* (LATN), *Ladesa*, and *Transportes Aéreos Militares* (TAM). Planes can be chartered. Domestic fares are subject to 2.5% tax.

Road The main roads are: **Route 1** from Asunción southeast to Paraguarí (Km 63), turning off as **Route 7** to Encarnación, 372 km from the capital, paved; **Route 2** from Asunción east to Coronel Oviedo, continuing to Ciudad del Este and the Iguazú falls, 362 km, paved; **Route 5** from Concepción east to the Brazilian frontier at Pedro Juan Caballero, 215 km, fully paved; **Route 8** which runs north from Coronel Bogado (junction with Route 1) via Coronel Oviedo (Route 2) to meet **Route 5** at Yby Yaú, paved; **Route 9** from Asunción northwest across the Río Paraguay at Remanso, continuing via Villa Hayes through the Chaco to Filadelfia and Bolivia, paved to Mariscal Estigarribia, 805 km.

Buses along the main roads will stop anywhere (on their route) for anyone, so all timings are approximate. For **motorists**, there are sufficient service stations, except in the Chaco area. Motorists should beware of stray cattle on the road at night. Gasoline/petrol is unleaded (some has sugar-cane alcohol added). Prices are: 95 octane US$0.64 per litre; 97 octane US$0.72 per litre; diesel US$0.40 per litre. Drivers are recommended to use diesel-powered vehicles as almost all the locals do. Motor fuel and oil are sold by the litre. To bring a private vehicle into Paraguay, temporary admission is usually given for 30 days. Entry is easier and faster with a *carnet de passage* or *libreta de pasos por aduana*. Motorcyclces do not need a *carnet*.

Car hire Weekly and free-km rates available. Rates start at US$75 a day, rising to US$200 for four-wheel drive.

Motor repairs A recommended mechanic is *Lauro C Noldin*, Dr Moleón Andreu 493 y 4ta Proyectada, Barrio Santa Librada, Asunción, T333933. He repairs Land Rover, Range Rover, Jaguar and all makes of British, European, American and Japanese cars, diesel and petrol engines, motorcycles, power generators for motor homes. For diesel service, *MBT* service garage at Av Eusebio Ayala y Lapacho Km 4, Asunción T553318. A recommended Land Rover parts source is *Euroimport López Moreira* at Herrera 604, Asunción. Mechanics at **Santo Domingo**, *Núñez y Farin*, very good for VWs and Japanese cars. Spares are available in Paraguay for all makes of car (European, North American, Asian); most makes of tyre are available.

The 441-km rail network has been closed since Feb 2001, but the early 19th-century steam **Train**
railway can still be visited at the station in the centre of Asunción (see page 1059), or at the
workshops in the small town of Sapucay (see page 1066).

The best maps, including ones of the Chaco, are available from **Instituto Geográfico** **Maps**
Militar, Av Artigas casi Av Perú, take passport (an *IGM* map of the country can be bought at
bookshops in Asunción). Small national maps, made by the Army, can be bought from the
TACP, at bookshops and bus terminals.

Keeping in touch

Few places provide internet access to the public, but the number of establishments with email is **Internet**
growing. Most of the main shopping centres have access to a free, 20-min internet connection.

Postal services are expensive and unreliable. A normal airmail letter to USA costs US$0.60 **Post**
and to Europe US$0.67. To register a letter costs US$0.70. Register important mail. Parcels
may be sent from the main post office on El Paraguayo Independiente, Asunción. Rates to
Europe by APR/SAL US$10 up to 1 kg, US$25 up to 5 kg; to USA US$7.60 and US$19 respectively. Airmail parcels cost US$14.30 to Europe and US$10 to USA for 1st kg. Packages under 2
kg should be handed in at the small packages window, over 2 kg at the 'Encomiendas' office
in the same building, but on corner of Alberdi and El Paraguayo Independiente. Customs
inspection of open parcel required.

The telephone service (few telephone boxes) links the main towns, and there is a telephone **Telephone**
service with most countries, operated by **Antelco**. Tokens for phone boxes are sold in shops
next to the box. Rates: to Europe US$2.90 per minute; USA, Canada, US$2.70 per min, 20
cheaper 1900-2400, 40 cheaper 2400-0800. To send a fax abroad costs US$2 for the first
page, plus US$1 for each subsequent page, in addition to the phone rate. To make a collect
call anywhere in the world, dial 0012. *Antelco* phone cards for calling other South American
countries cost US$3, and for 4 mins to USA or 3 mins to Europe US$9.25; can be used in any
phone box in Greater Asunción.

Newspapers *Ultima Hora*, www.ultimahora.com/, *Noticias*, www.diarionoticias.com.py, and **Media**
ABC Color, www.diarioabc.com.py, are published daily in Asunción. English-language papers
from Argentina and Brazil are sometimes available the following day at corner of Estrella and
Chile. German language paper *Aktuelle Rundschau*. CNN, in English, is available on Channel 8.

Food and drink

Typical local foods include *chipas*, cheese breads which come in a number of varieties: **Food**
almidón, made with yuca flour; *maíz*, made with corn flour; *guazú*, made with fresh corn; *Fruit is magnificent*
maní, made with peanuts (thery are always better warm than cold). *Chipa soo* is maize bread
with meat filling. *Sopa paraguaya* is a kind of dumpling of ground maize and cheese. *Soyo* is a
soup of different meats and vegetables, delicious; *albóndiga* a soup of meat balls; *bori bori*
another type of soup with diced meat, vegetables, and small balls of maize mixed with
cheese. *Palmitos* (palm hearts) should not be missed. The beef is excellent in better class restaurants (best cuts are *lomo* and *lomito*). Paraguayan *chorizos* (sausages) are good. *Parrillada*
completa is recommended and there are many *churrascarías* serving, as in Brazil, huge quantities of meat, with salad, vegetables and pasta. *Surubí*, a Paraná river fish, is prepared in many
different ways, and is delicious. Sugar-cane juice, greatly beloved, is known as *mosto*.

The national wine is not recommended (better is imported from Chile), but Baviera, a local **Drink**
lager beer is very good (beer is usually sold in litre bottles). *Cerveza de invierno* is Brazilian
black beer. The cane-sugar spirit, *caña* is good (the best is 'Aristocrata'; ask for 'Ari'). *Guaraná*
is a good local soft drink (originally from Brazil). Very typical of Paraguay is *tereré* (cold *mate*
with digestive herbs) for warm days and hot *mate* to warm you up on cold days.

Shopping

The famous *ñandutí* lace, made exclusively by the women of Itauguá (see page 1060). The local jewellery is also attractive. Handmade *aó po'í* (fine, unbleached cotton cloth) is suitable for shirts, blouses and tablecloths, and there are cotton thread belts in all colours. Bags, hammocks and blankets are also good. The *guampa* (wood or metal cup) and *bombilla* (metal straw) used for drinking *tereré* and *mate* make good souvenirs. The best place to buy these items is Villarrica. Also leather articles, the pottery and *palo santo* (small articles made from Paraguayan woods). See also Shopping, page 1057. Imported goods, especially cameras, film and tampons, are cheaper in Paraguay than in most other Latin American countries. The selection of all types of consumer goods is better in Ciudad del Este than Asunción, and there are good prices in Pedro Juan Caballero.

Holidays and festivals

1 January; 3 February; 1 March (anniversary of the death of former president Francisco Solano López); Maundy Thursday, Good Friday; 1, 14, 15 May; Corpus Christi, 12, 23 June; 15 (Day of the Child, in honour of the boys who died at the Battle of Acosta Ñu – see below), 25 August; 29 September; 12 October; 1 November; 8, 25 December.

Sport and special interest travel

Football is very popular. Fishing, basketball, tennis, horse-racing and rugby football are popular. There are two rowing and swimming clubs, and a motor-boat club, in Asunción. Swimming in the Río Paraguay is not recommended: beware stinging starfish where there is mud on the islands and beaches. Golf is played at the *Asunción Golf Club*, within the Jardín Botánico, and at the *Yacht y Golf Club Paraguayo*.

Paraguay is not developed, nor does it really have the geography for those sports generally termed adventure travel. Its main asset is wildlife, chiefly in the Chaco. In the Paraguayan Rural Tourism Association (PRTA), some 25 ranches in the Chaco invite visitors to participate in the work of the farm and enjoy typical food, horseriding, photo safaris and nature watching. Each ranch is different and you should be aware that few have purified drinking water (take your own) and that some do not have electricity. One-day tour prices start at about US$50; tours of 3 or more days for groups of 2-12, US$30-100, including food and drink (but not alcohol). Transport to and from these ranches from Asunción is sometimes included in the package. Contact **Solange Saguier**, Yegros 941, p2, Asunción, T446492/448651/674065, avanti@quanta.com, www.ecotur.com.py/html/turism.html

Health

Health/ disease risks
Be very careful over salad and tap water (bottled water is available)

Tuberculosis, typhoid, dysentery, and hepatitis are endemic. Hookworm is the most common disease in the country, and there is much venereal disease, goitre and leprosy. For vaccinations, see page 56. Local mosquito repellent, *Repel*, and pyrethrum coils are effective. Medical fees and medicine costs are high. The **Centro Paraguayo del Diagnóstico**, Gral Díaz 975 y Colón, Asunción, is recommended as inexpensive, foreign languages spoken. **Clínica Integral de Mujer**, Mcal Estigarribia 1085 y Brasil, Asunción, T494722, has been recommended as a good gynaecological clinic. Dentists can be found either at the centre, or at Odontología 3, Mcal Estigarribia 1414 y Pai Pérez, T200175, Asunción. Visitors are advised only to use private hospitals, many of which accept European and US health insurance.

Asunción

Asunción

Looking out over a bay on the eastern bank of the Río Paraguay, almost opposite its confluence with the Río Pilcomayo, Asunción's centre is a testament to 19th-century ideals, with names reflecting its heroes and battles. Tree-lined avenues, parks and squares break up the rigid grid system. In July and August the city is drenched in colour with the prolific pink bloom of the lapacho trees, which grow everywhere. Behind all the-21st century consumerism, there are quaint corners, top-class local restaurants and the nostalgia of harp and guitar music.

Phone code: 021
Colour map 6, grid C6
Population:
over 1.2 million

Getting there The international **airport** is 15 km northeast of the city, to which taxis, buses and an airport-to-hotel minibus service run. It takes from 30-45 mins from the airport to town. The **bus terminal** is south of the centre, also 30- 45 mins away. You can go by taxi or by city bus (see page 1058 for the correct one). Both the airport and bus terminal have tourist information desks. It is worth noting that, if you are heading out of the city, Asunción is very spread out and transport so slow that you need to allow 1½ hrs to get beyond its limits.

Ins and outs
For more detailed information see Transport, page 1057

    Getting around Most of the sights of interest are in a relatively small area by the river, so walking between them is not a problem. Similarly, there are many central hotels which can safely be reached on foot. Places outside this zone are easily reached by taxi or bus. The bus system is extensive and runs 0600-2400; buses stop at signs before every street corner.

    Tourist offices Dirección **General de Turismo**, Palma 468 esq Alberdi, open Mon-Fri 0800-2000, T441530, F491230, good free map (ask for it), information on all parts of Paraguay, but you may need to be persistent. Another map is sold in bookshops. **Oficina de Informaciones**, T494110 (0700-1900).

    Addresses Plaza de la Independencia is often referred to as Plaza Constitución, while Plaza de los Héroes is called Plaza Independencia on some sources, Plaza de la Democracia on others. Av España originally extended to Av San Martín, but the section between Av Kubitschek and Av Santísimo Sacramento was renamed Av Generalísimo Franco (not to be confused with Presidente Franco) and the remaining section between Av SS Sacramento and Av San Martín was renamed Av General Genes. It is often referred to as Av España for its entire length. On Sat morning, till 1200, Av Palma becomes a pedestrian area, with scores of stores selling anything that can be carried, or learnt.

Some street signs are misleading (pointing in the wrong direction, faulty numbering); if in doubt, ask

Paraguay

Background

Asunción, the capital and largest city in Paraguay, has over a quarter of the national population. Most of the public buildings are near the river, but none is older than the last half of the 19th century, most of them dating from the Presidencies of Carlos Antonio López and his son, Francisco Solano López. Dwelling houses are in a variety of styles; new villas in every kind of taste have replaced the traditional one-storey Spanish-Moorish type of house, except in the poorer quarters.

Sights

Most of the public buildings can be seen by following El Paraguayo Independiente southeast from the **Aduana** (Customs House). The first is the **Palacio de Gobierno**, built 1860-92 in the style of Versailles. It was the property of the López family. A platform has been built so that the side of the building facing the river may be viewed. ■ *Sun*. On the northwest side of the **Plaza de la Independencia** or **Constitución** is the **Antiguo Colegio Militar**, built in 1588 as a Jesuit College and now housing temporarily the congressional chamber while the **Congreso Nacional**, also on the Plaza, is falling into disrepair. The Museo Histórico Militar, formerly in the Antiguo Colegio, is in the Ministry of National Defense, Mcal López y 22 de Septiembre (surrender passport on entry). A new congress is under construction. On the southeast side of the Plaza is the **Cathedral**. Two blocks southwest, along C Chile, is **Plaza de los Héroes**, with the **Pantéon Nacional de los Héroes** based on Les Invalides in Paris, begun during the Triple Alliance War and finished in 1937. It contains the tombs of Carlos Antonio López, Mariscal Francisco Solano López, Mariscal Estigarribia, the victor of the Chaco War, an unknown child-soldier, and other national heroes. The child-soldiers honoured in the Panteón were boys aged 12-16 who fought at the battle of Acosta Ñu in the War of the Triple Alliance, 15 August 1869, as most able-bodied men had already been killed. Most of the boys died. Under the Plaza de los Héroes (in reality four squares) are parking areas. Four blocks southeast is the **Plaza Uruguaya** with the railway station nearby, built 1856, and a steam engine, the *Sapucai*, dating from 1861. The national cemetery (**Cementerio Recoleta**), resembling a miniature city with tombs in various architectural styles, is on Avenida Mariscal López, 3 km southeast of the centre. It contains the tomb of Eliza Lynch, the Irish mistress of Solano López (ask guide to show you the location), and, separately, the tomb of their baby daughter. Eliza Lynch's home at the corner of Yegros and Mcal Estigarribia was, until 1999, the Facultad de Derecho.

The best of several parks is **Parque Carlos Antonio López**, set high to the west along Colón and, if you can find a gap in the trees, with a grand view. Good views are also offered from Cerro de Lambaré, 7 km south (buses 9 and 29 from Gral Díaz). **Ñu Guazú** is a recreational park on the road out to the airport. It has two lakes, an 8-km track for walking and some modern art in stone. The **Jardín Botánico** (250 ha) is 6 km east, on Avenida Artigas y Primer Presidente. The gardens lie along the Río Paraguay, on the former estate of the López family. They are well-maintained, with signed walks, and contain only trees (no labels, but nice and shady), and an 18-hole golf course. In the gardens are the former residences of Carlos Antonio

Asunción

Sleeping		
1 Cecilia	4 Española	8 Paraná
2 Chaco	5 Gran Armele	9 Plaza
3 Embajador	6 Ñandutí	10 Zaphir
	7 Orly	

López, a one-storey typical Paraguayan country house with verandas, which now houses a natural history museum and library, and of Solano López, a two-storey European-inspired mansion which is now the Museo Indigenista. ■ *Getting there: by bus (Nos 2, 6, 23, and 40, US$0.15, about 35 mins from Luis A Herrera, or Nos 24, 35 or 44B from Oliva or Cerro Corá).* The beautiful church of **Santísima Trinidad** (on Santísimo Sacramento, parallel to Avenida Artigas), where Carlos Antonio López was originally buried, dating from 1854 with frescoes on the inside walls, is well worth a visit. The **Maca Indian reservation** (since 1985) is north of the Gardens. ■ *US$0.15, guide US$0.80. The Indians, who live in very poor conditions, expect you to photograph them (US$0.25). Getting there: take bus 42 or 44.*

Museo Nacional de Bellas Artes, Iturbe y Mcal Estigarribia, a good small collection of Spanish paintings (formerly privately owned) including works by Tintoretto and Murrillo; also an interesting selection of 20th-century Paraguayan art. ■ *Tue-Fri 0700-1900, Sat-Sun 0800-1200.* In the Jardín Botánico are the **Museo de Historia Natural** and the **Museo Indigenista**, neither in good condition. ■ *Mon-Sat 0730-1130, 1300-1730, Sun 0900-1300. Both free.* In the **Casa de la Independencia**, 14 de Mayo y Presidente Franco, is an interesting historical collection; this was where the 1811 anti-colonial revolution was plotted. ■ *Tue-Fri 0700-1200, 1430-1830, Sat and Sun 0800-1200, free.* **Panteón Nacional de los Héroes**, Palma y Chile. ■ *Daily.* **Museo Dr Andrés Barbero**, España y Mompox, is anthropological with a good collection of tools and weapons, etc, of the various Guaraní cultures. Recommended. ■ *Mon-Fri 0700-1100, and Mon, Wed, Fri 1500-1700, free.* **Museo Gral de Div Bernardino Caballero**, memorabilia and furniture. ■ *Parque Caballero. Mon-Fri 0800-1300, Sat 0800-1200.* **Centro de Artes Visuales** contains **Museo Paraguayo de Arte Contemporáneo**, with some striking murals, **Museo de Arte Indígeno** and **Museo de Barro**, containing ceramics. Highly recommended. ■ *Daily, except Sun and holidays, 1600-2030. Getting there: at Isla de Francia, access via Av Gral Genes, bus 30 or 44A from the centre.*

Museums

The town of **Luque** , near the airport, founded 1636 with some interesting colonial buildings, is famous for the making of Paraguayan harps (*Guitarras Sanabria* is one of the best-known firms, Km 13, T0212291), and for fine filigree work in silver and gold (ask around for Alberto Núñez). There are also many fine musical instrument shops on the road to Luque; get off the bus – No 30 – from Asunción just before the major roundabout. Mariscal López' house may be visited.

Excursions
Population: 24,917

Circuito de Oro Many towns close to Asunción can be visited on a day trip, for example Itauguá, San Bernardino and Aregua on Lago Ypacaraí (see page 1060) and Sapucay (see page 1066). For a longer look at the countryside, take a tour for US$45 from any travel agent (pick-up at your hotel – about US$100 with private taxi drivers) to drive the 'Circuito Central' also called 'Circuito

Paraguay (side text)

Map labels:
To Parque Caballero, Jardín Botánico, Puerto Falcón, Argentina & Chaco
To Airport & Luque
Museo Dr Andrés Barbero
Av España
Río Monday
Bogado (Rutas 1 & 2)
San Roque
9
Eligio Ayala
Plaza Uruguaya
Mcal Estigarribia
To Av Mcal López, Airport & Luque
25 de Mayo
1
Cerro Corá
Av Estados Unidos
Paraguarí
Antequera
Tacuary
To Itá Enramada

● **Eating**
1 Bolsi

de Oro': Asunción-San Lorenzo-Itá-Yaguarón-Paraguarí-Piribebuy-Caacupé-San Bernardino-Itauguá-Asunción. Some 200 km on paved roads, seven hours. The route goes through a range of hills, no more than 650 m high, which is very beautiful, with hidden waterfalls and a number of spas. Chololó, Pirareta (near Piribebuy) and Pinamar (between Piribebuy and Paraguarí) are the most developed for tourism.

Essentials

Sleeping
The hotel bill does not usually include a service charge. Check out time is usually 1000. Look out for special offers

Outside Asunción 12 km from town, at Lambaré, on its own beach on the Río Paraguay is **LL** *Hotel Casino Yacht y Golf Club Paraguayo*, PO Box 1795, T906117/121, www.hotelyacht.com.py 3 restaurants, super luxury, with pool, gym, golf, tennis, airport transfers, etc; many extras free and special deals. **In Asunción LL-L** *Granados Park*, Estrella y 15 de Agosto, T497921, www.granadospark.com.py New, luxury, top quality, with breakfast, all facilities. **L** *Chaco*, Caballero 285 y Estigarribia, T492066, F444223. With breakfast, parking nearby, rooftop swimming pool, good restaurant (US$15-20). **L** *Gran del Paraguay*, De La Residenta 902 y Padre Pucheau, T200051/3, F214098. In a wooded garden, with swimming pool, a nightclub on Fri, traditional dance show on Sat (recommended, food not as good), a former gentleman's club, full of character but getting rundown, English spoken, use of safe US$2. **L-AL** *Paramanta*, Av Aviadores del Chaco 3198, T607053, F607052, www.paraguay-hotel.de 4-star, mid-way between airport and centre, buses stop outside, with bath, TV, internet access, bar, restaurant, pool, gym, gardens, and many other services. English and German spoken. **AL** *Cecilia*, Estados Unidos 341, T210365, F497111. Very smart, comfortable, good restaurant. Recommended. **A** *Asunción Palace*, Colón 415, T/F492151-3. With breakfast, elegant, colonial style, laundry, colour TV, a few small, older rooms sometimes

available at backpacker rates, very helpful. **A** *Gran Armele*, Palma y Colón, T444455, F445903. With breakfast, good restaurant, a/c, used by tour groups. Recommended. **A** *El Lapacho*, República Dominicana 543, casi Av España, T210662. Family-run, welcoming, comfortable, convenient for local services, 10 mins from centre by bus, pool. **A** *Paraná*, Caballero y 25 de Mayo, T444236, F494793. With breakfast, central, secure, helpful, discounts negotiable, restaurant recommended, also short-stay. **B** *Orly*, Humaitá 209, T491497, F442307. Good value (**D** for stays over 2 months), *City* cafetería in lobby is good. **B** *Plaza*, Eligio Ayala 609, T444772, F448834. **D** without bath, spacious rooms, a/c, luggage stored, with breakfast, restaurant. Highly recommended. **B-C** *Embajador*, Pres Franco 514, T/F493393. With breakfast, a/c, **C** with fan, central, parking.

For German-speaking travellers L-A *Westfalenhaus*, M Benítez 1577 y Stma Trinidad, T292374, F291241, www.paraguay-hotel.com/guia, TV, comfortable, German run, swimming pool, a/c. **B** *Bavaria*, Chóferes del Chaco 1010, T600966. Comfortable, beautiful garden, pool, a/c, good value. **B** *Zaphir*, Estrella 955, T490025, F490721. Small, comfortable, good value. **C** *Ayuda Social Alemana*, España 202, T449485. With breakfast, double rooms only, a/c, fan, quiet, German and English spoken, interesting clientèle. **C** *Española*, Herrera y Yegros, T449280. Parking. Highly recommended. **C** *Miami*, México 449 (off Cerro Corá), T444950. With breakfast, a/c, attractive. Highly recommended. **C** *Ñandutí*, Pres Franco 551, T446780. With breakfast, comfortable, luggage stored. Recommended. **C** *Residencial Rufi*, Cerro Corá 660, T447751. Cheaper without bath, welcoming hot water, fans, dark rooms. Recommended. **C-E** *Sahara*, Oliva 920 y Montevideo, T494935, F493247. With breakfast, a/c, shared bath, popular, parking, small pool, large garden. **D** *Azara*, Azara 860, T449754. Attractive mansion but run down, with breakfast and a/c, parking, most rooms face an untended patio and pool. **D** *India*, General Díaz 934, near Av Montevideo, T493327. With breakfast and fan, pleasant, small beds, cheaper in old part. **D** *Viajero*, Antequera entre 25 de Mayo y Cerro Corá. Hot water, fan, Korean family, will store luggage. **D-E** *Oasis*, Azara 736, T495398. With bath, small rooms, no windows, Korean owned, safe. **E** *Atlántico*, Av México 572, T449919. Shared bath, hot water, fan, quiet, central. **E** *Residencial Itapúa*, Fulgencio R Moreno 943, T445121. Breakfast and a/c, quiet, comfortable, transport to airport.

Near Bus Terminal on Av F de la Mora C *2000*, No 2332, T551628. With breakfast, TV, small pool. **C** *Adelia*, on corner with Lapacho, T553083. With breakfast, modern. **C-D** *Yasy*, No 2390, T551623. With fan; all 3 are overpriced. Many more behind these in C Dolores eg **C-D** *Anahi*, T554943. With breakfast and fan. **F** pp *Yessika*, Lapacho y Encarnación, 10 mins' walk from terminal. With bath, basic, quiet.

Camping The pleasant site at the Jardín Botánico charges US$1.50 pp plus tent, cars also permitted, cold showers and 220v electricity, busy at weekends. If camping, take plenty of insect repellent. You can camp at rear of *Restaurant Westfalia*, T331772, owner speaks English, French, German, very knowledgeable, US$1 per night for car, hot showers, clothes washing facilities, noisy, animals. Take Av General Santos, towards Lambaré. *Rest Westfalia* is 5 km from Asunción (bus 19, 23 or 40). Buy camping supplies and gas canisters from *Safari Sport*, Montevideo 258, *Camping 44*, Pres Franco casi Ayolas, or *Unicentro*, Palma y 15 de Agosto.

Paraguay

Two good *churrascarías* are *Acuarela*, Mcal López casi San Martín, T609217, and *Paulista Grill*, San Martín casi Mcal López. *Amandau*, Rep Argentina y Boggiani. Not cheap but good. *Amstel*, Rep Argentina 1384. Good traditional food, expensive. *Arche Noah*, Tacuary 356. German run, good for meat, good value. *Baby Grill*, Villa Mora shopping plaza, open 1800-2400 (poorly signposted in building). Good food, pricey. *Bistro*, 15 de Agosto y Estrella. Excellent, US$25. *Bolsi*, Estrella 399. Wide choice of wines, good for breakfast, excellent food (open Sun 1200-1430), not cheap, snack bar next door also good; under same ownership *La Pergola Jardín*, Perú 240, excellent. *Boule Bar*, Caballero y 25 de Mayo, opposite Paraná. Tasteful setting, friendly. *Brasilera*, Mcal López casi San Martín. For barbecued meat. Recommended. *Hostería del Caballito Blanco*, Alberdi 631. Good food and service. *Colonial*, Plaza 25 de Mayo. French cuisine. *Mboricao*, Prof A Gonález Riobbó 737 y Chaco Boreal, T660048. Very good, fish, meat. *La Molleja*, Av Brasilia 604. Very good traditional grill. *Munich*, Eligio Ayala 163 (unsigned). Good German food, excellent value. *Oliver's* in *Hotel Presidente*. Very good, pricey, live music. *La Pipeta*, Oliva 476. Good value, occasional live

Eating
Open most days of the week, day and night. A few close at weekends, but may open at night. Average price of a good meal in quality restaurants: US$20-35

music. Recommended. *La Preferida*, Estados Unidos y 25 de Mayo 1005, T210641. US$25. Recommended (part of *Hotel Cecilia*). *Le Saint Tropez*, 25 de Mayo at Plaza Uruguay. Delicious French and Paraguayan food, good prices at lunchtime, higher prices in evening. *San Marcos*, Alberdi y Oliva. Part a/c, good food, reasonably priced, good for snacks in café. *San Roque*, Eligio Ayala y Tacuary. Traditional, turn-of-the-century atmosphere, inexpensive. Recommended. *Talleyrand*, Estigarribia 932, T441163. French. *Westfalia*, Bavarian style, see above under Camping.

Good Italian (and other) food at: *Buon Appetito*, 25 de Mayo y Constitución. *Da Vinci*, Estrella 695. Nice terrace. Recommended. *Navajo*, Av San Martín y del Maestro. Good pizzas. *La Piccola Góndola*, Av Mcal López y Juan de Motta. *Pizzapapa*, Perú 308 y Mcal Estigarribia. Good meat, good value.

Most cheap lunch places close around 1600

Cafés, snacks, etc *American Bar*, Estrella y 14 de Mayo. Self service open Sun, clean. *Amílcar*, Estados Unidos y 5a Proyectada. Cheap lunches. *Biggest*, 14 de Agosto y Estrella. Pizzas and café. *Chiquilín*, Av Perú y Estigarribia. Mostly pizza. *Copetín Micael*, Herrera y Yegros. Good coffee and *empanadas*. *Estrella*, Estrella y 15 de Agosto. Pizzas and *empanadas*. *La Flor de la Canela*, Tacuary 167 con Eligio Ayala. Cheap lunches. *Lido*, Plaza de los Héroes. Good for breakfast and *empanadas*, open Sun. *Lucho*, Estados Unidos 564. Good local food, cheap, try *churrasco* with *choclo* (maize). *El Molino*, España 382 near Brasil. Good value, downstairs for sandwiches and home-made pastries, upstairs for full meals in a nice setting, good service and food (particularly steaks) but pricey. Recommended. Also 2 outlets in *Super Centro* shopping, Palma 488. *Nick's Restaurant*, Azara 348 near Iturbe. Good for roast chicken, open Sun. *Pizza Hut* on Palma. A/c, reasonable prices. Many other fast food outlets. *Rincón Chilena*, Estados Unidos 314. Excellent *empanadas*. Also at Av 5, No 937, near Presidente Franco, open Sun. *Café San Francisco*, Brasil y Estigarribia. Good coffee, closed weekends. *Bar Victoria*, Chile y Oliva. Popular, cheap.

There are many good **oriental** restaurants including: *Corea*, Perú y Francia. Excellent. *Diamante*, San Martín casi España. Chinese. *Hiroshima*, Chóferes del Chaco y Av Moreno. Authentic Japanese. *Hoy*, Alberdi 642. Chinese. *Rico y Barato*, Oliva y 15 de Agosto. Pay by weight, good Chinese food. *Shangri La*, Av Aviadores del Chaco casi San Martín. Chinese. *Il Sik*, Perú 1091 y Colombia. Very good, open every day 1000-2300. *Sinorama*, Av Próceres de Mayo 262. Chinese. Plenty of Korean places around Perú y Francia.

Michael Bock, Pres Franco 828. Excellent bread and sweet shop. For **ice cream** try *Sugar's*, several branches including most Shopping Centres. Also *Heladería París*, Brasilia y Siria and San Martín casi Pacheco. Very popular. *Heladería Amandau*, Estrella 330. Plus coffee and cakes.

Yguazú, Chóferes del Chaco 1334 (San Lorenzo). Good meat. Paraguayan harp music, bottle dancing, reasonable food and service, but commercialized. Also in *El Gran Hotel Del Paraguay*, Sat only. Good Paraguayan harp/guitar group at *Churrasquería Sajón*, Av Carlos A López, bus 26 from centre. More central is *La Curva*, Av Próceres de Mayo 212. Reasonable food, several 'typical' groups play 2100-0300, check bill carefully. **Pubs**: *Summer Pub*, Cruz del Chaco 847. Good value, excellent meat. *Britannia Pub*, Cerro Corá 851. Evenings only, closed Tue, good variety of drinks, English spoken, popular, book exchange. *Austria Pub*, Austria 1783 y Viena, T604662. German run, brews own beer, popular. Recommended. *Pub Viejo Bavaria*, Estados Unidos 410. Good beer, chicken, sandwiches and burgers.

Entertainment **Cinema** Most Shopping Centres have between 3 and 6 *salas* where you can see current films at US$4.20 pp most days, except Wed, which is half price. *Centro Cultural de la Ciudad*, E V Haedo 347, for quality foreign films, US$1.50. Cinema programmes are given in the press; some offer 3 films at one price (US$2.50).

Theatre *Teatro Municipal*, Pres Franco, near Alberdi, is closed for restoration (2002). *Teatro Arlequin*, de Gaulle y Quesado, *Teatro Latino*, 16 de Julio y 16 de Agosto, and *Teatro El Lector*, San Martín y Austria have productions most of the year. Concerts are given at the *Teatro de las Américas*, J Bergés 297.

Nightclubs and discotheques *Asunción News*, Bertoni y José Ocampos. *Caracol Club*, Gen Santos y Porvenir. *Tabasco Club*, 1 de Marzo y Felicidad. *La Salsa*, Papa Juan XXIII y Oddone (Latin American Disco). There are floor shows in several hotels, eg

Paraguay

Hotel del Yacht (Scruples). *Coyote Night & Fun*, Sucre casi San Martín. *Face's, Mouse Cantina, Tequila Rock, Rapsodia, Muelle 69* and *Camaleón* all on Brasilia.

Bookshops *Librería Internacional*, Oliva 386, Estrella 723 and Palma 595, good for maps. Also '*Books*' at Mcal López 3971, at Villa Morra shopping centre, second-hand English language books, also magazines and newspapers. *El Lector* at Plaza Uruguaya y 25 de Mayo has a selection of foreign material. *Librería Alemana*, Av Luis A de Herrera 292, warmly recommended for German books and publications.

Shopping

    Crafts *Galería Colón 185* is recommended. For leather goods several places on Colón and on Montevideo including *Boutique Irene*, No 463; *La Casa Del Portafolio*, No 302 and *Boutique del Cuero*, No 329. *Casa Vera* at Estigarribia 470 for Paraguayan leatherwork, cheap and very good. *Artes de Madera* at Ayolas 222. Wooden articles and carvings. *Casa Overall 1*, Mcal Estigarribia y Caballero, and *2*, 25 de Mayo y Caballero. Good selection. *Folklore*, Mcal Estigarribia e Iturbe. Good for music, wood carvings and other items, a/c. *Victoria*, *Arte Artesanía*, Iturbe y Ayala, interesting selection of wood carvings, ceramics etc. Recommended. *Doña Miky*, O'Leary 215 y Pres Franco. Recommended. *La Plaza de la Democracia*, across the road from the old *Hotel Guaraní*, has a large variety of handicrafts. Outside Asunción, visit Luque (musical instruments and jewellery) – see page 1053, and Itauguá (lace) – see page 1060.

Colón, starting at the port, is lined with good tourist shops, and so are Pettirossi, Palma and Estrella. Check the quality of all handicrafts carefully, lower prices usually mean lower quality. Many leading tourist shops offer up to 15% discount for cash

    Markets The markets are worth a visit, especially the Pettirossi (food and ordinary clothes). There is a daily market on Av Dr Francia, best visited during the week, and a Sat one on Plaza de la Independencia, where the nuns from Villeta sell their hand-made clothing for children. There is a handicraft market on Plaza de los Héroes selling lace, *aó po'i* cotton clothing, jewellery, *guampas* and *bombillas* for *tereré* drinking, and items from Peru and Bolivia (bargain hard).

    Supermarkets and shopping centres Supermarkets are usually well stocked, especially with imported liquor; recommended are *Stock, Villa Morra, Ycau Bolaños, Superseis, Hiperseis* and the one at El Paraguayo Independiente y 14 de Mayo (open daily 0800-2100). Also opposite *Excelsior Hotel* at Chile 959. *Shopping del Sol* (Av Aviadores de Chaco esq DF de González) and *Shopping Mariscal López* are 2 of the best new shopping malls, with good stores, fashion and food halls, and they also contain the best cinemas in the city (*Sol* has 4 screens, *López* has 6, Wed and matinées half price). *Unicentro*, Palma y 15 de Agosto is another modern shopping centre. Malls selling more traditional items are on C Colón, between the port and Gral Díaz (safe by day, red light district by night). Prices of electronic goods in the Korean-run shops are very low.

Abysa, Azara 229, T441569, sells bus tickets in the centre of town. *Classic*, Independencia Nacional 921, T494262, classic@telesurf.com.py *Inter-Express* (Amex), Yegros 690, T490111, iexpres@conexion.com.py *Menno Travel*, Rep de Colombia 1042 y Brasil, T493504. German spoken. *Inter Tours*, Perú 436 y España, T211747, www.intertours.com.py Tours to Chaco and Jesuit missions. Recommended. *Lions Tours*, Alberdi 454, T490591. *Siboney*, 25 de Mayo 2140, T214018, F214004, siboney@pol.com.py *Time Tours*, 15 de Agosto y Díaz, T493527, fluent English. Recommended. Most agencies offer tours of the Circuito de Oro and the 'Triangle' (Encarnación, Jesuit Missions, Ciudad del Este, Itaipú and Iguazú), 3 days, 2 nights, US$185 double. For more information contact *Itra Travel*, Jejuí 733, T494302, itra98@conexion.com.py or *Dirección General de Turismo*.

Tour operators
All very helpful

Local Car rental: *Only Rent-a-Car*, 15 de Agosto 441, T492731, also airport. *Fast*, 15 de Agosto 588, T447069, F447112, good, helpful. See Essentials, page 48 for international rental agencies. See Motor repairs, page 1048.

Transport

    City buses: journeys within city US$0.40. For buses to the bus terminal, see below. Buses only recommended outside rush hours, with light luggage. Keep your ticket for inspection until you leave bus.

    Taxi: minimum fare in Asunción is US$0.70 plus US$0.05 for every 100 m. About 30-50 more at night. The average journey costs about US$2, there is an extra charge for luggage.

Paraguay

Hire by the hour; minimum US$10, up US$20 outside the city. *Radiotaxi* recommended, T550116, or 311080.

Long-distance Air: Silvio Pettirossi Airport, T206195. Several agencies have desks where you can book a taxi to your hotel, US$15. Bus 30 goes every 15 mins between the red bus stop outside the airport and Plaza de los Héroes, US$0.40, difficult with luggage, lots of hawkers and beggars. Minibus service from your hotel to airport run by *Tropical*, T424486, book in advance, US$8 (minimum 2 passengers, or pay for 2). The terminal has a tourist office (free city map and hotel information), bank (turn right as you leave customs), handicraft shop, restaurant and several travel agencies which can arrange hotel bookings and change money (very poor rates). Left luggage US$0.50 per piece.

There are many touts for bus companies at the terminal. Allow yourself time to choose the company you want and don't be bullied, or tricked, into buying the wrong ticket Main companies: Nuestra Señora de la Asunción, T551667 RYSA, T444244, rysa@rieder.com.py

Bus: Terminal, south of the centre at República Argentina y Fernando de la Mora (T551740), reached by taking local bus. No 8 is the only direct one from Oliva, which goes via Cerro Corá and Av Brasil from the centre, and stops outside the terminal, US$0.40. From the terminal to the centre it goes via Av Estados Unidos, Luis A Herrera, Antequera and E Ayala; get off at Chile y Díaz. Other buses Nos 10, 25, 31, 38 and 80, follow very circuitous routes. Taxi to/from centre, recommended if you have luggage, US$4, journey time depends on the amount of traffic, minimum 20 mins. The terminal has a bus information desk, free city/country map, restaurant (quite good), café, *casa de cambio* (poor rates) and shops. Bus company offices on the top floor are in 3 sections: short-distance, medium and long. Local departures, including for Yaguarón and Paraguarí from the basement. Hotels nearby: turn left from front of terminal, 2 mins' walk. Bus times and fares within Paraguay are given under destinations.

To Uruguay *COIT* (Eligio Ayala 693, T496197) runs to **Montevideo**, 0800, Sat and Wed, 20 hrs. *Brújula/Cynsa* (Pres Franco 995, T441720) Tue and Fri, with a third service in summer, US$70 (the route is Encarnación, Posadas, Paso de los Libres, Uruguaiana, Bella Unión, Salto, Paysandú – the only customs formalities are at Bella Unión; passport checks here and at Encarnación).

To Argentina There is a road north from Asunción (passing the Jardín Botánico on Primer Presidente) to a concrete arch span bridge (Puente Remanso – US$1 toll, pedestrian walkway on upstream side, 20 mins to cross) which leads to the border at Puerto Falcón (about 40 km) and then to **Clorinda** in Argentina. The border is open 24 hrs a day; local services are run by *Empresa Falcón* to Puerto Falcón (US$1, every hr, last bus from Falcón to the centre of Asunción 1830; from Falcón to Clorinda costs US$0.25), but it is cheaper to book direct from Asunción to Argentina. Buses don't wait for you to go through formalities: wait for the same company's next bus, or buy a new ticket.

Buses to Buenos Aires (18 hrs) daily, many companies, via Rosario and Santa Fe (average fare US$68 luxury, US$50 *diferencial*, US$48 *común*). To **Resistencia** (6 hrs, US$25) and **Formosa**, 4 a day, *Brújula/La Internacional* (US$10.50, plus US$1 luggage) many drug searches on this road; to **Córdoba** (US$55), *Brújula* 4 a week and *Cacorba* (3 times). To **Posadas**, *Singer,* 3 a week at midnight, or go to **Encarnación** (frequent service and cheaper) and cross the river. To **Salta**, *Stel*, T510757, Fri, 1300, 18 hrs, US$66.

To Brazil Many Paraguayan buses advertise that they go to destinations in Brazil, when, in fact you have to change buses and book again at the frontier. Note also that through services to **Campo Grande** (US$26) and **Corumbá** via Pedro Juan Caballero and Ponta Porã do not stop for immigration formalities. Check all details carefully. *Nuestra Señora* and *Rysa*, and the Brazilian companies *Pluma* and *Unesul*, have services to Ciudad del Este, continuing to **Foz do Iguaçu** (Brazil), US$11, 5-7 hrs, 6 direct buses a day in all. Seat reservations recommended. To **Curitiba**, with *Pluma*, buses daily, 15½ hrs. To **São Paulo**, *Rápido Yguazú*, *Pluma* and *Brújula*, 20 hrs, US$57 (*leito*, US$112). *Pluma* to **Rio de Janeiro**, US$70; to **Porto Alegre**, *Unesul*, 4 a week, US$35; *Nacional Expresso* to **Brasília** 3 a week. Services also to **Blumenau** (*Catarinense*, T551730) and **Florianópolis**, US$30 (*Pluma* and *Catarinense*).

To Bolivia Via the Chaco, to Santa Cruz, *Yacyretá*, T311156/551725, daily, some food provided, best to bring plenty of your own plus water, good service, frequent stops. Take toilet paper (no bathroom on the bus). Also *Bolpar*, 4 times a week (not recommended), US$65, also *Trans Suárez*. Advertised as 24 hrs, the trip can take 7 days if the bus breaks down. The buses can be very crowded. In summer the route can be very hot, but in winter, it can be cold at night. In the dry season it is very dusty; in the wet mud can cause serious delays. Foreigners must get an exit stamp in Pozo Colorado if leaving the country on this route. Don't wait until the border. Alternative route to Bolivia via Salta, Argentina (see above).

River boat: Sailings to Concepción every Mon, 27-30 hrs, US$27 1st class, US$17 2nd, US$11 deck space. Boats return Sun. Not very. Ferry to **Puerto Pilcomayo** (Argentina) about every 30 mins (US$0.50, 5 mins) from Itá Enramada (Paraguayan immigration), take bus 9 from Asunción (Argentine immigration closed at weekends for tourists).

On all sailings take food, water, toilet paper, warm clothes for the night (or mattress and blanket, or sleeping bag), mosquito repellent

Train: San Roque Station at Eligio Ayala y México, T447848. Pres Carlos Antonio López Railway to Encarnación: no trains were running in 2002. See page 1066 for the locomotive workshops at Sapucay.

Airline offices *Aerolíneas Argentinas*, Mcal López 706, T450577. *American Airlines*, Independencia Nacional 557, T443334. *Arpa*, Oliva 761 y Ayolas, T491040. *Iberia*, Mcal López 995, T214246. *LAB*, 14 de Mayo 563, of B, T441586, F448218. *LanChile*, 15 de Agosto 588, T491784. *Pluna*, Gral Díaz y 14 de Mayo, p 1, T490128. *TAM*, Oliva y Ayolas, T491040. *Varig*, 14 de Mayo y Gral Díaz, T448777.

Directory

Banks See Currency section in Essentials. *Lloyds TSB Bank*, Palma y O'Leary (and several other agencies in Greater Asunción). Accepts Visa. *Citibank*, Estrella y Chile. Will change Citibank TCs into US$ cash, and gives US$ cash on MasterCard. *Banco Alemán Paraguayo*, Estrella y 14 de Mayo. Fast service for money sent from Germany, paid by cheque which can be cashed into dollars at Cambio Guaraní. *Banco de Desarrollo*, VE Haedo y NS de la Asunción. Guaraníes only, US$200 limit. *Banco Real*, Estrella y Alberdi. Cash advances in guaraníes on Visa or MasterCard, no commission. Also Argentine, Brazilian and local banks. *Amex*, Yegros 690 y Herrera, but to change TCs you must go to *Banespa*, Independencia Nacional y Moreno, good rates, proof of purchase required. *ABN AMRO*, Haedo, entre NS de la Asunción e Independencia. Will give cash on MasterCard. Many *casas de cambio* on Palma, Estrella and nearby streets (open Mon-Fri 0730-1200, 1500-1830, Sat 0730-1200). Deutsche Marks can be changed at good rates, and all rates are better than at frontiers. Some will accept sterling notes. Some *casas de cambio* change only one type of dollar TC. Shop around as there are wide variations in commission. *Cambio Guaraní*, Palma 449, T90032/6, and in *Shopping del Sol*. Good, changes US$ TCs into US$ cash, Argentine pesos or reais, but small commission charged per cheque. *Cambios Yguazú*, 15 de Agosto 451, T490135, no commission.

Be careful to count money received from street money changers (Palma and surrounding area – their rates are poor when banks and cambios are closed)

Communications Internet: *Patio de Luz Internet Café*, Azara 248, T449741, pegaso@uninet.com.py Also bar, restaurant, occasional live music. *Planeta@ Café*, Shopping Mariscal López. Mon-Thu 1000-2200, Fri 1000-2300, Sat 1000-0100, Sun 1100-2300. **General Post Office:** Alberdi, between Benjamín Constant y El Paraguayo Independiente, T498112. A fine set of buildings around a colonnaded patio with plants and fountains. Open Mon-Fri 0700-2000, Sat 0700-1200. *Poste Restante* (ask at the Casillas section) charges about US$0.25 per item, but you may have to insist they double-check if you are expecting letters (*poste restante* closes 1100). Postcards for sale, but better ones in nearby bookshops. Post boxes throughout the city carry address of the nearest place to buy stamps. Register all important mail; you must go to main PO for this. There are sub-offices at the railway station and at the docks. **Telephone:** *Antelco*, Azara y Alberdi, Gral Bruguez y M Domínguez and at Terminal de Omnibus, all for international calls and fax, 24 hrs. Information T112.

Cultural centres Centro Cultural de la Ciudad, Haedo 347, organizes concerts, exhibitions and shows films. Casa de la Cultura, Plaza Independencia, organizes exhibitions and other activities, Mon-Fri 0830-1330, 1600-2000, Sat 0900- 1930, Sun 1000-1900. The US-Paraguay Cultural Centre has a good library at España 352 (open Mon-Fri 0900-2000, Sat 0900-1200, also has snack bar). Instituto Anglo-Paraguayo, Artigas 356 y Toledo, T225525, F203871, snack bar, library with British newspapers, book exchange, also US TV. Alianza Francesa, Mcal Estigarribia 1039, T210382, snack bar. Instituto Cultural Paraguayo Alemán, Juan de Salazar 310, T226242. Recommended. All these institutes have special events, film shows, etc. If you have the time, these institutes may be able to use volunteers to give classes/lectures in their subjects.

Embassies and consulates Argentine Consulate, España y Boquerón, T212320, www.embajada-argentina.org.py Visas issued at Edif Banco Nacional de Argentina, Palma 319, p1, T442151, open

Paraguay

0800-1300, 2-hr service, photo needed (if you require a multiple entry visa, get it in your country of residence). **Austrian Consulate**, Aviadores del Chaco 1690, T443910. **Belgian Consul**, Daniel Ceuppens, Ruta 2, Km 17, Capiatá, T028-33326. **Bolivian Consulate**, Eligio Ayala 2002 y Gral Bruguez, T203654, F210440. **Brazilian Consulate**, Edif Faro Internacional, Gral Díaz 523, p 3, open 0800-1200, Mon-Fri, US$22 for visa, T448084/069. **Canada**, Prof Ramírez 3, T227207, F227208. **Danish Consulate**, Nuestra Señora de la Asunción 766, T493160, T491539. **Dutch Consulate**, Chile 680, T492137, F445013. **Finnish Consulate**, Elias Ayola y Jasy, T291175. **France**, España 893, T213840, F211690. **German**, Av Venezuela 241,T214009, www.pla.net.py/embalem **Israel**, Yegros 437, Edif San Rafael, p8, T495097, F496355. **Italy**, Quesada 5871, T615620, F615622, ambasu@uninet.com.py **Japan**, Av Mcal López 2364, T604616, F606901. **Netherlands**, Chile 668, T448556, F445013. **Spain**, Yegros 435, p 6, T490686/7, F445394. **Swedish Consulate**, Perú y Artigas, T/F215141. **Switzerland**, O'Leary 409, p 4, of 423, T490848, swiemasu@pla.net.py **UK**, Av Boggiani 5848, Villa Mora (Casilla 404), T612611, F605007, brembasu@mail.pla.net.py Mon-Fri 0800-1300, holds mail. **Uruguay** , Boggiani 5832 y Boquerón, p 3, T602415. Visas processed immediately if exit ticket from Uruguay, overland travel to Uruguay and onward country visas can be shown, US$42 for Australians. **US Embassy and Consulate**, Av Mcal López 1776, T213715, F213728, delasu@usia.gov

Medical services Emergency/casualty: Brasil y FR Moreno, T204800. **Pharmacies:** *Farmacia Vicente Scavone*, Palma y 15 de Agosto, T490396. *Farmacia Catedral Centro*, Palme e Independencia Nacional, Plaza de los Héroes. Both reliable.

Useful addresses Immigration: O'Leary 625, p 8, T492908. Ministerio de Relaciones Exteriores, O'Leary y Pres Franco. **Mennonite Centre:** Colombia 1090, T200697. **Police:** T441111. To report theft go to *Comisaria Tercera*, Chile y Colombia.

East from Asunción

This area takes you through small towns with interesting local crafts, leading to jungle on the Brazilian border, Ciudad del Este and the attractions of the Itaipú dam and the nearby Iguazú Falls.

Route 2, the Mariscal Estigarribia Highway, passes **San Lorenzo** (Km 12, population 74,400), whose Museo Guido Boggiani is a social and artistic centre for Indians. Its collection of tribal items from the northern Chaco dates from the turn of the 19th/20th century. ■ *Bogado 888. Uncertain opening hours. Craft items for sale.* The national *Universidad de Agronomía* on the campus of the Universidad Nacional has natural history collections. ■ *Mon-Fri 0800-1530, free* and there is a small Museo Arqueológico near the cathedral.

Itauguá
Population: 5,400

At Km 30, founded in 1728, Itauguá is where the famous *ñandutí*, or spiderweb lace, is made. There are over 100 different designs. Prices are lower than in Asunción and the quality is better; try the *Taller Artesanal* (Km 29) or the *Mutual Tejedoras* (Km 28). To watch the lace being made, ask around. The old town lies two blocks from the main highway: the blocks of uniform dwellings around the plaza, with their red tile roofs projecting over the sidewalk and their lines of pillars, are very close to the descriptions we have of Guaraní Jesuit settlements. Worth seeing are the market, the church, the Museo de Historia Indígena (Km 25, beautiful collection of carvings of Guaraní myths. ■ *US$2* and the Museo Parroquial San Rafael, with a display of indigenous art and Franciscan artefacts. ■ *Daily 0800-1130, 1500-1800 except market – closed Sun. Frequent buses from Asunción, 1 hr, US$1.* There is a four-day festival in early-July, including processions and the crowning of Señorita Ñandutí.

Lago Ypacaraí

The lake, 24 km by 5 km, has facilities for swimming and watersports and a sandy beach. Ask locally about pollution levels in the water. There are frequent cruises from the pier during the tourist season, December-February, when it is crowded. At Capiatá (Route 2,

Km 20, fine colonial church), a left turn goes via a toll road (US$0.75) 7 km to **Aregua**, a pretty resort on the slopes above Lago Ypacaraí. It has an interesting ceramics co-operative, an attractive church at the highest point in town and convent. An increasing number of houses are being built around the lake. From here boat trips run across the lake at weekends to San Bernadino. ■ *Buses from Asunción, Transportes Ypacaraínse, every 30 mins, but do not leave from the terminal; alternatively take local bus to Capiatá and change.*

At Km 40 on Route 2 a branch road, 8 km long, leads off to **San Bernardino** (phone code 0512), known locally as 'San Be', on the east bank of Lago Ypacaraí. Boats can be hired and there is good walking in the neighbourhood, for example from San Bernardino to Altos, lake views, wooded hills and valleys, round trip about three hours. Shortly after the turn off from the main road towards San Bernardino is a sign to La Gruta; turn right here to a secluded national park. There are grottoes with still water and overhanging cliffs. ■ *Buses from Asunción, 56 km, 1-2 hours, US$1.70.*

Sleeping and eating **AL** *San Bernardino Pueblo*, Paseo del Pueblo y Mbocayá, T2195. Swimming pool, a/c, by the lake. **B** *Los Alpes*, Ruta Gral Morínigo Km 46.5, 3 km from town, T2083 or 0981-552066. A/c, cable TV, lovely gardens, 2 pools, excellent self-service restaurant, children's playground, beach 1 km away, frequent buses to centre. **B-C** *Del Lago*, lakeside in town, T2201. With breakfast, attractive 19th-century building but run down, pool, gardens. Next door is **LL** *Sol*, new, super luxury. **Camping** At Km 43 is *Casa Grande Camping Club* with all facilities. For information, Corfín Paraguaya, Ayolas 437 y Estrella, T492360/1, Asunción, or direct, T0511-649. There are many other hotels, many with restaurants serving good food at reasonable prices (eg *de Sol* and *los Alpes*) and other places to eat. Best to wander around and see what takes your fancy.

San Bernardino only comes alive at night and at the weekends. No buses run after 2000 and taxis are expensive

Around Asunción

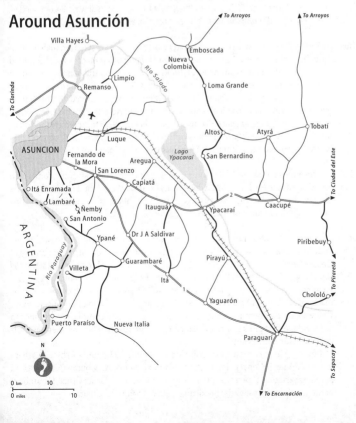

Paraguay

Caacupé

Phone code: 0511
Colour map 6, grid C6
Population: 9,105

At Km 54 on Route 2, this is a popular resort and religious centre on the Azcurra escarpment. Although the old church has been demolished, a small replica has been built about five blocks away. The centre is dominated by the modern Basilica of Our Lady of the Miracles, with copper roof, stained glass and polychrome stone esplanade, which was consecrated by the Pope in 1988. There is a market next to it. There is an ATM on the plaza between the supermarket and *Hotel El Mirador* (no other ATM accepts international credit cards between here and Asunción). ■ *Bus from Asunción US$1.40, get off at Basilica rather than Caacupé station.*

Prices are somewhat higher than normal in Paraguay. Go midweek if you can

Thousands of people from Paraguay, Brazil and Argentina flock to the shrine, especially for the **Feast of the Immaculate Conception** on 8 December. Besides fireworks and candlelit processions, pilgrims watch the agile gyrations of Paraguayan bottle-dancers; they weave in intricate measures whilst balancing bottles pyramided on their heads. The top bottle carries a spray of flowers and the more expert dancers never let drop a single petal.

Tobati, a town north of Caacupé which specializes in wood work, A *villa artesenal* is a short walk from the bus stop outside the house of Zenon Páez, a world famous sculptor whose pieces have strong local influence. There are some amazing rock formations on the way to Tobati. ■ *Getting there: take a bus from the corner below the park on the main Asunción road in Caacupé; ask the driver to let you off at Páez' house.*

A good town to stay in for exploring the area, cheaper than Lago Ypacaraí

Sleeping and eating B *Virgen Serrana*, on plaza, T2366. With a/c, **D** with fan. **D** *Katy María*, Eligio Ayala y Dr Pino, T2860/2441, beside Basílica. Well-kept, welcoming. Recommended. **D** *El Mirador*, on plaza. With bath. **D** *El Uruguayo*. Large rooms, a/c, hot water, parking, delightful restaurant but poor food, OK breakfast. And others. Chicken restaurant 1 block north of *El Uruguayo*, then 1 block east, on highway. Recommended. **Camping** *Club de Camping Melli*, 1 km east of town, all facilities, T2313.

Piribebuy

At Km 64 beyond Caacupé a paved road runs 13 km southeast to the small town of Piribebuy with **E** *Rincón Viejo*, reasonable and **F** *Pensión Santa Rosa*, basic, founded in 1640 and noted for its strong local drink, *caña*. In the central plaza is the church (1640), with fine sculptures, high altar and pulpit. The town was the site of a major battle in the War of the Triple Alliance (1869), commemorated by the Museo Histórico Pedro Juan Caballero, which also contains artefacts from the Chaco War. ■ *Free. Buses from Asunción by* Transportes Piribebuy. Near the town are the attractive small falls of Pirareta. The road goes on via Chololó, 13 km south, and reaches Route 1 at Paraguarí, 28 km from Piribebuy (see below, page 1066).

Vapor Cué National Park

A turn-off from Eusebio Ayala (Km 72) goes 23 km to Caraguatay, 5 km from which is the Vapor Cué National Park, where boats from the War of the Triple Alliance are preserved. Next to the museum is a pleasant hotel, also called *Vapor Cué* (T0521-395). Frequent buses run from Asunción to Caraguatay.

Coronel Oviedo

Phone code: 0521
Colour map 6, grid C6
Population: 21,800
The town is not worth a stop-over

An important route centre, situated 3 km south of the junction of west-east highway and the major north-south Route 8; buses drop passengers at the junction (El Cruce). There are various hotels (**D-F**), eg *Danubio*, T202385 (helpful and safe), *Del Rey* (Estigarribia 213, T2117) and *San Andrés* (Estigarribia y Humaitá, T2443) and good restaurants: *Churrasquería Internacional, Coqueta Tuyuti*. Excursions can be made to the village of Yataíty (reached by a turning 22 km south of Coronel Oviedo) where a local co-operative sells ponchos, fine weaving and embroidery. In June is a *feria artesanal* with folk music and dancing, exhibitions etc. There are German agricultural communities nearby.

Route 8 (paved) runs north to **Mbutuy**, continuing as Route 3 to Yby Yaú, where it meets Route 5 (Concepción to Pedro Juan Caballero). At Mbutuy (Km 56, good *parador*, restaurant, petrol station) Route 10 (paved as far as Cruce Carambey) branches off northeast to the Brazilian frontier at Saltos del Guaira.

Saltos del Guaira is named after the waterfalls now under the Itaipú lake. Here *Nowhere to change travellers' cheques* there is a 900 ha wildlife reserve. Saltos del Guaira, a free port, can also be reached by a paved road which runs north from Hernandarias, via Itaquyry to meet Route 10 at Cruce Carambey. There is **C-D** *Peralta*, T235, pleasant, with breakfast and bath, **E** without and a few others (**C-E**). ■ *Buses to Asunción, US$18; to Ciudad del Este, US$13.* **To Brazil** *Regular launches cross the lake to Guaíra, 20 mins, US$1. There is also an hourly bus/launch service, 30 mins, US$1. Buses also run north of the lake to Mondo Novo, where they connect with Brazilian services. Brazilian Consulate is at Destacamento de Caballería y Defensores del Chaco, T046-333.*

At Santa Rosa, 143 km north of Mbutuy, there is petrol, *pensión* and restaurants. Here a dirt road runs southwest for 27 km to **Nueva Germania** founded in 1866 by Bernhard Förster and Elisabeth Nietzsche (the philosopher's sister) as an attempt to establish a pure Aryan colony. This road goes on to San Pedro and Puerto Antequera on the Río Paraguay (88 km). A further 23 km north of Santa Rosa, a dirt road runs northeast through jungle to the interesting and tourist-free **Capitán Badó** (120 km) in the Cordillera Amambay which forms the frontier with Brazil. From here another road follows the frontier north to Pedro Juan Caballero (100 km). About 50 km north of the turn off to Capitán Badó is Yby Yaú, see page 1071.

Villarrica, 42 km south of Coronel Oviedo, is delightfully set on a hill rich with orange **Villarrica** trees. A very pleasant, friendly place, it has a fine cathedral, built in traditional style *Phone code: 0541* with veranda. The Plaza de los Héroes contains many statues and memorials, and a *Colour map 6, grid C6* battle-by-battle description of the Chaco War around the perimeter (walk clockwise). *Population: 21,210* There are other tree-filled plazas. The museum (closed weekends) behind the church *173 km SE of Asunción* has a foreign coin collection; please contribute. Products of the region are tobacco, *219 km N of* cotton, sugar, *yerba mate*, hides, meat and wine produced by German settlers. There is *Encarnación* a large student population, which makes it a lively place. Horse-drawn taxis.

Sleeping **C** *Ybytyruzú*, C A López y Dr Bottell, T2390, F2769. Best in town, with breakfast, more with a/c, restaurant. **D** *Asunción*, Thompson y Aquideban, T0541-2542. A/c, fan. **E** *Hospedaje El Porvenir*, Thompson 144. Basic, hospitable. **E** *Hospedaje La Guairana*, with restaurant, and next door, **E** *Pensión el Toro*, Mcal López 521, single beds only.

Eating Good restuarants are *La Tranquera*, *Asunción* and *La Cocina de Mamá*. At night *Many eating places* on the plaza with the Municipalidad stands sell delicious, cheap steaks. Two good discos are *on CA López and* *Monasterio* and *La Tirana*, great atmosphere. *Gral Díaz*

Transport Buses to **Coronel Oviedo**, US$1.50. To **Asunción**, frequent, US$5, 3 hrs (*Empresa Guaireña*). Also direct service to **Ciudad del Este**, 4 daily, US$6, 4 hrs.

Some 7 km north is a turn off to the east, then 20 km to **Colonia Independencia**, **German** which has some beautiful beaches on the river (popular in summer). **D** *Hotel Tilinski*, **colonies near** out of town, peaceful, German spoken, swimming pool (filled with river water), meals **Villarrica** for residents. *Che Valle Mi*, Sr Jacob Esslinger, Correo Melgarejo, T05418-241. Recommended. Next door is *Ulli y Klaus* restaurant, also recommended. Also a good restaurant, with German chalet style accommodation, *Hotel Restaurant Panorama*, set on top of a hill on the road 12 km from Colonia Independencia. It makes a good stop, especially for German-speaking travellers, who can also visit the German co-operative farms. There is camping nearby at Melgarejo with full facilities. ■ *Getting there: direct bus to Asunción, 3 daily (US$2.75, 4 hrs), as well as to Villarrica.*

From Villarrica Route 8 continues south 222 km (unpaved) through Caazapá to Coronel Bogado.

The paved Route 2 runs 195 km through cultivated areas and woods and across the **East from** Caaguazú hills to the spectacular 500-m single span 'Friendship Bridge' across the **Coronel** Paraná (to Brazil) at Ciudad del Este. **Oviedo**

Paraguay

Ciudad del Este

Phone code: 061
Colour map 7, grid C1
Population: 133,900

Originally founded as Ciudad Presidente Stroessner in 1957, this was the fastest growing city in the country until the completion of the Itaipú hydroelectric project, for which it is the centre of operations. Ciudad del Este has been described as the biggest shopping centre in Latin America, attracting Brazilian and Argentine visitors who find bargain prices for electrical goods, watches, perfumes etc. (Don't buy perfume at tempting prices on the street, it's only coloured water. Make sure that shops which package your goods pack what you actually bought.) Watch the exchange rates if you're a short-term visitor from Argentina or Brazil. It's dirty, unfriendly and hotels and restaurants are more expensive than elsewhere in Paraguay. The leather market is well worth a visit, be sure to bargain.

Excursions The **Monday** falls, where the Río Monday drops into the Paraná Gorge, are worth a visit. ■ *Taxi US$20 return.*

Sleeping **A** *Convair*, Adrián Jara y García, T500342. A/c, comfortable, cheaper rooms without bath. **A** *Executive*, Adrián Jara y Curupayty, T500942/3, F64430. Including a/c, breakfast – restaurant recommended. **A** *Residence de la Tour* at Paraná Country Club, 5 km from centre, T60316, F62193. Superb, Swiss-owned, excellent restaurant (US$12-16 pp), swimming pool, gardens, beautiful view. **B** *Catedral*, C A López 642, T500378, F62380. Including breakfast, TV, a/c, several blocks from commercial area, large, modern with swimming pool, restaurant. **B** *Gran Hotel Acaray*, 11 de Septiembre 826, T/F500252. Also has new extension, swimming pool, casino, nightclub, restaurant. **C** *Itaipú*, Rodríguez y Nanawa, T500371. Breakfast, a/c. **C** *Munich*, Fernández y Miranda, T500347. With breakfast, a/c, garage. Recommended. **C** *Puerta del Sol*, Rodríguez y Boquerón, T500798. A/c, just off main street. **C-D** *El Cid*, Recalde 425, T512221. Breakfast, a/c, cheaper with fan. **D** *Austria* (also known as *Viena*), Fernández 165, T504213/214, F500883. Above restaurant, with good breakfast, a/c, Austrian family, good views from upper floors, warmly recommended. **E** *Hotel Caribe*, Miranda y Fernández, opposite *Hotel Austria*, T62450. A/c, hot water, nice, garden, helpful owner. Recommended.

Eating *Coreio*, San Blas 125, T50448. Good Korean
Cheaper restaurants along García and in market. Many close on Sun
food. *Osaka*, Adrián Jara and, 100 m away, *New Tokyo*, Adrián Jara 202. Both good, authentic Japanese. *Seoul*, Curupayty y Adrián Jara. Good *parrillada*. *Mi Ranchero*, on Adrián Jara. Good food, service and prices, well-known. *Hotel Austria/Viena*, see above. Good Austrian food, clean, good value.

Transport **Air** Full jet airport. To **Asunción**, *Arpa* 3 flights Mon-Sat, 1 on Sun; also *TAM* daily en route to São Paulo. *TAM*, Edificio SABA, Monseñor Rodríguez, T506030. **Bus** Terminal is on the southern outskirts, T510421 (No 4 bus from centre, US$0.50, taxi US$3.50, recommended as it's not a safe area). Many buses (US$17.25 *rápido*, 4½ hrs, at night only; US$7.50 *común*, 5 hrs) to and from **Asunción**. *Nuestra Señora* recommended, *Rysa* and others. To **Villarrica**, 3 a day, last 0015, 4 hrs, US$6 (*San Juan Nepomuceno*).

Ciudad del Este

To Itaipú

To Asunción

Cap Miranda
Emiliano Fernández
Mongelos
Camilo Recalde
Cnel Toledo
Av San Blas
Ruta 7 Internacional
Av Mñor Rodríguez
Av Adrián Jara
Nanawa
Boquerón
Abay
Av Carlos López
Rgto Piribebuy
Rgto Ita Ybaté
García
Curupayty
Av Pai Pérez
Av Domingo Robledo
Francisco Cedzich
Pampliega
Av Mñor
Nicanor Pampliega
A Matiauda
Av Bernardino Caballero
Av Alejo García
Av Vicente
Pampliega
Carlos López
Oscar Ribas Ortellado

To Monday Falls

N

0 metres 100
0 yards 100

■ **Sleeping**
1 Austria
2 Catedral
3 Convair
4 El Cid
5 Executive
6 Itaipú
7 Munich
8 Puerta del Sol

Paraguay

To **Pedro Juan Caballero**, 7 hrs, US$19. To **Concepción**, *García*, 11 hrs, comfortable. To **Encarnación** (for Posadas and Argentina), along fully paved road, frequent, 3 hrs, US$7.50 (this is probably cheaper than via Foz do Iguaçu).

Banks *Banco Holandés Unido*, cash on MasterCard, 5 commission. Local banks (open Mon-Fri 0730-1100). Dollars and guaraníes can be changed into *reais* in town (in 2000 rates were better in Ciudad del Este than in Foz do Iguaçu). Several *Casas de Cambio*: **Cambio Guaraní**, Av Monseñor Rodríguez, changes TCs for US$0.50, branch on Friendship Bridge has good rates for many currencies including dollars and *reais*. **Tupi Cambios**, Adrián Jara 351. **Cambios Chaco**, Adrián Jara y Curupayty. *Casa de cambio* rates are better than street rates. **Communications** International Phone: Antelco, Alejo García y Pai Pérez, near centre on road to bus terminal.

Directory
Money changers (not recommended) operate at the bus terminal but not at the Brazilian end of the Friendship Bridge

Paraguay and Brazilian immigration formalities are dealt with on opposite sides of the bridge. **The border crossing over the Friendship Bridge** to Foz do Iguaçu is very informal but keep an eye on your luggage and make sure that you get necessary stamps – so great is the volume of traffic that it can be difficult to stop, especially with the traffic police moving you on. It is particularly busy on Wednesday and Saturday, with long queues of vehicles. Pedestrians from Brazil cross on the north side of the bridge allowing easier passage on the other side for those returning with bulky packages. There is a friendly tourist office in the customs building on the Paraguayan side of the bridge. The Brazilian consulate in Ciudad del Este, Pampliega 337, T500984, F500985, opens 0700 on weekdays to issue visas. Argentine visas are not available.

Border with Brazil
Adjust your watch to local time

Transport The international bus goes from outside the Ciudad del Este terminal to the *Rodoviária* in Foz. There are also local buses from the terminal and along Av Adrián Jara, every 15 mins, 0600-2000, US$1, which go to the city terminal (*terminal urbana*) in Foz. Most buses will not wait at immigration, so disembark to get your exit stamp, walk across the bridge (10 mins) and obtain your entry stamp; keep your ticket and continue to Foz on the next bus free. Paraguayan taxis cross freely to Brazil (US$18) but it is cheaper to walk across the bridge and then take a taxi, bargain hard. You can pay in either currency. **To Iguaçu Falls** If only visiting the Falls, immigration procedure on the Paraguayan and Brazilian sides of the Friendship Bridge is minimal, even for those normally requiring a visa to visit Brazil. If in doubt, obtain all necessary exit and entrance stamps.
To Argentina Direct buses to Puerto Iguazú, frequent service by several companies from outside the terminal, US$1, you need to get Argentine and Paraguayan stamps (not Brazilian), bus does not wait so keep ticket for next bus.

The **Itaipú** project is close to Ciudad del Este, and well worth a visit. ■ *Mon-Fri 0730-1200, 1330-1700. Sat, Sun and holidays 0800-1100. Bus tours start at 0800, 0900, 1400, 1500, 1600, Mon-Fri (morning only Sat, Sun and holidays), check times in advance. Free conducted tours of the project include a film show (versions in several languages – ask). Take passport. Getting there: any bus going to Hernandarias will drop you outside the Visitors' Centre.*

Itaipú
A huge hydroelectric project covering an area of 1,350 sq km

On the way to Itaipú is **Flora y Fauna Itaipú Binacional** containing animals and plants rescued from the area when the dam was built; it is about 2 km from the visitor's centre on the road back to Ciudad del Este. ■ *0830-1030, 1330-1630.*

Hernandarias, north of Ciudad del Este grew rapidly with the building of Itaipú. A paved road runs north to Cruce Carambey, where it meets Route 10 (see above, page 1062). From Hernandarias, boat trips on Lago Itaipú go to Puerto Guaraní where there is a museum. ■ *Getting there: frequent buses from Ciudad del Este, US$0.60.*

Paraguay

Asunción

South from Asunción

This is an attractive area of fertile landscapes, but especially notable for the Jesuit settlements, some of which have been extensively restored.

Route 1/7 runs through some of the old mission towns to Encarnación on the Alto Paraná. Itá (Km 37, population 9,310) is famous for rustic pottery.

Yaguarón   Founded in 1539, Yaguarón, Km 48, was the centre of the Franciscan missions in colonial times. It is set on a river at the foot of a hill in an orange-growing district. Most of Paraguay's petit-grain comes from the area. The town's famous church, San Buenaventura, in Hispano-Guaraní Baroque style, was built by the Franciscan order of Los Padres Alonso Buenaventura y Luis de Bolaños between 1755 and 1772. It was reconstructed in 1885 and was renovated in the late 20th century. The tints, made by the Indians from local plants, are still bright on the woodcarvings. The pulpit is particularly fine. Stations of the Cross behind the village lead to a good view of the surroundings. ■ *Daily 0700-1100, 1330-1630, except Sun when morning only.*

"The corridor, or outside walk under a projecting roof supported by pillars, is a typical feature of Paraguayan churches. Generally it runs all the way round the church, forming an entrance portico in front. An excellent example is the church at Yaguarón. It is the prototype of the mission sanctuaries of the early 18th century, when the structure was built with a sturdy wooden skeleton and the walls – simple screens of adobe or brick – had no function of support. The belfry is a modest little wooden tower somewhat apart from the church; in the missions it also served as a *mangrullo*, or watch tower," writes Paul Dony.

Museo Del Doctor Francia, 500 m down the road opposite the church, with artefacts from the life of Paraguay's first dictator, 'El Supremo', plus paintings and artefacts from the 18th century. The 18th-century single-storey adobe building with bamboo ceilings and tiled roof belonged to Francia's father. ■ *Tue-Sun 0730-1130. Free guided tour in Spanish.* Fiesta patronal is in mid-July. There are a few basic hotels (**E**). ■ *Getting there: buses every 15 mins from Asunción, US$0.70.*

Paraguarí   Founded 1775 (Km 63), the north entrance to the mission area, at the foot of a range
Colour map 6, grid C6   of hills with many streams. Its church, much restored, has two bell towers, both sep-
Population: 5,725   arate from the main structure. Buses between Asunción and Encarnación stop here. **D** *Hospedaje Alemán*, has vegetarian meals. There are a few basic hotels and excellent steaks at *Parador La Estación*. About 2½ km before the town is *La Frutería*, which has wide selection of fruit, outdoor seating and a restaurant serving *empanadas*, hamburgers, beer and fruit salad.

Supucay, 25 km east of Paraguarí, is the location of the workshops for the wood-burning steam locomotives. ■ *Mon-Fri. Take a bus from Asunción at 0700, 1200, 88 km, 3 hrs. There are cheap hospedajes.*

Northeast from Paraguarí 15 km is **Chololó**, with a small but attractive series of waterfalls and rapids with bathing facilities and walkways, mainly visited in the summer. (**B** *Parador Chololó*, T0531242, recommended). ■ *Getting there: it is a picturesque bus ride from Paraguarí, US$0.45.*

Parque   At **Carapeguá**, Km 84 (*hospedaje* on main street, basic, friendly; blankets and ham-
Nacional   mocks to rent along the main road, or buy your own, made locally and cheaper than
Ybicuy   elsewhere), a road turns off to Acahay, Ybicuy and the **Parque Nacional Ybicuy**, 67
One of the few   km southeast, one of the most accessible National Parks, if you have a car. Founded
remaining areas   in 1973, the 5,000 ha park includes one of the few remaining areas of rainforest in
of rainforest in
eastern Paraguay   eastern Paraguay. Good walks, a beautiful campsite (hardly used in the week, no

Paraguay (side tab)

lighting, some facilities may not be available) and lots of waterfalls. At the entrance is a well set out park and museum as well as the reconstructed remains of the country's first iron foundry (La Rosada). Crowded on Sunday but deserted the rest of the week. The only shops (apart from a small one at the entrance selling drinks, eggs, etc, and a good T-shirt stall which helps support the park) are at **Ybicuy**, 30 km northwest; **D** *Hotel Pytu'u Renda*, Avenida General Caballero 509, good food, cooking facilities; *Pensión Santa Rosa* and *San Juan*, both **E**, latter has no sign but is nice. ■ *Irregular buses from Ybicuy go to within 4 km of the park entrance, US$0.75. Hitching is easy. From Asunción take a bus to Acahay,* Transportes Emilio Cabrera, *8 daily and change, or bus to Ybicuy, 0630, US$2.*

At Km 161 is the Río Tebicuary which in colonial times formed the border between the Franciscan missionary areas to the north and the Jesuits to the south. At the crossing is **Villa Florida**, a holiday resort with various hotels and a pretty church. There is good swimming in the river; Playa Paraíso has changing rooms, US$1 per person. At Km 196 is the peaceful, prosperous town of **San Juan Bautista**, with cobbled streets and substantial houses. **E** *Waldorf*, pleasant rooms off a courtyard.

Km 226, a delightful town on the site of a Jesuit *reducción* (*guazú* is big in Guaraní). Several typical Hispano-Guaraní buildings survive. Each Sunday night at 2000 a folklore festival is held in the central plaza, free, very local, "fabulous". The **Museo Jesuítico**, housed in the former Jesuit art workshop, reputedly the oldest surviving civil building in Paraguay, contains an important collection of Guaraní art and sculpture from the missionary period. ■ *Daily 0800-1130, 1400-1730, US$1. Very knowledgeable attendant.* Nearby is the **Museo Histórico Sembranza de Héroes**, featuring displays on the Chaco War. ■ *Mon-Sat 0745-1145, 1400-1700, Sun 0800-1100.*

San Ignacio Guazú

Sleeping and eating **B** *Parador Piringó*, T082-262. Modern, on outskirts, with a/c, **E** pp without, recommended, restaurant open 24 hrs, most of the other places in town are *parrilladas*. **E** *Gran Katmandu*, Estigarribia e Iturbe (by plaza), T082-2001. A/c, hot water, pleasant, restaurant downstairs. **E** pp *Unión*, T082-544. With bath, a/c and breakfast. **E** *Hospedaje San Antonio*, T082-404. Fan, basic. Camping is possible outside the town.

Transport Regular bus services to/from **Asunción**, US$6 común, US$9 rápido; to **Encarnación**, frequent, US$7.50 común, US$10.50 rápido.

Santa María is 12 km to the northeast along a cobbled road. Here there is another fine museum in restored mission buildings containing some 60 Guaraní sculptures among the exhibits. ■ *0800-1130, 1330-1700 US$0.50.* The modern church has a lovely altar-piece of the Virgin and Child (the key is kept at a house on the opposite side of the plaza). Good local *artesanía* shop. **F** pp *Pensión San José*, basic. ■ *Getting there: bus from San Ignacio from the Esso station, 6 a day from 0500, 45 mins.*

At **Santa Rosa** (Km 248), founded 1698, only a chapel of the original church survived a fire. The chapel houses a museum; on the walls are frescoes in poor condition; exhibits include a sculpture of the Annunciation considered to be one of the great works of the Hispanic American Baroque (ask at the *parroquia* next door for entry). The former bell tower can also be visited. The plaza is the Plaza Mayor of mission-era Santa Rosa, surrounded by one-storey dwellings. The police station is a former *casa de indio*. One local hotel: **E** *Avenida*, on the outskirts. Buses from San Ignacio Guazú.

A road at Km 262 leads 52 km southwest to **Ayolas** and the Yacyretá hydroelectric scheme. At Km 18 **Santiago** is another important Jesuit centre (1669) with a modern church containing a fine wooden carving of Santiago slaying the saracens. More wooden statuary in the small museum next door (ask around the village for the key-holder). There is an annual Fiesta de la Tradición Misionera.

At Km 306 a road turns off the highway to **San Cosme y Damián**, 25 km south. When the Jesuits were expelled from Spanish colonies in 1767, the great church and ancillary buildings here were unfinished. A huge completion project has followed the original plans. ■ *0700-1130, 1300-1700 US$1. Some of the* casas de indios *are still in use. From Encarnación,* La Cosmeña *and* Perla del Sur *buses, US$4.25, 2½ hrs.*

Coronel Bogado (*Population*: 5,180), Km 319, is the southern limit of the mission area. Museum next door to the church, collection of wooden images from old church including reredos of San Francisco and San Felipe. At Carmen del Paraná, Km 331, the Alto Paraná is reached, 40 km west of Encarnación.

Encarnación

Phone code: 071
Colour map 6, grid C6
Population: 60,000
370 km SE of Asunción
The cost of living is higher than in most other parts of Paraguay, but tourist goods, electrical equipment and accommodation are cheaper than in Posadas

A bridge connects this busy port on the Alto Paraná (founded 1614) with the Argentine town of Posadas. The old town was badly neglected at one time as it was due to be flooded when the Yacyretá-Apipé dam was completed. Since the flooding, however, what is not under water has been restored and a modern town has been built higher up. This is less interesting than the lower part, which formed the main commercial area selling a wide range of cheap goods to visitors from Argentina and Brazil. The town exports the products of a rich area: timber, soya, *mate*, tobacco, cotton, and hides; it is fast losing its traditional, rural appearance. The town is a good centre for visiting the nearby Jesuit missions of San Cosmé y Damián, Trinidad and Jesús.

Sleeping
AL *Novotel Encarnación*, Villa Quiteria on outskirts Route 1, Km 2, T4222/4131. First class, comfortable, very well run. Highly recommended. **B** *Paraná*, Estigarribia 1414, T4440. Good breakfast, helpful. Recommended. **D** *Central*, Mcal López 542, Zona Baja, T3373. With breakfast, nice patio, German spoken. **D** *Germano*, Cabañas y C A López, opposite bus terminal, T3346. **E** without bath, German and Japanese spoken, small, very accommodating. Highly recommended. **D** *Itapúa*, C A López y Cabanas, T/F5045, opposite bus station. Dark rooms, modern. **D** *Hotel Liz*, Av Independencia 1746, T2609. Comfortable, restaurant, parking. Recommended. **D** *Viena*, PJ Caballero 568, T3486, beside Antelco. With breakfast, German-run, good food, garage. **E** *La Rueda*, C A López y Memmel near bus station. A bit run down but OK.

Eating
Buez Brasil, Av Irrazábal. Good, popular buffet. *Cuarajhy*, Estigarribia y Pereira. Terrace seating, good food, open 24 hrs. *Karanday*, Gral Caballero. Good grill. *Ñasaindy*, Estigarribia 900. Snacks. *Parrillada las Delicias*, Estigarribia 1694. Good steaks, comfortable, Chilean wines. *Rubi*, Mcal Estigarribia 519. Chinese, good. *Tokio*, Mcal Estigarribia 472. Good Japanese, real coffee.

Encarnación

0 metres 200
0 yards 200

Sleeping
1 Central
2 Cristal
3 Germano
4 Itapúa
5 La Rueda
6 Liz
7 Paraná
8 Viena

Paraguay

Bus The bus terminal is at Estigarribia y Memmel. Good cheap snacks. To/from **Asunción,** **Transport**
Alborada, Encarnaceña (recommended), *Flecha de Oro, Rysa, Nuestra Señora de la*
Asunción, all except last named at least 4 a day, 6 hrs, US$15. Stopping (*común*) buses US$9,
but much slower (6-7 hrs). To **Ciudad del Este,** US$7.50, several daily, 3 hrs.

Banks Most banks now in the upper town, eg *Banco Continental*, Mcal Estigarribia 1418, Visa   **Directory**
accepted. *Lloyds TSB Bank*, Mcal Estigarribia y Av G Caballero, Visa ATM, open Mon-Fri 0845-1215.   *Money changers at the*
Casas de cambio for cash on Mcal Estagarribia (eg *Cambios Guaraní* at No 307, *Cambio Iguazú* at No   *Paraguayan side of the*
211). **Communications** International Phone: Antelco, Capitán PJ Caballero y Mcal López,   *bridge but it is best to*
0700-2200, only Spanish spoken. **Consulates** Argentina, Mallorquín 788, T3446. Brazil, Memmel   *change money in town*
450, T3950. **Germany**, Memmel 631, T204041, F202682. **Japan**, C A López 1290, T2287, F5130. **Tourist**
offices Next to the Universidad Católica, very helpful, open 0800-1200; street map. In the afternoon a
map can be obtained from the Municipalidad, Estigarribia y Kreusser, oficina de planificación.

The new San Roque road bridge connects Encarnación with **Posadas**. Formalities   **Border with**
are conducted at respective ends of the bridge. Argentine side has different offices   **Argentina**
for locals and foreigners; Paraguay has one for both. **NB** Paraguay is one hour
behind Argentina, except during Paraguayan summer time.

Transport Take any 'Posadas/Argentina' bus from opposite bus terminal over the bridge,
US$1.50, 30 mins, *común* and US$3, *rápido* (faster treatment at the frontier). Bus passengers
should keep all luggage with them and should retain bus ticket; buses do not wait. After formalities (queues common), use ticket on next bus. Taxi costs US$5. Cycles are not allowed to
use the bridge, but officials may give cyclists a lift. A ferry still operates, but only for locals as
there are no immigration officials on the Argentine side.

Encarnación to Ciudad del Este

From Encarnación a paved road (Route 6) goes northeast to Ciudad del Este. At Km   **Jesuit Missions**
20, by Capitán Miranda, is **AL** *Hotel Tirol*, T071-202388, which has chalets, swim-   *50 km from the*
ming pools filled freezing cold spring water, restaurant with plain cuisine, and beau-   *Argentine border*
tiful views. On this road is **Trinidad**, the hilltop site of a Jesuit *reducción*, built
1706-60, now a UNESCO World Cultural Heritage Site. The Jesuit church, once
completely ruined, has been partially restored. Note the restored carved stone pulpit, the font and other masonry and relief sculpture. Also partially rebuilt is the
bell-tower which is near the original church (excellent views from the top). You can
also see another church, a college, workshops and the Indians' living quarters. It was
founded in 1706 by Padre Juan de Anaya; the architect was Juan Bautista Prímoli.
■ *US$1.* For information, or tours, ask at the Visitors' Centre. There is a good hotel
next to the entrance, **F** pp, or you can stay at the *Centro Social*, food and shower
available, take sleeping gear; camping permitted behind the souvenir stall, but
beware theft.

About 10 km northwest of Trinidad, along a rough road (which turns off 300 m
north from Trinidad entrance) is **Jesús**, now a small town where another group of
Jesuits finally settled in 1763. In the five years before they were expelled they commenced a massive construction programme including church, sacristy, *residencia*
and a baptistry, on one side of which is a square tower. There is a fine front façade
with three great arched portals in a Moorish style. ■ *Closed 1130-1330, US$1. Beau-*
tiful views in all directions. Camping permitted at entrance to ruins.

Transport Many buses go from Encarnación to and through **Trinidad**, take any bus from
the terminal marked Hohenau or Ciudad del Este, US$1 (beware overcharging). A taxi tour
from Encarnación costs about US$30. Bus direct Encarnación-**Jesús** 0800; buses run
Jesús-Trinidad every hr (30 mins, US$1), from where it is easy to get back to Encarnación, so
do Jesús first. Last bus Jesús-Trinidad 1700; also collective taxis, US$4.25. No buses on Sun.
Enquire locally as taxis try to overcharge.

Paraguay

From Trinidad the road goes through or near a number of German colonies including Hohenau (Km 36), Obligado, Santa Rita and Bella Vista (Km 42, **C** *Hotel Bella Vista Plaza*, Samaniego 1415, T0757-236. **B** *Papillón*, Km 44, T0757-235, a/c, pool, very pleasant, German, French, English, Flemish spoken). Some 200 km from Encarnación, 42 km before the Route 6 and 2 crossroads is **B** *Hotel Staufenberg*, T600756, good, restaurant. Route 6 meets Route 2 close to Ciudad del Este.

Asunción

North from Asunción

The Paraguay river, still a main trade route between Brazil and Argentina, dominates this section and a boat trip to Concepción is one of the easiest ways of seeing the country. The winding river is 400 m wide and is the main trade route for the products of northern Paraguay. Boats carry cattle, hides, yerba mate, tobacco, timber and quebracho, *a tree that provides the purest form of tannin.*

Asunción to Concepción North from Asunción by river, you pass Villa Hayes where the bridge marks the beginning of the Trans-Chaco Highway. Further upstream is Puerto Antequera and 100 km beyond is Concepción.

By road there are two alternative routes. One is via the Trans-Chaco Highway and Pozo Colorado. The Pozo Colorado-Concepción road, 146 km, is now completely paved. This route offers spectacular views of bird life.

Via Route 2 to Coronel Oviedo, Route 3/8 to Yby Yaú (paved) and thence west along Route 5 (paved). North of Coronel Oviedo, at San Estanislao, a road heads west to Rosario, from where you can visit the Mennonite community of **Colonia Volendam**, nine hours by bus from Asunción (two a day, *San Jorge*, US$5). German and Spanish are spoken here. **E** pp *Hotel Waldbrunner*, T0451-20175, with bath, **F** without a/c, good restaurant, recommended.

Concepción

Phone code: 0531
Colour map 6, grid B6
Population: 35,000
312 km N of Asunción

A free port for Brazil, Concepción stands on the east bank of the Río Paraguay. This pleasant, friendly, quiet and picturesque town is the trade centre of the north, doing a considerable business with Brazil. The *Brazilian Vice Consulate* is at Franco 972, T2655, Monday-Friday 0800-1200. The market is east of the main street, Agustín Pinedo; from here Avenida Pres Franco runs west to the port. The *Museo Municipal* is at Mcal López y Cerro Corá; it contains a collection of guns, religious art and other objects. ■ *Mon-Fri 0700-1230*. About 9 km south is a new bridge across the Río Paraguay, offering an interesting walk across the shallows and islands to the west bank, about one hour return trip, taxi US$9.

Sleeping **B** *Francés*, Franco y C A López, T2383. With a/c, **C-D** with fan, with breakfast, good value, restaurant. Recommended. **C-D** *Victoria*, Franco y Caballero, T2826. With a/c, **D** with fan, with breakfast, attractive old building, restaurant. Recommended. **E** *Boquerón*, Iturbe y Brasil. Basic, nice staff, dirty toilets, quiet area. **E** *Center*, Franco 240. With bath, hot water in hot weather, a/c on 2nd floor. **E** pp *Concepción*, Don Bosco y Colombia, T2506. With bath, breakfast and a/c, cheaper with fan, basic. **E** *Imperial*, Garay y Villarica. Fan, without bath, basic.

Eating The restaurants of *Hotels Victoria* and particularly *Francés* are good. Also, *Tedacar*, on Franco, good food, pleasant with seating in the garden behind. *Bar El Trébol*, in the centre, has *chamamé* and *polka paraguaya* music on Thu evening. *Heladería Amistad*, Franco y 31 de Mayo, good sandwiches and ice cream.

Paraguay

Air Asunción-**Concepción** flights are operated by *LATN, Aeronorte, Arpa* and *TAM* (which **Transport** tends to be cheapest). *TAM* to **Asunción** daily at 0800, 40 mins, book as early as possible (only 25 seats), free colectivo from *TAM* office on main street to airport. *Arpa* daily at 1530. On Mon, Wed and Fri at 0700 *TAM* flies from Asunción and Concepción to **Vallemí, Fuerte Olimpo** and **Bahía Negra**, all 3 villages to north of Concepción on the Río Paraguay. Air services to these places are irregular because runways are sometimes flooded.

Buses The terminal is on the outskirts, 8 blocks north along Gral Garay, but buses also stop in the centre. A shuttle bus (Línea 1) runs between the terminal and the port. Several companies to **Asunción**, most services overnight; most go via **Pozo Colorado**, 5½ hrs, US$18 *directo*, 6½ hrs, US$15 *semi-directo*, though a few go via **Yby Yaú** and **Coronel Oviedo**, 8 hrs, US$15 *semi-directo*. To **Pedro Juan Caballero**, *semi-directo* 6 hrs, US$6, *directo* 4 hrs, US$7. To **Horqueta**, 1 hr, US$1.50. To **Filadelfia**, 6 hrs.

Shipping To **Asunción**, 15 hrs, several companies (fares under Asunción River boats). For details of sailings ask at the **Agencia Marítima**, Nanawa 547, near dock.

There is a 215-km road (Route 5 – fully paved) from Concepción, eastwards to the **East of** Brazilian border. This road goes through Horqueta, Km 50, a cattle and lumber **Concepción** town of 10,000 people. Further on the road is very scenic. From Yby Yaú (junction with Route 8 south to Coronel Oviedo, fuel, restaurants) the road continues to Pedro Juan Caballero.

Six kilometres east of Yby Yaú a road branches off to the very pleasant, uncrowded **Parque Nacional Cerro Corá** (22,000 ha), which is the site of Mariscal Francisco Solano López' death and the final defeat of Paraguay in the War of the Triple Alliance. There is a monument to him and other national heroes; the site is constantly guarded. It has hills and cliffs (some with precolumbian caves and petroglyphs), camping facilities, swimming and hiking trails. The rocky outcrops are spectacular and the warden, Carmelo Rodríguez, is helpful and will provide free guides. When you have walked up the road and seen the line of leaders' heads, turn right and go up the track passing a dirty-looking shack (straight on leads to a military base). Administration office is at Km 180 on Ruta 5, 5 km east of the main entrance.

The Brazilian Border

This border town is separated from the Brazilian town of Ponta Porã, by a road **Pedro Juan** (Avenida Internacional): locals cross as they please (see below for immigration for- **Caballero** malities). The contrast between the two sides of the border is stark: most of the shops *Phone code: 036* are on the Paraguayan side, which is good for cheap liquor and electronics. Ponta *Colour map 7, grid B1* Porã has roads to São Paulo and the Atlantic coast and to Campo Grande. Near the *Population: 37,331* bus terminal at Teniente Herrero 998 y Estigarribia, is a natural history museum run by the Fundación Kayamo. ■ *Mon-Sat 0800-1200, 1300-1700, free.*

Sleeping and eating B *Casino Amambay*, Dr Francia 1, T2718. Luxury, good restaurant, close to border. **B** *Eiruzú*, Estigarribia 4-8, T2259. With breakfast, modern, swimming pool, good restaurant. Recommended. **D** *La Negra*, Mcal López 1346, T2324. Several others which are less good. Eating is mainly in hotels, or on the Brazilian side. *Parrillada El Galpón*, Mcal López 892, is recommended. *Nasaindy*, Av Internacional 778, not cheap. *Pepe*, Av Internacional 748, expensive, live music.

Transport Air: Daily flights to Asunción, twice on Tue and Fri (though they may be suspended after heavy rain). **Bus**: To **Concepción**, 4 hrs, US$7, *preferencial*, 5 hrs, US$6 *común*. To **Asunción**, direct, 7-7½ hrs, US$13.50-16.50 (US$24 deluxe sleeper) and slower buses, 9-10 hrs, eg *Cometa del Amambay* at 0900 and 1900, US$11. Most buses for **Campo Grande** leave from Ponta Porã.

Banks *Bancopar* changes TCs, at least 6 *casas de cambio* for TCs (also deal in European currencies) **Directory** including *Cambios Chaco*, Mcal López 1462. At weekends try *Game Centre Guaraní* or *Casa China*. **Communications Post Office**: at corner of 14 de Mayo y Cerro León.

Paraguay

Border with Brazil

To cross into Brazil officially, first obtain a Paraguayan exit stamp at Tte Herrero 2068, T2047, Monday-Friday 0700-1200, 1400-1700, Saturday 0700-1200. Then report to Brazilian federal police in Ponta Porã. It is essential to observe immigration formalities or you will run into problems later. The Brazilian consulate is at Dr José Rodríguez de Francia 830, T2218: go there first if you need a Brazilian visa.

There is another crossing to Brazil at Bella Vista on the Río Apá, northwest of PJ Caballero; buses run from the Brazilian border town of Bela Vista to Jardim and thence to Campo Grande.

Asuncion

The Chaco

This is a remarkable area of marshes and farmlands developed by German-speaking Mennonites, with a substantial population of Indian peoples. Birds are spectacular and common, while other wildlife is equally interesting but less frequently seen.

Ins & outs

Since this is a major smuggling route from Bolivia, it is unwise to stop for anyone in the night

The Paraguayan Chaco covers 24 million ha, but has fewer than 100,000 inhabitants, most of those living just across the Río Paraguay from Asunción (the average density is less than one person to the sq km). A single major highway, the Ruta Trans-Chaco, runs in a straight line northwest towards the Bolivian border. From Mariscal Estigarribia there are 2 routes to the frontier, the old road to Gral E A Garay, 20 km beyond Nueva Asunción, which continues to Boyuibe. The newer road takes a more southerly route, to Villamontes in Bolivia. As far as Mariscal Estigarribia, the paved surface is poor and beyond that point the dirt surface, after rain (Nov-Apr), is negotiable only by 4WD vehicles. The elevation rises very gradually from 50 m opposite Asunción to 450 m on the Bolivian border.

No expedition should leave the Trans-Chaco without plentiful supplies of water, food and fuel. No one should venture onto the dirt roads alone. In the Middle and Low Chaco, there are service stations at regular intervals along the highway, but none beyond Mariscal Estigarribia. There is almost no traffic in the High Chaco, and ill-equipped expeditions have had to be rescued by the army or have come to grief. Clear the area around your camp to deter poisonous snakes. Winter temperatures are warm by day, cooler by night, but summer heat and mosquitoes can make it very unpleasant (pyrethrum coils – *espirales* – are available throughout the region). The rapid improvement of the highway has opened the area to agricultural colonization, especially by foreigners.

The Low Chaco

Just west of Asunción across the Río Paraguay, this area is a picturesque palm savanna, much of which is permanently inundated because of the impenetrable clay beneath the surface, although there are 'islands' of high ground. Cattle ranching on gigantic *estancias* is the prevailing economic activity; some units lie several hundred kilometres down tracks off the highway. Remote *estancias* have their own airfields, and all are equipped with two-way radios.

The Middle Chaco

This region near Filadelfia has been settled by Mennonites, Anabaptist refugees of German extraction who began arriving in the late 1920s. There are three administratively distinct but adjacent colonies: Menno (from Russia via Canada and Mexico); Fernheim (directly from Russia) and Neuland (the last group to arrive, also from Russia, after the Second World War). Among themselves, the Mennonites speak 'plattdeutsch' ('Low German'), but they readily speak and understand 'hochdeutsch' ('High German'), which is the language of instruction in their schools. Increasingly, younger Mennonites speak Spanish and Guaraní, while English is not unknown. Altogether there are 118 villages with a population of about 10,000 Mennonites, 10,000 Indians and much smaller numbers of 'Paraguayans' and other immigrants. The natural vegetation is scrub forest, with a mixture of hardwoods, and cactus in the north. The *palo borracho* (bottle-tree) with its pear-shaped,

Paraguay

The People of the Chaco

The **Mennonites**, who run their own banks, schools, hospitals and agricultural cooperatives, have created a prosperous community in an area that has attracted few other settlers. They are mainly crop-farmers raising citrus, groundnuts, sorghum and cotton, but their dairy products are excellent and widely distributed throughout the country. About half the country's milk production comes from the Chaco.

Very few of the remaining **Chaco Indians**, most notably the Ayoreo, still rely on hunting and gathering for their livelihood to any great degree. Many have settled among or near Mennonite colonies, where they cultivate cotton and subsistence crops, and work as day labourers for the Mennonites or on Paraguayan cattle estancias. They speak a variety of indigenous languages, including Guaranj, but are often more likely to know German than Spanish. Controversial fundamentalist Christian missionaries proselytize actively among them.

water-conserving, trunk, the *palo santo*, with its green wood and beautiful scent, and the tannin-rich *quebracho* (axe-breaker) are the most important native species.

Parque Nacional Defensores del Chaco

From Filadelfia an alternative route goes north to this 780,000 ha park, where most of the country's remaining jaguars are found. Puma, tapir and peccary also inhabit the area, but none is commonly seen except, with great patience, around water holes at nightfall. This road is very rough and negotiable only by four-wheel drive vehicles; park rangers and very limited facilities can be found at Fortín Madrejón and Agua Dulce. Most settlements beyond the orbit of Filadelfia are under military jurisdiction and a letter of authorization or military introduction may be useful.

The High Chaco

Here, low dense thorn forest has created an impenetrable barricade of hard spikes and spiny branches resistant to fire, heat and drought, very tough on tyres. Occasional tracks lead off the Trans-Chaco for a short distance. Towards Bolivia cactus becomes more prevalent as rainfall decreases. There are a few *estancias* towards the south, where the brush is bulldozed into hedges and the trees left for shade. Summer temperatures often exceed 45°C.

To reach the Ruta Trans-Chaco, you leave Asunción by the route across the Río Paraguay to Villa Hayes. Birdlife is especially abundant and visible in the palm savanna, but other wild animals occur mostly as road kills. **Pirahú**, Km 252, is a good place to stop for a meal; it has a/c. At Km 271 is **Pozo Colorado**, the turning for Concepción (see page 1070) and the checkpoint for travellers en route to/from Bolivia. There are two restaurants, a basic hotel (**F** pp with fan, cheaper without), a service station and a military post; for hitching, try truck drivers at the truck stop. Toll point US$0.75. At this point, the tidy Mennonite homesteads, surrounded by flower gardens and citrus orchards, begin to appear. An acceptable place to stay or eat on the Trans-Chaco is **Cruce de los Pioneros**, at Km 415, a weekend excursion from Asunción where accommodation (**C** *Los Pioneros*, hot shower, a/c – reportedly, good breakfast), limited supermarket, a bank and fuel are available.

Filadelfia

The service centres of the Mennonite area are Filadelfia (Fernheim Colony), Loma Plata (Menno Colony), and Neu-Halbstadt (Neuland Colony). Filadelfia, 472 km from Asunción, is the largest of the three. A knowledge of German is very helpful in this area. Sieghart Friesen, Av Trébol, Filadelfia, recommended as guide, knowledgeable on the area, speaks Spanish and German. The **Unger Museum** provides a glimpse of pioneer life in the Chaco, as well as exhibiting artefacts of the aboriginal peoples of the region. ■ *US$1 admission including video. The Manager of the Hotel*

Colour map 6, grid B5

Paraguay

Florida will open the museum upon request, when things are not too busy. Next to the Unger Museum is a huge, well-stocked supermarket. In all the colonies the cooperatives can provide most essentials, especially dairy products. A craft shop, *Librería El Mensajero*, next to *Hotel Florida*, is run by Sra Penner, very helpful and informative.
■ *All services in the Mennonite areas, including fuel stations, close at 1130 on Sat. On weekdays everything closes by 2000. There is no bank for exchange so take sufficient guaraníes from Asunción. Buses from Asunción, Stel Turismo, Mon, Tue, Thu, Sun 2100, Sat 1230, 6 hrs, US$17. Nasa, Colombia 1050, T200697, 2200, Mon-Fri, Sat 1430, Sun 2000 7 hrs, US$14, better service (also calls at main terminal).*

Excursions **Loma Plata**, the centre of Menno Colony, is 25 km east of Filadelfia (**E** *Hotel Loma Plata*, a/c, friendly, clean, with restaurant). Good museum open on request; ask at nearby Secretariat building. Bus from Filadelfia, *Stel Turismo*, 1845, US$2.50. 33 km south of Filadelfia is **Neu-Halbstadt**, centre of Neuland Colony (**C** *Hotel Boquerón*, Av 10 de Febrero, T0951-311, with excellent restaurant and tasty ice cream). Neu-Halbstadt is a good place to purchase local Indian crafts. Bus, *Nasa*, leaves Filadelfia 1130, returns 1800.

Sleeping **C** *Florida*, T091-2151/5. Modern motel-style wing with a/c, breakfast, hot showers, TV, very
& eating comfortable, laundry service, good restaurant, pool (US$1.50), **E** pp in small annex (dirty,
Accommodation insecure), good German pastries available. **C** *Safari*. A/c, pool, comfortable. **E** *Edelweiss*.
in Filadelfia and Basic, fan. 5 km east of town, Parque Trébol has basic camping facilities at no charge, but
elsewhere in the Chaco lacks running water. *La Estrella* recommended for good ice cream and *asados*. Another
is heavily booked in good restaurant *El Girasol*, opposite. *Remi*, on same street, pizzas and ice cream. Plenty of
Sep when a national good, but basic home-made ice cream, more than welcome in the heat.
motor rally is in town

To Bolivia

Best to fill up with From Filadelfia there are sparse facilities (food, fuel) until **Mariscal Estigarribia**, Km
fuel and supplies at 540 (**D** *Hotel Alemán*, with breakfast, also cheaper rooms without bath; accommoda-
Filadelfia in the tion also available from *Ecmetur* Agency next to service station, US$8; the military post
Mennonite Co-op may provide a meal and bed; at Km 516, turn left and go 25 km to Rosaleda, to
supermarket **C** *Hotel-Restaurante Suizo*, with breakfast, shower, fan, clean, Swiss run). You can
Colour map 6, grid B5 change money at the supermarket *Chaparral*, and local German priests may offer you
a bed. (Daily bus from Filadelfia 1500, two hours, daily colectivo 1900; daily bus to
Asunción 0700. From Asunción *Ecmetur*, Monday-Friday 2115, Saturday 1330,
Sunday 2030, 9½ hours, US$14). Thereafter military outposts or *estancias* are the only
alternatives, with radio the only means of communication.

Identity checks Public transport, including trucks, now tends to take the Mariscal
numerous military Estigarribia-Fortín Infante Rivarola-Villamontes route. Backpackers should have
checkpoints are no special difficulties, but motorists should carry plenty of food and water since even
common, and photos small amounts of rain turn the highway into mud, causing major delays. Motorcy-
should be a good cling beyond Mariscal Estigarribia can be difficult because of deep sand and can be
likeness of the bearer dangerous in wet weather. Exit stamps should be obtained at Pozo Colorado, Km
270 (usually in the middle of the night). You must tell your bus driver that you have
to get an exit stamp, otherwise he will not stop: do not wait until the border, you will
be fined US$50 without a stamp. As well as this checkpoint, there are controls at the
bridge across the Río Paraguay and Río Verde, at either of which your documents
may be inspected and your bags searched.

For the continuation of the route into Bolivia, see under Boyuibe and
Villamontes, page 324. Take small denomination dollar notes as it is impossible to
buy bolivianos before reaching Bolivia (if entering from Bolivia street changers in
Santa Cruz sell Guaraníes at good rates).

Hitching is possible but traffic is sparse (fee US$10-15). Trucks travel into Bolivia and may take **Transport** passengers in Filadelfia; the Esso Station on Hindenburgstrasse and the police checkpoint are the most convenient places to ask, but Mariscal Estigarribia and other checkpoints on the Trans-Chaco are also possible: ask the police for help, but be prepared to wait up to a week.

If you wish to explore the remoter parts of the Chaco, contact the Paraguayan Rural Tour- **Tours from** ism Association (PRTA), see Sport and special interest travel, Essentials. Many agencies **Asunción** offer tours, staying for up to 6 days in Cruce de los Pioneros. Guides can be found in Asunción, often German speaking, for about US$100 per day. Most tours visit only Menno-nite communities.

Background

History

The disturbances in Buenos Aires in 1810-16, which led to independence from Spain, **Independence** enabled creole leaders in Asunción to throw off the rule of Buenos Aires as well as Madrid. **& dictatorship** The new republic was, however, subject to pressure from both Argentina, which blocked Paraguayan trade on the Río de la Plata, and Brazil. Following independence Paraguay was ruled by a series of dictators, the first of whom, Dr Gaspar Rodríguez de Francia (1814-40) known as 'El Supremo', imposed a policy of isolation and self-sufficiency. The opening of the Río de la Plata after the fall of the Argentine dictator Rosas enabled de Francia's successor, Carlos Antonio López (1840-62) to import modern technology: in 1856 a railway line between Asunción and Villarrica was begun; an iron foundry and telegraph system were also developed. Carlos López was succeeded by his son, Francisco Solano López (López II), who saw himself as the Napoleon of South America. Believing Paraguay to be threatened by Brazil and Argentina, Solano López declared war on Brazil in 1865. When Argentina refused permission to send troops through Misiones to attack Brazil, López declared war on Argentina. With Uruguay supporting Brazil and Argentina, the ensuing **War of the Triple Alliance** was disastrous for the Paraguayan forces who held on against overwhelming odds until the death of López at the Battle of Cerro Corá on 1 March 1870. Of a pre-war population of 400,000, only 220,000 survived the war, 28,000 of them males, mostly either very young or very old. In the peace settlement Paraguay lost territory to Brazil and Argentina, although rivalry between these neighbours prevented a worse fate.

After the war, Paraguay experienced political instability as civilian factions competed for power, often appealing to army officers for support. Although there were few policy differences between the two political parties (the National Republican Association, known as Colorados from its red banner, and the Liberal party who adopted the colour blue), rivalry was intense. Elections were held regularly, but whichever party was in government invariably intervened to fix the result and the opposition rarely participated.

While Paraguayan leaders were absorbed with domestic disputes, Bolivia began occupying **The Chaco** disputed parts of the Chaco in an attempt to gain access to the sea via the Río Paraguay. **War** Although Bolivian moves started in the late 19th century, the dispute was given new intensity by the discovery of oil in the 1920s. In the five-year Chaco War (1932-37) 56,000 Bolivians and 36,000 Paraguayans were killed. Despite general expectations Paraguayan troops under Mariscal Estigarribia pushed the Bolivian army out of most of the Chaco.

Victory in war only increased dissatisfaction in the army with the policies of pre-war governments. In February 1936 nationalist officers seized power and appointed the war hero, Colonel Rafael Franco as President. Although Franco was overthrown in a counter-coup in 1937, the so-called 'February Revolution' began major changes in Paraguay including the first serious attempt at land reform and legal recognition of the small labour movement. Between 1939 and 1954 Paraguayan politics were even more

Paraguay

☞ *The Chaco War*

In the 1920s the US Standard Oil Company was drilling for oil in the Bolivian Chaco. The company and the Bolivian government had designs on the Río Pilcomayo to transport the oil to the coast. It also seemed likely that there were further reserves in other parts of the inaccessible wilderness of the Chaco plain.

The problem was, however, that the Bolivian frontier with Paraguay had never been precisely defined. From 1928 there were border clashes with Paraguayan army patrols

and in 1932 the Chaco War broke out. The Paraguayan forces knew the terrain much better than the Bolivian soldiers, who were mostly from the Andes and unused to the intense heat and humidity. By 1935 Bolivia had lost the war, practically the whole of the Chaco and 56,000 lives, but it did keep the oil-fields. Paraguay, though, won no more than a symbolic victory as no oil has ever been found in the Chaco.

turbulent, as rival civilian factions and army officers vied for power. In 1946 civil war shook the country as army units based in Concepción fought to overthrow President Morínigo.

The Stroessner Years A military coup in May 1954 led to General Alfredo Stroessner becoming President. Stroessner retained power for 34 years, the most durable dictator in Paraguayan history. His rule was based on control over the army and the Colorado party, both of which were purged of opponents. While a network of spies informed on dissidents, party membership was made compulsory for most official posts including teachers and doctors. In fraudulent elections Stroessner was re-elected eight times. Paraguay became a centre for smuggling, gambling and drug-running, much of it controlled by Stroessner's supporters. Meanwhile the government spent large amounts of money on transportation and infrastructure projects, including the giant hydroelectric dam at Itaipú. Although these projects brought employment, the completion of Itaipú in 1982 coincided with recession in Brazil and Argentina on whose economies Paraguay was heavily dependent. Meanwhile rivalry intensified within the regime over the succession, with Stroessner favouring his son, Gustavo. Opposition focussed around Gen Andrés Rodríguez, who was married to Stroessner's daughter. When Stroessner tried to force Rodríguez to retire, troops loyal to Rodríguez overthrew the 75-year old Stroessner, who left to live in Brazil.

Liberalization Rodríguez, who became provisional president, easily won multi-party elections in May 1989. The commitment to greater democracy permitted opponents, who had previously boycotted, or been banned from elections, to gain an unprecedented number of seats in the legislative elections of the same date. Despite considerable scepticism over General Rodríguez's intentions, political liberalization became a reality. The presidential and congressional elections that he promised were held on 9 May 1993. The presidency was won by Juan Carlos Wasmosy of the Colorado Party and Domingo Laíno of the Authentic Radical Liberal Party came second. In congress the Colorados won the most seats, but insufficient to have a majority in either house.

The government's commitment to market reforms, privatization and to economic integration with Argentina and Brazil within Mercosur inspired protests from all quarters. 1994 saw the first general strike for 35 years. There were also demands for land reform. A worsening of relations between the military and the legislature in 1995 led to a critical few days in April 1996. Army commander General Lino Oviedo was dismissed for threatening a coup; Wasmosy offered him the defence ministry but then withdrew the offer after massive public protest. Oviedo was later arrested on charges of insurrection, but from jail he made many accusations about corruption at the highest level. To the dismay of the Colorado leadership, Oviedo was chosen as the party's candidate for the May 1998 presidential elections. This intensified the feud between Oviedo and Wasmosy who eventually succeeded in having Oviedo jailed by a military tribunal for 10 years for attempting a coup in 1996. A compromise ticket of Raúl Cubas Grau (Oviedo's running mate) and Luis María Argaña (Colorado party president and opponent of Wasmosy) won

Things go better with Coke

Coca was first cultivated in the warm valleys (Yungas) of the eastern Andes by the Aymara Indians many, many centuries ago. Awareness of coca in the First World is rather more recent, however. In 1862 German chemists had taken coca leaves brought by an Austrian scientific expedition from Peru and isolated an alkaloid, or nitrogen-based compound which they labelled cocain. By around 1880, it was being tried as a cure for opium addiction and alcoholism. The young Dr Sigmund Freud, reading of its effect on tired soldiers, took some himself and pronounced it a "magical substance", which was "wonderfully stimulating".

Today, there is a huge demand for this drug from the millions of North Americans and Europeans who snort, smoke or inject it. Supply on this scale is not a problem. Making cocaine hydrochloride is as easy as baking bread. The leaves go into a plastic pit with a solution of water and a little sulphuric acid where they are left to soak for a few days.

Then follows a succession of mixing and stirring with more chemicals until the liquid turns milky-white and then curdles, leaving tiny, ivory-coloured granules. This cocaine base is then transported to Colombia, where it is refined into the familiar white powder, before being shipped abroad. The costs involved to produce a kilo of the stuff are around US$5,000. The return on this investment can be as much as US$50,000.

Cocaine also has its legal uses. Patent medicines containing cocaine were popular – for hay fever, sinusitis and as a general tonic. Today, it is still used in hospitals worldwide as a local anaesthetic. Another legal use of cocaine is in soft drinks. The most famous soft drink in the world doesn't actually contain cocaine, but has something from the coca plant in it. Coca leaves from Peru and Bolivia are shipped to the USA where cocaine is extracted for medical use. From what's left comes a flavouring agent which goes into Coca-Cola, enjoyed in practically every country around the globe.

---

the election. Within a week of taking office in August 1998, Cubas released Oviedo from prison, provoking a constitutional crisis as the supreme court ruled that Oviedo should serve out his sentence. Matters came to a head when Vice President Argaña was shot in March 1999, just before the Senate was to vote on impeachment of Cubas. Intense diplomatic efforts, led by Paraguay's Mercosur partners, resulted in Cubas' resignation on 29 March. He was replaced by Luis González Macchi, the president of Congress. Cubas went into exile in Brazil, Oviedo in Argentina. In December 1999, Oviedo escaped from the Patagonian *estancia* where he was held and began verbal attacks on the government. Soldiers loyal to Oviedo staged an unsuccessful coup in May 2000, which González Macchi survived. In the following month Oviedo was arrested in Brazil. Subsequently, the González Macchi administration had to deal with an economy facing recession, high unemployment, strikes and social discontent. The economic downturn and its repercussions worsened in late 2001/early 2002 as a result of Argentina's financial crisis.

Government

A new Constitution was adopted in 1992. The country has 19 departments. Executive power rests with the president, elected for five years. There is a two-chamber Congress (Senate 45 seats, Chamber of Deputies 80). Voting is secret and obligatory for all over 18.

Culture

People

The total population in 2001 was 5.6 million, gowing at an average rate of 2.6 (1995-2000). Since Spanish influence was less than in many other parts of South America, most people are bilingual, speaking both Spanish and Guaraní. Outside Asunción, most people speak Guaraní by preference. There is a Guaraní theatre, it is taught in private schools, and books and periodicals are published in that tongue, which has official status as the second national language. According to official figures, the indigenous population is about 39,000; non-government sources put it as high as 99,000 (see *Return of the Indian* by Phillip Wearne, London 1996, page 212). Two-thirds of them are in the Chaco, and one-third in the rest of the country. There are 17 distinct ethnic groups with five different languages,

Forecast population growth 2000-2005: 2.5%
Urban population in 2000: 56%
Infant mortality: 37 per 1,000 live births

Paraguay

among which Guaraní predominates. The 1981 Law of Native Communities in theory guarantees Indian rights to ownership of their traditional lands and the maintenance of their culture. Contact Tierra Viva, Casilla de Correo 789, Asunción, T/F595-2185209.

Books

Así es el Paraguay (with maps and very useful information) and *Paraguay, Land of Lace and Legend* (1st published 1960, reprinted 1983, available from bookshops and Anglo-Paraguayan and US-Paraguay cultural institutes in Asunción); also *Green Hill, Far Away*, by **Peter Upton**. Books on the history of Paraguay include: *The Origins of the Paraguayan War* (2 vol) by **Pelham Horton Box**; *Tragedy of Paraguay* by **Gilbert Phelps**; *Portrait of a Dictator* by **RB Cunninghame-Grahame**, on López II; *Eliza Lynch, Regent of Paraguay*, by **Henry Lyon-Young**; *Seven Eventful Years in Paraguay* by **George F Masterman**, and *The Lost Paradise* by **Philip Caraman**, an account of the Jesuits in Paraguay 1607-1768, published in London in 1975. *Land Without Evil*, by **Richard Gott** (Verso 1993) is also on Jesuit history. For further reading on the origin and aftermath of the War of the Triple Alliance, see *Paraguay: un destino geopolítico*, by **Dra Julia Velilla Laconich de Aréllaga**; *Genocídio Americano: a Guerra do Paraguai*, by **Júlio José Chiavenalto**; *Woman on Horseback*, by **William E Barrett**. Michael Gonin has recommended, in addition, *The British in Paraguay* by **Josefina Plá**, for a complete study of this subject, and *Forgotten Fatherland* by **Ben MacIntyre**, about New Germany (Nueva Germania, page 1063) in Paraguay. **Graham Greene**'s *Travels With My Aunt* includes a voyage to Paraguay by a retired bank manager and his eccentric aunt. Paraguay's most renowned contemporary novelist is **Augusto Roa Bastos**: *Yo, el Supremo* and *Hijo de hombre*.

Peru

Cusco, navel of the Inca world, is now South America's gringo hangout, with its access to Machu Picchu and a buzzing nightlife. Not far away is magical Lake Titicaca, birthplace of the Inca myth. The adobe cities of the north coast, the mysterious cloud people of the northern highlands, the giant figures etched on the desert by the Nascans, are just a few of the pre-Inca cultures Peru has to offer. You can trek for ever amid high peaks and blue lakes, cycle down remote mountainsides, or surf the Pacific rollers. East of the Andes the jungles stretch towards the heart of the continent with some of the richest biodiversity on earth. And, should you tire of nature, there is always Lima, loud and brash, but with some of the best museums and liveliest nightlife in the country.

10

Peru

Essentials

Planning your trip

Lima, the sprawling capital, is daunting at first sight, but worth investigating for its museums, colonial architecture and nightlife. Routes radiate in every direction and great steps have been taken to improve major roads linking the Pacific with the highlands. Travelling overland does, however, take time, so if on a short visit, flying is the best option.

North of Lima it is only seven hours to Huaraz, in the Cordillera Blanca, the country's climbing and trekking centre. Mountaineering and hiking can be easily linked with the archaeological site at Chavín, east of Huaraz, or with the pre-Inca cities Sechín and Chan Chán, the latter close to the colonial city of Trujillo. Heading up the coast, there is plenty of evidence of precolumbian culture, particularly around Chiclayo, beaches for surfing (eg Chicama) or watching traditional fishing techniques, and wildlife parks in the far north near Tumbes. (Tumbes, and the nearby Piura-Sullana route are the gateways to Ecuador.) In the northern highlands, Cajamarca is a pleasant base for exploring more archaeological sites, thermal baths and beautiful countryside. From here, or by a route from Chiclayo, there is access to the remote Chachapoyas region where a bewildering number of prehispanic cities and cultures are beginning to be opened up to visitors. Going east from here is one of the less travelled roads into the jungle lowlands.

South of Lima are Peru's most deservedly famous tourist destinations. The chief focus is Cusco, where Spanish colonial and Inca architecture are united, and the Sacred Valley of the Incas, with the mountain-top city of Machu Picchu as the highlight of a historical and cultural treasure trove. Regular trips from Cusco extend to Puno on the shores of Lake Titicaca (on the overland route to Bolivia), in which islands are frequently visited to see a unique way of life. Arequipa, a fine city at the foot of El Misti volcano, gives access to the canyons of Colca and, for those with more time, the even deeper Cotahuasi. A much-travelled railway links Cusco, Puno and Arequipa, but the Cusco-Puno road has now been paved, offering new opportunities for exploring these high altitude regions.

On the southern coastal route is the Paracas Peninsula (near Pisco), reputed to be home to the largest sea-lion colony on earth, and offshore Ballestas islands, one of the best places to see marine birdlife in the world. The mysterious Nasca Lines, whose meanings still stir debate, etched in the stony desert, should not be missed if you are on the Lima-Arequipa road, or taking the Pan-American Highway south to Tacna and Chile.

The **Central Highlands** can be reached by roads from Lima, Pisco and Nasca, the main centres being Huancayo, Huancavelica and Ayacucho. There is much of historical interest here and the Mantaro Valley, near Huancayo, and Ayacucho are good areas for buying handicrafts. From Ayacucho you can continue to Cusco by plane or, if willing to rough it, by bus. Roads in this part of the Sierra are being improved considerably, but check conditions if going far off the beaten track.

Another route into the **Peruvian jungle** runs from the Central Highlands to Pucallpa, but the most popular journeys are by air to the Amazon city of Iquitos, from where boats can be taken to Brazil, or from Cusco to the spectacular Manu Biosphere Reserve and the Tambopata area (accessed from Puerto Maldonado). This has some of the highest levels of biodiversity in the world, providing wonderful opportunities for watchers of birds, butterflies and animals, and for plant lovers.

Peru

When to go Each of Peru's geographical zones has its own climate. The **coast**: from Dec to Apr summertime, temperatures from 25° to 35°C; hot and dry. These are the best months for swimming. Wintertime, May-Nov; the temperature drops a bit and it is cloudy. On the coast climate is determined by cold sea-water adjoining deserts: prevailing inshore winds pick up so little moisture over the cold Peruvian current that only from May to Nov does it condense. The resultant blanket of cloud and sea-mist extends from the south to about 200 km north of Lima. This *garúa* dampens isolated coastal zones of vegetation (called *lomas*) and they are grazed by livestock driven down from the mountains. During the *garúa* season, only the northern beaches near Tumbes are warm enough for pleasant swimming.

The **sierra**: from Apr to Oct is the dry season, hot and dry during the day, around 20°-25°C, cold and dry at night, often below freezing. From Nov to Apr is the wet season, dry and clear most mornings, some rainfall in the afternoon, with a small temperature drop (18°C) and not much difference at night (15°C).

Peru's high season is from Jun to Aug, which is the best time for hiking the Inca Trail or trekking and climbing elsewhere in the country. At this time the days are generally clear and sunny, though nights can be very cold at high altitude. The highlands can be visited at other times of the year, though during the wettest months from Nov to Apr some roads become impassable and hiking trails can be very muddy.

The **jungle**: Apr-Oct, dry season, temperatures up to 35°C. This is the best time to visit the jungle. In the jungle areas of the south, a cold front can pass through at night. Nov-Apr, wet season, heavy rainfall at any time, humid and hot. During the wet season, it only rains for a few hours at a time, which is not enough to spoil your trip, but enough to make some roads virtually impassable.

Finding out more

Tourism promotion and information is handled by **PromPerú**, Edificio Mitinci, located at the head of Av Carnaval y Moreyra in Corpac, 13th and 14th floor, San Isidro, T01-224 3279/224 3118/224 3395, F224 3323, iperu@promperu.gob.pe, www.peru.org.pe

There are offices in most towns, either run by the municipality, or independently, which provide tourist information. Outside Peru, tourist information can be obtained from Peruvian Embassies and Consulates (see box). **Indecopi** is the government-run consumer protection and tourist complaint bureau. They are friendly, professional and helpful. In Lima T224 7888, rest of Peru 0800-42579 (not available from payphones), tour@indecopi.gob.pe An excellent source of information is **South American Explorers**, in Lima (see page 1098) and Cusco. See also Essentials, page 26.

Websites www.planet.com.pe/aqpweb For Arequipa (Spansih).

www.cuscoweekly.com, www.cbc.org.pe For Cusco, former in English, latter in Spanish.

www.machupicchu.com For Machu Picchu.

www.machupicchu.org More than just Machu Picchu, a library of all things related to the Inca region and Peru.

www.yachay.com.pe/especiales/nasca, www.magicperu.com/MariaReiche Nasca lines (in Spanish).

www.perunorte.com Northern Peru (La Libertad, Cajamarca and Lambayeque)

www.yachay.com.pe Red Cientifica Peruana, click on Turismo to get to the travel page.

www.terra.com.pe/turismo/index1.shtml (in Spanish).

www.peru.com/turismo Peru.Com's travel page (Spanish and English).

www.traficoperu.com On-line travel agent with lots of useful information (Spanish and English).

www.andeantravelweb.com/peru Andean adventure travel, with advice, links and more (English and Spanish).

www.perurail.com Peru Rail.

www.conam.gob.pe National Environmental Commission (Spanish).

www.perucultural.org.pe For information on cultural activities, museums and Peruvian precolumbian textiles (Spanish).

Peru

www.adonde.com and www.perulinks.com/ Two portals, latter in Spanish and English.
www.best.com/~gibbons Andean culture (English).
Also www.magicperu.com (English and Spanish) and www.geocities.com/perutraveller/
(English).

The official language is Spanish. Quechua, the language of the Inca empire, has been given **Language**
some official status and there is much pride in its use. It is spoken by millions of people in the
Sierra who have little or no knowledge of Spanish. Another important indigenous language
is Aymara, used in the area around Lake Titicaca. The jungle is home to a plethora of
languages but Spanish is spoken in all but the remotest areas. English is not spoken widely,
except by those employed in the tourism industry.

Before you travel

Tourist cards: no visa is necessary for citizens of Western Europe, Asia, North or South America, **Visas &**
or citizens of Australia, New Zealand or South Africa. A Tourist Card is obtained free on flights **immigration**
arriving in Peru, or at border crossings for visits up to 90 days. Insist on getting the full 90 days,
at some borders cards valid for 60, or even only 30 days have been given. It is in duplicate, the
original given up on arrival and the copy on departure, and may be renewed (see below). A
new tourist card must be obtained for each re-entry or when an extension is given. If your
tourist card is stolen or lost, apply for a new one at **Migraciones**, Av España 700 y Av Huaraz,
Breña, Lima, 0900-1330, Mon-Frid; very helpful.

Tourist visas For citizens of countries not listed above, cost $9.60 (US$14 approximately)
or equivalent, for which you require a valid passport, a departure ticket from Peru (or a letter
of guarantee from a travel agency), two colour passport photos, one application form and
proof of economic solvency. All foreigners should be able to produce on demand some
recognizable means of identification, preferably a passport. You must present your passport
when reserving tickets for internal, as well as, international travel. An alternative is to
photocopy the important pages of your passport – including the immigration stamp, and
have it legalized by a 'Notario público' (US$1.50). This way you can avoid showing your
passport. We have received no reports of travellers being asked for an onward ticket at the
borders at Tacna, Aguas Verdes, La Tina, Yunguyo or Desaguadero. Travellers arriving by air are
not asked for an onward flight ticket at Lima airport, but it is quite possible that you will not
be allowed to board a plane in your home country without showing an onward ticket.

Renewals and extensions To extend a tourist card at Immigration in Lima (address
above), go to the third floor and enter the long narrow hall with many "teller" windows. Go to
window number 5 and present your passport and tourist card. The official will give you a
receipt for US$20 (the cost of a one-month extension) which you will pay at the Banco de la
Nación on the same floor. Then go back to the teller room and buy form F007 for S/.22
(US$6.35) from window 12. Fill out the form and return to window 5. Give the official the paid
receipt, the filled-out form, your passport and tourist card. Next, you will wait 10-15 minutes
for your passport to be stamped and signed. **NB** three extensions like this are permitted,
although it's unlikely that you will be allowed to buy more than one month at a time.
Peruvian law states that a tourist can remain in the country for a maximum of six months,
after which time you must leave. Crossing the border out of Peru and returning immediately
is acceptable. You will then receive another 90 days and the process begins all over again.

If you let your tourist visa expire you can be subject to a fine of US$20 per day, but this is up
to the discretion of the immigration official. You can extend your visa in Lima, Cusco, Puno,
Puerto Maldonado, and Iquitos, but in the provinces it can take more time.

Business visas If a visitor is going to receive money from Peruvian sources, he/she must
have a business visa: requirements are a valid passport, two colour passport photos, return
ticket and a letter from an employer or Chamber of Commerce stating the nature of business,
length of stay and guarantee that any Peruvian taxes will be paid. The visa costs US$31 (or
equivalent) and allows the holder to stay 90 days in the country. On arrival business visitors
must register with the *Dirección General de Contribuciones* for tax purposes.

Peru

Embassies and consulates

Australia, *40 Brisbane Avenue Suite 8, Ground Floor, Barton ACT 2600, Canberra, PO Box 106 Red Hill, T61-2-6273 8752, F61-2-6273 8754, www.embaperu.org.au Consulate in Sydney.*

Canada, *130 Albert Street, Suite 1901, Ottawa, Ontario K1P 5G4, T1-613-238 1777, F1-613-232 3062, emperuca@sprint.com Consulates in Montréal and Toronto.*

Finland, *Annankatu 31-33 C, 44, 00100, Helsinki, T358-9-693 3681, F358-9-693 3682, Embassy.peru@peruemb.inet.fi*

France, *50 Avenue Kleber, 75116 Paris, T33-1-5370 4200, F33-1-4704 3255, www.amb-perou.fr/*

Germany, *Godesberger Allee 125, 53175 Bonn, T49-228-373045, F49-228-379475, www.members.aol.com/perusipan Consulates in Berlin and Frankfurt.*

Israel, *37 Revov Ha-Marganit Shikun Vatikim, 52 584 Ramat Gan, Israel, T972-3-613 5591, F972-3-751 2286, emperu@netvision.net.il*

Italy, *Via Francesco Siacci N 4, 00197 Roma, T39-06-8069 1510, F39-06-8069 1777, amb.peru@agora.stm.it Consulate in Milan.*

Japan, *4-4-27 Higashi Shibuya-ku, Tokyo 150-0011, T81-3-3406 4243, F81-3-3409 7589, embperutokio@mb.meweb.ne.jp*

Netherlands, *Nassauplein 4, 2585 EA, The Hague, T31-70-365 3500, embperu@bart.nl*

New Zealand, *Level 8, 40 Mercer Street, Cigna House, Wellington, T64-4-499 8087, F64-4-499 8057, embassy.peru@xtra.co.nz*

South Africa, *Infotech Building, Suite 201, Arcadia Street, 1090 Hatfield, 0083 Pretoria, T27-12- 342 2390, F27-12-342 4944, emperu@iafrica.co*

Spain, *C Príncipe de Vergara 36, 5to Derecha, 28001 Madrid, T34-91-431 4242, F34-91-577 6861, embaperu@arrakis.es Consulate in Barcelona*

Sweden, *Brunnsgatan 21 B, 111 38 Stockholm, T46-8-440 8740, F46-8-205592, www.webmakers/peru*

Switzerland, *Thunstrasse No 36, CH-3005 Berne, T41-31-351 8555, F41-31-351 8570, lepruberna02@bluewin.ch Consulates in Geneva and Zurich.*

UK, *52 Sloane Street, London SW1X 9SP, T020-7235 1917, F020-7235 4463, www.peruembassy-uk.com*

USA, *1700 Massachusetts Avenue NW, Washington DC 20036, T1-202-833 9860, F1-202-659 8124, www.peruemb.org Consulates in Los Angeles, Miami, New York, Chicago, Houston, Puerto Rico, San Francisco.*

Student visas To obtain a one year student visa you must have: proof of adequate funds, affiliation to a Peruvian body, a letter of recommendation from your own and a Peruvian Consul, a letter of moral and economic guarantee from a Peruvian citizen and four photographs (frontal and profile). You must also have a health check certificate which takes four weeks to get and costs US$10. Also, to obtain a student visa, if applying within Peru, you have to leave the country and collect it in La Paz, Arica or Guayaquil from Peruvian immigration (it costs US$20).

Customs **Duty-free allowance**: 400 cigarettes or 50 cigars or 500 g of tobacco, three litres of alcoholic drinks, new articles for personal use or gifts up to value US$300. Five rolls of film, or five camcorder or video cassettes only are allowed duty-free; if taking in more, declare them and pay 20 import duty if you don't want to buy film in Peru.

Export ban No object of archaeological interest may be taken out of Peru.

Money

Currency The new sol (s/) is divided into 100 céntimos. Notes in circulation are: S/200, S/100, S/50, S/20
sol exchange rate with and S/10. Coins: S/5, S/2, S/1, S/0.50, S/0.20, S/0.10 and S/0.05 (being phased out). Some prices
US$: 3.64 are quoted in dollars in more expensive establishments, to avoid changes in the value of the sol. You can pay in soles, however. Try to break down large notes whenever you can.

Warning A large number of forged US dollar notes (especially US$20 and larger bills) are in circulation. Soles notes and coins are also forged. Always check your money when you change it, even in a bank (including ATMs). Hold notes up to the light to inspect the watermark and line which can be seen on the lefthand side of the bill spelling out the bill's

Peru

amount. There should also be tiny pieces of thread in the paper (not glued on). Posters in public places explain what to look for in forged soles. There is a shortage of change in museums, post offices, railway stations and even shops, while taxi drivers are notorious in this regard – one is simply told 'no change'. Do not accept this excuse.

Visa (by far the most widely-accepted card in Peru), MasterCard, American Express and Diners Club are all valid. There is often an 8-12% commission for all credit card charges. Most banks are affiliated with Visa/Plus system; those that you will find in almost every town and city are *Banco de Crédito, Banco Weise Sudameris, Banco Santander Central Hispano* (BSCH) and *Continental*. Not every branch offers the same services (even branches within the same city). *Banco de Crédito*'s ATM is *Telebanco 24 Horas* which accepts Visa and American Express cards. *Interbank* is affiliated with the Cirrus system. ATMs usually give dollars or soles and their use is widespread. Businesses displaying credit card symbols, on the other hand, are less lilkey to take foreign cards. Credit cards are not commonly accepted in smaller towns so go prepared with cash. For credit card loss: *MasterCard*, Porta 111, p 6, Miraflores, T242 2700, or 0800-307 7309; *Diners Club*, Canaval y Moreyra 535, San Isidro, T221 2050; *American Express*, T330 4482/5, Jr Belén 1040, Lima; *Visa* Travel Assistance, T108 and ask the operator for a collect call (por cobrar) to 410-581 9994/3836.

Credit cards
See Plastic, in Money section of Before you travel, Essentials, page 35

Exchange There are no restrictions on foreign exchange. Banks are the most discreet places to change travellers' cheques into soles. Some charge commission from 1% to 3%, some don't, and practice seems to vary from branch to branch, month to month. The services of the Banco de Crédito have been repeatedly recommended. Changing dollars at a bank always gives a lower rate than with *cambistas* (street changers) or *casas de cambio* (exchange houses). Always count your money in the presence of the cashier. US dollars are the most useful currency (take some small bills). Other currencies carry high commission fees. For changing into or out of small amounts of dollars cash, the street changers give the best rates avoiding paperwork and queuing, but they also employ many ruses to give you a bad deal (check your soles before handing over your dollars, check their calculators, etc, and don't change money in crowded areas). If using their services think about taking a taxi after changing, to avoid being followed. Street changers usually congregate near an office where the exchange 'wholesaler' operates; he will probably be offering better rates than on the street.

Soles can be exchanged into dollars at the exchange desks at Lima airport, and you can change soles for dollars at any border. Dollars can also be bought at the various borders.

NB No one, not even banks, will accept dollar bills that look 'old', or are in any way damaged or torn.

American Express will sell travellers' cheques to cardholders only, but will not exchange cheques into cash. *Amex* will hold mail for cardholders at the Lima branch only. They are also very efficient in replacing stolen cheques, though a police report is needed. Most of the main banks accept *American Express* travellers' cheques and *Banco de Crédito* and BSCH accept Visa travellers' cheques. *Citibank* in Lima and some BSCH branches handle *Citicorp* cheques. Travellers have reported great difficulty in cashing travellers' cheques in the jungle area, even Iquitos, and other remote areas. Always sign travellers' cheques in blue or black ink or ballpen.

Living costs in the provinces are from 20% to 50% below those in Lima, although Cusco is a little more expensive than other, less touristy provincial cities. For a lot of low income Peruvians, many items are simply beyond their reach. In 2002, the approximate budget was US$25-35 pp a day for living comfortably, including transport, or US$12-US$15 a day for low budget travel. Your budget will be higher the longer you stay in Lima and depending on how many flights you take between destinations. Accommodation rates range from US$3-4 pp for the most basic *alojamiento* to over US$150 for luxurious hotels in Lima and Cusco. For meal prices, see Food and drink.

Students can obtain very few reductions in Peru with an international students' card, except in and around Cusco. To be any use in Peru, it must bear the owner's photograph. An ISIC card can be obtained in Lima from *Intej*, Av San Martín 240, Barranco, T477 2864, F477 4105, or Portal de Comercio 141, p 2, Plaza de Armas, Cusco, T621351, www.intej.org for US$20.

Cost of travelling

Peru

Getting there

Air **From Europe** Direct flights Amsterdam (*KLM* via Aruba) and Barcelona and Madrid (*Iberia*) Though there are no direct flights from London, cheap options are available with *Avianca* via Bogotá (also the simplest connection from Paris), *Iberia* via Madrid and *KLM* via Amsterdam Alternatively, you can fly standby to Miami, then fly the airlines shown below. A little more expensive, but as convenient, are connections via Atlanta with *Delta*, or Houston with *Continental*. To avoid paying Peru's 18% tax on international air tickets, take your used outward ticket with you when buying return passage.

From North America Miami is the main gateway, together with Atlanta, Houston, Los Angeles and New York. Direct flights are available from Miami with *Aero Continente*, *American Airlines* (which also flies from Dallas), *Copa* and *Lan Perú*; through New York with *Continental*, which also flies from Houston, and Lan Chile; from Atlanta with Delta; and from Los Angeles with *Lacsa*, *Lan Chile* and *AeroMéxico*. Daily connections can be made from almost all major US cities.

From Latin America Regular flights from all South American countries and most Central American; in most cases, daily. *Avianca, Lan Chile* and *Lacsa/Taca* generally have the cheapest flights. Other airlines include *Aero Continente, Aerolíneas Argentinas, AeroMéxico, Avianca, Copa, Tame, LAB, Aeropostal* and *Varig*.

From Australia and New Zealand *Aerolíneas Argentinas* and *Qantas* fly twice a week from Sydney and Auckland to Buenos Aires, from where you can connect to a direct flight to Lima.

Road Peru has international bus links with Ecuador, Bolivia and Chile. Land borders with these countries are straightforward to cross with a private vehicle.

Boat River boats on the Amazon sail between Iquitos and the Brazil/Colombian border at Tabatinga and Leticia.

Touching down

Airport information **Airport departure taxes** There is a US$25 airport tax on international flight departures, payable in dollars or soles; 12 soles (US$3.45) on internal flights. 18% state tax is charged on air tickets; it is included in the price of the ticket.

There are ATMs between the national and international foyers accepting Visa, MasterCard and the Plus and Cirrus systems. There are 3 *Casas de Cambio* (money changing desks) in the airport. They are open 24 hrs and change all types of travellers' cheque (they claim) and most major currencies. There are also exchange facilities for cash in the international arrivals hall. *Banco de Crédito* stands, in the national and international foyers only collect the international or domestic airport tax that must be paid in order to get through the gate.

Public telephones are everywhere in and around the airport. There is also a *Telefónica del Peru* office in the international foyer, open 0700-2300 daily. Fax service is available. There are two post offices, one in the national foyer, the other at the far end of the international foyer.

There is a 24-hr pharmacy, on the second level to the left of the escalator near international departures, which offers everything from normal medication to yellow fever shots. Also opposite the departure gate is a First Aid post (not open in the early morning). The left luggage lock-up, located near international arrivals, offers safe 24-hr storage and retrieval for about US$3 per bag per day. Only official *Corpac* porters are allowed in the customs area.

Information desks can be found in the national and international foyers. There is also a helpful desk in the international arrivals hall. It can make hotel and transport reservations. The *Zeta* books kiosk in the international foyer and in the departure lounge have a good selection of English language guidebooks.

On the second level there are various cafés and restaurants, some accepting major credit cards. Food tends to be pricey and not very good. Safe to stay all night in 24 hr expresso-snack bar upstairs but expensive; also in VIP lounge, US$10.

Touching down

Official time 5 hrs behind GMT.

IDD code 51.

Business hours Shops: 0900 or 1000-1230 and 1500 or 1600-2000. In the main cities, supermarkets do not close for lunch and Lima has some that are open 24 hrs. Some are closed on Saturday and most are closed on Sunday. **Banks:** most banks around the country are open 0930 to 1200 and 1500 to 1800. Banks in Lima generally do not take a siesta so are open throughout the lunch hours. Many banks in Lima and Cusco have

Saturday morning hours from 0930 to 1230. **Offices:** 0830-1230, 1500-1800 all year round. Some have continuous hours 0900-1700 and most close on Saturday. **Government Offices:** Monday-Friday 0830-1130, January to March. The rest of year Monday-Friday 0900-1230, 1500-1700, but this changes frequently.

> **Voltage** 220 volts AC, 60 cycles throughout the country, except Arequipa (50 cycles).
>
> **Weights and measures** The metric system of weights and measures is compulsory.

Tipping

Restaurants: service is included in the bill (see below), but if someone goes out of his way to serve tips can be given. Taxi drivers, none (in fact, bargain the price down, then pay extra for good service if you get it). Cloakroom attendants and hairdressers (very high class only), US$0.50-US$1. Railway or airport porters, US$0.50. Usherettes, none. Car wash boys, US$0.30, car 'watch' boys, US$0.20. If going on a trek or tour, it is customary to tip the guide as well as the cook and porters.

Safety

The following notes on personal safety should not hide the fact that most Peruvians are hospitable and helpful.

For general hints on avoiding crime, please see the Security, Essentials, page 45. All the suggestions given there are valid for Peru. Snatch thieves in Lima are very fast, they often use beggars to distract you. The most common method of attack is bag-slashing. It is worth taking extra care during festivals when streets are crowded. The police presence in Lima, Arequipa, Puno and Cusco has been greatly stepped up. Nevertheless, there has been an alarming increase in aggressive assaults in centres along the Gringo Trail. Places like Arequipa, Puno and in particular Cusco have, at times, been plagued by waves of strangle muggings. Check with *South American Explorers* and/or the *Latin American Travel Advisor* (see page 26) for a current summary of the situation and how to keep safe. Outside the Jul-Aug peak holiday period, there is less tension, less risk of crime, and more friendliness. A friendly attitude on your part, smiling even when you've thwarted a thief's attempt, can help you out of trouble.

Although certain illegal drugs are readily available, anyone carrying any is almost automatically assumed to be a drug trafficker. If arrested on any charge the wait for trial in prison can take a year and is particularly unpleasant. Unfortunately, we have received reports of drug-planting, or mere accusation of drug-trafficking by the PNP on foreigners in Lima, with US$1,000 demanded for release. If you are asked by the narcotics police to go to the toilets to have your bags searched, insist on taking a witness. **Drugs use or purchase is punishable by up to 15 years' imprisonment. The number of foreigners in Peruvian prisons on drug charges is still increasing.**

Tricks employed to get foreigners into trouble over drugs include slipping a packet of cocaine into the money you are exchanging, being invited to a party or somewhere involving a taxi ride, or simply being asked on the street if you want to buy cocaine. In all cases, a plain clothes 'policeman' will discover the planted cocaine, in your money, at your feet in the taxi, and will ask to see your passport and money. He will then return them, minus a large part of your cash. Do not get into a taxi, do not show your money, and try not to be intimidated. Being in pairs is no guarantee of security, and single women may be particularly vulnerable. Beware also thieves dressed as policemen asking for your passport and wanting to search for drugs; **searching is only permitted if prior paperwork is done.**

Insurgency The guerrilla activities of Sendero Luminoso and MRTA seem to be a thing of the past, although it would be wrong to say that either organization was completely non-functional. It is still important to inform yourself of the latest situation before going, but in 2002 it was safe to travel to all parts of Peru except the Huallaga Valley and jungle areas east of Ayacucho because of drug trafficking and terrorism.

For up-to-date information contact the **Tourist Police**, see below, your embassy or consulate, fellow travellers, or *South American Explorers*, who issue the pamphlet 'How Not to Get Robbed in Peru' (T Lima 445 3306, Cusco 245484, or in Quito).

We have received new reports in 2002 of **nightclubs** denying entrance to people on the basis of skin colour and assumed economic status. This has happened in Lima and in Cusco. It is not possible to verify if this is the establishments' policy or merely that of certain doormen.

Tourist Protection Bureau (Indecopi) 24-hour hotline for travellers' complaints, T/F01-224 7888, or, outside Lima, toll free on 0800-42579 (not from pay phones), tour@indecopi.gob.pe At Jorge Chávez airport, Lima, T01-574 8000, T/F01-575 1434; in Cusco T/F084-252974, or, at the airport, T084-237364; In Arequipa, T054-212054; in Trujillo, T044-204146. This is run by the Tourist Bureau of Complaints and will help with complaints regarding customs, airlines, travel agencies, accommodation, restaurants, public authorities or if you have lost, or had stolen, documents. There is an office in every town as well as kiosks and information stands in airports and public buildings. They are very effective.

Tourist Police, Jr Moore 268, Magdalena at the 38th block of Av Brasil, T460 1060/460 0844, open daily 24 hrs. You should come here if you have had property stolen. They are friendly, helpful and speak English and some German

Where to stay

Hotels

See inside front cover of the book for our hotel price guide. At most airports and train stations, hotel representatives meet new arrivals with publicity for their employers

All deluxe and first class hotels charge 28% in taxes, which includes state tax and service charges; lower category hotels charge 18%. Few hotels have this surcharge included in their prices, but best check first. By law all places that offer accommodation now have a plaque outside bearing the letters H (Hotel), Hs (Hostal), HR (Hotel Residencial) or P (Pensión) according to type. A hotel has 51 rooms or more, a hostal 50 or fewer; the categories do not describe quality or facilities. Many hotels have safe parking for motor cycles. All hotels seem to be crowded during Christmas and Easter holidays, Carnival and at the end of Jul; Cusco in Jun is also very busy. Information on youth hostels and student accommodation can be obtained from *Intej*, Av San Martín 240, Barranco, Lima, T477 2864, F4774105, www.intej.org Also **Asociación Peruana de Albergues Turísticos Juveniles**, Av Casimiro Ulloa 328, San Antonio between San Isidro and Miraflores, Lima, T446 5488, F444 8187. Take a torch and candles, especially in remoter regions.

Camping

Camping is easy in Peru, especially along the coast. There can be problems with robbery when camping close to a small village. Avoid such a location, or ask permission to camp in a backyard or *chacra* (farmland). Most Peruvians are used to campers, but in some remote places, people have never seen a tent. Be casual about it, do not unpack all your gear, leave it inside your tent (especially at night) and never leave a tent unattended. Camping gas in little blue bottles is available in the main cities. Those with stoves designed for lead-free gasoline should use *ron de quemar*, available from hardware shops (*ferreterías*). White gas is called *bencina*, also available from hardware stores.

Getting around

Air

There are two main national carriers that serve the most travelled routes – Arequipa, Ayacucho, Cajamarca, Chiclayo, Cusco, Iquitos, Juliaca, Piura, Puerto Maldonado, Pucallpa, Tacna, Tarapoto, Trujillo and Tumbes; they are *AeroContinente* (www.aerocontinente.com.pe with its subsidiary *Aviandina*) and *Tans* (www.tans.com.pe). Both airlines generally cost the same, between US$39 and US$99 one-way anywhere in the country from Lima. For shorter flights it may cost a bit less (eg Cusco-Puerto Maldonado US$29). It is not unusual for the prices to go up at holiday times (Semana Santa, May Day, Inti Raymi, 28-29 Jul, Christmas and New Year), and for elections. During these times and the northern hemisphere summer seats can be hard to come by, especially on the Lima-Cusco-Lima route, so book early. *Lan Perú* (www.lanperu.com an offshoot of Lan Chile) offers services from Lima to Cusco, Arequipa and Juliaca. For remoter destinations in the highlands such as, Andahuaylas, Chachapoyas, Huánuco, and jungle airports such as Atalaya, Satipo, Tingo María and Tocache try *Aero Cóndor* (www.ascinsa.com/ AEROCONDOR), *TdobleA* and *Star-Up*. Ticketing for these airlines is not possible at many travel agencies, so it is better to contact the airline direct for information and reservations. See under Lima (page 1122) for airline phone numbers. Flight schedules and departure times change often and delays are common. In the rainy season cancellations occur. Flights into the mountains may well be put forward one hour if there are reports of bad weather. Flights to jungle regions are also unreliable. Always allow an extra day between national and international flights, especially in the rainy season. Internal flight prices are fixed in US dollars (but can be paid in soles) and have 18% tax added. If you have a choice, remember time-keeping tends to be better early morning than later. When buying an internal flight, check with travel agencies for occasional special deals, but scrutinize the ticket carefully.

NB If possible travel with hand luggage only (48 cm x 24 cm x 37 cm) so there is more chance of you and your baggage arriving at the same destination.

Flights must be reconfirmed in the town you will be leaving from 24 hours in advance, but 72 hours is advised. About 30 minutes before departure, the clerk is allowed by law to let standby passengers board, taking the reserved seats of those who haven't turned up.

Air Freight Luggage, packets, etc, are not handled with care; make sure there are no loose parts, or put your rucksack in a separate bag. Always lock your luggage when possible. Check that the correct destination label has been attached. Never put valuables into luggage to be checked in.

Road

The Pan-American Highway runs north-south through the coastal desert and is mostly in good condition. Also paved and well-maintained is the direct road which branches off the Pan-American at Pativilca and runs up to Huaraz and on to Caraz. The Northern route from Chiclayo through to Tarapoto is being paved. It is complete to Nueva Cajamarca, plus the spur to Jaén, and is being heavily worked on to Moyobamba and Tarapoto. Cajamarca is also going to have a smart new road connection to the coast to serve the Yanacocha mine. The Central Highway from Lima to Huancayo is mostly well-paved. It continues (mostly paved) to Pucallpa in the Amazon basin. South of Lima, there's the great new 'Liberatores' highway from Pisco to Ayacucho. From Nasca to Abancay is paved as far as Chalhuanca (about two-thirds of the way) and is being worked on for the rest of the route. When finished, this will be the main route from Lima to Cusco since Abancay-Cusco is paved. The Cusco-Puno stretch is paved and in good condition; it is now a fast, comfortable journey to rival the train. The paved road continues along the south shore of Lake Titicaca to Desasguadero on the Bolivian border. In the south, the road which runs into the Sierra to Arequipa is in good condition. From Arequipa the roads to Puno and Juliaca are under reconstruction, but the new route to Desaguadero from the coast via Moquegua is one of the nicest highways in the country. Roads from Arequipa to Mollendo and Matarani are also excellent.

Other roads in the mountains are of dirt, some good, some very bad. Each year they are affected by heavy rain and mud slides, especially those on the east slopes of the mountains. Repairs can be delayed because of a shortage of funds. Note that some of these roads can be dangerous or impassable in the rainy season. Check beforehand with locals (not with bus companies, who only want to sell tickets) as accidents are common at these times. Total road length is 71,400 km.

Toll roads in Peru include Aguas Verdes-Tumbes, many on the Pan-American Highway between Tumbes and Lima, Pativilca-Huaraz, Lima-Pucusana, Ica-Nasca, Lima (highway around city), Variante-Pacasmayo, which vary from US$1.50 to US$0.50. Ecuador to Chile/Bolivia on main roads comes to about US$20. (Motorcycles are exempt from road tolls: use the extreme righthand lane at toll gates.)

If you have to drive at night, do not go fast; many local vehicles have poor lights and street lighting is bad.

Car

Gasoline is sold by its equivalent octane rating. Leaded, 84 octane; and unleaded 90, 95, and 97 octane. Unleaded is widely available along the Panamericana and in cities with over

250,000 people. In the Central Highlands, however, unleaded fuel is rarely on sale. Diesel is referred to as "petróleo" and is marked on the price signs as D2. Prices are between US$2.50-US$3.50 for gasoline and around US$2 for diesel. The cost along the coast outside urban areas is slightly lower; and slightly higher in the highlands. Since the introduction in 1998 of the "Law of Amazonia" prices for fuel in the jungle are the cheapest in the country. Diesel, by far the fuel of choice, costs around US$1.50 thanks to governmental subsidies. Filling stations are called *grifos*.

Peruvian drivers tend to regard traffic lanes and traffic lights as recommendations, at most. In Lima never trust the green light. No-parking signs are painted at the roadside: illegally parked cars are towed away. Do not leave your vehicle on the street in Lima, always put it in a car park (called *playa*), usual charge US$0.75-1 per hour. If you want to sleep in your car, check with the local tourist police first. They may allow you to park near their office. Transit police in silver Landcruisers park beside the road everywhere. They check on vehicles frequently, so be prepared to pull over. Usually the police are friendly and helpful with dirrections.

Roads go to very high altitudes in Peru – make sure that the spark is properly adjusted and consider use of smaller carburettor jets if driving much at altitude. Avoid mountain travel between Nov and Apr. Take two planks of wood in case car gets stuck in soft soil when allowing other vehicles to pass. Never travel off the main roads without being self-sufficient. Always make sure your fuel tank is full when branching off a major highway, fill up whenever possible and make sure you do not receive diesel or kerosene. If you need mechanical assistance in the mountains ask for the nearest mining or road construction camp. Disadvantages of travelling in your own vehicle include the difficulties of getting insurance, theft, finding guarded parking lots, maintenance on appalling roads and nervous exhaustion, which may outweigh the advantages of mobility and independence.

Imported car spares are available and cheaper than in neighbouring countries. Makes with well-established dealerships are easiest to obtain (eg Volvo, Peugeot, VW). Many used Japanese and Korean vehicles are imported into Peru, so spares and service should be available for them, too. There is also a booming black market in motor parts involving both contraband and stolen parts.

You must have an international driving licence to drive in Peru, but if renting a car, your home driving licence will be accepted for up to six months. If bringing in your own vehicle a libreta de pasos por aduana or carnet de passages is officially required, as well as proof of ownership of the vehicle. To drive in Peru you must be over 21 and to rent a car over 25.

Bus Services along the coast to the north and south as well as inland to Huancayo, Ayacucho and Huaraz are very good. There are direct (*ejecutivo*) service buses to major centres (different companies use different titles for their top class or executive services, eg *Imperial, Ideal, Royal*). As well as *ejecutivo*, many bus companies have regular (local) service and the difference between the two is often great. Many buses have bathrooms, movies and reclining seats (*bus cama*). *Ormeño* and *Cruz del Sur* are the two bus lines generally thought to have the best service with the most routes. *Cruz del Sur* accepts Visa cards and gives 10% discount to ISIC and Under26 cardholders (you may have to insist). *Civa*, which has good buses, offer the most extensive coverage throughout the nation and are in a class just below *Ormeño* and *Cruz del Sur*. There are many smaller but still excellent bus lines that run only to specific areas. For bus lines, see Lima, Bus Companies. For long journeys take a water bottle. Blankets and emergency food are a **must** in the mountains. Where buses stop it is always possible to buy food on the roadside. With the better companies or *ejecutivo* service you will get a receipt for your luggage, which will be locked under the bus. On local buses there will be lots of people loading and unloading bags, so it's best to watch your luggage. Always carry your valuables with you, even when leaving the bus at a stop. If your bus breaks down and you are transferred to another line and have to pay extra, keep your original ticket for refund from the first company. If possible, on country buses avoid the back seats because of the bumpiness, and the left side because of exhaust fumes.

Combis operate between most small towns on 1-3-hour journeys. This makes it possible, in many cases, just to turn up and travel within an hour or two. On rougher roads, combis are minibuses (invariably Japanese), while on better roads there are also slightly more expensive and much faster car colectivos. Colectivos usually charge twice the bus fare. They leave only when full. They go almost anywhere in Peru; most firms have offices. Book one day in advance and they pick you up at your hotel or in the main plaza. Trucks are not always much cheaper than buses; wholly unpredictable, not for long hops, and comfort depends on the load. Always try to arrive at your destination in daylight: much safer.

NB Prices of bus tickets are raised by 60-100%, 2-3 days before Semana Santa, 28 Jul (Independence Day – Fiestas Patrias) and Christmas. Tickets are sold out 2-3 days in advance at this time and transport is hard to come by.

Hitchhiking

Hitchhiking is difficult. Freight traffic has to stop at the police *garitas* outside each town and these are the best places to try (also toll points, but these are further from towns). Drivers usually ask for money but don't always expect to get it. In mountain and jungle areas you usually have to pay drivers of lorries, vans and even private cars; ask the driver first how much he is going to charge, and then recheck with the locals. Private cars are very few and far between. Readers report that mining trucks are especially dirty to travel in, avoid if possible.

Taxi

Taxi prices are fixed in the mountain towns, about US$1.20 in the urban area. Fares are not fixed in Lima although some drivers work for companies that do have standard fares. Ask locals what the price should be and always set the price beforehand. The main cities have taxis which can be hired by phone, which charge a little more, but are reliable and safe.

Many taxi drivers work for commission from hotels. Choose your own hotel and get a taxi driver who is willing to take you there.

Taxis at airports are always more expensive; seek advice about the price in advance. In some places it is cheaper to walk out of the airport to the main road and flag down a cab.

Another common form of public transport is the mototaxi, a three-wheel motorcycle with an awning covering the double-seat behind the driver. Fares are about US$1.

Train

The railways of major interest to the traveller are Arequipa-Juliaca-Puno, Puno-Juliaca-Cusco, and Cusco-Machu Picchu. They are administered by *PerúRail SA*, which includes a tourist train to the Colca Canyon (Arequipa-Sumbay). For information, T084 (Cusco) 238722, reservations 221992, F221114, reservas@perurail.com, www.perurail.com The other main passenger service currently running is from Huancayo to Huancavelica in the Central Highlands. The service from Lima to Huancayo has been suspended indefinitely. In all there are in all 2,121 km of railway. Two rail lines run up the slopes of the Andes to the Sierra. Neither carries passengers. These railways run from Lima in the centre and the ports of Matarani and Mollendo in the south. From Lima a railway runs to La Oroya, at which point it splits, one section going to Cerro de Pasco and the other to Huancavelica, via Huancayo.

Maps

The **Touring y Automóvil Club del Perú**, Av César Vallejo 699, Lince, Lima (T221 2432), with offices in most provincial cities, gives news about the roads and hotels along the way (although for the most up-to-date information try the bus and colectivo offices). It sells a very good road map at US$5 (Mapa Vial del Perú, 1:3,000,000, Ed 1980) and route maps covering most of Peru (Hoja de Ruta, detail maps 1:1,000,000, very good but no information on road conditions). The *Guía Toyota* (Spanish), which is published annually, is one of the best guides for venturing off the beaten track. Lima 2000's *Mapa Vial del Perú* (1:2,200,000) is probably the best and most correct road map available for the country. Both can be obtained from the *South American Explorers*, who will give good advice on road conditions. Buy maps separately or in packages of eight. Other maps can be bought from street vendors in Colmena and Plaza San Martín, Lima. 'Westermanns Monatshefte; folio Ecuador, Peru, Bolivien' has excellent maps of Peru, especially the archaeological sites.

An excellent map of the Callejón de Huaylas and Cordillera Huayhuash, by Felipe Díaz, is available in many shops in Huaraz and at Casa de Guías. Hidrandina, the state hydroelectric company, at 27 de Noviembre 773, has dye-line maps of the Cordillera Blanca, open in morning only. Several guides and agencies have their own sketch maps of the most popular routes. Maps are also available by mail-order from *Latin American Travel Consultants*, PO Box 17-17-908, Quito, Ecuador, LATA@pi-pro.ec Maps of the Österreichischer Alpenverein, ÖAV, are good and can be bought in Peru, but are cheaper in Europe.

Peru

Keeping in touch

Internet You can find internet access everywhere. Centres with high tourism have internet cafés on every corner; many of them have net-phone. Internet cafés are listed in the travelling text under each town, except where there are too many to mention, like Lima. Internet cafés are incredibly cheap to use, often less than US$1 per hour. When they first open in the morning is often a good time to use cyber cafés, as they are less busy then. In addition, the system is often overloaded, so getting access to your server can take a long time. Internet access is more expensive in hotel business centres and in out of the way places. At branches of McDonalds you can use the internet for free.

Post The name of the postal system is *Serpost*. Sending mail and parcels can be done at any post office but Correo Central on the Plaza de Armas in Lima is the best place. The office is open Mon to Fri from 0730-1900, Sat 0730-1600. Stamps, envelopes and cloth sacks (to send bigger parcels in) can all be bought there. It costs US$1 to mail a letter anywhere in the Americas and US$1.20 to the rest of the world. You can also mail letters 'expreso' for about US$0.55 extra to the Americas, US$0.90 to the rest of the world, and they will arrive a little more quickly. Don't put tape on envelopes or packages, wait until you get to the post office and use the glue they have. It is very expensive to mail large packages out of Peru so it is best not to plan to send things home from here. For emergency or important documents, *DHL* and *Federal Express* are also options in Lima. Addresses of these agencies, and where to receive parcels, are given under Lima, **Communications**. To receive mail, letters can be sent to Poste Restante/General Delivery (*lista de correos*), your embassy, or, for cardholders, *American Express* offices. Members of the *South American Explorers* can have post and packages sent to them at either of the Peruvian offices.

Telephone *Telefónica* (or *Telser* in Cusco) offers the most comprehensive service that is of direct use for the traveller. The average cost for a three-minute call to North America or Western Europe is about US$6-7. Collect calls are possible to almost anywhere by ringing the international operator (108). You can also reach a variety of countries' operators direct if you wish to charge a call to your home calling card. 108 has the 0-800 numbers for the international direct options and they speak English. You can also receive calls at many *Telefónica* offices, the cost is usually around US$1 for 10 minutes. Net Phones are becoming increasingly popular, especially in Lima. Costs and service vary but can be as cheap as US$5 per hour to the USA. Calls to everywhere else are usually at least 50% more. Faxes cost about US$1.50 per page to North America, US$2 to most of Western Europe and US$2.50 to Israel. The cost to receive is about US$1 per page.

Media **Newspapers** Lima has several morning papers: *El Comercio* (good international news), www.elcomercioperu.com.pe; *La República* (liberal-left), www.larepublica.com.pe; *Expreso*, www.expreso.com.pe Also *Ojo. Gestión*, www.gestion.com.pe, is a business daily. The most widely-read weekly magazine is *Caretas*, www.caretas. com.pe Monthlies include *Business*, *Proceso Económico, Debate* and *Idede*. There is a weekly economic and political magazine in English, the *Andean Report*, with useful information and articles. *Rumbos* is a good bi-monthly magazine (English and Spanish) about tourism and culture, www.rumbos.delperu.com The *New World News* is a monthly publication in Cusco that is directed at the traveller. The main provincial cities have at least one newspaper each. The following websites have news coverage: www.perualdia.com or through www.yachay.com.pe; www.terra.com.pe; www.peru.com

Food and drink

Food **Coastal cuisine** The best coastal dishes are seafood based, the most popular being *ceviche*. This is a dish of white fish marinated in lemon juice, onion and hot peppers. Traditionally, *ceviche* is served with corn-on-the-cob, *cancha* (toasted corn), yucca and sweet potatoes. *Tiradito* is *ceviche* without onions made with plaice. Another mouth-watering fish dish is

Peru

escabeche – fish with onions, hot green pepper, red peppers, prawns (*langostinos*), cumin, hard-boiled eggs, olives, and sprinkled with cheese (it can also be made with chicken). For fish on its own, don't miss the excellent *corvina*, or white sea bass. You should also try *chupe de camarones*, which is a shrimp stew made with varying ingredients. Other fish dishes include *parihuela*, a popular bouillabaisse which includes *yuyo de mar*, a tangy seaweed, and *aguadito*, a thick rice and fish soup said to have rejuvenating powers.

A favourite northern coastal dish is *seco de cabrito*, roasted kid (baby goat) served with the ubiquitous beans and rice, or *seco de cordero* which uses lamb instead. Also good is *aji de gallina*, a rich and spicy creamed chicken, and duck is excellent. *Humitas* are small, stuffed dumplings made with maize. The *criollo* cooking of the coast has a strong tradition and can be found throughout the country. Two popular examples are *cau cau*, made with tripe, potatoes, peppers, and parsley and served with rice, and *anticuchos*, which are shish kebabs of beef heart with garlic, peppers, cumin seeds and vinegar.

Highland cuisine The staples of highland cooking, corn and potatoes, date back to Inca times and are found in a remarkable variety of shapes, sizes and colours.

Two good potato dishes are *Causa* and *carapulca*. Causa is made with yellow potatoes, lemons, pepper, hard-boiled eggs, olives, lettuce, sweet cooked corn, sweet cooked potato, fresh cheese, and served with onion sauce (it can be made with tuna, avocado or prawns). Another potato dish is *papa a la huancaina*, which is topped with a spicy sauce made with milk and cheese. *Ocopa* is a similar dish in which slices of potato are served with a sauce made from milk, herbs and pecan nuts. *Papa rellena* is a deep-fried mashed potato ball stuffed with vegetables, egg and meat. The most commonly eaten corn dishes are *choclo con queso*, corn on the cob with cheese, and *tamales*, boiled corn dumplings filled with meat and wrapped in a banana leaf.

Meat dishes are many and varied. *Ollucos con charqui* is a kind of potato with dried meat; *sancochado* is a meat and all kinds of vegetables stewed together and seasoned with ground garlic. A dish almost guaranteed to appear on every restaurant menu is *lomo saltado*, a kind of stir-fried beef with onions, vinegar, ginger, chilli, tomatoes and fried potatoes, served with rice. *Rocoto relleno* is spicy bell pepper stuffed with beef and vegetables, *palta rellena* is avocado filled with chicken salad, Russian salad or prawns. *Estofado de carne* is a stew which often contains wine and *carne en adobo* is a cut and seasoned steak. Others include *fritos*, fried pork, usually eaten in the morning, *chicharrones*, deep fried chunks of pork ribs and chicken or fish, and *lechón*, suckling pig. A delicacy in the highlands is *cuy*, guinea pig.

Very filling and good value are the many soups on offer, such as *yacu-chupe*, a green soup which has a basis of potato, with cheese, garlic, coriander leaves, parsley, peppers, eggs, onions, and mint, *and sopa a la criolla* containing thin noodles, beef heart, bits of egg and vegetables and pleasantly spiced.

Tropical cuisine The main ingredient in much jungle cuisine is fish, especially the succulent, dolphin-sized *paiche*, which comes with the delicious *palmito*, or palm-hearts, and the ever-present yucca and fried bananas. Another popular dish is *sopa de motelo* (turtle soup). *Juanes* are a jungle version of tamales, stuffed with chicken and rice.

Desserts Among the desserts and confections are *cocada al horno* – coconut, with yolk of egg, sesame seed, wine and butter; *picarones* – frittered cassava flour and eggs fried in fat and served with honey; *mazamorra morada* – purple maize, sweet potato starch, lemons, various dried fruits, sticks of ground cinnamon and cloves and perfumed pepper; *manjar blanco* – milk, sugar and eggs; *maná* – an almond paste with eggs, vanilla and milk; *alfajores* – shortbread biscuit with *manjar blanco*, pineapple, peanuts, etc; *pastelillos* – yuccas with sweet potato, sugar and anise fried in fat and powdered with sugar and served hot; and *zango de pasas*, made with maize, syrup, raisins and sugar. *Turrón*, the Lima nougat, is worth trying. *Tejas* are sugar candies wrapped in wax paper; the pecan-flavoured ones are tastiest. The various Peruvian fruits are of good quality: they include bananas, the citrus fruits, pineapples, dates, avocados (*paltas*), eggfruit (*lúcuma*), the custard apple (*chirimoya*) which can be as big as your head, quince, papaya, mango, guava, the passion-fruit (*maracuyá*) and the soursop (*guanábana*).

Peru

A normal lunch or dinner costs US$5-8, but can go up to about US$80 in a first-class restaurant, with drinks and wine included. Middle and high-class restaurants add 11% tax and 17% service to the bill (sometimes 18% and 13% respectively); this is not shown on the price list or menu, check in advance. Lower class restaurants charge only 5% tax, while cheap, local restaurants charge no taxes. Lunch is the main meal: dinner in restaurants is normally about 1900 onwards, but choice may be more limited than lunchtime. There are plenty of cheap and good restaurants around the centre of Lima and most offer a 'business lunch' called *menú* for US$1.50-3 for a three-course meal. There are many Chinese restaurants (*chifas*) in Peru which serve good food at reasonable prices. For really economically-minded people the *comedores populares* in most cities of Peru offer a standard three-course meal for US$1.25. Meals at this price, or little more, can be found under the name of *menú económico* at many restaurants throughout Peru.

NB. If asked to a party ask the hostess what time you are *really* expected unless the time is specified on the invitation card as *hora inglesa* – English time; Peruvians tend to ask guests for dinner at 2000.

Drink The most famous local drink is *pisco*, a brandy made in the Ica valley, from which pisco sour is made. Also popular are *chilcano*, a longer refreshing drink made with *guinda*, a local cherry brandy; and *algarrobina*, a sweet cocktail made with the syrup from the bark of the carob tree, egg whites, milk, pisco and cinnamon. The best wines are from Ica, Tacama and Ocucaje; both come in red, white and rosé, sweet and dry varieties. Tacama blancs de blancs and brut champagne have been recommended, also Gran Tinto Reserva Especial. Viña Santo Tomás, from Chincha, is reasonable and cheap. Casapalca is not recommended. Beer is best in lager and porter types, especially the *Cusqueña* and *Arequipeña* brands (lager) and *Trujillo Malta* (porter). In Lima only *Cristal* and *Pilsener* (not related to true Pilsen) are readily available, others have to be sought out. Look out for the sweetish 'maltina' brown ale, which makes a change from the ubiquitous pilsner–type beers. *Chicha de jora* is a maize beer, usually homemade and not easy to come by, refreshing but strong, and *chicha morada* is a soft drink made with purple maize. The local rival to Coca Cola, the fluorescent yellow *Inca Cola*, is made from lemon grass. Peruvian coffee is good, but the best is exported. Many cafés only serve coffee in liquid form or Nescafé. It is often brought to the table in a small jug accompanied by a mug of hot water to which you add the coffee essence. If you want coffee with milk, a mug of milk is brought. There are many different kinds of herb tea: the commonest are *manzanilla* (camomile) and *hierbaluisa* (lemon grass).

Shopping

It is possible to find any kind of handicraft in Lima. The prices are often the same as in the highlands, and the quality is high. Good buys are: silver and gold handicrafts; Indian hand-spun and hand-woven textiles; manufactured textiles in Indian designs; llama and alpaca wool products such as ponchos, rugs, hats, blankets, slippers, coats and sweaters; *arpilleras* (appliqué pictures of Peruvian life); and fine leather products which are mostly hand made. Another good buy is clothing made from high quality Pima cotton, which is grown in Peru.

The *mate burilado*, or engraved gourd found in every tourist shop, is cheap and one of the most genuine expressions of folk art in Peru. These are cheaper if bought in the villages of the Mantaro Valley near Huancayo in the Central Highlands. Alpaca clothing, such as sweaters, hats and gloves, is cheaper in the Sierra, especially in Puno. Another good source is Arequipa, where alpaca cloth for suits, coats, etc (mixed with 40% sheep's wool) can be bought cheaply from factories. Geniune alpaca is odourless wet or dry, wet llama 'stinks'.

One of the very best places in Peru to look for *artesanía* is Ayacucho in the Central Highlands. Here you'll find excellent woven textiles, as well as the beautifully intricate *retablos*, or Saint Mark's boxes. Cusco is one of the main weaving centres and a good place to shop for textiles, as well as excellent woodcarvings. Also recommended for textiles is Cajamarca. The island of Taquile on Lake Titicaca is a good place to buy *ch'uspas* (bags for coca leaves), *chumpis* (belts) and *chullos* (knitted conical hats).

Holidays and festivals

Two of the major festival dates are *Carnaval*, which is held over the weekend before Ash Wednesday, and *Semana Santa* (Holy Week), which ends on Easter Sunday. Carnival is celebrated in most of the Andes and Semana Santa throughout Peru. Another important festival is *Fiesta de la Cruz*, held on the first of May in much of the central and southern highlands and on the coast. In Cusco, the entire month of June is one huge *fiesta*, culminating in *Inti Raymi*, on 24 June, one of Peru's prime tourist attractions. Another national festival is *Todos los Santos* (All Saints) on **1 November**, and on **8 December** is *Festividad de la Inmaculada Concepción*. A full list of local festivals is listed under each town.

Apart from the festivals listed above, the main holidays are: **1 January**, New Year; **6 January**, *Bajada de Reyes*; **1 May**, Labour Day; **28-29 July**, Independence (Fiestas Patrias); **7 October**, Battle of Angamos; **24-25 December**, Christmas.

NB Most businesses such as banks, airline offices and tourist agencies close for the official holidays while supermarkets and street markets may be open. This depends a lot on where you are so ask around before the holiday. Sometimes holidays that fall during mid-week will be moved to the following Mon. The high season for foreign tourism in Peru is Jun to Sep while national tourism peaks at Christmas, Semana Santa and Fiestas Patrias. Prices rise and accommodation and bus tickets are harder to come by.

Sport and special interest travel

Birdwatching 18.5% of all the bird species in the world and 45% of all neotropical birds are found in Peru. A birding trip is possible during any month as birds breed all year round. The peak in breeding activity occurs just before the rains come in Oct, so it is easier to locate many birds between Sep and Christmas. Rainwear is recommended in the mountains, especially in the rainy season (Nov-Apr), but in the tropical lowlands it is better to take an umbrella. Besides binoculars, a telescope is useful in many areas.

There are many important sites, but the key ones are the Manu Biosphere Reserve, Tambopata-Candamo Reserved Zone, Iquitos, Paracas, Lomas de Lachay, the Colca Canyon and the Huascarán Biosphere Reserve. There are too many birds to mention, but from the tiny hummingbirds to flamingoes and the Andean condor, the range is totally rewarding for the beginner and the most experienced birder alike.

Climbing Peru offers plenty of possibilities. The Cordillera Blanca, with Huaraz as a base, is an ice climber's paradise. Over 50 summits are between 5,000 and 6,000 m and over 20 exceed 6,000 m. There is a wide range of difficulty and no peak fees are charged (although national park entrace has to paid in the Cordillera Blanca). The *Peruvian Mountain Guide Association* (AGMP) is located in the Casa de Guías, Huaraz. The Cordillera Huayhuash, southeast of Huaraz, is a bit more remote, with fewer facilities, but has some of the most spectacular ice walls in Peru. In the south of the country, the Cordilleras Vilcabamba and Vilcanota are the main destinations, but Cusco is not developed for climbing. Elsewhere in the Sierras are other peaks which are hardly ever climbed.

Rock climbing is becoming popular in the Huaraz area, at Monterrey (for beginners) and Quebrada de Llaca. Climbing equipment can be hired in Huaraz quite easily, but the quality can be poor.

Mountain biking This is a relatively new sport in Peru, but dedicated cyclists are beginning to open up routes which offer some magnificent possibilities. Peru has kilometre after kilometre of trails, dirt roads and single track, but very few maps to show you where to go. There is equipment for hire and tours in the Huaraz and Cusco areas and it may be a good idea to join an organized group to get the best equipment and guiding.

Rafting Peru has some of the finest whitewater rivers in the world. There are some spectacular places only accessible by this type of craft: desert canyons, jungle gorges, exotic rock formations and rare wildlife. Availability is almost year-round and all levels of difficulty can be enjoyed.

Cusco is probably the rafting capital and the Río Urubamba has some very popular trips. Further afield is the Río Apurímac, which has some of the best whitewater rafting anywhere, including a trip at the source of the Amazon.

Peru

In the southeastern jungle, a rafting trip on the Río Tambopata to the Tambopata-Candamo Reserved Zone involves four days of whitewater followed by two of drifting through virgin forest: an excellent adventure which must be booked up in advance.

Around Arequipa is some first-class, technical rafting in the Cotahuasi and Colca canyons and some less-demanding trips on the Río Majes. Other destinations are the Río Santa near Huaraz and the Río Cañete, south of Lima.

Swimming and surfing   Between Dec and Apr the entire coast of Peru offers good bathing, but during the rest of the year only the northern beaches near Tumbes provide pleasantly warm water. There are many bathing resorts near Lima (do not swim at, or even visit, these beaches alone). The current off the coast can be very strong, making it too dangerous to swim in places.

Trekking   Most walking is on trails well-trodden by local people, but some of the more popular routes are becoming damaged. Little is done to maintain the trails and no guards control them; a few conservation groups are trying to remedy this. If camping, ask permission from the landowner first, and do not leave litter anywhere.

There are some outstanding circuits around the peaks of the Cordilleras Blanca (eg Llanganuco to Santa Cruz, and the treks out of Caraz) and Huayhuash. The Ausangate trek near Cusco is also good. A second type of trek is walking among, or to, ruins. The prime example is the Inca Trail to Machu Picchu, but others include those to Vilcabamba (the Incas' last home) and Choquequirao, and the treks in the Chachapoyas region. The Colca and Cotahuasi canyons also offer superb trekking.

Walking   *South American Explorers* have good information and advice on trekking and sells books. See Books, Background, for suggested guide books.

Other adventure sports   These include kayaking, parapenting and hang gliding (on the coast and in the mountains), diving (in the sea and in caves) and fishing (deep sea off Ancón, trout and fly fishing in the lakes of the Andes near La Oroya, and trout fishing near Juliaca and in Lakes Titicaca and Arapa). Riding is a favourite recreation in the Sierra, where horses can be hired at reasonable rates.

Spectator sports   Association football is the most popular. Basketball and other sports are also played on the coast, particularly around Lima and Callao. Bullfights and cockfights are held throughout the country.

Health

See also Health in Essentials at the beginning of the book, page 56

Eating from street vendors is considered safe only if the food is boiled or can be peeled. Most middle-class restaurants are safe. Tap water should not be drunk anywhere unless it has been boiled or treated with iodine. Bottled water is available throughout Peru. If it cannot be found, note that at high altitudes boiling may be insufficient to purify water (since boiling point is less than 100°C); use additional forms of purification. Of the water purification tablets sold in local chemists, Certimil do not dissolve; Micropur are much better.

Typhoid and hepatitis are common. If buying gamma globulin in Peru note that it is valueless if it has not been kept under refrigeration.

In Lima, there is a **Centro de Antirrabia** (see page 1124) if you are unfortunate enough to be bitten by a rabid dog. In other cities, hospitals give anti-rabies injections (always have a check-up if bitten by a dog; rabies is not uncommon). Because of a TB epidemic, avoid non-pasteurized dairy products.

Further to the general advice about altitude sickness, note that, when walking at high altitude, the body needs sugar, which can be carried conveniently in the form of a block of crystallized pure cane sugar, called *chancaca*, and easily found in markets.

Hotels and chemists/pharmacies often let visitors use their toilets.

Lima

Lima's colonial centre and suburbs, shrouded in fog which lasts eight months of the year, are fringed by the pueblos jóvenes *which sprawl over the dusty hills overlooking the flat city. It has a great many historic buildings, some of the finest museums in the country and its food, drink and nightlife are second to none. Although not the most relaxing of South America's capitals, it is a good place to start before exploring the rest of the country.*

Phone code: 01
Colour map 3, grid C2
Population: 8 million
(metropolitan area)

Getting there All international flights land at Jorge Chávez **airport**, 16 km from the Plaza de Armas (a little further from the main suburbs of Miraflores and San Isidro). Transport into town by taxi or bus is easy if a little expensive. If arriving in the city by **bus**, most of the recommended companies have their terminals just south of the centre, many on Av Carlos Zavala. This is not a safe area and you should take a taxi to and from there.

Ins & outs
For more detailed information including getting from the airport, see Transport, page 1120

   Getting around Downtown Lima is not really suitable for exploring on foot, although the central hotels are quite close to some of the main sites. Miraflores is about 15 km south of the centre. Many of the better hotels and restaurants are here and in neighbouring San Isidro. Transport between the centre and the suburbs is not a problem. Three types of bus provide an extensive public transport system. All vehicles stop whenever flagged down. The system may look daunting, but the route of the bus is posted on a coloured sticker on the windscreen; ignore any destinations written on the side. **Taxis** do not use meters and anyone can drive one. You must agree the price of the journey beforehand and insist on being taken to the destination of your choice. Tips are not expected. On both buses and taxis be ready to pay the exact fare. At night, on Sun and public holidays a surcharge is made, 35-50% in taxis, less in buses.

   Addresses Several blocks, with their own names, make up a long street, a jirón (often abbreviated to Jr). Street corner signs bear both names, of the jirón and of the block. New and old names of streets are used interchangeably: Colmena is also Nicolás de Piérola, Wilson is Inca Garcilaso de la Vega, and Carabaya is also Augusto N Wiese. The city's urban motorway is often called 'El Zanjón' (the ditch) or Vía Expresa.

   Climate Only 12° south of the equator, one would expect a tropical climate, but Lima has two distinct seasons. The winter is from May to Nov, when a damp *garúa* (Scotch mist) hangs over the city, making everything look grey. It is damp and cold, 8-15°C. The sun breaks through around Nov and temperatures rise to as high as 30°C. Note that the temperature in the coastal suburbs is lower than the centre because of the sea's influence. Protect against the sun's rays when visiting the beaches around Lima, or elsewhere in Peru.

   Tourist information *Fertur Peru*, has lots of information, see under Tour operators. **Info Perú**, Jr de la Unión (Belén) 1066, of 102, T424 7963/431 0177, infoperu@yahoo.com

Peru

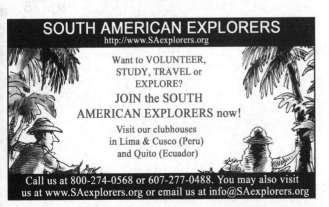

Very helpful, lots of good advice, English, French spoken, Mon-Fri 0930-1800, Sat 0930-1400 (may be moving in 2003). Ask for the helpful, free, *Peru Guide* published in English by *Lima Editora*, T444 0815, available at travel agencies or other tourist organizations. **South American Explorers**: Piura 135, (Casilla 3714), Miraflores, T/F445 3306 (dial 011-51-1 from USA) limaclub@saexplorers.org See also Essentials, page 26. **Federico Kauffmann-Doig** is a great source of information on Peruvian archaeology, for serious students and archaeologists. He is the director of the Instituto de Arqueología Amazónica, T449 0243, or (home) 449 9103. His book, *Historia del Perú: un nuevo perspectivo*, in two volumes (*Pre-Inca*, and *El Incario*) is available at better bookshops. The *Instituto Nacional de Cultura*, in the Museo de la Nación, should be contacted by archaeologists for permits and information.

History Lima, capital of Peru, is built on both sides of the Río Rímac, at the foot of Cerro San Cristóbal. It was originally named *La Ciudad de Los Reyes*, in honour of the Magi, at its founding by Spanish conquistador Francisco Pizarro in 1535. From then until the independence of the South American republics in the early 19th century, it was the chief city of Spanish South America. The name Lima, a corruption of the Quechua name *Rimac* (speaker), was not adopted until the end of the 16th century.

The Universidad de San Marcos was founded in 1551, and a printing press in 1595, both among the earliest of their kind in South America. Lima's first theatre

Peru

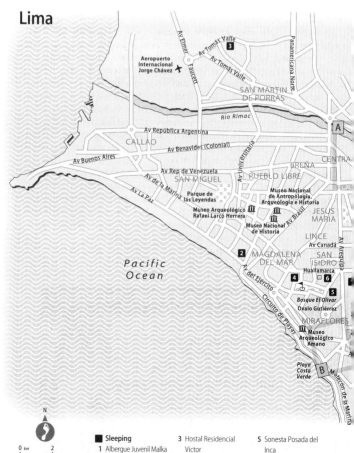

Lima

Related maps
A Lima centre,
page 1100
B Miraflores,
page 1105

0 km 2
0 miles 2

■ **Sleeping**
1 Albergue Juvenil Malka
2 Hostal Mami Panchita

3 Hostal Residencial Victor
4 Libertador

5 Sonesta Posada del Inca
6 Swissôtel Lima

opened in 1563, and the Inquisition was introduced in 1569 (it was not abolished until 1820). For some time the Viceroyalty of Peru embraced Colombia, Ecuador, Bolivia, Chile and Argentina. There were few cities in the Old World that could rival Lima's power, wealth and luxury, which was at its height during the 17th and early 18th centuries. The city's wealth attracted many freebooters and in 1670 a protecting wall 11 km long was built round it, then destroyed in 1869. The earthquake of 1746 destroyed all but 20 houses, killed 4,000 inhabitants and ended its pre-eminence. It was only comparatively recently, with the coming of industry, that Lima began to change into what it is today.

Modern Lima is seriously affected by smog for much of the year, and is surrounded by 'Pueblos Jóvenes', or settlements of squatters who have migrated from the Sierra. Villa El Salvador, a few kilometres southeast of Lima, may be the world's biggest 'squatters' camp' with 350,000 people building up an award-winning self-governing community since 1971.

Over the years the city has changed out of recognition. Many of the hotels and larger business houses have relocated to the fashionable suburbs of Miraflores and San Isidro, thus moving the commercial heart of the city away from the Plaza de Armas.

Half of the town-dwellers of Peru now live in Lima. The metropolitan area contains eight million people, nearly one-third of the country's total population, and two-thirds of its industries.

Sights

The traditional heart of the city, at least in plan, is still what it was in colonial days. Although parts of it are run down, much of the old centre is undergoing restoration and many colonial buildings have been cleaned up. It is well worth visiting the colonial centre to see the fine architecture and works of art. Most of the tourist attractions are in this area.

Plaza de Armas

One block south of the Río Rímac lies the Plaza de Armas (also called Plaza Mayor since 1998), which has been declared a World Heritage Site by UNESCO. Running along two sides are arcades with shops: Portal de Escribanos and Portal de Botoneros. In the centre of the Plaza is a bronze fountain dating from 1650.

The Palacio de Gobierno (Government Palace), on the north side of the Plaza, stands on the site of the original palace built by Pizarro. In 1937, the palace was totally rebuilt. The changing of the guard is at 1200. In order to take a tour of the Palace you must register at the office of public relations at Parque Pizarro, next to the Palace, a few days in advance. There is no charge.

The Cathedral, reduced to rubble in the earthquake of 1746, is a reconstruction on the lines of the original, completed 1755. Note the splendidly carved

Peru

stalls (mid-17th century), the silver-covered altars surrounded by fine woodwork, mosaic-covered walls bearing the coats of arms of Lima and Pizarro and an allegory of Pizarro's commanders, the 'Thirteen Men of Isla del Gallo'. The supposed remains of Franscisco Pizarro lie in a small chapel, the first on the right of the entrance, in a glass coffin, though later research indicates that they reside in the crypt. Museo de Arte Religioso in the cathedral, free guided tours (English available, give tip), ask to see the picture restoration room. ■ *To visitors Mon-Sat 1000-1430. All-inclusive entrance ticket is US$1.50.* Next to the cathedral is the **Archbishop's Palace**, rebuilt in 1924, with a superb wooden balcony.

Lima centre

Sleeping		
1 Europa	8 Hostal Roma	
2 Familia Rodríguez		& Café Carrara
3 Gran Hotel Continental	9 Hostal San Martín	
4 Gran Hotel Savoy	10 Kamana	
5 Granada	11 Lima Sheraton	
6 Hostal Belén &	12 Maury	
	Estrella de Belén	13 Pensión Ibarra
7 Hostal España	14 Plaza Francia Inn	

Eating	
1 Accllahuasy	
2 Chifas Wa Lok &	
	Chun Koc Sen
3 Cordano	
4 Heydi	
5 L'Eau Vive	
6 Machu Picchu	
7 Natur	

The Puente de Piedra, behind the Palacio de Gobierno, is a Roman-style stone bridge built in 1610, crossing the Río Rímac to the district of that name. On Jr Hualgayoc is the bullring in the **Plaza de Acho**, inaugurated on 20 January 1766, with the **Museo Taurino**. Apart from matador's relics, the museum contains good collections of paintings and engravings, some of the latter by Goya. ■ *Mon-Sat 0800-1800, US$1, students US$0.50, photography US$2, T482 3360, Hualgayoc 332.*

Around historic centre

The **Convento de Los Descalzos** on the Alameda de Los Descalzos in Rímac (founded 1592) contains over 300 paintings of the Cusco, Quito and Lima schools which line the four main cloisters and two ornate chapels. The chapel of El Carmen was constructed in 1730 and is notable for its baroque gold leaf altar. The museum shows the life of the Franciscan friars during colonial and early republican periods. The cellar, infirmary, pharmacy and a typical cell have been restored. ■ *Daily 1000-1300, 1500-1800, except Tue, US$1. Guided tour only, 45 mins in Spanish, worth it, T481 0441.*

Between Av Abancay and Jr Ayacucho is **Plaza Bolívar**, where General José de San Martín proclaimed Peru's independence. The plaza is dominated by the equestrian statue of the Liberator. Behind lies the Congress building which occupies the former site of the Universidad de San Marcos; visit recommended. Behind the Congress is Barrio Chino, with many *chifas* and small shops selling oriental items.

The Jr de La Unión, the main shopping street, runs to the Plaza de Armas. It has been converted into a pedestrian precinct which teems with life in the evening. In the two blocks south of Jr Unión, known as C Belén, several shops sell souvenirs and curios. The newer parts of the city are based on **Plaza San Martín**, south of Jr de la Unión, with a statue of San Martín in the centre. The plaza has been restored and is now a nice place to sit and relax. 1¼ km west is the **Plaza Dos de Mayo**. About 1 km due south of this again is the circular **Plaza Bolognesi**, from which many major avenues radiate.

At Jr Ucayali 363, is the **Palacio Torre Tagle** (1735), the city's best surviving example of secular colonial architecture. Today, it is used by the Foreign Ministry, but visitors are allowed to enter courtyards to inspect the fine, Moorish-influenced wood-carving in balconies and wrought iron work. ■ *Mon-Fri during working hours.* **Casa de la Rada**, or **Goyoneche**, Jr Ucayali 358, opposite, is a fine mid-18th-century French-style town house which now belongs to a bank. The patio and first reception room are open occasionally to the public.

Colonial Mansions

The late 16th-century **Casa de Jarava** or **Pilatos** is opposite San Francisco church, Jr Ancash 390. ■ *Mon-Fri 0830-1645.* **Casa La Riva**, Jr Ica 426, has an 18th-century porch and balconies, a small gallery with 20th-century paintings. ■ *1000-1300, 1400-1600, T428 2643.* **Casa de Oquendo** or **Osambela**, Conde de Superunda 298, stages art exhibitions. ■ *0900-1300.* **Casa de las Trece Monedas**, Jr Ancash 536, still has the original doors and window grills. The **Casa Aliaga**, Unión 224, is still occupied by the Aliaga family but has been opened to the public. *Lima Tours* has exclusive rights to include the house in its tours (T424 5110/7560/9386). The house contains what is said to be the oldest ceiling in Lima and is furnished entirely in the colonial style.

La Merced is in Plazuela de la Merced, Unión y Huancavelica. The first mass in Lima was said here on the site of the first church to be built. The restored façade is a fine example of colonial Baroque. Inside are some magnificent altars and the tilework on some of the walls is noteworthy. A door from the right of the nave leads into the Monastery. The cloister dates from 1546. ■ *Daily 0800-1200, 1600-2000; monastery daily 0800-1200 and 1500-1730, T427 8199.*

Churches
Churches open between 1830 and 2100 unless otherwise stated. Many are closed to visitors on Sun

Santo Domingo Church and Monastery is on the first block of Jr Camaná, built in 1549. The Cloister, one of the most attractive in the city, dates from 1603. The second Cloister is less elaborate. Beneath the sacristy are the tombs of San Martín de

Peru

Porres, one of Peru's most revered saints, and Santa Rosa de Lima (see below). In 1669, Pope Clement presented the alabaster statue of Santa Rosa in front of the altar. ■ *Monastery and tombs open Mon-Sat 0900-1300, 1500-1800; Sun and holidays morning only. US$0.75. T427 6793.*

San Francisco, first block of Jr Lampa, corner of Ancash: the baroque church, finished in 1674, withstood the 1746 earthquake. The nave and aisles are lavishly decorated in Mudéjar style. The monastery is famous for the Sevillian tilework and panelled ceiling in the cloisters (1620). The Catacombs under the church and part of the monastery are well worth seeing. ■ *Daily 0930-1745. Church and monastery US$1.50, US$0.50 children, only with guide, Spanish and English (recommended), T427 1381.*

San Pedro, third block of Jirón Ucayali, finished by Jesuits in 1638, has marvellous altars with Moorish-style balconies, rich gilded wood carvings in choir and vestry, and tiled throughout. Several Viceroys are buried here; the bell called La Abuelita, first rung in 1590, sounded the Declaration of Independence in 1821. ■ *Daily 0700-1200, 1700-1800.*

Santuario de Santa Rosa (Av Tacna, first block), small but graceful church. A pilgrimage centre; here are preserved the hermitage built by Santa Rosa herself, the house in which she was born, a section of the house in which she attended to the sick, her well, and other relics. ■ *Daily 0930-1300, 1500-1800, free to the grounds, T425 1279.*

Las Nazarenas Church, Av Tacna, 4th block, built around an image of Christ Crucified painted by a liberated slave in 1655. This, the most venerated image in Lima, and an oil copy of El Señor de los Milagros (Lord of Miracles), encased in a gold frame, are carried on a silver litter the whole weighing nearly a ton through the streets on 18, 19, and 28 October and again on 1 November (All Saints' Day). The whole city is decked out in purple. *El Comercio* newspaper and local pamphlets give details of times and routes. ■ *Daily 0700-1130, 1630-2000. T423 5718.*

San Agustín (Jr Ica 251), west of the Plaza de Armas: its façade (1720) is a splendid example of churrigueresque architecture. There are carved choir stalls and effigies, and a sculpture of Death, said to have frightened its maker into an early grave. The church has been sensitively restored after the last earthquake, but the sculpture of Death is in storage. ■ *Daily 0830-11300, 1630-1900, ring for entry, T427 7548.*

Museums

Some museums only open between 0900-1300 from Jan-Mar, and some close altogether in Jan. Some close early if there are few visitors

The famous Gold Museum is not featured here as last year it was revealed that the majority of the display were fakes

Museo de la Nación, on Javier Prado Este 2466, San Borja, in the huge *Banco de la Nación* building, is the museum for the exhibition and study of the art and history of the aboriginal races of Peru. It contains the **Museo Peruano de Ciencias de la Salud**, which has a collection of ceramics and mummies, plus an explanation of precolumbian lifestyle. There are good explanations in Spanish and English on Peruvian history, with ceramics, textiles and displays of almost every ruin in Peru. Guided tours in English/Spanish. It is arranged so that you can follow the development of Peruvian precolonial history through to the time of the Incas. A visit is recommended before you go to see the archaeological sites themselves. There are displays of the tomb of the Señor de Sipán, artefacts from Batán Grande near Chiclayo (Sicán culture), reconstructions of the friezes found at Huaca La Luna and Huaca El Brujo, near Trujillo, and of Sechín and other sites. Temporary exhibitions are held in the basement, where there is also an Instituto Nacional de Cultura bookshop. ■ *Tue-Sun 1000-1700, US$1.75. 50% discount with ISIC card, T476 9875/9878. Getting there: From Av Garcilaso de la Vega in downtown Lima take a combi with a "Javier Prado/Aviación" window sticker. Get off at the 21st block of Javier Prado at Av Aviación. From Miraflores take a bus down Av Arequipa to Av Javier Prado (27th block), then take a bus with a "Todo Javier Prado" or "Aviación" window sticker. Taxi from downtown Lima or Miraflores US$2. The museum has a cafetería.*

The original museum of anthropology and archaeology is **Museo Nacional de Antropología, Arqueología e Historia**, Plaza Bolívar in Pueblo Libre, not to be confused with Plaza Bolívar in the centre. On display are ceramics of the Chimú, Nasca, Mochica and Pachacámac cultures, various Inca curiosities and works of art, and interesting textiles. **Museo Nacional de Historia**, T463 2009, in a mansion occupied by San Martín (1821-22) and Bolívar (1823-26) is next door. It exhibits colonial and early republican paintings, manuscripts, portraits, uniforms, etc. ■ *Tue-Sat 0915-1700, Sun and holidays 1000-1700. US$3, photo permit US$5 (T463 5070), guides available, some displays in English. Take any public transportation vehicle on Av Brasil with a window sticker saying "Todo Brasil." Get off at the 21st block called Av Vivanco. Walk about 5 blocks down Vivanco. The museum will be on your left. Taxi from downtown Lima US$2; from Miraflores US$3 Follow the 'blue line' marked on the pavement to the Museo Arqueológico Rafael Larco Herrera (see below), 10 mins' walk.*

Museo Arqueológico Rafael Larco Herrera, Av Bolívar 1515, Pueblo Libre, T461 1312, www.museolarco.perucultural.org.pe Located in an 18th-century mansion, itself built on a seventh-century precolumbian pyramid, this museum has a collection which gives an excellent overview on the development of Peruvian cultures through their pottery. It has the world's largest collection of Moche, Sicán and Chimú pieces. There is a Gold and Silver of Ancient Peru pavilion, a magnificent textile collection and a fascinating erotica section. It is surrounded by beautiful gardens. ■ *Daily 0900-1800; texts in Spanish, English and French. US$4.50 (half price for students). Disabled access. Photography not permitted. Take any bus to the 15th block of Av Brasil. Then take a bus down Av Bolívar. Taxi from downtown, Miraflores or San Isidro, 15 mins, US$2-3. Follow the 'blue line' marked on the pavement to the Museo Nacional de Antropología, Arqueología e Historia (see above), 10 mins' walk.*

Museo Arqueológico Amano, Retiro 160, 11th block of Av Angamos Oeste, Miraflores: private collection of artefacts from the Chancay, Chimú and Nasca periods, owned by the late Mr Yoshitaro Amano. It has one of the most complete exhibits of Chancay weaving, and is particularly interesting for pottery and precolumbian textiles, all superbly displayed and lit. ■ *Visits are by appointment Mon-Fri in afternoons only, free (photography prohibited), T4412909. Getting there: Take a bus or colectivo to the corner of Av Arequipa y Av Angamos and another one to the 11th block of Av Angamos Oeste. Taxi from downtown US$2; from Parque Kennedy US$1.*

Museo Banco Central de Reserva, Av Ucayali 291 and Lampa, one block from San Pedro Church, on same side as Torre Tagle Palace. This is a large collection of pottery from the Vicus or Piura culture (AD 500-600) and gold objects from Lambayeque, as well as 19th and 20th-century paintings: both sections highly recommended. ■ *Tue-Fri 1000-1600, Sat-Sun 1000-1300. Photography prohibited, T427 6250, ext 2657.*

Museo Nacional de la Cultura Peruana, Av Alfonso Ugarte 650, Lima, T423 5892. The mock Tiahuanaco façade houses a rather disjointed collection of precolumbian and modern artefacts, including *mate burilado* (carved gourds), *retablos*, textiles, *keros* and *huacos*. There are examples of ceramics and cloth from some Amazonian tribes and a set of watercolours by Pancho Fierro, the 19th-century *costumbrista* artist. ■ *Tue-Sun 1000-1700, US$1, free guide in Spanish.*

Poli Museum, Lord Cochrane 466, Miraflores, is one of the best private collections of colonial and precolumbian artefacts in Peru, including material from Sipán. ■ *Guided tours (in Spanish only and delivered very fast) by Sr Poli or his son cost US$10 pp irrespective of the size of the group; allow 2 hrs. Phone in advance to arrange tours, T422 2437.*

Museo de Arte, 9 de Diciembre 125, in the Palacio de la Exposición, built in 1868 in Parque de la Exposición. There are more than 7,000 exhibits, giving a chronological history of Peruvian cultures and art from the Paracas civilization up to today. It includes excellent examples of 17th- and 18th-century Cusco paintings, a beautiful display of carved furniture, heavy silver and jewelled stirrups and also precolumbian pottery. ■ *Tue-Sun 1000-1700, US$2.30 , T423 4732. The Filmoteca (movie club) is on the premises and shows films just about every night. See the local paper for details, or look in the museum itself. Free guide, signs in English.* The **Gran Parque Cultural de Lima** is in the grounds. Inaugurated in January 2000, this large park has an

Peru

amphitheatre, Japanese garden, food court and children's activities. Relaxing strolls through this green, peaceful and safe oasis in the centre of Lima are recommended. ■ *0800-2030.*

Museo de Arte Italiano, Paseo de la República, second block, T423 9932, is in a wonderful neo-classical building, given by the Italian colony to Peru on the centenary of its independence. Note the remarkable mosaic murals on the outside. It consists of a large collection of Italian and other European works of art and houses the Instituto de Arte Contemporáneo, which has many exhibitions. ■ *Mon-Fri 0900-1630, US$1.*

Museo de Arte Colonial Pedro de Osma is on Av Pedro de Osma 421, Barranco, a private collection of colonial art of the Cusco, Ayacucho and Arequipa schools, ■ *Tue-Sun 1000-1330, 1430-1800, US$3. Only 10 visitors at any one time, T467 0141. Take bus 2, 54 or colectivo from Av Tacna.*

Museo del Tribunal de la Santa Inquisición, Plaza Bolívar, C Junín 548, near the corner of Av Abancay. The main hall, with a splendidly carved mahogany ceiling, remains untouched. The Court of Inquisition was held here from 1584; 1829-1938 it was used by the Senate. In the basement there is a recreation *in situ* of the gruesome tortures. A description in English is available at the desk. ■ *Mon-Sun 0900-1700, free. Students offer to show you round for a tip; good explanations in English.*

Museo de Historia Natural, Av Arenales 1256, Jesús María, T471 0117, belongs to Universidad de San Marcos. Exhibits of Peruvian flora and fauna. ■ *Mon-Fri 0900-1500, Sat 0900-1700, Sun 0900-1300, US$1 (students US$0.50).*

Philatelic Museum, at the Central Post Office, off Plaza de Armas. Incomplete collection of Peruvian stamps and information on the Inca postal system. ■ *Mon-Sun 0815-1300, 1400-1800. No charge to enter museum, T427 5060, ext 553. Stamp exchange in front of the museum every Sat and Sun, 0900-1300. Commemorative issues can be bought here.*

Cerro San Cristóbal dominates downtown Lima and can be visited in a one-hour tour, run by *Ofistur*, departing from in front of Santo Domingo, Jr Camaná. It includes a look at the run-down Rímac district, passes the Convento de los Descalzos (see above), ascends the hill through one of the city's oldest shanties with its brightly painted houses and spends about 20 minutes at the summit, where there is a small museum and café. Excellent views on a clear day. ■ *Sat and Sun 1000-2100; departures every 15 mins, US$1.50.*

Lima suburbs

The Av Arequipa connects the centre of Lima with Miraflores. Parallel to this is the Vía Expresa, a highway carrying fast traffic to the suburbs (six lanes for cars, two for buses).

San Isidro To the east of Av La República, down C Pancho Fierro, is **El Olivar**, an old olive grove planted by the first Spaniards which has been turned into a delightful park (best visited in daylight). There are many good hotels and restaurants in San Isidro; see Sleeping, page 1109 and Eating, page 1111.

Between San Isidro and Miraflores, at C Nicolás de Rivera 201 and Av Rosario, is **the Pan de Azúcar**, or **Huallamarca**, a restored adobe pyramid of the Maranga culture, dating from about AD 100-500. There is a small site museum. ■ *Daily 0900-1700, US$1.75. Take bus 1 from Av Tacna, or minibus 13 or 73 to Choquechaca, then walk.*

South of San Isidro is the rundown seaside resort of **Magdalena del Mar**, inland from which is **Pueblo Libre**, where many important museums are located (see under Museums, above).

Parque las Leyendas, is on the 24th block of Av de La Marina, Pueblo Libre, between Lima and Callao, T452 4282. It is arranged to represent the three regions of

Peru

Peru: the coast, the mountainous Sierra, and the tropical jungles of the Selva, with appropriate houses, animals and plants, children's playground. It gets very crowded at weekends. ■ *Daily 0900-1700, US$2. Getting there: Take bus 23 or colectivo on Av Abancay, or bus 135A or colectivo from Av La Vega.*

Av Arequipa continues to the coast, to the most important suburb of Lima (see **Miraflores** Sleeping, page, 1108, Youth hostel, page 1111 and eating, page 1111). Together with San Isidro and Barranco this is now the social centre of Lima.

Parque Kennedy, the Parque Central de Miraflores is located between Av Larco and Av Mcal Oscar Benavides (locally known as Av Diagonal). This extremely well kept park has a small open-air theatre with performances Thursday-Sunday and an arts and crafts market most evenings of the week. The house of the author **Ricardo Palma**, Gral Suárez 189, is now a museum. ■ *Mon-Fri 0915-1245, 1430-1700, small*

Peru

Miraflores

To Hostal Torreblanca (1 block)   To C'est si bon Restaurant (5 blocks)

To Miraflores Park Hotel (4 blocks) & Barranco   To Hotel Sipán (2½ blocks)

0 metres 50
0 yards 50

■ **Sleeping**
1 Albergue Turístico Juvenil Internacional *D3*
2 Antigua Miraflores *B1*
3 Casa de la Sra Jordan *C1*
4 Colonial Inn *A2*
5 Friend's House *C1*
6 Hospedaje Atahualpa *A3*
7 Hostal Bellavista de Miraflores *B2*
8 Hostal El Patio *C2*
9 Hostal Esperanza *C3*
10 Hostal Huaychulo *A2*
11 Hostal La Castellana *C2*
12 Hostal Lucerna *D1*
13 Hostal Señorial *D1*
14 José Antonio *C1*
15 La Hacienda *C1*
16 Residencial El Castillo Inn *C3*
17 San Antonio Abad *D3*

● **Eating**
1 Bircher Benner *C3*
2 Café Café *B2*
3 Café de la Paz *B2*
4 Café D'Oro *C2*
5 Café Tarata *C2*
6 Café Voltaire *B3*
7 Don Beta *A1*
8 Govinda *D2*
9 Haiti *B3*
10 Heladería 4D *A3*
11 La Gloria *B3*
12 La Palachinke & Media Naranja *B2*
13 Las Brujas de Cachiche *B1*
14 La Tiendecita Blanca *B3*
15 La Tranquera *B2*
16 La Trattoria *C3*
17 Las Tejas *C2*
18 Murphys *C3*
19 Pizza Street *B2*
20 Ricota *C2*
21 Vivaldi *B3*
22 Zugatti *C2*

entrance fee, T445 5836. The Miraflores branch of **Banco Wiese** has an exhibition of finds from El Brujo archaeological site north of Trujillo. ■ *Mon-Fri, 0900-1230, free.* At the end of Av Larco and running along the Malecón de la Reserva is the renovated **Parque Salazar** and the very modern shopping centre called Centro Comercial Larcomar. Here you will find expensive shops, fancy cafés and discos (including Hard Rock Café) and a wide range of restaurants, all with a beautiful ocean view. The 12-screen cinema is one of the best in Lima and even has a 'cine-bar' in the twelfth theatre. Don't forget to check out the Cosmic Bowling Alley with its black lights and fluorescent balls. A few hundred metres to the north is the famous **Parque del Amor** where on just about any night you'll see at least one wedding party taking photos of the newly married couple.

At Borgoña, eighth block s/n, turn off Av Arequipa at 45th block, is **Huaca Pucllana**, a fifth-century AD, pre-Inca site which is under excavation. Guided tours in Spanish only (give tip); small site museum but few objects from the site itself, handicrafts shop (see Eating, below). ■ *Free.*

Barranco This suburb further south was already a seaside resort by the end of the 17th century. Nowadays, a number of artists have their workshops here. The attractive public library, formerly the town hall, stands on the plaza. Nearby is the interesting *bajada*, a steep path leading down to the beach. **The Puente de los Suspiros** (Bridge of Sighs), leads towards the Malecón, with fine views of the bay. Barranco is quiet by day but comes alive at night (see Lima Eating and Bars) in the bars focused around the main plaza. Take a colectivo to Miraflores then another. Some run all the way to Barranco from Lima centre; check on the front window or ask, same fare. The 45 minute walk from Miraflores to Barranco along the Malecón is nice in summer.

Callao

Population: 588,600
Callao has a serious theft problem, avoid being there in the evening

Founded in 1537, Callao quickly became the main port for Spanish commerce in the Pacific. The merchants suffered English raids from Drake, Hawkins, and others. The 1746 earthquake caused a massive wave that completely destroyed the port.

Callao, although a continuation of Lima, is a separate province within the department of Lima. Shipyards, far from sea, load the fishing vessels they build on huge lorries and launch them into the ocean at Callao. The port handles 75 of the nation's imports and 25 of its exports. San Lorenzo island, a naval station, protects the roadstead from the south. The **Castillo del Real Felipe** is still a military post, and tourists are allowed to visit it. The **Museo Histórico Militar** is in the old barracks. There are many interesting military relics and the remains of the small Bleriot plane in which the Peruvian pilot, Jorge Chávez, made the first crossing of the Alps from Switzerland to Italy. ■ *Daily 0930-1400, US$2 including guide, no cameras allowed, T429 0532. Take bus 25, 74, 94 or colectivo from Av La Vega.* There is also the **Museo Naval** (Av Jorge Chávez 121, off Plaza Grau, T429 4793), with a collection of paintings, model ships, uniforms, etc. ■ *Tue-Sun 0900-1600, US$1.*

Boat trips: take a micro for La Punta and get off at Plaza Grau. At the foot of the steps to the sea (from where the liberty boats come and go to the Peruvian Navy ships anchored out in the bay) brightly painted pleasure boats, complete with life jackets, take trippers to the end of **La Punta** beach, on a spit of land stretching out to sea, and back. The journey is about 25 minutes and costs US$1. ■ *From Callao, Lima is at least 20 mins by car, colectivos US$0.30, bus US$0.25, taxi US$3-4 to the centre or Miraflores.*

Lima Beaches In summer (December-April) the city's beaches get very crowded at weekends and lots of activities are organized. Even though the water of the whole bay has been declared unsuitable for swimming, Limeños see the beach more as part of their culture than as a health risk. Do not camp on the beaches as robbery is a serious threat and, for the same reason, take care on the walkways down. Don't take any belongings with you to the beach, only what is really necessary.

The *Circuito de Playas*, which begins with Playa Arica (30 km from Lima) and ends with San Bartolo (45 km from Lima), has many great beaches for all tastes. If you want a beach that always is packed with people, there's El Silencio or Punta Rocas. Quieter options are Señoritas or Los Pulpos. Punta Hermosa has frequent surfing and volleyball tournaments.

Excursions

In the district of Chorrillos is the 396-ha wildlife sanctuary, **Pántanos de Villa**, an ecological wetland reserve with brackish water and abundant emergent vegetation. It provides the habitat for waterfowl typical of coastal Peru, including 17 species of migratory shorebirds. There are several species of fish, four types of reptile and over 50 species of water plants. Take binoculars. More information can be obtained from the municipal tourist office, T231 1325.

Pántanos de Villa

When the Spaniards arrived, Pachacámac in the Lurín valley was the largest city and ceremonial centre on the coast. A wooden statue of the creator-god, after whom the site is named, is in the site museum. Hernando Pizarro was sent here by his brother in 1533 in search of gold for Inca emperor Atahualpa's ransom. In their fruitless quest, the Spaniards destroyed images and killed the priests. The ruins encircle the top of a low hill, whose crest was crowned with a **Temple of the Sun**, now partially restored. Hidden from view is the reconstructed **House of the Mamaconas**, where the 'chosen women' spun fine cloth for the Inca and his court. An impression of the scale of the site can be gained from the top of the Temple of the Sun, or from walking or driving the 3-km circuit (the site is large and it is expected that tourists will be visiting by car – there are six parking spots). ■ *Daily 0900-1700; closed 1 May, US$1.75, includes the small site museum which sells soft drinks.*

Pachacámac
31 km from Lima

Transport Bus or colectivo from Lima: From the Pan American Highway (south-bound) take a combi with a sticker in the window reading "Pachacámac/Lurín" (US$0.85). Let the driver know you want to get off at the ruins. A taxi will cost approximately US$4.30, but if you don't ask the driver to wait for you (an extra cost), finding another to take you back to Lima may be a bit tricky. For organized tours contact one of the tour agencies listed above.

In the 19th and early 20th centuries, this was the smart seaside resort in Peru, but has now been deserted by the wealthy and in summer (January-March) is crowded with daytrippers. It has a mix of elegant 19th-century houses with wooden balconies and modern apartment blocks. ■ *Colectivo to Ancón from Plaza 2 de Mayo in Lima, US$0.60, returns 1 block from Ancón Cathedral.*

Ancón
30 km NW of Lima, on good paved highway

Essentials

All hotels and restaurants in the upper price brackets charge 18% state tax and 10% service on top of prices (neither is included in prices below). Many new 4- and 5-star hotels have opened, or are opening in the city. Such an abundance of high-class accommodation means that bargains can be found. The more expensive hotels charge in dollars according to the parallel rate of exchange at midnight. Consult the general Security section in the Essentials and see also the Warning under Transport. If arriving by air, especially at night, you can try the tourist office at the airport (beyond passport control) if you want to arrange a hotel room, but they may find you somewhere at a higher price than you wish to pay.

Sleeping
More visitors stay in Miraflores than in the centre, as it is more organized, cleaner and safer, but more expensive. Backpackers prefer cheaper hostales in the centre

Peru

There is a Holiday Inn and a Marriott in Miraflores. Apartments for two can be rented for US$50-150, check notices in Santa Isabel and Wong supermarkets, and El Comercio on Sun

Miraflores LL *Miraflores Park*, Av Malecón de la Reserva 1035, T242 3000, F242 3393, mira-park@peruorientexpress.com.pe An Orient Express hotel, excellent service and facilities, beautiful views over the ocean, top class. **L** *La Hacienda*, 28 de Julio 511 y Av Larco, T444 4346, lahacien@amauta.rcp.net.pe English spoken, excellent service, breakfast included, has casino. **AL** *Antigua Miraflores*, Av Grau 350 at C Francia, T241 6116, www.peru-hotels-inns.com A beautiful, small and elegant hotel in a quiet but central location, very friendly service, tastefully furnished and decorated, gym, cable TV, good restaurant. **AL** *Colonial Inn*, Cmdte Espinar 310, T241 7471, coloinn@terra.com.pe Colonial style, excellent service, noisy from traffic, parking, includes breakfast and tax. **AL** *José Antonio*, 28 de Julio 398 y C Colón, T 445 7743, T/F445 6870, j.antonio@amauta.rcp.net.pe Good in all respects, including the restaurant. **AL** *Sonesta Posada del Inca*, Alcanfores 490, T2417688. Part of the renowned chain of hotels (see San Isidro below). **A** *Alemán*, Arequipa 4704, T446 4045/241 2500, F447 3950. No sign, comfortable, quiet, garden, breakfast included, enquire about laundry service. **A** *Hostal Esperanza*, Esperanza 350, T444 2411/4909, F444 0834. Café, bar, TV, phone, pleasant, secure. **A** *Hostal La Castellana*, Grimaldo del Solar 222, T444 3530/4662, F446 8030. Pleasant, good value, nice garden, safe, expensive restaurant, laundry, English spoken, 10% discount for *South American Explorers* (SAE) members, price includes tax. **A** *Hostal Lucerna*, Las Dalias 276 (parallel with 12th block of Larco), T445 7321, F446 6050. Safe, quiet, cosy, excellent value, but drinks and restaurant are expensive. **A** *Hostal Señorial*, José González 567, T445 9724, F444 5755. Includes breakfast, comfortable, nice garden. **A** *Sipán*, Paseo de la República 6171, T447 0884/241 3758, F445 5298. Very pleasant, in a residential area, cable TV, fridge, security box, internet access, breakfast and tax included in price. **A** *Hostal Torreblanca*, Av José Pardo 1453, near the seafront, T447 0142, www.torreblancaperu.com Includes breakfast, quiet, safe, laundry, restaurant and bar, cosy rooms, will help with travel arrangements. **A** *San Antonio Abad*, Ramón Ribeyro 301, T447 6766, F446 4208, www.hotelsanantonioabad.com Secure, quiet, helpful, free airport transfer.

B *Hostal Bellavista de Miraflores*, Jr Bellavista 215, T445 7834, F444 2938. Excellent location, quiet, pleasant, price includes tax. **B** *Hostal Huaychulo*, Av Dos de Mayo 494, T241 3130. Secure, helpful, German owner-manager also speaks English. **B** *Hostal El Patio*, Diez Canseco 341, T444 2107. Includes breakfast, reductions for long stays, comfortable, English and French spoken, convenient. **B** *Villa Molina*, C Teruel 341, T440 4018, F222 5623, sbeleunde@electrodata.com.pe Beautiful house, quiet, breakfast and tax included.

C *Hospedaje Atahualpa*, Atahualpa 646c, T447 6601. Cheaper without bath, including breakfast, long-stay rates available, parking, hot water, cooking and laundry facilities, luggage stored, taxi service. **C** *Residencial El Castillo Inn*, Diez Canseco 580, T446 9501. All rooms with bath and hot water, family home, use of lounge, negotiate for longer stay.

D pp *Casa de La Sra Jordan*, Porta 724, near Parque del Amor, T445 9840. 8 rooms, reservations required, family home, quiet. **E** *Friend's House*, Jr Manco Cápac 368, T446 6248/3521. Hot water, cable TV, **F** in dormitory, use of kitchen at no cost, very popular with backpackers, near Larcomar shopping centre. **F** *Casa del Mochilero*, Jr Cesareo Chacaltana 130-A, p 2, T444 9089. Shared bath, kitchen, family atmosphere, a bit noisy at times.

Peru

San Isidro LL *Country Club*, Los Eucaliptos 590, T611 9000, F611 9002, www.accesoperu.com/countryclub Excellent, fine service, luxurious rooms, safes in rooms, cable TV, free internet for guests, good bar and restaurant, classically stylish. **LL** *Eko Hotel*, Av Paz Soldán 167, T221 108, F221 107, central@inkaterra.com 54 suites in this new hotel. **LL** *Sonesta Posada del Inca*, Pancho Fierro 194, T221 2121, F422-4345, www.sonesta.com Luxury, one of the top 5-star hotels in Lima, modern, restaurant, coffee shop, garden, swimming pool, quiet, popular with business visitors, price includes tax. **LL** *Swissôtel Lima*, Vía Central, Centro Empresarial Real, T421 4400, F421 4422, reservations.lima@swissotel.com Beautiful, superb restaurants including *Le Café*, excellent 5-star service. **L** *Libertador*, Los Eucaliptos 550, T421 6666, F442 3011, www.libertador.com.pe A Golden Tulip hotel, overlooking the Golf Course, full facilities for the business traveller, comfortable rooms, fine service, good restaurant. **L** *Sonesta Posada Del Inca*, Av Libertadores 490, T222 4373, F422 4345, www.sonesta.com Prices include all taxes, cable TV, restaurant, parking, very comfortable, excellent service. **AL** *Garden*, Rivera Navarrete 450, T442 1771, reservas@ gardenhotel.com.pe Includes tax and breakfast, good beds, small restaurant, ideal for business visitors, convenient, good value.

B *Sans Souci*, Av Arequipa 2670, T422 6035/441 7773, F441 7824. Breakfast and tax included, safe, good services and restaurant, garden, garage.

Barranco D *Hostal Los Girasoles*, Av Sáenz Peña 210, opposite Mutual FAP, T477 2843, losgirasoles@hotmail.com Very good. **F** pp *Mochileros Hostal*, Av Pedro de Osma 135, 1 block from main plaza, T477 4506, www.rcp.net.pe/backpacker Beautiful house, English-speaking owner, shared rooms, good pub, stone's throw from Barranco nightlife. **D-E** *Safe in Lima*, Enrique Barron 440, T728 2105, http://safeinlima.tripod.com.pe, new hostel.

Peru

Santa Beatriz, between San Isidro and Centre **B** *Hostal La Posada del Parque*, Parque Hernán Velarde 60, near 2nd block of Av Petit Thouars, T433 2412, www.incacountry.com Run by Sra Mónica Moreno and her husband Leo Rovayo who both speak good English, a charmingly refurbished old house in a safe area, elegant, cable TV, excellent bathrooms, breakfast US$3 extra, airport transfer 24 hrs for US$14 for up to 3 passengers, very good value. **C** *Renacimiento*, Parque Hernán Velarde 51, T433 2806/433 1917, hostalrenacimiento@hotmail.com **D** without bath, price includes taxes, snack bar for breakfast and lunch in vegetarian restaurant, quiet, parking, colonial building close to national stadium, helpful. **D** *Residencial Los Petirrojos*, Jr José Díaz 400, T433 5235, T987 7636 (Mob), Petirrojos@hotmail.com Spacious accommodation, price includes breakfast.

Pueblo Libre **E** *Guest House Marfil*, Parque Ayacucho 126, at the 3rd block of Bolívar, T463 3161, cosycoyllor@yahoo.com English spoken, breakfast, kitchen facilities and laundry free of charge, internet service, Spanish classes can be arranged, family atmosphere.

San Miguel **C** *Hostal Mami Panchita*, Av Federico Callese 198, T263 7203, raymi_travels@perusat.net.pe Dutch-Peruvian owned, English, French, Dutch, Spanish and German spoken, includes breakfast and welcome drink, comfortable rooms with bath, hot water, living room and bar, patio, email service, book exchange, *Raymi* Travel agency (good service), 15 mins from airport, 15 mins from Miraflores, 20 mins from historical centre.

Central Lima **LL** *Lima Sheraton*, Paseo de la República 170, T315 5022/5023, F315 5024. *Las Palmeras* coffee shop is good, daily buffet breakfast, good Italian restaurant, casino, all you'd expect of a 5-star hotel. **L-AL** *Maury*, Jr Ucayali 201, T428 8188/8174, hotmaury@amauta.rcp.net.pe Fancy, secure, breakfast included, most luxurious hotel in the historical centre. **A** *Kamana*, Jr Camaná 547, T426 7204, kamana@amauta. rcp.net.pe Price includes tax, TV, comfortable, safe, French and some English spoken, very helpful staff. **B** *Gran Hotel Continental*, Jr Puno 196, T427 5890, F426 1633. Price is for remodelled rooms (*ejecutivo*), also basic, *económico* rooms, **C**, 24-hr room service, safe. **B** *Gran Hotel Savoy*, Jr Cailloma 224, T428 3520. Includes taxes and breakfast, restaurant, cafeteria, bar, laundry, airport transfer, refurbished. **B** *Hostal San Martín*, Av Nicolás de Piérola 882, Plaza San Martín, T428 5337, F423 5744, hsanmartin@goalsnet.com.pe Includes poor breakfast served in room, a/c, modern, clean but run down, helpful, safe, not always hot water, money changing facilities, Japanese run, good restaurant.

    C *Granada*, Huancavelica 323, T/F427 9033. Includes breakfast and tax, hot water, English spoken, safe, laundry facilities. **C** *Hostal Roma*, Jr Ica 326, T/F427 7572, www.hostalroma.8m.com With bath **D** without, hot water all day, safe to leave luggage, basic but clean, often full, motorcycle parking (*Roma Tours*, helpful for trips, reservations, flight confirmations, Dante Reyes speaks English). **D** *Estrella de Belén*, Belén 1051, T428 6462. 3-star, good service, restaurant, takes credit cards. **D-E** *Hostal de las Artes*, Jr Chota 1460 near SAE, T433 0031/332 1868 (office), www.arteswelcome.tripod.com **F** without bath (no singles with bath), **G** pp in dormitory, Dutch owned, English spoken, safe luggage store, nice colonial building, usually hot water, book exchange, airport transfer US$12.

    F *Hostal Belén*, Belén 1049, just off San Martín, T427 8995. Discount for groups of 3 or more but give prior notice, Italian spoken, basic breakfast extra, hot water, basic, noisy. **F** *Europa*, Jr Ancash 376, T427 3351, opposite San Francisco church. Good, shared bath, excellent hot showers, also dormitory accommodation for **G** pp, great value, popular with backpackers. **E** *Hostal Iquique*, Jr Iquique 758, Breña(discount for SAE members), T423 3699, F433 4724, www.barrioperu.terra.com.pe/hiquique **F** without bath, noisy and draughty, otherwise good, use of kitchen, warm water, storage facilities, rooms on the top floor at the back are best. **D** *Plaza Francia Inn*, Jr Rufino Torrico 1117 (blue house, no sign, look for "Ecología es vida" mural opposite), near 9th block of Av Garcilaso de la Vega (aka Wilson), T330 6080, T945 4260 (Mob), franciasquareinn@yahoo.com Dormitory **E**, new, very cosy, hot water 24 hrs, safety box in each room for each bed, kitchen and laundry facilities, airport pick up for up to 4 people US$12 (send flight details in advance), discounts for ISIC cardholders, SAE members and readers of this Handbook, same owners as *Posada del Parque*.

F pp *Familia Rodríguez*, Av Nicolás de Piérola 730, 2nd floor, T423 6465, jotajot@terra.com.pe With breakfast, popular, some rooms noisy, will store luggage, also has dormitory accommodation with only one bathroom (same price), transport to airport US$10 pp for 2 people, US$4 pp for 3 or more, good information, secure. **F** *Pensión Ibarra*, Av Tacna 359, 14th-16th floor, T/F427 8603 (no sign). Breakfast US$2, discount for longer stay, use of kitchen, balcony with views of the city, very helpful owner, hot water, full board available (good small café next door).

   F *Hostal España*, Jr Azángaro 105, T427 9196, T/F428 5546, feertur@terra.com.pe **E** with bath (3 rooms), **G** pp in dormitory, fine old building, hot showers possible either very early or very late, run by a French-speaking Peruvian painter and his Spanish wife, English spoken, internet service, book exchange, motorcycle parking, luggage store (free), laundry service, don't leave valuables in rooms, roof garden, good café, can be very busy and attention suffers. **G** pp *Hospedaje Huaynapicchu*, Jr Pedro Ruiz 703 y Pasaje Echenique 1108, Breña, access from 11th block of Av Brazil, T431 2565, F447 9247, huaynapicc@business.com.pe Includes breakfast, shared bathroom, hot water all day, welcoming family, English spoken, internet access, laundry service, secure, great value.

Near the airport **B** *Hostal Residencial Victor*, Manuel Mattos 325, Urb San Amadeo de Garagay, Lima 31, T567 5107/5083, F568 9570, hostalvictor@terra.com.pe 5 mins from the airport by taxi, or phone or email in advance for free pick-up, large comfortable rooms, with bath, hot water, cable TV, free luggage store, American breakfast, evening meals can be ordered locally, *chifa* nearby, very helpful, owner Víctor Melgar has a free reservation service for Peru and Bolivia.

Youth hostel **F** pp *Albergue Turístico Juvenil Internacional*, Av Casimiro Ulloa 328, San Antonio, T446 5488, F444 8187. Youth hostel, dormitory accommodation, **C** in a double private room, basic cafeteria, travel information, cooking (minimal) and laundry facilities, swimming pool often empty, extra charge for kitchen facilities, safe, situated in a nice villa; 20 mins walk from the beach. GREATBus No 2 or colectivos pass Av Benavides to the centre; taxi to centre, US$2.50. **F** *Albergue Juvenil Malka*, Los Lirios 165 (near 4th block of Av Javier Prado Este), San Isidro, T442 0162, T/F222 5589, hostelmalka@ terra.com.pe Youth hostel, 20 discount with ISIC card, dormitory style, 4-8 beds per room, English spoken, cable TV, laundry, kitchen, nice café.

Menu prices fail to show that 18% state tax and 10% service will be added to your bill in middle and upper class restaurants. Chinese is often the cheapest at around US$5 including a drink. In **Miraflores** we recommend the following: **Expensive**: *Rosa Náutica*, T447 0057, built on old British-style pier (Espigón No 4), in Lima Bay. Delightful opulence, finest fish cuisine, experience the atmosphere by buying an expensive beer in the bar at sunset, open 1230-0200 daily. *Astrid y Gaston*, Cantuarias 175, T444 1496. Excellent local and international cuisine, one of the best. *Las Brujas de Cachiche*, Av Bolognesi 460, T447 1883. An old mansion converted into bars and dining rooms, traditional food (menu in Spanish and English), best Lomo Saltado in town, live *criollo* music. *Café Voltaire*, Av Dos de Mayo 220. International cuisine with emphasis on French dishes, beautifully-cooked food, pleasant ambience, good service. *Cuarto y Mitad*, Av Espinar 798. Popular Grill. *La Gloria*, Atahualpa 201. Very smart, excellent food and service. *Huaca Pucllana*, Gral Borgoña cuadra 8 s/n, alt cuadra 45 Av Arequipa, T4454042. Facing the archaeological site of the same name, contemporary Peruvian fusion cooking, very good food in an unusual setting. *Rincón Alemán*, Av Santa Cruz 982. Typical German food, authentic and good. *El Rincón Gaucho*, Av Armendáriz 580. Good grill. *Las Tejas*, Diez Canseco 340. Open 1100-2300 daily, good, typical Peruvian food. *La Tranquera*, Av Pardo 285. Argentine-owned steak house, very good. *La Trattoria*, Manuel Bonilla 106, 1 block from Parque Kennedy. Italian cuisine, popular, best cheesecake in Lima.

Peru

Eating

A cheap menú (set lunch) costs US$1.75-3.50, while a meal in a moderate café/bistro will cost US$15-20; in middle-range restaurants a meal costs US$25-30, rising to US$60-80 at the upper end of the range

Calle San Ramón, known as Pizza Street (across from Parque Kennedy), is a pedestrian walkway lined with restaurants specializing in Italian food. Very popular and open all night at weekends

Mid-range: *Bohemia*, Av Santa Cruz 805, on the Ovalo Gutiérrez. Large menu of international food, great salads and sandwiches. Also at Av El Polo 706, p 2, and at Pasaje Nicolás de Rivera 142, opposite the main post office near the Plaza de Armas, Lima centre, T427 5537.*Café de Paris*, Diez Canseco 180. Pleasant restaurant offering delicious soups, crepes etc, set 3-course meal for US$10, also good coffee. *Dalmacia*, San Fernando 401. Spanish-owned, casual gourmet restaurant, excellent. *Don Beta*, José Gálvez 667. Open 0800-2200 daily, good for seafood. *El Beduino*, Av 28 de Julio 1301. Good, authentic Arabic food. *Al Fresco*, Malecón Balta 790. Good *ceviche*, great cheap *sushi*, also in San Isidro. *Chifa Kun Fa*, San Martin 459 at Av Larco. Great Peruvian style Chinese food, excellent wan-tan soup. *Makoto Sushi Bar*, Larcomar shopping centre. Very good. *Il Postino*, Colina 401, T446 8381. Great Italian food. *La Palachinke*, Av Schell 120 at the bottom of Parque Kennedy. Recommended for pancakes. *Torero Sí Señor*, Av Angamos Oeste 598. Spanish food, fun, loud.

Cheap: *Big Apple Bagels*, Av Espinar 520 and Larcomar shopping centre, T441 4224 for delivery. The only bagels in Lima, surprisingly good. *Bocatta*, Av Benavides 1505. Great sandwiches.*Dino's Pizza*, Av Cdte Espinar 374. Great pizza at a good price, delivery service. *El Parquecito*, Diez Canseco 150. Good cheap menu. *Pardo's Chicken*, Av Benavides 730. Chicken and chips, very good and popular (branches throughout Lima).*Ricota*, Pasaje Tarata 248. Charming café on a pedestrian walkway, huge menu, big portions. On the same street, *Café Tarata*, No 260. Good atmosphere, family-run, good varied menu. *Rincón Arabe*, Independencia 633. Good cheap Arabic menu, fast-food style. *Sandwich.com*, Av Diagonal 234. Good, cheap sandwiches. *Super Rueda*, Porta 133, near the Cine Julieta, also Av Pardo 1224. Mexican food a-la Peru. *Whatta Burger*, Grau 120. American-style hamburgers. For cakes and sweets, *C'est si bon*, Av Cdte Espinar 663. Excellent cakes by the slice or whole, best in Lima. There are various small restaurants good for a cheap set meal along Los Pinos with Av Schell, at the bottom of Parque Kennedy.

Vegetarian *Bircher Benner*, Diez Canseco 487 y Grimaldo del Solar. Closed Sun, natural food store, slow service, good cheap *menú*. *Govinda*, Shell 634. Also sells natural products, good. *Madre Natura*, Chiclayo 815. Great natural foods shop. *El Paraíso*, Alcanfores 416, 2 blocks from Av Benavides. Natural foods/snacks, fruit salads, juices.

Cafés *Haiti*, Av Diagonal 160, Parque Kennedy. Open almost round the clock daily, great for people watching. *Vivaldi*, Av Ricardo Palma 260, 1 block from Parque Kennedy. Good, expensive.*La Tiendecita Blanca*, Av Larco 111 on Parque Kennedy. One of Miraflores' oldest, expensive, good people-watching, very good cakes, European-style food and delicatessen. *Café Café*, Martin Olaya 250, near the Parque Kennedy roundabout. Very popular, good atmosphere, over 100 different blends of coffee, good salads and sandwiches, very popular with 'well-to-do' Limeños. Also at Alvarez Calderón 198, San Isidro. *Café de la Paz*, middle of Parque Kennedy. Good outdoor café right on the park, expensive. *Café D'Oro*, Av Larco 763. Nice place for a sandwich or coffee. *Café 21*, Av José Pardo 4th block (ground floor of the *Las Américas Suites hotel*). Quiet and pleasant. *Café Milenium*, Av José Pardo 4th block (ground floor of the *El Pardo Hotel*). Busy at lunch and at night. *Café Olé*, Av Diagonal 322. Good, pricey. *San Antonio*, Av Angamos Oeste 1494, also Rocca de Vergallo 201, Magdalena del Mar and Av Primavera 373, San Borja. Fashionable *pastelería* chain, good, not too expensive.

Heladería 4D, Angamos Oeste 408. Open 1000-0100 daily, good Italian ice cream, at other locations throughout Lima.*Mi Abuela*, Angamos 393. Open 0900-2100 daily, probably the best yogurt in Lima, large selection of natural foods. *Zugatti*, Av Larco 361, across from Parque Kennedy. Good Italian gelato.

In San Isidro Expensive: *Antica Pizzería*, Av Dos de Mayo 728, T222 8437. Very popular, great ambience, excellent food, Italian owner. *Le Bistrot de mes Fils*, Av Conquistadores 510, T422 6308. Cosy French Bistrot, great food. *Chifa Royal*, Av Prescott 231, T421 0874. Excellent Sino-Peruvian food. *Valentino*, Manuel Bañon 215, T441 6174. One of Lima's best international restaurants.

Mid-range: *Al Fresco*, Santa Lucía 295. Seafood and *ceviche*, good cheap *sushi*. *Aromas Peruanos*, Av Guardia Civil 856. Typical Peruvian cuisine. *Chilis*, Ovalo Gutiérrez. American chain with a Peruvian twist. *Segundo Muelle*, Av Conquistadores 490, and Av

Peru

Canaval y Moreyra (aka Corpac) 605. Excellent ceviche, younger crowd. *Tierra Colombiana*, Av Conquistadores 585. Typical dishes from Colombia, good.

Cheap: *Delicass*, Miguel Dasso 131. Great deli with imported meats and cheeses, open late, slow service. *MiniMarket Kasher*, Av Pexet 1472. Kosher products, excellent, cheap *chala* bread every Fri. *Pits & Gloton*, 5th block of Av Espinar. Two back-to-back restaurants, popular late at night, chicken, sandwiches, etc, open 24 hrs.

Cafés *Mangos*, Ovalo Gutiérrez. Good, popular. *News Café*, Av Santa Luisa 110. Great salads and desserts, popular and expensive. *Café Oro Verde*, Vía Central 150 (behind Camino Real Shopping Centre). Excellent for coffee, lunch and snacks. *Café Olé*, Pancho Fierro 115 (1 block from *Hotel Olívar*). Huge selection of entrées and desserts.

In Barranco *Canta Rana*, Génova 101, T477 8934. Open daily 1200-1700, good *ceviche* but expensive, small portions. *La Costa Verde*, on Barranquito beach, T247 1244. Excellent fish and wine, expensive but recommended as the best by Limeños, open 1200-2400 daily, Sun buffet. *Domino's*, Av Grau 276. Open late, especially at the weekend. *Festín*, Av Grau 323, T477 3022. Huge menu, typical and international food. *El Hornito*, Av Grau 209, on corner of the main plaza, T477 2465. Pizzería and creole food. *Manos Morenas*, Av Pedro de Osma 409, T467 0421. Open 1230-1630, 1900-2300, creole cuisine with shows some evenings (cover charge for shows). *Las Mesitas*, Av Grau 341, T477 4199. Creole food and old sweet dishes which you won't find anywhere else.

In Pueblo Libre *Taberna Quierolo*, Av San Martín 1090, 2 blocks from Museo Nacional de Antropología y Arqueología. Old bar, good seafood and atmosphere, not open for dinner.

In Central Lima *L'Eau Vive*, Ucayali 370, T427 5612, across from the Torre Tagle Palace. Run by nuns, open Mon-Sat, 1230-1500 and 1930-2130, fixed-price lunch menu, Peruvian-style in interior dining room, or à la carte in either of dining rooms that open onto patio, excellent, profits go to the poor, Ave Maria is sung nightly at 2100. *Restaurant El Maurito*, Jr Ucayali 212, T426 2538. Peruvian/international, good pisco sours. *Chifa Cai*, Carabaya (Augusto N Wiese) y Ucayali. Clean, cheap, good fish dishes, ask about vegetarian if they're not too busy. *Heydi*, Puno 367. Good, cheap seafood, open daily 1100-2000, popular. *El Damero de Pizarro*, Jr de la Unión 543. Typical Peruvian food, huge helpings, popular with locals, loud music. *San Martín*, Av Nicolás de Piérola 890, off Plaza San Martín. Typical Peruvian food from both coast and highlands, good value, reasonably cheap. *Machu Picchu*, near *Hostal Europa* at Jr Ancash 312. Huge portions, grimy bathrooms (to say the least), yet very popular, closed for breakfast. *Manhatten*, Jr Miró Quesada 259. Open Mon-Fri 0700-1900, low end executive-type restaurant, local and international food from US$5-10, good. *La Colmena*, Av Nicolás de Piérola 742. Good set lunches, open 0800-2300. *Café Carrara*, Jr Ica 330, attached to *Hostal Roma*. Open daily until 2300, multiple breakfast combinations, pancakes, sandwiches, nice ambience, good. *Cafe-Restaurant Acclahuasy*, Jr Ancash 400, around the corner from *Hostal España*. Open 0700-2300, good. *Cordano*, Jr Ancash 202. Typical old Lima restaurant/watering hole, slow service and a bit grimy but full of character. Definitely worth the time it takes to drink a few beers. *Rincón Chileno*, Jr Camaná 234. Good food. *Jimmy's Baguetería y Pastelería*, Av Abancay 298 y Huallaga. Recommended, especially for sandwiches.

On Sat and Sun, 1100-1700, traditional dishes from all over Peru are served in Plaza Italia, plenty of seating, music, well-organized. Highly recommended

Vegetarian *Natur*, Moquegua 132, 1 block from Jr de la Unión, T427 8281. The owner, Humberto Valdivia, is also president of the *South American Explorers'* board of directors, good for food and casual conversation. *Centro de Medicina Natural*, Jr Chota 1462, next door to *Hostal de las Artes*. Very good.

Pasaje Olaya, on the Plaza de Armas between Jr de la Unión and Jr Carabaya, is a small pedestrian walkway with many nice restaurants frequented during lunch hours by executives. A bit on the pricey side but good.

In Breña *La Choza Náutica*, Jr Breña 204 behind Plaza Bolognesi. Good *ceviche* and friendly service. *D'Coco*, corner of Av Bolivia and Jr Iquique. Good, cheap *ceviche*. *Razato* Av Arica 298, 3 blocks from Plaza Bolognesi, T423 4369. Excellent and cheap Peruvian dishes.

Peru

In Chinatown There are many highly recommended *chifas* in the district of Barrios Altos. *Wa Lok*, Jr Paruro 864, T427 2656. Owner Liliana Com speaks fluent English, very friendly. *Salon Capon*, Jr Paruro 819. *Chun Koc Sen*, Jr Paruro 886, T427 5281. *Shanghai*, Jr Andahuaylas 685, T427 1560. *Fung Yen*, Jr Ucayali 744, T427 6567. *Chifa Capon*, Ucayali 774.

Bars & nightclubs

In Miraflores Bars: *Barra Brava*, Av Grau 192. Lot's of fun, sports bar(ish). *Media Naranja*, Schell 130, at the bottom of Parque Kennedy. Brazilian bar with typical drinks and food. *Murphys*, C Schell 627. Great Irish pub, "a must". *The Old Pub*, San Ramón 295 (Pizza Street). Cosy, with live music most days. *Pub Dionysos*, Av Dos de Mayo 385. Nice pub with Greek décor. *Rey David*, Av Benavides 567, Centro Comercial Los Duendes. Small café/bar. *Roca's Pub*, Bellavista 241. Cosy pub with late-night live shows.

Many places on Pizza St by Parque Kennedy

Nightclubs: *Downtown*, Los Pinos 162, at the 2nd block of Av Benavides. *Ministry*, Altos de D'Onofrio, opposite Parque Kennedy, T938 9231. Good music, performances and demonstrations of dance, exhibitions, tatooing, entry US$3. *Santa Sede*, Av 28 de Julio 441. Very popular, great music, fun crowd. *Satchmo*, Av La Paz 538, T442 8425. Live jazz, creole and blues shows. *Teatriz*, Larcomar shopping center, T242 3084/2358. Modern, expensive, very popular. *Tequila Rocks*, Diez Canseco 146, a half block from Parque Kennedy. Good music, very popular.

Watering holes and discos line both sides of Pasaje Sánchez Carrión, right off the main plaza. Av Grau, just across the street from the plaza, is also lined with bars

Barranco is the capital of Lima nightlife. The following is a brief selection. Bars: *Sargento Pimienta*, Bolognesi 755. Live music, always a favourite with Limeños. *Juanitos*, Av Grau, opposite the park. Barranco's oldest bar, and perfect to start the evening. *El Ekeko*, Av Grau 266. *La Estación*, Av Pedro de Osma 112. Live music, older crowd. *La Posada del Mirador*, near the *Puente de los Suspiros* (Bridge of Sighs). Beautiful view of the ocean, but you pay for the privilege. *Kitsch Bar*, Bolognesi 743. Decorated with flock wallpaper, dolls, religious icons, after midnight it becomes unbearably packed. *El Caserío*, Pasaje Sánchez Carrion 110. Great for dancing. *La Noche*, Bolognesi 307, at Pasaje Sánchez Carrión. A Lima institution. *Bar Quispe*, Plaza Raimondi, 1 block from Bolognesi. Photos of old Lima, large jar on the bar from which you can help yourself to peach brandy, wide range of music, popular at weekends. *El Grill de Costa Verde*, part of the *Costa Verde* restaurant on Barranco beach. Young crowd, packed at weekends. *Dirty Nelly's*, Av Pedro de Osma 135. Good craic Irish pub.

Many of the bars in this area turn into discos as the evening goes on

Nightclubs: *Noctambul*, Av Grau. Popular discotheque, large and modern. *Décimo Planeta*, Bolognesi 198. *My Place*, Domeyer 122. *Las Terrazas*, Av Grau 290.

In San Isidro *Palos de Moguer*, Av Emilio Cavenecia 129, T221 8363. Brews 4 different kinds of beer, typical bar food. *Punto G*, Av Conquistadores 512. Very popular, really small.

The centre of town, specifically Jr de la Unión, has many discos

In Central Lima *Queirolo Bar*, Jr Camaná 900 at Jr Quilca. Excellent for local colour, "a must". *Estadio Futbol Sports Bar*, Av Nicolás de Piérola 926 on the Plaza San Martín, T428 8866. Beautiful bar with a disco on the bottom floor, international football theme, good international and creole food. *El Rincón Cervecero*, Jr de la Unión (Belén) 1045. German pub without the beer, fun. *Piano Bar Munich*, Jr de la Unión 1044 (basement). Small and fun.

It's best to avoid the nightspots around the intersection of Av Tacna, Av Piérola and Av de la Vega. These places are rough and foreigners will receive much unwanted attention

Gay clubs: *Gitano*, Av Berlín 2nd block, Miraflores. Exclusively gay, good music. *Hedonismo*, Av Ignacio Merino 1700, Lince. Exclusively gay, good meeting place. *Imperio*, Jr Camaná 9th block, Lima centre. Exclusively gay, one of the older gay clubs in Lima, taxi recommended. *720 Downtown*, Av Uruguay 183, Lima centre. Exclusively gay, best in the centre, this is a rough neighbourhood so take a taxi to and from the club. *Kitsch Bar*, gay friendly, see Barranco bars. *Santa Sede*, very gay friendly, see Miraflores, Nightclubs.

Entertainment

Most films are in English with Spanish subtitles

Cinemas The newspaper *El Comercio* lists cinema information in the section called *Luces*. Most charge US$2 in the centre and around US$4-5 in Miraflores. Tue are reduced price at most cinemas. Cinemas in the centre tend to have poor sound quality. The best cinema chains in the city are *Cinemark*, *Cineplanet* and *UVK Multicines*. Among the best of the other movie theatres are *Cine Romeo y Julieta*, Pasaje Porta 115, at the bottom of Parque Kennedy, T447 5476, and *Multicine Starvision El Pacífico*, on the Ovalo by Parque Kennedy, T445 6990, both in Miraflores. Some *Cine Clubs* are: *Filmoteca de Lima*, Av 9 de Diciembre 125 (better known as Colón), T331 0126. *Cine Club Miraflores*, Av Larco 770, in the Miraflores Cultural Centre building, T446 2649. The cultural institutions (see below) usually show films once a week.

Peru

Peñas *Las Brisas de Titicaca*, Pasaje Walkuski 168, at 1st block of Av Brasil near Plaza Bolognesi, T332 1881. A Lima institution. *Sachun*, Av Del Ejército 657, Miraflores, T441 0123/4465. Great shows all week. *De Cajón*, C Merino 2nd block, near 6th block of Av Del Ejército, Miraflores. Good *música negra*. *Así Es Mi Perú*, Av Aviación 3390, San Borja, T476 2419.

In Barranco *Del Carajo*, San Ambrosio 328, T241 8904. *Don Porfirio*, C Manuel Segura 115, T447 3119. Traditional *peña*. *La Estación de Barranco*, at Pedro de Osma 112, T477 5030. Good, family atmosphere, varied shows. *Las Guitarras*, C Manuel Segura 295 (6th block of Av Grau), T247 3924. *Los Balcones*, Av Grau across from main plaza. Good, noisy and crowded. *Manos Morenas*, Av Pedro de Osma 409, T467 0421. Also a restaurant, older crowd, great shows beginning at 2230. *Peña Poggi*, Av Luna Pizarro 578, T247 5790/885 7619. 30 years old, traditional. *Perico's*, Av Pedro de Osma 1st block at the main plaza, T477 1311. *De Rompe y Raja*, Manuel Segura 127, T247 3271.

Theatre Most professional plays are staged at **Teatro Segura**, Jr Huancavelica 265, T427 9491. Many other theatres in the city. Occasional plays in English at **Teatro Británico**, C Bellavista 531, Miraflores, T447 9760.

The Luces section of El Comercio publishes theatre & cine details

Local festivals

18 Jan: Founding of Lima. **Semana Santa**, or Holy Week, is a colourful spectacle with processions. **28-29 Jul:** is Independence, with music and fireworks in the Plaza de Armas on the evening before. **30 Aug:** Santa Rosa de Lima. **Oct:** is the month of Our Lord of the Miracles; see Las Nazarenas church, above.

Prisons

Prisons hold several travellers, some imprisoned for up to one year without sentencing. For more information and details on visiting regulations, check with your embassy for prisoners from your own country, or ask at *South American Explorers* for the current list. A visit will be really appreciated!

Shopping

Silvania Prints, Conquistadores 915, San Isidro, also at Diéz Canseco 337A, Miraflores, sell modern silk-screen prints on Pima cotton with precolumbian designs. *La Casa de la Mujer Artesana*, Juan Pablo Ferandini 1550 (Av Brasil cuadra 15), Pueblo Libre, T423 8840, F423 4031, co-operative run by Movimiento Manuela Ramos, excellent quality work mostly from *pueblos jóvenes*, open Mon-Fri 0900-1300, 1400-1700. Miraflores is a good place for high quality, expensive handicrafts; there are many shops on and around Av La Paz. Recommended is *Kuntur Wasi*, Ocharan 182, T444 0557, English-speaking owner very knowledgeable about Peruvian textiles, frequently has exhibitions of fine folk art and crafts. *Antisuyo*, Tacna 460, at the 44th block of Av Arequipa, T241 6451, Mon-Fri 0900-1930, Sat 1030-1830, an indigenous co-operative run by an Englishwoman, sells handicrafts from all regions, reasonable prices (another outlet in Cusco). *Agua y Tierra*, Diez Canseco 298 y Alcanfores, Miraflores, T444 6980, fine crafts and indigenous art. *Centro Comercial El Alamo*, corner of La Paz y Diez Canseco, Miraflores, *artesanía* shops with good choice. *Las Pallas*, Cajamarca 212, 5th block of Av Grau, Barranco, T4774629, Mon-Sat 0900-1900, good quality handicrafts. In Lima centre: *Artesanía Santo Domingo*, Plaza Santo Domingo, by the church of that name, T428 9860. Good Peruvian crafts.

Since so many artisans have come to Lima, it is possible to find any kind of handicraft in the capital - quality is high

Alpaca 859, Av Larco 859, Miralflores, excellent quality alpaca and baby alpaca products. *Alpaca 111*, Av Larco 671, Miraflores, T447 1623, high quality alpaca, baby alpaca and vicuña items. *Royal Alpaca*, Pasaje El Suche, Av La Paz 646 no 14, Miraflores, T444 2150. Recommended for quality. *La Casa de la Alpaca*, Av La Paz 665, Miraflores, T447 6271. Open Mon-Fri 0930-2030. There are bargains in clothing made from high quality Pima cotton.

Bookshops *Libreria Mosca Azul*, Parque Salazar at Malecón de la Reserva 713, by Larcomar, Miraflores, T241 0675. Good selection of books in Spanish and some second hand English paperbacks. *Crisol*, Ovalo Gutiérrez, Av Santa Cruz 816, San Isidro, T221 1010, Below *Cine Planet*. Large bookshop with café, titles in English and French as well as Spanish. The *Virrey* chain has a great selection, but few in English: Larcomar Shopping Center (local 210), Miraflores, Pasaje Nicolás de Rivera, Lima centre behind the Municipalidad, T427 5080, and Miguel Dasso 141, San Isidro. *Special Book Services*, Av Angamos Oeste 301, Miraflores,

Foreign language books are subject to a high tax (US$12)

Peru

T242 4497, and at *Ibero Librerías*, Schell y Benavides, Miraflores, and Centro Comercial El Polo, Tienda B-115, Surco, T435 7597. Stocks Footprint Handbooks. *Zeta*, Av Cdte Espinar 219, T446 5139 and at airport. Stocks Footprint and other guide books. For magazines, whether in downtown Lima or Miraflores, almost all street kiosks sell up to date magazines in English such as *Time*, *Newsweek*, *People* etc. For the most recently published magazines and newspapers, try *Mallcco's* on Av Larco 175, on the Parque Kennedy roundabout, open daily 0800-2100. In front of *Café Haiti* by Parque Kennedy, men sell newspapers taken from arriving international flights; bargain hard.

It is recommended that you bring all camping and hiking gear from home

Camping equipment Camping gas (in small blue bottles) available from any large hardware store or bigger supermarket, about US$3. *Alpamayo*, Av Larco 345, Miraflores at Parque Kennedy, T445 1671. Sleeping mats, boots, rock shoes, climbing gear, water filters, tents, backpacks etc, very expensive but top quality equipment. The owner speaks fluent English and offers good information. *Todo Camping*, Av Angamos Oeste 350, Miraflores, near Av Arequipa, T447 6279. Sells 100% deet, bluet gas canisters, lots of accessories, tents, crampons and backpacks. *Camping Center*, Av Benavides 1620, Miraflores, T242 1779. Selection of tents, backpacks, stoves, camping and climbing gear. *Outdoor Peru*, Centro Comercial Chacarilla, store 211, on Av Caminos del Inca 257, Surco, T372 0428. Decent selection. *Huantzan*, Jr Tarapacá 384, Magdalena, T460 6101. Equipment sales and rentals, MSR stoves, backpacks, boots. *Mountain Worker*, Centro Comercial Camino Real, level A, store 17, San Isidro, T813 8367. Quality camping gear for all types of weather, made to order products as well. Recommended.

Wear long trousers and to take your passport when going to these places (except Lima 2000)

Maps Instituto Geográfico Nacional, Av Aramburú 1190, Surquillo, T475 9960/F475 3085. Open Mon-Fri 0830-1730. It has topographical maps of the whole country, mostly at 1:100,000, political and physical maps of all departments and satellite and aerial photographs. They also have a new series of tourist maps for trekking, eg of the Cordillera Blanca, the Cusco area, at 1:250,000. Ingemmet (Instituto Geológico Minero Y Metalúrgico), Av Canadá 1470, San Borja, T225 3128. Open Mon-Fri 0800-1300, 1400-1600. Sells a huge selection of geographic maps ranging from US$12 to US$112. Also satellite, aeromagnetic, geochemical and departmental mining maps. Enquire about new digital products. Aerial photographs are available at Servicio Aerofotográfico Nacional, Las Palmas Airforce Base, open Mon-Fri 0800-1400. Photos from mid-1950's aerial survey available, but they are expensive. Expect a waiting period as short as 1 day or as long as 2 weeks. Lima 2000, Av Arequipa 2625, Lince (near the intersection with Av Javier Prado), T440 3486, F440 3480, open Mon-Fri 0900-1300 and 1400-1800. Has an excellent street map of Lima (the only one worth buying), US$10, or US$14 in booklet form. Provincial maps and a country road map as well. Good for road conditions and distances, perfect for driving or cycling. Ministerio de Transporte, Av 28 de Julio 800, Lima centre, T433 7800. Open Mon-Fri 0800-1230, 1400-1600. Maps and plans of land communication routes, slow and bureaucratic. Ministerio de Agricultura, Av Salaverry y Húsares de Junín, Jesús María, T433 3034. Open Mon-Fri 0830-1300, 1400-1700. Complete set of 1:25,000 blueline maps, good service.

Markets Parque Kennedy, the main park of Miraflores, hosts a daily crafts market from 1700-2300. *Artesanía Carabaya*, Jr Carabaya 319 at the Plaza de Armas. There are crafts markets on **Av Petit Thouars** in Miraflores near Parque Kennedy. Av Petit Thouars runs parallel to Av Arequipa. At the 51st block you'll find an unnamed crafts market area with a large courtyard and lots of small flags. This is the largest crafts arcade in Miraflores. From here to Calle Ricardo Palma the street is lined with crafts markets. *La Portada del Sol*, on cuadra 54 of Petit Thouars, has a small café with reasonable prices and good coffee. All are open 7 days a week until late. On García Naranjo, La Victoria, just off Av Grau in the centre of town is *Polvos Azules*, the 'official' black market, sells just about anything; it is generally cheap and very interesting; beware pickpockets. Lima has 3 supermarket chains: *Santa Isabel*, *E Wong* and *Metro*. They all are well stocked and carry a decent supply of imported goods. The *Santa Isabel* on Av Benavides y Av Alcanfores in Miraflores is open 24 hrs. *Jockey Plaza*, Av Javier Prado Este, Surco, is a shopping, restaurant and cinema complex.

Bullfighting: there are 2 bullfight seasons: Oct to first week in Dec and during Jul. They **Sport**
are held in the afternoons on Sun and holidays. Tickets can be bought at Plaza Acho from
0930-1300 (T481 1467), or *Farmacia Dezza*, Av Conquistadores 1144, San Isidro, T440
8911/3798. Prices range from US$14 to US$90 (see page 1101). **Cycling**: Good shops
include: *Best Internacional*, Av Cdte Espinar 320, Miraflores, T446 4044 and Av Sucre
358, Magdalena, T470 1704. Open Mon-Sat 1000-1400, 1600-2000. Sells leisure and racing bikes, also repairs, parts and accessories. *Biclas*, Av Conquistadores 641, San Isidro,
T440 0890, F442 7548. Open Mon-Fri 1000-1300, 1600-2000, Sat 1000-1300. Knowledgeable staff, tours possible, good selection of bikes, repairs and accessories, cheap airline boxes for sale. *BikeMavil*, Av Aviación 4021, Surco, T449 8435. Open Mon-Sat
0930-2100. Rental service, repairs, excursions, selection of mountain and racing bicycles. *Casa Okuyama*, Jr Montevideo 785, Lima, T428 3444/426 3307. Open Mon-Fri
0900-1300, 1415-1800, Sat 0900-1300. Repairs, parts, try here for 28 inch tyres, excellent
service. *Cicloroni*, Las Casas 019, San Isidro, 32nd block of Petit Thouars, T222 6358, F442
3936. Open Mon-Sat 0900-2100, for repairs, parts and accessories, good information, ask
about Sat and Sun bike rides. *Cycling*, Av Tomás Marsano 2851, Higuereta-Surco, T/F271
0247. *Neuquén*, Av Aviación 3590, San Borja, T225 5219. For Shimano parts. *Perú Bike*,
Pedro de Osma 560, Barranco, T467 0757. Bike sales, repairs and accessories. *Willy Pro*
(Williams Arce), Av Javier Prado Este 3339, San Borja, T346 0468, F346 4082, warceleon@
misti.lared.net.pe Open Mon-Sat 0800-2000. Selection of specialized bikes, helpful
staff. **Contacts**: for information about all aspects of cycling in Lima and Peru, contact
Richard Fernandini at 442 1402/421 1226 (0900-1300, 1500-1800), he speaks English.
Diving: for information and equipment contact *Mundo Submarino*, Av Conquistadores
791, San Isidro, T4417604, Sr Alejandro Pez is a professional diver and arranges trips.
AquaSport, Av Conquistadores 645, San Isidro, T221 1548/7270, aquasport@
amauta.rcp.net.pe Owner is a CMAS instructor, gear for rent, tours and courses offered
and quality equipment for sale. *Peru Divers*, Av Huaylas 205, Chorrillos, T251 6231, open
Mon-Fri 0900-1900, Sat 0900-1700. Owner Lucho Rodríguez is a certified PADI instructor
who offers certification courses, tours and a wealth of good information. **Horse racing**:
Hipódromo Monterrico, on Tue and Thu evenings (1900) and Sat and Sun (1400) in summer, and in winter on Tue evening and Sat and Sun afternoons. For Caballos de Paso,
which move in 4-step amble, extravagantly paddling their forelegs, **National Paso
Association**, Miraflores, T447 6331. **Mountaineering**: *Asociación de Andinismo de la
Universidad de Lima*, Universidad de Lima, Javier Prado Este s/n, T437 6767. Meetings
on Wed 1800-2000, offers climbing courses. *Club de Montañeros Américo Tordoya*, Jr
Tarapacá 384, Magdalena, T460 6101. Meetings Thu 2000, contact Gonzalo Menacho.
Climbing excursions ranging from easy to difficult. *Grupo Cordillera*, T481 6649, cel 917
3832. Adventure tourism, weekly excursions. *Club de Ecoturismo*, T423 3329.
Parapenting: *Fly Adventure*, Jorge Chávez 658, Miraflores, T816 5461 (Mob) (Luis
Munarriz), 900 9150 (Eduardo Gómez). US$25 for 15-min tandem flight over the cliffs, 4
to 6-day courses US$250-350. Recommended. **Surfing**: *Focus*, Leonardo Da Vinci 208,
San Borja, T475 8459. Shaping factory and surf boards, knowledgeable about local spots
and conditions, rents boards. *Wayo Whiler*, Av 28 de Julio 287, Barranco, T247 6343
(workshop)/254 1344 (Wayo's house). For accessories, materials and repairs, can also
organize excursions. *O'Neills*, Av Santa Cruz 851, Miraflores, T445 0406. One of the best
surf shops in town. *Klimax*, José González 488, Miraflores, T447 1685. Sells new and secondhand boards, knowledgeable.

Peru

Tour operators

Do not conduct business anywhere other than in the agency's office and insist on a written contract. Bus offices or the airport are not the places to arrange and pay for tours. You may be dealing with representatives of companies that either do not exist or which fall far short of what is paid for

Most of those in Lima specialize in selling air tickets, or in setting up a connection in the place where you want to start a tour. Shop around and compare prices; also check all information carefully. It is best to use a travel agent in the town closest to the place you wish visit; it is cheaper and they are more reliable. See also *Fertur Peru* in the Tourist Office section. **Aracari Travel Consulting**, Av Pardo 610, No 802, Miraflores, T242 6673, F242 4856, www.aracari.com Regional tours throughout Peru, also 'themed' and activity tours. **Class Adventure Travel**, Av Grimaldo del Solar 463, Miraflores, T444 1652/2220, F241 8908, www.cat-travel.com Dutch-owned and run, one of the best. Highly recommended. **Coltur** Av José Pardo 138, Miraflores, T241 5551, F446 8073, www.coltur.com.pe With offices in Cusco and Arequipa, very helpful, well-organized. **Dasatour**, Jr Francisco Bolognesi 510 Miraflores, T447 7772, F447 0495, www.dasatariq.com Also in Cusco. **Explorandes**, C San Fernando 320, T445 8683/242 9527, F242 3496, Postmast@Exploran.com.pe Offers a wide range of adventure and cultural tours throughout the country. Also offices in Cusco and Huaraz (see page 1133). Highly recommended is Siduith Ferrer Herrera, CEO of **Fertur Peru**, Jr Junín 211 (main office) at the Plaza de Armas, T427 1958, T/F428 3247, fertur@ terra.com.pe Open 0900-1900. *Fertur* also has a satellite at *Hostal España*, Jr Azángaro 105, T427 9196. Her agency not only offers up to date, correct tourist information on a national level, but also great prices on national and international flights, discounts for those with ISIC and Youth cards and *South American Explorers* members (of which she is one). Other services include flight reconfirmations, hotel reservations and transfers to and from the airport or bus stations. Also tours. **Hada Tours**, 2 de Mayo 529, Miraflores, T446 8157, F446 2714, saleprom@hadatours.com.pe 20 years of experience. **Highland Peru Tours**, Atahualpa 197, Miraflores, T/F242 7189, sales@highlandperu.com **InkaNatura Travel**, Manuel Bañon 461, San Isidro, T420 2022, F422 9225, www.inkanatura.com Trips to Chachapoyas, north coast and southeastern jungle. **Inca Wasi**, Jr Porta 170, Miraflores, T445 9691, inkawasi@ lullitec.com.pe **Lima Tours**, Jr Belén 1040, Lima centre, T424 5110/756 0/6410, F424 6269. Recommended. Also has an office in San Isidro: Av Pardo y Alliaga 698, T222 2525, F222 5700. **Peru Expeditions**, Av Arequipa 5241 – 504, Lima 18, T447 2057, F445 7874, www.peru-expe-ditions.com Specialising in expeditions in 4x4 vehicles and Andes crossings. **Peru Travel Bureau**, Sebastián Tellería 45, San Isidro, T222 1909, F222 9250, postmast@ptb.com.pe Recommended. **Queen Adventures**, Jr Callao 301, near Plaza de Armas, qtours@terra.com.pe Good for arranging tours throughout the country. **Roma Tours**, Jr Ica 330, next to *Hostal Roma*, T/F427 7572, resroma@terra.com.pe, or dantereyes@hotmail.com Good and reliable. Administrator Dante Reyes is very friendly and speaks English. **Servicios Aéreos AQP SA**, Los Castaños 347, San Isidro, T222 3312, F222 5910, www.saaqp.com.pe Comprehensive service, tours offered throughout the country. **Victor's Travel Service**, Jr de la Unión (Belén) 1068, T431 4195/433 3367, F431 0046, 24 hr line 867 6341, victortravel@terra.com.pe Hotel reservations (no commission, free pick-up), free maps of Lima and Peru, Mon-Sat 0900-1800, very helpful. **Viento Sur**, Av Arequipa 4964, oficina 202, Miraflores, T242 6655, at night 449 1464, ecoturmar@yahoo.com Sailing boat and yacht tours to islands off the coast of Lima. Two 4-hr trips per day at 0930 and 1400, reservation required. **Viracocha**, Av Vasco Núñez de Balboa 191, Miraflores, T445 3986/447 5516, F447 2429. Very helpful, especially with flights. In addition

Private guides The following guides are certified by the **MITINCI** (Ministry of Industry Tourism, Integration and International Business) and most are members of **AGOTUR** (Asociación de Guías Oficiales de Turismo). Always book well in advance. All speak English unless indicated otherwise. **Ruben Cuneo**, T264 6092, T946 4949 (Mob), rubencuneo@ yahoo.com.uk Speaks Italian. **Lorena Duharte Arias**, T/F471 3728, T963 7608 (Mob), Italian and Flemish (no English). **Sra Goya**, T/F578 5937, T988 3773 (Mob), speaks Japanese. **Sr Gunnar**, T/F476 5016, kolibri@netaccessperu.net or gunnar_@algonet.se Specializes in bird watching, speaks Swedish. **Tino Guzmán Khang**, T/F at home 429 5779, T966 1363 (Mob), tino@amauta.rcp.net.pe Expert in Peruvian archeology and anthropology, private tours to all parts of the country. Member of *South American Explorers*, US$12 per hr. Also speaks French and some Chinese. Very highly recommended. **Sra Julia Huamán**, *Lima Tours* Official Guide, T531 1839, jhuaman@tsi.com.pe **Sra Nariko de Kana**, T442 4000, guide for

Kinjyo Travel. Speaks Japanese. ***Sra Elzinha de Mayer***, T445 0676, T975 8287 (Mob), elzinha@terra.com.pe Speaks Portuguese and French. ***Shoko Otani***, T221 2984, T969 2213 (Mob), Shoko-o@amauta. rcp.net.pe Speaks Japanese. ***Ernesto Riedner***, T446 1082, F446 6739, T909 4224 (Mob), eried@terra.com.pe Speaks German. ***Nila Soto***, T452 5483, T965-0951 (Mob), nilasoto@yahoo.com, or nilasoto@hotmail.com Speaks Italian. ***Anabella Velasco***, T/F433 7336, T993 1458 (Mob). Speaks German. ***Tessy Torres***, T/F422 8210, T975 8960 (Mob), jctc@terra.com.pe Speaks Portuguese, Italian and French. Also recommended: *Jaime Torres*, Los Algarrobos 1634, Urb Las Brisas, T337 6953, T917 3073 (Mob). Speaks fluent English, also taxi driver, very helpful.

Peru

Transport

Local Bus: the bus routes are shared by buses, combis (mid-size) and colectivos (mini-vans), the latter run from 0600-0100, and less frequently through the night, they are quicker and stop wherever requested. All charge US$0.35. On public holidays, Sun and from 2400 to 0500 every night, a small charge is added to the fare. The principal routes are from the centre of Lima to Miraflores, San Isidro, Pueblo Libre, central market and airport.

Buses to **Miraflores**: Av Arequipa runs 52 blocks between the downtown Lima area and Parque Kennedy in Miraflores. Public transport has "Todo Arequipa" on the windscreen. When heading towards downtown from Miraflores the window sticker should say "Wilson/Tacna". To get to Parque Kennedy from downtown look on the windshield for "Larco/Schell/Miraflores," "Chorrillos/ Huaylas" or "Barranco/ Ayacucho". On Vía Expresa, buses can be caught at Avs Tacna, Garcilaso de la Vega, Bolivia and Ugarte (faster than Av Arequipa, but watch for pickpockets). The main stop for Miraflores is Ricardo Palma, 4 blocks from Parque Kennedy. Taxi US$2.

It can be much cheaper to rent a car in a town in the Sierra for a few days than to drive all the way from Lima. Also, if there are any problems with the rental car, companies do not have a collection service

Car rental: most rental companies have an office at the airport, where you can arrange everything and pick up and leave the car. It's recommended to test-drive car before signing contract as quality varies. See Essentials for international rental agencies, page 48. Cars can be hired from: *Alamo Rent A Car*, Av Benavides 1180, Miraflores, T444 4122/444 3934/4443906, F241 7431. *Dollar Rent A Car*, Diez Canseco 236 no 201, Miraflores, T445 2239/444 5646, Cantuarias 341, Miraflores, T444 4920/3050, Airport T575 1719. *Inka's Rent a Car*, Cantuarias 160, Miraflores, T445 5716/447 2129, F447 2583, airport T/F575 1390, www.peruhot.com/ inkas   *Paz Rent A Car*, Av Diez Canseco 319, Miraflores, T446 4395, F242 4306. Prices range from US$40 to US$60 depending on type of car. Make sure that your car is in a locked garage at night.

Cycling: into or out of Lima is not recommended, difficult and dangerous.

Drivers don't expect tips; give them small change from the fare

Taxis: Fares: within city centre US$1.15-2; to Miraflores and most suburbs US$2-3.50; from outside airport terminal to centre US$4-6, San Isidro/Miraflores US$6-8, Breña US$3.50-4. Licensed taxis are yellow, but there are many other types. *Daewoo Ticos* are cheapest, the bigger black taxis charge US$15-20 from centre to suburbs. Licensed and phone taxis are safest. There are several reliable phone taxi companies, which can be called for immediate service, or booked in advance; prices are 2-3 times more than ordinary taxis; eg to the airport US$15-20, to suburbs US$7-8. Some are *Taxi América*, T265 1960; *Moli Taxi*, T479 0030; *Taxi Real*, T470 6263; *Taxi Tata*, T274 5151; *TCAM*, run by Carlos Astacio, T983 9305, safe, reliable. If hiring a taxi for over 1 hr agree on price per hr beforehand. To Callao, La Punta, San Miguel, Magdalena, Miraflores (US$4), Barranco, Chorrillos, by agreement, basis US$5 per hr. Recommended, knowledgeable drivers: Hugo Casanova Morella, T485 7708 (he lives in La Victoria), for city tours, travel to airport, etc. *Mónica Velásquez Carlich*, T425 5087, T943 0796 (Mob), vc_monica@hotmail.com   For airport pick-ups, tours, Speaks English, most helpful.

For international flight information T575 1712; domestic T574 5529. For services available at the airport, see Essentials, page 37

Long distance Air: Jorge Chávez Airport, 16 km from the centre of Lima. At the customs area, explain that you are a tourist and that your personal effects will not be sold in Peru; items such as laptops, cameras, bicycles, climbing equipment are exempt from taxes if they are not to be sold in Peru. **Transport from the airport** *Remise* taxi (*Mitsui* or *CMV*) from desks outside International Arrivals and National Arrivals, US$11.75 to centre, US$14.70 to San Isidro and Miraflores, US$17.65 to Barranco. There are many taxi drivers offering their services outside Arrivals with similar or higher prices (more at night). See above for other taxi fares. There is a service called *Urbanito*, from the airport to the centre, Breña and San Miguel US$3, Pueblo Libre, San Isidro and Miraflores US$4.40 (slow, as it calls at all hotels), T814 6932 (24 hrs)/425 1202/424 3650, urbanito@terra.com.pe Local buses and colectivos run between the airport perimeter and the city centre and suburbs, their routes are given on the front window (eg 'Miraflores' for Miraflores). Outside the pedestrian exit are the bus, colectivo and taxi stops, but there is more choice for buses at the roundabout by the car entrance. Luggage is not allowed on buses. Colectivo service from Av Tacna y Colmena (Nicolás de Piérola) 733, from 0600 to 2000, colectivos wait until they have 5 passengers,

US$0.35 pp, and US$0.25 for luggage. If you are feeling confident and not too jet-lagged, go to the car park exit and find a taxi outside the perimeter, by the roundabout. They charge US$3 to the city centre. The security guards may help you find a taxi. The big hotels have their own buses at the airport, and charge US$6-15.

Internal air services: to most destinations there are daily flights (most options are given in the text) but flights may be cancelled in the rainy season.

Bus: there are many different bus companies, but the larger ones are better organized, leave on time and do not wait until the bus is full. For approximate prices, frequency and duration of trip, see destinations. *Cruz del Sur*, Jr Quilca 531, Lima centre, T224 6200/424 1005, www.cruzdelsur.com.pe This terminal has routes to many destinations in Peru with *Ideal* service, quite comfortable buses and periodic stops for food and bathroom breaks, a cheap option with a quality company. The other *Ideal* terminal is at Av Paseo de la República 801, across the expressway from the National Stadium, T433 6765/332 4000/4330231. They go to: **Ica, Arequipa, Cusco, Puno, Chiclayo, Trujillo, Chincha, Cañete, Camana, Ilo, Moquegua, Pisco** and **Juliaca**. The other terminal is at Av Javier Prado Este 1109, San Isidro, T225 6163/6164. This terminal offers the *Imperial* service (luxury buses), more expensive and direct, with no chance of passengers in the aisle, and *Cruzero* service (super luxury buses). They go to: **Tumbes, Sullana, Huancayo, Piura, Chiclayo, Trujillo, Huaraz, Jauja, Camaná, Arequipa, Moquegua, Ilo, Tacna, Cusco** and **La Paz**. (Note this service is *Imperial* only to Arequipa, where you must transfer to an *Ideal* bus for the remaining leg of the trip). *Ormeño*, the following buses are all owned and operated by *Ormeño*: *Expreso Ancash* (routes to the **Huaraz area**), *Expreso Continental* (routes to **the north**), *Expreso San Cristóbal* (to **the southeast**), *Expreso Chinchano* (to the **south coast** and **Arequipa**) and *Expreso Internacional* (despite the name, to destinations throughout Peru).These depart from and arrive to: Av Carlos Zavala 177, Lima centre, T427 5679; also Av Javier Prado Este 1059, Santa Catalina, T472 1710, www.ascinsa.com/ORMENO/ *Ormeño* also offers *Royal Class* and *Business Class* service to certain destinations. These buses are very comfortable with bathrooms, hostess, etc. They arrive and depart from the Javier Prado terminal only.

Other companies include: *Móvil Tours*, Av Paseo de La República 656, Lima Centre near the national stadium, T332 0024. Very recommended service to **Huaraz**. Lots of leg room. *Expreso Molina*, Jr Ayacucho 1141, Lima Centre, T428 0617/4852. Good service to **Ayacucho** via Pisco. *Rodríguez*, Av Roosevelt 393, Lima Centre, T428 0506, terminal at Av Paseo de La República 749, opposite national stadium. **Huaraz, Caraz, Yungay, Carhuaz**. Recommended to arrive in Huaraz and then use local transportation to points beyond. Good. Various levels of bus service. *Mariscal Cáceres*, Av Carlos Zavala 211, Lima Centre, T427 2844, and Av 28 de Julio 2195, La Victoria, T474 6811/7850. To: **Huancayo** and **Jauja**. Very good. Service ranges from basic to deluxe. *Transportes Atahualpa*, Jr Sandia 266, Lima Centre, T428 7732. Direct to **Cajamarca** continuing on to **Celendín**. *Civa*, Av Carlos Zavala 211, Lima Centre, and Av 28 de Julio y Paseo de La República, T332 1754/428 5649. To **Cajamarca, Celendín, Chachapoyas** and **Bagua**; also to **Nasca**. Has *Servicio Imperial* (executive service). *Royal Tours*, Av Paseo de la República 3630, San Isidro, T440 6624. To **Huánuco, Tingo María** and **Pucallpa**. *Transportes León de Huánuco*, Av 28 de Julio 1520, La Victoria, T424 3893. Daily to **Huánuco, Tingo María** and **Pucallpa**. *Transportes Chanchamayo*, Av Manco Capac 1052, La Victoria, T265 6850/470 1189. To **Tarma, San Ramón** and **La Merced**.

International buses: *Ormeño*, Av Javier Prado 1059, Santa Catalina, T472 1710, F470 5454. To: **Guayaquil** (29 hrs, US$50), **Quito** (38 hrs), **Cali** (56 hrs), **Bogotá** (70 hrs), **Caracas** (100 hrs), **Santiago** (54 hrs, US$130), **Mendoza** (78 hrs), **Buenos Aires** (90 hrs, US$170). **NB** A maximum of 20 kg is allowed pp. Depending on the destination, extra weight penalties range from US$1-3 per kg. *El Rápido*, Av Rivera Navarrete 2650, Lince, T447 6101/441 6651. Service to Argentina and Uruguay only. Bear in mind that international buses are more expensive than travelling from one border to another on national buses.

Warning The area around the bus terminals is very unsafe; thefts and assaults are more common in this neighbourhood than elsewhere in the city. You are strongly advised to

In the weeks either side of 28/29 Jul (Independence), and of the Christmas/New Year holiday, it is practically impossible to get bus tickets out of Lima, unless you book in advance. Bus prices double at these times

Peru

To enter Peru, a ticket out of the country may be required. If you have to buy a bus ticket, be warned: they are not transferable or refundable

consider taking a taxi to and from your bus. Make sure your luggage is well guarded and put on the right bus. It is also important not to assume that buses leave from the place where you bought the tickets.

Directory **Airline offices Domestic**: *Aero Continente*, Av José Pardo 651, Miraflores; Av Larco 123, p 2, Miraflores, T242 4242; many other branches. **NB** *Aviandina* is a subisidiary of *Aero Continente* with an office opposite *Aero Continente*'s Av J Pardo office. *Aero Cóndor*, Juan de Arona 781, San Isidro, T442 5215/5663. *Lan Perú*, Av José Pardo 269, Miraflores, and C Paz Soldán 225, San Isidro, T213 8200. *Star Up*, Av Larco 101, oficina 1003, Miraflores, T447 7573. *Tans* (formerly *Grupo Ocho*, military airline), Jr Belén 1015, Lima centre, and Av Arequipa 5200, Miraflores, T241 8510. International *Aerolíneas Argentinas*, Av José Pardo 805, p 3, Miraflores, T241 3327/444 1387. *AeroMéxico*, Aristides Aljovín 472, Miraflores, T444 4441. *Air France*, Av José Pardo 601, Miraflores, T444 9285. *American Airlines*, Av Canaval y Moreyra 390, San Isidro, and in *Hotel Las Américas*, Av Benavides y Av Larco, Miraflores, T211 7000. *Avianca*, Av Paz Soldán 225, of C5, San Isidro, T221 7822. *Continental*, Víctor Belaúnde 147, oficina 101, San Isidro, and in the *Hotel Marriott*, 13th block of Av Larco, Miraflores, T221 4340/222 7080. *Copa*, Av 2 de Mayo 741, Miraflores, T444 7815/9776. *Delta*, Víctor Belaúnde 147, San Isidro, T211 9211. *Iberia*, Av Camino Real 390, p 9, San Isidro, T441 7801/421 4633. *KLM*, Av José Pardo 805, p 6, Miraflores, T242 1240/1241. *Lacsa*, Av Comandante Espinar 331, Miraflores, T444 4690. *Lan Chile*, Av José Pardo 269, Miraflores, T213 8200. *Lloyd Aéreo Boliviano*, Av José Pardo 231, Miraflores, T444 0510/241 5210. *Lufthansa*, Av Jorge Basadre 1330, San Isidro, T442 4466. *Tame*, Andalucía 174, Miraflores, T422 6600/1710. *Varig*, Av Camino Real 456, p 8, San Isidro, T442 1449/4163.

Banks *Interbank*, Jr de la Union 600, Lima Centre (main branch). Open Mon-Fri 0900-1800. Also Av Pardo 413, Av Larco 690 and in Larcomar, Miraflores, Av Grau 300, Barranco, Av Pezet 1405 and Av Pardo y Aliaga 634, San Isidro, and supermarkets *Wong* and *Metro*. Amex TCs only, ATM for MasterCard. *Banco de Crédito*, Jr Lampa 499, Lima Centre (main branch), Av Pardo 425 and Av Larco at Pasaje Tarata, Miraflores, Av Pardo y Aliaga at Av Camino Real, San Isidro). Open Mon-Fri 0900-1800, Sat 0930-1230. Amex TCs only, accepts Visa card and branches have Visa ATM. *Banco Santander Central Hispano (BSCH)*, Av Pardo 482 and Av Larco 479, Miraflores, Av Augusto Tamayo 120, San Isidro (main branch). Open Mon-Fri 0900-1800, Sat 0930-1230. TCs (Visa and Citicorp). ATM for Visa/Plus. *Banco de Comercio*, Av Pardo 272 and Av Larco 265, Miraflores, Jr Lampa 560, Lima Centre (main branch). Open Mon-Fri 0900-1800, Sat 0930-1200. Amex TCs only, ATM accepts Visa/Plus. *Banco Financiero*, Av Ricardo Palma 278, near Parque Kennedy (main branch). Open Mon-Fri 0900-1800, Sat 0930-1230. TCs (Amex), ATM for Visa/Plus. *Banco Continental*, corner of Av Larco and Av Benavides and corner of Av Larco and Pasaje Tarata, Miraflores, Jr Cusco 286, Lima Centre near Plaza San Martín. Open Mon-Fri 0900-1800, Sat 0930-1230. TCs (Amex), Visa ATM. *Banco Wiese Sudameris*, Av Diagonal 176 on Parque Kennedy, Av José Pardo 697, Miraflores, Av Alfonso Ugarte 1292, Breña, Miguel Dasso 286, San Isidro. Open Mon-Fri 0915-1800, Sat 0930-1230. TCs (Amex only), ATM for Visa/Plus. *Citibank*, in all *Blockbuster* stores, and at Av 28 de Julio 886, Av Benavides 23rd block and Av Emilio Cavenecia 175, Miraflores, Av Las Flores 205 and branch in Centro Comercial Camino Real, Av Camino Real 348, San Isidro. *Blockbuster* branches open Sat and Sun 1000-1900.

Exchange houses There are many *casas de cambio* on and around Jr Ocoña off the Plaza San Martín. On the corner of Ocoña and Jr Camaná is a large concentration of *cambistas* (street changers) with huge wads of dollars and soles in one hand and a calculator in the other. They should be avoided. Changing money on the street should only be done with official street changers wearing an identity card with a photo. This card doesn't *automatically* mean that they are legitimate but you're less likely to have a problem. Around Parque Kennedy and down Av Larco in Miraflores are dozens of official *cambistas* with ID cards and, usually, blue, sometimes green vest. There are also those who are independent, dressed in street clothes, but it's safer to use an official changer. There are a few places on Jr de la Unión at Plaza San Martín that will accept worn, ripped and old bills, but the exchange will be terrible. A repeatedly recommended *casa de cambio* is *LAC Dolar*, Jr Camaná 779, 1 block from Plaza San Martín, p 2, T428 8127, T/F427 3906, also at Av La Paz 211, Miraflores, T242 4069/4085. Open Mon-Sat 0900-1900, Sun and holidays 0900-1400, good rates, very helpful, safe, fast, reliable, 2 commission on cash and TCs (Amex, Citicorp, Thomas Cook, Visa), will come to your hotel if you're in a group. Another recommended *casa de cambio* is *Virgen P Socorro*, Jr Ocoña 184, T428 7748. Open daily 0830-2000, safe, reliable and friendly. *American Express*, Av Belén 1040 in the Lima Tours office, near Plaza San Martín. Official hours are Mon-Fri 0900-1700, Sat 0900-1300, but there is always someone there in case of emergencies. Replaces lost or stolen Amex cheques of any currency in the world. Can purchase Amex cheques with Amex card only. Also at Av Pardo y Aliaga 698, San Isidro,

T222 2525, F222 5700. *MasterCard*, Porta 111, p 6, Miraflores, T242 2700. *Moneygram*, Ocharan 260, Miraflores, T447 4044. Safe and reliable agency for sending and receiving money. Locations throughout Lima and the provinces. Exchanges most world currencies and TCs. *Western Union* Main branch: Av Petit Thouars 3595, San Isidro, T422 0036/9723/440 7934. Av Larco 826, Miraflores, T241 1220 (also *TNT* office). Jr Carabaya 693, Lima centre, T428 7624.

Communications Internet: Lima is completely inundated with internet cafés, so you will have absolutely no problem finding one regardless of where you are. An hour will cost you S/3-5 (US$0.85-1.50). **Post office:** The central post office is on Jr Camaná 195 in the centre of Lima near the Plaza de Armas. Mon-Fri 0730-1900 and Sat 0730-1600. Poste Restante is in the same building but is considered unreliable. In Miraflores the main post office is on Av Petit Thouars 5201 in Miraflores (same hours). There are many small branches around Lima, but they are less reliable. For express service: *DHL*, Los Castaños 225, San Isidro, T215-7500. *UPS*, Av del Ejército 2107, San Isidro, T264 0105. *Federal Express*, Av Jorge Chávez 475, T242 2280, Miraflores, C José Olaya 260, Miraflores. *EMS*, next to central post office in downtown Lima, T533 2020/2424/2005. When receiving parcels from other countries that weigh in over 1 kg, they will be automatically sent to one of Lima's two customs post offices. Take your passport and a lot of patience as the process can (but not always) take a long time: Teodoro Cárdenas 267, Santa Beatriz (12th block of Av Arequipa); and Av Tomás Valle, Los Olivos (near the Panamerican Highway). **NB** Long trousers must be worn when going to these offices. **Telephone:** There are many *Telefónica* offices all over Lima. Most allow collect calls but some don't. All offer fax service (sending and receiving). There are payphones all over the city. Some accept coins, some only phone cards and some honour both. Phone cards can often be purchased in the street near these booths. Some *Telefónica* offices are: Pasaje Tarata 280, Miraflores (near Av Alcanfores); Av Bolivia 347, Lima Centre; C Porta 139, Miraflores (near the bottom of Parque Kennedy). For full details on phone operation, see Telephones, Essentials, page 1092.

Cultural centres Peruvian-British Cultural Association, Av Arequipa 3495, T221 7550. English library and British newspapers, Mon-Fri 0800-1300, 1530-1930. **Instituto Cultural Peruano-Norteamericano**, Jr Cusco 446, Lima Centre, T428 3530, with library. Main branch at Av Arequipa 4798 y Angamos, Miraflores, T241 1940. Theatre productions and modern dance performances are just a couple of the activities the ICPNA offers. Also Spanish lessons; see Language schools, below. **Goethe Institute**, Jr Nasca 722, Jesús María, T433 3180. Mon-Fri 0800-2000, library, German papers. **Alianza Francesa**, Av Arequipa 4595, Miraflores, T241 7014. Various cultural activities, library.

Embassies and consulates Austria, Av Central 643, p 5, San Isidro, T442 0503, F442 8851. **Belgian Consulate**, Angamos Oeste 380, Miraflores, T241 7566, F241 6379. **Bolivian Consulate**, Los Castaños 235, San Isidro, T442 3826, postmast@emboli.org.pe (0900-1330), 24 hrs for visas (except those requiring clearance from La Paz). **Brazilian Consulate**, José Pardo 850, Miraflores, T421 5650, F445 2421, Mon-Fri 0930-1300. **Canada**, Libertad 130, Casilla 18-1126, Lima, T444 4015, F444 4347. **Chilean Consulate**, Javier Prado Oeste 790, San Isidro, T221 2080, embchile@mail.cosapidata.com.pe Open 0900-1300, need appointment. **Colombian Consulate**, Av Jorge Basadre 1580, San Isidro, T441 0954, F441 9806. Mon-Fri 0800-1400. **Ecuadorean Consulate**, Las Palmeras 356, San Isidro (6th block of Av Javier Prado Oeste), T440 9991, F442 4182, embjecua@amauta.rcp.net.pe **French Embassy**, Arequipa 3415, San Isidro, T221 7792, FRANCE.EMBAJADA@computextos.com.pe **Germany**, Av Arequipa 4210, Miraflores, T422 4919, F422 6475. **Israel**, Natalio Sánchez 125, p 6, Santa Beatriz, T433 4431, F433 8925. **Italy**, Av G Escobedo 298, Jesús María, T463 2727, F463 5317. **Japan**, Av San Felipe 356, Jesús María, T463 0000. **Netherlands Consulate**, Av Principal 190, Santa Catalina, La Victoria, T476 1069, F475 6536, open Mon-Fri 0900-1200. **New Zealand Consulate**, Av Camino Real 390, Torre Central, p 17 (Casilla 3553), San Isidro, T221 2833, F442 0155, reya@nzlatam.com Open Mon-Fri 0830-1300, 1400-1700. **Spain**, Jorge Basadre 498, San Isidro, T440 6998, open 0900-1300. **Sweden**, Camino Real 348, p 9, Torre del Pilar, San Isidro, T421 3400, F212 5805. **Switzerland**, Av Salaverry 3240, Magdalena, Lima 17, T264 0305, F264 1319, embsuiza@correo.tnet.com.pe **UK**, Torre Parque Mar, p 22, T617 3000, F617 3100, www.britemb.org.pe Open 1300-2130 (Dec-Apr to 1830 Mon and Fri, and Apr-Nov to 1830 Fri), good for security information and newspapers. **USA**, Av Encalada block 17, Surco, T434 3000, F434 3037, for emergencies after hrs T434 3032, the Consulate is in the same building.

During the summer, most embassies only open in the morning

Peru

Language schools *Instituto Cultural Peruano-Norteamericano*, Av Arequipa 4798, Miraflores, T241 1940/428 3530. Classes are on Mon-Fri from 0900 to 1100, US$80 per month, no private classes offered. *Instituto de Idiomas (Pontífica Universidad Católica del Perú)*, Av Camino Real 1037, San Isidro, T442 8761/442 6419. US$103 per month, classes Mon-Fri 1100-1300, private lessons possible.

Recommended. *Instituto de Idiomas (Universidad del Pacífico)*, Av Prescott 333, San Isidro, T421 2969. US$290 for 3 months, 3 days per week at 1½ hrs per lesson. Private classes possible for executive (business) level only. *Esit Idiomas*, Av Javier Prado Este 4457, Lima 33, T434 1060, www.esit-peru.com **Independent teachers** (enquire about rates): *Sra Lourdes Gálvez*, T435 3910. Highly recommended, also Quechua. *Sra Georgelina Sadastizágal*, T275 6460. Recommended. Also Sr Mariano Herrera and Sr Dante Herrera: all these four can be contacted through peruidiomas@ LatinMail.com *Srta Susy Arteaga*, T534 9289, T989 7271 (Mob), susyarteaga@hotmail.com, or susyarteaga@yahoo.com Recommended. *Srta Patty Félix*, T521 2559, patty_fel24@yahoo.com

For hospitals, doctors and dentists, contact your consulate for recommendations

Medical services Hospitals: **Clínica Anglo Americano**, Av Salazar 3rd block, San Isidro, a few blocks from Ovalo Gutiérrez, T221 3656. Stocks Yellow Fever for US$18 and Tetanus for US$3. Dr Luis Manuel Valdez recommended. **Clínica Internacional**, Jr Washington 1471 y Paseo Colón (9 de Diciembre), downtown Lima, T433 4306. Good, clean and professional, consultations up to US$35, no inoculations. **Instituto Médico Lince**, León Velarde 221, near 17th and 18th blocks of Av Arenales, Lince, T471 2238. Dr Alejandro Bussalleu Rivera speaks English, good for stomach problems, about US$28 for initial consultation. Repeatedly recommended. **Clínica San Borja**, Av Guardia Civil 337, San Borja (2 blocks from Av Javier Prado Este), T475 4000/475 3141. **Clínica Ricardo Palma**, Av Javier Prado Este 1066, San Isidro, T224 2224/224 2226. **Instituto de Ginecología y Reproducción**, part of Clínica Montesur, Av Monterrico 1045, Monterrico parallel to Av Polo, T434 2130/434 2426. Recommended Gynaecologists are **Dra Alicia García** and **Dr Ladislao Prasak**. **Instituto de Medicina Tropical**, Av Honorio Delgado near the Pan American Highway in the Cayetano Heredia Hospital, San Martín de Porres, T482 3903/482 3910. Cheap consultations, good for check-ups after jungle travel. Recommended. **Clínica del Niño**, Av Brasil 600 at 1st block of Av 28 de Julio, Breña, T330 0066/330 0033. **Centro Anti-Rabia de Lima**, Jr Austria 1300, Breña, T425 6313. Open Mon-Sat 0830-1830. Consultation is about US$2.50. **Clínica de Fracturas San Francisco**, Av San Felipe 142 at Av Brasil, Jesús María, T463 9855. **Clínica Padre Luis Tezza**, Av El Polo 570, Monterrico, T435 6990/6991, emergency 24 hrs T437 1310. Top quality clinic specializing in a wide variety of illnesses/disorders etc, expensive; for stomach or intestinal problems, ask for Dr Raul Morales (speaks some English, US$28 for first consultation). **Clínica Santa Teresa**, Av Los Halcones 410, Surquillo, T221 2027. **Dr José Luis Calderón**, general practitioner recommended. **International Chiropractors Center**, Av Santa Cruz 555, Miraflores, T221 4764. **Pharmacy:** Phramacy chains are modern, well-stocked, safe and very professional. They can be found throughout the city, often in or next to supermarkets. Some offer 24-hr delivery service. *Boticas Fasa*, T475 7070; *Boticas Torres de Limatambo*, T444 3022/214 1998; *Farmacentro Tassara*, T251 0600/442 7301; *Superfarma*, T440 9000. *Pharmax*, Av Salaverry 3100, San Isidro, Centro Comercial El Polo, Monterrico (near the US embassy). Pharmacy/hypermarket, with imported goods (Jewish food products sometimes available at Av Salaverry branch, which is open 24 hrs). *Farmacia Deza*, Av Conquistadores 1140, San Isidro. The same as *Pharmax*, also open 24 hrs.

Useful addresses Tourist Police, Jr Moore 268, Magdalena at the 38th block of Av Brasil, T460 1060/460 0844, open daily 24 hrs. They are friendly and very helpful, English spoken. It is recommended to visit when you have had property stolen. **Immigration:** Av España 700 y Jr Huaraz, Breña, open 0830-1500, but they only allow people to enter until 1300. Procedure for extensions is described on page 1083. Provides new entry stamps if passport is lost or stolen. **Intej**, Av San Martín 240, Barranco, T477 2864. They can extend student cards, change flight itineraries bought with student cards. **National library**, Av Abancay 4th block, with Jr Miró Quesada, T428 7690. Open Mon-Sat 0800-2000, Sun 0830-1330.

Lima

Huaraz and the Cordillera Blanca

From the coastal desert north of Lima a series of roads climb up to Huaraz, in the Callejón de Huaylas, gateway to Parque Nacional Huascarán in the spectacular Cordillera Blanca. This area of jewelled lakes and snowy mountain peaks attracts mountaineers and hikers in their thousands. Here also is one of Peru's most important pre-Inca sites, at Chavín de Huantar.

Lima to Huaraz

Between Lima and Pativilca there is a narrow belt of coastal land deposited at the mouths of the rivers and, from Pativilca to the mouth of the Río Santa, north of Chimbote, the Andes come down to the sea. Between Lima and Pativilca cotton and sugar-cane are grown, though the yield of sugar is less than it is further north where the sunshine is not interrupted by cloud. Much irrigated land grows vegetables and crops to supply Lima and Callao. Between June and October, cattle are driven down from the Highlands to graze the *lomas* on the mountain sides when the mists come.

The Pan-American Highway parallels the coast all the way to the far north, and feeder roads branch from it up the various valleys. Just north of Ancón (see page 1107), the Pasamayo sand dune, stretching for 20 km, comes right down to the seashore. The old road which snakes above the sea is spectacular, but is now closed except to commercial traffic. The toll road (US$0.85), which goes right over the top, is safer, with incredible views over the coast and valleys.

Huaura Valley The Pan-American Highway is four-lane (several tolls, US$0.75) to Km 101, at **Huacho**, 19 km east of **Puerto Huacho** (several hotels). The beaches south of the town are clean and deserted. ■ *Getting there: Bus from Lima 2½ hrs, US$2, or Comité 18, daily colectivos, US$2.50.*

The journey inland from Huacho, up the Huaura valley, is splendid. Beyond Sayán the road follows the Huaura valley which narrows almost to a gorge before climbing steeply to **Churín**, with hot, sulphurous springs which are used to cure a number of ailments, and various hotels and restaurants. The climate is dry, temperatures ranging from 10° to 32°C. The area makes a good excursion from Lima. It is famous for cheese, yoghurt and other natural products. Other hot springs nearby are **Huancahuasi**, **Picoy** (both new) and **Chiuchín** (neglected). ■ *Getting there: Estrella Polar, Espadín and Beteta have several buses a day from Lima, 4-5 hrs, US$5.*

Barranca & Paramonga Phone code: 034

At **Barranca** (Km 195) the beach is long, not too dirty, though windy. There are various hotels (**D-F**) and *Banco de la Nación* accepts travellers' cheques, good rates. A few km before Barranca (158 km from Lima) a turning to the right (east) leads to **Caral**, an ancient city 20 km from the coast in the Supe Valley whose date, about 2,600 BC, and monumental construction are overturning many of the accepted theories of Peruvian archaeology. It appears to be easily the oldest city in South America and to have flourished for 500 years. The evidence points to complex urban society beginning much earlier than previously thought and the city seems to have had a primarily religious, rather than warlike purpose (the only way to get there without your own transport would be to negotiate with a colectivo driver).

Peru

Transport Buses stop opposite the service station (*el grifo*) at the end of town. From **Lima to Barranca**, 3½ hrs, US$3. As bus companies have their offices in Barranca, buses will stop there rather than at Pativilca or Paramonga. Bus from Barranca to **Casma** 155 km, several daily, 3 hrs, US$3. From Barranca to Huaraz, 4 hrs, US$6, daily buses or trucks. The good, paved road to Huaraz turns off the Panamericana just past Pativilca.

Some 4 km beyond the turn-off to Huaraz, beside the Highway, are the well preserved ruins of the Chimú temple of **Paramonga**. Set on high ground with a view of the ocean, the fortress-like mound is reinforced by eight quadrangular walls rising in tiers to the top of the hill. ■ *US$1.20; caretaker may act as guide.*

Transport Buses run only to Paramonga port (3 km off the Highway, 4 km from the ruins, about 15 mins from Barranca). Taxi from Paramonga to the ruins and return after waiting, US$4.50, otherwise take a Barranca-Paramonga port bus, then a 3 km walk.

Casma

Phone code: 044
Colour map 3, grid B2

The town has a pleasant Plaza de Armas, several parks and two markets including a good food market. It is a base from where to explore one of the most important ruins on the Peruvian coast, **Sechín**, 5 km away. It consists of a large square temple completely faced with about 500 carved stone monoliths narrating, it is thought, a gruesome battle in graphic detail. The style is unique in Peru for its naturalistic vigour. The complex as a whole is associated with the pre-Chavín Sechín culture, dating from about 1500 BC. Three sides of the large stone temple have been excavated and restored, but you cannot see the earlier adobe buildings inside the stone walls because they were covered up and used as a base for a second storey, which has been completely destroyed.

■ *The site is open daily 0800-1700, photography best around midday, US$1.50 (children and students half price); ticket also valid for the Max Uhle Museum by the ruins and Pañamarca, an archaeological site in the Nepeña Valley, north of Casma. Getting there: To walk to the ruins from Casma, follow Av Ormeño east, at the circle turn right and follow the Pan-American Highway, walk about 3 km south to a well posted sign showing a left turn for Huaraz (this is at Km 370), then simply follow the road for 2 km to the ruins. Frequent colectivos leave from in front of the market in Casma, US$0.30 pp, or motorcycle taxi US$1.*

Sleeping & eating
Most hotels are on the Panamericana so rooms at the back will be quieter

In Casma **D** *Hostal El Farol*, Tupac Amaru 450, T711064. Cheaper in low season, breakfast extra, hot water, swimming pool, good restaurant, pleasant garden, parking, good local information. **E** *Hostal Ernesto's*, Garcilaso de la Vega y Gamarra, T711351. Modern, hot water, bakery downstairs. **E** *Indoamerica*, Av Huarmey 130, T711395. Cheaper without bath, hot water, good, changes cash. **E** *Gregori*, Luis Ormeño 530, T711073. Cheaper without bath, noisy. **E** *Las Dunas*, Luis Ormeño 505. Hot water, TV, can be noisy, internet café next door. **E** *Rebecca*, Huarmey 377. Modern. Recommended. **F** *Hostal Celene* Ormeño 595, T711065. Basic but with hot water, good rooms. *Sechín*, Nepeña y Mejía, near the plaza. Good set meal and chicken. *Tío Sam*, Huarmey 138. Chinese and *criollo* food. *Venecia*, Huarmey 204. Local dishes, popular. *Cevicherías* on Av Ormeño 600 block and cheap restaurants on Huarmey. The famous local ice-cream, *Caribe*, is sold on Avs Huarmey and Ormeño.

Transport **Buses** From **Lima**, 370 km, 5 hrs, US$5. Only *Transportes Vista Alegre* has buses direct to Lima, at 2300. Cheaper stopping buses pass through half-hourly from Trujillo and Chimbote and usually have a few spare seats. *Transportes Aguila* are the most frequent. Most offices in block 1 of Av Ormeño, opposite the petrol station. To **Chimbote**, 55 km, buses from Lima, if they have space, go to the Terminal Terrestre in Chimbote, or colectivos, when full, go to the centre of Chimbote. Both leave from the petrol station on Av Ormeño, less than 1 hr, US$1.50. To **Trujillo**, take transport to Chimbote terminal and then change to an *América Express* bus. To **Huaraz** (150 km), most buses go via Pativilca, good road, 6-7 hrs, US$6, *Transportes Huandoy* (Etseturh), Ormeño 158, T712336, *Turismo Chimbote* and *Trans Chinchaysuyo*. All run at night. Shorter in km but much tougher is the route via Pariacoto (see below) at 0800 and 210 with *Trans Huaraz* and *Empresa Tamara*, at 0900, 7 hrs, US$4.30. Also *Transportes Yungay Express* (4 a day) and *Trans San Pedro* (twice daily), starting from Chimbote. This difficult but beautiful trip is worth taking in daylight. From Casma the first 30 km are paved, a good dirt road follows for 30 km to **Pariacoto** (basic lodging). From here to the **Callán pass** (4,224 m) the road is rough (landslides in rainy season), but once the Cordillera Negra has been crossed, the wide, gravel road is better with spectacular views of the Cordillera Blanca (150 km in all to Huaraz).

Directory

Bank Good rates for cash and TCs, no commission, at *Banco de Crédito*, Bolívar 181. **Communications** Post office: at Fernando Loparte, ½ block from Plaza de Armas.

Chimbote

Phone code: 044
Colour map 3, grid B2
Population: 35,900

The port of Chimbote serves the national fishing industry and the smell of the fishmeal plants is overpowering. As well as being unpleasant it is also unsafe. Take extensive precautions, always use taxis from the bus station to your hotel and don't venture far from the hotel at night. The modern Municipal building has a small art gallery downstairs. ■ *0900-2000*. **NB** The main street, Av Víctor Raul Haya de la Torre, is also known by its old name, José Pardo. At weekends two-hour boat trips go around the bay to visit the cliffs and islands to see the marine birdlife and rock formations. www.laindustria.com (website of the local newspaper) has a section on Chimbote.

Sleeping & eating

Water shortages can be a problem, check your hotel has a tank before taking a room

AL *Gran Hotel Chimú*, José Gálvez 109, T/F321741. Including breakfast, safe parking. **B** *Ivansino Inn*, Haya de la Torre 738, T331395, F321927. Including breakfast, comfortable, modern. **B** *Presidente*, L Prado 536, T322411, F321988. Hot showers, safe parking (extra), poor snack bar. Recommended. **C** *Hostal Karol Inn*, Manuel Ruiz 277, T/F321216. Hot water, good, family run, laundry service, cafetería. **C-D** *Residencial El Parque*, E Palacios 309, on plaza, T323963. Converted old home, hot water, nice. **D** *Felic*, Haya de la Torre 552, T325901. **E** without bath, quiet. Recommended. **D** *San Felipe*, Haya de la Torre 514, T323401. Hot water, comfortable, restaurant. **E** *Hostal El Ensueño*, Sáenz Peña 268, 2 blocks from Plaza Central, T328662. **F** without bath, very good, safe, welcoming. **E** *Hostal Playa*, Malecón Miguel Grau 185. OK, safe. **F** *San Antonio*, Espinar 549. Simple, noisy, cold water, reasonable *chifa* downstairs. **F** *Sagitario*, José Gálvez 1174, T333676. Simple, good value.

Aquarius, Haya de la Torre 360. Vegetarian. *Chifa Pekín*, Haya de la Torre 600 block, 1 block from Plaza, T346273/323761. Good value, large portions, excellent. *Marisquito*, Bolognesi near Palacios. Good local food, disco at night. *Pizzería Corleone*, Bolognesi 175. All kinds of pizzas and pastas. *Pollo Gordo*, Prado y Aguirre. Good chicken and cold beer. An excellent bakery is *Delca*, at Haya de la Torre 568.

Tour operators

Chimbote Tours, Bolognesi 801, T325341, F324792, helpful and friendly, English spoken.

Transport

Warning: Under no circumstances should you walk to the centre: minibus costs US$0.25, taxi US$1.50. There are no hotels near the terminal; some bus companies have ticket offices in the centre

Taxis: radio taxis from T334433, T327777 and T322005. **Buses** The bus station is 4 km south on Av Meiggs. From **Lima**, to Chimbote, 420 km, 6 hrs, US$7-9, several buses daily, *Trans América Express* has the most frequent service. To **Trujillo**, 130 km, 2 hrs, US$2, buses leave every half hour. To **Tumbes**, 889 km, 13 hrs, US$11, *Continental* at 1630, *Cruz del Sur* at 2200. It is 8-10 hrs to Huaraz via the Santa Valley and spectacular Cañon del Pato (for a description of this route, see page 1138), US$7.15 with *Turismo Huaraz* minibus, office at Av José Pardo 1713, T321235, leaving Terminal Terrestre, stand 42, at 0800, passing the office at 0815, also every evening. Some companies go down the Panamericana to Pativilca, then up the paved highway to Huaraz. These include *Chinchaysuyo, Turismo Chimbote, Trans Huandoy, Yungay Express*, US$6. *Chinchaysuyo* continue to Caraz, US$6 also.

Directory

Banks *Banco de Crédito* and *Interbank*, both on Bolognesi and M Ruiz, for TCs and cash. *Casa Arroyo*, M Ruiz 292, cash only. There are other *casas* and street changers along M Ruiz between Bolognesi and VR Haya de la Torre. **Communications** Post: *Serpost*, Jr Tumbes behind market. **Telephone**: *Telefónica* main office, Tumbes 356, national and international fax and phone; also at Haya de la Torre 420 and M Ruiz 253.

Peru

Cordilleras Blanca, Negra and Callejón de Huaylas

Apart from the range of Andes running along the Chile-Argentina border, the highest mountains in South America lie along the Cordillera Blanca and are perfectly visible from many spots. From Huaraz alone, you can see over 23 snow-crested peaks of over 5,000 m, of which the most notable is Huascarán (6,768 m), the highest mountain in Peru. Although the snowline is receding, the Cordillera Blanca still contains the largest concentration of glaciers found in the world's tropical zone and the turquoise-coloured lakes, which form in the terminal moraines, are the jewels of the Andes.

Probably the easiest way to reach the Callejón de Huaylas is to take the paved road which branches east off the Pan-American Highway north of Pativilca (see page 1126), 203 km from Lima. The road climbs increasingly steeply to the chilly pass at 4,080 m (Km 120). Shortly after, Laguna **Conococha** comes into view, where the Río Santa rises. A dirt road branches off from Conococha to **Chiquián** (see page 1143) and the **Cordilleras Huayhuash** and **Raura** to the southeast. After crossing a high plateau the main road descends gradually for 47 km until **Catac**, where another road branches east to Chavín and on to the **Callejón de Conchucos**. Huaraz is 36 km further on and the road then continues north between the towering Cordillera Negra, snowless and rising to 4,600 m, and the snow-covered Cordillera Blanca. This valley, the Callejón de Huaylas, has many picturesque villages and small towns, with narrow cobblestone streets and odd-angled house roofs. The alternative routes to the Callejón de Huaylas are via the Callán pass from Casma to Huaraz (see page 1127), and from Chimbote to Caraz via the Cañon del Pato (page 1138).

Huaraz

Phone code: 044
Colour map 3, grid B2
Population: 80,000
Altitude: 3,091 m
420 km from Lima

The valley's focus is Huaraz, capital of Ancash department, and a major tourist centre, especially busy on market day (Thursday). It is a prime destination for hikers and a mecca for international climbers. It was almost completely destroyed in the earthquake of May 1970. The Plaza de Armas has been rebuilt, with a towering, white statue of Christ. A new Cathedral is still being built. The setting, at the foot of the Cordillera Blanca, is spectacular. For views of surrounding peaks visit the *Mirador Rataquenua* at the cross (visible from Huaraz) one hour's walk from the town (turn left past the cemetery and head uphill through a small forest). For an amazing view of the whole valley, continue to *Pukaventana*. **NB** Reports of armed hold-ups at the *Mirador*.

Museo Regional de Ancash, Instituto Nacional de Cultura, Plaza de Armas, contains stone monoliths and *huacos* from the Recuay culture, well labelled. ■ *Mon-Fri 0900-1700, Sat 0830-1700, Sun 0830-1400, US$1.45.* **Museo de Miniaturas del Perú**, in *Gran Hotel Huascarán*, Av Centenario block 10, north end of town, houses models of Huaraz and Yungay before the earthquake, plus Barbie dolls in Peruvian dress, strange but interesting. ■ *Mon-Sat, 0800-1300, 1500-2200, US$0.85.*

Excursions **Willkawain** About 8 km to the northeast is the Willkawain archaeological site. The ruins (AD 700 to 1000, Huari Empire) consist of three large two-storey structures with intact stone slab roofs and several small structures. ■ *US$1.50. Getting there: take a combi from 3 de Diciembre and Lúcar y Torre, US$0.55 direct to Willkawain. If walking, go past the Hotel Huascarán. After crossing a small bridge take a second right marked by a blue sign, it is about 2 hrs uphill walk; ask directions as there are many criss-crossing paths used regularly by local people. About 500 m past Willkawain is Ichiwillkawain with several similar but smaller structures. Take a torch if it's late. There is also an alternative road from the ruins to Monterrey.*

North of Huaraz, 6 km along the road to Caraz, are the thermal baths at **Monterrey** (*Altitude: 2,780 m*): the lower pool is US$0.85; the upper pool, which is nicer (closed Monday for cleaning), US$1.35; also individual and family tubs US$1.35 per person for 20 minutes; crowded at weekends and holidays. There are restaurants and hotels (**B-C**). ■ *Getting there: City buses along Av Luzuriaga go as far as Monterrey (US$0.22), until 1900; taxi US$2-3.*

Sleeping
Hotels fill up rapidly during high season (May-Sep), especially during public holidays and special events when prices rise (beware overcharging). Unless otherwise stated, all hotels listed are recommended

AL *Hostal Andino*, Pedro Cochachín 357, some way southeast from the centre (take a taxi after dark), T/F722830, andino@wayna.rcp.net.pe The best in town, expensive restaurant, safe parking, free internet for guests, Swiss run, 2nd floor rooms with balconies and views of Huascarán are more expensive, climbing and hiking gear for hire. **B** *Hostal Montañero*, Plaza Ginebra 30-B (ask at Casa de Guías), T/F722306. Hot water, modern, comfortable, good value, climbing equipment rental and sales. **B** *San Sebastián*, Jr Italia 1124, T726960, andeway@net.telematic.com.pe 2-star, very helpful, breakfast included, good views. **C** *Hostal Colomba*, Francisco de Zela 278, on Centenario across the river, T721501/727106, colomba@terra.com.pe Lovely old hacienda, bungalow, garden, safe car parking. **C** *Edward's Inn*, Bolognesi 121, T/F722692. Cheaper without bath, hot water, laundry, food available, popular, Edward speaks English and knows a lot about trekking and rents gear (not all guides share Edward's experience). **C** *El Tumi I*, San Martín 1121, T/F721784, in Lima T/F346 2725, hottumi@terra.com.pe Good restaurant (serves huge steaks), fairly good, advance reservations advised (**D** *El Tumi II*, San Martín 1089, T721784). **C** *Hostal Los Portales*, Raymondi 903, T/F728184. Hot water, parking, pleasant. **D** *Casablanca*, Tarapacá 138, near market, T722602, cashotel@telematic.edu.pe Pleasant, modern. **D** *Residencial Cataluña*, Av Raymondi 622, T722761. Hot water, TV, **E** for more basic rooms, restaurant open only in the high season, safe, noisy. **D** *Hostal Yanett*, Av Centenario 164, at the north end of town across the river, T727150. Hot water, large rooms, restaurant for breakfast. **D** *Schatzi*, Bolívar 419, near Raimondi, T723074. Nice courtyard, hot water, breakfast extra.

E *Hostal Chong Roca*, J de Morales 687, T721154. Hot water 24 hrs, huge rooms. **E** *Hostal Copa*, Jr Bolívar 615, T722071, F722619. Cheaper without bath, hot water, laundry facilities, owner's son Walter Melgarejo is a well-known guide, popular with trekkers, restaurant, travel agency with local tours. **E** *Hostal NG*, Pasaje Valenzuela 837, T721831. Family-run hostal set around a pleasant, small courtyard, hot water, breakfast included. **E** *Hostal Santa Anita*, Pasaje Valenzuela 933, T724500. Another small, family-run hostal with hot water, breakfast available. **E-F** *Casa Jansy's*, Jr Sucre 948. Hot water, meals, laundry, owner Jesús Rivera Lúcar is a mountain guide. Recommended. **E** *Hostal Estoico*, San Martín 635, T722371. Cheaper without bath, safe, hot water, laundry facilities, good value. **E** *Alojamiento El Rey*, Pasaje Olivera 919 near Plaza Belén, T721917. **G** pp with shared bath, basic, cooking and laundry facilities, family run, charming people, meals available. **E** *Hostal Gyula*, Parque Ginebra 632, opposite the Casa de Guías, T721567, hotelperu@ infoweb.com.pe Hot water, helpful but noisy at weekends, has good information on local tours, stores luggage. **E** *Hostal Galaxia*, Jr de la Cruz Romero 638, T722230. Cheaper without bath, hot water, laundry facilities, basic. **E** *Jo's Place*, Jr Daniel Villaizan 276, T725505. Safe, nice mountain views, garden, terrace, free tea and coffee, warm atmosphere. **E** *Oscar's Hostal*, La Mar 624, T/F722720, marciocoronel@hotmail.com Hot water, cheap breakfast next door, good beds, cheaper in low season, helpful. **E** *Hostal Quintana*, Mcal Cáceres 411, T726060. Cheaper without bath, hot shower, laundry facilities, basic, stores luggage, popular with trekkers. **E** *Hostal Tany*, Lúcar y Torre 468A, T722534. Cheaper without bath, hot water at night, spotless, money exchange, tours, café/restaurant.

F *Lodging Caroline*, Urb Avitentel Mz D-Lt 1, T722588, 20 min walk from centre. Free pick-up from anywhere in town, laundry, use of kitchen, warm family hospitality. **F** *Lodging Casa Sucre*, Sucre 1240, T722264, F721111. Private house, kitchen, laundry facilities, hot water, English and French spoken, mountaineering guide, Filiberto Rurush, can be contacated here. **F** *Hostal Continental*, 28 de Julio 586 near Plaza de Armas, T724171. Hot water, cafeteria serving breakfast. Recommended but avoid the rooms overlooking the street as there are 2 noisy *peñas* nearby. **F** *Alojamiento El Farolito*, Av Tarapacá 1466, T725792. Hot water, laundry service, good cafeteria. **F** *Hostal López*, Prolongación Alberto Gridilla s/n, Huarapampa, behind *Edward's Inn*, ask near the Estadio just off Av Bolognesi at the Santa river end. Lukewarm showers, washing facilities for clothes, beautiful garden and

Peru

Huaraz

Peru

*Related map
A Huaraz Centre,
page 1132*

Sleeping	
1	Albergue Churup *C3*
2	Alojamiento El Jacal *C3*
3	Alojamiento Soledad *C3*
4	Casa de Jaimes *C1*
5	Casa Jansy's *C2*
6	Casablanca *B1*
7	El Tumi I *D1*
8	El Tumi II *D1*
9	Hostal Andino *D3*

10	Hostal Colomba *A2*
11	Hostal Continental *C1*
12	Hostal Estoico *C1*
13	Hostal Galaxia *C1*
14	Hostal Los Portales *B2*
15	Hostal Mi Casa *C1*
16	Hostal Quintana *C1*
17	Hostal Rinconcito Huaracino *A2*
18	Hostal Yanett *A2*
19	Hostales NG & Santa Anita *D2*
20	La Cabaña *C3*
21	Lodging Casa Sucre *C3*
22	Residencial Cataluña *B1*
23	San Sebastián *B3*

Eating	
1	Aquelarre *D1*
2	Café Andino *C1*
3	Café Central *C1*
4	Fuente de Salud *B1*
5	Huaraz Querido *D2*
6	La Estación *D2*
7	Las Kenas *D1*
8	Las Puyas *B1*
9	Limón, Leña y Carbón *D1*
10	Pachamama *C1*
11	Pepe's Place *B1*
12	Pizza Bruno *D1*
13	Siam de Los Andes *C2*

Transport	
1	Chavín Express *C1*
2	Combis to Caraz *A1, A2*
3	Combis to Wilcawain *A2*
4	El Rápido *C1*
5	Los Andes y Turismo Huaraz *A2*
6	Terminal Terrestre Transportistas Zona Sur *C1*
7	Trans Rodríguez *C1*
8	Trans Sandoval *C1*
9	Virgen de Guadalupe *B2*
10	Yungay Express *A2*

restaurant, good views, luggage stored. **F** pp *Hostal Mi Casa*, Tarapacá 773 (Av 27 de Noviembre), T723375, www.eskimo.com/~pc22/BB/casa-ames.html, Includes breakfast, cheaper in low season, hot water, English spoken, very pleasant, owner Sr Ames is an expert on glaciers, his son is a climbing and rafting guide. **F** *Hostal Rinconcito Huaracino*, Fitzcarrald 226, T727591. Cheaper without bath, hot water, modern. **F-G** *Angeles Inn*, Av Gamarra 815, T722205, solandperu@yahoo.com No sign, look for *Sol Andino* travel agency in same building (www.solandino.com) New, kitchen and laundry facilities, small garden, hot water, owners Max and Saul Angeles are official guides, helpful with trekking and climbing, rent equipment. **F-G** *Alojamiento Marilla*, Sucre 1123, T728160/691956, alojamaril@latinmail.com Good views, modern, rooms with and without bath, also dormitory accommodation, hot water, laundry and breakfast available, kitchen facilities, luggage store, knowledgeable owners.

 G pp *La Cabaña*, Jr Sucre 1224, T723428. Shared and double rooms, hot showers, laundry, kitchen, computer, safe for parking, bikes and luggage. **F** pp *Albergue Churup*, Jr Amadeo Figueroa 1257, T722584, ring bell and wait for them to come from Jr Pedro Campos 735, churup@htmail.com Shared and double rooms, **F** without bath, hot water, breakfast, luggage store, trekking information, laundry, book exchange, use of kitchen at Pedro Campos 735, nice garden and fire in sitting room, internet access planned, English spoken, very heplful, motorcycle parking. **G** pp *Lodging House Ezama*, Mariano Melgar 623, Independencia, T723490, 15 mins' walk from Plaza de Armas (US$0.50 by taxi). Light, spacious rooms, hot water, safe, helpful. **G** pp *Casa de Familia Gómez Díaz*, Jr Eulogio del Río 1983, T723224. Hot water, quiet, family atmosphere, good beds. **G** pp *Alojamiento El Jacal*, Jr Sucre 1044, blue house with no sign. Cheaper without shower, hot water, very nice family. **G** pp *Hostal Imperio*, La Mar 520, T728539. Hot water, nice owners, great view from roof. **G** pp *Casa de Jaimes*, Alberto Gridilla 267, T722281, 2 blocks from the main plaza. Clean dormitory with hot showers, washing facilities, has maps and books of the region, use of kitchen, popular with Israelis. **G** *Alojamiento La Stancia*, Jr Huaylas 162, Centenario, T723183. With bath or shared shower, luggage store, safe motorcycle parking, good value. **G** *Casa de Familia Nelly Quito*, Bolognesi 507, T724021, ½ block from Av Tarapacá. Nice, family-run, hot water. **G** pp *Alojamiento Nemys*, Jr Figueroa 1135, T722949. Secure, hot shower, breakfast US$2.40, good for climbers, luggage store. **G** *Hostal Piscis*, Av Tarapacá 1452, T722362. Hot water, Family run, quiet, laundry service, can organize hiking and equipment hire. **G** pp *Alojamiento Soledad*, Jr Amadeo Figueroa 1267, T721196 (in Lima 242 8615), ajsoled@terra.com.pe Breakfast extra, laundry service, intermittent hot water, kitchen, family-run, cafeteria, secure.

 Youth Hostels **F** pp *Alojamiento Alpes Andes*, at Casa de Guías, Plaza Ginebra 28-g, T721811, F722306. Member of the Peruvian Youth Hostel Association, 1 dormitory with 14 beds and another with 6 beds, hot water, with very good restaurant (open 0700-1100, 1700-2300), laundry, free luggage store, the owner Sr López speaks English, French and German and is very helpful, he is the mountain guides administrator.

There are usually people waiting at the bus terminals offering cheap accommodation in their homes

Expensive: *Pizza Bruno*, Luzuriaga 834. "By far the best pizza", excellent crepes and pastries, good service, open from 1600-2300, French owner Bruno Reviron also has a 4WD with driver for hire. *Huaraz Querido*, Bolívar 981. Excellent cevichería. *Monte Rosa*, J de la Mar 661. Pizzería, also fondue and other Swiss specialities, open 1830-2300, Swiss owner is Victorinox representative, offering knives for sale and repair service, also has climbing and trekking books to read, excellent postcards for sale. *Créperie Patrick*, Luzuriaga 422 y Raymondi. Excellent crepes, fish, quiche, spaghetti and good wine. *Euskalerria*, Luzuriaga 406. Basque cuisine, good food and service, trekking information. *Siam de Los Andes*, Gamarra corner J de Morales. Authentic Thai cuisine, good food and atmosphere.

Eating

 Mid-range: *Alpes Andes*, Plaza Ginebra in Casa de Guías. Muesli, yoghurt etc in the morning, pastas and pizzas in the evening. *Bistro de los Andes*, J de Morales 823, T/F726249. Great food, owner speaks English, French and German. *La Familia* at Luzuriaga 431. Popular with gringos, vegetarian dishes, good for regional food such as cuy. *Fuente de Salud*, J de la Mar 562. Vegetarian, also meat and pasta dishes, good soups, breakfast. *Limón, Leña y Carbón*, Av Luzuriaga 1002. Typical dishes in the day, local grills at night, also seafood and fish dishes, bar, excellent food and value. *Pepe's Place*, Raymondi 624, good pizza, chicken, meat, warm atmosphere, run by Pepe from *Residencial Cataluña*. *Pizza B & B*, La Mar beside laundry of same name. Recommended for its traditional sauces for pizza. *Pizzería Landauro*, Sucre, on corner of Plaza de Armas. Very good for pizzas, Italian dishes, sandwiches, breakfasts, nice atmosphere, closed 1200-1800 and Sun. *Querubín's*, J de Morales 767. Good breakfast and set meals, also vegetarian, snacks and à la carte. *Rinconcito Minero*, J de Morales 757. Swiss-run, breakfast, lunch, vegetarian options, coffee and snacks. *Sabor Salud*, Luzuriaga 672, upstairs. Restaurant and pizzería specializing in vegetarian and Italian food.

Cheap: *La Estación*, 2 locations on Plazuela Belén. Video pub which serves a good lunch for only US$1, also good steaks, nice atmosphere. *Las Puyas*, Morales 535. Popular with gringos, *sopa criolla* and trout, also serves breakfast. *Piccolo*, J de Morales 632. Pizzería, very popular with gringos. *Pico de Oro*, San Martín 595. Good value Peruvian food. *Chifa Jim Hua*, Luzuriaga 645, upstairs, large, tasty portions, *menú* US$1.15, open Mon-Sat 0900-1500, 1800-2400, Sun 1800-2200. *Vegetarian Food*, Sucre y Av Bolívar. Excellent vegetarian, 3-course meal US$1.

Recreos specialize in typical local dishes, open only at weekends

Cafés *Café Andino*, 28 de Julio 562 at Luzuriaga, off Plaza de Armas. American-run café and bar, book exchange, library, a nice place to relax, great atmosphere, good meeting place, owner guides treks in Cordillera Huayhuash. *Café Central*, 28 de Julio 592. Good breakfast for US$1.30, great chocolate cake and apple pie. *Comedor 14*, San Martín 525. Good value breakfasts, sandwiches, teas, etc, honest.

Entertainment

Bars *The Bar and More*, J de Morales 747, modern interior, terrace, not cheap but worth it, popular. *Pachamama*, San Martín 687, T724200. Bar, café and restaurant, music, art gallery, garden, good toilets, nice place to relax, good information on treks, Swiss-owned. *Las Kenas*, Jr Gabino Uribe near Luzuriaga. Live Andean music, happy hour 2000-2200, good pisco sours. Next door, upstairs, is *Aquelarre*, popular with *gringos*, soft music, nice atmosphere, open 1900-0200. **Discos and peñas** *Imantata*, Luzuriaga 424, disco and folk music. *La Cueva del Oso*, Luzuriaga 674, taverna-style, good peña. *Taberna Tambo*, José de la Mar 776, folk music daily, disco, open 1000-1600, 2000-0200, knock on door to get in. *Monttrek Disco*, Sucre just off Plaza de Armas, in converted cinema, reasonable prices.

Local festivals Patron saints' day, *El Señor de la Soledad*, week starting **3 May**. *Semana del Andinismo*, in **Jun**, international climbing and skiing week. *San Juan* and *San Pedro* throughout the region during the last week of **Jun**.

Huaraz centre

Sleeping
1 Hostal Chong Roca
2 Hostal Copa
3 Hostal Gyula
4 Hostal Montañero
5 Hostal Tany
6 Oscar's Hostal
7 Schatzi

Eating
1 Chifa Jim Hua
2 Créperie Patrick
3 Imantata
4 La Familia
5 Monte Rosa
6 Monttrek Disco
7 Piccolo
8 Pizza B & B
9 Pizzería Landauro
10 Rinconcito Minero, The Bar and More, Querubin's
11 Sabor Salud
12 Taberna Tambo

Transport
1 Chinchaysuyo
2 Civa Cial
3 Cruz del Sur
4 Empresa 14
5 Expreso Ancash
6 Línea
7 Móvil Tours
8 Renzo

0 metres 20
0 yards 20

Peru

For local sweaters, hats, gloves and wall hangings at good value, Pasaje Mcal Cáceres, off **Shopping**
Luzuriaga, in the stalls off Luzuriaga between Morales and Sucre, Bolívar cuadra 6, and elsewhere. *Andean Expressions*, Jr J Arguedas 1246, near La Soledad church, T722951, olaza@
qnet.com.pe Open 0800-2200, run by Lucho, Mauro and Beto Olaza, recommended for
hand-printed clothing and gifts. Two well-stocked supermarkets are *Ortíz*, Luzuriaga 401
corner Raymondi (good selection) and *Militos*, Sucre 775. The central market offers a wide
variety of canned and dry goods, as well as fresh fruit and vegetables.

Climbing and trekking: the Cordillera Blanca is the main climbing and hiking centre of **Sport**
Peru. See below. **Mountain biking**: contact Julio Olaza at *Chakinani Perú*, Lúcar y Torre
538, T724259, www.chakinaniperu.com Also rents good quality bikes, highly recom-
mended, Julio speaks excellent English, US$20 for 5 hrs, various routes. Also rents rooms,
F pp. **River rafting and canoeing**: contact Carlos Ames, *River Runners*, via *Monttrek*, Av
Luzuriaga 646, see Tour operators below.

All agencies run conventional tours to Llanganuco, Pastoruri (both US$7.20 pp) and Chavín **Tour operators**
(US$8.65 pp), entry tickets not included. Many hire equipment (see Trekking and climbing in
the Cordillera Blanca) and also offer rafting on Río Santa (US$15 for half a day), climbing and
trekking tours and ski instruction. Most agencies provide transport, food, mules and guides.
NB Agencies shouldn't recommend Pastoruri as a first trip. It's best to go to Llanganuco first
to acclimatize. The following are recommended: *Andean Kingdom*, Luzuriaga 522. Most
helpful, free videos, English and some Hebrew spoken, information on treks, equipment
rental, climbing courses and other excursions organized. *Anden Sport Tours*, Luzuriaga 571,
T721612. Have a basic practice wall behind the office. They also organize mountain bike
tours, ski instruction and river rafting. *Baloo Tours*, Bolívar 471, T723928. Organizes tours
and rents gear. *Explorandes*, Av Centenario 489, T721960, F722850,
postmast@exploran.com.pe *Chavín Tours*, Luzuriaga 502, T721578, F724801 (Willy
Gordillo can also be found at *Hostal Casablanca*, address above, T722602). *Cordillera Blanca
Adventures*, owned and run by the Mejía Romero family, T724352. Experienced for trekking
and climbing, good guides and equipment. *Hirishanka Sport*, Sucre 802, T722562.
Climbing, trekking, horse riding, 4WD hire, they also rent rooms, **E** pp, with bath, hot water,
breakfast. *Kallpa*, Luzuriaga 479, T727868, kallpaperu@terra.com.pe Organizes treks, rents
gear, arranges *arrieros* and mules, very helpful. *Monttrek*, Luzuriaga 646, upstairs, T721124,
F726976. Trekking and climbing information, advice and maps, run ice and rock climbing
courses (at Monterrey), tours to Lago Churup and the 'spectacular' *Luna Llena* tour; they also
hire out mountain bikes, run ski instruction and trips, and river rafting. Next door in the
Pizzería is a climbing wall, maps, videos and slide shows. For new routes and maps contact
Porfirio Cacha Macedo, 'Pocho', at *Monttrek* or at Jr Corongo 307, T723930. *Pablo Tours*,
Luzuriaga 501, T721142/721145. For all local tours.

Taxi: standard fare in town is about US$0.90; radio taxis T721482 or 722512. **Transport**
　　Buses to/from Lima: 7 hrs, US$5.75-10. There is a large selection of ordinary service and
luxury coaches throughout the day. Many of the companies have their offices along Av
Raymondi and on Jr Lúcar y Torre. Some recommended companies are: *Cruz del Sur*, Lúcar y
Torre cuadra 4, T723532; *Transportes Rodríguez*, Tarapacá 622, T721353; *Expreso Ancash*
(Ormeño), Raymondi 845; *Civa Cial*, Morales opposite Lúcar y Torre; *Móvil Tours*, Bolívar
468, T722555; *Empresa 14*, Fitzcarrald 216, T721282, terminal at Bolívar 407.
　　Other long distance buses To **Casma** via the Callán pass (150 km) 6-7 hrs, US$4.30 (sit
on the left for best views): *Turismo Huaraz*, 13 de Diciembre y Lúcar y Torre, 0800, 2100, and
Empresa Tamara, 0900. *Chinchaysuyo* (Lúcar y Torre 487, T726417), *Turismo Chimbote*
and *Transportes Huandoy* (Fitzcarrald 261, T7272507 – terminal at Caraz 838), have night
buses to Casma via Pativilca, US$6. *Yungay Express*, same office and terminal as *Huandoy*, 4
a day, and *Trans San Pedro*, go to **Chimbote**, 185 km, via Casma. *Turismo Huaraz*, 13 de
Diciembre y Lúcar y Torre, twice daily (reduced to Sun, Tue and Thu at certain times),
T727362 to confirm, US$7.15, 10 hrs via Caraz and the Cañon del Pato (sit on the right for the
most exciting views) to Trujillo. Other companies go to **Chimbote** via Pativilca; US$7.20, 6

Peru

hrs (to **Pativilca**, 160 km, 4 hrs, US$3.50). Most continue to **Trujillo**, all buses go at night, 8-9 hrs, US$8.50: *Línea* (Raymondi y Ranrapalca, T726666), *Empresa 14* and, *Móvil Tours*, addresses above.

Within the Cordillera Blanca area Several buses and frequent minivans run daily, 0500-2000, between Huaraz and **Caraz**, 1½ hrs, US$1, from the parking area under the bridge on Fitzcarrald and from the open space beside the bridge on the other side of the river (beware of thieves here). To **Chavín**, 110 km, 4 hrs (sit on left side for best views), US$3: *Chavín Express*, Mcal Cáceres 338, T724652, daily at 0730, 0830, 1100 and 1400, Sun 1500; *Trans Sandóval*, 27 de Noviembre 582, T726930, 0800 and 1300; *Trans Río Mosne*, Cáceres 275, T726632, 0700 and 1300. All 3 companies have buses that go on to Huari, 6 hrs, US$5. To **Chacas** (US$4.35) and **San Luis** (US$5.75), at 0700 with *Virgen de Guadalupe*, Caraz 607, also to Yanama, US$5.75, Piscobamba, US$7.20, Pomabamba, US$7.20 at 0600, and La Unión, US$4.35 at 0700. *Renzo*, Raymondi 821, T724915, also runs to Chacas and San Luis (1300 Mon-Sat, 1500 Sun), Yanama, Piscobamba and Pomabamba (0630). *Los Andes*, 13 de Diciembre y Lúcar y Torre, goes daily at 0700 to Yungay, US$0.75, Lagunas de Llanganuco, US$3.45, Yanama, US$3.45, Piscobamba, US$5.20 and Pomabamba, US$5.75 (8 hrs). Colectivos to **Recuay**, US$0.45, and **Catac**, US$0.55, leave daily at 0500-2100, from Gridilla, just off Tarapacá (Terminal de Transportistas Zona Sur). To **Chiquián** for the Cordillera Huayhuash (see below). To **Huallanca** (Huánuco), via Pachacoto (see below), US$3.50. A fantastic journey which offers the option of travelling south, through the Sierra towards Cusco avoiding Lima. The route follows the Pastoruri valley passing through the Puyo Raimondi forest then climbs up above the glacier to 5,000 m. There are even more spectacular views of several other snow-capped massifs, including the Cordillera Huayhuash in the distance. In winter this route may be blocked by snow. The road then descends to the Vizcarra valley and between Huallanca and La Unión follows the river in the beautiful Vizcarra gorge. *Trans El Rápido*, Mcal Cáceres 312, T726437 (next to *Chavín Express*), 4½ hrs US$3.50, at 0630 and 1300; *Yungay Express* also at 1300. Some buses continue to La Unión, 5½ hrs, US$4.50. There are regular colectivos from Huallanca to La Unión from the corner of Comercio y 28 de Julio, 1 hr, US$0.75.

Directory **Banks** *Banco de Crédito*, on Plaza de Armas, closed 1300-1630, changes cash, 3.25% commission on TCs into soles, good rates, into cash dollars 5% commission, cash advance on Visa, Visa ATM. *Interbank*, on Plaza de Armas, np commission on TCs into soles, ATM. *Banco Wiese*, Sucre 766, changes cash and TCs. **Casa de Cambio** *Oh Na Nay*, opposite *Interbank*, cash only, good rates. Street changers and *casas de cambio* on Luzuriaga (be careful). **Communications** Internet: *Avance SRL*, Luzuriaga 672. 0700-2300 daily, US$3 per hr, US$1.75 per email message, US$1.75 to read or write a diskette, good equipment but expensive. There are several places with internet access in the centre, eg: one next to *Casa de Guías*, another opposite at Plaza Ginebra 630; *Portalnet*, Luzuriaga 999; *The H@ckers*, Luzuriaga y Pasaje Coral Vega; *Net Computer*, Av Fitzcarrald 320, interior, T728088, cgmacedo@latinmail.com, telephone office downstairs; *Fantasynet*, Caraz 601, of 102, fatasynet@lanet.com.pe Average price US$0.75 per hr. **Post office:** *Serpost*, Luzuriaga opposite Plaza de Armas, open 0800-2000 daily. **Telephone:** *Telefónica*, Sucre y Bolívar, Plaza de Armas, national and international phone and fax, open 0700-2300 daily. Many calling centres on Luzuriaga. **Tourist office** Basic tourist information is available from the *Policía de Turismo*, Jr Larrea y Loredo 716, T721341, ext 315. Mon-Fri 0900-1300, 1600-1900, Sat 0900-1300.

Parque Nacional Huascarán Established in July 1975, the park includes the entire Cordillera Blanca above 4,000 m, with a total area of 3,400 sq km. It is a UNESCO World Biosphere Reserve and part of the World Heritage Trust. The park's objectives are to protect the unique flora, fauna, geology, archaeological sites and extraordinary scenic beauty of the Cordillera. Please help by taking all your rubbish away with you when camping. The park administration charges visitors US$1.45 for a day visit. For visits of up to seven days (ie for trekking and climbing trips) a permit costing US$18 (65 soles) must be bought. If you stay longer than seven days, you will need another permit. The park office is in the Ministry of Agriculture, at the east end of Av Raymondi in Huaraz, open morning only, T722086; limited general information but useful for those planning specific research activities.

Trekking and climbing in the Cordillera Blanca

The Cordillera Blanca offers the most popular backpacking and trekking in Peru, with a network of trails used by the local people and some less well-defined mountaineers' routes. Most circuits can be hiked in five days. Although the trails are easily followed, they are rugged with very high passes, between 4,000 and nearly 5,000 m, so backpackers wishing to go it alone should be fit and acclimatized to the altitude, and carry all necessary equipment. Essential items are a tent, warm sleeping bag, stove, and protection against wind and rain (the weather is unreliable here and you cannot rule out rain and hail storms even in the dry season). Trekking demands less stamina since equipment can be carried by donkeys. For further reading on this region, including details of maps, see page 1295.

The season is from May to Sep, although conditions vary from year to year. The rainy season in Huaraz is Dec-Mar

Advice to climbers

The height of the Cordillera Blanca and the Callejón de Huaylas ranges and their location in the tropics create conditions different from the Alps or even the Himalayas. Fierce sun makes the mountain snow porous and glaciers move more rapidly. The British Embassy advises climbers to take at least six days for acclimatization, to move in groups of four or more, reporting to the Casa de Guías (see below) or the office of the guide before departing, giving the date at which a search should begin, and leaving your embassy's telephone number, with money for the call. In 1999 the **Policía Nacional de Perú** established *Unidad de Salvamento de Alta Montaña*, a 35-member rescue team (two of whom are women) in Yungay, with 24-hour phone service and vhf/uhf radio dispatch. They have two helicopters and trained search-and-rescue dogs. As of 2001 they will respond and effect rescues, "no questions asked" for anyone, at anytime, but will try to resolve costs, on a sliding scale basis, with the "rescued". T044-793327/333/327/291, F793292, usam@pnp.gob.pe

Be well prepared before setting out on a climb. Wait or cancel your trip when the weather is bad. Every year climbers are killed through failing to take weather conditions seriously. Climb only when and where you have sufficient experience.

NB A few hikers have been robbed; do not camp near a town or village or leave a campsite unattended; always hike with others when heading into remote districts.

On all treks in this area, respect the locals' property, leave no rubbish behind, do not give sweets or money to children who beg and remember your cooking utensils and tent would be very expensive for a *campesino*, so be sensitive and responsible.

Casa de Guías, Plaza Ginebra 28-g in Huaraz, T721811, F722306, agmp@ net.telematic.com.pe This is the climbers' and hikers' meeting place. It is useful with information, books, maps, arrangements for guides, *arrieros*, mules, etc. There is a notice board, postcards and posters for sale and language school. They provide rescue facilities (may be very expensive) and you can register here free of charge before heading out on your climb or trek. Be sure to advise of your return or any delay. ■ *Mon-Sat 0900-1300, 1600-1800, Sun 0900-1300.*

Guides
The Casa de Guías has a full list of all members of the Asociación de Guías de Montaña del Perú (AGMP) throughout the country.

Not necessarily members of AGMP

Recommended mountain guides: *Hugo Sifuentes Maguiña* and his brother *César* (speaks English and a little French), at *Trekperu*, Av Centenario 687, T728190/682616, trekperuhuaraz@terra.com.pe, or in the *Casa de Guías*. *Augusto Ortega*, Jr San Martín 1004, T724888, is the only Peruvian to have climbed Everest. *Filiberto Rurush Paucar*, Sucre 1240, T722264, speaks English, Spanish and Quechua.

Recommended trekking guides: *Tjen Verheye*, Jr Carlos Valenzuela 911, T722569, is Belgian and speaks Dutch, French, German, and reasonable English, runs trekking and conventional tours and is knowledgeable about the Chavín culture. *Irma Angeles*, T722205, speaks some English, knows the Huayhuash well. *Genaro Yanac Olivera*, T722825, speaks good English and some German, also a climbing guide. *Vladimiro Hinostrosa*, T692395, is a trekking guide with knowledge of the entire region. See also under Tour operators in Huaraz for organized trips.

Several of the agencies and **Casa de Guías** run **rock climbing** courses at Monterrey (behind *Hotel Baños Termales Monterrey*) and Huanchac (30 mins' walk from Huaraz). US$7.50-10 pp per day, including guide and transport.

Peru

Prices: The **Dirección de Turismo** issues qualified guides and *arrieros* (muleteers) with a photo ID. Always check for this when making arrangements; note down the name and card number in case you should have any complaints. Prices for specific services are set so enquire before hiring someone. Prices: *arriero*, US$10 per day; donkey or mule, US$5 per day; trekking guides US$30-50 per day; climbing guides US$60-90 per day, depending on the difficulty of the peak. In the low season guides' prices are about 20-30% less. You are required to provide or pay for food for all porters and guides.

Camping gear The following agencies are recommended for hiring gear: *Anden Sport Tours; Monttrek; Kallpa*. See under Tour operators in Huaraz for their addresses. *Casa de Guías* rents equipment and sells dried food. Also *Lobo*, Luzuriaga 557, T724646. On the 2nd floor of the *Hotel Residencial Cataluña*, Av Raymondi 622, T722761, *José Valle Espinosa*, 'Pepe', hires out equipment, organizes treks and pack animals, sells dried food, and is generally helpful and informative.

Check all camping and climbing equipment very carefully before taking it. Gear is usually of poor quality and mostly second hand, left behind by others. Also note that some items may not be available, so it's best to bring your own. All prices are standard, but not cheap, throughout town. All require payment in advance, passport or air ticket as deposit and will only give 50% of your money back if you return gear early. Several shops of the trekking agencies sell camping gaz cartridges. White gas is available from *ferreterías* on Raymondi below Luzuriaga and by Parque Ginebra. Campers have complained that campsites are dirty, toilet pits foul and guides and locals do not take their rubbish away with them

A Circuit of the Callejón de Huaylas

Huaraz to Chavín South of Huaraz is **Olleros** (*Altitude*: 3,450 m). The spectacular and relatively easy three-day hike to Chavín, along a precolumbian trail, starts from Olleros. Some basic meals and food supplies available. **C** *Altas Montañas*, at edge of village, T722569, altasmont@yahoo.es Small 3-star lodge, Belgian-run, with hot showers, good breakfast included, dinner available, bar, birdwatching, guided treks, information, laundry, recommended for start or end of trek, phone 24 hours in advance, preferably at 2000, to arrange free pick-up from Huaraz. ■ *You can get off at the main road and walk the 2 km to Olleros, or catch a truck or minibus from Tarapacá y Jr Cáceres to the village, 29 km, US$0.40.*

At 38 km via the main road from Huaraz is **Catac** (two basic hotels and a restaurant), where a road branches east for Chavín (first 10 km paved, then 20 km good gravel, then 40 km fair gravel). 7 km south of Catac on the main road is **Pachacoto** from where a road goes to **Huallanca** on the other side of the Cordillera Blanca (133 km, 4½ hrs).

A good place to see the impressive Puya Raimondi plants is the Pumapampa valley. 14 km gravel road from Pachacoto to park entrance (4,200 m), then 2 km to plants. Daily tours from Huaraz run to the **Pastoruri** valley, which is now a reserve with basic tourist facilities, to see the Puya Raimondi plants, lakes and the Pastoruri glacier, a steep one-hour walk up from the car park, US$7 per person, 0900-1800. Take extra clothing. You can hike up the trail from Pachacoto to the park entrance – 2½ hours – where there is a park office. You can spend the night here. Walking up the road from this point, you will see the gigantic plants, whose flower spike, which can reach 12 m in height, takes 100 years to develop. The final flowering (usually in May) is a spectacular sight. Another good spot, and less visited, is the **Queshque Gorge**. Follow the Río Queshque from Catac (see above); it's easy to find.

From Catac to Chavín is a magnificent journey, if frightening at times. The road passes Lago Querococha, has good views of the Yanamarey peaks and, at the top of the route, is cut through a huge rock face, entering the Cauish tunnel at 4,550 m. On the other side it descends the Tambillo valley, then the Río Mosna gorge before Chavín.

Chavín de Huantar, a fortress temple, was built about 800 BC. It is the only large **Chavín de** structure remaining of the Chavín culture which, in its heyday, is thought to have **Huantar** held influence in a region between Cajamarca and Chiclayo in the north to Ayacucho and Ica in the south. In December 1985, UNESCO designated Chavín a World Heritage Trust Site. The site is in good condition despite the effects of time and nature. The main attractions are the marvellous carved stone heads and designs in relief of symbolic figures and the many tunnels and culverts which form an extensive labyrinth throughout the interior of the structures. The carvings are in excellent condition, though many of the best sculptures are in Huaraz and Lima. The famous Lanzón dagger-shaped stone monolith of 800 BC is found inside one of the temple tunnels. In order to protect the site some areas are closed to visitors. All the galleries open to the public have electric lights. The guard is also a guide and gives excellent explanations of the ruins. There is a small museum at the entrance, with carvings and some Chavín pottery. ■ *Daily 0800-1700 (check if open Sun), US$3, students US$1.50. Camping is possible with permission from the guard. Go early to avoid the crowds between 1200-1700.*

The town of Chavín, just north of the ruins has a pleasant plaza with palm and pine *Colour map 3, grid B2* trees. There is nowhere to change money in town. Local *fiesta* July 13-20. Post office *Altitude: 3,140 m* and telephone, 17 de Enero 365N; open 0630-2200. Internet at *Restaurante Chavín Turístico*. There are hot sulphur baths (Baños Termales de Chavín) about 2 km south of Chavín at Km 68 in the village of Quercos. Camping is possible here. ■ *US$0.30; tip the boy who cleans the bath for you (he doesn't get paid).*

Sleeping and eating E *La Casona*, Wiracocha 130, Plaza de Armas, T754020. In a renovated *Day tours from* house with attractive courtyard, **F** without bath, warm water, no double beds, motorcycle *Huaraz last an* parking. Recommended. **E** *Hotel Chavín*, Tello y Inca Roca, T754009, F754055. Modern, hot *exhausting 10-12 hrs,* water, all rooms with bath and TV. Recommended. **E** *Inca*, Wiracocha 160. In a renovated *so it is definitely worth* house, **F** without bath, good beds, hot water on request, nice garden. **E** *Ri'kay*, on 17 de Enero *staying the night. That* 172N, T754068, F754027. Set around 2 patios, modern, best in town, TV, hot water, restaurant *way you avoid the* serving Italian food in the evening. Recommended. **F** pp *Montecarlo*, 17 de Enero 101S, *midday crowds, too* T754014. Shared bath, cold water, cold at night, member of the Peruvian Youth Hostel Association. **F** *Hostal Chavín*, Jr San Martín 141-151, half a block from the plaza, T/F754055. Pleasant courtyard, hot water, will provide breakfast for groups, best of the more basic hotels. **Camping** inside park gates for vehicles. Restaurants from north to south along the main street, 17 de Enero, are: *La Ramada*, regional dishes, also trout and set lunch. *Chavín Turístico*, the best in town, good *menú* and à la carte, delicious apple pie, nice courtyard, has internet. *Los Portales*, in an old house with tables set around a pleasant garden. Recommended.

Transport Buses from **Huaraz**, see under Huaraz. Only *Chavín Express* has buses direct from Chavín to Huaraz, at 1730 and 2130, often full, book the day before. *Transportes Sandoval*, *Río Mosna* and *Chavín Express* itself have buses coming from destinations further east, such as Huari, which pass through Chavín at 2200-2300. This makes visiting Chavín in a day by public transport very difficult. Buses also pass through between 2100-2400 heading for Lima which can drop you in Catac, 3 hrs, US$2.50, from where there are frequent combis to Huaraz, 1 hr, US$0.50. Avoid *Huari Express* (old buses, bad drivers). Huaraz travel agencies on tours to the ruins sometimes sell spare seats when they return at 1500-1700, US$5, 4 hrs. To **Lima**: 438 km, 12 hrs, US$9, with *Trans El Solitario* and *Perú Andino* daily. Most locals prefer to travel first to Huaraz and then take one of the better companies from there.

To other destinations in the Callejón de Conchucos, either use buses coming from Huaraz or Lima, or hop on and off combis which run between each town. To **San Marcos**, 8 km, and **Huari**, 38 km, take one of the combis which leave regularly from the main plaza in Chavín, 20 mins and 30 mins respectively. There are buses during the day from Lima and Huaraz which go on to Huari, with some going on to **San Luis**, a further 61 km, 3 hrs; **Piscobamba**, a further 62 km, 3 hrs; and **Pomabamba**, a further 22 km, 1 hr; such *as El Solitario* which passes through Chavín at 1800. Gasoline is available at north end of Chavín.

Peru

Chavín to Pomabamba

225 km in total, gravel road, parts rough

From Chavín one circuit by road back to Huaraz is via Huari, San Luis, Yanama and Yungay (see page 1141) but the bus service is infrequent. The road north from Chavín descends into the Mosna river canyon. The scenery is quite different from the other side of the Cordillera Blanca, very dry and hot. After 8 km it reaches **San Marcos**, a small, friendly town with a nice plaza and a few basic restaurants and *hostales*. Further on 32 km is **Huari**, perched on a hillside at 3,150 m, with various basic hotels (**F**) and restaurants. The post office is at Luzuriaga 324 by Parque Vigil. Telephone at Libertad 940, open 0700-2200 daily. *Fiesta of Nuestra Señora del Rosario* first two weeks of October. ■ *Bus companies have their offices around Parque Vigil. Getting there: To Huaraz, 5-6 hrs, US$3.75, departures through the day. Services also to San Luis and Lima.*

There is a spectacular 2-3 days' walk from Huari to Chacas via Laguna Purhuay. Alberto Cafferata of Caraz writes: "The Purhuay area is beautiful. It has splendid campsites, trout, exotic birds and, at its north end, a 'quenoal' forest. This is a microclimate at 3,500 m, where the animals, insects and flowers are more like a tropical jungle, fantastic for ecologists and photographers." A day walk to Laguna Purhuay is recommended for those who don't want the longer walk to Chacas.

In **Chacas**, 10 km south of San Luis, off the main road, is a fine church. The local *fiesta patronal* is in mid-August, with bullfights, a famous *carrera de cintas* and fireworks. Seek out the Taller Don Bosco, a woodcarving workshop run by an Italian priest. There are a few basic shops, restaurants, a small market and two or three basic hostels.

It is a two-day hike from Chacas to Marcará via the Quebradas Juytush and Honda (lots of condors to be seen). The Quebrada Honda is known as the Paraíso de las Cascadas because it contains at least seven waterfalls. From Huari the road climbs to the Huachacocha pass at 4,350 m and descends to **San Luis** at 3,130 m, 60 km from Huari (one basic hotel, **G**, a few basic restaurants, shops and a market).

Some 20 km north of San Luis, a road branches left to **Yanama**, 45 km from San Luis, at 3,400 m. It has one marked hotel outside and one unmarked hotel, **G**, on the plaza; ask at the pharmacy. Food is available, but no electricity in the village, which is beautifully surrounded by snow-capped peaks. A day's hike to the ruins above the town affords superb views. ■ *Daily bus between Yungay and Yanama over the 4,767 m Portachuelo de Llanganuco, continuing to Pomabamba. Trucks also go along this route.*

A longer circuit to Huaraz can be made by continuing from San Luis 62 km to **Piscobamba**. There is a basic, but clean and friendly hotel, and one other, both **G**; also a few shops and small restaurants.

Places like San Luis, Piscobamba, Pomabamba and Sihuas were on the royal Inca Road, that ran from Cusco to Quito

Beyond Piscobamba by 22 km, is **Pomabamba**, worth a visit for some very hot natural springs (the furthest are the hottest). There are various hotels (**F-G**) near the plaza and restaurants. *One Pyramid Travel*, Huaraz 209, T721283, run by Víctor Escudero, who speaks English, specializes in archaeological tours, including some little known, unspoilt places, recommended. ■ *Occasional buses run from San Luis. Bus to Lima twice a week via San Luis and Chavín. To Chimbote twice a week via Sihuas. See under Huaraz for bus services.*

Several good walks into the Cordillera Blanca start from near Pomabamba, via Palo Seco or Laurel to the Lagunas Safuna. From there you can go on to Nevado Alpamayo, dubbed 'the most beautiful mountain in the world'. The glacier of Alpamayo is an incredible sight. From there, continue down to Santa Cruz and Caraz for several days' hard walking in total.

Cañón del Pato to Huaraz

The route from Chimbote via the Santa Valley: just north of Chimbote, a road branches northeast off the Pan-American Highway and goes up the Santa valley following the route of the old Santa Corporation Railway which used to run as far as **Huallanca** (not to be confused with the town southeast of Huaraz), 140 km up the valley. At Chuquicara, three hours from Chimbote, is *Restaurante Rosales*, a good place to stop for a meal (US$1-1.30 – you can sleep here, too, but it's very rough). At Huallanca are *Hotel Huascarán*, good; *Koki's Hostal* and *Fantasy's Pollería*. Fuel is available. At the top of the valley by the hydroelectric centre, the road goes through the very narrow and spectacular **Cañon del Pato**. You pass under tremendous walls of bare rock and through 36 tunnels, but the flow of the river has been greatly reduced by the hydroelectric scheme. After this point the road is paved for all but a few km before the Callejón de Huaylas and the road south to Caraz and Huaraz.

An alternative road for cyclists (and vehicles with a permit) is the 50-km private road known as the 'Brasileños', used by the Brazilian company Odebrecht which has built a water channel for the Chavimochic irrigation scheme from the Río Santa to the coast. The turn-off is 35 km north of the Santa turning, 15 km south of the bridge in Chao, on the Pan-American Highway. It is a good all-weather road via Tanguche.

Caraz

This pleasant town is a good centre for walking, parasailing and the access point for many excellent treks and climbs. Tourist facilities are expanding as a more tranquil alternative to Huaraz, and there are great views of Huandoy and Huascarán as well as the northern Cordilleras in July and August. In other months, the mountains are often shrouded in cloud. Caraz has a milder climate than Huaraz and is more suited to day trips. **Museo del Traje Típico y Arte Religioso** explains the significance of traditional clothing. It is part of the Colegio Dos de Mayo. ■ *Av Noé Bazán, continuation of Sucre, US$0.30.* The ruins of **Tunshukaiko** are in the suburb of Cruz Viva, to the north about 400 m past the bridge over the Río Llullán on the left. There are seven platforms from the Huaraz culture, dating from around BC 500. On 20 January is the fiesta *Virgen de Chiquinquirá*. In the last week of July is *Semana Turística*.

Altitude: 2,250 m
Colour map 3, grid B2

Sleeping

C *Opal Inn*, Pativilca/Caraz Km 265.5, T044-791015. Scenic. Recommended. **D** *La Alameda*, Av Noé Bazán Peralta 262, T791177 (Lima 461 0541), jtorres@viabcp.com.pe Comfortable rooms, hot water, breakfast, parking, gardens. Recommended. **D** *La Perla de los Andes*, Plaza de Armas 179, T/F792007. Comfortable rooms, hot water, TV, helpful, good restaurant. Recommended. **E** *Caraz Dulzura*, Sáenz Peña 212, about 10 blocks from the city centre, follow San Martín uphill north from the plaza to 3rd block, at the statue at Av N Bazán Peralta turn left and take the right fork on to Sáenz Peña, T791523 (Lima 287 1253). Modern building in an old street, hot water, cheaper without bath and TV, comfortable, great service, airy rooms, breakfast extra. Recommended. **E** *Chavín*, San Martín 1135 just off the plaza, T791171, hostalchavin@latinmail.com Warm water, good service but a bit grubby, breakfast extra, guiding service, tourist information. **E** *Hostal La Casona*, Raymondi 319, 1 block east from the plaza, T791334. **F** without bath, hot water, lovely little patio. **E** *Regina*, Los Olivos s/n y Gálvez, at the south end of town, 1 block west of road to Yungay, T791520. Modern, hot water, good value. **F** *Restaurant Oasis*, Raymondi 425. Small, hot water, welcoming, good value, optional TV. **F** *Alojamiento Retama*, Sucre 712, T/F791932/715. 4 rooms, **G** in low season (Nov-Mar), hot water, patio, laundry facilities, safe for bicycles, breakfast extra. **G** pp *Alojamiento Caballero*, D Villar 485, T791637, or ask at *Pony's Expeditions* on the plaza. Shared bath, hot water, laundry facilities, stores luggage, basic, family run. **G** *Familia Aguilar*, San Martín 1143, next to *Chavín*, T791161. Basic, shared bath, owner is Prof Bernardino Aguilar Prieto, who has information on bee-keeping and trekking in the Cordillera Negra.

Youth Hostel G pp *Los Pinos*, Parque San Martín 103, 5 blocks from plaza, T791130, lospinos@terra.com.pe All rooms shared, except one, all with bath except one (which is cheaper), hot water, a member of the Peruvian Youth Hostel Assoc, discount for HI members, camping US$2 pp, use of internet US$2.75 per hr, safe, book exchange, information.

Eating

Jeny, Daniel Villar on the plaza. Good food at reasonable prices. *Caraz Dulzura*, D Villar on the plaza. Excellent home made ice cream, good value meals and set lunches (US$1), pastries. *La Punta Grande*, D Villar 595. Cheap local dishes, good, closes at 1900. *El Mirador*, Sucre 1202 on the plaza. Nice view from terrace, good set lunch and BBQ chicken at night, popular. Recommended. *Café de Rat*, Sucre 1266, above *Pony's Expeditions*. Serves breakfast, vegetarian dishes, pizzas, drinks and snacks, darts, travel books, nice atmosphere.

Many restaurants give pensión to engineers working at the Cañon del Pato hydroelectric scheme, so may be full at times

Peru

Recommended. *La Olla de Barro*, Sucre 1004. Good set meal. *Esmeralda*, Av Alfonso Ugarte 404. Good set meal, breakfast. Recommended.

Entertainment *Taberna Disco Huandy*, Mcal Cáceres 119, good atmosphere. *El Tabasco Taberna*, on San Francisco, 2 blocks from the plaza.

Shopping Shop for camping supplies, such as fresh food, in the market. Some dried camping food is available from *Pony's Expeditions*, who also sell camping gaz canisters and white gas.

Tour operators *Pony's Expeditions*, Sucre 1266, near the Plaza de Armas, T/F791642, T682848 (Mob), www.ponyexpeditions.com Open daily 0900-1300 and 1600-2100, English, French and Quechua spoken, excellent and reliable information about the area. Owners Alberto and Haydée Cafferata are very knowledgeable about treks and climbs. Local tours and trekking with guides are arranged, maps and books for sale, also equipment for hire, mountain bike rental (from US$5 for 1 hr up to US$25 for a full day), use of internet US$2.30 per hr. Highly recommended. Another trekking guide is Mariano Araya, who is also keen on photography and archaeology. Ask at the municipality.

Transport **Buses** From Caraz to **Lima**, 470 km, 5 companies on D Villar and Jr Córdova, daily, US$5.20 (*El Huaralino*) to US$5.75 (*Expreso Ancash*, T791509, *Móvil*, *Rodríguez*, T791184), 10-11 hrs. All go via Huaraz and Pativilca. To **Chimbote**, *Yungay Express* (D Villar 318), via Huaraz at 0800 and 1830 daily, US$5.75, 10 hrs; *Turismo Huaraz*, D Villar 410 (*Bar Café Thonyto*), T791143, via Huallanca and Cañon del Pato morning and evening (phone in advance), US$7, 8 hrs. To **Trujillo**, via Huaraz and Pativilca, *Chinchaysuyo* (D Villar 230, T791930), 1830 daily, US$8, 11-12 hrs, stops in Casma (US$5.20) and Chimbote (US$5.75). To **Huaraz**, combis leave 0400-1900, 1½ hrs, US$1, from all along Jr José Gálvez. To **Yungay**, 12 km, 15 mins, US$0.30. To the village of **Parón** (for trekking in Laguna Parón area) pickups from Santa Cruz y Grau by the market, Mon to Sat 0500 and 1300, Sun 0300 and 1300, 1 hr. They return from Parón at 0600 and 1400. To **Cashapampa** (Quebrada Santa Cruz) buses from Bolognesi, near the market, hourly from 0830 to 1530, 2 hrs, US$1.30. To **Huallanca** (for the Cañon del Pato), several buses daily from Manco Cápac y Grau, near the market (colectivos leave from the same place).

Directory **Banks** *Banco de Crédito*, D Villar 217, cash and TCs at good rates, no commission. *Comercial Fournier*, Sucre 907, cash only (if funds permit), daily 0800-1330, 1600-2000. *Pony's Expeditions* (see above) cash only. *Importaciones América*, Sucre 721, T791479 (Esteban), good rates and service, open weekends and evenings. **Communications** Internet: See *Los Pinos* and *Pony's Expeditions*, above. Also at Av 1 de Mayo 189, T791819. **Post Office:** at San Martín 909. **Telephone:** national and international phone and fax at Raymondi y Sucre. Also several others, eg at Sucre y Santa Cruz, and on Plaza de Armas next to *Jeny*. No collect calls can be made except from private lines. Very few of the coin boxes take phone cards. **Tourist office** At Plaza de Armas, in the municipality, T791029. Limited information.

Treks from Caraz A good day hike with good views of the Cordillera Blanca is to **Pueblo Libre** (about four hours round trip, or you can take a colectivo back to Caraz). A longer day walk about seven hours in total with excellent views of Huandoy and Huascarán follows the foothills of the Cordillera Blanca, from Caraz south (head for Punyan, from where transport goes back to Caraz).

Lago Parón From Caraz a narrow, rough road goes east 32 km to Lago Parón, in a cirque surrounded by several, massive snow-capped peaks, including Huandoy, Pirámide Garcilazo and Caraz. The water level has been lowered to protect Caraz, and the water from the lake is used for the Cañon del Pato hydroelectric scheme. The gorge leading to it is spectacular. It is about a two-day trek (25 km) up to the lake at 4,150 m, or a 3-4 hour walk from the village of Parón (you need to be acclimatized). If there is room, you can stay at the refuge run by Egenor (kitchen, bathroom); there is usually a charge for use of the facilities. ■ *From Caraz, colectivos go to the lake if there are enough passengers and only in the dry season, US$3-4 pp. Taxi from Caraz*

US$20 for 4, with 4 hrs wait. Pony's Expeditions in Caraz organize day-trips to the lake, Jun-Oct, for US$7 pp (minimum 6 people).

Santa Cruz Valley   The famous Llanganuco-Santa Cruz hike can be started at Cashapampa in the Santa Cruz valley (see transport above). It takes about four days, up the Santa Cruz Valley, over the pass of Punta Unión, to Colcabamba or Vaquería (see Llanganuco to Santa Cruz trek, page 1142). Many recommend this 'anticlockwise' route as the climb is gentler, giving more time to acclimatize, and the pass is easier to find. You can hire an *arriero* and mule, prices given in Trekking and Climbing, above. 3 km north of Cashapampa, 1-2 hours hike, are the hot baths of Huancarhuas. It is almost impossible to hitch from the end of the trail back to Yungay. ■ *Transport: Yanama to Yungay buses can be caught at Vaquería between 0800-0900, US$4, three hours. Also frequent combis Vaquería-Yungay US$2.25. Travellers describe this journey down to Yungay as exhilarating and terrifying. Prices for staying in the park are given under Huascarán National Park.*

A large stand of **Puya Raimondi** can be seen in the Cordillera Negra west of Caraz. Beyond Pueblo Libre the road which continues via Pamparomas and Moro is being upgraded to join the coastal highway between Casma and Chimbote. After 45 km (two hours) are the Puya Raymondi plants at a place called Wuinchus, with views of 120 km of the Cordillera Blanca and to the Pacific. ■ *To get there, hire a combi in Caraz for US$42.50 for eight people, plus US$7.20 for a guide. Alternatively take a combi for Pamparomas from Grau y Ugarte between 0800 and 0900 and get out at the Yuashtacruz pass at 4,300 m (also known as La Punta), US$2, 2½ hrs. From the pass it is a short walk to the plants. There is usually transport five days a week, ask beforehand. There are buses returning to Caraz only on some days. If there is no bus, you can walk back to Pueblo Libre in four hours, to Caraz in 6-8 hrs, but it is easy to get lost and there are not many people to ask directions along the way. Take warm clothing, food and water. You can also camp near the puyas and return the following day.*

Check that the plants are in flower before going, usually May or Oct

Yungay

The main road goes on 12 km south of Caraz to Yungay which was completely buried during the 1970 earthquake by a massive mudslide; a hideous tragedy in which 20,000 people lost their lives. The earthquake and its aftermath are remembered by many residents of the Callejón de Huaylas. The original site of Yungay, known as Yungay Viejo, desolate and haunting, has been consecrated as a *camposanto* (cemetery). The new settlement is on a hillside just north of the old town, and is growing gradually. It has a pleasant plaza and a concrete market, good on Thursday and Sunday. October 17 is the *Virgen del Rosario* fiesta and October 28 is the anniversary of the founding of the town. The tourist office is on the corner of the Plaza de Armas.

Colour map 3, grid B2

Peru

E pp *Complejo Turístico Yungay* (COMTURY), Prolongación 2 de Mayo 1019, 2.5 km south of the new town, 700 m east of main road in Aura, the only neighbourhood of old Yungay that survived, T691698/722578. Nice bungalows, pleasant country setting, hot water, fireplace, restaurant with regional specialities, camping possible. **E** *Hostal Gledel*, Av Arias Graziani, north past plaza, T793048. A few cheaper rooms available (**G**), owned by Sra Gamboa, who is hospitable and a good cook, shared bath, hot water, no towels or soap, excellent meals prepared on request, nice courtyard. Highly recommended. **E** *Hostal Yungay*, Jr Santo Domingo on plaza, T793053. Basic, shared bath. **F** *Hostal Blanco*, follow the hospital street at north end of plaza and continue up hill, there are signs, T793115. Shared bath, basic, nice views. There are several small *comedores* in and around market and by the plaza (eg *El Sabroso*, but better is *El Rosario*). *Alpamayo*, Av Arias Graziani s/n, at north entrance to town, good.

Sleeping & eating

Buses, colectivos and trucks run the whole day to **Caraz**, 12 km, US$0.30, and **Huaraz**, 54 km, 1½ hrs, US$1. To **Yanama**, via the Portachuelo de Llanganuco pass at 4,767 m, 58 km: buses and trucks leave Yungay daily from in front of the Policía Nacional, 1 block south of plaza, at

Transport

around 0800 but you may have to wait until they are full, 4-5 hrs, US$4.50. Some trucks continue to **San Luis**, a further 61 km, 3 hrs, US$2.50, **Huari** (61 km) and **Chavín** (38 km, 6 hrs, US$3.50); *Los Andes* buses, which go to Yanama via Llanganuco, continue north to **Piscobamba** and **Pomabamba** (US$5 Yungay-Pomabamba). Buses or colectivos will do the route to the **Llanganuco** lakes when full, and only in the dry season, 1 hr; colectivo US$4.50, combi US$2. Huaraz travel agencies organize trips to Llanganuco for about US$7.25.

Llanganuco to Santa Cruz Trek One of the finest treks is the 4-5 days route over the path by Huascarán and the lakes at **Llanganuco** (Orconcocha and Chinancocha) from Yungay to Piscobamba. The park office is situated below the lakes at 3,200 m, 19 km from Yungay. Accommodation is provided for trekkers who want to start from here, US$2 per person.

Although you can start hiking up the Llanganuco valley from the park office, most hikers continue by bus or truck to María Huayta (Km 66), 3 km from Vaquería, where the Llanganuco-Santa Cruz trail starts. From the park office to the lakes takes about five hours (a steep climb). For the last 1½ hours, take the Sendero María Josefa nature trail (sign on the road) to the western end of Chinancocha where there is a control post, descriptive trail and boat trips on the lake (a popular area for day-trippers). There is a campsite beyond Laguna Orconcocha, at Yurac Corral. From the lakes to the pass will take a further 2-3 hours, with perfect views of the surrounding peaks.

From the Portachuelo de Llanganuco down to **Vaquería** at 3,700 m, about 9 km, takes 2½ hours. The trail makes a short cut to **Colcabamba**, 4 km, three hours. Eugenio Dextre Sanches and Ricadenia Cruz Vidal let people sleep in their barn and provide food (**E**), first house on left after crossing the river to Vaquería and Colcabamba. There is basic lodging in Colcabamba; *Familia Calonge* recommended, friendly, good meals. You can arrange an *arriero* and mule for about US$15 per day.

From Colcabamba, the trail goes on to Huaripampa, Punta Pucaraju, then up the steep climb to the highest point, Punta Unión, 4,750 m. From here it is downhill through the Santa Cruz valley to Cashapampa (basic *hospedaje* **G**, 2 meals US$2; bus to Caraz, US$1.25, two hours, last one at 1400, also trucks) and the village of Santa Cruz, five hours' walk from Caraz.

Carhuaz *Colour map 3, grid B2* After Yungay, the main road goes to **Mancos** (8 km south, 30 minutes) at the foot of Huascarán. There is one *hostal*, some basic shops and restaurants.

From Mancos it is 14 km to Carhuaz, a friendly, quiet mountain town with a pleasant plaza. There is very good walking in the neighbourhood (eg to thermal baths; up the Ulta valley). Market days are Wednesday and Sunday (the latter is much larger). The local fiesta of *Virgen de las Mercedes*, September 14 to 24, is rated as among the best in the region.

Sleeping and eating C pp *Casa de Pocha*, 1 km out of town towards Hualcán, at foot of Nevado Hualcán, ask directions in town, T613058 (Mobl). Including breakfast and dinner, country setting, entirely solar and wind energy powered, hot water, sauna and pool, home-produced food (vegetarian available), horses for hire, camping possible, many languages spoken. Recommended. D pp *El Abuelo*, Jr 9 de Diciembre y Tumbes, T794149. Modern, comfortable, cafe, parking, ask at *Heladería El Abuelo* on main plaza. E *Hostal Residencial Carhuaz*, Av Progreso 586, T794312, just off plaza. Cheaper without bath, varying standards of rooms (check first), basic but pleasant, hot water, nice courtyard and garden. F *Hostal La Merced*, Ucayali 724, T794241/327 (Lima 442 3201). Hot water (usually), "like going back to the 1950s", luggage store. *El Palmero*, Av Progreso 490, good value. Several other restaurants on the plaza. *Café Heladería El Abuelo*, Plaza de Armas, D'Onofrio and local ice-cream, sweets, also sells regional maps and guides.

Transport All transport leaves from the main Plaza. There are trucks (only 1 or 2 a day) and one minivan (0800) going up the Ulta valley to **Chacas** (see page 1138), 87 km, 4-5 hrs, US$4.50. The road works its way up the Ulta valley to the pass at Punta Olímpica from where

here are excellent views. The dirt road is not in a very good condition owing to landslides every year (in the wet season it can be closed). The trucks continue to **San Luis** (see page 1138), a further 10 km, 1½ hrs. Each Thu, a bus (*Transportes Huandoy*) does the trip from Carhuaz to Chacas and returns, US$6 one way, 5 hrs. To **Huaraz**, colectivos and buses, 0500-2000, US$0.65, 40 mins; to **Caraz**, 0500-2000, US$0.75, 1 hr.

Cordillera Huayhuash

The Cordillera Huayhuash, lying south of the Cordillera Blanca, has azure trout-filled lakes interwoven with deep quebradas and high pastures around the hem of the range. You may see tropical parrakeets in the bottom of the gorges and condors circling the peaks. The complete circuit is very tough; allow 12 days. The trail head is at **Cuartel Huain**, between Matacancha and the **Punta Cacanan** pass (the continental divide at 4,700 m). There are up to eight passes over 4,600 m, depending on the route. A half-circuit is also possible, but there are many other options. Both ranges are approached from Chiquián in the north, **Oyón**, with links to Cerro de Pasco to the southeast, **Churín** in the south or Cajatambo to the southwest. The area offers fantastic scenery and insights into rural life.

Perhaps the most spectacular cordillera for its massive ice faces that seem to rise sheer out of the Puna's contrasting green

Chiquián is a town of narrow streets and overhanging eaves. An interesting feature is a public television mounted in a box on a pedestal which sits proudly in the Plaza de Armas. *Semana Turística*: first week of July. **Sleeping**: E *Gran Hotel Huayhuash*, Figueredo y 28 de Julio, T747049/747183. Private bathroom, hot water, TV, restaurant, laundry, parking, modern, great views. E *Hostal San Miguel*, Jr Comercio 233, T747001. Nice courtyard and garden, clean, many rooms, popular, much improved. G pp *Los Nogales de Chiquián*, Jr Comercio 1301, T747121 (in Lima T460 8037), hotel_nogales_chiquian@yahoo.com.pe Cheaper without bath, hot water, new, cable TV, cafeteria, parking. Recommended. *Yerupajá*, Jr Tarapacá 351, and *El Refugio de Bolognesi*, Tarapacá 471, offer basic set meals. There are several others. *Panificadora Santa Rosa*, Comercio 900, on the plaza, for good bread and sweets, has coin-operated phones and fax.

Buy all your food and supplies in Huaraz as there are only basic supplies in Chiquián and almost nothing in the hamlets along the route

Transport Coming from Huaraz, the road is paved from Conococha to within 23 km of Chiquián. More paving around Chiquián is in progress. Four bus companies run from **Huaraz** to Chiquián, 120 km, 2 hrs: *El Rápido*, at Cáceres 312, T726437, at 0600 (very crowded), 1330, 1900; *Virgen del Carmen*, around the corner from Huascarán on Raymondi; *Chiquián Tours*, on Tarapacá behind the market; and *El Amigo del Milenio*, opposite the Frigorífico de Huaraz on Bolognesi. From Chiquián to Huaraz: all buses leave the plaza at 0500 daily, and *El Rápido*, Jr Figueredo 216, T747049, at 0500 and 1500. US$1.75 (except *El Rápido*, US$2). There is also a connection from Chiquián to **Huallanca** (Huánuco) with buses coming up from Lima in the early morning and combis during the day, which leave when full, 3 hrs, US$2.50. From Huallanca there are regular combis on to **La Unión**, 1 hr, US$0.75, and from there transport to Huánuco. **Mule hire** It may take a day to bring the mules to your starting point from Llamac or Pocpa where they are kept. (Very basic supplies only can be bought in either village.) Ask for mules (US$5 per day) or horses (US$7 per day) at the hotels or restaurants in Chiquián. A guide for the Huayhuash is *Sr Delao Callupe*, ask for him in Chiquián.

Cajatambo is the southern approach to the Cordillera Huayhuash, a small, friendly market town. Electricity supply 1800-2200. There are various hotels (**F-G**) and some good restaurants around the plaza. ■ *Buses to Lima at 0600, US$8.80, daily with* Empresa Andia *(office on plaza next to Hostal Cajatambo),* Tour Bello *and* Turismo Cajatambo, *Jr Grau 120 (in Lima, Av Carlos Zavala 124 corner of Miguel Aljovin 449, T426 7238).*

Peru

Lima

Northern Peru

The north of Peru has been described as the Egypt of South America, as it is home to many ruined pre-Inca treasures. Many tourists pass through without stopping on their way to or from Ecuador, missing out on one of the most fascinating parts of the country. Along a seemingly endless stretch of desert coast lie many of the country's most important pre-Inca sites: Chan-Chán, the Moche pyramids, Túcume, Sipán, Batán Grande and El Brujo. The main city is Trujillo, while Chiclayo is more down-to-earth, with one of the country's largest witchdoctors' market. The coast is also famous for its deep-sea fishing, surfing, and the unique reed fishing boats at Huanchaco and Pimentel. Inland lies colonial Cajamarca, scene of Atahualpa's last stand. Further east, where the Andes meet the jungle, countless unexplored ancient ruins await the more adventurous traveller.

Trujillo

Phone code: 044
Colour map 3, grid B2
Population: 850,000
548 km to Lima

The capital of La Libertad Department disputes the title of second city of Peru with Arequipa. The compact colonial centre, though, has a small-town feel. The greenness surrounding the city is a delight against the backcloth of brown Andean foothills and peaks. Founded by Diego de Almagro in 1534 as an express assignment ordered by Francisco Pizarro, it was named after the latter's native town in Spain.

Ins & outs
For more detailed information, see Transport, page 1149

Getting there The **airport** is to the northwest of town; the entry to town is along Av Mansiche. There is no central bus terminal. **Bus stations** are spread out on three sides the city beyond the inner ring road, Av España. Companies are now moving to new premises north and south along the Panamericana. There is little accommodation around them, but there are lots of taxis and colectivos to take you to your hotel (insist on being taken to the hotel of your choice).

Getting around Trujillo is best explored on foot. Taxis around town charge US$0.75; always use official taxis, which are mainly yellow. The major sites outside the city, Chan Chán, the Moche pyramids and Huanchaco beach are easily reached by public transport, but care is needed when walking around. A number of recommended guides run expert tours to these and other places.

Tourist offices Tourist office, Independencia 626, **Caretur**, helpful, free information. Useful websites: www.xanga.com/TrujilloPeru Michael White and Clara Bravo's site, with loads of links and information (click on 'reviews'). www.laindustria.com/industria local newspaper in Spanish (click on 'ecoturismo'). www.bcrp.com/Espanol/Sucursales/trujillo *Banco Central de Reserva* site with information on colonial houses, folklore and economy in Spanish. Maps available from **Touring and Automobile Club**, Argentina 278, Urb El Recreo, T242101; also from *Librería Ayacucho*, Ayacucho 570.

Tourist Police have an office at Independencia 630, Casa Ganoza Chopitea, T291705. Open all year. They are provide useful information. Any complaints about tourist services should be addressed to **Indecopi**, Independencia 262, or the Ministerio de Industria y Turismo, Av España 1801, T245345/245794.

Peru

The focal point is the pleasant and spacious **Plaza Mayor**. The prominent sculpture represents agriculture, commerce, education, art, slavery, action and liberation, crowned by a young man holding a torch depicting liberty. Fronting it is the **Cathedral**, dating from 1666, with its museum of religious paintings and sculptures next door ■ *Museum closed in 2002.* Also on the Plaza are the *Hotel Libertador,* the colonial style Sociedad de Beneficencia Pública de Trujillo and the Municipalidad. The **Universidad de La Libertad**, second only to that of San Marcos at Lima, was founded in 1824. Two beautiful colonial mansions on the plaza have been taken over. The Banco Central de Reserva is in the Colonial-style **Casa Urquiaga (or Calonge)**, Pizarro 446, which contains valuable precolumbian ceramics. ■ *Mon-Sat 0930-1600, free, take passport.* The other is **Casa Bracamonte (or Lizarzaburu)**, at Independencia 441, with occasional exhibits. Opposite the Cathedral on Independencia, is the **Caja Rural** (officially known as Casa Garci Olguín), recently restored but boasting the oldest façade in the city and Moorish-style murals. The buildings that surround the Plaza, and many others in the vicinity, are painted in bright pastel colours. Near the Plaza de Armas, at Jr Pizarro 688, is the spacious 18th-century **Palacio Iturregui**, now occupied by the **Club Central**, an exclusive and social centre of Trujillo. It houses a private collection of ceramics. ■ *Mon-Sat 1100-1800. To enter the patio is free, but to see more of the palace and the ceramics collection costs US$1.45.*

Other mansions, still in private hands, include **Casa del Mayorazgo de Facalá**, Pizarro 314, now Banco Wiese. **Casa de la Emancipación**, Jr Pizarro 610 (Banco Continental), is where independence from Spain was planned and was the first seat of government and congress in Peru. ■ *Daily 0900-1300, 1700-2000.* The **Casa del Mariscal de Orbegoso**, Orbegoso 553, is the Museo de la República owned by *Banco Crédito.* ■ *Banking hours, free.* **Casa Ganoza Chopitea**, Independencia 630, architecturally the most representative house in the city.

One of the best churches is the 17th-century **La Merced** at Pizarro 550, with picturesque moulded figures below the dome. ■ *US$2.* **El Carmen** church and monastery at Colón y Bolívar has been described as the 'most valuable jewel of colonial art in Trujillo'. Next door is the Pinacoteca Carmelita. ■ *Mon-Sat 0900-1300, US$0.85. Church is open of rmass Sun 0700-0730.* **La Compañía**, near Plaza de Armas, once an auditorium for cultural events. Other churches include: **San Francisco** on the 6th block of Almagro; **Santa Clara** on the fourth block of Junín; **San Agustín**, Bolívar at the sixth block of Mcal Orbegoso; **Santa Ana** on the second block of the same street; and **Santo Domingo** on Bolognesi.

Museo de Arqueología in Casa Risco, Junín 662 y Ayacucho, houses a large and interesting collection of thematic exhibits. ■ *Mon 0930-1400, Tue-Fri 0915-1300, 1500-1900, Sat/Sun 0930-1600, US$2.85. www.unitru.edu.pe/arq/indice.html for good information.*

The basement of the **Cassinelli** garage on the fork of the Pan-American and Huanchaco roads contains a superb private collection of Mochica and Chimú pottery, recommended. Demonstrations of the whistling *huacos* are given. ■ *0915-1230, 1515-1830, US$1.50.*

Museo del Juguete, Independencia 705 y Junín, www.angelmira.com The toy museum contains examples from prehistoric times to 1950, collected by painter Gerardo Chávez. Downstairs is the Espacio Cultural Angelmira with a café bar; in a restored *casona*, worth a visit. ■ *Tue-Sat 1000-1800, Sun 1000-1300, 1500-1800, US$0.85, children US$0.30, café open 0800-2100.*

Museo de Zoología de Juan Ormea, Jr San Martín 349, has interesting displays of Peruvian animals. ■ *0800-1400, free (but donations welcome, and needed).*

For the archaeological sites near Trujillo, see page 1151.

Puerto Malabrigo (**Chicama**), is known by surfers as the best surf beach in Peru, claiming that it has the longest left-hand point-break in the world. It is 70 km north of Trujillo. There are several basic places to stay and eat.

Sights

The city is generally safe but be especially careful at bus stations when arriving or leaving. Also take care beyond the inner ring road, Av España, towards the hill and in the Sánchez Carrión district at night

Excursions

Peru

Trujillo

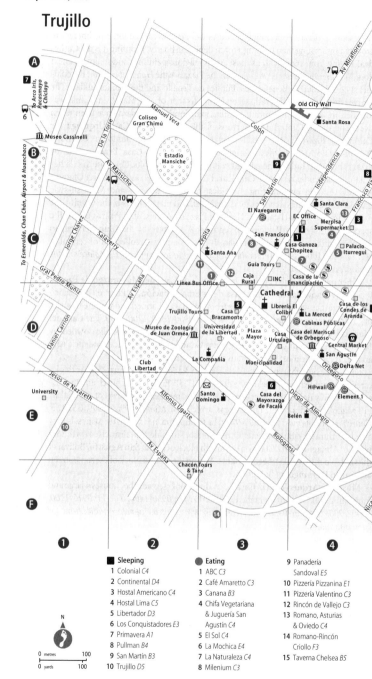

Sleeping
1 Colonial *C4*
2 Continental *D4*
3 Hostal Americano *C4*
4 Hostal Lima *C5*
5 Libertador *D3*
6 Los Conquistadores *E3*
7 Primavera *A1*
8 Pullman *B4*
9 San Martín *B3*
10 Trujillo *D5*

Eating
1 ABC *C3*
2 Café Amaretto *C3*
3 Canana *B3*
4 Chifa Vegetariana
  & Juguería San
  Agustín *C4*
5 El Sol *C4*
6 La Mochica *E4*
7 La Naturaleza *C4*
8 Milenium *C3*

9 Panadería
  Sandoval *E5*
10 Pizzería Pizzanina *E1*
11 Pizzería Valentino *C3*
12 Rincón de Vallejo *C3*
13 Romano, Asturias
  & Oviedo *C4*
14 Romano-Rincón
  Criollo *F3*
15 Taverna Chelsea *B5*

Peru

Transport

1 América Express, El Sol *F5*
2 Buses to Huaca del Sol y de la Luna *D6*
3 Buses to Huanchaco, Chan Chán, Huaca Arco Iris & Huaca La Esmeralda *D6*
4 Chinchaysuyo *B2*
5 Cruz del Sur *A5*
6 Empresa Díaz *B1*
7 Emtrafesa *A4*
8 Olano & Flores *A5*
9 Ormeño *A5*
10 Transportes Guadalupe *C2*

Sleeping
Trujillo has confusing double street names: the smaller printed name is that generally shown on maps, in guide books and in general use

L *Libertador*, Independencia 485 on Plaza de Armas, T232741, www.libertador.com.pe Including tax, pool (can be used by non-guests if they buy a drink), cafetería and restaurant, continental breakfast US$5, excellent buffet lunch on Sun. Recommended. **AL** *Gran Bolívar*, Bolívar 957, T223521, www.granbolivarhotel.com Price includes tax, breakfast, airport transfer and welcome drink, in converted 18th-century house. **AL** *El Gran Marqués*, Díaz de Cienfuegos 145-147, Urb La Merced, T/F249582. Including tax and breakfast, modern, pool, restaurant. Recommended. **AL** *Los Conquistadores*, Diego de Almagro 586, T203350, conquistadores@ computextos.com.pe Including tax and American breakfast, bar, restaurant, very comfortable. **B** *Pullman*, Jr Pizarro 879, T/F203624, hotelpullman@pmail.net Includes breakfast, cable TV, internet service, restaurant, bar, café, safe, free airport transfer disounts in low season. Recommended. **C** *Continental*, Gamarra 663, T241607, F249881. Opposite market, including tax, good, safe, cafetería recommended. **C** *Hostal Residencial Las Terrazas*, Av Manuel Vera Enríquez 874, Urb Primavera, behind *Hotel Primavera*, T232437. Hot water, phone, garage, cafetería, garden, pool, good value. **D** *Colonial*, Independencia 618, T/F258261. Attractive, helpful, central, good. **D** *San Martín*, San Martín 743-749, T234011. Cheaper without bath, good value, small restaurant, good breakfast, noisy. **D-E** *Primavera*, Av N de Piérola 872, Urb Primavera, T231915, F257399. Hot water, restaurant, bar, pool. **E** *Hostal Americano*, Pizarro 758, T241361. A vast, rambling old building, rooms without bath (**F**) are noisy and basic, most rooms without window (Nos 134 and 137, and those either side of 303, have windows, balconies and good views), safe, most popular backpackers' place, mixed reports. **E** *Familia Moreno*, Huáscar 247, near centre, cold water, quiet, safe. **E** *Trujillo*, Grau 581, T243921. **F** without bath or TV, hot water at times, good value but can be noisy. **E** pp *Hostal Wyllie's*, Raimondi 318, T205671. Hot water, good service, negotiate price. **F** pp *Clara Bravo and Michael White*, Cahuide 495, T243347, T662710 (Mob), T/F299997, microbewhite@ yahoo.com With bath, groups can be accommodated, meals on request, very helpful, loads of information available, many

Peru

languages spoken (see Guides, below). Recommended. There are several cheap hotels on Ayacucho, all of which are decaying and very basic, eg **G** *Hostal Lima*, Ayacucho 718, T244751, popular but dirty, baths terrible.

Eating

It's difficult to find a meal before 0800

Mid-range: *La Mochica*, Bolívar 462. Good typical food and occasional live music. *Romano*, Pizarro 725. International food, good *menú*, breakfasts, coffee and cakes, slow service. *Romano-Rincón Criollo*, Estados Unidos 162, Urb El Recreo, 10-min walk from centre. Northern Peruvian cuisine, good value *menú* for US$2, smart. *Pizzería Pizzanino*, Av Juan Pablo II 183, Urb San Andrés, opposite University. Recommended for pizzas, evening only. **Cheap**: *Asturias*, also No 725, café with excellent meals, good juices and snacks. *Los Luises*, Bolívar 526. Good, clean, sandwiches. *Juguería San Agustín*, Pizarro 691. Good juices, good *menú*, popular, excellent value. *La Selecta*, Pizarro 870. Set lunch for US$1.75, good value, also *heladería*. *ABC*, Orbegoso y San Martín 497. Good for chicken. *Rincón de Vallejo*, Orbegoso 303. Good *menú*. *Pizzería Valentino*, Orbegoso 224. Very good. **Vegetarian** (not exclusively): *Centro Naturista*, Bolívar 752. *Milenium*, Gamarra 316. *Natural*, Gamarra 439. *La Naturaleza*, Gamarra 455. Wide range of vegetarian dishes, unfriendly. *Oviedo*, Pizarro 725, next to *Asturias*. Good fresh salads, helpful. *El Sol*, Pizarro 660. The original and best, cheap set meals, also serves other dishes. *Chifa Vegetariana*, Pizarro 687. Also yoghurts and fruits. **Cafés** *Café Amaretto*, Gamarra 368. Smart, good selection of coffees, sweets, snacks and drinks. *Buenos Aires*, Pizarro 332. Very popular for sandwiches, closes at 1200. *Jano's*, Av España 195. Popular for sandwiches. *Kasumy*, Jr F Pizarro 857. Good value food and beer, beware overcharging. *Cafetería Oasis*, Gamarra y Grau. Good for breakfasts. *San Agustín*, Bolívar 522. Good for sandwiches.

There are several good, cheap seafood restaurants at Plazuela El Recreo, at the end of Pizarro, with outdoor seating (don't leave bags or cameras unattended). For really cheap meals try the market at Grau y Gamarra. Good selection of breads at *Panadería Sandoval*, Orbegoso 822, and *Panadería San José*, Ayacucho 561-65, behind Mercado Central.

Entertainment

Las Tinajas, Pizarro y Almagro, on Plaza Mayor, pub-disco, live rock music and *peña* on Sat. *Luna Rota*, América Sur 2119, at end of Huayna Capac, popular. *La Taberna*, Av Húsares de Junín 350, Urb La Merced, good for Andean folk music. *Taverna Chelsea*, Estete 675, smart bar and restaurant with live salsa at weekends, US$4. *Canana*, San Martín 791. Bars and restaurant, disco, live music at weekends, video. Recommended.

Festivals

The 2 most important festivals are the *National Marinera Contest* (end of Jan) and the *Festival Internacional de La Primavera* (last week of Sep), with cultural events, parades, beauty pageants and Trujillo's famous *Caballos de Paso*.

Shopping

Bookshops *Librería El Colibrí*, Pizarro 505, just off the Plaza. Has the best selection in town, ask for Sra Inés. **Markets** *Mercado Central* on Gamarra. *Mercado Mayorista* on Sinchi Roca. The best **supermarket** is *Merpisa*, Pizarro y Junín. **Pharmacies** *La Libertad*, Bolognesi 498. Good prices. Other places on either side of Belén hospital on Bolognesi.

Sport

Swimming *Academia Berendson*, Bolognesi 231, heated pool. There's an outdoor **swimming pool** next to Mansiche stadium, where buses leave for Chan Chán and Huanchaco. It's open 0900-1300 and 1600-1800, entry US$0.50.

Tour operators

Prices vary and competition is fierce so shop around for the best deal Few agencies run tours on Sun and often only at fixed times on other days

Chacón Tours, Av España 106-112, T255212. Open Sat afternoon and Sun morning. Recommended. *Guía Tours*, Independencia 527, T234856, F246353. Also Western Union agent. Recommended. *Trujillo Tours*, San Martín y Almagro 301, T233091, F257518, ttours@pol.com.pe Works with *Lima Tours*. To **Chan Chán**, **El Dragón** and **Huanchaco**, 3 hrs for US$15 pp. To **Huacas del Sol** and **de la Luna**, 2 hrs for US$13 pp. To **El Brujo**, US$20-25 pp. **City tours** cost US$6.50 pp (min of 2 people; discounts for 4 or more).

Guides: many hotels work on a commission basis with taxi drivers and travel agencies. If you decide on a guide, make your own direct approach. *Clara Bravo*, Cahuide 495, T243347, T662710 (Mob), T/F299997, www.xanga.com/TrujilloPeru An experienced tourist guide with her own transport, she speaks Spanish, German and understands Italian. She takes tourists on extended circuits of the region and is good for information (archaeological tour US$16 for 6 hrs, city tour US$7 pp, US$53 per car to El Brujo, with extension to Sipán, Brüning Museum and Túcume possible). Clara works with English chartered accountant *Michael White* (same address, microbewhite@yahoo.com, speaks German, French and Italian), who provides transport. He is very knowledgeable about tourist sites. They run tours any day of the week; 24-hr attention.

Zaby Miranda Acosta, Camelias 315, Huanchaco, T461246, T601102 (Mob), Zaby_miranda@hotmail.com Works at the tourist office, speaks German, Italian, US$10 per day. *Jannet Rojas Sánchez*, T401184, T602855 (Mob), jannarojas@hotmail.com Speaks English, enthusiastic, works independently and for *Guía Tours*. *José Soto Ríos*, Atahualpa 514, dpto 3, T251489. He speaks English and French. Other experienced guides are *Oscar and Gustavo Prada Marga*, Miguel Grau 169, Villa del Mar, or at Chan Chán. *Pedro Puerta* T609603 (Mob), works with *Guía Tours* and independently. *Celio Eduardo Roldán*, celioroldan@hotmail.com Helpful and informative taxi driver. The Tourist Police (see Directory) has a list of guides; average cost is US$7 per hr.

Local Bus and colectivos: on all routes, US$0.20-0.35; colectivos are safer as there are fewer people and fewer pick-pockets. **Taxi**: town trip, US$0.75. Chan Chán US$3 per car, to airport US$4; Huanchaco, US$5. Beware of overcharging, check fares with locals. Taxi from in front of *Hotel Libertador*, US$7 per hr, about the same rate as a tour with an independent guide or travel agent for 1-2 people. **Transport**

Long distance Air to Lima, 1 hr, daily flights with *Lan Perú*; *Aerocondor* daily to Cajamarca and Lima. Taxi to airport, US$4; or take bus or colectivo to Huanchaco and get out at airport turn-off (US$0.25) and walk 2 km. *Check flight times as they change frequently*

Buses to and from Lima, 561 km, 8 hrs in the better class buses, average fare US$21-15.75 in luxury classes, 10 hrs in the cheaper buses, US$8-10. There are many bus companies doing this route, among those recommended are: *Ormeño*, Av Ejército 233, T259782, 4 levels of service, normal 4 daily, also *super especial* (meal, drinks included); *Cruz del Sur*, Amazonas 437 near Av Ejército, T261801; *Empresa Díaz*, Nicolás de Piérola 1079 on Panamericana Norte, T232476, at 2130; *Línea*, Av América Sur 2855, T297000, ticket office at San Martín y Orbegoso, T245181, *bus cama* at 2200, others at 2230 and 2245, also to **Chimbote** hourly, **Huaraz** 2100, 9 hrs, US$8.65, **Cajamarca** 1030, 1030, US$5-8, 1st class at 2200, and **Piura**, 2300, US$5.75. Also *Flores* (Av Ejército 346, T208250), *Móvil Tours* (Av América Sur 3959 – Ovalo Larco, T286538), and *Trans Chiclayo* (Av América Norte 2404, T243345). *Trans Olano* (Oltursa), Av Ejército 342, T2603055, *bus cama* to Lima at 2300. All the cheaper, indirect buses use a southern terminal, 2 km south of the centre, about every 30 mins, when full.

Small buses leave regularly from the first block of Av Mansiche to **Pacasmayo**, 102 km, 2 hrs, US$1.50. To **Chiclayo**, another 118 km, 3 hrs from Trujillo, US$3-3.50, several companies. Among the best are *Emtrafesa*, Miraflores 127, T223981, on the half-hour every hour;

Peru

Vulkano/Línea (from Carrión by Av Mansiche), on the hour. *Móvil*'s Lima-Chiclayo-Chachapoyas service passes through Trujillo at 0130. To **Piura**, 278 km beyond Chiclayo, 6 hrs, US$6.50; and **Tumbes**, a further 282 km, US$7-12, 8-12 hrs. Companies include: *Transportes Dorado*, Av América Norte 2400, T242880, leave at 1830, 2000 to Piura and Sullana, US$5; and *Olano, Civa, Ormeño*, US$8.60; *Ormeño* also has US$12.85 (2215) and US$20 (2315) services.

Direct buses to **Huaraz**, 319 km, via Chimbote and Casma (169 km), with *Móvil* and *Línea*, 8 hrs, US$8.60 special. Also *Chinchaysuyo*, Av Mansiche entre Chávez y Carrión, at 2030; US$7, 10 hrs. There are several buses and colectivos to **Chimbote**, with *América Express* from Lloque 162, 135 km, 2 hrs, US$2.50, departures every 30 mins; then change at Chimbote (see above – leave Trujillo before 0600 to make a connection from 0800). *Turismo Huaraz/Expreso Yungay* depart at 0830 for Huaraz via the Cañon del Pato on Sun, Tue, Thu, sometimes daily, US$7, 8 hrs. Ask Clara Bravo and Michael White (see Guides) about transport to Caraz avoiding Chimbote (a very worthwhile trip via the Brasileños road and Cañon del Pato).

To **Cajamarca**, 300 km, 7-8 hrs, US$5-8: with *Línea* (see above), 1030, 2200; *Emtrafesa*, at 1000, *Empresa Cajamarca*, at 1300 (less good for seeing the scenery); and *Empresa Díaz* at 1300, 2200.

Transportes Guadalupe, Av Mansiche 331, has buses to **Tarapoto**, via Jaén and Moyobamba, 1000 daily, 24 hrs, US$20, continuing to **Yurimaguas**, US$25 (very exhausting, change buses 3 times); also *Turismo Tarapoto* to Tarapoto and *Ejetur* to Jaén.

Directory **Airline offices** *Aero Continente*, España opposite 1st block of San Martín, T244042. *Aerocondor*, T255212. **Banks** *Banco de Crédito*, Gamarra 562. No commission on cash into soles, but US$12 fee on TCs or changing into dollars, cash advance on Visa card, ATM (Visa). *Interbank*, Pizarro y Gamarra. Good rates for cash, no commission on Amex TCs into soles, reasonable rate, Visa cash advance, quick service, also has MasterCard ATM (doesn't close for lunch). *Banco Wiese Sudameris*, Pizarro 314, *Casa de Mayorazgo de Facalá*. Good rates for Amex TCs, 2% commission into soles or dollars, ATM for Visa/Plus. *BBV Continental*, Pizarro 620. Amex TCs and Visa card accepted, US$10 commission up to US$500. *Banco Santander Hispano*, Junín 479. Visa ATM. Note that banks close 1300-1615. There is little difference between the rates for cash dollars given by banks and street changers, *casas de cambio* and travel agencies. There are many *casas de cambio* and street changers on the plazoleta opposite the Casa de Condes de Aranda and all along the 600 block of Bolívar. *Western Union*, Almagro 581, España y Huayna Cápac, see also *Guía Tours*, above. **Communications** Internet: on Pizarro, *Internet Cabinas Públicas*, Nos 107, 154, 197, 508, and at No 551, 2nd floor. On Orbegoso, *Delta Net* at No 641 (relatively quick, efficient), *H@waii*, at corner with Ayacucho 493, and opposite *Element 1*, Ayacucho 496. *El Navegante*, San Martín 624, with café. *Leonardo da Vinci*, Av España 200, recommended. *Interc@ll*, Zepita 728, T246465, open 24 hrs. Many others, especially on Ayacucho, most slow or "stationary". Standard fee US$0.75 per hr. **Post Office:** Independencia 286 y Bolognesi. 0800-2000, stamps only on special request. *DHL*, Almagro 579. **Telephone:** *Telefónica*, headquarters at Bolívar 658, also Almagro 744. Private call centre at Pizarro 561 and others on 5th block of Bolívar for national and international phone calls and faxes. **Cultural centres** Alianza Francesa, San Martín 858-62, T204504/231232. Instituto de Cultura Peruano Norteamericano, Av Venezuela 125, Urb El Recreo, T261944, F261922. **Consulates** European Community, Independencia 630, behind *Caretur* office. *UK*, Honorary Consul, Mr Winston Barber, Jesús de Nazareth 312, T235548, F245935, winstonbarber@terra.com.pe Mon-Fri 0900-1700. **Medical services** Hospital: Hospital Belén, Bolívar 3rd block. Clínica Peruano Americana, Av Mansiche 702, T231261, English spoken, good. **Useful addresses** Immigration: Av Larco 1220, Urb Los Pinos. Gives 30-day visa extensions, US$20 (proof of funds and onward ticket required), plus US$1 for *formulario* in Banco de la Nación (fixers on the street will charge more).

Archaeological sites near Trujillo

These vast, unusually decorated crumbling ruins of the imperial city of the Chimú domains are the largest adobe city in the world. The ruins consist of nine great compounds built by Chimú kings. The 9-m high perimeter walls surrounded sacred enclosures with usually only one narrow entrance. Inside, rows of storerooms contained the agricultural wealth of the kingdom, which stretched 1,000 km along the coast from near Guayaquil to the Carabayllo Valley, north of Lima.

Chan Chán
*5 km from Trujillo
You need at least an
hour to gain a full
explanation of Chan
Chán and Huaca La
Luna; many tours only
allow 20 mins each*

Most of the compounds contain a huge walk-in well which tapped the ground water, raised to a high level by irrigation further up the valley. Each compound also included a platform mound which was the burial place of the king, with his women and his treasure, presumably maintained as a memorial. The Incas almost certainly copied this system and transported it to Cusco where the last Incas continued building huge enclosures. The Chimú surrendered to the Incas around 1471 after 11 years of siege and threats to cut the irrigation canals.

The dilapidated city walls enclose an area of 28 sq km containing the remains of palaces, temples, workshops, streets, houses, gardens and a canal. What is left of the adobe walls bears well-preserved moulded decorations of fish and other animals, and painted designs have been found on pottery unearthed from the debris of a city ravaged by floods, earthquakes, and *huaqueros* (grave looters) over the centuries. Owing to the damage, many of the interesting mouldings are closed to visitors. The **Ciudadela of Tschudi** has been restored (15 minutes walk from the road).

■ *0900-1630, but entry not permitted after 1600 (but it may be covered up if rain is expected). The site museum on the main road, 100 m before the turn-off, has a son-et-lumière display of the growth of Chan Chán as well as objects found in the area. A ticket which covers the entrance fees for Chan Chán, the site museum, Huaca El Dragón and Huaca La Esmeralda (for 2 days) costs US$3 (discount with ISIC card). A guide costs US$5.80 per hr; map and leaflet in English US$0.75.*

Getting there: For Chan Chán buses and combis leave from corner of Zela and Los Incas (114A – safer to catch bus at north corner of Huayna Cápac y Av Los Incas) or corner of España and Manuel Vera (114B) in Trujillo; US$0.35, 20 mins to the turn-off to the ruins. It is relatively safe to walk on the dirt track from turn-off to site, but go in a group, 20 mins; taxi, US$1. On no account walk the 4 km to, or on Buenos Aires beach near Chan Chán as there is serious danger of robbery, and of being attacked by dogs.

The partly-restored temple, **Huaca El Dragón**, dating from Huari to Chimú times (AD1000-1470), is also known as **Huaca Arco Iris** (rainbow), after the shape of friezes which decorate it. ■ *0900-1630. It is on the west side of the Pan-American Highway in the district of La Esperanza; combis from Av España y Manuel Vera marked 'Arco Iris/La Esperanza', taxi costs US$2.*

The poorly preserved **Huaca La Esmeralda** is at Mansiche, between Trujillo and Chan Chán, behind the church (not a safe area). Buses to Chan Chán and Huanchaco pass the church at Mansiche. The ticket to Chan Chán includes these ruins, but tickets are not sold here.

A few kilometres south of Trujillo are the huge and fascinating Moche pyramids, the **Huaca del Sol** and the **Huaca de la Luna**. ■ *0830-1600, US$3 (students half price, children US$0.30).* Until the Spaniards destroyed half of it in a vain search for treasure, Huaca del Sol was the largest man-made structure in the western hemisphere, at 45 m high. Huaca de la Luna, 500 m away, received scant attention until extensive polychrome moulded decorations were found throughout the 1990s. The colours on these remarkable geometric patterns and feline deities have faded little and can be easily viewed.

■ *Getting there: Taxi about US$10 return, including 1 hr wait. Combis (yellow and blue in colour) about half hourly from Suárez y Los Incas to the base of Huaca del Sol, every 30 mins, US$0.30. It's safer to catch the bus from Huayna Cápac, southeast of Av Los Incas.*

Peru

El Brujo   A complex considered one of the most important archaeological sites on the north coast is 60 km north of Trujillo. Covering 2 sq km, this complex is collectively known as El Brujo and was a ceremonial centre for perhaps 10 cultures, including the Moche. Huaca Cortada (or El Brujo) has a wall decorated with high relief stylized figures. Huaca Prieta is, in effect, a giant rubbish tip dating back 5,000 years, which once housed the very first settlers to this area. Huaca Cao Viejo has extensive friezes, polychrome reliefs up to 90 m long, 4 m high and on five different levels. In front of Cao Viejo are the remains of one of the oldest Spanish churches in the region. It was common practice for the Spaniards to build their churches near these ancient sites in order to counteract their religious importance.

■ *Excavations at the site will last many years, but part, extensively sheltered by awnings, is open to the public (entry US$1.85). As the nearest public transport stops 5 km away at Magdalena de Cao and individuals especially, but also tour groups, may not be allowed in without specific permission, it is best to go with a local tour guide. A guide may be able to arrange with the site guardian to view recent excavations. Tip the guardian if this opportunity arises; it will not be offered to lone visitors. Permission should be sought from The Wiese Foundation, The Regional Institute of Culture, INC (on Independencia block 5, Trujillo), or the University of Trujillo. The Director of Excavations may also deny access on windy days. The exhibition formerly at* Banco Wiese, *Pizarro 314, Trujillo, has been moved to the Chan Chán site museum but (mid-2002) is not yet on display. There are other exhibitions at* Banco Wiese *and* Museo de la Nación *in Lima, or visit a number of websites, including* www.unitru.edu.pe/arq/index.html *and* www.research.ibm.com/peru/brujo.htm *Road access is tricky, there is no public transport and there are no tourist facilities other than the ticket office.*

Huanchaco

An alternative to Trujillo is this fishing and surfing village, full of hotels, guest houses and restaurants. The beaches south of the pier are quite dirty, but are much cleaner northwards around the bay

This village is famous for its narrow pointed fishing rafts, known as *caballitos* (little horses) *de totora*, made of totora reeds and depicted on Mochica, Chimú and other cultures' pottery. Unlike those used on Lake Titicaca, they are flat, not hollow, and ride the breakers rather like surfboards (fishermen offer trips on their *caballitos* for US$1.50, be prepared to get wet; groups should contact Luis Gordillo, El Mambo, T461092). You can see fishermen returning in their reed rafts at about 0800 and 1400 when they stack the boats upright to dry in the fierce sun. Overlooking Huanchaco is a huge church from the belfry of which are extensive views. Post Office at Manco Capac 306, open 1100-1800 in theory.

Sleeping   **C** *Caballito de Totora*, Av La Rivera 219, T/F651828, totora@terra.com.pe   Includes taxes, **D** in low season, surfers' room **F**, pool, English spoken, nice garden, restaurant with good food and coffee, parking, good value, noisy. Recommended. **C** *Hostal Bracamonte*, Los Olivos 503, T461162, www.welcome.to/hostal_bracamonte   Comfortable, good, chalets with bath **B**, you can camp, pool, own water supply, emergency generator, rents bicycles, secure, good restaurant, English spoken. Highly recommended. **D** *Huanchaco Internacional*, Autopista a Huanchaco Km 13.5 (Playa Azul), T461754, www.perunorte.com/huanchacoint   Some distance from town, **B** in bungalows, also has bunk rooms, comfortable, hot water, internet, pool, restaurant, airport pick-up, tours arranged. Recommended. **D** *Hostal Huanchaco*, Larco 287 on Plaza, T461272, huanchaco@solui.com   With breakfast, TV, hot water, pool, good but expensive cafetería, video, pool table. Recommended. **D** *Hostal Los Esteros*, Av Larco 618, T461300. Hot water, restaurant, safe motorcycle parking. **D** *Las Brisas*, Raymondi 146, T461186, lasbrisas@hotmail.com Hot water, cafeteria, cable TV, comfortable. **E** *Naylamp*, Prolongación Víctor Larco 3, northern end of seafront in El Boquerón, T461022, naylamp@terra.com.pe   Peruvian-Swiss owned, rooms set around a courtyard, also dormitories **G** pp, hammocks, nice garden, good beds, hot water, camping US$1.45 with own tent, US$2.30 to hire tent, laundry facilities, safe, kitchen at campsite, English, German, French and Italian spoken, Italian food, good breakfasts. Highly recommended. **F** pp *Golden Club*, Av La

Peru

Rivera 217, T461306. Gym, pool, restaurant, use of kitchen, popular with surfers, laid back, excellent value, rooms on 1st floor cheaper. Recommended. **E** *El Malecón*, Av La Rivera 225, T461275. With hot shower, TV, excellent service, on the seafront. **F** pp *La Casa Suiza*, Los Pinos 451, T461285, www.huanchaco.net/casasuiza 3 blocks from the beach, run by Heidi and Oscar Stacher, speak German and English, cheaper with shared bath, hot water, nice roof balcony, excellent breakfast for US$1.50, family home (no drugs), surf boards to rent, book exchange, internet access. Highly recommended. **F** pp *Huanchacos Garden*, Av Circunvalación Mz 'U', lote 3, T461194, huanchacosgarden@huanchaco.znn.com Bungalows around a small pool, also rooms, 1 block from beach, TV, use of kitchen, hot water, many good reports. **F** *Mantram*, Ricardo Palma 491 y Larco, T461909. Cheaper without bath, camping, TV, kitchen and laundry facilities, beachwear rental, book exchange, massage, vegetarian restaurant. Recommended. **F** *Hostal Solange*, Los Ficus 484, 1 block from the beach, T461410, www.geocities.com/hostalsolange/solange.html Good food, laundry facilities, use of kitchen, popular meeting point.

Accommodation with families is easy to find for around US$2-3 a day, including meals. For example: *Casa Gaviotas*, Los Pinos 535, T461858; *Casa Jiménez*, Colón 378, T461844; *Sra Mabel Díaz de Aguilar*, near the football ground. *Sra Lola*, Manco Capac 136, basic, laundry, noisy at weekends. Opposite is *Sr Carlos Sánchez Leyton*, good, safe, cold water. *Sra Nelly Neyra de Facundo*, Las Palmeras 425, recommended.

Eating
Try picarones, the local speciality. Nowhere open for vegetarians on Mon lunchtime

Expensive: *Big Ben*, Víctor Larco 836, near A Sánchez, T461869. Seafood and international, very good. *Club Colonial*, Grau 272 on the plaza. Reputedly the best, run by Belgians, fish, chicken or meat, atmosphere of a traditional colonial dining club, but with private zoo. **Mid-range**: *El Tramboyo*, on the little plaza opposite the pier, good, helpful. Next door is *La Esquina*, C Unión 299, T461081, recommended (also has accommodation **G** pp). *Estrella Marina*, on the seafront. Great value. Good fish also at *La Barca*, *El Erizo*, La Rivera 269 (on seafront), *Pisagua*, just past the pier, and *El Caribe*, Atahualpa 291. *Mamma Mia*, on the seafront. Good value Italian food and delicious home-made pasta and ice-cream, English spoken by owner Fernando, closed Mon lunchtime, good lodging (**F**, shared showers) next door. *Sabes?*, V Larco 920, T461555, ysabes@yahoo.com Pub with food, internet café, popular, American run. *Wachake*, southern end of seafront road. Owned by Edgar who speaks English, good food, also has sleeping space for backpackers. **Cheap**: *Piccolo*, Los Abetos 142, 5 blocks from the plaza. Live folk music weekend evenings, excellent, closed Mon. Good seafood, including *ceviche*, at *El Suco*, north end of the beach.

Festivals

In the first week of **May** is the *Festival del Mar*, a celebration of the disembarkation of Taycanamo, the leader of the Chimú period. A procession is made in Totora boats. Also the annual *Olímpiadas Playeral* and *El Festival Internacional de la Primavera* (see Trujillo above). There are also surf competitions. Carnival and New Year are also popular celebrations.

Transport

Combis between Trujillo and Huanchaco include 114A or B. They both do an anti-clockwise circuit of Huanchaco and pass the roundabout on Av Mansiche, 3 blocks north of Av España in front of the Cassinelli museum, then A goes round the west side of Trujillo onto Av 28 de Julio and Av Los Incas, while B goes round the east side on Av Manuel Vera, España as far as Bolívar. At night they go only to España y Grau; they run till 2300 (later at weekends). Fare is US$0.30 for the 20-min journey. 'Micros' follow similar routes to América, but in daylight only; colectivos and some radio taxis run at night (US$4-6).

Peru

Trujillo to Cajamarca

To the northeast of Trujillo is Cajamarca, which can be reached by paved road via Pacasmayo, or by the old road via Huamachuco and Cajabamba. This latter road is terrible and (for cyclists especially) lonely, taking three days because buses do not interconnect (as opposed to 7-8 hours via Pacasmayo, see below), but it is more interesting, passing over the bare *puna* before dropping to the Huamachuco valley.

Huamachuco
Colour map 3, grid B2
Altitude: 3,180 m
181 km from Trujillo

This colonial town formerly on the royal Inca Road has a huge main plaza and a controversial modern cathedral. There is a colourful Sunday market and the Founding of Huamachuco festival, second week in August, with spectacular fireworks and the amazing, aggressive male dancers, called *turcos*. A three-hour walk (take the track which goes off to the right just after crossing the bridge on the road to Trujillo) takes you to the extensive ruins of hilltop pre-Inca fortifications, **Marcahuamachuco** (Alosio Rebaza, T441488, offers trips for up to 4 people, US$20-30). The Convento complex has been partially restored and the Castillo complex contains a remarkable circular construction. Nearby, beyond the local radio station, one hour's walk, are the pre-Inca ruins of **Wiracochapampa**, where the Waman Raymi festival is held on the first weekend in August. Inca legends are retold by people in costume. **Sleeping** There are various hotels (**E-F**), including *Noche Buena*, on the plaza adjoining the cathedral, with TV, *Hostal Huamachuco*, Castilla 354, T441393, and *Hostal Viracocha*, C Carmen La Troya, behind the market, safe, water problems. Among the restaurants, *Bar Michi Wasi*, San Román 461 on the plaza, open 1900-2400, is a good place to get information on ruins in the area. Internet at office of *Trans Horna*, C San Martín, off plaza.

Transport Air from Trujillo, *Air Líder*, T204470 (Trujillo). **Buses** from Trujillo, *Trans Sánchez López*, Vallejo 1390, T251270, *Trans Palacios*, España 1005, T222992, *Trans Negreiros*, Zarumilla 199, T210725, and *Trans Agreda*, Unión 149 (0800, 1800), spectacular journey through mining settlements, views of snow-capped peaks, over 4,100 m pass, US$5.80-8, 10 hrs, most buses at night (take warm clothing), try to go by day. *Trans Gran Turismo* and *Trans Anita* each have a daily bus to Cajabamba, 0400, 3 hrs, US$4, rough road, little other traffic.

Cajabamba is a small market town and stop-over point between Cajamarca and Huamachuco. **F** *Hostal Flores*, on the plaza, T851086, **G** without bath, hot water mornings only, pleasant courtyard. Restaurants include *El Cajabambino II*, Martínez 1193, next to market, trout and chicken dishes, and *Grau*, Grau 133, fresh fruit salads and *alfajores*. *Atahualpa* bus to Cajamarca US$2.85, six hours (*Rojas* run small, uncomfortable minibuses).

Pacasmayo
Colour map 3, grid A2
Population: 12,300
102 km N of Trujillo

Pacasmayo, port for the next oasis north is the main road connection from the coast to Cajamarca. The paved 180 km road branches off the Pan-American Highway soon after it crosses the Río Jequetepeque (bus Pacasmayo-Cajamarca US$4.30, five hours; to Chiclayo US$1.70, two hours). The river valley has terraced rice fields and mimosas may often be seen in bloom, brightening the otherwise dusty landscape.

A few kilometres northwest on the other side of Río Jequetepeque are the ruins of **Pacatnamú** comparable in size to Chan Chán pyramids, cemetery and living quarters of nobles and fishermen, possibly built in the Chavín or Moche periods. Taxi to Guadalupe (splendid church), 10 km from ruins (Ortiz family, Unión 6, T3166), US$20. Micros run in summer. Where the Pan-American Highway crosses the Jequetepeque are the well-signed ruins of **Farfán** (separate from those of Pacatnamú, but probably of the same period; no explanations at the site).

Sleeping F *Panamericano*, Leoncio Prado 18, T522521. With private cold shower, basic, small, safe, reasonable restaurant downstairs. **F** *San Francisco*, at No 21, opposite the *Panamericano*, T522021, is cleaner. Basic, OK. There are other places to stay, from 3-star down, and several cheap restaurants on the main street.

Some 103 km east of Pacasmayo is the mining town of Chilete, 21 km north of which on the road to San Pablo is **Kuntur Wasi**. The site was devoted to a feline cult and consists of a pyramid and stone monoliths. Extensive excavations are under way and significant new discoveries are being made. There is basic accommodation in San Pablo and two basic *hostales* in Chilete.

Cajamarca

This pleasant and attractive colonial town is surrounded by lovely countryside and is the commercial centre of the northern mountain area. Here Pizarro ambushed and captured Atahualpa, the Inca emperor. This was the first showdown between the Spanish and the Incas and, despite their huge numerical inferiority, the Spanish emerged victorious, executing Atahualpa in the process.

Phone code: 044
Colour map 3, grid B2
Population: 117,500
Altitude: 2,750 m

All museums are closed on Tue but open at weekends

The **Cuarto de Rescate** is not the actual chamber that Atahualpa filled with gold as ransom, but in fact the room where Atahualpa was held prisoner. The room was closed to the public for centuries and used by the nuns of Belén hospital. ■ *0900-1300, 1500-1745, Sat-Sun 0900-1245, closed Tue, US$1.15, entrance at Amalia Puga 750 (ticket also valid for Belén church and nearby museums).* The Plaza where Atahualpa was ambushed and the stone altar set high on **Santa Apolonia hill** where he is said to have reviewed his subjects can also be visited. ■ *US$0.30.* There is a road to the top, or you can walk up from C 2 de Mayo, using the steep stairway.

The **Plaza de Armas**, where Atahualpa was executed, has a 350-year-old fountain, topiary and gardens. The **Cathedral**, opened in 1776, is still missing its belfry (a legacy of a protest against a Spanish tax on completed churches). On the opposite side of the Plaza is the 17th-century **San Francisco Church**, older and more ornate than the Cathedral, with the **Museo de Arte Colonial**. A guided tour of the museum includes entry to the church's catacombs. ■ *Mon-Sat 1500-1800, US$0.85.*

The **Complejo Belén** comprises the Institute of Culture, a museum, art gallery and a beautifully ornate church, considered the city's finest. Connected to the church is the **Pinacoteca**, a gallery of local artists' work, which was once the kitchen of an 18th-century hospital for men. Across the street at Junín y Belén is a maternity hospital from the same era, now the **Archaeological Museum**. It houses a wide range of ceramics from all regions and civilizations of Peru, samples of local handicrafts and costumes used during the annual carnival celebrations.

Other churches well worth seeing are **San Pedro** (Gálvez y Junín), **San José** (M Iglesias y Angamos), **La Recoleta** (Maestro y Casanova) and **Capilla de La Dolorosa**, close to San Francisco.

The city has many old colonial houses with garden patios, and 104 elaborately carved doorways. See the **Bishop's Palace**, next to the Cathedral; the **Palace of the Condes de Uceda**, now occupied by the Banco de Crédito on Jr Apurímac 719; the house of **Toribio Casanova**, Jr José Gálvez 938; the house of the **Silva Santiesteban family**, Jr Junín 1123; and the houses of the **Guerrero** and **Castañeda** families.

The **Education Faculty of the University** has a museum at Del Batán 283 with objects of the pre-Inca Cajamarca culture, not seen in Lima. ■ *Mon-Sat 0700-1445, US$0.20 (guided tour), also offers tourist information.* The University maintains an experimental **arboretum** and agricultural station.

Excursions About 6 km away are the warm sulphurous thermal springs known as **Los Baños del Inca**, where there are baths whose temperature you can control. Atahualpa tried the effect of these waters on a festering war wound. The baths are cleaned after each user. There is also a flower garden with steaming ponds. ■ *Daily 0500-1930, old baths US$0.85-1.15, new baths US$1.45, sauna US$2.30, swimming pool US$0.60 (take your own towel). You are allowed 30 mins in the baths, which close at 2000. Buses and combis marked Baños del Inca every few minutes from Amazonas block 10, US$0.15, 15 mins.*

Other excursions include **Llacanora**, a typical Andean village in beautiful scenery (13 km southeast; nice walk downhill from Baños del Inca, two hours). **La Colpa**, a *hacienda* which is now a co-operative farm of the Ministry of Agriculture, breeds bulls and has a lake and gardens (11 km southeast). **Ventanillas de Otusco**, part of an old pre-Inca cemetery, has a gallery of secondary burial niches. ■ *US$0.85. Getting there: A 1-day round trip can be made, taking a bus from Del Batán to Ventanillas de Otusco (30 min) or colectivos leaving hourly from Revilla 170, US$0.15, walk to Baños del Inca (1½-2 hrs, 6 km); walk to Llacanora (1 hr, 7 km); then a further hour to La Colpa.*

Peru

A road goes to **Ventanillas de Combayo**, some 20 km past the burial niches of Otusco. These are more numerous and more spectacular, being located in an isolated, mountainous area, and are distributed over the face of a steep 200 m high hillside. ■ *Occasional combis on weekdays; more transport on Sun when a market is held nearby, 1 hr.*

Cumbe Mayo, a *pampa* on a mountain range, is 20 km southwest of Cajamarca. It is famous for its extraordinary, well-engineered pre-Inca channels, running for several kilometres across the mountain tops. It is said to be the oldest man-made construction in South America. The sheer scale of the scene is impressive and the huge rock formations are strange indeed, but take with a pinch of salt your guide's explanations. On the way to Cumbe Mayo is the Layzón ceremonial centre. There is a hostal at the site, **F** per person. ■ *There is no bus service; guided tour prices are about US$7 pp and run from 0900-1400 (recommended in order to see all the pre-Inca sites); taxi US$15. A milk truck goes daily to Cumbe Mayo leaving at 0400 from C Revilla 170. Ask Sr Segundo Malca, Jr Pisagua 482; small charge, dress warmly. To walk up takes 4 hrs. The trail starts from the hill of Santa Apolonia (Silla del Inca), and goes to Cumbe Mayo straight through the village and up the hill; at the top of the mountain, leave the trail and take the road to the right to the canal. The walk is not difficult and you do not need hiking boots. Take a good torch. The locals use the trail to bring their goods to market.*

Sleeping

During Oct there are many school trips, so most budget hotels are full at this time. Similarly at Carnival

Out of town: **L** *Posada del Puruay*, 5 km north of the city, T827928, F Lima 336 7835, postmast@p-puruay.com.pe Historic hacienda converted into a luxury hotel/museum, run on strong ecological lines. Recommended. **AL** *Laguna Seca*, Av Manco Capac 1098, Baños del Inca, T823149, hotel@lagunaseca.com.pe In pleasant surroundings, hot thermal baths in rooms, swimming pool with thermal water, restaurant, bar, disco, horses for hire, tours arranged. Recommended. **A** *El Ingenio*, Av Vía de Evitamiento 1611-1709, T/F827121/822003. With solar-heated water, spacious, very relaxed, fax service, helpful. Highly recommended. **A-B** *Hostal Hacienda San Vicente*, 2 km beyond Santa Apollonia, T822644, hacienda_san_vicente@yahoo.com In an old hacienda, totally remodelled in unique style, lovely surroundings, bar, restaurant, laundry service. **B** *Hostal Fundo Campero San Antonio*, 2 km off Baños road, T821237. An old *hacienda*, wonderfully restored, with open fireplaces and gardens, includes breakfast and a ride on the hotel's caballos de paso. Recommended. **D** *Hostal José Gálvez*, Av Manco Capac 552, at Baños del Inca, T821396. With private thermal bath, good value. There are other, cheaper *hostales* at Baños del Inca.

In town: **B** *Continental*, Jr Amazonas 760, T823036, F823024. Hot water, good restaurant, noisy. Recommended. **B-C** *Hostal Cajamarca*, in colonial house at Dos de Mayo 311, T/F821432, hotelcaj@

Cajamarca

To El Batán
Restaurant & Airport

To San Pedro Church

To Santa Apolonia Hill

To Cumbe Mayo

Tarapacá

Amalia Puga

Apurímac

José Sabogal

Central

University Museum

Cathedral

Del Batán

Municipalidad

Del Comercio

Plaza de Armas

Aero Continente

San Martín

Casa Silva Santiesteban

Aero Condor

San Francisco & Museo de Arte Colonial

Amazonas

Cuarto de Rescate

Dos de Mayo

Junín

Belén Church & Complejo Belén

Bellavista

Archaeological Museum

Belén

Guillermo Urrelo

Eten

Amalia Puga

To Bus Offices, Baños del Inca & the Coast

N

0 metres 100
0 yards 100

■ **Sleeping**
1 Casa Blanca
2 Continental
3 Hospedaje Los Jazmines
4 Hostal Cajamarca
5 Hostal Los Balcones de La Recoleta
6 Hostal Plaza

● **Eating**
1 Cascanuez Café Bar
2 El Cajamarqués
3 El Zarco
4 Salas
5 Up & Down

lanet.com.pe Hot water, phone, excellent food (see below), travel agency next door. Recommended. **B-C** *Hostal Los Pinos*, Jr La Mar 521, T/F825992. Including breakfast, lovely colonial-style house. **C** *Hostal Los Balcones de la Recoleta*, A Puga 1050, T823003, hcajama@correo.dnet.com.pe Restored 19th-century house, all rooms around lovely courtyard, period furniture. **C** *Casa Blanca*, Dos de Mayo 446 on Plaza de Armas, T/F822141. Safe, old building, garden, good restaurant. **C** *Hostal El Portal de Marqués*, Del Comercio 644, T/F828464, portalmarq@telematic.com.pe Also in converted colonial house, hot water, TV, safe, laundry, bar and restaurant. **D** *Hostal Atahualpa*, Pasaje Atahualpa 686, T822157. Hot water morning only, good value. **D** *Hospedaje Los Jazmines*, Amazonas 775, T821812. In a converted colonial house with a pleasant courtyard and café, some rooms with bath. Recommended. **D** *Hostal San Lorenzo*, Amazonas 1070, T822909, T/F926433. With hot water, helpful. **E** *Colonial Inn*, Av Los Héroes 350, T/F925300. Hot water, shared bath, English spoken, 24 hr attention. **E** *Hostal Delfort*, Apurímac 851. Near market, spacious, good value. **E** *Hostal Dos de Mayo*, Dos de Mayo 585, T822527. Shared bath, hot water morning and evening, good value *menú* in restaurant. Recommended. **E** *Hostal Plaza*, Plaza de Armas 669, T822058. Old building, mainly large rooms with many beds, private balcony (**F** without bath), hot water but poor supply, quiet. Recommended (especially rooms 4 and 12), with new annex (dirty but is open at 0200). **F** *Hostal La Merced*, Chanchamayo 140, T822171. Small, warm water on request, no towel, soap or paper, laundry facilities, good value. **F** *Hostal San José*, Angamos 358, T922002. Shared bath, basic, hot water, good value.

Mid-range: *El Batán Gran Bufet*, Del Batán 369. Great food, international dishes, good wine list, local dishes on non-tourist menu, some staff speak English, live music at weekends, art gallery on 2nd floor, Dutch owner, recommended. *El Cajamarqués*, Amazonas 770. Excellent, elegant colonial building, garden full of exotic birds. *Los Faroles*, Jr Dos de Mayo 311, in *Hostal Cajamarca*. Local specialities, informal. Recommended, *peña* in the evening. *Om-Gri*, San Martín 360, near Plaza de Armas, Italian dishes. Recommended. **Cheap**: *El Marengo*, Junín 1201. Pizzas from wood-burning oven. *Pizzería Vaca Loca*, San Martín 330. All types of Italian food, good, usually busy. *El Real Plaza*, Jr Dos de Mayo 569. Good. *Salas*, on Plaza, fast service, good, local food, best *tamales* in town. *Chifa Tenkentala*, Amalia Puga 531. Recommended Chinese. *El Zarco*, Jr Del Batán 170. Very popular, also has short *chifa* menu, good vegetarian dishes and fish. Unnamed restaurant at *Del Batán 368*, run by Sra Rosana D'Avila. Good value, tasty breakfasts and set lunches, also dinner.

Cafés and bars *Las Almendras*, Amazonas 801. Opens early for breakfast. *Cascanuez Café Bar*, Amalia Puga 554, near Cathedral. Great cakes, extensive menu including *humitas*. *Café Christian*, Del Comercio 719, 1 block from Plaza de Armas. Good value, cosy, TV. *Danubio*, San Sebastián 128, near Plaza Toribio Casanova. Good breakfast for US$1.45. *Los Maderos*, Amazonas 807, local specialities and *peña*, open 2100-0300 Mon-Sun. *Las Rocas*, Dos de Mayo 797. Excellent sandwiches, cheap. *Up & Down*, Tarapacá 782. Pub, *peña* and disco, lively Fri and Sat, open Thu-Sun, entry US$1.50 *Heladería Holanda*, Amalia Puga 657 on the Plaza de Armas, T830113. Dutch-owned, "easily the best ice-creams in Cajamarca, sit back and indulge". The area is renowned for its cheese, *manjar blanco*, butter, honey, etc: try *La Pauca* at Amazonas 713, *Manos Cajamarquiñas* at Tarapacá 628, or *La Colpa*, Amazonas 688.

Eating
For early breakfasts go to the market

The pre-Lent Carnival is very spectacular and regarded as one of the best in the country; it is also one of the most raucous. In Porcón, 16 km to the northwest, **Palm Sunday** processions are worth seeing. On **24 Jun**: is *San Juan* in Cajamarca, Chota, Llacanora, San Juan and Cutervo. An agricultural fair is held in **Jul** at Baños del Inca; on the first Sun in **Oct** is the *Festival Folklórico* in Cajamarca.

Festivals

Handicrafts are cheap, but bargain hard. Specialities including cotton and wool saddlebags (*alforjas*). Items can be made to order. The market on Amazonas is good for *artesanía*; also daily handicraft market on block 7 of Belén. Supermarket next to *El Cajamarqués* sells almost everything.

Shopping

Peru

Tour operators *Cumbemayo Tours*, Amalia Puga 635 on Plaza, T/F822938. Highly recommended, with tours to Ventanillas de Otusco (US$5 pp), Cumbe Mayo (US$6.50 pp), Porcón agricultural co-operative (US$7), Kuelap and Gran Vilaya (US$30 pp a day, 7-day tour). *Aventuras Cajamarca*, office next to *Hotel Casa Blanca*, T/F823610, run by Jorge Caballero. Recommended. *Inca Baths Tours*, Amalia Puga 807. Recommended for Cumbe Mayo (US$7 pp). Several travel agenices around the Plaza de Armas offer trips to local sites and beyond (eg Kuelap, normally a 5-day trip, US$200 pp). Recommended tour guides: *Rosa Díaz Vigo*, Av San Martín de Porras 425-33, Pueblo Libre, T824904. Specializes in ecotourism, offers trips to all parts of Peru. *Edwin Vásquez*. Ask for him in the *Cuarto de Rescate* or *Hostal Dos de Mayo*.

Transport **Local** Buses in town charge US$0.30. Taxis US$1 within city limits; US$2 to Baños del Inca. Mototaxis US$0.30.

Air *Aero Cóndor* (Dos de Mayo 323, T825674) fly daily to/from **Lima**. Airport 3 km from town; taxi US$1.75, mototaxi US$0.75.

   Buses To **Lima**, 856 km, 12-14 hrs, US$8-10, up to US$20-26 for Cruz del Sur's luxury service, several buses daily (see below). The road is paved. To **Pacasmayo**, 189 km, 5-6 hrs, US$7, several buses and colectivos daily. To **Trujillo**, 296 km, 6½ hrs, US$5-8, regular buses daily 0945-2230 most continue to Lima. To **Chiclayo**, 260 km, 6 hrs, US$4.30-7.20, several buses daily, most continuing to Piura (US$10.15) and Tumbes. To **Celendín**, 112 km, 4 hrs, US$3, at 0700 and 1300. The route follows a fairly good dirt road through beautiful countryside. Also to **Cajabamba**, 75 km, US$3.50, 5 hrs, several daily. Some buses and trucks go to **Hualgayoc, Bambamarca, Chota, Cochabamba, Cutervo** and on to **Batán Grande**, but it's not a well-travelled route.

   Among the bus companies are: *Trans Palacios*, Atahualpa 300, T825855 (Lima, Trujillo, Celendín – old, poor minibuses -and Bambamarca); *Línea*, Atahualpa 322, T823956 (Lima, Trujillo, Chiclayo); *Empresa Días*, Sucre 422, T827504 (to Lima, Chimbote, Trujillo, Chiclayo, Celendín and Bambamarca); *Virgen del Rosario*, Atahualpa 409, T823006 (to Cajabamba, buses not coming from Lima); *Atahualpa*, Atahualpa 299, T823060 (Lima, Celendín, Cajabamba, Bambamarca, Chota); *Emtrafesa*, Atahualpa 315, T829663 (to Trujillo); *Trans Mendoza*, Atahualpa 179, T828233 (to Chiclayo and Bambamarca); *El Cumbe*, Sucre 594, T823088 (to Chiclayo and Jaén). Companies which serve only Lima include: *Cruz del Sur*, Atahualpa 600, T822488; *Cial*, Atahualpa 300-C, T828701. The bus offices on Atahualpa and Independencia are 15-20 mins' walk south of the centre.

Directory **Banks** *Banco de Crédito*, Jr del Comercio 678. Changes TCs US$11.50 commission, cash advance on Visa, Visa ATM. *Banco Continental*, Tarapacá 721. Changes TCs US$10 commission minimum, Visa ATM. *Banco Wiese*, Del Comercio 257. MasterCard and Amex TCs, US$3 commission, cash advances on Visa, MasterCard and Diners Club. *Interbank*, 2 de Mayo 546. Changes TCs, US$5 commission, MasterCard ATM. Dollars can be changed in most banks, travel agencies and bigger hotels. Street changers on Jr Del Batán and Plaza de Armas offer better rates. **Communications** Internet: *Internet Café*, Amalia Puga 1062. Open Mon-Sat 0900-2100, Sun 0900-1300. Post Office: *Serpost*, Amazonas 443, 0800-2045. **Telephone:** *Telefónica del Perú* main office on Plaza de Armas, Jr Del Comercio s/n; also at Amalia Puga 1022, and Amazonas 518; for national and international calls. **Tourist offices** *PromPerú*, Belén 650, T822903. Helpful, open 0730-1300, 1415-1900 Mon-Fri. The University tourist office at Del Batán 289 offers free advice and leaflets, open 0700-1345 daily

The Chachapoyas Region

Cajamarca is a convenient starting point for the trip east to the province of Amazonas, which contains the archaeological riches of the Chachapoyans, also known as Sachupoyans. Here lie the great pre-Inca cities of Vilaya (not yet developed for tourism), Cerro Olán and the immense fortress of Kuelap, among many others. For details of further reading, see page 1295.

East from Cajamarca, this is the first town of note, with a pleasant plaza and cathedral. Festival 16 July (Virgen del Carmen). There is also an interesting local market on Sunday where you can buy cheap sandals and saddlebags.

Celendín
Phone code: 044
Colour map 3, grid B2
Population: 15,000
Altitude: 2,625 m

Sleeping and eating **E-F** *Hostal Celendín*, Jr Unión 305, on Plaza, T/F855239. Colonial, best value, limited hot water, good restaurant. **E** *Loyer's*, José Gálvez 410, T855210. Cheaper without bath, patio, nice. **F** *Amazonas*, J Gálvez, four blocks from plaza. OK, helpful. **F** *Hostal Maxmar*, Jr 2 de Mayo 349, T855414. Cheaper without bath, hot water, parking, good value, owner Francisco is very helpful. Eating places: *Bella Aurora*, Gran y José Gálvez, good. *Jalisco*, Jr Unión, on the Plaza. Good value breakfasts and other meals, but beware overcharging. *La Reserve*, José Gálvez 313, good quality and value. *Santa Isabel*, Jr José Gálvez 512. Clean, OK. There are several others.

Transport **Buses** To **Cajamarca**, 107 km, 4-5 hrs: with *Atahualpa*, 2 de Mayo 707, Plaza de Armas, T855256, at 0700 and 1300 daily, US$3; *Palacios*, Jr Unión 333, Plaza de Armas, at 0645 and 1300 daily, poor minibuses, US$3; *Turismo Días*, Pardo 456, Plaza de Armas, at 0715 and 1200 daily, US$3.50. To **Chachapoyas** via Balsas and Leymebamba, 12-14 hrs (may be much longer in the rainy season, take warm clothing, food and water): *Virgen del Carmen*, Cáceres 117, on Sun and Thu at 1100, US$7.20. Other local transport leaves from the market area.

It is common for buses to leave later than the set time, to break down and to suffer long delays (up to several days) in the wet season

The road is in bad condition to Chachapoyas, and barely passable in the rainy season because of landslides. It follows a winding course through the north Andes, crossing the wide and deep canyon of the Río Marañón at Balsas. The road climbs steeply with superb views of the mountains and the valleys below. The fauna and flora are spectacular as the journey alternates between high mountains and low rainforest.

Half of the bus journey is done at night

There are plenty of ruins around this pleasant town, many of them covered in vegetation. The *Comité Turístico* on the plaza is the place to go for all information on how to reach sites, including Laguna de los Cóndores (see below), for guides and horse hire. There are several basic hotels (**E-F**, eg *Laguna de los Cóndores*, Jr Amazonas, half a block from plaza, cheaper without bath, warm water) and restaurants (eg *Cely Pizza's* on the plaza, great for breakfast and evening meal – no pizzas though). ■ *Buses from Chachapoyas to Celendín pass Leymebamba about 4 hrs after departure; no guarantee of a seat. There are also combis, minibuses and trucks.*

Leymebamba

La Congona, a Chachapoyan site, is well worth the effort, with stupendous views. It consists of three hills: on the easterly, conical hill, the ruins are clustered in a small area, impossible to see until you are right above them. The other hills have been levelled. La Congona is the best preserved of three sites, with 30 decorated round stone houses (some with evidence of three storeys) and a watch tower. The two other sites, El Molinete and Pumahuanyuna, are nearby. ■ *It is a brisk three hours' walk from Leymebamba along a clearly marked trail which starts at the end of the street with the hotels. All three sites can be visited in a day but a guide is advisable; ask in the* Comité Turístico.

At **Laguna de los Cóndores** in 1996, a spectacular site consisting of six burial *chullpas*, containing 219 mummies and vast quantities of ceramics, textiles, woodwork, *quipus* and everyday utensils from the late Inca period, was discovered near a beautiful lake in a jungle setting. All the material was moved to a new museum at San Miguel (3 km south – 30-40 minutes' walk, take the footpath and ask directions constantly, the road is much longer). It is beautifully laid-out, very informative and, in one a/c room, has over 200 mummies. ■ *For further information contact Dr Sonia Guillén, Director, Centro Mallqui Bioanthropology Foundation, Av A Márquez 2014, Jesús María, Lima 11, T261 0095, F463 7875, mallqui@amauta.rcp.net.pe The trip to Laguna de los Cóndores takes 10-12 hrs on foot and horseback from Leymebamba, nine hrs return.*

The road to Chachapoyas crosses the Utcubamba River, passes through **Palmira** and heads north. Before Puente Santo Tomás there is a turn-off which heads east beyond **Duraznopampa** to the small town of **Montevideo**. Another Chachapoyan site is **Cerro Olán**, reached by colectivo to San Pedro de Utac, a small village beyond

Peru

Montevideo, then a 30 minute walk. From the Plaza a clear trail rises directly into the hills east of town to the ruins, which can be seen from the village. Here are the remains of towers which some archaeologists claim had roofs like mediaeval European castles.

Further north are the towns of **Yerbabuena** and **Puente Santo Tomás**, which is at the turn-off for the burial *Chullpas* of **Revash**, belonging to the Revash culture (AD 1250).

The attractive town of **Jalca Grande** (or La Jalca as it is known locally), at 2,600 m, lies between Montevideo and Tingo, up on the east side of the main valley. In the town itself, one block west of the Plaza de Armas, is the interesting and well-preserved Chachapoyan habitation of **Choza Redonda**, which was inhabited until 1964. There is one very basic *hostal*, otherwise ask the mayor. Take a torch. ■ *Combis from Chachapoyas at about 1300 daily (except Sat); 3½ hrs, US$1.85; return from La Jalca at 0500 daily. Or take transport to Ubilón, on the main road north to Tingo, from where it's a strenuous 3 hr walk uphill.*

Tingo

Phone code: 044
Colour map 3, grid B2
Altitude: 1,800 m
25 km from
Leymebamba
37 km S of
Chachapoyas
Market day Sun

Situated in the Utcubamba valley, much of this village was washed away in the floods of 1993. About 3½ km above Tingo in the hills is Tingo Nuevo. There is no running water or electricity in Tingo. **F** pp *Albergue León*, no sign, walk 50 m from police checkpoint to corner and turn left, it's the third house on left (righthand door), T999390. Basic, run by Lucho León, who is very knowledgeable. *Restaurant Kuelap*, at the junction of the main road with the road on the south bank of the Río Tingo. Two other eating places. ■ *For transport from Chachapoyas to Tingo, see Chachapoyas, Transport. There are several combis (from 0500) daily to Chachapoyas. Tingo to Leymebamba takes 2 hrs, US$1.75.*

Kuelap

Altitude: 3,000 m

Kuelap is a spectacular pre-Inca walled city which was re-discovered in 1843. It was built over a period of 200 years, from AD 900 to 1100 and contained three times more stone than the Great Pyramid at Giza in Egypt. The site lies along the summit of a mountain crest, more than 1 km in length. The massive stone walls, 585 m long by 110 m wide at their widest, are as formidable as those of any precolumbian city. Some reconstruction has taken place, mostly of small houses and walls, but the majority of the main walls on both levels are original, as is the inverted, cone-shaped dungeon. The structures have been left in their cloud forest setting, the trees covered in bromeliads and moss, the flowers visited by hummingbirds. ■ *0800-1700, US$3. The ruins are locked; the guardian, Gabriel Portocarrero, has the keys and accompanies visitors. He is very informative. Guides are available; pay them what you think appropriate. Getting there: there are four options: 1) Take a tour from Chachapoyas. 2) Hire a vehicle with driver in Chachapoyas, for example Sr Victor Torres, T777688, or ask at Salamanca y Grau. 3) Take a combi from Chachapoyas to María or Quizanga, US$2.85, or to Choctámal, the mid-point on the 36 km tortuous road from Tingo to Kuelap, which has been improved (see under Chachapoyas for details). You can stay in Choctámal with a family or at the Tambos Chachapoyanos lodge (see below), then walk 19 km (4-5 hrs) along the road to the site. 4) Take a combi from Chachapoyas to Tingo, spend the night, then take the 3½-4 hrs' strenuous walk uphill from Tingo; take waterproof, food and drink, and start early as it gets very hot. Only the fit should try to ascend and descend in one day on foot. In the rainy season it is advisable to wear boots; at other times it is hot and dry (take all your water with you as there is nothing on the way up). There are taxis between Tingo and Kuelap, US$10-20.*

Sleeping and guides Walking up from Tingo, the last house to the right of the track (*El Bebedero*) offers very basic accommodation (bed, breakfast and evening meal from US$6, good meals, friendly, helpful). The *Instituto Nacional de Cultura* (INC) hostel is 100 m below the ruins, with a dormitory for 12, US$1.75 pp, no running water, lovely setting, simple meals available from caretaker. Free camping.

At Choctámal: *Los Tambos Chachapoyanos* (**F** pp with sheets and towels, **G** pp with sleeping bag). Lovely setting, but cold at night. Check if it is open by asking in Choctámal for whoever has the key, or contact the address under Chachapoyas, Tour operators.

Chachapoyas

The capital of the Department of Amazonas, founded in 1538, was an important crossroads between coast and jungle until the 1940s. Archaeological and ecological tourism in the 1990s is slowly bringing in new economic benefits. The modern cathedral stands on the spacious Plaza de Armas.

Phone code: 044
Colour map 3, grid B2
Population: 25,000
Altitude: 2,234 m

Huancas, which produces rustic pottery, can be reached by a two-hour walk on the airport road. Colectivos leave from Jr Ortiz Arrieta y Salamanca; 20 minutes, US$0.45. Walk uphill from Huancas for a magnificent view into the deep canyon of the Río Sonche.

C *Gran Vilaya*, Ayacucho 755, T777664, vilaya@wayna.rcp.net.pe The best in town, comfortable rooms with firm beds, parking, English spoken, all services. **D** *Casa Vieja*, Chincha Alta 569, T777353, casavieja@terra.com.pe In a converted old house, very nicely decorated, family atmosphere, hot water, cable TV, *comedor*, continental breakfast, internet and library. Recommended. **D** *El Tejado*, Grau 534, Plaza de Armas. On first floor, same entrance as

Sleeping

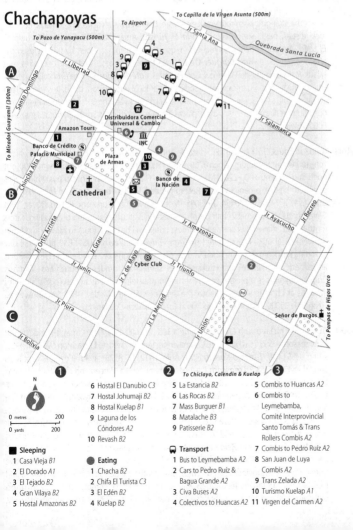

Chachapoyas

To Capilla de la Virgen Asunta (500m)
To Airport
To Pozo de Yanayacu (500m)
Jr Santa Ana
Quebrada Santa Lucía
Jr Libertad
Santo Domingo
Jr Salamanca
Distribuidora Comercial Universal & Cambio
Amazon Tours
Banco de Crédito
Palacio Municipal
Plaza de Armas
INC
Chincha Alta
Cathedral
Banco de la Nación
Jr Ayacucho
Jr Recreo
Jr Ortiz Arrieta
Jr Grau
Jr Amazonas
Jr Junín
Jr 2 de Mayo
Cyber Club
Jr Triunfo
Jr Piura
Jr La Merced
Jr Unión
Pol
To Pampas de Higos Urco
Señor de Burgos
Jr Bolivia
To Miradol Guayamil (300m)
Peru
To Chiclayo, Calendín & Kuelap

0 metres 200
0 yards 200

■ Sleeping
1 Casa Vieja *B1*
2 El Dorado *A1*
3 El Tejado *B2*
4 Gran Vilaya *B2*
5 Hostal Amazonas *B2*
6 Hostal El Danubio *C3*
7 Hostal Johumaji *B2*
8 Hostal Kuelap *B1*
9 Laguna de los Cóndores *A2*
10 Revash *B2*

● Eating
1 Chacha *B2*
2 Chifa El Turista *C3*
3 El Edén *B2*
4 Kuelap *B2*
5 La Estancia *B2*
6 Las Rocas *B2*
7 Mass Burguer *B1*
8 Matalache *B3*
9 Patisserie *B2*

▭ Transport
1 Bus to Leymebamba *A2*
2 Cars to Pedro Ruíz & Bagua Grande *A2*
3 Civa Buses *A2*
4 Colectivos to Huancas *A2*
5 Combis to Huancas *A2*
6 Combis to Leymebamba, Comité Interprovincial Santo Tomás & Trans Rollers Combis *A2*
7 Combis to Pedro Ruíz *A2*
8 San Juan de Luya Combis *A2*
9 Trans Zelada *A2*
10 Turismo Kuelap *A1*
11 Virgen del Carmen *A2*

restaurant, good, laundry. **D** *Revash*, Grau 517, Plaza de Armas, T777391, revash@tsi.com.pe Excellent hot showers, patio, helpful, laundry, sells local items, good local information. Recommended. **F** *Hostal Amazonas*, Grau 565, Plaza de Armas, T777199. Cheaper with shared bath, large rooms, nice patio, no breakfast, basic. **F** *Hostal El Danubio*, Tres Esquinas 193 y Junín 584, Plazuela Belén, some distance from centre, T777337. Hot water, cheaper with shared bath and cold water, meals can be ordered in advance. **E** *El Dorado*, Ayacucho 1062, T777047. Hot water, helpful. **F** *Hostal Johumaji*, Ayacucho 711, T777279, olvacha@ddm.com.pe Hot water, cheaper without TV, meals extra. **E** *Hostal Kuelap*, Amazonas 1057, T777136. Hot water, cheaper without TV, cheaper still with shared bath and cold water, parking. Recommended. **G** *Casa hospedaje Gutiérrez*, Ortiz Arrieta 371, T777513. Shared bath, basic. **G** *Laguna de los Cóndores*, Salamanca 941, T777492. Very basic, shared bath, cold water.

Eating *El Tejado*, upstairs at Grau 534, Plaza de Armas. Good quality, nice view and atmosphere. Recommended. *Chacha*, Grau 541, Plaza de Armas. Popular with locals, good, huge portions. Recommended. *Matalache*, Ayacucho 616. Also good and very popular. *La Estancia*, Amazonas 861. Grill and video pub. *Kuelap*, Ayacucho 832. Good for meat. Recommended. *Las Chozas de Marlissa*, Ayacucho 1133. Good for typical food, pub-type place at night, serves the strangest *pisco sour* you'll ever taste. *Las Rocas*, Ayacucho 932 on Plaza. Popular, local dishes, open Sun evening. *Chifa El Turista*, Amazonas 575. Reasonable, helpful. *El Edén*, Amazonas 828, p 2. Vegetarian, good, large helpings, open by 0830, closed Sat afternoon/evening. *Mass Burguer*, Ortiz Arrieta, Plaza de Armas. Excellent juices, cakes, fruit salads. *Patisserie*, Jr 2 de Mayo 558. Good pastries. *Café de Guías*, in *Hotel Gran Vilaya*, serves snacks, meals and organic coffee, also has lots of local information, good. It is run by Tom Gierasimczuk, a Canadian archaeologist. The bakery at Ayacucho 816 does good breakfasts, open Sun evening when many other places are shut. Try *Dulcería Santa Elena*, at Amazonas 800, for sweets.

Tour operators *Amazon Tours*, Ortiz Arrieta 520, Plaza de Armas, T778294, T999118 (Mob), F777615, amazon_tour@starmedia.com Open 0700-1300, 1500-1900, 2000-2200, Sun closes at 1400, but open Sun evening 2000-2200. Manager Lyndon Díaz Pizarro has a micro bus which takes people to Kuelap, organizes tours. Recommended. *Vilaya Tours*, c/o *Gran Hotel Vilaya*, Jr Grau 624, T777506, F778154, T999095 (Mob), www.vilayatours.com Robert Dover, Tom Gierasimczuk and Gumer Zegarra, long and short adventure trips, often challenging, caters for the 3-star market. Recommended. Most hotels will organize tours to Kuelap and other archaeological sites. Those offered by *Gran Vilaya* and *Revash*, US$11.50 pp for full day including lunch are recommended. The German ethnologist, *Dr Peter Lerche* (T/F778438) is an expert on culture and trekking; he sometimes guides groups. *Los Tambos Chachapoyanos* is a private project setting up hostels near the archaeological sites, for instance at Choctámal and Levanto; the director is Charles Motley, 1805 Swann Avenue, Orlando Fl 32809, USA, in Chachapoyas at Grau 534, www.kuelap.org

Transport **Buses** To **Chiclayo** with *Civa* (Ortiz Arrieta 368), at 1600 daily, 10 hrs (may be longer in the rainy season), US$5.75 (US$4.35 to Chamaya junction for Jaén); to **Lima**, Mon, Wed, Fri 0900, 22 hrs, US$14.40; *Turismo Kuelap* (Ortiz Arrieta 412, T778128), at 1500 daily, except Mon and Fri at 1700, US$7; *Transcarh* (La Libertad between La Merced and La Unión), also has buses to Chiclayo and Lima, 20 hrs, US$30. Also *Móvil* to Lima daily via Chiclayo and Trujillo, US$10. To **Celendín**, *Virgen del Carmen* (Av Salamanca y 2 de Mayo, in *El Aguila*), on Tue and Fri at 0700, 12-14 hrs, US$7.20. To **Pedro Ruíz**, for connections to Chiclayo or Tarapoto, combis (US$1.75, 0600-2000) and cars (US$2.60, US$5.20 to Bagua Grande) leave from either side of the corner of Grau and the small street between Salamanca and Libertad, 3 hrs. To **Mendoza** (86 km), *Trans Zelada* from Ortiz Arrieta 310 (also to Chiclayo, Trujillo and Lima); combis (1000 and 1400, 4½ hrs, US$3.45) and cars (leave when full, 3 hrs, US$5.20) leave from Comité Interprovincial Santo Tomás, Grau, by the cul-de-sac between Salamanca and Libertad. For **Kuelap**: if intending to walk up to the fortress, combis leave daily to **Tingo** between 0900 and 1600, Comité Interprovincial Santo Tomás, 2 hrs, US$1.45; alternatively,

Transportes Rollers, Grau 300 y Salamanca, has combis to **Choctámal** at 0300 ('dirección Yumal') and 0400 ('dirección María') daily, 3½ hrs, US$2, and to **Lónguita** and **María** at 0400, US$2.85, ask the María combi if it will take you to Quizango, the last village before the Kuelap car park. To **Leymebamba**, bus from Grau y Salamanca (vehicle parks on west side, if no one around knock on door opposite), at 1200 daily, 0300 Sun, 4 hrs, US$2. Cars for Leymebamba next to *Rollers* 1300 daily, except Sun, 2½ hrs, 3½ hrs in the wet. To **Jalca Grande**, Comité Interprovincial Santo Tomás, departures about 1300 onwards (few if any on Sat), US$1.75 (return in morning). To **Lamud**, from Comité Interprovincial Santo Tomás between 0600 and 1600, 1 hr, US$1.15, or from *San Juan de Luya*, Ortiz Arrieta 364, also to Luya, throughout the day till 1800, US$1.45. Taxis may be hired from the Plaza for any local destination, eg US$35 per vehicle to Kuelap, US$14.50 to Levanto, return.

Banks *Banco de Crédito*, on plaza, gives cash on Visa card, changes cash and TCs, Visa ATM. *Hostal Revash*, *Distribuidora Comercial Universal*, Ayacucho 940, Plaza de Armas, and the *Librería* at Amazonas 864, change cash. **Communications** Internet: *Cyber Club*, Triunfo 761, T778419. 2 terminals, closed Sun. *Lili@n's Explorer*, Jr 2 de Mayo 445, T778420, US$0.85 per hr. **Post Office:** Grau on Plaza de Armas. **Telephone:** Ayacucho 926, Plaza de Armas, and Grau 608.

Directory

Around Chachapoyas

The Spaniards built this, their first capital of the area, directly on top of the previous Chachapoyan structures. Although the capital was moved to Chachapoyas a few years later, Levanto still retained its importance, at least for a while, as it had been one of the seven great cities of the Chachapoyans as described by Cieza de León and Garcilaso de la Vega. Nowadays Levanto is a small, unspoilt, beautiful colonial village set on flat ground overlooking the massive canyon of the Utcubamba River. Kuelap can, on a clear day, be seen on the other side of the rift. Levanto is a good centre for exploring the many ruins around, being the centre of a network of ancient ruins, fortified redoubts and residential areas.

Levanto

A 30 minute walk from Levanto are the partly cleared ruins of **Yalape**. The local people will guide you to the ruins. Its scale, like that of Kuelap, can only be described as titanic, with many typical examples of Chachapoyan architecture and masonry.

Los Tambos Chachapoyanos have constructed a hostel, which can accommodate 12 people; hot shower, lounge with fireplace and kitchen. Small groups of travellers are welcome and beds and bedding are provided in the mayor's office and village meeting hall. There are two small bar-bodegas in the village.

■ *Levanto is 2 hrs by truck or 6 hrs walk from Chachapoyas by a very poor road. Trucks leave from the market in Chachapoyas most days at 0600, US$0.90; trucks and combis from outside* Bodega El Amigo *on Jr Hermosura at 1400. The nicest way to get there is by the Inca Road, 4-5 hrs. Take the heavy transit road out of Chachapoyas for 40 mins, then take the stone path on the left. It is in pretty good shape, with one 15-m long stone stairway in excellent condition. Ask in Chachapoyas market if anyone returning to Levanto will guide you for a small fee. A taxi from Chachapoyas to Levanto and back, including driver waiting while you look around, is US$14.50.*

On the road to Mendoza via Pipus and Cheto are the pre-Inca ruins of **Monte Peruvia** (known slocally as Purunllacta), hundreds of white stone houses with staircases, temples and palaces. The ruins have been cleared by local farmers and some houses have been destroyed. A guide is not necessary. If you get stuck in Pipus, ask to sleep at restaurant *Huaracina* or the police station next door. There are no hotels in Cheto but a house high up on the hill above the town with a balcony has cheap bed and board. The same family also has a house on the Plaza. The ruins are two-hour walk from Cheto. ■ *There is no direct transport from Chachapoyas. Take a combi at 0930 and 1500 from Jr Salamanca, 4th block down from market, to Pipus, at the turn-off to Cheto; 1½ hrs, US$1.35. A camioneta leaves Pipus for Cheto early morning, US$0.90; or a 2 hr walk on a rough road.*

East of Chachapoyas
40 km from Chachapoyas

Peru

The road east from Chachapoyas continues on to **Mendoza**, the starting point of an ethnologically interesting area in the Guayabamba Valley, where there is a high incidence of fair-skinned people. See *The Peru Handbook* for more information.

Northwest of Chachapoyas

On a turn-off on the road 37 km from Chachapoyas to Pedro Ruíz, is **Lamud**, which is a convenient base for several interesting sites, such as San Antonio and Pueblo de los Muertos. There is **D** *Hostal Kuelap*, Garcilaso de la Vega 452, on the plaza, and, a few doors down, *Restaurant María*, cheap, excellent value, popular, the owner's son is a good local guide and charges around US$10 per day. About 20 minutes' drive south of Lamud, on the same road, is the village of **Luya**, with *Hostal Jucusbamba*, under US$3. From here, more sites can be reached: Chipuric and Karajía, where remarkable, 2½-m high sarcophagi set into an impressive cliff face overlook the valley. Ask for directions in Luya. Best to take a local guide (US$3.50-5 a day). ■ *Buses and combis to Lamud and Luya are listed under Chachapoyas, Transport. The road is unpaved but in reasonable condition.*

Chachapoyas to the Amazon

From Chachapoyas the road heads north through the beautiful river canyon for 2-3 hours to a small crossroads, **Pedro Ruíz** (three hotels; basic restaurants), where you return to the coast or continue to Yurimaguas, making the spectacular descent from high Andes to high jungle. ■ *Many buses to and from Chiclayo, Tarapoto (9-10 hrs) and Chachapoyas all pass through town, mostly at night from 2000-2400. There is no way to reserve a seat and buses are usually full. Combis (US$1.75) and cars (US$2.30) go to Bagua Grande, 1½ hrs. Combis (US$1.75) and cars (US$2.60) also go to Chachapoyas, 3 hrs.*

Pedro Ruíz to **Rioja** (with basic hotels) is 198 km, on a recently improved road. In the rainy season, this and the continuation to Moyobamba and Tarapoto (which is being upgraded) can be subject to landslides. ■ *Pedro Ruíz to Nuevo Cajamarca, US$3.45 (combi), 4½ hrs, then a further 45 mins, US$1.15 to Rioja. There are regular combis to Moyobamba (US$0.85, 45 mins, or US$5.75 from Pedro Ruiz, 4 hrs) from where connections can be caught to Tarapoto.*

Moyobamba

Phone code: 094
Colour map 3, grid B2
Population: 14,000
Altitude: 915 m

Moyobamba is a pleasant town, in an attractive valley. Mosquito nets can be bought cheaply. This area has to cope with lots of rain in the wet season; in some years the whole area is flooded. A road with plenty of transport runs 21 km from Rioja to Moyobamba, capital of San Martín district.

Puerto Tahuiso is the town's harbour, where locals sell their produce at weekends. From **Morro de Calzada**, there is a good view of the area; take a truck to Calzada, 30 minutes, then walk up, 20 minutes. There are Baños Termales at San Mateo, 5 km from Moyobamba, which are worth a visit, and sulphur baths at Oromina, 6 km from town.

Sleeping

A *Puerto Mirador*, Jr Sucre, 1 km from the centre, T/F562050 (in Lima T442 3090, F442 4180, Av R Rivera Navarrete 889, of 208, San Isidro). Includes breakfast, nice location, pool, good restaurant. **C** *Marcoantonio*, Jr Pedro Canga 488, T/F562045/319. Smartest in town centre, hot water, TV, restaurant. **E** *Hostal Atlanta*, Alonso De Alvarado 865, T562063. Hot water, TV, fan, good but noisy, no breakfast. **E** *Hostal Country Club*, Manuel del Aguila 667, T562110. Hot water, comfortable, garden. Recommended. **E** *Hostal Royal*, Alonso de Alvarado 784, T562662, F562564. Hot water, TV (cheaper without), laundry, cafeteria. **G** pp *Hostal Cobos*, Jr Pedro Canga 404, T562153. With bath, cold water, simple but good.

Eating

La Olla de Barro, Pedro Canga y S Filomeno. Typical food, the most expensive but still good value. *Rocky's*, Pedro Canga 402. Typical food, good. Both open for breakfast. Also on Pedro Canga, No 451, is *Chifa Kikeku*. *Edén*, 3rd block of Callao. Vegetarian.

Buses Terminal Terrestre, about a dozen blocks from the centre on Av Grau, which leads out **Transport** of town (mototaxi to the centre US$0.30). To **Tarapoto** (many companies including *Turismo Tarapoto*, T563307), US$2.85, 3¼ hrs. Buses en route from Tarapoto to Pedro Ruíz and Chiclayo arrive at about 1400, except *Mejía*, which has a departure at 1100. **Combis** *Transportes y Turismo Selva*, Jr Callao entre Benavides y Varacadillo: to **Tarapoto** US$2.85, **Yurimaguas** US$6.35, **Rioja** US$0.85; departures 0530-1900. **Cars** to **Tarapoto** (3 hrs, US$6) and **Rioja** (30 mins, US$1.30) from Jr Pedro Canga.

Banks *Banco de Crédito*, Alonso de Alvarado 903 y San Martín. ATM for Visa/Plus. *BBV Continental*, **Directory** San Martín 494. **Tourist office** Dirección Regional de Turismo, Jr San Martín 301, on the plaza, T562043, dritinci-ctarsm@ddm.com.pe Helpful, some leaflets and a map. Information on excursions and hikes is available from the **Instituto Nacional de Cultura**, Jr Benavides 352, which also has a small departmental museum, entry US$0.35.

Tarapoto

Tarapoto is a very friendly place, eager to embrace tourism and agricultural development with a good local market 1½ blocks from Plaza de Armas on Av Raimondi. The road (La Carretera Marginal de la Selva) is in poor shape for much of the 109 km from Moyobamba to Tarapoto, although rebuilding is under way.

Phone code: 094
Colour map 3, grid B2
Rioja, Moyobamba and Tarapoto are growing centres of population, with much forest clearance beside the road.

At 35 km from Tarapoto towards Moyobamba a road leads off to **Lamas** where there is a small museum, with exhibits on local Indian community (Lamistas). ■ *US$0.60, custodian will show you round.* In the town, *Rolly's*, San Martín 925, just off the plaza, serves good food, Rolly is friendly. ■ *Getting there: Colectivo from Tarapoto, 30 mins, US$0.85, from Paradero Lamas on road to Moyobamba (take mototaxi from centre, US$0.45).*

About 14 km from Tarapoto on the spectacular road to Yurimaguas are the 50 m falls of **Ahuashiyacu**, which can be visited by tour from Tarapoto (US$4.50 by mototaxi). Entry is US$0.30 (toilets US$0.15). This is a popular place at lunchtimes and weekends. The entire falls can be seen from the *recreo turístico El Paraíso Verde*, with a restaurant serving typical food, drinks, toilets, swimming pool (US$0.60), also popular. There are many other waterfalls in the area.

A *Nilas*, Jr Moyobamba 173, T527331, nilas-tpto@terra.com.pe Modern, hot water, a/c, TV, **Sleeping** fridge, internet access, pool, jacuzzi, gym, airport transfer, very well appointed. **A** *Río Shilcayo*, Pasaje Las Flores 224, 1 km east of town in La Banda de Shilcayo, T522225, F524236 (in Lima T447 9359). Excellent meals, non-residents can use the swimming pool for a fee. **B** *Lily*, Jiménez Pimentel 405-407, T523154, F522394. Hot water, a/c, TV, includes breakfast and tax, laundry, sauna, restaurant. **C** *La Posada Inn*, San Martín 146, T522234, laposada@terra.com.pe Central, comfortable, hot water, fridge, TV, some rooms with a/c, nice atmosphere, breakfast and lunch. **D** *El Mirador*, Jr San Pablo de la Cruz 517, T522177. 5 blocks uphill from the plaza, cold water, fan, TV, very welcoming, laundry facilities, breakfast (US$2) and hammocks on roof terrace with good views, also offers tours. Recommended. **E** *Edinson*, Av Raimondi y Maynas, 10 m from Plaza Mayor, T523997, T/F524010. Cheaper without bath and a/c, cold water, breakfast, comfortable, karaoke bars and disco. **E** *July*, Jr Alegría Arias de Morey 205, T522087. Cold water, TV, fridge, no breakfast. **E** *Alojamiento Tarapoto*, Jr Grau 236, T522150, alojatarapoto@mixmail.com Cold water, TV, fan, nice rooms, no breakfast. **F** *Hostal San Antonio*, Jr Jiménez Pimentel 126, T522226. With TV, fan, courtyard, no breakfast. Noisy but recommended. **F** *Los Angeles*, Jr Moyobamba, near the Plaza, T525797. Good value, **G** without bath, laundry facilities, restaurant. **G** pp *Alojamiento Santa Juanita*, Av Salaverry 602, Morales (20 mins from centre). New, good beds, fan, spotless, family run, owner speaks English, safe.

The best are *Real* and *El Camarón*, in the same building on Moyobamba on the Plaza, **Eating** expensive. *Las Terrazas*, Ramírez Hurtado, also on the Plaza, typical food, recommended. *Chifa Lug Ming*, San Pablo de la Cruz, Chinese. *Pizza Selecta*, J Vargas 185, for pizza, lasagne

Peru

and chicken. Regional specialities: *cecina* (dried pork), *chorizo* (sausage – good and tasty), both usually served with *tocacho, juanes, inchicapi* and *ensalada de chonta* (see under Iquitos, Eating). Interesting juices are *cocona*, made with cloves and cinnamon, and *aguajina*, from the *aguaje* fruit (deep purple skin, orange inside, sold on street corners).

Transport **Air** US$1.75 per taxi airport to town, US$1.45 mototaxi (no bus service, but no problem to walk). To **Lima**, 1 hr, with *Aviandina* (Moyobamba y San Pablo de la Cruz, T524332), daily, and *Tans*, Plaza Mayor 491 (T525339), daily except Tue and Fri, who also fly to **Iquitos**. *Saosa*, M de Compagñón 468, has flights in small planes to **Pucallpa** and other places. **Buses** Buses to the west leave from Av Salaverry, Morales, 10 mins by mototaxi from the Plaza, except *Turismo Ejecutivo/Ejetur*, Cabo A Leveau in the centre. Many companies to **Moyobamba**, 116 km, US$2.85, 3¼ hrs, **Pedro Ruíz**, US$7.20 (US$8.65 *Turismo Tarapoto*, T523259, and *Paredes Estrella*, T523681), 11 hrs, Chiclayo, 690 km, 22 hrs, US$11.50, Trujillo, 25 hrs, and Lima, US$20. Combis to Moyobamba leave from *Turismo La Selva*, Av Salaverry. Cars to Moyobamba, US$5.75. Buses to **Yurimaguas** leave from the eastern side of Tarapoto, US$3.45, 5-6 hrs, several companies (same price by combi); pick-ups, daily, US$5.75 in front, US$2.85 in the back; cars US$7.20. Truck/pick-up leaves for Yurimaguas (usually 0800-0900, and in the afternoon) from Jorge Chávez 175, down Av Raimondi 2 blocks, then left along Av Pedro de Urzua.

Directory **Banks** *Banco de Crédito*, Maynas 134. Efficient, changes TCs, ATM for Plus/Visa. *BBV Continental*, Ramírez Hurtado, Plaza Mayor, with Visa/Plus ATM. *Interbank*, Grau 119, near the Plaza. Charges no commission on changing TCs for soles. There are many street changers near the corner of Maynas and Jiménez Pimentel, on the Plaza Mayor. **Communications** Internet: Four places close to each other: at San Martín y Arias de Morey, Arias de Morey 109 and 136, and San Martín 129. **Tourist offices** Some tourist information can be found at the **Casa del Turista**, Moyobamba on the Plaza Mayor, which is mostly a handicrafts shop, and at the **Cámara de Comercio**, Moyobamba y Manco Cápac.

Tarapoto to From Tarapoto to Yurimaguas on the Río Huallaga (129 km), the spectacular road
Yurimaguas can be very bad in the wet season, taking 6-8 hours for trucks (schedules above). Once the plains are reached, the road improves and there are more homes. From Yurimaguas on the Río Huallaga, launches ply to Iquitos.

Chachapoyas to the Coast

The road from Pedro Ruiz (see page 1164) goes west to Bagua Grande and then follows the Río Chamaya. It climbs to the Abra de Porculla (2,150 m) before descending to join the old Pan-American Highway at Olmos (see page 1173). The section Pedro Ruíz-Olmos is paved. From Olmos you can go southwest to Chiclayo, or northwest to Piura. **Bagua Grande** is the first town of note heading west and a busy, dusty place with many hotels on the main street. *Restaurant Central* at Av Chachapoyas 1553 is good. Cars (US$2.30) and combis (US$1.75) depart from Av Chachapoyas when full to Pedro Ruíz, 1½ hours.

Jaén Some 50 km west of Bagua Grande, a road branches northwest at Chamaya to **Jaén**, a
Phone code: 044 convenient stopover en route to the jungle. It is a modern city and a rice-growing
Colour map 3, grid B2 centre. Festival, *Nuestro Señor de Huamantanga*, 14 September.
Population: 25,000

Sleeping and eating **C** *El Bosque*, Mesones Muro 632, T/F731184. With fridge, pool, parking, gardens, best in town. **C** *Prim's*, Diego Palomino 1353, T731039, hotel prims@terra.com.pe Good service, comfortable, hot water, internet and computer service, small pool. Recommended. **D** *Hostal Cancún*, Diego Palomino 1413, T733511. Pleasant, hot water, fan, restaurant, pool. Recommended. **D** *Hostal Diana Gris*, Urreta 1136, T732127. Family run, TV, fan, laundry service, café. **E** *Hostal César*, Mesones Muro 168, T731277, F731491. Fan, phone, TV (cheaper without), parking, restaurant, nice. **E** *Hostal Bolívar*, Bolívar 1310, Plaza de Armas, T/F734077. With fan, TV, no breakfast. **E** *Santa Elena*, San Martín 1528, T732713. Basic. **F** *San Martín*, San Martín 1642. Basic, hot water, negligent staff. *La Cueva*, Pardo Miguel 304. Recommended restaurant. There are many others around the plaza.

Transport Bus to Chiclayo with *Civa*, Mariscal Ureta 1300 y V Pinillos (terminal at Bolívar 936), at 1030 and 2130 daily, 8 hrs, US$3.75. To **Lima** (US$17) on Mon, Wed and Fri, 1500, US$13-14.50. Many others to Chiclayo including *Ejetur*, Mesones Muro 410, at 2030, US$4.35, continuing to **Trujillo**, US$7.20; several from a terminal in the middle of the 4th block of Mesones Muro, and *Línea*, Mesones Muro 475, T733746, 1300 and 2300, US$4.35. To **Moyobamba** via Pedro Ruíz (the crossroads for Chachapoyas, 4 hrs) and Rioja: *Turismo Jaén*, R Castilla 421, T731615, US$7.20. Continuing to **Tarapoto**: *Ejetur*, US$10. Cars (US$2) run in the early morning and when full from *San Agustín*, Av Mesones Muro y Los Laureles to **Bagua Grande** (1 hr), where connections can be made for Pedro Ruíz. Combis do the same route (US$1.30) from *Servicentro San Martín de Porras*, Mesones Muro, 4th block.

To Ecuador A road runs north to **San Ignacio** (107 km), near the border with Ecuador (*fiesta* 31 Aug). Combis run from the *paradero* at the northern exit of Jaén, 3½-hrs, good, unmade road (US$3, from 0330 till the afternoon). From San Ignacio a minivan runs to Namballe, 3 hrs, 15 mins before the border (hotel, **G** pp); combis and pick-ups from the border to San Ignacio, 3½ hrs, US$3-4. The border post is called La Balsa, where you cross the river on a boat, US$0.15, until the new bridge is open. To leave Peru, knock loudly on the door of the new immigration building to summon the officer. It may be possible to change money in the immigration posts. Once through Ecuadorean immigration, you can take a *chiva* to Zumba, 3 a day, 1½ hrs on a bad road, US$1.50, and then a bus to Vilcabamba and Loja.

Directory Banks *Banco de Crédito*, Bolívar y V Pinillos. Cash only; ATM (Visa/Plus). *Banco Continental*, Ramón Castilla y San Martín. Cash, US$5 commission for TCs. *Cambios Coronel*, V Pinillos 360 (*Coronel 2* across the street at 339). Cash only, good rates. Others on plaza, next to public phones. Cash only. **Communications** Internet: *Fotocenter Erick*, Pardo Miguel 425. US$1.15 per hr.

Chiclayo

Chiclayo was founded in the 1560s as a rural Indian village by Spanish priests. It has become a major commercial hub, with a distinctive musical tradition (*Marinera*, *Tondero* and Afro-indian rhythms), and an unparalleled archaeological and ethnographic heritage (see Excursions).

Phone code: 074
Colour map 3, grid B1
Population: 280,000

On the Plaza de Armas is the 19th-century neoclassical **Cathedral**, designed by the English architect Andrew Townsend. The **Palacio Municipal** is at the junction of Av Balta, the main street and the Plaza. The private **Club de la Unión** is on the Plaza at the corner of Calle San José. Continue five blocks north on Balta to the **Mercado Modelo**, one of northern Peru's liveliest and largest daily markets. Don't miss the handicrafts stalls (see *Monsefú*) and the well-organized section (off C Arica on the south side) of ritual paraphernalia used by traditional curers and diviners (*curanderos*). Chiclayo's *mercado de brujos* (witch doctors' market) is said to be one of the most comprehensive in South America, filled with herbal medicines, folk charms, curing potions, and exotic objects including dried llama foetuses to cure all manner of real and imagined illnesses. At *Paseo de Artesanías*, 18 de Abril near Balta, stalls sell handicrafts in a quiet, custom-built open-air arcade.

L-AL *Gran Hotel Chiclayo*, Villareal 115, T234911, granhotel@lima.business.com.pe Including taxes and breakfast, a/c, pool, safe car park, changes dollars, jacuzzi, entertainments, restaurant. Recommended. **AL-A** *Garza*, Bolognesi 756, T228172, garzahot@ chiclayo.net A/c, excellent bar and restaurant, pool, car park, tourist office in lobby provides maps, information in English, vehicle hire, jacuzzi. Recommended. **C** *América*, Av L González 943, T229305, F270664. Comfortable, restaurant, good value but laundry and breakfast expensive. Recommended. **C** *Inca*, Av L González 622, T235931, incahotel@ kipurednorte.com.pe A/c, restaurant, garage, comfortable, helpful. **C** *Aristi*, Franciso Cabrera 102, T231074, F228673. TV, fan, comfortable, parking extra. **C** *Hostal Santa Victoria*, La Florida 586, Urb Santa Victoria, T225074. Hot water, restaurant, free parking, cash dollars exchanged, quiet, 15-20 mins' walk from the centre. **C-D** *Eras*, Vicente de la Vega 851, T236333, negotur@chiclayo.net Central, with TV, comfortable, good service, breakfast, laundry, price includes taxes. Recommended.

Sleeping
It is difficult to find decent cheap accommodation in Chiclayo

Peru

C-D *El Sol*, Elías Aguirre 119, T232120, F231070. Including tax, hot water, restaurant, pool, TV lounge, comfortable, free parking, good value. 3 hotels in a row, near the Mercado Modelo: **D** *Kalu*, Pedro Ruíz 1038, T/F229293, Kalu@Hotel.com.pe Comfortable, TV, laundry, safe, good. **D** *Paracas*, Pedro Ruíz 1046, T221611, T/F236433. With TV, good value. Recommended. **D-E** *Paraíso*, Pedro Ruíz 1064, T/F222070, hotelparaiso@terra.com.pe Also comfortable and well-appointed, but can be noisy. Recommended. **D** *Europa*, Elías Aguirre 466, T237919, F222066.Hot water, **F** without bath (single rooms small), restaurant, good value. **D** *Mochicas*, Torres Paz 429, T237217, mochcas1@hotmail.com Fan, TV, helpful, good service. **D** *Santa Rosa*, L González 935, T224411, F236242. Hot water, fan, laundry service, international phone service, good breakfast downstairs in snack bar. Recommended. **D** *Hostal Sicán*, MM Izaga 356, T237618, F233417. TV, comfortable, welcoming. Recommended. **E** *Sol Radiante*, Izaga 392, T237858, robertoiza@mixmail.com Hot water, comfortable, pleasant. **E** *Tumi de Oro*, L Prado 1145, T227108. Cheaper without bath, cold water, noisy but generally OK, good restaurant downstairs. **F** *Aries II*, Av Pedro Ruíz 937, T235235. Shared bath, cold water. **F** *Royal*, San José 787, on the Plaza, T233421. A big, rambling old building, a bit seedy and rundown, the rooms on the street have a balcony but are noisy. **F-G** *Hostal San José*, Juan Cuglievan 1370, 1 block from the Mercado Modelo. Basic, acceptable, cold water. There are many other cheap hotels near the

Chiclayo

To Combis to Tucúme (2 blocks)
To Combis to Batán Grande (1 block)

Peru

N

0 metres 100
0 yards 100

■ Sleeping
1 Adriático *B3*
2 América *B2*
3 Aristi *C1*
4 El Sol *B1*
5 Eras *B2*
6 Europa *B2*
7 Garza *C3*
8 Gran Chiclayo *B1*
9 Hostal San José *A2*
10 Hostal Sicán *C2*
11 Inca *B2*
12 Kalu *A3*
13 Paracas *A3*
14 Paraíso *A3*
15 Royal *B3*
16 Santa Rosa *B2*
17 Sol Radiante *C2*
18 Tumi de Oro *B3*

● Eating
1 Boulevar *B2*
2 D'Onofrio *C3*
3 El Rancho *B3*
4 Govinda *B3*
5 Hebrón *C3*
6 Kaprichos *A3*
7 La Panadería *B2*
8 La Parra *C3*
9 Las Américas *B3*
10 Mi Tía *B2*
11 Romana *C3*

🚌 Transport
1 Brüning Express to Lambayeque *B1*
2 Civa *C3*
3 Colectivos to Lambayeque *A2*
3 Colectivos to Monsefú *A3*
5 Colectivos to Puerto Etén *A3*
6 Combis to Pimental *A2, B1*
7 Cruz del Sur *C3*
8 Emtrafesa *C3*
9 Flores/Cial *C3*
10 Línea *C2*
11 Olano Oltursa *B1*
12 Paredes Estrella *C3*
13 Tepsa *C2*
14 Transportes Chiclayo *B1*

Mercado Modelo. **G** pp *Adriático*, Av Balta 1009. Fairly clean but basic, cold water.

Expensive: *Fiesta*, Av Salaverry 1820 in 3 de Octubre suburb, T201970. Local specialities, first **Eating**
class. *El Huaralino*, La Libertad 155, Santa Victoria. Wide variety, international and creole.
Mid-range: *Che Claudio*, Bolognesi 334, T237426. *Parrillada* with reasonable *empanadas* and
house wine. *Las Américas*, Aguirre 824. Open 0700-0200, good service. Recommended. For
more upmarket than average chicken, but also local food and *parrilla*, are *Hebrón*, Balta 605,
and *El Rancho*, Balta 1115 at Lora y Cordero. *Bar/Restaurante Roma*, Izaga 706. Wide choice.
Romana, Balta 512,T223598. First-class food, usually good breakfast, popular with locals.
Kaprichos, Pedro Ruíz 1059, T232721. Chinese, delicious, huge portions. *La Parra*, Izaga 752.
Chinese and creole, *parrillada*, very good, large portions. *Chifa Wong Kung*, Av Santa Victoria
475, Urb Santa Victoria. Good Chinese. **Cheap**: *El Algorrobo*, Av Sáenz Peña 1220. Good set
lunch for US$1.10. *Café Astoria*, Bolognesi 627. Breakfast, good value *menú*. *Boulevar* Colón
entre Izaga y Aguirre. Good, friendly, *menú* and à la carte. *La Plazuela*, San José 299, Plaza Elías
Aguirre. Good food, seats outside. *Mi Tía*, Aguirre 650, just off the plaza. Large portions, very
popular at lunchtime. In same block is *Greycy*, for good breakfasts, sandwiches and yoghurts.
Govinda, Balta 1029. Good vegetarian, open daily 0800-2000. *Lo Más Natural*, Luis González y
Arica, near market. Sells natural yoghurt, dried fruits, granola. *La Panadería*, Lapoint 847. Good
choice of breads, including *integral*, also snacks and soft drinks. *Snack Bar 775*, Ugarte 775.
Good breakfast, US$0.85. For great ice cream try *D'Onofrio*, Balta y Torres Paz.

6 Jan: *Reyes Magos* in **Mórrope**, **Illimo** and other towns, a recreation of a medieval pageant in **Festivals**
which precolumbian deities become the Wise Men. On **4 Feb**: *Túcume* devil dances (see
below). **Holy Week**, traditional Easter celebrations and processions in many villages. **2-7 Jun**:
Divine Child of the Miracle, Villa de Etén. **27-31 Jul**: *Fexticum* in **Monsefú**, traditional foods,
drink, handicrafts, music and dance. **5 Aug**: pilgrimage from the mountain shrine of **Chalpón**
to **Motupe**, 90 km north of Chiclayo; the cross is brought down from a cave and carried in procession through the village. At **Christmas** and **New Year**, processions and children dancers
(*pastorcitos* and *seranitas*) can be seen in many villages, eg **Ferreñafe**, **Mochumi**, **Mórrope**.

The Brüning Museum, Sipán and Túcume (see Around Chiclayo) can easily be visited by pub- **Tour operators**
lic transport. Expect to pay US$18-25 pp for a 3-hr tour to Sipán; US$25-35 pp for Túcume
and Brüning Museum (5 hrs); Batán Grande is US$45-55 pp for a full-day tour including
Ferreñafe and Pomac; to Zaña and coastal towns, US$35-55 pp. These prices are based on 2
people; discount for larger groups. *Indiana Tours*, Colón 556, T222991, F225751,
indianatours@terra.com.pe Daily tours to nearby archaeological sites and museums and a
variety of other daily and extended excursions with 4WD vehicles; English and Italian spoken,
Handbook users welcome, reservations for national flights and hotels. *InkaNatura Travel*, C
Las Begonias 137, Urb Los Parques, T209948, T/F270797.

Taxis Mototaxis are a cheap way to get around; US$0.50 anywhere in city. **Transport**
 Air José Abelardo Quiñones González airport 1 km from town, T233192; taxi from centre
US$1. Daily flights to/from **Lima**, with *Aviandina* and *Lan Perú*, who also fly to **Trujillo**.
 Buses No terminal terrestre; most buses stop outside their offices on Bolognesi. To **Lima**, *The cheapest buses*
770 km, US$8.65-13, US$15.85 for 1st class service and US$20 for *bus cama*: *Civa*, Av Bolognesi *may not be the*
714, T223434; *Cruz del Sur*, Bolognesi 888, T225508; *Ormeño*, Bolognesi 954A; *Las Dunas*, *most secure*
Bolognesi block 1, luxury service with a/c, toilet, meals, leaves at 2000; *Línea*, Bolognesi 638,
T233497, *especial* and *bus cama* service; *Olano Oltursa*, ticket office at Balta e Izaga, T2377789,
terminal at Vicente de la Vega 101, T225611; *Transportes Chiclayo*, Av L Ortiz 010, T237984.
Most companies leave from 1900 onwards. To **Trujillo**, 209 km, with *Emtrafesa*, Av Balta 110,
T234291, almost hourly from 0530-2015, US$3.45, and *Línea*, as above. To **Piura**, US$2.85, *Línea*
leaves 14 times a day; also *Emtrafesa* and *Cial*, Bolognesi, opposite *Hotel Garza* T205587. To
Sullana, US$4.35. To **Tumbes**, US$5.75, 9-10 hrs; with *Cial*, or *Transportes Chiclayo*; *Oltursa*
overnight service at 2015, arrives 0530 (good for crossing to Ecuador the next day), seats can be
reserved, unlike other companies which tend to arrive full from Lima late at night. Many buses
go on to the **Ecuadorean border** at **Aguas Verdes**. Go to the *Salida* on Elías Aguirre, mototaxi

drivers know where it is, be there by 1900. All buses stop here after leaving their terminals to try and fill empty seats, so discounts may be possible.

To **Cajamarca**, 260 km; *Línea*, normal 2200, US$5.20, *bus cama* 2245 US$7.20; many others from Tepsa terminal, Bolognesi y Colón, eg *El Cumbe*, T272245, 3 a day, US$4.30, *Días*, T224448. To **Chachapoyas**, 230 km: *Civa* 1630 daily, 10-11 hrs, US$5.75; *Turismo Kuelap*, in Tepsa station, 1830 daily, US$7. To **Jaén**, US$4.35: *Civa* at 1100, 2100, 8 hrs; *Señor de Huamantanga*, in Tepsa station, T274869, 1145, 2230 daily; *Turismo Jaén*, in Tepsa station, 7 a day. To **Tarapoto**, 18 hrs, US$11.50, and **Yurimaguas**, 25 hrs, with *Paredes Estrella*, T204879, in Cruz de Chalpón station, Balta y Bolognesi; also *Sol Peruano* in Tepsa station, T270913.

Directory

Beware of counterfeit bills, especially among street changers on 6th block of Balta, on Plaza de Armas and 7th block of MM Izaga

Airline offices *Aero Continente* and *Aviandina*, Elías Aguirre 712, T209916. **Banks** *Banco de Crédito*, Balta 630, no commission on TCs for US$100 or more (US$12 commission if less), cash on Visa, Visa ATM. *Banco Wiese Sudameris*, Balta 625, changes Amex TCs, cash advance on Visa card, ATM for Visa/Plus. *Banco Santander*, Izaga y Balta, changes Amex TCs. *Interbank*, on Plaza de Armas, no commission on TCs, OK rate, good rates for cash, MasterCard ATM. *NBK*, Elías Aguirre 275 on Plaza, Unicard ATM but no exchange facilities. **Communications** Internet: Lots of places, particularly on San José and Elías Aguirre, average price US$0.60 per hr. *Africa Café*, San José 473, T229431, with café downstairs. *Internet 20*, San José y Luis González. *Ciber Café Internet*, MM Izaga 716. **Post Office:** on 1 block of Aguirre, 6 blocks from Plaza. **Telephone:** *Telefónica*, headquarters at Aguirre 919; bank of phone booths on 7th block of 7 de Enero behind Cathedral for international and collect calls. Phone card sellers hang around here. **Cultural centres** Instituto Peruano Británico, Av 7 de Enero 256, T227521. **Instituto Nacional de la Cultura**, Av L González 375, T237261, occasional poetry readings, information on local archaeological sites, lectures, etc. **Instituto de Cultura Peruano-Norteamericana**, Av Izaga 807, T231241. **Alianza Francesa**, Cuglievan 644, T236013. **Medical services** Ambulance: *Max Salud*, 7 de Enero 185, T234032, F226501, maxsalud@telematic.edu.com **Tourist offices** Centro de Información Turística, CIT, Sáenz Peña 838, T238112. **Indecopi**, Av Balta 506, T209021, F238081, odicix@indecopi.gob.pe Mon-Fri 0800-1300, 1630-1930, for complaints and tourist protection. The **tourist police**, Av Sáenz Peña 830, T236700 ext 311, 24 hrs a day, are very helpful and may store luggage and take you to the sites themselves. There are tourist kiosks on the Plaza and outside *El Rancho* restaurant on Balta. For local news and occasional tourist information on specific places in Spanish, www.laindustria.com (website of the local newspaper). Another site to try is www.bcm.notrix.net/lambayeque

Around Chiclayo

Lambayeque

A multisite entrance ticket is available for US$4.35 covering most of the sites mentioned below. It can be bought at the INC in Chiclayo or any of the sites themselves

About 12 km northwest from Chiclayo is Lambayeque, its narrow streets lined by colonial and republican houses, many retaining their distinctive wooden balconies and wrought iron grill-work over the windows. For example, on 8 de Octubre are **Casona Iturregui Aguilarte**, No 410, and, at No 328, **Casona Cúneo** with the only decorated façade in the town; opposite is **Casona Descalzi**, perhaps the best preserved. On Calle 2 de Mayo see especially **Casa de la Logia o Montjoy/Munyeo**, whose 64 m long balcony is said to be the longest in the colonial Americas. Also of interest is the 16th-century **Complejo Religioso Monumental de San Pedro** and the baroque church of the same name which stands on the **Plaza de Armas 27 de Diciembre**.

The reason most people visit is the highly recommended **Brüning Archaeological Museum**, in an impressive modern building. It specializes in Mochica, Lambayeque/Sicán and Chimú cultures, and has a fine collection of Sipán and Lambayeque gold. The magnificent treasure from the tomb of a Moche warrior priest, the Lord of Sipán, and his physical remains found at Sipán in 1987 (see below), are housed here. ■ *Daily 0900-1700, US$2.85, guided tour in Spanish extra US$2.85, most exhibits labelled in English.* Three blocks east is a new **Museo de las Tumbas Reales de Sipán**, due open in late 2002.

There are four hotels in the town (*Jopami*, Grau 143, T282367, *Karla*, Huamachuco 758, T282930, *Lambayeque*, Tarapacá 261, T283474, all **E**, and **F** pp *La Posada*, Panamericana Norte Km 780, quiet, safe, cold water) and several good restaurants. ■ *Colectivos from Chiclayo US$0.50, 20 mins, leave from Pedro Ruíz at the junction with Av Ugarte. Also* Brüning Express *combis from Vicente de la Vega entre Angamos y Av L Ortiz, every 15 mins, US$0.20.*

Sipán

At this imposing complex a short distance east of Chiclayo, excavations since 1987 in one of three crumbling pyramids have brought to light a cache of funerary objects considered to rank among the finest examples of precolumbian art. Peruvian archaeologist Walter Alva, leader of the dig, continues to probe the immense mound that has revealed no less than 12 royal tombs filled with 1,800-year-old offerings worked in precious metals, stone, pottery and textiles of the Moche culture (circa AD 1-750). In the most extravagant Moche tomb discovered, El Señor de Sipán, a priest was found clad in gold (ear ornaments, breast plate, etc), with turquoise and other valuables. A site museum features photos and maps of excavations, technical displays and replicas of some finds.

Following the four-year restoration of the principal treasures in Germany, the Lord of Sipán's physical remains and extraordinary funerary paraphernalia spent some time in the Museo de la Nación in Lima before being returned to Lambayeque in 1999. In another tomb were found the remnants of what is thought to have been a priest, sacrificed llama and a dog, together with copper decorations. In 1989 another richly appointed, unlooted tomb contained even older metal and ceramic artefacts associated with what was probably a high-ranking shaman or spiritual leader, called 'The Old Lord of Sipán'. Tomb contents are being restored in the Brüning Museum. Three tombs are on display, containing replicas of the original finds. Replicas of the Old Lord and the Priest are awaited. You can wander around the previously excavated areas to get an idea of the construction of the burial mound and adjacent pyramids. For a good view, climb the large pyramid across from the Sipán excavation. Nearby is **F** *Parador Turística*, two rooms, meals possible, camping and use of facilities for US$1 per person.

■ *The site museum is open 0800-1700, entrance for tombs and museum is US$2.*
Getting there: Buses to Sipán leave from Terminal Este Sur-Nor Este on C Nicolás de

Chiclayo area

Piérola, east of the city (take a taxi there, US$1; it can be a dangerous area), US$0.40, 1 hr; guide at site US$2.85 (may not speak English). To visit the site takes about 3-4 hrs.

Túcume About 35 km north of Chiclayo, beside the old Panamericana to Piura, lie the ruins of this vast city built over 1,000 years ago. A short climb to the two *miradores* on **Cerro La Raya** (or **El Purgatorio**) offers the visitor an unparalleled panoramic vista of 26 major pyramids, platform mounds, walled citadels and residential compounds flanking a ceremonial centre and ancient cemeteries. One of the pyramids, Huaca Larga, where excavations were undertaken from 1987-92, is the longest adobe structure in the world, measuring 700 m long, 280 m wide and over 30 m high. There is no evidence of occupation of Túcume previous to the Lambayeque people who developed the site between AD 1000 and 1375 until the Chimú conquered the region, establishing a short reign until the arrival of the Incas around 1470. The Incas built on top of the existing structure of **Huaca Larga** using stone from Cerro La Raya. Among the other pyramids which make up this huge complex are: **Huaca El Mirador** (90 m by 65 m, 30 m high), **Huaca Las Estacas**, **Huaca Pintada** and **Huaca de las Balsas** which is thought to have housed people of elevated status such as priests. (Do not climb on the fragile adobe structures.)

Excavations at the site, which were once led by the late Norwegian explorer-archaeologist Thor Heyerdahl of *Kon-Tiki* fame, challenged many conventional views of ancient Peruvian culture. Some suspect that it will prove to be a civilization centre greater than Chan Chán. **A site museum** (same entrance as site), contains architectural reconstructions, photographs and drawings. ■ *Site closes at 1630, US$2; guides at the site charge, US$2.85.*

The town of Túcume is a 10-15 minute walk from the site. On the plaza is the interesting **San Pedro Church**. The surrounding countryside is pleasant for walks and swimming in the river. *Fiesta de la Purísima Concepción*, the festival of the town's patron saint, is eight days prior to Carnival in February, and also in September. ■ *Combis go from Chiclayo, Angamos y Manuel Pardo, US$1.50, 1 hr; a combi from Túcume to the village of Come passes the ruins, hourly. Chiclayo-Túcume transport passes the Brüning Museum; combi Túcume-Brüning Museum, US$0.35, 30 mins.*

Batán Grande, 50 km from Chiclayo, has revealed several sumptuous tombs dating to the middle Sicán period, AD 900-1100. The ruins comprise some 50 adobe pyramids, where some of the best examples of precolumbian gold artefacts, notably the 915-g Tumi (ceremonial knife), were found. The site, in 300 ha of desert-thorn forest of mezquite (*Prosopis pallida*), is now a national sanctuary and is protected by police. ■ *Getting there: colectivos, US$1.20, leave from 7 de Enero block 15 and J Fanning to the main square of the sugar cane co-operative (in which the ruins are set). You must get permission to visit the site from the co-operative (need to speak Spanish and to pay), and go with site archaeologist; Mon-Fri only; private car (taxi) from co-operative to site, US$7-9. Need full day to visit; impossible in wet season, Jan-Mar. Seek sound advice before you go or go with a tour company.*

The colonial town of **Ferreñafe**, northeast of Chiclayo, is worth a visit, especially for its new museum designed to house objects of the Sicán (Lambayeque) culture from Batán Grande (excellent exhibits, knowledgeable staff, but little English spoken). ■ *From the colectivo terminal ask driver to take you to the museum.* The traditional town of **Monsefú**, southwest, is known for handicrafts; good market, four blocks from the plaza. ■ *Handicraft stalls open when potential customers arrive (see also Festivals above).* **Mórrope**, on the Pan-American Highway north of Chiclayo still produces pottery using prehispanic techniques. The beautifully restored 16th-century **Capilla de la Ramada Las Animas** is on the plaza. The ruined Spanish town of **Zaña**, 51 km south of Chiclayo, was destroyed by floods in 1726, and sacked by English pirates on more than one occasion. There are ruins of five colonial churches and the convents of San Agustín, La Merced and San Francisco.

West of Chiclayo are three ports serving the Chiclayo area. The most southerly is **Puerto Etén**, a quaint port 24 km by road from Chiclayo. In the adjacent roadstead, Villa de Etén, panama hats are the local industry. **Pimentel**, north of Etén, is a beach resort which gets very crowded on Sunday. You can walk along the decaying pier for US$0.25. There are three hotels (**F**) and several seafood restaurants. The surfing between Pimentel and the Bayovar Peninsula is excellent, reached from Chiclayo (14½ km) by road branching off from the Pan-American Highway. Sea-going reed boats (*caballitos de totora*) are used by fishermen and may be seen returning in the late afternoon. At nearby **Santa Rosa**, fishermen use two groups of boats *caballitos* and *bolicheros* – pastel-painted craft which line the shore after the day's fishing. ■ *All 3 ports may be visited on a half-day trip. It is not safe to walk between Pimentel and Santa Rosa. Combis leave from Vicente de la Vega entre Angamos y Av L Ortiz, Chiclayo, to Pimentel; others leave from González y L Prado, 20 mins, US$0.25. Colectivos to Etén leave from 7 de Enero y Arica.*

On the old Pan-American Highway 885 km from Lima, **Olmos** is a tranquil place (several hotels and *Festival de Limón* last week in June). A paved road runs east from Olmos over the Porcuila Pass, branching north to Jaén and east to Bagua Grande (see page 1166). The old Pan-American Highway continues from Olmos to Cruz de Caña and Piura. At Lambayeque the new Pan-American Highway, which is in good condition, branches off the old road and drives 190 km straight across the Sechura Desert to Piura. There is also a coast road, narrow and scenic, between Lambayeque and Sechura via Bayovar.

North of Chiclayo

    The Sechura Desert is a large area of shifting sands separating the oases of Chiclayo and Piura. Water for irrigation comes from the Chira and Piura rivers, and from the Olmos and Tinajones irrigation projects which bring water from the Amazon watershed by means of tunnels (one over 16 km long) through the Andes to the Pacific coast. The northern river, the Chira, usually has a superabundance of water: along its irrigated banks large crops of Tangüis cotton are grown. A dam has been built at Poechos on the Chira to divert water to the Piura valley. In its upper course the Piura, whose flow is far less dependable, is mostly used to grow subsistence food crops, but around Piura, when there is enough water, the hardy long-staple Pima cotton is planted.

Solo cyclists should not cross the desert as muggings have occurred. Take the safer, inland route. In the desert, there is no water, no fuel and no accommodation. Do not attempt this alone

Piura

A proud and historic city, Piura was founded in 1532, three years before Lima, by the *conquistadores* left behind by Pizarro. There are two well-kept parks, Cortés and Pizarro (with a statue of the *conquistador*, also called Plaza de las Tres Culturas), and public gardens. Old buildings are kept in repair and new buildings blend with the Spanish style of the old city. Three bridges cross the Río Piura to Castilla, the oldest from C Huancavelica, for pedestrians, others from C Sánchez Cerro, from C Bolognesi, and the newest from Av Panamericana Norte, at west end of town. The winter climate, May-September, is very pleasant although nights can be cold and the wind piercing; December to March is very hot.

Phone code: 074
Colour map 3, grid A1
Population: 324,500
264 km from Chiclayo

Standing on the **Plaza de Armas** is the **cathedral**, with gold covered altar and paintings by Ignacio Merino. A few blocks away is **San Francisco**, where the city's independence from Spain was declared on 4 January 1821, nearly eight months before Lima. The colonial church of **Las Mercedes** has ornately carved balconies, three-tiered archway, hand-hewn supports and massive furnishings. **San Sebastián**, on Tacna y Moquegua, is also worth seeing. The birthplace of Admiral Miguel Grau, hero of the War of the Pacific with Chile, is **Casa Museo Grau**, on Jr Tacna 662, opposite the Centro Cívico. It is a museum and contains a model of the *Huáscar*, the largest Peruvian warship in the War of the Pacific, which was built in Britain. It also contains interesting old photographs. ■ *0800-1300, 1600-1900, free.* Interesting local craftwork is sold at the **Mercado**

Sights
Take care around the Plaza de Armas, well-dressed men offering help are reported to be thieves

Peru

Modelo. The small but interesting **Museo Complejo Cultural**, with archaeological and art sections, is on Sullana, near Huánuco.

Excursions **Catacaos**, 12 km to the southwest of Piura, is famous for its *chicha* (quality not always reliable), *picanterías* (local restaurants, some with music, *La Chayo*, San Francisco 493, recommended), tooled leather, gold and silver filigree jewellery, wooden articles, straw hats (expensive) and splendid celebrations in Holy Week. 2 km south of Catacaos is the **Narihualá** archaeological site. ■ *Combis to Catacaos leave when full from bus terminal at block 12 of Av Sánchez Cerro, US$0.25, 20 mins.*

Sleeping

Extremely difficult to find a room in late Jul due to Independence festivities. Water shortages are common

AL *Los Portales*, Libertad 875, Plaza de Armas, T322952, hoteles@peru.itete.com.pe A/c, hot water, pleasant terrace and patio, nice pool, good restaurant, buffet breakfast US$6, the city's social centre. **B** *Algarrobo Inn*, Av Los Cocos 389, Urb Club Grau, T307450, algarrobo@compunet.com.pe Variety of prices, hot water, includes breakfast, cheaper without a/c, TV, parking, restaurant in garden, safe. **C** *Esmeralda*, Loreto 235, T/F327109. Hot water, fan, comfortable, good, restaurant. **C** *Miraflores*, Cayetano Heredia 503 y Av Guardia Civil, Castilla, T327236. A/c, hot water, **E** with fan, comfortable, family run. **C** *San Miguel*, Lima y Apurímac, Plaza Pizarro, T305122. Modern, comfortable, TV, café. **C** *Vicus*, Av Guardia Civil B-3. In Castilla across river on Sánchez Cerro bridge, T322541, F325687. Hot water, fan,

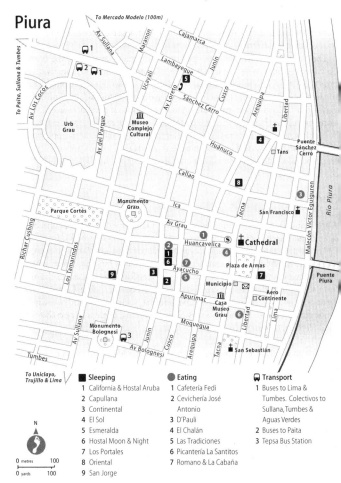

Piura

To Mercado Modelo (100m)

To Paita, Sullana & Tumbes

To Paita, Sullana & Tumbes

Av Sullana

Marañón

Cajamarca

Lambayeque

Ucayali

Av Loreto

Sánchez Cerro

Junín

Cusco

Arequipa

Libertad

Urb Grau

Av del Parque

Museo Complejo Cultural

Huánuco

Puente Sánchez Cerro

Tans

Callao

Parque Cortés

Richar Cushing

Monumento Grau

Ica

Tacna

San Francisco

Río Piura

Malecón Víctor Eguiguren

Av Grau

Los Tamarindos

Huancavelica

Cathedral

Plaza de Armas

Ayacucho

Apurímac

Municipio

Casa Museo Grau

Aero Continente

Puente Piura

Av Sullana

Monumento Bolognesi

Junín

Cusco

Moquegua

Arequipa

Tacna

Libertad

Lima

San Sebastián

Tumbes

Av Bolognesi

To Uniclayo, Trujillo & Lima

N

0 metres 100
0 yards 100

■ Sleeping	● Eating	⌐ Transport
1 California & Hostal Aruba	1 Cafetería Fedi	1 Buses to Lima &
2 Capullana	2 Cevichería José	Tumbes. Colectivos to
3 Continental	Antonio	Sullana, Tumbes &
4 El Sol	3 D'Pauli	Aguas Verdes
5 Esmeralda	4 El Chalán	2 Buses to Paita
6 Hostal Moon & Night	5 Las Tradiciones	3 Tepsa Bus Station
7 Los Portales	6 Picantería La Santitos	
8 Oriental	7 Romano & La Cabaña	
9 San Jorge		

Peru

quiet, parking. **C-D** *San Jorge*, Av Loreto 960, T327514, F322928. With fan, hot water. **D** *Cocos Inn*, José Olaya 197, Castilla, T329004. Including breakfast, cheaper with cold water, converted colonial home in quiet residential area, terrace. **D** *El Sol*, Sánchez Cerro 411, T324461, F326307. Hot water, small pool, snack bar, safe parking, accepts dollars cash or TCs but won't change them, helpful. **D** *Hostal Moon & Night*, Junín 899, T336174. Comfortable, modern, spacious, good value. **F** *Hostal Aruba*, Junín 851, T303067. Small rooms but comfortable, fan on request. Recommended. **F** *California*, Jr Junín 835, T328789. Shared bath, own water tank, mosquito netting on windows, roof terrace, pleasant, brightly decorated. Recommended. **E** *Capullana*, Junín 925. Some cheaper single rooms, welcoming. **E** *Continental*, Jr Junín 924, T334531. Some rooms with bath, comfortable. **E** *Oriental*, Callao 446, T328891. Cheaper without bath and fan, good value but very noisy, TV in reception.

Expensive: *Carburmer*, Apurimac 343 in Centro Comercial. Very good Italian, US$4-5 per dish. *La Cabaña*, Ayacucho 598. Pizzas and other good Italian food. *Café Concierto*, Cusco 933. Pleasant and popular. *Picantería La Santitos*, La Libertad 1014. Lunch only, wide range of traditional dishes in a renovated colonial house. **Mid-range**: *Gran Prix*, Loreto 395. Good food, reasonable prices. *La Carreta*, Huancavelica 726. One of the most popular places for roast chicken. *Chispita*, Sánchez Cerro 210, near the bridge. Good set meal, à la carte, fruit juices. *Cevichería José Antonio*, Junín y Huancavelica. Good traditional dishes and fish specialities. *Romano*, Ayacucho 580. Popular, extensive menu, set meal US$1.75. Recommended. *Las Tradiciones*, Ayacucho 579. Regional specialities, nice atmosphere, also an art gallery. **Cheap**: *Café-Café*, Jr Tacna 376, T301749. Good *menú*, good for breakfast. *Cafetería Fedi*, Arequipa 780. Homely tea-room, good pies, cakes and coffee. *Chifa Canton*, Libertad 377. Excellent, especially won ton soup and special rice, US$2.50 per dish, always busy. *Chifa Oriental*, on Huancavelica, 1 block west of the Plaza. Good. *Bar Román*, Ayacucho 580. Excellent set meal for US$1.75. Recommended. *Snack Bar*, Callao 536. Good fruit juices. *Ganímedes*, Sánchez Cerro y Lima. Good vegetarian, very popular set lunch, à la carte is slow but well worth it, try the excellent yoghurt and fruit. Two good places for sweets, cakes and ice-cream are: *El Chalán*, Tacna 520 on Plaza de Armas; and *D'Pauli*, Lima 541.

Eating
The market on Sánchez Cerro is good for fruit

Local specialities   *Majado de Yuca*, manioc root with pork; *Seco de Chavelo*, beef and plantain stew; *Carne Seca*, sun-dried meat. It's best-known sweet is the delicious *natilla*, made mostly of goats milk and molasses. The *natilla* factory on Sánchez Cerro, Miraflores, 4 blocks from bridge, sells *natilla* and *algarrobina* syrup. Try *pipa fría*, chilled coconut juice drunk from the nut with a straw.

Peru

There are several travel agents around the Plaza. Particularly helpful is *Piura Tours*, C Ayacucho 585, T328873, the manager Mario speaks very good English. Also helpful is *Amauta Tours*, Apurimac 580, T322976, F322277. *Tallan Tours*, Tacna 258, T334647.

Tour operators

Local   Car rental: daily rates range between US$40 for a small car and US$75 for a 4WD; book ahead as availability is limited. *Piura Rent-a-car*, Sánchez Cerro 425, T325510, F324658. *Sun Rent-a-car*, Arequipa 504, T/F325456. *S y S Rent-a-car*, Libertad 777, T/F326773. **Taxis**: *Radio Taxis*, T324509/324630. Taxis in town charge US$1, mototaxis US$0.50.

Transport

Long distance   Air: to **Lima** daily with *Aviandina*, 1¼ hrs. Taxi to airport, US$2 by day, US$3 at night. **Buses**: unless stated otherwise, companies are on Av Sánchez Cerro, blocks 11, 12 and 13. To **Lima**, 1,038 km, 14-16 hrs, US$13; most buses stop at the major cities en route. To **Chiclayo**, 190 km, 3 hrs, US$2.85, several buses daily. To **Trujillo**, 7 hrs, 487 km, US$6.50, only at night; to travel by day, change in Chiclayo. To **Tumbes**, 282 km, 4½ hrs, US$4.50, several buses daily, eg *Cruz del Sur*, La Libertad 1176, T337094, also to Lima; *Cial*, Bolognesi 817, T304250, also to Huaraz and Lima and *Emtrafesa*, Los Naranjos 235, T337093, also to Chiclayo and Trujillo; colectivos, US$8, 3½ hrs (very cramped). Bus to **Aguas Verdes** US$5.50 leaving 2300 arriving 0500. To **Sullana**, 39 km, 45 mins, frequent buses, US$0.50, and colectivos, US$1, from Roma y Sánchez Cerro and Loreto y Sánchez Cerro; to **La Tina** for Ecuadorean border, a further 122 km, 2-3 hrs, US$3; best to take an early bus to Sullana (start at 0630, every 20 mins), then a colectivo. Better to take the direct *Loja Internacional* buses between Piura and **Loja**, 3 a day, 9-10 hrs, US$8.25. The route is Sullana-La Tina-Macará-Loja.

Try not arrive by bus after dark

There is also a connecting colectivo to Vilcabamba from Loja. To **Talara**, US$1.75, 2 hrs, with *Talara Express* and *EPPO* (T331160). To **Máncora**, US$3.50, 3 hrs, with *EPPO*.

Directory **Airline offices** *Aero Continente*, Libertad 951, T325635. **Banks** *Banco de Crédito*, Grau y Tacna, cash and TCs (Visa, Amex, US$12 commission), TCs changed morning only, Visa. *Banco Continental*, Plaza de Armas, changes TCs (US$10 commission), Amex, helpful, open Sun. *Casas de cambio* are on Arequipa block 6; there is another at Ica 356; street changers on Grau and Arequipa. **Communications** Internet: *Compunet*, Grau 499 y Loreto. Also at University, Av Loreto near Huancavelica, and near junction of Tacna y Huánuco. **Post Office:** Libertad y Ayacucho on Plaza de Armas. **Telephone:** Loreto 259, national and international phone and fax; also at Ovalo Grau 483. **Consulates** Honorary British Consul, c/o American Airlines, Hancavelica 223, T305990, F333300. Mon-Fri 0900-1300, 1600-1900. **Honorary German Consul**, Jutta Moritz de Irazola, Las Amapolas K6, Urb Miraflores, Casilla 76, T332920, F320310. **Tourist offices** Information at the **Dirección Regional de Turismo**, Av Fortunato Chirichigno, Urb San Eduardo, T334328, at the north end of town, helpful when there are problems, open 0900-1300, 1600-1800.

Paita

Phone code: 074
Colour map 3, grid A1
Population: 51,500

The port for the area, 50 km from Piura, Paita exports cotton, cotton seed, wool and flax. Built on a small beach, flanked on three sides by a towering, sandy bluff, it is connected with Piura and Sullana by paved highways. It is a fishing port with a long history. Several colonial buildings survive, but in poor condition. Bolívar's mistress, Manuela Sáenz, lived the last 24 years of her life in Paita, after being exiled from Quito. She supported herself until her death in 1856 by weaving, embroidering and making candy, after refusing the fortune left her by her husband. Her house is on the road into town, adjoining a petrol station.

On a bluff looming over Paita is a small colonial fortress built to repel pirates. Paita was a port of call for Spanish shipping en route from Lima to Panama and Mexico. It was a frequent target for attack, from Drake (1579) to Anson (1741).

Sleeping and eating **E** *El Faro*, Junín 322, T611076. Small and clean. **E** *Hotel Las Brisas*, Aurora 201, T611023. On sea front, best, modern. **Chifa Hong Kong**, Jr Junín 358, renowned locally for authentic Chinese food. The restaurant on 2nd floor of Club Liberal building, Jorge Chávez 161, serves good fish, seafood and crêpes, good value.

Transport From Piura, *Trans Dora*, Sánchez Cerro 1387, every 20 mins, 1 hr, US$0.75; *Transportes San Fernando* and *Santiesteban*, close by, offer cheaper, slower stopping sevices.

Sullana

Phone code: 074
Colour map 3, grid A1
Population: 154,800
39 km N of Piura

Built on a bluff over the fertile Chira valley, this is a busy, modern place. San Martín is the main commercial street. Attractive parks and monuments were added in 1994/5. The local fiesta and agricultural fair is *Reyes*, held on 5-29 January.

Sleeping
Take care by the market and where colectivos leave for the border. Do not arrive in town at night

A *Hostal La Siesta*, Av Panamericana 400, T/F502264. At entrance to town, hot water, fan, **B** with cold water, pool, restaurant, laundry. **D** *El Churre*, Tarapacá 501, T507006. TV, laundry, café. Recommended. **E** *Hostal Lion's Palace*, Grau 1030, T502587. With fan, patio, pleasant, quiet. **E** *Hospedaje San Miguel*, C J Farfán 204, T502789. Without bath, basic, helpful, good showers, staff will spray rooms against mosquitoes, cafetería. **E** *Hostal Tarapacá*, Tarapacá 731, T503786. Quiet, good.

Eating *Bima Chopp*, Plaza de Armas. Excellent set menu for US$1.25, popular. *Chifa Kam Loy*, San Martín 925. Most authentic of several *chifas*. *Due Torri*, E Palacios 122. Italian and regional, popular with locals. *Pollería Ibáñez*, J de Lama 350. Grilled meats and chicken.

Tour operators *Pesa Tours*, Espinar 301 y Tarapacá, T/F502237, for airline tickets (flights from Piura) and information, helpful and friendly.

Peru

Local Taxis: *Radio Taxis*, T502210/504354. **Buses** Most bus companies are on Av José de Lama. To **Tumbes**, 244 km, 4-5 hrs US$5, several buses daily. **Piura**, 39 km, 45 mins, US$0.50, frequent buses, colectivos, US$1, taxi US$2. Combis to Piura and Paita, 1 hr, US$0.75, regularly from Av Lama. **Chiclayo** and **Trujillo** see under Piura. To **Lima**, 1,076 km, 14-16 hrs, US$9-18, several buses daily, most coming from Tumbes or Talara, luxury overnight via Trujillo with *Ittsa*, US$18; *Cruz del Sur*, Ugarte 1019; *Continental* (*Ormeño*), Tarapacá 1007. To Talara, *EPPO*, Callao y Piérola, 1 block from Av Lama block 3, 1 hr, US$1.25, faster service than *Emtrafesa*, Comercio, 1 block from Lama block 3, US$1, hourly. To **Máncora**, *EPPO*, 5 a day, 3 hrs, US$3.

Transport

Banks *Banco de Crédito*, San Martín 685, will change cash and TCs. *Casas de cambio* and street changers on San Martín by Tarapacá. **Communications** Post Office: at Farfán 326. **Telephone:** telephone and fax at Miró Quesada 213. **Useful addresses** Immigration: Grau 939.

Directory

North to Ecuador

At Sullana the Pan-American Highway forks. To the east it crosses the Peru-Ecuador border at La Tina and continues via Macará to Loja and Cuenca. The excellent paved road is very scenic. The more frequently used route to the border is the coastal road which goes from Sullana northwest towards the Talara oilfields, and then follows the coastline to Máncora and Tumbes.

The border crossing is described as problem-free and officials are helpful. The Peruvian immigration officer can be found at the nearby *cevichería* if not at his desk. The border is open 0800-1300, 1400-1800, better to cross in the morning. For Ecuadorean immigration, see page 980. A bank offers good rates on the Peruvian side. There is one basic hotel in Suyo and two in Las Lomas (75 km from Sullana), but none in La Tina.

Border at La Tina-Macará

Transport Combis leave from Sullana to the international bridge from Mercadillo Bellavista, Av Buenos Aires y Calle 4, which is a crowded market area. They leave between 0400 and 1300 when full, US$3 pp, 2 hrs. The Buenos Aires area is not safe, so it's best to take a taxi or mototaxi to and from here. From the border to Macará is 3 km: walk over the bridge and take one of the pick-ups or mototaxis which run from the border (10 mins, US$0.50). Buses leave the Ecuadorean side every few hours for Loja (5 hrs), so if you are not taking the through bus (see above under Piura), you can go from Sullana to Loja in 1 day.

A new crossing to Ecuador goes east from Piura or Sullana to Ayabaca (225 km northeast of Piura; several *hostales*; bus 6 hrs, US$7), home of El Señor Cautivo de Ayabaca whose shrine is the most famous in northern Peru. From Ayabaca it's 2 hrs to Samanguilla, or 2½ to the frontier bridge near the village of Espíndola (US$3 by public transport). Over the bridge it's 4 km to the Ecuadorean village of Jimbura, from where you can get a pick-up to Amaluza (45 mins).

New border crossing at Ayabaca

Talara, 112 km north of Piura, is the main centre of the coastal oil area. It has a State-owned, 60,000 barrel-a-day oil refinery and a fertilizer plant. Set in a desert oasis 5 km west of the Panamericana, the city is a triumph over formidable natural difficulties, with water piped 40 km from the Río Chira. La Peña beach, 2 km away, is unspoilt. Hotels include **A** *Gran Pacífico*, Av Aviación y Arica, T/F385450. Most luxurious, suites, hot water, pool, restaurant, bar, parking, pay in dollars. **D** *Res Grau*, Av Grau 77, T382841. Near main plaza, possible to park motor bike, owner changes dollars. **E** *Hostal Talara*, Av del Ejército 217, T382186. Comfortable. There are many cheap restaurants on the main plaza. ■ *Buses to Tumbes, 171 km, 3 hrs, US$3.50, most coming from Piura and stopping at major towns going north; several daily. To Piura, 2 hrs, US$1.75.*

To the border at Tumbes

Peru

Máncora

Máncora, a small, attractive resort stretching along 3 km of the Highway is a popular stop-off for travellers on the Peru-Ecuador route, with safe bathing on a long, sandy beach and excellent beaches being developed to the south. Surfing on this coast is best November-March and boards and suits can be hired from *Gondwanaland Café*, US$1.50 each per hour. It is 32 km north of the port of Cabo Blanco.

Sleeping & eating The better hotels are at the southern end of town. **B-C** *El Mar* and *Las Olas*, both on the beach, offer smart, cabin-style rooms with bath, hammocks and gardens, half and full-board rates available. **D** *Punta Ballenas*, south of Cabo Blanco bridge at the south entrance to town, T447 0437 (Lima), **B** in high season. Lovely setting on beach, garden with small pool, expensive restaurant, recommended. **D** *La Posada*, by Cabo Blanco bridge, follow the dry river bed away from the beach. **C** in high season, nice garden, hammocks, rooms for larger groups, meals on request, parking, camping possible, good local knowledge, owner sometimes does tours in the hinterland. **E** *Sol y Mar*, Piura cuadra 2. On beach, basic, restaurant, popular with surfers, shop, internet café. Recommended. **D** *Sausalito*, Piura block 4, T858058. Comfortable, quieter rooms at back, breakfast included. **E-E** *Hospedaje Crillon*, Paita 168, 1 block back from Panamericana in centre, T858001. Basic rooms with many beds, shared bath, plenty of water. Recommended. There are many small restaurants along the Panamericana in the centre which offer a range of fish dishes; even lobster is affordable. *Stephanies*, adjoining *Sol y Mar* overlooking beach, serves *fuentes*, huge plates big enough for two. *Regine's*, in town centre, good for fruit salads and breakfasts. *Café La Bajadita*, is the best place in the evening to hang out, eat chocolate cake or *manjarblanco* and listen to rock and reggae.

Prices can increase by up to 100% in high season (Dec-Mar)

Sport **Horse riding**: German Heidi Ritter hires horses at her ranch, US$4.50 pp for 2 hr guided tour through beautiful countryside, recommended. Take mototaxi or bicycle to El Angolo, then take main road north and turn right after the bridge. After about 1 km, just before the corrals on the right, turn right and you'll see a doorway which leads to Heidi's corrals.

Transport Talara to El Alto (Cabo Blanco), 32 km, 30 mins, US$0.75, continuing to Máncora, 28 km, 30 mins, US$0.75. To **Talara/Sullana/Piura** with *EPPO*, 5 a day, US$3, 3 hrs; to **Tumbes** (and points in between), combis leave when full, US$1.50, 2 hrs.

At 22 km further north of Máncora, at Km 1187, is the turn-off for **Punta Sal Grande**, 2 km, at the south end of beautiful Playa Punta Sal, a 3 km long sandy beach. The town is very quiet in the low season. Mototaxis go there from Cancas on the Panamericana, US$3. **Zorritos**, 27 km south of Tumbes, is an important fishing centre with a good beach (the water is not oily). The first South American oil well was sunk here in 1863. This is the only part of the Peruvian coast where the sea is warm all year. There is a good beach at **Caleta La Cruz**, 16 km southwest of Tumbes, where Pizarro landed in 1532. Regular colectivos, US$0.80 each way.

Sleeping in **Punta Sal**: **B** *Caballito del Mar*, at southern end of the bay, T Lima 442 6229. Very good, pool, restaurant. **D** *Hostal Hua*, on the beach. Older, rustic, camping possible, restaurant. Between Bocapán and Los Pinos, 30 km from Tumbes, is **E** pp *Casa Grillo Centro Ecoturistico Naturista*, Los Pinos 563, Youth Hostel, take colectivo from Tumbes market to Los Pinos, or get off bus on Pan-American Highway at Km 1236.5, T/F074-525207, T/F446 2233 (Lima). Excellent restaurant including vegetarian, great place to relax, 6 rooms for up to 4, made of local materials, shared bath, hot water, laundry, surfing, scuba diving, fishing, cycling, trekking, horse riding, camping available US$3 per tent, highly recommended.

Tumbes

The most northerly of Peruvian towns has a long promenade, the Malecón Benavides, beside the banks of the Río Tumbes. It is decorated with arches. There are some old houses in **Calle Grau**, and a colonial public library in the **Plaza de Armas** with a small museum. The **cathedral**, dating in its present incarnation from 1903, was restored in 1985. There are two pedestrian malls, Paseo de Los Libertadores on Bolívar and Paseo de la Concordia on San Martín, both leading north from the Plaza de Armas. Tumbes is a garrison town: do not photograph the military or their installations – they will destroy your film and probably detain you.

Phone code: 074
Colour map 3, grid A1
Population: 34,000
141 km N of Talara
265 km N of Piura
The water supply is poor

A *Costa del Sol*, San Martín 275, Plazuela Bolognesi, T523991, F525862. Best in town (but avoid noisy front rooms), hot water, minibar, fan, restaurant, good food and service, parking extra, nice garden with pool, helpful manager. **D** *Florián*, Piura 414 near El Dorado bus company, T522464, F524725. Fan. **D** *Lourdes*, Mayor Bodero 118, 1 block from main plaza, T522126, F522758. Fan, roof restaurant, slow service. Recommended. **E** *Amazonas*, Av Tumbes 317, T520629. With fan, noisy, water unreliable morning. **E** *Elica*, Tacna 319, T523870. With fan, quiet, good. **E** *Estoril*, Huáscar 317, 2 blocks from main plaza, T524906. With cold water, OK. **E** *Hostal Tumbes*, Grau 614, T522203. With cold water, fan, good value. Recommended. **E** *Toloa 1*, Av Tumbes 430, T523771. With fan, safe, helpful. **E** *Toloa 2*, Bolívar 458, T524135. With fan, OK. **F** *Cristina*, Mcal Castilla 758, near market, T521617. Basic. **F** *Sudamericano*, San Martín 130, Paseo de la Concordia. Shared bath, basic but good value. Many other cheap hotels by the market. **Camping** is possible near Rica Playa, by the waterfall on Río Tumbes. Ask at the tourist office.

Sleeping
Av Tumbes is still sometimes referred to by its old name of Teniente Vásquez At holiday times it can be very difficult to find a vacant room

Expensive: *Europa*, off Plaza de Armas. Recommended, particularly for omelettes. **Mid-range**: *Latino*, Bolívar 163, on Plaza de Armas. Good set meals (à la carte expensive), *peña* most evenings. *Cevichería El Sol Nato*, Bolívar 608. Delicious seafood dishes, lunch only. Highly recommended. *Río Tumbes*, Malecón Benavides s/n, at east end of seafront. Excellent views of river, pleasant atmosphere, seafood specialities. *Pollos a la Brasa Venezia*, Bolívar 237. Best roast chicken in Tumbes. *Chifa Wakay*, Huáscar 417. Smart, good. Recommended.

Eating

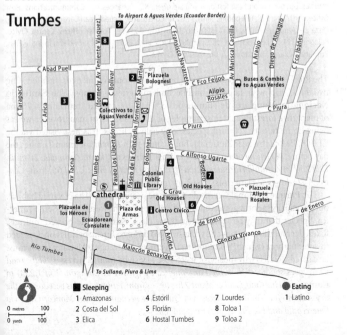

Tumbes

Peru

Sleeping				Eating
1 Amazonas	4 Estoril	7 Lourdes		1 Latino
2 Costa del Sol	5 Florián	8 Toloa 1		
3 Elica	6 Hostal Tumbes	9 Toloa 2		

Cheap: *Juliban*, Grau 704. Good, generous set meal. There are other inexpensive restaurants on the Plaza de Armas and near the markets. *Heladería La Suprema*, Paseo Libertadores 298. Great soya milk ice cream; next door at 296 is *Bam Bam*, for breakfast and snacks. Try *bolas de plátano*, soup with banana balls, meat, olives and raisins, and *sudado*, a local stew.

Tour operators Most companies offer day tours of the local area for US$20 pp, minimum 2, and US$35-50 pp to the hinterland. *Preferencial Tours*, Grau 427. Knowledgeable and friendly. *Rosillo Tours*, Tumbes 293, T/F523892. Information, tickets, Western Union agents.

Transport
A new bus terminal is planned on the north side of the city

Buses Daily to and from **Lima**, 1,320 km, 16-24 hrs, depending on stopovers, US$12 (normal service), US$18 (special), US$22 (luxury service), excellent paved road. Several buses daily, all on Av Tumbes: *Cial*, N 586; *Expreso Continental* (Ormeño group), 314; *Cruz del Sur*, 319, T526275; *Oltursa*, 324 and 359, daily 1330, recommended; *Tepsa*, Tacna 216, T522428, old buses, unsafe, often full, not recommended. For other companies, ask around; cheaper ones usually leave 1600-2100, more expensive ones 1200-1400. Except for luxury service, most buses to Lima stop at major cities en route, although you may be told otherwise. You can get tickets to anywhere between Tumbes and Lima quite easily, although buses are often booked well in advance, so if arriving from Ecuador you may have to stay overnight. Piura is a good place for connections in the daytime. To **Sullana**, 244 km, 3-4 hrs, US$4.50, several buses daily. To **Piura**, 4-5 hrs, 282 km, US$4.50 with *Empresa Chiclayo*, *Cruz del Sur*, *El Dorado* (Piura 459) 6 a day, *Dorado Express* (Tumbes 297); *Comité Tumbes/Piura* (Tumbes N 308, T525977), US$7 pp, fat cars, leave when full, 3½ hrs. To **Chiclayo**, 552 km, 6 hrs, US$5.75, several each day with *Cruz del Sur, El Dorado, Dorado Express, Emtrafesa* (Tumbes N 581), *Oltursa, Trans Chiclayo* (Tumbes N 466, T525260). To **Trujillo**, 769 km, 10-11 hrs, US$9-12, *Continental, Cruz del Sur, El Dorado, Dorado Express, Emtrafesa*. To **Chimbote**, 889 km, 13-14 hrs, US$11. Transport to the Border with Ecuador, see below.

Directory **Banks** *Banco Continental*, Bolívar 121, cash and Amex TCs only, US$5 commission. *Banco Regional*, 7 de Enero, Plaza de Armas, ATM, TCs exchanged. All banks close for lunch. Bad rates at the airport. *Cambios Internacionales*, Av Tumbes 245, cash only, good rates. Money changers on the street (on Bolívar, left of the Cathedral), some of whom are unscrupulous, give a much better rate than banks or *cambios*, but don't accept the first offer you are given. None changes TCs. **Communications** **Post Office**: San Martín 208. **Telephone**: San Martín 210. **Consulates** Ecuadorean Consulate, Bolívar 155, Plaza de Armas, T523022, 0900-1300 and 1400-1630, Mon-Fri. **Tourist offices** Centro Cívico, Bolognesi 194, 1st floor, on the plaza. Open 0800-1300, 1400-1800. Helpful, provides map and leaflets. *Pronaturaleza*, Av Tarapacá 4-16, Urb Fonavi, T523412.

Excursions from Tumbes
Mosquito repellent is a must for Tumbes area

The Río Tumbes is navigable by small boat to the mouth of the river, an interesting two hour trip with fantastic birdlife and mangrove swamps. The **Santuario Nacional los Manglares de Tumbes** protects 3,000 ha of Peru's remaining 4,750 ha of mangrove forest. It contains examples of all five species of mangroves as well as being home to over 200 bird species, especially pelicans. It is best visited via the CECODEM centre near Zarumilla, but arrange with *Pronaturaleza* in Tumbes the day before. ■ *Getting there: Combis run from Tumbes market to Zarumilla, 20 mins, US$0.50. In Zarumilla hire a mototaxi for the 7 km run (20 mins, US$1.50) to the Centre. A 2½-hr guided visit costs US$12, for up to six people.*

The **Parque Nacional Cerros de Amotape** protects 90,700 ha of varied habitat, but principally the best preserved area of dry forest on the west coast of South America. Species that may be sighted include the black parrot, white-backed squirrels, foxes, deer, tigrillos, pumas and white-winged turkeys. *Inrena* permission is needed to enter the area (which *Pronaturaleza* in Tumbes ca arrange). All water needs must be carried which is why most visitors choose to visit by tour. ■ *Access is via the road which goes southeast from the Pan-American Highway at Bocapán (Km 1,233) to Casitas and Huásimo, it takes about 2 hrs by car from Tumbes, and is best done in the dry season (Jul-Nov). Also access via Quebrada Fernández from Máncora and via Querecotilo and Los Encuentros from Sullana.*

The **Zona Reservada de Tumbes** (75,000 ha) lies northeast of Tumbes between the Ecuadorean border and Cerros de Amotape National Park. It protects dry equatorial forest and tropical rainforest. Wildlife includes monkeys, otters, wild boars, small cats and crocodiles. ■ *Access from Tumbes is via Cabuyal, Pampas de Hospital and El Caucho to the Quebrada Faical research station or via Zarumilla and Matapalo. The best accessible forest is around El Narango, which lies beyond the research station.* The Río Tumbes crocodile, which is a UN Red-data species, is found at the river's mouth, where there is a small breeding programme, and in its upper reaches. The Reserve is threatened by shrimp farming and intensive gold mining.

Immigration for those leaving Peru is at Zarumilla, at an office 3 km before the border; for those entering Peru, immigration is at the end of the international bridge, west side, at Aguas Verdes. PNP is on the east side. The border is open 24 hours a day and passports can be stamped on either side of the border at any time.

Border with Ecuador

Peruvian immigration formalities are reported as relatively trouble-free, but if you are asked for a bribe by police officers on the Peruvian side of the international bridge, be courteous but firm. You should ask for 90 days. Porters on either side of the border charge too much; don't be bullied and check price beforehand.

There are virtually no customs formalities at the border for passengers crossing on foot, but spot-checks sometimes take place

Exchange Changing money on either side of the border is a risky business. Rates are poor and cheating is common. Beware forged notes, especially soles. Change only enough money to get to a town with a reputable bank or cambio.

Sleeping If stuck overnight in the border area there is a hotel in **Aguas Verdes**: **E** *Hostal El Bosque*, at south end of town on Av República de Perú 402, shared bath, basic, mosquito nets. Aguas Verdes also has phone booths and airline ticket offices. There are 4 hotels in **Zarumilla**, at Km 1290 on the Pan-American Highway, 5 km south of Aguas Verdes.

Transport **Between Tumbes and the border**: colectivos leave from block 3 of Av Tumbes, US$1 pp or US$6 to hire car, and wait at the immigration office before continuing to the border, 30-40 mins. **Make sure the driver takes you all the way to the border and not just as far as the complex 3 km south of the bridge**. Returning from the border, some colectivos leave from near the bridge, but charge more than others which leave 2 blocks down along main street by a small plaza opposite the church. Combis leave from the market area along Mcal Castilla across from Calle Alipio Rosales, US$0.75, luggage on roof. They leave passengers at the immigration office. Old, slow city buses ply the same route as combis, US$0.40. Combis and buses return to Tumbes from an esplanade 3 blocks east of the colectivo stop, but don't wait at immigration. All vehicles only leave when full. From the border to Zarumilla by mototaxi costs US$0.50 pp. Taxi to Tumbes, including wait at immigration, US$6.

Lots of kids help with border crossing

Transport **Bus**: It is easier to take a colectivo to Tumbes and then a bus south, rather than trying to get on a bus from the border to a southern destination. **Car**: when driving into Peru, vehicle fumigation is not required, but there is one outfit who will attempt to fumigate your vehicle with water and charge US$10. Beware of officials claiming that you need a *carnet* to obtain your 90-day transit permit; this is not so, cite Decreto Supremo 015-87-ICTI/TUR. Frequent road tolls between Tumbes and Lima, approximately US$1 each.

Entering Peru

Peru

Lima

The South Coast

The mysterious Nazca lines, the Paracas bird reserve and Peru's main wine and pisco-producing area around Ica feature among the attractions along the desert coast south of the capital. The Pan-American Highway runs down to Chile, after heading inland towards Arequipa.

South from Lima

Most beaches have very strong currents and can be dangerous for swimming; if unsure, ask locals

The first 60 km from Lima are dotted with a series of seaside resort towns and clubs. **San Vicente de Cañete**, 150 km south of Lima on the Río Cañete, is a prosperous market centre set amid desert scenery. It is commonly called Cañete (festival last week in August). A paved road runs inland, mostly beside the Río Cañete to the Quebrada de Lunahuaná. After the town of **Lunahuaná** (40 km), the road continues unpaved to Huancayo up in the sierra; bus US$9 (see page 1257).

Lunahuaná is 8 km beyond the Inca ruins of **Incawasi**, which dominated the valley. It is interesting to visit the *bodegas* (wine cellars) in the valley and try the wine (the best-known is *Los Reyes*, in the *anexo* of Condoray). *Fiesta de la Vendimia*, grape harvest, first weekend in March. At the end of September/beginning October is the *Fiesta del Níspero* (medlar festival).

Several places offer rafting and kayaking: from November-April rafting is at levels 4-5. May-October is low water season with only boat trips possible (levels 1-2). Excellent kayaking is 2½ hours upriver. Rafting costs US$15 per person for 1½ hours. Annual championships and a festival of adventure sports are held every February. There are several hotels, ranging from **A-B** to **D-E**, and restaurants in Lunahuaná and surrounding districts.

Chincha Alta
Colour map 3, grid C3
35 km N of Pisco

Chincha is a fast-growing town where the negro/criollo culture is still alive. The famous festival, *Verano Negro*, is at the end of February while, in November, the *Festival de las Danzas Negras* is held in the black community of El Carmen, 10 km south. Chincha is a good place to sample locally produced wine and pisco. One of the best *bodegas* is the 100-year-old *Naldo Navarro*, Pasaje Santa Rosa, Sunampe, 100 m west of the Panamericana (free guided tours, including tasting). Other *bodegas* have guided tours.

Sleeping **B** *Hacienda San José*, 17th-century ranch-house, 9 km south of town in El Carmen district, T034-221458 (or book in Lima at Juan Fanning 328, of 202, Miraflores, T444 5242, hsanjose@bellnet.com.pe, credit card payment only). Full board, great lunch stop, buffet recommended, pool, garden, small church, colonial crafts, the tunnels believed to link up with other ranches and the catacombs, where many slaves were interred, can be visited, US$3 pp, very busy at weekends. Highly recommended. In Chincha are **C** *El Valle*, Panamericana in town centre, with excellent *Palacio de los Mariscos* restaurant; **F** *Hostal La Rueda*, near the plaza. Breakfast extra, hot showers, pool, lounge; several other hotels and restaurants.

Pisco

Phone code: 034
Colour map 3, grid C3
Population: 82,250
237 km S of Lima

The largest port between Callao and Matarani is a short distance to the west of the Pan-American Highway. The two parts of town, Pisco Pueblo with its colonial-style homes, and Pisco Puerto, which, apart from fisheries, has been replaced as a port by the deep-water Puerto General San Martín, have expanded into one.

In Pisco Pueblo, half a block west of the quiet Plaza de Armas, with its equestrian statue of San Martín, is the **Club Social Pisco**, Av San Martín 132, the headquarters of San Martín after he had landed at Paracas Bay. There is an old Jesuit church on San

Peru

Francisco, one block from the plaza, separated from the Municipalidad by a narrow park. The newer **Cathedral** is on the main plaza. Avenida San Martín runs from the Plaza de Armas to the sea.

B *Regidor*, Arequipa 201, T/F535220/219, regidor@mail.cosapidata.com.pe With TV, fan, **Sleeping** jacuzzi, café and restaurant, sauna, very good, price negotiable at quiet times. **D** *Posada Hispana Hostal*, Bolognesi 236, T536363, www.posadahispana.com Rooms with loft and bath, also rooms with shared bath (**G** pp), hot water, can accommodate groups, comfortable, breakfast extra, information service, English, French, Italian and Catalan spoken. Recommended. **E** *Hostal San Isidro*, San Clemente 103, T/F536471, hostalsanisidro@lettera.net Cheaper without bath, hot water 24 hrs, safe, laundry facilities, use of kitchen, English spoken, parking. **E** *Hostal Belén*, Arequipa 128, Plazuela Belén, T533046. Comfortable, hot water, recommended. **E** *El Condado*, Arequipa 136, Plazuela Belén, T533623. Hot water, cable TV, laundry, breakfast available, tours to Ballestas arranged. **E** *Pisco*, on Plaza de Armas, T532018, vonlignau@LatinMail.com **F** without bath, lower prices Nov-Mar, hot water, breakfast US$1.75, bar, agency arranges recommended tours to Ballestas and Paracas, parking for motorcycles. **E** *Hostal La Portada*, Alipio Ponce 250, T532098. Free coffee, hot water. Recommended. **F** *Colonial*, Comercio, pedestrianized part. Shared bath, large rooms with balcony overlooking plaza. **F** *Hostal Progreso*, Progreso 254. Communal bathrooms, water shortages, but recommended. **F** pp *Hostal Pisco Playa* (Youth Hostel), Jr José Balta 639, Pisco Playa, T532492. Kitchen and washing facilities, quite nice, breakfast US$1.50.

As de Oro, San Martín 472. Good, reasonable prices, closed Mon. *El Dorado*, main plaza oppo- **Eating** site Cathedral. Good value local dishes, popular. *Don Manuel*, Comercio 179, US$2-4 for main dish. Opposite is *Calamares*, which serves seafood and vegetarian options. *Chifa Chui Cheng*, Callao near Plaza. Soup and main course US$2, recommended. There are seafood restaurants along the shore between Pisco and San Andrés, and in San Andrés (buses from Plaza Belén, near *Hostal Perú*) there are: *La Fontana*, Lima 355, good food and pisco sours; *La Estrellita*; *Olimpia*, Grecia 200; and *Mendoza*, for fish and local dishes; all are recommended.

Taxis on Plaza de Armas. Combis from Repartición (see below), stop at Comercio by Plaza **Transport** Belén. **Buses** If arriving by bus, make sure it is going into town and will not leave you at the Repartición which is a 5-km, 10 min combi, US$0.50, or taxi ride, US$1, from the centre. To **Lima**, 242 km, 3½ hrs, US$3, buses and colectivos every hour. Company offices in Pisco are: *Ormeño*, San Francisco, 1 block from plaza, and *San Martín* at San Martín 199. To **Ayacucho**, 317 km, 8-10 hrs, US$7-10, several buses daily (*Expresos Molina* recommended), leave from San Clemente 10 km north on Panamericana Sur, take a colectivo (20 mins), book in advance to ensure seat and take warm clothing as it gets cold at night. To **Huancavelica**, 269 km, 12-14 hrs, US$7, with *Oropesa*, coming from Ica; also a few trucks. To **Ica** US$2 by colectivo, US$0.70 by bus, 45 mins, 70 km, 11 daily, with *Ormeño*, also *Saavedra* (Callao 181). To **Nasca**, 210 km, by bus, US$5, 3 hrs, via Ica, at 0830 with *Oropesa*, and 3 daily with *Ormeño*. To **Arequipa**, US$12, 10-12 hrs, 3 daily.

Banks ATMs at banks on Plaza, mostly Visa. *Banco de Crédito* on Plaza de Armas gives good rates, for **Directory** Amex and cash; also on Plaza, *Interbank*. **Communications** Internet: *Bill Gates Computer School*, San Francisco, next to church. **Telephone:** telephone and fax office on Plaza de Armas between Av San Martín y Callao.

Paracas National Reserve

Down the coast 15 km from Pisco Puerto is the bay of **Paracas**, sheltered by the Paracas peninsula. (The name means 'sandstorm' – they can last for three days, especially in August; the wind gets up every afternoon, peaking at around 1500.) Paracas can be reached by the coast road from San Andrés, passing the fishing port and a large proportion of Peru's fishmeal industry. Alternatively, go down the Pan-American Highway to 14.5 km past the Pisco turning and take the road to

One of the best marine reserves, with the highest concentration of marine birds in the world

Peru

Paracas across the desert. After 11 km turn left along the coast road and one km further on fork right to Paracas village. The peninsula, a large area of coast to the south and the Ballestas Islands are a National Reserve. ■ *Entrance US$1.70 pp.*

It's advisable to see the peninsula as part of a tour it is not safe to walk alone and it is easy to get lost

Return to the main road for the entrance to the Reserve (ask for a map here). There's an archaeological museum. ■ *Daily 0900-1700, US$1, a shop (guide books, film, drinks), a visitors' centre and a natural history museum.* You can walk down to the shore from the museum to see flamingoes feeding in Paracas bay (boat trips do not go to see flamingoes; in January-March the flamingoes go to the Sierra). The tiny fishing village of Lagunilla is 5 km from the museum across the neck of the peninsula; its beaches are free from sting rays but not very clean. The eating places tend to be overpriced, but *Rancho de la Tía Fela* is recommended. A network of firm dirt roads, reasonably well signed, crosses the peninsula (details from Park Office or ask for 'Hoja 28-K' map at Instituto Geográfico Militar in Lima). Other sights on the peninsula include Mirador de los Lobos at Punta El Arquillo, 6 km from Lagunilla, with view of sea lions; and a rock formation in the cliffs called La Catedral, 6 km from Lagunilla in the opposite direction.

About 14 km from the museum is the precolumbian Candelabra (**Candelabro** in Spanish) traced in the hillside, at least 50 m long, best seen from the sea. Condors may be seen (February/March) from the (bad) road between Paracas and Laguna Grande.

Sleeping & eating

Ask for permission to camp in the reserve, but note that there is no water. Do not camp alone as robberies occur

A *Paracas*, bungalows on beach (T Pisco 532220 or Lima T472 3850, F447 5073). Good food, not cheap, good buffet lunch on Sun US$25, fine grounds facing the bay, it is a good centre for excursions to the Peninsula and flights over Nasca, tennis courts, open-air pool (US$2 for non-residents), also houses the Masson ceramics collection which is worth seeing. 2-hr dune-buggy trips can be arranged for US$25 pp. **C** *El Mirador*, at the turn-off to El Chaco. Hot water, no phone, good service, boat trips arranged, meals available, sometimes full board only, reservations in Lima, T445 8496, ask for Sra Rosa. Camping is possible on the beach near the *Hotel Paracas* at a spot called La Muelle, no facilities, sea polluted. Excellent fried fish at open-sided restaurants at El Chaco (see below), eg *Jhonny y Jennifer*, friendly. *El Chorito*, close to *Hotel Paracas*.

Transport

No public transport on the peninsula

Taxi from Pisco to Paracas about US$3-4; combis to/from El Chaco beach (marked 'Chaco-Paracas-Museo') when full, US$0.50, 25 mins; some of them continue to the museum. The last one returns at about 2200.

Ballestas Islands

Trips to the **Islas Ballestas** leave from the jetty at El Chaco, the beach and fishing port by Paracas village. The islands are spectacular, eroded into numerous arches and caves (*ballesta* means bow, as in archery), which provide shelter for thousands of seabirds, some of which are very rare, and hundreds of sea lions. The book *Las Aves del Departamento de Lima* by Maria Koepcke is useful.

Beware scams, only book tours in company offices not in hotels, nor on the street

Tours For trips to Islas Ballestas: *Blue Sea Tours*, Chosica 320, San Andrés, Pisco, also at El Chaco, guides Jorge Espejo and Hubert Van Lomoen (speaks Dutch) are frequently recommended, no time limit on tours. On C San Francisco, Pisco: *Paseo Turístico Islas Ballestas*, No 109, multi-lingual guide, recommended. *Ballestas Travel Service*, No 251, T535564, recommended. *Paracas Tours*, No 257. *Paracas Islas Tours*, Comercio 128, T665872, recommended. *The Zarcillo Connection*, San Francisco 111, T262795, zarcillo@terraplus.com.pe, also good for Paracas National Reserve. The main hotels in Pisco and Paracas will also arrange tours (eg *Hotel Paracas*, US$18 in their own speedboat, 0900-1700). Full day tour of islands and peninsula US$20 pp ½-day boat tour to islands US$9-10 pp, usually starting at 0730, returning 1100 to avoid rougher seas in the afternoon; out of season tours are a lot cheaper. Few tours include Isla San Gallán, where there are thousands of sea lions. You will see, close up, thousands of inquisitive sea lions, guano birds, pelicans, penguins and, if you're lucky, dolphins swimming in the bay. All boats are speedboats with life jackets, some are very crowded; wear warm clothing and protect against the sun. The boats pass Puerto San Martín and the Candelabra en route to the islands.

A 317 km road goes to Ayacucho in the sierra, with a branch to Huancavelica. It is fully paved. At Castrovirreyna it reaches 4,600 m. The scenery on this journey is superb.

Tambo Colorado, one of the best-preserved Inca ruins in coastal Peru, is 48 km from Pisco, up the Pisco valley. It includes buildings where the Inca and his retinue would have stayed. Many of the walls retain their original colours. On the other side of the road is the public plaza and the garrison and messengers' quarters. The caretaker will act as a guide, he has a small collection of items found on the site. ■ *US$1.50. Getting there: Buses from Pisco, 0800, Oropesa, US$1.60, 3 hrs; also colectivos, US$1.20 pp. Alight 20 mins after the stop at Humay; the road passes right through the site. Return by bus to Pisco in the afternoon. For transport back to Pisco wait at the caretaker's house. Taxi from Pisco US$25. Tours from Pisco agencies US$10 with guide, minimum 2 people.*

Huaytará is four hours by bus from Pisco. The whole side of the church is a perfectly preserved Inca wall with niches and trapezoidal doorways. About 20 minutes from town are the ruins of **Incahuasi** with thermal baths. On 24 June is the Fiesta of San Juan Bautista, which involves a week of processions, fireworks, bullfights and dancing day and night. **D** *Hotel de Turistas*, lodging, food and tours. **E** *Municipal*, no restaurant, warm water. ■ *Bus from Pisco US$2.25 (US$5.50 for festival); also Molina from Lima, 6 hrs.*

Ica

Ica is Peru's chief wine centre and is famous for its *tejas*, a local sweet of *manjarblanco*. The **Museo Regional** has mummies, ceramics, textiles and trepanned skulls from the Paracas, Nasca and Inca cultures; a good, well-displayed collection of Inca counting strings (*quipus*) and clothes made of feathers. Behind the building is a scale model of the Nasca lines with an observation tower; a useful orientation before visiting the lines. The attendant paints copies of motifs from the ceramics and textiles in the original pigments (US$1), and sells his own good maps of Nasca for US$1.65. ■ *Mon-Sat 0745-1900, Sun 0900-1300, U S$2. Getting there: take bus 17 from the Plaza de Armas (US$0.50); moto-taxi from corner of plaza, US$0.40. Some tourist information is available at travel agencies. Also try* Touring y Automóvil Club del Perú, *Manzanilla 523.*

Phone code: 034
Colour map 3, grid C3
Population: 152,300
70 km SE of Pisco
Many people pass straight through as the town has a reputation for being inhospitable

Wine bodegas that you can visit are: **El Carmen**, on the right-hand side when arriving from Lima (has an ancient grape press made from a huge tree trunk). **Vista Alegre** (Spanish is essential), its shop is recommended. ■ *Official tours on Fri and Sat 0830-1130, T232919. Getting there: a local bus drops you at the entrance, or its a 10-15 min walk on the other side of the river.* **El Catador**, José Carrasco González, 10 km outside Ica, in the district of Subtanjalla, has a shop selling home-made wines and pisco, and traditional handicrafts associated with winemaking. In the evening it is a restaurant-bar with dancing and music, best visited during harvest, late February to early April, wine and pisco tasting usually possible. ■ *0800-1800. Getting there: bus No 6 from the 2nd block of Moquegua, every 30 mins, US$0.40.* Near El Catador is **Bodega Alvarez**, whose owner, Umberto Alvarez, is very hospitable and won the gold medal for the best pisco in Peru in 1995. Ask about *pisco de mosto verde* and the rarer, more expensive *pisco de limón*.

About 5 km from Ica, round a palm-fringed lake and amid amazing sand dunes, is the popular oasis and summer resort of **Huacachina**, a great place to relax. Its green sulphur waters are said to be curative and thousands of visitors come to swim here. In late 2001 the water and shore were reported to be dirty and polluted. **Sandboarding** on the dunes is a major pastime here; board hire US$1 per hour, from Manuel's restaurant, where you can also pitch a tent. **NB** For the inexperienced, sandboarding can be dangerous on the big dunes. ■ *Take a taxi from Ica for under US$1.* **L-AL** *Hotel Mossone* is at the east end of the lake, T034-213630,

Excursions

Peru

hmossone@derramajae.org.pe (Lima T221 7020). Full board available, lovely patio, pool, bicycles and sandboards for guests' use. Recommended. **F** pp *Casa de Arena*, T215439. Bungalow-style around a pool, **G** without bath, at foot of highest dune which is used for sandboarding, basic, bar, restaurant. Recommended. **G** pp *Hostal Rocha*, T222256. Rooms with bath (which need upgrading), family run, hot water, cooking and laundry facilities, popular, motorcycle parking, good breakfast extra, sandboards for hire US$1.45 per day, swimming pool, books tours to Nasca (good value). Camping possible at the end of the lake with toilets and showers, **G**. There are lots of eating places around the lake.

Sleeping
Hotels are fully booked during the harvest festival and prices rise greatly

AL *Las Dunas*, Av La Angostura 400, T231031, F231007, plus 18% tax and service, about 20% cheaper on weekdays. Highly recommended, in a complete resort with restaurant, swimming pool, horse riding and other activities, it has its own airstrip for flights over Nasca, 50 mins. Lima offices: Ricardo Rivera Navarrete 889, Oficina 208, San Isidro, Casilla 4410, Lima 100, T/F442 4180. **C** *Hostal Vylena*, Jr Ayacucho 505, T351292. Big rooms, helpful, safe, family-run, central. Highly recommended. **C-D** *Hostal Siesta I*, Independencia 160, T233249. Hot water, hospitable owner, noisy. *Siesta II*, T234633, similar. **D-E** *Princess*, Urb Santa María D-103, T/F215421, princesshotelos@yahoo.com A taxi ride from the main plaza, with hot water, TV, pool, tourist information, helpful, peaceful, very good. **E** *Confort*, La Mar 251, 4 blocks from plaza. Possible to park motorcycle. **E** *Hostal El Aleph*, Independencia 152. Good. **F** *Salaverry*, Salaverry 146, T214019. Basic but clean, shared bathroom, cold water. **F** *Lima*, Lima 262. Basic but quiet. **F** *Europa*, Independencia 258. Cold water, OK but unfriendly.

Eating
El Otro Peñoncito, Bolívar 255. Lunch US$6, friendly. *Chifa Karaoke Central*, Urb Los Viñedos de Santa María E-25, T221294. Excellent Chinese food. Good one at Ormeño bus terminal. *Pastelería La Spiga*, Lima 243. Recommended. *Pastelería Velazco*, on Plaza de Armas. Good service, recommended.

Festivals
Wine harvest festival in early **Mar**. The image of El Señor de Luren, in a fine church in Parque Luren, draws pilgrims from all Peru to the twice-yearly festivals in **Mar** and **Oct** (15-21), when there are all-night processions.

Transport
Beware of thieves when changing buses for Nasca and around the Plaza de Armas, even in daylight

Buses To **Pisco**, 70 km, several daily; *Saky* buses from opposite *Ormeño*, 45 mins to centre of Pisco, US$0.70. To **Lima**, 302 km, 4 hrs, US$5, several daily including *Soyuz*, *Flores* and *Ormeño* (at Lambayeque 180). See also Lima, Transport. All bus offices are on Lambayeque blocks 1 and 2 and Salaverry block 3. To **Nasca**, 140 km, 2 hrs, US$2, several buses and colectivos daily, including *Ormeño* (recommended), last bus 2100. To **Arequipa** the route goes via Nasca, see under Nasca. To **Huancavelica**, *Oropesa*, one per day, US$8. **Taxis** For trips in and around Ica, *Luis Andrade*, T222057, BETOSOUL812@hotmail.com US$4 per hr in an old Chevrolet.

Directory
Banks Avoid changing TCs if possible as commission is high. If necessary, use *Banco de Crédito*. **Communications** Post Office: at Callao y Moquegua. Telephone: at Av San Martín y Huánuco.

Nasca

Phone code: 034
Colour map 3, grid C3
Population: 50,000
Altitude: 619 m
140 km S of Ica via Pan-American Highway
444 km from Lima

Set in a green valley amid a perimeter of mountains, Nasca's altitude puts it just above any fog which may drift in from the sea. The sun blazes the year round by day and the nights are crisp. Nearby are the mysterious, world-famous Nasca Lines, which are described on page 1190. Overlooking the town is Cerro Blanco (2,078 m), the highest sand dune in the world, which is popular for sandboarding and parapenting. The large **Museo Antonini**, Av de la Cultura 600, at the eastern end of Jr Lima, houses the discoveries of Professor Orefici and his team from the huge pre-Inca city at Cahuachi (see below), which, Orefici believes, holds the key to the Nasca Lines. Many tombs survived the *huaqueros* and there are displays of ceramics, textiles, amazing *antaras* (panpipes) and photos of the excavations and the Lines.

■ *0900-1900, ring the bell to get in. US$3, including a local guide. A video is shown in the Conference Room. T523444. It is a 10-mins' walk from the plaza, or a short taxi ride. Recommended.* The **Maria Reiche Planetarium**, at the *Hotel Nasca Lines*, was opened in May 2000 in honour of Maria Reiche (see below). It is run by Edgardo Azabache, who speaks English, Italian and French, and Enrique Levano, who speaks English and Italian. Both give lectures every night about the Nasca Lines, based on Reiche's theories, which cover archaeology and astronomy. The show lasts about 45 minutes, after which visitors are able to look at the moon, planets and stars through sophisticated telescopes. ■ *Shows are usually at 1845 and 2045 nightly; US$6 (half price for students), T522293. Very good.* There is a small market at Lima y Grau and the Mercado Central at Arica y Tacna. Between 29 August-10 September is the *Virgen de la Guadalupe* festival.

Excursions

The Nasca area is dotted with over 100 cemeteries and the dry, humidity-free climate has perfectly preserved invaluable tapestries, cloth and mummies. At **Chauchilla** (30 km south of Nasca, last 12 km a sandy track), grave robbing *huaqueros* ransacked the tombs and left bones, skulls, mummies and pottery shards littering the desert. ■ *A tour takes about 2 hrs and should cost about US$7 pp with a minimum of 3 people.* Gold mining is one of the main local industries and a tour usually includes a visit to a small family processing shop where the techniques used are still very old-fashioned. Some tours also include a visit to a local potter's studio. That of Sr Andrés Calle Benavides, who makes Nasca reproductions, is particularly recommended.

To the Paredones ruins and aqueduct: the ruins, also called Cacsamarca, are Inca on a pre-Inca base. They are not well preserved. The underground aqueducts, built 300 BC-AD 700, are still in working order and worth seeing. By taxi it is about US$10 round trip, or go with a tour.

Cantalloc is a 30 minutes to one hour walk through Buena Fe, to see markings in the valley floor. These consist of a triangle pointing to a hill and a *tela* (cloth) with a spiral depicting the threads. Climb the mountain to see better examples.

Cahuachi, to the west of the Nasca Lines, comprises several pyramids and a site called **El Estaquería**. The latter is thought to have been a series of astronomical sighting posts, but more recent research suggests the wooden pillars were used to dry dead bodies and therefore it may have been a place of mummification. ■ *To visit the ruins of Cahuachi costs US$8, minimum 3 people. See also the Museo Antonini, above.*

Two hours out of Nasca is the **Reserva Nacional Pampas Galeras** at 4,100 m, which has a vicuña and museum. There is an interesting Museo del Sitio, also a military base and park guard here. It's best to go early as entry is free. At Km 155 is **Puquio** (**F** *Hostal Central*, Av Castilla 625, shared bath, hot water, restaurant, motorcycle parking). It's then another 185 km to **Chalhuanca** (**F** *Hostal Victoria*, Jr Arequipa 305, T321301, shared bath, clean and comfortable; one other on the main road between the plaza and the Wari bus stop, cheaper, very basic, dirty, has parking). There are wonderful views on this stretch, with lots of small villages, valleys and alpacas. Fuel is available in Puquio and Chalhuanca.

Peru

Sleeping

L-A *Maison Suisse*, opposite the airport, T/F522434. Comfortable, safe car park, expensive restaurant, pool, rooms with jacuzzi (dirty), accepts Amex, good giftshop, shows video of Nasca Lines. Also has camping facilities. **A** *Nasca Lines*, Jr Bolognesi, T522293, F522293. With a/c, comfortable, rooms with private patio, hot water, peaceful, restaurant, good but expensive meals, safe car park, pool (US$2.50 for non-guests, or free if having lunch), they can arrange package tours which include 2-3 nights at the hotel plus a flight over the lines and a desert trip for around US$250. Recommended. **A** *De La Borda*, an old hacienda at Majoro about 5 km from town past the airstrip, T522750. Lovely gardens, pool, excellent restaurant, quiet, helpful, English-speaking manageress. **C** *Nido del Cóndor*, opposite the airport, Panamericana Sur Km 447, T522424, acnasca@terra.com.pe Large rooms, hot water, good restaurant, bar, shop, videos, swimming pool, camping US$3, parking, English, Italian German spoken, free pick-up from town, reservation advised. **C-D** *Hostal Las Líneas*, Jr Arica

Those arriving by bus should beware being told that the hotel of their choice is closed, or full, and no longer runs tours. This applies particularly to Alegría. If you phone or email the hotel they will pick you up at the bus station free of charge day or night

299, T522488. Spacious, restaurant. Recommended. **D** *Internacional*, Av Maria Reiche, T522166. Hot water, garage, café, newer bungalows. **D** *Mirador*, Tacna 436, T523121, F523714. On main plaza, comfortable rooms with shower, cheaper with shared bath, hot water (unreliable at peak times), TV, new, modern, clean. Recommended. **E** pp *Alegría*, Jr Lima 168, T/F523775, T522444, T667381 (Mob), www.nazcaperu.com Has rooms with bath, carpet and a/c, continental breakfast and tax included, bungalows with hot shower, and rooms with shared bath (**G** pp), hot water, café, garden, manager (Efraín Alegría) speaks English and Hebrew, laundry facilities, safe luggage deposit (including for bus passengers not needing a hotel), book exchange, email facilities for US$2 per hr, netphone also US$2, free video on the Lines at 2100, very popular. Recommended. Efraín also runs a tour agency and guests are encouraged to buy tours (see Tour operators), flights and bus tickets arranged. *Alegría* gives 1 hr free internet use to those who email in advance. **E** *Estrella del Sur*, Callao 568, T522764. Welcoming, small rooms, includes breakfast. Recommended. **E** pp *Ex-Lima* (also calls itself *Alegría*, but is no relation), Av Los Incas 117, opposite *Ormeño* bus terminal, T522497. Basic, convenient for buses, cheaper without bath, hot water. **E** *Hostal Paramonga*, Juan Matta 880, T522576. With breakfast, good. **E** *Rancho Park*, on Panamericana 1 km from town towards the airport, T521153. On farmland, 2 swimming pools (one for children), entry to pools US$1, popular at weekends, good restaurant. **E** *Sol de Nasca*, Callao 586, T522730. Rooms with and without hot showers, TV, also has a restaurant, pleasant, don't leave valuables in luggage store. **E** *Hostal Restaurant Via Morburg*, JM Mejía 108, 3 blocks from Plaza de Armas, T/F522566 (in Lima T479 1467, F462 0932). With fan, hot water, small swimming pool, TV room, free pisco sour on arrival, excellent and cheap restaurant on top floor. Recommended.

F *Posada Guadalupe*, San Martín 225, T522249. Family run, lovely courtyard and garden, **G** without bath, hot water, good breakfast, relaxing (touts who try to sell tours are nothing to do with hotel). **F** pp *Hostal El Pajonal*, Jr Callao 911, near Plaza de Armas. With bath. Recommended. **F** *Nasca*, C Lima 438, T/F522085. Hot water, noisy, clothes washing facilities, luggage store, hard sell on tours and flights, mixed reports, safe motorcycle parking. **G** *Hostal Nuevo Milenio*, Arica 582. Hot water, use of kitchen, owner can book flights, tours and buses.

Eating *Aviance*, Arica 213. Recommended for *menú*. *Cañada*, Lima 160, nazcanada@yahoo.com Cheap, good *menú*, excellent pisco sours, nice wines, popular, display of local artists' work, email service, English spoken, owner Juan Carlos Fraola is very helpful. Recommended. *Concordia*, Lima 594. Good, also rents bikes at US$1 an hour. *Farita*, Bolognesi 388, 1 block from

Nasca

Sleeping	3 Ex-Lima (Alegría)	10 Sol de Nasca
1 Alegría	4 Hostal Las Líneas	11 Via Morburg
2 Estrella del Sur	5 Internacional	
	6 Mirador	**Eating**
	7 Nasca	1 Cañada
	8 Nasca Lines	2 Chifa Guang Zhou
	9 Posada Guadalupe	3 Chifa Nam Kug

4 El Puquio
5 Fuente de Soda Jumbory
6 La Púa
7 La Taberna
8 Los Angeles
9 Sudamérica

Peru

plaza. Typical Nasca breakfast (*tamales, chicharrones*, etc). *Chifa Guang Zhou*, Bolognesi 297, T522036. Very good. *Los Angeles*, Bolognesi 266. Good, cheap, try *sopa criolla*, and chocolate cake. *Chifa Nam Kug*, on Bolognesi near the plaza. Recommended. *La Púa*, Jr Lima, next to *Hotel Alegría*. Good. *El Puquio*, Bolognesi 50 m from plaza. Good food, especially pastas, pleasant atmsophere, good for drinks, popular. *Rico Pollo* opposite *Hostal Alegría*. Good local restaurant, cheap. *Sudamérica*, Lima 668. Good local food, especially meat. *La Taberna*, Jr Lima 321, T521411. Excellent food, live music, popular with gringos, it's worth a look just for the graffiti on the walls. *Fuente de Soda Jumbory*, near the cinema. Good *almuerzo*. *Panadería*, Bolognesi 387, opposite *Farita*.

All guides must be approved by the Ministry of Tourism and should have an official identity card. As more and more touts (*jaladores*) operate at popular hotels and the bus terminals, they are using false ID cards and fake hotel and tour brochures. They are all rip-off merchants who overcharge and mislead those who arrive by bus. Only conduct business with agencies at their office, or phone or email the company you want to deal with in advance. Some hotels are not above pressurising guests to purchase tours at inflated prices.

Tour operators
Do not take just any taxi on the plaza for a tour as they are unreliable and can lead to robbery. It is not dangerous to visit the sites if you go with a trustworthy person. Taxi drivers usually act as guides, but most speak only Spanish

Algería Tours, run by Efraín Alegría at *Hotel Alegría* offers inclusive tours which have been repeatedly recommended. Guides with radio contact and maps can be provided for hikes to nearby sites. They have guides who speak English, German, French and Italian. Tours go as far as Ica, Paracas and the Ballestas Islands. *Alegría* run a bus from Nasca to Pisco every day at 1000 (returns at 1000 from Pisco's Plaza de Armas), via Ica, Huacachina and *bodegas*. The *Fernández family*, who run the *Hotel Nasca*, also run local tours. Ask for the hotel owners and speak to them direct. Also ask Efraín Alegría or the Fernández family to arrange a taxi for you to one of the sites outside Nasca (eg US$50 to Sacaco, 30 mins at site). Juan Tohalino Vera of *Nasca Trails*, Bolognesi 550, T522858, nascatrails@terra.com.pe He speaks English, French, German and Italian. Recommended. *Nanasca Tours*, Jr Lima 160, T/F522917, T622054 (Mob), nanascatours@ yahoo.com Juan Carlos Iraola is very helpful. *Tour Perú*, Arica 285, Plaza de Armas. Efficient. *Viajes Nasca*, Jr Lima 185, T521027, Good, guide Susi is recommended.

Buses To Lima, 446 km, 6 hrs, several buses and colectivos daily. *Ormeño*, *Royal Class* at 1330 US$25, normal service, 4 a day, US$5; *Civa*, normal service at 2300, US$8. Ormeño's *Royal Class* arrives in Santa Catalina, a much safer area of Lima.
    Ormeño to **Ica**, 2 hrs, US$2, 3 a day, and to **Pisco** (210 km), 3 hrs, US$5, also 3 a day. *Royal Class* to **Paracas**, 2¾ hrs, and Pisco, both at 1330, US$15. Note that buses to Pisco stop 5 km outside town (see under Pisco, Transport). To **Arequipa**, 623 km, 9 hrs: *Ormeño* 1530, 2000, 2300, US$7.25, with *Royal* Class at 2130, US$30, 8 hrs. *Civa*, 1100, 1500, 2300, US$10, 9 hrs, with *Imperial* service at 1200, 9 hrs, US$20. Delays are possible out of Nasca because of drifting sand across the road or because of mudslides in the rainy season. Travel in daylight if possible. Book your ticket on previous day.
    Buses to **Cusco**, 659 km, 14 hrs, via **Chalhuanca** and **Abancay**. For a description of the road, see below. On the **Lima-Nasca-Abancay-Cusco** route *Expreso Wari* have normal services at 1600, 1800, and 2200, US$17, and *Imperial* service at 1200, US$20. Their offices are at the exit from Nasca on the road to Puquío. Also buses to Cusco with *Ormeño*, US$27, *Cruz del Sur*, 1630, 2400, US$20, and *Molina*. The highway from Nasca to Cusco is paved and is safe for bus travellers, drivers of private vehicles and motorcyclists.

Transport
It is worth paying the extra for a good bus Reports of robbery on the cheaper services Overbooking is common

Banks *Banco de Crédito*, Lima y Grau, changes cash and Visa TCs, cash advance on Visa, decent rates, Visa ATM. *Interbank*, on the Plaza de Armas, changes cash. Some street changers will change TCs for 8% commission. **Communications** Internet: Many places on Jr Bolognesi. *Lucy@com*, Bolognesi 298. US$0.75 per hr. *Migsu Net*, Arica 295, p 2. Open daily 0800-2400, good, fast machines, US$1 per hr. Facilities at *Hotel Alegría* and *Nasca Trails*. Post Office: at Fermín de Castillo 379, T522016. **Telephone:** *Telefónica* for international calls with coins on Plaza Bolognesi; also on Plaza de Armas and at Lima 359 where you can send or receive fax messages and make international collect calls. **Useful addresses** Police: at Av Los Incas.

Directory

Peru

Nasca Lines

Cut into the stony desert about 22 km north of Nasca, above the Ingenio valley on the Pampa de San José, along the Pan-American Highway, are the famous Nasca Lines. Large numbers of lines, not only parallels and geometrical figures, but also designs such as a dog, an enormous monkey, birds (one with a wing span of over 100 m), a spider and a tree. The lines, best seen from the air, are thought to have been etched on the Pampa Colorada sands by three different groups – the Paracas people 900-200 BC, the Nascas 200 BC-AD 600 and the Huari settlers from Ayacucho at about AD 630.

The Nascas had a highly developed civilization which reached its peak about AD 600. Their polychrome ceramics, wood carvings and adornments of gold are on display in many of Lima's museums. The Paracas was an early phase of the Nasca culture, renowned for the superb technical quality and stylistic variety in its weaving and pottery. The Huari empire, in conjunction with the Tiahuanaco culture, dominated much of Peru from AD 600-1000.

Origins of the lines The German expert, Dr Maria Reiche, who studied the lines for over 40 years, mostly from a step ladder, died in June 1998, aged 95. She maintained that they represent some sort of vast astronomical pre-Inca calendar. In 1976 Maria Reiche paid for a platform, the mirador, from which three of the huge designs can be seen – the hands, the Lizard and the Tree. Her book, *Mystery on the Desert*, is on sale for US$10 (proceeds to conservation work) in Nasca. In January 1994 Maria Reiche opened a small museum. ■ *US$1. 5 km from town at the Km 416 marker, take micro from in front of* Ormeño *terminal, US$0.70, frequent. Victoria Nikitzhi, a friend of Maria Reiche, gives lectures about the Nasca Lines, with a scale model, at 1900 at Jr San Martín 221; donations of US$2.85 requested. See the Planetarium, above. See also www.magicperu.com/MariaReiche Another good book is* Pathways to the Gods: the mystery of the Nasca Lines, *by Tony Morrison (Michael Russell, 1978), available in Lima.*

Other theories abound: Georg A von Breunig (1980) claims that the lines are the tracks of running contests, and a similar theory was proposed by the English astronomer Alan Sawyer; yet another is that they represent weaving patterns and yarns (Henri Stirlin) and that the plain is a map demonstrating the Tiahuanaco Empire (Zsoltan Zelko). *The Nazca Lines – a new perspective on their origin and meaning* (Editorial Los Pinos, Lima 18), by Dr Johan Reinhard, brings together ethnographic, historical and archaeological data, including current use of straight lines in Chile and Bolivia, to suggest that the Lines conform to fertility practices throughout the Andes.

Another theory is that the ancient Nascas flew in hot-air balloons; this is based on the fact that the lines are best seen from the air, and that there are pieces of ancient local pottery and tapestry showing balloonists, and local legends of flying men (see *Nasca, The flight of Condor 1*, by Jim Woodman, Murray, 1980, Pocket Books, NY 1977). This in part accords with the most recent research, carried out by the BBC series 'Ancient Voices'. The clues to the function of the lines are found in the highly advanced pottery and textiles of the ancient Nascans, some of which show a flying being emitting discharge from its nose and mouth. This is believed to portray the flight of the shaman who consumes certain psycho-active drugs that convince him he can fly and so enter the real world of spirits in order to rid sick people of evil spirits. In this way, the lines were not designed to be seen physically from above, but from the mind's eye of the flying shaman. This also explains the presence of creatures such as a monkey or killer whale which possess qualities needed by the shaman in his spirit journeys. Of the geometric figures, the straight lines are a feature of ancient Peruvian ritual behaviour, much like ley lines in Europe. They represent invisible paths of perceived energy, while the trapezoids are thought to have been ritual spaces where offerings were made to the gods.

Peru

Taxi-guides to the mirador, 0800-1200, cost US$4.35 pp, or you can hitch, but there is not always much traffic. Travellers suggest the view from the hill 500 m back to Nasca is better. *Ormeño* bus leaves for the lines at 0900 (US$1.75); hitch back, but have patience. Go by an early bus as the site gets very hot. Or take a taxi and arrive at 0745 before the buses.

Tours on land

Small planes take 3-5 passengers to see the Nasca Lines. Flights last 30-35 mins and are controlled by air traffic personnel at the airport to avoid congestion. Reservations should be made at the airport for flights with **Aerocóndor** (office opposite *Hotel Nasca Lines*). Flights can also be booked at *Hotel Alegría* with **Alas Peruanas** (experienced pilots fluent in English), *Hotel Nasca*, **AeroParacas**, T667231, F522688, or **Aero Ica** in Jr Lima and at the airport. These companies are recommended; there are others. The price for a flight is US$35 pp (special deals sometimes available, eg, *hostal* included; touts charge US$50; US$25, shorter flights on sale). You also have to pay US$2 airport tax. It is best to organize a flight with the airlines themselves at the airport. Flights are bumpy with many tight turns – many people are airsick so it's wise not to eat or drink just before a flight. Best times to fly are 0800-1000 and 1500-1630 when there is less turbulence and better light. *Alas Peruanas* also offer 1-hr flights over the Palpa and Llipata areas, where you can see more designs and other rare patterns (US$60 pp, minimum 3). They can also organize flights from Pisco (US$130) and Ica (US$120). All *Alas Peruanas* flights include the BBC film of Nasca. *Aerocóndor* in Lima (T442 5215/5663) and **Aero Ica** (T441 8614/8608) both offer flights over the lines from Lima in a 1-day tour (lunch in Nasca) for US$260 pp; or flights from Ica for US$130 pp. *Aero Ica* also offers a night in *Maison Suisse* plus flight for US$65, but book 48 hrs in advance. Taxi to airport, US$1.35, bus, US$0.10. Make sure you clarify everything before getting on the plane and ask for a receipt. Also let them know in advance if you have any special requests.

Tours by air

South of Nasca

Chala, 173 km from Nasca, is a friendly fishing village with beaches. **Sleeping**: **C** *Turistas*, T551111, cheaper without bath, hot water, restaurant, great sea view. Recommended. **F** *Hostal Grau*, T551009, rooms facing the ocean, use of kitchen, cheap meals on request; next door is *Hostal Evertyth*, T551095, similar, both good. All hotels are 10 minutes walk south down the Panamericana from where the buses stop (colectivo from Nasca, US$3.50). Dozens of restaurants, mostly catering for passing buses. Lima-Arequipa buses pass Chala about 0600.

About 10 km north of Chala are the large precolumbian ruins of **Puerto Inca** on the coast. This was the port for Cusco. The site is in excellent condition: the drying and store houses can be seen as holes in the ground (be careful where you walk). On the right side of the bay is a cemetery, on the hill a temple of reincarnation, and the Inca road from the coast to Cusco is clearly visible. The road was 240 km long, with a staging post every 7 km so that, with a change of runner at every post, messages could be sent in 24 hours. **Sleeping C** *Puerto Inka*, Km 603 Panamericana Sur (for reservations T691494, T/F054-258798). Bungalows on the beautiful beach, hammocks outside, great place to relax, boat hire, diving equipment rental, safe camping for US$2, discount for longer stay, very busy in summer. Recommended. The restaurant has not received the same consistently favourable reports as the hotel. ■ *Taxi from Chala US$5, or take Yauca colectivo, US$0.50, to Km 603 and walk down, 3 km, or walk from Chala, 2 hrs. 1-day tour from Nasca, US$10 pp.*

Peru

Arequipa and Lake Titicaca

Arequipa and Lake Titicaca share great local pride and major tourist popularity: colonial architecture in Arequipa; the tranquillity of Lake Titicaca and the bustling folklore of Puno. All are set in the southern cordilleras of the Peruvian Andes, with smoking volcanoes, deep canyons, bleak altiplano *and terraced valleys.*

Background   On 23 June 2001, an earthquake measuring 7.9 on the Richter Scale hit southern Peru. Its epicentre was in the Pacific Ocean about 82 km from Ocoña in Arequipa department. A tidal wave three-storeys high hit the coast, devastating resorts and agricultural land around Camaná. Inland, Arequipa itself, Moquegua, Cotahuasi, Tacna and parts of Ayacucho department were badly affected.

Arequipa

Phone code: 054
Colour map 6, grid A1
Population: 1 million
Altitude: 2,380 m
1,011 km from Lima
by road

The city of Arequipa stands in a beautiful valley at the foot of El Misti volcano, a snow-capped, perfect cone, 5,822 m high, guarded on either side by the mountains Chachani (6,075 m), and Pichu-Pichu (5,669 m). The city has fine Spanish buildings and many old and interesting churches built of sillar, a pearly white volcanic material almost exclusively used in the construction of Arequipa. The city was re-founded on 15 August 1540 by an emissary of Pizarro, but it had previously been occupied by Aymara Indians and the Incas. It is the main commercial centre for the south, and its people resent the general tendency to believe that everything is run from Lima. It has been declared a World Cultural Heritage site by UNESCO.

Ins & outs   **Getting there**   Transport to and from the **airport** (7 km west) is described below under
For more detailed   Transport. It takes about half an hour to town. The main **bus terminal** is south of the centre,
information, see   15 mins from the centre by colectivo, 10 mins by taxi.
Transport, page 1199   **Getting around**   The main places of interest and the hotels are within walking distance of the Plaza de Armas. If you are going to the suburbs, take a bus or taxi. A cheap tour of the city can be made in a *Vallecito* bus, 1½ hrs for US$0.30. It is a circular tour which goes down Calles Jerusalén and San Juan de Dios.

   Climate   The climate is delightful, with a mean temperature before sundown of 23°C, and after sundown of 14½°C. The sun shines on 360 days of the year. Annual rainfall is less than 150 mm.

   Tourist office   is in the Municipalidad on the south side of the Plaza de Armas, T211021, ext 113. Open 0800-1900. They are very helpful and friendly and give free street plans. **Oficina de Protección al Turista**, T0800-42579, 24 hrs, toll-free, or T212054, during office hours. **Tourist Police**, Jerusalén 315, T251270/239888, very helpful with complaints or giving directions. **Ministry of Tourism**, La Merced 117, T213116, will handle complaints. **Touring y Automóvil Club del Perú**, Av Goyeneche 313, T215631, mechanical assistance T215640.

The elegant **Plaza de Armas** is faced on three sides by arcaded buildings with many restaurants, and on the fourth by the Cathedral. Behind the Cathedral there is an attractive alley with handicraft shops and places to eat. The central **San Camilo market**, between Perú, San Camilo, Piérola and Alto de la Luna, is worth visiting, as is the Siglo XX market, to the east of the rail station. Arequipa is said to have the best preserved colonial architecture in Peru, apart from Cusco. The oldest district is **San Lázaro**, a collection of tiny climbing streets and houses quite close to the *Hotel Libertador*, where you can find the ancient **Capilla de San Lázaro**.

Sights

Theft can be a problem in the market area, especially after dark, in the park at Selva Alegre and on Calles San Juan de Dios and Alvarez Thomas, but the police are friendly conspicuous, and efficient Churches are usually open 0700-0900 and 1800-2000

Churches The massive **Cathedral**, founded in 1612 and largely rebuilt in the 19th century, is remarkable for having its façade along the whole length of the church (entrance on Santa Catalina and San Francisco). Inside is the fine Belgian organ and elaborately carved wooden pulpit. In the June 2001 earthquake, one of the cathedral's twin towers famously collapsed. Repairs are continuing and will not be completed until 2004. Visiting is fairly unaffected, other than the obvious annoyance of the outer scaffolding in photos!

At **La Compañía**, General Morán and Ejercicios, the main façade (1698) and side portal (1654) are striking examples of the florid Andean *mestizo* style. To the left of the sanctuary is the **Capilla Real** (Royal Chapel); its San Ignacio chapel has a beautiful polychrome cupola. ■ *Mon-Sat 0900-1240, 1500-1945, Sun 1700-1945, US$0.50.*

Also well worth seeing are the churches of **San Francisco** (Zela 103), **San Agustín** (corner of San Agustín y Sucre), the early 17th-century **La Merced** (La Merced 303), and **Santo Domingo** (Santo Domingo y Piérola).

La Recoleta, a Franciscan monastery built in 1647, stands on the other side of the river, on Recoleta. It contains several cloisters, a religious art museum, a precolumbian museum, an Amazon museum and a library with many rarities. ■ *Closed to visitors after the earthquake, but ask the staff if you can visit the library.*

Santa Catalina Convent is by far the most remarkable sight, opened in 1970 after four centuries of mystery. The convent has been beautifully refurbished, with period furniture, pictures of the Arequipa and Cusco schools and fully equipped kitchens. It is a complete miniature walled colonial town of over 2 ha in the middle of the city at Santa Catalina 301, where about 450 nuns lived in total seclusion, except for their women servants. The few remaining nuns have retreated to one section of the convent, allowing visitors to see a maze of cobbled streets and plazas bright with geraniums and other flowers, cloisters and buttressed houses. These have been painted in traditional white, orange, deep red and blue. ■ *0900-1600, US$7.25, T229798. The tour they offer you at the entrance is worthwhile; 1½ hrs, no set price, many of the guides speak English or German (a tip of US$2.85 is expected). There is a good café, which sells cakes made by the nuns and a special blend of tea.*

Colonial houses Arequipa has several fine seignorial houses with large carved tympanums over the entrances. Built as single-storey structures, they have mostly withstood earthquakes. They have small patios with no galleries, flat roofs and small windows, disguised by superimposed lintels or heavy grilles. Good examples are the 18th-century **Casa Tristán del Pozo**, or **Gibbs-Ricketts house**, with its fine portal and puma-head waterspouts (now *Banco Continental*), San Francisco 108 y San José. ■ *0915-1245, 1600-1830, Sat 0930-1230.*

Casa del Moral, or Williams house, with museum, *Banco Industrial*. ■ *Mon-Sat 0900-1700, Sun 0900-1300, US$1.40, US$0.90 for students, Moral 318 y Bolívar.*
Casa Goyeneche, La Merced 201 y Palacio Viejo (now an office of the *Banco Central de la Reserva*, ask the guards to let you view the courtyard and fine period rooms).

Museums Opposite the San Francisco church is the interesting **Museo Histórico Municipal** with much war memorabilia. ■ *Mon-Fri 0800-1800, US$0.50. Plaza San Francisco 407.* The **archaeological museum** at the Universidad de San Agustín, Av Independencia entre La Salle y Santa Rosa, has a good collection of ceramics and

Peru

mummies. ■ *Mon-Fri 0800-1400, US$1. Apply to Dr E Linares, the Director, T229719.*

The **Museo Santuarios Andinos** contains the frozen Inca mummies found on Mount Ampato by local climber Miguel Zarate and archaeologist Johan Reihard; the mummy known as 'Juanita' is fascinating as it is so well preserved. ■ *Mon-Sat 0900-1800, Sun 0900-1500, US$4.40 entry fee includes a 20-min video of the discovery in English followed by a guided tour in English, French, German, Italian or Spanish (tip the guide), discount with student card; www.ucsm.edu.pe~santury, T200345. Santa Catalina 210, corner of Ugarte, opposite the convent.*

Excursions **Climbing El Misti** At 5,822 m, **El Misti** volcano offers a relatively straightforward opportunity to scale a high peak. Start from the hydroelectric plant, after first registering with the police there, then you need one day to the Monte Blanco shelter, at 4,800 m. Start early for the 4-6 hours to the top, to get there by 1100 before the mists obscure the view. If you start back at 1200 you will reach the hydroelectric plant by 1800. Alternatively, take a jeep at 3,300 m to the end of the rough road, then 4-5 hours' hike to the campground at 4,600 m. Only space for three tents. Be sure to take plenty of food, water and protection against the weather; it takes two days to reach the crater. Remember that the summit is at a very high altitude and that this, combined with climbing on scree, makes it hard going for the untrained. Recent, unconfirmed reports of hold-ups of climbers make it inadvisable for you to go alone. Join a group or take a guide. Further information is available from travel agencies and Miguel and Carlos Zárate (address above, Climbing).

At **Yanahuara**, 2 km northwest, is a 1750 *mestizo*-style church, with a magnificent churrigueresque façade, all in *sillar*. ■ *1500. To get there cross the Puente Grau and turn right up Av Bolognesi.* On the same plaza is a *mirador*, through whose arches there is a fine view of El Misti with the city at its feet, a popular spot in the late afternoon.

In the hillside suburb of **Cayma** is the delightful 18th-century church (■ *Only until 1700*), and many old buildings associated with Bolívar and Garcilaso de la Vega. Many local buses go to Cayma.

Tingo, which has a very small lake and three swimming pools, should be visited on Sunday for local food; bus 7, US$0.20. 3 km past Tingo, beside the Río Sabandía on the Huasacanche road, is **La Mansión del Fundador**. Originally owned by the founder of Arequipa, Don Garcí Manuel de Carbajal, it has been restored as a museum with original furnishings and paintings. ■ *US$2.50, with cafetería and bar.*

About 8 km southeast of Arequipa is the **Molino de Sabandía**, the first stone mill in the area, built in 1621. It has been fully restored and the guardian diverts water to run the grinding stones when visitors arrive. The well-kept grounds have old willow trees and the surrounding countryside is pleasant. ■ *US$1.50; round trip by taxi US$4.* Adjoining Sabandía is **Yumina**, with many Inca terraces which are still in use and between Sabandía and Arequipa is Paucarpata, with an old church and views of terraces, El Misti and Chachani.

Sleeping

When arriving by bus, do not believe taxi drivers who say the hotel of your choice is closed or full. This applies to El Indio Dormido, La Reyna and Tambo Viejo in particular. Ring the door bell and check for yourself

AL *Maison d'Elise*, Av Bolognesi 104, T256185, F271935. Attractive Mediterranean-style village with pool, large rooms, also suites and apartments, helpful staff, pricey restaurant. **AL-A** *Libertador*, Plaza Simón Bolívar, Selva Alegre, T215110, F241933, arequipa@libertador.com.pe Safe, large comfortable rooms, good service, swimming pool (cold), gardens, good meals, pub-style bar, cocktail lounge, squash court. **A** *El Conquistador*, Mercaderes 409, T212916, F218987. Safe, lovely colonial atmosphere, owner speaks English, thin walls. **A** *Hostal Casa Grande*, García Calderón 125, Vallecito, T214000, F214021. Includes taxes, small, cosy, well-furnished, quiet, good services, restaurant. **B** *Casa de Melgar*, Melgar 108, T/F222459. Excellent rooms, 18th-century building, with bath, hot water (solar panel), safe, nice courtyard, good breakfast in café open in the morning and 1730-2100. **B** *Casa de Mi Abuela*, Jerusalén 606, T241206, F242761, casadmiabuela@ LaRed.net.pe Safe, hot water, laundry, cable TV, swimming pool, rooms at the back are quieter and overlook the garden, **D** without bath, self-catering if desired, English spoken, parking, internet access US$3 per hr, tours and transport organized in own agency (*Giardino*, T221345, F as above, giardinotours@chasqui.LaRed.net.pe), which has good information (expensive), small library of European books, breakfast or evening snacks on patio or in beautiful garden. **B** *Hostal Solar*, Ayacucho 108, T/F241793, solar@rh.com.pe Nice colonial building, TV, bath, hot water, includes good breakfast served in nice patio, sun lunge on roof, very secure, quiet.

C *Los Balcones de Moral y Santa Catalina*, Moral 217, T201291, F222555, losbalcones@ hotmail.com Convenient, 1 block from Plaza de Armas and close to Santa Catalina, large rooms, comfortable beds, with bath, hot water, laundry, café, tourist information. **C** *Miamaka*, San Juan de Dios 402, T241496, F227906. Excellent service, helpful, cable TV,

Arequipa

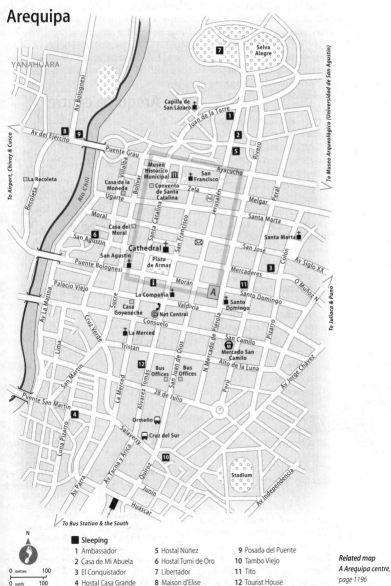

Sleeping
1 Ambassador
2 Casa de Mi Abuela
3 El Conquistador
4 Hostal Casa Grande
5 Hostal Núñez
6 Hostal Tumi de Oro
7 Libertador
8 Maison d'Elise
9 Posada del Puente
10 Tambo Viejo
11 Tito
12 Tourist House

0 metres 100
0 yards 100

Related map
A Arequipa centre,
page 1196

Peru

English spoken. **C** *Villa Baden Baden*, Manuel Ugarte 401, Selva Alegre, T222416. Run by Sra Bluemel de Castro, 6 rooms, breakfast included, German, French and English spoken, very informative about the area and climbing, safe. **D** *Hostal Le Foyer*, Ugarte 114 y San Francisco, T286473. Comfortable, hot water, laundry, luggage store, safe, helpful. **D** *Lluvia de Oro*, Jerusalén 308, T214252, F235730. Cheaper without bath, English-speaking, breakfast US$2, laundry service, good views. **D** *Las Torres de Ugarte*, Ugarte 401, T/F283532, torresdeugarte@lared.net.pe Next to Santa Catalina convent, hot water, cable TV, laundry service, roof terrace, parking, safe, luggage store. **D** *Hostal Tumi de Oro*, San Agustín 311A, 2½ blocks from the Plaza de Armas, T/F281319. French and English spoken, hot water, roof terrace, book exchange, tea/coffee facilities, safe. **D** *Posada de Sancho*, Santa Catalina 213 A and 223 A, near the convent, T/F287797. Hot showers (usually), cheaper without bath, safe, nice patio and terrace with a view of El Misti, good breakfast extra, English, French and German spoken, good travel information, offer cheap tours but rather pushy.

E *The Tourist House*, Alvarez Tomás 435, T211752. In an unsafe area, hot shower at any time, safe hotel, kitchen, TV lounge, offers tours. **E** *Ambassador*, Jerusalén 619, T281048. Hot water, TV, laundry, café, helpful, English-speaking staff. **E** *Hostal Núñez*, Jerusalén 528, T233268. Hot water, TV, laundry, safe, a bit neglected but still a good place to meet other travellers, small rooms, breakfast on roof terrace overlooking the city. **E** *Hostal Santa Catalina*, Santa Catalina 500, T233705. Hot water, TV, upper rooms quiet but elsewhere noisy, safe, luggage stored. **F** pp *Albergue El Misti*, Salaverry 302, 3 blocks from the rail station, T/F245760. Family rooms with bath, singles and shared rooms in an elegant old mansion, arranges cultural tours, also Spanish classes. **F** *Casa Itzhak*, Av Parra 97, T204596, T946643 (Mob). With and without bath, includes breakfast, cable TV, laundry service, restaurant, free transport to bus station, very helpful. **F** *Colonial House Inn*, Puente Grau 114, T/F223533, colonialhouseinn@hotmail.com Hot water, quieter rooms at the back, laundry facilities and service, kitchen facilities, roof terrace, good choice of breakfasts, owners speak English. **F** pp *El Indio Dormido*, Av Andrés Avelino Cáceres B-9, T427401, the_sleeping_indian@yahoo.com Close to bus terminal, free transport to centre, some rooms with bath, TV, very helpful. **F** *La Fiorentina*, Puente Grau 110, T202571. **G** without bath, hot water, comfortable, family atmosphere, tours arranged, laundry facilities, use of kitchen extra. **F** *Hostal La Portada del Mirador*, Portal de Flores 102, Plaza de Armas, T201209. Basic, shared bath, hot water, safe, will store luggage, great views from the roof. **F** *Hostal Regis*, Ugarte 202, T226111. Colonial house, French-style interior, hot water all day, cooking and laundry facilities, sun terrace with good views, safe deposit, luggage store, video rental, book exchange, very helpful, tours arranged.

Arequipa centre

12 Los Balcones de Moral y Santa Catalina

● Eating
1 Anushka
2 Ary Quepay
3 Bonanza
4 Bóveda San Agustín
5 Café Manolo
6 El Rincón Norteño
7 El Turko
8 Forum & Dejá Vu
9 Govinda
10 La Casita de José Antonio
11 Lakshmivan
12 Mandala
13 Pizzería Los Leños
14 Pizzería San Antonio
15 Zig Zag

■ Sleeping
1 Casa de Melgar
2 Colonial House Inn
3 Hostal La Portada del Mirador
4 Hostal La Reyna
5 Hostal Le Foyer
6 Hostal Posada de Sancho
7 Hostal Regis
8 Hostal Santa Catalina
9 Hostal Solar
10 La Fiorentina
11 Lluvia de Oro

Peru

F *Hostal La Reyna*, Zela 209, T286578. With or without bath, two more expensive rooms at the top of the house, hot water, the daughter speaks English, laundry, breakfast for US$1.15, pizza available at any hour, rooftop seating, will store luggage, ask about rips to the Colca Canyon and volcanoes. Less popular then it used to be. **F** pp *Tambo Viejo*, Av Malecón Socabaya 107, IV Centenario, T288195/206140, F284747, www.home.zonnet.nl/pcueva 5 blocks south of the plaza near the rail station. Cheaper with shared bath, **G** pp in shared room. English and Dutch spoken, walled garden, hot water 24 hrs (as long as demand isn't too great), expensive laundry service, cable TV, safe deposit, coffee shop, bar, book exchange (2 for 1), money changed, tourist information for guests, use of kitchen, phone for international calls, internet, bike rental, popular with young travellers, luggage store extra, tours arranged. For a small fee, you can use the facilities if passing through. Telephone the hostal and they will pick you up free of charge, day or night. **F** *Hospedaje Quilla*, Zela 313, T671520. Without bath, welcoming, parking. **F** *Tito*, Perú 105-B, T234424. Shared bathroom, good value. **G** *Hostal Moderno*, Alto de la Luna 106. Large rooms, laundry, hot water, safe. **G** pp *Hostal Wilson*, Puente Grau 306, T204097. Small, good views, good value.

Youth hostel D *Premier*, Av Quiroz 100, T/F241091, www.barrioperu.terra.com.pe/hotelpremier **F** pp in dormitory, HI-affiliated, cultural and other trips offered.

Camping Overnight vehicle parking at *Hostal Las Mercedes*, Av La Marina 1001, T/F213601. US$6 for 2 including use of toilet and shower.

Eating

Several restaurants overlook the Plaza de Armas on its west side; their staff may pounce on you good-naturedly as you walk by

Expensive *Anushka*, Santa Catalina 204. Open 1700-2100, or later if busy, occasional live music, German specialities, handicrafts for sale. *Ary Quepay*, Jerusalén 502. Excellent local meat and vegetarian dishes, open 1000-2400, slow service. *Picantería La Cantarilla*, Tahuaycani 106-108, Sachaca, T251515, southwest of the centre. Good Arequipeña and Peruvian dishes, including ostrich. *La Rueda*, Mercaderes 206. Excellent *parrilladas*. *Tradición Arequipeña*, Av Dolores 111, Paucarpata, T246467. Restaurant serving excellent food, popular with tourists and locals alike, also dance hall. There are many other restaurants and discos on this avenue.

Mid-range *Parrilla Andina*, Maruri 355. Excellent grill, good service. *Le Bistrot*, Santa Catalina 208. Excellent crepes, good value set lunch, also snacks, cocktails, coffee. *Café-Restaurante Bóveda San Agustín*, Portal San Agustín 127-129. Attractive, good value breakfasts and lunches, evening specials, opens at 0700. *El Camaroncito*, San Francisco y Ugarte. Recommended for seafood. *La Casita de José Antonio*, Plaza San Francisco 401 y Zela. *Cevichería*, fish and seafood. *Challwa*, Moral 113. Peruvian dishes, including *ceviche*, burgers, pasta, seafood, owner speaks English, tourist information. *El Fogón*, Santa Marta 112. Serves large steaks and chops, good. *Gianni*, San Francisco 304. Good value for pasta and pizza. *Los Guisos Arequipeños*, Av Pizarro 111, Lambramani. Good food, quick service, large, popular with locals. *Nómadas*, Melgar 306. Swiss and South American owned, breakfasts, wide menu including vegetarian, sandwiches. *Pizzería Los Leños*, Jerusalén 407. Excellent, good atmosphere, evenings only, popular, especially with tourists. *Pizzería Orcopampa*, Ugarte, opposite *Hotel Le Foyer*. Good food and atmosphere, warm. *Pizzería San Antonio*, Jerusalén y Santa Marta. Popular. *El Rincón Norteño*, San Francisco 300 B. Also for seafood *Zig Zag*, Zela 210, zigzagfood@mailcity.com In a colonial house, European (including Swiss) and local dishes, meats include ostrich and alpaca.

Cheap *Bonanza*, Jerusalén 114. Western-style food. *Café El Buho*, in Casona Chávez de la Rosa (UNSA), San Agustín. Evenings only. Recommended. *El Dólar*, San Juan de Dios 106. All meals available. Recommended. *Pizza Presto*, Gen Morán 108, Mercaderes 401 and other branches. Good. *El Turco*, San Francisco 216. Kebabs, coffee, breakfasts recommended, good sandwiches, open 0700-2200. Also *El Turco II*, San Francisco 315. Turkish, local and international, equally recommended.

Vegetarian *Casa Vegetariana*, Moral 205. Asian, typical local food and western dishes. *Come y Vive Mejor*, Nueva 410A. Cheap and good. *Govinda*, Santa Catalina 120, T285540. Set meal for US$1.25, themed each day, eg, Hindu, Italian, Arequipeño (mixed reports), good yoghurt and muesli, open Mon-Sat 0700-2100. *Lakshmivan*, Jerusalén 402. Set lunch for US$1.25 (small portions), pleasant courtyard. *Mandala*, Jerusalén 207, mandala26@correoweb.com Good value, breakfast, 3 set menus for lunch, buffet, dinner, friendly staff. Recommended.

Peru

Cafés *El Café*, San Francisco 125. Popular meeting place. *La Canasta*, Jerusalén 115. Bakes excellent baguettes twice daily, also serves breakfast and delicious apple and brazil nut pastries. *Café Manolo*, Mercaderes 107 and 113. Great cakes and coffee, also cheap lunches. *Pastelería Salón de Té*, Mercaderes 325. Very clean, open early, good breakfasts. *Café Suri*, on southeast corner of the Plaza. For sandwiches and pastries. Also on southeast corner of Plaza, *La Covacha* and *Da Vinci* (Portal de Flores 132, good). At Jerusalén 603, Jutta Grau and Carlos Gutiérrez bake wonderful German breads. They speak English, French and German and donate all profits to the disadvantaged.

Typical Arequipeño food is available at the San Camilo market. A good local speciality is Mejía cheese. You should also try the *queso helado*, which is frozen fresh milk mixed with sugar and a sprinkling of cinnamon. The local chocolate is excellent: *La Ibérica*, Jerusalén y Moral, is top quality, but expensive. The toffee and the fruit drinks called *papayada* and *tumbada* are also local specialities in the market and restaurants.

Entertainment
Watch out for the local folk-music group Chachani, said to be one of Peru's best

Bars *La Casa de Klaus*, Zela 207. German bar and restaurant, foreign beers, expensive but popular. *Forum*, San Francisco 317. Rock café, live music Thu-Sat 1800-0400, disco, pool tables, US$5 cover if band is playing, includes 1 drink, drinks US$1.50, popular. *Déjà Vu*, San Francisco 319-B. Café/restaurant and bar, good food, DJ evenings, shows movies, popular, 2000-2400. *Caktus*, Moral 223. Good music, concerts, excellent drinks and coffee. *Branighans*, Jerusalén 522-A. Blues-bar, live music Sat, nice atmosphere other nights. **Discos** *Qashwa*, Santa Catalina 200, below *Hospedaje Los Balcones Moral y Santa Catalina*. Fri and Sat 2200 live music. There are many good discos on Av Ejército in Yanahuara.

Local festivals
A full list of the department's many festivals is available locally

10 Jan: *Sor Ana de Los Angeles y Monteagudo*, festival for the patron saint of Santa Catalina monastery. **Mar-Apr:** *Semana Santa* celebrations involve huge processions every night, culminating in the burning of an effigy of Judas on Easter Sunday in the main plazas of Cayma and Yanahuara, and the reading of his will, containing criticisms of the city authorities. **27 Apr:** the celebration of the apostle Santiago. **May** is known as the *Mes de Las Cruces*, with ceremonies on hilltops throughout the city. **3 Aug:** a procession through the city bearing the images of Santo Domingo and San Francisco. **6-31 Aug:** *Fiesta Artesanal del Fundo El Fierro* is a sale and exhibition of *artesanía* from all parts of Peru, taking place near Plaza San Francisco. **6-17 Aug:** celebration of the city's anniversary (the 15th, many events including a mass ascent of El Misti). **2 Nov:** Day of the Dead celebrations in cemeteries.

Shopping

Casa Secchi, Av Víctor Andrés Belaunde 124, in Umacollo (near the aeroplane statue), sells good arts, crafts and clothing. *Alpaca 111*, Zela 212, T223238, recommended for high-quality alpaca and wool products, also in Claustros del Compañía, local 18. *Alpaca 21*, Jerusalén 115, of 125, T213425. Also recommended. *Colca Trading Company*, Santa Catalina 300B, T283737, pakucho@terra.com.pe Sells a wide variety of naturally coloured cotton and alpaca clothing for adults and children. The large *Fundo del Fierro* handicraft market behind the old prison on Plaza San Francisco is also worth a visit. Shop 14 sells alpaca-wool handicrafts from Callalli in the Colca canyon. The covered market opposite the Teatro Municipal in C Mercaderes is recommended for knitted goods, bags, etc. Also the market around Valdivia and N de Piérola. *Lanificio*, La Pampilla s/n, T225305, the factory for high-quality alpaca cloth at better prices than Lima outlets. *Sombrería El Triunfino*, N de Piérola 329-331, good selection of hats, but expensive. *El Zaguán*, Santa Catalina 105, good for handicrafts.

Bookshops For international magazines, look along C San Francisco, between Mercaderes and San José. *Librerías San Francisco* has branches at Portal de Flores 138, San Francisco 102-106 and 133-135. Books on Arequipa and Peru, some in English. *Special Book Services*, Rivero 115-A, Cercado, T205317. Stocks Footprint Handbooks.

Tour operators The following have been recommended as helpful and reliable. Most run tours to the Colca Canyon, some to Cotahuasi. *Castle Travel*, Santo Domingo 302, castle@castletravel.com.pe Good for local tours. *Conresa Tours*, Jerusalén 409, Casilla 563, T285420/247186/602355, conresatours@rch.com.pe Trips to the Colca Canyon, Toro Muerto petroglyphs, Las Salinas and Mejía lakes, and city tours. *Cusipata*, Jerusalén 408A. Specializes in rafting and kayaking in Cotahuasi. *Holley's Unusual Excursions*, T/F258459 (home) any day 1700-0700, or all day Sat and Sun, or Mon-Fri 0800-1600 T222525/225000 and leave a message, www.barrioperu.terra.com.pe/angocho Expat Englishman Anthony Holley runs trips in his Land Rover to El Misti, Toro Muerto, the desert and coast. *Ideal Travels SAC*, Urb San Isidro F-2, Vallecito, T244439, F242088, idealperu@terra.com.pe Open Mon-Fri 0800-1900, Sat 0830-1300, tours to Colca Canyon (2 days, 1 night, US$45-75, depending on accommodation, private service, all meals, rafting US$33), Cotahuasi Canyon, Andagua Volcanic valley, Majes River, Cotahuasi River, Toro Muerto, jeep and microbus rentals, excellent bilingual guides, international ticket reservations, accepts credit cards. *Illary Tours*, Santa Catalina 205, T220844. English-speaking guides, open daily 0800-1300, 1500-1930. *Inca Trail Tours*, Jerusalén 203. OK. *Naturaleza Activa*, Santa Catalina 211, T204182, naturactiva@yahoo.com Experienced guides, knowledgeable, climbing and trekking. *Santa Catalina Tours*, Santa Catalina 219-223, T216994. Offer unique tours of Collagua communities in the Colca Canyon, open daily 0800-1900. *Servicios Aéreos AQP SA*, head office in Lima, Los Castaños 347, San Isidro, T01-222 3312, F01-222 5910, tours@saaqp.com.pe Offers tours to Arequipa, Colca and to all parts of the country. *Transcontinential Arequipa*, Puente Bolognesi 132, of 5, T213843, F218608, transcontinental-aqp@terra.com.pe Cultural and wildlife tours in the Colca Canyon. *Volcanyon Travel*, C Villalba 414, T205078, mario-ortiz@terra.com.pe Trekking and some mountain bike tours in the Colca Canyon, also volcano climbing. Guide Jorg Krosel, T997971, joergkrosel@hotmail.com or contact through *Wasi Tours*, Santa Catalina 207. German guide who also speaks English, enthusiastic, efficient, trekking, oxygen carried on high-altitude trips, including Colca. **Climbing**: *Zárate Expeditions*, Santa Catalina 204, of 3, T202461/263107. Run by brothers Carlos and Miguel Zárate of the Mountaineering Club of Peru. They are mountaineers and explorers, who have information and advice and rent some equipment. A recommended guide for climbing, trekking, mountain biking and river rafting in the Colca Canyon is Vlado Soto, Jerusalén 401 B, T600170, F206217, colcatrek@hotmail.com He is knowledgeable and helpful and also rents equipment. Another climbing guide recommended as experienced and "full of energy" is *Julver Castro*, who has an agency called *Mountrekk*, T601833, julver_mountrekk@ hotmail.com

Many agencies on Jerusalén, Santa Catalina and around Plaza de Armas sell air, train and bus tickets and offer tours of Colca, Cotahuasi, Toro Muerto, Campiña and city. Prices vary greatly so shop around. As a general rule, you get what you pay for, so check carefully what is included in the cheapest of tours. Always settle the details before starting the tour and check that there are enough people for the tour to run. Travel agents frequently work together to fill buses (even the more expensive agencies may not have their own transport) and there are lots of touts. Many tourists prefer to contract tours through their hotel. If a travel agency puts you in touch with a guide, make sure he/she is official.

Local Car repairs: *FCI, Fidel Condorvilca*, Cacique Alpaca 205, Cayma, T271175. **Bicycle** **Transport** **repairs and equipment**: *Andes Bike*, Villalba 414, T205078 (see *Volcanyon Travel*, above). **Taxi**: US$4-5 airport to city (can be shared). US$0.70-0.85 around town, including to bus terminal. *Nova Taxi*, T252511; *Taxi 21*, T212121; *Telemóvil*, T221515; *Taxitur*, T422323; *Henry Málaga*, T655095, Spanish only.

Long distance Air: Rodríguez Ballón airport is 7 km from town, T443464. To and from **Lima**, 1 hr 10 mins, several daily with *Aero Continente/Aviandina, Lan Perú* and *Tans*. All serve **Juliaca**, 30 mins, while *Lan Perú* fly daily to **Cusco**, 40 mins, and *Lan Perú* and *Tans* fly to Tacna, 40 mins.

A reliable means of transport to and from the airport to the hotel of your choice is with *King Tours*, T243357/283037, US$1.30 pp; give 24 hrs notice for return pick-up from your hotel; journey takes 30-40 mins depending on traffic. Transport to the airport may be arranged when buying a ticket at a travel agency, US$1 pp, but not always reliable. Local buses go to about ½ km from the airport.

Buses There are two terminals at Av Andrés A Cáceres s/n, Parque Industrial, opposite *Inca Tops* factory, south of the centre; 15 mins from the centre by colectivo US$0.20, or taxi

US$1.75. The older terminal is Terminal Terrestre, which contains a tourist office, shops and places to eat. The newer terminal is Terrapuerto, the other side of the carpark, also with a tourist office (which makes hotel reservations) and its own hostal (**E** without breakfast), T421375. Terminal tax US$0.30. Buses may not depart from the terminal where you bought your ticket ("¿Por dónde me embarco, Terminal o Terrapuerto?") All the bus companies have their offices in Terminal Terrestre and several also have offices in Terrapuerto. Some companies also have offices around C San Juan de Dios (5-6 blocks from the Plaza de Armas), where tickets can be bought in advance. Addresses are given below.

Theft is a serious problem in the bus station area. Take a taxi to and from the bus station and do not wander around with your belongings

To **Lima**, 1,011 km, 16-18 hrs, 'normal' service US$8.70, 'imperial' US$17.40 (video, toilet, meals, comfortable seats, blankets), 'crucero' US$23-29 several daily; *Enlaces* (T430333, office only in Terrapuerto), *Ormeño* (T423975, or San Juan de Dios 657, T218885) and *Cruz del Sur* (T216625, or Av Salaverry 121, T213905) are recommended (prices quoted are of Cruz del Sur). The road is paved but drifting sand and breakdowns may prolong the trip.

To **Nasca**, 566 km, 9 hrs, US$7.25, several buses daily, mostly at night and most buses continue to Lima. Some bus companies charge the same fare to Nasca as to Lima. To **Moquegua**, 213 km, 3 hrs, US$3-5.85, several buses and colectivos daily. To **Tacna**, 320 km, 6-7 hrs, US$3.85-4.40, several buses daily, most with *Flores*.

To **Cusco**, 521 km, 12 bumpy hrs direct, eg with Carhuamayo at 0700, 1700 and 1800, US$7.25. Otherwise go via Juliaca or Puno. There is a new, quick paved road to **Juliaca**, via Yura amd Santa Lucía, cutting the Arequipa-Juliaca journey time to 5 hrs, US$5.80, and **Puno**, 6 hrs. Most buses and colectivos continue to Puno. Just about all bus companies are now using the new route. Another paved route runs Arequipa-Moquegua-Desaguadero-Puno-Juliaca: 12 hrs to **Puno** and 13 hrs to **Juliaca**.

Ormeño to **Santiago**, Tue and Sat, US$60.

If you feel bad on the train ask for the oxygen mask immediately

Trains: The railway system goes from Arequipa to Juliaca, where it divides, one line going north to Cusco, the other south to Puno. With the opening of the new Arequipa-Juliaca highway, the decreased demand for rail travel has lead to the end of regular passenger services on this route. *PerúRail* runs trains for private charter of for groups of over 40. There are plans to open the route for the peak season months of Jul and Aug, although this has not been confirmed. The service Puno-Juliaca-Cuzco is running as usual. The railway station is at Av Tacna y Arica 201, corner with Angamos.

Directory

Airline offices *Aero Continente* and *Aviandina*, Portal San Agustín 113, T207294. *LanPerú*, Santa Catalina 118-C, T 201100. *Tans*, Portal San Agustín 143A, T203637. Most tour agencies sell air tickets. **Banks** *Interbank*, Mercaderes 217, exchanges Citicorp dollar cheques. *Banco de Crédito*, San Juan de Dios 125, accepts Visa Card and gives good rates, no commission, Visa ATM. *Banco Continental*, San Francisco 108. Visa ATM. *BSCH*, C Jerusalén, close to Post Office, will change TCs, low rates, Visa ATM. *Banco Wiese*, Mercaderes 410. Also *cambios* on Jerusalén and San Juan de Dios, and several travel agencies. *Sergio A del Carpio D*, Jerusalén 126, T242987, good rates for dollars. *Via Tours*, Santo Domingo 114, good rates. *Casa de Cambio*, San Juan de Dios 109, T282528, good rates. It is almost impossible to change TCs on Sat afternoon or Sun; try to find a sympathetic street changer. Better rates for cash dollars in banks and *casas de cambio*. **Communications** Internet: *C@tedr@l*, Pasaje Catedral 101, T220622, internetcatedral@hotmail.com Open 0800-2400, fast machines, international phone calls. *Chips Internet*, San Francisco 202-A, chips@chips.com.pe *La Red Café Internet*, Jerusalén 306, café@LaRed.net.pe Good service, open 0830-2200, US$0.45 per hr, good for netphone. Also on Jerusalén: *Tienes un Email* at No 306B, and *Tr@vel Net*, No 218, US$0.75 per hr and international phone calls. *Líder Tours*, Portal San Agustín 105, Plaza de Armas, www.lider.lared.net.pe, US$0.75 per hr. *Net Central*, Alvarez Thomas 219, netcentral@netcentral. lared.net.pe Open 0900-2300, fast machines. *Cybercafé.com*, Santa Catalina 115-B, at *Easy Market*. US$0.75 per hr. Another at Puente Bolognesi 108, open 0700-2300.The central **Post Office** is at Moral 118, opposite *Hotel Crismar*. Letters can only be posted at the Post Office during opening hours: Mon-Sat, 0800-2000, Sun 0800-1400. **Telephone:** telephone and fax at Alvarez Thomas y Palacio Viejo. *DHL*, T234288/250045 for sending documents and money, also Western Union rep. *World Courier*, T241925, F218139. **Cultural centres** Instituto Cultural Peruano-Norte Americano, Casa de los Mendiburo, Melgar 109, T243201, has an **English Library**. Instituto Cultural Peruano Alemán, Ugarte 207, T228130. Instituto Regional de Cultura, Gen Morán 118 (altos), T213171. Instituto Nacional de Cultura,

Alameda San Lázaro 120, T213171. **Alianza Francesa**, Santa Catalina 208, T215579, F286777, aptdo 2724, www.ambafrancia.com.pe **Consulates Bolivia**, Mercaderes 212, of 405, T205703, Mon-Fri 0900-1400, 24 hrs for visa (except those needing clearance from La Paz), go early. **Chile**, Mercaderes 212, p 4, Of 401-402, Galerías Gameza, T/F233556/933556, entrance to lift 30 m down passageway down Mercaderes on left, open Mon-Fri 0900-1300, present passport 0900-1100 if you need a visa. **France**, Estadio Oeste 201-A, IV Centenario, T232119 (Sun T224915), Mon-Fri 1530-1900. **Germany**, in Colegio Max Uhle, Av Fernandini s/n, Sachaca, Mon-Fri 0900-1300, Casilla 743, T232921. **Italy**, La Salle D-5, T221444, open 1130-1300, in the afternoon T254686 (home). **Netherlands**, Mercaderes 410 (Banco Wiese), Sr Herbert Ricketts, T219567, F215437, Casilla 1, open Mon-Fri 0900-1300, 1630-1830. **Spain**, Ugarte 218, p 2, T214977 (home T224915), open Mon-Fri 1100-1300, Sat 0900-1300. **Sweden**, Av Villa Hermosa 803, Cerro Colorado, T259847/252868, open Mon-Fri 0830-1300, 1500-1730. **Switzerland**, Av Miguel Forga 348, Parque Industrial, T232723/229998. **UK**, Mr Roberts, Tacna y Arica 156, T241340, gerencia@roberts.rh.com.pe Mon-Fri 0830-1230, 1500-1830, reported as very friendly and helpful. **Language courses** Silvana Cornejo, 7 de Junio 118, Cerrito Los Alvarez, Cerro Colorado, T254985, US$6 per hr, negotiable for group, recommended, she speaks German fluently; her sister Roxanna charges US$3 per hr. Fidelia and Charo Sánchez, T224238, highly recommended, Fidelia speaks French, Charo English. *Centro de Intercambio Cultural Arequipa (CEICA)*, Urb Universitaria G-9, T/F231759. Classes at US$5 per hr, accommodation with families arranged, with or without board, also excursions. Also at Instituto Peruano-Norte Americano and Instituto Cultural Peruano Alemán. **Medical services Hospitals: Regional Honorio Delgado**, Av A Carrión s/n, T238465/231818 (inoculations). **General Base Goyeneche**, Av Goyeneche s/n, T211313. **Nacional del Sur**, Filtro y Peral s/n, T214430 in emergency. **Clinics: Clínica Arequipa SA**, esq Puente Grau y Av Bolognesi, T253424, fast and efficient with English-speaking doctors and all hospital facilities, consultation costs US$18, plus US$4 for sample analysis and around US$7 for a course of antibiotics. **San Juan de Dios**, Av Ejército 1020, Cayma, T252256/255544. **Monte Carmelo**, Gómez de la Torre 119, T231444, T/F287048. **Emergencies:** Ambulance T289800. **Pharmacy:** *Farmacia Libertad*, Piérola 108, owner speaks English.

Colca Canyon

The Colca Canyon is twice as deep as the Grand Canyon. The Río Colca descends from 3,500 m above sea level at Chivay to 2,200 m at Cabanaconde. The roads on either side of the canyon are at around 4,000 m. In the background looms the grey, smoking mass of Sabancaya, one of the most active volcanoes in the Americas, and its more docile neighbour, Ampato (6,288 m). Unspoiled Andean villages lie on both sides of the canyon, inhabited by the Cabana and Collagua peoples, and some of the extensive precolumbian terraced fields are still in use. High on anyone's list for visiting the canyon is an early-morning trip to the Cruz del Cóndor, to see these majestic birds at close quarters. From January to April is the rainy season, but this makes the area green, with lots of flowers. This is not the best time to see condors. May to December is the dry, cold season when there is more chance of seeing the birds.

Tours Travel agencies in Arequipa arrange a 'one-day' tour to the Mirador for US$18-20: depart Arequipa at 0400, arrive at the Cruz del Cóndor at 0800-0900, expensive lunch stop at Chivay and back to Arequipa by 2100; for many, especially for those with altitude problems, this is too much to fit into one day[the only advantage is that you don't have to sleep at high altitude]. Two-day tours start at US$20-30 pp with an overnight stop in Chivay; more expensive tours range from US$45 to US$75 with accommodation at the top of the range. Allow at least 2-3 days to appreciate the Colca Canyon fully, more if planning to do some trekking.

Local festivals Many in the Colca region: **2-3 Feb**: *Virgen de la Candelaria*, Chivay, Cabanaconde, Maca, Tapay. *Semana Santa*. **3 May**: *Cruz de la Piedra*, Tuti. **13 Jun**: *San Antonio*, Yanque, Maca. **14 Jun**: *San Juan*, Sibayo, Ichupampa. **21 Jun**: anniversary of Chivay. **29 Jun**: *San Pedro y San Pablo*, Sibayo. **14-17 Jul**: *La Virgen del Carmen*, Cabanaconde. **25 Jul**: *Santiago Apóstol*, Coporaque. **26 Jul-2 Aug**: *Virgen Santa Ana*, Maca. **15 Aug**: *Virgen de la Asunta*, Chivay. **8 Dec**: *Immaculada Concepción*, Yanque, Chivay. **25 Dec**: *Sagrada Familia*, Yanque. Many of these festivals last several days and involve traditional dances and customs.

Peru

Trekking There are many hiking possibilities in the area. Make sure to take enough water as it gets very hot and there is not a lot of water available. Moreover, sun protection is a must. Some treks are impossible if it rains heavily in the wet season, but this is very rare. Check beforehand. Ask locals for directions as there are hundreds of confusing paths going into the canyon. Buy food for longer hikes in Arequipa. Topographical maps are available at the *Instituto Geográfico Militar* in Lima, and good information from *South American Explorers*. From Chivay you can hike to Coporaque and Ichupampa, cross the river by the footbridge and climb up to Yanque, a 1-day hike. It is a 2-hr walk from the Mirador to Cabanaconde (or the other way round – horses can be hired) by a short cut, following the canyon instead of the road, which takes 3 hrs. It takes 2 days to walk from Chivay to Cabanaconde (70 km), you can camp along the route.

Two hours below Cabanaconde is Sangalle, an 'oasis' of palm trees, swimming areas and 2 campsites with toilets, US$1.50-3 (3-4½ hrs back up, ask for the best route in both directions, horses can be hired to carry your bag up, US$5.85), recommended. The hike from Cabanaconde to Tapay takes four hours; possible stay overnight in Tapay, or camp.

Chivay to A poor dirt road runs north from Arequipa, over the altiplano, to **Chivay** (3,600 m),
Cabanaconde the first village on the edge of the Canyon. About an hour out of Arequipa is the **Aguada Blanca National Vicuña Reserve**. If you're lucky, you can see herds of these rare animals near the road. This route affords fine views of the volcanoes Misti, Chachani, Ampato and Sabancaya. ■ *US$2 entrance fee to the canyon (not included in agency prices). Cyclists should use the new road via Yura; better condition and less of a climb at the start. The* PerúRail *train service from Arequipa to Juliaca and Puno stops at Sumbay, from where road transport continues to Chivay.*

Chivay is the linking point between the two sides of the canyon, as it has the only bridge over the river. The road continues northeast to **Tuti**, where there is a small handicrafts shop, and **Sibayo**, with a *pensión* and grocery store. A long circuit back to Arequipa heads south from Sibayo, passing through **Puente Callalli**, **Chullo** and **Sumbay**. This is a little-travelled road, but the views of fine landscapes with vicuña, llamas, alpacas and Andean duck are superb.

Crossing the river at Chivay going west to follow the canyon on the far side, you pass the villages of **Coporaque**, **Ichupampa** (where a footbridge crosses the river between the two villages and another connects with Achoma), **Lari**, **Madrigal** (footbridge to Maca) and **Tapay** (connected to Cabanaconde by a footbridge).

Chivay (3,600 m) is the gateway to the canyon. The hot springs of **La Calera** are 4-5 km away, regular colectivos (US$0.25) or a one hour walk from town, highly recommended after a hard day's trekking. ■ *US$1.25.*

From Chivay, the main road goes west along the Colca Canyon. The first village encountered is **Yanque** (8 km, excellent views), with an interesting church and a bridge to the villages on the other side of the canyon. A large thermal swimming pool is 20 minutes walk from the plaza, beside the renovated Inca bridge on the Yanque-Ichupampa road, US$0.75.

The road continues to **Achoma** and **Maca**, which barely survived an earthquake in November 1991. New housing has been built. The Mirador, or **Cruz del Cóndor**, is at the deepest point of the canyon. The view is wonderful and condors can be seen rising on the morning thermals (0900, arrive by 0800 to get a good spot) and sometimes in the late afternoon (1600-1800). Camping here is officially forbidden, but if you ask the tourist police in Chivay they may help. The 0500 bus from Chivay to Cabanaconde will stop here briefly at 0700 (if not, ask), US$0.75. Take the return bus from Cabanaconde (0730) and ask to be dropped off at the Mirador.

From the Mirador it is a 20-minute ride (or three-hour walk) to **Cabanaconde** (3,287 m), a friendly, typical basic, very basic (electricity 2000-2300, take a torch/flashlight). It is the last village in the Colca Canyon; it suffered badly in an earthquake in April 1998. The views are superb and condors can be seen from the hill just west of the village, a 15-minute walk from the plaza. A path winds down into the canyon and up to the village of Tapay.

Peru

Chivay C *Rumi Llacta*, 3 blocks from the plaza off the Arequipa road, T521098. Attractive cabins, hot showers, cosy bar/dining area. Recommended. **C** *Wasi Kolping*, 10 blocks south of town opposite Plaza de Toros, T521076. Comfortable cabins with hot shower, quiet, good views. **D** *El Posada del Inca*, Salaverry 330, T521032. Modern, with hot showers, carpeted rooms, safe. **E** *Hostal Anita*, north side of plaza. Small garden. Recommended. **E** *Inca*, Salavery, spacious rooms, good restaurant, vehicle parking. **F** *Hospedaje Jessy*, Zarumilla 218, 1 block from market. Simple, clean, excellent showers, **G** without bath, helpful, parking. **F** *Hospedaje Restaurant Los Portales*, Sucre, T521101. Good accommodation, breakfast US$0.75, same price for dinner in restaurant. **F** *La Casa de Lucila*, M Grau 131, T054-607086. Comfortable, coffee, guides available. **F** pp *Los Leños*, on Bolognesi. Safe, good breakfast and tomato soup. Recommended. **G** pp *Rumi Wasi*, C Sucre, 6 blocks from plaza (3 mins'walk). New, good rooms, breakfast included, hot water, helpful. *Casa Blanca*, on main plaza, good, main dishes US$2.50-7.50. *Fonda del Cazador*, north side of plaza, *Ricardito and Posada del Cóndor*, both on Salavery, are good places to eat. Local food can be found at *Don Angel*, near the health centre, and *La Pascana*, near the Plaza de Armas, both cheap. *Farren's*, bar owned by an Irishman, handmade Guinness sign outside, also bikes for hire. For bike hire and rafting tours, *Colca Adventures*, 22 de Agosto 101, T531137, rcordova@terra.com.pe Good machines and equipment, very helpful.

Between Chivay and Yanque AL *Parador del Colca*, paradorcolca@chasqui.lared.net.pe Built of local materials, comfortable suites, hot water, electricity, gardens, plenty of excursions, all meals available, price includes taxes. Recommended. **Yanque** itself has *Posada de Yanque*, run by Remi and Vitaliana Suyco. Nice rooms, traditional meals, guiding to local sites. Recommended. One other *Hostal*. **Coporaque** *Casa del Turista Mayta Capac*, on the plaza (Sr Mejía). Ask to see his collection of old pictures; he also knows some good excursions. **Between Coporaque and Ichupampa C** *Colca Lodge* (www.colca-lodge.com In Arequipa Zela 212, T212813). Very pleasant and relaxing, with beautiful hot springs beside the river, spend at least a day to make the most of the activities on offer. Recommended. **Ichupampa** *Casa del Turista Inca*, family lodging where Lourdes can act as a guide; in the morning, watch the bread being made and then taste it.

Cabanaconde E *Posada del Conde*, C San Pedro, T440197, F441197, T936809 (Mob). **G** in low season, new, with hot shower, excellent value, very good restaurant. **F** *Virgen del Carmen*, 5 blocks up from plaza. Hot showers, welcoming. **G** *Hostal San Pedro*, 2 blocks from plaza. Bright rooms, no shower. **G** *Hostal Valle del Fuego*, 1 and 2 blocks from the plaza, T280367 (Arequipa 203737). Good but basic, has two places, both with restaurants serving good meals for around US$3. The owner and his son, both Pablo Junco, is a wealth of information. There are several basic restaurants around the plaza, including *Rancho del Colca*, which is mainly vegetarian.

From Arequipa there are two routes to Chivay: the old route, via Cayma, called 'Cabreritas'; the new route, through Yura, following the railway, longer but quicker. *Cristo Rey*, *La Reyna* and *Andalucia* (recommended) have 7 departures daily from Arequipa to **Chivay**, continuing to **Cabanaconde** ; a further 75 km, 2 hrs, US$1. *La Reyna* has the quickest service, about 6 hrs, US$3.85, others US$3. It is a rough route and cold in the morning, reaching 4,825 m in the Pata Pampa pass, but the views are worth it. Buses return to Arequipa from the market. **Chivay-Cabanaconde** Combis run infrequently in each direction, none on Sun. Buses leave Cabanaconde for Arequipa from 0730 to 2300. It is difficult to go to Cusco from Chivay: you can take a colectivo to Puente Callalli, but the police there are unwilling to let passengers wait for a passing Cusco-bound bus, which may not stop anyway. Best to go back to Arequipa.

West of Arequipa, a dirt road branches off the Pan-American to Corire, Aplao and the Río Majes valley. The **world's largest field of petroglyphs** at Toro Muerto is near Corire, where there are several hotels and restaurants near the plaza. For Toro Muerto, turn-off on the right heading back out of Corire; one hour walk; ask directions. The higher you go, the more interesting the petroglyphs, though many have been ruined by graffiti. The designs range from simple llamas to elaborate human figures and animals. The sheer scale of the site is awe-inspiring and the view is

Sleeping & eating

Families in the Colca Canyon offer meals for about US$1 and lodging at US$2 Banco de la Nación on plaza will change dollars

Transport

Toro Muerto

Peru

wonderful (UNESCO World Heritage Site). Take plenty of water, sunglasses and protection against the sun. ■ *US$2; entrance 10 mins' drive from the petroglyphs. Buses to Corire leave from Arequipa main terminal hourly from 0500, 3 hrs, US$3. Ask to be let out at the beginning of the track to Toro Muerto, or from the plaza in Corire take a taxi, US$6-10 including 2-hr wait. If walking note that it takes 2 hrs to walk around the site, a lot in the heat.*

Cotahuasi Canyon

See www.lared.net.pe/ cotahuasi

Beyond Aplao the road heads north through **Chuquibamba** (festivals 20 January; 2-3 February; 15 May) traversing the western slopes of Nevado Coropuna (6,425 m), before winding down into **Cotahuasi** (*Population:* 4,000. *Altitude:* 2,683 m). The peaceful colonial town nestles in a sheltered hanging valley beneath Cerro Huinao. Its streets are narrow, the houses whitewashed. Local festival is 4 May.

Several kilometres away a canyon has been cut by the Río Cotahuasi, which flows into the Pacific as the Río Ocuña. At its deepest, at Ninochaca (just below the village of Quechualla), the canyon is 3,354 m deep, 163 m deeper than the Colca Canyon and the deepest in the world. From this point the only way down the canyon is by kayak and it is through kayakers' reports since 1994 that the area has come to the notice of tourists (it was declared a Zona de Reserva Turística in 1988). There is little agriculture apart from some citrus groves, but in Inca times the road linking Puerto Inca and Cusco ran along much of the canyon's course.

One of the main treks in the region follows the Inca trade road from Cotahuasi to Quechualla. From the football pitch the path goes through Piro, the gateway to the canyon, and Sipia (three hours, two suspension bridges to cross), near which are the powerful, 150 m high Cataratas de Sipia (take care near the falls if it is windy). The next three-hour stretch to Chaupo is not for vertigo sufferers as the path is barely etched into the canyon wall, 400 m above the river in places. At Chaupo ask permission to camp in the citrus groves; do not pick the fruit (it's a cash crop); water is available. Next is Velinga, then the dilapidated but extensive ruin of Huña, then **Quechualla**, a charming village and administrative capital of the district. Ask Sr Carmelo Velásquez Gálvez for permission to sleep in the schoolhouse. On the opposite side of the river are the ruined terraces of Maucullacta. If it rains, Quechualla can be cut off for days as sections where the river has to be waded become too deep and treacherous (eg just past Velinga).

Rafting It is possible to raft or kayak from a point on the Upper Cotahuasi, just past the town, almost to the Pacific (boats are usually taken out of the water at the village of Iquipi), a descent of 2,300 m. Season May-August; rapids class 3-5; some portaging unavoidable.

Sleeping & eating **F** *Alojamiento Chávez*, Jr Cabildo 125, T210222. Rooms around pleasant courtyard, friendly. Recommended, Sr José Chávez is helpful on places to visit, if a little vague on timings. And others. *Restaurant Ucho*, Jr Centenario, clean, good *menú*, also bar and hostal. 3 small restaurants/bars on Jr Arequipa offer basic fare. There are many well-stocked *tiendas*, particularly with fruit and vegetables.

Transport **Buses** 3 companies daily from Arequipa bus terminal, 12 hrs, US$9: *Alex*; *Cromotex*, at 1730; *Reyna* at 1700; all return from the plaza in Cotahuasi in the afternoon. To travel by day, take a *Sánchez* bus that goes to **Lima** at 0830 on Tue from Cotahuasi, or *Panorama*, Fri, 0800.

Directory **Useful services** No money exchange. *PNP*, on plaza; advisable to register with them on arrival and before leaving. **Maps:** some survey maps in Municipalidad and PNP; they may let you make photocopies (shop on the corner of the plaza and Arequipa). Sr Chávez has photocopies of the sheets covering Cotahuasi and surroundings.

South to Chile

Matarani 14½ km to the northwest has now replaced Mollendo as a port. Mollendo now depends partly upon the summer attraction of the beaches, during which time hotels can be full. There are three sandy beaches stretching down the coast, with the small beach nearest town the safest for swimming. The swimming pool on the beach is open January-March. The summer season starts on 6 January, which is the anniversary of the district. The small national reserve at the Lagunas de Mejía has 72 resident species of birds and 62 visiting species. ■ *US$1.50. Arrive early in the morning to see the birdlife at its best.*

Mollendo
Phone code: 054
Colour map 6, grid A1
Population: 30,000

Sleeping and eating **C** *Hostal Cabaña*, Comercio 240. Good. **D** *Hostal Willy*, Deán Valdivia 437-443. Hot water, modern, spacious, disco nearby. Recommended. There are several other cheap options in the **E-F** range on Arica. **F** *Hostal California*, Blondel 541, T535160. Best rooms at top, restaurant. Recommended. Several restaurants including *Cevichería Tío*, Comercio 208, excellent, cheap set meals. Several others on Comercio (eg *Tambo, Hong Kong Express*).

Transport **Buses** To **Arequipa**, 129 km, buses and colectivos daily, 3 hrs, US$3, many companies on Comercio opposite the church. To **Moquegua**, 156 km, 2 hrs, US$2-3, several buses and colectivos daily. To **Tacna**, 315 km, take colectivo from C Comercio early morning to El Fiscal, US$0.40, about 55 km, and connect with Arequipa-Tacna buses.

This peaceful town 213 km from Arequipa in the narrow valley of the Moquegua River enjoys a sub-tropical climate. The town was severely damaged by the earthquake of June 2001, but by the end of the year all services were operating. The old centre, a few blocks above the Pan-American Highway, has winding, cobbled streets and 19th-century buildings. The Plaza de Armas, with its mix of ruined and well-maintained churches, colonial and republican façades and fine trees, is one of the most interesting small-town plazas in the country. **Museo Contisuyo** on the Plaza de Armas, is within the ruins of the Iglesia Matriz. It covers the cultures which thrived in the Moquegua and Ilo valleys, including the Huari, Tiahuanaco, Chiribaya and Estuquiña, who were conquered by the Incas. Artefacts from the area are well-displayed and all the exhibits are clearly explained in Spanish and English. ■ *Mon-Sun 1000-1300, 1500-1730, except Tue 1000-1200, 1630-2000, US$0.45, T761844, www.members.aol.com/contisuyo/MuseoC.html Día de Santa Catalina*, 25 November, is the anniversary of the founding of the colonial city. There are several email offices in or near the Plaza de Armas. **Tourist offices** Jr Callao 121, in the Prefectura, is more administrative than service oriented, open 0830-1600.

A highly recommended excursion is to **Cerro Baúl**, 2,590 m, a tabletop mountain with marvellous views and many legends, which can be combined with the pleasant town of Torata, 24 km northeast (30 mins by colectivo, US$0.60).

Moquegua
Phone code: 054
Colour map 6, grid A1
Population: 110,000
Altitude: 1,412 m

Peru

Sleeping and eating **D** *Limoneros*, Jr Lima 441, T761649. Hot water, **E** without bath, helpful, car park, old house with basic rooms, nice garden (earthquake damage in 2001). **D** *Los Angeles*, Jr Torata 100-A, T762629. Cheaper without, hot water, TV, large comfortable rooms, market right outside, close to buses. Recommended. **D** *Hostal Adrianella*, Miguel Grau 239, T/F763469. Modern, hot water, TV, safe, helpful, tourist information, close to market and buses. Recommended. **E** *Hostal Carrera*, Jr Lima 320, T762113. Hot water (**F** shared bath, cold water), laundry facilities on roof. Recommended. **F** pp *Hospedaje Cornejo*, Tarapacá 281-A, T761034. Shared bath, hot water. The best place for meals is *Moraly*, Lima y Libertad. Breakfast, good lunches, *menú* US$1.75. Several other places, including *chifas*, in town.

Hotels do not serve breakfast

Transport **Buses**: All bus companies are on Av Ejército, 2 blocks north of the market at Jr Grau, except *Ormeño*, Av La Paz casi Balta. From **Lima**, US$23.50-11.75, 5 companies with executive and regular services. To **Tacna**, 159 km, 2 hrs, US$2, several buses and colectivos daily. To **Arequipa**, 3 hrs, US$3-5.85, several buses daily. To **Desaguadero**, 4 hrs, US$6 (11.75 *Ormeño*), and **Puno**, 5-6 hrs, US$7.35, several companies on the new road (see below). *Mily Tours*, Ev Ejército, T764000, run colectivos to Desaguadero, 3½ hrs, US$10. *Ormeño* continues to **La Paz**, US$30, and to Cusco, US$23.50, as does *Cruz del Sur*, US$17.65.

Moquegua to Desaguadero The Carretera Binacional, from Ilo to La Paz, has a breathtaking stretch from Moquegua to Desaguadero at the southeastern end of Lake Titicaca. It skirts Cerro Baúl and climbs through zones of ancient terraces to its highest point at 4,755 m. On the altiplano there are herds of llamas and alpacas, lakes with waterfowl, strange mountain formations and snow-covered peaks. At Mazo Cruz there is a PNP checkpoint where all documents and bags are checked. Approaching Desaguadero the Cordillera Real of Bolivia comes into view. The road is fully paved and should be taken in daylight.

Tacna

Phone code: 054
Colour map 6, grid A1
Population: 150,200
Altitude: 550 m
156 km S of Moquegua via the Pan-American Highway
1,292 km from Lima

Only 36 km from the Chilean border and 56 km from the international port of Arica, Tacna is fighting to gain free-trade status from the government. It is an important commercial centre and Chileans come for cheap medical and dental treatment. Around the city the desert is gradually being irrigated. The local economy includes olive groves, vineyards and fishing. Tacna was in Chilean hands from 1880 to 1929, when its people voted by plebiscite to return to Peru. Above the city (8 km away, just off the Panamericana Norte), on the heights, is the **Campo de la Alianza**, scene of a battle between Peru and Chile in 1880. The cathedral, designed by Eiffel, faces the Plaza de Armas, which contains huge bronze statues of Admiral Grau and Colonel Bolognesi. They stand at either end of the Arca de los Héroes, the triumphal arch which is the symbol of the city. The bronze fountain in the Plaza is said to be a

Peru

Tacna

N
0 metres 400
0 yards 400

■ **Sleeping**
1 Alameda
2 El Mesón
3 Hostal Bon Ami
4 Hostal HC
5 Gran Hotel Central
6 Gran Hotel Tacna
7 Lido
8 Lima & Phone Office

● **Eating**
1 Delfín Azul
2 Le Petit, El Sabor Criollo & Shaffie's House
3 Margarita's Café
4 Sociedad de Alimentación Vegetariana
5 Sur Perú
6 Vida y Salud

duplicate of the one in the Place de la Concorde (Paris) and was also designed by Eiffel. The **Parque de la Locomotora**, near the city centre, has a British-built locomotive, which was used in the War of the Pacific. There is a very good railway museum at the station. ■ *Daily 0700-1700, US$0.30; knock at the gate under the clock tower on Jr 2 de Mayo for entry.* The house of Francisco Zela, who gave the Cry of Independence on 20 July 1811, is a museum. ■ *Mon-Sat 0830-1230, 1530-1900, Zela 542.*

Sleeping & eating

Beware of pickpockets in the market area

A *Gran Hotel Tacna*, Av Bolognesi 300, T724193, F722015. Gardens, 2 swimming pools, safe car park, good breakfast for US$3-4, *menú* US$6, English spoken. **C** *Gran Hotel Central*, San Martín 561, T712281, F726031. With breakfast, central, secure, English spoken. Recommended. **C** *El Mesón*, Unánue 175, T725841, F721832, mesonhotel@terra.com.pe With breakfast, TV, central, modern, comfortable, safe, internet service. Recommended. **D-E** *Lima*, San Martín 442, T711912, on Plaza de Armas, american_tours@hotmail.com With breakfast, TV, hot water, bar, good restaurant, stores luggage. **E** *Alameda*, Bolognesi 780, T744978. **F** without bath or TV, good food. Recommended. **E** *Hostal Bon Ami*, 2 de Mayo 445, T711873. **F** without bath, hot water, secure. **E** *Hostal HC*, Zela 734, T742042. Hot water, TV, discounts available, cafetería next door, laundry service, videos. Recommended. **E** *Lido*, San Martín 876-A, near Plaza de Armas, T741598. With hot showers, no breakfast. Recommended. One recommended eating place is *Sur Perú*, Bolívar 380. Popular for lunch are *Shaffie's House*, Ayacucho 84-B, *El Sabor Criollo*, No 86-C, and *Le Petit*, No 88-A, US$2 *menú*. *Delfín Azul*, Zela 375. Good. *Margarita's Café*, Unánue 145, T711481. Excellent French pastry and desserts, nice inviting ambience, cheap, open 1600-2130. Recommended. Vegetarian: at *Vida y Salud*, Bolívar 335. Swiss-Peruvian owned and run, German, French and English spoken, yoghurts and juices, natural products for sale, also serves meat, good, open 0730-2030. *Sociedad de Alimentación Vegetariana*, Zela 495, T711037. Open Mon-Fri and Sun with reservation. *La Espiga*, San Martín 431. Good bakery and pastry shop.

Transport

Air To **Lima**, 1½ hrs; daily flights with *Aero Continente*, *Lan Perú* and *Tans*. To **Arequipa**, 40 mins with *Lan Perú* and *Tans*. Taxi to town and bus terminal US$3. It is possible to take a taxi from the airport to **Arica**, US$30 (can be shared), but the cheapest way is to take a taxi to the bus station, then take a colectivo.

Tickets can be purchased several days before departure and buses fill up quickly

Bus Two bus stations on Hipólito Unánue, 1 km from the plaza (colectivo US$0.25, taxi US$0.60 minimum). One terminal is for international services, the other for domestic, both are well-organized, local tax US$0.30, baggage store, easy to make connections to the border, Arequipa or Lima. To **Moquegua**, 159 km, 2 hrs, US$2, several buses and colectivos daily (colectivos also leave from the town exit, uphill from the terminal, eg *El Buen Samaritano*, 5 passengers, US$3, less than 2 hrs). There are no direct buses to **Mollendo**, so catch one of the frequent buses to El Fiscal (US$4, 4 hrs), then a colectivo to Mollendo. To **Arequipa**, 6 hrs, US$3.85-4.40, several buses daily, most with *Flores*, T725376. To **Nasca**, 793 km, 12 hrs, US$9, several buses daily, en route for Lima. Several companies daily to **Lima**, 1,239 km, 21-26 hrs, US$9-27, eg *Flores*, *Cruz del Sur* and *Ormeño*, recommended. To **Puno**, 395 km, go to Moquegua or Arequipa and change there.

At Tomasiri, 35 km north of Tacna, passengers' passports and luggage are checked, whether you have been out of the country or not. There is also a police control 10 km after the Camiara bridge (being rebuilt, near a military base), just before the Tacna/Moquegua departmental border (also called Camiara, 59 km from Tacna, 61 km from Moquegua).

Do not carry anything on the bus for a Peruvian, just your own belongings

To **La Paz**, the best route is via Moquegua and Desaguadero. The most direct service is *Ormeño's Royal* service, 1930, US$35, but you have to change buses in Moquegua. *Samericano* colectivos go direct to Desaguadero, otherwise take transport from Moquegua (see above). To **Santiago**, *Pullman Bus Internacional*, 6 a day, 28 hrs, US$25, *semi cama* with meals, to **Antofagasta**, 14 hrs, US$15. *Tramaca* also runs to **Santiago**.

Directory

Airline offices *Aero Continente*, Apurímac casi San Martín, T747300. *Lan Perú*, Apurímac y Bolívar, T743252. *Tans*, San Martín 611, T747002. **Banks** *Banco de Crédito*, San Martín 574, no commission for TCs (Amex, Citicorp) into soles. Similarly at *Banco Wiese*, San Martín 476. *Banco Santander*, Apurímac,

Peru

with exchange and ATM for Visa/Plus, MasterCard/Cirrus. *Interbank*, San Martín 646, has ATM for Visa/Plus, MasterCard/Cirrus and Amex. *Cambios Tacna* and *MoneyGram*, San Martín 612, T743607. Street changers stand outside the Municipalidad. **Communications Internet:**, many on San Martín, several open 24 hrs. Others around the centre. *F@stnet.com*, 2 de Mayo 380, open 0800-2400, also international phone calls, cheaper than others. *Tacna Net*, Av H Unánue at Plaza de Armas. Average price US$0.45 per hr, US$0.60 overnight. **Post office:** Av Bolognesi y Ayacucho. Open Mon-Sat 0800-2000. **Telephone:** public *locutorio* on Plaza de Armas, in same building as *Hostal Lima*. **Consulates** Chile, Presbítero Andía block 1, T 723063. Open Mon-Fri 0800-1300, closed holidays. **Tourist offices**: Dirección Regional de Indistria y Turismo, Gral Blondell 50, by the Centro Cultural Miculla, corner of Francisco Lazo, T722784. **Touring y Automóvil Club del Perú**, Av 2 de Mayo 55.

Border with Chile

Peruvian time is 1 hr earlier than Chilean time Mar-Oct; 2 hrs earlier Sep/Oct to Feb/Mar (varies annually) No fruit or vegetables are allowed into Chile or Tacna

There is a checkpoint before the border, which is open 0900-2200. Peruvian immigration is closed on public holidays. You need to obtain a Peruvian exit stamp and a Chilean entrance stamp; formalities are straightforward (see below). If you need a Chilean visa, you have to get it in Tacna (address above).

Crossing by private vehicle For those leaving Peru by car buy *relaciones de pasajeros* (official forms, US$0.45) from the kiosk at the border or from a bookshop; you will need four copies. Next, return your tourist card, visit the PNP office, return the vehicle permit and finally depart through the checkpoints.

Exchange Money changers are given under Banks, above. They can also be found at counters in the international bus terminal; rates are much the same as in town.

Transport **Road** 56 km, 1-2 hrs, depending on waiting time at the border. Buses to Arica charge US$1.50 and colectivo taxis US$3 pp. All leave from the international terminal in Tacna throughout the day. Colectivos (old Fords and Chevrolets which carry 5 passengers) only leave when full. As you approach the terminal you will be grabbed by a driver or his agent and told that the car is "just about to leave". This is hard to verify as you may not see the colectivo until you have filled in the paperwork. Once you have chosen a driver/agent, you will be rushed to his company's office where your passport will be taken from you and the details filled out on a Chilean entry form. You can change your remaining soles at the bus terminal while this is being done. It is 30 mins to the Peruvian border post at Santa Rosa, where all exit formalities are carried out. The driver will hustle you through all the procedures. A short distance beyond is the Chilean post at Chacalluta, where again the driver will show you what to do. All formalities take about 30 mins. It's a further 15 mins to Arica's bus terminal. A Chilean driver is more likely to take you to any address in Arica. **Train** At 0900 and 1600, US$1, Tacna-Arica; the train was not running in early 2002 as a bridge had been washed away.

The Titicaca region Newly paved roads climb from the coastal deserts and oases to the high plateau in which sits mystical Lake Titicaca, a huge inland sea which is the highest navigable lake in the world (Arequipa-Yura-Santa Lucía-Juliaca-Puno; Moquegua-Desaguadero-Puno). The steep ascents lead to wide open views of pampas with agricultural communities, desolate mountains, small lakes and salt flats. It is a rapid change of altitude, so be prepared for some discomfort and breathlessness.

Juliaca

Phone code: 054
Colour map 6, grid A2
Population: 134,700
Altitude: 3,825 m
289 km NE of Arequipa

Freezing cold at night, Juliaca is not particularly attractive. As the commercial focus of an area bounded by Puno, Arequipa and the jungle, it has grown very fast into a chaotic place with a large impermanent population, lots of contraband and counterfeiting and more *tricitaxis* than cars. Monday, market day, is the most disorganized of all. On the huge Plaza Melgar, several blocks from the main part of the town, is an interesting colonial church. At the large market in the plaza on Monday you can buy wool and alpaca goods. The handicrafts gallery, *Las Calceteras*, is on Plaza Bolognesi. Túpac Amaru market, on Moquegua seven blocks east of railway line, is a cheap market. There are several internet places in the centre.

Peru

The unspoiled little colonial town of **Lampa**, 31 km northwest of Juliaca is known as the 'Pink City'. It has a splendid church, La Inmaculada, containing a copy of Michelangelo's 'Pietà'. Also of interest is the Museo Kampac, Ugarte 462, a museum with sculptures and ceramics from the Lampa and Juli areas; the owner lives next door. It also has a good Sunday market. There is a basic *hostal*, **G** pp. Buses and trucks daily, one hour, US$0.65, from Plaza de Armas in Juliaca.

Excursions

AL-A *Suites Don Carlos*, Jr M Prado 335, on the outskirts of town, T321571/327270, www.tci.net.pe/doncarlos Prices include taxes, good facilities, continental breakfast US$6.50, lunch or dinner US$13. **B** *Hostal Don Carlos*, Jr 9 de Diciembre 114, Plaza Bolognesi, T323600, F322120. In same group, comfortable, modern facilities, hot water, TV, heater, good service, breakfast included, restaurant and room service. Recommended. **B** *Royal Inn*, San Román 158, T321561, Hotel_royal_inn@latinmail.com Decent accommodation with hot water, TV, safe, laundry, good restaurant *La Fonda del Royal* with *menú* US$1.50. Recommended. **D** *Karlo's Hostal*, Unión 317, T321817, lanzap@hotmail.com Comfortable, firm beds, hot water, TV, laundry, restaurant *Che Karlín* attached. **D** *Hostal Luquini*, San Román 409, Plaza Bolognesi, T321510. **E** without bath, breakfast included, comfortable, hot water, restaurant for all meals, *menú* US$1.50. Recommended. **E** *Yarur*, Jr M Núñez 414, T 321501. **F** without bath, hot water, safe, no breakfast. **F-G** *Hostal Ferrocarril*, San Martín 249. Shared and private rooms, shared bath, basic. For eating, try *Trujillo*, San Román 163. Extensive menu, daily specials, US$3-5.50 for main dishes, US$7.50 for fish. *Trujillo 2*, at No 175, serves chicken, sandwiches and snacks. Next door is *Ricos Pan*, bakery with café.

Sleeping & eating
There are water problems in town, especially in the dry season

Air Airport is small and well organized. To/from **Lima**, 2¼ hrs via **Arequipa** (30 mins), daily with *Aero Continente* (T328440) and *Aviandina*, 5 a week *Tans* (T321272), 4 a week *LanPerú* (T322228; also to Cusco). Minibuses 1-B, 6 and 14 to airport from 2 de Mayo at either Núñez or San Román, US$0.15; from airport to town they take you to your hotel. Taxi from Plaza Bolognesi, US$1.75. **Tourist buses** run direct from Puno to the airport and vice versa; US$1.50 pp, 1 hr. Also taxis, US$11.75. If taking a public colectivo from Puno to Juliaca for a flight, allow plenty of time as they drive around Puno looking for passengers to fill the vehicle first.

Transport

Buses New Terminal Terrestre is at Jr Mantaro y San Agustín: go down San Martín 10 blocks and cross Av Circunvalación. Lots of companies serve Desaguadero, Moquegua, Arequipa (US$5.80), Lima (US$10-17.65) and Cusco (US$4.40). To **Cusco**, 344 km, 5-6 hrs, with *Imexso* (in Terminal, T326389) and *Tour Perú* (tourperu@mixmail.com), day and night buses, prices as from Puno. *First Class* (www.firstclassperu.com) and *Inka Express* (inkaex@yahoo.com) have pullman tourist buses which stop for sightseeing and lunch, with guide, see under Puno. The road is paved and in good condition. To **Puno**, 44 km, 1 hr, US$0.45; small buses leave from Piérola y 18 de Noviembre, 2 companies. Combis to Puno leave from Terminal Terrestre on Plaza Bolognesi, also US$0.45. To **Huancané** (on the north side of Lake Titicaca), 51 km, and Moho, a further 40 km, *Santa Cruz* and *Joyas del Sur* companies, Moquegua 1019, at the corner with Ballón near the Túpac Amaru market, US$1.75, 3 hrs to Moho. It is paved to Huancané, then poor, but the views are wonderful. See below on how to get to the Bolivian border.

Trains See information under Puno or Cusco. The station at Juliaca is the junction for services between Arequipa (no regular passenger services), Puno and Cusco. Prices to Cusco are the same as from Puno. The ticket office, entrance on Plaza Bolognesi, opens 0700-1100, 1400-1800, except Tue 1400-1800, Thu 0600-1000, 1400-1800, Sat 0700-1100, Sun 0600-1000.

Peru

Puno

Phone code: 054
Colour map 6, grid A2
Population: 100,170
Altitude: 3,855 m
Puno gets bitterly cold at night: in June-August the temperature at night can fall to -25°C, but generally not below -5°C

On the northwest shore of Lake Titicaca, **Puno** is capital of its department and Peru's folklore centre with a vast array of handicrafts, festivals and costumes and a rich tradition of music and dance. The **Cathedral**, completed in 1657, has an impressive baroque exterior, but an austere interior. Beside the Cathedral is the **Balcony of the Conde de Lemos**, Deústua esquina Conde de Lemos, where Peru's Viceroy stayed when he first arrived in the city. A short walk up Independencia leads to the **Arco Deústua**, a monument honouring those killed in the battles of Junín and Ayacucho. Nearby, is a mirador giving fine views over the town, the port and the lake beyond. The walk from Jr Cornejo following the Stations of the Cross up a nearby hill, with fine views of Lake Titicaca, has been recommended, but be careful and don't go alone (the same applies to any of the hills around Puno, eg Huajsapata). The **Museo Municipal Dreyer** has been combined with the private collection of Sr Carlos Dreyer, Conde de Lemos 289. ■ *Mon-Fri 0730-1330, US$1.*

The *Yavari*, the **oldest ship on Lake Titicaca**, is berthed in the port and is now open as a museum and bar. She is moored next to the jetty from which the launches to Los Uros leave. The ship was built in England in 1862 and was shipped in kit form to Arica, then by rail to Tacna and by mule to Lake Titicaca. The journey took six years. The *Yavari* was eventually launched on Christmas Day 1870. The ship is being restored by an Anglo-Peruvian Association. Visitors are very welcome on board. ■ *US$2 to help with maintenance costs. Project addresses: England: 61 Mexfield Road, London, SW15 2RG, T/F44-20-8874 0583, info@yavari.org; Peru/Lima: Giselle Guldentops, c/o Lima Times, T0051-1-998 5071, Yavari.gulden@dwp.net In Puno: Asociación Yavari, c/o Capitán Carlos Saavedra, T0051-54-369329, F0051-54-352701, yavaricondor@viaexpresa.com.pe For general information, volunteering, donations, etc, visit www.yavari.org* Also in the harbour is Hull (UK)-built MS *Ollanta*, which sailed the lake from 1926 to the 1970s. *PerúRail* has restored the vessel with a view to starting twice-weekly cruises in 2002.

Excursions Anybody interested in religious architecture should visit the villages along the western shore of Lake Titicaca. An Inca sundial can be seen near the village of **Chucuíto** (19 km), which has an interesting church, La Asunción, and houses with carved stone doorways. Visits to Chucuíto usually include the Templo de la Fertilidad, **Inca Uyo**, which boasts many phalli and other fertility symbols. The authenticity and original location of these objects is the subject of debate. (**C** *Hostal Chucuíto*, 1 km north of town, includes breakfast, nice rooms, courtyard can be used for parking bicycles, hot water, negotiable in low season, T054-352108, leave message for Alfredo Sánchez. **E** *Albergue Juvenil Las Cabañas*, great little cottages, meals, highly recommended, T054-351276, will collect you from Puno bus station.)

Juli, 80 km, has some fine examples of religious architecture. **San Pedro** on the plaza, designated as the Cathedral, has been extensively restored. It contains a series of paintings of saints, with the Via Crucis scenes in the same frame, and gilt side altars above which some of the arches have baroque designs. No opening hours are displayed. **San Juan Letrán** has two sets of 17th-century paintings of the lives of St John the Baptist and of St Teresa, contained in sumptuous gilded frames. San Juan is a museum. ■ *Open mornings only; US$1.15; under restoration in late 2001.* It also has intricate *mestizo* carving in pink stone. **Santa Cruz** is partly roofless, with scaffolding and a shelter protecting what remains of the tower. It is completely closed to visitors, but there is a view of the lake from the plaza in front. The fourth church, **La Asunción**, is also a museum. The nave is empty, but its walls are lined with colonial paintings with no labels. The original painting on the walls of the transept is fading. Its fine bell tower was damaged by earthquake or lightning. Outside is an archway and atrium which date from the early 17th century. ■ *US$0.85.* Needlework, other weavings, handicrafts and antiques are offered for sale in town. Near Juli is a small colony of flamingoes. Many other birds can be seen from the road. Colectivo

Puno-Juli US$0.75; return from Juli outside market at Ilave 349. **F** pp *Municipal*, Jr Ilave 312, opposite market, **G** without bath, cold water, no restaurant. **G** pp *Hostal San Pedro*, on main plaza, basic, cold water, shared bath, restaurant.

A further 20 km along the lake is **Pomata** (US$0.30 from Juli), whose church of Santiago Apóstol is built of red sandstone. It has a beautiful interior, with superb carving and paintings. ■ *Daily 0700-1200, 1330-1600, free, but give a donation.* At **Zepita**, near Desaguadero, the 18th-century Dominican church is also worth a visit.

Near Puno are the *chullpas* (precolumbian funeral towers) of **Sillustani** in a beautiful setting on a peninsula in Lake Umayo, 32 km from Puno on an excellent road. John Hemming writes: "Most of the towers date from the period of Inca occupation in the 15th century, but they are burial towers of the Aymara-speaking Colla tribe. The engineering involved in their construction is more complex than anything the Incas built – it is defeating archaeologists' attempts to rebuild the tallest 'lizard' *chullpa*. Two are unfinished: one with a ramp still in place to raise blocks; the other with cut stones ready to go onto a very ambitious corbelled false dome." There is a museum and handicraft sellers wait at the exit. Photography is best in the afternoon light, though this is when the wind is strongest. The scenery is barren, but impressive. There is a small community at the foot of the promontory. ■ *US$2.25. Take an organized tour; about 3-4 hrs, leave 1430, about US$5; check that the entry fee is included in the price. Tours usually stop at a Colla house on the way, to see local products. Camping possible outside the museum (tip the guardian).*

Sleeping

Clean public showers near the football stadium. Puno sometimes has power and water shortages Check if breakfast is included in the price

L *Libertador Isla Esteves*, on an island linked by a causeway 5 km northeast of Puno (taxi US$3), T367780, www.libertador.com.pe Built on a Tiahuanaco-period site, spacious, good views, phone, bar, good restaurant, disco, good service, electricity and hot water all day, parking. **L** *Sonesta Posada del Inca*, Av Sesqui Centenario 610, Huaje, 5 km from Puno on the lakeshore, T364111, F363672, www.sonesta.com/peru_puno/ 62 rooms with heating, facilities for the disabled, welcoming, local textile decorations, good views, *Inkafé* restaurant has an Andean menu, folklore shows. **AL** *Plaza Mayor*, Deústua 342, T/F366089, reservas@plazamayorhostal.com New, comfortable, well-appointed and decorated, good big beds, buffet breakfast included, hot water, TV, laundry. Recommended. **A** *Colón Inn*, Tacna 290, T351432, www.titicaca-peru.com Colonial style, good rooms with hot shower, price includes tax and buffet breakfast, good service, safe, restaurant *Sol Naciente* and pizzería *Europa*, the Belgian manager Christian Nonis is well known, especially for his work on behalf of the people on Taquile island. Recommended. **A** *Hostal Hacienda*, Jr Deústua 297, T/F356109, hacienda@latinmail.com Refurbished colonial house, hot water, TV, includes breakfast, café, comfortable. Recommended. **A** *Sillustani*, Jr Lambayeque 195, T351881, sillustani@punonet.com Price includes breakfast and taxes, hot water, cable TV, safety deposit, heaters, internet, very good. **B** *Balsa Inn*, Cajamarca 555, T363144, www.balsainn.punored.com With breakfast, hot water, TV, comfortable, safe, heating, very helpful. **B** *Hospedaje Pukara*, Jr Libertad 328, T/F368448, pukara@terra.com.pe Excellent, English spoken, central, quiet, free coca tea in evening, breakfast included. Under same ownership is **B** *Tikarani*, Independencia 143, T365501, also recommended. **B-C** *Hostal Italia*, Teodoro Valcarcel 122, T352521, hitalia@peru-perured.net 2 blocks from the station. With breakfast, cheaper in low season, good, safe, hot water, good food, small rooms, staff helpful. **B-C** *El Buho*, Lambayeque 142, T/F354214, hotel_elbuho@yahoo.com Hot water, nice rooms with heaters, TV, restaurant, safe, special discount to Footprint Handbook owners, travel agency for excursions and flight reconfirmations. Recommended. **C** *Posada Don Giorgio*, Tarapacá 238, T363648, dongiorgio@titicacalake.com New, with breakfast, hot water, large rooms, nicely decorated, TV, comfortable. **C** *Hostal Imperial*, Teodoro Valcarcel 145, T352386. **D-E** In low season, hot water, helpful, stores luggage, comfortable, safe. **C-D** *Hostal Rubi 'Los Portales'*, Jr Cajamarca 152-154, T/F353384, hostalrubi@punonet.com Safe, breakfast US$2, hot water, safe, TV, good, tours arranged. **D** *Internacional*, Libertad 161, T352109. **E** without shower, hot water, TV, safe. **D** *Hostal Monterrey*, Lima 441, T351691, www.hostalmonterrey.com **E** without bath, better rooms with good showers, hot water, breakfast extra, secure for luggage, motorcycle parking US$0.50. **D** *Hostal Tumi*, Cajamarca 237, T353270, with *Tumi 2* next door. Both hotels are

Peru

secure, with hot water, breakfast available, some rooms are a bit dark and gloomy but most are big and comfortable, tours sold. **D** *Vylena*, Jr Ayacucho 505, T/F351292, hostalvylena@ hotmail.com Breakfast extra, hot water, quiet, safe, cheaper in low season. **D-E** *Hostal Arequipa*, Arequipa 153, T352071. Hot water, will change TCs at good rates, stores luggage, secure, arranges tours to the islands, OK. **D-E** *Manco Cápac Inn*, Av Tacna 227, T352985, mancocapacinn@punonet.com With hot water, luggage store, safe, average breakfast. **D-E** *Hostal Nesther*, Deústua 268, T351631. Also has triples, hot water. Recommended. **D-E** *Hostal Q'oñiwasi*, Av La Torre 135, opposite the rail station, T365784, qoniwasi@ mundomail.net **E** without bath and in low season, heating extra, hot water, laundry facilities and service, luggage store, breakfast extra, lunch available, safe, helpful. Recommended.

E *Hostal Europa*, Alfonso Ugarte 112, near the train station, T353023. Very popular, cheaper without bath, luggage may be stored, but don't leave your valuables in the room, hot water sometimes, garage space for motorcycles. **E** *Hostal Illampu*, Av La Torre 137-interior, T353284. Warm water, breakfast and TV extra, café, laundry, safe box, exchange money, arranges excursions (ask for Santiago). **E** *Los Uros*, Teodoro Valcarcel 135, T352141. Cheaper without bath, hot water, plenty of blankets, breakfast available, quiet at back, good value, small charge to leave luggage, laundry, often full, changes TCs a reasonable rate. Recommended. **E** *Pachacútec*, Arbulu 235. Comfortable, quiet and pleasant. **E-F** *Hostal Los Pinos*, Tarapacá 182, T/F367398, hostalpinos@hotmail.com Family run, hot showers, cheaper without bath, good breakfast, safe, luggage store, laundry facilities, helpful, cheap tours organized. Recommended. **F** *Hospedaje Don Julio*, Av Tacna 336, T363358. New, pleasant. **F** *Hospedaje El Trébol*, Deza 724, T352117. Big rooms, clean showers with hot water, good. **F** pp *Hospedaje Residencial Margarita*, Jr Tarapacá 130, T352820. Large building, family atmosphere, hot water most of the day, stores luggage, tours can be arranged. Recommended.

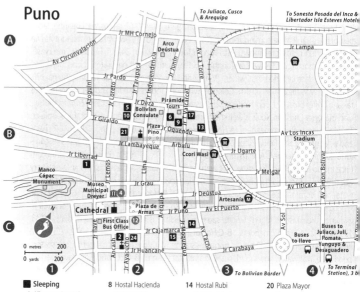

Puno

Sleeping

1 Albergue Juvenil Virgen de Copacabana *B1*
2 Balsa Inn *C2*
3 Colón Inn *Puno centre*
4 El Buho *Puno centre*
5 Hospedaje Residencial Margarita *B2*
6 Hostal Arequipa *B2*
7 Hostal Europa *Puno centre*
8 Hostal Hacienda *Puno centre*
9 Hostal Italia *B2*
10 Hostal Los Pinos *B2*
11 Hostal Monterrey *Puno centre*
12 Hostal Nesther *Puno centre*
13 Hostal Q'oñiwasi & Hostal Illampu *B3*
14 Hostal Rubi 'Los Portales' *C3*
15 Hostal Tumi & Tumi 2 *C2*
16 Internacional & Restaurant *Puno Centre*
17 Los Uros & Hostal Imperial *B3*
18 Manco Cápac Inn *Puno centre*
19 Pachacútec *Puno centre*
20 Plaza Mayor *Puno centre*
21 Posada Don Giorgio *B2*
22 Pukará *Puno centre*
23 Sillustani *Puno centre*
24 Vylena *C2*

Eating

1 Apu Salkantay & Pub Ekeko's *Puno centre*
2 Café Deliss *Puno Centre*

Youth Hostel: **F-G** pp *Albergue Juvenil Virgen de Copacabana*, Ilave 228, T354129 (no sign). Huge rooms, well-furnished, hot water, "awesome bathroom", good location, quiet, helpful owners, will wash your clothes for a reasonable fee, full breakfast for US$1.30, a real bargain. The passageway leading to the hostel is very dark and robbery has occurred; take great care at night (the hostel is as helpful as it can be).

On or near Jr Lima (all up to US$5 for main dish): *Fontana*, No 339. *Pizzería* and *trattoria*, good food. *Pizzería El Buho*, No 349 and at Jr Libertad 386. Excellent pizza, lively atmosphere, open 1800 onwards, pizzas US$2.35-3. *IncAbar*, No 356-A. Open for breakfast, lunch and dinner, interesting dishes in creative sauces, fish, pastas, curries, café and couch bar. *Apu Salkantay*, No 357 and in 400 block. Wide menu of meats, fish (more expensive), pastas, sandwiches, pizza, coffee, popular. *Don Piero*, No 360. Huge meals, live music, try their 'pollo coca-cola' (chicken in a sweet and sour sauce), slow service, popular, tax extra. *El Dorado*, No 371. Good for local fish, large portions. *La Casona*, No 521. Good for typical food, also Italian and pizzas. *Panq'arani*, Grau casi Lima. Closed Sat and some evenings, excellent typical dishes, breakfasts US$1.50-2, main dishes US$3.50-4. *Keros*, Lambayeque 131. Bar/restaurant with very good food, mostly Peruvian, good service, pleasant surroundings, good drinks. **Others**: **Mid-range**: *La Plaza*, Puno 425, Plaza de Armas. Good food, including fish. *Internacional*, Moquegua 201. Very popular, excellent trout, good pizzas, service variable. **Cheap**: *Adventista*, Jr Deza 349. Good, closed after lunch. *Chifa Fon Seng*, Arequipa 552. Good food, service and value, Chinese, popular. **Vegetarian**: *Sabor y Vigor*, Arequipa 508. Delicious meals. *Sol Interior*, Libertad 466, and *Vida Natural*, Libertad 449 (open for breakfast, salads, fruits, yoghurts). *El Milagro*, Arequipa 336. Natural food shop. **Cafés** *Casa del Corregidor*, Deústua 576, aptdo 2, T355694. In restored 17th-century building, sandwiches, good snacks, coffee, good music, nice surroundings with patio (exhibition space, library, handicrafts, internet to open in 2002). *Café Delisse*, Moquegua 200 corner with Libertad. Open from 0600 (closed Sat), espresso coffee, good vegetarian food, excellent set lunch US$1.50. *Cafetería Mercedes*, Jr Arequipa 351. Good *menú* US$1.50, also breads, cakes, snacks, juices and tea. *Ricos Pan*, Jr Lima 424. Café and bakery, great cakes, excellent coffees, juices and pastries, good breakfasts and other dishes, reasonable prices, great place to relax, open 0600-2300, closed Sun. Branches of their *panadería* at Av Titicaca 155 and Moquegua 330. *Panadería Una*, Lima 317 and Arequipa 144. For croissants, fresh bread and cakes. **Bars and nightclubs** *Dómino*, Libertad 443. "Megadisco", happy hour 2000-2130 Mon-Thu, good. *Peña Hostería*, Lima 501. Good music, also restaurant. Recommended. *Positive Vibrations*, Lima 445 y Grau. Good late night place (opens early evening) which serves food. Recommended. *Pub Ekeko's*, Jr Lima 355, p 2. Live music every night, happy hour 2000-2200.

Eating
Very cheap places in Jr Deústua for lunch or dinner. Many places on Lima, too many to list here, catering for the tourist market

Feb: at the *Fiesta de la Virgen de la Candelaria*, first 2 weeks in Feb, bands and dancers from all the local towns compete in a *Diablada*, or Devil Dance. The festivities are better at night on the streets than the official

Local festivals

no centre

Plaza Pino
bayeque
Edgar Adventures
Arbutu
All Ways Travel
Tour Perú
Imexso
Bus Office
Lan
Perú
Aero
Continente
Immigration
ourist
olice
Deústua

Lake
Titicaca

To Los Uros, Taquile & Amantaní

Yavari

estre (Bus
, turn left

Peru

functions in the stadium. Check the dates in advance as Candelaria may be moved if pre-Lentern carnival coincides with it. A candlelight procession through darkened streets takes place on **Good Friday**. **3 May:** *Invención de la Cruz*, an exhibition of local art. **29 Jun: Nov:** colourful festival of **San Pedro**, with a procession at Zepita (see page 1211); also 20 Jul. **4-5 Nov:** pageant dedicated to the founding of Puno and the emergence of Manco Cápac and Mama Ocllo from the waters of Lake Titicaca.

Shopping

Beware pickpockets in the market

In the covered part of the market mostly foodstuffs are sold (good cheeses), but there are also model reed boats, attractive carved stone amulets and Ekekos (household goods). This central market covers a large area and on Saturday it expands down to the stadium (mostly fruit and vegetables) and along Av Bolívar (potatoes and grains). The **Markets** between Av Los Incas and Arbulu (*Ccori Wasi*) and on the railway between Av Titicaca and Av El Puerto are two of the best places in Peru (or Bolivia) for llama and alpaca wool articles, but bargain hard, especially in the afternoon. You will be hassled on the street and outside restaurants to buy woollen goods, so take care.

Tour operators

Watch out for unofficial tour sellers, jalagringos, who offer hotels and tours at different rates, depending on how wealthy you look They are everywhere: train station, bus offices, airport and hotels. Ask to see their guide's ID card Only use agencies with named premises and compare prices

Agencies organize trips to the Uros floating islands (see page 1215) and the islands of Taquile and Amantaní, as well as to Sillustani, and other places. Make sure that you settle all details before embarking on the tour. Alternatively, you can go down to the lake and make your own arrangements with the boatmen. We have received good reports on the following: *Allways Travel*, Tacna 234, T/F355552, awtperu@terra.com.pe Very helpful, kind and reliable, speak German, French, English and Italian. They offer a unique cultural tour to the islands of Anapia and Yuspique in Lake Wiñaymarka, beyond the straits of Tiquina, "The Treasure of Wiñaymarka". *Arcobaleno*, Jr Lambayeque 175, T/F351052, arcobaleno@ titicacalake.com Local tours, Western Union representative. *Edgar Adventures*, Jr Lima 328, T/F353444 (office)/354811 (home), edgaradventures@terra.com.pe Run by Edgar Apaza F and Norka Flórez L who speak English, German and French, very helpful. *Ecoturismo Aventura*, Jr Lima 458, T355785. Very helpful. *Käfer Turismo*, Arequipa 179, T354742, F352701, kafer@inkanet.com.pe For local tours. *Kolla Tour*, Jr Moquegua 679, T352961, F354762. Sell airline tickets and have their own boat for tours on the lake. *Pirámide Tours*, Jr Deza 129 (at side of *Hotel Ferrocarril*), T/F367302, www.titikakalake.com Out of the ordinary and classic tours, flexible, personalized service, modern fast launches, very helpful. *Turpuno*, Lima 208, stand 8-II, upstairs in Gallery, T352001, F351431, www.turpuno.com Very good service for local tours, transfers and ticketing, DHL and Western Union agent.

Transport

In Puno, Juliaca and other Andean towns, 3-wheel 'Trici-Taxis', which costs about US$0.20 per km, are the best way to get around, even with heavy baggage Colectivos charge US$0.15 Bus prices to Cusco and La Paz have seasonal variations

Buses All long-distance buses, except some Cusco services and buses to La Paz (see below), leave from the new Terminal Terrestre, which is between Av Simón Bolívar and the lake, southeast of the centre. It has a tourist office, snack bars and toilets. Platform tax US$0.30. Small buses and colectivos for Juliaca, Ilave and towns on the lake shore between Puno and Desaguadero, including Yunguyo, leave from Av Bolívar between Jrs Carabaya and Palma. Daily buses to **Arequipa**, 6 hrs via Juliaca, 297 km, most buses are taking this route now, US$6. Or 11 hrs via Desaguadero and Moquegua, US$6-10 (*Cruz del Sur* – office also at Lima 442, *Best Way*, *Destinos*, *Julsa* – office also on Melgar 232, T369447, *Señor de Milagros*, or *Sur Oriente*, T368133, most have a morning and evening bus – better quality buses go at night). To **Moquegua**, US$4.50, and **Tacna**, US$5.30, *San Martín, Latino, Sagitario, Roel*. To **Lima**, 1,011 km, US$18, all buses go through Arequipa, sometimes with a change of bus. See under Arequipa. To **Juliaca**, 44 km, 45 mins, US$0.45.

If you wish to travel by bus and cannot get on a direct bus, it is no problem to take separate buses to Juliaca, then to Sicuani, then to Cusco

To **Cusco**, 388 km, 5-6 hrs, Imexso, Jr Libertad 115, T363909, 0800, 1930 (good buses), *Tour Perú*, at Terminal and Tacna 282, T352991, tourperu@mixmail.com, 0830, 2000, both US$8.75 (less in low season); *Libertad* at Terminal, T363694, 4 a day, *Cisnes*, at Terminal, T368674, 2 a day, *Pony Express* and others, US$4.40. *First Class* (Jr Puno 675, T365192, www.firstclassperu.com) and *Inka Express* (pick up at hotel, T/F365654, inkaex@yahoo.com), 0830 arriving 1800, US$25, daily, recommended. This service, while higher in price than the *turismo* train, leaves a little later and is comfortable, with a good lunch stop and visits to Pukará, La Raya, Raqchi and Andahuaylillas en route.

Trains The railway runs from Puno to Juliaca (44 km), where it divides, to Cusco (381 km) and Arequipa (279 km; no passenger service, 2002). To **Cusco** on Mon, Wed, Thu and Sat at 0800, arriving in Juliaca at 0910 and in Cusco at about 1800 (try to sit on the right hand side for the views). The train stops at La Raya. In the high season (Jun especially), tickets sell well in advance. In the wet season services may be cancelled for short periods. Always check. **Fares**: Puno-Cusco, *turismo*, US$12; *Inca* class, US$60 including meal. The ticket office is open from 0630-1030, 1600-1900 Mon-Sat, and on Sun in the afternoons only. Tickets can be bought in advance, or 1 hr before departure if there are any left. The station is well guarded by police and sealed off to those without tickets.

Boats on Lake Titicaca Boats to the islands leave from the rebuilt terminal in the harbour (see map); *trici-taxi* from centre, US$1.

Airline offices *Aero Continente*, Tacna y Libertad, T354870. *LanPerú*, also Tacna y Libertad.
Banks *Banco de Crédito*, Lima y Grau. Changes TCs before 1300 without commission, cash advance on Visa and Visa ATM. *Banco Continental*, *Interbank*, Lima y Libertador, changes TCs morning and afternoon, 0.5% commission, and *BSCH* have branches in town, but only **Continental**, Lima y Libertad, has an ATM (Visa). No bank in Puno accepts MasterCard. For cash go to the *cambios*, the travel agencies or the better hotels. Best rates with money changers on Jr Lima, many on 400 block, and on Tacna near the market, eg Arbulu y Tacna. Check your Peruvian soles carefully. Exchange rates from soles to bolivianos and vice versa are sometimes better in Puno than in Yunguyo; check with other travellers. **Communications** Internet: there are offices everywhere in the centre, upstairs and down. Many raise their prices from US$0.50 per hr in the morning to US$0.75 in the afternoon; many have overnights. Good ones include **CompuRed**, Jr Moquegua 189, 24 hrs; above *Fontana* restaurant, Lima 339; at *Pizzería Café Giorgio*, Lima 430; **Impacto's@net**, next to *Hostal Qoñi Wasi*, on Av La Torre (another one in the same block). **Post Office:** Jr Moquegua 267. **Telephone:** *Telefónica* at Puno y Moquegua for local and international calls. Another phone office at Lima 489. **Consulates** Bolivia, Jr Arequipa 120, T351251, consular visa on the spot, US$10, open 0830-1330 Mon to Fri. **Tourist offices** InfoTur, Jr Lima 549, near Plaza de Armas. They are friendly and helpful with general information, they sell a city guide and map for US$1.20. www.punored.com is a portal for the Puno area. www.punonet.com, has some information, with links to a number of establishments. Visit also www.titicacaalmundo.com, which has good information on Puno, sponsored by several local businesses (they also distribute a free CD-Rom). **Useful addresses** Immigration: Ayacucho 240, T352801, for renewing entry stamps, etc. The process is very slow and you must fill in 2 application forms at a bank, but there's nothing else to pay. **Touring Automóvil Club del Perú**, Arequipa 457.

Lake Titicaca

The Uros or the 'floating islands' have intermarried with the Aymara and no pure Uros exist. The present Puno Bay people fish, hunt birds and live off the lake plants, most important of which are the reeds they use for their boats, houses and the very foundations of their islands. Tourism has opened their lives to the scrutiny of cameras and camcorders, contributing to the erosion of their culture. Of the 42 islands on which the Uros live, just under half receive tourists. It is a very intensive tourism, but the islanders depend upon it now. The tourist islands are effectively floating souvenir stalls and some visitors find the 'peep show' nature of this type of tourism unsettling. There is no drinking water on the islands.

The influx of tourists to all the islands unfortunately prompts persistent requests for sweets,   **Responsible**
photographs and money, which irritates many travellers. Above all, stay good-humoured.   **tourism**
Gifts of fruit, torches (there is no electricity), moisturizer or sun block (the children suffer sore cheeks), pens, pencils or notebooks are appreciated. Buy their handicrafts instead of handing out sweets indiscriminately.

Motorboats from the dock charge US$3 pp for a 2-hr excursion. Boats go about every 30 mins   **Transport**
from about 0630 till 1000, or whenever there are 10 or more people to fill the boat. The earlier

Peru

you go the better, to beat the crowds of tourists. Out of season there are no regular boats, so either get a group together and rent a boat, or pay an agency US$15-20.

Taquile
45 km from Puno

Isla Taquile, on which there are numerous pre-Inca and Inca ruins, and Inca terracing, is only about 1 km wide, but 6-7 km long. Ask for the (unmarked) museum of traditional costumes, which is on the plaza, and also where you can see and photograph local weaving. There is a co-operative shop on the plaza that sells exceptional woollen goods, which are not cheap, but of very fine quality. Easter, from 2 to 7 June, the *Fiesta de Santiago* over two weeks in mid-July, and 1 and 2 August are the principal festival days, with many dances in between.

Plentiful accommodation in private houses but it is best to take warm clothes, a sleeping bag and hot water bottle

Sleeping and eating No previous arrangements can be made. There are two main entry points. The Puerto Principal at the south end has a very steep climb; the northern entry is longer but more gradual (remember you are at 3,800 m). On arrival you are greeted by a *jefe de alojamiento*, who oversees where you are going to stay. The system of assigning accommodation to visitors has fallen into disuse: you can either say where you are going, if you (or your guide) know where you want to stay, or the *jefe* can find you a room. Average rate for a bed is **G**, plus US$1.50 for breakfast. Other meals cost extra. Several families now have sizeable *alojamientos* (eg Pedro Huille, on the track up from the north entry, with showers under construction, proper loos). There are many small restaurants around the plaza and on the track to the Puerto Principal (eg Gerardo Hualta's *La Flor de Cantuta*, on the steps; *El Inca* on the main plaza). Meals are generally fish (the island has a trout farm), rice and chips, tortilla and *fiambre* – a local stew. Meat is rarely available and drinks often run out. Breakfast consists of pancakes and bread. Shops on the plaza sell film, postcards, water and dry goods. You are advised to take some food, particularly fruit, bread and vegetables, water, plenty of small-value notes, candles and a torch. Take precautions against sunburn.

Transport Boats leave Puno daily at 0700-0800; 3 hrs, return 1400/1430, US$5.80 one way. This doesn't leave enough time to appreciate the island fully. Organized tours can be arranged for about US$10-16 pp, but only give you about 2 hrs on the island. Tour boats usually call at Uros on the outward or return journey.

Amantaní

Another island worth visiting, is Amantaní, very beautiful and peaceful. There are six villages and ruins on both of the island's peaks, Pacha Tata and Pacha Mama, from which there are excellent views. There are also temples and on the shore there is a throne carved out of stone, the Inkatiana. On both hills, a fiesta is celebrated on 15 January (or thereabouts). The festivities are very colourful, musical and hard-drinking. There is also a festival the first Sunday in March with brass bands and colourful dancers. The residents make beautiful textiles and sell them quite cheaply at the Artesanía Cooperativa. They also make basketwork and stoneware. The people are Quechua speakers, but understand Spanish. There are no hotels, you stay with local

families. Ask your boat owner where you can stay. Accommodation, including three meals, is in our **G** range (a great deal for visitors, but artificially low). There is one restaurant, *Samariy*. Islanders arrange dances for tour groups (independent travellers can join in), visitors dress up in local clothes and join the dances. Small shops sell water and snacks, but more expensive than Puno.

Transport Boats leave from the harbour in Puno at 0700-0800 daily, return 0800, stopping at Taquile at 1430, US$5.80 one way. The journey takes 3½ hrs, take water and seasickness pills. A 1-day trip is not possible as the boats do not always return on the same day. Several tour operators in Puno offer 2-day excursions to Amantaní, Taquile and a visit to the floating islands, starting at US$12 pp (price depends on the season and size of group); including meals, 1 night on Amantaní and 3-4 hrs on Taquile. Despite what touts may tell you, it is possible to visit the islands independently and at your own pace. In this way the islands reap most of the reward from visitors; the majority of tour companies are owned in Puno. To visit both Taquile and Amantaní, it is better to go to Amantaní first; from there a boat goes to Taquile around 0800 when full, US$2.50 pp.

Llachón

At the eastern end of the Península de Capachica, which encloses the northern side of the Bahía de Puno, is **Llachón**, a farming village (population: 1,300) which is introducing community-based tourism. It has electricity and one phone. The scenery is very pretty, with sandy beaches, pre-Inca terracing, trees and flowers. The view of the sunset from the Auki Carus hill is reckoned to be better even than from Taquile. Visitors share in local activities and 70% of all produce served is from the residents' farms. The peninsula is good for hiking and mountain-biking and sailing boats can be hired. Neither Taquile not Amantaní are far away. Twelve families offer accommodation on a rotational basis (**G** per bed). Most meals are served in the house of Valentín Quispe, the organizer of tourism in Llachón: breakfast US$1.20, other meals US$2. There is a campsite towards the end of the peninsula. To contact Don Valentín, T360226/7, T680796 (Mob), llachon@yahoo.com or visit www.titicaca-peru.com/capachicae.htm

Transport Public boats leave Puno for Llachón on Fri, Sat and Sun only. Road transport runs on Wed and Sun; the unpaved road to the peninsula branches east from the main road half way between Puno and Juliaca. Tour operators in Puno arrange visits, about US$25 pp staying overnight, in groups of 10-15.

In the Peruvian part of the Lago Menor are the islands of **Anapia**, a friendly, Aymara-speaking community, and **Yuspique**, on which are ruins and vicuñas. The community has organized committees for tourism, motor boats, sailing boats and accommodation with families (*All Ways Travel*, see above, arranges tours which involve staying with families on Anapia, some community work and communal entertainment, highly worthwhile). To visit Anapia independently, take a colectivo from Yunguyo to Tinicachi and alight at Punta Hermosa, just after Unacachi. Boats to Anapia leave Punta Hermosa on Sunday and Thursday at 1300 (they leave Anapia for Yunguyo market on the same days at 0630). It's two hours each way by boat. On the island ask for José Flores, who is very knowledgeable about Anapia's history, flora and fauna. He sometimes acts as a guide.

Border with Bolivia

There are four different routes across the border. **NB** Peruvian time is one hour behind Bolivian time.

Puno-La Paz via Yunguyo & Copacabana

Peruvian immigration is five minutes' drive from **Yunguyo** and 100 m from the Bolivian post; open 24 hours a day (but Bolivian immigration is only open 0830-1930). Ninety days is normally given when entering Peru. Be aware of

Peru

corruption at customs and look out for official or unofficial people trying to charge you a fee, on either side of the border (say that you know it is illegal and ask why only gringos are approached to pay the 'embarkation tax').

Bolivian consulate is at Jr Grua 339, T856032, near the main plaza in Yunguyo, open Monday-Friday 0830-1500, for those who need a visa; some nationalities have to pay. For Bolivian immigration, see page 269. Good exchange rates are available for those entering Peru in the main plaza in Yunguyo, cash only. Travellers' cheques can be exchanged in the *cambio* here, poor rates. See also Puno, Banks.

Sleeping In **Yunguyo G** *Hostal Isabel*, San Francisco 110, near Plaza de Armas, T856019/856084, shared bath, hot water, modern, good value, will change money and arrange transport. A couple of others in **G** range .

Don't take a taxi Yunguyo-Puno without checking its reliability first, driver may pick up an accomplice to rob passengers

Transport The road is paved from Puno to Yunguyo and the scenery is interesting. In Puno 3 companies sell bus tickets for the direct route from Puno to La Paz, taking 6-8 hrs (fare does not include the Tiquina ferry crossing, US$0.25): *Colectur*, Tacna 221, T352302, 0730, US$6.50, combines with *Galería* in Bolivia; *Panamericano*, Tacna 245, T354001, 0700, US$7.35, combines with *Diana Tours*; *Tour Perú* (address under Puno Transport), 0800, US$8.75, combines with *Combi Tour* (fares rise at holiday times) They stop at the borders and 1 hr for lunch in Copacabana, arriving in La Paz at about 1700. You only need to change money into Bolivianos for lunch on this route. Bus fare Puno-Copacabana US$4.40-5.80. There are local buses and colectivos all day between Puno and Yunguyo, 3 hrs, US$1.20; they leave from Av Bolívar in Puno. From Yunguyo to the border (Kasani), colectivos charge US$0.25 pp. From the border it is a 20-min drive to Copacabana; colectivos and minibuses leave from just outside Bolivian immigration, US$0.50 pp. Taxi from Yunguyo to Copacabana costs about US$1.50 pp.

Puno-Desaguadero

Desaguadero is a scruffy, unscrupulous place, with poor restaurants and dubious accommodation. The best is **D-E** *Hostal Corona*, Av Panamericana 248, T851120, **F** without bath, TV, hot water, parking, luggage store, no meals. **F** *San Carlos*, without bath, extra for hot shower, basic, tiny rooms. There is no need to stopover in Desaguadero as all roads to it are paved and if you leave La Paz, Moquegua or Puno early enough you should be at your destination before nightfall. Colectivos and buses run Puno-Desaguadero, 2¼ hrs, US$1.50 by bus, every 30 minutes, last one around 1600. Border offices are open 0800-1200 and 1400-1930. Frequent buses run to Puno until 1930. It is easy to change money on the Peruvian side. This particular border crossing allows you to stop at Tiahuanaco en route.

To La Paz by Hydrofoil or Catamaran

There are luxury services from Puno/Juli to La Paz by *Crillon Tours* hydrofoil, with connections to tours, from La Paz, to Cusco and Machu Picchu. In Puno their office is at *Arcobaleno Tours* (see Tour operators), or contact head office in La Paz, see page 254 for details. The itinerary is: Puno-Copacabana by bus; Copacabana-Isla del Sol-Huatajata (Bolivia) by hydrofoil; Huatajata-La Paz by bus; 13 hrs. Similar services, by catamaran, are run by *Transturin*, whose dock is at Chúa, Bolivia; bookings through *Transturin*: offices in Puno at Libertad 176, T352771, F351316, leontours@terra.com.pe Or in La Paz.

Along the east side of Lake Titicaca

This is the most remote route, via **Huancané** (**F** *Hostal El Conquistador*, Puno y Castilla) and **Moho** (several *hostales*, **F-G**). Some walking may be involved as there is little traffic between Moho and **Puerto Acosta**, Bolivia. Make sure you get an exit stamp in Puno, post-dated by a couple of days. From Juliaca there are buses to Huancané and Moho (see Transport, above). From Moho, hitchhike to **Tilali**, the last village in Peru (3 hrs, basic accommodation). The road is very bad, but the views of the lake are stunning. Night buses to Tilali from Juliaca (6 hrs, only for certain on Mon, Tue, Fri and Sun) miss the scenery. From Tilali it is 15 mins' walk to the Peruvian immigration post, the border a further 30 mins and Puerto Acosta is a further 10 km. From there take a bus for 2½ hrs to Chaguaya, where there is a control post and immigration next door. Leave the bus to get a Bolivian entry stamp; the officials will help you get

Peru

transport to continue your journey. The road is good (paved from Escoma), several buses daily to La Paz.

The only tourist project on the north shore is **AL** *Albergue Rural Isla de Suasi*, T054-622709, or Puno T/F365968 (office, albergue@suasi.com) or 351417 (owner, Martha Giraldo, martha@suasi.com), or Lima 01-973 1404. The hotel is the only house on this tiny, tranquil island. There are beautiful terraced gardens, best Jan-Mar. The non-native eucalyptus trees are being replaced by native varieties. You can take a rowing boat around the island to see birds and the island has four vicuñas, a small herd of alpacas and one vizcacha. The sunsets from the highest point are beautiful. Facilities are spacious, comfortable and solar-powered, rooms with bath, hot water, hot water bottles. Price includes breakfast but other meals are extra, US$10-15; good food, lots of vegetables, all locally-produced. Private boats from Puno are expensive and take 4-6 hrs (2½ hrs by fast boat, US$450 up to 15 passengers), but you can call at the islands or Llachón en route. A car for 4 people will cost US$75. Otherwise take public transport from Juliaca to Moho and on to Cambría, near Conima, walk down to the shore and take a rowing boat to Suasi, 10 mins, US$1.50 pp.

Puno to Cusco

On the way from Puno to Cusco there is much to see from the train, which runs at an average altitude of 3,500 m. At the stations on the way, people sell food and local specialities, eg pottery bulls at Pucará (rooms available at the station); for Sicuani, see below; knitted alpaca ponchos and pullovers and miniature llamas at Santa Rosa (rooms available). There are three hotels in **Ayaviri**.

The railway crosses the altiplano, climbing to **La Raya**, the highest pass on the line; 210 km from Puno, at 4,321 m. Up on the heights breathing may be a little difficult, but the descent along the Río Vilcanota is rapid. To the right of **Aguas Calientes**, the next station, 10 km from La Raya, are steaming pools of hot water in the middle of the green grass; a startling sight. The temperature of the springs is 40° C, and they show beautiful deposits of red ferro-oxide. Communal bathing pools and a block of changing rooms have been opened. ■ *Entrance US$0.15.* At **Maranganí**, the river is wider and the fields greener, with groves of eucalyptus trees.

You can travel to Cusco from Puno by road which is paved all the way and consequently bus services are an acceptable alternative to the train.

At 38 km beyond La Raya pass is **Sicuani** (Altitude: 3,690 m), an important agricultural centre. Excellent items of llama and alpaca wool and skins are sold on the railway station and at the Sunday morning market. Around Plaza Libertad there are several hat shops. (For more information about places between Sicuani and Cusco, see page 1240.) Bus to Cusco, 137 km, US$1.25.

Sleeping and eating The bus terminal is in the newer part of town, which is separated from the older part and the Plaza by a pedestrian walkway and bridge. At the 'new' end of the bridge, but also close to the centre of town, are several *hostales* advertising hot water and private bathrooms. **E** *Royal Inti*, Av Centenario 116, T352730. West side of old pedestrian bridge, modern, good. Next door is **E** *Samariy*, No 138. Good value. **E** *Obada*, Tacna 104, T351214. Large, hot showers, has seen better days (basic dormitory at **G** *Hostal Obada*, on 2 de Mayo, nearby). **E** *Tairo*, Mejía 120, T351297. Modern, noisy. **G** *José's*, Av Arequipa 143, T351254. With bath, good. There are several eating places and nightspots. *Pizzería Ban Vino*, 2 de Mayo 129, p 2, good Italian, and *Viracocha*, west side of plaza, OK. *Pollerías* on C Zevallos.

Peru

Cusco

Phone code: 084
Colour map 3, grid C4
Altitude: 3,310 m

The ancient Inca capital is said to have been founded around AD1100, and since then has developed into a major commercial and tourism centre of 275,000 inhabitants, most of whom are Quechua. The city council has designated Qosqo (Cusco in Quechua) as the official spelling.

Today, colonial churches, monasteries and convents and extensive precolumbian ruins are interspersed with countless hotels, bars and restaurants that cater for the hundreds of thousands of visitors. Almost every central street has remains of Inca walls, arches and doorways; the perfect Inca stonework now serves as the foundations for more modern dwellings. This stonework is tapered upwards (battered); every wall has a perfect line of inclination towards the centre, from bottom to top. The curved stonework of the Temple of the Sun, for example, is probably unequalled in the world.

Ins & outs
For more detailed information, see Transport, page 1237

Getting there The **airport** is to the southeast of the city and the road into the centre goes close to Wanchac station, at which **trains** from Juliaca and Puno arrive. Cusco has a new **bus terminal** near the Pachacútec statue in Ttio district. Transport to your hotel is not a problem from any of these places by taxi or in transport arranged by hotel representatives.

Getting around The centre of Cusco is quite small and possible to explore on foot. Taxis in Cusco are cheap and recommended when arriving by air, train or bus and especially when returning to your hotel at night.

Cusco is only slightly lower than Puno, so respect the altitude: 2 or 3 hrs rest after arriving makes a great difference; avoid meat and smoking, eat lots of carbohydrates and drink plenty of clear, non-alcoholic liquid; remember to walk slowly. To see Cusco and the surrounding area properly – including Pisac, Ollantaytambo, Chinchero and Machu Picchu – you need five days to a week, allowing for slowing down because of altitude.

Tourist offices Official tourist information is at Portal Mantas 117-A, next to La Merced church, T263176, open 0800-2000. There is also a tourist information desk at the airport. The University is also a good source of information, especially on archaeological sites. They sell good videos of Cusco and surroundings. Other information sources include **South American Explorers**, Choquechaca 188, apto 4 (2 blocks behind the Cathedral), T245484, Aptdo postal 500, cuscoclub@saexplorers.org Open Mon-Fri 0930-1700, Sun 0930-1300, Sat 0930-1300. As with SAE's other clubhouses, this the place to go for specialized information, member-written trip reports and maps. For full details on *South American Explorers*, see page 26. **Automóvil Club del Perú**, Av Sol 457, p 3, next to *Banco Santander del Perú*, has some maps. Motorists beware; many streets end in flights of steps not marked as such. There are very few good maps of Cusco available. **Maps and guidebooks:** maps of the city, the Inca

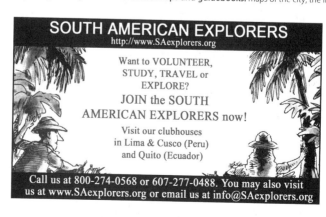
Peru

Trail and the Urubamba Valley are available at tour companies. There are lots of information booklets on Machu Picchu and the other ruins at the bookshops. *Cusco Weekly* is an English language newspaper, covering local and international news; www.cuscoweekly.com See Books, page 1295.

Visitors' tickets A combined entry ticket to most of the sites of main historical-cultural interest in and around the city, called *Boleto Turístico Unificado* (BTU), costs US$10 and is valid for 5-10 days. It permits entrance to: the Cathedral, San Blas, Santa Catalina Convent and Art Museum, Qoricancha or Temple of the Sun Museum (but not Santo Domingo/Qoricancha itself), Museo de Arte Religioso del Arzobispado, Museo Histórico Regional (Casa Inca Garcilazo de la Vega), Museo Palacio Municipal de Arte Contemporáneo; the archaeological sites of Sacsayhuaman, Qenqo, Puka Pukara, Tambo Machay, Pisac, Ollantaytambo, Chinchero, Tipón and Piquillacta. There is also a US$6, one-day ticket valid for Pisac, Chinchero and Ollantaytambo. They can be bought at the OFEC office (Casa Garcilazo), Plaza Regocijo, esquina Calle Garcilazo, Mon-Fri 0745-1800, Sat 0830-1300, or at any of the sites included in the ticket. There is a 50% discount for students, which is only available at the OFEC office (Casa Garcilazo) upon presentation of the ISIC card. Take your ISIC card when visiting the sites, as some may ask to see it. Photography is not allowed in the Cathedral, churches, and museums.

Entrance tickets for Santo Domingo/Qoricancha, the Inka Museum, El Palacio del Almirante, and La Merced are sold separately. Machu Picchu ruins and Inca trail entrance tickets are sold at the Instituto Nacional de Cultura (INC), San Bernardo s/n entre Mantas y Almagro, Mon-Fri 0900-1300, 1600-1800, Sat 0900-1100.

Security More police patrol the streets, trains and stations than in the past, which has led to an improvement in security, but one should still be vigilant. On no account walk back to your hotel after dark from a bar or club, strangle muggings and rape are frequent. For safety's sake, pay the US$1 taxi fare, but not just any taxi. Ask the club's doorman to get a taxi for you and make sure the taxi is licensed. The Santa Ana market (otherwise recommended); the San Cristóbal area and at out-of-the-way ruins. Also take special care during Inti Raymi.

The **Tourist Police** are on Calle Saphi, block 1, T221961. If you need a *denuncia* (a report for insurance purposes), which is available from the Banco de la Nación, they will type it out. Always go to the police when robbed, even though it will cost you a bit of time. The Tourist Protection Bureau (**Indecopi**) has been set up to protect the consumer rights of all tourists and will help with any problems or complaints. They can be very effective in dealing with tour agencies, hotels or restaurants. They are at Portal Carrizos, Plaza de Armas. T252974, or Lima 01-224 7888, or toll free 0800-42579 (24-hr hotline, not available from payphones).

Sights

The heart of the city in Inca days was *Huacaypata* (the place of tears) and *Cusipata* (the place of happiness), divided by a channel of the Saphi River. Today, Cusipata is Plaza Regocijo and Huacaypata is the Plaza de Armas, around which are colonial arcades and four churches. To the northeast is the early 17th-century baroque **Cathedral**, built on the site of the Palace of Inca Wiracocha (*Kiswarcancha*). The high altar is solid silver and the original altar *retablo* behind it is a masterpiece of Andean wood carving. The earliest surviving painting of the city can be seen, depicting Cusco during the 1650 earthquake. In the far right hand end of the church is an interesting local painting of the Last Supper replete with *cuy*, *chicha*, etc. In the sacristy are paintings of all the bishops of Cusco. The choir stalls, by a 17th-century Spanish priest, are a magnificent example of colonial baroque art. The elaborate pulpit and the sacristy are also notable. Much venerated is the crucifix of El Señor de los Temblores, the object of many pilgrimages and viewed all over Peru as a guardian against earthquakes. ■ *The Cathedral is open until 1000 for genuine worshippers – Quechua mass is held 0500-0600. Tourists may visit Tue, Wed, Fri, Sat 1000-1130, and Mon-Sun 1400-1730.* The tourist entrance to the Cathedral is through the church of **Jesús María** (1733), which stands to its left as you face it. Its gilt main altar has been renovated.

Peru

Inca society

Cusco was the capital of the Inca empire – one of the greatest planned societies the world has known – from its rise during the 11th century to its death in the early 16th century. (See John Hemming's Conquest of the Incas and B C Brundage's Lords of Cuzco and Empire of the Inca.) It was solidly based on other Peruvian civilizations which had attained great skill in textiles, building, ceramics and working in metal. Immemorially, the political structure of the Andean Indian had been the ayllu, the village community; it had its divine ancestor, worshipped household gods, was closely knit by ties of blood to the family and by economic necessity to the land, which was held in common. Submission to the ayllu was absolute, because it was only by such discipline that food could be obtained in an unsympathetic environment. All the domestic animals, the llama and alpaca and the dog, had long been tamed, and the great staple crops, maize and potatoes, established. What the Incas did – and it was a magnificent feat – was to conquer enormous territories and impose upon the variety of ayllus, through an unchallengeable central government, a willing spiritual and economic submission to the State. The common religion, already developed by the classical Tiwanaku culture, was worship of the Sun, whose vice-regent on earth was the absolute Sapa Inca. Around him, in the capital, was a religious and secular elite which never froze into a caste because it was open to talent. The elite was often recruited from chieftains defeated by the Incas; an effective way of reconciling local opposition. The mass of the people were subjected to rigorous planning. They were allotted land to work, for their group and for the State; set various tasks (the making of textiles, pottery, weapons, ropes, etc) from primary materials supplied by the functionaries, or used in enlarging the area of cultivation by building terraces on the hill-sides. Their political organization was simple but effective. The family, and not the individual, was the unit. Families were grouped in units of 10, 100, 500, 1,000, 10,000 and 40,000, each group with a leader responsible to the next largest group. The Sapa Inca crowned the political edifice; his four immediate counsellors were those to whom he allotted responsibility for the northern, southern, eastern and western regions (suyos) of the empire.

Equilibrium between production and consumption, in the absence of a free price mechanism and good transport facilities, must depend heavily upon statistical information. This the Incas raised to a high degree of efficiency by means of their quipus: a decimal system of recording numbers by knots in cords. Seasonal variations were guarded against by creating a system of state barns in which provender could be stored during years of plenty, to be used in years of scarcity. Statistical efficiency alone required that no one should be permitted to leave his home or his work. The loss of personal liberty was the price paid by the masses for economic security. In order to obtain information and to transmit orders quickly, the Incas built fine paved pathways along which couriers sped on foot. The whole system of rigorous control was completed by the greatest of all their monarchs, Pachacuti, who also imposed a common language, Quechua, as a further cementing force.

El Triunfo (1536), on its right of the Cathedral, is the first Christian church in Cusco, built on the site of the Inca Roundhouse (the *Suntur Huasi*). It has a statue of the Virgin of the Descent, reputed to have helped the Spaniards repel Manco Inca when he besieged the city in 1536.

On the southeast side of the plaza is the beautiful **La Compañía de Jesús**, built on the site of the Palace of the Serpents (*Amarucancha*, residence of Inca Huayna Capac) in the late 17th century. Its twin-towered exterior is extremely graceful, and the interior rich in fine murals, paintings and carved altars.

Much **Inca stonework** can be seen in the streets and most particularly in the Callejón Loreto, running southeast past La Compañía de Jesús from the main plaza. The walls of the *Acllahuasi* (House of the Chosen Women) are on one side, and of the *Amarucancha* on the other. There are also Inca remains in Calle San Agustín, to the east of the plaza. The famous stone of 12 angles is in Calle Hatun Rumiyoc half-way along its second block, on the right-hand side going away from the Plaza.

Between the centre and the airport on Alameda Pachacútec, the continuation of Av Sol, 20 minutes walk from the Plaza de Armas, there is a statue of the Inca Pachacútec placed on top of a lookout tower, from which there are excellent views of Cusco. ■ *1000-2000, free; small galleries and coffee shop.*

Churches **La Merced**, on Calle Márquez, was first built 1534 and rebuilt in the late 17th century. Attached is a very fine monastery with an exquisite cloister. Inside the church are buried Gonzalo Pizarro, half-brother of Francisco, and the two Almagros, father and son. The church is most famous for its jewelled monstrance, on view in the monastery's museum during visiting hours. ■ *The church is open 0830-1200, 1530-1730, except Sun; the monastery and museum are open 1430-1700. US$1.85.*

Many churches close to visitors on Sun; 'official' opening times are unreliable

San Francisco, on Plaza San Francisco, three blocks southwest of the Plaza de Armas, is an austere church reflecting many indigenous influences. Its monastery is being rebuilt and may be closed. ■ *The church is open 0600-0800, 1800-2000.* **Santa Catalina** church, convent and museum are on Arequipa at Santa Catalina Angosta. ■ *Daily 0900-1730, except Fri 0900-1500. There are guided tours by English-speaking students; tip expected.* **San Pedro**, in front of the Santa Ana market, was built in 1688. Its two towers were made from stones brought from an Inca ruin. ■ *Mon-Sat 1000-1200, 1400-1700.*

The smaller and less well-known church of **San Blas**, on Carmen Bajo, has a beautiful carved *mestizo* cedar pulpit, which is well worth seeing. ■ *Mon-Sat 1000-1130 (except Thu), Sun 1400-1730.* See Shopping Local crafts, below. Above Cusco, on the road up to Sacsayhuamán, is **San Cristóbal**, built to his patron saint by Cristóbal Paullu Inca. The church's atrium has been restored and there is a side-walk access to the Sacsayhuamán Archaeological Park. North of San Cristóbal, you can see the 11 doorway-sized niches of the great Inca wall of the Palacio de Colcampata, which was the residence of Manco Inca before he rebelled against the Spanish and fled to Vilcabamba.

Santo Domingo, southeast of the main Plaza, was built in the 17th century on the walls of the **Qoricancha**, **Temple of the Sun**, and from its stones. Excavation has revealed more of the five chambers of the Temple of the Sun, which shows the best Inca stonework to be seen in Cusco. The Temple of the Sun was awarded to Juan Pizarro, the younger brother of Francisco, who willed it to the Dominicans after he had been fatally wounded in the Sacsayhuaman siege. The baroque cloister has been gutted to reveal four of the original chambers of the great Inca temple – two on the west have been partly reconstructed in a good imitation of Inca masonry. The finest stonework is in the celebrated curved wall beneath the west end of Santo Domingo. This was rebuilt after the 1950 earthquake, at which time a niche that once contained a shrine was found at the inner top of the wall. Below the curved wall was a garden of gold and silver replicas of animals, maize and other plants. Excavations have revealed Inca baths below here, and more Inca retaining walls. The other superb stretch of late Inca stonework is in C Ahuacpinta outside the temple, to the east or left as you enter (John Hemming). ■ *Mon-Sat 0800-1700, Sun 1400-1600 (closed holidays). Santo Domingo US$1.15; English-speaking guides, tip of US$2-3 expected.*

Museo de Sitio Qorikancha (formerly Museo Arqueológico) on Av Sol, is under the garden below Santo Domingo. It contains a precolumbian collection, Spanish paintings of imitation Inca royalty dating from the 18th century, and photos of the excavation of Qoricancha. ■ *Mon-Fri 0800-1700, Sat 0900-1700, US$2; the staff will give a guided tour in Spanish but please give a tip.*

Colonial buildings The **Palacio del Almirante**, just north of the Plaza de Armas on Ataud, is impressive. It houses the **Museo Inka**, run by the Universidad San Antonio de Abad, which exhibits the development of culture in the region from pre-Inca, through Inca times to the present day: textiles, ceramics, metalwork,

No photographs allowed in any museums

Peru

jewellery, architecture, technology. See the colleciton of miniature turquoise figures and other offerings to the gods. Weaving demonstrations are given in the courtyard. ■ *Mon-Fri 0800-1730, Sat 0900-1700, US$1.40.*

The **Palacio Arzobispal** stands on Hatun Rumiyoc y Herrajes, two blocks north-east of Plaza de Armas. It was built on the site of the palace occupied in 1400 by the Inca Roca and was formerly the home of the Marqueses de Buena Vista. It contains the **Museo de Arte Religioso**, a fine collection of colonial paintings and furniture. The collection includes the paintings by the indigenous master, Diego Quispe Tito, of a 17th-century Corpus Christi procession that used to hang in the church of Santa Ana. ■ *Mon-Sat, 0830-1130, 1500-1730.*

The palace called **Casa de los Cuatro Bustos**, whose colonial doorway is at San Agustín 400, is now the *Hotel Libertador*. The general public can enter the Hotel from Plazoleta Santo Domingo, opposite the Temple of the Sun/Qoricancha. The **Convento de las Nazarenas**, on Plaza de las Nazarenas, is now an annex of Orient Express' *Monasterio* hotel. You can see the Inca-colonial doorway with a mermaid motif, but ask permission to view the lovely 18th-century frescos inside. Also on Plaza Nazarenas is **Casa Cabrera**, which is now a gallery and used by Banco Continental (free exhibition by indigenous photographer, Martín Chambi).

Museo de Historia Regional, in the Casa Garcilaso, Jr Garcilaso y Heladeros, tries to show the evolution of the Cuzqueño school of painting. It also contains Inca agricultural implements, colonial furniture and paintings. ■ *0730-1700.*

Excursions

Sacsayhuaman

Archaeologists are investigating the possibility of a tunnel between Qoricancha and Sacsayhuman, supporting the belief that the lost treasures of the Inca empire are buried beneath Cusco

There are some magnificent Inca walls in this ruined ceremonial centre, on a hill in the northern outskirts. The Incaic stones are hugely impressive. The massive rocks weighing up to 130 tons are fitted together with absolute perfection. Three walls run parallel for over 360 m and there are 21 bastions. Sacsayhuaman was thought for centuries to be a fortress, but the layout and architecture suggest a great sanctuary and temple to the Sun, which rises exactly opposite the place previously believed to be the Inca's throne – which was probably an altar, carved out of the solid rock. Broad steps lead to the altar from either side. The hieratic, rather than the military, hypothesis was supported by the discovery in 1982 of the graves of priests, who would have been unlikely to be buried in a fortress. The precise functions of the site, however, will probably continue to be a matter of dispute as very few clues remain, owing to its steady destruction. The site is about a 30-minute walk up Pumacurco from Plaza de las Nazarenas. ■ *Daily 0700-1730; free student guides, give them a tip.*

It is safest to visit the ruins in a group, especially if you wish to see them under a full moon. Take as few belongings as possible, and hide your camera

Along the road from Sacsayhuaman to Pisac, past a radio station, is the temple and amphitheatre of **Qenqo** with some of the finest examples of Inca stone carving *in situ*, especially inside the large hollowed-out stone that houses an altar. On the same road are **Cusilluchayoc** (K'usilluyuq), caves and Inca tunnels in a hillside (take a torch/flashlight); **Puka Pukara** (Red Fort, but more likely to have been a *tambo*, or post-house), wonderful views; and the spring shrine of **Tambo Machay**, which is in excellent condition. Water still flows by a hidden channel out of the masonry wall, straight into a little rock pool traditionally known as the Inca's bath. Take a guide to the sites and visit in the morning for the best photographs. Carry your multi-site ticket, there are roving ticket inspectors. You can visit the sites on foot, a pleasant walk of at least half a day through the countryside; take water, sun protection, and watch out for dogs. Alternatively, take the Pisac bus up to Tambo Machay (US$0.35) and walk back, or arrange a horseback tour with an agency (US$8 per person for four hours).

Peru

Essentials

Book more expensive hotels well in advance, particularly for the week or so around Inti Raymi, when prices are greatly increased. Prices given are for the high season in Jun-Aug. When there are fewer tourists hotels may drop their prices by as much as half. Always check for discounts. Train passengers are approached by unlicensed hotel agents for medium-priced hotels who are often misleading about details; their local nickname is *jalagringos* (gringo pullers), or *piratas*. Taxis and tourist minibuses meet the train and (should) take you to the hotel of your choice for US$0.50, but be insistent. Since it is cold here and many hotels have no heating, ask for an *estufa*, a space heater which some places will provide for an extra charge. The best are **L** *Libertador*, Plazoleta Santo Domingo 259 (see above), T231961, www.libertador.com.pe 5-star, price includes 28% tax and service and buffet breakfast, good, especially the service, warm and bright, *Inti Raymi* restaurant, excellent with folk music in the evening. **LL** *Monasterio*, Palacios 136, T241777, info@peruorientexpress.com.pe 5-star, beautifully restored Seminary of San Antonio Abad (a Peruvian National Historical Landmark), including the Baroque chapel, spacious comfortable rooms with all facilities, very helpful staff, price includes buffet breakfast (US$12 to non-residents, will fill you up for the rest of the day), good restaurants, lunch and dinner à la carte, business centre with email for guests (US$3 per hr) open 0930-1300, 1730-2130. **LL** *Novotel*, San Agustín 239, T228282, corphotelera@terra.com.pe 4-star, cheaper (still **LL**) in modern section, includes breakfast, converted from the colonial house of Miguel Sánchez Ponce who accompanied Pizarro, beautiful courtyard roofed in glass, spacious rooms with cable TV, central heating, 2 restaurants.

L *Picoaga*, Santa Teresa 344, T221269, www.computextos.com.pe/picoaga Very pleasant, comfortable, price includes buffet breakfast, courtyard, good location. **L** *Savoy Internacional*, Av Sol 954, T224322 (Lima T/F446 7965), www.cusco.net/savoyhotel One of the earliest modern hotels in the city, spacious rooms, with bath, heating,

Sleeping
The hotels in the list are recommended In Jun and other busy times, double-booking occurs so double-check reservations

Peru

full range of services, good view from Sky Room, bar, coffee shop, good food, many languages spoken, popular with groups. **L** *Sonesta Posada del Inca*, Portal Espinar 142, T227061, F248484, www.sonesta.com Full range of services, including taxes, central, excellent service, elevator, comfortable, popular with tour groups, internet for guests, book in advance. **AL** *Don Carlos IncaTambo Hacienda*, at Km 2, close to Sacsayhuaman, T221918, F222045 (Lima T224 0263, F224 8581), www.tci.net.pe/doncarlos Built on the site of Pizarro's original house, TV, heating, full services and facilities, horse riding in 60 ha of hotel grounds, 25% discount if booked through *Luzma Tours* (see below). **AL** *El Dorado Inn*, Av Sol 395, T231135, doratour@telser.com.pe 4-star, Full range of facilities, price includes breakfast, convenient location, excellent service, good restaurant (*Sky Room*), cafeteria open to the public, elevator. **AL** *Royal Inka I*, Plaza Regocijo 299, T231067, royalin@terra.com.pe (also

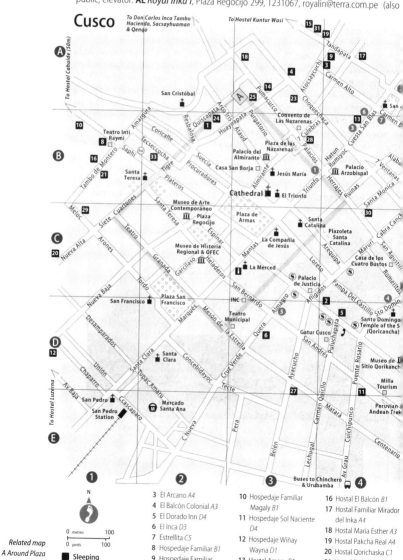

Cusco

Peru

N

| 0 metres | 100 |
| 0 yards | 100 |

Related map
A Around Plaza
de Armas,
page 1230

■ **Sleeping**
1 Albergue Municipal *B2*
2 Cristina *C4*

3 El Arcano *A4*
4 El Balcón Colonial *A3*
5 El Dorado Inn *D4*
6 El Inca *D3*
7 Estrellita *C5*
8 Hospedaje Familiar *B1*
9 Hospedaje Familiar
  Inti Quilla *A4*

10 Hospedaje Familiar
  Magaly *B1*
11 Hospedaje Sol Naciente
  D4
12 Hospedaje Wiñay
  Wayna *D1*
13 Hostal Amaru *B4*
14 Hostal Arqueólogo *A3*
15 Hostal Casa de Campo *A3*

16 Hostal El Balcón *B1*
17 Hostal Familiar Mirador
  del Inka *A4*
18 Hostal María Esther *A3*
19 Hostal Pakcha Real *A4*
20 Hostal Qorichaska *C1*
21 Hostal Rickch'airy *B1*
23 Hostal Rumi Punku *A3*
24 Hostal San Cristóbal *A3*

Royal Inka II on Santa Teresa, same price). Price includes taxes and breakfast, bar, dining room, good service. These hotels run a bus to Pisac at 1000 daily, returns 1800, free for guests. **A** *Pensión Alemana*, Tandapata 260, San Blas, T/F226861, pensioalemana@terra.Com.pe Swiss owned, welcoming, comfortable, price includes American breakfast, discount in low season. **A** *Hostal El Balcón*, Tambo de Montero 222, T236738, balcon1@terra.com.pe With breakfast, homely atmosphere, very welcoming, quiet, laundry, sauna, bar, meals on request, English spoken, wonderful views. **A** *Hostal Garcilaso*, Garcilaso de la Vega 233, T233031, hotelgarcilaso@hotmail.com Refurbished historic charm, safe for luggage, discount if booked through agents, helpful.

B *Hostal Cahuide*, Saphi 845, T222771, F222361. Discount for long stay, hot water, good rooms, quiet, good laundry service, storage facilities, helpful, good value breakfasts.

B *Hostal Casa de Campo*, Tandapata 296 (at the end of the street), T/F243069, www.hotelcasadecampo.com (or contact via *La Tertulia* café). Some of the highest rooms have a *lot* of steps up to them, hot water, includes Continental breakfast and airport/rail transfer with reservations, discount for longer stays and for students at the *Amauta* language school (see below), 10% discount for SAE members and Handbook owners, safe deposit box, sun terrace, quiet and relaxing, all rooms have great views, Dutch and English spoken, take a taxi there after dark. **B** *Hostal Corihuasi*, Suecia 561, T/F232233, www.corihuasi.com With breakfast, colonial house, laundry arranged, hot water, quiet, electric heaters, good views, popular with tour groups. **B** *Cristina*, Av Sol 341, T227233, hcristina@terra.com.pe Comfortable, hot water, breakfast available, reliable. **B-C** *Hostal Arqueólogo*, Pumacurco 408, T232569, F235126, www.hotelarqueologo.com Includes breakfast, hot water, helpful, French and English spoken, will store luggage, garden, cafeteria and kitchen. **B** *Hostal Monarca*, Pumapaccha 290, T/F226145, hostalesmonarca.com Breakfast included. **B** *Pensión Loreto*, Pasaje Loreto 115, Plaza de Armas, T226352, hostalloreto@telser.com.pe Rooms with Inca walls and electric heaters, a bit dark, cheap laundry service, comfortable and secure, taxis and other travel can be arranged, Lucio here is a good guide, safe luggage deposit. **B** *Los Marqueses*, Garcilaso 256, T232512, marqueseshotel@hotmail.com Lovely colonial house with a beautiful patio, room prices differ, heaters extra, in need of renovation. **B** *Los Portales*, Matará 322, T223500, portales01@terra.com.pe Includes airport pickup, modern facilities but plenty of character, very helpful, English spoken, safe deposit, luggage store.

Peru

25 Huaynapata *A3*
26 Libertador *C4*
27 Los Portales *D3*
28 Monasterio *B3*
29 Niños *C1*
30 Novotel *C4*
31 Pensión Alemana *A3*
32 Savoy Internacional *E5*
33 Suecia II *B2*

● **Eating**
1 A Mi Manera *B3*
2 Greens *A4*
3 Heidi Granja *B4*
4 Inkanato *C4*
5 Los Toldos *D3*
6 Macondo *A4*
7 Pacha-Papa *B4*

C *Hostal Amaru*, Cuesta San Blas 541, T/F225933, www.cusco.net/amaru Cheaper without bath, hot water, laundry, nice views, rooms in first courtyard are best. **C** *El Inca*, Quera 251, T/F221110, oscaralianza@yahoo.com **E** in the low season, heating, hot water variable, luggage store, restaurant, includes breakfast, Wilbur speaks English, and is helpful, noisy disco in basement till 0100. Otherwise recommended. **C** *Hostal Horeb*, San Juan de Dios 260, T236775. Hot showers, big rooms, family atmosphere, luggage stored. **C** *Huaynapata*, Huaynapata 369, T228034. Small rooms, quieter rooms at the back, family-run, hot water, stores luggage. **C** *Hostal Incawasi*, Portal de Panes 147, Plaza de Armas, T223992/228130, incawasi@telser.com.pe Hot water 0800-0900, 2000-2200, good beds, bargain for long stays, secure, helpful, good value (*Andes Grill* restaurant above). **C** *Hostal María Esther*, Pumacurco 516, T224382. Very comfortable, helpful, includes breakfast, garden. **C** *Niños Hotel*, Meloc 442, T/F231424, www.targetfound.nl.ninos Hot water, shared bath, restaurant, laundry service, luggage store, fax service, Dutch, English, German and French spoken,

run as part of the Dutch foundation *Niños Unidos Peruanos* and all profits are invested in projects to help street children. **C** *Hostal Pakcha Real*, Tandapata 300, San Blas, T237484, pakcharealhostal@hotmail.com Family run, hot water, cooking and laundry facilities, TV and video lounge, luggage stored, owner Edwin will arrange tours. **C** *Hostal Q'Awarina*, Suecia 757, T228130. Includes breakfast, group rates available, great views, great value.

D *El Arcano*, Carmen Alto 288, T/F232703. Cheaper in low season and with shared bath, hot water, safe to leave luggage, laundry, good beds, cheap breakfast. **D** *Hospedaje Familiar*, Saphi 661, T239353. **E** without bath, hot water, good beds, popular. **D** *Hostal Familiar Mirador del Inka*, Tandapata 160, off Plaza San Blas, T261384. Cheaper without bath, hot water, good beds, laundry, helpful family, son Edwin rents trekking equipment. **D** *Hostal Kuntur Wasi*, Tandapata 352-A, San Blas, T227570. Great views, **E** without bath, laundry service US$0.85 per kg, owner speaks a bit of English and is very helpful and welcoming, water not very warm, but excellent value. **D** *Hostal Royal Frankenstein*, San Juan de Dios 260 (next to *Horeb*), 200 m from the Plaza de Armas, T236999, ludwigroth@hotmail.com Eccentric, memorably-decorated, hot water, safe, cooking and laundry facilities, German-owned, German and English spoken.

E *Hostal Cáceres*, Plateros 368, 1 block from the Plaza de Armas. Hot water, big rooms (those at the back are warmer and quieter), luggage store, laundry service, book exchange, motorcycle parking in the patio. **E** *Hostal Casa Grande*, Santa Catalina Ancha 353, T264156. Wonderful location, hot water, **G** without bath, laundry service, café, good value. **E** *Qorichaska*, Nueva Alta 458, some distance from centre, T228974, F227094. Hot water, will store luggage, cafeteria open till 2100, safe, great value. **E** pp *Hospedaje Recoleta*, Jr Pumacahua 160, Tahuantinsuyo, T681095, hosperecoleta@usa.net Includes breakfast, hot water, comfortable, good service. **E-F** *Hostal Resbalosa*, Resbalosa 494, T224839. Cheaper without bath, hot water in the mornings and evenings, ask for a room with a view, luggage stored, laundry facilities, full breakfast for US$1.45. **E** *Suecia II*, Tecseccocha 465, T239757. **F** without bath, good security, breakfast US$1.40 from 0500, beautiful building, good meeting place, water not always hot or bathrooms clean, best to book in advance (but if full they will find alternative accommodation, which may not be as good). **E** *Hostal Tahuantinsuyo*, Jr Tupac Yupanqui 204, Urb Tahuantinsuyo (15-min walk from the Plaza de Armas), T/F261410, suya@ chaski.unsaac.edu.pe Cheaper without bath, includes breakfast, also drinks and snacks available, hot water, lovely atmosphere, very helpful, laundry service and facilities, secure parking for bikes and motorbikes, English, French and Italian spoken, can arrange tours. **E** *Posada del Viajero*, Santa Catalina Ancha 366, down lane next to *Rosie O'Grady's*. Variety of rooms, run by students, very good.

F pp *El Balcón Colonial*, Choquechaca 350, T238129. Accommodation for 16 people in 6 rooms, hot showers, breakfast extra, comfortable, safe, generous hosts. **F** *Hostal Luzerna*, Av Baja 205, near San Pedro train station (take a taxi at night), T232762/ 237591/227768. Hot water, safe to leave luggage, good beds, nice family, with breakfast, use of kitchen (Israeli hang-out). **F** *Hostal Rickch'airy*, Tambo de Montero 219, T236606. Shared bath (new rooms with bath **C**), hot water in the morning, laundry service, free luggage store, breakfast available, nice garden with good views, will collect guests from train station, tourist information, owned by Leo who is helpful. **F** *Hospedaje Sol Naciente*, Av Pardo 510, T228602. Hot water, comfortable, laundry facilities, luggage stored for a small fee, family-run. **F** *Tumi 1*, Siete Cuartones 245, 2 blocks from Plaza de Armas, T24413. Nice courtyard, hot water, good. **F** *Hospedaje Wiñay Wayna*, C Vitoque 628, just off Nueva Baja, miriamojeda@yahoo.com Price includes breakfast, family-run, homely, very good.

G *Estrellita*, Av Tullumayo 445, parte Alta, T234134, guesthouseestrellita@hotmail.com Includes breakfast, basic kitchen for guests, most rooms with shared bath, 2 with private bath, basic but excellent value, safe parking for bikes. **G** *Hospedaje Familiar Inti Quilla*, Atocsaycuchi 281, T252659. Shared rooms around a pleasant little courtyard, hot water 24 hrs. **G** *Hospedaje Familiar Magaly*, Saphi 739-2, T239099. Kind family, good beds. **G** *Hostal Pumacurco*, Pumacurco 336, Interior 329, T243347 (3 mins from the Plaza de Armas). In the newly restored part of a colonial house, hot water, owner Betty is very helpful, some large rooms, secure, laundry facilities. **G** pp *Hostal San Cristóbal*, Quiscapata 242, near San Cristóbal. Dormitory rooms, cooking and clothes-washing facilities, hot water, baggage deposit, reliable.

Peru

Around Plaza de Armas

Plateros detail

Peru

■ Sleeping
1 El Procurador *A2*
2 Hostal Cáceres
   Plateros detail
3 Hostal Casa Grande *C3*
4 Hostal Corihuasi *A3*
5 Hostal Garcilaso *B1*
6 Hostal Incawasi *B2*
7 Hostal Q'Awarina *A2*
8 Hostal Resbalosa *A3*
9 Hostal Royal
   Frankenstein &
   Hostal Horeb *B1*
10 Los Marqueses *B1*
11 Pensión Loreto *C2*
12 Picoaga *A1*
13 Posada del Viajero *C3*
14 Royal Inka I *B1*
15 Royal Inka II *A1*
16 Sonesta Posada
   del Inca *C2*
17 Tumi I *A1*

● Eating
1 Al Grano *C3*
2 Ama Lur *Plateros detail*
3 Auliya *B1*
4 Café Ayllu *B3*
5 Café Bagdad *B3*

6 Café Halliy
   Plateros detail
7 Chez Maggy Clave
   de Do *A2*
8 Chez Maggy El
   Corsario *B2*
9 Chez Maggy La
   Antigua *A2*
10 Chez Maggy
   Millenium
   Plateros detail
11 Eko *Plateros detail*
12 El Cuate *A2*
13 El Truco & Taberna
   del Truco *B1*
14 Govinda &
   Café Varayoc *B2*
15 Green's Juice Bar *A2*
16 Inka Grill *B2*
17 Kamikaze *B2*
18 Kintaro *B1*
19 Kusikuy
   Plateros detail
20 La Retama *B2*
21 La Tertulia *B2*
22 La Yunta *B3*
23 Los Perros *A2*
24 Mama Africa *C3*

25 Mesón de los
   Espaderos *B2*
26 Norton Rat's
   Tavern *C2*
27 Pachacútec Grill
   & Bar *B2*
28 Paddy O'Flaherty's *C3*
29 Paititi *C3*
30 Pizzería Americana
   Plateros detail
31 Pucará *Plateros detail*
32 Rosie O'Grady's *C3*
33 Tizziano Trattoria *A2*
34 Trotamundos *B2*
35 Tunupa & Cross
   Keys Pub *B2*
36 Ukuku's
   Plateros detail
37 Uptown *B3*
38 Victor Victoria *A2*

Youth hostel: F *Albergue Municipal*, Quiscapata 240, San Cristóbal, T252506. Dormitories, helpful staff, luggage store, great views, bar, cafeteria, laundry, safe deposit, discount for members. **F** *El Procurador*, Coricalle 440, Prolongación Procuradores, T243559, hostal-procurador-cusco@hotmail.com **G** without bath, includes breakfast, hot water, laundry, motorcycle parking.

Camping For renting equipment, there are several places around the Plaza area. Check the equipment carefully as it is common for parts to be missing. An example of prices per day: tent US$3-5, sleeping bag US$2 (down), US$1.50 (synthetic), stove US$1. A deposit of US$100 is asked, plus credit card, passport or plane ticket. *Soqllaq'asa Camping Service*, owned by English-speaking Sra Luzmila Bellota Miranda, at Plateros 365 No 2F, T252560, is recommended for equipment hire, also buy and sell camping gear and make alpaca jackets, open Mon-Sat 0900-1300, 1600-2030, Sun 1800-2030. White gas (*bencina*), US$1.50 per litre, can be bought at hardware stores, but check the purity. Stove spirit (*alcoól para quemar*) is available at pharmacies; blue gas canisters, costing US$5, can be found at some hardware stores and at shops which rent gear. You can also rent equipment through travel agencies.

Camping is not safe anywhere in the Cusco area

Eating

Expensive: *Inka Grill*, Portal de Panes 115, Plaza de Armas, T262992. According to many the best food in town, specializing in Novo Andino cuisine (the use of native ingredients and 'rescued' recipes), also homemade pastas, live music, breakfast from 0800 with excellent coffee and homemade pastries 'to go', very smart decor. *Mesón de los Espaderos*, Espaderos y Plaza de Armas, 2nd floor. Good *parrilladas* and other typical local dishes. *Mesón de los Portales*, Portal de Panes 163, Plaza de Armas, international and Peruvian cuisine. *Paititi*, Portal Carrizos 270, Plaza de Armas. Live music, good atmosphere, Inca masonry, excellent pizzas. *La Retama*, Portal de Panes 123, 2nd floor. Good food and service, live music and dance, art exhibitions. *Pachacútec Grill and Bar*, Portal de Panes 105, Plaza de Armas. International cuisine, including seafood and Italian specialities, folk music nightly. *El Truco*, Plaza Regocijo 261. Excellent local and international dishes, buffet lunch 1200-1500, nightly folk music at 2045, next door is *Taberna del Truco*, open 0900-0100. *Tunupa*, Portal Confiturias 233, p 2, Plaza de Armas (same entrance as *Cross Keys*). Large restaurant, small balcony overlooking Plaza, international, Peruvian and Novo Andino cuisine, good buffet for US$15, nicely decorated, cocktail lounge, live music and dance at 2030.

Mid-range: *Al Grano*, Santa Catalina Ancha 398, T228032. Authentic Asian dishes, menu changes daily, excellent food, best coffee in town, vegetarian choices, open 1000-2100, closed on Sun. *A Mi Manera*, Triunfo 393. Good food, service and balcony. *Greens*, Tandapata 700, behind the church on Plaza San Blas, T243820, greens_cusco@hotmail.com Good international food with some vegetarian, curries, Sunday roasts (reservation required), relaxing atmosphere, games, book exchange, popular. *Inkanato*, Plazoleta Santo Domingo 279, interior 2A, T222926. Good food, staff dressed in Inca and Amazonian outfits. *Kintaro*, Heladeros 149. Japanese and vegetarian, homemade and low fat food, good for high altitude, Japanese owner, closed Sun. *Macondo*, Cuesta San Blas 571, T229415, macondo@telser.com.pe Interesting restaurant with an imaginative menu, good food, well-furnished, gay friendly. *Pacha-Papa*, Plazoleta San Blas 120, opposite church of San Blas, T241318. Good typical Peruvian dishes, also international cuisine, beautiful setting with patio, Andean harp music. *Pizzería Americana*, Plateros 369, also does a good set meal for US$1.50. *Pucará*, Plateros 309. Peruvian and international food, open 1230-2200, closed Sun, nice atmosphere. *Tizziano Trattoria*, Tecseccocha 418. Good Italian food, homemade pasta, excellent value *menú* Tue-Sat 1200-1500 and daily 1800-2300, also vegetarian dishes. *Los Tomines*, Triunfo 384. Excellent 4-course set meal for US$5-6. *Los Toldos*, Almagro 171 and San Andrés 219. Grilled chicken, fries and salad bar, also *trattoria* with homemade pasta and pizza, delivery T229829. *Varayoc*, Almagro 136. Good brochettes and fast foods, see also *Café Literario Varayoc*.

Cheap: *Ama Lur*, Plateros 327. Very good *menú* for US$2. *La Barceloneta*, Procuradores 347. Spanish, Italian and Peruvian dishes, good value lunches, Spanish music Thu. *Chez Maggy*, 4 branches: *La Antigua* (the original) at Procuradores 365, *El Corsario* No 344 and *Clave de Do* No 374 (open at 0700 for buffet breakfast), plus *Millenium*, Plateros 348

The cheapest food can be found around the Mercado Santa Ana and San Pedro station

Peru

(opens 0700, buffet breakfast), all have good atmosphere, popular, freshly baked pizzas, pastas, Mexican food, soups, hotel delivery T234861 or 246316. *El Cuate*, Procuradores 386. Mexican food, great value, big portions, simple salads. *Fistuk*, Saphy 644, T251736. Good Israeli and Middle Eastern food, also travel agency. *Kusikuy*, Plateros 348, T262870. Open 0800-2300 Mon-Sat, local, national and international dishes, good service, set lunch unbeatable value at only US$2. *El Mexicanito*, Procuradores 392. Menus from US$2-3, good food. *El Nevado*, Plateros 345. Good set meals, also good soups and fish. *Víctor Victoria*, Tigre 130. Israeli and local dishes, first-class breakfasts, good value. *La Yunta*, Portal de Carnes, Plaza de Armas. Good salads, pancakes and juices, also vegetarian, popular with tourists, same owners as *Instinct Travel Agency*. Many good, cheap restaurants on Procuradores, Plateros (eg *Los Candiles*, No 323) and Tecseccocha.

Cafés: *Antojitos*, Marqués 284, 3 blocks from Plaza de Armas, T246334. Good tea and cakes, cheap (ignore the decor, though). *Café Ayllu*, Portal de Carnes 208. Classical/folk music, good atmosphere, superb range of milk products, wonderful apple pastries, good selection for breakfast, great juices, quick service. Next door upstairs is *Café Bagdad*. Good views of the plaza, cheap set lunch, good atmosphere, happy hour 1930-2130, German owner Florian Thurman speaks good English, service variable. *Café Halliy*, Plateros 363. Popular meeting place, especially for breakfast, good for comments on guides, has good snacks and 'copa Halliy' – fruit, muesli, yoghurt, honey and chocolate cake, also good vegetarian *menú* and set lunch. *Café Illary*, Procuradores 358. Open for breakfast at 0600, good. *Café Varayoc*, Espaderos 142, T232404. Good meeting place, excellent coffee, pizzas and chocolate cake, expensive. *Green's Juice Bar*, at the top of Procuradores. Tiny, choose from many fruits, drinks are huge, US$1.15, book exchange, English magazines. *Heidi Granja*, Cuesta San Blas 525. German owner Carlos serves up yoghurt, granola, ricotta cheese and honey and other great breakfast options, evening meals US$2.15. *Manu Café*, Av Pardo 1046. Good coffee and good food too. *Moni*, San Agustín 311. Peruvian/English owned, good fresh food and breakfast, British music, magazines, bright and clean. *La Tertulia*, Procuradores 50, 2nd floor. Run by Johanna and Alfredo of the *Amauta* Language School, excellent breakfast buffet for around US$3, vegetarian buffet 1800-2200 daily, set dinner and salad bar for US$3.50, also fondue and gourmet meals, book exchange, newspapers, classical music, open till 2300. *Trotamundos*, Portal Comercio 177, 2nd floor. Balcony overlooking the plaza, nice atmosphere, especially at night with open fire, good coffees and cakes, safe salads, internet service, open Mon-Sat 0800-2400. *Yaku Mama*, Procuradores 397. Good for breakfast, unlimited fruit and coffee. **Panaderías**: *Panadería El Buen Pastor*, Cuesta San Blas 579. Very good bread and pastries, proceeds go to a charity for orphans and street children. *Le Croissant*, Plaza San Francisco 134. French run, excellent pastries, good coffee. *La Dulcería*, Heladeros 167. Good for cakes, sandwiches, snacks and tea.

Vegetarian *Auliya*, Garcilaso 265, on 2nd floor. Beautifully-renovated colonial house, excellent, also stocks a wide range of dried food for trekking. *Frutos*, C Triunfo 393, p 2, tienda 202. Open Mon-Sat 0630-2200, Thu 0900-1500, excellent value set lunch. *Govinda*, Espaderos 128, just off the Plaza de Armas. Good value, especially the set meals. *La Naturaleza*, Procuradores 351. Cheap. *Paccha*, Portal de Panes 167. Good for breakfast, bookstore, posters for sale, English and French spoken.

Bars & nightclubs

Bars *Amaru Quechua Café Pub*, Plateros 325, 2nd floor, T246976. Bar with pizzería, games. *Cross Keys Pub*, Plaza de Armas, Portal Confiturías 233 (upstairs). Open 1100-0130, run by Barry Walker of *Manu Expeditions*, a Mancunian and ornithologist, darts, cable sports, pool, bar meals, plus daily half price specials Sun-Wed, great pisco sours, very popular, great atmosphere. *Keros Pub*, Procuradores at Plaza de Armas. Café until 1800, good, cheap breakfast, cakes, juices, good view of plaza, bar afterwards with live music every night. *Gypsy*, Carmen Alto 162-C. Great bar in San Blas. *Norton Rat's Tavern*, Loreto 115, p 2, same entrance as *Hostal Loreto*, T246204, nortonrats@yahoo.com Also serves meals, cable TV with BBC and CNN, popular, English spoken, fine balcony, pool, darts, motorcycle theme with information for motorcyclists from owner, Jeffrey Powers. *Paddy O'Flaherty's*, Triunfo 124 on the corner of the plaza. Irish theme pub, serves cans of Guinness, open 1300-0100, popular, good atmosphere and view. *Los Perros Bar*, Tecseccocha 436. Great place to chill out on comfy couches, excellent music, owner Tammy is English-speaking and very welcoming, good

Peru

coffee, tasty snacks available, book exchange, English and other magazines, board games, open 1100-0100. *Rosie O'Grady's*, Santa Catalina Ancha 360, T247935. Good music, tasty food, English and Russian spoken, good value, open 1100 till late (food served till midnight).

Nightclubs *Eko*, Plateros 334, 2nd floor. Bar with dancing, opens at 2100 till the early hours, free drink on presentation of Eko card obtainable at entrance, popular, great atmosphere, also has a couch lounge for quiet conversation, games and reading. *Kamikaze*, Plaza Regocijo 274, T233865. *Peña* at 2200, good old traditional rock music, candle-lit cavern atmosphere, entry US$2.50. *Mama Africa*, Portal Belén 115, 2nd floor. Live music at weekends, very popular, free entry with a pass which you can get on the plaza, free movies daily at 1630-1700, cybercafé (slow machines). *Ukuku's*, Plateros 316. US$1.35 entry, very popular, good atmosphere, good mix of music including live shows nightly, shows free movies around 1600-1700, also has a restaurant at Procuradores 398 (top end). *Uptown*, Suecia 302 on the corner of the plaza. Good music and atmosphere, very popular.

Cinema *Peliclub*, Tecseccocha 458, T246442, Tue-Sun 1500-2130, US$1.45, students US$0.85. **Folklore** Regular nightly folklore show at *Centro Qosqo de Arte nativo*, Av Sol 604, T227901. Show from 1900 to 2030, entrance fee US$3.50. *Teatro Inti Raymi*, Saphi 605, nightly at 1845, US$4.50, well worth it. There's a *peña* at *Inka's Restaurant Peña*, Portal de Panes 105, Plaza de Armas. Good menú at lunchtime for US$3. *Teatro Municipal*, C Mesón de la Estrella 149 (T227321 for information 0900-1300 and 1500-1900). Plays, dancing and shows, mostly Thu-Sun. They also run classes in music and dancing from Jan to Mar which are great value.

Entertainment

Carnival in Cusco is a messy affair with flour, water, cacti, bad fruit and animal manure thrown about in the streets (Carnival is lively along the length of the Sacred Valley). **Easter Monday:** procession of *El Señor de los Temblores* (Lord of the Earthquakes), starting at 1600 outside the Cathedral. A large crucifix is paraded through the streets, returning to the Plaza de Armas around 2000 to bless the tens of thousands of people who have assembled there. **2-3 May:** *Vigil of the Cross* takes place at all mountaintops with crosses on them, a boisterous affair. **Jun:** *Q'Olloriti*, the Snow Star Festival, is held at a 4,700 m glacier north of Ocongate (Ausangate) 150 km southeast of Cusco. Several agencies offer tours. (The date is moveable.) On *Corpus Christi* day, the Thu after Trinity Sunday, all the statues of the Virgin and of saints from Cusco's churches are paraded through the streets to the Cathedral. The Plaza de Armas is surrounded by tables with women selling *cuy* (guinea pig) and a mixed grill called *chiriuchu* (*cuy*, chicken, *tortillas*, fish eggs, water-weeds, maize, cheese and sausage) and lots of Cusqueña beer. **24 Jun:** the pageant of *Inti Raymi*, the Inca festival of the winter solstice, is enacted in Quechua at 1000 at the Qoricancha, moving on to Sacsayhuaman at 1300. Tickets for the stands can be bought a week in advance from the Emufec office, Santa Catalina Ancha 325, US$35. Standing places on the ruins are free but get there at about 1030 to defend your space. Travel agents can arrange the whole day for you, with meeting points, transport, reserved seats and packed lunch. Those who try to persuade you to buy a ticket for the right to film or take photos are being dishonest. On the night before Inti Raymi, the Plaza de Armas is crowded with processions and food stalls. Try to arrive in Cusco 15 days before Inti Raymi for the Cusqueña beer festival (US$6 entry) and other festivals, parades etc. **28 Jul:** Peruvian Independence Day. Prices shoot up during these celebrations. **Aug:** on the last Sun is the *Huarachicoy* festival at Sacsayhuaman, a spectacular re-enactment of the Inca manhood rite, performed in dazzling costumes by boys of a local school. **8 Sep:** *Day of the Virgin* is a colourful procession of masked dancers from the church of Almudena, at the southwest edge of Cusco, near Belén, to the Plaza de San Francisco. There is also a splendid fair at Almudena, and a free bull fight on the following day. **1 Nov:** *All Saints Day*, celebrated everywhere with bread dolls and traditional cooking. **8 Dec:** Cusco day, when churches and museums close at 1200. **24 Dec:** *Santuranticuy*, 'the buying of saints', with a big crafts market in the plaza, very noisy until early hours of the 25th.

Local festivals

Arts and crafts In the Plaza San Blas and the surrounding area, authentic Cusco crafts still survive. A market is held on Sat. Leading artisans who welcome visitors include

Shopping

Peru

Hilario Mendivil, Plazoleta San Blas 634, who makes Biblical figures from plaster, wheatflour and potatoes, and *Edilberta Mérida*, Carmen Alto 133, who makes earthenware figures showing the physical and mental anguish of the Indian peasant. *Víctor Vivero Holgado*, at Tandapata 172, is a painter of pious subjects, while *Antonio Olave Palomino*, Siete Angelitos 752, makes reproductions of precolumbian ceramics and colonial sculptures. *Maximiliano Palomino de la Sierra*, Triunfo 393, produces festive dolls and wood carvings, and *Santiago Rojas*, near San Blas, statuettes. *Luis Aguayo Revollar*, Cuesta del Almirante 256, T248661, aguayo@latinmail.com, makes fine woodcarvings

Cusco is the weaving centre of Peru, and excellent textiles can be found at good value. Be very careful of buying gold and silver objects and jewellery in and around Cusco

Mercado Artesanal, Av Sol, block 4, is good for cheap crafts. *Feria Artesanal Tesores del Inka*, Plateros 334B, open daily 0900-2300. *La Mamita*, Portal de Carnes 244, Plaza de Armas, sells the ceramics of Pablo Seminario (see under Urubamba), plus cotton, basketry, jewellery, etc. *Pedazo de Arte*, Plateros 334. A tasteful collection of Andean handicrafts, many designed by Japanese owner Miki Suzuki. *La Pérez*, Urb Mateo Pumacahua 598, Huanchac, T232186, is a big co-operative with a good selection; they will arrange a free pick-up from your hotel. For alpaca clothing and fabrics: *El Almacén – The Warehouse*, Av Ramón Zavaleta 110, Huanchac, T256565, almacensb@terra.co.pe Factory outlet for genuine camelid-fibre products, no commissions to guides, etc, at least 20% cheaper than tourist shops. *Alpaca 111*, Plaza Regocijo 202, T243233, *Alpaca 3*, Ruinas 472, and *Cuzmar II*, Portal Mantas 118T (English spoken). *Josefina Olivera*, Portal Comercio 169, Plaza de Armas, sells old textiles and weavings, expensive but worth it to save pieces being cut up to make other items, open daily 1100-2100. *Joyerías Peruanas*, Calle del Medio 130, gold, silver and other items in precolumbian, Inca and contemporary designs. *H Ormachea*, Plateros 372, T237061. Handmade gold and silver. *Ima Sumac*, Triunfo 338, T244722. Traditional Andean musical instruments. *Taki Museo de Música de los Andes*, Hatunrumiyoq 487-5. Shop and workshop selling and displaying musical instruments, knowledgeable owner. Visit *Nemesio Villasante*, Av 24 de Junio 415, T222915, for Paucartambo masks.

Bookshops *Jerusalem*, Heladeros 143, T235408, English books, guidebooks, music, postcards, book exchange. *Centro de Estudios Regionales Andinos Bartolomé de las Casas*, Heladeros 129A, good books on Peruvian history, archaeology, etc, Mon-Sat 1100-1400, 1600-1900. *Special Book Services*, Av El Sol 781-A, Wanchac, T248106. Stocks Footprint Handbooks.

General *Huanchac*, Av Garcilaso (southeast of centre) and *Santa Ana Market*, opposite Estación San Pedro, sell a variety of goods.

A good supermarket is *El Chinito*, Heladeros 109 and Matará 271. *Gato's Market*, Portal Belén 115. *Shop Market*, Plateros 352, open daily 1000-0300. *El Pepino*, Plaza San Francisco, Mon-Sat 0900-2000, closed lunchtime, wide variety of imported goods, delicatessen, etc.

Tour operators

For a list of recommended Tour operators for Manu, see page 1285

There are many travel agencies in Cusco. The sheer number and variety of tours on offer is bewildering and prices for the same tour can vary dramatically. Always remember that you get what you pay for. Always check details before making arrangements, shop around and be aware that overcharging and failing to keep to arrangements are common, especially in the high season. Also beware agencies quoting prices in dollars then converting to soles at an unfavourable rate when paying. Seek advice from visitors returning from trips for the latest information. In and around Cusco, and Machu Picchu, check the standard of your guide's English (or whichever language is required) as some have no more than a memorized spiel. The following agencies are those for which we have received favourable reports, which is not to say that those not listed are not recommended. Those listed under general tours (well established, more recently established and economical) offer a wide range of different tours, including Machu Picchu. The more expensive agencies generally offer a higher standard and quality of service. Most of the agencies speak English.

See below, under The Inca Trail, for new regulations concerning tour agencies

General tours **Well-established Expensive-mid range:** Most of these agencies have their main offices away from the centre, but have a local contact, cellular phone or hotel contact downtown. *APU Expediciones*, Hotel Savoy International, Av Sol 954, PO Box 24, T/F272442, www.geocities.com/TheTropics/Cabana/4037 Cultural, adventure, educational/academic programmes, nature tours and jungle packages to Manu and Tambopata, bilingual personnel, very knowledgeable, Andean textiles a speciality, run by Mariella Bernasconi Cillóniz. *Cóndor*, C Saphi 848, T225961, www.condortravel.com.pe Conventional tours all over Peru, also some trekking (good, but expensive), representative for most international airlines with ticket sales, connections, etc. *Explorandes*, Portal de Panes 236, Plaza de Armas, T244308, www.explorandes.com.pe Wide range of trekking, rafting and cultural tours in and around Cusco and throughout Peru. *Gatur Cusco*, Puluchapata 140 (a small street off Av Sol 3rd block), T223496, gatur@terra.com.pe Esoteric, ecotourism, and general tours, owner Dr José (Pepe) Altamirano, knowledgeable in Andean folk traditions, excellent conventional tours, bilingual guides and transportation. *Kantu Tours*, Portal Carrizos 258, T246372, T650202 (Mob), kantuperu@wayna.rcp.net.pe Good horse treks, adventure tours, river rafting, motorcycle excursions (also rental), enthusiastic and thorough. *Kinjyo Travel Service*, Av Sol 761, T231121, tes3@latiunmail.com Includes treks to weaving villages. *Lima Tours*, Av Machu Picchu D-24, Urb Mañuel Prado, T228431, www.limatours.com.pe/ Amex representative, gives TCs against Amex card, but no exchange, also DHL office, to receive a parcel you pay 35 of the marked value of customs tax. *Peruvian Andean Treks*, Av Pardo 705, T225701, www.andeantreks.com Manager Tom Hendrikson, adventure tour specialists. *Servicios Aéreos AQP SA*, Av Sol 675, www.saaqp.com.pe Offers a wide variety of tours within the country, agents for American, Continental, LAB and other airlines; head office in Lima, Los Castaños 347, San Isidro, T222 3312, F222 5910. *Southern Cross Adventures*, Portal de Panes 123, oficina 301, Plaza de Armas, T237649, southerncrosspaullo@terra.com.pe Specializes in horseback trips.

General tours More recently established All price ranges: *Andean Life*, C Plateros 341, T224227, www.andeanlife.com Tours and treks for small groups. *Destinos Turísticos*, Portal de Panes 123, oficina 101-102, Plaza de Armas, T/F228168, www.destinosturisticosperu.com.pe Owner speaks several languages, inforamtive and helpful. *Luzma Tours*, Garcilaso 265, of 1, T245677, luzmatours@latinmail.com Wide range of treks around Cusco, plus longer (2 weeks and more) organized tours all over Peru and to

Peru

Bolivia and Chile, very experienced, hotel reservations (with discounts), bus and air ticket bookings, also offers email, fax, phone and photocopying service, manager Luz Marina Anaya is very helpful. **SAS Travel**, Portal de Panes 143, T/F237292, www.sastravel.com Discount for SAE members and students, English speaking guides, responsible, good equipment and food. **Top Vacations**, Portal de Panes 109, of 6, T263278/624088, www.hikingperu.com Trekking on the Inca Trail, Choquequirao, Ausangate, Salkantay, Vilcabamba and elsewhere, good guides and arrangements. **Trekperu**, Pumacahua C-10, Wanchac, T252899, www.trekperu.com Experienced trek operator as well as other adventure sports and mountain biking.

General tours Economical: *Carla's Travel*, Plateros 320, T/F253018, carlastravel@telser.com.pe All tours. **Inca Explorers**, Suecia 339, www.incaexplorers.com Excellent service for all types of arrangement, good value. **K'uichy Light International**, Av Sol 814, of 219, T235536, rubenpal@yupi.mail.com Ruben E Palomino specializes in tours in Peru, Bolivia and Ecuador, good value. *Liz's Explorer*, Medio 114-B, T/F246619, www.geocities.com/lizexplorer/ Good tours and information; ask in advance if you need a guide who speaks a language other than English. **Naty's Travel**, Triunfo 338, p 2, T/F239437, natystravel@terra.com.pe All tours. **Peruvian Field Guides**, Portal Confiturías 265, interior oficina 1, Plaza de Armas, T243475. Well-organized and professional. *Q'ente*, Garcilaso 210, p 2, of 210B, T222535/247836, www.qente.com Adventure trips and equipment rental, very good, especially with children. **Sky Travel**, Santa Catalina Ancha 366, interior 3-C, T240141, www.skyperu.com General tours, good service (also have a branch in Arequipa). **United Mice**, Plateros 348, T221139, F238050. Discount with student card, good English-speaking guides, food and equipment.

Aerial adventures: **PerúFly**, El Comercio H11, Residencial Huancaro, T229439, T970 1547 (Mob) (in Lima: Jr Jorge Chávez 658, Miraflores, T444-5004, T970-1547 (Mob), www.perufly.com Bungee jumping, US$59 to see Peru upside down, jumping from a hot-air balloon! *Globos de los Andes*, T201143, T693812 (Mob), www.terra.perucultural.org.pe Hot-air ballooning and 4WD expeditions. **Viento Sur**, San Juan de Dios 278, T249128, viento-sur@terra.com.pe Paragliding tandem flights minimun 2 people US$50, initiation course US$120, and complete course UIS$400.

River rafting, mountain biking & trekking: *Amazonas Explorer*, PO Box 722, Cusco, T/F227137, www.amazonas-explorer.com In UK T01874-658125. Experienced, most bookings taken from overseas, also mountain biking and other adventure trips. **Apumayo**, C Garcilaso 265 interior 3, T246018 (Lima: T/F444 2320), www.cuscoperu.com/apumayo Rafting and hiking tours including in the Cotahuasi canyon. *Eric Adventures*, Plateros 324, T/F228475. www.ericadventures.com Good guides and food. **Instinct**, Procuradores 50, T233451, www.instinct.es.vg Also at Plaza de Armas, Ollantaytambo, T204045, Juan and Benjamín Muñiz speak good English and are recommended, also mountain bike hire. **Loreto Tours**, C del Medio 111, T228264, F236331. Adventure travel, strong on river rafting on the Urubamba, Apurímac and Tambopata, bicycle tours (good equipment). **Mayuc Expediciones**, Portal Confiturías 211, Plaza de Armas, T/F232666, www.mayuc.com Good equipment, one of the major river rafting adventure agencies, specializing in 3-day river rafting on the Río Apurímac and Tambopata/Candamo jungle rafting. **Pony's Expeditions**, Santa Catalina Ancha 353, 1 block from Plaza de Armas, at *Hotel Casa Grande*, T234887, www.ponyexpeditions.com New branch of trekking and tour company from Caraz, open Mon-Sat 0900-1300, 1600-2000, good quality camping gear for hire or sale, day tours, mountain bike tours, organizes and provides information for trekking in Salkantay, Ausangate and Inca Trail areas.

Cultural: *Milla Tourism*, Av Pardo 689, T231710, F231388, millaturismo@amauta.rcp.net.pe Tours of the artists' quarter in San Blas, also contact for details of the Centre for Andean Studies, which offers courses in Spanish, Quechua and Andean culture. **Mystic Inca Trail**, Unidad Vecinal Santiago, bloque 9, dpto 301, T/F221358, ivanndp@terra.com.pe Tours of sacred Inca sites and study of Andean spirituality. **Personal Travel Service**, Portal de Panes 123, oficina 109, T225518, F244036, ititoss@terra.com.pe Cultural tours in the Urubamba valley.

Other tour operators include *Viento Sur Adventure Club*, T20 1620, www.aventurasvientosur.com

Recommended private guides: Set prices: city tour US$15-20 per day; Urubamba/Sacred Valley US$25-30, Machu Picchu and other ruins US$40-50 per day. **Classic, standard tours** *Juana Pancorbo*, Av Los Pinos D-2, T227482. *Haydee Magrovejo*, T221907, Aymoa@hotmail.com *Mariella Lazo*, T264210, speaks German, experienced, also offers river rafting. *Mireya Bocángel*, mireyabocangel@latinmail.com Professional tour guide to Cusco and Machu Picchu. *José Cuba and Alejandra Cuba*, Urb Santa Rosa R Gibaja 182, T226179, T685187 (Mob), alecuba@Chaski.unsaac.edu.pe Both speak English, Alejandra speaks German and French, very good tours. *Boris Cárdenas*, boriscar@telser.com.pe Specializes in esoteric and cultural tourism. *Rómulo Lizarraga*, T239157, Spiritual tours and trekking. *Roberto Dargent*, Urb Zarumilla 5B-102, T247424, T622080 (Mob), turismo_inca@LatinMail.com Very helpful. **Adventure trips:** *Roger Valencia Espinoza*, José Gabriel Cosio 307, T251278, vroger@qenqo.rcp.net.pe

All of those listed are bilingual. At the end of 2000 new laws stated that guides may only operate through a registered agency, or independently after paying a high registration fee

Local Motorcycle mechanics: *Eric and Oscar Antonio Aranzábal*, Ejercicios 202, Tahuantinsuyo, T223397, highly recommended for repairs; also *Autocusa*, Av de la Cultura 730 (Sr Marco Tomaycouza), T240378. **Bicycle repair**: A good mechanic is *Eddy*, whose workshop is off Av Garcilaso (street between Tacna and Manco Inca). He welds, builds wheels, etc, but has no spares. For parts, cyclists must go to Arequipa or Lima, or try to use local parts.

Transport

Taxis: in Cusco are inexpensive and recommended when arriving by air, train or bus. They have fixed prices: in the centre US$0.60 (after 2200 US$0.85); to the suburbs US$0.85. Taxis on call are reliable but more expensive, in the centre US$1.25: *Ocarina* T247080, *Aló Cusco* T222222. Trips to Sacsayhuaman US$10; to the ruins of Tambo Machay US$15-20 (3-4 people); for a whole day trip US$40-70.

Touts will always quote much higher fares for taxis

Recommended taxi drivers: *Manuel Calanche*, T227368, T695402 (Mob). *Carlos Hirojosa*, T251160. *Angel Marcavillaca Palomino*, Av Regional 877, T251822, amarcavillaca@yahoo.com Helpful, patient, reasonable prices. *Movilidad Inmediata*, Juan Carlos Herrera Johnson, T623821 (Mob), local tours with English-speaking guide. *Ferdinand Pinares Cuadros*, Yuracpunco 155, Tahuantinsuyo, T225914, T681519 (Mob), English, French and German spoken, reasonable prices. *Angel Salazar*, Marcavalle 1-4 Huanchac, T224679 to leave messages, English speaking, helpful, arranges good tours. *Milton Velásquez*, T222638, T680730 (Mob), an anthropologist and tour guide who speaks English.

Long distance Air: the airport is at Quispiquilla, near the bus terminal, 1.6 km from centre. **NB** Sit on right side of the aircraft for the best view of the mountains when flying Cusco-Lima; check in 2 hrs before flight. Reconfirm 48 hrs before your flight departure. To **Lima**, 55 mins, daily flights with *Aero Continente, Tans, Taca, Lan Perú* and *Aviandina*. Flights are heavily booked on this route in the school holidays (May, Jul, Oct and Dec-Mar) and national holidays. To **Arequipa**, 30 mins daily with Lan Perú. To **Puerto Maldonado**, 30 mins, daily with *Aero Continente/Aviandina*, 3 a week with *Lan Perú*. To/from **La Paz** and **Santa Cruz**, *LAB* flies twice a week.

Cusco-Lima, flights may be delayed or cancelled during the wet season. Planes may leave early if the weather is bad

Taxi to and from the airport costs US$2-3 (US$3.50 by radio taxi), extra US$0.50 if you enter the car park. Colectivos cost US$0.20 from Plaza San Francisco or outside the airport car park. Many representatives of hotels and travel agencies operate at the airport, with transport to the hotel with which they are associated. Take your time to choose your hotel, at the price you can afford.

Airport information T222611/222601

Bus Terminal on Prolongación Pachacútec, about 4 blocks beyond Wanchac station, colectivo from centre US$0.15, taxi US$0.60. Platform tax US$0.30. To **Juliaca**, 344 km, 5-6 hrs, US$8.75, *Imexso* (Av Sol 818, T240801, terminal T229126), 0830, 2030. Also *Cisnes, Civa, Julsa, Libertad*, US$4.40, *Sur Oriente*, US$5.85-7.35, and *Ormeño* Royal class, US$14.70. All Juliaca buses continue to Puno. The road is fully paved, but after heavy rain buses may not run. To **Puno**, 44 km from Juliaca, *First Class* (Garcilaso 210, of 106, T240408, www.firstclassperu.com) and *Inka Express* (pick up at hotel, T/F247887, inkaex@yahoo.com), daily, 0700 or 0800, 9½ hrs, interesting stops *en route*, US$25; *Tour Perú*

Peru

morning and evening service, brief stop at La Raya, US$8.75, 6½-8 hrs. See under Puno for routes to La Paz. For services between Peru and Bolivia, call *Litoral*, T248989, which runs buses between the two countries, leaving Cusco at 2200, arriving La Paz 1200, US$30, including breakfast on bus and a/c. Travel agencies also sell this ticket.

To **Arequipa**, 521 km, 10-12 hrs direct, US$6-7.50 (eg *Carhuamayo*, 3 a day; *Cruz del Sur*, US$8.75). The new road leaves the Cusco-Puno road at Sicuani and runs close to the Colca Canyon, via Puente Callalli for Chivay; it is very rough in parts. Buses travel mostly at night and it's a very cold journey, so take a blanket. For Chivay, alight at 0400-0500 and wait till 0600-0700 (there is shelter) for first colectivo, US$1.20, 3 hrs. Some buses, eg *Cruz del Sur*, go via Puno, US$8.85. Direct buses to Lima (20 hrs) go via **Abancay**, 195 km, 5hrs (longer in the rainy season), paved to within an hour of Abancay, and **Nasca** (14 hrs). If prone to carsickness, be prepared on the road to Abancay, there are many, many curves, but the scenery is magnificent. From Abancay to Nasca via Puquío, the road is paved; a safe journey with some stunning scenery. At Abancay, the road forks, the other branch going to **Andahuaylas**, a further 138 km, 10-11 hrs from Cusco, and **Ayacucho**, another 261 km, 20 hrs from Cusco. On both routes at night, take a blanket or sleeping bag. All buses leave daily from the Terminal Terrestre. *Molina*, who also have an office on Av Pachacútec, just past the railway station, and *Expreso Wari* have buses on both routes. *Molina* twice a day, *Wari* 3 a day to Abancay, Nasca and Lima, both at 1900 to Abancay, Andahuaylas and Ayacucho (Andahuaylas-Ayacucho leg may be cancelled, requiring purchase of new ticket on another service, no refunds – best to buy ticket to Andahuaylas, then another). *San Jerónimo* has buses to Abancay and Andahuaylas at 1800. *Turismo Ampay*, *Turismo Abancay* and *Expreso Huamanga* go to Abancay. *Cruz del Sur* and *Ormeño* both run to Nasca and Lima. Fares: Abancay US$4.30, Andahuaylas US$5.75-7.20 (*Molina*), Ayacucho US$14.40, Nasca US$20, US$27 (*Imperial*), Lima US$21.60. After 2½ hrs buses pass a checkpoint at the Cusco/Apurímac departmental border. All foreigners must get out and show their passport. In Cusco you may be told that there are no buses in the day from Abancay to Andahuaylas; this is not so as *Señor de Huanca* does so. If you leave Cusco before 0800, with luck you'll make the onward connection at 1300, which is worth it for the scenery.

Buses to the Sacred Valley: From the outskirts of the city, near the Clorindo Matto de Turner school and Av de la Cultura: to **Pisac**, 32 km, 1 hr, US$0.65; to **Calca**, a further 18 km, 30 mins, US$0.10; to **Urubamba** a further 22 km, 45 mins, US$0.40. Colectivos, minibuses and buses leave when full, between 0600 and 1600; also trucks and pick-ups. Buses returning from Pisac are often full. The last one back leaves around 2000. An organized tour can be fixed up anytime with a travel agent for US$5 pp. Taxis charge about US$20 for the round trip. Combis and colectivos leave from 300 block of Av Grau, near Av Centenario for **Chinchero**, 23 km, 45 mins, US$0.45; and for **Urubamba** a further 25 km, 45 mins, US$0.45 (or US$0.85 Cusco-Urubamba direct, US$1.15 for a seat in a colectivo taxi). To **Ollantaytambo**, 0745, 1945, or catch a bus to Urubamba. Tours can also be arranged to Chinchero, Urubamba and Ollantaytambo with a Cusco travel agency. To Chinchero, US$6 pp; a taxi costs US$25 for the round trip. Usually only day tours are organized for visits to the valley; see under Tour Operators. Using public transport and staying overnight in Urubamba, Ollantaytambo or Pisac will allow much more time to see the ruins and markets.

Train There are 2 stations in Cusco. To Juliaca and Puno, trains leave from the Av Sol station, Estación Wanchac, T238722/221992. When arriving in Cusco, a tourist bus meets the train to take visitors to hotels whose touts offer rooms. Machu Picchu trains leave from Estación San Pedro, opposite the Santa Ana market.

The train to **Juliaca/Puno** leaves at 0800, Mon, Wed, Fri and Sat, arriving at Juliaca about 1635 (arrives Puno 1800), sit on the left for the best views. The train makes a stop to view the scenery at La Raya. Always check on whether the train is running, especially in the rainy season, when services may be cancelled. Fares are given under Puno, Transport. Ticket office is open Mon-Fri 0800-1700, Sat 0900-1200. Tickets sell out quickly and there are queues from 0400 before holidays in the dry season. In the low season tickets to Puno can be bought on the day of departure. You can buy tickets through the web (www.perurail.com) or through a travel agent. Meals are served on the train. To **Ollantaytambo** and **Machu Picchu**, see pages 1246 and 1251.

Airline offices *Aero Continente*, Portal de Carnes 254, Plaza de Armas, T235666, airport 235696 (toll free 0800-42420). *LAB*, Santa Catalina Angosta 160, T222990, airport 229220. *Lan Perú*, Portal Mantas 114, T225552. *Taca*, Av Sol 226, T249921, airport 246858 (toll free 0800-48222). *Tans*, San Agustín 315-17, T251000.

Banks Most of the banks are on Av Sol, and all have ATMs from which you can withdraw dollars or soles. *Banco de Crédito*, Av Sol 189, cash advances on Visa, changes TCs to soles with commission, 3% to dollars; Visa ATM. *Interbank*, Av Sol y Puluchapata, no commission on TCs, MasterCard. Next door *Banco Continental*, Visa ATM, US$5 commission on TCs. *BSCH*, Av Sol 459, Amex TCs, reasonable Rates, ATM for Visa. *Banco Wiese*, Maruri entre Pampa del Castillo y Pomeritos, gives cash advances on MasterCard in dollars. Many travel agencies and *casas de cambio* (eg on Portal de Comercio, Plaza de Armas, and Av Sol) change dollars; some of them change TCs as well, but charge 4-5% commission. The street changers hang around Av Sol, blocks 2-3, every day; they will also change TCs. In banks and on the street check the notes. Dollars are accepted at many restaurants and at the airport. *Western Union*, Santa Catalina Ancha 165, T233727, money transfers in 10 mins; also ar *DHL*, see below. Emergency number for lost **Visa** card: 0800-13333.

Communications Internet: Lots of places in the area around the Plaza de Armas. *@Internet*, Portal de Panes 123, Plaza de Armas at C procuradores, oficina 105. Fast machines, fair prices. *Internet Perú*, Portal de Comercio 141, Plaza de Armas. 10 computers, fast connection, helpful, spacious. *Internet Cusco*, at Galerías UNSAAC, Av Sol s/n beside Banco de Crédito, T238173. Open daily 0800-2400, 20 machines, no problem if you want more than an hour. *Telser*, at Telefónica del Perú, C del Medio 117, T242424, F242222. 15 machines, popular, difficult to get more than an hour, they have a café if you have to wait; also at Plazoleta Limacpampa, at Av Tullumayo and Arcopunco, T245505. *Worldnet*, Santa Catalina Ancha 315. Open 0800-2200, café, bar, music, net to phone, games, etc. Many more south of Plaza de Armas, rates average US$0.70 per hr. **Post Office:** Av Sol, block 5, Mon-Sat 0730-2000; 0800-1400 Sun and holidays. Stamps and postcards available. *Poste restante* is free and

Peru

helpful. *DHL*, Av Sol 627, T244167. **Telephone:** *Telefónica*, Av Sol 386, for telephone and fax, open Mon-Sat 0700-2300, 0700-1800 Sun and holidays. International calls by pay phone or go through the operator (long wait possible), deposit required.

Consulates **Belgium**, Av Sol 959, T221098, F221100. **France**, Jorge Escobar, C Michaela Bastidas 101 p4, T233610. **Germany**, Sra Maria-Sophia Júrgens de Hermoza, San Agustín 307, T235459, Casilla Postal 1128, Correo Central, open Mon-Fri, 1000-1200, appointments may be made by phone, also book exchange. **UK**, Barry Walker, Av Pardo 895, T239974, F236706, manuexpe+@amauta.rcp.net.pe **US Agent**, Dr Olga Villagarcía, Apdo 949, Cusco, T222183, F233541 or at the Binational Center (ICPNA), Av Tullumayo 125, Huanchaac.

Language schools *Amauta*, Suecia 480, p 2, T/F241422, PO Box 1164 (T020-8786 8081 in UK), www.amautaspanish.com Classes in Spanish and Quechua, US$6 per hr one-to-one, US$175 per week including accommodation in their *Hostal Casa de Campo* (see above), for one-to-one classes in your hotel, T270302, workshops in Peruvian cuisine, dance and music, arrange excursions, can help find voluntary work, owners also have *La Tertulia* café (see above) and a school in Urubamba. *Amerispan*, reservations: Albert Aguilera 26, 2 p -28015, Madrid, T0034 91 5912393, www.casadelenguas.com *English School*, Purgatorio 395 esq Huaynapata, T235830/235903. US$5 per hr for one-to-one Classes. Recommended. *Excel*, Cruz Verde 336, T235298, F232272, www.excel-spanishlanguageprograms-peru.org Very professional, US$3.50-7 per hr depending on group size, can arrange accommodation with local families. *Inca's Language School*, Saphi 652, www.orbita.starmedia.com/~incaslanguage Reliable and professional, can arrange lodging with families, salsa classes and other extras. Spanish classes are run by the *Acupari*, the German-Peruvian Cultural Association, San Agustín 307.

Medical services Clinics: *Hospital Regional*, Av de la Cultura, T227661, emergencies 223691. **Clínica Pardo**, Av de la Cultura 710, T240387, T930063 (Mob), www.clinicapardocusco.com 24 hrs daily, trained bilingual personnel, complete medical assistance coverage with international insurance companies, highly regarded. **Clínica Paredes**, Lechugal 405, T225269. Director: Dr Milagros Paredes, whose speciality is gynaecology. **Dr Ilya Gomon**, Av de la Cultura, Edif Santa Fe, of 207, T cel 651906. Canadian chiropractor, good, reasonable prices, available for hotel or home visits.

Useful addresses **Police:** National Police, C Saphi, block 4. **Migraciones** Av Sol s/n, block 6 close to post office, T222740, Mon-Fri 0800-1300, 1600-1800 (for extending stay in Peru.) **ISTC office**, Portal Comercio 141, p 2, T621351. Issues student cards.

The Sacred Valley

Cusco is at the west end of the gently sloping Cusco valley, which stretches 32 km east as far as Huambutío. This valley and the partly isolated basin of Anta, northwest of Cusco, are densely populated. Also densely populated is the Urubamba valley, stretching from Sicuani (on the railway to Puno) to the gorge of Torontoi, 600 m lower, to the northwest of Cusco. The region is full of archaeological sites, from Raqchi in the east, through the strategic fortresses of Pisac and Ollantaytambo, to the lost cities of Machu Picchu, Vilcabamba and Choquequirao in the west. There are vast stretches of Inca terracing, quaint colonial churches (Andahuaylillas, Huaro, Chinchero) and markets (Pisac, Chinchero), all in a landscape of sacred mountians and dramatic gorges. The best time to visit is April-May or October-November. The high season is June-September, but the rainy season, from December to March, is cheaper and pleasant enough.

Southeast from Cusco There are many interesting villages and ruins on this road. **Tipón** ruins, between the villages of Saylla and Oropesa, are extensive and include baths, terraces, irrigation systems, possibly an agricultural laboratory and a temple complex, accessible from a path leading from just above the last terrace (5 km climb from village; taqke a combi from Cusco to Oropesa, then a taxi, or taxi from Cusco US$6). **Oropesa** church contains a fine ornately carved pulpit.

At **Huambutío**, north of the village of Huacarpay, the road divides; northwest to Pisac and north to **Paucartambo**, on the eastern slope of Andes. This remote town, 80 km east of Cusco, has become a popular tourist destination. The *Fiesta de la Virgen del Carmen* is a major attraction, with masked dancers enacting rituals and folk tales: 15-17 July. (**G** *Quinta Rosa Marina*, near the bridge, and **G** *Albergue Municipal Carmen de la Virgen*, both basic.) From Paucartambo, in the dry season, you can go 44 km to **Tres Cruces**, along the Pilcopata road, turning left after 25 km. Tres Cruces gives a wonderful view of the sunrise in June and July: peculiar climactic conditions make it appear that three suns are rising. Tour agencies in Cusco can arrange transport and lodging. ■ *Getting there: Private car hire for a round trip Cusco-Paucartambo on 15-17 July, US$30; travel agencies in Cusco arrange this. A minibus leaves for Paucartambo from Av Huáscar in Cusco, every other day, US$4.50, 3-4 hrs; alternate days Paucartambo-Cusco. Trucks and a private bus leave from the Coliseo, behind Hospital Segura in Cusco, 5 hrs, US$2.50.*

Further on from Huacarpay are the Huari (pre-Inca) adobe wall ruins of **Piquillacta**, a large site, with some reconstruction in progress. Buses to Urcos from Av Huáscar in Cusco will drop you at the entrance on the north side of the complex, though this is not the official entry. ■ *Daily 0700-1730.* The Piquillacta Archaeological Park also contains the Laguna de Huacarpay (known as Muyna in ancient times) and the ruins that surround it: Kañarakay, Urpicancha and the huge gateway of Rumicolca. It's good to hike or cycle and birdwatch around the lake.

Andahuaylillas is a village 32 km southeast from Cusco, with a fine early 17th-century church (the 'Andean Sistine Chapel'), with beautiful frescoes, a splendid doorway and a gilded main altar. Taxis go there, as does the *Oropesa* bus (from Av Huáscar in Cusco) via Tipón, Piquillacta and Rumicolca. The next village, **Huaro**, also has a church whose interior is entirely covered with colourful frescoes.

Beyond Andahuaylillas is **Urcos**. There is accommodation in three very basic hostales. A spectacular road from Urcos crosses the Eastern Cordillera to Puerto Maldonado in the jungle (see page 1286). 47 km after passing the snow line Hualla-Hualla pass, at 4,820 m, the super-hot thermal baths of Marcapata, 173 km from Urcos, provide a relaxing break. ■ *US$0.10.*

Some 82 km from Urcos, at the base of **Nevado Ausangate** (6,384 m), is the town of **Ocongate**, which has two hotels on the Plaza de Armas. Beyond Ocongate is **Tinqui**, the starting point for hikes around Ausangate and in the Cordillera Vilcanota. On the flanks of the Nevado Ausangate is Q'Olloriti, where a church has been built close to the snout of a glacier. This place has become a place of pilgrimage (see Cusco, Local festivals, page 1233).

Hiking around Ausangate *Arrieros* and mules can be hired in Tinqui for US$10 per day for a chief *arriero*, US$5 for assistant, US$12 for a mule, US$15 for a saddle horse. *Arrieros* also expect food. Make sure you sign a contract with full details. The hike around the mountain of Ausangate takes about 5-6 days: spectacular, but quite hard, with 3 passes over 5,000 m, so you need to be acclimatized. Temperatures in high season (Apr-Oct) can drop well below zero at night. It is recommended to take a guide or *arriero*. Buy all food supplies in Cusco. Maps are available at the *IGM* in Lima or **South American Explorers**, who also have latest information. Some tour companies in Cusco have hike details.

Sleeping and transport **G** *Hostal Tinqui Guide*, on the right-hand side as you enter the village, meals available, the owner can arrange guides and horses; **G** *Ausangate*, very basic, warm, trekking tours organized. From Cusco, buses to **Tinqui** leave Mon-Sat 1000 from C Tomasatito Condemayta, near the Coliseo Cerrado; 172 km, 6-7 hrs, US$3.50.

From Urcos to Sicuani (see page 1219), the road passes **Cusipata** (with an Inca gate and wall), **Checacupe** (with a lovely church) and **Tinta**, 23 km from Sicuani (church

Peru

with brilliant gilded interior and an interesting choir vault). There are frequent buses and trucks to Cusco, or take the train from Cusco.

Colour map 3, grid C5

Continuing to Sicuani, **Raqchi** is the scene of the region's great folklore festival starting on 24 June, *Wiracocha*, when dancers come from all over Peru. Raqchi is also the site of the Viracocha Temple. John Hemming wrote: "What remains is the central wall, which is adobe above and Inca masonry below. This was probably the largest roofed building ever built by the Incas. On either side of the high wall, great sloping roofs were supported by rows of unusual round pillars, also of masonry topped by adobe. Nearby is a complex of barracks-like buildings and round store-houses. This was the most holy shrine to the creator god Viracocha, being the site of a miracle in which he set fire to the land – hence the lava flow nearby. There are also small Inca baths in the corner of a field beyond the temple and a straight row of ruined houses by a square. The landscape is extraordinary, blighted by huge piles of black volcanic rocks." ■ *Entrance to the site US$1.75. To reach Raqchi, take a bus or truck from Cusco towards Sicuani, US$1.50.*

Northwest from Cusco

Chinchero (3,762 m), is on a direct road to Urubamba. It has an attractive church built on an Inca temple. The church has been restored to reveal in all their glory the interior paintings. The ceiling, beams and walls are covered in beautiful floral and religious designs. The church is open on Sunday for mass and at festivals; ask in the tourist office in Cusco for other times. Recent excavations there have revealed many Inca walls and terraces. ■ *The site is open daily 0700-1730, on the combined entrance ticket (see page 1221).* The food market and the handicraft market are separate. The former is held every day, on your left as you come into town. The latter, on Sunday only, is up by the church, small, but attractive. On any day but Sunday there are few tourists. Fiesta, day of the Virgin, on 8 September (**F** *Hotel Inca*, with restaurant; *Restaurant Antabaraj*, just beyond ticket control, good view and food).

At **Moray**, there are three 'colosseums', used by the Incas, according to some theories, as a sort of open-air crop nursery, known locally as the laboratory of the Incas. The great depressions contain no ruined buildings, but are lined with fine terracing. Each level is said to have its own microclimate. It is a very atmospheric place which,

The Sacred Valley

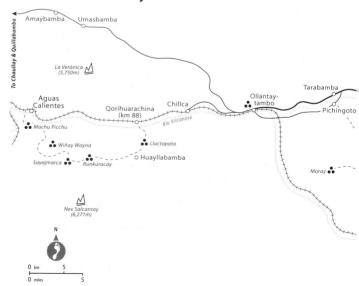

many claim, has mystical power. The scenery is absolutely stunning. ■ *Getting there: there is a paved road from the main road between Chinchero and Urubamba to the village of Maras and from there an unmade road in good condition leads to Moray, 9 km. Ask in Maras for the best route to walk, other than on the main road. There is public transport from Chinchero to Maras; it stops running between 1700 and 1800; US$0.60. The most interesting way to get to Moray is from Urubamba via the Pichingoto bridge over the Río Urubamba. The climb up from the bridge is fairly steep but easy. The path passes by the spectacular salt pans, still in production after thousands of years. Moray is about 1½ hrs further on. The* Hotel Incaland *in Urubamba can arrange horses and guide and a pick-up truck for the return; US$30-40 pp (see page 1245). There are no hotels at all in the area, so take care not to be stranded.*

Pisac

High above the town on the mountainside, 30 km north of Cusco, is a superb Inca *Colour map 3, grid C4* fortress. Pisac has a traditional Sunday morning market, at which local people sell their produce in exchange for essential goods. It is also a major draw for tourists who arrive after 0800 until 1700. Pisac has other, somewhat less crowded, less expensive, but more commercial markets on Tuesday and Thursday morning. Each Sunday at 1100 there is a Quechua mass. On the plaza are the church and a small interesting Museo Folklórico. The town is worth strolling around; look for the fine façade at Grau 485. There are many souvenir shops on Bolognesi. Local fiesta: 15 July.

The walk up to the ruins begins from the plaza (but see below), past the Centro de Salud and a new control post. The path goes through working terraces, giving the ruins a context. The first group of buildings is Pisaqa, with a fine curving wall. Climb then to the central part of the ruins, the Intihuatana group of temples and rock outcrops in the most magnificent Inca masonry. Here are the Reloj Solar ('Hitching Post of the Sun') – now closed because thieves stole a piece from it, palaces of the moon and stars, solstice markers, baths and water channels. From Intihuatana, a path leads around the hillside through a tunnel to Q'Allaqasa, the military area. Across the valley at this point, a large area of Inca tombs in holes in the hillside can be

Peru

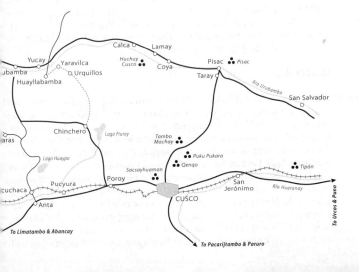

seen. The end of the site is Kanchiracay, where the agricultural workers were housed. Road transport approaches from this end. The descent takes 30 minutes. At dusk you will hear, if not see, the *pisaca* (partridges), after which the place is named. ■ *0700-1730. Guides charge about US$5. To appreciate the site fully, allow 5 hrs if going on foot. If you do not show your multi-site ticket on the way up, you will be asked to do so by the warden. There is transport up to the site on market days only so, at other times, you must walk, at least 1 hr uphill all the way. Horses are available for about US$3 pp, but travellers with a couple of dollars to spare should get a taxi from near the bridge up to the ruins and walk back down. A van from the plaza to the top costs about US$2.50 each way. Overnight parking allowed in the parking lot.*

Sleeping & eating
AL *Royal Inka Pisac*, Carretera Ruinas Km 1.5, T084-203064, F203067, royalin@terra.com.pe Including taxes and breakfast, converted hacienda with pool, sauna, very pleasant, provides guides. **E** pp *Pisaq*, at the corner of Pardo, on the Plaza in front of the church and marketplace, Casilla Postal 1179, Cusco, T084-203062, hotelpisaq@terra.com.pe **D** in the only room with bath, breakfast extra, excellent brownies, pizza served on Tue, Thu, Sat and Sun, hot water, pleasant decor, sauna, knowledgeable, English, German, French spoken. Recommended. **F** *Res Beho*, Intihuatana 642, T/F203001. Ask for room in main building, good breakfast for US$1, owner's son will act as guide to ruins at weekend. **G** pp *Parador*, on the Plaza, T203061. Shared bathrooms, breakfast extra, hot water, restaurant. *Doña Clorinda*, Bolognesi at the plaza, tasty food, including vegetarian. The bakery at Mcal Castilla 372 sells excellent cheese and onion *empanadas* for US$0.25, suitable for vegetarians, and good wholemeal bread.

Pisac to Urubamba
Calca, 2,900 m, is 18 km beyond Pisac. The plaza is divided in two: Urubamba buses stop on one side; and Cusco and Pisac buses on the other side of the dividing strip. *Fiesta de la Vírgen Asunta* 15-16 August. There are a couple of very basic hotels and **E** *Hostal Pitusiray*, on the edge of town. Recommended restaurant, *El Emperador*, Av Vilcanota 810, trout, good service.

About 3 km east of Urubamba, **Yucay** has two grassy plazas divided by the restored colonial church of Santiago Apóstol, with its oil paintings and fine altars. On the opposite side from Plaza Manco II is the adobe palace built for Sayri Túpac (Manco's son) when he emerged from Vilcabamba in 1558. In Yucay monks sell fresh milk, ham, eggs and other dairy produce from their farm on the hillside. **Sleeping** On the same plaza as the adobe palace is the **L-AL** *Sonesta Posada del Inca*, Plaza Manco II de Yucay 123, T084-201107, F201345, www.sonesta.com A converted 300-year-old monastery, it is like a little village with plazas, chapel, 69 comfortable, heated rooms, restaurant, conference facilities, price includes tax and buffet breakfast. Recommended. **AL** *Sonesta Posada del Inca Yucay II*, on same plaza, T201455, F201608. In the house where Simón Bolívar stayed in 1825, including tax and breakfast; balloon flights can be arranged here. **B-C** *Hostal Y'Llary*, on Plaza Manco II, T201112. Including breakfast.

Urubamba

Altitude: 2,863 m
Like many places along the valley, Urubamba is in a fine setting with snow-capped peaks in view. Calle Berriózabal, on the west edge of town, is lined with pisonay trees. The large market square is one block west of the main plaza. The main road skirts the town and the bridge for the road to Chinchero is just to the east of town. *Banco de la Nación* is on M Castilla at the start of the 2nd block; *Serpost* is on the Plaza de Armas. Visit **Seminario-Bejar Ceramic Studio** in the beautiful grounds of the former Urpihuasi hostal. They investigate and use precolumbian techniques and designs, highly recommended, Berriózabal 111, T201002, kupa@terra.com.pe For local festivals, May and June are the harvest months, with many processions following ancient schedules. Urubamba's main festival, *El Señor de Torrechayoc*, occupies the first week of June.

About 6 km west of Urubamba is **Tarabamba**, where a bridge crosses the Río Urubamba. Turn right after the bridge to **Pichingoto**, a tumbled-down village built under an overhanging cliff. Also, just over the bridge and before the town to the left of a small, walled cemetery is a salt stream. Follow the footpath beside the stream to Salinas, a small village below which are a mass of terraced Inca salt pans which are still in operation; there are over 5,000. The walk to the salt pans takes about 30 minutes. Take water as this side of the valley can be very hot and dry.

Sleeping

Out of town: **LL-AL** *Sol y Luna*, west of town, T201620, www.hotelsolyluna.com Nice bungalows set off the main road, pool, excellent buffet in restaurant. Has *Viento Sur* adventure travel agency, for horse riding, mountain biking, trekking and paragliding, www.aventurasvientosur.com **AL** *Incaland Hotel and Conference Center*, Av Ferrocarril s/n, 5 mins' walk from the centre, T/F201126/201117, www.incalandperu.com Special rates are also available, comfortable, spacious bungalows set in extensive gardens, English-owned, good restaurant serving buffet meals, bar, disco, 2 pools, also horse riding (eg to Moray), mountain biking, kayaking and rafting.

B *Perol Chico*, Casilla postal 59, Correo Central, T695188/624475, www.perolchico.com Dutch/Peruvian owned, private bungalows with fireplace and kitchen on a ranch, specializes in horse riding, 1 to 12-day trips out of Urubamba, good horses. Recommended. **C** *Las Chullpas*, 3 km from town, T685713, www.geocities.com/laschullpas Very peaceful, includes excellent breakfast, vegetarian meals, English and German spoken, Spanish classes, natural medicine, treks, riding, mountain biking, camping US$3 with hot shower.

In the town of Urubamba: **C** *Las Tres Marías*, Zavala 307, T201004 (Cusco 225252). New, hot water, welcoming, beautiful gardens. Recommended. **D** *Macha Wasi*, Jr Nicolás Barre, T201612, www.unsaac.edu.pe/machawasi Canadian owned, safe, lovely garden, comfortable rooms and dormitories, delicious breakfast extra, laundry, Spanish courses, treks. Recommended. **F** pp *Capulí*, Grau 222. With hot water and TV, or **G** per bed with shared bath. **F** *Hostal Urubamba*, Bolognesi 605. Basic, pleasant, cold water, **G** without bath.

Peru

Eating   *La Casa de la Abuela*, Bolívar 272. Fine restaurant around a courtyard, helpful, trout a speciality. Recommended. *Chez Mary*, Comercio y Grau, corner of main Plaza, T201003/201190. Excellent food, good pasta and pizzas, very cosy and comfortable, smart decor, good music, bar at night bar with live music. Mary Cuba, the owner, is a local Urubambina, very pleasant and helpful, she speaks good English. *El Fogón*, Parque Pintacha, T201534. Peruvian food. Recommended. On the main road, before the bridge, are: *Quinta los Geranios*, T201043. Regional dishes, excellent lunch with more than enough food, average price US$13. *El Maizal*, T201454. Country-style restaurant, buffet service with a variety of Novo Andino and international choices, beautiful gardens. Recommended.

Transport   **Bus terminal**, west of town almost opposite *Incaland*, about 3 km from centre. From Urubamba to **Calca**, **Pisac** (US$0.80, 1 hr) and **Cusco**, about 2 hrs, US$1, with Caminos del Inca, from 0530; also buses to Cusco via Chinchero. *El Señor de Huanca* combis run to Calca when full between 0700 and 1900; combis run to **Ollantaytambo**, 45 mins, US$0.30. Hotels such as the *Incaland* and *Posadas del Inca* (Yucay) run a twice-daily shuttle between Cusco airport and Urubamba for US$10. **Train**   See under Machu Picchu for the Sacred Valley Railway from Urubamba to Aguas Calientes, page 1251.

Ollantaytambo

Colour map 3, grid C4
Altitude: 2,800 m

The Inca town, or Llacta, on which the present-day town is based is clearly seen in the fine example of Inca *canchas* (blocks), which are almost entirely intact and still occupied behind the main plaza. Entering Ollantaytambo from Pisac, the road is built along the long wall of 100 niches. Note the inclination of the wall: it leans towards the road. Since it was the Inca's practice to build with the walls leaning towards the interiors of the buildings, it has been deduced that the road, much narrower then, was built inside a succession of buildings. The road out of the plaza leads across a bridge, down to the colonial church with its enclosed *recinto*. Beyond is a plaza (and car park) with entrances to the archaeological site. ■ *0700-1730*.

The so-called **Baño de la Ñusta** (bath of the princess) is of grey granite, and is in a small area between the town and the temple fortress. Some 200 m behind the Baño de la Ñusta along the face of the mountain are some small ruins known as Inca Misanca, believed to have been a small temple or observatory. A series of steps, seats and niches have been carved out of the cliff. There is a complete irrigation system, including a canal at shoulder level, some 6 ins deep, cut out of the sheer rock face (under renovation). The flights of terraces leading up above the town are superb, and so are the curving terraces following the contours of the rocks overlooking the Urubamba. These terraces were successfully defended by Manco Incas warriors against Hernando Pizarro in 1536. Manco Inca built the defensive wall above the site and another wall closing the Yucay valley against attack from Cusco. These are still visible on either side of the valley.

The temple itself was started by Pachacuti, using Colla Indians from Lake Titicaca – hence the similarities of the monoliths facing the central platform with the Tiahuanaco remains. The massive, highly finished granite blocks at the top are worth the climb to see. The Colla are said to have deserted half-way through the work, which explains the many unfinished blocks lying about the site. ■ *If possible arrive very early, 0700, before the tourists. Admission is by combined entrance ticket, which can be bought at the site.*

El Museo Catco, one block from plaza, has good displays of textiles, findings from local ruins, ethnographic and archaeological information. ■ *Tue-Sun 1000-1300, 1400-1600, US$1.75, T084-204034. Internet access US$2.85 per hr.*

On the west side of the main ruins, a two-dimensional 'pyramid' has been identified in the layout of the fields and walls of the valley. A fine 750 m wall aligns with the rays of the winter solstice on 21 June. It can be appreciated from a high point about 3.5 km from Ollantaytambo.

The real Pacaritambo?

Recently a 'pyramid' has been identified on the west side of the main ruins of Ollantaytambo. Its discoverers, Fernando and Edgar Elorietta, claim it is the real Pacaritambo, from where the four original Inca brothers emerged to found their empire (an alternative creation legend). Whether this is the case or not, it is still a first-class piece of engineering with great terraced fields and a fine 750 m wall aligned with the rays of the winter solstice, on 21 June. The mysterious 'pyramid', which covers 50-60 ha, can be seen properly from the other side of the river. This is a pleasant, easy one-hour walk, west from the Puente Inca, just outside the town. There are great views of the Sacred Valley, the river and the snowy peaks of the Verónica massif as a backdrop.

Sleeping & eating **A** *Pakaritambo*, C Ferrocarril s/n, T204020 (Cusco), 445 2803 (Lima). With bath, breakfast included, excellent quality and service. **A** *Hostal Sauce*, Plaza de Armas, T204044. Nice rooms, hot water, includes breakfast. **C** *Albergue Kapuly*, at the end of the station road, T204017. Quiet, spacious rooms with and without bath, cheaper in low season, garden. Recommended. Also on the road to the station is **C** *Hostal Munay Tika*, T204111, tika@latinmail.com Breakfast included, dinner by arrangement, sauna US$3 with prior notice, nice garden, good. **D** pp *El Albergue*, next to, and access via, the railway station, T/F084-204014 (or in Cusco at *Manu Expeditions*, T226671, Casilla 784, Cusco). Owned by North American Wendy Weeks, 6 rooms with shared bathrooms, "wonderful showers", charming, very relaxing, homely, with sauna, meals available on request, US$3 breakfast, US$10 lunch/dinner, convenient for Machu Picchu train, good place for information. Highly recommended. **E** pp *Las Orquídeas*, near the start of the road to the station, T204032. Good accommodation, meals available. **E** *Hostal La Ñusta*, up side street on right on way from Plaza de Armas towards ruins, T204035/077. Very good, hot showers, proprietor Rubén Ponce loves to share his knowledge of the ruins with guests, good view from terrace and some rooms, parking US$1.50 per day for those going to Machu Picchu. **F** pp *Hospedaje Los Andenes*, Plaza de Armas, T204095. Shared bath, continental breakfast included. **F** *Hostal Miranda*, between the main plaza and the ruins. With shower, basic.

There are several restaurants on the Plaza, such as **Ama Sumac, La Ñusta, Fortaleza Pizzería** (good), and **Pollería Bahía**. **Alcázar Café**, C del Medio. Good tourist menu, English spoken. **Café Sol del Oriente**, esquina Plaza de Ruinas, T204009. Soups, salads, vegetables, fish and meat, medium-priced, open for breakfast, lunch and dinner. Recommended. **Kusi Coyllor**, Plaza Ruinas, T246977 for delivery. Nice atmosphere, also bar. **Mayupata**, Jr Convención s/n, across the bridge on the way to the ruins, on the left, T (Cusco) 204083. International and Peruvian dishes, desserts, sandwiches, coffee, bar with fireplace, opens at 0600 for breakfast, relaxing atmosphere.

Festivals On the Sun following Inti Raymi, there is a colourful festival, the **Ollanta-Raymi**. On **6 Jan** there is the **Bajada de Reyes Magos** (the Magi), with music, dancing, processions. **29 Oct** there is the town's anniversary with lots of dancing in traditional costume and many local delicacies for sale.

Transport The station is 10-15 mins walk from the plaza. There are colectivos at the plaza for the station when trains are due. Check in advance the time trains pass through here (see also under trains to and from Machu Picchu, page 1251). You won't be allowed on the station unless you have previously bought a ticket (and it is best to buy tickets in Cusco).

The Inca Trail to Machu Picchu

The spectacular 3-5 day hike runs from Km 88, Qorihuayrachina (2,299 m), a point immediately after the first tunnel 22 km beyond Ollantaytambo station. A sturdy suspension bridge has now been built over the Río Urubamba. Guided tours often start at Km 82. New rules for hiking the trail are detailed below.

Peru

Equipment The trail is rugged and steep (beware of landslides), but the magnificent views compensate for any weariness which may be felt. It is cold at night, however, and weather conditions change rapidly, so it is important to take not only strong footwear, rain gear and warm clothing but also food, water, water purification for when you fill bottles from streams, insect repellent, a supply of plastic bags, coverings, a good sleeping bag, a torch/flashlight and a stove for preparing hot food and drink to ward off the cold at night. A stove using paraffin (kerosene) is preferable, as fuel can be bought in small quantities in markets. A tent is essential, but if you're hiring one in Cusco, check carefully for leaks. Walkers who have not taken adequate equipment have died of exposure. Caves marked on some maps are little better than overhangs, and are not sufficient shelter to sleep in.

All the necessary equipment can be rented; see page 1231 under Camping and page 1234 under Tour operators. Good maps of the Trail and area can be bought from *South American Explorers* in Lima or Cusco. If you have any doubts about carrying your own pack, reasonably priced porters/guides are available. Carry a day-pack for your water, snacks etc in case you walk faster than the porters and you have to wait for them to catch you up.

Tours Travel Agencies in Cusco arrange transport to the start, equipment, food, etc, for an all-in price, generally starting around US$135 pp, up to US$190 or more. All are subject to strict new rules introduced in 2001 and must be licensed. Tour operators taking clients on any of the Inca Trails leading to the Machu Picchu Historical Sanctuary have to pay an annual fee. Groups of up to 10 independent travellers who do not wish to use a tour operator will be allowed to hike the trails if they contact an independent, licensed guide to accompany them, as long as they do not contact any other persons such as porters or cooks. There is a maximum of 500 visitors per day allowed on the trail. Operators pay US$15 for each porter and other trail staff; porters are not be permitted to carry more than 20 kg. Littering is banned, as is carrying plastic water bottles (canteens only may be carried). Pets and pack animals are prohibited, but llamas are allowed as far as the first pass. Groups have to use approved campsites only. **Prices**: on all hiking trails adults must pay US$50 (students and children under 15 US$25), except Km 104 to Wiñay Wayna and Machu Picchu, where the fee is US$25 per adult (US$15 students and children), and Salkantay to Huayllabamba and Km 82, US$15. All tickets must be bought at the INC office on Calle San Bernardo in Cusco; none is sold without evidence that you are going with a licensed tour operator. None is sold at the entrance to any of the routes. Cheaper agencies tend to pool their clients together, so shop around for the cheapest there is (but remember that you get what you pay for – the cheapest tend not to pay the environment the respect the new rules were designed to instil). You can save a bit of money by arranging your own transport back to Ollantaytambo in advance, either for the last day of your tour, or by staying an extra night in Aguas Calientes and taking the early morning train, then take a bus back to Cusco. If you take your own tent and sleeping gear, some agencies give a discount. Make sure your return train ticket to Cusco has your name on it for the tourist train, otherwise you have to pay for any changes.

Timing & climate Four days would make a comfortable trip (though much depends on the weather) and you would not find yourself too tired to enjoy what you see. Allow a further day to see Machu Picchu when you have recovered from the hike. **NB** You are not allowed to walk back along the trail, though you can pay US$4.50 at Intipunku to be allowed to walk back as far as Wiñay-Wayna. You cannot take backpacks into Machu Picchu; leave them at ticket office, US$0.50.

NB The first 2 days of the Trail involve the stiffest climbing, so do not attempt it if you're feeling unwell. Leave all your valuables in Cusco and keep everything inside your tent, even your shoes. Security has, however, improved in recent years. Avoid the Jul-Aug high season and check the conditions in the rainy season from Nov to Apr (note that this can vary). In the wet it is cloudy and the paths are very muddy and difficult. Also watch out for coral snakes in this area (black, red, yellow bands).

The trail The trek to the sacred site begins either at Km 82, Piscacucho, or at Km 88, **Qorihuayrachina**, at 2,600 m. In order to reach Km 82 hikers are transported by their tour operator in a minibus on the road that goes to Quillabamba. From Piri onward the road follows the riverbank and ends at Km 82, where there is a bridge. You can depart as early as you like and arrive at Km 82 faster than going by train. The Inca Trail equipment, food, fuel and field personnel reach Km 82 (depending on the tour operator's logistics) for the Inrena staff to weigh each bundle before the group arrives. When several groups are leaving on the same day, it is more convenient to arrive early. Km 88 can only be reached by train, subject to schedule and baggage limitations. The train goes slower than a bus, but you start your walk nearer to Llaqtapata and Huayllabamba. Note that the route from Km 82 goes via **Cusichaca**, rather than Llaqtapata. (See below for details of variations in starting points for the Inca Trail.)

The walk to **Huayllabamba**, following the Cusichaca River, needs about 3 hrs and isn't too arduous. Beyond Huayllabamba, a popular camping spot for tour groups, there is a camping place about an hour ahead, at **Llulluchayoc** (3,200 m). A punishing 1½ hr climb further is **Llulluchapampa**, an ideal meadow for camping. If you have the energy to reach this point, it will make the second day easier because the next stage, the ascent to the first pass, **Warmiwañuska** (Dead Woman's Pass) at 4,200 m, is utterly exhausting, 2½ hrs.

Afterwards take the steep path downhill to the Pacamayo valley. Beware of slipping on the Inca steps after rain. You could camp by a stream at the bottom (1½ hrs from the first pass). It is no longer permitted to camp at **Runkuracay**, on the way up to the second pass (a much easier climb, 3,850 m). Magnificent views near the summit in clear weather. A good overnight place is about 30 mins past the Inca ruins at **Sayacmarca** (3,500 m), about an hour on after the top of the second pass.

A gentle 2-hr climb on a fine stone highway leads through an Inca tunnel to the third pass. Near the top there's a spectacular view of the entire Vilcabamba range. You descend to Inca ruins at **Phuyopatamarca** (3,650 m), well worth a long visit, even camping overnight. There is a 'tourist bathroom' here where water can be collected (but purify it before drinking).

From there steps go downhill to the impressive ruins of **Wiñay-Wayna** (2,700 m), with views of the recently cleared terraces of Intipata. Access is possible, but the trail is not easily visible. There is a basic hostel with bunk beds, **F** pp, showers and a small restaurant. There is a small campsite in front of the hostel. After Wiñay-Wayna there is no water and no camping till Machu Picchu.

The path from this point goes more or less level through jungle until the steep staircase up to the **Intipunku** (2 hrs), where there's a magnificent view of Machu Picchu, especially at dawn, with the sun alternately in and out, clouds sometimes obscuring the ruins, sometimes leaving them clear.

Get to Machu Picchu as early as possible, preferably before 0830 for best views but in any case before the tourist train arrives at 1030. **NB** Camping is not allowed at Intipunku; guards may confiscate your tent. You may only camp in the field by the river below Puente Ruinas station.

Alternative Inca routes

The **Camino Real de los Inkas** starts at Km 104, where a footbridge gives access to the ruins of Chachabamba and the trail which ascends through the ruins of Choquesuysuy to connect with the main trail at Wiñay-Wayna. This first part is a steady, continuous ascent of three hours (take water) and the trail is narrow and exposed in parts. Good hiking trails from Aguas Calientes (see page 1252) have been opened along the left bank of the Urubamba, for day hikes crossing the bridge of the hydroelectric plant to Choquesuysuy. A three-night trek goes from Km 82 to Km 88, then along the Río Urubamba to Pacaymayo Bajo and Km 104, from where you take the Camino Real de los Inkas.

Various treks involve routes from **Salkantay**: one joins the Inca Trail at Huayllabamba, then proceeds as before on the main Trail through Wiñay Wayna to Machu Picchu. To get to Salkantay, you have to start the trek in Mollepata, northwest of Cusco in the Apurímac valley. *Ampay* buses run from Arcopata on the Chinchero road, or you can take private transport to Mollepata (three hours from Cusco). Salkantay to Machu Picchu takes three nights. A four-night trek goes from

Peru

Paucarcancha, an important camping site on the trek from Salkantay, to Huayllabamba, then on the traditional Trail to Machu Picchu. Paucarcancha is an abandoned set of ruins on the descent from Pampacahuana, before the village of Huayllabamba on the main Inca Trail. Nearby there are some hot springs.

There are other routes which approach the Inca Trails to Machu Picchu, such as Km 77, Chillca, up the Sillque ravine in the Qente valley, which is commonly called the Lago Ancascocha route. Then there is another access through the Millpo Valley in the Salkantay area. From the Vilcabamba mountain range, one can reach Machu Picchu by hiking down from Huancacalle to Chaulla by road, getting to Santa Teresa and walking to the hydroelectric (Aobamba) train station. Then it's an hour's train ride on the local train to Aguas Calientes (tourists are allowed to ride the local train for this short section). Tour operators which specialize in trekking can advise on these routes.

Machu Picchu

Colour map 3, grid C4
Altitude: 2,380 m
42 km from
Ollantaytambo by rail

Machu Picchu is a complete Inca city. For centuries it was buried in jungle, until Hiram Bingham stumbled upon it in 1911. It was then explored by an archaeological expedition sent by Yale University. The ruins – staircases, terraces, temples, palaces, towers, fountains and the famous Intihuatana (the so-called 'Hitching Post of the Sun') – require at least a day. Take time to appreciate not only the masonry, but also the selection of large rocks for foundations, the use of water in the channels below the Temple of the Sun and the surrounding mountains.

Huayna Picchu, the mountain overlooking the site (on which there are also ruins), has steps to the top for a superlative view of the whole site, but it is not for those who are afraid of heights and you shouldn't leave the path. The climb takes up to 90 minutes but the steps are dangerous after bad weather. The path is open 0700-1300, with the latest return time being 1500; and you must register at a hut at the beginning of the trail. The other trail to Huayna Picchu, down near the Urubamba, is via the Temple of the Moon, in two caves, one above the other, with superb Inca niches inside, which have sadly been blemished by graffiti. For the trail to the Temple of the Moon: from the path to Huayna Picchu, take the marked trail to the left. It is in good shape, although it descends further than you think it should. After the Temple you may proceed to Huayna Picchu, but this path is overgrown, slippery in the wet and has a crooked ladder on an exposed part about 10 minutes before reaching the top (not for the faint-hearted). It is safer to return to the main trail to Huayna Picchu, although this adds about 30 minutes to the climb. The round trip takes about four hours. Before doing any trekking around Machu Picchu, check with an official which paths may be used, or which are one-way.

The famous Inca bridge is about 45 minutes along a well-marked trail south of the Royal Sector. The bridge – which is actually a couple of logs – is spectacularly sited, carved into a vertiginous cliff-face. East of the Royal Sector is the path leading up to **Intipunku** on the Inca Trail (45 minutes, fine views).

■ *The site is open from 0700 to 1730. Entrance fee is US$20, half price with ISIC card. If paying in dollars, only clean, undamaged notes will be accepted. You can deposit your luggage at the entrance for US$0.50 (reports of theft; remember where your luggage is, check for missing items and demand their return). Guides are available at the site, they are often very knowledgeable and worthwhile, US$30 for 2 hrs (but may take groups of up to 15). Site wardens are also informative, in Spanish only. Permission to enter the ruins before 0600 to watch the sunrise over the Andes, which is a spectacular experience, can be obtained from the Instituto Nacional de Cultura in Cusco, but it is often possible if you talk to the guards at the gate. After 1530 the ruins are quieter, but note that the last bus down from the ruins leaves at 1730. Mon and Fri are bad days because there is usually a crowd of people on guided tours who are going or have been to Pisac market on Sun, and too many people all want lunch at*

Peru

the same time. The hotel is located next to the entrance, with a self-service restaurant.
Take your own food and drink if you don't want to pay hotel prices, and take plenty of
drinking water. Note that food and drink are not officially allowed into the site. In the
dry season sandflies can be a problem, so take insect repellent and wear long clothes.
For further reading, see page 1295.

LL *Machu Picchu Sanctuary Lodge*, reservations as for the *Miraflores Park Hotel* in Lima, **Sleeping**
which is under the same management (Peru Orient Express Hotels) (T51 84 21 1039, F21
1053, info@peruorientexpress.com.pe Comfortable, good service, helpful staff, food
well-cooked and presented. Electricity and water 24 hrs a day, will accept American Express
traveller's cheques at the official rate, restaurant for residents only in the evening, but the
buffet lunch is open to all. The hotel, which was refurbished in 2001, is usually fully booked
well in advance, try Sun night as other tourists find Pisac market a greater attraction.

Trains *PerúRail* trains to Machu Picchu run from San Pedro station in Cusco. They pass **Transport**
through Poroy and Ollantaytambo to Aguas Calientes (the official name of this station is *Train schedules may*
'Machu Picchu'). The station for the tourist trains at Aguas Calientes is on the outskirts of *be affected by*
town, 200 m from the *Pueblo Hotel* and 50 m from where buses leave for Machu Picchu ruins. *mudslides in the rainy*
The ticket office is open 0630-1730; there is a guard on the gate. There is a paved road in poor *season. Delays occur*
condition between Aguas Calientes and the start of the road up to the ruins.

There are 3 classes of tourist train: *Vistadome*, *Inca* and *Backpacker*. The *Vistadome* costs
US$73 and *Inca* costs US$70 return; the *Backpacker* costs US$35 return. These trains depart
from Cusco. The new Sacred Valley Railway *Vistadome* service runs from Urubamba to Machu
Picchu and costs US$55 return, while there are further *Vistadomes* from Ollantaytambo to
Machu Picchu, also at US$55 return. The *Vistadome* leaves Cusco daily at 0600, stopping at
Ollantaytambo at 0805 and Machu Picchu at 0935. It returns from Machu Picchu at 1500,
passing Ollantaytambo at 1630, reaching Cusco at 1850. The *Inca* leaves at 0615,
Ollantaytambo at 0835, reaching Machu Picchu at 1000. It returns at 1525, passing
Ollantaytambo at 1700, getting to Cusco at 1925. The *Backpacker* leaves Cusco at 0630, pass-
ing Ollantaytambo at 0900 and Machu Picchu at 1030. It returns at 1610, passing
Ollantaytambo at 1750, getting to Cusco at 2030.The Sacred Valley Railway *Vistadome* leaves
Urubamba at 0600, reaching Machu Picchu at 0810, returning at 1700, reaching Urubamba
at 1915. The Ollantaytambo *Vistadomes* leave at 1010 and 1510, arriving at 1118 and 1630,
returning from Machu Picchu at 0825 and 1330, reaching Ollantaytambo at 0952 and 1444.
Seats can be reserved even if you're not returning the same day. The *Vistadome* and *Inca* tick-
ets include food in the price. These trains have toilets, video, snacks and drinks for sale.
Tickets for all trains should be bought at Wanchac station in Cusco, on Av Pachacútec. The
Sacred Valley Railway is to have ticket offices in Cusco, Lima and Urubamba (*Hotel Incaland*)
and tickets can be bought through *PerúRail*'s website, www.perurail.com

Tourist tickets: many people return by bus from Ollantaytambo, leaving the trains emp-
tier for the return trip to Cusco. Those trains that arrive in Cusco at night give a magical view
of the city lights. Tour agencies in Cusco sell various tourist tickets which include train fare,
round trip by bus up to the ruins, entrance fee and guide, but day trips (except those com-
mencing in Urubamba) are too rushed. They will pick you up from your hotel in Cusco and
take you to the train station.

The *Tren Local* or *Servicio Social* from Cusco and the *Cerrojo Social* from Ollantaytambo are
only for people who live along the route of the railway, Peruvian students and retired Peruvians. Tourists cannot buy tickets for these trains. If they do, and are found on board, they will
be sent back at their own expense. These trains are run by *PerúRail* as a public service, to support the local communities, and tourists purchasing seats will be depriving local people of
their only means of transport.

Buses leave Aguas Calientes for Machu Picchu every 30 mins from 0630 until 1300, 25 mins;
they return 1200-1730. US$9 return, valid 48 hrs. The walk up from Aguas Calientes takes
about 2½ hrs, following the Inca path.

Peru

Aguas Calientes Those with more time should spend the night here and visit the ruins early in the morning, when no one's around. Most hotels and restaurants are near the railway station, on the plaza, or on Av Pachacútec, which leads from the plaza to the thermal baths (a communal pool, rather smelly), 10 minutes walk from the town. They are open 0500-2030, US$1.50. You can rent towels and bathing costumes (US$0.65) at several places on the road to the baths; basic toilets and changing facilities and showers for washing *before* entering the baths; take soap and shampoo, and keep an eye on valuables.

Sleeping **LL** *Pueblo Hotel*, formerly *Machu Picchu Pueblo Hotel*, Km 110, 5 mins walk along the railway from the town. For reservations: Jr Andalucia 174, San Isidro, Lima, T01-422 6574, F422 4701; in Cusco at Julio C Tello C-13, Urb Santa Mónica, T245314, F244669, www.inkaterra.com Beautiful colonial-style bungalows in village compound surrounded by cloud forest, lovely gardens, pool, expensive restaurant, also campsite with hot showers at good rates, offer tours to Machu Picchu, several guided walks on the property, great buffet breakfasts for US$12. Also has the *Café Inkaterra* by the railway line. Recommended, but there are a lot of steps between the public areas and rooms. **AL-A** *Machu Picchu Inn*, Av Pachacútec 101, T211057, mapiinn@peruhotel.com.pe Includes breakfast, comfortable, good. **B** *Gringo Bill's* (*Hostal Q'oñi Unu*), Colla Raymi 104, T/F211046, gringobills@yahoo.com Cheaper without bath, relaxed, hot water, laundry, money exchange, good but expensive meals in *Villa Margarita* restaurant, breakfast from 0530, US$2 packed lunch, luggage stored, good beds, don't stay in the rooms nearest the entrance as they flood during heavy rain. **C** *Presidente*, at the old station, T211034 (Cusco T/F244598). Adjoining *Hostal Machu Picchu*, see below, better standard, rooms without river view cheaper, price includes breakfast and taxes. **D** *La Cabaña*, Av Pachacútec M20-3, T/F211048. Hot water, café, laundry service, popular with groups. **D** *Hostal Continental*, near the old train station, T211065. Good beds, hot showers. **D** *Las Orquídeas*, Urb Las Orquideas A-8, T211171. From Av Pachacútec, cross the bridge over the river to the football pitch, find a small dirt path on the right. With bath, hot water, quiet, pleasant. **D** *Hostal Machu Picchu*, at the old station, T211212. Functional, quiet, Wilber, the owner's son, has travel information, hot water, nice balcony over the Urubamba, grocery store, price includes breakfast and taxes. Recommended. **D** *Hostal Pachakúteq*, up the hill beyond *Hostal La Cabaña*, T211061. Hot water, good breakfast, quiet, family-run. Recommended. **D** *Hospedaje Quilla*, Av Pachacútec between Wiracocha and Tupac Inka Yupanki. Price includes breakfast, hot water, rents bathing gear for the hor springs. **D** *Hostal Wiracocha Inn*, C Wiracocha, T211088. Hot water, breakfast and soft drinks available, small garden, helpful, popular with groups. **D-E** *Rupa Wasi*, Collasuyo 110, T211101, rupawasi@hotmail.com Rooms and dormitories, hot water, traditional breakfasts, packed lunches and other meals, flexible, helpful, rooftop terrace, laundry, internet. Recommended. **E** pp *El Tambo*, at the old station, T211054. 4 rooms, hot water, breakfast included, also bar, *cambio*, restaurant serving pizzas and pasta. **F** pp *Las Bromelias*, Colla Raymi, just off Plaza before *Gringo Bill's*. Cheaper without bath, small, hot water. **F** *Hostal Samana Wasi*, C Tupac Inka Yupanki, T211170, quillavane@hotmail.com Hot water 24 hrs, cheaper without bath, pleasant place.

Camping: the only official campsite is in a field by the river, just below Puente Ruinas station. Do not leave your tent and belongings unattended.

Eating Pizza seems to be the most common dish in town, but many of the pizzerías serve other types of food as well. The old station and Av Pachútec are lined with eating places. At the station (where staff will try to entice you into their restaurant), are, among others: *Aiko*, recommended; *La Chosa Pizzería*, pleasant atmosphere, good value, mixed reports; *Las Quenas*, café and baggage store (US$0.30 per locker); and two branches of *Pizza Samana Wasi*. *Toto's House*, Av Imperio de los Incas. Good value and quality *menú*. *Clave de Sol*, Av Pachacútec 156. Same owner as *Chez Maggy* in Cusco, good cheap Italian food for under US$4, changes money, has vegetarian menu, great atmosphere, open 1200-1500, 1800-whenever. Also on this street: *Govinda*, by corner with Tupac Inka Yupanki. Vegetarian, cheap set lunch. Recommended. *Machu Picchu*. Good, friendly. *Inca Wasi*, very good;

Inka Machu Picchu, No 122, including vegetarian. *Inka's Pizza Pub*, on the plaza. Good pizzas, changes money, accepts traveller's cheques. Next door is *Illary*, popular. On Lloque Yupanqui are *Waisicha Pub*, good music and atmosphere, and *Indio Feliz*, T/F211090, great French cuisine, excellent value and service, set 3-course meal for US$10, good pisco sours. Highly recommended.

Qosqo Service, at the corner of Av Pachacútec and Mayta Capac, has postal service, *cambio* and **Directory** guiding service. The travel agency, *Rikuni Tours*, is at the old station, Av Imperio de los Incas 123, T/F211036, rikuni@chaski,unsaac.edu.pe Nydia is very helpful. They change money, have a postal service and sell postcards, maps and books (expensive). Email at *Yanantin Masintin* (US$3 per hr), which is part of the *Rikuni* group, as is *Tea House*, which is opposite, Av Imperio de los Incas 119. Both serve coffees, teas, snacks etc. *Serpost* (Post Office) agencies: just off the plaza, between the Centro Cultural Machu Picchu and *Galería de Arte Tunupa*. The telephone office is on Calle Collasuyo and there are plenty of phone booths around town. There are lots of places to choose from for exchange, shop around. The town has electricity 24 hrs a day.

Vitcos and Vilcabamba

The Incas' last stronghold is reached from **Chaullay**, a village on the road and railway between Ollantaytambo and Quillabamba. No trains run beyond Machu Picchu, so you must take the road which passes through Peña, a place of great beauty with snowy peaks on either side of the valley. Once out of Peña, the climb to the pass begins in earnest – on the right is a huge glacier. Soon on the left, Verónica begins to appear in all its huge and snowy majesty. After endless zig-zags and breathtaking views, you reach the Abra Málaga pass. The descent to the valley shows hillsides covered in lichen and Spanish moss. At Chaullay, the road crosses the river on the historic Choquechaca bridge (rebuilt in 2000). Another bridge at Maranura, 30 minutes downstream, also takes traffic over the river. ■ *Buses leave Cusco's new bus terminal for Quillabamba, taking 10 hrs for the 233 km:* Ampay *have a bus morning and evening,* Carhuamayo *in the evening only.*

From Chaullay you can drive, or take a daily bus or truck (4-7 hours) to the village of **Huancacalle**, the best base for exploring the nearby Inca ruins of **Vitcos**, with the palace of the last four Inca rulers from 1536 to 1572, and Yurac Rumi, the impressive sacred white stone of the Incas. There is a small hotel at Huancacalle, or villagers will accept travellers in their very basic homes (take sleeping bag). Vicente Macias has a three room *hostal* (no light or water, gets very busy on market days), and is also a guide for Vitcos, Ñustahispanan (a temple with holy waters), the sacred stone and the grave of Tupac Amaru. The Cobo family permits travellers to put up their tents on their property; Juvenal Cobo is a good guide and can supply mules for the trek to Vilcabamba Vieja (see below). Allow plenty of time for hiking to, and visiting Vitcos.

Peru

It takes one hour to walk from Huancacalle to Vitcos, 45 minutes Vitcos-Yurac Rumi, 45 minutes Yurac Rumi-Huancacalle. Horses can be hired if you wish.

The road from Chaullay continues to **Vilcabamba La Nueva**. You can also hike from Huancacalle; a three-hour walk through beautiful countryside with Inca ruins dotted around. There is a missionary building run by Italians, with electricity and running water, where you may be able to spend the night.

Vilcabamba Vieja Travellers with ample time can hike from Huancacalle to **Espíritu Pampa**, the site of the **Vilcabamba Vieja** ruins, a vast pre-Inca ruin with a neo-Inca overlay set in deep jungle at 1,000 m. The site is reached on foot or horseback from Pampaconas. From Chaullay, take a truck to Yupanca, Lucma or Pucyura: there rent horses or mules and travel through breathtaking countryside to Espíritu Pampa.

■ *To visit this area you must register with the police in Pucyura. You are advised to seek full information before travelling. Distances are considerable – it is at least 100 km from Chaullay to Espíritu Pampa – the going is difficult and maps appear to be very poor. Essential reading,* Sixpac Manco, *by Vincent R Lee (available in Cusco), has accurate maps of all archaeological sites in this area, and describes two expeditions into the region by the author and his party, following in the footsteps of Gene Savoy, who first identified the site in the 1960s. His book,* Antisuyo, *which describes this and other expeditions, is also recommended reading.*

Allow 5-8 days if going on foot. The best time of year is May to October. During the wet season be prepared to get very wet and very muddy. Insect repellent is essential, also pain-killers and other basic medicines.

West from Cusco Beyond Anta on the Abancay road, 2 km before Limatambo at the ruins of **Tarahuasi**, a few hundred metres from the road, is a very well-preserved **Inca temple platform**, with 28 tall niches, and a long stretch of fine polygonal masonry. The ruins are impressive, enhanced by the orange lichen which give the walls a honey colour.

Along the Abancay road 100 km from Cusco, is the exciting descent into the Apurímac canyon, near the former Inca suspension bridge that inspired Thornton Wilders' *The Bridge of San Luis Rey.* Also, 153 km along the road to Abancay from Cusco, near Curahuasi, is the stone of **Saihuite**, carved with animals, houses, etc, which appears to be a relief map of an Indian village. Unfortunately, 'treasure hunters' have defaced the stone. There are other interesting carvings in the area around the Saihuite stone. (In Curahuasi **G** *Hostal San Cristóbal*, pleasant, shared bath, cold shower. Ask the police for permission to camp.)

Choquequirao Choquequirao is another 'lost city of the Incas', built on a ridge spur almost 1,800 m above the Apurímac. Although only 30% has been uncovered, it is reckoned to be a larger site than Machu Picchu, but with fewer buildings. "Its utterly spectacular location... reminds one of Machu Picchu itself. The buildings around its central plaza represent extremely fine ceremonial and high-status residential architecture. There is a chain of ritual baths, an enormous, curving bank of fine terraces, numerous intriguing outlier groups of buildings... and a vast area of irrigated terracing on a nearby mountain slope, evidently designed to feed the local population." (Peter Frost, *Exploring Cusco*)

There are three ways in to Choquequirao. None is a gentle stroll. The shortest way is from **Cachora**, a village on the south side of the Apurímac, reached by a side road from the Cusco-Abancay highway, shortly after Saihuite. It is four hours by bus from Cusco to the turn-off, then a three-hour descent from the road to Cachora (from 3,695 m to 2,875 m). Buses run from Abancay to Cachora, but there is none arriving after 1100. Accommodation (eg *Hospedaje Judith Catherine*, T084-320202, **G** per bed), guides (Celestino Peña is the official guide) and mules are available in Cachora. From the village you need a day to descend to the Río Apurímac then seven hours to climb up to Choquequirao. Allow 1-2 days at the site then return the way you came. The second and third routes take a minimum of eight days and require thorough preparation. You can start either at Huancacalle, or at Santa Teresa, between Machu Picchu and Chaullay. Both routes involve an incredible number of strenuous ascents and descents. In each case you end the trail at Cachora. It is possible to start either of these long hikes at Cachora, continuing even from Choquequirao to Espíritu Pampa.

To much fanfare, the discovery of an Inca site near Choquequirao briefly fuelled stories of a new 'lost city'. **Corihuayrachina**, on Cerro Victoria (hence the nickname, 'Victoria's Secret') lies near an Inca road from Choquequirao to the interior of Vilcabamba, about 1½ days' hard walk from either Choqequirao or Santa Teresa. Controversy surrounded the announcement of the discovery (the 2001 expedition was led by Gary Ziegler, Peter Frost and Alfredo Valencia, with backing from the National Geographic Society), but it appears that the site was a support community for nearby mining operations, with a fluctuating population and no monumental structures.

The Central Highlands

Lima

The Central Andes are remote mountain areas with small, typical villages. The vegetation is low, but most valleys are cultivated. Roads, all dirt, are in poor condition, sometimes impassable in the rainy season; the countryside is beautiful with spectacular views and the people are friendly. The road into the central Andes has been improved and is paved throughout, offering fine views. Huancayo lies in a valley which produces many crafts; the festivals are very popular and not to be missed.

Lima to Huancayo

The Central Highway more or less parallels the course of the railway between Lima and Huanacayo (335 km). In 2002 no passenger service was running on this line and there seems to be little prospect of it recommencing. With the paving of roads from Pisco to Ayacucho and Nasca to Abancay, there are now more options for getting to the Sierra and the views on whichever ascent you choose are beyond compare. It is also becoming easier to reach the Central Highlands from Cusco (via Abancay and Andahuaylas) and from Huaraz (via La Unión and Huánuco), so Lima is not the sole point of access overland.

Much of the central highlands is reopening to tourism after the disruption caused by heavy terrorist activity in the 1980s and early 1990s. Knowledge of Spanish is essential, as is informing yourself regularly of the current political situation

Peru

Near the Central Highway, in the eastern outskirts of Lima, is **Puruchuco**, site of a major archaeological find, announced in 2002. Under a shanty town called Túpac Amaru, an Inca cemetery was found with over 2,000 intact mummy bundles. These, when unwrapped, should reveal a wealth of information about Inca society. Also at Puruchuco is the reconstructed palace of a pre-Inca Huacho noble, with a small museum.

Chosica (*Population*: 31,200. *Altitude*: 860 m) is the real starting place for the mountains, 40 km from Lima. It's warm and friendly and a great place to escape Lima's grey cloud. Beyond the town looms a precipitous range of hills almost overhanging the streets. There are four basic *hostales*, all with water problems. Recommended is **F** *Hospedaje Chosica*, Av 28 de Julio 134, T361 0841, rooms with and without bath, friendly family. **F** *La Posada*, Jr Trujillo y Salaverry, just off main road, comfortable, hot water. ■ *Colectivos for Chosica leave from Av Grau, Lima, when full, between 0600 and 2100, US$1. Most buses on the Lima-La Oroya route are full; colectivo taxi to La Oroya US$3.60, 3 hrs, very scenic, passing the highest railway in the world (see below).*

Marcahuasi Up the picturesque Santa Eulalia valley 40 km beyond Chosica, is **Marcahuasi**, a table mountain about 3 km by 3 km at 4,200 m, near the village of **San Pedro de Casta**. The *meseta* was investigated by the late Daniel Ruzo. There are three lakes, a 40 m high 'monumento a la humanidad', and other mysterious lines, gigantic figures, sculptures, astrological signs and megaliths which display non-American symbolism. Ruzo describes this pre-Incaic culture in his book, *La Culture Masma*, Extrait de l'Ethnographie, Paris, 1956. Others say that the formations are not man-made, but the result of wind erosion.

The trail starts behind the village of San Pedro, and bends to the left. It's three hours to the *meseta*; guides cost about US$3 a day and are advisable in misty weather. Mules for carrying bags cost US$4-8 to hire. There are three basic hotels in San Pedro, take sleeping bag; also two restaurants and good tourist information. Take all necessary camping equipment and use the authorized campsites (three); buy food in Chosica as there is little beyond that point. Take all the water you need as none is available. Tours can be arranged with travel agencies in Lima. ■ *Entry to the meseta US$3. Buses to San Pedro de Casta leave Chosica from Parque Echerique, opposite the market, twice daily, 4 hrs, US$2; return 0700 and 1400. The road is in a reasonable condition until the Callahuanca hydroelectric station.*

For a while, beyond Chosica, each successive valley looks greener and lusher, with a greater variety of trees and flowers. Between Río Blanco and **Chicla** (Km 127, 3,733 m), Inca contour-terraces can be seen quite clearly. After climbing up from **Casapalca** (Km 139, 4,154 m), there are glorious views of the highest peaks, and more mines, at the foot of a deep gorge. The road ascends to the Ticlio Pass, before the descent to **Morococha** and **La Oroya**. A large metal flag of Peru can be seen at the top of Mount Meiggs, not by any means the highest in the area, but through it runs Galera Tunnel, 1,175 m long, in which the Central Railway reaches its greatest altitude, 4,782 m.

La Oroya

Phone code: 064
Colour map 3, grid C3
Population: 36,000
Altitude: 3,755 m
187 km from Lima

The main smelting centre for the region's mining industry is full of vitality. It stands at the fork of the Yauli and Mantaro rivers. Asthmatics beware, the pollution from the heavy industry can cause severe problems. (For places to the east and north of La Oroya, see pages 1268 and 1270 respectively.)

Sleeping G pp *Hostal Regional*, Lima 112, T391017. Basic, hot water in morning. **F** *Hostal Inti*, Arequipa 117, T391098. Shared bath, warm water, basic. **F** *Hostal Chavín*, Tarma 281. Shared bath, cheap restaurant. *La Caracocha*, Lima 168. Cheap good *menú*. *Punta Arenas*, Zeballos 323. Good seafood, *chifa*. *El Tambo*, 2 km outside town on the road to Lima. Good trout and frogs, recommended as the best restaurant. There are lots of *pollerías* in front of the train station in C Lima.

Transport Buses To **Lima**, 4½ hrs, US$5.20. To **Jauja**, 80 km, 1½ hrs, US$1; and on to **Huancayo**, a further 44 km (paved), 1 hr, US$1. To **Tarma**, 1½ hrs, US$1.35. To **Cerro de Pasco**, 131 km, 3 hrs, US$2.20. To **Huánuco**, 236 km, 6 hr, US$4.35; on to **Tingo María**, 118 km, 3-4 hrs, US$1.75, and on to **Pucallpa**, 284 km, 7-9 hrs, US$7.85. Buses leave from Zeballos, adjacent to the train station. Colectivos also run on all routes (see under Lima).

Jauja

Phone code: 064
Colour map 3, grid C3
Population: 105,000
Altitude: 3,330 m
80 km SE of La Oroya

The old town of Jauja was Pizarro's provisional capital until the founding of Lima. It has a very colourful Wednesday and Sunday market. Jauja is a friendly, unspoilt town, in the middle of a good area for walking. There is an **archaeological museum**, which is recommended for the Huari culture. A modernized church retains three fine 17th-century altars. The **Cristo Pobre** church is claimed to have been modelled after Notre Dame and is something of a curiosity. On a hill above Jauja there is a fine line of Inca storehouses, and on hills nearby the ruins of hundreds of circular stone buildings from the Huanca culture (John Hemming). There are also ruins near the

Peru (side margin)

Paca lake, 3½ km away. The western shore is lined with restaurants, many of which offer boat trips at weekends, US$0.75 (combi from Av Pizarro US$0.30).

On the road to Huancayo 18 km to the south, is **Concepción** (*Altitude:* 3,251 m), with a market on Sunday. From Concepción a branch road (6 km) leads to the **Convent of Santa Rosa de Ocopa**, a Franciscan monastery set in beautiful surroundings. It was established in 1725 for training missionaries for the jungle. It contains a fine library with over 20,000 volumes, a biological museum and a large collection of paintings. ■ *0900-1200 and 1500-1800, closed Tue. 45-mins tours start on the hour, US$1.15. Colectivos from the market in Concepción, 15 mins, US$0.25.*

Sleeping and eating E pp *Hostal Manco Cápac*, Jr Manco Cápac 575, T361620. Central, good rooms, pleasant, beautiful patio, relaxing, good breakfast and coffee, German run. **E** *Hostal Francisco Pizarro*, Bolognesi 334, opposite the market, T362082. Shared bath, hot water, run down. **E** *Santa Rosa*, on main plaza. Modern, big rooms, restaurant. **F** *Ganso de Oro*, R Palma 249, T362165. **G** without bath, hot water, basic, good restaurant. **F** *Hostal Los Algarrobes*, Huancayo 264, T362633. Shared bath, hot water in the morning, very clean, good value. Eating places include *Marychris*, Jr Bolívar 1166, T362386. Lunch only, excellent. *La Rotunda*, Tarapacá 415. Tables in a pleasant courtyard or dining rooms, good lunch menú and pizzas in the evening. *Centro Naturista*, Huarancayo 138. Fruit salad, yoghurt, granola, etc.

Transport Buses To **Lima**: with *Mcal Cáceres*, daily 0800, 2300, *Etucsa* 0815, 1345, US$6, 6 hrs. Also *Sudamericano*. Most companies have their offices on the Plaza de Armas, but their buses leave from Av Pizarro. *Cruz del Sur*, Pizarro 220, direct to Lima, 5 hrs, US$8. **To Huancayo**, 44 km, takes 1 hr and costs US$1. To **Cerro de Pasco**, *Oriental* leave from 28 de Julio 156, and *Turismo Central* from 28 de Julio 150, 5 hrs, US$3.55. *Oriental* and *Turismo Central* also go to **Huánuco**, 7 hrs, US$5.35. To **Tarma**, US$2.25, hourly with *Canary Tours* and *ET San Juan* from Jr Tarma; the latter continues to **Chanchamayo**, US$4.50.

Directory Banks *Dollar Exchange Huarancayo*, on Jr Huarancayo, gives a much better rate than Banco de Crédito (no TCs). **Communications** Internet: *CSI*, Bolognesi 512. US$0.75 per hr. **Post office:** Jr Bolívar. **Telephone:** at Bolognesi 546, T064-362020, T/F361111; also at Ricardo Palma, opposite *Hotel Ganso de Oro*, T/F362395, better service and prices.

Huancayo

The city is in the beautiful Mantaro Valley. It is the capital of Junín Department and the main commercial centre for inland Peru. All the villages in the valley produce their own original crafts and celebrate festivals all year round. At the important festivals in Huancayo, people flock in from far and wide with an incredible range of food, crafts, dancing and music. The Sunday market gives a little taste of this every week (it gets going after 0900), but it is better to go to the villages for local handicrafts. Jr Huancavelica, 3 km long and four stalls wide, still sells clothes, fruit, vegetables, hardware, handicrafts and traditional medicines and goods for witchcraft. There is also an impressive daily market behind the railway station and a large handicrafts market between Ancash and Real, block 7, offering a wide selection.

Phone code: 064
Colour map 3, grid C3
Population: over 500,000
Altitude: 3,271 m

The museum at the Salesian school has over 5,000 pieces, including a large collection of jungle birds, animals and butterflies, insects, reptiles and fossils. ■ *Tue, Thu, Fri and Sun 0815-1100, 1415-1700, Wed 0815-1100, Sat 1415-1600, US$0.60. Recommended.* The **Parque de Identidad Wanka**, on Jr San Jorge in the Barrio San Carlos, is a fascinating mixture of surrealistic construction interwoven with indigenous plants and trees and the cultural history of the Mantaro Valley. ■ *Entry is free, but contributions are appreciated.*

Peru

Excursions

Keep an eye out for bagsnatchers and pickpockets. Beware of overcharging by taxi drivers, shopkeepers and the post office

The whole Mantaro valley is rich in culture. On the outskirts of town is **Torre-Torre**, impressive, eroded sandstone towers on the hillside. Take a bus to Cerrito de la Libertad and walk up. The ruins of **Warivilca** (15 km) are near **Huari**, with the remains of a pre-Inca temple of the Huanca tribe. Museum in the plaza, with deformed skulls, and modelled and painted pottery of successive Huanca and Inca occupations of the shrine. ■ *Ruins open 1000-1200, 1500-1700 (museum mornings only), US$0.15. Take a micro for Chilca from C Real.* Between Pilcomayo and Huayo (15 km) is the **Geophysical Institute of Huayo**, on the 'Magnetic Equator' 12½° south of the geographical equator (best to visit in the morning, or when the sun is shining). ■ *Take bus from Jr Giráldez to Chupaca, but get out by bridge before Chupaca, where the road splits, then take a colectivo.*

East of the Mantaro River The villages of **Cochas Chico** and **Cochas Grande**, 11 km away, are where the famous *mate burilado*, or gourd carving, is done. You can buy them cheaply direct from the manufacturers, but ask around. Beautiful views of the Valle de Mantaro and Huancayo. *Micros* leave from esq Amazonas y Giráldez, US$0.25.

Hualahoyo (11 km) has a little chapel with 21 colonial canvases. **San Agustín de Cajas** (8 km) makes fine hats, and **San Pedro** (10 km) makes wooden chairs; **Hualhuas** (12 km) fine alpaca weavings which you can watch being made. The weavers take special orders; small items can be finished in a day. Negotiate a price.

The town of **San Jerónimo** is renowned for the making of silver filigree jewellery; Wednesday market. Fiesta on the third Saturday in August. There are ruins 2-3 hours' walk above San Jerónimo, but seek advice before hiking to them.

Sleeping

Prices may be raised in Holy Week. Note that the Plaza de Armas is called Plaza Constitución

B *Turismo*, Ancash 729, T231072, hotelhyo@correo.dnet.com.pe Old building, some rooms small, quiet, good meals for US$3.50. **B** *Presidente*, C Real 1138, T231736, F231275, same email as *Turismo*. Helpful, safe, serves breakfast. Recommended. **C** *Santa Felicita*, Giráldez 145, Plaza Constitución, T235285. Hot water, good. **D** *El Dorado*, Piura 452, T223947. Hot water, some rooms with TV in **C** category. **D** *El Marqués*, Puno 294, T219026, F219202. Good value. **E** pp *Casa Alojamiento de Aldo y Soledad Bonilla*, Huánuco 332, half block from Mcal Cáceres bus station, T232103 (Lima 463 1141). **D** pp full board, colonial house, owners speak English, laundry, secure, relaxing, nice courtyard, can arrange tours, best to book ahead. **E** *La Casa de La Abuela*, Av Giráldez 693. Hot shower, price includes breakfast, drink in *La Cabaña* and 30-mins' free internet voucher, some rooms with antique beds, dormitory **F**, laundry facilities, meals available, mixed reports. **E** pp *Hospedaje César Ada*, Pasaje Santa Teresa 294, El Tambo-3 Esquinas, 5 km from centre, T235615 for pick-up, wadaycesar@latinmail.com Quiet, shared bath, garden, meals available, use of kitchen, breakfast included. **E** *Confort*, Ancash 231, 1 block from the main Plaza, T233601. Rooms with hot water are nicer, but more expensive than those with cold water, all rooms good value, safe for bicycles, car parking US$1. **E** *Hostal Huaracaya*, Amazonas 323. Hot water and TV, good value. **E** *Pussy Cat*, Giráldez 359, T231565. **F** without bath, hot water, safe, luggage stored, comfortable beds. **F** pp *Peru Andino Lodging & Excursions*, Pasaje San Antonio 113-115, 3 blocks from Av Centenario, 10-15 mins walk from the centre, T223956. Including breakfast, hot showers, several rooms with bath, safe area, cosy atmosphere, run by Sra Juana, daughter speaks some English, owner runs trekking and mountain bike tours, cooking and laundry facilities. Recommended. **F** *Hostal Santo Domingo*, Ica 655, T235461. Set around two pleasant patios, basic, good value. **G** pp *Hostal Baldeón*, Amazonas 543, T231634. Kitchen and laundry facilities, nice patio, hot shower on request, basic rooms, good value. **G** pp *Casa hospedaje*, Huamanmarca 125, T219980. Central, small, comfortable, hot water, shared showers, family run, nice atmosphere.

Peru

Mid-range: *El Inca*, Puno 530. Good value for salads and meals. *Huancahuasi*, Av Mcal Castilla 2222, T244826. Excellent traditional dishes, especially on Sun. *La Cabaña*, Av Giráldez 652. Pizzas, ice-cream, *calentitos*, and other dishes, folk music at weekends. *Incas del Perú* information office next door offers walking and biking tours, US$35, and visits to Huamancaca prison on Fri, US$10. They also have maps and a book exchange, bicycle hire (US$15 per day), www.incasdelperu.com *Pizzería Antojitos*, Puno 599. Attractive, atmospheric pizzería with live music some nights. *Pizzería La Colina*, Lima 151. Good quality. **Cheap**: *Chifa El Centro*, Giráldez 238. Chinese food, good service. *Chifa Rápido*, Arequipa 511. Authentic, good value and quality. *Mama Shanto*, Coliseo Cerrado 140 (Real block 8). Typical dishes such as *papa a la huancaína* and *ají de gallina*, beautifully decorated. *El Pino*, Real 539. Typical dishes for about US$2-3 and fixed price *menú*. Lots of cheap restaurants along Av Giráldez serving set *menú*, eg *The Waykyky*, close to Plaza and *Lalo's*, No 365.

Eating

Breakfast is served in Mercado Modelo from 0700.
Better class, more expensive restaurants, serving typical dishes for about US$4-5, plus 18% tax, drinks can be expensive

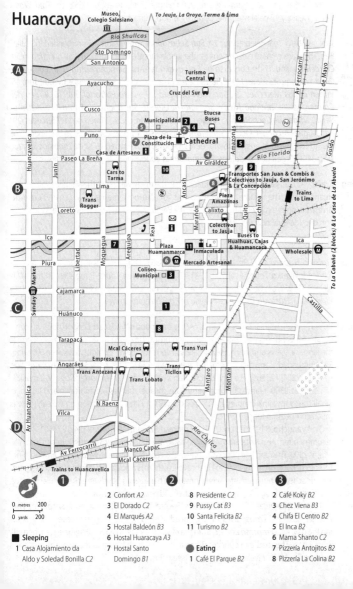

Huancayo

Peru

0 metres 200
0 yards 200

■ **Sleeping**
1 Casa Alojamiento da Aldo y Soledad Bonilla *C2*
2 Confort *A2*
3 El Dorado *C2*
4 El Marqués *A2*
5 Hostal Baldeón *B3*
6 Hostal Huaracaya *A3*
7 Hostal Santo Domingo *B1*
8 Presidente *C2*
9 Pussy Cat *B3*
10 Santa Felicita *B2*
11 Turismo *B2*

● **Eating**
1 Café El Parque *B2*
2 Café Koky *B2*
3 Chez Viena *B3*
4 Chifa El Centro *B2*
5 El Inca *B2*
6 Mama Shanto *C2*
7 Pizzería Antojitos *B2*
8 Pizzería La Colina *B2*

Cafés *Berisso*, Giráldez 258. Good for cakes and quiche, friendly. *Gustitos*, Real at corner of Plaza Constitución. Good service, huge burgers, real coffee. *Café Koky*, Ancash y Puno. Good for breakfasts and pastries during the day. Smart places to take coffee and cake: *Café El Parque*, Giráldez y Ancash, on the main plaza; and *Chez Viena*, Puno 125. Good, small, unnamed café at Puno 209, serves breakfast. **Vegetarian**: *El Lucero*, Arequipa 929. Good food, value and service. Other good ones at Arequipa 770, and Cajamarca 379. Vegetarian *chifa* at Huánuco 286. **Bars** *Café Billar*, Paseo de Breña 133. Open 0900-2400, serves beer and snacks, pool tables. *La Cereza*, Puno just below Plaza, near *Fuente de Soda El Inca*, good for late-night drinks, sandwiches, music videos, popular.

Entertainment **Discos** *A1A*, Bolognesi 299. Most discos open around 2000 and close at 0200. Some charge an entrance fee of US$3-4. **Peñas** All the *peñas* have folklore shows with dancing, open normally Fri, Sat and Sun from 1300 to 2200. Entrance fee is about US$2 pp. *Taki Wasi*, Huancavelica y 13 de Noviembre. *Ollantaytambo*, Puno, block 2.

Festivals **Jan:** 1-6, New Year celebrations; 20, *San Sebastián y San Fabián* (recommended in Jauja). **Feb:** there are carnival celebrations for the whole month, with highlights on 2, *Virgen de la Candelaria*, and 17-19 *Concurso de Carnaval*. **Mar-Apr:** *Semana Santa*, with impressive Good Friday processions. **May:** *Fiesta de las Cruces* throughout the whole month. **Jun:** 15 *Virgen de las Mercedes*; 24, *San Juan Bautista*; 29, *Fiesta Patronal*. **Jul:** 16, *Virgen del Carmen*; 24-25, *Santiago*. **Aug:** 4, *San Juan de Dios*; 16, *San Roque*; 30, *Santa Rosa de Lima*. **Sep:** 8, *Virgen de Cocharcas*; 15, *Virgen de la Natividad*; 23-24, *Virgen de las Mercedes*; 29, *San Miguel Arcángel*. **Oct:** 4, *San Francisco de Asís*; 18, *San Lucas*; 28-30 culmination of month-long celebrations for *El Señor de los Milagros*. **November:** 1, *Día de Todos los Santos*. **Dec:** 3-13, *Virgen de Guadalupe*; 8, *Inmaculada Concepción*; 25, *Navidad* (Christmas).

There are so many festivals in the Mantaro Valley that it is impossible to list all. Nearly every day of the year there is some sort of celebration in one of the villages. This is a selection

Shopping **Crafts** All crafts are made outside Huancayo in the many villages of the Mantaro Valley, or in Huancavelica. The villages are worth a visit to learn how the items are made. *Casa de Artesano*, on the corner of Real and Paseo La Breña, at Plaza Constitución, has a wide selection of good quality crafts.

Thieves in the market hand out rolled up pieces of paper and pick your pocket while you unravel them

Tour operators *Turismo Huancayo*, C Real 517 oficina 6, T233351. Organizes local tours and is recommended. *Wanka Tours*, Real 550, T231743, and *Peruvian Tours*, Puno 488, on the main plaza, T213069, are both reputable organizers of tours to a variety of places in the Mantaro Valley. Also, *Hurtado Tours* (see *Pizzería La Cabaña* entry above).

Transport **Bus** There are regular buses to **Lima**, 6-7 hrs on a good paved road, US$9-10 in more comfortable direct buses and US$6-7 in stopping buses. Travelling by day is recommended for the fantastic views and, of course, for safety. If you must travel by night, take warm clothing. Recommended companies: *Mcal Cáceres*, Real 1247, T234970/231621; *Cruz del Sur*, Ayacucho 281, T235650, 4 a day; *Etucsa*, Puno 220, 5 a day. *Transportes Rogger*, Lima 561, T212687, at 2300. Many other companies are cheaper, but less comfortable and less safe. Small buses for Lima congregate 15 blocks north of Plaza Constitución on C Real; there is much competition for passengers.

To **Ayacucho**, 319 km, 11 hrs, US$8. *Empresa Molina*, C Angaráes 334, T224501, 3 a day, recommended. Also *Antezana*, Arequipa 1301, at 2100, and *Transportes Lobato*, Omar Yali 148, at 2300. The road is in poor condition and is very difficult in the wet. Take warm clothing. After Izcuchaca, on the railway to Huancavelica, there is a good road to the Quichuas hydro-electric scheme, but thereafter it is narrow with hair-raising bends and spectacular bridges. The scenery is staggering. From Huanta the road descends into Ayacucho.

If driving to Ayacucho and beyond, roads are "amazingly rough". Don't go alone Count kilometres diligently to keep a record of where you are: road signs are poor

To **Huancavelica**, 147 km, 5 hrs, US$4. Several buses daily, including *Transportes Yuri*, Ancash 1220, and *Transportes Ticllos*, Ancash y Angaráes, both operate several buses during the day. Also *Empresa Zodiac*, from the *Mcal Cáceres* terminal, colectivos leave when full, 3 hrs, US$6. The road is in poor condition and takes much longer in the wet. The scenery is spectacular. Most travellers use the train (see below).

Peru

To **Cerro de Pasco**, 255 km, 5 hrs, US$4. *Turismo Central*, Ayacucho 274, T223128, at 1400, and *Transportes Salazar*, at 2100. Also *Transportes Javier*, 4 a day, US$3.50. Alternatively, take a bus to La Oroya which leaves when full, about every 20 mins, from Av Real about 10 blocks north of the main plaza. From La Oroya there are regular buses and colectivos to Cerro. The road to La Oroya and on to Cerro is in good condition. To Huánuco, 7 hrs, *Turismo Central* at 2100, US$6; *Transportes Rey*, Real 235, T237512, at 2130.

To **Chanchamayo**: *Empresa San Juan*, Ferrocarril 161 and Plaza Amazonas, and *Canary Tours* each have an hourly service via Jauja to Tarma, 3 hrs, US$2.50, some of which continue on to La Merced, 5 hrs, US$4.

Some trucks and a few buses travel to **Cañete**, 289 km, 10 hrs, US$4. It is a poor road, with beautiful mountain landscapes before dropping to the valley of Cañete.

To **Jauja**, 44 km, 1 hr. Colectivos and combis leave every few mins from Huamanmarca y Amazonas, and Plaza Amazonas, US$1.50. Ones via San Jerónimo and Concepción have 'Izquierda' on the front. Most buses to the Mantaro Valley leave from several places around the market area. Buses to **Hualhuas** and **Cajas** leave from block 3 of Pachiteca. Buses to **Cochas** leave from Amazonas y Giráldez.

Trains There are 2 unconnected railway stations. The Central station serves **Lima**, via La Oroya: no passenger services. From the small station in Chilca suburb (15 mins by taxi, US$1), trains run to **Huancavelica**, 142 km, narrow gauge 3 ft. There are 2 trains: the *autovagón* (*expreso*) at 0630 daily, US$3.50, has 1st class and Buffet carriages. The journey takes 4 hrs and has fine views, passing through typical mountain villages where vendors sell food and crafts. There are 38 tunnels and the line reaches 3,676 m. The local train leaves at 1300 daily and takes 5 hrs. There are 1st, US$2.25, 2nd, US$1.70, and Buffet, US$3.70, classes. You can buy tickets 1 day in advance, or an hour before departure. Services can be suspended in the rainy season.

Ask the driver if he'll let you ride in the engine

Directory

Banks *Banco de Crédito*, Real 1039, changes TCs with no commission, cash advance on Visa. *Banco Wiese*, Real casi Ica. ATM does not accept international cards, poor rates for TCs. *Western Union*, Ancash 540, Of 302, T224816/235655, open Mon-Fri 0900-1300 and 1600-2000; Sat 0900-1300. There are several *casas de cambio* on the 4th and 5th blocks of Real; street changers hang out there as well. Also travel agencies and banks will change dollars. **Communications** Internet: Numerous places round Plaza Constitución on Giráldez (eg *Alph@net*, No288), Paseo La Breña (eg *Cyberwanka*, No 173, very good) and Real; average price under US$1 per hr. **Language classes** *La Cabaña* (see Eating, above) organizes Spanish courses for beginners for US$100 per week, including accommodation with local families or at *La Casa de La Abuela*, as well as weaving, playing traditional music, Peruvian cooking and lots of other things. *Katia Cerna* is a recommended teacher, T225332, katiacerna@hotmail.com She can arrange home stays; her sister works in adventure tourism. **Tourist offices** Ministry of Tourism, C Real 481, junin@mitinci.gob.pe It has information about the area and is helpful; open 0900-1400, 1600-2000 Mon-Fri.

Between Huancayo and Huancavelica, **Izcuchaca** is the site of a bridge over the Río Mantaro. On the edge of town is a fascinating pottery workshop whose machinery is driven by a water turbine (plus a small shop). A nice hike is to the chapel on a hill overlooking the valley; about 1-1½ hours each way. Hotels: one is on the plaza, no bathroom, you have to use the public bath by the river; the other is just off the plaza, a yellow three-storey house, **G**, no shower, toilet suitable for men only, chamber pot supplied, only blankets on bed, cold. *Restaurant El Parque* on plaza, opens 0700, delicious food. ■ *Trains from Huancavelica arrive at 0800 and 1400-1430, then continue to Huancayo; US$1.15. Trains from Huancayo pass at around 0900 and 1600. They tend to be very crowded. Daily colectivo to Ayacucho at 1000-1100, 8 hrs.*

Huancavelica

Huancavelica is a friendly and attractive town, surrounded by huge, rocky mountains. It was founded in the 16th century by the Spanish to exploit rich deposits of mercury and silver. It is predominantly an indigenous town, and people still wear traditional costume. There are beautiful mountain walks in the neighbourhood. The Cathedral, located on the Plaza de Armas, has an altar considered to be one of the

Phone code: 064
Colour map 3, grid C3
Population: 37,500
Altitude: 3,680 m

Peru

finest examples of colonial art in Peru. Also very impressive are the five other churches in town. The church of San Francisco, for example, has no less than 11 altars. Sadly, though, most of the churches are closed to visitors.

Bisecting the town is the Río Huancavelica. South of the river is the main commercial centre. North of the river, on the hillside, are the thermal baths. ■ *US$0.15 for private rooms, water not very hot, US$0.10 for the hot public pool, also hot showers, take a lock for the doors, open 0600-1500.* There is a colourful daily market. Most handicrafts are transported directly to Lima, but you can still visit craftsmen in neighbouring villages. There is a daily food market at Muñoz y Barranca. The Potaqchiz hill, just outside the town, gives a fine view, about one hour walk up from San Cristóbal. *Instituto Nacional de la Cultura,* Plaza San Juan de Dios. Director Alfonso Zuasnabar, is a good source of information on festivals, archaeological sites, history, etc. Gives courses on music and dancing, and lectures some evenings. There is also an interesting but small archaeology and anthropology museum. ■ *Mon-Sat 1000-1300, 1500-1900.*

Sleeping & eating C *Presidente*, Plaza de Armas, T952760. Cheaper without bath, lovely colonial building, overpriced. **F** *Camacho*, Jr Carabaya 481. Best of the cheap hotels, **G** without bath, hot shower morning only, good value. **F** *Santo Domingo*, Av Barranca 366, T953086; and **F** *Savoy*, Av Muñoz 294, both very basic, shared bath, cold water. There are lots of cheap, basic restaurants on C Muñoz and Jr Virrey Toledo. All serve typical food, mostly with set *menú*, US$1.50. Better are: *Paquirri*, Jr Arequipa 137, good, expensive. *Mochica Sachún*, Av Virrey Toledo 303, great *menú* US$1.50, otherwise expensive, popular. *Pollería Joy*, Toledo y Arequipa, good for chicken; *La Casona*, Jr Virrey Toledo 230, cheap and good *menú*, also a *peña*. *Chifas* on Virrey Toledo: *Centro*, No 275, is better than *Imperio*.

Festivals The whole area is rich in culture. In **Sep** there is a tourist week with a huge crafts market, music and dancing. Typical festivals: **Jan:** *Niño Occe.* **12 Jan:** *Fiesta de Negritos*; carnival in Feb; *Palm Sunday* procession; *Semana Santa.* **Jun:** *Fiesta de Torre-Torre.* **Nov:** *Todos los Santos.* **25 Dec:** *Los Galos* .

Transport **Road** All bus companies have their offices on and leave from the east end of town on Muñoz and O'Donovan. To **Huancayo**, 147 km, 5 hrs, US$4, rough road, several buses a day, eg *Transportes Yuri* and *Transportes Ticllas* (O'Donovan 500). Also *Empresa Zodiac* colectivos, US$6. To **Lima** via Huancayo, 445 km, 13 hrs minimum, US$8. Most buses to Huancayo go on to Lima, there are several a day. To **Pisco**, 269 km, 12 hrs, US$7 and **Ica**, US$8, 1730 daily, with *Oropesa*, O'Donovan 599, near Parque Castilla. Arrives in Pisco 0230-0300 and Ica 0530-0600. Buy your ticket 1 day in advance. Some trucks also travel this route. The road is poor until it joins the Ayacucho-Pisco road, where it improves. The views are spectacular, but most of the journey is done at night. Be prepared for sub-zero temperatures in the early morning as the bus passes snowfields, then for temperatures of 25-30°C as the bus descends to the coast. **Trains** See under Huancayo; the *autovagón/expreso* leaves for Huancayo daily at 0630, the local train at 1230, daily.

Directory **Banks** *Banco de Crédito*, Virrey Toledo 300 block. **Communications** Internet:*Librería Municipal*, Plaza de Armas, US$0.60 per hr. **Post Office:** on Toledo, 1 block from the Plaza de Armas. **Telephone:** Carabaya y Virrey Toledo. **Tourist offices** Ministerio de Industria y Comercio, Turismo y Artesanías, Jr Nicolás de Piérola 180, open Mon-Fri 0730-1400, very helpful. *Citaq*, north side of Plaza de Armas, citaq@latinmail.com, run by Vidal Zarate, specializing in ecotourism and cultural and environmental excursions.

Huancavelica to Ayacucho The direct route from Huancavelica to Ayacucho (247 km) goes via **Santa Inés** (4,650 m), 78 km. Out of Huancavelica the road climbs steeply with switchbacks between herds of llamas and alpacas grazing on rocky perches. Around Pucapampa (Km 43) is one of the highest habitable *altiplanos* (4,500 m), where the rare and highly prized ash-grey alpaca can be seen. Snow-covered mountains are passed as the road climbs to 4,853 m at the Abra Chonta pass, 23 km before Santa Inés. By taking the turnoff to Huachocolpa at Abra Chonta and continuing for 3 km you'll reach the highest drivable pass in the world, at 5,059 m. In Santa Inés are *Alojamiento Andino*, a very friendly restaurant, *El Favorito*, where you can sleep, and several others. Nearby are two lakes (Laguna Choclacocha) which can be visited in 2½ hours. 52 km beyond Santa Inés at the Abra de Apacheta (4,750 m), 98 km from Ayacucho, the rocks are all the colours of the rainbow, and running through this fabulous scenery is a violet river. These incredible colours are all caused by oxides.

Transport Daily direct transport from Huancavelica to Ayacucho with *Ticllas* (address above), 0500, one stop for lunch, US$5, 7 hrs. *Expreso Turismo Nacional*, Cáceres 237, combi at 0500, US$5, 9 hrs. Buy tickets the day before. The road is good and new. The journey is a cold one but spectacular as it is the highest continuous road in the world, rarely dropping below 4,000 m for 150 km. Alternatives are: take the train to Izcuchaca, stay the night and take the colectivo (see above). Take a colectivo Huancavelica-Lircay, a small village with *Hostal El Paraíso*, **F** with bath, **G** without (*Transportes 5 de Mayo*, Av Sebastián Barranca y Cercado, US$3, 2 hrs, leave when full). The same company runs from Lircay Terminal Terrestre hourly from 0430 to Julcamarca (colonial church, *hostales* near plaza), 2½ hrs, then take a minibus from Julcamarca plaza to Ayacucho, US$2.50, 3 hrs; beautiful scenery all the way.

There is another route to Ayacucho from Huancayo, little used by buses, but which involves not so much climbing for cyclists. Cross the pass into the Mantaro valley on the road to **Quichuas** (**G** *Hostal Recreo Sol y Sombra*, charming, small courtyard, helpful, basic). Then to **Anco** (**G** *Hostal Gabi*, appalling, but better than anything else) and **Mayocc** (lodging). From here the road crosses a bridge after 10 km and in another 20 km reaches **Huanta** (see Ayacucho, Excursions). Then it's a paved road to Ayacucho.

Ayacucho

Ayacucho was founded on 9 January 1539. On the Pampa de Quinua, on 9 December 1824, the decisive Battle of Ayacucho was fought, bringing Spanish rule in Peru to an end. In the middle of the festivities, the Liberator Simón Bolívar decreed that the city be named Ayacucho, 'City of Blood', instead of its original name, Huamanga.

Phone code: 064
Colour map 3, grid C3
Population: 105,918
Altitude: 2,740 m

Peru

The city is built round Parque Sucre, the main plaza, with the Cathedral, Municipalidad and Palacio de Gobierno facing on to it. It is famous for its Semana Santa celebrations, its splendid market and its 33 churches. The climate is lovely, with warm, sunny days and pleasant balmy evenings.

Following the violence of Shining Path's most active period in the 1980s and early 1990s, peace has returned to this beautiful city, which is now eager to promote tourism.

For a fascinating insight into Quechua art and culture, a visit to **Barrio Santa Ana** is a must. The district is full of *artesanía* shops, galleries and workshops (eg *Galería Latina*, Plazuela de Santa Ana 605, and *Wari Art Gallery*, Jr Mcal Cáceres 302).

Sights

The **Mirador Turístico**, on Cerro Acuchimay, offers fine views over the city. Take a *micro* or bus from the corner of Jr 2 de Mayo and Jr C F Vivanco all the way there.

The **Cathedral**, built in 1612 has superb gold leaf altars. ■ *Daily 1730-1845.* See also San Cristóbal, the first church to be founded in the city; **La Merced**, whose high choir is a good example of the simplicity of the churches of the early period of the Viceroyalty; **La Compañía de Jesús** (1605), with a baroque façade guarded by two 18th-century towers. ■ *Daily 0900-1100.* **San Francisco de Asís** ■ *daily 0900-1100* and **Santa Teresa** (1683), both with magnificent gold-leafed altars heavily brocaded and carved in the churrigueresque style. ■ *Daily 1730-1900.* **Santa Clara** is renowned for its beautifully delicate coffered ceiling. ■ *Open only for the sale of sweets made by the nuns.* One of the city's most notable churches is **Santo Domingo** (1548). Its fine façade has triple Roman arches and Byzantine towers. ■ *Daily 0700-0800.*

To the north of Parque Sucre, on the corner of Portal de la Unión and Asamblea, are the **Casonas de los Marqueses de Mozobamba y del Pozo**, also called Velarde-Alvarez. **Casa Jaúregui** is situated opposite the church of La Merced, and **Casa Olano** is in C De la Compañía. On the 5th block of Jr Grau, before San Blas, is the house where Simón Bolívar and José Antonio de Sucre stayed. On the 5th block of 28 de Julio is **Casona Vivanco**, which now houses the **Museo Andrés A Cáceres**, displaying prehispanic, colonial, republican and contemporary art, as well exhibits on Mariscal Cáceres' battles in the War of the Pacific. ■ *Mon-Sat 0900-1230, 1400-1700, US$0.45.*

Museo Arqueológico Hipólito Unanue is opposite the University Residences, on Av Independencia, at the north end of town. It has many Huari artefacts and a small museum of printing and art. ■ *Mon-Fri 0800-1300, 1500-1700, Sat 0900-1300, US$0.75.*

Excursions The Inca ruins of **Vilcashuamán** are to the south, beyond Cangallo. John Hemming writes: "There is a five-tiered, stepped *usnu* platform faced in fine Inca masonry and topped by a monolithic two-seat throne. The parish church is built in part of the Inca sun temple and rests on stretches of Inca terracing. Vilcashuamán was an important provincial capital, the crossroads where the road from Cusco to the Pacific met the empire's north-south highway." Tours can be arranged with Travel Agencies in Ayacucho, US$13 per person, full day tour (0500-1800), including **Intihuatana** (Inca baths about one hour uphill from the village of Vischongo, one hour from Vilcashuamán, five from Ayacucho, also Puya Raimondi plants); alternatively stay overnight (three hotels, **G**, basic but clean). Market day is Wednesday. ■ *Buses and colectivos run from Av M Castilla, daily at 0400, 5-6 hrs, US$3.*

La Quinua village, 37 km northeast of Ayacucho, has a charming cobbled main plaza and many of the buildings have been restored. There is a small market on Sunday. Nearby, on the Pampa de Quinua, a 44 m-high obelisk commemorates the battle of Ayacucho. There is also a small, poorly displayed museum; US$1.40. The village's handicrafts are recommended, especially ceramics. Most of the houses have miniature ceramic churches on the roof. San Pedro Ceramics, at the foot of the hill leading to the monument, and Mamerto Sánchez, Jr Sucre, should be visited. *Fiesta de la Virgen de Cocharcas*, 7-8 September. It is a beautiful 18 km walk downhill from La Quinua to Huari, where trucks leave for Ayacucho until about 1700.

A good road going north from Ayacucho leads to **Huari**, dating from the 'Middle Horizon', when the Huari culture spread across most of Peru. This was the first urban walled centre in the Andes. The huge irregular stone walls are up to 12 m high and rectangular houses and streets can be made out. The most important activity here was artistic: ceramics, gold, silver, metal and alloys such as bronze, which was used for weapons and for decorative objects. The ruins now lie in an extensive *tuna* cactus forest. There is a museum at the site. ■ *Buses leave from Ovalo in Barrio Magdalena when full, from 0700 onwards. Buses go on to La Quinua, US$1, and Huanta, US$1.35 (see below). Trips can be arranged to Huari, La Quinua village and the battlefield; US$16-17 pp for 2 people (see Tour operators below).*

The Huanta valley is a picturesque region, 48 km northeast of Ayacucho. The town of Huanta is one hour from Ayacucho, on the road to Huancayo. From Huanta, several lakes can be visited (difficult in rainy season), also the valley of Luricocha, 5 km away, with its warm climate. Huanta celebrates the *Fiesta de las Cruces* during the first week of May. Its Sunday market is large and interesting. **E** *La Posada del Marqués*, Sáenz Peña 160, T831022, colonial, quiet, helpful, welcomes cyclists; **F** *Hospedaje Huanta*, Santillana 437, T832908, warm water, OK; good food at *Central* and *El Patio*, on Plaza de Armas.

On the road to Huanta 24 km from Ayacucho, is the site of perhaps the oldest known culture in South America, 20,000 years old, evidence of which was found in the cave of **Pikimachay**. The remains are now in Lima's museums.

AL *Plaza*, 9 de Diciembre 184, T814461, 812340. Beautiful colonial building but the rooms don't match up to the palatial splendour of the reception, comfortable, TV, some rooms overlook the plaza. **C** *Hostelería Santa Rosa*, Jr Lima 166, T814614. Lovely colonial court-yard, roof terrace (ask for room 40 at the top), hot water, car park, restaurant. Recommended. **D** *Colmena*, Jr Cusco 140, T812146. **E** without bath (poorer rooms), hot water 0700-0900, small rooms, secure, pleasant courtyard. **D** *Florida*, Jr Cusco 310, T812565, F816029. Small, pleasant, quiet, patio with flowers, TV, hot water in morning and on request. **D** *Hostal 3 Máscaras*, Jr 3 Máscaras 194, T814107. New rooms with bath better than the old ones with-out, nice colonial building with patio, hot water 0600-1100, car park. **D** *Samary*, Jr Callao 335, T/F812442. Discount for longer stay, safe, hot water in mornings, parking.

Sleeping

Ayacucho suffers from water shortages. There is usually no water between 0900 and 1500. Many hotels have their own water tanks

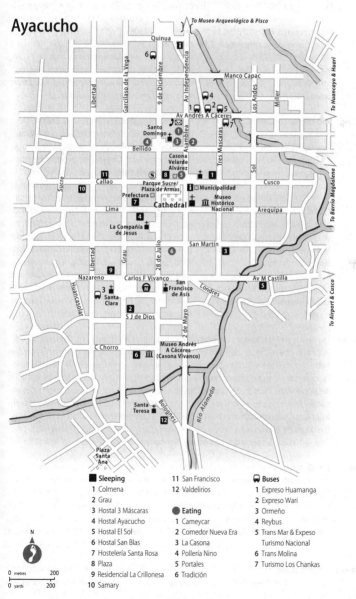

Ayacucho

Peru

Sleeping	Eating	Buses
1 Colmena	11 San Francisco	1 Expreso Huamanga
2 Grau	12 Valdelirios	2 Expreso Wari
3 Hostal 3 Máscaras		3 Ormeño
4 Hostal Ayacucho	**Eating**	4 Reybus
5 Hostal El Sol	1 Cameycar	5 Trans Mar & Expeso
6 Hostal San Blas	2 Comedor Nueva Era	Turismo Nacional
7 Hostelería Santa Rosa	3 La Casona	6 Trans Molina
8 Plaza	4 Pollería Nino	7 Turismo Los Chankas
9 Residencial La Crillonesa	5 Portales	
10 Samary	6 Tradición	

N

0 metres 200
0 yards 200

Recommended. **D** *San Francisco*, Jr Callao 290, T912959, 814501. Includes breakfast, hot water, comfortable, nice patio. Recommended. **D** *Valdelirios*, Bolognesi 520, T813908, 814014. Lovely colonial-style mansion, beautifully-furnished, pick-up from the airport for US$1.30, bar, reserve at least 24 hrs in advance. Recommended. **D** *Yáñez*, Av Cáceres 1210, T/F812464. With breakfast, cable TV, well-furnished rooms, it's a former hospital so the decor is slightly clinical. **E** *Hospedaje Central*, Av Cáceres 1048. Rooms without bath and TV are **F**, large rooms, hot water, good value. **E** *Residencial La Crillonesa*, Nazareno 165, T812350. **F** with shared bath, hot water, laundry facilities, discount for longer stay, great views from roof terrace. **E** *La Posada de Santa Inés*, Jr Chorro 139, T811670/819544. Hot water, TV, terrace with small swimming pool (ask in advance for it to be cleaned), good value. **E** *Hostal San Blas*, Jr Chorro 167, T814185/812712. Hot water, laundry facilities, nice rooms, cheap meals available, discount for longer stay, Carlos will act as a local tour guide and knows everyone. Recommended. **E** *Hostal Wari*, Mcal Cáceres 836, T813065. **F** with shared bath, hot water in the morning, basic, large rooms. **F** *Hostal El Sol*, Av Mcal Castilla 132, T813069. Hot water 0800-1000, 2000-2200, **G** in rooms with cold water, well-furnished large rooms. Recommended. **F** pp *Grau*, Jr San Juan de Dios 192, T812695. Rooms on 2nd floor are new, with bath (**G**), hot water, laundry facilities, good value, safe but noisy. Recommended. **F** *Guzmán*, Cusco 239, T816262. Small rooms, hot water, good restaurant, helpful owner.

Eating *Mid-range*: *La Casona*, Jr Bellido 463. Regional specialities. Recommended. *Lalo's Café*, Jr Lima 164. Open 0900-1300, 1600-2230 for coffee, teas, cakes, sandwiches and pizza. *Nino*, Jr Salvador Cavero 124. Recommended for local dishes. *Portales*, on plaza, Portal Unión. Popular. *Tradición*, San Martín 406. Popular, good cheap *menú*. **Cheap**: *Cameycar*, Jr Asamblea 261. Popular, good set menu. *Recreo Turístico Don Manuel*, Garcilaso 270. Open 0900 till late, they only serve *chicharrón, trucha* (trout) and *qapchi* (potato with *ají* and grated cheese), very good. *Café Dorado*, Jr Asamblea 310. Excellent value set menu in a pleasant setting. *Kutimuy*, Jr 28 de Julio 356, opposite police station. Looks like a copy shop, but serves good big breakfasts. *Mia Pizza*, San Martín, near *Tradición*. Good Italian meals. *Pollería Nino*, Jr 9 de Diciembre 205, opposite Santo Domingo church. Recommended for chicken. *Comedor Nueva Era*, Asamblea 204, 4th floor. Vegetarian, Mon-Sat 0700-2100, good. *Fuente de Soda María Auxiliadora*, 28 de Julio 151. Good for juices, cakes and snacks. Good bakery at Asamblea 237. Try *mondongo*, a soup made from meat, maize and mint, at the market near Santa Clara on Jr Carlos Vivanco. Sra Gallardo has been recommended. **Bars** *La Rumana Pizza Video Pub*, Cáceres 1045. Pizzas, drinks and music videos, if there aren't many customers the owner may let you rent a video to watch on the big screen, good sound.

Those wishing to try cuy should do so in Ayacucho as it's a lot cheaper than Cusco

Festivals The area is well-known for its festivals throughout the year. Almost every day there is a celebration in one of the surrounding villages. Check with the Ministry of Tourism. *Carnival* in **Feb** is reported as a wild affair. *Semana Santa* begins on the Fri before Holy Week. There follows one of the world's finest Holy Week celebrations, with candle-lit nightly processions, floral 'paintings' on the streets, daily fairs (the biggest on Easter Saturday), horse races and contests among peoples from all central Peru. All accommodation is fully booked for months in advance. Many people offer beds in their homes during the week. Look out for notices on the doors, especially on Jr Libertad. **25 Apr:** anniversary of the founding of Huamanga province. **4-10 Dec:** *Semana de la Libertad Americana*, to honour the Battle of Ayacucho.

Shopping **Handicrafts** Ayacucho is a good place to buy local crafts including filigree silver, which often uses *mudéjar* patterns. Also look out for little painted altars which show the manger scene, carvings in local alabaster, harps, or the pre-Inca tradition of carving dried gourds. The most famous goods are carpets and *retablos*. In both weaving and *retablos*, scenes of recent political strife have been added to more traditional motifs. For carpets, go to Barrio Santa Ana, *Familia Sulca*, Jr Mcal Cáceres 302 (see under Sights above); or *Familia Fernández*. In Barrio Belén, *Familia Pizarro*, Jr San Cristóbal 215, works in textiles and *piedra huamanga* (local alabaster), good quality.

Tour operators *ExplorMundo*, Jr 9 de Diciembre, T819518/812439, Explormundo@terra.com.pe Local tours with *Wari Tours*, Portal Independencia 70, T813115. Also handles Ormeño bus tickets and Western Union. Also *Urpillay Tours*, Portal Independencia 62. *Willy Tours*, Jr 9 de Diciembre 107, T812568, F814075.

Transport

Buses To **Lima**, 9-10 hrs on a good new paved road, via Ica (7 hrs). For **Pisco**, 332 km, 6 hrs, take a Ica/Lima bus and get out at San Clemente, 10 mins from Pisco, and take a bus or combi (same fare to San Clemente as for Ica). Companies include: *TransMar*, Av Mcal Cáceres 896; *Reybus*, Pasaje Cáceres 150; *Turismo Los Chankas*, Av Mcal Cáceres, opposite *Expreso Turismo Nacional*, which is at No 884. Average fare on these companies is US$5.80. More expensive are *Trans Molina*, Jr 9 de Diciembre 458-9, T812984, new terminal, US$8.70-11.60 (2 a day to Pisco, US$5.75-7.15); *Ormeño*, Jr Libertad, same block as Santa Clara, US$7.20; and *Cruz del Sur*, Av Mcal Cáceres 1264, US$11.60-14.40. To **Huancayo**, 319 km, 8-10 hrs, US$8. Daily with *Trans Molina*, 3 a day, and *Lobato* and *Antezana* (Av Manco Cápac 273), 1 each at night. The road is paved as far as Huanta, thereafter it is rough, especially in the wet season, but the views are breathtaking. For **Huancavelica**, *Ticllas*, 1700 daily, US$5, 7 hrs; *Expreso Turismo Nacional*, direct at 0630 daily, US$5.

To **Andahuaylas**, 261 km, 10 hrs (more in the rainy season). *Molina* 3 a day, *Wari* at 0500, both US$7.20, and *Expreso Turismo Nacional*, 0500, 1900, US$6, also *Los Chankas* (sometimes combines with *Turismo Nacional*). The first 3 continue to **Abancay**, a further 138 km, 6 hrs, US$9.30 from Ayacucho (US$8.65 with *Expreso Turismo Nacional*, only the 0500 bus continues), and **Cusco**, a further 195 km, 5 hrs, US$14.40. It takes 24 hrs to Cusco. There are no direct buses. Road conditions are terrible, and landslides a common occurrence in the wet season. The scenery, though, is stunning and makes up for it.

Directory

Banks *Banco de Crédito*, Callao, on Plaza de Armas, no commission on TCs, cash advance on Visa, Visa ATM. *Interbank*, opposite *Hotel Plaza* on Jr 9 de Diciembre. Opening hours 0915-1315, 1630-1830, Sat 0930-1230. Many street changers at Portal Constitución on Plaza, good rate for cash. *Casa de Cambio DMJ*, at Portal Constitución 4, good rates for cash, TCs at 1% commission, open Mon-Sat 0800-1900. **Communications** Internet: At Jr Lima 114, another next door. Others on Asamblea. Connections and machines are good, average price is US$0.60 per hr, some charge US$0.90 at night. All open 0800-2300 daily. **Post Office and Telephone:** Asamblea 293. **Tourist offices** Oficina de Información Turística de la Municipalidad Provincial de Huamanga, Portal Municipal 48, on the Plaza. Open Mon-Sat and holidays 0730-1800. **Dirección Rregional de Turismo** (DRITINCI), Asamblea 481, T812548. Open Mon-Fri 0800-1300, friendly and helpful. **Tourist Police**, Dos de Mayo y Arequipa.

Ayacucho to Cusco

The road towards Cusco goes through **Chincheros**, 158 km from Ayacucho and three hours from Andahuaylas. It's a picturesque town and a nice place to break the Andahuaylas-Ayacucho trip. Ask for the bakery with its outdoor oven. About 15 minutes from Chincheros, on the road from Andahuaylas, is Uripa with a good Sunday market. *Micros* regularly run between the two towns. There are a few hotels (F); also **G** *Hostal Zárate* in Uripa. ■ *A bus leaves for Ayacucho at 0400 and 1300. You may be able to hitch a lift with one of the trucks, if you're up before daybreak.*

Andahuaylas is 94 km further on, in a fertile valley. It offers few exotic crafts, poor transport, but beautiful scenery, great hospitality and a good market on Sunday. A large part of the town centre has electricity. The **tourist police** have an office on Av Perú. Some hotels have signs telling visitors to register with the tourist police, so that they know who is travelling in the area should a bus accident occur. Few people register, though. **Sleeping and eating D** *El Encanto de Oro*, Av Pedro Casafranca 424, T723066, F722555. Breakfast included, TV, hot water, laundry service, restaurant, organizes trips on request. **D** *Sol de Oro*, Jr Juan A Trelles 164, T721152/722815. Includes breakfast, hot water, TV, laundry service, restaurant. **D** *Turístico Andahuaylas*, Av Lázaro Carrillo 620, T721229. Hot water. **D** pp *Las Américas*, Jr Ramos. Hot water in the morning and on request, a bit run down. Recommended. **F** *Wari*, Ramos 427. Cold showers but clean. **G** *Hostal Waliman*, Av Andahuaylas 266, near where the buses leave for Cusco. Basic, cold water.

■ *Getting there: Daily buses to Ayacucho, a minimum of 10 very rough hours, US$7.20; Molina at 0700, 1100, 1500, and Wari at 0700; Expreso Turismo Nacional at 0800, 1000 and 1900, and Turismo Los Chankas at 0620, 0630 and 1900, both*

Peru

US$5.75. Molina *and* Wari's *Ayacucho buses continue to Lima, US$14.40. To Abancay, in addition to those on the Ayacucho-Cusco route (see above),* Señor de Huanca *at 0600, 1300 and 2000 daily, 6 hrs, US$4.30. To Cusco, in addition to those on the Ayacucho-Cusco route,* San Jerónimo, *via Abancay, 0630, US$7.20 (same price as* Molina, Wari *charges US$5.75). On all night buses, take a blanket.*

Nestled between mountains in the upper reaches of a glacial valley, the friendly town of **Abancay** (Phone code: 084) is first glimpsed when you are 62 km away. There is a petrol station. **B** *Hotel de Turismo Abancay*, Av Díaz Barcenas 500, T321017 (Cusco, 223339), old-fashioned house, overpriced, run down, poor hot water supply, but it does have internet, camping permitted US$3. There are various other hotels: **D-F** *Imperial*, Díaz Barcenas 517, T321578, great beds and hot water, spotless, helpful, parking. **F** *El Dorado*, Av Arenas 131-C, T322005, is good. *Elena*, on the same street as the bus companies, is a good place to eat. At Av Arena 170 is the restaurant of José (Pepe) Molero Ruiz, T684397, pepe_19g@yahoo.com He is knowledgeable about the area and encouraging all forms of tourism to sites near and farther afield.

■ *Several bus companies leave for Cusco (departing from Av Arenas near the market), Andahuaylas, Ayacucho, and Nasca on the Panamericana Sur, 464 km, via Chalhuanca and Puquío, continuing to Lima. All buses on the Lima-Nasca-Cusco route pass through Abancay at about midnight. Similarly, buses on the Ayacucho-Cusco route pass through Abancay 15 hrs after leaving Ayacucho, 10 hrs after Andahuaylas.* Señor de Huanca *runs between Abancay and Andahuaylas, leaving Abancay at 0600, 1300, 2000. The journey Abancay-Cusco takes 5 hrs, US$4.30. The scenery is dramatic, especially as it descends into the Apurímac valley and climbs out again. There is a checkpoint at the Apurímac border. Coming from Cusco, after the pass it takes an hour to zig-zag down to Abancay. See page 1254 for sites of interest between Abancay and Cusco. Buses from Cusco en route either to Andahuaylas/Ayacucho or Nasca/Lima leave Abancay 5-5½ hrs after departing from Cusco.*

East of La Oroya

Tarma
Colour map 3, grid C3
Population: 105,200
Altitude: 3,050 m
60 km from La Oroya

Founded in 1538, Tarma is now growing, with garish modern buildings, but still has a lot of charm. The Semana Santa celebrations are spectacular, with a very colourful Easter Sunday morning procession in the main plaza. Accommodation is hard to find at this time, but you can apply to the Municipalidad for rooms with local families. The town is also notable for its locally made fine flower-carpets. Good, friendly market around C Amazonas and Ucayali. The surrounding countryside is beautiful.

Excursions 8 km from Tarma, the small hillside town of **Acobamba** has fine *tapices* made in San Pedro de Cajas which depict the Crucifixion. **E** *Hotel Sumaq*, Chanchamayo 650, T341109, hot water, TV, good value. There are festivities during May. 2 km up beyond the town is the futuristic **Santuario de Muruhuay**, with a venerated picture painted on the rock behind the altar. **C** *Hostal Campestre Auberge Normandie*, beside the Sanctuary, T341028, or Lima 349 5440, hostalnormandie@yahoo.com 16 cabins with hot water, TV, bar, restaurant, fine views over the valley. ■ *Colectivos and yellow Canary buses from Tarma to Acobamba and up to Muruhuay every 10-20 mins, US$0.25.*

Sleeping and eating **AL** *Los Portales*, Av Castilla 512, T321411, F321410 (in Lima T421 7220). Out of town, hot water, heating, quiet, includes breakfast, good restaurant. **A** *La Florida*, 6 km from Tarma, T341041, F341358, kreida@yahoo.com (for reservations T Lima 344 1358). 18th-century, working hacienda, with hot water, includes breakfast, owned by German-Peruvian couple Inge and Pepe who arrange excursions. Highly recommended. Also camping for US$3. **D** *Hostal Internacional*, Dos de Mayo 307, T321830. With hot water in afternoon. **E** *Albania*, Amazonas 435. Small rooms, hot water. **E** *Hostal Central*, Huánuco 614, T321198. Shared bath, hot water, laundry facilities, a bit rundown but popular, has an observatory which opens Fri at 2000. **E** *La Colmena*, Jauja 618, T321157. Old building, convenient for Huancayo buses. **F** *Hostal Bolívar*, Huaraz 389, T321060. Old building, shared showers, hot water. Recommended. **F** *Hostal El Dorado*, Huánuco 488, T321598. Hot water, **G** without bath, rooms set round a patio, first floor rooms better, reasonable. *La Grima*, beneath Hostal Galaxia, on Plaza de Armas. Recommended for trout. *La Cabaña de Bryan*, Paucartambo 450. Good for meat dishes.*Lo Mejorcito de Tarma*, Huánuco 190, T320685. Good set menú US$1.50, local specialities, also has tourist information. Recommended. *El Sabor Criollo*, Huaraz y Callao. Local restaurant, cheap. *Señorial/Pollería Braserita*, Huánuco 138. Good *menú*. There are also several places on Lima, including a vegetarian. The *manjarblanco* of Tarma is famous, as well as *pachamanca, mondongo* and *picante de cuyes*. A good place to buy local produce is *El Tarmenito*, Lima 149.

Transport Buses to Lima, 231 km (paved), 6 hrs, US$4. *Transportes Chanchamayo*, Callao 1002, T321882, recommended, 3 a day, en route from Chanchamayo; *Turismo Imperial*, Callao 960, 4 a day, also coming from Chanchamayo. *Canary Tours* (0930 and 2130), *Transportes Sr de Muruhuay* (several daily) start in Tarma. To **Jauja** and **Huancayo**, *Transportes San Juan*, from the stadium hourly on the half hour, buses coming from Chanchamayo; *Canary Tours*, advertised as hourly but leave when full, 0500-2200, to Jauja 2 hrs, US$2. All buses continue to Huancayo, 3 hrs, US$2.50. Colectivos depart when full from Callao y Jauja, 2 hrs, US$4, and 3 hrs, US$6, respectively. To **Cerro de Pasco**, *Empresa Junín*, Amazonas 450, 4 a day, 3 hrs, US$2.50. also colectivos when full, 2 hrs, US$4. Buses to **La Oroya** leave from opposite the petrol station on Av Castilla block 5, 1 hr, US$1.25, while colectivos leave from the petrol station itself, 45 mins, US$2. To **Chanchamayo**, *Transportes San Juan* from the stadium every hour on the half hour, 1½ hrs, US$1.50 to San Ramón, and 2 hrs, US$2 to La Merced. Also, colectivos, 1-1¼ hrs, US$3 and US$3.50 respectively.

Directory **Banks** *Banco de Crédito*, Lima 407, changes Amex TCs. **Communications** Internet: Internet offices at Perené 292 and Paucartambo 632. **Telephone:** on the Plaza de Armas. **Tourist office** 2 de Mayo 775 on the Plaza, T321010, very helpful. Open Mon-Fri 0800-1300, 1600-1800, www.geocities.com/colqui_i/dos/htm

Beyond Tarma the road is steep and crooked but there are few places where cars cannot pass one another. In the 80 km between Tarma and La Merced the road, passing by great overhanging cliffs, drops 2,450 m and the vegetation changes dramatically from temperate to tropical. This is a really beautiful run.

The towns of San Ramón and La Merced are collectively known as **Chanchamayo** (*Population*: 7,000). **San Ramón** is 11 km before La Merced and has several hotels (**B-F**) and restaurants. Regular colectivos between the two towns, 15 minutes, US$0.25. ■ *Transport Air: flights leave from San Ramón. There is an 'air-colectivo' service to Puerto Bermúdez, 10 kg baggage allowance, US$5 per kg of excess luggage. The service continues to Atalaya, Satipo, Puerto Inca and Pucallpa. Air-colectivos go to Lima and to most places in the jungle region where there is an airstrip. Flights are cheap but irregular, and depend on technical factors, weather and goodwill.*

La Merced (*Population*: 15,000), lies in the fertile Chanchamayo valley. Campa Indians can usually be found around the central plaza selling bows, arrows, necklaces and trinkets. There is a festival in the last week of September. There are several hotels (**C-F**) and restaurants. ■ *Many buses go here from Lima:* Transportes Chanchamayo *is the best, also* Expreso Satipo; *7½ hrs, US$6.50. Also many buses from Tarma, US$2, 2½ hrs. To Puerto Bermúdez, 8 hrs, US$10, at 0330, 0430 with* Transdife *bus/truck, also* Fisel *buses, 0400.*

About 22 km north from La Merced is **San Luis de Shuaro**, from where the road has been extended over an intervening mountain range. A turn-off east leads to **Puerto Bermúdez** (**F** *Albergue Humboldt*, by the Río Pachitea at La Rampa, good, electricity 1800-2330, rooms, hammocks or tents, library, laundry, gardens, meals US$5 extra, Spanish cooking, T Lima 427 9196/428 5546, Humboldt49@

Peru

hotmail.com **F** *Hostal Tania*, opposite dock where motorized canoes tie up, clean; eating house opposite the airstrip). This is a great base for exploring further into the San Matías/San Carlos national reserve in the Selva Central Peruana, with trips upriver to the Ashininka communities. Tours arranged by *Albergue Humboldt* cost US$18-28 a day, depending on group size. Boat passages possible from passing traders. ■ *Getting there: to get to Pucallpa, there is transport via Puerto Palcazu, US$10.*

North of La Oroya

A paved road runs 130 km north from La Oroya to Cerro de Pasco. It runs up the Mantaro valley through narrow canyons to the wet and mournful Junín pampa at over 4,250 m, one of the world's largest high-altitude plains. An obelisk marks the battlefield where the Peruvians under Bolívar defeated the Spaniards in 1824. Blue peaks line the pampa in a distant wall. This windswept sheet of yellow grass is bitterly cold and the only signs of life are the youthful herders with their sheep and llamas. The road follows the east shores of the Lago de Junín. The town of **Junín** lies some distance south of the lake and has the somewhat desolate feel of a high puna town, bisected by the railway.

The **Lago Junín National Reserve** protects one of the best bird-watching sites in the central Andes where the giant coot and even flamingos may be spotted. It is easiest to visit from the village of Huayre, 5 km south of Carhuamayo, from which it is a 20-minute walk down to the lake. Fishermen are usually around to take visitors out on the lake. Carhuamayo is the best place to stay: *Gianmarco*, Maravillas 454, and *Patricia*, Tarapacá 862, are the best of several basic *hostales*. There are numerous restaurants along the main road.

Cerro de Pasco This long-established mining centre is not attractive, but is nevertheless very
Phone code: 064 friendly. Copper, zinc, lead, gold and silver are mined here, and coal comes from the
Population: 29,810 deep canyon of Goyllarisquisga, the 'place where a star fell', the highest coal mine in
Altitude: 4,330 m the world, 42 km north of Cerro de Pasco. The town is sited between Lago
130 km from La Oroya Patarcocha and the huge abyss of the mine above which its buildings and streets cling precariously. Nights are bitterly cold. *Banco de Crédito* is on Jr Bolognesi. Money changers can be found on Jr Bolognesi between the market and the Cathedral. A new town, San Juan de Pampa, has been built 1½ km away.

Southwest of Cerro de Pasco by 40 km is **Huayllay**, near which is the **Santuario Bosque de Piedras**, unique weathered limestone formations in the shape of a tortoise, elephant, alpaca, etc. At the Sanctuary (4,100-4,600 m), four tourist circuits through the spectacular rock formations have been laid out. ■ *Entrance fee US$1, payable only if the guides, Ernesto and Christian, are there. Camping is permitted within the Sanctuary. Take a bus from Cerro de Pasco and get off at El Cruce (Km 285). Any bus or colectivo for Carhuamayo, Junín or La Oroya can drop you there, 20 mins, US$0.50. Combis for Huallay wait at El Cruce and depart when full, about hourly, along a rough road, nearly 1 hr, US$1.*

Sleeping and eating D *Wong*, Carrión 99, T721918. Modern, hot water 24 hrs, TV, comfortable, attractive decorations. Recommended. **E** *Hostal Arenales*, Jr Arenales 162, near the bus station, T723088. Modern, TV, hot water in the morning. **E** *Welcome*, opposite the entrance to the bus station. Some rooms without window, hot water 24 hrs. **F** *El Viajero*, on the west side of the plaza, T722172. Hot water morning only. **F** *Santa Rosa*, on the north side of the plaza, T722120. Old building, large, hot water all day, basic. *Los Angeles*, Jr Libertad, near the market. Excellent *menú* for US$1.50. Recommended. *San Fernando* bakery in the plaza. Opens at 0700 for first-rate hot chocolate, bread and pastries.

Transport Buses: There is a large bus station. To **Lima** several companies including *Paraíso Tours*, 0730, 2100, *Carhuamayo* and *Transportes Apóstol San Pedro*, hourly 0800-1200, plus 4 departures 2030-2130, 8 hrs, US$4-5. If there are no convenient daytime buses, you could change buses in La Oroya. To **Carhuamayo, Junín** and **La Oroya**: buses leave when full, about every 20-30 mines, to Carhuamayo 1 hr, US$1; to Junín 1½ hrs, US$1; to La Oroya, 2½ hrs, US$2. Colectivos also depart with a similar frequency, 1½ hrs, US$2.50, to La Oroya. To **Tarma**, *Empresa Junín*, 0600, 1500, 3 hrs, $2.50. Colectivos also depart hourly, 1½ hrs, US$4. To **Huancayo**, *Transportes Javier*, 4 a day, 5 hrs, US$3.50; also *Trans Central* and *Salazar*, one each, US$4. To **Huánuco**, buses and cars leave when full, about half hourly, 2½ hrs and 1½ hrs, US$2 and US$4 respectively.

The Central Highway from Cerro de Pasco continues northeast another 528 km to Pucallpa, the limit of navigation for large Amazon river boats. The western part of this road (Cerro de Pasco-Huánuco) has been rebuilt into an all-weather highway.

The sharp descent along the nascent **Río Huallaga** is a tonic to travellers suffering from *soroche*. The road drops 2,436 m in the 100 km from Cerro de Pasco to Huánuco, and most of it is in the first 32 km. From the bleak high ranges the road plunges below the tree line offering great views. The only town of any size before Huánuco is **Ambo**.

NB The Huallaga valley is the country's main coca-growing area, with both drug-trafficking and guerrilla activity. The main centre of activity is between Tingo María and Tarapoto, so it is best to avoid the region at present. It does appear to be safe to visit Tingo María and Pucallpa, but as the area is under military control there are many checkpoints. Travelling during the day is advised and seek full information before going. (Huánuco and Tarapoto are safe to visit.)

Huánuco

This is an attractive Andean town on the Upper Huallaga with an interesting market. The two churches of **San Cristóbal** and **San Francisco** have both been much restored. The latter has some 16th-century paintings. The natural history museum, which claims to have 10,000 exhibits, is at Gen Prado 495, **Museo de Ciencias**. ■ *Mon-Fri 0900-1200, 1500-1800, Sat-Sun 1000-1200, US$0.50.*

Phone code: 064
Colour map 3, grid B3
Population: 118,814
Altitude: 1,894 m

About 5 km away on the road west to La Unión is **Kotosh** (*altitude:* 1,812 m), the Temple of Crossed Hands, the earliest evidence of a complex society and of pottery in Peru, dating from 2000 BC. ■ *US$0.75, including a guide (in Spanish) around a marked circuit which also passes through a small botanical garden of desert plants. Beware of the vicious black flies. Taxi US$5 from the centre, with 30 mins' wait.*

B *Gran Hotel Huánuco*, Jr D Beraun 775, T514222, F512410. Restaurant, pool, sauna, gym, parking. Recommended. **D** *Hostal Caribe*, Huánuco 546, T513645, F513753, and adjoining it **D** *Hostal Marino*, large modern hotels with big rooms, TV, as is **D** *Hostal Quintito*, 2 de Mayo 987. **D** *Cusco*, Huánuco 616, 2 blocks from the Plaza de Armas, T 513578, F514825. TV, cafetería, OK (couples using one bed only are charged single rate **E**). **E** *Hostal Residencial Huánuco*, Jr Huánuco, near the Plaza de Armas. Hot water, garden, use of kitchen, laundry facilities. Highly recommended. **E** *Las Vegas*, 28 de Julio 936, on Plaza de Armas, T/F512315. Small rooms, hot water, TV. Recommended. **E** *Hostal Miraflores*, Valdizan 564. Hot water, TV, quiet. **F** *El Roble*, Constitución 629. Slightly cheaper without bath, good value. **F** *Imperial*, Huánuco 581. With cold shower (intermittent water), reasonable value, quiet. *La Casona de Gladys*, Gen Prado 908, good, cheap local food. *La Casona*, Ayacucho 750, overlooking Plaza Santo Domingo. Specialises in anticuchos and steaks. Recommended. *Rinconcito Huanuqueño*, 2 de Mayo 175. Good cheap, local food. *Pizzería Don Sancho*, Prado 645. Best pizzas in town. There are vegetarian restaurants and cafés at Abtao 897, 2 de Mayo 751 and Prado 840. Good *chifas* on Beraun block 6. *Café Perú*, on the south side of the main plaza, is a traditional café serving good coffee, *humitas* and *tamales*. Highly recommended for breakfast.

Sleeping & eating

20-25 Jan: is *Carnaval Huanuqueño*. **3 May:** *La Cruz de Mayo*. **16 Jul:** *Fiesta de la Virgen del Carmen*. **12-18 Aug:** Tourist Week in Huánuco. **28-29 Oct:** *Fiesta del Rey y del Señor de Burgos*, the patron of Huánuco. **25 Dec:** *Fiesta de los Negritos*.

Festivals

Peru

Transport **Air** From **Lima**, *Aerocóndor*, Tue, Thu, Sat, 50 mins. There are connecting flights to Tingo María, Tocache, Juanjui, Pucallpa, Saposoa and other jungle towns. Check all flight details in advance. Flights may be cancelled in the rains or if not full.

    Buses To **Lima**, US$7-10, 8-10 hrs depending on the service (some are luxury). *León de Huánuco*, Malecón Alomía Robles 821 (28 de Julio 1520, La Victoria, Lima). Also *Etposa*, Valdizan block 7, *Transportes El Rey*, 28 de Julio 1201 (28 de Julio 1192, La Victoria, Lima), and *Trans G & M*, Tarapacá y 28 de Julio. The majority of buses of all companies leave 2030-2200, most also offer a bus at 0900-1000. A colectivo to Lima, costing US$20, leaves at 0400, arriving at 1400; book the night before at Gen Prado 607, 1 block from the plaza. Rec ommended. To **Cerro de Pasco**, 3 hrs, US$2, colectivos under 2 hrs, US$4. All leave when full from the Ovalo Carhuayna on the north side of the city, 3 km from the centre. To **Huancayo**, 6 hrs, US$5: *Turismo Central*, Tarapacá 530, at 2100, and *Transportes El Rey* at 2115. Colectivos run to **Tingo María**, from block 1 of Prado close to Puente Calicanto, 2½ hrs, US$5. Also *Etnasa*, 3-4 hrs, US2. For **Pucallpa**, take a colectivo to Tingo María, then a bus from there. This route has many checkpoints and robberies can occur. Travel by day and check on the current situation regarding safety. To **La Unión**, *Transportes El Niño*, Aguilar 530, colectivos, depart when full, 5 hrs, US$8. This is a rough road operated by old buses of which *Transportes Vitor*, Tarapacá 448, and *Transportes Rosario*, Tarapacá 330, 0730, 6 hrs, US$4, are the more reliable.

Directory **Banks** *Banco de Crédito*, at Dos de Mayo 1005, Visa ATM. **Communications** Internet: next to the Cathedral on the Plaza. **Post office**, block 9 of 2 de Mayo on the Plaza. Open 0800-2000 Mon-Sat, 0800-1400 Sun. **Telephone**: at 28 de Julio 1157. **Tourist offices** Gen Prado 716, on the Plaza de Armas. A good contact for adventure tours is *César Antezana*, Jr Pedro Puelles 261, T513622. A website giving local information is www.webhuanuco.com

From Huánuco, a spectacular but very poor dirt road leads to **La Unión**, capital of Dos de Mayo district. It's a friendly, fast developing town with a couple of hotels (**F**) and restaurants, but electricity can be a problem and it gets very cold at night. On the pampa above La Unión are the Inca ruins of **Huánuco Viejo**, a 2½ hour walk from the town, a great temple-fortress with residential quarters.

    Transport To Huánuco: *El Niño* colectivos, Jr Comercio 12, T064-515952, 5 hrs, US$8; bus companies leave at 0630, 5-6 hrs, US$4. To the Callejón de Huaylas there is reportedly a direct La Unión-Huaraz bus, 6 hrs, US$2. Alternatively go to **Huallanca (Huánuco)** (see Sleeping below): combis leave from the market, about half hourly, when full and follow the attractive Vizcarra valley, 1 hr, US$0.75. Then go to Pachacoto, 1 hr south of Huaraz. Alternatively, take a bus on the La Unión-Chiquián- Lima route and change at Chiquián or at the Conococha cross-roads, but check times to avoid being stranded in the dark. Huallanca is an attractive town, with mining projects nearby; **D** *Hotel Milán*, 28 de Julio 107, modern, TV and hot water in all rooms, best in town, good restaurant. **F** *Hostal Yesica*, L Prado 507, hot water, shared bathroom, the best of the basic ones. Check local political conditions before taking this route.

Amazon Basin

Cooled by winds sweeping down from the Andes but warmed by its jungle blanket, this region contains some of the most important tropical flora and fauna in the world. In the north of the region, Iquitos, on the Amazon itself, is the centre of jungle exploration. In southeastern Peru, the Manu Biosphere Reserve is reached by a short flight or a long road trip from Cusco, while the frontier town, Puerto Maldonado, only a 30-minute flight from Cusco, is the starting point for expeditions to one of the national parks at Tambopata or Heath.

It is a very varied landscape, with grasslands and tablelands of scrub-like vegetation, inaccessible swamps, and forests up to 2,000 m above sea level. The principal means of communication in the jungle is by its many rivers, the most important being the Amazon, which rises high up in the Andes as the Marañón, then joins the Ucayali to become the longest river in the world.

The journey to Tingo María from Huánuco, 135 km, is very dusty but gives a good view of the jungle. Some 25 km beyond Huánuco the road begins a sharp climb to the heights of Carpish (3,023 m). A descent of 58 km brings it to the Huallaga River again; it then continues along the river to Tingo María. The road is paved from Huánuco to Tingo María, including a tunnel through the Carpish hills. Landslides along this section are frequent and construction work causes delays. Although this route is reported to be relatively free from terrorism, robberies do occur and it is advisable to travel only by day.

Tingo María

Situated on the middle Huallaga, in the Ceja de Montaña, on the edge (literally 'eyebrow') of the mountains, Tingo María is isolated for days in the rainy season. The altitude prevents the climate from being oppressive. The Cordillera Azul, the front range of the Andes, covered with jungle-like vegetation to its top, separates it from the jungle lowlands to the east. The mountain which can be seen from all over the town is called La Bella Durmiente, the Sleeping Beauty. The meeting here of highlands and jungle makes the landscape extremely striking. Bananas, sugar cane, cocoa, rubber, tea and coffee are grown. The main crop of the area, though, is coca, grown on the *chacras* (smallholdings) in the countryside, and sold legitimately and otherwise in Tingo María.

Phone code: 064
Colour map 3, grid B2
Population: 20,560
Altitude: 655 m
Annual rainfall:
2,642 mm
This is a main narco-trafficking centre and although the town is generally safe, it is not safe to leave it at night. Always keep to the main routes

Peru

A small university outside the town, beyond the *Hotel Madera Verde*, has a little museum-cum-zoo; it also maintains botanical gardens in the town. ■ *Free but a small tip would help to keep things in order*. About 6½ km from Tingo, on a rough road, is a fascinating cave, the **Cueva de las Lechuzas**. There are many oilbirds in the cave and many small parakeets near the entrance. ■ *US$1.50 for the cave. Take a torch, and do not wear open shoes. Getting there: take a motorcycle-taxi from town, US$1.75; cross the Río Monzón by new bridge.*

Sleeping & eating

Hotels are often fully booked

A *Madera Verde*, Av Universitaria s/n, some way out of town on the road to Huánuco, near the University, T/F561800/562047 (in Lima Jr Colina 327, Miraflores, T445 4024, F445 9005) maverde@terra.com.pe Chalets in beautiful surroundings, with and without bath, restaurant, swimming pool. **E** *Hostal Marco Antonio*, Jr Monzón 364, T562201. Quiet, restaurant of the same name next door. **E** *Nueva York*, Av Alameda Perú 553, T562406. Cheaper without bath and TV, laundry, good value, restaurant. **F** *La Cabaña*, Raimondi 600 block. Fairly clean, good restaurant. **F** *Viena*, Jr Lamas. Good value. *El Antojito 2*, Jr Chiclayo 458, good local food. *Girasol*, Av Raimondi 253, T562065. Chicken, burgers, cakes and fruit juices.

Tour operators

Tingo María Travel Tours, Av Raimondi 460, T562501. For local excursions.

Transport

Watch out for thieves around the buses and do not leave luggage on the bus if you get off

Buses To **Huánuco**, 119 km, 3-4 hrs, US$2 with *Etnasa*; several micros daily and colectivos, US$5, 2 hrs. Direct buses continue to Lima, 12 hrs, with *Trans Rey*, US$15 *bus cama*, **León de Huánuco** and *Transmar*, US$11. To **Pucallpa**, 255 km, 12 hrs, US$5.50. Many of the big bus companies pass through Tingo María on their way to **Pucallpa**, from Lima, in the middle of the night. *Ucayali Express* colectivos leave from Raimondi y Callao. There are other colectivos and taxis, which all leave in the early morning in convoy.

North to Yurimaguas

The Río Huallaga winds northwards for 930 km. The Upper Huallaga is a torrent, dropping 15.8 m per km between its source and Tingo María. The Lower Huallaga moves through an enervation of flatness, with its main port, Yurimaguas, below the last rapids and only 150 m above the Atlantic Ocean, yet distant from that ocean by over a month's voyage. Between the Upper and Lower lies the Middle Huallaga: the third of the river which is downstream from Tingo María and upstream from Yurimaguas.

Yurimaguas

Phone code: 094
Colour map 3, grid A2
Population: 25,700

The Yurimaguas region was affected by guerrilla activity and anti-narcotics operations in the recent past. Seek the latest advice before going off the beaten track

Down-river of Tingo María, beyond Bellavista, the orientation is towards **Yurimaguas**, which is connected by road with the Pacific coast, via Tarapoto and Moyobamba (see page 1165). The town has a fine church of the Passionist Fathers, based on the Cathedral of Burgos, in Spain. A colourful market is held from 0600-0800, full of fruit and animals. Interesting excursions in the area include the gorge of Shanusi and the lakes of Mushuyacu and Sanango. To organize tours, go to the Municipalidad and ask for Jorge or Samuel (who speaks English). They can take visitors to meet people in the region, for instance the villages of Balsapuerto (70 km west) and Puerto Libre. Mopeds can be hired for US$2.35 per hour, including fuel. There is an *Interbank* or travel agents which charge poor rates and an internet cafe on Plaza de Armas, US$1.70 per hour. Tourist information is available from the Consejo Regional building on the main plaza. **Sleeping E** *Hostal Residencial El Naranjo*, Arica 318, T351560/352650, lillianarteaga@olva.com.pe or lillianarteaga@hotmail.com "The best in town," excellent value, with good restaurant. Recommended. **E** *Leo's Palace*, Plaza de Armas 104-6, good, reasonably priced, restaurant. **F** *Camus*, Manco Capac 201, no sign, cheap.

Transport To/from Tarapoto (a beautiful journey), several bus companies, 5-6 hrs, US$3.45, same price by combi; in a camioneta it costs US$5.75 up front, US$2.90 in the back. Cars charge US$7.20. By ferry to Iquitos takes two days and two nights. See General hints for river travel, page 1282. There are police inspections at each end of the trip. Fares usually include meals, US$17 for one bunk in a cabin. *Eduardo* company is best. To buy a hammock costs US$5.75-8.50 in Yurimaguas, on C Jáuregui.

The river journey to Iquitos can be broken at **Lagunas**, 12 hours from Yurimaguas. You can ask the local people to take you on a canoe trip into the jungle where you will see at very close range alligators, monkeys and a variety of birds, but only on trips of four days or so. Register with police on arrival. **Sleeping F** *Hostal La Sombra*, Jr Vásquez 1121, shared bath, basic, good food.

■ *Getting there: The* Constante *plies Yurimaguas to Lagunas 2-3 times a week (US$4.50); from there connections are difficult to Iquitos; you should confirm departures the day before by radio. Ask for details at police station on the plaza. The boats pass by the villages of Castilla and Nauta, where the Huallaga joins the Ucayali and becomes the Amazon.*

There are good jungle trips from Lagunas to the **Pacaya-Samiria Reserve**. A permit from INRENA in Lima or Iquitos is essential before going to Pacaya-Samiria. The main part of the reserve is off limits to tourists, who may only be taken to forest surrounding the reserve. Some guides penetrate Pacaya-Samiria illegally: if caught, the tourist may face stiff penalties for trespass. Do not join a tour that involves living off the land. ■ *Park entry costs US$20. Before entering the Reserve you pass through a village where you must pay US$4.50.* Trips are mostly on the river, sleeping in hammocks, and include fishing. At least 5 days is recommended to make the most of the park. Take water purifier and mosquito repellent.

Luiz and *Edinson* are recommended guides; ask for them at the *Hostal La Sombra* in Lagunas. Guides charge US$15 per day. Juan Huaycama, at Jáuregui 689, is highly recommended. Trips to Pacaya-Samiria can also be arranged in Iquitos with *Muyuna* (whose lodge is only 80 km from the reserve) and *Paseos Amazónicos*. Expeditions must be booked in advance, all equipment and food are provided.

From Tingo María to the end of the road at Pucallpa is 255 km, with a climb over the watershed – the Cordillera Azul – between the Huallaga and Ucayali rivers. The road is paved and good for 60-70 km after Tingo María and 70 km before Pucallpa. In between it is affected by mud and landslides in the rainy season. There are eight army checkpoints. When the road was being surveyed it was thought that the lowest pass over the Cordillera Azul was over 3,650 m high, but an old document stating that a Father Abad had found a pass through these mountains in 1757 was rediscovered, and the road now goes through the pass of Father Abad, a gigantic gap 4 km long and 2,000 m deep. At the top of the pass is a Peruvian Customs house; the jungle land to the east is a free zone. Coming down from the pass the road bed is along the floor of a magnificent canyon, the Boquerón Abad. It is a beautiful trip through luxuriant jungle, ferns and sheer walls of bare rock, punctuated by occasional waterfalls plunging into the roaring torrent below. East of the foot of the pass the all-weather road goes over the flat pampa, with few bends, to the village of **Aguaytía** (narcotics police checkpoint, gasoline, accommodation in the **F** *Hostal San Antonio*, clean, and two restaurants). From Aguaytía the road continues for 160 km to Pucallpa – five hours by bus. There are no service stations on the last half of the journey.

Pucallpa

Pucallpa is a rapidly expanding jungle town on the Río Ucayali, navigable by vessels of 3,000 tons from Iquitos, 533 nautical miles away. The town's newer sections have paved streets, sewers and lights, but much of the frontier atmosphere still exists. The floating ports of La Hoyada and Puerto Italia are about 5 km away and worth a visit to see the canoe traffic and open-air markets. The economy of the area includes sawmills, plywood factories, a paper mill, oil refinery, fishing and boat building. Large discoveries of oil and gas are being explored, and gold mining is underway nearby. Local festivals are February: *Carnival*. 24 June: *San Juan*. 5-20 October: Pucallpa's *Aniversario Political* and the Ucayali regional fair.

Phone code: 064
Colour map 3, grid B3
Population: 400, 000

The climate is tropical: dry during July and August; rainy October-November and February-March. The town is hot and dusty between June and November and muddy from December to May. **NB** There is much military control because of narcotics activity. The city itself is safe enough to visit, but don't travel at night.

Museo Regional, at Jr Inmaculada 999, has some good examples of Shibipo ceramics, as well as some delightful pickled snakes and other reptiles. ■ *0800-1200, 1600-1800, US$0.90.*

Excursions The Hospital Amazónico Albert Schweitzer, which serves the local Indians, is on picturesque Lake **Yarinacocha**, the main tourist attraction near Pucallpa. River dolphins can be seen in the lake. The Indian market of Moroti-Shobo ('The House of Selling and Buying') is a co-operative, organized by Shipibo-Conibo craftsmen. Fine handicrafts are sold in their shop; visit them in Yarinacocha; T571551. A good place to swim is at **San José**. Take the road out behind the power station round the lake. ■ *Yarinacocha is 20 mins by colectivo or bus from the market in Pucallpa, US$0.30, or 15 mins by taxi, US$2.*

San Francisco and **Santa Clara** can be visited at the far end of the lake on its western arm. Both are Shibipo villages still practising traditional ceramic and textile crafts. In San Francisco a nice place to spend the night is in the house of Alberto Sánchez Ríos, *Casa Artesanal Shibipo*, which is very friendly and warmly recommended. ■ *To reach these villages take one of the motorized canoes, peke-pekes, which leave from Puerto Callao when full, US$0.90.*

The beautifully located reserve, **Jardín Botánico Chullachaqui**, can be reached by boat from Puerto Callao, the port on Lake Yarinacocha, to Pueblo Nueva Luz de Fátima, 45 minutes, then one hour's walk to the garden. ■ *Free.* For information about traditional medicine contact Mateo Arevalomayna, San Francisco de Yarinacocha (president of the group Ametra; T573152, or ask at Moroti-Shobo).

Sleeping and eating in Yarinacocha: **B** *La Cabaña Lodge*, T616679, F579242. Full board, including transport to and from Yarinacocha harbour, run by Ruth and Leroy from USA, great food, jungle trips US$50 per day including boat, guide and food; next door is **B-C** pp *La Perla*, including all meals, German-Peruvian owned, English and German spoken, no electricity after 2100, good, jungle tours organized. **D-E** *Los Delfines*, T571129. With bath, fan, fridge, some with TV. **F** *El Pescador*, in Puerto Callao, cheapest in town, restaurant. There are many restaurants and bars on the waterfront and near the Plaza. *El Cucharón*, good food. *Grande Paraíso*, good view, also has a *peña* at night, popular with young people. *Orlando's*, Jr Aguaytía, good local food.

Sleeping **AL** *Sol del Oriente*, Av San Martín 552, T/F575510, www.peru-hotels.com/pucalsol.htm Pool, good restaurant. **D** *Arequipa*, Jr Progreso 573, T571348. Good. **D** *Mercedes*, Raimondi 601, T575120. Good, but noisy with good bar and restaurant attached, swimming pool. **E** *Barbtur*, Raimondi 670, T572532. **F** without bath, central, opposite the bus stop, good beds. **E** *Komby*, Ucayali 360, T57118. Comfortable, swimming pool, excellent value. **E** *Sun*, Ucayali 380. Cheaper without bath, good value, next to *Komby*. **F** *Marinhor*, Raimondi 699. Grubby but economical, helpful. **F** *Hostal Mori*, Jr Independencia 1114. Basic.

Eating *El Alamo*, Carretera Yarinacocha 2650. Good typical food. *El Sanguchón*, Jr Tarapacá 829. Near Banco de Crédito, clean, good sandwiches and coffee. *El Golf*, Jr Huáscar 545. *Cevichería. Jugos Don José*, Jr Ucayali 661. One of the oldest in town. *Cafetería Antonio*, Cnel Portillo 307, 2 blocks from the *Museo Regional*, good coffee.

Typical dishes *Patarashca* is barbecued fish wrapped in *bijao* leaves; *zarapatera*, a spicy soup made with turtle meat served in its shell, but consider the ecological implications of this dish; *chonta salad*, made with palm shoots; *juanes*, rice with chicken or fish served during the San Juan festival; *tacutacu* is banana and sauces. The local beer 'San Juan' has been recommended.

Artesanías La Selva, Jr Tarapacá 868, has a reasonable selection of indigenous craftwork. For local wood carvings visit the workshop of sculptor, *Agustín Rivas*, at Jr Tarapacá 861. Many Shibipo women carry and sell their products around Pucallpa and Yarinacocha.

Shopping

Laser Viajes y Turismo, Raymondi 470, T571120, T/F573776. Helpful, recommended for planning a jungle trip. If organizing a group tour with the boatmen on the waterfront, expect to pay around US$30 per day pp. Only use accredited guides.

Tour operators

Air To **Lima**, 1 hr, daily flights with *Aviandina* (Jr 7 de Junio 861, T575643), 5 a week with *Tans*. *Aviandina* and *Tans*' flights continue to/proceed from **Iquitos**. Airport to town, bus US$0.25; *motos* US$1; taxi US$2-3.

Transport

    Buses There are regular bus services to **Lima**, 812 km, 18-20 hrs (longer in the rainy season, Nov-Mar), US$11. To **Tingo María**, 255 km, 7-9 hrs, US$7.80, combis leave at 0600, 0700 and 0800 with *Ucayali Express*, 7 de Junio y San Martín. All buses have police guard and go in convoy. Take blankets as the crossing of the Cordillera at night is bitterly cold. It's recommended to cross the mountains by day as the views are wonderful.

    River Buses and colectivos go to the port, La Hoyada. In the dry season boats dock 3 km from the bus stop, it's a dusty walk, or taxi US$3. To **Iquitos**, some are better than others; only 3 boats with cabins, don't count on getting one (hammocks are cooler): *Florico*, *Carolina* and *Manuel*, trip takes 3-4 days, US$22 pp, US$27 inc cabin, with food.

    You can go to Puerto La Hoyada and Puerto Italia to find a smaller boat going to Iquitos; the Capitanía on the waterfront may give you information about sailings, but this is seldom reliable. Boats leave very irregularly. Avoid boats that will be loading en route, this can take up to 6 days. Do not pay for your trip before you board the vessel, and only pay the captain.

    NB Travellers to Iquitos may need confirmation from the PNP that their documents are in order, this must then be signed by the Capitanía otherwise no passenger can be accepted on a trip leaving Pucallpa. No such clearance is necessary when returning to Pucallpa. See General hints for river travel, page 1282.

Banks It is easy to change dollars cash at the banks, travel agencies, the better hotels and bigger stores. There are also lots of street changers (watch them carefully). *Banco de Crédito* is the only place to change TCs. Cash on Visa at *Banco de Crédito* and *Interbank*. **Communications** Internet: *Gibernet*, Jr Tarapacá 726. **Cultural centres** Art school: *Usko Ayar Amazonian School of Painting*, in the house of artist Pablo Amaringo, a former *vegetalista* (healer), Jr LM Sánchez, Cerro 465-467, www.egallery.com/pablo.html The school provides art classes for local people, and is financially dependent upon selling their art. The internationally renowned school welcomes overseas visitors for short or long stays to study painting and learn Spanish and/or teach English with Peruvian students. **Tourist offices** Dirección Regional de Turismo (MICTI), Raymondi block 2, T571506, helpful.

Directory

Peru

Iquitos

Iquitos stands on the west bank of the Amazon and is a chief town of Peru's jungle region. Some 800 km downstream from Pucallpa and 3,646 km from the mouth of the Amazon, the city is completely isolated except by air and river. Its first wealth came from the rubber boom (late 19th century to second decade of 20th century). It is now the centre for oil exploration in Peruvian Amazonia, and the main starting point for tourists wishing to explore Peru's northern jungle. See Excursions below and Tour operators.

Phone code: 064
Colour map 3, grid A4
Population: 600,000

The incongruous **Iron House** stands on the Plaza de Armas, designed by Eiffel for the Paris exhibition of 1889. It is said that the house was transported from Paris by a local rubber baron and is constructed entirely of iron trusses and sheets, bolted together and painted silver. It now houses a restaurant and snack bar.

Sights

    Belén, the picturesque, lively waterfront district, is worth visiting, but is not safe at night. Most of its huts are built on rafts to cope with the river's 10 m change of level during floods (January-July); now they're built on stilts. On Pasaje Paquito are bars serving local sugar cane rum. The main plaza has a bandstand made by Eiffel. In the high season canoes can be hired on the waterfront for a tour of Belén, US$3 per hour. The market at the end of the Malecón is well worth visiting, though you should get there before 0900 to see it in full swing.

Of special interest are the older buildings, faced with *azulejos* (glazed tiles). They date from the rubber boom of 1890 to 1912, when the rubber barons imported the tiles from Portugal and Italy and ironwork from England to embellish their homes. Werner Herzog's film *Fitzcarraldo* is a *cause célèbre* in the town and Fitzcarrald's house still stands on the Plaza de Armas. **Museo Amazónico**, in the renovated Prefectura, Malecón Tarapacá 386, has displays of native art. Next door to the tourist office on the Plaza is a **City Museum**, with items from the jungle in a lovely room with chandeliers, where rubber barons used to meet. ■ *Free*.

Excursions **Jungle tours from Iquitos** All agencies (see Tour operators) are under the control of the local office of the Ministry of Tourism. They arrange one day or longer trips to places of interest with guides speaking some English. The tourist office advises: it is always more expensive to buy a package at a lodge in your home country, over the internet or in Lima; negotiate all deals locally. Some agencies are reported as too easy going about their responsibilities on an organized trip, but many are conscientious. Take your time before making a decision and don't be bullied by the hustlers at the airport (they get paid a hefty commission). The Tourist Office in Iquitos has all the brochures and a list of illegal operators (see Directory); they give good advice. Shop around and deal direct with the lodge operators themselves at their own office, not any other address you may have been told about. In case of complaint contact *Indecopi*; T010-800 42579, tour@indecopi.gob.pe, or seek help at the tourist office, who can lead you through all the relevant procedures. Make sure your guide has a proper licence. Find out all the details of the trip and food arrangements before paying (a minimum of US$40-50 per day). **General information and advice** It is advisable to take a waterproof coat and shoes or light boots on such trips, and a good torch, as well as *espirales* to ward off the mosquitoes at night – they can be bought from drugstores in Iquitos. *Premier* is the most effective local insect repellent. The dry season is from Jul to Sep; Sep is the best month to see flowers and butterflies.

There is a beautiful white, sandy beach at **Bellavista**, which is safe for swimming and very popular at weekends in summer. Boats can be hired from here to see the meeting of the Nanay and Amazon rivers, and to visit villages en route. There are lots of food stalls selling typical local dishes. Take a bus from Jr Próspero to 'Bellavista Nanay', 15 minutes, US$0.40.

The beautiful **Lake Quistococha** in lush jungle is 13½ km south of the city, with a fish hatchery at the lakeside. There's a good two-hour walk through the surrounding jungle on a clearly marked trail. See particularly the *paiche*, a huge Amazonian fish whose steaks (*paiche a la loretana*) you can eat in Iquitos' restaurants. There are also bars and restaurants on the lakeside and a small beach. Boats are for hire on the lake and swimming is safe but the sandflies are vicious, so take insect repellent. US$1.30. Daily 0900-1700. ■ *Combis leave every hour until 1500 from Plaza 28 de Julio; the last one back leaves at 1700. Alternatively take a motocarro there and back with a 1 hr wait, which costs US$13. Perhaps the best option is to hire a motorbike and spend the day there. The road can be difficult after rain.*

L *El Dorado Plaza*, Napo 258 on main plaza, T222555, www.eldoradoplazahotel.com 5 star, very good accommodation and restaurant (*Mitos*), excellent service, bar, internet access, prices inlcude service, breakfast, welcome drink and transfer to/from airport. Recommended. **AL** *El Dorado*, Napo 362, T231742, F221985, dorado@tvs.com.pe Same ownership, pool (open to restaurant users), cable TV, bar and restaurant, prices include tax and service and airport transfer. Recommended. **A** *Victoria Regia*, Ricardo Palma 252, T231983, F232499. A/c, fridge, cable TV, free map of city, safe deposit boxes in rooms, good restaurant and pool. Recommended.

B *Amazonas*, Plaza de Armas, Arica 108, T242431. Modern, a/c, phone, fridge bar, TV. **B** *Hostal Ambassador*, Pevas 260, T233110. Includes tax, a/c, transport to and from airport, member of Peruvian Youth Hostel Association, cafeteria, owns *Sinchicuy Lodge* (see below). Recommended. **B** *Europa*, Brasil 222, T231123, F235483. A/c, cable TV, phone and fridge in every room, pleasant café/bar, good views from 5th floor. **B** *Jhuliana*, Putumayo 521, T/F233154. Includes tax and breakfast, nice pool, restaurant. Recommended. **C** *Internacional*, Próspero 835, T/F234684. A/c, TV, fridge, phone, secure, medium-priced restaurant, good value. Recommended. **D** *Hostal Bon Bini*, Pevas 386, T221058. With fridge, good value. Recommended. **D** *Hostal La Pascana*, Pevas 133, T231418. With cold shower, basic, fan, breakfast available, luggage store, TV lounge, luxuriant garden, relaxed, popular, book exchange, ask for Coby, a Dutch lady who will take tours on her houseboat, the *Miron Lenta*. Highly recommended.

Sleeping

Hotels are generally more expensive than the rest of the country, but discounts of 20% or more can be negotiated in the low season (Jan-Apr). Around Peruvian Independence Day (27 and 28 Jul) and Easter, Iquitos can get crowded and prices rise at this time

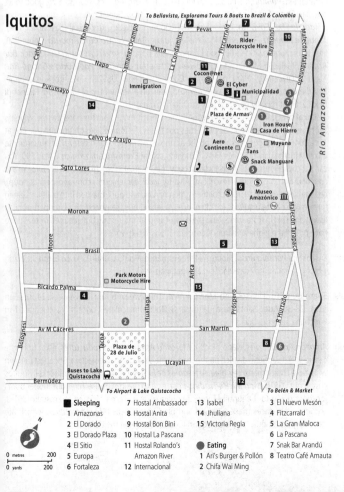

Iquitos

Peru

Sleeping	7 Hostal Ambassador	13 Isabel	3 El Nuevo Mesón
1 Amazonas	8 Hostal Anita	14 Jhuliana	4 Fitzcarrald
2 El Dorado	9 Hostal Bon Bini	15 Victoria Regia	5 La Gran Maloca
3 El Dorado Plaza	10 Hostal La Pascana		6 La Pascana
4 El Sitio	11 Hostal Rolando's	● Eating	7 Snak Bar Arandú
5 Europa	Amazon River	1 Ari's Burger & Pollón	8 Teatro Café Amauta
6 Fortaleza	12 Internacional	2 Chifa Wai Ming	

0 metres 200
0 yards 200

E *El Sitio*, Ricardo Palma 541, T234932. Fan, cafeteria. Highly recommended. **E** *Hostal Rolando's Amazon River*, Fitzcarrald y Nauta 307, T233979. With an, restaurant. **F** *Hostal Anita*, Ramírez Hurtado 742, T235354. No fan, basic. **F** *Pensión Económico*, Moore 1164, T265616. Large rooms, water all day, quiet, not central, no sign outside, breakfast on request. Recommended. **F** *Fortaleza*, Próspero 311, T234191. Basic, fan. **F** *Isabel*, Brasil 156, T234901. Good, but plug the holes in the walls, secure, often full.

Eating

Many private homes offer set lunch, look for the board outside

La Gran Maloca, Sargento Lores 170, opposite Banco Continental. A/c, high class. *Fitzcarrald*, Malecón Maldonado 103 y Napo. Smart, best pizza in town, also good pastas and salads. *El Dorado Inn*, C Huallaga 630. Good value and good menu. *Monte Carlo*, Napo 140-50, above casino. Excellent. *El Nuevo Mesón*, Malecón Maldonado 153. Local specialities include wild boar, alligator, turtle, tapir and other endangered species, has lots of regular dishes, too. *La Pascana*, Ramírez Hurtado 735. Good fish and *ceviche*, popular, try the *vientequatro raices*, 20% discount for *Handbook* users, open at lunchtimes only. *The Regal*, in the *Casa de Hierro*, Plaza de Armas, Próspero y Putumayo, 2nd floor. Nice location, good set lunch US$2.30. On the first floor is *El Copoasu*, a cafetería which serves malt beer with egg and fresh milk, a good pick-me-up. *Ari's Burger*, Plaza de Armas, Próspero 127. Medium-priced fast food, good breakfasts, popular with tourists. Next door is *Pollón*, chicken and chips, open in the daytime. *Hueng Teng*, Pucallpa y Nauta, Chinese, cheap. Recommended. *Paulina*, Tacna 591. Set lunch US$1.75, other dishes US$4.30-5.75, good food, popular. *Chifa Wai Ming*, San Martín at Plaza 28 de Julio. Good Chinese if a little expensive. *Heladería La Favorita*, Próspero 415. Good ice-cream (try local flavour *aguaje*). *Juguería Paladar*, Próspero 245. Excellent juices. **Bars** *Teatro Café Amauta*, Nauta 248. Live music, open 2200-2400, good atmosphere, popular, small exhibition hall. *Snack Bar Arandú*, Malecón Maldonado, good views of the Amazon river. *Papa Dan's Gringo Bar*, Napo y Fitzcarrald, Plaza de Armas. Good set menu, US$2.85, has book exchange. *La Ribereña*, Raymondi 453. With terraced seats on a newly-built plaza. *Tuspa*, Raimondi block 2. Light rock, livley, good place to listen to music.

Local specialities Try the local drink *chuchuhuasi*, made from the bark of a tree, which is supposed to have aphrodisiac properties but tastes like fortified cough tincture (for sale at Arica 1046), and *jugo de cocona*, and the alcoholic *cola de mono* and *siete raices* (aguardiente mixed with the bark of 7 trees and wild honey), sold at *Exquisita Amazónica*, Abtao 590. You can eat cheaply, especially fish and *ceviche*, at the 3 markets. Palm heart salad (*chonta*), or *a la Loretana* dish on menus is excellent. Also try *inchicapi* (chicken, corn and peanut soup), *cecina* (fried dried pork), *tacacho* (fried green banana and pork, mashed into balls and eaten for breakfast or tea), *juanes* (chicken, rice, olive and egg, seasoned and wrapped in bijao leaves and sold in restaurants) and the *camu-camu*, an interesting but acquired taste, said to have one of the highest vitamin C concentrations in the world.

Entertainment **Discos** *La Pantera Rosa*, Moore 434, free entrance, Mon-Sat until 0300. *La Estancia*, Napo 1 block, restaurant by day, dancing at night, popular.

Festivals **5 Jan:** founding of Iquitos. **Feb-Mar:** *Carnival.* **Third week in Jun:** tourist week. **24 Jun:** San Juan. **28-30 Aug:** Santa Rosa de Lima. **8 Dec:** Immaculate Conception, celebrated in Punchana, near the docks.

Shopping *Amazon Arts & Crafts*, Napo block 1. *Mercado Artesanal de Productores*, 4 km from the centre in the San Juan district, on the road to the airport, take a colectivo. Cheapest in town with more choice than elsewhere. *Artesanías de la Selva*, R Palma 190. Hammocks in Iquitos cost about US$10. *Mad Mick's Trading Post*, next to the Iron House, hires out rubber boots for those going to the jungle. There are pharmacies at Tacna 156 and at Próspero 361-3. Locals sell necklaces made with red and black rosary peas (*Abrus pecatorius*), which are extremely poisonous. They are illegal in Canada, but not in the USA.

Amazon Lodge & Safaris, Av La Marina 592A, T/F251078, amazonlodge@mixmail.com (attention Jorge and Elvira Lache); in Lima Av Alvarez Calderón 155, suite 304, San Isidro, T221 3341, F221 0974 (attention Gabriel Flores). 48 km down-river from Iquitos. Recommended as friendly and comfortable; 3 days/2 nights, US$200 pp for 2-4 people, US$50 pp for each additional night. *Amazon Tours and Cruises*, Requena 336, T231611/233931, F231265, amazontours.net In USA, 275 Fontainebleau Blvd, suite 173, Miami, FL 33172, T305 227 2266, toll free 800 423 2791, F305-227 1880, American-owned company. Various cruises available on the M/V *Arca* Iquitos-Leticia-Iquitos, US$595 pp, also MV *Marcelita*; and nature cruises on the M/V *Delfín*. Recommended. Also have **B** *Amazon Garden* in town, Pantoja 417 y Yavari, T236140, F231265, amazon@amazongardenhotel.com.pe Pleasant, 12 blocks out of town. *Cumaceba Lodge and Expeditions*, Putumayo 184 in the Iron House, T/F232229, www.manguare.com.pe/cumaceba Tours of 2-8 days to their lodges on the Amazon and Yarapa rivers, good birdwatching guides, 3 days/2 nights for US$120 pp. Very good all round.

Explorama Tours are highly recommended as the most efficient and, with over 35 years in existence, certainly the biggest and most established. Offices at Av La Marina 340, PO Box 446, T252526/252530, F252533; in USA, SACA, Toll Free, T800-707 5275, 781-581 0844, www.explorama.com They have 5 sites: *Explorama Inn*, 40 km (1½ hrs) from Iquitos, comfortable bungalows with cold water in a jungle setting. In the same reserve is *Ceiba Tops*, which provides "an adventure in luxury", 40 a/c rooms with electricity, hot showers, swimming pool with hydromassage and beautiful gardens. The food is good and, as in all Explorama's properties, is served communally. US$225 pp for 1 night/2 days, US$ 85 for each additional night (1-2 people). *Explorama Lodge* at Yanamono, 80 km from Iquitos, 2½ hrs from Iquitos, has palm-thatched accommodation with separate bathroom and shower facilities connected by covered walkways, cold water, no electricity, good food and service. US$325 for 3 days/2 nights and US$85 for each additional day (1-2 people). *Explornapo Lodge* at Llachapa on the Sucusai creek (a tributary of the Napo), is in the same style as Explorama Lodge, but is further away from Iquitos, 160 km (4 hrs), and is set in 105,000 ha of primary rainforest, so is better for seeing fauna. Nearby is the impressive canopy walkway 35 m above the forest floor and 500 m long, "a magnificent experience and not to be missed". It is associated with the *ACEER laboratory*, a scientific station, only 10 mins from the canopy walkway; the basic programme costs US$1,135 for 5 days/4 nights (2 people), the first and last nights are spent at Explorama Lodge. A US$25 donation to the Foundation for Conservation of Peruvian Amazon Biosphere (Conapac) is included if visiting the walkway. Each extra night to the basic programme costs US$98. Prices include transfers, advance reservations, etc. *Explor Tambos*, 2 hrs from *Explornapo*, more primitive accommodation, 8 shelters for 16 campers, bathing in the river, offers the best chance to see rare fauna. 15% discount to SAE members.

Muyuna Amazon Lodge and Expeditions, Putumayo 163, T242858, T937533 (Mob), www.muyuna.com 120 km from Iquitos, on the Yanayacu river, before San Juan village. Packages from 1 to 4 nights available, US$140-250 pp for 2-3 people, but users of this Handbook should make reservations in person for discounted price (similarly SAE members). Everything is included in the price (transport, good food, guides, excursions), personal service, flexible, radio contact, will collect passengers from airport if requested in advance. Highly recommended. *Paseos Amazónicos Ambassador*, Pevas 246, T/F231618, operates the *Amazonas Sinchicuy Lodge*, US$70 pp per night. The lodge is 1½ hrs from Iquitos on the Sinchicuy river, 25 mins by boat from the Amazon river. Cabins with bathroom, no electricity, good food, plenty activities, including visits to local villages. Recommended. They also organize visits to Lake Quistacocha. *Tahuayo Lodge*, *Amazonia Expeditions*, 10305 Riverburn Drive, Tampa, FL 33647, T toll free 800-262 9669, 813-907 8475, www.perujungle.com Near the Reserva Comunal de Tamshiyacu-Tahuayo on the Río Tahuayo, 145 km upriver from Iquitos, comfortable cabins with cold shower, buffet meals, good food, laundry service, wide range of excursions, excellent staff. A 7-day programme costs US$1,295, all inclusive, extra days US$100. Recommended. The lodge is associated with the Rainforest Conservation Fund (www.rainforestconservation.org), which works in Tamshiyacu-Tahuayo, one of the richest areas for primate species in the world, but also amphibians (there is a poison dart frog management programme), birds, other animals and plants.

Tour operators & jungle lodges
All prices are negotiable, except Muyuna, who do not take commissions

Peru

Yacumama Lodge, Sargento Lores 149, T/F235510 (Av Benavides 212, Oficina 1203, Miraflores, Lima). An excellent lodge on the Río Yarapa, 4 days/3 nights, US$389, 6 days/5 nights, US$559 (minimum 2 people), part of the fee is invested in local conservation. *Zungarococha Amazon Lodge*, Ricardo Palma 242, T/F231959, or Ricardo Rivera Navarrete 645E, San Isidro, Lima, T/F4424515. Comfortable lakeside bungalows reached by road (12 km), recreation centre with swimming pool, watersports, full day US$40, 1 night/2 days US$70. Also owns *Heliconia Lodge*, which is recommended (hot water, electricity for 3 hrs a day, good guiding and staff, rustic yet comfortable).

Guides *Pedro Alava Tuesta*, Av Grau 1770, T264224, pedroalava@hotmail.com Very experienced and reliable, all types of trip arranged. Recommended. *Percy Icomena*, Diego de Almagro 555, Puchana, bekeypp@operamail.com Freelance guide who can arrange any type of tour, including jungle survival, speaks English. Recommended. His brother, Louis, is also a guide, speaks English, French, Italian, German, Japanese, contact through Percy.

Transport **Motorcycle hire**: *Rider*, Pevas 219; *Park Motors*, Tacna 579, T/F231688. 2 others, addresses from tourist office, see Directory.

Air Francisco Secada Vigneta airport handles national and international flights, T260147. Airport departure tax is US$3.45. Taxi to the airport costs US$2.50 per car; *motocarro* (motorcycle with 2 seats), US$2.20. A bus from the airport, US$0.20, goes as far as the market area, about 12 blocks from the Plaza de Armas, a taxi from there is US$1.30. To **Lima**, daily; *Aero Continente, Aviandina* and *Tans*. *Aviandina* flies via **Pucallpa**, *Tans* direct and via either Pucallpa or Tarapoto. *Grupo 42* flies Mon, Wed, Sat to **Santa Rosa** for exit to Brazil (see below), returns to Iquitos Mon, Wed, Sat, 1½ hrs. At US$65 not much more than the fast boat and you won't be missing much wildlife as you see none from the boat. Flights are cancelled if the weather is bad. Iquitos flights are frequently delayed; be sure to reconfirm your flight in Iquitos, as they are often overbooked, especially over Christmas; check times in advance as itineraries frequently change.

From Jan to Jul the river rises and the port in Iquitos moves

Shipping **General hints for river travel on slow boats**: a hammock is essential. A double, of material (not string), provides one person with a blanket. Board the boat many hours in advance to guarantee hammock space. If going on the top deck, try to be first down the front; take rope for hanging your hammock, plus string and sarongs for privacy. On all boats, hang your hammock away from lightbulbs (they aren't switched off at night and attract all sorts of strange insects) and away from the engines, which usually emit noxious fumes. Guard your belongings from the moment you board. There is very little privacy; women travellers can expect a lot of attention. Stock up on drinking water, fruit and tinned food. Vegetarians must take their own supplies. On board, cabins are usually 4 berth and you have to buy both a first class ticket, which entitles you to food (whether you want it or not) and deck space to sling your hammock, and a cabin ticket if you want the 'luxury' of a berth. Adequate washing and toilet facilities, but the food is rice, meat and beans (and whatever can be picked up en route) cooked in river water. There is a good cheap bar on most boats. Take plenty of prophylactic enteritis tablets; many contract dysentery on the trip. Also take insect repellent and a mosquito net.

Upstream: river boats to **Pucallpa**, leave every second day, usually at 1700, 6/7 days when river is high, 3/4 days when low; price depends on demand, eg US$22 pp in hammock, US$27 pp with bed and cabin. To **Yurimaguas**, 3-4 days, longer if cargo is being carried, which is usually the case, US$18 pp, more or less daily. Information on boats and tickets at Bellavista, Malecón Tarapacá 596; or Puerto Masusa district of Puchana, Av La Marina y Masusa, bus from centre, 10 mins.

Downstream: boats to the border leave from one of two docks, Puerto de Servicio Masusa, or Embarcadero Turístico. There are no boats direct to Manaus, except a monthly luxury 54-passenger boat, *Río Amazonas*, operated by Amazon Tours and Cruises (see Jungle tours above), US$595 pp, return journey to Iquitos, Wed; also M/V *Arca*, US$500 pp, return journey Wed-Sat, and launch services. Fast boats, *rápidos*, leave from either port, but mostly Turístico. They leave most days at 0600; be at the port at 0445. *Expreso Turístico Loreto*, Próspero 441/Raimondi 384, T234084, US$50 (pay in dollars) to Tabatinga. Other operators are *Transtur* and *Transportes Pluma*, all charge the same and include a small breakfast, a reasonable lunch and mineral water (luggage limit 15 kg). Most travel agencies sell tickets. The trip takes 11 hrs (despite what you may be told). Hotels have details of sailings; ask around which boats are reliable. In dry season, going downstream can be as slow as going up if the river is very low. Regular boats, *lanchas*, leave almost every day to **Santa Rosa**, opposite Tabatinga (Brazil). The journey takes 2-3 days and costs US$25-30 pp with a cabin and meals (US$15-17.50 with a hammock). Passengers disembark at Santa Rosa, where immigration formalities take place (no exchange facilities), then take another US$1 boat to **Marco**, the port for **Tabatinga**. Most boats for **Manaus** depart from Marco.

Airline offices *Aero Continente*, Próspero 231, T233162, F233990; *Aviandina* in same office. *Grupo 42*, Sgto Lores 127, T234632. *Tans*, Próspero 215, open 0830-1300, 1530-1900, Sun 0830-1300. **Banks** *Banco de Crédito*, Plaza de Armas. For Visa, also cash and TCs at good rates, Visa ATM around the corner on Próspero. *BBV Continental*, Sgto Lores 171. For Visa, 1 commission on TCs. *Banco de la Nación*, Condamine 478. Good rates, changes Deutschmarks. *Banco Wiese Sudameris*, Próspero 282. *Banco del Trabajo*, Próspero 223. Unicard ATM for Visa and MasterCard. *Western Union*, Napo 359, T235182. **Communications Internet:** There are lots of internet places around the Plaza de Armas, eg: *Cocon@net*, Fitzcarrald 131, T232538, with snackbar. *El Cyber*, Fitzcarrald 120, T223608. *Inernet Satelite*, Putumayo 188, Mob 610642. *Manguaré*, Próspero 251, T242148. All average US$1.15 per hr. **Post Office:** on the corner of C Arica with Morona, near Plaza de Armas, open daily 0700-1700. **Telephone:** Arica 276. **Consulates Consulates: UK**, Casa de Hierro (Iron House), Putumayo 182A, T222732, F223607, Mon-Fri 1100-1200. **Colombia**, Nauta y Callao, T231461. **Spain**, Av La Marina, T232483. **France**, Napo 346, T232353. **Germany**, Max Drusche, Yavari 660, T232641, F236364. **NB** There is no Brazilian consulate. If you need a visa, you must get it in Lima. **Medical services** Clínica Loreto, Morona 471, T233752, 24-hr attention, recommended, but only Spanish spoken. **Hospital Iquitos**, Av Grau, emergency T231721. **Clínica Anna Stahl**, on Av La Marina (ask taxi driver); **Hospital Regional de Loreto**, 28 de Julio, emergency T235821. **Tourist offices** Napo 226, on the Plaza de Armas, in the Municipal building, T235621, T671633 (Mob), turismo.mpm@tvs.com.pe They have information on all operators offering tours to the jungle. They also have a list of contacts along the river should you need help in an emergency. They are very helpful and speak English. They also supply maps and general tourist literature; book exchange. If arriving at the airport, go straight to the tourist information desk at baggage claim for advice about hotels and touts and will provide a map. Open Mon-Fri 0800-2000, Sat-Sun 0900-1300. 5 languages spoken; luggage store, free water. **Useful addresses Immigration:** Napo 447, T235371. Quick service (may be moving to Nauta 4th block in 2001). **PARD**, Preservation of the Amazon River Dolphin, Pevas 253, T/F238585, Roxanne Kremer or Frank Aliaga for information. **Tourist police:** Sargento Lores 834, helpful with complaints. In emergency T241000 or 241001.

Directory
Don't change money on the streets.
The tourist office has the names of reliable money changers

Peru

Details on exit and entry formalities seem to change frequently, so when leaving Peru, check in Iquitos first at Immigration (see above) or with the Capitanía at the port. Boats stop in Santa Rosa for Peruvian exit formalities. All details are given in the Brazil chapter.

Border with Brazil

The Southeastern Jungle

The southern selva is in **Madre de Dios** department, which contains the **Manu National Park** (1,881,000 ha), the **Tambopata-Candamo Reserved Zone** (254,358 ha) and the Bahauja-Sonene National Park (1,091,416 ha).

The forest of this lowland region (*Altitude:* 260 m) is technically called Sub-tropical Moist Forest, which means that it receives less rainfall than tropical forest and is dominated by the floodplains of its meandering rivers. The most striking features are the former river channels that have become isolated as **ox-bow lakes**. These are home to **black caiman** and **giant otter**. Other rare species living in the forest are **jaguar, puma, ocelot** and **tapir**. There are also **howler monkeys, macaws, guans, currasows** and the **giant harpy eagle**. As well as containing some of the most important flora and fauna on Earth, the region also harbours gold-diggers, loggers, hunters, drug smugglers and oil-men, whose activities have endangered the unique rainforest. Various conservation groups are working to protect it.

Climate The climate is warm and humid, with a rainy season from Nov to Mar and a dry season from Apr to Oct. Cold fronts from the South Atlantic, called *friajes*, are characteristic of the dry season, when temperatures drop to 15-16° C during the day, and 13° at night. Always bring a sweater at this time. The best time to visit is during the dry season when there are fewer mosquitoes and the rivers are low, exposing the beaches. This is also a good time to see nesting and to view animals at close range, as they stay close to the rivers and are easily seen. Note that this is also the hottest time. A pair of binoculars is essential and insect repellent is a must.

Manu Biosphere Reserve

No other reserve can compare with Manu for the diversity of life forms; it holds over 850 species of birds and covers an altitudinal range from 200 to 4,100 m above sea-level. Giant otters, jaguars, ocelots and 13 species of primates abound in this pristine tropical wilderness, and uncontacted indigenous tribes are present in the more remote areas, as are indigenous groups with limited access.

Background The reserve is is one of the largest conservation units on Earth, encompassing the complete drainage of the Manu River. It is divided into the **Manu National Park** (1,532,000 ha), where only government sponsored biologists and anthropologists may visit with permits from the Ministry of Agriculture in Lima; the **Reserved Zone** of the Manu Biosphere reserve (257,000 ha), which is set aside for applied scientific research and ecotourism; and the **Multiple Use Zone** (92,000 ha), which contains acculturated native groups and colonists, where the locals still employ their traditional way of life. Among the ethnic groups in the Multiple Use Zone are the Harakmbut, Machiguenga and Yine in the Amarakaeri Reserved Zone, on the east bank of the Alto Madre de Dios. They have set up their own ecotourism activities. Associated with Manu are other areas protected by conservation groups, or local people (for example the Blanquillo reserved zone) and some cloud forest parcels along the road. The **Nahua-Kugapakori Reserved Zone**, set aside for these two nomadic native groups, is the area between the headwaters of the Río Manu and headwaters of the Río Urubamba, to the north of the alto Madre de Dios.

Access The multiple use zone is accessible to anyone and several lodges exist in the area (see Lodges in Manu below). The reserved zone of the Manu Biosphere Reserve is accessible by permit only. Entry is strictly controlled and visitors must visit the area under the auspices of an authorized operator with an authorized guide. Permits are limited and reservations should be made well in advance. In the reserved zone of the Manu Biosphere Reserve the only accommodation is in the comfortable Manu Lodge or in the comfortable but rustic Casa Machiguenga in the Cocha Salvador area. Several companies have tented safari camp infrastructures, some with shower and dining facilities, but all visitors sleep in tents. The entrance fee to the Reserved Zone is 150 soles pp (US$42 at the time of writing) and is included in package tour prices.

Useful addresses **In Lima** Asociación Peruana para la Conservación de la Naturaleza (APECO), Parque José Acosta 187, p 2, Magdalena del Mar. **Pronaturaleza** (FPCN), Av de los Rosales 255, San Isidro, www.pronaturaleza.com.pe
In Cusco Asociación para la Conservación de la Selva Sur (ACSS), Ricaldo Palma J-1, Santa Mónica (same office as *Peru Verde*), T243408, F226392, acss@telser.com.pe This is a local NGO that can help with information and has free video shows about Manu National Park and Tambopata-Candamo Reserve. They are friendly and helpful and also have information on programmes and research in the jungle area of Madre de Dios. Further information can be obtained from the **Manu National Park Office**, Av Micaela Bastidas 310, Cusco, T240898, pqnmanu@cosapidata.mail.com.pe, Casilla Postal 591, open 0800-1400. They issue a permit for the Reserved Zone which costs US$42.

Warning Beware of pirate operators on the streets of Cusco who offer trips to the Reserved Zone of Manu and end up halfway through the trip changing the route "due to emergencies", which, in reality means they have no permits to operate in the area. The following companies organize trips into the Multiple Use and Reserved Zones. Contact them for more details. *Manu Nature Tours*, Av Pardo 1046, Cusco, T252721, F234793, www.manuperu.com, owned by Boris Gómez Luna, run lodge-based trips, owners of *Manu Lodge* and part owners of *Manu Cloudforest Lodge*; *Manu* is the only lodge in the Reserved Zone, open all year, situated on an ox-bow lake, providing access to the forest, US$130 per night including meals, guides available; activities include river-rafting and canopy-climbing, highly recommended for experiencing the jungle in comfort. An 8-day trip bus/boat in and boat/plane out costs US$1,995 in high season (May-Oct), US$1,555 low season (Nov-Apr); 4-day trip with return flight US$1,382 high season, US$998 low season.

Manu Expeditions, Av Pardo 895, Cusco, T226671, F236706, www.ManuExpeditions.com, owned by ornithologist, Barry Walker, owners of *Manu Wildlife Centre* along with ACSS (see above), run 4-9 day trips in Safari camps and lodges and specialize in birdwatching trips (US$889 per 6 days), also trekking/horse riding trips off the beaten track. *InkaNatura*, in Cusco: C Plateros 361, T251173, in Lima: Manuel Bañón 461, San Isidro, T440 2022, T944 4272 (Mob) (Rodrigo Custodio), also with offices in Chiclayo and the US, www.inkanatura.com, tours to *Manu Wildlife*

Centre and *Sandoval Lake Lodge* (see below) and a unique tour into Machiguenga territory. *Pantiacolla Tours*, Plateros 360, Cusco, T238323, F252696, www.pantiacolla.com Run by Marianne Von Vlaardingen and Gustavo Moscoso. They have tours to the *Pantiacolla Lodge* (see below) and also 8-day camping trips. Pantiacolla has started a community-based ecotourism project, called the Yine Project, with the people of Diamante in the Multiple Use Zone. *Manu Ecological Adventures*, Plateros 356, T261640, F225562, www.manuadventures.com and *Expediciones Vilca*, Plateros 363, T/F381002, www.cbc.org.pe/manuvilca/ Both offer tours at economical prices (Vilca US$580 for 8 days, 3 nights in lodge, 3 camping).

Lodges in Manu *Manu Cloud Forest Lodge*, at Unión, at 1,800 m on the road from Paucartambo to Atalaya, owned by *Manu Nature Tours*, 6 rooms with 4 beds. *Cock of the Rock Lodge*, on the same road at 1,500 m, next to a Cock of the Rock *lek*, 8 double rooms and some private cabins, run by the ACSS group (see below). *Amazonia Lodge*, on the Río Alto Madre de Dios just across the river from Atalaya, an old tea hacienda run by the Yabar family, famous for its bird diversity and fine hospitality, a great place to relax, contact Santiago in advance and he'll arrange a pick-up. In Cusco at Matará 334, T/F231370, amazonia1@correo.dnet.com.pe *Pantiacolla Lodge*, 30 mins down-river from Shintuya. Owned by the Moscoso family. Book through *Pantiacolla Tours* (see above). *Manu Lodge*, situated on the Manu river, 3 hrs upriver from Boca Manu towards Cocha Salvador, run by *Manu Nature Tours* and only bookable as part of a full package deal with transport. *Manu Wildlife Centre*, 2 hrs down the Río Madre de Dios from Boca Manu, near the Blanquillo macaw lick and also counts on a Tapir lick and walk-up canopy tower. Book through Manu Expeditions or InkaNatura. 22 double cabins, all with private bathroom and hot water. Also canopy towers for birdwatching. *Erika Lodge*, on the Alto Madre de Dios, 25 mins from Atalaya, is a biological station used by Pronaturaleza (see above), which now accepts a small number of visitors. It offers basic accommodation and is cheaper than the other, more luxurious lodges. Contact *Manu Ecological Adventures*, Plateros 356, Cusco (see above), or Ernesto Yallico, Casilla 560, Cusco, T227765. *Casa Machiguenga* near Cocha Salvador, upriver from *Manu Lodge*. Machiguenga-style cabins run by local communities with NGO help. Contact Manu Expeditions or Apeco NGO, T225595.

Jungle routes to Puerto Maldonado and the Tambopata reserve

Cusco-Puerto Maldonado via Mazuko From Cusco take a bus to Urcos; one hour, US$2.25. Trucks leave from here for **Mazuko** around 1500-1600, arriving around 2400 the next day, US$6.65. Catch a truck early in the morning from here for Puerto Maldonado, US$4.50, 13-14 hours. It's a painfully slow journey on an appalling road; trucks frequently get stuck or break down. **Quincemil**, 240 km from Urcos on the road to Mazuko, is a centre for alluvial gold-mining with many banks. Accommodation is available in **F** *Hotel Toni*, friendly, clean, cold shower, good meals. Quincemil marks the half-way point and the start of the all-weather road. Gasoline is scarce in Quincemil because most road vehicles continue on 70 km to Mazuko, which is another mining centre, where they fill up with the cheaper gasoline of the jungle region.

The changing scenery is magnificent and worth the hardship and discomfort. The trucks only stop four times each day, for meals and a short sleeping period for the driver. You should take a mosquito net, repellent, sunglasses, sunscreen, a plastic sheet, a blanket, food and water.

To Puerto Maldonado via Pilcopata & Shintuya The arduous 255 km trip over the Andes from Cusco to Pilcopata takes about 12-15 hours by local truck (20-40 hours in the wet season). On this route, too, the scenery is magnificent. From Cusco you climb up to the pass before Paucartambo (very cold at night), before dropping down to this mountain village at the border between the departments of Cusco and Madre de Dios. The road then ascends to the second pass (also cold at night), after which it goes down to the cloud forest and then the rainforest, reaching **Pilcopata** at 650 m. At Pilcopata you can stay at the little *hostal* of Sra Rubella for US$2.50 per person, very basic, **F** pp *Gallito de las Rocas*, opposite the police checkpoint, or **F** *Albergue Eco Turístico Villa Carmen*.

Transport Trucks leave every Mon, Wed and Fri from the Coliseo Cerrado in Cusco at about 1000 (be there by 0800) to **Pilcopata** and **Shintuya** (passing Atalaya); US$7 to Shintuya. The journey takes at least 48 hrs and is rough and uncomfortable. They return the following day, but there is no service on Sun. There is also a bus service which leaves from the same place to **Pilcopata** on Mon and Fri, returns Tue and Sat. The journey takes 12 hrs in the dry season and costs US$8-10. Only basic supplies are available after leaving Cusco, so take all your camping and food essentials, including insect repellent. Transport can be disrupted in the wet season because the road is in poor condition (tour companies have latest details). Tour companies usually use their own vehicles for the overland trip from Cusco to Manu.

Pilcopata to Shintuya After Pilcopata, the route is hair-raising and breathtaking, passing through **Atalaya**, the first village on the Alto Madre de Dios River (basic accommodation). The route continues to Salvación, where the Park Office and the Park Entrance are situated. If you did not get a permit in Cusco, this is your last chance. There are basic hostals and restaurants. From Pilcopata, truck traffic is infrequent to Atalaya (one hour, US$8) and Shintuya (4-6 hours, US$10). Trucks leave in the morning between 0600 and 0900. Make sure you go with a recommended truck driver. Basic restaurants can be found in Pilcopata and Atalaya.

The end of the road is **Shintuya**, at 485 m, the starting point for river transport. The inhabitants are Masheos Indians. It is a commercial and social centre, as wood from the jungle is transported from here to Cusco. There are a few basic restaurants and you can camp (beware of thieves). The priest will let you stay in the dormitory rooms at the mission. Supplies are expensive.

Shintuya to Puerto Maldonado Cargo boats leave for the gold mining centre of Boca Colorado on the Río Madre de Dios, via Boca Manu, but only when the boat is fully laden; about 6-8 a week, nine hours, US$15. Very basic accommodation can be found here, but it is not recommended for lone women travellers. To Boca Manu is 3-4 hours, US$12. From Colorado you can catch a boat to Laberinto, 6-7 hours, US$20, from where regular combis run to Puerto Maldonado, 1½ hours. **NB** It is not possible to arrange trips to the Reserved Zone of the Biosphere Reserve from Shintuya, owing to park regulations. All arrangements must be made in Cusco.

Boca Manu is the connecting point between the rivers Alto Madre de Dios, Manu and Madre de Dios. It has a few houses, an air strip and some food supplies. It is also the entrance to the Manu Reserve and to go further you must be part of an organized group. ■ *The Park ranger station is located in Limonal. You need to show your permit here. Camping is allowed here if you have a permit. There are no regular flights from Cusco to Boca Manu. These are arranged the day before, if there are enough passengers. Contact Air Atlantic, at Maruri 228, oficina 208, Cusco, T084-245440; Trans Andes, T/F224638, or Malu Servicios, T/F242104, both at Cusco airport; or check with the tour operators in Cusco.*

To the Reserved Zone Upstream on the Río Manu you pass the *Manu Lodge* (see Manu Nature Tours), on the Cocha Juárez, 3-4 hours by boat. You can continue to Cocha Otorongo, 2½ hours and Cocha Salvador, 30 minutes, the biggest lake with plenty of wildlife. From here it is 2-3 hours to Pakitza, the entrance to the National Park Zone. This is only for biologists with a special permit.

Between Boca Manu and Colorado is **Blanquillo**, a private reserve (10,000 ha). Bring a good tent with you and all food if you want to camp and do it yourself, or alternatively accommodation is available at the *Tambo Blanquillo* (full board or accommodation only). Wildlife is abundant, especially macaws and parrots at the macaw lick near *Manu Wildlife Centre*. There are occasional boats to Blanquillo from Shintuya; US$10, 6-8 hours.

Peru

Puerto Maldonado

Phone code: 084
Colour map 3, grid C5
Population: 25,000
Altitude: 250 m

Puerto Maldonado is the dusty end of the line before stepping into the south eastern jungles of the Tambopata Reserve or departing for Bolivia. It overlooks the confluence of the rivers Tambopata and Madre de Dios and its isolation makes it a relatively expensive town and because of the gold mining and timber industries, the immediate surrounding jungle is now cultivated.

The beautiful and tranquil **Lago Sandoval** is a one-hour boat ride along the Río Madre de Dios, and then a 5-km walk into the jungle (parts of the first 3 km are a raised wooden walkway; boots are advisable). To visit the *Sandoval Lake Lodge*, contact *InkaNatura Travel* (see above), it is one of the few lodges with electricity and hot water; it has a camping platform on the Río Heath and is the only company to run trips there. **C** *Mejía Lodge*, T084-571428, is on the lakeshore, basic communal facilities, full board available. Boats can be hired at the Madre de Dios port for about US$20 a day, minimum 2 people (plus petrol) to go to Lago Sandoval, (don't pay the full cost in advance). The boat owner must accompany you. (See Tour operators.)

Sleeping
B *Wasai*, Billinghurst opposite the Capitanía, T/F571355 (or Cusco 084-572290), www.wasai.com In a beautiful location overlooking the Madre de Dios River, with forest surrounding cabin-style rooms, a/c, TV, shower, small pool with waterfall, good restaurant if slightly expensive (local fish a speciality). Highly recommended. They can organize local tours and also have a lodge on the Río Tambopata, 4 hrs upstream, 3-day trips US$110. **C** *Cabañaquinta*, Cusco 535, T571045, F571890. Fan, good restaurant, lovely garden, very comfortable, airport transfer. Recommended. **C** *Don Carlos*, Avda León Velarde 1271, T571029, T/F571323. Nice view over the Río Tambopata, a/c, restaurant, TV, phone, good. **D** *Libertador*, Libertad 433, 10 mins from the centre, T573860. Comfortable, with pool and garden, good restaurant. Recommended. **D** *Royal Inn*, 2 de Mayo 333, T571048. Modern and clean, very good. **E** pp *Hostal Iñapari*, 4 km from centre, 5 mins from the airport, T572575, F572155, joaquin@lullitec.com.pe Run by a Spanish couple Isabel and Javier, including breakfast and dinner, excellent food, very relaxing, recommended. **E** *Rey Port*, Av León Velarde 457, T571177. With bath, fan, front rooms noisy, good value. **E** *Wilson*, Jr González Prada 355, T572838. With bath, basic. **F** *Tambo de Oro*, Av Dos de Mayo 277, T572057. Cheap, basic, water 24 hrs. **F** *Hostal Moderno*, Billinghurst 357, T571063. Bright, quiet, welcoming, little privacy.

Eating
El Califa, Piura 266, some regional specialities, recommended. *Chez Maggy*, on the plaza, cosy atmosphere, good pizzas, very popular at weekends. *La Estrella*, Velarde 474, the smartest and best of the *pollos a la brasa* places. *Café Tu Dulce Espera*, Velarde 469, and *La Casa Nostra*, Velarde 515, sell huge glasses of fruit juice for US$0.50, as well as *tamales*, *papas rellenas* and enormous fancy cakes. The best **nightlife** is at *Witite* club, Velarde 153, open Fri, Sat 2300 onwards, US$1.50, wide range of Latin music, has a sophisticated sound system with speakers covered in huge spiders' webs.

Shopping
Artesanía Shabuya, Arequipa 279, south side of the plaza, 0900-1300, 1700-2200 Mon-Sat, sells a wide range of local handicrafts ranging from woven baskets to arrows to hammocks, plus jungle sound tapes and T-shirts.

Tour operators
Turismo de los Angeles, Jr Puno 657, T571070, run trips to Lago Sandoval (US$25 pp per day) and Lago Valencia. *Transtours*, G Prada 341, T572606. Reputable guides are Hernán Llave Cortez and Willy Wither, who can be contacted on arrival at the airport, if available. Also Javier Salazar of *Hostal Iñapari* is a reputable guide who specializes in trips up the remote Río Las Piedras. The *Guides Association* is at Fitzcarrald 341, T571413. The usual price for trips to Lago Sandoval is US$25 pp per day (minimum of 2 people), and US$35 pp per day for longer trips lasting 2-4 days (minimum of 4-6 people). All guides should have a Ministry of Tourism carnet for Lake Sandoval, which also verifies them as suitable guides for trips to other places and confirms their identity. Boat hire can be arranged through the Capitán del Puerto (Río Madre de Dios), T573003.

Peru

Motorcycle hire: scooters and mopeds can de hired from *Ocoñita*, on the corner of Puno **Transport** and G Prado for US$1 per hr or US$10 per day. This is the standard rate in town. Passport and driver's licence must be shown. **Air** To **Lima**, daily with *Tans* and *Aviandina* via Cusco. *Lan Perú* fly this route 3 times a week. *Aeroregional* flies to Cusco for US$35. A moto-taxi from town to the airport is US$1.50, 8 km. **Road and River** A standard journey by moto-taxi in town costs US$0.75, a ride on a motorbike US$0.30. Routes from Cusco are given above. Trucks for Cusco leave Puerto Maldonado usually between 1600 and 1900 from the market at León Velarde y Jr Troncoso. Most boats leave from **Laberinto**, 1½ hrs from Puerto Maldonado for Colorado, 8 hrs, US$12; from there you continue to Boca Manu and Shintuya, 9-10 hrs, US$15.

Airline offices *Aero Continente*, Velarde 506, T573702, F573704. *Tans*, Av León Velarde 160. **Directory** *Aeroregional*, Av León Velarde 525. **Banks** Open 0900-1300, 1700-1900. *Banco de Crédito*, cash advances with Visa, ATM, no commission on TCs. *Banco de la Nación*, cash on MasterCard, quite good rates for TCs. The best rates for cash are at the *casas de cambio* on Puno 6th block, eg *Cárdenas Hnos*, Puno 605. **Communications** Internet: on Velarde near Serpost. Serpost: at Velarde 6th block, 0800-2000, 0800-1500 Sun. **Telephone**: *Telefónica*, on Puno, 7th block. **Consulates** Bolivian **Consulate**, on the north side of the plaza. **Useful addresses** Peruvian immigration, is at 26 de Diciembre 356, 1 block from the plaza, get your exit stamp here.

Trips can be made to **Lago Valencia**, 60 km away near the Bolivian border, four **Jungle tours** hours there, eight hours back. It is an ox-bow lake with lots of wildlife. Many excel- **from Puerto** lent beaches and islands are located within an hour's boat ride. Mosquitoes are vora- **Maldonado** cious. If camping, take food and water.

It is quite easy to arrange a boat and guide from Puerto Maldonado (see Tour operators above) to the **Tambopata-Candamo Reserved Zone**, between the rivers Madre de Dios, Tambopata and Heath. Some superb ox-bow lakes can be visited and the birdwatching is wonderful. All visitors must pay *Inrena* (the protected areas institute) US$2 to enter the Zone if staying at a lodge, US$20 if camping. This is not always included in lodge packages, though they may organize the payment.

Some of the lodges along the Tambopata river offer guiding and research place-ments to biology and environmental science graduates. For more details send an SAE to TReeS: UK – J Forrest, PO Box 33153, London, NW3 4DR. USA – W Widdowson, PO Box 5668, Eureka, CA95502.

The **Bahuaja-Sonene National Park** was declared in 1996 and stretches from the Heath River across the Tambopata, incorporating the Río Heath National Sanctu-ary. It is closed to visitors.

Reserva Amazónica (formerly *Cusco Amazónico Pueblo Lodge*), 45 mins by boat down the **Jungle Lodges** Río Madre de Dios. Jungle tours available with multi-lingual guides, the lodge is surrounded by its own 10,000 ha but most tours are to Lago Sandoval, two package programmes: US$157 pp, or US$240 pp, a naturalists programme is also provided, negotiable out of sea-son, 50 rustic bungalows with private bathrooms, friendly staff, very good food, multi-lingual guides. The lodge has established (without full approval) its own trail to Lago Sandoval and its own Monkey Island. To book T/F422 6574, F422 4701, www.inkaterra.com, Lima. *Cuzco Tambo Lodge*, bungalows 15 km out on the northern bank of the Río Madre de Dios. 2, 3 and 4-day jungle programmes available, from US$90 pp in low season, tours visit Lago Sandoval. Book through *Cusco-Maldonado Tour*, Plateros 351 (T222332), Cusco.

Eco Amazonia Lodge, on the Madre de Dios, 1 hr down-river from Puerto Maldonado. Accommodation for up to 80 in basic bungalows and dormitories, good for birdwatching with viewing platforms and tree canopy access, US$150 for 3 days/2 nights. Book through their office in Cusco: Portal de Panes 109, oficina 6, T236159, F225068, ecolodge@ qenqo-unsaac.edu.pe **Explorers Inn**, the lodge is located adjoining the TCRZ, in the part where most research work has been done, 58 km from Puerto Maldonado. It's a 3-hr ride up the Río Tambopata (2 hrs return, in the early morning, so take warm clothes and rain gear), one of the best places in Peru for seeing jungle birds (580 plus species have been recorded

Peru

here), butterflies (1,230 plus species), also giant river otters, but you probably need more than a 2-day tour to benefit fully from the location. The guides are biologists and naturalists from around the world who undertake research in return for acting as guides. They provide interesting wildlife-treks, including to the macaw lick (*collpa*). US$180 for 3 days/2 nights, US$165 in the low season. Book through *Peruvian Safaris*, Alcanfores 459, Miraflores T4478888, F2418427, Lima, or Plateros 365, T4235342 Cusco, safaris@amauta.rcp.net.pe The office in Puerto Maldonado is at Fitzcarrald 136, T/F572078.

Posada Amazonas Lodge, on the Tambopata river, is located 2½ hrs upriver from Puerto Maldonado. A unique collaboration between a tour agency the local native community of Infierno. 24 large and attractive rooms with bathroom, visits to Lakes Cochacocha and Tres Chimbadas, with good birdwatching opportunities including the Tambopata *Collpa*. Prices start at US$190 for a 3 day/2 night package, or US$522 for 5 days/4 nights including the Tambopata Research Centre, the company's older, more spartan lodge, at which guests stay when visiting the macaw lick. Book through **Rainforest Expeditions**, Aramburú 166, of 4B, Miraflores, Lima 18, T421 8347, F421 8183, or Portal de Carnes 236, T246243, cusco@rainforest.com.pe, or Arequipa 401, Puerto Maldonado, T571056, or through www.perunature.com

Tambopata Jungle Lodge, on the Río Tambopata. Trips usually go to Lake Condenado, some to Lake Sachavacayoc, and to the *Collpa de Chuncho*, guiding mainly in English and Spanish, usual package US$160 pp for 3 days/2 nights (US$145 in the low season), naturalists programme provided. Make reservations at Av Pardo 705, Cusco, T225701, F238911, postmast@patcusco.com.pe **Wasai Lodge**, on the Río Tambopata, 80 km (4 hrs) upriver from Puerto Maldonado, 2 hrs return, same owners as *Hotel Wasai* in town; www.wasai.com Small lodge with 3 bungalows for 30 people, 15 km of trails around the lodge, guides in English and Spanish. The *Collpa de Chuncho*, one of the biggest macaw licks in the world, is only 1 hr up river; 3 day trips US$160, 7 days US$500.

Casa de Hospedaje Buenaventura, is a new intiative set up by long-term colonists living along the Tambopata river, 50-75 km upriver from Puerto Maldonado, 5-6 hrs by *peque-peque*. Accommodation for up to 10 in basic, rustic facilities, provides an insight into local lifestyles, minimum of 2 nights, from US$20-35 pp, includes transport to/from Tambopata dock, all food, mosquito net and Spanish-speaking guide, check if the package includes a trip to a *collpa*, in which case you'll also need a tent. Contact in advance via buenaventura50@hotmail.com There is usually a representative to meet incoming flights at Puerto Maldonado airport. *Sachavaca Inn*, associated with the same scheme, 2 bungalows for up to 20 people, located between *Explorer's Inn* and *Tambopata Jungle Lodge*. Visits are made to Lago Sachavacayoc. To book, T571883, F571297, Puerto Maldonado.

Take the boat to **Puerto Heath**, but get a tourist visa at the Bolivian immigration office in Puerto Maldonado. It can take several days to find a boat going all the way to the Bolivian border. Motorized dugout canoes go to Puerto Pardo on Peruvian side, 5 hrs, US$4.50 pp (no hotels or shops); wait here for a canoe to Puerto Heath. It is fairly hard to get a boat from the border to Riberalta (a wait of up to 3 days is not uncommon), 3 days, US$15-20; alternatively, travel to the naval base at América, then fly. **To the Bolivian border**

To Iberia and Iñapari

Daily public transport runs on the improved dirt road which begins across the Río Madre de Dios and runs to **Iberia** and **Iñapari** on the border with Brazil. In the wet season the road may only be passable with difficulty, especially between Iberia and Iñapari. In the dry, though, it is a fast road and dangerous for motorcyclists because of passing traffic. Along the road there remains no primary forest, only secondary growth and small farms (*chacras*). There are also picturesque *caseríos* (settlements) that serve as collecting and processing centres for the brazil nut. Approximately 70% of the inhabitants in the Madre de Dios are involved in the collection of this prized nut.

At **Planchón**, 40 km up the road, there is a hotel, **G**, which is clean, but has no mosquito nets, and two bar/restaurants. **Alegría** at Km 60 has a hotel/restaurant and Mavilla, at Km 80, a bar.

The hotel at **Alerta**, Km 115, is a room with four beds, **G**. The river is safe to swim in. If there is a boat here, it is the quickest route to Brasiléia (Brazil), apart from the plane. US$10-20 per person in a cargo canoe, or *peque-peque*, to Porvenir and then by road to Cobija (Bolivia), across the border from Brasiléia.

At **San Lorenzo**, Km 145, is the *Bolpebra* bar, which serves cheap food and drink and is generally lively.

Iberia, Km 168, has two hotels, the best is **F** *Hostal Aquino*, basic, cold shower, rooms serviced daily. Just outside the town the local rubber tappers association has set up an interesting Reserve and Information Centre.

Iñapari, at the end of the road, Km 235, has two basic hotels and a restaurant, but **Assis Brasil** across the border is much more attractive and has a much nicer basic hotel (**F**) on the main plaza. In the dry season it is possible to walk across the Rio Acre to Assis, otherwise take the ferry.

There is a road from Assis Brasil into Brazil and connections to Cobija in Bolivia from Brasileía. It can be cold travelling this road, so take a blanket or sleeping bag. There are no exchange facilities en route and poor exchange rates for Brazilian currency at Iñapari. Crossing between Peru and Bolivia on this route is not easy.

Exit stamps can be obtained in Iñapari. Check in advance that you do not need a consular visa for Brazil or Bolivia; they are not issued at the border. There is a daily bus at 0800 from the dock on the opposite side of the Madre de Dios from Puerto Maldonado to Iberia, five hours, US$3. A few colectivos also make this run each day, four hours, US$7. From Iberia to Iñapari there are occasional but regular colectivos, 2½ hours, US$7. Alternatively take a flight to Iberia and continue by road. Get a tourist visa at the Brazilian immigration in Iñapari. **Crossing to Brazil**

Peru

Background

History

Towards independence After the fatal Indian revolt of 1780, led by Túpac Amaru II, a further Indian rebellion in 1814 also failed. But this last flare-up had the sympathy of many of the locally born Spanish, who resented their status, inferior to the Spaniards born in Spain, the refusal to give them any but the lowest offices, the high taxation imposed by the home government, and the severe restrictions upon trade with any country but Spain.

Help came to them from the outside world: José de San Martín's Argentine troops, convoyed from Chile under the protection of Lord Cochrane's squadron, landed in southern Peru on 7 September 1820. San Martín proclaimed Peruvian independence at Lima on 28 July 1821, though most of the country was still in the hands of the Viceroy, José de La Serna. Bolívar, who had already freed Venezuela and Colombia, sent Antonio José de Sucre to Ecuador where, on 24 May 1822, he gained a victory over La Serna at Pichincha. San Martín, after a meeting with Bolívar at Guayaquil, left for Argentina and a self-imposed exile in France, while Bolívar and Sucre completed the conquest of Peru by defeating La Serna at the battle of Junín (6 August 1824) and the decisive battle of Ayacucho (9 December 1824). For over a year there was a last stand in the Real Felipe fortress at Callao by the Spanish troops under General Rodil before they capitulated on 22 January 1826. Bolívar was invited to stay in Peru, but left for Colombia in 1826.

Important subsequent events were a temporary confederation between Peru and Bolivia in the 1830s; the Peruvian-Spanish War (1866); and the War of the Pacific (1879-83), in which Peru and Bolivia were defeated by Chile and Peru lost its southern territory. A long-standing legacy of this was the Tacna-Arica dispute, which was not settled until 1929 (see under Tacna).

Modern Peru A reformist military Junta took over control of the country in October 1968. Under its first leader, Gen Juan Velasco Alvarado, the Junta instituted a series of measures to raise the personal status and standard of living of the workers and the rural Indians, by land reform, worker participation in industrial management and ownership, and nationalization of basic industries, exhibiting an ideology perhaps best described as 'military socialism'. In view of his failing health Gen Velasco was replaced in 1975 by Gen Francisco Morales Bermúdez and policy (because of a mounting economic crisis and the consequent need to seek financial aid from abroad) swung to the Right. Presidential and congressional elections were held on 18 May 1980, and Fernando Belaúnde Terry was elected President for the second time. His term was marked by growing economic problems and the appearance of the Maoist guerrilla movement Sendero Luminoso (Shining Path).

Initially conceived in the University of Ayacucho, the movement gained most support for its goal of overthrowing the whole system of Lima-based government from highland Indians and migrants to urban shanty towns. The activities of Sendero Luminoso and another guerrilla group, Túpac Amaru (MRTA), frequently disrupted transport and electricity supplies, although their strategies had to be reconsidered after the arrest of both their leaders in 1992. Víctor Polay of MRTA was arrested in June and Abimael Guzmán of Sendero Luminoso was captured in September; he was sentenced to life imprisonment. Although Sendero did not capitulate, many of its members in 1994-95 took advantage of the Law of Repentance, which guaranteed lighter sentences in return for surrender, and freedom in exchange for valuable information. Meanwhile, Túpac Amaru was thought to have ceased operations (see below).

The April 1985 elections were won by the APRA party leader Alán García Pérez. During his populist, left-wing presidency disastrous economic policies caused increasing poverty and civil instability. In presidential elections held over two rounds in 1990, Alberto Fujimori of the Cambio 90 movement defeated the novelist Mario Vargas Llosa, who belonged to the Fredemo (Democratic Front) coalition. Fujimori, without an established political network behind him, failed to win a majority in either the senate or the lower house. Lack of congressional support was one of the reasons behind the dissolution of congress and the suspension of the constitution on 5 April 1992. With massive popular support, President Fujimori declared that he needed a freer hand to introduce free-market reforms, combat terrorism and drug trafficking, and root out corruption.

Elections to a new, 80-member Democratic Constituent Congress (CCD) in November 1992 were boycotted by three major parties and Fujimori's Cambio 90/Nueva Mayoría coalition won a majority of seats. In municipal elections held in February 1993 the trend against mainstream political groups continued as independent candidates won the lion's share of council seats. A new constitution drawn up by the CCD was approved by a narrow majority of the electorate in October 1993. Among the new articles were the immediate re-election of the president (previously prohibited for one presidential term), the death penalty for terrorist leaders, the establishment of a single-chamber congress, the reduction of the role of the state, the designation of Peru as a market economy and the favouring of foreign investment. As expected, Fujimori stood for re-election on 9 April 1995 and beat his independent opponent, former UN General Secretary, Javier Pérez de Cuéllar, by a resounding margin. The coalition that supported him also won a majority in Congress.

The government's success in most economic areas did not accelerate the distribution of foreign funds for social projects. Furthermore, rising unemployment and the austerity imposed by economic policy continued to cause hardship for many. Economic progress also began to falter, casting further doubt on the government's ability to alleviate poverty. Dramatic events on 17 December 1996 thrust several of these issues into sharper focus. 14 Túpac Amaru guerrillas infiltrated a reception at the Japanese Embassy in Lima, taking 490 hostages and demanding the release of their imprisoned colleagues and new measures to raise living standards. Most of the hostages were released and negotiations were pursued during a stalemate that lasted until 22 April 1997. The president took sole responsibility for the successful, but risky assault which freed all the hostages (one died of heart failure) and killed all the terrorists. By not yielding to Túpac Amaru, Fujimori regained much popularity. But this masked the fact that no concrete steps had been taken to ease social problems. It also deflected attention from Fujimori's plans to stand for a third term following his unpopular manipulation of the law to persuade Congress that the new constitution did not apply to his first period in office. Until the last month of campaigning for the 2000 presidential elections, Fujimori had a clear lead over his main rivals. His opponents insisted that Fujimori that should not stand and local and international observers voiced increasing concern over the state domination of the media. Meanwhile, the popularity of Alejandro Toledo, a centrist and former World Bank official of humble origins, surged to such an extent that he and Fujimori were neck-and neck in the first poll. Toledo and his supporters claimed that Fujimori's slim majority was the result of fraud, a view echoed in the pressure put on the president, by the US government among others, to allow a second ballot. The run-off election, on 28 May 2000, was also contentious since foreign observers, including the Organization of American States, said the electoral system was unprepared and flawed, proposing a postponement. The authorities refused to delay. Toledo boycotted the election and Fujimori was returned unopposed, but with scant approval. Having won, he proposed to "strengthen democracy".

This pledge proved to be worthless following the airing of a secretly-shot video on 14 September 2000 of Fujimori's close aide and head of the National Intelligence Service (SIN), Vladimiro Montesinos, handing US$15,000 to a congressman, Alberto Kouri, to persuade him to switch allegiances to Fujimori's coalition. Fujimori's demise was swift. His initial reaction was to close down SIN and announce new elections, eventually set for 8 April 2001, at which he would not stand. Montesinos, declared a wanted man, fled to Panama, where he was denied asylum. He returned to Peru in October and Fujimori personally led the search parties to find his former ally. Peruvians watched in amazement as this game of cat-and-mouse was played out on their TV screens. While Montesinos himself successfully evaded capture, investigators began to uncover the extent of his empire, which held hundreds of senior figures in its web.

Peru

His activities encompassed extortion, money-laundering, bribery, intimidation, probably arms and drugs dealing and possibly links with the CIA and death squads. Swiss bank accounts in his name were found to contain about US$70 million, while other millions were discovered in accounts in the Cayman Islands and elsewhere. By early 2001 sightings of him were reported in Costa Rica, then Venezuela and Aruba. Meanwhile, Fujimori, apparently in pursuit of his presidential duties, made various overseas trips, including to Japan. Here, on 20 November, he sent Congress an email announcing his resignation. Congress rejected this, firing him instead on charges of being "morally unfit" to govern. An interim president, Valentín Paniagua, was sworn in, with ex-UN Secretary General Javier Pérez de Cuéllar as Prime Minister, and the government set about uncovering the depth of corruption associated with Montesinos and Fujimori. It also had to prepare for free and fair elections. Further doubt was cast over the entire Fujimori period by suggestions that he may not have been born in Peru, as claimed, but in Japan. His hosts certainly declared that, through his parents, he was a Japanese national and therefore exempt from extradition. If he was indeed Japanese by birth as well as ancestry, he should never have been entitled to stand for the highest office in Peru.

In the run-up to the 2001 elections, the front-runner was Alejandro Toledo, but with far from a clear majority. Other candidates included the right-winger Lourdes Flores, ex-Economy Minister Carlos Boloña, Fernando Olivera, who had made the Montesinos video public and ex-President Alan García. It was García who emerged as Toledo's main opponent, forcing a second ballot on 3 June. This was won by Toledo with 52% of the vote, compared to 48% for García. Toledo pledged to heal the wounds that had opened in Peru since his first electoral battle with the disgraced Fujimori, but his first year in office was marked by slow progress on both the political and economic fronts. In March 2002, just before US President George W Bush visited Lima for a regional summit, a car bomb exploded in Lima, killing several people. By June 2002, there had been no subsequent bombings, nor resurgence of terrorist movements.

In July 2002 Montesinos was convicted of usurping power and sentenced by the Peruvian anti-corruption court to nine years and four months in prison.

Government Under a new constitution (approved by plebiscite in October 1993), a single chamber, 80-seat congress replaced the previous, two-house legislature. Men and women over 18 are eligible to vote; registration and voting is compulsory until the age of 60. Those who do not vote are fined. The President, to whom is entrusted the Executive Power, is elected for five years and may, under the constitution which came into force on 1 January 1994, be re-elected for a second term.

Education Education is free and compulsory for both sexes between six and 14. There are public and private secondary schools and private elementary schools. There are 32 State and private universities, and five Catholic universities. A new educational system is being implemented as too many children fail to complete secondary school.

Culture

People Total population in 2001 was 26.1 million, with an annual average growth rate of 1.7 (1995-2000). The indigenous population of Peru is put at about three million Quechua and Aymara Indians in the Andean region and 200,000-250,000 Amazonian Indians from 40-50 ethnic groups. In the Andes, there are 5,000 Indian communities but few densely populated settlements. Their literacy rate is the lowest of any comparable group in South America and their diet is 50% below acceptable levels. About two million Indians speak no Spanish, their main tongue being Quechua, the language of the Incas; they are largely outside the money economy. The conflict between Sendero Luminoso guerrillas and the security forces caused the death of thousands of highland Indians. Many Indian groups are under threat from colonization, development and road-building projects. Some have been dispossessed and exploited for their labour.

Forecast population growth 2000-2005: 1.6%
Urban population in 2000: 73% of the total
Infant mortality: 37 per thousand live births

Peru

Books

See the *Peru Handbook* and *The Peru Reader*, edited by **Orin Starn**, **Carlos Iván Degregori** and **Robin Kirk** (Duke University Press; Durham and London, 1995). The latter contains history, culture and politics and is an excellent introduction to these topics; the anthology ranges from the precolonial to the present. *A Field Guide to the Birds of Peru*, by **James F Clements** and **Noam Shany** (Ibis, 2001); also *Birds of Colombia* (Princeton University) and *South American Birds*, by **John Dunning**, give the good coverage of birds of Peru; also *Birds of the High Andes* (University of Copenhagen, 1990) by **Nils Krabbe** and **Jon Fjeldsa**, which covers all Peruvian birds that occur above 3,000 m. *Ecotraveller's Wildlife Guide: Peru*, by **David L Person** and **Les Beletsky** (London: Academic Press, 2001).

Trekking in the Cordillera Blanca *South American Explorers* publishes a good map with additional notes on the popular Llanganuco to Santa Cruz loop. Guides currently in print: *Callejón de Huaylas y Cordillera Blanca*, by **Felipe Díaz** (Spanish, English and German editions), available locally, *La Cordillera Blanca de Los Andes*, by **Antonio Gómez** and **Juan José Tomé** (Desnivel, 1998, Spanish only, US$25) principally a climbing guide, but contains some trekking and general information, also available locally. **Juanjo Tomé** has also written *Escaladas en los Andes. Guía de la Cordillera Blanca* (Desnivel, 1999, Spanish only), a climbing guide. Another climbing guide is *Climbs of the Cordillera Blanca of Peru*, by **David Sharman** (1995), available locally, from *South American Explorers*, as well as from Cordee in the UK and Alpenbooks in the USA. **John Biggar**'s *The Andes. A Guide for Cllimbers* (BigR Publishing, 1999). *Parque Nacional Huascarán*, by **Jim Bartle**, is a beautiful soft-cover photo collection with English and Spanish text.

For an account of the Andean Inca road, see **Christopher Portway**, *Journey Along the Andes* (Impact Books, London, 1993). Also **Karin Muller**, *Along the Inca Road. A Woman's Journey into an Ancient Empire* (National Geographic Books, 2000). **Ricardo Espinosa**, *El Perú a toda Costa* (Editur, 1997), a walking guide covering the length of the country. The same company has published *Por los Caminos del Perú en Bicicleta*, by Omar Zarzar, www.caminanteperu.com

The Chachapoyas Region For studies of archaeological remains see **Henri and Paula Reichlen**, *Récherches archaeologiques dans les Andes du haut Utcubamba*, in *Journal des Américanistes*, includes an accurate map, and **Gene Savoy**, *Antisuyo*; **Kaufmann Doig** refers to the '12 Cities of the Condors' in his *Arqueología Peruana*. See also *The Cloud People, an Anthropological Survey* by **Morgan Davis**, and **Keith Muscutt**'s *Warriors of the Clouds: A Lost Civilization in the Upper Amazon of Peru* (New Mexico Press, 1998; www.chachapoyas.com).

Cusco and Machu Picchu See Footprint's *Cusco and the Inca Trail Handbook*. Also *Exploring Cusco*, by **Peter Frost**, which is available in Cusco bookshops. *Cusco Peru Tourist Guide*, published by Lima 2000. *The White Rock*, by **Hugh Thomson** (Phonenix paperback, 2002), describes Thomson's own travels in the Inca heartland, as well as the journeys of earlier explorers and the history of the region. *The Sacred Center*, by **Johan Reinhard**, explains Machu Picchu in archaeological terms. *The Machu Picchu Historical Sanctuary*, by **Peter Frost** (Nuevas Imagenes SA, with colour photographs). *Qosqo. The Navel of the World*, by **Tony Morrison** (Lima, 1997), describes Cusco's past and present with photographs of the city and its surroundings. Another book with photographs and text is **Max Milligan**'s *In the Realm of the Incas* (Harper Collins, 2001). *Apus and Incas*, by **Charles Brod**, describes cultural walks in and around Cusco, and treks in the Cordilleras Vilcabamba, Vilcanota and Urubamba, plus the Manu National Park (2nd edition, Inca Expeditions, 2323, Portland, USA. *Lost City of the Incas* by **Hiram Bingham** (available in Lima and Cusco, new illustrated edition, with an introduction by Hugh Thomson, Weidenfeld & Nicolson, London, 2002); *A Walking Tour of Machu Picchu* by **Pedro Sueldo Nava** – in several languages, available in Cusco. *South American Explorers* has detailed information on walks around Machu Picchu.

The southeastern jungle *Manu National Park*, by **Kim MacQuarrie** and **André and Cornelia Bartschi**, is a large, expensive and excellent book, with beautiful photographs. *Birds of Tambopata – a checklist, Mammals, Amphibians and Reptiles of*

Peru

Tambopata, Ecology of Tropical Rainforesets: a layman's guide and *Tambopata map guide*, all by TReeS, who also produce tapes of *Jungle Sounds* and *Bird Sounds of southeast Peru* (address on page 1289). *Madre de Dios Packet*, by *South American Explorers*, gives practical travel advice for the area.

A selection of books on history and culture: For the whole period of the Conquest John Hemming's *The Conquest of the Incas* is invaluable; Ann Kendall *Everyday Life of the Incas*, Batsford, London, 1978. Also *Oro y tragedia de los Incas* by **Manuel Portal Cabellos**, excellent on the division of the empire, civil war, the conquest and *huaqueros*. *The Incas and their Ancestors: The Archaeology of Peru*, Michael E Mosely; *Pyramids of Túcume*, Thor Heyerdahl, Daniel H Sandweiss & Alfredo Narváez (Thames & Hudson, 1995).

Travellers: Dervla Murphy, *Eight Feet in the Andes* (1983); Matthew Parris, *Inca-Kola* (1990); Tahir Shah, *Trail of Feathers* (2001); Ronald Wright, *Cut Stones and Crossroads: a Journey in Peru* (1984).

Fiction: Thornton Wilder, *The Bridge of San Luis Rey* (1927); Peter Mathiessen, *At Play in the Fields of the Lord* (1965); Nicholas Shakespeare, *The Vision of Elena Silves* (1989). Peruvian writers: **Clorinda Matto de Turner** (1854-1909) was the first writer of 'indigenist' fiction in Peru (see *Aves sin nido*) and others followed in attempting to use fiction to address the issues of the ethnic majority: eg **Ciro Alegría** (1909-67), *El mundo es ancho y ajeno/Broad and Alien is the World* (1941) and **José María Arguedas** (1911-69), *Los ríos profundos/Deep Rivers* (1958). Peru's best known novelist is Mario Vargas Llosa (1936-), who has written many internationally acclaimed books, eg *La ciudad y los perros/The Time of the Hero* (1962), *La casa verde/The Green House* (1965), *La guerra del fin del mundo/The War of the End of World* (1981) and, most recently, *La fiesta del chivo* (2000). **César Vallejo** (1892-1938) is Peru's outstanding 20th-century poet: his avant-garde collection *Trilce* (1922) is unlike anything before it in the Spanish language, but his work also has strong political commitment, as in *Poemas humanos* and *España, aparte de mí este cáliz*, both published posthumously.

Uruguay

Uruguay is a land of rolling hills, best explored on horseback, or by staying at the many estancias that have opened their doors to visitors. Fray Bentos, a town that lent its name to corned beef for generations, is now an industrial museum. Each summer, millions of holidaymakers flock to Punta del Este, one of the most famous resorts on the continent, but to avoid the crowds, go out of season, or venture up the Atlantic coast towards Brazil. West of Montevideo is Colonia del Sacramento, a former smuggling town turned gambling centre, and a colonial gem where race horses take their exercise in the sea.

11

Uruguay

Essentials

Planning your trip

Where to go

Montevideo, the capital, is the business heart of the country and has an interesting Ciudad Vieja (old city), which is being refurbished. The highlight here is Mercado del Puerto, the former dockside market, which has become an emporium for traditional food and drink. Within the city's limits are a number of beaches and, heading east up the coast, these continue along the north shore of the Río de la Plata and on to the Atlantic seaboard. The most famous resort is **Punta del Este** which, in season (Dec-Feb), is packed with Argentines, Brazilians and locals taking their summer break. Beyond Punta del Este, there are quieter beaches with less infrastructure, but with sand dunes and other natural features. A number of national parks have been set up to protect the environment on, and just inland from, the coast.

West of the capital is **Colonia del Sacramento**, a unique remnant of colonial building in this part of the continent. It is well preserved, standing on a small peninsula, and has one of the principal ferry ports for passenger traffic from Buenos Aires. Consequently it is a popular place, but well worth a visit. Continuing west you come to the confluence of the Río Uruguay with the Plata estuary. Up river are the last vestiges of the meat canning industry at **Fray Bentos**, which has a museum commemorating what used to be one of Uruguay's main businesses. Upriver are towns such as Paysandú and Salto, from which you can cross to Argentina, and the hot springs which have been developed into resorts.

The centre of the country is principally agricultural land, where livestock and a variety of crops are grown. Many *estancias* (farms) throughout the country accept visitors, some just for the day, others for longer stays. Daytrips out of Montevideo, Punta del Este, or Colonia, for instance, to an *estancia*, usually involve a meal, shopping for handicrafts, dairy produce, etc, and quite often an educational element. Those ranches which offer lodging let you take part in the daily work (as these are working farms) and the lifestyle of the countryside; you can do as much, or as little as you like. Horse riding is the main activity and there are usually horses to suit every level of ability.

When to go

The climate is temperate, if somewhat damp and windy, and summer heat is tempered by Atlantic breezes, but there are occasional large variations. In winter (Jun-Sep), when the average temperature is 10° to 16°C, the temperature can fall now and then to well below freezing. It is generally humid and hardly ever snows. Summer (Dec-Mar), with an average temperature of 21° to 27°C, has irregular dry periods. There is always some wind and for the most part the nights are relatively cool. The rainfall, with prolonged wet periods in Jul and Aug, averages about 1,200 mm at Montevideo and some 250 more in the north, but the amount varies yearly.

Most tourists visit during the summer, which is also high season, when prices are higher and hotels and transport should be booked in advance. Seasonal variations for Montevideo and Punta del Este are given on pages 1309 and 1319. In the low season on the coast many establishments close. Business visits can be made throughout the year, but it is best to avoid the tourist months.

Finding out more

The **Comisión Nacional de Turismo** information office, see under Montevideo Tourist offices, issues tourist literature. The **Ministry of Tourism** is at Av Libertador 1409, p 2, T900 4148. On the Internet, visit www.turismo.gub.uy A good Uruguayan portal worth investigating is www.eltimon.com A tourism portal is www.turismodeluruguay.com in English, Spanish and Portuguese.

Uruguay

Uruguayan embassies and consulates

Australia, *Suite 2, Level 4, Commerce House, 24 Brisbane Avenue, Barton ACT 2600, Canberra, T616-62739100, F616-6273-9099, urucan@austarmetro.com.au*

Canada, *130 Albert Street, Suite 1905 Ottawa, Ontario K1P 5G4, Canada, T1613-234-2727, F1613-234-2937, www.iosphere.net/-uruott/; 1315 Finch Avenue West, Suite 316, Toronto, Ontario M3J 2G6, T1416-6365454, F1416-6360351; 2nd floor, 827 West Pender Street, Vancouver BC V6C 3G8, T1604-6811377, F1604-7316775.*

Finland, *Lönnrotinkatu 7, 00120 Helsinki, T3580-61106, F3580-644836.*

France, *15 Le Sueur – 1ra étage 75.116, Paris, 1-45008137, F1-45012517, urugali@fr.inter.net*

Germany, *Budapesterstrasse 39, 10787 Berlin, T4930-263 9016, F4930-263 9017, urubrande@t-online.de*

Israel, *Nordau 73 Herzlta 'B', 46582 Tel Aviv, T9729-9569611, emrou@netvision.net.il*

Italy, *Via Vittorio Veneto 183, 5 floor, 00187 Roma, T3906-4821776, F3906-4823695, emb.uruguay@agora.stm.it*

Japan, *38 Kowa International Building, room 908, 4-12-24 Nishi Azabu, Minato-Ku, Tokyo 106, T813-34861750, F813-34869872, urujap@ad.il24.net*

Netherlands, *Mauritskade 33, 2de etage 2514 HD, The Hague, T3170-3609815, F3170-3562826, uruholan@wxs.nl*

New Zealand, *Davis Ogilvie & Partners Ltd, PO Box 549, 4th floor BNZ Building, 137 Armagh Street, Christchurch, T643-366 1653, F643-379 2348, emma@dop.co.nz*

Norway, *Kongens gt 16, 0153, T47-93404293, F47-22335301.*

Spain, *Pase del Pintor Rosales, No 32, p 1, D Madrid 28008, T91-758 0475, urumatri@urumatri.com*

Sweden *(also for Denmark), Kommendoersgatan 114.58, Stockholm, Sweden, T6603196, F6653166, urustoc@uruemb.se*

UK, *140 Brompton Road, 2nd Floor, London SW3 1HY, T020-75898835, F020-75819585, urubri@demon.co.uk*

USA, *2715 M Street NW, 3rd floor, Washington DC 20007, T1202-3311313, F1202-3318142, uruguay@erols.com; 1077 Ponce de León Boulevard, Suite B Coral Gables, FL 33134, Miami, T1305-4439764, F1305-4437802, urumia@bellsouth.net; 564 Market Street, Suite 221, San Francisco CA 94104, T1415-9865222, F1415-9894502.*

Before you travel

Visas & immigration A passport is necessary for entry except for nationals of most Latin American countries and citizens of the USA, who can get in with national identity documents for stays of up to 90 days. Visas are not required for a stay of less than 3 months by nationals of Argentina, Australia, Austria, Bahamas, Barbados, Belgium, Belize, Bolivia, Brazil, Canada, Colombia, Costa Rica, Chile, Croatia, Cyprus, Czech Republic, Denmark, Dominican Republic, Ecuador, El Salvador, Finland, France, Germany, Greece, Guatemala, Guyana, Honduras, Hungary, Italy, Israel, Iceland, Jamaica, Republic of Ireland, Japan, Luxembourg, Liechtenstein, Lithuania, Malaysia, Malta, Mexico, Netherlands, New Zealand, Nicaragua, Norway, Panama, Paraguay, Peru, Poland, Portugal, Slovenia, South Africa, Spain, Sweden, Switzerland, Seychelles, Trinidad and Tobago, Turkey, UK, USA, Venezuela. Visas cost £27 (or equivalent), and you need a passport photograph and to show a ticket out of Uruguay. Tourist cards (obligatory for all tourists, obtainable on entry) are valid for three months, extendable for a similar period. For extensions (small fee) go to Migraciones office, Calle Misiones 1513, T916 0471/916 1094.

Customs **Duty-free allowance**: duties are not usually charged on a reasonable quantity of goods brought in obviously for the traveller's own use. 400 cigarettes or 50 cigars or 250 g of tobacco are admitted duty-free; so are two litres of alcoholic drink, three small bottles of perfume and gifts up to the value of US$5.

Currency The currency is the *peso uruguayo*. Bank notes issued are for 10, 50, 100, 200 (do not confuse with old peso 2,000 notes – pre-1993, which are now worth 2 pesos), 500 (don't confuse with 50), 1,000, 5,000 and 10,000 pesos uruguayos. Coins: 50 centavos; one, two pesos. Any amount of currency can be taken in or out.

Banks No restriction on foreign exchange transactions (ie an excellent place to stock up with US\$ bills, though American Express and some banks refuse to do this for credit cards; most places charge 3% commission for such transactions). Those banks which give US\$ cash against a credit card are given in the text. Dollars cash can be purchased when leaving the country. Changing Argentine pesos into Uruguayan pesos is usually a marginally worse rate than for dollars. Brazilian *reais* get a much worse rate. US\$ notes are widely accepted.

Credit cards There is a 10% charge on the use of credit cards. Visa and MasterCard ATMs can be found at branches of Redbanc and ABN Amro. Many other banks have Visa ATMs, including Bancos Comercial, de Crédito, Francés, Santander and Sudameris, BankBoston and Citibank. Many shopkeepers are unaware of this but a phone call will confirm it. Credit card hotline: T0900-2020. MasterCard emergency line call collect to USA, T1-314-542 7111. Most hotels outside Montevideo do not accept credit cards.

Cost of travelling Uruguay is expensive, but not as expensive as Argentina. Prices vary considerably between summer and winter, Punta del Este being the most expensive summer resort in Latin America. Some Argentines find that generally prices and quality of clothing, for instance, are better in Montevideo than Buenos Aires. Someone staying in a cheap hotel, eating the *menú del día* and travelling by bus, should allow US\$25-35 per day.

Money
Rates change frequently because of the floating exchange rate and inflation differentials against the US dollar; peso exchange rate with US\$ in July 2002: 18.73

Getting there

From Europe Direct flights by Pluna (Madrid, twice a week via Rio de Janeiro). From the UK, connecting flights via São Paulo daily. Flying by other carriers, a change must be made at Rio, São Paulo or Buenos Aires.

From North America United Airlines daily from Chicago and American daily from Dallas, both via Miami and Buenos Aires.

To Uruguay from South America From Argentina: ferry and hydrofoil services (Montevideo and Colonia to Buenos Aires) and launch services (Carmelo to Tigre) are given in the text. *Aerolíneas Argentinas*, ARG (ex-Lapa), *Pluna* and other carriers have several flights a day between Aeroparque in Buenos Aires and Carrasco Airport, flights can be very full, especially in high season. Service intensified during holiday period. Also flights to Punta del Este from Buenos Aires. There are bus/plane services via Colonia to Buenos Aires. Buses run across the Paysandú and Fray Bentos bridges. Direct bus between Buenos Aires and Montevideo via Fray Bentos takes about 10 hours. Ferries cross the Río Uruguay between Salto and Concordia. **From Bolivia** *TAM/Mercosur* 3 times a week from Santa Cruz via Asunción and Buenos Aires. **From Brazil** There are regular daily flights from Rio de Janeiro and São Paulo with *Pluna* and *Varig* (joint operation). *Pluna/Varig* includes a stopover at Porto Alegre on two of their daily Rio-Montevideo flights. By road: the Pan-American Highway runs 2,880 km from Rio de Janeiro to Montevideo and on to Colonia. It is poorly surfaced in parts. There are several bus services. See under Brazil, How to get to Brazil: By Air, for the Mercosur airpass. **From Chile** Pluna (5 a week) and *LanChile* (daily) from Santiago. **From Paraguay** Daily with either *TAM/Mercosur* or *Pluna*. Also regular buses between Asunción and Montevideo.

Air

Touching down

Airport tax US\$6 on all air travellers leaving Uruguay for Buenos Aires, Aeroparque (but US\$12 to Ezeiza); US\$12 for all other countries (payable in US dollars or local currency), US\$0.50 on internal flights, and a tax of 3% on all tickets issued and paid for in Uruguay.

Airport information

Normally all hotel and restaurant bills include a percentage service charge plus 23% value-added tax, but an additional small tip is expected. In other cases give 10% of the total bill. Porters at the airport expect about US\$1 per piece of luggage. Taxi drivers are tipped 10%

Tipping

Uruguay

Touching down

Business hours *Department stores generally are open 0900 to 1200 (or 1230), 1400 (or 1430) to 1900, but 0900 to 1230 on Saturday.* **Businesses**: *most work from 0830 to 1200, 1430 to 1830 or 1900, according to whether they open on Saturday.* **Banks**: *1300 to 1700 in Montevideo; there are special summer hours (1 December-15 March) in Montevideo (1330-1730), in the interior (0800-1200) and in Punta del Este, Maldonado and other resorts (1600-2000);*

banks are closed on Saturday. **Government offices**: *mid-March to mid-November, 1300 to 1830 from Monday to Friday; rest of the year, 0700 to 1230 (not Saturday).*
IDD 598 *Long equal tones with long equal pauses means it is ringing; short equal tones with short pauses indicates engaged.*
Voltage *220 volts 50 cycles AC.*
Weights and measures *Metric units alone are legal.*

of the fare. Tips at cafés are about 10%. Cinema ushers get a small tip, as do cloakroom attendants and hairdressers (10-15%).

Safety Personal security offers few problems in most of Uruguay to travellers who are reasonably prudent. Since 1997 there has been a rise in gang robbery in Montevideo, so you should not show any signs of obvious wealth there. The Policía Turística patrol the streets of the capital.

Where to stay

Camping There are lots of sites. Most towns have municipal sites (quality varies). Many sites along the Ruta Interbalnearia, but most of these close off season. The Tourist Office in Montevideo issues a good guide to campsites and youth hostels; see references in main text. Methylated spirits, called *alcohol de quemar*, is sold in *Dispensas*.

Youth hostels Asociación de Alberguistas del Uruguay, Calle Pablo de María 1583, Montevideo. Open Mon-Fri 1130-1900, T4004245, F4001326 (www.internet.com.uy/aau) operates hostels (HI members only) at 16 locations around the country. Many of the hostels are poorly equipped. A 10% rebate is available with HI membership on *Lapa* plane tickets between Colonia and Buenos Aires, and rebates have also been reported (10-20%) for bus fares and hotel prices.

Getting around

Air Internal flights are very cheap with Pluna and Aviasur (addresses under Montevideo). Provincial airports are given in the text. **Road** There are 52,000 km of roads, 23 of them paved and a further 60 (approximately) all-weather. Roads are generally in good condition. Motorists should drive with their headlights on, especially on major roads, even in daylight. The *Comisión Nacional de Turismo* will help to plan itineraries by car. **NB Hitchhiking** is not easy. **Bus** Bus services are given in the text.

Motoring
Care is needed at night since vehicle lights do not always work. Vehicles do not stop, nor is there a right of way, at uncontrolled intersections

Drivers in Montevideo are generally courteous towards pedestrians, but if driving yourself, take care. Outside Montevideo there is little traffic and few filling stations (many close at weekends). There are many ancient cars (1920s and 1930s models are called *cachilas* and skilled mechanics keep them on the road). Insurance is not required by law. Gasoline prices are US$1.03 per litre *eco supra*, US$0.97 per litre *super*, US$0.84 per litre *común*; diesel is US$0.45 per litre. Automóvil Club del Uruguay has a fuel and service station for its members only at Yí y Colonia, Montevideo, T902 1691 (head office is Av Libertador General Lavalleja 1532, T902 4792). Reciprocity with foreign automobile clubs is available all year round, members do not have to pay for affiliation. To bring a private car into Uruguay, 90-day temporary admission is usually given without any problems, as long as the customs officer is satisfied with your genuine tourist intentions. A new sedan may arouse suspicions of illegal import. Entry is easier and faster with a *carnet de passages*, but it is not essential. Without it you will be given a temporary import paper which must be surrendered on leaving the country. Car spares are expensive. The area around Galicia and Yí in Montevideo is recommended for new parts.

Train The only passenger services in operation are Tacuarembó-Rivera and commuter services Montevideo – 25 de Agosto (in Florida department). There are plans to resume services to Minas and Río Branco (on the Brazilian border).

Maps **Automóvil Club del Uruguay**, Av Libertador General Lavalleja 1532, Montevideo, T908 4710, publishes road maps of the city and country, and so do *Esso* and *Ancap* at about US$2 each. *ITM* of Vancouver also publish a map of Uruguay (1:800,000). Official maps are issued by **Instituto Geográfico Militar**, Abreu y 8 de Octubre, open 0800-1230, T801 6868.

Keeping in touch

The use of email is becoming more common, but cybercafés are not plentiful. **Internet**

Postal services are very unreliable; all items should be registered and sent by air mail to avoid **Post** delay (probably better to go direct to airport, avoiding chaos of the sorting office). Rates to USA and Europe, up to 20 g US$1, up to 100 g US$3; to South Africa and Asia up to 20 g US$1.40, up to 100 g US$3.70. Courier services are used increasingly: to Europe US$30-40, USA US$25, South Africa US$35, Middle East US$45, Buenos Aires US$12.

Provided by *Antel* (see under Montevideo). Direct dialling to any country abroad is **Telephone** straightforward – public phones cannot receive incoming calls. Collect calls available to most countries (collect calls are the cheapest way of phoning USA and Canada). US$1 per min to Mercosur countries, US$0.75 reduced rate. For the rest of the world, US$2.85 for the 1st min, US$1.10 for each subsequent min, US$2.15 and 0.85 respectively, reduced rate. Reduced rate operates 2100 to 0900 and all weekend. Fax from *Antel*, first sheet costs US$1 more than a minute's phone call to USA, Europe and Australia (US$0.50 more to Argentina and Brazil).

Newspapers Montevideo newspapers: *El País*, www3.diarioelpais.com/edicion/ *La* **Media** *República*, www.diariolarepublica.com *El Observador*, www.observa.com.uy and *La Mañana*, www.lm.com.uy and *El Diario* and *Ultimas Noticias* which come out in the evening. *Búsqueda* and *Ambito Financiero* are published weekly. The town of Paysandú has *El Telégrafo*, www.paysandu.com At about 1000 the main Buenos Aires papers, including the *Buenos Aires Herald*, can be bought in Montevideo.

Radio and television There are 35 radio stations (8 private FM) in Montevideo and 65 in the rest of the country. Of the 20 colour-TV stations, 4 transmit from Montevideo (channel 12 is the most popular). Also satellite and cable TV.

Food and drink

Beef is eaten at almost all meals. The majority of restaurants are *parrilladas* (grills) where the **Food** staple is beef. *Asado* (barbecued beef) is popular; the main cuts are *asado de tira* (ribs); *pulpa* (no *Dinner in 'top class* bones), *lomo* (fillet steak) and entrecote. To get a lean piece of *asado*, ask for *asado flaco*. *Costilla* *restaurants' is served* (chop) and *milanesa* (veal cutlet) are also popular; usually eaten with mixed salad or chips. *from 2000 to 0100.* *Chivitos* are Uruguayan steak burgers; *chivitos canadienses* are sandwiches filled with slices of *In less formal* meat, lettuce, tomato, egg, etc (normally over US$2 – very filling). Two other good local dishes *restaurants service* are *puchero* (beef with vegetables, bacon, beans and sausages) and the local varieties of pizza. *starts at 1930.* Other specialities are barbecued pork, grilled chicken in wine, *cazuela* (or stew) usually with *Restaurants usually* *mondongo* (tripe) or sea foods (for example squid, shark – *cazón*, mussels – *mejillones*). The *charge cubierto* sausages are very good and spicy (*chorizos, morcillas, salchichas*). *Morcilla dulce*, a sweet black *(bread), ranging from* sausage, made from blood, orange peel and walnuts, has been highly praised; so has the *US$0.30 to US$1 in* *morcilla salada*, which is savoury. For snacks, *media lunas mixtas* are a type of croissant filled with *Punta del Este* ham and cheese, either hot or cold; toasted sandwiches are readily available; *panchos* are hot dogs, *húngaros* are spicy sausage hot dogs. *Preparación* is a selection of crisps, nuts, vol-au-vent, etc. An excellent dessert is *chajá*, from Paysandú, a type of sponge-cake ball with cream and jam inside, also with peaches – very sweet; others are *massini* (a cream sponge), *Martín Fierro* (*dulce* *de membrillo* with cheese) and the common lemon pie. Pastries are very good indeed, and crystallized egg-yolks, known as *yemas*, are popular sweets. Ice cream is excellent everywhere.

Drink

Local wines are very varied, not only from bodega to bodega, but also from vintage to vintage. 'Del museo' indicates the bodega's vintage reserve

The beers are good. Imported drinks are freely available in Montevideo, for example whisky and Chilean wines. *Mate* is a favourite drink between meal hours. The local spirits are *caña* and *grappa*; some find the locally-made whisky and gin acceptable. In the Mercado del Puerto, Montevideo, a *medio medio* is half still white wine, half sparkling white (a must! Elsewhere a *medio medio* is half *caña* and half whisky). *Espillinar* is a cross between whisky and rum. Try the *clérico*, a tasty mixture of wine, fruit juices and fruits. Coffee is good: a *cortado* is strong, white coffee, *café con leche* is milk with a little coffee. Milk is available, in plastic sacs.

Holidays and festivals

Holidays

1 January, 6 January; Carnival (see below); Easter week; 19 April; 1, 18 May; 19 June; 18 July; 25 August; 12 October; 2 November; 25 December. (8 December is a religious holiday which also marks the official start of the summer holiday.) *Carnival* week is officially the Monday and Tuesday immediately preceding Ash Wednesday, but a great many firms close for the whole of the week.

Business comes to a standstill also during **Holy Week**, which coincides with *La Semana Criolla* (horse-breaking, stunt riding by cowboys, dances and song, many Argentine visitors). Department stores close only from Good Friday. Banks and offices close Thursday-Sunday. Easter Monday is not a holiday.

Sport and special interest travel

Association football is played intensively. **Rugby football** is also played, and there is an annual championship. There are two good 18-hole **golf** links, Cerro and Punta Carretas. There are several **lawn tennis** clubs, and two for **polo**. **Horse racing** at Las Piedras, 4 days a week. Uruguay has 3 important **yacht clubs**, the Uruguayo, the Nautilus and the Punta del Este.

There are 3 main elements to tourism in Uruguay: the beaches (the beach itself is more popular than the water); thermal resorts; and rural and ecological tourism. It is in the last of these that special interest holidays fall, with the emphasis being on areas which are relatively undisturbed. In Uruguay, though, nature tourism seldom means being in the wilderness as the majority of the land is farmed and nature reserves are small. Most important is *estancia* **tourism**, which has already been mentioned in Where to go, at the beginning of the chapter. There is a **Sociedad Uruguaya de Turismo Rural**, Av Uruguay 864, 11100 Montevideo, T323 6854, M 099-610939. Information on *estancias* can be found here, or at the tourist offices in Montevideo (see page 332), general travel agencies and those that specialize in this field: **Estancias Gauchas**, Cecilia Regules Viajes, Bacacay 1334, Montevideo, T/F916 3011, regulesv@adinet.com.uy or uy21333@antel.com.uy (agent for an organization of 80 *estancias* offering lunch and/or lodging, English, French and Portuguese spoken), recommended; **Estancias de Turismo**, Río Branco 1407, apto 306, T/F901 0698. There is a full list of estancias at www.turismo.gub.uy/estancias/operadores_s.html

Fishing is a popular sport, freshwater and sea angling. The best rivers are the Uruguay and the Negro. There is also hunting, but it is controlled by the Ministerio de Ganadería, Agricultura y Pesca. Uruguay is an ideal country for **cycle** touring. Adventure **tourism** The Ríos Uruguay and Negro, again, are the best for **canoeing**, while other outdoor activities include guided and non-guided trekking, horse riding and hang gliding. **Nature tourism** Birdwatching is best in the east of the country, where a number of national parks have been set up in a variety of habitats. These include coastal zones, such as the sand dunes at Cabo Polonio, lakes, marshes and forest reserves on the Atlantic, Santa Teresa (which also contains important historical sites), and offshore islands.

Health

Milk and tap water can be drunk and fresh salads eaten fairly freely throughout the country. Medical services are reported to be expensive. See also Health, Essentials.

Montevideo

Montevideo

Phone code: 02
Colour map 8, grid B6
Population: 1,311,976

Montevideo is many cities rolled into one. It is an international port at its western end and, in the east, a seaside resort with sandy streets and pine forests. In between are the faded Old City, the country's financial heart and the posh residential areas along the coast. Everything blends together: a multitude of architectural styles; café society and tango music; pizza, parrillada and wines; outdoor markets and indoor malls; agricultural fairs; football and traffic. This is where all the elements of Uruguay meet on the shores of the Río de la Plata.

Montevideo, the capital, was founded in 1726. The original site is on a promontory between the Río de la Plata and an inner bay, though the fortifications have been destroyed. In addition to some colonial Spanish and Italian architecture, French and Art Deco styles can be seen. Many buildings in the centre exhibit fine stone and ironwork. The city not only dominates the country's commerce and culture: it accounts for 70% of industrial production and handles almost 90% of imports and exports. It is also a summer resort and the point of departure for a string of seaside resorts to the east (see East from Montevideo).

Getting there Carrasco international **airport** is east of the centre, to which connections by bus or taxi are easy. It takes about 50 mins by bus, 30 mins by taxi, but there is a longer route, by the coast, which may have fewer delays, but is more expensive (ask for the quick route if you want it). Many visitors arrive in Montevideo by boat from Buenos Aires. The **ferry terminal** is in the heart of the city, at the docks not far from the Mercado del Puerto. The **bus terminal**, Tres Cruces, is 10-15 mins by city bus from the centre. It has good facilities and is used by all bus companies.

Getting around The Ciudad Vieja can be explored on foot as it is not large. From there it is not far to Plazas de la Independencia, Fabini and Cagancha, but buses are plentiful along Avenida 18 de Julio, connecting all these places. To get to other parts of the city and the beach districts there are many buses, some running on express routes. There are two types of taxis, the ordinary ones, which are not expensive, but which charge more on Sun and holidays, and *remises*, which operate out of offices and from the airport, and are more expensive. Full details are given in Local Transport, below.

Tourist offices Tourist information is at the Tres Cruces bus terminal (T409 7399) and in the middle of the plaza outside Palacio Municipal, 18 de Julio y Ejido (open daily in high season), both helpful. Also at Carrasco international airport, T601 1757. The *Guía del Ocio*, a weekly guide with Fri edition of *El País*, gives information on museums, cultural events, nightlife and entertainment, including addresses. Recommended. See also www.eltimon.com, for entertainment details. The website of the municipality is www.montevideo.gub.uy **Maps:** best street maps of Montevideo are at the beginning of the *Guía Telefónica* (both white and yellow page volumes). *Eureka Guía De Montevideo* is recommended for streets, sector by sector, with index and bus routes (US$4.75 from bookshops). Kiosks sell the *Atlas* bus guide.

Ins & outs
Some streets have changed name recently but this may not be marked on all maps: Michelini was Cuareim; Hector Gutiérrez Ruiz was Ibicuy; Convención was Latorre; Wilson Ferreira Aldunate was Río Branco

For more detailed information see Transport, page 1314

Uruguay

Sights

In the **Ciudad Vieja** is the oldest square in Montevideo: the **Plaza de la Constitución**, also known as the Plaza Matriz. Here on one side is the **Catedral** (1790-1804), with the historic **Cabildo** (1808) opposite at Gómez y Sarandí (**Museo Histórico Nacional**. ■ *Tue-Sun 1430-1900, T915 9685*. On the south side is the **Club Uruguay** (built 1888, now crumbling), which is worth a look inside. See also the unusual fountain, dating from 1881, made by Italians who misspelt the Spanish inscription at the base.

In the old city a considerable amount of renovation is being done. The Ciudad Vieja is deserted at night and therefore not very safe

Still further west along Calle Rincón is the small **Plaza Zabala**, with a monument to Zabala, founder of the city. North of this Plaza are: the **Banco de la República** (Cerrito y Zabala), the **Aduana** (Rambla 25 de Agosto). Several historic houses belong to the Museo Histórico Nacional: **Casa de Montero**, **Museo Romántico**, 25 de Mayo 428, first built in 1728, rebuilt by Antonio Montero in 1831, contains late 19th, early 20th century furniture, furnishings and portraits. ■ *Tue-Fri 1300-1800, Sun 1400-1800 T915 5361.* **Museo Casa Rivera**, Rincón 437, is a 19th-century mansion. Its rooms are dedicated to various stages of Uruguayan history. ■ *Mon-Fri 1300-1700, T915 1051.* The other houses belonging to the Museo Histórico Nacional in the Ciudad Vieja, **Museo Casa Lavalleja**, Zabala 1469, **Casa de Giró**, Cerrito 584-6, and **Casa del Gral José Garibaldi,** 25 de Mayo 314, have all been closed by municipal directive. Also in the Ciudad Vieja is the **Palacio Taranco, Museo de Artes Decorativos**, 25 de Mayo y 1 de Mayo, garden overlooking Plaza Zabala, a palatial mansion in turn-of-the-century French style, sumptuously-decorated ground floor rooms, museum of Islamic and Classical pottery and glass in the basement. It was first built as a theatre in 1793; in 1908 it was purchased by the Ortiz de Taranco family. ■ *Tue-Sat 1000-1800, Sun 1400-1800, T915 6060, free.*

Three blocks north of Plaza Zabala are the docks, while three blocks south is the Río de la Plata. The seafront road, the Rambla, has been opened round the point to the port. In the port (which one can visit on Saturday from 1300 till sunset and on Sunday from 0800 till sunset), the ship's bell of HMS *Ajax* has been set up to commemorate the scuttling of the *Graf Spee*; it is in an open-air museum on the opposite side of the road from the Port Administration, 50 m to the right next to a large military building. The anchor of the *Graf Spee* was erected inside the port area in 1964 to commemorate the 25th anniversary of the battle. The old railway station (by the port, at end of Río Negro) is a romantic old building with an old train on display. In the Ciudad Vieja, many of the street names have descriptive plaques, but a number of the old buildings are in a poor state of repair.

Uruguay

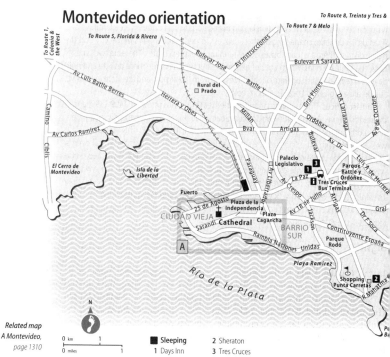

Montevideo orientation

Related map
A Montevideo,
page 1310

■ Sleeping	
1 Days Inn	2 Sheraton
	3 Tres Cruces

Between the Ciudad Vieja and the new city is the largest of Montevideo's squares, **Plaza de la Independencia**, a short distance east of Plaza de la Constitución along the pedestrianized Calle Sarandí. In the middle is the marble mausoleum of Artigas. Just west of the plaza is **Museo Torres García**, Sarandí 683, has an exhibition of the paintings of Joaquín Torres García (1874-1949), one of Uruguay's foremost contributors to the modern art movements of the 20th century. ■ *Mon-Fri 1500-1900, bookshop, T916 2663.* At the eastern end is the **Palacio Salvo**, a major landmark. On the southern side is the **Casa de Gobierno Histórico** (Palacio Estévez). The modern block to the west of the Casa de Gobierno is the new Palacio de Justicia. The Casa de Gobierno itself is now used for ceremonial purposes only as the executive offices have been moved to the Edificio Libertad, far from the centre. Just off the plaza to the west is the splendid, renovated **Teatro Solís** (1856), in a wing of which is the **Museo de Historia Natural**, Buenos Aires 652. ■ *Mon-Fri 1400-1800 (library 1230-1730), T916 0908.*

The Avenida 18 de Julio, whose pavements are always thronged, runs east from Plaza de la Independencia. The **Museo del Gaucho y de la Moneda** is at Avenida 18 de Julio 998, Edificio Banco de la República. ■ *Tue-Fri 0930-1200, 1600-1900 Sat, Sun 1600-1900, T900 8764, free.* Museo de la Moneda has a survey of Uruguayan currency and a collection of Roman coins; Museo del Gaucho is a fascinating history of the Uruguayan gaucho, highly recommended, but closed Sunday; also temporary exhibitions. Between Julio Herrera and Río Negro is the **Plaza Fabini**, or **del Entrevero**, with a statue of a group of *gauchos* engaged in battle, the last big piece of work by sculptor José Belloni. Beneath the plaza is the **Salón Municipal de Exposiciones**, temporary exhibitions of contemporary art, photography, etc. ■ *Daily 1700-2100, free.* In the **Plaza Cagancha** (or Plaza Libertad) is a statue of Liberty. The **Palacio Municipal** (La Intendencia) is on the south side of Avenida 18 de Julio, just before it bends north, at the statue of **El Gaucho**. The best view of the city is from the top of the Palacio Municipal; external glass elevators take you up to a *mirador* (glass-fronted terrace) on the 22nd floor. ■ *1230-2230, US$0.45. Entrance at the back of the building on Soriano, between Ejido and Santiago de Chile. The road which forks south from the Gaucho is Constituyente, and leads to the beach at Pocitos.* **Museo de Historia de Arte**, at Palacio Municipal (18 de Julio 1360). ■ *Tue-Sun 1430-2000, T908 0456.* **Centro de Exposiciones**, Palacio Municipal (Soriano entrance). ■ *Mon-Sat 1600-2000.* Temporary exhibitions of contemporary art.

The immense **Palacio Legislativo** was built between 1908 and 1925 from local marble: there are 55 colours of Uruguayan marble in the Salón de los Pasos Perdidos, 12 types of wood in the library. Other rooms are beautiful. ■ *Mon-Fri 0830-1830, free; free tours in English and Spanish every hour on the ½ hour.* The Palacio is reached from Plaza Fabini along Avenida del Libertador Brig Gen Juan Lavalleja (normally known as Avenida Libertador), five blocks east of Plaza de la Independencia (buses 150, 173, 175 from Calle Mercedes). Some 6-7 blocks northeast of the Palacio is the **Barrio Reus**, with beautiful pastel-painted houses.

Uruguay

Museums outside the centre

Museo Nacional de Antropología, Avenue de las Instrucciones 948, ex-Quinta de Mendilaharsu, a modest but well-presented anthropological collection in the hall of a superb, late 19th century mansion (see, among other things, the Music Room with its huge Chinese silk tapestry). ■ *Mon-Fri 1300-1900, Sat, Sun and holidays 1000-1900, T305 1480. Getting there: bus 149 from Ejido.* **Museo Municipal de Bellas Artes Juan Manuel Blanes**, Millán 4014 esq Arroyo, ex-Quinta Raffo (late 19th century mansion) dedicated to the work of the artist Blanes (1830-1901), plus a room of the works of Pedro Figari (1861-1938), a lawyer who painted strange, naive pictures of peasant life and negro ceremonies, also work by other Uruguayan artists; has a room with paintings by Courbet, Vlaminck, Utrillo, Dufy, etchings by Orozco and engravings by Goya; temporary exhibitions. ■ *Tue-Sun 1300-1900, T336 2248, free. Getting there: buses 146, 148, 149, 150 from Mercedes.* **Museo Zoológico**, Rambla República de Chile 4215, Buceo, is well-displayed and arranged, recommended, great for children too. ■ *Tue-Sun 1000-1700, T622 0258, free. Getting there: bus 104 from 18 de Julio.*

The **Panteón Nacional**, Av Gonzalo Ramírez y Aquiles Lanza (in the Cementerio Central), houses the burial monuments of local families, many with sculptured façades and inscriptions.

Museo Naval, Rambla Costanera y Luis A de Herrera, small display of naval history from War of Independence onwards, documentation on Battle of the River Plate and sinking of the *Graf Spee*, and on the sailing ship *Capitán Miranda*, which circumnavigated the globe in 1937-8 and is now in the port (can be visited Saturday and Sunday), bus 104 from 18 de Julio. ■ *0800-1200, 1400-1800, closed Thu, T622 1084, free.* **Museo Aeronáutico**, Plaza de la Aviación, Larrañaga 4045, has a collection of vintage planes. ■ *Sat, Sun and holidays, 1500-1800, T215 2039, US$0.15. Getting there: bus 71, 79 from Mercedes.*

Parks & gardens

In **Parque Batlle y Ordóñez** (reached by a continuation eastwards of Avenida 18 de Julio), are several statues: the most interesting group is the very well-known **La Carreta** monument, by José Belloni, showing three yoke of oxen drawing a wagon. In the grounds is the **Estadio Centenario**, the national football stadium with a seating capacity of 70,000 and a football museum, a field for athletics and a bicycle race-track (bus 107). The **Planetarium** (adjacent to the Jardín Zoológico) is southeast of this park at Avenida Gral Rivera 3254 (buses 141, 142 or 144 from San José). ■ *The planetarium (free) gives good, 40-min shows on Thu at 1730, Sat and Sun at 1630 and 1730.*

From the Palacio Legislativo, Avenida Agraciada runs northwest to **Parque Prado**, the oldest of the city's many parks, situated about 5 km from Avenida 18 de Julio (bus 125 and others). Among fine lawns, trees and lakes is a rose garden planted with 850 varieties, the monument of **La Diligencia** (the stage coach), the Círculo de Tenís and the Sociedad Rural premises. Part of the park is the adjacent **Jardín Botánico** which is in fine condition. ■ *Mon-Sat 0900-1900. Visits with a guide Mon-Fri, without a guide Sat, T3094422. It is reached via Avenida 19 de Abril (bus 522 from Ejido next to Palacio Municipal), or via Avenida Dr LA de Herrera (bus 147 from Paysandú).* The largest and most popular park is **Parque Rodó**, on Rambla Presidente Wilson. Here are an open-air theatre, an amusement park, and a boating lake studded with islands. At the eastern end is the **Museo Nacional de Artes Visuales**, Tomás Garibaldi 2283, a collection of contemporary plastic arts, plus a room devoted to Blanes. Recommended. ■ *Wed-Sun 1500-1900. T711 6124, free.*

Among the main seaside residential areas are **Pocitos** and **Carrasco**, a delightful semi-rural place behind the beach of the same name at the end of the Rambla Sur, backed by the forest of the **Parque Nacional Roosevelt**, a green belt stretching north to the marshes of Carrasco (which are being drained). The city itself is expanding beyond Roosevelt. The international airport is nearby. The express bus DI runs every 30 minutes along Av 18 de Julio; by using this service, which costs slightly more (US$1.20) about 30 minutes are saved on the journey time to Carrasco.

At the western end of the bay is the **Cerro**, or hill, 139 m high (from which Montevideo gets its name), with the Fortaleza General Artigas, an old fort, on the top. It is now the **Museo Militar**, historical momentos, documentation of War of Independence. ■ *Mon-Fri 1300-1800, Sat, Sun and holidays 1000-1800, T487 3121, free. Getting there: bus 125 from Mercedes goes near.* The Cerro is surmounted by the oldest lighthouse in the country (1804). Bus from centre to Cerro: 125 'Cerro' from Mercedes, and others, or boat Saturday and Sunday 1500-1900, US$5, T601 8601/2.

Nine sandy bathing beaches stretch along almost the whole of the metropolitan water front, from Playa Ramírez in the west to Playa Carrasco in the east. Along the whole waterfront runs the Rambla Naciones Unidas, named along its several stretches in honour of various nations. Bus 104 from Aduana, which goes along Avenida 18 de Julio, gives a pleasant ride (further inland in winter) past Pocitos, Punta Gorda and all the beaches to Playa Miramar, beyond Carrasco, total journey time from Pocitos to Carrasco, 35 minutes. The seawater, despite its muddy colour (sediment stirred up by the Río de la Plata), is safe to bathe in and the beaches are clean. Lifeguards are on duty during the summer months.

The beaches

Essentials

During the tourist season, 15 Dec-15 Mar, hotels should be booked in advance. At the beaches many hotels offer full board only during the season. After 1 Apr prices are greatly reduced and some hotel dining rooms shut down. For Carnival week, on the other hand, prices are raised by 20%. The city is visited by many Argentines at weekends: many hotels increase prices. In midweek, though, many hotel prices are lower than those posted. Always ask in advance. When not included, breakfast (*café completo*) costs US$4 or more in a hotel.

The tourist office has information only on more expensive hotels. For more information and reservations contact **Asociación de Hoteles y Restaurantes del Uruguay**, Gutiérrez Ruiz 1213, T900 0346, F908 0141.

Sleeping
Hotels add a 14% charge to bills, on top of which there is 23% VAT

In the Ciudad Vieja LL *Plaza Fuerte*, Bartolomé Mitre 1361, esq Sarandí, T915 9563, F915 9569. Each room with different design, a/c, many other facilities, restaurant, bar, all in a historic building. **AL** *Columbia Palace*, Reconquista 470, T916 0001, F916 0192. 1st class, breakfast, IDD phone in every room, minibar, TV, restaurant, sauna, mixed music show. **B-D** *Solís*, Bartolomé Mitre 1314, T915 0279, hotelsolis@hotmail.com A variety of rooms, some with bath, a/c, others without, pleasant old house, safe, helpful, bike rental, excursions, internet, bar. **C** *Palacio*, Bartolomé Mitre 1364, T916 3612, fpelaez@internet.com.uy With bath, safe, balconies, TV. Highly recommended. **D** *City House*, Buenos Aires 462 (opposite Correos), T915 6427. With bath, bar, remodelled, good value (prices rise at weekend). **D** *Príncipe*, Juncal 1434, T908 5310, F902 6167. A/c, fridge, café, parking, prices rise on Fri and Sat. **E** *Hospedaje Pensión Roy*, Colón 135, T915 5328. Budget hotel with long-term residents, access to dirty kitchen, dirty shared baths, laundry facilities.

Centre, east of Ciudad Vieja There are many hotels in this area. **LL** *Radisson Victoria Plaza*, Plaza Independencia 759, T908 1048, F902 1628. A/c, excellent restaurant (rooftop, fine views), less formal restaurant in lobby, luxurious casino in basement, new 5-star wing fully open, business centre (for guests only).

AL *Oxford*, Paraguay 1286, T902 0046, F902 3792. Good breakfast. Recommended. **A** *Balfer*, Z Michelini 1328, T902 1418, F902 4228. Good, TV, safe deposit, excellent breakfast. **A** *Facal*, Paseo Yí y 18 de Julio 1363, T902 8833, F902 8828. A/c, safe, TV, convenient, pleasant, terrace restaurant. **A** *Lancaster*, Plaza Cagancha 1334, T902 1054, F902 1117. A/c, with breakfast and fridge/bar, good service. **A** *London Palace*, Río Negro 1278, T902 0024, F902 1633. With breakfast, garage, parking.

B *Aramaya*, Av 18 de Julio 1103, T902 1058, F902 9039. Old, comfortable. **B** *Mediterráneo*, Paraguay 1486, T900 5090. With breakfast, TV, comfortable. **B** *Montevideo*, Aquiles Lanza 1309, T902 4634. Recommended. Small garage.

Uruguay

C *Arapey*, Av Uruguay 925, near Convención, T900 7032, F600 2758, mfer@adinet.com.uy Good location, on bus roiute to airport, with bath, no breakfast. **C** *Casablanca*, San José 1039, T901 0918. Good value. **C** *Ecology Europa*, Colonia 1341, T902 1222. Good. **C** *Itá Residencial*, San José 1160, T901 3363. Quiet, 10% discount if you stay more than a week. **B** *Royal*, Soriano 1120, T908 3115. Without breakfast, dark rooms. Recommended.

D *Cifre* (10% discount on stays of over 2 weeks) Mercedes 1166, **E** with shared bath, use of kitchen. **D** *Ideal*, Colonia 914, T901 6389. Hot water, cheaper without bath, no breakfast, higher rates on Sat. **E** *Hospedaje del Centro*, Soriano 1126, T900 1419. Cooking facilities. Recommended. **D** *Nueva Pensión Ideal*, Soriano 1073. Laundry facilities, no breakfast. **D-E** *Windsor*, Michelini 1260, T901 5080. Simple, good location, helpful, hot water, pleasant, noisy front door buzzer can be disturbing.

Near Tres Cruces bus terminal AL *Days Inn*, Acevedo Díaz 1821-23, T400 4840, www.daysinnn.com.uy A/c, TV, with breakfast, safe, coffee shop and health club. **A** *Tres Cruces*, Miguelete 2356 esq Acevedo Díaz, T402 3474, www.hoteltrescruces.com A/c, TV, safe, coffee shop.

Suburbs east of centre LL *Sheraton*, Victor Saliño 349, T710 2121, www.sheraton.com Beside Shopping Punta Carretas, all facilities, good views, access to Golf Club. **LL** *Belmont House*, Av Rivera 6512, Carrasco, T600 0430, www.belmonthouse.com.uy 5-star, small, beautifully furnished, top quality, excellent restaurant and service, pub/bar *Memories*, pool, 4 blocks from beach. Highly recommended. **L** *Hostería del Lago*, Arizona 9637, T601 2210, www.hosteriadellago.com.uy East of Carrasco, Depto de Canelones, excellent. **AL** *Oceania*, Mar Artico 1227, Playa Los Ingleses, T600 0444, F600 2273. Pleasant view, good restaurant and night club. Highly recommended. **AL** *Pedro Figari*, Rambla Rep de México 6535, Carrasco, T600 8824, www.hotelpedrofigari.com A/c, buffet breakfast, cable TV, very pleasant. **AL** *Villa Biarriz*, Francisco Vidal 613, T711 2543/711 6491.

Montevideo

Sleeping
1 Aramaya B5
2 Balfer B6
3 City House B3
4 Columbia Palace B3
5 Ecology Europa A6
6 Facal B6
7 Hospedaje del Centro B5
8 Ideal B4
9 Itá Residencial B5
10 Lancaster B5
11 London Palace B5
12 Mediterráneo A5
13 Montevideo B6
14 Nueva Pensión Ideal B5
15 Oxford B5
16 Palacio B3

Recommended. **D** *Riviera*, Rambla Rep de México 6095, Carrasco. Built in 1926 in Louis XV style, must be seen, pleasant, good service.

Youth hostel The headquarters of the Association are at Pablo de María 1583, apartment 008, T400 4245/400 0581, F400 1326, www.internet.com.uy/aau Open 1130-1900 Mon-Fri. Hostel (members only) is at Canelones 935, T908 1324/400 4245. Open all year. US$10 pp (with seasonal variations, breakfast included, sheets US$1 extra), doors locked at 2400 (but security lax), friendly, clean, dormitory style, cooking facilities, plenty of hot water, shortage of bathrooms, closed Sat and Sun 1000-1700.

Camping Parque Roosevelt, near Carrasco, US$5 pp, free, hot showers, safe, no electricity, 15 km from centre, open all year. For vans and caravans only at Punta Ramírez on Rambla República Argentina, free for stays under 48 hrs, central, basic facilities, 24 hr security.

Eating

Don't miss eating at the ***Mercado del Puerto***, the 19th-century market building, opposite the Aduana, on Calle Piedras, between Maciel and Pérez Castellano (take 'Aduana' bus), closed Sun, delicious grills cooked on huge charcoal grates (menus are limited to meat). It is best to go at lunchtime, especially Sat; the atmosphere is great, including buskers outside. *La Estancia del Puerto* (No 34, 36), *Río Alegre* (No 33), *La Proa* (touristy), ***Cabaña Verónica*** (No 38) and ***Las Tablitas*** (No 46, also at Costa Rica 2105, Carrasco) have been recommended. All mid-range. *Roldós*, specializes in sandwiches and is where most people start with a *medio medio* (half still, half sparkling white wine).

Expensive restaurants at the centre are *La Silenciosa*, Ituzaingó 1426, T915 9409. In a converted Jesuit convent (18th-century), later a prestigious fashion house (19th-century), now an historical monument, excellent food, international and French, open Mon-Fri for lunch and Thu-Sat for dinner. Highly recommended. **Mid-range**: On C Bacacay, between pedestrianized part of Sarandí and Teatro Solís, are small cafés and restaurants serving anything from a coffee to a full meal; recommended are *Café Bacacay*, Bacacay 1310 y Buenos Aires, good music and atmosphere, food served, try the specials, and *Roma Amor*, Bacacay 1331. Closed Sun, excellent antipasti lunchtime buffet.

In the central Plaza Cagancha district Mid-range: *Anticuario*, Maldonado 1602. Atmospheric, fish and *parrilla*. *Las Brasas*, San José 909. Good typical food. *El Fogón*, San José 1080. Good value, very friendly, always full (also Ellauri 350, Shopping Punta Carretas). *La Genovesa* (Spanish), San José 1242. Excellent, *marisquería* and *parrillada*. *Viejo Sancho*, San José 1229. Excellent, popular, complimentary sherry or vermouth to early arrivals, tearoom by day. **Cheap**: Chinese: *Gran China*, San José 1077. Friendly, good. *Cantón Chino*, at Tres Cruces bus terminal, also at Roque Graseras 740, Pocitos, and Shopping Punta Carretas. Good. A reasonable place for lunch is restaurant on 6th floor of YMCA building, Colonia 1870, good views, ask for the Asociación Cristiana de Jóvenes.

Vegetarian Cheap: *Vegetariana*, Av Brasil 3086, Pocitos, and other locations (eg Yí 1334 and 25 de Mayo 462). Closed every day 1500-1900, 2000 on Sat, Sun open

Uruguay

1200-1500. Excellent, self-service buffet. *Vida Natural*, San José 1184. Basic menu US$6.

Many good restaurants in and around Pocitos: **Expensive**: *Doña Flor*, Artigas 1034. Classy French restaurant, limited menu but good, moves to Punta del Este in summer. *Spaghetería 23*, Scosería 2584. Tue-Sun, very good Italian. **Mid-range**: *El Entrevero*, 21 de Septiembre 2774. Excellent value, beef, take bus 522 from the centre. *El Puesto de Joaquín*, Williman 637. Popular, good atmosphere, varied menu.

In Carrasco, **expensive**: *Bungalow Suizo*, Camino a Carrasco 16.500, T601 1073. Very good. **Mid-range**: *La Casa Violeta*, P Murillo 6566 (and other branches in the city, eg Rambla Armenia 3676, Pocitos Nuevo). Help yourself, fixed price. *Dackel*, Dr Gabriel Otero 6438, T6006211. German/Swiss/Austrian food, good prices.

Confiterías A *confitería* is an informal eating/drinking place which serves meals at any time, as opposed to a *restaurante*, which serves meals at set times. A *confitería* may describe itself as a *cafetería, bar, repostería, cervecería, coctelería, sandwichería, grill, pizzería, salón de té* or *whiskería*. Many serve *preparación*, a collection of hors d'oeuvres. There are a great many; the following is a selection: on Av 18 de Julio, *Lusitano*, esq Paraguay; *Lion d'Or*, No 1981; *Soko's*, No 1250, popular, good if expensive food, good coffee, open till 0100, 0400 on Sat; *Sorocabana*, No 1008, open 1400-2330. *Cake's*, José Ellauri 1067, Pocitos. Expensive. Recommended. *Conaprole*, Solano Antuña 2996. *Oro del Rhin*, Convención 1403. Open 0830-2100, good cakes. *Universal Bar*, Piedras y Gómez. Last of the real dock bars, worth a visit.

Ice cream parlours produce very good, unusual ice creams in the summer

Heladerías Try *La Cigale*, R Graseras 845 (Pocitos), Ejido 1368 and several other locations. *Las Delicias*, Schroeder 6454, Carrasco. *Batuk*, 26 de Marzo y Pérez, Pocitos, and at 18 de Julio y Yí. Both open daily 1000-0200. *Papitos*, 18 de Julio 1060. Excellent but pricey.

Entertainment **Boliches** (Café-Concerts/Peñas/Folk-Pubs, offering the most typical local night-life) *Amarcor*, Julio Herrera y Obes 1321. Thu-Sat 2100 onwards, traditional pop music. *Clyde's*, Costa Rica y Rivera. Lively, live music. *Flannagans Pub*, Luis B Cavia 3082, Pocitos. Young, lively, pop, rock and salsa. *Fun-Fun*, Ciudadela 1229. Amateur and local music. *Lobizón*, Michelini 1329. Good food, good price. *Pizza Sing*, Schroeder 6411, Carrasco. Good, karaoke. *Subterráneo Magallanes*, Gonzalo Ramírez 1701, T419 1075. Daily 0800-2400, Fri and Sat 2230-0315, book in advance. *Taj Mahal*, Andes 1255. Sangria, good food.

Cinema Very popular. Price is almost the same in all cinemas, at US$7 (US$4 on Tue and Wed). During the week no cinemas open before 1730. Classic and serious films at Cinemateca film club (3 separate cinemas – at L Carnelli 1311, Soriano 1227 and A Chucarro 1036), monthly membership US$6, and Cine Universitario (2 halls, Lumière and Chaplin, Canelones 1280). Films are released quite soon after the UK and USA, and often before they get to Buenos Aires. Details in *Guía del Ocio* and monthly *Cinemateca Uruguaya* (free). At least half of Montevideo's cinemas show blue films – marked *sexo explícito*.

Discos *Boites* are the more expensive discos which provide live music for dancing; prices, US$15-30. There are many discos in the city. See www.eltimon.com and entertainments magazines for latest recommendations.

Music Every Sat, from midnight to Sun morning, thousands of dancers crowd into the *Palacio Sud América*, Yatay 1429, near Palacio Legislativo, 3 dance salons, Caribbean music on 1st floor, Tango on 2nd, tickets half price if bought before 2400.

Tanguerías *La Vieja Cumparsita*, C Gardel 1811. Nightly 2330-0500, no singles admitted, also has *candombe* shows, book ahead. Besides tango and *candombe*, other popular music forms in Montevideo are Música Campestre-Folklórica (of gaucho origin), Música del Caribe by Uruguayan orchestras dedicated to dance music from Puerto Rico, and "the best New Orleans Dixieland Jazz Bands" in Latin America writes John Raspey.

Theatres *Solís*, Buenos Aires 678. Two auditoria, home of the Comedia Nacional; free classical concerts most Mon evenings Apr-Nov. About 10 others present professional productions. *Teatro Millington-Drake* at the Anglo (see Cultural centres) puts on occasional productions, as do the theatres of the Alianza Uruguay-Estados Unidos and the Alianza Francesa (addresses below). Many theatres close during Jan and Feb.

The main shopping area is Av 18 de Julio. Suede and leather are good buys. Try *Casa Mario*, Piedras 641 (expensive). Several shops and workshops around Plaza Independencia *Montevideo Leather Factory*, No 832. Recommended. For leather and woollen goods, *Artesanal*, Av 18 de Julio 1197, Río Negro 1320 L 2, good prices. Amethysts, topazes, agate and quartz are mined and polished in Uruguay and are also good buys. Recommended is *Benito Sityá*, Sarandí 650 (Ciudad Vieja) and *Cuarzos del Uruguay*, Sarandí 604. For woollen wall hangings see *Manos del Uruguay*, which also sells floor cushions, crafts, high quality woollen goods, etc at Reconquista 587, in an old colonial-style house, in Montevideo and Punta Carretas Shopping Centers (see below), and at San José 1111. Other good craftwork (cheaper) in daily covered craft market *Mercado de los Artesanos* of the *Asociación Uruguaya de Artesanos*, between Paraguay 1368 and Plaza Cagancha, and at Mercado de la Abundancia, San José 1312, T901 0550, auda@minetuy.com

On Sun, 0800-1400, there is a large, crowded street market on Tristán Narvaja (good for silver and copper, and all sorts of collectibles) opposite Facultad de Derecho on 18 de Julio. A small Sat morning market and a Sun antique fair are held in Plaza de la Constitución; there is also a big market, Villa Biarritz, on Vásquez Ledesma near Parque Rodó, Pocitos, selling fruit, vegetables, clothes and shoes (Tue and Sat 0900-1500, and on Sun in Parque Rodó, 0800-1400).

The Montevideo Shopping Center on the east edge of Pocitos (Herrera 1290 y Galanza, 1 block south of Rivera): it is open daily 1000-2100 and has a self-service restaurant, a cinema and *confiterías*. It also has wide range of shops selling leather goods, *Foto Martín*, *Bookshop*, supermarkets and more (bus 141 or 142 from San José). Outside is a *McDonalds*, serving economical breakfasts. *Punta Carretas Shopping*, Ellauri 306, close to Playa Pocitos in the former prison, open 0900-2200, is large, modern, with all types of shop, also cinema complex and good food patio, popular. Take bus 117 or 121 from Calle San José. Other shopping centres at Portones in Carrasco, the Tres Cruces bus station and Plaza Arozena Shopping Mall.

Bookshops The following have English and American books: *Plaza Libros*, Av 18 de Julio 892, has a wide range of international books, travel guides, and gay literature. Also at 1185 on the same avenue. *Librería Barreiro y Ramos*, 25 de Mayo y JC Gómez, 18 de Julio 937, 21 de Septiembre (Pocitos) and Av Arocena 1599 (Carrasco). *Ibana*, International Book and News Agency, Convención 1479, specializes in foreign publications. *Librería Británica*, Sarandí 580, specializes in language and children's books. Others include *Librería Mosca Hermanos*, Av 18 de Julio 1578 and Av Arocena 1576 (Carrasco). *Linardi y Risso*, Juan Carlos Gómez 1435, lyrbooks@linardiyrisso.com *Roberto Cataldo*, Juan Carlos Gómez 1327, elgaleon@netgate.com.uy *Feria del Libro*, Av 18 de Julio y Río Negro. *Palacio del Libro*, 25 de Mayo 577, and *Fundación de Cultura Universitaria* at No 568, in the Ciudad Vieja. For books on Uruguay in Spanish and Uruguayan music, *Mercado de Todo la Cultura Uruguaya* Plaza Fabini. *Librería Oriente Occidente*, Cerrito 477 and *Librería El Aleph*, Bartolomé Mitre 1358, both sell used and rare books (former has English books, also exchange of books in perfect condition). The only shop with exclusively English stock is *Bookshop SRL*, JE Rodó 1671 (at Minas y Constituyente), T400 9954, Cristina Mosca, very friendly staff, also at Montevideo Shopping Center; specializes in travel. The Sun market on Paysandú is good for second-hand books.

Many international newspapers can be bought on the east side of Plaza Independencia

Exprinter, Sarandí 700, T902 0829, PO Box 6447. Also does exchange. *Freeway*, Colonia 994, T900 8931/33. *Golden Tours*, Colonia 1221, T902 2617. English spoken. *JP Santos*, Colonia 951, T902 0300, and *Jetmar*, Plaza de la Independencia 725-7, T902 0793. Both helpful. *Jorge Martínez*, Río Branco y Colonia 949, T902 1844. *Orientur*, Río Negro 1358, Plaza Fabini, T908 3369. *Rumbos*, Galería del Libertador, Rio Branco 1377, p 7, T900 2407, rumbouno@adinet.com.uy Also at World Trade Center, Luis A de Herrera 1248, T628 5555, rumbodos@adinet.com.uy Caters specifically for independent travellers, very helpful. *Turisport Ltda*, San José 930, T902 0829. American Express for travel and mail services, good; sells Amex dollar TCs on Amex card and personal cheque at 1 commission. 1-day tours of Punta del Este are organized by many travel agents and run from several hotels, US$40-100 including meals. Bilingual guide: Marian Whitaker, T700 6842, F701 5411, for tours of Montevideo and Uruguay, riding, hiking, camping, fishing, also visits to Santa Sofia *estancia* in Río Negro. The Palacio Municipal organizes city tours, Sat-Sun, US$5, T903 0648/9, Mon-Fri 1000-1800.

Uruguay

Transport

Local Bus: US$0.70 (pay the conductor on board); express buses D2 US$0.70, D3, 5, 8, 10, 11 US$0.90, D1 (see Sights Carrasco, above) US$1.20. There are many buses to all parts from 18 de Julio; from other parts to the centre or old city, look for those marked 'Aduana'. For Pocitos from city centre take bus No 121 from Calle San José. **Car hire**: without chauffeur, from US$36 to US$85 per 24 hrs (insurance included), plus extra per km if only hiring for the day; guarantee of US$500 required. Hire for 3-day weekend start at US$118 (rates are much lower out of season and vary according to size of vehicle). Cheaper weekly rates available. Best to make reservations before arrival. Collision damage waiver (amounting to US$1,000), US$15 per day. *Punta Car*, Cerro Largo 1383, T900 2772, also at Aeropuerto Carrasco. *Snappy*, Andes 1363, T900 7728 or 099-660660. *Sudancar*, Piedras 533, T915 8150; many others. See Essentials, page 48 for international agencies. **Remises**: US$8 per hr; **Remises Montevideo**, Joaquín Requena 1303, F401 1149; **Libertad**, Plaza Cagancha 1126, T902 4393; **Juan Mastroianni**, T099-639865 (mob), good, safe, reasonably-priced; **Guillermo Muñoz**, Bartolito Mitre 2636, T707 3928. Recommended.

Beware of taxi drivers telling you that long-distance buses are full and offering to take you instead; this is unlikely to be true

Taxis: US$0.90 for first 600 m, and US$0.21 for each 140 m afterwards; on holidays and Sun, 20 more; charge per hr US$15. Average fare Pocitos to old city US$3. Fares are shown on the meter by a number which determines the cost according to a table; make sure the meter starts at zero, even in radio taxis. There is a small charge for each piece of luggage, but tipping is not expected. Taxis now have a glass screen between driver and passengers, which gives the driver more security but the passenger reduced leg room.

If making an advance hotel reservation, ask them to send a taxi to meet you; it's cheaper than taking an airport taxi

Long distance Air: the main airport, is at Carrasco, 21 km outside the city, T601 1757; with coffee shop and children's play area in departure lounge; left luggage about US$1 per day per item; good rates at the exchange facilities, but if closed, buses will accept dollars for fares to town. To Montevideo 30 mins by taxi or *remise* (US$19-32, depending on destination in the city – may be able to charge it to hotel bill if without cash); about 50 mins by bus. Buses, Nos 700, 701, 704, 710 and 711, from Terminal Brun, Río Branco y Galicia, go to the airport US$1 (crowded before and after school hours); dark brown 'Copsa' bus terminates at the airport. *COT* buses connect airport and Punta del Este, US$5. *Pluna* has a bus service from *Hotel Victoria Plaza*, Plaza Independencia to airport at 30 mins past the hour (only for *Pluna* and *Varig* passengers). *IBAT* bus service T601 0209/0943 2373. *Concorde Travel* (Robert Mountford), Germán Barbato 1358, apto 1302, T902 6346/8, has a service from hotel to plane (almost) US$10-25.

Air services to Argentina: for the Puente Aéreo to Buenos Aires, check in at Montevideo airport, pay departure tax and go to immigration to fill in an Argentine entry form before going through Uruguayan immigration. Get your stamp out of Uruguay, surrender the tourist card you received on entry and get your stamp into Argentina. There are no immigration checks on arrival at Aeroparque, Buenos Aires. For flights via Colonia see page 1330.

Road Buses within Uruguay: excellent terminal, Tres Cruces, Bulevar Artigas y Av Italia, T401 8998 (10-15 mins by bus from the centre, Nos 21, 64, 180, 187, 188); it has a shopping mall, tourist office, restaurants, left luggage (free for 4 hrs at a time, if you have a ticket for that day), post and phone offices, toilets, good medical centre, *Banco de Montevideo* and *Indumex* cambio (accepts MasterCard). For nearby hotels, see Sleeping, above. All buses leave from here and bus company offices are here, too. During the summer holiday season buses are booked heavily; it is recommended to book in advance (also for Fri and weekend travel all year round). Fares and journey times from the capital are given under destinations.

You need a passport when buying international tickets. On through buses to Brazil and Argentina, you can expect full luggage checks both by day and night

To Argentina: Ferries and buses Direct to Buenos Aires: *Buquebus*, at the docks, in old customs hall, T902 0670/916 8801, Río Negro 1400, T902 0170 and Terminal Las Cruces, Local B29, T408 8146, 3 daily, 2 hrs 5 mins or 2½ hrs, US$59 tourist class, US$72 1st class (bus service from *Hotel Carrasco* 1½ hrs before sailings). At Montevideo dock, go to Preembarque 30 mins before departure, present ticket and pay exit tax; then go to Migración for Uruguayan exit and Argentine entry formalities. The terminal has been redesigned like an airport. On board there is duty-free shopping, video and expensive food and drinks. **Services via Colonia**: bus/ferry services by *Buquebus*: 4 crossings daily 45 mins or 2½ hrs,

Uruguay

US$32 tourist, US$38 1st class on the fast ship, US$20 tourist, US$27 1st class on the slow ship, bus Montevideo-Colonia from Tres Cruces 3½ hrs earlier, US$7 extra. *Buquebus* on either route carries cars, US$101-125 Montevideo, US$46-78 (depending on size of vehicle and boat) Colonia. Schedules and fares can be checked on www.buquebus.com Fares increase in high season, Dec-Jan, when there are more sailings. *Ferryturismo*, Río Branco 1368, T900 0045, and at Tres Cruces local 27, T409 8198, *Sea Cat* 4 hrs Montevideo-Buenos Aires via Colonia: 4 a day, 3 on Sat-Sun, bus leaves Montevideo 3 hrs before catamaran sails, US$39, 30 from Colonia (cars US$71-88. Break of journey in Colonia on all services is allowed; cheaper, if you do this, to buy bus ticket only in Montevideo, and then ferry ticket in Colonia. Services **via Carmelo and Tigre** (interesting trip): bus/motor launch service by Cacciola, 0100, 1200, 1300 on Sun, Tres Cruces T401 9350, Plaza Cagancha 1326, T901 0755, US$20. Bus service **via Fray Bentos**, *Bus de la Carrera*, 1000 and 2200 daily, US$25.20, 8½ hrs, and *dormibus* at 2300, US$28, 9 hrs, slow journey. Bus services to Paraná (US$35), Santa Fe (US$36), Rosario (US$39), Córdoba (US$50) and Mendoza (US$63) are operated by *EGA* (see above). Advanced booking is advisable on all services at busy periods.

To Paraguay, Brazil, Chile   To **Asunción**, Paraguay, US$67, 18 hrs: twice a week (Wed and Sat, plus Mon in summer) by *COIT*, Río Branco 1389, T908 6469, or *Tres Cruces*, T401 5628, and 2 a week by *Brújula*, T901 5143, both services recommended, meals served. Alternatively take bus to **Santa Fe**, Argentina (US$36), via Paysandú bridge, for easy access to Asunción. The through bus route is via Paysandú, Salto, Bella Unión, Uruguaiana, Paso de los Libros, Posadas, Encarnación, to Asunción (there are no passport or customs formalities except passport checks at Bella Unión and at Encarnación). There are very comfortable buses to **Porto Alegre** (US$44, 10 hrs, daily) and **São Paulo** (US$96, 32 hrs via Florianópolis, US$65, Camboriú, US$68, a good place to stop over, and Curitiba, US$79, Wed, Fri, Sun at 1600) with *EGA* (recommended), *Tres Cruces*, T4025164, or *Río Branco* 1409, T902 5335, egakeg@andinet.com.uy *TTL* (*Tres Cruces* or *Río Branco* 1375, T901 7142/401 1410) also serves São Paulo, Florianópolis and Porto Alegre. A cheaper alternative route (which also avoids the risk of being stranded at the border by through-bus drivers) is to Chuy, eg *COIT*, T409 4949, or *Plaza Cagancha* 1124, T902 4004 (US$13, 4½ hrs), then catch an onward bus to Porto Alegre (7½ hrs, US$13 if paid in reais), either direct or via Pelotas.

If intending to travel through Uruguay to Brazil, do not forget to have Uruguayan entry stamped in your passport when crossing from Argentina. Without it you will not be able to cross the Brazilian border

Train: the station is at the north end of Calle Río Negro (with Cerro Largo). Fine building with information office, post office, restaurants and historical display. Commuter trains run north to 25 de Agosto (Florida), Mon-Fri depart 25 de Agosto 4 times between 0440 and 0655, returning from Montevideo 4 times 1728-1930, 1 hr 50 mins, US$1.90. On Sat, depart 25 de Agosto 0440, 0530, return 1320, 1420. You can take the train to Santa Lucía, the stop before 25 de Agosto, and return by bus (2 hrs); the train goes via Canelones also. *Ferrotransporte* (T924 1387) arrange return trips to Florida, with lunch and tours, US$15.80 for the train ride.

Airline offices   *Aerolíneas Argentinas*, Convención 1343, p 3, T901 9466. *American Airlines*, Sarandí 699 bis y Plaza Independencia, T916 3979. *ASATEJ Uruguay*, Student Flight Centre, Río Negro 1354, p 2, of 1/2, T908 0509. *Aviasur*, at airport, T601 4618. *Iberia*, Colonia 673/75, T908 1032, F902 3284. *KLM*, Andes 1217, T902 5057. *Pluna* (www.pluna.com.uy) and *Varig*, office on south side of Plaza Independencia, Fast Track check-in and bus at *Victoria Plaza* hotel, Plaza Independencia, near the driveway off Florida, T902 1414/600 0750. *United*, Plaza Independencia 831, p 5, T902 4630. For information on all flight arrivals and departures, T601 1991.

Directory

Information: 141
Emergency medical assistance: T105
Fire service: T104
Police patrol: T999-109

Banks   *Casas de cambio* on Plaza Cagancha open daily until 2200, including Sun, but banks open only from 1230 to 1730. Many banks give cash advances against Visa and MasterCard. Airport bank open every day 0700-2200. *Lloyds TSB Bank*, Calle Zabala 1500, and 11 city agencies. *Citibank*, Colonia 1329 and 26 de Marzo 3509, no commission on own cheques, Visa ATM. *ABN Amro*, 25 de Mayo 501 and 18 de Julio 1300 (MasterCard and Visa ATM); 22 other branches. 2 branches of *Redbanc* for Visa and MasterCard ATMs: Colonia 758, *Victoria Plaza*, and Galicia 963 y Río Branco. Branches of *Banco de Crédito* take Visa, with ATM, eg Río Branco 1450 y Mercedes. *Banco Comercial*, Cerrito 400 and Av Libertador (up to US$1,000 available on MasterCard or Visa, best rates for deutschemark cheques), Visa ATM. *American Express Bank*, Rincón 473, T916 0092/916 1162, does

Don't trust black market money changers offering temptingly good rates, many are experienced confidence tricksters

Uruguay

not change cash or TCs (see Turisport under Tour operators). *Western Union*, Río Negro y 18 de Julio opposite *McDonalds*. The MasterCard office is in Edif Torre Libertad, Plaza Cagancha 1335, p 3. There are exchange houses, especially along 18 de Julio, eg *Almar* at 1077, *La Favorita* (Amex agents) a 1459, *Suizo* at 1190, *Zito* at 1841, but shop around for best rates (rates for cash are better than for TCs, but both are often better than in banks, and quicker service). *Exprinter* on Plaza Independencia (also travel agency – see below), *Brimar*, Misiones 1476; *Durazno*, 25 de Mayo 481, *Delta*, Río Negro 1341, and *Cambio Indumex*, Rincón 464, 18 de Julio 1128, Tres Cruces bus terminal and at Buquebus terminal, have been recommended.

Communications Internet:*Café Net*, Paraguay 1325, local 13, in mall. *Cyber Café Nueva Dimensión* Paraguay 1444, T902 6963, neuvadim@adinet.com.uy Mon-Fri, 0930-2200, only 2 terminals, US$4 per hr, coffee, music, also photographic studio. *Cyber Café Uruguay*, Colonia 1955. Also pub and dancing. **Post Office**: Misiones 1328 y Buenos Aires; 0800-1800 Mon-Fri, 0800-1300 Sat and holidays; philatelic bureau on 1st floor sells back issues. *Poste restante* at main post office will keep mail for 1 month, 2 if authorized in advance by administrator. Next to Pluna office on Av Libertador, next to Montevideo Shopping Center, 0800-1300, and under Intendencia at corner of Av 18 de Julio and Ejido. **Telephone**: *Antel*, Fernández Crespo 1534 (headquarters) and at San José 1102 (Plaza), Arocena 1666 (Carrasco), Ariel 4914 (Sayago), Cádiz 3280 (Mercado Modelo), Garzón 1806 (Colón), José Belloni 4445 (Piedras Blancas); for international phone calls (including USA Direct Express), telex, fax, cables, etc, open 0800-2000 daily. Long distance operator 120; for Latin America 0007, other countries 0008; special service 124.

Cultural centres Alianza Cultural Uruguay-Estados Unidos, Paraguay 1217, T901 5234, library open Mon-Fri, 1400-2000, US publications and books (excellent selection), theatre, art gallery. Instituto Cultural Anglo-Uruguayo (known as the 'Anglo'), San José 1426, T900 8468 (theatre, recommended, library open Mon-Fri 0930-1200, 1430-1930); café at No 1227. **Alliance Française**, Soriano 1180, T901 1979 (theatre, concerts, exhibitions in French and Spanish, library, excellent bookshop). **Goethe Institut**, Canelones 1524, T400 5813/409 3499, F404432 (open Mon, Tue, Thu, Fri 1000-1300, 1600-1930). **Casa Cultural Uruguay-Suecia**, Ejido 1444, T900 0067. **Instituto Italiano de Cultura**, Paraguay 1177, T900 3354.

Embassies and consulates Argentine Consulate, Michelini 1470, T902 8166, www.emb-uruguay.mrecic.gov.ar/index1.htm Open 1400-1900, visa US$15, 1 day wait, English spoken. **Austrian Consulate-General**, Misiones 1372, T916 0152/916 0718, F915 1283. **Belgium**, Leyenda Patria 2880, Apt 202, T710 1265. **Brazilian Consulate**, Bulevar Artigas 1328, T707 2115, F707 2086, www.brasmont.org.uy Consulate: Convención 1343, piso 6, T900 6282, F900 0348, Open 0930-1230, 1430-1730 (service for visas takes 24 hrs and the procedure is more complicated than Buenos Aires – need photo, onward ticket, entry ticket, proof of finances). **Canada**, Plaza Independencia 749, of 102, T902 2030, F902 2029, www.dfait-maeci.gc.ca/montevideo **Chile**, Andes 1365, T902 6316. Open 0900-1400, visa US$5, same day. **France**, Uruguay 853, T902 0077, www.amb-montevideo.fr/ **Germany**, La Cumparsita 1417-35, T902 5222, F902 3422, www.emb-alemania.com Open 0930-1230. **Israel**, Blvd Gral Artigas 1585, T400 4164. **Italy**, JB Lamas 2857, T708 4916, F708 4148, www.ambitalia.com.uy **Netherlands**, Leyenda Patria 2880, Apt 202, T700 1631. **New Zealand Consulate**, Bulevar Artigas 1074, T785925, F780509. **Paraguayan Consulate**, Blvd Artigas 1191, T408 5810. Open 0900-1200 summer, 1400-1730 winter. **Portugal**, Av Dr F Soca 1128. **Spanish Consulate**, Libertad 2750, T708 0048. **Sweden**, Av Brasil 3079, piso 6, Pocitos, T708 0088. **Switzerland**, Ing Federico Abadie 2934-40, T710 4315. **UK**, Marco Bruto 1073, T622 3630, F622 7815, bemonte@internet.com.uy **US Embassy** and **Consulate**, Lauro Muller 1776, T408 777, F418 8611, www.embeeuu.gub.uy

Medical services Hospital Británico, Av Italia 2420, T400 9011. Recommended.

Uruguay

East from Montevideo

Montevideo

This beautiful coast consists of an endless succession of small bays, beaches and promontories, set among hills and woods. Punta del Este, 139 km from Montevideo, is a major international resort. From Punta del Este to the Brazilian frontier is much less developed. The bird watching in the coastal lagoons is good.

Two paved roads go to Punta del Este. The northern branch via Pando and Soca, is Route 8 (toll just before Route 9 branch); at Km 75 Route 8 continues northeast towards Minas (see page 1325), while Route 9 branches off to San Carlos (14½ km north of Maldonado and 19 km north of Punta del Este) through beautiful rolling country with views of the Laguna del Sauce. The other road, the 'Interbalnearia', runs largely along the coast, with short branches to some of the resorts, such as Atlántida, Solís and Las Flores. It has been made into a dual carriageway. There are toll posts (US$4) at Arroyo Pando and at Arroyo Solís Grande (you are charged only on the way out from Montevideo). For the first 15 km or so out of Montevideo an alternative road to the Interbalnearia runs parallel between it and the coast (recommended during heavy traffic to avoid dangerous junctions).

The beach season is from Dec to the end of Feb

Piriápolis

This resort set among hills is laid out with an abundance of shady trees, and the district is rich in pine, eucalyptus and acacia woods. It has a good beach, a yacht harbour, a country club, a motor-racing track and is particularly popular with Argentines. It was, in fact, founded in the 1890s as a bathing resort for residents of Buenos Aires. The tourist office, *Asociación de Turismo*, is at Rambla de los Argentinos 1348, which closes at 2100, T22560. Good-value excursions can be arranged at *Inmobiliaria Piriápolis*, Edificio Piria, Rambla de los Argentinos, T22596.

Phone code: 043
Colour map 8, grid B6
Population: 6,000
101 km from Montevideo

About 6 km north on the R37 is Cerro Pan de Azúcar (Sugar Loaf Hill), crowned by a tall cross with a circular stairway inside; there is only a steep path, marked by red arrows, up to the cross. Just north of Piriápolis R 37 passes the La Cascada Municipal park (open all year) which contains the Museo Castillo de Piria, the house of Francisco Piria, the founder of the resort, open daily in summer, weekends in winter, 1200-2000. ■ *Take bus 'Cerro Pan de Azúcar' and get off after 6 km.* About 4 km beyond Cerro Pan de Azúcar is the village of Pan de Azúcar, which has a Museo al Aire Libre de Pintura where the walls of the buildings have been decorated by Uruguayan and Argentine painters, designers and writers with humorous and tango themes (direct bus every hour from Piriápolis).

AL *Argentino*, Rambla de los Argentinos y Armenia, T22791. A fine hotel designed by Piria with casino, 2 restaurants and medicinal springs, ice rink and pool open to public for US$3.50, also sauna. **B** *Danae*, Rambla 1270 y Freire, T22594. **D** out of season, bath, breakfast, heating. **B** *Rivadavia*, Rambla 1208, T22543. Open all year (**C** in winter), hot water. Many others in our price ranges **C** and up. The Centro de Hoteles y Anexos de Piriápolis runs a reservation office at Edificio Piria on Rambla de los Argentinos. **Youth hostel** *Albergue de Piriápolis*, behind *Hotel Argentino*, Simón del Pino 1106/1136, T20394. US$10 pp (open all year), 322 beds, hot showers, cooking facilities, student cards accepted. **Camping** International YMCA camp on the slope of Cerro del Toro, double rooms in bungalows, and tents. Site at Misiones y Niza. Poor showers, smelly toilets, US$6. Many small restaurants near the harbour, for example *Don Anselmo*, between Puntas Fría and Colorada (shellfish, excellent, overlooking sea) and *Náutico*, both recommended. Also *Posada de los Reyes*, Gorlero 629, *Taberna Barlovento*, T22837. Good for paella, US$15 for two.

Sleeping & eating
Many hotels situated along the sea front. Most close end-Feb until mid-Dec. Reservation advisable in high season

Uruguay

Transport **Road** Piriápolis may be reached either by following the very beautiful R10 from the end of the Interbalnearia, or by taking the original access road (R37) from Pan de Azúcar, which crosses the R93. The shortest route from Piriápolis to Punta del Este is by the Camino de las Bases which runs parallel to the R37 and joins the R93 some 4 km east of the R37 junction. **Bus**: to/from **Montevideo**, US$4, 1½ hrs. To **Punta del Este**, US$2.50. To **Maldonado**, US$2. For **Rocha**, **La Paloma** and **Chuy**, take bus to Pan de Azúcar and change.

To Buenos Aires: *Buquebus* has a ferry service Buenos Aires-Piriápolis in summer twice a day (Sun only in winter), US$56 tourist class, US$76 1st class, cars US$124-165, 3 hr crossing. Bus to Punta del Este US$4 extra.

Portezuelo & R93 runs between the coast and the Laguna del Sauce to Portezuelo, which has good
Punta Ballena beaches. The **Arboreto Lussich** (T78077, open 1030-1630) on the west slope of the Sierra de la Ballena (north of R93) contains a unique set of native and exotic trees. There are footpaths, or you can drive through; two *miradores*, worth a visit. From Portezuelo it is possible to drive north towards the R9 by way of the R12 which then continues, unpaved, to Minas. Just off R12 is *El Sosiego*, T042-20000, F20303, a dairy farm open to the public, selling goats' cheese, *dulce de leche* and other products.

At Punta Ballena there is a wide crescent beach, calm water and very clean sand. The place is a residential resort but is still quiet. At the top of Punta Ballena there is a panoramic road 2½ km long with remarkable views of the coast. **Casa Pueblo**, the house and gallery of Uruguayan artist Carlos Páez Villaro, is built in a Spanish-Moroccan style on a cliff over the sea; the gallery can be visited (US$5), there are paintings, collages and ceramics on display, and for sale; season: 1 November to 1 April. Walk downhill towards the sea for a good view of the house.

Sleeping There is a hotel at **LL** *Casa Pueblo*, T579386, F578818. Highly recommended. Also time-share apartments, restaurant and, lower down the hill, a *parrillada*. **LL** *Solana del Mar*, Km 126.5, T578888, F578045. Modern, restaurant on the beach, full board. **LL** *Cumbres de Ballena*, Ruta 12 Km 3.9, T578689, www.cumbres.com.uy Hotel, some rooms **L** out of season, restaurant and tea room (very expensive but popular). Campsite near Arboreto Lussich, turn off at Km 128 on Interbalnearia, T427 8902/24181, or Montevideo 480 1662. US$5.60 for 2 with tent, many facilities, very clean.

Maldonado

Phone code: 042 The capital of Maldonado Department is a peaceful town, sacked by the British in
Colour map 8, grid B6 1806, now a dormitory suburb of Punta del Este, but it has many colonial remains.
Population: 33,000 Worth seeing is the El Vigia watch tower; Gorriti y Pérez del Puerto; the Cathedral
140 km E of (started 1801, completed 1895), on Plaza San Fernando; the windmill; the Cuartel
Montevideo de Dragones exhibition centre (Pérez del Puerto y 18 de Julio, by Plaza San Fernando) and the Cachimba del Rey (an old well on the continuation of 3 de Febrero, almost Artigas – local legend claims that those who drink from the well will never leave Maldonado). **Museo Mazzoni**, Ituzaingó 787, has regional items, indigenous, Spanish, Portuguese and English. ■ *Tue-Fri 1800-2200, T21107.* **Museo de Arte Americano**, José Dodera 648 y Treinta y Tres, private museum of national and international art, interesting. ■ *Summer only 1800-2200, T22276.* For information on concerts and exhibitions in summer T222276. Tourist information at bus station, T225701.

Sleeping **C** *Hospedaje Isla de Gorriti*, Michelini 884, T225223. Recommended. **C** *Celta*, Ituzaingó 839,
& eating T/F230139. Helpful, Irish owner, No 7 bus stop outside. **Camping** In Parque El Placer,
Hotel accommodation T270034, free. **Restaurants** *Piano-Bar JR Pizzetas*, Rincón y Gutiérrez Ruiz, pizzas and
is scarce in summer pasta, under US$12 pp. *Taberna Patxi*, Florida 828. Basque specialities, good, reaonable prices, open all year. Best ice cream at *Popy's*, 2 branches.

Transport

Buses to/from **Montevideo**, US$5.75; to **Minas**, 2 hrs, 5 a day, US$3.75. To **San Carlos** take a local bus 3 blocks from the main bus station, US$0.80.

Directory

Banks *Banco Pan de Azúcar*, accepts MasterCard. *Cambio Bacacay*, Florida 803, good rates, TCs.

An old town on Route 9, 14½ km north of Maldonado; of interest are the church, dating from 1722, heavily reconstructed, and the regional museum (L Olivera y C Reyles, closed Monday). There are two cambios which exchange travellers' cheques. **D** *Hospedaje*, on main plaza (limited hot water, good but cold and damp in winter). **E** *Hospedaje Terminal Carlitos*, at bus terminal. *El Amanecer*, Treinta y Tres 634, free camping, with poor facilities, in municipal park. ■ *San Carlos is a good point for connections to La Paloma (2 buses a day), and Chuy on the Brazilian border (US$7.40). Buses from Plaza Artigas run to Maldonado every 15 mins.*

San Carlos
Colour map 8, grid B6
Population: 20,000

Punta del Este

About 7 km from Maldonado and 139 km from Montevideo (a little less by dual carriageway), facing the bay on one side and the open waters of the Atlantic on the other, lies the largest and best known of the resorts, **Punta del Este**, which is particularly popular among Argentines. The narrow peninsula of Punta del Este has been entirely built over. On the land side, the city is flanked by large planted forests of eucalyptus, pine and mimosa. Two blocks from the sea, at the tip of the peninsula, is the historic monument of El Faro (lighthouse); in this part of the city no building may exceed its height. On the ocean side of the peninsula, at the end of Calle 25 (Arrecifes), is a shrine to the first mass said by the Conquistadores on this coast, 2 February 1515. Three blocks from the shrine is Plaza General Artigas, which has a *feria artesanal* (handicraft market); along its side runs Av Gorlero, the main street. There are a golf course, two casinos and many beautiful holiday houses. **Museo Ralli** of Contemporary Latin American Art, Barrio Beverly Hills, Curupay y Los Arachanes. ■ *Tue-Sun 1700-2100 in Jan-Feb, Sat-Sun 1400-1800 rest of year, free, T483476. Worth a visit but a car is needed to get there.*

Phone code: 042
Colour map 8, grid B6
139 km from
Montevideo

High season is 15
Dec-28 Feb; mid
season 1 Oct-15 Dec;
low season 1 Mar-
30 Sep. From 10 Mar to
Easter and from Easter
onwards the place is
deserted and on sunny
days it is still warm
enough to swim

Punta del Este has excellent bathing beaches, the calm *playa mansa* on the bay side, the rough *playa brava* on the ocean side. There are some small beaches hemmed in by rocks on this side of the peninsula, but most people go to where the extensive *playa brava* starts, opposite the *Hotel Playa*. Papa Charlie beach on the Atlantic (Parada 13) is preferred by families with small children as it is safe.

There is an excellent yacht marina, yacht and fishing clubs. There is good fishing both at sea and in three nearby

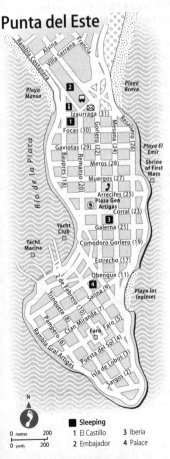

Punta del Este

Rambla Costanera
Alsina
Villa Serrana
Francia

Playa Mansa

Izaurraga (31)
Focas (30)
Gorlero (32)
Mesana (24)
Resalsero (26)
Playa Brava

Gaviotas (29)
Baupres (18)
Remanso (20)
Meros (28)
Muergos (27)
Playa El Emir
Shrine of First Mass

Arrecifes (25)
Plaza Gen Artigas
Corral (23)

Yacht Club
Galerna (21)
Comodoro Gorlero (19)

Yacht Marina
Estrecho (17)

Obenque (11)
Salina (9)
2 de Febrero
Trinquete (10)
Ctan Miranda (7)
Playa los Ingleses

Pampero (8)
Faro (5)
Faro
Rambla Gral Artigas
Puesta del Sol (4)
Isla de Lobos (3)
Sargos (2)

R í o   d e   l a   P l a t a

N
0 metres 200
0 yards 200

Sleeping
1 El Castillo
2 Embajador
3 Iberia
4 Palace

Uruguay

lakes and the Río Maldonado. The *Muriel*, a late-19th-century yacht, makes three sailings daily, lasting three hours US$35.

Isla de Gorriti, visited by explorers including Solís, Magellan and Drake, was heavily fortified by the Spanish in the 1760's to keep the Portuguese out. The island, densely wooded and with superb beaches, is an ideal spot for campers (boats from 0800-1700, return 0915-1715, US$7, T441716; *Don Quico*, also does fishing trips, T443963). On **Isla de Lobos**, which is a government reserve within sight of the town, there is a huge sea-lion colony; excursions, US$30. Ticket should be booked in advance (T441716).

Sleeping

Streets on the peninsula have names and numbers; lowest numbers at the tip

Very many, but expensive: we list only those with positive confirmations. Rates in those few hotels that are open after the end of Mar are as much as halved. In the high season, for which prices below apply, it is better to find a hotel in Maldonado and commute, or look for a hotel that is rebuilding, so that you can negotiate on prices. Visitors without a car are forced to take a hotel on the peninsula, unless they want to spend a fortune on taxis.

On the peninsula **L** *Embajador*, C Risso, parada 1, by bus terminal, T481008, F486750. Good.**L** *Palace*, Av Gorlero esq 11, T441919, F444695 (**AL** in Mar, closed in winter). Breakfast only (expensive restaurant, *La Stampa*, in the hotel), lovely courtyard, colonial style, well kept. **AL** *Iberia*, C 24, No 685, T440405, F445422. About centre-peninsula, **A** out of season, pleasant, breakfast included, open all year, good covered garage opposite.

Bed and breakfast at **B** pp *Alicia Lorenzo*, Parada 5, T480781. Nice room with bath, barbecue. Recommended. **Youth hostel** *El Castillo*, C 31 entre 20y 18, 100 m from bus station, across the road from the Information Centre (ask there for details).US$10 pp off season, **B** in double room, very good, close to beaches.

Eating

In Punta del Este, expensive = over US$20 pp, mid-range = US$12-20, cheap = under US$12

Expensive (usually very): *La Bourgogne*, Av del Mar y Pedragosa Sierra. French, excellent restaurant and afternoon tea in stylish surroundings, the most expensive and chic. *Bungalow Suizo*, Av Roosevelt y Parada 8. Excellent Swiss, must book. *Lo de Charlie*, 12 y La Salina. For fish. *Lo de Tere*, 20 y 21. Good local food, open all year. *La Lutèce*, Los Sauces casi Pedragosa Sierra. French cuisine, superb. *Mariskonea*, Calle 26, No 650. One of the oldest establishments, fish and seafood, very good quality and service. *Martín Fierro*, Rambla Artigas y 14. Good Argentine food. *Portofino*, Rambla Artigas entre 10 y 12. Good Italian. *Rosario*, Av Francia esq Lensina. Excellent but expensive coffee shop, pastries, sandwiches. *Yatch Club Uruguayo*, Gral Artigas y 8. Very good, fish, seafood, continental, views over the port, the exclusive Yacht Club. **Mid-range**: *Blue Cheese*, Rambla y 23. For steaks and unlimited salads, good value. *Los Caracoles*, Calle 20 y 28. Excellent food (international, *parrilla*, seafood) at good prices. *El Ciclista*, Calle 20 y 27. One of the oldest restaurants, international, Italian, *parrilla* and seafood. *La Estación*, C El Pinar esq San Francisco y California. *Parrilla* and salad bar, good, popular. *Gure-etxe* (also in La Coronilla), Calle 9 y 12. Seafood and Basque. *El Mejillón*, Rambla Portuaria y 11. *Confitería*, snack bar, popular. *Viejo Marino*, Calle 11 entre 14 y 15, Las Palmeras. Fish restaurant, very busy so go early. **Cheap**: *Avenida Rotisería*, Calle 21 (La Galerna). Good. *Il Barreto*, C 18 y 28. Italian vegetarian, good value, live music some evenings. *La Fragata*, Gorlero y 27. Open 24 hrs all year, a good meeting place for pastas, meat and *confitería*. *La Hamburguesa*, Calle 27 entre Gorlero y 24. For burgers and other dishes. *Jade Gardens*, Paso de la Cadena y Roosevelt parada 8. Chinese, nice place. *El Metejón*, Gorlero 578 y 19. International, *parrilla* and seafood, good value. *Mónaco*, 12 y 11. Good value fixed-price meals (*tenedor libre*) or expensive à la carte (10% discount for cash), also patisserie. *Tutto Sapori*, Parada 2 y Francia. Italian specialities, eat on terrace, accordion music in evening. Many enticing ice cream parlours on Gorlero.

Entertainment **Discos** Often don't begin till 0200. Entry US$25-50 for a couple, including 2 drinks. The UK club, *Cream* owns a beachfront bar in Punta del Este, www.cream.co.uk **Sport Riding**: *Nueva Escuela de Equitación* at *Cantegril Country Club*, Av Saravia, T423211, classes, guided rides, all levels and ages catered for.

Madrid, T441654, excursions from US$12, car hire, fishing trips and to islands. *Turisport*, Gorlero y 21, T445500, AmEx representative, also banking services here. *Tuttie*, local 1 de Servicio de Tráfico de Lanchas, T442594, for trips to islands and fishing.

Tour operators

Local Car hire: *Punta Car*, Continuación Gorlero s/n, *Hotel Playa*, T482112, puntacar@ puntacar.com.uy *Uno*, Gorlero y 21, T445018, unonobat@movinet.com.uy And others. See *Madrid Viajes* above and Essentials, for international agencies. **Scooter hire**: US$10 per hr, US$25 per day, with drivers licence (US$50 fine if caught without it) and ID documents, one place opposite bus terminal, others on same street as *Taller Los Angeles*, Parada 2 casi Blvr Artigas, T486732. *Los Angeles* rents scooters and bicycles (US$1.50-US$2.20 per hr, US$5.15-US$6 per day depending on number of gears, padlock and chain included, leave ID as deposit).

Transport
Traffic is directed by a one-way system; town bus services start from C 5 (El Faro), near the lighthouse

    Long distance Air Direct daily Boeing 737 flights from Buenos Aires to Punta del Este airport during the high season. *Laguna del Sauce*, Capitán Curbelo (T559777), which handles flights to Buenos Aires (*AR*, *Pluna*, *ARG* and *Southern Winds*, 40 mins). Airport tax US$15. Exchange facilities, tax-free shopping. Regular bus service to airport from Punta del Este bus station, US$4, 90 mins before departure, also connects with arriving flights. Taxi US$25; *remise* US$18-US$38 depending on destination (T441269 or Punta del Este 443221). El Jagüel airport is used by private planes. **Buses** Terminal at Av Gorlero, Blvd Artigas and C 32, T489467 (served by local bus No 7); has toilets, left luggage at *COT*, newsagent, café. To/from **Montevideo**, *COT* (T486810) or *Copsa* (T489205), US$6.50, just over 2 hrs, frequent in the summer; *COT* to Carrasco airport, US$5 (check about bus times to connect with flights). To **Piriápolis**, US$2.50. To **San Carlos** (US$2.25) for connections to Porto Alegre, Rocha, La Paloma, Chuy. Direct to **Chuy**, 4 hrs, US$7.50. Local bus fare about US$0.60. For transport Montevideo-Buenos Aires, *Buquebus* T484995/488380, at bus terminal, and *Ferryturismo* T442820, Galeria Sagasti local 16-17, Av Gorlero.

Airline offices *Aerolíneas Argentinas*, Galería Santos Dumont locales 2 y 3, T441976, Laguna del Sauce, T559782; *ARG*, Laguna del Sauce T559003; *Pluna-Varig*, Av Roosevelt y Parada 9, T441922. **Banks** Best rates of exchange from *Banco de la República Oriental de Uruguay*, which opens earlier and closes later than the other banks and accepts MasterCard, but no TCs. Many ATMs at banks on the peninsula and at Punta Shopping (Roosevelt). Also *casas de cambio*, eg *Indumex*, Av Gorlero y 28, *Brimar*, C 31 No 610. **Communications** Internet: *Cybermix Café*, Gorlero y 30, T447158, US$5 per hr. *Spot*, Gorlero y 30, T447290, open 0900-0200, US$6 per hr. **Post Office**: Av Gorlero entre 31 y 32, 0900-1400, 1600-1900, daily (shorter hours out of season). **Telephone**: telephone and fax on Calle 24 at Calle 25, by the square. *Telefónica* phones at Ancap station, Gorlero y C 30, T/F446018. **Tourist offices** Tourist information at *Liga de Fomento*, Parada 1, T441914/440514, open 0800-2000, or at airports. See the websites www.puntaweb.com, www.puntadeleste.com and www.vivapunta.com *Qué hacemos hoy* weekly magazine lists restaurants, entertainments, etc.

Directory

Around Punta del Este

Uruguay

Between the Peninsula and the mouth of the Río Maldonado, a road runs along the coast, passing luxurious houses, dunes and pines. At **Playa San Rafael**, there is an 18-hole golf course. The river is crossed by a unique undulating bridge, like a shallow M, to **La Barra**, a fashionable place with beaches, art galleries, bars and restaurants (taxi from Punta del Este US$15). The new **Museo del Mar** has an excellent collection on the subject of the sea, its life and history. ■ *In summer open daily 1000-2030; winter Sat, Sun and holidays 1030-1800, T771817, www.vivapunta.com/museomar* The coast road climbs a headland here before descending to the beaches further north,

Beaches east of Punta del Este

Montoya and **Manantiales** (reached by Condesa bus; taxi US$23). Some 30 km from Punta del Este is the fishing village of **Faro José Ignacio**, with a lighthouse, a beach club and other new developments, now the road is paved. ■ *Fri-Sun 1700-1900.* Coastal R10 runs some way east of José Ignacio, but there is no through connection to La Paloma as a new bridge across the mouth of the Lago Garzón is not operational. A car ferry sometimes runs, but rowing boats will take pedestrians and cyclists across.

Sleeping & eating
At San Rafael L *San Marcos*, Av Mar del Plata 191, T482251, F487870. Very pleasant. **L** *La Capilla*, Viña del Mar y Blvd Artigas, T484059, F487953. Cheaper out of season, gardens, good. *Camping San Rafael*, T486715. Good facilities, US$7, bus 5 from Maldonado. *Gitana*, good beach restaurant (open Christmas to end-Feb). **At La Barra L** *La Posta del Cangrejo* hotel and restaurant, Ruta 10 Km 160, T770021, F770173. Nice location, smart, if a bit old. Recommended. There are 2 campsites after the bridge, the second is cheaper, US$9.75, good showers and toilets. **B-D** *Backpacker de La Barra*, C 9, No 2306, T/F772272, www.vivapunta.com/backpacker/ Youth hostel style, price depends on what's included (eg **B** is full board, bicycle hire), café and restaurant, cybercafé, laundry. **Restaurants** *Lo de Miguel*, Ruta 10 y C 7. Excellent, small, booking essential (US$30 pp). *Pizza Bruja*, Ruta 10, just across the bridge. Crêpes, pizzas and pasta. *Yenny's*, Ruta 10, good seafood. Other *pizzerías* and restaurants up the hill. **At Manantiales LL-L** *Las Dunas*, Ruta 10 Km 163, T771211, F771210. Good rooms, but no breakfast, meals US$25-US$30, opulent. *Nueva Puebla Youth Hostel*, US$5, kitchen and washing facilities, small. **At Faro José Ignacio AL** *Parador Renner*, T0486-2056. With breakfast, good dining room. *Parador Santa Teresita*, T0486-2004, very popular, US$25 pp. Many other small restaurants, eg *Los Negros Franceses*, *La Gamba*, T0486-2055. Very good, popular, expensive.

Rocha
Population: 52,000
211 km from Montevideo

The capital of Rocha Department has groves of palms dotted about the fields, giving the area an unusual beauty. The city has an interesting central plaza and cathedral. There is a cinema on the plaza and the Club Social has dancing. Tourist information: T0598-472 8202. Portal on the web for Rocha Department: **C** *Municipal*, on 19 de Abril, very good. Good *confitería* on the plaza. Try also *Titar Grill* opposite old Onda bus terminal. ■ *Buses to* Montevideo, *3 hrs, US$8 (COT); to* Chuy, *US$6.25. No direct services to Punta del Este, but easy connections at San Carlos.*

La Paloma

Phone code: 0473
Colour map 8, grid B6
Population: 5,000
28 km from Rocha

Protected by an island and a sandspit, this is a good port for yachts. The surrounding scenery is attractive, with extensive wetlands nearby. You can walk for miles along the beach. The freshwater and sea fishing are good and the pace is more relaxed than Punta del Este. ■ *Frequent buses run to and from* Rocha, *and to and from the capital (5 hrs, US$9.20). 4 buses daily to Chuy, US$4.35, 3½ hrs, 2 a day to San Carlos, Pan de Azúcar and Aguas Dulces, all with* Rutas del Sol *company.*

Sleeping & eating
In nearby La Aguada, *Palma de Mallorca*, on Playa La Aguada, luxury hotel, T0479-6739, right on the ocean. Family discounts and 7-day packages offered, heated pool. **B** *Bungalows de Piemonte*, Costanera, T6096. **Youth hostel** At Parque Andresito, T6396, 40 beds, US$10 pp, clean, friendly, good meals available, kitchen facilities, open 1 Dec to 15 Apr. **Camping** In Parque Andresito, T6107, US$11.75. Overpriced, thatched *cabañas* for rent, US$22-38 per day with maid and kitchen facilities, sleep 4-6. *Grill del Camping* for *parrillas*, La Aguada, T6239, 2 km east of town, US$5. Good, each site with own barbecue, tap, sink, water and electricity. *La Marea*, near tourist office. Very popular, has outstanding seafood. *Arrecife*, on main street, first class. Excellent bread at *Confitería La Farola*.

Directory
Tourist office on Av Solari at entrance to town, very helpful, T6088. **Useful services** Bike rental opposite the casino, US$3.50 a day; horses can be hired. One bank which changes TCs; also a supermarket and post office.

Coastal R10 runs to Aguas Dulces (regular bus services along this route). About 10 km from La Paloma is **La Pedrera**, a beautiful village with sandy beaches. Beyond La Pedrera the road runs near pleasant fishing villages which are rapidly being developed with holiday homes, for example **Barra de Valizas**, 50 minutes north. At **Cabo Polonio**, visits to the islands of Castillos and Wolf can be arranged to see sea lions and penguins. It has a great beach ('old hippy' atmosphere), interesting rock formations with crashing waves, souvenir stands and haphazard development. All-terrain vehicles run across the dunes from a number of stops on the main road (several companies, US$6). Ask locally in Valizas about walking there, either 8 km over the dunes (very interesting, but hot, unless you go early), or along a dirt road off the main road (at Km 257), through woods, then 2-3 km across the dunes. From **Aguas Dulces** the road runs inland to the town of **Castillos** (easy bus connections to Chuy), where it rejoins R9. There is a tourist office at the Aguas Dulces/Castillos crossroads on R9; they have details on accommodation. At Km 298 there is a turn off for **Punta del Diablo**, a fishing village in dramatic surroundings, again with fine beaches, some tranquil, some rough.

Northeast of La Paloma

From Castillos it is 16 km to the **Bosque de Ombúes**, woods containing *ombú* trees (Phytolacca dioica – the national tree), *coronilla* (Scutia buxifolia) and *canelón* (Rapanea laetevirens). The woods are reached by turning off at Castillos along R16 to Aguas Dulces, just before which you turn onto R10 to the bridge. Take a boat from here, 30 minutes along the river, US$5 including guided tour (*Monte Grande* recommended as they visit both sides of the river).

At La Pedrera A*Hotel La Pedrera*, T0479-2001, F0479-2062, www.mayoral.com.uy/hpedrera.htm Swimming pool, tennis, comfortable rooms, charming, good food. Recommended. **Campsite** *La Palomita*, 8 blocks from the sea. Wooded, electricity, US$5, open summer only. **At Barra de Valizas A***Posada Eirete*. Small, tasteful, good breakfasts, owned by painter María Beloso. Recommended. Ask around for cottage rental at US$25 per day, sleeps 4, fully equipped. Youth Hostel, T094-414561, US$10 pp, open 1 Dec-14 Apr, reserve in Montevideo first. Free campsite, no facilities; fresh fish available if you ask. No electricity. **At Cabo Polonio** A few basic restaurants, eg *Estación Central* for local seafood, two *hosterías* **B** *Mariemar*, nice owners, own electricity generator, only hotel open off-season. Recommended. Also **A** *La Perla*, T0470-5125, T099-872360 (mob), www.mayoral.com.uy/laperla.htm Meals US$8-11. Houses or rooms to rent; informal camping at your own risk. No electricity, cooking gas, or phone. **At Aguas Dulces** *Hotel Gainford*, with restaurant, and others, **D-E** including breakfast. Lots of cheap cabins for rent. *Restaurant La Terraza*. *Chivito Veloz*, good, large portions for US$5. Camping fairly organized. About 2 km from Aguas Dulces is the private *Reserva Ecológica La Laguna*, T099-602410/0475-2118, on a 25 ha lake, with cabins for 4-6 (**B**), youth hostel (**D-E**) meals extra, HI affiliated, open all year, English, German, French, Italian, Spanish spoken, pick-up from bus stop in jeep or horse-drawn carriage, tours arranged, riding, boating on lake, sandboarding, birdwatching, credit cards accepted (Rutas del Sol bus from Montevideo, US$10). At Km 280.5, 17 km north of Castillos is *Camping Esmeralda*. **At Castillos** Several hotels including **D** *Hotel A Mi Gente*, Acosta 1235. Several restaurants including *La Strada* on 19 de Abril. **At Punta del Diablo A** *Hostería del Pescador*, T0472-1611 LD17. Private houses for rent US$50 per day for 4. Several restaurants, for example *La Posada*, excellent food. Highly recommended. Food and fish shops and handmade jewellery for sale.

Sleeping & eating

Parque Nacional Santa Teresa

This park has curving, palm-lined avenues and plantations of many exotic trees. It also contains botanical gardens, fresh-water pools for bathing and beaches which stretch for many kilometres (the surf is too rough for swimming). It is the site of the impressive colonial fortress of Santa Teresa, begun by the Portuguese in 1762 and seized by the Spanish in 1793. The fortress houses a museum of artefacts from the wars of independence. ■ *1000-1700 except Mon (winter hours shorter). US$0.30.*

100 km from Rocha 308 km from Montevideo

Uruguay

Tickets from restaurant La Posada del Viajero, *opposite. Recommended.* On the inland side of Route 9, the strange and gloomy Laguna Negra and the marshes of the Bañado de Santa Teresa support large numbers of wild birds.

Park services Park entry is US$1.20 (check opening times, maybe 1300 on weekdays). There are countless campsites (open all year), and a few cottages to let in the summer (which are usually snapped up quickly). At the *capatacia*, or administrative headquarters, campers pay US$2 pp for 3 nights (tickets are collected for each night stayed). Here there are also a small supermarket, greengrocer, butcher, bakery, medical clinic, petrol station, auto mechanic, post and telephone offices, and the *Club Santa Teresa*, where drinks and meals are available, but expensive. Practically every amenity is closed off-season. Tour by taxi (US$12, daily) can be made to Santa Teresa fortress, Laguna Negra, and the collection of native and exotic plants from the bathing resort of **La Coronilla** (10 km north of Santa Teresa, 20 south of Chuy; several hotels and restaurants most closed in winter). Montevideo-Chuy buses stop at La Coronilla.

Chuy

Phone code: 0474
Colour map 7, inset
Population: 9,000
340 km from
Montevideo

At Chuy the Brazilian frontier runs along the main street, Avenida Internacional, which is called Avenida Brasil in Uruguay and Avenida Uruguaí in Brasil. There are duty-free shops in Chuy and tourists from Uruguay may buy limited amounts of manufactured goods on the Brazilian side without formalities. There is also a casino. A tourist kiosk at the Uruguayan border post (see below) is not always open. For details on the Brazilian town of **Chuí**, see Brazil chapter, page 459. ■ *Buses to Montevideo (COT, Cynsa, Rutas del Sol, Turismar) US$13, 5 hrs, may have to change buses in San Carlos; to Maldonado US$7.50. To Treinta y Tres,* Transportes Puentes.

On the Uruguayan side, on a promontory overlooking Laguna Merín and the gaúcho landscape of southern Brazil, stands the restored fortress of **San Miguel**, dating from 1752 and surrounded by a moat. It is set in a park in which many plants and animals are kept. (Bus from Chuy US$0.45, entry US$0.20, closed Mon.) The hotel nearby, **AL** *Parador San Miguel*, is excellent, beautiful rooms, fine food and service. Highly recommended. Tours (US$9 from Chuy) end for the season after 31 March.

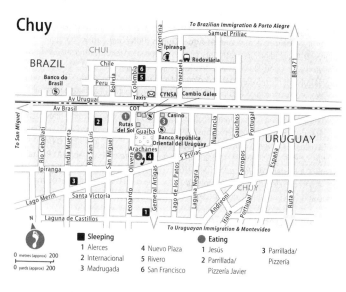

Chuy

■ Sleeping
1 Alerces
2 Internacional
3 Madrugada
4 Nuevo Plaza
5 Rivero
6 San Francisco

● Eating
1 Jesús
2 Parrillada/
 Pizzería Javier
3 Parrillada/
 Pizzería

Uruguay

B *Nuevo Hotel Plaza*, Artigas y Arachanes, T/F2309. On plaza, bath, breakfast, TV, very help- ful, good, restaurant *El Mesón del Plaza*. **C** *Alerces*, Laguna de Castillos 578, T/F2260, 4 blocks from border. Bath, TV, breakfast, heater, nice. **C** *International*, Río San Luis 121, T2055, by the border avenue. Breakfast extra. **D** *Madrugada*, Calle S Priliac e India Muerta, T2346, on a quiet corner. Pleasant. **Camping** From Chuy buses run every 2 hrs to the Barra del Chuy campsite, Ruta 9 Km 331, turn right 13 km, T2425. Good bathing, many birds. *Cabañas* for up to 4 persons cost US$20 daily or less, depending on amenities. **Restaurants** *Restaurant Jesús*, Av Brasil y L Olivera. Good value and quality. *Parrillada/Pizzería Javier*, Arachanes on plaza. Quite good. Also *Parrillada/Pizzería Los Leños*, Artigas entre Brasil y Arachanes. Casino open till 0400.

Banks Several *cambios* on Av Brasil, eg *Gales*, Artigas y Brasil, open Mon-Fri 0830-1200, 1330-1800, Sat 0830-1200, and in World Trade Center, open 1000-2200; on either side of *Gales* are *Aces* and *Val*. All give similar rates, charging US$1 plus 1% commission on TCs, dollars, pesos and reais exchanged. On Sun, try the casino, or look for someone on the street outside the *cambios*. *Banco de la República Oriental Uruguay*, Gen Artigas, changes TCs. **Communications** Post Office: On Gen Artigas. Telephone: *Antel*, S Priliac almost Artigas, open 0700-2300.

Uruguayan passport control is 2½ km before the border on Ruta 9 into Chuy, US$2 by taxi, 20 minutes' walk, or take a town bus; officials friendly and cooperative. Ministry of Tourism kiosk here is helpful, especially for motorists. If travelling by bus, make sure the driver knows you want to stop at Uruguayan immigration, as passengers are not expected to disembark. All formalities must be carried out at passport control immediately prior to leaving Uruguay, so if you stay in town you must go back to immigration. Tourists may freely cross the border in either direction as long as they do not go beyond either country's border post. Taking a car into Brazil is no problem, especially if the car is not registered in Brazil or Uruguay. From the border post, Ruta 9 bypasses the town, becoming BR-471 on the Brazilian side, leading to Brazilian immigration, also outside town. The Brazilian consulate is at Tito Fernández esq Laguna Merín, T2040, F2910, Chuy. ■ *For buses to Brazilian destinations, go to the rodoviária in Chuí (details in the Brazil chapter, page 459. **NB** From Oct to Feb, Uruguay is 1 hr behind Brazil.*

Entering Uruguay To enter Uruguay, you must have a Brazilian exit stamp and a Uruguayan entry stamp, otherwise you will not be permitted to proceed (for example at the customs post between Chuy and San Miguel fortress, on Route 19 toward Treinta y Tres). Those requiring a visa must have a medical examination before a visa can be issued in Chuí, cost about US$20 and US$10 respectively.

Montevideo north to Brazil

Montevideo

Two roads run towards Melo, heart of cattle-ranching country: Route 8 and Route 7, the latter running for most of its length through the Cuchilla Grande, a range of hills with fine views. Route 8 via Minas and Treinta y Tres, is the more important of these two roads to the border and it is completely paved.

Minas

This picturesque small town is set in wooded hills, which supply granite, marble and other minerals. Juan Lavalleja, the leader of the Thirty-Three who brought independence to the country, was born here (equestrian statue), and there is an equestrian statue to Artigas, said to be the largest such in the world, on the Cerro Artigas just out of town. The church's portico and towers, some caves in the neighbourhood, and the countryside around are worth seeing. In March and April you can buy

Phone code: 0442
Colour map 8, grid B6
Population: 34,000
120 km N of Montevideo

butea palm fruit, which is grape size, orange and tastes bitter-sweet. Good confectionery is made in Minas; the largest firm, opposite *Hotel Verdun*, shows tourists round its premises. *Lloyds TSB Bank* and national banks are open 1300-1700 Monday-Friday. There is a tourist office at the bus station. ■ *Buses to Montevideo, US$6 (*Núñez, Rutas del Plata*), US$4.60 (*Minuano, CUT*), 2½ hrs. To* Maldonado, *US$3.75, 5 a day, 2 hrs.*

Excursions The Parque Salus, on the slopes of Sierras de las Animas, is 8 km to the south and very attractive; take the town bus marked 'Cervecería Salus' from plaza to the Salus brewery, then walk 2 km to the mineral spring and bottling plant (**C** pp *Parador Salus*, half board, good; reasonable set lunch). It is a beautiful three-hour walk back to Minas from the springs. The Cascada de Agua del Penitente waterfall, about 11 km east off Route 8, is interesting and you may see wild rheas (protected) nearby. It is difficult to get to the falls in the off-season.

Sleeping **D** *Ramos*, 18 de Julio near bus station. Basic (discount for HI members). **D-E** *Las Sierras*, 18 de
& eating Julio 486, T3631. Including breakfast, very good value. **Youth hostel** *Chalet Las Chafas*, Route 8, Km 145, in small village of Villa Serrana, US$5 pp a night (open all year), 28 km beyond Minas on road to Treinta y Tres. Basic, poor facilities, take plenty of food and drink as there is no shop. Direct bus from Montevideo or Minas, ask driver to set you down and walk 3 km to Villa Serrana; essential to book through Montevideo office. **Camping** *Arequita*, T161170, beautiful surroundings, US$6. Recommended eating places are *San Francisco*, 25 de Mayo 586, and *El Portal*, Aníbal del Campo 743, for *parrillada*. The best pastry shop is *Irisarri*, Calle Treinta y Tres 618, known for *yemas* (egg candy) and *damasquitos* (apricot sweets).

To the Route 8 continues north via **Treinta y Tres** (*Population*: 28,000) to Melo, near
Brazilian Aceguá close to the border. At Km 307.5, Ruta 8 is **D** pp *Cañada del Brujo*, Sierra del
Border Yerbal, 34 km north of Treinta y Tres, T0452-2837, M099-297448,
For road traffic, cdelbrujo@latinmail.com An isolated hostel without electricity, basic but "fantas-
the frontier at tic", dormitory accommodation, local food, owner Pablo Rado drives you there,
Chuy is better than canoeing, trekking on foot or horseback, trips to Quebrada de los Cuervos. In **Melo**
Río Branco or Aceguá (*Population*: 42,000. *Phone code*: 0462), there is **L** *Gran Hotel Virrey*, J Muñiz 727,
T2411, better rooms in new part, TV, minibar, good café. Exchange rates are usually better in Melo than at the frontier. ■ **NB** *Melo is also reached direct from the capital by Route 7, which runs for most of its length through the hills of the Cuchilla Grande. Bus from Montevideo US$15.30 (*Núñez*). Several buses daily to Río Branco.*

At 12 km southeast of Melo is the Posta del Chuy (2 km off Route 26). This house, bridge and toll gate (built 1851 by two Frenchmen) was once the only safe crossing place on the main road between Uruguay and Brazil. Nowadays it houses a display of gaucho paintings and artefacts relating to its history.

Río Branco was founded in 1914, on the Río Yaguarón. The 1 km-long Mauá bridge across the river leads to the Brazilian town of Jaguarão. **D** *Italiano*, with bath. *Oasis* has good *pollo a la brasa*. The Brazilian consulate is at 10 de Junio 379, T2003, F2816.

An alternative route to Brazil is via Route 5, the 509-km road from Montevideo to the border town of Rivera, which runs almost due north, bypassing Canelones and Florida before passing through Durazno. After crossing the Río Negro, it goes to Tacuarembó. South of the Río Negro is gently rolling cattle country, vineyards, orchards, orange, lemon and olive groves. North is hilly countryside with steep river valleys and cattle ranching. The road is dual carriageway as far as Canelones. There is a toll 68 km north of Montevideo. If driving this route, note that on the narrow bridges on the single carriageway traffic coming from the north has preference.

Uruguay

Situated on the Río Yí, Durazno is a friendly provincial town with tree-lined avenues and an airport. There is a good view of the river from the western bridge. There are a few hotels (**C-D**) and a youth hostel at Sarabia y Dr Penza, T2835. Camping is at 33 Orientales, in park of same name by river, T2806, nice beach, hot showers, toilets, laundry sinks. **Tourism Farm** *Estancia Albergue El Silencio*, Ruta 14 Km 166, 10 km west of Durazno, T2014 (or T0360-2270, member of IH), silencio@adinet.com.uy About 15 minutes walk east of bridge over Río Yí where bus will stop: basic, clean rooms, simple tasty food, very friendly, riding, swimming, fishing, bird watching, can help the gauchos. Recommended. ■ *Buses from Montevideo US$7.30, Núñez, US$6.80, Turismar, Nossar.*

Durazno
Phone code: 0362
Colour map 8, grid B6
Population: 28,000
182 km from Montevideo

Dams on the Río Negro have created an extensive network of lakes near **Paso de los Toros** (Population: 13,000; 66 km north of Durazno, bus from Montevideo US$9.55), with camping and sports facilities. Some 43 km north of Paso de los Toros a 55-km road turns east to **San Gregorio de Polanco**, at the eastern end of Lago Rincón del Bonete. The beach by the lake is excellent, with opportunities for boat trips, horse riding and other sports. **Sleeping A** *Los Médanos*, T0369-4013, with breakfast, nicely furnished, swimming pool, jacuzzi, good value, its restaurant is across the road.

This is an agro-industrial town and major route centre. **A** *Tacuarembó*, 18 de Julio 133, T2104, breakfast, central. *Hospedaje 25*, 25 de Mayo 358, basic, garden. There are campsites 1 km out of town in the Parque Laguna de las Lavanderas, T4761, and 7 km north on R26 at Balneario Iporá. *Restaurante Parrilla La Rueda*, W Beltrán 251, good. ■ *Buses from Montevideo, US$15 (Turil, Núñez). Train service to Rivera at 0600 (see below).*

Tacuarembó
Phone code: 0632
Colour map 8, grid B6
Population: 40,000
390 km N of Montevideo

Rivera (*Population*: 55,400. *Phone code*: 0622) is divided by a street from the Brazilian town of Santa Ana do Livramento. Points of interest are the park, the Plaza Internacional, and the dam of Cañapirú. There are a casino, many duty-free shops and plenty of exchange offices. Uruguayan immigration is in the new Complejo Turístico at Sarandí y Viera, 14 blocks, 2 km, from the border (take bus along Agraciada). There is also a tourist office here, T5899. Luggage is inspected when boarding buses out of Rivera; there are also 3 checkpoints on the road out of town. The Brazilian consulate is at Ceballos 1159, T3278, F4470 and the Argentine one is at Ituzaingó 524, T3257. **NB** This is not a straightforward border crossing by public transport. Remember that you must have a Uruguayan exit stamp to enter Brazil and a Brazilian exit stamp to enter Uruguay.

The Brazilian Border

Sleeping A *Casablanca*, Sarandí 484, T3221. Shower, breakfast, a/c, comfortable, pleasant. **B-C** *Comercio*, Artigas 115. Comfortable, **C** without bath. **B-C** *Sarandí*, Sarandí 777, T3521. Fan, good, **C** without bath. **C** *Uruguay-Brasil*, Sarandí 440, T3068. A/c, breakfast. **D** *Ferrocarril*, Lavalleja y Uruguay, T3389. Without bath, basic, quiet. **Youth hostel** *Hotel Nuevo*, Ituzaingó 411, T0622-3039. Open all year, family rooms, canteen, no cooking facilities. **Camping** In Municipal site near AFE station, T3803, and in the Parque Gran Bretaña 7 km south along Route 27.

Transport Air *Aviasur* from Montevideo; *Pluna*, Paysandú 1079, T3404. **Train** Passenger service to Tacuarembó leaves Rivera 1700, Mon-Sat, 3½ hrs; depart Tacuarembó 0600, US$3. The train goes through beautiful countryside abundant with animal life. **Bus** Terminal at Uruguay y Viera (1½ km from the terminal in Santa Ana). To/from **Montevideo**, US$19.25 (*Turil, Núñez*). To **Fray Bentos** and **Durazno**. To **Paysandú**, *Copay* at 0330, 1600, US$15. To **Tacuarembó**, US$4.50 (*Núñez, Turil*), no connections for Paysandú. To **Salto**, Mon and Fri 1630, 6 hrs, US$16. For **Artigas**, take bus in Livramento to Quaraí, then cross bridge.

Uruguay

Montevideo

West from Montevideo

Route 1, part of the Pan-American Highway, runs west from Montevideo, lined with ribbon development for the first 50 km. Roads lead off to several beaches, notably Pascual, Kiyú and Boca del Cufre.

Colonias Valdense & Suiza At Km 121 from Montevideo the road passes Colonia Valdense, a colony of Waldensians who still cling to some of the old customs of the Piedmontese Alps. Tourist information T055-88412. A road branches off north here to Colonia Suiza, a town of Swiss settlement also known as **Nueva Helvecia** (*Population*: 9,000. *Phone code*: 0552). The Swiss national day is celebrated with great enthusiasm.

The area is famous for its cheeses and other dairy produce

Sleeping and eating L *Nirvana*, Av Batlle y Ordóñez, T44081, F44175, www.ciu.com.uy/nirvana/index.html Restaurant (Swiss and traditional cuisine), sports facilities, gardens. Recommended. **A** *Granja Hotel Suizo*, T4002. Fine restaurant. Recommended. **C** *Del Prado* – Youth Hostel – open all year, huge buffet breakfast, T45812, F44169. Campsite in a park at the turnoff for Col Suiza, on main road, free, toilets (locked after 2100), no showers. Snack Bar/Restaurant *Don Juan*, main plaza, excellent food, pastries and bread. **Tourism Farms** *El Terruño*, Ruta 1, Km 140, 35 km before Colonia, T/F0550-6004, full day tours US$20, including rural safari, lunch. *Estancia Los Macachines*, Km 93.5, Ruta 1, T0340-9074 (or Montevideo 600 1950, Nariño 1604, CP 11500), overnight stay **AL** pp, typical meals, horse riding, sports, *estancia* tours, attended by the owners, day rate US$45. Recommended. **A** pp *Estancia Don Miguel*, Ruta 1 Km 121 y Ruta 52, T0550-2041, esmiguel@adinet.com.uy Book through *Cecilia Regules Viajes*, see page 1304. Rustic, working farm, full board, transport extra, good activities including milking, riding, walking, adequate food, little English spoken. Recommended.

Transport Buses Montevideo-Colonia Suiza, frequent, with *COT*, 2½ hrs, US$5; *Turil*, goes to Colonia Suiza and Valdense; to **Colonia del Sacramento**, frequent, 1 hr, US$1.85. Local services between Colonia Valdense and Nueva Helvecia connect with Montevideo/Colonia del Sacramento buses.

Colonia del Sacramento

Phone code: 052, from Bs As: 022 Colour map 8, grid B5 Population: 22,000

Founded by Portuguese settlers from Brazil in 1680, Colonia del Sacramento was an important centre for smuggling British goods across the Río de la Plata into the Spanish colonies throughout the 17th century. The small historic section juts into the Río de la Plata, while the modern town extends around a bay. It is a charming, lively place with streets lined with plane trees, a pleasant Plaza 25 de Agosto and a grand Intendencia Municipal (Méndez y Av Gen Flores – the main street). The whole town is kept very trim. The best beach is Playa Ferrando, 2 km to the east (buses from Gen Flores every two hours). There are regular sea and air connections with Buenos Aires and a free port. In the old city, visit the *Mercado Artesanal*, del Comercio y de la Playa and the *Rincón del Turista*, Santa Rita. In the third week of January, festivities are held marking the founding of Colonia.

The **Barrio Histórico**, with its narrow streets (see Calle de los Suspiros), colonial buildings and reconstructed city walls, is interesting because there are few such examples in this part of the continent. It has been declared Patrimonio Cultural de la Humanidad by UNESCO. The **Plaza Mayor** is especially picturesque. Grouped around it are the **Museo Municipal** in the former house of Almirante Brown (with indigenous archaeology, historical items, paleontology, natural history), the **Casa Nacarello** next door, the **Casa del Virrey**, the **Museo Portugués** and the

Uruguay

ruins of the Convento de San Francisco, to which is attached the **Faro** (lighthouse, entry US$1). At the eastern end is the **Puerta del Campo**, the restored city gate and drawbridge. Just north of the Plaza Mayor is the **Archivo Regional**. The **Iglesia Matriz**, on Calle Vasconcellos (beside the Plaza de Armas/Manuel Lobo), is the oldest church in Uruguay. At the end of Calle Misiones de los Tapes, the Casa Portuguesa is now the tiny **Museo del Azulejo**. The house of Gen Mitre, Calles de San José y España, now houses the **Museo Español**. At the north edge, the fortifications of the **Bastión del Carmen** can be seen; nearby is the Teatro Bastión del Carmen, Rivadavia 223. ■ *All museums open 1130-1830, entry by combined ticket bought from Museo Municipal, US$1; not all may be open on the same day.*

Around the bay (5 km, take blue bus from Avenida Gen Flores y A Méndez, 30 minutes, US$0.40), is **Real de San Carlos**, an unusual, once grand but now sad tourist complex, built by Nicolás Mihanovic between 1903-12. The elegant bull-ring, in use for a mere two years, is falling apart (it is closed to visitors but a local guide will take you through a gap in the fence). The casino, the nearest to Buenos Aires (where gambling was prohibited), failed when a special tax was imposed on Mihanovic's excursions; it and its hotel are decaying. A huge Frontón court can still be used, but the building is rotting. Only the racecourse (Hipódromo) is still operational (US$1 for men, women free) and you can see the horses exercising and swimming in the sea. Also in Real de San Carlos is a Museo Municipal; by the beach are two restaurants. At Parada 20, about seven stops before Real de San Carlos, is the Capilla de San Benito.

Tourist offices Flores y Rivera, T26141/23700, good maps of the Barrio Histórico. ■ *Mon-Fri 0800-1830, Sat and Sun 0900-2200.* Also at passenger terminal at the dock, T24897, www.colonianet.com, and www.guiacolonia.com.uy

Sleeping

In Barrio Histórico L-AL *Plaza Mayor*, Del Comercio 111, T25316, F23193, plazamayor@colonianet.com Lovely, English spoken. **AL** *Posada del Gobernador*, 18 de Julio 205, T22918, www.colonianet.com/governador/index.htm With breakfast, charming. Recommended.

In the centre AL *Beltrán*, Gral Flores 311, T22955, www.guiacolonia.com.uy/Beltran With bath, comfortable. **AL** *Esperanza*, Gral Flores 237, T/F22922 (**B** weekdays). Charming. **AL** *Posada Los Linajes*, Washington Barbot 191, T28300, www.guiacolonia.com.uy/loslinajes Central, a/c, TV, cafeteria. Warmly recommended. **A** *Italiano*, Lobo 341, T22103. **B** without bath, good restaurant, hot water but no heating. Recommended. **A** *Leoncia*, Rivera 214, T22369, F22049, www.guiacolonia.com.uy/Leoncia/index.htm A/c, modern, good. **B** *Hostal de los Poetas*, Mangarelli 675, T/F25457. With bath, quiet, pleasant. Recommended. **B** *Los Angeles*, Roosevelt 213, T22335. Small rooms, no restaurant, English spoken. **B** *Royal*, General Flores 340, T22169, www.guiacolonia.com.uy/royal/index.htm With breakfast, comfortable, good restaurant, pool, noisy a/c but recommended. **C** *Blanca y Juan Carlos*, Lobo 430, T24304. One double room, one shared room **G** pp, shared bath, hot water, welcoming, convenient, lovely wild garden, vegetarian restaurant opposite. Recommended. **C-D** *Hospedaje Colonial*, Flores 436, T22906. HI affiliated, restaurant below. Recommended but noisy. **D** pp *La Casa de Charo*, Alberto Méndez 163, T23373. **D-E** pp without bath, with breakfast, TV, antique furnuiture, full of character. Recommended. **D** *Señora Raquel Suárez*, T22916. Spacious rooms to rent, good value. **E** pp *Español*, Lobo 377, www.guiacolonia.com.uy/espanol/espanol.htm Without bath, courtyard, good value, breakfast US$2, meals US$5. Recommended. Family *hospedajes* are good value, eg **E** pp *18 de Julio 481*, T25813. With breakfast, bath, cable TV. The municipal sports complex has 2 dormitories with 80 beds, which are sometimes available – ask at the tourist office.

Camping Municipal site at Real de San Carlos, T24444, US$3.50 pp, **C** in mini-cabañas, electric hook-ups, 100 m from beach, hot showers, open all year, safe, excellent. Recommended.

Eating

El Aljibe, Flores 248 e Ituzaingó. Good fish dishes. *Almacén del Túnel*, Flores 227. Good meat dishes, but encourages eating of fresh vegetables. *El Asador*, Ituzaingó 168. Good *parrillada* and pasta, nice atmosphere, value for money. *Club Colonial*, Gen Flores 382. Good value. *El Drugstore*, Vasconcellos 179 y Portugal, on Plaza Menor. Popular. *El Frijol Mágico*, Manuel Lobo y Méndez. Good vegetarian food, 1130-1400. *Pulpería Los Faroles*, Misiones

Uruguay

de los Tapes 101, just off Plaza Mayor, old town. *La Torre*, Av Gral Flores y San Gabriel, in old town. Bar and restaurant, loud disco music, but fine panoramic views especially at sunset. *La Ventana de Marcelo M*, C Real 147 y de la Playa, Plaza Mayor. Historic house, good food, 1 internet terminal. Recommended, friendly. *El Viejo Galeón*, Ituzaingó y 18 de Julio. *Yacht Club* (at Puerto de Yates) and *Esperanza* (at hotel) are good. *Arcoiris*, Av Gral Flores. For very good ice cream.

Transport **Car hire:** *Budget*, Flores 91, budget@colonianet.com; *Punta*, Paseo de la Estación L3, on

Book in advance for all sailings and flights in summer, especially at weekends

Méndez near Flores; also car hire at airport. Motorcycle and bicycle hire at Flores y Rivera and outside ferry dock, US$5 per hr, US$15 per day, recommended as a good way of seeing the town, traffic is slow. **Air** Flights to Aeroparque, Buenos Aires, most days, fare includes connecting bus services to/from Montevideo, generally quicker than hydrofoil. The airport is 17 km out of town along Route 1; for taxi to Colonia, buy ticket in building next to arrivals, US$2.

Road From Colonia to Punta del Este bypassing Montevideo: take Ruta 11 at Ecilda Paullier, passing through San José de Mayo, Santa Lucía and Canelones, joining the Ruta Interbalnearia at Km 46. **Bus:** All leave from a new bus terminal between the ferry port and the petrol station (free luggage lockers). to **Montevideo**, 2½ hrs, *COT* (slower, several stops

Colonia del Sacramento

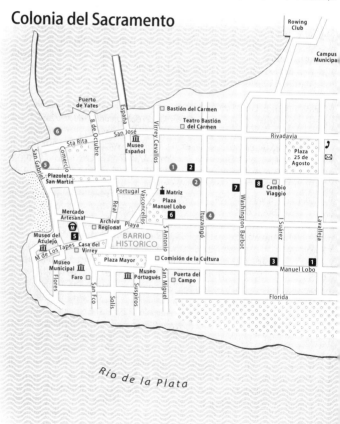

	Sleeping	4 Leoncia	7 Posada Los Linajes	Eating
	1 Español	5 Plaza Mayor	8 Royal	1 Almacén del Túnel
	2 Esperanza	6 Posada del		2 El Aljibe
Not to scale	3 Italiano	Gobernador		3 El Frijol Mágico

Uruguay

en route) and *Turil*, half-hourly service between the two, US$5-6; *Chadre* US$8. *Turil* to Col Valdense, US$2.35. To **Carmelo**, 1½ hrs, *Tauriño*, 4 a day (not Sun), US$2.50. *Chadre/Agencia Central* to Carmelo, **Salto**, 8 hrs, US$18.75 and on to **Bella Unión** en route from the capital. *Turil* to **Tacuarembó**, US$14.85, **Rivera**, US$19.10, and **Artigas**, US$23.40.

Sea To Buenos Aires: up to 10 crossings daily, 45 mins with *Buquebus* (T052-22975/23364), cars carried, and *Ferryturismo*, fares and schedules given under Montevideo.

Banks Banks open in afternoon only. *Banco Comerical*, on plaza, gives cash against Visa. *Cambio Viaggio*, Flores 350 y Suárez, T22070, Mon-Sat 0900-1200, 1300-1800, Sun 1000-1300 (also outside the ferry dock, with car hire). *Cambio Colonia* and *Banco de la República Oriental del Uruguay* at the ferry port (dollars and South American currencies). Exchange rates at the ferry port are far worse than in town. Many establishements accept Argentine pesos. **Communications Post Office**: on main plaza. **Telephone**: *Antel*, Rivadavia 420, open till 2300, does not accept foreign money. **Consulates** Argentine Consulate, Flores 215, T22091, open weekdays 1200-1700. **Directory**

The Rio Uruguay marks the frontier with Argentina (international crossings at Fray Bentos, Paysandú and Salto). On the Uruguayan side are rolling hills crossed by a network of rivers. At all the major towns on the Uruguay are beaches and campsites and there are thermal springs at Guaviyú, Daymán and Arapey.

To Real de San Carlos
Cnl Arroyo
Av Gen Artigas
Alberto Méndez
Rivera
Dr D Fosalba
V García
To Playa Ferrando (2 km)
Budget
Intendencia
☐ Municipal
4
Plaza de Deportes
To Montevideo
To Real de San Carlos
Av General Flores
☐ Punta Rent a Car
18 de Julio
AV F D Roosevelt
PUERTO
Ⓢ
▼ To Buenos Aires

4 El Viejo Galeón
5 La Torre
6 Yacht Club

Carmelo
Phone code: 0542
Population: 18,000
74 km from Colonia del Sacramento

From Colonia, Route 21 heads north then northwest to reach **Carmelo**, on the banks of Arroyo Las Vacas. A fine avenue of trees leads to the river, crossed by the first swing bridge built in Uruguay. Across the bridge is the Rambla de los Constituyentes, with terraces and the Fuente de las Tentaciones. The town is pleasant, with the church, museum and archive of El Carmen on Plaza Artigas (named after the founder of the city). In the Casa de Cultura, 19 de Abril 246, is a tourist office and museum. Banks will only exchange bills and not travellers' cheques. The Argentine consulate is at FD Roosevelt 318.

Sleeping D *San Fernando*, 19 de Abril 161, T2503. Full of character, temperamental showers. Recommended. **Camping** At Playa Seré, hot showers.

Transport Buses To **Montevideo**, US$9.20, *Intertur*, US$10, *Chadre*. To **Fray Bentos**, **Salto**, from main plaza 0710, 1540. To **Colonia**, *Tauriño*, 4 a day, 1½ hrs, US$2.50. **To Argentina**: via Tigre, across the Paraná delta, a most interesting bus/boat ride past innumerable islands: *Cacciola* 3 a day; office in Carmelo, Constituyente 263, T0542-8062, see under Montevideo for more details, page 1314.

Uruguay

Mercedes

This livestock centre and resort on the Río Negro is best reached by Route 2 from the main Colonia-Montevideo highway. Founded in 1788, this pleasant town is a yachting and fishing centre during the season. Its charm (it is known as 'the city of flowers') derives from its Spanish-colonial appearance, though it is not as old as the older parts of Colonia. There is a pleasant *costanera* (riverside drive). Some 4 km west of town is the Parque Mauá, dating from 1757. It has a mansion which contains the Museum of Palaeontology on the ground floor, well-presented collection. ■ *Daily 1100-1800. Free.* The building is worth wandering around to see the exterior, upper apartments and stable block. There are also picnic tables, barbecues, camping possible in season. It takes 45 minutes to walk to the park, a pleasant route passing Calera Real on the river bank, dating back to 1722, the oldest industrial ruins in the country (lime kilns hewn out of the sandstone). The tourist office is at *Colón*, on the plaza, maps and hotel lists available.

Sleeping & eating

D *Club de Remeros*, Youth Hostel, on riverside, T2534. Kitchen and laundry facilities. Good food at *La Brasa*, Artigas 426, and at *Círculo Policial*, C 25 de Mayo. *El Emporio de los Panchos*, Roosevelt 711. Good range of dishes. **Camping** Site at Mercedes, on an island in mid-river, reached by a small road, toilets, showers, US$2.20. **Tourism Farm** *Estancia La Sirena Marinas del Río Negro*, Ruta 14, Km 4, T0530-2017, *estancia* dating from 1830, very picturesque, on the river, birdwatching, fishing, waterskiing, accommodation, meals, attended by Rodney, Lucia and Patricia Bruce, its friendly owners: all information from Calle Pittaluga 6396, Montevideo 11500, T02-600 7029/401 4446. www.lasirena.com.uy

Tranport

Bus To **Paysandú**, with *Sabelín*, Sánchez 782, T3937, 2½ hrs, US$6.25; also *Chadre* on the Montevideo-Bella Unión route US$11.50. Bus to **Argentina** and **Montevideo**, *CUT*, Artigas (on plaza).

Directory

Banks *Cambio Fagalde*, Giménez 709. *Banco Comercial* on Colón (just off plaza) and *Banco de la República*, on plaza.

Fray Bentos

Route 2 continues westwards (34 km) to Fray Bentos, the main port on the east bank of Río Uruguay. Here in 1865 the Liebig company built its first factory producing meat extract. The original plant, much extended and known as **El Anglo**, has been restored as the Museo de La Revolución Industrial, and business park (there is a restaurant, *Wolves*, and a disco, *Fuel Oil*). ■ *Daily except Mon, entry by guided tour only, US$1, 1000, 1430 (1000, 1130 and 1700 in summer), tour 1½ hrs in Spanish, may provide leaflet in English, T3607.* The office block in the factory has been preserved complete with its original fittings. Many machines can be seen. Within the complex is the Barrio Inglés, where workers were housed, and La Casa Grande, where the director lived. For exchange, there is *Cambio Fagalde*, Plaza Constitución, open Mon-Fri 0800-1900, Sat 0800-1230. The tourist office is at Puente General San Martín, T2369.

There are beaches to the northeast and southwest and also at *Las Cañas*, 8 km south, where there is a tourist complex. Entry US$1; pleasant, but crowded in summer. **B** in motel rooms with kitchenette and bath, cheaper without kitchen, all with a/c, TV, fridge. Camping US$8.50 per day minimum, T2224.

Sleeping & eating

B *Plaza*, 18 de Julio y 25, T2363. Comfortable. **E** *Colonial*, 25 de Mayo 3293, T2260. Attractive old building with patio. **E** pp *25 de Mayo*, 25 de Mayo y Lavalleja, T2586. Basic. **Camping** At the *Club Remeros*, near the river and at Colegio Laureles, 1 km from centre, T2236. *Olla*, 18 de Julio near Plaza Constitución. Seafood and pasta, good value. Several other cafés and pizzerias on 18 de Julio near Plaza Constitución.

Terminal at 18 de Julio y Blanes, buses call here, but do not alight as buses also call at company **Transport** offices around Plaza Constitución. To/from **Montevideo**, *CUT*, 4½ hrs, 6 a day, US$11.75, also Chadre, US$12.50. To **Mercedes**, *ETA*, US$1, frequent, 30 mins. To **Paysandú**, US$4.75.

About 9 km upriver from Fray Bentos is the San Martín International Bridge, the **Crossing to** most popular overland route with Argentina, toll US$4 per car (tourist office). Bicy- **Argentina** cles are not allowed to cross, but officials will give you a lift if there is no other traffic. Formalities are separate, at opposite ends of the bridge. The Argentine consulate is at Sarandí 3195, Fray Bentos. ■ *Buses to Gualeguaychú (Argentina), ETA, 2 a day, 1 hr, US$5, passports inspected on bus. To Buenos Aires, 3½ hrs, US$18.*

Paysandú

North of Fray Bentos 130 km is this city on the east bank of the Río Uruguay, along *Phone code: 072* Route 24. Temperatures in summer can rise as high as 42°C. There is a golf club, and *Colour map 8, grid A5* a rowing club which holds regattas. The cathedral is 19th-century. The cemetery on *Population: 100,000* the outskirts is worth a look. **Museo de la Tradición**, north of town at the Balneario *480 km from* Municipal, gaucho articles, is also worth a visit. ■ *Tue-Fri from 1630, Sat 0900-1200,* *Montevideo* *Sun 1330-1700, reached by bus to Zona Industrial.* **Museo Salesiano**, Florida 1278, attached to Cathedral, interesting. ■ *Mon-Fri 0830-1130.*

    Excursions To the **Río Quequay waterfalls**, 25 km to the north; the **Termas del Guaviyú** thermal springs 50 km north (1½ hours by bus, US$2.50, four a day) with four pools, restaurant, motel accommodation and excellent cheap camping facilities (can be noisy and crowded in high season, good bakery), entrance to springs US$0.50. Also to the **Meseta de Artigas**, 90 km north of Paysandú, 13 km off the highway to Salto. The Meseta, 45 m above the Río Uruguay, which here narrows and forms whirl-pools at the rapids of El Hervidero, was used as a base by General Artigas during the struggle for independence. A terrace commands a fine view, but the rapids are not visi-ble from the Meseta. The statue, with Artigas' head topping a tall shaft, is very original.

L *Gran Hotel Paysandú*, 18 de Julio y 19 de Abril, T23400. A/c, with breakfast, comfortable. **Sleeping** **AL** *Casa Grande*, Florida 1221 at Plaza Constitución, T24994. A/c, welcoming, parking, very *Book hotels in advance* good. **A** *Lobato*, Gómez 1415, T22241. With breakfast, a/c, modern, good. **B-C** *Rafaela*, 18 *during Holy Week* de Julio 1181, T25053. With breakfast, large rooms, modern. **C** *Concordia*, 18 de Julio 984, T22417. **D** without bath, old-fashioned, pleasant patio. **D** *Sarandí*, Sarandí 931, T23465. Good, comfortable. **E** pp *Victoria*, 18 de Julio 979, T24320. Cheaper without bath, very help-ful. Highly recommended. **Youth hostel C** *Hotel La Posada*, José Pedro Varela 566, T27879. Open all year except 25 Dec and 1 Jan, family rooms available, no cooking facilities. **Camping** Balneario Municipal, 2 km north of centre, by the river, no facilities. Also at the Parque Municipal, south of centre, some facilities.

Artemio, 18 de Julio 1248. Has "best food in town". *Don Diego*, 19 Av España 1474. **Eating** *Parrillada*, very good.

Viñar Turismo, Artigas 1163. Helpful. **Tour operators**

Air *Aviasur* flights to **Montevideo** (US$80 return; *Pluna*, Florida 1249, T23071). **Bus** Terminal **Transport** at San Martín y Artigas. To/from **Montevideo**, US$14.50 (*Núñez, Copay*), 5-6 hrs, also *Chadre/Agencia Central*, US$15.25, many buses. To **Salto** US$5, 6 a day. To **Rivera**, US$15. To **Fray Bentos**, 4 a day, 1½ hrs direct, 4 hrs via Young, US$5. To **Paso de los Toros** 1430 (return 0430), US$6.25, or by *Alonso* bus to **Guichón** at 0600, 1100, 1430 and change. To **Colonia** by *Chadre*, 1700, 6 hrs, US$7.50. It can be difficult to get a seat on long-distance buses going north.

Banks Several *casas de cambio* on 18 de Julio, including *Cambio Fagalde*, No 1004; *Cambio Bacacay*, **Directory** No 1008; both change TCs, open Sat 0830-1230. Also *Banco de la República*, 18 de Julio y 19 de Abril, and others on 18 de Julio. **Communications** Post Office: 18 de Julio y Montevideo. **Telephone:**

Antel, Montevideo 875. **Embassies and consulates** Argentina, Gómez 1084, T22253, Mon-Fri 0800-1300. **Tourist office** on Plaza de Constitución, 18 de Julio 1226, T26221 (Mon-Fri 0800-1900, Sat-Sun 0800-1800), and at the Puente Gen Artigas.

Tourism Farm   **L** *La Calera*, near Guichón, 89 km east of Paysandú (T Montevideo 916 3011, or 0740-2292, Mara Morán, Colonia 881, piso 10, www.lacalera.com.uy). Cheaper Mon-Thu, 20 luxurious suites with fireplace, full board, dining room with home made food, swimming pool, riding, rodeo, conference facilities. Highly recommended.

Crossing to Argentina   The José Artigas international bridge connects with Colón, Argentina (toll US$4 per car), about 8 km away. ■ *Buses to* Colón *and* Concepción del Uruguay, *5 a day, 2 on Sun, US$3 to Colón, US$4 to Concepción.*

Salto

Phone code: 073
Colour map 8, grid A5
Population: 80,000

A centre for cultivating and processing oranges and other citrus fruit, Salto is a beautifully-kept town 120 km by paved road north of Paysandú. The town's commercial area is on Calle Uruguay, between Plazas Artigas and Treinta y Tres. Next to the Club Uruguay, Calle Uruguay, is the *Farmacia Fénix*, "la más antigua de Salto", over 100 years old. See the beautiful but run down **Parque Solari** (on Ruta Gral Artigas, northeast of the centre) and the **Parque Harriague** (south of the centre) with an open air theatre. The **Museo de Bellas Artes y Artes Decorativas** in the French style mansion of a rich *estanciero* (Palacio Gallino), Uruguay 1067, opens at 1400, well worth a visit. There is a Shrove Tuesday carnival.

The most popular tourist site in the area is the large **Salto Grande** dam and hydroelectric plant 20 km from Salto, built jointly by Argentina and Uruguay; a tour can be arranged with the tourist office, US$5, minimum five people, every 30 minutes, 0700-1400. A road runs along the top of the dam to Argentina. By launch to the **Salto Chico** beach, fishing, camping. Nearby is the resort **AL** *Hotel Horacio Quiroga*, T34411, hquiroga@adinet.com.uy Sports facilities, staffed by nearby catering school, special packages offered in season.

Sleeping   **AL-A** *Los Cedros*, Uruguay 657, T33984, F34235, www.hotelloscedros.com.uy With breakfast, a/c, comfortable. **A** *Gran Hotel Salto*, 25 de Agosto 5, T34333, F33251, www.saltoweb.com.uy/granhotelsalto/ With breakfast, a/c, good restaurant, reasonably priced. Recommended. **B** *Argentina*, Uruguay 892, T29931. With breakfast, a/c, cafetería, comfortable. **C** *Artigas Plaza*, Artigas 1146, T34824 (no sign). Run down, log fire in winter, some rooms without windows. **D** *Pensión 33*, Treinta y Tres 269. Basic, central. **D** pp *Plaza*, Plaza Treinta y Tres, T33744. Includes breakfast, fans, good location, simple, old-fashioned. Recommended. **Youth hostel**   *Club Remeros de Salto*, Rambla Gutiérrez y Belén (by the river) T33418. Open all year, no cooking facilities, pool (US$5 per day), US$5, US$6.50 without HI card, poor value.

Eating   *La Caldera*, Uruguay 221, T24648. Good *parillada*. *Pizzería Las Mil y Una*, Uruguay 906. Popular, good atmosphere. *Pizzería La Farola*, Uruguay y Julio Delgado. *Don Diego*, Chiazzaro 20. Pasta. *Club de Uruguay*, Uruguay 754. Good breakfast and good value meals.

Transport   **Air** *Aviasur* flights to/from the capital. *Pluna*, Uruguay 657, T2724. Bus to airport, US$2. **Buses** Terminal 6 blocks south of centre at Latorre y Larrañaga. To/from **Montevideo**, 7½ hrs, US$19 (*Bus del Norte*, *Núñez* and *Chadre*). To **Termas del Arapey**, 2 hrs, daily, US$5.25. **Paysandú** US$5, 2 hrs, 6 a day. To **Rivera**, US$16. To **Bella Unión**, 2 hrs, US$6, 6 a day. To **Colonia** by *Chadre*, 0555, 1555, 8 hrs, US$18.75; to **Fray Bentos**, same times, US$10.

Directory   **Banks** *Banco Pan de Azúcar* does cash advances on Visa and MasterCard. *Banco de Crédito*. Both on Uruguay, several exchange houses on Uruguay. **Communications** Post Office: Treinta y Tres y Artigas. **Tourist offices** at Uruguay 1052, T34096, open 0800-2000, Sun 0800-1200, free map, and at the international bridge, T28933.

North of the town, at the Salto Grande dam, there is an international bridge to Concordia, Argentina. **Immigration** is carried out on the bus. The Argentine consul is at Artigas 1162, T32931, open Monday-Friday 1300-1700.

Crossing to Argentina

Transport Buses To **Concordia**, *Chadre* and *Flecha Bus*, 2 a day each, not Sun, US$3. To **Buenos Aires**, US$29, *Flecha Bus*. To **Posadas** night buses only, to **Puerto Iguazú**, 12 hrs, US$44. **Ferry** To Concordia, *Sanchristobal/Río Lago* joint service, 5 a day, Mon-Fri, 4 Sat, 2 Sun, US$4, depart from port on C Brasil, 20 mins.

Medicinal springs at Fuente Salto, 6 km north of the city. About 10 km south of Salto, reached by bus No 4 every 30 minutes from Calle Artigas (US$0.15) are **Termas del Daymán**, beautifully laid out with 14 swimming pools (entrance US$2.50; it is cheaper to buy combined bus/entrance ticket in Salto). Three hotels: *Hotel Termas Daymán*, in front of the public spa; next door is *El Tritón*, T073-52250, open 0700 for breakfast. Highly recommended. *La Posta del Daymán*, Ruta 3, Km 487, T29701, F28618, a/c, half-board, thermal swimming pool, good restaurant, discounts for long stay. Recommended. This hotel also has a hydrothermal complex offering hydrotherapy, sauna and massage. **D** *Youth hostel La Canela* on Route 3, Km 488.3, T073-32121 (open all year), good value. *Complejo San Francisco*, clean, cheap accommodation on the main road. Campsite at *Estancia San Niconos*, 12 km from Termas de Daymán, good facilities, pools.

Hot springs

The road to **Termas del Arapey** branches off the partially paved Route 3 to Bella Unión, at 61 km north of Salto, and then runs 35 km east and then south. Pampa birds, rheas and metre-long lizards in evidence. Termas del Arapey is on the Arapey river south of Isla Cabellos (Baltazar Brum). The waters at these famous thermal baths (five pools) contain bicarbonated salts, calcium and magnesium. There is a hotel with pool, **L-B** *Hotel Termas del Arapey*, price depends on cabin size and facilities, very simple *parador* (meals only) and good restaurant. Book ahead at tourist offices in Salto or Montevideo. Camping US$2 per person, good facilities (beware of theft at campsite. Take food as local markets very expensive).

To the Brazilian border

Route 3 runs north, 144 km from Salto, to the little town of **Bella Unión** near the confluence of the Ríos Uruguay and Cuaraim. The Brazilian frontier, nearby, is crossed by the Barra del Cuaraim bridge. Bella Unión has three hotels and a campsite in the Parque Fructuoso Rivera (T0642-2261), insect repellent needed.

Bella Unión
Colour map 8, grid A5
Population: 12,000

Uruguay

Transport Bus from **Salto**, US$6, 2 hrs. From **Montevideo**, US$24.50, *Bus del Norte*, US$29.25, *Chadre*. Launches go from Bella Unión to Monte Caseros. Buses to Barra del Cuaraim (the 'town') leave every 30 mins, US$0.60, from Plaza 25 de Agosto. If entering from Brazil by car take plenty of fuel as there are few service stations on the roads south.

From near Bella Unión Route 30 runs east to Artigas, a frontier town in a cattle raising and agricultural area (excellent swimming upstream from the bridge). The town is known for its good quality amethysts. There is a bridge across the Río Cuaraim to the Brazilian town of Quaraí. The Brazilian consul is at Lecueder 432, T5414, F5404.

Artigas
Phone code: 0642
Colour map 8, grid A6
Population: 40,000

Sleeping and eating Youth hostel *Club Deportivo Artigas*, Pte Berreta and LA de Herrera, 4 km from city, T0772-3860/2532. Open all year, communal room, camping, restaurant, no cooking facilities, closes early. **Camping** At Paseo 7 de Septiembre (by river), T2261, and at Club Zorrilla, T4341. *Donatello*, Lecueder. Good bar, pizza. *Deportivo*, Herrera. Good value.

Transport Air Airport at Bella Unión (*Tamu* to Montevideo US$30); *Pluna*, Garzón y Baldomir, T2545. **Buses** To **Salto**, 225 km, Oribe 279, US$6.85. *Turil* and others from **Montevideo** via Durazno, Paso de los Toros and Tacuarembó, US$23.30.

Background

History

Struggle for independence

In 1808 Montevideo declared its independence from Buenos Aires. In 1811, the Brazilians attacked from the north, but the local patriot, José Gervasio Artigas, rose in arms against them. In the early stages he had some of the Argentine provinces for allies, but soon declared the independence of Uruguay from both Brazil and Argentina. Buenos Aires invaded again in 1812 and was able to enter Montevideo in June 1814. In January the following year the Orientales (Uruguayans) defeated the Argentines at Guayabos and regained Montevideo. The Portuguese then occupied all territory south of the Río Negro except Montevideo and Colonia. The struggle continued from 1814 to 1820, but Artigas had to flee to Paraguay when Brazil took Montevideo in 1820. In 1825 General Juan Lavalleja, at the head of 33 patriots (the Treinta y Tres Orientales), crossed the river and returned to Uruguay, with Argentine aid, to harass the invaders. After the defeat of the Brazilians at Ituzaingó on 20 February 1827, Britain intervened, both Argentina and Brazil relinquished their claims on the country, and independence was finally achieved in 1828.

19th-century upheavals

The early history of the republic was marked by a civil war (known as the Guerra Grande) which began as a conflict between two rival leaders, José Fructuoso Rivera with his Colorados and Manuel Oribe with his Blancos; these are still two of the three main parties today. Oribe was helped by the Argentine dictator, Juan Manuel de Rosas, but was overthrown in 1838. Blanco forces, backed by Rosas, besieged Montevideo between 1843 and 1851. Although Rosas fell from power in 1852, the contest between Colorados and Blancos continued. A Colorado, General Venancio Flores, helped by Argentina, became president and, in 1865, Uruguay was dragged into the war of the Triple Alliance against the Paraguayan dictator, López. Flores was assassinated in 1868 three days after his term as president ended.

Batlle y Ordóñez

The country, wracked by civil war, dictatorship and intrigue, only emerged from its long political turmoil in 1903, when another Colorado, a great but controversial man, José Batlle y Ordóñez was elected president. During Batlle y Ordóñez' two terms as president, 1903-07 and 1911-15, Uruguay became within a short space of time the only 'welfare state' in Latin America. Its workers' charter provides free medical service, old age and service pensions and unemployment pay. Education is free and compulsory, capital punishment abolished, and the church disestablished.

Guerrillas & Military rule

As the country's former prosperity has ebbed away since the 1960s, the welfare state has become increasingly fictitious. The military promised to reduce bureaucracy and spend more on the poor and development after the turmoil of 1968-73, the period in which the Tupamaros urban guerrilla movement was most active. In practice the military, which effectively wiped out the Tupamaros by 1972, expanded state spending by raising military and security programmes. Real wages fell to less than half their 1968 level and only the very wealthy benefited from the military regime's attempted neo-liberal economic policies. Less than 10% of the unemployed received social security payments. Montevideo began to sprout shanty towns, once unheard of in this corner of the hemisphere. Nevertheless, the country's middle class remains very large, if impoverished, and the return to democracy in 1985 raised hopes that the deterioration in the social structure would be halted. Almost 10% of the population emigrated for economic or political reasons during the 1960s and 1970s: the unemployed continue to leave, but the political and artistic exiles have returned.

Uruguay

Allying himself with the Armed Forces in 1973, the elected president, Juan M Bordaberry, dissolved Congress and stayed on to rule as the military's figurehead until 1976. Scheduled elections were cancelled in that year, and a further wave of political and trade union repression instituted. Unable to convince the population to vote for a new authoritarian constitution in 1980, the military became increasingly anxious to hand back power to conservative politicians.

Return to democracy

In August 1984 agreement was reached finally on the legalization of most of the banned leftist parties and elections were held in November. Under the moderate government of Julio María Sanguinetti (of the Colorado party) the process of national reconstruction and political reconciliation began with a widespread political amnesty (endorsed by referendum in April 1989). The moderate conservative Partido Nacional (Blancos) won November 1989 presidential and congressional elections and Luis Alberto Lacalle became president. There was considerable opposition to plans for wage restraint, spending cuts, social reforms and privatization. As a result, his Blanco Party lost the November 1994 elections: Colorado ex-president Sanguinetti was again victorious over the Blancos and the Frente Amplio, a broad left front. Each party won about a third of the seats in Congress. Soon after taking office in March 1995, President Sanguinetti managed to forge an alliance with the Blancos to introduce economic restructuring and steps towards implementing much needed social security reforms. While the coalition worked together to reduce the influence of the public sector, the Frente Amplio gained support for its aim of maintaining the welfare state.

In December 1996 a referendum was held on constitutional reforms, including changes to the presidential selection process which would restrict political parties to a single candidate for each election and the introduction of a second ballot for the presidency. The Blancos and Colorados were in favour of the changes, but the Frente, fearing that the two main parties would maintain their cooperation to keep it from power, was opposed. The electorate voted in favour of the changes. The first elections under the new system were held at the end of 1999 and the Frente Amplio candidate, Tabaré Vásquez, was narrowly defeated in the second ballot by Jorge Batlle of the Colorados. Batlle needed the support of Blanco voters anxious to keep the left from power. In congress, however, the Frente Amplio, in coalition with Encuentro Progresista, was the single party with the largest number of seats.

After his predecessor had implemented essential reforms of the social security system, such as ending the state monopoly in insurance and pensions, incoming president Jorge Batlle planned to bring new impetus to the economy through diversification away from wool and beef and opening new export markets. Unfortunately, the recession that began in 1999 continued through 2000 and 2001 into 2002, largely as a result of high international interest rates, rising oil prices and economic stagnation in Argentina, plus severe drought affecting domestic agriculture. In consequence, internal demand fell and unemployment rose to almost 15% of the workforce by the end of 2000. By April 2002 it was evident that Argentina's economic collapse would continue to exert a strong negative influence with little immediate improvement in either the economy or living standards. Farmers, among others, protested at the government's failure to introduce measures to pull the sector out of recession.

Government

Uruguay is a republic with a bicameral legislature: a Senate with 31 seats and a Chamber of Representatives with 99 seats. The president, who is head of state and of the government, holds office for five years. The country is divided into 19 provinces.

Uruguay

Culture

People

Forecast population growth 2000-2005: 0.7%
Urban population in 2000: 91% of the total
Infant mortality rate: 13 per 1,000 live births

Total population in 2001 was 3.4 million. Population growth 1995-2000 was 0.7%. Uruguayans are virtually all European, mostly of Spanish and Italian stock. A small percentage in parts of Montevideo and near the Brazilian border are of mixed African and European descent. Less than 10% are mestizos.

There was little Spanish settlement in the early years and, for a long time, the area was inhabited mainly by groups of nomadic *gauchos* who trailed after the herds of cattle killing them for food and selling their hides only. Organized commerce began with the arrival of cattle buyers from Buenos Aires who found it profitable to hire herdsmen to look after cattle in defined areas around their headquarters. By about 1800 most of the land had been parcelled out into large *estancias*. The only commercial farming was around Montevideo, where small *chacras* grew vegetables, wheat and maize for the near-by town. Only after 1828 did immigration begin on any scale. Montevideo was then a small town of 20,000 inhabitants. Between 1836 and 1926 about 648,000 immigrants arrived in Uruguay, mostly from Italy and Spain, some into the towns, some to grow crops and vegetables round Montevideo. The native Uruguayans remained pastoralists, leaving commercial farming to the immigrants. More recent immigrants, however, Jewish, Armenian, Lebanese and others have chosen to enter the retail trades, textiles and leather production rather than farming.

Books

Satius Guiatur publishes a *Guía de Montevideo* in Spanish and English, with factual and cultural information, and a guide to Uruguay. *Pirelli* of Argentina publishes a good guide to Uruguay (1996), written by **Diego Bigongiari**. Uruguay has a strong tradition of critical writing, for example **José Enrique Rodó** (*Ariel*, 1900), **Angel Rama** and **Eduardo Galeano** (*Venas abiertas de América Latina, Memoria del fuego, Días y noches de amor y de guerra*, etc). Two novelists who have gained international fame are *Juan Carlos Onetti* and *Mario Benedetti* (also a poet and critic).

Uruguay

venezuela

Venezuela is where the Andes meet the Caribbean. The Orinoco river separates great plains from the table-top mountains of the Gran Sabana, where waterfalls tumble in sheer drops into the forest and lost worlds are easy to imagine. More recent innovations – cablecars up to the high peaks, hang gliders for jumping off them – are now part of the scene at Mérida, capital of Venezuela's Andes. Descend from the highlands to the Llanos for some superlative birdwatching, or move up the coast for beautiful beaches, tropical islands and the rhythms of the drums of San Juan.

12

Venezuela

Essentials

Planning your trip

Venezuela falls into four distinct zones: the Caribbean coast; the northeastern arm of the Andean mountain chain; the low-lying *llanos* east of the mountains and north of the Río Orinoco; the region south of the Orinoco with both the Gran Sabana, savannas dotted with table-top mountains (*tepuis*), and Amazon-type rainforest. To experience all four requires time, but any combination of zones makes for a rewarding visit.

The country's main gateway for flights is Caracas, although there are other international airports, such as Maracaibo in the west and Porlamar on Isla de Margarita (chiefly for holiday-makers to this Caribbean island). Venezuela is the starting point for the long trek south through the continent (or the end for those going north) and there is a well trodden route through Santa Elena de Uairén to Brazil, leading by road to Manaus on the Amazon. The main overland routes to Colombia are through San Antonio/Cúcuta in the Andes, which is less problematic than the Maicao crossing in the far northwest.

The Caribbean coast Venezuela has the longest coastline in the Caribbean with numerous palm-fringed beaches of white sand. **Caracas** is just a short drive (in kilometre terms, if not in time), from the sea. The capital is hidden from the Caribbean by Monte Avila, one of Venezuela's national parks. The central coast, nearest to Caracas, was devastated by flash floods and landslides in 1999, but you don't have to go too far east or west to find good beaches. Only a few hours west of the capital are some lovely little beaches, ideal if you have a few spare days before flying out, or on arrival. Further west is the Parque Nacional Morrocoy, with many islands close to the shore. North of Morrocoy is the historic town of Coro, surrounded by sand dunes, and the Paranaguá Peninsula. There are some excellent beaches in the Parque Nacional Mochima, east of Caracas, which also has a multitude of islets for exploring on or beneath the water. Further east are unrivalled beaches on the Paria Peninsula, but they are harder to reach. Besides those islands already mentioned, there is Isla de Margarita, one of the country's principal destinations for local and foreign tourists. The Islas Los Roques, 166 km due north of the central coast, is a beautiful archipelago, still quite unspoilt despite the growth in tourist interest.

The Andes Venezuela's Andes have some gorgeous scenery, with snow-capped peaks and remote villages. The main centre for visitors is Mérida, in the middle of the Sierra Nevada of the same name. It is well provided with accommodation, other services and tour companies which can help with arranging treks, climbing and other excursions. Two of its claims to fame are the highest cable car in the world, ascending the 4,776-m Pico Espejo, and the shop selling the largest number of ice cream flavours in the world.

The Llanos Life in the *llanos* revolves around the cycle of wet and dry seasons; the movement of cattle, the mainstay of the region's economy, depends on it. In the flat grasslands are slow running rivers which flood in the rainy season, creating a huge inland sea. When the rains cease, the whole area dries out completely. South of the cattle lands are forests and the tributaries of the Río Orinoco. Just after the May-November wet season, this is a paradise for nature lovers, with a spectacular variety of birds, monkeys (especially in the gallery forest along the riverbanks), big cats, anaconda, river dolphins, caiman and capybara. Tours to the *llanos* are run from Mérida and there are ecotourism ranches which offer you the chance to get to know the lifestyle of the plains.

Where to go

Venezuela

Guayana and the Orinoco This huge area comprises the Gran Sabana, the delta of the Orinoco itself and the Amazon region. Above the grasslands of the savanna rise *tepuis* flat-topped mountains from which spring magnificent waterfalls and rivers. The Angel Falls, the highest in the world, are one such wonder, usually seen from a plane, but also reachable by a 2-3 day trip upriver. There are many other falls in the Gran Sabana and a few places to stay, the most popular being Canaima camp on a lagoon on the Río Carrao. Where Venezuela meets Brazil and Guyana is Mount Roraima, one of the candidates for Arthur Conan-Doyle's 'Lost World' and one of the most adventurous excursions to be made in the country. The Orinoco delta is a remote part of the country, but trips can be made into it from the small town of Tucupita. Amazonas too, is well off the beaten track, but here again trips can be made from Puerto Ayacucho. Much of the rainforest is protected and permission from the authorities is required to visit areas beyond the reach of a tour company.

When to go The climate is tropical, with changes between the seasons being a matter of wet and dry, rather than hot and cold. Temperature is determined by altitude. The dry season in Caracas is Dec to Apr, with Jan and Feb the coolest months (there is a great difference between day and night temperatures at this time). The hottest months are Jul and Aug. The Caribbean coast is generally dry and rain is particularly infrequent in the states of Sucre, in the east, and Falcón, in the northwest. The lowlands of Maracaibo are very hot all year round; the least hot months are Jul to Sep. South of the Orinoco, in the Gran Sabana and Parque Nacional Canaima, the dry season is Nov to May. The same months are dry in the *llanos*, but the best time to visit is just after the rains, when the rivers and channels are still full of water and the humidity is not too high. In the Andes, the dry season is Oct to May, and this is the best time for climbing or hiking. The days are clear, but the nights are very cold. The rains usually begin in Jun, but in the mountains there is no guarantee that the weather will not change from day to day. Also remember when planning a visit that at holiday times, hotels and transport are heavily booked. Details of festivals are given in the text.

Finding out more Tourist information is handled by the Venezuelan Tourist Board, **Corporacion de Turismo Venezuela** (Corpoturismo), p 37, Torre Oeste, Parque Central, Apartado 50.200, Caracas, T0212-574 1968, corpoturismo@platino.gov.ve Outside Venezuela, tourist information can be obtained from Venezuelan embassies and consulates (for addresses, see box).

National Parks Venezuela has 35 national parks and 15 smaller national monuments, some of which are mentioned in the text. A full list is published by the **Instituto Nacional de Parques** (Inparques), Museo de Transporte, Edif Sur, Avenida Rómulo Gallegos, Parque del Este (exit Parque del Este metro opposite park, turn left, office is a few hundred metres further on up a slight incline), T284 1956/234 7331, F234 4238 (Caracas). Each park has a regional director and its own guards (*guardaparques*). Permits (free) are required to stay in the parks (up to five), although this is not usually necessary for those parks visited frequently. For further information on the national parks system, visit the **Ministerio del Ambiente y de los Recursos Naturales Renovables** (MARNR), Centro Simón Bolívar, Torre Sul, p 19, Caracas 1010, T483 3164/1071, www.marnr.gov.ve The book *Guía de los Parques Nacionales y Monumentos Naturales de Venezuela*, is obtainable in Audubon headquarters, 0900-1230 and 1430-1800, Las Mercedes shopping centre, Las Mercedes, Caracas in the La Cuadra sector next to the car parking area (it is difficult to find), www.audubondevenezuela,org (and also at *Librería Noctúa*, Villa Mediterránea, in the Centro Plaza shopping centre). The society will plan itineraries and make reservations. Another website with relevant material is **www.webmediaven.com/fundanatura/** (in Spanish, which concentrates on nature and tourism). Ecotourism portal: **www.ecoportal.venezuela.com**, for ecotourism, sports, national parks and places to stay.

Websites The official government site is **www.venezuela.gov.ve**; Asociación Venezolana de Agencias de Viajes: **www.viajes-venezuela.com/avavit**; websites with useful information and links are **www.auyantepuy.com** and **www.terra.com.ve**

Before you travel

Entry is by passport and visa, or by passport and tourist card. Tourist cards (*tarjetas de ingreso*) are issued by most airlines to visitors from: Andorra, Antigua and Barbuda, Argentina, Australia, Austria, Barbados, Belgium, Brazil, Canada, Chile, Costa Rica, Dominica, Denmark, Finland, France, Germany, Ireland, Italy, Iceland, Japan, Liechtenstein, Luxembourg, Lithuania, Malaysia, Mexico, Monaco, Norway, Netherlands, New Zealand, Paraguay, Portugal, St Kitts/Nevis, St Lucia, San Marino, St Vincent, South Africa, Spain, Sweden, Switzerland, Taiwan, Trinidad and Tobago, UK, Uruguay, and USA. Valid for 60 days, tourist cards are not extendable. Overstaying your 60 days can lead to arrest and a fine when you try to depart.

To enter the country overland or by sea, you must obtain a tourist visa in advance. Apply to a Venezuela consulate prior to arrival. For a Tourist Visa, you need two passport photos, passport valid for six months, references from bank and employer, onward or return ticket, completed and signed application form. The fee in the UK is £22 (costs vary from country to country). For extensions go to **DIEX**, Avenida Baralt on Plaza Miranda in Caracas, T483 2744, take passport, tourist visa, photographs and return ticket; opens 0800, passport with extension returned at end of day. DIEX offices in many cities do not offer extensions. Transit visas, valid for 72 hours are also available, mostly the same requirements and cost (inward and onward tickets needed). DIEX in Caracas will not exchange a transit for a tourist visa. It appears that you cannot get a visa in advance in the USA, or Canada, so to apply for an overland visa in Colombia or Brazil you need: passport, one photo and an onward ticket. In Manaus you also need a yellow fever inoculation certificate. Consuls may give a one-year visa if a valid reason can be given. To change a tourist visa to a business visa, to obtain or to extend the latter, costs £42 in UK.

Visas to work in Venezuela also cost £42 and require authorization from the **Dirección General Sectorial de Identificación y Control de Extranjeros** in Caracas. Student visas require a letter of acceptance from the Venezuelan institution, proof of means of support, medical certificate, passport photo, passport and £42. It generally takes two days to issue any visa.

Nationals of countries not listed above must obtain a consular visa in advance. All travellers to Venezuela are advised to check with the consulate before leaving home as regulations are subject to change.

NB Carry your passport with you all the time you are in Venezuela as the police mount frequent spot checks and anyone found without identification is immediately detained (carrying a certified copy for greater safety is permissible, though not always accepted by officials). There are many military checkpoints, especially in border areas, at which all transport is stopped. Have your documents ready and make sure you know what entry permits you need; the soldiers may be unfamiliar with regulations for foreigners. Border searches are very thorough.

Business visitors on short visits are strongly advised to enter the country as tourists, otherwise they will have to obtain a tax clearance certificate (solvencia) before they can leave.
Do not lose the carbon copy of your visa as this has to be surrendered when leaving the country

Duty free allowance You may bring into Venezuela, free of duty, 25 cigars and 200 cigarettes, two litres of alcoholic drinks, four small bottles of perfume, and gifts at the inspector's discretion. New items to the value of US$1,000 may be brought in.

Inoculation against typhoid and yellow fever, and protection against malaria, is recommended for the Orinoco and other swampy or forest regions.

Tropical weight in normal city colours is best for business, otherwise, clothing is less formal, but smart dress (jackets and ties) is required in the most exclusive restaurants and clubs. In Maracaibo and hot, humid coastal and low-lying areas, regular washable tropical clothing is best. The climate in the Andes is cooler, especially at night, so you'll need warmer clothing. Cinemas may not admit men in shorts or anyone in flip-flops. Chloroquine is available, free; alternatively, bring malaria tablets with you. Factor 15 suntan cream is available.

Venezuela

Money

bolívar exchange rate in July 2002 with US$: 1,381

Currency The unit of currency is the bolívar, which is divided into 100 céntimos (owing to devaluation, céntimos are not in use). There are coins for 1, 2, 5, 25, 50, 100 and 500 bolívares, and notes for 5, 10, 20, 50, 100, 500, 1,000, 2,000, 5,000 and 10,000 bolívares. There is a shortage of small coinage and small notes and many people are reluctant to take 5,000 and 10,000 bolívar notes because these denominations are frequently forged.

Exchange Dollars cash and TCs can be changed in banks and *casas de cambio*. To convert unused bolívares back into dollars upon leaving, you must present the original exchange receipt (up to 30% of original amount changed); only banks and authorized *casas de cambio* can legally sell bolívares. Rates of exchange in hotels are generally poor. *Casas de cambio* may change TCs more readily than banks, but they always insist on photocopying your passport, may ask for proof of purchase and will photograph you. Beware of forged Amex TCs and US$ notes.

Credit cards Visitors are strongly advised to use Visa or MasterCard. There are cash machines for Visa, MasterCard and Amex at Simón Bolívar airport although these may give a receipt but no cash. You should be wary of using cash machines throughout the country as Visa and MasterCard transactions inside banks offer good rates and, although slower, are much safer (machines are often old or tampered with and queues at ATM machines attract thieves). Corp Banca is affiliated with American Express, no commission, some branches cash personal cheques from abroad on an Amex card; *American Express* travel services are handled by *Italcambio* and *Quo Vadis* agencies around the country. Banco Unión and Banco de Venezuela handle Visa and ATM transactions, including cash advances, and Banco Mercantil handles MasterCard. MasterCard assistance T8001-002902. Visa assistance T8001-2169.

Cost of travelling On the cheapest possible budget you can get by on around US$20 pp per day, depending on which part of the country you visit. A less basic budget would be about US$35 per day, rising to US$100 and upwards for first class travel. VAT/IVA is 14.5%.

Getting there

Air **From Europe** There are regular flights from London, Paris, Amsterdam, Frankfurt, Madrid, Milan and Lisbon.

From North America Cities which have direct flights to Caracas are New York, Miami, Chicago, Atlanta, Dallas and Houston.

From Latin America and the Caribbean South American cities from which there are direct flights to Caracas are Bogotá, Buenos Aires, Santa Cruz (Bolivia), Rio de Janeiro, São Paulo, Manaus, Santiago de Chile, Lima, Quito and Guayaquil. From Central America there are flights from Mexico City (daily), San José and Panama City (*Lacsa*). Caribbean cities with flights to Venezuela are Santo Domingo (Dominican Republic), San Juan (Puerto Rico), Curaçao, Aruba, Port of Spain, Fort-de-France (Martinique – *Air France* twice a week), and Havana.

Boat See Shipping, Essentials, for agencies that can arrange cruises to Venezuela on cargo vessels. Ferries from/to Aruba can be found in the text under Coro, and from/to Trinidad under Güiria.

Yacht Do not try and clear Customs and Immigration without an agent in a commercial port. Well worth the fee. Get your tourist card at a Venezuelan embassy before arriving, although if you arrive during a major storm officials may make an exception. During the busy hurricane season, **security** problems increase; thieves arrive by night in boats with bolt cutters and fast engines and steal dinghies, motors and other items left on deck. Best security is in marinas. Porlamar even has trouble with swimmers during the day. Fewer problems in the outer islands of La Blanquilla, La Tortuga, Los Roques, Los Aves and Los Testigos, but trouble reported in coastal anchorages, eg Cumaná, Mochima, Morrocoy, Puerto La Cruz. Take all precautions possible.

Embassies and consulates

Australia *5 Culgoa Circuit O'Malley, ACT 2606, Canberra, T61-2-6290 2967, F6290 2911, www.venezuela-emb.org.au*
Canada *32 Range Road, Ottawa, ON-K1N8J4, T1-613-235 5151, F235 3205.*
Denmark *Holbergsgade 14, 3th, 1070 Copenhagen K, T3393 6311, F3315 6911, www.home7.inet.tele.dk/emvendk/*
France *11 rue Copernic, 75116 Paris, T33-1-4553 2998, F4755 6456, www.embavenez-paris.com*
Germany *Grosse Wienmeisterstrasse 53, 1 44 69 Potsdam, T49-331-231 0920, F231 0977, www.botschaft-venezuela.de*
Italy *Via Nicolò Tartaglia 11, 00197 Roma, T39-6-807 9797, F808 4410, www.users.iol.it/embaveit*
Japan *38 Kowa Building, Room 703, 12-24, Nishi Azabu, 4 Chome, Minato-Ku, Tokyo-106, T81-3-3409 1501, F3409 1505,*
www.sunsite.sut.ac.jp/venemb/embvenez.html
Netherlands *Nassaulaan 2, 2514 JS The Hague, T31-70-352 3851, F365 6954, embvene@xs4a11.nl*
Spain *C Capitán Haya 1, 13, Torrre EuroCentro, 28020 Madrid, T34-91-598 1200, F597 1583, www.univernet.net/embavenez/index.htm*
Sweden *Engelbrektsgaten 35B, S-114, 31 Stockholm, T46-8-411 0996, F213100.*
Switzerland *Morillonstrasse 9, 3007 Bern, T41-31-371 3282, F371 0424, embavenez@span.ch*
UK *Venezuelan consulate, 56 Grafton Way, London W1T 5DL, T44-020-7387 6727, F020-7383 4857, www.venezlon.demon.co.uk*
USA *1099 30th Street, NW, Washington DC 20007, T1-202-3422214, F3426820, www.embavenez-us.org*

Touching down

Airport information

Passengers leaving Caracas on international flights must reconfirm their reservations not less than 72 hours in advance; it is safer to do so in person than by telephone; not less than 24 hours for national flights: if you fail to do this, you lose all rights to free accommodation, food, transport, etc if your flight is cancelled and may lose your seat if the plane is fully booked. Beware of counterfeit tickets; buy only from agencies. If told by an agent that a flight is fully booked, try at the airport anyway. International passengers must check in two hours before departure or they may lose their seat to someone on a waiting list. Handling charge for your luggage US$0.50. See Caracas, Travel, Long Distance Air, for information and advice on taxis.

Airport & other taxes

All passengers on international flights pay a combined airport and exit tax of approximately US$50 (payable in bolívares, cash only). Minors under 12 years of age do not pay the exit tax. There is a 1% tax on the cost of all domestic flights, plus an airport tax which varies according to the airport. Exit stamps for overland travellers, US$2 (exept US$5 Maracaibo-Maicao and US$15 San Antonia-Cúcuta, Colombia). Correct taxes are not advertised and travellers have experienced overcharging.

Tipping

Taxi drivers are tipped if the taxi has a meter (hardly anywhere), but not if you have agreed the fare in advance. Usherettes are not tipped. Hotel porters, US$0.50; airport porters US$0.50 per piece of baggage. Restaurants, between 5% and 10% of bill.

Safety

Visitors to Caracas find it a very uncomfortable city, largely because of acute levels of poverty and hardship, but also because it is dirty. Levels of crime are high and you should be on the lookout from the moment you arrive: there are many pirate taxis and rip-off merchants operating at the international airport. There was a considerable amount of political tension in Caracas in 2002, but this did not affect foreigners directly. Carry handbags, cameras etc on the side away from the street as motor-cycle purse-snatchers are notorious, especially in Caracas. Outside the capital, the atmosphere is much more relaxed, but as in any country you should take care to protect your valuables and belongings in the cities.

Venezuela

Touching down

Hours of business Banks 0830 to 1530 Monday to Friday only. **Government offices** 0800-1200 are usual morning hours, although they vary. Officials have fixed hours, usually 0900-1000 or 1500-1600, for receiving visitors. **Businesses** 0800 to 1800 with a midday break. **Shops** 0900-1300, 1500-1900, Monday-Saturday. Generally speaking, Venezuelans start work early, and by 0700 in the morning everything is in full swing. Most

firms and offices close on Saturday.
IDD 58. Long equal tones with equal long pauses mean it is ringing. Short equal tones with equal pauses mean it is engaged.
Official time Four hours behind GMT, one hour ahead of EST.
Voltage 110 volts, 60 cycles, throughout the country.
Weights and measures Weights and measures are metric.

Where to stay

Sleeping

See inside front cover of the book for our hotel grade price guide

Officially controlled prices exist for one-star and two-star hotels. Hotels of our B price category upwards are often heavily booked up, especially in Caracas; advance reservations are advisable. Prices for singles are often not much less than doubles. There is a tax of 16.5% on hotel rooms; 10% service may also be added.

Camping

Equipment is available at sports-goods shops in Caracas. It is illegal to refill portable gas cylinders. Even the higher octane fuels will cause blockages of fuel jets in gasoline stoves. Camping in Venezuela is a popular recreation, for spending a weekend at the beach, on the islands, in the *llanos* and in the mountains. Camping, with or without a vehicle, is not possible at the roadside. If camping on the beach, for the sake of security, pitch your tent close to others, even though they play their radios loud.

Getting around

Air

Most places of importance are served by *Aeropostal, Aereotuy, Air Venezuela, Aserca, Avensa, Avior, LAI, Laser, Santa Bárbara* and *Servivensa*, which fly to a variety of destinations. Apart from *Aserca*, which has been recommended, none is perfect. Lost luggage is a frequent problem. Internal airlines offer special family discounts and student discount but practice is variable, photocopies of ISIC card are useful as it allows officials to staple one to the ticket. Beware of overbooking during holiday time, especially at Caracas airport; it is recommended that you check in two hours before departure, particularly at Easter.

Bus & taxi

Buses are relatively cheap, but the quality of long-distance travel varies a lot. There are numerous services between the major cities and many services bypass Caracas, so you dopn't have to change buses in the capital. Buses stop frequently, but there may not always be a toilet at the stop. For night journeys in a/c buses take a sleeping bag or similar because the temperature is set to freezing. Also take earplugs against the loud stereo systems. The colectivo taxis and minibuses, known as *por puesto*, seem to monopolize transport to and from smaller towns and villages. For longer journeys they are normally twice as expensive as buses, but faster. They may be reluctant to take luggage and the ill-kempt. If first on board, wait for other passengers to arrive, do not take a *por puesto* on your own unless you want to pay for the whole vehicle. Outside Caracas, town taxis are relatively expensive. At peak periods *revendedores* (touts) will try to sell tickets at 2-3 times face value.

Car

A tourist can bring in a car without paying duty. A *carnet de passages* is required (it may be possible to enter from Brazil without one, but it's at the discretion of the customs officer). An entry permit for a car costs US$10 and requires one photograph (takes 24 hours); ask for a permit for six months, or unspecified time. Entry from Colombia is not easy. In the border area with Colombia, police checks are frequent; make sure you have all your papers.

Venezuela

The *Touring y Automóvil Club de Venezuela* (addresses under Caracas, Useful addresses, and San Cristóbal, Tourist offices – the Maracaibo office only deals through Caracas) issues the *Libreta de Pasos por Aduana* for taking foreign-registered cars into other South American countries. Takes 24 hours and your vehicle must be presented to the club. Before shipping your vehicle to Venezuela, go to a Venezuelan consul to obtain all necessary documentation, including visa, to allow you to enter the country prior to getting the *libreta*. You must also go to a Venezuelan consul in the country in which you land your car if other than Venezuela.

All visitors to Venezuela can drive if they are over 18 and have a valid driving licence from their own country; an international driving licence is preferred. It is a good idea to hire a car; many of the best places are off the beaten track. Some companies such as National have a wide network of offices in towns and airports allowing fly-drive, using a number of different vehicles. You have to have a credit card to rent a vehicle. Car hire with insurance varies from company to company: basic rates for a car are from US$20-50 per day depending on make; government tax of 16.5% is also added. Rates tend to be the same in all cities, except on Margarita, which is more expensive. If you book and prepay outside the country, most major companies give unlimited mileage. Car and personal insurance (US$10-17.50 per day) is strongly recommended as you will be lucky to survive two or three days as a newcomer, especially in Caracas traffic, without a dent or a scrape. All cars should be checked carefully as most have some defect or other, and insist on a short test drive. If you have an accident and someone is injured, you will be detained as a matter of routine, even if you are not at fault. Do not drive at night if you can help it (if you do have to, don't drive fast). Carry insect spray if you do; if you stop and get out, the car will fill with biting insects.

The roads in Venezuela are generally poor, except for the four-lane autopistas. Motoring restrictions in Caracas include a ban on parking in front of a bank; motorcycles may not be driven at night; pillion passengers may not be carried on motorcycles if of the same sex as the driver. You are more likely to be penalized for infringing these rules than for driving through a red light; they are designed to improve security for banks and pedestrians. In addition, motorcyclists are obliged to wear a crash helmet but it must not be of a type which obscures the face. Use private car-parks whenever possible as break-ins on streets are common in Caracas and all large cities.

There are three grades of **gasoline**: 87, 91 and 95 octane (average cost US$0.10-0.16 a litre). Diesel (US$0.10 a litre) is used by most goods vehicles, available from many filling stations in Caracas. Oil costs US$0.60 a litre. Service stations are open 0500-2100, Monday-Saturday, except those on highways which are open longer hours. Only those designated to handle emergencies are open on Sunday. In the event of breakdown, Venezuelans are usually very helpful. There are many garages, even in rural areas; service charges are not high, nor are tyres, oil or accessories expensive, but being able to speak Spanish will greatly assist in sorting out problems. Carry spare battery water, fan belts, the obligatory breakdown triangle, a jack and spanners. **Warning** There is an automatic US$20 fine for running out of fuel.

Hitchhiking

Hitchhiking (*Cola*) is not very easy and not very safe in coastal regions, but elsewhere the Venezuelans are usually friendly and helpful if you know some Spanish. The best places to try are Guardia Nacional posts outside cities (may get free bus rides from them). It is illegal on toll roads and, theoretically, for non-family members in the back of pick up trucks. Some drivers may ask for money for the lift, especially if on a bus route, common in the Gran Sabana.

Maps

The official mapping agency is the **Ministerio del Ambiente y de los Recursos Naturales Renovables**, Dirección de Cartografía Nacional, Edificio Camejo, 1st floor, Avenida Este 6, Colón, south side; the office is not in the same building as the Ministry's other departments (Centro Simón Bolívar). 1:50,000, 1:100,000, 1:200,000 and 1:250,000 sheets covering most of Venezuela north of the Orinoco, plus some state maps and a 1:500,000 series. Guía Vial de Venezuela 2000, edited by **Miro Popic** (Caracas 1999), US$25, is a motoring guide with road maps and tourist information. The best road map is published by *Lagoven* and a similar version by *Corpoven* but at twice the scale and with a very good street plan of Caracas on the back, available from most service stations (not just Lagoven's), latest edition 1995, US$2. The best country map is the late Kevin Healey's, published by *International Travel Maps*, Vancouver, BC, Canada; available at good travel agents (for example, in Mérida).

Keeping in touch

Internet Email is becoming more common and public access to the internet is fairly widespread with cybercafés in both large and small towns. The best places for cybercafés are Caracas and Mérida.

Post *Ipostel*, the national postal service, offers an international express mail service (EMS), which guarantees delivery in 2-3 days, depending on the country of destination. It costs from US$20 for up to 1 kg. Normal airmail letters cost US$0.90 for up to 10 g and usually take 2-3 days to the USA. *Ipostel* also offer EEE, which is a domestic express mail service, guaranteeing next day delivery to all major cities. An alternative to DHL or other courier companies is offered by *Grupo Zoom*, who sell A5 or A4 envelopes for international postage, guaranteed delivery arriving in 3-4 days. The envelopes are meant for correspondence, but small gifts or photographs may also be sent; cost US$10-15.

Telephone
Phone numbers throughout Venezuela have been changed in 2002, with the introduction of 7-digit numbers for all cities

All international and long distance calls are operated by CANTV and can be dialled direct. Major cities are linked by direct dialling (*Discado Directo*), with a three-figure prefix for each town in Venezuela. There are CANTV offices for long-distance and international calls. Collect calls are possible to some countries, at least from Caracas, though staff in offices may not be sure of this. Most public phones operate on prepaid CANTV cards (*tarjetas*) in denominations of 3,000 and 5,000 bolívares. Buy them from CANTV or numerous small shops bearing the CANTV logo, or a scrap of card reading '¡Si! ¡hay *tarjetas*!' They are also sold by street vendors. Make sure they are still in their clear plastic wrapper with an unbroken red seal. Many small shops impose a 25% handling charge and *tarjetas* may be out of stock particularly outside Caracas or larger towns. When making international calls from a public booth, ensure that it has a globe symbol on the side. International calls can be made with a *tarjeta*, minimum needed Bs 5,000, but you get little more than one minute to Europe. To make an international call, dial 00 plus country code etc. Canada direct: 800-11100. For UK, BT Direct, 800-11440 (BT chargecard works from any phone). For collect calls to Germany, T800-11490. International calls are charged by a series of bands, ranging from about US$1 per minute to USA and Canada, to US$2 to UK, to US$2.15 elsewhere. There are various reduced and economy rates according to band. Fax rates are as for phones.

Media **Newspapers** Caracas: *El Universal*, www.el-universal.com, *El Nacional*, www.el-nacional.com and *El Diario de Caracas, La Religión, Ultimas Noticias*. The *Daily Journal* (English), *El Mundo* and *2001* (evening), *Número* (weekly), *Resumen* (weekly), *Elite* (weekly), *Momento* (weekly), *Venezuela Gráfica* (weekly), *Páginas* (weekly), *Semana* (weekly), *Ve Venezuela*, tourist bi-monthly. Maracaibo: *Panorama, La Crítica*. Puerto La Cruz: *El Tiempo*. For economic news, *El Globo* (daily), *Economía Hoy* (daily) and *Reporte* (three times a week). The Sun edition of *Hoy* contains the UK *Guardian Weekly*.

Food and drink

Food There is excellent local fish (for example *pargo* or red snapper), crayfish, small oysters and prawns. Sometimes there is turtle, though it is a protected species. Turtle may appear on menus in the Península de Paraguaná as *ropa especial*. Of true Venezuelan food there is *sancocho* (a stew of vegetables, especially yuca, with meat, chicken or fish); *arepas*, a kind of white maize bread, very bland in flavour; toasted *arepas* served with a wide selection of relishes, fillings or the local somewhat salty white cheese are cheap, filling and nutritious; *cachapas*, a maize pancake wrapped around white cheese; *pabellón*, made of shredded meat, beans, rice and fried plantains (vegetarian versions available); and *empanadas*, maize-flour pies containing cheese, meat or fish. At Christmas only there are *hallacas*, maize pancakes stuffed with chicken, pork, olives, etc boiled in a plantain leaf (but don't eat the leaf). A *muchacho* (boy) on the menu is a cut of beef. *Ganso* is also not goose but beef. *Solomo* and *lomito* are other cuts of beef. *Hervido* is chicken or beef with vegetables. *Contorno* with a meat or fish dish is a choice of fried chips, boiled potatoes, rice or yuca. *Caraotas* are beans; *cachitos* are filled *croissants*. *Pasticho* is what the Venezuelans call Italian *lasagne*. The main fruits are bananas, oranges, grapefruit, mangoes, pineapple and pawpaws. **NB** Some Venezuelan variants of names for fruit: *lechosa* is papaya, *patilla* water melon, *parchita* passion fruit, and *cambur* a small banana. Excellent strawberries are grown at Colonia Tovar, 90 minutes from Caracas. Delicious sweets are *huevos chimbos* – egg yolk boiled and bottled in sugar syrup, and *quesillo* – made with milk, egg and caramel. The Caracas *Daily Journal* (in English) lists many reliable restaurants in Caracas and Maracaibo. Venezuelans dine late.

Drink Venezuelan rum is very good; recommended brands are *Cacique, Pampero* and *Santa Teresa*. There are five good beers: *Polar* (the most popular), *Regional* (with a strong flavour of hops), *Cardenal* and *Nacional* (a *lisa* is a glass of keg beer; for a bottle of beer ask for a *tercio*); Brazilian *Brahma* beer (lighter than *Polar*) is now brewed in Venezuela. There are also mineral waters and gin. There is a good, local wine in Venezuela. The *Polar* brewery joined with Martell (France) to build a winery in Carora. Wines produced are 'Viña Altagracia' and 'Bodegas Pomar'. 'Bodegas Pomar' also produces a sparkling wine in the traditional champagne style. Liqueurs are cheap, try the local *ponche crema*. The coffee is excellent and very cheap (*café con leche* has a lot of milk, *café marrón* much less, *café negro* for black coffee, which, though obvious, is not common in the rest of Latin America); visitors should also try a *merengada*, a delicious drink made from fruit pulp, ice, milk and sugar; a *batido* is the same but with water and a little milk; *jugo* is the same but with water. A *plus-café* is an after-dinner liqueur. Water is free in all restaurants even if no food is bought. Bottled water in *cervecerías* is often from the tap; no deception is intended, bottles are simply used as convenient jugs. Insist on seeing the bottle opened if you want mineral water. *Chicha de arroz* is a sweet drink made of milk, rice starch, sugar and vanilla; fruit juices are very good.

Holidays and festivals

Holidays applying to all businesses include: 1 January, Carnival on the Monday and Tuesday before Ash Wednesday (everything shuts down Saturday-Tuesday; make sure accommodation is booked in advance), Thursday-Saturday of Holy Week, 19 April, 1 May, 24 June (the feast day of San Juan Bautista, a particularly popular festival celebrated along the central coast where there were once large concentrations of plantation slaves who considered San Juan their special Saint; some of the best-known events are in villages between Puerto Cabello, and Chuspa, to the east, such as Chuao, Cata and Ocumare de la Costa), 5 and 24 July, 24 September, 12 October, 25 December. From 24 December-1 January, most restaurants are closed and there is no long-distance public transport. On New Year's Eve, everything closes and does not open for a least a day. Queues for tickets, and traffic jams, are long. Business travellers should not visit during Holy Week or Carnival. Holidays for banks and insurance companies only include all the above and also: 19 March and the nearest Monday to 6 January, Ascension Day, 29 June, 15 August, 1 November and 8 December. There are also holidays applying to certain occupations such as Doctor's Day or Traffic Policeman's Day.

Sport and special interest travel

Climbing Although there are some opportunities for climbing in the Gran Sabana, these are mostly hard to get to and are technically very challenging. The heart of Venezuelan **mountaineering** and **trekking** is the Andes, with Mérida as the base. A number of important peaks can be scaled and there are some superb hikes in the highlands. Bear in mind that high altitudes will be reached and acclimatization is essential. Similarly, suitable equipment is necessary and you may wish to consider bringing your own. Also in the Sierra Nevada you can find the following sports: **mountain biking, white water rafting, hang-gliding, paragliding** and **horse riding.**

Watersports Diving Venezuela's waters are not as famous as those off neighbouring Bonaire, but they have excellent opportunities for seeing underwater flora, fauna and shipwrecks. The main areas are the national parks of Morrocoy, Mochima and Islas Los Roques (best for experienced divers), a number of sites to the east and west of Caracas, and in the waters off

Isla de Margarita. **Deep sea fishing** mainly for white and blue marlin, is exceptional in the Venezuelan Caribbean, but there is also good fishing closer to shore. Here again, Los Roques is a good destination, while Macuto and Río Chico on the mainland are popular. Freshwater fishing is possible in the lakes in the Andes and in the rivers in the *llanos*. **Sailing** Venezuela is a frequent destination for yachts sailing in the southern Caribbean. **Windsurfing** is also popular with a number of centres around Margarita and on the central coast.

Nature tourism The *llanos* are a prime wildlife destination, and if you intend to go there you should plan the timing carefully to make the most of your trip. Amazonas and the Orinoco delta also offer wildlife possibilities, but in the latter case tours can be expensive and poorly organized, so choose with caution. The Gran Sabana does not have quite the extent of wildlife that you will find in the *llanos*, but for lovers of open landscapes the area is unmatched. In the Andes, too, the scenery is the key, and throughout the *páramo* (open grasslands with small pockets of cloud forest above 2,500-3,000 m), the unusual *frailejón* plant (felt-leaved and with a yellow bloom) is a common sight. You may also be lucky enough to see the condor. Another significant birdwatching site is the Parque Nacional Henri Pittier in the coastal mountains between Maracay and the Caribbean. For marine birdlife, the Cuare Wildlife Sanctuary, north of Morrocoy, is an important nesting area. Finally, a much visited attraction is the Cueva del Guácharo, a cave near Caripe in the east.

Health

Water in all main towns is heavily chlorinated, so is safe to drink, although most people drink bottled water. Medical attention is good and state health care is free (the *Clínica Metropolitana* in Caracas has been recommended). A doctor's consultation costs about US$10. Some rivers are infected with bilharzia and in some areas there are warning signs check before bathing. Protect against mosquito bites as dengue fever has been present since 1995. Malaria tablets may be obtained in Caracas from Hospital Padre Machado (left-hand building as you face it), no charge; or **Ministerio de Sanidad y Asistencia Social** (MSAS), Torre del Silencio (southwest corner of Plaza Caracas), División de Malariología, free, English spoken, yellow fever vaccinations also given, free (also at MSAS, 'La Pastora', Avenida Baralt 36, Caracas); also at **Instituto de Malariología**, C El Degredo y Avenida Roosevelt, open 0900-1200, 1330-1600, metro to Maternidad and taxi, US$4, not easy to find. On the coast from Cumaná eastwards precautions against vampire bat bite are warranted since they can be rabies-carriers. Lights over hatches and windows are used by local fishermen to deter bats from entering boats and shore cabins. If bitten seek medical advice. When travelling to the mountainous areas, beware of altitude sickness. It is a good idea to acclimatize for a few days before embarking on mountain treks. If you need a hospital, ask for a *clínica*, which is private; a *hospital* is government-run and often will be short of basic medication, and hygiene standards can be low; a taxi is usually faster than an ambulance.

Venezuela

Caracas

Caracas is not the gentlest of introductions to South America. Founded in 1567, it lies in a rift in thickly forested mountains which rise abruptly from a lush green coast to heights of 2,000-3,000 m. The small basin in which the capital lies runs some 24 km east and west. By way of escape, there are several nearby excursions to mountain towns, the Parque Nacional Monte Avila, beaches and Los Roques, a beautiful Caribbean atoll.

Getting there The **airport** is 28 km from Caracas, near the port of La Guaira: Maiquetía and Aeropuerto Auxiliar for national flights and Simón Bolívar for international flights. There are 3 main **bus terminals** in different parts of the city; where you arrive depends upon where you travelled from.

Getting around The metro is a/c, clean, well-patrolled, safe and more comfortable and quicker than any other form of city transport. Buses are overcrowded in rush hour and charge an additional fare after 2100. On longer runs these buses are probably more comfortable for those with luggage than a *por puesto* minibus. Minibuses are known as *carmelitas*. *Por puestos* run on regular routes; fares depend on the distance travelled within the city and rise for journeys outside. Many *por puesto* services start in El Silencio.

Orientation Caracas' growth since the Second World War has been greater than that of any other Latin American capital. Colonial buildings have given way to modern multi-storeyed edifices and many visitors find the metropolis lacking in character, as there is no single centre. A broad strip some 10 km from west to east, fragmented by traffic-laden arteries, contains several centres, for example Plaza Bolívar, Plaza Venezuela, Sabana Grande, Chacaíto, Altamira, La Floresta, Boleíta.

Tourist offices Corpoturismo, p 37, Torre Oeste, Parque Central (metro Bellas Artes is closest), T574 1968; open Mon-Fri 0830-1200, 1400-1630, helpful but not much information or maps. There is a smaller office at the airport (see below). A website covering Caracas is www.une.edu.ve/caracas/

Security It is advisable not to arrive in Caracas at night and not to walk down narrow streets or in parks after dark. Avoid certain areas such as all suburbs from the El Silencio monument to Propatria, other than main roads, the area around the *teleférico*, Chapellín near the Country Club, and Petare. Street crime is on the increase, even armed robbery in daylight. Even in a crowded place like Sabana Grande, bag slashing and mugging are not uncommon. Take care at all times and never carry valuables. Car theft is common. Police searches are frequent and thorough, especially around Av Las Acacias after dark and in airports; always carry ID. If you have entered overland from Colombia, you can expect thorough investigation (once you've left the border, better to say you flew in).

Ins & outs
Phone code: 0212
Colour map 1, grid A6
Population:
nearly 5 million
(city 1,825,000)
Altitude: 960 m
Climate:
maximum 32°C
Jul-Aug,
minimum 9°C Jan-Feb
For full details see
Transport, page 1359.
In the centre each
street corner has a
name. Addresses are
generally given as, for
example, 'Santa
Capilla a Mijares',
rather than the official
'Calle Norte 2, No 26'

Venezuela

Sights

The shady **Plaza Bolívar**, with its fine equestrian statue of the Liberator and pleasant colonial cathedral, is still the official centre of the city, though no longer geographically so. In the **Capitolio Nacional** the Elliptical Salon has some impressive paintings by the Venezuelan artist Martín Tovar y Tovar and a bronze urn containing the 1811 Declaration of Independence. ■ *Tue-Sun, 0900-1200, 1500-1700.* The present **Cathedral** dating from 1674 has a beautiful façade, gilded altar, the Bolívar family chapel and paintings by Michelena, Murillo and an alleged Rubens 'Resurrection'. **San Francisco**, Avenida Universidad y San Francisco (one block southwest of Plaza Bolívar), should be seen for its colonial altars and Murillo's 'San Agustín' (oldest church in Caracas, rebuilt 1641). **Santa Teresa**, between La Palma and Santa Teresa, just southeast of the Centro Simón Bolívar, has good interior chapels and a supposedly miraculous portrait of Nazareno de San Pablo (popular and solemn devotions on Good Friday).

Panteón Nacional The remains of Simón Bolívar, the Liberator, lie here in the Plaza Panteón, Avenida Norte y Avenida Panteón. The tomb of Francisco Miranda (the Precursor of Independence), who died in a Spanish prison, has been left open to await the return of his body, likewise the tomb of Antonio José de Sucre, who was assassinated in Colombia. Every 25 years the President opens Bolívar's casket to verify that the remains are still there. Daniel O'Leary, Bolívar's Irish aide-de camp, is buried alongside. The changing of the guard takes place at 1430 daily. ■ *Tue-Sun 0900-1200,1430-1700.*

Modern Caracas The **Ciudad Universitaria** is an enormous and coherent complex in which paintings, sculpture and stained glass are completely integrated with the architecture (which is now showing signs of wear). South of the university, reached by Autopista El Valle, is **Paseo de los Próceres** with its twin monoliths and other monuments to the heroes of independence. Beside the Avenida de los Próceres is the magnificent **Círculo Militar**.

Museums

Museums and art galleries in Venezuela close Mon. Many museums refuse entry to anyone wearing shorts

Museo de Bellas Artes, Plaza Morelos in Parque Los Caobos, the oldest museum in Caracas, designed by Carlos Raúl Villanueva. ■ *Tue-Fri 0900-1200, 1500-1730, Sat-Sun 1000-1700.* Paintings include an El Greco among works by mainly Venezuelan artists. Adjacent is the Galería de Arte Nacional, T571 0176, same opening hours, which also houses the Cinemateca Nacional. ■ *Tue-Sun 1830 and 2130, Sun 1100 for children's films.* **Museo de Ciencias Naturales**, Plaza Morelos: archaeological, particularly precolumbian, zoological and botanical exhibits. ■ *Tue-Fri 0900-1200, 1500-1730, weekend 1000-1700.*

Museo de Arte Colonial, Quinta Anauco, Avenida Panteón, San Bernardino, take *por puesto* from Bellas Artes metro (at the same stop as the metro bus), those bound for San Bernardino go past Quinta Anauco. A delightful house built in 1720, the residence of the Marqués del Toro. ■ *Mon-Fri 0900-1130, 1400-1630, Sat-Sun 1000-1700. Closed 20 Dec-10 Jan. Guided tour compulsory: in Spanish every 30 mins, in English by arrangement. Chamber concerts most Sat at 1800.*

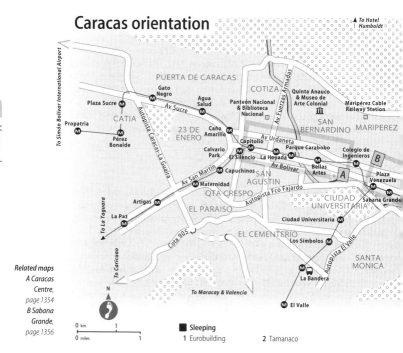

Caracas orientation

Related maps
A Caracas
Centre,
page 1354
B Sabana
Grande,
page 1356

■ Sleeping
1 Eurobuilding   2 Tamanaco

Casa Natal del Libertador: a reconstruction of the house where Bolívar was born (on 24 July 1783) on Sur 1 y Este 2, Jacinto a Traposos. It contains interesting pictures and furniture. The first house, of adobe, was destroyed by an earthquake. The second became a stable, and was later pulled down. ■ *Tue-Fri 0900-1200, 1430-1700, Sun and holidays 1000-1700.* **The Museo Bolivariano** is alongside the Casa Natal and contains the Liberator's war relics. **Cuadra Bolívar**, Bárcenas y Las Piedras, eight blocks south of Plaza Bolívar; 'El Palmar', the Bolívar family's summer home, a beautifully preserved colonial country estate. ■ *Tue-Sat 0900-1300, 1430-1700; Sun and holidays 0900-1700.*

Museo de Transporte, Parque Nacional del Este (to which it is connected by a pedestrian overpass), includes a large collection of locomotives and old cars. ■ *Sat-Sun 0900-1600, US$0.10.*

In the **Parque Central**, between Avenida Lecuna (east end) and the elevated section of Avenida Bolívar there are four museums in a complex which includes two octagonal towers (56 floors each – ask the security guard to let you go up to the roof, leave passport and they will guide you, not Monday) and four large apartment buildings with shopping below: **Museo de Arte Contemporáneo**, Parque Central, Cuadra Bolívar, entrance beside *Anauco Hilton*, very good, European and Venezuelan painters, a room devoted to Picasso pen and ink drawings, and interesting modern sculptures. ■ *Tue-Sun 1000-1800, free.* **Museo de los Niños**, Parque Central, next to east Tower, a highly sophisticated modern science museum, extremely popular. ■ *Wed-Sun and holidays, 0900-1200, 1400-1700, US$0.75 (adults).* Also in the Parque Central complex, **Museo Audiovisual**, ■ *Tue-Fri 0900-1700, US$1*, and **Museo del Teclado** (keyboard instruments).

Museo Histórico Fundación John Boulton, Torre El Chorro, 11th floor, Avenida Universidad y Sur 3, entre El Chorro y Dr Díaz, previously in La Guaira, contains many unique historical items and a library of 19th-century research material and commercial records of the Casa Boulton (easy access, free). ■ *Mon-Fri 0800-1200, 1300-1700, 2 tours a day by knowledgeable guides; underground parking on presentation of ID.*

The Consejo Municipal (City Hall) on Plaza Bolívar contains three museums: a collection of the paintings of Emilio Boggio, a Venezuelan painter; the Raúl Santana Museum of the Creole Way of Life, a collection of miniature figures in costumes and poses characteristic of Venezuelan life, all handmade by Raúl Santana; and the Sala de Arqueología Gaspar Marcano, exhibiting ceramics, mostly discovered on the coast. ■ *All 3 open Tue-Fri 0930-1200, 1500-1800; Sat and Sun 0930-1800. Informative guides are available.*

Parks **Jardín Botánico**, near Plaza Venezuela, entrance by Ciudad Universitaria, is worth a visit. There are extensive plant collections and a small area of 'natural forest'. Here you can see the world's largest palm tree (*Corypha Sp*) and the Elephant Apple with its huge edible fruit. ■ *Tue-Sun 0800-1630, US$0.30, guide US$1 in English. You need permission to take photographs.* **Parque Los Caobos** is peaceful and has a cafeteria in the middle. By the entrance in Avenida México is the cultural centre, **Ateneo de Caracas**, with a theatre, art gallery, concert room, bookshop and the imposing Teresa Carreño theatre complex. **Parque Nacional del Este** is a popular place to relax, especially at weekends. ■ *Closed Mon, opens 0530 for joggers, 0800 for others, till 1730 (reached from Parque del Este metro station). US$0.15.* There is a boating lake, a replica of Columbus' Santa María (being renovated since 1991), the Humboldt Planetarium (weekend shows, US$0.25), a number of different sunken lakes featuring caiman and turtles, monkeys, two frustratingly caged jaguars, many types of water birds, a terrarium (open Sat-Sun, US$0.05). The heavily wooded **Parque Caricuao** is at the southwest end of the Metro line, and forms part of the Parque Nacional Macuro. Recommended for a pleasant day out. ■ *Tue-Sun 0900-1700, US$0.20. Take metro to*

Caracas centre

	Sleeping		
	1 Avenida	4 Inter	7 Plaza Catedral
	2 Caracas Hilton	5 La Neve	8 Renovación
	3 Hospedaje Fidelina	6 Palas	

Caricuao Zoológico, then 5 min walk up Av Principal La Hacienda. The **Parque Los Chorros** at the foot of the mountain has impressive waterfalls, also recommended. ■ *US$0.05. Take bus marked Petare and La Urbina.* **El Calvario**, west of El Silencio, with the Arch of Confederation at the entrance, has a good view of Centro Simón Bolívar, but muggings have been reported. It has a small Museo Ornitológico, botanical gardens and a picturesque chapel.

Essentials

Sleeping
■ *on maps,
pages 1354 and 1356
Price codes:
see inside front cover*

Cheap pensiones are usually full of long-stay residents and have very few rooms available for travellers. In the centre all cheap hotels take only short stay customers on Fri afternoon. The cheapest hotels are in the downtown area, but this is not a safe part of town at night, or even in the day with a backpack. It is better to spend a little more and stay in Sabana Grande. Hotels in the following list are recommended, apart from any minor points mentioned. Hotel prices below do not include 16.5% tax. Hotels tend to be full at weekends and in Jul and Aug. **Hotel reservations** The airport tourist office is very helpful and will book hotel rooms. If you book from abroad, make sure you receive confirmation before beginning your journey. For apartment rental, consult *El Universal* daily paper, small ads columns.

Chuao/Las Mercedes LL *Tamanaco Inter-Continental*, Av Principal Las Mercedes, PO Box 467, Caracas 1060A, T909 7111, caracas@interconti.com The best hotel in Caracas, superb pool, luxury business hotel, difficult to get rooms as it is normally fully booked (includes service, tax 15%, rooms are priced in dollars), courteous staff, good facilities, changes TCs for guests only. **L** *Eurobuilding*, C La Guairita, Chuao, T902 1111,

Business/commercial district SE of centre, not on metro

Venezuela

ventas01@ven.net 5-star, modern, has all-suite wing, well-furnished, a/c, includes breakfast, efficient service, large pool, gym, restaurants, many services, weekend rates available; **AL** *Best Western CCT*, Centro Ciudad Comercial Tamanaco, T900 8006, www.bestwestern.com/thisco/bw/77401/77401_b.html Smart business hotel with a pool terrace, approached through shopping mall, not that easy to find. **C** *Nostrum*, Av Orinoco y final C al lado de Pollos Riviera, T92 7646. Noisy, safe, enclosed parking.

Respectable area, **Near Altamira metro station L** *Continental*, Av San Juan Bosco, T261 0644, *east of centre* www.hotel-continental.org Smart, gardens front and rear and a good, private swimming pool. **AL** *El Cid*, Av San Felipe, between 1a and 2a, T263 2611, F263 5578. Spanish style interior, large suites with living area, breakfast rooms, kitchenette ensuite, a/c, good value.

Many restaurants and **Sabana Grande/ Chacaíto L** *Gran Meliá*, Av Casanova y El Recreo, T762 8111, *shops, convenient for* www.solmelia.es/cgi-bin/solmelia/dirdinamic/hotelhtml?45832 Business centre, restau-
metro and safest area rants (including Japanese and pizzería), gym, piano bar. **L-AL** *Cumberland*, 2da Av de las
for cheap hotels Delicias, T762 9961, www.hotelescumberland.com Very good, nice restaurant, taxi service
to airport. **AL** *Las Américas*, C Los Cerritos, T951 7133, www.hotellasamericas.com.ve A
Many hotels in the Av modern tower, with new block attached, tiny roof pool and restaurant, taxi service to airport,
Las Acacias/Av good value. **AL** *Tampa*, Av Francisco Solano López, T762 3771, F762 0112. Comfy but noisy
Casanova area, but the a/c, plain interior, interesting bodega-style restaurant. **A** *Atlántida*, Av la Salle, Los Caobos, 2
majority are short-stay blocks up from Av Libertador, T793 3211, F781 3696. Safe, noisy, a/c, restaurant. **AL** *Coliseo*,
Av Casanova y Coromoto, T762 7916, www.hotelcoliseo.com.ve A/c, good breakfast, 100 m
from Sabana Grande metro station. **B** *Crillon*, Av Libertador, esq Av Las Acacias, T761 4411,
hotelcrillon@cantv.net Highrise block, good service, comfortable, good bar, accepts credit
cards. **A** *Kursaal*, Av Casanova y El Colegio, T762 2922. Safe, a/c, cheap taxi service to airport.
A *Plaza Palace*, Av Los Mangos, Las Delicias, T762 4821. Very good value. **A** *Savoy*, Av Francisco Solano López y Av Las Delicias, T762 1971, www.hotelssavoycaraacas.com Good food,
efficient, secure vehicle park, taxi service to airport. **B** *El Cóndor*, Av Las Delicias, T762 9911.
Comfortable but plain, outstanding restaurant in Spanish bodega style. **B** *Montpark*, Los
Cerritos, Bello Monte, T951 0240, F951 7437. Quiet, spotless. **C** *Cristal*, Pasaje Asunción, just

Sabana Grande

To Atlántida Hotel & Los Caobos

	Sleeping	4	Cumberland	8	Odeon	12	Tampa
1	Coliseo	5	Escorial	9	Plaza Palace		
2	Crillón	6	Gran Meliá	10	Ritz		
3	Cristal	7	Kursaal	11	Savoy		

Venezuela

off Av Abraham Lincoln, near Sabana Grande metro, T761 9131. A/c, comfortable, safe, good value, disco at weekends, restaurant. **C** *Escorial*, Av El Colegio, T762 8820, F762 7505. A/c, secure, mediocre restaurant and bar, fax service, cheap taxi service to airport, good value. **C** *Odeon*, Las Acacias y Av Casanova, T793 1322, F781 9380. Modern, stores luggage, restaurant serves Colombian food, good value but cockroaches. **C** *Ritz*, Av Las Palmas y Av Libertador, near Plaza Venezuela, T793 7811. A/c, safe provided, good beds, luggage store, restaurant, secure free parking. **D** *Nuestro*, C Colegio and Av Casanova. With fan, secure, basic but good value. Used by short stay couples but rents rooms to backpackers as well.

San Bernardino L *Avila*, Av Jorge Washington T555 3000, www.viajes-venezuela.com/ hotelavila Set in tranquil, park-like gardens some distance from the centre, very pleasant, good service, most of staff speak English and German, fans, mosquito screens, pool, Metrobus nearby, very good restaurant and poolside bar, helpful travel agency, phones which accept Visa/MasterCard. **C** *Waldorf*, Av Industria, T571 4733. Hot water erratic, restaurant, English sometimes spoken, good value, will store luggage.

Residential area 2 km N of Bellas Artes metro

Central area L *Caracas Hilton*, Av Sur 25 with Av Mexico, T503 5000, www.hiltoncaracas.com.ve Ageing luxury hotel, excellent business centre, spectacular city views, especially at night, noisy (traffic and a/c), useful long-term luggage deposit and good breakfast, nice pool, fax service open to non-residents, very helpful, good sushi bar. Just across the road is the *Anauco Hilton*, Av Lecuna, Torre Este, Parque Central (an area of tower blocks, concrete walkways and underpasses, near metro Bellas Artes), T573 4111, F573 7724, an annex to the main hotel with rooms for longer stays. **A** *Plaza Catedral*, Blvd Plaza Bolívar, next to Cathedral, T564 2111, F564 1797. Beautiful location in the colonial part of town, Amex accepted, a/c, some English spoken, good restaurant. **C** *Limón*, C Este 10, No 228, near metro Bellas Artes. Safe, parking, often recommended. **C** *Palas*, Sur 4, Pilita a Glorieta, T482 5731, F484 6815. Modern, a/c, helpful, luggage stored, good restaurant. **C** *Renovación*, Av Este 2 No 154, near Los Caobos and Bellas Artes Metro, T571 0133, www.usuarios.lycos.es/hotelrenovacion With a/c, modern, lots of restaurants nearby. **D** *Avenida*, C Sur 4 y Av Vicente Lecuna, T482 6440. Hot water sporadic, a/c, safe, also short stay. **D** *Caroní*, Av Baralt, between Muñoz and Piñango. Popular, safe but a bit noisy, not very clean, bar, restaurant. **D** *Hospedaje Fidelina*, Sur 4 No 120, T482 8769. Safe, fan, **E** with shared bath/toilet. **D** *Inter*, Animas a Calero, on corner of Av Urdaneta, near Nuevo Circo, T564 0251. Helpful, English spoken, very popular, poor restaurant, accepts credit cards. **D** *La Neve*, Sur 4, Pilita a Glorieta No 126 – Sur 4, near Metro Capitolio. A/c or fan, good, safe, quiet, good restaurant.

Cheapest hotels around the Nuevo Circo bus terminal (not a safe area)

Eating

Midday is the most economical time to eat the main meal of the day and about the only opportunity to find fresh vegetables. Particularly good value is the 3-course 'menú ejecutivo' or 'cubierto'. Breakfast in your hotel is likely to be poor. It is better and cheaper in a *fuente de soda* and cheaper still in a *pastelería* or *arepería*. Food on display in a bar is free with your drink if they offer it as a *pasapalo*, but will be charged for if offered as a *ración*. You can save on the service charge by eating at the bar and not at a table.

● *on map, pages 1354 and 1356 Guides to eating including Guía gastronómica de Venezuela, available in most bookshops*

Venezuela

There is a wide selection of good restaurants around Av Urdaneta and in the districts of **Altamira**, **Las Mercedes**, **Sabana Grande** (see below) and **La Castellana** (eg *La Estancia*, Av Principal La Castellana, esq Urdaneta, near Altamira metro, very good beef in traditional style and popular; next door is *Primi*, Italian/Creole cuisine, quite chic and friendly, plenty of vegetarian dishes).

Central area There are plenty of eating places around Plaza Bolívar: *Plaza Mayor*, Torre a Veroes, northeast corner of Plaza Bolívar, very good. *El Paso*, Hospital a Glorieta, Ed Atlántico, Plaza La Concordia, Chinese, cheap, good. Seafood at *Las Vegas* near *Hotel Plaza Catedral*. *Casa de Italia*, in the Italia building, next to *Waldorf Hotel*, best Italian food for the price, excellent service, view and bar.

Full of cafés, bars (tascas) and restaurants to suit all tastes and budgets. Open-air tables on Av Abraham Lincoln, but it's expensive and waiters overcharge, check prices first

Sabana Grande Among the recommended restaurants *Tivoli*, El Colegio between Lincoln and Casanova, good pasta dishes from US$1.70-2.50. *Caserío*, on Fco Solano, and *Urrutia*, Fco Solano y Los Mangos, both very good for national dishes. *Bohío Habanero*, in La Previsora, Cuban food, recommended. *La Buca* in *Hotel Kursaal*, international food. *Pizzeria Colisseo*, Blvd Sabana Grande (Av Lincoln) y El Colegio. Cheap, good food and drinks, terrace bar. *Victor's Pollo*, Av F Solano y El Bosque (Chacaíto end), has 20 different chicken dishes. *Shorthorn*, Av Libertador y El Bosque, very good. There is a good selection of Arabic, Chinese and Hindu restaurants on C Villa Flor and all Arabic restaurants have vegetarian options. For example *Comida Arabe*, Colegio, near *Hotel Kursaal*, excellent.

Vegetarian *Buffet Vegetariano*, Av Los Jardines. *El Acuarino*, Truco a Caja de Agua; neither open for dinner. *Almuerzo*, Hoyo a Sta Rosalía, good, cheap. *Sabas Nieves*, Pascual Navarro 12, Sabana Grande, open 1130-1500. *Delicatesses Indú*, specializes in southern Indian dishes, good quality, small portions, on C Villaflor, in Sabana Grande just off Av Abraham Lincoln between metro stations Sabana Grande and Plaza Venezuela.

Fast foods There are many burger and pizza places. *Arturo's*, is a chain of clean, modern, chicken-and-chips style restaurants in various locations. *El Arepazo*, 1 block south of Chacaíto metro station, has every kind of arepa filling you could wish for. *El Coco*, in the Centro Comercial Chacaíto, has very good Venezuelan food at much lower prices than the sidewalk cafés on nearby Sabana Grande.

Entertainment There are frequent Sun morning concerts in the *Teatro Municipal*, 1100. Concerts, ballet, theatre and film festivals at the *Ateneo de Caracas*, Paseo Colón, Plaza Morelos; and similar events, including foreign artists, at the *Complejo Cultural Teresa Carreño*, see Parks above. For details of cinemas and other events, see the newspapers, *El Universal*, *El Nacional* and *Daily Journal*, and the Sun issue of *El Diario de Caracas*.

Nightclubs Caracas is a lively city by night. Caraqueños dine at home around 2000, and in restaurants from 2100 to 2300, so nightclubs don't usually come to life until after 2300, and then go on to all hours of the morning. *Un Solo Pueblo*, typical Venezuelan music, 3rd Transversal, Altamira (there are many small clubs, restaurants and bars on Plaza Altamira Sur); opposite is *Café Rajatabla*, in the Ateneo cultural complex, young crowd and often has live music. *El Maní es Así*, C El Cristo, 1 block up from Av Fco Solano, good for live salsa and dancing, US$6 after 2200. 1 block east of Nuevo Circo, opposite the filling station, *Rica Arepa*, an arepería, has traditional Venezuelan folk music, free, on Fri, Sat, Sun nights.

Discos: Most permit entry to couples only. One that admits singles is *Palladium*, in CCCT shopping centre, popular, big.

Sport **Baseball**: season is Oct-Jan. **Clubs**: The Social Centre of the **British Commonwealth Association**, Quinta Alborada, Av 7 with Transversal 9, Altamira, T261 3060, bar and swimming pool, British and Commonwealth visitors only, entry fee according to length of stay. The sports club run by the *Tamanaco Hotel* is open to non-guests and suitable for people staying a short time.

Festivals 3 May, *Velorio de la Cruz de Mayo* still celebrated with dances and parties in some districts. 18-25 Dec, Yuletide masses at different churches leading up to Christmas. Traditional creole dishes served at breakfasts.

Venezuela

For gems and fine jewellery, try **Labady**, Sabana Grande 98, beautifully made gold jewellery, **Shopping**
English spoken. **Pro-Venezuela Exposición y Venta de Arte Popular**, on Gran Avenida, Plaza
Venezuela (opposite Torre La Previsora), sells Venezuelan crafts, very crowded, no prices, bargain hard. Good quality Sun craft market between Museo de Bellas Artes and Museo de Historia
Natural (metro Bellas Artes). Indian market on southwest corner of Plaza Chacaíto has selection
of Venezuelan, Peruvian and Ecuadorean crafts. The **CCCT shopping centre** is worth a visit, as
is the **Centro Comercial Plaza Las Americanas**, mostly for fashion stores and beach wear.
Centro Plaza Altamira, between metro stations Altamira and Parque del Este, has shops, cafés,
tascas and the **Centro Mediterráneo**, with boutiques and cafés and a good quality cinema.

   Bookshops American Bookshop, Av San Juan Bosco, Edif Belveder, T263 5455/267
4134, near Altamira metro, Mon-Fri 0900-1730, Sat 0900-1400, good selection of second-hand English books; also available in bookstalls in the street. **Audobon Society of Venezuela**, in the basement of Paseo Las Mercedes, T993 2525, sells guidebooks and gives
information, closed Sat. **Librería del Este**, Av Francisco de Miranda 52, Edif Galipán, and
Librería Unica, Centro Capriles, ground floor local 13N, Plaza Venezuela, have foreign language books. **Librería Washington**, La Torre a Veroes No 25, good service.
Librería Ecológica, Plaza Caracas, between Torres Norte and Sur, Centro Simón Bolívar, near
CANTV office, for environmental books, also has some maps. A French bookshop is
Librería La France, Centro Comercial Chacaíto. Italian bookshop, **El Libro Italiano**, Pasaje La
Concordia (between Sabana Grande pedestrian street and Av Fco Solano López). For Ger-
man books, **Librería Alemana** (Oscar Todtmann), Centro El Bosque, Av Libertador, T763
0881, open Tue-Sat, 0900-1230, 1500-1800.

Cacao Travel, C Andromeda, Qta Orquidea, El Peñón, Caracas, T977 1234, F977 0110, reser- **Tour operators**
vation@cacaotravel.com Tours and lodges throughout Venezuela. **Candes Turismo**, office
in lobby of *Hilton* and Edif Celeste, Av Abraham Lincoln, T953 4710, F953 6755,
www.candesturismo.com.ve Helpful, English, Italian, German spoken. **Condor Verde**, Av
Caura, Torre Humboldt, Prados del Este, Caracas, T975 4306, F975 2385, www.con-
dor-verde.com Operate throughout the country. **Delfino Tours**, Aptdo Postal 61.800,
Chacao, 1060 Caracas, T267 5175, www.delfinotours.com Contact Elizabeth Klar, specialize
in tours to Los Roques archipelago. Recommended. **KuMeKa Tours**, Torre Altocentro, C
Negrín, p 1, T762 8356, F761 8538, kumekatours@cantv.net Tours throughout Venezuela,
helpful. **Lost World Adventures**, Edif 3-H, p 6, Oficina 62, Av Abraham Lincoln, Caracas 1050,
T761 1108, F761 7538, lwaccs@cantv.net Tours to Roraima and Canaima. **Orinoco Tours**,
Edif Galerías Bolívar, p 7, Av Abraham Lincoln, Caracas 1050-A, PO Box 51505, T761 7662,
F761 6801, orinocotours.com Flights and tours, very helpful. **Selma Viajes**, Av Blandín,
Centro San Ignacio, Torre Este, p 3, La Castellana, T266 6489, F263 9695,
www.selma.com.ve Run recommended excursions to Canaima.

Local Buses: See Getting around, page 1351 **Transport**
   Driving: Self-drive cars (*Hertz, Avis, Volkswagen, Budget, Dollar, ACO*) are available at the
airport (offices open 0700-2100, *Avis* till 2300, good service) and in town. They are cheaper
than guided excursions for less than full loads. Rates are given on page 1347. **Garage**:
Yota-Box, 3a Transversal Mis Encantos, Quinta Morava, No 1 15, Chacao, owner Gerardo
Ayala, recommended, especially for Toyota. **Bel-Cro**, Av Intercomunal de Antímano, very
good for VWs, also sells new and used parts, very cheap and highly recommended.

   Motorcycle repairs: **Industrial Amanfini**, El Progreso 14, El Hatillo, Caracas, T963 6110, *Motorcycles may*
F963 4117, Spanish only, good service, but expensive. *not be ridden in*
   Taxis are required by law to install and use taxi-meters, but they either never use them or *Caracas between*
remove them. Fares must be negotiated in advance. Most city trips are US$1 absolute mini- *2300 and 0500*
mum during the day (most fares US$2). Taxi drivers are authorized to charge an extra 20% on
night trips after 1800, on Sun and all holidays, and US$0.45 for answering telephone calls.
After 1800 drivers are selective about where they want to go. Beware of taxi drivers trying to
renegotiate fixed rates because your destination is in 'a difficult area'. The sign on the roof of
a taxi reads 'Libre'. See NB under Air about pirate taxis. Never tell a taxi driver it is your first visit
to Caracas. See yellow pages for radio taxis.

Venezuela

Metro Operates 0530-2300, no smoking, no luggage allowed. There are 3 lines: Line 1 (west-east) from Propatria to Palo Verde; Line 2 (north-south), from Capitolio to Las Adjuntas, with connection to Caricuao Zoológico; Line 3, south from Plaza Venezuela to El Valle, plus metrobus El Valle-Los Teques. Tickets cost US$0.45 per journey; 10-journey tickets (Multi Abono) are available. Student discounts are available with ISIC card. Metrobuses connect with the Metro system: get transfer tickets (*boleto integrado*, US$0.20) for services to southern districts, route maps displayed at stations – retain ticket after exit turnstile. Good selection of maps at shop in La California station.

Airport: 28 km from Caracas at La Guaira port. Flight enquiries T031-355 2858; passenger assistance T355 1310 Police T355 1226

Long distance Air: The airport has 3 terminals, Maiquetía (national), Simón Bolívar (international), which are 5 mins' walk apart, and Auxiliar (national), which is 400 m from Maiquetía – taxis take a circular route, fare US$2.25; airport authorities run shuttle buses every 10 mins from 0700. The Tourist Office at the international airport has good maps, helpful; some English spoken, open 0700-2400; will book hotels, reconfirm flights, English spoken, better service than Corpoturismo head office. Many facilities close 1 Jan, including duty free and money exchanges. Duty free shops close 2230. At Simón Bolívar: several *casas de cambio* open 24 hrs (good rates at *Italcambio*, outside duty-free area, but count notes carefully); also *Banco Industrial* branch in international terminal and another, less crowded, in baggage reclaim area. If changing TCs you may be asked for your receipt of purchase; commission 2.5%. There are cash machines for Visa, Amex and MasterCard. Pharmacy, bookshops, basement café (good value meals and snacks, open 0600-2400, hard to find); cafés and bars on 1st floor viewing terrace also good value. No official left luggage; ask for Paulo at the mini bar on the 1st floor. Look after your belongings in both terminals. Direct dial phone calls to USA from AT&T booth in international departure lounge. CANTV at Gates 15 and 24, open 0700-2100, long-distance, international and fax services, including receipt of faxes.

Always allow plenty of time when going to the airport, whatever means of transport you are using: the route can be very congested (2 hrs in daytime, but only 30 mins at 0430). Allow at least 2 hrs checking-in time before your flight. Official prices are listed at the airport: US$11 to Caracas city centre, US$30 if late at night. Although fares are supposed to be controlled, it is essential to negotiate with the driver. In practice taxi fares from airport to Caracas cost on average US$18 minimum, depending on the quality of the taxi, the part of city, or on the number of stars of your hotel (give the name of a cheaper hotel nearby). After 2200 and at weekends a surcharge may be added and the fare may go up to US$40. Overcharging is rife and taxi drivers can be aggressive in seeking passengers. Drivers may only surcharge you for luggage (US$0.50 per large bag). From the city centre to the airport is around US$10-12. If you think the licensed taxi driver is overcharging you, make a complaint to Corpoturismo or tell him you will report him to the Departamento de Protección del Consumidor. **NB** Beware of pirate taxis as we have received reports of travellers being robbed at gunpoint in these unlicensed cabs which may have a sign but no yellow number plates. If you have any doubts about your driver or the car, or if a first-time visitor on your own, then it is best to call a radio taxi. *Teletaxi*, T753 4155 have been recommended; they have an office inside the airport. Airport police, T355 1226 for reporting crimes.

Caracas Metro

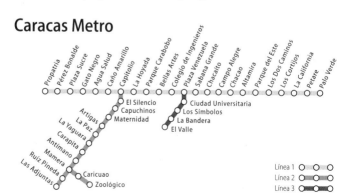

Propatria · Pérez Bonalde · Plaza Sucre · Gato Negro · Agua Salud · Caño Amarillo · Capitolio · La Hoyada · Parque Carabobo · Bellas Artes · Colegio de Ingenieros · Plaza Venezuela · Sabana Grande · Chacaíto · Campo Alegre · Chacao · Altamira · Parque del Este · Los Dos Caminos · Los Cortijos · La California · Petare · Palo Verde

El Silencio
Capuchinos
Maternidad

Ciudad Universitaria
Los Símbolos
La Bandera
El Valle

Artigas · La Paz · La Yaguara · Carapita · Antímano · Mamera · Ruíz Pineda · Las Adjuntas · Caricuao · Zoológico

Línea 1
Línea 2
Línea 3

Venezuela

The airport shuttle bus (blue and white with 'Aeropuerto Internacional' on the side) leaves from east end of terminal, left out of exit. To airport catch it under the flyover at Bolívar and Av Sur 17, 250 m from Bellas Artes metro (poorly lit at night, not recommended to wait here in the dark); regular service from 0700 to 2300, bus leaves when there are enough passengers, 1 hr, US$3.50. If heading for a hotel in Sabana Grande on arrival, ask to be dropped off at Gato Negro metro station (same fare) and take metro from there to Plaza Venezuela or Sabana Grande. The shuttle bus or *por puesto* to airport can also be caught at Gato Negro metro station.

Buses: The **Terminal Oriente** at Guarenas for **eastern destinations** is clean, modern and safe. City buses leave Nuevo Circo bullring every 30 mins, US$0.30, 45 mins, 1 hr in rush hour; or take *por puesto* from Petare metro station, an easier option but take care at night. Taxi to terminal US$4. Bus from terminal to centre: turn left outside main entrance towards main parking area where buses wait; get off at Bellas Artes or El Silencio, US$0.50.

The new La Bandera terminal for all **western** destinations is a 500 m, unsafe walk from La Bandera or Los Símbolos stations on metro line 3. City buses that pass are prominently marked 'La Bandera'. Give yourself plenty of time to find the bus you need although there are bus agents who will assist in finding a ticket for your destination. Tickets are sold in advance except for nearby destinations such as **Maracay** and **Valencia**, which leave as soon as full from a separate section (turn right on entering the terminal). For long distance buses use the stairs just inside the terminal entrance. Those first on get the best seats so it is advisable to arrive an hour before departure. Buses may also leave early. There is a left luggage office, telephone office, cash machines and a restaurant and many food and drink kiosks.

Buses for places close to Caracas leave from across the road from the old Nuevo Circo bus station, via the underpass (eg **Los Teques, Higuerote, Catia La Mar, La Guaira**). From La Hoyada metro, do not go under the bridge, but walk straight down the road for 300 m.

On public holidays buses are usually fully booked leaving Caracas and drivers often make long journeys without stopping. Sat and Sun morning are also bad for travel into/out of Caracas, no problem on journeys of 4 hrs or less. Always take identification when booking a long-distance journey. Times and fares of buses are given under destinations. Buses going west on the Panamericana route are not recommended because the old road suffers from many accidents. Autoexpresos Ejecutivos, terminal at Av Principal de Bello Campo, Quinta Marluz (between Chacao and Altamira metro stops), T266 2321, F266 9011, aeroexpresos.com.ve, to **Maracay, Valencia, Barquisimeto, Maracaibo, Maturín** and **Puerto La Cruz**, reserve 2 days in advance, except for buses leaving on Fri (no left luggage). Fares are 3-4 times higher than other companies, but worth it.

International buses *Ormeño* (T/F471 7205) has buses to **Bogotá** (US$75), **Cali** (US$90), **Quito** (US$130), **Guayaquil** (US$140), **Lima** (US$190), **Santiago** (US$270), **Mendoza** (US$330) and **Buenos Aires** (US$340); safe, comfortable, a/c, video, toilet; terminal at Final Av San Martín, Sector Oeste, C Sucre con C Nueva, near Metro La Paz.

Airline offices Domestic: *Aeropostal*, 22nd floor, Torre Polar, Av Paseo Colón, Plaza Venezuela, T708 6222. *Aereotuy*, Edif Gran Sabana, p 5, Av Lincoln y Blvd Sabana Grande (T763 8043, F762 5254). *Avensa*, Edif Atlántida, Av Universidad (Metro La Hoyada), T561 3366 (domestic airport T355 1609, international airport T355 1889). International: *Aerolíneas Argentinas*, Centro Altamira, p 4, Av San Juan Bosco, Altamira, T355 2749. *Air France*, Parque Cristal, Torre Este, p 2, Los Palos Grandes, T283 5855. *Alitalia*, Edif Atlantic, p 5, Av Andrés Bello, Los Palos Grandes, T285 6108. *American*, Torre ING Bank, p 7, Centro Letonia, T209 8111. *Avianca*, Av F de Miranda, Edif Roraima, T953 7254. *British Airways*, Torre Copérnico (oeste), p 3, oficina 03-03, La Castellana, T266 0122. *BWIA*, Edif Exa, p 8, oficinas 803-804, Av Libertador y C Alameda, T953 6666. *Cubana*, Edif Atlantic, p 4, oficina 5, Av Andrés Bello l 1ra Tranversal, T286 8639. *Iberia*, Centro Altamira, p 4, Av San Juan Bosco, Altamira, T267 8666. *KLM*, Torre KLM, Av R Gallegos, T285 3333. *Lufthansa*, Centro Torre Conaisa, p 1, Av San Felipe, La Castellana, T285 2113. *United*, Edif Parque Canaima, p 8, Av F de Miranda, Los Palos Grandes, T278 4545. *Varig*, Centro Emp Los Ruices, p 3, oficinas 316-317, Av Principal de Los Ruices, T238 2111.

Banks *Citibank*, Av Urdaneta, Carmelitas a Altagracia, T806 2211, also Torre Banaven, Av La Estancia, Chuao, and Seguros Venezuela, Av Francisco de Miranda, Chacaíto. ATM and will exchange Citicorp cheques. *Banco Unión* branches for *Visa* transactions and ATM. Also for Visa ATMs, brances of

Directory

See also Currency, page 1344

Venezuela

Banco de Venezuela.For cash advances on *MasterCard*, and ATM go to branches of *Banco Mercantil*. To change *American Express* TCs, try *Corp Banca*, Av Principal de La Castellana entre Blandón y Los Chaguaramas, Torre Corp Banca, La Castellana, T206 2677, mornings and afternoons. They usually ask for ID and proof of purchase. For **exchange** and Amex travel services go to *Italcambio*. They also cahnge Visa TCs, require proof of TC purchase, commission 0.50%, open Mon-Fri till 1630, Sat till 1200. You can also buy TCs with bolívares. Offices at: Av Urdanata esq Animas y Platanal, T563 3633 (or *Visesta CA* opposite, highly recommended, accepts Eurocheques, also for travel arrangements, Walter Kleebinder speaks several languages and is very helpful, T562 4698/5333); Av Casanova entre 1 y 2 C Bello Monte (Sabana Grande), T761 8244; Edif Belmont, Av L Roche (Altaira Sur), T267 3389; Las Mercedes, C California, qta Las Churrucas, T993 0255; Simón Bolívar Airport (may limit transaction to US$100, open public holidays), T288 7877, www.italviajes.com Amex services also at *Quo Vadis*, Av Principoal La Castellana, Banco Lara p 8, T261 7782, mmassimo@quovadis.com.ve *La Moneda*, Centro Financiero Latino, Urdaneta, p 8, and Av Fco Solano, 1 block from Plaza Venezuela metro, opposite El Molino Rosso restaurant and next to Banco Profesional, open Mon-Fri only. *Confinanzas*, Centro Comercial Paseo Las Mercedes, Local PA-CI, open 0800-1200, 1400-1700, 1% commission usually charged on TCs. *MVS Cambios*, Av Francisco Solano López, between C El Cristo and Los Manguitos, Edif Torre Oasis, Sabana Grande, less waiting, good rates. *Viajes Febres Parra*, Av Fco de Miranda, basement of Centro Lido (not well signed). Good rates for US$ and TCs, no queues.

Communications Internet: *Cyber Café 2000*, Galerías Bolívar, Blvd Sabana Grande, 0900-1900. *Cybercafé Madrid*, Acuario floor, Centro Sambil, Chacao. *Torre Capriles*, ground floor, Plaza Venezuela, Mon-Fri 0900-1800. **Post Office** Central at Urdaneta y Norte 4, close to Plaza Bolívar. Efficient overseas package service but packages should be ready to send. *Lista de correos* costs US$0.30, Mon-Fri 0700-1945, Sat 0800-1700, Sun 0800-1200. Ipostel office in Centro Comercial Cediaz, on Av Casanova between C Villaflor and San Jerónimo, open Mon-Fri office hrs, Sat till 1200; also at airport. **Telephone:** *CANTV*, on 1st floor of Centro Plaza on Francisco Miranda in the east (corner of Andrés Bello between metros Parque del Este and Altamira), open Mon-Sat 0800-1945, T284 7932, phone cards sold here. Also public phones in the Metro stations and along Blvd Sabana Grande (Abraham Lincoln). Phone and fax at *Cables Internacionales*, Santa Capilla a Mijares, Edif San Mauricio, planta baja, Mon-Sat 0700-1900, near Capitolio Metro, 1 block east of main Post Office then ½ block north.

Cultural centres **British Council**, Torre Credicard, p 3, Av Principal del Bosque, Chacaíto, T952 9965, F952 9651, www.britcoun.org **El Centro Venezolano-Americano**, Av Principal, Las Mercedes, good free library of books in English, and free concerts. Also Spanish courses, 8 different levels, each lasts 17 days and costs US$50, highly recommended. **Asociación Cultural Humboldt (Goethe Institut)**, Av Juan Germán Roscio, San Bernardino, T552 7634, library, lectures, films, concerts, Spanish courses.

Embassies and consulates Australia, 'Yolanda', Av Luis Roche, between transversal 6 and 7, Altamira, T261 4632, F261 3448, www.venezuela.embassy.gov.au **Austria**, Edif Plaza C PH, Londres entre Caroni y Nueva York, Las Mercedes, T993 9844. www.internet.ve/austria **Brazil**, Edif 'Centro Gerencial Mohedano', p 6, between C Los Chaguaramas and Av Mohedano, La Castellano, T261 5505, F261 9601, Mon-Fri 0830-1230. Visa (valid for 3 months maximum) costs US$15, you need a photo, and it takes 24 hrs. **Canada**, Av Francisco de Miranda con Altamira Sur, Altamira, T264 0833, www.dfait-maeci.gc.ca/caracas/ **Colombia**, Torre Credival, p 11, 2nd Av Campo Alegre with Av Fco de Miranda, T261 5584, F261 1358. Mon-Fri 0800-1400 for visas, you need a photo and US$12.50, the process can take anything from 10 mins to 1 day. **Denmark**, Av Venezuela, esquina C Mohedano, Edif Centuria, p 7, El Rosal, near Chacaítio Metro station, T951 4618, F951 5278. Mon-Thu 0800-1600, Fri 0800-1300. **Finland**, Torre C, p 14, Centro Plaza, Av Fco de Miranda, T284 5013. **France**, C Madrid and Av Trinidad, Las Mercedes, T993 6666. **Germany**, Edif Panavén, p 2, Av San Juan Bosco, Altamira, T265 2827, open Mon-Fri 0900-1300. **Guyana**, Quinta Roraima, Av El Paseo, Prados del Este, T977 1158. Open for visa Mon, Wed and Fri, 0830-1200, issued on the same day if you're early, need passport, airline ticket, yellow fever certificate and 2 photos. **Israel**, Av Fco de Miranda, Centro Empresario Miranda, p 4, T239 4511, F239 4320. **Italy**, Ed Atrium, C Sorocaima entre Avs Tamanaco y Venezuela, El Rosal, T952 7311, F952 4960. **Japan**, Av San Juan Bosco, between 8th and 9th Transversal, Altamira, T261 8333. **Netherlands**, Edif San Juan, p 9, San Juan Bosco and Av Transversal 2, Altamira, T263 3622 (Apdo Postal 62286, Caracas 1060a). **New Zealand consulate**, c/o New Zealand Milk Products Venezuela, Torre La Noria, p 10, of 10-B4, Paseo Henrique Eraso, San Ramón, T292 4332, F292 3571. **Spain**, Edif Bancaracas, p 7, Plaza La Castellana, T266 0222. **Sweden**, Centro Coinasa, p 2, Av San Felipe, La Castellana, T266 2968. **Switzerland**, Centro Letonia, Torre ING-Bank, p 15, La Castellana (Apdo 62.555, 1060-A Caracas), T267 9585, F267 7745, swissemcar@compuserve.com Open 0900-1200.

Suriname, 4a Av, between 7a and 8a Transversal, Urb Altaira, T261 2724. **Trinidad**, beside the Suriname Embassy, Quinta Serrana, 4a Av, between 7a and 8a Transversal, Altaira, T261 5796. Visa costs US$20, you need 2 photos, it can take up to 1 week. **UK**, Torre Las Mercedes, 3rd floor, Av La Estancia, Chuao, T993 4111 for appointment, emergency number outside office hrs, T0416-262973 (mob) (they can issue a new passport in 5 days, best in the morning), F993 9989, www.britain.org.ve **USA**, C F with C Suapure, Colinas de Valle Arriba, take metro to Chacaíto then taxi, US$5, T977 2011, F977 0843, PO Box 62291, www.embajadausa.org.ve

Medical services Hospital de Clínicas, Av Panteón y Av Alameda, San Bernardino, T574 2011.

Useful addresses DIEX for visa renewal, Av Baralt, El Silencio, T483 2744. **Touring y Automóvil Club de Venezuela**, Torre Phelps, p 15, of A y C, Plaza Venezuela, T781 7481, ask for Sr Oscar Giménez Landínez (treasurer, speaks some English), or Zonaida R Mendoza (Secretary to the Club President).

Don't believe anyone who tells you visa extensions are not available

Around Caracas

The 85,192 ha **Parque Nacional El Avila** forms the northern boundary of Caracas. The green slopes rise steeply from both the city and from the central Caribbean coast. Despite being so close to the capital, the fauna is said to include red howler monkeys, jaguar and puma. There are also several species of poisonous snake. Access to the park is from Caracas where there are several marked entrances along Cota Mil (Avenida Boyacá), which are designed for hikers. Access from the old Caracas-La Guaira road which crosses the park from north to south on the western side was damaged by the heavy rains of December 1999. The Caribbean side of the national park was worst affected, but all parts of the park are open.

Monte Avila
Colour map 1, grid A6

The cable railway (*teleférico*) up Monte Avila from Avenida Perimetral de Maripérez, after years of inaction, reopened in 2001. The modern, eight-passenger cabin, runs 0800-2000 daily. The future of the *Humboldt Hotel* on the summit has not been decided. Camping is possible with permission. A dirt road runs from La Puerta section of San Bernardino to the summit, 45 minutes in four-wheel drive vehicle. A recommended trip is to ride up in a vehicle and hike back down (note that it is cold at the summit, average temperature 13° C).

Listed below are three good places to start a hike in the park. Hikers should go in groups of at least three, from the point of view of both mountain and personal safety (Monte Avila is not a dangerous place, but the occasional thief lurks there). Always take water and something for the cold at altitude. The unfit should not attempt any of the hikes. Full descriptions of the hiking routes are given in the *Venezuela Handbook*.

Pico Naiguatá This is a very strenuous hike. Take the metro to La California, then a bus going up Avenida Sanz, ask for the Centro Comercial El Marqués. From there walk up Avenida Sanz towards Cota Mil (Avenida Boyacá), about four blocks. At the end of Avenida Sanz, underneath the bridge, is the entrance to the Naiguatá trail. In about 40 minutes you reach La Julia *guardaparques* station, where you have to state your destination and pay US$0.50 entrance.

2,765 m

Pico Oriental From the Altamira metro station take a bus to 'La entrada de Sabas Nieves', where the *Tarzilandia* restaurant is. From here a dirt road leads up to the Sabas Nieves *guardaparques* station (about 40 minutes). The path to Pico Oriental starts at the back of Sabas Nieves and is extremely easy to follow.

2,600 m

Hotel Humboldt This is a relatively easy route of three hours. Take the metro bus from Bellas Artes station to El Avila stop, US$0.25; opposite is a grocery. Turn the corner and walk two blocks up towards the mountain. At the top of the street turn left; almost immediately on your right is the park entrance. **NB** This area is not safe before 0800 or after dark. Plenty of people take this route, starting 0830-0900, giving plenty of time to get up and down safely and in comfort.

2,150 m

Agencies The hiking club, **Centro Excursionista de Caracas**, Parcela Zona Verde, C Chivacao con Yare, San Ramón, Aptdo postal 50766, Sabana Grande 1050, T235 3155/985

Venezuela

3210 (Sr Contreras, President), or Sr Barcón (T573 8515), meets Sat 1430, arranges day and weekend hikes, very welcoming; some English and German spoken.

Colonia Tovar

Phone code: 0244
Population: 10,000
Altitude: 1,890 m

This mountain town was founded in 1843 by German immigrants from Kaiserstuhl in the Black Forest; a small museum tells the history of the founding pioneers. ■ *1000-1800, Sat and Sun, and holidays.* They retained their customs and isolation until a paved road reached the settlement in 1963. It is now very touristy, but the blond hair, blue eyes and Schwartzwald-accented German of the inhabitants are still much in evidence. *Tovarenses* make great bread, blackberry jam and bratwurst, and grow strawberries, coffee, garlic, rhubarb and flowers for the Caracas market. Colonia Tovar offers delightful landscapes, mild climate, old architecture and dignified hospitality.

Sleeping and eating There are many hotels, all of which are normally full at weekends. Rates, which are not below our **B** category, include good, German-style food. Half-board prices are usually **AL**. Credit cards are widely accepted. Restaurants: *El Molino*, on C Molino next to the historic old mill (worth a visit), great *jugo de fresas*, wide selection of German dishes, open 0900-1000, 1200-1600, 1800-1900, Mon 0900-1400, highly recommended. Other recommended restaurants: *El Codazzi*, in centre on C Codazzi, traditional German and Hungarian dishes, strudel and biscuits, open 1100-1600, closed Mon and Tue. *Café Munstall*, opposite the church, interesting location in oldest house in Colonia Tovar, pastry and coffee at weekends. Local fruit, vegetables and flowers sold at *Frutería Bergman* next to Lagoven station at east entrance to town; across the street is *Panadería Tovar* for delicious bread; many food stalls on weekends along Av Codazzi.

Transport Road The 1½ hrs' drive up from Caracas on Ruta 4, through Antímano and El Junquito, is easy during the week, but murder on weekends – long traffic jams, difficult to find picnic spots or accommodation, definitely not recommended. It is generally easy to get a lift if there are no buses. Taxi fare for the round trip from Caracas to Colonia Tovar (driver will wait) is about US$30. **Buses:** from Av Sur 9 y El Rosario, next to Nuevo Circo, or, easier, from La Yaguara metro station, to El Junquito (1 hr, US$0.75), then change for Colonia Tovar (1 hr, US$1). *Por puesto* from Plaza Catia or O'Leary (more frequently), Caracas, 1 hr, US$1.75. Alternatively, take a *por puesto* from Plaza Capuchino to El Junquito, then one from there to Colonia Tovar, US$1.75. If changing *por puesto*, make sure the driver stops at the right place. Last bus to Caracas 1800.

From Colonia Tovar, Ruta 4 continues (well-paved but hair-raising) south down the slopes for 34 km to La Victoria on the Caracas – Valencia Highway (see below); bus US$2.50; glorious scenery.

In **San Francisco de Yare** (*Phone code:* 0239; 90 km from Caracas), a celebration is held at Corpus Christi in early June. Some 80 male 'Diablos' of all ages, dressed all in red and wearing horned masks, dance to the sound of their own drums and rattles. From Santa Teresa make a detour to the beautiful and little frequented **Parque Nacional Guatopo** on the road to Altagracia de Orituco (bus from Nuevo Circo marked 'El Popular', US$2.50). You must return to Santa Teresa to continue your journey to Yare. At the Parque Guatopo are various convenient places to picnic on the route through the forest and a number of good nature trails. Take insect repellent. Free camping at Hacienda La Elvira; take jeep from Altagracia de Orituco (US$0.75) and ask to be let off at the turn-off to the Hacienda. A permit must be obtained at the Inparques office, which has some accommodation, or baggage can be stored temporarily while walking in the park.

The Coast –
Central Litoral

The Central Litoral is the name given to the stretch of Caribbean Coast directly north of Caracas. A paved road runs east from Catia La Mar, past the airport and then through the towns of Maiquetía, La Guaira and Macuto. This became the state of

Vargas in January 1999 and in December that year was the focus of Venezuela's worst natural disaster of the 20th century. Prolonged heavy rains on deforested hillsides caused flash floods and landslides, killing and causing to disappear an estimated 26,000 people and leaving 400,000 homeless. The zone's famous beach tourism has been lost as the beaches remain effectively closed. A few hotels are open, but nothing on the pre-1999 scale. It is planned to turn the whole area into a national park.

La Guaira Venezuela's main port dates back to 1567. It achieved its greatest *Colour map 1, grid A6* importance in the 18th century when the Basque Guipuzcoana Company held the royal trading monopoly. Much of the city was severely damaged in the 1999 floods.

Macuto About 5 km east of La Guaira and founded in 1740, Macuto used to be a pleasant alternative to Caracas when arriving or before flying out before 1999's disaster. The coastal promenade (Paseo la Playa) was badly hit, with almost all the hotels closed, **La Guzmanía**, the coastal residence of the President, built by Guzmán Blanco, washed away, and many other old buildings destroyed.

West from Caracas

Caracas

The Central Highlands run through this varied region. North of the highlands is the Caribbean, with secluded coves, popular resorts and two coastal national parks: Morrocoy, which lies offshore, and Los Médanos, around the old city of Coro. Straddling the mountains is the birders' paradise of Parque Nacional Henri Pittier. The great basin in which lies the Lago de Valencia and the industrial towns of Maracay and Valencia is 100 km west of Caracas. The basin, which is only 450 m above sea-level, receives plenty of rain and is one of the most important agricultural areas in the country.

Founded in 1703 and capital of Miranda state, this city is a mixture of skyscrapers and colonial buildings around Plaza Guaicaipuro (statue of the Carib chief who fought the Spaniards here) and Plaza Bolívar, with several attractive parks. Parque El Encanto in the mountains nearby, is reached by a 20-minute ride aboard an 1891 German locomotive and antique carriages from the old Los Teques station, 2 km south of the town beside the highway (it is also the terminus for buses from Caracas); ■ *3 trips on weekdays, 9 at weekends, first 0900, last return 1800, adults US$2.50, children US$1.25 return.*

Los Teques
Phone code: 0212
Colour map 1, grid A6
Population: 200,000
Altitude: 1,180 m
25 km from Caracas

At 24 km beyond Los Teques on the way down into the fertile valleys of Aragua, you can either join the Caracas-Valencia tollway or take the older road through several attractive towns such as La Victoria. Venezuela's oldest bullring is here. Despite the surrounding industrial zones the city retains much of its 18th-century charm; visit the beautiful Nuestra Señora de la Victoria church.

La Victoria
Phone code: 0244
Population: 105,000

The Quinta de Bolívar is at San Mateo, between La Victoria and Maracay. The Liberator spent much of his youth here and the museum is a must for anyone interested in Simón Bolívar. ■ *0800-1200, 1400-1700 except Mon.* The rich San Mateo church is also worth a visit. Soon after San Mateo, Highway 11 leads off south (45 km) to **San Juan de Los Morros**.

San Mateo

Maracay

This is a hot, humid, thriving industrial city. It is the centre of an important agricultural area, and the school and experimental stations of the Ministry of Agriculture are worth visiting. San José festival is on 16-25 March.

In its heyday it was the favourite city of Gen Juan Vicente Gómez (dictator, 1909-35) and some of his most fantastic whims are still there. **Jardín Las Delicias**

Phone code: 0243
Colour map 1, grid A6
Population: 600,000
Altitude: 445 m

Venezuela

(on Avenida Las Delicias, en route to Choroní; take an Ocumare bus from terminal) with its beautiful zoological garden (closed Monday), park and fountain, built for his revels. The **Gómez mausoleum** (C Mariño), built in his honour, has a huge triumphal arch. The heart of the city is **Plaza Girardot**, on which is the attractive, white **Cathedral**, dating back almost to the city's foundation in 1701. There is an interesting collection of prehispanic artefacts in the museum of the **Instituto de Antropología e Historia** on the south side of the plaza. ■ *Tue-Fri 0800-1530, Sat and Sun 0900-1200, free.* The opposite end of the same building has rooms dedicated to Gómez and Bolívar. At the rear end of the building is the **Biblioteca de Historia** whose walls are lined with portraits of Bolívar. **Plaza Bolívar**, said to be the largest such-named plaza in Latin America, is 500 m east. On one side is the **Palacio del Gobierno**, originally the *Hotel Jardín*, built by Gómez in 1924. Also here are the **Palacio Legislativo** and the modern **opera house** (1973).

Sleeping & eating

Budget hotels are located in the streets around Plaza Girardot

AL *Italo*, Av Las Delicias, Urb La Soledad, T232 1576, www.hotelitalo.com.ve A/c, 4-star, on bus route, very pleasant, small rooftop pool, good Italian restaurant, *El Fornaio*. Recommended. **B** *Posada El Limón*, Calle de Pinal 64, El Limón suburb, near Parque Nacional Henri Pittier, T283 4925, T0414-444 1915 (mob), cariben@telcel.net.ve Dutch owned, relaxed, family atmosphere, a/c, laundry, pool, restaurant, internet, excursions. **C** *Princesa Plaza*, Av Miranda Este entre Fuerzas Aéreas y Av Bermúdez, T232 2052, www.hotelprincesaplaza.com Commercial hotel, 1 block east of Plaza Bolívar, convenient, inexpensive restaurant. **C** *Caroní*, Ayacucho Norte 197, Bolívar, T554 4465. A/c, hot showers, comfortable. Recommended. **D** *San Luis*, Carabobo Sur 13, off the main shopping street. Well-kept, welcoming. **D** *Central*, Av Santos Michelena 6, T245 2834. Safe and central.

Many excellent restaurants in the Av Las Delicias area; many are American style drive-up, fast-food outlets. *Biergarten Park*, on east side of Plaza Bolívar, a pleasant, covered terrace with bar and restaurant, some German and Italian specialities, cheap and good. *El Indio Maecho*, Av 10 de Diciembre 114. Good cheap food, entertaining owner. Recommended. Many reliable Chinese restaurants and *loncherías*, *tascas* and inexpensive restaurants in the streets around Plaza Girardot.

Transport

Airport is 5 km from centre
Bus station is 2 km SE of centre, taxi US$3

Air *Avior* flights to Maracaibo, Mérida and Porlamar. **Buses** *Por puesto* marked 'Terminal' for the bus station and 'Centro' for the town centre (Plaza Girardot). To **Maracaibo, *Expresos los Llanos***, US$14. **Valencia**, US$0.75, 1 hr. **Caracas**, US$1.50, 1½ hrs, *por puesto* US$5. **Barinas**, US$5.50, 7 hrs, *Expresos Los Llanos*. **Mérida** at 0800 and 2000, 1'2 hrs; **Ciudad Bolívar**, US$15, 10 hrs. To **Coro**, US$9, 7¾ hrs. Oriente destinations including **Margarita** served by *Expresos Ayacucho*, T234 9765, daily departure to Margarita, 1400, US$25 (including first class ferry crossing). Many buses to every part of the country, most leave 0600-0900 and 1800-2300.

Directory

Banks *Italcambio* (American Express), Av Aragua con C Bermúdez, C C Maracay Plaza, loc 10K, T235 6867. *Cambio* in *Air March* travel agency, ground floor of CADA Centro Comercial, Av 19 de Abril, Local 20, 2 blocks north of Plaza Girardot. 2.5 commission. **Communications** Internet On Av 19 de Abril, opposite bullring and *Casa de Cultura* (art and cultural exhibitions, 2 blocks northwest of Plaza Bolívar).

Parque Nacional Henri Pittier

A land of steep rugged hills and tumbling mountain streams, the 107,800 ha park rises from sea-level in the north to 2,430 m at Pico Cenizo, descending to 450 m towards the Lago de Valencia. Established in 1937, this park is the oldest in the country. It extends from the north of Maracay to the Caribbean, excluding the coastal towns of Ocumare, Cata and Choroní, and south to the valleys of Aragua and the villages of Vigírima, Mariara and Turmero. The dry season runs from December-March and the rainy season (although still agreeable) is from April-November. The variation in altitude gives great variety of vegetation, including lower and upper cloud forests. For further information refer to *Parque Nacional de Henri Pittier – Lista de Aves*, by Miguel Lentino and Mary Lou Goodwin, 1993. ■ *Park entrance fee US$0.65 pp.*

Two paved roads cut through the Park. The Ocumare road climbs to the 1,128 m high Portachuelo pass, guarded by twin peaks (38 km from Maracay). At the pass is Rancho Grande, the uncompleted palace/hotel Gómez was building when he died (in a state of disrepair). It is close to the migratory routes, September and October are the best months. There are many trails in the vicinity. ■ *Permits to visit the park and walk the trails near the Rancho Grande biological research station are available here. There are plenty of beds for those wishing to stay at the station, US$5 pp per night, use of kitchen facilities, take warm sleeping bag, candles and food; nearest supplies at El Limón, 20 km before Rancho Grande.* Another option is El Cocuy Mountain Refuge, **F** *for accommodation only,* **A** *full board. T0416-747 3833, F0243-991 1106, www.geocities.com/elcocuytours/index Sleeping in hammocks, tours arranged with bi-lingual Spanish/ English guides.*

■ *Getting there: A taxi can be hired at Maracay for a day's outing in the park for about US$40 (bargain hard). Buses depart from Maracay Terminal; pay full fare to Ocumare or hitch from El Limón Alcabala.*

578 bird species
7 different eagles
and 8 kites
43 of all species
in Venezuela
5.4 different species
for every sq km.
One of the highest
densities recorded
in the world

The Aragua Coast

The road to the coast from Rancho Grande goes through **Ocumare de la Costa** (*Population*: 6,140, 48 km from Maracay), to La Boca de Ocumare and **El Playón** (hotels and restaurants at both places); bus from Maracay, 2-2½ hours, US$2. A few kilometres east is **Bahía de Cata**, now overdeveloped, particularly at the west end, while the smaller beach at **Catita** is reached by fishing boat ferries (10 minutes, US$1). In Cata town (5 km inland, *population* of town and beach 3,120) is the small colonial church of San Francisco; devil dancers here fulfil an ancient vow by dancing non-stop through the morning of 27 July each year. **Sleeping AL** *De La Costa Eco-Lodge*, Ocumare de la Costa, T/F993 1986, dlcecolodge@hotmail.com With bath, outdoor bar serving food, excursions, tours included in price, equipment hire, specialist bilingual guides. ■ *Por puesto to Cata from Ocumare US$1; from El Playón US$0.35 from plaza.* Cuyagua beach, unspoilt, is 23 km further on at the end of the road. Good surfing, dangerous rips for swimmers. Devil dancers here too, on movable date in July or August.

To Cata & Cuyagua

The second road through the Parque Nacional Henri Pittier is spectacular and goes over a more easterly pass (1,830 m), to Santa Clara de Choroní, a beautiful colonial town. The Fiesta de San Juan on 31 May is worth seeing.

To Choroní

Choroní is a good base for walking in the park. There are numerous opportunities for exploring the unmarked trails, many of them originate in picturesque spots such as the river pools, 'pozos', of El Lajao (beware of the dangerous whirlpool), and Los Colores, 6 km above Choroní. Other recommended 'pozos' are La Virgen, 10 km from Choroní and La Nevera, 11 km away. **Sleeping A** *Choroní*, colonial building on plaza, T0212-977 1234 (Caracas). Bed and breakfast, dinners available, basic, attractive, small, shared bath. **B** *Hacienda La Aljorra*, T0212-237 7462 (Caracas). Breakfast and dinner included, 9 colonial rooms in 62 ha of wooded hillside. **B** *La Gran Posada*, 5 km north of Choroní on a steep hillside above Maracay road, T0243-991 1207. Neat, pleasant bar and restaurant, short walks in the park. ■ *Maracay-Choroní, beautiful journey, every 2 hrs from around 0630-1700, more at the weekend, US$2, 2½ hrs.*

Puerto Colombia

Just beyond Choroní is the fishing village of Puerto Colombia, with the dazzling white beach of Playa Grande, five minutes' walk across the river. Bus journeys start and end here. At weekends the beach is crowded and littered; if swimming, beware the strong undertow. The usually deserted three beaches of Diario are a 50-minute walk.

Nowhere to make international phone calls in Pto Colombia

Venezuela

Excursions Many fishing boats for hire in the harbour, US$55 for a day trip to one of the several nearby beaches. Launches to Cepe, 30 minutes east, US$10-15 per person depending on numbers, boats usually take 6-10 people. Beautiful unspoiled beach and accommodation at **A** *Posada Puerto Escondido*. Includes three meals, drinks and boat from Puerto Colombia, four clean, spacious rooms, with bath, hot water and fan, peaceful and homely atmosphere, owner Freddy Fisher organizes fishing and scuba diving trips, with guide and equipment to explore the only bit of coral on this stretch of the Venezuelan coast.

Sleeping & eating Recommended hotels are: **A** *Mesón Xuchytlan*, T991 1234. Beautiful, immaculate rooms, a/c, good bathrooms, huge buffet breakfast. **A** *Posada Pittier*, on road to Choroní, T/F0243-991 1028, or Caracas 0212-573 7848, F577 4410. 8 small but immaculate rooms, a/c, good meals, Sat night add US$10, helpful, garden. **B** *Posada La Parchita*, near *Posada Los Guanches* (see below). Including breakfast, 5 rooms set around a lovely patio, very nice. **D** *Posada Alfonso*, T991 1037. German owner, quiet, hammocks, laundry facilities. **B** *Costa Brava*, near Malecón, T/F991 1057. Cheaper without bath, basic, ceiling fans, laundry facilities, good food, English spoken, family-run. **C** *Lemon Tree 2*. German run, clean, nice atmosphere, internet, English spoken. **D** *La Montañita*, near Malecón, malecon@telcel.net.ve Popular, nice courtyard, charming owners, packages available (**B** including all meals). **D** *Habitaciones Playa Grande*, above *Tasca Bahía*, T991 1054. With a/c, **E** with shared bath and fan, 6 rooms. **D** *Hostal Colonial*, opposite the bus stop, T991 1087, or 0212-963 2155, hcolonial@hotmail.com With fan, laundry facilities, German owner, good value. **D-E** *Posada Los Guanches*, C Trino Ranchel, off C Colón near plaza, T991 1209. Costs more at weekends, 9 rooms, cold water, fan, good. **E** *La Abuela*, near bridge to Playa Grande. Basic, fan. Camping possible on the beach; beware of theft.

For eating, try **Araguaney**, near bridge to Playa Grande, large portions, breakfast for US$1, main gringo hangout but poor food and service, changes cash at poor rates and gives cash against credit cards, US$600 maximum, passport required. Cash and TCs can also be changed at the same rate at *licorería* on opposite side beside the bridge. *El Abuelo*, just before bridge to Playa Grande, very good food, prices OK.

Transport Buses from Maracay bus terminal leave from platform 5. Taxi from Maracay US$20 for 4. Buses for **Maracay** depart from the park near the police checkpoint every hour or so from 0500, last one at 1700, US$4.

Valencia

Phone code: 0241
Colour map 1, grid A5
Population: 1,350,000
Altitude: 480 m
Mean temperature: 24°C

Founded in 1555, the capital of Carabobo State is Venezuela's third largest city, the centre of its most developed agricultural region, and the most industrialized. It stands on the west bank of the Río Cabriales, which empties into the Lago de Valencia (352 sq km, the second largest in the country, with no outlet, consequently it is polluted). It is 50 km to the west of Maracay, via a road through low hills thickly planted with citrus, coffee and sugar. The valley is hot and humid; annual rainfall, 914 mm. In late March is Valencia Week, while on 15 November the Patrocinales de NS del Perpetuo Socorro are celebrated (one week Valencia Fair), with bullfights.

Sights
Most of the interesting sights are closed on Mon

The **Cathedral**, built in 1580, is on the east side of **Plaza Bolívar**. The statue of the Virgen del Socorro (1550) in the left transept is the most valued treasure; on the second Sunday in November (during the Valencia Fair) it is paraded with a richly jewelled crown. ■ *Daily 0630-1130, 1500-1830, Sun 0630-1200, 1500-1900*. See also **El Capitolio** (Páez, between Díaz Moreno y Montes de Oca), the **Teatro Municipal** (Colombia y Avenida Carabobo), the old **Carabobo University** building and the handsome **Plaza de Toros** (south end of Avenida Constitución beyond the ring road) which is the second largest in Latin America after Mexico City. At Páez y Boyacá is the magnificent former **residence of General Páez** (hero of the Carabobo battle), now a museum. ■ *Mon-Fri, free.* Equally attractive is the **Casa de Célis** (1766), which houses the Museo de Arte e Historia, C 98 y Avenida 104, with precolumbian exhibits. ■ *Tue-Sat 0800-1400.* Like its Spanish namesake, Valencia is famous for its oranges.

Near Valencia are several groups of petroglyphs: most important is **Parque** **Excursions** **Nacional Piedras Pintadas** where lines of prehispanic stone slabs, many bearing swirling glyphs, march up the ridges of Cerro Pintado. The new Museo Parque Arqueológico Piedra Pintada, at the foot of Cerro Las Rosas, contains 165 examples of rock art and menhirs (parking, café). ■ *Navy-blue buses run to Vigírima 20 km northeast of Valencia at regular intervals (US$1), ask to get off at the 'Cerro Pintado' turnoff. Driving from Vigírima, turn left at a small blue 'Cadafe Tronconero' sign, then a further 3 km.*

Other extensive ancient petroglyphs have been discovered at **La Taimata** near Güigüe, 34 km east of Valencia on the lake's southern shore. There are more sites along the west shore, and on the rocks by the Río Chirgua, reached by a 10-km paved road from Highway 11 (turn north at La Mona Maraven gas station), 50 km west of Valencia. About 5 km past Chirgua, at the Hacienda Cariaprima, is the country's only geoglyph, a remarkable 35 m-tall humanoid figure carved into a steep mountain slope at the head of the valley.

At 30 km southwest of Valencia on the highway to San Carlos is the site of the **Carabobo** battlefield, an impressive historical monument surrounded by splendid gardens. The view over the field from the *mirador* where the Liberator directed the battle in 1814 is impressive. Historical explanations Wednesday, weekends and holidays. ■ *Buses to Carabobo leave from bottom of Av Bolívar Sur y C 75, or from Plaza 5 de Julio, US$0.25, ask for Parque Carabobo (1¼ hrs).*

Some 18 km from Valencia, the road passes the decaying spa of **Las** *Population: 1,350* **Trincheras**, which has three baths (hot, hotter, very hot), a mud bath and a *2nd hottest sulphur* Turkish bath; delightful setting. ■ *Facilities open 0800-1800 daily, US$1.50. Fre-* *springs in the world* *quent buses from Valencia.* *(98° C)*

AL pp *Hacienda Guataparo*, 20 mins from centre. Owned by Vestey family, 9,000 ha peace- **Sleeping** ful farm, all meals, riding and mountain bikes, good birding, must be booked in advance **& eating** through *Last Frontiers*, UK (see Tour operators in Essentials page 24.) **B** *Continental*, Av Boyacá 101-70, T857 1004. Restaurant, good value. There are many hotels across the price range on Av Bolívar, but it is a long avenue, so don't attempt to walk it. **B** *Marconi*, Av Bolívar 141-65, T823 4843. A/c, helpful, safe, laundry, recommended (next to a petrol station), take bus or colectivo from bus station to stop after 'El Elevado' bridge. **C** *Carabobo*, C Libertad 100-37, esq Plaza Bolívar, T858 8860. OK, with large a/c lobby. **E** *Caracas*, Plaza Bolívar. Tatty but spacious, with bath, ice water. For eating, try *Fego*, Av Bolívar 102-75, recommended. *El Bosque*, opposite *Hotel Marconi*, cheap. *La Rinconada*, Plaza Bolívar, recommended, open Sun. *Caballo Blanco*, Av 97 Farriar, cheap and good food, clean, well-lit, Italian run.

Air *Aeropostal* flights daily except Sat to **Caracas**, also to **Barcelona, Maracaibo, Miami** **Transport** (daily), **Porlamar** and **San Antonio.** The airport is 6 km southeast of centre. *Aserca* flies to Caracas daily, and Aruba. *Santa Bárbara* flies to Aruba, Barcelona, Barquisimeto and Mérida. *Servensa* daily to Miami. *Dutch Caribbean Airlines* to Curaçao. **Buses** Terminal is 4 km east of centre, part of shopping mall *Big-Low* (24-hr restaurants). Entry to platforms by *ficha* (token), US$0.05. Left luggage store. Minibus to centre, frequent and cheap, but slow and confusing route at peak times; taxi from bus station to centre, US$4 (official drivers wear identity badges). To **Caracas**, US$3, *por puesto* US$6, *Autoexpresos Ejecutivos* (T0414-940 5010 (mob)), US$10, 8-9 a day. **Mérida**, 10-12 hrs, US$15; to **San Cristóbal**, 10 hrs, US$17.50. **Barquisimeto**, US$3.80, 3 hrs. **Maracay**, 1 hr, US$0.75. **Puerto Cabello**, US$1.25, 1 hr. **Tucacas**, US$2.50, or US$5 by frequent *por puesto* service. To **Coro** US$7.25, 4½ hrs. To **Ciudad Bolívar**, US$15, 10 hrs.

Venezuela

Directory   **Banks** *Corp Banca*, C 100 y Moreno. Amex TCs changed. *Italcambio*, Av Bolívar Norte, Edif Talia, loc 2, T824 9043. Amex travel services, Visa TCs, a long way from centre in Urbanización Los Sauces, get off bus at junction with C 132; also at airport. **Communications** Internet: *Web Universe*, Edif Reda, Las 4 Avenidas de Prebo, Zona Norte. Telephone: *CANTV*, Plaza Bolívar, for international calls. **Consulates** British Honorary Consul, Agropecuaria Flora, C143 No 100-227, Urb La Ceiba, T823 8401, agrflora@viptel.com

Puerto Cabello, 55 km from Valencia, is Venezuela's second most important port (*Phone code*: 0242, *Population*: 185,000). The **Museo de Historia** is in one of the few remaining colonial houses (1790) on C Los Lanceros (No 43), in the tangle of small streets between the Plaza Bolívar and the seafront. ■ *Mon-Fri 0800-1200, 1500-1800, Sat-Sun 0800-1200*. A recommended hike is on the old, cobbled **Camino Real** from Valencia to the village of San Esteban, 8 km inland from Puerto Cabello. To the east is **Bahía de Patanemo**, a beautiful horseshoe-shaped beach shaded by palms (**C** *La Churuata*, T617535, family-run hotel, without bath, English, French, Spanish, Italian spoken, pool, horses, excellent food and drink, local excursions, highly recommended).

Parque Nacional Morrocoy

Colour map 1, grid A5
Hundreds of coral reefs, palm-studded islets, secluded beaches

The largest, cleanest and most popular of the islands within the park is **Cayo Sombrero**. It's very busy at weekends but has some deserted beaches, with trees to sling a hammock. **Playuela** is beautiful and better for snorkelling (beware of mosquitoes in the mangrove swamps), while **Playa del Sol** has no good beach and no palm trees. **Bocaseca** is more exposed to the open sea than other islands and thus has fewer

Playa Sur and other areas are not safe; muggings reported

mosquitoes. **Cayo Borracho** is one of the nicest islands. With appropriate footwear it is possible to walk between some of the islands. Calm waters here are ideal for water-skiing and snorkelling while scuba diving is best suited to beginners. As much of the coral was destroyed in 1996, advanced divers will find little of interest.

Adjoining the park to the north is a vast nesting area for scarlet ibis, flamingoes and herons, the **Cuare Wildlife Sanctuary**. Most of the flamingoes are in and around the estuary next to Chichiriviche, which is too shallow for boats but you can walk there or take a taxi. Birds are best watched early morning or late afternoon.

Camping   You may camp on the islands but must first make a reservation with **Inparques** (National Parks), T800 8487, Mon-Sun 0800-2000; reserve at least 8 working days in advance giving all details; US$2.50 pp per night, 7 nights maximum, pay in full in advance (very complicated procedure). Very few facilities and no fresh water; Cayo Sombrero and Paiclas have restaurants, Boca Seca has a small café (closed Mon); Sombrero, Playa Azul and Paiclas have ecological toilets. At weekends and holidays it is very crowded and litter-strewn (beware rats).

Transport   **From Tucacas**: prices per boat range from US$20 return to Paiclas to US$40 return to Cayo
See below for description of Tucacas and Chichiriviche Sombrero (maximum 7 per boat). Ticket office is to the left of the car entrance to the Park. Recommended boatmen are Orlando and Pepe. **From Chichiriviche**: prices per boat vary according to distance; eg, US$15 to Cayo Muerto, US$50 to Cayo Sombrero. A 3-4 hr trip is US$50 per boat; 5-6 hr trip US$70 (maximum 8 per boat); bargaining essential. There are 2 ports; one close to the centre and Playa Sur. The latter has a ticket system which is supposed to guarantee that you will not be cheated and that you will be picked up on time for return trip.

Tucacas   This is a hot, busy, dirty and expensive town, where bananas and other fruit are loaded
Phone code: 0259 for Curaçao and Aruba. **Sleeping** The only accommodation **within the park** is
Colour map 1, grid A5 **AL** pp *Villa Mangrovia* on the Lizardo Spit between Tucacas and Chichiriviche, 3 rooms, excellent food and service, charming owner, book through *Last Frontiers*, UK (01296-658650) or *Journey Latin America*, UK (T020-8747 8315/0161-832 1441). **B** *Manaure*, Av Silva, T812 1011. A/c, hot water, pool, good restaurant. **D** *La Suerte* on main street, T812 1332. A/c, **E** with fan, small shop. Next door is **E** *Las Palmas*.

With shower, basic, fan, kitchen and laundry facilities, helpful, cheap boat trips to islands. Recommended. Cheap accommodation is difficult to find, especially in high season and at weekends. **Camping** Gas available in Tucacas or Puerto Cabello.

Diving: equipment can be hired from near the harbour. *Submatur*, C Ayacucho 6, T812 0082. Owner Mike Osborn, 4-day PADI course US$330, 1 day trip 2 dives US$65 (US$45 with own equipment); also rents rooms, **E**, fan and cooking facilities. **Bicycles**: can be hired in town. There's *Unibanca*, which gives cash advance on credit cards only. Hotels and travel agents will change money but at very low rates, if they have enough cash. ■ *Frequent por puesto from Valencia, US$5, bus US$2.50; Coro, US$5.*

A few kilometres beyond Tucacas, towards Coro, is this popular and expensive beach resort, which gets very crowded at holidays and weekends. Chichiriviche is gaining a reputation for rip-offs and robberies. **Sleeping** Recommended hotels: **A** *La Garza*, Av Principal, T818 6711. Attractive, pool, restaurant, with breakfast, comfortable, popular, post box in lobby, daily collection, changes cash. **C** *Capri*, C Zamora, T818 6026. Near docks, shower, fan or a/c, pleasant, Italian owner, good restaurant and supermarket. **D** *Posada La Perrera*, C Riera, near centre, 150 m from bus stop. Quiet, fan, laundry facilities, patio, hammocks, luggage stored, Italian owner, tours arranged, very good. **D** *Res Delia*, C Mariño 30, 1 block from Gregoria, T818 6089. Including breakfast, shared bath, organizes tours. **D** *Posada Villa Gregoria*, C Mariño, 1 block north of the bus stop behind the large water tank. Spanish-run, very helpful, good value, fan, laundry facilities, parking. **E** *Posada Alemania*, Cementos Coro, T815 0912, posadaalemania@cantv.net German-run, runs tours, rents snorkel gear, 200 m from Playa Sur, nice garden. **E** *Morena's Place*, Sector Playa Norte, 10 mins walk from the bus stop, T/F815 0936. Beautifully decorated house, fan, hammocks, hepful hosts, English spoken. Recommended. **Eating** *Cafetín*, Av Zamora 10, 2 blocks from beach. Argentine-run, good fruit juices, internet, safe, very helpful. *Taverna de Pablo*, opposite Banco Industrial. Good pizzas, seafood etc. *Veracruz*, at top of main street overlooking beach. Good fish.

Diving: *Centro de Buceo Caribe*, Playa Sur. Runs PADI courses for US$360, 1 day diving trip US$65, rents equipment, rooms for rent, **D**, with cooking facilities.

■ *Getting there: To Puerto Cabello, frequent por puestos, 2 hrs, US$3.50; to Barquisimeto, 3 hrs; to Valera, 9 hrs. Direct buses from Valencia or take bus from Morón to Coro and get out at turnoff, 1½ hrs, US$1.75.*

Chichiriviche
Phone code: 0259
Population: 7,000

Coro

Founded in 1527, Coro is clean and well kept and the colonial part is lovely with many beautiful buildings and shaded plazas. The **Cathedral**, a national monument, was begun in 1583. **San Clemente** church has a wooden cross in the plaza in front, said to mark the site of the first mass said in Venezuela; it is believed to be the country's oldest such monument. It is undergoing reconstruction. There are several intseresting colonial houses: **Los Arcaya**, Zamora y Federación, one of the best examples of 18th-century architecture (see Museo de Cerámica below); **Los Senior**, Talavera y Hernández, where Bolívar stayed in 1827; **Las Ventanas de Hierro**, Zamora y Colón, built in 1764/65, now a museum of period furniture. ■ *Tue-Sat 0900-1200 and 1500-1800, Sun 0900-1300, US$0.20.* Opposite is the **Casa del Tesoro**, an art gallery showing local artists' work. ■ *Free.* The **Jewish cemetery**, on C 23 de Enero esq C Zamora, is the oldest on the continent.

The **Museo de Coro 'Lucas Guillermo Castillo'**, C Zamora opposite Plaza San Clemente, is in an old monastery, and has a good collection of church relics, recommended. ■ *Tue-Sat 0900-1200,1500-1800, Sun 0900-1400, US$0.20.* **Museo de Cerámica**, housed in Los Arcaya (see above), small but interesting, beautiful garden. ■ *Tue-Sat 0900-1200,1500-1800, Sun 0900-1400,US$0.10.*

Phone code: 0268
Colour map 1, grid A5
Population: 158,760
Mean temperature: 28°C
177 km from Tucacas

Venezuela

Excursions Coro is surrounded by sand dunes, **Los Médanos de Coro**, which form a **national park**. The place is guarded by police and generally safe to visit but stay close to the entrance and on no account wander off across the dunes. Kiosk at entrance sells drinks and snacks; open till 2400. ■ *Getting there: Take bus marked 'Carabobo' from Avenida Falcón, it goes past the road leading to the Médanos on Av Independencia (look out for sign saying Santa Ana de Coro); from here walk 500 m to entrance, or take a taxi.*

On the road to the town's port, **La Vela de Coro**, near the turnoff, is the **Jardín Botánico Xerofito Dr León Croisart**, which has plants from Africa, Australia, etc. ■ *Very interesting, guided tours in Spanish Mon-Fri 1430-1730, Sat 1000-1500, Sun 0830-1200, free. Take Vela bus from corner of C Falcón, opposite Banco Coro, and ask to be let off at Pasarela del Jardín Botánico – the bridge over the road.*

Sleeping & eating
AL-A *Miranda Cumberland*, Av Josefa Camejo, opposite old airport, T252 3322, www.hotelescumberland.com Beautiful hotel, good value, restaurant, lovely swimming pool. **C** *Falcón*, Av Los Médanos, T251 6076. A/c, fridge, good restaurant, 15 mins walk to centre. **C** *Intercaribe*, Av Manaure entre Zamora y Urdaneta, T251 1844. Expensive food, good, pool, a/c. Recommended. **D** *Coro*, Av Independencia, ½ block from Av Los Médanos, T251 3421. Helpful, a/c, accepts credit cards. **D** *Zamora*, on C Zamora, 2 blocks from Av Manaure, T251 6005. With cold water but no shortages, a/c, TV, huge rooms with table and chairs, modern. **E** pp *Colonial*, Paseo Talavera. Beside the cathedral, with bath, a/c, OK value. **G** pp *El Gallo*, Federación 26, T252 9481. French owned, relaxed atmosphere, courtyard with hammocks, use of kitchen, see Eric for tours. Recommended. **Camping** About 30 km west of Coro at *La Cumara*, nice, good beach and dunes, US$1.20 per person.

Restaurants Mid-range: *Don Luis*, opposite airport, near *Miranda Cumberland*. Good fish. Recommended. *Mersi*, C Toledo 36A, off C Zamora, 1 block down from *Hotel Venezia*. Good pizzas. Recommended. *Pasta della Nonna*, C Falcón. Varied menu, good food. **Cheap:** *Chupulún*, Av Manaure esq C Monzón. Recommended for lunch, homemade *chicha*. *La Colmea*, Comercio, between Garcés and Buchivaca. Mexican food, good, small portions, patio. *Makokas Café*, on the boulevard between Plaza Falcón and Cathedral. Recommended for breakfast. *Dulzura y algo más*, on corner of Paseo Alameda. Good ice cream and typical sweets. *Panadería Costa Nova*, Av Manaure, opposite *Hotel Intercaribe*. Good bread and pastries, poor coffee.

Festivals 26 Jul, Coro Week. 9-12 Oct, state fair. 24-25 Dec, *Tambor Coriano* and *Parranda de San Benito* (Coro, La Vela and Puerto Cumarebo). Aug Regatta, Curaçao to La Vela, competitors from USA, Holland, Caribbean take part, ask at Capitanía (Port Captain's office) for information.

Tour operators *Kuriana Travel*, C Zamora, opposite Cathedral, Edif Avila, p 2, oficina 2B, T251 3055. Local tours with English-speaking guide; ask for Mercedes Medina, who has an excellent campsite nearby (*Llano Largo*), highly recommended, specializing in ecotourism. *Aeromar*, C Ciencias, CC Miranda, local 4, T251 3187, tremont1@cantv.net

Coro

Sleeping
1 Miranda Cumberland

Eating
1 Dulzura y algo más

Air Airport is 10 mins walk from centre; good restaurant on 1st floor, no money changing facilities. Flights to Caracas with *Avior*. Ask at airport for details of private flights to Curaçao (see also Las Piedras, below). **Buses** Buses to terminal go up C Falcón, US$0.17, taxi US$2. To/from **Caracas** US$15-20, 10 hrs; **Maracaibo**, US$7, 4½ hrs, *por puesto* US$14; **Tucacas**, US$5, 3 hrs; **Punto Fijo**, *por puesto* US$2. *Expreso Occidente* has its own terminal on Av Manaure entre Libertad y Monzón, T251 2356, daily bus to San Cristóbal, 1900, 12 hrs, US$18, also to Caracas, Maracaibo, Valencia, Punto Fijo. **Sea** The port of La Vela de Coro is called Muaco, 3 km east of town. Ferry services to Aruba resumed in Mar 2002. The *Josefa Camejo* sails Thu-Mon 0700, 3 hrs (returns from Aruba 1100), VIP class US$90 return, ordinary US$70, cars US$150. For details contact *Maduro Travel*, Rockefellerstraat 1, Oranjestad, Aruba, T011-297-825995, F011-297-826676, travel@selmaduro.com

Banks *Banco Unión*, C Churuguara, Visa ATM. Try hotels and travel agents for cash and TCs; eg *Hotel Sahara*, C 20, 1 block from Av Manaure, and *Kuriana Travel* (see above). *CorpBanca*, C Zamora, same building as *Hotel Zamora*. Changes Amex TCs without commission. **Communications** Internet: *El Dish* Punta del Sol p 1, C Falcon y Av Maure. US$2 per half hour. **Telephone:** *CANTV* is in the very fine Casa de las 100 Ventanas, has internet; international calls from the Centro de Monedas on Plaza Sucre, opposite the jail. **Tourist offices** On Paseo Alameda, English spoken, helpful, free maps. Office at airport will help to find a hotel. See the website www.coroweb.com, in Spanish, English and French.

Paraguaná Peninsula

This area is a must for windsurfers and is a great place for walking and fla-mingo-spotting. The western side of the peninsula is industrialized, with oil refiner-ies at Cardón and Amuay connected by pipeline to the Lago de Maracaibo oilfields. The main town is **Punto Fijo**, a busy, unappealing place. 5 km away is the residential area of **Judibana**, a much nicer place to stay, with shopping centre, cinema and res-taurants. Beaches around Los Taques are at least 30 minutes north of Punto Fijo, many are accessible by car, few visitors, good camping but no shade or facilities.

**Around
Punto Fijo**
Phone code: 0269
Colour map 1, grid A5
Population: 125,000

Sleeping and eating Punto Fijo: D *Comercio*, Av Bolívar with C Carnevali, near terminal, T246 5430. With a/c, good *panadería* opposite. Highly recommended. **E** *Miami*, C Falcón entre Av México y Bolivia, T245 8532. Recommended. A recommended and cheap restau-rant is *Colonial*, C Libertad entre Colombia y Ecuador. **Judibana: C** *Jardín*, on Av Mariscal y C Falcón, near airport, T246 1727. A/c, adequate rooms, pool, restaurant, accepts credit cards, changes US$ cash. **C** *Luigi*, C 10 next to Banco de Venezuela, T246 0970. A/c, pleasant, good restaurant, changes US$ cash, accepts credit cards.

Transport Air: Airport is at **Las Piedras**: *por puestos* from C Garcés y Av Bolívar; taxi from Punto Fijo US$6; from Coro US$40. 8 flights a day to **Aruba**, various companies. Domestic flights to **Caracas** and **Maracaibo**. **Buses** Terminal on C Peninsular entre Colombia y Ecuador; *por puestos* to **Pueblo Nuevo**, **Adícora**, **Coro**, **Valencia** and **Maracaibo**. To **Maracay**, **Barquisimeto**, **Barinas**, **Mérida**, **Maracaibo**, **Puerto La Cruz** and **Caracas**: *Expresos Occidente*, on C Comercio entre Ecuador y Bolivia; *Expresos San Cristóbal*, C Carnevali just behind *Hotel Comercio*; *Expresos Alianza*, on Av Colombia between Carnevali and Democracia.

Directory Banks: *Corp Banca*, Av Bolívar y C Zamora. Only place to get cash on Visa or MasterCard. *Banco Mercantil*, Av Bolívar y C Girardot. Changes Citicorp TCs. *Casa Fukayama*, Av Bolívar entre C Altagracia y Girardot. Changes US$ cash. **Communications** *CANTV* at C Falcón y Av México. *Ipostel* at C Páez y Av Panamá, collection every 10 days. **Consulates** Dutch Consul in Judibana at Urb La Laguna, C Mucubaji 38, Roque Hernández, T460430, open weekdays 1600-1700.

This is a quiet little resort on the east side. The beaches are very windswept and not great but Adícora is a good base for exploring the peninsula. There are three wind-surfing schools in town.

Cerro Santa Ana (830 m) is the only hill on the peninsula and commands spec-tacular views. ■ *Entrance is at El Moruy; take bus to Pueblo Nuevo (0730-0800),*

Adícora
A must for windsurfers

then take one to Punto Fijo and ask to be dropped off at the entrance to Santa Ana. From the plaza walk back to the signpost for Pueblo Nuevo and take the dirt road going past a white building; 20 m to the left is Restaurant La Hija. Walk 1 km through scrubby vegetation (watch out for dogs) to the Inparques *office (closed Mon-Fri but busy at weekends). Register here before attempting the steep 3-hr climb. It's safer to go at weekends.*

Laguna Boca de Caño (also known as Laguna Tiraya) is a nature reserve north of Adícora, inland from Supi, along a dirt track normally fit for all vehicles. Bird life here is abundant, particularly flamingoes. It is the only mangrove zone on the east side of the peninsula. **Sleeping C** *Posada Kritzburger*, on Malecón. Fan, German owners, no single rooms, good restaurant. Recommended. **D** *Posada La Caratoña*, C Comercio, 1 block from beach. Clean, full of mosquitos, owner organizes boat trips. ■ *There are several buses daily to and from Coro, from 0630-1830, US$1.25, 50 mins; to and from Pueblo Nuevo and Punto Fijo, several daily from 0600-1730.*

Sierra de San Luis

Colour map 1, grid A5

A paradise for nature lovers and hikers, with tropical forest, caves and waterfalls

South of Coro, on the road to Barquisimeto, the Sierra includes the **Parque Nacional Juan C Falcón**. The picturesque village of **Curimagua** is best for visiting the park; jeeps leave from Coro terminal, US$2. The lovely colonial town of **Cabure** is the capital of the Sierra. Jeeps leave from Coro terminal, US$2.75. A few kilometres up the road is a huge series of waterfalls, Cataratas de Hueque. **The Spanish Road** is a fantastic three-hour walk through orange groves and tropical forest from Curimagua to Cabure. Take water. Ask at any of the hotels listed below.

Sleeping Curimagua: **E-F** *Finca El Monte*, 5 km from the village. Run by a Swiss couple on an ecological basis, hot water, meals, Ernesto takes tours round the park. Highly recommended. Also *Falconese* and *Apolo* (both **C**, restaurant, run tours in park) and *El Trapichito* (**D**, 2 km outside Curimagua, good). **Cabure**: 20 mins uphill from village is **D** *Hotel El Duende*. A beautiful old posada, restaurant. Recommended. In town are **D** *Camino Viejo*, and **E** *La Montaña*. Also restaurants, bars, bakery, supermarket, pharmacy.

Barquisimeto

Phone code: 0251
Colour map 1, grid A5
Population: 900,000
Altitude: 565 m
Mean temperature: 25°C

Venezuela's fourth largest city was largely destroyed by an earthquake in 1812, but is a nice enough place to spend a few days when visiting the area. Many fascinating corners have been preserved and a law prohibiting demolition of older buildings means that more are being restored. The **Museo de Barquisimeto**, at Avenida 15 between C 25 and 26, displays the town's history, also contemporary art. ■ *Tue-Fri 0900-1700, Sat-Sun 1000-1700, free.* More old buildings are a block away around **Plaza Jacinto Lara**. The **San Francisco church** faces the plaza. On the opposite side is the small **Anteneo gallery**, Carrera 17 y C 23, which has temporary exhibitions in an 18th-century house. ■ *Mon-Fri 0830-1200, 1500-1830, Sat 0900-1200, free. Also restaurant, occasional evening concerts.* The **Cathedral**, C 30 y Carrera 26 (Venezuela), is a modern structure of reinforced concrete and glass. At the heart of the old city is **Plaza Bolívar**, with a heroic statue of the Liberator and the white-painted **Iglesia Concepción** on the south side. Also on the plaza, the **Palacio Municipal**, Carrera 17 y C 25, is an attractive modern building. On Carrera 15 (Avenida Francisco de Miranda) between C 41-43 there is **Parque Ayacucho**, with lush vegetation, paths, fountains and a bronze statue of Mcal Sucre.

Excursions

About 24 km southwest of Barquisimeto is the busy agricultural centre of **Quíbor** (*Phone code*: 0253. *Population*: 53,525). Festivals on 18 January (NS de Altagracia) and 12 June (San Antonio de Padua). The Centro Antropológico de Quíbor exhibits work of the Indians who used to live in the region. South of Quíbor and 40 minutes from Barquisimeto is **Sanaré** (1,360 m), on the edge of the **Parque Nacional Yacambu**, where you can hike through tropical forest up the Fumerola, a sleeping volcano. **E-D** *Posada Turística El Cerrito*, Sanaré, T0253-49016, manager speaks

Venezuela

English, small restaurant and bar, tours to local sights and Yacambu, highly recommended. About 60 km east of Barquisimeto is **Chivacoa** (*Population*: 40,400). South of the town is the sacred mountain of the Voodoo-like María-Lionza cult, practised throughout Venezuela. Celebrations are held there mostly at weekends with 12 October (Día de la Raza) being the most important day. There is a Catholic festival, La Inmaculada Concepción, from 8-14 December.

B *Príncipe*, Av 18 entre C 22 y C 23, T231 2344. Pool, restaurant. Recommended. **C** *Hevelin*, Av Vargas entre 20 y 21. Hot water, a/c, good value. Recommended. **C** *Yacambú*, Av Vargas, between C 19 and 20, T251 3229. Pool, a/c. **D** *La Casona*, Av 17 con C 27 near Plaza Bolívar, T231 5311. A/c, hot water, parking, restaurant. **D** *Lido*, Av 15 entre C26 y 27. Hot water, a/c or fan. *Barquipán*, C 26 entre Cras 17 y 18. Good breakfasts, snacks. *Sabor Vegetariano*, on C 24 entre Av 20 y 21, next to *El Rincón Griego* restaurant. Vegetarian snacks. *Majestic*, Av 19 con C 31. Good breakfast and vegetarian meals.

Sleeping & eating

On **28 Dec** (morning) is the fiesta of *La Zaragoza*, when colourfully clad participants and children pass through the streets accompanied by music and dancing. Huge crowds are attracted to the procession of *La Divina Pastora* in early **Jan**, when an image of the Virgin Mary is carried from the shrine at Santa Rosa village into the city.

Festivals

Air Jacinto Lara international airport is 8 km southwest of the centre, 10 mins, US$5 by taxi. Local buses stop outside, US$0.20. *Santa Bárbara* to **Aruba** Fri and Sun. Flights also to **Caracas**, **Mérida**, **Porlamar**, **San Antonio** and **Valencia**.
　　Buses Terminal is on the edge of the city at Carrera 25 y C 44: to **Mérida**, 3-4 a day, at 1020 and several between 2000 and 0200, 8 hrs via Agua Viva and El Vigía, US$12; to **Acarigua** (see page 1413), 1 hr, US$3. To **Valera** *por puesto*, 3½ hrs, US$8.75. To **Tucacas** every 2 hrs; to **Coro** at 1200 and by night, 7 hrs, US$8.75. To **Caracas**, US$8.75, 6 hrs. For **renting cars** (Volkswagen best), Av Pedro León Torres y C 56, also at airport.

Transport

Banks *Banco Provincial*, Av 20 entre C 31 y 32 and C 23 entre Avs 18 y 19, for Visa and MasterCard. *Banco Unión*, Av Vargas entre 21 y 22 (and othr branches) and *Banco de Venezuela*, Av 20 y C 31, No 31-08 (and other branches), Visa ATMs. *Capital Express*, Av Los Leones, Centro Comercial Paseo, next to Caffe 90. Changes US$ cash at low rates. *Italcambio*, Av Los Leones, C C París, loc 1-40, T254 9790, and at airport for Amex. **Communications** **Post Office:** Av 17 con C 25. **Telephone:** C 30 entre Avs 24 y 25. **Tourist office** División de Turismo y Recreación, Av Libertador, Edif Fundalara p 2, T537544 (take a No 12 bus).

Directory

Maracaibo

For most Venezuelans, this part of their country can be summed up in three letters – oil. For others, it can be summed up in four letters – heat. Both are certainly true. This is the main oil producing region as well as being one of the hottest places in all of Latin America. At times you could swear that the vast quantities of oil produced here are being used to fuel some giant blast furnace that reduces everyone to a little puddle of perspiration.

Phone code: 0261
Colour map 1, grid A4
Population: 1,800,000

*　　Not too many tourists find their way here. Those that do are usually on their way to Colombia via the border crossing on the Guajira Peninsula to the north. If you've got the time, though, and can handle the heat, the state of Zulia is worth a detour. Maracaibo is the only town or city in Venezuela where you'll see indigenous people in traditional dress going about their business. Just north of the regional capital is a lagoon where you can see the same houses built on stilts that inspired the first Spanish invaders to christen it "Little Venice". In the southwest is the Catatumbo delta, a huge swamp brimming with wildlife and one of the most fascinating trips in the whole country.*

Venezuela's second largest city, capital of the State of Zulia, is Venezuela's oil capital, with 70% of the nation's output coming from the Lago de Maracaibo area. It's a

Background

Venezuela

modern commercial city with wide, clean streets and, apart from the intense heat, is pleasant to walk around, especially around Plaza Bolívar. The hottest months are July, August and September, but there is usually a sea breeze from 1500 until morning.

Ins & outs The **airport**, La Chinita, is 25 km southwest of city centre. Taxis charge between US$8-10,
For more detailed there are no *por puestos*. The **bus station** is 15 mins walk from centre, 1 km south of the old
information see town. Ask for buses into town, local services are confusing.
Transport, page 1378

Sights The traditional city centre is **Plaza Bolívar**, on which stand the **Cathedral** (at east
The old part of the end), the **Casa de Gobierno**, the **Asamblea Legislativa** and the **Casa de la**
city is not safe after **Capitulación** (or Casa Morales), a colonial building and national monument, tour
1700 and even requires free. The Casa has an extensive library dedicated to the Liberator. ■ *Mon-Fri,*
care in daylight *0800-1600.* Next door is the 19th-century **Teatro Baralt**. Running west of Plaza
Bolívar is the **Paseo de las Ciencias**, a 1970s development which levelled all the old
buildings in the area. Only the **Iglesia de Santa Bárbara** stands in the Paseo. **Calle
Carabobo** (one block north of the Paseo de las Ciencias) is a very good example of a
colonial Maracaibo street. One block south of the Paseo is **Plaza Baralt** on Avenida
6, stretching to C 100 and the old waterfront market (**Mercado de Pulgas**). The
Centro de Arte de Maracaibo Lía Bermúdez is housed in the 19th-century
Mercado de Pulgas building, where the work of national artists is displayed (it is a/c,
a good place to escape the midday heat and makes a good starting place for a walking
tour of the city centre). The new part of the city round **Bella Vista** and towards the
University is in vivid contrast with the **old town** near the docks. The latter, with narrow streets and brightly-painted, colonial style adobe houses, has hardly changed
from the last century, although many buildings are in an advanced state of decay.
The buildings facing **Parque Urdaneta** (three blocks north of Paseo de las Ciencias)
have been well-restored. Also well-preserved are the church of **Santa Lucía** and the
streets around. This old residential area is a short ride (or long walk) north from the
old centre. **Parque La Marina**, on the shores of the lake, contains sculptures by the
Venezuelan artist, Jesús Soto. More of his work can be seen in the **Galería de Arte
Brindhaven** (free), near Santa Lucía, where he is often in residence.

Excursions **Paseo de Maracaibo**, or del Lago, is a lakeside park built in the late 1970s, near the
Hotel del Lago. It offers walks along the shores of the Lake at its narrowest point,
spectacular views of the Rafael Urdaneta bridge and of oil tankers sailing to the
Caribbean. The park attracts a wide variety of birds. ■ *Getting there: Take a* Milagro
*bus northbound from the Mercado de los Guajiros, and ask the driver to let you off at
the entrance, which is well-marked.*

Sleeping **AL** *Kristoff*, Av 8 Santa Rita entre C 68 y 69, T797 2911, www.hotelkristoff.com A/c, nice pool
It is difficult to open to non-residents US$6, disco, laundry service, restaurant, changes US$ cash at terrible
obtain rooms without rates. **A** *Gran Hotel Delicias*, Av 15 esq C 70, T797 6111, F797 3037. A/c, recommended restau-
making reservations rant, good value, pool, disco, accepts credit cards, changes dollars. **C** *Doral*, C 75 y Av 14A, T797
well in advance 8385. A/c, helpful. Recommended. **C** *Paraíso*, Av 93, No 82-70, sector Veritas, T797 6149. With
small sitting room, a/c, cable TV. **D** *Almería*, Av 3H No 74-78, T791 4424. A/c, hot water.
D *Astor*, south side of Plaza de la República, Bella Vista, T791 4510. A/c, popular. **D** *Novedades*,
C 78 (also known as Dr Portillo) No 9-43, Bella Vista, T797 5766. A/c, shower, safe, small rooms,
safe parking, basic. **D** *San Martín*, Av 3Y (San Martín) con C 80, T791 5097. A/c, restaurant next
door, accepts credit cards. **E** *Victoria*, Plaza Baralt. With bath, no hot water, a/c.

Eating *Pizzería Napoletana*, C 77 near Av 4. Excellent food but poor service, closed Tue.
Most restaurants *Mi Vaquita*, Av 3H con C 76. Texan steak house, popular with locals, good atmosphere, rec-
are closed on Sun ommended. *El Carite*, C 78, No 8-35, T71878. Excellent selection of fish and seafood, delicious and moderately-priced. *La Habana*, Av Bella Vista (Av 4) near C 76. Good salads and
milkshakes, open 24 hrs. *La Friulana*, C 95 con Av 3. Good cheap meal, closes 1900. Repeatedly recommended *San José*, Av 3Y (San Martín), 82-29. Good. *El Gaucho*, Plaza Banderas.

Venezuela

Argentine-style, good. *Larga Vida*, Av 13A entre C 75 y C 76. Health food store. *Bambi*, Av 4, 78-70. Italian run with good capuccino, pastries, recommended, cheap. 1 block away, near C 76, is *Panadería Bella Vista*, recommended for *quesillo* and *tiramisu*. On C Carabobo (see above) *Zaguán* serves traditional regional cooking, expensive and difficult to find at night. There are good restaurants around the Plaza de la República (C77/5 de Julio and Av 31, Bella Vista), such as *Chips*, Av 31 opposite Centro Comercial Salto Angel, regional fast food, *tequeños* and *patacones*. Recommended. Also many restaurants on *palafitos* (stilts) in Santa Rosa de Agua district, good for fish (*por puesto* US$0.35 to get there).

Virgen del Rosario, 5 Oct; 24 Oct; 18 Nov, *NS de Chiquimquira* (La Chinita), processions, bullfights – the main regional religious festival. **Festivals**

Maracaibo orientation

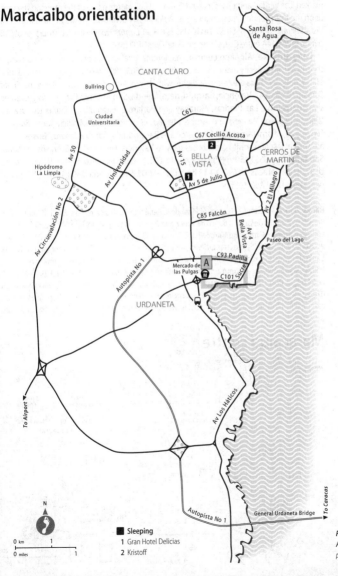

■ Sleeping
1 Gran Hotel Delicias
2 Kristoff

0 km   1
0 miles   1

Related map
A Maracaibo centre,
page 1378

Venezuela

Shopping The outdoor market, *Las Pulgas*, is enormous, mostly clothes, shoes, and general household goods, south side of C 100 entre Av 10 y 14. *El Mercado de las Indias Guajiras*, open market at C 96 y Av 2 (El Milagro), a few crafts, some pottery, hammocks, etc. Most of the shops on C Carabobo sell regional crafts, eg *La Salita*. **Foto Bella Vista**, Av Bella Vista, C 78, recommended service. **Bookshops** *Librería Universal*, Av 5 de Julio y Av 4. Maps, stationery, Caracas newspapers but poor selection of books. *Librería Cultural*, Av 5 de Julio. Best Spanish language bookstore in town. *Librería Italiana*, Av 5 de Julio, Ed Centro América. Postcards and foreign publications (including US). Staff at the public library, Av 2, are helpful to tourists.

Transport **Local** *Por puestos* go up and down Av 4 from the old centre to Bella Vista. Ruta 6 goes up and down C 67 (Cecilia Acosta). The San Jacinto bus goes along Av 15 (Las Delicias). Buses from Las Delicias also go to the centre and terminal. From C 76 to the centre *por puestos* marked 'Las Veritas' and buses marked 'Ziruma'. Look for the name of the route on the roof, or on the front window, passenger's side. A ride from downtown to Av 5 de Julio in a 'Bella Vista' *por puesto* costs US$0.35. **Taxis**: US$2.50-3.50. *Luquis Taxis* will do city tours for US$10 per hr; on Av 14A entre C 76 y 77, near *Hotel Doral*, T971556.

    Long distance **Air:**Airport terminal has international and national lounges. Good bookshop in arrivals sells city map; *casa de cambio* open 0600-1800 daily, no commission; car hire offices outside. There are frequent flights with *Aserca, Avensa, Aeropostal, Avior* and *Santa Bárbara* to **Caracas, Valencia, Barquisimeto, Mérida, San Antonio** (be early to guarantee seat), **Barcelona, Las Piedras, Maracay** and **Porlamar**. International flights to **Curaçao** (*Dutch Caribbean Airlines*) and **Aruba** (*Aeropostal, Royal Aruban Airlines, Santa Bárbara, Servivensa*), **Miami** (*American, Aeropostal*) and **Barranquilla** (*Santa Bárbara*). **Buses**: There are several fast and comfortable buses daily to **Valencia**, US$13.50 by *Expresos del Lago*. **San Cristóbal**, US$11.50, 6-8 hrs, *por puesto*, US$23. **Barquisimeto**, 5½ hrs, US$8.75. **Coro** US$7, 4 hrs. **Caracas**, US$20, 10-13 hrs, *por puesto* US$40. **Mérida**, 2300, US$12, 5-7 hrs, or *por puesto*, US$17.50, 6½ hrs.

Directory **Banks** *Banco Mercantil*, on corner of Plaza de la República. Cash advance on Visa and MasterCard. Branches of *Banco Unión* and *Banco de Venezuela*, including at airport, for Visa ATMs. Best for dollars and TCs is *Casa de Cambio de Maracaibo*, C 78 con Av 9B. *Italcambio*, C C Montielco, loc PA 1-1, entre Av 20 y C 72, T7832682, Amex rep. *Citibank*, Av 15 (Las Delicias) con C 77 (5 de Julio) for Citicorp TCs. All banks shut at 1630, exchange morning only. *Cambio* at bus terminal will change Colombian pesos into bolívares into bolívares at a poor rate. **Communications** Internet *Cyber Estudio*, Av 10 No 66-110, 1100-2300, US$3 per hr. Post Office: Av Libertador y Av 3. **Telephone:** *CANTV*, C 76 near Av 3E, Bella Vista, open 0700-2330, Mon-Fri. *Servicio de Telecomunicaciones de Venezuela*, C 99, esq Av 3. Payphones for local calls only. If offices are closed, phone cards are available at the desk of the nearby *Hotel Astor*, south side

Venezuela

Maracaibo centre

of Plaza de la República. **Consulates** France, Av 3F y C70, T791 2921. **Germany**, C77 No 3C-24, Edif Los Cerros p 9, T791 2406, F791 2506. **Italy**, Av 3H No 69-79, T791 9903. **Netherlands**, Av 3C y C67, La Lago, Unicentro Virginia, office 6, p 2, T/F792 2885. **Norway**, Km 1 Carretera a Perijá, Sector Plaza Las Banderas-Los Haticos. **Spain**, Av Sabaneta y C El Prado No 9B-55. **Sweden**, Av 15 Las Delicias No 88-78. **Switzerland**, Av 9B No 75-95. **UK**, Av 2G No 67-49, Sector El Lago, Urbanización Virginia, T791 5589, F791 3487, georgep@inspecciones.com open 0800-1230. **Medical services** Doctors: *Dr García, Hospital Coromoto*, Av 3C and C 72, T912222, speaks English, as does *Dr Carlos Febres*, a dentist, Av 8, No 84-129, Mon-Fri 0900-1200, 1500-1800, T221504.

About one hour north is the Río Limón. Take a bus (US$0.70, from terminal or Avenida 15 entre C 76 y 77) to **El Moján**, riding with the Guajira Indians as they return to their homes on the peninsula. From El Moján, *por puestos* go to **Sinamaica** (US$1.40; taxi US$5). Beyond Sinamaica, a paved road passes the Sinamaica Lagoon and leads to the border with Colombia. Along the way you see Guajira Indians, the men with bare legs, on horseback; the women with long, black, tent-shaped dresses and painted faces, wearing the sandals with big wool pom-poms which they make and sell, more cheaply than in the tourist shops. The men do nothing: women do all the work, tending sheep and goats, selling slippers and raising very little on the dry, hot, scrubby Guajira Peninsula.

Maracaibo to Colombia
Because of the proximity of the border, across which drug trafficking occurs, it is best not to stay in this area after 1600

The border opens at 0800. Ask for 90 days on entering Colombia. For information on entering Colombia, see page 833. **Buses** Maracaibo-Maicao by colectivo taxi from Maracaibo bus terminal (5 passengers), US$10 per person, plus US$2 road toll. Lots of police checks en route, but no luggage checks; a straightforward crossing.

    To enter Venezuela by land a visa may be asked for, even for those who don't officially require one. Only 72-hour transit visas are issued at this border; *tarjetas de turismo* must be obtained from *DIEX* in Maracaibo – not an easy task. Get a visa in advance. You can expect searches at the border and en route to Maracaibo.

Border with Colombia
Colombia is 1 hr behind Venezuela

The Andes

Caracas

Venezuela's high Andes offer hiking and mountaineering, and fishing in lakes and rivers. The main tourist centre is Mérida, but there are many interesting rural villages. The Transandean Highway runs through the Sierra to the border with Colombia, while the Pan-American Highway runs along the foot of the Andes through El Vigía and La Fría to join the Transandean at San Cristóbal.

    The **Sierra Nevada de Mérida,** *running from south of Maracaibo to the Colombian frontier, is the only range in Venezuela where snow lies permanently on the higher peaks. Several basins lying between the mountains are actively cultivated; the inhabitants are concentrated mainly in valleys and basins at between 800 m and 1,300 m above sea level. The three towns of Mérida, Valera and San Cristóbal are in this zone. There are two distinct rainy and dry seasons in the year. Two crops of the staple food, maize, can be harvested annually up to an elevation of about 2,000 m.*

This is the most important town in the State of Trujillo. Here, you can choose between two roads over the Sierra, either via Timotes and Mucuchíes to Mérida, or via Boconó and down to the Llanos at Guanare. Agricultural and industrial fair in August. There is *Corp Banca*, Avenida Bolívar con C 5, changes Amex TCs, no commission and *Banco de Venezuela*, C 7 con Avenida 10, cash on Visa and MasterCard, very efficient and helpful. **Sleeping and eating** A *Camino Real*, Av Independencia, near terminal, T2251704. A/c, restaurant, bar, parking. B *Valera*, Av Maya, 4 blocks from terminal, T225 7511, F225 7937. Including taxes, a/c, restaurant, parking. D *Posada del Guerrero*, C 9 No 5-38. Cell-like rooms, fan, cable TV, hospitable, OK for a night. There are lots of Italian restaurants, eg *Aurora*, Av Bolívar between C 9

Valera
*Phone code: 0271
Colour map 1, grid A5
Population: 130,000*

Venezuela

and 10. Good, cheap. *Italio* opposite *Hotel Valera*. Recommended. *Fuente de Soda Bulevar*, Av Bolívar between C 11 and 12. Good breakfast and juices.

■ *Getting there: To Caracas daily flights with* Avior. *The bus terminal is on the edge of town. To Boconó, US$4 3 hrs; to Trujillo, regular por puestos, 30 mins, US$0,75; to Caracas, 9 hrs, US$12 (direct at 2230 with* Expresos Mérida*); to Mérida, 4 daily with* Empresa Barinas *(0800, 1000, 1300, 1500), US$4.50, 4½ hrs; por puestos to Mérida, 3 hrs, US$9, leave when full; to Maracaibo, micros every 30 mins until 1730, 4 hrs, US$6.50.*

Trujillo

Phone code: 0272
Colour map 1, grid A5
Population: 44,460
Altitude: 805 m

From Valera a road runs via the restored colonial village of **La Plazuela** to the state capital, Trujillo. This beautiful historic town consists basically of two streets running uphill from the Plaza Bolívar. It's a friendly place with a warm, sub-tropical climate. The **Centro de Historia de Trujillo**, on Avenida Independencia, is a restored colonial house, now a museum. Bolívar lived there and signed the 'proclamation of war to the death' in the house. A monument to the **Virgen de la Paz** (47 m high, with elevator) was built in 1983; it stands at 1,608 m, 2½ hours walk from town. ■ *Jeeps leave when full from opposite* Hotel Trujillo*, 20 mins, US$1.40 pp; open 0900-1700, US$0.75 entry, good views to Lake Maracaibo but go early. Banco Provincial, on main plaza, cash on Visa and MasterCard. Banco de Venezuela, one block down from cathedral, has ATM.* **Sleeping and eating B** Country, 1 km uphill from Plaza Bolívar on Av Independencia, T236 3942. A/c, pool, restaurant, international phone calls. **C** *La Paz*, Av Caracas behind *Country*, T236 5157. Spacious apartments for up to 4, hot water, TV, some with fridge. **D** *Los Gallegos*, Av Independencia 5-65, T/F236 3193. With hot water. *Tasca Restaurant La Gran City*, Av Independencia. Good, disco. *Café D'Adria*, next to *Hotel los Gallegos*. Good lunches and breakfast. *Momento's*, Av Independencia, between *Hotel Los Gallegos* and *Restaurante Gran City*. Patio, cheap, friendly staff. ■ *Getting there: bus to Caracas, 9 hrs, US$12, at 2000, 2100 and 2130; to Barinas and Mérida, at 0700; to Boconó, regular por puestos from Plaza Bolívar, US$2.75.*

Boconó

Phone code: 0272
Population: 50,500
Altitude: 1,225 m
93 km from Trujillo

From Trujillo there is a high, winding, spectacular paved road to the town built on steep mountain sides and famed for its crafts. The Centro de Acopio Artesanal Tiscachic is highly recommended for *artesanía* (turn left just before bridge at entrance to town and walk 300-400 m). It has three basic hotels and **C** *Estancia de Mosquey*, at Mosquey, 10 km from Boconó towards Biscucuy, family run, great views, good beds, good restaurant, pool, recommended. From Boconó you can continue down to Guanare (see page 1413; bus US$3.50, 3½ hours) in the Llanos via **Biscucuy** (*Population: 27,000*). See also transport, Trujillo.

Niquitao

Population: 4,400
Altitude: 1,917 m

Founded in 1625, this small town is one hour southwest of Boconó. It is still relatively unspoilt, colonial-style, celebrating many festivals, particularly Holy Week, when paper is rolled out in the streets for children to create a giant painted mural. As well as three basic hotels with food available, there is **D** *Posada Turística de Niquitao* and **D** *Na Delia*, on a hill 500 m out of town, both have restaurants. *La Estancia*, Plaza Bolívar, owner Golfredo Pérez, helpful, kind, knows area well, excellent pizzas.

Excursions can be made to the Teta de Niquitao (4,007 m), two hours by jeep, the waterfalls and pools known as Las Pailas, and a nearby lake. Southwest of Niquitao, by partly-paved road is **Las Mesitas**; continue up towards **Tuñame**, turn left on a good gravel road (no signs), cross pass and descend to **Pueblo Llano** (one basic hotel and restaurant), from where you can climb to the Parque Nacional Sierra Nevada at 3,600 m, passing Santo Domingo. Good hiking in the area; Johnny Olivio at the video shop on Plaza Bolívar is a knowledgeable guide.

Valera to Mérida

4,007 m
best seen early morning, frequently in the clouds

After Timotes (two good hotels: **C** *Las Truchas*, T0271-828 9158, **D** *Carambay*, Avenida Bolívar 41, T0271-828 9261) the road climbs through increasingly wild, barren and rugged country and through the windy pass of **Pico El Aguila**. This is the way Bolívar went when crossing the Andes to liberate Colombia, and on the peak is the statue of a condor. At the pass is the tourist restaurant *Páramo Aguila*, reasonably

Venezuela

priced with open fire; also food stalls, souvenir sellers and horses for hire. Across from the monument is a small chapel with fine views. A paved road leads from here 2 km to a *CANTV* microwave tower (4,118 m), continuing north as a lonely track to the **Piñango lakes** (45 km) and the traditional village of **Piñango** (2,480 m). Great views for miles around. The Aranjo family provides food and lodging and hires horses.

Santo Domingo, with good handicraft shops and fishing, is on the spectacular road up from Barinas to Mérida, before the Parque Nacional Sierra Nevada. Festival: 30 September, San Gerónimo. The tourist office is on the right leaving town, 10 minutes from the centre. **Sleeping AL** *La Trucha Azul*, east end of town, T898 8066, F898 8067. Rooms with open fireplace, expensive for what it offers. **C** *Cabañas Halcón de Oro*, T898 8044. Cheap rooms for rent next door, opposite *Panadería Santo Domingo*. **B** *Hotel Moruco*, T898 8155, F898 8225, out of town. Beautiful, good value, food very good, bar expensive. **C** *Santo Domingo*, 20 mins from town centre, T898 8144, F898 8277. Log cabins for up to 4 people, log fireplace, games room, hot water, excellent restaurant with good selection of wines. ■ *Buses or busetas pass through in either direction at approximately 2 hr intervals through the day. Mérida 2 hrs, US$4 por puesto; Barinas 1½ hrs, US$4.25.*

Phone code 0274
Population: 6,000
Altitude: 2,178 m

Between Santo Domingo and Laguna Mucubají is the beautiful former monastery, **A** *Los Frailes*, at 3,700 m, international menus, expensive wines. Book through *Hoturvensa*, T0212-907 8130, F907 8140, hoturvensa@cantv.net, but pay at hotel. On the other side of the river is **B** *Paso Real*, almost as good.

Parque Nacional Sierra Nevada (North)

The Transandean highway snakes its way through the rugged mountain landscape, past neat, little towns of red-tiled roofs, steep fields and terraces of maize and

Venezuela

potatoes. The snow-tipped peaks of the high sierras watch over this bucolic scene, with Pico Bolívar, at 5,000 m, lording it over them all.

A few kilometres before the road from Barinas meets the road from Valera is the entrance to the **Parque Nacional Sierra Nevada** (*Trans Barinas* bus, two hours, or *por puesto* from Mérida US$3.50, two hours, 60 km). At the turn-off to the park is a motel, restaurant (good coffee and *arepas*) and shop. The park is clean and very well kept. Near the entrance is **Laguna Mucubají**, at 3,600 m, with free but insecure campsite (visitors' centre, bookshop, good maps, interesting museum). A 1½-hour walk takes you to Laguna Negra. A permit is required from *Inparques* office at the entrance. Be prepared for near-freezing temperatures if camping out. A further 1½-hour walk from Laguna Negra is the very beautiful Laguna Los Patos. Horses can be hired (US$5 per person including guide). Guides (not absolutely necessary) can be found at Laguna Mucubají or at the hotels in Santo Domingo. (See Parque Nacional Sierra Nevada (South)). Throughout the park you will see a plant with curious felt-like leaves of pale grey-green, the *frailejón* (or great friar), which blooms with yellow flowers from September to December.

Apartaderos
Phone code: 0274
Population: 5,000
Altitude: 3,342 m

The road then dips rapidly through Apartaderos (12½ km), a scattered, town at the junction of Route 7 and the road over the Sierra Nevada to Barinas. It's a bit of a tourist trap and not very appealing. **B** *Hotel y Restaurante Mifafi*, T888 0131, good food, beautiful, no heating. **B** *Parque Turístico*, T888 0094, attractive modern chalet-style building, heating, very hot showers, helpful owner, expensive but recommended restaurant. **E** *Posada Viejo Apartaderos*, T888 0015, good value, good restaurant with reasonable prices. Several places to eat. ■ *Buses to Mérida US$2; bus to Barinas on the road over the Sierra Nevada is unreliable, best to catch it in Mérida.*

About 3 km above Apartaderos, a narrow paved road (signposted) turns west off the highway at 'Escuela Estatal 121' and winds its way to **Llano del Hato** (at 3,510 m, the highest place in Venezuela served by road) and on to the three-domed Centro de Investigaciones de Astronomía at 3,600 m. At least two viewing points on the way in give great views of the Lake Mucubají plateau. ■ *CIDA's 4 telescopes and modern facilities are open to visitors daily 1000-2230 during school holidays, Easter Week, and in Aug and Dec; otherwise open Sat 1000-2230, Sun 1000-1630, US$1.75, www.cida.ve* About 2 km beyond the turnoff to CIDA is a dirt road to the left, marked by a large Inparques sign, leading to the Museo del Cóndor (3,740 m). A video is shown and other items of interest. At weekends and on holidays there is open-air bird show. ■ *Daily, free but donations welcome. 4WD necessary.* A good paved road descends 7 km from Llano del Hato to the Mérida highway at La Toma, just above Mucuchíes. Many prehispanic terraces and irrigation systems, adobe houses and ox-ploughed fields (*poyos*) are visible from this road.

From Apartaderos the road to Mérida (two hours), follows the Río Chama valley and drops 1,850 m. This is the heart of the cultivated highlands and the fields extend up to the edge of the *páramo*, clinging to the steepest slopes. The road leads up to **San Rafael de Mucuchíes** (*Altitude*: 3,140 m), said to be the highest village in Venezuela. You should visit the remarkable church, pieced together from thousands of stones, by the late Juan Félix Sánchez and Epifania Gil. **E** *El Rosal*, hot water, good.

Mucuchíes
Population: 9,175
Altitude: 2,980 m

A few kilometres beyond San Rafael is Mucuchíes, where there is a trout farm. Beside the Liberator on the statue in Plaza Bolívar is a representation of the Indian boy, Tinajaca, and the Mucuchíes dog, Snowy, given to Bolívar in 1813 and, according to legend, devoted to him until their deaths on the same day at the Battle of Boyacá. The patron saint of Mucuchíes is San Benito; his festival on 29 December is celebrated by participants wearing flower-decorated hats and firing blunderbusses continuously. Tourist office on C 9 as you enter from Mérida; internet at C 9 Independencia. **C** *Los Conquistadores*, Avenida Carabobo 14, T/F872 0350, good hotel with lots of facilities including pool and bicycle hire, ATM. **D** *Los Andes*, T872 0151, old house above

Venezuela

plaza, four rooms, hot water, shared bathrooms, excellent restaurant (closes 2030), highly recommended.

Before Mérida is **Los Aleros**, a reconstruction of a 1930s town; entry US$5. Staff wear appropriate rustic costume (the drunks are not acting; they're paid by the government). Restaurant *El Caney*, colonial style, in front of bus stop, cheap, highly recommended, busy at weekends.

From Plaza Bolívar in Tabay a jeep can be taken to the cloud forest at **La Mucuy** and to Aguas Calientes (or Termales), two warm pools in a stream (US$1 entry). On the Mérida road 1½ km from the plaza is **D** *La Casona de Tabay*, T0274-283 0089, a beautiful colonial-style hotel, surrounded by mountains, comfortable, home cooking, family-run, highly recommended, take *por puesto*, two signposts. **F** *Posada de la Mano Poderosa*, dormitory rooms, lovely, quiet, hot showers, good food, great value, get off at La Plazuela then walk 15 minutes towards Vivero Tutti Flor. For eating, try *El Morichal*, 50 m from plaza, good, cheap. ■ *Regular por puesto service, buses from Mérida C 19 entre Avs 3 y 4. Gasoline in Tabay.*

Tabay
10 km from Mérida

Mérida

The road continues to descend through increasingly lush, tropical vegetation until the city of Mérida becomes visible. It stands on an alluvial terrace - a kind of giant shelf - 15 km long, 2½ km wide, surrounded by cliffs and plantations and within sight of Pico Bolívar, the highest in Venezuela, crowned with a bust of Bolívar. Mérida (founded 1558), the capital of Mérida State, retains some colonial buildings. From here the Parque Nacional Sierra Nevada can be visited.

Phone code: 0274
Colour map 1, grid A4
Population: 300,000
Altitude: 1,640 m
674 km from Caracas

The **airport** is on the main highway, 5 km from the centre. *Por puesto* into town US$0.20, taxi US$4. The **bus terminal** is about 3 km from the centre of town on the west side of the valley, connected by a frequent minibus service to Calle 25 entre Avenidas 2 y 3. Taxi from bus station to town centre at night US$4.50.

Tourist offices Corporación Merideña de Turismo, Av Urdaneta y C 45, next to the airport. Low season 0800-1200, 1400-1800, high season 0800-1800, closed Sun. They supply a useful map of the state and town (US$0.30). Also at the airport in the waiting lounge, very informative, same low season hours, 0730-1330 in high season; in the bus terminal, same hours, have a map of the city (US$0.30). At Jardín Acuario, Av Andrés Bello, low season 0800-1200, 1400-1800, high season 0830-1830. **Inparques** (National Parks) office at Av Las Américas, map of Parque Nacional Sierra Nevada (mediocre) US$1; also at Teleférico for permits. Two good websites for information on Mérida are www.andes.net/index.html and www.frailejon.com

Ins & outs
For more detailed information see Transport, page 1387. Mérida may seem a safe place, but theft and robbery does occur. Avoid the Pueblo Nuevo area by the river at the foot of the stairs leading down from Av 2, as well as Av 2 itself and Viaducto Miranda

Mérida is known for its 33 parks and many statues. **Parque de las Cinco Repúblicas** (C 13, between Avs 4 and 5), beside the barracks, had the first monument in the world to Bolívar (1842, replaced in 1988) and contains soil from each of the five countries he liberated (photography strictly prohibited). Three of the peaks known as the Five White Eagles (Bolívar, 5,007 m, Toro, 4,755 m, and León 4,740 m) can be clearly seen from here. The **Parque La Isla** contains orchids, basketball and tennis courts, an amphitheatre and fountains. In the **Plaza Beethoven**, a different melody from Beethoven's works is chimed every hour; *por puestos/busetas*, run along Avenida 5, marked 'Santa María' or 'Chorro de Milla', US$0.25. **Jardín Acuario**, beside the aquarium, is an exhibition centre, mainly devoted to the way of life and the crafts of the Andean *campesinos*, ■ *Tue-Sun 0800-1200, 1400-2000, US$0.10; (busetas leave from Av 4 y C 25, US$0.20, passing airport).*

Sights

Museo de Arte Colonial. ■ *Daily, except Mon 0800-1200, 1400-1800, Sun 1900-1300, US$0.80, Av 4, Casa 20-8, T252 7860.* More interesting is the small **Museo Arqueológico** with precolombian exhibits from the Andean region.

Venezuela

■ *Tue-Fri 0800-1200, 1400-1800, Sat-Sun 1500-1900, Av 3, Edif del Rectorado de la Universidad de los Andes, just off Plaza Bolívar.* **Museo de Arte Moderno**, Centro Cultural Don Tulio Febres Cordero, between Avenidas 2 and 3, diagonally opposite Plaza Bolívar (check here for cultural events). Roger Manrique has an impressive butterfly collection (over 10,000), also knowledgeable about Andean wildlife, contact through *Arassari Trek*, see Tour operators.

Sleeping

Difficult to get rooms during school holidays and the Feria del Sol. It is advisable to book in advance. Just about every hotel has a link on www.andes.net or www.frailejon.net

The following are recommended hotels. **AL** *El Tisure*, Av 4 entre C 17 y 18, T252 6072, www.andes.net/tisure/ Modern colonial-style building, very pleasant, disco. **A** *Pedregosa*, off Av Los Próceres, T266 3181, www.andes.net/pedregosa/ On the edge of town, laid out like an Andean village with guests' cottages, pool, restaurant, good for families with children, safe, armed guards, National car hire office, horse riding, rowing boats and bicycle rental nearby. **B** *Mintoy*, C 25 (Ayacucho), No 8-130, T252 0340, www.anes.net/mintoy/ 10% discount for cash, comfortably furnished, poor breakfast, good value, parking, suites with separate sitting area (sleeps 5). **C** *Apart Hotel Central*, Av 3 entre C 16 y 17, T252 7629. Good apartments for 4 or 8 with TV and kitchen. **C** *La Casona de Margot*, Av 4 entre C 15 y C 16,

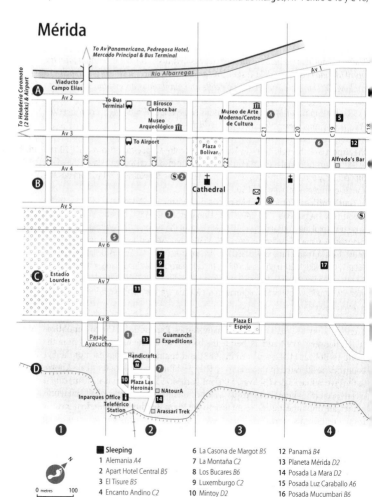

Mérida

To Av Panamericana, Pedregosa Hotel,
Mercado Principal & Bus Terminal

To Heladería Coromoto
(2 blocks) & Airport

A Viaducto Campo Elías

Río Albarregas

Av 1

Av 2

To Bus Terminal

Birosco Carioca bar

Museo Arqueológico

Museo de Arte Moderno/Centro de Cultura

Av 3

To Airport

Plaza Bolívar

Alfredo's Bar

B

Av 4

Cathedral

Av 5

Av 6

C Estadio Lourdes

Av 7

Av 8

Plaza El Espejo

Pasaje Ayacucho

Guamanchi Expeditions

Handicrafts

D

Plaza Las Heroinas

Inparques Office
Teleférico Station

NAtourA

Arassari Trek

1   **2**   **3**   **4**

0 metres 100
0 yards 100

■ Sleeping
1 Alemania *A4*
2 Apart Hotel Central *B5*
3 El Tisure *B5*
4 Encanto Andino *C2*
5 Italia *A4*

6 La Casona de Margot *B5*
7 La Montaña *C2*
8 Los Bucares *B6*
9 Luxemburgo *C2*
10 Mintoy *D2*
11 Montecarlo *C2*

12 Panamá *B4*
13 Planeta Mérida *D2*
14 Posada La Mara *D2*
15 Posada Luz Caraballo *A6*
16 Posada Mucumbari *B6*
17 Residencial San Pedro *C4*

T/F252 3312. Hot water, parking. **C** *La Montaña*, C 24 No 6-47 entre Av 6 y 7, T252 5977, F252 7055. With laundry, English spoken, excellent restaurant. **C** *Posada Casa Sol*, Av 4 entre C15 y C16, T2524164, www.posadacasasol.com Bed and breakfast under the same ownership as *La Casona de Margot*. **C** *Posada Luz Caraballo*, Av 2 No 13-80, opposite La Plaza de Milla, T252 5441, www.andes.net/luzcaraballo Excellent cheap restaurant, good bar, hot water, colonial style old building. **C** *Montecarlo*, Av 7 entre C 24 y C 25, T252 5981, F252 5910. Safe, parking, hot water, restaurant, ask for a back room with mountain view. **C** *Posada Mucumbari*, Av 3 entre C 14 y 15, T252 6015, carnaval@telcel.net.ve German, English and French spoken, shared bath, hot water, often full, laundry, breakfast and snack bar, travel agency. **C** *Posada Doña Pumpa*, Av 5 y C 14, T/F252 7286, www.megadataweb.com/donapumpa Good showers, spacious rooms, cable TV, quiet, very comfortable, English-speaking owner.

D *Alemania*, Av 2 entre C 17 y 18, No 17-76, T252 4067, aleven@telcel.net.ve **E** without bath, quiet, family atmosphere, nice patio, busy, German owner runs excursions. **D** *Los Bucares*, Av 4 No 15-5, T252 2841. Quiet, hot showers, TV, family rooms **B**, nice patio with occasional live music, garage, safe. **D** *Luxemburgo*, C 24, between Avs 6-7, T252 6865. Cold water, annex guesthouse used when hotel is full, safe. **D** *Posada Encanto Andino*, C 24 No 6-53, entre Avs 6 y 7, T252 6929, F252 3580. Cheaper without bath, fully-equipped kitchen. **E** *Italia*, C 19 entre Av 2 y 3, T252 5737. Hot water, **F** in smaller rooms without bath, laundry facilities, post box, travel agency, speak English and French, changes dollars. **E** *Res de Rafael Cuevas*, Av 8 entre C 20 y 21, No 20-49. Helpful. **E** *Res San Pedro*, C 19, No 6-36, entre Avs 6 y 7, T252 2735. Family run, fully equipped, cheaper without bath, hot water, laundry facilities, kitchen, luggage store. **E** *Panamá*, Av 3 entre 18 y 19, T252 9156. Hot water, popular with students and backpackers, changes dollars and TCs. On Plaza las Heroínas: **E** *Planeta Mérida*, C 24 y Av 8, T252 6844. Opposite *Guamanchi Tours*, luggage store, laundry, good. **E** *Posada La Mara*, C 24 No 8-215, T252 5507. Pleasant.

Houses for rent *Finca La Trinitaria*, a beautiful farm with a 3-bedroom colonial house, 10 mins from the town centre towards the Hechicera. Sleeps 6 in comfort, self-catering, well-furnished and equipped, US$50 per night, contact Ian and Mary Woodward, T244 0760, IanWdwrd@netscape.net

Eating
Many places offer student set lunches for US$1-1.50

La Buona Pizza, Av 7, C 24 y 25. Good food reasonably priced. *Café Atico*, C 25 near Plaza Las Heroínas. Excellent lunch for US$4. Recommended. *Cheo's Pizzería*, 3 separate restaurants on Plaza Las Heroínas serving the best pizzas in town. *Chino*, Av Los Chorros de Milla, a few hundred metres before Parque Chorros de Milla, 15 mins by bus. Excellent Chinese. *Chipen*, Av 5, C 24/C 23. Good meat. *D'Angelos Pizzería*, Edif El Col, Paseo Las Ferias. Excellent. *La Esquina*

● **Eating**
1 Café Atico *D2*
2 Café Rodos *B2*
3 Chipen *B2*
4 Fortune *A3*
5 La Esquina de Pajarito *C2*
6 La Mamma *B4*
7 Tatuy *D2*
8 Vegetariano *B4*

Av 1 Rodríguez Picón

Av 2 Lora

C17 C16

Plaza de Milla

C15 C14

15

To Barinas & Valera

Av 3 Independencia

2 **16**

Av 4 Bolívar

6 **8**

DIEX

Museo de te Colonial

Av 5 Zerpa

Av 6 Rodríguez Xuárez

Av 7 Maldonado

Plaza Belén

Av 8 Paredes

Parque Rincón de los Poetas

5 **6**

Venezuela

de Pajarito, C 25 esquina Av 6. Simple but good Venezuelan food, cheap set lunch. *Fortune*, C 21 entre Av 2 y 3. Good Chinese food, English and German spoken. *La Mamma*, Av 3 and C 19. Good pizza, pasta and set lunches, excellent salad bar, popular in the evening, live music at weekends, very cheap local wine. *La Montaña*, C 24 between Maldonado and R Suárez. Good, cheap food, pleasant setting. *El Museo*, Av 3, C12-13. Nice patio, nostalgic decorations, lots of graffiti, good food, pleasant place for a drink. *El Sabor de los Quesos*, C 13, Av 1-2 and Av 3 on Plaza de Milla. Very good and cheap pizzería. *Tatuy*, C 24, No 8-197, Plaza Las Heroínas. Expensive but good, try filled trout with seafood. *Trattoria da Luna*, Pasaje Ayacucho. Italian food, very good pasta, pleasant setting. The *Heladería La Coromoto*, Av 3 y C 29, T523525, open 1400-2200, closed Mon, offers 750 flavours of ice cream, at least 60 choices each day, eg, trout, avocado, garlic, spaghetti! *Lonchería Joseph*, C 23 entre Av 4 y 5. Good *batidos*, cheap set meal, friendly Lebanese owner speaks French. *Café Rodos*, Av 4 esquina C 23 near Plaza Bolívar. Good location and coffee, but watch belongings. *Panadería Roma*, Calle 24. Breakfast and picnic shopping.

Vegetarian restaurants *El Vegeteriano*, Av 4 y C 18. Set lunch US$2.25, good service, recommended, run by Hare Krishnas. Next door but one is a great snack bar with excellent *empanadas*. *Federico's*, Av 3, C27-28. Vegetarian lunches, pizza in the evening. *Fonda Vegetariana*, C 29/Av 4. Recommended. *Picasso*, C 19, Av 3-4. Good. Unnamed place on Av 2, C 28-29. Small, family-run, hard to find.

Bars & nightclubs *La Basura*, Comercial Alto Chama on the road to Parroquía. *La Jungla*, Av 4 y C 36. Very popular. *Birosca Carioca*, Av 2 y C 24. Popular, with live music. Disco in *Hotel Pedregosa* (see above) open later than others and recommended. *Alfredo's*, C 19 y Av 4. Bar, very popular. There is no cover charge for nightclubs but always take your passport or a copy.

Festivals For 2 weeks leading up to Christmas there are daily song contests between local students on Plaza Bolívar, 1700-2200. *Feria del Sol*, held on the week preceding Ash Wednesday. This is also the peak bullfighting season. 1-2 Jan, *Paradura del Niño*; 15 May, *San Isidro*.

Shopping Handicraft market on La Plaza de Las Heroínas, by *teleférico*, good café. Market on C 26 near Av T Febres Cordero has expensive but beautiful and unusual jewellery. *Mercado Principal* on Av las Américas (buses for bus station pass by), has many small shops, top floor restaurant has regional *comida típica*, bargaining possible. Good record shop *Discoteca Internacional*, Av 3, Edif Trujillo. The up-market *Centro Comercial Las Tapias* has shops, disco (La Cucarracha), multi cinema (films are shown in English), 1½ km southwest of the airport on Av Andrés Bello, opposite Jardín Acuario, taxi US$2. Cheaper is the *Centro Comercial Viaducto*, Av Las Américas at Viaducto 26.

Bookshops *Libros Usados*, J Santos, Av 6, 21-45, very good prices, including some second-hand English, German and French books. *Librería Universidad*, Av 3 C 29/30, superb.

Tour operators

Several agencies offer paragliding courses. Beginners must recognize that this is a dangerous sport and conditions in Mérida (lots of wind and thermals) are much better suited to those with experience. Accidents are not uncommon. A recommended instructor is Raul Penso (contact through Arassari Trek)

Arassari Trek, C 24 No 8-301 (beside the teleférico), T/F252 5879, www.arassari.com Run by Tom and Raquel Evenou, English, French and German spoken, good tours with great guides at fair prices, very helpful and hospitable, highly recommended for trekking and climbing in the Sierra Nevada, horse riding, mountain biking, canyoning, caving, parapenting, rafting and canoeing. They also have a book exchange and cybercafé with excellent food. Angel Barreto can arrange domestic flights. Their Llanos tour (US$160-190 for 4 days) is excellent with many different activities. English-speaking guide Alan Highton is highly recommended for the tours of the Llanos and the Río Catatumbo. *Colibrí Expediciones*, in *Posada Alemania* (see above) to whom they are affiliated, T252 4961, aleven@telcel.net.ve Tours in Mérida, Llanos and Amazonas. *Guaguanco Tours*, C24 No 8-181, Parque Las Heroínas, T/F252 3709, guaguancotours@cantv.net English speaking guide. *Guamanchi Tours* (owned by John Peña), C 24, No 8-39, T/F252 2080, info@guamanchi.com German, French and English spoken, recommended for hiking, paragliding, horse riding, biking, equipment hire, exchange, information, mountain climbing, also tours to Llanos, Amazonia and Angel Falls, email service, free to customers. *Montaña Adventure*, Edif Las Américas PB, Av Las Américas, Mérida,

T/F266 1448, Apdo Postal 645, also at airport, ask for Gustavo García-Quintana. Recommended guide, especially in Andes, offers climbing holidays, horseriding, birdwatching, hang gliding, mountain biking, trout fishing, trips elsewhere in Venezuela, English-speaking guides. *NAtourA*, C 24 No 8-237 beside the teleférico, T252 4216, www.natoura.com Open Mon-Sun 0830-1900, friendly company organizing tours throughout Venezuela, run by José Luis Troconis and Renate Reiners, English, French, German and Italian spoken, climbing, trekking, rafting, horse riding, mountain biking, birdwatching and equipment hire. Repeatedly recommended. Ponciano Dugarte Sánchez, T266 5096/252 8416, recommended for jeep hire, English, German and Italian spoken. Also Lucio (T252 8416) and Nicolás Savedra (T271 2618) and Juan Medina, *Yagrumo*, mostalla@hotmail.com.

Local Car hire: several companies at the airport, including *Mérida Rent a Car*, T263 0722, ask for José Félix Rangel, or *Dávila Tours*, Av Los Próceres opposite Urb la Trinidad, T266 0711, or airport T263 4510. **Taxis**: in town about US$3.50; from bus terminal to centre US$4. *Línea Tibisay*, outside *Park Hotel*, T263 7930, recommended.

Transport

Long distance Air: Daily flights to *Caracas* (1 hr direct), with *Avior* and *Santa Bárbara* (T263 2723); also to *Maracaibo, Barquisimeto, Maracay, Porlamar* and *Valencia*. In the rainy season, especially on afternoon flights, planes may be diverted to San Antonio (3-5 hrs by road), or El Vigía (2½ hrs away). Airport tax US$1. *Casa de cambio* (see Banks below). **Buses**: To call a taxi ring bell on left just outside entrance as you leave. A small exit tax of US$0.10 is charged at the information desk, make sure you pay, officials check buses before departure. On interstate buses, it is essential to book in advance; for buses within the state you pay on board. **Bus companies**: *Expresos Occidente*, daily direct to *Caracas* at 0830, US$20, 12 hrs; via Valencia and Maracay at 0800, US$19; to *Coro/Punto Fijo* at 0700, US$19, 12-14 hrs. *Expresos San Cristóbal* (T263 1881), daily direct to Caracas at 1930, 12 hrs, via Valencia and Maracay at 1700, 2030; to *Maracaibo*, at 1930, 8 hrs, US$8.75-12.50. *Expresos Mérida* (T263 3430/263 9918), to Caracas hourly from 1800, some direct others via Valencia and Maracay (US$15, 10-11 hrs); also to *Barquisimeto* (US$12, 8 hrs), Maracaibo and Punto Fijo. *Transportes Barinas* (T263 4651), 4 daily to *Barinas* via Santo Domingo, US$3.50, 5 hrs; 3 to *Valera*, US$2.60, 5 hrs. *Expresos Unidos* (T263 1592), to *San Cristóbal* (US$14, 6 hrs), direct to San Antonio at 0300. *Expresos Los Llanos* (T265 5927), to Caracas at 1900; to *San Fernando de Apure*, via Valencia and San Juan, at 2045, 18 hrs, US$30. Also *por puestos* leave from upper level of terminal to: Jají, Chiguará, Apartaderos (US$3.50), Barinas (US$6, 4 hrs), Maracaibo (US$17.50), Barquisimeto, Caracas, El Vigía, San Cristóbal (US$12), Valera (US$9).

You can save a lot of time by checking in the day before flight

Banks *Banco Unión*, Av 4, No 27-67. Visa ATM. Also at branches of *Banco de Venezuela*, including Av 4 y C 23. Cash advance on Visa and MasterCard. *Corp Banca*, Av Las Américas, 1 block from Mercado Principal. Only bank for Amex TCs (no commission). *Banco Mercantil*, Av 5 y C 15. ATM takes Cirrus (commission lower than Visa). *Italcambio* at airport; this is often the easiest place to change cash and TCs. **Communications** Internet: About US$2 per hr. *La Abadía*, Av 3 between C 17-18, very nice atmosphere and building. *Arassari Trek* (see above). Others at C 35 y Av 3 and ON Las Américas between Viaducto Campo Elias and Mercado Principal (professional). *Zanzibar*, Av 4 No 19-35. Post Office and telephone: *Ipostel*, C 21 entre Avs 4 y 5, 0800-1900 daily. *CANTV*, C 21 y Av 5, Mon-Sat 0800-1930. Post office also in bus terminal, 0800-1200, 1400-1700, weekdays only. **Consulates Colombia**, Av Las Américas, CC Mamayeya, p 5, T244 8607, open 0800-1400. Visas take 10 min. **UK**, Professor Robert Kirby, honorary vice-Consul, Edif Don Chabelo, Apto PH-4, in front of Urb Humboldt, T266 2022, F266 3369. **Medical services** Doctor: *Dra María Yuraima C de Kirby* at *Clínica Médica*, C 22 (opposite Cultural Centre), T521859. Speaks English. Recommended. **Language schools** *Iowa Institute*, Av 4 y C 18, T252 6404, www.ing.ula.ve/~iowainst/ Run by Cathy Jensen de Sánchez, competitive prices, fully qualified teachers, homestays arranged. Recommended. *Latinoamericano de Idiomas*, CC Mamayeya, p 4, of C-5-38, T/F244 7808. Contact Marinés Asprino, Conjunto Residencial Andrés Bello, Torre C, p 5, Apt 6-1, T271 1209 for private lessons and cheap accommodation. Recommended. *María Eugenia Olívar* (also Renjifo and Nora), Av 2 con C 19, Edif Chiquinquirá No 19-11 Apt 3, T252 0845. Recommended. Many tutors place ads in *posadas* and bars. **Useful addresses** Immigration Office: DIEX, Av 4 y C 16. Tourist police: The **Cuerpo Técnico de Policía Judicial** (PTJ), will provide a *constancia* reporting the crime and listing the losses. Their office is on Av

Directory

Most banks won't change cash dollars. Some shops advertise that they change dollars, or try travel agencies. Cash is less welcome than Tcs and rates are poor

Venezuela

Las Américas, just below the Mercado Principal. Open daily but won't issue a *constancia* on Sun. To get there, take any bus marked 'Terminal Sur' or 'Mercado' leaving from C 25. You can also get a *constancia* from the *Prefectura Civil del Municipio Libertador*, but it can take all day and is only valid for a limited period of time; at Av 4 No 21-69, just off Plaza Bolívar; opening hours variable. The Tourist Offices are probably a better bet than the police if you need to register a theft report for insurance purposes.

Parque Nacional Sierra Nevada (South)

Close to Mérida is the popular hiking area around Los Nevados, with the added attraction of the highest cable car in the world (if it's running). The further you go from Mérida, the greater the off-the-beaten-track possibilities for hiking and exploration that arise.

Information Since this is a national park, you need a permit to hike and camp overnight. It must be obtained from the *Inparques* (National Parks) office in Mérida (see Ins & outs). Permits are not given to single hikers (except to Los Nevados): a minimum of two people is required. It costs US$0.20 per person. Have your passport available. Return permit after your hike. If camping, remember that the area is between 3,500 and 4,200 m so acclimatization is necessary, as is warm clothing for night-time. (See Altitude, Health, Essentials, at the beginning of the book.) Some treks are very difficult so be sure to check with the tourist office before leaving. Water purification is also recommended. See also Mérida Tour operators and Parque Nacional Sierra Nevada (North) page 1381.

Pico Espejo The world's highest and longest aerial cableway (built by the French in 1958) runs to Pico Espejo (4,776 m) in four stages. In 2002 it was running only intermittently (closed in June 2002 with administrative problems). When operating, its final station is at Pico Espejo, with a change of car at Loma Redonda, the penultimate station, at 4,045 m. It is not know if/when normal service will be resumed.

Los Nevados An alternative to the cableway is to take a jeep as far as the little hamlet of Los
Altitude: 2,711 m Nevados. Recommended *posadas* are *Posada Bella Vista*, Sánchez family, **D** pp including breakfast and dinner, behind church. *El Buen Jesús* **F** pp. *Posada Guamanchi*, owned by travel agency of same name in Mérida, solar power, great views but no heating or hot water, sleeping bag advisable. *La Posada de Florencia*, run by Omar and Rosa, private rooms and dormitories, with breakfast and supper, **F** pp. All *posadas* will arrange food and mules for climbing to El Alto de la Cruz or to Loma Redonda. ■ *Jeep Los Nevados-Mérida, late afternoon (depart 0700 from Plaza Las Heroínas in Mérida), 4-6 hrs, US$10 pp, US$50 per jeep, very rough and narrow but spectacular.*

From Los Nevados, it is a very testing two-day trek to **Pico Espejo**; strong possibility of altitude sickness as the ascent is more than 1,600 m. It is best done early in the morning (before 0830 ideally), before the clouds spoil the view, and from November to June. In summer the summit, with its statue to Nuestra Señora de las Nieves, is clouded and covered with snow and there is no view. It is a one-day return to Mérida. **It is not recommended to attempt Pico Espejo alone; better to go with a guide as it is easy to get lost**. Reputable trekking companies provide suitable clothing, temperatures can be as low as 0° C. August is the coldest month on the peaks. The glacier on Pico Bolívar can be seen clearly; so can Picos Humboldt and Bompland (4,883 m), forming the Corona, and to the east, on a clear day, the blue haze of the llanos.

From Los Nevados to **Loma Redonda** takes 5-7 hours (14 km). The hike is not too difficult; breathtaking views; be prepared for cold rain in the afternoon, start very early. Mules do the journey daily, four hours; US$8 per mule.

You can walk down from Loma Redonda to **La Aguada** station (3,452 m) on a rough path, two hours; wear boots, walk slowly, not for children or the elderly, take water. From La Aguada you can walk to the main road to Mérida (3-5 hours) and catch a *por puesto* to town. It is a 30-minute walk from La Aguada to Los Calderones' farm (accommodation and horses for hire). From La Aguada to the next station down, **La Montaña** (2,442 m), it's a tough 2½ hours walk (wet and overgrown). From La Montaña, the penultimate station on the way down, it's a 2½-3½ hour walk to Mérida.

The walk from Los Nevados to the village of **El Morro** (24 km) takes 7-9 hours (very steep in parts). Sr Oviller Ruiz provides information on the history of the church and Indian cemetery. *Posada* run by Doña Chepa, as you enter from Los Nevados, warm, highly recommended. **F** pp *Posada El Orégano*, including meals, basic, good food, recommended.

47 km to Mérida; jeeps do the trip daily

A recommended hike from Pico Espejo, is to the cloud forest at La Mucuy (see page 1383), 2-3 days walking at over 4,000 m altitude, passing spectacular snow peaks and several lakes. A tent and a warm sleeping bag are essential, as is a good map (local guides may lend theirs to photocopy). The refuge at the foot of **Pico Humboldt** (4,942 m) is in disrepair but there is a camping area at Laguna Verde (water available here).

Jají is famous for its colonial architecture, including an attractive main plaza. The plaza and adjoining streets are mainly given over to *artesanías* from all over the continent. There are a few basic hotels and good walking in the hills. *Buseta* from Terminal Sur, Mérida, hourly, 50 minutes, US$1. Off the road to Jají, 20 minutes from Mérida, is *Venezuela de Anteayer*, where regional culture is recreated in a series of displays, includes typical music and food, US$8. *Por puesto* from C 26, Mérida.

Southwest of Mérida
Phone code: 0274
43 km from Mérida

Continuing for 62 km – narrow, but mostly paved – beyond Jají, the Panamericana is reached 37 km east of El Vigía (several gas stations on the way). Transandean Route 7 leaves Mérida and passes through the Chama valley, heading for Lagunillas and Bailadores.

Believed to be the first site of Mérida, **San Juan de Lagunillas** has a striking church and is noted for its craftwork especially weaving. Fiestas from Christmas to Candlemas (2 February), three weeks in May (14 and 15 the highpoint) and in July. From San Juan, or from further along Route 7, Lagunillas can be reached. On the edge of Lagunillas is **Jamu**, a reconstructed Indian village where demonstrations of weaving and other skills are given. ■ *US$1.20.*

Phone code:0274
Altitude: 1,070 m

Tovar is a nice little town with pleasant excursions, from where you can rejoin the Panamericana via Zea, itself a pleasant village, or tackle the wild and beautiful old mountain road over the Páramo de La Negra to San Cristóbal. **D** *Hostería Sabaneta*, Cra 3, T873 0611, with bath. **F** *Pensión Ideal*, basic, laundry facilities. *Restaurant Kek Duna*, Hungarian owner speaks six languages and serves interesting food. ■ *From Mérida to Tovar, bus US$2.50.* From Tovar the road continues to **Bailadores** (fiesta from Christmas to Candlemas, bus US$1.25), and **La Grita**, a pleasant town (Sunday market, fiesta 6 August).

Phone code: 0275)
96 km from Mérida

San Cristóbal

The capital of Táchira State was founded in 1561 and has been restored in the colonial style. A good road runs over the mountains to San Antonio (see below) towards the Colombian border, which is 55 km from San Cristóbal. Fiesta de San Sebastián, 7-30 January.

Phone code: 0276
Colour map 1, grid B4
Population: 290,900
Altitude: 830 m
Mean temp: 22°C

A *Círculo Militar De Ferias El Tamá*, Av 19 de Abril, overlooking the town, T356 1870. Safe, spacious, good pool and gymnasium. Recommended. **D** *Del Rey*, Av Ferrero Tamayo, T343 0561. Good showers, fridge, quiet. Recommended. **D** *Machirí*, C 7 No 4-30. Hot water, central. **E** *Ejecutivo*, C 6, No 3-45. Old and basic but clean and central. **E** *Tropicana*, next to bus

Sleeping & eating

Venezuela

terminal. Basic, noisy. **E** *Río*, outside bus station. Big rooms, hot shower. **E** *Unisa*, also near bus terminal. OK. There are several cheap hotels on Av 6A, just off the central plaza, and around Avs 5-7, C 4-8; **F** category. *Fuente de Soda La Bohème*, Av García de Hevia y 7 Av, Centro Cívico. Expensive, breakfasts all day. *El Rancho de Esteban*, 500 m from *Hotel Del Rey*. Open-air with fine view over city, special barbecue dishes. Highly recommended.

Transport

The bus station is well-equipped the information booth has little useful information

Air Airport at Santo Domingo, 40 km away. Taxi to San Cristóbal US$19, or walk 30 mins to highway and catch bus, 1 hr, US$0.55. Daily flights to/from Caracas with *Aeropostal* and *Aserca*. **Buses** To Maracaibo, 6-8 hrs, US$11.50, *por puesto*, US$23. To **Mérida**, US$14, 6 hrs, US$25 by *por puesto*. To/from **Bailadores** US$2.50. To **Caracas**, US$20, 15 hrs (*Expresos Occidente*), executive service US$23.50; **Valencia**, US$17.50. To **San Antonio**, 2½ hrs by bus, US$2, or *por puesto*, US$4, which continues to **Cúcuta**, stopping at Immigration in both countries, runs every 20 mins. By taxi to Cúcuta: US$19 to San Antonio, US$8 to wait at border, then US$12 to Cúcuta. To **Guasdualito**, US$10, 0650 bus connects with 1200 from Guasdualito to San Fernando de Apure.

Directory **Banks** *Corp Banca* (American Express), 5a Av, Edif Torre east. **Communications** **Post Office:** Palacio Municipal, next to Cathedral. *CANTV*, on Carrera 23, C 10 y Pasaje Acueducto. **Consulates** German, Edif Torovega, Carrera 8, La Concordia, T347 1644, F347 0544, aveco@telcel.net.ve **UK**, Aveco, Britannia House, Av Rotaria esq Parque Exposición, La Concordia, T347 1644, F347 0544, aveco@telcel.net.ve **Tourist offices** Cotatur, Pabellones de Exposición, Av España, Pueblo Nuevo, T357 9655, very helpful, José Gregorio speaks English, good map and hotel list. **Inparques**, Parque Metropolitano, Av 19 de Abril. **Touring y Automóvil Club,** Av Libertador C y Av Principal Las Lomas, Edif Olga, (Sr Hernán Sojo González.)

San Antonio

Colour map 1, grid B4
Population: 42,630

The border town of San Antonio is connected by international bridge with Cúcuta on the Colombian side (about 16 km); continue by road or air to Bogotá. San Antonio has an attractive colonial cathedral and some pleasant parks, but is not tourist-oriented. San Antonio festival is on 13-20 May. There is Amex at *Corp Banca*, both on main plaza. TCs are difficult to change. *Casas de cambio* near the international bridge will not all change cheques and some will only change Colombian pesos, not even US$ cash. The exchange rate for bolívares to pesos is the same in San Antonio as in Cúcuta. **Sleeping and eating** **C** *Neveri*, C 3, No 3-11, esq Carrera 3, T771 5702. A/c, TV, safe, parking nearby, by border. **D** *Terepaima*, Carrera 8, No 1-37, T771 1763. Safe, good meals. Recommended. **E** *Frontera*, C 2 y Carrera 9, No 8-70. Pleasant, good value. Many hotels near town centre. Eating places include *Refugio de Julio*, Carrera 10. good value pizzas. *La Giralda de Sevilla*, next door to *Hotel Neveri* (above). Very good, only place open on Sun evenings.

■ *Getting there: The airport has exchange facilities (mainly for Colombian pesos). Taxis run to* DIEX *(immigration) in town, and on to Cúcuta airport, US$15. Por puesto to airport, US$0.35. Internal flights: to Caracas, Aeropostal, Aserca; Aeropostal and Santa Bárbara to Maracaibo and Valencia, Santa Bárbara to Barquisimeto. Buses Caracas-San Antonio US$23.50, a/c, to Caracas at 1600 and 1800, 12 hrs.*

Border with Colombia

Venezuelan time is 1 hr ahead of Colombian

Get a Venezuelan exit stamp at *DIEX*, Carrera 9 y Avenida 1 de Mayo, San Antonio. The Colombian consulate is at 10 Centro Cívico San Antonio, p 2, open 0800-1400; better to go to Mérida for visas. For entry into **Colombia**, see page 810.

Entering Venezuela, go to *DIEX* before buying a bus ticket to San Cristóbal. If Venezuelan customs is closed at weekends, it is not possible to cross from Cúcuta. There is a customs post 5 km after San Antonio; be prepared for strip searches and for further searches between San Cristóbal and Mérida.

If crossing by private vehicle, car documents are checked at *DIEX*. You must have a visa and a *carnet de passages* (but see page 1346). See Cúcuta, **Colombia**, page 810, for details on exit formalities. Once in Venezuela, you may find that police are ignorant of requirements for foreign cars.

Venezuela

Transport Air: It is cheaper, but slower, to fly Caracas-San Antonio, take a taxi to Cúcuta, then take an internal Colombian flight, than to fly direct Caracas-Colombia. The airport transfer at San Antonio is well-organized and taxi drivers make the 25-min trip with all necessary stops. Air tickets out of Cúcuta can be reserved in advance in a Venezuelan travel agency. **Buses**: San Antonio to border bridge US$1.75, in bolívares or pesos. Taxi to Cúcuta, US$12. On any form of transport that crosses the border, make sure that the driver knows that you need to stop to obtain stamps. *Por puesto* drivers may refuse to wait. Taxi drivers will stop at all the right offices. Just to visit Cúcuta, no documents are needed.

The East Coast

Beautiful beaches, islands, forested slopes and a strong colonial influence all help to make this one of the most visited parts of the country. The eastern part, with mountain summits rising to 2,000 m, has abundant rainfall in its tropical forest. The western part, which is comparatively dry, has most of the inhabitants and the two main cities, Cumaná and Barcelona.

It is five hours from Caracas to Barcelona by road through Caucagua, from which there is a 58 km road northeast to Higuerote. The partly-paved coastal road from Los Caracas also goes to Higuerote; beautiful views, many beaches. Surrounded by sandy beaches and currently the focus of large-scale tourist projects, Higuerote is expensive, especially during the festival of the Tambores de San Juan (23-26 June). There is a good fruit and vegetable market as well as banks with ATMs.

Higuerote
Phone code: 0234
Population: 13,700

At 14 km before Higuerote on the road from Caucagua is Tacarigua de Mamporal, where you can turn off to the **Parque Nacional Laguna de Tacarigua**. The 18,400 ha national park enclosing the lagoon is an important ecological reserve, with mangroves, good fishing and many water birds, including flamingoes (usually involving a day-long boat trip to see them, best time to see them 1700-1930; permit from *Inparques* required, US$0.50). Boats leave from *Muelle Ciudad Tablita*; also from Inparques *muelle* (but overcharging is common here). Agencies have offices in Sector Belén in the fishing village of **Tacarigua de la Laguna**; fixed price of US$30 for two. Boats can be hired to anywhere in the Park and to *Club Miami* beach resort, **B**, includes two meals, on the Caribbean side of the eastern sandspit. The beaches beyond here are unspoilt and relaxing, but mosquitoes are a problem after sunset. **Sleeping and eating** E *Casa de Ivan Pastuch*, 200 m from the Inparques *muelle*. Quiet, fan, use of cooker and fridge, German spoken. Recommended. About 3 km before the village on the road is **B** *Villa del Río*, apart-hotel. Price for 1-7 persons, bath, kitchen facilities, fan, connected with *Remigios Tours*, transfer to and from Tacarigua for US$20. Good fish at *Bar-Restaurant Poleo Lebranche Asado*.

Parque Nacional Laguna de Tacarigua

Barcelona

Barcelona, founded in 1671, straddles the Río Neveri, 5 km from the sea. Its colonial streets and old buildings are pleasant if a little run down, and a more peaceful alternative to neighbouring Puerto La Cruz, 12 km away by 4-lane highway (Avenida Intercomunal), which has surpassed it touristically and commercially. Between the two towns is the residential resort of **Lechería**, which is the place for clubbing. ■ *Take a por puesto to the beach, from Barcelona or Puerto La Cruz, or a taxi from either town.*

On **Plaza Boyacá** are the Palacio de Gobierno and San Cristóbal **Cathedral** (started 1748, rebuilt 1773), which contains the embalmed remains of the Italian martyr, San Celestino. ■ *0600-1200, 1500-1930.* Several blocks north on Avenida 5

Phone code: 0281
Colour map 2, grid A1
Population: 266,750
Mean temp: 27° C

Venezuela

de Julio are the twin **plazas of Bolívar** (with statue) and **Miranda**. Facing Plaza Bolívar are the ruins of the **Casa Fuerte**, a national monument, where 1600 of Bolívar's followers were massacred in 1817. Details of this and other historic epics can be found next door in the **public library**, weekdays only. **Museo de la Tradición**, C Juncal, in a 1671 building once the centre of the slave trade, houses a wide collection of indigenous and Spanish religious art. ■ *Mon-Fri 0800-1200, 1400-1700, weekends 0900-1500.* Next to the *por puesto* station on Avenida San Carlos, over 1 km south of Plaza Boyacá, is the **Mercado Libre**, for food and just about anything else.

Sleeping & eating **C** *Barcelona*, Av 5 de Julio, 1 block from Cathedral, T277 1065, F277 1076. TV, parking, 6th floor restaurant (good fish). **C** *Neveri*, Av Fuerzas Armadas, T277 2376. Similar, good restaurant *Castillo del Oriente*. **D** *Madrid*, just behind cathedral, T277 4043. With restaurant. **D** *Plaza*, C Juncal opposite Cathedral, T277 2843. In a colonial building. Recommended. **D** *Toledo*, Juncal y Av 5 de Julio. Basic, good value. There is a wide variety of restaurants in town, including *Bueno Pollo*, Av Miranda y C 5 Maturín. Good grilled chicken, pleasant atmosphere. *Lucky*, Av Miranda No 4-26, north of Plaza Bolívar. Chinese.

Transport **Air** The airport is 3 km south; also serves Puerto La Cruz. Many flights daily to Caracas, 40 mins, Porlamar, 30 mins, and daily flights to Maracaibo, Puerto Ordaz, and Valencia. *Oficambio* exchange facilities (no TCs), *artesanía* shops, small museum, car rental agencies, *Corpoturismo* booth (stays open late for some incoming flights, few handouts, friendly, cannot book hotels, a city map can be scrounged from *National Car Rental*). Taxi to airport from bus station US$3.50; taxi to Puerto La Cruz US$8-10.

Take care around bus terminals **Buses** The Terminal de Pasajeros next to the Mercado Libre is used mostly by *por puestos*, with regular departures to Anaco, El Tigre, Maturín, Cumaná and other nearby destinations. Buses go to **Caracas** (5 hrs, 3 daily, US$8.75); **San Félix** (Ciudad Guayana); **Ciudad Bolívar** (6 daily); **Maturín** (2 daily). Buses for **Puerto La Cruz** (40 mins) run every few mins from another Terminal de Pasajeros, along Av 5 de Julio, past Plaza Bolívar.

Directory **Tourist office** Carrera 13, No 3-7, just off Plaza Boyacá; open weekdays only.

Puerto La Cruz

Phone code: 0281
Colour map 2, grid A1
Population: 220,000

Originally a fishing village, Puerto La Cruz is now a major oil refining town and busy, modern holiday resort. Tourist facilities are above average, if expensive, but the sea is polluted. The seafront avenue, Paseo Colón, extends to the eastern extremity of a broad bay. To the west the bay ends at the prominent El Morro headland. Most hotels, restaurants, bars and clubs are along Paseo Colón, from where you get excellent views of the Bahía de Pozuelas and the islands of the Parque Nacional Mochima (see below). Vendors of paintings, jewellery, leather and hammocks are on Paseo Colón in the evening, cheaper than the souvenir shops. The *Santa Cruz* festival is on 3 May, while 8 September is the *Virgen del Valle*, when boats cruise the harbour clad in palms and balloons; afternoon party at El Faro, Chimana, lots of salsa and beer.

Excursions
Excellent snorkelling, fishing and swimming

The main attractions of Puerto La Cruz lie offshore on the many islands of the beautiful **Parque Nacional Mochima** and in the surrounding waters. Bring your own food as the island restaurants are expensive. Three companies offer trips to the islands: *Transtupuerto*, on Paseo Colón, between Buenos Aires y Sucre, T667138, trips to closest islands (Islas Chimanas and Las Borrachas) for US$8, day tour around several islands with stops US$30-40, includes snorkelling equipment and soft drinks; *Transporte Turístico Virgen del Valle*, offers similar deals (food extra); *Transtupaco*, next to *Hotel Hesperia*, no tours, they act as a taxi to the islands.

Alternatively, you can reach the islands with the *Embarcadero de Peñeros*, on Paseo Colón, behind the *Tejas Restaurant*. Departures from 0900-1000, return at 1600-1630; US$6 per person. Tourist office in Puerto La Cruz provides tour

Venezuela

operators for day trips to various islands for swimming or snorkelling; six-hour trip to four islands costs US$25 per person, including drinks. The islands to the east (Isla de Plata, Monos, Picuda Grande and Chica and the beaches of Conoma and Conomita) are best reached from the port at **Guanta** (taxi from town, or *por puesto* from C Freites between Avenida 5 de Julio and C Democracia, and ask to be dropped off at the Urb Pamatacualito). **NB** Boat trips to the islands are cheaper from **Santa Fe** or **Mochima** (see below).

The following are recommended. **L** *Hesperia*, on Paseo Colón, at the eastern edge of the centre, T265 3611, F265 3117. Best in this part of town, luxury hotel with all services and facilities. **A** *Rasil*, Paseo Colón y Rodriguez, T267 2535, F267 3121. Rooms, suites and bungalows, 3 restaurants, bar, pool, gym, money exchange, car rental and other facilities, a little run down but convenient for ferries and buses. **A** *Cristal Park*, Buenos Aires entre Libertad y Honduras, T267 0744, F265 3105. A/c, laundry service, changes money at a better rate than *casas de cambio*. **A** *Gaeta*, Paseo Colón y Maneiro, T265 0411, www.enoriente.com/gaeta Very modern, a/c, good location but very small rooms, restaurant, scooter rentals, *casa de cambio* (good rates). **A** *Senador*, Miranda y Bolívar, T267 3522. A/c, back rooms quieter, phone, restaurant with good view, parking. **B** *Caribbean Inn*, Freites, T267 2811. Big rooms, very well kept with quiet a/c, small pool, very good service. **B** *La Marina*, Andrés Eloy Blanco, at the new ferry terminal. A/c, good views, expensive waterside restaurant, parking for those using the Margarita ferry. **B** *Riviera*, Paseo Colón between Maneiro y Freites, T265 1394. Seafront hotel, noisy a/c, some rooms have balcony, phone, bar, watersports, very good location, poor breakfast. **B** *Aparthotel Cristián del Valle*, Maneiro 15, T265 0925. Trinidadian owner speaks English, a/c, fans, dining room, kitchen. **C** *Comercio*, Maneiro, 1 block from Paseo Colón, T262 3465. Phones, cold water only, a/c, safe. **C** *Puerto La Cruz*, Av 5 de Julio, T262 1698. Phone, good. **D** *Pippo*, Freites y Municipal, T268 8810. Cold water, some rooms with TV, very noisy.

Sleeping

Newer, up-market hotels are at Lechería (see above) and El Morro; cheaper hotels are concentrated in the centre, though it's not easy to find a cheap hotel

Puerto La Cruz

Venezuela

0 metres 200
0 yards 200

Eating Many on **Paseo Colón** , eg *El Parador*, 2nd floor, excellent food and service. *Da Luigi*, Italian, good. *Big Garden*, delicious sea food. *Casa Nápoli*, cheap, recommended. *Reale*, No 69
pizzería, good for breakfast. *Ristorante O Sole Mio*, cheap, excellent, wide variety.
Las Cabañas, very good value and service. *El Guatacarauzo*, near Pizza Hut, live music,
salsa, good atmosphere and good value. *Heladería 4D*, best ice cream. *Sourdough Bakery
and Grill*, indoor and outdoor seating, some vegetarian options, excellent. *La Taberna de
Guácharo*, C Carabobo, east end of Paseo Colón. Excellent cheap Venezuelan cuisine, good
service. Highly recommended. *Maroco*, Av 5 de Julio 103. Good seafood. *El Teide*, Av 5 de
Julio No 153, near Plaza Bolívar. Good and cheap local food, closes at 2000. *El Farao*, east corner of main bus station. Excellent, authentic, spicy Arabic food.

Vegetarian *Celeri*, on Av Municipal, 1 block from Guamaché. Open weekdays
1130-1530. Recommended. Also try *La Colmena*, next to *Hotel Riviera*; and *La Granela*, at
Miranda and Honduras.

Gamblers nightclub, Paseo Colón, near Burger King. Excellent music, free entry.
Christophers, La Marina, 1 block from Paseo Colón. An informal cellar-type bar, Canadian-owned, book exchange, open from 1600 till late.

Sport **Diving**: several companies run diving courses and trips and rent equipment, mostly on Paseo
Colón. They're a bit more expensive than comparable courses on offer in Santa Fe and
Mochima. We have received favourable reports on the following: *Explosub*, Hotel Hesperia,
T265 3611, F267 3256, PO Box 4784. Efficient, helpful, will dive with 1 person, US$75 for 2 dives.
Lolo's Diving Center, at Guanta, T268 3052 (or contact Eddy Revelant T0414-980 1543 (mob)).
Very experienced, English spoken, collect you from hotel and provide lunch, US$60 for 2 dives,
2-3 person minimum, 4-day PADI course US$300. Hotels and travel agents also organize trips.
The nearest recompression chamber is on Isla Margarita. **Kayaking**: *Jakera*, CC Tropical
Shopping Center, loc 8, p 1, C Bolívar, T267 3112, www.jakera.com Sea kayaks for rent at Playa
Colorada, trips to whole country arranged, Chris and Joanna helpful, English spoken.

Transport **Buses** Bus terminal to the east of town; *por puesto* terminal at Av Juncal y Democracia. To
Caracas, 5 hrs, US$8-14, at least 15 through the night, *Expresos Los Llanos* (T671373, recommended, a/c, movies), *Sol de Margarita* (recommended), *por puesto*, depart 1550, 4 hrs,
US$30; *Autoexpresos Ejecutivos* to/from Caracas 4 a day, US$22 (T678855, next to ferry terminal), highly recommended (also to Maracay, Valencia, Barquisimeto and Maturín). To
Mérida, US$30, 16 hrs. To **Ciudad Bolívar** US$8; to **Ciudad Guayana** US$13.50. To
Cumaná, US$5, *Expresos Guayanesa*, recommended, *por puesto* US$10, 1½ hrs. To **Barce-
lona**, US$1.75, 40 mins. To **Carúpano**, US$7, 5 hrs. *Por puesto* to Playa Colorada US$2 and to
Santa Fe about US$3. There are also services to San Félix, Maracay, Valencia, Barinas, San
Cristóbal, Güiria. Along Av 5 de Julio runs a bus marked 'Intercomunal'. It links Puerto La Cruz
with Barcelona and intervening points. Another Barcelona bus is marked 'Ruta Alternativa'
and uses the inland highway via the Puerto La Cruz Golf and Country Club and Universidad
de Oriente, US$0.20. For details of **Ferries** to **Isla Margarita**, see page 1408.

Directory **Banks** Corpbanca (American Express TCs), Av 5 de Julio, Local No 43. *Italcambio*, C C Paseo Mar, loc 6,
C Sucre y Paseo Colón, T267 3623. Amex representative. *Oficambio*, Maneiro y Libertad, no
commission on TCs, best rates, open 0800-1200, 1400-1730 Mon-Fri, or on the sea front between
Buenos Aires and Sucre, Mon-Fri 0800-2100. **Communications** Internet: On C Bolívar entre Sucre y
Buenos Aires, next to Plaza Bolívar, open Sun. *North American Connection*, CC Paseo Plaza, C
Carabobo, ½ block south of *Hotel Puerto La Cruz*. Fax and scanning facility as well as internet.
CANTV and Ipostel, Freites y Bolívar, 1 block from Paseo Colón. Telephone office accepts Visa for calls,
will hold faxes, F651266. **Consulates** UK, *Hotel Maremares*, Av Américo Vespucio y Av R17, T811011,
F814494. **Tourist offices** Coranztur on Paseo Colón, entre Buenos Aires y Sucre, French, English,
Italian and Dutch spoken, very helpful and friendly, open Mon-Fri 0800-2100. Useful website:
www.enoriente.com Do not buy tours from wandering salesmen not affiliated with a registered tour
company If in doubt, go to *Coranztur*.

Parque Nacional Mochima

Hundreds of islands in the Caribbean Sea, a seemingly endless series of beaches backed by some of Venezuela's most beautiful scenery and tiny coves tucked into bays make this one of the country's most beautiful regions.

At Christmas, Carnival and Easter this part of the coast becomes extremely congested so patience is needed as long queues of traffic can develop. Accommodation is very hard to find. It can also become littered and polluted, especially on the islands. Robbery may be a problem, but if you take care and use common sense the risk is minimal. Camping on the islands in Parque Nacional Mochima is not advisable.

Starting east from Puerto La Cruz is the Costa Azul, with the islands of the Parque Nacional Mochima offshore. Highway 9 follows the shore for much of the 85 km to Cumaná. The road is spectacular but if driving take great care between Playa Colorada and Cumaná. It passes the 'paradise-like' beaches of **Conoma** and **Conomita** (see Excursions under Puerto La Cruz). Further along is **Playa Arapito** (*posada*, **D**, restaurant, parking extra). Here boats can be hired to **La Piscina**, a beautiful coral reef near some small islands, for good snorkelling (lots of dolphins); US$15 per boat.

Playa Colorada is a popular beach (Km 32) with beautiful red sands and palm trees (*por puesto* from corner of terminal in Puerto La Cruz, US$2, or hitch). Nearby are **Playa Vallecito** (camping free, security guard, car US$1, bar with good food and bottled water on sale, plenty of palm trees for hammock-slinging) and **Playa Santa Cruz**. At **Playa Los Hicacos** is a lovely coral reef.

In Sucre State 40 km from Puerto La Cruz is **Santa Fe** (*phone code:* 0293), larger and noisier than Mochima, but a good place to relax. The attractive beach is cleaned daily. It has a market on Saturday. Jeep, boat or diving tours available. Fishermen offer trips but their prices are usually high. Boat trips to Playas Colorada or Blanca cost US$15 per person; better to hire your own boat for half the price, or hitch down the road to Colorada. ■ *Getting there: from Cumaná, take por puesto 1 block down from the Redonda del Indio, along Av Perimetral, US$1.75. It may be difficult to get a bus from Puerto La Cruz to stop at Santa Fe, take a por puesto or taxi, US$23 including wait (depart from terminal, US$2, 1 hr).*

The little village of **Mochima** beyond Santa Fe, is 4 km off the main road (hitching difficult). It's busy at weekends but almost deserted through the week. The sea is dirty near the town. Boats take tourists to nearby beaches, such as Playa Marita and Playa Blanca (excellent snorkelling, take own equipment). Both have restaurants, but bring food and water to be safe. Boats to the islands cost US$12-15 (up to six people), depending on distance. Arrange with the boatman what time he will collect you. The tourist office arranges six hour, four-island trips with snorkelling and swimming, US$15. Canoeing trips are available and walks on local trails and to caves (ask for information, eg from Carlos Hernández, or Rodolfo Plaza – see Diving, below). ■ *Getting there: from Cumaná take bus from centre going to Redoma del Indio and walk back along Av Arismendi (via centro) 1 block to small green plaza; jeeps to Mochima depart from here, daily until around 1800 (until 1500-1600 on Sun), US$1.50, luggage extra. No buses between Santa Fe and Mochima, take a por puesto, bargain hard on the price, US$15-21 is reasonable. Bus to Cumaná, 1400, US$1.40.*

Playa Colorada **B** *Colorado Bungalos Hotel Club*. Delightful, split-level mini-apartments with fan, fully-equipped kitchen, small pool, garden. **D** *Villas Turísticas Playa Colorada*, Av Principal, T0416-681 6365 (mob). Clean pool, comfortable rooms, also trailers for 4 (**B**), good restaurant, Apdo 61355, Caracas 1060-A, T0212-952 1393, no credit cards. **D** *Quinta Jaly*, Quinta Jali, C Marchant, Playa Colorada, T0416-681 8113 (mob). Run by Lynn and Jack Allard, they have another house 4 blocks away, a/c, shared bathroom, hot water, very quiet, smaller rooms **E**, family atmosphere, English and French spoken, laundry facilities, German books, good breakfast (US$4), dinner is also served on request. Recommended. Opposite *Jali* is **D** *Villa Nirvana*, run by Sra Rita who is Swiss, T0414-803 0101. Rooms with fan, also mini-apartments with kitchen for 2-4 people. *Sra Mónica* lets rooms, **D**, Av Principal, 3 min walk from the beach, T0416-681 6465 (mob). A/c and use of kitchen, French spoken. *Daniel's Barraca*, at east end of the beach, is good. **D** *Posada Lemus*, Carretera Nacional, 200 m from entrance to town. Very clean, laundry, excellent food. Highly recommended. **D** *Carmita*, Apdo 46/7, on road from beach to village. Excellent breakfast included, very helpful German-speaking local owner. Highly recommended.

Santa Fe B *Playa Santa Fe Resort and Dive Center*, T0414-773 3777, Santafe@ telcel.net.ve Renovated *posada* with various rooms and suites, laundry service, restaurant, owner Jerry Canaday speaks English, diving trips US$65, transport to beaches, mountain bike rental. **C** *Café del Mar*. 1st hotel on beach, fan, good restaurant, tours to islands US$5-10 per person, also to Gran Sabana, Orinoco Delta, owner Matthias Sauter, German spoken. **C** *Siete Delfines*, on beach, dolphins@cantv.net **D** without breakfast, safe, fan, terrace where you can cook, bar, laundry service, ask here for information, water sports and beach games, owner speaks German, English, Italian and some French. **D** *Bahía del Mar*. Pleasant rooms with fan, upstairs rooms have a cool breeze, French and English spoken. **D** *Las Palmeras*, T0414-773 6152. Behind *Cochaima*, fan, room for 5 with fridge and cooker, French spoken. **D** *Posada Los Angeles*, T0414-775 5445. With fan, room for 4 with fridge and cooker, Italian restaurant. **D** *La Sierra Inn*, near *Café del Mar*. Comfortable rooms with fans, self-contained garden suite with fridge and cooker, run by Sr José Vivas, English spoken, helpful, tours to islands from US$10 pp, recommended. **E** *Cochaima*, on beach. Run by Margot, noisy, popular, fan, next to restaurant of same name (slow service), safe. Recommended. **E** *El Portugués, Sr Julio César*, last *posada* on beach. Cooking facilities, very helpful. Recommended. **F** *Posada Lodging*, opposite *Club Naútico*. Basic, shared bath. Other places to eat: *Club Naútico*, fish and Venezuelan dishes, open for lunch and dinner. *Los Molinos (Julios)*, open all day from 0800, beach bar serves sandwiches, hamburgers, beer and cocktails.

Mochima B *Posada Gaby*, at end of road with its own pier next to sea, T0414-773 1104. A/c or fan, breakfast available, lovely place, take guests to islands for US$6-7 per person. **D** *Posada Mochimero*, on main street in front of *Restaurant Mochimero*. A/c or fan. **D** *Villa Vicenta*, Av Principal, T0414-993 5877. Basic rooms with cold water, owner Otilio is helpful. **E** *Posada Beatriz*, T0414-773 2262. Run by Sr Juan Remez, fan, use of kitchen. Sr César Bareto rents rooms for 2 and house for 4 or more, **D**. A highly recommended restaurant is *El Mochimero*, on waterfront 5 mins from jetty, lunch and dinner. *Brisas de Mochima*, at the end of the main road behind the statue. Fish dishes, lunch and dinner. *Dulce y Salado*, next to jetty. Delicious *pastelitos* and *empanadas*, homemade cakes and juices. *Mi Compay*, close to jetty. Hearty breakfasts, *arepas*, juices and coffee.

Sport **Mochima Diving**: *Rodolfo Plaza* runs a diving school for beginners and hires equipment, also walking and canoeing trips around Mochima; contact him in Caracas (Los Palos Grandes, Av Andrés Bello entre 3a y 4a transversal, T0212-961 2531). *Francisco García* (2 doors down from Rodolfo), also runs a diving school (PADI courses) and shop. *Fantasea Dive Center*, scuba24@hotmail.com PADI courses all levels, including 4-day PADI certification course US$300, also basic **D** accommodation.

Cumaná

Phone code: 0293
Colour map 2, grid A1
Population: 280,000
Average temperature:
27°C

Cumaná is possibly the oldest Hispanic city on the South American mainland, founded in 1521 to exploit the nearby pearl fisheries. It straddles both banks of the Río Manzanares. Because of a succession of devastating earthquakes (the last in 1997), only a few historic sites remain. Cumaná is a charming place with its mixture of old and new, but the port area (1½ km from the centre) is not safe at night. Main festivals are 22 January, Santa Inés, a pre-Lenten carnival throughout the state of Sucre and 2 November, the Santos y Fideles Difuntos festival at El Tacal.

A long public beach, **San Luis**, is a short bus ride from the centre of town; take the San Luis/Los Chaimas' bus. The least spoilt part is the end by the *Hotel Los Bordones*.

The **Castillo de San Antonio de la Eminencia** (1686) has 16 mounted cannons, a drawbridge and dungeons from which there are said to be underground tunnels leading to the Santa Inés church. Restored in 1975, it is flood-lit at night (but don't go there after dark, it's not safe). The **Castillo de Santa María de la Cabeza** (1669) is a rectangular fortress with a panoramic view of San Antonio and the elegant homes below. **Convento de San Francisco**, the original Capuchin mission of 1514, was the first school on the continent; its remains are on the Plaza Badaracco Bermúdez. The **Church of Santa Inés** (1637) was the base of the Franciscan missionaries; earthquakes have caused it to be rebuilt five times. A tiny 400-year-old statue of the Virgen de Candelaria is in the garden. The **home of Andrés Eloy Blanco** (1896-1955), one of Venezuela's greatest poets and politicians, on Plaza Bolívar, has been nicely restored to its turn-of-the-century elegance. ■ *Mon-Fri 0800-1200, 1600-2000, Sat and Sun 0900-1200, 1600-2000, free.* On the opposite side of the plaza is **La Gobernación** around a courtyard lined by cannon from Santa María de la Cabeza; note the gargoyles and other colonial features. There are markets selling handicrafts and food on both sides of the river.

The **Museo Gran Mariscal de Ayacucho** in the old Consejo Municipal in Parque Ayacucho commemorates the 150th anniversary of the battle of Ayacucho: mainly portraits, relics and letters of Bolívar and José Antonio Sucre (Bolívar's first lieutenant). ■ *Tue-Fri 0845-1130, 1545-1830; free guided tours.* **Museo del Mar**, has good exhibits of tropical marine life, at the old airport, Avenida Universidad with Avenida Industrial. ■ *Tue-Sun 0830-1130, 1500-1800, US$0.60. Take San Luis minibus from outside the cathedral.*

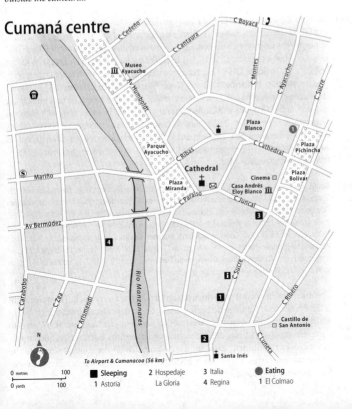

Cumaná centre

To Airport & Cumanacoa (56 km)

| 0 metres | 100 |
| 0 yards | 100 |

■ **Sleeping**
1 Astoria
2 Hospedaje La Gloria
3 Italia
4 Regina

● **Eating**
1 El Colmao

Venezuela

Sleeping Recommended hotels **AL** *Barceló Nuevo Toledo*, end of Av Universidad, close to San Luis beach, T451 8118. A/c, hot water, TV, pool, beach bar, good value all-inclusive deals. **AL** *Los Bordones*, at end of Av Universidad on the beach, T451 1898. A/c, pool, excellent restaurant. **B** *Bubulina's*, Callejón Santa Inés, half a block west of Santa Inés church. In the historic centre, this colonial building has been beautifully restored, a/c, TV, hot water, good service, good restaurant with Venezuelan food. **B** *Gran Hotel*, on Av Universidad near San Luis beach, T451 0671, F451 2677. A/c, pool, restaurant. **C** *Mariño*, Mariño y Junín, T432 0751. Central, a/c, hot water, reasonable restaurant. **C** *Posada San Francisco*, C Sucre near *Hotel Astoria*. Swiss owned, fan. **C** *Regina*, Arismendi y Av Bermúdez, T431 1073. Hot water, a/c, restaurant, very helpful, safe for valuables.

Cheaper hotels can be found across the river, around Plaza Ayacucho, especially on C Sucre: **E-F** *Astoria*, T433 2708. A/c 2300-0600, shower, basic, bar and restaurant with good food cooked to order, tours arranged. **E** *Italia*, esq Plaza Bolívar, T433 3678. Dirty, with fan, or a/c with bath, safe, cheap restaurant. **E** *Hospedaje La Gloria*, opposite Sta Inés church. A/c or fan, basic, helpful.

Eating *El Colmao* on Plaza Pichincha, C Sucre. Very good fish, charming service, not expensive. *All central restaurants close Sun lunchtime.* *Ali Baba*, Av Bermúdez near corner with C Castellón. Excellent, cheap, middle eastern food. Recommended. *Ducheff*, C Sucre. Good pizza. *Jardín de Sport*, Plaza Bolívar. Outdoor café, good food, good but noisy atmosphere. Recommended. For excellent cheap lunches, fish and seafood, try *El Mercadito* at Redoma del Indio. There is a vegetarian restaurant on the 2nd floor of the Centro Comercial Ciudad Cumaná on Av Mariño. *Panadería Cathy*, C Arismendi next to *Hotel Regina*. Good choice of fruit juices. A good *tasca* is *La Casa Tomada*, just off Plaza Bolívar on Sucre. Good atmosphere, reasonable prices.

Good restaurants on Av Perimetral near La Savoia Hotel

Tour operators *Ancar*, C Bolívar 29, T433 3821. Several others.

Transport **Air** New airport 10 km east of centre (taxi fare US$2.50). Daily flights to **Caracas, Porlamar** and **Güiria** (except Sun). **Buses** Terminal 3 km northwest of the centre on Av Las Palomas, just before the junction with the peripheral road (has information office, a little English spoken). Local bus into centre US$0.15, taxi US$2. *Por puesto* to **Puerto La Cruz**, US$10, bus US$5, 1½ hrs. To **Güiria**, US$6, 1230, *por puesto* US$12 (5 hrs), beware of overcharging, often stop in Carúpano. To **Caripe**, 0730 and 1230, US$3.50, 4 hrs. To **Caracas**, US$12 upwards depending on company (7-8 hrs), frequent service but not all advertised buses run; many daily to **Ciudad Guayana** and **Ciudad Bolívar**, US$18 and 15 respectively with *Expresos Guayanesa*, 6 hrs. Other destinations including Maracay, Valencia, Carúpano (US$5), Maturín and Barcelona. **Sea** To **Mariquari** 15 mins, $1, frequent service in covered boat. To **Araya**, infrequent, 1 hr in calm seas, $1.30 for cars or foot passengers. For Ferries to **Isla Margarita**, see page 1408.

Directory **Banks** For cash advance on Visa and MasterCard *Banco Caribe*, Mariño y Junín. *Banco Venezuela*, at Mariño y Rojas, Visa ATM. *Corp Banca*, Av Bermúdez. Amex TCs changed at good rates, no commission. *Oficambio*, Mariño y Carabobo, Edif Funcal, 1 block from Plaza Estudiante. Cash and TCs at official rate (take passport and proof of purchase, may limit exchange to US$200), open weekdays 0800-1130 and 1415-1730, Sat 0830-1130. **Communications** Internet: *Comiti*, Edif Arismendi p2, Av Arismendi. Post and telephone: *Ipostel*, next to Cathedral on C Paraíso. *CANTV*, on C Montés con Boyacá, 2 blocks from Plaza Blanco. **Tourist offices** Dirección de Turismo, C Sucre 49, T431 2232. Very helpful, English spoken, information not always accurate, only open in morning.

Araya Peninsula The main settlement is Araya which has an airport and a ferry dock. The major sight is the Fortaleza de Santiago de León, built by Spain to protect the salt mines, but of which very little now remains. Construction began in 1622 and it took 47 years to complete, most work being done at night to avoid the heat. Entry is free, but the only facilities are a refreshment stand and a picnic area. Today the mines are exploited by a Government-owned corporation, ENSAL. Windsurfing here is excellent, but only for experienced windsurfers.

An area of desert landscapes and pink salt lakes

Venezuela

Sleeping and eating **C-D** *Araya*, difficult to get to without a car. A/c, hot water, with bath, good restaurant, offers tours to the Salinas and around Araya. **D** *Araya's Wind*, beside the Fortaleza in front of beach. Fan, some rooms with bath, cold water, good restaurant, recommended. Next door is **D-E** *Posada Helen*. Fan, cold water. In front of *Posada Helen* is **Parador Turístico Eugenia** for good value meals. *La Monaguense*, 2 blocks from dock. Good value Venezuelan food. *El Delfín*, at the dock. Good food and service. Hamburger stalls around the dock and 2 *panaderías*. Eat early as most places close before 2000.

Transport Cumaná-Araya ferry *la palita* shuttles back and forth from 0600 till 1700, US$0.75, takes cars. At weekends it usually makes only 1 trip each way. Also *Araya Express*, 5 a day. To get to ferry terminal take Conferry bus from **parador del centro**, just up from **CANTV**, in Cumaná (avoid walking; it can be dangerous). Alternatively, take a *tapadito* (passeger ferry in a converted fishing boat) to Manicuare and *camioneta* from there to Araya (15 mins). Return ferries from Araya depart from main wharf at end of Avenida Bermúdez. Ferries to Isla de Margarita, *tapaditos* depart from **Chacopata** (1 hr, US$10 one way).

A paved road runs to Araya from Cariaco, 78 km east on the Cumaná-Carúpano highway; no public transport. The highway from Cumaná, meanwhile, goes on to the port of Carúpano, on the Paría Peninsula (135 km). The coastal route as far as Villa Frontado is beautiful, running along the Golfo de Cariaco past a succession of attractive beaches and small villages. After Cariaco (*population*: 25,350, gas/petrol station), the road winds inland over the Paría Ridge to Carúpano. An alternative road between Cariaco and Carúpano heads due north for 17 km, reaching the coast at **Saucedo**, then runs east for 38 km. The beaches on this coast are covered with shells, which make swimming less attractive, but good sand can be found at Saucedo and the **Balneario Costa Azul** (2 km east of the village of Guaca).

Carúpano

This is a colonial town dating back to 1647, from which 70% of Venezuela's cocoa is shipped. The area around Plaza Santa Rosa has been declared a national and international heritage site by UNESCO. Buildings include the **Museo Histórico**, containing a comprehensive data base on the city, the **Casa del Cable**, location of the first telecommunications link with Europe, and the **Iglesia Santa Rosa**. Carúpano is famous throughout Venezuela as the last place still celebrating a traditional pre-Lenten Carnival: days of dancing, rum drinking, with completely masked women in black (*negritas*). Book accommodation ahead at this time (February). Other local festivals are 3 May, Velorios de la Cruz (street dances); 15 August, Asunción de la Virgen.

Phone code: 0294
Colour map 2, grid A1
Population: 120,000

Sleeping

On the outskirts of Carúpano at **Playa Copey** (ask the *por puesto*/bus to drop you at Playa Copey if arriving from Cumaná or other westerly points, or take a taxi from town, US$5): **C** *Posada Nena*, 1 block from the beach. Fan, hot water, games room, good restaurant, public phone, good service, German spoken, owner Volker Alsen offers day trips to Cueva del Guácharo, Mochima, Medina and Pui Puy, US$25 pp. Recommended. **C-D** *Posada Casa Blanca*, 5 mins from *Posada Nena*. Fan, hot water, safe, good family atmosphere, private stretch of beach illuminated at night, Spanish restaurant, German spoken, discounts for long stays. Recommended.

In **Carúpano**: **B** *Posada El Colibrí*, at the 1st roundabout on entering town, follow the bypass to the right, then left into Av Sur. Cabins beside a pool, in tropical gardens, hot water, fan, TV, fully-equipped kitchen, various personal touches, restaurant service by arrangement, English, German and Dutch spoken, owners Polly and Gunter Hoffman. Recommended. **B** *Posada La Colina*, on hill behind *Hotel Victoria*. A/c, TV, hot water, includes breakfast, pool, restaurant and bar, beautiful view. **C** *Hotel Lilma*, T331 1361, Av Independencia, 3 blocks from Plaza Colón. A/c, hot water in some rooms, TV, restaurant, *tasca*, cinema. **C** *San Francisco*, Av Juncal y Las Margaritas. A/c, no hot water, TV, parking, restaurant, *tasca*. **D** *Posada Zahuco*, next door. A/c, TV, hot water, use of kitchen and lounge. **D** *Centro*, Carabobo, close

Venezuela

to Iglesia Santa Catalina. A/c or fan, TV. **E** *Bologna,* Av Independencia, 1 block from Plaza Santa Rosa. Basic but clean, cheap restaurant.

Eating *La Madriguera,* Av Independencia close to Plaza Santa Rosa. Good Italian food, some vegetarian dishes, Italian and English spoken. *El Fogón de La Petaca,* Av Perimetral on the seafront. Traditional Venezuelan dishes, including fish. *Bam Bam,* kiosk at the end of Plaza Miranda, close to seafront. Tasty hotdogs and hamburgers. *La Flor de Oriente,* Av Libertad, 4 blocks from Plaza Colón. Open from 0800, arepas, fruit juice and main meals, good, large portions, reasonable prices, very busy at lunchtime. *El Oasis,* Juncal in front of Plaza Bolívar. Open from 1800, best Arabic food in Carúpano. Other options include the food stalls in the market, especially the one located next to the carpark, and the *empanadas* in the Plaza Santa Rosa.

Tour operators *Corpomedina,* T331 5241, F331 3021, at the airport, reservations for cabins at Medina or Pui Puy beach: at Medina US$143 for 2, US$250 for 4, including meals, but not alcoholic beverages or transport; at Pui Puy US$51 for 2, US$80 for 4, including breakfast. Transport from the airport to Medina and return for 2 people US$95,to Pui Puy US$110. *Mar y Luna,* louisa@cantv.net Offer day trips to Medina, Pui Puy, Caripe, El Pilar, Los Pozos, specialist surfing and diving packages, walking and hiking in the Paria Peninsula, reconfirmation of international flights, reservations for national flights, reservations for *posadas,* reception of fax and email, general information and advice, English, French, Portuguese and a little Italian spoken.

Transport **Air** The airport is 15 mins' walk from the centre, US$5 by taxi. *Avior* flies daily to Caracas and Porlamar, and less frequently to Barcelona, Güiria and Tucupita.

    Bus To **Caracas,** US$15, 8 hrs, *Rodovías* directly into central Caracas close to Metro Colegio de Ingenieros. Most other buses only go as far as Terminal de Oriente. To **Maracay, Valencia,** US$20, 10 hrs. For other destinations such as **Cumaná,** US$5, 2 hrs, **Puerto La Cruz,** US$7, 4 hrs (Mochima/Santa Fé), **Güiria,** US$5, 2½ hrs *por puestos* are a better option. They run more frequently and make fewer stops. Buses do not go from Carúpano to Caripe, but can be taken from Cumaná or Maturín. **Ferry** A passenger ferry leaves Carúpano at 0700 daily for **Margarita,** returning at 1600, US$10, 1½ hrs. To get to Chacopata from Carúpano for *tapadito* to Margarita (see above), take a *por puesto* at the stop diagonal to the market entrance (where the fish is unloaded), US$5, 1½ hrs.

Directory **Banks** It is not easy to change foreign currency in Carúpano. American Express TCs can be changed until 1400 at *CorpBanca,* next to Plaza Colón. Cash advance on Visa or MasterCard at *Banco Caribe,* Av Independencia, 4 blocks from Plaza Santa Rosa. *Banco Unión,* Independencia y Güiria, Visa ATM. ATMs are unreliable for European cards. It may be possible to change dollars in *Hotels Lilma, San Francisco* or *Victoria,* but rates are not good. **Communications** Internet: at *Milenium,* Av Independencia 136, and *Cyber Café* at No 158. Both *Ipostel* and *CANTV* are at the end of Carabobo, 1 block up from Plaza Santa Rosa.

Paria Peninsula

A finger of land stretches out to the most easterly point on Venezuela's Caribbean coast. It contains peaceful, coastal towns, beaches and forest.

Río Caribe

Phone code: 0294
Population: 25,100
20 km E of Carúpano

This lovely fishing village used to be a major cacao-exporting port. It is a good jumping-off point for the beautiful beaches of Playa Medina (in an old coconut plantation, 25 km east) and Pui Puy, both famous for their crystal-clear water and golden sands.

    To get to Playa Medina, take a taxi with *Línea San Miguel* (Rivero y Mariño, T61107), departing in morning till 1000, returning around 1500, US$30-35 return trip per car, US$35-40 to Pui Puy. Also *camioneta* departs from opposite petrol station at exit to village (US$0.70, one hour), drops you at entrance to beaches, but it's 1½ hours walk from there (further to Pui Puy). Further east is the delightful village of **San Juan de las Galdonas** and some great beaches.

Río Caribe: **B** *Posada Caribana*, Av Bermúdez 25. Beautifully restored colonial house, tastefully decorated, some a/c, otherwise fans, with breakfast, restaurant, bar, excursions. **C** *La Posada de Arlet*, 24 de Julio 22. Including breakfast, a/c, laundry service, French and German spoken, bar, offers day trips to local beaches and rents mountain bikes. Recommended. **C** *Mar Caribe*, corner of boulevard next to pier. A/c, hot water, pool, restaurant. **E** *Posada Vanexa*, on right as you enter village. Basic but clean, use of cooker. **F** *Pensón Papagayo*, 14 de Febrero, 1 block from police station, opposite *liceo*. Charming house and garden, fan, shared bath with hot water, use of kitchen, German spoken, nice atmosphere, owner Cristina Castillo leads tours in the area. Also private, unmarked pensions; ask around.

In **San Juan de las Galdonas**: **B** *Las Pioneras*. 4 star overlooking the main beach, fan or a/c, hot water, bar/restaurant, swimming pool, jacuzzi, parking. **C** *Posada Las Tres Carabelas*, T0416-894 0914 (mob), carabelas3@hotmail.com Fans and mosquito nets, restaurant, bar, wonderful view, managers Santiago Roch and Mónica Pérez have extensive knowledge of the local area and can arrange hikes and excursions. **C** *Habitat Paria*, T0414-779 7955, www.habitatparia.vzla.org With breakfast and supper, fan, hot water in some rooms, bar/restaurant, terraces, garden, ask for Juliano, Nicol or Angel. The *posada* is right behind Barlovento beach on the right hand side of San Juan. Also run day trips by boat US$30 pp per minimum 5 passengers, soft drinks and packed lunch included.

Buses direct from Caracas (Terminal del Oriente) to Río Caribe at 0730 and 0930 (check times in advance), 10 hrs. Buses depart Río Caribe from the other Plaza Bolívar, 7 blocks up from pier. There are no exchange facilities in Río Caribe. Jeep Carúpano-San Juan de las Galdonas 1100, 1½ hrs; camioneta from Río Caribe from stop near petrol station, 0600 till 1300.

Güiria

At Bohordal, the paved road from Río Caribe across the mountains meets Route 9, which continues to the pleasant town of Irapa (*Population*: 11,500; hotels, bus connections). The paved highway continues 42 km to Güiria, a friendly, peaceful town and a littered beach. Feria de la Pesca, 14 July. Roads end here, but gasoline is available.

Phone code: 0294
Colour map 2, grid A2
Population: 30,000

C *El Digno*, Av Miranda, on way out of town towards beach. Best in town, expensive trips to Trinidad. **C** *La Posada de Chuchu*, C Bideau, 2 blocks from plaza. Good *creole* restaurant. Recommended. **C** *Playa Paraíso*, 10 mins from town on dirty beach. OK (but has caged toucan), trips to Pedernales and Trinidad. **D** *Miramar*, Turiparin, close to Banco República. A/c, cheaper with fan. **E** *Plaza*, esq Plaza Bolívar. Basic, restaurant, luggage store. Restaurants include *El Milagro*, corner of Plaza Bolívar. OK. *Rincón Güireño*, corner of Plaza Sucre. Recommended for breakfast (also rents rooms, **D-E**). Everywhere closed Sun, except for kiosks on Plaza Bolívar.

Buses Depart Plaza Sucre, at top end of C Bolívar: *Expresos Maturín* to Maturín (US$6, 6 hrs), Caripito, San Félix, Cumaná, Puerto La Cruz and Caracas; also *Expresos Los Llanos* (recommended). **Boats** To **Macuro**: Mon-Sat, possibly Sun, at 1000 from pier 1½ blocks from *Hotel Miramar* (US$2.50-5, take sunblock and plastic sheeting – ask for Don Pedro), return 0530, 3 hrs; to **Pedernales**, depart daily 1100-1200 from the Playita, for fares, see below. **Travel to Trinidad** A ferry leaves every Wed at 1500 for Chaguaramas, Trinidad (leaves Trinidad at 0900, Wed), 3½ hrs, US$47.50 one way (US$95 return). There is a US$23 exit tax from Venezuela (US$12.35 from Trinidad). Talk to Siciliano Bottini at the *Agencia Naviera* for other ships to Trinidad. Fishing boats and trading vessels can often be persuaded to take passengers.

Banks *Corp Banca* for American Express TCs, good rates, no commission. *La Librería* changes cash at poor rates. **Useful services** Immigration: visas can't be arranged in Güiria, should you need one; maximum length of stay 14 days (but check). For more than 14 days, get visa in Caracas. Remember to get exit stamp before leaving Venezuela. Officially, to enter Trinidad and Tobago you need a ticket to your home country, but a return to Venezuela is usually enough.

Macuro
Population: 1,500

A quiet town on the tip of the Peninsula, Macuro is accessible only by boat (two hours from Güiria). It was around here Columbus made the first recorded European landing on the continent on 5 August 1498. Locals like to believe the landing took place at Macuro, and the town's official new name is Puerto Colón. A big party is held here every year on 12 October to mark the official 'discovery' of America. The beach is unattractive but the coast on the north side of the peninsula is truly wonderful; crystal-clear water and dazzling sands backed by dense jungle. A highly recommended trip for the adventurous is the hike to **Uquire** and **Don Pedro** on the north coast; 4-6 hours walk, places to hang a hammock or pitch a tent. In Uquire ask for Nestor Mata, the Inparques guard, very helpful. **NB** This part of the peninsula is a national park; you need a permit from Inparques in Caracas. A highly recommended guide is Eduardo Rothe, who put together, and lives at, the Museo de Macuro on Calle Bolívar, one block from *Posada Beatriz*. He'll take you on walking tours to the north coast, US$10-15 per person per day, or boat trips (US$60 per boat), or fishing trips (US$30 per person per day, including mangroves). **Sleeping and eating** E *Posada Beatriz*, C Mariño y Carabobo. Basic, clean, with bath, fan. F *Posada Marlo*, C Mariño. Shared bath, fan. Restaurants only open weekends. Good food at Sra Mercedes, on C Carabobo, round corner from *Posada Beatriz* (blue house). Also a few basic shops and pharmacy. Boat to Güiria at 0500, arrive early, US$2.50-5 per person.

Güiria to the Orinoco delta

You can visit the Orinoco delta from Güiria. There are motor boats trading between Güiria and **Pedernales** (*Population: 3,100*), a small, largely indigenous village in the delta. Accommodation here is basic in the extreme. The store on the riverbank has rooms with cooking facilities, **F**; also at the blue house opposite, **G**. For a shower, ask Jesús, who runs a fish-freezing business. Pedernales is only accessible by boat. From Güiria, about five hours, US$13, check for boats at the harbour (the *Guadeloupe*, *Verónica* and *Mil del Valle*), the *Hotel Fortuna*, the *Hotel Plaza*, or ask for Andrecito, who lives on north side of small plaza nearest harbour entrance. Cargo boats operated by men from Pedernales, known in Güiria as 'Los Indios', charge US$7.50-10 negotiable according to number of passengers, no seats, deck space in open only, can be rough. From **Tucupita** (see page 1424) boats are easier to find. To Tucupita, locals pay US$5, but you may get asked for US$40 (ask for Juan but be prepared to bargain hard), leave at daybreak, 6-7 hours, recommended as the boat stops in some of the villages, where you can buy hammocks (*chinchorros*), fish, cheese, and some beautiful carved animal figures made of balsa wood (see also page 1425). Many birds and river dolphins may be seen en route.

Maturín

Phone code: 0291
Colour map 2, grid A1

The capital of Monagas State is a thriving and fast-growing petrol town, with relatively expensive accommodation and facilities.

Sleeping & eating

C *Chaima Inn*, Final Av Raúl Leoni, T641 6062. Pool, satellite TV, good restaurant with buffet lunch. Recommended. C *Paris*, Av Bolívar 183, T641 4028. A/c, hot water, safe, central. Recommended. C *Sur Oriente*, C 28 No 28. A/c, TV, cheaper with fan, good, safe, family hotel. E *El Terminal*, at bus terminal, just out of town on road to Barcelona. Very convenient, a/c, drinking water supplied, helpful owner. Recommended. For eating, try *Yarúa*, behind the Cathedral. Most expensive, seafood and grilled meat. *Pizzería Mamma Mia*, opposite *Hotel Sur Oriente*. Good.

Venezuela

Air Flights to Caracas (*Aeropostal, Avior*). *Avior* also to **Porlamar** and *Aeropostal* to Cumaná. Good restaurant upstairs in airport. **Buses** Main terminal at end of Av Bolívar. Buses leave 3 times a day for **Caracas** (US$11, 8 hrs, *por puesto* US$22); buses for **Ciudad Guayana, San Félix** (0815, 3 hrs, US$7, including ferry) and **El Dorado** leave from terminal near the airport. To **Puerto La Cruz** or **Barcelona**, take a *por puesto* to Cumaná and change, 2 hrs, US$7.25. Bus only to **Ciudad Bolívar**, US$7.50, change in Ciudad Guyana-San Félix (no *por puesto*). Bus to **Carúpano**, at 1000, US$5, 3 hrs. To **Caripe**, 2½ hrs, US$2, *por puesto*, 2 hrs, US$4.50. Bus to **Río Caribe**, US$5, 4 hrs, at 1100 with *Expresos Maturín*, ticket does not guarantee a seat or even transport. Bus to **Tucupita** at 1100, US$5 with *Expresos Guayanesa*, 3-4 hrs. Bus to **Güiria**, US$6, 6 hrs, *Expresos Maturín*; to **Irapa** 1230, 4½ hrs, US$7.

Transport
Travelling between the airport and town: por puesto Nos 1, 5, 6 (US$0.35), or bus from main road outside airport (US$0.20). Taxis from the Responsable de Venezuela office will try to charge much more

Banks *Italcambio* (American Express), C C Portofino, Av Bolívar con Cra 8, T291 642 2901. *Banco Mercantil*, C Monagas and opposite central market, most likely to accept TCs. *Banco Unión*, Cra 7 y Juncal, and *Banco de Venezuela*, Bolívar y Casualidad, Visa ATMs. **Communications** Internet: *Gelatos y Algo Más*, Av Principal de la Floresta, between C$ and 5.

Directory

Caripe

At San Francisco, on the Maturín-Cumaná road (212 km, all paved but twisty; beautiful tropical mountain scenery), is a branch road running 22½ km northeast to Caripe, an attractive town set in beautiful mountain scenery. A good place to escape from the beaches and especially good for walking and biking. There is also a paved road between Carúpano and Caripe via Santa Cruz and Santa María, 2 hours. *Feria de las Flores* is on 2-12 August and *NS del Pilar* is 10-12 October.

Phone code: 0292
Population: 23,880

C *Hacienda Campo Claro*, at Teresén, T551013. Cabins with cooking facilities and bath, can provide meals, horseriding. **D** *Samán*, Enrique Chaumer 29, T/F545 1183, oscargh@cantv.net **C** full board, hot water, pool, good restaurant, free internet access, runs local tours (US$10 to Cueva del Guácharo), ask for Oscar at reception, English spoken. **E** *Venezia*, Av Enrique Chaumer 118, 5 mins from centre, T545 1875. No sheets on beds, very good restaurant, owner speaks English. **E** *San Francisco*, opposite church on Plaza Bolívar. Hot water, not very clean. **F** *La Posada*, next to *San Francisco*. Restaurant closes at 2000. Recommended. **F** *La Fogata*, opposite *San Francisco*. Shared bath, large rooms, good value.

Sleeping

Bus terminal 1 block south of main plaza. Bus from Caripe to **Caracas** at 1800 stops in Cumaná, pick up at San Remo Sur office, next to *Hotel San Francisco*. Caracas direct leaves at 2000. Bus to **Maturín** direct, 0600, 2½ hrs, US$2. *Por puesto* to Ciudad Bolívar 1500, 1½ hrs, US$3.50. Bus between **Cumaná** and Caripe leaves at 0730 and 1130, 3 hrs.

Transport

This remarkable cave was discovered by Humboldt and has since been penetrated 10½ km along a small, crystal-clear stream. First come the caves in which live about 18,000 *guácharos* (oil birds) with an in-built radar system for sightless flight. Their presence supports a variety of wildlife in the cave: blind mice, fish and crabs in the stream, yellow-green plants, crickets, ants, etc. For two hours at dusk (about 1900) the birds pour out of the cave's mouth. Through a very narrow entrance is the *Cueva del Silencio* (Cave of Silence). About 2 km in is the *Pozo del Viento* (Well of the Wind).

Cueva del Guácharo
12 km from Caripe

Wear old clothes, stout shoes and be prepared to get wet. In the wet season it can be a bit slippery; tours into the cave may be shortened or even closed in August-September because of rising water level. There is a caving museum with a leaflet in English, US$0.80; good cafeteria. Opposite the road is a paved path to **Salto Paila**, a 25 m waterfall, about 30 minutes' walk, guides available. A beautiful path, built by Inparqes, starts at the caving museum, with some nice shelters for picnics. Camping is allowed by the cave for US$5, or you can sleep without a tent under the roof by the café for free. ■ *The cave is open 0800-1700, US$2 entry with compulsory guide in Spanish, US$6 with English speaking guide. Last tour at 1600. Tour maybe shortened at busy times. Leave backpacks at the ticket office. Tape recorders and cameras are*

Venezuela

allowed, the guides inform you when you can use a flash. To go further than 1½ km into the caves, permits from Inparques in Caracas and special equipment are needed.

Transport There are frequent buses from Caripe to the caves. If staying in Caripe, take a por puesto (a jeep marked Santa María – Muelle), at 0800, US$5, see the caves and waterfall and catch the Cumaná bus which goes past the caves between 1200 and 1230. Taxis from Caripe (US$8.75), hitching difficult. Bus from Cumaná direct to the Cueva del Guácharo leaves at 0715, US$3.50 and stops right in front of the caves. Por puesto from Cumaná US$12.50, 2 hrs. Private tours can be organized from Cumaná for about US$15 per person, with guide.

Isla de Margarita

Margarita is the country's main Caribbean holiday destination. Some parts are crowded but there are undeveloped beaches and colonial villages. Despite the property boom and frenetic building on much of the coast and in Porlamar, much of the island has been given over to natural parks. Of these the most striking is the Laguna La Restinga.

Isla de Margarita is in fact one island whose two sections are linked by the 18 km sandspit which separates the sea from the Restinga lagoon. At its largest, Margarita is about 32 km from north to south and 67 km from east to west. Isla de Margarita and two close neighbours, Coche and Cubagua, form the state of Nueva Esparta. Most of its people live in the developed eastern part, which has some wooded areas and fertile valleys.

The western part, the Península de Macanao, is hotter and more barren, with scrub, sand dunes and marshes. Wild deer, goats and hares roam the interior, but four-wheel drive vehicles are needed to penetrate it. The entrance to the Península de Macanao is a pair of hills known as **Las Tetas de María Guevara**, a national monument covering 1,670 ha. There are mangroves in the **Laguna de las Marites**

Isla de Margarita

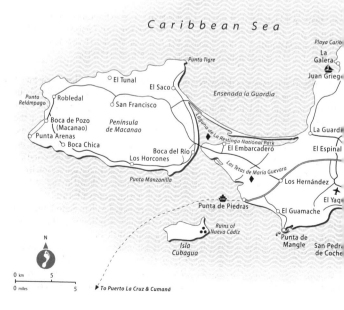

natural monument, west of Porlamar. Other parks are **Cerro El Copey**, 7,130 ha, and **Cerro Matasiete y Guayamurí**, 1,672 ha (both reached from La Asunción).

The climate is exceptionally good; very little rain. The roads are good, and a bridge connects the two parts. Nueva Esparta's population is over 250,000, of whom 85,000 live in the main city, Porlamar. The capital is La Asunción.

Margarita's status as a duty-free zone attracts Venezuelan shoppers, who go in droves for clothing, electronic goods and other consumer items. Gold and gems are good value, but many things are not. Its popularity means that various packages are on offer, sometimes at good value, especially off-season.

Getting there & around
See transport, page 1407, for further details

There are many flights from Caracas and other Venezuelan cities, as well as international scheduled services. There also ferries from Puerto La Cruz and Cumaná in Venezuela. Car hire is a cheap way of getting around. The roads are generally good and most are paved. A bridge connects the 2 parts. Sign posts are often non-existent or poorly-positioned. It is best not to drive outside Porlamar after dark. Beware of robbery of hired vehicles. Public transport is available if you don't want to drive.

Tourist offices

The private **Cámara de Turismo** (T2639024) is located at the seaward end of Av Santiago Mariño in Porlamar. They have free maps and are very helpful. A tourist information booth on Av 4 de Mayo, opposite the *Dugout* sports bar, has a good map, coupon booklet and *La Vista* tourist magazine. Travel agencies can also provide a tourist guide to Margarita. *MultiGuía de Margarita* (US$4) is published yearly and is a useful directory of tourist information and can be found in kiosks, *panaderías*, cafés, and bookshops. A good English-language newspaper, *Mira*, is published on the island, the editor/publisher acts also as an inexpensive tour guide; Av Santiago Mariño, Ed Carcaleo Suites, Apartamento 2-A, Porlamar (T261 3351). The best map is available from *Corpoven*. Websites: www.islamargarita.com and www.margaritaonline.com

Safety

Don't wander around late at night, wherever you are on the island, without asking if the area is safe. Women alone should avoid the centre after dark.

Festivals on Margarita

Many religious festivals on the island, including **19 Mar** at Paraguachí (*Feria de San José*, 10 days); **26 Jul** at Punta de Piedras; **31 Jul** (Batalla de Matasiete) and **15 Aug** (Asunción de la Virgen) at La Asunción; **1-8 Sep** at El Valle; **4-11 Nov** at Boca del Río, **4-30 Nov** at Boca del Pozo; **5-6 Dec** at Porlamar; **27 Dec-3 Jan** at Juan Griego. See map for locations.

Porlamar

Most of the hotels are at Porlamar. If you're seeking sun and sand, then head for the north coast towns. Porlamar's beaches are nothing special, but it makes up for what it lacks in this department with its shops. The trendy Avenida Santiago Mariño and surroundings are the place for designer labels, but decent copies can be found on Blvds Guevara and Gómez and around Plaza Bolívar in the centre. For super bargains on denims,

*Phone code: 0295
20 km from airport
28 km from Punta de Piedra, where ferries dock*

Venezuela

t-shirts, shorts, swimming gear, bikinis, towels, and underwear, take a bus to the *Conejeros* market. At Igualdad y Díaz is the Museo de Arte Francisco Narváez, displaying the work of this contemporary local sculptor. At night everything closes by 2300.

Excursions Ferries go to the **Isla de Coche** (11 km by 6), which has 4,500 inhabitants and one of the richest salt mines in the country (see Transport). They also go, or hire only, to **Isla de Cubagua**, which is totally deserted, but you can visit the ruins of Nueva Cádiz (which have been excavated). Large private yachts and catamarans take tourists on day trips to Coche.

Sleeping

There is both a C Mariño and Av Santiago Mariño in the centre. Almost all of the luxury hotels are grouped in the Costa Azul suburb to the east of Porlamar

Most hotels and tour operators work on a high season/low season price system. High season prices (Christmas, Easter and Jun-Aug) can be as much as 25% higher. Flights and hotels are usually fully booked at this time. In low season, bargaining is possible.

The following are all recommended. **AL** *Bella Vista*, Av Santiago Mariño, T261 7222, www.hbellavista.com Luxury hotel with all expected services, also beach, car hire, French restaurant, and restaurant serving *comida criolla*. **AL** *Hilton*, Los Uveros, Costa Azul, T2621132, res-margarita@hilton.com Luxury services plus beach, parasailing, car hire, casino. **A** *Margarita Princess*, Av 4 de Mayo, T261 8732, www.margaritaprincess.com Large, comfortable rooms, balcony, restaurant, small pool, *Highberg Tours* (see below). **A** *For You*, Av Santiago Mariño, T263 8635, F261 8708. Large rooms, breakfast (and welcome cocktail) included, excellent service and roof restaurant, bar. **A** *Colibrí*, Av Santiago Mariño, T261 6346, www.hotelcolibri.com.ve Good rooms, breakfast included, *cambio*, car hire, travel agency. **C** *Imperial*, Prolongación de Marcano y Campos, T261 6420, F261 5056. Best rooms in front have sea view, comfortable, safe, a/c, hot water, parking, English spoken. **C** *Posada Lutecia*, Campos Cedeño a Marcano, T/F263 8526. Lovely rooms with personal touch, a/c, hot water, TV, French-owned, café with outdoor seating. **C** *Tamaca*, Prolongación de Marcano y Campos, near the sea, T261 1602. Popular, a/c, OK, **D** with fan, good atmosphere, German-run *tasca*. **D** *Brasilia*, San Nicolás. Quiet, nice new rooms at back. **D** *Malecón*, Marina y Arismendi, T263 5723. Sea view from front rooms, very helpful and generous, dangerous area at night, best to take a taxi. **G** *Porto Viejo*, La Marina y Fajardo, T263 8480. Simple hostel in colonial building, basic, not overly friendly, take care at night. Many others around Plaza Bolívar, but none is particularly salubrious or good value.

Eating

Upmarket dining such as Japanese food in Urb Costa Azul on Av Bolívar

Plenty of eating places on Campos and 4 de Mayo, including Mediterráneo Café, Italian, and *Flaco's Ribs*, Tex-Mex. On 4 de Mayo: *El Picadilly*, good, cheap lunch; *Dragón Chino*, great Chinese food. *Doña Martha*, Velázquez near Hernández. Colombian food, good, inexpensive. *El Punto Criollo*, Igualdad near *Hotel Porlamar*. Excellent value *comida margariteña*. *Rancho Grande*, C Guevara, near Playa El Agua bus stop. Colombian, good value. *El Pollo de Carlitos*, Marcano y Martínez. Nice location, live music most nights, good food and value. *Bahía* bar-restaurant, Av Raúl Leoni y Vía El Morro. Excellent value, live music. *Los 3 Delfines*, Cedeño 26-9. Good seafood. *La Isla*, Mariño y Cedeño. 8 fast food counters ranging from hamburgers to sausages from around the world. *Dino's Grill*, Igualdad y Martínez. Open 0700-1400, buffet lunch, indoor/outdoor seating, grill, home-made sausages, wood-fired pizza oven, cheap, good service.

Entertainment

Mosquito Coast Club, behind *Bella Vista Hotel*. Good merengue and rock music, bar outside, also does excellent Mexican meals (beware of overcharging on simple items like water). *Village Club*, Av Santiago Mariño. Recommended disco, expensive drinks, cover charge. *Doce 34*, Av 4 de Mayo. 2 dance floors. Highly recommended. Also *Woody's Bar*, Av 4 de Mayo. A spit and sawdust venue that's good for a drink and a dance. In the Centro Comercial Costal Azul on Av Bolívar there are 3 bar/clubs, including the popular *Señor Frogs*. *Cheers*, Av Santiago Mariño y Tubores and *Dugout*, Av 4 de Mayo, are popular sports bars. Many of the hotels in Urb Costa Azul have relatively inexpensive casinos; the best are the *Casino del Sol* at the *Hotel Marina Bay*, and *Gran Casino Hilton*. Porlamar has many illegal casinos, too.

Besides all the duty-free shops, *Del Bellorín*, Cedeño, near Av Santiago Mariño, is good for **Shopping**
handicrafts. Street sellers lay out their handicrafts on Av Santiago Mariño during the afternoon. Good selection of jewellery at *Sonia Gems*, on Cedeño. When purchasing jewellery,
bargain hard, don't pay by credit card (surcharges are imposed), get a detailed guarantee of
the item.

Esparta Tours, Final de Av Santiago Mariño, near *Hotel Bella Vista*, T261 5524. **Jeep tours**   **Tour operators**
around Margarita from: *Highberg Tours*, *Hotel Margarita Princess*, Av 4 de Mayo, T/F263   **& sport**
1170, jeepsafari@telcel.net US$50 pp, guides in English, German, and Polish; *CC Tours*, El   *Most tours can be*
Colegio, T264 2003, taking in Cerro El Copey and La Restinga national parks, off-roading in   *arranged through*
Macanao Peninsula, and a couple of beaches, including food and drinks. Porlamar is a good   *travel agents of which*
place to book **scuba diving** and **snorkelling** trips: most go to Los Frailes, a small group of   *there are plenty*
islands to the north of Playa Agua, and reputedly the best diving and snorkelling in
Margarita, but it's also possible to dive at Parque Nacional La Restinga and Isla Cubagua.
Enomis' Divers, at *Hotel Margarita Dynasty*, Los Uveros, and Caribbean Center Mall, Av
Bolívar, T/F262 2977 enomisdivers@hotmail.com Recommended. *Octopus*, at *Hotel Hilton*,
Los Uveros, and Av Bolívar 13, T264 6272, octopus@cantv.net *Margarita Divers*, at the
Marina Concorde, T264 2350. Offer ½ and 1-day dives and PADI courses. Prices from US$85
pp for an all-inclusive full day (2 dives), but bargaining is possible if you have a group of 4 or
more. Snorkelling is always about half the price of scuba diving. The private yachts *Viola Festi-
val* and *Moon Dancer*, and the catamarans *Yemaya* and *Catatumbo* all can be hired for mini
cruises to the island of Coche or Isla Cubagua. Contact *Viola Turismo*, Caribbean Center Mall,
Av Bolívar, T267 0552, *Enomis' Divers* (see above), or *Octopus* (see above). Expect to pay
US$35-40 pp. They can also arrange fishing trips. *Moony Shuttle Service*, T263 5418, runs
treks in Cerro El Copey. **Bicycles** can be hired for US$6 per day from *Bicimanía*, Caribbean
Center Mall, Av Bolívar T/F262 9116, bicimania@cantv.net

Local Car hire: a cheap way of getting around the island; several offices at the airport and   **Transport**
larger hotels. *Ramcar II*, at airport and *Hotel Bella Vista*, recommended as cheap and reliable,
non- deductible insurance (others on Av Santiago Mariño). In all cases, check the brakes and
bodywork and check conditions and terms of hire thoroughly. Scooters can also be hired.
Maruba Motor Rentals, La Mariña. English spoken, good maps, US$16 bikes for 2, US$13
bikes for one. Highly recommended. Motor cycles may not be ridden between 2000 and
0500. **NB** Make sure to fill up before leaving Porlamar as service stations become scarce the
further away you get.
   Driving on Isla Margarita: the roads are generally good and most are paved. Signposts are
often non-existent, confusing, or poorly-positioned. Although the free maps of the island are
sometimes just as confusing, it is a good idea to have one with you before you start driving. It
is best not to drive outside Porlamar after dark. Also beware of robbery of hired vehicles.
   Public: *Por Puestos* serve most of the island: to Punta de Piedras, from Maneiro, Mariño a
Arismendi, US$0.75; Airport, from Centro Comercial AB, Av Bolívar (0530 and 2000 every
day), US$1; La Asunción, from Fajardo, Igualdad a Marcano, US$0.35; Pampatar, from Fajardo
y La Marina, US$0.25; La Restinga, from Mariño, La Marina a Maneiro, US$1; Playa El Agua,
from Guevara, Marcano a Cedeño; Juan Griego, from Av Miranda, Igualdad a Marcano,
US$0.65; El Valle, from Av Miranda, Igualdad a Marcano; Playa Guacuco, from Fraternidad, La
Marina a Mérito (mornings), from Fajardo, Igualdad a Velásquez (afternoons); El Conejeros,
Fraternidad, Igualidad a Velásquez.
   Taxi: fares published by *Mira* but not uniformly applied by drivers. To hire a taxi for a day
costs US$10-15 per hour. Always fix fare in advance; 30% surcharge after 2100.

Long distance Air: Gen Santiago Mariño Airport, between Porlamar and Punta de Piedras,   *There are too many*
has the international and national terminals at either end. Taxi from Porlamar US$10. There   *flight options to list*
are scheduled flights to Miami, Dusseldorf and Frankfurt, Port of Spain, Grenada and St Lucia,   *here: check with local*
and internal flights to almost all Venezuela's airports. All national airlines have routes to   *offices for details*
Margarita. Many daily flights to/from **Caracas**, with *Avensa, Aeropostal, Laser, Aserca, Avior*,
LAI, and *Air Venezuela*, 45 mins flight; tickets are much cheaper if purchased in Venezuela in

Venezuela

local currency. Reservations made from outside Venezuela are not always honoured. To Canaima and to **Los Roques** with *Aereotuy* and *Rutaca*.

Very busy at weekends and Mon

Ferries: From **Puerto La Cruz** to Margarita (**Punta de Piedras**): *Conferry*, Los Cocos terminal, Puerto La Cruz, T0281-267 7847/267 7129, F0281-267 7090 www.conferry.com Ferries to Margarita, depart 4 times a day (check times, extras when busy), 5 hrs, passengers US$16.50 one-way 1st class, US$12.50 2nd, children and pensioners half price, cars US$30. A fast ferry, *Margarita Express*, takes 2 hrs, US$40, cars US$70. Also from Terminal Marítimo, La Guaira, near Caracas, T/F331 2433. Fares are twice the price. Ferries not always punctual. Don't believe taxi drivers at bus terminal who may tell you there's a ferry about to leave. To get to terminal in Puerto La Cruz, take 'Bello Monte' *por puesto* from Libertad y Anzoátegui, 2 blocks from Plaza Bolívar. From **Cumaná**, Conferry Terminal, Puerto Sucre, T/F0293-431 1462, twice a day, US$10 one way for passengers. *Conferry* freefone number for reservations 0800-337 7900. *Gran Cacique II* is a passenger-only hydrofoil service that also runs from Puerto La Cruz, T0800-227 2600 (2 daily, US$19, 2 hrs), and Cumaná, T0293-432 0011 (2 daily, US$16, 2 hrs). A ferry operated by *Conferry* from Punta de Piedras to Coche sails once a day, US$1.50, 1 hr.

Road: Several bus companies in Caracas sell through tickets from Caracas to Porlamar, arriving about midday. Buses return to Caracas from La Paralela bus station in Porlamar.

Directory

Banks are open 0830-1130, 1400-1630

Airline offices *Aeropostal*, Hotel Hilton, Los Uveros, T264 5877, T0800-284 6637. *Aereotuy*, Av Santiago Mariño, T263 0367. *Air Venezuela*, Hotel Plaza Royal, Fermín, T263 0367. *Aserca*, CC Margarita Plaza, Av Santiago Mariño, near Hotel Bella Vista, T261 6186, T0800-648 8356. *Avensa*, at airport, T269 1315. *Avior*, at airport, T269 1314. *LAI*, at airport, T269 1352. *Laser*, Edif Bahía de Guaraguao, Av Santiago Mariño, T269 1216, T0800-527 3700. *Rutaca*, Galería La Rosa, Cedeño, T269 9236. **Banks** National banks on Avs Santiago Mariño and 4 de Mayo. **Casas de cambio**: *Cambio Cussco* at Velásquez y Av Santiago Mariño. *Italcambio*, CC Jumbo, Av 4 de Mayo, Nivel Ciudad. **Communications** Internet: *Cyber Café Jumbo Margarita*, CC Jumbo, Av 4 de Mayo, Nivel Fiesta. *Neon's Chat & Play*, Marcano, A Hernández a C Narváez. *News Café*, 4 de Mayo, open 0800-midnight. Post Office: on Maneiro. **Telephone**: *CANTV*, Av Bolívar, Fajardo a Fraternidad. **Consulates** Canada, Final Av Santiago Mariño, next to *Aserca*, T261 3475, **Denmark**, Prolongación Av 4 de Mayo, T262 4002, josemendoza@enlared.net **France**, Autopista El Valle, T287 0660, max@aguanuestra.com **Spain**, Av 4 de Mayo, T264 1771. **UK**, Douglas Weller, Av Aldonza Manrique, Playa el Angel, Pampatar, T/F262 4665, dw@enlared.net

La Asunción

Population: 30,000

The capital is a few kilometres inland from Porlamar. It has several colonial buildings, a cathedral, and the fort of Santa Rosa, with a famous bottle dungeon. ■ *Mon 0800-1500, other days 0800-1800*. There is a museum in the Casa Capitular, and a local market, good for handicrafts. Nearby is the Cerro Matasiete historical site, where the defeat of the Spanish on 31 July 1817 led to their evacuation of the island. **Sleeping B** *Ciudad Colonial*, C La Margarita, T242 3086. Upmarket, pleasant. **D** *Hotel Asunción*, C Unión, 2 blocks from Plaza Bolívar, T242 0902. With a/c, fridge, room prices vary. Frequent *por puesto* service stops in front of hotel.

Beaches on Margarita

There are wild, isolated beaches, long white stretches of sand bordered by palms, developed beaches with restaurants and sunshades for hire, and beaches where you can surf or snorkel. Sunscreen is essential. The beaches of Porlamar suffer from their popularity at weekends. The *Bella Vista* beach, although crowded, is kept clean; lots of restaurants. Playa Concorde is small, sheltered and tucked away to the side of the marina. Playa Morena is a long, barren strip of sand serving the Costa Azul hotel zone to the east of the city. La Caracola is a very popular beach for the younger crowd.

The beaches on the east coast are divided into ocean and calm beaches, according to their location in relation to the open sea. The former tend to be rougher (good surfing and windsurfing) and colder. Water is clear and unpolluted. Restaurants, *churuatas* (bars built like native huts), sunshades and deckchairs are widespread. Hire charges are about US$5.

For a more Venezuelan atmosphere go northeast to **Pampatar**, which is set around a bay favoured by yachtsmen as a summer anchorage. Pampatar has the island's largest fort, San Carlos de Borromeo, built in 1662 after the Dutch destroyed the original. Visit also the church of Cristo del Buen Viaje, the Library/Museum and the customs house. There is an amusement park to the southwest of Pampatar, called Isla Aventura. ■ *Fri-Sat 1800-2400, Sun 1700-2400, more frequently in peak holiday season. US$5 adults, US$3.35 children, all rides included (low season US$0.50 and each ride US$0.30-0.60.* Jet skis can be hired on the clean and pretty beach. A scale model of Columbus' Santa María is used for taking tourists on trips. A fishing boat can be hired for US$20 for 2½ hrs, 4-6 passengers; shop around for best price, good fun and fishing.

Pampatar
Population: 25,000

Sleeping and eating AL pp *Flamingo Beach*, T262 4822, F262 0271. 5-star, all-inclusive, food, drinks, entertainment, service, taxes, casino, good value. Beach restaurant *Antonio's*, recommended; also *Trimar*, good value. *El Farallón*, beside the Castillo. Excellent seafood. There is a language school: *Centro de Linguistica Aplicada*, Corocoro Qta, CELA Urb. Playa El Angel. T262 8198, http://cela-ve.com

Reached from La Asunción by a road through the Guayamurí reserve, this is a popular local beach with a lot of surf, fairly shallow, palm trees, restaurants and parking lot; excellent horseriding here or up into the hills, US$30 for two hours, contact Harry Padrón at the ranch in Agua de Vaca, or phone travel agent on 261 1311. Playa Parguito further up the east coast is best for surfing (strong waves; full public services).

Playa Guacuco

Sleeping (High season prices) **A** *Guacuco Resort*, Sabana de Guacuco, T242 3040, www.guacucoresort.com Apartments for up to 4 people (prices quoted for 2), 1 km from the beach and 300 m off the road, a/c, self-catering facilities, tranquil, beautiful gardens, pool and bar. **D** pp *Posada Isla Dorada*, near *Hotel Guacuco Resort*, well signposted, T416 3132. Simple rooms with a/c, meals extra.

Here there are 4 km of stone-free white sand with many *kioskos*, which have palm-leaf shade areas. The sea is very rough for children, but fairly shallow (beware the strong cross current when you are about waist deep). This beach gets overcrowded at Venezuelan holiday times. The fashionable part is at the south end. Horseriding can be arranged with *Altos de Cimarrón*. It's possible to see the island by Ultralight from here at weekends. Contact Omar Contreras, T261 7632 or José-Antonio Fernández 262 3519, English spoken.

Playa El Agua
45 mins by bus from Porlamar (US$0.45) Many restaurants stay open till 2200. Best to stay off the beach after the restaurants close

Sleeping and eating A *Coco Paraíso*, Av Principal, T249 0117, www.cocoparaiso.cjb.net Very pleasant, large rooms, a/c, pool, 3 mins from beach, German spoken. **A** *Costa Linda*, Miragua, T/F249 1229, www.hotelcostalinda.com Very nice rooms in colonial-style house

Venezuela

with a/c, TV, safe, pool, restaurant and bar, includes breakfast, accepts credit cards, changes TCs and US$, English and German spoken. **A** *Trudel's Garden Vacation Homes*, Miragua, www.islamargarita.com/trudel.htm 6 large 2-bedroom houses set in a beautiful garden, 200 m from beach, fully equipped kitchens. **A** *Chalets de Belén*, Miragua 3, next to *El Agua*, T249 1707. 2 chalets for 4 and 6, kitchen facilities, good value, no towels provided, parking, laundry service, also 2 double rooms, **C** (discounts in low season). **B** *Res Miramar*, Av 31 de Julio-Carretera Manzanillo, esq Miragua. 3 mins from beach, 1 min from supermarket (expensive), family-run, self-catering apartments, comfortable, barbecue. Recommended. **C** *Res Vacacional El Agua*, T249 1975, T0414-797 3221 (mob). Fully equipped, self-catering bungalows for 4, 6 and 8 with fan, run down, but good value, 1 double room, **E**. **D** *Hostería El Agua*, Av 31 de Julio vía Manzanillo, T249 1297, hosteriaelagua@hotmail.com Simple, a/c, hot water, safe, laundry facilities, restaurant/bar, 4 mins' walk from beach, English and Italian spoken. For eating, try *El Paradiso*, south end. Rents out cabins, small but comfortable. *Kiosko El Agua*. Helpful, English spoken. *Posada Shangri-Lá*. Recommended. *Casa Vieja*. Seafood. *La Dorada*. French owned by Gérard and Hilda, with good beach view. Recommended as good value. *Mini Golf Café*, from the corner of *Miramar* turn left after 300 m. Run by Matthias, ask for special dishes cooked by Yvonne, internet access (good rates). Every Fri there is dancing at *Marlin Bar & Restaurant* on Blvd Playa El Agua.

Manzanillo
Population: 2,000

This is a picturesque bay between the mountains on the northeast point of the island. Hotels and apartments in our **A** and **B** ranges, beach houses and places to eat. Playa Escondida is at the far end. **Puerto Fermín**/El Tirano is where Lope de Aguirre, the infamous conquistador, landed in 1561 on his flight from Peru; **El Caserío** handicrafts museum is nearby. **A-B** *Hostería Marymonte*, T234 8066, www.marymonte.compucen.com Beachfront, 8 cottages with hot water, mosquito net, fan or a/c, bar, pool, English spoken, price depends on season.

The coast road is interesting, with glimpses of the sea and beaches to one side. There are a number of clifftop look-out points. The road improves radically beyond Manzanillo, winding from one beach to the next. Playa Puerto la Cruz (wide and windy) adjoins **Pedro González** (*Population:* 3,700), with a broad sweeping beach, running from a promontory (easy to climb) to scrub and brush that reach down almost to the water's edge. **Playa Caribe** is a fantastic curve of white sand with moderate surf. Chairs and umbrellas can be hired from the many beach bars. **L-AL** pp *Casa Chiara*, contact through *Delfino Tours*, T Caracas 267 5175, or www.web.tiscalinet.it/casa_chiara Eight private villas built with adobe and hardwood with small gardens that back on to a large pool, a huge *churuata* houses bar, restaurant and seating area, Italian owners, Paolo and Chiara, are great hosts, exceptional food, highly recommended.

Juan Griego
Population: 8,300

Further west is Juan Griego, a small, sleepy town whose picturesque bay is full of fishing boats. It's a good place for cheap shopping (quieter and safer than Porlamar). The little fort of La Galera is on a promontory at the northern side, beyond which is a bay of the same name with a narrow strip of beach and many seafront restaurants. Cash can be changed in most shops. Banco del Orinoco is the only bank for Tcs.

Sleeping and eating B *El Yare*, El Fuerte, T253 0835, 1 block from beach. Some suites with kitchen, owner speaks English. Recommended. **D** *Hotel Nuevo Juan Griego*, next to beach. English spoken, book echange, very popular. Recommended. **D** *Aparthotel y Res El Apurano*, La Marina y El Fuerte, T253 0901. English-speaking manager, 2-bedroom apartments, hot water, a/c, but no utensils or towels (because of theft). **D** *Patrick's*, El Fuerte, next to *Hotel Fortín*, T/F253 4089. French-run, a/c rooms with fine sunset views, excellent restaurant and bar. Recommended. **E** *Res Carmencita*, Guevara 20, T253 5561. A/c. Recommended. **E** *Fortín*, opposite beach. A/c, cold water, most rooms have good views, good restaurant and tables on the beach. **E** *La Posada de Clary*, Los Mártires, T253 0037. Restaurant, also apartments for 4, **D**, a/c, kitchen, parking. Recommended. *Restaurant Mi Isla* is

Venezuela

recommended. *Viña del Mar*, opposite *Hotel Fortín*. A/c, attractive, excellent food. *Juan Griego Steak House*, same building as *Hotel El Yare*. Good value. Recommended. Also *Viejo Muelle*, good restaurant, live music, outside beach bar.

Playa El Yaque on the south coast, near the airport, is a Mecca for windsurfers. Most come on package deals and therefore accommodation is expensive, but cheaper places can be found. There is no public transport; a taxi from Porlamar costs US$8. Sailboards, kite surf and kayaks can be hired on the beach from at least five well-equipped companies, who also offer lessons. Half day costs US$30, full day US$35-40 for sailboard; US$25 per hour for kite surf. English, German, French and Portuguese spoken. *Cholymar* travel agency will change money and there is *casa de cambio* in the *Hotel California*. Passages to Coche island cost US$14 from *Hotel Yaque Paradise*. Mary Luz offers Spanish lessons, T0416-474 9172 (mob), maryluz2008@hotmail.com

The winds are perfect from mid-Jun to mid-Oct and the water is shallow enough to satnd when you fall off

Sleeping and eating **AL** *Hotel Yaque Paradise*, T263 9810, yaque@grupoparadise.com Upmarket, good rooms, English and German spoken, includes breakfast. **C** *El Yaque Motion*, T263 9742, www.elyaquemotion.com Next to *La Casa de Migelina*, 400 m from beach. Fan, kitchen, laundry, cheaper with shared bath, English and German spoken. **D** *La Casa de Migelina*, orange house behind the police checkpoint at entrance to town. A/c, also very handsome, self-catering apartments, for maximum 5, **A**, fully equipped kitchen, a/c, sitting room, TV, discounts for long stay. **D** *Sail Fast Shop*, T/F263 7486, sailfastshop@hotmail.com Basic rooms 300 m from the beach, ask for Herbert Novak at the Sail Fast Shop opposite *Hotel Yaque Paradise*. Several other hotels, all with restaurants. For eating, try *Fuerza 6* and *Gabi's Grill*, main meals US$6. Several beach bars; best bar is *Los Surf Piratas*, drinks and dancing from 2130.

La Restinga is a 22-km sandbar of broken seashells that joins the eastern and western parts of Margarita. Behind the *restinga* is the eponymous national park, designated a wetland of international importance. Over 100 species of birds live here, including the blue-crowned parakeet, which is endemic to Margarita. There are also marine turtles and other reptiles, dolphins, deer, ocelots, seahorses and oysters. *Lanchas* can be taken into the fascinating lagoon and mangrove swamps to the beach from landing stages at the eastern end (US$18 per person for an hour trip, plus US$0.35 entrance fee to park). Bus from Porlamar US$1. On La Restinga beach you can look for shellfish in the shallows (protection against the sun essential), the delicious oysters can be bought for around US$1 a dozen.

The **Peninsula de Macanao**, over the road bridge from La Restinga is mountainous, arid, barely populated and a peaceful place to get away from the holidaymakers on the main part of Margarita. It also has some good beaches that are often deserted. Punta Arenas, a pleasant beach with calm water is the most popular and has some restaurants, chairs and sunshades. Further on is the wilder Playa Manzanillo. There is no accommodation at these beaches, but in nearby Robledal is **B** *Auberge L'Oasis*, T291 5339 charles@enlared.net A/c or fan, hot water, TV, sea view, garden, restaurant. Playa La Pared is an impressive beach bounded by steep cliff walls. There is a *parador turístico* at the top of the cliff and lodging at the eccentric **A** *Makatao*, T/F263 6647, www.makatao.iespana.es Run by Dr Alexis Vásquez, price includes transfer, food, natural drinks and lodging in the singular rooms. The doctor runs health, 'eco-relax' and therapy programs, and there are mud baths at the *campamento*. You can go horseriding on the peninsula at *Hato San Francisco*, *Cabatucan Ranch* (T0416-681 9348 (mob), cabatucan@telcel.net.ve) and at El Saco with *Rancho Negro* (T242 3197, T0414-995 1103 (mob)). Prices US$35-US$45 pp. At *Cabatucan Ranch*, 2 km from Guayacancito on the road to Punta Arenas, is the charming **A** *Posada Río Grande*, T416 8111, www.posadariogrande.com Attractive rooms with a/c, hot water, full board available, will also arrange all-inclusive

Venezuela

scuba diving (US$57) and snorkelling trips (US$27) to Isla Cubagua. Boca del Río, near the road bridge has a museum featuring excellent collections of marine life, organized by ecosystem, and a small aquarium. T291 3231, www.fpolar.org.ve/museomarino *US$2 adults, US$1 children 0900-1630 every day.*

Islas Los Roques

Phone code: 0212.
Colour map 1, grid A6
Long stretches of white beaches and over 20 km of coral reef with crystal-clear water ideal for snorkelling

These islands lie 150 km due north of Caracas; the atoll, of about 340 islets and reefs, constitutes one of Venezuela's loveliest national parks (225,153 ha). There are many bird nesting sites (eg the huge gull colonies on Francisqui and the pelicans, boobies and frigates on Selenqui); May is nesting time at the gull colonies. For more information write to La Fundación Científica Los Roques, Apdo No 1, Avenida Carmelitas, Caracas 1010. This is one of the least visited diving spots in the Caribbean; best visited midweek as Venezuelans swarm here on long weekends and at school holidays. (Low season is Easter to July.) Snorkelling is best at the southern part of the archipelago. There are at least seven main dive sites offering caves, cliffs, coral and, at Nordesqui, shipwrecks. There area many fish to be see, including sharks at the caves of Olapa de Bavusqui. Prices are higher than the mainland and infrastructure is limited but the islands are beautiful and unspoiled. Camping is free, but campers need a permit from Inparques, T234 7331, F234 4238, or the office in Gran Roque. Average temp 29° C with coolish nights. You will need strong sunblock as there is no shade. ■ *Park entry US$12.*

Population: 900

Gran Roque is the main and only permanently inhabited island. The airport is here, as is the national guard, three grocery stores and a good craft shop, public phones, medical facilities, a few restaurants and accommodation. There is nowhere to change travellers' cheques. Park Headquarters are in the scattered fishing village. Tourist information is available free of charge from the very helpful *Angel & Oscar Shop*, directly in front as you leave the airstrip.

You can negotiate with local fishermen for transport to other islands: you will need to take your own tent, food and (especially) water. Gran Roque's main beach was washed away in a hurricane in late 1999; the offshore coral was unaffected, though. **Madrisqui** has nine summer houses. **Francisqui** is three islands joined by sandspits, with calm lagoon waters to the south and rolling surf to the north (there is one *posada*, T793 0694, F793 9579. **A-B**, full board including drinks, good food, friendly staff, nice beach, snorkelling gear, water and light 24 hours, fan, bargaining possible if you stay for several days; also hammock sites and camping).

Sleeping
In most places, breakfast and dinner are included in the price

On Gran Roque **L** pp *Piano y Papaya*, near Plaza Bolívar towards seafront, T0414-281 0104 (mob). Very tasteful, run by Italian artist, with fan, **AL** pp for bed and breakfast, credit cards and TCs accepted, Italian and English spoken. **L** pp *Posada Caracol*, on seafront near airstrip, T0414-313 0101 (mob), or Caracas T0212-267 5175, info@posadacaracol.com Delightful, half-board and bed and breakfast options available, **AL** pp, credit cards and TCs accepted, Italian and English spoken, good boats. **C** pp *El Botuto*, on seafront near *Supermercado W Salazar*, T0414-373 0002 (mob). Nice airy rooms with fan, meals extra. **C** pp *Posada Doña Magalys*, Plaza Bolívar, T0414-373 1993 (mob). Simple, with fan, cheaper with shared bath. **C** pp *Roquelusa*, behind *Supermercado W Salazar*, T0414-369 6401 (mob). Probably the cheapest option on Gran Roque, basic, with fan, some with a/c. There are over 60 *posadas* on Gran Roque (some bookable through *Aereotuy*), ranging from **B** to **LL**. Bargaining is advisable (especially in low season) if you intend to stay more than 2 nights. **Yachts** Fully equipped yachts can be chartered for US$120 per day, all inclusive, highly recommended as a worthwhile way of getting some shade on the treeless beaches. Ask at *Angel & Oscar Shop*, or *Posada Pez Ratón*.

Sport
For health reasons you must allow 12 hrs to elapse between diving and flying back to the mainland

Scuba diving: *Ecobuzos*, 3 blocks from the airstrip, T221 1235, T0416-895 8082 (mob), fobtours1@cantv.net, and *Sesto Continente*, past Inparques at the far end of town, T/F9241853, scdrgerencia@telcel.net.ve Both offer 2 dives for US$85. PADI courses and beginner dives also available. **Snorkelling**: Cayo de Agua and Francisqui recommended for snorkelling. Boats can be arranged through your posada, *Angel & Oscar Shop*, or independent fishermen. **Windsurfing**: *Happy Surf*, Francisqui, US$35.50 half day; US$50 full day, ask for Elías. **Ultralight flights**: Hernando Arnal, at the airport and Plaza Bolívar, US$40 for 12 mins, US$60 for 25 mins, speaks English, incredible views.

Transport

Flights from Maiquetía or Porlamar. *Aereotuy*, *Aeroejecutivos*, *Chapi Air* and *Sol De Américas* all fly from Maiquetía (Aeropuerto Auxiliar) once a day, 40 mins, US$110. *Aereotuy* offer 1, 2 and 3-day packages (return flight, accommodation, meals, drinks, catamaran excursion with snorkelling and diving equipment), from US$300 pp (1-day from Margarita US$150).

Directory

Banks *Banesco*, Plaza Bolívar, Mon-Fri 0830-1230, 1430-1700. Cash advances on Visa up to US$500 per day. **Communications** **Public telephone**: Plaza Bolívar and Guardia National on seafront.

The Llanos

Caracas

A spectacular route descends from the Sierra Nevada to the flat llanos, one of the best places in the world to see birds and animals. This vast, sparsely populated wilderness of 300,000 sq km – one third of the country's area – lies between the Andes to the west and the Orinoco to the south and east.

Background

The *llanos* are veined by numerous slow running rivers, forested along their banks. The flat plain is only varied here and there by *mesas*, or slight upthrusts of the land. About five million of the country's 6.4 million cattle are in the *llanos*, but only around 10% of the human population. When the whole plain is periodically under water, the *llaneros* drive their cattle into the hills or through the flood from one *mesa* to another. When the plain is parched by the sun and the savanna grasses become inedible they herd the cattle down to the damper region of the Apure and Orinoco. Finally they drive them into the valley of Valencia to be fattened.

Around October/November, when the vast plains are still partially flooded, wildlife abounds. Among the animals that can be seen are capybara, caiman, monkeys, anacondas, river dolphins, pumas and countless varieties of birds. Though it's possible to explore this huge region independently, towns are few and far between and distances involved are very great. Much better to visit the *llanos* as part of a tour from Mérida (see Tour operators, page 1386), or stay at one of the ecotourism *hatos*, or ranches (see below).

Guanare
Phone code: 0257
Colour map 1, grid B5
Population: 32,500

An excellent road goes to the western *llanos* of Barinas from Valencia. It goes through San Carlos, Acarigua (an agricultural centre and the largest city in Portuguesa state) and Guanare, which is a national place of pilgrimage with an old parish church containing the much venerated relic of the Virgin of Coromoto. Pilgrimages to Coromoto are on 2 January and 8 September and Candlemas is 1 February. **C** *Italia*, Carrera 5, No 19-60, a/c, bar and restaurant, offstreet parking. **D** *Colina*, near the river at bottom of town, motel-style, comfortable, restaurant. *Restaurante Turístico La Casa Vieja*, good food and value. *El Paisano*, popular restaurant.

Venezuela

Barinas

Phone code: 0273
Colour map 1, grid A5
Population: 240,000

The road continues to Barinas, the hot, sticky capital of the cattle-raising and oil-rich State of Barinas. The shady Parque Universitario has a botanical garden open Monday to Friday. *Banco Italo* for MasterCard or Visa cash withdrawals. *Banco Unión* and *Banco de Venezuela* for Visa ATMs. The tourist office on Plaza Bolívar is helpful, local maps available, no English spoken.

Sleeping & eating

On Av 23 de Enero, all recommended, near the airport: **B** *Bristol*, T552 0911, a/c, safe; **D** *Motel La Media Avenida*, T552 2278, cold showers, bar, restaurant, parking. **C** *Internacional*, C Arzobispo Méndez on Plaza Zamora, T552 2343. A/c, safe, good restaurant. **Opposite bus terminal D** *Palacio*, a/c, good value; **E** pp *Lisboa*, basic, fan.

Don Enrique, opposite *Hotel Palacio*. Good, cheap. *Yoanna*, Av 7, 16-47, corner of Márques del Pumar. Arab owner, excellent. *El Estribo*, C Apure entre Av Garguera y Andrés Varela. Roast and barbecued local meat, good, open 1100-2400.

Transport

Air Aeropuerto Nacional, Av 23 de Enero. Daily flights to **Caracas** with *Avior*.

Buses To **Mérida**, 6 a day with *Transportes Barinas*, US$3.25, spectacular ride through the mountains, 5-7 hrs (sit on right for best views); *por puesto*, US$6; also to **Valera** at 0730, US$5, 7 hrs. To **Caracas**, US$12.50, 8 hrs, several companies go direct or via **Maracay** (US$5.50, 7 hrs) and **Valencia**, regularly 0730-2300. To **San Cristóbal**, several daily, US$8.50, 5 hrs; to **San Fernando de Apure**, US$10, 9 hrs with *Expresos Los Llanos* at 0900, 2300; the same company also goes to **Maracaibo** (at 2000 and 2200, US$10, 8 hrs), **San Antonio** (at 2330) and **Puerto La Cruz** (1330, 1445 and 2130, US$25, 16 hrs).

From Barinas there is a beautifully scenic road to Apartaderos, in the Sierra Nevada de Mérida (see page 1382). Motorists travelling east to Ciudad Bolívar can either go across the *llanos* or via San Carlos, Tinaco, El Sombrero, Chaguaramas, Valle de la Pascua (see below) and El Tigre. The latter route requires no ferry crossings and has more places with accommodation.

Staying at a tourist ranch

An alternative to travelling independently or arranging a tour from Mérida is to stay at one of the tourist ranches. Most of these are in Apure state and can be reached from Barinas or San Fernando de Apure.

LL-L pp *Hato Piñero*, is a safari-type lodge at a working ranch near El Baúl (turn off Tinaco-El Sombrero road at El Cantón). Fully inclusive price, per day, packages can include return overland or air transport from Caracas. Free drinks, good room, bi-lingual nature guide for excellent bird- and animal-watching trips. Highly recommended. Address: Hato Piñero, Edif Gen de Seguros, p 6, Ofic 6B, Avenida La Estancia, Chuao, Caracas 1060, T0212-991 8935, F991 6668, www.branger.com/pinero.html No public transport to ranch but ask police in El Baúl for ride with Hato Piñero workers. From Caracas the direct route is six hours; from Ciudad Bolívar nine hours.

On the road to El Baúl at Km 93 (next to Hato Piñero turn off) is the *Reserva Privada de Flora y Fauna Mataclara*, lodging with full board, horse riding, fishing and animal watching trips costs US$50 per person a day. Address: Prof Antonio González-Fernández, Universidad de Los Llanos 'Unellez', Mesa de Caracas, Guanare 3323, Estado de Portuguesa.

About 30 minutes by bus from Mantecal (see below) is **LL** *Hato El Cedral*, a 53,000-ha ranch where hunting is banned. Fully inclusive price, a/c, hot water, land and river safaris, pool. Address: Avenida La Salle, edif Pancho p 5, of 33, Los Caobos, Caracas, T0212-781 8995, F793 6082, www.hatocedral.com Also in this area: *Doña Bárbara*, ranch, book through *Doña Bárbara* travel agency, Paseo Libertador, Edif Hotel La Torraca, PB y Mezzanina, Apdo 55, San Fernando de Apure, T0247-341 3463, F341 2235, barbara@sfapure.c-com.net Also *Hato El Frío*, office in Achaguas, elfrio@cantv.net Both also **LL** per person per night including three meals, two tours per day, bath, a/c or fan, clean, comfortable, or US$45 for a daytime visit. **B** pp *Río Caiman Camp* is reached from Bruzual (see below), by road or by boat in the wet season (US$5). Fully inclusive, except horse riding and river rafting, accommodation in hammocks or tents, lots of excursions, multilingual guides (mostly English and German). Contact Alexis Léon Rojas, Sector La Plazuela, San Rafael de Tabay, Mérida, T0414-974 5099, leontours@hotmail.com

San Fernando de Apure

At Lagua, 16 km east of Maracay, a good road leads south to San Fernando de Apure. It passes through San Juan de los Morros, which has natural hot springs; Ortiz, near the crossroads with the San Carlos-El Tigre road; the Guárico lake and Calabozo. 132 km south of Calabozo, San Fernando is the hot and sticky capital of the state of Apure and a fast-growing trade and transport hub for the region. There is *Corp Banca* for American Express, Avenida Miranda, and *Bano Unión*, Avenida Boulevard entre Sucre y Muñoz, with Visa ATM. From San Fernando you can travel east to Ciudad Bolívar (see below), or south to Puerto Ayacucho (see page 1435).

Phone code: 0247
Colour map 1, grid A6
Population: 135,000

Sleeping & eating

B *Gran Hotel Plaza*, C Bolívar, T342 1746, 2 blocks from the bus terminal. A/c, good. **C** pp *El Río*, Av María Nieves, near the bus terminal, T341 1928. With a/c, good value. **C-D** *La Fuente*, Miranda y Libertador. A/c, TV, phone, safe. **D** *Trinacria*, Av Miranda, near bus terminal, T342 3578. Huge rooms, a/c. **D** *La Torraca*, Av Boulevard y Paseo Libertador by Plaza Bolívar, T342 2777. Excellent rooms, a/c, balcony overlooking centre of town. Recommended. **F** *Hospedaje Central*, C Bolívar 98, T342 4120. With bath, colonial-style, basic. Most hotels are within 1 block of the intersection of Paseo Libertador and Av Miranda. Eating places include *Punto Criollo*, Av Miranda. Good value. *Gran Imperio Romano*, along Av Boulevard from *Europa*. Small, popular, good and cheap. *Comedor* in building beside CANTV. Has good *menú*, Mon-Fri, 1100-1200.

Transport

Air Aeropuerto Las Flecheras, Av 1 de Mayo, T342 3356. Flights to **Caracas** with *Avior*, daily.

Buses Terminal is modern and clean, not far from centre; US$2 taxi ride. To **Caracas**, US$11, 7 hrs; to **Barinas**, *Expresos Zamora*, 5 daily, 7 hrs (take food and drink), rough ride, day and night bus, US$10; to **Maracay**, US$7; to **Puerto Ayacucho**, US$15, 6½ hrs; to **Calabozo**, 1½ hrs, US$2.50.

San Fernando to Barinas

From San Fernando a road heads to head west to Barinas (468 km). It's a beautiful journey, but the road is in terrible condition between Mantecal, La Ye junction and Bruzual, a town just south of the Puente Nutrias on the Río Apure. In the early morning, many animals and birds can be seen, and in the wet season caiman (alligators) cross the road. **Mantecal** is a friendly cattle-ranching town with hotels (*El Nilo*, basic but convenient for buses) and restaurants. *Fiesta*, 23-26 February. ■ *San Fernando de Apure-Mantecal 3½ hrs, US$4.50; Mantecal-Barinas, 4 hrs, US$6.*

Venezuela

Caracas

Guayana, the Orinoco delta and Amazonas

The historic Ciudad Bolívar on the Río Orinoco is a good starting place for the superb landscapes further south, notably the table-top mountains and waterfalls in Parque Nacional Canaima. Here, you'll find the spectacular Angel Falls, the highest in the world, and the mysterious "Lost World" of Roraima. Further east the Orinoco Delta is opening up to tourism, and in the southwest, on the banks of the Orinoco, Puerto Ayacucho is the gateway to the jungles of Venezuela.

Background Guayana, south of the Orinoco River, constitutes half of Venezuela, comprising rounded forested hills and narrow valleys, rising to flat-topped tablelands on the borders of Brazil. These savannahs interspersed with semi-deciduous forest are very sparsely populated. So far, communications have been the main difficulty, but a road that leads to Manaus has now been opened to Santa Elena de Uairén on the Brazilian frontier (see page 1429). The area is Venezuela's largest gold and diamond source, but its immense reserves of iron ore, manganese and bauxite are of far greater economic importance.

To Ciudad Bolívar from the coast & the Llanos Ciudad Bolívar can be reached easily by roads south from Caracas and Puerto La Cruz. The Caracas route, via Valle de la Pascua, and the Puerto La Cruz route, via Anaco, meet at El Tigre (*population*: 105,000), which has good hotels and services. From the *llanos*, from **Chaguaramas** turn south through Las Mercedes (basic hotel) to **Cabruta** (*Population*: 4,300), 179 km, road in extremely bad shape, daily bus to Caracas, US$11, basic hotel. Then take a ferry from opposite the airport to **Caicara** (ferry for cars 1½ hours, *lanchas* for pedestrians 25 minutes). Alternatively, from San Fernando de Apure take a bus to Calabozo and *por puesto* from there to El Sombrero (US$2), where you can catch the Ciudad Bolívar bus at 1700.

Ciudad Bolívar

Phone code: 0285
Colour map 2, grid A1
Population: 300,000
640 km to Caracas
Mean temperature: 29°C

Ciudad Bolívar is on the narrows of the Orinoco, some 300 m wide, which gave the town its old name of Angostura. It is 400 km from the Orinoco delta. It was here that Bolívar came after defeat to reorganize his forces, and the British Legionnaires joined him. At Angostura he was declared President of the Gran Colombia he had yet to build, and which was to fragment before his death.

At the Congress of Angostura, 15 February 1819, the representatives of the present day Venezuela, Colombia and Ecuador met to proclaim Gran Colombia. The building, on **Plaza Bolívar**, built 1766-76 by Manuel Centurión, the provincial governor, houses a museum, the **Casa del Congreso de Angostura** ■ *Guides in Spanish only*. Also on this historic plaza is the **Cathedral** (started 1764, completed 1840), the **Casa de Los Gobernadores de la Colonia** (also built by Centurión in 1766), the **Real Intendencia**, and the **Casa de la Cultura**. Also on the north side of the plaza, at Bolívar 33, is the house where Gen Manuel Piar, the Liberator of Guayana from the Spanish, was held prisoner before being executed by Bolívar on 16 October 1817, for refusing to put himself under Bolívar's command. The restored **Plaza Miranda**, up C Carabobo, has an art centre, formerly a theatre. The present legislative assembly and **Consejo Municipal** are between Plaza Bolívar and Plaza Miranda. In 1824, when the town was still known as Angostura a Prussian physician to Bolívar's troops invented the famous bitters ; the factory moved to Port of Spain in 1875.

Venezuela

Launches take passengers across the river (US$0.25), but there are no other passenger boat services. The Paseo Orinoco leading west out of town goes to the **Angostura Bridge**, which can be seen from town. This is the only bridge across the Orinoco, 1,668 m long (over a mile), opened in 1967 (toll US$0.80; cyclists and walkers are not allowed to cross, you must flag down a car or truck). The **Zamuro hill fort** (1902), on another hill in the centre, dominates the city. ■ *Closed 1200-1400. Entrance on Paseo Heres.*

West of the centre is **El Zanjón**, an area of vegetation typical of the region. East is **Parque El Porvenir**, with botanical gardens. Outside the airport is the *Río Caroní* aeroplane, which Jimmy Angel landed on top of Auyán Tepuy (see page 1421).

The **Museo Soto**, Avenida Germania, some distance from the centre in pleasant gardens, has works by Venezuela's Jesús Rafael Soto and other modern artists. Recommended. ■ *Tue-Sun 1000-1700, free, guide in Spanish only.* Museum at **Casa del Correo del Orinoco**, Paseo Orinoco y Carabobo, modern art and some exhibits of history of the city. **Museo Casa San Isidro**, a mansion where Simón Bolívar stayed. ■ *Tue-Sat 0930-1200, 1430-1700, Sun 0930-1200; Av Táchira.*

Near airport B *Laja Real*, Av Andrés Bello y Jesús Soto, opposite airport, T632 7911, F632 8778, lajareal@telcel.net.ve Comfortable rooms, a/c, hot water, TV, fridge, pool open to non-residents for US$5 per day, excellent restaurant, sauna, gym, disco, parking, casa de cambio in lobby. **C** *Valentina*, Av Maracay 55, T632 2145, F632 9311. Quiet, a/c, hot water, TV, comfortable, very good restaurant. **D** *Da Gino*, Av Jesús Soto, opposite airport, T632 0313, F632 5454. A/c, hot water, TV, good service and restaurant, changes US$ cash. **D** *Laja City*, Av Táchira y Av Bolívar, T/F632 9910. Quiet, a/c, hot water, TV, restaurant. **In the centre C** *Posada Angostura*, C Boyacá 8, T0414-851 2295 (mob). Handsome rooms in old colonial house, a/c, fan, hot water, restaurant, and travel agency. **D** *Colonial*, Paseo Orinoco, T632 4402, F632 3649. Has seen better days but good value, a/c, *Neckar* travel agency, nice restaurant on balcony overlooking river. **E-F** *Caracas*, Paseo Orinoco y Roscio, T/F632 8512.

Sleeping
Recommended hotels, unless stated otherwise

Venezuela

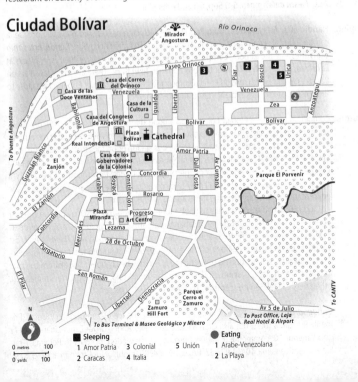

Ciudad Bolívar

■ **Sleeping**
1 Amor Patria   3 Colonial   5 Unión
2 Caracas   4 Italia

● **Eating**
1 Arabe-Venezolana
2 La Playa

0 metres 100
0 yards 100

Fan, no hot water, pool table, table tennis, table football, gift shop and a restaurant on the balcony overlooking river, changes TCs and US$ cash, luggage store, English, German, Italian spoken, *Expediciones Dearunes* (see below) based here. Many people stay here; in 2001 most reports were uncomplimentary. **E** *Unión*, C Urica 11, T632 3374. A/c, good value, **F** with fan. **F** *Amor Patrio*, Amor Patria 30, T632 8819, plazabolivar@hotmail.com Renovated colonial house, fan, shared bathrooms, use of kitchen, hammocks can be rented, **G**. German and English spoken, *Soana Travel* (see below) based here. Recommended. **Near the bus terminal D** *Universo*, Av República, 2 blocks left out of terminal, T654 3732. A/c, hot water, TV, restaurant, accepts credit cards. **Outside of town E** *Posada La Casita*, Av Ligia Pulido, Urb 24 de Julio, PO Box 118, T617 0832, T0414-850 0989 (mob), F632 6883. Very nice rooms, with cold water, fan, hammock with mosquito net can be rented, **G**, space for tents, **G**. Beautiful gardens, pool, laundry service, good food and drinks available, German and English spoken. Free pick up from airport or bus terminal (ring in advance). Free shuttle service into town. The owner runs *Gekko Tours* (see below).

Eating *Savoy*, Venezuela y Dalla Costa. Good value breakfast. *Mi Casa*, C Venezuela. Open-air, good value. *América*, Paseo Orinoco esq Roscio. Good food, dishes US$3-5, open late. *Arabe-Venezolano*, on Cumaná near Bolívar. Clean, a/c, good Arabic food, not cheap. Good breakfast at *Lonchería Ché*, next to *Hotel Colonial*. *La Playa*, on C Urica between Venezuela and Zea. Good for fish, reasonable prices. *Lonchería Caribe*, C Libertad y Bolívar, close to the cathedral. Good, cheap, popular with locals. *Tasca de la Playa*, Urica between Zea and Venezuela. Good food, cheap, popular with locals. *Lonchería Urica*, Urica, next to *Hotel Unión*. Good lunch for US$1.25, get there early. *La Carioca*, at the end of Paseo Orinoco, has a series of small, cheap restaurants. *Pizzeria La Casita* Venezuela, opposite *La Casa de las Doce Ventanas*. Good value pizza and ice cream, views over Puente Angostura. *Restaurant Vegetariano* Amor Patria y Dalla Costa. Lunch only. *Mirador* Paseo Orinoco. *Comida criolla* with views over the river.

Festivals Aug, *Fiesta del Orinoco*, 5-8 Sep, fair and exhibition.

Shopping **Handicrafts** Arts and crafts from Bolívar state, including basketry from the Orinoco Delta can be found in *La Carioca* market, at the end of Paseo Orinoco and *Tienda Artesanía Guayanesa* at the airport. **Camping equipment** White gas (stove fuel) is available at *Lubriven*, Av República 16, near the bus terminal. **Jewellery** There are many jewellers on Pasaje Guayana, which runs off Paseo Orinoco and near *Hotel Colonial*. Supermarket close to the Museo Soto on Av Germania, large and well-stocked.

Tour operators Competition is stiff in Ciudad Bolívar, and among the genuine companies roam phoney salesmen. You are more than likely to have someone attempt to sell you a tour at the bus station. Do not pay any money to anyone in the bus station or on the street. Always ask to be taken to the office. Always ask for a receipt (and make sure that it comes on paper bearing the company logo). Be suspicious of people offering tours that start in another town or city. If you are unfortunate enough to fall prey to a con artist, be sure to make a *denuncio* at the police station and inform genuine travel agents where you can.

Ciudad Bolívar is the best place to book a tour to Canaima, but you may pick up cheaper deals for trips to Roraima and the Gran Sabana from Santa Elena. There are 2 main tours operators in Canaima who offer tours at backpacker prices – *Bernal Tours* and *Tiuna Tours*. Most agents in Ciudad Bolívar sell one of these two options, but sometimes add commission. Always ask who will be running the actual tour – it may be cheaper to book from the tour operator directly. Reports of most tour operators are conflicting, some highly recommended, others very critical. Service seems to change with the seasons.

Cunaguaro Tours, T632 7810, Carlos at *Hotel Italia* entrance (Paseo Orinoco y Urica). Primarily Río Caura tours, but also Gran Sabana and Salto Angel, driver Lenin Linares is very good, friendly. Recommended. *Miguel Gasca* is recommended for tours to Roraima, Gran Sabana and Canaima, T0414-923 5210/0166-629 4600 (mob), or look for him at *Hotel Italia*.

Expediciones Dearuna, Javier Cubillos at *Hotel Caracas*, T/F632 8512, T0414-854 6807 (mob), expediciones_dearuna@yahoo.com All the usual tours at competitive prices. *Gekko Tours*, run by Pieter Rothfuss at airport (also *Posada La Casita*), T632 3223, T0414-985 1683 (mob), www.gekkotours-venezuela.de Gran Sabana, Canaima, Roraima, Orinoco Delta, rafting and river trips. *Sapito Tours (Bernal Tours)*, at airport, T0414-854 8234 (mob), bernaltours@terra.com.ve Canaima tours slightly more expensive, Indian guides. Also offer tours to Roraima, Gran Sabana, Orinoco Delta, Kavác and Río Caura. *Soana Travel*, run by Martin Haars at *Hospedaje Amor Patrio*, T632 8819, T0414 852 0373 (mob), soanatravel@gmx.de Tours to Río Caura, Canaima and Gran Sabana, English and German spoken. *Tiuna Tours*, at airport, T632 8697, www.mitrompo.com/tiunatours Cheapest option for Canaima, have a camp that takes 180 people. Guides speak English, German and Italian. *Turi Express*, at airport, T652 9764, T0414-893 9078 (mob), turiexpress@cantv.net Usual range of tours plus Guri dam and fishing tours, good English. Recommended. For 3 days/2 nights tours to Canaima expect to pay around US$190-230 pp; 4 days/3 nights to Gran Sabana US$250. 5 days/4 nights; Río Caura US$250-300.

Local Taxis: US$1.50-2 to virtually anywhere in town. US$2.25-3.50 from bus station to **Transport** town centre.

Long distance Air: Minibuses and buses (Ruta 2) marked Terminal to town centre. Taxi to Paseo Orinoco US$2.25. To Caracas daily with *Avior* and *LAI*, US$80 1½ hrs. *Rutaca* and *Comeravia* fly daily to Canaima and Santa Elena, US$55. Airport tax US$0.50. There are international phones at the airport, a good restaurant and car hire (Budget). Check where tours start from as some fly from Ciudad Guayana (*Turi Tours*), and charge passengers for taxi transfers. **Buses**: Terminal at junction of Av República and Av Sucre. To get there take bus marked Terminal going west along Paseo Orinoco (US$0.25). 10 daily to **Caracas** US$15 (student discount available, night bus $17.50), 8-9 hrs, with *Expresos Los Llanos*, *Rodovias*, and *Rapidos de Guayanesa*, *por puesto* US$40. 10 daily to **Puerto La Cruz**, US$8 (student discount available), 5 hrs, with *Caribe* and *Expresos San Cristobal*, *por puesto*, US$17.50. 1 daily to **Cumaná** US$15, 7 hrs with *Caribe*. Several daily to **Maracay**, US$15, and **Valencia**, via Maracay, US$15, 8-9 hrs, with *Expresos Los Llanos* and *Rodovias*. **Tumeremo** US$9; Tumeremo bus through to El Dorado US$9.50, 3 daily. To **Santa Elena de Uairén** direct with *Caribe* US$21 (3 daily), *Expresos San Cristobal*, US$16.50 (2 daily), stopping en route with *Línea Orinoco, Transportes Mundial* (5 daily), spectacular views of Gran Sabana, 12-13 hrs. 1 daily to **Boa Vista** with *Caribe*, US$33, 20 hrs. To **Ciudad Guayana** hourly from 0700, US$2, 1½ hrs, *por puesto*, US$5.50, 1½ hrs. To **Ciudad Piar**, US$4, 3 hrs, and **La Paragua**, US$8, 4 hrs, with *Coop Gran Mcal Sucre*. 2 daily to **Caicara**, US$6.50 (including 2 ferry crossings), 7-8 hrs, with *Coop Gran Mcal Sucre*. To **Maturín** with **Unión Maturín**. 2 daily to **Puerto Ayacucho**, US$12, 10-12 hrs with **Coop Gran Mcal Sucre** (*por puesto* US$20), take food.

Banks *Corp Banca*, Paseo Meneses, Edif Johanna, C Bolívar. Amex TCs. *Banco de Venezuela*, near **Directory** Hotel Colonial. Cash on Visa, ATM. *Banco Mercantil*, east end of Paseo Orinoco. Changes TCs, has ATM. *TCs difficult to change* *Banco Provincial*,west end of Av Jesús Soto, opposite Mobil petrol station. Cash on Visa, ATM. *ATMs open only in* **Communications** Internet: *Galaxia.com*, C C Abboud Centre, Paseo Orinoco. *Galaxy Computer*, Av *banking hours* República y Jesús Soto, behind Mobil petrol station. **Post Office**: Av Táchira, 15 mins walk from centre. **Telephone**: *CANTV*, Av 5 de Julio, 100 m from Av Táchira (closed Sun). **Consulates** Denmark, Av Táchira, Quinta Maninata 50, of 319, T632 3490, 0800-1200, 1500-1700. **Italy**, Av 17 de Diciembre, Edif Terepaima, Local 1, T/F654 4335. **Tourist office** Dirección de Turismo, Av Bolívar, Quinta Yeita, T632 2362, F632 4525, helpful, English spoken. Open weekdays 0800-1200, 1400-1730.

Parque Nacional Canaima

The Angel Falls, the highest fall in the world (979 m – its longest single drop is 807 m) *Colour map 2, grid B1* and **Canaima**, 70 km down-river, are best reached from Caracas, Ciudad Bolívar or *One of the 6 largest* Ciudad Guayana, by air. At Canaima camp, the Río Carrao tumbles spectacularly *parks in the world* over six waterfalls into the lagoon below, which has beautiful tannin-stained water with soft beige beaches. There are several tourist lodges at Canaima and many package tours now visit on day trips. ■ *Park entry US$8 pp paid to* Inparques *on arrival.* Do not forget swimming costumes, insect repellent and sun cream; waterproof clothing may be advisable. There are dangerous undercurrents in the lagoon; people have drowned while swimming near the falls. Do not walk barefoot as there are chiggers, or *niguas*, in the lagoon's sand beaches.

Tours You can do walking expeditions into the jungle to Indian villages with a guide, but bargain hard on the price. Other excursions are to the Mayupa Falls, including a canoe ride on the Río Carrao (US$45, half day), to Yuri Falls by jeep and boat (US$25, half day); to Isla Orquídea (US$65, full day, good boat ride, beach barbecue); to Saltos de Sapo and Sapito, 3 hrs, US$20.

Sleeping **LL** *Campamiento Canaima*, T0212-907 8130, F907 8053, PO Box 943, Caracas 1010. Comfortable cabins, with shower and toilet. Meals are poor value, but drinks are at regular prices. Tours are well organized. 1 night, US$355 (high season price, 1 Dec-30 Apr), pp in double room, including transfers, meals, boat trip and flight over the Angel Falls, weather permitting. The airfare is not included. Although the quickest and most convenient way to visit Canaima is on a package tour, it is much cheaper to travel independently. **L** *Parakaupa Lodge*, 5 mins from airport, T0286-961 4963, parakaupa@etheron.net Attractive rooms with bath, hammocks outside rooms, views over the lagoon and falls, restaurant, full board. **AL** *Campamiento Ucaima*, T0286-962 2359, www.ucaima.com Run by the daughter of the late 'Jungle' Rudy Truffino, full board available, 2 hrs walk from Canaima above Hacha Falls. **B** *Kusary* is close to *Parakaupa Lodge*, near the airport, T0286-962 0443. Basic but clean, with bath, fan, food available, ask for Claudio at *Tienda Canaima*. **D** *Camp Wey Tüpü*, in the village, T0414-884 0993 (mob). Ring direct to the camp if you wish to reserve lodgings only, *Roymar* in Caracas handle reservations of all-inclusive packages run from the camp, T/F0212-576 5655, roymar@cantv.net Fan, shower, bar. Some families in the village rent hammocks for US$5-10 per person. Travel agencies also rent hammocks for US$3-5 per person a night; ask at the airport. There may be space free to rent a hammock at *Campamento Tomas Bernal* (*Bernal Tours*) on Anatoly Island, T0414-854 8562 (mob), or at *Campamento*

Parque Nacional Canaima

Tiuna (*Tiuna Tours*). **Camping** Camp for free; fires are not permitted. Ask *Inparques* at the airport. No tents available for hire.

Food is expensive at the *Campamiento Canaima* restaurant. A cheaper option is *Simon's* restaurant in the village which is used by many of the agencies, US$3-4 pp. It is advisable to take food, though the village near Canaima has a small store selling mainly canned foods. A *fuente de soda* overlooks the lagoon. There is an expensive snack bar at the airport; also souvenir shop.

Eating

Bernal Tours, with its own camp on an island in the lagoon, beds and hammocks, popular with travellers, contact in Canaima or in Ciudad Bolívar (see above). *Kamaracoto Tours*, *Tiuna Tours*, and *Mario Rojas* (Chilean) for trips to Salto Sapo, Kaváč, Salto Angel; they will also help with finding accommodation. There is fierce competition at the airport but agencies pretty much offer the same thing at the same price.

Guides in Canaima

Some package tours to Canaima are listed under Caracas and Ciudad Bolívar Tour operators. Agents may tell you that guides speak English: some do, but many don't.

The full airfare from Caracas is US$220. *Avior* flies daily from Caracas, 1 hr 40 mins direct. Do not rely on being able to change the return date on your flight and be even more wary of getting an open return. The airlines are quite happy to change your ticket, but the next available seat could be in 5 days time and Canaima is a very expensive place to kill time. Arrangements are best made through travel agencies. *Aereotuy* runs 1 day excursions by 19-seat Dornier aircraft out of Ciudad Bolívar, landing at Canaima. There is a connecting *Aereotuy* flight from Isla Margarita (0900, returning 1500) and direct excursions from Margarita (0730 departure returning 1800). They have a new camp near the foot of Nonon Tepuy, bookable only through *Aereotuy*, recommended (T0212-763 8043, F762 5254). Various companies offer day excursions in 5-seater Cessnas to Canaima from Ciudad Bolívar, book early, 0630-0700 at airport, US$180 pp, including flight over Angel Falls, boat across lagoon, lunch and trip to Salto Sapo; flight only, US$55 one way with *Rutaca* and *Ciaca*, 2 hrs. Reductions are available for parties. Note that you may not even see the falls from the air in the rainy season – the additional cost of a trip to the Angel Falls may well bring the cost of your journey up to that of a package. Flight to **Santa Elena** from Canaima costs US$55, one way. Tours can also be made to **Kaváč** (see Kaváč section).

Transport

The Falls are named after Jimmy Angel, the US airman who first reported their existence in 1935. Two years later he returned and crash-landed his plane, the *Río Caroní*, on top of Auyán Tepuy. The site is now marked with a plaque. The sheer rock face was climbed in 1971 by three Americans and an Englishman, David Nott, who recounted the 10-day adventure in his book *Angels Four* (Prentice-Hall).

Angel Falls
Colour map 2, grid B1
NB The Falls face east so only receive sun in the morning

Trips by boat upriver to the Angel Falls operate May-January, depending on the level of the water in the rivers. All trips make an overnight stop on one of the islands, continuing to the Falls the next day. 12-hour day trips cost around US$150. More relaxing, but showing nothing different, are 44-hour, 'three day' trips, US$260. If you have a *permiso de excursionistas* from *Inparques*, you may be able to go on one tour and come back with another, giving yourself more time at the Falls, but you may have to pay extra to do this, up to US$50 (take all food and gear). Trips can be arranged with agencies in Ciudad Bolívar (see above) or at Canaima airport. All *curiaras* (dugouts) must carry first aid, life jackets, etc. Take wet weather gear, swimwear, mosquito net for hammock and insect repellent, lots of film and a plastic bag to protect your camera.

The cheapest way to fly over the falls is on scheduled flights from Ciudad Bolívar with Rutaca or Ciaca (see above). From Canaima a 45-minute flight costs US$45 per person and does some circuits over and alongside the falls.

The largest of the tepuis, **Auyán Tepuy** (700 sq km) is also one of the more accessible. **Kamarata** is a friendly Indian settlement with a Capuchin mission on the plain at the east foot of the tepuy. It has a well-stocked shop but no real hotels; basic rooms

Kamarata

Venezuela

can be found for about US$6 per person, camping also possible at the mission (mosquito nets necessary and anti-malarial pills advised). Take food, although there is one place to eat, and locals may sell you dinner. *Aereotuy, Rutaca* and *Comeravia* fly from Ciudad Bolívar (US$80 one way, 2 hrs), and *Rutaca* and *Comeravia* fly from Santa Elena de Uairén (US$140 one way).

Pemón families in Kamarata have formed co-operatives and can arrange *curiaras*, tents and porters for various excursions: *Macunaima Tours* (Tito Abati), *Excursiones Pemón* (Marino Sandoval), and Jorge and Antonio Calcaño. The whole area is within the Parque Nacional Canaima. For details on climbing Auyán Tepuy, contact *Kamadac* in Santa Elena, run by Andreas Hauer (T0289-995 1583, T0414-850 9604 (mob), or *Alechiven*, run by Edith Rogge, which has a base and radio at Kamarata, T0414-211828. *Alechiven* and Pemón co-operatives run six-day river trips from Kamarata to Angel Falls (May-December), descending the **Río Akanán** to the Carrao by motorized dugout then turning south up the 'Devil's Canyon' to the Falls; the tours continue downriver to Canaima. It costs about US$450 for the *curiara* (minimum 4 persons), not including flights to Kamarata or food – supply your own food. River trips in this region are easier in the rainy season. Guides for Auyán Tepuy can be hired here for about US$25 per day, if you have your own equipment. Contact Andreas Hauer at *Kamadac*.

Kaváck About a two-hour walk northwest of Kamarata, this a new Indian-run resort consisting of a dozen thatched huts (*churuatas*) for guests, a small shop, and an excitingly short airstrip serviced by Cessnas from Ciudad Bolívar, Santa Elena, and Isla Margarita; flights from the north provide excellent views of Angel Falls and Auyán Tepuy. There is a vehicle connection with Kamarata but it is expensive because all fuel has to be flown in. The prime local excursion is to **Kaváck Canyon** and its waterfall known as La Cueva, which can be reached by joining a group or by setting out early west up the Río Kaváck. A natural jacuzzi is encountered after a 30-minute wade/scramble along the sparkling stream, after which the gorge narrows dramatically until the falls are reached. Go in the morning to avoid groups of day-trippers from Porlamar. The sun's rays illuminate the vertical walls of the canyon only for a short time around 1100. Be prepared to get wet; bathing suits and shoes with good grip, plus a dry change of clothing are recommended; also insect repellent, since there is a mosquito invasion around dusk. Late afternoon winds off the savannah can make conditions chilly. It costs US$16 per person to stay at the camp (cheaper in hammocks). The price includes the tour to the canyon. Take food with you.

A day excursion by light plane to Kaváck from Canaima (45 minutes' flight) can be made with any of the tour operators at the airport, and costs around US$130-140 per person depending on number of passengers. Flight only from Ciudad Bolívar to Kaváck or Kamarata costs US$80 per person one way. Trips from Ciudad Bolívar can be arranged with tour agencies in town or at airport; around US$250 per person including flight via Angel Falls, meals, and one night's accommodation.

Ciudad Guayana

Phone code: 0286
Colour map 2, grid A2
Population: 700,000
105 km downriver
from Ciudad Bolívar

In an area rich in natural resources an entirely new metropolis, known as Ciudad Guayana, is still being built. It is on the south bank of the Orinoco and both sides of the Caroní River before it spills into the Orinoco. Four separate centres, San Félix, Palúa, Puerto Ordaz and Matanzas, are being forged into one. East of the Caroní are the commercial port of **San Félix** (work in progress to make a riverside walk and park) and the Palúa iron-ore terminal of the railway from El Pao. Across the Caroní by the 470 m concrete bridge is **Puerto Ordaz** (airport), the iron-ore loading port connected by rail with the famous Cerro Bolívar open-cast iron mine. The iron-tinted waterfall in the pretty Parque Cachamay (20 minutes' walk from centre; closes 1700) is worth a visit.

Excursions Just up the Caroní is the Macagua hydroelectric plant; there are some truly beautiful cataracts called **Salto Llovizna** as you enter the grounds (known as **Parque La Llovizna**, take a taxi, US$5). There is grand facility on the dam itself housing an archaeological museum and exhibits on the construction of the dam (free entry), as well as a coffee shop. ■ *1000-2100 daily, except Mon.* Higher up the river is the massive **Guri dam**, the world's second-largest artificial reservoir. The trip to Guri takes 90 minutes by taxi; the plant is open daily 0900-1030, 1415-1515, take your passport; the area gets very full during holidays, Easter or carnival. You can also visit the rest of the complex including the hotel (**C**, a/c, comfortable). *Por puesto* from Ciudad Bolívar, Route 70, US$20 one way; for return, ask at Alcabala Río Claro (gatehouse) if they can get you a free lift.

Los Castillos, said to be where Sir Walter Raleigh's son was killed in the search for El Dorado, are two old forts down the Orinoco from San Félix (one hour by *por puesto*, US$2.50, or take a tour).

In Puerto Ordaz B *Dos Ríos*, México esq Ecuador, T923 3092. Being renovated, newer rooms with new a/c, hot water, TV, older rooms with a/c, without hot water, **C**, pool, restaurant, *loncheria*, hairdresser, helpful. **E** in the house of Rolf and Rosa Kampen, C Surinam 03-07, Villa Antillana, 3 km from central Pto Ordaz, T/F923 0516. Room for 6 people, free pick up (best to contact by fax), breakfast US$5, dinner can be arranged. Rolf speaks English, German and Dutch. Recommended. **E** with Wolfgang Löffler of *Lobo Tours*, C Zambia 2, Africana Manzana 39, T961 6286, F961 7708. Room for 8 people, free transfer from airport. 'El Lobo' speaks English and German. Recommended. There are plenty of restaurants and cafés on Cras Tumeremo and Upata, off Av Las Américas. There is a very good *churrascaría* on Av Las Américas 15 mins walk from *Hotel Guyana* towards the airport, in an old hacienda building on the left, next to a *cervecería*, recommended. Fast food and upmarket eateries in Ciudad Comercial Altavista and surrounding streets.

Sleeping & eating

Anaconda Tours, PB, loc 2, CC Anto, Av Las Américas, T923 7966, T/F922 6572, anaconda2@cantv.net Trips to Castillos de Guayana (US$25 pp) and Guri dam (US$70 pp). Also organize tours to Orinoco Delta, Gran Sabana, Canaima, and Los Roques. *Bagheera Tours*, p 2, of 86, C C Gran Sabana, Paseo Caroní, near airport, T952 9481, F952 8767, bagheera@telcel.net.ve Tours to Gran Sabana, Angel Falls, Caura River and Orinoco Delta. *Lobo Tours*, C Zambia No 2, Villa Africana Manzana 39, T961 6286, F961 7708. Wolfgang Löffler will tailor his tours to fit your demands. Trips generally organized to the Gran Sabana and Orinoco Delta, but will put together other excursions. Very helpful. US$70 pp per day all-inclusive, excellent cooking. English and German spoken. Recommended. *Piranha Tours*, at *Hotel Inter Continental*, T920 1111, F923 6487. River trips on the Caroní, to see the Cachamay Falls, and the confluence of the Caroní and Orinoco rivers, US$20-25 pp. *Sacoroco Tours*, T961 5526, T0414-895 3948 (mob), sacoroco@cantv.net Roger Ruffenach organizes tours into the less-frequented southern parts of the Orinoco Delta (very basic facilities), leaving from Piacoa, approximate cost US$250 pp. German spoken. Recommended guide: *Richard Brandt*, T/F922 4370 (or in Santa Elena de Uairén, T922 0078/922 6813), has his own car, speaks English and tailors trips to your requirements, including Roraima, from US$50-80 per person a day.

Tour operators

The massive *Ciudad Comercial Altavista*, in Altavista, has all the high-street shops you might hope for. *Librería Orinoco*, Centro Cívico, C El Tocuyo y Carrera Upata, stocks international magazines and paperbacks in English. *Barro Lindo*, Macro Centro, Altavista, sells pottery and artesanía.

Shopping

Local Car hire: Many different operators at the airport, *Margarita Rentals* cars recommended, expect to pay US$50-60 per day; *Hertz*, Puerto Ordaz, rents 4WD vehicles. A car is very useful in this area, especially for visiting the Cerro Bolívar mine and Guri dam, or taking a road trip through the Gran Sabana to Brazil. **Taxis**: San Félix-Puerto Ordaz US$2.50, Puerto Ordaz-airport US$3.25, airport-bus terminal US$12, San Félix bus terminal-Puerto Ordaz bus terminal US$5, bus terminal-town centre US$3, town centre-San Félix bus terminal US$3.50.

Transport

Venezuela

Long distance Air: Daily flights from Puerto Ordaz to Caracas, Porlamar and Barcelona. Walk 600 m to gas station on main road for buses to San Félix or Puerto Ordaz. **Buses**: Terminals at San Félix and close to Puerto Ordaz airport; long distance buses pass through both. Minibuses are fast, frequent and cheap; San Félix-Puerto Ordaz, US$0.85; buses run until about 2100. Several buses daily to **Santa Elena de Uairén** (via El Callao), US$18, 10 hrs, with *Caribe* (recommended) and *Turgar* (or overnight bus, which misses the fine scenery, 9 hrs). **El Callao** (US$6.50), **Tumeremo** (US$8), El Dorado (US$9.50) and Km 88with *Turgar*. **Ciudad Bolívar** US$3 (*por puesto* US$5.50), 1 hr. Bus to **Maturín** US$7, 2½ hrs. 8 daily to **Caracas**, US$15 (night bus US$17.50), 10 hrs, with *Rodovias* and *Expresos Occidente*. 8 daily to **Barcelona** and **Puerto La Cruz**, US$13.50, 6 hrs, with *Caribe*. 2 daily to **Cumaná**, US$18, 8 hrs, with *Caribe*. 5 daily to **Valencia**, US$16.50, 10 hrs, with *Rodovias* and *Expresos Occidente*. To **Tucupita**, US$9, 3 hrs, leaving from San Felix bus terminal with *Expresos Guayanesa*, booking office opens 1 hr before departure, be there early, passport check just before Tucupita. San Felix bus terminal is not a safe place, especially at night. **International buses**: 1 bus daily to **Brazil**, US$33,14 hrs including 3 refreshment stops, departs 2130, arrives Boa Vista 1130,, with *Caribe* recommended, buses have a/c (take warm clothes), toilets and reclining seats.

Directory **Banks** *Corp Banca* (American Express), C Urbana, Edif Don Andrés. *Banco de Venezuela*, Av Las Américas y Av Monseñor Zabaleta. Banks will not exchange Brazilian currency. **Communication** Internet: *Planet Web Café*, Carrera Tumeremo, *Cyberarepa*, an unanticipated fusion of global and Venezuelan culture, CC Altavista. **Consulates** Brazil, Av Las Américas, near CANTV, T923 5243, F923 7105, 0900-1700. Friendly, helpful, visa issued in 1 hr, no onward ticket requested (some nationalities have to pay, eg Australians US$45), good information. **Norway**, Calle El Callao, Residencias Cachamay, Local 1, T922 9364, F922 5619. **Spain** UD-33-21, Parcela 6-7, Zona Industrial Matanza, Core 8, T/F994 1118. **Medical Services** Clinic Chilemex, Av Las Américas.

Orinoco Delta

Tucupita
Phone code: 0287
Colour map 2, grid A2
Population: 81,820
Climate: very humid

A worthwhile side trip along asphalted roads can be made to Tucupita, on the Orinoco delta. Though capital of Delta Amacuro state and the main commercial centre of the delta, there's a one-horse feel about it. There is a tourist office at C Dalla Costa beside Sonido Color 2000. Tourists should go here first for information on tours. **NB** Banks won't change travellers' cheques.

Sleeping and eating **C** *Rivera*, 500 m south of centre. Safe, bar. **D** *Gran Hotel Amacuro*, Bolívar 23, T721 0404. A/c, big rooms, dubious, **E** with fan. **D** *Sans Souci*, Centurión 30, T721 0132, F721 6221. Safe, a/c, OK, **E** with fan. French spoken. **E** *Pequeño*, La Paz, T721 0523. Basic but clean, fan, good value, safe, stores luggage, orchid garden, Israelis stay free of charge, closes at 2200. **E** *Residencias San Cristobal*, San Cristobal 50, T7214529. New, fan, parking. *Mi Tasca*, C Dalla Costa. Popular, varied menu, large portions. Recommended. On Paseo Manamo *Refresquería La Cascada*, English spoken; and *Capri*, very good.

Transport *Por puesto* from **Maturín** about US$10, 2-3 hrs; bus to Maturín, US$5, 3-4 hrs, with *Expresos Guayanesa*, US$6 with *Expresos Los Llanos* recommended. 2 daily to **San Félix**, US$4, 3 hrs, with *Expresos La Guayanesa*. 2 daily to **Caracas**, US$15, 12-13 hrs, with *Expresos Los Llanos* recommended. **Maracay** and **Valencia**, US$16, 12-13 hrs, with *Expresos Los Llanos*. **Puerto La Cruz**, US$10, 6 hrs.

Delta Trips For a 3-4 day trip to see the delta, its fauna and the indigenous *Warao*, either arrange boats through the tourist office, or contact Juan Carrión (all the taxi drivers know him, but he is very expensive). Boats are not easy to come by and are expensive except for large groups. Bargain hard and never pay up front.

Excursions often only travel on the main river, not in the *caños* where wildlife is most often be seen. To avoid disappointment, be sure to determine where your guide intends to take you before you leave. Alternatively, take a *por puesto* from

Plaza Bolívar to the peaceful village of **La Horqueta** on the banks of the Orinoco (US$0.50, 45 minutes), where a boat may be found. There are no hotels, but there are shops selling drinks and dry foodstuffs. If the river level rises after a downpour, arrangements may be cancelled. On all trips agree in advance exactly what is included, especially that there is enough food and water for you and your guide. Hammocks and mosquito repellents are essential. You can buy hammocks and local handicrafts. Passports must be shown leaving La Horqueta.

Tour operators

Recent favourable reports received: Delta Sur, C Mariño and C Pativilca, T/F721 2666, established company run by Sr Abelardo, US$200-250 pp for 3 day tour, English spoken. *Aventura Turística Delta*, C Centurión 62, opposite cathedral, T721 0837, T/F7210835, also at the bus station, a_t_d_1973@hotmail.com 1-5 day trips to the Delta Orinoco, Nicolás and Vidalig are very helpful, they speak French and English, they charge US$100 per person per day (price per person decreases with more people in the group, eg $80 pp per day for a group of 6). *Tucupita Expeditions*, opposite hospital, T721 0801, www.orinocodelta.com US$255 pp for 3-day tour. *Mis Palafitos*, in the centro comercial near the *Fondo Común* bank on Plaza Bolívar, and at *Hotel Saxxi* (T721 2112) on the road into town, mispalafitos@cantv.net, www.deltaorinocomispalafitos.com The luxury option, tours cost US$110 per day. These four are registered with the tourist board and have insurance. *Romero Ildemaro* (ask at *Bar Warauno*, or C Tucupita 19), US$50 pp per day, basic but watertight accommodation, good food, hammocks and mosquito nets, recommended. Raúl at the *Gran Hotel Amacuro* runs a one-day trip for up to four, including food and drink, visit to *Warao* village. Some boat owners visit hotels in the evenings looking for clients and may negotiate a price. Ask Pieter Rothfuss at *Posada La Casita* in Ciudad Bolívar about a trip through the southern part of the delta and into the Sierra Imataca highlands.

Directory

Banks *Unibanca* C Petión, Delta a La Paz, cash advances against Visa. *Banco de Venezuela*, Paseo Manamo, Delta a La Paz, ATM and cash advances. **Communication** Internet: *Compucenter.com*, in the same centro comercial as *Mis Palafitos*, Plaza Bolívar. *Delta Microsystems*, C Pativilca.

Barrancas
Colour map 2, grid A2
Population: 13,000

An interesting and friendly village is Barrancas. Founded in 1530, it is one of the oldest villages in the Americas. Situated on the Orinoco, it can be reached by road from Tucupita (63 km, US$1.50, buses return at 0945 and 1700) or from Maturín. It has one basic hotel. The village has a large community of Guyanese people who speak English. It is possible to take a boat to the *Warao* villages of **Curiapo** and **Amacuro** (near Guyana border), check at harbour.

Warning Avoid boats that are carrying suspicious goods, those that do not have adequate shelter from the rain and those that do not stop in Curiapo, as this is the only place to get an exit stamp out of Venezuela.

South to Brazil

Travelling South from Ciudad Guayana to the Brazilian border is becoming an increasingly popular excursion for Venezuelan tourists, as well as for overland travellers heading into Brazil via Boa Vista. The road to the border at Santa Elena de Uairén passes over the beautiful Gran Sabana and is completely paved, with all bridges in place.

Getting there

If hitchhiking note that if you're dropped away from a base there will be no shade. Camping is possible but a tent with good waterproofing is essential (see also above, under Parque Nacional Canaima). Insect repellent and long-sleeved/trousered clothes are needed against *puri-puri* (small, black, vicious biting insects) and mosquitoes (especially in El Dorado, at Km 88 and at Icabarú); or use baby oil mixed with vitamin B12. 5-day/4-night tours of the Gran Sabana can be arranged in Caracas, or in Ciudad Bolívar, which is cheaper and easier.

A 4WD is only necessary if you wander off the main road, particularly in the rainy season. It is highly recommended to take spare tanks of gasoline (spare tanks are available at Km 88,

Venezuela

but better and cheaper to get one earlier). All petrol pumps have fuel, but not all octane levels. It is also advisable to carry extra water and plenty of food. There are Guardia Nacional checks at the Río Cuyuní (Km 8), at Km 126, and at San Ignacio de Yuruaní (Km 259), and a military checkpoint at Luepa (Km 143); all driving permits, car registration papers, and identification must be shown.

South from Ciudad Guayana Highway 10 is a four-lane *autopista* as far as **Upata** (*Phone code:* 0288; *Population*: 51,500). There's a good place to buy provisions opposite the petrol station. **C** *Andrea*, Plaza Miranda, T221 3618, F221 3736. Decent rooms, a/c, hot water, TV, fridge in some rooms. Credit cards accepted, Chinese restaurant, safe parking, good. **E** *Comercio*, C Ayacucho, excellent, as is its restaurant. **NB** Water is rationed in Upata and hot water in hotels is rare south of Ciudad Guayana.

From Upata to Km 88 the road is partly resurfaced and has some broad hard shoulders. At 18 km beyond **Guasipati** (*Population*: 8,600. **C** *Hotel La Reina*, Avenida Orinoco, a/c, good; also **D** *Hotel Venezuela*, Plaza Bolívar, opposite is a café serving excellent coffee; **E** *Residencias El Agua*, southern end of town, basic, a/c, OK) is **El Callao** on the south bank of the Río Yuruari, off the highway, a small, clean, bright town (*Population*: 7,400) whose Trinidadian inhabitants add a touch of calypso to its pre-Lenten carnival. The gold mine, 8 km away in El Perú, can be visited, the director will show you around. The town has many jewellery shops and several restaurants. You may be able to change US$ cash in *Banco de Venezuela* on main plaza, but not travellers' cheques. **C** *New Millenium*, Plaza Bolívar, T762 0995. New, nice rooms, a/c, TV, laundry, parking, cheaper without hot water. Recommended. **D** *Arte Dorado*, C Roscio 51, 5 minutes from Plaza Bolívar, T762 0535. A/c, TV, parking, cheaper without hot water, good. **E** *Isidora*, on the road to El Perú but in town, T762 0290. A/c. **E** *Callao*, C Bolívar, 2 blocks from the plaza. Shared bath, laundry facilities, very welcoming owners, recommended. **F** *Italia City*, C Ricuarte off Plaza Bolívar, T762 0770. Basic, a/c. **F** *Ritz*, C Ricuart, T762 0730. Basic, serves cold beer. There is a chronic water shortage, check when it is available in your hotel. All prices rise for the carnival in February.

Tumeremo
Colour map 2, grid A2
Population: 25,000

On another 41 km is Tumeremo, recommended as the best place to buy provisions. There is *Unibanca* (Visa), *Banco de Orinoco* (Amex, after 1500, US$5 commission), and gasoline (all grades) at a normal price (better than El Dorado). About 5 km from Tumeremo towards the Fuerte Tarabay is the beautiful artificial lake of San Pedro with free campsite.

Sleeping and eating D *Cacique*. Very good, noisy, excellent shower. Recommended. **D***Sinfonies*, C El Dorado, 1 block down from *Leocar*. Good value, good beds, a/c, TV, bath, nice. **E** *Leocar*, next to the bus stop. Poor value, noisy, with bath, fan and a/c, some rooms with fridges, restaurant. **E** *Central*, near plaza, T710 2064. Fan, good, bakery and snackbar. **F** *Francia*, C Bolívar, T711 1477. Clean, a/c, TV friendly owner. **F** *Hospedaje Tumeremo*, on C El Dorado. Fan, clean bathroom, good. *El Esturión*, C El Dorado, Edif Bolívar. Good, friendly restaurant. *Restaurante Turístico*. Expensive but OK. *Restaurante Las Cuevas*, near plaza. Popular, average food and prices, service slow, check your bill.

Transport Buses: To **Santa Elena**, US$15, 8-10 hrs, with *Líneas Orinoco*, 2 blocks from plaza near *Leocar*); **El Dorado**, US$2, 1½ hrs. Bus to **Ciudad Bolívar**, US$9.25, 6 a day, 6½ hrs or *por puesto* (via San Félix and Puerto Ordaz). Bus to **San Félix** (Ciudad Guayana), US$3.60, *por puesto* US$8.75. To **Caracas**, US$20, direct service at 1600, 14 hrs.

The road between Tumeremo and El Dorado is in poor repair, but is passable with care.

This hot, dirty and very noisy miners' supply centre in dense forest is 76 km from Tumeremo, 7 km off the road on the Río Cuyuní. On an island in the river stands the regional prison made famous by Papillon's stay there in 1945, in use again after renovation. It is possible to get police permission to cross the river (free) and land on the island. The local gold seams have been largely exhausted but mining still continues and the town's nightlife is entirely for the miners, violence is in the air after nightfall. El Dorado's other economic mainstay is its gas station (open 0800-1900, daily). There is a *Banco de Venezuela*, which accepts Visa and MasterCard; exchange is possible with the gold buyer on the main street, cash only, poor rates. Yesenia at *Agua Selva* and Bruno and Vanessa at *El Encanto Cuyuní* can organize boat trips and trips into the jungle. Dugout canoes (*curiaras*) are generally rented at around US$150 (maximum 9 persons).

El Dorado
Phone code: 0288
Colour map 2, grid B2
Population: 4,000
278 km from
Ciudad Guayana

Sleeping and eating E *Universo*, C Cuyuní, running parallel to the river, T991 1151. Clean, safe, a/c, geared towards tourists, some rooms have TV, safe parking. Recommended. F *Agua Selva*, on right when entering town, T991 1093. Rustic camp, with shared bathrooms, fan, includes breakfast, dinner available at extra cost. Hammocks also available for rent, G including breakfast. Welcoming owner, tours organized. Recommended. Another camp is F *El Encanto Cuyuní*, 3 km down the road at the Puente Río Cuyuní, T0289-808 1024. Will prepare food. G *San Antonio*, Edif Ceferino, next to bus stop. Electricity intermittent, prefers to let by the hour, fan, questionable safety. G *Mirador*, basic, noisy at weekends, rents by the hour, but good. *La Brasa*, on left when entering town, excellent food but small portions. *El Caney*, on right just down from *Agua Selva*, good food. Recommended. *Archiven*, Plaza Bolívar, good, helpful owner. Restaurant beside church serves delicious *criolla* food.

All hotels have problems with running water and there is no lack of accommodation for short-stay clients

Transport Buses: From **Caracas**, *Expresos del Oriente*, at 1830 daily, US$20, 14½ hrs, return at 1400 (925 km). The Orinoco bus line connects with **Ciudad Bolívar** (6 hrs) and Santa Elena, as does *Transmundial* (better buses, leaving 1100, US$9.50 to **Santa Elena**, US$5.50 to San Félix, 4 hrs). From El Dorado a bus runs to **San Martín** on the Guyanese border (see above). Buses also to **Caicara**. All buses stop on main plaza.

The turn-off to El Dorado is marked Km 0; distances are measured from here by green signs 1 km apart. About 3 km south of the turnoff to El Dorado, is the Río Cuyuní crossed by a bridge. From here it is possible to take boat trips to the gold mines, for example Payapal one hour 40 minutes each way, US$25 per person, beautiful trip; can also be visited by car, leaving from central plaza every hour or so, 30-minutes journey, US$8 return, people are friendly and will let you look into the 30-m deep mines.

El Dorado to Santa Elena de Uairén

At Km 88 (also called **San Isidro**), there is gasoline (the last before Santa Elena – rarely 92 octane), a garage, the last telephone before Santa Elena and Banco Guayana. Everything is expensive; better food shops at Km 85.

Sleeping and eating At Km 84.5 is **AL** *La Barquilla de Fresa* run by Henry Cleve, English and German spoken. Book through Alba Betancourt in Caracas T0212-256 4162, T0416-709 7205 (mob), barquilladefresa@cantv.net It specializes in bird watching tours and the inventory of bird species for the jungle here has reached more than 300 species. US$70 pp per day, full board (reservations and deposit required). **Las Claritas**, a gold-miners' town at Km 85: **B** *Campamento Turístico Anaconda*, T0286-923 7996, anaconda@cantv.net Cabins with bath, fan, well-furnished, bar, including breakfast and dinner, reserved for tour groups (**C** in low season). **D** *Landolfi*, left turn in the centre of town towards the indigenous village of San Lucia de Inaway. A/c, **E** with fan. Also restaurant, big market for food and gold, safe parking at Las Hermanitas de las Pobres (Convent), which can be better reached by the track from Km 88. **Km 88**: **D** *El Parador del Viajero*, restaurant, OK. **F** *La Pilonera*, opposite Vargas store, with fan, safe parking, some rooms with bath, restaurant with good fruit drinks; good food next door at the *Fuente de Soda*; *Restaurant Internacional*, grotty exterior but excellent and cheap. Rooms for rent, **E**, with bath, fan, clean, ask at *farmacia*.

Venezuela

Transport Bus Km 88-Caracas, US$20; to Ciudad Bolívar wait at gas station for buses from Las Claritas (depart 0900, 1100, 1500, 1800). Frequent *por puestos* from El Dorado to Km 88, 1 hr, US$3.50. The only reliable public transport out of Km 88 is the bus from Ciudad Bolívar, which stops at 1400 daily, 6 hrs to **Santa Elena**, US$7.75; the alternative is to get a ride with passing jeeps and trucks (very little passes after 1030).

The wall of the Gran Sabana looms above Km 88 and the highway climbs steeply in sharp curves for 40 km before reaching the top. The road is in very good condition and presents no problem for conventional cars. Four-wheel drives may be better in the wet season (May-October). At Km 100 the huge **Piedra de la Virgen** (sandy coloured with black streaks) is passed before the steepest climb (La Escalera) enters the beautiful **Parque Nacional Canaima** (see page 1419).

Characteristic of this area are the large abrupt tepuis (flat-topped mountains or mesas), hundreds of waterfalls, and the silence of one of the oldest plateaus on earth

The landscape is essentially savannah, with clusters of trees, moriche palms and bromeliads. At Km 119 (sign can only be seen going north) a short trail leads to the 40 m **Danto ('Tapir') Falls**, a powerful fall wreathed in mosses and mist. If you are paying for your ride, try to persuade the driver to make a short stop; the falls are close to the road (about five minutes slippery walk down on the left-hand side), but not visible from it. (Buses cannot be flagged down here because of dangerous bends.) The **Monumento al Soldado Pionero** (Km 137) commemorates the army engineers who built the road up from the lowlands, finally opened in 1973; barbecues, toilets, shelters. Some 4 km beyond is **Luepa**; all travellers must stop at the *ciudadela* (military checkpoint) a little way south. There is a popular camping place at Luepa, on the right going south which belongs to a tour company. An informative guide on duty will rent you a tent or you can hang a hammock in an open-sided shelter (very cold at night, no water or facilities, possible to buy a meal from a tour group, but expensive). There is a breakfast place, US$4. The Inparques station at Luepa has some guestrooms which are intended for visitors of Inparques, but they may let you stay for a small fee. There is a kitchen at the station and a cafetería for employees of Inparques and Edelca.

Some 8 km beyond Luepa, a graded gravel road leads 70 km west to **Kavanayén** (little traffic, best to have your own vehicle with high clearance, especially during the wet season, take plenty of snacks; the road can be cycled but is slow, lots of soft, sandy places). Accommodation is at the Franciscan mission, **F**, very friendly, also in private homes; cash travellers' cheques at a better rate than in Santa Elena. One of the two grocery stores will prepare food, or the restaurant opposite serves cheap breakfasts and dinners, order in advance. Medical post near the airstrip.

The settlement is surrounded by *tepuis*. Bargain with pilots at the airstrip to fly you over the Gran Sabana: a tour of Auyán Tepuy, Angel Falls, Canaima and back to Kavanayén; US$200 for five passengers. Off the road to Kavanayén are the falls of **Torón Merú** and **Chinak-Merú** (also called Aponwao), 110 m high and very impressive. Neither is a straightforward detour, so get full instructions before setting out. Chinak-Merú is reached via the very friendly Pemón village of **Iboribó**.

For the remaining 180 km to Santa Elena de Uairén few people and only a handful of Pemón Indian villages are to be seen. Kampirán, **Rápidos de Kamoirán** (Km 172, rooms to let **D**, clean, with fan, cold water, camping US$$2, also restaurant, gasoline, and picnic spot by the rapids) and Oriwarai are passed. The 5-m Kawí falls at the **Kama** River are at Km 195, while at Km 201.5 are the impressive 55 m high **Kama Merú** falls can be seen (nominal US$0.60 to walk to the bottom of the falls). Also a small lake, local handicrafts for sale, a small shop for supplies, canoe trips US$1.50 per hour per person. Cabins and *churuatas* can be rented for about US$3 pp, camping at US$2 per tent. *Puri-puri* flies descend at dusk. Buses can be flagged down going south or north three times a day; check times in advance.

At Km 237 the Río Yuruaní cascades over the charming **Quebrada Arepán** (Pacheco); pools nearby where you can swim. Tour groups often stop here. A path up the opposite side of the main falls leads to an isolated natural swimming pool 20 minutes walk away, in the middle of the savannah. A 15-minute hike to the Yuruaní waterfall leaves the main road 250 m after the crossing, turn left. A new camp is being built between Kama Merú and Quebrada Arepán. There are plans for lodging, a restaurant, an indigenous cultural centre, and to offer excursions in the savannah. Contact Oscar Romero on T0414-886 2034 (mob). Next is **Balneario Suruape** (Km 249), a good place for swimming and picnics, natural whirlpool, restaurant, 10 minutes downriver is a natural waterslide. Then, at Km 250, comes the Pemón village of San Francisco de Yuruaní (see page 1433), whose falls can be seen from the road bridge, followed, 9 km of bends later, by the smaller village of **San Ignacio de Yuruaní** (strict military checkpoint; excellent regional food).

A trail at Km 275 leads to the **Quebrada de Jaspe** where a river cuts through striated cliffs and pieces of jasper glitter on the banks. Visit at midday when the sun shines best on the jasper, or at 1500 when the colour changes from red to orange, dazzlingly beautiful.

Between Km 277 and 278 a 3 km dirt road (high-clearance only) leads to **La Ventana/La Puerta del Cielo** at Agua Fría. A waterfall roars into a steep canyon whose walls seem to form a window, through which there is an endless view of the Gran Sabana. Another trail goes to a waterfall with a beautiful natural pool.

Sleeping Km 201.5 (Kama Merú) There is accommodation, **F**, with bath, cold water, or pitch your tent in the camping area, under US$2; no facilities, take water purification tablets, also a good value restaurant and a small shop. **Km 249** Cabins with hammocks for up to 12, **D**, cooking facilities. **Quebrada de Jaspe** Campsite beside the river, no facilities, bad drainage and exposed, not recommended.

Santa Elena de Uairén

This booming, pleasant frontier town was established by Capuchin Monks in 1931. Thanks to its relaxed atmosphere and plentiful supply of hotels, Santa Elena is an agreeable place in which to spend time. Gold is a better buy here than in Ciudad Bolívar. The local festival is on 9-19 August, featuring music, dance and handicrafts.

Phone code: 0289
Colour map 2, grid B2
Population: 15,000

Sleeping

A *Gran Sabana*, outside town, 10 km from border, T995 1810, www.hotelgransaban.com Most luxurious in town, good service. Recommended. **C** *Villa Fairmont*, Urb Akurimá, T995 1022, at north edge of town, a few mins' drive from bus station, large, comfortable rooms, a/c, hot water, TV, restaurant, small craft shop. Nearby is **C** *Cabañas Roraima*, up road behind bus terminal, T996 1164. A/c, hot water, fridge, also has cabins for up to 8, near supermarket. **C** *Lucas*, Km 320, Urb Brisas de Uairén, C La Cancha, T995 1018. Breakfast included, with bar and restaurant, pool. **C** *Ya-Koo Ecological Camp*, 2 km on unpaved road to Sampai Indian community, up the mountain behind Santa Elena, T995 1742, www.ya-koo.com *Cabañas* with all facilities in beautiful 10-ha site, full board, spacious rooms, hot water, natural swimming pool. Prices 20% more expensive in high season. Recommended if you have a car. **D** pp *Cabañas Friedenau*, Av Ppal de Cielo Azul, off Av Perimetral, T995 1353, friedenau@cantv.net Self-contained chalets, price includes breakfast, pleasant grounds, caters for groups, vegetarian food, parking, transfer to Puerto Ordaz, bicycles and horseback trips, also run trips to Roraima (see below), English and German spoken. Recommended. **D** *Lucrecia*, Av Perimetral, T/F995 1105, near terminal. A/c or fan, TV, restaurant, helpful, OK. **D** *Los Castaños*, C Mcal Sucre, near the bus terminal, T995 1450. A/c, TV, **F** with fan only. **D** *Tres Naciones*, on C Zea, T995 1190. Basic, with a/c, hot water, restaurant, parking. **D** *Panzarelli*, C Bolívar, near plaza, T995 1196. Hot water, fans, nice rooms, good value. **E** *Villa Apoipo*, on the road to the airport, turn left at the *Hotel Gran Sabana*, T0414-886 2049 (mob). Very nice rooms, hot water, fan. Set up to receive groups but will take independent travellers if you ring ahead. Use of kitchen or full board option. Bunk beds or hammocks available in large *churuata*, **G**. **E** *La Posada Aventura*, above *Adventure Tours* on Av Perimetral, T995 1574.

Venezuela

Hot water, fan. Good. **E** *Las 5 Jotas*, near *Cabañas Roraima*. Comfortable, good value. **E** *Jaspe*, on C Mcal Sucre, T995 1379, 150 m from bus terminal on opposite side. Hot water, fan, TV, free coffee. **F** *Casa de Gladys*, Urdaneta 187, T995 1171. The irrepressible Gladys' haphazard family house, fan, cooking and washing facilities, continuous coffee, internet, tourist information, day trips, luggage stored for a fee, **G** in a dormitory or hammock. **F** *Luz*, C Peña, 2 mins' walk from Plaza Bolívar. Basic, dark, no hot water, fan, good meeting point, mixed reports about security. If hotel's full, owner will help to find a room in a private home. **G** *Michelle*, C Urdaneta, next to *Café Goldfieber*, T995 1415, hotelmichelle@cantv.net Spotless clean, hot water, fan, spacious room, very helpful, laundry, good value. Credit cards accepted, cash advances on Visa if you are desperate. Recommended.

Eating *El Rincon Cubano*, Av Perimetral. Excellent breakfasts and superb Cuban dinners at good prices. Fantastic cocktails made by the owner, once 'second-best cocktail mixer in Cuba'. Highly recommended. *La Bohemia*, behind bus station. European style, coffee, sandwiches, etc. *Venezuela Primera*, Av Perimetral, chicken, meat, and seafood. *Café Goldfieber*, C Urdaneta, next to *Tommy Town* Chinese restaurant. Makes good breakfasts, also dinners, and internet. Good place to form tour groups with other travellers. *Panadería Rico Pan*, next to *Hotel Augusta* on C Bolívar. Good breakfasts and coffee. There are several restaurants on Mcal Sucre, one of these *El Ranchón Criollo* serves good *criolla* fare.

Tour operators The tours industry in Santa Elena is burgeoning, with more and more operators popping up every day, and freelance guides in the street. Bargains are to be had if you shop around, form larger groups, and haggle. Santa Elena is becoming the most economical place to book tours of the Gran Sabana, Roraima, and other tepuis. Many tour operators will tailor their tours to fit your needs, contact by e-mail to discuss plans before arriving. *Adventure Tours*, Av Perimetral at the end of C Urdaneta, T/F995 1861 adventure3tours@hotmail.com Tours of

Santa Elena de Uairén

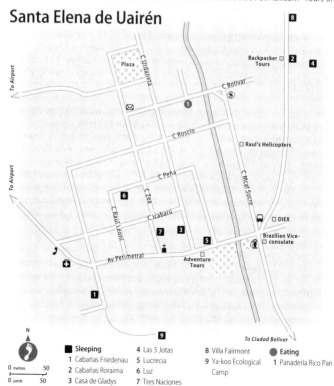

Sleeping ■	4 Las 5 Jotas	8 Villa Fairmont	Eating ●
1 Cabañas Friedenau	5 Lucrecia	9 Ya-koo Ecological	1 Panadería Rico Pan
2 Cabañas Roraima	6 Luz	Camp	
3 Casa de Gladys	7 Tres Naciones		

0 metres 50
0 yards 50

Gran Sabana or El Pauji, US$25 per person per day guide and transport only, or US$50 per person per day all included, group discounts, 6 days to Roraima US$236 per person all included (minimum 4 persons). Sleeping bags and camping mats available for hire (US$19 for Roraima tour). *Backpacker Tours*, Urb Akurimá, opposite *Cabañas Roraima*, T995 1524, T0414-8864022 (mob), www.venezuela-tours.de Eric Buschbell runs 1-5 day, all-inclusive jeep tours through the Gran Sabana, visiting little-known falls in the Kavanayen area, US$60 pp. Trekking to the nearby Churikayen Tepuy, 3-4 days and to Roraima, US$50 pp per day (minimum 4 persons). Equipment hire included in price of tour. German and English spoken. Recommended. *Expediciones Dearuna*, of Ciudad Bolívar are on C Urdaneta, next to *Casa de Gladys*. They offer the same tours as their office in Bolívar (T/F632 8512, T0414-854 6807 (mob)) expediciones_dearuna@yahoo.com *Kamadac*, C Urdaneta, opposite *Café Goldfieber*, T995 1583, T0414-850 9604 (mob), www.abenteuer-venezuela.de Run by Andreas Hauer, tours of Gran Sabana, US$100 per day for jeep (maximum 4 persons), El Pauji area (includes gold-washing), US$120, 2 days, all-inclusive (minimum 4 persons), and Pemón-style fishing trips. 6-day, all-inclusive tour to Roraima, US$250 pp (for 4-6 persons), sleeping bag and camping mat US$25 extra, and also more adventurous tours to; Auyán Tepuy from which Angel Falls cascades (7-8 days, approximately US$70 pp per day for 5-6 people), difficult; Acopan Tepuy, virgin territory in the Chimantá massif (5-6 days, approximately US$400 pp, groups of 3-4, or 7-8); Kamarata Falls, from Kavác by *curiara* (4 days, $400 pp for 4 persons). Andreas is happy to share his knowledge of the Gran Sabana. German and English spoken. Recommended. *Mount Roraima Tours*, Ana Mathilde López, T/F995 1826, T0414-886 3870 (mob), www.roraimatours.com *New Frontiers Adventure*, also on C Urdaneta next to *Tommy Town*, T995 1584, T0414-927 7140 (mob), www.newfrontiersadventures.com Affiliated to the International Ecotourism Society, Claude Saint-Pierre and the 4 other guides of *New Frontiers* specialize in ecotours and tours for small groups. They offer all the usual tours at standard prices, but more interestingly offer 4-day, all-inclusive walking tours at US$40 pp per day, taking in the different ecosystems of the Gran Sabana, and staying in Pemón villages. English, French, and German spoken. Recommended. *Petoi Tours*, Ricardo Arreaza, T0414-886 1721 (mob), petoitours@cantv.net *Radical Tours*, C Urdaneta y Icabarú, T414 5294, T0414-854 8094 (mob), radicaltours@cantv.net The newest tour operator in town with swanky new jeeps. Offers usual tours at standard prices. *Ruta Salvaje*, the faux-indigenous *churuata* at the entrance to the town, across from the bus terminal, T995 1134, T0414-886 3833 (mob), www.geocities.com/rutagransabana A tourist information service and private agency. Usual tours, standard prices. Also rafting (US$40 pp per day) and bicycle hire (US$10 per day). *Tayukasen Tours*, C Urdaneta, opposite *Expediciones Dearuna*, T995 1505, www.lagransabana.com/tayukasen 1-5 day tours of Gran Sabana, US$25 pp per day (minimum 4 persons), 6 day treks to Roraima US$230 pp all included, also trips to El Pauji and the gold mines, Canaima, Angel Falls and Kavác. English and Portuguese spoken. Recommended guides: *Rawllins* and his brother, *Guyanese* who speak English, excellent cooks, T0414-886 2669 (mob), rawllins@yahoo.com Ray Sanson, T0414-864 6969 (mob), raysteven71@hotmail.com Speaks English, Spanish and local dialects, tours to Roraima, jungle and fishing trips. *Raúl's Helicopters*, on left at the top of the rise before entering town or at the 5-star *Hotel Gran Sabana*, T995 1159. This option is for those with deep pockets – flights over tepuis start around US$1,400 per hr.

Air Airport, 8 km from the centre. *Rutaca* is the only company currently serving the airstrip in Santa Elena. Their 5-seater Cessnas leave once or twice a day for destinations that include Ciudad Bolívar, Canaima, Kavác, Kamarata, and Kavanayen (US$70 one way), Wonken (US$40 one way), and El Pauji and Icabarú (US$25 one way). To calculate the price of chartering an airplane from Santa Elena to any destination, take the cost per passenger and multiply by 5.

    Road PDV gas station on C Mcal Sucre (road out of town), open 0800-1900. **Jeeps** To **El Pauji** (US$10), **Canta Rana** (US$15), and **Icabarú** (US$20) leave early (about 0700) from Plaza Bolívar. They can also be caught at the *Panadería Gran Café* on C Icabarú. **Buses** Terminal on C Mcal Sucre y Av Perimetral. From **Caracas** it is best to go to Ciudad Bolívar and take a bus direct to Boa Vista, or Santa Elena. 10 buses daily from Santa Elena to **Ciudad Bolívar**,

Transport

Venezuela

US$21, with *Expresos Los Llanos* (recommended), *San Cristobal*, and *Línea Orinoco*, 10-12 hrs. 10 daily to **Ciudad Guayana** and **San Félix**, US$18, 10-11 hrs, with *Caribe* (recommended), *Turgar*, and *Línea Orinoco*. 10 daily to **Puerto La Cruz**, US$21, 14 hrs, with *Caribe* (recommended), *Turgar*, and *Línea Orinoco*. *Expresos Maturín* goes to Maturín daily. *Expresos Los Llanos* go to **Maracay** and **Valencia** 3 times a day, US$22, 18-20 hrs. 1 bus daily to **Boa Vista**, US$15, 4 hrs, with *Caribe*. Take warm clothing for buses with a/c (the driver may even insist that the shades be closed throughout the journey, so as not to affect the a/c).

Hitchhiking North from Santa Elena is said to be easy. Stand at the roadside at the garage just opposite the terminal. Expect a small charge, up to US$5.

Directory **Banks** *Banco Industrial* C Bolívar. Cash advances on Visa. Try the shops in the centre for dollars cash, reais or TCs, eg *Casa de Los Cóchamos*, the gold shop south of main plaza, which changes TCs at lower rate than bank. *Inversiones Fortaleza*, C Urdaneta on plaza, cash dollars, TCs or Brazilian currency. *La Boutique Zapatería* also changes TCs and cash at reasonable rates. Also grocery store *El Gordito*, next to *La Abuela* on C Urdaneta, for Brazilian currency (English and French spoken). Try at border with Brazilians entering Venezuela. Generally the rates are poor; check with travellers going in opposite direction what rates should be. For better rates you must wait until Ciudad Guayana, or Boa Vista if going to Brazil (change some money into Brazilian currency before the bus leaves). **Communications** Internet: *Global de Communicaciones*, C Icabarú y Urdaneta. *Café Goldfieber*, C Urdaneta. **Telephone:** *Global de Communicaciones*, *CANTV* office, on Av Perimetral, next to hospital at west end of C Icabarú, for international calls, but not all day. **Useful addresses** Mechanic: Antonio Mejías, good, cheap, a miracle-worker. *Parks Auto Parts*, next to *Hotel Fronteras*, run by Floyd Park from Texas, USA, helpful.

Border with Brazil The 16 km road to the border is paved. The entire road links Caracas with Manaus in four days with hard driving; see Northern Brazil, page 555, for a description of the road from the border and Brazilian immigration formalities. DIEX immigration office is at the frontier; opens at 0730-1230 and 1400-1800. All passports and car documents must be stamped here on entry or exit. Staff at the Ministry of Justice uphill behind the bus terminal, and the Guardia Nacional headquarters have been recommended as helpful with entry/exit difficulties. The Brazilian consulate is near the bus terminal opposite PDV gas station; open 0800-1200 and 1400-1800. You can get a visa here.

For entry to Venezuela, most nationalities who cross the border from Boa Vista, Brazil must have a visa, which costs US$75 (not required by western Europeans – passport must be valid for one year). Venezuelan consulates are given in the Brazil chapter. Ask well in advance what health requirements are in force (yellow fever vaccination certificate is required, malaria test certificate and medical check-up may also be necessary). Entering by car, make sure to keep photocopies of your license, the Brazilian permission to leave and Venezuelan entry stamp. Allow two hours to undertake all formalities when crossing by private vehicle and don't cross during the lunch hour. Border officials may insist upon US$20 per day for your stay. Fresh fruit and vegetables may not be brought into Venezuela. There are frequent road checks.

El Pauji A road leaves the highway 8 km south of Santa Elena and after passing through a tunnel of jungle vegetation emerges onto rolling savannah dotted with *tepuis*. The unpaved road has been considerably improved since the era when it took three hours to arrive. Now, it is passable in a normal car, although with care. Take advice before setting out, as rain can rapidly degrade the quality of the road. At Km 58 is a Guardia Nacional checkpoint at Paraitepuí, waterfall nearby. At Km 68 is *Shailili-ko* camp, English, Italian and French spoken, recommended.

El Pauji, 17 km further on, is an agricultural settlement with a growing number of foreign residents. At *La Bodega* general store, Victoriano has information on guides for tourists. At Solís, 15 km from El Pauji, Arquimedes and Philippe have a tourist camp and organize tours. El Pauji is in a lovely area, with good walking. Excellent sights: **Chirica Tepuy**, huge, beautiful, jet black, surrounded by rolling savannah;

Río Surucun, where the largest diamond in Venezuela was found; **Salto Catedral**, beautiful small hollow, lovely falls, bright red water below because of the tree roots, excellent for swimming; **Salto La Gruta**, very impressive falls, but very slippery; and **Pozo Esmeralda**, just outside El Pauji, fine rapids, waterfall you can stand under and pools for swimming. It is 20 minutes to Los Saltos de Pauji, good for a bath. A good walk is to the small hill, 2 km from El Pauji beyond the airfield; views from the crest over **El Abismo**, the plunging wall of rock that marks the end of the Gran Sabana highlands and the beginning of the Amazon rain forest. The thick green carpet of the jungle stretches as far as the eye can see. It takes about an hour to reach the top, and the walk is highly recommended. Guides, though not strictly necessary, can be found in the village. A recommended guide is German-speaking Marco.

Apiculture is the primary activity of El Pauji and there is an International Honey Festival every summer. The honey made in this region is divine and ought to be sampled. It can be purchased from the shop in El Pauji or at Salto Catedral, en route.

Sleeping and eating A pp *Campamento Amariba*, 3½ km outside El Pauji on rod from Santa Elena, transport usually available from air strip, reservations in Caracas T0212-753 9314, amariba@cantv.net Comfortable cabins with mosquito nets, separate bathrooms with good facilities, full board, kitchen, tours arranged, very hospitable. **C** pp *Chimanta* and *Manoa*, T995 1431. Cozy rooms, restaurant serving vegan food, run by Louise Scott. **C** *Campamento El Pauji*, 3½ km outside El Pauji on road from Santa Elena, transport usually available from airstrip, T995 1431. Beautiful cabins with spectacular views over the Gran Sabana, food available, camping US$6 per tent. Recommended. **D** *Hospedaje Maripak Tepuy*, near the airstrip and small store, T/F995 1562, or reserve in Caracas T0212-234 3661. Run by Mariela Gil, cabins for 2/3 with bathroom, US$10 per meal, good food, organizes tours, camping US$6 per tent. **E** *Hospedaje Karaware*, run by Nelson and Elizabeth, helpful. **F** *El Caminante* tourist camp, just after the bridge coming from Santa Elena. Run by Danielle, trips arranged, camping US$2 per tent. Just before the bridge is *El Merendero* restaurant. 25 km from the town is the **F** *Canta Rana* tourist camp with basic accommodation, breakfast and dinner included in the price, owners, Alfonso and Barbara Borrero, speak German, English and Spanish, waterfall and lovely surroundings. The store has few supplies and prices are double elsewhere.

Transport Air: El Pauji to Santa Elena (see above). **Road** To get further than El Pauji – to Canta Rana and Icabarú – a 4WD vehicle is necessary. From Santa Elena, US$13-17 by jeep if full, more if not, daily at around 0600-0700 and 1500-1600 from Plaza Bolívar, or *Panadería Gran Café* on C Icabarú, 3 hrs; ask for Sr Manriques. Taxi US$6-10. Hitching from the airport is possible, but normally ends in tears of frustration. You may get lucky. Jeep hire in El Pauji, US$50 per day.

Mount Roraima

An exciting trek is to the summit of Mt Roraima, believed to be the '**Lost World**' made famous by Arthur Conan Doyle's novel. Roraima is a word in the Pemón Indian language meaning 'The great, ever fruitful mother of streams'. Owing to the tough terrain and extreme weather conditions, this hike is only suitable for the fit. Supplies for a week or more should be bought in Santa Elena. If your food is being supplied by a tour company, check what food you will be eating; often vegetarians go hungry.

Altitude: 2,810 m

The starting point is this Pemón village, 9 km north of the San Ignacio military checkpoint (at which you are required to register). **E** *El Caney de Yuruaní*, T995 1307. Clean, basic rooms, fan, retaurant. **F** *Posada*, run by *Roraima Tours* (see below), dormitories, usually full. **G** *Arapena Posada*, T0141-890 3314 (mob). Run by Arepena Tours (see below), small, basic rooms. Sr Casilda Rodriguez has a *churuata* where you can sling a hammock. Camping is permitted just about anywhere, free. Plenty of mosquitos at night. There are three small shops selling basic

San Francisco de Yuruaní
60 km N of Santa Elena

Venezuela

goods but not enough for Roraima hike. Meals are available and tents can be hired, US$3 each per day, quality of tents and stoves is poor, try to get hold of good equipment. ■ *Buses from Santa Elena will let you off here and pick up passengers en route northwards. A jeep to Paraitepuí is around US$100. Cheapest is Oscar Mejías Hernández, ask for him in village.*

Paraitepuí The badly eroded track to Paraitepuí (signposted), the nearest village to the mountain, leaves the highway 1 km south of San Francisco. Very little traffic; difficult to hitch. In the rain many vehicles get stuck on the last stretch and the authorities are tired of pulling them out; the full 25 km can be walked in seven hours. You can sleep free in the village if hiring a guide; camping is permitted. Few supplies available; one small shop sells soft drinks and biscuits. The villagers speak Tauripán, the local dialect, but now most of them also speak Spanish.

Climbing Roraima The foot trail winds back and forth on a more direct line than the little-used jeep track; it is comparatively straightforward and adequately marked descending from the heights just past Paraitepuí across rolling hills and numerous clear streams. The goal, Roraima, is the mountain on the right, the other massive outcrop on the left is Mata Hui (known as Kukenán after the river which rises within it). If leaving the village early enough in the day, you may reach the Río Cuquenán crossing by early afternoon (good camping here). Three hours' walk brings you to a lovely bird-filled meadow below the foothills of the massif, another perfect camping spot known as *campamento base* (10 hours to base camp from Paraitepuí). The footpath now climbs steadily upwards through the cloud forest at the mountain's base and becomes an arduous scramble over tree trunks and damp rocks until the cliff is reached. From here it is possible to ascend to the plateau along the 'easy' rock ledge which is the only route to the top. Walkers in good health should take about four hours from the meadow to the top. The summit is an eerie world of stone and water, difficult to move around easily. There are not many good spots to camp; best is *El Hotel* – a sandy patch under an overhanging ledge – to which red painted arrows lead the way to the right after reaching the summit. From *El Hotel* a marked track leads to the survey pillar near the east cliff where Guyana, Brazil and Venezuela meet; allow a day as the track is very rough.

The whole trip can take anywhere between five days and two weeks. The dry season for trekking is November-May (with annual variations); June-August Roraima is usually enveloped in cloud. Do not remove crystals from the mountain; on the spot fines up to US$100 may be charged. Thorough searches are now made on your return.

Guides & tours The National Guard requires all visitors to have a guide beyond Paraitepuí, otherwise you will be fined. It is not recommended to go alone; best to go with a guide from Santa Elena or from a tour company in San Francisco (those hired on the street or in Paraitepuí have no accident insurance cover). A guide can be of great assistance for the hike's final stages (it is very easy to get lost) and for knowing best places to camp. **In San Francisco de Yuruaní** *Roraima Tours*, T808 1037, T0414-886 3405 (mob), recommended, Ana Fernández is very helpful, all-inclusive tour (group rates can be arranged), or US$45 per day for guide only. Guides in San Francisco charge about US$35-40 a day, more if they carry your supplies; you must pay for guide's food. *Arapena Tours*, T0414-890 3314 (mob), arapenatours@ latinmail.com Ovelio Rodriguez runs tours to Roraima and Kavurin, US$40 per day for guide. **In Paraitepuí** guides available here from US$12 a day and carriers for US$15, Spanish speaking guides available. The *Ayuso* brothers are the best-known guides. Ask for El Capitán, he is in charge of guides.

Camping Full camping equipment including stove is essential (an igloo-type tent with a plastic sheet for the floor is best for the summit, where it can rain a lot), wear thick socks and boots to protect legs from snakes, also essential are warm clothes for the summit (much mist, rain squalls and lightning at night: beware) and effective insect repellent – biting *plaga (blackflies)* infest the grasslands. The water on the summit and around the foot of Roraima is very pure, but as more tourists do the trek, the waters are becoming dirtied. Bring bottled water or a purifier for the savannah. Fires must not be lit on top of Roraima, only gas or liquid fuel stoves. Litter is beginning to appear along the trail; please take care of the environment.

Amazonas

Due south of San Fernando de Apure is **Puerto Páez** (*Population*: 2,600; *Phone code*: 0247) at the confluence of the Meta and Orinoco rivers; here there are crossings to Puerto Carreño in Colombia (see below), and to El Burro west of the Caicara-Puerto Ayacucho road. A road is being built from San Fernando to Puerto Páez; for 134 km it is paved, then from the Río Capanaparo it is dirt (two buses a day San Fernando-Puerto Páez, dry season, four ferry crossings). Between the Capanaparo and Cinaruco rivers is the **Parque Nacional Cinaruco-Capanaparo** (also called **Santos Luzardo**), reached only from this road. If this road is closed, to get to Puerto Ayacucho from San Fernando involves a 15-hour (minimum) detour via the Caicara ferry.

San Fernando to Puerto Ayacucho

From Caicara a new paved road runs 370 km southwest to Puerto Ayacucho. The turn off to **El Burro**, where the boat crosses the Orinoco to Puerto Páez (ferry US$1, also to Puerto Carreño, Colombia), is 88 km north of Puerto Ayacucho (*taxi* El Burro-Puerto Ayacucho, two hours US$8).

On arrival in the Amazonas territory, it is necessary to register at a Guardia Nacional checkpoint about 20 km before Puerto Ayacucho. Around this area the national guard can be very strict and travellers are likely to be searched.

Puerto Ayacucho

This is the capital of the State of Amazonas, which has an area of 175,000 sq km and a population of 80,000. At the end of the dry season (April), it is very hot and sticky. It is deep in the wild, but no direct boats do the five day journey up river. **Museo Etnológico**, Monseñor Enzo Ceccarelli, opposite church, has a library and collection of regional exhibits, recommended. ■ *Tue-Sat, Sun morning. US$0.80.* In front of the museum is a market, open every day, where Indians sell handicrafts. One block away is the cathedral. The Salesian Mission House and boys' school on Plaza Bolívar may also be visited. Prices in Puerto Ayacucho are generally higher than north of the Orinoco. **NB** Malaria is prevalent in this area; take precautions.

Phone code: 0248
Colour map 1, grid B6
Population: 73,660
800 km via Orinoco
from Ciudad Bolívar

Locals recommend October to December as the best time for trips, when the rivers are high but the worst of the rains has passed. In the low season, May-June, it may be difficult to organize tours for only a few days.

Excursions

You can walk up **Cerro Perico** for good views of the town, or go to the Mirador, about 1 km from centre, which offers good views of the Ature rapids. A recommended trip is to the small village of Pintado (12 km south), where petroglyphs described by Humboldt can be seen on the huge rock called **Cerro Pintado**. This the most easily accessible petroglyph site of the hundreds scattered throughout Amazonas.

Some 35 km south on the road to Samariapo is the **Parque Tobogán de la Selva**, a pleasant picnic area with tables and refreshments based around a steeply inclined, smooth rock over which the Río Maripures cascades. This water-slide is great fun in the wet season; crowded on Sunday, take swimsuit, bathing shoes and food and drink (stick to the right to avoid crashing into the barrier, there are some painful rocks to the left near the bottom; few locals slide right from the top; also beware of broken glass). A small trail leads up from the slide to a natural jacuzzi after about 20 minutes. Taxi to Cerro Pintado and Parque Tobogán, US$15-20 return (be sure to organize your return with the driver, otherwise you may face a lengthy hike). Agencies in town arrange tours; easier but more expensive.

Venezuela

The well-paved road from Puerto Ayacucho to Samariapo (63 km) was built to bypass the rapids which here interrupt the Orinoco, dividing it into 'Upper' and 'Lower'; the powerful Maripures Rapids are very impressive.

Sleeping **A** *Oriniquia Lodge*, on the Río Orinoco, 20 mins from airport, book through Cacao Travel, cacaotravel@cantv.net Nice setting, comfortable rooms. **C** *City Center*, on roundabout at entrance to town, T521 0691. Pleasant, safe parking, takes credit cards. **C** *Apure*, Av Orinoco 28, T521 0516, less than 1 km from centre. A/c, good restaurant. Recommended. **C** *Guacharo's Amazonas Resort Hotel*, at end of Av Evelio Roa, 2 blocks from Av Río Negro. A/c, restaurant, attractive sitting room. **C** *Tobogán*, Av Orinoco con Av Evelio Roa. With a/c, TV lounge, laundry facilities, helpful staff, English spoken, popular. **E** *Res Internacional*, Av Aguerrevere 18. A/c (cheaper without), comfortable, shower, locked parking, safe but basic, not very clean, good place to find tour information and meet other travellers, if no room available you can sling up your hammock, bus drivers stay here and will drive you to the terminal for early morning journeys. **E** *Res La Cueva*, Av 23 de Enero, 1 block from the Redoma (traffic roundabout, petrol station). A/c, luggage stored. Recommended. **F** *Res Ayacucho*, Urb Pedro Camejo, 2 blocks off Amazonas behind *Guacharo's Amazonas Hotel*. Bath, fan, cheapest in town.

Eating *Las Palmeras*, Av 23 de Enero, 2 blocks from the Redoma. Pizzas and fast food. *El Padrino*, in Urb Andrés Eloy Blanco on Av Belisio Pérez off Av 23 de Enero. Good Italian. *El Espagetazo*, Av Aguerrevere. Mainly pasta, most dishes cost US$3, popular with locals. *Cherazad*, Aguerrevere y Av Orinoco. Arabic food, expensive. *Capi Fuente de Soda*, on Av Evelio Roa behind *gobernación*. Vegetarian and other dishes.

Shopping Good *artesanía* in the Plaza del Indio; also in *Artes Amazonas* on Av Evelio Roa, next to *Wayumi*, and in *Topocho* just up from Plaza del Indio. Many tourist souvenirs are on offer and Vicente Barletta, of *Típico El Casique*, Av Principal 583, Urb Andrés Eloy Blanco, has a good collection of masks (free); he also works as a guide, recommended, take own food and equipment.

Transport **Air** Airport 7 km southeast along Av Orinoco. *Santa Bárbara* daily to Caracas, 1½ hrs.
  Road **Vehicle hire**: *Servicio Amazonas de Alquiler*, Av Aguerrevere. **Buses**: *Expresos del Valle* to Cuidad Bolívar (US$12, 10 hrs; take something to eat, bus stops once for early lunch), Caicara, Puerto Ordaz and San Félix; *Cooperativa Cacique* to San Fernando de Apure, US$15, 6½ hrs; both companies in bus terminal. *Expresos La Prosperidad* to Caracas and Maracay from Urb Alto Parima. Bus from Caracas, 2030, 2230 daily, US$21, 12 hrs (but much longer in wet season). *Por puesto* to Ciudad Bolívar, 3 daily, US$20, 10-12 hrs (Caicara Amazonas).
  River Ferry across the Orinoco, US$0.30. Boat to Caicara, 1½ days, US$18.75 including food, but bargain; repellent and hammock required.

Directory **Banks** *Banco Unión*, Av Orinoco No 37, has Visa ATM. Changing dollars is difficult; try *Hotel Tobogán* or *Hotel Orinoco*. **Communications** Post office: *Ipostel* on Av Aguerrevere 3 blocks up from Av Orinoco. **Telephone:** international calls from *CANTV*, on Av Orinoco next to *Hotel Apure*; also from *Las Churuwatas* on Av Aguerrevere y C Amazonas, 1 block from Plaza del Indio.

Border with Colombia Some 88 km north of Puerto Ayacucho a paved branch road leads west to El Burro, from where a ferry-barge crosses to Puerto Páez. On the south bank of the Meta opposite is Puerto Carreño in Colombia. Do not cross this border without first finding out what the security situation is on either side of the border. It is not recommended to enter the Llanos of Colombia at this time.

Tours in Amazonas

Much of Amazonas is stunningly beautiful and untouched, but access is only by river. For starting out, the best base is Puerto Ayacucho. Do not travel alone. By ascending the Autana or Sipapo rivers, for example, you can see **Autana-tepuy**, a

1,200 m-high soaring mass of rock which no-one has yet climbed from the base. There are other *tepuis* in the region, including the great mass of the Sierra de la Neblina on the Brazilian border.

San Juan de Manapiare (*Population*: 3,700) is the regional centre for the middle Ventuari. A beautiful track winds around the Cerro Guanay to get there. The road starts at Caicara and goes through Guaniamo and Sabana de Cardona.

There are a number of private river camps on the upper Orinoco but they do not welcome casual guests; the most welcoming is *Yutajé Camp*, located on a tributary of the Río Manapiare due east of Puerto Ayacucho. The camp accommodates 30, with restaurant and bar, full board (in theory), fishing, canoes, horses, airboats, excursions to Indian villages, expensive but professional. Reached by plane from Puerto Ayacucho or boat up the Ríos Manapiare and Corocoro (take something soft to sit on). Also in the area is the *Campamento Camani*, in a forest clearing on the banks of the Río Alto Ventuari, 2 hrs by launch from San Juan de Manapiare. From Puerto Ayacucho the daily aerotaxi takes 50 mins. Maximum 26 guests at any one time, mosquito nets provided, all amenities, excursions available. Both are in the **LL** bracket, but for 3 day/2 night packages. Near Puerto Ayacucho, in mixed jungle and dry forest setting, is *Jungle Camp Calypso*, run by *Calypso Tours*, T Caracas 0212-545 0024, F541 3036, **LL** pp for 2 days including food, basic cabin accommodation, highly recommended, excursions in canoes. **B** *Canturama Amazonas Resort*, T Caracas 0212-941 8813, F943 5160, 20 mins by vehicle south of town, on the banks of the Orinoco, 40 km from nearest jungle, highly recommended accommodation and food but beware biting insects by the river, full day tours US$10. **B** *Dantos Adventure*, very basic jungle refuge, accommodation and canoe tours, probably cheapest option available, also space for camping, run by English-speaking guide Reni Barrio, recommended, ask at *Aguas Bravas* (see below).

Sleeping

It is strongly recommended to go on tours organized by tour agents or guides registered in the **Asocación de Guías**, in the Cámara de Turismo, Casa de la Piedra, on the Arteria Vial de la Av Orinoco with Av Principal (the house on top of the large rock). Some independent guides may not have permission to visit Amazonas. Tours generally cost US$50-120 pp per day. Those listed below will arrange permits and insurance but shop around: *Tobogán Tours*, Av 23 de Enero 24, near *Instituto del Menor*, T521 4865. *Autana Aventura*, Av Aguerrevere, 1 block from Av Orinoco. Owned by Julián Jaramillo. *Coyote Expediciones*, Av Aguirrevere 75. Helpful, professional, English spoken, organizes trips staying in Indian villages. *Guaharibo CA*, C Evelio Roa 39, in same building as *Wayumi*, T Caracas 952 6996, F953 0092, manager Levis Olivo. *Yutajé Tours*, in Urb Monte Bello, 1 block from Av Orinoco, past the Mercadito going out of town, T521 0664, turismoamazonas@cantv.net Good value for money but organization erratic. *Expediciones Aguas Bravas Venezuela*, Av Río Negro, No 32-2, in front of Plaza Rómulo Betancourt. Whitewater rafting, 2 daily from 0900-1200 and 1500-1800, 3-13 people per boat, reservations required at peak times, take insect repellent, sun protector, light shoes and swimsuit, US$35 pp.

Tour operators

Venezuela

Background

History

After Independence Despite being at the heart of Simón Bolívar's cherished Gran Colombia (together with Ecuador, Colombia and Panama), Venezuela under General Páez became an independent nation in 1830, before Bolívar's death. Páez was either president, or the power behind the presidency from 1831 to 1848, a time of stability and economic progress. In the second half of the 19th century, though, the rise of the Liberal Party in opposition to the ruling Conservatives led to conflicts and social upheaval. In 1870 a Liberal politician-general, Antonio Guzmán Blanco, came to power. Even though his term was peaceful, it marked the entry of the army into Venezuelan politics, a role which it did not relinquish for almost a century.

20th century In the first half of the century presidents of note were Juan Vicente Gómez (1909-35), a brutal but efficient dictator, and Isaías Medina Angarita, who introduced the oil laws. There was much material progress under the six-year dictatorship of Gen Marcos Pérez Jiménez (1952-58), but his Gómez-like methods led to his overthrow in January 1958. A largely stable democracy has been created since, with regular presidential elections every five years. Carlos Andrés Pérez of the centre-left Democratic Action party (AD) took office in 1974, presiding over a period of rapid development following the first great oil-price rise, and was succeeded in 1979 by Luis Herrera Campins of the Christian Democratic party, Copei. Jaime Lusinchi of Democratic Action was elected president in 1983, to be followed by Carlos Andrés Pérez, who began his second term in 1989.

1990s: instability & economic crisis Pérez' second term was marked by protests against economic adjustment and growing levels of poverty. In 1992 there were two unsuccessful coup attempts by military officers, including Colonel Hugo Chávez Frías, who became president by legitimate means in 1999. Among reforms designed to root out corruption, the Supreme Court and Central Bank were given greater independence. Both bodies were instrumental in the decision that Pérez himself be tried on corruption charges in 1993. The president was suspended from office, arrested and, after two years of house arrest, was found guilty in May 1996. An interim president, Senator Ramón José Velázquez, took office until the presidential elections of December 1993, in which Rafael Caldera, standing as an independent, was re-elected to office (as a member of Copei, he was president 1969-74). Many of his aims, such as improvement in social conditions, tax reform and the control of inflation, had to be postponed, even reversed, in favour of solving an economic and financial crisis which began in 1994. This helped him to conclude an agreement with the IMF, but caused public protest at declining salaries and deteriorating public services.

Presidential elections in December 1998 were won by Hugo Chávez, by an overwhelming majority. On taking office in February 1999, Chávez called for a complete overhaul of Venezuela's political system in order to root out corruption and inefficiency. He obtained special powers from Congress to reduce the budget deficit and diversify the economy away from oil. These were first steps towards his aim of eradicating poverty and restoring real incomes, which had fallen by two thirds in 15 years. He set up a constituent assembly which drew up a new constitution and 70% of the electorate approved it in a plebiscite in December 1999. New elections, scheduled for May 2000 but postponed until end-July as the electoral commission failed to make the necessary preparations, were won comfortably by Chávez. Opposition parties did, however, increase their share of seats in Congress as the middle and upper classes supported Chávez' main challenger, Francisco Arias Calderón, while the president held on to his heartland in the poverty-stricken slums. The goals of the 'Chávez revolution' remained unchanged, but a referendum in late 2000 to reform labour unions and remove their supposedly corrupt leaders, while winning a majority, had very low voter turnout and was bitterly attacked at home and abroad.

Through 2001 and into 2002 Chávez succeeded in annoying many sections of society. Dissident military officers repeatedly called for his resignation, calling the president "tyrannical". His policies and pronouncements frequently antagonized the business sector, the Roman Catholic Church and the press. The middle classes, office workers and trades unionists blamed him for mismanaging the economy. Pro- and anti-Chávez street demonstrations became a regular event in Caracas. The final straw was the reform of PDVSA, the state oil company, which Chávez believed should be contributing more to the overall economy. When he replaced PDVSA executives with his own allies, the value of the bolívar slumped against the dollar and oil workers went on strike. This led to a 48-hour general strike in early April and, during the protests, 16 people were killed. On 12 April it was announced that Chávez had been replaced as president after being arrested by the military high command. His successor was businessman Pedro Carmona, who dissolved Congress and cancelled the constitution, only to resign a day later in the face of pro-Chávez demonstrations equally as strong as those that had ousted the president. On 14 April, Chávez was restored to office, backed by the lower ranks of the army. He was also supported by most Latin American leaders, who condemned the undemocratic removal of the president. In contrast, the US administration initially welcomed Carmona's take-over, although it denied any encouragement for, or involvement in the coup. On his return, Chávez promised dialogue with his opponents, but this was greeted with some scepticism.

The 2002 coup

Venezuela is a federal republic of 23 states, a Federal District and federal dependencies of over 70 islands. There is one legislative house, a chamber of deputies with 199 members who are elected every five years. A referendum was held on 15 December 1999 which voted to change the constitution and allow immediate reelection of the president. The resulting constitution came into force on 30 December 1999. The country's name was changed to the Bolivarian Republic of Venezuela.

Government

Culture

In 2001 the total population was 24.6 million. Population growth between 1995 and 2000 averaged 2.0% annually. A large number are of mixed Spanish and Indian origin. There are some pure Africans and a strong element of African descent along the coast, particularly at the ports. The arrival of 800,000 European immigrants, mostly in the 1950s, has greatly modified the racial make-up in Venezuela. One in six of all Venezuelans is foreign born.

   A very small proportion of the population (150,000) is Indian. Among the best-known are the Yanomami, who live in Amazonas, and the Bari in the Sierra de Perijá (on the northwest border with Colombia). An Indian Reserve gives the Bari effective control of their own land, but this has not prevented infringement from mining, plantation or settlers. Other groups do not have title to their territory. These groups include the Wayuu (in the Guajira), the Panare and the Piaroa.

   Venezuela, despite its wealth, still faces serious social problems. Many rural dwellers have drifted to the cities; one result of this exodus is that Venezuelan farmers do not provide all the food the nation needs and imports of foodstuffs are necessary, even for items such as beans and rice.

   Elementary schools are free, and education is compulsory from the age of seven to the completion of the primary grade.

People
Forecast population growth 2000-2005: 1.8%
Urban population in 2000: 87% of total
Infant mortality: 19 per 1,000 live births

Venezuela

Books

Venezuela Handbook by **Alan Murphy & Mick Day** (Footprint Handbooks, £10.99). The *Guide to Venezuela* (925 pages), by **Janice Bauman**, **Leni Young** and others, in English (available in Caracas) is a mine of information and maps (US$11). **Elizabeth Kline**'s *Guide to Camps, Posadas and Cabins/Guía de campamentos, posadas y cabañas in/en*

Venezuela is published every other year and gives a comprehensive survey of these establishments throughout the country (Apartado 63089, Caracas 1067-A, Venezuela, T0212-945 1543, ekline@cantv.net). There are many fine coffee-table books on the various regions of Venezuela, for example Charles Brewer-Carias' books on Roraima and Venezuela as a whole. *Venezuela in Focus* (**Latin America Bureau**, £5.99), a guide to the history, politics, economy and culture of the country. The best known of all Venezuelan writers is **Rómulo Gallegos** (1884-1969), who was president briefly in 1947. Among his novels are *Doña Bárbara* (1929) and *Canaima* (1935). Another early 20th-century writer, still regarded as the country's best woman writer, is **Teresa de la Parra** (1890-1936). Other novelists worth looking out for are **Arturo Uslar Pietri**, who died in February 2001 (eg *Las lanzas coloradas*, 1931), **Miguel Otero Silva**, **Julián Padrón** and **Adriano González León**. In the 1970s a new literary form known as *Testimonios* developed, incorporating genuine recorded material (usually dramatic social and political issues) into a semi-fictional account of a real event, eg *Soy un delincuente*, by **Ramón Antonio Brizuela**, or *Aquí no pasa nada* by **Angela Zayo**. Among non-Venezuelan writers whose works are worth consulting are **Alexander von Humboldt**, whose *Travels* were written after five years in South America (1799-1804); **Sir Arthur Conan Doyle**'s *The Lost World* (1912) is reputed to be set on Mount Roraima and the Costaguana of **Joseph Conrad**'s *Nostromo* (1904) is said to be modelled on Venezuela; **W H Hudson** set *Green Mansions* (1904) in Venezuela. See also **Alejo Carpentier**'s *Los pasos perdidos* (1953), **Lisa St Aubin de Teran**'s *The Keepers of the House* (1982) and *The Tiger* (1985) and **Isabel Allende**'s *Eva Luna* (1987). For an entertaining and sometimes alarming account of travelling in Venezuela, read **Redmond O'Hanlon**'s *In Trouble Again. A Journey between the Orinoco and the Amazon* (1988).

Guianas

Guyana's coastal region is dominated by a mixture of Calypso music, Hindu temples, rice and Demerara sugar. Leaving the sea behind, travelling by riverboat or by plane, it is a land of waterfalls and rainforest, which gives way to wildlife-rich savannahs and isolated ranches. Suriname, too, has the intriguing combination of Dutch, Asian and African, which influences the culture, food and street life. And, like its neighbour, when you head inland, you enter a different world of jungles and Amerindian villages. Guyane has a famous old penal colony circled by sharks, a European space programme whose launches can be witnessed and jungle adventure, all within the context of a corner of South America which is an overseas department of France.

13

Guianas

Guyana

Essentials

Planning your trip

Where to go Despite being located on the Atlantic, Georgetown, capital of Guyana, is known as the 'Garden City of the Caribbean'. This gives some idea of the country's orientation, in trade and cultural terms. The coast, where most of the population live, is a strange mix of coconut palms and calypso music, Dutch place names and techniques for draining the land, Hindu temples and Islamic mosques, all of which reflect the chequered history of the country. The thinly populated interior is different again, with life revolving around the rivers through the tropical forest, or, further south, the scattered ranches of the Rupununi Savanna. The main tourist potential is in the largely untouched interior, where places of interest are so spread out that they are best reached by river boat or plane. Highlights include the Kaieteur Falls, among the highest in the world, the Orinduik Falls on the border with Brazil and the Iwokrama Rain Forest Programme. Travelling on any of the rivers, many of which have excellent beaches, is the most interesting way to get around. On the coast there are no beaches for bathing, but in the far northwest is Shell Beach, a protected area for marine turtles and birdlife.

When to go Although hot, the climate is not unhealthy. Mean shade temperature throughout the year is 27° C; the mean maximum is about 31° C and the mean minimum 24° C. The heat is greatly tempered by cooling breezes from the sea and is most felt from Aug to Oct. There are two wet seasons in the north of the country, from May to Jun, and from Dec to the end of Jan, although they may extend into the months either side. The south and the Rupununi receive one wet season, May to Jul. Rainfall averages 2,300 mm a year in Georgetown. Note that the Republic Day celebrations (23 Feb) last about a week: during this time hotels in Georgetown are very full. Hotels are also very full during international cricket.

Finding out more The **Ministry of Trade, Tourism and Industry** has a Tourism Department which can provide information through its office at 229 South Road near Camp St, Georgetown, T226 2505/226 3182, F225 4370, www.sdnp.org.gy/mtti The Ministry has a booth (often closed) at Timehri Airport. The private sector **Tourism and Hospitality Association of Guyana** (THAG – office and information desk at 157 Waterloo St, T225 0807, F225 0817, www.exploreguyana.com 24-hour emergency hotline, T225 6699), covers all areas of tourism. The THAG produces a 46-page, full-colour magazine called *Explore Guyana*, which may be obtained from the Association at PO Box 101147, Georgetown, or phone the above number. Online tourist guide www.turq.com/guyana

Before you travel

Documents The following countries do not need a visa to visit Guyana: Australia, Belgium, Canada, Denmark, Finland, France, Germany, Greece, Ireland, Italy, Japan, Korea, Luxembourg, the Netherlands, New Zealand, Norway, Portugal, Spain, Sweden, UK, USA, and the Commonwealth countries. Visitors are advised to check with the nearest embassy, consulate or travel agent for further changes. All visitors require a passport with six months' validity and all nationalities, apart from those above, require visas. To obtain a visa, three photos, evidence of sufficient funds, a travel itinerary and, if coming from a country with yellow fever, a yellow fever certificate are required. Tourist visas cost US$30, one-entry business visas US$40, multiple entry business visas US$50. Visitors from those countries where they are required arriving without visas are refused entry, unless a tour operator has obtained permission for the visitor to get a visa on arrival. To fly in to Guyana, an exit ticket is required, at land borders an onward ticket is usually not asked for.

Guyana's representation overseas: High Commission to the UK, 3 Palace Court, Bayswater, W2 4LP, T020-7229 7684, F020-7727 9809, ghc.1@ic24.net **Embassy in USA**: 2490 Tracy Place, NW, Washington DC 20008, T265 6900, F232 1297, **New York Consulate General**,

866 United Nations Plaza, suite 304, T212-527 3215-6, F212-527 3229. **High Commission to Canada**, Burnside Building, 151 Slater St, suite 309, Ottawa, Ontario, K1P 5H3, T613-235 7249, F613-235 1447, guyanahcott@travel-net.com

Customs Baggage examination can be very thorough. Duties are high on goods imported in commercial quantities.

What to take A good torch/flashlight and batteries (for the interior, but also in case of electricity cuts) is essential. Items such as batteries, good quality toiletries, etc, are readily

Guyana

Sleeping
1 Dadanawa Ranch
2 Karanambu Ranch
3 Rock View Lodge
4 Shanklands

0 km 50
0 miles 50

available in Georgetown, but if travelling in the interior and staying in places other than resorts, you should take your own. Protection against sun, rain and insects are essential.

Money   Currency: the unit is the Guyanese dollar. There are notes for 20, 100, 500 and 1,000 dollars. Coins are for 1, 5 and 10 dollars.

   Exchange: the official exchange rate is adjusted weekly in line with the rate offered by licensed exchange houses (*cambios*). In July 2002, this was G$179.6 = US$1. No *cambio* changes travellers' cheques. They only buy US or Canadian dollars and pounds sterling. Most *cambios* accept drafts (subject to verification) and telegraphic transfers, but not credit cards. Rates vary slightly between *cambios* and from day to day and some *cambios* offer better rates for changing over US$100. Rates for changing travellers' cheques are good on the black market. Banks which accept travellers' cheques are *Bank of Nova Scotia*, *Demerara Bank* (South Road and Camp Street), *Guyana Bank of Trade and Industry*, *National Bank of Industry and Commerce* and *GNBC*. Banks which accept euros are *Demerara Bank* and *NBIC*. Note that to sell Guyanese dollars on leaving the country, you will need to produce your *cambio* receipt. The illegal black market on America St ('Wall Street') in Georgetown still operates, but the rates offered are not significantly better than the *cambio* rate. To avoid being robbed or cheated on the black market, or if you need to change money when *cambios* are closed, go by taxi and ask someone (preferably a friend) to negotiate for you. The black market also operates in Molson Creek/Springlands, the entry point from Suriname.

Cost of travelling: the devaluation means that, for foreigners, prices for food and drink are low at present. Even imported goods may be cheaper than elsewhere and locally produced goods such as fruit are very cheap. Hotels, tours and services in the interior are subject to electricity and fuel surcharges, which make them less cheap.

Air   There are no direct flights to Guyana from Europe, but *BWIA*'s flights from London to Barbados and Port of Spain have daily direct connections. From North America *BWIA* flies daily from New York, Miami and Toronto. Most *BWIA* flights involve a change of plane in Port of Spain (check baggage allowance carefully because it is different on each leg and many bags are lost in Trinidad). See www.bwee.com   *North American Airlines* fly five days a week to New York. *BWIA* flies to Guyana from Trinidad twice a day, more when demand is high. *LIAT* and *BWIA* fly daily from Barbados; *BWIA* flies daily from Antigua and Kingston via Port of Spain. *Surinam Airways* (176 Middle Street, at *Wilderness Explorers* – see below) fly Mon to Friday to Suriname with connections on to Guiane and Belém (Brazil). Also connects with KLM in Surinam and Air France in Guiane for connections to Europe. Bookings can be made by e mailing surinamairways@wilderness-explorers.com Arrangements can be made for tickets to be available for pickup in any country SLM flies to. *BWIA* have flights from Caracas, Venezuela, to Georgetown via Port of Spain three times a week. *Meta* flies between Boa Vista (Brazil) and Guyana, 3 days a week, with connections to Manaus.

Getting there

Guianas

Touching down

Flights are often booked weeks in advance, especially at Christmas and in August when overseas Guyanese return to visit relatives. Flights are frequently overbooked, so it is essential to reconfirm your outward flight within 72 hours of arrival, which can take some time, and difficult to change your travel plans at the last minute. A number of travel agents are now computerized, making reservations and reconfirmations easier. Foreigners must pay for airline tickets in US$ (most airlines do not accept US$100 bills), or other specified currencies. Luggage should be securely locked as theft from checked-in baggage is common.

Sea See Getting there by Sea in Essentials, at the front of the book, for travel agents and websites dealing with passages to South America.

Touching down **Airport information** Cheddi Jagan International Airport is at Timehri, 40 km south of Georgetown. Check in three hours before most flights and you should contact the airline the day before your flight to hear if it has been delayed, or even brought forward. There are three duty-free shops. Some spirits are more expensive than downtown. There is also an exchange house, open usual banking hours; if closed, plenty of parallel traders outside (signboard in the exchange house says what the rate is). It is difficult to pay for flight tickets at the airport with credit cards or travellers' cheques. The exchange desk will change travellers' cheques for flight ticket purchases.

Where to stay *See inside front cover of the book for our hotel grade price guide* The largest hotels in Georgetown have their own emergency electricity generators and water pumps to deal with any interruptions in supply. Other hotels usually provide a bucket of water in your room, fill this up when water is available. When booking an a/c room, ensure it also has natural ventilation. A 10% tax applies to hotels with more than 16 rooms.

Getting around **Air** For scheduled flights between Georgetown and Lethem, and services to Kaieteur and Rupununi, see below. Scheduled services to many parts of Guyana are offered by *Trans Guyana Airways*, *TGA* (158-9 Charlotte St, T227 3010), and *Roraima Airways*, *RAL* (T225 9648), from Ogle airstrip, just outside Georgetown. Domestic airlines are very strict on baggage allowance on internal flights: 15 pounds pp (TGA) and 25 pounds (Roraima).

Road Most coastal towns are linked by a good 296-km road from Springlands in the east to Charity in the west; the Berbice and Essequibo rivers are crossed by ferries, the Demerara by a toll bridge, which, besides closing at high tide for ships to pass through (2-3 hours) is subject to frequent closures (when an alternative ferry service runs). Apart from a good road connecting Timehri and Linden, continuing as good dirt to Mabura Hill, and the new Georgetown-Lethem road, most other roads in the interior are very poor. **Car hire** is available from several firms, see under Georgetown. **Motoring**: there are shortages of car spares. Gasoline costs about US$1.72 a gallon. Traffic drives on the left. Minibuses and collective taxis, an H on their number plate, run between Georgetown and the entire coast from Charity to Corriverton; also to Linden. All taxis also have an H on their number plate. No *carnet de passages* is required for driving a private vehicle in Guyana.

Guianas

River There are over 960 km of navigable river, which provide an important means of communication. Ferries and river boats are referred to in this chapter, but contact the Transport and Harbours Department, Water St, Georgetown for details. Six-seater river boats are called *ballahoos*, 3-4 seaters *corials*; they provide the transport in the forest. The ferry across the Corentyne to Suriname carries vehicles.

Maps Maps of country and Georgetown (US$6) from **Department of Lands and Surveys**, Homestreet Ave, Durban Backland (take a taxi). T226 0524/9 in advance, poor stock. *Kojac Marketing* has a tour map and business guide of Georgetown, US$3. Rivers and islands change frequently according to water levels, so maps can only give you a general direction. A local guide can be more reliable. City and country maps are sold at *Pegasus* and *Tower* hotels. City maps also from *Guyana Store*, Water St, next to the ice house (take a taxi). Georgetown and Guyana maps in *Explore Guyana*. Guyana ITMB map is recommended.

Internet There are a few cyber cafés in Georgetown and some hotels have business suites for guests to use.

Keeping in touch

Post Overseas postal rates are cheap: a postcard to anywhere in the world costs G$20 (US$0.11). Parcels sent abroad have to be weighed and checked by customs before sealing. Take all materials and passport; choose between ordinary and registered service.

Telephone In 2001 the telephone system was changed. City codes have been eliminated and all numbers in the country are seven-digit. It is possible to dial direct to any country in the world. Blue public telephones in Georgetown only allow collect calls overseas; phone booths have overseas, three-digit codes printed inside. Yellow phones are for calls to local areas, G$3 per call. Some businesses and hotels may allow you to use their phone for local calls if you are buying something – usual charge about US$0.05. Overseas calls can be made from the *Guyana Telephone and Telegraph Company* office behind the *Bank of Guyana* building; open daily till 2000 (arrive early and be prepared for a long wait). To Canada US$0.80 per minute; USA US$1 per minute; to UK US$1.15 per minute. Calls are subject to 10 tax. Travel agencies may allow you to make overseas collect calls when buying tickets. Hotels add high extra charges to phone bills. Canada Direct, dial 0161; UK direct 169. Fax rates are in line with phone rates. Most hotels have faxes.

Media Newspapers: *The Chronicle*, daily. *The Mirror*, weekly PPP-run. *The Stabroek News*, daily, independent, www.stabroeknews.com *The Catholic Standard*, weekly, well-respected and widely read. **Radio** State-run GBC Radio; Hot FM, 98.1. **Television** The 14 TV channels mainly broadcast programmes from US satellite television. Local content is increasing.

Local food The blend of different national influences – Indian, African, Chinese, Creole, English, Portuguese, Amerindian, North American – gives a distinctive flavour to Guyanese cuisine. One well-known dish, traditional at Christmas, is pepper-pot, meat cooked in bitter cassava (casareep) juice with peppers and herbs. Seafood is plentiful and varied, as is the wide variety of tropical fruits and vegetables. The staple food is rice. In the interior wild meat is often available – try wild cow, or else *labba* (a small rodent).

Food & drink

Drink Rum is the most popular drink. There is a wide variety of brands, all cheap, including the best which are very good and cost US$3 a bottle. Demerara Distillers' produces two prize-winning brands, the 12-year-old King of Diamonds premium rum, and the 15-year-old El Dorado (voted the best rum in the world in 1999, 2000 and 2001, US$30 in Georgetown, US$20 at duty free in the airport). High wine is a strong local rum. There is also local brandy and whisky (Diamond Club), which are worth trying. The local beer, Banks, made partly from rice is good and cheap. There is a wide variety of fruit juices. D'Aguiar's Cream Liqueur, produced and bottled by Banks DIH Ltd, is excellent (and strong).

Guianas

Public holidays 1 January, New Years' Day; 23 February, Republic Day and Mashramani festival; Good Friday, Easter Monday; Labour Day, 1 May; Independence Day, 26 May (instigated in 1996); Caricom Day, first Monday in July; Freedom Day, first Monday in August; Christmas Day, 25 December, and Boxing Day, 26 December. Hindu and Muslim festivals follow a lunar calendar, and dates should be checked as required: Phagwah, usually March; Eid el Fitr, end of Ramadan; Eid el Azah; Youm un Nabi; Deepavali, usually November.

Holidays & festivals

Sport The national indoor sport is dominoes. In Georgetown, there are clubs for cricket, tennis, football, rugby, hockey, riding, swimming, cycling, athletics, badminton, volley ball, netball, snooker, pool, golf, boxing, ballroom dancing and rifle shooting. At Easter there are kite flying competitions. The Guyanese enjoy songbird (finch) contests, called 'rackling', or 'racing'.

Health
See also Health in
Essentials at the
beginning of the book

Health/disease risks There is a high risk of both types of malaria in some parts of the interior, especially in the wet season. Seek expert advice on suitable prophylaxis. There are reports of chloroquine-resistant malaria. If travelling to the interior for long periods carry drugs for treatment as these may not be available. Sleep under a mosquito net. Although there are plenty of mosquitoes on the coast, they are not malarial.

There is some risk of typhoid and water-borne diseases (eg cholera) owing to low water pressure. Purification is a good idea. Tap water is usually brown and contains sediment. Bottled water (many brands) must be bought for drinking. In the interior, use purification. The Georgetown Hospital has a new outpatient block. It remains understaffed even though facilities have improved. Well-equipped private hospitals include **St Joseph's** on Parade St, Kingston; **Prashad's** on Thomas Street, doctor on call at weekends, 24-hour malaria clinic, T226 7214/9 (US$2 to US$8 per day; medical consultations cost US$2 to US$4). If admitted to hospital you are expected to provide sheets and food (St Joseph's provides these). Recommended doctor, **Dr Clarence Charles**, 254 Thomas Street, surgery 1200-1400 hours.

In the interior, travellers should examine shower pipes, bedding, shoes and clothing for snakes and spiders. In most towns there is neither a hospital nor police. If travelling independently, you are on your own. Take iodine to treat wounds and prevent infection (can also be used for water purification), a hammock with rope for securing it, and a machete, especially if in the jungle. Remember to drink plenty of water.

Georgetown

Colour map 2, grid B3
Population: 200,000

Guyana's capital, and chief town and port, is on the east bank of the mouth of the Demerara river. The climate is tropical, with a mean temperature of 27° C, but the trade winds provide welcome relief. The city is built on a grid plan, with wide tree-lined streets and drainage canals following the layout of the old sugar estates. Parts of the city are very attractive, with white-painted wooden 19th century houses raised on stilts and a profusion of flowering trees. In the evening the sea wall is crowded with strollers and at Easter it is a mass of colourful kites.

Ins & outs
For more detailed
information, see
Transport, page 1453

Getting there From the airport, take minibus No 42 to Georgetown US$1 (from Georgetown leaves from next to Parliament building); for a small charge they will take you to your hotel (similarly for groups going to the airport). A taxi costs US$15-20 (use approved airport taxis). Internal flights go from Ogle airstrip, 8 km from Georgetown; minibus from Market to Ogle US$0.20.

Getting around Minibuses run regularly to most parts of the city, mostly from Stabroek market or Ave of the Republic, standard fare G$30 (US$0.16) very crowded. It is difficult to get a seat during rush hours. Taxis: charge US$1.20 for short journeys, US$2.20 for longer runs, with higher rates at night (a safe option) and outside the city limits. Collective taxis ply set routes at a fixed fare; they stop at any point on request. Certain hand signals are used on some routes to indicate the final destination (ask). Special taxis at hotels and airports, marked 'special' on the windscreen, charge US$1.25 around town, stops and waiting time extra, or you can negotiate a 'by the hour' deal, usually US$6.

Security Despite the delights of this beautiful city, normal security precautions should be taken. Don't walk the streets at night. Check where it is safe to go with your hotel and in particular avoid Albouystown (south of the centre) and the Tiger Bay area, 1 block west of Main St. Leave your valuables in your hotel.

Sights Although part of the old city centre was destroyed by fire in 1945, there are some fine 19th century buildings, particularly on or near High Street and the Avenue of the Republic. **St George's Anglican Cathedral**, which dates from 1889 (consecrated

Guianas

1894), is 44 m high and is reputed to be the tallest wooden building in the world (it was designed by Sir Arthur Blomfield). Above the altar is a chandelier given by Queen Victoria. The Gothic-style **City Hall** dates from 1888; its interior has been recently restored and may be viewed. Other fine buildings on High Street are the City Engineer's Office, the Victoria Law Courts (1887) and the Magistrates' Court. The **Public Buildings**, on Brickdam, which house Parliament, are an impressive

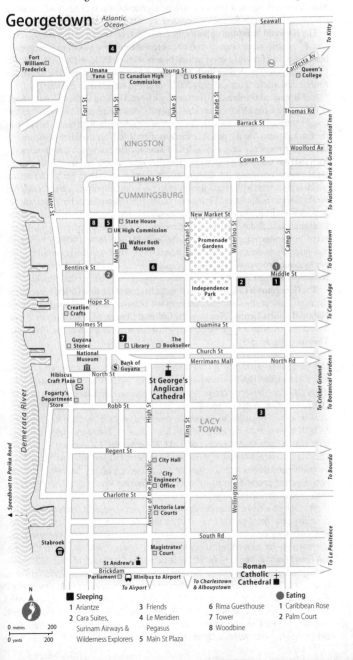

Georgetown

Atlantic Ocean

Seawall

To Kitty

Fort William Frederick

Umana Yana

Canadian High Commission

US Embassy

Young St

Carifesta Av

Queen's College

Fort St

High St

Duke St

Parade St

Thomas Rd

To National Park & Grand Coastal Inn

Barrack St

KINGSTON

Woolford Av

Cowan St

Lamaha St

CUMMINGSBURG

Water St

New Market St

State House

UK High Commission

Walter Roth Museum

Carmichael St

Waterloo St

Promenade Gardens

Camp St

To Queenstown

Bentinck St

Main St

Middle St

To Cara Lodge

Hope St

Independence Park

Creation Crafts

Holmes St

Quamina St

Guyana Stores

Library

The Bookseller

Church St

National Museum

Bank of Guyana

Merrimans Mall

North Rd

To Cricket Ground

To Botanical Gardens

Hibiscus Craft Plaza

North St

St George's Anglican Cathedral

Fogarty's Department Store

Robb St

High St

King St

LACY TOWN

To Bourda

Demerara River

Regent St

City Hall

City Engineer's Office

Avenue of the Republic

Wellington St

Charlotte St

Victoria Law Courts

Speedboat to Parika Road

Stabroek

South Rd

To La Penitence

Magistrates' Court

Brickdam Parliament

St Andrew's

Minibus to Airport

To Airport

To Charlestown & Albouystown

Roman Catholic Cathedral

N

0 metres 200
0 yards 200

Guianas

■ **Sleeping**
1 Ariantze
2 Cara Suites, Surinam Airways & Wilderness Explorers
3 Friends
4 Le Meridien Pegasus
5 Main St Plaza
6 Rima Guesthouse
7 Tower
8 Woodbine

● **Eating**
1 Caribbean Rose
2 Palm Court

neo-classical structure built in 1839. Opposite, is **St Andrew's Presbytery** (18th century). **State House** on Main St is the residence of the president. Much of the city centre is dominated by the imposing tower above **Stabroek market** (1880). At the head of Brickdam is an aluminium arch commemorating independence. Nearby is a monument to the 1763 slave rebellion, surmounted by an impressive statue of Cuffy, its best-known leader. Near *Le Meridien Pegasus Hotel* on Seawall Rd is the **Umana Yana**, a conical thatched structure built by a group of Wai Wai Amerindians using traditional techniques for the 1972 conference of the Non-Aligned Movement.

The **National Museum**, opposite the post office, houses an idiosyncratic collection of exhibits from Guyana and elsewhere, including a model of Georgetown before the 1945 fire and a good natural history section. ■ *Mon-Fri 0900-1700, Sat 0900-1200, free*. The **Walter Roth Museum of Anthropology**, on Main Street, has Amerindian artefacts (closed early 2002, but due to reopen later that year).

The **Botanical Gardens** (20 minutes walk from Anglican Cathedral, entry free), covering 50 ha, have Victorian bridges and pavilions, palms and lily-ponds (undergoing continual improvements). The gardens are safe in daylight hours, but keep to the marked paths. Do not go to the gardens after dark. Near the southwest corner is the former residence of the president, Castellani House, which now houses the **National Art Collection** (open after extensive renovation), and there is also a large mausoleum containing the remains of the former president, Forbes Burnham, which is decorated with reliefs depicting scenes from his political career. Look out for the rare cannonball tree (*Couroupita Guianensis*), named after the appearance of its poisonous fruit. The **zoo** (poor condition but being upgraded) has a collection of local animals including manatees. The zoo also boasts a breeding centre for endangered birds which are released into the wild. ■ *0800-1800, US$0.55 for adults, half-price for children; to use personal video US$11*. There also beautiful tropical plants in the **Promenade Gardens** (frequently locked) on Middle Street and in the **National Park** on Carifesta Avenue, which has a good public running track.

The **Georgetown Cricket Club** at Bourda has one of the finest cricket grounds in the tropics. Near the southeast corner of the Botanic Gardens is a well-equipped **National Sports Centre**. Nearby is the **Cultural Centre**, an impressive air-conditioned theatre with a large stage. Performances are also given at the **Playhouse Theatre** in Parade St.

Sleeping **LL-L** *Cara Suites*, 176 Middle St, T226 1612/5, F226 1541. Luxurious, secure, self-contained rooms with kitchen, Irish Bar serving Guinness and Irish and Scotch whiskies, grocery, shoeshine, laundry, business centre, internet access, no restaurant, airport pick-up. **LL-L** *Le Méridien Pegasus*, Seawall Rd, PO Box 101147, T225 2856, F225 3703, www.lemeridien-pegasus.com Completely renovated, very safe, a/c, comfortable, fridge, cable TV, lovely swimming pool, gym, tennis, business centre, 24-hr back up electricity, organizes tours to *Timberhead*, see Eating, below. **LL-AL** *Cara Lodge*, 294 Quamina St, T225 5301, F225 5310, www.carahotels.com A Heritage House hotel, 150-year-old converted mansion, 14 rooms, good service, superb, restaurant, bar, taxi service, laundry, business centre with internet access, pool and conference room. **LL-AL** *Cara Inn*, Pere St, Kitty, T225 0811, F225 0808. Lovely surroundings on Seawall just over 3 km from city centre, self-contained apartments and bedrooms with bath, laundry, restaurant (see below), pool, tennis court, also has dormitory with shared bath at **C** pp plus 10% tax. **L-AL** *Tower*, 74-75 Main St, T227 2015, F225 6021, hoteltower@solutions2000.net A/c, lively bar, *Main Street Café*, swimming pool (membership for non-residents), gym, business centre, 24-hr electricity back up. **L-A** *Grand Coastal Inn*, 2 Area M Le Ressouvenir, 5 km out of city, T220 1091, www.grandcoastal.cjb.net New, 3 standards of room, with breakfast and drinking water, dining room, laundry, business centre with internet, car rental, tours, good. **AL** *Brandsville's Apratments*, 89 Pike St, Campbellville, T226 1133, bransvil@guyana.net.gy New apartments, good standard. **AL-A** *Ariantze*, 176 Middle St, T226 5363/227 0115, Hughes@caribsurf.com Fans, or a/c in deluxe rooms and suites, including breakfast, see Eating, below, very good. **AL** *Main Street Plaza*, 45 Main St, T225 7775, F225 7666, www.mainstplaza.com Self-contained suites with kitchen, café, *Shutters* restaurant, small pool, welcoming, business facilities, safe. **A-C** *Friends*, 82 Robb St, T227 2383, F227 0762. Renovated with bath, a/c, TV, kitchenette, hot water, safe, cheaper without kitchen or a/c, mosquito net, bar, restaurant with Creole dishes, travel agency (domestic and international). **A-C** *Woodbine*, 41-42 New Market St, T225 9404, F225 8406, just off Main St. A/c or fan, bar, breakfast extra, restaurant, health club, overpriced. **A-D** *Hotel Glow*, 23 Queen St, Kitty, T227 0863. Clean, a/c or fan, with and without TV, 24-hour restaurant, breakfast extra, taxi or mini-bus to centre. **B** *Campala*, Camp St, T225 2951, 226 1920/225 1620. Modern, a/c, TV, cheaper without fridge, near prison (breakfast extra, lunch US$4, dinner US$6). **B** *Waterchris*, Waterloo St, between Murray and Church Sts, T227 1980. A/c, TV, hot water, phone (**C** with fan), good restaurant, breakfast extra.

There are also many smaller, cheaper hotels. Recommended are: **B-C** *Day Star*, 314 Sheriff St, Campbellville, T225 4425, F226 2665. Various rooms, bath, fan, mosquito net, no restaurant but several nearby, breakfast available, laundry, 15-20 mins from centre. **C** *Demico*, near Stabroek Market, T225 6372. A/c, TV, fridge, small rooms cheaper, no breakfast, lunch US$5. **C-D** *Rima Guest House*, 92 Middle St, T225 7401. Good area, modernized, well-run, popular with backpackers, good value, central, safe, mosquito nets, restaurant (breakfast US$4.45, lunch and dinner US$5.55). Highly recommended. **D-E** *Florentene's*, 3 North Rd, Lacytown, T226 2283. **E-F** *Tropicana*, Waterloo and Middle Sts. Very basic, some rooms self-contained. Many small hotels and guesthouses are full of long-stay residents, while some are rented by the hour. Try to book in advance. If in doubt, go to a larger hotel for first night and look around next day in daylight.

Resorts near Georgetown **L** pp *Timberhead*, operated by *Le Meridien Pegasus Hotel* in the Santa Amerindian Reserve (founded 1858), situated on a sandy hill overlooking Savannah and the Pokerero Creek, 3 beautiful native lodges with bath and kitchen facilities, well-run, good food, lovely trip up the Kamuni River to get there, much wildlife to be seen, 212 species of bird have been recorded, activities include swimming, fishing, jungle trails, visit to Santa Mission Arawak village, volleyball, US$61 pp for a day trip (minimum 2 people), US$116 pp per night (including all transport, meals, bar, guide, accommodation). Recommended. **L** pp *Arrowpoint Nature Resort*, just up the river from *Timberhead*, similar construction, US$60 pp day trip, US$110 pp overnight (minimum 5 people). *Double 'B' Exotic Gardens*, 58 Lamaha Gardens, Georgetown, T225 2023, F226 0997, contact Boyo Ramsaroop, near Timehri Airport, birdwatching, gardens specializing in heliconias, day tours only for groups of 30-40 people. **AL** *Emerald Tower Rainforest Lodge*, Madewini on Demerara River, T227 2011, F225 6021, minibus from Georgetown, day tour US$11-14 (US$5-6 without meals), overnight stays US$85-95 double (includes lodging, 3 meals, soft drinks, higher prices at weekends), cabins for day rental US$10, meals cost US$10, breakfast US$5, activities include swimming, bicycle and nature trails, birdwatching, archery. *Splashmin's*, a water fun park on Linden Highway, 1 hr from Georgetown, adults US$8, children (8-14) US$4.50, infants free, price includes coach from Georgetown hourly 0900-1300, office: 48 High St, Kingston, T223 7301, F225 6052, info@splashmins.com

Eating

10% service may be added to the bill. Many restaurants are closed on public holidays Restaurants are categorized according to their most expensive dishes. All have much cheaper options on menus

At hotels: **Expensive**: At *Le Meridien*: *El Dorado*, good atmosphere, Caribbean, Continental and Guyanese, *Browne's Old Café*, full English breakfast, lunch and dinner, *Poolside* BBQ and pizza with live bands. *Bottle Bar and Restaurant* at *Cara Lodge*. Very good, pleasant surroundings, must book, also open for breakfast. *Pasta Bowl*, at *Cara Inn*. The only Italian restaurant in Georgetown. *Sidewalk Café and Jazz Club* in *Ariantze Hotel*, Middle St. Buffet lunches Mon-Sat. **Mid-range**: *Main Street Café*, at *Tower Hotel*. Good breakfast and other meals. **Cheap**: Very good breakfast at *Waterchris*, also lunch and dinner.

Restaurants: **Expensive**: *Arawak Steak House*, in roof garden above *Demico Hotel*. Casual atmosphere, busy in evening, good value, closes 2200. *Caribbean Rose*, opposite *Ariantze*. West Indian and creole food, slow service, up 4 flights of stairs and on the roof, the open sides will cool you down, credit cards not accepted but will take US$ or Guyanese dollars. *Coalpot* in New Town. Good lunches starting at US$4, up to US$12.45 (no shorts allowed, cheaper cafetería). *Golden Coast*, Main and Middle Sts. New Chinese, good food. *New Thriving*, Camp and Brickdam Sts. Very good Chinese. *Palm Court*, Main St. Mixed

Guianas

menu, good food and service. *Royal Castle*, Hadfield and Lombard Sts, opposite Stabroek. Good chicken, fish, etc. *Calypso*, Regent St, *Forest Hills*, Camp St, and *Hing Loon*, Main St, all serve fast food, snacks, etc, prices from S$13.50 down to US$2.50. **Mid-range**: Wild meats and seafood at *Anchor*, 136 Waterloo St. *Brazil Churrascaria*, 208 Alexander St, Lacytown. All you can eat for US$5.40, great place. *Hack's Hallal*, 5 Commerce St, T225 6798. Specializing in West Indian food, with some vegetarian and sweet dishes. *Yue Yuan*, Robb St. Good Chinese. For fast food, try: *Arapaima*, Main St; *Creole Hot Pot*, 37C Cummings St, exclusively Guyanese dishes; *Demico House*, Stabroek Market, convenient, but poor service; *Idaho*, Brickdam; or *Kwality Foods*, in *Kwality Supermarket*, Camp and Regent Sts, a/c. *KFC* at Stabroek Market, on Vlissengen Rd, on Mandel Ave and near Harbour Bridge. *Pizza Hut* on Vlissengen Rd, near *KFC*. *Subway* on Water Street, near *Fogarty's*. *VIP*, Barr St, Kitty, and corner of King St and North Rd (opposite St George's Cathedral). Good subs, chicken, burgers. **Cheap**: *Back to Eden*, Middle St opposite hospital. Recommended vegetarian. Fresh daily baking at *Jerries*, 228 Camp St. Ice cream at *Igloo*, Camp and Middle Sts. *Brown Betty's*, near Stabroek. Excellent fruit juices at *Organic Juices*, Croal St, Bourda. *Juice Power*, Middle St, past the hospital, also sells drinking water. *Beacon Foundation*, 3 branches in Georgetown (ask for directions), charitable organization for the homeless and terminally ill; food at reasonable prices.

Entertainment

Surprisingly lively at night, mainly with gold miners, traders and overseas Guyanese throwing US$ around. Take care walking home at night

Nightlife *Club Nite Life*, Camp St, disco and beer garden, entry US$1.65-2.75, lively. Also on Camp St *Rumours Bar*, no cover charge. *Latino Bar*, at *Le Meridien Pegasus*. Fri and Sat night, Cuban theme, very popular, lively, no cover charge. *Nightflight*, 62 Main St, entry US$8. *Palm Court*, Main St, popular bar/café (French style), very lively Fri evening (entry US$2.75) and holidays, no entrance fee on other days. *Sidewalk Café and Jazz Club* in *Ariantze Hotel*, Middle St, US$2 on Thu, major international artists US$3.50-7. *Trump Card*, Church St, near St George's, sometimes has a live band. Near the Kitty Market are *Jazzy Jacks*, Alexander St (open till 0400 at weekends), and *Wee Place*, Lamaha St, both US$3 entry, but this area is unsafe unless you go with locals. *Zone Restaurant and Pub*, 232 Middle St, T225 5505, no cover charge. Sheriff St is some way from the centre but is 'the street that never sleeps' full of late night Chinese restaurants and has some good bars including *Tennessee Lounge* (no cover charge), *Burns Beat* (US$5.50 for night club section), *Buddy's Pool Hall and Nightclub* (No 137), and *Sheriff* (no cover charge unless they have a show, live band, go-go dancers, US$3). Most nightclubs sell imported, as well as local Banks beer; many sell drinks by the bottle rather than shot, this works out cheaper. You can visit the steel pan yards and watch practice sessions. There are 2 theatres. **Cinemas** *Astor*, Waterloo and Church Sts; *Strand*, Charlotte St; 1 on Main St; all worth a visit, US$0.90 for a double bill (protect against mosquitoes).

Shopping

The main shopping area is Regent St. The 2 main department stores are *Guyana Stores* in Church St, and *Fogarty's*, both of which stock a wide range of goods. Most Guyanese do their regular shopping at the 4 big markets: Stabroek (don't take valuables), Bourda, La Penitence and Kitty. Craft items are a good buy: Amerindian basketwork, hammocks, wood carvings, pottery, and small figures made out of Balata, a rubbery substance tapped from trees in the interior. *Houseproud*, 6 Ave of the Republic, has a good selection of expensive craftwork. Many other craft shops including *Creations Craft*, Water St, *Amerindian Hostel*, Princess St, *Hibiscus Craft Plaza*, outside General Post Office. Others are advertised in the papers. Good T-shirts are sold at *Guyana Stores* and in the markets. Gold is sold widely, often at good prices but make sure you know what you are buying. Do not buy it on the street. Films over ASA400 are normally not available; bring your own stock. **Bookshops** Some interesting books in *Houseproud*. Try also *GNTC* on Water St, *Argosy* and *Kharg* both on Regent St, *Dimension* on Cummings St, as well as *Guyana Stores* and *Fogarty's*. *The Bookseller*, Church St, wide selection. *Universal Bookstore* on Water St, near *Fogarty's*, has a good selection of books and greetings cards.

Tour operators

Try Mr Mendoza at *Frandec Travel Service*, Main St, repeatedly recommended (no tours to the interior). *H and R Ramdehol*, 215 South Rd, Lacytown. *Connections Travel* on Ave of the Republic, above *Houseproud*. The tourism sector is promoting ecotourism in the form of environmentally friendly resorts and camps on Guyana's rivers and in the rainforest (see below). There is much tropical wildlife to be seen.

Earth Tours Ltd, 106 Lamaha St, North Cummingsburg, T225 4020/226 5340, www.angelfire.com/ga3/earthtours Tours to Iwokrama, Kaieteur Falls and fishing trips to the east coast, Demerara River, Canal no 1 and Canal no 2. *Evergreen Adventures*, 185 Shribasant St, Prashad Nagar, T225 1048, www.baganara.com Tours on the Essequibo River to Baganara Island. *Greenheart Tours*, 36 Craig St, Campbellville, T/F225 8219, jpgon_7nov@yahoo.com Itineraries for any group size, tours. *Nature Tours*, Kingston Business Centre, 45 High St, T223 7713/226 6108, naturetour60@hotmail.com Contact Joanie Bastian, offers tours to Kaieteur, Orinduik, Santa Mission and the Essequibo River. *Outdoor Expeditions*, 307 'I' Stone Av, Campbellville, T/F225 2315, outdoor_expeditionsguyana@yahoo.com Contact Paul Waldron and Zenise Hartley; camping and trekking trips, guiding and custom-designed itineraries. *Shell Beach Adventures*, office at *Le Meridien Pegasus*, T225 4483/4, F226 0532 (after hours T227 4732), www.sbadventures.com Trips to Shell Beach in northwest Guyana, 3-day trip US$450 pp using light aircraft and camping on beach (minimum 2 people, cheaper rates for larger groups), day and overland trips to Kaieteur, custom-designed trips to inland resorts and other locations. *Rainforest Tours*, Frank Singh, 33 Barrack St, Kingston, T/F227 5632/227 2011. Day and overland trips to Kaieteur, Santa Mission, Essequibo/Mazaruni; also Pakaraima Mountain hike, Kukubara to Orinduik, five days from one Amerindian village to another. *Roraima Airways*, 101 Cummings St, Bourda, T225 9648, F225 9646. Day trips to Kaieteur and Orinduik Falls. *Torong Guyana*, 56 Coralita Av, Bel Air Park, T225 0876/226 5298, F225 0749, toronggy@networksgy.com Margaret and Malcolm Chan-a-Sue provide air, land and river advice and logistical support to any and all destinations in Guyana, for small and large groups. *Whitewater Adventure Tours*, Lot no 3 Sandy Babb St, Kitty, T226 6614, F226 5225. Daytrips to Baracara Island on the Mazaruni River from US$60; trips to Marshall Falls (rapids) available, uses two jetboats for tours. *Wilderness Explorers*, Cara Suites, 176 Middle St, T227 7698, T/F226 2085, www.wilderness-explorers.com Offer ready-made or custom-designed itineraries for any group size. Tours available to all of Guyana's interior resorts, day and overland tours to Kaieteur Falls, horse trekking, hiking and general tours in the Rupununi (agents for *Ranches of the Rupununi*) and rainforest (trips to Iwokrama Rain Forest Programme, see page 1460). Tours also in Suriname, Guyane, Brazil, Venezuela, Barbados, St Vincent and the Grenadines and Trinidad and Tobago. Specialists in nature, adventure and birdwatching tours. Free tourism information, booklet and advice available. Wilderness Explorers are general sales agents for Surinam Airways and Trans Guyana Airways. Recommended. *Wonderland Tours*, 158 Waterloo St, T225 3122, T/F225 9795 (24 hrs), day trips to Kaieteur and Orinduik Falls, Santa Mission, Essequibo and Mazaruni rivers, city tours; special arrangements for overnight stays available, recommended.

Bus There are regular services by minibuses and collective taxis to most coastal towns from the Stabroek Market. To **Moleson Creek** for the crossing to Suriname, No 65 from opposite the City Hall, Ave of the Republic between Regent and Charlotte Sts, leaves when full, US$5.50.If, by mistake, you get on a bus going only as far as **Springlands**, 15 mins before Moleson Creek, the driver will probably take you for a little extra money (check with the driver in Georgetown where his bus is going); to **Rossignol**, US$2.75; to **Parika**, No 32, US$1.10; to **Linden**, No 43, US$2.75. Ask other passengers what the fare should be. **Car hire**: available through numerous companies (page 18 of Guyana Telephone Book gives details). *Budget* at *Ocean View Hotel*, US$105, plus US$250 deposit for minimum of 3 days. Shivraj, 98 Hadfield St, Werk-en-Rust, T226 0550/225 4785, F226 0531, carl@solution.com US$54.65 plus US$220 deposit. A permit is needed from local police; rental agencies can advise.

Transport

Guianas

NB For visiting many parts of the interior, particularly Amerindian districts, permits are required in advance from the *Ministry of Home Affairs* and the *Minister of Amerindian Affairs* in the office of the president, New Garden St in Georgetown. If venturing out of Georgetown on your own, check beforehand whether you need a permit for where you intend to visit. Permits can be difficult to obtain and may require some time. Apply before arrival in Guyana. *Wilderness Explorers* offer a service for obtaining permits.

Directory **Banks** *National Bank of Industry and Commerce*, *Guyana Bank of Trade and Industry*, *Bank of Baroda*, *Bank of Nova Scotia* (2 branches) will give cash advance on Visa card. **Exchange houses:** (*cambios*) in shops may be open longer hrs. A good, safe *cambio* is *Kayman Sankar*, Lamaha St. There is a *cambio* next to *Rima Guest House*, Middle St. Roving *cambios* at entrance to Stabroek Market, take care. To buy Suriname guilders, go to *Swiss House*, a *cambio* in the unsafe market area around Water Street and America Street, known locally as 'Wall Street'. **Communications** Internet: *Byte 'N' Surf*, 288 Middle Street, South Cummingsburg, T225 6481, US$2.15 per hr. *Internet World*, 16 'B' Duncan St, Newton Kitty, T227 1051, US$1.90 per hr. *Solutioins 2000*, 167 Waterloo St, South Cummingsburg, T225 2653/1436, USA$2.15 per hr. **Post Office:** main 1 on North St. **Embassies and consulates** Brazilian Embassy, 308 Church St, Queenstown, T225 7970, bragetown@ solutions2000.net Visa issued next day, 90 days, 1 photo, US$12.75. **Canadian High Commission**, High and Young Sts, T227 2081-5, F225 8380, www.dfait-maeci.gc.ca/guyana **Honorary French Consul** , 7 Sherriff St, T226 5238. **Suriname Embassy**, 171 Peter Rose and Crown St, Queenstown, T226 7844/225 3467, F225 0759. Consular section open Mon, Wed, Fri morning only, but visa application can be handed in at any time. **UK High Commission**, 44 Main St, T592-226 5881/4, www.britain-in-guyana.org **US Embassy**, 99-100 Young and Duke Sts, Kingston, T225 4902, F225 8497, www.usembguyana.com **Venezuelan Embassy**, 296 Thomas St, South Cummingsburg, T226 6749/227 2162, F226 0841. **Medical services** See page 1448.

Southeast to Suriname

Linden
Colour map 2, grid B3
Population: 60,000
112 km S of Georgetown

The second-largest town in Guyana, is a bauxite mining town on both banks of the Demerara River. The two towns are connected by a good road (slow for the first part to Timehri); the police checks are to stop drug and gun running. Linden is a company mining town. The opencast mine is 60-90 m deep and is said to have the world's longest boom walking dragline. The town is dominated by a disused alumina plant and scarred by old bauxite pits. In town, there is the lovely colonial guesthouse on the Demerara River, run by the mining company. **B** *Hotel Star Bonnett*, 671 Industrial Area, 1¾ km out of town on Georgetown Rd, T444 6505, F444 6829. Various standards of room, all with a/c and TV, clean, good lunches. Nearby**C-E** *Summit Hotel*, 6 Industrial Area, McKenzie, T444 6500. Cheaper shared rooms available, breakfast extra.

From Linden rough roads suitable for four-wheel drive vehicles run south to the bauxite mining towns of **Ituni** and **Kwakwani**. The road south to the logging centre at Mabura Hill is in excellent condition; from here a good road runs west to Mahdia, with a pontoon crossing of the Essequibo, and another road continues south from Mabura Hill to Kurupukari, but four-wheel drive is needed on this stretch. A good road goes west from Linden to Rockstone ferry on the Essequibo River. From Rockstone roads run north to Bartica (bad) and southwest to Issano (being improved).

New Amsterdam
Colour map 2, grid B4
Population: 25,000
104 km SE of Georgetown

On the east bank of the Berbice River, near its mouth, is the picturesque New Amsterdam. From Georgetown, take a minibus (44, or express No 50) or collective taxi to Rosignol on the west bank of the Berbice, US$1.10, then cross the river by the ferry, 15 mins crossing, but add another 45 mins for loading/unloading (US$0.30; also takes vehicles). **A** *Church View Guest House*, 3 Main and King Sts, T333 6439, F333 2880. Including breakfast and 1 hr in gym, A/C, phone, TV, clean. Recommended. **A** *Little Rock*, 65 Vrymans Erven, self-contained, hot water, a/c, TV, phone, fridge, breakfast US$3.25 extra. **A** *Parkway*, 4 Main St, T333 3928, F333 2028. Clean, **C** without a/c, safe, with bath. Recommended but no breakfast. **C** *Astor*, 7 Strand. All rooms self-contained, breakfast US$2.45.

Berbice resorts **A** pp *Dubalay Ranch*, a working ranch on the Berbice River, 147 km from the river mouth, has forest, savanna and swamp habitats, with some 300 bird species, deer, large cats, water buffalo and Dutch colonial remains (eg graves, bottles). Activities include boat trips (US$25 with guide), riding (US$15 for first hr, then US$10 per hr), birdwatching (US$15), jeep tours (US$30), nighttime wildlife trips (US$50), custom-made packages, or just relaxing. Price is **C** for scientists or students, includes 3 meals and soft drinks/juices, but not transport to the

Guianas

ranch (US$230 return from/to Georgetown) or activities. Small parties preferred; advance booking essential. Contact *Shell Beach Adventures* or *Wilderness Explorers*, see Tours and tour operators, Georgetown. *Lu-lu's Wilderness Resort*, on the Berbice savannas, T226 6208.

The road continues east from New Amsterdam (minibus, No 50, US$1.75-2.50), to **Springlands** and **Skeldon** at the mouth of the Corentyne River. In Skeldon there is **A** *Par Park*, with bath and a/c, hot water, TV, no meals available. **B** *Mahogany*, with bath, TV, fridge, hot water, clean, lunch/dinner US$2.60-3.25. Recommended. Good Indian food at *Mansoor*. The two towns are officially known as **Corriverton** (Corentyne River Town). Springlands is 2 km long, so you need to know where you want to get off the bus. **E** pp *Swiss Guest House*, T339 2329. Pakistani run, with bath and fan, no meals, helpful, simple accommodation. Several good Chinese restaurants within a few blocks of Springlands town centre. There are the *National Bank of Industry and Commerce* and the *Guyana National Commercial Bank*. Suriname guilders can officially be changed into Guyanese dollars.

Corriverton
Colour map 2, grid B4
Population: 31, 000

Transport   Ferry to Suriname: a ferry from Moleson, or Crabwood Creek, 13 km south of Springlands, to South Drain (40 km south of Nieuw-Nickerie) runs daily at 1000, US$8 single, bicycles free, motorbikes US$5, cars US$15, pick-ups US$20, 30 min crossing. Immigration forms are handed out on board. At the ferry point is a hut/bar where you can buy Suriname guilders. There are direct buses Georgetown-Moleson Creek. Check visa requirements for Suriname before travelling.

West from Georgetown

Travelling west from Georgetown, the road crosses the 2 km long floating Demerara bridge (opens often for shipping, US$0.25 toll, pedestrians free). Speedboats cross the Demerara from Stabroek market, US$0.30 every 30 minutes. The road continues 42 km, past rice paddies, *kokers* and through villages to **Parika**, a growing town on the east bank of the Essequibo River (minibus US$1). It has a Sunday market, 0600-1100, and three banks. From here ferries cross the river to **Adventure** on the west bank at 1700 daily and 0830 Wednesday and Friday, returning at 0300 daily and 1330 Wednesday and Friday; or speedboat US$2.40.

The northwest coastal area is mainly accessible by boat only. Speedboats cross from Parika to Supenaam, US$5.50 (very wet). From Supenaam minibuses or taxis (US$5.50 per person) go to Charity. From Adventure a road runs north through Anna Regina. Nearby there is a resort at **Lake Mainstay**. You can visit a hot and cold lake, which varies in temperature from one place to another, and the Wayaka Mainstay Amerindian Community, 13 km from Anna Regina. Mainstay is 2½ hours by road and ferry from Georgetown (depending on tides), 17 minutes by plane from Ogle (US$35). The road goes on to **Charity**, a pleasant little town with two small hotels and a lively market on Monday (quiet at other times). **AL** *Lake Mainstay Resort*, T226 2975, F226 2755 (or T771 4960/4963/4959, F771 4951). Completely refurbished, 40 cabins with a/c, cheaper without lake view, also single rooms, beachfront on the lake, restaurant, bars, swimming, boating, other sports, birdwatching and nature trails; special events and entertainment. Breakfast US$3.85, lunch and dinner US$7.20. Day trips can be arranged for US$51 per person (1-7 passengers), US$31 (eight and over) including entrance fees, road and boat transport, breakfast and lunch, but no drinks. Transport only is US$27.75 Georgetown-Parika return, US$83 return Parika-Supenaam in a regular speed boat, up to 10 people, US$33 return Supenaam-Lake Mainstay for up to four passengers.

Near the border with Venezuela are the small ports of **Morawhanna** (Morajuana to the Venezuelans) and **Mabaruma**. Mabaruma has replaced Morawhanna as capital of the region since it is less at risk from flooding. There is a Government Guest House, two rooms with bath, others with shared bath, clean, friendly staff, book in

Border with Venezuela

Guianas

advance. **D** *Kumaka Tourist Resort*, Maburama, contact *Somwaru Travel Agency*, Georgetown, T225 9276, meals, bath, balcony, hammocks, run down; offers trips to Hosororo Falls, Babarima Amerindian settlement, rainforest, early examples of Amerindian art. ■ *TGA flies from Georgetown Mon, Wed, Fri, Sat, US$66 one way, US$128 return. A ferry runs every other Tue from Georgetown at 1500 (US$8.35) to Mabaruma. The journey is surprisingly rough and 'you will have to fight for hammock space and watch your possessions like a hawk'. For assistance with transport contact Mr Prince through the Government Guest House.*

Shell Beach Part of a protected area of Atlantic coastline, Shell Beach is some 145 km long, from the Pomeroon River to the Venezuelan border. It safeguards the nesting grounds of leatherback, green, hawksbill and olive Ridley turtles. Nesting activity begins in late March and continues, with hatching, until mid-August. Former turtle hunters have been retrained to patrol and identify nest sites, which are logged using global positioning satellite equipment. The whole project is supported by the Florida Audubon Society. The coast consists of large areas of mangrove swamps with intermittent beaches formed entirely of eroded shell particles. There are large flocks of stunning scarlet ibis. Other birds include Amazon parrots, macaws, toucans, woodpeckers, crab hawks and many others. Iguanas are usually seen in the mangroves, with occasional sightings of rare river dolphin on the narrower stretches of river.

The camp consists of a thatched dining area and huts for the staff and igloo-type tents for guests, with fly-sheets and mosquito netting. Showers and toilets are very simple. Food is very good (Venezuelan fishermen exchange fresh fish for ice). An Arawak family runs the camp and offers daily activities of fishing and birdwatching. They are excellent guides and speak English. Turtle watching is available in season.

Transport Fly Georgetown-Mabaruma, then take a motorized canoe to Shell Beach, 1 hr (good trip in the early morning for birdwatching); the last 20 mins is from the mouth of the Waini River along coast to Shell Beach camp, which can be a jolting ride. Or from Georgetown by canoe along some very interesting waterways. Allow 3-4 days. For information, contact *Shell Beach Adventures* or *Wilderness Explorers*, see Tours and tour operators, Georgetown.

Southwest from Georgetown: to Brazil

Fort Island & Bartica From Parika there's a vehicle ferry up the Essequibo River to Bartica on Monday, Thursday and Saturday, returning next day, US$1.50 one way. The 58 km journey *Colour map 2, grid B3* takes six hours, stopping at **Fort Island**; boats come out from riverside settlements to load up with fruit. On Fort Island is a Dutch fort (built 1743, restored by Raleigh International in 1991) and the Dutch Court of Policy, built at the same time. There is also a small village; the rest of the island is dairy farms. Speedboats do the journey any time, US$4.25 per person, 1-2 hours, depending on horsepower.

Bartica, at the junction of the Essequibo and Mazaruni rivers, is the 'take-off' town for the gold and diamond fields and the interior generally. Opposite Bartica, at the mouth of the Mazaruni, is Kaow Island, with a lumber mill. The *stelling* (wharf) and market in Bartica are very colourful; *Crystal Crest* has a huge sound system and will play requests. Easter regatta, mostly power boats. A good boatman and guide is B Balkarran, 2 Triangle Street, T455 2544. *Essequibo Adventure Tours*, 52 First Avenue, Bartica, T455 2441/455 2253, F455 2956, sbell@guyananet.gy Jet boat and other tours on the Essequibo/Mazaruni and Cuyuni Rivers.

Sleeping and eating B *Marin Hotel*, 19 Second Ave, T455 2243. **A** with a/c, with bath, TV, phone, fridge, meals available (breakfast US$2.45, lunch and dinner US$6.40). **E** *Modern*, 9 First Ave, T455 2301, near ferry. 2 luxury rooms **C**, others basic, with bath and fan. Recommended. Good food, book ahead if possible. Also on First Ave, **E** *Hi-Lo*, self-contained suites, also very basic rooms under US$3, crowded, no bath, claustrophobic. Mrs Payne's daughter, Third Ave

Guianas

next to Hospital, rooms basic, clean. *Riverview Beach Bar*, at Goshan near Bartica (Camp Silo bible study centre), popular hotel and bar, disco, videos, nice beach, safe swimming.

Resorts near Bartica LL *Shanklands*, booking office in *Cara Suites*, 176 Middle St, T226 8907, F225 1586, www.shanklands.com **L** in low season, dormitory accommodation available. Beautifully located on a cliff overlooking the Essequibo, 5 colonial style cottages with verandah set in lawns and trees, activities include swimming, walking, birdwatching, croquet, fishing, watersports, first class, US$55 pp for day trip (minimum 4 people), excellent service, good food. *Shanklands* can be reached by boat from Parika or Bartica; the Baganara Island airstrip is not far away; private transport by road can be arranged from *Timberhead* (see above). **AL** pp *Baracara Resort*, on an island opposite the confluence of the Cuyuni and Mazaruni rivers, 10 mins by boat from Bartika, T/F226 5225, whitewateradv@ solutions2000.net Day trips using jet boat US$60 (minimum 10) pp, 9 rooms with bath, mosquito net, balcony; popular on Sun and in Jun-Aug. Buffet meals, swimming, short boat ride to nature trail and waterfall. Contact *Whitewater Adventure Tours*. **LL-AL** *Baganara Island Resort*, beautiful house on Baganara Island in Essequibo River a few miles south of Bartica, everg@solutions2000.net Price depends on season and standard of room, full board, private beach, watersports, airstrip; day trips US$60 pp (minimum 10), with meals, bar and activities. Transport to resort US$25 pp return.

South of Bartica

The Essequibo is navigable to large boats for some miles upstream Bartica. The Cuyuni flows into the Mazaruni three miles above Bartica, and above this confluence the Mazaruni is impeded for 190 km by thousands of islands, rapids and waterfalls. To avoid this stretch of treacherous river a road has been built from Bartica to Issano, where boats can be taken up the more tranquil upper Mazaruni. At the confluence of the Mazaruni and Cuyuni rivers are the ruins of the Dutch stronghold **Kyk-over-al**, once the seat of government for the Dutch county of Essequibo. Nearby are the **Marshall Falls** (30-60 minutes by boat from Bartica, US$50 per boat, return), which are beautiful, but too dangerous for swimming. You can swim in the nearby bay, part of the Rainbow River Marshall Falls property.

Sleeping A *Rainbow River Safari*, a 16,800 acre, independent conservation site on the Mazaruni River at Marshall Falls, accommodation is very simple (softwood cabins, basic bedding, pit latrines, washing in river), cooking over woodfire. Trails in unspoilt forest, waterfalls, wildlife watching, gold and diamond panning, swimming and other activities. Day trippers have to pay G$1,000. For prices, other tours and development plans contact *Mr E Sabat*, tedsabat@aol.com or tedsabat@yahoo.com, www.hometown.aol.com/ tedsabat/rainbowrivermarshallfallsguyana.html

Kaieteur National Park

Kaieteur Falls rank with the Niagara, Victoria, and Iguazú Falls in majesty and beauty, but have the added attraction of being surrounded by unspoilt forest

The Kaieteur Falls, on the Potaro River, nearly five times the height of Niagara, with a sheer drop of 228 m, are almost 100 m wide. They are unspoilt because of their isolation. The Kaieteur Falls lie within the **Kaieteur National Park**, where there is a variety of wildlife: tapirs, ocelots, monkeys, armadillos, anteaters, and jungle and river birds. At the Falls themselves, one can see the magnificent silver fox, often near the rest house, the cock-of-the-rock and the Kaieteur swift, which lives behind the falls. At dusk the swifts swoop in and out of the gorge before passing through the deluge to roost behind the water. Tiny golden frogs live in the tank bromeliads. Permission to enter park must be obtained from the National Parks Commission in Georgetown, T225 9142 (arranged by tour operators). In the dry months, April and October, the flow of the falls is reduced; in January and June/July the flow is fullest, but in June, the height of the wet season, the overland route is impassable.

A trip to the Kaieteur Falls costs US$210 with most operators, minimum five people (can be negotiated lower for larger groups, for example US$195 for nine with Roraima Airways). The trip includes two hours at Kaieteur Falls, two hours at Orinduik Falls, lunch, drinks, park entrance fee and guide; sit on left for best views, take swimming gear. Trips depend on the charter plane being filled; there is normally at least one flight per week. Cancellations only occur in bad weather or if there are

Guianas

insufficient passengers. Operators offering this service are *Wilderness Explorers*, *Wonderland Tours* (Richard Ousman), *Torang Guyana*, *Shell Beach Adventures*, *Rainforest Tours*, and *Nature Tours*. To charter a plane privately costs US$1,200 to Kaieteur and Orinduik. *Air Services Ltd* offer a Kaieteur only flight on Sat and Sun for US$99 (includes national park registration); flight must be full, last minute cancellations not uncommon. *Wilderness Explorers* and *Rainforest Tours* in Georgetown offer overland trips to Kaieteur for US$625 for minimum of three people; rate includes all transport, meals, camping gear, guides and flight back to Georgetown. Minibuses run daily from Georgetown as far as Mahdia, via Mabura Hill.

The Pakaraima Mountains stretch from Kaieteur westwards to include the highest peak in Guyana, **Mount Roraima**, the possible inspiration for Conan Doyle's *Lost World*. Roraima is very difficult to climb from the Guyanese side, but *Wilderness Explorers* offer trips via Brazil and Venezuela.

Sleeping E The rest house at the top of the Falls is open for guests, but is very basic; enquire and pay first at the National Parks Commission, Georgetown, T225 9142 (if planning to stay overnight, you must be self-sufficient, whether the guest-house is open or not; take your own food and a hammock, it can be cold and damp at night; the warden is not allowed to collect money).

Orinduik Falls Orinduik Falls are on the Ireng River, which forms the border with Brazil; the river pours over steps and terraces of jasper, with a backdrop of the grass-covered Pakaraima Mountains. There is good swimming at the falls which are a 25-minute flight from Kaieteur. Vincent and Rose Cheong run a tourist shelter and are full of information about the area. *Wilderness Explorers* offer four trips per year from Orinduik north on the Ireng in dugout canoes with Amerindian guides.

Rupununi Savanna This is an extensive area of dry grassland in the far southwest of Guyana, with scattered trees, termite mounds and wooded hills. The rivers, creeks and ponds, lined with Ite palms and other trees, are good for seeing wildlife. Among a wide variety of birds, look out for macaws, toucan, parrots, parakeets, osprey, hawks and jabiru storks (take binoculars). Many of the animals are nocturnal and seldom seen. The region is scattered with occasional Amerindian villages and a few large cattle ranches which date from the late 19th century: the descendants of some of the Scots settlers still live here. Links with Brazil are much closer than with the Guyanese coast; many people speak Portuguese and most trade is with Brazil.

Avoid the Rupununi in the wet season (mid-May to August); much of the Savanna floods and malaria mosquitoes and *kabura*/sandflies are widespread. The best time is October to April. River bathing is good, but beware of dangerous stingrays and black caiman. Note that a permit from the Home Affairs Ministry is usually required to visit Rupununi, unless you go with a tour operator. Check in advance if your passport is sufficient. A separate permit to visit Amerindian villages is needed from the Minister of Amerindian Affairs, the President's office in Georgetown.

Lethem
Colour map 2, grid B3
A small but scattered town on the Brazilian border (see below), this is the service centre for the Rupununi and for trade with Brazil. There are many small stores, a small hospital (T772 2006), a police station (T772 2011) and government offices. A big event at Easter is the rodeo, visited by cowboys from all over the Rupununi. Prices are about twice as high as in Georgetown. About 2½ km south of town at St Ignatius there is a Jesuit mission dating from 1911. In the nearby mountains there is good birdwatching and there are waterfalls to visit.

Sleeping and eating A number of places take guests, full board, organize tours and transport. **B-C** *Savannah Inn*, attached to General Store, T772 2035 (Georgetown 227 6203), or book through *Wilderness Explorers*. Including breakfast, a/c cabins with bath (cheaper with fan), phone, TV, fridge, good, clean, helpful, bar, good food, breakfast US$3.25, lunch or dinner US$4.30, changes reais into Guyanese dollars, tours arranged, will take you to airport.

Guianas

B-E *Takutu Guest House*, T772 2084. Cheapest in single room without a/c, with bath, fridge, clean, breakfast US$2.15-4.30. Lunch/dinner US$3.80-5.40 (has information on trucks to Georgetown). **D** *Cacique Guest House*, T772 2083. With bath, fan, clean, pleasant, good, breakfast US$2.15-2.70. At the *Airport Shop*, T772 2085, the *Penthouse* is for backpackers, bathroom outside, safe, can tie up hammock, basic; Don and Shirley Melville provide the most comprehensive information and assistance service in the Rupununi. The *Manari Ranch Hotel*, 11 km north of Lethem on a creek (good swimming). US$60 per day, can accommodate about 20 people. *Foo Foods*, T772 2010. Highly recommended for snacks. The *Airport Shop*, good snacks, bar.

　　Resorts L pp *Dadanawa Ranch*, Duane and Sandy de Freitas, 96 km south of Lethem, 1 of the world's largest ranches, each bedroom has verandah (being upgraded). They can organize recommended trekking and horse riding trips, also camping with *vaqueros*. **L** pp *Karanambu Ranch*, Dianne McTurk, 96 km northeast of Lethem, on the Rupununi River, unique old home, cottages with bath, mosquito net, toiletries, good meals, fishing, excellent birdwatching and boat rides with guides. 24 km from Yupukari Amerindian village, trips possible. Dianne McTurk rears and rehabilitates orphaned giant river otters. For both ranches contact *Wilderness Explorers*. All transport is arranged.

Transport Local: The Airport Shop can arrange horse hire for US$8 per hour, and Land Rovers and trucks at US$3 per mile. *Savannah Inn* has good 4WD vehicles for hire with driver. For birdwatching trips and transport contact Loris Franklin through the Airport Shop. Best time to ask about vehicle hire (with driver), or horse is when plane arrives, the only time when lots of people are around. Car hire is expensive.

　　Transport around the Rupununi is difficult; there are a few 4WD vehicles, but ox-carts and bicycles are more common on the rough roads. From Lethem transport can be hired for day-trips to the Moco-Moco Falls and the Kumu Falls and to the Kanuku Mountains (4WD and driver to Moco-Moco US$72.50, long, rough ride and walk, but worth it). Trucks may also be hired to visit Annai, 130 km northeast (see below) along a poor road, 4 hrs journey, US$200. All trucks leaving town must check with the police.

　　Long distance: The road from Georgetown to Lethem via Mabura Hill and Kurupukari is good in the dry season (more difficult in the wet). It provides a through route from Georgetown to Boa Vista (Brazil). After Linden, the 100 km to Mabura Hill is good. The next 50 km, to Frenchman's Creek, is a hard, rocky rollercoaster (4WD needed), then, to the Essequibo, it is "a mixture of white sand and badly-rutted, metre-deep puddles edged with razor grass". This stretch is very hard for cyclists and motorcyclists, best to hitch a ride with a truck, and motorists should tag along with a lorry too (Jason Uribe, Hindhead, UK). After the river and Iwokrama (see below) the road goes through jungle to Annai. Trucks often make a pit stop on the way at Annai, where food, washing facilities and accommodation are available at *Rock View* (see below). Then it is hard earth and gravel across the Rupununi (largely flooded after the rains). Truck Georgetown-Lethem: contact **Ministry of Regional Development**, Georgetown; Eddie Singh, 137 Herstelling, near Providence police station, 5 miles south of Georgetown, T226 2672; *Ng-a-fook*, on Church St, between Camp St and Waterloo St. Trip takes 18-24 hrs, can take longer, US$28 pp 1 way, no seat but share truck with load, take food, lots of water and hammock. (Care is needed on this route, but it is exciting, through savanna and rainforest.). **Air**: *TGA* flies Georgetown-Lethem-Georgetown daily, and *RAL*, Tue, Wed, Fri and Sun from Ogle airstrip. Stops are available at Annai and Karanambu Ranch. The *TGA* fare is US$109 one way, US$211 return Georgetown to Lethem, Karanambu or Annai. *RAL* fares are US$100 one way, US$195 return to Lethem, US$111 one way, US$222 return to Karanambu and Annai.

Annai is a remote Amerindian village in the northern savannas, south of the **Annai** Iwokrama Rainforest Programme. It is possible to trek over the plains to the Rupununi River, or through dense jungle to the mountains. About 1-2 hours on foot are the villages of Kwatamang and Wowetta where Raleigh International built a Health and Community Resource Centre in 1995. Some 25 km north of Annai is the Amerindian village of **Surama** which organizes its own ecotourism activities

Guianas

through the village council and can accommodate guests in the new guest house (**E** pp, meals extra). Birdwatching (US$6), night trekking (US$9), boating (US$30-60) and Land Rover trips (US$30) arranged; every visitor pays a village fee of US$3. In Georgetown all bookings are made through *Wilderness Explorers*, who have formed a partnership with Surama community to develop tourism, www.wilderness-explorers.com; 10 packages on offer.

Resorts L *The Rock View Lodge*, Annai, Colin Edwards and family, guest house with 8 self-contained rooms, bars, zoo, natural rock swimming pool; in the Pakaraima foothills, where the savanna meets the Iwokrama Rainforest Programme (see below); www.rockviewlodge.com T226 5412, F225 5310 to book, or through *Wilderness Explorers*. Pony treks to nearby foothills, nature tours with for painting, photography and fishing, regional Amerindian and other local cooking, full board. Recommended. TGA agent in Annai is Colin Edwards and the Lodge is beside the airstrip. Rock View-Georgetown by Land Rover US$70 return. From *Karanambu* to *Rock View* by boat and jeep costs US$195 for up to 4 people, a fascinating trip.

Iwokrama Rainforest Programme
Exceptionally good wildlife, including macaws, toucans, black curacow, peccary, and howler monkeys. One of the best places to see jaguar in the wild

This is a 388,000 ha project, set up by Guyana and the Commonwealth to conserve about 2 of Guyana's tropical forest. In addition to conservation, the Programme will involve studies on the sustainable use of the rainforest and ecotourism. It is hoped that the results will provide a database for application worldwide. The Field Station is at Kurukupari, on the northern boundary of the reserve. You can meet research teams, take boat trips and stay at satellite camps deep in the forest (Clearwater on the Burro-burro, Kabocalli and Turtle Mountain on the Essequibo). Fishing is good, especially for peacock bass. Well-trained rangers escort visitors through the forest on many trails. One goes to Turtle Mountain (45 minutes by boat, then 1½ hours walk), go early for great views of the forest canopy. Another trek is to the top of Mount Iwokrama, a difficult 20 km round trip; for the less fit there is a 10 km trail to the foot of the mountain to a pleasant stream and Amerindian petroglyphs. There are set rates for boat and Land Rover use and for field assistants to accompany you. Tourists stay in cabins at the Field Station, paying a fee for the bed and a user fee. Three of the five cabins are very comfortable, with veranda. Meals served in huge thatched dining research area with fine views of the river. For charges, which change frequently, contact The Administrator, Iwokrama International Centre for Rainforest Conservation and Development, 67 Bel Air, Georgetown, PO Box 10630, T225 1504, F225 9199. All meals cost US$5 (take your own alcoholic drinks). ■ *Iwokrama is 3 hrs by road from Annai, 2 hrs from Surama. Coming from Georgetown, you have to cross the Essequibo at Kurupukari; ferry runs 0800-1700, hoot for service, US$9 for a pick-up, US$18 for truck. Wilderness Explorers can arrange standard and custom-designed packages to Iwokrama.*

Camps *Maparri Wilderness Camp* is on the Maparri River, in the Kanuku Mountains, recognized by Conservation International as one of the few remaining pristine Amazonian areas, rich in flora and fauna. It is easy to watch macaws, herons, toucans, kingfisherm, maybe harpy eagles. With luck, you can see tayra, labba, ocelot, agouti, monkeys, tapir, even jaguar. Various treks are arranged. It can only be reached by a combination of air and river. *Maparri Camp* is built of wood, with open sides, and has hammocks with mosquito nets. The site overlooks a waterfall; the river water is crystal clear (unlike most rivers in Guyana) and the fall and surrounding pools are safe for swimming. The camp is merely a framework. Simple, nutritional meals, supplemented by fish from the river, are prepared over an open fire. Contact *Wilderness Explorers* for rates and bookings.

Border with Brazil
The Takutu River separates Lethem from Bonfim in Brazil. The crossing is about 1.6 km north of Lethem (taxis, or pickups, US$2) and 2½ km from Bonfim. Small boats ferry foot passengers (US$0.25); vehicles cross by pontoon on demand, US$4 return. A bridge is under construction. Formalities are generally lax on both sides of the border, but it is important to observe them as people not having the correct

papers and stamps will have problems further into either country. All procedures for exit and entry are carried out by immigration at Lethem airport (not at the police station). If arriving from Brazil, buy some Guyanese dollars in Boa Vista as there are not exchange facilities in Lethem. ■ *Buses from Bonfim to Boa Vista (Brazil) about 6 a day, 2½ hrs, US$6; colectivos charge US$18.*

Background

The country was first partially settled between 1616 and 1621 by the Dutch West India Company, who erected a fort and depot at Fort Kyk-over-al (County of Essequibo). The first English attempt at settlement was made by Captain Leigh on the Oiapoque River (now French Guyane) in 1604, but he failed to establish a permanent settlement. Lord Willoughby, famous in the early history of Barbados, founded a settlement in 1663 at Suriname, which was captured by the Dutch in 1667 and ceded to them at the Peace of Breda in exchange for New York. The Dutch held the three colonies till 1796 when they were captured by a British fleet. The territory was restored to the Dutch in 1802, but in the following year was retaken by Great Britain, which finally gained it in 1814, when the three counties of Essequibo, Berbice and Demerara were merged to form British Guiana.

History

During the 17th century the Dutch and English settlers established posts upriver, in the hills, mostly as trading points with the Amerindian natives. Plantations were laid out and worked by African slaves. Poor soil defeated this venture, and the settlers retreated with their slaves to the coastal area in mid-18th century: the old plantation sites can still be detected from the air. Coffee and cotton were the main crops until the late 18th century, but sugar had become the dominant crop by 1820. In 1834 slavery was abolished. Many slaves scattered as small landholders, and settlers had to find another source of labour: indentured workers from India, a few Chinese, and some Portuguese labourers from the Azores and Madeira. At the end of their indentures many settled in Guyana.

The end of the colonial period was politically turbulent, with rioting between the mainly Indo-Guyanese People's Progressive Party (PPP), led by Dr Cheddi Jagan, and the mainly Afro-Guyanese People's National Congress (PNC), under Mr Forbes Burnham. The PNC, favoured over the PPP by the colonial authorities, formed a government in 1964 and retained office until 1992. Guyana is one of the few countries in the Caribbean where political parties have used race as an election issue. As a result, tension between the main ethnic groups has manifested itself mainly at election time.

On 26 May 1966 Guyana gained independence, and on 23 February 1970 it became a co-operative republic within the Commonwealth, adopting a new constitution. Another new constitution was adopted in 1980; this declared Guyana to be in transition from capitalism to socialism. Many industries, including bauxite and sugar, were nationalized in the 1970s and close relations with the USSR and Eastern Europe were developed. Following the death of President Forbes Burnham in August 1985, Desmond Hoyte became president. Since then, relations with the United States have improved.

Regular elections to the National Assembly and to the presidency since independence were widely criticized as fraudulent. Having been delayed since May 1991, national assembly and presidential elections were finally held on 5 October 1992. In the polling, declared free and fair by international observers, the PPP/Civic party, led by Dr Jagan, won power after 28 years in opposition. The installation of a government by democratic means was greeted with optimism and prompted foreign investors to study potential opportunities in Guyana. An economic recovery programme, part of an IMF Enhanced Structural Adjustment Facility, stimulated several years of positive gdp growth, but also seriously eroded workers' real income and hit the middle classes very hard.

In March 1997, President Jagan died after a heart attack. New elections were held on 15 December 1997, in which the PPP/Civic alliance was re-elected to power. Janet Jagan, Jagan's widow, was elected as president. The PNC, led by Desmond Hoyte, disputed the results and a brief period of violent demonstrations was ended when a Caricom (Caribbean Common Market) mission agreed to mediate between the two sides. Even though the PPP/Civic was sworn in to office on 24 December 1997, agreeing to review the constitution and hold new elections within three years, Hoyte refused to recognize Jagan as president. In August 1999 President Jagan resigned because of ill health and Minister of Finance, Bharrat Jagdeo was appointed in her place. Elections were scheduled for January 2001, but the elections commission was unprepared so the poll was postponed until 19 March 2001. During the delay, a high court judge, Claudette Singh, ruled in January 2001 that the 1997 elections had been invalid, but the opposition's delight at this news was quashed when she ruled that the PPP/Civic should continue to govern until the March vote. The PPP/Civic alliance was subsequently returned to office, with Jagdeo remaining as president.

Government A Prime Minister and cabinet are responsible to the National Assembly, which has 65 members elected for a maximum term of five years. The president is Head of State. The country is divided into 10 administrative regions.

People Total population in 2001 was estimated at 763,000, of whom just over a third were urban-based (principally Georgetown, Linden and Nieuw Amsterdam). Population growth rate between 1993 and 1998 was 0.3%. Until the 1920s there was little natural increase in population, but the eradication of malaria and other diseases has since led to rapid expansion, particularly among the East Indians (Asian), who, according to most estimates comprise about 50% of the population. Infant mortality is put at 52 per thousand live births. The 1992 census showed the following ethnic distribution: East Indian 48.3%; black 32.7%; mixed 12.2%; Amerindian 6.3%; white 0.3%; Chinese 0.2%; other 0.02%. Descendants of the original Amerindian inhabitants are divided into nine ethnic groups, including the Akawaio, Makuxi and Pemon. Some have lost their isolation and moved to the urban areas, others keenly maintain aspects of their traditional culture and identity.

Books *Jungle Cowboy* by **Stanley E Brock** (1972). *Guyana Fragile Frontier* by **Marcus Colchester** (Latin American Bureau, World Rainforest Movement and Ian Randle, 1997). *Three singles to Adventure* by **Gerald Durrell**. *The Ventriloquist's Tale* by **Pauline Melville** (1997) and works by novelists such as **Wilson Harris**, **Roy Heath** and **Fred D'Aguiar**.

Suriname

Essentials

Planning your trip **Where to go** Like its neighbours, Suriname has been influenced by a variety of cultures, African, Asian, European and Amerindian. Markets, customs, festivals and food all reflect this. In Paramaribo, the capital, there is some fine wooden architecture, dating from the Dutch colony, and important Jewish monuments. Colonial buildings can be seen elsewhere. Probably the main attraction is the tropical flora and fauna in this very sparsely populated country. Much of the interior is untouched, and infrastructure is limited. Nature reserves, such as the Central Suriname Nature Reserve, formed by the Raleigh Falls, Eilerts de Haan and Tafelberg reserves, Brownsberg, Wia-Wia and Galibi are given in the text below. You can also take trips on the rivers of the interior and visit Amerindian and Maroon (descendants of slaves) villages. See below for agencies specializing in such tours. There are no beaches to speak of; the sea and rivers around the coast are muddy, and mosquitoes can be a problem.

The high seasons, when everything is more expensive, are 15 Mar-15 May, Jul-Sep and 15 Dec-15 Jan

When to go The climate is tropical and moist, but not very hot, since the northeast trade wind makes itself felt during the whole year. In the coastal area the temperature varies on an average from 23° to 31° C, during the day; the annual mean is 27° C, and the monthly mean ranges from 26° to 28° C. The mean annual rainfall is about 2,340 mm for Paramaribo and 1,930 mm for the western division. The seasons are: minor rainy season, Nov-Feb; minor dry season, Feb-Apr; main rainy season, Apr-Aug; main dry season, Aug-Nov. None of these seasons is, however, usually either very dry or very wet. The degree of cloudiness is fairly high and the average humidity is 82. The climate of the interior is similar but with higher rainfall.

Guianas

Suriname Embassies and consulates

Belgium, *Avenue Louise 379, 1050 Brussels*, *T6401172, F6463962*.
Brazil, *SHIS-Q1, Conjunto 1, casa 6*, *71600 Brasília, T2483995, F2483791*.
Guyana, *304 Church Street, Georgetown*, *PO Box 334, T02-67844, F02-53476*.
Guyane, *38 ter Rue Christoph Colomb*, *Cayenne, T317645, F300461*.
Netherlands: *Embassy, Alexander Gogelweg 2, 2517 JH Den Haag, T3650844, F3617445; Consulate, De Cuserstraat 11, 1081 CK Amsterdam (for visas), T206-426137, F206-465311*.

Trinidad, *11 Maraval Road, 5th floor*, *Tatil Building, Port of Spain*, *T868-6280704, F868-6280086*.
USA: *Embassy, Van Ness Center*, *4301 Connecticut, NW Suite 108*, *Washington DC, 20008, T202-2447590*, *F202-2445878; Consulate, 7235 NW 19th Street, Suite A, Miami, FLA 33126*, *T305-5932163, F305-5991034*.
Venezuela, *entre 7 y 8a Transversal 41*, *Qta Los Milagros, Altamira, Caracas 1060A*, *T2631554, F2612724*.

Finding out more For information about Suriname, contact Suriname representatives abroad (see box), **Suriname Tourism Foundation**, Dr J F Nassylaan 2, T410357, stsur@sr.net, www.sr.net/users/stsur or *Stinasu* or *NV Mets*, address of both above. The *Suriname Planatlas* is out of print, but can be consulted at the National Planning office on Dr Sophie Redmondstraat; maps with natural environment and economic development topics, each with commentary in Dutch and English.

Useful websites A good starting point with lots of links is the University of Texas site http://lanic.utexas.edu/la/sa/suriname/ Many similar links can be found on www.worldskip.com/suriname/ Two useful portals are **www.surinameindex.com**, for general information on Suriname, and **www.surilinks.com/sr**, both in Dutch and English. There is also Suriname Resources at http://ourworld.compuserve.com/homepages/ OPKemp/ For news, information, forums, etc **www.surinam.net** **www.sr.net** (in Dutch and English, Suriname in general). For travel and other information try: **www.surinfo.org** (in English and Dutch), **www.surinametourism.com** (in English), **www.suriname.ch** (in German). Most portals are in Dutch, **www.sraga.com** **www.sranan.com** **www.suriname -network.com** **www.waterkant.net** **www.parbo.com** (English and Dutch) is Paramaribo-based **www.nickerie.com** is Marlon Romeo's webpage on the district of Nickerie, in English **www.moengo.com** is the webpage of the district of Moengo, in Dutch **www.conservation.org** (Conservation International) has information on Suriname.

Language The official language is Dutch. The native language, called Sranan Tongo, originally the speech of the Creoles, is now a *lingua franca* understood by all groups, and English is widely used. The Asians, Maroons and Amerindians still speak their own languages among themselves.

Getting in Documents: Visitors must have a valid passport and a visa. Nationalities which do not need a visa are: Brazil, Chile, Costa Rica, Gambia, Israel, Japan, Malaysia, Philippines, Switzerland and the Caricom countries. To obtain a visa in advance, apply to a Surinamese Embassy or Consulate (see box). You need to fill an application and present passport, a passport photo and an onward ticket (or confirmation). Procedures at consulates vary. Visas issued at the consulate in Cayenne normally take one day; two passport photos are required. In Georgetown, visa applications can be given in at any time, but only collected when the consular section is open on Monday, Wednesday and Friday morning. If applying when the consulate is open, visas are usually processed on the same day. A visa costs US$30, but costs may vary per nationality and where visa is bought. On entry to Suriname (by land or air) your passport will be stamped by the military police indicating a brief period (usually 7-10 days) for which you can remain in the country, regardless of the length of stay authorized by your visa. If you are considering a longer visit, or want a multiple entry visa (US$60), you should go as soon as possible to the Immigration Office in Paramaribo to get a second stamp in your passport and to apply for a 'blue card' (foreigner registration card): Immigration Office, van 't

Before you travel

Guianas

Hogerhuysstraat, Nieuwe Haven, Paramaribo. To get this you need a receipt for Sf10 from the Commissariat Combé, Van Sommelsdijkstraat, opposite *Torarica Hotel*, take passport and two passport photos, allow a week to get it. Mon-Fri, 0700-1430. The procedure is relatively quick and painless and you will generally be authorized a three month stay (once again the length of your entry visa seems irrelevant). If you stay more than two weeks, you should return to Immigration at that time, to collect your blue card which you can carry instead of your passport (it is prudent to carry both). You must also return here for any further extensions and for an exit authorization stamp (called 'stamp out') two days before you leave the country. The final exit stamp is again given by the military police at the airport or land border. These procedures are not usually explained to visitors on arrival. **NB** Brazilians need a certificate of vaccination against yellow fever to be allowed entry.

Customs Duty-free imports include 400 cigarettes or 100 cigars or ½ a kg of tobacco, two litres of spirits and four litres of wine, 50 g of perfume and one litre of toilet water, eight rolls of still film and 60 m of cinefilm, 100 m of recording tape, and other goods up to a value of Sf40. Personal baggage is free of duty. Customs examination of baggage can be very thorough.

What to take Lightweight tropical clothing is best, shorts and T-shirts. An umbrella is very useful. Take protection against the sun, including sunglasses. For health advice if going to the interior, see below.

Suriname

♦ **National Park**	6 Eilerts de Haan	13 Wia-Wia
1 Brownsberg	7 Galibi	
	8 Peruvia	♦ **Multiple Use Area**
♦ **Nature Reserves**	9 Raleighvallen	14 Bigi-Pan
2 Boven-Coesewijne	Voltzberg	
3 Brink-Heuvel	10 Sipaliwini	Area in dispute with
4 Copi	11 Tafelberg	Guyana & Guyane
5 Coppename Mondingh	12 Wanekreek	

0 km   50
0 miles   50

Touching down

Business hours *Shops and businesses:*
Monday-Friday 0900-1630, Saturday
0900-1300. **Government offices:**
Monday-Thursday 0700-1500, Friday
0700-1430. **Banks:** *Monday-Friday 0900-1400*
(airport bank is open when flights operate).
Official time *Three hours behind GMT.*
Voltage *110/127 volts AC, 60 cycles. Plug*
fittings: usually 2-pin round (European
continental type). Lamp fittings: screw type.

Weights and measures *The metric system*
is in general use.
IDD *597. Equal tones separated by long*
pauses mean it is ringing. Equal tones with
equal pauses mean it is engaged.
Useful telephone numbers *Police*
emergency: T115. *Other police numbers.*
T471111/7777/3101. **First Aid centre:**
Academic Hospital, T442222. **Fire Brigade:**
T473333/491111/451111.

Money **Currency:** the unit of currency is the Suriname guilder (Sf) divided into 100 cents. There are notes for 5, 10, 25, 100, 500, 1,000, 2,000, 5,000, 10,000 and 25,000 guilders. Coins are for 1 and 2.50 guilders and 1, 5, 10 and 25 cents (the 25-cent coin is usually known as a *kwartje,* 10-cent *dubbeltje,* 5-cent *stuiver* and Sf2.50 *doller*). **Exchange:** in July 1994 all exchange rates were unified and a floating rate was established at Sf183 = US\$1. In July 2002 the rate was Sf2,167 = US\$1. Dutch guilders and French francs are readily exchanged in banks and on the black market, cash only in the latter case. It is, however, illegal to change money on the black market; police pretend to be black marketeers. On arrival, change a little money at the bank in the Johan Adolf Pengel Airport (where rates are poorer than in the city), then go to the main banks, or one of the many *cambios* (exchange houses) in Paramaribo for further exchange. Officially visitors must declare their foreign currency on arrival. When arriving by land, visitors' funds are rarely checked, but you should be prepared for it. If entering Suriname from Guyana, you can change money at one of several banks in Nieuw-Nickerie. If arriving via Albina, the nearest bank, *Surinaamsche Bank,* is in Moengo, otherwise *Hakrinbank* at Tamanredjo (Commewijne), or *Multitrack Money Exchange* not far from the Jules Albert Wijdenbosch bridge in Meerzorg Commewijne. On departure, make sure you have no Suriname guilders left, they are not accepted anywhere else.

Getting there

Air *Surinam Airways* (www.slm.firm.sr) flies four times a week from Amsterdam (joint operation with *KLM*), Miami (twice a week), Belém (four times a week), Port of Spain (twice), Curaçao (twice, and *Dutch Caribbean Airlines* twice), Cayenne (four times), and Georgetown (five times a week). *Universal Airlines* flies three times a week from New York via Port of Spain. Many people go to Cayenne to take advantage of cheap *Air France* tickets to Europe as well as increased seat availability. Internal services are run by *SLM* and *Gum Air* (T498888, F497670), two small air charter firms. *Heli Jets* is a helicopter charter company at Zorg en Hoop airport.
Boat *Fyffes* banana boats sail from Portsmouth, UK, and Flushing, Holland, to Paramaribo on 13-14 day schedule, sometimes calling at Georgetown.

Touching down

Airport information **Airport tax:** There is an exit tax of US\$10, plus a terminal fee from the Departure Hall of US\$5 (ie US\$15 in total).
Safety Street crime in Paramaribo is rising: take the usual precautions with cameras, watches, etc. Avoid downtown and market areas at night unless accompanied by a local. Do not photograph military installations. If in doubt, ask first. Those travelling to the interior should ask in the capital about the safety situation in the areas they plan to visit.

Where to stay
See inside front cover for hotel grade guide

Hotels and restaurants are rare outside the capital, and you usually have to supply your own hammock and mosquito net, and food. A tent is less useful in this climate. Travelling is cheap if you change cash dollars on the black market; taking hammock and food will reduce costs.

Getting around

Air There are no scheduled flights, only charters, with *Surinam Airways, Gum Air* and *Heli Jets* helicopters. Bush flights are operated by *Surinam Airways* and *Gum Air* to several Amerindian and Maroon villages. Most settlements have an airstrip, but internal air services are limited. These flights are on demand.

Guianas

Motoring There are 2,500 km of main roads, of which 850 km are paved. East-west roads: From Albina to Paramaribo to Nieuw-Nickerie is open; buses and taxis are available (details in the text below). North-south: the road Paramaribo-Paranam-Afobaka-Pokigron is open. The road to the western interior, Zanderij-Apura, crosses the Coppename River; thereafter small bridges are in poor shape (take planks to bridge gaps). On the unpaved Moengo-Blakawatra road (eastern Suriname), the bridge across the Commewijne River is closed to traffic. **Self-Drive Cars** *Avis*, Fred O'Kirkstraat, T450447/807090, F456392; *Hertz* at *Real Car*, Van 't Hogerhuysstraat 19, T402833, ckcmotor@sr.net, *U-Drive* Car rental, T490803, and other agencies such as *City Taxi*, *Purperhart*, *Kariem*, *Intercar*. All driving licences accepted, but you need a stamp from the local police and a deposit. There is a 24 hour emergency service for motorists: *Wegenwacht*, Sr Winston Churchillweg 123, T484691/487540. Gasoline/petrol is sold as diesel, 'regular', unleaded, or super unleaded (more expensive). **Bicycles** can be bought from *A Seymonson*, Rijwielhersteller, Rust en Vredestraat. Recommended rides from Paramaribo include to Nieuw-Amsterdam, Marienburg, Alkmaar and back via Tamanredjo in the Javanese Commewijne district or from Rust en Werk to Spieringshoek to Reijnsdorp (3½ hours) and return to Leonsberg via ferry, whence it is a 30 minutes to Paramaribo. Driving is on the left, but many vehicles have left-hand drive. To drive a foreign registered vehicle requires no *carnet* or other papers. People wishing to travel from Suriname to either Guyana of Guiane by car need special vehicle insurance, available from *Assuria Insurance Company*, Gravenstraat 5-7, Paramaribo. T473400, www.assuria.sr

NB Although an international driver's license is accepted in both Suriname and Guyana, a special permit is required to drive a vehicle in the two countries for longer than one month.

Hitchhiking This is not common, but it is possible.

Ferry The ferries across the main rivers operate only in daytime (the Paramaribo-Meerzorg ferry until 2200; the new Jules Albert Wijdenbosch bridge across the Suriname River is open, but the ferry still runs). The *Suriname Navigation Co* (SMS) has a daily service, leaving 0700, on the Commewijne River (a nice four hour trip; one can get off at *De Nieuwe Grond*, a plantation owned by an English couple, and stay overnight). The *SMS* ferry to Alliance/Reynsdorp leaves on Wednesday, Friday, Saturday or Sunday at 0700. SMS also has infrequent services on other rivers (Wayombo and Cottica).

NB It is advisable to check the weather conditions and probabilities of returning on schedule before you set out on a trip to the interior. Heavy rains can make it impossible for planes to land in some jungle areas; little or no provision is made for such delays and it can be a long and hungry wait for better conditions.

Keeping in touch

Internet *Telesur* (see below) offers internet services at its several branches, except the head office. Another important supplier of internet services is *Carib*, with branches in the synagogue at the Heerenstraat, the Hermitage Mall, Kwattaweg, Lelydorp and in Commewijne.

Post Post is quick and reliable. *Surpost*, surpost@sr.net or havenpost@sr.net Letters must be franked at the post office and posted the same day (no stamps sold). Both postal and telecommunications charges are very low at the black market exchange rate. *DHL*, Van 't Hogerhuysstraat 55, Paramaribo, T474007, 473990, dhl@sr.net *Federal Express*, Hermitage Mall, Lalla Rookweg at Uitvlugt, Paramaribo, T474436, F474696.

Telephone Telephone cards for international, local and cellular calls can be bought at the local phone company, *Telesur*, Heiligenweg 1, Paramaribo (near the fountain, downtown) and its branches, or in supermarkets nationwide, T474242, www.sr.net For information, open 0700-1500, Monday-Friday. *AT&T's* USA Direct is available for collect calls from any phone; dial 156, 24 hour service. For Dutch *PTT Holland Direct*, dial 157, 24 hours. Send or receive faxes through *Telesur*, T151 for information, 0700-2400 daily. Cellular phones with *Telesur*-ready connection can be purchased via *Telesur*, Nieuwe Haven, and its outlets in Paramaribo, such as *Cell Star* (Saramaccastraat) and *Boembox* (opposite *Hotel Krasnapolsky*). Public telephone booths are widely available in Paramaribo. They do not accept coins, but phone cards for cellular, local and international calls.

Media Newspapers: These are in Dutch, *De Ware Tijd* (morning, articles in English on www.dwt.net) and De West *DeWest* (evening), www.dewestonline.com **Radio**: Radio Zon

Guianas

(107.5 FM) has news bulletins in English at 1800. Radio Paramaribo (89.7 FM) broadcasts Voice of America after 0100 daily. Zon and Paramaribo broadcast 24 hours, as do Apintie (www.apintie.sr), ABC (www.abcsuriname.com), Trishul (www.trishul.sr), Radio SRS, Radio Garuda (broadcasts in Javanese), Radio Kankantrie, B104 (popular music), Radio Sangeet Mala (broadcasts in *sarnami*, the local Hindu language), and Radio 10. **Television**: There are 11 stations, ABC (www.abcsuriname.com), ATV (24 hours, www.atv.sr), STVS (1500-2400, www.stvs.info.sr), SCCN and Apintie (1800-2400), broadcasting in Dutch and English; RBN, Radhika, Trishul (24 hours www.trishul.sr), Ramasha Media Group (RMG) and Sangeet Mala broadcasting in *sarnami*; and Garuda TV broadcasting in Javanese. In Nickerie the TV station is RTV. All are in colour. ATV, ABC and STVS have good coverage of international sports, especially football; ATV, ABC, Apintie and Trishul carry CNN in English and Trishul carries BBC World. Cable TV available. ATV, ABC, Trishul, Apintie offer live stream broadcasts via internet through their respective web pages.

Surinamese cuisine is as rich and varied as the country's ethnic makeup. Rice is the main **Food & drink** staple and of very high quality. Cassava, sweet potatoes, plantain, and hot red peppers are widely used. *Pom* is a puree of the tayer root (a relative of cassava) tastily spiced and served with *kip* (chicken). *Moksie Alesie* is rice mixed with meat, chicken, white beans, tomatoes, peppers and spices. *Pindasoep* (peanut soup with plantain dumplings, also with plantain noodles) and *okersoep met tayerblad* (gumbo and cassava soup) are both worth a try. *Petjil* are vegetables cooked in peanut sauce. Well known Indonesian dishes include *bami* (fried noodles) and *nassie goreng* (fried rice), both spicy with a slightly sweet taste. Among the Hindustani dishes are *roti* (a crêpe wrapped around curried potatoes, vegetables and chicken), *somosa* (fried pastry filled with spicy potatoes and vegetables), and *phulawri* (fried chick-pea balls). Among the many tropical fruits of Suriname, palm nuts such as the orange coloured awarra and the cone shaped brown maripa are most popular.

Public holidays 1 January, *New Year*; *Holi Phagwa* (Hindu spring festival, date varies each **Holidays &** year, generally in March, very interesting but watch out for throwing of water, paint, talc and **festivals** coloured powder); Good Friday; Easter (two days); 1 May (*Labour Day*); 1 July (*Emancipation Day*); Diwali (Hindu Festival of Light in October); 25 November (*Independence Day*); Christmas (two days). For Moslem holidays see note under Guyana. **Festivals** Avond Vierdaagse starts on the first Wednesday after Easter, a carnival parade of the young and old dressed in traditional costume or simple clothes; it is organized by Bedrijven Vereniging Sport en Spel (BVVS), Johannes Mungrastraat 48, Paramaribo, T461020. Surifesta (www.surifesta.com) is a year-end festival, from mid-December to the first week of January, with shows, street parties, flower markets, culminating in *Het Vat* (www.vat.cq-link.sr) on 31 December.

Boil or purify water, even in the capital, as water-borne diseases are present. Otherwise, no **Health** special precautions necessary except for a trip to the malarial interior; for free malaria *See also Health in* prophylaxis contact the Public Health Department (BOG, 15 Rode Kruislaan), but better to *Essentials at the* take your own. *METS, Stinasu* and *Suriname Safari Tours* provide malaria prophylaxis on their *beginning of the book* package tours. Chloroquine-resistant malaria occurs in the interior. Mosquito nets should be used at night over beds in rooms not air-conditioned or screened. In some coastal districts there is a risk of bilharzia (schistosomiasis). Ask before bathing in lakes and rivers. Vaccinations: yellow fever and tetanus advisable, typhoid only for trips into the interior. Swim only in running water because of poisonous fish. There is good swimming on the Marowijne and Coppename Rivers. There are four hospitals in Paramaribo, best is **St Vincentius**, Koninginnestraat 4, T471212, F473148.

Guianas

Paramaribo

Colour map 2, grid B5
Population: 257,000

The capital and chief port, lies on the Suriname River, 12 km from the sea. There are many attractive colonial buildings. The **Governor's Mansion** (now the Presidential Palace) is on Onafhankelijkheidsplein (also called Eenheidsplein and, originally, Oranjeplein). Many beautiful 18th and 19th century buildings in Dutch (neo-Normanic) style are in the same area. A few have been restored but much of the old city is sadly decaying.

Ins & outs

*For more detailed
information see
Transport, page 1472*

Getting there The airport is 47 km south. Minibuses charge Sf2,000 and taxis Sf10,000 to the city. There is no central bus station; see **Transport**, below, for details.

Getting around There are very few regular **buses**; the few services that are left leave from Heiligenweg. There are privately run 'wild buses', also known as 'numbered buses' which run on fixed routes around the city; they are minivans and are severely overcrowded. **Taxis** generally have no meters. The price should be agreed on beforehand to avoid trouble. If hiring a taxi for touring, beware of overcharging. If you're a hotel guest, let the hotel make arrangements.

There is a **tourist information centre** next to the Cabinet office of the President on Zeelaniaweg by the entrance of the Fort Zeelandia complex. It has information on the country, tour operators and advice on tours.

Sights

Fort Zeelandia houses the Suriname Museum, restored to this purpose after being repossessed by the military. The whole complex has been opened to the public again and its historic buildings can be visited. The fort itself now belongs to the Stichting (foundation) Surinaams Museum, and is generally in good condition. The old wooden officers' houses in the same complex have been restored with Dutch finance. Very few exhibits remain in the old museum in the residential suburb of Zorg en Hoop, Commewijnestraat. ■ *0700-1300, US$0.75, guided tours on Sat at*

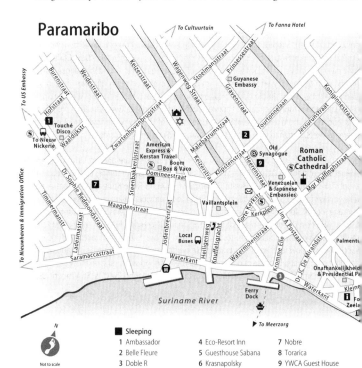

Paramaribo

Sleeping ■		
1 Ambassador	4 Eco-Resort Inn	7 Nobre
2 Belle Fleure	5 Guesthouse Sabana	8 Torarica
3 Doble R	6 Krasnapolsky	9 YWCA Guest House

Guianas

1100 and 1200. Look for Mr F H R Lim A Postraat if you wish to see what Paramaribo looked like only a comparatively short time ago. The 19th century **Roman Catholic St Peter and Paul Cathedral** (1885), built entirely of wood, is said to be the largest wooden building in the Americas, but it has been closed indefinitely for repairs since 1993. Much of the old town, dating from the 19th century, and the churches have been restored. Other things to see are the colourful **market** and the waterfront, **Hindu temples** in Koningstraat and Wanicastraat (finally completed after years of construction), one of the Caribbean's largest **mosques** at Keizerstraat (magnificent photos of it can be taken at sunset). There are two **synagogues**: one next to the mosque at Keizerstraat 88, the other (1854) on the corner of Klipstenstraat and Heerenstraat (closed, now houses an internet café and IT business unit). A new harbour has been constructed about 1½ km upstream. Two pleasant parks are the **Palmentuin**, with a stage for concerts, and the **Cultuurtuin** (with poorly-kept zoo owing to lack of funds, US$1.20, busy on Sunday), the latter is a 20 minute walk from the centre. National dress is normally only worn by the Asians on national holidays and at wedding parties, but some Javanese women still go about in sarong and klambi. A university (Anton de Kom Universiteit van Suriname) was opened in 1968. There is one public swimming pool at Weidestraat, US$0.60 per person. There is an exotic Asian flavour the market area.

An interesting custom practised throughout Suriname is the birdsong competitions, held in parks and plazas on Sunday and holidays. People carrying their songbird (usually a small black tua-tua) in a cage are frequently seen; on their way to and from work, to a 'training session', or simply taking their pet for a stroll!

L-AL *Torarica*, Mr Rietbergplein, T471500, PO Box 1514, www.torarica.com Best in town, very pleasant, book ahead, swimming pool and other sports facilities, sauna, casino, nightclub, tropical gardens, a/c, central, 3 expensive restaurants (*Plantation Room*, European; *Saramacca Bar*, with live entertainment; good poolside buffet on Fri evening), superb breakfast, business centre with internet, fax facilities. **L-AL** *Krasnapolsky*, Domineestraat 39, T475050, www.krasnapolsky.sr A/c, central, travel agency, shopping centre, exhibition hall in the lobby, good breakfast and buffet, *Atrium* restaurant for local and international cuisine (mid-range), *Rumours Grand Café* (with jazz jam sessions on Tue and Fri), poolside bar, business centre with internet, fax facilities, takes Amex, swimming pool.

A-B *Ambassador*, Dr Sophie Redmondstraat 66-68, T477555, F477688. A/c, including breakfast, good 24 hr restaurant (mid-range), casino. **A** *De Luifel*, Gondastraat 13 (about 15 mins from centre), T439933, F439930. A/c, warm water, cable TV, mid-priced European restaurant, special `business-to-business' deal: 1 night with breakfast, laundry, airport transfer, car hire and taxes included, US$99, Amex accepted. **A** *Eco-Resort Inn*, Cornelis Jongbawstraat 16, PO Box 2998, T425522, www.ecores.com Use of *Torarica* facilities, restaurant (mid-range), bar, Ms Maureen Libanon is very helpful, business centre, with internet and fax. **A** *Shereday*, Cornelis Prinsstraat 87, T434564, F463844, 5 km from centre.

Sleeping
Service charge at hotels is 5-10%
Beware: many cheap hotels not listed are 'hot pillow' establishments

● **Eating**
1 La Bastille
2 'T VAT
3 Warungs & Uncle Ray

Guianas

Exercise floor, swimming pool, restaurant/bar (mid-range), good reports. **A** *Residence Inn*, Anton Dragtenweg 7, T472387, www.metsresorts.com TV, minibar, laundry, including breakfast, credit cards accepted, in a residential area, pool, tennis court, a/c bar and *Atlantis* restaurant, European and Surinamese food (mid-range).

B *Guesthouse Amice*, Gravenberchstraat 5 (10 mins from centre), T434289, www.guest-house-amice.sr (in Netherlands, Robijndrift 47, 3436 BR Nieuwegein, T030-294 5229, amice@worldonline.nl). Room with balcony more expensive, quiet neighbourhood, a/c, comfortable, email/internet facilities, breakfast, airport transfer and tours available.

C *Doble R*, Kleine Waterstraat opposite *Torarica*, T473592. A/c, good value, but noisy bar downstairs, cheap restaurant, often full. The Suriname Museum in Zorg-en-Hoop now has a good guest house; book in advance. **C** *Guesthouse Sabana*, Kleine Waterstraat 7, T424158, F310022, opposite *Torarica*. A/c, safe, helpful.

D *Belle Fleure*, Heerenstraat 28, T424370/453318. Very clean. For budget travellers, best is **D** *YWCA Guesthouse* at Heerenstraat 14-16, T476981. Cheaper weekly rates, full of permanent residents, essential to book in advance (office open 0800-1400), safe, cheap local snackbar.

Otherwise, try **E** *Fanna*, Prinsessestraat 31, T476789. From a/c with bath to basic, breakfast extra, safe, family run, English spoken. **E** *Mivimost*, Anamoestraat 23, 3 km from centre, T451002. A/c, cheaper with fan, toilet, safe. Recommended.

F *Nobre*, Dr Sophie Redmondstraat 24, T420277, F424147. Central, withfan, cheap self-service restaurant (food sold by weight), bar, good. *Mrs Robles' Guesthouse*, Rooseveltkade 20, T474770. Family run. *Balden*, Kwattaweg 183, 2 km from centre on the road to Nickerie is probably the cheapest available accommodation; its Chinese restaurant serves cheap meals. A religious organization, Stadszending, Burenstraat 17-19, T47307, **F**, good location, best to reserve. The *Salvation Army*, Saramaccastraat, will give the hard up a bed for a minimal price. Mrs Rudia Shair-Ali, Toenalaan 29, 20 min walk from centre, not a hotel but a large private house: Mrs Shair-Ali charges US$1-2 a night, free use of kitchen.

Eating

Unless otherwise stated, restaurants listed are mid-range, US$5-12 Meat and noodles from stalls in the market are very cheap

There are some good restaurants, mainly Indonesian and Chinese dishes. Blauwgrond is the area for typical Indonesian food, served in *warungs* (the Indonesian name for restaurants, cheap). Try a *rijsttafel* in an **Indonesian** restaurant, eg *Sarinah* (open-air dining), Verlengde Gemenelandsweg 187. *Bali*, Ma Retraiteweg 3, T422325. Very good food, service and atmosphere, check bill. *Jawa*, Kasabaholoweg 7. Famous Indonesian restaurant. *De Smaak*, Sommelsdijckstraat 38 (cheap). Javanese foodstalls on Waterkant are excellent and varied, lit at night by candles. Try *bami* (spicy noodles) and *petjil* (vegetables), especially recommended on Sun when the area is busiest. In restaurants a dish to try is *gadogado*, an Indonesian vegetable and peanut concoction. **Others**: *La Bastille*, Kleine Waterstraat, opposite *Torarica*, T473991. Also opposite *Torarica*, **Restaurant 'T VAT'**. *Golden Dragon*, Anamoestraat 22. *Golden Crown*, David Simmonstraat. *Fa Tai*, Maagdenstraat 64. A/c. *Oriental Foods*, Gravenstraat 118. *Chi Min*, Cornelis Jongbawstraat 83. For well-prepared Chinese food. Recommended. Many other Chinese restaurants. *Tori Oso* (literally 'Chat House'), Rust en Vredestraat 76. Popular venue for good conversation. *Natura*, Rust en Vredestraat between Keizerstraat and Weidestraat. Whole-grain bread and natural foods. **Cheap**: *Grand Café Vaillant* and *Un Patu* in *Un Mall*, opposite *Telesur* in Vaillantsplein. *Roja's*, corner of Mahonielaan and Grote Combéweg. Good places for lunch include *Cartousj Terras*, Domineestraat. For breakfast, try *Klein Maar Fijn*, Watermolenstraat. **Fast food**: *Kentucky Fried Chicken*, Wilhelminastraat 62 and Waterkant 74-76, *McDonalds*, Keizerstraat 62-64, *Pizza Hut*, Wilhelminastraat 62 (expensive), *Popeye's*, in *Hotel Krasnapolsky* building, Domineestraat 39, and Texaco Station near Jules Albert Wijdenbosch bridge across Suriname River. *Power Smoothie*, Zwartenhovenbrugstraat and Wilhelminastraat (next to *Pizza Hut*), specializing in healthy fast food. *Royal Castle*, Jodenbreestraat. Trinidadian fast food. *Naskip*, Gravenstraat near 's Lands Hopsitaal, and *Shelly's*, Tourtonnelaan and Latour. Both for local fast food. *Uncle Ray* at Waterkant by the Javanese *warungs*, opposite Central Bank of Suriname. Local Creole food. The local **beer** is called *Parbo*; imported *Heineken* is more expensive. The local **rums** are *Borgoe* (popular), and *Black Cat*.

Discos: *Touché*, Waaldijk/Dr Sophie Redmondstraat 60. Fri and Sat only 2300, small restaurant and the best disco. Other discos are *Millennium*, H J de Vriesstraat, near *Pizza Hut*, popular with `mature' clientele, has *The Grill Eatery*, mid-priced fast food. *Club Baya*, next to *Pizza Hut*, `mature' clientele, and *Energy*, Hermitageweg, Paramaribo-Zuid, younger crowd. There are many Brazilian girls seeking European husbands and several nightclubs cater for this trade. A good one where it is not blatant is *El Condor*, Zwartenhovenbrugstraat 158, not far from *Ambassador Hotel*. A/c, clean, restaurant, soft music, often full. Many other clubs. There are many **casinos** in the city, including at major hotels. **Cinema** *Un Kino*, new, showing US, European, Indian and Chinese films. In *Un Mall*, opposite *Telesur* in Vaillantsplein. Also *Tower* (Heerenstraat), showing local productions.

Entertainment

Crafts of Amerindian and Maroon origin. **Arts & Crafts**, Neumanpad 13a. Amerindian goods, batik prints, carvings, basket work, drums are attractive. *Cultuurwinkel*, Anton de Komstraat. Bosneger carvings, also available at *Hotel Torarica*. Carvings are better value at the workshops on Nieuwe Domineestraat and the Neumanpad. Many jewellers' shops in the centre sell good pieces at reasonable prices. Local ceramics are sold on the road between the airport and Paranam, but they are rather brittle. The following sell international and local music on CD (the latter is heavily influenced by Caribbean styles): *Disco Amigo*, Wagenwegstraat, opposite Theater Star, *Boom Box*, Domineestraat, opposite *Krasnapolsky Hotel* and *Beat Street* in the H J de Vries mall. Old Dutch bottles are sold. **Bookshops**: the 2 main bookshops are *Vaco* (opposite *Krasnapolsky*) and *Kersten*, both on Domineestraat, and both sell English-language books. Also *Hoeksteen* (Gravenstraat 17) and the kiosk in *Krasnapolsky Hotel*. *Boekhandel Univers NV*, Gravenstraat 61, is recommended for nature, linguistic and scholarly books on Suriname. Second-hand books, English and Dutch, are bought and sold in the market. Maps are hard to find, but try *Vaco*. Cheap film at *Photo Max*, 37 Domineestraat, next to *Krasnapolsky Hotel*.

Shopping

NV Mets (Movement for Eco-Tourism in Suriname), PO Box 9080, Anton Dragtenweg 7, Paramaribo, T477088, mets@sr.net, www.metsresorts.com Also in Cayenne, 15 rue Louis Blanc, T317298, F305786; in Georgetown contact *Wilderness Explorers* (see page 1453), the general sales agent for Surinam Airways and Mets in Guyana. Organizes trips to the interior at reasonable rates. Tours offered are City Tour, Rivercruise, Santigron (all day trips); 4/5 day trips to Tukunari Island; 4/5-day trips to Palumeu (see below) staying in lodges; 8-day trip to Mount Kasikasima in remote southern Suriname (all transport, food and guides – good – included, US$625).
   Stinasu is the Foundation for Nature Preservation in Suriname, Cornelis Jongbawstraat 14, T476597/421683/427102, F422555, PO Box 12252, Paramaribo, fnps@sr.net, www.stinasu.sr It offers reasonably priced accommodation and provides tour guides on the extensive nature reserves throughout the country. One can see 'true wilderness and wildlife' with them. Recommended.
   Amar's Tours, Estabrielstraat 16, T400372. History and cultural tours to Jodensavanne, Brownsberg, Braamspunt, Raleighvallen, Blanche Marievallen Falls. *Arinze Tours*, Prinsessestraat 2c, T425960, arinze@sr.net, www.arinzetours.com Tours to Maroon villages of Santigron, manager George Lazo. *Cardy Adventures*, Cornelis Jongbawstraat 31, T422518, www.cardytours.com Bicycle rental (bikerental@cardytours.com) and tours to Commewijne district, and tours to Brownsberg, Raleigh Falls, Matapica and jungle survival trips, English spoken, very helpful and efficient, excellent food. *Libase Tours*, van Idsingastraat 101, T480180, libase@sr.net (Bernard Abia). Specializes in tours to the interior (villages such as Jaw Jaw, Gunsi). *Ma-Ye-Du*, Matoeliestraat 22, T/F410348. For tours to Maroon villages in the Marowijne River. *Paradise*, Keizerstraat 15, T424122. Eco tours, trips to Albina Amerindian communities. *Ram's Tours & Travel Service*, Neumanpad 30, T476011, F472411. Tours in Suriname and abroad. *Saramaccan Jungle Safaris* (John Ligeon), PO Box 676, Zwartenhovenbrugstraat 19. For visits by canoe to Saramaccan Maroon villages and wildlife tours. *Sun and Forest Tours*, Gravenstraat 155, T478383, www.surinamesunforest.com Specializes in tours to the interior (office in the Netherlands, 1020 Mk Amsterdam, PO Box 36401, T206 373103, F204 923601). *Suriname Safari Tours*, Dr

Tour operators

Guianas

S S Kaffiludistraat 27, T400925, F455768. Has excursions to the interior. *Waldo's Travel Service*, Heerenstraat 8, T422530, F424844, www.waldostravel.sr For all tours within Suriname. *Wild Coast Expeditions*, Prinsessestraat 37, T454522, wildexp@sr.net Boat tours to Jodensavanne, Galibi, New Amsterdam, Matapica and Braamspunt. At the same address is *Access Suriname Travel*, T424522, www.surinametravel.com, which sells all major tours in Suriname and can supply general travel information on the country, manager Syrano Zalman is helpful.

NB If intending to take a tour to the jungle and either Amerindian or Maroon villages, check how much time is spent in the jungle itself and on the conditions in the villages. One such trip is to Palumeu, an Amerindian village (Trio, Wajana and Akurio peoples) due south of Paramaribo, not far from the Brazilian border. Four-day, three-night packages include flights, food, accommodation, jungle hikes and boat trips.

Transport **Long distance** **Air**: The Johan Pengel International Airport is 47 km south of Paramaribo. Minibus to town costs Sf2,000 (eg *De Paarl*, T403610); taxi costs Sf10,000/US$14 (*Ashruf*, T454451), but negotiate. *Hotel Torarica, Eco Resort Inn* and *Residence Inn* offer free transfers to and from the international airport for guests with room reservation. *Surinam Airways*, Dr Sophie Redmondstraat 219, T432700, F434723. (At Pengel Airport T03-25181, F03-25292.) There is a guest house near the airport. Internal flights leave from Zorg en Hoop airfield in a suburb of Paramaribo (take minibus 8 or 9 from Steenbakkerijstraat).

Verify all fares in advance and beware of overcharging

Buses: To **Nickerie** from Dr Sophie Redmondstraat, near *Hotel Ambassador*, minibuses leave when full between 0500 and 1000. There are also buses after 1200, but the price then depends on the driver, 4-5 hrs, extra for large bag. Taxis from the same area are slightly faster. Buses to **Albina** from Paramaribo cross the new bridge; bus station located near ferry service in Paramaribo (take an APB or PBA bus, which has a plainclothes policeman on board). Taxis are available, but dishonest (usually). There are irregular bus services to other towns. For full details ask drivers or enquire at the tourist office. There is much jostling in the queues and pure mayhem when boarding vehicles. They are all minivans and have no luggage space. Try to put bags under your seat or you will have to hold it in your lap.

Directory **Banks** *Finabank*, Dr Sophie Redmondstraat 61, opposite *Ambassador Casino*. *Hakrinbank*, Dr Sophie
Don't use money changers in the market and on the street, who approach you calling 'wissel' (exchange) They are illegal and many visitors have been robbed or cheated
Redmondstraat 11-13, www.hakrinbank.com 0700-1400. *Royal Bank of Trinidad and Tobago, RBTT*, Kerkplein 1, www.rbtt.com Cash on Visa *Surinaamsche Bank*, Gravenstraat 26-30, www.dsbbank.sr Cash on Visa. *Surinaamse Postspaar Bank*, Heiligenweg near bus station. *Volks Crediet Bank*, Waterkant 104. All banks except *Finabank* are closed on Sat. Amex agent is C Kersten and Co, NV, in Kersten Travel building opposite *Hotel Krasnapolsky*, T477148. *Cambios* for exchange, open evenings and on Sat: *De Vries*, Waterkant 92-94; *Dallex*, Keizerstraat 8; *Surichange*, Dr Sophie Redmondstraat 71, *Yokohama Drive Through*, Saramaccastraat (open Sun), *Surora Drive Through*, Gravenstraat opposite 's Lands Hospitaal. There is also a *cambio* opposite *Hotel Torarica* (open Sun).
Embassies and consulates Brazil, Maratakkastraat 2, T400200, F400205, brasaemb1@sr.net **British Honorary Consul**, c/o VSH United Buildings, PO Box 1300, Van't Hogerhuysstraat 9-11, T402870, F403515, united@sr.net **Canadian consulate**, Wagenwegstraat 50b, 1st floor, PO Box 1449, T424527, F425962, cantim@sr.net **Netherlands**, Roseveltkade 5, T477211, F477792, nlgovprm@sr.net **France**, Gravenstraat 5-7, T476455. **Guyana**, Gravenstraat 82, T477895, F472679, guyembassy@ sr.net **Japan**, Gravenstraat 23-25, T474860, F412208, eojparbo@sr.net **USA**, Dr Sophie Redmondstraat 129, PO Box 1821, T472900, F410025, consul F425788, embsur@erols.com **Venezuela**, Gravenstraat 23-25, T475401, F475602, resvensu@sr.net

Excursions **Accaribo** resort, about one hour by car from the capital on the Suriname River, near the villages of La Vigilantia and Accaribo: seven rooms with bath, visit Amerindian settlement, pottery making, swimming in the river, Creole and Javanese cultures. **Powaka**, about 90 minutes outside the capital, is a primitive village of thatched huts but with electric light and a small church. In the surrounding forest one can pick mangoes and other exotic fruit. An interesting half, or full day excursion is to take minibus 4, or taxi, to **Leonsberg** on the Suriname River (*Stardust Hotel*, www-hotelstardust.com with mid-priced restaurant, coffee shop, swimming pool,

Guianas

games; restaurant *Rusty Pelikan* on waterfront; at *Leonsberg* restaurant try *saoto* soup and other Javanese specialities, overlooking the river), then ferry to **Nieuw-Amsterdam**, the capital of the predominantly Javanese district of Commewijne. There is an open-air museum inside the old fortress which guarded the confluence of the Suriname and Commewijne rivers (badly rundown, open only in mornings except Friday, 1700-1900). There are some interesting old plantation mansions left in the Commewijne district.

Braamspunt, a peninsula with nice beaches at the mouth of the Suriname River, is 10 km from Paramaribo. Boats from the Leonsberg scaffold go down river.

You can go by private car to **Jodensavanne** (Jews' Savanna, established 1639), south of Paramaribo on the opposite bank of the Suriname River, where a cemetery and the foundations of one of the oldest synagogues in the Western Hemisphere have been restored. There is no public transport and taxis won't go because of the bad road. It is still only 1½ hours with a suitable vehicle (see above for tours). There is a bridge across the Suriname River to Jodensavanne. **Blakawatra** is said to be one of the most beautiful spots in all Suriname (shame about the amount of rubbish strewn around). This was the scene of much fighting in the civil war. A full day trip to Jodensavanne and Blakawatra, returning to Paramaribo via Moengo, has been recommended if you can arrange the transport. Bus to Blakawatra at 0800, three hours, Sf500. Some 5 km from the International Airport there is a resort called **Colakreek**, so named for the colour of the water, but good for swimming (busy at weekends), lifeguards, water bicycles, children's village, restaurant, bar, tents or huts for overnight stay, entry Sf500. The village Bersaba, 40 km from Paramaribo close to the road to the airport, is popular area for the Coropinakreek. Many people go there and the neighbouring village of Republiek at weekends and on holidays. At Bersaba are the fully-furnished **AL-B** *Hendrison Bungalows*, contact address Andresietsstraat 4, Paramaribo T/F457391 (Rodenryselaan 403, 3037 XG Rotterdam, T104-66414, F104-664132), www.hendrison.com

Approximately 30 km southwest of Paramaribo, via **Lelydorp** (*Hotel De Lely*, Sastrodisomoweg 41; *The Lely Hills* casino), is the Bush Negro village of **Santigron**, on the east bank of the Saramacca River. Minibuses leave Paramaribo at 0530 and 1500, two hours, Sf200. They return as soon as they drop off passengers in the village, so make sure you will have a bus to return on; there is no accommodation in Santigron. Nearby is the Amerindian village of **Pikin Poika**. The two make a good independent day trip. Tour agencies also visit the area about twice a month, including canoe rides on the Saramacca River and a Bush Negro dance performance.

By bus or car to **Afobakka**, where there is a large hydroelectric dam on the Suriname River. There is a government guest house (price includes three meals a day) in nearby **Brokopondo**. Victoria is an oil-palm plantation in the same area.

The hills of **Brownsberg National Park**, an hour by car from Brokopondo, overlook the Professor Dr Ir van Blommensteinmeer reservoir. It features good walking and three impressive waterfalls. ■ *US$1.20*. Stinasu run all-inclusive tours from Paramaribo (one and three-day tours, price includes transport, accommodation, food, and guide). Independent visits are possible. Buses for Brownsweg leave Paramaribo daily at 0800, two hours, rate not fixed. Go to Stinasu at least 24 hours in advance and pay for accommodation in their guest houses (US$35, or US$5 to camp) or to arrange for a vehicle to pick you up in Brownsweg (US$30). Take your own food.

Tukunari Island, in van Blommesteinmeer lake, is about three hours drive from Paramaribo to Brokopondo then a two hours canoe ride. The island is near the village of Lebi Doti, where Aucaner Maroons live. Tours with NV Mets include fishing, visits to villages, jungle treks and visits to rapids.

Raleighvallen/Voltzberg Nature Reserve (78,170 ha) is a rainforest park, southwest of Paramaribo, on the Coppename River. It includes Foengoe Island in the river and Voltzberg peak; climbing the mountain at sunrise is unforgettable. The reserve can be reached by air, or by road (180 km) followed by a 3-4 hour boat ride. This reserve has been joined with Tafelberg and Eilerts de Haan reserves to create the Central Suriname Nature Reserve (1.592 million ha – 9.7% of Suriname's total land area). The Reserve is now part of the Unesco's World Heritage List (www.unesco.org). New tourist facilities have been opened. Stinasu does a US$10 tour, or can arrange all-inclusive tours with accommodation, transport, food and guides. **Stoelmanseiland**, on the Lawa River in the interior, and the Maroon villages and rapids in the area can be visited on an organized tour. Price US$170 per person for three days (five persons, minimum). They are, however, more easily reached by river from St-Laurent du Maroni and Maripasoula in Guyane.

West of Paramaribo

A narrow but paved road leads through the citrus and vegetable growing areas of **Wanica** and **Saramaca**, linked by a bridge over the Saramaca River. At **Boskamp** (90 km from Paramaribo) is the Coppename River. The Coppename bridge crosses to **Jenny** on the west bank. The **Coppename Estuary** is a national park, protecting many bird colonies.

A further 50 km is **Totness**, where there was once a Scottish settlement. It is the largest village in the Coronie district, along the coast between Paramaribo and Nieuw-Nickerie on the Guyanese border. There is a good government guesthouse. The road (bad, liable to flooding) leads through an extensive forest of coconut palms. Bus to Paramaribo at 0600. 40 km further west, 5 km south of the main road is **Wageningen**, a modern little town, the centre of the Suriname rice-growing area. The road from Nickerie has been renewed. One of the largest fully mechanized rice farms in the world is found here (*Hotel de Wereld*, T0251544). The **Bigi-Pan** area of mangroves is a birdwatchers' paradise; boats may be hired from local fishermen.

Nieuw-Nickerie
Colour map 2, grid B4
Population: over 8,000
(district 45,000,
mostly East Indian)
237 km from
Paramaribo

Situated on the south bank of the Nickerie River 5 km from its mouth, opposite Guyana, is the main town and port of the Nickerie district and is distinguished for its ricefields. It is a clean and ordered town, but there are a lot of mosquitoes. There are five banks on the park, R P Bharosstraat with Landingstraat, and at the corner of Gouverneurstraat and Oost-Kanaalstraat. *Finabank* is in the *Residence Inn Nickerie* building. Post and Telephone offices are on Oost-Kanaalstraat, between Gouverneurstraat and R P Bharosstraat. Business hours are 0700-1500, shops 0800-1300, 1600-1900. **NB** If phoning within town, omit 0 from prefix. ■ *For bus services, see under Paramaribo. The bus station is next to the market on G G Maynardstraat.*

Sleeping and eating A-B *Residence Inn*, R P Bharosstraat 84, PO Box 4330, T0210950/1, F0210954, www.metsresorts.com Best in town, prices higher at weekend, central, a/c, bath, hot water, TV, business centre with email (US$5 per hr), internet access (US$7 per hr), fax (US$0.35 national only), laundry, good restaurants (*De Palm* and *Café de Tropen*, both mid-range), bar. **C** *Ameerali*, Maynardstraat 32-36, T0231212, F31066. A/c, good, mid-priced restaurant/bar. **C** *De Vesting*, Balatastraat 6, T0231265. **E** *De President*, Gouverneurstraat. Cheaper without bath, a/c, good value. **F** *Tropical*, Gouverneurstraat 114, T231796. Noisy bar downstairs. **Discos**: *Zeppelin* is the best, on the road out towards Paramaribo.

Tour operators *Manoetje Tours*, Crownstraat 11, Nieuw-Nickerie, T231991 (Hans Overeem). Boat tours to, among other places, Apura, Orealla, Corantijn.

Border with Guyana
Suriname is 1 hr
ahead of Guyana

Ferry to Springlands From South Drain (Suriname, 40 km from Nieuw-Nickerie) to Moleson/Crabwood Creek (Guyana). The 30-minute crossing is at 1000 only, US$8, cars US$15, pick ups US$20. (Immigration forms are handed out on the boat.) Bus Paramaribo-South Drain: *Le Grand Baldew*, Tourtonnelaan 59, Paramaribo, T474713, F421164, www.baldew.com (can organize trips through to Georgetown, four hours, US$6-8, higher price at night, and Cayenne), Master Card accepted. Also *Lambada Bus Service*, Keizerstraat 162. T411073, for bus services to South Drain and Georgetown. The illegal 'Back Track' speedboat runs from a point 10 minutes from town, by a café on the beach. Seek local advice before using this route.

Apura on the Corantijn can be reached by sea-going vessels (**C** with three meals, advance booking from Paramaribo advisable, good). **Blanche Marie Falls**, 320 km from Paramaribo on the Apura road, is a popular destination. There is a guesthouse, **B** *Dubois*, contact Eldoradolaan 22, Paramaribo T476904/2. **Washabo** near Apura, which has an airstrip, is an Amerindian village. ■ *No public transport from Paramaribo to the Apura-Bakhuis area, but frequent charter flights to the Washabo airstrip. Irregular small boats from Apura to Nieuw-Nickerie and to Springlands (Guyana).*

East of Paramaribo to Guyane

Eastern Suriname was the area most severely damaged during the civil war. A paved road connects Meerzorg (bridge across the river, but the vehicle ferry from Paramaribo still runs) with Albina, passing through the districts of Commewijne and Marowijne. There is little population or agriculture left here. **Moengo**, 160 km up the Cottica River from Paramaribo, was a bauxite mining and loading centre for Suralco. It can be reached by medium draught ships and by cars. The new bauxite mining centre is at Coermotibo, not far from Moengo.

Two **nature reserves** are located on the northeast coast of Suriname. Known primarily as a major nesting site for sea turtles (five species including the huge leatherback turtle come ashore to lay their eggs), **Wia-Wia Nature Reserve** (36,000 ha) also has nesting grounds for some magnificent birds. The nesting activity of sea turtles is best observed April-July (July is a good month to visit as you can see adults coming ashore to lay eggs and hatchlings rushing to the sea at high tide). Since the beaches and consequently the turtles have shifted westwards out of the reserve, accommodation is now at **Matapica** beach, not in the reserve itself. (After a visit to the reserves please send any comments to Stinasu. Your support is needed to keep the reserves functioning.) There may also be mosquitoes and sandflies, depending on the season. The SMS riverboat from Paramaribo stops at Alliance on its journey up the Commewijne River. You then transfer to a Stinasu motorboat for a one hour ride to Matapica. The motorboat costs US$50 for four people, round trip; a guide is the same price. Suitable waterproof clothing should be worn. Fishermen make the crossing for US$3-4. Book accommodation and boat through Stinasu or other agencies; keep your receipts or you will be refused entry. Early booking is essential as Matapica is very popular. Stinasu has a lodge at Matapica. It can accommodate 8 people, facilities are basic and it costs US$53.

The **Galibi Nature Reserve**, where there are more turtle-nesting places, is near the mouth of the Marowijne River. There are Carib Indian villages. From Albina it is a 3 hour (including 30 minutes on the open sea) boat trip to Galibi. There is new tourist lodge here: it has cooking facilities, a refrigerator, rooms with shower and toilet, powered mostly by solar energy. Make arrangements through Stinasu who run all-inclusive tours. Galibi can be seen on the net at www.biotopic.demon.nl/suriname/suriname.htm

East of Moengo, the scars of war are most obvious. **Albina** is on the Marowijne River, the frontier with Guyane. Once a thriving, pleasant town and then a bombed-out wreck, it is now showing signs of recovery with new buildings, shops, a market and several restaurants. *The Creek Hotel* (eight rooms) is on the northern outskirts of town; the owner speaks English.

Border with Guyane

Customs and immigration on both sides close at 1900, but in Albina staff usually leave by 1700. Be wary of local information on exchange rates and transport (both the ferry and buses to Paramaribo). Changing money on the Suriname side of the border is illegal; see **Currency**, page 1465. Suriname guilders are not recognized in Guyane; when crossing to Suriname, pay for the ferry in francs, or get the minivan driver to pay and he will stop at a cambio before reaching Paramaribo so you can change money and pay him. ■ *A passenger and vehicle ferry leaves Albina for St-Laurent du Maroni Mon, Thu, 0800, 1000, 1500, 1700, Tue, Wed, Sat, 0800, 1000, Sun 1630, 1700, 30 min voyage; the fare is US$4 pp, which is the same charged by pirogues, US$20 for cars.*

Guianas

Background

History Although Amsterdam merchants had been trading with the 'wild coast' of Guiana as early as 1613 (the name Parmurbo-Paramaribo was already known) it was not until 1630 that 60 English settlers came to Suriname under Captain Marshall and planted tobacco. The real founder of the colony was Lord Willoughby of Parham, governor of Barbados, who sent an expedition to Suriname in 1651 under Anthony Rowse to find a suitable place for settlement. Willoughbyland became an agricultural colony with 500 little sugar plantations, 1,000 white inhabitants and 2,000 African slaves. Jews from Holland and Italy joined them, as well as Dutch Jews ejected from Brazil after 1654. On 27 February 1667, Admiral Crynssen conquered the colony for the states of Zeeland and Willoughbyfort became the present Fort Zeelandia. By the Peace of Breda, 31 July 1667, it was agreed that Suriname should remain with the Netherlands, while Nieuw-Amsterdam (New York) should be given to England. The colony was conquered by the British in 1799, only to be restored to the Netherlands with the Treaty of Paris in 1814. Slavery was forbidden in 1818 and formally abolished in 1863. Indentured labour from China and Indonesia (Java) took its place.

On 25 November 1975, the country became an independent republic, which signed a treaty with the Netherlands for an economic aid programme worth US$1.5bn until 1985. A military coup on 25 February 1980 overthrew the elected government. The military leader, Lieutenant-Colonel Desi Bouterse, and his associates came under pressure from the Dutch and the USA as a result of dictatorial tendencies. After the execution of 15 opposition leaders on 8 December 1982, the Netherlands broke off relations and suspended its aid programme, although bridging finance was restored in 1988.

The ban on political parties was lifted in late 1985 and a new constitution was drafted. In 1986 guerrilla rebels (the Jungle Commando), led by a former bodyguard of Lieutenant-Colonel Bouterse, Ronny Brunswijk, mounted a campaign to overthrow the government, disrupting both plans for political change and the economy. Nevertheless, elections for the National Assembly were held in November 1987. A three-party coalition (the Front for Democracy and Development) gained a landslide victory over the military, winning 40 of the 51 seats, but conflicts between Assembly President Ramsewak Shankar and Lieutenant-Colonel Bouterse led to the deposition of the government in a bloodless coup on 24 December 1990 (the 'telephone coup'). A military-backed government under the presidency of Johan Kraag was installed and elections for a new national assembly were held on 25 May 1991. The New Front of three traditional parties and the Surinamese Labour Party (SPA) won 30 Assembly seats. Twelve went to the army-backed National Democratic Party (NDP, led by Lieutenant-Colonel Bouterse) and nine to the Democratic Alternative, which favours closer links with The Netherlands. New Front Ronald Venetiaan was elected president on 6 September 1991. Meetings between Suriname and the Netherlands ministers after the 1991 elections led to the renewal of aid in 1992. In August 1992, a peace treaty was signed between the government and the Jungle Commando.

It was only after the 1990 coup and a 25% fall in the price of alumina in 1991 that pressing economic issues such as unifying the complex system of exchange rates, reducing state involvement in the economy and cutting the huge budget deficit began to be addressed. In 1992 a Structural Adjustment Programme (SAP) was drawn up as a forerunner to a 1994-8 Multi-Year Development Programme. A unified floating rate was introduced in 1994, but apart from that the New Front Government failed to reap any benefit from the SAP. New Front's popularity slumped as its handling of the economy foundered and corruption scandals undermined its claim to introduce 'clean politics'. Because of wide ideological differences, the opposition parties presented no concerted campaign against the New Front until the 23 May 1996 general election. Until then, much greater impetus was given to popular discontent by the economic decline, which reached catastrophic proportions by 1995. Although the New Front won a small majority in the National Assembly, Venetiaan did not hold enough seats to become president. Several parties defected to the NDP with the result that, in September 1996, the United Peoples Assembly elected by secret ballot Jules Wijdenbosch as president. Wijdenbosch, who had been a vice-president during Bouterse's regime, formed a coalition government of his own

NDP and five other parties. Bouterse, for whom the special post of Councillor of State had been created in 1997, was dismissed by Wijdenbosch in April 1999 for failing to 'contribute to a healthy political climate'. At the same time Bouterse was tried *in absentia* in the Netherlands on suspicion of drug trafficking; he was convicted in July (Ronnie Brunswijk was convicted *in absentia* on similar charges in April). @BTM2 = Protests and strikes at the government's handling of the economy erupted in 1998-99 and Wijdenbosch's position became precarious following the collapse of his coalition. After losing a vote of confidence in parliament in June 1999, he was forced to bring forward elections from 2001 to 25 May 2000. Wijdenbosch was humiliated by the electorate, gaining a mere 9% of the vote, while the New Front coalition led by ex-president Ronald Venetiaan won 47%. Venetiaan was sworn in as president in August 2000 and his most urgent priority was to stabilize the economy. Between 1995 and 1998 some improvement in the economy had been noticeable, with positive gdp growth rates, inflation under 20%, increases in earnings, little fluctuation in the exchange rate and no major expansion of debt. By 2000,, though, all these trends had been reversed. Dutch aid was terminated and the economy went into recession. Real wages fell by about 14%, tax revenues declined and domestic and external debt mushroomed. In this grim economic climate, there was little chance of improvement for the 64% of the population estimated by the United Nations to be living in poverty.

Government

There is one legislative house, the National Assembly, which has 51 members. The President is both head of state and government. Suriname is divided into 10 districts, of which the capital is one.

People

The estimated composition of the population is: Indo-Pakistanis (known locally as Hindustanis), 37%; Creoles (European-African and other descent), 31%; Javanese, 15%; Bush Negroes, called locally 'Maroons' (retribalized descendants of slaves who escaped in the 17th century, living on the upper Saramacca, Suriname and Marowijne rivers), 10%; Europeans, Chinese and others, 3%; Amerindians, 3% (some sources say only 1%). About 90% of the existing population live in or around Paramaribo or in the coastal towns; the remainder, mostly Carib and Arawak Indians and Maroons, are widely scattered.

Population 2001: 419,000 population growth 1995-2000: 0.4% Infant mortality per 1,000 live births: 26

The Asian people originally entered the country as contracted estate labourers, and settled in agriculture or commerce after completion of their term. They dominate the countryside, whereas Paramaribo is racially very mixed. Although some degree of racial tension exists between all the different groups, Creole-Hindustani rivalry is not as fundamental an issue as in Guyana, for example. Many Surinamese, of all backgrounds, pride themselves on their ability to get along with one another in such a heterogeneous country.

Land & environment

Principal rivers are the Marowijne in the east, the Corantijn in the west, and the Suriname, Commewijne (with its tributary, the Cottica), Coppename, Saramacca and Nickerie. The country is divided into topographically quite diverse natural regions: the northern lowlands, 25 km wide in the east and 80 km wide in the west, have clay soil covered with swamps. There follows a region, 5-6 km wide, of a loamy and very white sandy soil, then an undulating region, about 30 km wide. It is mainly savanna, mostly covered with quartz sand, and overgrown with grass and shrubs. South of this lies the interior highland, almost entirely overgrown with dense tropical forest, intersected by streams. At the southern boundary with Brazil there are savannas. A large area in the southwest is in dispute between Guyana and Suriname; a less serious border dispute with Guyane is in the southeast.

Land area: 163,820 sq km

Guianas

Books

Tales of a Shaman's Apprentice, by **M J Plotkin** (1993). An ethnobotanist's search for shamans' knowledge in the rainforests of Suriname and other Amazonian regions.

Guyane

Essentials

Planning your trip

Where to go Guyane is an Overseas Department of France, upon which it is heavily dependent. The capital, Cayenne, is on an island at the mouth of the river of the same name. Like its neighbours, Guyane has a populated coastal strip and much of the country remains sparsely populated and underdeveloped despite French aid. The department is known internationally for its space station at Kourou, home to the European Ariane space programme, where economic activity and investment is concentrated. The site has been used to launch over half the world's commercial satellites and over 20,000 foreigners are employed there. Tourism is slowly being developed, but the lack of good beaches and the proximity of the Amazon which muddies the water has deterred many. About 10,000 tourists visit annually, mainly for adventure trips into the forests, but their numbers are dwarfed by the 60,000 other visitors, businessmen and those who work in the space programme. An unusual attraction is the remains of the former penal colony, notably the Iles du Salut.

Best months to visit are between Aug-Nov, the usual months for trips to the jungle

When to go The climate is tropical with very heavy rainfall. Average temperature at sea-level is 27° C, and fairly constant at that. Night and day temperatures vary more in the highlands. The rainy season is from Nov to Jul, with (sometimes) a short dry interruption in Feb and Mar. The great rains begin in May.

Tour operators Two specialist travel agents in Paris are *Fleuves de Monde*, 17 rue de la Bûcherie, 75005 Paris, T44321285, www.fleuves-du-monde.com and *Soleil Plus*, IBP – Bâtiment Héra, 74160 Archamps, T04-50315215, www.soleilplus.com Other operators in France run tours.

Finding out more The French Government tourist offices generally have leaflets on Guyane; also **Comité du Tourisme de la Guyane**, 1 rue Clapeyron, 75008 Paris, T33-1-42941516, F42941465, guyanaparis@wanadoo.fr In Guyane: **Comité du Tourisme de la Guyane**, 12 rue Lallouette, BP 801, 97338 Cayenne, T05-94-296500, F05-94-296501, ctginfo@tourisme-guyane.gf www.tourisme-guyane.gf

NB The Amerindian villages in the Haut-Maroni and Haut-Oyapock areas may only be visited with permission from the Préfecture in Cayenne *before* arrival in Guyane.

Before you travel

Getting in Documents: Passports are not required by nationals of France and most French-speaking African countries carrying identity cards. For EU visitors, documents are the same as for Metropolitan France (that is no visa, no exit ticket required – check with a consulate in advance). No visa required for most nationalities (except for those of Brazil, Guyana, Suriname, some Eastern European countries, and Asian – not Japan – and other African countries) for a stay of up to three months, but an exit ticket out of the country is essential (a ticket out of one of the other Guianas is not sufficient); a deposit is required otherwise. If you stay more than three months, income tax clearance is required before leaving the country. A visa costs £15-20, or equivalent (US$22-30).

Vaccinations Inoculation against yellow-fever is obligatory for all and you may not be allowed to board your flight without a valid certificate. Tropical diseases, dysentery, malaria, etc, occur, but the country is fairly healthy. Malaria prophylaxis recommended.

Money The currency is the Euro. Try to take Euro with you as the exchange rate for dollars is low (In July 2002: 1.01), many banks do not offer exchange facilities and most places demand cash. A better rate can be obtained by using Visa or MasterCard (less common) to withdraw cash from any bank in Cayenne, Kourou and St-Laurent du Maroni. American Express, Eurocard and Carte Bleue cards are also accepted.

Getting there

Air *Air France* flies daily direct to Cayenne from Paris Charles de Gaulle. It also flies from Pointe-à-Pitre (Guadeloupe) and Fort-de-France (Martinique), and daily except Sunday from

Touching down

Business hours *Hours vary widely between different offices, shops and even between different branches of the same bank or supermarket. There seem to be different business hours for every day of the week, but they are usually posted. Most shops and offices close for a few hours around midday.*
Official time *Three hours behind GMT.*
Weights and measures *Metric is used.*
IDD *594. Equal tones separated by long pauses mean it's ringing. Equal tones with equal pauses mean it 's engaged.*

Port-au-Prince (Haiti), and Miami. Penta flies except Sunday daily from Belém and Macapá. Surinam Airways flies from Belém and Paramaribo twice a week.

Boat *Compagnie Général Maritime* runs a monthly passenger service to France via Martinique and a freight service every three months. To Brazil from St-Georges to Oiapoque, see text below.

Airport information Cayenne-Rochambeau (T353882/89) is 16 km from Cayenne, 20 minutes by taxi, and 67 km from Kourou (US$60-80). There is a cambio changing US dollars and Brazilian reais as well as Cirrus and Visa Plus cashpoints for withdrawing French francs. No public transport; only taxis (US$25 daytime, US$30 night, but you can probably bargain or share). The cheapest route to town is taxi to Matoury US$10, then bus to centre US$2. Cheapest method of return to airport is by collective taxi from corner of Avenue de la Liberté and rue Malouet to Matoury (10 km) for US$2.40, then hitch or walk. On departure at the airport, once through the gate, there are no facilities (no duty free, exchange or restaurant). **Touching down**

Details of hotels are given in the text. The **Comité du Tourisme de la Guyane** (see Finding out more above) has addresses of furnished apartments for rent (*Locations Clévacances*) and *Gîtes*, which are categorized as *Gîtes d'Amazonie*, with accommodation in hammocks or *carbets* (imitation Amerindian huts), *Carbets d'Hôtes*, which include breakfast, and *Gîtes Panda Tropiques Label*, which are approved by the WWF. **Where to stay**
For our hotel grade price guide, see inside front cover

Air Internal air services are by *Air Guyane*. These flights are always heavily booked, so be prepared to wait, or write or telephone *Air Guyane*, address under Airline offices, Cayenne. There are daily connections to Maripasoula, at 0930 and 1430, Saül at 1200 and St-Georges at 0745 and 1430. Baggage allowance 10 kg. *Guyane Aéro Services*, T356162, F358450, operates an air taxi service to Camopi, Grand-Santi, Ouanary, Régina and St-Laurent. **Getting around**

Bus There is a lack of public transport.

Car/car hire Car hire can be a great convenience (there are 14 agencies in Cayenne; those at the airport open only for flight arrivals). *Avis, Budget* and *Hertz* have offices (see page 48 for websites). A local agency is *Jasmin*, T308490, www.jasminrent-a-car.gf All types of car available, from economy to luxury to pick-ups and jeeps. Cheapest rates are about US$50 a day, US$385 per week. Check insurance details carefully; the excess is very high. **Motorcycle hire** at Av Pasteur and Dr Gippet, from US$30-US$35 per day, also a good way to get around. Gasoline/petrol costs about US$0.85 a litre; diesel US$0.55 a litre. **Motoring:** There are no railways, and about 1,000 km of road. The main road, narrow, but now paved, runs for 130 km from Pointe Macouris, on the roadstead of Cayenne, to Iracoubo. Another 117 km takes it to Mana and St-Laurent. It also runs to Régina and Cacao, but the last stretch has rough patches. There are no formalities for bringing a private car across the Guyane-Suriname border.

Ferry 1-3 ton boats which can be hauled over the rapids are used by the gold-seekers, the forest workers, and the rosewood establishments. Ferries are free. Trips by motor-canoe (*pirogue*) up-river from Cayenne into the jungle can be arranged.

Hitchhiking Hitching is reported to be easy and widespread.

Guianas

Keeping in touch

The official language is French, with officials not usually speaking anything else. Créole is more commonly spoken

Internet There are cybercafés in Cayenne and many businesses have email. **Telephone services** International calls can be made direct to any country from any phone: dial 00 + country code. Public telephones are widely installed and used. They take phonecards of 50 or 120 units (about US$5.35 or US$12), which can be bought at tobacconists, bookshops or supermarkets. How to use the phone is displayed in each phone booth in French, English, Italian and Spanish. To call the USA, one unit buys 3.6 seconds, to EU 2.5 seconds; discounts at weekends and between 1700 and 0700. The system is totally interconnected with the French system. Communication radios, satellite and mobile phones (GSM) can be bought or hired from *Compu' Phone*, 38 Av Léopold Héder, T256200, F252001 or their branch at the airport. **Media Newspapers**: *La Presse de la Guyane* is the daily paper (circulation 1,500). *France-Guyane-Antilles* is a weekly newspaper with a good information page for the tourist.

Shopping

The best buys are handicrafts in wood in the Saramaca village (Kourou) and along the road in the west of the country, and in St-Laurent du Maroni; also white rum. Hmong embroidery is sold at Sunday markets in Cacao and Jahourey.

Holidays & festivals

Public holidays These are the same as in Metropolitan France, with the addition of *Slavery Day*, **10 June**. Carnaval (February or March). Although not as famous as those of its neighbours in Brazil or the Caribbean, Guyane's Carnaval is joyous and interesting. It is principally a Créole event, but there is some participation by all the different cultural groups in the department (best known are the contributions of the Brazilian and Haitian communities). Celebrations begin in January, with festivities every weekend, and culminate in colourful parades, music, and dance during the four days preceding Ash Wednesday. Each day has its own motif and the costumes are very elaborate. On Saturday night, a dance called 'Chez Nana – Au Soleil Levant' is held, for which the women disguise themselves beyond recognition as 'Touloulous', and ask the men to dance. They are not allowed to refuse. On Sunday there are parades in downtown Cayenne. Lundi Gras (Fat Monday) is the day to ridicule the institution of marriage, with mock wedding parties featuring men dressed as brides and women as grooms. 'Vaval', the devil and soul of Carnaval, appears on Mardi Gras (Fat Tuesday) with dancers sporting red costumes, horns, tails, pitch-forks, et cetera. He is burnt that night (in the form of a straw doll) on a large bonfire in the Place des Palmistes. Ash Wednesday is a time of sorrow, with participants in the final parades dressed in black and white.

Health

Recommended specialist in tropical diseases, *Dr P Chesneau*, Place Europe, T321105, Kourou. Dentists: *R Fournier*, 115 Lot Moucayou, Matoury, T356499; J-P Brugerie, Impasse France Equinociale, Kourou, T321258. See also Health, in Essentials at the beginning of the book.

Cayenne

Population: 52,000-60,000 (est) 645 km from Georgetown (Guyana) 420 km from Paramaribo (Suriname) by sea Colour map 2, grid B6

The capital and the chief port is on the island of Cayenne at the mouth of the Cayenne River. There is an interesting museum, the **Musée Départemental Franconie**, 1 rue de Rémire, near the Place de Palmistes, which contains quite a mixture of exhibits, from pickled snakes to the trunk of the 'late beloved twin-trunked palm' of the Place de Palmistes. There is a good entomological collection and excellent paintings of convict life. ■ *Mon and Wed 0800-1300, Tue and Fri 1500-1800, Thu 1030-1330, Sat 0830-1200, US$2.25, T295913*. Next door is the municipal library. **L'Orstom** (scientific research institute), Route de Montabo, has a research library and permanent exhibits on ecosystems and archaeological finds in Guyane. ■ *Mon and Fri 0700-1330, 1500-1800, Tue-Thu 0700-1300*. Also worth a visit are **La Crique**, the colourful but dangerous area around the Canal Laussat (built by Malouet in 1777); the Jesuit-built residence (circa 1890) of the Prefect (**L'Hôtel-de-Ville**) in the Place de Grenoble; the **Place des Amandiers** (also known as the **Place Auguste-Horth**) by the sea; the Place des Palmistes, with assorted palms; a swimming pool and five cinemas. The **fruit and vegetable market** on Monday, Wednesday, Friday and Saturday mornings has a Caribbean flavour, but it is expensive. There are bathing beaches (water rather muddy) around the island, the

Guianas

best is Montjoly, but watch out for sharks. Minibuses run from the terminal to Rémire-Montjoly for beaches. They leave when full – check when the last one returns. There is a walking trail called '**Rorota**' which follows the coastline and can be reached from Montjoly or the Gosselin beaches. Another trail, '**Habitation Vidal**' in Rémire, passes through former sugar cane plantations and ends at the remains of 19th century sugar mills.

Some 43 km southwest of Cayenne is Montsinéry, with a zoo featuring Amazonian flora and fauna (open daily 1000-1900), an orchid and a walking trail, 'Bagne des Annamites', through remains of a camp where prisoners from Indochina were interned in the 1930s.

Tourist offices **Comité du Tourisme de la Guyane**, 12 rue Lallouette, BP 801, 97300 Cayenne, T296500, F296501, ctginfo@tourisme-guyane.gf Open 0800-1200, 1500-1800.

Ins & outs
For more detailed information see Transport, page 1482

Most hotels do not add tax and service to their bill, but stick to prices posted outside or at the desk. Bed and breakfast accommodation (gîte) is available for about US$60 a night (breakfast included) – contact the tourist office for details. **AL** *Hotel des Amandiers*, Place Auguste-Horth, T302600, F307484. A/c, excellent restaurant. **AL** *Best Western Amazonia*, 28 Av Gen de Gaulle,T310000, www.amazonia-hotel.com Good, a/c, luggage stored, pool, central location, good buffet breakfast extra. **A** *Central Hotel*, corner rue Molé and rue Becker, T256565, centralhotel@wanadoo.fr Downtown, a/c, good value. **A** *La Bodega*, 42 Av Gen de Gaulle, T302513, www.labodega.fr A/c or cheaper with fan and without bath, hammock space, noisy, central, snack bar. **B** *Ajoupa*, Route de Cabassou (Camp de Tigre), 2 km from town, T303308, hotel.ajoupa@wanadoo.fr Helpful. **B** *Ket-Tai*, Av de la Liberté corner Blvd Jubelin, T301100, F309976. Modern, a/c, reasonable, Chinese restaurant.

About 10 km from Cayenne in Rémire-Montjoly are: **A** *Beauregard*, Km 9.2 Route de Rémire, T354100, criccrac@nplus.gf Recommended for business visitors, pool, tennis, squash, sauna, *Cric-Crac* restaurant (see below) and nightclub. **A** *Motel du Lac*, T380800, F381034, Chemin Poupon, Route de Montjoly. Pool, bar, restaurant, good business hotel.

Sleeping
Hotel rooms are expensive – it is hard to find a room under US$40 a night double. Amex cards are often not accepted but Visa is OK

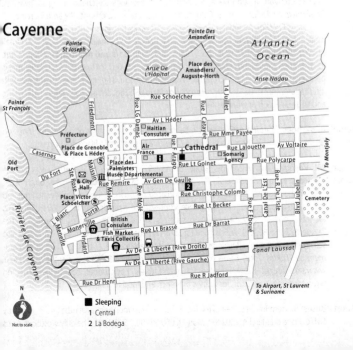

Cayenne

Pointe St Joseph

Pointe Des Amandiers

Atlantic Ocean

Anse Nadau

Anse De L'Hôpital

Place des Amandiers/ Auguste-Horth

Pointe St François

Rue Schoelcher

14 Juillet

Rue Catayée

Préfecture

Av L Héder

Haitian Consulate

Rue Mme Payée

Av Voltaire

Place de Grenoble & Place L Héder

Caserness

Air France

Rue F Arago

Cathedral

Rue Lalouette

Somarig Agency

Rue Polycarpe

Friedmont

Rue Lg Damas

Rue Lt Goinet

Old Port

Du Fort

Ste Rose

Maissin

Place des Palmistes

Musée Départemental

Av Gen de Gaulle

Rue Christophe Colomb

Rue R De L'Isle

Canal De L'Est

Blvd Jubelin

To Montjoly

Guianas

City Hall

Rue Remire

Place Victor Schoelcher

Malouet

Molé

Rue Lt Becker

Rue F Eboué

Cemetery

L Blanc

Menelle

Monerville

Portal

British Consulate

Rue Dr Barrat

Pindard

Fish Market & Taxis Collectifs

Rue Lt Brassé

Av De La Liberté (Rive Droite)

Av De La Liberté (Rive Gauche)

Canal Laussat

Rivière de Cayenne

Rue Dr Henri

Rue R Jadford

To Airport, St Laurent & Suriname

N

Not to scale

■ **Sleeping**
1 Central
2 La Bodega

Near Matoury and the airport are: **A** *La Chaumiere*, Chemin de la Chaumière (off the road to Kourou), 97351 Matoury, T255701, lachaumiere@wanadoo.fr Set in gardens with thatched huts, restaurant, pool. **B** *Le Grillardin*, Km 6 Route de Matoury, 4 km from airport, T356390, F358605. A/c, good value, helpful, good restaurant.

Apartment rentals include: *Mme Castor*, 4 rue du Dr Gippet, T309180, Raymonde.CASTOR@wanadoo.fr A/c, from US$225 per week. *M Benoit*, 117 rue Ch Colomb, T314281. From US$185 per week.

Eating   Main **hotels**: *Hostellerie 'Les Amandiers'*, Place Auguste-Horth. Excellent, French, expensive (US$38). *Cric-Crac* at *Motel Beauregard*, Créole cooking, lovely atmosphere. *Le Grillardin*, very good Créole cooking. **French and Créole**: *Au Vieux Genois*, 89 rue Christophe Colomb. Very good, French with local products, fish specialities, good business lunches. *La Caravelle*, 21 rue Christophe Colomb. French and Créole food *Le Vesuvio*, route Montabo. Very good. *Le Patriarche*, rues Voltaire and Samuel Lubin. Considered the best for French and regional food. Recommended. *Tournesol*, rue Lt Goinet. Real French food, fine wines, expensive. Highly recommended. *Paris-Cayenne*, 59 rue de Lalouette. French, very good, nice décor. **Others**: *Porta Verde*, 58 rue Lt Goinet. Brazilian buffet, US$12 per kg. Recommended. *La Baie des Iles*, Km 10 Route des Plages, Rémire-Montjoly, T386020. On the beach, good value seafood, 1000-midnight, closed Mon evening and Tue. Recommended. *Mille Pâtes*, 16 rue Felix Eboué. Good value. *Bar des Palmistes*, Place des Palmistes. Good daily menu, US$17, breakfast US$4. Central and spacious. *Fish & Chips*, 8 rue de Rémire. Good value and service, set meals at lunchtime (no fish and chips!). *Le Traiteur de la Fôret*, Blvd Jubelin. Friendly, good. *Marveen Snack Bar*, rue Christophe Colomb, near Canal de L'Est. Food and staff pleasant, the patrons are very helpful regarding air travel and excursions (the elder of the 2 is a pilot for the Guyane Flying Club). **Oriental**: *Ko Fei*, 18 rue Lalouette, T312888. Good Chinese. *Apsara*, 95 rue Christophe Colomb. Chinese, good value. *La Rose d'Asie*, 20 rue Samuel Lubin. Very good Vietnamese. *Thang-Long Vietnamese*, 1 rue Mentel. Good Vietnamese food. *Hindu-Creol*, rue J Catayée. Indian, good. Along the Canal Laussant there are Javanese snack bars; try *bami* (spicy noodles) or *saté* (barbecued meat in a spicy peanut sauce). Also along the canal are small, cheap Créole restaurants, not very clean. **Snacks etc**: Vans around Place des Palmistes in evenings sell cheap, filling sandwiches. *Delifrance*, Av de Gaulle at rue Catayée. Hot chocolate and croissants. *Le Snack Créole*, 17 rue Eboué. *Epi D'or*, Av Jubelin. Good sweets and cakes. Recommended. Food is about 38% more expensive than Metropolitan France: it is hard to find a meal for under US$7.50 (small Chinese restaurants charge US$7.50-12 for a full meal). **Bars and nightclubs** *Pacha Club*, 45 Av Gen de Gaulle (above Maracana Sport). Bar from 1700, disco from 2300 (US$15 entry) is particularly good for Zouk. *Acropolys*, Route de Cabassou, 3 km from town. Nightclub with international music, US$15 entry. *Harry's Bar*, 20 rue Rouget de l'Isle. Jazz, blues, Latin music and large selection of whiskies.

Shopping   **Bookshops**: *Librairie AJC*, 31 Blvd Jubelin, has an excellent stock of books and maps on Guyane (in French), There is a branch in *Drugstore des Palmistes*, Place des Palmistes.

Tour   *JAL Voyages*, 26 Av Gen de Gaulle, BP 110297334, T316820, F301101, www.jal-voy-
operators   ages.com For a wide range of tours on the Mahury, Mana, Approuague rivers, on a house-boat on the Kaw marshes (US$85, very good accommodation, food and birdwatching) and to Devil's Island. Recommended. *Agence Sainte-Claire*, 8 rue de Rémire, T300038, F300682, for travel outside Guyane (including charters to Caracas and Cuba). *Somarig*, 32 rue Lalouette, T302980, F305766, is good for South American and European airline tickets. It also sells boat tickets to Ile Royale as well as meal tickets for the Auberge, which are recommended. *Takari Tour*, 8 rue du Capitaine Bernard, BP 051397332, T311960, F315470, www.takaritour.gf Recommended for inland tours. Look under Tours Opérateurs on www.tourisme-guyane.gf for listings of French and local tour operators.

Transport   **Buses** Bus terminal at corner of rue Molé and Av de la Liberté. Regular urban services run by *SMTC*, Place du Marché, T302100, Mon-Fri 0800-1200, 1500-1700. The only westbound bus is run by *Ruffinel & Cie*, 8 Av Galmot, T312666 (Kourou US$12, St Laurent US$25) leaves 0530 (not Sun). Minibuses to St-Laurent du Maroni leave when full from the terminal, 0400-1200, 3 hrs, US$25. Service to **Mana** Mon and Thu only. To Kaw, Wed. Otherwise transport is by shared taxis (collectifs), which leave from the *gare routière* by the Canal Laussat early in the morning (Kourou US$12, St Laurent US$30-38). Other taxis can be found at the stand on Place des Palmistes, at the corner of Av Gen de Gaulle and Molé.

Airline offices *Air France*, 17-19 rue Lalouette, BP 33, Cayenne, T298787, F298790. *Air Guyane*, 2 rue Lalouette, 97300 Cayenne, T293630, F293631. *Penta*, Sainte Claire Voyages, Centre Commercial Katoury, 97300 Cayenne, T303910, F309000. *Surinam Airways*, 15 rue Louis Blanc, T293001, F305786. **Banks** *Banque Nationale de Paris-Guyane (BNPG)*, 2 Place Schoelcher; no exchange facilities on Sat. *Banque Française Commerciale (BFC)*, 2 Place des Palmistes (best bank exchange rates). *Crédit Populaire Guyanais*, 93 rue Lalouette. Most banks have ATMs for cash withdrawals on Visa, sometimes MasterCard, never Amex. *Banque Populaire*, 5 Av Gen de Gaulle, Cirrus/MasterCard ATM. *Crédit Mutuel*, 13 rue Léon Damas, Visa/Plus and Cirrus/MasterCard ATM. *Cambio Caraïbe*, Av Gen de Gaulle near Catayée (best rates for US$). *Guyane Change*, Av Gen de Gaulle near rue F Eboué. The Post Office exchanges cash and TCs at good rates, but complicated and time-consuming. There is an exchange facility at the airport (see Airport information, above). Central drugstore may help when banks are closed. Almost impossible to change dollars outside Cayenne or Kourou. **Communications** Internet: *Cybercafé des Palmistes*, 1 Av Gen de Gaulle, US$15 per hr. **Post Office:** Route de Baduel, 2 km out from town (US$2.25 by taxi or 20 mins on foot), crowded. Poste Restante letters are only kept for 2 weeks maximum. Also Poste Cayenne Cépéron, Place L Héder. **Embassies and consulates** British (Honorary), Mr Nouh-Chaia, 16 Ave Monnerville (BP 664, Cayenne 97300), T311034, F304094. **Brazilian**, 23 Res St Antoine, T296010, www.nplus.gf/~cbrascay **Danish/Belgian**, Imm Simeg Zi, Dégrad de Cannes, 97358 Rémire, T354649. **Dutch** (Honorary), Batiment Sogudem, Port of Dégrad des Cannes, BP139, Cayenne 97323, T354931, F354671. **Haitian**, 12 rue L Héder, at corner of Place des Palmistes, T311858, F312065, closed Sat. **Suriname**, 38 ter rue C Colomb, T300461, Mon-Fri 0900-1200. For USA and Canada, apply to embassies in Paramaribo, Suriname.

Directory

West to Suriname

This is where the main French space centre (Centre Spatial Guyanais), used for the European Space Agency's Ariane programme, is located. It is referred to by the Guyanais as 'white city' because of the number of metropolitan French families living there. Tourist attractions include bathing, fishing, sporting and aero club, and a variety of organized excursions. The tourist office is *Syndicat d'Initiative de Kourou*, T324884.

Kourou
Population: 20,000
56 km W of Cayenne
Colour map 2, grid B6

The space centre occupies an area of about 4 km deep along some 30 km of coast, bisected by the Kourou River. Public guided tours are given Monday-Thursday at 0745 and 1300 (Friday 0745 only). Tours are free and last 3-4 hours; children younger than nine are not admitted. Advance reservations must be made several days beforehand, T326123, F321745, Monday-Friday 0800-1200. No tours during a launch or on the days before or after. The Musée de l'Espace, T334347, can be visited without reservation, open Monday-Friday 1000-1800, Saturday 1400-1800, US$6.50. No public transport, take a taxi or hitch. To watch a launch you must write to CNES – Centre Spatial Guyanais, Relations Publiques, BP 726, 97387 Kourou Cedex, T334482, F334719, saying you want to attend; phone or fax to find out when launches take place. Supply full names and ID; ask for your invitation from Centre d'acceuil du CSG, or Syndicat d'Initiative de Cayenne, 7 Avenue G Monnerville, 97300 Cayenne (T324884). Invitations must be collected 2-3 days before the launch; if you hear nothing, it's probably full, but you can try wait-listing (arrive early). There are five viewing sites: Toucan (for VIPs, but wait-listing, or enquiries, possible), Kikiwi, Colibri (both good), Agami (OK) and Ibis (not recommended). Alternatively, you can watch the launch for free, from 10 km, at Montagne Carapa at Pariacabo.

Guianas

Sleeping L *Mercure Ariatel*, Av de St-Exupéry, Lac Bois Diable, T328900, h1592@accor-hotels.com Good restaurant and pool with snack bar. **AL** *Hôtel des Roches*, Pointe des Roches, T320066, F320328. Fair, a/c, includes breakfast, pool with bar, beach, good restaurant, cybercafé. **AL** *Mercure Inn Atlantis*, near Lac Bois Diable, T321300, h1538@accor-hotels.com A/c, modern, pool, good restaurant, best value for business visitors. **A** *Les Jardins D'Hermes*, 56 rue Duchesne, T324206, F325208, in heart of old Kourou. A/c, modern, good, restaurant. **B** *Ballahou*, 2-3 rue Amet Martial, T220022. A/c, TV, nice, modern, good restaurant. At Km 17.5 south of Kourou on the Saramaca road is *Les Maripas*, tourist camp, T325548, F323660. River and overland excursions, **D** for tent, book at Guyane Excursion, 7 quartier Simarouba, near *Restaurant Saramaca*.

Eating Many, especially on Av Gen de Gaulle, offer US$10 menu (Créole or Chinese) including *Le Catouri*, *Cachiri Combo* (No 3, T324464, also has basic rooms, **C**). *La Grillade*, Av Berlioz. *L'Enfer Vert*, Av G Monnerville. *Le Paradisier* in *Hotel des Roches* (see above). *L'Hydromel*, rue Raymond Cresson. Good pancakes. *Le Provence*, 11 passage G Monnerville. Best French, expensive. *Ballahou* (see Hotels), best for fish and seafood (try *Guyabaisse*). Pizza at *Le Valentino*, 4 place Galilé. Pizzas, seafood Fri. *Le Saramaca*, place du Marché. *La Pirogue*, Quartier de l'Europe, 20 m from post office. At US$10 good value. In same area, *Le Citron Vert*, *Le Moaï*, *Le Roc*, *Le Gourbi*, *Viet Nam*, *Le Colibri* (good chicken) and *Bar des Sports* (beside Post Office, US$7.50). Many cheap Chinese (also takeaway): *Le Chinatown*, rue Duchesne. Recommended. *Kong Loong*, rue du Levant. Many vans sell sandwiches filled with Créole food, good. *Le Glacier des 2 Lacs*, 68 ave des 2 Lacs. Ice cream, cakes, teas, very good.

Entertainment Nightclubs: *3ème Dimension* (Créole style), *Le Vieux Montmartre*, both on de Gaulle. *Clibertown*, quartier de l'Anse, very good.
Bars: *La Nouvelle Dimension* (Créole and European style). *American Bar* in *Hotel des Roches* (see Hotels). *Le Forban*, rue Dreyfus, district 205, worth seeing the murals (also for the lonely, many young Brazilian women).

Tour operators *Espace Amazonie*, 7 Centre Commercial Simarouba, T323430, www.espace-amazonie.com *Guyanespace Voyages*, A Hector Berlioz, T223101, www.guyanespace.com

Transport Taxi US$10, Lopez T320560, Gilles TT320307, Kourou T321444. To **Cayenne**, bus leaves Shell service station, corner Av de France, Av Vermont Polycarpe. Bus to **St-Laurent du Maroni** from same place, 2 between 0600 and 0700, US$30. *Taxis collectifs*, 0600, 0630, 0700, 1330, US$12 to Cayenne. Taxi to Cayenne or airport, US$60 (US$85 at night). To St-Laurent du Maroni US$25 by *taxi collectif* (irregular) or by minibus from Shell station.

Directory Banks *Banque National de Paris Guyane*, near the Mairie. *Banque Française Commerciale*, Place Jeanne d'Arc. *Crédit Populaire Guyanais*, Simarouba. *Crédit Martiniqueis*, Ave G Monnerville. **Communications** Post Office: Ave des Frères Kennedy.

The **Iles du Salut** (many visitors at weekends), opposite Kourou, include the Ile Royale, the Ile Saint-Joseph, and the Ile du Diable. They were the scene of the notorious convict settlement built in 1852; the last prisoners left in 1953.One of their most famous residents was Henri Charrière, who eventually made a miraculous escape to Venezuela. He later recounted the horrors of the penal colony and his hair-raising escape attempts in his book *Papillon*. The Ile du Diable ('Devil's Island'), a rocky palm-covered islet almost inaccessible from the sea, was where political prisoners, including Alfred Dreyfus, were held. There is a 60-bed hotel on Ile Royale, **A** *Auberge Iles du Salut* (postal address BP 324, 97378 Kourou, T321100, F324223), **AL** full board, also hammock space US$20 per person; former guard's bungalow, main meals (excellent), minimum US$36, breakfast US$6; gift shop with high prices (especially when a cruise ship is in), good English guide book for sale. Camping is possible, but suitable sites are limited (try the northeastern end of Ile Royale), the strong-hearted may try the old prison barracks; take food and water (you can also sling a hammock in the open, take a plastic sheet to protect yourself from morning mist); bread and water (check bottle is sealed) can be bought from the hotel stall. You can see monkeys, agoutis, turtles, hummingbirds and macaws, and there are many coconut palms. Take a torch for visiting the ruins. Paintings of prison life are on show in the tiny church. Visit the children's graveyard, hospital, mental asylum and death cells. These, and the church, are not always open. Little is being done to stop the deterioration of the buildings. Guided tours, in French, are given three times a week.

Transport Boat from Kourou's port at the end of Av Gen de Gaulle, 4 km from the old centre US$37 return (children under 12 half price), leaves 0800 daily, returns from island at 1700 (book in advance, T320995/321100), additional sailing Sat and in high season, 1 hr each way. Advance bookings are imperative in Jul and Aug. Tickets may be obtained from *Somarig Voyages*, address under Cayenne **Tour operators**; *Air Guyane Voyages*, 2 rue Lalouette, T317200; in Kourou from au Carbet des Roches, cash only. Getting back to Cayenne late in the afternoon after the boat docks may be a problem if you don't have your own transport: ask other tourists for a lift. There are no regular boats from Ile Royale to Ile Saint-Joseph, which is wilder and more beautiful, with a small beach (this island had solitary-confinement cells and the warders' graveyard). It may be possible to hire a private boat at the ferry dock, or ask for James on the Kourou-Ile Royale ferry. There are no sailings between Ile Royale and Ile du Diable by law.

Between Kourou and Iracoubo, on the road west to St-Laurent, is **Sinnamary** (116 km from Cayenne), a pleasant town where Galibi Indians at a mission make artificial flowers from feathers, for sale to tourists. Scarlet ibis can be seen in numbers on the Sinnamary estuary at Iracoubo. (Tours at 1500, T345310, Amoida Georges, US$16.50.) Also at Iracoubo is a pretty church with paintings by a convict. *Chez Floria*, 14 rue Ronda Silva, T346385, F326378, furnished rooms.

Sinnamary & St-Laurent du Maroni

    St-Laurent du Maroni (*population* 25,000), formerly a penal transportation camp, is now a quiet colonial town 250 km from Cayenne on the river Maroni, bordering Suriname. It can be visited as a day tour from Cayenne if you hire a car. The old Camp de Transportation (the original penal centre) can be wandered round at will, but a guide is needed to enter the cells (an absolute must if visiting the country). Guided tours of Les Bagnes (prison camps) Tuesday-Friday, 0815-1115, 1515-1715, Saturday 0915-1115, 1515-1715, Sunday and holidays 0915-1115, chilling, buy tickets from tourist office, US$2.50. ■ *Closed Mon.* Here also is the tourist office, *Office du Tourisme et Syndicat d'Initiative*, 1 Blvd Malouet, 97393 St-Laurent du Maroni, T342398, F342883. ■ *Mon-Fri 0730-1800, Sat 0800-1200, 1500-1800, Sun 0900-1200.* The tourist office can also arrange a tour to a rum factory, or T340909.

Sleeping Sinnamary: **AL** *Hôtel du Fleuve*, 11 rue Léon Mine, T345400, www.hoteldufleuve.com Gardens, restaurant, internet access, pool, expensive. *Restaurant Madras*, good Créole; ask for *Gaya Baru*, Indonesian restaurant in an Indonesian village. Wood carvings and jewellery are on sale here and the workshops can be visited. There are 3-5 day excursions up the Sinnamarie River. **St-Laurent**: **AL** *Le Relais des 3 Lacs*, 19-23 Domaine du Lac Bleu, T340505, 23lacs@nplus.gf A/c, cheaper with fan, shuttle to town centre, restaurant, gardens, pool. **A** *La Tentiaire*, 12 Av Franklin Roosevelt, T342600, rioual.robert@wanadoo.fr A/c, the best, breakfast extra, phone, pool, secure parking. **A** *Star Hotel*, 109 rue Thiers, T341084. A/c, pool, cheaper rooms poor value, cheap restaurant. **B** *Chez Julienne*, 6 Route des Malgaches, T341153. A/c, TV, shower, good. In the countryside not far from St-Laurent is **C** *Auberge Bois Diable*, PK8 Acarouany, T/F341935. 1 bedroom, hammock space US$6, meals US$16, breakfast US$4, good food, hospitable, tours arranged, a good place to stay for walking, or for trips to see turtles at Les Hattes (see below).

    Eating St-Laurent: *Restaurants Vietnam* and *La Goelette*, T342897, are recommended. The latter is French/Brazilian, closed Sun evening, Mon, also has kayak and canoe tours. *Loe*, near hospital, Créole, excellent. Many cheap Chinese. **Bars** *Jean Solis*, opposite Catholic church. Recommended.

Guianas

Tour operators *Ouest Guyane*, 10 rue Féliz Eboué, T344444, F344446, ouestguyane@
wanadoo.fr

Transport Minibuses to Cayenne meet the ferry from Suriname, leaving when full, 3 hrs
(maybe not until 1830 or 1900), US$25. Bus to Cayenne, US$33, US$30 to Kourou, 0500 daily,
tickets and information at *Hotel Star*; taxis *collectifs* to and from Cayenne, 8 people, US$25 a
head, 3½ hr trip. Freight *pirogues* sometimes take passengers inland along the Maroni River;
alternatively a group can hire a *pirogue* at about US$200 a day.

Directory Banks *BFC*, 11 Av Félix Eboué, open Tue-Fri, Sat morning. *Cambio COP*, 19 rue Montravel,
near BNP, T343823, changes Dutch and Suriname guilders, dollars.

Border with
Suriname
Make sure you obtain proper entry stamps from immigration, not the police, to
avoid problems when leaving. Customs and immigration close at 1900. There are
many aggressive exchange touts on the St-Laurent and Albina piers. It is best to
change money in the Village Chinois in St-Laurent (dangerous area); although rates
are lower than in Paramaribo, it is illegal to change money in Albina. Beware theft at
St-Laurent's black market. ■ *Ferry for vehicles and passengers to Albina Mon, Thu,
0700, 0900, 1400, 1600, Tue, Wed, Sat 0700, 0900, Sun, 1530, 1600, 30 mins. Passengers US$4 one-way, car US$20 one-way. Speedboats US$3.50-US$4.75. Minibuses
and taxis for Paramaribo meet the Albina ferry.*

About 3 km from St-Laurent, along the Paul Isnard road, is Saint-Maurice, where
the rum distillery of the same name can be visited, Monday-Friday 0730-1130. At
Km 70 on the same dirt road is access to **Voltaire Falls**, 1½ hours walk from the road
(**A** *Auberge des Chutes Voltaires*, T342716). 7 km south of St-Laurent on the road to
St-Jean du Maroni is the Amerindian village of **Terre Rouge**; canoes can be hired for
day trips up the Maroni River (see Maripasoula below). These can be arranged with
Youkaliba (*Maroni*) *Expeditions*, 3 rue Simon, T341645/312398. For example
one-night trip to Apatou, US$140; to Saut Anana on Mana River, 10 days, US$655.

Some 40 km north of St-Laurent du Maroni is **Mana**, a delightful town with rustic
architecture near the coast (nuns next to the church rent beds and hammocks,
US$8, clean and simple, T348270, F348415, Communauté des Soeurs de St-Joseph
de Cluny, 1 rue Bourguignon; **C** *Le Bougainvillier*, 3 rue des Frères, T342082,
F348295, a/c, **D** with shared bath; *Gîte Angoulême*, Mme Maryse Buira, 59 route de
St Maurice, 97320 St-Laurent, T342855, beside the river Mana, hammock space
US$6, gîte **AL** for weekend, breakfast US$4.50, meals US$24). 20 km west of Mana
following the river along a single track access road is **Les Hattes**, or Yalimapo, an
Amerindian village (three *gîtes*: *Chez Jeanne*, T342982, F342071; *Chez Judith et
Denis*, T342438; *Amazonie Détente*, T325228, F328252 Kourou; restaurant *Au
Paradis des Acajous*; Indian restaurant near beach). About 4 km further on is Les
Hattes beach where leatherback turtles lay their eggs at night; season April-August
with May-June peak. No public transport to Les Hattes and its beach, but hitching
possible at weekends; take food and water and mosquito repellent. Despite the
dryish climate Mana is a malaria region. The freshwater of the Maroni and Mana
rivers makes sea bathing very pleasant. It is very quiet during the week.

Aouara, or Awala, an Amerindian village with hammock places, is 16 km west of
Les Hattes. It also has a beach where leatherback turtles lay their eggs; they take
about three hours over it. Take mosquito nets, hammock and insect repellent.

There are daily flights from Cayenne to **Maripasoula**; details in Air transport, page
1479, local office T372141 (**D** *Auberge Chez Dedè*, Av Leonard, T372005, US$4 per
extra person; **AL** *Campement Touristique de Saut Sonnelle*, T344945, full board). It
is up the Maroni from St-Laurent (2-4 day journey up river in *pirogue*). There may
be freight canoes which take passengers (US$40) or private boats (US$150) which
leave from St-Laurent; 5-6 day tours and other options with *Takari Tour* or other

Guianas

tour operators in Cayenne. Maripasoula has 5,000 inhabitants in town and its surroundings. Many bush negros live here.

This remote gold-mining settlement in the 'massif central' is the geographical centre **Saül** of Guyane. The main attractions are for the nature-loving tourist. Beautiful undisturbed tropical forests are accessible by a very well-maintained system of 90 km of marked trails, including several circular routes. The place has running water, a radio-telephone, and electricity. Ten-day expeditions are run by Christian Ball, '*Vie Sauvage*', 97314 Saül, US$86 (30% in advance) per day with meals, maps of local trails provided, own hammock and bedding useful but not essential. It can be cold at night. Another fascinating overland route goes from Roura (see below) up the Comte River to Belizon, followed by a 14-16-day trek through the jungle to Saül, visiting many villages en route, guide recommended. **E** per person *Larozaly*, a tourist camp in Saül, has running water, solar electricity, cooking facilities, and is a good place to stay. Meals are arranged by the *mairée* at *Restaurant Pinot*. Two markets sell food. 7 km north of Saül on foot is *Les Eaux Claires – Horizons Secrets*, tourist camp, T415379, **AL** full board, **C** in hammock including breakfast and dinner (drinks extra).

Transport Air service with *Air Guyane* from Cayenne or via Maripasoula (see Air transport, above; local office T309111). Try at airport even if flight said to be full. By *pirogue* from Mana up Mana River, 9-12 days, then 1 day's walk to Saül, or from St-Laurent via Maripasoula along Moroni and Inini rivers, 15 days and 1 day's walk to Saül, both routes expensive.

Southeast to Brazil

About 28 km southeast of Cayenne is the small town of **Roura**, which has an interesting church. An excursion may be made to the Fourgassier Falls several kilometres away (*L'Auberge des Cascades*, excellent restaurant). From Cayenne the road crosses a new bridge over the Comte River. Excursions can be arranged along the Comte River. For information about the area contact the *Syndicat D'Initiative de Roura*, T311104. Nearby is Dacca, a Laotian village, which has *La Crique Gabrielle*, T/F280104, a restaurant which also has rooms.

From Roura a paved road, RD06, runs southeast towards the village of Kaw. 29 km from Roura is **C** *Auberge du Camp Caïman* (tourist camp, **F** to hang hammock), T376034, tours arranged to watch caiman in the swamps. At Km 36 from Cayenne is the **C** *Hotel Relais de Patawa* (T280395), or sling your hammock for US$4, cheaper rates for longer stays, highly recommended. The owners, M and Mme Baloup, who are entomologists, will show you their collection, take you on guided tours of local sights and introduce you to their pet anaconda and boa constrictors. **Kaw** is on an island amid swamps which are home to much rare wildlife including caimans. The village is reached from where the Roura road ends at the river at Approuague. Basic accommodation available; *Jacana Tour*, T380795, excursions by day or night on the river; take insect repellent.

At Km 53 on another road southeast to Régina is the turn-off to **Cacao** (a further 13 km), a small, quiet village, where Hmong refugees from Laos are settled; they are farmers and produce fine traditional handicrafts. The main attraction is the Sunday morning market with local produce, Laotian food, embroidery. **C** *Restaurant La Lan*, one room, good value, good food; M Levessier, T305122, has hammocks, **E**. Best restaurant is *Chez By et David*, Laotian food; also good is *Degrad Cacao*. Canoe and kayak rental behind the *Degrad Cacao*, US$2.50 per hour, US$8.50 per day, good wildlife trips upriver. Minibus from Cayenne, Monday 1200; Friday 1800, return Monday 0730, Friday 1400. Halfway along the side road is the *Belle Vue* restaurant, which lives up to its name, because of the superb view over the tropical forest; the restaurant is open at weekends. Consult the Comité du Tourisme de la Guyane for *gîtes* in the area.

Guianas

Southwest of Kaw on the river Approuague is **Régina**, linked with Cayenne by a paved road. A good trip is on the river to Athanase with G Frétique, T304551. An unmade road, built by the French army, runs from Régina to St-Georges de l'Oyapock (difficult during the rainy season).

Border with Brazil

St-Georges de l'Oyapock, with its small detachment of the French Foreign Legion who parade on Bastille Day, is 15 minutes down river from Oiapoque in Brazil, US$4 per person by motorized canoe, bargain for a return fare. The tourist office is in the library to the left of the town hall. Thierry Beltran, Rue Henri Sulny, T370259, offers guided river and forest tours. A pleasant day trip is to the **Saut Maripa** rapids (not very impressive with high water), located about 30 minutes upstream along the Oiapock River, past the Brazilian towns of Oiapoque and Clevelândia do Norte. Hire a motorized *pirogue* (canoe) to take you to a landing downstream from the rapids. Then walk along the trolley track (used to move heavy goods around the rapids) for 20 minutes to the rundown huts by the rapids (popular and noisy at weekends). There are more rapids further upstream on the way to Camopi.

Immigration (*gendarmerie*) for entry/exit stamps at eastern end of town, follow signs, open daily 0700-1200, 1500-1800 (sometimes not open after early morning on Sunday, in which case try the police at the airport); French and Portuguese spoken. One of the Livre Service supermarkets and *Hotel Chez Modestine* will sometimes change dollars cash into euros at very poor rates; if entering the country here, change money before arriving in St-Georges. Brazilian currency is accepted in shops at poor rates.

Also bars, restaurants, supermarkets with French specialities, post office and public telephones which take phone cards

Sleeping **B** *Caz Cale*, rue E Elfort, 1 street back from the riverfront, just east of the main square, T/F370054. A/c, cheaper with fan. **B** *Chez Modestine*, on the main square, T370013, F370214. A/c or fan, restaurant. **C** *Le Tamarin*, rue Joseph Léandre, on the riverfront near the main square, T370884. With bath, fan, bar and good restaurant.

Transport There are no passenger services by boat from St-Georges to Cayenne. Other than driving on the unmade road from Regina, flying is the only option. For *Air Guyane* flights to Cayenne see Air transport in Essentials. *Air Guyane* office at airport open 0700-0730, 1400-1430 for check in, open 0800-1100 for reservations, T/F370360. Flights are fully booked several days in advance; you must check in at stated times. Extra flights are sometimes added. The police check that those boarding flights who have arrived from Brazil have obtained their entry stamp; also thorough baggage search.

Background

History Several French and Dutch expeditions attempted to settle along the coast in the early 17th century, but were driven off by the native population. The French finally established a settlement at Sinnamary in the early 1660s but this was destroyed by the Dutch in 1665 and seized by the British two years later. Under the Treaty of Breda, 1667, Guyane was returned to France. Apart from a brief occupation by the Dutch in 1676, it remained in French hands until 1809 when a combined Anglo-Portuguese naval force captured the colony and handed it over to the Portuguese (Brazilians). Though the land was restored to France by the Treaty of Paris in 1814, the Portuguese remained until 1817. Gold was discovered in 1853, and disputes arose about the frontiers of the colony with Suriname and Brazil. These were settled by arbitration in 1891, 1899, and 1915. By the law of 19 March 1946, the Colony of Cayenne, or Guyane Française, became the Department of Guyane, with the same laws, regulations, and administration as a department in metropolitan France. The seat of the Prefect and of the principal courts is at Cayenne. The colony was used as a prison for French convicts with camps scattered throughout the country; Saint-Laurent was the port of entry. After serving prison terms convicts spent an equal number of years in exile and were usually unable to earn their return passage to France. Majority opinion seems to be in favour of greater autonomy and there was some civil

Guianas

Alexander von Humboldt

Von Humboldt is known principally for the cold current that flows northwards off the coast of Chile and Peru, which he discovered, measured and bears his name. This is a minor achievement of a man who was one of the great explorers of the world and had a important impact on many branches of natural science.

He was born in Berlin (Prussia) in 1769, the same year as Napoleon. He trained as a mining engineer, and worked for a time in the gold and copper mines near Bayreuth, but his main passion was botany and he had his eye on South America, which had never been open to scientific investigation. After much frustration, he finally obtained permission from Charles IV to go with the French botanist, Aimé, Bonpland, to Spanish America in 1799. During the next five years they travelled 10,000 km on foot, horseback and in canoes in South and Central America.

From 1804 to 1827 von Humboldt analysed and published his conclusions from the mass of data he had brought back from his travels. Apart from the basis he created for the area's botany, he made important contributions to world meteorology, to the study of vulcanism and the earth's crust and the connection between climate and flora. One of his spectacular achievements was to make the first ascent of several volcanoes including Chimborazo in Ecuador, where he and Bonpland reached the summit bergschrund (where the glacier meets the summit rocks) but not the top. Nevertheless, no one recorded a higher ascent anywhere for 30 years, and as a result of this climb, he correctly concluded that mountain sickness was caused by a lack of oxygen at high altitudes.

Von Humboldt even used his astronomical skills to make the first reliable maps of the continent, most notably of the course of the Orinoco River.

Humboldt's sense of adventure came from his dissatisfaction with home life. In 1801, he wrote: "I was spurred on by an uncertain longing for what is distant and unknown, for whatever excited: danger at sea, the desire for adventures, to be transported from a boring daily life to a marvellous world". His yearning for travel was based on the premise that few scientists had made dangerous journeys into the interior of South America. Only by the risk of travelling could the scientist make observations and comparisons with his own eyes, ensuring that science advances beyond dogma and hypothesis.

It is virtually impossible to overestimate the importance and influence of Humboldt on the world of science. He was a major inspiration for a certain young Charles Darwin and Johann Wolfgang Goethe (1749-1832). However, his fame spread beyond the confines of science. In France, writers and painters like Balzac, Victor Hugo, Chateaubriand, Gerard and Flaubert admired his descriptive prose. The North American poet and philosopher, Ralph Waldo Emerson called Humboldt the "Encyclopaedia of Science", and Lord Byron satirized his precise empirical investigation in 'Don Juan' (1821) by referring to the cynometer - an instrument for measuring the blueness of the sky.

The recently independent Spanish American intellectuals and politicians especially revered Humboldt. The Liberator, Simón Bolívar, no less, spoke of his debts to his friend: "Baron Humboldt did more for the Americas than all the conquistadores".

He spent the last 25 years writing Kosmos, an account of his scientific findings. A measure of its importance and readability is that, within a few years, the book had been translated into nearly all European languages. In spite of the illnesses and strains of his explorations, he lived to the ripe old age of 90, a good omen for ardent travellers.

Humboldt's account of his journey, documented in his Personal Narrative is not only a scientific journal but also the first objective travel book on South America. (Personal Narrative of a Journey to the Equinoctial Regions of the New Continent, published by Penguin Books, 1995).

Guianas

unrest in 2000 caused by a minority calling for change in the relationship with Metropolitan France. The French government has shown no inclination to alter the department's status. There is an independence movement, but it does not have a significant following.

Rhum, by the French Guyanese writer Blaise Cendrars, is worth reading for its descriptions of the country's distinctive customs and traditions.

Government The head of state is the president of France; the local heads of government are Le Préfet (the Prefect), for France, and the presidents of the local General and Regional Councils. The General Council (19 seats) and the Regional Council (31 seats) are the two legislative houses. The two main parties in the regional council are the Parti Socialiste Guyanais and the Front Democratique Guyanais. Guyane sends one representative to the French Senate and one to the National Assembly in Paris.

People The total population in 2000 was estimated at 181,000, with an annual average growth rate of 4% (1993-98). There are widely divergent estimates for the ethnic composition of the population. Calculations vary according to the number included of illegal immigrants, attracted by social benefits and the high living standards. By some measures, over 40% of the population are Créoles, with correspondingly low figures for Europeans, Asians and Brazilians (around 17% in total). Other estimates put the Créole proportion at 36%, with Haitians 26%, Europeans 10% (of whom about 95% are from France), Brazilians 8%, Asians 4.7% (3.2% from Hong Kong, 1.5% from Laos), about 4% from Suriname and 2.5% from Guyana. The Amerindian population is put at 3.6% (over 4% by some estimates). The main groups are Galibis (1,700), Arawak (400), Wayanas (600), Palikours (500), Wayampis-Oyampis (600) and Emerillons (300). There are also bush negroes (Bonis, Saramacas, Djukas), who live mostly in the Maroni area, and others (Dominicans, St Lucians, etc) at 0.7%. The language is French, with officials not usually speaking anything else. Créole is also widely spoken. The religion is predominantly Roman Catholic.

Falkland Islands

These remote South Atlantic outposts, where there are more penguins than people, are the only part of South America where UK sterling is the currency, and the British monarch's head appears on the stamps. Windswept they may be, but the islands are a haven for wildlife and a paradise for those who wish to see it: albatross nest in the tussac grass, sea lions breed on the beaches and Orca whales cruise off the coast.

14

Falkland Islands

Falkland Islands/ Islas Malvinas

Essentials

In accordance with the practice suggested by the UN, we are calling the islands by both their English and Spanish names.

Where to go

About 640 km (400 miles) east of the South American mainland, the Falklands Islands/Islas Malvinas are made up of two large islands, surrounded by hundreds of smaller ones. For anyone interested in marine mammals and birdlife, this is the place to go. The islands' remoteness adds to the charm of being able to see elephant seals, dolphins, whales, albatross and, above all, penguins at close range. There are said to be 494,500 breeding pairs of five types of penguin here (that's about 415 birds per human inhabitant). The capital, Stanley, is a small, modern town, with reminders of its seafaring past in the hulks of sailing ships in the bay. To visit the camp, as the land outside Stanley is known, four-wheel-drive vehicles make tours, or you can fly to farming outposts for warm hospitality, huge skies and unparalleled nature watching.

When to go

Although the *Sunday Express* once referred to a mutton freezer in the Falklands as a Colonial Development project near the South Pole (8 March 1953), the Islands are in the same latitude south as London is north. The climate is cool and oceanic, dominated by persistent westerly winds which average 16 knots. Long periods of calm are rare except in winter. Though not always inclement, weather is very changeable but temperatures vary relatively little. At Stanley, the capital, the mean temperature in summer (Jan/Feb) is 10° C and in winter (Jun/Jul) 3° C. Stanley's annual rainfall of about 600 mm is slightly higher than London's. In the drier camp, outside Stanley, summer drought sometimes threatens local water supplies. Snowfall is rare although a dusting may occur at any time of the year. Spring, autumn and winter clothing, as used in the UK, is suitable.

Best months to visit are Oct-Mar. Wind-protective clothing is recommended. Sunblock is essential. Lipsalve recommended

Before you travel

Getting in All travellers must have full passports to visit the Falkland Islands/Islas Malvinas. Citizens of the European Union, the Commonwealth, USA, Argentina and other Mercosur countries, Andorra, Cyprus, Finland, Iceland, Israel, Japan, Republic of Korea, Liechtenstein, Norway, San Marino, Sweden, Switzerland and the Vatican are permitted to visit the islands without a visa, as are holders of UN and International Committee of the Red Cross passports. Other nationals should apply for a visa from *Falkland House* in London (see Getting there, below), the Immigration Department in Stanley (see Stanley, Useful addresses), or a British Embassy or Consulate. All visitors require a one-month visitor permit, normally provided on arrival upon presentation of a return ticket. Visitors are also asked to have pre-booked accommodation and sufficient funds to cover their stay. Work permits are not available. Do not stay beyond the valid period of your visa without applying to the Immigration Office for an extension.

Money Currency: The local pound (£) is on a par with sterling. Local notes and coins. UK notes and coins are also legal tender. Currency from Ascension Island, where the RAF Tri-Star stops for refuelling, or Santa Helena, is not accepted, nor are Falklands notes or coins legal in the UK. Foreign currency may be changed at *Standard Chartered Bank*, Ross Road, Stanley, but while some establishments accept US dollars non-British visitors are advised to bring only pounds sterling cash or travellers' cheques as exchange rates are poor (UK cheques can be cashed here up to the value of guarantee card, £2 commission). Visa and MasterCard credit cards are widely accepted in Stanley. American Express and Diners Club are accepted in very few places. There are no ATMs on the islands.

Cost of living About the same as in Britain. Freight adds to the price of imported groceries. Since the construction of a hydroponic market garden near Stanley, fresh produce

Falkland Islands

such as lettuce, tomatoes and aubergines are available year-round. There is no value added tax; only tobacco, wine, spirits and beer pay import duty. Small luxury goods on which freight is correspondingly low are sometimes cheaper than in the UK.

Air Flights from Santiago, via Puerto Montt and Punta Arenas with *LanChile* go every **Getting there**
Saturday and, once a month, stop at Río Gallegos in Argentina on both the outward and return flight. 2002 fares: return from Santiago US$680, Puerto Montt US$630, Punta Arenas US$490. Package tours from the UK via Santiago are available for £1,071 including tax.

The RAF usually operates six-seven Tri-Star flights a month from Brize Norton, Oxfordshire, to Mount Pleasant airport. The fare is £2,490 return, but there are also cheaper APEX (£1,530) and group rates (£1,290 for six or more). Falkland Islands residents receive a discount (£1,079). All flights are subject to £20 tax. Confirm your seat 12 hours before departure to avoid disappointment from overbooking or lost reservations. Flight time is 18 hours, but diversions to Montevideo owing to bad weather are not uncommon. Enquiries about passages can be addressed to Travel Co-ordinator, **Falkland Islands Government London Office**, Falkland House, 14 Broadway, Westminster, London SW1H 0BH. T020-7222 2542, F7222 2375, travel@figo.u-net.com or visit www.falklands.gov.fk The **Falkland Islands Tourist Board** (same address and phone number) answers enquiries about the islands themselves and gives information on organized tours; www.tourism.org.fk, tourism@fidc.co.fk

Boat *MV Tamar FI*, of Byron Marine Ltd, Stanley, T22245, byron@horizon.co.kf sails every 6-8 weeks Stanley-Punta Arenas-Stanley, 2½-3½ days, £180 per person, two cabins, two passengers per cabin, cramped though the ship is, relatively modern and a good sea-goer. Make reservations well in advance. Cruise ships from Europe and the USA visit the islands; a full list is given on www.tourism.org.fk

Airport information Mount Pleasant, 35 miles from Stanley, is built to international **Touching** specifications. *Falkland Islands Tours and Travel*, 6 Pioneer Row, Stanley, T/F21775, **down** astewart@horizon.co.fk transports passengers and luggage to and from the capital for £13 single. Departing passengers should make reservations. Also, *Lowes Taxi*, T21381, for transport between Stanley and the airport (£50), and within Stanley (£2), and *Stanley Cabs* T22600.

Business hours Office hours, including all government departments, are Mon-Fri 0800-1200, 1300-1630. Banking hours are 0830-1500. **Duty free allowance** is as for the UK, for those arriving from outside the EU. **Electricity supply** is 220/240 volts at 50 cycles. **Official time**: four hours behind GMT in winter, three in summer.

Internet Internet is widely used and there is an internet café with high-speed, permanent **Keeping** connections. **Post** Since the opening of Mount Pleasant, there is direct and dependable air **in touch** mail service from the United Kingdom. Heavy parcels come by sea from the UK every month. There is also a weekly in and out-bound DHL service operated through the Falkland Islands Chamber of Commerce, T22264, F22265, commerce@horizon.co.fk Inter-island mail service is carried out by FIGAS and by the vessel *Tamar* (see above). **Telephone** IDD code is 500. There is no mobile phone service. The local satellite service is incompatible with US and UK handsets.

Stanley

The capital, Stanley, on East Falkland, is the major population centre. Its residents *Population: 1,989* live mostly in brightly-painted houses, many of which have corrugated iron roofs. Surrounded by rolling moorland, Stanley resembles parts of the Hebrides. The outer harbour of Port William is larger but less protected. East Cove, 30 miles southeast of the capital, is the principal port for the new military installations at Mount Pleasant.

The Museum at Britannia House, Ross Road West, merits a visit. ■ *Tue-Fri, 1000-1200, 1400-1600, Sat-Sun, 1400-1600, £2.* Mr John Smith, the curator, is knowledgeable on the islands' maritime history. Government House, the Anglican Cathedral (most southerly in the world, built in 1892), and monuments commemorating the naval battle of 1914 and the 1982 liberation are also worth seeing. At the public jetty, the **Jetty Visitors Centre** has permanent and temporary exhibitions, an information service, toilets and public phones. The public library has a good selection of books on travel and on flora and fauna; in the same building is a public swimming pool and some good gym machines, for public use. During the December holidays, the annual sports meeting at the race course attracts visitors from all over the Islands. The equally popular West and East Falkland sports, at the end of the shearing season in February or March, rotate among various settlements.

Ins & outs

For more detailed information see Transport, page 1497

Tourist offices Falkland Islands Tourist Board (FITB), Shackleton House, West Hillside, Stanley, representative, John Fowler, Stanley, T010-500-22215, F22619, www.tourism.org.fk Will provide all information on holidays on the islands. Bookings for lodgings and for fishing, riding, vehicle hire, tours, inter-island travel are handled by *Stanley Services Ltd*, Airport Rd, Stanley, T22622, F22623, abedford@stanley-services.co.fk See above, under Getting there, for the Falklands Islands Tourist Board's London Office. **Falklands Conservation**, PO Box 571, Stanley, T22247, F22288, www.falklandsconservation.com Publishes *A Visitors Guide to the Falklands* (November 2001).

Sleeping & eating

In all cases, advance reservation of room is essential

L pp *Malvina House*, 3 Ross Rd, T21355, malvina@horizon.co.fk Very good, full board, power showers, hot drinks, central heating, TV, nice restaurant, bar, spa, laundry. **L** *Upland Goose Hotel*, 20-22 Ross Rd, T21455, fic@horizon.co.fk Some cheaper rooms, full board, lounge bar and restaurant. **B** *Dolphins Guest House and Tea Rooms*, T/F 22950, commersons@horizon.co.fk Central location, bed and breakfast, lunches and evening meals are also available. *Emma's Guest House*, 36 Ross Rd, emmas@horizon.co.fk Being refurbished mid-2002. **C** pp *Kay MacCallum's*, bed and breakfast, 14 Drury St, T/F21071, F21148. Dinner £5, lunch £2-3, excellent value, good food. Highly recommended (will permit camping in her grounds). *Isabel Short*, 2 Brisbane Road, T25155, pwshort@horizon.co.fk Very central but quiet position, bed and breakfast. All Stanley B&Bs are priced at around £25 pp or under. Fish and chips and pizza at *Woodbine Café*, 29 Fitzroy Rd, T21102. Closed Sun and Mon. *Deanos* bistro, bar snacks on John St, including vegetarian menu. *Shortys Diner*, Snake Hill. 1100-2100, closed Wed. *Falklands Brasserie*, Philomel St, centrally located 1 min from the Public Jetty, T21159, brasserie@horizon.co.fk Offers innovative cooking using local produce, opens 1100 and serves lunch, afternoon tea, and evening meal. *Lighthouse Seamans Centre*, over the bridge next to FIPASS. Serves tea, coffee, snacks, home cooking and lunches, open all day, all are welcome. *Stanley Bakery*, T22692. Mon-Fri, 0830-1530, Sat 0900-1230. **Bars** The few pubs, the *Globe* near the

Stanley

0 metres 100
0 yards 100

■ **Sleeping**
1 Emma's
2 Upland Goose

● **Eating**
1 Globe Pub
2 Shorty's Dine
3 Victory Pub

public jetty, the *Victory* on Philomel Hill, *Deanos* on Dean St, the *Stanley Arms* at west end of Stanley, John Biscoe Rd, and the *Ship* behind the *Upland Goose Hotel* are popular meeting places (open all day, except Sun only from 1200 to 1400, and 1900-2200).

There are some well-stocked stores, open daily. *Falkland Printz* photo shop at Mt Pleasant Airport, £6.55 (24 hrs for 36 exposures, plus £1.50 1 hr, sells slide film), films can be deposited at *Pastimes* in town for no extra charge (only available for the overnight service).

Shopping

International Tours and Travel, Beauchene Shopping Centre, Stanley, T22041, F22042, int.travel@horizon.co.fk Handle inbound tourist bookings, book FIGAS flights, arrange tours etc and are the Falkland Island agents for *LanChile*. Recommended. *Sulivan Shipping Services Ltd*, Davis St, Stanley, T22626, F22625, sulivan@horizon.co.fk Deal principally with cruise ship passengers. *Stanley Services Ltd Travel Division*, see Tourist offices, above. Offer inbound tourist services, FIGAS flights, excursions etc.

Tour operators

Rentals: The *Falkland Islands Company* (FIC), The West Shore, Stanley, T27633, F27626, fic@horizon.co.fk Rents a range of 4WD vehicles from Suzuki jeeps to Land Rover Discoveries for road use only. Also Jeff and Tracy Porter, T/F21574, tporter@horizon.co.fk Carol and Dave Eynon, *South Atlantic Marine Services*, PO Box 140, Stanley, T21145, F22674, sams@horizon.co.fk Offer adventure tourism, overland tours, boat trips, safaris and have a dive centre with deck recompression chamber (PADI courses). *Falkland Images* (SAMS) produce videos and still photographs for sale, plus the book *Beneath Falkland Waters*. Tony Smith of *Discovery Tours* (T21027, F22304, discovery@horizon.co.fk), *Montana Short* (T/F21076) and Sharon Halford of *Tenacres Tours* (T21155, F21950, tenacres@horizon.co.fk) all offer overland four-wheel drive excursions from Stanley to various sights. Neil Rowlands of *Hebe Tours*, T/F21561, nrowlands@horizon.co.fk Offers overland and boat tours, and can act as a fishing guide. Boats may be hired from *Sulivan Shipping*, T22626, or the FIC.

Transport

Communications Internet: *Hard Disk*, Fitzroy Rd, £10 per hour. **Post Office:** *Philatelic Bureau* (they sell stamps from South Georgia and the Antarctic Territories). **Telephones:** Cable and Wireless, Ross Rd, operate overseas telephone, fax, telegraph and telex services. The islands' telephone system has direct dialling worldwide. **Medical services Hospitals:** Stanley has an excellent hospital. Dental services are also available. **Useful addresses Immigration:** Customs and Immigration Department, West Hilside, Stanley, T27340, F27342, customs.fig@ horizon.co.fk Library and some other government services are in Town Hall, Ross Rd. Other government offices are in the nearby Secretariat.

Directory

Outside Stanley

On arrival, visitors are given a guide to respecting the Falklands wildlife and its habitat, with a checklist of breeding birds and mammals. Available from *Falklands Conservation*, see above, is a checklist of breeding birds and mammals together with a guide to behaviour near wildlife. Make allowance for unpredictable weather. Always wear or carry waterproof clothing; wear good boots and a peaked hat to protect the eyes from rain or hail. Outside Stanley, there is a major road to the airport at Mount Pleasant, but great care should nevertheless be taken on it. Roads connect Stanley with San Carlos (70 miles), Port San Carlos (75 miles) and Goose Green (64 miles). On West Falkland a new road connects most of the settlements. Elsewhere, tracks require four-wheel drive or motorbikes. Remember to phone farms in the camp for permission to drive across private land. Off-road driving in the boggy terrain is a skill not easily learned by short-term visitors. Near Stanley and a few farm settlements there are still some clearly-marked and fenced minefields from the 1982 war. Visitors should *never* enter these areas and should report suspicious objects to the police or military authorities in Stanley. Free minefield maps are available from the Bomb Disposal Office, Ross Road, Stanley. Ordnance Survey maps of the Islands are available from the Secretariat, £2.50 each for the 1:50,000 sheets; there is also a two-sheet, 1:250,000 map suitable for most purposes.

For wildlife enthusiasts, especially ornithologists, the Islands are an exceptional destination

Falkland Islands

Carcass Island and New Island

On Carcass Island the farm at Settlement Harbour is home to the McGills. The farm is surrounded by an arbour, alive with Black-crowned Night Herons. A group of Dusky Dolphins often play in the harbour. Patagonian Crested Ducks, with their deep wine-red eyes, can be seen spinning in courtship displays in the shallows while brilliant white male Kelp Geese and their less conspicuous female partners pick their way along the shore. Like the other islands, Carcass is an idyllic place to explore on foot; the long white beaches and colonies of penguins and albatrosses, Upland Geese grazing in the fields and Military Starlings, with their crimson breasts, marching among the tussock. Anyone who pauses will soon be befriended by the small brown tussock bird, indigenous to the Falklands. There are lovely views to West Falkland.

The tussock grass in the southern sector of New Island is home to one of the largest colonies of Prions; it is magical at nightfall when the prions return in huge, cackling, flocks to feed their young. There is also a colony of Black-browed Albatrosses. These birds once seen are never forgotten, overwhelmingly graceful in flight, endearingly serene on the nest or in courtship, and amazingly comical when landing. Adjacent to the albatrosses there is a colony of Rockhopper Penguins. These aptly named birds are often considered the punks of the penguin world with erect yellow crests. Both of these species are at present declining: Rockhoppers are being considered for the globally threatened list; and Black-browed Albatross populations are being closely monitored. It is a privilege and incredibly rewarding to sit quietly near the edge of one of these colonies.

Kim Crosbie, Scott Polar Research Institute, Cambridge, UK.

Travel outside the vicinity of Stanley and the road to Goose Green is mainly by air. The Falkland Islands Government Air Service (FIGAS, T27219, figas.fig@horizon.co.fk) operates three Islander aircraft to farm settlements and settled outer islands according to bookings, seat availability, and weather. To book a seat, visitors should telephone FIGAS no later than the morning of the day before travelling; flight schedules are announced that evening on local radio (airfares are about £1 per minute for non-islanders, luggage limit 14 kg/30 pounds, high excess charge). FIGAS tickets are also available from *Stanley Services Travel*, address under Tourist offices. Also from *International Tours and Travel Ltd*, see Tour operators, above. Regular service operates seven days a week. Flights leave from Stanley Airport, three miles east of town on the Cape Pembroke peninsula. Passengers arriving on LanChile can fly with FIGAS directly to Port Howard or Pebble Island with prior arrangement.

Sights

Battlefield visits, to some of the sites associated with the 1982 conflict, can be arranged

Sparrow Cove, Kidney Cove, and adjacent areas, only a short distance across Stanley Harbour by boat and out into Port William, are good areas to see penguins and other wildlife; dolphins often follow in the wake of your boat near The Narrows. Gypsy Cove, walking distance from Stanley, features a colony of burrowing Magellanic penguins and other shorebirds. Leopard seals, elephant seals and the occasional killer whale visit the area. Observe minefield fences which prevent close inspection of the penguins (they are not unduly inhibiting, though). At Cape Pembroke, around the town airport and the renovated lighthouse one can see Gentoo penguins and ground-nesting birds such as dotterels, snipe, and Upland geese.

Of particular interest are the hulks of old sailing ships at Stanley and Darwin. Examples at Stanley are the *Jhelum* (built in 1839 for the East India Company) near Government House, the *Charles Cooper* (the last US sailing packet to sail out of New York Harbour; in the Islands since 1866), and the iron-built *Lady Elizabeth* at the far end of the harbour (228 ft long, with three masts still standing). A Maritime History Trail has been set up around Port Stanley (self-guided with interpretive panels at key points, and guide book available at FITB; a book describing the Stanley wrecks is sold by the museum). At Darwin are the *Vicar of Bray* (last survivor of the California Gold Rush fleet), and another old iron ship, the *Garland*. Some of these hulks are still used for storage. There are interesting old French buildings and ruins at Port Louis (the road between Stanley and Port Louis is a boulder-strewn clay track, very tricky when wet).

From the Beaver hanger opposite Strathcarron, Ross Road west, walk past the various ships and monuments, along the harbour, up to the Falkland Islands Company offices. Here it is possible to walk onto the jetty and visit the after section of a 19th-century sailing vessel that is still being used as a warehouse. Also below the jetty you will see a couple of 19th-century Welsh colliers. From here go east until you reach B slip, used by the British Forces during the 1982 conflict. Carry on east, past the floating harbour and around the head of the bay to the iron barque *Lady Elizabeth*. At low tide it is possible to walk out to her. Follow the bay round and eventually you will come to various penguin rookeries and Gypsy Cove.

Volunteer Point, north of Stanley, is a wildlife sanctuary. It contains the only substantial nesting colony of King penguins outside of South Georgia. Gentoo penguins, Magellanic penguins, geese, ducks, and elephant seals are very tame and easily photographed. The sanctuary is open at the discretion of the landowner.

Sea Lion Island in the southeast is a delightful place to explore and relax. Throughout the austral summer the lodge, run by Jenny Luxton, accommodates a maximum of 15 visitors. Many Southern Sea Lions breed on the beaches; Southern Elephant Seals also breed here. A pod of Orca whales is seen almost daily cruising the kelp beds in search of an unsuspecting meal. The island also has magnificent bird life: Gentoo, Magellanic and Rockhopper Penguins, Giant Petrels (known locally as stinkers), King Cormorants, the incredible flightless Steamer Duck, Black-crowned Night Herons, the friendly Tussock Bird, Oystercatcher (Magellanic and Black) and the rare Striated Caracara. Also on the island is the HMS *Sheffield* memorial.

Sea-trout fishing is excellent on the islands. The season runs from 1 Sep to 30 Apr. A licence costs £10 per year

The smaller islands off West Falkland, such as Carcass and New Island, are the most spectacular and attractive for wildlife and scenery. New Island is divided into two distinct properties, both of which are run as nature reserves. The New Island South, on the extreme west of the archipelago, is run as a nature reserve by Ian and Maria Strange. The northern half, owned by Tony Chater, has a small sheep farm. The island has a grass airstrip and is served by FIGAS on flights limited to three passengers (owing to the length of the strip). Carcass can be visited more easily and has two self-catering cottages (see below). Cruise ships stop here *en route* to Antarctica, but only for a few hours. **Saunders Island**, besides a representative sample of wildlife, contains the ruins of the 18th century British outpost at Port Egmont. It is run by Susan and David Pole-Evans (T41298, F41296, davidpe@horizon.co.fk). There is a small group of King Penguins at the Neck, about three-hour walk, 45 minutes by jeep from the settlement. Gentoo, Magellanic, Rock Hoppers and albatross can also be seen here (**B** pp in a self-catering Portakabin at the Neck, including transport, basic). A further 1½-2 hours walk goes to the point where sea elephants can be seen. Another good place is the bay just north of the settlement with many Gentoo and Magellanic penguins and other wildlife. At the settlement is a self-catering cottage, **D** per person per night.

Sleeping

The comfortable tourist lodges at Sea Lion Island, the most southerly inhabited island of the group (35 mins flight from Stanley), and Pebble Island (40 mins flight) are good bases to view wildlife. Each lodge has a long wheelbase Land Rover for transport to the airstrip and points of interest nearby. **On Sea Lion Island**: **L-AL** pp *Sea Lion Lodge*, T32004, F32003, www.sealionisland.com Price depends on season, full board, some rooms shared bath, modern, central heating, all rooms with phone and internet. **At Port Howard**: **AL** pp*Port Howard Lodge*, T/F42187, www.port-howard.com Price depends on season, all rooms ensuite, central heating, excursions extra, rod hire, Land Rover hire. This scenic lodge, on West Falkland, offers excellent trout fishing, a small but interesting war museum, and an opportunity to see the operations of a traditional large sheep station. **On Pebble Island**: **AL** *Pebble Island Hotel*, T/F 41093, pebblehotel@horizon.co.fk or 21 St Mary's Walk, Stanley, T21439, vsteen@horizon.co.fk Ensuite rooms, central heating, full board. **On Carcass Island**: **B** *Carcass Island Cottages*, Mr and Mrs McGill, Ross Rd East, T41106, F41107, on West Falkland. Price per cottage,

Falkland Islands

on one of the wild-life jewels of the Falklands, open summer only. **On New Island**: There are basic self-catering facilities; enquiries should be addressed to Ian and Maria Strange, Snake Hill, Stanley, T21185, F21186; on New Island 42017. **On Weddell Island: A** pp *Mountain View House*, Karen Taylor, T42398, F42399. **A-B** pp *Weddell House* and **C** pp *Hamilton Cottages*, full board available; for all see www.weddell.island.com

Also **D** pp *Salvador* (Gibraltar Station, East Falkland, T31199/31193, F31194), children half price, also has camping. *Darwin House*, T32255, darwin.h@horizon.co.uk Close to Goose Green, the British and Argentine cemeteries and only 35 mins' drive from Mount Pleasant Airport, an excellent base for the start of a holiday. Offers fully-catered accommodation in the lodge and has 2 cottages available for self-catering.

Camping: is not encouraged on outer islands because of the very real risk of fire and disturbance to wildlife. However the following locations do welcome campers, subject to farm work: *Port Sussex*, T32203, F32204; *Estancia*, T31042; *Rincon Grande*, T31119, F31149; *Bold Cove*, T42178, F42177; *West Lagoons*, T/F41194; *Spring Point*, T/F42001; and the *Falkland Landholdings Farms*, T22698, F22699, fhl@horizon.co.fk

Background

History Records of early voyages are ambiguous, but Dutchman Sebald de Weert made the first universally acknowledged sighting in 1598. (An earlier sighting in 1592 is said to have been made by English sailor John Davis.) The Englishman John Strong landed in 1690 and named the Falkland Sound for a British peer; this name was later applied to the entire group. The Islands acquired their French appellation, Iles Malouines, from 17th-century seafarers from the channel port of St Malo. This in turn became the Spanish Islas Malvinas.

In 1764 France established a small colony of Acadians at Port Louis under Bougainville. Two years later France sold the settlement to Spain, under which it became a military garrison and penal colony. At about the same time as France, Britain had built an outpost at Saunders Island, West Falkland, whose occupants Spain discovered and expelled in 1770. Restored in the following year after threat of war, the post was abandoned in 1774.

Deserted by Spain in 1811, during the South American wars of independence, the Islands lacked formal authority until 1820, when the United Provinces of the River Plate (later part of Argentina) raised their flag at Port Louis (Soledad). In 1831, a US warship destroyed a promising colonization project under the auspices of a German-born merchant from Buenos Aires, who had arrested and imprisoned US sealers operating in the area. After British warships expelled a token Buenos Aires force in 1833, the Islands experienced nearly 150 years of stability until April 1982, when Argentina invaded and occupied. Britain's counter invasion recaptured the Islands by June of that year. After extensive talks including representatives from the Islands, a joint statement was signed in London by the Argentine and British governments on 14 July 1999. This agreement ended the ban on travel to the Islands by Argentine citizens, planned for co-operation in the conservation of fish stocks and gave permission for a war memorial in the Argentine cemetery among other confidence building measures. Flights from Chile were resumed and flights from the Argentine mainland began in October 1999. After a fishery zone was established in 1986, giving the islands the opportunity to sell fishing rights, they have become economically self-sufficient in all areas except defence. Sheep's wool is therefore no longer the dominant sector of the economy. Tourism has also grown, with 30,000 visitors estimated for the 2001-02 season, both land-based and on cruise ships.

People The population, according to the 2001 census, was 2,379. 60% of the residents were Falklands-born. Slightly more than a quarter live and work on sheep farms.

Education A Junior and Senior Community School in Stanley cater to the needs of town children and rural children who board in the School Hostel. Instruction to GCSE Level is available locally (compulsory to the age of 16), but higher education requires overseas travel, usually to Britain. Rural children receive attention from settlement instructors or travelling teachers. Radio is used to keep in contact with the more isolated farms.

The islands are internally self-governing. Decisions are made by an elected Legislative Council. The Islands Constitution provides for a Governor, appointed from London.

Administration

The Falkland Islands/Islas Malvinas comprise about 420 islands in two groups: East Falkland (Isla Soledad) with its adjacent islands, about 2,600 square miles; and West Falkland (Gran Malvina), with its islands, about 2,100 square miles. Approximately 480 miles northeast of Cape Horn, the Islands lie between latitudes 51 and 53 south and between longitudes 57 and 62 west. Nearly all land combat during the 1982 war was confined to the northern half of East Falkland; its southern peninsula of Lafonia, and West Falkland were little affected.

Land & environment

The main islands are covered by acidic peaty soil of low fertility, though at higher elevations (over 500 m) the peat gives way to stony and clay soils. Large areas of the major islands are covered by oceanic heathlands, consisting of White Grass, dwarf shrubs, Mountain Berry and Christmas Bush. These heathlands support little fauna, but where they are crossed by small streams the valleys are covered by rich grasslands which attract several species, among them Upland and Ruddy Headed Geese. Tussac grass, which was common on the larger islands until the introduction of livestock farming, covers about 270 of the smaller islands. Tussac grass, which grows to 3m in height and has leaves up to 2m long, thrives in marine environments subject to sea spray and moisture-laden atmospheres with a high salt content. It provides ideal nesting for birds: 46 of the 62 species which regularly breed on the islands use tussac grass as a nesting or feeding habitat. There are few trees on the islands and only where these have been introduced and carefully cultivated at settlements such as Hill Cove.

South Georgia

South Georgia, in latitude 54½° south and longitude 36° to 38° west, has an area of about 3,755 sq km, and a small transient population of soldiers and British Antarctic Survey scientists. During the summer months, tourists may sometimes book a passage on a Royal Fleet Auxiliary vessel at Stanley for £520 return, but weather conditions sometimes prevent landings. Intending visitors must submit a request through the Commissioner in Stanley. The Island was briefly occupied by Argentina in April 1982 (21 days).

South Georgia is a mass of high, snow-covered mountains and glaciers. Between 1951 and 1980 at King Edward Point, at sea level, snow fell an average of nearly 200 days per annum, but the coastal area is free from snow and partially covered by vegetation in summer. Wildlife consists of most of the same species found in the Falkland Islands/Islas Malvinas, but in much larger numbers. Reindeer, introduced by Norwegian whalers in 1909, have flourished. Other points of interest are seven abandoned whaling stations, the little white church, and many wrecks. A South Georgia Whaling Museum has been established at Grytviken. If it is unmanned access may be obtained from the Magistrate (Garrison Commander) at King Edward Point, 1 km away. The museum has a display of artefacts, photographs and other items about the old Antarctic whaling and sealing industry. Local administration of South Georgia is by the magistrate, who also runs the island's post office with its distinctive stamps.

Antarctica

Antarctica, the fifth largest continent, is 99.8% covered with perpetual ice. Although very inaccessible, approximately 12,000 tourists visit annually and it is well known for extraordinary scenery, wildlife, scientific stations, and historic sites. The weather may also be spectacularly severe, thus visits are confined to the brief summer. Presently 17 countries operate 43 scientific stations with wintering personnel there, and about 18 stations are open for summer only. A wintering population of about 1,000 lives in a continent larger than Europe. The governmental stations are expensive to maintain thus, with only minor exceptions, they make no provision for visitors not connected with their work. The Antarctic Heritage Trust and some other organizations maintain several historical huts of great interest where organized groups are admitted and many current research stations

There is a vast amount of specialist and general books about Antarctica, but the current best single source of information is Antarctica: great stories from the frozen continent by Reader's Digest (first published Sydney 1985, with several later editions)

allow visitors for a tour of a couple of hours. Of the historic huts, the one at Port Lockroy, established in 1944 and now a museum, has recently become the most visited site.

Governance of Antarctica is principally through the Antarctic Treaty (1959) signed by all countries operating there (45 countries were parties to the Treaty in 2002, these represent over 75% of the Earth's population). Most visitors will be affected by several provisions of the Treaty, in particular those of the Environmental Protocol of 1991. Seven countries have territorial claims over parts of Antarctica and three of these overlap (Antártida Argentina, British Antarctic Territory, and Territorio Chileno Antártico); the Treaty has neutralized these with provision of free access to citizens of contracting states. Some display of sovereignty is legitimate; many stations operate a Post Office where philatelic items and various souvenirs are sold.

www.spri.cam.ac.uk
General information
including links to
other sites found
at the Scott Polar
Research Institute
site

The region south of South America is the most accessible part of the Antarctic, therefore over half the scientific stations are there and on adjacent islands. Coincidentally it is one of the most spectacular areas with many mountains, glaciers and fjords closely approachable by sea. Two ice-breaker, several other large ships, as many as 16 private yachts, and an air company carry passengers there every austral summer. Three ports are used: Stanley (Falkland Islands/Islas Malvinas), Punta Arenas (Chile), and Ushuaia (Argentina), the last is the major base for yachts. Vessels sailing from one may return to another or go farther to South Africa, New Zealand, or Australia. Most are fully booked well in advance by luxury class passengers but sometimes late opportunistic vacancies can be secured by local agencies (on the basis that any vacant cabin is a loss). During the 2001-2002 austral summer 16 passenger vessels made several visits each to Antarctica carrying between 50 to 120 tourists who land at several sites during a fortnight's voyage. Some much larger vessels also visit; these generally do not land passengers but merely cruise around the coasts.

Voyages from South America and the Falkland Islands/Islas Malvinas involve at least two days each way, crossing the Drake Passage where sea conditions may be very uncomfortable. No guarantee of landings, views or wildlife is possible and delays due to storms are not exceptional. Conversely, on a brilliant day, some of the most spectacular sights and wildlife anywhere can be seen. All visitors should be well prepared for adverse conditions with warm clothing, windproofs and waterproofs, and good boots for wet landings. Weather and state of the sea can change quickly without warning.

In 1991 the **International Association of Antarctica Tour Operators** was formed (PO Box 2178, Basalt, Colorado, US, 81621; T+1-970-7041047, F+1-970-7049660, www. iaato.org) which represents the majority of companies and can provide details of most Antarctic voyages planned during an austral summer (there is much annual variation). Many vessels have a principal contractor and a number of other companies bring smaller groups, thus it is advantageous to contact the principal. *Adventure Network International* (4800 North Federal Highway, Suite 307 D, Boca Raton, FL 33431, USA; T+1-561-237 2359, F+1-561-347 7523, www.adventure-network.com), provides flights to Antarctica which depart from Punta Arenas where there is a local office (935 Arauco, Punta Arenas, Chile; T+56-61-247735, F226167). Wheeled aircraft fly as far as a camp at Patriot Hills (80° 19S, 81° 20W) whence ski-aircraft proceed to the South Pole, vicinity of Vinson Massif (4,897 m, Antarctica's highest peak), and elsewhere. Tickets start at about US$12,000; services may become overloaded and delayed, thus no guarantee of reaching one's destination is practicable. This company also flies occasionally from Cape Town to Dronning Maud Land and *Safair* is proposing to start similar flights. One day overflights are operated by *Qantas* from Sydney, Melbourne and Perth in Australia.

More opportunistic travel is possible aboard some private yachts which carry passengers (including mountaineers and other adventurers). These voyages are not co-ordinated but enquiries on the waterside at Ushuaia, or the other ports listed may secure a passage. Similarly opportunities to travel with the Argentine, Chilean or Russian supply ships occur but are virtually impossible to arrange other than at the departure ports. Comfort and prices are usually much less than for the cruise ships. Many tourist ships and some yachts also visit South Georgia; there are other possibilities for reaching this Antarctic island described above.

RK Headland, Scott Polar Research Institute, Cambridge.

Background

15

Background

History

It is generally accepted that the earliest settlers in South America were related to people who had crossed the Bering Straits from Asia and drifted through the Americas from about 50,000 BC. Alternative theories of early migrations from across the Pacific and Atlantic have been rife since Thor Heyerdahl's raft expeditions in 1947 and 1969-70. The earliest evidence of human presence has been found at various sites: in the Central Andes (with a radiocarbon date between 12000 and 9000 BC), northern Venezuela (11000 BC), southeast Brazil, south-central Chile and Argentine Patagonia (from at least 10000 BC). After the Pleistocene Ice Age, 8000-7000 BC, rising sea levels and climatic changes introduced new conditions as many mammal species became extinct and coastlands were drowned. A wide range of crops was brought into cultivation and camelids and guinea pigs were domesticated. It seems that people lived nomadically in small groups, mainly hunting and gathering but also cultivating some plants seasonally, until villages with effective agriculture began to appear between 2500-1500 BC. The earliest ceramic-making in the western hemisphere was thought to have come from what is now Colombia and Ecuador, around 4000 BC, but fragments of painted pottery were found near Santarém, Brazil, in 1991 with dates of 6000-5000 BC.

The coast of central Peru was where settled life began to develop most rapidly. The abundant wealth of marine life produced by the Humboldt Current, especially north of today's Lima, boosted population growth and settlement in this area. Around 2000 BC climatic change dried up the *lomas* ('fog meadows'), and drove sea shoals into deeper water. People turned more to farming and began to spread inland along river valleys. As sophisticated irrigation and canal systems were developed, farming productivity increased and communities had more time to devote to building and producing ceramics and textiles. The development of pottery also led to trade and cultural links with other communities.

The earliest buildings constructed by organized group labour were *huacas*, adobe platform mounds, centres of some cult or sacred power dating from the second millennium BC onwards. During this period, however, much more advanced architecture was being built at Kotosh, in the central Andes near Huánuco, now in Peru. Japanese archaeological excavations there in the 1960s revealed a temple with ornamental niches and friezes. Some of the earliest pottery was also found here, showing signs of influence from southern Ecuador and the tropical lowlands, adding weight to theories of Andean culture originating in the Amazon. Radiocarbon dates of some Kotosh remains are as early as 1850 BC.

Chavín and Sechín For the next 1,000 years or so up to c900 BC, communities grew and spread inland from the north coast and south along the north highlands. Farmers still lived in simple adobe or rough stone houses but built increasingly large and complex ceremonial centres. As farming became more productive and pottery more advanced, commerce grew and states began to develop throughout central and north-central Peru, with the associated signs of social structure and hierarchies.

Around 900 BC a new era was marked by the rise of two important centres; Chavín de Huántar in the central Andes and Sechín Alto, inland from Casma on the north coast, both now in Peru. The chief importance of Chavín de Huántar was not so much in its highly advanced architecture as in the influence of its cult, coupled with the artistic style of its ceramics and other artefacts. The founders of Chavín may have originated in the tropical lowlands, as some of its carved monoliths show representations of monkeys and felines.

The Chavín cult This was paralleled by the great advances made in this period in textile production and in some of the earliest examples of metallurgy. The origins of metallurgy have been attributed to some gold, silver and copper ornaments found in graves in Chongoyape, near Chiclayo, which show Chavín-style features. But earlier evidence has been discovered at Kuntur Wasi (some 120 km east of the coast at Pacasmayo) where 4,000-year old gold has been found, and in the Andahuaylas region, dating from 1800-900 BC. The religious symbolism of gold and other precious metals and stones is thought to have been an inspiration behind some of the beautiful artefacts found in the central Andean area.

The cultural brilliance of Chavín de Huántar was complemented by its contemporary, Sechín which may have combined forces, with Sechín as the military power that spread the cultural word of Chavín. Their influence did not reach far to the south where the Paracas and Tiwanaku cultures held sway. The Chavín hegemony broke up around 500 BC, soon after which the Nasca culture began to bloom in southern Peru. This period, up to about AD 500, was a time of great social and cultural development. Sizable towns of 5-10,000 inhabitants grew on the south coast, populated by artisans, merchants, government administrators and religious officials.

Paracas-Nasca Nasca origins are traced back to about the second century BC, to the Paracas Cavernas and Necropolis, on the coast in the national park near Pisco in Peru. The extreme dryness of the desert here has preserved remarkably the textiles and ceramics in the mummies' tombs excavated. The technical quality and stylistic variety in weaving and pottery rank them among the world's best, and many of the finest examples can be seen in the museums of Lima. The famous Nasca Lines are a feature of the region. Straight lines, abstract designs and outlines of animals are scratched in the dark desert surface forming a lighter contrast that can be seen clearly from the air. There are many theories of how and why the lines were made but no definitive explanation has yet been able to establish their place in South American history. There are similarities between the style of some of the line patterns and that of the pottery and textiles of the same period. In contrast to the quantity and quality of the Nasca artefacts found, relatively few major buildings belonging to this period have been uncovered in the southern desert. Alpaca hair found in Nasca textiles, however, indicates that there must have been strong trade links with highland people.

Moche culture Nasca's contemporaries on the north coast were the militaristic Moche who, from about AD 100-800, built up an empire whose traces stretch from Piura in the north to Huarmey, in the south. The Moche built their capital outside present day Trujillo. The huge pyramid temples of the Huaca del Sol and Huaca de la Luna mark the remains of this city. Moche roads and system of way stations are thought to have been an early inspiration for the Inca network. The Moche increased the coastal population with intensive irrigation projects. Skilful engineering works were carried out, such as the La Cumbre canal, still in use today, and the Ascope aqueduct, both on the Chicama River. The Moche's greatest achievement, however, was its artistic genius. Exquisite ornaments in gold, silver and precious stones were made by its craftsmen. Moche pottery progressed through five stylistic periods, most notable for the stunningly lifelike portrait vases. A wide variety of everyday scenes were created in naturalistic ceramics, telling us more about Moche life than is known about other earlier cultures, and perhaps used by them as 'visual aids' to compensate for the lack of a written language. A spectacular discovery of a Moche royal tomb at Sipán, made in February 1987 by Walter Alva, director of the Brüning Archaeological Museum, Lambayeque, included semi-precious stones brought from Chile and Argentina, and seashells from Ecuador. The Moche were great navigators.

The cause of the collapse of the Moche Empire around AD 600-700 is unknown, but it may have been started by a 30-year drought at the end of the sixth century, followed by one of the periodic El Niño flash floods (identified by meteorologists from ice thickness in the Andes) and finished by the encroaching forces of the Huari Empire. The decline of the Moche signalled a general tipping of the balance of power in Peru from the north coast to the south sierra.

Huari-Tiwanaku The ascendant Huari-Tiwanaku movement, from AD 600-1000, combined the religious cult of the Tiwanaku site in the Titicaca basin, with the military dynamism of the Huari, based in the central highlands. The two cultures developed independently but they are generally thought to have merged compatibly. Up until their own demise around AD 1440, the Huari-Tiwanaku had spread their empire and influence across much of south Peru, north Bolivia and Argentina. They made considerable gains in art and technology, building roads, terraces and irrigation canals across the country. The Huari-Tiwanaku ran their empire with efficient labour and administrative systems that were later adopted and refined by the Incas. Labour tribute for state projects practised by the Moche were further developed. But the empire could not contain regional kingdoms who began to fight for land and power. As control broke down, rivalry and coalitions emerged, and the system collapsed. With the country once again fragmented, the scene was set for the rise of the Incas.

Chachapoyas and Chimú cultures After the decline of the Huari Empire, the unity that had been imposed on the Andes was broken. A new stage of autonomous regional or local political organizations began. Among the cultures corresponding to this period were the Chachapoyas in northern highlands (see page 1158) and the Chimú. The Chachapoyas people were not so much an empire as a loose-knit 'confederation of ethnic groups with no recognized capital' (Morgan Davis 'Chachapoyas: The Cloud People', Ontario, 1988). But the culture did develop into an advanced society with great skill in road and monument building. Their fortress at Kuelap was known as the most impregnable in the Peruvian Andes. The Chimú culture had two centres. To the north was Lambayeque, near Chiclayo, while to the south, in the Moche valley near present-day Trujillo, was the great adobe walled city of Chan Chán. Covering 20 sq km, this was the largest pre-Hispanic Peruvian city. Chimú has been classified as a despotic state that based its power on wars of conquest. Rigid social stratification existed and power rested in the hands of the great lord *Siquic* and the lord *Alaec*. These lords were followed in social scale by a group of urban couriers who enjoyed a certain degree of economic power. At the bottom were the peasants and slaves. In 1450, the Chimú kingdom was conquered by the Inca Túpac Yupanqui, the son and heir of the Inca ruler Pachacuti Inca Yupanqui.

Cultures of the northern Andes What is today Ecuador was a densely populated region with a variety of peoples. One of the most important of these was the **Valdivia culture** (3500-1500 BC) on the coast, from which remains of buildings and earthenware figures have been found. A rich mosaic of cultures developed in the period 500 BC to AD 500, after which integration of groups occurred. In the mid-15th century, the relentless expansion of the Inca empire reached Ecuador. The **Cañaris** resisted until 1470 and the Quitu/Caras were defeated in 1492. Further north, most of the peoples who occupied Colombia were primitive hunters or nomad agriculturists, but one part of the country, the high basins of the Eastern Cordillera, was densely occupied by **Chibcha Indians** who had become sedentary farmers. Their staple foods were maize and the potato, and they had no domestic animal save the dog; the use they could make of the land was therefore limited. Other cultures present in Colombia in the precolumbian era were the **Tayrona, Quimbaya, Sinú** and **Calima**. Exhibits of theirs and the Chibcha (Muisca) Indians' gold-work can be seen at the Gold Museum in Bogotá and other cities.

The southern Andes Although there was some influence in southern Bolivia, northern Chile and northern Argentina from cultures such as Tiwanaku, most of the southern Andes was an area of autonomous peoples, probably living in fortified settlements by the time the Incas arrived in the mid-15th century. The conquerors from Peru moved south to the Río Maule in Chile where they encountered the fierce **Mapuches** (Araucanians) who halted their advance. Archaeological evidence from the Amazon basin and Brazil is more scanty than from the Andes or Pacific because the materials used for house building, clothing and decoration were perishable and did not survive the warm, humid conditions of the jungle. Ceramics have been found on Marajó island at the mouth of the Amazon while on the coast much evidence comes from huge shell mounds, called *sambaquis*. Although structured societies developed and population was large, no political groupings of the scale of those of the Andes formed. The Incas made few inroads into the Amazon so it was the arrival of the Portuguese in 1500 which initiated the greatest change on the Atlantic side of the continent.

The origins of the Inca Dynasty are shrouded in mythology and shaky evidence. The best known story reported by the Spanish chroniclers talks about Manco Cápac and his sister rising out of Lake Titicaca, created by the sun as divine founders of a chosen race. This was in approximately AD 1200. Over the next 300 years the small tribe grew to supremacy as leaders of the largest empire ever known in the Americas, the four territories of

The Inca Dynasty

Background

Tawantinsuyo, united by Cusco as the umbilicus of the Universe (the four quarters of Tawantinsuyo, all radiating out from Cusco, were Chinchaysuyo, north and northwest; Cuntisuyo, south and west; Collasuyo, south and east; Antisuyo, east).

At its peak, just before the Spanish Conquest, the Inca Empire stretched from the Río Maule in central Chile, north to the present Ecuador-Colombia border, contained most of Ecuador, Peru, west Bolivia, north Chile and northwest Argentina. The area was roughly equivalent to France, Belgium, Holland, Luxembourg, Italy and Switzerland combined, 980,000 sq km. For a brief description of **Inca Society**, see under Cusco. The first Inca ruler, Manco Cápac, moved to the fertile Cusco region, and established Cusco as his capital. Successive generations of rulers were fully occupied with local conquests of rivals, such as the Colla and Lupaca to the south, and the Chanca to the northwest. At the end of Inca Viracocha's reign the hated Chanca were finally defeated, largely thanks to the heroism of one of his sons, Pachacuti Inca Yupanqui, who was subsequently crowned as the new ruler.

From the start of Pachacuti's own reign in 1438, imperial expansion grew in earnest. With the help of his son and heir, Topa Inca, territory was conquered from the Titicaca basin south into Chile, and all the north and central coast down to the Lurin Valley. In 1460-71, the Incas also laid siege to the Chimú. Typical of the Inca method of government, some of the Chimú skills were assimilated into their own political and administrative system, and some Chimú nobles were even given positions in Cusco.

Perhaps the pivotal event in Inca history came in 1527 with the death of the ruler, Huayna Cápac. Civil war broke out in the confusion over his rightful successor. One of his legitimate sons, Huáscar, ruled the southern part of the empire from Cusco. Atahualpa, Huáscar's half-brother, governed Quito, the capital of Chinchaysuyo. In 1532, soon after Atahualpa had won the civil war, Francisco Pizarro arrived in Tumbes with 179 *conquistadores*, many on horseback. Atahualpa's army was marching south, probably for the first time, when he clashed with Pizarro at Cajamarca. **Francisco Pizarro**'s only chance against the formidable imperial army he encountered at Cajamarca was a bold stroke. He drew Atahualpa into an ambush, slaughtered his guards, promised him liberty if a certain room were filled with treasure, and finally killed him on the pretext that an Inca army was on its way to free him. Pushing on to Cusco, he was at first hailed as the executioner of a traitor: Atahualpa had ordered the death of Huáscar in 1533, while himself captive of Pizarro, and his victorious generals were bringing the defeated Huáscar to see his half-brother. Panic followed when the *conquistadores* set about sacking the city, and they fought off with difficulty an attempt by Manco Inca to recapture Cusco in 1536.

The Spanish conquest

Pizarro's arrival in Peru had been preceded by Columbus' landfall on the Paria Peninsula (Venezuela) on 5 August 1498 and Spanish reconaissance of the Pacific coast in 1522. Permanent Spanish settlement was established at Santa Marta (Colombia) in 1525 and Cartagena was founded in 1533. Gonzalo Jiménez de Quesada conquered the Chibcha kingdom and founded Bogotá in 1538. Pizarro's lieutenant, Sebastián de Belalcázar, was sent north through Ecuador; he captured Quito with Diego de Almagro in 1534. Gonzalo Pizarro, Francisco's brother, took over control of Quito in 1538 and, during his exploration of the Amazon lowlands, he sent Francisco de Orellana to prospect downriver. Orellana did not return, but drifted down the Amazon, finally reaching the river's mouth in 1542, the first European to cross the continent in this way. Belalcázar pushed north, founding Pasto, Cali and Popayán (Colombia) in 1536, arriving in Bogotá in 1538. Meanwhile, wishing to secure his communications with Spain, Pizarro founded Lima, near the ocean, as his capital in 1535. The same year Diego de Almagro set out to conquer Chile. Unsuccessful, he returned to Peru, quarrelled with Pizarro, and in 1538 fought a pitched battle with Pizarro's men at the Salt Pits, near Cusco. He was defeated and put to death. Pizarro, who had not been at the battle, was assassinated in his palace in Lima by Almagro's son three years later. In 1541, Pedro de Valdivia founded Santiago de Chile after a renewed attempt to conquer Chile. Like the Incas before them, the Spaniards were unable to master the Mapuches; Valdivia was killed in 1553 and a defensive barrier along the Río Biobío had to be built to protect the colony.

Since 1516 European seafarers had visited the Río de la Plata, first Juan de Solís, then Sebastian Cabot and his rival Diego García in 1527. An expedition led by Pedro de Mendoza founded Buenos Aires in 1536, but it was abandoned in 1541. Mendoza sent Juan

Background

The Jesuits

Between 1609, when they built their first reducción or mission in the region of Guaíra in present day Brazil, and 1767, when they were expelled from Spanish America, the Jesuits founded about 50 missions around the upper reaches of the Ríos Paraná, Paraguay and Uruguay. In 1627, the northern missions around Guaíra were attacked by slave-hunting Bandeirantes from São Paulo, forcing them to flee southwards. Some 10,000 converts, led by their priests, floated 700 rafts down the Río Parapanema into the Paraná, only to find their route blocked by the Guaíra Falls. Pushing on for eight days through dense forest, they built new boats below the Falls and continued their journey to reestablish their missions 725 km from their original homes.

Efficiently organized and strictly laid out, the missions prospered, growing indigenous and European crops and herding cattle. Their

success and economic power attracted many enemies, from the Spanish crown to local landowners and traders. When, in 1750, Spain and Portugal settled their South American border dispute, seven missions were placed under Portuguese control. This the Jesuits resisted with arms, fuelling further the suspicion of the order's excessive power. Under highest secrecy, King Carlos III sent instructions to South America in 1767 to expel the Jesuits. 2,000 were shipped to Italy, their property was auctioned and their schools and colleges were taken over by the Franciscans and Dominicans. By the early 19th century, many of the missions had fallen into disrepair.

Only four missions show signs of their former splendour: San Ignacio Miní in Argentina; Jesús and Trinidad in Paraguay; and São Miguel in Brazil.

---

de Ayolas up the Río Paraná to reach Peru from the east. It is not known for certain what happened to Ayolas, but his lieutenant Domingo Martínez de Irala founded Asunción on the Paraguay in 1537. This was the base from which the Spaniards relaunched their conquest of the Río de la Plata and Buenos Aires was refounded in 1580.

Treasure hunt   As Spanish colonization built itself around new cities, the *conquistadores* set about finding the wealth which had lured them to South America in the first place. The great prize came in 1545 when the hill of silver at Potosí (Bolivia) was discovered. Other mining centres grew up and the trade routes to supply them and carry out the riches were established. The Spanish crown soon imposed political and administrative jurisdiction over its new empire, replacing the power of the *conquistadores* with that of governors and bureaucrats. The Viceroyalty of Peru became the major outlet for the wealth of the Americas, but each succeeding representative of the Kingdom of Spain was faced with the twofold threat of subduing the Inca successor state of Vilcabamba, north of Cusco, and unifying the fierce Spanish factions. Francisco de Toledo (appointed 1568) solved both problems during his 14 years in office: Vilcabamba was crushed in 1572 and the last reigning Inca, Túpac Amaru, put to death. For the next 200 years the Viceroys closely followed Toledo's system, if not his methods. The Major Government – the Viceroy, the *Audiencia* (High Court), and *corregidores* (administrators) – ruled through the Minor Government – Indian chiefs put in charge of large groups of natives: a rough approximation to the original Inca system.

The Indians of Peru rose in 1780, under the leadership of an Inca noble who called himself Túpac Amaru II. He and many of his lieutenants were captured and put to death under torture at Cusco. Another Indian leader in revolt suffered the same fate in 1814, but this last flare-up had the sympathy of many of the locally born Spanish, who resented their status: inferior to the Spaniards born in Spain, the refusal to give them any but the lowest offices, the high taxation imposed by the home government, and the severe restrictions upon trade with any country but Spain. This was a complaint common to all parts of the Spanish empire and it fostered a twin-pronged independence movement. Given impetus by Napoleon's invasion of Spain in 1808, Simón Bolívar, El Libertador, led a revolution in the north and José de San Martín, with his Army of the Andes, led an uprising through Argentina and Chile. Both converged on Peru.

Towards independence

The Bandeirantes

Reviled in some quarters for their appalling treatment of Indians, revered in others for their determination and willingness to withstand extreme hardship in the pursuit of their goals, the bandeirantes are an indispensible element in the formation of Brazil.

The Portuguese knew that South America held great riches; their Spanish rivals were shipping vast quantities back to Europe from Peru. Legends proliferated of mountains of precious stones, golden lakes and other marvels, also of terrifying places, all in the mysterious interior. Regardless of the number of expeditions sent into the sertão which returned empty-handed, or failed to return at all, there was always the promise of silver, emeralds or other jewels to lure the adventurous beyond the coast.

The one thing that Brazil had in abundance was Indians. Throughout the colony there was a demand for slaves to work the plantations and farms, especially in the early 17th century when Portugal temporarily lost its African possession of Angola.

The men who settled in São Paulo proved themselves expert at enslaving Indians. Without official sanction, and certainly not blessed by the Jesuits, these adventurers formed themselves into expeditions which would set out often for years at a time, to capture slaves for the internal market. The Guaraní Indians who had been organized into reducciones by the Jesuits around the Río Paraguay were the top prize and there developed an intense rivalry between the bandeirantes and the Jesuits. The priests regarded the Paulistas as murderous and inhumane; the slavers felt they had some justification in attacking the missions because they were in Spanish territory and, in the 17th century, the entire western boundary of Brazil was in dispute.

This was one side of the coin. The other was that the bandeirantes were incredibly resourceful, trekking for thousands of kilometres, withstanding great hardships, travelling light, inspired not just by the desire to get rich, but also by a fierce patriotism. To uncover the sertão's riches, they demystified it, trekking into Minas Gerais, Goiás and Mato Grosso looking for precious metals. Through their efforts, the Minas Gerais gold rush began. In the bandeirantes' footsteps came settlers and cattle herders who took over the lands that had been emptied of their Indian population. Although Indians were exploited as labour and became a source of income for the Paulistas, they also intermarried with the Europeans, hastening the miscegenation process which became so evident throughout Brazil.

Bolívar, born in Venezuela in 1783, was involved in the early struggle to free the region from Spanish rule. In 1811 Venezuela declared itself an independent republic, only to be defeated by Spain in 1812. Bolívar led a new revolt in 1813, which was crushed in 1815. He went into exile in Jamaica and Haiti, to return in 1816 with a new army which, in a bold move, he led over the Andes from Venezuela to liberate Nueva Granada (as Colombia was called) at the Battle of Boyacá in 1819. He proclaimed a new republic, Gran Colombia, taking in Colombia, Venezuela and Ecuador. Venezuela was freed at the Battle of Carabobo in 1821.

San Martín's Argentine troops, convoyed from Chile under the protection of the English admiral, Lord Cochrane, landed in southern Peru on 7 September 1820. San Martín proclaimed Peruvian independence at Lima on 28 July 1821, though most of the country was still in the hands of the Viceroy, José de La Serna. Bolívar sent Antonio José de Sucre to Ecuador where, on 24 May 1822, he gained a victory over La Serna at Pichincha. San Martín, after a meeting with Bolívar at Guayaquil, left for Argentina and a self-imposed exile in France, while Bolívar and Sucre completed the conquest of Peru by defeating La Serna at the battle of Junín (6 August 1824) and the decisive battle of Ayacucho (9 December 1824). For over a year there was a last stand in the Real Felipe fortress at Callao by the Spanish troops under General Rodil before they capitulated on 22 January 1826. Bolívar was invited to stay in Peru, but in 1826 he left for Colombia where he tried to hold Gran Colombia together as a single state. He failed as internal divisions and political ambitions pulled the three new republics apart. While heading for exile, Bolívar died in 1830.

The Portuguese, Pedro Álvares Cabral, landed in Brazil on 22 April, 1500. He left after a week, shortly followed by Amérigo Vespucci who had been sent to explore further. The first system of government adopted by the Portuguese was a Capitania, a kind of feudal principality – there were 13 of them, but these were replaced in 1572 by a Viceroyalty. In the same year it was decided to divide the colony into two, north and south, with capitals at Salvador and Rio; it was not until 1763 that Rio became the sole capital.

Three centuries under the paternal eye of Portugal had ill-prepared the colonists for independent existence, except for the experience of Dutch invasion (1624 in Salvador, and 1630-54 in Recife). The colonists ejected the Dutch from Brazil with little help from Portugal, and Brazilians date the birth of their national sentiment from these events. Resentment against Portuguese government and trade intervention led to the **Inconfidência**, the first revolution, masterminded by **Tiradentes** with 11 other citizens of Minas Gerais. They were unsuccessful (Tiradentes was executed), but when France invaded Portugal in 1807, King João VI was shipped to safety in Brazil, escorted by the British navy. Rio was temporarily declared the capital of the Portuguese Empire. The British, as a price for their assistance in the Portuguese war, forced the opening of Brazil's ports to non-Portuguese trade. King João VI returned to the mother country in 1821, leaving his son, the handsome young Pedro, as Regent. Pedro refused to return control of Brazil to the Portuguese Côrtes (parliament), and on 13 May 1822, by popular request, he agreed to stay and assumed the title of 'Perpetual Defender and Protector of Brazil'. On 7 September he declared Brazil's independence with the cry 'Independence or Death' by the Rio Ipiranga; on 12 October he was proclaimed constitutional emperor of Brazil, and on 1 December he was crowned in Rio.

Brazil: from colony to independence

Background

Land and environment

The dominant feature of South America's geography is the Andes mountain range which defines the western, Pacific, side of the continent from 12°N to 56°S, with tablelands and older mountains stretching east to the Atlantic Ocean. The highest peaks of the Andes have no rivals outside the Himalaya. Dominant to the east are the vast river basins of the Orinoco, the Paraná and above all the Amazon. At least part of every country (except Uruguay) is in the tropics, though the southernmost tips of Chile and Argentina are close to Antarctica. No wonder the variety of scenery, climate and vegetation is immense.

The Andean countries

Four ranges of the Andes (*cordilleras*) run from north to south. Between the ranges run deep longitudinal valleys. Roughly half of Colombia consists of these deep north-south valleys of the Andes and the coastal fringes along the Pacific and Caribbean shorelines. The remaining 620,000 sq km east of the Andes consists of the hot plains (*llanos*) to the north, running down to the Orinoco River, and the Amazon forests to the south. Near the foot of the Andes, the *llanos* are used for cattle ranching, but beyond is jungle. Except for the northwest corner where oil has been found, islands of settlement are connected with the rest of the country only by air and river; the few roads are impassable most of the year.

The Cordilleras, the main Andes ranges, run northwards for 800 km from the borders of Ecuador to the Caribbean lowlands. A few peaks in the Western Cordillera are over 4,000 m but none reaches the snowline. The Central Cordillera, 50-65 km wide, is much higher; several of its peaks, snow clad, rise above 5,000 m and its highest, the volcano cone of Huila, is 5,750 m. The Eastern Cordillera extends north across the border into Venezuela (see below), and includes the spectacular Cucuy ranges. Apart from the peaks (a few are active volcanoes), there are large areas of high undulating plateaux, cold, treeless and inhospitable, dissected by deep river gorges. They have interesting flora and fauna and many of these regions are protected as national parks. In a high basin of the Eastern Cordillera, 160 km east of the Río Magdalena, the Spaniards in 1538 founded the city of Bogotá at 2,560 m, now the national capital. The great rural activity here is the growing of food: cattle, wheat, barley, maize and potatoes. **The Valleys** between the Cordilleras are deep and dominated by the Magdalena

Colombia
Almost all Colombians live in the western 50% of the country
Land area: 1,242,568 sq km

and Cauca Rivers. The upper sections are filled with volcanic ash and are very fertile. With the tropical range of temperature and rainfall, this is very productive land. Coffee dominates but almost every known tropical fruit and vegetable grows here. In the upper parts of the valleys, the climate is more temperate, with another wide range of crops. There is cattle production everywhere; sugar, cotton, rice and tobacco are common.

The Caribbean Lowlands include three centres of population, Cartagena, Barranquilla and Santa Marta, behind which lies a great lowland, the floodplain of the Magdalena, Cauca and their tributaries. During the dry season from October to March great herds of cattle are grazed there, but for the rest of the year much of it is a network of swamps and lagoons with very little land that can be cultivated except for a few ranges of low hills near the coast. **The Northeast** includes one more mountain group in Colombia, the Sierra Nevada de Santa Marta, standing isolated from the other ranges on the shores of the Caribbean. This is the highest range of all: its snow-capped peaks rise to 5,800 m within 50 km of the coast. Further northeast, is La Guajira, a strange region of semi-desert, salt-pans, flamingos and unusual micro-climates. **The Pacific Coast** stretches for 1,300 km. Along the coast north of Buenaventura runs the Serranía de Baudó, the shortest of the Cordilleras, thickly forested. East of it is a low trough before the land rises to the slopes of the Western Cordillera. The trough is drained southwards into the Pacific by the Río San Juan, and northwards into the Caribbean by the Río Atrato, both are partly navigable. The climate is hot and torrential rain falls daily. The inhabitants are mostly black. The 320 km south of the port of Buenaventura to the border with Ecuador is a wide, marshy, and sparsely inhabited coastal lowland.

Ecuador

Land area: 272,045 sq km

The Andes, running from north to south, form a mountainous backbone to the country. There are two main ranges, the Central Cordillera and the Western Cordillera, separated by a 400-km long Central Valley, whose rims are about 50 km apart. The rims are joined together, like the two sides of a ladder, by hilly rungs, and between each pair of rungs lies an intermont basin with a dense cluster of population. These basins are drained by rivers which cut through the rims to run either west to the Pacific or east to join the Amazon. Both rims of the Central Valley are lined with the cones of more than 50 volcanoes. Several of them have long been extinct, for example, Chimborazo, the highest (6,310 m). At least eight, however, are still active including Cotopaxi (5,897 m), which had several violent eruptions in the 19th century; Pichincha (4,794 m), which re-entered activity in 1998 and expelled a spectacular mushroom cloud in October 1999; and Sangay (5,230 m), one of the world's most active volcanoes, continuously emitting fumes and ash.

Ecuador's active volcanoes, fumeroles and hot springs are evidence of unstable geological conditions. Earthquakes too are common

The Sierra, as the central trough of the Andes in known, is home to about 47% of the people of Ecuador, the majority of whom are indigenous. Some of the land is still held in large private estates worked by the Indians, but a growing proportion is now made up of small family farms or is held by native communities, run as cooperatives. Some communities live at subsistence level, others have developed good markets for products using traditional skills in embroidery, pottery, jewellery, knitting, weaving, and carving.

The Costa is mostly lowland at an altitude of less than 300 m, apart from a belt of hilly land which runs northwest from Guayaquil to the coast, where it turns north and runs parallel to the shore to Esmeraldas. In the extreme north there is a typical tropical rain forest, severely endangered by uncontrolled logging. The forests thin out in the more southern lowlands and give way to tropical dry forest. The main agricultural exports come from the lowlands to the southeast and north of Guayaquil. The heavy rains, high temperature and humidity suit the growth of tropical crops. Bananas and mango are grown here while rice is farmed on the natural levees of this flood plain. The main crop comes from the alluvial fans at the foot of the mountains rising out of the plain. Coffee is grown on the higher ground. Shrimp farming was typical of the coast until this was damaged by disease in 1999. The Guayas lowland is also a great cattle-fattening area in the dry season. South of Guayaquil the rainfall is progressively less, mangroves disappear and by the border with Peru, it is semi-arid.

The Oriente is east of the Central Cordillera where the forest-clad mountains fall sharply to a chain of foothills (the Eastern Cordillera) and then the jungle through which meander the tributaries of the Amazon. This east lowland region makes up 36% of Ecuador's total territory, but is only sparsely populated by indigenous and agricultural colonists from the highlands. In total, the region has only 5% of the national population, but colonization is now proceeding rapidly owing to population pressure and in the wake of an oil boom in the northern Oriente. There is gold and other minerals in the south. **The Galápagos** are about 1,000 km west of Ecuador, on the Equator, and are not structuraly connected to the mainland. They mark the junction between two tectonic plates on the Pacific floor where basalt has escaped to form massive volcanoes, only the tips of which are above sea level. Several of the islands have volcanic activity today. Their isolation from any other land has led to their unique flora and fauna.

The whole of Peru's west seaboard with the Pacific is desert on which rain seldom falls. From this coastal shelf the Andes rise steeply to a high Sierra which is studded with massive groups of soaring mountains and gouged with deep canyons. The highland slopes more gradually east and is deeply forested and ravined. Eastward from these mountains lie the vast jungle lands of the Amazon basin.

Peru
Land area:
1,285,216 sq km

The Highlands (or Sierra), at an average altitude of 3,000 m, cover 26% of the country and contain about 50% of the people, mostly Indian, an excessive density on such poor land. Here, high-level land of gentle slopes is surrounded by towering ranges of high peaks including the most spectacular range of the continent, the Cordillera Blanca. This has several ice peaks over 6,000 m; the highest, Huascarán, is 6,768 m and is a mecca for mountaineers. There are many volcanoes in the south. The north and east highlands are heavily forested up to a limit of 3,350 m: the grasslands are between the forest line and the snowline, which rises from 5,000 m in the latitude of Lima to 5,800 m in the south. Most of the Sierra is covered with grasses and shrubs, with Puna vegetation (bunch grass mixed with low, hairy-leaved plants) from north of Huaraz to the south. Here the indigenous graze llamas, alpacas and sheep providing meat, clothing, transport and even fuel from the animals' dung. Some potatoes and cereals (*quinua, kiwicha* and *kañiwa*) are grown at altitude, but the deep valley basins contain the best land for arable farming. Most of the rivers which rise in these mountains flow east to the Amazon and cut through the plateau in canyons, sometimes 1,500 m deep, in which the climate is tropical. A few go west to the Pacific including the Colca and Cotahuasi in the south, which have created dramatic canyons over 3,000 m deep from rim to water level.

The Coast, a narrow ribbon of desert 2,250 km long, takes up 11% of the country and holds about 45% of the population. It is the economic heart of Peru, consuming most of the imports and supplying half of the exports. When irrigated, the river valleys are extremely fertile, creating oases which grow cotton throughout the country, sugar-cane, rice and export crops such as asparagus in the north, grapes, fruit and olives in the south. At the same time, the coastal current teems with fish and Peru has in the past had the largest catch in the world. **The Jungle** covers the forested eastern half of the Andes and the tropical forest beyond, altogether 62% of the country's area, but with only about 5% of the population who are crowded on the river banks in the cultivable land – a tiny part of the area. The few roads have to cope with dense forest, deep valleys, and sharp eastern slopes ranging from 2,150 m in the north to 5,800 m east of Lake Titicaca. Rivers are the main highways, though navigation is hazardous. The economic potential of the area includes reserves of timber, excellent land for rubber, jute, rice, tropical fruits and coffee and the breeding of cattle. The vast majority of Peru's oil and gas reserves are also east of the Andes.

Bolivia is the only South American country with no coastline or even navigable river to the sea. It is dominated by the Andes and has five distinct geographical areas. **The Andes** are at their widest in Bolivia, a maximum of 650 km. The Western Cordillera, which separates Bolivia from Chile, has high peaks of between 5,800 m and 6,500 m and a number of active volcanoes along its crest. The Eastern Cordillera also rises to giant massifs, with several peaks over 6,000 m in the Cordillera Real section to the north. The far sides of the Cordillera Real fall away very sharply to the northeast, towards the Amazon basin.

Bolivia
Land area:
1,098,581 sq km

Background

A harsh, strange land, a dreary grey solitude except for the bursts of green after rain. The air is unbelievably clear – the whole landscape is a bowl of luminous light

Background

The Altiplano lies between the Cordilleras, a bleak, treeless, windswept plateau, much of it 4,000 m above sea-level. Its surface is by no means flat, and the Western Cordillera sends spurs dividing it into basins. The more fertile northern part has more inhabitants; the southern part is parched desert and almost unoccupied, save for a mining town here and there. Nearly 70% of the population lives on it; over half of the people in towns. **Lake Titicaca**, at the northern end of the Altiplano, is an inland sea of 8,965 sq km at 3,810 m, the highest navigable water in the world. Its depth, up to 280 m in some places, keeps the lake at an even all-year-round temperature of 10° C. This modifies the extremes of winter and night temperatures on the surrounding land, which supports a large Aymara indigenous population, tilling the fields and the hill terraces, growing potatoes and cereals, tending their sheep, alpaca and llamas, and using the resources of the lake. **The Yungas and the Puna** are to the east of the Altiplano. The heavily forested northeastern slopes of the Cordillera Real are deeply indented by the fertile valleys of the Yungas, drained into the Amazon lowlands by the Río Beni and its tributaries, where cacao, coffee, sugar, coca and tropical fruits are grown. Further south, from a point just north of Cochabamba, the Eastern Cordillera rises abruptly in sharp escarpments from the Altiplano and then flattens out to an easy slope east to the plains: an area known as the Puna. The streams which flow across the Puna cut increasingly deep incisions as they gather volume until, to the east, the Puna is eroded to little more than a high remnant between the river valleys. In these valleys a variety of grain crops and fruits is grown.

The Tropical Lowlands stretch from the foothills of the Eastern Cordillera to the borders with Brazil, Paraguay and Argentina. They take up 70% of the total area of Bolivia, but contain only about 20% of its population. In the north and east the Oriente has dense tropical forest. Open plains covered with rough pasture, swamp and scrub occupy the centre. Before the expulsion of the Jesuits in 1767 this was a populous land of plenty; for 150 years Jesuit missionaries had controlled the area and guided it into a prosperous security. Decline followed but in recent years better times have returned. Meat is now shipped from Trinidad, capital of Beni Department, and from airstrips in the area, to the urban centres of La Paz, Oruro, and Cochabamba. Further south, the forests and plains beyond the Eastern Cordillera sweep down towards the Río Pilcomayo, which drains into the Río de la Plata, getting progressively less rain and merging into a comparatively dry land of scrub forest and arid savanna. The main city of this area is Santa Cruz de la Sierra, founded in the 16th century, now the second city of Bolivia and a large agricultural centre.

The Southern Cone

Chile

Land area: 756, 626 sq km

Chile is a ribbon of land lying between the Andes and the Pacific. The Andes and a coastal range of highland take up from a third to a half of its width. There are wide variations of soil and vast differences of climate; these profoundly affect the density of population. Down virtually the whole length, between the Andes and the coastal ranges, is a longitudinal depression. For 1,050 km south of the capital Santiago this is a great valley stretching as far as Puerto Montt. South of Puerto Montt the sea has broken through the coastal range and drowned the valley, and there is a bewildering assortment of archipelagos and channels. The Andes, with many snow-capped peaks over 6,000 m, culminate near Santiago with several of almost 7,000 m. They diminish in height from Santiago southwards, but throughout the range are spectacular volcanoes right down to the southern seas, where the Strait of Magellan gives access to the Atlantic. Associated with the mountains are geological faults and earthquakes are common.

From north to south the country falls into five sharply contrasted zones: The first 1,250 km from the Peruvian frontier to Copiapó is a rainless hot desert of brown hills and plains devoid of vegetation, with a few oases. Here lie nitrate deposits and several copper mines. There is almost no rain, just occasional mists from coastal condensation. From Copiapó to Illapel (600 km) is semi-desert; there is a slight winter rainfall, but great tracts of land are without vegetation most of the year. Valley bottoms are cultivated under irrigation. From Illapel to Concepción is Chile's heartland, where the vast majority of its people live. Here there is abundant rainfall in the winter, but the summers are perfectly dry. Great farms and vineyards cover the country, which is exceptionally beautiful. The fourth zone, between Concepción and Puerto Montt, is a country of lakes and rivers, with heavy rainfall through much of the year. Cleared and cultivated land alternates with mountains and primeval forests. The fifth zone, from Puerto Montt to Cape Horn, stretches for 1,600 km. This is archipelagic Chile, a sparsely populated region of wild forests and mountains, glaciers, fjords, islands and channels. Rainfall is torrential, and the climate cold and stormy. South of Puerto Montt, the Camino Austral provides almost unbroken road access for more than 1,000 km. Chilean Patagonia is in the extreme south of this zone. A subdivision of the fifth zone is Atlantic Chile – that part which lies along the Magellan Strait to the east of the Andes, including the Chilean part of Tierra del Fuego island. There is a cluster of population here raising sheep and mining coal. Large offshore oilfields have now been discovered in the far south, and the area is developing rapidly.

Argentina occupies most of the southern cone of the continent. There are four main physical areas: the Andes, the north and Mesopotamia, the Pampas, and Patagonia. Much of the country is comparatively flat which made modern communications easy. **The Andes** run the full length of Argentina, low and deeply glaciated in the Patagonian south, high and dry in the prolongation in northwest Argentina adjoining the Bolivian Altiplano. Though of modest height, Cerro Fitzroy and other peaks on the fringes of the Patagonia icecap are amongst the most dramatic on the continent, while many peaks in the north are over 6,000 m, including Aconcagua, the highest outside the Himalayas. To the east, in the shadow of the Andes, it is dry. Oases strung along the eastern foot of the Andes from Jujuy to San Rafael, including Tucumán and Mendoza, were the first places to be colonized by the Spaniards. Further south is the beautiful Lake District, with Bariloche at its heart. The mountain ridges and the many lakes created by the glaciers are now withdrawing under the impact of global warming. **The North and Mesopotamia** contains the vast plains of the Chaco and the floodplain lying between the rivers Paraná and Uruguay. Rice growing and ranching are widespread. The Province of Misiones in the northeast lies on the great Paraná plateau while the northwest Chaco has some of the highest temperatures in the continent.

    The Pampas make up the heart of the country. These vast, rich plains lie south of the Chaco, and east of the Andes down to the Río Colorado. Buenos Aires lies on the northeast corner of the Pampas and is the only part of the country which has a dense population – about 40% of Argentines live in and around the capital. The Pampas stretch for hundreds of kilometres in almost unrelieved flatness, but get progressively wetter going east. Cattle and cereal growing dominate. **Patagonia** lies south of the Río Colorado – a land of arid, wind-swept plateaux cut across by ravines. In the deep south the wind is wilder and more continuous. There is no real summer, but the winters are rarely severe.

Unlike all other South American countries, Uruguay is compact, accessible and homogeneous. **The coast** along the Atlantic consists of bays, beaches and off-shore islands, lagoons and bars, the sand brought by currents north from the River Plate. Behind is a narrow plain which fringes most of the coast (but not near Montevideo). Behind is a line of mainly wooded hills (called *cuchillas*), the whole area extensively farmed with grain and cattle *estancias*. **Central Uruguay** up to the Brazilian border is pleasant, rolling country dissected by the Río Negro which rises in Brazil and on which a number of dams have been built. North of the river is agricultural and pasture country dominated by sheep. Near Minas there are stone quarries and other mining activity. **Western Uruguay** is dominated by the River Plate from Montevideo round to Colonia, then north up the Río Uruguay which provides the frontier with Argentina. It consists of an alluvial flood plain stretching north to Fray Bentos where the first road crossing can be made. Thereafter, the general character of the land is undulating, with little forest except on the banks of its rivers and streams. The long grass slopes rise gently to far-off hills, but none of these is higher than 600 m. Five rivers flow westwards across the country to drain into the Río Uruguay, including the Río Negro. Cattle and wheat are the main traditional products.

Paraguay is landlocked and is divided into two by the Río Paraguay. The Río Paraná forms part of the eastern and southern boundaries of the country but the rivers are so difficult to navigate that communication with Buenos Aires, 1,450 km from Asunción, has been mainly on land.

    Eastern Paraguay is the 40% of the country east of the Río Paraguay, a rich land of rolling hills in which most of the population live. An escarpment runs north from the Río Alto Paraná,

Argentina
Land area:
2, 780, 092 sq km

Uruguay
Uruguay is the smallest Hispanic country in South America; land area:
406,752 sq km

Paraguay
Land area:
406, 752 sq km

Background

Background

west of Encarnación, to the Brazilian border. East of this escarpment the Paraná Plateau extends across neighbouring parts of Argentina and Brazil. The Plateau, which is crossed by the Río Paraná, ranges from 300-600 m in height, was originally forest and enjoys relatively high levels of rainfall. West and south of the escarpment and stretching to the Río Paraguay lies a fertile plain with wooded hills, drained by several tributaries of the Río Paraná. Most of the population of Paraguay lives in these hilly lands, stretching southeast from the capital, to Encarnación. The area produces timber, cotton, hides and semi-tropical products. Closer to the rivers, much of the plain is flooded once a year; it is wet savanna, treeless, but covered with coarse grasses. **The Chaco**, about 60% of the country's area, is a flat, infertile plain stretching north along the west bank of the Río Paraguay. The marshy, unnavigable Río Pilcomayo, which flows southeast across the Chaco to join the Río Paraguay near Asunción, forms the frontier with Argentina. The landscape is dominated by the alluvial material brought down in the past by the rivers from the Andes. As the rainfall diminishes westwards, the land can naturally support little more than scrub and cacti. The arrival of the Mennonites has led to some intense production of fruit and other crops.

Brazil

Land area: 8,547,404 sq km

The heavy Amazon rain comes from the daily cycle of intense evaporation plus the saturated air brought by winds from the northeast and southeast, losing their moisture as they approach the Andes

Brazil is one of the largest countries of the world. It stretches over 4,300 km across the continent but is one of the few in South America that does not reach the Andes. The two great river basins, the Amazon and the River Plate, account for about three-fifths of Brazil's area.

The Amazon Basin, in northern and western Brazil, takes up more than a third of the whole country. The basin borders the Andes and funnels narrowly to the Atlantic, recalling the geological period, before the uplift of the Andes, when the Amazon flowed into the Pacific Ocean. Most of the drained area has an elevation of less than 250 m. The rainfall is heavy: some few places receive from 3,750 to 5,000 mm a year, though over most of the area it is no more than from 1,500 to 2,500 mm. Much of the basin suffers from annual floods. The region was covered by tropical forest, with little undergrowth except along the watercourses; it is now being rapidly cut down. The climate is hot and the humidity high throughout the year. **The Brazilian Highlands** lying southeast of the Amazon and northeast of the River Plate Basin form a tableland of from 300 to 900 m high, but here and there, mostly in southeast Brazil, mountain ranges rise from it. The highest temperature recorded was 42°C, in the dry northeastern states. The highest peak in southern Brazil, the Pico da Bandeira, northeast of Rio, is 2,898 m. **The Great Escarpment** is where the Brazilian Highlands cascade sharply down to the Atlantic, leaving a narrow coastal strip which is the economic heartland of the country. It runs from south of Salvador as far as Porto Alegre and in only a few places is this Escarpment breached by deeply cut river beds, for example those of the Rio Doce and the Rio Paraíba. Along most of its course, the Great Escarpment falls to the sea in parallel steps, each step separated by the trough of a valley making for difficult communication with the interior. The few rivers rising on the Escarpment, which flow direct into the Atlantic, do so precipitously and are not navigable. Most of the rivers flow west, deep into the interior. Those in southern Brazil rise almost within sight of the sea, but run westward through the vast interior to join the Paraná, often with falls as they leave the Escarpment, including the spectacular Iguaçú. In the central area the Escarpment rivers run away from the sea to join the São Francisco River, which flows northwards parallel to the coast for 2,900 km, to tumble over the Paulo Afonso Falls on its eastward course to the Atlantic.

The River Plate Basin, in the southern part of Brazil, has a more varied surface and is less heavily forested than the Amazon Basin. The land is higher and the climate a little cooler. **The Guiana Highlands**, north of the Amazon, are ancient rock structures, some of the oldest in the world. The area is partly forested, partly hot stony desert. Slopes that face the northeast trade winds get heavy rainfall, but the southern areas are drier. The highest peak in all Brazil, the Pico da Neblina, 3,014 m, is on the Venezuelan border.

Guyane

Land area: 83,900-86, 504 sq km (estimate); one sixth the size of France

Guyane has its eastern frontier with Brazil formed partly by the river Oiapoque (Oyapock in French) and its southern, also with Brazil, formed by the Tumuc-Humac mountains (the only range of importance). The western frontier with Suriname is along the river Maroni-Litani. To the north is the Atlantic coastline of 320 km. The land rises gradually from a coastal strip some 15-40 km wide to the higher slopes and plains or savannahs, about 80 km inland. Forests cover the hills and valleys of the interior, and the territory is well watered, for over 20 rivers run to the Atlantic.

Like its neighbours, Suriname has a coastline on the Atlantic to the north. The principal rivers are the Marowijne in the east, the Corantijn in the west, and the Suriname, Commewijne (with its tributary, the Cottica), Coppename, Saramacca and Nickerie. The country is divided into topographically quite diverse natural regions: the northern lowlands, 25 km wide in the east and 80 km wide in the west, have clay soil covered with swamps. There follows a region, 5-6 km wide, of a loamy and very white sandy soil, then an undulating region, about 30 km wide. It is mainly savanna, mostly covered with quartz sand, and overgrown with grass and shrubs. South of this lies the interior highland, almost entirely overgrown with dense tropical forest, intersected by streams. At the southern boundary with Brazil there are savannas.

Guyana has an area of 215,083 sq km, nearly the size of Britain, but only about 2.5% is cultivated. About 90% of the population lives on the narrow coastal plain, either in Georgetown, the capital, or in villages along the main road running from Charity in the west to the Suriname border. The rivers give some access to the interior beyond which are the jungles and highlands towards the border with Brazil.

The Coastal Plain is mostly below sea level. Large wooden houses stand on stilts above ground level. A sea wall keeps out the Atlantic and the fertile clay soil is drained by a system of dykes; sluice gates, *kokers* are opened to let out water at low tide. Separate channels irrigate fields in dry weather. Most of the western third of the coastal plain is undrained and uninhabited. Four **Major Rivers** cross the coastal plain, from west to east they are the Essequibo, the Demerara, the Berbice, and the Corentyne (which forms the frontier with Suriname). Only the Demerara is crossed by bridges. Elsewhere ferries must be used. At the mouth of the Essequibo River, 34 km wide, are islands the size of Barbados. The lower reaches of these rivers are navigable; but waterfalls and rapids prevent them being used by large boats to reach the interior. **The Jungles and the Highlands** inland from the coastal plain, are mainly thick rain forest, although in the east there is a large area of grassland. Towards Venezuela the rain forest rises in a series of steep escarpments, with spectacular waterfalls, the highest and best known of which are the Kaieteur Falls on the Potaro River. In the southwest is the Rupununi Savanna, an area of grassland more easily reached from Brazil than from Georgetown.

Venezuela has 2,800 km of coastline on the Caribbean Sea and many islands. The Andes run up north-eastwards from Colombia, along the coast eastwards past Caracas, ending up as the north coast of the Caribbean island of Trinidad. In the northwest corner is the Maracaibo basin. South of the Andean spine is the vast plain of the Orinoco which reaches the sea near the Guyana border and to the southeast of that are the ancient rocks known as the Guayana Highlands.

The Andes are highest near the Colombian border where they are known as the Sierra Nevada de Mérida. Beyond they broaden out into the Segovia Highlands north of Barquisimeto, and then turn east in parallel ridges along the coast to form the Central Highlands, dipping into the Caribbean Sea only to rise again into the North Eastern Highlands of the peninsulas of Araya and Paria. This region has an agreeable climate and is well populated with most of the main towns. **The Maracaibo Lowlands** are around the fresh water lake of Maracaibo, the largest lake in South America, is 12,800 sq km. Considerable rainfall feeds the lake and many rivers flow through thick forest to create swamps on its southern shore. The area is dominated by the oil producing fields on both sides of the lake and beneath its surface. To the west, the Sierra de Perijá forms the boundary with Colombia and outside the lake to the east is the most northerly point of the country the peninsular of Paraguaná, virtually desert.

The Llanos, as the Orinoco plains are called, cover about one third of the country. They are almost flat and are a vast cattle range. The Orinoco river itself is part of Latin America's third largest river system. Many significant rivers flow from the Andes and Guayana Highlands to join the Orinoco, whose delta is made up of innumerable channels and thousands of forest-covered islands. **The Guayana Highlands**, which take up almost half the country, are south of the Orinoco. This is an area of ancient crystalline rocks that extend along the top of the continent towards the mouth of the Amazon and form the northern part of Brazil. In Venezuela they are noted for huge, precipitous granite blocks known as *tepuys*, many of which have their own unique flora, and create many high waterfalls including the Angel Falls, the world's highest.

Suriname
Land area:
163,820 sq km
A large area in the southwest is in dispute with Guyana. A less serious border dispute with Guyane is in the southeast

Background

Guyana
Land area:
215,083 sq km

The area west of the Essequibo River, about 70% of the national territory, is claimed by Venezuela

Venezuela
Land area:
912, 050 sq km

Culture

Music and dance

Argentina Buenos Aires contains almost half of the country's population and its music is the Tango. Although also sung and played, the Tango was born as a dance just before the turn of the 20th century. The exact moment of the birth was not recorded by any contemporary observer and continues to be a matter of debate, though the roots can be traced. The name 'Tango' predates the dance and was given to the carnivals (and dances) of the black inhabitants of the Río de la Plata in the early 19th century. Elements of the black tradition were taken over by whites, as the black population declined into insignificance. However, the name 'Tango Americano' was also given to the Habanera (a Cuban descendant of the English Country Dance) which became the rage in Spain and bounced back into the Río de la Plata in the middle of the 19th century, not only as a fashionable dance, together with the polka, mazurka, waltz and cuadrille, but also as a song form in the very popular 'Zarzuelas', or Spanish operettas. However, the Habanera led not a double, but a triple life, by also infiltrating the lowest levels of society directly from Cuba via sailors who arrived in the ports of Montevideo and Buenos Aires. Here it encountered the Milonga, originally a Gaucho song style, but by 1880 a dance, especially popular with the so-called 'Compadritos' and 'Orilleros', who frequented the port area and its brothels, whence the Argentine Tango emerged around the turn of the century to dazzle the populace with its brilliant, personalized footwork, which could not be accomplished without the partners staying glued together. As a dance it became the rage and, as the infant recording industry grew by leaps and bounds, it also became popular as a song and an instrumental genre, with the original violins and flutes being eclipsed by the bandoneón button accordion, then being imported from Germany. In 1911 the new dance took Paris by storm and returned triumphant to Buenos Aires. It achieved both respectability and notoriety, becoming a global phenomenon after the First World War. The golden voice of the renowned Carlos Gardel soon gave a wholly new dimension to the music of the Tango until his death in 1935. After losing some popularity in Argentina, it came to the forefront again in the 1940s (1920-50 is considered the real golden age). Its resurgence was assisted by Perón's decree that 50% of all music played on the radio must be Argentine, only to suffer a second, much more serious decline in the face of rock music over the past two decades. Fortunately, it has experienced another revival in recent years and the Tango and Milonga can once again be seen being danced in Buenos Aires. Apart from Carlos Gardel, other great names connected with the Tango are Francisco Canaro (Uruguayan), Osvaldo Pugliese and Astor Piazzolla, who has modernized it by fusion with jazz styles (nuevo tango).

If the Tango represents the soul of Buenos Aires, this is not the case in the rest of the country. The provinces have a very rich and attractive heritage of folk dances, mainly for couples, with arms held out and fingers clicked or handkerchiefs waved, with the 'Paso Valseado' as the basic step. Descended from the Zamacueca, and therefore a cousin of the Chilean Cueca and Peruvian Marinera, is the slow and stately Zamba, where the handkerchief is used to greatest effect. Equally popular throughout most of the country are the faster Gato, Chacarera and Escondido. These were the dances of the Gaucho and their rhythm evokes that of a cantering horse. Guitar and the bombo drum provide the accompaniment. Particularly spectacular is the Malambo, where the Gaucho shows off his dextrous footwork, the spurs of his boots adding a steely note to the rhythm.

Different regions of the country have their own specialities. The music of Cuyo in the west is sentimental and very similar to that of neighbouring Chile, with its Cuecas for dance and Tonadas for song. The northwest on the other hand is Andean, with its musical culture closer to that of Bolivia, particularly on the Puna, where the Indians play the quena and charango and sound mournful notes on the great long erke. Here the dances are Bailecitos and Carnavalitos, while the songs are Vidalitas and the extraordinary high pitched Bagualas, the very essence of primeval pain. In the northeast provinces of Corrientes and Misiones, the music shares cultural similarities with Paraguay. The Polca and Galopa are danced and the local Chamamé is sung, to the accordion or the harp, the style being sentimental. Santiago del Estero is the heartland of the Chacarera and the lyrics are often part Spanish and part Quichua, a local dialect of the Andean Quechua language. Down in the Province of Buenos Aires you are more likely to hear the Gauchos singing their Milongas, Estilos and Cifras and challenging each other to a Payada or rhymed duel. Argentina experienced a great folk revival in the 50's and 60's and some of the most celebrated groups are still drawing enthusiastic audiences today. These groups include Los Chalchaleros and Los Fronterizos, the perennial virtuoso singer and guitarist, Eduardo Falú and, more recently, León Gieco from Santa Fe.

Bolivia

The heart of Bolivia is the Altiplano and it is the music of the Quechua and Aymara-speaking Indians of this area that provides the most distinctive Bolivian musical sound. Although there is much that is of Spanish colonial origin in the Indians' dances, the music itself has more Amerindian style and content than that of any other country in South America. It is rare to find an Indian who cannot play an instrument and it is these instruments, both wind and percussion, that are quintessentially Bolivian. The clear sounds of the quena and pinkullo, the deeper, breathier notes of the tarka, pututo and sicuri accompanied by huankaré, pululu and caja drums can be heard all over the Altiplano, the charango (a small, G-stringed guitar) being virtually the only instrument of European origin. The Indian dances are mainly collective and take place at religious fiestas. The dancers wear colourful costumes with elaborate, plumed headdresses and some of them still parody their ex-Spanish colonial masters.

The principal popular dances that can be regarded as 'national' in their countrywide appeal are the Cueca and Huayño. The Bolivian Cueca is a close relative of the Chilean national dance of the same name and they share a mutual origin in the Zamacueca, itself derived from the Spanish Fandango. The Huayño is of Indian origin and involves numerous couples, who whirl around or advance down the street, arm-in-arm, in a 'Pandilla'. Justly celebrated is the great carnival Diablada of Oruro, with its hordes of grotesquely masked devils, a spectacle comparable to those of Rio in Brazil and Barranquilla in Colombia. The region of Tarija near the Argentine border has a distinctive musical tradition of its own, based on religious processions that culminate with that of San Roque on the first Sunday in September. There are many professional folk groups on record, the best known being *Grupo Aymara, Los Runas, Los Laris, Los Masis, Kolla Marka* and *Bolivia Manta,* some of which have now established themselves in Europe and North America.

Brazil

Perhaps because of its sheer size, Brazil has a greater musical inventory than any other Latin American country, not only reflected in the immense regional spread of folk music but also in its successive waves of urban popular music. The Brazilian expresses themselves through music and dance to an extraordinary degree and the music covers the whole spectrum from the utmost rural simplicity to the ultimate state-of-the-art commercial sophistication.

The South In Paraná, Santa Catarina and Rio Grande do Sul, the music is strictly European in origin, rhythm and instrumentation. Rio Grande do Sul shares Gaucho dances such as the Pericom and song styles such as the Milonga, Trova and Pajada with neighbouring Uruguay and Argentina. The Chula is a competitive dance for men to show off (comparable to the Argentine Malambo), while the Pexinho is for men and women. The guitar and the accordion are favourite instruments, also true for Santa Catarina and Paraná, where the names of the dances denote their European origins: Mazurkas, Valsas, Chotes, Polquinhas and Rancheiras. The Chimarrita is a song style that came straight from the Azores. If you are feeling sentimental, you sing a Toada, if energetic, you stamp your feet to a Fandango. Except for the Batuque de Rio Grande do Sul in Porto Alegre, closely related to the Candombe of nearby Montevideo, there is no African influence in the music of this region and none of that classic Brazilian syncopation.

São Paulo, Rio de Janeiro, Minas Gerais Moving north into São Paulo, we enter an area rich in traditional folk dances and music, with the African admixture beginning to show up. At many religious festivals will be found the Congadas (European 'Moors and Christians', but danced by blacks) and Moçambique (a stick dance for men), while the Samba de Lenço, Fandango and Batuque are recreational dances for one or more couples. The instrumental accompaniment branches out into shakers (the ganzá), drums (caixas and tambores) and above all the guitar (viola). Try the great pilgrimage church at Aparecida do Norte on a Sunday. You might well see a group of religious dances. In the hinterland of Rio de Janeiro the Folias de Reis are out on the street from Christmas to Epiphany, singing from house to house, accompanying themselves on the caixa and adufe drums and the guitar, while in the old coastal towns of Paraty and Angra dos Reis are to be found the Dança de Velhos (the old men), performed to the accordion. The Jongo is a dance of African origin for men and women, naturally with a drum accompaniment. And there is hardly need to mention Rio at carnival and its Samba Schools. Further north again, we come to the states of Espírtu Santo, Minas Gerais and Goiás. In colonial Ouro Preto, in Minas, you can hear the old Modinha sung to the Portuguese guitar as a serenade and be transported into the past. Espírtu Santo is home to the Ticumbi, a kind of Congada, danced to the guitar and shakers (chocalhos). Goiás shares with Minas Gerais a very rich heritage of Portuguese derived religious folk song and dance, centred on Folias, Modas and Calangos.

Bahia Bahia is the heart of African Brazil and a very musical heart it is, born of the Yoruba religion that came with the slaves from what is now Nigeria. The resulting syncretic religion is known as Candomblé in Bahia and the gods or 'Orixás' are worshipped through song, dance and possession in the 'Terreiros', directed by the priests (Pais-de-Santo) and priestesses (Mães-de-Santo). The mainly female adepts, dressed entirely in white, circle gracefully to the background chant of 'Pontos' and the thunderous pounding of the atabaques, the tall drums. The two most revered priestesses are Mãe Olga de Alakêto and Mãe Menininha de Gantois. Similar syncretic African religions are found elsewhere in Brazil. Another vital African element in Bahian folk music is the spectacular dance-cum-martial arts form of Capoeira. Bodies whirl and cartwheel around each other to the sound of the berimbau (a one-stringed bow with resonator) and the accompanying chant. Related to the Capoeira is the stick dance Maculelê. Two of the best berimbau groups on record are *Camaféu de Oxóssi* and the *Cordão de Ouro*. Bahia has a carnival almost as celebrated as that of Rio and here you can see the Afoxé, a serious religious dance, performed to drums alone.

The North East North of Bahia is the Nordeste, with music that runs the whole gamut from black African to mediaeval Portuguese. In colonial times the church directed the peoples' musical energies into religious plays, songs and dances and a large number of these are still performed. The Bumba-Meu-Boi is a folk drama in the course of which a bull is killed and then brought back to life. Particularly popular in Piauí and Maranhão, its variants are found as far afield as Amazônia, where it is called the Boi-Bumbá, and Paraná in the far south, where it is known as Boi-Mamão. Also popular along the coast from Ceará to Paraíba is a nautical drama of Portuguese origin called Marujada or Nau Catarineta, a version of Moors and Christians, accompanied by Portuguese guitar (violão), drums and the ganzá scraper. In Alagoas, Sergipe and Pernambuco we find the sword dance called Reisado, danced after Christmas, the Caboclinhos, who are dressed like Indians and dance with bows and arrows, and the Guerreiros Alagoanos, a mixture of both. The last named are accompanied by the classical northeastern musical group called Terno de Pífanos, with the pífano vertical flute, accompanied by maracas and ganzá. The Banda de Pífanos of Caruaru in Pernambuco can be found on record. Recreational dance music in the Nordeste goes under the generic name of 'Forró', said to be derived from the expression 'For All', because the English companies operating at the turn of the century organized weekend dances for their workmen to which all comers were invited. Four very popular recreational folk dances of this region are the Ciranda (a round dance), the Coco, the Bate-Coxa (where the dancers bump bellies) and the Bambelô. Carnival in Recife, the largest city, is when and where to see the energetic and gymnastic Frevo, danced by young men with an umbrella in their hands, and the very stately and superbly costumed Maracatu dancers, with their queen and king. The Nordeste is equally rich in song styles, notably the Desafios, Emboladas, Cocos and Aboios. The Desafios are performed by so-called Repentistas or Violeiros, who accompany themselves on the Portuguese guitar and whose repertoire includes a large inventory of verse styles. They will sing about individual spectators, who then pay willingly for the compliment. The Emboladas and Cocos are similar, but faster and accompanied solely by tambourines, while the Aboios are haunting songs related to cattle and cattlemen. Repentistas and Emboladores can normally be found at work in markets throughout the region. The premier Repentista is Otacílio Batista do Pajeú, who sang to the Pope during the latter's visit to Brazil. The music of the Nordeste has also been well propagated by more sophisticated groups that have based themselves on folk roots, such as the Quinteto Violado, Ariano Suassuna's Orchestra Armorial and Cussy de Almeida's Quinteto Armorial, not forgetting the veteran accordionist Luiz Gonzaga and the popular Alceu Valença. As a result of the huge migration of nordestinos to the urban south, moreover, it is just as easy to hear this regional music in São Paulo as it is in Recife.

Pará and the Amazon Finally to Pará and the Amazon in the far north, where the music has been heavily influenced from the Caribbean. The most popular musical genre here is the Carimbó, danced to a Merengue-type rhythm and played on drums, wind or brass (usually the clarinet) and strings, particularly the banjo. Notable performers are Pinduca ('O Rei do Carimbó'), Veriquete and Vieira. It is the latter who thought up the term 'Lambada' for his particular version of the Carimbó, and the spectacular, thigh-entwining dance form introduced to the world in Paris by Karakos and Lorsac in 1988 had already been popular among young people at 'Forrós' throughout the region for some years. The very traditional island of Marajó in the mouth of the Amazon has preserved versions of 18th century dances, such as the Lundú and Chula.

Urban popular music The vast range of Brazilian regional folk music is only equalled by the chronological depth of its urban popular music, which surges like endless waves on a beach. For the origins we have to go back to Jesuit missions and Portuguese folk music, influenced and blended by African slaves, from which emerged the 19th century Lundús, Polcas and Maxixes that in turn gave way to the romantic and sentimental Choro song genre (from chorar, to weep), accompanied by guitar, flute and cavaquinho (small guitar), which became all the rage and indeed still has its adepts in Brazil today. A key figure in urban music was Ernesto Nazaré, composer and pianist, who occupied a special niche somewhere between popular and light classical, composing between 1880 and 1930 a vast number of Tangos Brasileiros (not to be confused with the Argentine variety), Mazurkas, Polcas, Waltzes and other popular songs.

Around the turn of the century the instrumentation turned to brass and Rio's urban Samba was born, a birth that was announced by the recording in 1917 of Donga's 'Pelo Telefone'. Names from this early period are Pixinguinha, Sinhô, Heitor dos Prazeres, Ary Barroso, Noel Rosa and of course Carmen Miranda, who took the Samba to Hollywood and the rest of the world. It also became intimately connected with the carnival in the form of Marcha Ranchos and Sambas de Enredo as the first samba schools were formed, of which Salgueiro, Mangueira, Partido Alto, Portela, Mocidade Independente and Beija-Flor are some of the most famous. With the Escolas de Samba came the Batucada or percussion groups playing the pandeiro (tambourine), atabaque and tamborim (drum), agogô (cowbell), reco-reco, chocalho, afoxê and cuíca. This is the real engine room of Samba. Listen to Lúcio Perrone or Mocidade Independente de Padre Miguel. A new phase was ushered in with an invasion from Bahia and the Nordeste in the early 1950s. From Bahia came Dorival Caymmi, who dropped his fishermen's songs in favour of the Samba, and Luiz Gonzaga, who brought his accordion, zabumba drum and triangulo, with which to play his Baiãos (his 'Asa Branca' is a classic) and almost put the Samba itself into eclipse for several years. Almost, but not quite, for out of the ashes there soon arose Bossa Nova – white, middle class and silky smooth. Vinícius de Moraes and Tom Jobim were its heroes; 1958 to 1964 the years; Copacabana, Ipanema and Leblon the scene; 'Samba de uma Nota Só', 'A Garota de Ipanema' and 'Desafinado' the songs and Nara Leão, Baden Powell, Toquinho, João Gilberto, Luis Bonfá and Astrud Gilberto the main performers. Stan Getz, the American jazz saxophonist, helped export it to the world. What was now being called MPB (Música Popular Brasileira) then took off in several directions. Chico Buarque, Edu Lobo and Milton Nascimento were protest singers. Out of Bahia emerged 'Tropicalismo' in the persons of Gilberto Gil, Caetano Veloso and his sister Maria Bethânia, Gal Costa, João Gilberto and 'Som Livre'. The words were important, but the rhythm was still there. Brazilian rock also now appeared, with such stars as Roberto Carlos, Elis Regina, Rita Lee, and Ney Mattogrosso. Heavy metal is a popular genre that continues to evolve as exemplified by the band *Sepultura*. Recently, in turning towards international black consciousness, the Bahianos have mixed Reggae and Samba to produce 'axê'. Still, Samba has survived, although now called 'Pagode' and amazingly, 40% of all Brazilian records sold are of Música Sertaneja, a highly commercialized pseudo-folk genre which is closer to American Country and Western than to most other Brazilian music. Listen to the 'Duplas' of Tonico and Tinoco, Jacó e Jacozinho, Vieira and Vieirinha, or Leonardo and Leandro (who died in 1998) and you'll see. In the meantime a series of brilliant Brazilian instrumentalists have become international names and often live abroad – Sérgio Mendes, the guitarist Sebastião Tapajós, flautist Hermêto Paschoal, saxophonist Paulo Moura, accordionist Sivuca, percussionists Airto Moreira and Nana Vasconcelos, singer Flora Purim and all-rounder Egberto Gismonti are but a few. On the top of a huge recording industry, we're now a long way from the grassroots and the haunting flute music of the forest Indians.

Chile At the very heart of Chilean music is the Cueca, a courting dance for couples, both of whom make great play with a handkerchief waved aloft in the right hand. The man's knees are slightly bent and his body arches back. It is lively and vigorous, seen to best advantage when performed by a Huaso wearing spurs. Guitar and harp are the accompanying instruments, while handclapping and shouts of encouragement add to the atmosphere. The dance has a common origin with the Argentine Zamba and Peruvian Marinera via the early 19th century Zamacueca, in turn descended from the Spanish Fandango. For singing only is the Tonada, with its variants the Glosa, Parabienes, Romance, Villancico (Christmas carol) and Esquinazo (serenade) and the Canto a lo Poeta, which can be in the form of a Contrapunto or Controversia, a musical duel. Among the most celebrated groups are Los Huasos Quincheros, Silvia Infante with Los Condores and the Conjunto Millaray. Famous folk singers in this genre are the Parra Family from Chillán, Hector Pávez and Margot Loyola. In the north of the country the music is Amerindian and closely related to that of Bolivia. Groups called 'Bailes' dance the Huayño, Taquirari, Cachimbo or Rueda at carnival and other festivities and precolumbian rites like the Cauzulor and Talatur. Instruments are largely wind and percussion, including zampoñas (pan pipes), lichiguayos, pututos (conch shells) and clarines. There are some notable religious festivals that attract large crowds of pilgrims and include numerous groups of costumed dancers. The most outstanding of these festivals are those of the Virgen de La Tirana near Iquique, San Pedro de Atacama, the Virgen de la Candelaria of Copiapó and the Virgen de Andacollo. In the south the Mapuche nation, the once greatly feared and admired 'Araucanos', who kept the Spaniards and Republicans at bay for 400 years, have their own songs, dance-songs and magic and collective dances, accompanied by wind instruments like the great long trutruca horn, the shorter pifilka and the kultrun drum. Further south still, the island of Chiloé, which remained in the hands of pro-Spanish loyalists after the rest of the country had become independent, has its own unique musical expression. Wakes and other religious social occasions include collective singing, while the recreational dances, all of Spanish origin, such as the Vals, Pavo, Pericona and Nave have a heavier and less syncopated beat than in central Chile. Accompanying instruments here are the rabel (fiddle), guitar and accordion.

Colombia No South American country has a greater variety of music than Colombia, strategically placed where the Andes meet the Caribbean. The four major musical areas are (a) the mountain heartland (b) the Pacific coast (c) the Caribbean coast and (d) the Llanos or eastern plains. The mountain heartland covers the Andean highlands and intervening valleys of the Cauca and Magdalena and includes the country's three largest cities, Bogotá, Cali and Medellín. It is relatively gentle and sentimental music, accompanied largely by string instruments, with an occasional flute and a chucho or carángano shaker to lay down the rhythm. The preferred instrument of the highlands and by extension Colombia's national instrument, is the tiple, a small 12-stringed guitar, most of which are manufactured at Chiquinquirá in Boyacá. The national dance is the Bambuco, whose lilting sounds are said to have inspired Colombian troops at the Battle of Ayacucho in 1824. It is to be found throughout the countrys heartland for dancing, singing and instrumentalizing and has long transcended its folk origins. The choreography is complex, including many figures, such as la Invitación, Los Ochos, Los Codos, Los Coqueteos, La Perseguida and La Arrodilla. Other related dances are the Torbellino, where the woman whirls like a top, the more stately Guabina, the Pasillo, Bunde, Sanjuanero and the picaresque Rajaleña. Particularly celebrated melodies are the 'Guabina Chiquinquireña' and the 'Bunde Tolimense'. The following fiestas, among others, provide a good opportunity of seeing the music and dance: La Fiesta del Campesino, ubiquitous on the first Sunday in June, the Fiesta del Bambuco in Neiva and Festival Folklórico Colombiano in Ibagué later in the month, the Fiesta Nacional de la Guabina y el Tiple, held in Vélez in early August, the Desfile de

Silleteros in Medellín in the same month and Las Fiestas de Pubenza in Popayán just after the New Year, where the Conjuntos de Chirimía process through the streets.

On Colombia's tropical Pacific coast (and extending down into Esmeraldas, Ecuador) is to be found some of the most African sounding black music in all South America. The Currulao and its variants, the Berejú and Patacoré, are extremely energetic recreational dances and the vocals are typically African-style call- and-response. This is the home of the marimba and the music is very percussion driven, including the upright cununo drum plus bombos and redoblantes. Wakes are important in this region and at these the Bundes, Arrullos and Alabaos are sung. Best known is the 'Bunde de San Antonio'. The Jota Chocoana is a fine example of a Spanish dance taken by black people and turned into a satirical weapon against their masters. The regional fiestas are the Festival Folklórico del Litoral at Buenaventura in July and San Francisco de Asís at Quibdó on 4 August. Quibdó also features a Fiesta de los Indios at Easter.

The music of Colombia's Caribbean coast became popular for dancing throughout Latin America more than 30 years ago under the name of 'Música Tropical' and has much more recently become an integral part of the Salsa repertoire. It can be very roughly divided into 'Cumbia' and 'Vallenato'. The Cumbia is a heavily black influenced dance form for several couples, the men forming an outer circle and the women an inner one. The men hold aloft a bottle of rum and the women a bundle of slim candles called 'espermas'. The dance probably originated in what is now Panama, moved east into Cartagena, where it is now centred and quite recently further east to Barranquilla and Santa Marta. The most celebrated Cumbias are those of Ciénaga, Mompós, Sampués, San Jacinto and Sincelejo. The instrumental accompaniment consists of gaitas or flautas de caña de millo, backed by drums. The gaitas ('male' and 'female') are vertical cactus flutes with beeswax heads, while the cañas de millo are smaller transverse flutes. The most famous conjuntos are the Gaiteros de San Jacinto, the Cumbia Soledeña and the Indios Selectos. Variants of the Cumbia are the Porro, Gaita, Puya, Bullerengue and Mapalé, these last two being much faster and more energetic. Lately Cumbia has also become very much part of the Vallenato repertoire and is therefore often played on the accordion. Vallenato music comes from Valledupar in the Department of César and is of relatively recent origin. It is built around one instrument, the accordion, albeit backed by guacharaca rasps and caja drums. The most popular rhythms are the Paseo and the Merengue, the latter having arrived from the Dominican Republic, where it is the national dance. Perhaps the first virtuoso accordionist was the legendary 'Francisco El Hombre', playing around the turn of the century. Today's best known names are those of Rafael Escalona, Alejandro Durán and Calixto Ochoa. In April the Festival de la Leyenda Vallenata is held in Valledupar and attended by thousands. Barranquilla is the scene of South America's second most celebrated Carnival, after that of Rio de Janeiro, with innumerable traditional masked groups, such as the Congos, Toros, Diablos and Caimanes. The Garabato is a dance in which death is defeated. Barranquilla's carnival is less commercialized and more traditional than that of Rio and should be a must for anyone with the opportunity to attend. Other important festivals in the region are the Corralejas de Sincelejo with its bullfights in January, La Candelaria in Cartagena on 2 February, the Festival de la Cumbia in El Banco in June, Fiesta del Caiman in Ciénaga in January and Festival del Porro in San Pelayo (Córdoba). To complete the music of the Caribbean region, the Colombian islands of San Andrés and Providencia, off the coast of Nicaragua, have a fascinating mix of mainland Colombian and Jamaican island music, with the Calypso naturally a prominent feature.

The fourth musical region is that of the great eastern plains, the so-called Llanos Orientales between the Ríos Arauca and Guaviare, a region where there is really no musical frontier between the two republics of Colombia and Venezuela. Here the Joropo reigns supreme as a dance, with its close relatives the Galerón, the slower and more romantic Pasaje and the breathlessly fast Corrido and Zumba que Zumba. These are dances for couples, with a lot of heel tapping, the arms hanging down loosely to the sides. Arnulfo Briceño and Pentagrama Llanera are the big names and the harp is the only instrument that matters, although normally backed by cuatro, guitar, tiple and maracas. The place to see and hear it all is at the Festival Nacional del Joropo at Villavicencio in December.

Culturally, ethnically and geographically, Ecuador is very much two countries – the Andean highlands with their centre at Quito and the Pacific lowlands behind Guayaquil. In spite of

Ecuador

this, the music is relatively homogeneous and it is the Andean music that would be regarded as 'typically Ecuadorean'. The principal highland rhythms are the Sanjuanito, Cachullapi, Albaza, Yumbo and Danzante, danced by Indian and mestizo alike. These may be played by brass bands, guitar trios or groups of wind instruments, but it is the rondador, a small panpipe, that provides the classic Ecuadorean sound, although of late the Peruvian quena has been making heavy inroads via pan-Andean groups and has become a threat to the local instrument. The coastal region has its own song form, the Amorfino, but the most genuinely 'national' song and dance genres, both of European origin, are the Pasillo (shared with Colombia) in waltz time and the Pasacalle, similar to the Spanish Pasodoble. Of Ecuador's three best loved songs, 'El Chulla Quiteño', 'Romántico Quito' and 'Vasija de Barro', the first two are both Pasacalles. Even the Ecuadorean mestizo music has a melancholy quality not found in Peruvian 'Música Criolla', perhaps due to Quito being in the mountains, while Lima is on the coast. Music of the highland Indian communities is, as elsewhere in the region, related to religious feasts and ceremonies and geared to wind instruments such as the rondador, the pinqullo and pifano flutes and the great long guarumo horn with its mournful note. The guitar is also usually present and brass bands with well worn instruments can be found in even the smallest villages. Among the most outstanding traditional fiestas are Inti Raymi in Cayambe and Ingapirca, the Pase del Niño in Cuenca and other cities, the Mama Negra of Latacunga, carnival in Guaranda, the Yamor in Otavalo, the Fiesta de las Frutas y las Flores in Ambato, plus Corpus Cristi and the Feast of Saint John all over the highlands. Among the best known musical groups who have recorded are Los Embajadores (whose 'Tormentos' is superb) and the Duo Benítez-Valencia for guitar. There is one totally different cultural area, that of the black inhabitants of the Province of Esmeraldas and the highland valley of the Río Chota in Imbabura. The former is a southern extension of the Colombian Pacific coast negro culture, centred round the marimba xylophone. The musical genres are also shared with black Colombians, including the Bunde, Bambuco, Caderona, Torbellino and Currulao dances and this music is some of the most African sounding in the whole of South America. The Chota Valley is an inverted oasis of desert in the Andes and here the black people dance the Bomba. It is also home to the unique Bandas Mochas, whose primitive instruments include leaves that are doubled over and blown through.

Paraguay   The music of Paraguay is a curiosity. Although this is the only South American country, the majority of whose population still speak the original native tongue, the music is totally European in origin. The 17th and 18th century Jesuits found the Guaraní people to be highly musical and when their missions were established, the natives were immediately and totally indoctrinated into European music, of which they became fine performers, albeit not composers or innovators. A good example is Cristóbal Pirioby (1764-94), who changed his name to José Antonio Ortiz and moved to Buenos Aires to perform. At his death he left a large collection of musical instruments and sheet music of works by Haydn, Boccherini, etc. After the disastrous War of the Triple Alliance there was an abandonment of things national and even the national anthem was composed by a Uruguayan. Although black slaves were introduced to the country, they became quickly absorbed and there is no trace of black influence in the music. Neither is there any Guaraní element, nor infusion from Brazil or Argentina. Virtually the only popular instruments are the guitar and harp and it is the latter in particular that has come to be the hallmark of all that is musically Paraguayan, with the assistance of such brilliant performers as Félix Pérez Cardoso and Digno García. Paraguayan songs are notably languid and extremely sentimental and the present repertoire is not 'traditional', but of 20th century origin and by known composers. Of the three principal musical genres, two are slow and for singing, while one is lively and purely for dancing. The two singing genres are the Canción Paraguaya (or Purajhéi) and the Guarania, the former being a slow polka, of which the earliest and most famous example is 'Campamento Cerro León' about the War of the Triple Alliance. The Guarania was developed by José Asunción Flores as recently as the 1920s and includes most of the country's best loved and oft-repeated songs, such as 'India', 'Mi Dicha Lejana' and 'Recuerdos de Ypacaraí'. Equally celebrated and far more vigorous is that favourite of harp virtuosos, the wordless but onomatopeic 'Pájaro Campana'.

For dancing there are the lively Polca Paraguaya and Polca Galopada, first mentioned in print in 1858. They have similarities with the Argentine 'Gato' for instance and are not a true polka nor a gallop, the names of these popular European dances having been attached to an existing Paraguayan dance of unknown name. The Polca is a dance for couples, whilst the even livelier Galopa is usually danced by groups of women, the so-called 'Galoperas', who swing round barefoot, balancing a bottle or jar on their heads. This in turn has developed into the 'Danza de la Botella' or bottle dance, a more recent variant for virtuoso individual performance. Other less well known dances are the Valseadas (a local variant of the waltz), the Chopi or Santa Fé (for three couples), the Taguato, Golondrina, Palomita and Solito, the last named a kind of 'musical chairs'. Paraguayan music first came to global attention soon after the second world war and a number of artists such as Luis Alberto del Paraná and Los Paraguayos have achieved world fame. At the other end of the spectrum the four barefoot old men of the Banda Peteke Peteke from Guajayvity near Yaguarón play their own traditional music on two mimby flutes and two little drums, a small idiosyncratic island in an ocean of harp music.

Peru

Peru is the Andean heartland. Its musicians, together with those of Bolivia, have appeared on the streets of cities all over Europe and North America. However, the costumes they wear, the instruments they play, notably the quena and charango, are not typical of Peru as a whole, only of the Cusco region. Peruvian music divides at a very basic level into that of the highlands ('Andina') and that of the coast ('Criolla'). The highlands are immensely rich in terms of music and dance, with over 200 dances recorded. Every village has its fiestas and each fiesta has its communal and religious dances. Those of Paucartambo and Coylloriti (Q'olloriti) in the Cusco region moreover attract innumerable groups of dancers from far and wide. The highlands themselves can be very roughly subdivided into some half dozen major musical regions, of which perhaps the most characteristic are Ancash and the north, the Mantaro Valley, Cusco, Puno and the Altiplano, Ayacucho and Parinacochas.

There is one recreational dance and musical genre, the Huayno, that is found throughout the whole of the Sierra, and has become ever more popular and commercialized to the point where it is in danger of swamping and indeed replacing the other more regional dances. Nevertheless, still very popular among Indians and/or Mestizos are the Marinera, Carnaval, Pasacalle, Chuscada (from Ancash), Huaylas, Santiago and Chonguinada (all from the Mantaro) and Huayllacha (from Parinacochas). For singing only are the mestizo Muliza, popular in the Central Region, and the soulful lament of the Yaravi, originally Indian, but taken up and developed early in the 19th century by the poet and hero of independence Mariano Melgar, from Arequipa.

The Peruvian Altiplano shares a common musical culture with that of Bolivia and dances such as the Auqui-Auqui and Sicuris, or Diabladas, can be found on either side of the border. The highland instrumentation varies from region to region, although the harp and violin are ubiquitous. In the Mantaro area the harp is backed by brass and wind instruments, notably the clarinet, in Cusco it is the charango and quena and on the Altiplano the sicu panpipes. Two of the most spectacular dances to be seen are the Baile de las Tijeras ('scissor dance') from the Ayacucho/Huancavelica area, for men only and the pounding, stamping Huaylas for both sexes. Huaylas competitions are held annually in Lima and should not be missed. Indeed, owing to the overwhelming migration of peasants into the barrios of Lima, most types of Andean music and dance can be seen in the capital, notably on Sunday at the so-called 'Coliseos', which exist for that purpose. Were a Hall of Fame to be established, it would have to include the Ancashino singers La Pastorcita Huaracina and El Jilguero del Huascarán, the charango player Jaime Guardia, the guitar virtuoso Raul García from Ayacucho and the Lira Paucina trio from Parinacochas.

The flood of migration to the cities has meant that the distinct styles of regional and ethnic groups have become blurred. One example is Chicha, a hybrid of Huayno music and the Colombian Cumbia rhythm which comes from the pueblos jóvenes. More recent is Tecno-cumbia, which originated in the jungle region with groups such as Rossy War, from Puerto Maldonado, and Euforia, from Iquitos. It is a vibrant dance music which has gained much greater popularity across Peruvian society than chicha music ever managed.

The 'Música Criolla' from the coast could not be more different from that of the Sierra. Here the roots are Spanish and African. The immensely popular Valsesito is a syncopated waltz that would certainly be looked at askance in Vienna; the Polca has also suffered an attractive sea change, but reigning over all is the Marinera, Peru's national dance, a splendidly rhythmic and graceful courting encounter, a close cousin of Chile's and Bolivia's Cueca and the Argentine Zamba, all of them descended from the Zamacueca. The Marinera has its 'Limeña' and 'Norteña' versions and a more syncopated relative, the Tondero, found in the north coastal regions, is said to have been influenced by slaves brought from Madagascar. All these dances are accompanied by guitars and frequently the *cajón*, a resonant wooden box on which the player sits, pounding it with his hands. Some of the great names of 'Música Criolla' are the singer/composers Chabuca Granda and Alicia Maguiña, the female singer Jesús Vásquez and the groups Los Morochucos and Hermanos Zañartu.

Also on the coast is to be found the music of the small black community, the 'Música Negroide' or 'Afro-Peruano', which had virtually died out when it was resuscitated in the 50s, but has since gone from strength to strength. It has all the qualities to be found in black music from the Caribbean - a powerful, charismatic beat, rhythmic and lively dancing, and strong percussion provided by the *cajón* and the *quijada de burro*, a donkey's jaw with the teeth loosened. Some of the classic dances in the black repertoire are the Festejo, Son del Diablo, Toro Mata, Landó and Alcatraz. In the Alcatraz one of the partners dances behind the other with a candle, trying to set light to a piece of paper tucked into the rear of the other partner's waist. Nicomedes and Victoria Santa Cruz have been largely responsible for popularizing this black music, and Peru Negro is another excellent professional group. Finally, in the Peruvian Amazon region around Iquitos, local variants of the Huayno and Marinera are danced, as well as the Changanacui, accompanied by flute and drum.

Uruguay

One of the best known of all tangos, 'La Cumparsita', was composed by the Uruguayan Gerardo Matos Rodríguez in Montevideo in 1917

Most musical influences came with the European immigrants who arrived after the disappearance of the Amerindian population. The folk songs and dances are very closely related to those of the Argentine pampas, except in the north, where they are shared with the neighbouring Brazilian state of Rio Grande do Sul. The major song genres are the Estilo, Cifra, Milonga and Vidalita, whilst the 'national' dance is the stately Pericón for six or more couples. The Milonga is also danced, as are the Tango, Cielito, Media Caña and Ranchera. The guitar is the instrument that accompanies most country music and as in Argentina, the gauchos like to engage in Payadas de Contrapunto, where two singers vie with each other, alternating improvised verses. 19th century Europe introduced other popular dances into Uruguay, such as the polca, waltz, chotis and mazurca, all of which were given a local touch. In the northern departments a number of dances are shared with Brazil, such as the Chimarrita, Carangueijo and Tirana, which are also sung, either in Spanish or Portuguese or a mixture of both. There were many black slaves in the Río de la Plata during colonial times and the African ritual of the Candombe was practised in Montevideo until late in the 19th century. Less than 3% of the population is black and the only musical remains of African origin are to be found in the presence during carnival of the Morenada groups of up to 50 Candomberos, who take part in the procession, playing their tamboril drums, while smaller groups take part in these so-called 'Llamadas' from December through to Holy Week. There are four sizes of drums – chico, repique, piano and bajo – and the complex polyrhythms produced by the mass of drummers advancing down the street is both unexpected and impressive.

Venezuela

Venezuelan music is more homogenous than that of some of the other republics. Its highly distinctive sound is based on an instrumental combination of harp, cuatro (a small, four stringed guitar) and maracas. Many of the rhythms have a very fast, almost headlong pace to them, stimulating both to the senses and to the feet, music here being almost inseparable from dance. The recipe for Venezuelan music is a classic European/African/Amerindian mix. The country's national dance is the Joropo, a name deriving from the Arab 'Xarop', meaning syrup and which originally meant a country dance. This is a dance for couples with several sequences, such as the Valseao, Zapatiao, Escobillao and Toriao. Closely related to the Joropo are the Corrido, with a ballad content, Galerón (slow for singing or fast for dancing), Pasaje (lyrical, very popular in the Llanos) and Golpe, from the State of Lara, to all of which styles the Joropo may be danced in different parts of the country. Note that the little cuatro is normally referred to as 'guitarra' while the Spanish guitar is called the 'guitarra grande'. Some of the dance rhythms have been imported from abroad or are shared with neighbouring countries, such as the urban Merengue (introduced into Caracas in the 1920s), the Jota and Malagueña of Anzoátegui State, the Pasillo (shared with Colombia and Ecuador), the Polo of the Oriente and Isla Margarita and the Bambuco, found in Lara and Táchira states near the border with Colombia.

There is a wealth of dances and musical forms found in particular towns or states at religious festivities. Outstanding among these is the Tamunangue of Lara State, danced in the second fortnight of June to the accompaniment of drums and small guitars and made up of seven individual dances, varying from the 'Batalla', where men battle with sticks, to the 'Bella', a flirtatious dance for couples. Corpus Cristi is the time to visit San Francisco de Yare in Miranda State, 90 km from Caracas, and see the 80 or so male 'Diablos' of all ages, dressed entirely in red and wearing large horned masks, who dance in the streets to the sound of their own drums and rattles. The Bailes de Tambor take place among the largely black people of the Barlovento coast during the feasts of San Juan and San Pedro and at Christmas. This is brilliant polyrhythm on huge drums (cumacos, minas and curvetas) held between the legs. Also in Barlovento, but in May, can be heard the Fulias, chant-and-response songs addressed to a venerated saint or cross, to the accompaniment of cuatro, tambora drum and maracas. Christmas is a great period for music from the Gaitas of Zulia to the ubiquitous Aguinaldos, both in Merengue rhythm, with solo verses responded to by a chorus and varied instrumental accompaniment. Notable in the eastern states are the folk theatre dances of the Pájaro Guarandol (a hunter shoots a large bird that is brought back to life), Carite (from Margarita, using a large model fish), Chiriguare (a monster that is duly despatched) and Burriquita (a hobby horse). More surprising is to find the Calipso, played on steel bands by the black inhabitants of El Callao in the Orinoco region, whose ancestors came from Trinidad and who also perform the Limbo.

Venezuelans enjoy Salsa as much as other Hispanic peoples around the Caribbean, but they are also very keen on their own music, whether rustic 'folk' or urban 'popular'. The virtuoso harpist Juan Vicente Torrealba has performed with his group Los Torrealberos for more than three decades, usually with Mario Suárez as vocal soloist. Another famous singer is Simón Díaz. Outstanding among the folk groups who strive for authenticity are Un Solo Pueblo, Grupo Vera and Grupo Convenezuela. Choral and contrapuntal singing of native music in a more sophisticated style has also been perfected by Quinteto Contrapunto and Serenata Guayanesa.

Films

The following list includes a number of films with a South American theme, from The Second World War to the present:

1939   *Only Angels Have Wings* (**Howard Hawks**). Cary Grant and Jean Arthur star in a drama about flying mail planes in the treacherous mountains of the Peruvian Andes.

1945   *The Three Caballeros* (**Walt Disney**). Donald Duck goes to Rio with two Latino chums, José Carioca and Panchito.

1946   *Notorious* (**Alfred Hitchcock**). Cary Grant (again) and Ingrid Bergman track neo-Nazis in Brazil; the plot is complicated by a cache of uranium on the chief baddie's estate.

1959   *Orfeu Negro* (Balck Orpheus) (**Marcel Camus**). The Orpheus and Eurydice legend retold during Rio Carnaval; music by Antônio Carlos Jobim and Luiz Bonfa.

1963   *Vidas Secas* (Barren Lives) (**Nelson Pereira dos Santos**). Based on Graciliano Ramos' novel of the same name, about a family's efforts to survive in Brazil's drought-stricken *sertão*.

1966-68   *La hora de los hornos* (The Hour of the Furnaces) (**Fernando Solanas**). A four-hour documentary about Argentina, with a strong political message about radical Peronism, highly influential in cinematic terms.

1969   *Macunaíma* (Jungle Freaks) (**Joaquim Pedro de Andrade**). Adapted from the novel by Mário de Andrade, this anarchic Brazilian film tells of the crazy adventures of an Afro-Brazilian who becomes white, gets involved in urban terrorism and battles evil.

1969   *Butch Cassidy and the Sundance Kid* (**Roy Hill**). Contains scenes in Patagonia and Bolivia of the outlaws' last years; Paul Newman and Robert Redford's first big adventure together.

1969   *The Royal Hunt of the Sun* (**Irving Lerner**). Based on the play of the same name, about the Spanish conquest of the Incas.

1972   *Aguirre Wrath of God* (**Werner Herzog**). About Lope de Aguirre, the murderous conquistador and his journey down the Amazon; Klaus Kinski stars.

1973   *Papillon* (**Franklin J Schaffner**). Set on the notorious French convict island off Guyane and one man's attempts to escape, with Dustin Hoffman and Steve McQueen.

1978   *The Boys from Brazil* (**Franklin J Schaffner**). Thriller about Nazi hunter Laurence Olivier and his efforts to stop Gregory Peck's Josef Mengele filling the world with cloned Hitlers.

1981   *Pixote, a Lei do Mais Fraco* (Pixote) (**Hector Babenco**). Harrowing film about Brazil's homeless children.

1982   *Missing* (**Constantin Costa Gavras**). An American activist goes missing in an unspecified South American country. His wife, Sissy Spacek, and father, Jack Lemmon, set out to find him, despite the country's dictator and the US consul's opposition.

1982   *Fitzcarraldo* (**Werner Herzog**). The epic story of one man's obsession (Klaus Kinski again) to build an opera house in the Peruvian jungle; includes the remarkable attempt to haul a 300-ton ship over a mountain. See also *Burden of Dreams* (1982, Les Blank), which documents Herzog's obsession in making of *Fitzcarraldo*.

1983   *The Honorary Consul* (also called *Beyond the Limit*) (**John MacKenzie**). Set in Corrientes, Argentina, based on the novel by Graham Greene, the film stars Richard Gere and Michael Caine.

1983   *Romancing the Stone* (**Robert Zemeckis**). Michael Douglas and Kathleen Turner chase a bag of emeralds in Colombia.

1984   *Camila* (**María Luisa Bemberg**) Argentine film retelling the life of a 19th-century aristocratic woman's love for a Catholic priest, which ends with her execution.

1984   *The Emerald Forest* (**John Boorman**). In the Amazon jungle of Brazil a western engineer tries to find his son who has been kidnapped by forest Indians.

1985   *A Hora da Estrela* (The Hour of the Star) (**Suzana Amaral**). Adapted from Clarice Lispector's novel about a country girl trying to make a living as a typist in Rio.

1985   *Kiss of the Spider Woman* (O Beijo da Mulher Aranha) (**Hector Babenco**). Based on the novel by Manuel Puig, a two-hander between a homosexual and a terrorist in a prison cell.

1986   *The Mission* (**Roland Joffé**). Robert de Niro and Jeremy Irons as Jesuit priests in the Missions in Argentina and Paraguay at the time of the expulsion of the order from South America accompanied by a beautiful Ennio Morricone score.

1986   *La historia oficial* (The Official Version) (**Luis Puenzo**) The first Argentine film to win an Oscar, set in the period of the Dirty War.

1987   *Chronicle of a Death Foretold* (**Francesco Rosi**). Based on the novel by Gabriel García Márquez, set in northern Colombia, depicting the events surrounding a murder in a small town.

1988   *Sur* (South) (**Fernando Solanas**) A political prisoner is released from jail as Argentina emerges from military dictatorship.

1992   *Alive* (**Frank Marshall**). How members of the Uruguayan rugby team survived an air crash in the Argentine Andes (includes cannibalism).

1993   *The House of Spirits* (**Bille August**). Family saga based on Chilean Isabel Allende's novel of the same name.

1994   *Death and the Maiden* (**Roman Polanski**). Taken from Ariel Dorfman's play of the same name, this is a grim story of a woman (Sigourney Weaver) taking revenge on the man (Ben Kingsley) who, she believes, was her torturer several years earlier (country unnamed) .

1994   *The Postman* (Il Postino) (**Michael Radford**) Taken from Antonio Skármeta's novel, *El cartero de Neruda* (originally called *Ardiente paciencia*); it weaves the story of a Chilean postman's love for a barmaid with the death of Pablo Neruda and the fall of Salvador Allende.

1998   *Central do Brasil* (Central Station) (**Walter Salles**). An Oscar-winning Brazilian movie telling of the hardships faced by a young boy and the woman who takes him under her wing as he tries to find his father.

2001   *Behind the Sun* (**Walter Salles**). The tale of a blood feud between two sugar-growing families in northeast Brazil and two brothers' efforts to break it.

Footnotes

16

Footnotes

Useful words and phrases

Greetings & courtesies	**Spanish**	**Portuguese**
hello/good morning	hola/buenos días	oi/bom dia
good afternoon/evening/night	buenas tardes/noches	boa tarde/boa noite
goodbye	adiós/chao	adeus/tchau
see you later	hasta luego	até logo
how are you?	¿cómo está/cómo estás?	como vai você?/tudo bem?
		tudo bom?
I'm fine	estoy bien	tudo bem /tudo bom
pleased to meet you	mucho gusto/encantado	um prazer
please	por favor	por favor/faz favor
thank you (very much)	(muchas) gracias	(muito) obrigado (man speaking)
		/obrigada (woman speaking)
yes/no	sí/no	sim/não
excuse me/I beg your pardon	permiso	com licença
I don't understand	no entiendo	não entendo
please speak slowly	hable despacio por favor	fale devagar por favor
what's your name?/	¿cómo se llama?/me llamo_	Qual é seu nome?/ O meu
I'm called_		nome é_
Go away!	¡Váyase!	Vai embora!

Basic questions		
where is_?	¿dónde está_?	onde está/onde fica?
how much does it cost?	¿cuánto cuesta?	quanto custa?
when?	¿cuándo?	quando?
when does the bus leave/	¿a qué hora sale/llega el	qa que hora sai/chega o
arrive?	autobus?	ônibus?
why?	¿por qué?	por que?
how do I get to_?	¿cómo llegar a_?	para chegar a_?

Basics		
police (policeman)	la policía (el policía)	a polícia (o policía)
hotel	el hotel (la pensión, el	o hotel (a pensão,
	residencial, el alojamiento)	a hospedaria)
room	el cuarto/la habitación	o quarto
single/double	sencillo/doble	(quarto de) solteiro
with two beds	con dos camas	com duas camas
bathroom/toilet	el baño	o banheiro
hot/cold water	agua caliente/fría	água quente/fria
toilet paper	el papel higiénico	o papel higiênico
restaurant	el restaurante	o restaurante (o lanchonete)
post office/telephone office	el correo/el centro de llamadas	o correio/o centro telefônico
supermarket/market	el supermercado/el mercado	o supermercado/o mercado
bank/exchange house	el banco/la casa de cambio	o banco/a casa de câmbio
exchange rate	la tasa de cambio	a taxa de câmbio
travellers' cheques	los travelers/los cheques de	os travelers/os cheques de viagem
	viajero	
cash	el efectivo	o dinheiro
breakfast/lunch	el desayuno/el almuerzo	o café de manhã/o almoço
dinner/supper	la cena	o jantar
meal/drink	la comida/la bebida	a refeição/a bebida
mineral water	el agua mineral	a água mineral
beer	la cerveza	a cerveja
without sugar/without meat	sin azúcar/sin carne	sem açúcar/sem carne

Getting around

on the left/right	*a la izquierda/derecha*	*á esquerda/á direita*
straight on	*derecho*	*direito*
bus station	*la terminal (terrestre)*	*a rodoviária*
bus stop	*la parada*	*a parada*
bus	*el bus/el autobus/la flota/ el colectivo/el micro*	*o ônibus*
train/train station	*el tren/la estación (de tren/ferrocarril)*	*o trem*
airport/aeroplane	*el aeropuerto/el avión*	*o aeroporto/o avião*
ticket/ticket office	*el boleto/la taquilla*	*o bilhete/a bilheteria*

Time

What time is it?	*¿Qué hora es?*	*Que horas são?*
at half past two/two thirty	*a las dos y media*	*as dois e meia*
it's one o'clock/ it's seven o'clock	*es la una/son las siete*	*é uma/são as sete*
ten minutes/five hours	*diez minutos/cinco horas*	*dez minutos/cinco horas*

Numbers

1	*uno/una*	*um/uma*
2	*dos*	*dois/duas*
3	*tres*	*três*
4	*cuatro*	*quatro*
5	*cinco*	*cinco*
6	*seis*	*seis*
7	*siete*	*sete*
8	*ocho*	*oito*
9	*nueve*	*nove*
10	*diez*	*dez*
11	*once*	*onze*
12	*doce*	*doze*
13	*trece*	*treze*
14	*catorce*	*catorze*
15	*quince*	*quinze*
16	*dieciseis*	*dezesseis*
17	*diecisiete*	*dezessete*
18	*dieciocho*	*dezoito*
19	*diecinueve*	*dezenove*
20	*veinte*	*vinte*
21	*veintiuno*	*vinte e um*
30	*treinte*	*trinta*
40	*cuarenta*	*quarenta*
50	*cincuenta*	*cinqüenta*
60	*sesenta*	*sessenta*
70	*setenta*	*setenta*
80	*ochenta*	*oitenta*
90	*noventa*	*noventa*
100	*cien, ciento*	*cem, cento*
1000	*mil*	*mil*

See also Language in Essentials, page 48.

Shorts index

Footnotes

Map index

Footnotes

Advertisers' index

Footnotes

Index

Footprint – how it all happened

It was 1921
Ireland had just been partitioned, the British miners were striking for more pay and the federation of British industry had an idea. Exports were booming in South America – how about a Handbook for businessmen trading in that far away continent? The *Anglo-South American Handbook* was born that year, written by W Koebel, the most prolific writer on Latin America of his day.

1924
Two editions later the book was 'privatised' and in 1924, in the hands of Royal Mail, the steamship company for South America, became the *South American Handbook*, subtitled 'South America in a nutshell'. This annual publication became the 'bible' for generations of travellers to South America and remains so to this day. In the early days travel was by sea and the Handbook gave all the details needed for the long voyage from Europe. What to wear for dinner; how to arrange a cricket match with the Cable & Wireless staff on the Cape Verde Islands and a full account of the journey from Liverpool up the Amazon to Manaus: 5898 miles without changing cabin!

1939
As the continent opened up, the *South American Handbook* reported the new Pan Am flying boat services, and the fortnightly airship service from Rio to Europe on the Graf Zeppelin. For reasons still unclear but with extraordinary determination, the annual editions continued through World War 2.

1970
From the 1970s, jet aircraft transformed travel. Many more people discovered South America and the backpacking trail started to develop. All the while the Handbook was gathering fans including literary vagabonds such as Paul Theroux and Graham Greene who once sent some updates addressed to **'The publishers of the best travel guide in the world, Bath, England'**.

1990s
During the 1990s Patrick and James Dawson, the publishers of the *South American Handbook* set about developing a new travel guide series using this legendary title as the flagship. By 1997 there were over a dozen guides in the series and the Footprint imprint was launched.

2002
There are now over 70 Footprint travel guides covering more than 145 destinations in Latin America and the Caribbean, Africa, the Indian sub-continent, Southeast Asia, the Middle East, Australasia and Europe. In addition Footprint are launching a new series of pocket format guides focusing on European short-break cities.

The future
There are many more Handbooks and pocket Handbooks in the pipeline. To keep up-to-date with the latest releases check out the Footprint website for all the latest news and information, **www.footprintbooks.com**

Acknowledgements

A great many people have helped in the preparation of this book. Thanks are due in particular to Sara Smith and Wendy Baldwin, who prepared the update files from the travellers' letters, and all at Footprint, especially Rachel, Claire, Sarah, Emma, Rob and Alan.

Argentina: Nicolás Kugler (Buenos Aires), who would like to thank María José Solís, Julio Giustozzi, Román Gueijman and Lautaro Lafleur for their help. Christine Fox (Río Gallegos). Herbert Levi (Buenos Aires). Federico Kirbus (Buenos Aires).

Bolivia: Roger Perkins and Kate Hannay (UK, Researchers, Footprint's *Bolivia Handbook*).

Brazil: Jane Egginton (UK, writer, Footprint's *Brazil Handbook*). Fábio Sombra (Rio de Janeiro). Beatrix Boscardin (Curitiba).

Chile: Toby Green (UK, writer, Footprint's *Chile Handbook*). Janak Jani (Valparaíso). Jean-Charles (Charlie) de Keyser (Arica).

Colombia: Peter Pollard (UK, writer, Footprint's *Colombia Handbook*), who wishes to thank Mark Duffy (Bogotá), Tim Dowling (Medellín) and Mike Esposito (USA).

Ecuador: Robert and Daisy Kunstaetter (writers, Footprint's *Ecuador Handbook*), who would like to offer special thanks to Jean Brown as well as Grace and Marcelo Naranjo for their valuable ongoing assistance. They are also grateful to the following contributors: Guido and Jeaneth Abad, Santiago Cabascango, Marco Cruz, Miguel Falk, Joana May, Marcelo Muñoz, Popkje van der Ploeg, Michael Resch, William Reyes, Iván Suárez and Delia María Torres.

Peru: Ben Box visited Peru and Northern Chile in late 2001. For their help in Peru and for assistance with the Peru chapter in this edition, Ben is most grateful to: Ibeth Acuña, Alessia di Paolo (and Greg), María del Rocío Vesga, María del Pilar Lazarte Conroy and Walter Vizareta of *PromPerú*, especially for the opportunity to visit Manu, also John Melton and Jorge Quiñones of *Inkanatura* and Frida Pérez of *Inti Tour* (Cusco). At *South American Explorers*, Fiona Cameron (Cusco), who would like to thank Shawn Navis and David Ugarte for their help with research; Simon Atkinson (Lima), Julia Levanton and Tara Aleck. In Lima: Mónica Moreno, Leo Rovayo, Marcelina and Mauro (*Posada del Parque*); Cecilia Kamiche; Víctor Melgar; Kato, Lucho and Michael of *Fly Adventure*. In Puno: Víctor and Maruja Pauca and all the staff at *All Ways Travel*; Martha Giraldo (*Suasi*), Edwin Giraldo; Miguel Vera (*Pirámide Tours*); Edgar and Norka (*Edgar Adventures*); Valentín Quispe (Llachón). In Cusco: Rafael Carbone (*Inka Grill*); Stephen Light. Many thanks also to Andre Vltchek (Hanoi, travelling in South America).

Venezuela: Dan Green (writer, Footprint's *Venezuela Handbook*); Steve Chew (UK).

Guyana: Tony Thorne (Georgetown).

Suriname: Jerry A-Kum (Paramaribo and Georgetown).

Falklands/Malvinas: Geraldine Anthony, Travel Coordinator, FIGO, London.

Antarctica: Robert Headland (Scott Polar Research Institute, Cambridge, UK).

Land and environment: Peter Pollard

Adventure Highs in South America: Katie Moore (France).

Specialist contributors: John Lewis for business travel; Ashley Rawlings for motorcycling; Hallam Murray for cycling; Hilary Bradt for hiking and trekking; Richard Robinson for world wide radio information; Journey Latin America for flight details; Mark Eckstein for responsible travel and Dr Charlie Easmon for health. The health section was written by **Dr Charlie Easmon** MBBS MRCP MSc Public Health DTM&H DOccMed Director of *Travel Screening Services*.

Travellers who have written are acknowledged on page 1548.

Footnotes

Travellers' letters

Daniel Aderhold (Per); Stephan Aerni, Switzerland (Bol, Bra, Ecu, Per); Toni Ajoksenmaki, Finland (Bol, Bra,Chi, Col, Per); Lorraine Alcock (Per); Alvaro Allende, Chile (Chi); Liz Anderson (Bol); Ingvar Andersson, Sweden (Bol, Chi); Jochen R Andritzky, Germany (Bol, Chi, Per); Lukas Aufschlaeger, Switzerland (Chi); Dirk Bachmann (Bol, Col, Ecu, Ven); Erich Baechler, Switzerland (Arg); Mandy Ball, UK (Per); Peter Balwin, Switzerland (Chi); Eran Barlev, Israel (Arg, Chi); André Bause, Germany (Per); Stefan Beck, Germany (Col); William Becker, UK (Per); Tomas Berrin (Per); Andrea Bieder, Switzerland (Bol, Chi, Ecu, Per); Kees Biekart, Netherlands (Chi); Vidar Birkeland, Norway (Chi); Dr Michael Bohndorf, Germany (Bra); Alex Boughton (Ven); Christopher Brown (Bra); Hannah Brown, UK (Per); Paterson Brown (Per); Friederike Buchner-Kaufholdt, Germany (Bol); Daniel Buck, USA (Bol); Lorraine & Rob Callery (Per); Mike and Amy Capelle, USA (Bol); Jaime Carrera Nóritz (Ecu); Lars & Dora Clausen, Denmark (Bra); Richard Coetzee, South Africa (Ven); Phillip Colin, Belgium (Arg); Stefan & Rozemarijn Cornelissen (Bol, Ecu, Per); Tara Crete (Per); Adrian Croft (Ecu, Per); Jacqueline Cullen (Per); Elly Day, UK (Bra, Uru); Eyal Dayan, Israel (Arg); Daniel De Backer, Belgium (Bol); Walter De Boef, The Netherlands (Bra); Michele De Oliveira Carvalho, Switzerland (Bra); David De-Fina, Australia (Arg, Bol, Bra, Chi, Per); Hilary Dennison (Bol); Richard Derichs, Germany (Ven); Dan Doliner, Israel (Arg, Bol, Bra, Ecu, Par, Per, Ven); Maurus & Manuela Dosch, Switzerland (Arg, Bol, Chi, Per); Ryan Elliott, USA (Chi); Donat and Birgit Elsener, Switzerland (Bol,Per); Hilary Emberton, USA (Per); Sam Eyde, Norway (Bra); Natasha Fanshawe, UK (Per); Jacqueline Feetz (Bol, Ecu, Per); Michael Ferguson, Peru (Per); David Fern (Per); DWA Fisher, UK (Bol); Gloria Fisher, USA (Per); Erlend Fossedal Olsen, Norway (Ecu); Pauline Fox, Pauline (Ecu); Bryan & Sonja Fraser (Bol); Dr Valerie Fraser, UK (Bra); Klaus Fritscher, Brazil (Bol, Bra, Chi); Michel Gagnon (Per); Yair Galler, Israel (Chi); Alvaro Garcia, Uruguay (Ven); David Gilcrist (Bra); Ingrid Glatz, Germany (Arg); Cecelia Gnos, Switzerland (Ecu); Ingrid & Andreas Gökeler, Germany (Bol, Bra, Ecu, Per); Amanda Grant, UK (Chi); Mark Greenwood, Brazil (Bra, Par); Nico Gurtner, Switzerland (Arg, Bol, Chi); Anne Habets, Belgium (Chi); Simon Haenni, Switzerland (Chi); Peter Haenseler, Switzerland (Ecu, Per); Naylah Hamour, UK (Ecu); Olivia Hanley, UK (Ecu); Egli Hannes (Per); Heidi Heinzerling (Bol); Anna Henningsen, Denmark (Bol); Rado Hnath, Slovakia (Ecu); Toby Hofton (Chi); Anne Hook (Arg, Par, Per, Uru); Ned Hopkins, USA (Bra); Chris Horton (Arg, Bra, Chi, Par); Patricia Houton (Per); Manfred Imiela (Ecu, Per); Tamsin Irving, UK (Ecu); Marco Isella, Switzerland (Chi); D R James, UK (Per); Silvana Jastreb, Mexico (Arg); Ian Jenkins, UK (Col); Ann Johnson (Chi); Todd Johnson, USA (Guy); Dr & Mrs RG Jones (Ecu); Robert Jones, Latacunga (Ecu); Daniel Kast, Switzerland (Ecu); Els & Frank Kerckhof, Belgium (Bol); Hee Joung Kimmel, S Korea (Bol, Bra, Chi, Ecu, Per); John-Paul Kimmel, Peru (Per); Helen King, UK (Ecu, Per); Rachel King, UK (Ecu, Per); Yonatan Klein, Israel (Bol, Ecu, Per); Joachim Kleinwächter, Germany (Ven); Roman Klotsvog, Israel (Per); Marc Knaff, Switzerland (Ven); Joe Kopp (Ecu, Per); Doreen Krueger, Germany (Bra); Dietmar Kuhrt, Germany (Ven); Lars Peter Kuipers (Arg); Oskar Kullingsjo, Sweden (Bol); Andreas Kurschat, Germany (Per); Silvia Lavalle, Peru (Per); Rob Lawrence, New Zealand (Arg, Bol, Chi, Ecu, Per); Sarah Lawson, UK (Bra); Jessaca Leinaweaver, Peru (Per); Irene and Alain Leiser, Switzerland (Ecu); Roman Leone, Argentina (Bra); Herbert Levi, Argentina (Arg, Chi, Ecu, Par, Per, Uru); Daniel Levy (Per); Anne Lindley, France (Per); Thomas Löliger (Chi); Iris Luechinger (Bol); Anna Luginbuehl, Switzerland (Chi); Maria Macarena, New Zealand (Arg); Wolfram Madlener, Germany (Per); Cinzia Mainini (Chi); Sarah Malin (Ecu); Magdalena Mandy, Mauritius (Arg, Bra); Simone Marzoll, Switzerland (Arg, Bol, Bra, Col, Ecu, Per, Uru, Ven); Paul Mason, UK (Chi); Iain McGhee, UK (Col); Steve McGilchrist (Bol, Bra); Lynn McMahon (Ecu); Andreas Meese, Germany (Ecu); Thomas Mehis, Germany (Bol, Ecu, Per); Ilse Michielsen, Belgium (Ecu, Per); Ashley Milne-Tyte (Chi); Roberto Morán, Argentina (Chi); Tony Morgan (Chi); Nathan Morris, USA (Chi); Maor Moses (Per); Roger Murcia (Ven); Hadas Nachum, Israel (Per); Ishay Nadler, Israel (Bol, Chi, Per); Bernhard Nanninga, The

Netherlands (Bol,Bra); Catherine & Peter Newman, UK (Bol); Elizabeth Newstead, Brazil (Bra); Hugo Nisbett (Bra); Marianne Noulet, France (Arg); Nahum and Dave Ofir (Chi); Olly Ogg, UK (Bol, Bra, Chi, Per); Nick Oliver, UK (Per); Notman Parlane, New Zealand (Arg, Chi, Ecu); Massimo Passera, Switzerland (Bra); David Paul, USA (Bra); Gerard Paul-Clark, S Korea (Bol, Bra, Chi, Ecu, Per); Jeanette Pauli, Switzerland (Arg, Chi); Uffe Pedersen, Denmark (Per); David Pohl (Chi); Natasha Porter, UK (Bra); Wolfgang Pössl (Bol, Par); Lucia Postelnicu, Germany (Col); Chris Preager (Arg, Chi); Russell Price (Per); Wolfgang Prince (Ven); Sybille Pringot, Belgium (Per); Sarah Prior, UK (Chi); Janette and Tom Purves, UK (Ecu); Mr E Quiroga, UK (Arg); Martha Radice, UK (Arg, Bol, Chi, Per, Uru); Jeremy Raiz, Australia (Chi); Chris Ratcliffe (Ven); Christopher Ratcliffe, UK (Arg, Bra, Chi); Albert Recknagel, Germany (Per); Janet Reese, USA (Ecu); Marco Reinhoudt (Bol, Bra); Peter Rendle, UK (Per); Anke Restin (Chi); Hannah Richardson, UK (Ecu); Ole Riis Simonsen, Norway (Arg); Rik Rik (Ecu); Peter Ritschard (Chi); Camillo Roberti, UK (Bra); Will Robinson, Australia (Arg); Jay Rossiter, USA (Per); Tammy Rothenberg, UK (Per); Jeff Rothman (Bra); Hans Rudolf Ruchti, Switzerland (Bra, Col, Par); Marie Sansom (Chi); Charles Sarasin, Switzerland (Chi, Per, Ven); Scott Saunders, UK (Per); M Sayer (Ven); Kees Schaapveld, Netherlands (Bol, Bra, Par); Jeremy Scholes, UK (Ecu); Claudia Schreier, Switzerland (Ven); Verena Senter, USA (Chi); Yishai Shimoni, Israel (Per); Amit Shur, Israel (Arg, Bol, Bra, Chi, Col, Ecu, Per, Uru); Fred Smith (Bol); Kate Smith, UK (Bol, Bra, Chi, Per); Teresa Soop, Teresa, Sweden (Bra, Ecu); Barbara Spycher, Switzerland (Ecu); Paul Steele, Brazil (Bra); Richard Steele, UK (Arg); Peter Stricker, Switzerland (Bol); Peter Sweeny (Ecu); Bastiaan te Wierik, Netherlands (Arg); Nele Teich, Germany (Bol, Par); Reto Thalmann, Switzerland (Bol, Chi, Per); David Thom (Chi, Ecu, Per); Marie Thompson, Marie (Ecu, Per); Andreas Tröndle (Per); Tim Tucker (Chi, Ecu, Per); Boaz Tzur, Israel (Arg, Chi, Per); Erik Uddenbergt, Sweden (Fal); Janet Um, USA (Per); David Van Den Berghe, Belgium (Arg, Chi, Ecu); Kris van der Starren, Canada (Ecu, Par, Uru); Rob VanHoudt (Ven); Eva Varga (Ecu); Paul Verhoosel, The Netherlands (Bra); Evert Vink (Bra); Tim Vivian, UK (Ecu); Kath Vlcek, UK (Per); Hannah Völkering, Germany (Per); Ulrich von Werder (Arg); Patrick Vuylsteek, Belgium (Ecu); Ute Waditschatka, Austria (Bra); Hans K Wagner, Switzerland (Chi); Marek Wakar, Marek (Uru); Margot Walet, Netherlands (Bra); Melanie Wartho (Bol); Robert Watson, UK (Arg); Richard Webber, UK (Bol); Hurni, Mirjam, & Thomas Weber, Switzerland (Per); Petra Wendeler, USA (Chi); Richard & others Whitaker (Bol, Per); Glen Widmer, Argentina (Arg, Chi); Anders Wienecke, Sweden (Per); Chris Wille (Arg, Bol); Christoph Wille (Arg, Bol, Bra); Andre Wilting, Netherlands (Chi); Nadine Wincke, Germany (Arg); Neil Wray (Chi); Rachel Wrench, UK (Bol); Tom Wynne-Powell, UK (Per); Anat Zimmermann, Israel (Per); Andy , UK (Bra); Astrid and Bernd (Arg, Bol, Chi, Per); Ben , Israel (Col); Betty , Canada (Arg); Christopher, UK (Bra); Danny & Meytal (Bol); Isabel and Bigna , Switzerland (Ecu); Josef & Claudia, Switzerland (Arg, Chi); Juan (Bra); Judith , Switzerland (Ecu); Klaus (Bra); Natalie , Australia (Per).

Climatic tables

The following tables have been very kindly furnished by Mr R K Headland. Each weather station is given with its altitude in metres (m). Temperatures (Centigrade) are given as averages for each month; the first line is the maximum and the second the minimum. The third line is the average number of wet days encountered in each month.

	Jan	Feb	Mar	Apr	May	Jun	Jul	Aug	Sep	Oct	Nov	Dec
Arica, Chile	26	26	25	23	21	19	19	18	19	21	22	24
29 m	18	18	17	16	14	14	12	13	13	14	16	17
	0	0	0	0	0	0	0	0	0	0	0	0
Asunción, Par	34	34	33	28	25	22	24	25	27	29	31	33
64 m	22	22	21	18	14	13	14	14	16	17	19	21
	7	6	9	7	5	4	4	4	6	5	6	7
Bariloche, Arg	21	21	18	14	10	7	6	8	10	11	16	18
825 m	8	8	6	4	2	1	0	0	1	3	5	6
	2	3	5	7	11	13	11	11	8	6	4	4
Barranquilla, Col	31	31	32	33	34	33	33	33	33	32	32	30
12 m	22	22	23	24	25	25	25	25	25	24	24	23
	0	0	0	1	4	8	5	6	8	11	6	4
Belém, Braz	31	30	30	31	31	32	32	32	32	32	32	32
24 m	23	23	23	23	23	23	22	22	22	22	22	22
	24	26	25	22	24	15	14	15	13	10	11	14
Belo Horizonte	27	27	27	27	25	24	24	25	27	27	27	26
857 m	18	18	17	16	12	10	10	12	14	16	17	18
	15	13	9	4	4	2	2	1	2	10	12	14
Bogotá	21	21	21	20	20	19	19	19	20	20	20	21
2,560 m	7	7	9	10	10	9	8	8	8	9	8	7
	9	7	10	18	16	10	16	10	13	18	16	13
Brasília	27	28	28	28	27	26	26	28	30	29	27	27
912 m	18	18	18	17	15	13	13	14	16	18	18	18
	19	16	15	9	3	1	0	2	4	11	15	20
Buenos Aires	30	29	26	22	18	15	15	16	18	21	25	29
25 m	18	17	15	12	9	6	6	6	8	11	13	16
	5	5	6	6	4	4	5	6	5	7	7	7
Caracas	26	26	28	28	28	27	26	27	28	27	27	26
1,035 m	15	15	16	17	18	18	17	17	17	17	17	16
	4	3	2	4	8	13	13	11	11	11	8	6
Córdoba, Arg	32	31	28	25	21	19	19	20	23	26	28	31
425 m	17	16	14	11	7	4	4	5	8	11	13	16
	8	9	9	6	4	2	2	1	3	7	9	10
Cusco	20	21	21	22	21	21	21	21	22	22	23	22
3310 m	7	7	7	4	2	1	-1	1	4	6	6	7
	18	13	11	8	3	2	2	2	7	8	12	16
Guayaquil	31	31	32	31	31	29	28	29	30	29	30	31
6 m	22	22	23	23	22	21	20	20	20	21	21	22
	12	13	15	10	4	1	0	0	0	1	0	2
La Paz, Bol	18	18	18	19	17	17	17	17	18	19	19	19
3632 m	6	6	6	5	3	2	1	2	3	5	6	6
	21	18	16	9	5	2	2	4	9	9	11	18

	Jan	Feb	Mar	Apr	May	Jun	Jul	Aug	Sep	Oct	Nov	Dec
Lima	25	26	26	24	21	19	17	17	17	19	20	23
137 m	19	20	19	18	16	15	14	13	13	14	16	17
	1	0	0	0	1	1	1	2	1	0	0	0
Manaus	30	30	30	30	31	31	32	33	33	33	32	31
48 m	23	23	23	23	24	23	23	24	24	24	24	24
	20	18	21	20	18	12	12	5	7	4	12	16
Montevideo	28	28	26	22	18	15	14	15	17	20	23	26
22 m	17	16	15	12	9	6	6	6	8	9	12	15
	6	5	5	6	6	5	6	7	6	6	6	7
Porto Alegre, Braz	31	30	29	25	22	20	20	21	22	24	27	29
10 m	20	20	19	16	13	11	10	11	13	15	17	18
	9	10	10	6	6	8	8	8	11	10	8	8
Punta Arenas,	15	14	13	9	6	4	3	4	7	10	12	14
Chile	7	7	6	4	2	1	1	1	2	3	4	6
28 m	6	5	7	9	6	8	6	5	5	5	5	8
Quito	21	21	20	21	21	21	21	22	22	21	21	21
2,818 m	8	8	8	8	8	7	7	7	7	8	8	8
	9	11	11	15	10	9	3	3	8	13	13	7
Recife, Braz	30	30	30	30	29	28	27	27	28	29	30	30
56 m	24	25	24	23	23	22	21	21	22	23	24	24
	7	8	10	11	17	16	17	14	7	3	4	4
Rio de Janeiro	30	30	29	27	26	25	25	25	25	26	28	28
30 m	23	23	23	21	20	18	18	18	19	20	20	22
	13	11	9	9	6	5	5	4	5	11	10	12
Salvador (Bahia)	29	29	29	28	27	26	26	26	27	28	28	29
8 m	23	23	24	23	22	21	21	21	21	22	23	23
	6	9	17	19	22	23	18	15	10	8	9	11
Santa Cruz, Bol	30	31	30	28	25	23	24	28	29	30	31	31
437 m	21	21	20	19	16	15	15	16	19	20	20	21
	14	10	12	9	11	8	5	4	5	7	8	11
Santiago de Chile	29	29	27	23	18	14	15	17	19	22	26	28
520 m	12	11	9	7	5	3	3	4	6	7	9	11
	0	0	1	1	5	6	6	5	3	3	1	0
São Paulo	28	28	27	25	23	22	21	23	25	25	25	26
792 m	18	18	17	15	13	11	10	11	13	14	15	16
	15	13	12	6	3	4	4	3	5	12	11	14

Sources: H.M.S.O. Meteorological Reports   K.L.M. Climatic Data Publication

Footprint feedback

We try as hard as we can to make each Footprint Handbook as up-to-date and accurate as possible but, of course, things always change. Many people email or write to us with corrections, new information, or simply comments. If you want to let us know about your experiences and adventures – be they good, bad or ugly – then don't delay; we're dying to hear from you. And please try to include all the relevant details and juicy bits. Your help will be greatly appreciated, especially by other travellers. In return we will send you details about our special guidebook offer.

email Footprint at:
SAH 2003_online@footprintbooks.com

or write to:
Elizabeth Taylor
Footprint Handbooks
6 Riverside Court
Lower Bristol Road
Bath   BA2 3DZ
UK